As the rain and the snow
come down from heaven,
and do not return to it
without watering the earth
and making it bud and flourish,
so that it yields seed for the sower and
bread for the eater,
so is my word that goes out from my
mouth:

It will not return to me empty,
but will accomplish what I desire
and achieve the purpose for which I
sent it.

— Isaiah 55:10-11

Reading the World's Greatest Story

The heart and soul of the Bible is its story. It is the real saga of a particular people, how God called them and intended for them to bring blessing to all people.

Story is also the word that best describes our own lives. While we may or may not follow the right rules, investigate certain facts and attempt to live wisely, none of these activities provides the central way we make sense of our lives. Stories give context and provide meaning.

All the different parts of the Bible come together as one narrative.

To understand the Bible you must get to know its characters, understand its setting and follow its plot.

The climax and ultimate resolution will make sense only if you've followed the earlier parts as a story. Learn to feel the tension and wrestle with its major conflict. Lose yourself in this story the way you do with a good novel.

We present here an abbreviated version of the story of the Bible as a drama in five acts.

Act I: Creation

The drama begins with God already on the stage. He is creating the world. He makes a man, Adam and places him in the Garden of Eden to work in it and take care of it. God's intention is for humanity to be in close relationship with him and in harmony with the rest of creation around them. God is described in these early chapters of the Bible as dwelling in the garden together with the first human beings, Adam and Eve. At the end of the first chapter of Genesis, God gives his own assessment of his work:

> *God saw all that he had made, and it was very good* (v. 31).

Later, God's people celebrated God's creative work:

> *"Blessed be your glorious name, and may it be exalted above all blessing and praise. You alone are the Lord. You made the heavens, even the highest heavens, and all their starry host, the earth and all that is on it, the seas and all that is in them. You give life to everything, and the multitudes of heaven worship you"* (Nehemiah 9:5–6).

Act I reveals God's desire for people and provides the setting for all the action that follows.

Act II: The Fall

Tension is introduced in the story when Adam and Eve decide to go their own way and seek their own wisdom. They listen to the deceptive voice of God's enemy, Satan, and doubt God's trustworthiness.

As a result of this rebellion:

> *The Lord God banished him [Adam] from the Garden of Eden to work the ground from which he had been taken. After he drove the man out, he placed on the east side of the Garden of Eden cherubim and a flaming sword flashing back and forth to guard the way to the tree of life* (Genesis 3:23–24).

God's intention in creation is known, but part of his own creation has put his plan off course. Can God regain his relationship with humanity and remove the curse from creation? Or did God's enemy effectively end the plan and subvert the story?

Acts I and II take only the first few pages in the Bible to be completed. Yet they introduce the struggle that dominates the rest of the story.

Act III: Israel

> *The Lord had said to Abram, "Leave your country, your people and your father's household and go to the land I will show you.*
>
> *"I will make you into a great nation*
> *and I will bless you;*
> *I will make your name great,*
> *and you will be a blessing.*
> *I will bless those who bless you,*
> *and whoever curses you I will curse;*
> *and all peoples on earth*
> *will be blessed through you."*
>
> —Genesis 12:1–3

In calling Abram (God later renamed him Abraham) and promising to make him into a great nation, God is narrowing his focus and concentrating on one group of people for a period of time. But the ultimate goal remains the same: to bless all the peoples on earth, remove the curse from creation and restore the original relationship that existed in the garden.

When Abraham's descendants are later enslaved in Egypt, a central pattern in the story is set: God returns to his people, frees them and restores them to the land promised to them. God makes a covenant with this new nation of Israel at Mt. Sinai. He appoints Moses to be their leader during their liberation from Egypt—the Exodus. As part of the covenant, God makes it clear that if his people remain true to him and faithfully follow his ways, he will bless them in their new land and make it like the original Garden of Eden.

However, if Israel is not faithful to the covenant, God warns them that he will send them out of the land, just as he did with Adam and Eve. Sadly, and in spite of God's repeated warnings and pleadings, they are determined to go their own way. They break the covenant, follow the false gods of the nations that surround them and bring the judgment of God down upon themselves.

Abraham's descendants, chosen to reverse the failure of Adam, have now apparently failed themselves. Along the way, however, God has planted the seeds of a different outcome. One of Israel's kings, David, is noted for being *"a man after God's own heart."* So God promises to send another king to Israel, a son of David, who will lead Israel wisely, bring the nation back to God and be the agent of blessing to the peoples of the world.

So while Act III ends tragically, with God apparently absent, the hope of a promise remains.

Act IV: Jesus

Four centuries later, the people of Israel are suffering under Roman occupation and waiting for God to return. An angel of God comes to a young woman named Mary and announces,

> *"You will be with child and give birth to a son, and you are to give him the name Jesus. He will be great and will be called the Son of the Most High. The Lord God will give him the throne of his father David, and he will reign over the house of Jacob forever; his kingdom will never end"* (Luke 1:31–33).

Jesus' arrival is introduced with the claim that God is keeping his promise.

So Jesus begins his mission. He heals sickness and disease among the people. He confronts God's enemies in the spiritual realm, the demons, and forcefully orders them to leave the people whom they torment. Jesus forgives the sins of those who humbly come to him. He proclaims the gospel, or good news, that:

> *"The time has come. The kingdom of God is near.*
> *Repent and believe the good news!"* (Mark 1:15).

The very heart of Jesus' message is the good news of the coming of God's reign. God is coming back to dwell with his people. This is why Jesus is called Immanuel, which means "God with us."

But Jesus' message receives mixed responses. Some people believe, and out of these Jesus chooses twelve disciples or followers. But most people simply watch him with amazement, never knowing quite what to make of him. The established religious leaders quickly become hostile toward him. Eventually this conflict escalates to the breaking point and the religious leaders conspire to have Jesus arrested and killed on a cross.

But this defeat is actually God's greatest victory. Jesus' death turns the tables on God's enemy and turns the world upside down. By willingly giving up his life as a sacrifice, Jesus takes onto himself God's judgment for our wrongdoing. As the early Christian leader Paul later wrote:

> *God made you alive with Christ. He forgave us all our sins, having canceled the written code, with its regulations, that was against us and that stood opposed to us; he took it away, nailing it to the cross. And having disarmed the powers and authorities, he made a public spectacle of them, triumphing over them by the cross* (Colossians 2:13–15).

Jesus speaks the message of God as Israel's true prophet. He defeats the very power behind all evil as Israel's true king, the son of David. He gives up his own life as a sacrifice for his people as Israel's true priest. He leads his people to a new Exodus, through death to a new life. In all of this Jesus shows himself to be the promised child of Abraham who reconciles humanity with God. It is through Jesus that Israel can finally fulfill its role, the purpose for which God called Abraham.

This account of Jesus is the focal point of the Bible's entire story. The key struggle with God's enemy, the desperate attempts to correct what has gone wrong at the very heart of things, comes to a head in the life of Jesus. He is the one and only hero of the story.

Act V: The New People of God

If the key victory has already been secured, why is there an Act V? God wants the victory of Jesus to spread to all the nations of the world. Those who follow Jesus are being built into God's new temple, the place where God's Spirit lives. God is gathering these people from all around the world and forming them into his church. When this is complete, Jesus will return and the reign of God will become a reality throughout God's creation (1 Corinthians 15:24–25). The curse imposed during Act II will be removed (Revelation 22:3).

The task of bringing blessing to the peoples of the world has been given again to the descendants of Abraham. According to the New Testament, all those who belong to Christ are true children of Abraham (Galatians 3:29). Act V emphasizes the mission of Christ-followers: to proclaim and live out the liberating message of the good news of Christ's kingdom.

Act V moves through history to our own time, enveloping us in its drama. The message of Christ and his kingdom has now come to us. The challenge of a decision now confronts us too. What will we do? How will we fit into this story?

The story of the Bible is the true account of the central conflict winding its way through the history of the world. Will we be a part of God's mission of re-creation—of restoring the world around us—and making the world (including ourselves) new?

What Now?

The most important thing you can do is to read these Scriptures carefully. God's Spirit uses them actively and powerfully to accomplish his purposes—in you and through you to impact the world.

The Bible is not necessarily an easy book to read. Some passages are difficult for everyone to understand. But if you stick with it, if you are committed to learning more about God and the story he's given us in the Bible, it will guide you, change you and keep you close to God.

Finding Your Place in the Story

The story of Jesus offers a new beginning for humanity and confronts each of us with a personal choice. If you haven't begun to follow the way that Jesus provided for restoring your relationship with God, this section will help you to understand what this means. If you are following Jesus, these ideas are valuable in helping you realize what you have been given through Christ.

Soon after Christ had given his mission to his followers and returned to heaven, Peter (who was a disciple of Jesus and a leader in the early church) was speaking to a gathering of Jews. He recounts the story of Jesus' life, death and resurrection, then challenges them to make the right response to what God has done for them:

> *"Repent, then, and turn to God, so that your sins may be wiped out, that times of refreshing may come from the Lord, and that he may send the Christ, who has been appointed for you—even Jesus. He must remain in heaven until the time comes for God to restore everything, as he promised long ago through his holy prophets.*
>
> *..."Indeed, all the prophets from Samuel on, as many as have spoken, have foretold these days. And you are heirs of the prophets and of the covenant God made with your fathers. He said to Abraham, 'Through your offspring all peoples on earth will be blessed.' When God raised up his servant, he sent him first to you to bless you by turning each of you from your wicked ways"* (Acts 3:19–26).

Peter connects Jesus' sacrifice to the ancient promise made to Abraham. He makes clear that now is the time for the blessing to occur. God has made a way for you to turn away from your wrongdoing and return to him.

As a son or daughter of Adam, you were born separated from God and the close, trusting relationship he desires to have with you. Jesus is the one who can bring you back to God. Your sins can be forgiven and your life can be renewed when you personally accept Christ's sacrifice on your behalf. As John's account of the story of Jesus puts it:

> *"For God so loved the world that he gave his one and only Son, that whoever believes in him shall not perish but have eternal life"* (John 3:16).

Your life's story can be rewritten within the storyline of the Bible. You can join with God's people from all over the world who are living out Act V today. For this to happen, though, you must turn away from your sins and commit to trust and follow Jesus.

Getting Started

Perhaps you don't know where to start reading in this book. Although this is not an exhaustive list, the following passages will give you a helpful overview of God's story.

Act I: Creation

The creation, Genesis 1—2:3 (p. 1)

Praise God for his creation, Psalm 8 (p. 379)

Praise to the Creator of all things, Psalm 104 (p. 421)

Praise God for creating me, Psalm 139 (p. 437)

Act II: The Fall

The fall into sin, Genesis 3 (p. 2)

Noah, the flood and the ark, Genesis 6—9:17 (p. 4)

A prayer of repentance, Psalm 51 (p. 398)

No one is righteous, Romans 3:9–26 (page 782)

Act III: Israel

God's covenant with Abraham, Genesis 12:1–9 (p. 8); 15:1–21 (p. 9)

Abraham almost sacrifices his son Isaac, Genesis 22:1–19 (p. 14)

Jacob receives his father's blessing, Genesis 27:1–40 (p. 19)

Jacob's (Israel's) family, Genesis 29:16—30:24

Joseph the dreamer, Genesis 37:2–36 (p. 27); 39—50 (p. 29)

Moses is born in Egypt, Exodus 1—2:10 (p. 39)

Ten plagues, Exodus 7:14—11:10 (p. 44)

The Passover, Exodus 12:1–17 (p. 47)

The Israelites leave Egypt, Exodus 12:18—15:21 (p. 48)

God's covenant with Israel, Exodus 19—20; 24 (p. 52)

God keeps his promise, Joshua 23—24 (p. 165)

Rahab the prostitute hides the Israelite spies, Joshua 2 (p. 149)

David kills Goliath, 1 Samuel 17 (p. 199)

David becomes king, 2 Samuel 5:1–5 (p. 213)

God's promise to David, 2 Samuel 7 (p. 215)

David and Bathsheba, 2 Samuel 11—12:25 (p. 217)

The Lord is my shepherd, Psalm 23 (p. 385)

A prayer of thanksgiving, Psalm 100 (p. 419)

Israel sent into exile, 2 Chronicles 36:15–23 (p. 327)

Queen Esther saves her people, Esther (p. 347)

Messiah's birth prophesied, Isaiah 9:1–7 (p. 481)

God's promise to return, Isaiah 52:1–12 (p. 514)

Daniel's dream of God's kingdom, Daniel 7 (p. 621)

Act IV: JESUS

The birth of Jesus, Luke 1—2 (p. 710)

The temptation of Jesus, Matthew 4:1–11 (p. 670); Luke 4:1–13 (p. 713)

The Sermon on the Mount, Matthew 5—6 (p. 671)

Jesus shares his calling with the people, Luke 4:16–30 (p. 713)

Jesus' teaching on prayer, Luke 11:1–13 (p. 721)

The prodigal (lost) son, Luke 15 (p. 726)

New birth, John 3 (p. 737)

Jesus is the resurrection and the life, John 11 (p. 746)

Three prayers of Jesus, John 17 (p. 751)

The Lord's Supper, Luke 22:7–38, (p. 732); 1 Corinthians 11:17–34 (p. 797)

The death of Jesus, Luke 23:26–56 (p. 734); John 19:16–42 (p. 753)

The resurrection of Jesus, Luke 24 (p. 734); John 20 (p. 754)

Jesus ascends into heaven, Acts 1:1–11 (p. 755)

Act V: THE NEW PEOPLE OF GOD

The Great Commission from Jesus, Matthew 28:16–20 (p. 694)

The coming of the Holy Spirit, Acts 2:1–21 (p. 756)

"Repent and be baptized," Acts 2:22–47 (p. 757)

Jesus, the fulfillment of Abraham's covenant, Acts 3 (p. 757)

Salvation in Jesus alone, Acts 4 (p. 758)

Paul's conversion, Acts 9:1–31 (p. 763)

Paul's testimony before King Agrippa, Acts 25:23—26:32 (p. 777)

What real love is, 1 Corinthians 13 (p. 798)

The fruit of the Holy Spirit, Galatians 5:22–23 (p. 810)

The armor of God, Ephesians 6:10–18 (p. 813)

Imitating Christ, Philippians 2:1–11 (p. 815)

Heroes of the faith, Hebrews 11 (p. 834)

Faith in action, James 2:14–26 (p. 837)

The return of Christ, 1 Thessalonians 4:13–18 (p. 820); 2 Peter 3:3–14 (p. 843)

The new heaven and earth, Revelation 21—22 (p. 860)

How to Read this Story

Can you read the Bible like other stories? Not exactly. The Bible is a collection of books, 66 in all, that were written over a long period of time. They tell the story of how God is working to set things right in our world. But these books were written in a different time than ours, and that means you will need to keep some important things in mind as you read.

The key to reading the Bible is to remember two questions: *What did it mean then?* and *What does it mean now?* The first step in reading the Bible is to discover what the original author was saying. Once this is clear, ask yourself what it means for you today.

Here are some keys to finding what a Bible story or passage originally meant:

- ✦ What kind of literature is being used: is it historical story? law? psalm (song)? letter? wisdom saying? Answering this question correctly will help you to interpret the passage correctly.
- ✦ Where are you reading in the story? Where did these people live? What is happening around them? What is God telling them now? What happened before? What are they expecting to happen next? As in all stories, some things change and some things stay the same as the story progresses.
- ✦ How does this passage fit into the message of other passages around it? It is critical to read the Bible in context. As with any story, if you pull isolated sayings out of context, you may change the meaning entirely.

As you move into thinking about what a Bible passage means for you today, keep these in mind:

- ✦ Use common sense. God is not trying to trick us or hide secret meanings in the Bible. Some parts of the Bible are difficult, yet in most places the meaning can be discerned clearly. Look for the plain meaning of the text, then focus on what your response should be.
- ✦ Keep in mind the cultural differences between the Bible times and ours today. When God is teaching an important principle for living, the way that principle gets lived out may look very different in our day from what it looked like in the ancient world.
- ✦ Remember where you are in the story. We are living after the death and resurrection of the Messiah Jesus, which is the climax of the Bible's whole story. The main event has happened. God has shown us what he is like by sending Jesus to us. Everything you read should be shaped by that fact.

The Bible is not primarily about you. It is the ancient story of God, the world and the people he called. Yet, this story has a place for you. In fact, the reason this story was saved and written down is so that people like you could read it and find the true meaning for their lives . Our prayer is that you will read it and discover within it the life that is truly life (1 Timothy 6:19).

The

Holy Bible

New International Version

INTERNATIONAL BIBLE SOCIETY®

The purpose and passion of International Bible Society® is to faithfully translate and reach out with God's Word so that people around the world may become disciples of Jesus Christ and members of his Body.

To receive a free catalog featuring hundreds of Scripture ministry products, contact International Bible Society®:

In US and Canada, contact:
Phone: 800-524-1588 **Fax:** 719-867-2870
Internet: IBSDirect.com **E-mail:** IBSDirectService@ibs.org
Mail: 1820 Jet Stream Drive, Colorado Springs, CO 80921-3696

INTERNATIONAL BIBLE SOCIETY®
1820 Jet Stream Drive, Colorado Springs, CO 80921-3696

Eng. Bible NIV 921/923/927/929/933/BB013/CC168 11/08
IBS08-160000/160000/140000/90000/100000/100000/2500 Printed in U.S.A.
921: ISBN 978-1-56320-518-7 923: ISBN 978-1-56320-519-4
927: ISBN 978-1-56320-521-7 929: ISBN 978-1-56320-478-4
933: ISBN 978-1-56320-479-1

Contents

Reading the World's Greatest Story A2
Finding Your Place in the Story A7
Getting Started A8
How to Read this Story A10
A Word about the *NIV* A14

THE BOOKS OF THE OLD TESTAMENT

Genesis 1
Exodus 39
Leviticus 69
Numbers 91
Deuteronomy 122
Joshua 149
Judges 166
Ruth 184
1 Samuel 187
2 Samuel 210
1 Kings 231
2 Kings 254
1 Chronicles 277
2 Chronicles 302
Ezra 328
Nehemiah 336
Esther 347
Job 352
Psalms 377
Proverbs 441
Ecclesiastes 464
Song of Songs 470
Isaiah 475
Jeremiah 525
Lamentations 572
Ezekiel 577
Daniel 615
Hosea 626
Joel 634
Amos 637
Obadiah 643
Jonah 644
Micah 645
Nahum 650
Habakkuk 652
Zephaniah 654
Haggai 656
Zechariah 658
Malachi 664

THE BOOKS OF THE NEW TESTAMENT

Matthew 669
Mark 694
Luke 709
John 736
Acts 755
Romans 780
1 Corinthians 791
2 Corinthians 801
Galatians 807
Ephesians 811
Philippians 814
Colossians 816
1 Thessalonians 819
2 Thessalonians 821
1 Timothy 822
2 Timothy 825
Titus 827
Philemon 828
Hebrews 829
James 837
1 Peter 839
2 Peter 842
1 John 844
2 John 847
3 John 847
Jude 848
Revelation 848

Table of Weights and Measures
Dictionary/Concordance

A Word About the *NIV*

The New International Version is a completely new translation of the Holy Bible made by over a hundred scholars working directly from the best available Hebrew, Aramaic and Greek texts. It had its beginning in 1965 when, after several years of exploratory study by committees from the Christian Reformed Church and the National Association of Evangelicals, a group of scholars met at Palos Heights, Illinois, and concurred in the need for a new translation of the Bible in contemporary English. This group, though not made up of official church representatives, was transdenominational. Its conclusion was endorsed by a large number of leaders from many denominations who met in Chicago in 1966.

Responsibility for the new version was delegated by the Palos Heights group to a self-governing body of fifteen, the Committee on Bible Translation, composed for the most part of biblical scholars from colleges, universities and seminaries. In 1967 the New York Bible Society (now the International Bible Society) generously undertook the financial sponsorship of the project—a sponsorship that made it possible to enlist the help of many distinguished scholars. The fact that participants from the United States, Great Britain, Canada, Australia and New Zealand worked together gave the project its international scope. That they were from many denominations—including Anglican, Assemblies of God, Baptist, Brethren, Christian Reformed, Church of Christ, Evangelical Free, Lutheran, Methodist, Nazarene, Presbyterian, Wesleyan and other churches—helped to safeguard the translation from sectarian bias.

How it was made helps to give the New International Version its distinctiveness. The translation of each book was assigned to a team of scholars. Next, one of the Intermediate Editorial Committees revised the initial translation, with constant reference to the Hebrew, Aramaic or Greek. Their work then went to one of the General Editorial Committees, which checked it in detail and made another thorough revision. This revision in turn was carefully reviewed by the Committee on Bible Translation, which made further changes and then released the final version for publication. In this way the entire Bible underwent three revisions, during each of which the translation was examined for its faithfulness to the original languages and for its English style.

All this involved many thousands of hours of research and discussion regarding the meaning of the texts and the precise way of putting them into English. It may well be that no other translation has been made by a more thorough process of review and revision from committee to committee than this one.

From the beginning of the project, the Committee on Bible Translation held to certain goals for the New International Version: that it would be an accurate translation and one that would have clarity and literary quality and so prove suitable for public and private reading, teaching, preaching, memorizing and liturgical use. The Committee also sought to preserve some measure of continuity with the long tradition of translating the Scriptures into English.

In working toward these goals, the translators were united in their commitment to the authority and infallibility of the Bible as God's Word in written form. They believe that it contains the divine answer to the deepest needs of humanity, that it sheds unique light on our path in a dark world, and that it sets forth the way to our eternal well-being.

The first concern of the translators has been the accuracy of the translation and its fidelity to the thought of the biblical writers. They have weighed the significance of the lexical and grammatical details of the Hebrew, Aramaic and Greek texts. At the same time, they have striven for more than a word-for-word translation. Because thought patterns and syntax differ from language to language, faithful communication of the meaning of the writers of the Bible demands frequent modifications in sentence structure and constant regard for the contextual meanings of words.

A sensitive feeling for style does not always accompany scholarship. Accordingly the Committee on Bible Translation submitted the developing version to a number of stylistic consultants. Two of them read every book of both the Old and New Testaments twice—once before and once after the last major revision—and made valuable suggestions. Samples of the translation were tested for clarity and ease of reading by various kinds of people—young and old, highly educated and less well educated, ministers and laymen.

Concern for clear and natural English—that the New International Version should be idiomatic but not idiosyncratic, contemporary but not dated—motivated the translators and consultants. At the same time, they tried to reflect the differing styles of the biblical writers. In view of the international use of English, the translators sought to avoid obvious Americanisms on the one hand and obvious Anglicanism on the other. A British edition reflects the comparatively few differences of significant idiom and of spelling.

As for the traditional pronouns "thou," "thee" and "thine" in reference to the Deity, the translators judged that to use these archaisms (along with the old verb forms such as "doest," "wouldest" and "hadst") would violate accuracy in translation. Neither Hebrew, Aramaic nor Greek uses special pronouns for the persons of the Godhead. A present-day translation is not enhanced by forms that in the time of the King James Version were used in everyday speech, whether referring to God or man.

For the Old Testament the standard Hebrew text, the Masoretic Text as published in the latest editions of *Biblia Hebraica*, was used throughout. The Dead Sea Scrolls contain material bearing on an earlier stage of the Hebrew text. They were consulted, as were the Samaritan Pentateuch and the ancient scribal traditions relating to textual changes. Sometimes a variant Hebrew reading in the margin of the Masoretic Text was followed instead of the text itself. Such instances, being variants within the Masoretic tradition, are not specified by footnotes. In rare cases, words in the consonantal text were divided differently from the way they appear in the Masoretic Text. Footnotes indicate this. The translators also consulted the more important early versions—Septuagint; Aquila, Symmachus and Theodotion; the Vulgate; the Syriac Peshitta; the Targums; and for the Psalms the *Juxta Hebraica* of Jerome. Readings from these versions were occasionally followed where the Masoretic Text seemed doubtful and where accepted principles of textual criticism showed that one or more of these textual witnesses appeared to provide the correct reading. Such instances are footnoted. Sometimes the vowel letters and vowel signs did not, in the judgment of the translators, represent the correct vowels for the original consonantal text. Accordingly some words were read with a different set of vowels. These instances are usually not indicated by footnotes.

The Greek text used in translating the New Testament was an eclectic one. No other piece of ancient literature has such an abundance of manuscript witnesses as does the New Testament. Where existing manuscripts differ, the translators made their choice of readings according to accepted principles of New Testament textual criticism. Footnotes call attention to places where there was uncertainty about what the original text was. The best current printed texts of the Greek New Testament were used.

There is a sense in which the work of translation is never wholly finished. This applies to all great literature and uniquely so to the Bible. In 1973 the New Testament in the New International Version was published. Since then, suggestions for corrections and revisions have been received from various sources. The Committee on Bible Translation carefully considered the suggestions and adopted a number of them. These were incorporated in the first printing of the entire Bible in 1978. Some additional revisions were made by the Committee on Bible Translation in 1983 and appear in printings after that date.

As in other ancient documents, the precise meaning of the biblical texts is sometimes uncertain. This is more often the case with the Hebrew and Aramaic texts than with the Greek text. Although archaeological and linguistic discoveries in this century aid in understanding difficult passages, some uncertainties remain. The more significant of these have been called to the reader's attention in the footnotes.

In regard to the divine name *YHWH*, commonly referred to as the *Tetragrammaton*, the translators adopted the device used in most English versions of rendering that name as "LORD" in capital letters to distinguish it from *Adonai*, another Hebrew word rendered "Lord," for which small letters are used. Wherever the two names stand together in the Old Testament as a compound name of God, they are rendered "Sovereign LORD."

Because for most readers today the phrases "The LORD of hosts" and "God of hosts" have little meaning, this version renders them "the LORD Almighty" and "God Almighty." These renderings convey the sense of the Hebrew, namely, "he who is sovereign over all the 'hosts' (powers) in heaven and on earth, especially over the 'hosts' (armies) of Israel." For readers unacquainted with Hebrew this does not make clear the distinction between *Sabaoth* ("hosts" or "Almighty") and *Shaddai* (which can also be translated "Almighty"), but the latter occurs infrequently and is always footnoted. When *Adonai* and *YHWH Sabaoth* occur together, they are rendered "the Lord, the LORD Almighty."

As for other proper nouns, the familiar spellings of the King James Version are generally retained. Names traditionally spelled with "ch," except where it is final, are usually spelled in this translation with "k" or "c," since the biblical languages do not have the sound that "ch" frequently indicates in English—for example, in *chant*. For well-known names such as

Zechariah, however, the traditional spelling has been retained. Variation in the spelling of names in the original languages has usually not been indicated. Where a person or place has two or more different names in the Hebrew, Aramaic or Greek texts, the more familiar one has generally been used, with footnotes where needed.

To achieve clarity the translators sometimes supplied words not in the original texts but required by the context. If there was uncertainty about such material, it is enclosed in brackets. Also for the sake of clarity or style, nouns, including some proper nouns, are sometimes substituted for pronouns, and vice versa. And though the Hebrew writers often shifted back and forth between first, second and third personal pronouns without change of antecedent, this translation often makes them uniform, in accordance with English style and without the use of footnotes.

Poetical passages are printed as poetry, that is, with indentation of lines and with separate stanzas.These are generally designed to reflect the structure of Hebrew poetry. This poetry is designed to reflect the structure of Hebrew poetry. This poetry is normally characterized by parallelism in balanced lines. Most of the poetry in the Bible is in the Old Testament, and scholars differ regarding the scansion of Hebrew lines. The translators determined the stanza divisions for the most part by analysis of the subject matter. The stanzas there fore serve as poetic paragraphs.

As an aid to the reader, italicized sectional headings are inserted in most of the books. They are not to be regarded as part of the NIV text, are not for oral reading, and are not intended to dictate the interpretation of the sections they head.

The footnotes in this version are of several kinds, most of which need no explanation. Those giving alternative translations begin with "Or" and generally introduce the alternative with the last word preceding it in the text, except when it is a single-word alternative; in poetry quoted in a footnote a slant mark indicates a line division. Footnotes introduced by "Or" do not have uniform significance. In some cases two possible translations were considered to have about equal validity. In other cases, though the translators were convinced that the translation in the text was correct, they judged that another interpretation was possible and of sufficient importance to be represented in a footnote.

In the New Testament, footnotes that refer to uncertainty regarding the original text are introduced by "Some manuscripts" or similar expressions. In the Old Testament, evidence for the reading chosen is given first and evidence for the alternative is added after a semicolon (for example: Septuagint; Hebrew *father*). In such notes the term "Hebrew" refers to the Masoretic Text.

It should be noted that minerals, flora and fauna, architectural details, articles of clothing and jewelry, musical instruments and other articles cannot always be identified with precision. Also measures of capacity in the biblical period are particularly uncertain (see the table of weights and measures following the text).

Like all translations of the Bible, made as they are by imperfect man, this one undoubtedly falls short of its goals. Yet we are grateful to God for the extent to which he has enabled us to realize these goals and for the strength he has given us and our colleagues to complete our task. We offer this version of the Bible to him in whose name for whose glory it has been made. We pray that it will lead many into a better understanding of the Holy Scriptures and a fuller knowledge of Jesus Christ the incarnate Word, of whom the Scriptures so faithfully testify.

The Committee on Bible Translation
June 1978
(Revised August 1983)

Names of the translators and editors may be secured from:

International Bible Society
1820 Jet Stream Drive
Colorado Springs, CO 80921-3696

The Old Testament

Genesis

The Beginning

1 In the beginning God created the heavens and the earth. 2Now the earth was[a]
formless and empty, darkness was over the
surface of the deep, and the Spirit of God
was hovering over the waters.

3And God said, "Let there be light," and there
was light. 4God saw that the light was
good, and he separated the light from the
darkness. 5God called the light "day," and
the darkness he called "night." And there
was evening, and there was morning—the
first day.
6And God said, "Let there be an expanse between the waters to separate water from
water." 7So God made the expanse and
separated the water under the expanse from
the water above it. And it was so. 8God
called the expanse "sky." And there was
evening, and there was morning—the second day.
9And God said, "Let the water under the
sky be gathered to one place, and let dry
ground appear." And it was so. 10God
called the dry ground "land," and the gathered waters he called "seas." And God saw
that it was good.
11Then God said, "Let the land produce
vegetation: seed-bearing plants and trees
on the land that bear fruit with seed in it,
according to their various kinds." And it
was so. 12The land produced vegetation:
plants bearing seed according to their kinds
and trees bearing fruit with seed in it according to their kinds. And God saw that it
was good. 13And there was evening, and
there was morning—the third day.
14And God said, "Let there be lights in the
expanse of the sky to separate the day from
the night, and let them serve as signs to
mark seasons and days and years, 15and let
them be lights in the expanse of the sky to
give light on the earth." And it was so.
16God made two great lights—the greater
light to govern the day and the lesser light
to govern the night. He also made the stars.
17God set them in the expanse of the sky to
give light on the earth, 18to govern the day
and the night, and to separate light from
darkness. And God saw that it was good.
19And there was evening, and there was
morning—the fourth day.
20And God said, "Let the water teem with living creatures, and let birds fly above the
earth across the expanse of the sky." 21So
God created the great creatures of the sea
and every living and moving thing with
which the water teems, according to their
kinds, and every winged bird according to
its kind. And God saw that it was good.
22God blessed them and said, "Be fruitful
and increase in number and fill the water in
the seas, and let the birds increase on the
earth." 23And there was evening, and there
was morning—the fifth day.
24And God said, "Let the land produce living
creatures according to their kinds: livestock, creatures that move along the
ground, and wild animals, each according
to its kind." And it was so. 25God made the
wild animals according to their kinds, the
livestock according to their kinds, and all
the creatures that move along the ground
according to their kinds. And God saw that
it was good.
26Then God said, "Let us make man in
our image, in our likeness, and let them
rule over the fish of the sea and the birds
of the air, over the livestock, over all the
earth,[b] and over all the creatures that move
along the ground."

27So God created man in his own image,
in the image of God he created him;
male and female he created them.

28God blessed them and said to them,
"Be fruitful and increase in number; fill the
earth and subdue it. Rule over the fish of
the sea and the birds of the air and over
every living creature that moves on the
ground."
29Then God said, "I give you every
seed-bearing plant on the face of the whole
earth and every tree that has fruit with seed
in it. They will be yours for food. 30And to
all the beasts of the earth and all the birds
of the air and all the creatures that move on
the ground—everything that has the breath
of life in it—I give every green plant for
food." And it was so.
31God saw all that he had made, and it
was very good. And there was evening, and
there was morning—the sixth day.

2 Thus the heavens and the earth were
completed in all their vast array.

2By the seventh day God had finished the
work he had been doing; so on the seventh
day he rested[c] from all his work. 3And
God blessed the seventh day and made it
holy, because on it he rested from all the
work of creating that he had done.

Adam and Eve

4This is the account of the heavens and the
earth when they were created.

When the LORD God made the earth and the
heavens— 5and no shrub of the field had yet

[a]2 Or possibly *became* [b]26 Hebrew; Syriac *all the wild animals* [c]2 Or *ceased*; also in verse 3

appeared on the earth[a] and no plant of the field
had yet sprung up, for the LORD God had not
sent rain on the earth[a] and there was no man
to work the ground, 6but streams[b] came up
from the earth and watered the whole surface
of the ground— 7the LORD God formed the
man[c] from the dust of the ground and breathed
into his nostrils the breath of life, and the man
became a living being.

8Now the LORD God had planted a garden in
the east, in Eden; and there he put the man he
had formed. 9And the LORD God made all
kinds of trees grow out of the ground—trees
that were pleasing to the eye and good for
food. In the middle of the garden were the tree
of life and the tree of the knowledge of good
and evil.

10A river watering the garden flowed from
Eden; from there it was separated into four
headwaters. 11The name of the first is the Pi-
shon; it winds through the entire land of Havilah, where there is gold. 12(The gold of that
land is good; aromatic resin[d] and onyx are also
there.) 13The name of the second river is the
Gihon; it winds through the entire land of
Cush.[e] 14The name of the third river is the
Tigris; it runs along the east side of Asshur.
And the fourth river is the Euphrates.

15The LORD God took the man and put him
in the Garden of Eden to work it and take care
of it. 16And the LORD God commanded the
man, "You are free to eat from any tree in the
garden; 17but you must not eat from the tree of
the knowledge of good and evil, for when you
eat of it you will surely die."

18The LORD God said, "It is not good for the
man to be alone. I will make a helper suitable
for him."

19Now the LORD God had formed out of the
ground all the beasts of the field and all the
birds of the air. He brought them to the man to
see what he would name them; and whatever
the man called each living creature, that was its
name. 20So the man gave names to all the livestock, the birds of the air and all the beasts of
the field.

But for Adam[f] no suitable helper was
found. 21So the LORD God caused the man to
fall into a deep sleep; and while he was sleeping, he took one of the man's ribs[g] and closed
up the place with flesh. 22Then the LORD God
made a woman from the rib[h] he had taken out
of the man, and he brought her to the man.

23The man said,

"This is now bone of my bones
  and flesh of my flesh;
she shall be called 'woman,[i]'
  for she was taken out of man."

24For this reason a man will leave his father
and mother and be united to his wife, and they
will become one flesh.

25The man and his wife were both naked,
and they felt no shame.

The Fall of Man

3 Now the serpent was more crafty than any
of the wild animals the LORD God had
made. He said to the woman, "Did God really
say, 'You must not eat from any tree in the
garden'?"

2The woman said to the serpent, "We may
eat fruit from the trees in the garden, 3but God
did say, 'You must not eat fruit from the tree
that is in the middle of the garden, and you
must not touch it, or you will die.' "

4"You will not surely die," the serpent said
to the woman. 5"For God knows that when you
eat of it your eyes will be opened, and you will
be like God, knowing good and evil."

6When the woman saw that the fruit of the
tree was good for food and pleasing to the eye,
and also desirable for gaining wisdom, she
took some and ate it. She also gave some to her
husband, who was with her, and he ate it.
7Then the eyes of both of them were opened,
and they realized they were naked; so they
sewed fig leaves together and made coverings
for themselves.

8Then the man and his wife heard the sound
of the LORD God as he was walking in the
garden in the cool of the day, and they hid
from the LORD God among the trees of the
garden. 9But the LORD God called to the man,
"Where are you?"

10He answered, "I heard you in the garden,
and I was afraid because I was naked; so I
hid."

11And he said, "Who told you that you were
naked? Have you eaten from the tree that I
commanded you not to eat from?"

12The man said, "The woman you put here
with me—she gave me some fruit from the
tree, and I ate it."

13Then the LORD God said to the woman,
"What is this you have done?"

The woman said, "The serpent deceived me,
and I ate."

14So the LORD God said to the serpent, "Because you have done this,

"Cursed are you above all the livestock
  and all the wild animals!
You will crawl on your belly
  and you will eat dust
  all the days of your life.
15And I will put enmity
  between you and the woman,
  and between your offspring[j] and hers;
he will crush[k] your head,
  and you will strike his heel."

16To the woman he said,

"I will greatly increase your pains in
    childbearing;

[a]5 Or *land*; also in verse 6 [b]6 Or *mist* [c]7 The Hebrew for *man (adam)* sounds like and may be related to the Hebrew for *ground (adamah)*; it is also the name *Adam* (see Gen. 2:20). [d]12 Or *good; pearls* [e]13 Possibly southeast Mesopotamia [f]20 Or *the man* [g]21 Or *took part of the man's side* [h]22 Or *part* [i]23 The Hebrew for *woman* sounds like the Hebrew for *man.* [j]15 Or *seed* [k]15 Or *strike*

with pain you will give birth to
children.
Your desire will be for your husband,
and he will rule over you."

17To Adam he said, "Because you listened
to your wife and ate from the tree about which
I commanded you, 'You must not eat of it,'

"Cursed is the ground because of you;
through painful toil you will eat of it
all the days of your life.
18It will produce thorns and thistles for you,
and you will eat the plants of the field.
19By the sweat of your brow
you will eat your food
until you return to the ground,
since from it you were taken;
for dust you are
and to dust you will return."

20Adam[a] named his wife Eve,[b] because she
would become the mother of all the living.
21The LORD God made garments of skin for
Adam and his wife and clothed them. 22And
the LORD God said, "The man has now become
like one of us, knowing good and evil. He must
not be allowed to reach out his hand and take
also from the tree of life and eat, and live forever." 23So the LORD God banished him from
the Garden of Eden to work the ground from
which he had been taken. 24After he drove the
man out, he placed on the east side[c] of the
Garden of Eden cherubim and a flaming sword
flashing back and forth to guard the way to the
tree of life.

Cain and Abel

4 Adam[a] lay with his wife Eve, and she became pregnant and gave birth to Cain.[d]
She said, "With the help of the LORD I have
brought forth[e] a man." 2Later she gave birth to
his brother Abel.
Now Abel kept flocks, and Cain worked the
soil. 3In the course of time Cain brought some
of the fruits of the soil as an offering to the
LORD. 4But Abel brought fat portions from
some of the firstborn of his flock. The LORD
looked with favor on Abel and his offering,
5but on Cain and his offering he did not look
with favor. So Cain was very angry, and his
face was downcast.
6Then the LORD said to Cain, "Why are you
angry? Why is your face downcast? 7If you do
what is right, will you not be accepted? But if
you do not do what is right, sin is crouching at
your door; it desires to have you, but you must
master it."
8Now Cain said to his brother Abel, "Let's
go out to the field."[f] And while they were in
the field, Cain attacked his brother Abel and
killed him.
9Then the LORD said to Cain, "Where is
your brother Abel?"
"I don't know," he replied. "Am I my brother's keeper?"
10The LORD said, "What have you done?
Listen! Your brother's blood cries out to me
from the ground. 11Now you are under a curse
and driven from the ground, which opened its
mouth to receive your brother's blood from
your hand. 12When you work the ground, it
will no longer yield its crops for you. You will
be a restless wanderer on the earth."
13Cain said to the LORD, "My punishment is
more than I can bear. 14Today you are driving
me from the land, and I will be hidden from
your presence; I will be a restless wanderer on
the earth, and whoever finds me will kill me."
15But the LORD said to him, "Not so[g]; if
anyone kills Cain, he will suffer vengeance
seven times over." Then the LORD put a mark
on Cain so that no one who found him would
kill him. 16So Cain went out from the LORD's
presence and lived in the land of Nod,[h] east of
Eden.
17Cain lay with his wife, and she became
pregnant and gave birth to Enoch. Cain was
then building a city, and he named it after his
son Enoch. 18To Enoch was born Irad, and Irad
was the father of Mehujael, and Mehujael was
the father of Methushael, and Methushael was
the father of Lamech.
19Lamech married two women, one named
Adah and the other Zillah. 20Adah gave birth
to Jabal; he was the father of those who live in
tents and raise livestock. 21His brother's name
was Jubal; he was the father of all who play the
harp and flute. 22Zillah also had a son, Tubal-
Cain, who forged all kinds of tools out of[i]
bronze and iron. Tubal-Cain's sister was Naamah.
23Lamech said to his wives,

"Adah and Zillah, listen to me;
wives of Lamech, hear my words.
I have killed[j] a man for wounding me,
a young man for injuring me.
24If Cain is avenged seven times,
then Lamech seventy-seven times."

25Adam lay with his wife again, and she
gave birth to a son and named him Seth,[k] saying, "God has granted me another child in
place of Abel, since Cain killed him." 26Seth
also had a son, and he named him Enosh.
At that time men began to call on[l] the name
of the LORD.

From Adam to Noah

5 This is the written account of Adam's line.

When God created man, he made him in the
likeness of God. 2He created them male and

[a]*20,1* Or *The man* [b]*20* *Eve* probably means *living.* [c]*24* Or *placed in front* [d]*1* *Cain* sounds like the Hebrew for *brought forth* or *acquired.* [e]*1* Or *have acquired* [f]*8* Samaritan Pentateuch, Septuagint, Vulgate and Syriac; Masoretic Text does not have *"Let's go out to the field."* [g]*15* Septuagint, Vulgate and Syriac; Hebrew *Very well* [h]*16* *Nod* means *wandering* (see verses 12 and 14). [i]*22* Or *who instructed all who work in* [j]*23* Or *I will kill* [k]*25* *Seth* probably means *granted.* [l]*26* Or *to proclaim*

female and blessed them. And when they were created, he called them "man.[a]"

3When Adam had lived 130 years, he had a son in his own likeness, in his own image; and he named him Seth. 4After Seth was born, Adam lived 800 years and had other sons and daughters. 5Altogether, Adam lived 930 years, and then he died.

6When Seth had lived 105 years, he became the father[b] of Enosh. 7And after he became the father of Enosh, Seth lived 807 years and had other sons and daughters. 8Altogether, Seth lived 912 years, and then he died.

9When Enosh had lived 90 years, he became the father of Kenan. 10And after he became the father of Kenan, Enosh lived 815 years and had other sons and daughters. 11Altogether, Enosh lived 905 years, and then he died.

12When Kenan had lived 70 years, he became the father of Mahalalel. 13And after he became the father of Mahalalel, Kenan lived 840 years and had other sons and daughters. 14Altogether, Kenan lived 910 years, and then he died.

15When Mahalalel had lived 65 years, he became the father of Jared. 16And after he became the father of Jared, Mahalalel lived 830 years and had other sons and daughters. 17Altogether, Mahalalel lived 895 years, and then he died.

18When Jared had lived 162 years, he became the father of Enoch. 19And after he became the father of Enoch, Jared lived 800 years and had other sons and daughters. 20Altogether, Jared lived 962 years, and then he died.

21When Enoch had lived 65 years, he became the father of Methuselah. 22And after he became the father of Methuselah, Enoch walked with God 300 years and had other sons and daughters. 23Altogether, Enoch lived 365 years. 24Enoch walked with God; then he was no more, because God took him away.

25When Methuselah had lived 187 years, he became the father of Lamech. 26And after he became the father of Lamech, Methuselah lived 782 years and had other sons and daughters. 27Altogether, Methuselah lived 969 years, and then he died.

28When Lamech had lived 182 years, he had a son. 29He named him Noah[c] and said, "He will comfort us in the labor and painful toil of our hands caused by the ground the LORD has cursed." 30After Noah was born, Lamech lived 595 years and had other sons and daughters. 31Altogether, Lamech lived 777 years, and then he died.

32After Noah was 500 years old, he became the father of Shem, Ham and Japheth.

The Flood

6 When men began to increase in number on the earth and daughters were born to them, 2the sons of God saw that the daughters of men were beautiful, and they married any of them they chose. 3Then the LORD said, "My Spirit will not contend with[d] man forever, for he is mortal[e]; his days will be a hundred and twenty years."

4The Nephilim were on the earth in those days—and also afterward—when the sons of God went to the daughters of men and had children by them. They were the heroes of old, men of renown.

5The LORD saw how great man's wickedness on the earth had become, and that every inclination of the thoughts of his heart was only evil all the time. 6The LORD was grieved that he had made man on the earth, and his heart was filled with pain. 7So the LORD said, "I will wipe mankind, whom I have created, from the face of the earth—men and animals, and creatures that move along the ground, and birds of the air—for I am grieved that I have made them." 8But Noah found favor in the eyes of the LORD.

9This is the account of Noah.

Noah was a righteous man, blameless among the people of his time, and he walked with God. 10Noah had three sons: Shem, Ham and Japheth.

11Now the earth was corrupt in God's sight and was full of violence. 12God saw how corrupt the earth had become, for all the people on earth had corrupted their ways. 13So God said to Noah, "I am going to put an end to all people, for the earth is filled with violence because of them. I am surely going to destroy both them and the earth. 14So make yourself an ark of cypress[f] wood; make rooms in it and coat it with pitch inside and out. 15This is how you are to build it: The ark is to be 450 feet long, 75 feet wide and 45 feet high.[g] 16Make a roof for it and finish[h] the ark to within 18 inches[i] of the top. Put a door in the side of the ark and make lower, middle and upper decks. 17I am going to bring floodwaters on the earth to destroy all life under the heavens, every creature that has the breath of life in it. Everything on earth will perish. 18But I will establish my covenant with you, and you will enter the ark—you and your sons and your wife and your sons' wives with you. 19You are to bring into the ark two of all living creatures, male and female, to keep them alive with you. 20Two of every kind of bird, of every kind of animal and of every kind of creature that moves along the ground will come to you to be kept alive. 21You are to take every kind of food that is to

[a]2 Hebrew *adam* [b]6 *Father* may mean *ancestor*; also in verses 7-26. [c]29 *Noah* sounds like the Hebrew for *comfort.* [d]3 Or *My spirit will not remain in* [e]3 Or *corrupt* [f]14 The meaning of the Hebrew for this word is uncertain. [g]15 Hebrew *300 cubits long, 50 cubits wide and 30 cubits high* (about 140 meters long, 23 meters wide and 13.5 meters high) [h]16 Or *Make an opening for light by finishing* [i]16 Hebrew *a cubit* (about 0.5 meter)

be eaten and store it away as food for you and for them."

22Noah did everything just as God commanded him.

7 The LORD then said to Noah, "Go into the ark, you and your whole family, because I have found you righteous in this generation. 2Take with you seven[a] of every kind of clean animal, a male and its mate, and two of every kind of unclean animal, a male and its mate, 3and also seven of every kind of bird, male and female, to keep their various kinds alive throughout the earth. 4Seven days from now I will send rain on the earth for forty days and forty nights, and I will wipe from the face of the earth every living creature I have made."

5And Noah did all that the LORD commanded him.

6Noah was six hundred years old when the floodwaters came on the earth. 7And Noah and his sons and his wife and his sons' wives entered the ark to escape the waters of the flood. 8Pairs of clean and unclean animals, of birds and of all creatures that move along the ground, 9male and female, came to Noah and entered the ark, as God had commanded Noah. 10And after the seven days the floodwaters came on the earth.

11In the six hundredth year of Noah's life, on the seventeenth day of the second month—on that day all the springs of the great deep burst forth, and the floodgates of the heavens were opened. 12And rain fell on the earth forty days and forty nights.

13On that very day Noah and his sons, Shem, Ham and Japheth, together with his wife and the wives of his three sons, entered the ark. 14They had with them every wild animal according to its kind, all livestock according to their kinds, every creature that moves along the ground according to its kind and every bird according to its kind, everything with wings. 15Pairs of all creatures that have the breath of life in them came to Noah and entered the ark. 16The animals going in were male and female of every living thing, as God had commanded Noah. Then the LORD shut him in.

17For forty days the flood kept coming on the earth, and as the waters increased they lifted the ark high above the earth. 18The waters rose and increased greatly on the earth, and the ark floated on the surface of the water. 19They rose greatly on the earth, and all the high mountains under the entire heavens were covered. 20The waters rose and covered the mountains to a depth of more than twenty feet.[b,c] 21Every living thing that moved on the earth perished—birds, livestock, wild animals, all the creatures that swarm over the earth, and all mankind. 22Everything on dry land that had the breath of life in its nostrils died. 23Every living thing on the face of the earth was wiped out; men and animals and the creatures that move along the ground and the birds of the air were wiped from the earth. Only Noah was left, and those with him in the ark.

24The waters flooded the earth for a hundred and fifty days.

8 But God remembered Noah and all the wild animals and the livestock that were with him in the ark, and he sent a wind over the earth, and the waters receded. 2Now the springs of the deep and the floodgates of the heavens had been closed, and the rain had stopped falling from the sky. 3The water receded steadily from the earth. At the end of the hundred and fifty days the water had gone down, 4and on the seventeenth day of the seventh month the ark came to rest on the mountains of Ararat. 5The waters continued to recede until the tenth month, and on the first day of the tenth month the tops of the mountains became visible.

6After forty days Noah opened the window he had made in the ark 7and sent out a raven, and it kept flying back and forth until the water had dried up from the earth. 8Then he sent out a dove to see if the water had receded from the surface of the ground. 9But the dove could find no place to set its feet because there was water over all the surface of the earth; so it returned to Noah in the ark. He reached out his hand and took the dove and brought it back to himself in the ark. 10He waited seven more days and again sent out the dove from the ark. 11When the dove returned to him in the evening, there in its beak was a freshly plucked olive leaf! Then Noah knew that the water had receded from the earth. 12He waited seven more days and sent the dove out again, but this time it did not return to him.

13By the first day of the first month of Noah's six hundred and first year, the water had dried up from the earth. Noah then removed the covering from the ark and saw that the surface of the ground was dry. 14By the twenty-seventh day of the second month the earth was completely dry.

15Then God said to Noah, 16"Come out of the ark, you and your wife and your sons and their wives. 17Bring out every kind of living creature that is with you—the birds, the animals, and all the creatures that move along the ground—so they can multiply on the earth and be fruitful and increase in number upon it."

18So Noah came out, together with his sons and his wife and his sons' wives. 19All the animals and all the creatures that move along the ground and all the birds—everything that moves on the earth—came out of the ark, one kind after another.

20Then Noah built an altar to the LORD and, taking some of all the clean animals and clean birds, he sacrificed burnt offerings on it. 21The LORD smelled the pleasing aroma and said in his heart: "Never again will I curse the ground because of man, even though[d] every inclina-

[a]2 Or *seven pairs*; also in verse 3 [b]20 Hebrew *fifteen cubits* (about 6.9 meters) [c]20 Or *rose more than twenty feet, and the mountains were covered* [d]21 Or *man, for*

tion of his heart is evil from childhood. And never again will I destroy all living creatures, as I have done.

22"As long as the earth endures,
seedtime and harvest,
cold and heat,
summer and winter,
day and night
will never cease."

God's Covenant With Noah

9 Then God blessed Noah and his sons, saying to them, "Be fruitful and increase in number and fill the earth. 2The fear and dread of you will fall upon all the beasts of the earth and all the birds of the air, upon every creature that moves along the ground, and upon all the fish of the sea; they are given into your hands. 3Everything that lives and moves will be food for you. Just as I gave you the green plants, I now give you everything.

4"But you must not eat meat that has its lifeblood still in it. 5And for your lifeblood I will surely demand an accounting. I will demand an accounting from every animal. And from each man, too, I will demand an accounting for the life of his fellow man.

6"Whoever sheds the blood of man,
by man shall his blood be shed;
for in the image of God
has God made man.

7As for you, be fruitful and increase in number; multiply on the earth and increase upon it."

8Then God said to Noah and to his sons with him: 9"I now establish my covenant with you and with your descendants after you 10and with every living creature that was with you—the birds, the livestock and all the wild animals, all those that came out of the ark with you—every living creature on earth. 11I establish my covenant with you: Never again will all life be cut off by the waters of a flood; never again will there be a flood to destroy the earth."

12And God said, "This is the sign of the covenant I am making between me and you and every living creature with you, a covenant for all generations to come: 13I have set my rainbow in the clouds, and it will be the sign of the covenant between me and the earth. 14Whenever I bring clouds over the earth and the rainbow appears in the clouds, 15I will remember my covenant between me and you and all living creatures of every kind. Never again will the waters become a flood to destroy all life. 16Whenever the rainbow appears in the clouds, I will see it and remember the everlasting covenant between God and all living creatures of every kind on the earth."

17So God said to Noah, "This is the sign of the covenant I have established between me and all life on the earth."

The Sons of Noah

18The sons of Noah who came out of the ark were Shem, Ham and Japheth. (Ham was the father of Canaan.) 19These were the three sons of Noah, and from them came the people who were scattered over the earth.

20Noah, a man of the soil, proceeded[a] to plant a vineyard. 21When he drank some of its wine, he became drunk and lay uncovered inside his tent. 22Ham, the father of Canaan, saw his father's nakedness and told his two brothers outside. 23But Shem and Japheth took a garment and laid it across their shoulders; then they walked in backward and covered their father's nakedness. Their faces were turned the other way so that they would not see their father's nakedness.

24When Noah awoke from his wine and found out what his youngest son had done to him, 25he said,

"Cursed be Canaan!
The lowest of slaves
will he be to his brothers."

26He also said,

"Blessed be the LORD, the God of Shem!
May Canaan be the slave of Shem.[b]
27May God extend the territory of Japheth[c];
may Japheth live in the tents of Shem,
and may Canaan be his[d] slave."

28After the flood Noah lived 350 years. 29Altogether, Noah lived 950 years, and then he died.

The Table of Nations

10 This is the account of Shem, Ham and Japheth, Noah's sons, who themselves had sons after the flood.

The Japhethites

2The sons[e] of Japheth:
Gomer, Magog, Madai, Javan, Tubal, Meshech and Tiras.
3The sons of Gomer:
Ashkenaz, Riphath and Togarmah.
4The sons of Javan:
Elishah, Tarshish, the Kittim and the Rodanim.[f] 5(From these the maritime peoples spread out into their territories by their clans within their nations, each with its own language.)

The Hamites

6The sons of Ham:
Cush, Mizraim,[g] Put and Canaan.
7The sons of Cush:
Seba, Havilah, Sabtah, Raamah and Sabteca.
The sons of Raamah:

[a]20 Or *soil, was the first* [b]26 Or *be his slave* [c]27 *Japheth* sounds like the Hebrew for *extend.* [d]27 Or *their* [e]2 *Sons* may mean *descendants* or *successors* or *nations*; also in verses 3, 4, 6, 7, 20-23, 29 and 31. [f]4 Some manuscripts of the Masoretic Text and Samaritan Pentateuch (see also Septuagint and 1 Chron. 1:7); most manuscripts of the Masoretic Text *Dodanim* [g]6 That is, Egypt; also in verse 13

Sheba and Dedan.

8Cush was the father[a] of Nimrod, who grew to be a mighty warrior on the earth. 9He was a mighty hunter before the LORD; that is why it is said, "Like Nimrod, a mighty hunter before the LORD." 10The first centers of his kingdom were Babylon, Erech, Akkad and Calneh, in[b] Shinar.[c] 11From that land he went to Assyria, where he built Nineveh, Rehoboth Ir,[d] Calah 12and Resen, which is between Nineveh and Calah; that is the great city.

13Mizraim was the father of
the Ludites, Anamites, Lehabites, Naphtuhites, 14Pathrusites, Casluhites (from whom the Philistines came) and Caphtorites.
15Canaan was the father of
Sidon his firstborn,[e] and of the Hittites, 16Jebusites, Amorites, Girgashites, 17Hivites, Arkites, Sinites, 18Arvadites, Zemarites and Hamathites.

Later the Canaanite clans scattered 19and the borders of Canaan reached from Sidon toward Gerar as far as Gaza, and then toward Sodom, Gomorrah, Admah and Zeboiim, as far as Lasha.

20These are the sons of Ham by their clans and languages, in their territories and nations.

The Semites

21Sons were also born to Shem, whose older brother was[f] Japheth; Shem was the ancestor of all the sons of Eber.

22The sons of Shem:
Elam, Asshur, Arphaxad, Lud and Aram.
23The sons of Aram:
Uz, Hul, Gether and Meshech.[g]
24Arphaxad was the father of[h] Shelah,
and Shelah the father of Eber.
25Two sons were born to Eber:
One was named Peleg,[i] because in his time the earth was divided; his brother was named Joktan.
26Joktan was the father of
Almodad, Sheleph, Hazarmaveth, Jerah, 27Hadoram, Uzal, Diklah, 28Obal, Abimael, Sheba, 29Ophir, Havilah and Jobab. All these were sons of Joktan.

30The region where they lived stretched from Mesha toward Sephar, in the eastern hill country.

31These are the sons of Shem by their clans and languages, in their territories and nations.

32These are the clans of Noah's sons, according to their lines of descent, within their nations. From these the nations spread out over the earth after the flood.

The Tower of Babel

11 Now the whole world had one language and a common speech. 2As men moved eastward,[j] they found a plain in Shinar[c] and settled there.

3They said to each other, "Come, let's make bricks and bake them thoroughly." They used brick instead of stone, and tar for mortar. 4Then they said, "Come, let us build ourselves a city, with a tower that reaches to the heavens, so that we may make a name for ourselves and not be scattered over the face of the whole earth."

5But the LORD came down to see the city and the tower that the men were building. 6The LORD said, "If as one people speaking the same language they have begun to do this, then nothing they plan to do will be impossible for them. 7Come, let us go down and confuse their language so they will not understand each other."

8So the LORD scattered them from there over all the earth, and they stopped building the city. 9That is why it was called Babel[k]—because there the LORD confused the language of the whole world. From there the LORD scattered them over the face of the whole earth.

From Shem to Abram

10This is the account of Shem.

Two years after the flood, when Shem was 100 years old, he became the father[l] of Arphaxad. 11And after he became the father of Arphaxad, Shem lived 500 years and had other sons and daughters.

12When Arphaxad had lived 35 years, he became the father of Shelah. 13And after he became the father of Shelah, Arphaxad lived 403 years and had other sons and daughters.[m]

14When Shelah had lived 30 years, he became the father of Eber. 15And after he became the father of Eber, Shelah lived 403 years and had other sons and daughters.

16When Eber had lived 34 years, he became the father of Peleg. 17And after he became the father of Peleg, Eber lived 430 years and had other sons and daughters.

18When Peleg had lived 30 years, he became the father of Reu. 19And after he became the father of Reu, Peleg lived 209 years and had other sons and daughters.

20When Reu had lived 32 years, he became

[a]8 *Father* may mean *ancestor* or *predecessor* or *founder*; also in verses 13, 15, 24 and 26. [b]10 Or *Erech and Akkad—all of them in* [c]10,2 That is, Babylonia [d]11 Or *Nineveh with its city squares* [e]15 Or *of the Sidonians, the foremost* [f]21 Or *Shem, the older brother of* [g]23 See Septuagint and 1 Chron. 1:17; Hebrew *Mash* [h]24 Hebrew; Septuagint *father of Cainan, and Cainan was the father of* [i]25 *Peleg* means *division.* [j]2 Or *from the east*; or *in the east* [k]9 That is, Babylon; *Babel* sounds like the Hebrew for *confused.* [l]10 *Father* may mean *ancestor*; also in verses 11-25. [m]12,13 Hebrew; Septuagint (see also Luke 3:35, 36 and note at Gen. 10:24) *35 years, he became the father of Cainan. 13And after he became the father of Cainan, Arphaxad lived 430 years and had other sons and daughters, and then he died. When Cainan had lived 130 years, he became the father of Shelah. And after he became the father of Shelah, Cainan lived 330 years and had other sons and daughters*

the father of Serug. 21And after he became the
father of Serug, Reu lived 207 years and had
other sons and daughters.
22When Serug had lived 30 years, he became the father of Nahor. 23And after he became the father of Nahor, Serug lived 200
years and had other sons and daughters.
24When Nahor had lived 29 years, he became the father of Terah. 25And after he became the father of Terah, Nahor lived 119
years and had other sons and daughters.
26After Terah had lived 70 years, he became
the father of Abram, Nahor and Haran.

27This is the account of Terah.

Terah became the father of Abram, Nahor
and Haran. And Haran became the father of
Lot. 28While his father Terah was still alive,
Haran died in Ur of the Chaldeans, in the land
of his birth. 29Abram and Nahor both married.
The name of Abram's wife was Sarai, and the
name of Nahor's wife was Milcah; she was the
daughter of Haran, the father of both Milcah
and Iscah. 30Now Sarai was barren; she had no
children.
31Terah took his son Abram, his grandson
Lot son of Haran, and his daughter-in-law Sarai, the wife of his son Abram, and together
they set out from Ur of the Chaldeans to go to
Canaan. But when they came to Haran, they
settled there.
32Terah lived 205 years, and he died in Haran.

The Call of Abram

12 The LORD had said to Abram, "Leave
your country, your people and your father's household and go to the land I will show
you.

2"I will make you into a great nation
and I will bless you;
I will make your name great,
and you will be a blessing.
3I will bless those who bless you,
and whoever curses you I will curse;
and all peoples on earth
will be blessed through you."

4So Abram left, as the LORD had told him;
and Lot went with him. Abram was seventy-
five years old when he set out from Haran. 5He
took his wife Sarai, his nephew Lot, all the
possessions they had accumulated and the people they had acquired in Haran, and they set
out for the land of Canaan, and they arrived
there.
6Abram traveled through the land as far as
the site of the great tree of Moreh at Shechem.
At that time the Canaanites were in the land.
7The LORD appeared to Abram and said, "To
your offspring[a] I will give this land." So he
built an altar there to the LORD, who had appeared to him.
8From there he went on toward the hills east
of Bethel and pitched his tent, with Bethel on
the west and Ai on the east. There he built an
altar to the LORD and called on the name of the
LORD. 9Then Abram set out and continued toward the Negev.

Abram in Egypt

10Now there was a famine in the land, and
Abram went down to Egypt to live there for a
while because the famine was severe. 11As he
was about to enter Egypt, he said to his wife
Sarai, "I know what a beautiful woman you
are. 12When the Egyptians see you, they will
say, 'This is his wife.' Then they will kill me
but will let you live. 13Say you are my sister,
so that I will be treated well for your sake and
my life will be spared because of you."
14When Abram came to Egypt, the Egyptians saw that she was a very beautiful woman.
15And when Pharaoh's officials saw her, they
praised her to Pharaoh, and she was taken into
his palace. 16He treated Abram well for her
sake, and Abram acquired sheep and cattle,
male and female donkeys, menservants and
maidservants, and camels.
17But the LORD inflicted serious diseases
on Pharaoh and his household because of
Abram's wife Sarai. 18So Pharaoh summoned
Abram. "What have you done to me?" he said.
"Why didn't you tell me she was your wife?
19Why did you say, 'She is my sister,' so that
I took her to be my wife? Now then, here is
your wife. Take her and go!" 20Then Pharaoh
gave orders about Abram to his men, and they
sent him on his way, with his wife and everything he had.

Abram and Lot Separate

13 So Abram went up from Egypt to the
Negev, with his wife and everything he
had, and Lot went with him. 2Abram had become very wealthy in livestock and in silver
and gold.
3From the Negev he went from place to
place until he came to Bethel, to the place between Bethel and Ai where his tent had been
earlier 4and where he had first built an altar.
There Abram called on the name of the LORD.
5Now Lot, who was moving about with
Abram, also had flocks and herds and tents.
6But the land could not support them while
they stayed together, for their possessions were
so great that they were not able to stay together. 7And quarreling arose between Abram's
herdsmen and the herdsmen of Lot. The Canaanites and Perizzites were also living in the
land at that time.
8So Abram said to Lot, "Let's not have any
quarreling between you and me, or between
your herdsmen and mine, for we are brothers.
9Is not the whole land before you? Let's part
company. If you go to the left, I'll go to the
right; if you go to the right, I'll go to the left."
10Lot looked up and saw that the whole
plain of the Jordan was well watered, like the
garden of the LORD, like the land of Egypt,

[a]7 Or *seed*

toward Zoar. (This was before the LORD destroyed Sodom and Gomorrah.) 11So Lot chose
for himself the whole plain of the Jordan and
set out toward the east. The two men parted
company: 12Abram lived in the land of Canaan, while Lot lived among the cities of the
plain and pitched his tents near Sodom. 13Now
the men of Sodom were wicked and were sinning greatly against the LORD.

14The LORD said to Abram after Lot had
parted from him, "Lift up your eyes from
where you are and look north and south, east
and west. 15All the land that you see I will give
to you and your offspring[a] forever. 16I will
make your offspring like the dust of the earth,
so that if anyone could count the dust, then
your offspring could be counted. 17Go, walk
through the length and breadth of the land, for
I am giving it to you."

18So Abram moved his tents and went to
live near the great trees of Mamre at Hebron,
where he built an altar to the LORD.

Abram Rescues Lot

14 At this time Amraphel king of Shinar,[b]
Arioch king of Ellasar, Kedorlaomer
king of Elam and Tidal king of Goiim 2went to
war against Bera king of Sodom, Birsha king
of Gomorrah, Shinab king of Admah, Sheme-
ber king of Zeboiim, and the king of Bela (that
is, Zoar). 3All these latter kings joined forces
in the Valley of Siddim (the Salt Sea[c]). 4For
twelve years they had been subject to Kedorlaomer, but in the thirteenth year they rebelled.

5In the fourteenth year, Kedorlaomer and
the kings allied with him went out and defeated the Rephaites in Ashteroth Karnaim, the
Zuzites in Ham, the Emites in Shaveh Kiriathaim 6and the Horites in the hill country of
Seir, as far as El Paran near the desert. 7Then
they turned back and went to En Mishpat (that
is, Kadesh), and they conquered the whole territory of the Amalekites, as well as the Amorites who were living in Hazazon Tamar.

8Then the king of Sodom, the king of Gomorrah, the king of Admah, the king of Zeboiim and the king of Bela (that is, Zoar) marched
out and drew up their battle lines in the Valley
of Siddim 9against Kedorlaomer king of Elam,
Tidal king of Goiim, Amraphel king of Shinar
and Arioch king of Ellasar—four kings against
five. 10Now the Valley of Siddim was full of
tar pits, and when the kings of Sodom and
Gomorrah fled, some of the men fell into them
and the rest fled to the hills. 11The four kings
seized all the goods of Sodom and Gomorrah
and all their food; then they went away. 12They
also carried off Abram's nephew Lot and his
possessions, since he was living in Sodom.

13One who had escaped came and reported
this to Abram the Hebrew. Now Abram was
living near the great trees of Mamre the Amorite, a brother[d] of Eshcol and Aner, all of
whom were allied with Abram. 14When Abram
heard that his relative had been taken captive,
he called out the 318 trained men born in his
household and went in pursuit as far as Dan.
15During the night Abram divided his men to
attack them and he routed them, pursuing them
as far as Hobah, north of Damascus. 16He recovered all the goods and brought back his
relative Lot and his possessions, together with
the women and the other people.

17After Abram returned from defeating Kedorlaomer and the kings allied with him, the
king of Sodom came out to meet him in the
Valley of Shaveh (that is, the King's Valley).

18Then Melchizedek king of Salem[e]
brought out bread and wine. He was priest of
God Most High, 19and he blessed Abram, saying,

"Blessed be Abram by God Most High,
 Creator[f] of heaven and earth.
20And blessed be[g] God Most High,
 who delivered your enemies into your
  hand."

Then Abram gave him a tenth of everything.
21The king of Sodom said to Abram, "Give
me the people and keep the goods for yourself."

22But Abram said to the king of Sodom, "I
have raised my hand to the LORD, God Most
High, Creator of heaven and earth, and have
taken an oath 23that I will accept nothing belonging to you, not even a thread or the thong
of a sandal, so that you will never be able to
say, 'I made Abram rich.' 24I will accept nothing but what my men have eaten and the share
that belongs to the men who went with me—to
Aner, Eshcol and Mamre. Let them have their
share."

God's Covenant With Abram

15 After this, the word of the LORD came
to Abram in a vision:

"Do not be afraid, Abram.
 I am your shield,[h]
 your very great reward.[i]"

2But Abram said, "O Sovereign LORD, what
can you give me since I remain childless and
the one who will inherit[j] my estate is Eliezer
of Damascus?" 3And Abram said, "You have
given me no children; so a servant in my
household will be my heir."

4Then the word of the LORD came to him:
"This man will not be your heir, but a son
coming from your own body will be your
heir." 5He took him outside and said, "Look up
at the heavens and count the stars—if indeed
you can count them." Then he said to him, "So
shall your offspring be."

6Abram believed the LORD, and he credited
it to him as righteousness.

7He also said to him, "I am the LORD, who

[a]*15* Or *seed*; also in verse 16 [b]*1* That is, Babylonia; also in verse 9 [c]*3* That is, the Dead Sea
[d]*13* Or *a relative*; or *an ally* [e]*18* That is, Jerusalem [f]*19* Or *Possessor*; also in verse 22 [g]*20* Or *And praise be to* [h]*1* Or *sovereign* [i]*1* Or *shield; / your reward will be very great* [j]*2* The meaning of the Hebrew for this phrase is uncertain.

brought you out of Ur of the Chaldeans to give
you this land to take possession of it."
8But Abram said, "O Sovereign LORD, how
can I know that I will gain possession of it?"
9So the LORD said to him, "Bring me a heifer, a goat and a ram, each three years old,
along with a dove and a young pigeon."
10Abram brought all these to him, cut them
in two and arranged the halves opposite each
other; the birds, however, he did not cut in
half. 11Then birds of prey came down on the
carcasses, but Abram drove them away.
12As the sun was setting, Abram fell into a
deep sleep, and a thick and dreadful darkness
came over him. 13Then the LORD said to him,
"Know for certain that your descendants will
be strangers in a country not their own, and
they will be enslaved and mistreated four hundred years. 14But I will punish the nation they
serve as slaves, and afterward they will come
out with great possessions. 15You, however,
will go to your fathers in peace and be buried
at a good old age. 16In the fourth generation
your descendants will come back here, for the
sin of the Amorites has not yet reached its full
measure."
17When the sun had set and darkness had
fallen, a smoking firepot with a blazing torch
appeared and passed between the pieces. 18On
that day the LORD made a covenant with
Abram and said, "To your descendants I give
this land, from the river[a] of Egypt to the great
river, the Euphrates— 19the land of the Kenites, Kenizzites, Kadmonites, 20Hittites, Perizzites, Rephaites, 21Amorites, Canaanites,
Girgashites and Jebusites."

Hagar and Ishmael

16 Now Sarai, Abram's wife, had borne
him no children. But she had an Egyp-
tian maidservant named Hagar; 2so she said to
Abram, "The LORD has kept me from having
children. Go, sleep with my maidservant; perhaps I can build a family through her."
Abram agreed to what Sarai said. 3So after
Abram had been living in Canaan ten years,
Sarai his wife took her Egyptian maidservant
Hagar and gave her to her husband to be his
wife. 4He slept with Hagar, and she conceived.
When she knew she was pregnant, she began to despise her mistress. 5Then Sarai said to
Abram, "You are responsible for the wrong I
am suffering. I put my servant in your arms,
and now that she knows she is pregnant, she
despises me. May the LORD judge between you
and me."
6"Your servant is in your hands," Abram
said. "Do with her whatever you think best."
Then Sarai mistreated Hagar; so she fled from
her.
7The angel of the LORD found Hagar near a
spring in the desert; it was the spring that is
beside the road to Shur. 8And he said, "Hagar,
servant of Sarai, where have you come from,
and where are you going?"
"I'm running away from my mistress Sarai,"
she answered.
9Then the angel of the LORD told her, "Go
back to your mistress and submit to her."
10The angel added, "I will so increase your
descendants that they will be too numerous to
count."
11The angel of the LORD also said to her:

"You are now with child
  and you will have a son.
You shall name him Ishmael,[b]
  for the LORD has heard of your misery.
12He will be a wild donkey of a man;
  his hand will be against everyone
  and everyone's hand against him,
and he will live in hostility
  toward[c] all his brothers."

13She gave this name to the LORD who
spoke to her: "You are the God who sees me,"
for she said, "I have now seen[d] the One who
sees me." 14That is why the well was called
Beer Lahai Roi[e]; it is still there, between Kadesh and Bered.
15So Hagar bore Abram a son, and Abram
gave the name Ishmael to the son she had
borne. 16Abram was eighty-six years old when
Hagar bore him Ishmael.

The Covenant of Circumcision

17 When Abram was ninety-nine years
old, the LORD appeared to him and said,
"I am God Almighty[f]; walk before me and be
blameless. 2I will confirm my covenant between me and you and will greatly increase
your numbers."
3Abram fell facedown, and God said to him,
4"As for me, this is my covenant with you:
You will be the father of many nations. 5No
longer will you be called Abram[g]; your name
will be Abraham,[h] for I have made you a father of many nations. 6I will make you very
fruitful; I will make nations of you, and kings
will come from you. 7I will establish my covenant as an everlasting covenant between me
and you and your descendants after you for the
generations to come, to be your God and the
God of your descendants after you. 8The whole
land of Canaan, where you are now an alien, I
will give as an everlasting possession to you
and your descendants after you; and I will be
their God."
9Then God said to Abraham, "As for you,
you must keep my covenant, you and your
descendants after you for the generations to
come. 10This is my covenant with you and
your descendants after you, the covenant you
are to keep: Every male among you shall be
circumcised. 11You are to undergo circumcision, and it will be the sign of the covenant
between me and you. 12For the generations to

[a] 18 Or *Wadi* [b] 11 *Ishmael* means *God hears.* [c] 12 Or *live to the east of* [d] 13 Or *seen the back of* [e] 14 *Beer Lahai Roi* means *well of the Living One who sees me.* [f] 1 Hebrew *El-Shaddai* [g] 5 *Abram* means *exalted father.* [h] 5 *Abraham* means *father of many.*

come every male among you who is eight days
old must be circumcised, including those born
in your household or bought with money from
a foreigner—those who are not your offspring.
13 Whether born in your household or bought
with your money, they must be circumcised.
My covenant in your flesh is to be an everlasting covenant. 14 Any uncircumcised male, who
has not been circumcised in the flesh, will be
cut off from his people; he has broken my
covenant."

15 God also said to Abraham, "As for Sarai
your wife, you are no longer to call her Sarai;
her name will be Sarah. 16 I will bless her and
will surely give you a son by her. I will bless
her so that she will be the mother of nations;
kings of peoples will come from her."

17 Abraham fell facedown; he laughed and
said to himself, "Will a son be born to a man
a hundred years old? Will Sarah bear a child at
the age of ninety?" 18 And Abraham said to
God, "If only Ishmael might live under your
blessing!"

19 Then God said, "Yes, but your wife Sarah
will bear you a son, and you will call him
Isaac.[a] I will establish my covenant with him
as an everlasting covenant for his descendants
after him. 20 And as for Ishmael, I have heard
you: I will surely bless him; I will make him
fruitful and will greatly increase his numbers.
He will be the father of twelve rulers, and I
will make him into a great nation. 21 But my
covenant I will establish with Isaac, whom
Sarah will bear to you by this time next year."
22 When he had finished speaking with Abraham, God went up from him.

23 On that very day Abraham took his son
Ishmael and all those born in his household
or bought with his money, every male in his
household, and circumcised them, as God told
him. 24 Abraham was ninety-nine years old
when he was circumcised, 25 and his son Ishmael was thirteen; 26 Abraham and his son Ishmael were both circumcised on that same day.
27 And every male in Abraham's household, including those born in his household or bought
from a foreigner, was circumcised with him.

The Three Visitors

18 The LORD appeared to Abraham near
the great trees of Mamre while he was
sitting at the entrance to his tent in the heat of
the day. 2 Abraham looked up and saw three
men standing nearby. When he saw them, he
hurried from the entrance of his tent to meet
them and bowed low to the ground.

3 He said, "If I have found favor in your
eyes, my lord,[b] do not pass your servant by.
4 Let a little water be brought, and then you
may all wash your feet and rest under this tree.
5 Let me get you something to eat, so you can
be refreshed and then go on your way—now
that you have come to your servant."

"Very well," they answered, "do as you
say."

6 So Abraham hurried into the tent to Sarah.
"Quick," he said, "get three seahs[c] of fine
flour and knead it and bake some bread."

7 Then he ran to the herd and selected a
choice, tender calf and gave it to a servant,
who hurried to prepare it. 8 He then brought
some curds and milk and the calf that had been
prepared, and set these before them. While
they ate, he stood near them under a tree.

9 "Where is your wife Sarah?" they asked
him.

"There, in the tent," he said.

10 Then the LORD[d] said, "I will surely return
to you about this time next year, and Sarah
your wife will have a son."

Now Sarah was listening at the entrance to
the tent, which was behind him. 11 Abraham
and Sarah were already old and well advanced
in years, and Sarah was past the age of childbearing. 12 So Sarah laughed to herself as she
thought, "After I am worn out and my master[e]
is old, will I now have this pleasure?"

13 Then the LORD said to Abraham, "Why
did Sarah laugh and say, 'Will I really have a
child, now that I am old?' 14 Is anything too
hard for the LORD? I will return to you at the
appointed time next year and Sarah will have
a son."

15 Sarah was afraid, so she lied and said, "I
did not laugh."

But he said, "Yes, you did laugh."

Abraham Pleads for Sodom

16 When the men got up to leave, they looked
down toward Sodom, and Abraham walked
along with them to see them on their way.
17 Then the LORD said, "Shall I hide from
Abraham what I am about to do? 18 Abraham
will surely become a great and powerful nation, and all nations on earth will be blessed
through him. 19 For I have chosen him, so that
he will direct his children and his household
after him to keep the way of the LORD by
doing what is right and just, so that the LORD
will bring about for Abraham what he has
promised him."

20 Then the LORD said, "The outcry against
Sodom and Gomorrah is so great and their sin
so grievous 21 that I will go down and see if
what they have done is as bad as the outcry
that has reached me. If not, I will know."

22 The men turned away and went toward
Sodom, but Abraham remained standing before the LORD.[f] 23 Then Abraham approached
him and said: "Will you sweep away the righteous with the wicked? 24 What if there are fifty
righteous people in the city? Will you really
sweep it away and not spare[g] the place for the
sake of the fifty righteous people in it? 25 Far be
it from you to do such a thing—to kill the
righteous with the wicked, treating the righ-

[a] 19 *Isaac* means *he laughs.* [b] 3 Or *O Lord* [c] 6 That is, probably about 20 quarts (about 22 liters)
[d] 10 Hebrew *Then he* [e] 12 Or *husband* [f] 22 Masoretic Text; an ancient Hebrew scribal tradition *but the LORD remained standing before Abraham* [g] 24 Or *forgive*; also in verse 26

teous and the wicked alike. Far be it from you! Will not the Judge[a] of all the earth do right?"

26 The LORD said, "If I find fifty righteous people in the city of Sodom, I will spare the whole place for their sake."

27 Then Abraham spoke up again: "Now that I have been so bold as to speak to the Lord, though I am nothing but dust and ashes, 28 what if the number of the righteous is five less than fifty? Will you destroy the whole city because of five people?"

"If I find forty-five there," he said, "I will not destroy it."

29 Once again he spoke to him, "What if only forty are found there?"

He said, "For the sake of forty, I will not do it."

30 Then he said, "May the Lord not be angry, but let me speak. What if only thirty can be found there?"

He answered, "I will not do it if I find thirty there."

31 Abraham said, "Now that I have been so bold as to speak to the Lord, what if only twenty can be found there?"

He said, "For the sake of twenty, I will not destroy it."

32 Then he said, "May the Lord not be angry, but let me speak just once more. What if only ten can be found there?"

He answered, "For the sake of ten, I will not destroy it."

33 When the LORD had finished speaking with Abraham, he left, and Abraham returned home.

Sodom and Gomorrah Destroyed

19 The two angels arrived at Sodom in the evening, and Lot was sitting in the gateway of the city. When he saw them, he got up to meet them and bowed down with his face to the ground. 2 "My lords," he said, "please turn aside to your servant's house. You can wash your feet and spend the night and then go on your way early in the morning."

"No," they answered, "we will spend the night in the square."

3 But he insisted so strongly that they did go with him and entered his house. He prepared a meal for them, baking bread without yeast, and they ate. 4 Before they had gone to bed, all the men from every part of the city of Sodom—both young and old—surrounded the house. 5 They called to Lot, "Where are the men who came to you tonight? Bring them out to us so that we can have sex with them."

6 Lot went outside to meet them and shut the door behind him 7 and said, "No, my friends. Don't do this wicked thing. 8 Look, I have two daughters who have never slept with a man. Let me bring them out to you, and you can do what you like with them. But don't do anything to these men, for they have come under the protection of my roof."

9 "Get out of our way," they replied. And they said, "This fellow came here as an alien, and now he wants to play the judge! We'll treat you worse than them." They kept bringing pressure on Lot and moved forward to break down the door.

10 But the men inside reached out and pulled Lot back into the house and shut the door. 11 Then they struck the men who were at the door of the house, young and old, with blindness so that they could not find the door.

12 The two men said to Lot, "Do you have anyone else here—sons-in-law, sons or daughters, or anyone else in the city who belongs to you? Get them out of here, 13 because we are going to destroy this place. The outcry to the LORD against its people is so great that he has sent us to destroy it."

14 So Lot went out and spoke to his sons-in-law, who were pledged to marry[b] his daughters. He said, "Hurry and get out of this place, because the LORD is about to destroy the city!" But his sons-in-law thought he was joking.

15 With the coming of dawn, the angels urged Lot, saying, "Hurry! Take your wife and your two daughters who are here, or you will be swept away when the city is punished."

16 When he hesitated, the men grasped his hand and the hands of his wife and of his two daughters and led them safely out of the city, for the LORD was merciful to them. 17 As soon as they had brought them out, one of them said, "Flee for your lives! Don't look back, and don't stop anywhere in the plain! Flee to the mountains or you will be swept away!"

18 But Lot said to them, "No, my lords,[c] please! 19 Your[d] servant has found favor in your[d] eyes, and you[d] have shown great kindness to me in sparing my life. But I can't flee to the mountains; this disaster will overtake me, and I'll die. 20 Look, here is a town near enough to run to, and it is small. Let me flee to it—it is very small, isn't it? Then my life will be spared."

21 He said to him, "Very well, I will grant this request too; I will not overthrow the town you speak of. 22 But flee there quickly, because I cannot do anything until you reach it." (That is why the town was called Zoar.[e])

23 By the time Lot reached Zoar, the sun had risen over the land. 24 Then the LORD rained down burning sulfur on Sodom and Gomorrah—from the LORD out of the heavens. 25 Thus he overthrew those cities and the entire plain, including all those living in the cities—and also the vegetation in the land. 26 But Lot's wife looked back, and she became a pillar of salt.

27 Early the next morning Abraham got up and returned to the place where he had stood before the LORD. 28 He looked down toward Sodom and Gomorrah, toward all the land of the plain, and he saw dense smoke rising from the land, like smoke from a furnace.

[a] 25 Or *Ruler* [b] 14 Or *were married to* [c] 18 Or *No, Lord*; or *No, my lord* [d] 19 The Hebrew is singular.
[e] 22 *Zoar* means *small.*

29So when God destroyed the cities of the plain, he remembered Abraham, and he brought Lot out of the catastrophe that overthrew the cities where Lot had lived.

Lot and His Daughters

30Lot and his two daughters left Zoar and settled in the mountains, for he was afraid to stay in Zoar. He and his two daughters lived in a cave. 31One day the older daughter said to the younger, "Our father is old, and there is no man around here to lie with us, as is the custom all over the earth. 32Let's get our father to drink wine and then lie with him and preserve our family line through our father."

33That night they got their father to drink wine, and the older daughter went in and lay with him. He was not aware of it when she lay down or when she got up.

34The next day the older daughter said to the younger, "Last night I lay with my father. Let's get him to drink wine again tonight, and you go in and lie with him so we can preserve our family line through our father." 35So they got their father to drink wine that night also, and the younger daughter went and lay with him. Again he was not aware of it when she lay down or when she got up.

36So both of Lot's daughters became pregnant by their father. 37The older daughter had a son, and she named him Moab[a]; he is the father of the Moabites of today. 38The younger daughter also had a son, and she named him Ben-Ammi[b]; he is the father of the Ammonites of today.

Abraham and Abimelech

20 Now Abraham moved on from there into the region of the Negev and lived between Kadesh and Shur. For a while he stayed in Gerar, 2and there Abraham said of his wife Sarah, "She is my sister." Then Abimelech king of Gerar sent for Sarah and took her.

3But God came to Abimelech in a dream one night and said to him, "You are as good as dead because of the woman you have taken; she is a married woman."

4Now Abimelech had not gone near her, so he said, "Lord, will you destroy an innocent nation? 5Did he not say to me, 'She is my sister,' and didn't she also say, 'He is my brother'? I have done this with a clear conscience and clean hands."

6Then God said to him in the dream, "Yes, I know you did this with a clear conscience, and so I have kept you from sinning against me. That is why I did not let you touch her. 7Now return the man's wife, for he is a prophet, and he will pray for you and you will live. But if you do not return her, you may be sure that you and all yours will die."

8Early the next morning Abimelech summoned all his officials, and when he told them all that had happened, they were very much afraid. 9Then Abimelech called Abraham in and said, "What have you done to us? How have I wronged you that you have brought such great guilt upon me and my kingdom? You have done things to me that should not be done." 10And Abimelech asked Abraham, "What was your reason for doing this?"

11Abraham replied, "I said to myself, 'There is surely no fear of God in this place, and they will kill me because of my wife.' 12Besides, she really is my sister, the daughter of my father though not of my mother; and she became my wife. 13And when God had me wander from my father's household, I said to her, 'This is how you can show your love to me: Everywhere we go, say of me, "He is my brother." ' "

14Then Abimelech brought sheep and cattle and male and female slaves and gave them to Abraham, and he returned Sarah his wife to him. 15And Abimelech said, "My land is before you; live wherever you like."

16To Sarah he said, "I am giving your brother a thousand shekels[c] of silver. This is to cover the offense against you before all who are with you; you are completely vindicated."

17Then Abraham prayed to God, and God healed Abimelech, his wife and his slave girls so they could have children again, 18for the LORD had closed up every womb in Abimelech's household because of Abraham's wife Sarah.

The Birth of Isaac

21 Now the LORD was gracious to Sarah as he had said, and the LORD did for Sarah what he had promised. 2Sarah became pregnant and bore a son to Abraham in his old age, at the very time God had promised him. 3Abraham gave the name Isaac[d] to the son Sarah bore him. 4When his son Isaac was eight days old, Abraham circumcised him, as God commanded him. 5Abraham was a hundred years old when his son Isaac was born to him.

6Sarah said, "God has brought me laughter, and everyone who hears about this will laugh with me." 7And she added, "Who would have said to Abraham that Sarah would nurse children? Yet I have borne him a son in his old age."

Hagar and Ishmael Sent Away

8The child grew and was weaned, and on the day Isaac was weaned Abraham held a great feast. 9But Sarah saw that the son whom Hagar the Egyptian had borne to Abraham was mocking, 10and she said to Abraham, "Get rid of that slave woman and her son, for that slave woman's son will never share in the inheritance with my son Isaac."

11The matter distressed Abraham greatly because it concerned his son. 12But God said to him, "Do not be so distressed about the boy and your maidservant. Listen to whatever Sarah tells you, because it is through Isaac that

[a]*37 Moab* sounds like the Hebrew for *from father.* [b]*38 Ben-Ammi* means *son of my people.* [c]*16* That is, about 25 pounds (about 11.5 kilograms) [d]*3 Isaac* means *he laughs.*

your offspring[a] will be reckoned. 13I will make the son of the maidservant into a nation also, because he is your offspring."

14Early the next morning Abraham took some food and a skin of water and gave them to Hagar. He set them on her shoulders and then sent her off with the boy. She went on her way and wandered in the desert of Beersheba.

15When the water in the skin was gone, she put the boy under one of the bushes. 16Then she went off and sat down nearby, about a bowshot away, for she thought, "I cannot watch the boy die." And as she sat there nearby, she[b] began to sob.

17God heard the boy crying, and the angel of God called to Hagar from heaven and said to her, "What is the matter, Hagar? Do not be afraid; God has heard the boy crying as he lies there. 18Lift the boy up and take him by the hand, for I will make him into a great nation."

19Then God opened her eyes and she saw a well of water. So she went and filled the skin with water and gave the boy a drink.

20God was with the boy as he grew up. He lived in the desert and became an archer. 21While he was living in the Desert of Paran, his mother got a wife for him from Egypt.

The Treaty at Beersheba

22At that time Abimelech and Phicol the commander of his forces said to Abraham, "God is with you in everything you do. 23Now swear to me here before God that you will not deal falsely with me or my children or my descendants. Show to me and the country where you are living as an alien the same kindness I have shown to you."

24Abraham said, "I swear it."

25Then Abraham complained to Abimelech about a well of water that Abimelech's servants had seized. 26But Abimelech said, "I don't know who has done this. You did not tell me, and I heard about it only today."

27So Abraham brought sheep and cattle and gave them to Abimelech, and the two men made a treaty. 28Abraham set apart seven ewe lambs from the flock, 29and Abimelech asked Abraham, "What is the meaning of these seven ewe lambs you have set apart by themselves?"

30He replied, "Accept these seven lambs from my hand as a witness that I dug this well."

31So that place was called Beersheba,[c] because the two men swore an oath there.

32After the treaty had been made at Beersheba, Abimelech and Phicol the commander of his forces returned to the land of the Philistines. 33Abraham planted a tamarisk tree in Beersheba, and there he called upon the name of the LORD, the Eternal God. 34And Abraham stayed in the land of the Philistines for a long time.

Abraham Tested

22 Some time later God tested Abraham. He said to him, "Abraham!"

"Here I am," he replied.

2Then God said, "Take your son, your only son, Isaac, whom you love, and go to the region of Moriah. Sacrifice him there as a burnt offering on one of the mountains I will tell you about."

3Early the next morning Abraham got up and saddled his donkey. He took with him two of his servants and his son Isaac. When he had cut enough wood for the burnt offering, he set out for the place God had told him about. 4On the third day Abraham looked up and saw the place in the distance. 5He said to his servants, "Stay here with the donkey while I and the boy go over there. We will worship and then we will come back to you."

6Abraham took the wood for the burnt offering and placed it on his son Isaac, and he himself carried the fire and the knife. As the two of them went on together, 7Isaac spoke up and said to his father Abraham, "Father?"

"Yes, my son?" Abraham replied.

"The fire and wood are here," Isaac said, "but where is the lamb for the burnt offering?"

8Abraham answered, "God himself will provide the lamb for the burnt offering, my son." And the two of them went on together.

9When they reached the place God had told him about, Abraham built an altar there and arranged the wood on it. He bound his son Isaac and laid him on the altar, on top of the wood. 10Then he reached out his hand and took the knife to slay his son. 11But the angel of the LORD called out to him from heaven, "Abraham! Abraham!"

"Here I am," he replied.

12"Do not lay a hand on the boy," he said. "Do not do anything to him. Now I know that you fear God, because you have not withheld from me your son, your only son."

13Abraham looked up and there in a thicket he saw a ram[d] caught by its horns. He went over and took the ram and sacrificed it as a burnt offering instead of his son. 14So Abraham called that place The LORD Will Provide. And to this day it is said, "On the mountain of the LORD it will be provided."

15The angel of the LORD called to Abraham from heaven a second time 16and said, "I swear by myself, declares the LORD, that because you have done this and have not withheld your son, your only son, 17I will surely bless you and make your descendants as numerous as the stars in the sky and as the sand on the seashore. Your descendants will take possession of the cities of their enemies, 18and through your offspring[a] all nations on earth will be blessed, because you have obeyed me."

19Then Abraham returned to his servants,

[a]*12,18* Or *seed* [b]*16* Hebrew; Septuagint *the child* [c]*31* *Beersheba* can mean *well of seven* or *well of the oath.* [d]*13* Many manuscripts of the Masoretic Text, Samaritan Pentateuch, Septuagint and Syriac; most manuscripts of the Masoretic Text *a ram behind ⌊him⌋*

and they set off together for Beersheba. And Abraham stayed in Beersheba.

Nahor's Sons

20Some time later Abraham was told, "Milcah is also a mother; she has borne sons to your brother Nahor: 21Uz the firstborn, Buz his brother, Kemuel (the father of Aram), 22Kesed, Hazo, Pildash, Jidlaph and Bethuel." 23Bethuel became the father of Rebekah. Milcah bore these eight sons to Abraham's brother Nahor. 24His concubine, whose name was Reumah, also had sons: Tebah, Gaham, Tahash and Maacah.

The Death of Sarah

23 Sarah lived to be a hundred and twenty-seven years old. 2She died at Kiriath Arba (that is, Hebron) in the land of Canaan, and Abraham went to mourn for Sarah and to weep over her.

3Then Abraham rose from beside his dead wife and spoke to the Hittites.[a] He said, 4"I am an alien and a stranger among you. Sell me some property for a burial site here so I can bury my dead."

5The Hittites replied to Abraham, 6"Sir, listen to us. You are a mighty prince among us. Bury your dead in the choicest of our tombs. None of us will refuse you his tomb for burying your dead."

7Then Abraham rose and bowed down before the people of the land, the Hittites. 8He said to them, "If you are willing to let me bury my dead, then listen to me and intercede with Ephron son of Zohar on my behalf 9so he will sell me the cave of Machpelah, which belongs to him and is at the end of his field. Ask him to sell it to me for the full price as a burial site among you."

10Ephron the Hittite was sitting among his people and he replied to Abraham in the hearing of all the Hittites who had come to the gate of his city. 11"No, my lord," he said. "Listen to me; I give[b] you the field, and I give[b] you the cave that is in it. I give[b] it to you in the presence of my people. Bury your dead."

12Again Abraham bowed down before the people of the land 13and he said to Ephron in their hearing, "Listen to me, if you will. I will pay the price of the field. Accept it from me so I can bury my dead there."

14Ephron answered Abraham, 15"Listen to me, my lord; the land is worth four hundred shekels[c] of silver, but what is that between me and you? Bury your dead."

16Abraham agreed to Ephron's terms and weighed out for him the price he had named in the hearing of the Hittites: four hundred shekels of silver, according to the weight current among the merchants.

17So Ephron's field in Machpelah near Mamre—both the field and the cave in it, and all the trees within the borders of the field—was deeded 18to Abraham as his property in the presence of all the Hittites who had come to the gate of the city. 19Afterward Abraham buried his wife Sarah in the cave in the field of Machpelah near Mamre (which is at Hebron) in the land of Canaan. 20So the field and the cave in it were deeded to Abraham by the Hittites as a burial site.

Isaac and Rebekah

24 Abraham was now old and well advanced in years, and the LORD had blessed him in every way. 2He said to the chief[d] servant in his household, the one in charge of all that he had, "Put your hand under my thigh. 3I want you to swear by the LORD, the God of heaven and the God of earth, that you will not get a wife for my son from the daughters of the Canaanites, among whom I am living, 4but will go to my country and my own relatives and get a wife for my son Isaac."

5The servant asked him, "What if the woman is unwilling to come back with me to this land? Shall I then take your son back to the country you came from?"

6"Make sure that you do not take my son back there," Abraham said. 7"The LORD, the God of heaven, who brought me out of my father's household and my native land and who spoke to me and promised me on oath, saying, 'To your offspring[e] I will give this land'—he will send his angel before you so that you can get a wife for my son from there. 8If the woman is unwilling to come back with you, then you will be released from this oath of mine. Only do not take my son back there." 9So the servant put his hand under the thigh of his master Abraham and swore an oath to him concerning this matter.

10Then the servant took ten of his master's camels and left, taking with him all kinds of good things from his master. He set out for Aram Naharaim[f] and made his way to the town of Nahor. 11He had the camels kneel down near the well outside the town; it was toward evening, the time the women go out to draw water.

12Then he prayed, "O LORD, God of my master Abraham, give me success today, and show kindness to my master Abraham. 13See, I am standing beside this spring, and the daughters of the townspeople are coming out to draw water. 14May it be that when I say to a girl, 'Please let down your jar that I may have a drink,' and she says, 'Drink, and I'll water your camels too'—let her be the one you have chosen for your servant Isaac. By this I will know that you have shown kindness to my master."

15Before he had finished praying, Rebekah came out with her jar on her shoulder. She was the daughter of Bethuel son of Milcah, who was the wife of Abraham's brother Nahor. 16The girl was very beautiful, a virgin; no man

[a]3 Or *the sons of Heth*; also in verses 5, 7, 10, 16, 18 and 20 [b]11 Or *sell* [c]15 That is, about 10 pounds (about 4.5 kilograms) [d]2 Or *oldest* [e]7 Or *seed* [f]10 That is, Northwest Mesopotamia

had ever lain with her. She went down to the
spring, filled her jar and came up again.
17The servant hurried to meet her and said,
"Please give me a little water from your jar."
18"Drink, my lord," she said, and quickly
lowered the jar to her hands and gave him a
drink.
19After she had given him a drink, she said,
"I'll draw water for your camels too, until they
have finished drinking." 20So she quickly emptied her jar into the trough, ran back to the well
to draw more water, and drew enough for all
his camels. 21Without saying a word, the man
watched her closely to learn whether or not the
LORD had made his journey successful.
22When the camels had finished drinking,
the man took out a gold nose ring weighing a
beka[a] and two gold bracelets weighing ten
shekels.[b] 23Then he asked, "Whose daughter
are you? Please tell me, is there room in your
father's house for us to spend the night?"
24She answered him, "I am the daughter of
Bethuel, the son that Milcah bore to Nahor."
25And she added, "We have plenty of straw
and fodder, as well as room for you to spend
the night."
26Then the man bowed down and worshiped
the LORD, 27saying, "Praise be to the LORD, the
God of my master Abraham, who has not
abandoned his kindness and faithfulness to my
master. As for me, the LORD has led me on the
journey to the house of my master's relatives."
28The girl ran and told her mother's household about these things. 29Now Rebekah had a
brother named Laban, and he hurried out to the
man at the spring. 30As soon as he had seen the
nose ring, and the bracelets on his sister's
arms, and had heard Rebekah tell what the man
said to her, he went out to the man and found
him standing by the camels near the spring.
31"Come, you who are blessed by the LORD,"
he said. "Why are you standing out here? I
have prepared the house and a place for the
camels."
32So the man went to the house, and the
camels were unloaded. Straw and fodder were
brought for the camels, and water for him and
his men to wash their feet. 33Then food was set
before him, but he said, "I will not eat until I
have told you what I have to say."
"Then tell us," ⌊Laban⌋ said.
34So he said, "I am Abraham's servant.
35The LORD has blessed my master abundantly, and he has become wealthy. He has given
him sheep and cattle, silver and gold, menservants and maidservants, and camels and donkeys. 36My master's wife Sarah has borne him
a son in her[c] old age, and he has given him
everything he owns. 37And my master made
me swear an oath, and said, 'You must not get
a wife for my son from the daughters of the
Canaanites, in whose land I live, 38but go to
my father's family and to my own clan, and get
a wife for my son.'
39"Then I asked my master, 'What if the
woman will not come back with me?'
40"He replied, 'The LORD, before whom I
have walked, will send his angel with you and
make your journey a success, so that you can
get a wife for my son from my own clan and
from my father's family. 41Then, when you go
to my clan, you will be released from my oath
even if they refuse to give her to you—you
will be released from my oath.'
42"When I came to the spring today, I said,
'O LORD, God of my master Abraham, if you
will, please grant success to the journey on
which I have come. 43See, I am standing beside this spring; if a maiden comes out to draw
water and I say to her, "Please let me drink a
little water from your jar," 44and if she says to
me, "Drink, and I'll draw water for your camels too," let her be the one the LORD has chosen for my master's son.'
45"Before I finished praying in my heart,
Rebekah came out, with her jar on her shoulder. She went down to the spring and drew
water, and I said to her, 'Please give me a
drink.'
46"She quickly lowered her jar from her
shoulder and said, 'Drink, and I'll water your
camels too.' So I drank, and she watered the
camels also.
47"I asked her, 'Whose daughter are you?'
"She said, 'The daughter of Bethuel son of
Nahor, whom Milcah bore to him.'
"Then I put the ring in her nose and the
bracelets on her arms, 48and I bowed down and
worshiped the LORD. I praised the LORD, the
God of my master Abraham, who had led me
on the right road to get the granddaughter of
my master's brother for his son. 49Now if you
will show kindness and faithfulness to my
master, tell me; and if not, tell me, so I may
know which way to turn."
50Laban and Bethuel answered, "This is
from the LORD; we can say nothing to you one
way or the other. 51Here is Rebekah; take her
and go, and let her become the wife of your
master's son, as the LORD has directed."
52When Abraham's servant heard what they
said, he bowed down to the ground before the
LORD. 53Then the servant brought out gold and
silver jewelry and articles of clothing and gave
them to Rebekah; he also gave costly gifts to
her brother and to her mother. 54Then he and
the men who were with him ate and drank and
spent the night there.
When they got up the next morning, he said,
"Send me on my way to my master."
55But her brother and her mother replied,
"Let the girl remain with us ten days or so;
then you[d] may go."
56But he said to them, "Do not detain me,
now that the LORD has granted success to my
journey. Send me on my way so I may go to
my master."
57Then they said, "Let's call the girl and ask

[a] *22* That is, about 1/5 ounce (about 5.5 grams) [b] *22* That is, about 4 ounces (about 110 grams)
[c] *36* Or *his* [d] *55* Or *she*

her about it." 58So they called Rebekah and asked her, "Will you go with this man?"

"I will go," she said.

59So they sent their sister Rebekah on her way, along with her nurse and Abraham's servant and his men. 60And they blessed Rebekah and said to her,

"Our sister, may you increase
  to thousands upon thousands;
may your offspring possess
  the gates of their enemies."

61Then Rebekah and her maids got ready and mounted their camels and went back with the man. So the servant took Rebekah and left.

62Now Isaac had come from Beer Lahai Roi, for he was living in the Negev. 63He went out to the field one evening to meditate,[a] and as he looked up, he saw camels approaching. 64Rebekah also looked up and saw Isaac. She got down from her camel 65and asked the servant, "Who is that man in the field coming to meet us?"

"He is my master," the servant answered. So she took her veil and covered herself.

66Then the servant told Isaac all he had done. 67Isaac brought her into the tent of his mother Sarah, and he married Rebekah. So she became his wife, and he loved her; and Isaac was comforted after his mother's death.

The Death of Abraham

25 Abraham took[b] another wife, whose name was Keturah. 2She bore him Zimran, Jokshan, Medan, Midian, Ishbak and Shuah. 3Jokshan was the father of Sheba and Dedan; the descendants of Dedan were the Asshurites, the Letushites and the Leummites. 4The sons of Midian were Ephah, Epher, Hanoch, Abida and Eldaah. All these were descendants of Keturah.

5Abraham left everything he owned to Isaac. 6But while he was still living, he gave gifts to the sons of his concubines and sent them away from his son Isaac to the land of the east.

7Altogether, Abraham lived a hundred and seventy-five years. 8Then Abraham breathed his last and died at a good old age, an old man and full of years; and he was gathered to his people. 9His sons Isaac and Ishmael buried him in the cave of Machpelah near Mamre, in the field of Ephron son of Zohar the Hittite, 10the field Abraham had bought from the Hittites.[c] There Abraham was buried with his wife Sarah. 11After Abraham's death, God blessed his son Isaac, who then lived near Beer Lahai Roi.

Ishmael's Sons

12This is the account of Abraham's son Ishmael, whom Sarah's maidservant, Hagar the Egyptian, bore to Abraham.

13These are the names of the sons of Ishmael, listed in the order of their birth: Nebaioth the firstborn of Ishmael, Kedar, Adbeel, Mibsam, 14Mishma, Dumah, Massa, 15Hadad, Tema, Jetur, Naphish and Kedemah. 16These were the sons of Ishmael, and these are the names of the twelve tribal rulers according to their settlements and camps. 17Altogether, Ishmael lived a hundred and thirty-seven years. He breathed his last and died, and he was gathered to his people. 18His descendants settled in the area from Havilah to Shur, near the border of Egypt, as you go toward Asshur. And they lived in hostility toward[d] all their brothers.

Jacob and Esau

19This is the account of Abraham's son Isaac.

Abraham became the father of Isaac, 20and Isaac was forty years old when he married Rebekah daughter of Bethuel the Aramean from Paddan Aram[e] and sister of Laban the Aramean.

21Isaac prayed to the LORD on behalf of his wife, because she was barren. The LORD answered his prayer, and his wife Rebekah became pregnant. 22The babies jostled each other within her, and she said, "Why is this happening to me?" So she went to inquire of the LORD.

23The LORD said to her,

"Two nations are in your womb,
  and two peoples from within you will
    be separated;
one people will be stronger than the other,
  and the older will serve the younger."

24When the time came for her to give birth, there were twin boys in her womb. 25The first to come out was red, and his whole body was like a hairy garment; so they named him Esau.[f] 26After this, his brother came out, with his hand grasping Esau's heel; so he was named Jacob.[g] Isaac was sixty years old when Rebekah gave birth to them.

27The boys grew up, and Esau became a skillful hunter, a man of the open country, while Jacob was a quiet man, staying among the tents. 28Isaac, who had a taste for wild game, loved Esau, but Rebekah loved Jacob.

29Once when Jacob was cooking some stew, Esau came in from the open country, famished. 30He said to Jacob, "Quick, let me have some of that red stew! I'm famished!" (That is why he was also called Edom.[h])

31Jacob replied, "First sell me your birthright."

32"Look, I am about to die," Esau said. "What good is the birthright to me?"

33But Jacob said, "Swear to me first." So he swore an oath to him, selling his birthright to Jacob.

[a]*63* The meaning of the Hebrew for this word is uncertain. [b]*1* Or *had taken* [c]*10* Or *the sons of Heth* [d]*18* Or *lived to the east of* [e]*20* That is, Northwest Mesopotamia [f]*25* *Esau* may mean *hairy*; he was also called Edom, which means *red.* [g]*26* *Jacob* means *he grasps the heel* (figuratively, *he deceives*). [h]*30* *Edom* means *red.*

34Then Jacob gave Esau some bread and
some lentil stew. He ate and drank, and then
got up and left.
So Esau despised his birthright.

Isaac and Abimelech

26 Now there was a famine in the land—
besides the earlier famine of Abraham's
time—and Isaac went to Abimelech king of
the Philistines in Gerar. 2The LORD appeared
to Isaac and said, "Do not go down to Egypt;
live in the land where I tell you to live. 3Stay
in this land for a while, and I will be with you
and will bless you. For to you and your descendants I will give all these lands and will confirm the oath I swore to your father Abraham.
4I will make your descendants as numerous as
the stars in the sky and will give them all these
lands, and through your offspring[a] all nations
on earth will be blessed, 5because Abraham
obeyed me and kept my requirements, my
commands, my decrees and my laws." 6So
Isaac stayed in Gerar.
7When the men of that place asked him
about his wife, he said, "She is my sister,"
because he was afraid to say, "She is my wife."
He thought, "The men of this place might kill
me on account of Rebekah, because she is
beautiful."
8When Isaac had been there a long time,
Abimelech king of the Philistines looked down
from a window and saw Isaac caressing his
wife Rebekah. 9So Abimelech summoned
Isaac and said, "She is really your wife! Why
did you say, 'She is my sister'?"
Isaac answered him, "Because I thought I
might lose my life on account of her."
10Then Abimelech said, "What is this you
have done to us? One of the men might well
have slept with your wife, and you would have
brought guilt upon us."
11So Abimelech gave orders to all the people: "Anyone who molests this man or his wife
shall surely be put to death."
12Isaac planted crops in that land and the
same year reaped a hundredfold, because the
LORD blessed him. 13The man became rich,
and his wealth continued to grow until he became very wealthy. 14He had so many flocks
and herds and servants that the Philistines envied him. 15So all the wells that his father's
servants had dug in the time of his father Abraham, the Philistines stopped up, filling them
with earth.
16Then Abimelech said to Isaac, "Move
away from us; you have become too powerful
for us."
17So Isaac moved away from there and encamped in the Valley of Gerar and settled
there. 18Isaac reopened the wells that had been
dug in the time of his father Abraham, which
the Philistines had stopped up after Abraham
died, and he gave them the same names his
father had given them.
19Isaac's servants dug in the valley and discovered a well of fresh water there. 20But the
herdsmen of Gerar quarreled with Isaac's
herdsmen and said, "The water is ours!" So he
named the well Esek,[b] because they disputed
with him. 21Then they dug another well, but
they quarreled over that one also; so he named
it Sitnah.[c] 22He moved on from there and dug
another well, and no one quarreled over it. He
named it Rehoboth,[d] saying, "Now the LORD
has given us room and we will flourish in the
land."
23From there he went up to Beersheba.
24That night the LORD appeared to him and
said, "I am the God of your father Abraham.
Do not be afraid, for I am with you; I will bless
you and will increase the number of your
descendants for the sake of my servant Abraham."
25Isaac built an altar there and called on the
name of the LORD. There he pitched his tent,
and there his servants dug a well.
26Meanwhile, Abimelech had come to him
from Gerar, with Ahuzzath his personal adviser and Phicol the commander of his forces.
27Isaac asked them, "Why have you come to
me, since you were hostile to me and sent me
away?"
28They answered, "We saw clearly that the
LORD was with you; so we said, 'There ought
to be a sworn agreement between us'—between us and you. Let us make a treaty with
you 29that you will do us no harm, just as we
did not molest you but always treated you well
and sent you away in peace. And now you are
blessed by the LORD."
30Isaac then made a feast for them, and they
ate and drank. 31Early the next morning the
men swore an oath to each other. Then Isaac
sent them on their way, and they left him in
peace.
32That day Isaac's servants came and told
him about the well they had dug. They said,
"We've found water!" 33He called it Shibah,[e]
and to this day the name of the town has been
Beersheba.[f]
34When Esau was forty years old, he married Judith daughter of Beeri the Hittite, and
also Basemath daughter of Elon the Hittite.
35They were a source of grief to Isaac and
Rebekah.

Jacob Gets Isaac's Blessing

27 When Isaac was old and his eyes were
so weak that he could no longer see, he
called for Esau his older son and said to him,
"My son."
"Here I am," he answered.
2Isaac said, "I am now an old man and don't
know the day of my death. 3Now then, get
your weapons—your quiver and bow—and go
out to the open country to hunt some wild
game for me. 4Prepare me the kind of tasty

[a]4 Or *seed* [b]20 *Esek* means *dispute.* [c]21 *Sitnah* means *opposition.* [d]22 *Rehoboth* means *room.*
[e]33 *Shibah* can mean *oath* or *seven.* [f]33 *Beersheba* can mean *well of the oath* or *well of seven.*

food I like and bring it to me to eat, so that I
may give you my blessing before I die."
5Now Rebekah was listening as Isaac spoke
to his son Esau. When Esau left for the open
country to hunt game and bring it back, 6Re-
bekah said to her son Jacob, "Look, I overheard your father say to your brother Esau,
7'Bring me some game and prepare me some
tasty food to eat, so that I may give you my
blessing in the presence of the LORD before I
die.' 8Now, my son, listen carefully and do
what I tell you: 9Go out to the flock and bring
me two choice young goats, so I can prepare
some tasty food for your father, just the way he
likes it. 10Then take it to your father to eat, so
that he may give you his blessing before he
dies."
11Jacob said to Rebekah his mother, "But
my brother Esau is a hairy man, and I'm a man
with smooth skin. 12What if my father touches
me? I would appear to be tricking him and
would bring down a curse on myself rather
than a blessing."
13His mother said to him, "My son, let the
curse fall on me. Just do what I say; go and get
them for me."
14So he went and got them and brought them
to his mother, and she prepared some tasty
food, just the way his father liked it. 15Then
Rebekah took the best clothes of Esau her older son, which she had in the house, and put
them on her younger son Jacob. 16She also
covered his hands and the smooth part of his
neck with the goatskins. 17Then she handed to
her son Jacob the tasty food and the bread she
had made.
18He went to his father and said, "My father."
"Yes, my son," he answered. "Who is it?"
19Jacob said to his father, "I am Esau your
firstborn. I have done as you told me. Please sit
up and eat some of my game so that you may
give me your blessing."
20Isaac asked his son, "How did you find it
so quickly, my son?"
"The LORD your God gave me success," he
replied.
21Then Isaac said to Jacob, "Come near so I
can touch you, my son, to know whether you
really are my son Esau or not."
22Jacob went close to his father Isaac, who
touched him and said, "The voice is the voice
of Jacob, but the hands are the hands of Esau."
23He did not recognize him, for his hands were
hairy like those of his brother Esau; so he
blessed him. 24"Are you really my son Esau?"
he asked.
"I am," he replied.
25Then he said, "My son, bring me some of
your game to eat, so that I may give you my
blessing."
Jacob brought it to him and he ate; and he
brought some wine and he drank. 26Then his
father Isaac said to him, "Come here, my son,
and kiss me."
27So he went to him and kissed him. When
Isaac caught the smell of his clothes, he
blessed him and said,

"Ah, the smell of my son
is like the smell of a field
that the LORD has blessed.
28May God give you of heaven's dew
and of earth's richness—
an abundance of grain and new wine.
29May nations serve you
and peoples bow down to you.
Be lord over your brothers,
and may the sons of your mother bow
down to you.
May those who curse you be cursed
and those who bless you be blessed."

30After Isaac finished blessing him and Jacob had scarcely left his father's presence, his
brother Esau came in from hunting. 31He too
prepared some tasty food and brought it to his
father. Then he said to him, "My father, sit up
and eat some of my game, so that you may
give me your blessing."
32His father Isaac asked him, "Who are
you?"
"I am your son," he answered, "your firstborn, Esau."
33Isaac trembled violently and said, "Who
was it, then, that hunted game and brought it to
me? I ate it just before you came and I blessed
him—and indeed he will be blessed!"
34When Esau heard his father's words, he
burst out with a loud and bitter cry and said to
his father, "Bless me—me too, my father!"
35But he said, "Your brother came deceitfully and took your blessing."
36Esau said, "Isn't he rightly named Jacob[a]? He has deceived me these two times:
He took my birthright, and now he's taken my
blessing!" Then he asked, "Haven't you reserved any blessing for me?"
37Isaac answered Esau, "I have made him
lord over you and have made all his relatives
his servants, and I have sustained him with
grain and new wine. So what can I possibly do
for you, my son?"
38Esau said to his father, "Do you have only
one blessing, my father? Bless me too, my father!" Then Esau wept aloud.
39His father Isaac answered him,

"Your dwelling will be
away from the earth's richness,
away from the dew of heaven above.
40You will live by the sword
and you will serve your brother.
But when you grow restless,
you will throw his yoke
from off your neck."

Jacob Flees to Laban

41Esau held a grudge against Jacob because
of the blessing his father had given him. He
said to himself, "The days of mourning for my

[a]36 *Jacob* means *he grasps the heel* (figuratively, *he deceives*).

father are near; then I will kill my brother Jacob."
42When Rebekah was told what her older
son Esau had said, she sent for her younger son
Jacob and said to him, "Your brother Esau is
consoling himself with the thought of killing
you. 43Now then, my son, do what I say: Flee
at once to my brother Laban in Haran. 44Stay
with him for a while until your brother's fury
subsides. 45When your brother is no longer angry with you and forgets what you did to him,
I'll send word for you to come back from
there. Why should I lose both of you in one
day?"
46Then Rebekah said to Isaac, "I'm disgust-
ed with living because of these Hittite women.
If Jacob takes a wife from among the women
of this land, from Hittite women like these, my
life will not be worth living."
28 So Isaac called for Jacob and blessed[a]
him and commanded him: "Do not marry a Canaanite woman. 2Go at once to Paddan
Aram,[b] to the house of your mother's father
Bethuel. Take a wife for yourself there, from
among the daughters of Laban, your mother's
brother. 3May God Almighty[c] bless you and
make you fruitful and increase your numbers
until you become a community of peoples.
4May he give you and your descendants the
blessing given to Abraham, so that you may
take possession of the land where you now live
as an alien, the land God gave to Abraham."
5Then Isaac sent Jacob on his way, and he
went to Paddan Aram, to Laban son of Bethuel
the Aramean, the brother of Rebekah, who was
the mother of Jacob and Esau.
6Now Esau learned that Isaac had blessed
Jacob and had sent him to Paddan Aram to
take a wife from there, and that when he
blessed him he commanded him, "Do not marry a Canaanite woman," 7and that Jacob had
obeyed his father and mother and had gone to
Paddan Aram. 8Esau then realized how displeasing the Canaanite women were to his father Isaac; 9so he went to Ishmael and married
Mahalath, the sister of Nebaioth and daughter
of Ishmael son of Abraham, in addition to the
wives he already had.

Jacob's Dream at Bethel

10Jacob left Beersheba and set out for Haran. 11When he reached a certain place, he
stopped for the night because the sun had set.
Taking one of the stones there, he put it under
his head and lay down to sleep. 12He had a
dream in which he saw a stairway[d] resting on
the earth, with its top reaching to heaven, and
the angels of God were ascending and descending on it. 13There above it[e] stood the
LORD, and he said: "I am the LORD, the God of
your father Abraham and the God of Isaac. I
will give you and your descendants the land on
which you are lying. 14Your descendants will
be like the dust of the earth, and you will
spread out to the west and to the east, to the
north and to the south. All peoples on earth
will be blessed through you and your offspring. 15I am with you and will watch over
you wherever you go, and I will bring you
back to this land. I will not leave you until I
have done what I have promised you."
16When Jacob awoke from his sleep, he
thought, "Surely the LORD is in this place, and
I was not aware of it." 17He was afraid and
said, "How awesome is this place! This is none
other than the house of God; this is the gate of
heaven."
18Early the next morning Jacob took the
stone he had placed under his head and set it
up as a pillar and poured oil on top of it. 19He
called that place Bethel,[f] though the city used
to be called Luz.
20Then Jacob made a vow, saying, "If God
will be with me and will watch over me on this
journey I am taking and will give me food to
eat and clothes to wear 21so that I return safely
to my father's house, then the LORD[g] will be
my God 22and[h] this stone that I have set up as
a pillar will be God's house, and of all that you
give me I will give you a tenth."

Jacob Arrives in Paddan Aram

29 Then Jacob continued on his journey
and came to the land of the eastern peoples. 2There he saw a well in the field, with
three flocks of sheep lying near it because the
flocks were watered from that well. The stone
over the mouth of the well was large. 3When
all the flocks were gathered there, the shepherds would roll the stone away from the
well's mouth and water the sheep. Then they
would return the stone to its place over the
mouth of the well.
4Jacob asked the shepherds, "My brothers,
where are you from?"
"We're from Haran," they replied.
5He said to them, "Do you know Laban,
Nahor's grandson?"
"Yes, we know him," they answered.
6Then Jacob asked them, "Is he well?"
"Yes, he is," they said, "and here comes his
daughter Rachel with the sheep."
7"Look," he said, "the sun is still high; it is
not time for the flocks to be gathered. Water
the sheep and take them back to pasture."
8"We can't," they replied, "until all the
flocks are gathered and the stone has been
rolled away from the mouth of the well. Then
we will water the sheep."
9While he was still talking with them, Rachel came with her father's sheep, for she was
a shepherdess. 10When Jacob saw Rachel
daughter of Laban, his mother's brother, and
Laban's sheep, he went over and rolled the
stone away from the mouth of the well and
watered his uncle's sheep. 11Then Jacob kissed

[a] *1* Or *greeted* [b] *2* That is, Northwest Mesopotamia; also in verses 5, 6 and 7 [c] *3* Hebrew *El-Shaddai*
[d] *12* Or *ladder* [e] *13* Or *There beside him* [f] *19* *Bethel* means *house of God.* [g] *20,21* Or *Since God . . . father's house, the LORD* [h] *21,22* Or *house, and the LORD will be my God, 22then*

Rachel and began to weep aloud. 12He had told Rachel that he was a relative of her father and a son of Rebekah. So she ran and told her father.

13As soon as Laban heard the news about Jacob, his sister's son, he hurried to meet him. He embraced him and kissed him and brought him to his home, and there Jacob told him all these things. 14Then Laban said to him, "You are my own flesh and blood."

Jacob Marries Leah and Rachel

After Jacob had stayed with him for a whole month, 15Laban said to him, "Just because you are a relative of mine, should you work for me for nothing? Tell me what your wages should be."

16Now Laban had two daughters; the name of the older was Leah, and the name of the younger was Rachel. 17Leah had weak[a] eyes, but Rachel was lovely in form, and beautiful. 18Jacob was in love with Rachel and said, "I'll work for you seven years in return for your younger daughter Rachel."

19Laban said, "It's better that I give her to you than to some other man. Stay here with me." 20So Jacob served seven years to get Rachel, but they seemed like only a few days to him because of his love for her.

21Then Jacob said to Laban, "Give me my wife. My time is completed, and I want to lie with her."

22So Laban brought together all the people of the place and gave a feast. 23But when evening came, he took his daughter Leah and gave her to Jacob, and Jacob lay with her. 24And Laban gave his servant girl Zilpah to his daughter as her maidservant.

25When morning came, there was Leah! So Jacob said to Laban, "What is this you have done to me? I served you for Rachel, didn't I? Why have you deceived me?"

26Laban replied, "It is not our custom here to give the younger daughter in marriage before the older one. 27Finish this daughter's bridal week; then we will give you the younger one also, in return for another seven years of work."

28And Jacob did so. He finished the week with Leah, and then Laban gave him his daughter Rachel to be his wife. 29Laban gave his servant girl Bilhah to his daughter Rachel as her maidservant. 30Jacob lay with Rachel also, and he loved Rachel more than Leah. And he worked for Laban another seven years.

Jacob's Children

31When the LORD saw that Leah was not loved, he opened her womb, but Rachel was barren. 32Leah became pregnant and gave birth to a son. She named him Reuben,[b] for she said, "It is because the LORD has seen my misery. Surely my husband will love me now."

33She conceived again, and when she gave birth to a son she said, "Because the LORD heard that I am not loved, he gave me this one too." So she named him Simeon.[c]

34Again she conceived, and when she gave birth to a son she said, "Now at last my husband will become attached to me, because I have borne him three sons." So he was named Levi.[d]

35She conceived again, and when she gave birth to a son she said, "This time I will praise the LORD." So she named him Judah.[e] Then she stopped having children.

30 When Rachel saw that she was not bearing Jacob any children, she became jealous of her sister. So she said to Jacob, "Give me children, or I'll die!"

2Jacob became angry with her and said, "Am I in the place of God, who has kept you from having children?"

3Then she said, "Here is Bilhah, my maidservant. Sleep with her so that she can bear children for me and that through her I too can build a family."

4So she gave him her servant Bilhah as a wife. Jacob slept with her, 5and she became pregnant and bore him a son. 6Then Rachel said, "God has vindicated me; he has listened to my plea and given me a son." Because of this she named him Dan.[f]

7Rachel's servant Bilhah conceived again and bore Jacob a second son. 8Then Rachel said, "I have had a great struggle with my sister, and I have won." So she named him Naphtali.[g]

9When Leah saw that she had stopped having children, she took her maidservant Zilpah and gave her to Jacob as a wife. 10Leah's servant Zilpah bore Jacob a son. 11Then Leah said, "What good fortune!"[h] So she named him Gad.[i]

12Leah's servant Zilpah bore Jacob a second son. 13Then Leah said, "How happy I am! The women will call me happy." So she named him Asher.[j]

14During wheat harvest, Reuben went out into the fields and found some mandrake plants, which he brought to his mother Leah. Rachel said to Leah, "Please give me some of your son's mandrakes."

15But she said to her, "Wasn't it enough that you took away my husband? Will you take my son's mandrakes too?"

"Very well," Rachel said, "he can sleep with you tonight in return for your son's mandrakes."

16So when Jacob came in from the fields that evening, Leah went out to meet him. "You must sleep with me," she said. "I have hired

[a]*17* Or *delicate* [b]*32* *Reuben* sounds like the Hebrew for *he has seen my misery*; the name means *see, a son.* [c]*33* *Simeon* probably means *one who hears.* [d]*34* *Levi* sounds like and may be derived from the Hebrew for *attached.* [e]*35* *Judah* sounds like and may be derived from the Hebrew for *praise.* [f]*6* *Dan* here means *he has vindicated.* [g]*8* *Naphtali* means *my struggle.* [h]*11* Or *"A troop is coming!"* [i]*11* *Gad* can mean *good fortune* or *a troop.* [j]*13* *Asher* means *happy.*

you with my son's mandrakes." So he slept
with her that night.
17God listened to Leah, and she became
pregnant and bore Jacob a fifth son. 18Then
Leah said, "God has rewarded me for giving
my maidservant to my husband." So she
named him Issachar.[a]
19Leah conceived again and bore Jacob a
sixth son. 20Then Leah said, "God has presented me with a precious gift. This time my husband will treat me with honor, because I have
borne him six sons." So she named him Zebulun.[b]
21Some time later she gave birth to a daughter and named her Dinah.
22Then God remembered Rachel; he listened
to her and opened her womb. 23She became
pregnant and gave birth to a son and said,
"God has taken away my disgrace." 24She
named him Joseph,[c] and said, "May the LORD
add to me another son."

Jacob's Flocks Increase

25After Rachel gave birth to Joseph, Jacob
said to Laban, "Send me on my way so I can
go back to my own homeland. 26Give me my
wives and children, for whom I have served
you, and I will be on my way. You know how
much work I've done for you."
27But Laban said to him, "If I have found
favor in your eyes, please stay. I have learned
by divination that[d] the LORD has blessed me
because of you." 28He added, "Name your
wages, and I will pay them."
29Jacob said to him, "You know how I have
worked for you and how your livestock has
fared under my care. 30The little you had before I came has increased greatly, and the
LORD has blessed you wherever I have been.
But now, when may I do something for my
own household?"
31"What shall I give you?" he asked.
"Don't give me anything," Jacob replied.
"But if you will do this one thing for me, I will
go on tending your flocks and watching over
them: 32Let me go through all your flocks today and remove from them every speckled or
spotted sheep, every dark-colored lamb and
every spotted or speckled goat. They will be
my wages. 33And my honesty will testify for
me in the future, whenever you check on the
wages you have paid me. Any goat in my possession that is not speckled or spotted, or any
lamb that is not dark-colored, will be considered stolen."
34"Agreed," said Laban. "Let it be as you
have said." 35That same day he removed all the
male goats that were streaked or spotted, and
all the speckled or spotted female goats (all
that had white on them) and all the dark-
colored lambs, and he placed them in the care
of his sons. 36Then he put a three-day journey
between himself and Jacob, while Jacob continued to tend the rest of Laban's flocks.
37Jacob, however, took fresh-cut branches
from poplar, almond and plane trees and made
white stripes on them by peeling the bark and
exposing the white inner wood of the branches.
38Then he placed the peeled branches in all the
watering troughs, so that they would be directly in front of the flocks when they came to
drink. When the flocks were in heat and came
to drink, 39they mated in front of the branches.
And they bore young that were streaked or
speckled or spotted. 40Jacob set apart the
young of the flock by themselves, but made the
rest face the streaked and dark-colored animals
that belonged to Laban. Thus he made separate
flocks for himself and did not put them with
Laban's animals. 41Whenever the stronger fe-
males were in heat, Jacob would place the
branches in the troughs in front of the animals
so they would mate near the branches, 42but if
the animals were weak, he would not place
them there. So the weak animals went to Laban
and the strong ones to Jacob. 43In this way the
man grew exceedingly prosperous and came to
own large flocks, and maidservants and menservants, and camels and donkeys.

Jacob Flees From Laban

31 Jacob heard that Laban's sons were saying, "Jacob has taken everything our father owned and has gained all this wealth from
what belonged to our father." 2And Jacob noticed that Laban's attitude toward him was not
what it had been.
3Then the LORD said to Jacob, "Go back to
the land of your fathers and to your relatives,
and I will be with you."
4So Jacob sent word to Rachel and Leah to
come out to the fields where his flocks were.
5He said to them, "I see that your father's attitude toward me is not what it was before, but
the God of my father has been with me. 6You
know that I've worked for your father with all
my strength, 7yet your father has cheated me
by changing my wages ten times. However,
God has not allowed him to harm me. 8If he
said, 'The speckled ones will be your wages,'
then all the flocks gave birth to speckled
young; and if he said, 'The streaked ones will
be your wages,' then all the flocks bore
streaked young. 9So God has taken away your
father's livestock and has given them to me.
10"In breeding season I once had a dream in
which I looked up and saw that the male goats
mating with the flock were streaked, speckled
or spotted. 11The angel of God said to me in
the dream, 'Jacob.' I answered, 'Here I am.'
12And he said, 'Look up and see that all the
male goats mating with the flock are streaked,
speckled or spotted, for I have seen all that
Laban has been doing to you. 13I am the God
of Bethel, where you anointed a pillar and
where you made a vow to me. Now leave this
land at once and go back to your native land.' "
14Then Rachel and Leah replied, "Do we

[a] 18 *Issachar* sounds like the Hebrew for *reward.* [b] 20 *Zebulun* probably means *honor.* [c] 24 *Joseph* means *may he add.* [d] 27 Or possibly *have become rich and*

still have any share in the inheritance of our father's estate? 15 Does he not regard us as foreigners? Not only has he sold us, but he has used up what was paid for us. 16 Surely all the wealth that God took away from our father belongs to us and our children. So do whatever God has told you."

17 Then Jacob put his children and his wives on camels, 18 and he drove all his livestock ahead of him, along with all the goods he had accumulated in Paddan Aram,[a] to go to his father Isaac in the land of Canaan.

19 When Laban had gone to shear his sheep, Rachel stole her father's household gods. 20 Moreover, Jacob deceived Laban the Aramean by not telling him he was running away. 21 So he fled with all he had, and crossing the River,[b] he headed for the hill country of Gilead.

Laban Pursues Jacob

22 On the third day Laban was told that Jacob had fled. 23 Taking his relatives with him, he pursued Jacob for seven days and caught up with him in the hill country of Gilead. 24 Then God came to Laban the Aramean in a dream at night and said to him, "Be careful not to say anything to Jacob, either good or bad."

25 Jacob had pitched his tent in the hill country of Gilead when Laban overtook him, and Laban and his relatives camped there too. 26 Then Laban said to Jacob, "What have you done? You've deceived me, and you've carried off my daughters like captives in war. 27 Why did you run off secretly and deceive me? Why didn't you tell me, so I could send you away with joy and singing to the music of tambourines and harps? 28 You didn't even let me kiss my grandchildren and my daughters good-by. You have done a foolish thing. 29 I have the power to harm you; but last night the God of your father said to me, 'Be careful not to say anything to Jacob, either good or bad.' 30 Now you have gone off because you longed to return to your father's house. But why did you steal my gods?"

31 Jacob answered Laban, "I was afraid, because I thought you would take your daughters away from me by force. 32 But if you find anyone who has your gods, he shall not live. In the presence of our relatives, see for yourself whether there is anything of yours here with me; and if so, take it." Now Jacob did not know that Rachel had stolen the gods.

33 So Laban went into Jacob's tent and into Leah's tent and into the tent of the two maidservants, but he found nothing. After he came out of Leah's tent, he entered Rachel's tent. 34 Now Rachel had taken the household gods and put them inside her camel's saddle and was sitting on them. Laban searched through everything in the tent but found nothing.

35 Rachel said to her father, "Don't be angry, my lord, that I cannot stand up in your presence; I'm having my period." So he searched but could not find the household gods.

36 Jacob was angry and took Laban to task. "What is my crime?" he asked Laban. "What sin have I committed that you hunt me down? 37 Now that you have searched through all my goods, what have you found that belongs to your household? Put it here in front of your relatives and mine, and let them judge between the two of us.

38 "I have been with you for twenty years now. Your sheep and goats have not miscarried, nor have I eaten rams from your flocks. 39 I did not bring you animals torn by wild beasts; I bore the loss myself. And you demanded payment from me for whatever was stolen by day or night. 40 This was my situation: The heat consumed me in the daytime and the cold at night, and sleep fled from my eyes. 41 It was like this for the twenty years I was in your household. I worked for you fourteen years for your two daughters and six years for your flocks, and you changed my wages ten times. 42 If the God of my father, the God of Abraham and the Fear of Isaac, had not been with me, you would surely have sent me away empty-handed. But God has seen my hardship and the toil of my hands, and last night he rebuked you."

43 Laban answered Jacob, "The women are my daughters, the children are my children, and the flocks are my flocks. All you see is mine. Yet what can I do today about these daughters of mine, or about the children they have borne? 44 Come now, let's make a covenant, you and I, and let it serve as a witness between us."

45 So Jacob took a stone and set it up as a pillar. 46 He said to his relatives, "Gather some stones." So they took stones and piled them in a heap, and they ate there by the heap. 47 Laban called it Jegar Sahadutha,[c] and Jacob called it Galeed.[d]

48 Laban said, "This heap is a witness between you and me today." That is why it was called Galeed. 49 It was also called Mizpah,[e] because he said, "May the LORD keep watch between you and me when we are away from each other. 50 If you mistreat my daughters or if you take any wives besides my daughters, even though no one is with us, remember that God is a witness between you and me."

51 Laban also said to Jacob, "Here is this heap, and here is this pillar I have set up between you and me. 52 This heap is a witness, and this pillar is a witness, that I will not go past this heap to your side to harm you and that you will not go past this heap and pillar to my side to harm me. 53 May the God of Abraham and the God of Nahor, the God of their father, judge between us."

So Jacob took an oath in the name of the Fear of his father Isaac. 54 He offered a sacrifice there in the hill country and invited his

[a] *18* That is, Northwest Mesopotamia [b] *21* That is, the Euphrates [c] *47* The Aramaic *Jegar Sahadutha* means *witness heap.* [d] *47* The Hebrew *Galeed* means *witness heap.* [e] *49* *Mizpah* means *watchtower.*

relatives to a meal. After they had eaten, they spent the night there.

55Early the next morning Laban kissed his grandchildren and his daughters and blessed them. Then he left and returned home.

Jacob Prepares to Meet Esau

32 Jacob also went on his way, and the angels of God met him. 2When Jacob saw them, he said, "This is the camp of God!" So he named that place Mahanaim.[a]

3Jacob sent messengers ahead of him to his brother Esau in the land of Seir, the country of Edom. 4He instructed them: "This is what you are to say to my master Esau: 'Your servant Jacob says, I have been staying with Laban and have remained there till now. 5I have cattle and donkeys, sheep and goats, menservants and maidservants. Now I am sending this message to my lord, that I may find favor in your eyes.' "

6When the messengers returned to Jacob, they said, "We went to your brother Esau, and now he is coming to meet you, and four hundred men are with him."

7In great fear and distress Jacob divided the people who were with him into two groups,[b] and the flocks and herds and camels as well. 8He thought, "If Esau comes and attacks one group,[c] the group[c] that is left may escape."

9Then Jacob prayed, "O God of my father Abraham, God of my father Isaac, O LORD, who said to me, 'Go back to your country and your relatives, and I will make you prosper,' 10I am unworthy of all the kindness and faithfulness you have shown your servant. I had only my staff when I crossed this Jordan, but now I have become two groups. 11Save me, I pray, from the hand of my brother Esau, for I am afraid he will come and attack me, and also the mothers with their children. 12But you have said, 'I will surely make you prosper and will make your descendants like the sand of the sea, which cannot be counted.' "

13He spent the night there, and from what he had with him he selected a gift for his brother Esau: 14two hundred female goats and twenty male goats, two hundred ewes and twenty rams, 15thirty female camels with their young, forty cows and ten bulls, and twenty female donkeys and ten male donkeys. 16He put them in the care of his servants, each herd by itself, and said to his servants, "Go ahead of me, and keep some space between the herds."

17He instructed the one in the lead: "When my brother Esau meets you and asks, 'To whom do you belong, and where are you going, and who owns all these animals in front of you?' 18then you are to say, 'They belong to your servant Jacob. They are a gift sent to my lord Esau, and he is coming behind us.' "

19He also instructed the second, the third and all the others who followed the herds: "You are to say the same thing to Esau when you meet him. 20And be sure to say, 'Your servant Jacob is coming behind us.' " For he thought, "I will pacify him with these gifts I am sending on ahead; later, when I see him, perhaps he will receive me." 21So Jacob's gifts went on ahead of him, but he himself spent the night in the camp.

Jacob Wrestles With God

22That night Jacob got up and took his two wives, his two maidservants and his eleven sons and crossed the ford of the Jabbok. 23After he had sent them across the stream, he sent over all his possessions. 24So Jacob was left alone, and a man wrestled with him till daybreak. 25When the man saw that he could not overpower him, he touched the socket of Jacob's hip so that his hip was wrenched as he wrestled with the man. 26Then the man said, "Let me go, for it is daybreak."

But Jacob replied, "I will not let you go unless you bless me."

27The man asked him, "What is your name?"

"Jacob," he answered.

28Then the man said, "Your name will no longer be Jacob, but Israel,[d] because you have struggled with God and with men and have overcome."

29Jacob said, "Please tell me your name."

But he replied, "Why do you ask my name?" Then he blessed him there.

30So Jacob called the place Peniel,[e] saying, "It is because I saw God face to face, and yet my life was spared."

31The sun rose above him as he passed Peniel,[f] and he was limping because of his hip. 32Therefore to this day the Israelites do not eat the tendon attached to the socket of the hip, because the socket of Jacob's hip was touched near the tendon.

Jacob Meets Esau

33 Jacob looked up and there was Esau, coming with his four hundred men; so he divided the children among Leah, Rachel and the two maidservants. 2He put the maidservants and their children in front, Leah and her children next, and Rachel and Joseph in the rear. 3He himself went on ahead and bowed down to the ground seven times as he approached his brother.

4But Esau ran to meet Jacob and embraced him; he threw his arms around his neck and kissed him. And they wept. 5Then Esau looked up and saw the women and children. "Who are these with you?" he asked.

Jacob answered, "They are the children God has graciously given your servant."

6Then the maidservants and their children approached and bowed down. 7Next, Leah and her children came and bowed down. Last of all came Joseph and Rachel, and they too bowed down.

[a]2 *Mahanaim* means *two camps.* [b]7 Or *camps*; also in verse 10 [c]8 Or *camp* [d]28 *Israel* means *he struggles with God.* [e]30 *Peniel* means *face of God.* [f]31 Hebrew *Penuel,* a variant of *Peniel*

8 Esau asked, "What do you mean by all these droves I met?"

"To find favor in your eyes, my lord," he said.

9 But Esau said, "I already have plenty, my brother. Keep what you have for yourself."

10 "No, please!" said Jacob. "If I have found favor in your eyes, accept this gift from me. For to see your face is like seeing the face of God, now that you have received me favorably. 11 Please accept the present that was brought to you, for God has been gracious to me and I have all I need." And because Jacob insisted, Esau accepted it.

12 Then Esau said, "Let us be on our way; I'll accompany you."

13 But Jacob said to him, "My lord knows that the children are tender and that I must care for the ewes and cows that are nursing their young. If they are driven hard just one day, all the animals will die. 14 So let my lord go on ahead of his servant, while I move along slowly at the pace of the droves before me and that of the children, until I come to my lord in Seir."

15 Esau said, "Then let me leave some of my men with you."

"But why do that?" Jacob asked. "Just let me find favor in the eyes of my lord."

16 So that day Esau started on his way back to Seir. 17 Jacob, however, went to Succoth, where he built a place for himself and made shelters for his livestock. That is why the place is called Succoth.[a]

18 After Jacob came from Paddan Aram,[b] he arrived safely at the[c] city of Shechem in Canaan and camped within sight of the city. 19 For a hundred pieces of silver,[d] he bought from the sons of Hamor, the father of Shechem, the plot of ground where he pitched his tent. 20 There he set up an altar and called it El Elohe Israel.[e]

Dinah and the Shechemites

34 Now Dinah, the daughter Leah had borne to Jacob, went out to visit the women of the land. 2 When Shechem son of Hamor the Hivite, the ruler of that area, saw her, he took her and violated her. 3 His heart was drawn to Dinah daughter of Jacob, and he loved the girl and spoke tenderly to her. 4 And Shechem said to his father Hamor, "Get me this girl as my wife."

5 When Jacob heard that his daughter Dinah had been defiled, his sons were in the fields with his livestock; so he kept quiet about it until they came home.

6 Then Shechem's father Hamor went out to talk with Jacob. 7 Now Jacob's sons had come in from the fields as soon as they heard what had happened. They were filled with grief and fury, because Shechem had done a disgraceful thing in[f] Israel by lying with Jacob's daughter—a thing that should not be done.

8 But Hamor said to them, "My son Shechem has his heart set on your daughter. Please give her to him as his wife. 9 Intermarry with us; give us your daughters and take our daughters for yourselves. 10 You can settle among us; the land is open to you. Live in it, trade[g] in it, and acquire property in it."

11 Then Shechem said to Dinah's father and brothers, "Let me find favor in your eyes, and I will give you whatever you ask. 12 Make the price for the bride and the gift I am to bring as great as you like, and I'll pay whatever you ask me. Only give me the girl as my wife."

13 Because their sister Dinah had been defiled, Jacob's sons replied deceitfully as they spoke to Shechem and his father Hamor. 14 They said to them, "We can't do such a thing; we can't give our sister to a man who is not circumcised. That would be a disgrace to us. 15 We will give our consent to you on one condition only: that you become like us by circumcising all your males. 16 Then we will give you our daughters and take your daughters for ourselves. We'll settle among you and become one people with you. 17 But if you will not agree to be circumcised, we'll take our sister[h] and go."

18 Their proposal seemed good to Hamor and his son Shechem. 19 The young man, who was the most honored of all his father's household, lost no time in doing what they said, because he was delighted with Jacob's daughter. 20 So Hamor and his son Shechem went to the gate of their city to speak to their fellow townsmen. 21 "These men are friendly toward us," they said. "Let them live in our land and trade in it; the land has plenty of room for them. We can marry their daughters and they can marry ours. 22 But the men will consent to live with us as one people only on the condition that our males be circumcised, as they themselves are. 23 Won't their livestock, their property and all their other animals become ours? So let us give our consent to them, and they will settle among us."

24 All the men who went out of the city gate agreed with Hamor and his son Shechem, and every male in the city was circumcised.

25 Three days later, while all of them were still in pain, two of Jacob's sons, Simeon and Levi, Dinah's brothers, took their swords and attacked the unsuspecting city, killing every male. 26 They put Hamor and his son Shechem to the sword and took Dinah from Shechem's house and left. 27 The sons of Jacob came upon the dead bodies and looted the city where[i] their sister had been defiled. 28 They seized their flocks and herds and donkeys and everything else of theirs in the city and out in the fields. 29 They carried off all their wealth and all their women and children, taking as plunder everything in the houses.

[a] *17 Succoth* means *shelters.* [b] *18* That is, Northwest Mesopotamia [c] *18* Or *arrived at Shalem, a* [d] *19* Hebrew *hundred kesitahs*; a kesitah was a unit of money of unknown weight and value. [e] *20 El Elohe Israel* can mean *God, the God of Israel* or *mighty is the God of Israel.* [f] *7* Or *against* [g] *10* Or *move about freely*; also in verse 21 [h] *17* Hebrew *daughter* [i] *27* Or *because*

30Then Jacob said to Simeon and Levi, "You have brought trouble on me by making me a stench to the Canaanites and Perizzites, the people living in this land. We are few in number, and if they join forces against me and attack me, I and my household will be destroyed."

31But they replied, "Should he have treated our sister like a prostitute?"

Jacob Returns to Bethel

35 Then God said to Jacob, "Go up to Bethel and settle there, and build an altar there to God, who appeared to you when you were fleeing from your brother Esau."

2So Jacob said to his household and to all who were with him, "Get rid of the foreign gods you have with you, and purify yourselves and change your clothes. 3Then come, let us go up to Bethel, where I will build an altar to God, who answered me in the day of my distress and who has been with me wherever I have gone." 4So they gave Jacob all the foreign gods they had and the rings in their ears, and Jacob buried them under the oak at Shechem. 5Then they set out, and the terror of God fell upon the towns all around them so that no one pursued them.

6Jacob and all the people with him came to Luz (that is, Bethel) in the land of Canaan. 7There he built an altar, and he called the place El Bethel,[a] because it was there that God revealed himself to him when he was fleeing from his brother.

8Now Deborah, Rebekah's nurse, died and was buried under the oak below Bethel. So it was named Allon Bacuth.[b]

9After Jacob returned from Paddan Aram,[c] God appeared to him again and blessed him. 10God said to him, "Your name is Jacob,[d] but you will no longer be called Jacob; your name will be Israel.[e]" So he named him Israel.

11And God said to him, "I am God Almighty[f]; be fruitful and increase in number. A nation and a community of nations will come from you, and kings will come from your body. 12The land I gave to Abraham and Isaac I also give to you, and I will give this land to your descendants after you." 13Then God went up from him at the place where he had talked with him.

14Jacob set up a stone pillar at the place where God had talked with him, and he poured out a drink offering on it; he also poured oil on it. 15Jacob called the place where God had talked with him Bethel.[g]

The Deaths of Rachel and Isaac

16Then they moved on from Bethel. While they were still some distance from Ephrath, Rachel began to give birth and had great difficulty. 17And as she was having great difficulty in childbirth, the midwife said to her, "Don't be afraid, for you have another son." 18As she breathed her last—for she was dying—she named her son Ben-Oni.[h] But his father named him Benjamin.[i]

19So Rachel died and was buried on the way to Ephrath (that is, Bethlehem). 20Over her tomb Jacob set up a pillar, and to this day that pillar marks Rachel's tomb.

21Israel moved on again and pitched his tent beyond Migdal Eder. 22While Israel was living in that region, Reuben went in and slept with his father's concubine Bilhah, and Israel heard of it.

Jacob had twelve sons:

23The sons of Leah:
Reuben the firstborn of Jacob,
Simeon, Levi, Judah, Issachar and Zebulun.
24The sons of Rachel:
Joseph and Benjamin.
25The sons of Rachel's maidservant Bilhah:
Dan and Naphtali.
26The sons of Leah's maidservant Zilpah:
Gad and Asher.

These were the sons of Jacob, who were born to him in Paddan Aram.

27Jacob came home to his father Isaac in Mamre, near Kiriath Arba (that is, Hebron), where Abraham and Isaac had stayed. 28Isaac lived a hundred and eighty years. 29Then he breathed his last and died and was gathered to his people, old and full of years. And his sons Esau and Jacob buried him.

Esau's Descendants

36 This is the account of Esau (that is, Edom).

2Esau took his wives from the women of Canaan: Adah daughter of Elon the Hittite, and Oholibamah daughter of Anah and granddaughter of Zibeon the Hivite— 3also Basemath daughter of Ishmael and sister of Nebaioth.

4Adah bore Eliphaz to Esau, Basemath bore Reuel, 5and Oholibamah bore Jeush, Jalam and Korah. These were the sons of Esau, who were born to him in Canaan.

6Esau took his wives and sons and daughters and all the members of his household, as well as his livestock and all his other animals and all the goods he had acquired in Canaan, and moved to a land some distance from his brother Jacob. 7Their possessions were too great for them to remain together; the land where they were staying could not support them both because of their livestock. 8So Esau (that is, Edom) settled in the hill country of Seir.

[a] 7 *El Bethel* means *God of Bethel.* [b] 8 *Allon Bacuth* means *oak of weeping.* [c] 9 That is, Northwest Mesopotamia; also in verse 26 [d] 10 *Jacob* means *he grasps the heel* (figuratively, *he deceives*). [e] 10 *Israel* means *he struggles with God.* [f] 11 Hebrew *El-Shaddai* [g] 15 *Bethel* means *house of God.* [h] 18 *Ben-Oni* means *son of my trouble.* [i] 18 *Benjamin* means *son of my right hand.*

[9]This is the account of Esau the father of the Edomites in the hill country of Seir.

[10]These are the names of Esau's sons:
Eliphaz, the son of Esau's wife Adah, and Reuel, the son of Esau's wife Basemath.
[11]The sons of Eliphaz:
Teman, Omar, Zepho, Gatam and Kenaz.
[12]Esau's son Eliphaz also had a concubine named Timna, who bore him Amalek. These were grandsons of Esau's wife Adah.
[13]The sons of Reuel:
Nahath, Zerah, Shammah and Mizzah. These were grandsons of Esau's wife Basemath.
[14]The sons of Esau's wife Oholibamah daughter of Anah and granddaughter of Zibeon, whom she bore to Esau:
Jeush, Jalam and Korah.

[15]These were the chiefs among Esau's descendants:
The sons of Eliphaz the firstborn of Esau:
Chiefs Teman, Omar, Zepho, Kenaz, [16]Korah,[a] Gatam and Amalek. These were the chiefs descended from Eliphaz in Edom; they were grandsons of Adah.
[17]The sons of Esau's son Reuel:
Chiefs Nahath, Zerah, Shammah and Mizzah. These were the chiefs descended from Reuel in Edom; they were grandsons of Esau's wife Basemath.
[18]The sons of Esau's wife Oholibamah:
Chiefs Jeush, Jalam and Korah. These were the chiefs descended from Esau's wife Oholibamah daughter of Anah.

[19]These were the sons of Esau (that is, Edom), and these were their chiefs.

[20]These were the sons of Seir the Horite, who were living in the region:
Lotan, Shobal, Zibeon, Anah, [21]Dishon, Ezer and Dishan. These sons of Seir in Edom were Horite chiefs.
[22]The sons of Lotan:
Hori and Homam.[b] Timna was Lotan's sister.
[23]The sons of Shobal:
Alvan, Manahath, Ebal, Shepho and Onam.
[24]The sons of Zibeon:
Aiah and Anah. This is the Anah who discovered the hot springs[c] in the desert while he was grazing the donkeys of his father Zibeon.
[25]The children of Anah:
Dishon and Oholibamah daughter of Anah.
[26]The sons of Dishon[d]:
Hemdan, Eshban, Ithran and Keran.
[27]The sons of Ezer:
Bilhan, Zaavan and Akan.
[28]The sons of Dishan:
Uz and Aran.
[29]These were the Horite chiefs:
Lotan, Shobal, Zibeon, Anah, [30]Dishon, Ezer and Dishan. These were the Horite chiefs, according to their divisions, in the land of Seir.

The Rulers of Edom

[31]These were the kings who reigned in Edom before any Israelite king reigned[e]:
[32]Bela son of Beor became king of Edom. His city was named Dinhabah.
[33]When Bela died, Jobab son of Zerah from Bozrah succeeded him as king.
[34]When Jobab died, Husham from the land of the Temanites succeeded him as king.
[35]When Husham died, Hadad son of Bedad, who defeated Midian in the country of Moab, succeeded him as king. His city was named Avith.
[36]When Hadad died, Samlah from Masrekah succeeded him as king.
[37]When Samlah died, Shaul from Rehoboth on the river[f] succeeded him as king.
[38]When Shaul died, Baal-Hanan son of Acbor succeeded him as king.
[39]When Baal-Hanan son of Acbor died, Hadad[g] succeeded him as king. His city was named Pau, and his wife's name was Mehetabel daughter of Matred, the daughter of Me-Zahab.

[40]These were the chiefs descended from Esau, by name, according to their clans and regions:
Timna, Alvah, Jetheth, [41]Oholibamah, Elah, Pinon, [42]Kenaz, Teman, Mibzar, [43]Magdiel and Iram. These were the chiefs of Edom, according to their settlements in the land they occupied.

This was Esau the father of the Edomites.

Joseph's Dreams

37 Jacob lived in the land where his father had stayed, the land of Canaan.

[2]This is the account of Jacob.

Joseph, a young man of seventeen, was tending the flocks with his brothers, the sons of Bilhah and the sons of Zilpah, his father's

[a]16 Masoretic Text; Samaritan Pentateuch (see also Gen. 36:11 and 1 Chron. 1:36) does not have *Korah.*
[b]22 Hebrew *Hemam,* a variant of *Homam* (see 1 Chron. 1:39) [c]24 Vulgate; Syriac *discovered water;* the meaning of the Hebrew for this word is uncertain. [d]26 Hebrew *Dishan,* a variant of *Dishon*
[e]31 Or *before an Israelite king reigned over them* [f]37 Possibly the Euphrates [g]39 Many manuscripts of the Masoretic Text, Samaritan Pentateuch and Syriac (see also 1 Chron. 1:50); most manuscripts of the Masoretic Text *Hadar*

wives, and he brought their father a bad report about them.

[3]Now Israel loved Joseph more than any of his other sons, because he had been born to him in his old age; and he made a richly ornamented[a] robe for him. [4]When his brothers saw that their father loved him more than any of them, they hated him and could not speak a kind word to him.

[5]Joseph had a dream, and when he told it to his brothers, they hated him all the more. [6]He said to them, "Listen to this dream I had: [7]We were binding sheaves of grain out in the field when suddenly my sheaf rose and stood upright, while your sheaves gathered around mine and bowed down to it."

[8]His brothers said to him, "Do you intend to reign over us? Will you actually rule us?" And they hated him all the more because of his dream and what he had said.

[9]Then he had another dream, and he told it to his brothers. "Listen," he said, "I had another dream, and this time the sun and moon and eleven stars were bowing down to me."

[10]When he told his father as well as his brothers, his father rebuked him and said, "What is this dream you had? Will your mother and I and your brothers actually come and bow down to the ground before you?" [11]His brothers were jealous of him, but his father kept the matter in mind.

Joseph Sold by His Brothers

[12]Now his brothers had gone to graze their father's flocks near Shechem, [13]and Israel said to Joseph, "As you know, your brothers are grazing the flocks near Shechem. Come, I am going to send you to them."

"Very well," he replied.

[14]So he said to him, "Go and see if all is well with your brothers and with the flocks, and bring word back to me." Then he sent him off from the Valley of Hebron.

When Joseph arrived at Shechem, [15]a man found him wandering around in the fields and asked him, "What are you looking for?"

[16]He replied, "I'm looking for my brothers. Can you tell me where they are grazing their flocks?"

[17]"They have moved on from here," the man answered. "I heard them say, 'Let's go to Dothan.' "

So Joseph went after his brothers and found them near Dothan. [18]But they saw him in the distance, and before he reached them, they plotted to kill him.

[19]"Here comes that dreamer!" they said to each other. [20]"Come now, let's kill him and throw him into one of these cisterns and say that a ferocious animal devoured him. Then we'll see what comes of his dreams."

[21]When Reuben heard this, he tried to rescue him from their hands. "Let's not take his life," he said. [22]"Don't shed any blood. Throw him into this cistern here in the desert, but don't lay a hand on him." Reuben said this to rescue him from them and take him back to his father.

[23]So when Joseph came to his brothers, they stripped him of his robe—the richly ornamented robe he was wearing— [24]and they took him and threw him into the cistern. Now the cistern was empty; there was no water in it.

[25]As they sat down to eat their meal, they looked up and saw a caravan of Ishmaelites coming from Gilead. Their camels were loaded with spices, balm and myrrh, and they were on their way to take them down to Egypt.

[26]Judah said to his brothers, "What will we gain if we kill our brother and cover up his blood? [27]Come, let's sell him to the Ishmaelites and not lay our hands on him; after all, he is our brother, our own flesh and blood." His brothers agreed.

[28]So when the Midianite merchants came by, his brothers pulled Joseph up out of the cistern and sold him for twenty shekels[b] of silver to the Ishmaelites, who took him to Egypt.

[29]When Reuben returned to the cistern and saw that Joseph was not there, he tore his clothes. [30]He went back to his brothers and said, "The boy isn't there! Where can I turn now?"

[31]Then they got Joseph's robe, slaughtered a goat and dipped the robe in the blood. [32]They took the ornamented robe back to their father and said, "We found this. Examine it to see whether it is your son's robe."

[33]He recognized it and said, "It is my son's robe! Some ferocious animal has devoured him. Joseph has surely been torn to pieces."

[34]Then Jacob tore his clothes, put on sackcloth and mourned for his son many days. [35]All his sons and daughters came to comfort him, but he refused to be comforted. "No," he said, "in mourning will I go down to the grave[c] to my son." So his father wept for him.

[36]Meanwhile, the Midianites[d] sold Joseph in Egypt to Potiphar, one of Pharaoh's officials, the captain of the guard.

Judah and Tamar

38 At that time, Judah left his brothers and went down to stay with a man of Adullam named Hirah. [2]There Judah met the daughter of a Canaanite man named Shua. He married her and lay with her; [3]she became pregnant and gave birth to a son, who was named Er. [4]She conceived again and gave birth to a son and named him Onan. [5]She gave birth to still another son and named him Shelah. It was at Kezib that she gave birth to him.

[6]Judah got a wife for Er, his firstborn, and her name was Tamar. [7]But Er, Judah's first-

[a]*3* The meaning of the Hebrew for *richly ornamented* is uncertain; also in verses 23 and 32. [b]*28* That is, about 8 ounces (about 0.2 kilogram) [c]*35* Hebrew *Sheol* [d]*36* Samaritan Pentateuch, Septuagint, Vulgate and Syriac (see also verse 28); Masoretic Text *Medanites*

born, was wicked in the LORD's sight; so the LORD put him to death.

[8]Then Judah said to Onan, "Lie with your brother's wife and fulfill your duty to her as a brother-in-law to produce offspring for your brother." [9]But Onan knew that the offspring would not be his; so whenever he lay with his brother's wife, he spilled his semen on the ground to keep from producing offspring for his brother. [10]What he did was wicked in the LORD's sight; so he put him to death also.

[11]Judah then said to his daughter-in-law Tamar, "Live as a widow in your father's house until my son Shelah grows up." For he thought, "He may die too, just like his brothers." So Tamar went to live in her father's house.

[12]After a long time Judah's wife, the daughter of Shua, died. When Judah had recovered from his grief, he went up to Timnah, to the men who were shearing his sheep, and his friend Hirah the Adullamite went with him.

[13]When Tamar was told, "Your father-in-law is on his way to Timnah to shear his sheep," [14]she took off her widow's clothes, covered herself with a veil to disguise herself, and then sat down at the entrance to Enaim, which is on the road to Timnah. For she saw that, though Shelah had now grown up, she had not been given to him as his wife.

[15]When Judah saw her, he thought she was a prostitute, for she had covered her face. [16]Not realizing that she was his daughter-in-law, he went over to her by the roadside and said, "Come now, let me sleep with you."

"And what will you give me to sleep with you?" she asked.

[17]"I'll send you a young goat from my flock," he said.

"Will you give me something as a pledge until you send it?" she asked.

[18]He said, "What pledge should I give you?"

"Your seal and its cord, and the staff in your hand," she answered. So he gave them to her and slept with her, and she became pregnant by him. [19]After she left, she took off her veil and put on her widow's clothes again.

[20]Meanwhile Judah sent the young goat by his friend the Adullamite in order to get his pledge back from the woman, but he did not find her. [21]He asked the men who lived there, "Where is the shrine prostitute who was beside the road at Enaim?"

"There hasn't been any shrine prostitute here," they said.

[22]So he went back to Judah and said, "I didn't find her. Besides, the men who lived there said, 'There hasn't been any shrine prostitute here.' "

[23]Then Judah said, "Let her keep what she has, or we will become a laughingstock. After all, I did send her this young goat, but you didn't find her."

[24]About three months later Judah was told, "Your daughter-in-law Tamar is guilty of prostitution, and as a result she is now pregnant."

Judah said, "Bring her out and have her burned to death!"

[25]As she was being brought out, she sent a message to her father-in-law. "I am pregnant by the man who owns these," she said. And she added, "See if you recognize whose seal and cord and staff these are."

[26]Judah recognized them and said, "She is more righteous than I, since I wouldn't give her to my son Shelah." And he did not sleep with her again.

[27]When the time came for her to give birth, there were twin boys in her womb. [28]As she was giving birth, one of them put out his hand; so the midwife took a scarlet thread and tied it on his wrist and said, "This one came out first." [29]But when he drew back his hand, his brother came out, and she said, "So this is how you have broken out!" And he was named Perez.[a] [30]Then his brother, who had the scarlet thread on his wrist, came out and he was given the name Zerah.[b]

Joseph and Potiphar's Wife

39 Now Joseph had been taken down to Egypt. Potiphar, an Egyptian who was one of Pharaoh's officials, the captain of the guard, bought him from the Ishmaelites who had taken him there.

[2]The LORD was with Joseph and he prospered, and he lived in the house of his Egyptian master. [3]When his master saw that the LORD was with him and that the LORD gave him success in everything he did, [4]Joseph found favor in his eyes and became his attendant. Potiphar put him in charge of his household, and he entrusted to his care everything he owned. [5]From the time he put him in charge of his household and of all that he owned, the LORD blessed the household of the Egyptian because of Joseph. The blessing of the LORD was on everything Potiphar had, both in the house and in the field. [6]So he left in Joseph's care everything he had; with Joseph in charge, he did not concern himself with anything except the food he ate.

Now Joseph was well-built and handsome, [7]and after a while his master's wife took notice of Joseph and said, "Come to bed with me!"

[8]But he refused. "With me in charge," he told her, "my master does not concern himself with anything in the house; everything he owns he has entrusted to my care. [9]No one is greater in this house than I am. My master has withheld nothing from me except you, because you are his wife. How then could I do such a wicked thing and sin against God?" [10]And though she spoke to Joseph day after day, he refused to go to bed with her or even be with her.

[11]One day he went into the house to attend to his duties, and none of the household servants was inside. [12]She caught him by his

[a]29 *Perez* means *breaking out.* [b]30 *Zerah* can mean *scarlet* or *brightness.*

cloak and said, "Come to bed with me!" But he left his cloak in her hand and ran out of the house.

13When she saw that he had left his cloak in her hand and had run out of the house, 14she called her household servants. "Look," she said to them, "this Hebrew has been brought to us to make sport of us! He came in here to sleep with me, but I screamed. 15When he heard me scream for help, he left his cloak beside me and ran out of the house."

16She kept his cloak beside her until his master came home. 17Then she told him this story: "That Hebrew slave you brought us came to me to make sport of me. 18But as soon as I screamed for help, he left his cloak beside me and ran out of the house."

19When his master heard the story his wife told him, saying, "This is how your slave treated me," he burned with anger. 20Joseph's master took him and put him in prison, the place where the king's prisoners were confined.

But while Joseph was there in the prison, 21the LORD was with him; he showed him kindness and granted him favor in the eyes of the prison warden. 22So the warden put Joseph in charge of all those held in the prison, and he was made responsible for all that was done there. 23The warden paid no attention to anything under Joseph's care, because the LORD was with Joseph and gave him success in whatever he did.

The Cupbearer and the Baker

40 Some time later, the cupbearer and the baker of the king of Egypt offended their master, the king of Egypt. 2Pharaoh was angry with his two officials, the chief cupbearer and the chief baker, 3and put them in custody in the house of the captain of the guard, in the same prison where Joseph was confined. 4The captain of the guard assigned them to Joseph, and he attended them.

After they had been in custody for some time, 5each of the two men—the cupbearer and the baker of the king of Egypt, who were being held in prison—had a dream the same night, and each dream had a meaning of its own.

6When Joseph came to them the next morning, he saw that they were dejected. 7So he asked Pharaoh's officials who were in custody with him in his master's house, "Why are your faces so sad today?"

8"We both had dreams," they answered, "but there is no one to interpret them."

Then Joseph said to them, "Do not interpretations belong to God? Tell me your dreams."

9So the chief cupbearer told Joseph his dream. He said to him, "In my dream I saw a vine in front of me, 10and on the vine were three branches. As soon as it budded, it blossomed, and its clusters ripened into grapes. 11Pharaoh's cup was in my hand, and I took the grapes, squeezed them into Pharaoh's cup and put the cup in his hand."

12"This is what it means," Joseph said to him. "The three branches are three days. 13Within three days Pharaoh will lift up your head and restore you to your position, and you will put Pharaoh's cup in his hand, just as you used to do when you were his cupbearer. 14But when all goes well with you, remember me and show me kindness; mention me to Pharaoh and get me out of this prison. 15For I was forcibly carried off from the land of the Hebrews, and even here I have done nothing to deserve being put in a dungeon."

16When the chief baker saw that Joseph had given a favorable interpretation, he said to Joseph, "I too had a dream: On my head were three baskets of bread.[a] 17In the top basket were all kinds of baked goods for Pharaoh, but the birds were eating them out of the basket on my head."

18"This is what it means," Joseph said. "The three baskets are three days. 19Within three days Pharaoh will lift off your head and hang you on a tree.[b] And the birds will eat away your flesh."

20Now the third day was Pharaoh's birthday, and he gave a feast for all his officials. He lifted up the heads of the chief cupbearer and the chief baker in the presence of his officials: 21He restored the chief cupbearer to his position, so that he once again put the cup into Pharaoh's hand, 22but he hanged[c] the chief baker, just as Joseph had said to them in his interpretation.

23The chief cupbearer, however, did not remember Joseph; he forgot him.

Pharaoh's Dreams

41 When two full years had passed, Pharaoh had a dream: He was standing by the Nile, 2when out of the river there came up seven cows, sleek and fat, and they grazed among the reeds. 3After them, seven other cows, ugly and gaunt, came up out of the Nile and stood beside those on the riverbank. 4And the cows that were ugly and gaunt ate up the seven sleek, fat cows. Then Pharaoh woke up.

5He fell asleep again and had a second dream: Seven heads of grain, healthy and good, were growing on a single stalk. 6After them, seven other heads of grain sprouted—thin and scorched by the east wind. 7The thin heads of grain swallowed up the seven healthy, full heads. Then Pharaoh woke up; it had been a dream.

8In the morning his mind was troubled, so he sent for all the magicians and wise men of Egypt. Pharaoh told them his dreams, but no one could interpret them for him.

9Then the chief cupbearer said to Pharaoh, "Today I am reminded of my shortcomings. 10Pharaoh was once angry with his servants, and he imprisoned me and the chief baker in the house of the captain of the guard. 11Each of

[a]*16* Or *three wicker baskets* [b]*19* Or *and impale you on a pole* [c]*22* Or *impaled*

us had a dream the same night, and each dream
had a meaning of its own. 12Now a young Hebrew was there with us, a servant of the captain
of the guard. We told him our dreams, and he
interpreted them for us, giving each man the
interpretation of his dream. 13And things
turned out exactly as he interpreted them to us:
I was restored to my position, and the other
man was hanged.[a]"

14So Pharaoh sent for Joseph, and he was
quickly brought from the dungeon. When he
had shaved and changed his clothes, he came
before Pharaoh.

15Pharaoh said to Joseph, "I had a dream,
and no one can interpret it. But I have heard it
said of you that when you hear a dream you
can interpret it."

16"I cannot do it," Joseph replied to Pharaoh, "but God will give Pharaoh the answer he
desires."

17Then Pharaoh said to Joseph, "In my
dream I was standing on the bank of the Nile,
18when out of the river there came up seven
cows, fat and sleek, and they grazed among the
reeds. 19After them, seven other cows came
up—scrawny and very ugly and lean. I had
never seen such ugly cows in all the land of
Egypt. 20The lean, ugly cows ate up the seven
fat cows that came up first. 21But even after
they ate them, no one could tell that they had
done so; they looked just as ugly as before.
Then I woke up.

22"In my dreams I also saw seven heads of
grain, full and good, growing on a single stalk.
23After them, seven other heads sprouted—
withered and thin and scorched by the east
wind. 24The thin heads of grain swallowed up
the seven good heads. I told this to the magicians, but none could explain it to me."

25Then Joseph said to Pharaoh, "The dreams
of Pharaoh are one and the same. God has
revealed to Pharaoh what he is about to do.
26The seven good cows are seven years, and
the seven good heads of grain are seven years;
it is one and the same dream. 27The seven lean,
ugly cows that came up afterward are seven
years, and so are the seven worthless heads of
grain scorched by the east wind: They are sev-
en years of famine.

28"It is just as I said to Pharaoh: God has
shown Pharaoh what he is about to do. 29Seven
years of great abundance are coming throughout the land of Egypt, 30but seven years of
famine will follow them. Then all the abundance in Egypt will be forgotten, and the famine will ravage the land. 31The abundance in
the land will not be remembered, because the
famine that follows it will be so severe. 32The
reason the dream was given to Pharaoh in two
forms is that the matter has been firmly decided by God, and God will do it soon.

33"And now let Pharaoh look for a discerning and wise man and put him in charge of the
land of Egypt. 34Let Pharaoh appoint commissioners over the land to take a fifth of the harvest of Egypt during the seven years of abundance. 35They should collect all the food of
these good years that are coming and store up
the grain under the authority of Pharaoh, to be
kept in the cities for food. 36This food should
be held in reserve for the country, to be used
during the seven years of famine that will
come upon Egypt, so that the country may not
be ruined by the famine."

37The plan seemed good to Pharaoh and to
all his officials. 38So Pharaoh asked them,
"Can we find anyone like this man, one in
whom is the spirit of God[b]?"

39Then Pharaoh said to Joseph, "Since God
has made all this known to you, there is no one
so discerning and wise as you. 40You shall be
in charge of my palace, and all my people are
to submit to your orders. Only with respect to
the throne will I be greater than you."

Joseph in Charge of Egypt

41So Pharaoh said to Joseph, "I hereby put
you in charge of the whole land of Egypt."
42Then Pharaoh took his signet ring from his
finger and put it on Joseph's finger. He dressed
him in robes of fine linen and put a gold chain
around his neck. 43He had him ride in a chariot
as his second-in-command,[c] and men shouted
before him, "Make way[d]!" Thus he put him in
charge of the whole land of Egypt.

44Then Pharaoh said to Joseph, "I am Pharaoh, but without your word no one will lift
hand or foot in all Egypt." 45Pharaoh gave Joseph the name Zaphenath-Paneah and gave
him Asenath daughter of Potiphera, priest of
On,[e] to be his wife. And Joseph went throughout the land of Egypt.

46Joseph was thirty years old when he entered the service of Pharaoh king of Egypt.
And Joseph went out from Pharaoh's presence
and traveled throughout Egypt. 47During the
seven years of abundance the land produced
plentifully. 48Joseph collected all the food produced in those seven years of abundance in
Egypt and stored it in the cities. In each city he
put the food grown in the fields surrounding it.
49Joseph stored up huge quantities of grain,
like the sand of the sea; it was so much that he
stopped keeping records because it was beyond measure.

50Before the years of famine came, two sons
were born to Joseph by Asenath daughter of
Potiphera, priest of On. 51Joseph named his
firstborn Manasseh[f] and said, "It is because
God has made me forget all my trouble and all
my father's household." 52The second son he
named Ephraim[g] and said, "It is because God
has made me fruitful in the land of my suffering."

53The seven years of abundance in Egypt
came to an end, 54and the seven years of fam-

[a] *13* Or *impaled* [b] *38* Or *of the gods* [c] *43* Or *in the chariot of his second-in-command*; or *in his second chariot* [d] *43* Or *Bow down* [e] *45* That is, Heliopolis; also in verse 50 [f] *51* *Manasseh* sounds like and may be derived from the Hebrew for *forget.* [g] *52* *Ephraim* sounds like the Hebrew for *twice fruitful.*

ine began, just as Joseph had said. There was
famine in all the other lands, but in the whole
land of Egypt there was food. 55When all
Egypt began to feel the famine, the people
cried to Pharaoh for food. Then Pharaoh told
all the Egyptians, "Go to Joseph and do what
he tells you."
56When the famine had spread over the
whole country, Joseph opened the storehouses
and sold grain to the Egyptians, for the famine
was severe throughout Egypt. 57And all the
countries came to Egypt to buy grain from Joseph, because the famine was severe in all the
world.

Joseph's Brothers Go to Egypt

42 When Jacob learned that there was grain
in Egypt, he said to his sons, "Why do
you just keep looking at each other?" 2He continued, "I have heard that there is grain in
Egypt. Go down there and buy some for us, so
that we may live and not die."
3Then ten of Joseph's brothers went down to
buy grain from Egypt. 4But Jacob did not send
Benjamin, Joseph's brother, with the others,
because he was afraid that harm might come to
him. 5So Israel's sons were among those who
went to buy grain, for the famine was in the
land of Canaan also.
6Now Joseph was the governor of the land,
the one who sold grain to all its people. So
when Joseph's brothers arrived, they bowed
down to him with their faces to the ground.
7As soon as Joseph saw his brothers, he recognized them, but he pretended to be a stranger
and spoke harshly to them. "Where do you
come from?" he asked.
"From the land of Canaan," they replied, "to
buy food."
8Although Joseph recognized his brothers,
they did not recognize him. 9Then he remembered his dreams about them and said to them,
"You are spies! You have come to see where
our land is unprotected."
10"No, my lord," they answered. "Your servants have come to buy food. 11We are all the
sons of one man. Your servants are honest
men, not spies."
12"No!" he said to them. "You have come to
see where our land is unprotected."
13But they replied, "Your servants were
twelve brothers, the sons of one man, who
lives in the land of Canaan. The youngest is
now with our father, and one is no more."
14Joseph said to them, "It is just as I told
you: You are spies! 15And this is how you will
be tested: As surely as Pharaoh lives, you will
not leave this place unless your youngest
brother comes here. 16Send one of your number to get your brother; the rest of you will be
kept in prison, so that your words may be tested to see if you are telling the truth. If you are
not, then as surely as Pharaoh lives, you are
spies!" 17And he put them all in custody for
three days.
18On the third day, Joseph said to them, "Do
this and you will live, for I fear God: 19If you
are honest men, let one of your brothers stay
here in prison, while the rest of you go and
take grain back for your starving households.
20But you must bring your youngest brother to
me, so that your words may be verified and
that you may not die." This they proceeded
to do.
21They said to one another, "Surely we are
being punished because of our brother. We
saw how distressed he was when he pleaded
with us for his life, but we would not listen;
that's why this distress has come upon us."
22Reuben replied, "Didn't I tell you not to
sin against the boy? But you wouldn't listen!
Now we must give an accounting for his
blood." 23They did not realize that Joseph
could understand them, since he was using an
interpreter.
24He turned away from them and began to
weep, but then turned back and spoke to them
again. He had Simeon taken from them and
bound before their eyes.
25Joseph gave orders to fill their bags with
grain, to put each man's silver back in his sack,
and to give them provisions for their journey.
After this was done for them, 26they loaded
their grain on their donkeys and left.
27At the place where they stopped for the
night one of them opened his sack to get feed
for his donkey, and he saw his silver in the
mouth of his sack. 28"My silver has been returned," he said to his brothers. "Here it is in
my sack."
Their hearts sank and they turned to each
other trembling and said, "What is this that
God has done to us?"
29When they came to their father Jacob in
the land of Canaan, they told him all that had
happened to them. They said, 30"The man who
is lord over the land spoke harshly to us and
treated us as though we were spying on the
land. 31But we said to him, 'We are honest
men; we are not spies. 32We were twelve
brothers, sons of one father. One is no more,
and the youngest is now with our father in
Canaan.'
33"Then the man who is lord over the land
said to us, 'This is how I will know whether
you are honest men: Leave one of your brothers here with me, and take food for your starving households and go. 34But bring your youngest brother to me so I will know that you are
not spies but honest men. Then I will give your
brother back to you, and you can trade[a] in the
land.' "
35As they were emptying their sacks, there
in each man's sack was his pouch of silver!
When they and their father saw the money
pouches, they were frightened. 36Their father
Jacob said to them, "You have deprived me of
my children. Joseph is no more and Simeon is
no more, and now you want to take Benjamin.
Everything is against me!"

[a]34 Or *move about freely*

37Then Reuben said to his father, "You may
put both of my sons to death if I do not bring
him back to you. Entrust him to my care, and
I will bring him back."
38But Jacob said, "My son will not go down
there with you; his brother is dead and he is the
only one left. If harm comes to him on the
journey you are taking, you will bring my gray
head down to the grave[a] in sorrow."

The Second Journey to Egypt

43 Now the famine was still severe in the
land. 2So when they had eaten all the
grain they had brought from Egypt, their father
said to them, "Go back and buy us a little more
food."
3But Judah said to him, "The man warned us
solemnly, 'You will not see my face again unless your brother is with you.' 4If you will send
our brother along with us, we will go down and
buy food for you. 5But if you will not send
him, we will not go down, because the man
said to us, 'You will not see my face again
unless your brother is with you.' "
6Israel asked, "Why did you bring this trouble on me by telling the man you had another
brother?"
7They replied, "The man questioned us
closely about ourselves and our family. 'Is
your father still living?' he asked us. 'Do you
have another brother?' We simply answered
his questions. How were we to know he would
say, 'Bring your brother down here'?"
8Then Judah said to Israel his father, "Send
the boy along with me and we will go at once,
so that we and you and our children may live
and not die. 9I myself will guarantee his safety;
you can hold me personally responsible for
him. If I do not bring him back to you and set
him here before you, I will bear the blame
before you all my life. 10As it is, if we had not
delayed, we could have gone and returned
twice."
11Then their father Israel said to them, "If it
must be, then do this: Put some of the best
products of the land in your bags and take
them down to the man as a gift—a little balm
and a little honey, some spices and myrrh,
some pistachio nuts and almonds. 12Take double the amount of silver with you, for you must
return the silver that was put back into the
mouths of your sacks. Perhaps it was a mistake. 13Take your brother also and go back to
the man at once. 14And may God Almighty[b]
grant you mercy before the man so that he will
let your other brother and Benjamin come back
with you. As for me, if I am bereaved, I am
bereaved."
15So the men took the gifts and double the
amount of silver, and Benjamin also. They
hurried down to Egypt and presented themselves to Joseph. 16When Joseph saw Benjamin with them, he said to the steward of his
house, "Take these men to my house, slaughter
an animal and prepare dinner; they are to eat
with me at noon."
17The man did as Joseph told him and took
the men to Joseph's house. 18Now the men
were frightened when they were taken to his
house. They thought, "We were brought here
because of the silver that was put back into our
sacks the first time. He wants to attack us and
overpower us and seize us as slaves and take
our donkeys."
19So they went up to Joseph's steward and
spoke to him at the entrance to the house.
20"Please, sir," they said, "we came down here
the first time to buy food. 21But at the place
where we stopped for the night we opened our
sacks and each of us found his silver—the exact weight—in the mouth of his sack. So we
have brought it back with us. 22We have also
brought additional silver with us to buy food.
We don't know who put our silver in our
sacks."
23"It's all right," he said. "Don't be afraid.
Your God, the God of your father, has given
you treasure in your sacks; I received your
silver." Then he brought Simeon out to them.
24The steward took the men into Joseph's
house, gave them water to wash their feet and
provided fodder for their donkeys. 25They prepared their gifts for Joseph's arrival at noon,
because they had heard that they were to eat
there.
26When Joseph came home, they presented
to him the gifts they had brought into the
house, and they bowed down before him to the
ground. 27He asked them how they were, and
then he said, "How is your aged father you told
me about? Is he still living?"
28They replied, "Your servant our father is
still alive and well." And they bowed low to
pay him honor.
29As he looked about and saw his brother
Benjamin, his own mother's son, he asked, "Is
this your youngest brother, the one you told me
about?" And he said, "God be gracious to you,
my son." 30Deeply moved at the sight of his
brother, Joseph hurried out and looked for a
place to weep. He went into his private room
and wept there.
31After he had washed his face, he came
out and, controlling himself, said, "Serve the
food."
32They served him by himself, the brothers
by themselves, and the Egyptians who ate with
him by themselves, because Egyptians could
not eat with Hebrews, for that is detestable to
Egyptians. 33The men had been seated before
him in the order of their ages, from the firstborn to the youngest; and they looked at each
other in astonishment. 34When portions were
served to them from Joseph's table, Benjamin's portion was five times as much as anyone else's. So they feasted and drank freely
with him.

[a]*38* Hebrew *Sheol* [b]*14* Hebrew *El-Shaddai*

A Silver Cup in a Sack

44 Now Joseph gave these instructions to
the steward of his house: "Fill the men's
sacks with as much food as they can carry, and
put each man's silver in the mouth of his sack.
2Then put my cup, the silver one, in the mouth
of the youngest one's sack, along with the silver for his grain." And he did as Joseph said.
3As morning dawned, the men were sent on
their way with their donkeys. 4They had not
gone far from the city when Joseph said to his
steward, "Go after those men at once, and
when you catch up with them, say to them,
'Why have you repaid good with evil? 5Isn't
this the cup my master drinks from and also
uses for divination? This is a wicked thing you
have done.' "
6When he caught up with them, he repeated
these words to them. 7But they said to him,
"Why does my lord say such things? Far be it
from your servants to do anything like that!
8We even brought back to you from the land of
Canaan the silver we found inside the mouths
of our sacks. So why would we steal silver or
gold from your master's house? 9If any of your
servants is found to have it, he will die; and the
rest of us will become my lord's slaves."
10"Very well, then," he said, "let it be as you
say. Whoever is found to have it will become
my slave; the rest of you will be free from
blame."
11Each of them quickly lowered his sack to
the ground and opened it. 12Then the steward
proceeded to search, beginning with the oldest
and ending with the youngest. And the cup was
found in Benjamin's sack. 13At this, they tore
their clothes. Then they all loaded their donkeys and returned to the city.
14Joseph was still in the house when Judah
and his brothers came in, and they threw themselves to the ground before him. 15Joseph said
to them, "What is this you have done? Don't
you know that a man like me can find things
out by divination?"
16"What can we say to my lord?" Judah replied. "What can we say? How can we prove
our innocence? God has uncovered your servants' guilt. We are now my lord's slaves—we
ourselves and the one who was found to have
the cup."
17But Joseph said, "Far be it from me to do
such a thing! Only the man who was found to
have the cup will become my slave. The rest of
you, go back to your father in peace."
18Then Judah went up to him and said:
"Please, my lord, let your servant speak a word
to my lord. Do not be angry with your servant,
though you are equal to Pharaoh himself. 19My
lord asked his servants, 'Do you have a father
or a brother?' 20And we answered, 'We have
an aged father, and there is a young son born
to him in his old age. His brother is dead, and
he is the only one of his mother's sons left, and
his father loves him.'
21"Then you said to your servants, 'Bring
him down to me so I can see him for myself.'
22And we said to my lord, 'The boy cannot
leave his father; if he leaves him, his father
will die.' 23But you told your servants, 'Unless
your youngest brother comes down with you,
you will not see my face again.' 24When we
went back to your servant my father, we told
him what my lord had said.
25"Then our father said, 'Go back and buy a
little more food.' 26But we said, 'We cannot go
down. Only if our youngest brother is with us
will we go. We cannot see the man's face unless our youngest brother is with us.'
27"Your servant my father said to us, 'You
know that my wife bore me two sons. 28One of
them went away from me, and I said, "He has
surely been torn to pieces." And I have not
seen him since. 29If you take this one from me
too and harm comes to him, you will bring my
gray head down to the grave[a] in misery.'
30"So now, if the boy is not with us when I
go back to your servant my father and if my
father, whose life is closely bound up with the
boy's life, 31sees that the boy isn't there, he
will die. Your servants will bring the gray head
of our father down to the grave in sorrow.
32Your servant guaranteed the boy's safety to
my father. I said, 'If I do not bring him back to
you, I will bear the blame before you, my father, all my life!'
33"Now then, please let your servant remain
here as my lord's slave in place of the boy, and
let the boy return with his brothers. 34How can
I go back to my father if the boy is not with
me? No! Do not let me see the misery that
would come upon my father."

Joseph Makes Himself Known

45 Then Joseph could no longer control
himself before all his attendants, and he
cried out, "Have everyone leave my presence!"
So there was no one with Joseph when he
made himself known to his brothers. 2And he
wept so loudly that the Egyptians heard him,
and Pharaoh's household heard about it.
3Joseph said to his brothers, "I am Joseph! Is
my father still living?" But his brothers were
not able to answer him, because they were terrified at his presence.
4Then Joseph said to his brothers, "Come
close to me." When they had done so, he said,
"I am your brother Joseph, the one you sold
into Egypt! 5And now, do not be distressed and
do not be angry with yourselves for selling me
here, because it was to save lives that God sent
me ahead of you. 6For two years now there has
been famine in the land, and for the next five
years there will not be plowing and reaping.
7But God sent me ahead of you to preserve for
you a remnant on earth and to save your lives
by a great deliverance.[b]
8"So then, it was not you who sent me here,
but God. He made me father to Pharaoh, lord
of his entire household and ruler of all Egypt.
9Now hurry back to my father and say to him,

[a] *29* Hebrew *Sheol*; also in verse 31 [b] *7* Or *save you as a great band of survivors*

'This is what your son Joseph says: God has
made me lord of all Egypt. Come down to me;
don't delay. 10You shall live in the region of
Goshen and be near me—you, your children
and grandchildren, your flocks and herds, and
all you have. 11I will provide for you there,
because five years of famine are still to come.
Otherwise you and your household and all who
belong to you will become destitute.'
12"You can see for yourselves, and so can
my brother Benjamin, that it is really I who am
speaking to you. 13Tell my father about all the
honor accorded me in Egypt and about everything you have seen. And bring my father
down here quickly."
14Then he threw his arms around his brother
Benjamin and wept, and Benjamin embraced
him, weeping. 15And he kissed all his brothers
and wept over them. Afterward his brothers
talked with him.
16When the news reached Pharaoh's palace
that Joseph's brothers had come, Pharaoh and
all his officials were pleased. 17Pharaoh said to
Joseph, "Tell your brothers, 'Do this: Load
your animals and return to the land of Canaan,
18and bring your father and your families back
to me. I will give you the best of the land of
Egypt and you can enjoy the fat of the land.'
19"You are also directed to tell them, 'Do
this: Take some carts from Egypt for your children and your wives, and get your father and
come. 20Never mind about your belongings,
because the best of all Egypt will be yours.' "
21So the sons of Israel did this. Joseph gave
them carts, as Pharaoh had commanded, and
he also gave them provisions for their journey.
22To each of them he gave new clothing, but to
Benjamin he gave three hundred shekels[a] of
silver and five sets of clothes. 23And this is
what he sent to his father: ten donkeys loaded
with the best things of Egypt, and ten female
donkeys loaded with grain and bread and other
provisions for his journey. 24Then he sent his
brothers away, and as they were leaving he
said to them, "Don't quarrel on the way!"
25So they went up out of Egypt and came
to their father Jacob in the land of Canaan.
26They told him, "Joseph is still alive! In fact,
he is ruler of all Egypt." Jacob was stunned; he
did not believe them. 27But when they told him
everything Joseph had said to them, and when
he saw the carts Joseph had sent to carry him
back, the spirit of their father Jacob revived.
28And Israel said, "I'm convinced! My son Joseph is still alive. I will go and see him before
I die."

Jacob Goes to Egypt

46 So Israel set out with all that was his,
and when he reached Beersheba, he offered sacrifices to the God of his father Isaac.
2And God spoke to Israel in a vision at night
and said, "Jacob! Jacob!"
"Here I am," he replied.
3"I am God, the God of your father," he
said. "Do not be afraid to go down to Egypt,
for I will make you into a great nation there. 4I
will go down to Egypt with you, and I will
surely bring you back again. And Joseph's
own hand will close your eyes."
5Then Jacob left Beersheba, and Israel's
sons took their father Jacob and their children
and their wives in the carts that Pharaoh had
sent to transport him. 6They also took with
them their livestock and the possessions they
had acquired in Canaan, and Jacob and all his
offspring went to Egypt. 7He took with him to
Egypt his sons and grandsons and his daughters and granddaughters—all his offspring.

8These are the names of the sons of Israel
(Jacob and his descendants) who went to
Egypt:

Reuben the firstborn of Jacob.
9The sons of Reuben:
Hanoch, Pallu, Hezron and Carmi.
10The sons of Simeon:
Jemuel, Jamin, Ohad, Jakin, Zohar
and Shaul the son of a Canaanite
woman.
11The sons of Levi:
Gershon, Kohath and Merari.
12The sons of Judah:
Er, Onan, Shelah, Perez and Zerah
(but Er and Onan had died in the land
of Canaan).
The sons of Perez:
Hezron and Hamul.
13The sons of Issachar:
Tola, Puah,[b] Jashub[c] and Shimron.
14The sons of Zebulun:
Sered, Elon and Jahleel.
15These were the sons Leah bore to Jacob in
Paddan Aram,[d] besides his daughter Dinah.
These sons and daughters of his were thirty-
three in all.

16The sons of Gad:
Zephon,[e] Haggi, Shuni, Ezbon, Eri,
Arodi and Areli.
17The sons of Asher:
Imnah, Ishvah, Ishvi and Beriah.
Their sister was Serah.
The sons of Beriah:
Heber and Malkiel.
18These were the children born to Jacob by
Zilpah, whom Laban had given to his daughter
Leah—sixteen in all.

19The sons of Jacob's wife Rachel:
Joseph and Benjamin. 20In Egypt,
Manasseh and Ephraim were born to
Joseph by Asenath daughter of Po-
tiphera, priest of On.[f]
21The sons of Benjamin:
Bela, Beker, Ashbel, Gera, Naaman,

[a]22 That is, about 7 1/2 pounds (about 3.5 kilograms) [b]13 Samaritan Pentateuch and Syriac (see also 1 Chron. 7:1); Masoretic Text *Puvah* [c]13 Samaritan Pentateuch and some Septuagint manuscripts (see also Num. 26:24 and 1 Chron. 7:1); Masoretic Text *Iob* [d]15 That is, Northwest Mesopotamia [e]16 Samaritan Pentateuch and Septuagint (see also Num. 26:15); Masoretic Text *Ziphion* [f]20 That is, Heliopolis

Ehi, Rosh, Muppim, Huppim and Ard.
22These were the sons of Rachel who were
born to Jacob—fourteen in all.

23The son of Dan:
Hushim.
24The sons of Naphtali:
Jahziel, Guni, Jezer and Shillem.
25These were the sons born to Jacob by Bilhah, whom Laban had given to his daughter
Rachel—seven in all.

26All those who went to Egypt with Jacob—
those who were his direct descendants, not
counting his sons' wives—numbered sixty-six
persons. 27With the two sons[a] who had been
born to Joseph in Egypt, the members of Jacob's family, which went to Egypt, were seventy[b] in all.

28Now Jacob sent Judah ahead of him to
Joseph to get directions to Goshen. When they
arrived in the region of Goshen, 29Joseph had
his chariot made ready and went to Goshen to
meet his father Israel. As soon as Joseph appeared before him, he threw his arms around
his father[c] and wept for a long time.
30Israel said to Joseph, "Now I am ready to
die, since I have seen for myself that you are
still alive."
31Then Joseph said to his brothers and to his
father's household, "I will go up and speak to
Pharaoh and will say to him, 'My brothers and
my father's household, who were living in the
land of Canaan, have come to me. 32The men
are shepherds; they tend livestock, and they
have brought along their flocks and herds and
everything they own.' 33When Pharaoh calls
you in and asks, 'What is your occupation?'
34you should answer, 'Your servants have
tended livestock from our boyhood on, just as
our fathers did.' Then you will be allowed to
settle in the region of Goshen, for all shepherds
are detestable to the Egyptians."

47 Joseph went and told Pharaoh, "My father and brothers, with their flocks and
herds and everything they own, have come
from the land of Canaan and are now in Goshen." 2He chose five of his brothers and presented them before Pharaoh.
3Pharaoh asked the brothers, "What is your
occupation?"
"Your servants are shepherds," they replied
to Pharaoh, "just as our fathers were." 4They
also said to him, "We have come to live here
awhile, because the famine is severe in Canaan
and your servants' flocks have no pasture. So
now, please let your servants settle in Goshen."
5Pharaoh said to Joseph, "Your father and
your brothers have come to you, 6and the land
of Egypt is before you; settle your father and
your brothers in the best part of the land. Let
them live in Goshen. And if you know of any
among them with special ability, put them in
charge of my own livestock."
7Then Joseph brought his father Jacob in
and presented him before Pharaoh. After Jacob
blessed[d] Pharaoh, 8Pharaoh asked him, "How
old are you?"
9And Jacob said to Pharaoh, "The years of
my pilgrimage are a hundred and thirty. My
years have been few and difficult, and they do
not equal the years of the pilgrimage of my
fathers." 10Then Jacob blessed[e] Pharaoh and
went out from his presence.
11So Joseph settled his father and his brothers in Egypt and gave them property in the best
part of the land, the district of Rameses, as
Pharaoh directed. 12Joseph also provided his
father and his brothers and all his father's
household with food, according to the number
of their children.

Joseph and the Famine

13There was no food, however, in the whole
region because the famine was severe; both
Egypt and Canaan wasted away because of the
famine. 14Joseph collected all the money that
was to be found in Egypt and Canaan in payment for the grain they were buying, and he
brought it to Pharaoh's palace. 15When the
money of the people of Egypt and Canaan was
gone, all Egypt came to Joseph and said, "Give
us food. Why should we die before your eyes?
Our money is used up."
16"Then bring your livestock," said Joseph.
"I will sell you food in exchange for your livestock, since your money is gone." 17So they
brought their livestock to Joseph, and he gave
them food in exchange for their horses, their
sheep and goats, their cattle and donkeys. And
he brought them through that year with food in
exchange for all their livestock.
18When that year was over, they came to
him the following year and said, "We cannot
hide from our lord the fact that since our money is gone and our livestock belongs to you,
there is nothing left for our lord except our
bodies and our land. 19Why should we perish
before your eyes—we and our land as well?
Buy us and our land in exchange for food, and
we with our land will be in bondage to Pharaoh. Give us seed so that we may live and not
die, and that the land may not become desolate."
20So Joseph bought all the land in Egypt for
Pharaoh. The Egyptians, one and all, sold their
fields, because the famine was too severe for
them. The land became Pharaoh's, 21and Joseph reduced the people to servitude,[f] from
one end of Egypt to the other. 22However, he
did not buy the land of the priests, because
they received a regular allotment from Pharaoh
and had food enough from the allotment Pharaoh gave them. That is why they did not sell
their land.

[a]27 Hebrew; Septuagint *the nine children* [b]27 Hebrew (see also Exodus 1:5 and footnote); Septuagint (see also Acts 7:14) *seventy-five* [c]29 Hebrew *around him* [d]7 Or *greeted* [e]10 Or *said farewell to*
[f]21 Samaritan Pentateuch and Septuagint (see also Vulgate); Masoretic Text *and he moved the people into the cities*

23Joseph said to the people, "Now that I
have bought you and your land today for Pharaoh, here is seed for you so you can plant the
ground. 24But when the crop comes in, give a
fifth of it to Pharaoh. The other four-fifths you
may keep as seed for the fields and as food for
yourselves and your households and your children."

25"You have saved our lives," they said.
"May we find favor in the eyes of our lord; we
will be in bondage to Pharaoh."

26So Joseph established it as a law concerning land in Egypt—still in force today—that a
fifth of the produce belongs to Pharaoh. It was
only the land of the priests that did not become
Pharaoh's.

27Now the Israelites settled in Egypt in the
region of Goshen. They acquired property
there and were fruitful and increased greatly in
number.

28Jacob lived in Egypt seventeen years, and
the years of his life were a hundred and forty-
seven. 29When the time drew near for Israel to
die, he called for his son Joseph and said to
him, "If I have found favor in your eyes, put
your hand under my thigh and promise that
you will show me kindness and faithfulness.
Do not bury me in Egypt, 30but when I rest
with my fathers, carry me out of Egypt and
bury me where they are buried."

"I will do as you say," he said.

31"Swear to me," he said. Then Joseph
swore to him, and Israel worshiped as he
leaned on the top of his staff.[a]

Manasseh and Ephraim

48 Some time later Joseph was told, "Your
father is ill." So he took his two sons
Manasseh and Ephraim along with him.
2When Jacob was told, "Your son Joseph has
come to you," Israel rallied his strength and sat
up on the bed.

3Jacob said to Joseph, "God Almighty[b] appeared to me at Luz in the land of Canaan, and
there he blessed me 4and said to me, 'I am
going to make you fruitful and will increase
your numbers. I will make you a community of
peoples, and I will give this land as an everlasting possession to your descendants after you.'

5"Now then, your two sons born to you in
Egypt before I came to you here will be reckoned as mine; Ephraim and Manasseh will be
mine, just as Reuben and Simeon are mine.
6Any children born to you after them will be
yours; in the territory they inherit they will be
reckoned under the names of their brothers.
7As I was returning from Paddan,[c] to my sorrow Rachel died in the land of Canaan while
we were still on the way, a little distance from
Ephrath. So I buried her there beside the road
to Ephrath" (that is, Bethlehem).

8When Israel saw the sons of Joseph, he
asked, "Who are these?"

9"They are the sons God has given me
here," Joseph said to his father.

Then Israel said, "Bring them to me so I
may bless them."

10Now Israel's eyes were failing because of
old age, and he could hardly see. So Joseph
brought his sons close to him, and his father
kissed them and embraced them.

11Israel said to Joseph, "I never expected to
see your face again, and now God has allowed
me to see your children too."

12Then Joseph removed them from Israel's
knees and bowed down with his face to the
ground. 13And Joseph took both of them,
Ephraim on his right toward Israel's left hand
and Manasseh on his left toward Israel's right
hand, and brought them close to him. 14But
Israel reached out his right hand and put it on
Ephraim's head, though he was the younger,
and crossing his arms, he put his left hand on
Manasseh's head, even though Manasseh was
the firstborn.

15Then he blessed Joseph and said,

"May the God before whom my fathers
    Abraham and Isaac walked,
the God who has been my shepherd
    all my life to this day,
16the Angel who has delivered me from all
        harm
    —may he bless these boys.
May they be called by my name
    and the names of my fathers Abraham
        and Isaac,
and may they increase greatly
    upon the earth."

17When Joseph saw his father placing his
right hand on Ephraim's head he was displeased; so he took hold of his father's hand to
move it from Ephraim's head to Manasseh's
head. 18Joseph said to him, "No, my father,
this one is the firstborn; put your right hand on
his head."

19But his father refused and said, "I know,
my son, I know. He too will become a people,
and he too will become great. Nevertheless, his
younger brother will be greater than he, and his
descendants will become a group of nations."
20He blessed them that day and said,

"In your[d] name will Israel pronounce this
        blessing:
    'May God make you like Ephraim and
        Manasseh.' "

So he put Ephraim ahead of Manasseh.

21Then Israel said to Joseph, "I am about to
die, but God will be with you[e] and take you[e]
back to the land of your[e] fathers. 22And to
you, as one who is over your brothers, I give
the ridge of land[f] I took from the Amorites
with my sword and my bow."

[a]31 Or *Israel bowed down at the head of his bed* [b]3 Hebrew *El-Shaddai* [c]7 That is, Northwest Mesopotamia [d]20 The Hebrew is singular. [e]21 The Hebrew is plural. [f]22 Or *And to you I give one portion more than to your brothers—the portion*

Jacob Blesses His Sons

49 Then Jacob called for his sons and said: "Gather around so I can tell you what will happen to you in days to come.

2"Assemble and listen, sons of Jacob;
listen to your father Israel.

3"Reuben, you are my firstborn,
my might, the first sign of my strength,
excelling in honor, excelling in power.
4Turbulent as the waters, you will no longer excel,
for you went up onto your father's bed,
onto my couch and defiled it.

5"Simeon and Levi are brothers—
their swords[a] are weapons of violence.
6Let me not enter their council,
let me not join their assembly,
for they have killed men in their anger
and hamstrung oxen as they pleased.
7Cursed be their anger, so fierce,
and their fury, so cruel!
I will scatter them in Jacob
and disperse them in Israel.

8"Judah,[b] your brothers will praise you;
your hand will be on the neck of your enemies;
your father's sons will bow down to you.
9You are a lion's cub, O Judah;
you return from the prey, my son.
Like a lion he crouches and lies down,
like a lioness—who dares to rouse him?
10The scepter will not depart from Judah,
nor the ruler's staff from between his feet,
until he comes to whom it belongs[c]
and the obedience of the nations is his.
11He will tether his donkey to a vine,
his colt to the choicest branch;
he will wash his garments in wine,
his robes in the blood of grapes.
12His eyes will be darker than wine,
his teeth whiter than milk.[d]

13"Zebulun will live by the seashore
and become a haven for ships;
his border will extend toward Sidon.

14"Issachar is a rawboned[e] donkey
lying down between two saddlebags.[f]
15When he sees how good is his resting place
and how pleasant is his land,
he will bend his shoulder to the burden
and submit to forced labor.

16"Dan[g] will provide justice for his people
as one of the tribes of Israel.
17Dan will be a serpent by the roadside,
a viper along the path,
that bites the horse's heels
so that its rider tumbles backward.

18"I look for your deliverance, O LORD.

19"Gad[h] will be attacked by a band of raiders,
but he will attack them at their heels.

20"Asher's food will be rich;
he will provide delicacies fit for a king.

21"Naphtali is a doe set free
that bears beautiful fawns.[i]

22"Joseph is a fruitful vine,
a fruitful vine near a spring,
whose branches climb over a wall.[j]
23With bitterness archers attacked him;
they shot at him with hostility.
24But his bow remained steady,
his strong arms stayed[k] limber,
because of the hand of the Mighty One of Jacob,
because of the Shepherd, the Rock of Israel,
25because of your father's God, who helps you,
because of the Almighty,[l] who blesses you
with blessings of the heavens above,
blessings of the deep that lies below,
blessings of the breast and womb.
26Your father's blessings are greater
than the blessings of the ancient mountains,
than[m] the bounty of the age-old hills.
Let all these rest on the head of Joseph,
on the brow of the prince among[n] his brothers.

27"Benjamin is a ravenous wolf;
in the morning he devours the prey,
in the evening he divides the plunder."

28All these are the twelve tribes of Israel, and this is what their father said to them when he blessed them, giving each the blessing appropriate to him.

The Death of Jacob

29Then he gave them these instructions: "I am about to be gathered to my people. Bury me with my fathers in the cave in the field of Ephron the Hittite, 30the cave in the field of Machpelah, near Mamre in Canaan, which Abraham bought as a burial place from Ephron the Hittite, along with the field. 31There Abraham and his wife Sarah were buried, there Isaac and his wife Rebekah were buried, and there I buried Leah. 32The field and the cave in it were bought from the Hittites.[o]"
33When Jacob had finished giving instruc-

[a]5 The meaning of the Hebrew for this word is uncertain. [b]8 *Judah* sounds like and may be derived from the Hebrew for *praise*. [c]10 Or *until Shiloh comes*; or *until he comes to whom tribute belongs* [d]12 Or *will be dull from wine, / his teeth white from milk* [e]14 Or *strong* [f]14 Or *campfires* [g]16 *Dan* here means *he provides justice.* [h]19 *Gad* can mean *attack* and *band of raiders.* [i]21 Or *free; / he utters beautiful words* [j]22 Or *Joseph is a wild colt, / a wild colt near a spring, / a wild donkey on a terraced hill* [k]23,24 Or *archers will attack . . . will shoot . . . will remain . . . will stay* [l]25 Hebrew *Shaddai* [m]26 Or *of my progenitors, / as great as* [n]26 Or *the one separated from* [o]32 Or *the sons of Heth*

tions to his sons, he drew his feet up into the
bed, breathed his last and was gathered to his
people.
50 Joseph threw himself upon his father
and wept over him and kissed him.
2Then Joseph directed the physicians in his
service to embalm his father Israel. So the physicians embalmed him, 3taking a full forty
days, for that was the time required for em-
balming. And the Egyptians mourned for him
seventy days.
4When the days of mourning had passed,
Joseph said to Pharaoh's court, "If I have
found favor in your eyes, speak to Pharaoh for
me. Tell him, 5'My father made me swear an
oath and said, "I am about to die; bury me in
the tomb I dug for myself in the land of Canaan." Now let me go up and bury my father;
then I will return.' "
6Pharaoh said, "Go up and bury your father,
as he made you swear to do."
7So Joseph went up to bury his father. All
Pharaoh's officials accompanied him—the
dignitaries of his court and all the dignitaries
of Egypt— 8besides all the members of Joseph's household and his brothers and those
belonging to his father's household. Only their
children and their flocks and herds were left in
Goshen. 9Chariots and horsemen[a] also went
up with him. It was a very large company.
10When they reached the threshing floor of
Atad, near the Jordan, they lamented loudly
and bitterly; and there Joseph observed a
seven-day period of mourning for his father.
11When the Canaanites who lived there saw
the mourning at the threshing floor of Atad,
they said, "The Egyptians are holding a solemn
ceremony of mourning." That is why that place
near the Jordan is called Abel Mizraim.[b]
12So Jacob's sons did as he had commanded
them: 13They carried him to the land of Canaan
and buried him in the cave in the field of
Machpelah, near Mamre, which Abraham had
bought as a burial place from Ephron the Hittite, along with the field. 14After burying his
father, Joseph returned to Egypt, together with
his brothers and all the others who had gone
with him to bury his father.

Joseph Reassures His Brothers

15When Joseph's brothers saw that their father was dead, they said, "What if Joseph holds
a grudge against us and pays us back for all the
wrongs we did to him?" 16So they sent word to
Joseph, saying, "Your father left these instructions before he died: 17'This is what you are to
say to Joseph: I ask you to forgive your brothers the sins and the wrongs they committed in
treating you so badly.' Now please forgive the
sins of the servants of the God of your father."
When their message came to him, Joseph
wept.
18His brothers then came and threw themselves down before him. "We are your slaves,"
they said.
19But Joseph said to them, "Don't be afraid.
Am I in the place of God? 20You intended to
harm me, but God intended it for good to accomplish what is now being done, the saving
of many lives. 21So then, don't be afraid. I will
provide for you and your children." And he
reassured them and spoke kindly to them.

The Death of Joseph

22Joseph stayed in Egypt, along with all his
father's family. He lived a hundred and ten
years 23and saw the third generation of Ephraim's children. Also the children of Makir son
of Manasseh were placed at birth on Joseph's
knees.[c]
24Then Joseph said to his brothers, "I am
about to die. But God will surely come to your
aid and take you up out of this land to the land
he promised on oath to Abraham, Isaac and
Jacob." 25And Joseph made the sons of Israel
swear an oath and said, "God will surely come
to your aid, and then you must carry my bones
up from this place."
26So Joseph died at the age of a hundred and
ten. And after they embalmed him, he was
placed in a coffin in Egypt.

Exodus

The Israelites Oppressed

1 These are the names of the sons of Israel
who went to Egypt with Jacob, each with
his family: 2Reuben, Simeon, Levi and Judah;
3Issachar, Zebulun and Benjamin; 4Dan and
Naphtali; Gad and Asher. 5The descendants of
Jacob numbered seventy[d] in all; Joseph was
already in Egypt.
6Now Joseph and all his brothers and all that
generation died, 7but the Israelites were fruitful and multiplied greatly and became exceedingly numerous, so that the land was filled
with them.
8Then a new king, who did not know about
Joseph, came to power in Egypt. 9"Look," he
said to his people, "the Israelites have become
much too numerous for us. 10Come, we must
deal shrewdly with them or they will become

[a] 9 Or *charioteers* [b] 11 *Abel Mizraim* means *mourning of the Egyptians.* [c] 23 That is, were counted as his
[d] 5 Masoretic Text (see also Gen. 46:27); Dead Sea Scrolls and Septuagint (see also Acts 7:14 and note at
Gen. 46:27) *seventy-five*

even more numerous and, if war breaks out, will join our enemies, fight against us and leave the country."

11So they put slave masters over them to oppress them with forced labor, and they built Pithom and Rameses as store cities for Pharaoh. 12But the more they were oppressed, the more they multiplied and spread; so the Egyptians came to dread the Israelites 13and worked them ruthlessly. 14They made their lives bitter with hard labor in brick and mortar and with all kinds of work in the fields; in all their hard labor the Egyptians used them ruthlessly.

15The king of Egypt said to the Hebrew midwives, whose names were Shiphrah and Puah, 16"When you help the Hebrew women in childbirth and observe them on the delivery stool, if it is a boy, kill him; but if it is a girl, let her live." 17The midwives, however, feared God and did not do what the king of Egypt had told them to do; they let the boys live. 18Then the king of Egypt summoned the midwives and asked them, "Why have you done this? Why have you let the boys live?"

19The midwives answered Pharaoh, "Hebrew women are not like Egyptian women; they are vigorous and give birth before the midwives arrive."

20So God was kind to the midwives and the people increased and became even more numerous. 21And because the midwives feared God, he gave them families of their own.

22Then Pharaoh gave this order to all his people: "Every boy that is born[a] you must throw into the Nile, but let every girl live."

The Birth of Moses

2 Now a man of the house of Levi married a Levite woman, 2and she became pregnant and gave birth to a son. When she saw that he was a fine child, she hid him for three months. 3But when she could hide him no longer, she got a papyrus basket for him and coated it with tar and pitch. Then she placed the child in it and put it among the reeds along the bank of the Nile. 4His sister stood at a distance to see what would happen to him.

5Then Pharaoh's daughter went down to the Nile to bathe, and her attendants were walking along the river bank. She saw the basket among the reeds and sent her slave girl to get it. 6She opened it and saw the baby. He was crying, and she felt sorry for him. "This is one of the Hebrew babies," she said.

7Then his sister asked Pharaoh's daughter, "Shall I go and get one of the Hebrew women to nurse the baby for you?"

8"Yes, go," she answered. And the girl went and got the baby's mother. 9Pharaoh's daughter said to her, "Take this baby and nurse him for me, and I will pay you." So the woman took the baby and nursed him. 10When the child grew older, she took him to Pharaoh's daughter and he became her son. She named him Moses,[b] saying, "I drew him out of the water."

Moses Flees to Midian

11One day, after Moses had grown up, he went out to where his own people were and watched them at their hard labor. He saw an Egyptian beating a Hebrew, one of his own people. 12Glancing this way and that and seeing no one, he killed the Egyptian and hid him in the sand. 13The next day he went out and saw two Hebrews fighting. He asked the one in the wrong, "Why are you hitting your fellow Hebrew?"

14The man said, "Who made you ruler and judge over us? Are you thinking of killing me as you killed the Egyptian?" Then Moses was afraid and thought, "What I did must have become known."

15When Pharaoh heard of this, he tried to kill Moses, but Moses fled from Pharaoh and went to live in Midian, where he sat down by a well. 16Now a priest of Midian had seven daughters, and they came to draw water and fill the troughs to water their father's flock. 17Some shepherds came along and drove them away, but Moses got up and came to their rescue and watered their flock.

18When the girls returned to Reuel their father, he asked them, "Why have you returned so early today?"

19They answered, "An Egyptian rescued us from the shepherds. He even drew water for us and watered the flock."

20"And where is he?" he asked his daughters. "Why did you leave him? Invite him to have something to eat."

21Moses agreed to stay with the man, who gave his daughter Zipporah to Moses in marriage. 22Zipporah gave birth to a son, and Moses named him Gershom,[c] saying, "I have become an alien in a foreign land."

23During that long period, the king of Egypt died. The Israelites groaned in their slavery and cried out, and their cry for help because of their slavery went up to God. 24God heard their groaning and he remembered his covenant with Abraham, with Isaac and with Jacob. 25So God looked on the Israelites and was concerned about them.

Moses and the Burning Bush

3 Now Moses was tending the flock of Jethro his father-in-law, the priest of Midian, and he led the flock to the far side of the desert and came to Horeb, the mountain of God. 2There the angel of the LORD appeared to him in flames of fire from within a bush. Moses saw that though the bush was on fire it did not burn up. 3So Moses thought, "I will go over and see this strange sight—why the bush does not burn up."

4When the LORD saw that he had gone over to look, God called to him from within the bush, "Moses! Moses!"

[a]22 Masoretic Text; Samaritan Pentateuch, Septuagint and Targums *born to the Hebrews* [b]10 *Moses* sounds like the Hebrew for *draw out.* [c]22 *Gershom* sounds like the Hebrew for *an alien there.*

And Moses said, "Here I am."

5"Do not come any closer," God said. "Take off your sandals, for the place where you are standing is holy ground." 6Then he said, "I am the God of your father, the God of Abraham, the God of Isaac and the God of Jacob." At this, Moses hid his face, because he was afraid to look at God.

7The LORD said, "I have indeed seen the misery of my people in Egypt. I have heard them crying out because of their slave drivers, and I am concerned about their suffering. 8So I have come down to rescue them from the hand of the Egyptians and to bring them up out of that land into a good and spacious land, a land flowing with milk and honey—the home of the Canaanites, Hittites, Amorites, Perizzites, Hivites and Jebusites. 9And now the cry of the Israelites has reached me, and I have seen the way the Egyptians are oppressing them. 10So now, go. I am sending you to Pharaoh to bring my people the Israelites out of Egypt."

11But Moses said to God, "Who am I, that I should go to Pharaoh and bring the Israelites out of Egypt?"

12And God said, "I will be with you. And this will be the sign to you that it is I who have sent you: When you have brought the people out of Egypt, you[a] will worship God on this mountain."

13Moses said to God, "Suppose I go to the Israelites and say to them, 'The God of your fathers has sent me to you,' and they ask me, 'What is his name?' Then what shall I tell them?"

14God said to Moses, "I AM WHO I AM.[b] This is what you are to say to the Israelites: 'I AM has sent me to you.' "

15God also said to Moses, "Say to the Israelites, 'The LORD,[c] the God of your fathers—the God of Abraham, the God of Isaac and the God of Jacob—has sent me to you.' This is my name forever, the name by which I am to be remembered from generation to generation.

16"Go, assemble the elders of Israel and say to them, 'The LORD, the God of your fathers—the God of Abraham, Isaac and Jacob—appeared to me and said: I have watched over you and have seen what has been done to you in Egypt. 17And I have promised to bring you up out of your misery in Egypt into the land of the Canaanites, Hittites, Amorites, Perizzites, Hivites and Jebusites—a land flowing with milk and honey.'

18"The elders of Israel will listen to you. Then you and the elders are to go to the king of Egypt and say to him, 'The LORD, the God of the Hebrews, has met with us. Let us take a three-day journey into the desert to offer sacrifices to the LORD our God.' 19But I know that the king of Egypt will not let you go unless a mighty hand compels him. 20So I will stretch out my hand and strike the Egyptians with all the wonders that I will perform among them. After that, he will let you go.

21"And I will make the Egyptians favorably disposed toward this people, so that when you leave you will not go empty-handed. 22Every woman is to ask her neighbor and any woman living in her house for articles of silver and gold and for clothing, which you will put on your sons and daughters. And so you will plunder the Egyptians."

Signs for Moses

4 Moses answered, "What if they do not believe me or listen to me and say, 'The LORD did not appear to you'?"

2Then the LORD said to him, "What is that in your hand?"

"A staff," he replied.

3The LORD said, "Throw it on the ground."

Moses threw it on the ground and it became a snake, and he ran from it. 4Then the LORD said to him, "Reach out your hand and take it by the tail." So Moses reached out and took hold of the snake and it turned back into a staff in his hand. 5"This," said the LORD, "is so that they may believe that the LORD, the God of their fathers—the God of Abraham, the God of Isaac and the God of Jacob—has appeared to you."

6Then the LORD said, "Put your hand inside your cloak." So Moses put his hand into his cloak, and when he took it out, it was leprous,[d] like snow.

7"Now put it back into your cloak," he said. So Moses put his hand back into his cloak, and when he took it out, it was restored, like the rest of his flesh.

8Then the LORD said, "If they do not believe you or pay attention to the first miraculous sign, they may believe the second. 9But if they do not believe these two signs or listen to you, take some water from the Nile and pour it on the dry ground. The water you take from the river will become blood on the ground."

10Moses said to the LORD, "O Lord, I have never been eloquent, neither in the past nor since you have spoken to your servant. I am slow of speech and tongue."

11The LORD said to him, "Who gave man his mouth? Who makes him deaf or mute? Who gives him sight or makes him blind? Is it not I, the LORD? 12Now go; I will help you speak and will teach you what to say."

13But Moses said, "O Lord, please send someone else to do it."

14Then the LORD's anger burned against Moses and he said, "What about your brother, Aaron the Levite? I know he can speak well. He is already on his way to meet you, and his heart will be glad when he sees you. 15You shall speak to him and put words in his mouth; I will help both of you speak and will teach

[a] 12 The Hebrew is plural. [b] 14 Or *I WILL BE WHAT I WILL BE* [c] 15 The Hebrew for *LORD* sounds like and may be derived from the Hebrew for *I AM* in verse 14. [d] 6 The Hebrew word was used for various diseases affecting the skin—not necessarily leprosy.

you what to do. 16He will speak to the people for you, and it will be as if he were your mouth and as if you were God to him. 17But take this staff in your hand so you can perform miraculous signs with it."

Moses Returns to Egypt

18Then Moses went back to Jethro his father-in-law and said to him, "Let me go back to my own people in Egypt to see if any of them are still alive."

Jethro said, "Go, and I wish you well."

19Now the LORD had said to Moses in Midian, "Go back to Egypt, for all the men who wanted to kill you are dead." 20So Moses took his wife and sons, put them on a donkey and started back to Egypt. And he took the staff of God in his hand.

21The LORD said to Moses, "When you return to Egypt, see that you perform before Pharaoh all the wonders I have given you the power to do. But I will harden his heart so that he will not let the people go. 22Then say to Pharaoh, 'This is what the LORD says: Israel is my firstborn son, 23and I told you, "Let my son go, so he may worship me." But you refused to let him go; so I will kill your firstborn son.' "

24At a lodging place on the way, the LORD met ⌊Moses⌋[a] and was about to kill him. 25But Zipporah took a flint knife, cut off her son's foreskin and touched ⌊Moses'⌋ feet with it.[b] "Surely you are a bridegroom of blood to me," she said. 26So the LORD let him alone. (At that time she said "bridegroom of blood," referring to circumcision.)

27The LORD said to Aaron, "Go into the desert to meet Moses." So he met Moses at the mountain of God and kissed him. 28Then Moses told Aaron everything the LORD had sent him to say, and also about all the miraculous signs he had commanded him to perform.

29Moses and Aaron brought together all the elders of the Israelites, 30and Aaron told them everything the LORD had said to Moses. He also performed the signs before the people, 31and they believed. And when they heard that the LORD was concerned about them and had seen their misery, they bowed down and worshiped.

Bricks Without Straw

5 Afterward Moses and Aaron went to Pharaoh and said, "This is what the LORD, the God of Israel, says: 'Let my people go, so that they may hold a festival to me in the desert.' "

2Pharaoh said, "Who is the LORD, that I should obey him and let Israel go? I do not know the LORD and I will not let Israel go."

3Then they said, "The God of the Hebrews has met with us. Now let us take a three-day journey into the desert to offer sacrifices to the LORD our God, or he may strike us with plagues or with the sword."

4But the king of Egypt said, "Moses and Aaron, why are you taking the people away from their labor? Get back to your work!" 5Then Pharaoh said, "Look, the people of the land are now numerous, and you are stopping them from working."

6That same day Pharaoh gave this order to the slave drivers and foremen in charge of the people: 7"You are no longer to supply the people with straw for making bricks; let them go and gather their own straw. 8But require them to make the same number of bricks as before; don't reduce the quota. They are lazy; that is why they are crying out, 'Let us go and sacrifice to our God.' 9Make the work harder for the men so that they keep working and pay no attention to lies."

10Then the slave drivers and the foremen went out and said to the people, "This is what Pharaoh says: 'I will not give you any more straw. 11Go and get your own straw wherever you can find it, but your work will not be reduced at all.' " 12So the people scattered all over Egypt to gather stubble to use for straw. 13The slave drivers kept pressing them, saying, "Complete the work required of you for each day, just as when you had straw." 14The Israelite foremen appointed by Pharaoh's slave drivers were beaten and were asked, "Why didn't you meet your quota of bricks yesterday or today, as before?"

15Then the Israelite foremen went and appealed to Pharaoh: "Why have you treated your servants this way? 16Your servants are given no straw, yet we are told, 'Make bricks!' Your servants are being beaten, but the fault is with your own people."

17Pharaoh said, "Lazy, that's what you are—lazy! That is why you keep saying, 'Let us go and sacrifice to the LORD.' 18Now get to work. You will not be given any straw, yet you must produce your full quota of bricks."

19The Israelite foremen realized they were in trouble when they were told, "You are not to reduce the number of bricks required of you for each day." 20When they left Pharaoh, they found Moses and Aaron waiting to meet them, 21and they said, "May the LORD look upon you and judge you! You have made us a stench to Pharaoh and his officials and have put a sword in their hand to kill us."

God Promises Deliverance

22Moses returned to the LORD and said, "O Lord, why have you brought trouble upon this people? Is this why you sent me? 23Ever since I went to Pharaoh to speak in your name, he has brought trouble upon this people, and you have not rescued your people at all."

6 Then the LORD said to Moses, "Now you will see what I will do to Pharaoh: Because of my mighty hand he will let them go; because of my mighty hand he will drive them out of his country."

2God also said to Moses, "I am the LORD. 3I appeared to Abraham, to Isaac and to Jacob as

[a]24 Or ⌊*Moses' son*⌋; Hebrew *him* [b]25 Or *and drew near* ⌊*Moses'*⌋ *feet*

God Almighty,[a] but by my name the LORD[b] I did not make myself known to them.[c] 4I also established my covenant with them to give them the land of Canaan, where they lived as aliens. 5Moreover, I have heard the groaning of the Israelites, whom the Egyptians are enslaving, and I have remembered my covenant.

6"Therefore, say to the Israelites: 'I am the LORD, and I will bring you out from under the yoke of the Egyptians. I will free you from being slaves to them, and I will redeem you with an outstretched arm and with mighty acts of judgment. 7I will take you as my own people, and I will be your God. Then you will know that I am the LORD your God, who brought you out from under the yoke of the Egyptians. 8And I will bring you to the land I swore with uplifted hand to give to Abraham, to Isaac and to Jacob. I will give it to you as a possession. I am the LORD.' "

9Moses reported this to the Israelites, but they did not listen to him because of their discouragement and cruel bondage.

10Then the LORD said to Moses, 11"Go, tell Pharaoh king of Egypt to let the Israelites go out of his country."

12But Moses said to the LORD, "If the Israelites will not listen to me, why would Pharaoh listen to me, since I speak with faltering lips[d]?"

Family Record of Moses and Aaron

13Now the LORD spoke to Moses and Aaron about the Israelites and Pharaoh king of Egypt, and he commanded them to bring the Israelites out of Egypt.

14These were the heads of their families[e]:

The sons of Reuben the firstborn son of Israel were Hanoch and Pallu, Hezron and Carmi. These were the clans of Reuben.

15The sons of Simeon were Jemuel, Jamin, Ohad, Jakin, Zohar and Shaul the son of a Canaanite woman. These were the clans of Simeon.

16These were the names of the sons of Levi according to their records: Gershon, Kohath and Merari. Levi lived 137 years.

17The sons of Gershon, by clans, were Libni and Shimei.

18The sons of Kohath were Amram, Izhar, Hebron and Uzziel. Kohath lived 133 years.

19The sons of Merari were Mahli and Mushi.

These were the clans of Levi according to their records.

20Amram married his father's sister Jochebed, who bore him Aaron and Moses. Amram lived 137 years.

21The sons of Izhar were Korah, Nepheg and Zicri.

22The sons of Uzziel were Mishael, Elzaphan and Sithri.

23Aaron married Elisheba, daughter of Amminadab and sister of Nahshon, and she bore him Nadab and Abihu, Eleazar and Ithamar.

24The sons of Korah were Assir, Elkanah and Abiasaph. These were the Korahite clans.

25Eleazar son of Aaron married one of the daughters of Putiel, and she bore him Phinehas.

These were the heads of the Levite families, clan by clan.

26It was this same Aaron and Moses to whom the LORD said, "Bring the Israelites out of Egypt by their divisions." 27They were the ones who spoke to Pharaoh king of Egypt about bringing the Israelites out of Egypt. It was the same Moses and Aaron.

Aaron to Speak for Moses

28Now when the LORD spoke to Moses in Egypt, 29he said to him, "I am the LORD. Tell Pharaoh king of Egypt everything I tell you."

30But Moses said to the LORD, "Since I speak with faltering lips, why would Pharaoh listen to me?"

7 Then the LORD said to Moses, "See, I have made you like God to Pharaoh, and your brother Aaron will be your prophet. 2You are to say everything I command you, and your brother Aaron is to tell Pharaoh to let the Israelites go out of his country. 3But I will harden Pharaoh's heart, and though I multiply my miraculous signs and wonders in Egypt, 4he will not listen to you. Then I will lay my hand on Egypt and with mighty acts of judgment I will bring out my divisions, my people the Israelites. 5And the Egyptians will know that I am the LORD when I stretch out my hand against Egypt and bring the Israelites out of it."

6Moses and Aaron did just as the LORD commanded them. 7Moses was eighty years old and Aaron eighty-three when they spoke to Pharaoh.

Aaron's Staff Becomes a Snake

8The LORD said to Moses and Aaron, 9"When Pharaoh says to you, 'Perform a miracle,' then say to Aaron, 'Take your staff and throw it down before Pharaoh,' and it will become a snake."

10So Moses and Aaron went to Pharaoh and did just as the LORD commanded. Aaron threw his staff down in front of Pharaoh and his officials, and it became a snake. 11Pharaoh then summoned wise men and sorcerers, and the Egyptian magicians also did the same things by their secret arts: 12Each one threw down his staff and it became a snake. But Aaron's staff swallowed up their staffs. 13Yet Pharaoh's

[a]3 Hebrew *El-Shaddai* [b]3 See note at Exodus 3:15. [c]3 Or *Almighty, and by my name the LORD did I not let myself be known to them?* [d]12 Hebrew *I am uncircumcised of lips*; also in verse 30 [e]14 The Hebrew for *families* here and in verse 25 refers to units larger than clans.

heart became hard and he would not listen to them, just as the LORD had said.

The Plague of Blood

14Then the LORD said to Moses, "Pharaoh's heart is unyielding; he refuses to let the people go. 15Go to Pharaoh in the morning as he goes out to the water. Wait on the bank of the Nile to meet him, and take in your hand the staff that was changed into a snake. 16Then say to him, 'The LORD, the God of the Hebrews, has sent me to say to you: Let my people go, so that they may worship me in the desert. But until now you have not listened. 17This is what the LORD says: By this you will know that I am the LORD: With the staff that is in my hand I will strike the water of the Nile, and it will be changed into blood. 18The fish in the Nile will die, and the river will stink; the Egyptians will not be able to drink its water.' "

19The LORD said to Moses, "Tell Aaron, 'Take your staff and stretch out your hand over the waters of Egypt—over the streams and canals, over the ponds and all the reservoirs'—and they will turn to blood. Blood will be everywhere in Egypt, even in the wooden buckets and stone jars."

20Moses and Aaron did just as the LORD had commanded. He raised his staff in the presence of Pharaoh and his officials and struck the water of the Nile, and all the water was changed into blood. 21The fish in the Nile died, and the river smelled so bad that the Egyptians could not drink its water. Blood was everywhere in Egypt.

22But the Egyptian magicians did the same things by their secret arts, and Pharaoh's heart became hard; he would not listen to Moses and Aaron, just as the LORD had said. 23Instead, he turned and went into his palace, and did not take even this to heart. 24And all the Egyptians dug along the Nile to get drinking water, because they could not drink the water of the river.

The Plague of Frogs

25Seven days passed after the LORD struck

8 the Nile. 1Then the LORD said to Moses, "Go to Pharaoh and say to him, 'This is what the LORD says: Let my people go, so that they may worship me. 2If you refuse to let them go, I will plague your whole country with frogs. 3The Nile will teem with frogs. They will come up into your palace and your bedroom and onto your bed, into the houses of your officials and on your people, and into your ovens and kneading troughs. 4The frogs will go up on you and your people and all your officials.' "

5Then the LORD said to Moses, "Tell Aaron, 'Stretch out your hand with your staff over the streams and canals and ponds, and make frogs come up on the land of Egypt.' "

6So Aaron stretched out his hand over the waters of Egypt, and the frogs came up and covered the land. 7But the magicians did the same things by their secret arts; they also made frogs come up on the land of Egypt.

8Pharaoh summoned Moses and Aaron and said, "Pray to the LORD to take the frogs away from me and my people, and I will let your people go to offer sacrifices to the LORD."

9Moses said to Pharaoh, "I leave to you the honor of setting the time for me to pray for you and your officials and your people that you and your houses may be rid of the frogs, except for those that remain in the Nile."

10"Tomorrow," Pharaoh said.

Moses replied, "It will be as you say, so that you may know there is no one like the LORD our God. 11The frogs will leave you and your houses, your officials and your people; they will remain only in the Nile."

12After Moses and Aaron left Pharaoh, Moses cried out to the LORD about the frogs he had brought on Pharaoh. 13And the LORD did what Moses asked. The frogs died in the houses, in the courtyards and in the fields. 14They were piled into heaps, and the land reeked of them. 15But when Pharaoh saw that there was relief, he hardened his heart and would not listen to Moses and Aaron, just as the LORD had said.

The Plague of Gnats

16Then the LORD said to Moses, "Tell Aaron, 'Stretch out your staff and strike the dust of the ground,' and throughout the land of Egypt the dust will become gnats." 17They did this, and when Aaron stretched out his hand with the staff and struck the dust of the ground, gnats came upon men and animals. All the dust throughout the land of Egypt became gnats. 18But when the magicians tried to produce gnats by their secret arts, they could not. And the gnats were on men and animals.

19The magicians said to Pharaoh, "This is the finger of God." But Pharaoh's heart was hard and he would not listen, just as the LORD had said.

The Plague of Flies

20Then the LORD said to Moses, "Get up early in the morning and confront Pharaoh as he goes to the water and say to him, 'This is what the LORD says: Let my people go, so that they may worship me. 21If you do not let my people go, I will send swarms of flies on you and your officials, on your people and into your houses. The houses of the Egyptians will be full of flies, and even the ground where they are.

22" 'But on that day I will deal differently with the land of Goshen, where my people live; no swarms of flies will be there, so that you will know that I, the LORD, am in this land. 23I will make a distinction[a] between my people and your people. This miraculous sign will occur tomorrow.' "

24And the LORD did this. Dense swarms of

[a]23 Septuagint and Vulgate; Hebrew *will put a deliverance*

flies poured into Pharaoh's palace and into the houses of his officials, and throughout Egypt the land was ruined by the flies.

25Then Pharaoh summoned Moses and Aaron and said, "Go, sacrifice to your God here in the land."

26But Moses said, "That would not be right. The sacrifices we offer the LORD our God would be detestable to the Egyptians. And if we offer sacrifices that are detestable in their eyes, will they not stone us? 27We must take a three-day journey into the desert to offer sacrifices to the LORD our God, as he commands us."

28Pharaoh said, "I will let you go to offer sacrifices to the LORD your God in the desert, but you must not go very far. Now pray for me."

29Moses answered, "As soon as I leave you, I will pray to the LORD, and tomorrow the flies will leave Pharaoh and his officials and his people. Only be sure that Pharaoh does not act deceitfully again by not letting the people go to offer sacrifices to the LORD."

30Then Moses left Pharaoh and prayed to the LORD, 31and the LORD did what Moses asked: The flies left Pharaoh and his officials and his people; not a fly remained. 32But this time also Pharaoh hardened his heart and would not let the people go.

The Plague on Livestock

9 Then the LORD said to Moses, "Go to Pharaoh and say to him, 'This is what the LORD, the God of the Hebrews, says: "Let my people go, so that they may worship me." 2If you refuse to let them go and continue to hold them back, 3the hand of the LORD will bring a terrible plague on your livestock in the field—on your horses and donkeys and camels and on your cattle and sheep and goats. 4But the LORD will make a distinction between the livestock of Israel and that of Egypt, so that no animal belonging to the Israelites will die.' "

5The LORD set a time and said, "Tomorrow the LORD will do this in the land." 6And the next day the LORD did it: All the livestock of the Egyptians died, but not one animal belonging to the Israelites died. 7Pharaoh sent men to investigate and found that not even one of the animals of the Israelites had died. Yet his heart was unyielding and he would not let the people go.

The Plague of Boils

8Then the LORD said to Moses and Aaron, "Take handfuls of soot from a furnace and have Moses toss it into the air in the presence of Pharaoh. 9It will become fine dust over the whole land of Egypt, and festering boils will break out on men and animals throughout the land."

10So they took soot from a furnace and stood before Pharaoh. Moses tossed it into the air, and festering boils broke out on men and animals. 11The magicians could not stand before Moses because of the boils that were on them and on all the Egyptians. 12But the LORD hardened Pharaoh's heart and he would not listen to Moses and Aaron, just as the LORD had said to Moses.

The Plague of Hail

13Then the LORD said to Moses, "Get up early in the morning, confront Pharaoh and say to him, 'This is what the LORD, the God of the Hebrews, says: Let my people go, so that they may worship me, 14or this time I will send the full force of my plagues against you and against your officials and your people, so you may know that there is no one like me in all the earth. 15For by now I could have stretched out my hand and struck you and your people with a plague that would have wiped you off the earth. 16But I have raised you up[a] for this very purpose, that I might show you my power and that my name might be proclaimed in all the earth. 17You still set yourself against my people and will not let them go. 18Therefore, at this time tomorrow I will send the worst hailstorm that has ever fallen on Egypt, from the day it was founded till now. 19Give an order now to bring your livestock and everything you have in the field to a place of shelter, because the hail will fall on every man and animal that has not been brought in and is still out in the field, and they will die.' "

20Those officials of Pharaoh who feared the word of the LORD hurried to bring their slaves and their livestock inside. 21But those who ignored the word of the LORD left their slaves and livestock in the field.

22Then the LORD said to Moses, "Stretch out your hand toward the sky so that hail will fall all over Egypt—on men and animals and on everything growing in the fields of Egypt." 23When Moses stretched out his staff toward the sky, the LORD sent thunder and hail, and lightning flashed down to the ground. So the LORD rained hail on the land of Egypt; 24hail fell and lightning flashed back and forth. It was the worst storm in all the land of Egypt since it had become a nation. 25Throughout Egypt hail struck everything in the fields—both men and animals; it beat down everything growing in the fields and stripped every tree. 26The only place it did not hail was the land of Goshen, where the Israelites were.

27Then Pharaoh summoned Moses and Aaron. "This time I have sinned," he said to them. "The LORD is in the right, and I and my people are in the wrong. 28Pray to the LORD, for we have had enough thunder and hail. I will let you go; you don't have to stay any longer."

29Moses replied, "When I have gone out of the city, I will spread out my hands in prayer to the LORD. The thunder will stop and there will be no more hail, so you may know that the earth is the LORD's. 30But I know that you and your officials still do not fear the LORD God."

[a]16 Or *have spared you*

31(The flax and barley were destroyed, since
the barley had headed and the flax was in
bloom. 32The wheat and spelt, however, were
not destroyed, because they ripen later.)
33Then Moses left Pharaoh and went out of
the city. He spread out his hands toward the
LORD; the thunder and hail stopped, and the
rain no longer poured down on the land.
34When Pharaoh saw that the rain and hail and
thunder had stopped, he sinned again: He and
his officials hardened their hearts. 35So Pharaoh's heart was hard and he would not let the
Israelites go, just as the LORD had said through
Moses.

The Plague of Locusts

10 Then the LORD said to Moses, "Go to
Pharaoh, for I have hardened his heart
and the hearts of his officials so that I may
perform these miraculous signs of mine among
them 2that you may tell your children and
grandchildren how I dealt harshly with the
Egyptians and how I performed my signs
among them, and that you may know that I am
the LORD."
3So Moses and Aaron went to Pharaoh and
said to him, "This is what the LORD, the God
of the Hebrews, says: 'How long will you refuse to humble yourself before me? Let my
people go, so that they may worship me. 4If
you refuse to let them go, I will bring locusts
into your country tomorrow. 5They will cover
the face of the ground so that it cannot be seen.
They will devour what little you have left after
the hail, including every tree that is growing in
your fields. 6They will fill your houses and
those of all your officials and all the Egyptians—something neither your fathers nor your
forefathers have ever seen from the day they
settled in this land till now.' " Then Moses
turned and left Pharaoh.
7Pharaoh's officials said to him, "How long
will this man be a snare to us? Let the people
go, so that they may worship the LORD their
God. Do you not yet realize that Egypt is ruined?"
8Then Moses and Aaron were brought back
to Pharaoh. "Go, worship the LORD your God,"
he said. "But just who will be going?"
9Moses answered, "We will go with our
young and old, with our sons and daughters,
and with our flocks and herds, because we are
to celebrate a festival to the LORD."
10Pharaoh said, "The LORD be with you—if
I let you go, along with your women and children! Clearly you are bent on evil.[a] 11No!
Have only the men go; and worship the LORD,
since that's what you have been asking for."
Then Moses and Aaron were driven out of
Pharaoh's presence.
12And the LORD said to Moses, "Stretch
out your hand over Egypt so that locusts will
swarm over the land and devour everything
growing in the fields, everything left by the
hail."
13So Moses stretched out his staff over
Egypt, and the LORD made an east wind blow
across the land all that day and all that night.
By morning the wind had brought the locusts;
14they invaded all Egypt and settled down in
every area of the country in great numbers.
Never before had there been such a plague of
locusts, nor will there ever be again. 15They
covered all the ground until it was black. They
devoured all that was left after the hail—everything growing in the fields and the fruit on
the trees. Nothing green remained on tree or
plant in all the land of Egypt.
16Pharaoh quickly summoned Moses and
Aaron and said, "I have sinned against the
LORD your God and against you. 17Now forgive my sin once more and pray to the LORD
your God to take this deadly plague away
from me."
18Moses then left Pharaoh and prayed to the
LORD. 19And the LORD changed the wind to a
very strong west wind, which caught up the
locusts and carried them into the Red Sea.[b]
Not a locust was left anywhere in Egypt. 20But
the LORD hardened Pharaoh's heart, and he
would not let the Israelites go.

The Plague of Darkness

21Then the LORD said to Moses, "Stretch out
your hand toward the sky so that darkness will
spread over Egypt—darkness that can be felt."
22So Moses stretched out his hand toward the
sky, and total darkness covered all Egypt for
three days. 23No one could see anyone else or
leave his place for three days. Yet all the Israelites had light in the places where they lived.
24Then Pharaoh summoned Moses and said,
"Go, worship the LORD. Even your women and
children may go with you; only leave your
flocks and herds behind."
25But Moses said, "You must allow us to
have sacrifices and burnt offerings to present
to the LORD our God. 26Our livestock too must
go with us; not a hoof is to be left behind. We
have to use some of them in worshiping the
LORD our God, and until we get there we will
not know what we are to use to worship the
LORD."
27But the LORD hardened Pharaoh's heart,
and he was not willing to let them go. 28Phar-
aoh said to Moses, "Get out of my sight! Make
sure you do not appear before me again! The
day you see my face you will die."
29"Just as you say," Moses replied, "I will
never appear before you again."

The Plague on the Firstborn

11 Now the LORD had said to Moses, "I
will bring one more plague on Pharaoh
and on Egypt. After that, he will let you go
from here, and when he does, he will drive you
out completely. 2Tell the people that men and
women alike are to ask their neighbors for articles of silver and gold." 3(The LORD made the
Egyptians favorably disposed toward the peo-

[a] *10* Or *Be careful, trouble is in store for you!* [b] *19* Hebrew *Yam Suph*; that is, Sea of Reeds

ple, and Moses himself was highly regarded in
Egypt by Pharaoh's officials and by the people.)
4So Moses said, "This is what the LORD
says: 'About midnight I will go throughout
Egypt. 5Every firstborn son in Egypt will die,
from the firstborn son of Pharaoh, who sits on
the throne, to the firstborn son of the slave girl,
who is at her hand mill, and all the firstborn of
the cattle as well. 6There will be loud wailing
throughout Egypt—worse than there has ever
been or ever will be again. 7But among the
Israelites not a dog will bark at any man or
animal.' Then you will know that the LORD
makes a distinction between Egypt and Israel.
8All these officials of yours will come to me,
bowing down before me and saying, 'Go, you
and all the people who follow you!' After that
I will leave." Then Moses, hot with anger, left
Pharaoh.
9The LORD had said to Moses, "Pharaoh will
refuse to listen to you—so that my wonders
may be multiplied in Egypt." 10Moses and
Aaron performed all these wonders before
Pharaoh, but the LORD hardened Pharaoh's
heart, and he would not let the Israelites go out
of his country.

The Passover

12 The LORD said to Moses and Aaron in
Egypt, 2"This month is to be for you the
first month, the first month of your year. 3Tell
the whole community of Israel that on the
tenth day of this month each man is to take a
lamb[a] for his family, one for each household.
4If any household is too small for a whole
lamb, they must share one with their nearest
neighbor, having taken into account the number of people there are. You are to determine
the amount of lamb needed in accordance with
what each person will eat. 5The animals you
choose must be year-old males without defect,
and you may take them from the sheep or the
goats. 6Take care of them until the fourteenth
day of the month, when all the people of the
community of Israel must slaughter them at
twilight. 7Then they are to take some of the
blood and put it on the sides and tops of the
doorframes of the houses where they eat
the lambs. 8That same night they are to eat the
meat roasted over the fire, along with bitter
herbs, and bread made without yeast. 9Do not
eat the meat raw or cooked in water, but roast
it over the fire—head, legs and inner parts.
10Do not leave any of it till morning; if some
is left till morning, you must burn it. 11This is
how you are to eat it: with your cloak tucked
into your belt, your sandals on your feet and
your staff in your hand. Eat it in haste; it is the
LORD's Passover.
12"On that same night I will pass through
Egypt and strike down every firstborn—both
men and animals—and I will bring judgment
on all the gods of Egypt. I am the LORD. 13The
blood will be a sign for you on the houses
where you are; and when I see the blood, I will
pass over you. No destructive plague will
touch you when I strike Egypt.
14"This is a day you are to commemorate;
for the generations to come you shall celebrate
it as a festival to the LORD—a lasting ordinance. 15For seven days you are to eat bread
made without yeast. On the first day remove
the yeast from your houses, for whoever eats
anything with yeast in it from the first day
through the seventh must be cut off from Israel. 16On the first day hold a sacred assembly,
and another one on the seventh day. Do no
work at all on these days, except to prepare
food for everyone to eat—that is all you
may do.
17"Celebrate the Feast of Unleavened Bread,
because it was on this very day that I brought
your divisions out of Egypt. Celebrate this day
as a lasting ordinance for the generations to
come. 18In the first month you are to eat bread
made without yeast, from the evening of the
fourteenth day until the evening of the twenty-
first day. 19For seven days no yeast is to be
found in your houses. And whoever eats anything with yeast in it must be cut off from the
community of Israel, whether he is an alien or
native-born. 20Eat nothing made with yeast.
Wherever you live, you must eat unleavened
bread."
21Then Moses summoned all the elders of
Israel and said to them, "Go at once and select
the animals for your families and slaughter the
Passover lamb. 22Take a bunch of hyssop, dip
it into the blood in the basin and put some of
the blood on the top and on both sides of the
doorframe. Not one of you shall go out the
door of his house until morning. 23When
the LORD goes through the land to strike down
the Egyptians, he will see the blood on the top
and sides of the doorframe and will pass over
that doorway, and he will not permit the destroyer to enter your houses and strike you
down.
24"Obey these instructions as a lasting ordinance for you and your descendants. 25When
you enter the land that the LORD will give you
as he promised, observe this ceremony. 26And
when your children ask you, 'What does this
ceremony mean to you?' 27then tell them, 'It is
the Passover sacrifice to the LORD, who passed
over the houses of the Israelites in Egypt and
spared our homes when he struck down the
Egyptians.' " Then the people bowed down
and worshiped. 28The Israelites did just what
the LORD commanded Moses and Aaron.
29At midnight the LORD struck down all the
firstborn in Egypt, from the firstborn of Pharaoh, who sat on the throne, to the firstborn of
the prisoner, who was in the dungeon, and the
firstborn of all the livestock as well. 30Pharaoh
and all his officials and all the Egyptians got
up during the night, and there was loud wailing
in Egypt, for there was not a house without
someone dead.

[a] *3* The Hebrew word can mean *lamb* or *kid*; also in verse 4.

The Exodus

31During the night Pharaoh summoned Moses and Aaron and said, "Up! Leave my people, you and the Israelites! Go, worship the LORD as you have requested. 32Take your flocks and herds, as you have said, and go. And also bless me."

33The Egyptians urged the people to hurry and leave the country. "For otherwise," they said, "we will all die!" 34So the people took their dough before the yeast was added, and carried it on their shoulders in kneading troughs wrapped in clothing. 35The Israelites did as Moses instructed and asked the Egyptians for articles of silver and gold and for clothing. 36The LORD had made the Egyptians favorably disposed toward the people, and they gave them what they asked for; so they plundered the Egyptians.

37The Israelites journeyed from Rameses to Succoth. There were about six hundred thousand men on foot, besides women and children. 38Many other people went up with them, as well as large droves of livestock, both flocks and herds. 39With the dough they had brought from Egypt, they baked cakes of unleavened bread. The dough was without yeast because they had been driven out of Egypt and did not have time to prepare food for themselves.

40Now the length of time the Israelite people lived in Egypt[a] was 430 years. 41At the end of the 430 years, to the very day, all the LORD's divisions left Egypt. 42Because the LORD kept vigil that night to bring them out of Egypt, on this night all the Israelites are to keep vigil to honor the LORD for the generations to come.

Passover Restrictions

43The LORD said to Moses and Aaron, "These are the regulations for the Passover:

"No foreigner is to eat of it. 44Any slave you have bought may eat of it after you have circumcised him, 45but a temporary resident and a hired worker may not eat of it.

46"It must be eaten inside one house; take none of the meat outside the house. Do not break any of the bones. 47The whole community of Israel must celebrate it.

48"An alien living among you who wants to celebrate the LORD's Passover must have all the males in his household circumcised; then he may take part like one born in the land. No uncircumcised male may eat of it. 49The same law applies to the native-born and to the alien living among you."

50All the Israelites did just what the LORD had commanded Moses and Aaron. 51And on that very day the LORD brought the Israelites out of Egypt by their divisions.

Consecration of the Firstborn

13 The LORD said to Moses, 2"Consecrate to me every firstborn male. The first offspring of every womb among the Israelites belongs to me, whether man or animal."

3Then Moses said to the people, "Commemorate this day, the day you came out of Egypt, out of the land of slavery, because the LORD brought you out of it with a mighty hand. Eat nothing containing yeast. 4Today, in the month of Abib, you are leaving. 5When the LORD brings you into the land of the Canaanites, Hittites, Amorites, Hivites and Jebusites—the land he swore to your forefathers to give you, a land flowing with milk and honey—you are to observe this ceremony in this month: 6For seven days eat bread made without yeast and on the seventh day hold a festival to the LORD. 7Eat unleavened bread during those seven days; nothing with yeast in it is to be seen among you, nor shall any yeast be seen anywhere within your borders. 8On that day tell your son, 'I do this because of what the LORD did for me when I came out of Egypt.' 9This observance will be for you like a sign on your hand and a reminder on your forehead that the law of the LORD is to be on your lips. For the LORD brought you out of Egypt with his mighty hand. 10You must keep this ordinance at the appointed time year after year.

11"After the LORD brings you into the land of the Canaanites and gives it to you, as he promised on oath to you and your forefathers, 12you are to give over to the LORD the first offspring of every womb. All the firstborn males of your livestock belong to the LORD. 13Redeem with a lamb every firstborn donkey, but if you do not redeem it, break its neck. Redeem every firstborn among your sons.

14"In days to come, when your son asks you, 'What does this mean?' say to him, 'With a mighty hand the LORD brought us out of Egypt, out of the land of slavery. 15When Pharaoh stubbornly refused to let us go, the LORD killed every firstborn in Egypt, both man and animal. This is why I sacrifice to the LORD the first male offspring of every womb and redeem each of my firstborn sons.' 16And it will be like a sign on your hand and a symbol on your forehead that the LORD brought us out of Egypt with his mighty hand."

Crossing the Sea

17When Pharaoh let the people go, God did not lead them on the road through the Philistine country, though that was shorter. For God said, "If they face war, they might change their minds and return to Egypt." 18So God led the people around by the desert road toward the Red Sea.[b] The Israelites went up out of Egypt armed for battle.

19Moses took the bones of Joseph with him because Joseph had made the sons of Israel swear an oath. He had said, "God will surely come to your aid, and then you must carry my bones up with you from this place."[c]

20After leaving Succoth they camped at

[a]40 Masoretic Text; Samaritan Pentateuch and Septuagint *Egypt and Canaan* [b]18 Hebrew *Yam Suph*; that is, Sea of Reeds [c]19 See Gen. 50:25.

Etham on the edge of the desert. 21By day the
LORD went ahead of them in a pillar of cloud
to guide them on their way and by night in a
pillar of fire to give them light, so that they
could travel by day or night. 22Neither the pillar of cloud by day nor the pillar of fire by
night left its place in front of the people.

14 Then the LORD said to Moses, 2"Tell the
Israelites to turn back and encamp near
Pi Hahiroth, between Migdol and the sea. They
are to encamp by the sea, directly opposite
Baal Zephon. 3Pharaoh will think, 'The Israelites are wandering around the land in confusion, hemmed in by the desert.' 4And I will
harden Pharaoh's heart, and he will pursue
them. But I will gain glory for myself through
Pharaoh and all his army, and the Egyptians
will know that I am the LORD." So the Israelites did this.

5When the king of Egypt was told that the
people had fled, Pharaoh and his officials
changed their minds about them and said,
"What have we done? We have let the Israelites go and have lost their services!" 6So he
had his chariot made ready and took his army
with him. 7He took six hundred of the best
chariots, along with all the other chariots of
Egypt, with officers over all of them. 8The
LORD hardened the heart of Pharaoh king of
Egypt, so that he pursued the Israelites, who
were marching out boldly. 9The Egyptians—
all Pharaoh's horses and chariots, horsemen[a]
and troops—pursued the Israelites and overtook them as they camped by the sea near Pi
Hahiroth, opposite Baal Zephon.

10As Pharaoh approached, the Israelites
looked up, and there were the Egyptians,
marching after them. They were terrified and
cried out to the LORD. 11They said to Moses,
"Was it because there were no graves in Egypt
that you brought us to the desert to die? What
have you done to us by bringing us out of
Egypt? 12Didn't we say to you in Egypt,
'Leave us alone; let us serve the Egyptians'? It
would have been better for us to serve the
Egyptians than to die in the desert!"

13Moses answered the people, "Do not be
afraid. Stand firm and you will see the deliverance the LORD will bring you today. The Egyptians you see today you will never see again.
14The LORD will fight for you; you need only
to be still."

15Then the LORD said to Moses, "Why are
you crying out to me? Tell the Israelites to
move on. 16Raise your staff and stretch out
your hand over the sea to divide the water so
that the Israelites can go through the sea on dry
ground. 17I will harden the hearts of the Egyptians so that they will go in after them. And I
will gain glory through Pharaoh and all his
army, through his chariots and his horsemen.
18The Egyptians will know that I am the LORD
when I gain glory through Pharaoh, his chariots and his horsemen."

19Then the angel of God, who had been traveling in front of Israel's army, withdrew and
went behind them. The pillar of cloud also
moved from in front and stood behind them,
20coming between the armies of Egypt and Israel. Throughout the night the cloud brought
darkness to the one side and light to the other
side; so neither went near the other all night
long.

21Then Moses stretched out his hand over
the sea, and all that night the LORD drove the
sea back with a strong east wind and turned it
into dry land. The waters were divided, 22and
the Israelites went through the sea on dry
ground, with a wall of water on their right and
on their left.

23The Egyptians pursued them, and all Pharaoh's horses and chariots and horsemen followed them into the sea. 24During the last
watch of the night the LORD looked down from
the pillar of fire and cloud at the Egyptian
army and threw it into confusion. 25He made
the wheels of their chariots come off[b] so that
they had difficulty driving. And the Egyptians
said, "Let's get away from the Israelites! The
LORD is fighting for them against Egypt."

26Then the LORD said to Moses, "Stretch out
your hand over the sea so that the waters may
flow back over the Egyptians and their chariots
and horsemen." 27Moses stretched out his hand
over the sea, and at daybreak the sea went back
to its place. The Egyptians were fleeing toward[c] it, and the LORD swept them into the
sea. 28The water flowed back and covered the
chariots and horsemen—the entire army of
Pharaoh that had followed the Israelites into
the sea. Not one of them survived.

29But the Israelites went through the sea on
dry ground, with a wall of water on their right
and on their left. 30That day the LORD saved
Israel from the hands of the Egyptians, and
Israel saw the Egyptians lying dead on the
shore. 31And when the Israelites saw the great
power the LORD displayed against the Egyptians, the people feared the LORD and put their
trust in him and in Moses his servant.

The Song of Moses and Miriam

15 Then Moses and the Israelites sang this
song to the LORD:

"I will sing to the LORD,
  for he is highly exalted.
The horse and its rider
  he has hurled into the sea.
2The LORD is my strength and my song;
  he has become my salvation.
He is my God, and I will praise him,
  my father's God, and I will exalt him.
3The LORD is a warrior;
  the LORD is his name.
4Pharaoh's chariots and his army
  he has hurled into the sea.
The best of Pharaoh's officers

[a]9 Or *charioteers*; also in verses 17, 18, 23, 26 and 28 [b]25 Or *He jammed the wheels of their chariots* (see Samaritan Pentateuch, Septuagint and Syriac) [c]27 Or *from*

are drowned in the Red Sea.[a]
5The deep waters have covered them;
they sank to the depths like a stone.

6"Your right hand, O LORD,
was majestic in power.
Your right hand, O LORD,
shattered the enemy.
7In the greatness of your majesty
you threw down those who opposed
you.
You unleashed your burning anger;
it consumed them like stubble.
8By the blast of your nostrils
the waters piled up.
The surging waters stood firm like a wall;
the deep waters congealed in the heart
of the sea.

9"The enemy boasted,
'I will pursue, I will overtake them.
I will divide the spoils;
I will gorge myself on them.
I will draw my sword
and my hand will destroy them.'
10But you blew with your breath,
and the sea covered them.
They sank like lead
in the mighty waters.

11"Who among the gods is like you,
O LORD?
Who is like you—
majestic in holiness,
awesome in glory,
working wonders?
12You stretched out your right hand
and the earth swallowed them.

13"In your unfailing love you will lead
the people you have redeemed.
In your strength you will guide them
to your holy dwelling.
14The nations will hear and tremble;
anguish will grip the people of Philistia.
15The chiefs of Edom will be terrified,
the leaders of Moab will be seized with
trembling,
the people[b] of Canaan will melt away;
16 terror and dread will fall upon them.
By the power of your arm
they will be as still as a stone—
until your people pass by, O LORD,
until the people you bought[c] pass by.
17You will bring them in and plant them
on the mountain of your inheritance—
the place, O LORD, you made for your
dwelling,
the sanctuary, O Lord, your hands
established.
18The LORD will reign
for ever and ever."

19When Pharaoh's horses, chariots and
horsemen[d] went into the sea, the LORD
brought the waters of the sea back over them,
but the Israelites walked through the sea on dry
ground. 20Then Miriam the prophetess, Aaron's sister, took a tambourine in her hand, and
all the women followed her, with tambourines
and dancing. 21Miriam sang to them:

"Sing to the LORD,
for he is highly exalted.
The horse and its rider
he has hurled into the sea."

The Waters of Marah and Elim

22Then Moses led Israel from the Red Sea
and they went into the Desert of Shur. For
three days they traveled in the desert without
finding water. 23When they came to Marah,
they could not drink its water because it was
bitter. (That is why the place is called Marah.[e]) 24So the people grumbled against Moses, saying, "What are we to drink?"
25Then Moses cried out to the LORD, and the
LORD showed him a piece of wood. He threw
it into the water, and the water became sweet.
There the LORD made a decree and a law for
them, and there he tested them. 26He said, "If
you listen carefully to the voice of the LORD
your God and do what is right in his eyes, if
you pay attention to his commands and keep
all his decrees, I will not bring on you any of
the diseases I brought on the Egyptians, for I
am the LORD, who heals you."
27Then they came to Elim, where there were
twelve springs and seventy palm trees, and
they camped there near the water.

Manna and Quail

16 The whole Israelite community set out
from Elim and came to the Desert of
Sin, which is between Elim and Sinai, on the
fifteenth day of the second month after they
had come out of Egypt. 2In the desert the
whole community grumbled against Moses
and Aaron. 3The Israelites said to them, "If
only we had died by the LORD's hand in
Egypt! There we sat around pots of meat and
ate all the food we wanted, but you have
brought us out into this desert to starve this
entire assembly to death."
4Then the LORD said to Moses, "I will rain
down bread from heaven for you. The people
are to go out each day and gather enough for
that day. In this way I will test them and see
whether they will follow my instructions. 5On
the sixth day they are to prepare what they
bring in, and that is to be twice as much as they
gather on the other days."
6So Moses and Aaron said to all the Israelites, "In the evening you will know that it was
the LORD who brought you out of Egypt, 7and
in the morning you will see the glory of the
LORD, because he has heard your grumbling
against him. Who are we, that you should
grumble against us?" 8Moses also said, "You
will know that it was the LORD when he gives
you meat to eat in the evening and all the bread
you want in the morning, because he has heard

[a]4 Hebrew *Yam Suph*; that is, Sea of Reeds; also in verse 22 [b]15 Or *rulers* [c]16 Or *created*
[d]19 Or *charioteers* [e]23 *Marah* means *bitter.*

your grumbling against him. Who are we? You
are not grumbling against us, but against the
LORD."
9Then Moses told Aaron, "Say to the entire
Israelite community, 'Come before the LORD,
for he has heard your grumbling.' "
10While Aaron was speaking to the whole
Israelite community, they looked toward the
desert, and there was the glory of the LORD
appearing in the cloud.
11The LORD said to Moses, 12"I have heard
the grumbling of the Israelites. Tell them, 'At
twilight you will eat meat, and in the morning
you will be filled with bread. Then you will
know that I am the LORD your God.' "
13That evening quail came and covered the
camp, and in the morning there was a layer of
dew around the camp. 14When the dew was
gone, thin flakes like frost on the ground appeared on the desert floor. 15When the Israelites saw it, they said to each other, "What is
it?" For they did not know what it was.
Moses said to them, "It is the bread the
LORD has given you to eat. 16This is what the
LORD has commanded: 'Each one is to gather
as much as he needs. Take an omer[a] for each
person you have in your tent.' "
17The Israelites did as they were told; some
gathered much, some little. 18And when they
measured it by the omer, he who gathered
much did not have too much, and he who gathered little did not have too little. Each one
gathered as much as he needed.
19Then Moses said to them, "No one is to
keep any of it until morning."
20However, some of them paid no attention
to Moses; they kept part of it until morning,
but it was full of maggots and began to smell.
So Moses was angry with them.
21Each morning everyone gathered as much
as he needed, and when the sun grew hot, it
melted away. 22On the sixth day, they gathered
twice as much—two omers[b] for each person—and the leaders of the community came
and reported this to Moses. 23He said to them,
"This is what the LORD commanded: 'Tomorrow is to be a day of rest, a holy Sabbath to the
LORD. So bake what you want to bake and boil
what you want to boil. Save whatever is left
and keep it until morning.' "
24So they saved it until morning, as Moses
commanded, and it did not stink or get maggots in it. 25"Eat it today," Moses said, "because today is a Sabbath to the LORD. You will
not find any of it on the ground today. 26Six
days you are to gather it, but on the seventh
day, the Sabbath, there will not be any."
27Nevertheless, some of the people went out
on the seventh day to gather it, but they found
none. 28Then the LORD said to Moses, "How
long will you[c] refuse to keep my commands
and my instructions? 29Bear in mind that the
LORD has given you the Sabbath; that is why
on the sixth day he gives you bread for two
days. Everyone is to stay where he is on the
seventh day; no one is to go out." 30So the
people rested on the seventh day.
31The people of Israel called the bread manna.[d] It was white like coriander seed and tasted
like wafers made with honey. 32Moses said,
"This is what the LORD has commanded: 'Take
an omer of manna and keep it for the generations to come, so they can see the bread I gave
you to eat in the desert when I brought you out
of Egypt.' "
33So Moses said to Aaron, "Take a jar and
put an omer of manna in it. Then place it before the LORD to be kept for the generations to
come."
34As the LORD commanded Moses, Aaron
put the manna in front of the Testimony, that
it might be kept. 35The Israelites ate manna
forty years, until they came to a land that was
settled; they ate manna until they reached the
border of Canaan.
36(An omer is one tenth of an ephah.)

Water From the Rock

17 The whole Israelite community set out
from the Desert of Sin, traveling from
place to place as the LORD commanded. They
camped at Rephidim, but there was no water
for the people to drink. 2So they quarreled with
Moses and said, "Give us water to drink."
Moses replied, "Why do you quarrel with
me? Why do you put the LORD to the test?"
3But the people were thirsty for water there,
and they grumbled against Moses. They said,
"Why did you bring us up out of Egypt to
make us and our children and livestock die of
thirst?"
4Then Moses cried out to the LORD, "What
am I to do with these people? They are almost
ready to stone me."
5The LORD answered Moses, "Walk on
ahead of the people. Take with you some of the
elders of Israel and take in your hand the staff
with which you struck the Nile, and go. 6I will
stand there before you by the rock at Horeb.
Strike the rock, and water will come out of it
for the people to drink." So Moses did this in
the sight of the elders of Israel. 7And he called
the place Massah[e] and Meribah[f] because the
Israelites quarreled and because they tested the
LORD saying, "Is the LORD among us or not?"

The Amalekites Defeated

8The Amalekites came and attacked the Israelites at Rephidim. 9Moses said to Joshua,
"Choose some of our men and go out to fight
the Amalekites. Tomorrow I will stand on top
of the hill with the staff of God in my hands."
10So Joshua fought the Amalekites as Moses
had ordered, and Moses, Aaron and Hur went
to the top of the hill. 11As long as Moses held
up his hands, the Israelites were winning, but
whenever he lowered his hands, the Amalek-

[a] *16* That is, probably about 2 quarts (about 2 liters); also in verses 18, 32, 33 and 36 [b] *22* That is, probably about 4 quarts (about 4.5 liters) [c] *28* The Hebrew is plural. [d] *31* *Manna* means *What is it?* (see verse 15). [e] *7* *Massah* means *testing.* [f] *7* *Meribah* means *quarreling.*

ites were winning. 12When Moses' hands grew tired, they took a stone and put it under him and he sat on it. Aaron and Hur held his hands up—one on one side, one on the other—so that his hands remained steady till sunset. 13So Joshua overcame the Amalekite army with the sword.

14Then the LORD said to Moses, "Write this on a scroll as something to be remembered and make sure that Joshua hears it, because I will completely blot out the memory of Amalek from under heaven."

15Moses built an altar and called it The LORD is my Banner. 16He said, "For hands were lifted up to the throne of the LORD. The[a] LORD will be at war against the Amalekites from generation to generation."

Jethro Visits Moses

18 Now Jethro, the priest of Midian and father-in-law of Moses, heard of everything God had done for Moses and for his people Israel, and how the LORD had brought Israel out of Egypt.

2After Moses had sent away his wife Zipporah, his father-in-law Jethro received her 3and her two sons. One son was named Gershom,[b] for Moses said, "I have become an alien in a foreign land"; 4and the other was named Eliezer,[c] for he said, "My father's God was my helper; he saved me from the sword of Pharaoh."

5Jethro, Moses' father-in-law, together with Moses' sons and wife, came to him in the desert, where he was camped near the mountain of God. 6Jethro had sent word to him, "I, your father-in-law Jethro, am coming to you with your wife and her two sons."

7So Moses went out to meet his father-in-law and bowed down and kissed him. They greeted each other and then went into the tent. 8Moses told his father-in-law about everything the LORD had done to Pharaoh and the Egyptians for Israel's sake and about all the hardships they had met along the way and how the LORD had saved them.

9Jethro was delighted to hear about all the good things the LORD had done for Israel in rescuing them from the hand of the Egyptians. 10He said, "Praise be to the LORD, who rescued you from the hand of the Egyptians and of Pharaoh, and who rescued the people from the hand of the Egyptians. 11Now I know that the LORD is greater than all other gods, for he did this to those who had treated Israel arrogantly." 12Then Jethro, Moses' father-in-law, brought a burnt offering and other sacrifices to God, and Aaron came with all the elders of Israel to eat bread with Moses' father-in-law in the presence of God.

13The next day Moses took his seat to serve as judge for the people, and they stood around him from morning till evening. 14When his father-in-law saw all that Moses was doing for the people, he said, "What is this you are doing for the people? Why do you alone sit as judge, while all these people stand around you from morning till evening?"

15Moses answered him, "Because the people come to me to seek God's will. 16Whenever they have a dispute, it is brought to me, and I decide between the parties and inform them of God's decrees and laws."

17Moses' father-in-law replied, "What you are doing is not good. 18You and these people who come to you will only wear yourselves out. The work is too heavy for you; you cannot handle it alone. 19Listen now to me and I will give you some advice, and may God be with you. You must be the people's representative before God and bring their disputes to him. 20Teach them the decrees and laws, and show them the way to live and the duties they are to perform. 21But select capable men from all the people—men who fear God, trustworthy men who hate dishonest gain—and appoint them as officials over thousands, hundreds, fifties and tens. 22Have them serve as judges for the people at all times, but have them bring every difficult case to you; the simple cases they can decide themselves. That will make your load lighter, because they will share it with you. 23If you do this and God so commands, you will be able to stand the strain, and all these people will go home satisfied."

24Moses listened to his father-in-law and did everything he said. 25He chose capable men from all Israel and made them leaders of the people, officials over thousands, hundreds, fifties and tens. 26They served as judges for the people at all times. The difficult cases they brought to Moses, but the simple ones they decided themselves.

27Then Moses sent his father-in-law on his way, and Jethro returned to his own country.

At Mount Sinai

19 In the third month after the Israelites left Egypt—on the very day—they came to the Desert of Sinai. 2After they set out from Rephidim, they entered the Desert of Sinai, and Israel camped there in the desert in front of the mountain.

3Then Moses went up to God, and the LORD called to him from the mountain and said, "This is what you are to say to the house of Jacob and what you are to tell the people of Israel: 4'You yourselves have seen what I did to Egypt, and how I carried you on eagles' wings and brought you to myself. 5Now if you obey me fully and keep my covenant, then out of all nations you will be my treasured possession. Although the whole earth is mine, 6you[d] will be for me a kingdom of priests and a holy nation.' These are the words you are to speak to the Israelites."

7So Moses went back and summoned the

[a]16 Or *"Because a hand was against the throne of the LORD, the LORD will be at war against the Amalekites from generation to generation."* — *the*

[a]16 Or *"Because a hand was against the throne of the LORD, the* ... *an alien there.*

elders of the people and set before them all the
words the LORD had commanded him to speak.
[8]The people all responded together, "We will
do everything the LORD has said." So Moses
brought their answer back to the LORD.
[9]The LORD said to Moses, "I am going to
come to you in a dense cloud, so that the people will hear me speaking with you and will
always put their trust in you." Then Moses told
the LORD what the people had said.
[10]And the LORD said to Moses, "Go to the
people and consecrate them today and tomorrow. Have them wash their clothes [11]and be
ready by the third day, because on that day the
LORD will come down on Mount Sinai in the
sight of all the people. [12]Put limits for the people around the mountain and tell them, 'Be
careful that you do not go up the mountain
or touch the foot of it. Whoever touches the
mountain shall surely be put to death. [13]He
shall surely be stoned or shot with arrows; not
a hand is to be laid on him. Whether man or
animal, he shall not be permitted to live.' Only
when the ram's horn sounds a long blast may
they go up to the mountain."
[14]After Moses had gone down the mountain
to the people, he consecrated them, and they
washed their clothes. [15]Then he said to the
people, "Prepare yourselves for the third day.
Abstain from sexual relations."
[16]On the morning of the third day there was
thunder and lightning, with a thick cloud over
the mountain, and a very loud trumpet blast.
Everyone in the camp trembled. [17]Then Moses
led the people out of the camp to meet with
God, and they stood at the foot of the mountain. [18]Mount Sinai was covered with smoke,
because the LORD descended on it in fire. The
smoke billowed up from it like smoke from a
furnace, the whole mountain[a] trembled violently, [19]and the sound of the trumpet grew
louder and louder. Then Moses spoke and the
voice of God answered him.[b]
[20]The LORD descended to the top of Mount
Sinai and called Moses to the top of the mountain. So Moses went up [21]and the LORD said to
him, "Go down and warn the people so they do
not force their way through to see the LORD
and many of them perish. [22]Even the priests,
who approach the LORD, must consecrate
themselves, or the LORD will break out against
them."
[23]Moses said to the LORD, "The people cannot come up Mount Sinai, because you yourself warned us, 'Put limits around the mountain and set it apart as holy.' "
[24]The LORD replied, "Go down and bring
Aaron up with you. But the priests and the
people must not force their way through to
come up to the LORD, or he will break out
against them."
[25]So Moses went down to the people and
told them.

The Ten Commandments

20 And God spoke all these words:

[2]"I am the LORD your God, who
brought you out of Egypt, out of the
land of slavery.

[3]"You shall have no other gods before[c] me.

[4]"You shall not make for yourself an idol
in the form of anything in heaven
above or on the earth beneath or in
the waters below. [5]You shall not
bow down to them or worship
them; for I, the LORD your God, am
a jealous God, punishing the children for the sin of the fathers to the
third and fourth generation of those
who hate me, [6]but showing love to
a thousand ⌊generations⌋ of those
who love me and keep my commandments.

[7]"You shall not misuse the name of the
LORD your God, for the LORD will
not hold anyone guiltless who mis-
uses his name.

[8]"Remember the Sabbath day by keeping
it holy. [9]Six days you shall labor
and do all your work, [10]but the seventh day is a Sabbath to the LORD
your God. On it you shall not do
any work, neither you, nor your son
or daughter, nor your manservant
or maidservant, nor your animals,
nor the alien within your gates.
[11]For in six days the LORD made
the heavens and the earth, the sea,
and all that is in them, but he rested
on the seventh day. Therefore the
LORD blessed the Sabbath day and
made it holy.

[12]"Honor your father and your mother, so
that you may live long in the land
the LORD your God is giving you.

[13]"You shall not murder.

[14]"You shall not commit adultery.

[15]"You shall not steal.

[16]"You shall not give false testimony
against your neighbor.

[17]"You shall not covet your neighbor's
house. You shall not covet your
neighbor's wife, or his manservant
or maidservant, his ox or donkey,
or anything that belongs to your
neighbor."

[18]When the people saw the thunder and
lightning and heard the trumpet and saw the
mountain in smoke, they trembled with fear.
They stayed at a distance [19]and said to Moses,
"Speak to us yourself and we will listen. But
do not have God speak to us or we will die."
[20]Moses said to the people, "Do not be
afraid. God has come to test you, so that the

[a] *18* Most Hebrew manuscripts; a few Hebrew manuscripts and Septuagint *all the people* [b] *19* Or *and God answered him with thunder* [c] *3* Or *besides*

fear of God will be with you to keep you from
sinning."
21The people remained at a distance, while
Moses approached the thick darkness where
God was.

Idols and Altars

22Then the LORD said to Moses, "Tell the
Israelites this: 'You have seen for yourselves
that I have spoken to you from heaven: 23Do
not make any gods to be alongside me; do not
make for yourselves gods of silver or gods of
gold.
24" 'Make an altar of earth for me and sacrifice on it your burnt offerings and fellowship
offerings,[a] your sheep and goats and your cattle. Wherever I cause my name to be honored,
I will come to you and bless you. 25If you
make an altar of stones for me, do not build it
with dressed stones, for you will defile it if you
use a tool on it. 26And do not go up to my altar
on steps, lest your nakedness be exposed
on it.'

21 "These are the laws you are to set before
them:

Hebrew Servants

2"If you buy a Hebrew servant, he is to serve
you for six years. But in the seventh year, he
shall go free, without paying anything. 3If he
comes alone, he is to go free alone; but if
he has a wife when he comes, she is to go with
him. 4If his master gives him a wife and she
bears him sons or daughters, the woman and
her children shall belong to her master, and
only the man shall go free.
5"But if the servant declares, 'I love my
master and my wife and children and do not
want to go free,' 6then his master must take
him before the judges.[b] He shall take him to
the door or the doorpost and pierce his ear with
an awl. Then he will be his servant for life.
7"If a man sells his daughter as a servant,
she is not to go free as menservants do. 8If she
does not please the master who has selected
her for himself,[c] he must let her be redeemed.
He has no right to sell her to foreigners, because he has broken faith with her. 9If he selects her for his son, he must grant her the
rights of a daughter. 10If he marries another
woman, he must not deprive the first one of her
food, clothing and marital rights. 11If he does
not provide her with these three things, she is
to go free, without any payment of money.

Personal Injuries

12"Anyone who strikes a man and kills him
shall surely be put to death. 13However, if he
does not do it intentionally, but God lets it
happen, he is to flee to a place I will designate.
14But if a man schemes and kills another man
deliberately, take him away from my altar and
put him to death.
15"Anyone who attacks[d] his father or his
mother must be put to death.
16"Anyone who kidnaps another and either
sells him or still has him when he is caught
must be put to death.
17"Anyone who curses his father or mother
must be put to death.
18"If men quarrel and one hits the other with
a stone or with his fist[e] and he does not die but
is confined to bed, 19the one who struck the
blow will not be held responsible if the other
gets up and walks around outside with his
staff; however, he must pay the injured man
for the loss of his time and see that he is completely healed.
20"If a man beats his male or female slave
with a rod and the slave dies as a direct result,
he must be punished, 21but he is not to be
punished if the slave gets up after a day or two,
since the slave is his property.
22"If men who are fighting hit a pregnant
woman and she gives birth prematurely[f] but
there is no serious injury, the offender must be
fined whatever the woman's husband demands
and the court allows. 23But if there is serious
injury, you are to take life for life, 24eye for
eye, tooth for tooth, hand for hand, foot for
foot, 25burn for burn, wound for wound, bruise
for bruise.
26"If a man hits a manservant or maidservant in the eye and destroys it, he must let the
servant go free to compensate for the eye.
27And if he knocks out the tooth of a manservant or maidservant, he must let the servant go
free to compensate for the tooth.
28"If a bull gores a man or a woman to
death, the bull must be stoned to death, and its
meat must not be eaten. But the owner of the
bull will not be held responsible. 29If, however, the bull has had the habit of goring and the
owner has been warned but has not kept it
penned up and it kills a man or woman, the
bull must be stoned and the owner also must be
put to death. 30However, if payment is demanded of him, he may redeem his life by
paying whatever is demanded. 31This law also
applies if the bull gores a son or daughter. 32If
the bull gores a male or female slave, the owner must pay thirty shekels[g] of silver to the
master of the slave, and the bull must be
stoned.
33"If a man uncovers a pit or digs one and
fails to cover it and an ox or a donkey falls into
it, 34the owner of the pit must pay for the loss;
he must pay its owner, and the dead animal
will be his.
35"If a man's bull injures the bull of another
and it dies, they are to sell the live one and
divide both the money and the dead animal
equally. 36However, if it was known that the
bull had the habit of goring, yet the owner did
not keep it penned up, the owner must pay,

[a]24 Traditionally *peace offerings* [b]6 Or *before God* [c]8 Or *master so that he does not choose her*
[d]15 Or *kills* [e]18 Or *with a tool* [f]22 Or *she has a miscarriage* [g]32 That is, about 12 ounces (about 0.3 kilogram)

animal for animal, and the dead animal will be
his.

Protection of Property

22 “If a man steals an ox or a sheep and
slaughters it or sells it, he must pay back
five head of cattle for the ox and four sheep for
the sheep.
2“If a thief is caught breaking in and is
struck so that he dies, the defender is not guilty
of bloodshed; 3but if it happens[a] after sunrise,
he is guilty of bloodshed.
“A thief must certainly make restitution, but
if he has nothing, he must be sold to pay for his
theft.
4“If the stolen animal is found alive in his
possession—whether ox or donkey or sheep—
he must pay back double.
5“If a man grazes his livestock in a field or
vineyard and lets them stray and they graze in
another man’s field, he must make restitution
from the best of his own field or vineyard.
6“If a fire breaks out and spreads into thornbushes so that it burns shocks of grain or
standing grain or the whole field, the one who
started the fire must make restitution.
7“If a man gives his neighbor silver or goods
for safekeeping and they are stolen from the
neighbor’s house, the thief, if he is caught,
must pay back double. 8But if the thief is not
found, the owner of the house must appear
before the judges[b] to determine whether he
has laid his hands on the other man’s property.
9In all cases of illegal possession of an ox, a
donkey, a sheep, a garment, or any other lost
property about which somebody says, ‘This is
mine,’ both parties are to bring their cases before the judges. The one whom the judges
declare[c] guilty must pay back double to his
neighbor.
10“If a man gives a donkey, an ox, a sheep
or any other animal to his neighbor for safekeeping and it dies or is injured or is taken
away while no one is looking, 11the issue between them will be settled by the taking of an
oath before the LORD that the neighbor did not
lay hands on the other person’s property. The
owner is to accept this, and no restitution is
required. 12But if the animal was stolen from
the neighbor, he must make restitution to the
owner. 13If it was torn to pieces by a wild
animal, he shall bring in the remains as evidence and he will not be required to pay for the
torn animal.
14“If a man borrows an animal from his
neighbor and it is injured or dies while the
owner is not present, he must make restitution.
15But if the owner is with the animal, the borrower will not have to pay. If the animal was
hired, the money paid for the hire covers the
loss.

Social Responsibility

16“If a man seduces a virgin who is not
pledged to be married and sleeps with her, he
must pay the bride-price, and she shall be his
wife. 17If her father absolutely refuses to give
her to him, he must still pay the bride-price for
virgins.
18“Do not allow a sorceress to live.
19“Anyone who has sexual relations with an
animal must be put to death.
20“Whoever sacrifices to any god other than
the LORD must be destroyed.[d]
21“Do not mistreat an alien or oppress him,
for you were aliens in Egypt.
22“Do not take advantage of a widow or an
orphan. 23If you do and they cry out to me, I
will certainly hear their cry. 24My anger will
be aroused, and I will kill you with the sword;
your wives will become widows and your children fatherless.
25“If you lend money to one of my people
among you who is needy, do not be like a
moneylender; charge him no interest.[e] 26If you
take your neighbor’s cloak as a pledge, return
it to him by sunset, 27because his cloak is the
only covering he has for his body. What else
will he sleep in? When he cries out to me, I
will hear, for I am compassionate.
28“Do not blaspheme God[f] or curse the ruler of your people.
29“Do not hold back offerings from your
granaries or your vats.[g]
“You must give me the firstborn of your
sons. 30Do the same with your cattle and your
sheep. Let them stay with their mothers for
seven days, but give them to me on the eighth
day.
31“You are to be my holy people. So do not
eat the meat of an animal torn by wild beasts;
throw it to the dogs.

Laws of Justice and Mercy

23 “Do not spread false reports. Do not
help a wicked man by being a malicious
witness.
2“Do not follow the crowd in doing wrong.
When you give testimony in a lawsuit, do not
pervert justice by siding with the crowd, 3and
do not show favoritism to a poor man in his
lawsuit.
4“If you come across your enemy’s ox or
donkey wandering off, be sure to take it back
to him. 5If you see the donkey of someone who
hates you fallen down under its load, do not
leave it there; be sure you help him with it.
6“Do not deny justice to your poor people in
their lawsuits. 7Have nothing to do with a false
charge and do not put an innocent or honest
person to death, for I will not acquit the guilty.
8“Do not accept a bribe, for a bribe blinds
those who see and twists the words of the righteous.

[a] *3* Or *if he strikes him* [b] *8* Or *before God*; also in verse 9 [c] *9* Or *whom God declares* [d] *20* The Hebrew term refers to the irrevocable giving over of things or persons to the LORD, often by totally destroying them.
[e] *25* Or *excessive interest* [f] *28* Or *Do not revile the judges* [g] *29* The meaning of the Hebrew for this phrase is uncertain.

9“Do not oppress an alien; you yourselves know how it feels to be aliens, because you were aliens in Egypt.

Sabbath Laws

10“For six years you are to sow your fields and harvest the crops, 11but during the seventh year let the land lie unplowed and unused. Then the poor among your people may get food from it, and the wild animals may eat what they leave. Do the same with your vineyard and your olive grove.

12“Six days do your work, but on the seventh day do not work, so that your ox and your donkey may rest and the slave born in your household, and the alien as well, may be refreshed.

13“Be careful to do everything I have said to you. Do not invoke the names of other gods; do not let them be heard on your lips.

The Three Annual Festivals

14“Three times a year you are to celebrate a festival to me.

15“Celebrate the Feast of Unleavened Bread; for seven days eat bread made without yeast, as I commanded you. Do this at the appointed time in the month of Abib, for in that month you came out of Egypt.

“No one is to appear before me empty-handed.

16“Celebrate the Feast of Harvest with the firstfruits of the crops you sow in your field.

“Celebrate the Feast of Ingathering at the end of the year, when you gather in your crops from the field.

17“Three times a year all the men are to appear before the Sovereign LORD.

18“Do not offer the blood of a sacrifice to me along with anything containing yeast.

“The fat of my festival offerings must not be kept until morning.

19“Bring the best of the firstfruits of your soil to the house of the LORD your God.

“Do not cook a young goat in its mother’s milk.

God’s Angel to Prepare the Way

20“See, I am sending an angel ahead of you to guard you along the way and to bring you to the place I have prepared. 21Pay attention to him and listen to what he says. Do not rebel against him; he will not forgive your rebellion, since my Name is in him. 22If you listen carefully to what he says and do all that I say, I will be an enemy to your enemies and will oppose those who oppose you. 23My angel will go ahead of you and bring you into the land of the Amorites, Hittites, Perizzites, Canaanites, Hivites and Jebusites, and I will wipe them out. 24Do not bow down before their gods or worship them or follow their practices. You must demolish them and break their sacred stones to pieces. 25Worship the LORD your God, and his blessing will be on your food and water. I will take away sickness from among you, 26and none will miscarry or be barren in your land. I will give you a full life span.

27“I will send my terror ahead of you and throw into confusion every nation you encounter. I will make all your enemies turn their backs and run. 28I will send the hornet ahead of you to drive the Hivites, Canaanites and Hittites out of your way. 29But I will not drive them out in a single year, because the land would become desolate and the wild animals too numerous for you. 30Little by little I will drive them out before you, until you have increased enough to take possession of the land.

31“I will establish your borders from the Red Sea[a] to the Sea of the Philistines,[b] and from the desert to the River.[c] I will hand over to you the people who live in the land and you will drive them out before you. 32Do not make a covenant with them or with their gods. 33Do not let them live in your land, or they will cause you to sin against me, because the worship of their gods will certainly be a snare to you.”

The Covenant Confirmed

24 Then he said to Moses, “Come up to the LORD, you and Aaron, Nadab and Abihu, and seventy of the elders of Israel. You are to worship at a distance, 2but Moses alone is to approach the LORD; the others must not come near. And the people may not come up with him.”

3When Moses went and told the people all the LORD’s words and laws, they responded with one voice, “Everything the LORD has said we will do.” 4Moses then wrote down everything the LORD had said.

He got up early the next morning and built an altar at the foot of the mountain and set up twelve stone pillars representing the twelve tribes of Israel. 5Then he sent young Israelite men, and they offered burnt offerings and sacrificed young bulls as fellowship offerings[d] to the LORD. 6Moses took half of the blood and put it in bowls, and the other half he sprinkled on the altar. 7Then he took the Book of the Covenant and read it to the people. They responded, “We will do everything the LORD has said; we will obey.”

8Moses then took the blood, sprinkled it on the people and said, “This is the blood of the covenant that the LORD has made with you in accordance with all these words.”

9Moses and Aaron, Nadab and Abihu, and the seventy elders of Israel went up 10and saw the God of Israel. Under his feet was something like a pavement made of sapphire,[e] clear as the sky itself. 11But God did not raise his hand against these leaders of the Israelites; they saw God, and they ate and drank.

12The LORD said to Moses, “Come up to me on the mountain and stay here, and I will give

[a] *31* Hebrew *Yam Suph*; that is, Sea of Reeds [b] *31* That is, the Mediterranean [c] *31* That is, the Euphrates
[d] *5* Traditionally *peace offerings* [e] *10* Or *lapis lazuli*

you the tablets of stone, with the law and commands I have written for their instruction."
13Then Moses set out with Joshua his aide,
and Moses went up on the mountain of God.
14He said to the elders, "Wait here for us until
we come back to you. Aaron and Hur are with
you, and anyone involved in a dispute can go
to them."
15When Moses went up on the mountain, the
cloud covered it, 16and the glory of the LORD
settled on Mount Sinai. For six days the cloud
covered the mountain, and on the seventh day
the LORD called to Moses from within the
cloud. 17To the Israelites the glory of the LORD
looked like a consuming fire on top of the
mountain. 18Then Moses entered the cloud as
he went on up the mountain. And he stayed on
the mountain forty days and forty nights.

Offerings for the Tabernacle

25 The LORD said to Moses, 2"Tell the Israelites to bring me an offering. You are
to receive the offering for me from each man
whose heart prompts him to give. 3These are
the offerings you are to receive from them:
gold, silver and bronze; 4blue, purple and scarlet yarn and fine linen; goat hair; 5ram skins
dyed red and hides of sea cows[a]; acacia wood;
6olive oil for the light; spices for the anointing
oil and for the fragrant incense; 7and onyx
stones and other gems to be mounted on the
ephod and breastpiece.
8"Then have them make a sanctuary for me,
and I will dwell among them. 9Make this tabernacle and all its furnishings exactly like the
pattern I will show you.

The Ark

10"Have them make a chest of acacia
wood—two and a half cubits long, a cubit and
a half wide, and a cubit and a half high.[b]
11Overlay it with pure gold, both inside and
out, and make a gold molding around it. 12Cast
four gold rings for it and fasten them to its four
feet, with two rings on one side and two rings
on the other. 13Then make poles of acacia
wood and overlay them with gold. 14Insert the
poles into the rings on the sides of the chest to
carry it. 15The poles are to remain in the rings
of this ark; they are not to be removed. 16Then
put in the ark the Testimony, which I will give
you.
17"Make an atonement cover[c] of pure
gold—two and a half cubits long and a cubit
and a half wide.[d] 18And make two cherubim
out of hammered gold at the ends of the cover.
19Make one cherub on one end and the second
cherub on the other; make the cherubim of one
piece with the cover, at the two ends. 20The
cherubim are to have their wings spread upward, overshadowing the cover with them. The
cherubim are to face each other, looking toward the cover. 21Place the cover on top of the
ark and put in the ark the Testimony, which I
will give you. 22There, above the cover between the two cherubim that are over the ark of
the Testimony, I will meet with you and give
you all my commands for the Israelites.

The Table

23"Make a table of acacia wood—two cubits
long, a cubit wide and a cubit and a half high.[e]
24Overlay it with pure gold and make a gold
molding around it. 25Also make around it a rim
a handbreadth[f] wide and put a gold molding
on the rim. 26Make four gold rings for the table
and fasten them to the four corners, where the
four legs are. 27The rings are to be close to the
rim to hold the poles used in carrying the table.
28Make the poles of acacia wood, overlay them
with gold and carry the table with them. 29And
make its plates and dishes of pure gold, as well
as its pitchers and bowls for the pouring out of
offerings. 30Put the bread of the Presence on
this table to be before me at all times.

The Lampstand

31"Make a lampstand of pure gold and hammer it out, base and shaft; its flowerlike cups,
buds and blossoms shall be of one piece with
it. 32Six branches are to extend from the sides
of the lampstand—three on one side and three
on the other. 33Three cups shaped like almond
flowers with buds and blossoms are to be on
one branch, three on the next branch, and the
same for all six branches extending from the
lampstand. 34And on the lampstand there are to
be four cups shaped like almond flowers with
buds and blossoms. 35One bud shall be under
the first pair of branches extending from the
lampstand, a second bud under the second pair,
and a third bud under the third pair—six
branches in all. 36The buds and branches shall
all be of one piece with the lampstand, hammered out of pure gold.
37"Then make its seven lamps and set them
up on it so that they light the space in front of
it. 38Its wick trimmers and trays are to be of
pure gold. 39A talent[g] of pure gold is to be
used for the lampstand and all these accessories. 40See that you make them according to
the pattern shown you on the mountain.

The Tabernacle

26 "Make the tabernacle with ten curtains
of finely twisted linen and blue, purple
and scarlet yarn, with cherubim worked into
them by a skilled craftsman. 2All the curtains
are to be the same size—twenty-eight cubits
long and four cubits wide.[h] 3Join five of the
curtains together, and do the same with the
other five. 4Make loops of blue material along

[a]5 That is, dugongs [b]10 That is, about 3 3/4 feet (about 1.1 meters) long and 2 1/4 feet (about 0.7 meter) wide and high [c]17 Traditionally *a mercy seat* [d]17 That is, about 3 3/4 feet (about 1.1 meters) long and 2 1/4 feet (about 0.7 meter) wide [e]23 That is, about 3 feet (about 0.9 meter) long and 1 1/2 feet (about 0.5 meter) wide and 2 1/4 feet (about 0.7 meter) high [f]25 That is, about 3 inches (about 8 centimeters) [g]39 That is, about 75 pounds (about 34 kilograms) [h]2 That is, about 42 feet (about 12.5 meters) long and 6 feet (about 1.8 meters) wide

the edge of the end curtain in one set, and do the same with the end curtain in the other set. 5Make fifty loops on one curtain and fifty loops on the end curtain of the other set, with the loops opposite each other. 6Then make fifty gold clasps and use them to fasten the curtains together so that the tabernacle is a unit.

7"Make curtains of goat hair for the tent over the tabernacle—eleven altogether. 8All eleven curtains are to be the same size—thirty cubits long and four cubits wide.[a] 9Join five of the curtains together into one set and the other six into another set. Fold the sixth curtain double at the front of the tent. 10Make fifty loops along the edge of the end curtain in one set and also along the edge of the end curtain in the other set. 11Then make fifty bronze clasps and put them in the loops to fasten the tent together as a unit. 12As for the additional length of the tent curtains, the half curtain that is left over is to hang down at the rear of the tabernacle. 13The tent curtains will be a cubit[b] longer on both sides; what is left will hang over the sides of the tabernacle so as to cover it. 14Make for the tent a covering of ram skins dyed red, and over that a covering of hides of sea cows.[c]

15"Make upright frames of acacia wood for the tabernacle. 16Each frame is to be ten cubits long and a cubit and a half wide,[d] 17with two projections set parallel to each other. Make all the frames of the tabernacle in this way. 18Make twenty frames for the south side of the tabernacle 19and make forty silver bases to go under them—two bases for each frame, one under each projection. 20For the other side, the north side of the tabernacle, make twenty frames 21and forty silver bases—two under each frame. 22Make six frames for the far end, that is, the west end of the tabernacle, 23and make two frames for the corners at the far end. 24At these two corners they must be double from the bottom all the way to the top, and fitted into a single ring; both shall be like that. 25So there will be eight frames and sixteen silver bases—two under each frame.

26"Also make crossbars of acacia wood: five for the frames on one side of the tabernacle, 27five for those on the other side, and five for the frames on the west, at the far end of the tabernacle. 28The center crossbar is to extend from end to end at the middle of the frames. 29Overlay the frames with gold and make gold rings to hold the crossbars. Also overlay the crossbars with gold.

30"Set up the tabernacle according to the plan shown you on the mountain.

31"Make a curtain of blue, purple and scarlet yarn and finely twisted linen, with cherubim worked into it by a skilled craftsman. 32Hang it with gold hooks on four posts of acacia wood overlaid with gold and standing on four silver bases. 33Hang the curtain from the clasps and place the ark of the Testimony behind the curtain. The curtain will separate the Holy Place from the Most Holy Place. 34Put the atonement cover on the ark of the Testimony in the Most Holy Place. 35Place the table outside the curtain on the north side of the tabernacle and put the lampstand opposite it on the south side.

36"For the entrance to the tent make a curtain of blue, purple and scarlet yarn and finely twisted linen—the work of an embroiderer. 37Make gold hooks for this curtain and five posts of acacia wood overlaid with gold. And cast five bronze bases for them.

The Altar of Burnt Offering

27 "Build an altar of acacia wood, three cubits[e] high; it is to be square, five cubits long and five cubits wide.[f] 2Make a horn at each of the four corners, so that the horns and the altar are of one piece, and overlay the altar with bronze. 3Make all its utensils of bronze—its pots to remove the ashes, and its shovels, sprinkling bowls, meat forks and firepans. 4Make a grating for it, a bronze network, and make a bronze ring at each of the four corners of the network. 5Put it under the ledge of the altar so that it is halfway up the altar. 6Make poles of acacia wood for the altar and overlay them with bronze. 7The poles are to be inserted into the rings so they will be on two sides of the altar when it is carried. 8Make the altar hollow, out of boards. It is to be made just as you were shown on the mountain.

The Courtyard

9"Make a courtyard for the tabernacle. The south side shall be a hundred cubits[g] long and is to have curtains of finely twisted linen, 10with twenty posts and twenty bronze bases and with silver hooks and bands on the posts. 11The north side shall also be a hundred cubits long and is to have curtains, with twenty posts and twenty bronze bases and with silver hooks and bands on the posts.

12"The west end of the courtyard shall be fifty cubits[h] wide and have curtains, with ten posts and ten bases. 13On the east end, toward the sunrise, the courtyard shall also be fifty cubits wide. 14Curtains fifteen cubits[i] long are to be on one side of the entrance, with three posts and three bases, 15and curtains fifteen cubits long are to be on the other side, with three posts and three bases.

16"For the entrance to the courtyard, provide a curtain twenty cubits[j] long, of blue, purple and scarlet yarn and finely twisted linen—the work of an embroiderer—with four posts and four bases. 17All the posts around the courtyard are to have silver bands and hooks, and

[a] *8* That is, about 45 feet (about 13.5 meters) long and 6 feet (about 1.8 meters) wide [b] *13* That is, about 1 1/2 feet (about 0.5 meter) [c] *14* That is, dugongs [d] *16* That is, about 15 feet (about 4.5 meters) long and 2 1/4 feet (about 0.7 meter) wide [e] *1* That is, about 4 1/2 feet (about 1.3 meters) [f] *1* That is, about 7 1/2 feet (about 2.3 meters) long and wide [g] *9* That is, about 150 feet (about 46 meters); also in verse 11 [h] *12* That is, about 75 feet (about 23 meters); also in verse 13 [i] *14* That is, about 22 1/2 feet (about 6.9 meters); also in verse 15 [j] *16* That is, about 30 feet (about 9 meters)

bronze bases. 18The courtyard shall be a hundred cubits long and fifty cubits wide,[a] with
curtains of finely twisted linen five cubits[b]
high, and with bronze bases. 19All the other
articles used in the service of the tabernacle,
whatever their function, including all the tent
pegs for it and those for the courtyard, are to be
of bronze.

Oil for the Lampstand

20"Command the Israelites to bring you
clear oil of pressed olives for the light so that
the lamps may be kept burning. 21In the Tent
of Meeting, outside the curtain that is in front
of the Testimony, Aaron and his sons are to
keep the lamps burning before the LORD from
evening till morning. This is to be a lasting
ordinance among the Israelites for the generations to come.

The Priestly Garments

28 "Have Aaron your brother brought to
you from among the Israelites, along
with his sons Nadab and Abihu, Eleazar and
Ithamar, so they may serve me as priests.
2Make sacred garments for your brother Aaron, to give him dignity and honor. 3Tell all the
skilled men to whom I have given wisdom in
such matters that they are to make garments
for Aaron, for his consecration, so he may
serve me as priest. 4These are the garments
they are to make: a breastpiece, an ephod, a
robe, a woven tunic, a turban and a sash. They
are to make these sacred garments for your
brother Aaron and his sons, so they may serve
me as priests. 5Have them use gold, and blue,
purple and scarlet yarn, and fine linen.

The Ephod

6"Make the ephod of gold, and of blue, purple and scarlet yarn, and of finely twisted lin-
en—the work of a skilled craftsman. 7It is to
have two shoulder pieces attached to two of its
corners, so it can be fastened. 8Its skillfully
woven waistband is to be like it—of one piece
with the ephod and made with gold, and with
blue, purple and scarlet yarn, and with finely
twisted linen.
9"Take two onyx stones and engrave on
them the names of the sons of Israel 10in the
order of their birth—six names on one stone
and the remaining six on the other. 11Engrave
the names of the sons of Israel on the two
stones the way a gem cutter engraves a seal.
Then mount the stones in gold filigree settings
12and fasten them on the shoulder pieces of the
ephod as memorial stones for the sons of Israel. Aaron is to bear the names on his shoulders
as a memorial before the LORD. 13Make gold
filigree settings 14and two braided chains of
pure gold, like a rope, and attach the chains to
the settings.

The Breastpiece

15"Fashion a breastpiece for making decisions—the work of a skilled craftsman. Make
it like the ephod: of gold, and of blue, purple
and scarlet yarn, and of finely twisted linen.
16It is to be square—a span[c] long and a span
wide—and folded double. 17Then mount four
rows of precious stones on it. In the first row
there shall be a ruby, a topaz and a beryl; 18in
the second row a turquoise, a sapphire[d] and an
emerald; 19in the third row a jacinth, an agate
and an amethyst; 20in the fourth row a chrysolite, an onyx and a jasper.[e] Mount them in
gold filigree settings. 21There are to be twelve
stones, one for each of the names of the sons
of Israel, each engraved like a seal with the
name of one of the twelve tribes.
22"For the breastpiece make braided chains
of pure gold, like a rope. 23Make two gold
rings for it and fasten them to two corners of
the breastpiece. 24Fasten the two gold chains to
the rings at the corners of the breastpiece,
25and the other ends of the chains to the two
settings, attaching them to the shoulder pieces
of the ephod at the front. 26Make two gold
rings and attach them to the other two corners
of the breastpiece on the inside edge next to
the ephod. 27Make two more gold rings and
attach them to the bottom of the shoulder
pieces on the front of the ephod, close to the
seam just above the waistband of the ephod.
28The rings of the breastpiece are to be tied to
the rings of the ephod with blue cord, connecting it to the waistband, so that the breastpiece
will not swing out from the ephod.
29"Whenever Aaron enters the Holy Place,
he will bear the names of the sons of Israel
over his heart on the breastpiece of decision
as a continuing memorial before the LORD.
30Also put the Urim and the Thummim in the
breastpiece, so they may be over Aaron's heart
whenever he enters the presence of the LORD.
Thus Aaron will always bear the means of
making decisions for the Israelites over his
heart before the LORD.

Other Priestly Garments

31"Make the robe of the ephod entirely of
blue cloth, 32with an opening for the head in its
center. There shall be a woven edge like a
collar[f] around this opening, so that it will not
tear. 33Make pomegranates of blue, purple and
scarlet yarn around the hem of the robe, with
gold bells between them. 34The gold bells and
the pomegranates are to alternate around the
hem of the robe. 35Aaron must wear it when he
ministers. The sound of the bells will be heard
when he enters the Holy Place before the LORD
and when he comes out, so that he will not die.
36"Make a plate of pure gold and engrave on
it as on a seal: HOLY TO THE LORD. 37Fasten a
blue cord to it to attach it to the turban; it is to

[a] *18* That is, about 150 feet (about 46 meters) long and 75 feet (about 23 meters) wide [b] *18* That is, about 7 1/2 feet (about 2.3 meters) [c] *16* That is, about 9 inches (about 22 centimeters) [d] *18* Or *lapis lazuli* [e] *20* The precise identification of some of these precious stones is uncertain. [f] *32* The meaning of the Hebrew for this word is uncertain.

be on the front of the turban. 38It will be on Aaron's forehead, and he will bear the guilt involved in the sacred gifts the Israelites consecrate, whatever their gifts may be. It will be on Aaron's forehead continually so that they will be acceptable to the LORD.

39"Weave the tunic of fine linen and make the turban of fine linen. The sash is to be the work of an embroiderer. 40Make tunics, sashes and headbands for Aaron's sons, to give them dignity and honor. 41After you put these clothes on your brother Aaron and his sons, anoint and ordain them. Consecrate them so they may serve me as priests.

42"Make linen undergarments as a covering for the body, reaching from the waist to the thigh. 43Aaron and his sons must wear them whenever they enter the Tent of Meeting or approach the altar to minister in the Holy Place, so that they will not incur guilt and die.

"This is to be a lasting ordinance for Aaron and his descendants.

Consecration of the Priests

29 "This is what you are to do to consecrate them, so they may serve me as priests: Take a young bull and two rams without defect. 2And from fine wheat flour, without yeast, make bread, and cakes mixed with oil, and wafers spread with oil. 3Put them in a basket and present them in it—along with the bull and the two rams. 4Then bring Aaron and his sons to the entrance to the Tent of Meeting and wash them with water. 5Take the garments and dress Aaron with the tunic, the robe of the ephod, the ephod itself and the breastpiece. Fasten the ephod on him by its skillfully woven waistband. 6Put the turban on his head and attach the sacred diadem to the turban. 7Take the anointing oil and anoint him by pouring it on his head. 8Bring his sons and dress them in tunics 9and put headbands on them. Then tie sashes on Aaron and his sons.[a] The priesthood is theirs by a lasting ordinance. In this way you shall ordain Aaron and his sons.

10"Bring the bull to the front of the Tent of Meeting, and Aaron and his sons shall lay their hands on its head. 11Slaughter it in the LORD's presence at the entrance to the Tent of Meeting. 12Take some of the bull's blood and put it on the horns of the altar with your finger, and pour out the rest of it at the base of the altar. 13Then take all the fat around the inner parts, the covering of the liver, and both kidneys with the fat on them, and burn them on the altar. 14But burn the bull's flesh and its hide and its offal outside the camp. It is a sin offering.

15"Take one of the rams, and Aaron and his sons shall lay their hands on its head. 16Slaughter it and take the blood and sprinkle it against the altar on all sides. 17Cut the ram into pieces and wash the inner parts and the legs, putting them with the head and the other pieces. 18Then burn the entire ram on the altar. It is a burnt offering to the LORD, a pleasing aroma, an offering made to the LORD by fire.

19"Take the other ram, and Aaron and his sons shall lay their hands on its head. 20Slaughter it, take some of its blood and put it on the lobes of the right ears of Aaron and his sons, on the thumbs of their right hands, and on the big toes of their right feet. Then sprinkle blood against the altar on all sides. 21And take some of the blood on the altar and some of the anointing oil and sprinkle it on Aaron and his garments and on his sons and their garments. Then he and his sons and their garments will be consecrated.

22"Take from this ram the fat, the fat tail, the fat around the inner parts, the covering of the liver, both kidneys with the fat on them, and the right thigh. (This is the ram for the ordination.) 23From the basket of bread made without yeast, which is before the LORD, take a loaf, and a cake made with oil, and a wafer. 24Put all these in the hands of Aaron and his sons and wave them before the LORD as a wave offering. 25Then take them from their hands and burn them on the altar along with the burnt offering for a pleasing aroma to the LORD, an offering made to the LORD by fire. 26After you take the breast of the ram for Aaron's ordination, wave it before the LORD as a wave offering, and it will be your share.

27"Consecrate those parts of the ordination ram that belong to Aaron and his sons: the breast that was waved and the thigh that was presented. 28This is always to be the regular share from the Israelites for Aaron and his sons. It is the contribution the Israelites are to make to the LORD from their fellowship offerings.[b]

29"Aaron's sacred garments will belong to his descendants so that they can be anointed and ordained in them. 30The son who succeeds him as priest and comes to the Tent of Meeting to minister in the Holy Place is to wear them seven days.

31"Take the ram for the ordination and cook the meat in a sacred place. 32At the entrance to the Tent of Meeting, Aaron and his sons are to eat the meat of the ram and the bread that is in the basket. 33They are to eat these offerings by which atonement was made for their ordination and consecration. But no one else may eat them, because they are sacred. 34And if any of the meat of the ordination ram or any bread is left over till morning, burn it up. It must not be eaten, because it is sacred.

35"Do for Aaron and his sons everything I have commanded you, taking seven days to ordain them. 36Sacrifice a bull each day as a sin offering to make atonement. Purify the altar by making atonement for it, and anoint it to consecrate it. 37For seven days make atonement for the altar and consecrate it. Then the altar will be most holy, and whatever touches it will be holy.

38"This is what you are to offer on the altar regularly each day: two lambs a year old. 39Of-

[a]9 Hebrew; Septuagint *on them* [b]28 Traditionally *peace offerings*

fer one in the morning and the other at twilight. 40 With the first lamb offer a tenth of an ephah[a] of fine flour mixed with a quarter of a hin[b] of oil from pressed olives, and a quarter of a hin of wine as a drink offering. 41 Sacrifice the other lamb at twilight with the same grain offering and its drink offering as in the morning—a pleasing aroma, an offering made to the LORD by fire.

42 "For the generations to come this burnt offering is to be made regularly at the entrance to the Tent of Meeting before the LORD. There I will meet you and speak to you; 43 there also I will meet with the Israelites, and the place will be consecrated by my glory.

44 "So I will consecrate the Tent of Meeting and the altar and will consecrate Aaron and his sons to serve me as priests. 45 Then I will dwell among the Israelites and be their God. 46 They will know that I am the LORD their God, who brought them out of Egypt so that I might dwell among them. I am the LORD their God.

The Altar of Incense

30 "Make an altar of acacia wood for burning incense. 2 It is to be square, a cubit long and a cubit wide, and two cubits high[c]—its horns of one piece with it. 3 Overlay the top and all the sides and the horns with pure gold, and make a gold molding around it. 4 Make two gold rings for the altar below the molding—two on opposite sides—to hold the poles used to carry it. 5 Make the poles of acacia wood and overlay them with gold. 6 Put the altar in front of the curtain that is before the ark of the Testimony—before the atonement cover that is over the Testimony—where I will meet with you.

7 "Aaron must burn fragrant incense on the altar every morning when he tends the lamps. 8 He must burn incense again when he lights the lamps at twilight so incense will burn regularly before the LORD for the generations to come. 9 Do not offer on this altar any other incense or any burnt offering or grain offering, and do not pour a drink offering on it. 10 Once a year Aaron shall make atonement on its horns. This annual atonement must be made with the blood of the atoning sin offering for the generations to come. It is most holy to the LORD."

Atonement Money

11 Then the LORD said to Moses, 12 "When you take a census of the Israelites to count them, each one must pay the LORD a ransom for his life at the time he is counted. Then no plague will come on them when you number them. 13 Each one who crosses over to those already counted is to give a half shekel,[d] according to the sanctuary shekel, which weighs twenty gerahs. This half shekel is an offering to the LORD. 14 All who cross over, those twenty years old or more, are to give an offering to the LORD. 15 The rich are not to give more than a half shekel and the poor are not to give less when you make the offering to the LORD to atone for your lives. 16 Receive the atonement money from the Israelites and use it for the service of the Tent of Meeting. It will be a memorial for the Israelites before the LORD, making atonement for your lives."

Basin for Washing

17 Then the LORD said to Moses, 18 "Make a bronze basin, with its bronze stand, for washing. Place it between the Tent of Meeting and the altar, and put water in it. 19 Aaron and his sons are to wash their hands and feet with water from it. 20 Whenever they enter the Tent of Meeting, they shall wash with water so that they will not die. Also, when they approach the altar to minister by presenting an offering made to the LORD by fire, 21 they shall wash their hands and feet so that they will not die. This is to be a lasting ordinance for Aaron and his descendants for the generations to come."

Anointing Oil

22 Then the LORD said to Moses, 23 "Take the following fine spices: 500 shekels[e] of liquid myrrh, half as much (that is, 250 shekels) of fragrant cinnamon, 250 shekels of fragrant cane, 24 500 shekels of cassia—all according to the sanctuary shekel—and a hin[f] of olive oil. 25 Make these into a sacred anointing oil, a fragrant blend, the work of a perfumer. It will be the sacred anointing oil. 26 Then use it to anoint the Tent of Meeting, the ark of the Testimony, 27 the table and all its articles, the lampstand and its accessories, the altar of incense, 28 the altar of burnt offering and all its utensils, and the basin with its stand. 29 You shall consecrate them so they will be most holy, and whatever touches them will be holy.

30 "Anoint Aaron and his sons and consecrate them so they may serve me as priests. 31 Say to the Israelites, 'This is to be my sacred anointing oil for the generations to come. 32 Do not pour it on men's bodies and do not make any oil with the same formula. It is sacred, and you are to consider it sacred. 33 Whoever makes perfume like it and whoever puts it on anyone other than a priest must be cut off from his people.' "

Incense

34 Then the LORD said to Moses, "Take fragrant spices—gum resin, onycha and galbanum—and pure frankincense, all in equal amounts, 35 and make a fragrant blend of incense, the work of a perfumer. It is to be salted and pure and sacred. 36 Grind some of it to powder and place it in front of the Testimony in the Tent of Meeting, where I will meet with you. It shall be most holy to you. 37 Do not

a40 That is, probably about 2 quarts (about 2 liters) *b40* That is, probably about 1 quart (about 1 liter)
c2 That is, about 1 1/2 feet (about 0.5 meter) long and wide and about 3 feet (about 0.9 meter) high
d13 That is, about 1/5 ounce (about 6 grams); also in verse 15 *e23* That is, about 12 1/2 pounds (about 6 kilograms) *f24* That is, probably about 4 quarts (about 4 liters)

make any incense with this formula for yourselves; consider it holy to the LORD. 38 Whoever makes any like it to enjoy its fragrance must be cut off from his people."

Bezalel and Oholiab

31 Then the LORD said to Moses, 2 "See, I have chosen Bezalel son of Uri, the son of Hur, of the tribe of Judah, 3 and I have filled him with the Spirit of God, with skill, ability and knowledge in all kinds of crafts— 4 to make artistic designs for work in gold, silver and bronze, 5 to cut and set stones, to work in wood, and to engage in all kinds of craftsmanship. 6 Moreover, I have appointed Oholiab son of Ahisamach, of the tribe of Dan, to help him. Also I have given skill to all the craftsmen to make everything I have commanded you: 7 the Tent of Meeting, the ark of the Testimony with the atonement cover on it, and all the other furnishings of the tent— 8 the table and its articles, the pure gold lampstand and all its accessories, the altar of incense, 9 the altar of burnt offering and all its utensils, the basin with its stand— 10 and also the woven garments, both the sacred garments for Aaron the priest and the garments for his sons when they serve as priests, 11 and the anointing oil and fragrant incense for the Holy Place. They are to make them just as I commanded you."

The Sabbath

12 Then the LORD said to Moses, 13 "Say to the Israelites, 'You must observe my Sabbaths. This will be a sign between me and you for the generations to come, so you may know that I am the LORD, who makes you holy.[a]

14 " 'Observe the Sabbath, because it is holy to you. Anyone who desecrates it must be put to death; whoever does any work on that day must be cut off from his people. 15 For six days, work is to be done, but the seventh day is a Sabbath of rest, holy to the LORD. Whoever does any work on the Sabbath day must be put to death. 16 The Israelites are to observe the Sabbath, celebrating it for the generations to come as a lasting covenant. 17 It will be a sign between me and the Israelites forever, for in six days the LORD made the heavens and the earth, and on the seventh day he abstained from work and rested.' "

18 When the LORD finished speaking to Moses on Mount Sinai, he gave him the two tablets of the Testimony, the tablets of stone inscribed by the finger of God.

The Golden Calf

32 When the people saw that Moses was so long in coming down from the mountain, they gathered around Aaron and said, "Come, make us gods[b] who will go before us. As for this fellow Moses who brought us up out of Egypt, we don't know what has happened to him."

2 Aaron answered them, "Take off the gold earrings that your wives, your sons and your daughters are wearing, and bring them to me." 3 So all the people took off their earrings and brought them to Aaron. 4 He took what they handed him and made it into an idol cast in the shape of a calf, fashioning it with a tool. Then they said, "These are your gods,[c] O Israel, who brought you up out of Egypt."

5 When Aaron saw this, he built an altar in front of the calf and announced, "Tomorrow there will be a festival to the LORD." 6 So the next day the people rose early and sacrificed burnt offerings and presented fellowship offerings.[d] Afterward they sat down to eat and drink and got up to indulge in revelry.

7 Then the LORD said to Moses, "Go down, because your people, whom you brought up out of Egypt, have become corrupt. 8 They have been quick to turn away from what I commanded them and have made themselves an idol cast in the shape of a calf. They have bowed down to it and sacrificed to it and have said, 'These are your gods, O Israel, who brought you up out of Egypt.'

9 "I have seen these people," the LORD said to Moses, "and they are a stiff-necked people. 10 Now leave me alone so that my anger may burn against them and that I may destroy them. Then I will make you into a great nation."

11 But Moses sought the favor of the LORD his God. "O LORD," he said, "why should your anger burn against your people, whom you brought out of Egypt with great power and a mighty hand? 12 Why should the Egyptians say, 'It was with evil intent that he brought them out, to kill them in the mountains and to wipe them off the face of the earth'? Turn from your fierce anger; relent and do not bring disaster on your people. 13 Remember your servants Abraham, Isaac and Israel, to whom you swore by your own self: 'I will make your descendants as numerous as the stars in the sky and I will give your descendants all this land I promised them, and it will be their inheritance forever.' " 14 Then the LORD relented and did not bring on his people the disaster he had threatened.

15 Moses turned and went down the mountain with the two tablets of the Testimony in his hands. They were inscribed on both sides, front and back. 16 The tablets were the work of God; the writing was the writing of God, engraved on the tablets.

17 When Joshua heard the noise of the people shouting, he said to Moses, "There is the sound of war in the camp."

18 Moses replied:

"It is not the sound of victory,
 it is not the sound of defeat;
 it is the sound of singing that I hear."

19 When Moses approached the camp and saw the calf and the dancing, his anger burned and he threw the tablets out of his hands, breaking them to pieces at the foot of the

[a] 13 Or *who sanctifies you*; or *who sets you apart as holy* [b] 1 Or *a god*; also in verses 23 and 31
[c] 4 Or *This is your god*; also in verse 8 [d] 6 Traditionally *peace offerings*

mountain. 20And he took the calf they had made and burned it in the fire; then he ground it to powder, scattered it on the water and made the Israelites drink it.

21He said to Aaron, "What did these people do to you, that you led them into such great sin?"

22"Do not be angry, my lord," Aaron answered. "You know how prone these people are to evil. 23They said to me, 'Make us gods who will go before us. As for this fellow Moses who brought us up out of Egypt, we don't know what has happened to him.' 24So I told them, 'Whoever has any gold jewelry, take it off.' Then they gave me the gold, and I threw it into the fire, and out came this calf!"

25Moses saw that the people were running wild and that Aaron had let them get out of control and so become a laughingstock to their enemies. 26So he stood at the entrance to the camp and said, "Whoever is for the LORD, come to me." And all the Levites rallied to him.

27Then he said to them, "This is what the LORD, the God of Israel, says: 'Each man strap a sword to his side. Go back and forth through the camp from one end to the other, each killing his brother and friend and neighbor.' " 28The Levites did as Moses commanded, and that day about three thousand of the people died. 29Then Moses said, "You have been set apart to the LORD today, for you were against your own sons and brothers, and he has blessed you this day."

30The next day Moses said to the people, "You have committed a great sin. But now I will go up to the LORD; perhaps I can make atonement for your sin."

31So Moses went back to the LORD and said, "Oh, what a great sin these people have committed! They have made themselves gods of gold. 32But now, please forgive their sin—but if not, then blot me out of the book you have written."

33The LORD replied to Moses, "Whoever has sinned against me I will blot out of my book. 34Now go, lead the people to the place I spoke of, and my angel will go before you. However, when the time comes for me to punish, I will punish them for their sin."

35And the LORD struck the people with a plague because of what they did with the calf Aaron had made.

33 Then the LORD said to Moses, "Leave this place, you and the people you brought up out of Egypt, and go up to the land I promised on oath to Abraham, Isaac and Jacob, saying, 'I will give it to your descendants.' 2I will send an angel before you and drive out the Canaanites, Amorites, Hittites, Perizzites, Hivites and Jebusites. 3Go up to the land flowing with milk and honey. But I will not go with you, because you are a stiff-necked people and I might destroy you on the way."

4When the people heard these distressing words, they began to mourn and no one put on any ornaments. 5For the LORD had said to Moses, "Tell the Israelites, 'You are a stiff-necked people. If I were to go with you even for a moment, I might destroy you. Now take off your ornaments and I will decide what to do with you.' " 6So the Israelites stripped off their ornaments at Mount Horeb.

The Tent of Meeting

7Now Moses used to take a tent and pitch it outside the camp some distance away, calling it the "tent of meeting." Anyone inquiring of the LORD would go to the tent of meeting outside the camp. 8And whenever Moses went out to the tent, all the people rose and stood at the entrances to their tents, watching Moses until he entered the tent. 9As Moses went into the tent, the pillar of cloud would come down and stay at the entrance, while the LORD spoke with Moses. 10Whenever the people saw the pillar of cloud standing at the entrance to the tent, they all stood and worshiped, each at the entrance to his tent. 11The LORD would speak to Moses face to face, as a man speaks with his friend. Then Moses would return to the camp, but his young aide Joshua son of Nun did not leave the tent.

Moses and the Glory of the LORD

12Moses said to the LORD, "You have been telling me, 'Lead these people,' but you have not let me know whom you will send with me. You have said, 'I know you by name and you have found favor with me.' 13If you are pleased with me, teach me your ways so I may know you and continue to find favor with you. Remember that this nation is your people."

14The LORD replied, "My Presence will go with you, and I will give you rest."

15Then Moses said to him, "If your Presence does not go with us, do not send us up from here. 16How will anyone know that you are pleased with me and with your people unless you go with us? What else will distinguish me and your people from all the other people on the face of the earth?"

17And the LORD said to Moses, "I will do the very thing you have asked, because I am pleased with you and I know you by name."

18Then Moses said, "Now show me your glory."

19And the LORD said, "I will cause all my goodness to pass in front of you, and I will proclaim my name, the LORD, in your presence. I will have mercy on whom I will have mercy, and I will have compassion on whom I will have compassion. 20But," he said, "you cannot see my face, for no one may see me and live."

21Then the LORD said, "There is a place near me where you may stand on a rock. 22When my glory passes by, I will put you in a cleft in the rock and cover you with my hand until I have passed by. 23Then I will remove my hand and you will see my back; but my face must not be seen."

The New Stone Tablets

34 The LORD said to Moses, "Chisel out
two stone tablets like the first ones, and
I will write on them the words that were on the
first tablets, which you broke. 2Be ready in the
morning, and then come up on Mount Sinai.
Present yourself to me there on top of the
mountain. 3No one is to come with you or be
seen anywhere on the mountain; not even the
flocks and herds may graze in front of the
mountain."
4So Moses chiseled out two stone tablets
like the first ones and went up Mount Sinai
early in the morning, as the LORD had commanded him; and he carried the two stone tablets in his hands. 5Then the LORD came down
in the cloud and stood there with him and proclaimed his name, the LORD. 6And he passed
in front of Moses, proclaiming, "The LORD,
the LORD, the compassionate and gracious
God, slow to anger, abounding in love and
faithfulness, 7maintaining love to thousands,
and forgiving wickedness, rebellion and sin.
Yet he does not leave the guilty unpunished;
he punishes the children and their children for
the sin of the fathers to the third and fourth
generation."
8Moses bowed to the ground at once and
worshiped. 9"O Lord, if I have found favor in
your eyes," he said, "then let the Lord go with
us. Although this is a stiff-necked people, forgive our wickedness and our sin, and take us as
your inheritance."
10Then the LORD said: "I am making a covenant with you. Before all your people I will
do wonders never before done in any nation in
all the world. The people you live among will
see how awesome is the work that I, the LORD,
will do for you. 11Obey what I command you
today. I will drive out before you the Amorites,
Canaanites, Hittites, Perizzites, Hivites and
Jebusites. 12Be careful not to make a treaty
with those who live in the land where you are
going, or they will be a snare among you.
13Break down their altars, smash their sacred
stones and cut down their Asherah poles.[a]
14Do not worship any other god, for the LORD,
whose name is Jealous, is a jealous God.
15"Be careful not to make a treaty with those
who live in the land; for when they prostitute
themselves to their gods and sacrifice to them,
they will invite you and you will eat their sacrifices. 16And when you choose some of their
daughters as wives for your sons and those
daughters prostitute themselves to their gods,
they will lead your sons to do the same.
17"Do not make cast idols.
18"Celebrate the Feast of Unleavened Bread.
For seven days eat bread made without yeast,
as I commanded you. Do this at the appointed
time in the month of Abib, for in that month
you came out of Egypt.
19"The first offspring of every womb belongs to me, including all the firstborn males
of your livestock, whether from herd or flock.
20Redeem the firstborn donkey with a lamb,
but if you do not redeem it, break its neck.
Redeem all your firstborn sons.
"No one is to appear before me empty-
handed.
21"Six days you shall labor, but on the seventh day you shall rest; even during the plowing season and harvest you must rest.
22"Celebrate the Feast of Weeks with the
firstfruits of the wheat harvest, and the Feast of
Ingathering at the turn of the year.[b] 23Three
times a year all your men are to appear before
the Sovereign LORD, the God of Israel. 24I will
drive out nations before you and enlarge your
territory, and no one will covet your land when
you go up three times each year to appear before the LORD your God.
25"Do not offer the blood of a sacrifice to
me along with anything containing yeast, and
do not let any of the sacrifice from the Passover Feast remain until morning.
26"Bring the best of the firstfruits of your
soil to the house of the LORD your God.
"Do not cook a young goat in its mother's
milk."
27Then the LORD said to Moses, "Write
down these words, for in accordance with
these words I have made a covenant with you
and with Israel." 28Moses was there with the
LORD forty days and forty nights without eating bread or drinking water. And he wrote on
the tablets the words of the covenant—the Ten
Commandments.

The Radiant Face of Moses

29When Moses came down from Mount Sinai with the two tablets of the Testimony in his
hands, he was not aware that his face was radiant because he had spoken with the LORD.
30When Aaron and all the Israelites saw Moses, his face was radiant, and they were afraid
to come near him. 31But Moses called to them;
so Aaron and all the leaders of the community
came back to him, and he spoke to them. 32Af-
terward all the Israelites came near him, and he
gave them all the commands the LORD had
given him on Mount Sinai.
33When Moses finished speaking to them,
he put a veil over his face. 34But whenever he
entered the LORD's presence to speak with
him, he removed the veil until he came out.
And when he came out and told the Israelites
what he had been commanded, 35they saw that
his face was radiant. Then Moses would put
the veil back over his face until he went in to
speak with the LORD.

Sabbath Regulations

35 Moses assembled the whole Israelite
community and said to them, "These are
the things the LORD has commanded you to do:
2For six days, work is to be done, but the seventh day shall be your holy day, a Sabbath of
rest to the LORD. Whoever does any work on

[a]13 That is, symbols of the goddess Asherah [b]22 That is, in the fall

it must be put to death. 3Do not light a fire in any of your dwellings on the Sabbath day."

Materials for the Tabernacle

4Moses said to the whole Israelite community, "This is what the LORD has commanded: 5From what you have, take an offering for the LORD. Everyone who is willing is to bring to the LORD an offering of gold, silver and bronze; 6blue, purple and scarlet yarn and fine linen; goat hair; 7ram skins dyed red and hides of sea cows[a]; acacia wood; 8olive oil for the light; spices for the anointing oil and for the fragrant incense; 9and onyx stones and other gems to be mounted on the ephod and breastpiece.

10"All who are skilled among you are to come and make everything the LORD has commanded: 11the tabernacle with its tent and its covering, clasps, frames, crossbars, posts and bases; 12the ark with its poles and the atonement cover and the curtain that shields it; 13the table with its poles and all its articles and the bread of the Presence; 14the lampstand that is for light with its accessories, lamps and oil for the light; 15the altar of incense with its poles, the anointing oil and the fragrant incense; the curtain for the doorway at the entrance to the tabernacle; 16the altar of burnt offering with its bronze grating, its poles and all its utensils; the bronze basin with its stand; 17the curtains of the courtyard with its posts and bases, and the curtain for the entrance to the courtyard; 18the tent pegs for the tabernacle and for the courtyard, and their ropes; 19the woven garments worn for ministering in the sanctuary—both the sacred garments for Aaron the priest and the garments for his sons when they serve as priests."

20Then the whole Israelite community withdrew from Moses' presence, 21and everyone who was willing and whose heart moved him came and brought an offering to the LORD for the work on the Tent of Meeting, for all its service, and for the sacred garments. 22All who were willing, men and women alike, came and brought gold jewelry of all kinds: brooches, earrings, rings and ornaments. They all presented their gold as a wave offering to the LORD. 23Everyone who had blue, purple or scarlet yarn or fine linen, or goat hair, ram skins dyed red or hides of sea cows brought them. 24Those presenting an offering of silver or bronze brought it as an offering to the LORD, and everyone who had acacia wood for any part of the work brought it. 25Every skilled woman spun with her hands and brought what she had spun—blue, purple or scarlet yarn or fine linen. 26And all the women who were willing and had the skill spun the goat hair. 27The leaders brought onyx stones and other gems to be mounted on the ephod and breastpiece. 28They also brought spices and olive oil for the light and for the anointing oil and for the fragrant incense. 29All the Israelite men and women who were willing brought to the LORD freewill offerings for all the work the LORD through Moses had commanded them to do.

Bezalel and Oholiab

30Then Moses said to the Israelites, "See, the LORD has chosen Bezalel son of Uri, the son of Hur, of the tribe of Judah, 31and he has filled him with the Spirit of God, with skill, ability and knowledge in all kinds of crafts—32to make artistic designs for work in gold, silver and bronze, 33to cut and set stones, to work in wood and to engage in all kinds of artistic craftsmanship. 34And he has given both him and Oholiab son of Ahisamach, of the tribe of Dan, the ability to teach others. 35He has filled them with skill to do all kinds of work as craftsmen, designers, embroiderers in blue, purple and scarlet yarn and fine linen, and weavers—all of them master craftsmen

36 and designers. 1So Bezalel, Oholiab and every skilled person to whom the LORD has given skill and ability to know how to carry out all the work of constructing the sanctuary are to do the work just as the LORD has commanded."

2Then Moses summoned Bezalel and Oholiab and every skilled person to whom the LORD had given ability and who was willing to come and do the work. 3They received from Moses all the offerings the Israelites had brought to carry out the work of constructing the sanctuary. And the people continued to bring freewill offerings morning after morning. 4So all the skilled craftsmen who were doing all the work on the sanctuary left their work 5and said to Moses, "The people are bringing more than enough for doing the work the LORD commanded to be done."

6Then Moses gave an order and they sent this word throughout the camp: "No man or woman is to make anything else as an offering for the sanctuary." And so the people were restrained from bringing more, 7because what they already had was more than enough to do all the work.

The Tabernacle

8All the skilled men among the workmen made the tabernacle with ten curtains of finely twisted linen and blue, purple and scarlet yarn, with cherubim worked into them by a skilled craftsman. 9All the curtains were the same size—twenty-eight cubits long and four cubits wide.[b] 10They joined five of the curtains together and did the same with the other five. 11Then they made loops of blue material along the edge of the end curtain in one set, and the same was done with the end curtain in the other set. 12They also made fifty loops on one curtain and fifty loops on the end curtain of the other set, with the loops opposite each other. 13Then they made fifty gold clasps and used

[a]7 That is, dugongs; also in verse 23 [b]9 That is, about 42 feet (about 12.5 meters) long and 6 feet (about 1.8 meters) wide

them to fasten the two sets of curtains together so that the tabernacle was a unit.

14They made curtains of goat hair for the tent over the tabernacle—eleven altogether. 15All eleven curtains were the same size—thirty cubits long and four cubits wide.[a] 16They joined five of the curtains into one set and the other six into another set. 17Then they made fifty loops along the edge of the end curtain in one set and also along the edge of the end curtain in the other set. 18They made fifty bronze clasps to fasten the tent together as a unit. 19Then they made for the tent a covering of ram skins dyed red, and over that a covering of hides of sea cows.[b]

20They made upright frames of acacia wood for the tabernacle. 21Each frame was ten cubits long and a cubit and a half wide,[c] 22with two projections set parallel to each other. They made all the frames of the tabernacle in this way. 23They made twenty frames for the south side of the tabernacle 24and made forty silver bases to go under them—two bases for each frame, one under each projection. 25For the other side, the north side of the tabernacle, they made twenty frames 26and forty silver bases—two under each frame. 27They made six frames for the far end, that is, the west end of the tabernacle, 28and two frames were made for the corners of the tabernacle at the far end. 29At these two corners the frames were double from the bottom all the way to the top and fitted into a single ring; both were made alike. 30So there were eight frames and sixteen silver bases—two under each frame.

31They also made crossbars of acacia wood: five for the frames on one side of the tabernacle, 32five for those on the other side, and five for the frames on the west, at the far end of the tabernacle. 33They made the center crossbar so that it extended from end to end at the middle of the frames. 34They overlaid the frames with gold and made gold rings to hold the crossbars. They also overlaid the crossbars with gold.

35They made the curtain of blue, purple and scarlet yarn and finely twisted linen, with cherubim worked into it by a skilled craftsman. 36They made four posts of acacia wood for it and overlaid them with gold. They made gold hooks for them and cast their four silver bases. 37For the entrance to the tent they made a curtain of blue, purple and scarlet yarn and finely twisted linen—the work of an embroiderer; 38and they made five posts with hooks for them. They overlaid the tops of the posts and their bands with gold and made their five bases of bronze.

The Ark

37 Bezalel made the ark of acacia wood—two and a half cubits long, a cubit and a half wide, and a cubit and a half high.[d] 2He overlaid it with pure gold, both inside and out, and made a gold molding around it. 3He cast four gold rings for it and fastened them to its four feet, with two rings on one side and two rings on the other. 4Then he made poles of acacia wood and overlaid them with gold. 5And he inserted the poles into the rings on the sides of the ark to carry it.

6He made the atonement cover of pure gold—two and a half cubits long and a cubit and a half wide.[e] 7Then he made two cherubim out of hammered gold at the ends of the cover. 8He made one cherub on one end and the second cherub on the other; at the two ends he made them of one piece with the cover. 9The cherubim had their wings spread upward, overshadowing the cover with them. The cherubim faced each other, looking toward the cover.

The Table

10They[f] made the table of acacia wood—two cubits long, a cubit wide, and a cubit and a half high.[g] 11Then they overlaid it with pure gold and made a gold molding around it. 12They also made around it a rim a handbreadth[h] wide and put a gold molding on the rim. 13They cast four gold rings for the table and fastened them to the four corners, where the four legs were. 14The rings were put close to the rim to hold the poles used in carrying the table. 15The poles for carrying the table were made of acacia wood and were overlaid with gold. 16And they made from pure gold the articles for the table—its plates and dishes and bowls and its pitchers for the pouring out of drink offerings.

The Lampstand

17They made the lampstand of pure gold and hammered it out, base and shaft; its flowerlike cups, buds and blossoms were of one piece with it. 18Six branches extended from the sides of the lampstand—three on one side and three on the other. 19Three cups shaped like almond flowers with buds and blossoms were on one branch, three on the next branch and the same for all six branches extending from the lampstand. 20And on the lampstand were four cups shaped like almond flowers with buds and blossoms. 21One bud was under the first pair of branches extending from the lampstand, a second bud under the second pair, and a third bud under the third pair—six branches in all. 22The buds and the branches were all of one piece with the lampstand, hammered out of pure gold.

23They made its seven lamps, as well as its wick trimmers and trays, of pure gold. 24They

[a] *15* That is, about 45 feet (about 13.5 meters) long and 6 feet (about 1.8 meters) wide [b] *19* That is, dugongs [c] *21* That is, about 15 feet (about 4.5 meters) long and 2 1/4 feet (about 0.7 meter) wide
[d] *1* That is, about 3 3/4 feet (about 1.1 meters) long and 2 1/4 feet (about 0.7 meter) wide and high [e] *6* That is, about 3 3/4 feet (about 1.1 meters) long and 2 1/4 feet (about 0.7 meter) wide [f] *10* Or *He*; also in verses 11-29 [g] *10* That is, about 3 feet (about 0.9 meter) long, 1 1/2 feet (about 0.5 meter) wide, and 2 1/4 feet (about 0.7 meter) high [h] *12* That is, about 3 inches (about 8 centimeters)

made the lampstand and all its accessories
from one talent[a] of pure gold.

The Altar of Incense

25They made the altar of incense out of acacia wood. It was square, a cubit long and a
cubit wide, and two cubits high[b]—its horns of
one piece with it. 26They overlaid the top and
all the sides and the horns with pure gold, and
made a gold molding around it. 27They made
two gold rings below the molding—two on
opposite sides—to hold the poles used to carry
it. 28They made the poles of acacia wood and
overlaid them with gold.

29They also made the sacred anointing oil
and the pure, fragrant incense—the work of a
perfumer.

The Altar of Burnt Offering

38 They[c] built the altar of burnt offering of
acacia wood, three cubits[d] high; it was
square, five cubits long and five cubits wide.[e]
2They made a horn at each of the four corners,
so that the horns and the altar were of one
piece, and they overlaid the altar with bronze.
3They made all its utensils of bronze—its pots,
shovels, sprinkling bowls, meat forks and firepans. 4They made a grating for the altar, a
bronze network, to be under its ledge, halfway
up the altar. 5They cast bronze rings to hold the
poles for the four corners of the bronze grating.
6They made the poles of acacia wood and
overlaid them with bronze. 7They inserted the
poles into the rings so they would be on the
sides of the altar for carrying it. They made it
hollow, out of boards.

Basin for Washing

8They made the bronze basin and its bronze
stand from the mirrors of the women who
served at the entrance to the Tent of Meeting.

The Courtyard

9Next they made the courtyard. The south
side was a hundred cubits[f] long and had curtains of finely twisted linen, 10with twenty
posts and twenty bronze bases, and with silver
hooks and bands on the posts. 11The north side
was also a hundred cubits long and had twenty
posts and twenty bronze bases, with silver
hooks and bands on the posts.

12The west end was fifty cubits[g] wide and
had curtains, with ten posts and ten bases, with
silver hooks and bands on the posts. 13The east
end, toward the sunrise, was also fifty cubits
wide. 14Curtains fifteen cubits[h] long were on
one side of the entrance, with three posts and
three bases, 15and curtains fifteen cubits long
were on the other side of the entrance to the
courtyard, with three posts and three bases.
16All the curtains around the courtyard were of
finely twisted linen. 17The bases for the posts
were bronze. The hooks and bands on the posts
were silver, and their tops were overlaid with
silver; so all the posts of the courtyard had
silver bands.

18The curtain for the entrance to the courtyard was of blue, purple and scarlet yarn and
finely twisted linen—the work of an embroiderer. It was twenty cubits[i] long and, like the
curtains of the courtyard, five cubits[j] high,
19with four posts and four bronze bases. Their
hooks and bands were silver, and their tops
were overlaid with silver. 20All the tent pegs of
the tabernacle and of the surrounding courtyard were bronze.

The Materials Used

21These are the amounts of the materials
used for the tabernacle, the tabernacle of the
Testimony, which were recorded at Moses'
command by the Levites under the direction of
Ithamar son of Aaron, the priest. 22(Bezalel
son of Uri, the son of Hur, of the tribe of
Judah, made everything the LORD commanded
Moses; 23with him was Oholiab son of Ahisamach, of the tribe of Dan—a craftsman and
designer, and an embroiderer in blue, purple
and scarlet yarn and fine linen.) 24The total
amount of the gold from the wave offering
used for all the work on the sanctuary was 29
talents and 730 shekels,[k] according to the
sanctuary shekel.

25The silver obtained from those of the community who were counted in the census was
100 talents and 1,775 shekels,[l] according to
the sanctuary shekel— 26one beka per person,
that is, half a shekel,[m] according to the sanctuary shekel, from everyone who had crossed
over to those counted, twenty years old or
more, a total of 603,550 men. 27The 100 talents[n] of silver were used to cast the bases for
the sanctuary and for the curtain—100 bases
from the 100 talents, one talent for each base.
28They used the 1,775 shekels[o] to make the
hooks for the posts, to overlay the tops of the
posts, and to make their bands.

29The bronze from the wave offering was 70
talents and 2,400 shekels.[p] 30They used it to
make the bases for the entrance to the Tent of
Meeting, the bronze altar with its bronze grating and all its utensils, 31the bases for the surrounding courtyard and those for its entrance
and all the tent pegs for the tabernacle and
those for the surrounding courtyard.

[a] *24* That is, about 75 pounds (about 34 kilograms) [b] *25* That is, about 1 1/2 feet (about 0.5 meter) long and wide, and about 3 feet (about 0.9 meter) high [c] *1* Or *He*; also in verses 2-9 [d] *1* That is, about 4 1/2 feet (about 1.3 meters) [e] *1* That is, about 7 1/2 feet (about 2.3 meters) long and wide [f] *9* That is, about 150 feet (about 46 meters) [g] *12* That is, about 75 feet (about 23 meters) [h] *14* That is, about 22 1/2 feet (about 6.9 meters) [i] *18* That is, about 30 feet (about 9 meters) [j] *18* That is, about 7 1/2 feet (about 2.3 meters) [k] *24* The weight of the gold was a little over one ton (about 1 metric ton). [l] *25* The weight of the silver was a little over 3 3/4 tons (about 3.4 metric tons). [m] *26* That is, about 1/5 ounce (about 5.5 grams) [n] *27* That is, about 3 3/4 tons (about 3.4 metric tons) [o] *28* That is, about 45 pounds (about 20 kilograms) [p] *29* The weight of the bronze was about 2 1/2 tons (about 2.4 metric tons).

The Priestly Garments

39 From the blue, purple and scarlet yarn they made woven garments for ministering in the sanctuary. They also made sacred garments for Aaron, as the LORD commanded Moses.

The Ephod

2They[a] made the ephod of gold, and of blue, purple and scarlet yarn, and of finely twisted linen. 3They hammered out thin sheets of gold and cut strands to be worked into the blue, purple and scarlet yarn and fine linen—the work of a skilled craftsman. 4They made shoulder pieces for the ephod, which were attached to two of its corners, so it could be fastened. 5Its skillfully woven waistband was like it—of one piece with the ephod and made with gold, and with blue, purple and scarlet yarn, and with finely twisted linen, as the LORD commanded Moses.

6They mounted the onyx stones in gold filigree settings and engraved them like a seal with the names of the sons of Israel. 7Then they fastened them on the shoulder pieces of the ephod as memorial stones for the sons of Israel, as the LORD commanded Moses.

The Breastpiece

8They fashioned the breastpiece—the work of a skilled craftsman. They made it like the ephod: of gold, and of blue, purple and scarlet yarn, and of finely twisted linen. 9It was square—a span[b] long and a span wide—and folded double. 10Then they mounted four rows of precious stones on it. In the first row there was a ruby, a topaz and a beryl; 11in the second row a turquoise, a sapphire[c] and an emerald; 12in the third row a jacinth, an agate and an amethyst; 13in the fourth row a chrysolite, an onyx and a jasper.[d] They were mounted in gold filigree settings. 14There were twelve stones, one for each of the names of the sons of Israel, each engraved like a seal with the name of one of the twelve tribes.

15For the breastpiece they made braided chains of pure gold, like a rope. 16They made two gold filigree settings and two gold rings, and fastened the rings to two of the corners of the breastpiece. 17They fastened the two gold chains to the rings at the corners of the breastpiece, 18and the other ends of the chains to the two settings, attaching them to the shoulder pieces of the ephod at the front. 19They made two gold rings and attached them to the other two corners of the breastpiece on the inside edge next to the ephod. 20Then they made two more gold rings and attached them to the bottom of the shoulder pieces on the front of the ephod, close to the seam just above the waistband of the ephod. 21They tied the rings of the breastpiece to the rings of the ephod with blue cord, connecting it to the waistband so that the breastpiece would not swing out from the ephod—as the LORD commanded Moses.

Other Priestly Garments

22They made the robe of the ephod entirely of blue cloth—the work of a weaver— 23with an opening in the center of the robe like the opening of a collar,[e] and a band around this opening, so that it would not tear. 24They made pomegranates of blue, purple and scarlet yarn and finely twisted linen around the hem of the robe. 25And they made bells of pure gold and attached them around the hem between the pomegranates. 26The bells and pomegranates alternated around the hem of the robe to be worn for ministering, as the LORD commanded Moses.

27For Aaron and his sons, they made tunics of fine linen—the work of a weaver— 28and the turban of fine linen, the linen headbands and the undergarments of finely twisted linen. 29The sash was of finely twisted linen and blue, purple and scarlet yarn—the work of an embroiderer—as the LORD commanded Moses.

30They made the plate, the sacred diadem, out of pure gold and engraved on it, like an inscription on a seal: HOLY TO THE LORD. 31Then they fastened a blue cord to it to attach it to the turban, as the LORD commanded Moses.

Moses Inspects the Tabernacle

32So all the work on the tabernacle, the Tent of Meeting, was completed. The Israelites did everything just as the LORD commanded Moses. 33Then they brought the tabernacle to Moses: the tent and all its furnishings, its clasps, frames, crossbars, posts and bases; 34the covering of ram skins dyed red, the covering of hides of sea cows[f] and the shielding curtain; 35the ark of the Testimony with its poles and the atonement cover; 36the table with all its articles and the bread of the Presence; 37the pure gold lampstand with its row of lamps and all its accessories, and the oil for the light; 38the gold altar, the anointing oil, the fragrant incense, and the curtain for the entrance to the tent; 39the bronze altar with its bronze grating, its poles and all its utensils; the basin with its stand; 40the curtains of the courtyard with its posts and bases, and the curtain for the entrance to the courtyard; the ropes and tent pegs for the courtyard; all the furnishings for the tabernacle, the Tent of Meeting; 41and the woven garments worn for ministering in the sanctuary, both the sacred garments for Aaron the priest and the garments for his sons when serving as priests.

42The Israelites had done all the work just as the LORD had commanded Moses. 43Moses inspected the work and saw that they had done it just as the LORD had commanded. So Moses blessed them.

[a] *2* Or *He*; also in verses 7, 8 and 22 [b] *9* That is, about 9 inches (about 22 centimeters) [c] *11* Or *lapis lazuli* [d] *13* The precise identification of some of these precious stones is uncertain. [e] *23* The meaning of the Hebrew for this word is uncertain. [f] *34* That is, dugongs

Setting Up the Tabernacle

40 Then the LORD said to Moses: 2“Set up the tabernacle, the Tent of Meeting, on the first day of the first month. 3Place the ark of the Testimony in it and shield the ark with the curtain. 4Bring in the table and set out what belongs on it. Then bring in the lampstand and set up its lamps. 5Place the gold altar of incense in front of the ark of the Testimony and put the curtain at the entrance to the tabernacle.

6“Place the altar of burnt offering in front of the entrance to the tabernacle, the Tent of Meeting; 7place the basin between the Tent of Meeting and the altar and put water in it. 8Set up the courtyard around it and put the curtain at the entrance to the courtyard.

9“Take the anointing oil and anoint the tabernacle and everything in it; consecrate it and all its furnishings, and it will be holy. 10Then anoint the altar of burnt offering and all its utensils; consecrate the altar, and it will be most holy. 11Anoint the basin and its stand and consecrate them.

12“Bring Aaron and his sons to the entrance to the Tent of Meeting and wash them with water. 13Then dress Aaron in the sacred garments, anoint him and consecrate him so he may serve me as priest. 14Bring his sons and dress them in tunics. 15Anoint them just as you anointed their father, so they may serve me as priests. Their anointing will be to a priesthood that will continue for all generations to come.” 16Moses did everything just as the LORD commanded him.

17So the tabernacle was set up on the first day of the first month in the second year. 18When Moses set up the tabernacle, he put the bases in place, erected the frames, inserted the crossbars and set up the posts. 19Then he spread the tent over the tabernacle and put the covering over the tent, as the LORD commanded him.

20He took the Testimony and placed it in the ark, attached the poles to the ark and put the atonement cover over it. 21Then he brought the ark into the tabernacle and hung the shielding curtain and shielded the ark of the Testimony, as the LORD commanded him.

22Moses placed the table in the Tent of Meeting on the north side of the tabernacle outside the curtain 23and set out the bread on it before the LORD, as the LORD commanded him.

24He placed the lampstand in the Tent of Meeting opposite the table on the south side of the tabernacle 25and set up the lamps before the LORD, as the LORD commanded him.

26Moses placed the gold altar in the Tent of Meeting in front of the curtain 27and burned fragrant incense on it, as the LORD commanded him. 28Then he put up the curtain at the entrance to the tabernacle.

29He set the altar of burnt offering near the entrance to the tabernacle, the Tent of Meeting, and offered on it burnt offerings and grain offerings, as the LORD commanded him.

30He placed the basin between the Tent of Meeting and the altar and put water in it for washing, 31and Moses and Aaron and his sons used it to wash their hands and feet. 32They washed whenever they entered the Tent of Meeting or approached the altar, as the LORD commanded Moses.

33Then Moses set up the courtyard around the tabernacle and altar and put up the curtain at the entrance to the courtyard. And so Moses finished the work.

The Glory of the LORD

34Then the cloud covered the Tent of Meeting, and the glory of the LORD filled the tabernacle. 35Moses could not enter the Tent of Meeting because the cloud had settled upon it, and the glory of the LORD filled the tabernacle.

36In all the travels of the Israelites, whenever the cloud lifted from above the tabernacle, they would set out; 37but if the cloud did not lift, they did not set out—until the day it lifted. 38So the cloud of the LORD was over the tabernacle by day, and fire was in the cloud by night, in the sight of all the house of Israel during all their travels.

Leviticus

The Burnt Offering

1 The LORD called to Moses and spoke to him from the Tent of Meeting. He said, 2“Speak to the Israelites and say to them: ‘When any of you brings an offering to the LORD, bring as your offering an animal from either the herd or the flock.

3“ ‘If the offering is a burnt offering from the herd, he is to offer a male without defect. He must present it at the entrance to the Tent of Meeting so that it[a] will be acceptable to the LORD. 4He is to lay his hand on the head of the burnt offering, and it will be accepted on his behalf to make atonement for him. 5He is to slaughter the young bull before the LORD, and then Aaron’s sons the priests shall bring the blood and sprinkle it against the altar on all sides at the entrance to the Tent of Meeting. 6He is to skin the burnt offering and cut it into pieces. 7The sons of Aaron the priest are to put fire on the altar and arrange wood on the fire. 8Then Aaron’s sons the priests shall arrange

[a] 3 Or *he*

the pieces, including the head and the fat, on
the burning wood that is on the altar. 9He is to
wash the inner parts and the legs with water,
and the priest is to burn all of it on the altar. It
is a burnt offering, an offering made by fire, an
aroma pleasing to the LORD.

10" 'If the offering is a burnt offering from
the flock, from either the sheep or the goats, he
is to offer a male without defect. 11He is to
slaughter it at the north side of the altar before
the LORD, and Aaron's sons the priests shall
sprinkle its blood against the altar on all sides.
12He is to cut it into pieces, and the priest shall
arrange them, including the head and the fat,
on the burning wood that is on the altar. 13He
is to wash the inner parts and the legs with
water, and the priest is to bring all of it and
burn it on the altar. It is a burnt offering, an
offering made by fire, an aroma pleasing to the
LORD.

14" 'If the offering to the LORD is a burnt
offering of birds, he is to offer a dove or a
young pigeon. 15The priest shall bring it to the
altar, wring off the head and burn it on the
altar; its blood shall be drained out on the side
of the altar. 16He is to remove the crop with its
contents[a] and throw it to the east side of the
altar, where the ashes are. 17He shall tear it
open by the wings, not severing it completely,
and then the priest shall burn it on the wood
that is on the fire on the altar. It is a burnt
offering, an offering made by fire, an aroma
pleasing to the LORD.

The Grain Offering

2 " 'When someone brings a grain offering
to the LORD, his offering is to be of fine
flour. He is to pour oil on it, put incense on it
2and take it to Aaron's sons the priests. The
priest shall take a handful of the fine flour and
oil, together with all the incense, and burn this
as a memorial portion on the altar, an offering
made by fire, an aroma pleasing to the LORD.
3The rest of the grain offering belongs to Aaron and his sons; it is a most holy part of the
offerings made to the LORD by fire.

4" 'If you bring a grain offering baked in an
oven, it is to consist of fine flour: cakes made
without yeast and mixed with oil, or[b] wafers
made without yeast and spread with oil. 5If
your grain offering is prepared on a griddle, it
is to be made of fine flour mixed with oil, and
without yeast. 6Crumble it and pour oil on it;
it is a grain offering. 7If your grain offering is
cooked in a pan, it is to be made of fine flour
and oil. 8Bring the grain offering made of these
things to the LORD; present it to the priest, who
shall take it to the altar. 9He shall take out the
memorial portion from the grain offering and
burn it on the altar as an offering made by fire,
an aroma pleasing to the LORD. 10The rest of
the grain offering belongs to Aaron and his
sons; it is a most holy part of the offerings
made to the LORD by fire.

11" 'Every grain offering you bring to the
LORD must be made without yeast, for you are
not to burn any yeast or honey in an offering
made to the LORD by fire. 12You may bring
them to the LORD as an offering of the firstfruits, but they are not to be offered on the altar
as a pleasing aroma. 13Season all your grain
offerings with salt. Do not leave the salt of the
covenant of your God out of your grain offerings; add salt to all your offerings.

14" 'If you bring a grain offering of firstfruits to the LORD, offer crushed heads of new
grain roasted in the fire. 15Put oil and incense
on it; it is a grain offering. 16The priest shall
burn the memorial portion of the crushed grain
and the oil, together with all the incense, as an
offering made to the LORD by fire.

The Fellowship Offering

3 " 'If someone's offering is a fellowship offering,[c] and he offers an animal from the
herd, whether male or female, he is to present
before the LORD an animal without defect. 2He
is to lay his hand on the head of his offering
and slaughter it at the entrance to the Tent of
Meeting. Then Aaron's sons the priests shall
sprinkle the blood against the altar on all sides.
3From the fellowship offering he is to bring a
sacrifice made to the LORD by fire: all the fat
that covers the inner parts or is connected to
them, 4both kidneys with the fat on them near
the loins, and the covering of the liver, which
he will remove with the kidneys. 5Then Aaron's sons are to burn it on the altar on top of
the burnt offering that is on the burning wood,
as an offering made by fire, an aroma pleasing
to the LORD.

6" 'If he offers an animal from the flock as
a fellowship offering to the LORD, he is to offer
a male or female without defect. 7If he offers
a lamb, he is to present it before the LORD. 8He
is to lay his hand on the head of his offering
and slaughter it in front of the Tent of Meeting.
Then Aaron's sons shall sprinkle its blood
against the altar on all sides. 9From the fellowship offering he is to bring a sacrifice made to
the LORD by fire: its fat, the entire fat tail cut
off close to the backbone, all the fat that covers
the inner parts or is connected to them, 10both
kidneys with the fat on them near the loins, and
the covering of the liver, which he will remove
with the kidneys. 11The priest shall burn them
on the altar as food, an offering made to the
LORD by fire.

12" 'If his offering is a goat, he is to present
it before the LORD. 13He is to lay his hand on
its head and slaughter it in front of the Tent of
Meeting. Then Aaron's sons shall sprinkle its
blood against the altar on all sides. 14From
what he offers he is to make this offering to the
LORD by fire: all the fat that covers the inner
parts or is connected to them, 15both kidneys

[a] *16* Or *crop and the feathers*; the meaning of the Hebrew for this word is uncertain. [b] *4* Or *and*
[c] *1* Traditionally *peace offering*; also in verses 3, 6 and 9

with the fat on them near the loins, and the covering of the liver, which he will remove with the kidneys. 16The priest shall burn them on the altar as food, an offering made by fire, a pleasing aroma. All the fat is the LORD's.

17" 'This is a lasting ordinance for the generations to come, wherever you live: You must not eat any fat or any blood.' "

The Sin Offering

4 The LORD said to Moses, 2"Say to the Israelites: 'When anyone sins unintentionally and does what is forbidden in any of the LORD's commands—

3" 'If the anointed priest sins, bringing guilt on the people, he must bring to the LORD a young bull without defect as a sin offering for the sin he has committed. 4He is to present the bull at the entrance to the Tent of Meeting before the LORD. He is to lay his hand on its head and slaughter it before the LORD. 5Then the anointed priest shall take some of the bull's blood and carry it into the Tent of Meeting. 6He is to dip his finger into the blood and sprinkle some of it seven times before the LORD, in front of the curtain of the sanctuary. 7The priest shall then put some of the blood on the horns of the altar of fragrant incense that is before the LORD in the Tent of Meeting. The rest of the bull's blood he shall pour out at the base of the altar of burnt offering at the entrance to the Tent of Meeting. 8He shall remove all the fat from the bull of the sin offering—the fat that covers the inner parts or is connected to them, 9both kidneys with the fat on them near the loins, and the covering of the liver, which he will remove with the kidneys—10just as the fat is removed from the ox[a] sacrificed as a fellowship offering.[b] Then the priest shall burn them on the altar of burnt offering. 11But the hide of the bull and all its flesh, as well as the head and legs, the inner parts and offal— 12that is, all the rest of the bull—he must take outside the camp to a place ceremonially clean, where the ashes are thrown, and burn it in a wood fire on the ash heap.

13" 'If the whole Israelite community sins unintentionally and does what is forbidden in any of the LORD's commands, even though the community is unaware of the matter, they are guilty. 14When they become aware of the sin they committed, the assembly must bring a young bull as a sin offering and present it before the Tent of Meeting. 15The elders of the community are to lay their hands on the bull's head before the LORD, and the bull shall be slaughtered before the LORD. 16Then the anointed priest is to take some of the bull's blood into the Tent of Meeting. 17He shall dip his finger into the blood and sprinkle it before the LORD seven times in front of the curtain. 18He is to put some of the blood on the horns of the altar that is before the LORD in the Tent of Meeting. The rest of the blood he shall pour out at the base of the altar of burnt offering at the entrance to the Tent of Meeting. 19He shall remove all the fat from it and burn it on the altar, 20and do with this bull just as he did with the bull for the sin offering. In this way the priest will make atonement for them, and they will be forgiven. 21Then he shall take the bull outside the camp and burn it as he burned the first bull. This is the sin offering for the community.

22" 'When a leader sins unintentionally and does what is forbidden in any of the commands of the LORD his God, he is guilty. 23When he is made aware of the sin he committed, he must bring as his offering a male goat without defect. 24He is to lay his hand on the goat's head and slaughter it at the place where the burnt offering is slaughtered before the LORD. It is a sin offering. 25Then the priest shall take some of the blood of the sin offering with his finger and put it on the horns of the altar of burnt offering and pour out the rest of the blood at the base of the altar. 26He shall burn all the fat on the altar as he burned the fat of the fellowship offering. In this way the priest will make atonement for the man's sin, and he will be forgiven.

27" 'If a member of the community sins unintentionally and does what is forbidden in any of the LORD's commands, he is guilty. 28When he is made aware of the sin he committed, he must bring as his offering for the sin he committed a female goat without defect. 29He is to lay his hand on the head of the sin offering and slaughter it at the place of the burnt offering. 30Then the priest is to take some of the blood with his finger and put it on the horns of the altar of burnt offering and pour out the rest of the blood at the base of the altar. 31He shall remove all the fat, just as the fat is removed from the fellowship offering, and the priest shall burn it on the altar as an aroma pleasing to the LORD. In this way the priest will make atonement for him, and he will be forgiven.

32" 'If he brings a lamb as his sin offering, he is to bring a female without defect. 33He is to lay his hand on its head and slaughter it for a sin offering at the place where the burnt offering is slaughtered. 34Then the priest shall take some of the blood of the sin offering with his finger and put it on the horns of the altar of burnt offering and pour out the rest of the blood at the base of the altar. 35He shall remove all the fat, just as the fat is removed from the lamb of the fellowship offering, and the priest shall burn it on the altar on top of the offerings made to the LORD by fire. In this way the priest will make atonement for him for the sin he has committed, and he will be forgiven.

5 " 'If a person sins because he does not speak up when he hears a public charge

[a] *10* The Hebrew word can include both male and female.

[b] *10* Traditionally *peace offering*; also in verses 26, 31 and 35

to testify regarding something he has seen or
learned about, he will be held responsible.
2“ ‘Or if a person touches anything ceremonially unclean—whether the carcasses of
unclean wild animals or of unclean livestock
or of unclean creatures that move along the
ground—even though he is unaware of it, he
has become unclean and is guilty.
3“ ‘Or if he touches human uncleanness—
anything that would make him unclean—even
though he is unaware of it, when he learns of
it he will be guilty.
4“ ‘Or if a person thoughtlessly takes an
oath to do anything, whether good or evil—in
any matter one might carelessly swear about—
even though he is unaware of it, in any case
when he learns of it he will be guilty.
5“ ‘When anyone is guilty in any of these
ways, he must confess in what way he has
sinned 6and, as a penalty for the sin he has
committed, he must bring to the LORD a female
lamb or goat from the flock as a sin offering;
and the priest shall make atonement for him
for his sin.
7“ ‘If he cannot afford a lamb, he is to bring
two doves or two young pigeons to the LORD
as a penalty for his sin—one for a sin offering
and the other for a burnt offering. 8He is to
bring them to the priest, who shall first offer
the one for the sin offering. He is to wring its
head from its neck, not severing it completely,
9and is to sprinkle some of the blood of the sin
offering against the side of the altar; the rest of
the blood must be drained out at the base of the
altar. It is a sin offering. 10The priest shall then
offer the other as a burnt offering in the prescribed way and make atonement for him for
the sin he has committed, and he will be forgiven.
11“ ‘If, however, he cannot afford two doves
or two young pigeons, he is to bring as an
offering for his sin a tenth of an ephah[a] of fine
flour for a sin offering. He must not put oil or
incense on it, because it is a sin offering. 12He
is to bring it to the priest, who shall take a
handful of it as a memorial portion and burn it
on the altar on top of the offerings made to the
LORD by fire. It is a sin offering. 13In this way
the priest will make atonement for him for any
of these sins he has committed, and he will be
forgiven. The rest of the offering will belong to
the priest, as in the case of the grain offering.’ ”

The Guilt Offering

14The LORD said to Moses: 15“When a person commits a violation and sins unintentionally in regard to any of the LORD’s holy things,
he is to bring to the LORD as a penalty a ram
from the flock, one without defect and of the
proper value in silver, according to the sanctuary shekel.[b] It is a guilt offering. 16He must
make restitution for what he has failed to do in
regard to the holy things, add a fifth of the
value to that and give it all to the priest, who
will make atonement for him with the ram as
a guilt offering, and he will be forgiven.
17“If a person sins and does what is forbidden in any of the LORD’s commands, even
though he does not know it, he is guilty and
will be held responsible. 18He is to bring to the
priest as a guilt offering a ram from the flock,
one without defect and of the proper value. In
this way the priest will make atonement for
him for the wrong he has committed unintentionally, and he will be forgiven. 19It is a guilt
offering; he has been guilty of[c] wrongdoing
against the LORD.”
6 The LORD said to Moses: 2“If anyone sins
and is unfaithful to the LORD by deceiving
his neighbor about something entrusted to him
or left in his care or stolen, or if he cheats him,
3or if he finds lost property and lies about it, or
if he swears falsely, or if he commits any such
sin that people may do— 4when he thus sins
and becomes guilty, he must return what he
has stolen or taken by extortion, or what was
entrusted to him, or the lost property he found,
5or whatever it was he swore falsely about. He
must make restitution in full, add a fifth of the
value to it and give it all to the owner on the
day he presents his guilt offering. 6And as a
penalty he must bring to the priest, that is, to
the LORD, his guilt offering, a ram from the
flock, one without defect and of the proper
value. 7In this way the priest will make atonement for him before the LORD, and he will be
forgiven for any of these things he did that
made him guilty.”

The Burnt Offering

8The LORD said to Moses: 9“Give Aaron
and his sons this command: ‘These are the regulations for the burnt offering: The burnt offering is to remain on the altar hearth throughout
the night, till morning, and the fire must be
kept burning on the altar. 10The priest shall
then put on his linen clothes, with linen undergarments next to his body, and shall remove
the ashes of the burnt offering that the fire has
consumed on the altar and place them beside
the altar. 11Then he is to take off these clothes
and put on others, and carry the ashes outside
the camp to a place that is ceremonially clean.
12The fire on the altar must be kept burning; it
must not go out. Every morning the priest is to
add firewood and arrange the burnt offering on
the fire and burn the fat of the fellowship offerings[d] on it. 13The fire must be kept burning on
the altar continuously; it must not go out.

The Grain Offering

14“ ‘These are the regulations for the grain
offering: Aaron’s sons are to bring it before the
LORD, in front of the altar. 15The priest is to
take a handful of fine flour and oil, together
with all the incense on the grain offering, and
burn the memorial portion on the altar as an
aroma pleasing to the LORD. 16Aaron and his

[a] *11* That is, probably about 2 quarts (about 2 liters) [b] *15* That is, about 2/5 ounce (about 11.5 grams)
[c] *19* Or *has made full expiation for his* [d] *12* Traditionally *peace offerings*

sons shall eat the rest of it, but it is to be eaten without yeast in a holy place; they are to eat it in the courtyard of the Tent of Meeting. 17It must not be baked with yeast; I have given it as their share of the offerings made to me by fire. Like the sin offering and the guilt offering, it is most holy. 18Any male descendant of Aaron may eat it. It is his regular share of the offerings made to the LORD by fire for the generations to come. Whatever touches them will become holy.[a]' "

19The LORD also said to Moses, 20"This is the offering Aaron and his sons are to bring to the LORD on the day he[b] is anointed: a tenth of an ephah[c] of fine flour as a regular grain offering, half of it in the morning and half in the evening. 21Prepare it with oil on a griddle; bring it well-mixed and present the grain offering broken[d] in pieces as an aroma pleasing to the LORD. 22The son who is to succeed him as anointed priest shall prepare it. It is the LORD's regular share and is to be burned completely. 23Every grain offering of a priest shall be burned completely; it must not be eaten."

The Sin Offering

24The LORD said to Moses, 25"Say to Aaron and his sons: 'These are the regulations for the sin offering: The sin offering is to be slaughtered before the LORD in the place the burnt offering is slaughtered; it is most holy. 26The priest who offers it shall eat it; it is to be eaten in a holy place, in the courtyard of the Tent of Meeting. 27Whatever touches any of the flesh will become holy, and if any of the blood is spattered on a garment, you must wash it in a holy place. 28The clay pot the meat is cooked in must be broken; but if it is cooked in a bronze pot, the pot is to be scoured and rinsed with water. 29Any male in a priest's family may eat it; it is most holy. 30But any sin offering whose blood is brought into the Tent of Meeting to make atonement in the Holy Place must not be eaten; it must be burned.

The Guilt Offering

7 " 'These are the regulations for the guilt offering, which is most holy: 2The guilt offering is to be slaughtered in the place where the burnt offering is slaughtered, and its blood is to be sprinkled against the altar on all sides. 3All its fat shall be offered: the fat tail and the fat that covers the inner parts, 4both kidneys with the fat on them near the loins, and the covering of the liver, which is to be removed with the kidneys. 5The priest shall burn them on the altar as an offering made to the LORD by fire. It is a guilt offering. 6Any male in a priest's family may eat it, but it must be eaten in a holy place; it is most holy.

7" 'The same law applies to both the sin offering and the guilt offering: They belong to the priest who makes atonement with them. 8The priest who offers a burnt offering for anyone may keep its hide for himself. 9Every grain offering baked in an oven or cooked in a pan or on a griddle belongs to the priest who offers it, 10and every grain offering, whether mixed with oil or dry, belongs equally to all the sons of Aaron.

The Fellowship Offering

11" 'These are the regulations for the fellowship offering[e] a person may present to the LORD:

12" 'If he offers it as an expression of thankfulness, then along with this thank offering he is to offer cakes of bread made without yeast and mixed with oil, wafers made without yeast and spread with oil, and cakes of fine flour well-kneaded and mixed with oil. 13Along with his fellowship offering of thanksgiving he is to present an offering with cakes of bread made with yeast. 14He is to bring one of each kind as an offering, a contribution to the LORD; it belongs to the priest who sprinkles the blood of the fellowship offerings. 15The meat of his fellowship offering of thanksgiving must be eaten on the day it is offered; he must leave none of it till morning.

16" 'If, however, his offering is the result of a vow or is a freewill offering, the sacrifice shall be eaten on the day he offers it, but anything left over may be eaten on the next day. 17Any meat of the sacrifice left over till the third day must be burned up. 18If any meat of the fellowship offering is eaten on the third day, it will not be accepted. It will not be credited to the one who offered it, for it is impure; the person who eats any of it will be held responsible.

19" 'Meat that touches anything ceremonially unclean must not be eaten; it must be burned up. As for other meat, anyone ceremonially clean may eat it. 20But if anyone who is unclean eats any meat of the fellowship offering belonging to the LORD, that person must be cut off from his people. 21If anyone touches something unclean—whether human uncleanness or an unclean animal or any unclean, detestable thing—and then eats any of the meat of the fellowship offering belonging to the LORD, that person must be cut off from his people.' "

Eating Fat and Blood Forbidden

22The LORD said to Moses, 23"Say to the Israelites: 'Do not eat any of the fat of cattle, sheep or goats. 24The fat of an animal found dead or torn by wild animals may be used for any other purpose, but you must not eat it. 25Anyone who eats the fat of an animal from which an offering by fire may be[f] made to the LORD must be cut off from his people. 26And wherever you live, you must not eat the blood of any bird or animal. 27If anyone eats blood, that person must be cut off from his people.' "

[a] *18* Or *Whoever touches them must be holy*; similarly in verse 27 [b] *20* Or *each* [c] *20* That is, probably about 2 quarts (about 2 liters) [d] *21* The meaning of the Hebrew for this word is uncertain.
[e] *11* Traditionally *peace offering*; also in verses 13-37 [f] *25* Or *fire is*

The Priests' Share

28The LORD said to Moses, 29"Say to the
Israelites: 'Anyone who brings a fellowship
offering to the LORD is to bring part of it as his
sacrifice to the LORD. 30With his own hands he
is to bring the offering made to the LORD by
fire; he is to bring the fat, together with the
breast, and wave the breast before the LORD as
a wave offering. 31The priest shall burn the fat
on the altar, but the breast belongs to Aaron
and his sons. 32You are to give the right thigh
of your fellowship offerings to the priest as a
contribution. 33The son of Aaron who offers
the blood and the fat of the fellowship offering
shall have the right thigh as his share. 34From
the fellowship offerings of the Israelites, I have
taken the breast that is waved and the thigh
that is presented and have given them to Aaron
the priest and his sons as their regular share
from the Israelites.' "

35This is the portion of the offerings made to
the LORD by fire that were allotted to Aaron
and his sons on the day they were presented to
serve the LORD as priests. 36On the day they
were anointed, the LORD commanded that the
Israelites give this to them as their regular
share for the generations to come.

37These, then, are the regulations for the
burnt offering, the grain offering, the sin offering, the guilt offering, the ordination offering
and the fellowship offering, 38which the LORD
gave Moses on Mount Sinai on the day he
commanded the Israelites to bring their offerings to the LORD, in the Desert of Sinai.

The Ordination of Aaron and His Sons

8 The LORD said to Moses, 2"Bring Aaron
and his sons, their garments, the anointing
oil, the bull for the sin offering, the two rams
and the basket containing bread made without
yeast, 3and gather the entire assembly at the
entrance to the Tent of Meeting." 4Moses did
as the LORD commanded him, and the assembly gathered at the entrance to the Tent of
Meeting.

5Moses said to the assembly, "This is what
the LORD has commanded to be done." 6Then
Moses brought Aaron and his sons forward
and washed them with water. 7He put the tunic
on Aaron, tied the sash around him, clothed
him with the robe and put the ephod on him.
He also tied the ephod to him by its skillfully
woven waistband; so it was fastened on him.
8He placed the breastpiece on him and put the
Urim and Thummim in the breastpiece. 9Then
he placed the turban on Aaron's head and set
the gold plate, the sacred diadem, on the front
of it, as the LORD commanded Moses.

10Then Moses took the anointing oil and
anointed the tabernacle and everything in it,
and so consecrated them. 11He sprinkled some
of the oil on the altar seven times, anointing
the altar and all its utensils and the basin with
its stand, to consecrate them. 12He poured
some of the anointing oil on Aaron's head and
anointed him to consecrate him. 13Then he
brought Aaron's sons forward, put tunics on
them, tied sashes around them and put headbands on them, as the LORD commanded Moses.

14He then presented the bull for the sin offering, and Aaron and his sons laid their hands
on its head. 15Moses slaughtered the bull and
took some of the blood, and with his finger he
put it on all the horns of the altar to purify the
altar. He poured out the rest of the blood at the
base of the altar. So he consecrated it to make
atonement for it. 16Moses also took all the fat
around the inner parts, the covering of the liver, and both kidneys and their fat, and burned
it on the altar. 17But the bull with its hide and
its flesh and its offal he burned up outside the
camp, as the LORD commanded Moses.

18He then presented the ram for the burnt
offering, and Aaron and his sons laid their
hands on its head. 19Then Moses slaughtered
the ram and sprinkled the blood against the
altar on all sides. 20He cut the ram into pieces
and burned the head, the pieces and the fat.
21He washed the inner parts and the legs with
water and burned the whole ram on the altar as
a burnt offering, a pleasing aroma, an offering
made to the LORD by fire, as the LORD commanded Moses.

22He then presented the other ram, the ram
for the ordination, and Aaron and his sons laid
their hands on its head. 23Moses slaughtered
the ram and took some of its blood and put it
on the lobe of Aaron's right ear, on the thumb
of his right hand and on the big toe of his right
foot. 24Moses also brought Aaron's sons forward and put some of the blood on the lobes of
their right ears, on the thumbs of their right
hands and on the big toes of their right feet.
Then he sprinkled blood against the altar on all
sides. 25He took the fat, the fat tail, all the fat
around the inner parts, the covering of the liver, both kidneys and their fat and the right
thigh. 26Then from the basket of bread made
without yeast, which was before the LORD, he
took a cake of bread, and one made with oil,
and a wafer; he put these on the fat portions
and on the right thigh. 27He put all these in the
hands of Aaron and his sons and waved them
before the LORD as a wave offering. 28Then
Moses took them from their hands and burned
them on the altar on top of the burnt offering
as an ordination offering, a pleasing aroma, an
offering made to the LORD by fire. 29He also
took the breast—Moses' share of the ordination ram—and waved it before the LORD as a
wave offering, as the LORD commanded Moses.

30Then Moses took some of the anointing oil
and some of the blood from the altar and sprinkled them on Aaron and his garments and on
his sons and their garments. So he consecrated
Aaron and his garments and his sons and their
garments.

31Moses then said to Aaron and his sons,
"Cook the meat at the entrance to the Tent of
Meeting and eat it there with the bread from
the basket of ordination offerings, as I com-

manded, saying,[a] 'Aaron and his sons are to
eat it.' 32Then burn up the rest of the meat and
the bread. 33Do not leave the entrance to the
Tent of Meeting for seven days, until the days
of your ordination are completed, for your ordination will last seven days. 34What has been
done today was commanded by the LORD to
make atonement for you. 35You must stay at
the entrance to the Tent of Meeting day and
night for seven days and do what the LORD
requires, so you will not die; for that is what I
have been commanded." 36So Aaron and his
sons did everything the LORD commanded
through Moses.

The Priests Begin Their Ministry

9 On the eighth day Moses summoned Aaron
and his sons and the elders of Israel. 2He
said to Aaron, "Take a bull calf for your sin
offering and a ram for your burnt offering,
both without defect, and present them before
the LORD. 3Then say to the Israelites: 'Take
a male goat for a sin offering, a calf and a
lamb—both a year old and without defect—
for a burnt offering, 4and an ox[b] and a ram for
a fellowship offering[c] to sacrifice before the
LORD, together with a grain offering mixed
with oil. For today the LORD will appear to
you.' "

5They took the things Moses commanded to
the front of the Tent of Meeting, and the entire
assembly came near and stood before the
LORD. 6Then Moses said, "This is what the
LORD has commanded you to do, so that
the glory of the LORD may appear to you."

7Moses said to Aaron, "Come to the altar
and sacrifice your sin offering and your burnt
offering and make atonement for yourself and
the people; sacrifice the offering that is for the
people and make atonement for them, as the
LORD has commanded."

8So Aaron came to the altar and slaughtered
the calf as a sin offering for himself. 9His sons
brought the blood to him, and he dipped his
finger into the blood and put it on the horns of
the altar; the rest of the blood he poured out at
the base of the altar. 10On the altar he burned
the fat, the kidneys and the covering of the
liver from the sin offering, as the LORD commanded Moses; 11the flesh and the hide he
burned up outside the camp.

12Then he slaughtered the burnt offering.
His sons handed him the blood, and he sprinkled it against the altar on all sides. 13They
handed him the burnt offering piece by piece,
including the head, and he burned them on the
altar. 14He washed the inner parts and the legs
and burned them on top of the burnt offering
on the altar.

15Aaron then brought the offering that was
for the people. He took the goat for the people's sin offering and slaughtered it and offered it for a sin offering as he did with the first
one.

16He brought the burnt offering and offered
it in the prescribed way. 17He also brought the
grain offering, took a handful of it and burned
it on the altar in addition to the morning's
burnt offering.

18He slaughtered the ox and the ram as the
fellowship offering for the people. His sons
handed him the blood, and he sprinkled it
against the altar on all sides. 19But the fat portions of the ox and the ram—the fat tail, the
layer of fat, the kidneys and the covering of the
liver— 20these they laid on the breasts, and
then Aaron burned the fat on the altar. 21Aaron
waved the breasts and the right thigh before
the LORD as a wave offering, as Moses commanded.

22Then Aaron lifted his hands toward the
people and blessed them. And having sacrificed the sin offering, the burnt offering and
the fellowship offering, he stepped down.

23Moses and Aaron then went into the Tent
of Meeting. When they came out, they blessed
the people; and the glory of the LORD appeared
to all the people. 24Fire came out from the
presence of the LORD and consumed the burnt
offering and the fat portions on the altar. And
when all the people saw it, they shouted for joy
and fell facedown.

The Death of Nadab and Abihu

10 Aaron's sons Nadab and Abihu took
their censers, put fire in them and added
incense; and they offered unauthorized fire before the LORD, contrary to his command. 2So
fire came out from the presence of the LORD
and consumed them, and they died before the
LORD. 3Moses then said to Aaron, "This is
what the LORD spoke of when he said:

" 'Among those who approach me
I will show myself holy;
in the sight of all the people
I will be honored.' "

Aaron remained silent.

4Moses summoned Mishael and Elzaphan,
sons of Aaron's uncle Uzziel, and said to them,
"Come here; carry your cousins outside the
camp, away from the front of the sanctuary."
5So they came and carried them, still in their
tunics, outside the camp, as Moses ordered.

6Then Moses said to Aaron and his sons
Eleazar and Ithamar, "Do not let your hair become unkempt,[d] and do not tear your clothes,
or you will die and the LORD will be angry
with the whole community. But your relatives,
all the house of Israel, may mourn for those the
LORD has destroyed by fire. 7Do not leave the
entrance to the Tent of Meeting or you will die,
because the LORD's anointing oil is on you."
So they did as Moses said.

8Then the LORD said to Aaron, 9"You and
your sons are not to drink wine or other fermented drink whenever you go into the Tent of
Meeting, or you will die. This is a lasting ordi-

[a] 31 Or *I was commanded:* [b] 4 The Hebrew word can include both male and female; also in verses 18 and 19. [c] 4 Traditionally *peace offering*; also in verses 18 and 22 [d] 6 Or *Do not uncover your heads*

nance for the generations to come. 10You must distinguish between the holy and the common, between the unclean and the clean, 11and you must teach the Israelites all the decrees the LORD has given them through Moses."

12Moses said to Aaron and his remaining sons, Eleazar and Ithamar, "Take the grain offering left over from the offerings made to the LORD by fire and eat it prepared without yeast beside the altar, for it is most holy. 13Eat it in a holy place, because it is your share and your sons' share of the offerings made to the LORD by fire; for so I have been commanded. 14But you and your sons and your daughters may eat the breast that was waved and the thigh that was presented. Eat them in a ceremonially clean place; they have been given to you and your children as your share of the Israelites' fellowship offerings.[a] 15The thigh that was presented and the breast that was waved must be brought with the fat portions of the offerings made by fire, to be waved before the LORD as a wave offering. This will be the regular share for you and your children, as the LORD has commanded."

16When Moses inquired about the goat of the sin offering and found that it had been burned up, he was angry with Eleazar and Ithamar, Aaron's remaining sons, and asked, 17"Why didn't you eat the sin offering in the sanctuary area? It is most holy; it was given to you to take away the guilt of the community by making atonement for them before the LORD. 18Since its blood was not taken into the Holy Place, you should have eaten the goat in the sanctuary area, as I commanded."

19Aaron replied to Moses, "Today they sacrificed their sin offering and their burnt offering before the LORD, but such things as this have happened to me. Would the LORD have been pleased if I had eaten the sin offering today?" 20When Moses heard this, he was satisfied.

Clean and Unclean Food

11 The LORD said to Moses and Aaron, 2"Say to the Israelites: 'Of all the animals that live on land, these are the ones you may eat: 3You may eat any animal that has a split hoof completely divided and that chews the cud.

4" 'There are some that only chew the cud or only have a split hoof, but you must not eat them. The camel, though it chews the cud, does not have a split hoof; it is ceremonially unclean for you. 5The coney,[b] though it chews the cud, does not have a split hoof; it is unclean for you. 6The rabbit, though it chews the cud, does not have a split hoof; it is unclean for you. 7And the pig, though it has a split hoof completely divided, does not chew the cud; it is unclean for you. 8You must not eat their meat or touch their carcasses; they are unclean for you.

9" 'Of all the creatures living in the water of the seas and the streams, you may eat any that have fins and scales. 10But all creatures in the seas or streams that do not have fins and scales—whether among all the swarming things or among all the other living creatures in the water—you are to detest. 11And since you are to detest them, you must not eat their meat and you must detest their carcasses. 12Anything living in the water that does not have fins and scales is to be detestable to you.

13" 'These are the birds you are to detest and not eat because they are detestable: the eagle, the vulture, the black vulture, 14the red kite, any kind of black kite, 15any kind of raven, 16the horned owl, the screech owl, the gull, any kind of hawk, 17the little owl, the cormorant, the great owl, 18the white owl, the desert owl, the osprey, 19the stork, any kind of heron, the hoopoe and the bat.[c]

20" 'All flying insects that walk on all fours are to be detestable to you. 21There are, however, some winged creatures that walk on all fours that you may eat: those that have jointed legs for hopping on the ground. 22Of these you may eat any kind of locust, katydid, cricket or grasshopper. 23But all other winged creatures that have four legs you are to detest.

24" 'You will make yourselves unclean by these; whoever touches their carcasses will be unclean till evening. 25Whoever picks up one of their carcasses must wash his clothes, and he will be unclean till evening.

26" 'Every animal that has a split hoof not completely divided or that does not chew the cud is unclean for you; whoever touches ⌊the carcass of⌋ any of them will be unclean. 27Of all the animals that walk on all fours, those that walk on their paws are unclean for you; whoever touches their carcasses will be unclean till evening. 28Anyone who picks up their carcasses must wash his clothes, and he will be unclean till evening. They are unclean for you.

29" 'Of the animals that move about on the ground, these are unclean for you: the weasel, the rat, any kind of great lizard, 30the gecko, the monitor lizard, the wall lizard, the skink and the chameleon. 31Of all those that move along the ground, these are unclean for you. Whoever touches them when they are dead will be unclean till evening. 32When one of them dies and falls on something, that article, whatever its use, will be unclean, whether it is made of wood, cloth, hide or sackcloth. Put it in water; it will be unclean till evening, and then it will be clean. 33If one of them falls into a clay pot, everything in it will be unclean, and you must break the pot. 34Any food that could be eaten but has water on it from such a pot is unclean, and any liquid that could be drunk from it is unclean. 35Anything that one of their carcasses falls on becomes unclean; an oven or cooking pot must be broken up. They are unclean, and you are to regard them as unclean.

[a]*14* Traditionally *peace offerings* [b]*5* That is, the hyrax or rock badger [c]*19* The precise identification of some of the birds, insects and animals in this chapter is uncertain.

36A spring, however, or a cistern for collecting water remains clean, but anyone who touches one of these carcasses is unclean. 37If a carcass falls on any seeds that are to be planted, they remain clean. 38But if water has been put on the seed and a carcass falls on it, it is unclean for you.

39" 'If an animal that you are allowed to eat dies, anyone who touches the carcass will be unclean till evening. 40Anyone who eats some of the carcass must wash his clothes, and he will be unclean till evening. Anyone who picks up the carcass must wash his clothes, and he will be unclean till evening.

41" 'Every creature that moves about on the ground is detestable; it is not to be eaten. 42You are not to eat any creature that moves about on the ground, whether it moves on its belly or walks on all fours or on many feet; it is detestable. 43Do not defile yourselves by any of these creatures. Do not make yourselves unclean by means of them or be made unclean by them. 44I am the LORD your God; consecrate yourselves and be holy, because I am holy. Do not make yourselves unclean by any creature that moves about on the ground. 45I am the LORD who brought you up out of Egypt to be your God; therefore be holy, because I am holy.

46" 'These are the regulations concerning animals, birds, every living thing that moves in the water and every creature that moves about on the ground. 47You must distinguish between the unclean and the clean, between living creatures that may be eaten and those that may not be eaten.' "

Purification After Childbirth

12 The LORD said to Moses, 2"Say to the Israelites: 'A woman who becomes pregnant and gives birth to a son will be ceremonially unclean for seven days, just as she is unclean during her monthly period. 3On the eighth day the boy is to be circumcised. 4Then the woman must wait thirty-three days to be purified from her bleeding. She must not touch anything sacred or go to the sanctuary until the days of her purification are over. 5If she gives birth to a daughter, for two weeks the woman will be unclean, as during her period. Then she must wait sixty-six days to be purified from her bleeding.

6" 'When the days of her purification for a son or daughter are over, she is to bring to the priest at the entrance to the Tent of Meeting a year-old lamb for a burnt offering and a young pigeon or a dove for a sin offering. 7He shall offer them before the LORD to make atonement for her, and then she will be ceremonially clean from her flow of blood.

" 'These are the regulations for the woman who gives birth to a boy or a girl. 8If she cannot afford a lamb, she is to bring two doves or two young pigeons, one for a burnt offering and the other for a sin offering. In this way the priest will make atonement for her, and she will be clean.' "

Regulations About Infectious Skin Diseases

13 The LORD said to Moses and Aaron, 2"When anyone has a swelling or a rash or a bright spot on his skin that may become an infectious skin disease,[a] he must be brought to Aaron the priest or to one of his sons[b] who is a priest. 3The priest is to examine the sore on his skin, and if the hair in the sore has turned white and the sore appears to be more than skin deep,[c] it is an infectious skin disease. When the priest examines him, he shall pronounce him ceremonially unclean. 4If the spot on his skin is white but does not appear to be more than skin deep and the hair in it has not turned white, the priest is to put the infected person in isolation for seven days. 5On the seventh day the priest is to examine him, and if he sees that the sore is unchanged and has not spread in the skin, he is to keep him in isolation another seven days. 6On the seventh day the priest is to examine him again, and if the sore has faded and has not spread in the skin, the priest shall pronounce him clean; it is only a rash. The man must wash his clothes, and he will be clean. 7But if the rash does spread in his skin after he has shown himself to the priest to be pronounced clean, he must appear before the priest again. 8The priest is to examine him, and if the rash has spread in the skin, he shall pronounce him unclean; it is an infectious disease.

9"When anyone has an infectious skin disease, he must be brought to the priest. 10The priest is to examine him, and if there is a white swelling in the skin that has turned the hair white and if there is raw flesh in the swelling, 11it is a chronic skin disease and the priest shall pronounce him unclean. He is not to put him in isolation, because he is already unclean.

12"If the disease breaks out all over his skin and, so far as the priest can see, it covers all the skin of the infected person from head to foot, 13the priest is to examine him, and if the disease has covered his whole body, he shall pronounce that person clean. Since it has all turned white, he is clean. 14But whenever raw flesh appears on him, he will be unclean. 15When the priest sees the raw flesh, he shall pronounce him unclean. The raw flesh is unclean; he has an infectious disease. 16Should the raw flesh change and turn white, he must go to the priest. 17The priest is to examine him, and if the sores have turned white, the priest shall pronounce the infected person clean; then he will be clean.

18"When someone has a boil on his skin and it heals, 19and in the place where the boil was,

[a]2 Traditionally *leprosy*; the Hebrew word was used for various diseases affecting the skin—not necessarily leprosy; also elsewhere in this chapter. [b]2 Or *descendants* [c]3 Or *be lower than the rest of the skin*; also elsewhere in this chapter

a white swelling or reddish-white spot appears, he must present himself to the priest.
20The priest is to examine it, and if it appears
to be more than skin deep and the hair in it has
turned white, the priest shall pronounce him
unclean. It is an infectious skin disease that has
broken out where the boil was. 21But if, when
the priest examines it, there is no white hair in
it and it is not more than skin deep and has
faded, then the priest is to put him in isolation
for seven days. 22If it is spreading in the skin,
the priest shall pronounce him unclean; it is
infectious. 23But if the spot is unchanged and
has not spread, it is only a scar from the boil,
and the priest shall pronounce him clean.
24"When someone has a burn on his skin
and a reddish-white or white spot appears in
the raw flesh of the burn, 25the priest is to
examine the spot, and if the hair in it has
turned white, and it appears to be more than
skin deep, it is an infectious disease that has
broken out in the burn. The priest shall pronounce him unclean; it is an infectious skin
disease. 26But if the priest examines it and
there is no white hair in the spot and if it is not
more than skin deep and has faded, then the
priest is to put him in isolation for seven days.
27On the seventh day the priest is to examine
him, and if it is spreading in the skin, the priest
shall pronounce him unclean; it is an infectious
skin disease. 28If, however, the spot is unchanged and has not spread in the skin but has
faded, it is a swelling from the burn, and the
priest shall pronounce him clean; it is only a
scar from the burn.
29"If a man or woman has a sore on the head
or on the chin, 30the priest is to examine the
sore, and if it appears to be more than skin
deep and the hair in it is yellow and thin, the
priest shall pronounce that person unclean; it is
an itch, an infectious disease of the head or
chin. 31But if, when the priest examines this
kind of sore, it does not seem to be more than
skin deep and there is no black hair in it, then
the priest is to put the infected person in isolation for seven days. 32On the seventh day the
priest is to examine the sore, and if the itch has
not spread and there is no yellow hair in it and
it does not appear to be more than skin deep,
33he must be shaved except for the diseased
area, and the priest is to keep him in isolation
another seven days. 34On the seventh day the
priest is to examine the itch, and if it has not
spread in the skin and appears to be no more
than skin deep, the priest shall pronounce him
clean. He must wash his clothes, and he will be
clean. 35But if the itch does spread in the skin
after he is pronounced clean, 36the priest is to
examine him, and if the itch has spread in the
skin, the priest does not need to look for yellow hair; the person is unclean. 37If, however,
in his judgment it is unchanged and black hair
has grown in it, the itch is healed. He is clean,
and the priest shall pronounce him clean.
38"When a man or woman has white spots
on the skin, 39the priest is to examine them,
and if the spots are dull white, it is a harmless
rash that has broken out on the skin; that person is clean.
40"When a man has lost his hair and is bald,
he is clean. 41If he has lost his hair from the
front of his scalp and has a bald forehead, he
is clean. 42But if he has a reddish-white sore
on his bald head or forehead, it is an infectious
disease breaking out on his head or forehead.
43The priest is to examine him, and if the swollen sore on his head or forehead is reddish-
white like an infectious skin disease, 44the man
is diseased and is unclean. The priest shall pronounce him unclean because of the sore on his
head.
45"The person with such an infectious disease must wear torn clothes, let his hair be
unkempt,[a] cover the lower part of his face and
cry out, 'Unclean! Unclean!' 46As long as he
has the infection he remains unclean. He must
live alone; he must live outside the camp.

Regulations About Mildew

47"If any clothing is contaminated with mildew—any woolen or linen clothing, 48any woven or knitted material of linen or wool, any
leather or anything made of leather— 49and if
the contamination in the clothing, or leather, or
woven or knitted material, or any leather article, is greenish or reddish, it is a spreading
mildew and must be shown to the priest. 50The
priest is to examine the mildew and isolate the
affected article for seven days. 51On the seventh day he is to examine it, and if the mildew
has spread in the clothing, or the woven or
knitted material, or the leather, whatever its
use, it is a destructive mildew; the article is
unclean. 52He must burn up the clothing, or the
woven or knitted material of wool or linen, or
any leather article that has the contamination
in it, because the mildew is destructive; the
article must be burned up.
53"But if, when the priest examines it, the
mildew has not spread in the clothing, or the
woven or knitted material, or the leather article, 54he shall order that the contaminated article be washed. Then he is to isolate it for another seven days. 55After the affected article
has been washed, the priest is to examine it,
and if the mildew has not changed its appearance, even though it has not spread, it is unclean. Burn it with fire, whether the mildew
has affected one side or the other. 56If, when
the priest examines it, the mildew has faded
after the article has been washed, he is to tear
the contaminated part out of the clothing, or
the leather, or the woven or knitted material.
57But if it reappears in the clothing, or in the
woven or knitted material, or in the leather
article, it is spreading, and whatever has the
mildew must be burned with fire. 58The clothing, or the woven or knitted material, or any
leather article that has been washed and is rid

[a]45 Or *clothes, uncover his head*

of the mildew, must be washed again, and it will be clean."

59These are the regulations concerning contamination by mildew in woolen or linen clothing, woven or knitted material, or any leather article, for pronouncing them clean or unclean.

Cleansing From Infectious Skin Diseases

14 The LORD said to Moses, 2"These are the regulations for the diseased person at the time of his ceremonial cleansing, when he is brought to the priest: 3The priest is to go outside the camp and examine him. If the person has been healed of his infectious skin disease,[a] 4the priest shall order that two live clean birds and some cedar wood, scarlet yarn and hyssop be brought for the one to be cleansed. 5Then the priest shall order that one of the birds be killed over fresh water in a clay pot. 6He is then to take the live bird and dip it, together with the cedar wood, the scarlet yarn and the hyssop, into the blood of the bird that was killed over the fresh water. 7Seven times he shall sprinkle the one to be cleansed of the infectious disease and pronounce him clean. Then he is to release the live bird in the open fields.

8"The person to be cleansed must wash his clothes, shave off all his hair and bathe with water; then he will be ceremonially clean. After this he may come into the camp, but he must stay outside his tent for seven days. 9On the seventh day he must shave off all his hair; he must shave his head, his beard, his eyebrows and the rest of his hair. He must wash his clothes and bathe himself with water, and he will be clean.

10"On the eighth day he must bring two male lambs and one ewe lamb a year old, each without defect, along with three-tenths of an ephah[b] of fine flour mixed with oil for a grain offering, and one log[c] of oil. 11The priest who pronounces him clean shall present both the one to be cleansed and his offerings before the LORD at the entrance to the Tent of Meeting.

12"Then the priest is to take one of the male lambs and offer it as a guilt offering, along with the log of oil; he shall wave them before the LORD as a wave offering. 13He is to slaughter the lamb in the holy place where the sin offering and the burnt offering are slaughtered. Like the sin offering, the guilt offering belongs to the priest; it is most holy. 14The priest is to take some of the blood of the guilt offering and put it on the lobe of the right ear of the one to be cleansed, on the thumb of his right hand and on the big toe of his right foot. 15The priest shall then take some of the log of oil, pour it in the palm of his own left hand, 16dip his right forefinger into the oil in his palm, and with his finger sprinkle some of it before the LORD seven times. 17The priest is to put some of the oil remaining in his palm on the lobe of the right ear of the one to be cleansed, on the thumb of his right hand and on the big toe of his right foot, on top of the blood of the guilt offering. 18The rest of the oil in his palm the priest shall put on the head of the one to be cleansed and make atonement for him before the LORD.

19"Then the priest is to sacrifice the sin offering and make atonement for the one to be cleansed from his uncleanness. After that, the priest shall slaughter the burnt offering 20and offer it on the altar, together with the grain offering, and make atonement for him, and he will be clean.

21"If, however, he is poor and cannot afford these, he must take one male lamb as a guilt offering to be waved to make atonement for him, together with a tenth of an ephah[d] of fine flour mixed with oil for a grain offering, a log of oil, 22and two doves or two young pigeons, which he can afford, one for a sin offering and the other for a burnt offering.

23"On the eighth day he must bring them for his cleansing to the priest at the entrance to the Tent of Meeting, before the LORD. 24The priest is to take the lamb for the guilt offering, together with the log of oil, and wave them before the LORD as a wave offering. 25He shall slaughter the lamb for the guilt offering and take some of its blood and put it on the lobe of the right ear of the one to be cleansed, on the thumb of his right hand and on the big toe of his right foot. 26The priest is to pour some of the oil into the palm of his own left hand, 27and with his right forefinger sprinkle some of the oil from his palm seven times before the LORD. 28Some of the oil in his palm he is to put on the same places he put the blood of the guilt offering—on the lobe of the right ear of the one to be cleansed, on the thumb of his right hand and on the big toe of his right foot. 29The rest of the oil in his palm the priest shall put on the head of the one to be cleansed, to make atonement for him before the LORD. 30Then he shall sacrifice the doves or the young pigeons, which the person can afford, 31one[e] as a sin offering and the other as a burnt offering, together with the grain offering. In this way the priest will make atonement before the LORD on behalf of the one to be cleansed."

32These are the regulations for anyone who has an infectious skin disease and who cannot afford the regular offerings for his cleansing.

Cleansing From Mildew

33The LORD said to Moses and Aaron, 34"When you enter the land of Canaan, which I am giving you as your possession, and I put a spreading mildew in a house in that land, 35the owner of the house must go and tell the priest, 'I have seen something that looks like mildew in my house.' 36The priest is to order

[a] *3* Traditionally *leprosy;* the Hebrew word was used for various diseases affecting the skin—not necessarily leprosy; also elsewhere in this chapter. [b] *10* That is, probably about 6 quarts (about 6.5 liters) [c] *10* That is, probably about 2/3 pint (about 0.3 liter); also in verses 12, 15, 21 and 24 [d] *21* That is, probably about 2 quarts (about 2 liters) [e] *31* Septuagint and Syriac; Hebrew *31such as the person can afford, one*

the house to be emptied before he goes in to examine the mildew, so that nothing in the house will be pronounced unclean. After this the priest is to go in and inspect the house. 37 He is to examine the mildew on the walls, and if it has greenish or reddish depressions that appear to be deeper than the surface of the wall, 38 the priest shall go out the doorway of the house and close it up for seven days. 39 On the seventh day the priest shall return to inspect the house. If the mildew has spread on the walls, 40 he is to order that the contaminated stones be torn out and thrown into an unclean place outside the town. 41 He must have all the inside walls of the house scraped and the material that is scraped off dumped into an unclean place outside the town. 42 Then they are to take other stones to replace these and take new clay and plaster the house.

43 "If the mildew reappears in the house after the stones have been torn out and the house scraped and plastered, 44 the priest is to go and examine it and, if the mildew has spread in the house, it is a destructive mildew; the house is unclean. 45 It must be torn down—its stones, timbers and all the plaster—and taken out of the town to an unclean place.

46 "Anyone who goes into the house while it is closed up will be unclean till evening. 47 Anyone who sleeps or eats in the house must wash his clothes.

48 "But if the priest comes to examine it and the mildew has not spread after the house has been plastered, he shall pronounce the house clean, because the mildew is gone. 49 To purify the house he is to take two birds and some cedar wood, scarlet yarn and hyssop. 50 He shall kill one of the birds over fresh water in a clay pot. 51 Then he is to take the cedar wood, the hyssop, the scarlet yarn and the live bird, dip them into the blood of the dead bird and the fresh water, and sprinkle the house seven times. 52 He shall purify the house with the bird's blood, the fresh water, the live bird, the cedar wood, the hyssop and the scarlet yarn. 53 Then he is to release the live bird in the open fields outside the town. In this way he will make atonement for the house, and it will be clean."

54 These are the regulations for any infectious skin disease, for an itch, 55 for mildew in clothing or in a house, 56 and for a swelling, a rash or a bright spot, 57 to determine when something is clean or unclean.

These are the regulations for infectious skin diseases and mildew.

Discharges Causing Uncleanness

15 The LORD said to Moses and Aaron, 2 "Speak to the Israelites and say to them: 'When any man has a bodily discharge, the discharge is unclean. 3 Whether it continues flowing from his body or is blocked, it will make him unclean. This is how his discharge will bring about uncleanness:

4 " 'Any bed the man with a discharge lies on will be unclean, and anything he sits on will be unclean. 5 Anyone who touches his bed must wash his clothes and bathe with water, and he will be unclean till evening. 6 Whoever sits on anything that the man with a discharge sat on must wash his clothes and bathe with water, and he will be unclean till evening.

7 " 'Whoever touches the man who has a discharge must wash his clothes and bathe with water, and he will be unclean till evening.

8 " 'If the man with the discharge spits on someone who is clean, that person must wash his clothes and bathe with water, and he will be unclean till evening.

9 " 'Everything the man sits on when riding will be unclean, 10 and whoever touches any of the things that were under him will be unclean till evening; whoever picks up those things must wash his clothes and bathe with water, and he will be unclean till evening.

11 " 'Anyone the man with a discharge touches without rinsing his hands with water must wash his clothes and bathe with water, and he will be unclean till evening.

12 " 'A clay pot that the man touches must be broken, and any wooden article is to be rinsed with water.

13 " 'When a man is cleansed from his discharge, he is to count off seven days for his ceremonial cleansing; he must wash his clothes and bathe himself with fresh water, and he will be clean. 14 On the eighth day he must take two doves or two young pigeons and come before the LORD to the entrance to the Tent of Meeting and give them to the priest. 15 The priest is to sacrifice them, the one for a sin offering and the other for a burnt offering. In this way he will make atonement before the LORD for the man because of his discharge.

16 " 'When a man has an emission of semen, he must bathe his whole body with water, and he will be unclean till evening. 17 Any clothing or leather that has semen on it must be washed with water, and it will be unclean till evening. 18 When a man lies with a woman and there is an emission of semen, both must bathe with water, and they will be unclean till evening.

19 " 'When a woman has her regular flow of blood, the impurity of her monthly period will last seven days, and anyone who touches her will be unclean till evening.

20 " 'Anything she lies on during her period will be unclean, and anything she sits on will be unclean. 21 Whoever touches her bed must wash his clothes and bathe with water, and he will be unclean till evening. 22 Whoever touches anything she sits on must wash his clothes and bathe with water, and he will be unclean till evening. 23 Whether it is the bed or anything she was sitting on, when anyone touches it, he will be unclean till evening.

24 " 'If a man lies with her and her monthly flow touches him, he will be unclean for seven days; any bed he lies on will be unclean.

25 " 'When a woman has a discharge of blood for many days at a time other than her monthly period or has a discharge that continues beyond her period, she will be unclean as

long as she has the discharge, just as in the days of her period. 26Any bed she lies on while her discharge continues will be unclean, as is her bed during her monthly period, and anything she sits on will be unclean, as during her period. 27Whoever touches them will be unclean; he must wash his clothes and bathe with water, and he will be unclean till evening.

28" 'When she is cleansed from her discharge, she must count off seven days, and after that she will be ceremonially clean. 29On the eighth day she must take two doves or two young pigeons and bring them to the priest at the entrance to the Tent of Meeting. 30The priest is to sacrifice one for a sin offering and the other for a burnt offering. In this way he will make atonement for her before the LORD for the uncleanness of her discharge.

31" 'You must keep the Israelites separate from things that make them unclean, so they will not die in their uncleanness for defiling my dwelling place,[a] which is among them.' "

32These are the regulations for a man with a discharge, for anyone made unclean by an emission of semen, 33for a woman in her monthly period, for a man or a woman with a discharge, and for a man who lies with a woman who is ceremonially unclean.

The Day of Atonement

16 The LORD spoke to Moses after the death of the two sons of Aaron who died when they approached the LORD. 2The LORD said to Moses: "Tell your brother Aaron not to come whenever he chooses into the Most Holy Place behind the curtain in front of the atonement cover on the ark, or else he will die, because I appear in the cloud over the atonement cover.

3"This is how Aaron is to enter the sanctuary area: with a young bull for a sin offering and a ram for a burnt offering. 4He is to put on the sacred linen tunic, with linen undergarments next to his body; he is to tie the linen sash around him and put on the linen turban. These are sacred garments; so he must bathe himself with water before he puts them on. 5From the Israelite community he is to take two male goats for a sin offering and a ram for a burnt offering.

6"Aaron is to offer the bull for his own sin offering to make atonement for himself and his household. 7Then he is to take the two goats and present them before the LORD at the entrance to the Tent of Meeting. 8He is to cast lots for the two goats—one lot for the LORD and the other for the scapegoat.[b] 9Aaron shall bring the goat whose lot falls to the LORD and sacrifice it for a sin offering. 10But the goat chosen by lot as the scapegoat shall be presented alive before the LORD to be used for making atonement by sending it into the desert as a scapegoat.

11"Aaron shall bring the bull for his own sin offering to make atonement for himself and his household, and he is to slaughter the bull for his own sin offering. 12He is to take a censer full of burning coals from the altar before the LORD and two handfuls of finely ground fragrant incense and take them behind the curtain. 13He is to put the incense on the fire before the LORD, and the smoke of the incense will conceal the atonement cover above the Testimony, so that he will not die. 14He is to take some of the bull's blood and with his finger sprinkle it on the front of the atonement cover; then he shall sprinkle some of it with his finger seven times before the atonement cover.

15"He shall then slaughter the goat for the sin offering for the people and take its blood behind the curtain and do with it as he did with the bull's blood: He shall sprinkle it on the atonement cover and in front of it. 16In this way he will make atonement for the Most Holy Place because of the uncleanness and rebellion of the Israelites, whatever their sins have been. He is to do the same for the Tent of Meeting, which is among them in the midst of their uncleanness. 17No one is to be in the Tent of Meeting from the time Aaron goes in to make atonement in the Most Holy Place until he comes out, having made atonement for himself, his household and the whole community of Israel.

18"Then he shall come out to the altar that is before the LORD and make atonement for it. He shall take some of the bull's blood and some of the goat's blood and put it on all the horns of the altar. 19He shall sprinkle some of the blood on it with his finger seven times to cleanse it and to consecrate it from the uncleanness of the Israelites.

20"When Aaron has finished making atonement for the Most Holy Place, the Tent of Meeting and the altar, he shall bring forward the live goat. 21He is to lay both hands on the head of the live goat and confess over it all the wickedness and rebellion of the Israelites—all their sins—and put them on the goat's head. He shall send the goat away into the desert in the care of a man appointed for the task. 22The goat will carry on itself all their sins to a solitary place; and the man shall release it in the desert.

23"Then Aaron is to go into the Tent of Meeting and take off the linen garments he put on before he entered the Most Holy Place, and he is to leave them there. 24He shall bathe himself with water in a holy place and put on his regular garments. Then he shall come out and sacrifice the burnt offering for himself and the burnt offering for the people, to make atonement for himself and for the people. 25He shall also burn the fat of the sin offering on the altar.

26"The man who releases the goat as a scapegoat must wash his clothes and bathe himself with water; afterward he may come into the camp. 27The bull and the goat for the sin offerings, whose blood was brought into the Most Holy Place to make atonement, must

[a]31 Or *my tabernacle* [b]8 That is, the goat of removal; Hebrew *azazel*; also in verses 10 and 26

be taken outside the camp; their hides, flesh
and offal are to be burned up. 28The man who
burns them must wash his clothes and bathe
himself with water; afterward he may come
into the camp.

29"This is to be a lasting ordinance for you:
On the tenth day of the seventh month you
must deny yourselves[a] and not do any work—
whether native-born or an alien living among
you— 30because on this day atonement will be
made for you, to cleanse you. Then, before the
LORD, you will be clean from all your sins. 31It
is a sabbath of rest, and you must deny yourselves; it is a lasting ordinance. 32The priest
who is anointed and ordained to succeed his
father as high priest is to make atonement. He
is to put on the sacred linen garments 33and
make atonement for the Most Holy Place, for
the Tent of Meeting and the altar, and for the
priests and all the people of the community.

34"This is to be a lasting ordinance for you:
Atonement is to be made once a year for all the
sins of the Israelites."

And it was done, as the LORD commanded
Moses.

Eating Blood Forbidden

17 The LORD said to Moses, 2"Speak to
Aaron and his sons and to all the Israelites and say to them: 'This is what the LORD
has commanded: 3Any Israelite who sacrifices
an ox,[b] a lamb or a goat in the camp or outside
of it 4instead of bringing it to the entrance to
the Tent of Meeting to present it as an offering
to the LORD in front of the tabernacle of the
LORD—that man shall be considered guilty of
bloodshed; he has shed blood and must be cut
off from his people. 5This is so the Israelites
will bring to the LORD the sacrifices they are
now making in the open fields. They must
bring them to the priest, that is, to the LORD, at
the entrance to the Tent of Meeting and sacrifice them as fellowship offerings.[c] 6The priest
is to sprinkle the blood against the altar of the
LORD at the entrance to the Tent of Meeting
and burn the fat as an aroma pleasing to the
LORD. 7They must no longer offer any of their
sacrifices to the goat idols[d] to whom they
prostitute themselves. This is to be a lasting
ordinance for them and for the generations to
come.'

8"Say to them: 'Any Israelite or any alien
living among them who offers a burnt offering
or sacrifice 9and does not bring it to the entrance to the Tent of Meeting to sacrifice it to
the LORD—that man must be cut off from his
people.

10" 'Any Israelite or any alien living among
them who eats any blood—I will set my face
against that person who eats blood and will cut
him off from his people. 11For the life of a
creature is in the blood, and I have given it to
you to make atonement for yourselves on the
altar; it is the blood that makes atonement for
one's life. 12Therefore I say to the Israelites,
"None of you may eat blood, nor may an alien
living among you eat blood."

13" 'Any Israelite or any alien living among
you who hunts any animal or bird that may be
eaten must drain out the blood and cover it
with earth, 14because the life of every creature
is its blood. That is why I have said to the
Israelites, "You must not eat the blood of any
creature, because the life of every creature is
its blood; anyone who eats it must be cut off."

15" 'Anyone, whether native-born or alien,
who eats anything found dead or torn by wild
animals must wash his clothes and bathe with
water, and he will be ceremonially unclean till
evening; then he will be clean. 16But if he does
not wash his clothes and bathe himself, he will
be held responsible.' "

Unlawful Sexual Relations

18 The LORD said to Moses, 2"Speak to the
Israelites and say to them: 'I am the
LORD your God. 3You must not do as they do
in Egypt, where you used to live, and you must
not do as they do in the land of Canaan, where
I am bringing you. Do not follow their practices. 4You must obey my laws and be careful
to follow my decrees. I am the LORD your
God. 5Keep my decrees and laws, for the man
who obeys them will live by them. I am the
LORD.

6" 'No one is to approach any close relative
to have sexual relations. I am the LORD.

7" 'Do not dishonor your father by having
sexual relations with your mother. She is your
mother; do not have relations with her.

8" 'Do not have sexual relations with your
father's wife; that would dishonor your father.

9" 'Do not have sexual relations with your
sister, either your father's daughter or your
mother's daughter, whether she was born in
the same home or elsewhere.

10" 'Do not have sexual relations with your
son's daughter or your daughter's daughter;
that would dishonor you.

11" 'Do not have sexual relations with the
daughter of your father's wife, born to your
father; she is your sister.

12" 'Do not have sexual relations with your
father's sister; she is your father's close relative.

13" 'Do not have sexual relations with your
mother's sister, because she is your mother's
close relative.

14" 'Do not dishonor your father's brother
by approaching his wife to have sexual relations; she is your aunt.

15" 'Do not have sexual relations with your
daughter-in-law. She is your son's wife; do
not have relations with her.

16" 'Do not have sexual relations with your
brother's wife; that would dishonor your
brother.

17" 'Do not have sexual relations with both

[a]29 Or *must fast*; also in verse 31 [b]3 The Hebrew word can include both male and female.
[c]5 Traditionally *peace offerings* [d]7 Or *demons*

a woman and her daughter. Do not have sexual
relations with either her son's daughter or her
daughter's daughter; they are her close relatives. That is wickedness.
18" 'Do not take your wife's sister as a rival
wife and have sexual relations with her while
your wife is living.
19" 'Do not approach a woman to have sexual relations during the uncleanness of her
monthly period.
20" 'Do not have sexual relations with your
neighbor's wife and defile yourself with her.
21" 'Do not give any of your children to be
sacrificed[a] to Molech, for you must not profane the name of your God. I am the LORD.
22" 'Do not lie with a man as one lies with
a woman; that is detestable.
23" 'Do not have sexual relations with an
animal and defile yourself with it. A woman
must not present herself to an animal to have
sexual relations with it; that is a perversion.
24" 'Do not defile yourselves in any of these
ways, because this is how the nations that I am
going to drive out before you became defiled.
25Even the land was defiled; so I punished it
for its sin, and the land vomited out its inhabitants. 26But you must keep my decrees and my
laws. The native-born and the aliens living
among you must not do any of these detestable
things, 27for all these things were done by the
people who lived in the land before you, and
the land became defiled. 28And if you defile
the land, it will vomit you out as it vomited out
the nations that were before you.
29" 'Everyone who does any of these detestable things—such persons must be cut off
from their people. 30Keep my requirements
and do not follow any of the detestable customs that were practiced before you came and
do not defile yourselves with them. I am the
LORD your God.' "

Various Laws

19 The LORD said to Moses, 2"Speak to the
entire assembly of Israel and say to
them: 'Be holy because I, the LORD your God,
am holy.
3" 'Each of you must respect his mother and
father, and you must observe my Sabbaths. I
am the LORD your God.
4" 'Do not turn to idols or make gods of cast
metal for yourselves. I am the LORD your God.
5" 'When you sacrifice a fellowship offering[b] to the LORD, sacrifice it in such a way that
it will be accepted on your behalf. 6It shall be
eaten on the day you sacrifice it or on the next
day; anything left over until the third day must
be burned up. 7If any of it is eaten on the third
day, it is impure and will not be accepted.
8Whoever eats it will be held responsible because he has desecrated what is holy to the
LORD; that person must be cut off from his
people.
9" 'When you reap the harvest of your land,
do not reap to the very edges of your field or
gather the gleanings of your harvest. 10Do not
go over your vineyard a second time or pick up
the grapes that have fallen. Leave them for the
poor and the alien. I am the LORD your God.
11" 'Do not steal.
" 'Do not lie.
" 'Do not deceive one another.
12" 'Do not swear falsely by my name and
so profane the name of your God. I am the
LORD.
13" 'Do not defraud your neighbor or rob
him.
" 'Do not hold back the wages of a hired
man overnight.
14" 'Do not curse the deaf or put a stumbling
block in front of the blind, but fear your God.
I am the LORD.
15" 'Do not pervert justice; do not show partiality to the poor or favoritism to the great, but
judge your neighbor fairly.
16" 'Do not go about spreading slander
among your people.
" 'Do not do anything that endangers your
neighbor's life. I am the LORD.
17" 'Do not hate your brother in your heart.
Rebuke your neighbor frankly so you will not
share in his guilt.
18" 'Do not seek revenge or bear a grudge
against one of your people, but love your
neighbor as yourself. I am the LORD.
19" 'Keep my decrees.
" 'Do not mate different kinds of animals.
" 'Do not plant your field with two kinds of
seed.
" 'Do not wear clothing woven of two kinds
of material.
20" 'If a man sleeps with a woman who is a
slave girl promised to another man but who
has not been ransomed or given her freedom,
there must be due punishment. Yet they are not
to be put to death, because she had not been
freed. 21The man, however, must bring a ram
to the entrance to the Tent of Meeting for a
guilt offering to the LORD. 22With the ram of
the guilt offering the priest is to make atonement for him before the LORD for the sin he
has committed, and his sin will be forgiven.
23" 'When you enter the land and plant any
kind of fruit tree, regard its fruit as forbidden.[c]
For three years you are to consider it forbidden[c]; it must not be eaten. 24In the fourth year
all its fruit will be holy, an offering of praise to
the LORD. 25But in the fifth year you may eat
its fruit. In this way your harvest will be increased. I am the LORD your God.
26" 'Do not eat any meat with the blood still
in it.
" 'Do not practice divination or sorcery.
27" 'Do not cut the hair at the sides of your
head or clip off the edges of your beard.
28" 'Do not cut your bodies for the dead or
put tattoo marks on yourselves. I am the LORD.
29" 'Do not degrade your daughter by making her a prostitute, or the land will turn to
prostitution and be filled with wickedness.

[a]21 Or *to be passed through* ⌊*the fire*⌋ [b]5 Traditionally *peace offering* [c]23 Hebrew *uncircumcised*

30“ ‘Observe my Sabbaths and have reverence for my sanctuary. I am the LORD.
31“ ‘Do not turn to mediums or seek out
spiritists, for you will be defiled by them. I am
the LORD your God.
32“ ‘Rise in the presence of the aged, show
respect for the elderly and revere your God. I
am the LORD.
33“ ‘When an alien lives with you in your
land, do not mistreat him. 34The alien living
with you must be treated as one of your native-
born. Love him as yourself, for you were
aliens in Egypt. I am the LORD your God.
35“ ‘Do not use dishonest standards when
measuring length, weight or quantity. 36Use
honest scales and honest weights, an honest
ephah[a] and an honest hin.[b] I am the LORD
your God, who brought you out of Egypt.
37“ ‘Keep all my decrees and all my laws
and follow them. I am the LORD.’ ”

Punishments for Sin

20 The LORD said to Moses, 2“Say to the
Israelites: ‘Any Israelite or any alien
living in Israel who gives[c] any of his children
to Molech must be put to death. The people of
the community are to stone him. 3I will set my
face against that man and I will cut him off
from his people; for by giving his children to
Molech, he has defiled my sanctuary and profaned my holy name. 4If the people of the community close their eyes when that man gives
one of his children to Molech and they fail to
put him to death, 5I will set my face against
that man and his family and will cut off from
their people both him and all who follow him
in prostituting themselves to Molech.
6“ ‘I will set my face against the person who
turns to mediums and spiritists to prostitute
himself by following them, and I will cut him
off from his people.
7“ ‘Consecrate yourselves and be holy, because I am the LORD your God. 8Keep my
decrees and follow them. I am the LORD, who
makes you holy.[d]
9“ ‘If anyone curses his father or mother, he
must be put to death. He has cursed his father
or his mother, and his blood will be on his own
head.
10“ ‘If a man commits adultery with another
man’s wife—with the wife of his neighbor—
both the adulterer and the adulteress must be
put to death.
11“ ‘If a man sleeps with his father’s wife,
he has dishonored his father. Both the man and
the woman must be put to death; their blood
will be on their own heads.
12“ ‘If a man sleeps with his daughter-in-
law, both of them must be put to death. What
they have done is a perversion; their blood will
be on their own heads.
13“ ‘If a man lies with a man as one lies with
a woman, both of them have done what is detestable. They must be put to death; their blood
will be on their own heads.
14“ ‘If a man marries both a woman and her
mother, it is wicked. Both he and they must be
burned in the fire, so that no wickedness will
be among you.
15“ ‘If a man has sexual relations with an
animal, he must be put to death, and you must
kill the animal.
16“ ‘If a woman approaches an animal to
have sexual relations with it, kill both the
woman and the animal. They must be put to
death; their blood will be on their own heads.
17“ ‘If a man marries his sister, the daughter
of either his father or his mother, and they have
sexual relations, it is a disgrace. They must be
cut off before the eyes of their people. He has
dishonored his sister and will be held responsible.
18“ ‘If a man lies with a woman during her
monthly period and has sexual relations with
her, he has exposed the source of her flow, and
she has also uncovered it. Both of them must
be cut off from their people.
19“ ‘Do not have sexual relations with the
sister of either your mother or your father, for
that would dishonor a close relative; both of
you would be held responsible.
20“ ‘If a man sleeps with his aunt, he has
dishonored his uncle. They will be held responsible; they will die childless.
21“ ‘If a man marries his brother’s wife, it
is an act of impurity; he has dishonored his
brother. They will be childless.
22“ ‘Keep all my decrees and laws and follow them, so that the land where I am bringing
you to live may not vomit you out. 23You must
not live according to the customs of the nations
I am going to drive out before you. Because
they did all these things, I abhorred them.
24But I said to you, “You will possess their
land; I will give it to you as an inheritance, a
land flowing with milk and honey.” I am the
LORD your God, who has set you apart from
the nations.
25“ ‘You must therefore make a distinction
between clean and unclean animals and between unclean and clean birds. Do not defile
yourselves by any animal or bird or anything
that moves along the ground—those which I
have set apart as unclean for you. 26You are to
be holy to me[e] because I, the LORD, am holy,
and I have set you apart from the nations to be
my own.
27“ ‘A man or woman who is a medium or
spiritist among you must be put to death. You
are to stone them; their blood will be on their
own heads.’ ”

Rules for Priests

21 The LORD said to Moses, “Speak to the
priests, the sons of Aaron, and say to
them: ‘A priest must not make himself ceremonially unclean for any of his people who

[a]36 An ephah was a dry measure. [b]36 A hin was a liquid measure. [c]2 Or *sacrifices*; also in verses 3 and 4 [d]8 Or *who sanctifies you*; or *who sets you apart as holy* [e]26 Or *be my holy ones*

die, 2except for a close relative, such as his mother or father, his son or daughter, his brother, 3or an unmarried sister who is dependent on him since she has no husband—for her he may make himself unclean. 4He must not make himself unclean for people related to him by marriage,[a] and so defile himself.

5" 'Priests must not shave their heads or shave off the edges of their beards or cut their bodies. 6They must be holy to their God and must not profane the name of their God. Because they present the offerings made to the LORD by fire, the food of their God, they are to be holy.

7" 'They must not marry women defiled by prostitution or divorced from their husbands, because priests are holy to their God. 8Regard them as holy, because they offer up the food of your God. Consider them holy, because I the LORD am holy—I who make you holy.[b]

9" 'If a priest's daughter defiles herself by becoming a prostitute, she disgraces her father; she must be burned in the fire.

10" 'The high priest, the one among his brothers who has had the anointing oil poured on his head and who has been ordained to wear the priestly garments, must not let his hair become unkempt[c] or tear his clothes. 11He must not enter a place where there is a dead body. He must not make himself unclean, even for his father or mother, 12nor leave the sanctuary of his God or desecrate it, because he has been dedicated by the anointing oil of his God. I am the LORD.

13" 'The woman he marries must be a virgin. 14He must not marry a widow, a divorced woman, or a woman defiled by prostitution, but only a virgin from his own people, 15so he will not defile his offspring among his people. I am the LORD, who makes him holy.[d]' "

16The LORD said to Moses, 17"Say to Aaron: 'For the generations to come none of your descendants who has a defect may come near to offer the food of his God. 18No man who has any defect may come near: no man who is blind or lame, disfigured or deformed; 19no man with a crippled foot or hand, 20or who is hunchbacked or dwarfed, or who has any eye defect, or who has festering or running sores or damaged testicles. 21No descendant of Aaron the priest who has any defect is to come near to present the offerings made to the LORD by fire. He has a defect; he must not come near to offer the food of his God. 22He may eat the most holy food of his God, as well as the holy food; 23yet because of his defect, he must not go near the curtain or approach the altar, and so desecrate my sanctuary. I am the LORD, who makes them holy.[e]' "

24So Moses told this to Aaron and his sons and to all the Israelites.

22 The LORD said to Moses, 2"Tell Aaron and his sons to treat with respect the sacred offerings the Israelites consecrate to me, so they will not profane my holy name. I am the LORD.

3"Say to them: 'For the generations to come, if any of your descendants is ceremonially unclean and yet comes near the sacred offerings that the Israelites consecrate to the LORD, that person must be cut off from my presence. I am the LORD.

4" 'If a descendant of Aaron has an infectious skin disease[f] or a bodily discharge, he may not eat the sacred offerings until he is cleansed. He will also be unclean if he touches something defiled by a corpse or by anyone who has an emission of semen, 5or if he touches any crawling thing that makes him unclean, or any person who makes him unclean, whatever the uncleanness may be. 6The one who touches any such thing will be unclean till evening. He must not eat any of the sacred offerings unless he has bathed himself with water. 7When the sun goes down, he will be clean, and after that he may eat the sacred offerings, for they are his food. 8He must not eat anything found dead or torn by wild animals, and so become unclean through it. I am the LORD.

9" 'The priests are to keep my requirements so that they do not become guilty and die for treating them with contempt. I am the LORD, who makes them holy.[g]

10" 'No one outside a priest's family may eat the sacred offering, nor may the guest of a priest or his hired worker eat it. 11But if a priest buys a slave with money, or if a slave is born in his household, that slave may eat his food. 12If a priest's daughter marries anyone other than a priest, she may not eat any of the sacred contributions. 13But if a priest's daughter becomes a widow or is divorced, yet has no children, and she returns to live in her father's house as in her youth, she may eat of her father's food. No unauthorized person, however, may eat any of it.

14" 'If anyone eats a sacred offering by mistake, he must make restitution to the priest for the offering and add a fifth of the value to it. 15The priests must not desecrate the sacred offerings the Israelites present to the LORD 16by allowing them to eat the sacred offerings and so bring upon them guilt requiring payment. I am the LORD, who makes them holy.' "

Unacceptable Sacrifices

17The LORD said to Moses, 18"Speak to Aaron and his sons and to all the Israelites and say to them: 'If any of you—either an Israelite or an alien living in Israel—presents a gift for a burnt offering to the LORD, either to fulfill a vow or as a freewill offering, 19you must

a4 Or *unclean as a leader among his people* b8 Or *who sanctify you*; or *who set you apart as holy* c10 Or *not uncover his head* d15 Or *who sanctifies him*; or *who sets him apart as holy* e23 Or *who sanctifies them*; or *who sets them apart as holy* f4 Traditionally *leprosy*; the Hebrew word was used for various diseases affecting the skin—not necessarily leprosy. g9 Or *who sanctifies them*; or *who sets them apart as holy*; also in verse 16

present a male without defect from the cattle, sheep or goats in order that it may be accepted on your behalf. 20Do not bring anything with a defect, because it will not be accepted on your behalf. 21When anyone brings from the herd or flock a fellowship offering[a] to the LORD to fulfill a special vow or as a freewill offering, it must be without defect or blemish to be acceptable. 22Do not offer to the LORD the blind, the injured or the maimed, or anything with warts or festering or running sores. Do not place any of these on the altar as an offering made to the LORD by fire. 23You may, however, present as a freewill offering an ox[b] or a sheep that is deformed or stunted, but it will not be accepted in fulfillment of a vow. 24You must not offer to the LORD an animal whose testicles are bruised, crushed, torn or cut. You must not do this in your own land, 25and you must not accept such animals from the hand of a foreigner and offer them as the food of your God. They will not be accepted on your behalf, because they are deformed and have defects.' "

26The LORD said to Moses, 27"When a calf, a lamb or a goat is born, it is to remain with its mother for seven days. From the eighth day on, it will be acceptable as an offering made to the LORD by fire. 28Do not slaughter a cow or a sheep and its young on the same day.

29"When you sacrifice a thank offering to the LORD, sacrifice it in such a way that it will be accepted on your behalf. 30It must be eaten that same day; leave none of it till morning. I am the LORD.

31"Keep my commands and follow them. I am the LORD. 32Do not profane my holy name. I must be acknowledged as holy by the Israelites. I am the LORD, who makes[c] you holy[d] 33and who brought you out of Egypt to be your God. I am the LORD."

23 The LORD said to Moses, 2"Speak to the Israelites and say to them: 'These are my appointed feasts, the appointed feasts of the LORD, which you are to proclaim as sacred assemblies.

The Sabbath

3" 'There are six days when you may work, but the seventh day is a Sabbath of rest, a day of sacred assembly. You are not to do any work; wherever you live, it is a Sabbath to the LORD.

The Passover and Unleavened Bread

4" 'These are the LORD's appointed feasts, the sacred assemblies you are to proclaim at their appointed times: 5The LORD's Passover begins at twilight on the fourteenth day of the first month. 6On the fifteenth day of that month the LORD's Feast of Unleavened Bread begins; for seven days you must eat bread made without yeast. 7On the first day hold a sacred assembly and do no regular work. 8For seven days present an offering made to the LORD by fire. And on the seventh day hold a sacred assembly and do no regular work.' "

Firstfruits

9The LORD said to Moses, 10"Speak to the Israelites and say to them: 'When you enter the land I am going to give you and you reap its harvest, bring to the priest a sheaf of the first grain you harvest. 11He is to wave the sheaf before the LORD so it will be accepted on your behalf; the priest is to wave it on the day after the Sabbath. 12On the day you wave the sheaf, you must sacrifice as a burnt offering to the LORD a lamb a year old without defect, 13together with its grain offering of two-tenths of an ephah[e] of fine flour mixed with oil—an offering made to the LORD by fire, a pleasing aroma—and its drink offering of a quarter of a hin[f] of wine. 14You must not eat any bread, or roasted or new grain, until the very day you bring this offering to your God. This is to be a lasting ordinance for the generations to come, wherever you live.

Feast of Weeks

15" 'From the day after the Sabbath, the day you brought the sheaf of the wave offering, count off seven full weeks. 16Count off fifty days up to the day after the seventh Sabbath, and then present an offering of new grain to the LORD. 17From wherever you live, bring two loaves made of two-tenths of an ephah of fine flour, baked with yeast, as a wave offering of firstfruits to the LORD. 18Present with this bread seven male lambs, each a year old and without defect, one young bull and two rams. They will be a burnt offering to the LORD, together with their grain offerings and drink offerings—an offering made by fire, an aroma pleasing to the LORD. 19Then sacrifice one male goat for a sin offering and two lambs, each a year old, for a fellowship offering.[a] 20The priest is to wave the two lambs before the LORD as a wave offering, together with the bread of the firstfruits. They are a sacred offering to the LORD for the priest. 21On that same day you are to proclaim a sacred assembly and do no regular work. This is to be a lasting ordinance for the generations to come, wherever you live.

22" 'When you reap the harvest of your land, do not reap to the very edges of your field or gather the gleanings of your harvest. Leave them for the poor and the alien. I am the LORD your God.' "

Feast of Trumpets

23The LORD said to Moses, 24"Say to the Israelites: 'On the first day of the seventh month you are to have a day of rest, a sacred assembly commemorated with trumpet blasts. 25Do no regular work, but present an offering made to the LORD by fire.' "

[a]21,19 Traditionally *peace offering* [b]23 The Hebrew word can include both male and female. [c]32 Or *made* [d]32 Or *who sanctifies you*; or *who sets you apart as holy* [e]13 That is, probably about 4 quarts (about 4.5 liters); also in verse 17 [f]13 That is, probably about 1 quart (about 1 liter)

Day of Atonement

26The LORD said to Moses, 27"The tenth day of this seventh month is the Day of Atonement. Hold a sacred assembly and deny yourselves,[a] and present an offering made to the LORD by fire. 28Do no work on that day, because it is the Day of Atonement, when atonement is made for you before the LORD your God. 29Anyone who does not deny himself on that day must be cut off from his people. 30I will destroy from among his people anyone who does any work on that day. 31You shall do no work at all. This is to be a lasting ordinance for the generations to come, wherever you live. 32It is a sabbath of rest for you, and you must deny yourselves. From the evening of the ninth day of the month until the following evening you are to observe your sabbath."

Feast of Tabernacles

33The LORD said to Moses, 34"Say to the Israelites: 'On the fifteenth day of the seventh month the LORD's Feast of Tabernacles begins, and it lasts for seven days. 35The first day is a sacred assembly; do no regular work. 36For seven days present offerings made to the LORD by fire, and on the eighth day hold a sacred assembly and present an offering made to the LORD by fire. It is the closing assembly; do no regular work.

37(" 'These are the LORD's appointed feasts, which you are to proclaim as sacred assemblies for bringing offerings made to the LORD by fire—the burnt offerings and grain offerings, sacrifices and drink offerings required for each day. 38These offerings are in addition to those for the LORD's Sabbaths and[b] in addition to your gifts and whatever you have vowed and all the freewill offerings you give to the LORD.)

39" 'So beginning with the fifteenth day of the seventh month, after you have gathered the crops of the land, celebrate the festival to the LORD for seven days; the first day is a day of rest, and the eighth day also is a day of rest. 40On the first day you are to take choice fruit from the trees, and palm fronds, leafy branches and poplars, and rejoice before the LORD your God for seven days. 41Celebrate this as a festival to the LORD for seven days each year. This is to be a lasting ordinance for the generations to come; celebrate it in the seventh month. 42Live in booths for seven days: All native-born Israelites are to live in booths 43so your descendants will know that I had the Israelites live in booths when I brought them out of Egypt. I am the LORD your God.' "

44So Moses announced to the Israelites the appointed feasts of the LORD.

Oil and Bread Set Before the LORD

24 The LORD said to Moses, 2"Command the Israelites to bring you clear oil of pressed olives for the light so that the lamps may be kept burning continually. 3Outside the curtain of the Testimony in the Tent of Meeting, Aaron is to tend the lamps before the LORD from evening till morning, continually. This is to be a lasting ordinance for the generations to come. 4The lamps on the pure gold lampstand before the LORD must be tended continually.

5"Take fine flour and bake twelve loaves of bread, using two-tenths of an ephah[c] for each loaf. 6Set them in two rows, six in each row, on the table of pure gold before the LORD. 7Along each row put some pure incense as a memorial portion to represent the bread and to be an offering made to the LORD by fire. 8This bread is to be set out before the LORD regularly, Sabbath after Sabbath, on behalf of the Israelites, as a lasting covenant. 9It belongs to Aaron and his sons, who are to eat it in a holy place, because it is a most holy part of their regular share of the offerings made to the LORD by fire."

A Blasphemer Stoned

10Now the son of an Israelite mother and an Egyptian father went out among the Israelites, and a fight broke out in the camp between him and an Israelite. 11The son of the Israelite woman blasphemed the Name with a curse; so they brought him to Moses. (His mother's name was Shelomith, the daughter of Dibri the Danite.) 12They put him in custody until the will of the LORD should be made clear to them.

13Then the LORD said to Moses: 14"Take the blasphemer outside the camp. All those who heard him are to lay their hands on his head, and the entire assembly is to stone him. 15Say to the Israelites: 'If anyone curses his God, he will be held responsible; 16anyone who blasphemes the name of the LORD must be put to death. The entire assembly must stone him. Whether an alien or native-born, when he blasphemes the Name, he must be put to death.

17" 'If anyone takes the life of a human being, he must be put to death. 18Anyone who takes the life of someone's animal must make restitution—life for life. 19If anyone injures his neighbor, whatever he has done must be done to him: 20fracture for fracture, eye for eye, tooth for tooth. As he has injured the other, so he is to be injured. 21Whoever kills an animal must make restitution, but whoever kills a man must be put to death. 22You are to have the same law for the alien and the native-born. I am the LORD your God.' "

23Then Moses spoke to the Israelites, and they took the blasphemer outside the camp and stoned him. The Israelites did as the LORD commanded Moses.

The Sabbath Year

25 The LORD said to Moses on Mount Sinai, 2"Speak to the Israelites and say to them: 'When you enter the land I am going to give you, the land itself must observe a sabbath

[a]27 Or *and fast*; also in verses 29 and 32 [b]38 Or *These feasts are in addition to the LORD's Sabbaths, and these offerings are* [c]5 That is, probably about 4 quarts (about 4.5 liters)

to the LORD. 3For six years sow your fields, and for six years prune your vineyards and gather their crops. 4But in the seventh year the land is to have a sabbath of rest, a sabbath to the LORD. Do not sow your fields or prune your vineyards. 5Do not reap what grows of itself or harvest the grapes of your untended vines. The land is to have a year of rest. 6Whatever the land yields during the sabbath year will be food for you—for yourself, your manservant and maidservant, and the hired worker and temporary resident who live among you, 7as well as for your livestock and the wild animals in your land. Whatever the land produces may be eaten.

The Year of Jubilee

8" 'Count off seven sabbaths of years—seven times seven years—so that the seven sabbaths of years amount to a period of forty-nine years. 9Then have the trumpet sounded everywhere on the tenth day of the seventh month; on the Day of Atonement sound the trumpet throughout your land. 10Consecrate the fiftieth year and proclaim liberty throughout the land to all its inhabitants. It shall be a jubilee for you; each one of you is to return to his family property and each to his own clan. 11The fiftieth year shall be a jubilee for you; do not sow and do not reap what grows of itself or harvest the untended vines. 12For it is a jubilee and is to be holy for you; eat only what is taken directly from the fields.

13" 'In this Year of Jubilee everyone is to return to his own property.

14" 'If you sell land to one of your countrymen or buy any from him, do not take advantage of each other. 15You are to buy from your countryman on the basis of the number of years since the Jubilee. And he is to sell to you on the basis of the number of years left for harvesting crops. 16When the years are many, you are to increase the price, and when the years are few, you are to decrease the price, because what he is really selling you is the number of crops. 17Do not take advantage of each other, but fear your God. I am the LORD your God.

18" 'Follow my decrees and be careful to obey my laws, and you will live safely in the land. 19Then the land will yield its fruit, and you will eat your fill and live there in safety. 20You may ask, "What will we eat in the seventh year if we do not plant or harvest our crops?" 21I will send you such a blessing in the sixth year that the land will yield enough for three years. 22While you plant during the eighth year, you will eat from the old crop and will continue to eat from it until the harvest of the ninth year comes in.

23" 'The land must not be sold permanently, because the land is mine and you are but aliens and my tenants. 24Throughout the country that you hold as a possession, you must provide for the redemption of the land.

25" 'If one of your countrymen becomes poor and sells some of his property, his nearest relative is to come and redeem what his countryman has sold. 26If, however, a man has no one to redeem it for him but he himself prospers and acquires sufficient means to redeem it, 27he is to determine the value for the years since he sold it and refund the balance to the man to whom he sold it; he can then go back to his own property. 28But if he does not acquire the means to repay him, what he sold will remain in the possession of the buyer until the Year of Jubilee. It will be returned in the Jubilee, and he can then go back to his property.

29" 'If a man sells a house in a walled city, he retains the right of redemption a full year after its sale. During that time he may redeem it. 30If it is not redeemed before a full year has passed, the house in the walled city shall belong permanently to the buyer and his descendants. It is not to be returned in the Jubilee. 31But houses in villages without walls around them are to be considered as open country. They can be redeemed, and they are to be returned in the Jubilee.

32" 'The Levites always have the right to redeem their houses in the Levitical towns, which they possess. 33So the property of the Levites is redeemable—that is, a house sold in any town they hold—and is to be returned in the Jubilee, because the houses in the towns of the Levites are their property among the Israelites. 34But the pastureland belonging to their towns must not be sold; it is their permanent possession.

35" 'If one of your countrymen becomes poor and is unable to support himself among you, help him as you would an alien or a temporary resident, so he can continue to live among you. 36Do not take interest of any kind[a] from him, but fear your God, so that your countryman may continue to live among you. 37You must not lend him money at interest or sell him food at a profit. 38I am the LORD your God, who brought you out of Egypt to give you the land of Canaan and to be your God.

39" 'If one of your countrymen becomes poor among you and sells himself to you, do not make him work as a slave. 40He is to be treated as a hired worker or a temporary resident among you; he is to work for you until the Year of Jubilee. 41Then he and his children are to be released, and he will go back to his own clan and to the property of his forefathers. 42Because the Israelites are my servants, whom I brought out of Egypt, they must not be sold as slaves. 43Do not rule over them ruthlessly, but fear your God.

44" 'Your male and female slaves are to come from the nations around you; from them you may buy slaves. 45You may also buy some of the temporary residents living among you and members of their clans born in your country, and they will become your property. 46You can will them to your children as inherited

[a] *36* Or *take excessive interest*; similarly in verse 37

property and can make them slaves for life, but you must not rule over your fellow Israelites ruthlessly.

[47]“ ‘If an alien or a temporary resident among you becomes rich and one of your countrymen becomes poor and sells himself to the alien living among you or to a member of the alien’s clan, [48]he retains the right of redemption after he has sold himself. One of his relatives may redeem him: [49]An uncle or a cousin or any blood relative in his clan may redeem him. Or if he prospers, he may redeem himself. [50]He and his buyer are to count the time from the year he sold himself up to the Year of Jubilee. The price for his release is to be based on the rate paid to a hired man for that number of years. [51]If many years remain, he must pay for his redemption a larger share of the price paid for him. [52]If only a few years remain until the Year of Jubilee, he is to compute that and pay for his redemption accordingly. [53]He is to be treated as a man hired from year to year; you must see to it that his owner does not rule over him ruthlessly.

[54]“ ‘Even if he is not redeemed in any of these ways, he and his children are to be released in the Year of Jubilee, [55]for the Israelites belong to me as servants. They are my servants, whom I brought out of Egypt. I am the LORD your God.

Reward for Obedience

26 “ ‘Do not make idols or set up an image or a sacred stone for yourselves, and do not place a carved stone in your land to bow down before it. I am the LORD your God.

[2]“ ‘Observe my Sabbaths and have reverence for my sanctuary. I am the LORD.

[3]“ ‘If you follow my decrees and are careful to obey my commands, [4]I will send you rain in its season, and the ground will yield its crops and the trees of the field their fruit. [5]Your threshing will continue until grape harvest and the grape harvest will continue until planting, and you will eat all the food you want and live in safety in your land.

[6]“ ‘I will grant peace in the land, and you will lie down and no one will make you afraid. I will remove savage beasts from the land, and the sword will not pass through your country. [7]You will pursue your enemies, and they will fall by the sword before you. [8]Five of you will chase a hundred, and a hundred of you will chase ten thousand, and your enemies will fall by the sword before you.

[9]“ ‘I will look on you with favor and make you fruitful and increase your numbers, and I will keep my covenant with you. [10]You will still be eating last year’s harvest when you will have to move it out to make room for the new. [11]I will put my dwelling place[a] among you, and I will not abhor you. [12]I will walk among you and be your God, and you will be my people. [13]I am the LORD your God, who brought you out of Egypt so that you would no longer be slaves to the Egyptians; I broke the bars of your yoke and enabled you to walk with heads held high.

Punishment for Disobedience

[14]“ ‘But if you will not listen to me and carry out all these commands, [15]and if you reject my decrees and abhor my laws and fail to carry out all my commands and so violate my covenant, [16]then I will do this to you: I will bring upon you sudden terror, wasting diseases and fever that will destroy your sight and drain away your life. You will plant seed in vain, because your enemies will eat it. [17]I will set my face against you so that you will be defeated by your enemies; those who hate you will rule over you, and you will flee even when no one is pursuing you.

[18]“ ‘If after all this you will not listen to me, I will punish you for your sins seven times over. [19]I will break down your stubborn pride and make the sky above you like iron and the ground beneath you like bronze. [20]Your strength will be spent in vain, because your soil will not yield its crops, nor will the trees of the land yield their fruit.

[21]“ ‘If you remain hostile toward me and refuse to listen to me, I will multiply your afflictions seven times over, as your sins deserve. [22]I will send wild animals against you, and they will rob you of your children, destroy your cattle and make you so few in number that your roads will be deserted.

[23]“ ‘If in spite of these things you do not accept my correction but continue to be hostile toward me, [24]I myself will be hostile toward you and will afflict you for your sins seven times over. [25]And I will bring the sword upon you to avenge the breaking of the covenant. When you withdraw into your cities, I will send a plague among you, and you will be given into enemy hands. [26]When I cut off your supply of bread, ten women will be able to bake your bread in one oven, and they will dole out the bread by weight. You will eat, but you will not be satisfied.

[27]“ ‘If in spite of this you still do not listen to me but continue to be hostile toward me, [28]then in my anger I will be hostile toward you, and I myself will punish you for your sins seven times over. [29]You will eat the flesh of your sons and the flesh of your daughters. [30]I will destroy your high places, cut down your incense altars and pile your dead bodies on the lifeless forms of your idols, and I will abhor you. [31]I will turn your cities into ruins and lay waste your sanctuaries, and I will take no delight in the pleasing aroma of your offerings. [32]I will lay waste the land, so that your enemies who live there will be appalled. [33]I will scatter you among the nations and will draw out my sword and pursue you. Your land will be laid waste, and your cities will lie in ruins. [34]Then the land will enjoy its sabbath years all the time that it lies desolate and you are in the

[a] *11* Or *my tabernacle*

country of your enemies; then the land will rest and enjoy its sabbaths. 35All the time that it lies desolate, the land will have the rest it did not have during the sabbaths you lived in it.

36" 'As for those of you who are left, I will make their hearts so fearful in the lands of their enemies that the sound of a windblown leaf will put them to flight. They will run as though fleeing from the sword, and they will fall, even though no one is pursuing them. 37They will stumble over one another as though fleeing from the sword, even though no one is pursuing them. So you will not be able to stand before your enemies. 38You will perish among the nations; the land of your enemies will devour you. 39Those of you who are left will waste away in the lands of their enemies because of their sins; also because of their fathers' sins they will waste away.

40" 'But if they will confess their sins and the sins of their fathers—their treachery against me and their hostility toward me, 41which made me hostile toward them so that I sent them into the land of their enemies—then when their uncircumcised hearts are humbled and they pay for their sin, 42I will remember my covenant with Jacob and my covenant with Isaac and my covenant with Abraham, and I will remember the land. 43For the land will be deserted by them and will enjoy its sabbaths while it lies desolate without them. They will pay for their sins because they rejected my laws and abhorred my decrees. 44Yet in spite of this, when they are in the land of their enemies, I will not reject them or abhor them so as to destroy them completely, breaking my covenant with them. I am the LORD their God. 45But for their sake I will remember the covenant with their ancestors whom I brought out of Egypt in the sight of the nations to be their God. I am the LORD.' "

46These are the decrees, the laws and the regulations that the LORD established on Mount Sinai between himself and the Israelites through Moses.

Redeeming What Is the LORD's

27 The LORD said to Moses, 2"Speak to the Israelites and say to them: 'If anyone makes a special vow to dedicate persons to the LORD by giving equivalent values, 3set the value of a male between the ages of twenty and sixty at fifty shekels[a] of silver, according to the sanctuary shekel[b]; 4and if it is a female, set her value at thirty shekels.[c] 5If it is a person between the ages of five and twenty, set the value of a male at twenty shekels[d] and of a female at ten shekels.[e] 6If it is a person between one month and five years, set the value of a male at five shekels[f] of silver and that of a female at three shekels[g] of silver. 7If it is a person sixty years old or more, set the value of a male at fifteen shekels[h] and of a female at ten shekels. 8If anyone making the vow is too poor to pay the specified amount, he is to present the person to the priest, who will set the value for him according to what the man making the vow can afford.

9" 'If what he vowed is an animal that is acceptable as an offering to the LORD, such an animal given to the LORD becomes holy. 10He must not exchange it or substitute a good one for a bad one, or a bad one for a good one; if he should substitute one animal for another, both it and the substitute become holy. 11If what he vowed is a ceremonially unclean animal—one that is not acceptable as an offering to the LORD—the animal must be presented to the priest, 12who will judge its quality as good or bad. Whatever value the priest then sets, that is what it will be. 13If the owner wishes to redeem the animal, he must add a fifth to its value.

14" 'If a man dedicates his house as something holy to the LORD, the priest will judge its quality as good or bad. Whatever value the priest then sets, so it will remain. 15If the man who dedicates his house redeems it, he must add a fifth to its value, and the house will again become his.

16" 'If a man dedicates to the LORD part of his family land, its value is to be set according to the amount of seed required for it—fifty shekels of silver to a homer[i] of barley seed. 17If he dedicates his field during the Year of Jubilee, the value that has been set remains. 18But if he dedicates his field after the Jubilee, the priest will determine the value according to the number of years that remain until the next Year of Jubilee, and its set value will be reduced. 19If the man who dedicates the field wishes to redeem it, he must add a fifth to its value, and the field will again become his. 20If, however, he does not redeem the field, or if he has sold it to someone else, it can never be redeemed. 21When the field is released in the Jubilee, it will become holy, like a field devoted to the LORD; it will become the property of the priests.[j]

22" 'If a man dedicates to the LORD a field he has bought, which is not part of his family land, 23the priest will determine its value up to the Year of Jubilee, and the man must pay its value on that day as something holy to the LORD. 24In the Year of Jubilee the field will revert to the person from whom he bought it, the one whose land it was. 25Every value is to be set according to the sanctuary shekel, twenty gerahs to the shekel.

26" 'No one, however, may dedicate the firstborn of an animal, since the firstborn already belongs to the LORD; whether an ox[k] or

[a]*3* That is, about 1 1/4 pounds (about 0.6 kilogram); also in verse 16 [b]*3* That is, about 2/5 ounce (about 11.5 grams); also in verse 25 [c]*4* That is, about 12 ounces (about 0.3 kilogram) [d]*5* That is, about 8 ounces (about 0.2 kilogram) [e]*5* That is, about 4 ounces (about 110 grams); also in verse 7 [f]*6* That is, about 2 ounces (about 55 grams) [g]*6* That is, about 1 1/4 ounces (about 35 grams) [h]*7* That is, about 6 ounces (about 170 grams) [i]*16* That is, probably about 6 bushels (about 220 liters) [j]*21* Or *priest*
[k]*26* The Hebrew word can include both male and female.

a sheep, it is the LORD's. 27If it is one of the unclean animals, he may buy it back at its set value, adding a fifth of the value to it. If he does not redeem it, it is to be sold at its set value.

28" 'But nothing that a man owns and devotes[a] to the LORD—whether man or animal or family land—may be sold or redeemed; everything so devoted is most holy to the LORD.

29" 'No person devoted to destruction[b] may be ransomed; he must be put to death.

30" 'A tithe of everything from the land, whether grain from the soil or fruit from the trees, belongs to the LORD; it is holy to the LORD. 31If a man redeems any of his tithe, he must add a fifth of the value to it. 32The entire tithe of the herd and flock—every tenth animal that passes under the shepherd's rod—will be holy to the LORD. 33He must not pick out the good from the bad or make any substitution. If he does make a substitution, both the animal and its substitute become holy and cannot be redeemed.' "

34These are the commands the LORD gave Moses on Mount Sinai for the Israelites.

Numbers

The Census

1 The LORD spoke to Moses in the Tent of Meeting in the Desert of Sinai on the first day of the second month of the second year after the Israelites came out of Egypt. He said: 2"Take a census of the whole Israelite community by their clans and families, listing every man by name, one by one. 3You and Aaron are to number by their divisions all the men in Israel twenty years old or more who are able to serve in the army. 4One man from each tribe, each the head of his family, is to help you. 5These are the names of the men who are to assist you:

from Reuben, Elizur son of Shedeur;
6from Simeon, Shelumiel son of Zurishaddai;
7from Judah, Nahshon son of Amminadab;
8from Issachar, Nethanel son of Zuar;
9from Zebulun, Eliab son of Helon;
10from the sons of Joseph:
from Ephraim, Elishama son of Ammihud;
from Manasseh, Gamaliel son of Pedahzur;
11from Benjamin, Abidan son of Gideoni;
12from Dan, Ahiezer son of Ammishaddai;
13from Asher, Pagiel son of Ocran;
14from Gad, Eliasaph son of Deuel;
15from Naphtali, Ahira son of Enan."

16These were the men appointed from the community, the leaders of their ancestral tribes. They were the heads of the clans of Israel.

17Moses and Aaron took these men whose names had been given, 18and they called the whole community together on the first day of the second month. The people indicated their ancestry by their clans and families, and the men twenty years old or more were listed by name, one by one, 19as the LORD commanded Moses. And so he counted them in the Desert of Sinai:

20From the descendants of Reuben the firstborn son of Israel:

All the men twenty years old or more who were able to serve in the army were listed by name, one by one, according to the records of their clans and families. 21The number from the tribe of Reuben was 46,500.

22From the descendants of Simeon:

All the men twenty years old or more who were able to serve in the army were counted and listed by name, one by one, according to the records of their clans and families. 23The number from the tribe of Simeon was 59,300.

24From the descendants of Gad:

All the men twenty years old or more who were able to serve in the army were listed by name, according to the records of their clans and families. 25The number from the tribe of Gad was 45,650.

26From the descendants of Judah:

All the men twenty years old or more who were able to serve in the army were listed by name, according to the records of their clans and families. 27The number from the tribe of Judah was 74,600.

28From the descendants of Issachar:

All the men twenty years old or more who were able to serve in the army were listed by name, according to the records of their clans and families. 29The number from the tribe of Issachar was 54,400.

[a]28 The Hebrew term refers to the irrevocable giving over of things or persons to the LORD.
[b]29 The Hebrew term refers to the irrevocable giving over of things or persons to the LORD, often by totally destroying them.

30From the descendants of Zebulun:
All the men twenty years old or more who were able to serve in the army were listed by name, according to the records of their clans and families.
31The number from the tribe of Zebulun was 57,400.

32From the sons of Joseph:
From the descendants of Ephraim:
All the men twenty years old or more who were able to serve in the army were listed by name, according to the records of their clans and families.
33The number from the tribe of Ephraim was 40,500.

34From the descendants of Manasseh:
All the men twenty years old or more who were able to serve in the army were listed by name, according to the records of their clans and families.
35The number from the tribe of Manasseh was 32,200.

36From the descendants of Benjamin:
All the men twenty years old or more who were able to serve in the army were listed by name, according to the records of their clans and families.
37The number from the tribe of Benjamin was 35,400.

38From the descendants of Dan:
All the men twenty years old or more who were able to serve in the army were listed by name, according to the records of their clans and families.
39The number from the tribe of Dan was 62,700.

40From the descendants of Asher:
All the men twenty years old or more who were able to serve in the army were listed by name, according to the records of their clans and families.
41The number from the tribe of Asher was 41,500.

42From the descendants of Naphtali:
All the men twenty years old or more who were able to serve in the army were listed by name, according to the records of their clans and families.
43The number from the tribe of Naphtali was 53,400.

44These were the men counted by Moses
and Aaron and the twelve leaders of Israel,
each one representing his family. 45All the Israelites twenty years old or more who were
able to serve in Israel's army were counted
according to their families. 46The total number
was 603,550.
47The families of the tribe of Levi, however,
were not counted along with the others. 48The
LORD had said to Moses: 49"You must not
count the tribe of Levi or include them in the
census of the other Israelites. 50Instead, appoint the Levites to be in charge of the tabernacle of the Testimony—over all its furnishings
and everything belonging to it. They are to
carry the tabernacle and all its furnishings;
they are to take care of it and encamp around
it. 51Whenever the tabernacle is to move, the
Levites are to take it down, and whenever the
tabernacle is to be set up, the Levites shall do
it. Anyone else who goes near it shall be put to
death. 52The Israelites are to set up their tents
by divisions, each man in his own camp under
his own standard. 53The Levites, however, are
to set up their tents around the tabernacle of
the Testimony so that wrath will not fall on the
Israelite community. The Levites are to be responsible for the care of the tabernacle of the
Testimony."
54The Israelites did all this just as the LORD
commanded Moses.

The Arrangement of the Tribal Camps

2 The LORD said to Moses and Aaron: 2"The
Israelites are to camp around the Tent of
Meeting some distance from it, each man under his standard with the banners of his family."

3On the east, toward the sunrise, the
divisions of the camp of Judah are to encamp under their standard. The leader of
the people of Judah is Nahshon son of
Amminadab. 4His division numbers
74,600.
5The tribe of Issachar will camp next to
them. The leader of the people of Issachar
is Nethanel son of Zuar. 6His division
numbers 54,400.
7The tribe of Zebulun will be next. The
leader of the people of Zebulun is Eliab
son of Helon. 8His division numbers
57,400.
9All the men assigned to the camp of
Judah, according to their divisions, number 186,400. They will set out first.

10On the south will be the divisions of
the camp of Reuben under their standard.
The leader of the people of Reuben is Elizur son of Shedeur. 11His division numbers 46,500.
12The tribe of Simeon will camp next
to them. The leader of the people of Simeon is Shelumiel son of Zurishaddai. 13His
division numbers 59,300.
14The tribe of Gad will be next. The
leader of the people of Gad is Eliasaph
son of Deuel.[a] 15His division numbers
45,650.
16All the men assigned to the camp
of Reuben, according to their divisions,
number 151,450. They will set out second.

17Then the Tent of Meeting and the
camp of the Levites will set out in the

[a] *14* Many manuscripts of the Masoretic Text, Samaritan Pentateuch and Vulgate (see also Num. 1:14); most manuscripts of the Masoretic Text *Reuel*

middle of the camps. They will set out in
the same order as they encamp, each in
his own place under his standard.

18On the west will be the divisions of
the camp of Ephraim under their standard.
The leader of the people of Ephraim is
Elishama son of Ammihud. 19His division
numbers 40,500.

20The tribe of Manasseh will be next to
them. The leader of the people of Manasseh is Gamaliel son of Pedahzur. 21His
division numbers 32,200.

22The tribe of Benjamin will be next.
The leader of the people of Benjamin is
Abidan son of Gideoni. 23His division
numbers 35,400.

24All the men assigned to the camp
of Ephraim, according to their divisions,
number 108,100. They will set out third.

25On the north will be the divisions of
the camp of Dan, under their standard.
The leader of the people of Dan is Ahiezer son of Ammishaddai. 26His division
numbers 62,700.

27The tribe of Asher will camp next to
them. The leader of the people of Asher is
Pagiel son of Ocran. 28His division numbers 41,500.

29The tribe of Naphtali will be next.
The leader of the people of Naphtali is
Ahira son of Enan. 30His division num-
bers 53,400.

31All the men assigned to the camp of
Dan number 157,600. They will set out
last, under their standards.

32These are the Israelites, counted according to their families. All those in the
camps, by their divisions, number
603,550. 33The Levites, however, were
not counted along with the other Israelites, as the LORD commanded Moses.

34So the Israelites did everything the LORD
commanded Moses; that is the way they encamped under their standards, and that is the
way they set out, each with his clan and family.

The Levites

3 This is the account of the family of Aaron
and Moses at the time the LORD talked
with Moses on Mount Sinai.

2The names of the sons of Aaron were Nadab the firstborn and Abihu, Eleazar and Ithamar. 3Those were the names of Aaron's sons,
the anointed priests, who were ordained to
serve as priests. 4Nadab and Abihu, however,
fell dead before the LORD when they made an
offering with unauthorized fire before him in
the Desert of Sinai. They had no sons; so only
Eleazar and Ithamar served as priests during
the lifetime of their father Aaron.

5The LORD said to Moses, 6"Bring the tribe
of Levi and present them to Aaron the priest to
assist him. 7They are to perform duties for him
and for the whole community at the Tent of
Meeting by doing the work of the tabernacle.
8They are to take care of all the furnishings of
the Tent of Meeting, fulfilling the obligations
of the Israelites by doing the work of the tabernacle. 9Give the Levites to Aaron and his sons;
they are the Israelites who are to be given
wholly to him.[a] 10Appoint Aaron and his sons
to serve as priests; anyone else who approaches the sanctuary must be put to death."

11The LORD also said to Moses, 12"I have
taken the Levites from among the Israelites in
place of the first male offspring of every Israelite woman. The Levites are mine, 13for all
the firstborn are mine. When I struck down all
the firstborn in Egypt, I set apart for myself
every firstborn in Israel, whether man or animal. They are to be mine. I am the LORD."

14The LORD said to Moses in the Desert of
Sinai, 15"Count the Levites by their families
and clans. Count every male a month old or
more." 16So Moses counted them, as he was
commanded by the word of the LORD.

17These were the names of the sons of
Levi:
Gershon, Kohath and Merari.
18These were the names of the Gershonite
clans:
Libni and Shimei.
19The Kohathite clans:
Amram, Izhar, Hebron and Uzziel.
20The Merarite clans:
Mahli and Mushi.

These were the Levite clans, according to
their families.

21To Gershon belonged the clans of the Lib-
nites and Shimeites; these were the Gershonite
clans. 22The number of all the males a month
old or more who were counted was 7,500.
23The Gershonite clans were to camp on the
west, behind the tabernacle. 24The leader of the
families of the Gershonites was Eliasaph son
of Lael. 25At the Tent of Meeting the Gershonites were responsible for the care of the tabernacle and tent, its coverings, the curtain at the
entrance to the Tent of Meeting, 26the curtains
of the courtyard, the curtain at the entrance to
the courtyard surrounding the tabernacle and
altar, and the ropes—and everything related to
their use.

27To Kohath belonged the clans of the Amramites, Izharites, Hebronites and Uzzielites;
these were the Kohathite clans. 28The number
of all the males a month old or more was
8,600.[b] The Kohathites were responsible for
the care of the sanctuary. 29The Kohathite
clans were to camp on the south side of the
tabernacle. 30The leader of the families of the
Kohathite clans was Elizaphan son of Uzziel.
31They were responsible for the care of the ark,

[a]9 Most manuscripts of the Masoretic Text; some manuscripts of the Masoretic Text, Samaritan Pentateuch and Septuagint (see also Num. 8:16) *to me* [b]28 Hebrew; some Septuagint manuscripts *8,300*

the table, the lampstand, the altars, the articles of the sanctuary used in ministering, the curtain, and everything related to their use. 32 The chief leader of the Levites was Eleazar son of Aaron, the priest. He was appointed over those who were responsible for the care of the sanctuary.

33 To Merari belonged the clans of the Mahlites and the Mushites; these were the Merarite clans. 34 The number of all the males a month old or more who were counted was 6,200. 35 The leader of the families of the Merarite clans was Zuriel son of Abihail; they were to camp on the north side of the tabernacle. 36 The Merarites were appointed to take care of the frames of the tabernacle, its crossbars, posts, bases, all its equipment, and everything related to their use, 37 as well as the posts of the surrounding courtyard with their bases, tent pegs and ropes.

38 Moses and Aaron and his sons were to camp to the east of the tabernacle, toward the sunrise, in front of the Tent of Meeting. They were responsible for the care of the sanctuary on behalf of the Israelites. Anyone else who approached the sanctuary was to be put to death.

39 The total number of Levites counted at the LORD's command by Moses and Aaron according to their clans, including every male a month old or more, was 22,000.

40 The LORD said to Moses, "Count all the firstborn Israelite males who are a month old or more and make a list of their names. 41 Take the Levites for me in place of all the firstborn of the Israelites, and the livestock of the Levites in place of all the firstborn of the livestock of the Israelites. I am the LORD."

42 So Moses counted all the firstborn of the Israelites, as the LORD commanded him. 43 The total number of firstborn males a month old or more, listed by name, was 22,273.

44 The LORD also said to Moses, 45 "Take the Levites in place of all the firstborn of Israel, and the livestock of the Levites in place of their livestock. The Levites are to be mine. I am the LORD. 46 To redeem the 273 firstborn Israelites who exceed the number of the Levites, 47 collect five shekels[a] for each one, according to the sanctuary shekel, which weighs twenty gerahs. 48 Give the money for the redemption of the additional Israelites to Aaron and his sons."

49 So Moses collected the redemption money from those who exceeded the number redeemed by the Levites. 50 From the firstborn of the Israelites he collected silver weighing 1,365 shekels,[b] according to the sanctuary shekel. 51 Moses gave the redemption money to Aaron and his sons, as he was commanded by the word of the LORD.

The Kohathites

4 The LORD said to Moses and Aaron: 2 "Take a census of the Kohathite branch of the Levites by their clans and families. 3 Count all the men from thirty to fifty years of age who come to serve in the work in the Tent of Meeting.

4 "This is the work of the Kohathites in the Tent of Meeting: the care of the most holy things. 5 When the camp is to move, Aaron and his sons are to go in and take down the shielding curtain and cover the ark of the Testimony with it. 6 Then they are to cover this with hides of sea cows,[c] spread a cloth of solid blue over that and put the poles in place.

7 "Over the table of the Presence they are to spread a blue cloth and put on it the plates, dishes and bowls, and the jars for drink offerings; the bread that is continually there is to remain on it. 8 Over these they are to spread a scarlet cloth, cover that with hides of sea cows and put its poles in place.

9 "They are to take a blue cloth and cover the lampstand that is for light, together with its lamps, its wick trimmers and trays, and all its jars for the oil used to supply it. 10 Then they are to wrap it and all its accessories in a covering of hides of sea cows and put it on a carrying frame.

11 "Over the gold altar they are to spread a blue cloth and cover that with hides of sea cows and put its poles in place.

12 "They are to take all the articles used for ministering in the sanctuary, wrap them in a blue cloth, cover that with hides of sea cows and put them on a carrying frame.

13 "They are to remove the ashes from the bronze altar and spread a purple cloth over it. 14 Then they are to place on it all the utensils used for ministering at the altar, including the firepans, meat forks, shovels and sprinkling bowls. Over it they are to spread a covering of hides of sea cows and put its poles in place.

15 "After Aaron and his sons have finished covering the holy furnishings and all the holy articles, and when the camp is ready to move, the Kohathites are to come to do the carrying. But they must not touch the holy things or they will die. The Kohathites are to carry those things that are in the Tent of Meeting.

16 "Eleazar son of Aaron, the priest, is to have charge of the oil for the light, the fragrant incense, the regular grain offering and the anointing oil. He is to be in charge of the entire tabernacle and everything in it, including its holy furnishings and articles."

17 The LORD said to Moses and Aaron, 18 "See that the Kohathite tribal clans are not cut off from the Levites. 19 So that they may live and not die when they come near the most holy things, do this for them: Aaron and his

[a] *47* That is, about 2 ounces (about 55 grams) [b] *50* That is, about 35 pounds (about 15.5 kilograms)
[c] *6* That is, dugongs; also in verses 8, 10, 11, 12, 14 and 25

sons are to go into the sanctuary and assign to each man his work and what he is to carry. 20 But the Kohathites must not go in to look at the holy things, even for a moment, or they will die."

The Gershonites

21 The LORD said to Moses, 22 "Take a census also of the Gershonites by their families and clans. 23 Count all the men from thirty to fifty years of age who come to serve in the work at the Tent of Meeting.

24 "This is the service of the Gershonite clans as they work and carry burdens: 25 They are to carry the curtains of the tabernacle, the Tent of Meeting, its covering and the outer covering of hides of sea cows, the curtains for the entrance to the Tent of Meeting, 26 the curtains of the courtyard surrounding the tabernacle and altar, the curtain for the entrance, the ropes and all the equipment used in its service. The Gershonites are to do all that needs to be done with these things. 27 All their service, whether carrying or doing other work, is to be done under the direction of Aaron and his sons. You shall assign to them as their responsibility all they are to carry. 28 This is the service of the Gershonite clans at the Tent of Meeting. Their duties are to be under the direction of Ithamar son of Aaron, the priest.

The Merarites

29 "Count the Merarites by their clans and families. 30 Count all the men from thirty to fifty years of age who come to serve in the work at the Tent of Meeting. 31 This is their duty as they perform service at the Tent of Meeting: to carry the frames of the tabernacle, its crossbars, posts and bases, 32 as well as the posts of the surrounding courtyard with their bases, tent pegs, ropes, all their equipment and everything related to their use. Assign to each man the specific things he is to carry. 33 This is the service of the Merarite clans as they work at the Tent of Meeting under the direction of Ithamar son of Aaron, the priest."

The Numbering of the Levite Clans

34 Moses, Aaron and the leaders of the community counted the Kohathites by their clans and families. 35 All the men from thirty to fifty years of age who came to serve in the work in the Tent of Meeting, 36 counted by clans, were 2,750. 37 This was the total of all those in the Kohathite clans who served in the Tent of Meeting. Moses and Aaron counted them according to the LORD's command through Moses.

38 The Gershonites were counted by their clans and families. 39 All the men from thirty to fifty years of age who came to serve in the work at the Tent of Meeting, 40 counted by their clans and families, were 2,630. 41 This was the total of those in the Gershonite clans who served at the Tent of Meeting. Moses and Aaron counted them according to the LORD's command.

42 The Merarites were counted by their clans and families. 43 All the men from thirty to fifty years of age who came to serve in the work at the Tent of Meeting, 44 counted by their clans, were 3,200. 45 This was the total of those in the Merarite clans. Moses and Aaron counted them according to the LORD's command through Moses.

46 So Moses, Aaron and the leaders of Israel counted all the Levites by their clans and families. 47 All the men from thirty to fifty years of age who came to do the work of serving and carrying the Tent of Meeting 48 numbered 8,580. 49 At the LORD's command through Moses, each was assigned his work and told what to carry.

Thus they were counted, as the LORD commanded Moses.

The Purity of the Camp

5 The LORD said to Moses, 2 "Command the Israelites to send away from the camp anyone who has an infectious skin disease[a] or a discharge of any kind, or who is ceremonially unclean because of a dead body. 3 Send away male and female alike; send them outside the camp so they will not defile their camp, where I dwell among them." 4 The Israelites did this; they sent them outside the camp. They did just as the LORD had instructed Moses.

Restitution for Wrongs

5 The LORD said to Moses, 6 "Say to the Israelites: 'When a man or woman wrongs another in any way[b] and so is unfaithful to the LORD, that person is guilty 7 and must confess the sin he has committed. He must make full restitution for his wrong, add one fifth to it and give it all to the person he has wronged. 8 But if that person has no close relative to whom restitution can be made for the wrong, the restitution belongs to the LORD and must be given to the priest, along with the ram with which atonement is made for him. 9 All the sacred contributions the Israelites bring to a priest will belong to him. 10 Each man's sacred gifts are his own, but what he gives to the priest will belong to the priest.' "

The Test for an Unfaithful Wife

11 Then the LORD said to Moses, 12 "Speak to the Israelites and say to them: 'If a man's wife goes astray and is unfaithful to him 13 by sleeping with another man, and this is hidden from her husband and her impurity is undetected (since there is no witness against her and she has not been caught in the act), 14 and if feelings of jealousy come over her husband and he suspects his wife and she is impure—or if he

[a] 2 Traditionally *leprosy*; the Hebrew word was used for various diseases affecting the skin—not necessarily leprosy. [b] 6 Or *woman commits any wrong common to mankind*

is jealous and suspects her even though she is not impure— 15 then he is to take his wife to the priest. He must also take an offering of a tenth of an ephah[a] of barley flour on her behalf. He must not pour oil on it or put incense on it, because it is a grain offering for jealousy, a reminder offering to draw attention to guilt.

16 " 'The priest shall bring her and have her stand before the LORD. 17 Then he shall take some holy water in a clay jar and put some dust from the tabernacle floor into the water. 18 After the priest has had the woman stand before the LORD, he shall loosen her hair and place in her hands the reminder offering, the grain offering for jealousy, while he himself holds the bitter water that brings a curse. 19 Then the priest shall put the woman under oath and say to her, "If no other man has slept with you and you have not gone astray and become impure while married to your husband, may this bitter water that brings a curse not harm you. 20 But if you have gone astray while married to your husband and you have defiled yourself by sleeping with a man other than your husband"— 21 here the priest is to put the woman under this curse of the oath—"may the LORD cause your people to curse and denounce you when he causes your thigh to waste away and your abdomen to swell.[b] 22 May this water that brings a curse enter your body so that your abdomen swells and your thigh wastes away.[c]"

" 'Then the woman is to say, "Amen. So be it."

23 " 'The priest is to write these curses on a scroll and then wash them off into the bitter water. 24 He shall have the woman drink the bitter water that brings a curse, and this water will enter her and cause bitter suffering. 25 The priest is to take from her hands the grain offering for jealousy, wave it before the LORD and bring it to the altar. 26 The priest is then to take a handful of the grain offering as a memorial offering and burn it on the altar; after that, he is to have the woman drink the water. 27 If she has defiled herself and been unfaithful to her husband, then when she is made to drink the water that brings a curse, it will go into her and cause bitter suffering; her abdomen will swell and her thigh waste away,[d] and she will become accursed among her people. 28 If, however, the woman has not defiled herself and is free from impurity, she will be cleared of guilt and will be able to have children.

29 " 'This, then, is the law of jealousy when a woman goes astray and defiles herself while married to her husband, 30 or when feelings of jealousy come over a man because he suspects his wife. The priest is to have her stand before the LORD and is to apply this entire law to her. 31 The husband will be innocent of any wrongdoing, but the woman will bear the consequences of her sin.' "

The Nazirite

6 The LORD said to Moses, 2 "Speak to the Israelites and say to them: 'If a man or woman wants to make a special vow, a vow of separation to the LORD as a Nazirite, 3 he must abstain from wine and other fermented drink and must not drink vinegar made from wine or from other fermented drink. He must not drink grape juice or eat grapes or raisins. 4 As long as he is a Nazirite, he must not eat anything that comes from the grapevine, not even the seeds or skins.

5 " 'During the entire period of his vow of separation no razor may be used on his head. He must be holy until the period of his separation to the LORD is over; he must let the hair of his head grow long. 6 Throughout the period of his separation to the LORD he must not go near a dead body. 7 Even if his own father or mother or brother or sister dies, he must not make himself ceremonially unclean on account of them, because the symbol of his separation to God is on his head. 8 Throughout the period of his separation he is consecrated to the LORD.

9 " 'If someone dies suddenly in his presence, thus defiling the hair he has dedicated, he must shave his head on the day of his cleansing—the seventh day. 10 Then on the eighth day he must bring two doves or two young pigeons to the priest at the entrance to the Tent of Meeting. 11 The priest is to offer one as a sin offering and the other as a burnt offering to make atonement for him because he sinned by being in the presence of the dead body. That same day he is to consecrate his head. 12 He must dedicate himself to the LORD for the period of his separation and must bring a year-old male lamb as a guilt offering. The previous days do not count, because he became defiled during his separation.

13 " 'Now this is the law for the Nazirite when the period of his separation is over. He is to be brought to the entrance to the Tent of Meeting. 14 There he is to present his offerings to the LORD: a year-old male lamb without defect for a burnt offering, a year-old ewe lamb without defect for a sin offering, a ram without defect for a fellowship offering,[e] 15 together with their grain offerings and drink offerings, and a basket of bread made without yeast—cakes made of fine flour mixed with oil, and wafers spread with oil.

16 " 'The priest is to present them before the LORD and make the sin offering and the burnt offering. 17 He is to present the basket of unleavened bread and is to sacrifice the ram as a fellowship offering to the LORD, together with its grain offering and drink offering.

18 " 'Then at the entrance to the Tent of Meeting, the Nazirite must shave off the hair that he dedicated. He is to take the hair and put it in the fire that is under the sacrifice of the fellowship offering.

[a] *15* That is, probably about 2 quarts (about 2 liters) [b] *21* Or *causes you to have a miscarrying womb and barrenness* [c] *22* Or *body and cause you to be barren and have a miscarrying womb* [d] *27* Or *suffering; she will have barrenness and a miscarrying womb* [e] *14* Traditionally *peace offering*; also in verses 17 and 18

19“ ‘After the Nazirite has shaved off the hair of his dedication, the priest is to place in his hands a boiled shoulder of the ram, and a cake and a wafer from the basket, both made without yeast. 20The priest shall then wave them before the LORD as a wave offering; they are holy and belong to the priest, together with the breast that was waved and the thigh that was presented. After that, the Nazirite may drink wine.

21“ ‘This is the law of the Nazirite who vows his offering to the LORD in accordance with his separation, in addition to whatever else he can afford. He must fulfill the vow he has made, according to the law of the Nazirite.’ ”

The Priestly Blessing

22The LORD said to Moses, 23“Tell Aaron and his sons, ‘This is how you are to bless the Israelites. Say to them:

24“ ‘ “The LORD bless you
and keep you;
25the LORD make his face shine upon you
and be gracious to you;
26the LORD turn his face toward you
and give you peace.” ’

27“So they will put my name on the Israelites, and I will bless them.”

Offerings at the Dedication of the Tabernacle

7 When Moses finished setting up the tabernacle, he anointed it and consecrated it and all its furnishings. He also anointed and consecrated the altar and all its utensils. 2Then the leaders of Israel, the heads of families who were the tribal leaders in charge of those who were counted, made offerings. 3They brought as their gifts before the LORD six covered carts and twelve oxen—an ox from each leader and a cart from every two. These they presented before the tabernacle.

4The LORD said to Moses, 5“Accept these from them, that they may be used in the work at the Tent of Meeting. Give them to the Levites as each man’s work requires.”

6So Moses took the carts and oxen and gave them to the Levites. 7He gave two carts and four oxen to the Gershonites, as their work required, 8and he gave four carts and eight oxen to the Merarites, as their work required. They were all under the direction of Ithamar son of Aaron, the priest. 9But Moses did not give any to the Kohathites, because they were to carry on their shoulders the holy things, for which they were responsible.

10When the altar was anointed, the leaders brought their offerings for its dedication and presented them before the altar. 11For the LORD had said to Moses, “Each day one leader is to bring his offering for the dedication of the altar.”

12The one who brought his offering on the first day was Nahshon son of Amminadab of the tribe of Judah.

13His offering was one silver plate weighing a hundred and thirty shekels,[a] and one silver sprinkling bowl weighing seventy shekels,[b] both according to the sanctuary shekel, each filled with fine flour mixed with oil as a grain offering; 14one gold dish weighing ten shekels,[c] filled with incense; 15one young bull, one ram and one male lamb a year old, for a burnt offering; 16one male goat for a sin offering; 17and two oxen, five rams, five male goats and five male lambs a year old, to be sacrificed as a fellowship offering.[d] This was the offering of Nahshon son of Amminadab.

18On the second day Nethanel son of Zuar, the leader of Issachar, brought his offering.

19The offering he brought was one silver plate weighing a hundred and thirty shekels, and one silver sprinkling bowl weighing seventy shekels, both according to the sanctuary shekel, each filled with fine flour mixed with oil as a grain offering; 20one gold dish weighing ten shekels, filled with incense; 21one young bull, one ram and one male lamb a year old, for a burnt offering; 22one male goat for a sin offering; 23and two oxen, five rams, five male goats and five male lambs a year old, to be sacrificed as a fellowship offering. This was the offering of Nethanel son of Zuar.

24On the third day, Eliab son of Helon, the leader of the people of Zebulun, brought his offering.

25His offering was one silver plate weighing a hundred and thirty shekels, and one silver sprinkling bowl weighing seventy shekels, both according to the sanctuary shekel, each filled with fine flour mixed with oil as a grain offering; 26one gold dish weighing ten shekels, filled with incense; 27one young bull, one ram and one male lamb a year old, for a burnt offering; 28one male goat for a sin offering; 29and two oxen, five rams, five male goats and five male lambs a year old, to be sacrificed as a fellowship offering. This was the offering of Eliab son of Helon.

30On the fourth day Elizur son of Shedeur, the leader of the people of Reuben, brought his offering.

31His offering was one silver plate weighing a hundred and thirty shekels, and one silver sprinkling bowl weighing seventy shekels, both according to the sanctuary shekel, each filled with fine flour mixed with oil as a grain offering; 32one gold dish weighing ten shekels, filled with in-

[a] *13* That is, about 3 1/4 pounds (about 1.5 kilograms); also elsewhere in this chapter [b] *13* That is, about 1 3/4 pounds (about 0.8 kilogram); also elsewhere in this chapter [c] *14* That is, about 4 ounces (about 110 grams); also elsewhere in this chapter [d] *17* Traditionally *peace offering*; also elsewhere in this chapter

cense; 33one young bull, one ram and one
male lamb a year old, for a burnt offering;
34one male goat for a sin offering; 35and
two oxen, five rams, five male goats and
five male lambs a year old, to be sacrificed as a fellowship offering. This was
the offering of Elizur son of Shedeur.

36On the fifth day Shelumiel son of Zurishaddai, the leader of the people of Simeon,
brought his offering.

37His offering was one silver plate weighing a hundred and thirty shekels, and one
silver sprinkling bowl weighing seventy
shekels, both according to the sanctuary
shekel, each filled with fine flour mixed
with oil as a grain offering; 38one gold
dish weighing ten shekels, filled with incense; 39one young bull, one ram and one
male lamb a year old, for a burnt offering;
40one male goat for a sin offering; 41and
two oxen, five rams, five male goats and
five male lambs a year old, to be sacrificed as a fellowship offering. This was
the offering of Shelumiel son of Zurishaddai.

42On the sixth day Eliasaph son of Deuel, the
leader of the people of Gad, brought his offering.

43His offering was one silver plate weighing a hundred and thirty shekels, and one
silver sprinkling bowl weighing seventy
shekels, both according to the sanctuary
shekel, each filled with fine flour mixed
with oil as a grain offering; 44one gold
dish weighing ten shekels, filled with incense; 45one young bull, one ram and one
male lamb a year old, for a burnt offering;
46one male goat for a sin offering; 47and
two oxen, five rams, five male goats and
five male lambs a year old, to be sacrificed as a fellowship offering. This was
the offering of Eliasaph son of Deuel.

48On the seventh day Elishama son of Ammihud, the leader of the people of Ephraim,
brought his offering.

49His offering was one silver plate weighing a hundred and thirty shekels, and one
silver sprinkling bowl weighing seventy
shekels, both according to the sanctuary
shekel, each filled with fine flour mixed
with oil as a grain offering; 50one gold
dish weighing ten shekels, filled with incense; 51one young bull, one ram and one
male lamb a year old, for a burnt offering;
52one male goat for a sin offering; 53and
two oxen, five rams, five male goats and
five male lambs a year old, to be sacrificed as a fellowship offering. This was
the offering of Elishama son of Ammihud.

54On the eighth day Gamaliel son of Pedahzur,
the leader of the people of Manasseh, brought
his offering.

55His offering was one silver plate weighing a hundred and thirty shekels, and one
silver sprinkling bowl weighing seventy
shekels, both according to the sanctuary
shekel, each filled with fine flour mixed
with oil as a grain offering; 56one gold
dish weighing ten shekels, filled with incense; 57one young bull, one ram and one
male lamb a year old, for a burnt offering;
58one male goat for a sin offering; 59and
two oxen, five rams, five male goats and
five male lambs a year old, to be sacrificed as a fellowship offering. This was
the offering of Gamaliel son of Pedahzur.

60On the ninth day Abidan son of Gideoni, the
leader of the people of Benjamin, brought his
offering.

61His offering was one silver plate weighing a hundred and thirty shekels, and one
silver sprinkling bowl weighing seventy
shekels, both according to the sanctuary
shekel, each filled with fine flour mixed
with oil as a grain offering; 62one gold
dish weighing ten shekels, filled with incense; 63one young bull, one ram and one
male lamb a year old, for a burnt offering;
64one male goat for a sin offering; 65and
two oxen, five rams, five male goats and
five male lambs a year old, to be sacrificed as a fellowship offering. This was
the offering of Abidan son of Gideoni.

66On the tenth day Ahiezer son of Ammishaddai, the leader of the people of Dan, brought
his offering.

67His offering was one silver plate weighing a hundred and thirty shekels, and one
silver sprinkling bowl weighing seventy
shekels, both according to the sanctuary
shekel, each filled with fine flour mixed
with oil as a grain offering; 68one gold
dish weighing ten shekels, filled with incense; 69one young bull, one ram and one
male lamb a year old, for a burnt offering;
70one male goat for a sin offering; 71and
two oxen, five rams, five male goats and
five male lambs a year old, to be sacrificed as a fellowship offering. This was
the offering of Ahiezer son of Ammishaddai.

72On the eleventh day Pagiel son of Ocran, the
leader of the people of Asher, brought his offering.

73His offering was one silver plate weighing a hundred and thirty shekels, and one
silver sprinkling bowl weighing seventy
shekels, both according to the sanctuary
shekel, each filled with fine flour mixed
with oil as a grain offering; 74one gold
dish weighing ten shekels, filled with incense; 75one young bull, one ram and one
male lamb a year old, for a burnt offering;
76one male goat for a sin offering; 77and
two oxen, five rams, five male goats and
five male lambs a year old, to be sacrificed as a fellowship offering. This was
the offering of Pagiel son of Ocran.

78On the twelfth day Ahira son of Enan, the

leader of the people of Naphtali, brought his offering.

79His offering was one silver plate weighing a hundred and thirty shekels, and one silver sprinkling bowl weighing seventy shekels, both according to the sanctuary shekel, each filled with fine flour mixed with oil as a grain offering; 80one gold dish weighing ten shekels, filled with incense; 81one young bull, one ram and one male lamb a year old, for a burnt offering; 82one male goat for a sin offering; 83and two oxen, five rams, five male goats and five male lambs a year old, to be sacrificed as a fellowship offering. This was the offering of Ahira son of Enan.

84These were the offerings of the Israelite leaders for the dedication of the altar when it was anointed: twelve silver plates, twelve silver sprinkling bowls and twelve gold dishes. 85Each silver plate weighed a hundred and thirty shekels, and each sprinkling bowl seventy shekels. Altogether, the silver dishes weighed two thousand four hundred shekels,[a] according to the sanctuary shekel. 86The twelve gold dishes filled with incense weighed ten shekels each, according to the sanctuary shekel. Altogether, the gold dishes weighed a hundred and twenty shekels.[b] 87The total number of animals for the burnt offering came to twelve young bulls, twelve rams and twelve male lambs a year old, together with their grain offering. Twelve male goats were used for the sin offering. 88The total number of animals for the sacrifice of the fellowship offering came to twenty-four oxen, sixty rams, sixty male goats and sixty male lambs a year old. These were the offerings for the dedication of the altar after it was anointed.

89When Moses entered the Tent of Meeting to speak with the LORD, he heard the voice speaking to him from between the two cherubim above the atonement cover on the ark of the Testimony. And he spoke with him.

Setting Up the Lamps

8 The LORD said to Moses, 2"Speak to Aaron and say to him, 'When you set up the seven lamps, they are to light the area in front of the lampstand.' "

3Aaron did so; he set up the lamps so that they faced forward on the lampstand, just as the LORD commanded Moses. 4This is how the lampstand was made: It was made of hammered gold—from its base to its blossoms. The lampstand was made exactly like the pattern the LORD had shown Moses.

The Setting Apart of the Levites

5The LORD said to Moses: 6"Take the Levites from among the other Israelites and make them ceremonially clean. 7To purify them, do this: Sprinkle the water of cleansing on them; then have them shave their whole bodies and wash their clothes, and so purify themselves. 8Have them take a young bull with its grain offering of fine flour mixed with oil; then you are to take a second young bull for a sin offering. 9Bring the Levites to the front of the Tent of Meeting and assemble the whole Israelite community. 10You are to bring the Levites before the LORD, and the Israelites are to lay their hands on them. 11Aaron is to present the Levites before the LORD as a wave offering from the Israelites, so that they may be ready to do the work of the LORD.

12"After the Levites lay their hands on the heads of the bulls, use the one for a sin offering to the LORD and the other for a burnt offering, to make atonement for the Levites. 13Have the Levites stand in front of Aaron and his sons and then present them as a wave offering to the LORD. 14In this way you are to set the Levites apart from the other Israelites, and the Levites will be mine.

15"After you have purified the Levites and presented them as a wave offering, they are to come to do their work at the Tent of Meeting. 16They are the Israelites who are to be given wholly to me. I have taken them as my own in place of the firstborn, the first male offspring from every Israelite woman. 17Every firstborn male in Israel, whether man or animal, is mine. When I struck down all the firstborn in Egypt, I set them apart for myself. 18And I have taken the Levites in place of all the firstborn sons in Israel. 19Of all the Israelites, I have given the Levites as gifts to Aaron and his sons to do the work at the Tent of Meeting on behalf of the Israelites and to make atonement for them so that no plague will strike the Israelites when they go near the sanctuary."

20Moses, Aaron and the whole Israelite community did with the Levites just as the LORD commanded Moses. 21The Levites purified themselves and washed their clothes. Then Aaron presented them as a wave offering before the LORD and made atonement for them to purify them. 22After that, the Levites came to do their work at the Tent of Meeting under the supervision of Aaron and his sons. They did with the Levites just as the LORD commanded Moses.

23The LORD said to Moses, 24"This applies to the Levites: Men twenty-five years old or more shall come to take part in the work at the Tent of Meeting, 25but at the age of fifty, they must retire from their regular service and work no longer. 26They may assist their brothers in performing their duties at the Tent of Meeting, but they themselves must not do the work. This, then, is how you are to assign the responsibilities of the Levites."

The Passover

9 The LORD spoke to Moses in the Desert of Sinai in the first month of the second year after they came out of Egypt. He said, 2"Have the Israelites celebrate the Passover at the appointed time. 3Celebrate it at the appointed

[a]85 That is, about 60 pounds (about 28 kilograms) [b]86 That is, about 3 pounds (about 1.4 kilograms)

time, at twilight on the fourteenth day of this month, in accordance with all its rules and regulations."

4So Moses told the Israelites to celebrate the Passover, 5and they did so in the Desert of Sinai at twilight on the fourteenth day of the first month. The Israelites did everything just as the LORD commanded Moses.

6But some of them could not celebrate the Passover on that day because they were ceremonially unclean on account of a dead body. So they came to Moses and Aaron that same day 7and said to Moses, "We have become unclean because of a dead body, but why should we be kept from presenting the LORD's offering with the other Israelites at the appointed time?"

8Moses answered them, "Wait until I find out what the LORD commands concerning you."

9Then the LORD said to Moses, 10"Tell the Israelites: 'When any of you or your descendants are unclean because of a dead body or are away on a journey, they may still celebrate the LORD's Passover. 11They are to celebrate it on the fourteenth day of the second month at twilight. They are to eat the lamb, together with unleavened bread and bitter herbs. 12They must not leave any of it till morning or break any of its bones. When they celebrate the Passover, they must follow all the regulations. 13But if a man who is ceremonially clean and not on a journey fails to celebrate the Passover, that person must be cut off from his people because he did not present the LORD's offering at the appointed time. That man will bear the consequences of his sin.

14" 'An alien living among you who wants to celebrate the LORD's Passover must do so in accordance with its rules and regulations. You must have the same regulations for the alien and the native-born.' "

The Cloud Above the Tabernacle

15On the day the tabernacle, the Tent of the Testimony, was set up, the cloud covered it. From evening till morning the cloud above the tabernacle looked like fire. 16That is how it continued to be; the cloud covered it, and at night it looked like fire. 17Whenever the cloud lifted from above the Tent, the Israelites set out; wherever the cloud settled, the Israelites encamped. 18At the LORD's command the Israelites set out, and at his command they encamped. As long as the cloud stayed over the tabernacle, they remained in camp. 19When the cloud remained over the tabernacle a long time, the Israelites obeyed the LORD's order and did not set out. 20Sometimes the cloud was over the tabernacle only a few days; at the LORD's command they would encamp, and then at his command they would set out. 21Sometimes the cloud stayed only from evening till morning, and when it lifted in the morning, they set out. Whether by day or by night, whenever the cloud lifted, they set out. 22Whether the cloud stayed over the tabernacle for two days or a month or a year, the Israelites would remain in camp and not set out; but when it lifted, they would set out. 23At the LORD's command they encamped, and at the LORD's command they set out. They obeyed the LORD's order, in accordance with his command through Moses.

The Silver Trumpets

10 The LORD said to Moses: 2"Make two trumpets of hammered silver, and use them for calling the community together and for having the camps set out. 3When both are sounded, the whole community is to assemble before you at the entrance to the Tent of Meeting. 4If only one is sounded, the leaders—the heads of the clans of Israel—are to assemble before you. 5When a trumpet blast is sounded, the tribes camping on the east are to set out. 6At the sounding of a second blast, the camps on the south are to set out. The blast will be the signal for setting out. 7To gather the assembly, blow the trumpets, but not with the same signal.

8"The sons of Aaron, the priests, are to blow the trumpets. This is to be a lasting ordinance for you and the generations to come. 9When you go into battle in your own land against an enemy who is oppressing you, sound a blast on the trumpets. Then you will be remembered by the LORD your God and rescued from your enemies. 10Also at your times of rejoicing—your appointed feasts and New Moon festivals—you are to sound the trumpets over your burnt offerings and fellowship offerings,[a] and they will be a memorial for you before your God. I am the LORD your God."

The Israelites Leave Sinai

11On the twentieth day of the second month of the second year, the cloud lifted from above the tabernacle of the Testimony. 12Then the Israelites set out from the Desert of Sinai and traveled from place to place until the cloud came to rest in the Desert of Paran. 13They set out, this first time, at the LORD's command through Moses.

14The divisions of the camp of Judah went first, under their standard. Nahshon son of Amminadab was in command. 15Nethanel son of Zuar was over the division of the tribe of Issachar, 16and Eliab son of Helon was over the division of the tribe of Zebulun. 17Then the tabernacle was taken down, and the Gershonites and Merarites, who carried it, set out.

18The divisions of the camp of Reuben went next, under their standard. Elizur son of Shedeur was in command. 19Shelumiel son of Zurishaddai was over the division of the tribe of Simeon, 20and Eliasaph son of Deuel was over the division of the tribe of Gad. 21Then the Kohathites set out, carrying the holy things.

[a] *10* Traditionally *peace offerings*

The tabernacle was to be set up before they
arrived.
22The divisions of the camp of Ephraim
went next, under their standard. Elishama son
of Ammihud was in command. 23Gamaliel son
of Pedahzur was over the division of the tribe
of Manasseh, 24and Abidan son of Gideoni
was over the division of the tribe of Benjamin.
25Finally, as the rear guard for all the units,
the divisions of the camp of Dan set out, under
their standard. Ahiezer son of Ammishaddai
was in command. 26Pagiel son of Ocran was
over the division of the tribe of Asher, 27and
Ahira son of Enan was over the division of
the tribe of Naphtali. 28This was the order of
march for the Israelite divisions as they set out.
29Now Moses said to Hobab son of Reuel
the Midianite, Moses' father-in-law, "We are
setting out for the place about which the LORD
said, 'I will give it to you.' Come with us and
we will treat you well, for the LORD has promised good things to Israel."
30He answered, "No, I will not go; I am
going back to my own land and my own people."
31But Moses said, "Please do not leave us.
You know where we should camp in the
desert, and you can be our eyes. 32If you come
with us, we will share with you whatever good
things the LORD gives us."
33So they set out from the mountain of the
LORD and traveled for three days. The ark of
the covenant of the LORD went before them
during those three days to find them a place to
rest. 34The cloud of the LORD was over them
by day when they set out from the camp.
35Whenever the ark set out, Moses said,

"Rise up, O LORD!
May your enemies be scattered;
may your foes flee before you."

36Whenever it came to rest, he said,

"Return, O LORD,
to the countless thousands of Israel."

Fire From the LORD

11 Now the people complained about their
hardships in the hearing of the LORD,
and when he heard them his anger was
aroused. Then fire from the LORD burned
among them and consumed some of the outskirts of the camp. 2When the people cried out
to Moses, he prayed to the LORD and the fire
died down. 3So that place was called Taberah,[a] because fire from the LORD had burned
among them.

Quail From the LORD

4The rabble with them began to crave other
food, and again the Israelites started wailing
and said, "If only we had meat to eat! 5We
remember the fish we ate in Egypt at no cost—
also the cucumbers, melons, leeks, onions and
garlic. 6But now we have lost our appetite; we
never see anything but this manna!"
7The manna was like coriander seed and
looked like resin. 8The people went around
gathering it, and then ground it in a handmill or
crushed it in a mortar. They cooked it in a pot
or made it into cakes. And it tasted like something made with olive oil. 9When the dew settled on the camp at night, the manna also came
down.
10Moses heard the people of every family
wailing, each at the entrance to his tent. The
LORD became exceedingly angry, and Moses
was troubled. 11He asked the LORD, "Why
have you brought this trouble on your servant?
What have I done to displease you that you put
the burden of all these people on me? 12Did I
conceive all these people? Did I give them
birth? Why do you tell me to carry them in my
arms, as a nurse carries an infant, to the land
you promised on oath to their forefathers?
13Where can I get meat for all these people?
They keep wailing to me, 'Give us meat to
eat!' 14I cannot carry all these people by myself; the burden is too heavy for me. 15If this is
how you are going to treat me, put me to death
right now—if I have found favor in your
eyes—and do not let me face my own ruin."
16The LORD said to Moses: "Bring me seventy of Israel's elders who are known to you as
leaders and officials among the people. Have
them come to the Tent of Meeting, that they
may stand there with you. 17I will come down
and speak with you there, and I will take of the
Spirit that is on you and put the Spirit on them.
They will help you carry the burden of the
people so that you will not have to carry it
alone.
18"Tell the people: 'Consecrate yourselves
in preparation for tomorrow, when you will eat
meat. The LORD heard you when you wailed,
"If only we had meat to eat! We were better off
in Egypt!" Now the LORD will give you meat,
and you will eat it. 19You will not eat it for just
one day, or two days, or five, ten or twenty
days, 20but for a whole month—until it comes
out of your nostrils and you loathe it—because
you have rejected the LORD, who is among
you, and have wailed before him, saying,
"Why did we ever leave Egypt?" ' "
21But Moses said, "Here I am among six
hundred thousand men on foot, and you say, 'I
will give them meat to eat for a whole month!'
22Would they have enough if flocks and herds
were slaughtered for them? Would they have
enough if all the fish in the sea were caught for
them?"
23The LORD answered Moses, "Is the
LORD's arm too short? You will now see
whether or not what I say will come true for
you."
24So Moses went out and told the people
what the LORD had said. He brought together
seventy of their elders and had them stand
around the Tent. 25Then the LORD came down
in the cloud and spoke with him, and he took
of the Spirit that was on him and put the Spirit

[a]3 *Taberah* means *burning.*

on the seventy elders. When the Spirit rested
on them, they prophesied, but they did not do
so again.[a]

26However, two men, whose names were Eldad and Medad, had remained in the camp.
They were listed among the elders, but did not
go out to the Tent. Yet the Spirit also rested on
them, and they prophesied in the camp. 27A
young man ran and told Moses, "Eldad and
Medad are prophesying in the camp."

28Joshua son of Nun, who had been Moses'
aide since youth, spoke up and said, "Moses,
my lord, stop them!"

29But Moses replied, "Are you jealous for
my sake? I wish that all the LORD's people
were prophets and that the LORD would put his
Spirit on them!" 30Then Moses and the elders
of Israel returned to the camp.

31Now a wind went out from the LORD and
drove quail in from the sea. It brought them[b]
down all around the camp to about three feet[c]
above the ground, as far as a day's walk in any
direction. 32All that day and night and all the
next day the people went out and gathered
quail. No one gathered less than ten homers.[d]
Then they spread them out all around the
camp. 33But while the meat was still between
their teeth and before it could be consumed,
the anger of the LORD burned against the people, and he struck them with a severe plague.
34Therefore the place was named Kibroth Hattaavah,[e] because there they buried the people
who had craved other food.

35From Kibroth Hattaavah the people traveled to Hazeroth and stayed there.

Miriam and Aaron Oppose Moses

12 Miriam and Aaron began to talk against
Moses because of his Cushite wife, for
he had married a Cushite. 2"Has the LORD spoken only through Moses?" they asked. "Hasn't
he also spoken through us?" And the LORD
heard this.

3(Now Moses was a very humble man, more
humble than anyone else on the face of the
earth.)

4At once the LORD said to Moses, Aaron and
Miriam, "Come out to the Tent of Meeting, all
three of you." So the three of them came out.
5Then the LORD came down in a pillar of
cloud; he stood at the entrance to the Tent and
summoned Aaron and Miriam. When both of
them stepped forward, 6he said, "Listen to my
words:

"When a prophet of the LORD is among
you,
I reveal myself to him in visions,
I speak to him in dreams.
7But this is not true of my servant Moses;
he is faithful in all my house.
8With him I speak face to face,
clearly and not in riddles;
he sees the form of the LORD.
Why then were you not afraid
to speak against my servant Moses?"

9The anger of the LORD burned against
them, and he left them.

10When the cloud lifted from above the
Tent, there stood Miriam—leprous,[f] like
snow. Aaron turned toward her and saw that
she had leprosy; 11and he said to Moses,
"Please, my lord, do not hold against us the sin
we have so foolishly committed. 12Do not let
her be like a stillborn infant coming from its
mother's womb with its flesh half eaten away."

13So Moses cried out to the LORD, "O God,
please heal her!"

14The LORD replied to Moses, "If her father
had spit in her face, would she not have been
in disgrace for seven days? Confine her outside the camp for seven days; after that she can
be brought back." 15So Miriam was confined
outside the camp for seven days, and the people did not move on till she was brought back.

16After that, the people left Hazeroth and
encamped in the Desert of Paran.

Exploring Canaan

13 The LORD said to Moses, 2"Send some
men to explore the land of Canaan,
which I am giving to the Israelites. From each
ancestral tribe send one of its leaders."

3So at the LORD's command Moses sent
them out from the Desert of Paran. All of them
were leaders of the Israelites. 4These are their
names:

from the tribe of Reuben, Shammua son
of Zaccur;
5from the tribe of Simeon, Shaphat son of
Hori;
6from the tribe of Judah, Caleb son of
Jephunneh;
7from the tribe of Issachar, Igal son of
Joseph;
8from the tribe of Ephraim, Hoshea son
of Nun;
9from the tribe of Benjamin, Palti son of
Raphu;
10from the tribe of Zebulun, Gaddiel son
of Sodi;
11from the tribe of Manasseh (a tribe of
Joseph), Gaddi son of Susi;
12from the tribe of Dan, Ammiel son of
Gemalli;
13from the tribe of Asher, Sethur son of
Michael;
14from the tribe of Naphtali, Nahbi son
of Vophsi;
15from the tribe of Gad, Geuel son of
Maki.

16These are the names of the men Moses sent
to explore the land. (Moses gave Hoshea son
of Nun the name Joshua.)

17When Moses sent them to explore Canaan,
he said, "Go up through the Negev and on into

[a]25 Or *prophesied and continued to do so* [b]31 Or *They flew* [c]31 Hebrew *two cubits* (about 1 meter)
[d]32 That is, probably about 60 bushels (about 2.2 kiloliters) [e]34 *Kibroth Hattaavah* means *graves of
craving.* [f]10 The Hebrew word was used for various diseases affecting the skin—not necessarily leprosy.

the hill country. 18See what the land is like and whether the people who live there are strong or weak, few or many. 19What kind of land do they live in? Is it good or bad? What kind of towns do they live in? Are they unwalled or fortified? 20How is the soil? Is it fertile or poor? Are there trees on it or not? Do your best to bring back some of the fruit of the land." (It was the season for the first ripe grapes.)

21So they went up and explored the land from the Desert of Zin as far as Rehob, toward Lebo[a] Hamath. 22They went up through the Negev and came to Hebron, where Ahiman, Sheshai and Talmai, the descendants of Anak, lived. (Hebron had been built seven years before Zoan in Egypt.) 23When they reached the Valley of Eshcol,[b] they cut off a branch bearing a single cluster of grapes. Two of them carried it on a pole between them, along with some pomegranates and figs. 24That place was called the Valley of Eshcol because of the cluster of grapes the Israelites cut off there. 25At the end of forty days they returned from exploring the land.

Report on the Exploration

26They came back to Moses and Aaron and the whole Israelite community at Kadesh in the Desert of Paran. There they reported to them and to the whole assembly and showed them the fruit of the land. 27They gave Moses this account: "We went into the land to which you sent us, and it does flow with milk and honey! Here is its fruit. 28But the people who live there are powerful, and the cities are fortified and very large. We even saw descendants of Anak there. 29The Amalekites live in the Negev; the Hittites, Jebusites and Amorites live in the hill country; and the Canaanites live near the sea and along the Jordan."

30Then Caleb silenced the people before Moses and said, "We should go up and take possession of the land, for we can certainly do it."

31But the men who had gone up with him said, "We can't attack those people; they are stronger than we are." 32And they spread among the Israelites a bad report about the land they had explored. They said, "The land we explored devours those living in it. All the people we saw there are of great size. 33We saw the Nephilim there (the descendants of Anak come from the Nephilim). We seemed like grasshoppers in our own eyes, and we looked the same to them."

The People Rebel

14 That night all the people of the community raised their voices and wept aloud. 2All the Israelites grumbled against Moses and Aaron, and the whole assembly said to them, "If only we had died in Egypt! Or in this desert! 3Why is the LORD bringing us to this land only to let us fall by the sword? Our wives and children will be taken as plunder. Wouldn't it be better for us to go back to Egypt?" 4And they said to each other, "We should choose a leader and go back to Egypt."

5Then Moses and Aaron fell facedown in front of the whole Israelite assembly gathered there. 6Joshua son of Nun and Caleb son of Jephunneh, who were among those who had explored the land, tore their clothes 7and said to the entire Israelite assembly, "The land we passed through and explored is exceedingly good. 8If the LORD is pleased with us, he will lead us into that land, a land flowing with milk and honey, and will give it to us. 9Only do not rebel against the LORD. And do not be afraid of the people of the land, because we will swallow them up. Their protection is gone, but the LORD is with us. Do not be afraid of them."

10But the whole assembly talked about stoning them. Then the glory of the LORD appeared at the Tent of Meeting to all the Israelites. 11The LORD said to Moses, "How long will these people treat me with contempt? How long will they refuse to believe in me, in spite of all the miraculous signs I have performed among them? 12I will strike them down with a plague and destroy them, but I will make you into a nation greater and stronger than they."

13Moses said to the LORD, "Then the Egyptians will hear about it! By your power you brought these people up from among them. 14And they will tell the inhabitants of this land about it. They have already heard that you, O LORD, are with these people and that you, O LORD, have been seen face to face, that your cloud stays over them, and that you go before them in a pillar of cloud by day and a pillar of fire by night. 15If you put these people to death all at one time, the nations who have heard this report about you will say, 16'The LORD was not able to bring these people into the land he promised them on oath; so he slaughtered them in the desert.'

17"Now may the Lord's strength be displayed, just as you have declared: 18'The LORD is slow to anger, abounding in love and forgiving sin and rebellion. Yet he does not leave the guilty unpunished; he punishes the children for the sin of the fathers to the third and fourth generation.' 19In accordance with your great love, forgive the sin of these people, just as you have pardoned them from the time they left Egypt until now."

20The LORD replied, "I have forgiven them, as you asked. 21Nevertheless, as surely as I live and as surely as the glory of the LORD fills the whole earth, 22not one of the men who saw my glory and the miraculous signs I performed in Egypt and in the desert but who disobeyed me and tested me ten times— 23not one of them will ever see the land I promised on oath to their forefathers. No one who has treated me with contempt will ever see it. 24But because my servant Caleb has a different spirit and follows me wholeheartedly, I will bring him into the land he went to, and his descendants will

[a]21 Or *toward the entrance to* [b]23 *Eshcol* means *cluster*; also in verse 24.

inherit it. 25Since the Amalekites and Canaanites are living in the valleys, turn back tomorrow and set out toward the desert along the route to the Red Sea.[a]"

26The LORD said to Moses and Aaron: 27"How long will this wicked community grumble against me? I have heard the complaints of these grumbling Israelites. 28So tell them, 'As surely as I live, declares the LORD, I will do to you the very things I heard you say: 29In this desert your bodies will fall—every one of you twenty years old or more who was counted in the census and who has grumbled against me. 30Not one of you will enter the land I swore with uplifted hand to make your home, except Caleb son of Jephunneh and Joshua son of Nun. 31As for your children that you said would be taken as plunder, I will bring them in to enjoy the land you have rejected. 32But you—your bodies will fall in this desert. 33Your children will be shepherds here for forty years, suffering for your unfaithfulness, until the last of your bodies lies in the desert. 34For forty years—one year for each of the forty days you explored the land—you will suffer for your sins and know what it is like to have me against you.' 35I, the LORD, have spoken, and I will surely do these things to this whole wicked community, which has banded together against me. They will meet their end in this desert; here they will die."

36So the men Moses had sent to explore the land, who returned and made the whole community grumble against him by spreading a bad report about it— 37these men responsible for spreading the bad report about the land were struck down and died of a plague before the LORD. 38Of the men who went to explore the land, only Joshua son of Nun and Caleb son of Jephunneh survived.

39When Moses reported this to all the Israelites, they mourned bitterly. 40Early the next morning they went up toward the high hill country. "We have sinned," they said. "We will go up to the place the LORD promised."

41But Moses said, "Why are you disobeying the LORD's command? This will not succeed! 42Do not go up, because the LORD is not with you. You will be defeated by your enemies, 43for the Amalekites and Canaanites will face you there. Because you have turned away from the LORD, he will not be with you and you will fall by the sword."

44Nevertheless, in their presumption they went up toward the high hill country, though neither Moses nor the ark of the LORD's covenant moved from the camp. 45Then the Amalekites and Canaanites who lived in that hill country came down and attacked them and beat them down all the way to Hormah.

Supplementary Offerings

15 The LORD said to Moses, 2"Speak to the Israelites and say to them: 'After you enter the land I am giving you as a home 3and you present to the LORD offerings made by fire, from the herd or the flock, as an aroma pleasing to the LORD—whether burnt offerings or sacrifices, for special vows or freewill offerings or festival offerings— 4then the one who brings his offering shall present to the LORD a grain offering of a tenth of an ephah[b] of fine flour mixed with a quarter of a hin[c] of oil. 5With each lamb for the burnt offering or the sacrifice, prepare a quarter of a hin of wine as a drink offering.

6" 'With a ram prepare a grain offering of two-tenths of an ephah[d] of fine flour mixed with a third of a hin[e] of oil, 7and a third of a hin of wine as a drink offering. Offer it as an aroma pleasing to the LORD.

8" 'When you prepare a young bull as a burnt offering or sacrifice, for a special vow or a fellowship offering[f] to the LORD, 9bring with the bull a grain offering of three-tenths of an ephah[g] of fine flour mixed with half a hin[h] of oil. 10Also bring half a hin of wine as a drink offering. It will be an offering made by fire, an aroma pleasing to the LORD. 11Each bull or ram, each lamb or young goat, is to be prepared in this manner. 12Do this for each one, for as many as you prepare.

13" 'Everyone who is native-born must do these things in this way when he brings an offering made by fire as an aroma pleasing to the LORD. 14For the generations to come, whenever an alien or anyone else living among you presents an offering made by fire as an aroma pleasing to the LORD, he must do exactly as you do. 15The community is to have the same rules for you and for the alien living among you; this is a lasting ordinance for the generations to come. You and the alien shall be the same before the LORD: 16The same laws and regulations will apply both to you and to the alien living among you.' "

17The LORD said to Moses, 18"Speak to the Israelites and say to them: 'When you enter the land to which I am taking you 19and you eat the food of the land, present a portion as an offering to the LORD. 20Present a cake from the first of your ground meal and present it as an offering from the threshing floor. 21Throughout the generations to come you are to give this offering to the LORD from the first of your ground meal.

Offerings for Unintentional Sins

22" 'Now if you unintentionally fail to keep any of these commands the LORD gave Moses— 23any of the LORD's commands to you through him, from the day the LORD gave them

[a]25 Hebrew *Yam Suph*; that is, Sea of Reeds [b]4 That is, probably about 2 quarts (about 2 liters) [c]4 That is, probably about 1 quart (about 1 liter); also in verse 5 [d]6 That is, probably about 4 quarts (about 4.5 liters) [e]6 That is, probably about 1 1/4 quarts (about 1.2 liters); also in verse 7 [f]8 Traditionally *peace offering* [g]9 That is, probably about 6 quarts (about 6.5 liters) [h]9 That is, probably about 2 quarts (about 2 liters); also in verse 10

and continuing through the generations to come— 24and if this is done unintentionally without the community being aware of it, then the whole community is to offer a young bull for a burnt offering as an aroma pleasing to the LORD, along with its prescribed grain offering and drink offering, and a male goat for a sin offering. 25The priest is to make atonement for the whole Israelite community, and they will be forgiven, for it was not intentional and they have brought to the LORD for their wrong an offering made by fire and a sin offering. 26The whole Israelite community and the aliens living among them will be forgiven, because all the people were involved in the unintentional wrong.

27" 'But if just one person sins unintentionally, he must bring a year-old female goat for a sin offering. 28The priest is to make atonement before the LORD for the one who erred by sinning unintentionally, and when atonement has been made for him, he will be forgiven. 29One and the same law applies to everyone who sins unintentionally, whether he is a native-born Israelite or an alien.

30" 'But anyone who sins defiantly, whether native-born or alien, blasphemes the LORD, and that person must be cut off from his people. 31Because he has despised the LORD's word and broken his commands, that person must surely be cut off; his guilt remains on him.' "

The Sabbath-Breaker Put to Death

32While the Israelites were in the desert, a man was found gathering wood on the Sabbath day. 33Those who found him gathering wood brought him to Moses and Aaron and the whole assembly, 34and they kept him in custody, because it was not clear what should be done to him. 35Then the LORD said to Moses, "The man must die. The whole assembly must stone him outside the camp." 36So the assembly took him outside the camp and stoned him to death, as the LORD commanded Moses.

Tassels on Garments

37The LORD said to Moses, 38"Speak to the Israelites and say to them: 'Throughout the generations to come you are to make tassels on the corners of your garments, with a blue cord on each tassel. 39You will have these tassels to look at and so you will remember all the commands of the LORD, that you may obey them and not prostitute yourselves by going after the lusts of your own hearts and eyes. 40Then you will remember to obey all my commands and will be consecrated to your God. 41I am the LORD your God, who brought you out of Egypt to be your God. I am the LORD your God.' "

Korah, Dathan and Abiram

16 Korah son of Izhar, the son of Kohath, the son of Levi, and certain Reubenites—Dathan and Abiram, sons of Eliab, and On son of Peleth—became insolent[a] 2and rose up against Moses. With them were 250 Israelite men, well-known community leaders who had been appointed members of the council. 3They came as a group to oppose Moses and Aaron and said to them, "You have gone too far! The whole community is holy, every one of them, and the LORD is with them. Why then do you set yourselves above the LORD's assembly?"

4When Moses heard this, he fell facedown. 5Then he said to Korah and all his followers: "In the morning the LORD will show who belongs to him and who is holy, and he will have that person come near him. The man he chooses he will cause to come near him. 6You, Korah, and all your followers are to do this: Take censers 7and tomorrow put fire and incense in them before the LORD. The man the LORD chooses will be the one who is holy. You Levites have gone too far!"

8Moses also said to Korah, "Now listen, you Levites! 9Isn't it enough for you that the God of Israel has separated you from the rest of the Israelite community and brought you near himself to do the work at the LORD's tabernacle and to stand before the community and minister to them? 10He has brought you and all your fellow Levites near himself, but now you are trying to get the priesthood too. 11It is against the LORD that you and all your followers have banded together. Who is Aaron that you should grumble against him?"

12Then Moses summoned Dathan and Abiram, the sons of Eliab. But they said, "We will not come! 13Isn't it enough that you have brought us up out of a land flowing with milk and honey to kill us in the desert? And now you also want to lord it over us? 14Moreover, you haven't brought us into a land flowing with milk and honey or given us an inheritance of fields and vineyards. Will you gouge out the eyes of[b] these men? No, we will not come!"

15Then Moses became very angry and said to the LORD, "Do not accept their offering. I have not taken so much as a donkey from them, nor have I wronged any of them."

16Moses said to Korah, "You and all your followers are to appear before the LORD tomorrow—you and they and Aaron. 17Each man is to take his censer and put incense in it—250 censers in all—and present it before the LORD. You and Aaron are to present your censers also." 18So each man took his censer, put fire and incense in it, and stood with Moses and Aaron at the entrance to the Tent of Meeting. 19When Korah had gathered all his followers in opposition to them at the entrance to the Tent of Meeting, the glory of the LORD appeared to the entire assembly. 20The LORD said to Moses and Aaron, 21"Separate yourselves from this assembly so I can put an end to them at once."

22But Moses and Aaron fell facedown and cried out, "O God, God of the spirits of all

[a] 1 Or *Peleth—took ⌞men⌟*   [b] 14 Or *you make slaves of*; or *you deceive*

mankind, will you be angry with the entire
assembly when only one man sins?"
23Then the LORD said to Moses, 24"Say to
the assembly, 'Move away from the tents of
Korah, Dathan and Abiram.' "
25Moses got up and went to Dathan and Abiram, and the elders of Israel followed him.
26He warned the assembly, "Move back from
the tents of these wicked men! Do not touch
anything belonging to them, or you will be
swept away because of all their sins." 27So
they moved away from the tents of Korah,
Dathan and Abiram. Dathan and Abiram had
come out and were standing with their wives,
children and little ones at the entrances to their
tents.
28Then Moses said, "This is how you will
know that the LORD has sent me to do all these
things and that it was not my idea: 29If these
men die a natural death and experience only
what usually happens to men, then the LORD
has not sent me. 30But if the LORD brings about
something totally new, and the earth opens its
mouth and swallows them, with everything
that belongs to them, and they go down alive
into the grave,[a] then you will know that these
men have treated the LORD with contempt."
31As soon as he finished saying all this, the
ground under them split apart 32and the earth
opened its mouth and swallowed them, with
their households and all Korah's men and all
their possessions. 33They went down alive into
the grave, with everything they owned; the
earth closed over them, and they perished and
were gone from the community. 34At their
cries, all the Israelites around them fled, shouting, "The earth is going to swallow us too!"
35And fire came out from the LORD and consumed the 250 men who were offering the incense.
36The LORD said to Moses, 37"Tell Eleazar
son of Aaron, the priest, to take the censers out
of the smoldering remains and scatter the coals
some distance away, for the censers are holy—
38the censers of the men who sinned at the cost
of their lives. Hammer the censers into sheets
to overlay the altar, for they were presented
before the LORD and have become holy. Let
them be a sign to the Israelites."
39So Eleazar the priest collected the bronze
censers brought by those who had been burned
up, and he had them hammered out to overlay
the altar, 40as the LORD directed him through
Moses. This was to remind the Israelites that
no one except a descendant of Aaron should
come to burn incense before the LORD, or he
would become like Korah and his followers.
41The next day the whole Israelite community grumbled against Moses and Aaron. "You
have killed the LORD's people," they said.
42But when the assembly gathered in opposition to Moses and Aaron and turned toward
the Tent of Meeting, suddenly the cloud covered it and the glory of the LORD appeared.
43Then Moses and Aaron went to the front of
the Tent of Meeting, 44and the LORD said to
Moses, 45"Get away from this assembly so I
can put an end to them at once." And they fell
facedown.
46Then Moses said to Aaron, "Take your
censer and put incense in it, along with fire
from the altar, and hurry to the assembly to
make atonement for them. Wrath has come out
from the LORD; the plague has started." 47So
Aaron did as Moses said, and ran into the
midst of the assembly. The plague had already
started among the people, but Aaron offered
the incense and made atonement for them.
48He stood between the living and the dead,
and the plague stopped. 49But 14,700 people
died from the plague, in addition to those who
had died because of Korah. 50Then Aaron returned to Moses at the entrance to the Tent of
Meeting, for the plague had stopped.

The Budding of Aaron's Staff

17 The LORD said to Moses, 2"Speak to the
Israelites and get twelve staffs from
them, one from the leader of each of their ancestral tribes. Write the name of each man on
his staff. 3On the staff of Levi write Aaron's
name, for there must be one staff for the head
of each ancestral tribe. 4Place them in the Tent
of Meeting in front of the Testimony, where I
meet with you. 5The staff belonging to the man
I choose will sprout, and I will rid myself of
this constant grumbling against you by the Israelites."
6So Moses spoke to the Israelites, and their
leaders gave him twelve staffs, one for the
leader of each of their ancestral tribes, and
Aaron's staff was among them. 7Moses placed
the staffs before the LORD in the Tent of the
Testimony.
8The next day Moses entered the Tent of the
Testimony and saw that Aaron's staff, which
represented the house of Levi, had not only
sprouted but had budded, blossomed and produced almonds. 9Then Moses brought out all
the staffs from the LORD's presence to all the
Israelites. They looked at them, and each man
took his own staff.
10The LORD said to Moses, "Put back Aaron's staff in front of the Testimony, to be kept
as a sign to the rebellious. This will put an end
to their grumbling against me, so that they will
not die." 11Moses did just as the LORD commanded him.
12The Israelites said to Moses, "We will die!
We are lost, we are all lost! 13Anyone who
even comes near the tabernacle of the LORD
will die. Are we all going to die?"

Duties of Priests and Levites

18 The LORD said to Aaron, "You, your
sons and your father's family are to bear
the responsibility for offenses against the sanctuary, and you and your sons alone are to bear
the responsibility for offenses against the
priesthood. 2Bring your fellow Levites from

[a]30 Hebrew *Sheol*; also in verse 33

your ancestral tribe to join you and assist you when you and your sons minister before the Tent of the Testimony. 3They are to be responsible to you and are to perform all the duties of the Tent, but they must not go near the furnishings of the sanctuary or the altar, or both they and you will die. 4They are to join you and be responsible for the care of the Tent of Meeting—all the work at the Tent—and no one else may come near where you are.

5"You are to be responsible for the care of the sanctuary and the altar, so that wrath will not fall on the Israelites again. 6I myself have selected your fellow Levites from among the Israelites as a gift to you, dedicated to the LORD to do the work at the Tent of Meeting. 7But only you and your sons may serve as priests in connection with everything at the altar and inside the curtain. I am giving you the service of the priesthood as a gift. Anyone else who comes near the sanctuary must be put to death."

Offerings for Priests and Levites

8Then the LORD said to Aaron, "I myself have put you in charge of the offerings presented to me; all the holy offerings the Israelites give me I give to you and your sons as your portion and regular share. 9You are to have the part of the most holy offerings that is kept from the fire. From all the gifts they bring me as most holy offerings, whether grain or sin or guilt offerings, that part belongs to you and your sons. 10Eat it as something most holy; every male shall eat it. You must regard it as holy.

11"This also is yours: whatever is set aside from the gifts of all the wave offerings of the Israelites. I give this to you and your sons and daughters as your regular share. Everyone in your household who is ceremonially clean may eat it.

12"I give you all the finest olive oil and all the finest new wine and grain they give the LORD as the firstfruits of their harvest. 13All the land's firstfruits that they bring to the LORD will be yours. Everyone in your household who is ceremonially clean may eat it.

14"Everything in Israel that is devoted[a] to the LORD is yours. 15The first offspring of every womb, both man and animal, that is offered to the LORD is yours. But you must redeem every firstborn son and every firstborn male of unclean animals. 16When they are a month old, you must redeem them at the redemption price set at five shekels[b] of silver, according to the sanctuary shekel, which weighs twenty gerahs.

17"But you must not redeem the firstborn of an ox, a sheep or a goat; they are holy. Sprinkle their blood on the altar and burn their fat as an offering made by fire, an aroma pleasing to the LORD. 18Their meat is to be yours, just as the breast of the wave offering and the right thigh are yours. 19Whatever is set aside from the holy offerings the Israelites present to the LORD I give to you and your sons and daughters as your regular share. It is an everlasting covenant of salt before the LORD for both you and your offspring."

20The LORD said to Aaron, "You will have no inheritance in their land, nor will you have any share among them; I am your share and your inheritance among the Israelites.

21"I give to the Levites all the tithes in Israel as their inheritance in return for the work they do while serving at the Tent of Meeting. 22From now on the Israelites must not go near the Tent of Meeting, or they will bear the consequences of their sin and will die. 23It is the Levites who are to do the work at the Tent of Meeting and bear the responsibility for offenses against it. This is a lasting ordinance for the generations to come. They will receive no inheritance among the Israelites. 24Instead, I give to the Levites as their inheritance the tithes that the Israelites present as an offering to the LORD. That is why I said concerning them: 'They will have no inheritance among the Israelites.' "

25The LORD said to Moses, 26"Speak to the Levites and say to them: 'When you receive from the Israelites the tithe I give you as your inheritance, you must present a tenth of that tithe as the LORD's offering. 27Your offering will be reckoned to you as grain from the threshing floor or juice from the winepress. 28In this way you also will present an offering to the LORD from all the tithes you receive from the Israelites. From these tithes you must give the LORD's portion to Aaron the priest. 29You must present as the LORD's portion the best and holiest part of everything given to you.'

30"Say to the Levites: 'When you present the best part, it will be reckoned to you as the product of the threshing floor or the winepress. 31You and your households may eat the rest of it anywhere, for it is your wages for your work at the Tent of Meeting. 32By presenting the best part of it you will not be guilty in this matter; then you will not defile the holy offerings of the Israelites, and you will not die.' "

The Water of Cleansing

19 The LORD said to Moses and Aaron: 2"This is a requirement of the law that the LORD has commanded: Tell the Israelites to bring you a red heifer without defect or blemish and that has never been under a yoke. 3Give it to Eleazar the priest; it is to be taken outside the camp and slaughtered in his presence. 4Then Eleazar the priest is to take some of its blood on his finger and sprinkle it seven times toward the front of the Tent of Meeting. 5While he watches, the heifer is to be burned—its hide, flesh, blood and offal. 6The priest is to take some cedar wood, hyssop and

[a] *14* The Hebrew term refers to the irrevocable giving over of things or persons to the LORD. [b] *16* That is, about 2 ounces (about 55 grams)

scarlet wool and throw them onto the burning heifer. 7After that, the priest must wash his clothes and bathe himself with water. He may then come into the camp, but he will be ceremonially unclean till evening. 8The man who burns it must also wash his clothes and bathe with water, and he too will be unclean till evening.

9"A man who is clean shall gather up the ashes of the heifer and put them in a ceremonially clean place outside the camp. They shall be kept by the Israelite community for use in the water of cleansing; it is for purification from sin. 10The man who gathers up the ashes of the heifer must also wash his clothes, and he too will be unclean till evening. This will be a lasting ordinance both for the Israelites and for the aliens living among them.

11"Whoever touches the dead body of anyone will be unclean for seven days. 12He must purify himself with the water on the third day and on the seventh day; then he will be clean. But if he does not purify himself on the third and seventh days, he will not be clean. 13Whoever touches the dead body of anyone and fails to purify himself defiles the LORD's tabernacle. That person must be cut off from Israel. Because the water of cleansing has not been sprinkled on him, he is unclean; his uncleanness remains on him.

14"This is the law that applies when a person dies in a tent: Anyone who enters the tent and anyone who is in it will be unclean for seven days, 15and every open container without a lid fastened on it will be unclean.

16"Anyone out in the open who touches someone who has been killed with a sword or someone who has died a natural death, or anyone who touches a human bone or a grave, will be unclean for seven days.

17"For the unclean person, put some ashes from the burned purification offering into a jar and pour fresh water over them. 18Then a man who is ceremonially clean is to take some hyssop, dip it in the water and sprinkle the tent and all the furnishings and the people who were there. He must also sprinkle anyone who has touched a human bone or a grave or someone who has been killed or someone who has died a natural death. 19The man who is clean is to sprinkle the unclean person on the third and seventh days, and on the seventh day he is to purify him. The person being cleansed must wash his clothes and bathe with water, and that evening he will be clean. 20But if a person who is unclean does not purify himself, he must be cut off from the community, because he has defiled the sanctuary of the LORD. The water of cleansing has not been sprinkled on him, and he is unclean. 21This is a lasting ordinance for them.

"The man who sprinkles the water of cleansing must also wash his clothes, and anyone who touches the water of cleansing will be unclean till evening. 22Anything that an unclean person touches becomes unclean, and anyone who touches it becomes unclean till evening."

Water From the Rock

20 In the first month the whole Israelite community arrived at the Desert of Zin, and they stayed at Kadesh. There Miriam died and was buried.

2Now there was no water for the community, and the people gathered in opposition to Moses and Aaron. 3They quarreled with Moses and said, "If only we had died when our brothers fell dead before the LORD! 4Why did you bring the LORD's community into this desert, that we and our livestock should die here? 5Why did you bring us up out of Egypt to this terrible place? It has no grain or figs, grapevines or pomegranates. And there is no water to drink!"

6Moses and Aaron went from the assembly to the entrance to the Tent of Meeting and fell facedown, and the glory of the LORD appeared to them. 7The LORD said to Moses, 8"Take the staff, and you and your brother Aaron gather the assembly together. Speak to that rock before their eyes and it will pour out its water. You will bring water out of the rock for the community so they and their livestock can drink."

9So Moses took the staff from the LORD's presence, just as he commanded him. 10He and Aaron gathered the assembly together in front of the rock and Moses said to them, "Listen, you rebels, must we bring you water out of this rock?" 11Then Moses raised his arm and struck the rock twice with his staff. Water gushed out, and the community and their livestock drank.

12But the LORD said to Moses and Aaron, "Because you did not trust in me enough to honor me as holy in the sight of the Israelites, you will not bring this community into the land I give them."

13These were the waters of Meribah,[a] where the Israelites quarreled with the LORD and where he showed himself holy among them.

Edom Denies Israel Passage

14Moses sent messengers from Kadesh to the king of Edom, saying:

> "This is what your brother Israel says: You know about all the hardships that have come upon us. 15Our forefathers went down into Egypt, and we lived there many years. The Egyptians mistreated us and our fathers, 16but when we cried out to the LORD, he heard our cry and sent an angel and brought us out of Egypt.
>
> "Now we are here at Kadesh, a town on the edge of your territory. 17Please let us pass through your country. We will not go through any field or vineyard, or drink water from any well. We will travel along the king's highway and not turn to the

[a]13 *Meribah* means *quarreling.*

right or to the left until we have passed through your territory."

18But Edom answered:

"You may not pass through here; if you try, we will march out and attack you with the sword."

19The Israelites replied:

"We will go along the main road, and if we or our livestock drink any of your water, we will pay for it. We only want to pass through on foot—nothing else."

20Again they answered:

"You may not pass through."

Then Edom came out against them with a large and powerful army. 21Since Edom refused to let them go through their territory, Israel turned away from them.

The Death of Aaron

22The whole Israelite community set out from Kadesh and came to Mount Hor. 23At Mount Hor, near the border of Edom, the LORD said to Moses and Aaron, 24"Aaron will be gathered to his people. He will not enter the land I give the Israelites, because both of you rebelled against my command at the waters of Meribah. 25Get Aaron and his son Eleazar and take them up Mount Hor. 26Remove Aaron's garments and put them on his son Eleazar, for Aaron will be gathered to his people; he will die there."

27Moses did as the LORD commanded: They went up Mount Hor in the sight of the whole community. 28Moses removed Aaron's garments and put them on his son Eleazar. And Aaron died there on top of the mountain. Then Moses and Eleazar came down from the mountain, 29and when the whole community learned that Aaron had died, the entire house of Israel mourned for him thirty days.

Arad Destroyed

21 When the Canaanite king of Arad, who lived in the Negev, heard that Israel was coming along the road to Atharim, he attacked the Israelites and captured some of them. 2Then Israel made this vow to the LORD: "If you will deliver these people into our hands, we will totally destroy[a] their cities." 3The LORD listened to Israel's plea and gave the Canaanites over to them. They completely destroyed them and their towns; so the place was named Hormah.[b]

The Bronze Snake

4They traveled from Mount Hor along the route to the Red Sea,[c] to go around Edom. But the people grew impatient on the way; 5they spoke against God and against Moses, and said, "Why have you brought us up out of Egypt to die in the desert? There is no bread! There is no water! And we detest this miserable food!"

6Then the LORD sent venomous snakes among them; they bit the people and many Israelites died. 7The people came to Moses and said, "We sinned when we spoke against the LORD and against you. Pray that the LORD will take the snakes away from us." So Moses prayed for the people.

8The LORD said to Moses, "Make a snake and put it up on a pole; anyone who is bitten can look at it and live." 9So Moses made a bronze snake and put it up on a pole. Then when anyone was bitten by a snake and looked at the bronze snake, he lived.

The Journey to Moab

10The Israelites moved on and camped at Oboth. 11Then they set out from Oboth and camped in Iye Abarim, in the desert that faces Moab toward the sunrise. 12From there they moved on and camped in the Zered Valley. 13They set out from there and camped alongside the Arnon, which is in the desert extending into Amorite territory. The Arnon is the border of Moab, between Moab and the Amorites. 14That is why the Book of the Wars of the LORD says:

". . . Waheb in Suphah[d] and the ravines,
the Arnon 15and[e] the slopes of the ravines
that lead to the site of Ar
and lie along the border of Moab."

16From there they continued on to Beer, the well where the LORD said to Moses, "Gather the people together and I will give them water."

17Then Israel sang this song:

"Spring up, O well!
Sing about it,
18about the well that the princes dug,
that the nobles of the people sank—
the nobles with scepters and staffs."

Then they went from the desert to Mattanah, 19from Mattanah to Nahaliel, from Nahaliel to Bamoth, 20and from Bamoth to the valley in Moab where the top of Pisgah overlooks the wasteland.

Defeat of Sihon and Og

21Israel sent messengers to say to Sihon king of the Amorites:

22"Let us pass through your country. We will not turn aside into any field or vineyard, or drink water from any well. We will travel along the king's highway until we have passed through your territory."

23But Sihon would not let Israel pass

[a]2 The Hebrew term refers to the irrevocable giving over of things or persons to the LORD, often by totally destroying them; also in verse 3. [b]3 *Hormah* means *destruction.* [c]4 Hebrew *Yam Suph*; that is, Sea of Reeds [d]14 The meaning of the Hebrew for this phrase is uncertain. [e]14,15 Or *"I have been given from Suphah and the ravines / of the Arnon [15]to*

through his territory. He mustered his entire
army and marched out into the desert against
Israel. When he reached Jahaz, he fought with
Israel. 24Israel, however, put him to the sword
and took over his land from the Arnon to the
Jabbok, but only as far as the Ammonites, because their border was fortified. 25Israel captured all the cities of the Amorites and occupied them, including Heshbon and all its
surrounding settlements. 26Heshbon was the
city of Sihon king of the Amorites, who had
fought against the former king of Moab and
had taken from him all his land as far as the
Arnon.
27That is why the poets say:

"Come to Heshbon and let it be rebuilt;
let Sihon's city be restored.

28"Fire went out from Heshbon,
a blaze from the city of Sihon.
It consumed Ar of Moab,
the citizens of Arnon's heights.
29Woe to you, O Moab!
You are destroyed, O people of
Chemosh!
He has given up his sons as fugitives
and his daughters as captives
to Sihon king of the Amorites.

30"But we have overthrown them;
Heshbon is destroyed all the way to
Dibon.
We have demolished them as far as
Nophah,
which extends to Medeba."

31So Israel settled in the land of the Amorites.
32After Moses had sent spies to Jazer, the
Israelites captured its surrounding settlements
and drove out the Amorites who were there.
33Then they turned and went up along the road
toward Bashan, and Og king of Bashan and his
whole army marched out to meet them in battle
at Edrei.
34The LORD said to Moses, "Do not be
afraid of him, for I have handed him over to
you, with his whole army and his land. Do to
him what you did to Sihon king of the Amorites, who reigned in Heshbon."
35So they struck him down, together with
his sons and his whole army, leaving them no
survivors. And they took possession of his
land.

Balak Summons Balaam

22 Then the Israelites traveled to the plains
of Moab and camped along the Jordan
across from Jericho.[a]
2Now Balak son of Zippor saw all that Israel
had done to the Amorites, 3and Moab was terrified because there were so many people. Indeed, Moab was filled with dread because of
the Israelites.
4The Moabites said to the elders of Midian,
"This horde is going to lick up everything
around us, as an ox licks up the grass of the
field."
So Balak son of Zippor, who was king of
Moab at that time, 5sent messengers to summon Balaam son of Beor, who was at Pethor,
near the River,[b] in his native land. Balak said:

"A people has come out of Egypt; they
cover the face of the land and have settled
next to me. 6Now come and put a curse on
these people, because they are too powerful for me. Perhaps then I will be able to
defeat them and drive them out of the
country. For I know that those you bless
are blessed, and those you curse are
cursed."

7The elders of Moab and Midian left, taking
with them the fee for divination. When they
came to Balaam, they told him what Balak had
said.
8"Spend the night here," Balaam said to
them, "and I will bring you back the answer
the LORD gives me." So the Moabite princes
stayed with him.
9God came to Balaam and asked, "Who are
these men with you?"
10Balaam said to God, "Balak son of Zippor,
king of Moab, sent me this message: 11'A people that has come out of Egypt covers the face
of the land. Now come and put a curse on them
for me. Perhaps then I will be able to fight
them and drive them away.' "
12But God said to Balaam, "Do not go with
them. You must not put a curse on those people, because they are blessed."
13The next morning Balaam got up and said
to Balak's princes, "Go back to your own
country, for the LORD has refused to let me go
with you."
14So the Moabite princes returned to Balak
and said, "Balaam refused to come with us."
15Then Balak sent other princes, more numerous and more distinguished than the first.
16They came to Balaam and said:

"This is what Balak son of Zippor says:
Do not let anything keep you from coming to me, 17because I will reward you
handsomely and do whatever you say.
Come and put a curse on these people
for me."

18But Balaam answered them, "Even if Balak gave me his palace filled with silver and
gold, I could not do anything great or small to
go beyond the command of the LORD my God.
19Now stay here tonight as the others did,
and I will find out what else the LORD will
tell me."
20That night God came to Balaam and said,
"Since these men have come to summon you,
go with them, but do only what I tell you."

Balaam's Donkey

21Balaam got up in the morning, saddled his
donkey and went with the princes of Moab.

[a] *1* Hebrew *Jordan of Jericho*; possibly an ancient name for the Jordan River [b] *5* That is, the Euphrates

22But God was very angry when he went, and
the angel of the LORD stood in the road to
oppose him. Balaam was riding on his donkey,
and his two servants were with him. 23When
the donkey saw the angel of the LORD standing
in the road with a drawn sword in his hand, she
turned off the road into a field. Balaam beat
her to get her back on the road.

24Then the angel of the LORD stood in a
narrow path between two vineyards, with walls
on both sides. 25When the donkey saw the angel of the LORD, she pressed close to the wall,
crushing Balaam's foot against it. So he beat
her again.

26Then the angel of the LORD moved on
ahead and stood in a narrow place where there
was no room to turn, either to the right or to the
left. 27When the donkey saw the angel of the
LORD, she lay down under Balaam, and he was
angry and beat her with his staff. 28Then the
LORD opened the donkey's mouth, and she
said to Balaam, "What have I done to you to
make you beat me these three times?"

29Balaam answered the donkey, "You have
made a fool of me! If I had a sword in my
hand, I would kill you right now."

30The donkey said to Balaam, "Am I not
your own donkey, which you have always ridden, to this day? Have I been in the habit of
doing this to you?"

"No," he said.

31Then the LORD opened Balaam's eyes,
and he saw the angel of the LORD standing in
the road with his sword drawn. So he bowed
low and fell facedown.

32The angel of the LORD asked him, "Why
have you beaten your donkey these three
times? I have come here to oppose you because your path is a reckless one before me.[a]
33The donkey saw me and turned away from
me these three times. If she had not turned
away, I would certainly have killed you by
now, but I would have spared her."

34Balaam said to the angel of the LORD, "I
have sinned. I did not realize you were standing in the road to oppose me. Now if you are
displeased, I will go back."

35The angel of the LORD said to Balaam,
"Go with the men, but speak only what I tell
you." So Balaam went with the princes of Balak.

36When Balak heard that Balaam was coming, he went out to meet him at the Moabite
town on the Arnon border, at the edge of his
territory. 37Balak said to Balaam, "Did I not
send you an urgent summons? Why didn't you
come to me? Am I really not able to reward
you?"

38"Well, I have come to you now," Balaam
replied. "But can I say just anything? I must
speak only what God puts in my mouth."

39Then Balaam went with Balak to Kiriath
Huzoth. 40Balak sacrificed cattle and sheep,
and gave some to Balaam and the princes who
were with him. 41The next morning Balak took
Balaam up to Bamoth Baal, and from there he
saw part of the people.

Balaam's First Oracle

23 Balaam said, "Build me seven altars
here, and prepare seven bulls and seven
rams for me." 2Balak did as Balaam said, and
the two of them offered a bull and a ram on
each altar.

3Then Balaam said to Balak, "Stay here beside your offering while I go aside. Perhaps the
LORD will come to meet with me. Whatever he
reveals to me I will tell you." Then he went off
to a barren height.

4God met with him, and Balaam said, "I
have prepared seven altars, and on each altar I
have offered a bull and a ram."

5The LORD put a message in Balaam's
mouth and said, "Go back to Balak and give
him this message."

6So he went back to him and found him
standing beside his offering, with all the
princes of Moab. 7Then Balaam uttered his oracle:

"Balak brought me from Aram,
  the king of Moab from the eastern
    mountains.
'Come,' he said, 'curse Jacob for me;
  come, denounce Israel.'
8How can I curse
  those whom God has not cursed?
How can I denounce
  those whom the LORD has not
    denounced?
9From the rocky peaks I see them,
  from the heights I view them.
I see a people who live apart
  and do not consider themselves one of
    the nations.
10Who can count the dust of Jacob
  or number the fourth part of Israel?
Let me die the death of the righteous,
  and may my end be like theirs!"

11Balak said to Balaam, "What have you
done to me? I brought you to curse my enemies, but you have done nothing but bless
them!"

12He answered, "Must I not speak what the
LORD puts in my mouth?"

Balaam's Second Oracle

13Then Balak said to him, "Come with me to
another place where you can see them; you
will see only a part but not all of them. And
from there, curse them for me." 14So he took
him to the field of Zophim on the top of Pisgah, and there he built seven altars and offered
a bull and a ram on each altar.

15Balaam said to Balak, "Stay here beside
your offering while I meet with him over
there."

16The LORD met with Balaam and put a
message in his mouth and said, "Go back to
Balak and give him this message."

[a]32 The meaning of the Hebrew for this clause is uncertain.

17So he went to him and found him standing
beside his offering, with the princes of Moab.
Balak asked him, "What did the LORD say?"
18Then he uttered his oracle:

"Arise, Balak, and listen;
hear me, son of Zippor.
19God is not a man, that he should lie,
nor a son of man, that he should change
his mind.
Does he speak and then not act?
Does he promise and not fulfill?
20I have received a command to bless;
he has blessed, and I cannot change it.

21"No misfortune is seen in Jacob,
no misery observed in Israel.[a]
The LORD their God is with them;
the shout of the King is among them.
22God brought them out of Egypt;
they have the strength of a wild ox.
23There is no sorcery against Jacob,
no divination against Israel.
It will now be said of Jacob
and of Israel, 'See what God has done!'
24The people rise like a lioness;
they rouse themselves like a lion
that does not rest till he devours his prey
and drinks the blood of his victims."

25Then Balak said to Balaam, "Neither curse
them at all nor bless them at all!"
26Balaam answered, "Did I not tell you I
must do whatever the LORD says?"

Balaam's Third Oracle

27Then Balak said to Balaam, "Come, let
me take you to another place. Perhaps it will
please God to let you curse them for me from
there." 28And Balak took Balaam to the top of
Peor, overlooking the wasteland.
29Balaam said, "Build me seven altars here,
and prepare seven bulls and seven rams for
me." 30Balak did as Balaam had said, and offered a bull and a ram on each altar.

24 Now when Balaam saw that it pleased
the LORD to bless Israel, he did not re-
sort to sorcery as at other times, but turned his
face toward the desert. 2When Balaam looked
out and saw Israel encamped tribe by tribe, the
Spirit of God came upon him 3and he uttered
his oracle:

"The oracle of Balaam son of Beor,
the oracle of one whose eye sees
clearly,
4the oracle of one who hears the words of
God,
who sees a vision from the Almighty,[b]
who falls prostrate, and whose eyes are
opened:

5"How beautiful are your tents, O Jacob,
your dwelling places, O Israel!

6"Like valleys they spread out,
like gardens beside a river,
like aloes planted by the LORD,
like cedars beside the waters.
7Water will flow from their buckets;
their seed will have abundant water.

"Their king will be greater than Agag;
their kingdom will be exalted.

8"God brought them out of Egypt;
they have the strength of a wild ox.
They devour hostile nations
and break their bones in pieces;
with their arrows they pierce them.
9Like a lion they crouch and lie down,
like a lioness—who dares to rouse
them?

"May those who bless you be blessed
and those who curse you be cursed!"

10Then Balak's anger burned against Balaam. He struck his hands together and said to
him, "I summoned you to curse my enemies,
but you have blessed them these three times.
11Now leave at once and go home! I said I
would reward you handsomely, but the LORD
has kept you from being rewarded."
12Balaam answered Balak, "Did I not tell
the messengers you sent me, 13'Even if Balak
gave me his palace filled with silver and gold,
I could not do anything of my own accord,
good or bad, to go beyond the command of the
LORD—and I must say only what the LORD
says'? 14Now I am going back to my people,
but come, let me warn you of what this people
will do to your people in days to come."

Balaam's Fourth Oracle

15Then he uttered his oracle:

"The oracle of Balaam son of Beor,
the oracle of one whose eye sees
clearly,
16the oracle of one who hears the words of
God,
who has knowledge from the Most
High,
who sees a vision from the Almighty,
who falls prostrate, and whose eyes are
opened:

17"I see him, but not now;
I behold him, but not near.
A star will come out of Jacob;
a scepter will rise out of Israel.
He will crush the foreheads of Moab,
the skulls[c] of[d] all the sons of Sheth.[e]
18Edom will be conquered;
Seir, his enemy, will be conquered,
but Israel will grow strong.
19A ruler will come out of Jacob
and destroy the survivors of the city."

Balaam's Final Oracles

20Then Balaam saw Amalek and uttered his
oracle:

[a]21 Or *He has not looked on Jacob's offenses / or on the wrongs found in Israel.* [b]4 Hebrew *Shaddai*; also in verse 16 [c]17 Samaritan Pentateuch (see also Jer. 48:45); the meaning of the word in the Masoretic Text is uncertain. [d]17 Or possibly *Moab, / batter* [e]17 Or *all the noisy boasters*

"Amalek was first among the nations,
but he will come to ruin at last."

21Then he saw the Kenites and uttered his
oracle:

"Your dwelling place is secure,
your nest is set in a rock;
22yet you Kenites will be destroyed
when Asshur takes you captive."

23Then he uttered his oracle:

"Ah, who can live when God does this?[a]
24 Ships will come from the shores of
Kittim;
they will subdue Asshur and Eber,
but they too will come to ruin."

25Then Balaam got up and returned home
and Balak went his own way.

Moab Seduces Israel

25 While Israel was staying in Shittim, the
men began to indulge in sexual immorality with Moabite women, 2who invited them
to the sacrifices to their gods. The people ate
and bowed down before these gods. 3So Israel
joined in worshiping the Baal of Peor. And the
LORD's anger burned against them.
4The LORD said to Moses, "Take all the
leaders of these people, kill them and expose
them in broad daylight before the LORD, so
that the LORD's fierce anger may turn away
from Israel."
5So Moses said to Israel's judges, "Each of
you must put to death those of your men who
have joined in worshiping the Baal of Peor."
6Then an Israelite man brought to his family
a Midianite woman right before the eyes of
Moses and the whole assembly of Israel while
they were weeping at the entrance to the Tent
of Meeting. 7When Phinehas son of Eleazar,
the son of Aaron, the priest, saw this, he left
the assembly, took a spear in his hand 8and
followed the Israelite into the tent. He drove
the spear through both of them—through the
Israelite and into the woman's body. Then the
plague against the Israelites was stopped; 9but
those who died in the plague numbered
24,000.
10The LORD said to Moses, 11"Phinehas son
of Eleazar, the son of Aaron, the priest, has
turned my anger away from the Israelites; for
he was as zealous as I am for my honor among
them, so that in my zeal I did not put an end to
them. 12Therefore tell him I am making my
covenant of peace with him. 13He and his
descendants will have a covenant of a lasting
priesthood, because he was zealous for the
honor of his God and made atonement for the
Israelites."
14The name of the Israelite who was killed
with the Midianite woman was Zimri son of
Salu, the leader of a Simeonite family. 15And
the name of the Midianite woman who was put
to death was Cozbi daughter of Zur, a tribal
chief of a Midianite family.
16The LORD said to Moses, 17"Treat the
Midianites as enemies and kill them, 18because
they treated you as enemies when they deceived you in the affair of Peor and their sister
Cozbi, the daughter of a Midianite leader, the
woman who was killed when the plague came
as a result of Peor."

The Second Census

26 After the plague the LORD said to Moses and Eleazar son of Aaron, the priest,
2"Take a census of the whole Israelite community by families—all those twenty years old or
more who are able to serve in the army of
Israel." 3So on the plains of Moab by the Jordan across from Jericho,[b] Moses and Eleazar
the priest spoke with them and said, 4"Take a
census of the men twenty years old or more, as
the LORD commanded Moses."

These were the Israelites who came out of
Egypt:

5The descendants of Reuben, the firstborn son
of Israel, were:
through Hanoch, the Hanochite clan;
through Pallu, the Palluite clan;
6through Hezron, the Hezronite clan;
through Carmi, the Carmite clan.
7These were the clans of Reuben; those numbered were 43,730.
8The son of Pallu was Eliab, 9and the sons
of Eliab were Nemuel, Dathan and Abiram.
The same Dathan and Abiram were the community officials who rebelled against Moses
and Aaron and were among Korah's followers
when they rebelled against the LORD. 10The
earth opened its mouth and swallowed them
along with Korah, whose followers died when
the fire devoured the 250 men. And they
served as a warning sign. 11The line of Korah,
however, did not die out.

12The descendants of Simeon by their clans
were:
through Nemuel, the Nemuelite clan;
through Jamin, the Jaminite clan;
through Jakin, the Jakinite clan;
13through Zerah, the Zerahite clan;
through Shaul, the Shaulite clan.
14These were the clans of Simeon; there were
22,200 men.

15The descendants of Gad by their clans were:
through Zephon, the Zephonite clan;
through Haggi, the Haggite clan;
through Shuni, the Shunite clan;
16through Ozni, the Oznite clan;
through Eri, the Erite clan;
17through Arodi,[c] the Arodite clan;
through Areli, the Arelite clan.
18These were the clans of Gad; those numbered were 40,500.

[a]23 Masoretic Text; with a different word division of the Hebrew *A people will gather from the north.*
[b]3 Hebrew *Jordan of Jericho*; possibly an ancient name for the Jordan River; also in verse 63
[c]17 Samaritan Pentateuch and Syriac (see also Gen. 46:16); Masoretic Text *Arod*

19Er and Onan were sons of Judah, but they died in Canaan.
20The descendants of Judah by their clans were:
through Shelah, the Shelanite clan;
through Perez, the Perezite clan;
through Zerah, the Zerahite clan.
21The descendants of Perez were:
through Hezron, the Hezronite clan;
through Hamul, the Hamulite clan.
22These were the clans of Judah; those numbered were 76,500.

23The descendants of Issachar by their clans were:
through Tola, the Tolaite clan;
through Puah, the Puite[a] clan;
24through Jashub, the Jashubite clan;
through Shimron, the Shimronite clan.
25These were the clans of Issachar; those numbered were 64,300.

26The descendants of Zebulun by their clans were:
through Sered, the Seredite clan;
through Elon, the Elonite clan;
through Jahleel, the Jahleelite clan.
27These were the clans of Zebulun; those numbered were 60,500.

28The descendants of Joseph by their clans through Manasseh and Ephraim were:

29The descendants of Manasseh:
through Makir, the Makirite clan (Makir was the father of Gilead);
through Gilead, the Gileadite clan.
30These were the descendants of Gilead:
through Iezer, the Iezerite clan;
through Helek, the Helekite clan;
31through Asriel, the Asrielite clan;
through Shechem, the Shechemite clan;
32through Shemida, the Shemidaite clan;
through Hepher, the Hepherite clan.
33(Zelophehad son of Hepher had no sons; he had only daughters, whose names were Mahlah, Noah, Hoglah, Milcah and Tirzah.)
34These were the clans of Manasseh; those numbered were 52,700.

35These were the descendants of Ephraim by their clans:
through Shuthelah, the Shuthelahite clan;
through Beker, the Bekerite clan;
through Tahan, the Tahanite clan.
36These were the descendants of Shuthelah:
through Eran, the Eranite clan.
37These were the clans of Ephraim; those numbered were 32,500.
These were the descendants of Joseph by their clans.

38The descendants of Benjamin by their clans were:
through Bela, the Belaite clan;
through Ashbel, the Ashbelite clan;
through Ahiram, the Ahiramite clan;
39through Shupham,[b] the Shuphamite clan;
through Hupham, the Huphamite clan.
40The descendants of Bela through Ard and Naaman were:
through Ard,[c] the Ardite clan;
through Naaman, the Naamite clan.
41These were the clans of Benjamin; those numbered were 45,600.

42These were the descendants of Dan by their clans:
through Shuham, the Shuhamite clan.
These were the clans of Dan: 43All of them
were Shuhamite clans; and those numbered were 64,400.

44The descendants of Asher by their clans were:
through Imnah, the Imnite clan;
through Ishvi, the Ishvite clan;
through Beriah, the Beriite clan;
45and through the descendants of Beriah:
through Heber, the Heberite clan;
through Malkiel, the Malkielite clan.
46(Asher had a daughter named Serah.)
47These were the clans of Asher; those numbered were 53,400.

48The descendants of Naphtali by their clans were:
through Jahzeel, the Jahzeelite clan;
through Guni, the Gunite clan;
49through Jezer, the Jezerite clan;
through Shillem, the Shillemite clan.
50These were the clans of Naphtali; those numbered were 45,400.

51The total number of the men of Israel was 601,730.

52The LORD said to Moses, 53"The land is to
be allotted to them as an inheritance based on
the number of names. 54To a larger group give
a larger inheritance, and to a smaller group a
smaller one; each is to receive its inheritance
according to the number of those listed. 55Be
sure that the land is distributed by lot. What
each group inherits will be according to the
names for its ancestral tribe. 56Each inheritance is to be distributed by lot among the
larger and smaller groups."

57These were the Levites who were counted by their clans:
through Gershon, the Gershonite clan;
through Kohath, the Kohathite clan;

[a]23 Samaritan Pentateuch, Septuagint, Vulgate and Syriac (see also 1 Chron. 7:1); Masoretic Text *through Puvah, the Punite* [b]39 A few manuscripts of the Masoretic Text, Samaritan Pentateuch, Vulgate and Syriac (see also Septuagint); most manuscripts of the Masoretic Text *Shephupham* [c]40 Samaritan Pentateuch and Vulgate (see also Septuagint); Masoretic Text does not have *through Ard.*

through Merari, the Merarite clan.
58These also were Levite clans:
the Libnite clan,
the Hebronite clan,
the Mahlite clan,
the Mushite clan,
the Korahite clan.
(Kohath was the forefather of Amram; 59the name of Amram's wife was Jochebed, a descendant of Levi, who was born to the Levites[a] in Egypt. To Amram she bore Aaron, Moses and their sister Miriam. 60Aaron was the father of Nadab and Abihu, Eleazar and Ithamar. 61But Nadab and Abihu died when they made an offering before the LORD with unauthorized fire.)

62All the male Levites a month old or more numbered 23,000. They were not counted along with the other Israelites because they received no inheritance among them.

63These are the ones counted by Moses and Eleazar the priest when they counted the Israelites on the plains of Moab by the Jordan across from Jericho. 64Not one of them was among those counted by Moses and Aaron the priest when they counted the Israelites in the Desert of Sinai. 65For the LORD had told those Israelites they would surely die in the desert, and not one of them was left except Caleb son of Jephunneh and Joshua son of Nun.

Zelophehad's Daughters

27 The daughters of Zelophehad son of Hepher, the son of Gilead, the son of Makir, the son of Manasseh, belonged to the clans of Manasseh son of Joseph. The names of the daughters were Mahlah, Noah, Hoglah, Milcah and Tirzah. They approached 2the entrance to the Tent of Meeting and stood before Moses, Eleazar the priest, the leaders and the whole assembly, and said, 3"Our father died in the desert. He was not among Korah's followers, who banded together against the LORD, but he died for his own sin and left no sons. 4Why should our father's name disappear from his clan because he had no son? Give us property among our father's relatives."

5So Moses brought their case before the LORD 6and the LORD said to him, 7"What Zelophehad's daughters are saying is right. You must certainly give them property as an inheritance among their father's relatives and turn their father's inheritance over to them.

8"Say to the Israelites, 'If a man dies and leaves no son, turn his inheritance over to his daughter. 9If he has no daughter, give his inheritance to his brothers. 10If he has no brothers, give his inheritance to his father's brothers. 11If his father had no brothers, give his inheritance to the nearest relative in his clan, that he may possess it. This is to be a legal requirement for the Israelites, as the LORD commanded Moses.' "

Joshua to Succeed Moses

12Then the LORD said to Moses, "Go up this mountain in the Abarim range and see the land I have given the Israelites. 13After you have seen it, you too will be gathered to your people, as your brother Aaron was, 14for when the community rebelled at the waters in the Desert of Zin, both of you disobeyed my command to honor me as holy before their eyes." (These were the waters of Meribah Kadesh, in the Desert of Zin.)

15Moses said to the LORD, 16"May the LORD, the God of the spirits of all mankind, appoint a man over this community 17to go out and come in before them, one who will lead them out and bring them in, so the LORD's people will not be like sheep without a shepherd."

18So the LORD said to Moses, "Take Joshua son of Nun, a man in whom is the spirit,[b] and lay your hand on him. 19Have him stand before Eleazar the priest and the entire assembly and commission him in their presence. 20Give him some of your authority so the whole Israelite community will obey him. 21He is to stand before Eleazar the priest, who will obtain decisions for him by inquiring of the Urim before the LORD. At his command he and the entire community of the Israelites will go out, and at his command they will come in."

22Moses did as the LORD commanded him. He took Joshua and had him stand before Eleazar the priest and the whole assembly. 23Then he laid his hands on him and commissioned him, as the LORD instructed through Moses.

Daily Offerings

28 The LORD said to Moses, 2"Give this command to the Israelites and say to them: 'See that you present to me at the appointed time the food for my offerings made by fire, as an aroma pleasing to me.' 3Say to them: 'This is the offering made by fire that you are to present to the LORD: two lambs a year old without defect, as a regular burnt offering each day. 4Prepare one lamb in the morning and the other at twilight, 5together with a grain offering of a tenth of an ephah[c] of fine flour mixed with a quarter of a hin[d] of oil from pressed olives. 6This is the regular burnt offering instituted at Mount Sinai as a pleasing aroma, an offering made to the LORD by fire. 7The accompanying drink offering is to be a quarter of a hin of fermented drink with each lamb. Pour out the drink offering to the LORD at the sanctuary. 8Prepare the second lamb at twilight, along with the same kind of grain offering and drink offering that you prepare in the morning. This is an offering made by fire, an aroma pleasing to the LORD.

[a] 59 Or *Jochebed, a daughter of Levi, who was born to Levi* [b] 18 Or *Spirit* [c] 5 That is, probably about 2 quarts (about 2 liters); also in verses 13, 21 and 29 [d] 5 That is, probably about 1 quart (about 1 liter); also in verses 7 and 14

Sabbath Offerings

9" 'On the Sabbath day, make an offering of
two lambs a year old without defect, together
with its drink offering and a grain offering of
two-tenths of an ephah[a] of fine flour mixed
with oil. 10This is the burnt offering for every
Sabbath, in addition to the regular burnt offering and its drink offering.

Monthly Offerings

11" 'On the first of every month, present to
the LORD a burnt offering of two young bulls,
one ram and seven male lambs a year old, all
without defect. 12With each bull there is to be
a grain offering of three-tenths of an ephah[b] of
fine flour mixed with oil; with the ram, a grain
offering of two-tenths of an ephah of fine flour
mixed with oil; 13and with each lamb, a grain
offering of a tenth of an ephah of fine flour
mixed with oil. This is for a burnt offering, a
pleasing aroma, an offering made to the LORD
by fire. 14With each bull there is to be a drink
offering of half a hin[c] of wine; with the ram,
a third of a hin[d]; and with each lamb, a quarter
of a hin. This is the monthly burnt offering to
be made at each new moon during the year.
15Besides the regular burnt offering with its
drink offering, one male goat is to be presented
to the LORD as a sin offering.

The Passover

16" 'On the fourteenth day of the first month
the LORD's Passover is to be held. 17On the
fifteenth day of this month there is to be a
festival; for seven days eat bread made without
yeast. 18On the first day hold a sacred assembly and do no regular work. 19Present to the
LORD an offering made by fire, a burnt offering of two young bulls, one ram and seven
male lambs a year old, all without defect.
20With each bull prepare a grain offering of
three-tenths of an ephah of fine flour mixed
with oil; with the ram, two-tenths; 21and with
each of the seven lambs, one-tenth. 22Include
one male goat as a sin offering to make atonement for you. 23Prepare these in addition to the
regular morning burnt offering. 24In this way
prepare the food for the offering made by fire
every day for seven days as an aroma pleasing
to the LORD; it is to be prepared in addition to
the regular burnt offering and its drink offering. 25On the seventh day hold a sacred assembly and do no regular work.

Feast of Weeks

26" 'On the day of firstfruits, when you
present to the LORD an offering of new grain
during the Feast of Weeks, hold a sacred assembly and do no regular work. 27Present a
burnt offering of two young bulls, one ram and
seven male lambs a year old as an aroma pleasing to the LORD. 28With each bull there is to be
a grain offering of three-tenths of an ephah of
fine flour mixed with oil; with the ram, two-
tenths; 29and with each of the seven lambs,
one-tenth. 30Include one male goat to make
atonement for you. 31Prepare these together
with their drink offerings, in addition to the
regular burnt offering and its grain offering. Be
sure the animals are without defect.

Feast of Trumpets

29 " 'On the first day of the seventh month
hold a sacred assembly and do no regular work. It is a day for you to sound the trumpets. 2As an aroma pleasing to the LORD, prepare a burnt offering of one young bull, one
ram and seven male lambs a year old, all without defect. 3With the bull prepare a grain offering of three-tenths of an ephah[e] of fine flour
mixed with oil; with the ram, two-tenths[f];
4and with each of the seven lambs, one-tenth.[g]
5Include one male goat as a sin offering to
make atonement for you. 6These are in addition to the monthly and daily burnt offerings
with their grain offerings and drink offerings
as specified. They are offerings made to the
LORD by fire—a pleasing aroma.

Day of Atonement

7" 'On the tenth day of this seventh month
hold a sacred assembly. You must deny yourselves[h] and do no work. 8Present as an aroma
pleasing to the LORD a burnt offering of one
young bull, one ram and seven male lambs a
year old, all without defect. 9With the bull
prepare a grain offering of three-tenths of an
ephah of fine flour mixed with oil; with the
ram, two-tenths; 10and with each of the seven
lambs, one-tenth. 11Include one male goat as a
sin offering, in addition to the sin offering for
atonement and the regular burnt offering with
its grain offering, and their drink offerings.

Feast of Tabernacles

12" 'On the fifteenth day of the seventh
month, hold a sacred assembly and do no regular work. Celebrate a festival to the LORD for
seven days. 13Present an offering made by fire
as an aroma pleasing to the LORD, a burnt offering of thirteen young bulls, two rams and
fourteen male lambs a year old, all without
defect. 14With each of the thirteen bulls prepare a grain offering of three-tenths of an
ephah of fine flour mixed with oil; with each
of the two rams, two-tenths; 15and with each
of the fourteen lambs, one-tenth. 16Include one
male goat as a sin offering, in addition to the
regular burnt offering with its grain offering
and drink offering.

17" 'On the second day prepare twelve
young bulls, two rams and fourteen male
lambs a year old, all without defect. 18With the

[a] *9* That is, probably about 4 quarts (about 4.5 liters); also in verses 12, 20 and 28 [b] *12* That is, probably about 6 quarts (about 6.5 liters); also in verses 20 and 28 [c] *14* That is, probably about 2 quarts (about 2 liters) [d] *14* That is, probably about 1 1/4 quarts (about 1.2 liters) [e] *3* That is, probably about 6 quarts (about 6.5 liters); also in verses 9 and 14 [f] *3* That is, probably about 4 quarts (about 4.5 liters); also in verses 9 and 14 [g] *4* That is, probably about 2 quarts (about 2 liters); also in verses 10 and 15 [h] *7* Or *must fast*

bulls, rams and lambs, prepare their grain offerings and drink offerings according to the number specified. 19 Include one male goat as a sin offering, in addition to the regular burnt offering with its grain offering, and their drink offerings.

20 " 'On the third day prepare eleven bulls, two rams and fourteen male lambs a year old, all without defect. 21 With the bulls, rams and lambs, prepare their grain offerings and drink offerings according to the number specified. 22 Include one male goat as a sin offering, in addition to the regular burnt offering with its grain offering and drink offering.

23 " 'On the fourth day prepare ten bulls, two rams and fourteen male lambs a year old, all without defect. 24 With the bulls, rams and lambs, prepare their grain offerings and drink offerings according to the number specified. 25 Include one male goat as a sin offering, in addition to the regular burnt offering with its grain offering and drink offering.

26 " 'On the fifth day prepare nine bulls, two rams and fourteen male lambs a year old, all without defect. 27 With the bulls, rams and lambs, prepare their grain offerings and drink offerings according to the number specified. 28 Include one male goat as a sin offering, in addition to the regular burnt offering with its grain offering and drink offering.

29 " 'On the sixth day prepare eight bulls, two rams and fourteen male lambs a year old, all without defect. 30 With the bulls, rams and lambs, prepare their grain offerings and drink offerings according to the number specified. 31 Include one male goat as a sin offering, in addition to the regular burnt offering with its grain offering and drink offering.

32 " 'On the seventh day prepare seven bulls, two rams and fourteen male lambs a year old, all without defect. 33 With the bulls, rams and lambs, prepare their grain offerings and drink offerings according to the number specified. 34 Include one male goat as a sin offering, in addition to the regular burnt offering with its grain offering and drink offering.

35 " 'On the eighth day hold an assembly and do no regular work. 36 Present an offering made by fire as an aroma pleasing to the LORD, a burnt offering of one bull, one ram and seven male lambs a year old, all without defect. 37 With the bull, the ram and the lambs, prepare their grain offerings and drink offerings according to the number specified. 38 Include one male goat as a sin offering, in addition to the regular burnt offering with its grain offering and drink offering.

39 " 'In addition to what you vow and your freewill offerings, prepare these for the LORD at your appointed feasts: your burnt offerings, grain offerings, drink offerings and fellowship offerings.[a]' "

40 Moses told the Israelites all that the LORD commanded him.

[a]39 Traditionally *peace offerings*

Vows

30 Moses said to the heads of the tribes of Israel: "This is what the LORD commands: 2 When a man makes a vow to the LORD or takes an oath to obligate himself by a pledge, he must not break his word but must do everything he said.

3 "When a young woman still living in her father's house makes a vow to the LORD or obligates herself by a pledge 4 and her father hears about her vow or pledge but says nothing to her, then all her vows and every pledge by which she obligated herself will stand. 5 But if her father forbids her when he hears about it, none of her vows or the pledges by which she obligated herself will stand; the LORD will release her because her father has forbidden her.

6 "If she marries after she makes a vow or after her lips utter a rash promise by which she obligates herself 7 and her husband hears about it but says nothing to her, then her vows or the pledges by which she obligated herself will stand. 8 But if her husband forbids her when he hears about it, he nullifies the vow that obligates her or the rash promise by which she obligates herself, and the LORD will release her.

9 "Any vow or obligation taken by a widow or divorced woman will be binding on her.

10 "If a woman living with her husband makes a vow or obligates herself by a pledge under oath 11 and her husband hears about it but says nothing to her and does not forbid her, then all her vows or the pledges by which she obligated herself will stand. 12 But if her husband nullifies them when he hears about them, then none of the vows or pledges that came from her lips will stand. Her husband has nullified them, and the LORD will release her. 13 Her husband may confirm or nullify any vow she makes or any sworn pledge to deny herself. 14 But if her husband says nothing to her about it from day to day, then he confirms all her vows or the pledges binding on her. He confirms them by saying nothing to her when he hears about them. 15 If, however, he nullifies them some time after he hears about them, then he is responsible for her guilt."

16 These are the regulations the LORD gave Moses concerning relationships between a man and his wife, and between a father and his young daughter still living in his house.

Vengeance on the Midianites

31 The LORD said to Moses, 2 "Take vengeance on the Midianites for the Israelites. After that, you will be gathered to your people."

3 So Moses said to the people, "Arm some of your men to go to war against the Midianites and to carry out the LORD's vengeance on them. 4 Send into battle a thousand men from each of the tribes of Israel." 5 So twelve thousand men armed for battle, a thousand from each tribe, were supplied from the clans of

Israel. [6]Moses sent them into battle, a thousand
from each tribe, along with Phinehas son of
Eleazar, the priest, who took with him articles
from the sanctuary and the trumpets for signal-
ing.
[7]They fought against Midian, as the LORD
commanded Moses, and killed every man.
[8]Among their victims were Evi, Rekem, Zur,
Hur and Reba—the five kings of Midian. They
also killed Balaam son of Beor with the sword.
[9]The Israelites captured the Midianite women
and children and took all the Midianite herds,
flocks and goods as plunder. [10]They burned all
the towns where the Midianites had settled, as
well as all their camps. [11]They took all the
plunder and spoils, including the people and
animals, [12]and brought the captives, spoils and
plunder to Moses and Eleazar the priest
and the Israelite assembly at their camp on the
plains of Moab, by the Jordan across from Jericho.[a]
[13]Moses, Eleazar the priest and all the leaders of the community went to meet them outside the camp. [14]Moses was angry with the
officers of the army—the commanders of
thousands and commanders of hundreds—who
returned from the battle.
[15]"Have you allowed all the women to
live?" he asked them. [16]"They were the ones
who followed Balaam's advice and were the
means of turning the Israelites away from the
LORD in what happened at Peor, so that a
plague struck the LORD's people. [17]Now kill
all the boys. And kill every woman who has
slept with a man, [18]but save for yourselves
every girl who has never slept with a man.
[19]"All of you who have killed anyone or
touched anyone who was killed must stay outside the camp seven days. On the third and
seventh days you must purify yourselves and
your captives. [20]Purify every garment as well
as everything made of leather, goat hair or
wood."
[21]Then Eleazar the priest said to the soldiers
who had gone into battle, "This is the requirement of the law that the LORD gave Moses:
[22]Gold, silver, bronze, iron, tin, lead [23]and
anything else that can withstand fire must be
put through the fire, and then it will be clean.
But it must also be purified with the water of
cleansing. And whatever cannot withstand fire
must be put through that water. [24]On the seventh day wash your clothes and you will be
clean. Then you may come into the camp."

Dividing the Spoils

[25]The LORD said to Moses, [26]"You and Eleazar the priest and the family heads of the
community are to count all the people and animals that were captured. [27]Divide the spoils
between the soldiers who took part in the battle
and the rest of the community. [28]From the soldiers who fought in the battle, set apart as tribute for the LORD one out of every five hundred,
whether persons, cattle, donkeys, sheep or
goats. [29]Take this tribute from their half share
and give it to Eleazar the priest as the LORD's
part. [30]From the Israelites' half, select one out
of every fifty, whether persons, cattle, donkeys, sheep, goats or other animals. Give them
to the Levites, who are responsible for the care
of the LORD's tabernacle." [31]So Moses and Eleazar the priest did as the LORD commanded
Moses.
[32]The plunder remaining from the spoils that
the soldiers took was 675,000 sheep, [33]72,000
cattle, [34]61,000 donkeys [35]and 32,000 women
who had never slept with a man.
[36]The half share of those who fought in the
battle was:

337,500 sheep, [37]of which the tribute for the LORD was 675;
[38]36,000 cattle, of which the tribute for the LORD was 72;
[39]30,500 donkeys, of which the tribute for the LORD was 61;
[40]16,000 people, of which the tribute for the LORD was 32.

[41]Moses gave the tribute to Eleazar the
priest as the LORD's part, as the LORD commanded Moses.
[42]The half belonging to the Israelites, which
Moses set apart from that of the fighting
men— [43]the community's half—was 337,500
sheep, [44]36,000 cattle, [45]30,500 donkeys [46]and
16,000 people. [47]From the Israelites' half, Moses selected one out of every fifty persons and
animals, as the LORD commanded him, and
gave them to the Levites, who were responsible for the care of the LORD's tabernacle.
[48]Then the officers who were over the units
of the army—the commanders of thousands
and commanders of hundreds—went to Moses
[49]and said to him, "Your servants have counted the soldiers under our command, and not
one is missing. [50]So we have brought as an
offering to the LORD the gold articles each of
us acquired—armlets, bracelets, signet rings,
earrings and necklaces—to make atonement
for ourselves before the LORD."
[51]Moses and Eleazar the priest accepted
from them the gold—all the crafted articles.
[52]All the gold from the commanders of thousands and commanders of hundreds that Moses
and Eleazar presented as a gift to the LORD
weighed 16,750 shekels.[b] [53]Each soldier had
taken plunder for himself. [54]Moses and Eleazar the priest accepted the gold from the commanders of thousands and commanders of
hundreds and brought it into the Tent of Meeting as a memorial for the Israelites before the
LORD.

The Transjordan Tribes

32 The Reubenites and Gadites, who had
very large herds and flocks, saw that the
lands of Jazer and Gilead were suitable for

[a]12 Hebrew *Jordan of Jericho*; possibly an ancient name for the Jordan River [b]52 That is, about 420 pounds (about 190 kilograms)

livestock. 2So they came to Moses and Eleazar the priest and to the leaders of the community, and said, 3"Ataroth, Dibon, Jazer, Nimrah, Heshbon, Elealeh, Sebam, Nebo and Beon— 4the land the LORD subdued before the people of Israel—are suitable for livestock, and your servants have livestock. 5If we have found favor in your eyes," they said, "let this land be given to your servants as our possession. Do not make us cross the Jordan."

6Moses said to the Gadites and Reubenites, "Shall your countrymen go to war while you sit here? 7Why do you discourage the Israelites from going over into the land the LORD has given them? 8This is what your fathers did when I sent them from Kadesh Barnea to look over the land. 9After they went up to the Valley of Eshcol and viewed the land, they discouraged the Israelites from entering the land the LORD had given them. 10The LORD's anger was aroused that day and he swore this oath: 11'Because they have not followed me wholeheartedly, not one of the men twenty years old or more who came up out of Egypt will see the land I promised on oath to Abraham, Isaac and Jacob— 12not one except Caleb son of Jephunneh the Kenizzite and Joshua son of Nun, for they followed the LORD wholeheartedly.' 13The LORD's anger burned against Israel and he made them wander in the desert forty years, until the whole generation of those who had done evil in his sight was gone.

14"And here you are, a brood of sinners, standing in the place of your fathers and making the LORD even more angry with Israel. 15If you turn away from following him, he will again leave all this people in the desert, and you will be the cause of their destruction."

16Then they came up to him and said, "We would like to build pens here for our livestock and cities for our women and children. 17But we are ready to arm ourselves and go ahead of the Israelites until we have brought them to their place. Meanwhile our women and children will live in fortified cities, for protection from the inhabitants of the land. 18We will not return to our homes until every Israelite has received his inheritance. 19We will not receive any inheritance with them on the other side of the Jordan, because our inheritance has come to us on the east side of the Jordan."

20Then Moses said to them, "If you will do this—if you will arm yourselves before the LORD for battle, 21and if all of you will go armed over the Jordan before the LORD until he has driven his enemies out before him— 22then when the land is subdued before the LORD, you may return and be free from your obligation to the LORD and to Israel. And this land will be your possession before the LORD.

23"But if you fail to do this, you will be sinning against the LORD; and you may be sure that your sin will find you out. 24Build cities for your women and children, and pens for your flocks, but do what you have promised."

25The Gadites and Reubenites said to Moses, "We your servants will do as our lord commands. 26Our children and wives, our flocks and herds will remain here in the cities of Gilead. 27But your servants, every man armed for battle, will cross over to fight before the LORD, just as our lord says."

28Then Moses gave orders about them to Eleazar the priest and Joshua son of Nun and to the family heads of the Israelite tribes. 29He said to them, "If the Gadites and Reubenites, every man armed for battle, cross over the Jordan with you before the LORD, then when the land is subdued before you, give them the land of Gilead as their possession. 30But if they do not cross over with you armed, they must accept their possession with you in Canaan."

31The Gadites and Reubenites answered, "Your servants will do what the LORD has said. 32We will cross over before the LORD into Canaan armed, but the property we inherit will be on this side of the Jordan."

33Then Moses gave to the Gadites, the Reubenites and the half-tribe of Manasseh son of Joseph the kingdom of Sihon king of the Amorites and the kingdom of Og king of Bashan— the whole land with its cities and the territory around them.

34The Gadites built up Dibon, Ataroth, Aroer, 35Atroth Shophan, Jazer, Jogbehah, 36Beth Nimrah and Beth Haran as fortified cities, and built pens for their flocks. 37And the Reubenites rebuilt Heshbon, Elealeh and Kiriathaim, 38as well as Nebo and Baal Meon (these names were changed) and Sibmah. They gave names to the cities they rebuilt.

39The descendants of Makir son of Manasseh went to Gilead, captured it and drove out the Amorites who were there. 40So Moses gave Gilead to the Makirites, the descendants of Manasseh, and they settled there. 41Jair, a descendant of Manasseh, captured their settlements and called them Havvoth Jair.[a] 42And Nobah captured Kenath and its surrounding settlements and called it Nobah after himself.

Stages in Israel's Journey

33 Here are the stages in the journey of the Israelites when they came out of Egypt by divisions under the leadership of Moses and Aaron. 2At the LORD's command Moses recorded the stages in their journey. This is their journey by stages:

> 3The Israelites set out from Rameses on the fifteenth day of the first month, the day after the Passover. They marched out boldly in full view of all the Egyptians, 4who were burying all their firstborn, whom the LORD had struck down among them; for the LORD had brought judgment on their gods.
>
> 5The Israelites left Rameses and camped at Succoth.
>
> 6They left Succoth and camped at Etham, on the edge of the desert.

[a]41 Or *them the settlements of Jair*

7They left Etham, turned back to Pi Hahiroth, to the east of Baal Zephon, and
camped near Migdol.
8They left Pi Hahiroth[a] and passed
through the sea into the desert, and when
they had traveled for three days in the
Desert of Etham, they camped at Marah.
9They left Marah and went to Elim,
where there were twelve springs and seventy palm trees, and they camped there.
10They left Elim and camped by the
Red Sea.[b]
11They left the Red Sea and camped in
the Desert of Sin.
12They left the Desert of Sin and
camped at Dophkah.
13They left Dophkah and camped at
Alush.
14They left Alush and camped at Rephidim, where there was no water for the
people to drink.
15They left Rephidim and camped in
the Desert of Sinai.
16They left the Desert of Sinai and
camped at Kibroth Hattaavah.
17They left Kibroth Hattaavah and
camped at Hazeroth.
18They left Hazeroth and camped at
Rithmah.
19They left Rithmah and camped at
Rimmon Perez.
20They left Rimmon Perez and camped
at Libnah.
21They left Libnah and camped at Rissah.
22They left Rissah and camped at Kehelathah.
23They left Kehelathah and camped at
Mount Shepher.
24They left Mount Shepher and camped
at Haradah.
25They left Haradah and camped at
Makheloth.
26They left Makheloth and camped at
Tahath.
27They left Tahath and camped at Terah.
28They left Terah and camped at Mithcah.
29They left Mithcah and camped at
Hashmonah.
30They left Hashmonah and camped at
Moseroth.
31They left Moseroth and camped at
Bene Jaakan.
32They left Bene Jaakan and camped
at Hor Haggidgad.
33They left Hor Haggidgad and camped
at Jotbathah.
34They left Jotbathah and camped at
Abronah.
35They left Abronah and camped at
Ezion Geber.
36They left Ezion Geber and camped at
Kadesh, in the Desert of Zin.
37They left Kadesh and camped at
Mount Hor, on the border of Edom. 38At
the LORD's command Aaron the priest
went up Mount Hor, where he died on the
first day of the fifth month of the fortieth
year after the Israelites came out of
Egypt. 39Aaron was a hundred and
twenty-three years old when he died on
Mount Hor.
40The Canaanite king of Arad, who
lived in the Negev of Canaan, heard that
the Israelites were coming.
41They left Mount Hor and camped at
Zalmonah.
42They left Zalmonah and camped at
Punon.
43They left Punon and camped at
Oboth.
44They left Oboth and camped at Iye
Abarim, on the border of Moab.
45They left Iyim[c] and camped at Dibon
Gad.
46They left Dibon Gad and camped at
Almon Diblathaim.
47They left Almon Diblathaim and
camped in the mountains of Abarim, near
Nebo.
48They left the mountains of Abarim
and camped on the plains of Moab by the
Jordan across from Jericho.[d] 49There on
the plains of Moab they camped along
the Jordan from Beth Jeshimoth to Abel
Shittim.

50On the plains of Moab by the Jordan
across from Jericho the LORD said to Moses,
51"Speak to the Israelites and say to them:
'When you cross the Jordan into Canaan,
52drive out all the inhabitants of the land before you. Destroy all their carved images and
their cast idols, and demolish all their high
places. 53Take possession of the land and settle
in it, for I have given you the land to possess.
54Distribute the land by lot, according to your
clans. To a larger group give a larger inheritance, and to a smaller group a smaller one.
Whatever falls to them by lot will be theirs.
Distribute it according to your ancestral tribes.
55" 'But if you do not drive out the inhabitants of the land, those you allow to remain
will become barbs in your eyes and thorns in
your sides. They will give you trouble in the
land where you will live. 56And then I will do
to you what I plan to do to them.' "

Boundaries of Canaan

34 The LORD said to Moses, 2"Command
the Israelites and say to them: 'When
you enter Canaan, the land that will be allotted

[a]8 Many manuscripts of the Masoretic Text, Samaritan Pentateuch and Vulgate; most manuscripts of the Masoretic Text *left from before Hahiroth* [b]10 Hebrew *Yam Suph*; that is, Sea of Reeds; also in verse 11
[c]45 That is, Iye Abarim [d]48 Hebrew *Jordan of Jericho*; possibly an ancient name for the Jordan River; also in verse 50

to you as an inheritance will have these boundaries:

3" 'Your southern side will include some of the Desert of Zin along the border of Edom. On the east, your southern boundary will start from the end of the Salt Sea,[a] 4cross south of Scorpion[b] Pass, continue on to Zin and go south of Kadesh Barnea. Then it will go to Hazar Addar and over to Azmon, 5where it will turn, join the Wadi of Egypt and end at the Sea.[c]

6" 'Your western boundary will be the coast of the Great Sea. This will be your boundary on the west.

7" 'For your northern boundary, run a line from the Great Sea to Mount Hor 8and from Mount Hor to Lebo[d] Hamath. Then the boundary will go to Zedad, 9continue to Ziphron and end at Hazar Enan. This will be your boundary on the north.

10" 'For your eastern boundary, run a line from Hazar Enan to Shepham. 11The boundary will go down from Shepham to Riblah on the east side of Ain and continue along the slopes east of the Sea of Kinnereth.[e] 12Then the boundary will go down along the Jordan and end at the Salt Sea.

" 'This will be your land, with its boundaries on every side.' "

13Moses commanded the Israelites: "Assign this land by lot as an inheritance. The LORD has ordered that it be given to the nine and a half tribes, 14because the families of the tribe of Reuben, the tribe of Gad and the half-tribe of Manasseh have received their inheritance. 15These two and a half tribes have received their inheritance on the east side of the Jordan of Jericho,[f] toward the sunrise."

16The LORD said to Moses, 17"These are the names of the men who are to assign the land for you as an inheritance: Eleazar the priest and Joshua son of Nun. 18And appoint one leader from each tribe to help assign the land. 19These are their names:

Caleb son of Jephunneh,
from the tribe of Judah;
20Shemuel son of Ammihud,
from the tribe of Simeon;
21Elidad son of Kislon,
from the tribe of Benjamin;
22Bukki son of Jogli,
the leader from the tribe of Dan;
23Hanniel son of Ephod,
the leader from the tribe of Manasseh son of Joseph;
24Kemuel son of Shiphtan,
the leader from the tribe of Ephraim son of Joseph;
25Elizaphan son of Parnach,
the leader from the tribe of Zebulun;
26Paltiel son of Azzan,
the leader from the tribe of Issachar;
27Ahihud son of Shelomi,
the leader from the tribe of Asher;
28Pedahel son of Ammihud,
the leader from the tribe of Naphtali."

29These are the men the LORD commanded to assign the inheritance to the Israelites in the land of Canaan.

Towns for the Levites

35 On the plains of Moab by the Jordan across from Jericho,[g] the LORD said to Moses, 2"Command the Israelites to give the Levites towns to live in from the inheritance the Israelites will possess. And give them pasturelands around the towns. 3Then they will have towns to live in and pasturelands for their cattle, flocks and all their other livestock.

4"The pasturelands around the towns that you give the Levites will extend out fifteen hundred feet[h] from the town wall. 5Outside the town, measure three thousand feet[i] on the east side, three thousand on the south side, three thousand on the west and three thousand on the north, with the town in the center. They will have this area as pastureland for the towns.

Cities of Refuge

6"Six of the towns you give the Levites will be cities of refuge, to which a person who has killed someone may flee. In addition, give them forty-two other towns. 7In all you must give the Levites forty-eight towns, together with their pasturelands. 8The towns you give the Levites from the land the Israelites possess are to be given in proportion to the inheritance of each tribe: Take many towns from a tribe that has many, but few from one that has few."

9Then the LORD said to Moses: 10"Speak to the Israelites and say to them: 'When you cross the Jordan into Canaan, 11select some towns to be your cities of refuge, to which a person who has killed someone accidentally may flee. 12They will be places of refuge from the avenger, so that a person accused of murder may not die before he stands trial before the assembly. 13These six towns you give will be your cities of refuge. 14Give three on this side of the Jordan and three in Canaan as cities of refuge. 15These six towns will be a place of refuge for Israelites, aliens and any other people living among them, so that anyone who has killed another accidentally can flee there.

16" 'If a man strikes someone with an iron object so that he dies, he is a murderer; the murderer shall be put to death. 17Or if anyone has a stone in his hand that could kill, and he strikes someone so that he dies, he is a murderer; the murderer shall be put to death. 18Or if anyone has a wooden object in his hand that could kill, and he hits someone so that he dies, he is a murderer; the murderer shall be put to

[a] 3 That is, the Dead Sea; also in verse 12 [b] 4 Hebrew *Akrabbim* [c] 5 That is, the Mediterranean; also in verses 6 and 7 [d] 8 Or *to the entrance to* [e] 11 That is, Galilee [f] 15 *Jordan of Jericho* was possibly an ancient name for the Jordan River. [g] 1 Hebrew *Jordan of Jericho*; possibly an ancient name for the Jordan River [h] 4 Hebrew *a thousand cubits* (about 450 meters) [i] 5 Hebrew *two thousand cubits* (about 900 meters)

death. 19The avenger of blood shall put the murderer to death; when he meets him, he shall put him to death. 20If anyone with malice aforethought shoves another or throws something at him intentionally so that he dies 21or if in hostility he hits him with his fist so that he dies, that person shall be put to death; he is a murderer. The avenger of blood shall put the murderer to death when he meets him.

22" 'But if without hostility someone suddenly shoves another or throws something at him unintentionally 23or, without seeing him, drops a stone on him that could kill him, and he dies, then since he was not his enemy and he did not intend to harm him, 24the assembly must judge between him and the avenger of blood according to these regulations. 25The assembly must protect the one accused of murder from the avenger of blood and send him back to the city of refuge to which he fled. He must stay there until the death of the high priest, who was anointed with the holy oil.

26" 'But if the accused ever goes outside the limits of the city of refuge to which he has fled 27and the avenger of blood finds him outside the city, the avenger of blood may kill the accused without being guilty of murder. 28The accused must stay in his city of refuge until the death of the high priest; only after the death of the high priest may he return to his own property.

29" 'These are to be legal requirements for you throughout the generations to come, wherever you live.

30" 'Anyone who kills a person is to be put to death as a murderer only on the testimony of witnesses. But no one is to be put to death on the testimony of only one witness.

31" 'Do not accept a ransom for the life of a murderer, who deserves to die. He must surely be put to death.

32" 'Do not accept a ransom for anyone who has fled to a city of refuge and so allow him to go back and live on his own land before the death of the high priest.

33" 'Do not pollute the land where you are. Bloodshed pollutes the land, and atonement cannot be made for the land on which blood has been shed, except by the blood of the one who shed it. 34Do not defile the land where you live and where I dwell, for I, the LORD, dwell among the Israelites.' "

Inheritance of Zelophehad's Daughters

36 The family heads of the clan of Gilead son of Makir, the son of Manasseh, who were from the clans of the descendants of Joseph, came and spoke before Moses and the leaders, the heads of the Israelite families. 2They said, "When the LORD commanded my lord to give the land as an inheritance to the Israelites by lot, he ordered you to give the inheritance of our brother Zelophehad to his daughters. 3Now suppose they marry men from other Israelite tribes; then their inheritance will be taken from our ancestral inheritance and added to that of the tribe they marry into. And so part of the inheritance allotted to us will be taken away. 4When the Year of Jubilee for the Israelites comes, their inheritance will be added to that of the tribe into which they marry, and their property will be taken from the tribal inheritance of our forefathers."

5Then at the LORD's command Moses gave this order to the Israelites: "What the tribe of the descendants of Joseph is saying is right. 6This is what the LORD commands for Zelophehad's daughters: They may marry anyone they please as long as they marry within the tribal clan of their father. 7No inheritance in Israel is to pass from tribe to tribe, for every Israelite shall keep the tribal land inherited from his forefathers. 8Every daughter who inherits land in any Israelite tribe must marry someone in her father's tribal clan, so that every Israelite will possess the inheritance of his fathers. 9No inheritance may pass from tribe to tribe, for each Israelite tribe is to keep the land it inherits."

10So Zelophehad's daughters did as the LORD commanded Moses. 11Zelophehad's daughters—Mahlah, Tirzah, Hoglah, Milcah and Noah—married their cousins on their father's side. 12They married within the clans of the descendants of Manasseh son of Joseph, and their inheritance remained in their father's clan and tribe.

13These are the commands and regulations the LORD gave through Moses to the Israelites on the plains of Moab by the Jordan across from Jericho.[a]

Deuteronomy

The Command to Leave Horeb

1 These are the words Moses spoke to all Israel in the desert east of the Jordan—that is, in the Arabah—opposite Suph, between Paran and Tophel, Laban, Hazeroth and Dizahab. 2(It takes eleven days to go from Horeb to Kadesh Barnea by the Mount Seir road.)

3In the fortieth year, on the first day of the eleventh month, Moses proclaimed to the Israelites all that the LORD had commanded him

a13 Hebrew *Jordan of Jericho*; possibly an ancient name for the Jordan River

concerning them. 4This was after he had defeated Sihon king of the Amorites, who reigned in Heshbon, and at Edrei had defeated Og king of Bashan, who reigned in Ashtaroth.

5East of the Jordan in the territory of Moab, Moses began to expound this law, saying:

6The LORD our God said to us at Horeb, "You have stayed long enough at this mountain. 7Break camp and advance into the hill country of the Amorites; go to all the neighboring peoples in the Arabah, in the mountains, in the western foothills, in the Negev and along the coast, to the land of the Canaanites and to Lebanon, as far as the great river, the Euphrates. 8See, I have given you this land. Go in and take possession of the land that the LORD swore he would give to your fathers—to Abraham, Isaac and Jacob—and to their descendants after them."

The Appointment of Leaders

9At that time I said to you, "You are too heavy a burden for me to carry alone. 10The LORD your God has increased your numbers so that today you are as many as the stars in the sky. 11May the LORD, the God of your fathers, increase you a thousand times and bless you as he has promised! 12But how can I bear your problems and your burdens and your disputes all by myself? 13Choose some wise, understanding and respected men from each of your tribes, and I will set them over you."

14You answered me, "What you propose to do is good."

15So I took the leading men of your tribes, wise and respected men, and appointed them to have authority over you—as commanders of thousands, of hundreds, of fifties and of tens and as tribal officials. 16And I charged your judges at that time: Hear the disputes between your brothers and judge fairly, whether the case is between brother Israelites or between one of them and an alien. 17Do not show partiality in judging; hear both small and great alike. Do not be afraid of any man, for judgment belongs to God. Bring me any case too hard for you, and I will hear it. 18And at that time I told you everything you were to do.

Spies Sent Out

19Then, as the LORD our God commanded us, we set out from Horeb and went toward the hill country of the Amorites through all that vast and dreadful desert that you have seen, and so we reached Kadesh Barnea. 20Then I said to you, "You have reached the hill country of the Amorites, which the LORD our God is giving us. 21See, the LORD your God has given you the land. Go up and take possession of it as the LORD, the God of your fathers, told you. Do not be afraid; do not be discouraged."

22Then all of you came to me and said, "Let us send men ahead to spy out the land for us and bring back a report about the route we are to take and the towns we will come to."

23The idea seemed good to me; so I selected twelve of you, one man from each tribe. 24They left and went up into the hill country, and came to the Valley of Eshcol and explored it. 25Taking with them some of the fruit of the land, they brought it down to us and reported, "It is a good land that the LORD our God is giving us."

Rebellion Against the LORD

26But you were unwilling to go up; you rebelled against the command of the LORD your God. 27You grumbled in your tents and said, "The LORD hates us; so he brought us out of Egypt to deliver us into the hands of the Amorites to destroy us. 28Where can we go? Our brothers have made us lose heart. They say, 'The people are stronger and taller than we are; the cities are large, with walls up to the sky. We even saw the Anakites there.' "

29Then I said to you, "Do not be terrified; do not be afraid of them. 30The LORD your God, who is going before you, will fight for you, as he did for you in Egypt, before your very eyes, 31and in the desert. There you saw how the LORD your God carried you, as a father carries his son, all the way you went until you reached this place."

32In spite of this, you did not trust in the LORD your God, 33who went ahead of you on your journey, in fire by night and in a cloud by day, to search out places for you to camp and to show you the way you should go.

34When the LORD heard what you said, he was angry and solemnly swore: 35"Not a man of this evil generation shall see the good land I swore to give your forefathers, 36except Caleb son of Jephunneh. He will see it, and I will give him and his descendants the land he set his feet on, because he followed the LORD wholeheartedly."

37Because of you the LORD became angry with me also and said, "You shall not enter it, either. 38But your assistant, Joshua son of Nun, will enter it. Encourage him, because he will lead Israel to inherit it. 39And the little ones that you said would be taken captive, your children who do not yet know good from bad—they will enter the land. I will give it to them and they will take possession of it. 40But as for you, turn around and set out toward the desert along the route to the Red Sea.[a]"

41Then you replied, "We have sinned against the LORD. We will go up and fight, as the LORD our God commanded us." So every one of you put on his weapons, thinking it easy to go up into the hill country.

42But the LORD said to me, "Tell them, 'Do not go up and fight, because I will not be with you. You will be defeated by your enemies.' "

43So I told you, but you would not listen. You rebelled against the LORD's command and in your arrogance you marched up into the hill country. 44The Amorites who lived in those hills came out against you; they chased you

[a]40 Hebrew *Yam Suph*; that is, Sea of Reeds

like a swarm of bees and beat you down from
Seir all the way to Hormah. 45You came back
and wept before the LORD, but he paid no attention to your weeping and turned a deaf ear
to you. 46And so you stayed in Kadesh many
days—all the time you spent there.

Wanderings in the Desert

2 Then we turned back and set out toward
the desert along the route to the Red Sea,[a]
as the LORD had directed me. For a long time
we made our way around the hill country of
Seir.
2Then the LORD said to me, 3"You have
made your way around this hill country long
enough; now turn north. 4Give the people these
orders: 'You are about to pass through the
territory of your brothers the descendants of
Esau, who live in Seir. They will be afraid of
you, but be very careful. 5Do not provoke them
to war, for I will not give you any of their land,
not even enough to put your foot on. I have
given Esau the hill country of Seir as his own.
6You are to pay them in silver for the food you
eat and the water you drink.' "
7The LORD your God has blessed you in all
the work of your hands. He has watched over
your journey through this vast desert. These
forty years the LORD your God has been with
you, and you have not lacked anything.
8So we went on past our brothers the
descendants of Esau, who live in Seir. We
turned from the Arabah road, which comes
up from Elath and Ezion Geber, and traveled
along the desert road of Moab.
9Then the LORD said to me, "Do not harass
the Moabites or provoke them to war, for I will
not give you any part of their land. I have
given Ar to the descendants of Lot as a possession."
10(The Emites used to live there—a people
strong and numerous, and as tall as the Anakites. 11Like the Anakites, they too were considered Rephaites, but the Moabites called
them Emites. 12Horites used to live in Seir, but
the descendants of Esau drove them out. They
destroyed the Horites from before them and
settled in their place, just as Israel did in the
land the LORD gave them as their possession.)
13And the LORD said, "Now get up and cross
the Zered Valley." So we crossed the valley.
14Thirty-eight years passed from the time
we left Kadesh Barnea until we crossed the
Zered Valley. By then, that entire generation
of fighting men had perished from the camp, as
the LORD had sworn to them. 15The LORD's
hand was against them until he had completely
eliminated them from the camp.
16Now when the last of these fighting men
among the people had died, 17the LORD said to
me, 18"Today you are to pass by the region of
Moab at Ar. 19When you come to the Ammonites, do not harass them or provoke them to
war, for I will not give you possession of any
land belonging to the Ammonites. I have given
it as a possession to the descendants of Lot."
20(That too was considered a land of the
Rephaites, who used to live there; but the Ammonites called them Zamzummites. 21They
were a people strong and numerous, and as tall
as the Anakites. The LORD destroyed them
from before the Ammonites, who drove them
out and settled in their place. 22The LORD had
done the same for the descendants of Esau,
who lived in Seir, when he destroyed the Horites from before them. They drove them out
and have lived in their place to this day. 23And
as for the Avvites who lived in villages as
far as Gaza, the Caphtorites coming out from
Caphtor[b] destroyed them and settled in their
place.)

Defeat of Sihon King of Heshbon

24"Set out now and cross the Arnon Gorge.
See, I have given into your hand Sihon the
Amorite, king of Heshbon, and his country.
Begin to take possession of it and engage him
in battle. 25This very day I will begin to put the
terror and fear of you on all the nations under
heaven. They will hear reports of you and will
tremble and be in anguish because of you."
26From the desert of Kedemoth I sent messengers to Sihon king of Heshbon offering
peace and saying, 27"Let us pass through your
country. We will stay on the main road; we
will not turn aside to the right or to the left.
28Sell us food to eat and water to drink for their
price in silver. Only let us pass through on
foot— 29as the descendants of Esau, who live
in Seir, and the Moabites, who live in Ar, did
for us—until we cross the Jordan into the land
the LORD our God is giving us." 30But Sihon
king of Heshbon refused to let us pass through.
For the LORD your God had made his spirit
stubborn and his heart obstinate in order to
give him into your hands, as he has now done.
31The LORD said to me, "See, I have begun
to deliver Sihon and his country over to you.
Now begin to conquer and possess his land."
32When Sihon and all his army came out to
meet us in battle at Jahaz, 33the LORD our God
delivered him over to us and we struck him
down, together with his sons and his whole
army. 34At that time we took all his towns and
completely destroyed[c] them—men, women
and children. We left no survivors. 35But the
livestock and the plunder from the towns we
had captured we carried off for ourselves.
36From Aroer on the rim of the Arnon Gorge,
and from the town in the gorge, even as far as
Gilead, not one town was too strong for us.
The LORD our God gave us all of them. 37But
in accordance with the command of the LORD
our God, you did not encroach on any of the
land of the Ammonites, neither the land along
the course of the Jabbok nor that around the
towns in the hills.

[a]1 Hebrew *Yam Suph*; that is, Sea of Reeds [b]23 That is, Crete [c]34 The Hebrew term refers to the irrevocable giving over of things or persons to the LORD, often by totally destroying them.

Defeat of Og King of Bashan

3 Next we turned and went up along the road toward Bashan, and Og king of Bashan with his whole army marched out to meet us in battle at Edrei. 2The LORD said to me, "Do not be afraid of him, for I have handed him over to you with his whole army and his land. Do to him what you did to Sihon king of the Amorites, who reigned in Heshbon."

3So the LORD our God also gave into our hands Og king of Bashan and all his army. We struck them down, leaving no survivors. 4At that time we took all his cities. There was not one of the sixty cities that we did not take from them—the whole region of Argob, Og's kingdom in Bashan. 5All these cities were fortified with high walls and with gates and bars, and there were also a great many unwalled villages. 6We completely destroyed[a] them, as we had done with Sihon king of Heshbon, destroying[a] every city—men, women and children. 7But all the livestock and the plunder from their cities we carried off for ourselves.

8So at that time we took from these two kings of the Amorites the territory east of the Jordan, from the Arnon Gorge as far as Mount Hermon. 9(Hermon is called Sirion by the Sidonians; the Amorites call it Senir.) 10We took all the towns on the plateau, and all Gilead, and all Bashan as far as Salecah and Edrei, towns of Og's kingdom in Bashan. 11(Only Og king of Bashan was left of the remnant of the Rephaites. His bed[b] was made of iron and was more than thirteen feet long and six feet wide.[c] It is still in Rabbah of the Ammonites.)

Division of the Land

12Of the land that we took over at that time, I gave the Reubenites and the Gadites the territory north of Aroer by the Arnon Gorge, including half the hill country of Gilead, together with its towns. 13The rest of Gilead and also all of Bashan, the kingdom of Og, I gave to the half tribe of Manasseh. (The whole region of Argob in Bashan used to be known as a land of the Rephaites. 14Jair, a descendant of Manasseh, took the whole region of Argob as far as the border of the Geshurites and the Maacathites; it was named after him, so that to this day Bashan is called Havvoth Jair.[d]) 15And I gave Gilead to Makir. 16But to the Reubenites and the Gadites I gave the territory extending from Gilead down to the Arnon Gorge (the middle of the gorge being the border) and out to the Jabbok River, which is the border of the Ammonites. 17Its western border was the Jordan in the Arabah, from Kinnereth to the Sea of the Arabah (the Salt Sea[e]), below the slopes of Pisgah.

18I commanded you at that time: "The LORD your God has given you this land to take possession of it. But all your able-bodied men, armed for battle, must cross over ahead of your brother Israelites. 19However, your wives, your children and your livestock (I know you have much livestock) may stay in the towns I have given you, 20until the LORD gives rest to your brothers as he has to you, and they too have taken over the land that the LORD your God is giving them, across the Jordan. After that, each of you may go back to the possession I have given you."

Moses Forbidden to Cross the Jordan

21At that time I commanded Joshua: "You have seen with your own eyes all that the LORD your God has done to these two kings. The LORD will do the same to all the kingdoms over there where you are going. 22Do not be afraid of them; the LORD your God himself will fight for you."

23At that time I pleaded with the LORD: 24"O Sovereign LORD, you have begun to show to your servant your greatness and your strong hand. For what god is there in heaven or on earth who can do the deeds and mighty works you do? 25Let me go over and see the good land beyond the Jordan—that fine hill country and Lebanon."

26But because of you the LORD was angry with me and would not listen to me. "That is enough," the LORD said. "Do not speak to me anymore about this matter. 27Go up to the top of Pisgah and look west and north and south and east. Look at the land with your own eyes, since you are not going to cross this Jordan. 28But commission Joshua, and encourage and strengthen him, for he will lead this people across and will cause them to inherit the land that you will see." 29So we stayed in the valley near Beth Peor.

Obedience Commanded

4 Hear now, O Israel, the decrees and laws I am about to teach you. Follow them so that you may live and may go in and take possession of the land that the LORD, the God of your fathers, is giving you. 2Do not add to what I command you and do not subtract from it, but keep the commands of the LORD your God that I give you.

3You saw with your own eyes what the LORD did at Baal Peor. The LORD your God destroyed from among you everyone who followed the Baal of Peor, 4but all of you who held fast to the LORD your God are still alive today.

5See, I have taught you decrees and laws as the LORD my God commanded me, so that you may follow them in the land you are entering to take possession of it. 6Observe them carefully, for this will show your wisdom and understanding to the nations, who will hear about all these decrees and say, "Surely this great nation is a wise and understanding people." 7What other nation is so great as to have their gods near them the way the LORD our God is near us

[a]6 The Hebrew term refers to the irrevocable giving over of things or persons to the LORD, often by totally destroying them. [b]11 Or *sarcophagus* [c]11 Hebrew *nine cubits long and four cubits wide* (about 4 meters long and 1.8 meters wide) [d]14 Or *called the settlements of Jair* [e]17 That is, the Dead Sea

whenever we pray to him? 8And what other nation is so great as to have such righteous decrees and laws as this body of laws I am setting before you today?

9Only be careful, and watch yourselves closely so that you do not forget the things your eyes have seen or let them slip from your heart as long as you live. Teach them to your children and to their children after them. 10Remember the day you stood before the LORD your God at Horeb, when he said to me, "Assemble the people before me to hear my words so that they may learn to revere me as long as they live in the land and may teach them to their children." 11You came near and stood at the foot of the mountain while it blazed with fire to the very heavens, with black clouds and deep darkness. 12Then the LORD spoke to you out of the fire. You heard the sound of words but saw no form; there was only a voice. 13He declared to you his covenant, the Ten Commandments, which he commanded you to follow and then wrote them on two stone tablets. 14And the LORD directed me at that time to teach you the decrees and laws you are to follow in the land that you are crossing the Jordan to possess.

Idolatry Forbidden

15You saw no form of any kind the day the LORD spoke to you at Horeb out of the fire. Therefore watch yourselves very carefully, 16so that you do not become corrupt and make for yourselves an idol, an image of any shape, whether formed like a man or a woman, 17or like any animal on earth or any bird that flies in the air, 18or like any creature that moves along the ground or any fish in the waters below. 19And when you look up to the sky and see the sun, the moon and the stars—all the heavenly array—do not be enticed into bowing down to them and worshiping things the LORD your God has apportioned to all the nations under heaven. 20But as for you, the LORD took you and brought you out of the iron-smelting furnace, out of Egypt, to be the people of his inheritance, as you now are.

21The LORD was angry with me because of you, and he solemnly swore that I would not cross the Jordan and enter the good land the LORD your God is giving you as your inheritance. 22I will die in this land; I will not cross the Jordan; but you are about to cross over and take possession of that good land. 23Be careful not to forget the covenant of the LORD your God that he made with you; do not make for yourselves an idol in the form of anything the LORD your God has forbidden. 24For the LORD your God is a consuming fire, a jealous God.

25After you have had children and grandchildren and have lived in the land a long time—if you then become corrupt and make any kind of idol, doing evil in the eyes of the LORD your God and provoking him to anger, 26I call heaven and earth as witnesses against you this day that you will quickly perish from the land that you are crossing the Jordan to possess. You will not live there long but will certainly be destroyed. 27The LORD will scatter you among the peoples, and only a few of you will survive among the nations to which the LORD will drive you. 28There you will worship man-made gods of wood and stone, which cannot see or hear or eat or smell. 29But if from there you seek the LORD your God, you will find him if you look for him with all your heart and with all your soul. 30When you are in distress and all these things have happened to you, then in later days you will return to the LORD your God and obey him. 31For the LORD your God is a merciful God; he will not abandon or destroy you or forget the covenant with your forefathers, which he confirmed to them by oath.

The LORD Is God

32Ask now about the former days, long before your time, from the day God created man on the earth; ask from one end of the heavens to the other. Has anything so great as this ever happened, or has anything like it ever been heard of? 33Has any other people heard the voice of God[a] speaking out of fire, as you have, and lived? 34Has any god ever tried to take for himself one nation out of another nation, by testings, by miraculous signs and wonders, by war, by a mighty hand and an outstretched arm, or by great and awesome deeds, like all the things the LORD your God did for you in Egypt before your very eyes?

35You were shown these things so that you might know that the LORD is God; besides him there is no other. 36From heaven he made you hear his voice to discipline you. On earth he showed you his great fire, and you heard his words from out of the fire. 37Because he loved your forefathers and chose their descendants after them, he brought you out of Egypt by his Presence and his great strength, 38to drive out before you nations greater and stronger than you and to bring you into their land to give it to you for your inheritance, as it is today.

39Acknowledge and take to heart this day that the LORD is God in heaven above and on the earth below. There is no other. 40Keep his decrees and commands, which I am giving you today, so that it may go well with you and your children after you and that you may live long in the land the LORD your God gives you for all time.

Cities of Refuge

41Then Moses set aside three cities east of the Jordan, 42to which anyone who had killed a person could flee if he had unintentionally killed his neighbor without malice aforethought. He could flee into one of these cities and save his life. 43The cities were these: Bezer in the desert plateau, for the Reubenites;

[a]33 Or *of a god*

Ramoth in Gilead, for the Gadites; and Golan
in Bashan, for the Manassites.

Introduction to the Law

44This is the law Moses set before the Israelites. 45These are the stipulations, decrees and
laws Moses gave them when they came out of
Egypt 46and were in the valley near Beth Peor
east of the Jordan, in the land of Sihon king of
the Amorites, who reigned in Heshbon and
was defeated by Moses and the Israelites as
they came out of Egypt. 47They took possession of his land and the land of Og king of
Bashan, the two Amorite kings east of the Jordan. 48This land extended from Aroer on the
rim of the Arnon Gorge to Mount Siyon[a] (that
is, Hermon), 49and included all the Arabah east
of the Jordan, as far as the Sea of the Arabah,[b]
below the slopes of Pisgah.

The Ten Commandments

5 Moses summoned all Israel and said:
Hear, O Israel, the decrees and laws I declare in your hearing today. Learn them and be
sure to follow them. 2The LORD our God made
a covenant with us at Horeb. 3It was not with
our fathers that the LORD made this covenant,
but with us, with all of us who are alive here
today. 4The LORD spoke to you face to face out
of the fire on the mountain. 5(At that time I
stood between the LORD and you to declare to
you the word of the LORD, because you were
afraid of the fire and did not go up the mountain.) And he said:

6"I am the LORD your God, who
brought you out of Egypt, out of the
land of slavery.

7"You shall have no other gods before[c] me.

8"You shall not make for yourself an idol
in the form of anything in heaven
above or on the earth beneath or in
the waters below. 9You shall not
bow down to them or worship
them; for I, the LORD your God, am
a jealous God, punishing the children for the sin of the fathers to the
third and fourth generation of those
who hate me, 10but showing love to
a thousand ⌞generations⌟ of those
who love me and keep my commandments.

11"You shall not misuse the name of the
LORD your God, for the LORD will
not hold anyone guiltless who mis-
uses his name.

12"Observe the Sabbath day by keeping it
holy, as the LORD your God has
commanded you. 13Six days you
shall labor and do all your work,
14but the seventh day is a Sabbath
to the LORD your God. On it you
shall not do any work, neither you,
nor your son or daughter, nor your
manservant or maidservant, nor
your ox, your donkey or any of
your animals, nor the alien within
your gates, so that your manservant
and maidservant may rest, as you
do. 15Remember that you were
slaves in Egypt and that the LORD
your God brought you out of there
with a mighty hand and an outstretched arm. Therefore the LORD
your God has commanded you to
observe the Sabbath day.

16"Honor your father and your mother, as
the LORD your God has command-
ed you, so that you may live long
and that it may go well with you in
the land the LORD your God is giving you.

17"You shall not murder.

18"You shall not commit adultery.

19"You shall not steal.

20"You shall not give false testimony
against your neighbor.

21"You shall not covet your neighbor's
wife. You shall not set your desire
on your neighbor's house or land,
his manservant or maidservant, his
ox or donkey, or anything that belongs to your neighbor."

22These are the commandments the LORD
proclaimed in a loud voice to your whole assembly there on the mountain from out of the
fire, the cloud and the deep darkness; and he
added nothing more. Then he wrote them on
two stone tablets and gave them to me.
23When you heard the voice out of the darkness, while the mountain was ablaze with fire,
all the leading men of your tribes and your
elders came to me. 24And you said, "The LORD
our God has shown us his glory and his majesty, and we have heard his voice from the fire.
Today we have seen that a man can live even
if God speaks with him. 25But now, why
should we die? This great fire will consume us,
and we will die if we hear the voice of the
LORD our God any longer. 26For what mortal
man has ever heard the voice of the living God
speaking out of fire, as we have, and survived?
27Go near and listen to all that the LORD our
God says. Then tell us whatever the LORD our
God tells you. We will listen and obey."
28The LORD heard you when you spoke to
me and the LORD said to me, "I have heard
what this people said to you. Everything they
said was good. 29Oh, that their hearts would be
inclined to fear me and keep all my commands
always, so that it might go well with them and
their children forever!
30"Go, tell them to return to their tents.
31But you stay here with me so that I may give
you all the commands, decrees and laws you
are to teach them to follow in the land I am
giving them to possess."
32So be careful to do what the LORD your
God has commanded you; do not turn aside to

[a] *48* Hebrew; Syriac (see also Deut. 3:9) *Sirion* [b] *49* That is, the Dead Sea [c] *7* Or *besides*

the right or to the left. 33Walk in all the way that the LORD your God has commanded you, so that you may live and prosper and prolong your days in the land that you will possess.

Love the LORD Your God

6 These are the commands, decrees and laws the LORD your God directed me to teach you to observe in the land that you are crossing the Jordan to possess, 2so that you, your children and their children after them may fear the LORD your God as long as you live by keeping all his decrees and commands that I give you, and so that you may enjoy long life. 3Hear, O Israel, and be careful to obey so that it may go well with you and that you may increase greatly in a land flowing with milk and honey, just as the LORD, the God of your fathers, promised you.

4Hear, O Israel: The LORD our God, the LORD is one.[a] 5Love the LORD your God with all your heart and with all your soul and with all your strength. 6These commandments that I give you today are to be upon your hearts. 7Impress them on your children. Talk about them when you sit at home and when you walk along the road, when you lie down and when you get up. 8Tie them as symbols on your hands and bind them on your foreheads. 9Write them on the doorframes of your houses and on your gates.

10When the LORD your God brings you into the land he swore to your fathers, to Abraham, Isaac and Jacob, to give you—a land with large, flourishing cities you did not build, 11houses filled with all kinds of good things you did not provide, wells you did not dig, and vineyards and olive groves you did not plant—then when you eat and are satisfied, 12be careful that you do not forget the LORD, who brought you out of Egypt, out of the land of slavery.

13Fear the LORD your God, serve him only and take your oaths in his name. 14Do not follow other gods, the gods of the peoples around you; 15for the LORD your God, who is among you, is a jealous God and his anger will burn against you, and he will destroy you from the face of the land. 16Do not test the LORD your God as you did at Massah. 17Be sure to keep the commands of the LORD your God and the stipulations and decrees he has given you. 18Do what is right and good in the LORD's sight, so that it may go well with you and you may go in and take over the good land that the LORD promised on oath to your forefathers, 19thrusting out all your enemies before you, as the LORD said.

20In the future, when your son asks you, "What is the meaning of the stipulations, decrees and laws the LORD our God has commanded you?" 21tell him: "We were slaves of Pharaoh in Egypt, but the LORD brought us out of Egypt with a mighty hand. 22Before our eyes the LORD sent miraculous signs and wonders—great and terrible—upon Egypt and Pharaoh and his whole household. 23But he brought us out from there to bring us in and give us the land that he promised on oath to our forefathers. 24The LORD commanded us to obey all these decrees and to fear the LORD our God, so that we might always prosper and be kept alive, as is the case today. 25And if we are careful to obey all this law before the LORD our God, as he has commanded us, that will be our righteousness."

Driving Out the Nations

7 When the LORD your God brings you into the land you are entering to possess and drives out before you many nations—the Hittites, Girgashites, Amorites, Canaanites, Perizzites, Hivites and Jebusites, seven nations larger and stronger than you— 2and when the LORD your God has delivered them over to you and you have defeated them, then you must destroy them totally.[b] Make no treaty with them, and show them no mercy. 3Do not intermarry with them. Do not give your daughters to their sons or take their daughters for your sons, 4for they will turn your sons away from following me to serve other gods, and the LORD's anger will burn against you and will quickly destroy you. 5This is what you are to do to them: Break down their altars, smash their sacred stones, cut down their Asherah poles[c] and burn their idols in the fire. 6For you are a people holy to the LORD your God. The LORD your God has chosen you out of all the peoples on the face of the earth to be his people, his treasured possession.

7The LORD did not set his affection on you and choose you because you were more numerous than other peoples, for you were the fewest of all peoples. 8But it was because the LORD loved you and kept the oath he swore to your forefathers that he brought you out with a mighty hand and redeemed you from the land of slavery, from the power of Pharaoh king of Egypt. 9Know therefore that the LORD your God is God; he is the faithful God, keeping his covenant of love to a thousand generations of those who love him and keep his commands. 10But

those who hate him he will repay to their
 face by destruction;
he will not be slow to repay to their
 face those who hate him.

11Therefore, take care to follow the commands, decrees and laws I give you today.

12If you pay attention to these laws and are careful to follow them, then the LORD your God will keep his covenant of love with you, as he swore to your forefathers. 13He will love you and bless you and increase your numbers.

[a]*4* Or *The LORD our God is one LORD*; or *The LORD is our God, the LORD is one*; or *The LORD is our God, the LORD alone* [b]*2* The Hebrew term refers to the irrevocable giving over of things or persons to the LORD, often by totally destroying them; also in verse 26. [c]*5* That is, symbols of the goddess Asherah; here and elsewhere in Deuteronomy

He will bless the fruit of your womb, the crops
of your land—your grain, new wine and oil—
the calves of your herds and the lambs of your
flocks in the land that he swore to your forefathers to give you. 14You will be blessed more
than any other people; none of your men or
women will be childless, nor any of your livestock without young. 15The LORD will keep
you free from every disease. He will not inflict
on you the horrible diseases you knew in
Egypt, but he will inflict them on all who hate
you. 16You must destroy all the peoples the
LORD your God gives over to you. Do not look
on them with pity and do not serve their gods,
for that will be a snare to you.

17You may say to yourselves, "These nations are stronger than we are. How can we
drive them out?" 18But do not be afraid of
them; remember well what the LORD your God
did to Pharaoh and to all Egypt. 19You saw
with your own eyes the great trials, the miraculous signs and wonders, the mighty hand and
outstretched arm, with which the LORD your
God brought you out. The LORD your God will
do the same to all the peoples you now fear.
20Moreover, the LORD your God will send the
hornet among them until even the survivors
who hide from you have perished. 21Do not be
terrified by them, for the LORD your God, who
is among you, is a great and awesome God.
22The LORD your God will drive out those nations before you, little by little. You will not be
allowed to eliminate them all at once, or the
wild animals will multiply around you. 23But
the LORD your God will deliver them over to
you, throwing them into great confusion until
they are destroyed. 24He will give their kings
into your hand, and you will wipe out their
names from under heaven. No one will be able
to stand up against you; you will destroy them.
25The images of their gods you are to burn in
the fire. Do not covet the silver and gold on
them, and do not take it for yourselves, or you
will be ensnared by it, for it is detestable to the
LORD your God. 26Do not bring a detestable
thing into your house or you, like it, will be set
apart for destruction. Utterly abhor and detest
it, for it is set apart for destruction.

Do Not Forget the LORD

8 Be careful to follow every command I am
giving you today, so that you may live and
increase and may enter and possess the land
that the LORD promised on oath to your forefathers. 2Remember how the LORD your God led
you all the way in the desert these forty years,
to humble you and to test you in order to know
what was in your heart, whether or not you
would keep his commands. 3He humbled you,
causing you to hunger and then feeding
you with manna, which neither you nor your
fathers had known, to teach you that man does
not live on bread alone but on every word that
comes from the mouth of the LORD. 4Your
clothes did not wear out and your feet did not
swell during these forty years. 5Know then in
your heart that as a man disciplines his son, so
the LORD your God disciplines you.

6Observe the commands of the LORD your
God, walking in his ways and revering him.
7For the LORD your God is bringing you into a
good land—a land with streams and pools of
water, with springs flowing in the valleys and
hills; 8a land with wheat and barley, vines and
fig trees, pomegranates, olive oil and honey; 9a
land where bread will not be scarce and you
will lack nothing; a land where the rocks are
iron and you can dig copper out of the hills.

10When you have eaten and are satisfied,
praise the LORD your God for the good land he
has given you. 11Be careful that you do not
forget the LORD your God, failing to observe
his commands, his laws and his decrees that I
am giving you this day. 12Otherwise, when you
eat and are satisfied, when you build fine
houses and settle down, 13and when your herds
and flocks grow large and your silver and gold
increase and all you have is multiplied, 14then
your heart will become proud and you will
forget the LORD your God, who brought you
out of Egypt, out of the land of slavery. 15He
led you through the vast and dreadful desert,
that thirsty and waterless land, with its venomous snakes and scorpions. He brought you water out of hard rock. 16He gave you manna to
eat in the desert, something your fathers had
never known, to humble and to test you so that
in the end it might go well with you. 17You
may say to yourself, "My power and the
strength of my hands have produced this
wealth for me." 18But remember the LORD
your God, for it is he who gives you the ability
to produce wealth, and so confirms his covenant, which he swore to your forefathers, as it
is today.

19If you ever forget the LORD your God and
follow other gods and worship and bow down
to them, I testify against you today that you
will surely be destroyed. 20Like the nations the
LORD destroyed before you, so you will be
destroyed for not obeying the LORD your God.

Not Because of Israel's Righteousness

9 Hear, O Israel. You are now about to cross
the Jordan to go in and dispossess nations
greater and stronger than you, with large cities
that have walls up to the sky. 2The people are
strong and tall—Anakites! You know about
them and have heard it said: "Who can stand
up against the Anakites?" 3But be assured today that the LORD your God is the one who
goes across ahead of you like a devouring fire.
He will destroy them; he will subdue them
before you. And you will drive them out and
annihilate them quickly, as the LORD has
promised you.

4After the LORD your God has driven them
out before you, do not say to yourself, "The
LORD has brought me here to take possession
of this land because of my righteousness." No,
it is on account of the wickedness of these
nations that the LORD is going to drive them
out before you. 5It is not because of your righ-

teousness or your integrity that you are going in to take possession of their land; but on account of the wickedness of these nations, the LORD your God will drive them out before you, to accomplish what he swore to your fathers, to Abraham, Isaac and Jacob. **6**Understand, then, that it is not because of your righteousness that the LORD your God is giving you this good land to possess, for you are a stiff-necked people.

The Golden Calf

7Remember this and never forget how you provoked the LORD your God to anger in the desert. From the day you left Egypt until you arrived here, you have been rebellious against the LORD. **8**At Horeb you aroused the LORD's wrath so that he was angry enough to destroy you. **9**When I went up on the mountain to receive the tablets of stone, the tablets of the covenant that the LORD had made with you, I stayed on the mountain forty days and forty nights; I ate no bread and drank no water. **10**The LORD gave me two stone tablets inscribed by the finger of God. On them were all the commandments the LORD proclaimed to you on the mountain out of the fire, on the day of the assembly.

11At the end of the forty days and forty nights, the LORD gave me the two stone tablets, the tablets of the covenant. **12**Then the LORD told me, "Go down from here at once, because your people whom you brought out of Egypt have become corrupt. They have turned away quickly from what I commanded them and have made a cast idol for themselves."

13And the LORD said to me, "I have seen this people, and they are a stiff-necked people indeed! **14**Let me alone, so that I may destroy them and blot out their name from under heaven. And I will make you into a nation stronger and more numerous than they."

15So I turned and went down from the mountain while it was ablaze with fire. And the two tablets of the covenant were in my hands.[a] **16**When I looked, I saw that you had sinned against the LORD your God; you had made for yourselves an idol cast in the shape of a calf. You had turned aside quickly from the way that the LORD had commanded you. **17**So I took the two tablets and threw them out of my hands, breaking them to pieces before your eyes.

18Then once again I fell prostrate before the LORD for forty days and forty nights; I ate no bread and drank no water, because of all the sin you had committed, doing what was evil in the LORD's sight and so provoking him to anger. **19**I feared the anger and wrath of the LORD, for he was angry enough with you to destroy you. But again the LORD listened to me. **20**And the LORD was angry enough with Aaron to destroy him, but at that time I prayed for Aaron too. **21**Also I took that sinful thing of yours, the calf you had made, and burned it in the fire. Then I crushed it and ground it to powder as fine as dust and threw the dust into a stream that flowed down the mountain.

22You also made the LORD angry at Taberah, at Massah and at Kibroth Hattaavah.

23And when the LORD sent you out from Kadesh Barnea, he said, "Go up and take possession of the land I have given you." But you rebelled against the command of the LORD your God. You did not trust him or obey him. **24**You have been rebellious against the LORD ever since I have known you.

25I lay prostrate before the LORD those forty days and forty nights because the LORD had said he would destroy you. **26**I prayed to the LORD and said, "O Sovereign LORD, do not destroy your people, your own inheritance that you redeemed by your great power and brought out of Egypt with a mighty hand. **27**Remember your servants Abraham, Isaac and Jacob. Overlook the stubbornness of this people, their wickedness and their sin. **28**Otherwise, the country from which you brought us will say, 'Because the LORD was not able to take them into the land he had promised them, and because he hated them, he brought them out to put them to death in the desert.' **29**But they are your people, your inheritance that you brought out by your great power and your outstretched arm."

Tablets Like the First Ones

10 At that time the LORD said to me, "Chisel out two stone tablets like the first ones and come up to me on the mountain. Also make a wooden chest.[b] **2**I will write on the tablets the words that were on the first tablets, which you broke. Then you are to put them in the chest."

3So I made the ark out of acacia wood and chiseled out two stone tablets like the first ones, and I went up on the mountain with the two tablets in my hands. **4**The LORD wrote on these tablets what he had written before, the Ten Commandments he had proclaimed to you on the mountain, out of the fire, on the day of the assembly. And the LORD gave them to me. **5**Then I came back down the mountain and put the tablets in the ark I had made, as the LORD commanded me, and they are there now.

6(The Israelites traveled from the wells of the Jaakanites to Moserah. There Aaron died and was buried, and Eleazar his son succeeded him as priest. **7**From there they traveled to Gudgodah and on to Jotbathah, a land with streams of water. **8**At that time the LORD set apart the tribe of Levi to carry the ark of the covenant of the LORD, to stand before the LORD to minister and to pronounce blessings in his name, as they still do today. **9**That is why the Levites have no share or inheritance among their brothers; the LORD is their inheritance, as the LORD your God told them.)

10Now I had stayed on the mountain forty days and nights, as I did the first time, and the

[a] *15* Or *And I had the two tablets of the covenant with me, one in each hand* [b] *1* That is, an ark

LORD listened to me at this time also. It was not his will to destroy you. 11"Go," the LORD said to me, "and lead the people on their way, so that they may enter and possess the land that I swore to their fathers to give them."

Fear the LORD

12And now, O Israel, what does the LORD your God ask of you but to fear the LORD your God, to walk in all his ways, to love him, to serve the LORD your God with all your heart and with all your soul, 13and to observe the LORD's commands and decrees that I am giving you today for your own good?

14To the LORD your God belong the heavens, even the highest heavens, the earth and everything in it. 15Yet the LORD set his affection on your forefathers and loved them, and he chose you, their descendants, above all the nations, as it is today. 16Circumcise your hearts, therefore, and do not be stiff-necked any longer. 17For the LORD your God is God of gods and Lord of lords, the great God, mighty and awesome, who shows no partiality and accepts no bribes. 18He defends the cause of the fatherless and the widow, and loves the alien, giving him food and clothing. 19And you are to love those who are aliens, for you yourselves were aliens in Egypt. 20Fear the LORD your God and serve him. Hold fast to him and take your oaths in his name. 21He is your praise; he is your God, who performed for you those great and awesome wonders you saw with your own eyes. 22Your forefathers who went down into Egypt were seventy in all, and now the LORD your God has made you as numerous as the stars in the sky.

Love and Obey the LORD

11 Love the LORD your God and keep his requirements, his decrees, his laws and his commands always. 2Remember today that your children were not the ones who saw and experienced the discipline of the LORD your God: his majesty, his mighty hand, his outstretched arm; 3the signs he performed and the things he did in the heart of Egypt, both to Pharaoh king of Egypt and to his whole country; 4what he did to the Egyptian army, to its horses and chariots, how he overwhelmed them with the waters of the Red Sea[a] as they were pursuing you, and how the LORD brought lasting ruin on them. 5It was not your children who saw what he did for you in the desert until you arrived at this place, 6and what he did to Dathan and Abiram, sons of Eliab the Reubenite, when the earth opened its mouth right in the middle of all Israel and swallowed them up with their households, their tents and every living thing that belonged to them. 7But it was your own eyes that saw all these great things the LORD has done.

8Observe therefore all the commands I am giving you today, so that you may have the strength to go in and take over the land that you are crossing the Jordan to possess, 9and so that you may live long in the land that the LORD swore to your forefathers to give to them and their descendants, a land flowing with milk and honey. 10The land you are entering to take over is not like the land of Egypt, from which you have come, where you planted your seed and irrigated it by foot as in a vegetable garden. 11But the land you are crossing the Jordan to take possession of is a land of mountains and valleys that drinks rain from heaven. 12It is a land the LORD your God cares for; the eyes of the LORD your God are continually on it from the beginning of the year to its end.

13So if you faithfully obey the commands I am giving you today—to love the LORD your God and to serve him with all your heart and with all your soul— 14then I will send rain on your land in its season, both autumn and spring rains, so that you may gather in your grain, new wine and oil. 15I will provide grass in the fields for your cattle, and you will eat and be satisfied.

16Be careful, or you will be enticed to turn away and worship other gods and bow down to them. 17Then the LORD's anger will burn against you, and he will shut the heavens so that it will not rain and the ground will yield no produce, and you will soon perish from the good land the LORD is giving you. 18Fix these words of mine in your hearts and minds; tie them as symbols on your hands and bind them on your foreheads. 19Teach them to your children, talking about them when you sit at home and when you walk along the road, when you lie down and when you get up. 20Write them on the doorframes of your houses and on your gates, 21so that your days and the days of your children may be many in the land that the LORD swore to give your forefathers, as many as the days that the heavens are above the earth.

22If you carefully observe all these commands I am giving you to follow—to love the LORD your God, to walk in all his ways and to hold fast to him— 23then the LORD will drive out all these nations before you, and you will dispossess nations larger and stronger than you. 24Every place where you set your foot will be yours: Your territory will extend from the desert to Lebanon, and from the Euphrates River to the western sea.[b] 25No man will be able to stand against you. The LORD your God, as he promised you, will put the terror and fear of you on the whole land, wherever you go.

26See, I am setting before you today a blessing and a curse— 27the blessing if you obey the commands of the LORD your God that I am giving you today; 28the curse if you disobey the commands of the LORD your God and turn from the way that I command you today by following other gods, which you have not known. 29When the LORD your God has brought you into the land you are entering to possess, you are to proclaim on Mount Geri-

[a]4 Hebrew *Yam Suph*; that is, Sea of Reeds [b]24 That is, the Mediterranean

zim the blessings, and on Mount Ebal the curses. 30As you know, these mountains are across the Jordan, west of the road,[a] toward the setting sun, near the great trees of Moreh, in the territory of those Canaanites living in the Arabah in the vicinity of Gilgal. 31You are about to cross the Jordan to enter and take possession of the land the LORD your God is giving you. When you have taken it over and are living there, 32be sure that you obey all the decrees and laws I am setting before you today.

The One Place of Worship

12 These are the decrees and laws you must be careful to follow in the land that the LORD, the God of your fathers, has given you to possess—as long as you live in the land. 2Destroy completely all the places on the high mountains and on the hills and under every spreading tree where the nations you are dispossessing worship their gods. 3Break down their altars, smash their sacred stones and burn their Asherah poles in the fire; cut down the idols of their gods and wipe out their names from those places.

4You must not worship the LORD your God in their way. 5But you are to seek the place the LORD your God will choose from among all your tribes to put his Name there for his dwelling. To that place you must go; 6there bring your burnt offerings and sacrifices, your tithes and special gifts, what you have vowed to give and your freewill offerings, and the firstborn of your herds and flocks. 7There, in the presence of the LORD your God, you and your families shall eat and shall rejoice in everything you have put your hand to, because the LORD your God has blessed you.

8You are not to do as we do here today, everyone as he sees fit, 9since you have not yet reached the resting place and the inheritance the LORD your God is giving you. 10But you will cross the Jordan and settle in the land the LORD your God is giving you as an inheritance, and he will give you rest from all your enemies around you so that you will live in safety. 11Then to the place the LORD your God will choose as a dwelling for his Name—there you are to bring everything I command you: your burnt offerings and sacrifices, your tithes and special gifts, and all the choice possessions you have vowed to the LORD. 12And there rejoice before the LORD your God, you, your sons and daughters, your menservants and maidservants, and the Levites from your towns, who have no allotment or inheritance of their own. 13Be careful not to sacrifice your burnt offerings anywhere you please. 14Offer them only at the place the LORD will choose in one of your tribes, and there observe everything I command you.

15Nevertheless, you may slaughter your animals in any of your towns and eat as much of the meat as you want, as if it were gazelle or deer, according to the blessing the LORD your God gives you. Both the ceremonially unclean and the clean may eat it. 16But you must not eat the blood; pour it out on the ground like water. 17You must not eat in your own towns the tithe of your grain and new wine and oil, or the firstborn of your herds and flocks, or whatever you have vowed to give, or your freewill offerings or special gifts. 18Instead, you are to eat them in the presence of the LORD your God at the place the LORD your God will choose—you, your sons and daughters, your menservants and maidservants, and the Levites from your towns—and you are to rejoice before the LORD your God in everything you put your hand to. 19Be careful not to neglect the Levites as long as you live in your land.

20When the LORD your God has enlarged your territory as he promised you, and you crave meat and say, "I would like some meat," then you may eat as much of it as you want. 21If the place where the LORD your God chooses to put his Name is too far away from you, you may slaughter animals from the herds and flocks the LORD has given you, as I have commanded you, and in your own towns you may eat as much of them as you want. 22Eat them as you would gazelle or deer. Both the ceremonially unclean and the clean may eat. 23But be sure you do not eat the blood, because the blood is the life, and you must not eat the life with the meat. 24You must not eat the blood; pour it out on the ground like water. 25Do not eat it, so that it may go well with you and your children after you, because you will be doing what is right in the eyes of the LORD.

26But take your consecrated things and whatever you have vowed to give, and go to the place the LORD will choose. 27Present your burnt offerings on the altar of the LORD your God, both the meat and the blood. The blood of your sacrifices must be poured beside the altar of the LORD your God, but you may eat the meat. 28Be careful to obey all these regulations I am giving you, so that it may always go well with you and your children after you, because you will be doing what is good and right in the eyes of the LORD your God.

29The LORD your God will cut off before you the nations you are about to invade and dispossess. But when you have driven them out and settled in their land, 30and after they have been destroyed before you, be careful not to be ensnared by inquiring about their gods, saying, "How do these nations serve their gods? We will do the same." 31You must not worship the LORD your God in their way, because in worshiping their gods, they do all kinds of detestable things the LORD hates. They even burn their sons and daughters in the fire as sacrifices to their gods.

32See that you do all I command you; do not add to it or take away from it.

[a]30 Or *Jordan, westward*

Worshiping Other Gods

13 If a prophet, or one who foretells by dreams, appears among you and announces to you a miraculous sign or wonder, 2and if the sign or wonder of which he has spoken takes place, and he says, "Let us follow other gods" (gods you have not known) "and let us worship them," 3you must not listen to the words of that prophet or dreamer. The LORD your God is testing you to find out whether you love him with all your heart and with all your soul. 4It is the LORD your God you must follow, and him you must revere. Keep his commands and obey him; serve him and hold fast to him. 5That prophet or dreamer must be put to death, because he preached rebellion against the LORD your God, who brought you out of Egypt and redeemed you from the land of slavery; he has tried to turn you from the way the LORD your God commanded you to follow. You must purge the evil from among you.

6If your very own brother, or your son or daughter, or the wife you love, or your closest friend secretly entices you, saying, "Let us go and worship other gods" (gods that neither you nor your fathers have known, 7gods of the peoples around you, whether near or far, from one end of the land to the other), 8do not yield to him or listen to him. Show him no pity. Do not spare him or shield him. 9You must certainly put him to death. Your hand must be the first in putting him to death, and then the hands of all the people. 10Stone him to death, because he tried to turn you away from the LORD your God, who brought you out of Egypt, out of the land of slavery. 11Then all Israel will hear and be afraid, and no one among you will do such an evil thing again.

12If you hear it said about one of the towns the LORD your God is giving you to live in 13that wicked men have arisen among you and have led the people of their town astray, saying, "Let us go and worship other gods" (gods you have not known), 14then you must inquire, probe and investigate it thoroughly. And if it is true and it has been proved that this detestable thing has been done among you, 15you must certainly put to the sword all who live in that town. Destroy it completely,[a] both its people and its livestock. 16Gather all the plunder of the town into the middle of the public square and completely burn the town and all its plunder as a whole burnt offering to the LORD your God. It is to remain a ruin forever, never to be rebuilt. 17None of those condemned things[a] shall be found in your hands, so that the LORD will turn from his fierce anger; he will show you mercy, have compassion on you, and increase your numbers, as he promised on oath to your forefathers, 18because you obey the LORD your God, keeping all his commands that I am giving you today and doing what is right in his eyes.

Clean and Unclean Food

14 You are the children of the LORD your God. Do not cut yourselves or shave the front of your heads for the dead, 2for you are a people holy to the LORD your God. Out of all the peoples on the face of the earth, the LORD has chosen you to be his treasured possession.

3Do not eat any detestable thing. 4These are the animals you may eat: the ox, the sheep, the goat, 5the deer, the gazelle, the roe deer, the wild goat, the ibex, the antelope and the mountain sheep.[b] 6You may eat any animal that has a split hoof divided in two and that chews the cud. 7However, of those that chew the cud or that have a split hoof completely divided you may not eat the camel, the rabbit or the coney.[c] Although they chew the cud, they do not have a split hoof; they are ceremonially unclean for you. 8The pig is also unclean; although it has a split hoof, it does not chew the cud. You are not to eat their meat or touch their carcasses.

9Of all the creatures living in the water, you may eat any that has fins and scales. 10But anything that does not have fins and scales you may not eat; for you it is unclean.

11You may eat any clean bird. 12But these you may not eat: the eagle, the vulture, the black vulture, 13the red kite, the black kite, any kind of falcon, 14any kind of raven, 15the horned owl, the screech owl, the gull, any kind of hawk, 16the little owl, the great owl, the white owl, 17the desert owl, the osprey, the cormorant, 18the stork, any kind of heron, the hoopoe and the bat.

19All flying insects that swarm are unclean to you; do not eat them. 20But any winged creature that is clean you may eat.

21Do not eat anything you find already dead. You may give it to an alien living in any of your towns, and he may eat it, or you may sell it to a foreigner. But you are a people holy to the LORD your God.

Do not cook a young goat in its mother's milk.

Tithes

22Be sure to set aside a tenth of all that your fields produce each year. 23Eat the tithe of your grain, new wine and oil, and the firstborn of your herds and flocks in the presence of the LORD your God at the place he will choose as a dwelling for his Name, so that you may learn to revere the LORD your God always. 24But if that place is too distant and you have been blessed by the LORD your God and cannot carry your tithe (because the place where the LORD will choose to put his Name is so far away), 25then exchange your tithe for silver, and take the silver with you and go to the place the LORD your God will choose. 26Use the sil-

[a] *15,17* The Hebrew term refers to the irrevocable giving over of things or persons to the LORD, often by totally destroying them. [b] *5* The precise identification of some of the birds and animals in this chapter is uncertain.
[c] *7* That is, the hyrax or rock badger

ver to buy whatever you like: cattle, sheep, wine or other fermented drink, or anything you wish. Then you and your household shall eat there in the presence of the LORD your God and rejoice. 27And do not neglect the Levites living in your towns, for they have no allotment or inheritance of their own.

28At the end of every three years, bring all the tithes of that year's produce and store it in your towns, 29so that the Levites (who have no allotment or inheritance of their own) and the aliens, the fatherless and the widows who live in your towns may come and eat and be satisfied, and so that the LORD your God may bless you in all the work of your hands.

The Year for Canceling Debts

15 At the end of every seven years you must cancel debts. 2This is how it is to be done: Every creditor shall cancel the loan he has made to his fellow Israelite. He shall not require payment from his fellow Israelite or brother, because the LORD's time for canceling debts has been proclaimed. 3You may require payment from a foreigner, but you must cancel any debt your brother owes you. 4However, there should be no poor among you, for in the land the LORD your God is giving you to possess as your inheritance, he will richly bless you, 5if only you fully obey the LORD your God and are careful to follow all these commands I am giving you today. 6For the LORD your God will bless you as he has promised, and you will lend to many nations but will borrow from none. You will rule over many nations but none will rule over you.

7If there is a poor man among your brothers in any of the towns of the land that the LORD your God is giving you, do not be hardhearted or tightfisted toward your poor brother. 8Rather be openhanded and freely lend him whatever he needs. 9Be careful not to harbor this wicked thought: "The seventh year, the year for canceling debts, is near," so that you do not show ill will toward your needy brother and give him nothing. He may then appeal to the LORD against you, and you will be found guilty of sin. 10Give generously to him and do so without a grudging heart; then because of this the LORD your God will bless you in all your work and in everything you put your hand to. 11There will always be poor people in the land. Therefore I command you to be openhanded toward your brothers and toward the poor and needy in your land.

Freeing Servants

12If a fellow Hebrew, a man or a woman, sells himself to you and serves you six years, in the seventh year you must let him go free. 13And when you release him, do not send him away empty-handed. 14Supply him liberally from your flock, your threshing floor and your winepress. Give to him as the LORD your God has blessed you. 15Remember that you were slaves in Egypt and the LORD your God redeemed you. That is why I give you this command today.

16But if your servant says to you, "I do not want to leave you," because he loves you and your family and is well off with you, 17then take an awl and push it through his ear lobe into the door, and he will become your servant for life. Do the same for your maidservant.

18Do not consider it a hardship to set your servant free, because his service to you these six years has been worth twice as much as that of a hired hand. And the LORD your God will bless you in everything you do.

The Firstborn Animals

19Set apart for the LORD your God every firstborn male of your herds and flocks. Do not put the firstborn of your oxen to work, and do not shear the firstborn of your sheep. 20Each year you and your family are to eat them in the presence of the LORD your God at the place he will choose. 21If an animal has a defect, is lame or blind, or has any serious flaw, you must not sacrifice it to the LORD your God. 22You are to eat it in your own towns. Both the ceremonially unclean and the clean may eat it, as if it were gazelle or deer. 23But you must not eat the blood; pour it out on the ground like water.

Passover

16 Observe the month of Abib and celebrate the Passover of the LORD your God, because in the month of Abib he brought you out of Egypt by night. 2Sacrifice as the Passover to the LORD your God an animal from your flock or herd at the place the LORD will choose as a dwelling for his Name. 3Do not eat it with bread made with yeast, but for seven days eat unleavened bread, the bread of affliction, because you left Egypt in haste—so that all the days of your life you may remember the time of your departure from Egypt. 4Let no yeast be found in your possession in all your land for seven days. Do not let any of the meat you sacrifice on the evening of the first day remain until morning.

5You must not sacrifice the Passover in any town the LORD your God gives you 6except in the place he will choose as a dwelling for his Name. There you must sacrifice the Passover in the evening, when the sun goes down, on the anniversary[a] of your departure from Egypt. 7Roast it and eat it at the place the LORD your God will choose. Then in the morning return to your tents. 8For six days eat unleavened bread and on the seventh day hold an assembly to the LORD your God and do no work.

Feast of Weeks

9Count off seven weeks from the time you begin to put the sickle to the standing grain. 10Then celebrate the Feast of Weeks to the LORD your God by giving a freewill offering in proportion to the blessings the LORD your God has given you. 11And rejoice before the LORD

[a]6 Or *down, at the time of day*

your God at the place he will choose as a
dwelling for his Name—you, your sons and
daughters, your menservants and maidservants, the Levites in your towns, and the
aliens, the fatherless and the widows living
among you. 12Remember that you were slaves
in Egypt, and follow carefully these decrees.

Feast of Tabernacles

13Celebrate the Feast of Tabernacles for sev-
en days after you have gathered the produce of
your threshing floor and your winepress. 14Be
joyful at your Feast—you, your sons and
daughters, your menservants and maidservants, and the Levites, the aliens, the fatherless
and the widows who live in your towns. 15For
seven days celebrate the Feast to the LORD
your God at the place the LORD will choose.
For the LORD your God will bless you in all
your harvest and in all the work of your hands,
and your joy will be complete.

16Three times a year all your men must appear before the LORD your God at the place he
will choose: at the Feast of Unleavened Bread,
the Feast of Weeks and the Feast of Tabernacles. No man should appear before the LORD
empty-handed: 17Each of you must bring a gift
in proportion to the way the LORD your God
has blessed you.

Judges

18Appoint judges and officials for each of
your tribes in every town the LORD your God
is giving you, and they shall judge the people
fairly. 19Do not pervert justice or show partiality. Do not accept a bribe, for a bribe blinds the
eyes of the wise and twists the words of the
righteous. 20Follow justice and justice alone,
so that you may live and possess the land the
LORD your God is giving you.

Worshiping Other Gods

21Do not set up any wooden Asherah pole[a]
beside the altar you build to the LORD your
God, 22and do not erect a sacred stone, for
these the LORD your God hates.

17 Do not sacrifice to the LORD your God
an ox or a sheep that has any defect or
flaw in it, for that would be detestable to him.

2If a man or woman living among you in
one of the towns the LORD gives you is found
doing evil in the eyes of the LORD your God in
violation of his covenant, 3and contrary to my
command has worshiped other gods, bowing
down to them or to the sun or the moon or the
stars of the sky, 4and this has been brought to
your attention, then you must investigate it
thoroughly. If it is true and it has been proved
that this detestable thing has been done in Israel, 5take the man or woman who has done this
evil deed to your city gate and stone that person to death. 6On the testimony of two or three
witnesses a man shall be put to death, but no
one shall be put to death on the testimony of
only one witness. 7The hands of the witnesses
must be the first in putting him to death, and
then the hands of all the people. You must
purge the evil from among you.

Law Courts

8If cases come before your courts that are
too difficult for you to judge—whether bloodshed, lawsuits or assaults—take them to the
place the LORD your God will choose. 9Go to
the priests, who are Levites, and to the judge
who is in office at that time. Inquire of them
and they will give you the verdict. 10You must
act according to the decisions they give you at
the place the LORD will choose. Be careful to
do everything they direct you to do. 11Act according to the law they teach you and the decisions they give you. Do not turn aside from
what they tell you, to the right or to the left.
12The man who shows contempt for the judge
or for the priest who stands ministering there
to the LORD your God must be put to death.
You must purge the evil from Israel. 13All the
people will hear and be afraid, and will not be
contemptuous again.

The King

14When you enter the land the LORD your
God is giving you and have taken possession
of it and settled in it, and you say, "Let us set
a king over us like all the nations around us,"
15be sure to appoint over you the king the
LORD your God chooses. He must be from
among your own brothers. Do not place a foreigner over you, one who is not a brother Israelite. 16The king, moreover, must not acquire
great numbers of horses for himself or make
the people return to Egypt to get more of them,
for the LORD has told you, "You are not to go
back that way again." 17He must not take many
wives, or his heart will be led astray. He must
not accumulate large amounts of silver and
gold.

18When he takes the throne of his kingdom,
he is to write for himself on a scroll a copy of
this law, taken from that of the priests, who are
Levites. 19It is to be with him, and he is to read
it all the days of his life so that he may learn
to revere the LORD his God and follow carefully all the words of this law and these decrees
20and not consider himself better than his
brothers and turn from the law to the right or
to the left. Then he and his descendants will
reign a long time over his kingdom in Israel.

Offerings for Priests and Levites

18 The priests, who are Levites—indeed
the whole tribe of Levi—are to have no
allotment or inheritance with Israel. They shall
live on the offerings made to the LORD by fire,
for that is their inheritance. 2They shall have
no inheritance among their brothers; the LORD
is their inheritance, as he promised them.

3This is the share due the priests from the
people who sacrifice a bull or a sheep: the
shoulder, the jowls and the inner parts. 4You
are to give them the firstfruits of your grain,
new wine and oil, and the first wool from the

[a]21 Or *Do not plant any tree dedicated to Asherah*

shearing of your sheep, 5for the LORD your
God has chosen them and their descendants
out of all your tribes to stand and minister in
the LORD's name always.
6If a Levite moves from one of your towns
anywhere in Israel where he is living, and
comes in all earnestness to the place the LORD
will choose, 7he may minister in the name of
the LORD his God like all his fellow Levites
who serve there in the presence of the LORD.
8He is to share equally in their benefits, even
though he has received money from the sale of
family possessions.

Detestable Practices

9When you enter the land the LORD your
God is giving you, do not learn to imitate the
detestable ways of the nations there. 10Let no
one be found among you who sacrifices his
son or daughter in[a] the fire, who practices divination or sorcery, interprets omens, engages
in witchcraft, 11or casts spells, or who is a
medium or spiritist or who consults the dead.
12Anyone who does these things is detestable
to the LORD, and because of these detestable
practices the LORD your God will drive out
those nations before you. 13You must be
blameless before the LORD your God.

The Prophet

14The nations you will dispossess listen to
those who practice sorcery or divination. But
as for you, the LORD your God has not permitted you to do so. 15The LORD your God will
raise up for you a prophet like me from among
your own brothers. You must listen to him.
16For this is what you asked of the LORD your
God at Horeb on the day of the assembly when
you said, "Let us not hear the voice of the
LORD our God nor see this great fire anymore,
or we will die."
17The LORD said to me: "What they say is
good. 18I will raise up for them a prophet like
you from among their brothers; I will put my
words in his mouth, and he will tell them everything I command him. 19If anyone does not
listen to my words that the prophet speaks in
my name, I myself will call him to account.
20But a prophet who presumes to speak in my
name anything I have not commanded him to
say, or a prophet who speaks in the name of
other gods, must be put to death."
21You may say to yourselves, "How can we
know when a message has not been spoken by
the LORD?" 22If what a prophet proclaims in
the name of the LORD does not take place or
come true, that is a message the LORD has not
spoken. That prophet has spoken presumptu-
ously. Do not be afraid of him.

Cities of Refuge

19 When the LORD your God has destroyed
the nations whose land he is giving you,
and when you have driven them out and settled
in their towns and houses, 2then set aside for
yourselves three cities centrally located in the
land the LORD your God is giving you to possess. 3Build roads to them and divide into three
parts the land the LORD your God is giving you
as an inheritance, so that anyone who kills a
man may flee there.
4This is the rule concerning the man who
kills another and flees there to save his life—
one who kills his neighbor unintentionally,
without malice aforethought. 5For instance, a
man may go into the forest with his neighbor
to cut wood, and as he swings his ax to fell a
tree, the head may fly off and hit his neighbor
and kill him. That man may flee to one of these
cities and save his life. 6Otherwise, the avenger of blood might pursue him in a rage, overtake him if the distance is too great, and kill
him even though he is not deserving of death,
since he did it to his neighbor without malice
aforethought. 7This is why I command you to
set aside for yourselves three cities.
8If the LORD your God enlarges your territory, as he promised on oath to your forefathers,
and gives you the whole land he promised
them, 9because you carefully follow all these
laws I command you today—to love the LORD
your God and to walk always in his ways—
then you are to set aside three more cities.
10Do this so that innocent blood will not be
shed in your land, which the LORD your God is
giving you as your inheritance, and so that you
will not be guilty of bloodshed.
11But if a man hates his neighbor and lies in
wait for him, assaults and kills him, and then
flees to one of these cities, 12the elders of his
town shall send for him, bring him back from
the city, and hand him over to the avenger of
blood to die. 13Show him no pity. You must
purge from Israel the guilt of shedding innocent blood, so that it may go well with you.
14Do not move your neighbor's boundary
stone set up by your predecessors in the inheritance you receive in the land the LORD your
God is giving you to possess.

Witnesses

15One witness is not enough to convict a
man accused of any crime or offense he may
have committed. A matter must be established
by the testimony of two or three witnesses.
16If a malicious witness takes the stand to
accuse a man of a crime, 17the two men involved in the dispute must stand in the presence of the LORD before the priests and the
judges who are in office at the time. 18The
judges must make a thorough investigation,
and if the witness proves to be a liar, giving
false testimony against his brother, 19then do
to him as he intended to do to his brother. You
must purge the evil from among you. 20The
rest of the people will hear of this and be
afraid, and never again will such an evil thing
be done among you. 21Show no pity: life for
life, eye for eye, tooth for tooth, hand for hand,
foot for foot.

[a] *10* Or *who makes his son or daughter pass through*

Going to War

20 When you go to war against your enemies and see horses and chariots and an army greater than yours, do not be afraid of them, because the LORD your God, who brought you up out of Egypt, will be with you. 2When you are about to go into battle, the priest shall come forward and address the army. 3He shall say: "Hear, O Israel, today you are going into battle against your enemies. Do not be fainthearted or afraid; do not be terrified or give way to panic before them. 4For the LORD your God is the one who goes with you to fight for you against your enemies to give you victory."

5The officers shall say to the army: "Has anyone built a new house and not dedicated it? Let him go home, or he may die in battle and someone else may dedicate it. 6Has anyone planted a vineyard and not begun to enjoy it? Let him go home, or he may die in battle and someone else enjoy it. 7Has anyone become pledged to a woman and not married her? Let him go home, or he may die in battle and someone else marry her." 8Then the officers shall add, "Is any man afraid or fainthearted? Let him go home so that his brothers will not become disheartened too." 9When the officers have finished speaking to the army, they shall appoint commanders over it.

10When you march up to attack a city, make its people an offer of peace. 11If they accept and open their gates, all the people in it shall be subject to forced labor and shall work for you. 12If they refuse to make peace and they engage you in battle, lay siege to that city. 13When the LORD your God delivers it into your hand, put to the sword all the men in it. 14As for the women, the children, the livestock and everything else in the city, you may take these as plunder for yourselves. And you may use the plunder the LORD your God gives you from your enemies. 15This is how you are to treat all the cities that are at a distance from you and do not belong to the nations nearby.

16However, in the cities of the nations the LORD your God is giving you as an inheritance, do not leave alive anything that breathes. 17Completely destroy[a] them—the Hittites, Amorites, Canaanites, Perizzites, Hivites and Jebusites—as the LORD your God has commanded you. 18Otherwise, they will teach you to follow all the detestable things they do in worshiping their gods, and you will sin against the LORD your God.

19When you lay siege to a city for a long time, fighting against it to capture it, do not destroy its trees by putting an ax to them, because you can eat their fruit. Do not cut them down. Are the trees of the field people, that you should besiege them?[b] 20However, you may cut down trees that you know are not fruit trees and use them to build siege works until the city at war with you falls.

Atonement for an Unsolved Murder

21 If a man is found slain, lying in a field in the land the LORD your God is giving you to possess, and it is not known who killed him, 2your elders and judges shall go out and measure the distance from the body to the neighboring towns. 3Then the elders of the town nearest the body shall take a heifer that has never been worked and has never worn a yoke 4and lead her down to a valley that has not been plowed or planted and where there is a flowing stream. There in the valley they are to break the heifer's neck. 5The priests, the sons of Levi, shall step forward, for the LORD your God has chosen them to minister and to pronounce blessings in the name of the LORD and to decide all cases of dispute and assault. 6Then all the elders of the town nearest the body shall wash their hands over the heifer whose neck was broken in the valley, 7and they shall declare: "Our hands did not shed this blood, nor did our eyes see it done. 8Accept this atonement for your people Israel, whom you have redeemed, O LORD, and do not hold your people guilty of the blood of an innocent man." And the bloodshed will be atoned for. 9So you will purge from yourselves the guilt of shedding innocent blood, since you have done what is right in the eyes of the LORD.

Marrying a Captive Woman

10When you go to war against your enemies and the LORD your God delivers them into your hands and you take captives, 11if you notice among the captives a beautiful woman and are attracted to her, you may take her as your wife. 12Bring her into your home and have her shave her head, trim her nails 13and put aside the clothes she was wearing when captured. After she has lived in your house and mourned her father and mother for a full month, then you may go to her and be her husband and she shall be your wife. 14If you are not pleased with her, let her go wherever she wishes. You must not sell her or treat her as a slave, since you have dishonored her.

The Right of the Firstborn

15If a man has two wives, and he loves one but not the other, and both bear him sons but the firstborn is the son of the wife he does not love, 16when he wills his property to his sons, he must not give the rights of the firstborn to the son of the wife he loves in preference to his actual firstborn, the son of the wife he does not love. 17He must acknowledge the son of his unloved wife as the firstborn by giving him a double share of all he has. That son is the first sign of his father's strength. The right of the firstborn belongs to him.

A Rebellious Son

18If a man has a stubborn and rebellious son who does not obey his father and mother and

[a] *17* The Hebrew term refers to the irrevocable giving over of things or persons to the LORD, often by totally destroying them. [b] *19* Or *down to use in the siege, for the fruit trees are for the benefit of man.*

will not listen to them when they discipline him, **19**his father and mother shall take hold of him and bring him to the elders at the gate of his town. **20**They shall say to the elders, "This son of ours is stubborn and rebellious. He will not obey us. He is a profligate and a drunkard." **21**Then all the men of his town shall stone him to death. You must purge the evil from among you. All Israel will hear of it and be afraid.

Various Laws

22If a man guilty of a capital offense is put to death and his body is hung on a tree, **23**you must not leave his body on the tree overnight. Be sure to bury him that same day, because anyone who is hung on a tree is under God's curse. You must not desecrate the land the LORD your God is giving you as an inheritance.

22 If you see your brother's ox or sheep straying, do not ignore it but be sure to take it back to him. **2**If the brother does not live near you or if you do not know who he is, take it home with you and keep it until he comes looking for it. Then give it back to him. **3**Do the same if you find your brother's donkey or his cloak or anything he loses. Do not ignore it.

4If you see your brother's donkey or his ox fallen on the road, do not ignore it. Help him get it to its feet.

5A woman must not wear men's clothing, nor a man wear women's clothing, for the LORD your God detests anyone who does this.

6If you come across a bird's nest beside the road, either in a tree or on the ground, and the mother is sitting on the young or on the eggs, do not take the mother with the young. **7**You may take the young, but be sure to let the mother go, so that it may go well with you and you may have a long life.

8When you build a new house, make a parapet around your roof so that you may not bring the guilt of bloodshed on your house if someone falls from the roof.

9Do not plant two kinds of seed in your vineyard; if you do, not only the crops you plant but also the fruit of the vineyard will be defiled.[a]

10Do not plow with an ox and a donkey yoked together.

11Do not wear clothes of wool and linen woven together.

12Make tassels on the four corners of the cloak you wear.

Marriage Violations

13If a man takes a wife and, after lying with her, dislikes her **14**and slanders her and gives her a bad name, saying, "I married this woman, but when I approached her, I did not find proof of her virginity," **15**then the girl's father and mother shall bring proof that she was a virgin to the town elders at the gate. **16**The girl's father will say to the elders, "I gave my daughter in marriage to this man, but he dislikes her. **17**Now he has slandered her and said, 'I did not find your daughter to be a virgin.' But here is the proof of my daughter's virginity." Then her parents shall display the cloth before the elders of the town, **18**and the elders shall take the man and punish him. **19**They shall fine him a hundred shekels of silver[b] and give them to the girl's father, because this man has given an Israelite virgin a bad name. She shall continue to be his wife; he must not divorce her as long as he lives.

20If, however, the charge is true and no proof of the girl's virginity can be found, **21**she shall be brought to the door of her father's house and there the men of her town shall stone her to death. She has done a disgraceful thing in Israel by being promiscuous while still in her father's house. You must purge the evil from among you.

22If a man is found sleeping with another man's wife, both the man who slept with her and the woman must die. You must purge the evil from Israel.

23If a man happens to meet in a town a virgin pledged to be married and he sleeps with her, **24**you shall take both of them to the gate of that town and stone them to death—the girl because she was in a town and did not scream for help, and the man because he violated another man's wife. You must purge the evil from among you.

25But if out in the country a man happens to meet a girl pledged to be married and rapes her, only the man who has done this shall die. **26**Do nothing to the girl; she has committed no sin deserving death. This case is like that of someone who attacks and murders his neighbor, **27**for the man found the girl out in the country, and though the betrothed girl screamed, there was no one to rescue her.

28If a man happens to meet a virgin who is not pledged to be married and rapes her and they are discovered, **29**he shall pay the girl's father fifty shekels of silver.[c] He must marry the girl, for he has violated her. He can never divorce her as long as he lives.

30A man is not to marry his father's wife; he must not dishonor his father's bed.

Exclusion From the Assembly

23 No one who has been emasculated by crushing or cutting may enter the assembly of the LORD.

2No one born of a forbidden marriage[d] nor any of his descendants may enter the assembly of the LORD, even down to the tenth generation.

3No Ammonite or Moabite or any of his descendants may enter the assembly of the LORD, even down to the tenth generation. **4**For they did not come to meet you with bread and water on your way when you came out of Egypt, and they hired Balaam son of Beor

[a] *9* Or *be forfeited to the sanctuary* [b] *19* That is, about 2 1/2 pounds (about 1 kilogram) [c] *29* That is, about 1 1/4 pounds (about 0.6 kilogram) [d] *2* Or *one of illegitimate birth*

from Pethor in Aram Naharaim[a] to pronounce a curse on you. 5However, the LORD your God would not listen to Balaam but turned the curse into a blessing for you, because the LORD your God loves you. 6Do not seek a treaty of friendship with them as long as you live.

7Do not abhor an Edomite, for he is your brother. Do not abhor an Egyptian, because you lived as an alien in his country. 8The third generation of children born to them may enter the assembly of the LORD.

Uncleanness in the Camp

9When you are encamped against your enemies, keep away from everything impure. 10If one of your men is unclean because of a nocturnal emission, he is to go outside the camp and stay there. 11But as evening approaches he is to wash himself, and at sunset he may return to the camp.

12Designate a place outside the camp where you can go to relieve yourself. 13As part of your equipment have something to dig with, and when you relieve yourself, dig a hole and cover up your excrement. 14For the LORD your God moves about in your camp to protect you and to deliver your enemies to you. Your camp must be holy, so that he will not see among you anything indecent and turn away from you.

Miscellaneous Laws

15If a slave has taken refuge with you, do not hand him over to his master. 16Let him live among you wherever he likes and in whatever town he chooses. Do not oppress him.

17No Israelite man or woman is to become a shrine prostitute. 18You must not bring the earnings of a female prostitute or of a male prostitute[b] into the house of the LORD your God to pay any vow, because the LORD your God detests them both.

19Do not charge your brother interest, whether on money or food or anything else that may earn interest. 20You may charge a foreigner interest, but not a brother Israelite, so that the LORD your God may bless you in everything you put your hand to in the land you are entering to possess.

21If you make a vow to the LORD your God, do not be slow to pay it, for the LORD your God will certainly demand it of you and you will be guilty of sin. 22But if you refrain from making a vow, you will not be guilty. 23Whatever your lips utter you must be sure to do, because you made your vow freely to the LORD your God with your own mouth.

24If you enter your neighbor's vineyard, you may eat all the grapes you want, but do not put any in your basket. 25If you enter your neighbor's grainfield, you may pick kernels with your hands, but you must not put a sickle to his standing grain.

24 If a man marries a woman who becomes displeasing to him because he finds something indecent about her, and he writes her a certificate of divorce, gives it to her and sends her from his house, 2and if after she leaves his house she becomes the wife of another man, 3and her second husband dislikes her and writes her a certificate of divorce, gives it to her and sends her from his house, or if he dies, 4then her first husband, who divorced her, is not allowed to marry her again after she has been defiled. That would be detestable in the eyes of the LORD. Do not bring sin upon the land the LORD your God is giving you as an inheritance.

5If a man has recently married, he must not be sent to war or have any other duty laid on him. For one year he is to be free to stay at home and bring happiness to the wife he has married.

6Do not take a pair of millstones—not even the upper one—as security for a debt, because that would be taking a man's livelihood as security.

7If a man is caught kidnapping one of his brother Israelites and treats him as a slave or sells him, the kidnapper must die. You must purge the evil from among you.

8In cases of leprous[c] diseases be very careful to do exactly as the priests, who are Levites, instruct you. You must follow carefully what I have commanded them. 9Remember what the LORD your God did to Miriam along the way after you came out of Egypt.

10When you make a loan of any kind to your neighbor, do not go into his house to get what he is offering as a pledge. 11Stay outside and let the man to whom you are making the loan bring the pledge out to you. 12If the man is poor, do not go to sleep with his pledge in your possession. 13Return his cloak to him by sunset so that he may sleep in it. Then he will thank you, and it will be regarded as a righteous act in the sight of the LORD your God.

14Do not take advantage of a hired man who is poor and needy, whether he is a brother Israelite or an alien living in one of your towns. 15Pay him his wages each day before sunset, because he is poor and is counting on it. Otherwise he may cry to the LORD against you, and you will be guilty of sin.

16Fathers shall not be put to death for their children, nor children put to death for their fathers; each is to die for his own sin.

17Do not deprive the alien or the fatherless of justice, or take the cloak of the widow as a pledge. 18Remember that you were slaves in Egypt and the LORD your God redeemed you from there. That is why I command you to do this.

19When you are harvesting in your field and you overlook a sheaf, do not go back to get it. Leave it for the alien, the fatherless and the widow, so that the LORD your God may bless you in all the work of your hands. 20When you beat the olives from your trees, do not go over

[a]4 That is, Northwest Mesopotamia [b]18 Hebrew *of a dog* [c]8 The Hebrew word was used for various diseases affecting the skin—not necessarily leprosy.

the branches a second time. Leave what remains for the alien, the fatherless and the widow. 21When you harvest the grapes in your
vineyard, do not go over the vines again.
Leave what remains for the alien, the fatherless
and the widow. 22Remember that you were
slaves in Egypt. That is why I command you to
do this.

25 When men have a dispute, they are to
take it to court and the judges will decide the case, acquitting the innocent and condemning the guilty. 2If the guilty man deserves
to be beaten, the judge shall make him lie
down and have him flogged in his presence
with the number of lashes his crime deserves,
3but he must not give him more than forty
lashes. If he is flogged more than that, your
brother will be degraded in your eyes.

4Do not muzzle an ox while it is treading out
the grain.

5If brothers are living together and one of
them dies without a son, his widow must not
marry outside the family. Her husband's brother shall take her and marry her and fulfill the
duty of a brother-in-law to her. 6The first son
she bears shall carry on the name of the dead
brother so that his name will not be blotted out
from Israel.

7However, if a man does not want to marry
his brother's wife, she shall go to the elders at
the town gate and say, "My husband's brother
refuses to carry on his brother's name in Israel.
He will not fulfill the duty of a brother-in-law
to me." 8Then the elders of his town shall summon him and talk to him. If he persists in saying, "I do not want to marry her," 9his brother's widow shall go up to him in the presence
of the elders, take off one of his sandals, spit
in his face and say, "This is what is done to the
man who will not build up his brother's family
line." 10That man's line shall be known in Israel as The Family of the Unsandaled.

11If two men are fighting and the wife of one
of them comes to rescue her husband from his
assailant, and she reaches out and seizes him
by his private parts, 12you shall cut off her
hand. Show her no pity.

13Do not have two differing weights in your
bag—one heavy, one light. 14Do not have two
differing measures in your house—one large,
one small. 15You must have accurate and honest weights and measures, so that you may live
long in the land the LORD your God is giving
you. 16For the LORD your God detests anyone
who does these things, anyone who deals dis-
honestly.

17Remember what the Amalekites did to you
along the way when you came out of Egypt.
18When you were weary and worn out, they
met you on your journey and cut off all who
were lagging behind; they had no fear of God.
19When the LORD your God gives you rest
from all the enemies around you in the land he
is giving you to possess as an inheritance, you
shall blot out the memory of Amalek from under heaven. Do not forget!

Firstfruits and Tithes

26 When you have entered the land the
LORD your God is giving you as an inheritance and have taken possession of it and
settled in it, 2take some of the firstfruits of all
that you produce from the soil of the land the
LORD your God is giving you and put them in
a basket. Then go to the place the LORD your
God will choose as a dwelling for his Name
3and say to the priest in office at the time, "I
declare today to the LORD your God that I have
come to the land the LORD swore to our forefathers to give us." 4The priest shall take the
basket from your hands and set it down in front
of the altar of the LORD your God. 5Then you
shall declare before the LORD your God: "My
father was a wandering Aramean, and he went
down into Egypt with a few people and lived
there and became a great nation, powerful and
numerous. 6But the Egyptians mistreated us
and made us suffer, putting us to hard labor.
7Then we cried out to the LORD, the God of our
fathers, and the LORD heard our voice and saw
our misery, toil and oppression. 8So the LORD
brought us out of Egypt with a mighty hand
and an outstretched arm, with great terror and
with miraculous signs and wonders. 9He
brought us to this place and gave us this land,
a land flowing with milk and honey; 10and now
I bring the firstfruits of the soil that you,
O LORD, have given me." Place the basket before the LORD your God and bow down before
him. 11And you and the Levites and the aliens
among you shall rejoice in all the good things
the LORD your God has given to you and your
household.

12When you have finished setting aside a
tenth of all your produce in the third year, the
year of the tithe, you shall give it to the Levite,
the alien, the fatherless and the widow, so that
they may eat in your towns and be satisfied.
13Then say to the LORD your God: "I have
removed from my house the sacred portion and
have given it to the Levite, the alien, the fatherless and the widow, according to all you
commanded. I have not turned aside from your
commands nor have I forgotten any of them.
14I have not eaten any of the sacred portion
while I was in mourning, nor have I removed
any of it while I was unclean, nor have I offered any of it to the dead. I have obeyed the
LORD my God; I have done everything you
commanded me. 15Look down from heaven,
your holy dwelling place, and bless your people Israel and the land you have given us as
you promised on oath to our forefathers, a land
flowing with milk and honey."

Follow the LORD's Commands

16The LORD your God commands you this
day to follow these decrees and laws; carefully
observe them with all your heart and with all
your soul. 17You have declared this day that
the LORD is your God and that you will walk
in his ways, that you will keep his decrees,
commands and laws, and that you will obey

him. 18And the LORD has declared this day that
you are his people, his treasured possession as
he promised, and that you are to keep all his
commands. 19He has declared that he will set
you in praise, fame and honor high above all
the nations he has made and that you will be a
people holy to the LORD your God, as he promised.

The Altar on Mount Ebal

27 Moses and the elders of Israel commanded the people: "Keep all these
commands that I give you today. 2When you
have crossed the Jordan into the land the LORD
your God is giving you, set up some large
stones and coat them with plaster. 3Write on
them all the words of this law when you have
crossed over to enter the land the LORD your
God is giving you, a land flowing with milk
and honey, just as the LORD, the God of your
fathers, promised you. 4And when you have
crossed the Jordan, set up these stones on
Mount Ebal, as I command you today, and coat
them with plaster. 5Build there an altar to the
LORD your God, an altar of stones. Do not use
any iron tool upon them. 6Build the altar of the
LORD your God with fieldstones and offer
burnt offerings on it to the LORD your God.
7Sacrifice fellowship offerings[a] there, eating
them and rejoicing in the presence of the LORD
your God. 8And you shall write very clearly all
the words of this law on these stones you have
set up."

Curses From Mount Ebal

9Then Moses and the priests, who are Levites, said to all Israel, "Be silent, O Israel, and
listen! You have now become the people of the
LORD your God. 10Obey the LORD your God
and follow his commands and decrees that I
give you today."

11On the same day Moses commanded the
people:

12When you have crossed the Jordan, these
tribes shall stand on Mount Gerizim to bless
the people: Simeon, Levi, Judah, Issachar, Joseph and Benjamin. 13And these tribes shall
stand on Mount Ebal to pronounce curses:
Reuben, Gad, Asher, Zebulun, Dan and Naphtali.

14The Levites shall recite to all the people of
Israel in a loud voice:

> 15"Cursed is the man who carves an
> image or casts an idol—a thing detestable
> to the LORD, the work of the craftsman's
> hands—and sets it up in secret."
> Then all the people shall say,
> "Amen!"
>
> 16"Cursed is the man who dishonors his
> father or his mother."
> Then all the people shall say,
> "Amen!"
>
> 17"Cursed is the man who moves his
> neighbor's boundary stone."
> Then all the people shall say,
> "Amen!"
>
> 18"Cursed is the man who leads the
> blind astray on the road."
> Then all the people shall say,
> "Amen!"
>
> 19"Cursed is the man who withholds
> justice from the alien, the fatherless or the
> widow."
> Then all the people shall say,
> "Amen!"
>
> 20"Cursed is the man who sleeps with
> his father's wife, for he dishonors his fa-
> ther's bed."
> Then all the people shall say,
> "Amen!"
>
> 21"Cursed is the man who has sexual
> relations with any animal."
> Then all the people shall say,
> "Amen!"
>
> 22"Cursed is the man who sleeps with
> his sister, the daughter of his father or the
> daughter of his mother."
> Then all the people shall say,
> "Amen!"
>
> 23"Cursed is the man who sleeps with
> his mother-in-law."
> Then all the people shall say,
> "Amen!"
>
> 24"Cursed is the man who kills his
> neighbor secretly."
> Then all the people shall say,
> "Amen!"
>
> 25"Cursed is the man who accepts a
> bribe to kill an innocent person."
> Then all the people shall say,
> "Amen!"
>
> 26"Cursed is the man who does not up-
> hold the words of this law by carrying
> them out."
> Then all the people shall say,
> "Amen!"

Blessings for Obedience

28 If you fully obey the LORD your God
and carefully follow all his commands I
give you today, the LORD your God will set
you high above all the nations on earth. 2All
these blessings will come upon you and accompany you if you obey the LORD your God:

> 3You will be blessed in the city and
> blessed in the country.
>
> 4The fruit of your womb will be
> blessed, and the crops of your land and
> the young of your livestock—the calves
> of your herds and the lambs of your
> flocks.
>
> 5Your basket and your kneading trough
> will be blessed.
>
> 6You will be blessed when you come in
> and blessed when you go out.

7The LORD will grant that the enemies who
rise up against you will be defeated before you.

[a]7 Traditionally *peace offerings*

They will come at you from one direction but flee from you in seven.

8The LORD will send a blessing on your barns and on everything you put your hand to. The LORD your God will bless you in the land he is giving you.

9The LORD will establish you as his holy people, as he promised you on oath, if you keep the commands of the LORD your God and walk in his ways. 10Then all the peoples on earth will see that you are called by the name of the LORD, and they will fear you. 11The LORD will grant you abundant prosperity—in the fruit of your womb, the young of your livestock and the crops of your ground—in the land he swore to your forefathers to give you.

12The LORD will open the heavens, the storehouse of his bounty, to send rain on your land in season and to bless all the work of your hands. You will lend to many nations but will borrow from none. 13The LORD will make you the head, not the tail. If you pay attention to the commands of the LORD your God that I give you this day and carefully follow them, you will always be at the top, never at the bottom. 14Do not turn aside from any of the commands I give you today, to the right or to the left, following other gods and serving them.

Curses for Disobedience

15However, if you do not obey the LORD your God and do not carefully follow all his commands and decrees I am giving you today, all these curses will come upon you and overtake you:

> 16You will be cursed in the city and cursed in the country.
> 17Your basket and your kneading trough will be cursed.
> 18The fruit of your womb will be cursed, and the crops of your land, and the calves of your herds and the lambs of your flocks.
> 19You will be cursed when you come in and cursed when you go out.

20The LORD will send on you curses, confusion and rebuke in everything you put your hand to, until you are destroyed and come to sudden ruin because of the evil you have done in forsaking him.[a] 21The LORD will plague you with diseases until he has destroyed you from the land you are entering to possess. 22The LORD will strike you with wasting disease, with fever and inflammation, with scorching heat and drought, with blight and mildew, which will plague you until you perish. 23The sky over your head will be bronze, the ground beneath you iron. 24The LORD will turn the rain of your country into dust and powder; it will come down from the skies until you are destroyed.

25The LORD will cause you to be defeated before your enemies. You will come at them from one direction but flee from them in seven, and you will become a thing of horror to all the kingdoms on earth. 26Your carcasses will be food for all the birds of the air and the beasts of the earth, and there will be no one to frighten them away. 27The LORD will afflict you with the boils of Egypt and with tumors, festering sores and the itch, from which you cannot be cured. 28The LORD will afflict you with madness, blindness and confusion of mind. 29At midday you will grope about like a blind man in the dark. You will be unsuccessful in everything you do; day after day you will be oppressed and robbed, with no one to rescue you.

30You will be pledged to be married to a woman, but another will take her and ravish her. You will build a house, but you will not live in it. You will plant a vineyard, but you will not even begin to enjoy its fruit. 31Your ox will be slaughtered before your eyes, but you will eat none of it. Your donkey will be forcibly taken from you and will not be returned. Your sheep will be given to your enemies, and no one will rescue them. 32Your sons and daughters will be given to another nation, and you will wear out your eyes watching for them day after day, powerless to lift a hand. 33A people that you do not know will eat what your land and labor produce, and you will have nothing but cruel oppression all your days. 34The sights you see will drive you mad. 35The LORD will afflict your knees and legs with painful boils that cannot be cured, spreading from the soles of your feet to the top of your head.

36The LORD will drive you and the king you set over you to a nation unknown to you or your fathers. There you will worship other gods, gods of wood and stone. 37You will become a thing of horror and an object of scorn and ridicule to all the nations where the LORD will drive you.

38You will sow much seed in the field but you will harvest little, because locusts will devour it. 39You will plant vineyards and cultivate them but you will not drink the wine or gather the grapes, because worms will eat them. 40You will have olive trees throughout your country but you will not use the oil, because the olives will drop off. 41You will have sons and daughters but you will not keep them, because they will go into captivity. 42Swarms of locusts will take over all your trees and the crops of your land.

43The alien who lives among you will rise above you higher and higher, but you will sink lower and lower. 44He will lend to you, but you will not lend to him. He will be the head, but you will be the tail.

45All these curses will come upon you. They will pursue you and overtake you until you are destroyed, because you did not obey the LORD your God and observe the commands and decrees he gave you. 46They will be a sign and a wonder to you and your descendants forever.

[a]20 Hebrew *me*

47Because you did not serve the LORD your God joyfully and gladly in the time of prosperity, 48therefore in hunger and thirst, in nakedness and dire poverty, you will serve the enemies the LORD sends against you. He will put an iron yoke on your neck until he has destroyed you.

49The LORD will bring a nation against you from far away, from the ends of the earth, like an eagle swooping down, a nation whose language you will not understand, 50a fierce-looking nation without respect for the old or pity for the young. 51They will devour the young of your livestock and the crops of your land until you are destroyed. They will leave you no grain, new wine or oil, nor any calves of your herds or lambs of your flocks until you are ruined. 52They will lay siege to all the cities throughout your land until the high fortified walls in which you trust fall down. They will besiege all the cities throughout the land the LORD your God is giving you.

53Because of the suffering that your enemy will inflict on you during the siege, you will eat the fruit of the womb, the flesh of the sons and daughters the LORD your God has given you. 54Even the most gentle and sensitive man among you will have no compassion on his own brother or the wife he loves or his surviving children, 55and he will not give to one of them any of the flesh of his children that he is eating. It will be all he has left because of the suffering your enemy will inflict on you during the siege of all your cities. 56The most gentle and sensitive woman among you—so sensitive and gentle that she would not venture to touch the ground with the sole of her foot—will begrudge the husband she loves and her own son or daughter 57the afterbirth from her womb and the children she bears. For she intends to eat them secretly during the siege and in the distress that your enemy will inflict on you in your cities.

58If you do not carefully follow all the words of this law, which are written in this book, and do not revere this glorious and awesome name—the LORD your God— 59the LORD will send fearful plagues on you and your descendants, harsh and prolonged disasters, and severe and lingering illnesses. 60He will bring upon you all the diseases of Egypt that you dreaded, and they will cling to you. 61The LORD will also bring on you every kind of sickness and disaster not recorded in this Book of the Law, until you are destroyed. 62You who were as numerous as the stars in the sky will be left but few in number, because you did not obey the LORD your God. 63Just as it pleased the LORD to make you prosper and increase in number, so it will please him to ruin and destroy you. You will be uprooted from the land you are entering to possess.

64Then the LORD will scatter you among all nations, from one end of the earth to the other. There you will worship other gods—gods of wood and stone, which neither you nor your fathers have known. 65Among those nations you will find no repose, no resting place for the sole of your foot. There the LORD will give you an anxious mind, eyes weary with longing, and a despairing heart. 66You will live in constant suspense, filled with dread both night and day, never sure of your life. 67In the morning you will say, "If only it were evening!" and in the evening, "If only it were morning!"—because of the terror that will fill your hearts and the sights that your eyes will see. 68The LORD will send you back in ships to Egypt on a journey I said you should never make again. There you will offer yourselves for sale to your enemies as male and female slaves, but no one will buy you.

Renewal of the Covenant

29 These are the terms of the covenant the LORD commanded Moses to make with the Israelites in Moab, in addition to the covenant he had made with them at Horeb.

2Moses summoned all the Israelites and said to them:

Your eyes have seen all that the LORD did in Egypt to Pharaoh, to all his officials and to all his land. 3With your own eyes you saw those great trials, those miraculous signs and great wonders. 4But to this day the LORD has not given you a mind that understands or eyes that see or ears that hear. 5During the forty years that I led you through the desert, your clothes did not wear out, nor did the sandals on your feet. 6You ate no bread and drank no wine or other fermented drink. I did this so that you might know that I am the LORD your God.

7When you reached this place, Sihon king of Heshbon and Og king of Bashan came out to fight against us, but we defeated them. 8We took their land and gave it as an inheritance to the Reubenites, the Gadites and the half-tribe of Manasseh.

9Carefully follow the terms of this covenant, so that you may prosper in everything you do. 10All of you are standing today in the presence of the LORD your God—your leaders and chief men, your elders and officials, and all the other men of Israel, 11together with your children and your wives, and the aliens living in your camps who chop your wood and carry your water. 12You are standing here in order to enter into a covenant with the LORD your God, a covenant the LORD is making with you this day and sealing with an oath, 13to confirm you this day as his people, that he may be your God as he promised you and as he swore to your fathers, Abraham, Isaac and Jacob. 14I am making this covenant, with its oath, not only with you 15who are standing here with us today in the presence of the LORD our God but also with those who are not here today.

16You yourselves know how we lived in Egypt and how we passed through the countries on the way here. 17You saw among them their detestable images and idols of wood and stone, of silver and gold. 18Make sure there is no man or woman, clan or tribe among you

today whose heart turns away from the LORD
our God to go and worship the gods of those
nations; make sure there is no root among you
that produces such bitter poison.
19When such a person hears the words of
this oath, he invokes a blessing on himself and
therefore thinks, "I will be safe, even though I
persist in going my own way." This will bring
disaster on the watered land as well as the
dry.[a] 20The LORD will never be willing to forgive him; his wrath and zeal will burn against
that man. All the curses written in this book
will fall upon him, and the LORD will blot out
his name from under heaven. 21The LORD will
single him out from all the tribes of Israel for
disaster, according to all the curses of the covenant written in this Book of the Law.
22Your children who follow you in later
generations and foreigners who come from
distant lands will see the calamities that have
fallen on the land and the diseases with which
the LORD has afflicted it. 23The whole land
will be a burning waste of salt and sulfur—
nothing planted, nothing sprouting, no vegetation growing on it. It will be like the destruction of Sodom and Gomorrah, Admah and
Zeboiim, which the LORD overthrew in fierce
anger. 24All the nations will ask: "Why has the
LORD done this to this land? Why this fierce,
burning anger?"
25And the answer will be: "It is because this
people abandoned the covenant of the LORD,
the God of their fathers, the covenant he made
with them when he brought them out of Egypt.
26They went off and worshiped other gods and
bowed down to them, gods they did not know,
gods he had not given them. 27Therefore the
LORD's anger burned against this land, so that
he brought on it all the curses written in this
book. 28In furious anger and in great wrath the
LORD uprooted them from their land and thrust
them into another land, as it is now."
29The secret things belong to the LORD our
God, but the things revealed belong to us and
to our children forever, that we may follow all
the words of this law.

Prosperity After Turning to the LORD

30 When all these blessings and curses I
have set before you come upon you and
you take them to heart wherever the LORD
your God disperses you among the nations,
2and when you and your children return to the
LORD your God and obey him with all your
heart and with all your soul according to everything I command you today, 3then the LORD
your God will restore your fortunes[b] and have
compassion on you and gather you again from
all the nations where he scattered you. 4Even if
you have been banished to the most distant
land under the heavens, from there the LORD
your God will gather you and bring you back.
5He will bring you to the land that belonged to
your fathers, and you will take possession of it.
He will make you more prosperous and numerous than your fathers. 6The LORD your God
will circumcise your hearts and the hearts of
your descendants, so that you may love him
with all your heart and with all your soul, and
live. 7The LORD your God will put all these
curses on your enemies who hate and persecute you. 8You will again obey the LORD and
follow all his commands I am giving you today. 9Then the LORD your God will make you
most prosperous in all the work of your hands
and in the fruit of your womb, the young of
your livestock and the crops of your land. The
LORD will again delight in you and make you
prosperous, just as he delighted in your fathers,
10if you obey the LORD your God and keep his
commands and decrees that are written in this
Book of the Law and turn to the LORD your
God with all your heart and with all your soul.

The Offer of Life or Death

11Now what I am commanding you today is
not too difficult for you or beyond your reach.
12It is not up in heaven, so that you have to ask,
"Who will ascend into heaven to get it and
proclaim it to us so we may obey it?" 13Nor is
it beyond the sea, so that you have to ask,
"Who will cross the sea to get it and proclaim
it to us so we may obey it?" 14No, the word is
very near you; it is in your mouth and in your
heart so you may obey it.
15See, I set before you today life and prosperity, death and destruction. 16For I command
you today to love the LORD your God, to walk
in his ways, and to keep his commands, decrees and laws; then you will live and increase,
and the LORD your God will bless you in the
land you are entering to possess.
17But if your heart turns away and you are
not obedient, and if you are drawn away to
bow down to other gods and worship them, 18I
declare to you this day that you will certainly
be destroyed. You will not live long in the land
you are crossing the Jordan to enter and possess.
19This day I call heaven and earth as witnesses against you that I have set before you
life and death, blessings and curses. Now
choose life, so that you and your children may
live 20and that you may love the LORD your
God, listen to his voice, and hold fast to him.
For the LORD is your life, and he will give you
many years in the land he swore to give to your
fathers, Abraham, Isaac and Jacob.

Joshua to Succeed Moses

31 Then Moses went out and spoke these
words to all Israel: 2"I am now a hundred and twenty years old and I am no longer
able to lead you. The LORD has said to me,
'You shall not cross the Jordan.' 3The LORD
your God himself will cross over ahead of you.
He will destroy these nations before you, and
you will take possession of their land. Joshua
also will cross over ahead of you, as the LORD
said. 4And the LORD will do to them what he

[a] *19* Or *way, in order to add drunkenness to thirst."* [b] *3* Or *will bring you back from captivity*

did to Sihon and Og, the kings of the Amorites, whom he destroyed along with their land. 5The LORD will deliver them to you, and you must do to them all that I have commanded you. 6Be strong and courageous. Do not be afraid or terrified because of them, for the LORD your God goes with you; he will never leave you nor forsake you."

7Then Moses summoned Joshua and said to him in the presence of all Israel, "Be strong and courageous, for you must go with this people into the land that the LORD swore to their forefathers to give them, and you must divide it among them as their inheritance. 8The LORD himself goes before you and will be with you; he will never leave you nor forsake you. Do not be afraid; do not be discouraged."

The Reading of the Law

9So Moses wrote down this law and gave it to the priests, the sons of Levi, who carried the ark of the covenant of the LORD, and to all the elders of Israel. 10Then Moses commanded them: "At the end of every seven years, in the year for canceling debts, during the Feast of Tabernacles, 11when all Israel comes to appear before the LORD your God at the place he will choose, you shall read this law before them in their hearing. 12Assemble the people—men, women and children, and the aliens living in your towns—so they can listen and learn to fear the LORD your God and follow carefully all the words of this law. 13Their children, who do not know this law, must hear it and learn to fear the LORD your God as long as you live in the land you are crossing the Jordan to possess."

Israel's Rebellion Predicted

14The LORD said to Moses, "Now the day of your death is near. Call Joshua and present yourselves at the Tent of Meeting, where I will commission him." So Moses and Joshua came and presented themselves at the Tent of Meeting.

15Then the LORD appeared at the Tent in a pillar of cloud, and the cloud stood over the entrance to the Tent. 16And the LORD said to Moses: "You are going to rest with your fathers, and these people will soon prostitute themselves to the foreign gods of the land they are entering. They will forsake me and break the covenant I made with them. 17On that day I will become angry with them and forsake them; I will hide my face from them, and they will be destroyed. Many disasters and difficulties will come upon them, and on that day they will ask, 'Have not these disasters come upon us because our God is not with us?' 18And I will certainly hide my face on that day because of all their wickedness in turning to other gods.

19"Now write down for yourselves this song and teach it to the Israelites and have them sing it, so that it may be a witness for me against them. 20When I have brought them into the land flowing with milk and honey, the land I promised on oath to their forefathers, and when they eat their fill and thrive, they will turn to other gods and worship them, rejecting me and breaking my covenant. 21And when many disasters and difficulties come upon them, this song will testify against them, because it will not be forgotten by their descendants. I know what they are disposed to do, even before I bring them into the land I promised them on oath." 22So Moses wrote down this song that day and taught it to the Israelites.

23The LORD gave this command to Joshua son of Nun: "Be strong and courageous, for you will bring the Israelites into the land I promised them on oath, and I myself will be with you."

24After Moses finished writing in a book the words of this law from beginning to end, 25he gave this command to the Levites who carried the ark of the covenant of the LORD: 26"Take this Book of the Law and place it beside the ark of the covenant of the LORD your God. There it will remain as a witness against you. 27For I know how rebellious and stiff-necked you are. If you have been rebellious against the LORD while I am still alive and with you, how much more will you rebel after I die! 28Assemble before me all the elders of your tribes and all your officials, so that I can speak these words in their hearing and call heaven and earth to testify against them. 29For I know that after my death you are sure to become utterly corrupt and to turn from the way I have commanded you. In days to come, disaster will fall upon you because you will do evil in the sight of the LORD and provoke him to anger by what your hands have made."

The Song of Moses

30And Moses recited the words of this song from beginning to end in the hearing of the whole assembly of Israel:

32 Listen, O heavens, and I will speak;
hear, O earth, the words of my mouth.
2Let my teaching fall like rain
and my words descend like dew,
like showers on new grass,
like abundant rain on tender plants.

3I will proclaim the name of the LORD.
Oh, praise the greatness of our God!
4He is the Rock, his works are perfect,
and all his ways are just.
A faithful God who does no wrong,
upright and just is he.

5They have acted corruptly toward him;
to their shame they are no longer his children,
but a warped and crooked generation.[a]
6Is this the way you repay the LORD,
O foolish and unwise people?
Is he not your Father, your Creator,[b]
who made you and formed you?

[a]5 Or *Corrupt are they and not his children, / a generation warped and twisted to their shame*
[b]6 Or *Father, who bought you*

7Remember the days of old;
consider the generations long past.
Ask your father and he will tell you,
your elders, and they will explain to you.
8When the Most High gave the nations their inheritance,
when he divided all mankind,
he set up boundaries for the peoples
according to the number of the sons of Israel.[a]
9For the LORD's portion is his people,
Jacob his allotted inheritance.

10In a desert land he found him,
in a barren and howling waste.
He shielded him and cared for him;
he guarded him as the apple of his eye,
11like an eagle that stirs up its nest
and hovers over its young,
that spreads its wings to catch them
and carries them on its pinions.
12The LORD alone led him;
no foreign god was with him.

13He made him ride on the heights of the land
and fed him with the fruit of the fields.
He nourished him with honey from the rock,
and with oil from the flinty crag,
14with curds and milk from herd and flock
and with fattened lambs and goats,
with choice rams of Bashan
and the finest kernels of wheat.
You drank the foaming blood of the grape.

15Jeshurun[b] grew fat and kicked;
filled with food, he became heavy and sleek.
He abandoned the God who made him
and rejected the Rock his Savior.
16They made him jealous with their foreign gods
and angered him with their detestable idols.
17They sacrificed to demons, which are not God—
gods they had not known,
gods that recently appeared,
gods your fathers did not fear.
18You deserted the Rock, who fathered you;
you forgot the God who gave you birth.

19The LORD saw this and rejected them
because he was angered by his sons and daughters.
20"I will hide my face from them," he said,
"and see what their end will be;
for they are a perverse generation,
children who are unfaithful.
21They made me jealous by what is no god
and angered me with their worthless idols.
I will make them envious by those who are not a people;
I will make them angry by a nation that has no understanding.
22For a fire has been kindled by my wrath,
one that burns to the realm of death[c] below.
It will devour the earth and its harvests
and set afire the foundations of the mountains.

23"I will heap calamities upon them
and spend my arrows against them.
24I will send wasting famine against them,
consuming pestilence and deadly plague;
I will send against them the fangs of wild beasts,
the venom of vipers that glide in the dust.
25In the street the sword will make them childless;
in their homes terror will reign.
Young men and young women will perish,
infants and gray-haired men.
26I said I would scatter them
and blot out their memory from mankind,
27but I dreaded the taunt of the enemy,
lest the adversary misunderstand
and say, 'Our hand has triumphed;
the LORD has not done all this.' "

28They are a nation without sense,
there is no discernment in them.
29If only they were wise and would understand this
and discern what their end will be!
30How could one man chase a thousand,
or two put ten thousand to flight,
unless their Rock had sold them,
unless the LORD had given them up?
31For their rock is not like our Rock,
as even our enemies concede.
32Their vine comes from the vine of Sodom
and from the fields of Gomorrah.
Their grapes are filled with poison,
and their clusters with bitterness.
33Their wine is the venom of serpents,
the deadly poison of cobras.

34"Have I not kept this in reserve
and sealed it in my vaults?
35It is mine to avenge; I will repay.
In due time their foot will slip;
their day of disaster is near
and their doom rushes upon them."

36The LORD will judge his people
and have compassion on his servants
when he sees their strength is gone
and no one is left, slave or free.
37He will say: "Now where are their gods,
the rock they took refuge in,
38the gods who ate the fat of their sacrifices

[a]8 Masoretic Text; Dead Sea Scrolls (see also Septuagint) *sons of God* [b]15 *Jeshurun* means *the upright one*, that is, Israel. [c]22 Hebrew *to Sheol*

and drank the wine of their drink
offerings?
Let them rise up to help you!
Let them give you shelter!

39"See now that I myself am He!
There is no god besides me.
I put to death and I bring to life,
I have wounded and I will heal,
and no one can deliver out of my hand.
40I lift my hand to heaven and declare:
As surely as I live forever,
41when I sharpen my flashing sword
and my hand grasps it in judgment,
I will take vengeance on my adversaries
and repay those who hate me.
42I will make my arrows drunk with blood,
while my sword devours flesh:
the blood of the slain and the captives,
the heads of the enemy leaders."

43Rejoice, O nations, with his people,[a, b]
for he will avenge the blood of his
servants;
he will take vengeance on his enemies
and make atonement for his land and
people.

44Moses came with Joshua[c] son of Nun and
spoke all the words of this song in the hearing
of the people. 45When Moses finished reciting
all these words to all Israel, 46he said to them,
"Take to heart all the words I have solemnly
declared to you this day, so that you may command your children to obey carefully all the
words of this law. 47They are not just idle
words for you—they are your life. By them
you will live long in the land you are crossing
the Jordan to possess."

Moses to Die on Mount Nebo

48On that same day the LORD told Moses,
49"Go up into the Abarim Range to Mount
Nebo in Moab, across from Jericho, and view
Canaan, the land I am giving the Israelites as
their own possession. 50There on the mountain
that you have climbed you will die and be
gathered to your people, just as your brother
Aaron died on Mount Hor and was gathered to
his people. 51This is because both of you broke
faith with me in the presence of the Israelites
at the waters of Meribah Kadesh in the Desert
of Zin and because you did not uphold my
holiness among the Israelites. 52Therefore, you
will see the land only from a distance; you will
not enter the land I am giving to the people of
Israel."

Moses Blesses the Tribes

33 This is the blessing that Moses the man
of God pronounced on the Israelites before his death. 2He said:

"The LORD came from Sinai
and dawned over them from Seir;
he shone forth from Mount Paran.
He came with[d] myriads of holy ones
from the south, from his mountain
slopes.[e]
3Surely it is you who love the people;
all the holy ones are in your hand.
At your feet they all bow down,
and from you receive instruction,
4the law that Moses gave us,
the possession of the assembly of Jacob.
5He was king over Jeshurun[f]
when the leaders of the people
assembled,
along with the tribes of Israel.

6"Let Reuben live and not die,
nor[g] his men be few."

7And this he said about Judah:

"Hear, O LORD, the cry of Judah;
bring him to his people.
With his own hands he defends his cause.
Oh, be his help against his foes!"

8About Levi he said:

"Your Thummim and Urim belong
to the man you favored.
You tested him at Massah;
you contended with him at the waters of
Meribah.
9He said of his father and mother,
'I have no regard for them.'
He did not recognize his brothers
or acknowledge his own children,
but he watched over your word
and guarded your covenant.
10He teaches your precepts to Jacob
and your law to Israel.
He offers incense before you
and whole burnt offerings on your altar.
11Bless all his skills, O LORD,
and be pleased with the work of his
hands.
Smite the loins of those who rise up
against him;
strike his foes till they rise no more."

12About Benjamin he said:

"Let the beloved of the LORD rest secure
in him,
for he shields him all day long,
and the one the LORD loves rests
between his shoulders."

13About Joseph he said:

"May the LORD bless his land
with the precious dew from heaven
above
and with the deep waters that lie below;
14with the best the sun brings forth
and the finest the moon can yield;
15with the choicest gifts of the ancient
mountains

[a]43 Or *Make his people rejoice, O nations* [b]43 Masoretic Text; Dead Sea Scrolls (see also Septuagint) *people, / and let all the angels worship him /* [c]44 Hebrew *Hoshea,* a variant of *Joshua* [d]2 Or *from* [e]2 The meaning of the Hebrew for this phrase is uncertain. [f]5 *Jeshurun* means *the upright one,* that is, Israel; also in verse 26. [g]6 Or *but let*

and the fruitfulness of the everlasting
hills;
16with the best gifts of the earth and its
fullness
and the favor of him who dwelt in the
burning bush.
Let all these rest on the head of Joseph,
on the brow of the prince among[a] his
brothers.
17In majesty he is like a firstborn bull;
his horns are the horns of a wild ox.
With them he will gore the nations,
even those at the ends of the earth.
Such are the ten thousands of Ephraim;
such are the thousands of Manasseh."

18About Zebulun he said:

"Rejoice, Zebulun, in your going out,
and you, Issachar, in your tents.
19They will summon peoples to the
mountain
and there offer sacrifices of
righteousness;
they will feast on the abundance of the
seas,
on the treasures hidden in the sand."

20About Gad he said:

"Blessed is he who enlarges Gad's
domain!
Gad lives there like a lion,
tearing at arm or head.
21He chose the best land for himself;
the leader's portion was kept for him.
When the heads of the people assembled,
he carried out the LORD's righteous
will,
and his judgments concerning Israel."

22About Dan he said:

"Dan is a lion's cub,
springing out of Bashan."

23About Naphtali he said:

"Naphtali is abounding with the favor of
the LORD
and is full of his blessing;
he will inherit southward to the lake."

24About Asher he said:

"Most blessed of sons is Asher;
let him be favored by his brothers,
and let him bathe his feet in oil.
25The bolts of your gates will be iron and
bronze,
and your strength will equal your days.

26"There is no one like the God of Jeshurun,
who rides on the heavens to help you
and on the clouds in his majesty.
27The eternal God is your refuge,
and underneath are the everlasting arms.
He will drive out your enemy before you,
saying, 'Destroy him!'
28So Israel will live in safety alone;
Jacob's spring is secure
in a land of grain and new wine,
where the heavens drop dew.
29Blessed are you, O Israel!
Who is like you,
a people saved by the LORD?
He is your shield and helper
and your glorious sword.
Your enemies will cower before you,
and you will trample down their high
places.[b]"

The Death of Moses

34 Then Moses climbed Mount Nebo from
the plains of Moab to the top of Pisgah,
across from Jericho. There the LORD showed
him the whole land—from Gilead to Dan, 2all
of Naphtali, the territory of Ephraim and Manasseh, all the land of Judah as far as the western sea,[c] 3the Negev and the whole region
from the Valley of Jericho, the City of Palms,
as far as Zoar. 4Then the LORD said to him,
"This is the land I promised on oath to Abraham, Isaac and Jacob when I said, 'I will give
it to your descendants.' I have let you see it
with your eyes, but you will not cross over
into it."
5And Moses the servant of the LORD died
there in Moab, as the LORD had said. 6He buried him[d] in Moab, in the valley opposite Beth
Peor, but to this day no one knows where his
grave is. 7Moses was a hundred and twenty
years old when he died, yet his eyes were not
weak nor his strength gone. 8The Israelites
grieved for Moses in the plains of Moab thirty
days, until the time of weeping and mourning
was over.
9Now Joshua son of Nun was filled with the
spirit[e] of wisdom because Moses had laid his
hands on him. So the Israelites listened to him
and did what the LORD had commanded Moses.
10Since then, no prophet has risen in Israel
like Moses, whom the LORD knew face to face,
11who did all those miraculous signs and wonders the LORD sent him to do in Egypt—to
Pharaoh and to all his officials and to his
whole land. 12For no one has ever shown the
mighty power or performed the awesome
deeds that Moses did in the sight of all Israel.

[a]16 Or *of the one separated from* [b]29 Or *will tread upon their bodies* [c]2 That is, the Mediterranean
[d]6 Or *He was buried* [e]9 Or *Spirit*

Joshua

The LORD Commands Joshua

1 After the death of Moses the servant of the
LORD, the LORD said to Joshua son of Nun,
Moses' aide: 2“Moses my servant is dead.
Now then, you and all these people, get ready
to cross the Jordan River into the land I am
about to give to them—to the Israelites. 3I will
give you every place where you set your foot,
as I promised Moses. 4Your territory will extend from the desert to Lebanon, and from
the great river, the Euphrates—all the Hittite
country—to the Great Sea[a] on the west. 5No
one will be able to stand up against you all the
days of your life. As I was with Moses, so I
will be with you; I will never leave you nor
forsake you.

6“Be strong and courageous, because you
will lead these people to inherit the land I
swore to their forefathers to give them. 7Be
strong and very courageous. Be careful to obey
all the law my servant Moses gave you; do not
turn from it to the right or to the left, that you
may be successful wherever you go. 8Do not
let this Book of the Law depart from your
mouth; meditate on it day and night, so that
you may be careful to do everything written in
it. Then you will be prosperous and successful.
9Have I not commanded you? Be strong and
courageous. Do not be terrified; do not be discouraged, for the LORD your God will be with
you wherever you go.”

10So Joshua ordered the officers of the people: 11“Go through the camp and tell the people, ‘Get your supplies ready. Three days from
now you will cross the Jordan here to go in and
take possession of the land the LORD your God
is giving you for your own.’ ”

12But to the Reubenites, the Gadites and the
half-tribe of Manasseh, Joshua said, 13“Remember the command that Moses the servant
of the LORD gave you: ‘The LORD your God is
giving you rest and has granted you this land.’
14Your wives, your children and your livestock
may stay in the land that Moses gave you east
of the Jordan, but all your fighting men, fully
armed, must cross over ahead of your brothers.
You are to help your brothers 15until the LORD
gives them rest, as he has done for you, and
until they too have taken possession of the land
that the LORD your God is giving them. After
that, you may go back and occupy your own
land, which Moses the servant of the LORD
gave you east of the Jordan toward the sunrise.”

16Then they answered Joshua, “Whatever
you have commanded us we will do, and wherever you send us we will go. 17Just as we fully
obeyed Moses, so we will obey you. Only may
the LORD your God be with you as he was with
Moses. 18Whoever rebels against your word
and does not obey your words, whatever you
may command them, will be put to death. Only
be strong and courageous!”

Rahab and the Spies

2 Then Joshua son of Nun secretly sent two
spies from Shittim. “Go, look over the
land,” he said, “especially Jericho.” So they
went and entered the house of a prostitute[b]
named Rahab and stayed there.

2The king of Jericho was told, “Look! Some
of the Israelites have come here tonight to spy
out the land.” 3So the king of Jericho sent this
message to Rahab: “Bring out the men who
came to you and entered your house, because
they have come to spy out the whole land.”

4But the woman had taken the two men and
hidden them. She said, “Yes, the men came to
me, but I did not know where they had come
from. 5At dusk, when it was time to close the
city gate, the men left. I don't know which way
they went. Go after them quickly. You may
catch up with them.” 6(But she had taken them
up to the roof and hidden them under the stalks
of flax she had laid out on the roof.) 7So the
men set out in pursuit of the spies on the road
that leads to the fords of the Jordan, and as
soon as the pursuers had gone out, the gate was
shut.

8Before the spies lay down for the night, she
went up on the roof 9and said to them, “I know
that the LORD has given this land to you and
that a great fear of you has fallen on us, so that
all who live in this country are melting in fear
because of you. 10We have heard how the
LORD dried up the water of the Red Sea[c] for
you when you came out of Egypt, and what
you did to Sihon and Og, the two kings of the
Amorites east of the Jordan, whom you completely destroyed.[d] 11When we heard of it, our
hearts melted and everyone's courage failed
because of you, for the LORD your God is God
in heaven above and on the earth below.
12Now then, please swear to me by the LORD
that you will show kindness to my family, because I have shown kindness to you. Give me
a sure sign 13that you will spare the lives of my
father and mother, my brothers and sisters, and
all who belong to them, and that you will save
us from death.”

14“Our lives for your lives!” the men assured her. “If you don't tell what we are doing,
we will treat you kindly and faithfully when
the LORD gives us the land.”

15So she let them down by a rope through
the window, for the house she lived in was part

[a] *4* That is, the Mediterranean [b] *1* Or possibly *an innkeeper* [c] *10* Hebrew *Yam Suph*; that is, Sea of Reeds
[d] *10* The Hebrew term refers to the irrevocable giving over of things or persons to the LORD, often by totally destroying them.

of the city wall. 16Now she had said to them, "Go to the hills so the pursuers will not find you. Hide yourselves there three days until they return, and then go on your way."

17The men said to her, "This oath you made us swear will not be binding on us 18unless, when we enter the land, you have tied this scarlet cord in the window through which you let us down, and unless you have brought your father and mother, your brothers and all your family into your house. 19If anyone goes outside your house into the street, his blood will be on his own head; we will not be responsible. As for anyone who is in the house with you, his blood will be on our head if a hand is laid on him. 20But if you tell what we are doing, we will be released from the oath you made us swear."

21"Agreed," she replied. "Let it be as you say." So she sent them away and they departed. And she tied the scarlet cord in the window.

22When they left, they went into the hills and stayed there three days, until the pursuers had searched all along the road and returned without finding them. 23Then the two men started back. They went down out of the hills, forded the river and came to Joshua son of Nun and told him everything that had happened to them. 24They said to Joshua, "The LORD has surely given the whole land into our hands; all the people are melting in fear because of us."

Crossing the Jordan

3 Early in the morning Joshua and all the Israelites set out from Shittim and went to the Jordan, where they camped before crossing over. 2After three days the officers went throughout the camp, 3giving orders to the people: "When you see the ark of the covenant of the LORD your God, and the priests, who are Levites, carrying it, you are to move out from your positions and follow it. 4Then you will know which way to go, since you have never been this way before. But keep a distance of about a thousand yards[a] between you and the ark; do not go near it."

5Joshua told the people, "Consecrate yourselves, for tomorrow the LORD will do amazing things among you."

6Joshua said to the priests, "Take up the ark of the covenant and pass on ahead of the people." So they took it up and went ahead of them.

7And the LORD said to Joshua, "Today I will begin to exalt you in the eyes of all Israel, so they may know that I am with you as I was with Moses. 8Tell the priests who carry the ark of the covenant: 'When you reach the edge of the Jordan's waters, go and stand in the river.' "

9Joshua said to the Israelites, "Come here and listen to the words of the LORD your God. 10This is how you will know that the living God is among you and that he will certainly drive out before you the Canaanites, Hittites, Hivites, Perizzites, Girgashites, Amorites and Jebusites. 11See, the ark of the covenant of the Lord of all the earth will go into the Jordan ahead of you. 12Now then, choose twelve men from the tribes of Israel, one from each tribe. 13And as soon as the priests who carry the ark of the LORD—the Lord of all the earth—set foot in the Jordan, its waters flowing downstream will be cut off and stand up in a heap."

14So when the people broke camp to cross the Jordan, the priests carrying the ark of the covenant went ahead of them. 15Now the Jordan is at flood stage all during harvest. Yet as soon as the priests who carried the ark reached the Jordan and their feet touched the water's edge, 16the water from upstream stopped flowing. It piled up in a heap a great distance away, at a town called Adam in the vicinity of Zarethan, while the water flowing down to the Sea of the Arabah (the Salt Sea[b]) was completely cut off. So the people crossed over opposite Jericho. 17The priests who carried the ark of the covenant of the LORD stood firm on dry ground in the middle of the Jordan, while all Israel passed by until the whole nation had completed the crossing on dry ground.

4 When the whole nation had finished crossing the Jordan, the LORD said to Joshua, 2"Choose twelve men from among the people, one from each tribe, 3and tell them to take up twelve stones from the middle of the Jordan from right where the priests stood and to carry them over with you and put them down at the place where you stay tonight."

4So Joshua called together the twelve men he had appointed from the Israelites, one from each tribe, 5and said to them, "Go over before the ark of the LORD your God into the middle of the Jordan. Each of you is to take up a stone on his shoulder, according to the number of the tribes of the Israelites, 6to serve as a sign among you. In the future, when your children ask you, 'What do these stones mean?' 7tell them that the flow of the Jordan was cut off before the ark of the covenant of the LORD. When it crossed the Jordan, the waters of the Jordan were cut off. These stones are to be a memorial to the people of Israel forever."

8So the Israelites did as Joshua commanded them. They took twelve stones from the middle of the Jordan, according to the number of the tribes of the Israelites, as the LORD had told Joshua; and they carried them over with them to their camp, where they put them down. 9Joshua set up the twelve stones that had been[c] in the middle of the Jordan at the spot where the priests who carried the ark of the covenant had stood. And they are there to this day.

10Now the priests who carried the ark remained standing in the middle of the Jordan until everything the LORD had commanded

[a]4 Hebrew *about two thousand cubits* (about 900 meters) [b]16 That is, the Dead Sea [c]9 Or *Joshua also set up twelve stones*

Joshua was done by the people, just as Moses had directed Joshua. The people hurried over, 11and as soon as all of them had crossed, the ark of the LORD and the priests came to the other side while the people watched. 12The men of Reuben, Gad and the half-tribe of Manasseh crossed over, armed, in front of the Israelites, as Moses had directed them. 13About forty thousand armed for battle crossed over before the LORD to the plains of Jericho for war.

14That day the LORD exalted Joshua in the sight of all Israel; and they revered him all the days of his life, just as they had revered Moses.

15Then the LORD said to Joshua, 16"Command the priests carrying the ark of the Testimony to come up out of the Jordan."

17So Joshua commanded the priests, "Come up out of the Jordan."

18And the priests came up out of the river carrying the ark of the covenant of the LORD. No sooner had they set their feet on the dry ground than the waters of the Jordan returned to their place and ran at flood stage as before.

19On the tenth day of the first month the people went up from the Jordan and camped at Gilgal on the eastern border of Jericho. 20And Joshua set up at Gilgal the twelve stones they had taken out of the Jordan. 21He said to the Israelites, "In the future when your descendants ask their fathers, 'What do these stones mean?' 22tell them, 'Israel crossed the Jordan on dry ground.' 23For the LORD your God dried up the Jordan before you until you had crossed over. The LORD your God did to the Jordan just what he had done to the Red Sea[a] when he dried it up before us until we had crossed over. 24He did this so that all the peoples of the earth might know that the hand of the LORD is powerful and so that you might always fear the LORD your God."

Circumcision at Gilgal

5 Now when all the Amorite kings west of the Jordan and all the Canaanite kings along the coast heard how the LORD had dried up the Jordan before the Israelites until we had crossed over, their hearts melted and they no longer had the courage to face the Israelites.

2At that time the LORD said to Joshua, "Make flint knives and circumcise the Israelites again." 3So Joshua made flint knives and circumcised the Israelites at Gibeath Haaraloth.[b]

4Now this is why he did so: All those who came out of Egypt—all the men of military age—died in the desert on the way after leaving Egypt. 5All the people that came out had been circumcised, but all the people born in the desert during the journey from Egypt had not. 6The Israelites had moved about in the desert forty years until all the men who were of military age when they left Egypt had died, since they had not obeyed the LORD. For the LORD had sworn to them that they would not see the land that he had solemnly promised their fathers to give us, a land flowing with milk and honey. 7So he raised up their sons in their place, and these were the ones Joshua circumcised. They were still uncircumcised because they had not been circumcised on the way. 8And after the whole nation had been circumcised, they remained where they were in camp until they were healed.

9Then the LORD said to Joshua, "Today I have rolled away the reproach of Egypt from you." So the place has been called Gilgal[c] to this day.

10On the evening of the fourteenth day of the month, while camped at Gilgal on the plains of Jericho, the Israelites celebrated the Passover. 11The day after the Passover, that very day, they ate some of the produce of the land: unleavened bread and roasted grain. 12The manna stopped the day after[d] they ate this food from the land; there was no longer any manna for the Israelites, but that year they ate of the produce of Canaan.

The Fall of Jericho

13Now when Joshua was near Jericho, he looked up and saw a man standing in front of him with a drawn sword in his hand. Joshua went up to him and asked, "Are you for us or for our enemies?"

14"Neither," he replied, "but as commander of the army of the LORD I have now come." Then Joshua fell facedown to the ground in reverence, and asked him, "What message does my Lord[e] have for his servant?"

15The commander of the LORD's army replied, "Take off your sandals, for the place where you are standing is holy." And Joshua did so.

6 Now Jericho was tightly shut up because of the Israelites. No one went out and no one came in.

2Then the LORD said to Joshua, "See, I have delivered Jericho into your hands, along with its king and its fighting men. 3March around the city once with all the armed men. Do this for six days. 4Have seven priests carry trumpets of rams' horns in front of the ark. On the seventh day, march around the city seven times, with the priests blowing the trumpets. 5When you hear them sound a long blast on the trumpets, have all the people give a loud shout; then the wall of the city will collapse and the people will go up, every man straight in."

6So Joshua son of Nun called the priests and said to them, "Take up the ark of the covenant of the LORD and have seven priests carry trumpets in front of it." 7And he ordered the people, "Advance! March around the city, with the armed guard going ahead of the ark of the LORD."

8When Joshua had spoken to the people, the seven priests carrying the seven trumpets be-

[a]23 Hebrew *Yam Suph*; that is, Sea of Reeds [b]3 *Gibeath Haaraloth* means *hill of foreskins.* [c]9 *Gilgal* sounds like the Hebrew for *roll.* [d]12 Or *the day* [e]14 Or *lord*

fore the LORD went forward, blowing their trumpets, and the ark of the LORD's covenant followed them. 9The armed guard marched ahead of the priests who blew the trumpets, and the rear guard followed the ark. All this time the trumpets were sounding. 10But Joshua had commanded the people, "Do not give a war cry, do not raise your voices, do not say a word until the day I tell you to shout. Then shout!" 11So he had the ark of the LORD carried around the city, circling it once. Then the people returned to camp and spent the night there.

12Joshua got up early the next morning and the priests took up the ark of the LORD. 13The seven priests carrying the seven trumpets went forward, marching before the ark of the LORD and blowing the trumpets. The armed men went ahead of them and the rear guard followed the ark of the LORD, while the trumpets kept sounding. 14So on the second day they marched around the city once and returned to the camp. They did this for six days.

15On the seventh day, they got up at daybreak and marched around the city seven times in the same manner, except that on that day they circled the city seven times. 16The seventh time around, when the priests sounded the trumpet blast, Joshua commanded the people, "Shout! For the LORD has given you the city! 17The city and all that is in it are to be devoted[a] to the LORD. Only Rahab the prostitute[b] and all who are with her in her house shall be spared, because she hid the spies we sent. 18But keep away from the devoted things, so that you will not bring about your own destruction by taking any of them. Otherwise you will make the camp of Israel liable to destruction and bring trouble on it. 19All the silver and gold and the articles of bronze and iron are sacred to the LORD and must go into his treasury."

20When the trumpets sounded, the people shouted, and at the sound of the trumpet, when the people gave a loud shout, the wall collapsed; so every man charged straight in, and they took the city. 21They devoted the city to the LORD and destroyed with the sword every living thing in it—men and women, young and old, cattle, sheep and donkeys.

22Joshua said to the two men who had spied out the land, "Go into the prostitute's house and bring her out and all who belong to her, in accordance with your oath to her." 23So the young men who had done the spying went in and brought out Rahab, her father and mother and brothers and all who belonged to her. They brought out her entire family and put them in a place outside the camp of Israel.

24Then they burned the whole city and everything in it, but they put the silver and gold and the articles of bronze and iron into the treasury of the LORD's house. 25But Joshua spared Rahab the prostitute, with her family and all who belonged to her, because she hid the men Joshua had sent as spies to Jericho—and she lives among the Israelites to this day.

26At that time Joshua pronounced this solemn oath: "Cursed before the LORD is the man who undertakes to rebuild this city, Jericho:

"At the cost of his firstborn son
 will he lay its foundations;
at the cost of his youngest
 will he set up its gates."

27So the LORD was with Joshua, and his fame spread throughout the land.

Achan's Sin

7 But the Israelites acted unfaithfully in regard to the devoted things[c]; Achan son of Carmi, the son of Zimri,[d] the son of Zerah, of the tribe of Judah, took some of them. So the LORD's anger burned against Israel.

2Now Joshua sent men from Jericho to Ai, which is near Beth Aven to the east of Bethel, and told them, "Go up and spy out the region." So the men went up and spied out Ai.

3When they returned to Joshua, they said, "Not all the people will have to go up against Ai. Send two or three thousand men to take it and do not weary all the people, for only a few men are there." 4So about three thousand men went up; but they were routed by the men of Ai, 5who killed about thirty-six of them. They chased the Israelites from the city gate as far as the stone quarries[e] and struck them down on the slopes. At this the hearts of the people melted and became like water.

6Then Joshua tore his clothes and fell facedown to the ground before the ark of the LORD, remaining there till evening. The elders of Israel did the same, and sprinkled dust on their heads. 7And Joshua said, "Ah, Sovereign LORD, why did you ever bring this people across the Jordan to deliver us into the hands of the Amorites to destroy us? If only we had been content to stay on the other side of the Jordan! 8O Lord, what can I say, now that Israel has been routed by its enemies? 9The Canaanites and the other people of the country will hear about this and they will surround us and wipe out our name from the earth. What then will you do for your own great name?"

10The LORD said to Joshua, "Stand up! What are you doing down on your face? 11Israel has sinned; they have violated my covenant, which I commanded them to keep. They have taken some of the devoted things; they have stolen, they have lied, they have put them with their own possessions. 12That is why the Israelites cannot stand against their enemies; they turn their backs and run because they have been made liable to destruction. I will not be with

[a] *17* The Hebrew term refers to the irrevocable giving over of things or persons to the LORD, often by totally destroying them; also in verses 18 and 21. [b] *17* Or possibly *innkeeper*; also in verses 22 and 25
[c] *1* The Hebrew term refers to the irrevocable giving over of things or persons to the LORD, often by totally destroying them; also in verses 11, 12, 13 and 15. [d] *1* See Septuagint and 1 Chron. 2:6; Hebrew *Zabdi*; also in verses 17 and 18. [e] *5* Or *as far as Shebarim*

you anymore unless you destroy whatever among you is devoted to destruction.

13“Go, consecrate the people. Tell them, ‘Consecrate yourselves in preparation for tomorrow; for this is what the LORD, the God of Israel, says: That which is devoted is among you, O Israel. You cannot stand against your enemies until you remove it.

14“ ‘In the morning, present yourselves tribe by tribe. The tribe that the LORD takes shall come forward clan by clan; the clan that the LORD takes shall come forward family by family; and the family that the LORD takes shall come forward man by man. 15He who is caught with the devoted things shall be destroyed by fire, along with all that belongs to him. He has violated the covenant of the LORD and has done a disgraceful thing in Israel!’ ”

16Early the next morning Joshua had Israel come forward by tribes, and Judah was taken. 17The clans of Judah came forward, and he took the Zerahites. He had the clan of the Zerahites come forward by families, and Zimri was taken. 18Joshua had his family come forward man by man, and Achan son of Carmi, the son of Zimri, the son of Zerah, of the tribe of Judah, was taken.

19Then Joshua said to Achan, “My son, give glory to the LORD,[a] the God of Israel, and give him the praise.[b] Tell me what you have done; do not hide it from me.”

20Achan replied, “It is true! I have sinned against the LORD, the God of Israel. This is what I have done: 21When I saw in the plunder a beautiful robe from Babylonia,[c] two hundred shekels[d] of silver and a wedge of gold weighing fifty shekels,[e] I coveted them and took them. They are hidden in the ground inside my tent, with the silver underneath.”

22So Joshua sent messengers, and they ran to the tent, and there it was, hidden in his tent, with the silver underneath. 23They took the things from the tent, brought them to Joshua and all the Israelites and spread them out before the LORD.

24Then Joshua, together with all Israel, took Achan son of Zerah, the silver, the robe, the gold wedge, his sons and daughters, his cattle, donkeys and sheep, his tent and all that he had, to the Valley of Achor. 25Joshua said, “Why have you brought this trouble on us? The LORD will bring trouble on you today.”

Then all Israel stoned him, and after they had stoned the rest, they burned them. 26Over Achan they heaped up a large pile of rocks, which remains to this day. Then the LORD turned from his fierce anger. Therefore that place has been called the Valley of Achor[f] ever since.

Ai Destroyed

8 Then the LORD said to Joshua, “Do not be afraid; do not be discouraged. Take the whole army with you, and go up and attack Ai. For I have delivered into your hands the king of Ai, his people, his city and his land. 2You shall do to Ai and its king as you did to Jericho and its king, except that you may carry off their plunder and livestock for yourselves. Set an ambush behind the city.”

3So Joshua and the whole army moved out to attack Ai. He chose thirty thousand of his best fighting men and sent them out at night 4with these orders: “Listen carefully. You are to set an ambush behind the city. Don’t go very far from it. All of you be on the alert. 5I and all those with me will advance on the city, and when the men come out against us, as they did before, we will flee from them. 6They will pursue us until we have lured them away from the city, for they will say, ‘They are running away from us as they did before.’ So when we flee from them, 7you are to rise up from ambush and take the city. The LORD your God will give it into your hand. 8When you have taken the city, set it on fire. Do what the LORD has commanded. See to it; you have my orders.”

9Then Joshua sent them off, and they went to the place of ambush and lay in wait between Bethel and Ai, to the west of Ai—but Joshua spent that night with the people.

10Early the next morning Joshua mustered his men, and he and the leaders of Israel marched before them to Ai. 11The entire force that was with him marched up and approached the city and arrived in front of it. They set up camp north of Ai, with the valley between them and the city. 12Joshua had taken about five thousand men and set them in ambush between Bethel and Ai, to the west of the city. 13They had the soldiers take up their positions—all those in the camp to the north of the city and the ambush to the west of it. That night Joshua went into the valley.

14When the king of Ai saw this, he and all the men of the city hurried out early in the morning to meet Israel in battle at a certain place overlooking the Arabah. But he did not know that an ambush had been set against him behind the city. 15Joshua and all Israel let themselves be driven back before them, and they fled toward the desert. 16All the men of Ai were called to pursue them, and they pursued Joshua and were lured away from the city. 17Not a man remained in Ai or Bethel who did not go after Israel. They left the city open and went in pursuit of Israel.

18Then the LORD said to Joshua, “Hold out toward Ai the javelin that is in your hand, for into your hand I will deliver the city.” So Joshua held out his javelin toward Ai. 19As soon as he did this, the men in the ambush rose quickly from their position and rushed forward. They entered the city and captured it and quickly set it on fire.

20The men of Ai looked back and saw the

[a] *19* A solemn charge to tell the truth [b] *19* Or *and confess to him* [c] *21* Hebrew *Shinar* [d] *21* That is, about 5 pounds (about 2.3 kilograms) [e] *21* That is, about 1 1/4 pounds (about 0.6 kilogram) [f] *26* *Achor* means *trouble*.

smoke of the city rising against the sky, but they had no chance to escape in any direction, for the Israelites who had been fleeing toward the desert had turned back against their pursuers. 21For when Joshua and all Israel saw that the ambush had taken the city and that smoke was going up from the city, they turned around and attacked the men of Ai. 22The men of the ambush also came out of the city against them, so that they were caught in the middle, with Israelites on both sides. Israel cut them down, leaving them neither survivors nor fugitives. 23But they took the king of Ai alive and brought him to Joshua.

24When Israel had finished killing all the men of Ai in the fields and in the desert where they had chased them, and when every one of them had been put to the sword, all the Israelites returned to Ai and killed those who were in it. 25Twelve thousand men and women fell that day—all the people of Ai. 26For Joshua did not draw back the hand that held out his javelin until he had destroyed[a] all who lived in Ai. 27But Israel did carry off for themselves the livestock and plunder of this city, as the LORD had instructed Joshua.

28So Joshua burned Ai and made it a permanent heap of ruins, a desolate place to this day. 29He hung the king of Ai on a tree and left him there until evening. At sunset, Joshua ordered them to take his body from the tree and throw it down at the entrance of the city gate. And they raised a large pile of rocks over it, which remains to this day.

The Covenant Renewed at Mount Ebal

30Then Joshua built on Mount Ebal an altar to the LORD, the God of Israel, 31as Moses the servant of the LORD had commanded the Israelites. He built it according to what is written in the Book of the Law of Moses—an altar of uncut stones, on which no iron tool had been used. On it they offered to the LORD burnt offerings and sacrificed fellowship offerings.[b] 32There, in the presence of the Israelites, Joshua copied on stones the law of Moses, which he had written. 33All Israel, aliens and citizens alike, with their elders, officials and judges, were standing on both sides of the ark of the covenant of the LORD, facing those who carried it—the priests, who were Levites. Half of the people stood in front of Mount Gerizim and half of them in front of Mount Ebal, as Moses the servant of the LORD had formerly commanded when he gave instructions to bless the people of Israel.

34Afterward, Joshua read all the words of the law—the blessings and the curses—just as it is written in the Book of the Law. 35There was not a word of all that Moses had commanded that Joshua did not read to the whole assembly of Israel, including the women and children, and the aliens who lived among them.

The Gibeonite Deception

9 Now when all the kings west of the Jordan heard about these things—those in the hill country, in the western foothills, and along the entire coast of the Great Sea[c] as far as Lebanon (the kings of the Hittites, Amorites, Canaanites, Perizzites, Hivites and Jebusites)— 2they came together to make war against Joshua and Israel.

3However, when the people of Gibeon heard what Joshua had done to Jericho and Ai, 4they resorted to a ruse: They went as a delegation whose donkeys were loaded[d] with worn-out sacks and old wineskins, cracked and mended. 5The men put worn and patched sandals on their feet and wore old clothes. All the bread of their food supply was dry and moldy. 6Then they went to Joshua in the camp at Gilgal and said to him and the men of Israel, "We have come from a distant country; make a treaty with us."

7The men of Israel said to the Hivites, "But perhaps you live near us. How then can we make a treaty with you?"

8"We are your servants," they said to Joshua.

But Joshua asked, "Who are you and where do you come from?"

9They answered: "Your servants have come from a very distant country because of the fame of the LORD your God. For we have heard reports of him: all that he did in Egypt, 10and all that he did to the two kings of the Amorites east of the Jordan—Sihon king of Heshbon, and Og king of Bashan, who reigned in Ashtaroth. 11And our elders and all those living in our country said to us, 'Take provisions for your journey; go and meet them and say to them, "We are your servants; make a treaty with us." ' 12This bread of ours was warm when we packed it at home on the day we left to come to you. But now see how dry and moldy it is. 13And these wineskins that we filled were new, but see how cracked they are. And our clothes and sandals are worn out by the very long journey."

14The men of Israel sampled their provisions but did not inquire of the LORD. 15Then Joshua made a treaty of peace with them to let them live, and the leaders of the assembly ratified it by oath.

16Three days after they made the treaty with the Gibeonites, the Israelites heard that they were neighbors, living near them. 17So the Israelites set out and on the third day came to their cities: Gibeon, Kephirah, Beeroth and Kiriath Jearim. 18But the Israelites did not attack them, because the leaders of the assembly had sworn an oath to them by the LORD, the God of Israel.

[a]*26* The Hebrew term refers to the irrevocable giving over of things or persons to the LORD, often by totally destroying them. [b]*31* Traditionally *peace offerings* [c]*1* That is, the Mediterranean [d]*4* Most Hebrew manuscripts; some Hebrew manuscripts, Vulgate and Syriac (see also Septuagint) *They prepared provisions and loaded their donkeys*

The whole assembly grumbled against the
leaders, 19but all the leaders answered, "We
have given them our oath by the LORD, the
God of Israel, and we cannot touch them now.
20This is what we will do to them: We will let
them live, so that wrath will not fall on us for
breaking the oath we swore to them." 21They
continued, "Let them live, but let them be
woodcutters and water carriers for the entire
community." So the leaders' promise to them
was kept.

22Then Joshua summoned the Gibeonites
and said, "Why did you deceive us by saying,
'We live a long way from you,' while actually
you live near us? 23You are now under a curse:
You will never cease to serve as woodcutters
and water carriers for the house of my God."

24They answered Joshua, "Your servants
were clearly told how the LORD your God had
commanded his servant Moses to give you the
whole land and to wipe out all its inhabitants
from before you. So we feared for our lives
because of you, and that is why we did this.
25We are now in your hands. Do to us whatever seems good and right to you."

26So Joshua saved them from the Israelites,
and they did not kill them. 27That day he made
the Gibeonites woodcutters and water carriers
for the community and for the altar of the
LORD at the place the LORD would choose.
And that is what they are to this day.

The Sun Stands Still

10 Now Adoni-Zedek king of Jerusalem
heard that Joshua had taken Ai and totally destroyed[a] it, doing to Ai and its king as
he had done to Jericho and its king, and that
the people of Gibeon had made a treaty of
peace with Israel and were living near them.
2He and his people were very much alarmed at
this, because Gibeon was an important city,
like one of the royal cities; it was larger than
Ai, and all its men were good fighters. 3So
Adoni-Zedek king of Jerusalem appealed to
Hoham king of Hebron, Piram king of Jarmuth, Japhia king of Lachish and Debir king of
Eglon. 4"Come up and help me attack Gibeon," he said, "because it has made peace with
Joshua and the Israelites."

5Then the five kings of the Amorites—the
kings of Jerusalem, Hebron, Jarmuth, Lachish
and Eglon—joined forces. They moved up
with all their troops and took up positions
against Gibeon and attacked it.

6The Gibeonites then sent word to Joshua in
the camp at Gilgal: "Do not abandon your servants. Come up to us quickly and save us!
Help us, because all the Amorite kings from
the hill country have joined forces against us."

7So Joshua marched up from Gilgal with his
entire army, including all the best fighting
men. 8The LORD said to Joshua, "Do not be
afraid of them; I have given them into your
hand. Not one of them will be able to withstand you."

9After an all-night march from Gilgal, Joshua took them by surprise. 10The LORD threw
them into confusion before Israel, who defeated them in a great victory at Gibeon. Israel
pursued them along the road going up to Beth
Horon and cut them down all the way to Azekah and Makkedah. 11As they fled before Israel on the road down from Beth Horon to Azekah, the LORD hurled large hailstones down on
them from the sky, and more of them died
from the hailstones than were killed by the
swords of the Israelites.

12On the day the LORD gave the Amorites
over to Israel, Joshua said to the LORD in the
presence of Israel:

"O sun, stand still over Gibeon,
O moon, over the Valley of Aijalon."
13So the sun stood still,
and the moon stopped,
till the nation avenged itself on[b] its
enemies,

as it is written in the Book of Jashar.

The sun stopped in the middle of the sky and
delayed going down about a full day. 14There
has never been a day like it before or since, a
day when the LORD listened to a man. Surely
the LORD was fighting for Israel!

15Then Joshua returned with all Israel to the
camp at Gilgal.

Five Amorite Kings Killed

16Now the five kings had fled and hidden in
the cave at Makkedah. 17When Joshua was
told that the five kings had been found hiding
in the cave at Makkedah, 18he said, "Roll large
rocks up to the mouth of the cave, and post
some men there to guard it. 19But don't stop!
Pursue your enemies, attack them from the rear
and don't let them reach their cities, for the
LORD your God has given them into your
hand."

20So Joshua and the Israelites destroyed
them completely—almost to a man—but the
few who were left reached their fortified cities.
21The whole army then returned safely to Joshua in the camp at Makkedah, and no one uttered a word against the Israelites.

22Joshua said, "Open the mouth of the cave
and bring those five kings out to me." 23So
they brought the five kings out of the cave—
the kings of Jerusalem, Hebron, Jarmuth, Lachish and Eglon. 24When they had brought
these kings to Joshua, he summoned all the
men of Israel and said to the army commanders who had come with him, "Come here and
put your feet on the necks of these kings." So
they came forward and placed their feet on
their necks.

25Joshua said to them, "Do not be afraid; do
not be discouraged. Be strong and courageous.
This is what the LORD will do to all the ene-

[a] *1* The Hebrew term refers to the irrevocable giving over of things or persons to the LORD, often by totally destroying them; also in verses 28, 35, 37, 39 and 40. [b] *13* Or *nation triumphed over*

mies you are going to fight." 26Then Joshua struck and killed the kings and hung them on five trees, and they were left hanging on the trees until evening.

27At sunset Joshua gave the order and they took them down from the trees and threw them into the cave where they had been hiding. At the mouth of the cave they placed large rocks, which are there to this day.

28That day Joshua took Makkedah. He put the city and its king to the sword and totally destroyed everyone in it. He left no survivors. And he did to the king of Makkedah as he had done to the king of Jericho.

Southern Cities Conquered

29Then Joshua and all Israel with him moved on from Makkedah to Libnah and attacked it. 30The LORD also gave that city and its king into Israel's hand. The city and everyone in it Joshua put to the sword. He left no survivors there. And he did to its king as he had done to the king of Jericho.

31Then Joshua and all Israel with him moved on from Libnah to Lachish; he took up positions against it and attacked it. 32The LORD handed Lachish over to Israel, and Joshua took it on the second day. The city and everyone in it he put to the sword, just as he had done to Libnah. 33Meanwhile, Horam king of Gezer had come up to help Lachish, but Joshua defeated him and his army—until no survivors were left.

34Then Joshua and all Israel with him moved on from Lachish to Eglon; they took up positions against it and attacked it. 35They captured it that same day and put it to the sword and totally destroyed everyone in it, just as they had done to Lachish.

36Then Joshua and all Israel with him went up from Eglon to Hebron and attacked it. 37They took the city and put it to the sword, together with its king, its villages and everyone in it. They left no survivors. Just as at Eglon, they totally destroyed it and everyone in it.

38Then Joshua and all Israel with him turned around and attacked Debir. 39They took the city, its king and its villages, and put them to the sword. Everyone in it they totally destroyed. They left no survivors. They did to Debir and its king as they had done to Libnah and its king and to Hebron.

40So Joshua subdued the whole region, including the hill country, the Negev, the western foothills and the mountain slopes, together with all their kings. He left no survivors. He totally destroyed all who breathed, just as the LORD, the God of Israel, had commanded. 41Joshua subdued them from Kadesh Barnea to Gaza and from the whole region of Goshen to Gibeon. 42All these kings and their lands Joshua conquered in one campaign, because the LORD, the God of Israel, fought for Israel.

43Then Joshua returned with all Israel to the camp at Gilgal.

Northern Kings Defeated

11 When Jabin king of Hazor heard of this, he sent word to Jobab king of Madon, to the kings of Shimron and Acshaph, 2and to the northern kings who were in the mountains, in the Arabah south of Kinnereth, in the western foothills and in Naphoth Dor[a] on the west; 3to the Canaanites in the east and west; to the Amorites, Hittites, Perizzites and Jebusites in the hill country; and to the Hivites below Hermon in the region of Mizpah. 4They came out with all their troops and a large number of horses and chariots—a huge army, as numerous as the sand on the seashore. 5All these kings joined forces and made camp together at the Waters of Merom, to fight against Israel.

6The LORD said to Joshua, "Do not be afraid of them, because by this time tomorrow I will hand all of them over to Israel, slain. You are to hamstring their horses and burn their chariots."

7So Joshua and his whole army came against them suddenly at the Waters of Merom and attacked them, 8and the LORD gave them into the hand of Israel. They defeated them and pursued them all the way to Greater Sidon, to Misrephoth Maim, and to the Valley of Mizpah on the east, until no survivors were left. 9Joshua did to them as the LORD had directed: He hamstrung their horses and burned their chariots.

10At that time Joshua turned back and captured Hazor and put its king to the sword. (Hazor had been the head of all these kingdoms.) 11Everyone in it they put to the sword. They totally destroyed[b] them, not sparing anything that breathed, and he burned up Hazor itself.

12Joshua took all these royal cities and their kings and put them to the sword. He totally destroyed them, as Moses the servant of the LORD had commanded. 13Yet Israel did not burn any of the cities built on their mounds—except Hazor, which Joshua burned. 14The Israelites carried off for themselves all the plunder and livestock of these cities, but all the people they put to the sword until they completely destroyed them, not sparing anyone that breathed. 15As the LORD commanded his servant Moses, so Moses commanded Joshua, and Joshua did it; he left nothing undone of all that the LORD commanded Moses.

16So Joshua took this entire land: the hill country, all the Negev, the whole region of Goshen, the western foothills, the Arabah and the mountains of Israel with their foothills, 17from Mount Halak, which rises toward Seir, to Baal Gad in the Valley of Lebanon below Mount Hermon. He captured all their kings and struck them down, putting them to death. 18Joshua waged war against all these kings for a long time. 19Except for the Hivites living in

[a]2 Or *in the heights of Dor* [b]11 The Hebrew term refers to the irrevocable giving over of things or persons to the LORD, often by totally destroying them; also in verses 12, 20 and 21.

Gibeon, not one city made a treaty of peace
with the Israelites, who took them all in battle.
20For it was the LORD himself who hardened
their hearts to wage war against Israel, so that
he might destroy them totally, exterminating
them without mercy, as the LORD had commanded Moses.
21At that time Joshua went and destroyed
the Anakites from the hill country: from Hebron, Debir and Anab, from all the hill country
of Judah, and from all the hill country of Israel.
Joshua totally destroyed them and their towns.
22No Anakites were left in Israelite territory;
only in Gaza, Gath and Ashdod did any survive. 23So Joshua took the entire land, just as
the LORD had directed Moses, and he gave it as
an inheritance to Israel according to their tribal
divisions.
Then the land had rest from war.

List of Defeated Kings

12 These are the kings of the land whom
the Israelites had defeated and whose
territory they took over east of the Jordan,
from the Arnon Gorge to Mount Hermon, including all the eastern side of the Arabah:

2Sihon king of the Amorites,
who reigned in Heshbon. He ruled from
Aroer on the rim of the Arnon Gorge—
from the middle of the gorge—to the Jabbok River, which is the border of the Ammonites. This included half of Gilead.
3He also ruled over the eastern Arabah
from the Sea of Kinnereth[a] to the Sea of
the Arabah (the Salt Sea[b]), to Beth Jeshimoth, and then southward below the
slopes of Pisgah.

4And the territory of Og king of Bashan,
one of the last of the Rephaites, who
reigned in Ashtaroth and Edrei. 5He ruled
over Mount Hermon, Salecah, all of Bashan to the border of the people of Geshur
and Maacah, and half of Gilead to the
border of Sihon king of Heshbon.

6Moses, the servant of the LORD, and the
Israelites conquered them. And Moses the servant of the LORD gave their land to the Reubenites, the Gadites and the half-tribe of Manasseh to be their possession.
7These are the kings of the land that Joshua
and the Israelites conquered on the west side of
the Jordan, from Baal Gad in the Valley of
Lebanon to Mount Halak, which rises toward
Seir (their lands Joshua gave as an inheritance
to the tribes of Israel according to their tribal
divisions— 8the hill country, the western foothills, the Arabah, the mountain slopes, the
desert and the Negev—the lands of the Hittites, Amorites, Canaanites, Perizzites, Hivites
and Jebusites):

9the king of Jericho	one
the king of Ai (near Bethel)	one
10the king of Jerusalem	one
the king of Hebron	one
11the king of Jarmuth	one
the king of Lachish	one
12the king of Eglon	one
the king of Gezer	one
13the king of Debir	one
the king of Geder	one
14the king of Hormah	one
the king of Arad	one
15the king of Libnah	one
the king of Adullam	one
16the king of Makkedah	one
the king of Bethel	one
17the king of Tappuah	one
the king of Hepher	one
18the king of Aphek	one
the king of Lasharon	one
19the king of Madon	one
the king of Hazor	one
20the king of Shimron Meron	one
the king of Acshaph	one
21the king of Taanach	one
the king of Megiddo	one
22the king of Kedesh	one
the king of Jokneam in Carmel	one
23the king of Dor (in Naphoth Dor[c])	one
the king of Goyim in Gilgal	one
24the king of Tirzah	one

thirty-one kings in all.

Land Still to Be Taken

13 When Joshua was old and well advanced in years, the LORD said to him,
"You are very old, and there are still very large
areas of land to be taken over.

2"This is the land that remains: all the
regions of the Philistines and Geshurites:
3from the Shihor River on the east of
Egypt to the territory of Ekron on the
north, all of it counted as Canaanite (the
territory of the five Philistine rulers in
Gaza, Ashdod, Ashkelon, Gath and Ekron—that of the Avvites); 4from the
south, all the land of the Canaanites, from
Arah of the Sidonians as far as Aphek, the
region of the Amorites, 5the area of the
Gebalites[d]; and all Lebanon to the east,
from Baal Gad below Mount Hermon to
Lebo[e] Hamath.

6"As for all the inhabitants of the mountain
regions from Lebanon to Misrephoth Maim,
that is, all the Sidonians, I myself will drive
them out before the Israelites. Be sure to allo-
cate this land to Israel for an inheritance, as I
have instructed you, 7and divide it as an inheritance among the nine tribes and half of the
tribe of Manasseh."

Division of the Land East of the Jordan

8The other half of Manasseh,[f] the Reubenites

[a] 3 That is, Galilee [b] 3 That is, the Dead Sea [c] 23 Or *in the heights of Dor* [d] 5 That is, the area of Byblos [e] 5 Or *to the entrance to* [f] 8 Hebrew *With it* (that is, with the other half of Manasseh)

and the Gadites had received the inheritance that Moses had given them east of the Jordan, as he, the servant of the LORD, had assigned it to them.

9It extended from Aroer on the rim of the Arnon Gorge, and from the town in the middle of the gorge, and included the whole plateau of Medeba as far as Dibon, 10and all the towns of Sihon king of the Amorites, who ruled in Heshbon, out to the border of the Ammonites. 11It also included Gilead, the territory of the people of Geshur and Maacah, all of Mount Hermon and all Bashan as far as Salecah— 12that is, the whole kingdom of Og in Bashan, who had reigned in Ashtaroth and Edrei and had survived as one of the last of the Rephaites. Moses had defeated them and taken over their land. 13But the Israelites did not drive out the people of Geshur and Maacah, so they continue to live among the Israelites to this day.

14But to the tribe of Levi he gave no inheritance, since the offerings made by fire to the LORD, the God of Israel, are their inheritance, as he promised them.

15This is what Moses had given to the tribe of Reuben, clan by clan:

16The territory from Aroer on the rim of the Arnon Gorge, and from the town in the middle of the gorge, and the whole plateau past Medeba 17to Heshbon and all its towns on the plateau, including Dibon, Bamoth Baal, Beth Baal Meon, 18Jahaz, Kedemoth, Mephaath, 19Kiriathaim, Sibmah, Zereth Shahar on the hill in the valley, 20Beth Peor, the slopes of Pisgah, and Beth Jeshimoth 21—all the towns on the plateau and the entire realm of Sihon king of the Amorites, who ruled at Heshbon. Moses had defeated him and the Midianite chiefs, Evi, Rekem, Zur, Hur and Reba—princes allied with Sihon—who lived in that country. 22In addition to those slain in battle, the Israelites had put to the sword Balaam son of Beor, who practiced divination. 23The boundary of the Reubenites was the bank of the Jordan. These towns and their villages were the inheritance of the Reubenites, clan by clan.

24This is what Moses had given to the tribe of Gad, clan by clan:

25The territory of Jazer, all the towns of Gilead and half the Ammonite country as far as Aroer, near Rabbah; 26and from Heshbon to Ramath Mizpah and Betonim, and from Mahanaim to the territory of Debir; 27and in the valley, Beth Haram, Beth Nimrah, Succoth and Zaphon with the rest of the realm of Sihon king of Heshbon (the east side of the Jordan, the territory up to the end of the Sea of Kinnereth[a]). 28These towns and their villages were the inheritance of the Gadites, clan by clan.

29This is what Moses had given to the half-tribe of Manasseh, that is, to half the family of the descendants of Manasseh, clan by clan:

30The territory extending from Mahanaim and including all of Bashan, the entire realm of Og king of Bashan—all the settlements of Jair in Bashan, sixty towns, 31half of Gilead, and Ashtaroth and Edrei (the royal cities of Og in Bashan). This was for the descendants of Makir son of Manasseh—for half of the sons of Makir, clan by clan.

32This is the inheritance Moses had given when he was in the plains of Moab across the Jordan east of Jericho. 33But to the tribe of Levi, Moses had given no inheritance; the LORD, the God of Israel, is their inheritance, as he promised them.

Division of the Land West of the Jordan

14 Now these are the areas the Israelites received as an inheritance in the land of Canaan, which Eleazar the priest, Joshua son of Nun and the heads of the tribal clans of Israel allotted to them. 2Their inheritances were assigned by lot to the nine-and-a-half tribes, as the LORD had commanded through Moses. 3Moses had granted the two-and-a-half tribes their inheritance east of the Jordan but had not granted the Levites an inheritance among the rest, 4for the sons of Joseph had become two tribes—Manasseh and Ephraim. The Levites received no share of the land but only towns to live in, with pasturelands for their flocks and herds. 5So the Israelites divided the land, just as the LORD had commanded Moses.

Hebron Given to Caleb

6Now the men of Judah approached Joshua at Gilgal, and Caleb son of Jephunneh the Kenizzite said to him, "You know what the LORD said to Moses the man of God at Kadesh Barnea about you and me. 7I was forty years old when Moses the servant of the LORD sent me from Kadesh Barnea to explore the land. And I brought him back a report according to my convictions, 8but my brothers who went up with me made the hearts of the people melt with fear. I, however, followed the LORD my God wholeheartedly. 9So on that day Moses swore to me, 'The land on which your feet have walked will be your inheritance and that of your children forever, because you have followed the LORD my God wholeheartedly.'[b]

10"Now then, just as the LORD promised, he has kept me alive for forty-five years since the time he said this to Moses, while Israel moved about in the desert. So here I am today, eighty-

[a]27 That is, Galilee [b]9 Deut. 1:36

five years old! 11 I am still as strong today as
the day Moses sent me out; I'm just as vigorous to go out to battle now as I was then.
12 Now give me this hill country that the LORD
promised me that day. You yourself heard then
that the Anakites were there and their cities
were large and fortified, but, the LORD helping
me, I will drive them out just as he said."
13 Then Joshua blessed Caleb son of Jephunneh and gave him Hebron as his inheritance.
14 So Hebron has belonged to Caleb son of Jephunneh the Kenizzite ever since, because he
followed the LORD, the God of Israel, wholeheartedly. 15 (Hebron used to be called Kiriath
Arba after Arba, who was the greatest man
among the Anakites.)
Then the land had rest from war.

Allotment for Judah

15 The allotment for the tribe of Judah,
clan by clan, extended down to the territory of Edom, to the Desert of Zin in the extreme south.

2 Their southern boundary started from
the bay at the southern end of the Salt
Sea,[a] 3 crossed south of Scorpion[b] Pass,
continued on to Zin and went over to the
south of Kadesh Barnea. Then it ran past
Hezron up to Addar and curved around to
Karka. 4 It then passed along to Azmon
and joined the Wadi of Egypt, ending at
the sea. This is their[c] southern boundary.
5 The eastern boundary is the Salt Sea
as far as the mouth of the Jordan.
The northern boundary started from the
bay of the sea at the mouth of the Jordan,
6 went up to Beth Hoglah and continued
north of Beth Arabah to the Stone of Bohan son of Reuben. 7 The boundary then
went up to Debir from the Valley of
Achor and turned north to Gilgal, which
faces the Pass of Adummim south of the
gorge. It continued along to the waters of
En Shemesh and came out at En Rogel.
8 Then it ran up the Valley of Ben Hinnom
along the southern slope of the Jebusite
city (that is, Jerusalem). From there it
climbed to the top of the hill west of the
Hinnom Valley at the northern end of the
Valley of Rephaim. 9 From the hilltop
the boundary headed toward the spring of
the waters of Nephtoah, came out at the
towns of Mount Ephron and went down
toward Baalah (that is, Kiriath Jearim).
10 Then it curved westward from Baalah to
Mount Seir, ran along the northern slope
of Mount Jearim (that is, Kesalon), continued down to Beth Shemesh and crossed
to Timnah. 11 It went to the northern slope
of Ekron, turned toward Shikkeron,
passed along to Mount Baalah and
reached Jabneel. The boundary ended at
the sea.
12 The western boundary is the coastline
of the Great Sea.[d]
These are the boundaries around the people of
Judah by their clans.

13 In accordance with the LORD's command
to him, Joshua gave to Caleb son of Jephunneh
a portion in Judah—Kiriath Arba, that is, Hebron. (Arba was the forefather of Anak.)
14 From Hebron Caleb drove out the three Anakites—Sheshai, Ahiman and Talmai—descendants of Anak. 15 From there he marched
against the people living in Debir (formerly
called Kiriath Sepher). 16 And Caleb said, "I
will give my daughter Acsah in marriage to the
man who attacks and captures Kiriath Sepher."
17 Othniel son of Kenaz, Caleb's brother, took
it; so Caleb gave his daughter Acsah to him in
marriage.
18 One day when she came to Othniel, she
urged him[e] to ask her father for a field. When
she got off her donkey, Caleb asked her,
"What can I do for you?"
19 She replied, "Do me a special favor. Since
you have given me land in the Negev, give me
also springs of water." So Caleb gave her the
upper and lower springs.

20 This is the inheritance of the tribe of Judah, clan by clan:

21 The southernmost towns of the tribe of Judah
in the Negev toward the boundary of Edom
were:
Kabzeel, Eder, Jagur, 22 Kinah, Dimo-
nah, Adadah, 23 Kedesh, Hazor, Ithnan,
24 Ziph, Telem, Bealoth, 25 Hazor Hadat-
tah, Kerioth Hezron (that is, Hazor),
26 Amam, Shema, Moladah, 27 Hazar Gad-
dah, Heshmon, Beth Pelet, 28 Hazar Shual,
Beersheba, Biziothiah, 29 Baalah, Iim,
Ezem, 30 Eltolad, Kesil, Hormah, 31 Ziklag, Madmannah, Sansannah, 32 Lebaoth,
Shilhim, Ain and Rimmon—a total of
twenty-nine towns and their villages.

33 In the western foothills:
Eshtaol, Zorah, Ashnah, 34 Zanoah, En
Gannim, Tappuah, Enam, 35 Jarmuth,
Adullam, Socoh, Azekah, 36 Shaaraim,
Adithaim and Gederah (or Gederothaim)[f]—fourteen towns and their villages.
37 Zenan, Hadashah, Migdal Gad, 38 Dil-
ean, Mizpah, Joktheel, 39 Lachish, Bozkath, Eglon, 40 Cabbon, Lahmas, Kitlish,
41 Gederoth, Beth Dagon, Naamah and
Makkedah—sixteen towns and their villages.
42 Libnah, Ether, Ashan, 43 Iphtah, Ashnah, Nezib, 44 Keilah, Aczib and Mareshah—nine towns and their villages.
45 Ekron, with its surrounding settlements and villages; 46 west of Ekron, all
that were in the vicinity of Ashdod, together with their villages; 47 Ashdod, its

[a] *2* That is, the Dead Sea; also in verse 5 [b] *3* Hebrew *Akrabbim* [c] *4* Hebrew *your* [d] *12* That is, the Mediterranean; also in verse 47 [e] *18* Hebrew and some Septuagint manuscripts; other Septuagint manuscripts (see also note at Judges 1:14) *Othniel, he urged her* [f] *36* Or *Gederah and Gederothaim*

surrounding settlements and villages; and
Gaza, its settlements and villages, as far
as the Wadi of Egypt and the coastline of
the Great Sea.

48 In the hill country:
Shamir, Jattir, Socoh, 49 Dannah, Kiriath Sannah (that is, Debir), 50 Anab, Esh-
temoh, Anim, 51 Goshen, Holon and Gi-
loh—eleven towns and their villages.
52 Arab, Dumah, Eshan, 53 Janim, Beth
Tappuah, Aphekah, 54 Humtah, Kiriath
Arba (that is, Hebron) and Zior—nine
towns and their villages.
55 Maon, Carmel, Ziph, Juttah, 56 Jezreel, Jokdeam, Zanoah, 57 Kain, Gibeah and
Timnah—ten towns and their villages.
58 Halhul, Beth Zur, Gedor, 59 Maarath,
Beth Anoth and Eltekon—six towns and
their villages.
60 Kiriath Baal (that is, Kiriath Jearim)
and Rabbah—two towns and their villages.

61 In the desert:
Beth Arabah, Middin, Secacah, 62 Nib-
shan, the City of Salt and En Gedi—six
towns and their villages.
63 Judah could not dislodge the Jebusites,
who were living in Jerusalem; to this day the
Jebusites live there with the people of Judah.

Allotment for Ephraim and Manasseh

16 The allotment for Joseph began at
the Jordan of Jericho,[a] east of the
waters of Jericho, and went up from there
through the desert into the hill country of
Bethel. 2 It went on from Bethel (that is,
Luz),[b] crossed over to the territory of the
Arkites in Ataroth, 3 descended westward
to the territory of the Japhletites as far as
the region of Lower Beth Horon and on to
Gezer, ending at the sea.
4 So Manasseh and Ephraim, the descendants
of Joseph, received their inheritance.

5 This was the territory of Ephraim, clan by
clan:
The boundary of their inheritance went
from Ataroth Addar in the east to Upper
Beth Horon 6 and continued to the sea.
From Micmethath on the north it curved
eastward to Taanath Shiloh, passing by it
to Janoah on the east. 7 Then it went down
from Janoah to Ataroth and Naarah,
touched Jericho and came out at the Jordan. 8 From Tappuah the border went west
to the Kanah Ravine and ended at the sea.
This was the inheritance of the tribe of the
Ephraimites, clan by clan. 9 It also included all the towns and their villages that
were set aside for the Ephraimites within
the inheritance of the Manassites.
10 They did not dislodge the Canaanites living
in Gezer; to this day the Canaanites live among
the people of Ephraim but are required to do
forced labor.

17 This was the allotment for the tribe of
Manasseh as Joseph's firstborn, that is,
for Makir, Manasseh's firstborn. Makir was
the ancestor of the Gileadites, who had received Gilead and Bashan because the Makirites were great soldiers. 2 So this allotment was
for the rest of the people of Manasseh—the
clans of Abiezer, Helek, Asriel, Shechem, Hepher and Shemida. These are the other male
descendants of Manasseh son of Joseph by
their clans.
3 Now Zelophehad son of Hepher, the son of
Gilead, the son of Makir, the son of Manasseh,
had no sons but only daughters, whose names
were Mahlah, Noah, Hoglah, Milcah and Tirzah. 4 They went to Eleazar the priest, Joshua
son of Nun, and the leaders and said, "The
LORD commanded Moses to give us an inheritance among our brothers." So Joshua gave
them an inheritance along with the brothers
of their father, according to the LORD's command. 5 Manasseh's share consisted of ten
tracts of land besides Gilead and Bashan east
of the Jordan, 6 because the daughters of the
tribe of Manasseh received an inheritance
among the sons. The land of Gilead belonged
to the rest of the descendants of Manasseh.
7 The territory of Manasseh extended
from Asher to Micmethath east of Shechem. The boundary ran southward from
there to include the people living at En
Tappuah. 8 (Manasseh had the land of
Tappuah, but Tappuah itself, on the
boundary of Manasseh, belonged to the
Ephraimites.) 9 Then the boundary continued south to the Kanah Ravine. There
were towns belonging to Ephraim lying
among the towns of Manasseh, but the
boundary of Manasseh was the northern
side of the ravine and ended at the sea.
10 On the south the land belonged to
Ephraim, on the north to Manasseh. The
territory of Manasseh reached the sea and
bordered Asher on the north and Issachar
on the east.
11 Within Issachar and Asher, Manasseh
also had Beth Shan, Ibleam and the people of Dor, Endor, Taanach and Megiddo,
together with their surrounding settlements (the third in the list is Naphoth[c]).
12 Yet the Manassites were not able to occupy
these towns, for the Canaanites were determined to live in that region. 13 However, when
the Israelites grew stronger, they subjected the
Canaanites to forced labor but did not drive
them out completely.
14 The people of Joseph said to Joshua,
"Why have you given us only one allotment
and one portion for an inheritance? We are a
numerous people and the LORD has blessed us
abundantly."
15 "If you are so numerous," Joshua an-

[a] *1 Jordan of Jericho* was possibly an ancient name for the Jordan River. [b] *2* Septuagint; Hebrew *Bethel to Luz* [c] *11* That is, Naphoth Dor

swered, "and if the hill country of Ephraim is too small for you, go up into the forest and clear land for yourselves there in the land of the Perizzites and Rephaites."

16The people of Joseph replied, "The hill country is not enough for us, and all the Canaanites who live in the plain have iron chariots, both those in Beth Shan and its settlements and those in the Valley of Jezreel."

17But Joshua said to the house of Joseph—to Ephraim and Manasseh—"You are numerous and very powerful. You will have not only one allotment 18but the forested hill country as well. Clear it, and its farthest limits will be yours; though the Canaanites have iron chariots and though they are strong, you can drive them out."

Division of the Rest of the Land

18 The whole assembly of the Israelites gathered at Shiloh and set up the Tent of Meeting there. The country was brought under their control, 2but there were still seven Israelite tribes who had not yet received their inheritance.

3So Joshua said to the Israelites: "How long will you wait before you begin to take possession of the land that the LORD, the God of your fathers, has given you? 4Appoint three men from each tribe. I will send them out to make a survey of the land and to write a description of it, according to the inheritance of each. Then they will return to me. 5You are to divide the land into seven parts. Judah is to remain in its territory on the south and the house of Joseph in its territory on the north. 6After you have written descriptions of the seven parts of the land, bring them here to me and I will cast lots for you in the presence of the LORD our God. 7The Levites, however, do not get a portion among you, because the priestly service of the LORD is their inheritance. And Gad, Reuben and the half-tribe of Manasseh have already received their inheritance on the east side of the Jordan. Moses the servant of the LORD gave it to them."

8As the men started on their way to map out the land, Joshua instructed them, "Go and make a survey of the land and write a description of it. Then return to me, and I will cast lots for you here at Shiloh in the presence of the LORD." 9So the men left and went through the land. They wrote its description on a scroll, town by town, in seven parts, and returned to Joshua in the camp at Shiloh. 10Joshua then cast lots for them in Shiloh in the presence of the LORD, and there he distributed the land to the Israelites according to their tribal divisions.

Allotment for Benjamin

11The lot came up for the tribe of Benjamin, clan by clan. Their allotted territory lay between the tribes of Judah and Joseph:

12On the north side their boundary began at the Jordan, passed the northern slope of Jericho and headed west into the hill country, coming out at the desert of Beth Aven. 13From there it crossed to the south slope of Luz (that is, Bethel) and went down to Ataroth Addar on the hill south of Lower Beth Horon.

14From the hill facing Beth Horon on the south the boundary turned south along the western side and came out at Kiriath Baal (that is, Kiriath Jearim), a town of the people of Judah. This was the western side.

15The southern side began at the outskirts of Kiriath Jearim on the west, and the boundary came out at the spring of the waters of Nephtoah. 16The boundary went down to the foot of the hill facing the Valley of Ben Hinnom, north of the Valley of Rephaim. It continued down the Hinnom Valley along the southern slope of the Jebusite city and so to En Rogel. 17It then curved north, went to En Shemesh, continued to Geliloth, which faces the Pass of Adummim, and ran down to the Stone of Bohan son of Reuben. 18It continued to the northern slope of Beth Arabah[a] and on down into the Arabah. 19It then went to the northern slope of Beth Hoglah and came out at the northern bay of the Salt Sea,[b] at the mouth of the Jordan in the south. This was the southern boundary.

20The Jordan formed the boundary on the eastern side.

These were the boundaries that marked out the inheritance of the clans of Benjamin on all sides.

21The tribe of Benjamin, clan by clan, had the following cities:

Jericho, Beth Hoglah, Emek Keziz, 22Beth Arabah, Zemaraim, Bethel, 23Avvim, Parah, Ophrah, 24Kephar Ammoni, Ophni and Geba—twelve towns and their villages.

25Gibeon, Ramah, Beeroth, 26Mizpah, Kephirah, Mozah, 27Rekem, Irpeel, Taralah, 28Zelah, Haeleph, the Jebusite city (that is, Jerusalem), Gibeah and Kiriath—fourteen towns and their villages.

This was the inheritance of Benjamin for its clans.

Allotment for Simeon

19 The second lot came out for the tribe of Simeon, clan by clan. Their inheritance lay within the territory of Judah. 2It included:

Beersheba (or Sheba),[c] Moladah, 3Hazar Shual, Balah, Ezem, 4Eltolad, Bethul, Hormah, 5Ziklag, Beth Marcaboth, Hazar Susah, 6Beth Lebaoth and Sharuhen—thirteen towns and their villages;

7Ain, Rimmon, Ether and Ashan—four towns and their villages— 8and all the

[a] *18* Septuagint; Hebrew *slope facing the Arabah* [b] *19* That is, the Dead Sea [c] *2* Or *Beersheba, Sheba*; 1 Chron. 4:28 does not have *Sheba.*

villages around these towns as far as Baalath Beer (Ramah in the Negev).

This was the inheritance of the tribe of the Simeonites, clan by clan. 9The inheritance of the Simeonites was taken from the share of Judah, because Judah's portion was more than they needed. So the Simeonites received their inheritance within the territory of Judah.

Allotment for Zebulun

10The third lot came up for Zebulun, clan by clan:

The boundary of their inheritance went as far as Sarid. 11Going west it ran to Maralah, touched Dabbesheth, and extended to the ravine near Jokneam. 12It turned east from Sarid toward the sunrise to the territory of Kisloth Tabor and went on to Daberath and up to Japhia. 13Then it continued eastward to Gath Hepher and Eth Kazin; it came out at Rimmon and turned toward Neah. 14There the boundary went around on the north to Hannathon and ended at the Valley of Iphtah El. 15Included were Kattath, Nahalal, Shimron, Idalah and Bethlehem. There were twelve towns and their villages.

16These towns and their villages were the inheritance of Zebulun, clan by clan.

Allotment for Issachar

17The fourth lot came out for Issachar, clan by clan. 18Their territory included:

Jezreel, Kesulloth, Shunem, 19Hapharaim, Shion, Anaharath, 20Rabbith, Kishion, Ebez, 21Remeth, En Gannim, En Haddah and Beth Pazzez. 22The boundary touched Tabor, Shahazumah and Beth Shemesh, and ended at the Jordan. There were sixteen towns and their villages.

23These towns and their villages were the inheritance of the tribe of Issachar, clan by clan.

Allotment for Asher

24The fifth lot came out for the tribe of Asher, clan by clan. 25Their territory included:

Helkath, Hali, Beten, Acshaph, 26Allammelech, Amad and Mishal. On the west the boundary touched Carmel and Shihor Libnath. 27It then turned east toward Beth Dagon, touched Zebulun and the Valley of Iphtah El, and went north to Beth Emek and Neiel, passing Cabul on the left. 28It went to Abdon,[a] Rehob, Hammon and Kanah, as far as Greater Sidon. 29The boundary then turned back toward Ramah and went to the fortified city of Tyre, turned toward Hosah and came out at the sea in the region of Aczib, 30Ummah, Aphek and Rehob. There were twenty-two towns and their villages.

31These towns and their villages were the inheritance of the tribe of Asher, clan by clan.

Allotment for Naphtali

32The sixth lot came out for Naphtali, clan by clan:

33Their boundary went from Heleph and the large tree in Zaanannim, passing Adami Nekeb and Jabneel to Lakkum and ending at the Jordan. 34The boundary ran west through Aznoth Tabor and came out at Hukkok. It touched Zebulun on the south, Asher on the west and the Jordan[b] on the east. 35The fortified cities were Ziddim, Zer, Hammath, Rakkath, Kinnereth, 36Adamah, Ramah, Hazor, 37Kedesh, Edrei, En Hazor, 38Iron, Migdal El, Horem, Beth Anath and Beth Shemesh. There were nineteen towns and their villages.

39These towns and their villages were the inheritance of the tribe of Naphtali, clan by clan.

Allotment for Dan

40The seventh lot came out for the tribe of Dan, clan by clan. 41The territory of their inheritance included:

Zorah, Eshtaol, Ir Shemesh, 42Shaalabbin, Aijalon, Ithlah, 43Elon, Timnah, Ekron, 44Eltekeh, Gibbethon, Baalath, 45Jehud, Bene Berak, Gath Rimmon, 46Me Jarkon and Rakkon, with the area facing Joppa.

47(But the Danites had difficulty taking possession of their territory, so they went up and attacked Leshem, took it, put it to the sword and occupied it. They settled in Leshem and named it Dan after their forefather.)

48These towns and their villages were the inheritance of the tribe of Dan, clan by clan.

Allotment for Joshua

49When they had finished dividing the land into its allotted portions, the Israelites gave Joshua son of Nun an inheritance among them, 50as the LORD had commanded. They gave him the town he asked for—Timnath Serah[c] in the hill country of Ephraim. And he built up the town and settled there.

51These are the territories that Eleazar the priest, Joshua son of Nun and the heads of the tribal clans of Israel assigned by lot at Shiloh in the presence of the LORD at the entrance to the Tent of Meeting. And so they finished dividing the land.

Cities of Refuge

20 Then the LORD said to Joshua: 2"Tell the Israelites to designate the cities of refuge, as I instructed you through Moses, 3so that anyone who kills a person accidentally and unintentionally may flee there and find protection from the avenger of blood.

4"When he flees to one of these cities, he is to stand in the entrance of the city gate and state his case before the elders of that city. Then they are to admit him into their city and

[a]28 Some Hebrew manuscripts (see also Joshua 21:30); most Hebrew manuscripts *Ebron* [b]34 Septuagint; Hebrew *west, and Judah, the Jordan,* [c]50 Also known as *Timnath Heres* (see Judges 2:9)

give him a place to live with them. 5If the
avenger of blood pursues him, they must not
surrender the one accused, because he killed
his neighbor unintentionally and without malice aforethought. 6He is to stay in that city until
he has stood trial before the assembly and until
the death of the high priest who is serving at
that time. Then he may go back to his own
home in the town from which he fled."

7So they set apart Kedesh in Galilee in the
hill country of Naphtali, Shechem in the hill
country of Ephraim, and Kiriath Arba (that is,
Hebron) in the hill country of Judah. 8On the
east side of the Jordan of Jericho[a] they designated Bezer in the desert on the plateau in the
tribe of Reuben, Ramoth in Gilead in the tribe
of Gad, and Golan in Bashan in the tribe of
Manasseh. 9Any of the Israelites or any alien
living among them who killed someone accidentally could flee to these designated cities
and not be killed by the avenger of blood prior
to standing trial before the assembly.

Towns for the Levites

21 Now the family heads of the Levites
approached Eleazar the priest, Joshua
son of Nun, and the heads of the other tribal
families of Israel 2at Shiloh in Canaan and said
to them, "The LORD commanded through Moses that you give us towns to live in, with
pasturelands for our livestock." 3So, as the
LORD had commanded, the Israelites gave the
Levites the following towns and pasturelands
out of their own inheritance:

4The first lot came out for the Kohathites,
clan by clan. The Levites who were descendants of Aaron the priest were allotted thirteen
towns from the tribes of Judah, Simeon and
Benjamin. 5The rest of Kohath's descendants
were allotted ten towns from the clans of the
tribes of Ephraim, Dan and half of Manasseh.

6The descendants of Gershon were allotted
thirteen towns from the clans of the tribes of
Issachar, Asher, Naphtali and the half-tribe of
Manasseh in Bashan.

7The descendants of Merari, clan by clan,
received twelve towns from the tribes of Reuben, Gad and Zebulun.

8So the Israelites allotted to the Levites
these towns and their pasturelands, as the
LORD had commanded through Moses.

9From the tribes of Judah and Simeon they
allotted the following towns by name 10(these
towns were assigned to the descendants of
Aaron who were from the Kohathite clans of
the Levites, because the first lot fell to them):

11They gave them Kiriath Arba (that is,
Hebron), with its surrounding pastureland, in the hill country of Judah. (Arba
was the forefather of Anak.) 12But the
fields and villages around the city they
had given to Caleb son of Jephunneh as
his possession.

13So to the descendants of Aaron the
priest they gave Hebron (a city of refuge
for one accused of murder), Libnah, 14Jat-
tir, Eshtemoa, 15Holon, Debir, 16Ain, Juttah and Beth Shemesh, together with their
pasturelands—nine towns from these two
tribes.

17And from the tribe of Benjamin they
gave them Gibeon, Geba, 18Anathoth and
Almon, together with their pasturelands—four towns.

19All the towns for the priests, the descendants
of Aaron, were thirteen, together with their
pasturelands.

20The rest of the Kohathite clans of the Levites
were allotted towns from the tribe of Ephraim:

21In the hill country of Ephraim they
were given Shechem (a city of refuge for
one accused of murder) and Gezer, 22Kib-
zaim and Beth Horon, together with their
pasturelands—four towns.

23Also from the tribe of Dan they received Eltekeh, Gibbethon, 24Aijalon and
Gath Rimmon, together with their pasturelands—four towns.

25From half the tribe of Manasseh they
received Taanach and Gath Rimmon, together with their pasturelands—two
towns.

26All these ten towns and their pasturelands
were given to the rest of the Kohathite clans.

27The Levite clans of the Gershonites were
given:
from the half-tribe of Manasseh,
Golan in Bashan (a city of refuge for one
accused of murder) and Be Eshtarah, together with their pasturelands—two
towns;
28from the tribe of Issachar,
Kishion, Daberath, 29Jarmuth and En
Gannim, together with their pasturelands—four towns;
30from the tribe of Asher,
Mishal, Abdon, 31Helkath and Rehob, together with their pasturelands—four
towns;
32from the tribe of Naphtali,
Kedesh in Galilee (a city of refuge for one
accused of murder), Hammoth Dor and
Kartan, together with their pasturelands—three towns.

33All the towns of the Gershonite clans were
thirteen, together with their pasturelands.

34The Merarite clans (the rest of the Levites)
were given:
from the tribe of Zebulun,
Jokneam, Kartah, 35Dimnah and Nahalal,
together with their pasturelands—four
towns;
36from the tribe of Reuben,
Bezer, Jahaz, 37Kedemoth and Mephaath,
together with their pasturelands—four
towns;
38from the tribe of Gad,
Ramoth in Gilead (a city of refuge for one

[a]8 *Jordan of Jericho* was possibly an ancient name for the Jordan River.

accused of murder), Mahanaim, 39Hesh-
bon and Jazer, together with their pasturelands—four towns in all.
40All the towns allotted to the Merarite clans,
who were the rest of the Levites, were twelve.
41The towns of the Levites in the territory
held by the Israelites were forty-eight in all,
together with their pasturelands. 42Each of
these towns had pasturelands surrounding it;
this was true for all these towns.

43So the LORD gave Israel all the land he had
sworn to give their forefathers, and they took
possession of it and settled there. 44The LORD
gave them rest on every side, just as he had
sworn to their forefathers. Not one of their enemies withstood them; the LORD handed all
their enemies over to them. 45Not one of all the
LORD's good promises to the house of Israel
failed; every one was fulfilled.

Eastern Tribes Return Home

22 Then Joshua summoned the Reubenites,
the Gadites and the half-tribe of Manasseh 2and said to them, "You have done all that
Moses the servant of the LORD commanded,
and you have obeyed me in everything I commanded. 3For a long time now—to this very
day—you have not deserted your brothers but
have carried out the mission the LORD your
God gave you. 4Now that the LORD your God
has given your brothers rest as he promised,
return to your homes in the land that Moses the
servant of the LORD gave you on the other side
of the Jordan. 5But be very careful to keep the
commandment and the law that Moses the servant of the LORD gave you: to love the LORD
your God, to walk in all his ways, to obey his
commands, to hold fast to him and to serve
him with all your heart and all your soul."
6Then Joshua blessed them and sent them
away, and they went to their homes. 7(To the
half-tribe of Manasseh Moses had given land
in Bashan, and to the other half of the tribe
Joshua gave land on the west side of the Jordan
with their brothers.) When Joshua sent them
home, he blessed them, 8saying, "Return to
your homes with your great wealth—with
large herds of livestock, with silver, gold,
bronze and iron, and a great quantity of clothing—and divide with your brothers the plunder from your enemies."
9So the Reubenites, the Gadites and the
half-tribe of Manasseh left the Israelites at Shiloh in Canaan to return to Gilead, their own
land, which they had acquired in accordance
with the command of the LORD through Moses.
10When they came to Geliloth near the Jordan in the land of Canaan, the Reubenites, the
Gadites and the half-tribe of Manasseh built
an imposing altar there by the Jordan. 11And
when the Israelites heard that they had built the
altar on the border of Canaan at Geliloth near
the Jordan on the Israelite side, 12the whole
assembly of Israel gathered at Shiloh to go to
war against them.
13So the Israelites sent Phinehas son of Eleazar, the priest, to the land of Gilead—to Reuben, Gad and the half-tribe of Manasseh.
14With him they sent ten of the chief men, one
for each of the tribes of Israel, each the head of
a family division among the Israelite clans.
15When they went to Gilead—to Reuben,
Gad and the half-tribe of Manasseh—they said
to them: 16"The whole assembly of the LORD
says: 'How could you break faith with the God
of Israel like this? How could you turn away
from the LORD and build yourselves an altar in
rebellion against him now? 17Was not the sin
of Peor enough for us? Up to this very day we
have not cleansed ourselves from that sin, even
though a plague fell on the community of the
LORD! 18And are you now turning away from
the LORD?
" 'If you rebel against the LORD today, tomorrow he will be angry with the whole community of Israel. 19If the land you possess is
defiled, come over to the LORD's land, where
the LORD's tabernacle stands, and share the
land with us. But do not rebel against the LORD
or against us by building an altar for yourselves, other than the altar of the LORD our
God. 20When Achan son of Zerah acted unfaithfully regarding the devoted things,[a] did
not wrath come upon the whole community of
Israel? He was not the only one who died for
his sin.' "
21Then Reuben, Gad and the half-tribe of
Manasseh replied to the heads of the clans of
Israel: 22"The Mighty One, God, the LORD!
The Mighty One, God, the LORD! He knows!
And let Israel know! If this has been in rebellion or disobedience to the LORD, do not spare
us this day. 23If we have built our own altar to
turn away from the LORD and to offer burnt
offerings and grain offerings, or to sacrifice
fellowship offerings[b] on it, may the LORD
himself call us to account.
24"No! We did it for fear that some day your
descendants might say to ours, 'What do you
have to do with the LORD, the God of Israel?
25The LORD has made the Jordan a boundary
between us and you—you Reubenites and
Gadites! You have no share in the LORD.' So
your descendants might cause ours to stop
fearing the LORD.
26"That is why we said, 'Let us get ready
and build an altar—but not for burnt offerings
or sacrifices.' 27On the contrary, it is to be a
witness between us and you and the generations that follow, that we will worship the
LORD at his sanctuary with our burnt offerings,
sacrifices and fellowship offerings. Then in the
future your descendants will not be able to say
to ours, 'You have no share in the LORD.'
28"And we said, 'If they ever say this to us,
or to our descendants, we will answer: Look at
the replica of the LORD's altar, which our fa-

[a]20 The Hebrew term refers to the irrevocable giving over of things or persons to the LORD, often by totally destroying them. [b]23 Traditionally *peace offerings*; also in verse 27

thers built, not for burnt offerings and sacrifices, but as a witness between us and you.'
29"Far be it from us to rebel against the
LORD and turn away from him today by building an altar for burnt offerings, grain offerings
and sacrifices, other than the altar of the LORD
our God that stands before his tabernacle."
30When Phinehas the priest and the leaders
of the community—the heads of the clans of
the Israelites—heard what Reuben, Gad and
Manasseh had to say, they were pleased. 31And
Phinehas son of Eleazar, the priest, said to
Reuben, Gad and Manasseh, "Today we know
that the LORD is with us, because you have not
acted unfaithfully toward the LORD in this matter. Now you have rescued the Israelites from
the LORD's hand."
32Then Phinehas son of Eleazar, the priest,
and the leaders returned to Canaan from their
meeting with the Reubenites and Gadites in
Gilead and reported to the Israelites. 33They
were glad to hear the report and praised God.
And they talked no more about going to war
against them to devastate the country where
the Reubenites and the Gadites lived.
34And the Reubenites and the Gadites gave
the altar this name: A Witness Between Us that
the LORD is God.

Joshua's Farewell to the Leaders

23 After a long time had passed and the
LORD had given Israel rest from all their
enemies around them, Joshua, by then old and
well advanced in years, 2summoned all Israel—their elders, leaders, judges and officials—and said to them: "I am old and well
advanced in years. 3You yourselves have seen
everything the LORD your God has done to all
these nations for your sake; it was the LORD
your God who fought for you. 4Remember
how I have allotted as an inheritance for your
tribes all the land of the nations that remain—
the nations I conquered—between the Jordan
and the Great Sea[a] in the west. 5The LORD
your God himself will drive them out of your
way. He will push them out before you, and
you will take possession of their land, as the
LORD your God promised you.
6"Be very strong; be careful to obey all that
is written in the Book of the Law of Moses,
without turning aside to the right or to the left.
7Do not associate with these nations that remain among you; do not invoke the names of
their gods or swear by them. You must not
serve them or bow down to them. 8But you are
to hold fast to the LORD your God, as you have
until now.
9"The LORD has driven out before you great
and powerful nations; to this day no one has
been able to withstand you. 10One of you routs
a thousand, because the LORD your God fights
for you, just as he promised. 11So be very careful to love the LORD your God.
12"But if you turn away and ally yourselves
with the survivors of these nations that remain
among you and if you intermarry with them
and associate with them, 13then you may be
sure that the LORD your God will no longer
drive out these nations before you. Instead,
they will become snares and traps for you,
whips on your backs and thorns in your eyes,
until you perish from this good land, which the
LORD your God has given you.
14"Now I am about to go the way of all the
earth. You know with all your heart and soul
that not one of all the good promises the LORD
your God gave you has failed. Every promise
has been fulfilled; not one has failed. 15But just
as every good promise of the LORD your God
has come true, so the LORD will bring on you
all the evil he has threatened, until he has destroyed you from this good land he has given
you. 16If you violate the covenant of the LORD
your God, which he commanded you, and go
and serve other gods and bow down to them,
the LORD's anger will burn against you, and
you will quickly perish from the good land he
has given you."

The Covenant Renewed at Shechem

24 Then Joshua assembled all the tribes of
Israel at Shechem. He summoned the
elders, leaders, judges and officials of Israel,
and they presented themselves before God.
2Joshua said to all the people, "This is what
the LORD, the God of Israel, says: 'Long ago
your forefathers, including Terah the father of
Abraham and Nahor, lived beyond the River[b]
and worshiped other gods. 3But I took your
father Abraham from the land beyond the River and led him throughout Canaan and gave
him many descendants. I gave him Isaac, 4and
to Isaac I gave Jacob and Esau. I assigned the
hill country of Seir to Esau, but Jacob and his
sons went down to Egypt.
5" 'Then I sent Moses and Aaron, and I afflicted the Egyptians by what I did there, and
I brought you out. 6When I brought your fathers out of Egypt, you came to the sea, and the
Egyptians pursued them with chariots and
horsemen[c] as far as the Red Sea.[d] 7But they
cried to the LORD for help, and he put darkness
between you and the Egyptians; he brought the
sea over them and covered them. You saw with
your own eyes what I did to the Egyptians.
Then you lived in the desert for a long time.
8" 'I brought you to the land of the Amorites
who lived east of the Jordan. They fought
against you, but I gave them into your hands.
I destroyed them from before you, and you
took possession of their land. 9When Balak son
of Zippor, the king of Moab, prepared to fight
against Israel, he sent for Balaam son of Beor
to put a curse on you. 10But I would not listen
to Balaam, so he blessed you again and again,
and I delivered you out of his hand.
11" 'Then you crossed the Jordan and came
to Jericho. The citizens of Jericho fought

[a]4 That is, the Mediterranean [b]2 That is, the Euphrates; also in verses 3, 14 and 15 [c]6 Or *charioteers*
[d]6 Hebrew *Yam Suph*; that is, Sea of Reeds

against you, as did also the Amorites, Perizzites, Canaanites, Hittites, Girgashites, Hivites and Jebusites, but I gave them into your hands. [12]I sent the hornet ahead of you, which drove them out before you—also the two Amorite kings. You did not do it with your own sword and bow. [13]So I gave you a land on which you did not toil and cities you did not build; and you live in them and eat from vineyards and olive groves that you did not plant.'

[14]"Now fear the LORD and serve him with all faithfulness. Throw away the gods your forefathers worshiped beyond the River and in Egypt, and serve the LORD. [15]But if serving the LORD seems undesirable to you, then choose for yourselves this day whom you will serve, whether the gods your forefathers served beyond the River, or the gods of the Amorites, in whose land you are living. But as for me and my household, we will serve the LORD."

[16]Then the people answered, "Far be it from us to forsake the LORD to serve other gods! [17]It was the LORD our God himself who brought us and our fathers up out of Egypt, from that land of slavery, and performed those great signs before our eyes. He protected us on our entire journey and among all the nations through which we traveled. [18]And the LORD drove out before us all the nations, including the Amorites, who lived in the land. We too will serve the LORD, because he is our God."

[19]Joshua said to the people, "You are not able to serve the LORD. He is a holy God; he is a jealous God. He will not forgive your rebellion and your sins. [20]If you forsake the LORD and serve foreign gods, he will turn and bring disaster on you and make an end of you, after he has been good to you."

[21]But the people said to Joshua, "No! We will serve the LORD."

[22]Then Joshua said, "You are witnesses against yourselves that you have chosen to serve the LORD."

"Yes, we are witnesses," they replied.

[23]"Now then," said Joshua, "throw away the foreign gods that are among you and yield your hearts to the LORD, the God of Israel."

[24]And the people said to Joshua, "We will serve the LORD our God and obey him."

[25]On that day Joshua made a covenant for the people, and there at Shechem he drew up for them decrees and laws. [26]And Joshua recorded these things in the Book of the Law of God. Then he took a large stone and set it up there under the oak near the holy place of the LORD.

[27]"See!" he said to all the people. "This stone will be a witness against us. It has heard all the words the LORD has said to us. It will be a witness against you if you are untrue to your God."

Buried in the Promised Land

[28]Then Joshua sent the people away, each to his own inheritance.

[29]After these things, Joshua son of Nun, the servant of the LORD, died at the age of a hundred and ten. [30]And they buried him in the land of his inheritance, at Timnath Serah[a] in the hill country of Ephraim, north of Mount Gaash.

[31]Israel served the LORD throughout the lifetime of Joshua and of the elders who outlived him and who had experienced everything the LORD had done for Israel.

[32]And Joseph's bones, which the Israelites had brought up from Egypt, were buried at Shechem in the tract of land that Jacob bought for a hundred pieces of silver[b] from the sons of Hamor, the father of Shechem. This became the inheritance of Joseph's descendants.

[33]And Eleazar son of Aaron died and was buried at Gibeah, which had been allotted to his son Phinehas in the hill country of Ephraim.

Judges

Israel Fights the Remaining Canaanites

1 After the death of Joshua, the Israelites asked the LORD, "Who will be the first to go up and fight for us against the Canaanites?"

[2]The LORD answered, "Judah is to go; I have given the land into their hands."

[3]Then the men of Judah said to the Simeonites their brothers, "Come up with us into the territory allotted to us, to fight against the Canaanites. We in turn will go with you into yours." So the Simeonites went with them.

[4]When Judah attacked, the LORD gave the Canaanites and Perizzites into their hands and they struck down ten thousand men at Bezek. [5]It was there that they found Adoni-Bezek and fought against him, putting to rout the Canaanites and Perizzites. [6]Adoni-Bezek fled, but they chased him and caught him, and cut off his thumbs and big toes.

[7]Then Adoni-Bezek said, "Seventy kings with their thumbs and big toes cut off have picked up scraps under my table. Now God has paid me back for what I did to them." They brought him to Jerusalem, and he died there.

[8]The men of Judah attacked Jerusalem also

[a]*30* Also known as *Timnath Heres* (see Judges 2:9) [b]*32* Hebrew *hundred kesitahs*; a kesitah was a unit of money of unknown weight and value.

and took it. They put the city to the sword and set it on fire.

9After that, the men of Judah went down to fight against the Canaanites living in the hill country, the Negev and the western foothills. 10They advanced against the Canaanites living in Hebron (formerly called Kiriath Arba) and defeated Sheshai, Ahiman and Talmai.

11From there they advanced against the people living in Debir (formerly called Kiriath Sepher). 12And Caleb said, "I will give my daughter Acsah in marriage to the man who attacks and captures Kiriath Sepher." 13Othniel son of Kenaz, Caleb's younger brother, took it; so Caleb gave his daughter Acsah to him in marriage.

14One day when she came to Othniel, she urged him[a] to ask her father for a field. When she got off her donkey, Caleb asked her, "What can I do for you?"

15She replied, "Do me a special favor. Since you have given me land in the Negev, give me also springs of water." Then Caleb gave her the upper and lower springs.

16The descendants of Moses' father-in-law, the Kenite, went up from the City of Palms[b] with the men of Judah to live among the people of the Desert of Judah in the Negev near Arad.

17Then the men of Judah went with the Simeonites their brothers and attacked the Canaanites living in Zephath, and they totally destroyed[c] the city. Therefore it was called Hormah.[d] 18The men of Judah also took[e] Gaza, Ashkelon and Ekron—each city with its territory.

19The LORD was with the men of Judah. They took possession of the hill country, but they were unable to drive the people from the plains, because they had iron chariots. 20As Moses had promised, Hebron was given to Caleb, who drove from it the three sons of Anak. 21The Benjamites, however, failed to dislodge the Jebusites, who were living in Jerusalem; to this day the Jebusites live there with the Benjamites.

22Now the house of Joseph attacked Bethel, and the LORD was with them. 23When they sent men to spy out Bethel (formerly called Luz), 24the spies saw a man coming out of the city and they said to him, "Show us how to get into the city and we will see that you are treated well." 25So he showed them, and they put the city to the sword but spared the man and his whole family. 26He then went to the land of the Hittites, where he built a city and called it Luz, which is its name to this day.

27But Manasseh did not drive out the people of Beth Shan or Taanach or Dor or Ibleam or Megiddo and their surrounding settlements, for the Canaanites were determined to live in that land. 28When Israel became strong, they pressed the Canaanites into forced labor but never drove them out completely. 29Nor did Ephraim drive out the Canaanites living in Gezer, but the Canaanites continued to live there among them. 30Neither did Zebulun drive out the Canaanites living in Kitron or Nahalol, who remained among them; but they did subject them to forced labor. 31Nor did Asher drive out those living in Acco or Sidon or Ahlab or Aczib or Helbah or Aphek or Rehob, 32and because of this the people of Asher lived among the Canaanite inhabitants of the land. 33Neither did Naphtali drive out those living in Beth Shemesh or Beth Anath; but the Naphtalites too lived among the Canaanite inhabitants of the land, and those living in Beth Shemesh and Beth Anath became forced laborers for them. 34The Amorites confined the Danites to the hill country, not allowing them to come down into the plain. 35And the Amorites were determined also to hold out in Mount Heres, Aijalon and Shaalbim, but when the power of the house of Joseph increased, they too were pressed into forced labor. 36The boundary of the Amorites was from Scorpion[f] Pass to Sela and beyond.

The Angel of the LORD at Bokim

2 The angel of the LORD went up from Gilgal to Bokim and said, "I brought you up out of Egypt and led you into the land that I swore to give to your forefathers. I said, 'I will never break my covenant with you, 2and you shall not make a covenant with the people of this land, but you shall break down their altars.' Yet you have disobeyed me. Why have you done this? 3Now therefore I tell you that I will not drive them out before you; they will be ⌊thorns⌋ in your sides and their gods will be a snare to you."

4When the angel of the LORD had spoken these things to all the Israelites, the people wept aloud, 5and they called that place Bokim.[g] There they offered sacrifices to the LORD.

Disobedience and Defeat

6After Joshua had dismissed the Israelites, they went to take possession of the land, each to his own inheritance. 7The people served the LORD throughout the lifetime of Joshua and of the elders who outlived him and who had seen all the great things the LORD had done for Israel.

8Joshua son of Nun, the servant of the LORD, died at the age of a hundred and ten. 9And they buried him in the land of his inheritance, at Timnath Heres[h] in the hill country of Ephraim, north of Mount Gaash.

10After that whole generation had been gathered to their fathers, another generation grew up, who knew neither the LORD nor what he had done for Israel. 11Then the Israelites did

[a] *14* Hebrew; Septuagint and Vulgate *Othniel, he urged her* [b] *16* That is, Jericho [c] *17* The Hebrew term refers to the irrevocable giving over of things or persons to the LORD, often by totally destroying them.
[d] *17* *Hormah* means *destruction.* [e] *18* Hebrew; Septuagint *Judah did not take* [f] *36* Hebrew *Akrabbim*
[g] *5* *Bokim* means *weepers.* [h] *9* Also known as *Timnath Serah* (see Joshua 19:50 and 24:30)

evil in the eyes of the LORD and served the Baals. 12They forsook the LORD, the God of their fathers, who had brought them out of Egypt. They followed and worshiped various gods of the peoples around them. They provoked the LORD to anger 13because they forsook him and served Baal and the Ashtoreths. 14In his anger against Israel the LORD handed them over to raiders who plundered them. He sold them to their enemies all around, whom they were no longer able to resist. 15Whenever Israel went out to fight, the hand of the LORD was against them to defeat them, just as he had sworn to them. They were in great distress.

16Then the LORD raised up judges,[a] who saved them out of the hands of these raiders. 17Yet they would not listen to their judges but prostituted themselves to other gods and worshiped them. Unlike their fathers, they quickly turned from the way in which their fathers had walked, the way of obedience to the LORD's commands. 18Whenever the LORD raised up a judge for them, he was with the judge and saved them out of the hands of their enemies as long as the judge lived; for the LORD had compassion on them as they groaned under those who oppressed and afflicted them. 19But when the judge died, the people returned to ways even more corrupt than those of their fathers, following other gods and serving and worshiping them. They refused to give up their evil practices and stubborn ways.

20Therefore the LORD was very angry with Israel and said, "Because this nation has violated the covenant that I laid down for their forefathers and has not listened to me, 21I will no longer drive out before them any of the nations Joshua left when he died. 22I will use them to test Israel and see whether they will keep the way of the LORD and walk in it as their forefathers did." 23The LORD had allowed those nations to remain; he did not drive them out at once by giving them into the hands of Joshua.

3 These are the nations the LORD left to test all those Israelites who had not experienced any of the wars in Canaan 2(he did this only to teach warfare to the descendants of the Israelites who had not had previous battle experience): 3the five rulers of the Philistines, all the Canaanites, the Sidonians, and the Hivites living in the Lebanon mountains from Mount Baal Hermon to Lebo[b] Hamath. 4They were left to test the Israelites to see whether they would obey the LORD's commands, which he had given their forefathers through Moses.

5The Israelites lived among the Canaanites, Hittites, Amorites, Perizzites, Hivites and Jebusites. 6They took their daughters in marriage and gave their own daughters to their sons, and served their gods.

Othniel

7The Israelites did evil in the eyes of the LORD; they forgot the LORD their God and served the Baals and the Asherahs. 8The anger of the LORD burned against Israel so that he sold them into the hands of Cushan-Rishathaim king of Aram Naharaim,[c] to whom the Israelites were subject for eight years. 9But when they cried out to the LORD, he raised up for them a deliverer, Othniel son of Kenaz, Caleb's younger brother, who saved them. 10The Spirit of the LORD came upon him, so that he became Israel's judge[d] and went to war. The LORD gave Cushan-Rishathaim king of Aram into the hands of Othniel, who overpowered him. 11So the land had peace for forty years, until Othniel son of Kenaz died.

Ehud

12Once again the Israelites did evil in the eyes of the LORD, and because they did this evil the LORD gave Eglon king of Moab power over Israel. 13Getting the Ammonites and Amalekites to join him, Eglon came and attacked Israel, and they took possession of the City of Palms.[e] 14The Israelites were subject to Eglon king of Moab for eighteen years.

15Again the Israelites cried out to the LORD, and he gave them a deliverer—Ehud, a left-handed man, the son of Gera the Benjamite. The Israelites sent him with tribute to Eglon king of Moab. 16Now Ehud had made a double-edged sword about a foot and a half[f] long, which he strapped to his right thigh under his clothing. 17He presented the tribute to Eglon king of Moab, who was a very fat man. 18After Ehud had presented the tribute, he sent on their way the men who had carried it. 19At the idols[g] near Gilgal he himself turned back and said, "I have a secret message for you, O king."

The king said, "Quiet!" And all his attendants left him.

20Ehud then approached him while he was sitting alone in the upper room of his summer palace[h] and said, "I have a message from God for you." As the king rose from his seat, 21Ehud reached with his left hand, drew the sword from his right thigh and plunged it into the king's belly. 22Even the handle sank in after the blade, which came out his back. Ehud did not pull the sword out, and the fat closed in over it. 23Then Ehud went out to the porch[i]; he shut the doors of the upper room behind him and locked them.

24After he had gone, the servants came and found the doors of the upper room locked. They said, "He must be relieving himself in the inner room of the house." 25They waited to the point of embarrassment, but when he did not open the doors of the room, they took a key and unlocked them. There they saw their lord fallen to the floor, dead.

26While they waited, Ehud got away. He

[a] *16* Or *leaders*; similarly in verses 17-19 [b] *3* Or *to the entrance to* [c] *8* That is, Northwest Mesopotamia [d] *10* Or *leader* [e] *13* That is, Jericho [f] *16* Hebrew *a cubit* (about 0.5 meter) [g] *19* Or *the stone quarries*; also in verse 26 [h] *20* The meaning of the Hebrew for this phrase is uncertain. [i] *23* The meaning of the Hebrew for this word is uncertain.

passed by the idols and escaped to Seirah.
27 When he arrived there, he blew a trumpet in
the hill country of Ephraim, and the Israelites
went down with him from the hills, with him
leading them.

28 "Follow me," he ordered, "for the LORD
has given Moab, your enemy, into your
hands." So they followed him down and, taking possession of the fords of the Jordan that
led to Moab, they allowed no one to cross
over. 29 At that time they struck down about ten
thousand Moabites, all vigorous and strong;
not a man escaped. 30 That day Moab was made
subject to Israel, and the land had peace for
eighty years.

Shamgar

31 After Ehud came Shamgar son of Anath,
who struck down six hundred Philistines with
an oxgoad. He too saved Israel.

Deborah

4 After Ehud died, the Israelites once again
did evil in the eyes of the LORD. 2 So the
LORD sold them into the hands of Jabin, a king
of Canaan, who reigned in Hazor. The commander of his army was Sisera, who lived in
Harosheth Haggoyim. 3 Because he had nine
hundred iron chariots and had cruelly oppressed the Israelites for twenty years, they
cried to the LORD for help.

4 Deborah, a prophetess, the wife of Lappi-
doth, was leading[a] Israel at that time. 5 She
held court under the Palm of Deborah between
Ramah and Bethel in the hill country of Ephraim, and the Israelites came to her to have their
disputes decided. 6 She sent for Barak son of
Abinoam from Kedesh in Naphtali and said to
him, "The LORD, the God of Israel, commands
you: 'Go, take with you ten thousand men of
Naphtali and Zebulun and lead the way to
Mount Tabor. 7 I will lure Sisera, the commander of Jabin's army, with his chariots and
his troops to the Kishon River and give him
into your hands.' "

8 Barak said to her, "If you go with me, I will
go; but if you don't go with me, I won't go."

9 "Very well," Deborah said, "I will go with
you. But because of the way you are going
about this,[b] the honor will not be yours, for the
LORD will hand Sisera over to a woman." So
Deborah went with Barak to Kedesh, 10 where
he summoned Zebulun and Naphtali. Ten
thousand men followed him, and Deborah also
went with him.

11 Now Heber the Kenite had left the other
Kenites, the descendants of Hobab, Moses'
brother-in-law,[c] and pitched his tent by the
great tree in Zaanannim near Kedesh.

12 When they told Sisera that Barak son of
Abinoam had gone up to Mount Tabor, 13 Sisera gathered together his nine hundred iron
chariots and all the men with him, from Harosheth Haggoyim to the Kishon River.

14 Then Deborah said to Barak, "Go! This is
the day the LORD has given Sisera into your
hands. Has not the LORD gone ahead of you?"
So Barak went down Mount Tabor, followed
by ten thousand men. 15 At Barak's advance,
the LORD routed Sisera and all his chariots and
army by the sword, and Sisera abandoned his
chariot and fled on foot. 16 But Barak pursued
the chariots and army as far as Harosheth Haggoyim. All the troops of Sisera fell by the
sword; not a man was left.

17 Sisera, however, fled on foot to the tent of
Jael, the wife of Heber the Kenite, because
there were friendly relations between Jabin
king of Hazor and the clan of Heber the Kenite.

18 Jael went out to meet Sisera and said to
him, "Come, my lord, come right in. Don't be
afraid." So he entered her tent, and she put a
covering over him.

19 "I'm thirsty," he said. "Please give me
some water." She opened a skin of milk, gave
him a drink, and covered him up.

20 "Stand in the doorway of the tent," he told
her. "If someone comes by and asks you, 'Is
anyone here?' say 'No.' "

21 But Jael, Heber's wife, picked up a tent
peg and a hammer and went quietly to him
while he lay fast asleep, exhausted. She drove
the peg through his temple into the ground, and
he died.

22 Barak came by in pursuit of Sisera, and
Jael went out to meet him. "Come," she said,
"I will show you the man you're looking for."
So he went in with her, and there lay Sisera
with the tent peg through his temple—dead.

23 On that day God subdued Jabin, the Canaanite king, before the Israelites. 24 And the
hand of the Israelites grew stronger and stronger against Jabin, the Canaanite king, until
they destroyed him.

The Song of Deborah

5 On that day Deborah and Barak son of
Abinoam sang this song:

2 "When the princes in Israel take the lead,
when the people willingly offer
themselves—
praise the LORD!

3 "Hear this, you kings! Listen, you rulers!
I will sing to[d] the LORD, I will sing;
I will make music to[e] the LORD, the
God of Israel.

4 "O LORD, when you went out from Seir,
when you marched from the land of
Edom,
the earth shook, the heavens poured,
the clouds poured down water.
5 The mountains quaked before the LORD,
the One of Sinai,
before the LORD, the God of Israel.

6 "In the days of Shamgar son of Anath,

[a] 4 Traditionally *judging* [b] 9 Or *But on the expedition you are undertaking* [c] 11 Or *father-in-law*
[d] 3 Or *of* [e] 3 Or / *with song I will praise*

in the days of Jael, the roads were
abandoned;
travelers took to winding paths.
7Village life[a] in Israel ceased,
ceased until I,[b] Deborah, arose,
arose a mother in Israel.
8When they chose new gods,
war came to the city gates,
and not a shield or spear was seen
among forty thousand in Israel.
9My heart is with Israel's princes,
with the willing volunteers among the
people.
Praise the LORD!

10"You who ride on white donkeys,
sitting on your saddle blankets,
and you who walk along the road,
consider 11the voice of the singers[c] at the
watering places.
They recite the righteous acts of the
LORD,
the righteous acts of his warriors[d] in
Israel.

"Then the people of the LORD
went down to the city gates.
12'Wake up, wake up, Deborah!
Wake up, wake up, break out in song!
Arise, O Barak!
Take captive your captives, O son of
Abinoam.'

13"Then the men who were left
came down to the nobles;
the people of the LORD
came to me with the mighty.
14Some came from Ephraim, whose roots
were in Amalek;
Benjamin was with the people who
followed you.
From Makir captains came down,
from Zebulun those who bear a
commander's staff.
15The princes of Issachar were with
Deborah;
yes, Issachar was with Barak,
rushing after him into the valley.
In the districts of Reuben
there was much searching of heart.
16Why did you stay among the campfires[e]
to hear the whistling for the flocks?
In the districts of Reuben
there was much searching of heart.
17Gilead stayed beyond the Jordan.
And Dan, why did he linger by the
ships?
Asher remained on the coast
and stayed in his coves.
18The people of Zebulun risked their very
lives;
so did Naphtali on the heights of the
field.

19"Kings came, they fought;
the kings of Canaan fought
at Taanach by the waters of Megiddo,
but they carried off no silver, no
plunder.
20From the heavens the stars fought,
from their courses they fought against
Sisera.
21The river Kishon swept them away,
the age-old river, the river Kishon.
March on, my soul; be strong!
22Then thundered the horses' hoofs—
galloping, galloping go his mighty
steeds.
23'Curse Meroz,' said the angel of the
LORD.
'Curse its people bitterly,
because they did not come to help the
LORD,
to help the LORD against the mighty.'

24"Most blessed of women be Jael,
the wife of Heber the Kenite,
most blessed of tent-dwelling women.
25He asked for water, and she gave him
milk;
in a bowl fit for nobles she brought him
curdled milk.
26Her hand reached for the tent peg,
her right hand for the workman's
hammer.
She struck Sisera, she crushed his head,
she shattered and pierced his temple.
27At her feet he sank,
he fell; there he lay.
At her feet he sank, he fell;
where he sank, there he fell—dead.

28"Through the window peered Sisera's
mother;
behind the lattice she cried out,
'Why is his chariot so long in coming?
Why is the clatter of his chariots
delayed?'
29The wisest of her ladies answer her;
indeed, she keeps saying to herself,
30'Are they not finding and dividing the
spoils:
a girl or two for each man,
colorful garments as plunder for Sisera,
colorful garments embroidered,
highly embroidered garments for my
neck—
all this as plunder?'

31"So may all your enemies perish,
O LORD!
But may they who love you be like the
sun
when it rises in its strength."

Then the land had peace forty years.

Gideon

6 Again the Israelites did evil in the eyes of
the LORD, and for seven years he gave
them into the hands of the Midianites. 2Be-

[a]*7* Or *Warriors* [b]*7* Or *you* [c]*11* Or *archers*; the meaning of the Hebrew for this word is uncertain.
[d]*11* Or *villagers* [e]*16* Or *saddlebags*

cause the power of Midian was so oppressive, the Israelites prepared shelters for themselves in mountain clefts, caves and strongholds. 3Whenever the Israelites planted their crops, the Midianites, Amalekites and other eastern peoples invaded the country. 4They camped on the land and ruined the crops all the way to Gaza and did not spare a living thing for Israel, neither sheep nor cattle nor donkeys. 5They came up with their livestock and their tents like swarms of locusts. It was impossible to count the men and their camels; they invaded the land to ravage it. 6Midian so impoverished the Israelites that they cried out to the LORD for help.

7When the Israelites cried to the LORD because of Midian, 8he sent them a prophet, who said, "This is what the LORD, the God of Israel, says: I brought you up out of Egypt, out of the land of slavery. 9I snatched you from the power of Egypt and from the hand of all your oppressors. I drove them from before you and gave you their land. 10I said to you, 'I am the LORD your God; do not worship the gods of the Amorites, in whose land you live.' But you have not listened to me."

11The angel of the LORD came and sat down under the oak in Ophrah that belonged to Joash the Abiezrite, where his son Gideon was threshing wheat in a winepress to keep it from the Midianites. 12When the angel of the LORD appeared to Gideon, he said, "The LORD is with you, mighty warrior."

13"But sir," Gideon replied, "if the LORD is with us, why has all this happened to us? Where are all his wonders that our fathers told us about when they said, 'Did not the LORD bring us up out of Egypt?' But now the LORD has abandoned us and put us into the hand of Midian."

14The LORD turned to him and said, "Go in the strength you have and save Israel out of Midian's hand. Am I not sending you?"

15"But Lord,[a]" Gideon asked, "how can I save Israel? My clan is the weakest in Manasseh, and I am the least in my family."

16The LORD answered, "I will be with you, and you will strike down all the Midianites together."

17Gideon replied, "If now I have found favor in your eyes, give me a sign that it is really you talking to me. 18Please do not go away until I come back and bring my offering and set it before you."

And the LORD said, "I will wait until you return."

19Gideon went in, prepared a young goat, and from an ephah[b] of flour he made bread without yeast. Putting the meat in a basket and its broth in a pot, he brought them out and offered them to him under the oak.

20The angel of God said to him, "Take the meat and the unleavened bread, place them on this rock, and pour out the broth." And Gideon did so. 21With the tip of the staff that was in his hand, the angel of the LORD touched the meat and the unleavened bread. Fire flared from the rock, consuming the meat and the bread. And the angel of the LORD disappeared. 22When Gideon realized that it was the angel of the LORD, he exclaimed, "Ah, Sovereign LORD! I have seen the angel of the LORD face to face!"

23But the LORD said to him, "Peace! Do not be afraid. You are not going to die."

24So Gideon built an altar to the LORD there and called it The LORD is Peace. To this day it stands in Ophrah of the Abiezrites.

25That same night the LORD said to him, "Take the second bull from your father's herd, the one seven years old.[c] Tear down your father's altar to Baal and cut down the Asherah pole[d] beside it. 26Then build a proper kind of[e] altar to the LORD your God on the top of this height. Using the wood of the Asherah pole that you cut down, offer the second[f] bull as a burnt offering."

27So Gideon took ten of his servants and did as the LORD told him. But because he was afraid of his family and the men of the town, he did it at night rather than in the daytime.

28In the morning when the men of the town got up, there was Baal's altar, demolished, with the Asherah pole beside it cut down and the second bull sacrificed on the newly built altar!

29They asked each other, "Who did this?"

When they carefully investigated, they were told, "Gideon son of Joash did it."

30The men of the town demanded of Joash, "Bring out your son. He must die, because he has broken down Baal's altar and cut down the Asherah pole beside it."

31But Joash replied to the hostile crowd around him, "Are you going to plead Baal's cause? Are you trying to save him? Whoever fights for him shall be put to death by morning! If Baal really is a god, he can defend himself when someone breaks down his altar." 32So that day they called Gideon "Jerub-Baal,[g]" saying, "Let Baal contend with him," because he broke down Baal's altar.

33Now all the Midianites, Amalekites and other eastern peoples joined forces and crossed over the Jordan and camped in the Valley of Jezreel. 34Then the Spirit of the LORD came upon Gideon, and he blew a trumpet, summoning the Abiezrites to follow him. 35He sent messengers throughout Manasseh, calling them to arms, and also into Asher, Zebulun and Naphtali, so that they too went up to meet them.

36Gideon said to God, "If you will save Israel by my hand as you have promised— 37look, I will place a wool fleece on the threshing

[a] *15* Or *sir* [b] *19* That is, probably about 3/5 bushel (about 22 liters) [c] *25* Or *Take a full-grown, mature bull from your father's herd* [d] *25* That is, a symbol of the goddess Asherah; here and elsewhere in Judges [e] *26* Or *build with layers of stone an* [f] *26* Or *full-grown*; also in verse 28 [g] *32* *Jerub-Baal* means *let Baal contend.*

floor. If there is dew only on the fleece and all the ground is dry, then I will know that you will save Israel by my hand, as you said." 38And that is what happened. Gideon rose early the next day; he squeezed the fleece and wrung out the dew—a bowlful of water.

39Then Gideon said to God, "Do not be angry with me. Let me make just one more request. Allow me one more test with the fleece. This time make the fleece dry and the ground covered with dew." 40That night God did so. Only the fleece was dry; all the ground was covered with dew.

Gideon Defeats the Midianites

7 Early in the morning, Jerub-Baal (that is, Gideon) and all his men camped at the spring of Harod. The camp of Midian was north of them in the valley near the hill of Moreh. 2The LORD said to Gideon, "You have too many men for me to deliver Midian into their hands. In order that Israel may not boast against me that her own strength has saved her, 3announce now to the people, 'Anyone who trembles with fear may turn back and leave Mount Gilead.' " So twenty-two thousand men left, while ten thousand remained.

4But the LORD said to Gideon, "There are still too many men. Take them down to the water, and I will sift them for you there. If I say, 'This one shall go with you,' he shall go; but if I say, 'This one shall not go with you,' he shall not go."

5So Gideon took the men down to the water. There the LORD told him, "Separate those who lap the water with their tongues like a dog from those who kneel down to drink." 6Three hundred men lapped with their hands to their mouths. All the rest got down on their knees to drink.

7The LORD said to Gideon, "With the three hundred men that lapped I will save you and give the Midianites into your hands. Let all the other men go, each to his own place." 8So Gideon sent the rest of the Israelites to their tents but kept the three hundred, who took over the provisions and trumpets of the others.

Now the camp of Midian lay below him in the valley. 9During that night the LORD said to Gideon, "Get up, go down against the camp, because I am going to give it into your hands. 10If you are afraid to attack, go down to the camp with your servant Purah 11and listen to what they are saying. Afterward, you will be encouraged to attack the camp." So he and Purah his servant went down to the outposts of the camp. 12The Midianites, the Amalekites and all the other eastern peoples had settled in the valley, thick as locusts. Their camels could no more be counted than the sand on the seashore.

13Gideon arrived just as a man was telling a friend his dream. "I had a dream," he was saying. "A round loaf of barley bread came tumbling into the Midianite camp. It struck the tent with such force that the tent overturned and collapsed."

14His friend responded, "This can be nothing other than the sword of Gideon son of Joash, the Israelite. God has given the Midianites and the whole camp into his hands."

15When Gideon heard the dream and its interpretation, he worshiped God. He returned to the camp of Israel and called out, "Get up! The LORD has given the Midianite camp into your hands." 16Dividing the three hundred men into three companies, he placed trumpets and empty jars in the hands of all of them, with torches inside.

17"Watch me," he told them. "Follow my lead. When I get to the edge of the camp, do exactly as I do. 18When I and all who are with me blow our trumpets, then from all around the camp blow yours and shout, 'For the LORD and for Gideon.' "

19Gideon and the hundred men with him reached the edge of the camp at the beginning of the middle watch, just after they had changed the guard. They blew their trumpets and broke the jars that were in their hands. 20The three companies blew the trumpets and smashed the jars. Grasping the torches in their left hands and holding in their right hands the trumpets they were to blow, they shouted, "A sword for the LORD and for Gideon!" 21While each man held his position around the camp, all the Midianites ran, crying out as they fled.

22When the three hundred trumpets sounded, the LORD caused the men throughout the camp to turn on each other with their swords. The army fled to Beth Shittah toward Zererah as far as the border of Abel Meholah near Tabbath. 23Israelites from Naphtali, Asher and all Manasseh were called out, and they pursued the Midianites. 24Gideon sent messengers throughout the hill country of Ephraim, saying, "Come down against the Midianites and seize the waters of the Jordan ahead of them as far as Beth Barah."

So all the men of Ephraim were called out and they took the waters of the Jordan as far as Beth Barah. 25They also captured two of the Midianite leaders, Oreb and Zeeb. They killed Oreb at the rock of Oreb, and Zeeb at the winepress of Zeeb. They pursued the Midianites and brought the heads of Oreb and Zeeb to Gideon, who was by the Jordan.

Zebah and Zalmunna

8 Now the Ephraimites asked Gideon, "Why have you treated us like this? Why didn't you call us when you went to fight Midian?" And they criticized him sharply.

2But he answered them, "What have I accomplished compared to you? Aren't the gleanings of Ephraim's grapes better than the full grape harvest of Abiezer? 3God gave Oreb and Zeeb, the Midianite leaders, into your hands. What was I able to do compared to you?" At this, their resentment against him subsided.

4Gideon and his three hundred men, exhausted yet keeping up the pursuit, came to the Jordan and crossed it. 5He said to the men of

Succoth, "Give my troops some bread; they are worn out, and I am still pursuing Zebah and Zalmunna, the kings of Midian."

6But the officials of Succoth said, "Do you already have the hands of Zebah and Zalmunna in your possession? Why should we give bread to your troops?"

7Then Gideon replied, "Just for that, when the LORD has given Zebah and Zalmunna into my hand, I will tear your flesh with desert thorns and briers."

8From there he went up to Peniel[a] and made the same request of them, but they answered as the men of Succoth had. 9So he said to the men of Peniel, "When I return in triumph, I will tear down this tower."

10Now Zebah and Zalmunna were in Karkor with a force of about fifteen thousand men, all that were left of the armies of the eastern peoples; a hundred and twenty thousand swordsmen had fallen. 11Gideon went up by the route of the nomads east of Nobah and Jogbehah and fell upon the unsuspecting army. 12Zebah and Zalmunna, the two kings of Midian, fled, but he pursued them and captured them, routing their entire army.

13Gideon son of Joash then returned from the battle by the Pass of Heres. 14He caught a young man of Succoth and questioned him, and the young man wrote down for him the names of the seventy-seven officials of Succoth, the elders of the town. 15Then Gideon came and said to the men of Succoth, "Here are Zebah and Zalmunna, about whom you taunted me by saying, 'Do you already have the hands of Zebah and Zalmunna in your possession? Why should we give bread to your exhausted men?' " 16He took the elders of the town and taught the men of Succoth a lesson by punishing them with desert thorns and briers. 17He also pulled down the tower of Peniel and killed the men of the town.

18Then he asked Zebah and Zalmunna, "What kind of men did you kill at Tabor?"

"Men like you," they answered, "each one with the bearing of a prince."

19Gideon replied, "Those were my brothers, the sons of my own mother. As surely as the LORD lives, if you had spared their lives, I would not kill you." 20Turning to Jether, his oldest son, he said, "Kill them!" But Jether did not draw his sword, because he was only a boy and was afraid.

21Zebah and Zalmunna said, "Come, do it yourself. 'As is the man, so is his strength.' " So Gideon stepped forward and killed them, and took the ornaments off their camels' necks.

Gideon's Ephod

22The Israelites said to Gideon, "Rule over us—you, your son and your grandson—because you have saved us out of the hand of Midian."

23But Gideon told them, "I will not rule over you, nor will my son rule over you. The LORD will rule over you." 24And he said, "I do have one request, that each of you give me an earring from your share of the plunder." (It was the custom of the Ishmaelites to wear gold earrings.)

25They answered, "We'll be glad to give them." So they spread out a garment, and each man threw a ring from his plunder onto it. 26The weight of the gold rings he asked for came to seventeen hundred shekels,[b] not counting the ornaments, the pendants and the purple garments worn by the kings of Midian or the chains that were on their camels' necks. 27Gideon made the gold into an ephod, which he placed in Ophrah, his town. All Israel prostituted themselves by worshiping it there, and it became a snare to Gideon and his family.

Gideon's Death

28Thus Midian was subdued before the Israelites and did not raise its head again. During Gideon's lifetime, the land enjoyed peace forty years.

29Jerub-Baal son of Joash went back home to live. 30He had seventy sons of his own, for he had many wives. 31His concubine, who lived in Shechem, also bore him a son, whom he named Abimelech. 32Gideon son of Joash died at a good old age and was buried in the tomb of his father Joash in Ophrah of the Abiezrites.

33No sooner had Gideon died than the Israelites again prostituted themselves to the Baals. They set up Baal-Berith as their god and 34did not remember the LORD their God, who had rescued them from the hands of all their enemies on every side. 35They also failed to show kindness to the family of Jerub-Baal (that is, Gideon) for all the good things he had done for them.

Abimelech

9 Abimelech son of Jerub-Baal went to his mother's brothers in Shechem and said to them and to all his mother's clan, 2"Ask all the citizens of Shechem, 'Which is better for you: to have all seventy of Jerub-Baal's sons rule over you, or just one man?' Remember, I am your flesh and blood."

3When the brothers repeated all this to the citizens of Shechem, they were inclined to follow Abimelech, for they said, "He is our brother." 4They gave him seventy shekels[c] of silver from the temple of Baal-Berith, and Abimelech used it to hire reckless adventurers, who became his followers. 5He went to his father's home in Ophrah and on one stone murdered his seventy brothers, the sons of Jerub-Baal. But Jotham, the youngest son of Jerub-Baal, escaped by hiding. 6Then all the citizens of Shechem and Beth Millo gathered beside the great tree at the pillar in Shechem to crown Abimelech king.

[a] 8 Hebrew *Penuel,* a variant of *Peniel*; also in verses 9 and 17 [b] 26 That is, about 43 pounds (about 19.5 kilograms) [c] 4 That is, about 1 3/4 pounds (about 0.8 kilogram)

7When Jotham was told about this, he climbed up on the top of Mount Gerizim and shouted to them, "Listen to me, citizens of Shechem, so that God may listen to you. 8One day the trees went out to anoint a king for themselves. They said to the olive tree, 'Be our king.'

9"But the olive tree answered, 'Should I give up my oil, by which both gods and men are honored, to hold sway over the trees?'

10"Next, the trees said to the fig tree, 'Come and be our king.'

11"But the fig tree replied, 'Should I give up my fruit, so good and sweet, to hold sway over the trees?'

12"Then the trees said to the vine, 'Come and be our king.'

13"But the vine answered, 'Should I give up my wine, which cheers both gods and men, to hold sway over the trees?'

14"Finally all the trees said to the thornbush, 'Come and be our king.'

15"The thornbush said to the trees, 'If you really want to anoint me king over you, come and take refuge in my shade; but if not, then let fire come out of the thornbush and consume the cedars of Lebanon!'

16"Now if you have acted honorably and in good faith when you made Abimelech king, and if you have been fair to Jerub-Baal and his family, and if you have treated him as he deserves— 17and to think that my father fought for you, risked his life to rescue you from the hand of Midian 18(but today you have revolted against my father's family, murdered his seventy sons on a single stone, and made Abimelech, the son of his slave girl, king over the citizens of Shechem because he is your brother)— 19if then you have acted honorably and in good faith toward Jerub-Baal and his family today, may Abimelech be your joy, and may you be his, too! 20But if you have not, let fire come out from Abimelech and consume you, citizens of Shechem and Beth Millo, and let fire come out from you, citizens of Shechem and Beth Millo, and consume Abimelech!"

21Then Jotham fled, escaping to Beer, and he lived there because he was afraid of his brother Abimelech.

22After Abimelech had governed Israel three years, 23God sent an evil spirit between Abimelech and the citizens of Shechem, who acted treacherously against Abimelech. 24God did this in order that the crime against Jerub-Baal's seventy sons, the shedding of their blood, might be avenged on their brother Abimelech and on the citizens of Shechem, who had helped him murder his brothers. 25In opposition to him these citizens of Shechem set men on the hilltops to ambush and rob everyone who passed by, and this was reported to Abimelech.

26Now Gaal son of Ebed moved with his brothers into Shechem, and its citizens put their confidence in him. 27After they had gone out into the fields and gathered the grapes and trodden them, they held a festival in the temple of their god. While they were eating and drinking, they cursed Abimelech. 28Then Gaal son of Ebed said, "Who is Abimelech, and who is Shechem, that we should be subject to him? Isn't he Jerub-Baal's son, and isn't Zebul his deputy? Serve the men of Hamor, Shechem's father! Why should we serve Abimelech? 29If only this people were under my command! Then I would get rid of him. I would say to Abimelech, 'Call out your whole army!' "[a]

30When Zebul the governor of the city heard what Gaal son of Ebed said, he was very angry. 31Under cover he sent messengers to Abimelech, saying, "Gaal son of Ebed and his brothers have come to Shechem and are stirring up the city against you. 32Now then, during the night you and your men should come and lie in wait in the fields. 33In the morning at sunrise, advance against the city. When Gaal and his men come out against you, do whatever your hand finds to do."

34So Abimelech and all his troops set out by night and took up concealed positions near Shechem in four companies. 35Now Gaal son of Ebed had gone out and was standing at the entrance to the city gate just as Abimelech and his soldiers came out from their hiding place.

36When Gaal saw them, he said to Zebul, "Look, people are coming down from the tops of the mountains!"

Zebul replied, "You mistake the shadows of the mountains for men."

37But Gaal spoke up again: "Look, people are coming down from the center of the land, and a company is coming from the direction of the soothsayers' tree."

38Then Zebul said to him, "Where is your big talk now, you who said, 'Who is Abimelech that we should be subject to him?' Aren't these the men you ridiculed? Go out and fight them!"

39So Gaal led out[b] the citizens of Shechem and fought Abimelech. 40Abimelech chased him, and many fell wounded in the flight—all the way to the entrance to the gate. 41Abimelech stayed in Arumah, and Zebul drove Gaal and his brothers out of Shechem.

42The next day the people of Shechem went out to the fields, and this was reported to Abimelech. 43So he took his men, divided them into three companies and set an ambush in the fields. When he saw the people coming out of the city, he rose to attack them. 44Abimelech and the companies with him rushed forward to a position at the entrance to the city gate. Then two companies rushed upon those in the fields and struck them down. 45All that day Abimelech pressed his attack against the city until he had captured it and killed its people. Then he destroyed the city and scattered salt over it.

[a]29 Septuagint; Hebrew *him." Then he said to Abimelech, "Call out your whole army!"* [b]39 Or *Gaal went out in the sight of*

46On hearing this, the citizens in the tower
of Shechem went into the stronghold of the
temple of El-Berith. 47When Abimelech heard
that they had assembled there, 48he and all his
men went up Mount Zalmon. He took an ax
and cut off some branches, which he lifted to
his shoulders. He ordered the men with him,
"Quick! Do what you have seen me do!" 49So
all the men cut branches and followed Abimelech. They piled them against the stronghold
and set it on fire over the people inside. So all
the people in the tower of Shechem, about a
thousand men and women, also died.

50Next Abimelech went to Thebez and besieged it and captured it. 51Inside the city,
however, was a strong tower, to which all the
men and women—all the people of the city—
fled. They locked themselves in and climbed
up on the tower roof. 52Abimelech went to the
tower and stormed it. But as he approached the
entrance to the tower to set it on fire, 53a woman dropped an upper millstone on his head and
cracked his skull.

54Hurriedly he called to his armor-bearer,
"Draw your sword and kill me, so that they
can't say, 'A woman killed him.' " So his servant ran him through, and he died. 55When the
Israelites saw that Abimelech was dead, they
went home.

56Thus God repaid the wickedness that
Abimelech had done to his father by murdering his seventy brothers. 57God also made the
men of Shechem pay for all their wickedness.
The curse of Jotham son of Jerub-Baal came
on them.

Tola

10 After the time of Abimelech a man of
Issachar, Tola son of Puah, the son of
Dodo, rose to save Israel. He lived in Shamir,
in the hill country of Ephraim. 2He led[a] Israel
twenty-three years; then he died, and was buried in Shamir.

Jair

3He was followed by Jair of Gilead, who led
Israel twenty-two years. 4He had thirty sons,
who rode thirty donkeys. They controlled thirty towns in Gilead, which to this day are called
Havvoth Jair.[b] 5When Jair died, he was buried
in Kamon.

Jephthah

6Again the Israelites did evil in the eyes of
the LORD. They served the Baals and the Ashtoreths, and the gods of Aram, the gods of
Sidon, the gods of Moab, the gods of the Ammonites and the gods of the Philistines. And
because the Israelites forsook the LORD and no
longer served him, 7he became angry with
them. He sold them into the hands of the Philistines and the Ammonites, 8who that year
shattered and crushed them. For eighteen years
they oppressed all the Israelites on the east side
of the Jordan in Gilead, the land of the Amorites. 9The Ammonites also crossed the Jordan
to fight against Judah, Benjamin and the house
of Ephraim; and Israel was in great distress.
10Then the Israelites cried out to the LORD,
"We have sinned against you, forsaking our
God and serving the Baals."

11The LORD replied, "When the Egyptians,
the Amorites, the Ammonites, the Philistines,
12the Sidonians, the Amalekites and the Maon-
ites[c] oppressed you and you cried to me for
help, did I not save you from their hands?
13But you have forsaken me and served other
gods, so I will no longer save you. 14Go and
cry out to the gods you have chosen. Let them
save you when you are in trouble!"

15But the Israelites said to the LORD, "We
have sinned. Do with us whatever you think
best, but please rescue us now." 16Then they
got rid of the foreign gods among them and
served the LORD. And he could bear Israel's
misery no longer.

17When the Ammonites were called to arms
and camped in Gilead, the Israelites assembled
and camped at Mizpah. 18The leaders of the
people of Gilead said to each other, "Whoever
will launch the attack against the Ammonites
will be the head of all those living in Gilead."

11 Jephthah the Gileadite was a mighty
warrior. His father was Gilead; his
mother was a prostitute. 2Gilead's wife also
bore him sons, and when they were grown up,
they drove Jephthah away. "You are not going
to get any inheritance in our family," they said,
"because you are the son of another woman."
3So Jephthah fled from his brothers and settled
in the land of Tob, where a group of adventurers gathered around him and followed him.

4Some time later, when the Ammonites
made war on Israel, 5the elders of Gilead went
to get Jephthah from the land of Tob.
6"Come," they said, "be our commander, so
we can fight the Ammonites."

7Jephthah said to them, "Didn't you hate me
and drive me from my father's house? Why do
you come to me now, when you're in trouble?"

8The elders of Gilead said to him, "Nevertheless, we are turning to you now; come with
us to fight the Ammonites, and you will be our
head over all who live in Gilead."

9Jephthah answered, "Suppose you take me
back to fight the Ammonites and the LORD
gives them to me—will I really be your head?"

10The elders of Gilead replied, "The LORD is
our witness; we will certainly do as you say."
11So Jephthah went with the elders of Gilead,
and the people made him head and commander
over them. And he repeated all his words before the LORD in Mizpah.

12Then Jephthah sent messengers to the Ammonite king with the question: "What do you
have against us that you have attacked our
country?"

13The king of the Ammonites answered
Jephthah's messengers, "When Israel came up

[a]2 Traditionally *judged*; also in verse 3 [b]4 Or *called the settlements of Jair* [c]12 Hebrew; some Septuagint manuscripts *Midianites*

out of Egypt, they took away my land from the Arnon to the Jabbok, all the way to the Jordan. Now give it back peaceably."

[14]Jephthah sent back messengers to the Ammonite king, [15]saying:

> "This is what Jephthah says: Israel did not take the land of Moab or the land of the Ammonites. [16]But when they came up out of Egypt, Israel went through the desert to the Red Sea[a] and on to Kadesh. [17]Then Israel sent messengers to the king of Edom, saying, 'Give us permission to go through your country,' but the king of Edom would not listen. They sent also to the king of Moab, and he refused. So Israel stayed at Kadesh.
>
> [18]"Next they traveled through the desert, skirted the lands of Edom and Moab, passed along the eastern side of the country of Moab, and camped on the other side of the Arnon. They did not enter the territory of Moab, for the Arnon was its border.
>
> [19]"Then Israel sent messengers to Sihon king of the Amorites, who ruled in Heshbon, and said to him, 'Let us pass through your country to our own place.' [20]Sihon, however, did not trust Israel[b] to pass through his territory. He mustered all his men and encamped at Jahaz and fought with Israel.
>
> [21]"Then the LORD, the God of Israel, gave Sihon and all his men into Israel's hands, and they defeated them. Israel took over all the land of the Amorites who lived in that country, [22]capturing all of it from the Arnon to the Jabbok and from the desert to the Jordan.
>
> [23]"Now since the LORD, the God of Israel, has driven the Amorites out before his people Israel, what right have you to take it over? [24]Will you not take what your god Chemosh gives you? Likewise, whatever the LORD our God has given us, we will possess. [25]Are you better than Balak son of Zippor, king of Moab? Did he ever quarrel with Israel or fight with them? [26]For three hundred years Israel occupied Heshbon, Aroer, the surrounding settlements and all the towns along the Arnon. Why didn't you retake them during that time? [27]I have not wronged you, but you are doing me wrong by waging war against me. Let the LORD, the Judge,[c] decide the dispute this day between the Israelites and the Ammonites."

[28]The king of Ammon, however, paid no attention to the message Jephthah sent him.

[29]Then the Spirit of the LORD came upon Jephthah. He crossed Gilead and Manasseh, passed through Mizpah of Gilead, and from there he advanced against the Ammonites. [30]And Jephthah made a vow to the LORD: "If you give the Ammonites into my hands, [31]whatever comes out of the door of my house to meet me when I return in triumph from the Ammonites will be the LORD's, and I will sacrifice it as a burnt offering."

[32]Then Jephthah went over to fight the Ammonites, and the LORD gave them into his hands. [33]He devastated twenty towns from Aroer to the vicinity of Minnith, as far as Abel Keramim. Thus Israel subdued Ammon.

[34]When Jephthah returned to his home in Mizpah, who should come out to meet him but his daughter, dancing to the sound of tambourines! She was an only child. Except for her he had neither son nor daughter. [35]When he saw her, he tore his clothes and cried, "Oh! My daughter! You have made me miserable and wretched, because I have made a vow to the LORD that I cannot break."

[36]"My father," she replied, "you have given your word to the LORD. Do to me just as you promised, now that the LORD has avenged you of your enemies, the Ammonites. [37]But grant me this one request," she said. "Give me two months to roam the hills and weep with my friends, because I will never marry."

[38]"You may go," he said. And he let her go for two months. She and the girls went into the hills and wept because she would never marry. [39]After the two months, she returned to her father and he did to her as he had vowed. And she was a virgin.

From this comes the Israelite custom [40]that each year the young women of Israel go out for four days to commemorate the daughter of Jephthah the Gileadite.

Jephthah and Ephraim

12 The men of Ephraim called out their forces, crossed over to Zaphon and said to Jephthah, "Why did you go to fight the Ammonites without calling us to go with you? We're going to burn down your house over your head."

[2]Jephthah answered, "I and my people were engaged in a great struggle with the Ammonites, and although I called, you didn't save me out of their hands. [3]When I saw that you wouldn't help, I took my life in my hands and crossed over to fight the Ammonites, and the LORD gave me the victory over them. Now why have you come up today to fight me?"

[4]Jephthah then called together the men of Gilead and fought against Ephraim. The Gileadites struck them down because the Ephraimites had said, "You Gileadites are renegades from Ephraim and Manasseh." [5]The Gileadites captured the fords of the Jordan leading to Ephraim, and whenever a survivor of Ephraim said, "Let me cross over," the men of Gilead asked him, "Are you an Ephraimite?" If he replied, "No," [6]they said, "All right, say 'Shibboleth.' " If he said, "Sibboleth," because he could not pronounce the word correctly, they

[a]*16* Hebrew *Yam Suph*; that is, Sea of Reeds [b]*20* Or *however, would not make an agreement for Israel*
[c]*27* Or *Ruler*

seized him and killed him at the fords of the Jordan. Forty-two thousand Ephraimites were killed at that time.

7Jephthah led[a] Israel six years. Then Jephthah the Gileadite died, and was buried in a town in Gilead.

Ibzan, Elon and Abdon

8After him, Ibzan of Bethlehem led Israel. 9He had thirty sons and thirty daughters. He gave his daughters away in marriage to those outside his clan, and for his sons he brought in thirty young women as wives from outside his clan. Ibzan led Israel seven years. 10Then Ibzan died, and was buried in Bethlehem.

11After him, Elon the Zebulunite led Israel ten years. 12Then Elon died, and was buried in Aijalon in the land of Zebulun.

13After him, Abdon son of Hillel, from Pirathon, led Israel. 14He had forty sons and thirty grandsons, who rode on seventy donkeys. He led Israel eight years. 15Then Abdon son of Hillel died, and was buried at Pirathon in Ephraim, in the hill country of the Amalekites.

The Birth of Samson

13 Again the Israelites did evil in the eyes of the LORD, so the LORD delivered them into the hands of the Philistines for forty years.

2A certain man of Zorah, named Manoah, from the clan of the Danites, had a wife who was sterile and remained childless. 3The angel of the LORD appeared to her and said, "You are sterile and childless, but you are going to conceive and have a son. 4Now see to it that you drink no wine or other fermented drink and that you do not eat anything unclean, 5because you will conceive and give birth to a son. No razor may be used on his head, because the boy is to be a Nazirite, set apart to God from birth, and he will begin the deliverance of Israel from the hands of the Philistines."

6Then the woman went to her husband and told him, "A man of God came to me. He looked like an angel of God, very awesome. I didn't ask him where he came from, and he didn't tell me his name. 7But he said to me, 'You will conceive and give birth to a son. Now then, drink no wine or other fermented drink and do not eat anything unclean, because the boy will be a Nazirite of God from birth until the day of his death.' "

8Then Manoah prayed to the LORD: "O Lord, I beg you, let the man of God you sent to us come again to teach us how to bring up the boy who is to be born."

9God heard Manoah, and the angel of God came again to the woman while she was out in the field; but her husband Manoah was not with her. 10The woman hurried to tell her husband, "He's here! The man who appeared to me the other day!"

11Manoah got up and followed his wife. When he came to the man, he said, "Are you the one who talked to my wife?"

"I am," he said.

12So Manoah asked him, "When your words are fulfilled, what is to be the rule for the boy's life and work?"

13The angel of the LORD answered, "Your wife must do all that I have told her. 14She must not eat anything that comes from the grapevine, nor drink any wine or other fermented drink nor eat anything unclean. She must do everything I have commanded her."

15Manoah said to the angel of the LORD, "We would like you to stay until we prepare a young goat for you."

16The angel of the LORD replied, "Even though you detain me, I will not eat any of your food. But if you prepare a burnt offering, offer it to the LORD." (Manoah did not realize that it was the angel of the LORD.)

17Then Manoah inquired of the angel of the LORD, "What is your name, so that we may honor you when your word comes true?"

18He replied, "Why do you ask my name? It is beyond understanding.[b]" 19Then Manoah took a young goat, together with the grain offering, and sacrificed it on a rock to the LORD. And the LORD did an amazing thing while Manoah and his wife watched: 20As the flame blazed up from the altar toward heaven, the angel of the LORD ascended in the flame. Seeing this, Manoah and his wife fell with their faces to the ground. 21When the angel of the LORD did not show himself again to Manoah and his wife, Manoah realized that it was the angel of the LORD.

22"We are doomed to die!" he said to his wife. "We have seen God!"

23But his wife answered, "If the LORD had meant to kill us, he would not have accepted a burnt offering and grain offering from our hands, nor shown us all these things or now told us this."

24The woman gave birth to a boy and named him Samson. He grew and the LORD blessed him, 25and the Spirit of the LORD began to stir him while he was in Mahaneh Dan, between Zorah and Eshtaol.

Samson's Marriage

14 Samson went down to Timnah and saw there a young Philistine woman. 2When he returned, he said to his father and mother, "I have seen a Philistine woman in Timnah; now get her for me as my wife."

3His father and mother replied, "Isn't there an acceptable woman among your relatives or among all our people? Must you go to the uncircumcised Philistines to get a wife?"

But Samson said to his father, "Get her for me. She's the right one for me." 4(His parents did not know that this was from the LORD, who was seeking an occasion to confront the Philistines; for at that time they were ruling over Israel.) 5Samson went down to Timnah togeth-

[a] 7 Traditionally *judged*; also in verses 8-14 [b] 18 Or *is wonderful*

er with his father and mother. As they approached the vineyards of Timnah, suddenly a
young lion came roaring toward him. 6The
Spirit of the LORD came upon him in power so
that he tore the lion apart with his bare hands
as he might have torn a young goat. But he told
neither his father nor his mother what he had
done. 7Then he went down and talked with the
woman, and he liked her.
8Some time later, when he went back to
marry her, he turned aside to look at the lion's
carcass. In it was a swarm of bees and some
honey, 9which he scooped out with his hands
and ate as he went along. When he rejoined his
parents, he gave them some, and they too ate it.
But he did not tell them that he had taken the
honey from the lion's carcass.
10Now his father went down to see the woman. And Samson made a feast there, as was
customary for bridegrooms. 11When he appeared, he was given thirty companions.
12"Let me tell you a riddle," Samson said to
them. "If you can give me the answer within
the seven days of the feast, I will give you
thirty linen garments and thirty sets of clothes.
13If you can't tell me the answer, you must
give me thirty linen garments and thirty sets of
clothes."
"Tell us your riddle," they said. "Let's
hear it."
14He replied,

"Out of the eater, something to eat;
out of the strong, something sweet."

For three days they could not give the answer.
15On the fourth[a] day, they said to Samson's
wife, "Coax your husband into explaining the
riddle for us, or we will burn you and your
father's household to death. Did you invite us
here to rob us?"
16Then Samson's wife threw herself on him,
sobbing, "You hate me! You don't really love
me. You've given my people a riddle, but you
haven't told me the answer."
"I haven't even explained it to my father or
mother," he replied, "so why should I explain
it to you?" 17She cried the whole seven days of
the feast. So on the seventh day he finally told
her, because she continued to press him. She in
turn explained the riddle to her people.
18Before sunset on the seventh day the men
of the town said to him,

"What is sweeter than honey?
What is stronger than a lion?"

Samson said to them,

"If you had not plowed with my heifer,
you would not have solved my riddle."

19Then the Spirit of the LORD came upon
him in power. He went down to Ashkelon,
struck down thirty of their men, stripped them
of their belongings and gave their clothes to
those who had explained the riddle. Burning
with anger, he went up to his father's house.
20And Samson's wife was given to the friend
who had attended him at his wedding.

Samson's Vengeance on the Philistines

15 Later on, at the time of wheat harvest,
Samson took a young goat and went to
visit his wife. He said, "I'm going to my wife's
room." But her father would not let him go in.
2"I was so sure you thoroughly hated her,"
he said, "that I gave her to your friend. Isn't
her younger sister more attractive? Take her
instead."
3Samson said to them, "This time I have a
right to get even with the Philistines; I will
really harm them." 4So he went out and caught
three hundred foxes and tied them tail to tail in
pairs. He then fastened a torch to every pair of
tails, 5lit the torches and let the foxes loose in
the standing grain of the Philistines. He burned
up the shocks and standing grain, together with
the vineyards and olive groves.
6When the Philistines asked, "Who did
this?" they were told, "Samson, the Timnite's
son-in-law, because his wife was given to his
friend."
So the Philistines went up and burned her
and her father to death. 7Samson said to them,
"Since you've acted like this, I won't stop until
I get my revenge on you." 8He attacked them
viciously and slaughtered many of them. Then
he went down and stayed in a cave in the rock
of Etam.
9The Philistines went up and camped in Judah, spreading out near Lehi. 10The men of
Judah asked, "Why have you come to
fight us?"
"We have come to take Samson prisoner,"
they answered, "to do to him as he did to us."
11Then three thousand men from Judah went
down to the cave in the rock of Etam and said
to Samson, "Don't you realize that the Philistines are rulers over us? What have you done
to us?"
He answered, "I merely did to them what
they did to me."
12They said to him, "We've come to tie you
up and hand you over to the Philistines."
Samson said, "Swear to me that you won't
kill me yourselves."
13"Agreed," they answered. "We will only
tie you up and hand you over to them. We will
not kill you." So they bound him with two new
ropes and led him up from the rock. 14As he
approached Lehi, the Philistines came toward
him shouting. The Spirit of the LORD came
upon him in power. The ropes on his arms
became like charred flax, and the bindings
dropped from his hands. 15Finding a fresh jawbone of a donkey, he grabbed it and struck
down a thousand men.
16Then Samson said,

"With a donkey's jawbone
I have made donkeys of them.[b]

[a] 15 Some Septuagint manuscripts and Syriac; Hebrew *seventh*
[b] 16 Or *made a heap or two*; the Hebrew for *donkey* sounds like the Hebrew for *heap*.

With a donkey's jawbone
 I have killed a thousand men."

17When he finished speaking, he threw away the jawbone; and the place was called Ramath Lehi.[a]

18Because he was very thirsty, he cried out to the LORD, "You have given your servant this great victory. Must I now die of thirst and fall into the hands of the uncircumcised?" 19Then God opened up the hollow place in Lehi, and water came out of it. When Samson drank, his strength returned and he revived. So the spring was called En Hakkore,[b] and it is still there in Lehi.

20Samson led[c] Israel for twenty years in the days of the Philistines.

Samson and Delilah

16 One day Samson went to Gaza, where he saw a prostitute. He went in to spend the night with her. 2The people of Gaza were told, "Samson is here!" So they surrounded the place and lay in wait for him all night at the city gate. They made no move during the night, saying, "At dawn we'll kill him."

3But Samson lay there only until the middle of the night. Then he got up and took hold of the doors of the city gate, together with the two posts, and tore them loose, bar and all. He lifted them to his shoulders and carried them to the top of the hill that faces Hebron.

4Some time later, he fell in love with a woman in the Valley of Sorek whose name was Delilah. 5The rulers of the Philistines went to her and said, "See if you can lure him into showing you the secret of his great strength and how we can overpower him so we may tie him up and subdue him. Each one of us will give you eleven hundred shekels[d] of silver."

6So Delilah said to Samson, "Tell me the secret of your great strength and how you can be tied up and subdued."

7Samson answered her, "If anyone ties me with seven fresh thongs[e] that have not been dried, I'll become as weak as any other man."

8Then the rulers of the Philistines brought her seven fresh thongs that had not been dried, and she tied him with them. 9With men hidden in the room, she called to him, "Samson, the Philistines are upon you!" But he snapped the thongs as easily as a piece of string snaps when it comes close to a flame. So the secret of his strength was not discovered.

10Then Delilah said to Samson, "You have made a fool of me; you lied to me. Come now, tell me how you can be tied."

11He said, "If anyone ties me securely with new ropes that have never been used, I'll become as weak as any other man."

12So Delilah took new ropes and tied him with them. Then, with men hidden in the room, she called to him, "Samson, the Philistines are upon you!" But he snapped the ropes off his arms as if they were threads.

13Delilah then said to Samson, "Until now, you have been making a fool of me and lying to me. Tell me how you can be tied."

He replied, "If you weave the seven braids of my head into the fabric ⌊on the loom⌋ and tighten it with the pin, I'll become as weak as any other man." So while he was sleeping, Delilah took the seven braids of his head, wove them into the fabric 14and[f] tightened it with the pin.

Again she called to him, "Samson, the Philistines are upon you!" He awoke from his sleep and pulled up the pin and the loom, with the fabric.

15Then she said to him, "How can you say, 'I love you,' when you won't confide in me? This is the third time you have made a fool of me and haven't told me the secret of your great strength." 16With such nagging she prodded him day after day until he was tired to death.

17So he told her everything. "No razor has ever been used on my head," he said, "because I have been a Nazirite set apart to God since birth. If my head were shaved, my strength would leave me, and I would become as weak as any other man."

18When Delilah saw that he had told her everything, she sent word to the rulers of the Philistines, "Come back once more; he has told me everything." So the rulers of the Philistines returned with the silver in their hands. 19Having put him to sleep on her lap, she called a man to shave off the seven braids of his hair, and so began to subdue him.[g] And his strength left him.

20Then she called, "Samson, the Philistines are upon you!"

He awoke from his sleep and thought, "I'll go out as before and shake myself free." But he did not know that the LORD had left him.

21Then the Philistines seized him, gouged out his eyes and took him down to Gaza. Binding him with bronze shackles, they set him to grinding in the prison. 22But the hair on his head began to grow again after it had been shaved.

The Death of Samson

23Now the rulers of the Philistines assembled to offer a great sacrifice to Dagon their god and to celebrate, saying, "Our god has delivered Samson, our enemy, into our hands."

24When the people saw him, they praised their god, saying,

"Our god has delivered our enemy
 into our hands,
the one who laid waste our land
 and multiplied our slain."

25While they were in high spirits, they shouted, "Bring out Samson to entertain us."

[a] 17 *Ramath Lehi* means *jawbone hill.* [b] 19 *En Hakkore* means *caller's spring.* [c] 20 Traditionally *judged*
[d] 5 That is, about 28 pounds (about 13 kilograms) [e] 7 Or *bowstrings*; also in verses 8 and 9 [f] 13,14 Some Septuagint manuscripts; Hebrew *"⌊I can⌋ if you weave the seven braids of my head into the fabric ⌊on the loom⌋." 14So she* [g] 19 Hebrew; some Septuagint manuscripts *and he began to weaken*

So they called Samson out of the prison, and
he performed for them.
When they stood him among the pillars,
26Samson said to the servant who held his
hand, "Put me where I can feel the pillars that
support the temple, so that I may lean against
them." 27Now the temple was crowded with
men and women; all the rulers of the Philistines were there, and on the roof were about
three thousand men and women watching
Samson perform. 28Then Samson prayed to the
LORD, "O Sovereign LORD, remember me.
O God, please strengthen me just once more,
and let me with one blow get revenge on the
Philistines for my two eyes." 29Then Samson
reached toward the two central pillars on
which the temple stood. Bracing himself
against them, his right hand on the one and his
left hand on the other, 30Samson said, "Let me
die with the Philistines!" Then he pushed with
all his might, and down came the temple on the
rulers and all the people in it. Thus he killed
many more when he died than while he lived.
31Then his brothers and his father's whole
family went down to get him. They brought
him back and buried him between Zorah and
Eshtaol in the tomb of Manoah his father. He
had led[a] Israel twenty years.

Micah's Idols

17 Now a man named Micah from the hill
country of Ephraim 2said to his mother,
"The eleven hundred shekels[b] of silver that
were taken from you and about which I heard
you utter a curse—I have that silver with me;
I took it."
Then his mother said, "The LORD bless you,
my son!"
3When he returned the eleven hundred shekels of silver to his mother, she said, "I solemnly consecrate my silver to the LORD for my son
to make a carved image and a cast idol. I will
give it back to you."
4So he returned the silver to his mother, and
she took two hundred shekels[c] of silver and
gave them to a silversmith, who made them
into the image and the idol. And they were put
in Micah's house.
5Now this man Micah had a shrine, and he
made an ephod and some idols and installed
one of his sons as his priest. 6In those days
Israel had no king; everyone did as he saw fit.
7A young Levite from Bethlehem in Judah,
who had been living within the clan of Judah,
8left that town in search of some other place to
stay. On his way[d] he came to Micah's house in
the hill country of Ephraim.
9Micah asked him, "Where are you from?"
"I'm a Levite from Bethlehem in Judah," he
said, "and I'm looking for a place to stay."
10Then Micah said to him, "Live with me
and be my father and priest, and I'll give you
ten shekels[e] of silver a year, your clothes and
your food." 11So the Levite agreed to live with
him, and the young man was to him like one of
his sons. 12Then Micah installed the Levite,
and the young man became his priest and lived
in his house. 13And Micah said, "Now I know
that the LORD will be good to me, since this
Levite has become my priest."

Danites Settle in Laish

18 In those days Israel had no king.
And in those days the tribe of the Danites was seeking a place of their own where
they might settle, because they had not yet
come into an inheritance among the tribes of
Israel. 2So the Danites sent five warriors from
Zorah and Eshtaol to spy out the land and explore it. These men represented all their clans.
They told them, "Go, explore the land."
The men entered the hill country of Ephraim
and came to the house of Micah, where they
spent the night. 3When they were near Micah's
house, they recognized the voice of the young
Levite; so they turned in there and asked him,
"Who brought you here? What are you doing
in this place? Why are you here?"
4He told them what Micah had done for him,
and said, "He has hired me and I am his
priest."
5Then they said to him, "Please inquire of
God to learn whether our journey will be successful."
6The priest answered them, "Go in peace.
Your journey has the LORD's approval."
7So the five men left and came to Laish,
where they saw that the people were living in
safety, like the Sidonians, unsuspecting and secure. And since their land lacked nothing, they
were prosperous.[f] Also, they lived a long way
from the Sidonians and had no relationship
with anyone else.[g]
8When they returned to Zorah and Eshtaol,
their brothers asked them, "How did you find
things?"
9They answered, "Come on, let's attack
them! We have seen that the land is very good.
Aren't you going to do something? Don't hesitate to go there and take it over. 10When you
get there, you will find an unsuspecting people
and a spacious land that God has put into your
hands, a land that lacks nothing whatever."
11Then six hundred men from the clan of the
Danites, armed for battle, set out from Zorah
and Eshtaol. 12On their way they set up camp
near Kiriath Jearim in Judah. This is why the
place west of Kiriath Jearim is called Mahaneh
Dan[h] to this day. 13From there they went on to
the hill country of Ephraim and came to Micah's house.
14Then the five men who had spied out the
land of Laish said to their brothers, "Do you
know that one of these houses has an ephod,
other household gods, a carved image and a
cast idol? Now you know what to do." 15So

[a] *31* Traditionally *judged* [b] *2* That is, about 28 pounds (about 13 kilograms) [c] *4* That is, about 5 pounds (about 2.3 kilograms) [d] *8* Or *To carry on his profession* [e] *10* That is, about 4 ounces (about 110 grams) [f] *7* The meaning of the Hebrew for this clause is uncertain. [g] *7* Hebrew; some Septuagint manuscripts *with the Arameans* [h] *12* *Mahaneh Dan* means *Dan's camp.*

they turned in there and went to the house of the young Levite at Micah's place and greeted him. 16The six hundred Danites, armed for battle, stood at the entrance to the gate. 17The five men who had spied out the land went inside and took the carved image, the ephod, the other household gods and the cast idol while the priest and the six hundred armed men stood at the entrance to the gate.

18When these men went into Micah's house and took the carved image, the ephod, the other household gods and the cast idol, the priest said to them, "What are you doing?"

19They answered him, "Be quiet! Don't say a word. Come with us, and be our father and priest. Isn't it better that you serve a tribe and clan in Israel as priest rather than just one man's household?" 20Then the priest was glad. He took the ephod, the other household gods and the carved image and went along with the people. 21Putting their little children, their livestock and their possessions in front of them, they turned away and left.

22When they had gone some distance from Micah's house, the men who lived near Micah were called together and overtook the Danites. 23As they shouted after them, the Danites turned and said to Micah, "What's the matter with you that you called out your men to fight?"

24He replied, "You took the gods I made, and my priest, and went away. What else do I have? How can you ask, 'What's the matter with you?' "

25The Danites answered, "Don't argue with us, or some hot-tempered men will attack you, and you and your family will lose your lives." 26So the Danites went their way, and Micah, seeing that they were too strong for him, turned around and went back home.

27Then they took what Micah had made, and his priest, and went on to Laish, against a peaceful and unsuspecting people. They attacked them with the sword and burned down their city. 28There was no one to rescue them because they lived a long way from Sidon and had no relationship with anyone else. The city was in a valley near Beth Rehob.

The Danites rebuilt the city and settled there. 29They named it Dan after their forefather Dan, who was born to Israel—though the city used to be called Laish. 30There the Danites set up for themselves the idols, and Jonathan son of Gershom, the son of Moses,[a] and his sons were priests for the tribe of Dan until the time of the captivity of the land. 31They continued to use the idols Micah had made, all the time the house of God was in Shiloh.

A Levite and His Concubine

19 In those days Israel had no king.

Now a Levite who lived in a remote area in the hill country of Ephraim took a concubine from Bethlehem in Judah. 2But she was unfaithful to him. She left him and went back to her father's house in Bethlehem, Judah. After she had been there four months, 3her husband went to her to persuade her to return. He had with him his servant and two donkeys. She took him into her father's house, and when her father saw him, he gladly welcomed him. 4His father-in-law, the girl's father, prevailed upon him to stay; so he remained with him three days, eating and drinking, and sleeping there.

5On the fourth day they got up early and he prepared to leave, but the girl's father said to his son-in-law, "Refresh yourself with something to eat; then you can go." 6So the two of them sat down to eat and drink together. Afterward the girl's father said, "Please stay tonight and enjoy yourself." 7And when the man got up to go, his father-in-law persuaded him, so he stayed there that night. 8On the morning of the fifth day, when he rose to go, the girl's father said, "Refresh yourself. Wait till afternoon!" So the two of them ate together.

9Then when the man, with his concubine and his servant, got up to leave, his father-in-law, the girl's father, said, "Now look, it's almost evening. Spend the night here; the day is nearly over. Stay and enjoy yourself. Early tomorrow morning you can get up and be on your way home." 10But, unwilling to stay another night, the man left and went toward Jebus (that is, Jerusalem), with his two saddled donkeys and his concubine.

11When they were near Jebus and the day was almost gone, the servant said to his master, "Come, let's stop at this city of the Jebusites and spend the night."

12His master replied, "No. We won't go into an alien city, whose people are not Israelites. We will go on to Gibeah." 13He added, "Come, let's try to reach Gibeah or Ramah and spend the night in one of those places." 14So they went on, and the sun set as they neared Gibeah in Benjamin. 15There they stopped to spend the night. They went and sat in the city square, but no one took them into his home for the night.

16That evening an old man from the hill country of Ephraim, who was living in Gibeah (the men of the place were Benjamites), came in from his work in the fields. 17When he looked and saw the traveler in the city square, the old man asked, "Where are you going? Where did you come from?"

18He answered, "We are on our way from Bethlehem in Judah to a remote area in the hill country of Ephraim where I live. I have been to Bethlehem in Judah and now I am going to the house of the LORD. No one has taken me into his house. 19We have both straw and fodder for our donkeys and bread and wine for ourselves your servants—me, your maidservant, and the young man with us. We don't need anything."

20"You are welcome at my house," the old man said. "Let me supply whatever you need. Only don't spend the night in the square." 21So he took him into his house and fed his don-

[a]*30* An ancient Hebrew scribal tradition, some Septuagint manuscripts and Vulgate; Masoretic Text *Manasseh*

keys. After they had washed their feet, they had something to eat and drink.

22While they were enjoying themselves, some of the wicked men of the city surrounded the house. Pounding on the door, they shouted to the old man who owned the house, "Bring out the man who came to your house so we can have sex with him."

23The owner of the house went outside and said to them, "No, my friends, don't be so vile. Since this man is my guest, don't do this disgraceful thing. 24Look, here is my virgin daughter, and his concubine. I will bring them out to you now, and you can use them and do to them whatever you wish. But to this man, don't do such a disgraceful thing."

25But the men would not listen to him. So the man took his concubine and sent her outside to them, and they raped her and abused her throughout the night, and at dawn they let her go. 26At daybreak the woman went back to the house where her master was staying, fell down at the door and lay there until daylight.

27When her master got up in the morning and opened the door of the house and stepped out to continue on his way, there lay his concubine, fallen in the doorway of the house, with her hands on the threshold. 28He said to her, "Get up; let's go." But there was no answer. Then the man put her on his donkey and set out for home.

29When he reached home, he took a knife and cut up his concubine, limb by limb, into twelve parts and sent them into all the areas of Israel. 30Everyone who saw it said, "Such a thing has never been seen or done, not since the day the Israelites came up out of Egypt. Think about it! Consider it! Tell us what to do!"

Israelites Fight the Benjamites

20 Then ail the Israelites from Dan to Beersheba and from the land of Gilead came out as one man and assembled before the LORD in Mizpah. 2The leaders of all the people of the tribes of Israel took their places in the assembly of the people of God, four hundred thousand soldiers armed with swords. 3(The Benjamites heard that the Israelites had gone up to Mizpah.) Then the Israelites said, "Tell us how this awful thing happened."

4So the Levite, the husband of the murdered woman, said, "I and my concubine came to Gibeah in Benjamin to spend the night. 5During the night the men of Gibeah came after me and surrounded the house, intending to kill me. They raped my concubine, and she died. 6I took my concubine, cut her into pieces and sent one piece to each region of Israel's inheritance, because they committed this lewd and disgraceful act in Israel. 7Now, all you Israelites, speak up and give your verdict."

8All the people rose as one man, saying, "None of us will go home. No, not one of us will return to his house. 9But now this is what we'll do to Gibeah: We'll go up against it as the lot directs. 10We'll take ten men out of every hundred from all the tribes of Israel, and a hundred from a thousand, and a thousand from ten thousand, to get provisions for the army. Then, when the army arrives at Gibeah[a] in Benjamin, it can give them what they deserve for all this vileness done in Israel." 11So all the men of Israel got together and united as one man against the city.

12The tribes of Israel sent men throughout the tribe of Benjamin, saying, "What about this awful crime that was committed among you? 13Now surrender those wicked men of Gibeah so that we may put them to death and purge the evil from Israel."

But the Benjamites would not listen to their fellow Israelites. 14From their towns they came together at Gibeah to fight against the Israelites. 15At once the Benjamites mobilized twenty-six thousand swordsmen from their towns, in addition to seven hundred chosen men from those living in Gibeah. 16Among all these soldiers there were seven hundred chosen men who were left-handed, each of whom could sling a stone at a hair and not miss.

17Israel, apart from Benjamin, mustered four hundred thousand swordsmen, all of them fighting men.

18The Israelites went up to Bethel[b] and inquired of God. They said, "Who of us shall go first to fight against the Benjamites?"

The LORD replied, "Judah shall go first."

19The next morning the Israelites got up and pitched camp near Gibeah. 20The men of Israel went out to fight the Benjamites and took up battle positions against them at Gibeah. 21The Benjamites came out of Gibeah and cut down twenty-two thousand Israelites on the battlefield that day. 22But the men of Israel encouraged one another and again took up their positions where they had stationed themselves the first day. 23The Israelites went up and wept before the LORD until evening, and they inquired of the LORD. They said, "Shall we go up again to battle against the Benjamites, our brothers?"

The LORD answered, "Go up against them."

24Then the Israelites drew near to Benjamin the second day. 25This time, when the Benjamites came out from Gibeah to oppose them, they cut down another eighteen thousand Israelites, all of them armed with swords.

26Then the Israelites, all the people, went up to Bethel, and there they sat weeping before the LORD. They fasted that day until evening and presented burnt offerings and fellowship offerings[c] to the LORD. 27And the Israelites inquired of the LORD. (In those days the ark of the covenant of God was there, 28with Phine-

[a]10 One Hebrew manuscript; most Hebrew manuscripts *Geba,* a variant of *Gibeah* [b]18 Or *to the house of God*; also in verse 26 [c]26 Traditionally *peace offerings*

has son of Eleazar, the son of Aaron, ministering before it.) They asked, "Shall we go up again to battle with Benjamin our brother, or not?"

The LORD responded, "Go, for tomorrow I will give them into your hands."

29Then Israel set an ambush around Gibeah. 30They went up against the Benjamites on the third day and took up positions against Gibeah as they had done before. 31The Benjamites came out to meet them and were drawn away from the city. They began to inflict casualties on the Israelites as before, so that about thirty men fell in the open field and on the roads—the one leading to Bethel and the other to Gibeah.

32While the Benjamites were saying, "We are defeating them as before," the Israelites were saying, "Let's retreat and draw them away from the city to the roads."

33All the men of Israel moved from their places and took up positions at Baal Tamar, and the Israelite ambush charged out of its place on the west[a] of Gibeah.[b] 34Then ten thousand of Israel's finest men made a frontal attack on Gibeah. The fighting was so heavy that the Benjamites did not realize how near disaster was. 35The LORD defeated Benjamin before Israel, and on that day the Israelites struck down 25,100 Benjamites, all armed with swords. 36Then the Benjamites saw that they were beaten.

Now the men of Israel had given way before Benjamin, because they relied on the ambush they had set near Gibeah. 37The men who had been in ambush made a sudden dash into Gibeah, spread out and put the whole city to the sword. 38The men of Israel had arranged with the ambush that they should send up a great cloud of smoke from the city, 39and then the men of Israel would turn in the battle.

The Benjamites had begun to inflict casualties on the men of Israel (about thirty), and they said, "We are defeating them as in the first battle." 40But when the column of smoke began to rise from the city, the Benjamites turned and saw the smoke of the whole city going up into the sky. 41Then the men of Israel turned on them, and the men of Benjamin were terrified, because they realized that disaster had come upon them. 42So they fled before the Israelites in the direction of the desert, but they could not escape the battle. And the men of Israel who came out of the towns cut them down there. 43They surrounded the Benjamites, chased them and easily[c] overran them in the vicinity of Gibeah on the east. 44Eighteen thousand Benjamites fell, all of them valiant fighters. 45As they turned and fled toward the desert to the rock of Rimmon, the Israelites cut down five thousand men along the roads. They kept pressing after the Benjamites as far as Gidom and struck down two thousand more.

46On that day twenty-five thousand Benjamite swordsmen fell, all of them valiant fighters. 47But six hundred men turned and fled into the desert to the rock of Rimmon, where they stayed four months. 48The men of Israel went back to Benjamin and put all the towns to the sword, including the animals and everything else they found. All the towns they came across they set on fire.

Wives for the Benjamites

21 The men of Israel had taken an oath at Mizpah: "Not one of us will give his daughter in marriage to a Benjamite."

2The people went to Bethel,[d] where they sat before God until evening, raising their voices and weeping bitterly. 3"O LORD, the God of Israel," they cried, "why has this happened to Israel? Why should one tribe be missing from Israel today?"

4Early the next day the people built an altar and presented burnt offerings and fellowship offerings.[e]

5Then the Israelites asked, "Who from all the tribes of Israel has failed to assemble before the LORD?" For they had taken a solemn oath that anyone who failed to assemble before the LORD at Mizpah should certainly be put to death.

6Now the Israelites grieved for their brothers, the Benjamites. "Today one tribe is cut off from Israel," they said. 7"How can we provide wives for those who are left, since we have taken an oath by the LORD not to give them any of our daughters in marriage?" 8Then they asked, "Which one of the tribes of Israel failed to assemble before the LORD at Mizpah?" They discovered that no one from Jabesh Gilead had come to the camp for the assembly. 9For when they counted the people, they found that none of the people of Jabesh Gilead were there.

10So the assembly sent twelve thousand fighting men with instructions to go to Jabesh Gilead and put to the sword those living there, including the women and children. 11"This is what you are to do," they said. "Kill every male and every woman who is not a virgin." 12They found among the people living in Jabesh Gilead four hundred young women who had never slept with a man, and they took them to the camp at Shiloh in Canaan.

13Then the whole assembly sent an offer of peace to the Benjamites at the rock of Rimmon. 14So the Benjamites returned at that time and were given the women of Jabesh Gilead who had been spared. But there were not enough for all of them.

15The people grieved for Benjamin, because the LORD had made a gap in the tribes of Israel.

[a]33 Some Septuagint manuscripts and Vulgate; the meaning of the Hebrew for this word is uncertain.
[b]33 Hebrew *Geba,* a variant of *Gibeah* [c]43 The meaning of the Hebrew for this word is uncertain.
[d]2 Or *to the house of God* [e]4 Traditionally *peace offerings*

16 And the elders of the assembly said, "With the women of Benjamin destroyed, how shall we provide wives for the men who are left? 17 The Benjamite survivors must have heirs," they said, "so that a tribe of Israel will not be wiped out. 18 We can't give them our daughters as wives, since we Israelites have taken this oath: 'Cursed be anyone who gives a wife to a Benjamite.' 19 But look, there is the annual festival of the LORD in Shiloh, to the north of Bethel, and east of the road that goes from Bethel to Shechem, and to the south of Lebonah."

20 So they instructed the Benjamites, saying, "Go and hide in the vineyards 21 and watch. When the girls of Shiloh come out to join in the dancing, then rush from the vineyards and each of you seize a wife from the girls of Shiloh and go to the land of Benjamin. 22 When their fathers or brothers complain to us, we will say to them, 'Do us a kindness by helping them, because we did not get wives for them during the war, and you are innocent, since you did not give your daughters to them.' "

23 So that is what the Benjamites did. While the girls were dancing, each man caught one and carried her off to be his wife. Then they returned to their inheritance and rebuilt the towns and settled in them.

24 At that time the Israelites left that place and went home to their tribes and clans, each to his own inheritance.

25 In those days Israel had no king; everyone did as he saw fit.

Ruth

Naomi and Ruth

1 In the days when the judges ruled,[a] there was a famine in the land, and a man from Bethlehem in Judah, together with his wife and two sons, went to live for a while in the country of Moab. 2 The man's name was Elimelech, his wife's name Naomi, and the names of his two sons were Mahlon and Kilion. They were Ephrathites from Bethlehem, Judah. And they went to Moab and lived there.

3 Now Elimelech, Naomi's husband, died, and she was left with her two sons. 4 They married Moabite women, one named Orpah and the other Ruth. After they had lived there about ten years, 5 both Mahlon and Kilion also died, and Naomi was left without her two sons and her husband.

6 When she heard in Moab that the LORD had come to the aid of his people by providing food for them, Naomi and her daughters-in-law prepared to return home from there. 7 With her two daughters-in-law she left the place where she had been living and set out on the road that would take them back to the land of Judah.

8 Then Naomi said to her two daughters-in-law, "Go back, each of you, to your mother's home. May the LORD show kindness to you, as you have shown to your dead and to me. 9 May the LORD grant that each of you will find rest in the home of another husband."

Then she kissed them and they wept aloud 10 and said to her, "We will go back with you to your people."

11 But Naomi said, "Return home, my daughters. Why would you come with me? Am I going to have any more sons, who could become your husbands? 12 Return home, my daughters; I am too old to have another husband. Even if I thought there was still hope for me—even if I had a husband tonight and then gave birth to sons— 13 would you wait until they grew up? Would you remain unmarried for them? No, my daughters. It is more bitter for me than for you, because the LORD's hand has gone out against me!"

14 At this they wept again. Then Orpah kissed her mother-in-law good-by, but Ruth clung to her.

15 "Look," said Naomi, "your sister-in-law is going back to her people and her gods. Go back with her."

16 But Ruth replied, "Don't urge me to leave you or to turn back from you. Where you go I will go, and where you stay I will stay. Your people will be my people and your God my God. 17 Where you die I will die, and there I will be buried. May the LORD deal with me, be it ever so severely, if anything but death separates you and me." 18 When Naomi realized that Ruth was determined to go with her, she stopped urging her.

19 So the two women went on until they came to Bethlehem. When they arrived in Bethlehem, the whole town was stirred because of them, and the women exclaimed, "Can this be Naomi?"

20 "Don't call me Naomi,[b]" she told them. "Call me Mara,[c] because the Almighty[d] has made my life very bitter. 21 I went away full, but the LORD has brought me back empty. Why call me Naomi? The LORD has afflicted[e] me; the Almighty has brought misfortune upon me."

22 So Naomi returned from Moab accompanied by Ruth the Moabitess, her daughter-in-law, arriving in Bethlehem as the barley harvest was beginning.

[a] *1* Traditionally *judged* [b] *20* *Naomi* means *pleasant*; also in verse 21. [c] *20* *Mara* means *bitter.*
[d] *20* Hebrew *Shaddai*; also in verse 21 [e] *21* Or *has testified against*

Ruth Meets Boaz

2 Now Naomi had a relative on her husband's side, from the clan of Elimelech, a man of standing, whose name was Boaz.

2And Ruth the Moabitess said to Naomi, "Let me go to the fields and pick up the leftover grain behind anyone in whose eyes I find favor."

Naomi said to her, "Go ahead, my daughter." 3So she went out and began to glean in the fields behind the harvesters. As it turned out, she found herself working in a field belonging to Boaz, who was from the clan of Elimelech.

4Just then Boaz arrived from Bethlehem and greeted the harvesters, "The LORD be with you!"

"The LORD bless you!" they called back.

5Boaz asked the foreman of his harvesters, "Whose young woman is that?"

6The foreman replied, "She is the Moabitess who came back from Moab with Naomi. 7She said, 'Please let me glean and gather among the sheaves behind the harvesters.' She went into the field and has worked steadily from morning till now, except for a short rest in the shelter."

8So Boaz said to Ruth, "My daughter, listen to me. Don't go and glean in another field and don't go away from here. Stay here with my servant girls. 9Watch the field where the men are harvesting, and follow along after the girls. I have told the men not to touch you. And whenever you are thirsty, go and get a drink from the water jars the men have filled."

10At this, she bowed down with her face to the ground. She exclaimed, "Why have I found such favor in your eyes that you notice me—a foreigner?"

11Boaz replied, "I've been told all about what you have done for your mother-in-law since the death of your husband—how you left your father and mother and your homeland and came to live with a people you did not know before. 12May the LORD repay you for what you have done. May you be richly rewarded by the LORD, the God of Israel, under whose wings you have come to take refuge."

13"May I continue to find favor in your eyes, my lord," she said. "You have given me comfort and have spoken kindly to your servant—though I do not have the standing of one of your servant girls."

14At mealtime Boaz said to her, "Come over here. Have some bread and dip it in the wine vinegar."

When she sat down with the harvesters, he offered her some roasted grain. She ate all she wanted and had some left over. 15As she got up to glean, Boaz gave orders to his men, "Even if she gathers among the sheaves, don't embarrass her. 16Rather, pull out some stalks for her from the bundles and leave them for her to pick up, and don't rebuke her."

17So Ruth gleaned in the field until evening. Then she threshed the barley she had gathered, and it amounted to about an ephah.[a] 18She carried it back to town, and her mother-in-law saw how much she had gathered. Ruth also brought out and gave her what she had left over after she had eaten enough.

19Her mother-in-law asked her, "Where did you glean today? Where did you work? Blessed be the man who took notice of you!"

Then Ruth told her mother-in-law about the one at whose place she had been working. "The name of the man I worked with today is Boaz," she said.

20"The LORD bless him!" Naomi said to her daughter-in-law. "He has not stopped showing his kindness to the living and the dead." She added, "That man is our close relative; he is one of our kinsman-redeemers."

21Then Ruth the Moabitess said, "He even said to me, 'Stay with my workers until they finish harvesting all my grain.' "

22Naomi said to Ruth her daughter-in-law, "It will be good for you, my daughter, to go with his girls, because in someone else's field you might be harmed."

23So Ruth stayed close to the servant girls of Boaz to glean until the barley and wheat harvests were finished. And she lived with her mother-in-law.

Ruth and Boaz at the Threshing Floor

3 One day Naomi her mother-in-law said to her, "My daughter, should I not try to find a home[b] for you, where you will be well provided for? 2Is not Boaz, with whose servant girls you have been, a kinsman of ours? Tonight he will be winnowing barley on the threshing floor. 3Wash and perfume yourself, and put on your best clothes. Then go down to the threshing floor, but don't let him know you are there until he has finished eating and drinking. 4When he lies down, note the place where he is lying. Then go and uncover his feet and lie down. He will tell you what to do."

5"I will do whatever you say," Ruth answered. 6So she went down to the threshing floor and did everything her mother-in-law told her to do.

7When Boaz had finished eating and drinking and was in good spirits, he went over to lie down at the far end of the grain pile. Ruth approached quietly, uncovered his feet and lay down. 8In the middle of the night something startled the man, and he turned and discovered a woman lying at his feet.

9"Who are you?" he asked.

"I am your servant Ruth," she said. "Spread the corner of your garment over me, since you are a kinsman-redeemer."

10"The LORD bless you, my daughter," he replied. "This kindness is greater than that which you showed earlier: You have not run after the younger men, whether rich or poor. 11And now, my daughter, don't be afraid. I will do for you all you ask. All my fellow townsmen know that you are a woman of no-

[a] *17* That is, probably about 3/5 bushel (about 22 liters)

[b] *1* Hebrew *find rest* (see Ruth 1:9)

ble character. 12Although it is true that I am
near of kin, there is a kinsman-redeemer nearer than I. 13Stay here for the night, and in the
morning if he wants to redeem, good; let him
redeem. But if he is not willing, as surely as
the LORD lives I will do it. Lie here until morning."

14So she lay at his feet until morning, but
got up before anyone could be recognized; and
he said, "Don't let it be known that a woman
came to the threshing floor."

15He also said, "Bring me the shawl you are
wearing and hold it out." When she did so, he
poured into it six measures of barley and put it
on her. Then he[a] went back to town.

16When Ruth came to her mother-in-law,
Naomi asked, "How did it go, my daughter?"

Then she told her everything Boaz had done
for her 17and added, "He gave me these six
measures of barley, saying, 'Don't go back to
your mother-in-law empty-handed.' "

18Then Naomi said, "Wait, my daughter, until you find out what happens. For the man will
not rest until the matter is settled today."

Boaz Marries Ruth

4 Meanwhile Boaz went up to the town gate
and sat there. When the kinsman-redeemer
he had mentioned came along, Boaz said,
"Come over here, my friend, and sit down." So
he went over and sat down.

2Boaz took ten of the elders of the town and
said, "Sit here," and they did so. 3Then he said
to the kinsman-redeemer, "Naomi, who has
come back from Moab, is selling the piece of
land that belonged to our brother Elimelech. 4I
thought I should bring the matter to your attention and suggest that you buy it in the presence
of these seated here and in the presence of the
elders of my people. If you will redeem it, do
so. But if you[b] will not, tell me, so I will
know. For no one has the right to do it except
you, and I am next in line."

"I will redeem it," he said.

5Then Boaz said, "On the day you buy the
land from Naomi and from Ruth the Moabitess, you acquire[c] the dead man's widow, in
order to maintain the name of the dead with his
property."

6At this, the kinsman-redeemer said, "Then
I cannot redeem it because I might endanger
my own estate. You redeem it yourself. I cannot do it."

7(Now in earlier times in Israel, for the redemption and transfer of property to become
final, one party took off his sandal and gave it
to the other. This was the method of legalizing
transactions in Israel.)

8So the kinsman-redeemer said to Boaz,
"Buy it yourself." And he removed his sandal.

9Then Boaz announced to the elders and all
the people, "Today you are witnesses that I
have bought from Naomi all the property of
Elimelech, Kilion and Mahlon. 10I have also
acquired Ruth the Moabitess, Mahlon's widow, as my wife, in order to maintain the name
of the dead with his property, so that his name
will not disappear from among his family or
from the town records. Today you are witnesses!"

11Then the elders and all those at the gate
said, "We are witnesses. May the LORD make
the woman who is coming into your home like
Rachel and Leah, who together built up the
house of Israel. May you have standing in Ephrathah and be famous in Bethlehem. 12Through
the offspring the LORD gives you by this young
woman, may your family be like that of Perez,
whom Tamar bore to Judah."

The Genealogy of David

13So Boaz took Ruth and she became his
wife. Then he went to her, and the LORD enabled her to conceive, and she gave birth to a
son. 14The women said to Naomi: "Praise be to
the LORD, who this day has not left you without a kinsman-redeemer. May he become famous throughout Israel! 15He will renew your
life and sustain you in your old age. For your
daughter-in-law, who loves you and who is
better to you than seven sons, has given him
birth."

16Then Naomi took the child, laid him in her
lap and cared for him. 17The women living
there said, "Naomi has a son." And they
named him Obed. He was the father of Jesse,
the father of David.

18This, then, is the family line of Perez:

Perez was the father of Hezron,
19Hezron the father of Ram,
Ram the father of Amminadab,
20Amminadab the father of Nahshon,
Nahshon the father of Salmon,[d]
21Salmon the father of Boaz,
Boaz the father of Obed,
22Obed the father of Jesse,
and Jesse the father of David.

[a] *15* Most Hebrew manuscripts; many Hebrew manuscripts, Vulgate and Syriac *she* [b] *4* Many Hebrew manuscripts, Septuagint, Vulgate and Syriac; most Hebrew manuscripts *he* [c] *5* Hebrew; Vulgate and Syriac *Naomi, you acquire Ruth the Moabitess,* [d] *20* A few Hebrew manuscripts, some Septuagint manuscripts and Vulgate (see also verse 21 and Septuagint of 1 Chron. 2:11); most Hebrew manuscripts *Salma*

1 Samuel

The Birth of Samuel

1 There was a certain man from Ramathaim, a Zuphite[a] from the hill country of Ephraim, whose name was Elkanah son of Jeroham, the son of Elihu, the son of Tohu, the son of Zuph, an Ephraimite. 2He had two wives; one was called Hannah and the other Peninnah. Peninnah had children, but Hannah had none.

3Year after year this man went up from his town to worship and sacrifice to the LORD Almighty at Shiloh, where Hophni and Phinehas, the two sons of Eli, were priests of the LORD. 4Whenever the day came for Elkanah to sacrifice, he would give portions of the meat to his wife Peninnah and to all her sons and daughters. 5But to Hannah he gave a double portion because he loved her, and the LORD had closed her womb. 6And because the LORD had closed her womb, her rival kept provoking her in order to irritate her. 7This went on year after year. Whenever Hannah went up to the house of the LORD, her rival provoked her till she wept and would not eat. 8Elkanah her husband would say to her, "Hannah, why are you weeping? Why don't you eat? Why are you downhearted? Don't I mean more to you than ten sons?"

9Once when they had finished eating and drinking in Shiloh, Hannah stood up. Now Eli the priest was sitting on a chair by the doorpost of the LORD's temple.[b] 10In bitterness of soul Hannah wept much and prayed to the LORD. 11And she made a vow, saying, "O LORD Almighty, if you will only look upon your servant's misery and remember me, and not forget your servant but give her a son, then I will give him to the LORD for all the days of his life, and no razor will ever be used on his head."

12As she kept on praying to the LORD, Eli observed her mouth. 13Hannah was praying in her heart, and her lips were moving but her voice was not heard. Eli thought she was drunk 14and said to her, "How long will you keep on getting drunk? Get rid of your wine."

15"Not so, my lord," Hannah replied, "I am a woman who is deeply troubled. I have not been drinking wine or beer; I was pouring out my soul to the LORD. 16Do not take your servant for a wicked woman; I have been praying here out of my great anguish and grief."

17Eli answered, "Go in peace, and may the God of Israel grant you what you have asked of him."

18She said, "May your servant find favor in your eyes." Then she went her way and ate something, and her face was no longer downcast.

19Early the next morning they arose and worshiped before the LORD and then went back to their home at Ramah. Elkanah lay with Hannah his wife, and the LORD remembered her. 20So in the course of time Hannah conceived and gave birth to a son. She named him Samuel,[c] saying, "Because I asked the LORD for him."

Hannah Dedicates Samuel

21When the man Elkanah went up with all his family to offer the annual sacrifice to the LORD and to fulfill his vow, 22Hannah did not go. She said to her husband, "After the boy is weaned, I will take him and present him before the LORD, and he will live there always."

23"Do what seems best to you," Elkanah her husband told her. "Stay here until you have weaned him; only may the LORD make good his[d] word." So the woman stayed at home and nursed her son until she had weaned him.

24After he was weaned, she took the boy with her, young as he was, along with a three-year-old bull,[e] an ephah[f] of flour and a skin of wine, and brought him to the house of the LORD at Shiloh. 25When they had slaughtered the bull, they brought the boy to Eli, 26and she said to him, "As surely as you live, my lord, I am the woman who stood here beside you praying to the LORD. 27I prayed for this child, and the LORD has granted me what I asked of him. 28So now I give him to the LORD. For his whole life he will be given over to the LORD." And he worshiped the LORD there.

Hannah's Prayer

2 Then Hannah prayed and said:

"My heart rejoices in the LORD;
 in the LORD my horn[g] is lifted high.
My mouth boasts over my enemies,
 for I delight in your deliverance.

2"There is no one holy[h] like the LORD;
 there is no one besides you;
 there is no Rock like our God.

3"Do not keep talking so proudly
 or let your mouth speak such arrogance,
for the LORD is a God who knows,
 and by him deeds are weighed.

4"The bows of the warriors are broken,
 but those who stumbled are armed with strength.
5Those who were full hire themselves out for food,

[a] *1* Or *from Ramathaim Zuphim* [b] *9* That is, tabernacle [c] *20* *Samuel* sounds like the Hebrew for *heard of God.* [d] *23* Masoretic Text; Dead Sea Scrolls, Septuagint and Syriac *your* [e] *24* Dead Sea Scrolls, Septuagint and Syriac; Masoretic Text *with three bulls* [f] *24* That is, probably about 3/5 bushel (about 22 liters) [g] *1* *Horn* here symbolizes strength; also in verse 10. [h] *2* Or *no Holy One*

but those who were hungry hunger no
more.
She who was barren has borne seven
children,
but she who has had many sons pines
away.

6 “The LORD brings death and makes alive;
he brings down to the grave[a] and raises
up.
7 The LORD sends poverty and wealth;
he humbles and he exalts.
8 He raises the poor from the dust
and lifts the needy from the ash heap;
he seats them with princes
and has them inherit a throne of honor.

“For the foundations of the earth are the
LORD’s;
upon them he has set the world.
9 He will guard the feet of his saints,
but the wicked will be silenced in
darkness.

“It is not by strength that one prevails;
10 those who oppose the LORD will be
shattered.
He will thunder against them from heaven;
the LORD will judge the ends of the
earth.

“He will give strength to his king
and exalt the horn of his anointed.”

11 Then Elkanah went home to Ramah, but
the boy ministered before the LORD under Eli
the priest.

Eli’s Wicked Sons

12 Eli’s sons were wicked men; they had no
regard for the LORD. 13 Now it was the practice
of the priests with the people that whenever
anyone offered a sacrifice and while the meat
was being boiled, the servant of the priest
would come with a three-pronged fork in his
hand. 14 He would plunge it into the pan or
kettle or caldron or pot, and the priest would
take for himself whatever the fork brought up.
This is how they treated all the Israelites who
came to Shiloh. 15 But even before the fat was
burned, the servant of the priest would come
and say to the man who was sacrificing, “Give
the priest some meat to roast; he won’t accept
boiled meat from you, but only raw.”

16 If the man said to him, “Let the fat be
burned up first, and then take whatever you
want,” the servant would then answer, “No,
hand it over now; if you don’t, I’ll take it by
force.”

17 This sin of the young men was very great
in the LORD’s sight, for they[b] were treating the
LORD’s offering with contempt.

18 But Samuel was ministering before the
LORD—a boy wearing a linen ephod. 19 Each
year his mother made him a little robe and took
it to him when she went up with her husband
to offer the annual sacrifice. 20 Eli would bless
Elkanah and his wife, saying, “May the LORD
give you children by this woman to take the
place of the one she prayed for and gave to the
LORD.” Then they would go home. 21 And
the LORD was gracious to Hannah; she conceived and gave birth to three sons and two
daughters. Meanwhile, the boy Samuel grew
up in the presence of the LORD.

22 Now Eli, who was very old, heard about
everything his sons were doing to all Israel and
how they slept with the women who served at
the entrance to the Tent of Meeting. 23 So he
said to them, “Why do you do such things? I
hear from all the people about these wicked
deeds of yours. 24 No, my sons; it is not a good
report that I hear spreading among the LORD’s
people. 25 If a man sins against another man,
God[c] may mediate for him; but if a man sins
against the LORD, who will intercede for him?”
His sons, however, did not listen to their father’s rebuke, for it was the LORD’s will to put
them to death.

26 And the boy Samuel continued to grow in
stature and in favor with the LORD and with
men.

Prophecy Against the House of Eli

27 Now a man of God came to Eli and said to
him, “This is what the LORD says: ‘Did I not
clearly reveal myself to your father’s house
when they were in Egypt under Pharaoh? 28 I
chose your father out of all the tribes of Israel
to be my priest, to go up to my altar, to burn
incense, and to wear an ephod in my presence.
I also gave your father’s house all the offerings
made with fire by the Israelites. 29 Why do
you[d] scorn my sacrifice and offering that I
prescribed for my dwelling? Why do you hon-
or your sons more than me by fattening yourselves on the choice parts of every offering
made by my people Israel?’

30 “Therefore the LORD, the God of Israel,
declares: ‘I promised that your house and your
father’s house would minister before me forever.’ But now the LORD declares: ‘Far be it from
me! Those who honor me I will honor, but
those who despise me will be disdained. 31 The
time is coming when I will cut short your
strength and the strength of your father’s
house, so that there will not be an old man in
your family line 32 and you will see distress in
my dwelling. Although good will be done to
Israel, in your family line there will never be
an old man. 33 Every one of you that I do not
cut off from my altar will be spared only to
blind your eyes with tears and to grieve your
heart, and all your descendants will die in the
prime of life.

34 “ ‘And what happens to your two sons,
Hophni and Phinehas, will be a sign to you—
they will both die on the same day. 35 I will
raise up for myself a faithful priest, who will
do according to what is in my heart and mind.
I will firmly establish his house, and he will
minister before my anointed one always.
36 Then everyone left in your family line will

[a] 6 Hebrew *Sheol* [b] 17 Or *men* [c] 25 Or *the judges* [d] 29 The Hebrew is plural.

come and bow down before him for a piece of silver and a crust of bread and plead, "Appoint me to some priestly office so I can have food to eat." ' "

The LORD Calls Samuel

3 The boy Samuel ministered before the LORD under Eli. In those days the word of the LORD was rare; there were not many visions.

2One night Eli, whose eyes were becoming so weak that he could barely see, was lying down in his usual place. 3The lamp of God had not yet gone out, and Samuel was lying down in the temple[a] of the LORD, where the ark of God was. 4Then the LORD called Samuel.

Samuel answered, "Here I am." 5And he ran to Eli and said, "Here I am; you called me."

But Eli said, "I did not call; go back and lie down." So he went and lay down.

6Again the LORD called, "Samuel!" And Samuel got up and went to Eli and said, "Here I am; you called me."

"My son," Eli said, "I did not call; go back and lie down."

7Now Samuel did not yet know the LORD: The word of the LORD had not yet been revealed to him.

8The LORD called Samuel a third time, and Samuel got up and went to Eli and said, "Here I am; you called me."

Then Eli realized that the LORD was calling the boy. 9So Eli told Samuel, "Go and lie down, and if he calls you, say, 'Speak, LORD, for your servant is listening.' " So Samuel went and lay down in his place.

10The LORD came and stood there, calling as at the other times, "Samuel! Samuel!"

Then Samuel said, "Speak, for your servant is listening."

11And the LORD said to Samuel: "See, I am about to do something in Israel that will make the ears of everyone who hears of it tingle. 12At that time I will carry out against Eli everything I spoke against his family—from beginning to end. 13For I told him that I would judge his family forever because of the sin he knew about; his sons made themselves contemptible,[b] and he failed to restrain them. 14Therefore, I swore to the house of Eli, 'The guilt of Eli's house will never be atoned for by sacrifice or offering.' "

15Samuel lay down until morning and then opened the doors of the house of the LORD. He was afraid to tell Eli the vision, 16but Eli called him and said, "Samuel, my son."

Samuel answered, "Here I am."

17"What was it he said to you?" Eli asked. "Do not hide it from me. May God deal with you, be it ever so severely, if you hide from me anything he told you." 18So Samuel told him everything, hiding nothing from him. Then Eli said, "He is the LORD; let him do what is good in his eyes."

19The LORD was with Samuel as he grew up, and he let none of his words fall to the ground. 20And all Israel from Dan to Beersheba recognized that Samuel was attested as a prophet of the LORD. 21The LORD continued to appear at Shiloh, and there he revealed himself to Samuel through his word.

4 And Samuel's word came to all Israel.

The Philistines Capture the Ark

Now the Israelites went out to fight against the Philistines. The Israelites camped at Ebenezer, and the Philistines at Aphek. 2The Philistines deployed their forces to meet Israel, and as the battle spread, Israel was defeated by the Philistines, who killed about four thousand of them on the battlefield. 3When the soldiers returned to camp, the elders of Israel asked, "Why did the LORD bring defeat upon us today before the Philistines? Let us bring the ark of the LORD's covenant from Shiloh, so that it[c] may go with us and save us from the hand of our enemies."

4So the people sent men to Shiloh, and they brought back the ark of the covenant of the LORD Almighty, who is enthroned between the cherubim. And Eli's two sons, Hophni and Phinehas, were there with the ark of the covenant of God.

5When the ark of the LORD's covenant came into the camp, all Israel raised such a great shout that the ground shook. 6Hearing the uproar, the Philistines asked, "What's all this shouting in the Hebrew camp?"

When they learned that the ark of the LORD had come into the camp, 7the Philistines were afraid. "A god has come into the camp," they said. "We're in trouble! Nothing like this has happened before. 8Woe to us! Who will deliver us from the hand of these mighty gods? They are the gods who struck the Egyptians with all kinds of plagues in the desert. 9Be strong, Philistines! Be men, or you will be subject to the Hebrews, as they have been to you. Be men, and fight!"

10So the Philistines fought, and the Israelites were defeated and every man fled to his tent. The slaughter was very great; Israel lost thirty thousand foot soldiers. 11The ark of God was captured, and Eli's two sons, Hophni and Phinehas, died.

Death of Eli

12That same day a Benjamite ran from the battle line and went to Shiloh, his clothes torn and dust on his head. 13When he arrived, there was Eli sitting on his chair by the side of the road, watching, because his heart feared for the ark of God. When the man entered the town and told what had happened, the whole town sent up a cry.

14Eli heard the outcry and asked, "What is the meaning of this uproar?"

The man hurried over to Eli, 15who was

[a]*3* That is, tabernacle [b]*13* Masoretic Text; an ancient Hebrew scribal tradition and Septuagint *sons blasphemed God* [c]*3* Or *he*

ninety-eight years old and whose eyes were set so that he could not see. 16He told Eli, "I have just come from the battle line; I fled from it this very day."

Eli asked, "What happened, my son?"

17The man who brought the news replied, "Israel fled before the Philistines, and the army has suffered heavy losses. Also your two sons, Hophni and Phinehas, are dead, and the ark of God has been captured."

18When he mentioned the ark of God, Eli fell backward off his chair by the side of the gate. His neck was broken and he died, for he was an old man and heavy. He had led[a] Israel forty years.

19His daughter-in-law, the wife of Phinehas, was pregnant and near the time of delivery. When she heard the news that the ark of God had been captured and that her father-in-law and her husband were dead, she went into labor and gave birth, but was overcome by her labor pains. 20As she was dying, the women attending her said, "Don't despair; you have given birth to a son." But she did not respond or pay any attention.

21She named the boy Ichabod,[b] saying, "The glory has departed from Israel"—because of the capture of the ark of God and the deaths of her father-in-law and her husband. 22She said, "The glory has departed from Israel, for the ark of God has been captured."

The Ark in Ashdod and Ekron

5 After the Philistines had captured the ark of God, they took it from Ebenezer to Ashdod. 2Then they carried the ark into Dagon's temple and set it beside Dagon. 3When the people of Ashdod rose early the next day, there was Dagon, fallen on his face on the ground before the ark of the LORD! They took Dagon and put him back in his place. 4But the following morning when they rose, there was Dagon, fallen on his face on the ground before the ark of the LORD! His head and hands had been broken off and were lying on the threshold; only his body remained. 5That is why to this day neither the priests of Dagon nor any others who enter Dagon's temple at Ashdod step on the threshold.

6The LORD's hand was heavy upon the people of Ashdod and its vicinity; he brought devastation upon them and afflicted them with tumors.[c] 7When the men of Ashdod saw what was happening, they said, "The ark of the god of Israel must not stay here with us, because his hand is heavy upon us and upon Dagon our god." 8So they called together all the rulers of the Philistines and asked them, "What shall we do with the ark of the god of Israel?"

They answered, "Have the ark of the god of Israel moved to Gath." So they moved the ark of the God of Israel.

9But after they had moved it, the LORD's hand was against that city, throwing it into a great panic. He afflicted the people of the city, both young and old, with an outbreak of tumors.[d] 10So they sent the ark of God to Ekron.

As the ark of God was entering Ekron, the people of Ekron cried out, "They have brought the ark of the god of Israel around to us to kill us and our people." 11So they called together all the rulers of the Philistines and said, "Send the ark of the god of Israel away; let it go back to its own place, or it[e] will kill us and our people." For death had filled the city with panic; God's hand was very heavy upon it. 12Those who did not die were afflicted with tumors, and the outcry of the city went up to heaven.

The Ark Returned to Israel

6 When the ark of the LORD had been in Philistine territory seven months, 2the Philistines called for the priests and the diviners and said, "What shall we do with the ark of the LORD? Tell us how we should send it back to its place."

3They answered, "If you return the ark of the god of Israel, do not send it away empty, but by all means send a guilt offering to him. Then you will be healed, and you will know why his hand has not been lifted from you."

4The Philistines asked, "What guilt offering should we send to him?"

They replied, "Five gold tumors and five gold rats, according to the number of the Philistine rulers, because the same plague has struck both you and your rulers. 5Make models of the tumors and of the rats that are destroying the country, and pay honor to Israel's god. Perhaps he will lift his hand from you and your gods and your land. 6Why do you harden your hearts as the Egyptians and Pharaoh did? When he[f] treated them harshly, did they not send the Israelites out so they could go on their way?

7"Now then, get a new cart ready, with two cows that have calved and have never been yoked. Hitch the cows to the cart, but take their calves away and pen them up. 8Take the ark of the LORD and put it on the cart, and in a chest beside it put the gold objects you are sending back to him as a guilt offering. Send it on its way, 9but keep watching it. If it goes up to its own territory, toward Beth Shemesh, then the LORD has brought this great disaster on us. But if it does not, then we will know that it was not his hand that struck us and that it happened to us by chance."

10So they did this. They took two such cows and hitched them to the cart and penned up their calves. 11They placed the ark of the LORD on the cart and along with it the chest containing the gold rats and the models of the tumors. 12Then the cows went straight up toward Beth Shemesh, keeping on the road and lowing all

[a]*18* Traditionally *judged* [b]*21* *Ichabod* means *no glory.* [c]*6* Hebrew; Septuagint and Vulgate *tumors. And rats appeared in their land, and death and destruction were throughout the city* [d]*9* Or *with tumors in the groin* (see Septuagint) [e]*11* Or *he* [f]*6* That is, God

the way; they did not turn to the right or to the
left. The rulers of the Philistines followed them
as far as the border of Beth Shemesh.

13Now the people of Beth Shemesh were
harvesting their wheat in the valley, and when
they looked up and saw the ark, they rejoiced
at the sight. 14The cart came to the field of
Joshua of Beth Shemesh, and there it stopped
beside a large rock. The people chopped up the
wood of the cart and sacrificed the cows as a
burnt offering to the LORD. 15The Levites took
down the ark of the LORD, together with the
chest containing the gold objects, and placed
them on the large rock. On that day the people
of Beth Shemesh offered burnt offerings and
made sacrifices to the LORD. 16The five rulers
of the Philistines saw all this and then returned
that same day to Ekron.

17These are the gold tumors the Philistines
sent as a guilt offering to the LORD—one each
for Ashdod, Gaza, Ashkelon, Gath and Ekron.
18And the number of the gold rats was according to the number of Philistine towns belonging to the five rulers—the fortified towns with
their country villages. The large rock, on
which[a] they set the ark of the LORD, is a witness to this day in the field of Joshua of Beth
Shemesh.

19But God struck down some of the men of
Beth Shemesh, putting seventy[b] of them to
death because they had looked into the ark of
the LORD. The people mourned because of the
heavy blow the LORD had dealt them, 20and the
men of Beth Shemesh asked, "Who can stand
in the presence of the LORD, this holy God? To
whom will the ark go up from here?"

21Then they sent messengers to the people
of Kiriath Jearim, saying, "The Philistines
have returned the ark of the LORD. Come down
7 and take it up to your place." 1So the men
of Kiriath Jearim came and took up the ark
of the LORD. They took it to Abinadab's house
on the hill and consecrated Eleazar his son to
guard the ark of the LORD.

Samuel Subdues the Philistines at Mizpah

2It was a long time, twenty years in all, that
the ark remained at Kiriath Jearim, and all the
people of Israel mourned and sought after the
LORD. 3And Samuel said to the whole house of
Israel, "If you are returning to the LORD with
all your hearts, then rid yourselves of the foreign gods and the Ashtoreths and commit
yourselves to the LORD and serve him only,
and he will deliver you out of the hand of the
Philistines." 4So the Israelites put away their
Baals and Ashtoreths, and served the LORD
only.

5Then Samuel said, "Assemble all Israel at
Mizpah and I will intercede with the LORD for
you." 6When they had assembled at Mizpah,
they drew water and poured it out before the
LORD. On that day they fasted and there they
confessed, "We have sinned against the
LORD." And Samuel was leader[c] of Israel at
Mizpah.

7When the Philistines heard that Israel had
assembled at Mizpah, the rulers of the Philistines came up to attack them. And when the
Israelites heard of it, they were afraid because
of the Philistines. 8They said to Samuel, "Do
not stop crying out to the LORD our God for us,
that he may rescue us from the hand of the
Philistines." 9Then Samuel took a suckling
lamb and offered it up as a whole burnt offering to the LORD. He cried out to the LORD on
Israel's behalf, and the LORD answered him.

10While Samuel was sacrificing the burnt
offering, the Philistines drew near to engage
Israel in battle. But that day the LORD thundered with loud thunder against the Philistines
and threw them into such a panic that they
were routed before the Israelites. 11The men of
Israel rushed out of Mizpah and pursued the
Philistines, slaughtering them along the way to
a point below Beth Car.

12Then Samuel took a stone and set it up
between Mizpah and Shen. He named it Ebenezer,[d] saying, "Thus far has the LORD helped
us." 13So the Philistines were subdued and did
not invade Israelite territory again.

Throughout Samuel's lifetime, the hand of
the LORD was against the Philistines. 14The
towns from Ekron to Gath that the Philistines
had captured from Israel were restored to her,
and Israel delivered the neighboring territory
from the power of the Philistines. And there
was peace between Israel and the Amorites.

15Samuel continued as judge over Israel all
the days of his life. 16From year to year he
went on a circuit from Bethel to Gilgal to Mizpah, judging Israel in all those places. 17But he
always went back to Ramah, where his home
was, and there he also judged Israel. And he
built an altar there to the LORD.

Israel Asks for a King

8 When Samuel grew old, he appointed his
sons as judges for Israel. 2The name of his
firstborn was Joel and the name of his second
was Abijah, and they served at Beersheba.
3But his sons did not walk in his ways. They
turned aside after dishonest gain and accepted
bribes and perverted justice.

4So all the elders of Israel gathered together
and came to Samuel at Ramah. 5They said to
him, "You are old, and your sons do not walk
in your ways; now appoint a king to lead[e] us,
such as all the other nations have."

6But when they said, "Give us a king to lead
us," this displeased Samuel; so he prayed to
the LORD. 7And the LORD told him: "Listen to
all that the people are saying to you; it is not
you they have rejected, but they have rejected
me as their king. 8As they have done from the

[a] *18* A few Hebrew manuscripts (see also Septuagint); most Hebrew manuscripts *villages as far as Greater Abel, where* [b] *19* A few Hebrew manuscripts; most Hebrew manuscripts and Septuagint *50,070*
[c] *6* Traditionally *judge* [d] *12* *Ebenezer* means *stone of help.* [e] *5* Traditionally *judge*; also in verses 6 and 20

day I brought them up out of Egypt until this day, forsaking me and serving other gods, so they are doing to you. 9Now listen to them; but warn them solemnly and let them know what the king who will reign over them will do."

10Samuel told all the words of the LORD to the people who were asking him for a king. 11He said, "This is what the king who will reign over you will do: He will take your sons and make them serve with his chariots and horses, and they will run in front of his chariots. 12Some he will assign to be commanders of thousands and commanders of fifties, and others to plow his ground and reap his harvest, and still others to make weapons of war and equipment for his chariots. 13He will take your daughters to be perfumers and cooks and bakers. 14He will take the best of your fields and vineyards and olive groves and give them to his attendants. 15He will take a tenth of your grain and of your vintage and give it to his officials and attendants. 16Your menservants and maidservants and the best of your cattle[a] and donkeys he will take for his own use. 17He will take a tenth of your flocks, and you yourselves will become his slaves. 18When that day comes, you will cry out for relief from the king you have chosen, and the LORD will not answer you in that day."

19But the people refused to listen to Samuel. "No!" they said. "We want a king over us. 20Then we will be like all the other nations, with a king to lead us and to go out before us and fight our battles."

21When Samuel heard all that the people said, he repeated it before the LORD. 22The LORD answered, "Listen to them and give them a king.'

Then Samuel said to the men of Israel, "Everyone go back to his town."

Samuel Anoints Saul

9 There was a Benjamite, a man of standing, whose name was Kish son of Abiel, the son of Zeror, the son of Becorath, the son of Aphiah of Benjamin. 2He had a son named Saul, an impressive young man without equal among the Israelites—a head taller than any of the others.

3Now the donkeys belonging to Saul's father Kish were lost, and Kish said to his son Saul, "Take one of the servants with you and go and look for the donkeys." 4So he passed through the hill country of Ephraim and through the area around Shalisha, but they did not find them. They went on into the district of Shaalim, but the donkeys were not there. Then he passed through the territory of Benjamin, but they did not find them.

5When they reached the district of Zuph, Saul said to the servant who was with him, "Come, let's go back, or my father will stop thinking about the donkeys and start worrying about us."

6But the servant replied, "Look, in this town there is a man of God; he is highly respected, and everything he says comes true. Let's go there now. Perhaps he will tell us what way to take."

7Saul said to his servant, "If we go, what can we give the man? The food in our sacks is gone. We have no gift to take to the man of God. What do we have?"

8The servant answered him again. "Look," he said, "I have a quarter of a shekel[b] of silver. I will give it to the man of God so that he will tell us what way to take." 9(Formerly in Israel, if a man went to inquire of God, he would say, "Come, let us go to the seer," because the prophet of today used to be called a seer.)

10"Good," Saul said to his servant. "Come, let's go." So they set out for the town where the man of God was.

11As they were going up the hill to the town, they met some girls coming out to draw water, and they asked them, "Is the seer here?"

12"He is," they answered. "He's ahead of you. Hurry now; he has just come to our town today, for the people have a sacrifice at the high place. 13As soon as you enter the town, you will find him before he goes up to the high place to eat. The people will not begin eating until he comes, because he must bless the sacrifice; afterward, those who are invited will eat. Go up now; you should find him about this time."

14They went up to the town, and as they were entering it, there was Samuel, coming toward them on his way up to the high place.

15Now the day before Saul came, the LORD had revealed this to Samuel: 16"About this time tomorrow I will send you a man from the land of Benjamin. Anoint him leader over my people Israel; he will deliver my people from the hand of the Philistines. I have looked upon my people, for their cry has reached me."

17When Samuel caught sight of Saul, the LORD said to him, "This is the man I spoke to you about; he will govern my people."

18Saul approached Samuel in the gateway and asked, "Would you please tell me where the seer's house is?"

19"I am the seer," Samuel replied. "Go up ahead of me to the high place, for today you are to eat with me, and in the morning I will let you go and will tell you all that is in your heart. 20As for the donkeys you lost three days ago, do not worry about them; they have been found. And to whom is all the desire of Israel turned, if not to you and all your father's family?"

21Saul answered, "But am I not a Benjamite, from the smallest tribe of Israel, and is not my clan the least of all the clans of the tribe of Benjamin? Why do you say such a thing to me?"

22Then Samuel brought Saul and his servant into the hall and seated them at the head of

[a] *16* Septuagint; Hebrew *young men* [b] *8* That is, about 1/10 ounce (about 3 grams)

those who were invited—about thirty in number. 23Samuel said to the cook, "Bring the
piece of meat I gave you, the one I told you to
lay aside."
24So the cook took up the leg with what was
on it and set it in front of Saul. Samuel said,
"Here is what has been kept for you. Eat, because it was set aside for you for this occasion,
from the time I said, 'I have invited guests.' "
And Saul dined with Samuel that day.
25After they came down from the high place
to the town, Samuel talked with Saul on the
roof of his house. 26They rose about daybreak
and Samuel called to Saul on the roof, "Get
ready, and I will send you on your way." When
Saul got ready, he and Samuel went outside
together. 27As they were going down to the
edge of the town, Samuel said to Saul, "Tell
the servant to go on ahead of us"—and the
servant did so—"but you stay here awhile, so
that I may give you a message from God."
10 Then Samuel took a flask of oil and
poured it on Saul's head and kissed him,
saying, "Has not the LORD anointed you leader
over his inheritance?[a] 2When you leave me
today, you will meet two men near Rachel's
tomb, at Zelzah on the border of Benjamin.
They will say to you, 'The donkeys you set out
to look for have been found. And now your
father has stopped thinking about them and is
worried about you. He is asking, "What shall I
do about my son?" '
3"Then you will go on from there until you
reach the great tree of Tabor. Three men going
up to God at Bethel will meet you there. One
will be carrying three young goats, another
three loaves of bread, and another a skin of
wine. 4They will greet you and offer you two
loaves of bread, which you will accept from
them.
5"After that you will go to Gibeah of God,
where there is a Philistine outpost. As you approach the town, you will meet a procession of
prophets coming down from the high place
with lyres, tambourines, flutes and harps being
played before them, and they will be prophesying. 6The Spirit of the LORD will come upon
you in power, and you will prophesy with
them; and you will be changed into a different
person. 7Once these signs are fulfilled, do
whatever your hand finds to do, for God is
with you.
8"Go down ahead of me to Gilgal. I will
surely come down to you to sacrifice burnt
offerings and fellowship offerings,[b] but you
must wait seven days until I come to you and
tell you what you are to do."

Saul Made King

9As Saul turned to leave Samuel, God
changed Saul's heart, and all these signs were
fulfilled that day. 10When they arrived at Gibeah, a procession of prophets met him; the Spirit
of God came upon him in power, and he joined
in their prophesying. 11When all those who
had formerly known him saw him prophesying
with the prophets, they asked each other,
"What is this that has happened to the son of
Kish? Is Saul also among the prophets?"
12A man who lived there answered, "And
who is their father?" So it became a saying: "Is
Saul also among the prophets?" 13After Saul
stopped prophesying, he went to the high
place.
14Now Saul's uncle asked him and his servant, "Where have you been?"
"Looking for the donkeys," he said. "But
when we saw they were not to be found, we
went to Samuel."
15Saul's uncle said, "Tell me what Samuel
said to you."
16Saul replied, "He assured us that the donkeys had been found." But he did not tell his
uncle what Samuel had said about the kingship.
17Samuel summoned the people of Israel to
the LORD at Mizpah 18and said to them, "This
is what the LORD, the God of Israel, says: 'I
brought Israel up out of Egypt, and I delivered
you from the power of Egypt and all the kingdoms that oppressed you.' 19But you have now
rejected your God, who saves you out of all
your calamities and distresses. And you have
said, 'No, set a king over us.' So now present
yourselves before the LORD by your tribes and
clans."
20When Samuel brought all the tribes of Israel near, the tribe of Benjamin was chosen.
21Then he brought forward the tribe of Benjamin, clan by clan, and Matri's clan was chosen. Finally Saul son of Kish was chosen. But
when they looked for him, he was not to be
found. 22So they inquired further of the LORD,
"Has the man come here yet?"
And the LORD said, "Yes, he has hidden
himself among the baggage."
23They ran and brought him out, and as he
stood among the people he was a head taller
than any of the others. 24Samuel said to all the
people, "Do you see the man the LORD has
chosen? There is no one like him among all the
people."
Then the people shouted, "Long live the
king!"
25Samuel explained to the people the regulations of the kingship. He wrote them down on
a scroll and deposited it before the LORD. Then
Samuel dismissed the people, each to his own
home.
26Saul also went to his home in Gibeah, accompanied by valiant men whose hearts God
had touched. 27But some troublemakers said,
"How can this fellow save us?" They despised
him and brought him no gifts. But Saul kept
silent.

[a] *1* Hebrew; Septuagint and Vulgate *over his people Israel? You will reign over the LORD's people and save them from the power of their enemies round about. And this will be a sign to you that the LORD has anointed you leader over his inheritance:* [b] *8* Traditionally *peace offerings*

Saul Rescues the City of Jabesh

11 Nahash the Ammonite went up and besieged Jabesh Gilead. And all the men
of Jabesh said to him, "Make a treaty with us,
and we will be subject to you."
2But Nahash the Ammonite replied, "I will
make a treaty with you only on the condition
that I gouge out the right eye of every one of
you and so bring disgrace on all Israel."
3The elders of Jabesh said to him, "Give
us seven days so we can send messengers
throughout Israel; if no one comes to rescue us,
we will surrender to you."
4When the messengers came to Gibeah of
Saul and reported these terms to the people,
they all wept aloud. 5Just then Saul was returning from the fields, behind his oxen, and he
asked, "What is wrong with the people? Why
are they weeping?" Then they repeated to him
what the men of Jabesh had said.
6When Saul heard their words, the Spirit of
God came upon him in power, and he burned
with anger. 7He took a pair of oxen, cut them
into pieces, and sent the pieces by messengers
throughout Israel, proclaiming, "This is what
will be done to the oxen of anyone who does
not follow Saul and Samuel." Then the terror
of the LORD fell on the people, and they turned
out as one man. 8When Saul mustered them at
Bezek, the men of Israel numbered three hundred thousand and the men of Judah thirty
thousand.
9They told the messengers who had come,
"Say to the men of Jabesh Gilead, 'By the time
the sun is hot tomorrow, you will be delivered.' " When the messengers went and reported this to the men of Jabesh, they were elated.
10They said to the Ammonites, "Tomorrow we
will surrender to you, and you can do to us
whatever seems good to you."
11The next day Saul separated his men into
three divisions; during the last watch of the
night they broke into the camp of the Ammonites and slaughtered them until the heat of the
day. Those who survived were scattered, so
that no two of them were left together.

Saul Confirmed as King

12The people then said to Samuel, "Who
was it that asked, 'Shall Saul reign over us?'
Bring these men to us and we will put them to
death."
13But Saul said, "No one shall be put to
death today, for this day the LORD has rescued
Israel."
14Then Samuel said to the people, "Come,
let us go to Gilgal and there reaffirm the kingship." 15So all the people went to Gilgal and
confirmed Saul as king in the presence of the
LORD. There they sacrificed fellowship offerings[a] before the LORD, and Saul and all the
Israelites held a great celebration.

Samuel's Farewell Speech

12 Samuel said to all Israel, "I have listened to everything you said to me and
have set a king over you. 2Now you have a
king as your leader. As for me, I am old and
gray, and my sons are here with you. I have
been your leader from my youth until this day.
3Here I stand. Testify against me in the presence of the LORD and his anointed. Whose ox
have I taken? Whose donkey have I taken?
Whom have I cheated? Whom have I oppressed? From whose hand have I accepted a
bribe to make me shut my eyes? If I have done
any of these, I will make it right."
4"You have not cheated or oppressed us,"
they replied. "You have not taken anything
from anyone's hand."
5Samuel said to them, "The LORD is witness
against you, and also his anointed is witness
this day, that you have not found anything in
my hand."
"He is witness," they said.
6Then Samuel said to the people, "It is the
LORD who appointed Moses and Aaron and
brought your forefathers up out of Egypt.
7Now then, stand here, because I am going to
confront you with evidence before the LORD as
to all the righteous acts performed by the LORD
for you and your fathers.
8"After Jacob entered Egypt, they cried to
the LORD for help, and the LORD sent Moses
and Aaron, who brought your forefathers out
of Egypt and settled them in this place.
9"But they forgot the LORD their God; so he
sold them into the hand of Sisera, the commander of the army of Hazor, and into the
hands of the Philistines and the king of Moab,
who fought against them. 10They cried out to
the LORD and said, 'We have sinned; we have
forsaken the LORD and served the Baals and
the Ashtoreths. But now deliver us from the
hands of our enemies, and we will serve you.'
11Then the LORD sent Jerub-Baal,[b] Barak,[c]
Jephthah and Samuel,[d] and he delivered you
from the hands of your enemies on every side,
so that you lived securely.
12"But when you saw that Nahash king of
the Ammonites was moving against you, you
said to me, 'No, we want a king to rule over
us'—even though the LORD your God was
your king. 13Now here is the king you have
chosen, the one you asked for; see, the LORD
has set a king over you. 14If you fear the LORD
and serve and obey him and do not rebel
against his commands, and if both you and the
king who reigns over you follow the LORD
your God—good! 15But if you do not obey the
LORD, and if you rebel against his commands,
his hand will be against you, as it was against
your fathers.
16"Now then, stand still and see this great
thing the LORD is about to do before your eyes!
17Is it not wheat harvest now? I will call upon
the LORD to send thunder and rain. And you

[a] *15* Traditionally *peace offerings* [b] *11* Also called *Gideon* [c] *11* Some Septuagint manuscripts and Syriac; Hebrew *Bedan* [d] *11* Hebrew; some Septuagint manuscripts and Syriac *Samson*

will realize what an evil thing you did in the eyes of the LORD when you asked for a king."

18Then Samuel called upon the LORD, and that same day the LORD sent thunder and rain. So all the people stood in awe of the LORD and of Samuel.

19The people all said to Samuel, "Pray to the LORD your God for your servants so that we will not die, for we have added to all our other sins the evil of asking for a king."

20"Do not be afraid," Samuel replied. "You have done all this evil; yet do not turn away from the LORD, but serve the LORD with all your heart. 21Do not turn away after useless idols. They can do you no good, nor can they rescue you, because they are useless. 22For the sake of his great name the LORD will not reject his people, because the LORD was pleased to make you his own. 23As for me, far be it from me that I should sin against the LORD by failing to pray for you. And I will teach you the way that is good and right. 24But be sure to fear the LORD and serve him faithfully with all your heart; consider what great things he has done for you. 25Yet if you persist in doing evil, both you and your king will be swept away."

Samuel Rebukes Saul

13 Saul was ⌊thirty⌋[a] years old when he became king, and he reigned over Israel ⌊forty-⌋[b] two years.

2Saul[c] chose three thousand men from Israel; two thousand were with him at Micmash and in the hill country of Bethel, and a thousand were with Jonathan at Gibeah in Benjamin. The rest of the men he sent back to their homes.

3Jonathan attacked the Philistine outpost at Geba, and the Philistines heard about it. Then Saul had the trumpet blown throughout the land and said, "Let the Hebrews hear!" 4So all Israel heard the news: "Saul has attacked the Philistine outpost, and now Israel has become a stench to the Philistines." And the people were summoned to join Saul at Gilgal.

5The Philistines assembled to fight Israel, with three thousand[d] chariots, six thousand charioteers, and soldiers as numerous as the sand on the seashore. They went up and camped at Micmash, east of Beth Aven. 6When the men of Israel saw that their situation was critical and that their army was hard pressed, they hid in caves and thickets, among the rocks, and in pits and cisterns. 7Some Hebrews even crossed the Jordan to the land of Gad and Gilead.

Saul remained at Gilgal, and all the troops with him were quaking with fear. 8He waited seven days, the time set by Samuel; but Samuel did not come to Gilgal, and Saul's men began to scatter. 9So he said, "Bring me the burnt offering and the fellowship offerings.[e]" And Saul offered up the burnt offering. 10Just as he finished making the offering, Samuel arrived, and Saul went out to greet him.

11"What have you done?" asked Samuel.

Saul replied, "When I saw that the men were scattering, and that you did not come at the set time, and that the Philistines were assembling at Micmash, 12I thought, 'Now the Philistines will come down against me at Gilgal, and I have not sought the LORD's favor.' So I felt compelled to offer the burnt offering."

13"You acted foolishly," Samuel said. "You have not kept the command the LORD your God gave you; if you had, he would have established your kingdom over Israel for all time. 14But now your kingdom will not endure; the LORD has sought out a man after his own heart and appointed him leader of his people, because you have not kept the LORD's command."

15Then Samuel left Gilgal[f] and went up to Gibeah in Benjamin, and Saul counted the men who were with him. They numbered about six hundred.

Israel Without Weapons

16Saul and his son Jonathan and the men with them were staying in Gibeah[g] in Benjamin, while the Philistines camped at Micmash. 17Raiding parties went out from the Philistine camp in three detachments. One turned toward Ophrah in the vicinity of Shual, 18another toward Beth Horon, and the third toward the borderland overlooking the Valley of Zeboim facing the desert.

19Not a blacksmith could be found in the whole land of Israel, because the Philistines had said, "Otherwise the Hebrews will make swords or spears!" 20So all Israel went down to the Philistines to have their plowshares, mattocks, axes and sickles[h] sharpened. 21The price was two thirds of a shekel[i] for sharpening plowshares and mattocks, and a third of a shekel[j] for sharpening forks and axes and for repointing goads.

22So on the day of the battle not a soldier with Saul and Jonathan had a sword or spear in his hand; only Saul and his son Jonathan had them.

Jonathan Attacks the Philistines

23Now a detachment of Philistines had gone out to the pass at Micmash.

14 1One day Jonathan son of Saul said to the young man bearing his armor, "Come, let's go over to the Philistine outpost on the other side." But he did not tell his father.

2Saul was staying on the outskirts of Gibeah

[a]*1* A few late manuscripts of the Septuagint; Hebrew does not have *thirty.* [b]*1* See the round number in Acts 13:21; Hebrew does not have *forty-.* [c]*1,2* Or *and when he had reigned over Israel two years, 2he*
[d]*5* Some Septuagint manuscripts and Syriac; Hebrew *thirty thousand* [e]*9* Traditionally *peace offerings*
[f]*15* Hebrew; Septuagint *Gilgal and went his way; the rest of the people went after Saul to meet the army, and they went out of Gilgal* [g]*16* Two Hebrew manuscripts; most Hebrew manuscripts *Geba,* a variant of *Gibeah*
[h]*20* Septuagint; Hebrew *plowshares* [i]*21* Hebrew *pim*; that is, about 1/4 ounce (about 8 grams) [j]*21* That is, about 1/8 ounce (about 4 grams)

under a pomegranate tree in Migron. With him
were about six hundred men, 3among whom
was Ahijah, who was wearing an ephod. He
was a son of Ichabod's brother Ahitub son of
Phinehas, the son of Eli, the LORD's priest in
Shiloh. No one was aware that Jonathan had
left.
4On each side of the pass that Jonathan intended to cross to reach the Philistine outpost
was a cliff; one was called Bozez, and the other Seneh. 5One cliff stood to the north toward
Micmash, the other to the south toward Geba.
6Jonathan said to his young armor-bearer,
"Come, let's go over to the outpost of those
uncircumcised fellows. Perhaps the LORD will
act in our behalf. Nothing can hinder the LORD
from saving, whether by many or by few."
7"Do all that you have in mind," his armor-
bearer said. "Go ahead; I am with you heart
and soul."
8Jonathan said, "Come, then; we will cross
over toward the men and let them see us. 9If
they say to us, 'Wait there until we come to
you,' we will stay where we are and not go up
to them. 10But if they say, 'Come up to us,' we
will climb up, because that will be our sign that
the LORD has given them into our hands."
11So both of them showed themselves to the
Philistine outpost. "Look!" said the Philistines.
"The Hebrews are crawling out of the holes
they were hiding in." 12The men of the outpost
shouted to Jonathan and his armor-bearer,
"Come up to us and we'll teach you a lesson."
So Jonathan said to his armor-bearer,
"Climb up after me; the LORD has given them
into the hand of Israel."
13Jonathan climbed up, using his hands and
feet, with his armor-bearer right behind him.
The Philistines fell before Jonathan, and his
armor-bearer followed and killed behind him.
14In that first attack Jonathan and his armor-
bearer killed some twenty men in an area of
about half an acre.[a]

Israel Routs the Philistines

15Then panic struck the whole army—those
in the camp and field, and those in the outposts
and raiding parties—and the ground shook. It
was a panic sent by God.[b]
16Saul's lookouts at Gibeah in Benjamin
saw the army melting away in all directions.
17Then Saul said to the men who were with
him, "Muster the forces and see who has left
us." When they did, it was Jonathan and his
armor-bearer who were not there.
18Saul said to Ahijah, "Bring the ark of
God." (At that time it was with the Israelites.)[c]
19While Saul was talking to the priest, the tumult in the Philistine camp increased more and
more. So Saul said to the priest, "Withdraw
your hand."
20Then Saul and all his men assembled and
went to the battle. They found the Philistines in
total confusion, striking each other with their
swords. 21Those Hebrews who had previously
been with the Philistines and had gone up with
them to their camp went over to the Israelites
who were with Saul and Jonathan. 22When all
the Israelites who had hidden in the hill country of Ephraim heard that the Philistines were
on the run, they joined the battle in hot pursuit.
23So the LORD rescued Israel that day, and the
battle moved on beyond Beth Aven.

Jonathan Eats Honey

24Now the men of Israel were in distress that
day, because Saul had bound the people under
an oath, saying, "Cursed be any man who eats
food before evening comes, before I have
avenged myself on my enemies!" So none of
the troops tasted food.
25The entire army[d] entered the woods, and
there was honey on the ground. 26When they
went into the woods, they saw the honey ooz-
ing out, yet no one put his hand to his mouth,
because they feared the oath. 27But Jonathan
had not heard that his father had bound the
people with the oath, so he reached out the end
of the staff that was in his hand and dipped it
into the honeycomb. He raised his hand to his
mouth, and his eyes brightened.[e] 28Then one
of the soldiers told him, "Your father bound
the army under a strict oath, saying, 'Cursed be
any man who eats food today!' That is why the
men are faint."
29Jonathan said, "My father has made trouble for the country. See how my eyes brightened[f] when I tasted a little of this honey.
30How much better it would have been if the
men had eaten today some of the plunder they
took from their enemies. Would not the
slaughter of the Philistines have been even
greater?"
31That day, after the Israelites had struck
down the Philistines from Micmash to Aijalon,
they were exhausted. 32They pounced on the
plunder and, taking sheep, cattle and calves,
they butchered them on the ground and ate
them, together with the blood. 33Then someone
said to Saul, "Look, the men are sinning
against the LORD by eating meat that has blood
in it."
"You have broken faith," he said. "Roll a
large stone over here at once." 34Then he said,
"Go out among the men and tell them, 'Each
of you bring me your cattle and sheep, and
slaughter them here and eat them. Do not sin
against the LORD by eating meat with blood
still in it.' "
So everyone brought his ox that night and
slaughtered it there. 35Then Saul built an altar
to the LORD; it was the first time he had done
this.
36Saul said, "Let us go down after the Philistines by night and plunder them till dawn, and
let us not leave one of them alive."

[a] *14* Hebrew *half a yoke*; a "yoke" was the land plowed by a yoke of oxen in one day. [b] *15* Or *a terrible panic* [c] *18* Hebrew; Septuagint *"Bring the ephod." (At that time he wore the ephod before the Israelites.)* [d] *25* Or *Now all the people of the land* [e] *27* Or *his strength was renewed* [f] *29* Or *my strength was renewed*

"Do whatever seems best to you," they replied.
But the priest said, "Let us inquire of God
here."
37 So Saul asked God, "Shall I go down after
the Philistines? Will you give them into Israel's hand?" But God did not answer him that
day.
38 Saul therefore said, "Come here, all you
who are leaders of the army, and let us find out
what sin has been committed today. 39 As surely as the LORD who rescues Israel lives, even
if it lies with my son Jonathan, he must die."
But not one of the men said a word.
40 Saul then said to all the Israelites, "You
stand over there; I and Jonathan my son will
stand over here."
"Do what seems best to you," the men replied.
41 Then Saul prayed to the LORD, the God of
Israel, "Give me the right answer."[a] And Jonathan and Saul were taken by lot, and the men
were cleared. 42 Saul said, "Cast the lot between me and Jonathan my son." And Jonathan was taken.
43 Then Saul said to Jonathan, "Tell me what
you have done."
So Jonathan told him, "I merely tasted a
little honey with the end of my staff. And now
must I die?"
44 Saul said, "May God deal with me, be it
ever so severely, if you do not die, Jonathan."
45 But the men said to Saul, "Should Jonathan die—he who has brought about this great
deliverance in Israel? Never! As surely as the
LORD lives, not a hair of his head will fall to
the ground, for he did this today with God's
help." So the men rescued Jonathan, and he
was not put to death.
46 Then Saul stopped pursuing the Philistines, and they withdrew to their own land.
47 After Saul had assumed rule over Israel,
he fought against their enemies on every side:
Moab, the Ammonites, Edom, the kings[b] of
Zobah, and the Philistines. Wherever he
turned, he inflicted punishment on them.[c]
48 He fought valiantly and defeated the Amalekites, delivering Israel from the hands of
those who had plundered them.

Saul's Family

49 Saul's sons were Jonathan, Ishvi and
Malki-Shua. The name of his older daughter
was Merab, and that of the younger was Michal. 50 His wife's name was Ahinoam daughter of Ahimaaz. The name of the commander
of Saul's army was Abner son of Ner, and Ner
was Saul's uncle. 51 Saul's father Kish and Abner's father Ner were sons of Abiel.
52 All the days of Saul there was bitter war
with the Philistines, and whenever Saul saw a
mighty or brave man, he took him into his
service.

The LORD Rejects Saul as King

15 Samuel said to Saul, "I am the one the
LORD sent to anoint you king over his
people Israel; so listen now to the message
from the LORD. 2 This is what the LORD Almighty says: 'I will punish the Amalekites for
what they did to Israel when they waylaid
them as they came up from Egypt. 3 Now go,
attack the Amalekites and totally destroy[d] everything that belongs to them. Do not spare
them; put to death men and women, children
and infants, cattle and sheep, camels and donkeys.' "
4 So Saul summoned the men and mustered
them at Telaim—two hundred thousand foot
soldiers and ten thousand men from Judah.
5 Saul went to the city of Amalek and set an
ambush in the ravine. 6 Then he said to the
Kenites, "Go away, leave the Amalekites so
that I do not destroy you along with them; for
you showed kindness to all the Israelites when
they came up out of Egypt." So the Kenites
moved away from the Amalekites.
7 Then Saul attacked the Amalekites all the
way from Havilah to Shur, to the east of Egypt.
8 He took Agag king of the Amalekites alive,
and all his people he totally destroyed with the
sword. 9 But Saul and the army spared Agag
and the best of the sheep and cattle, the fat
calves[e] and lambs—everything that was good.
These they were unwilling to destroy completely, but everything that was despised and
weak they totally destroyed.
10 Then the word of the LORD came to Samuel: 11 "I am grieved that I have made Saul
king, because he has turned away from me and
has not carried out my instructions." Samuel
was troubled, and he cried out to the LORD all
that night.
12 Early in the morning Samuel got up and
went to meet Saul, but he was told, "Saul has
gone to Carmel. There he has set up a monument in his own honor and has turned and gone
on down to Gilgal."
13 When Samuel reached him, Saul said,
"The LORD bless you! I have carried out the
LORD's instructions."
14 But Samuel said, "What then is this bleat-
ing of sheep in my ears? What is this lowing of
cattle that I hear?"
15 Saul answered, "The soldiers brought
them from the Amalekites; they spared the best
of the sheep and cattle to sacrifice to the LORD
your God, but we totally destroyed the rest."
16 "Stop!" Samuel said to Saul. "Let me tell
you what the LORD said to me last night."
"Tell me," Saul replied.
17 Samuel said, "Although you were once

[a] *41* Hebrew; Septuagint *"Why have you not answered your servant today? If the fault is in me or my son Jonathan, respond with Urim, but if the men of Israel are at fault, respond with Thummim."* [b] *47* Masoretic Text; Dead Sea Scrolls and Septuagint *king* [c] *47* Hebrew; Septuagint *he was victorious* [d] *3* The Hebrew term refers to the irrevocable giving over of things or persons to the LORD, often by totally destroying them; also in verses 8, 9, 15, 18, 20 and 21. [e] *9* Or *the grown bulls*; the meaning of the Hebrew for this phrase is uncertain.

small in your own eyes, did you not become the head of the tribes of Israel? The LORD anointed you king over Israel. 18And he sent you on a mission, saying, 'Go and completely destroy those wicked people, the Amalekites; make war on them until you have wiped them out.' 19Why did you not obey the LORD? Why did you pounce on the plunder and do evil in the eyes of the LORD?"

20"But I did obey the LORD," Saul said. "I went on the mission the LORD assigned me. I completely destroyed the Amalekites and brought back Agag their king. 21The soldiers took sheep and cattle from the plunder, the best of what was devoted to God, in order to sacrifice them to the LORD your God at Gilgal."

22But Samuel replied:

"Does the LORD delight in burnt offerings
and sacrifices
as much as in obeying the voice of the
LORD?
To obey is better than sacrifice,
and to heed is better than the fat of
rams.
23For rebellion is like the sin of divination,
and arrogance like the evil of idolatry.
Because you have rejected the word of the
LORD,
he has rejected you as king."

24Then Saul said to Samuel, "I have sinned. I violated the LORD's command and your instructions. I was afraid of the people and so I gave in to them. 25Now I beg you, forgive my sin and come back with me, so that I may worship the LORD."

26But Samuel said to him, "I will not go back with you. You have rejected the word of the LORD, and the LORD has rejected you as king over Israel!"

27As Samuel turned to leave, Saul caught hold of the hem of his robe, and it tore. 28Samuel said to him, "The LORD has torn the kingdom of Israel from you today and has given it to one of your neighbors—to one better than you. 29He who is the Glory of Israel does not lie or change his mind; for he is not a man, that he should change his mind."

30Saul replied, "I have sinned. But please honor me before the elders of my people and before Israel; come back with me, so that I may worship the LORD your God." 31So Samuel went back with Saul, and Saul worshiped the LORD.

32Then Samuel said, "Bring me Agag king of the Amalekites."

Agag came to him confidently,[a] thinking, "Surely the bitterness of death is past."

33But Samuel said,

"As your sword has made women
childless,
so will your mother be childless among
women."

And Samuel put Agag to death before the LORD at Gilgal.

34Then Samuel left for Ramah, but Saul went up to his home in Gibeah of Saul. 35Until the day Samuel died, he did not go to see Saul again, though Samuel mourned for him. And the LORD was grieved that he had made Saul king over Israel.

Samuel Anoints David

16 The LORD said to Samuel, "How long will you mourn for Saul, since I have rejected him as king over Israel? Fill your horn with oil and be on your way; I am sending you to Jesse of Bethlehem. I have chosen one of his sons to be king."

2But Samuel said, "How can I go? Saul will hear about it and kill me."

The LORD said, "Take a heifer with you and say, 'I have come to sacrifice to the LORD.' 3Invite Jesse to the sacrifice, and I will show you what to do. You are to anoint for me the one I indicate."

4Samuel did what the LORD said. When he arrived at Bethlehem, the elders of the town trembled when they met him. They asked, "Do you come in peace?"

5Samuel replied, "Yes, in peace; I have come to sacrifice to the LORD. Consecrate yourselves and come to the sacrifice with me." Then he consecrated Jesse and his sons and invited them to the sacrifice.

6When they arrived, Samuel saw Eliab and thought, "Surely the LORD's anointed stands here before the LORD."

7But the LORD said to Samuel, "Do not consider his appearance or his height, for I have rejected him. The LORD does not look at the things man looks at. Man looks at the outward appearance, but the LORD looks at the heart."

8Then Jesse called Abinadab and had him pass in front of Samuel. But Samuel said, "The LORD has not chosen this one either." 9Jesse then had Shammah pass by, but Samuel said, "Nor has the LORD chosen this one." 10Jesse had seven of his sons pass before Samuel, but Samuel said to him, "The LORD has not chosen these." 11So he asked Jesse, "Are these all the sons you have?"

"There is still the youngest," Jesse answered, "but he is tending the sheep."

Samuel said, "Send for him; we will not sit down[b] until he arrives."

12So he sent and had him brought in. He was ruddy, with a fine appearance and handsome features.

Then the LORD said, "Rise and anoint him; he is the one."

13So Samuel took the horn of oil and anointed him in the presence of his brothers, and from that day on the Spirit of the LORD came upon David in power. Samuel then went to Ramah.

[a] *32* Or *him trembling, yet* [b] *11* Some Septuagint manuscripts; Hebrew *not gather around*

David in Saul's Service

14Now the Spirit of the LORD had departed
from Saul, and an evil[a] spirit from the LORD
tormented him.

15Saul's attendants said to him, "See, an evil
spirit from God is tormenting you. 16Let our
lord command his servants here to search for
someone who can play the harp. He will play
when the evil spirit from God comes upon you,
and you will feel better."

17So Saul said to his attendants, "Find someone who plays well and bring him to me."

18One of the servants answered, "I have
seen a son of Jesse of Bethlehem who knows
how to play the harp. He is a brave man and a
warrior. He speaks well and is a fine-looking
man. And the LORD is with him."

19Then Saul sent messengers to Jesse and
said, "Send me your son David, who is with
the sheep." 20So Jesse took a donkey loaded
with bread, a skin of wine and a young goat
and sent them with his son David to Saul.

21David came to Saul and entered his service. Saul liked him very much, and David
became one of his armor-bearers. 22Then Saul
sent word to Jesse, saying, "Allow David to
remain in my service, for I am pleased with
him."

23Whenever the spirit from God came upon
Saul, David would take his harp and play.
Then relief would come to Saul; he would feel
better, and the evil spirit would leave him.

David and Goliath

17 Now the Philistines gathered their
forces for war and assembled at Socoh
in Judah. They pitched camp at Ephes Dammim, between Socoh and Azekah. 2Saul and
the Israelites assembled and camped in the
Valley of Elah and drew up their battle line to
meet the Philistines. 3The Philistines occupied
one hill and the Israelites another, with the
valley between them.

4A champion named Goliath, who was from
Gath, came out of the Philistine camp. He was
over nine feet[b] tall. 5He had a bronze helmet
on his head and wore a coat of scale armor of
bronze weighing five thousand shekels[c]; 6on
his legs he wore bronze greaves, and a bronze
javelin was slung on his back. 7His spear shaft
was like a weaver's rod, and its iron point
weighed six hundred shekels.[d] His shield bearer went ahead of him.

8Goliath stood and shouted to the ranks of
Israel, "Why do you come out and line up for
battle? Am I not a Philistine, and are you not
the servants of Saul? Choose a man and have
him come down to me. 9If he is able to fight
and kill me, we will become your subjects; but
if I overcome him and kill him, you will become our subjects and serve us." 10Then the
Philistine said, "This day I defy the ranks of
Israel! Give me a man and let us fight each
other." 11On hearing the Philistine's words,
Saul and all the Israelites were dismayed and
terrified.

12Now David was the son of an Ephrathite
named Jesse, who was from Bethlehem in Judah. Jesse had eight sons, and in Saul's time he
was old and well advanced in years. 13Jesse's
three oldest sons had followed Saul to the war:
The firstborn was Eliab; the second, Abinadab;
and the third, Shammah. 14David was the
youngest. The three oldest followed Saul, 15but
David went back and forth from Saul to tend
his father's sheep at Bethlehem.

16For forty days the Philistine came forward
every morning and evening and took his stand.

17Now Jesse said to his son David, "Take
this ephah[e] of roasted grain and these ten
loaves of bread for your brothers and hurry to
their camp. 18Take along these ten cheeses to
the commander of their unit.[f] See how your
brothers are and bring back some assurance[g]
from them. 19They are with Saul and all the
men of Israel in the Valley of Elah, fighting
against the Philistines."

20Early in the morning David left the flock
with a shepherd, loaded up and set out, as Jesse
had directed. He reached the camp as the army
was going out to its battle positions, shouting
the war cry. 21Israel and the Philistines were
drawing up their lines facing each other. 22Da-
vid left his things with the keeper of supplies,
ran to the battle lines and greeted his brothers.
23As he was talking with them, Goliath, the
Philistine champion from Gath, stepped out
from his lines and shouted his usual defiance,
and David heard it. 24When the Israelites saw
the man, they all ran from him in great fear.

25Now the Israelites had been saying, "Do
you see how this man keeps coming out? He
comes out to defy Israel. The king will give
great wealth to the man who kills him. He will
also give him his daughter in marriage and will
exempt his father's family from taxes in Israel."

26David asked the men standing near him,
"What will be done for the man who kills this
Philistine and removes this disgrace from Israel? Who is this uncircumcised Philistine that
he should defy the armies of the living God?"

27They repeated to him what they had been
saying and told him, "This is what will be done
for the man who kills him."

28When Eliab, David's oldest brother, heard
him speaking with the men, he burned with
anger at him and asked, "Why have you come
down here? And with whom did you leave
those few sheep in the desert? I know how
conceited you are and how wicked your heart
is; you came down only to watch the battle."

29"Now what have I done?" said David.
"Can't I even speak?" 30He then turned away

[a] *14* Or *injurious*; also in verses 15, 16 and 23 [b] *4* Hebrew *was six cubits and a span* (about 3 meters)
[c] *5* That is, about 125 pounds (about 57 kilograms) [d] *7* That is, about 15 pounds (about 7 kilograms)
[e] *17* That is, probably about 3/5 bushel (about 22 liters) [f] *18* Hebrew *thousand* [g] *18* Or *some token*; or
some pledge of spoils

to someone else and brought up the same matter, and the men answered him as before. 31 What David said was overheard and reported to Saul, and Saul sent for him.

32 David said to Saul, "Let no one lose heart on account of this Philistine; your servant will go and fight him."

33 Saul replied, "You are not able to go out against this Philistine and fight him; you are only a boy, and he has been a fighting man from his youth."

34 But David said to Saul, "Your servant has been keeping his father's sheep. When a lion or a bear came and carried off a sheep from the flock, 35 I went after it, struck it and rescued the sheep from its mouth. When it turned on me, I seized it by its hair, struck it and killed it. 36 Your servant has killed both the lion and the bear; this uncircumcised Philistine will be like one of them, because he has defied the armies of the living God. 37 The LORD who delivered me from the paw of the lion and the paw of the bear will deliver me from the hand of this Philistine."

Saul said to David, "Go, and the LORD be with you."

38 Then Saul dressed David in his own tunic. He put a coat of armor on him and a bronze helmet on his head. 39 David fastened on his sword over the tunic and tried walking around, because he was not used to them.

"I cannot go in these," he said to Saul, "because I am not used to them." So he took them off. 40 Then he took his staff in his hand, chose five smooth stones from the stream, put them in the pouch of his shepherd's bag and, with his sling in his hand, approached the Philistine.

41 Meanwhile, the Philistine, with his shield bearer in front of him, kept coming closer to David. 42 He looked David over and saw that he was only a boy, ruddy and handsome, and he despised him. 43 He said to David, "Am I a dog, that you come at me with sticks?" And the Philistine cursed David by his gods. 44 "Come here," he said, "and I'll give your flesh to the birds of the air and the beasts of the field!"

45 David said to the Philistine, "You come against me with sword and spear and javelin, but I come against you in the name of the LORD Almighty, the God of the armies of Israel, whom you have defied. 46 This day the LORD will hand you over to me, and I'll strike you down and cut off your head. Today I will give the carcasses of the Philistine army to the birds of the air and the beasts of the earth, and the whole world will know that there is a God in Israel. 47 All those gathered here will know that it is not by sword or spear that the LORD saves; for the battle is the LORD's, and he will give all of you into our hands."

48 As the Philistine moved closer to attack him, David ran quickly toward the battle line to meet him. 49 Reaching into his bag and taking out a stone, he slung it and struck the Philistine on the forehead. The stone sank into his forehead, and he fell facedown on the ground.

50 So David triumphed over the Philistine with a sling and a stone; without a sword in his hand he struck down the Philistine and killed him.

51 David ran and stood over him. He took hold of the Philistine's sword and drew it from the scabbard. After he killed him, he cut off his head with the sword.

When the Philistines saw that their hero was dead, they turned and ran. 52 Then the men of Israel and Judah surged forward with a shout and pursued the Philistines to the entrance of Gath[a] and to the gates of Ekron. Their dead were strewn along the Shaaraim road to Gath and Ekron. 53 When the Israelites returned from chasing the Philistines, they plundered their camp. 54 David took the Philistine's head and brought it to Jerusalem, and he put the Philistine's weapons in his own tent.

55 As Saul watched David going out to meet the Philistine, he said to Abner, commander of the army, "Abner, whose son is that young man?"

Abner replied, "As surely as you live, O king, I don't know."

56 The king said, "Find out whose son this young man is."

57 As soon as David returned from killing the Philistine, Abner took him and brought him before Saul, with David still holding the Philistine's head.

58 "Whose son are you, young man?" Saul asked him.

David said, "I am the son of your servant Jesse of Bethlehem."

Saul's Jealousy of David

18 After David had finished talking with Saul, Jonathan became one in spirit with David, and he loved him as himself. 2 From that day Saul kept David with him and did not let him return to his father's house. 3 And Jonathan made a covenant with David because he loved him as himself. 4 Jonathan took off the robe he was wearing and gave it to David, along with his tunic, and even his sword, his bow and his belt.

5 Whatever Saul sent him to do, David did it so successfully[b] that Saul gave him a high rank in the army. This pleased all the people, and Saul's officers as well.

6 When the men were returning home after David had killed the Philistine, the women came out from all the towns of Israel to meet King Saul with singing and dancing, with joyful songs and with tambourines and lutes. 7 As they danced, they sang:

"Saul has slain his thousands,
 and David his tens of thousands."

8 Saul was very angry; this refrain galled him. "They have credited David with tens of thousands," he thought, "but me with only thousands. What more can he get but the king-

[a] 52 Some Septuagint manuscripts; Hebrew *a valley* [b] 5 Or *wisely*

dom?" 9And from that time on Saul kept a
jealous eye on David.

10The next day an evil[a] spirit from God
came forcefully upon Saul. He was prophesying in his house, while David was playing the
harp, as he usually did. Saul had a spear in his
hand 11and he hurled it, saying to himself, "I'll
pin David to the wall." But David eluded him
twice.

12Saul was afraid of David, because the
LORD was with David but had left Saul. 13So
he sent David away from him and gave him
command over a thousand men, and David led
the troops in their campaigns. 14In everything
he did he had great success,[b] because the
LORD was with him. 15When Saul saw how
successful[c] he was, he was afraid of him.
16But all Israel and Judah loved David, because he led them in their campaigns.

17Saul said to David, "Here is my older
daughter Merab. I will give her to you in marriage; only serve me bravely and fight the battles of the LORD." For Saul said to himself, "I
will not raise a hand against him. Let the Philistines do that!"

18But David said to Saul, "Who am I, and
what is my family or my father's clan in Israel,
that I should become the king's son-in-law?"
19So[d] when the time came for Merab, Saul's
daughter, to be given to David, she was given
in marriage to Adriel of Meholah.

20Now Saul's daughter Michal was in love
with David, and when they told Saul about it,
he was pleased. 21"I will give her to him," he
thought, "so that she may be a snare to him and
so that the hand of the Philistines may be
against him." So Saul said to David, "Now you
have a second opportunity to become my son-
in-law."

22Then Saul ordered his attendants: "Speak
to David privately and say, 'Look, the king is
pleased with you, and his attendants all like
you; now become his son-in-law.' "

23They repeated these words to David. But
David said, "Do you think it is a small matter
to become the king's son-in-law? I'm only a
poor man and little known."

24When Saul's servants told him what David
had said, 25Saul replied, "Say to David, 'The
king wants no other price for the bride than a
hundred Philistine foreskins, to take revenge
on his enemies.' " Saul's plan was to have David fall by the hands of the Philistines.

26When the attendants told David these
things, he was pleased to become the king's
son-in-law. So before the allotted time
elapsed, 27David and his men went out and
killed two hundred Philistines. He brought
their foreskins and presented the full number
to the king so that he might become the king's
son-in-law. Then Saul gave him his daughter
Michal in marriage.

28When Saul realized that the LORD was
with David and that his daughter Michal loved
David, 29Saul became still more afraid of him,
and he remained his enemy the rest of his days.

30The Philistine commanders continued to
go out to battle, and as often as they did, David
met with more success[e] than the rest of Saul's
officers, and his name became well known.

Saul Tries to Kill David

19 Saul told his son Jonathan and all the
attendants to kill David. But Jonathan
was very fond of David 2and warned him, "My
father Saul is looking for a chance to kill you.
Be on your guard tomorrow morning; go into
hiding and stay there. 3I will go out and stand
with my father in the field where you are. I'll
speak to him about you and will tell you what
I find out."

4Jonathan spoke well of David to Saul his
father and said to him, "Let not the king do
wrong to his servant David; he has not
wronged you, and what he has done has bene-
fited you greatly. 5He took his life in his hands
when he killed the Philistine. The LORD won a
great victory for all Israel, and you saw it and
were glad. Why then would you do wrong to
an innocent man like David by killing him for
no reason?"

6Saul listened to Jonathan and took this
oath: "As surely as the LORD lives, David will
not be put to death."

7So Jonathan called David and told him the
whole conversation. He brought him to Saul,
and David was with Saul as before.

8Once more war broke out, and David went
out and fought the Philistines. He struck them
with such force that they fled before him.

9But an evil[a] spirit from the LORD came
upon Saul as he was sitting in his house with
his spear in his hand. While David was playing
the harp, 10Saul tried to pin him to the wall
with his spear, but David eluded him as Saul
drove the spear into the wall. That night David
made good his escape.

11Saul sent men to David's house to watch it
and to kill him in the morning. But Michal,
David's wife, warned him, "If you don't run
for your life tonight, tomorrow you'll be
killed." 12So Michal let David down through a
window, and he fled and escaped. 13Then Michal took an idol[f] and laid it on the bed, covering it with a garment and putting some goats'
hair at the head.

14When Saul sent the men to capture David,
Michal said, "He is ill."

15Then Saul sent the men back to see David
and told them, "Bring him up to me in his bed
so that I may kill him." 16But when the men
entered, there was the idol in the bed, and at
the head was some goats' hair.

17Saul said to Michal, "Why did you deceive me like this and send my enemy away so
that he escaped?"

Michal told him, "He said to me, 'Let me get
away. Why should I kill you?' "

[a] *10,9* Or *injurious* [b] *14* Or *he was very wise* [c] *15* Or *wise* [d] *19* Or *However,* [e] *30* Or *David acted more wisely* [f] *13* Hebrew *teraphim*; also in verse 16

18When David had fled and made his escape, he went to Samuel at Ramah and told him all that Saul had done to him. Then he and Samuel went to Naioth and stayed there. 19Word came to Saul: "David is in Naioth at Ramah"; 20so he sent men to capture him. But when they saw a group of prophets prophesying, with Samuel standing there as their leader, the Spirit of God came upon Saul's men and they also prophesied. 21Saul was told about it, and he sent more men, and they prophesied too. Saul sent men a third time, and they also prophesied. 22Finally, he himself left for Ramah and went to the great cistern at Secu. And he asked, "Where are Samuel and David?"

"Over in Naioth at Ramah," they said.

23So Saul went to Naioth at Ramah. But the Spirit of God came even upon him, and he walked along prophesying until he came to Naioth. 24He stripped off his robes and also prophesied in Samuel's presence. He lay that way all that day and night. This is why people say, "Is Saul also among the prophets?"

David and Jonathan

20 Then David fled from Naioth at Ramah and went to Jonathan and asked, "What have I done? What is my crime? How have I wronged your father, that he is trying to take my life?"

2"Never!" Jonathan replied. "You are not going to die! Look, my father doesn't do anything, great or small, without confiding in me. Why would he hide this from me? It's not so!"

3But David took an oath and said, "Your father knows very well that I have found favor in your eyes, and he has said to himself, 'Jonathan must not know this or he will be grieved.' Yet as surely as the LORD lives and as you live, there is only a step between me and death."

4Jonathan said to David, "Whatever you want me to do, I'll do for you."

5So David said, "Look, tomorrow is the New Moon festival, and I am supposed to dine with the king; but let me go and hide in the field until the evening of the day after tomorrow. 6If your father misses me at all, tell him, 'David earnestly asked my permission to hurry to Bethlehem, his hometown, because an annual sacrifice is being made there for his whole clan.' 7If he says, 'Very well,' then your servant is safe. But if he loses his temper, you can be sure that he is determined to harm me. 8As for you, show kindness to your servant, for you have brought him into a covenant with you before the LORD. If I am guilty, then kill me yourself! Why hand me over to your father?"

9"Never!" Jonathan said. "If I had the least inkling that my father was determined to harm you, wouldn't I tell you?"

10David asked, "Who will tell me if your father answers you harshly?"

11"Come," Jonathan said, "let's go out into the field." So they went there together.

12Then Jonathan said to David: "By the LORD, the God of Israel, I will surely sound out my father by this time the day after tomorrow! If he is favorably disposed toward you, will I not send you word and let you know? 13But if my father is inclined to harm you, may the LORD deal with me, be it ever so severely, if I do not let you know and send you away safely. May the LORD be with you as he has been with my father. 14But show me unfailing kindness like that of the LORD as long as I live, so that I may not be killed, 15and do not ever cut off your kindness from my family—not even when the LORD has cut off every one of David's enemies from the face of the earth."

16So Jonathan made a covenant with the house of David, saying, "May the LORD call David's enemies to account." 17And Jonathan had David reaffirm his oath out of love for him, because he loved him as he loved himself.

18Then Jonathan said to David: "Tomorrow is the New Moon festival. You will be missed, because your seat will be empty. 19The day after tomorrow, toward evening, go to the place where you hid when this trouble began, and wait by the stone Ezel. 20I will shoot three arrows to the side of it, as though I were shooting at a target. 21Then I will send a boy and say, 'Go, find the arrows.' If I say to him, 'Look, the arrows are on this side of you; bring them here,' then come, because, as surely as the LORD lives, you are safe; there is no danger. 22But if I say to the boy, 'Look, the arrows are beyond you,' then you must go, because the LORD has sent you away. 23And about the matter you and I discussed—remember, the LORD is witness between you and me forever."

24So David hid in the field, and when the New Moon festival came, the king sat down to eat. 25He sat in his customary place by the wall, opposite Jonathan,[a] and Abner sat next to Saul, but David's place was empty. 26Saul said nothing that day, for he thought, "Something must have happened to David to make him ceremonially unclean—surely he is unclean." 27But the next day, the second day of the month, David's place was empty again. Then Saul said to his son Jonathan, "Why hasn't the son of Jesse come to the meal, either yesterday or today?"

28Jonathan answered, "David earnestly asked me for permission to go to Bethlehem. 29He said, 'Let me go, because our family is observing a sacrifice in the town and my brother has ordered me to be there. If I have found favor in your eyes, let me get away to see my brothers.' That is why he has not come to the king's table."

30Saul's anger flared up at Jonathan and he said to him, "You son of a perverse and rebellious woman! Don't I know that you have sided with the son of Jesse to your own shame and to the shame of the mother who bore you? 31As long as the son of Jesse lives on this earth, neither you nor your kingdom will be

[a]25 Septuagint; Hebrew *wall. Jonathan arose*

established. Now send and bring him to me,
for he must die!”
32“Why should he be put to death? What has
he done?” Jonathan asked his father. 33But
Saul hurled his spear at him to kill him. Then
Jonathan knew that his father intended to kill
David.
34Jonathan got up from the table in fierce
anger; on that second day of the month he did
not eat, because he was grieved at his father’s
shameful treatment of David.
35In the morning Jonathan went out to the
field for his meeting with David. He had a
small boy with him, 36and he said to the boy,
“Run and find the arrows I shoot.” As the boy
ran, he shot an arrow beyond him. 37When the
boy came to the place where Jonathan’s arrow
had fallen, Jonathan called out after him, “Isn’t
the arrow beyond you?” 38Then he shouted,
“Hurry! Go quickly! Don’t stop!” The boy
picked up the arrow and returned to his master.
39(The boy knew nothing of all this; only Jonathan and David knew.) 40Then Jonathan gave
his weapons to the boy and said, “Go, carry
them back to town.”
41After the boy had gone, David got up from
the south side ⌊of the stone⌋ and bowed down
before Jonathan three times, with his face to
the ground. Then they kissed each other and
wept together—but David wept the most.
42Jonathan said to David, “Go in peace, for
we have sworn friendship with each other in
the name of the LORD, saying, ‘The LORD is
witness between you and me, and between
your descendants and my descendants forever.’ ” Then David left, and Jonathan went back
to the town.

David at Nob

21 David went to Nob, to Ahimelech the
priest. Ahimelech trembled when he
met him, and asked, “Why are you alone? Why
is no one with you?”
2David answered Ahimelech the priest,
“The king charged me with a certain matter
and said to me, ‘No one is to know anything
about your mission and your instructions.’ As
for my men, I have told them to meet me at a
certain place. 3Now then, what do you have on
hand? Give me five loaves of bread, or whatever you can find.”
4But the priest answered David, “I don’t
have any ordinary bread on hand; however,
there is some consecrated bread here—provided the men have kept themselves from
women.”
5David replied, “Indeed women have been
kept from us, as usual whenever[a] I set out. The
men’s things[b] are holy even on missions that
are not holy. How much more so today!” 6So
the priest gave him the consecrated bread,
since there was no bread there except the bread
of the Presence that had been removed from
before the LORD and replaced by hot bread on
the day it was taken away.
7Now one of Saul’s servants was there that
day, detained before the LORD; he was Doeg
the Edomite, Saul’s head shepherd.
8David asked Ahimelech, “Don’t you have a
spear or a sword here? I haven’t brought my
sword or any other weapon, because the king’s
business was urgent.”
9The priest replied, “The sword of Goliath
the Philistine, whom you killed in the Valley
of Elah, is here; it is wrapped in a cloth behind
the ephod. If you want it, take it; there is no
sword here but that one.”
David said, “There is none like it; give it
to me.”

David at Gath

10That day David fled from Saul and went to
Achish king of Gath. 11But the servants of
Achish said to him, “Isn’t this David, the king
of the land? Isn’t he the one they sing about in
their dances:

“ ‘Saul has slain his thousands,
and David his tens of thousands’?”

12David took these words to heart and was
very much afraid of Achish king of Gath. 13So
he pretended to be insane in their presence;
and while he was in their hands he acted like
a madman, making marks on the doors of the
gate and letting saliva run down his beard.
14Achish said to his servants, “Look at the
man! He is insane! Why bring him to me?
15Am I so short of madmen that you have to
bring this fellow here to carry on like this in
front of me? Must this man come into my
house?”

David at Adullam and Mizpah

22 David left Gath and escaped to the cave
of Adullam. When his brothers and his
father’s household heard about it, they went
down to him there. 2All those who were in
distress or in debt or discontented gathered
around him, and he became their leader. About
four hundred men were with him.
3From there David went to Mizpah in Moab
and said to the king of Moab, “Would you let
my father and mother come and stay with you
until I learn what God will do for me?” 4So he
left them with the king of Moab, and they
stayed with him as long as David was in the
stronghold.
5But the prophet Gad said to David, “Do not
stay in the stronghold. Go into the land of Judah.” So David left and went to the forest of
Hereth.

Saul Kills the Priests of Nob

6Now Saul heard that David and his men
had been discovered. And Saul, spear in hand,
was seated under the tamarisk tree on the hill
at Gibeah, with all his officials standing
around him. 7Saul said to them, “Listen, men
of Benjamin! Will the son of Jesse give all of
you fields and vineyards? Will he make all of
you commanders of thousands and command-

[a]5 Or *from us in the past few days since* [b]5 Or *bodies*

ers of hundreds? 8Is that why you have all conspired against me? No one tells me when my son makes a covenant with the son of Jesse. None of you is concerned about me or tells me that my son has incited my servant to lie in wait for me, as he does today."

9But Doeg the Edomite, who was standing with Saul's officials, said, "I saw the son of Jesse come to Ahimelech son of Ahitub at Nob. 10Ahimelech inquired of the LORD for him; he also gave him provisions and the sword of Goliath the Philistine."

11Then the king sent for the priest Ahimelech son of Ahitub and his father's whole family, who were the priests at Nob, and they all came to the king. 12Saul said, "Listen now, son of Ahitub."

"Yes, my lord," he answered.

13Saul said to him, "Why have you conspired against me, you and the son of Jesse, giving him bread and a sword and inquiring of God for him, so that he has rebelled against me and lies in wait for me, as he does today?"

14Ahimelech answered the king, "Who of all your servants is as loyal as David, the king's son-in-law, captain of your bodyguard and highly respected in your household? 15Was that day the first time I inquired of God for him? Of course not! Let not the king accuse your servant or any of his father's family, for your servant knows nothing at all about this whole affair."

16But the king said, "You will surely die, Ahimelech, you and your father's whole family."

17Then the king ordered the guards at his side: "Turn and kill the priests of the LORD, because they too have sided with David. They knew he was fleeing, yet they did not tell me."

But the king's officials were not willing to raise a hand to strike the priests of the LORD.

18The king then ordered Doeg, "You turn and strike down the priests." So Doeg the Edomite turned and struck them down. That day he killed eighty-five men who wore the linen ephod. 19He also put to the sword Nob, the town of the priests, with its men and women, its children and infants, and its cattle, donkeys and sheep.

20But Abiathar, a son of Ahimelech son of Ahitub, escaped and fled to join David. 21He told David that Saul had killed the priests of the LORD. 22Then David said to Abiathar: "That day, when Doeg the Edomite was there, I knew he would be sure to tell Saul. I am responsible for the death of your father's whole family. 23Stay with me; don't be afraid; the man who is seeking your life is seeking mine also. You will be safe with me."

David Saves Keilah

23 When David was told, "Look, the Philistines are fighting against Keilah and are looting the threshing floors," 2he inquired of the LORD, saying, "Shall I go and attack these Philistines?"

The LORD answered him, "Go, attack the Philistines and save Keilah."

3But David's men said to him, "Here in Judah we are afraid. How much more, then, if we go to Keilah against the Philistine forces!"

4Once again David inquired of the LORD, and the LORD answered him, "Go down to Keilah, for I am going to give the Philistines into your hand." 5So David and his men went to Keilah, fought the Philistines and carried off their livestock. He inflicted heavy losses on the Philistines and saved the people of Keilah. 6(Now Abiathar son of Ahimelech had brought the ephod down with him when he fled to David at Keilah.)

Saul Pursues David

7Saul was told that David had gone to Keilah, and he said, "God has handed him over to me, for David has imprisoned himself by entering a town with gates and bars." 8And Saul called up all his forces for battle, to go down to Keilah to besiege David and his men.

9When David learned that Saul was plotting against him, he said to Abiathar the priest, "Bring the ephod." 10David said, "O LORD, God of Israel, your servant has heard definitely that Saul plans to come to Keilah and destroy the town on account of me. 11Will the citizens of Keilah surrender me to him? Will Saul come down, as your servant has heard? O LORD, God of Israel, tell your servant."

And the LORD said, "He will."

12Again David asked, "Will the citizens of Keilah surrender me and my men to Saul?"

And the LORD said, "They will."

13So David and his men, about six hundred in number, left Keilah and kept moving from place to place. When Saul was told that David had escaped from Keilah, he did not go there.

14David stayed in the desert strongholds and in the hills of the Desert of Ziph. Day after day Saul searched for him, but God did not give David into his hands.

15While David was at Horesh in the Desert of Ziph, he learned that Saul had come out to take his life. 16And Saul's son Jonathan went to David at Horesh and helped him find strength in God. 17"Don't be afraid," he said. "My father Saul will not lay a hand on you. You will be king over Israel, and I will be second to you. Even my father Saul knows this." 18The two of them made a covenant before the LORD. Then Jonathan went home, but David remained at Horesh.

19The Ziphites went up to Saul at Gibeah and said, "Is not David hiding among us in the strongholds at Horesh, on the hill of Hakilah, south of Jeshimon? 20Now, O king, come down whenever it pleases you to do so, and we will be responsible for handing him over to the king."

21Saul replied, "The LORD bless you for your concern for me. 22Go and make further preparation. Find out where David usually goes and who has seen him there. They tell me he is very crafty. 23Find out about all the hiding places he uses and come back to me with definite information.[a] Then I will go with you; if he is in the area, I will track him down among all the clans of Judah."

24So they set out and went to Ziph ahead of Saul. Now David and his men were in the Desert of Maon, in the Arabah south of Jeshimon. 25Saul and his men began the search, and when David was told about it, he went down to the rock and stayed in the Desert of Maon. When Saul heard this, he went into the Desert of Maon in pursuit of David.

26Saul was going along one side of the mountain, and David and his men were on the other side, hurrying to get away from Saul. As Saul and his forces were closing in on David and his men to capture them, 27a messenger came to Saul, saying, "Come quickly! The Philistines are raiding the land." 28Then Saul broke off his pursuit of David and went to meet the Philistines. That is why they call this place Sela Hammahlekoth.[b] 29And David went up from there and lived in the strongholds of En Gedi.

David Spares Saul's Life

24 After Saul returned from pursuing the Philistines, he was told, "David is in the Desert of En Gedi." 2So Saul took three thousand chosen men from all Israel and set out to look for David and his men near the Crags of the Wild Goats.

3He came to the sheep pens along the way; a cave was there, and Saul went in to relieve himself. David and his men were far back in the cave. 4The men said, "This is the day the LORD spoke of when he said[c] to you, 'I will give your enemy into your hands for you to deal with as you wish.' " Then David crept up unnoticed and cut off a corner of Saul's robe.

5Afterward, David was conscience-stricken for having cut off a corner of his robe. 6He said to his men, "The LORD forbid that I should do such a thing to my master, the LORD's anointed, or lift my hand against him; for he is the anointed of the LORD." 7With these words David rebuked his men and did not allow them to attack Saul. And Saul left the cave and went his way.

8Then David went out of the cave and called out to Saul, "My lord the king!" When Saul looked behind him, David bowed down and prostrated himself with his face to the ground. 9He said to Saul, "Why do you listen when men say, 'David is bent on harming you'? 10This day you have seen with your own eyes how the LORD delivered you into my hands in the cave. Some urged me to kill you, but I spared you; I said, 'I will not lift my hand against my master, because he is the LORD's anointed.' 11See, my father, look at this piece of your robe in my hand! I cut off the corner of your robe but did not kill you. Now understand and recognize that I am not guilty of wrongdoing or rebellion. I have not wronged you, but you are hunting me down to take my life. 12May the LORD judge between you and me. And may the LORD avenge the wrongs you have done to me, but my hand will not touch you. 13As the old saying goes, 'From evildoers come evil deeds,' so my hand will not touch you.

14"Against whom has the king of Israel come out? Whom are you pursuing? A dead dog? A flea? 15May the LORD be our judge and decide between us. May he consider my cause and uphold it; may he vindicate me by delivering me from your hand."

16When David finished saying this, Saul asked, "Is that your voice, David my son?" And he wept aloud. 17"You are more righteous than I," he said. "You have treated me well, but I have treated you badly. 18You have just now told me of the good you did to me; the LORD delivered me into your hands, but you did not kill me. 19When a man finds his enemy, does he let him get away unharmed? May the LORD reward you well for the way you treated me today. 20I know that you will surely be king and that the kingdom of Israel will be established in your hands. 21Now swear to me by the LORD that you will not cut off my descendants or wipe out my name from my father's family."

22So David gave his oath to Saul. Then Saul returned home, but David and his men went up to the stronghold.

David, Nabal and Abigail

25 Now Samuel died, and all Israel assembled and mourned for him; and they buried him at his home in Ramah.

Then David moved down into the Desert of Maon.[d] 2A certain man in Maon, who had property there at Carmel, was very wealthy. He had a thousand goats and three thousand sheep, which he was shearing in Carmel. 3His name was Nabal and his wife's name was Abigail. She was an intelligent and beautiful woman, but her husband, a Calebite, was surly and mean in his dealings.

4While David was in the desert, he heard that Nabal was shearing sheep. 5So he sent ten young men and said to them, "Go up to Nabal at Carmel and greet him in my name. 6Say to him: 'Long life to you! Good health to you and your household! And good health to all that is yours!

7" 'Now I hear that it is sheep-shearing time. When your shepherds were with us, we did not mistreat them, and the whole time they were at Carmel nothing of theirs was missing. 8Ask your own servants and they will tell you. Therefore be favorable toward my young men, since we come at a festive time. Please give your servants and your son David whatever you can find for them.' "

[a]23 Or *me at Nacon* [b]28 *Sela Hammahlekoth* means *rock of parting.* [c]4 Or *"Today the LORD is saying*
[d]1 Some Septuagint manuscripts; Hebrew *Paran*

9When David's men arrived, they gave Nabal this message in David's name. Then they waited.

10Nabal answered David's servants, "Who is this David? Who is this son of Jesse? Many servants are breaking away from their masters these days. 11Why should I take my bread and water, and the meat I have slaughtered for my shearers, and give it to men coming from who knows where?"

12David's men turned around and went back. When they arrived, they reported every word. 13David said to his men, "Put on your swords!" So they put on their swords, and David put on his. About four hundred men went up with David, while two hundred stayed with the supplies.

14One of the servants told Nabal's wife Abigail: "David sent messengers from the desert to give our master his greetings, but he hurled insults at them. 15Yet these men were very good to us. They did not mistreat us, and the whole time we were out in the fields near them nothing was missing. 16Night and day they were a wall around us all the time we were herding our sheep near them. 17Now think it over and see what you can do, because disaster is hanging over our master and his whole household. He is such a wicked man that no one can talk to him."

18Abigail lost no time. She took two hundred loaves of bread, two skins of wine, five dressed sheep, five seahs[a] of roasted grain, a hundred cakes of raisins and two hundred cakes of pressed figs, and loaded them on donkeys. 19Then she told her servants, "Go on ahead; I'll follow you." But she did not tell her husband Nabal.

20As she came riding her donkey into a mountain ravine, there were David and his men descending toward her, and she met them. 21David had just said, "It's been useless—all my watching over this fellow's property in the desert so that nothing of his was missing. He has paid me back evil for good. 22May God deal with David,[b] be it ever so severely, if by morning I leave alive one male of all who belong to him!"

23When Abigail saw David, she quickly got off her donkey and bowed down before David with her face to the ground. 24She fell at his feet and said: "My lord, let the blame be on me alone. Please let your servant speak to you; hear what your servant has to say. 25May my lord pay no attention to that wicked man Nabal. He is just like his name—his name is Fool, and folly goes with him. But as for me, your servant, I did not see the men my master sent.

26"Now since the LORD has kept you, my master, from bloodshed and from avenging yourself with your own hands, as surely as the LORD lives and as you live, may your enemies and all who intend to harm my master be like Nabal. 27And let this gift, which your servant has brought to my master, be given to the men who follow you. 28Please forgive your servant's offense, for the LORD will certainly make a lasting dynasty for my master, because he fights the LORD's battles. Let no wrongdoing be found in you as long as you live. 29Even though someone is pursuing you to take your life, the life of my master will be bound securely in the bundle of the living by the LORD your God. But the lives of your enemies he will hurl away as from the pocket of a sling. 30When the LORD has done for my master every good thing he promised concerning him and has appointed him leader over Israel, 31my master will not have on his conscience the staggering burden of needless bloodshed or of having avenged himself. And when the LORD has brought my master success, remember your servant."

32David said to Abigail, "Praise be to the LORD, the God of Israel, who has sent you today to meet me. 33May you be blessed for your good judgment and for keeping me from bloodshed this day and from avenging myself with my own hands. 34Otherwise, as surely as the LORD, the God of Israel, lives, who has kept me from harming you, if you had not come quickly to meet me, not one male belonging to Nabal would have been left alive by daybreak."

35Then David accepted from her hand what she had brought him and said, "Go home in peace. I have heard your words and granted your request."

36When Abigail went to Nabal, he was in the house holding a banquet like that of a king. He was in high spirits and very drunk. So she told him nothing until daybreak. 37Then in the morning, when Nabal was sober, his wife told him all these things, and his heart failed him and he became like a stone. 38About ten days later, the LORD struck Nabal and he died.

39When David heard that Nabal was dead, he said, "Praise be to the LORD, who has upheld my cause against Nabal for treating me with contempt. He has kept his servant from doing wrong and has brought Nabal's wrongdoing down on his own head."

Then David sent word to Abigail, asking her to become his wife. 40His servants went to Carmel and said to Abigail, "David has sent us to you to take you to become his wife."

41She bowed down with her face to the ground and said, "Here is your maidservant, ready to serve you and wash the feet of my master's servants." 42Abigail quickly got on a donkey and, attended by her five maids, went with David's messengers and became his wife. 43David had also married Ahinoam of Jezreel, and they both were his wives. 44But Saul had given his daughter Michal, David's wife, to Paltiel[c] son of Laish, who was from Gallim.

[a] *18* That is, probably about a bushel (about 37 liters) [b] *22* Some Septuagint manuscripts; Hebrew *with David's enemies* [c] *44* Hebrew *Palti*, a variant of *Paltiel*

David Again Spares Saul's Life

26 The Ziphites went to Saul at Gibeah and said, "Is not David hiding on the hill of Hakilah, which faces Jeshimon?"

2So Saul went down to the Desert of Ziph, with his three thousand chosen men of Israel, to search there for David. 3Saul made his camp beside the road on the hill of Hakilah facing Jeshimon, but David stayed in the desert. When he saw that Saul had followed him there, 4he sent out scouts and learned that Saul had definitely arrived.[a]

5Then David set out and went to the place where Saul had camped. He saw where Saul and Abner son of Ner, the commander of the army, had lain down. Saul was lying inside the camp, with the army encamped around him.

6David then asked Ahimelech the Hittite and Abishai son of Zeruiah, Joab's brother, "Who will go down into the camp with me to Saul?"

"I'll go with you," said Abishai.

7So David and Abishai went to the army by night, and there was Saul, lying asleep inside the camp with his spear stuck in the ground near his head. Abner and the soldiers were lying around him.

8Abishai said to David, "Today God has delivered your enemy into your hands. Now let me pin him to the ground with one thrust of my spear; I won't strike him twice."

9But David said to Abishai, "Don't destroy him! Who can lay a hand on the LORD's anointed and be guiltless? 10As surely as the LORD lives," he said, "the LORD himself will strike him; either his time will come and he will die, or he will go into battle and perish. 11But the LORD forbid that I should lay a hand on the LORD's anointed. Now get the spear and water jug that are near his head, and let's go."

12So David took the spear and water jug near Saul's head, and they left. No one saw or knew about it, nor did anyone wake up. They were all sleeping, because the LORD had put them into a deep sleep.

13Then David crossed over to the other side and stood on top of the hill some distance away; there was a wide space between them. 14He called out to the army and to Abner son of Ner, "Aren't you going to answer me, Abner?"

Abner replied, "Who are you who calls to the king?"

15David said, "You're a man, aren't you? And who is like you in Israel? Why didn't you guard your lord the king? Someone came to destroy your lord the king. 16What you have done is not good. As surely as the LORD lives, you and your men deserve to die, because you did not guard your master, the LORD's anointed. Look around you. Where are the king's spear and water jug that were near his head?"

17Saul recognized David's voice and said, "Is that your voice, David my son?"

David replied, "Yes it is, my lord the king." 18And he added, "Why is my lord pursuing his servant? What have I done, and what wrong am I guilty of? 19Now let my lord the king listen to his servant's words. If the LORD has incited you against me, then may he accept an offering. If, however, men have done it, may they be cursed before the LORD! They have now driven me from my share in the LORD's inheritance and have said, 'Go, serve other gods.' 20Now do not let my blood fall to the ground far from the presence of the LORD. The king of Israel has come out to look for a flea—as one hunts a partridge in the mountains."

21Then Saul said, "I have sinned. Come back, David my son. Because you considered my life precious today, I will not try to harm you again. Surely I have acted like a fool and have erred greatly."

22"Here is the king's spear," David answered. "Let one of your young men come over and get it. 23The LORD rewards every man for his righteousness and faithfulness. The LORD delivered you into my hands today, but I would not lay a hand on the LORD's anointed. 24As surely as I valued your life today, so may the LORD value my life and deliver me from all trouble."

25Then Saul said to David, "May you be blessed, my son David; you will do great things and surely triumph."

So David went on his way, and Saul returned home.

David Among the Philistines

27 But David thought to himself, "One of these days I will be destroyed by the hand of Saul. The best thing I can do is to escape to the land of the Philistines. Then Saul will give up searching for me anywhere in Israel, and I will slip out of his hand."

2So David and the six hundred men with him left and went over to Achish son of Maoch king of Gath. 3David and his men settled in Gath with Achish. Each man had his family with him, and David had his two wives: Ahinoam of Jezreel and Abigail of Carmel, the widow of Nabal. 4When Saul was told that David had fled to Gath, he no longer searched for him.

5Then David said to Achish, "If I have found favor in your eyes, let a place be assigned to me in one of the country towns, that I may live there. Why should your servant live in the royal city with you?"

6So on that day Achish gave him Ziklag, and it has belonged to the kings of Judah ever since. 7David lived in Philistine territory a year and four months.

8Now David and his men went up and raided the Geshurites, the Girzites and the Amalekites. (From ancient times these peoples had lived in the land extending to Shur and Egypt.) 9Whenever David attacked an area, he did not leave a man or woman alive, but took sheep

[a]4 Or *had come to Nacon*

and cattle, donkeys and camels, and clothes. Then he returned to Achish.

10When Achish asked, "Where did you go raiding today?" David would say, "Against the Negev of Judah" or "Against the Negev of Jerahmeel" or "Against the Negev of the Kenites." 11He did not leave a man or woman alive to be brought to Gath, for he thought, "They might inform on us and say, 'This is what David did.' " And such was his practice as long as he lived in Philistine territory. 12Achish trusted David and said to himself, "He has become so odious to his people, the Israelites, that he will be my servant forever."

Saul and the Witch of Endor

28 In those days the Philistines gathered their forces to fight against Israel. Achish said to David, "You must understand that you and your men will accompany me in the army."

2David said, "Then you will see for yourself what your servant can do."

Achish replied, "Very well, I will make you my bodyguard for life."

3Now Samuel was dead, and all Israel had mourned for him and buried him in his own town of Ramah. Saul had expelled the mediums and spiritists from the land.

4The Philistines assembled and came and set up camp at Shunem, while Saul gathered all the Israelites and set up camp at Gilboa. 5When Saul saw the Philistine army, he was afraid; terror filled his heart. 6He inquired of the LORD, but the LORD did not answer him by dreams or Urim or prophets. 7Saul then said to his attendants, "Find me a woman who is a medium, so I may go and inquire of her."

"There is one in Endor," they said.

8So Saul disguised himself, putting on other clothes, and at night he and two men went to the woman. "Consult a spirit for me," he said, "and bring up for me the one I name."

9But the woman said to him, "Surely you know what Saul has done. He has cut off the mediums and spiritists from the land. Why have you set a trap for my life to bring about my death?"

10Saul swore to her by the LORD, "As surely as the LORD lives, you will not be punished for this."

11Then the woman asked, "Whom shall I bring up for you?"

"Bring up Samuel," he said.

12When the woman saw Samuel, she cried out at the top of her voice and said to Saul, "Why have you deceived me? You are Saul!"

13The king said to her, "Don't be afraid. What do you see?"

The woman said, "I see a spirit[a] coming up out of the ground."

14"What does he look like?" he asked.

"An old man wearing a robe is coming up," she said.

Then Saul knew it was Samuel, and he bowed down and prostrated himself with his face to the ground.

15Samuel said to Saul, "Why have you disturbed me by bringing me up?"

"I am in great distress," Saul said. "The Philistines are fighting against me, and God has turned away from me. He no longer answers me, either by prophets or by dreams. So I have called on you to tell me what to do."

16Samuel said, "Why do you consult me, now that the LORD has turned away from you and become your enemy? 17The LORD has done what he predicted through me. The LORD has torn the kingdom out of your hands and given it to one of your neighbors—to David. 18Because you did not obey the LORD or carry out his fierce wrath against the Amalekites, the LORD has done this to you today. 19The LORD will hand over both Israel and you to the Philistines, and tomorrow you and your sons will be with me. The LORD will also hand over the army of Israel to the Philistines."

20Immediately Saul fell full length on the ground, filled with fear because of Samuel's words. His strength was gone, for he had eaten nothing all that day and night.

21When the woman came to Saul and saw that he was greatly shaken, she said, "Look, your maidservant has obeyed you. I took my life in my hands and did what you told me to do. 22Now please listen to your servant and let me give you some food so you may eat and have the strength to go on your way."

23He refused and said, "I will not eat."

But his men joined the woman in urging him, and he listened to them. He got up from the ground and sat on the couch.

24The woman had a fattened calf at the house, which she butchered at once. She took some flour, kneaded it and baked bread without yeast. 25Then she set it before Saul and his men, and they ate. That same night they got up and left.

Achish Sends David Back to Ziklag

29 The Philistines gathered all their forces at Aphek, and Israel camped by the spring in Jezreel. 2As the Philistine rulers marched with their units of hundreds and thousands, David and his men were marching at the rear with Achish. 3The commanders of the Philistines asked, "What about these Hebrews?"

Achish replied, "Is this not David, who was an officer of Saul king of Israel? He has already been with me for over a year, and from the day he left Saul until now, I have found no fault in him."

4But the Philistine commanders were angry with him and said, "Send the man back, that he may return to the place you assigned him. He must not go with us into battle, or he will turn against us during the fighting. How better could he regain his master's favor than by taking the heads of our own men? 5Isn't this the David they sang about in their dances:

[a]13 Or *see spirits*; or *see gods*

" 'Saul has slain his thousands,
and David his tens of thousands'?"

6So Achish called David and said to him,
"As surely as the LORD lives, you have been
reliable, and I would be pleased to have you
serve with me in the army. From the day you
came to me until now, I have found no fault in
you, but the rulers don't approve of you. 7Turn
back and go in peace; do nothing to displease
the Philistine rulers."
8"But what have I done?" asked David.
"What have you found against your servant
from the day I came to you until now? Why
can't I go and fight against the enemies of my
lord the king?"
9Achish answered, "I know that you have
been as pleasing in my eyes as an angel of
God; nevertheless, the Philistine commanders
have said, 'He must not go up with us into
battle.' 10Now get up early, along with your
master's servants who have come with you,
and leave in the morning as soon as it is light."
11So David and his men got up early in the
morning to go back to the land of the Philistines, and the Philistines went up to Jezreel.

David Destroys the Amalekites

30 David and his men reached Ziklag on
the third day. Now the Amalekites had
raided the Negev and Ziklag. They had attacked Ziklag and burned it, 2and had taken
captive the women and all who were in it, both
young and old. They killed none of them, but
carried them off as they went on their way.
3When David and his men came to Ziklag,
they found it destroyed by fire and their wives
and sons and daughters taken captive. 4So David and his men wept aloud until they had no
strength left to weep. 5David's two wives had
been captured—Ahinoam of Jezreel and Abigail, the widow of Nabal of Carmel. 6David
was greatly distressed because the men were
talking of stoning him; each one was bitter in
spirit because of his sons and daughters. But
David found strength in the LORD his God.
7Then David said to Abiathar the priest, the
son of Ahimelech, "Bring me the ephod." Abiathar brought it to him, 8and David inquired of
the LORD, "Shall I pursue this raiding party?
Will I overtake them?"
"Pursue them," he answered. "You will certainly overtake them and succeed in the rescue."
9David and the six hundred men with him
came to the Besor Ravine, where some stayed
behind, 10for two hundred men were too exhausted to cross the ravine. But David and four
hundred men continued the pursuit.
11They found an Egyptian in a field and
brought him to David. They gave him water to
drink and food to eat— 12part of a cake of
pressed figs and two cakes of raisins. He ate
and was revived, for he had not eaten any food
or drunk any water for three days and three
nights.
13David asked him, "To whom do you belong, and where do you come from?"
He said, "I am an Egyptian, the slave of an
Amalekite. My master abandoned me when I
became ill three days ago. 14We raided the
Negev of the Kerethites and the territory belonging to Judah and the Negev of Caleb. And
we burned Ziklag."
15David asked him, "Can you lead me down
to this raiding party?"
He answered, "Swear to me before God that
you will not kill me or hand me over to my
master, and I will take you down to them."
16He led David down, and there they were,
scattered over the countryside, eating, drinking
and reveling because of the great amount of
plunder they had taken from the land of the
Philistines and from Judah. 17David fought
them from dusk until the evening of the next
day, and none of them got away, except four
hundred young men who rode off on camels
and fled. 18David recovered everything the
Amalekites had taken, including his two
wives. 19Nothing was missing: young or old,
boy or girl, plunder or anything else they had
taken. David brought everything back. 20He
took all the flocks and herds, and his men
drove them ahead of the other livestock, saying, "This is David's plunder."
21Then David came to the two hundred men
who had been too exhausted to follow him and
who were left behind at the Besor Ravine.
They came out to meet David and the people
with him. As David and his men approached,
he greeted them. 22But all the evil men and
troublemakers among David's followers said,
"Because they did not go out with us, we will
not share with them the plunder we recovered.
However, each man may take his wife and
children and go."
23David replied, "No, my brothers, you must
not do that with what the LORD has given us.
He has protected us and handed over to us the
forces that came against us. 24Who will listen
to what you say? The share of the man who
stayed with the supplies is to be the same as
that of him who went down to the battle. All
will share alike." 25David made this a statute
and ordinance for Israel from that day to this.
26When David arrived in Ziklag, he sent
some of the plunder to the elders of Judah, who
were his friends, saying, "Here is a present for
you from the plunder of the LORD's enemies."
27He sent it to those who were in Bethel,
Ramoth Negev and Jattir; 28to those in Aroer,
Siphmoth, Eshtemoa 29and Racal; to those in
the towns of the Jerahmeelites and the Kenites;
30to those in Hormah, Bor Ashan, Athach
31and Hebron; and to those in all the other
places where David and his men had roamed.

Saul Takes His Life

31 Now the Philistines fought against Israel; the Israelites fled before them, and
many fell slain on Mount Gilboa. 2The Philistines pressed hard after Saul and his sons, and
they killed his sons Jonathan, Abinadab and

Malki-Shua. 3The fighting grew fierce around Saul, and when the archers overtook him, they wounded him critically.

4Saul said to his armor-bearer, "Draw your sword and run me through, or these uncircumcised fellows will come and run me through and abuse me."

But his armor-bearer was terrified and would not do it; so Saul took his own sword and fell on it. 5When the armor-bearer saw that Saul was dead, he too fell on his sword and died with him. 6So Saul and his three sons and his armor-bearer and all his men died together that same day.

7When the Israelites along the valley and those across the Jordan saw that the Israelite army had fled and that Saul and his sons had died, they abandoned their towns and fled. And the Philistines came and occupied them.

8The next day, when the Philistines came to strip the dead, they found Saul and his three sons fallen on Mount Gilboa. 9They cut off his head and stripped off his armor, and they sent messengers throughout the land of the Philistines to proclaim the news in the temple of their idols and among their people. 10They put his armor in the temple of the Ashtoreths and fastened his body to the wall of Beth Shan.

11When the people of Jabesh Gilead heard of what the Philistines had done to Saul, 12all their valiant men journeyed through the night to Beth Shan. They took down the bodies of Saul and his sons from the wall of Beth Shan and went to Jabesh, where they burned them. 13Then they took their bones and buried them under a tamarisk tree at Jabesh, and they fasted seven days.

2 Samuel

David Hears of Saul's Death

1 After the death of Saul, David returned from defeating the Amalekites and stayed in Ziklag two days. 2On the third day a man arrived from Saul's camp, with his clothes torn and with dust on his head. When he came to David, he fell to the ground to pay him honor.

3"Where have you come from?" David asked him.

He answered, "I have escaped from the Israelite camp."

4"What happened?" David asked. "Tell me."

He said, "The men fled from the battle. Many of them fell and died. And Saul and his son Jonathan are dead."

5Then David said to the young man who brought him the report, "How do you know that Saul and his son Jonathan are dead?"

6"I happened to be on Mount Gilboa," the young man said, "and there was Saul, leaning on his spear, with the chariots and riders almost upon him. 7When he turned around and saw me, he called out to me, and I said, 'What can I do?'

8"He asked me, 'Who are you?'

" 'An Amalekite,' I answered.

9"Then he said to me, 'Stand over me and kill me! I am in the throes of death, but I'm still alive.'

10"So I stood over him and killed him, because I knew that after he had fallen he could not survive. And I took the crown that was on his head and the band on his arm and have brought them here to my lord."

11Then David and all the men with him took hold of their clothes and tore them. 12They mourned and wept and fasted till evening for Saul and his son Jonathan, and for the army of the LORD and the house of Israel, because they had fallen by the sword.

13David said to the young man who brought him the report, "Where are you from?"

"I am the son of an alien, an Amalekite," he answered.

14David asked him, "Why were you not afraid to lift your hand to destroy the LORD's anointed?"

15Then David called one of his men and said, "Go, strike him down!" So he struck him down, and he died. 16For David had said to him, "Your blood be on your own head. Your own mouth testified against you when you said, 'I killed the LORD's anointed.' "

David's Lament for Saul and Jonathan

17David took up this lament concerning Saul and his son Jonathan, 18and ordered that the men of Judah be taught this lament of the bow (it is written in the Book of Jashar):

19"Your glory, O Israel, lies slain on your
heights.
How the mighty have fallen!

20"Tell it not in Gath,
proclaim it not in the streets of
Ashkelon,
lest the daughters of the Philistines be
glad,
lest the daughters of the uncircumcised
rejoice.

21"O mountains of Gilboa,
may you have neither dew nor rain,
nor fields that yield offerings ⌞of grain⌟.
For there the shield of the mighty was
defiled,
the shield of Saul—no longer rubbed
with oil.

22From the blood of the slain,
from the flesh of the mighty,
the bow of Jonathan did not turn back,
the sword of Saul did not return
unsatisfied.

23"Saul and Jonathan—
in life they were loved and gracious,
and in death they were not parted.
They were swifter than eagles,
they were stronger than lions.

24"O daughters of Israel,
weep for Saul,
who clothed you in scarlet and finery,
who adorned your garments with
ornaments of gold.

25"How the mighty have fallen in battle!
Jonathan lies slain on your heights.
26I grieve for you, Jonathan my brother;
you were very dear to me.
Your love for me was wonderful,
more wonderful than that of women.

27"How the mighty have fallen!
The weapons of war have perished!"

David Anointed King Over Judah

2 In the course of time, David inquired of the
LORD. "Shall I go up to one of the towns of
Judah?" he asked.

The LORD said, "Go up."

David asked, "Where shall I go?"

"To Hebron," the LORD answered.

2So David went up there with his two wives,
Ahinoam of Jezreel and Abigail, the widow of
Nabal of Carmel. 3David also took the men
who were with him, each with his family, and
they settled in Hebron and its towns. 4Then the
men of Judah came to Hebron and there they
anointed David king over the house of Judah.

When David was told that it was the men of
Jabesh Gilead who had buried Saul, 5he sent
messengers to the men of Jabesh Gilead to say
to them, "The LORD bless you for showing this
kindness to Saul your master by burying him.
6May the LORD now show you kindness and
faithfulness, and I too will show you the same
favor because you have done this. 7Now then,
be strong and brave, for Saul your master is
dead, and the house of Judah has anointed me
king over them."

War Between the Houses of David and Saul

8Meanwhile, Abner son of Ner, the commander of Saul's army, had taken Ish-Bosheth
son of Saul and brought him over to Mahanaim. 9He made him king over Gilead, Ashuri[a]
and Jezreel, and also over Ephraim, Benjamin
and all Israel.

10Ish-Bosheth son of Saul was forty years
old when he became king over Israel, and he
reigned two years. The house of Judah, however, followed David. 11The length of time David
was king in Hebron over the house of Judah
was seven years and six months.

12Abner son of Ner, together with the men
of Ish-Bosheth son of Saul, left Mahanaim and
went to Gibeon. 13Joab son of Zeruiah and
David's men went out and met them at the
pool of Gibeon. One group sat down on one
side of the pool and one group on the other
side.

14Then Abner said to Joab, "Let's have
some of the young men get up and fight hand
to hand in front of us."

"All right, let them do it," Joab said.

15So they stood up and were counted off—
twelve men for Benjamin and Ish-Bosheth son
of Saul, and twelve for David. 16Then each
man grabbed his opponent by the head and
thrust his dagger into his opponent's side, and
they fell down together. So that place in Gibeon was called Helkath Hazzurim.[b]

17The battle that day was very fierce, and
Abner and the men of Israel were defeated by
David's men.

18The three sons of Zeruiah were there:
Joab, Abishai and Asahel. Now Asahel was as
fleet-footed as a wild gazelle. 19He chased Abner, turning neither to the right nor to the left
as he pursued him. 20Abner looked behind him
and asked, "Is that you, Asahel?"

"It is," he answered.

21Then Abner said to him, "Turn aside to the
right or to the left; take on one of the young
men and strip him of his weapons." But Asahel
would not stop chasing him.

22Again Abner warned Asahel, "Stop chasing me! Why should I strike you down? How
could I look your brother Joab in the face?"

23But Asahel refused to give up the pursuit;
so Abner thrust the butt of his spear into Asahel's stomach, and the spear came out through
his back. He fell there and died on the spot.
And every man stopped when he came to the
place where Asahel had fallen and died.

24But Joab and Abishai pursued Abner, and
as the sun was setting, they came to the hill of
Ammah, near Giah on the way to the wasteland of Gibeon. 25Then the men of Benjamin
rallied behind Abner. They formed themselves
into a group and took their stand on top of a
hill.

26Abner called out to Joab, "Must the sword
devour forever? Don't you realize that this will
end in bitterness? How long before you order
your men to stop pursuing their brothers?"

27Joab answered, "As surely as God lives, if
you had not spoken, the men would have continued the pursuit of their brothers until morning.[c]"

28So Joab blew the trumpet, and all the men
came to a halt; they no longer pursued Israel,
nor did they fight anymore.

29All that night Abner and his men marched
through the Arabah. They crossed the Jordan,

[a]9 Or *Asher* [b]16 *Helkath Hazzurim* means *field of daggers* or *field of hostilities.* [c]27 Or *spoken this morning, the men would not have taken up the pursuit of their brothers*; or *spoken, the men would have given up the pursuit of their brothers by morning*

continued through the whole Bithron[a] and came to Mahanaim.

30Then Joab returned from pursuing Abner and assembled all his men. Besides Asahel, nineteen of David's men were found missing. 31But David's men had killed three hundred and sixty Benjamites who were with Abner. 32They took Asahel and buried him in his father's tomb at Bethlehem. Then Joab and his men marched all night and arrived at Hebron by daybreak.

3 The war between the house of Saul and the house of David lasted a long time. David grew stronger and stronger, while the house of Saul grew weaker and weaker.

2Sons were born to David in Hebron:

His firstborn was Amnon the son of Ahinoam of Jezreel;
3his second, Kileab the son of Abigail the widow of Nabal of Carmel;
the third, Absalom the son of Maacah daughter of Talmai king of Geshur;
4the fourth, Adonijah the son of Haggith;
the fifth, Shephatiah the son of Abital;
5and the sixth, Ithream the son of David's wife Eglah.
These were born to David in Hebron.

Abner Goes Over to David

6During the war between the house of Saul and the house of David, Abner had been strengthening his own position in the house of Saul. 7Now Saul had had a concubine named Rizpah daughter of Aiah. And Ish-Bosheth said to Abner, "Why did you sleep with my father's concubine?"

8Abner was very angry because of what Ish-Bosheth said and he answered, "Am I a dog's head—on Judah's side? This very day I am loyal to the house of your father Saul and to his family and friends. I haven't handed you over to David. Yet now you accuse me of an offense involving this woman! 9May God deal with Abner, be it ever so severely, if I do not do for David what the LORD promised him on oath 10and transfer the kingdom from the house of Saul and establish David's throne over Israel and Judah from Dan to Beersheba." 11Ish-Bosheth did not dare to say another word to Abner, because he was afraid of him.

12Then Abner sent messengers on his behalf to say to David, "Whose land is it? Make an agreement with me, and I will help you bring all Israel over to you."

13"Good," said David. "I will make an agreement with you. But I demand one thing of you: Do not come into my presence unless you bring Michal daughter of Saul when you come to see me." 14Then David sent messengers to Ish-Bosheth son of Saul, demanding, "Give me my wife Michal, whom I betrothed to myself for the price of a hundred Philistine foreskins."

15So Ish-Bosheth gave orders and had her taken away from her husband Paltiel son of Laish. 16Her husband, however, went with her, weeping behind her all the way to Bahurim. Then Abner said to him, "Go back home!" So he went back.

17Abner conferred with the elders of Israel and said, "For some time you have wanted to make David your king. 18Now do it! For the LORD promised David, 'By my servant David I will rescue my people Israel from the hand of the Philistines and from the hand of all their enemies.' "

19Abner also spoke to the Benjamites in person. Then he went to Hebron to tell David everything that Israel and the whole house of Benjamin wanted to do. 20When Abner, who had twenty men with him, came to David at Hebron, David prepared a feast for him and his men. 21Then Abner said to David, "Let me go at once and assemble all Israel for my lord the king, so that they may make a compact with you, and that you may rule over all that your heart desires." So David sent Abner away, and he went in peace.

Joab Murders Abner

22Just then David's men and Joab returned from a raid and brought with them a great deal of plunder. But Abner was no longer with David in Hebron, because David had sent him away, and he had gone in peace. 23When Joab and all the soldiers with him arrived, he was told that Abner son of Ner had come to the king and that the king had sent him away and that he had gone in peace.

24So Joab went to the king and said, "What have you done? Look, Abner came to you. Why did you let him go? Now he is gone! 25You know Abner son of Ner; he came to deceive you and observe your movements and find out everything you are doing."

26Joab then left David and sent messengers after Abner, and they brought him back from the well of Sirah. But David did not know it. 27Now when Abner returned to Hebron, Joab took him aside into the gateway, as though to speak with him privately. And there, to avenge the blood of his brother Asahel, Joab stabbed him in the stomach, and he died.

28Later, when David heard about this, he said, "I and my kingdom are forever innocent before the LORD concerning the blood of Abner son of Ner. 29May his blood fall upon the head of Joab and upon all his father's house! May Joab's house never be without someone who has a running sore or leprosy[b] or who leans on a crutch or who falls by the sword or who lacks food."

30(Joab and his brother Abishai murdered Abner because he had killed their brother Asahel in the battle at Gibeon.)

31Then David said to Joab and all the people with him, "Tear your clothes and put on sack-

[a]29 Or *morning*; or *ravine*; the meaning of the Hebrew for this word is uncertain. [b]29 The Hebrew word was used for various diseases affecting the skin—not necessarily leprosy.

cloth and walk in mourning in front of Abner." King David himself walked behind the bier. 32They buried Abner in Hebron, and the king wept aloud at Abner's tomb. All the people wept also.

33The king sang this lament for Abner:

"Should Abner have died as the lawless
die?
34 Your hands were not bound,
your feet were not fettered.
You fell as one falls before wicked men."

And all the people wept over him again.

35Then they all came and urged David to eat something while it was still day; but David took an oath, saying, "May God deal with me, be it ever so severely, if I taste bread or anything else before the sun sets!"

36All the people took note and were pleased; indeed, everything the king did pleased them. 37So on that day all the people and all Israel knew that the king had no part in the murder of Abner son of Ner.

38Then the king said to his men, "Do you not realize that a prince and a great man has fallen in Israel this day? 39And today, though I am the anointed king, I am weak, and these sons of Zeruiah are too strong for me. May the LORD repay the evildoer according to his evil deeds!"

Ish-Bosheth Murdered

4 When Ish-Bosheth son of Saul heard that Abner had died in Hebron, he lost courage, and all Israel became alarmed. 2Now Saul's son had two men who were leaders of raiding bands. One was named Baanah and the other Recab; they were sons of Rimmon the Beerothite from the tribe of Benjamin—Beeroth is considered part of Benjamin, 3because the people of Beeroth fled to Gittaim and have lived there as aliens to this day.

4(Jonathan son of Saul had a son who was lame in both feet. He was five years old when the news about Saul and Jonathan came from Jezreel. His nurse picked him up and fled, but as she hurried to leave, he fell and became crippled. His name was Mephibosheth.)

5Now Recab and Baanah, the sons of Rimmon the Beerothite, set out for the house of Ish-Bosheth, and they arrived there in the heat of the day while he was taking his noonday rest. 6They went into the inner part of the house as if to get some wheat, and they stabbed him in the stomach. Then Recab and his brother Baanah slipped away.

7They had gone into the house while he was lying on the bed in his bedroom. After they stabbed and killed him, they cut off his head. Taking it with them, they traveled all night by way of the Arabah. 8They brought the head of Ish-Bosheth to David at Hebron and said to the king, "Here is the head of Ish-Bosheth son of Saul, your enemy, who tried to take your life. This day the LORD has avenged my lord the king against Saul and his offspring."

9David answered Recab and his brother Baanah, the sons of Rimmon the Beerothite, "As surely as the LORD lives, who has delivered me out of all trouble, 10when a man told me, 'Saul is dead,' and thought he was bringing good news, I seized him and put him to death in Ziklag. That was the reward I gave him for his news! 11How much more—when wicked men have killed an innocent man in his own house and on his own bed—should I not now demand his blood from your hand and rid the earth of you!"

12So David gave an order to his men, and they killed them. They cut off their hands and feet and hung the bodies by the pool in Hebron. But they took the head of Ish-Bosheth and buried it in Abner's tomb at Hebron.

David Becomes King Over Israel

5 All the tribes of Israel came to David at Hebron and said, "We are your own flesh and blood. 2In the past, while Saul was king over us, you were the one who led Israel on their military campaigns. And the LORD said to you, 'You will shepherd my people Israel, and you will become their ruler.' "

3When all the elders of Israel had come to King David at Hebron, the king made a compact with them at Hebron before the LORD, and they anointed David king over Israel.

4David was thirty years old when he became king, and he reigned forty years. 5In Hebron he reigned over Judah seven years and six months, and in Jerusalem he reigned over all Israel and Judah thirty-three years.

David Conquers Jerusalem

6The king and his men marched to Jerusalem to attack the Jebusites, who lived there. The Jebusites said to David, "You will not get in here; even the blind and the lame can ward you off." They thought, "David cannot get in here." 7Nevertheless, David captured the fortress of Zion, the City of David.

8On that day, David said, "Anyone who conquers the Jebusites will have to use the water shaft[a] to reach those 'lame and blind' who are David's enemies.[b]" That is why they say, "The 'blind and lame' will not enter the palace."

9David then took up residence in the fortress and called it the City of David. He built up the area around it, from the supporting terraces[c] inward. 10And he became more and more powerful, because the LORD God Almighty was with him.

11Now Hiram king of Tyre sent messengers to David, along with cedar logs and carpenters and stonemasons, and they built a palace for David. 12And David knew that the LORD had established him as king over Israel and had exalted his kingdom for the sake of his people Israel.

[a]8 Or *use scaling hooks* [b]8 Or *are hated by David* [c]9 Or *the Millo*

13After he left Hebron, David took more concubines and wives in Jerusalem, and more sons and daughters were born to him. 14These are the names of the children born to him there: Shammua, Shobab, Nathan, Solomon, 15Ibhar, Elishua, Nepheg, Japhia, 16Elishama, Eliada and Eliphelet.

David Defeats the Philistines

17When the Philistines heard that David had been anointed king over Israel, they went up in full force to search for him, but David heard about it and went down to the stronghold. 18Now the Philistines had come and spread out in the Valley of Rephaim; 19so David inquired of the LORD, "Shall I go and attack the Philistines? Will you hand them over to me?"

The LORD answered him, "Go, for I will surely hand the Philistines over to you."

20So David went to Baal Perazim, and there he defeated them. He said, "As waters break out, the LORD has broken out against my enemies before me." So that place was called Baal Perazim.[a] 21The Philistines abandoned their idols there, and David and his men carried them off.

22Once more the Philistines came up and spread out in the Valley of Rephaim; 23so David inquired of the LORD, and he answered, "Do not go straight up, but circle around behind them and attack them in front of the balsam trees. 24As soon as you hear the sound of marching in the tops of the balsam trees, move quickly, because that will mean the LORD has gone out in front of you to strike the Philistine army." 25So David did as the LORD commanded him, and he struck down the Philistines all the way from Gibeon[b] to Gezer.

The Ark Brought to Jerusalem

6 David again brought together out of Israel chosen men, thirty thousand in all. 2He and all his men set out from Baalah of Judah[c] to bring up from there the ark of God, which is called by the Name,[d] the name of the LORD Almighty, who is enthroned between the cherubim that are on the ark. 3They set the ark of God on a new cart and brought it from the house of Abinadab, which was on the hill. Uzzah and Ahio, sons of Abinadab, were guiding the new cart 4with the ark of God on it,[e] and Ahio was walking in front of it. 5David and the whole house of Israel were celebrating with all their might before the LORD, with songs[f] and with harps, lyres, tambourines, sistrums and cymbals.

6When they came to the threshing floor of Nacon, Uzzah reached out and took hold of the ark of God, because the oxen stumbled. 7The LORD's anger burned against Uzzah because of his irreverent act; therefore God struck him down and he died there beside the ark of God.

8Then David was angry because the LORD's wrath had broken out against Uzzah, and to this day that place is called Perez Uzzah.[g]

9David was afraid of the LORD that day and said, "How can the ark of the LORD ever come to me?" 10He was not willing to take the ark of the LORD to be with him in the City of David. Instead, he took it aside to the house of Obed-Edom the Gittite. 11The ark of the LORD remained in the house of Obed-Edom the Gittite for three months, and the LORD blessed him and his entire household.

12Now King David was told, "The LORD has blessed the household of Obed-Edom and everything he has, because of the ark of God." So David went down and brought up the ark of God from the house of Obed-Edom to the City of David with rejoicing. 13When those who were carrying the ark of the LORD had taken six steps, he sacrificed a bull and a fattened calf. 14David, wearing a linen ephod, danced before the LORD with all his might, 15while he and the entire house of Israel brought up the ark of the LORD with shouts and the sound of trumpets.

16As the ark of the LORD was entering the City of David, Michal daughter of Saul watched from a window. And when she saw King David leaping and dancing before the LORD, she despised him in her heart.

17They brought the ark of the LORD and set it in its place inside the tent that David had pitched for it, and David sacrificed burnt offerings and fellowship offerings[h] before the LORD. 18After he had finished sacrificing the burnt offerings and fellowship offerings, he blessed the people in the name of the LORD Almighty. 19Then he gave a loaf of bread, a cake of dates and a cake of raisins to each person in the whole crowd of Israelites, both men and women. And all the people went to their homes.

20When David returned home to bless his household, Michal daughter of Saul came out to meet him and said, "How the king of Israel has distinguished himself today, disrobing in the sight of the slave girls of his servants as any vulgar fellow would!"

21David said to Michal, "It was before the LORD, who chose me rather than your father or anyone from his house when he appointed me ruler over the LORD's people Israel—I will celebrate before the LORD. 22I will become even more undignified than this, and I will be humiliated in my own eyes. But by these slave girls you spoke of, I will be held in honor."

23And Michal daughter of Saul had no children to the day of her death.

[a] *20 Baal Perazim* means *the lord who breaks out.* [b] *25* Septuagint (see also 1 Chron. 14:16); Hebrew *Geba*
[c] *2* That is, Kiriath Jearim; Hebrew *Baale Judah,* a variant of *Baalah of Judah* [d] *2* Hebrew; Septuagint and Vulgate do not have *the Name.* [e] *3,4* Dead Sea Scrolls and some Septuagint manuscripts; Masoretic Text *cart* [4]*and they brought it with the ark of God from the house of Abinadab, which was on the hill*
[f] *5* See Dead Sea Scrolls, Septuagint and 1 Chronicles 13:8; Masoretic Text *celebrating before the LORD with all kinds of instruments made of pine.* [g] *8 Perez Uzzah* means *outbreak against Uzzah.* [h] *17* Traditionally *peace offerings*; also in verse 18

God's Promise to David

7 After the king was settled in his palace and
the LORD had given him rest from all his
enemies around him, 2he said to Nathan the
prophet, "Here I am, living in a palace of cedar, while the ark of God remains in a tent."
3Nathan replied to the king, "Whatever you
have in mind, go ahead and do it, for the LORD
is with you."
4That night the word of the LORD came to
Nathan, saying:

> 5"Go and tell my servant David, 'This
> is what the LORD says: Are you the one to
> build me a house to dwell in? 6I have not
> dwelt in a house from the day I brought
> the Israelites up out of Egypt to this day.
> I have been moving from place to place
> with a tent as my dwelling. 7Wherever I
> have moved with all the Israelites, did I
> ever say to any of their rulers whom
> I commanded to shepherd my people Isra-
> el, "Why have you not built me a house of
> cedar?" '
> 8"Now then, tell my servant David,
> 'This is what the LORD Almighty says: I
> took you from the pasture and from fol-
> lowing the flock to be ruler over my peo-
> ple Israel. 9I have been with you wherever
> you have gone, and I have cut off all your
> enemies from before you. Now I will
> make your name great, like the names of
> the greatest men of the earth. 10And I will
> provide a place for my people Israel and
> will plant them so that they can have a
> home of their own and no longer be dis-
> turbed. Wicked people will not oppress
> them anymore, as they did at the begin-
> ning 11and have done ever since the time
> I appointed leaders[a] over my people Isra-
> el. I will also give you rest from all your
> enemies.
> " 'The LORD declares to you that the
> LORD himself will establish a house for
> you: 12When your days are over and you
> rest with your fathers, I will raise up your
> offspring to succeed you, who will come
> from your own body, and I will establish
> his kingdom. 13He is the one who will
> build a house for my Name, and I will
> establish the throne of his kingdom forev-
> er. 14I will be his father, and he will be my
> son. When he does wrong, I will punish
> him with the rod of men, with floggings
> inflicted by men. 15But my love will nev-
> er be taken away from him, as I took it
> away from Saul, whom I removed from
> before you. 16Your house and your king-
> dom will endure forever before me[b]; your
> throne will be established forever.' "

17Nathan reported to David all the words of
this entire revelation.

David's Prayer

18Then King David went in and sat before
the LORD, and he said:

> "Who am I, O Sovereign LORD, and
> what is my family, that you have brought
> me this far? 19And as if this were not
> enough in your sight, O Sovereign LORD,
> you have also spoken about the future of
> the house of your servant. Is this your
> usual way of dealing with man,
> O Sovereign LORD?
> 20"What more can David say to you?
> For you know your servant, O Sovereign
> LORD. 21For the sake of your word and
> according to your will, you have done this
> great thing and made it known to your
> servant.
> 22"How great you are, O Sovereign
> LORD! There is no one like you, and there
> is no God but you, as we have heard with
> our own ears. 23And who is like your peo-
> ple Israel—the one nation on earth that
> God went out to redeem as a people for
> himself, and to make a name for himself,
> and to perform great and awesome won-
> ders by driving out nations and their gods
> from before your people, whom you re-
> deemed from Egypt?[c] 24You have estab-
> lished your people Israel as your very
> own forever, and you, O LORD, have be-
> come their God.
> 25"And now, LORD God, keep forever
> the promise you have made concerning
> your servant and his house. Do as you
> promised, 26so that your name will be
> great forever. Then men will say, 'The
> LORD Almighty is God over Israel!' And
> the house of your servant David will be
> established before you.
> 27"O LORD Almighty, God of Israel,
> you have revealed this to your servant,
> saying, 'I will build a house for you.' So
> your servant has found courage to offer
> you this prayer. 28O Sovereign LORD, you
> are God! Your words are trustworthy, and
> you have promised these good things to
> your servant. 29Now be pleased to bless
> the house of your servant, that it may
> continue forever in your sight; for you,
> O Sovereign LORD, have spoken, and
> with your blessing the house of your ser-
> vant will be blessed forever."

David's Victories

8 In the course of time, David defeated the
Philistines and subdued them, and he took
Metheg Ammah from the control of the Philistines.
2David also defeated the Moabites. He made
them lie down on the ground and measured
them off with a length of cord. Every two
lengths of them were put to death, and the third
length was allowed to live. So the Moabites

[a]*11* Traditionally *judges* [b]*16* Some Hebrew manuscripts and Septuagint; most Hebrew manuscripts *you*
[c]*23* See Septuagint and 1 Chron. 17:21; Hebrew *wonders for your land and before your people, whom you redeemed from Egypt, from the nations and their gods.*

became subject to David and brought tribute.
3 Moreover, David fought Hadadezer son of
Rehob, king of Zobah, when he went to restore
his control along the Euphrates River. 4 David
captured a thousand of his chariots, seven
thousand charioteers[a] and twenty thousand
foot soldiers. He hamstrung all but a hundred
of the chariot horses.
5 When the Arameans of Damascus came to
help Hadadezer king of Zobah, David struck
down twenty-two thousand of them. 6 He put
garrisons in the Aramean kingdom of Damascus, and the Arameans became subject to him
and brought tribute. The LORD gave David victory wherever he went.
7 David took the gold shields that belonged
to the officers of Hadadezer and brought them
to Jerusalem. 8 From Tebah[b] and Berothai,
towns that belonged to Hadadezer, King David
took a great quantity of bronze.
9 When Tou[c] king of Hamath heard that David had defeated the entire army of Hadadezer,
10 he sent his son Joram[d] to King David to
greet him and congratulate him on his victory
in battle over Hadadezer, who had been at war
with Tou. Joram brought with him articles of
silver and gold and bronze.
11 King David dedicated these articles to the
LORD, as he had done with the silver and gold
from all the nations he had subdued: 12 Edom[e]
and Moab, the Ammonites and the Philistines,
and Amalek. He also dedicated the plunder
taken from Hadadezer son of Rehob, king of
Zobah.
13 And David became famous after he returned from striking down eighteen thousand
Edomites[f] in the Valley of Salt.
14 He put garrisons throughout Edom, and all
the Edomites became subject to David. The
LORD gave David victory wherever he went.

David's Officials

15 David reigned over all Israel, doing what
was just and right for all his people. 16 Joab son
of Zeruiah was over the army; Jehoshaphat son
of Ahilud was recorder; 17 Zadok son of Ahitub
and Ahimelech son of Abiathar were priests;
Seraiah was secretary; 18 Benaiah son of Jehoiada was over the Kerethites and Pelethites; and
David's sons were royal advisers.[g]

David and Mephibosheth

9 David asked, "Is there anyone still left of
the house of Saul to whom I can show
kindness for Jonathan's sake?"
2 Now there was a servant of Saul's household named Ziba. They called him to appear
before David, and the king said to him, "Are
you Ziba?"
"Your servant," he replied.
3 The king asked, "Is there no one still left of
the house of Saul to whom I can show God's
kindness?"
Ziba answered the king, "There is still a son
of Jonathan; he is crippled in both feet."
4 "Where is he?" the king asked.
Ziba answered, "He is at the house of Makir
son of Ammiel in Lo Debar."
5 So King David had him brought from Lo
Debar, from the house of Makir son of Ammiel.
6 When Mephibosheth son of Jonathan, the
son of Saul, came to David, he bowed down to
pay him honor.
David said, "Mephibosheth!"
"Your servant," he replied.
7 "Don't be afraid," David said to him, "for
I will surely show you kindness for the sake of
your father Jonathan. I will restore to you all
the land that belonged to your grandfather
Saul, and you will always eat at my table."
8 Mephibosheth bowed down and said,
"What is your servant, that you should notice
a dead dog like me?"
9 Then the king summoned Ziba, Saul's servant, and said to him, "I have given your master's grandson everything that belonged to
Saul and his family. 10 You and your sons and
your servants are to farm the land for him and
bring in the crops, so that your master's grandson may be provided for. And Mephibosheth,
grandson of your master, will always eat at my
table." (Now Ziba had fifteen sons and twenty
servants.)
11 Then Ziba said to the king, "Your servant
will do whatever my lord the king commands
his servant to do." So Mephibosheth ate at David's[h] table like one of the king's sons.
12 Mephibosheth had a young son named
Mica, and all the members of Ziba's household
were servants of Mephibosheth. 13 And Mephibosheth lived in Jerusalem, because he always ate at the king's table, and he was crippled in both feet.

David Defeats the Ammonites

10 In the course of time, the king of the
Ammonites died, and his son Hanun
succeeded him as king. 2 David thought, "I will
show kindness to Hanun son of Nahash, just as
his father showed kindness to me." So David
sent a delegation to express his sympathy to
Hanun concerning his father.
When David's men came to the land of the
Ammonites, 3 the Ammonite nobles said to Hanun their lord, "Do you think David is honoring your father by sending men to you to express sympathy? Hasn't David sent them to

[a]*4* Septuagint (see also Dead Sea Scrolls and 1 Chron. 18:4); Masoretic Text *captured seventeen hundred of his charioteers* [b]*8* See some Septuagint manuscripts (see also 1 Chron. 18:8); Hebrew *Betah.* [c]*9* Hebrew *Toi,* a variant of *Tou;* also in verse 10 [d]*10* A variant of *Hadoram* [e]*12* Some Hebrew manuscripts, Septuagint and Syriac (see also 1 Chron. 18:11); most Hebrew manuscripts *Aram* [f]*13* A few Hebrew manuscripts, Septuagint and Syriac (see also 1 Chron. 18:12); most Hebrew manuscripts *Aram* (that is, Arameans) [g]*18* Or *were priests* [h]*11* Septuagint; Hebrew *my*

you to explore the city and spy it out and overthrow it?" 4So Hanun seized David's men,
shaved off half of each man's beard, cut off
their garments in the middle at the buttocks,
and sent them away.
5When David was told about this, he sent
messengers to meet the men, for they were
greatly humiliated. The king said, "Stay at Jericho till your beards have grown, and then
come back."
6When the Ammonites realized that they
had become a stench in David's nostrils, they
hired twenty thousand Aramean foot soldiers
from Beth Rehob and Zobah, as well as the
king of Maacah with a thousand men, and also
twelve thousand men from Tob.
7On hearing this, David sent Joab out with
the entire army of fighting men. 8The Ammonites came out and drew up in battle formation
at the entrance to their city gate, while the
Arameans of Zobah and Rehob and the men of
Tob and Maacah were by themselves in the
open country.
9Joab saw that there were battle lines in
front of him and behind him; so he selected
some of the best troops in Israel and deployed
them against the Arameans. 10He put the rest
of the men under the command of Abishai his
brother and deployed them against the Ammonites. 11Joab said, "If the Arameans are too
strong for me, then you are to come to my
rescue; but if the Ammonites are too strong for
you, then I will come to rescue you. 12Be
strong and let us fight bravely for our people
and the cities of our God. The LORD will do
what is good in his sight."
13Then Joab and the troops with him advanced to fight the Arameans, and they fled
before him. 14When the Ammonites saw that
the Arameans were fleeing, they fled before
Abishai and went inside the city. So Joab returned from fighting the Ammonites and came
to Jerusalem.
15After the Arameans saw that they had
been routed by Israel, they regrouped. 16Had-
adezer had Arameans brought from beyond the
River[a]; they went to Helam, with Shobach
the commander of Hadadezer's army leading
them.
17When David was told of this, he gathered
all Israel, crossed the Jordan and went to Helam. The Arameans formed their battle lines to
meet David and fought against him. 18But they
fled before Israel, and David killed seven hundred of their charioteers and forty thousand of
their foot soldiers.[b] He also struck down Shobach the commander of their army, and he died
there. 19When all the kings who were vassals
of Hadadezer saw that they had been defeated
by Israel, they made peace with the Israelites
and became subject to them.
So the Arameans were afraid to help the
Ammonites anymore.

David and Bathsheba

11 In the spring, at the time when kings go
off to war, David sent Joab out with the
king's men and the whole Israelite army. They
destroyed the Ammonites and besieged Rabbah. But David remained in Jerusalem.
2One evening David got up from his bed and
walked around on the roof of the palace. From
the roof he saw a woman bathing. The woman
was very beautiful, 3and David sent someone
to find out about her. The man said, "Isn't this
Bathsheba, the daughter of Eliam and the wife
of Uriah the Hittite?" 4Then David sent messengers to get her. She came to him, and he
slept with her. (She had purified herself from
her uncleanness.) Then[c] she went back home.
5The woman conceived and sent word to David, saying, "I am pregnant."
6So David sent this word to Joab: "Send me
Uriah the Hittite." And Joab sent him to David.
7When Uriah came to him, David asked him
how Joab was, how the soldiers were and how
the war was going. 8Then David said to Uriah,
"Go down to your house and wash your feet."
So Uriah left the palace, and a gift from the
king was sent after him. 9But Uriah slept at the
entrance to the palace with all his master's
servants and did not go down to his house.
10When David was told, "Uriah did not go
home," he asked him, "Haven't you just come
from a distance? Why didn't you go home?"
11Uriah said to David, "The ark and Israel
and Judah are staying in tents, and my master
Joab and my lord's men are camped in the
open fields. How could I go to my house to eat
and drink and lie with my wife? As surely as
you live, I will not do such a thing!"
12Then David said to him, "Stay here one
more day, and tomorrow I will send you back."
So Uriah remained in Jerusalem that day and
the next. 13At David's invitation, he ate and
drank with him, and David made him drunk.
But in the evening Uriah went out to sleep on
his mat among his master's servants; he did
not go home.
14In the morning David wrote a letter to
Joab and sent it with Uriah. 15In it he wrote,
"Put Uriah in the front line where the fighting
is fiercest. Then withdraw from him so he will
be struck down and die."
16So while Joab had the city under siege, he
put Uriah at a place where he knew the strongest defenders were. 17When the men of the
city came out and fought against Joab, some of
the men in David's army fell; moreover, Uriah
the Hittite died.
18Joab sent David a full account of the battle. 19He instructed the messenger: "When you
have finished giving the king this account of
the battle, 20the king's anger may flare up, and
he may ask you, 'Why did you get so close to
the city to fight? Didn't you know they would
shoot arrows from the wall? 21Who killed

[a]*16* That is, the Euphrates [b]*18* Some Septuagint manuscripts (see also 1 Chron. 19:18); Hebrew *horsemen*
[c]*4* Or *with her. When she purified herself from her uncleanness,*

Abimelech son of Jerub-Besheth[a]? Didn't a woman throw an upper millstone on him from the wall, so that he died in Thebez? Why did you get so close to the wall?' If he asks you this, then say to him, 'Also, your servant Uriah the Hittite is dead.' "

22 The messenger set out, and when he arrived he told David everything Joab had sent him to say. 23 The messenger said to David, "The men overpowered us and came out against us in the open, but we drove them back to the entrance to the city gate. 24 Then the archers shot arrows at your servants from the wall, and some of the king's men died. Moreover, your servant Uriah the Hittite is dead."

25 David told the messenger, "Say this to Joab: 'Don't let this upset you; the sword devours one as well as another. Press the attack against the city and destroy it.' Say this to encourage Joab."

26 When Uriah's wife heard that her husband was dead, she mourned for him. 27 After the time of mourning was over, David had her brought to his house, and she became his wife and bore him a son. But the thing David had done displeased the LORD.

Nathan Rebukes David

12 The LORD sent Nathan to David. When he came to him, he said, "There were two men in a certain town, one rich and the other poor. 2 The rich man had a very large number of sheep and cattle, 3 but the poor man had nothing except one little ewe lamb he had bought. He raised it, and it grew up with him and his children. It shared his food, drank from his cup and even slept in his arms. It was like a daughter to him.

4 "Now a traveler came to the rich man, but the rich man refrained from taking one of his own sheep or cattle to prepare a meal for the traveler who had come to him. Instead, he took the ewe lamb that belonged to the poor man and prepared it for the one who had come to him."

5 David burned with anger against the man and said to Nathan, "As surely as the LORD lives, the man who did this deserves to die! 6 He must pay for that lamb four times over, because he did such a thing and had no pity."

7 Then Nathan said to David, "You are the man! This is what the LORD, the God of Israel, says: 'I anointed you king over Israel, and I delivered you from the hand of Saul. 8 I gave your master's house to you, and your master's wives into your arms. I gave you the house of Israel and Judah. And if all this had been too little, I would have given you even more. 9 Why did you despise the word of the LORD by doing what is evil in his eyes? You struck down Uriah the Hittite with the sword and took his wife to be your own. You killed him with the sword of the Ammonites. 10 Now, therefore, the sword will never depart from your house, because you despised me and took the wife of Uriah the Hittite to be your own.'

11 "This is what the LORD says: 'Out of your own household I am going to bring calamity upon you. Before your very eyes I will take your wives and give them to one who is close to you, and he will lie with your wives in broad daylight. 12 You did it in secret, but I will do this thing in broad daylight before all Israel.' "

13 Then David said to Nathan, "I have sinned against the LORD."

Nathan replied, "The LORD has taken away your sin. You are not going to die. 14 But because by doing this you have made the enemies of the LORD show utter contempt,[b] the son born to you will die."

15 After Nathan had gone home, the LORD struck the child that Uriah's wife had borne to David, and he became ill. 16 David pleaded with God for the child. He fasted and went into his house and spent the nights lying on the ground. 17 The elders of his household stood beside him to get him up from the ground, but he refused, and he would not eat any food with them.

18 On the seventh day the child died. David's servants were afraid to tell him that the child was dead, for they thought, "While the child was still living, we spoke to David but he would not listen to us. How can we tell him the child is dead? He may do something desperate."

19 David noticed that his servants were whispering among themselves and he realized the child was dead. "Is the child dead?" he asked.

"Yes," they replied, "he is dead."

20 Then David got up from the ground. After he had washed, put on lotions and changed his clothes, he went into the house of the LORD and worshiped. Then he went to his own house, and at his request they served him food, and he ate.

21 His servants asked him, "Why are you acting this way? While the child was alive, you fasted and wept, but now that the child is dead, you get up and eat!"

22 He answered, "While the child was still alive, I fasted and wept. I thought, 'Who knows? The LORD may be gracious to me and let the child live.' 23 But now that he is dead, why should I fast? Can I bring him back again? I will go to him, but he will not return to me."

24 Then David comforted his wife Bathsheba, and he went to her and lay with her. She gave birth to a son, and they named him Solomon. The LORD loved him; 25 and because the LORD loved him, he sent word through Nathan the prophet to name him Jedidiah.[c]

26 Meanwhile Joab fought against Rabbah of the Ammonites and captured the royal citadel. 27 Joab then sent messengers to David, saying, "I have fought against Rabbah and taken its water supply. 28 Now muster the rest of the troops and besiege the city and capture it. Oth-

[a] 21 Also known as *Jerub-Baal* (that is, Gideon)
[b] 14 Masoretic Text; an ancient Hebrew scribal tradition *this you have shown utter contempt for the LORD*
[c] 25 *Jedidiah* means *loved by the LORD.*

erwise I will take the city, and it will be named after me."

29So David mustered the entire army and went to Rabbah, and attacked and captured it. 30He took the crown from the head of their king[a]—its weight was a talent[b] of gold, and it was set with precious stones—and it was placed on David's head. He took a great quantity of plunder from the city 31and brought out the people who were there, consigning them to labor with saws and with iron picks and axes, and he made them work at brickmaking.[c] He did this to all the Ammonite towns. Then David and his entire army returned to Jerusalem.

Amnon and Tamar

13 In the course of time, Amnon son of David fell in love with Tamar, the beautiful sister of Absalom son of David.

2Amnon became frustrated to the point of illness on account of his sister Tamar, for she was a virgin, and it seemed impossible for him to do anything to her.

3Now Amnon had a friend named Jonadab son of Shimeah, David's brother. Jonadab was a very shrewd man. 4He asked Amnon, "Why do you, the king's son, look so haggard morning after morning? Won't you tell me?"

Amnon said to him, "I'm in love with Tamar, my brother Absalom's sister."

5"Go to bed and pretend to be ill," Jonadab said. "When your father comes to see you, say to him, 'I would like my sister Tamar to come and give me something to eat. Let her prepare the food in my sight so I may watch her and then eat it from her hand.' "

6So Amnon lay down and pretended to be ill. When the king came to see him, Amnon said to him, "I would like my sister Tamar to come and make some special bread in my sight, so I may eat from her hand."

7David sent word to Tamar at the palace: "Go to the house of your brother Amnon and prepare some food for him." 8So Tamar went to the house of her brother Amnon, who was lying down. She took some dough, kneaded it, made the bread in his sight and baked it. 9Then she took the pan and served him the bread, but he refused to eat.

"Send everyone out of here," Amnon said. So everyone left him. 10Then Amnon said to Tamar, "Bring the food here into my bedroom so I may eat from your hand." And Tamar took the bread she had prepared and brought it to her brother Amnon in his bedroom. 11But when she took it to him to eat, he grabbed her and said, "Come to bed with me, my sister."

12"Don't, my brother!" she said to him. "Don't force me. Such a thing should not be done in Israel! Don't do this wicked thing. 13What about me? Where could I get rid of my disgrace? And what about you? You would be like one of the wicked fools in Israel. Please speak to the king; he will not keep me from being married to you." 14But he refused to listen to her, and since he was stronger than she, he raped her.

15Then Amnon hated her with intense hatred. In fact, he hated her more than he had loved her. Amnon said to her, "Get up and get out!"

16"No!" she said to him. "Sending me away would be a greater wrong than what you have already done to me."

But he refused to listen to her. 17He called his personal servant and said, "Get this woman out of here and bolt the door after her." 18So his servant put her out and bolted the door after her. She was wearing a richly ornamented[d] robe, for this was the kind of garment the virgin daughters of the king wore. 19Tamar put ashes on her head and tore the ornamented[e] robe she was wearing. She put her hand on her head and went away, weeping aloud as she went.

20Her brother Absalom said to her, "Has that Amnon, your brother, been with you? Be quiet now, my sister; he is your brother. Don't take this thing to heart." And Tamar lived in her brother Absalom's house, a desolate woman.

21When King David heard all this, he was furious. 22Absalom never said a word to Amnon, either good or bad; he hated Amnon because he had disgraced his sister Tamar.

Absalom Kills Amnon

23Two years later, when Absalom's sheepshearers were at Baal Hazor near the border of Ephraim, he invited all the king's sons to come there. 24Absalom went to the king and said, "Your servant has had shearers come. Will the king and his officials please join me?"

25"No, my son," the king replied. "All of us should not go; we would only be a burden to you." Although Absalom urged him, he still refused to go, but gave him his blessing.

26Then Absalom said, "If not, please let my brother Amnon come with us."

The king asked him, "Why should he go with you?" 27But Absalom urged him, so he sent with him Amnon and the rest of the king's sons.

28Absalom ordered his men, "Listen! When Amnon is in high spirits from drinking wine and I say to you, 'Strike Amnon down,' then kill him. Don't be afraid. Have not I given you this order? Be strong and brave." 29So Absalom's men did to Amnon what Absalom had ordered. Then all the king's sons got up, mounted their mules and fled.

30While they were on their way, the report came to David: "Absalom has struck down all the king's sons; not one of them is left." 31The king stood up, tore his clothes and lay down on the ground; and all his servants stood by with their clothes torn.

[a] *30* Or *of Milcom* (that is, Molech) [b] *30* That is, about 75 pounds (about 34 kilograms) [c] *31* The meaning of the Hebrew for this clause is uncertain. [d] *18* The meaning of the Hebrew for this phrase is uncertain. [e] *19* The meaning of the Hebrew for this word is uncertain.

32But Jonadab son of Shimeah, David's brother, said, "My lord should not think that they killed all the princes; only Amnon is dead. This has been Absalom's expressed intention ever since the day Amnon raped his sister Tamar. 33My lord the king should not be concerned about the report that all the king's sons are dead. Only Amnon is dead."

34Meanwhile, Absalom had fled.

Now the man standing watch looked up and saw many people on the road west of him, coming down the side of the hill. The watchman went and told the king, "I see men in the direction of Horonaim, on the side of the hill."[a]

35Jonadab said to the king, "See, the king's sons are here; it has happened just as your servant said."

36As he finished speaking, the king's sons came in, wailing loudly. The king, too, and all his servants wept very bitterly.

37Absalom fled and went to Talmai son of Ammihud, the king of Geshur. But King David mourned for his son every day.

38After Absalom fled and went to Geshur, he stayed there three years. 39And the spirit of the king[b] longed to go to Absalom, for he was consoled concerning Amnon's death.

Absalom Returns to Jerusalem

14 Joab son of Zeruiah knew that the king's heart longed for Absalom. 2So Joab sent someone to Tekoa and had a wise woman brought from there. He said to her, "Pretend you are in mourning. Dress in mourning clothes, and don't use any cosmetic lotions. Act like a woman who has spent many days grieving for the dead. 3Then go to the king and speak these words to him." And Joab put the words in her mouth.

4When the woman from Tekoa went[c] to the king, she fell with her face to the ground to pay him honor, and she said, "Help me, O king!"

5The king asked her, "What is troubling you?"

She said, "I am indeed a widow; my husband is dead. 6I your servant had two sons. They got into a fight with each other in the field, and no one was there to separate them. One struck the other and killed him. 7Now the whole clan has risen up against your servant; they say, 'Hand over the one who struck his brother down, so that we may put him to death for the life of his brother whom he killed; then we will get rid of the heir as well.' They would put out the only burning coal I have left, leaving my husband neither name nor descendant on the face of the earth."

8The king said to the woman, "Go home, and I will issue an order in your behalf."

9But the woman from Tekoa said to him, "My lord the king, let the blame rest on me and on my father's family, and let the king and his throne be without guilt."

10The king replied, "If anyone says anything to you, bring him to me, and he will not bother you again."

11She said, "Then let the king invoke the LORD his God to prevent the avenger of blood from adding to the destruction, so that my son will not be destroyed."

"As surely as the LORD lives," he said, "not one hair of your son's head will fall to the ground."

12Then the woman said, "Let your servant speak a word to my lord the king."

"Speak," he replied.

13The woman said, "Why then have you devised a thing like this against the people of God? When the king says this, does he not convict himself, for the king has not brought back his banished son? 14Like water spilled on the ground, which cannot be recovered, so we must die. But God does not take away life; instead, he devises ways so that a banished person may not remain estranged from him.

15"And now I have come to say this to my lord the king because the people have made me afraid. Your servant thought, 'I will speak to the king; perhaps he will do what his servant asks. 16Perhaps the king will agree to deliver his servant from the hand of the man who is trying to cut off both me and my son from the inheritance God gave us.'

17"And now your servant says, 'May the word of my lord the king bring me rest, for my lord the king is like an angel of God in discerning good and evil. May the LORD your God be with you.' "

18Then the king said to the woman, "Do not keep from me the answer to what I am going to ask you."

"Let my lord the king speak," the woman said.

19The king asked, "Isn't the hand of Joab with you in all this?"

The woman answered, "As surely as you live, my lord the king, no one can turn to the right or to the left from anything my lord the king says. Yes, it was your servant Joab who instructed me to do this and who put all these words into the mouth of your servant. 20Your servant Joab did this to change the present situation. My lord has wisdom like that of an angel of God—he knows everything that happens in the land."

21The king said to Joab, "Very well, I will do it. Go, bring back the young man Absalom."

22Joab fell with his face to the ground to pay him honor, and he blessed the king. Joab said, "Today your servant knows that he has found favor in your eyes, my lord the king, because the king has granted his servant's request."

23Then Joab went to Geshur and brought

[a]*34* Septuagint; Hebrew does not have this sentence. [b]*39* Dead Sea Scrolls and some Septuagint manuscripts; Masoretic Text *But ⌊the spirit of⌋ David the king* [c]*4* Many Hebrew manuscripts, Septuagint, Vulgate and Syriac; most Hebrew manuscripts *spoke*

Absalom back to Jerusalem. 24But the king
said, "He must go to his own house; he must
not see my face." So Absalom went to his own
house and did not see the face of the king.

25In all Israel there was not a man so highly
praised for his handsome appearance as Absalom. From the top of his head to the sole of his
foot there was no blemish in him. 26Whenever
he cut the hair of his head—he used to cut his
hair from time to time when it became too
heavy for him—he would weigh it, and its
weight was two hundred shekels[a] by the royal
standard.

27Three sons and a daughter were born to
Absalom. The daughter's name was Tamar,
and she became a beautiful woman.

28Absalom lived two years in Jerusalem
without seeing the king's face. 29Then Absalom sent for Joab in order to send him to the
king, but Joab refused to come to him. So he
sent a second time, but he refused to come.
30Then he said to his servants, "Look, Joab's
field is next to mine, and he has barley there.
Go and set it on fire." So Absalom's servants
set the field on fire.

31Then Joab did go to Absalom's house and
he said to him, "Why have your servants set
my field on fire?"

32Absalom said to Joab, "Look, I sent word
to you and said, 'Come here so I can send you
to the king to ask, "Why have I come from
Geshur? It would be better for me if I were still
there!" ' Now then, I want to see the king's
face, and if I am guilty of anything, let him put
me to death."

33So Joab went to the king and told him this.
Then the king summoned Absalom, and he
came in and bowed down with his face to the
ground before the king. And the king kissed
Absalom.

Absalom's Conspiracy

15 In the course of time, Absalom provided
himself with a chariot and horses and
with fifty men to run ahead of him. 2He would
get up early and stand by the side of the road
leading to the city gate. Whenever anyone
came with a complaint to be placed before the
king for a decision, Absalom would call out to
him, "What town are you from?" He would
answer, "Your servant is from one of the tribes
of Israel." 3Then Absalom would say to him,
"Look, your claims are valid and proper, but
there is no representative of the king to hear
you." 4And Absalom would add, "If only I
were appointed judge in the land! Then everyone who has a complaint or case could come to
me and I would see that he gets justice."

5Also, whenever anyone approached him to
bow down before him, Absalom would reach
out his hand, take hold of him and kiss him.
6Absalom behaved in this way toward all the
Israelites who came to the king asking for justice, and so he stole the hearts of the men of
Israel.

7At the end of four[b] years, Absalom said to
the king, "Let me go to Hebron and fulfill a
vow I made to the LORD. 8While your servant
was living at Geshur in Aram, I made this vow:
'If the LORD takes me back to Jerusalem, I will
worship the LORD in Hebron.[c]' "

9The king said to him, "Go in peace." So he
went to Hebron.

10Then Absalom sent secret messengers
throughout the tribes of Israel to say, "As soon
as you hear the sound of the trumpets, then
say, 'Absalom is king in Hebron.' " 11Two
hundred men from Jerusalem had accompanied Absalom. They had been invited as guests
and went quite innocently, knowing nothing
about the matter. 12While Absalom was offering sacrifices, he also sent for Ahithophel the
Gilonite, David's counselor, to come from Gi-
loh, his hometown. And so the conspiracy
gained strength, and Absalom's following kept
on increasing.

David Flees

13A messenger came and told David, "The
hearts of the men of Israel are with Absalom."

14Then David said to all his officials who
were with him in Jerusalem, "Come! We must
flee, or none of us will escape from Absalom.
We must leave immediately, or he will move
quickly to overtake us and bring ruin upon us
and put the city to the sword."

15The king's officials answered him, "Your
servants are ready to do whatever our lord the
king chooses."

16The king set out, with his entire household
following him; but he left ten concubines to
take care of the palace. 17So the king set out,
with all the people following him, and they
halted at a place some distance away. 18All his
men marched past him, along with all the Kerethites and Pelethites; and all the six hundred
Gittites who had accompanied him from Gath
marched before the king.

19The king said to Ittai the Gittite, "Why
should you come along with us? Go back and
stay with King Absalom. You are a foreigner,
an exile from your homeland. 20You came
only yesterday. And today shall I make you
wander about with us, when I do not know
where I am going? Go back, and take your
countrymen. May kindness and faithfulness be
with you."

21But Ittai replied to the king, "As surely as
the LORD lives, and as my lord the king lives,
wherever my lord the king may be, whether
it means life or death, there will your servant be."

22David said to Ittai, "Go ahead, march on."
So Ittai the Gittite marched on with all his men
and the families that were with him.

23The whole countryside wept aloud as all
the people passed by. The king also crossed the

[a] *26* That is, about 5 pounds (about 2.3 kilograms) [b] *7* Some Septuagint manuscripts, Syriac and Josephus; Hebrew *forty* [c] *8* Some Septuagint manuscripts; Hebrew does not have *in Hebron.*

Kidron Valley, and all the people moved on toward the desert.

24Zadok was there, too, and all the Levites who were with him were carrying the ark of the covenant of God. They set down the ark of God, and Abiathar offered sacrifices[a] until all the people had finished leaving the city.

25Then the king said to Zadok, "Take the ark of God back into the city. If I find favor in the LORD's eyes, he will bring me back and let me see it and his dwelling place again. 26But if he says, 'I am not pleased with you,' then I am ready; let him do to me whatever seems good to him."

27The king also said to Zadok the priest, "Aren't you a seer? Go back to the city in peace, with your son Ahimaaz and Jonathan son of Abiathar. You and Abiathar take your two sons with you. 28I will wait at the fords in the desert until word comes from you to inform me." 29So Zadok and Abiathar took the ark of God back to Jerusalem and stayed there.

30But David continued up the Mount of Olives, weeping as he went; his head was covered and he was barefoot. All the people with him covered their heads too and were weeping as they went up. 31Now David had been told, "Ahithophel is among the conspirators with Absalom." So David prayed, "O LORD, turn Ahithophel's counsel into foolishness."

32When David arrived at the summit, where people used to worship God, Hushai the Arkite was there to meet him, his robe torn and dust on his head. 33David said to him, "If you go with me, you will be a burden to me. 34But if you return to the city and say to Absalom, 'I will be your servant, O king; I was your father's servant in the past, but now I will be your servant,' then you can help me by frustrating Ahithophel's advice. 35Won't the priests Zadok and Abiathar be there with you? Tell them anything you hear in the king's palace. 36Their two sons, Ahimaaz son of Zadok and Jonathan son of Abiathar, are there with them. Send them to me with anything you hear."

37So David's friend Hushai arrived at Jerusalem as Absalom was entering the city.

David and Ziba

16 When David had gone a short distance beyond the summit, there was Ziba, the steward of Mephibosheth, waiting to meet him. He had a string of donkeys saddled and loaded with two hundred loaves of bread, a hundred cakes of raisins, a hundred cakes of figs and a skin of wine.

2The king asked Ziba, "Why have you brought these?"

Ziba answered, "The donkeys are for the king's household to ride on, the bread and fruit are for the men to eat, and the wine is to refresh those who become exhausted in the desert."

3The king then asked, "Where is your master's grandson?"

Ziba said to him, "He is staying in Jerusalem, because he thinks, 'Today the house of Israel will give me back my grandfather's kingdom.' "

4Then the king said to Ziba, "All that belonged to Mephibosheth is now yours."

"I humbly bow," Ziba said. "May I find favor in your eyes, my lord the king."

Shimei Curses David

5As King David approached Bahurim, a man from the same clan as Saul's family came out from there. His name was Shimei son of Gera, and he cursed as he came out. 6He pelted David and all the king's officials with stones, though all the troops and the special guard were on David's right and left. 7As he cursed, Shimei said, "Get out, get out, you man of blood, you scoundrel! 8The LORD has repaid you for all the blood you shed in the household of Saul, in whose place you have reigned. The LORD has handed the kingdom over to your son Absalom. You have come to ruin because you are a man of blood!"

9Then Abishai son of Zeruiah said to the king, "Why should this dead dog curse my lord the king? Let me go over and cut off his head."

10But the king said, "What do you and I have in common, you sons of Zeruiah? If he is cursing because the LORD said to him, 'Curse David,' who can ask, 'Why do you do this?' "

11David then said to Abishai and all his officials, "My son, who is of my own flesh, is trying to take my life. How much more, then, this Benjamite! Leave him alone; let him curse, for the LORD has told him to. 12It may be that the LORD will see my distress and repay me with good for the cursing I am receiving today."

13So David and his men continued along the road while Shimei was going along the hillside opposite him, cursing as he went and throwing stones at him and showering him with dirt. 14The king and all the people with him arrived at their destination exhausted. And there he refreshed himself.

The Advice of Hushai and Ahithophel

15Meanwhile, Absalom and all the men of Israel came to Jerusalem, and Ahithophel was with him. 16Then Hushai the Arkite, David's friend, went to Absalom and said to him, "Long live the king! Long live the king!"

17Absalom asked Hushai, "Is this the love you show your friend? Why didn't you go with your friend?"

18Hushai said to Absalom, "No, the one chosen by the LORD, by these people, and by all the men of Israel—his I will be, and I will remain with him. 19Furthermore, whom should I serve? Should I not serve the son? Just as I served your father, so I will serve you."

[a]24 Or *Abiathar went up*

20Absalom said to Ahithophel, "Give us your advice. What should we do?"

21Ahithophel answered, "Lie with your father's concubines whom he left to take care of the palace. Then all Israel will hear that you have made yourself a stench in your father's nostrils, and the hands of everyone with you will be strengthened." 22So they pitched a tent for Absalom on the roof, and he lay with his father's concubines in the sight of all Israel.

23Now in those days the advice Ahithophel gave was like that of one who inquires of God. That was how both David and Absalom regarded all of Ahithophel's advice.

17 Ahithophel said to Absalom, "I would[a] choose twelve thousand men and set out tonight in pursuit of David. 2I would[b] attack him while he is weary and weak. I would[b] strike him with terror, and then all the people with him will flee. I would[b] strike down only the king 3and bring all the people back to you. The death of the man you seek will mean the return of all; all the people will be unharmed." 4This plan seemed good to Absalom and to all the elders of Israel.

5But Absalom said, "Summon also Hushai the Arkite, so we can hear what he has to say." 6When Hushai came to him, Absalom said, "Ahithophel has given this advice. Should we do what he says? If not, give us your opinion."

7Hushai replied to Absalom, "The advice Ahithophel has given is not good this time. 8You know your father and his men; they are fighters, and as fierce as a wild bear robbed of her cubs. Besides, your father is an experienced fighter; he will not spend the night with the troops. 9Even now, he is hidden in a cave or some other place. If he should attack your troops first,[c] whoever hears about it will say, 'There has been a slaughter among the troops who follow Absalom.' 10Then even the bravest soldier, whose heart is like the heart of a lion, will melt with fear, for all Israel knows that your father is a fighter and that those with him are brave.

11"So I advise you: Let all Israel, from Dan to Beersheba—as numerous as the sand on the seashore—be gathered to you, with you yourself leading them into battle. 12Then we will attack him wherever he may be found, and we will fall on him as dew settles on the ground. Neither he nor any of his men will be left alive. 13If he withdraws into a city, then all Israel will bring ropes to that city, and we will drag it down to the valley until not even a piece of it can be found."

14Absalom and all the men of Israel said, "The advice of Hushai the Arkite is better than that of Ahithophel." For the LORD had determined to frustrate the good advice of Ahithophel in order to bring disaster on Absalom.

15Hushai told Zadok and Abiathar, the priests, "Ahithophel has advised Absalom and the elders of Israel to do such and such, but I have advised them to do so and so. 16Now send a message immediately and tell David, 'Do not spend the night at the fords in the desert; cross over without fail, or the king and all the people with him will be swallowed up.' "

17Jonathan and Ahimaaz were staying at En Rogel. A servant girl was to go and inform them, and they were to go and tell King David, for they could not risk being seen entering the city. 18But a young man saw them and told Absalom. So the two of them left quickly and went to the house of a man in Bahurim. He had a well in his courtyard, and they climbed down into it. 19His wife took a covering and spread it out over the opening of the well and scattered grain over it. No one knew anything about it.

20When Absalom's men came to the woman at the house, they asked, "Where are Ahimaaz and Jonathan?"

The woman answered them, "They crossed over the brook."[d] The men searched but found no one, so they returned to Jerusalem.

21After the men had gone, the two climbed out of the well and went to inform King David. They said to him, "Set out and cross the river at once; Ahithophel has advised such and such against you." 22So David and all the people with him set out and crossed the Jordan. By daybreak, no one was left who had not crossed the Jordan.

23When Ahithophel saw that his advice had not been followed, he saddled his donkey and set out for his house in his hometown. He put his house in order and then hanged himself. So he died and was buried in his father's tomb.

24David went to Mahanaim, and Absalom crossed the Jordan with all the men of Israel. 25Absalom had appointed Amasa over the army in place of Joab. Amasa was the son of a man named Jether,[e] an Israelite[f] who had married Abigail,[g] the daughter of Nahash and sister of Zeruiah the mother of Joab. 26The Israelites and Absalom camped in the land of Gilead.

27When David came to Mahanaim, Shobi son of Nahash from Rabbah of the Ammonites, and Makir son of Ammiel from Lo Debar, and Barzillai the Gileadite from Rogelim 28brought bedding and bowls and articles of pottery. They also brought wheat and barley, flour and roasted grain, beans and lentils,[h] 29honey and curds, sheep, and cheese from cows' milk for David and his people to eat. For they said, "The people have become hungry and tired and thirsty in the desert."

Absalom's Death

18 David mustered the men who were with him and appointed over them com-

[a]1 Or *Let me* [b]2 Or *will* [c]9 Or *When some of the men fall at the first attack* [d]20 Or *"They passed by the sheep pen toward the water."* [e]25 Hebrew *Ithra,* a variant of *Jether* [f]25 Hebrew and some Septuagint manuscripts; other Septuagint manuscripts (see also 1 Chron. 2:17) *Ishmaelite* or *Jezreelite* [g]25 Hebrew *Abigal,* a variant of *Abigail* [h]28 Most Septuagint manuscripts and Syriac; Hebrew *lentils, and roasted grain*

manders of thousands and commanders of
hundreds. 2David sent the troops out—a third
under the command of Joab, a third under
Joab's brother Abishai son of Zeruiah, and a
third under Ittai the Gittite. The king told the
troops, "I myself will surely march out with
you."
3But the men said, "You must not go out; if
we are forced to flee, they won't care about us.
Even if half of us die, they won't care; but you
are worth ten thousand of us.[a] It would be
better now for you to give us support from the
city."
4The king answered, "I will do whatever
seems best to you."
So the king stood beside the gate while all
the men marched out in units of hundreds and
of thousands. 5The king commanded Joab,
Abishai and Ittai, "Be gentle with the young
man Absalom for my sake." And all the troops
heard the king giving orders concerning Absalom to each of the commanders.
6The army marched into the field to fight
Israel, and the battle took place in the forest of
Ephraim. 7There the army of Israel was defeated by David's men, and the casualties that day
were great—twenty thousand men. 8The battle
spread out over the whole countryside, and the
forest claimed more lives that day than the
sword.
9Now Absalom happened to meet David's
men. He was riding his mule, and as the mule
went under the thick branches of a large oak,
Absalom's head got caught in the tree. He was
left hanging in midair, while the mule he was
riding kept on going.
10When one of the men saw this, he told
Joab, "I just saw Absalom hanging in an oak
tree."
11Joab said to the man who had told him
this, "What! You saw him? Why didn't you
strike him to the ground right there? Then I
would have had to give you ten shekels[b] of
silver and a warrior's belt."
12But the man replied, "Even if a thousand
shekels[c] were weighed out into my hands, I
would not lift my hand against the king's son.
In our hearing the king commanded you and
Abishai and Ittai, 'Protect the young man Absalom for my sake.[d]' 13And if I had put my
life in jeopardy[e]—and nothing is hidden from
the king—you would have kept your distance
from me."
14Joab said, "I'm not going to wait like this
for you." So he took three javelins in his hand
and plunged them into Absalom's heart while
Absalom was still alive in the oak tree. 15And
ten of Joab's armor-bearers surrounded Absalom, struck him and killed him.
16Then Joab sounded the trumpet, and the
troops stopped pursuing Israel, for Joab halted
them. 17They took Absalom, threw him into a
big pit in the forest and piled up a large heap
of rocks over him. Meanwhile, all the Israelites
fled to their homes.
18During his lifetime Absalom had taken a
pillar and erected it in the King's Valley as a
monument to himself, for he thought, "I have
no son to carry on the memory of my name."
He named the pillar after himself, and it is
called Absalom's Monument to this day.

David Mourns

19Now Ahimaaz son of Zadok said, "Let me
run and take the news to the king that the LORD
has delivered him from the hand of his enemies."
20"You are not the one to take the news
today," Joab told him. "You may take the news
another time, but you must not do so today,
because the king's son is dead."
21Then Joab said to a Cushite, "Go, tell the
king what you have seen." The Cushite bowed
down before Joab and ran off.
22Ahimaaz son of Zadok again said to Joab,
"Come what may, please let me run behind the
Cushite."
But Joab replied, "My son, why do you want
to go? You don't have any news that will bring
you a reward."
23He said, "Come what may, I want to run."
So Joab said, "Run!" Then Ahimaaz ran by
way of the plain[f] and outran the Cushite.
24While David was sitting between the inner
and outer gates, the watchman went up to the
roof of the gateway by the wall. As he looked
out, he saw a man running alone. 25The watchman called out to the king and reported it.
The king said, "If he is alone, he must have
good news." And the man came closer and
closer.
26Then the watchman saw another man running, and he called down to the gatekeeper,
"Look, another man running alone!"
The king said, "He must be bringing good
news, too."
27The watchman said, "It seems to me that
the first one runs like Ahimaaz son of Zadok."
"He's a good man," the king said. "He
comes with good news."
28Then Ahimaaz called out to the king, "All
is well!" He bowed down before the king with
his face to the ground and said, "Praise be to
the LORD your God! He has delivered up the
men who lifted their hands against my lord the
king."
29The king asked, "Is the young man Absalom safe?"
Ahimaaz answered, "I saw great confusion
just as Joab was about to send the king's servant and me, your servant, but I don't know
what it was."
30The king said, "Stand aside and wait
here." So he stepped aside and stood there.

[a]3 Two Hebrew manuscripts, some Septuagint manuscripts and Vulgate; most Hebrew manuscripts *care; for now there are ten thousand like us* [b]11 That is, about 4 ounces (about 115 grams) [c]12 That is, about 25 pounds (about 11 kilograms) [d]12 A few Hebrew manuscripts, Septuagint, Vulgate and Syriac; most Hebrew manuscripts may be translated *Absalom, whoever you may be.* [e]13 Or *Otherwise, if I had acted treacherously toward him* [f]23 That is, the plain of the Jordan

31Then the Cushite arrived and said, "My lord the king, hear the good news! The LORD has delivered you today from all who rose up against you."

32The king asked the Cushite, "Is the young man Absalom safe?"

The Cushite replied, "May the enemies of my lord the king and all who rise up to harm you be like that young man."

33The king was shaken. He went up to the room over the gateway and wept. As he went, he said: "O my son Absalom! My son, my son Absalom! If only I had died instead of you—O Absalom, my son, my son!"

19 Joab was told, "The king is weeping and mourning for Absalom." 2And for the whole army the victory that day was turned into mourning, because on that day the troops heard it said, "The king is grieving for his son." 3The men stole into the city that day as men steal in who are ashamed when they flee from battle. 4The king covered his face and cried aloud, "O my son Absalom! O Absalom, my son, my son!"

5Then Joab went into the house to the king and said, "Today you have humiliated all your men, who have just saved your life and the lives of your sons and daughters and the lives of your wives and concubines. 6You love those who hate you and hate those who love you. You have made it clear today that the commanders and their men mean nothing to you. I see that you would be pleased if Absalom were alive today and all of us were dead. 7Now go out and encourage your men. I swear by the LORD that if you don't go out, not a man will be left with you by nightfall. This will be worse for you than all the calamities that have come upon you from your youth till now."

8So the king got up and took his seat in the gateway. When the men were told, "The king is sitting in the gateway," they all came before him.

David Returns to Jerusalem

Meanwhile, the Israelites had fled to their homes. 9Throughout the tribes of Israel, the people were all arguing with each other, saying, "The king delivered us from the hand of our enemies; he is the one who rescued us from the hand of the Philistines. But now he has fled the country because of Absalom; 10and Absalom, whom we anointed to rule over us, has died in battle. So why do you say nothing about bringing the king back?"

11King David sent this message to Zadok and Abiathar, the priests: "Ask the elders of Judah, 'Why should you be the last to bring the king back to his palace, since what is being said throughout Israel has reached the king at his quarters? 12You are my brothers, my own flesh and blood. So why should you be the last to bring back the king?' 13And say to Amasa, 'Are you not my own flesh and blood? May God deal with me, be it ever so severely, if from now on you are not the commander of my army in place of Joab.' "

14He won over the hearts of all the men of Judah as though they were one man. They sent word to the king, "Return, you and all your men." 15Then the king returned and went as far as the Jordan.

Now the men of Judah had come to Gilgal to go out and meet the king and bring him across the Jordan. 16Shimei son of Gera, the Benjamite from Bahurim, hurried down with the men of Judah to meet King David. 17With him were a thousand Benjamites, along with Ziba, the steward of Saul's household, and his fifteen sons and twenty servants. They rushed to the Jordan, where the king was. 18They crossed at the ford to take the king's household over and to do whatever he wished.

When Shimei son of Gera crossed the Jordan, he fell prostrate before the king 19and said to him, "May my lord not hold me guilty. Do not remember how your servant did wrong on the day my lord the king left Jerusalem. May the king put it out of his mind. 20For I your servant know that I have sinned, but today I have come here as the first of the whole house of Joseph to come down and meet my lord the king."

21Then Abishai son of Zeruiah said, "Shouldn't Shimei be put to death for this? He cursed the LORD's anointed."

22David replied, "What do you and I have in common, you sons of Zeruiah? This day you have become my adversaries! Should anyone be put to death in Israel today? Do I not know that today I am king over Israel?" 23So the king said to Shimei, "You shall not die." And the king promised him on oath.

24Mephibosheth, Saul's grandson, also went down to meet the king. He had not taken care of his feet or trimmed his mustache or washed his clothes from the day the king left until the day he returned safely. 25When he came from Jerusalem to meet the king, the king asked him, "Why didn't you go with me, Mephibosheth?"

26He said, "My lord the king, since I your servant am lame, I said, 'I will have my donkey saddled and will ride on it, so I can go with the king.' But Ziba my servant betrayed me. 27And he has slandered your servant to my lord the king. My lord the king is like an angel of God; so do whatever pleases you. 28All my grandfather's descendants deserved nothing but death from my lord the king, but you gave your servant a place among those who eat at your table. So what right do I have to make any more appeals to the king?"

29The king said to him, "Why say more? I order you and Ziba to divide the fields."

30Mephibosheth said to the king, "Let him take everything, now that my lord the king has arrived home safely."

31Barzillai the Gileadite also came down from Rogelim to cross the Jordan with the king and to send him on his way from there. 32Now Barzillai was a very old man, eighty years of age. He had provided for the king during his stay in Mahanaim, for he was a very wealthy

man. 33The king said to Barzillai, “Cross over
with me and stay with me in Jerusalem, and I
will provide for you.”
34But Barzillai answered the king, “How
many more years will I live, that I should go up
to Jerusalem with the king? 35I am now eighty
years old. Can I tell the difference between
what is good and what is not? Can your servant
taste what he eats and drinks? Can I still hear
the voices of men and women singers? Why
should your servant be an added burden to my
lord the king? 36Your servant will cross over
the Jordan with the king for a short distance,
but why should the king reward me in this
way? 37Let your servant return, that I may die
in my own town near the tomb of my father
and mother. But here is your servant Kimham.
Let him cross over with my lord the king. Do
for him whatever pleases you.”
38The king said, “Kimham shall cross over
with me, and I will do for him whatever
pleases you. And anything you desire from me
I will do for you.”
39So all the people crossed the Jordan, and
then the king crossed over. The king kissed
Barzillai and gave him his blessing, and Barzillai returned to his home.
40When the king crossed over to Gilgal,
Kimham crossed with him. All the troops of
Judah and half the troops of Israel had taken
the king over.
41Soon all the men of Israel were coming to
the king and saying to him, “Why did our
brothers, the men of Judah, steal the king away
and bring him and his household across the
Jordan, together with all his men?”
42All the men of Judah answered the men of
Israel, “We did this because the king is closely
related to us. Why are you angry about it?
Have we eaten any of the king’s provisions?
Have we taken anything for ourselves?”
43Then the men of Israel answered the men
of Judah, “We have ten shares in the king; and
besides, we have a greater claim on David than
you have. So why do you treat us with contempt? Were we not the first to speak of bringing back our king?”

But the men of Judah responded even more
harshly than the men of Israel.

Sheba Rebels Against David

20 Now a troublemaker named Sheba son
of Bicri, a Benjamite, happened to be
there. He sounded the trumpet and shouted,

“We have no share in David,
no part in Jesse’s son!
Every man to his tent, O Israel!”

2So all the men of Israel deserted David to
follow Sheba son of Bicri. But the men of Judah stayed by their king all the way from the
Jordan to Jerusalem.
3When David returned to his palace in Jerusalem, he took the ten concubines he had left
to take care of the palace and put them in a
house under guard. He provided for them, but
did not lie with them. They were kept in con-
finement till the day of their death, living as
widows.
4Then the king said to Amasa, “Summon the
men of Judah to come to me within three days,
and be here yourself.” 5But when Amasa went
to summon Judah, he took longer than the time
the king had set for him.
6David said to Abishai, “Now Sheba son of
Bicri will do us more harm than Absalom did.
Take your master’s men and pursue him, or he
will find fortified cities and escape from us.”
7So Joab’s men and the Kerethites and Pelethites and all the mighty warriors went out under the command of Abishai. They marched
out from Jerusalem to pursue Sheba son of
Bicri.
8While they were at the great rock in Gibeon, Amasa came to meet them. Joab was wearing his military tunic, and strapped over it at
his waist was a belt with a dagger in its sheath.
As he stepped forward, it dropped out of its
sheath.
9Joab said to Amasa, “How are you, my
brother?” Then Joab took Amasa by the beard
with his right hand to kiss him. 10Amasa was
not on his guard against the dagger in Joab’s
hand, and Joab plunged it into his belly, and
his intestines spilled out on the ground. Without being stabbed again, Amasa died. Then
Joab and his brother Abishai pursued Sheba
son of Bicri.
11One of Joab’s men stood beside Amasa
and said, “Whoever favors Joab, and whoever
is for David, let him follow Joab!” 12Amasa
lay wallowing in his blood in the middle of the
road, and the man saw that all the troops came
to a halt there. When he realized that everyone
who came up to Amasa stopped, he dragged
him from the road into a field and threw a
garment over him. 13After Amasa had been
removed from the road, all the men went on
with Joab to pursue Sheba son of Bicri.
14Sheba passed through all the tribes of Israel to Abel Beth Maacah[a] and through the entire region of the Berites, who gathered together and followed him. 15All the troops with Joab
came and besieged Sheba in Abel Beth Maacah. They built a siege ramp up to the city, and
it stood against the outer fortifications. While
they were battering the wall to bring it down,
16a wise woman called from the city, “Listen!
Listen! Tell Joab to come here so I can speak
to him.” 17He went toward her, and she asked,
“Are you Joab?”

“I am,” he answered.

She said, “Listen to what your servant has to
say.”

“I’m listening,” he said.

18She continued, “Long ago they used to
say, ‘Get your answer at Abel,’ and that settled
it. 19We are the peaceful and faithful in Israel.
You are trying to destroy a city that is a mother

[a]14 Or *Abel, even Beth Maacah*; also in verse 15

in Israel. Why do you want to swallow up the LORD's inheritance?"

20"Far be it from me!" Joab replied, "Far be it from me to swallow up or destroy! 21That is not the case. A man named Sheba son of Bicri, from the hill country of Ephraim, has lifted up his hand against the king, against David. Hand over this one man, and I'll withdraw from the city."

The woman said to Joab, "His head will be thrown to you from the wall."

22Then the woman went to all the people with her wise advice, and they cut off the head of Sheba son of Bicri and threw it to Joab. So he sounded the trumpet, and his men dispersed from the city, each returning to his home. And Joab went back to the king in Jerusalem.

23Joab was over Israel's entire army; Benaiah son of Jehoiada was over the Kerethites and Pelethites; 24Adoniram[a] was in charge of forced labor; Jehoshaphat son of Ahilud was recorder; 25Sheva was secretary; Zadok and Abiathar were priests; 26and Ira the Jairite was David's priest.

The Gibeonites Avenged

21 During the reign of David, there was a famine for three successive years; so David sought the face of the LORD. The LORD said, "It is on account of Saul and his blood-stained house; it is because he put the Gibeonites to death."

2The king summoned the Gibeonites and spoke to them. (Now the Gibeonites were not a part of Israel but were survivors of the Amorites; the Israelites had sworn to ⌊spare⌋ them, but Saul in his zeal for Israel and Judah had tried to annihilate them.) 3David asked the Gibeonites, "What shall I do for you? How shall I make amends so that you will bless the LORD's inheritance?"

4The Gibeonites answered him, "We have no right to demand silver or gold from Saul or his family, nor do we have the right to put anyone in Israel to death."

"What do you want me to do for you?" David asked.

5They answered the king, "As for the man who destroyed us and plotted against us so that we have been decimated and have no place anywhere in Israel, 6let seven of his male descendants be given to us to be killed and exposed before the LORD at Gibeah of Saul—the LORD's chosen one."

So the king said, "I will give them to you."

7The king spared Mephibosheth son of Jonathan, the son of Saul, because of the oath before the LORD between David and Jonathan son of Saul. 8But the king took Armoni and Mephibosheth, the two sons of Aiah's daughter Rizpah, whom she had borne to Saul, together with the five sons of Saul's daughter Merab,[b] whom she had borne to Adriel son of Barzillai the Meholathite. 9He handed them over to the Gibeonites, who killed and exposed them on a hill before the LORD. All seven of them fell together; they were put to death during the first days of the harvest, just as the barley harvest was beginning.

10Rizpah daughter of Aiah took sackcloth and spread it out for herself on a rock. From the beginning of the harvest till the rain poured down from the heavens on the bodies, she did not let the birds of the air touch them by day or the wild animals by night. 11When David was told what Aiah's daughter Rizpah, Saul's concubine, had done, 12he went and took the bones of Saul and his son Jonathan from the citizens of Jabesh Gilead. (They had taken them secretly from the public square at Beth Shan, where the Philistines had hung them after they struck Saul down on Gilboa.) 13David brought the bones of Saul and his son Jonathan from there, and the bones of those who had been killed and exposed were gathered up.

14They buried the bones of Saul and his son Jonathan in the tomb of Saul's father Kish, at Zela in Benjamin, and did everything the king commanded. After that, God answered prayer in behalf of the land.

Wars Against the Philistines

15Once again there was a battle between the Philistines and Israel. David went down with his men to fight against the Philistines, and he became exhausted. 16And Ishbi-Benob, one of the descendants of Rapha, whose bronze spearhead weighed three hundred shekels[c] and who was armed with a new ⌊sword⌋, said he would kill David. 17But Abishai son of Zeruiah came to David's rescue; he struck the Philistine down and killed him. Then David's men swore to him, saying, "Never again will you go out with us to battle, so that the lamp of Israel will not be extinguished."

18In the course of time, there was another battle with the Philistines, at Gob. At that time Sibbecai the Hushathite killed Saph, one of the descendants of Rapha.

19In another battle with the Philistines at Gob, Elhanan son of Jaare-Oregim[d] the Bethlehemite killed Goliath[e] the Gittite, who had a spear with a shaft like a weaver's rod.

20In still another battle, which took place at Gath, there was a huge man with six fingers on each hand and six toes on each foot—twenty-four in all. He also was descended from Rapha. 21When he taunted Israel, Jonathan son of Shimeah, David's brother, killed him.

22These four were descendants of Rapha in Gath, and they fell at the hands of David and his men.

David's Song of Praise

22 David sang to the LORD the words of this song when the LORD delivered him

[a]*24* Some Septuagint manuscripts (see also 1 Kings 4:6 and 5:14); Hebrew *Adoram* [b]*8* Two Hebrew manuscripts, some Septuagint manuscripts and Syriac (see also 1 Samuel 18:19); most Hebrew and Septuagint manuscripts *Michal* [c]*16* That is, about 7 1/2 pounds (about 3.5 kilograms) [d]*19* Or *son of Jair the weaver* [e]*19* Hebrew and Septuagint; 1 Chron. 20:5 *son of Jair killed Lahmi the brother of Goliath*

from the hand of all his enemies and from the
hand of Saul. 2He said:

"The LORD is my rock, my fortress and my deliverer;
3 my God is my rock, in whom I take refuge,
my shield and the horn[a] of my salvation.
He is my stronghold, my refuge and my savior—
from violent men you save me.
4 I call to the LORD, who is worthy of praise,
and I am saved from my enemies.

5 "The waves of death swirled about me;
the torrents of destruction overwhelmed me.
6 The cords of the grave[b] coiled around me;
the snares of death confronted me.
7 In my distress I called to the LORD;
I called out to my God.
From his temple he heard my voice;
my cry came to his ears.

8 "The earth trembled and quaked,
the foundations of the heavens[c] shook;
they trembled because he was angry.
9 Smoke rose from his nostrils;
consuming fire came from his mouth,
burning coals blazed out of it.
10 He parted the heavens and came down;
dark clouds were under his feet.
11 He mounted the cherubim and flew;
he soared[d] on the wings of the wind.
12 He made darkness his canopy around him—
the dark[e] rain clouds of the sky.
13 Out of the brightness of his presence
bolts of lightning blazed forth.
14 The LORD thundered from heaven;
the voice of the Most High resounded.
15 He shot arrows and scattered ⌊the enemies⌋,
bolts of lightning and routed them.
16 The valleys of the sea were exposed
and the foundations of the earth laid bare
at the rebuke of the LORD,
at the blast of breath from his nostrils.

17 "He reached down from on high and took hold of me;
he drew me out of deep waters.
18 He rescued me from my powerful enemy,
from my foes, who were too strong for me.
19 They confronted me in the day of my disaster,
but the LORD was my support.
20 He brought me out into a spacious place;
he rescued me because he delighted in me.

21 "The LORD has dealt with me according to my righteousness;
according to the cleanness of my hands
he has rewarded me.
22 For I have kept the ways of the LORD;
I have not done evil by turning from my God.
23 All his laws are before me;
I have not turned away from his decrees.
24 I have been blameless before him
and have kept myself from sin.
25 The LORD has rewarded me according to my righteousness,
according to my cleanness[f] in his sight.

26 "To the faithful you show yourself faithful,
to the blameless you show yourself blameless,
27 to the pure you show yourself pure,
but to the crooked you show yourself shrewd.
28 You save the humble,
but your eyes are on the haughty to bring them low.
29 You are my lamp, O LORD;
the LORD turns my darkness into light.
30 With your help I can advance against a troop[g];
with my God I can scale a wall.

31 "As for God, his way is perfect;
the word of the LORD is flawless.
He is a shield
for all who take refuge in him.
32 For who is God besides the LORD?
And who is the Rock except our God?
33 It is God who arms me with strength[h]
and makes my way perfect.
34 He makes my feet like the feet of a deer;
he enables me to stand on the heights.
35 He trains my hands for battle;
my arms can bend a bow of bronze.
36 You give me your shield of victory;
you stoop down to make me great.
37 You broaden the path beneath me,
so that my ankles do not turn.

38 "I pursued my enemies and crushed them;
I did not turn back till they were destroyed.
39 I crushed them completely, and they could not rise;
they fell beneath my feet.
40 You armed me with strength for battle;
you made my adversaries bow at my feet.
41 You made my enemies turn their backs in flight,
and I destroyed my foes.

[a]3 *Horn* here symbolizes strength. [b]6 Hebrew *Sheol* [c]8 Hebrew; Vulgate and Syriac (see also Psalm 18:7) *mountains* [d]11 Many Hebrew manuscripts (see also Psalm 18:10); most Hebrew manuscripts *appeared* [e]12 Septuagint and Vulgate (see also Psalm 18:11); Hebrew *massed* [f]25 Hebrew; Septuagint and Vulgate (see also Psalm 18:24) *to the cleanness of my hands* [g]30 Or *can run through a barricade* [h]33 Dead Sea Scrolls, some Septuagint manuscripts, Vulgate and Syriac (see also Psalm 18:32); Masoretic Text *who is my strong refuge*

42 They cried for help, but there was no one
to save them—
to the LORD, but he did not answer.
43 I beat them as fine as the dust of the
earth;
I pounded and trampled them like mud
in the streets.

44 "You have delivered me from the attacks
of my people;
you have preserved me as the head of
nations.
People I did not know are subject to me,
45 and foreigners come cringing to me;
as soon as they hear me, they obey me.
46 They all lose heart;
they come trembling[a] from their
strongholds.

47 "The LORD lives! Praise be to my Rock!
Exalted be God, the Rock, my Savior!
48 He is the God who avenges me,
who puts the nations under me,
49 who sets me free from my enemies.
You exalted me above my foes;
from violent men you rescued me.
50 Therefore I will praise you, O LORD,
among the nations;
I will sing praises to your name.
51 He gives his king great victories;
he shows unfailing kindness to his
anointed,
to David and his descendants forever."

The Last Words of David

23 These are the last words of David:

"The oracle of David son of Jesse,
the oracle of the man exalted by the
Most High,
the man anointed by the God of Jacob,
Israel's singer of songs[b]:

2 "The Spirit of the LORD spoke through
me;
his word was on my tongue.
3 The God of Israel spoke,
the Rock of Israel said to me:
'When one rules over men in
righteousness,
when he rules in the fear of God,
4 he is like the light of morning at sunrise
on a cloudless morning,
like the brightness after rain
that brings the grass from the earth.'

5 "Is not my house right with God?
Has he not made with me an everlasting
covenant,
arranged and secured in every part?
Will he not bring to fruition my salvation
and grant me my every desire?
6 But evil men are all to be cast aside like
thorns,
which are not gathered with the hand.
7 Whoever touches thorns
uses a tool of iron or the shaft of a
spear;
they are burned up where they lie."

David's Mighty Men

8 These are the names of David's mighty
men:
Josheb-Basshebeth,[c] a Tahkemonite,[d] was
chief of the Three; he raised his spear against
eight hundred men, whom he killed[e] in one
encounter.
9 Next to him was Eleazar son of Dodai the
Ahohite. As one of the three mighty men, he
was with David when they taunted the Philistines gathered ⌊at Pas Dammim⌋[f] for battle.
Then the men of Israel retreated, 10 but he stood
his ground and struck down the Philistines till
his hand grew tired and froze to the sword. The
LORD brought about a great victory that day.
The troops returned to Eleazar, but only to
strip the dead.
11 Next to him was Shammah son of Agee
the Hararite. When the Philistines banded together at a place where there was a field full of
lentils, Israel's troops fled from them. 12 But
Shammah took his stand in the middle of the
field. He defended it and struck the Philistines
down, and the LORD brought about a great victory.
13 During harvest time, three of the thirty
chief men came down to David at the cave of
Adullam, while a band of Philistines was encamped in the Valley of Rephaim. 14 At that
time David was in the stronghold, and the Philistine garrison was at Bethlehem. 15 David
longed for water and said, "Oh, that someone
would get me a drink of water from the well
near the gate of Bethlehem!" 16 So the three
mighty men broke through the Philistine lines,
drew water from the well near the gate of
Bethlehem and carried it back to David. But he
refused to drink it; instead, he poured it out
before the LORD. 17 "Far be it from me,
O LORD, to do this!" he said. "Is it not the
blood of men who went at the risk of their
lives?" And David would not drink it.
Such were the exploits of the three mighty
men.
18 Abishai the brother of Joab son of Zeruiah
was chief of the Three.[g] He raised his spear
against three hundred men, whom he killed,
and so he became as famous as the Three.
19 Was he not held in greater honor than the
Three? He became their commander, even
though he was not included among them.
20 Benaiah son of Jehoiada was a valiant
fighter from Kabzeel, who performed great ex-

[a]46 Some Septuagint manuscripts and Vulgate (see also Psalm 18:45); Masoretic Text *they arm themselves.*
[b]1 Or *Israel's beloved singer* [c]8 Hebrew; some Septuagint manuscripts suggest *Ish-Bosheth,* that is, *Esh-Baal* (see also 1 Chron. 11:11 *Jashobeam*). [d]8 Probably a variant of *Hacmonite* (see 1 Chron. 11:11)
[e]8 Some Septuagint manuscripts (see also 1 Chron. 11:11); Hebrew and other Septuagint manuscripts *Three; it was Adino the Eznite who killed eight hundred men* [f]9 See 1 Chron. 11:13; Hebrew *gathered there.*
[g]18 Most Hebrew manuscripts (see also 1 Chron. 11:20); two Hebrew manuscripts and Syriac *Thirty*

ploits. He struck down two of Moab's best
men. He also went down into a pit on a snowy
day and killed a lion. 21 And he struck down a
huge Egyptian. Although the Egyptian had a
spear in his hand, Benaiah went against him
with a club. He snatched the spear from the
Egyptian's hand and killed him with his own
spear. 22 Such were the exploits of Benaiah son
of Jehoiada; he too was as famous as the three
mighty men. 23 He was held in greater honor
than any of the Thirty, but he was not included
among the Three. And David put him in charge
of his bodyguard.

24 Among the Thirty were:
Asahel the brother of Joab,
Elhanan son of Dodo from Bethlehem,
25 Shammah the Harodite,
Elika the Harodite,
26 Helez the Paltite,
Ira son of Ikkesh from Tekoa,
27 Abiezer from Anathoth,
Mebunnai[a] the Hushathite,
28 Zalmon the Ahohite,
Maharai the Netophathite,
29 Heled[b] son of Baanah the Netophathite,
Ithai son of Ribai from Gibeah in Benjamin,
30 Benaiah the Pirathonite,
Hiddai[c] from the ravines of Gaash,
31 Abi-Albon the Arbathite,
Azmaveth the Barhumite,
32 Eliahba the Shaalbonite,
the sons of Jashen,
Jonathan 33 son of[d] Shammah the Hararite,
Ahiam son of Sharar[e] the Hararite,
34 Eliphelet son of Ahasbai the Maacathite,
Eliam son of Ahithophel the Gilonite,
35 Hezro the Carmelite,
Paarai the Arbite,
36 Igal son of Nathan from Zobah,
the son of Hagri,[f]
37 Zelek the Ammonite,
Naharai the Beerothite, the armor-bearer of Joab son of Zeruiah,
38 Ira the Ithrite,
Gareb the Ithrite
39 and Uriah the Hittite.
There were thirty-seven in all.

David Counts the Fighting Men

24 Again the anger of the LORD burned
against Israel, and he incited David
against them, saying, "Go and take a census of
Israel and Judah."
2 So the king said to Joab and the army commanders[g] with him, "Go throughout the tribes
of Israel from Dan to Beersheba and enroll the
fighting men, so that I may know how many
there are."
3 But Joab replied to the king, "May the
LORD your God multiply the troops a hundred
times over, and may the eyes of my lord the
king see it. But why does my lord the king
want to do such a thing?"
4 The king's word, however, overruled Joab
and the army commanders; so they left the
presence of the king to enroll the fighting men
of Israel.
5 After crossing the Jordan, they camped
near Aroer, south of the town in the gorge, and
then went through Gad and on to Jazer. 6 They
went to Gilead and the region of Tahtim Hod-
shi, and on to Dan Jaan and around toward
Sidon. 7 Then they went toward the fortress of
Tyre and all the towns of the Hivites and Canaanites. Finally, they went on to Beersheba in
the Negev of Judah.
8 After they had gone through the entire land,
they came back to Jerusalem at the end of nine
months and twenty days.
9 Joab reported the number of the fighting
men to the king: In Israel there were eight
hundred thousand able-bodied men who could
handle a sword, and in Judah five hundred
thousand.
10 David was conscience-stricken after he
had counted the fighting men, and he said to
the LORD, "I have sinned greatly in what I have
done. Now, O LORD, I beg you, take away the
guilt of your servant. I have done a very foolish thing."
11 Before David got up the next morning, the
word of the LORD had come to Gad the prophet, David's seer: 12 "Go and tell David, 'This is
what the LORD says: I am giving you three
options. Choose one of them for me to carry
out against you.' "
13 So Gad went to David and said to him,
"Shall there come upon you three[h] years of
famine in your land? Or three months of fleeing from your enemies while they pursue you?
Or three days of plague in your land? Now
then, think it over and decide how I should
answer the one who sent me."
14 David said to Gad, "I am in deep distress.
Let us fall into the hands of the LORD, for his
mercy is great; but do not let me fall into the
hands of men."
15 So the LORD sent a plague on Israel from
that morning until the end of the time designated, and seventy thousand of the people from
Dan to Beersheba died. 16 When the angel
stretched out his hand to destroy Jerusalem, the
LORD was grieved because of the calamity and
said to the angel who was afflicting the people,
"Enough! Withdraw your hand." The angel of

[a]27 Hebrew; some Septuagint manuscripts (see also 1 Chron. 11:29) *Sibbecai* [b]29 Some Hebrew manuscripts and Vulgate (see also 1 Chron. 11:30); most Hebrew manuscripts *Heleb* [c]30 Hebrew; some Septuagint manuscripts (see also 1 Chron. 11:32) *Hurai* [d]33 Some Septuagint manuscripts (see also 1 Chron. 11:34); Hebrew does not have *son of.* [e]33 Hebrew; some Septuagint manuscripts (see also 1 Chron. 11:35) *Sacar* [f]36 Some Septuagint manuscripts (see also 1 Chron. 11:38); Hebrew *Haggadi* [g]2 Septuagint (see also verse 4 and 1 Chron. 21:2); Hebrew *Joab the army commander* [h]13 Septuagint (see also 1 Chron. 21:12); Hebrew *seven*

the LORD was then at the threshing floor of Araunah the Jebusite.

17When David saw the angel who was striking down the people, he said to the LORD, "I am the one who has sinned and done wrong. These are but sheep. What have they done? Let your hand fall upon me and my family."

David Builds an Altar

18On that day Gad went to David and said to him, "Go up and build an altar to the LORD on the threshing floor of Araunah the Jebusite." 19So David went up, as the LORD had commanded through Gad. 20When Araunah looked and saw the king and his men coming toward him, he went out and bowed down before the king with his face to the ground.

21Araunah said, "Why has my lord the king come to his servant?"

"To buy your threshing floor," David answered, "so I can build an altar to the LORD, that the plague on the people may be stopped."

22Araunah said to David, "Let my lord the king take whatever pleases him and offer it up. Here are oxen for the burnt offering, and here are threshing sledges and ox yokes for the wood. 23O king, Araunah gives all this to the king." Araunah also said to him, "May the LORD your God accept you."

24But the king replied to Araunah, "No, I insist on paying you for it. I will not sacrifice to the LORD my God burnt offerings that cost me nothing."

So David bought the threshing floor and the oxen and paid fifty shekels[a] of silver for them. 25David built an altar to the LORD there and sacrificed burnt offerings and fellowship offerings.[b] Then the LORD answered prayer in behalf of the land, and the plague on Israel was stopped.

1 Kings

Adonijah Sets Himself Up as King

1 When King David was old and well advanced in years, he could not keep warm even when they put covers over him. 2So his servants said to him, "Let us look for a young virgin to attend the king and take care of him. She can lie beside him so that our lord the king may keep warm."

3Then they searched throughout Israel for a beautiful girl and found Abishag, a Shunammite, and brought her to the king. 4The girl was very beautiful; she took care of the king and waited on him, but the king had no intimate relations with her.

5Now Adonijah, whose mother was Haggith, put himself forward and said, "I will be king." So he got chariots and horses[c] ready, with fifty men to run ahead of him. 6(His father had never interfered with him by asking, "Why do you behave as you do?" He was also very handsome and was born next after Absalom.)

7Adonijah conferred with Joab son of Zeruiah and with Abiathar the priest, and they gave him their support. 8But Zadok the priest, Benaiah son of Jehoiada, Nathan the prophet, Shimei and Rei[d] and David's special guard did not join Adonijah.

9Adonijah then sacrificed sheep, cattle and fattened calves at the Stone of Zoheleth near En Rogel. He invited all his brothers, the king's sons, and all the men of Judah who were royal officials, 10but he did not invite Nathan the prophet or Benaiah or the special guard or his brother Solomon.

11Then Nathan asked Bathsheba, Solomon's mother, "Have you not heard that Adonijah, the son of Haggith, has become king without our lord David's knowing it? 12Now then, let me advise you how you can save your own life and the life of your son Solomon. 13Go in to King David and say to him, 'My lord the king, did you not swear to me your servant: "Surely Solomon your son shall be king after me, and he will sit on my throne"? Why then has Adonijah become king?' 14While you are still there talking to the king, I will come in and confirm what you have said."

15So Bathsheba went to see the aged king in his room, where Abishag the Shunammite was attending him. 16Bathsheba bowed low and knelt before the king.

"What is it you want?" the king asked.

17She said to him, "My lord, you yourself swore to me your servant by the LORD your God: 'Solomon your son shall be king after me, and he will sit on my throne.' 18But now Adonijah has become king, and you, my lord the king, do not know about it. 19He has sacrificed great numbers of cattle, fattened calves, and sheep, and has invited all the king's sons, Abiathar the priest and Joab the commander of the army, but he has not invited Solomon your servant. 20My lord the king, the eyes of all Israel are on you, to learn from you who will sit on the throne of my lord the king after him. 21Otherwise, as soon as my lord the king is laid to rest with his fathers, I and my son Solomon will be treated as criminals."

[a]24 That is, about 1 1/4 pounds (about 0.6 kilogram) [b]25 Traditionally *peace offerings* [c]5 Or *charioteers*
[d]8 Or *and his friends*

22While she was still speaking with the king, Nathan the prophet arrived. 23And they told the king, "Nathan the prophet is here." So he went before the king and bowed with his face to the ground.

24Nathan said, "Have you, my lord the king, declared that Adonijah shall be king after you, and that he will sit on your throne? 25Today he has gone down and sacrificed great numbers of cattle, fattened calves, and sheep. He has invited all the king's sons, the commanders of the army and Abiathar the priest. Right now they are eating and drinking with him and saying, 'Long live King Adonijah!' 26But me your servant, and Zadok the priest, and Benaiah son of Jehoiada, and your servant Solomon he did not invite. 27Is this something my lord the king has done without letting his servants know who should sit on the throne of my lord the king after him?"

David Makes Solomon King

28Then King David said, "Call in Bathsheba." So she came into the king's presence and stood before him.

29The king then took an oath: "As surely as the LORD lives, who has delivered me out of every trouble, 30I will surely carry out today what I swore to you by the LORD, the God of Israel: Solomon your son shall be king after me, and he will sit on my throne in my place."

31Then Bathsheba bowed low with her face to the ground and, kneeling before the king, said, "May my lord King David live forever!"

32King David said, "Call in Zadok the priest, Nathan the prophet and Benaiah son of Jehoiada." When they came before the king, 33he said to them: "Take your lord's servants with you and set Solomon my son on my own mule and take him down to Gihon. 34There have Zadok the priest and Nathan the prophet anoint him king over Israel. Blow the trumpet and shout, 'Long live King Solomon!' 35Then you are to go up with him, and he is to come and sit on my throne and reign in my place. I have appointed him ruler over Israel and Judah."

36Benaiah son of Jehoiada answered the king, "Amen! May the LORD, the God of my lord the king, so declare it. 37As the LORD was with my lord the king, so may he be with Solomon to make his throne even greater than the throne of my lord King David!"

38So Zadok the priest, Nathan the prophet, Benaiah son of Jehoiada, the Kerethites and the Pelethites went down and put Solomon on King David's mule and escorted him to Gihon. 39Zadok the priest took the horn of oil from the sacred tent and anointed Solomon. Then they sounded the trumpet and all the people shouted, "Long live King Solomon!" 40And all the people went up after him, playing flutes and rejoicing greatly, so that the ground shook with the sound.

41Adonijah and all the guests who were with him heard it as they were finishing their feast. On hearing the sound of the trumpet, Joab asked, "What's the meaning of all the noise in the city?"

42Even as he was speaking, Jonathan son of Abiathar the priest arrived. Adonijah said, "Come in. A worthy man like you must be bringing good news."

43"Not at all!" Jonathan answered. "Our lord King David has made Solomon king. 44The king has sent with him Zadok the priest, Nathan the prophet, Benaiah son of Jehoiada, the Kerethites and the Pelethites, and they have put him on the king's mule, 45and Zadok the priest and Nathan the prophet have anointed him king at Gihon. From there they have gone up cheering, and the city resounds with it. That's the noise you hear. 46Moreover, Solomon has taken his seat on the royal throne. 47Also, the royal officials have come to congratulate our lord King David, saying, 'May your God make Solomon's name more famous than yours and his throne greater than yours!' And the king bowed in worship on his bed 48and said, 'Praise be to the LORD, the God of Israel, who has allowed my eyes to see a successor on my throne today.' "

49At this, all Adonijah's guests rose in alarm and dispersed. 50But Adonijah, in fear of Solomon, went and took hold of the horns of the altar. 51Then Solomon was told, "Adonijah is afraid of King Solomon and is clinging to the horns of the altar. He says, 'Let King Solomon swear to me today that he will not put his servant to death with the sword.' "

52Solomon replied, "If he shows himself to be a worthy man, not a hair of his head will fall to the ground; but if evil is found in him, he will die." 53 Then King Solomon sent men, and they brought him down from the altar. And Adonijah came and bowed down to King Solomon, and Solomon said, "Go to your home."

David's Charge to Solomon

2 When the time drew near for David to die, he gave a charge to Solomon his son.

2"I am about to go the way of all the earth," he said. "So be strong, show yourself a man, 3and observe what the LORD your God requires: Walk in his ways, and keep his decrees and commands, his laws and requirements, as written in the Law of Moses, so that you may prosper in all you do and wherever you go, 4and that the LORD may keep his promise to me: 'If your descendants watch how they live, and if they walk faithfully before me with all their heart and soul, you will never fail to have a man on the throne of Israel.'

5"Now you yourself know what Joab son of Zeruiah did to me—what he did to the two commanders of Israel's armies, Abner son of Ner and Amasa son of Jether. He killed them, shedding their blood in peacetime as if in battle, and with that blood stained the belt around his waist and the sandals on his feet. 6Deal with him according to your wisdom, but do not let his gray head go down to the grave[a] in peace.

7"But show kindness to the sons of Barzillai of Gilead and let them be among those who eat at your table. They stood by me when I fled from your brother Absalom.

8"And remember, you have with you Shimei son of Gera, the Benjamite from Bahurim, who called down bitter curses on me the day I went to Mahanaim. When he came down to meet me at the Jordan, I swore to him by the LORD: 'I will not put you to death by the sword.' 9But now, do not consider him innocent. You are a man of wisdom; you will know what to do to him. Bring his gray head down to the grave in blood."

10Then David rested with his fathers and was buried in the City of David. 11He had reigned forty years over Israel—seven years in Hebron and thirty-three in Jerusalem. 12So Solomon sat on the throne of his father David, and his rule was firmly established.

Solomon's Throne Established

13Now Adonijah, the son of Haggith, went to Bathsheba, Solomon's mother. Bathsheba asked him, "Do you come peacefully?"

He answered, "Yes, peacefully." 14Then he added, "I have something to say to you."

"You may say it," she replied.

15"As you know," he said, "the kingdom was mine. All Israel looked to me as their king. But things changed, and the kingdom has gone to my brother; for it has come to him from the LORD. 16Now I have one request to make of you. Do not refuse me."

"You may make it," she said.

17So he continued, "Please ask King Solomon—he will not refuse you—to give me Abishag the Shunammite as my wife."

18"Very well," Bathsheba replied, "I will speak to the king for you."

19When Bathsheba went to King Solomon to speak to him for Adonijah, the king stood up to meet her, bowed down to her and sat down on his throne. He had a throne brought for the king's mother, and she sat down at his right hand.

20"I have one small request to make of you," she said. "Do not refuse me."

The king replied, "Make it, my mother; I will not refuse you."

21So she said, "Let Abishag the Shunammite be given in marriage to your brother Adonijah."

22King Solomon answered his mother, "Why do you request Abishag the Shunammite for Adonijah? You might as well request the kingdom for him—after all, he is my older brother—yes, for him and for Abiathar the priest and Joab son of Zeruiah!"

23Then King Solomon swore by the LORD: "May God deal with me, be it ever so severely, if Adonijah does not pay with his life for this request! 24And now, as surely as the LORD lives—he who has established me securely on the throne of my father David and has founded a dynasty for me as he promised—Adonijah shall be put to death today!" 25So King Solomon gave orders to Benaiah son of Jehoiada, and he struck down Adonijah and he died.

26To Abiathar the priest the king said, "Go back to your fields in Anathoth. You deserve to die, but I will not put you to death now, because you carried the ark of the Sovereign LORD before my father David and shared all my father's hardships." 27So Solomon removed Abiathar from the priesthood of the LORD, fulfilling the word the LORD had spoken at Shiloh about the house of Eli.

28When the news reached Joab, who had conspired with Adonijah though not with Absalom, he fled to the tent of the LORD and took hold of the horns of the altar. 29King Solomon was told that Joab had fled to the tent of the LORD and was beside the altar. Then Solomon ordered Benaiah son of Jehoiada, "Go, strike him down!"

30So Benaiah entered the tent of the LORD and said to Joab, "The king says, 'Come out!' "

But he answered, "No, I will die here."

Benaiah reported to the king, "This is how Joab answered me."

31Then the king commanded Benaiah, "Do as he says. Strike him down and bury him, and so clear me and my father's house of the guilt of the innocent blood that Joab shed. 32The LORD will repay him for the blood he shed, because without the knowledge of my father David he attacked two men and killed them with the sword. Both of them—Abner son of Ner, commander of Israel's army, and Amasa son of Jether, commander of Judah's army—were better men and more upright than he. 33May the guilt of their blood rest on the head of Joab and his descendants forever. But on David and his descendants, his house and his throne, may there be the LORD's peace forever."

34So Benaiah son of Jehoiada went up and struck down Joab and killed him, and he was buried on his own land[b] in the desert. 35The king put Benaiah son of Jehoiada over the army in Joab's position and replaced Abiathar with Zadok the priest.

36Then the king sent for Shimei and said to him, "Build yourself a house in Jerusalem and live there, but do not go anywhere else. 37The day you leave and cross the Kidron Valley, you can be sure you will die; your blood will be on your own head."

38Shimei answered the king, "What you say is good. Your servant will do as my lord the king has said." And Shimei stayed in Jerusalem for a long time.

39But three years later, two of Shimei's slaves ran off to Achish son of Maacah, king of Gath, and Shimei was told, "Your slaves are in Gath." 40At this, he saddled his donkey and

[a]6 Hebrew *Sheol*; also in verse 9 [b]34 Or *buried in his tomb*

went to Achish at Gath in search of his slaves.
So Shimei went away and brought the slaves
back from Gath.
41When Solomon was told that Shimei had
gone from Jerusalem to Gath and had returned,
42the king summoned Shimei and said to him,
"Did I not make you swear by the LORD and
warn you, 'On the day you leave to go anywhere else, you can be sure you will die'? At
that time you said to me, 'What you say is
good. I will obey.' **43**Why then did you not
keep your oath to the LORD and obey the command I gave you?"
44The king also said to Shimei, "You know
in your heart all the wrong you did to my father David. Now the LORD will repay you for
your wrongdoing. **45**But King Solomon will be
blessed, and David's throne will remain secure
before the LORD forever."
46Then the king gave the order to Benaiah
son of Jehoiada, and he went out and struck
Shimei down and killed him.
The kingdom was now firmly established in
Solomon's hands.

Solomon Asks for Wisdom

3 Solomon made an alliance with Pharaoh
king of Egypt and married his daughter. He
brought her to the City of David until he finished building his palace and the temple of the
LORD, and the wall around Jerusalem. **2**The
people, however, were still sacrificing at the
high places, because a temple had not yet been
built for the Name of the LORD. **3**Solomon
showed his love for the LORD by walking according to the statutes of his father David, except that he offered sacrifices and burned incense on the high places.
4The king went to Gibeon to offer sacrifices,
for that was the most important high place, and
Solomon offered a thousand burnt offerings on
that altar. **5**At Gibeon the LORD appeared to
Solomon during the night in a dream, and God
said, "Ask for whatever you want me to give
you."
6Solomon answered, "You have shown
great kindness to your servant, my father David, because he was faithful to you and righteous and upright in heart. You have continued
this great kindness to him and have given him
a son to sit on his throne this very day.
7"Now, O LORD my God, you have made
your servant king in place of my father David.
But I am only a little child and do not know
how to carry out my duties. **8**Your servant is
here among the people you have chosen, a
great people, too numerous to count or number. **9**So give your servant a discerning heart to
govern your people and to distinguish between
right and wrong. For who is able to govern this
great people of yours?"
10The Lord was pleased that Solomon had
asked for this. **11**So God said to him, "Since
you have asked for this and not for long life or
wealth for yourself, nor have asked for the
death of your enemies but for discernment in
administering justice, **12**I will do what you
have asked. I will give you a wise and discerning heart, so that there will never have been
anyone like you, nor will there ever be.
13Moreover, I will give you what you have not
asked for—both riches and honor—so that in
your lifetime you will have no equal among
kings. **14**And if you walk in my ways and obey
my statutes and commands as David your father did, I will give you a long life." **15**Then
Solomon awoke—and he realized it had been
a dream.
He returned to Jerusalem, stood before the
ark of the Lord's covenant and sacrificed burnt
offerings and fellowship offerings.[a] Then he
gave a feast for all his court.

A Wise Ruling

16Now two prostitutes came to the king and
stood before him. **17**One of them said, "My
lord, this woman and I live in the same house.
I had a baby while she was there with me.
18The third day after my child was born, this
woman also had a baby. We were alone; there
was no one in the house but the two of us.
19"During the night this woman's son died
because she lay on him. **20**So she got up in the
middle of the night and took my son from my
side while I your servant was asleep. She put
him by her breast and put her dead son by my
breast. **21**The next morning, I got up to nurse
my son—and he was dead! But when I looked
at him closely in the morning light, I saw that
it wasn't the son I had borne."
22The other woman said, "No! The living
one is my son; the dead one is yours."
But the first one insisted, "No! The dead one
is yours; the living one is mine." And so they
argued before the king.
23The king said, "This one says, 'My son is
alive and your son is dead,' while that one
says, 'No! Your son is dead and mine is
alive.' "
24Then the king said, "Bring me a sword."
So they brought a sword for the king. **25**He
then gave an order: "Cut the living child in two
and give half to one and half to the other."
26The woman whose son was alive was
filled with compassion for her son and said to
the king, "Please, my lord, give her the living
baby! Don't kill him!"
But the other said, "Neither I nor you shall
have him. Cut him in two!"
27Then the king gave his ruling: "Give the
living baby to the first woman. Do not kill him;
she is his mother."
28When all Israel heard the verdict the king
had given, they held the king in awe, because
they saw that he had wisdom from God to
administer justice.

Solomon's Officials and Governors

4 So King Solomon ruled over all Israel.
2And these were his chief officials:

[a] *15* Traditionally *peace offerings*

Azariah son of Zadok—the priest;
3Elihoreph and Ahijah, sons of Shisha—
secretaries;
Jehoshaphat son of Ahilud—recorder;
4Benaiah son of Jehoiada—commander
in chief;
Zadok and Abiathar—priests;
5Azariah son of Nathan—in charge of the
district officers;
Zabud son of Nathan—a priest and personal adviser to the king;
6Ahishar—in charge of the palace;
Adoniram son of Abda—in charge of
forced labor.

7Solomon also had twelve district governors
over all Israel, who supplied provisions for the
king and the royal household. Each one had to
provide supplies for one month in the year.
8These are their names:

Ben-Hur—in the hill country of
Ephraim;
9Ben-Deker—in Makaz, Shaalbim, Beth
Shemesh and Elon Bethhanan;
10Ben-Hesed—in Arubboth (Socoh and
all the land of Hepher were his);
11Ben-Abinadab—in Naphoth Dor[a] (he
was married to Taphath daughter of
Solomon);
12Baana son of Ahilud—in Taanach and
Megiddo, and in all of Beth Shan next
to Zarethan below Jezreel, from Beth
Shan to Abel Meholah across to Jok-
meam;
13Ben-Geber—in Ramoth Gilead (the settlements of Jair son of Manasseh in
Gilead were his, as well as the district
of Argob in Bashan and its sixty large
walled cities with bronze gate bars);
14Ahinadab son of Iddo—in Mahanaim;
15Ahimaaz—in Naphtali (he had married
Basemath daughter of Solomon);
16Baana son of Hushai—in Asher and in
Aloth;
17Jehoshaphat son of Paruah—in Issachar;
18Shimei son of Ela—in Benjamin;
19Geber son of Uri—in Gilead (the country of Sihon king of the Amorites and
the country of Og king of Bashan). He
was the only governor over the district.

Solomon's Daily Provisions

20The people of Judah and Israel were as
numerous as the sand on the seashore; they ate,
they drank and they were happy. 21And Solomon ruled over all the kingdoms from the River[b] to the land of the Philistines, as far as the
border of Egypt. These countries brought tribute and were Solomon's subjects all his life.
22Solomon's daily provisions were thirty
cors[c] of fine flour and sixty cors[d] of meal,
23ten head of stall-fed cattle, twenty of
pasture-fed cattle and a hundred sheep and
goats, as well as deer, gazelles, roebucks and
choice fowl. 24For he ruled over all the kingdoms west of the River, from Tiphsah to Gaza,
and had peace on all sides. 25During Solomon's lifetime Judah and Israel, from Dan to
Beersheba, lived in safety, each man under his
own vine and fig tree.
26Solomon had four[e] thousand stalls for
chariot horses, and twelve thousand horses.[f]
27The district officers, each in his month,
supplied provisions for King Solomon and all
who came to the king's table. They saw to it
that nothing was lacking. 28They also brought
to the proper place their quotas of barley and
straw for the chariot horses and the other
horses.

Solomon's Wisdom

29God gave Solomon wisdom and very great
insight, and a breadth of understanding as measureless as the sand on the seashore. 30Solo-
mon's wisdom was greater than the wisdom of
all the men of the East, and greater than all the
wisdom of Egypt. 31He was wiser than any
other man, including Ethan the Ezrahite—wiser than Heman, Calcol and Darda, the sons of
Mahol. And his fame spread to all the surrounding nations. 32He spoke three thousand
proverbs and his songs numbered a thousand
and five. 33He described plant life, from the
cedar of Lebanon to the hyssop that grows out
of walls. He also taught about animals and
birds, reptiles and fish. 34Men of all nations
came to listen to Solomon's wisdom, sent by
all the kings of the world, who had heard of his
wisdom.

Preparations for Building the Temple

5 When Hiram king of Tyre heard that Solomon had been anointed king to succeed his
father David, he sent his envoys to Solomon,
because he had always been on friendly terms
with David. 2Solomon sent back this message
to Hiram:

3"You know that because of the wars
waged against my father David from all
sides, he could not build a temple for the
Name of the LORD his God until the LORD
put his enemies under his feet. 4But now
the LORD my God has given me rest on
every side, and there is no adversary or
disaster. 5I intend, therefore, to build a
temple for the Name of the LORD my
God, as the LORD told my father David,
when he said, 'Your son whom I will put
on the throne in your place will build the
temple for my Name.'
6"So give orders that cedars of Lebanon be cut for me. My men will work
with yours, and I will pay you for your
men whatever wages you set. You know

[a]*11* Or *in the heights of Dor* [b]*21* That is, the Euphrates; also in verse 24 [c]*22* That is, probably about 185 bushels (about 6.6 kiloliters) [d]*22* That is, probably about 375 bushels (about 13.2 kiloliters) [e]*26* Some Septuagint manuscripts (see also 2 Chron. 9:25); Hebrew *forty* [f]*26* Or *charioteers*

that we have no one so skilled in felling timber as the Sidonians."

7 When Hiram heard Solomon's message, he was greatly pleased and said, "Praise be to the LORD today, for he has given David a wise son to rule over this great nation."

8 So Hiram sent word to Solomon:

> "I have received the message you sent me and will do all you want in providing the cedar and pine logs. 9 My men will haul them down from Lebanon to the sea, and I will float them in rafts by sea to the place you specify. There I will separate them and you can take them away. And you are to grant my wish by providing food for my royal household."

10 In this way Hiram kept Solomon supplied with all the cedar and pine logs he wanted, 11 and Solomon gave Hiram twenty thousand cors[a] of wheat as food for his household, in addition to twenty thousand baths[b,c] of pressed olive oil. Solomon continued to do this for Hiram year after year. 12 The LORD gave Solomon wisdom, just as he had promised him. There were peaceful relations between Hiram and Solomon, and the two of them made a treaty.

13 King Solomon conscripted laborers from all Israel—thirty thousand men. 14 He sent them off to Lebanon in shifts of ten thousand a month, so that they spent one month in Lebanon and two months at home. Adoniram was in charge of the forced labor. 15 Solomon had seventy thousand carriers and eighty thousand stonecutters in the hills, 16 as well as thirty-three hundred[d] foremen who supervised the project and directed the workmen. 17 At the king's command they removed from the quarry large blocks of quality stone to provide a foundation of dressed stone for the temple. 18 The craftsmen of Solomon and Hiram and the men of Gebal[e] cut and prepared the timber and stone for the building of the temple.

Solomon Builds the Temple

6 In the four hundred and eightieth[f] year after the Israelites had come out of Egypt, in the fourth year of Solomon's reign over Israel, in the month of Ziv, the second month, he began to build the temple of the LORD.

2 The temple that King Solomon built for the LORD was sixty cubits long, twenty wide and thirty high.[g] 3 The portico at the front of the main hall of the temple extended the width of the temple, that is twenty cubits,[h] and projected ten cubits[i] from the front of the temple. 4 He made narrow clerestory windows in the temple. 5 Against the walls of the main hall and inner sanctuary he built a structure around the building, in which there were side rooms. 6 The lowest floor was five cubits[j] wide, the middle floor six cubits[k] and the third floor seven.[l] He made offset ledges around the outside of the temple so that nothing would be inserted into the temple walls.

7 In building the temple, only blocks dressed at the quarry were used, and no hammer, chisel or any other iron tool was heard at the temple site while it was being built.

8 The entrance to the lowest[m] floor was on the south side of the temple; a stairway led up to the middle level and from there to the third. 9 So he built the temple and completed it, roofing it with beams and cedar planks. 10 And he built the side rooms all along the temple. The height of each was five cubits, and they were attached to the temple by beams of cedar.

11 The word of the LORD came to Solomon: 12 "As for this temple you are building, if you follow my decrees, carry out my regulations and keep all my commands and obey them, I will fulfill through you the promise I gave to David your father. 13 And I will live among the Israelites and will not abandon my people Israel."

14 So Solomon built the temple and completed it. 15 He lined its interior walls with cedar boards, paneling them from the floor of the temple to the ceiling, and covered the floor of the temple with planks of pine. 16 He partitioned off twenty cubits[h] at the rear of the temple with cedar boards from floor to ceiling to form within the temple an inner sanctuary, the Most Holy Place. 17 The main hall in front of this room was forty cubits[n] long. 18 The inside of the temple was cedar, carved with gourds and open flowers. Everything was cedar; no stone was to be seen.

19 He prepared the inner sanctuary within the temple to set the ark of the covenant of the LORD there. 20 The inner sanctuary was twenty cubits long, twenty wide and twenty high.[o] He overlaid the inside with pure gold, and he also overlaid the altar of cedar. 21 Solomon covered the inside of the temple with pure gold, and he extended gold chains across the front of the inner sanctuary, which was overlaid with gold. 22 So he overlaid the whole interior with gold. He also overlaid with gold the altar that belonged to the inner sanctuary.

23 In the inner sanctuary he made a pair of cherubim of olive wood, each ten cubits[i] high. 24 One wing of the first cherub was five cubits long, and the other wing five cubits—ten cubits from wing tip to wing tip. 25 The second

[a] *11* That is, probably about 125,000 bushels (about 4,400 kiloliters) [b] *11* Septuagint (see also 2 Chron. 2:10); Hebrew *twenty cors* [c] *11* That is, about 115,000 gallons (about 440 kiloliters) [d] *16* Hebrew; some Septuagint manuscripts (see also 2 Chron. 2:2, 18) *thirty-six hundred* [e] *18* That is, Byblos [f] *1* Hebrew; Septuagint *four hundred and fortieth* [g] *2* That is, about 90 feet (about 27 meters) long and 30 feet (about 9 meters) wide and 45 feet (about 13.5 meters) high [h] *3,16* That is, about 30 feet (about 9 meters) [i] *3,23* That is, about 15 feet (about 4.5 meters) [j] *6* That is, about 7 1/2 feet (about 2.3 meters); also in verses 10 and 24 [k] *6* That is, about 9 feet (about 2.7 meters) [l] *6* That is, about 10 1/2 feet (about 3.1 meters) [m] *8* Septuagint; Hebrew *middle* [n] *17* That is, about 60 feet (about 18 meters) [o] *20* That is, about 30 feet (about 9 meters) long, wide and high

cherub also measured ten cubits, for the two cherubim were identical in size and shape. 26The height of each cherub was ten cubits. 27He placed the cherubim inside the innermost room of the temple, with their wings spread out. The wing of one cherub touched one wall, while the wing of the other touched the other wall, and their wings touched each other in the middle of the room. 28He overlaid the cherubim with gold.

29On the walls all around the temple, in both the inner and outer rooms, he carved cherubim, palm trees and open flowers. 30He also covered the floors of both the inner and outer rooms of the temple with gold.

31For the entrance of the inner sanctuary he made doors of olive wood with five-sided jambs. 32And on the two olive wood doors he carved cherubim, palm trees and open flowers, and overlaid the cherubim and palm trees with beaten gold. 33In the same way he made four-sided jambs of olive wood for the entrance to the main hall. 34He also made two pine doors, each having two leaves that turned in sockets. 35He carved cherubim, palm trees and open flowers on them and overlaid them with gold hammered evenly over the carvings.

36And he built the inner courtyard of three courses of dressed stone and one course of trimmed cedar beams.

37The foundation of the temple of the LORD was laid in the fourth year, in the month of Ziv. 38In the eleventh year in the month of Bul, the eighth month, the temple was finished in all its details according to its specifications. He had spent seven years building it.

Solomon Builds His Palace

7 It took Solomon thirteen years, however, to complete the construction of his palace. 2He built the Palace of the Forest of Lebanon a hundred cubits long, fifty wide and thirty high,[a] with four rows of cedar columns supporting trimmed cedar beams. 3It was roofed with cedar above the beams that rested on the columns—forty-five beams, fifteen to a row. 4Its windows were placed high in sets of three, facing each other. 5All the doorways had rectangular frames; they were in the front part in sets of three, facing each other.[b]

6He made a colonnade fifty cubits long and thirty wide.[c] In front of it was a portico, and in front of that were pillars and an overhanging roof.

7He built the throne hall, the Hall of Justice, where he was to judge, and he covered it with cedar from floor to ceiling.[d] 8And the palace in which he was to live, set farther back, was similar in design. Solomon also made a palace like this hall for Pharaoh's daughter, whom he had married.

9All these structures, from the outside to the great courtyard and from foundation to eaves, were made of blocks of high-grade stone cut to size and trimmed with a saw on their inner and outer faces. 10The foundations were laid with large stones of good quality, some measuring ten cubits[e] and some eight.[f] 11Above were high-grade stones, cut to size, and cedar beams. 12The great courtyard was surrounded by a wall of three courses of dressed stone and one course of trimmed cedar beams, as was the inner courtyard of the temple of the LORD with its portico.

The Temple's Furnishings

13King Solomon sent to Tyre and brought Huram,[g] 14whose mother was a widow from the tribe of Naphtali and whose father was a man of Tyre and a craftsman in bronze. Huram was highly skilled and experienced in all kinds of bronze work. He came to King Solomon and did all the work assigned to him.

15He cast two bronze pillars, each eighteen cubits high and twelve cubits around,[h] by line. 16He also made two capitals of cast bronze to set on the tops of the pillars; each capital was five cubits[i] high. 17A network of interwoven chains festooned the capitals on top of the pillars, seven for each capital. 18He made pomegranates in two rows[j] encircling each network to decorate the capitals on top of the pillars.[k] He did the same for each capital. 19The capitals on top of the pillars in the portico were in the shape of lilies, four cubits[l] high. 20On the capitals of both pillars, above the bowl-shaped part next to the network, were the two hundred pomegranates in rows all around. 21He erected the pillars at the portico of the temple. The pillar to the south he named Jakin[m] and the one to the north Boaz.[n] 22The capitals on top were in the shape of lilies. And so the work on the pillars was completed.

23He made the Sea of cast metal, circular in shape, measuring ten cubits[e] from rim to rim and five cubits high. It took a line of thirty cubits[o] to measure around it. 24Below the rim, gourds encircled it—ten to a cubit. The gourds were cast in two rows in one piece with the Sea.

25The Sea stood on twelve bulls, three facing north, three facing west, three facing south and three facing east. The Sea rested on top of them, and their hindquarters were toward the

[a]*2* That is, about 150 feet (about 46 meters) long, 75 feet (about 23 meters) wide and 45 feet (about 13.5 meters) high [b]*5* The meaning of the Hebrew for this verse is uncertain. [c]*6* That is, about 75 feet (about 23 meters) long and 45 feet (about 13.5 meters) wide [d]*7* Vulgate and Syriac; Hebrew *floor* [e]*10,23* That is, about 15 feet (about 4.5 meters) [f]*10* That is, about 12 feet (about 3.6 meters) [g]*13* Hebrew *Hiram,* a variant of *Huram*; also in verses 40 and 45 [h]*15* That is, about 27 feet (about 8.1 meters) high and 18 feet (about 5.4 meters) around [i]*16* That is, about 7 1/2 feet (about 2.3 meters); also in verse 23 [j]*18* Two Hebrew manuscripts and Septuagint; most Hebrew manuscripts *made the pillars, and there were two rows* [k]*18* Many Hebrew manuscripts and Syriac; most Hebrew manuscripts *pomegranates* [l]*19* That is, about 6 feet (about 1.8 meters); also in verse 38 [m]*21* *Jakin* probably means *he establishes.* [n]*21* *Boaz* probably means *in him is strength.* [o]*23* That is, about 45 feet (about 13.5 meters)

center. 26It was a handbreadth[a] in thickness, and its rim was like the rim of a cup, like a lily blossom. It held two thousand baths.[b]

27He also made ten movable stands of bronze; each was four cubits long, four wide and three high.[c] 28This is how the stands were made: They had side panels attached to uprights. 29On the panels between the uprights were lions, bulls and cherubim—and on the uprights as well. Above and below the lions and bulls were wreaths of hammered work. 30Each stand had four bronze wheels with bronze axles, and each had a basin resting on four supports, cast with wreaths on each side. 31On the inside of the stand there was an opening that had a circular frame one cubit[d] deep. This opening was round, and with its basework it measured a cubit and a half.[e] Around its opening there was engraving. The panels of the stands were square, not round. 32The four wheels were under the panels, and the axles of the wheels were attached to the stand. The diameter of each wheel was a cubit and a half. 33The wheels were made like chariot wheels; the axles, rims, spokes and hubs were all of cast metal.

34Each stand had four handles, one on each corner, projecting from the stand. 35At the top of the stand there was a circular band half a cubit[f] deep. The supports and panels were attached to the top of the stand. 36He engraved cherubim, lions and palm trees on the surfaces of the supports and on the panels, in every available space, with wreaths all around. 37This is the way he made the ten stands. They were all cast in the same molds and were identical in size and shape.

38He then made ten bronze basins, each holding forty baths[g] and measuring four cubits across, one basin to go on each of the ten stands. 39He placed five of the stands on the south side of the temple and five on the north. He placed the Sea on the south side, at the southeast corner of the temple. 40He also made the basins and shovels and sprinkling bowls.

So Huram finished all the work he had undertaken for King Solomon in the temple of the LORD:

41the two pillars;
the two bowl-shaped capitals on top of the pillars;
the two sets of network decorating the two bowl-shaped capitals on top of the pillars;
42the four hundred pomegranates for the two sets of network (two rows of pomegranates for each network, decorating the bowl-shaped capitals on top of the pillars);
43the ten stands with their ten basins;
44the Sea and the twelve bulls under it;
45the pots, shovels and sprinkling bowls.

All these objects that Huram made for King Solomon for the temple of the LORD were of burnished bronze. 46The king had them cast in clay molds in the plain of the Jordan between Succoth and Zarethan. 47Solomon left all these things unweighed, because there were so many; the weight of the bronze was not determined.

48Solomon also made all the furnishings that were in the LORD's temple:

the golden altar;
the golden table on which was the bread of the Presence;
49the lampstands of pure gold (five on the right and five on the left, in front of the inner sanctuary);
the gold floral work and lamps and tongs;
50the pure gold basins, wick trimmers, sprinkling bowls, dishes and censers;
and the gold sockets for the doors of the innermost room, the Most Holy Place, and also for the doors of the main hall of the temple.

51When all the work King Solomon had done for the temple of the LORD was finished, he brought in the things his father David had dedicated—the silver and gold and the furnishings—and he placed them in the treasuries of the LORD's temple.

The Ark Brought to the Temple

8 Then King Solomon summoned into his presence at Jerusalem the elders of Israel, all the heads of the tribes and the chiefs of the Israelite families, to bring up the ark of the LORD's covenant from Zion, the City of David. 2All the men of Israel came together to King Solomon at the time of the festival in the month of Ethanim, the seventh month.

3When all the elders of Israel had arrived, the priests took up the ark, 4and they brought up the ark of the LORD and the Tent of Meeting and all the sacred furnishings in it. The priests and Levites carried them up, 5and King Solomon and the entire assembly of Israel that had gathered about him were before the ark, sacrificing so many sheep and cattle that they could not be recorded or counted.

6The priests then brought the ark of the LORD's covenant to its place in the inner sanctuary of the temple, the Most Holy Place, and put it beneath the wings of the cherubim. 7The cherubim spread their wings over the place of the ark and overshadowed the ark and its carrying poles. 8These poles were so long that their ends could be seen from the Holy Place in front of the inner sanctuary, but not from outside the Holy Place; and they are still there

[a] *26* That is, about 3 inches (about 8 centimeters) [b] *26* That is, probably about 11,500 gallons (about 44 kiloliters); the Septuagint does not have this sentence. [c] *27* That is, about 6 feet (about 1.8 meters) long and wide and about 4 1/2 feet (about 1.3 meters) high [d] *31* That is, about 1 1/2 feet (about 0.5 meter) [e] *31* That is, about 2 1/4 feet (about 0.7 meter); also in verse 32 [f] *35* That is, about 3/4 foot (about 0.2 meter) [g] *38* That is, about 230 gallons (about 880 liters)

today. 9There was nothing in the ark except the two stone tablets that Moses had placed in it at Horeb, where the LORD made a covenant with the Israelites after they came out of Egypt.

10When the priests withdrew from the Holy Place, the cloud filled the temple of the LORD. 11And the priests could not perform their service because of the cloud, for the glory of the LORD filled his temple.

12Then Solomon said, "The LORD has said that he would dwell in a dark cloud; 13I have indeed built a magnificent temple for you, a place for you to dwell forever."

14While the whole assembly of Israel was standing there, the king turned around and blessed them. 15Then he said:

> "Praise be to the LORD, the God of Israel, who with his own hand has fulfilled what he promised with his own mouth to my father David. For he said, 16'Since the day I brought my people Israel out of Egypt, I have not chosen a city in any tribe of Israel to have a temple built for my Name to be there, but I have chosen David to rule my people Israel.'
>
> 17"My father David had it in his heart to build a temple for the Name of the LORD, the God of Israel. 18But the LORD said to my father David, 'Because it was in your heart to build a temple for my Name, you did well to have this in your heart. 19Nevertheless, you are not the one to build the temple, but your son, who is your own flesh and blood—he is the one who will build the temple for my Name.'
>
> 20"The LORD has kept the promise he made: I have succeeded David my father and now I sit on the throne of Israel, just as the LORD promised, and I have built the temple for the Name of the LORD, the God of Israel. 21I have provided a place there for the ark, in which is the covenant of the LORD that he made with our fathers when he brought them out of Egypt."

Solomon's Prayer of Dedication

22Then Solomon stood before the altar of the LORD in front of the whole assembly of Israel, spread out his hands toward heaven 23and said:

> "O LORD, God of Israel, there is no God like you in heaven above or on earth below—you who keep your covenant of love with your servants who continue wholeheartedly in your way. 24You have kept your promise to your servant David my father; with your mouth you have promised and with your hand you have fulfilled it—as it is today.
>
> 25"Now LORD, God of Israel, keep for your servant David my father the promises you made to him when you said, 'You shall never fail to have a man to sit before me on the throne of Israel, if only your sons are careful in all they do to walk before me as you have done.' 26And now, O God of Israel, let your word that you promised your servant David my father come true.
>
> 27"But will God really dwell on earth? The heavens, even the highest heaven, cannot contain you. How much less this temple I have built! 28Yet give attention to your servant's prayer and his plea for mercy, O LORD my God. Hear the cry and the prayer that your servant is praying in your presence this day. 29May your eyes be open toward this temple night and day, this place of which you said, 'My Name shall be there,' so that you will hear the prayer your servant prays toward this place. 30Hear the supplication of your servant and of your people Israel when they pray toward this place. Hear from heaven, your dwelling place, and when you hear, forgive.
>
> 31"When a man wrongs his neighbor and is required to take an oath and he comes and swears the oath before your altar in this temple, 32then hear from heaven and act. Judge between your servants, condemning the guilty and bringing down on his own head what he has done. Declare the innocent not guilty, and so establish his innocence.
>
> 33"When your people Israel have been defeated by an enemy because they have sinned against you, and when they turn back to you and confess your name, praying and making supplication to you in this temple, 34then hear from heaven and forgive the sin of your people Israel and bring them back to the land you gave to their fathers.
>
> 35"When the heavens are shut up and there is no rain because your people have sinned against you, and when they pray toward this place and confess your name and turn from their sin because you have afflicted them, 36then hear from heaven and forgive the sin of your servants, your people Israel. Teach them the right way to live, and send rain on the land you gave your people for an inheritance.
>
> 37"When famine or plague comes to the land, or blight or mildew, locusts or grasshoppers, or when an enemy besieges them in any of their cities, whatever disaster or disease may come, 38and when a prayer or plea is made by any of your people Israel—each one aware of the afflictions of his own heart, and spreading out his hands toward this temple— 39then hear from heaven, your dwelling place. Forgive and act; deal with each man according to all he does, since you know his heart (for you alone know the hearts of all men), 40so that they will fear you all the time they live in the land you gave our fathers.
>
> 41"As for the foreigner who does not belong to your people Israel but has come from a distant land because of your name— 42for men will hear of your great

name and your mighty hand and your outstretched arm—when he comes and prays toward this temple, 43then hear from heaven, your dwelling place, and do whatever the foreigner asks of you, so that all the peoples of the earth may know your name and fear you, as do your own people Israel, and may know that this house I have built bears your Name.

44"When your people go to war against their enemies, wherever you send them, and when they pray to the LORD toward the city you have chosen and the temple I have built for your Name, 45then hear from heaven their prayer and their plea, and uphold their cause.

46"When they sin against you—for there is no one who does not sin—and you become angry with them and give them over to the enemy, who takes them captive to his own land, far away or near; 47and if they have a change of heart in the land where they are held captive, and repent and plead with you in the land of their conquerors and say, 'We have sinned, we have done wrong, we have acted wickedly'; 48and if they turn back to you with all their heart and soul in the land of their enemies who took them captive, and pray to you toward the land you gave their fathers, toward the city you have chosen and the temple I have built for your Name; 49then from heaven, your dwelling place, hear their prayer and their plea, and uphold their cause. 50And forgive your people, who have sinned against you; forgive all the offenses they have committed against you, and cause their conquerors to show them mercy; 51for they are your people and your inheritance, whom you brought out of Egypt, out of that iron-smelting furnace.

52"May your eyes be open to your servant's plea and to the plea of your people Israel, and may you listen to them whenever they cry out to you. 53For you singled them out from all the nations of the world to be your own inheritance, just as you declared through your servant Moses when you, O Sovereign LORD, brought our fathers out of Egypt."

54When Solomon had finished all these prayers and supplications to the LORD, he rose from before the altar of the LORD, where he had been kneeling with his hands spread out toward heaven. 55He stood and blessed the whole assembly of Israel in a loud voice, saying:

56"Praise be to the LORD, who has given rest to his people Israel just as he promised. Not one word has failed of all the good promises he gave through his servant Moses. 57May the LORD our God be with us as he was with our fathers; may he never leave us nor forsake us. 58May he turn our hearts to him, to walk in all his ways and to keep the commands, decrees and regulations he gave our fathers. 59And may these words of mine, which I have prayed before the LORD, be near to the LORD our God day and night, that he may uphold the cause of his servant and the cause of his people Israel according to each day's need, 60so that all the peoples of the earth may know that the LORD is God and that there is no other. 61But your hearts must be fully committed to the LORD our God, to live by his decrees and obey his commands, as at this time."

The Dedication of the Temple

62Then the king and all Israel with him offered sacrifices before the LORD. 63Solomon offered a sacrifice of fellowship offerings[a] to the LORD: twenty-two thousand cattle and a hundred and twenty thousand sheep and goats. So the king and all the Israelites dedicated the temple of the LORD.

64On that same day the king consecrated the middle part of the courtyard in front of the temple of the LORD, and there he offered burnt offerings, grain offerings and the fat of the fellowship offerings, because the bronze altar before the LORD was too small to hold the burnt offerings, the grain offerings and the fat of the fellowship offerings.

65So Solomon observed the festival at that time, and all Israel with him—a vast assembly, people from Lebo[b] Hamath to the Wadi of Egypt. They celebrated it before the LORD our God for seven days and seven days more, fourteen days in all. 66On the following day he sent the people away. They blessed the king and then went home, joyful and glad in heart for all the good things the LORD had done for his servant David and his people Israel.

The LORD Appears to Solomon

9 When Solomon had finished building the temple of the LORD and the royal palace, and had achieved all he had desired to do, 2the LORD appeared to him a second time, as he had appeared to him at Gibeon. 3The LORD said to him:

"I have heard the prayer and plea you have made before me; I have consecrated this temple, which you have built, by putting my Name there forever. My eyes and my heart will always be there.

4"As for you, if you walk before me in integrity of heart and uprightness, as David your father did, and do all I command and observe my decrees and laws, 5I will establish your royal throne over Israel forever, as I promised David your father when I said, 'You shall never fail to have a man on the throne of Israel.'

6"But if you[c] or your sons turn away from me and do not observe the com-

[a]63 Traditionally *peace offerings*; also in verse 64 [b]65 Or *from the entrance to* [c]6 The Hebrew is plural.

mands and decrees I have given you[a] and go off to serve other gods and worship them, 7then I will cut off Israel from the land I have given them and will reject this temple I have consecrated for my Name. Israel will then become a byword and an object of ridicule among all peoples. 8And though this temple is now imposing, all who pass by will be appalled and will scoff and say, 'Why has the LORD done such a thing to this land and to this temple?' 9People will answer, 'Because they have forsaken the LORD their God, who brought their fathers out of Egypt, and have embraced other gods, worshiping and serving them—that is why the LORD brought all this disaster on them.' "

Solomon's Other Activities

10At the end of twenty years, during which Solomon built these two buildings—the temple of the LORD and the royal palace— 11King Solomon gave twenty towns in Galilee to Hiram king of Tyre, because Hiram had supplied him with all the cedar and pine and gold he wanted. 12But when Hiram went from Tyre to see the towns that Solomon had given him, he was not pleased with them. 13"What kind of towns are these you have given me, my brother?" he asked. And he called them the Land of Cabul,[b] a name they have to this day. 14Now Hiram had sent to the king 120 talents[c] of gold.

15Here is the account of the forced labor King Solomon conscripted to build the LORD's temple, his own palace, the supporting terraces,[d] the wall of Jerusalem, and Hazor, Megiddo and Gezer. 16(Pharaoh king of Egypt had attacked and captured Gezer. He had set it on fire. He killed its Canaanite inhabitants and then gave it as a wedding gift to his daughter, Solomon's wife. 17And Solomon rebuilt Gezer.) He built up Lower Beth Horon, 18Baalath, and Tadmor[e] in the desert, within his land, 19as well as all his store cities and the towns for his chariots and for his horses[f]—whatever he desired to build in Jerusalem, in Lebanon and throughout all the territory he ruled.

20All the people left from the Amorites, Hittites, Perizzites, Hivites and Jebusites (these peoples were not Israelites), 21that is, their descendants remaining in the land, whom the Israelites could not exterminate[g]—these Solomon conscripted for his slave labor force, as it is to this day. 22But Solomon did not make slaves of any of the Israelites; they were his fighting men, his government officials, his officers, his captains, and the commanders of his chariots and charioteers. 23They were also the chief officials in charge of Solomon's projects—550 officials supervising the men who did the work.

24After Pharaoh's daughter had come up from the City of David to the palace Solomon had built for her, he constructed the supporting terraces.

25Three times a year Solomon sacrificed burnt offerings and fellowship offerings[h] on the altar he had built for the LORD, burning incense before the LORD along with them, and so fulfilled the temple obligations.

26King Solomon also built ships at Ezion Geber, which is near Elath in Edom, on the shore of the Red Sea.[i] 27And Hiram sent his men—sailors who knew the sea—to serve in the fleet with Solomon's men. 28They sailed to Ophir and brought back 420 talents[j] of gold, which they delivered to King Solomon.

The Queen of Sheba Visits Solomon

10 When the queen of Sheba heard about the fame of Solomon and his relation to the name of the LORD, she came to test him with hard questions. 2Arriving at Jerusalem with a very great caravan—with camels carrying spices, large quantities of gold, and precious stones—she came to Solomon and talked with him about all that she had on her mind. 3Solomon answered all her questions; nothing was too hard for the king to explain to her. 4When the queen of Sheba saw all the wisdom of Solomon and the palace he had built, 5the food on his table, the seating of his officials, the attending servants in their robes, his cupbearers, and the burnt offerings he made at[k] the temple of the LORD, she was overwhelmed.

6She said to the king, "The report I heard in my own country about your achievements and your wisdom is true. 7But I did not believe these things until I came and saw with my own eyes. Indeed, not even half was told me; in wisdom and wealth you have far exceeded the report I heard. 8How happy your men must be! How happy your officials, who continually stand before you and hear your wisdom! 9Praise be to the LORD your God, who has delighted in you and placed you on the throne of Israel. Because of the LORD's eternal love for Israel, he has made you king, to maintain justice and righteousness."

10And she gave the king 120 talents[c] of gold, large quantities of spices, and precious stones. Never again were so many spices brought in as those the queen of Sheba gave to King Solomon.

11(Hiram's ships brought gold from Ophir; and from there they brought great cargoes of almugwood[l] and precious stones. 12The king used the almugwood to make supports for the temple of the LORD and for the royal palace, and to make harps and lyres for the musicians.

[a] *6* The Hebrew is plural. [b] *13* *Cabul* sounds like the Hebrew for *good-for-nothing*. [c] *14,10* That is, about 4 1/2 tons (about 4 metric tons) [d] *15* Or *the Millo*; also in verse 24 [e] *18* The Hebrew may also be read *Tamar*. [f] *19* Or *charioteers* [g] *21* The Hebrew term refers to the irrevocable giving over of things or persons to the LORD, often by totally destroying them. [h] *25* Traditionally *peace offerings* [i] *26* Hebrew *Yam Suph*; that is, Sea of Reeds [j] *28* That is, about 16 tons (about 14.5 metric tons) [k] *5* Or *the ascent by which he went up to* [l] *11* Probably a variant of *algumwood*; also in verse 12

So much almugwood has never been imported or seen since that day.)

13 King Solomon gave the queen of Sheba all she desired and asked for, besides what he had given her out of his royal bounty. Then she left and returned with her retinue to her own country.

Solomon's Splendor

14 The weight of the gold that Solomon received yearly was 666 talents,[a] 15 not including the revenues from merchants and traders and from all the Arabian kings and the governors of the land.

16 King Solomon made two hundred large shields of hammered gold; six hundred bekas[b] of gold went into each shield. 17 He also made three hundred small shields of hammered gold, with three minas[c] of gold in each shield. The king put them in the Palace of the Forest of Lebanon.

18 Then the king made a great throne inlaid with ivory and overlaid with fine gold. 19 The throne had six steps, and its back had a rounded top. On both sides of the seat were armrests, with a lion standing beside each of them. 20 Twelve lions stood on the six steps, one at either end of each step. Nothing like it had ever been made for any other kingdom. 21 All King Solomon's goblets were gold, and all the household articles in the Palace of the Forest of Lebanon were pure gold. Nothing was made of silver, because silver was considered of little value in Solomon's days. 22 The king had a fleet of trading ships[d] at sea along with the ships of Hiram. Once every three years it returned, carrying gold, silver and ivory, and apes and baboons.

23 King Solomon was greater in riches and wisdom than all the other kings of the earth. 24 The whole world sought audience with Solomon to hear the wisdom God had put in his heart. 25 Year after year, everyone who came brought a gift—articles of silver and gold, robes, weapons and spices, and horses and mules.

26 Solomon accumulated chariots and horses; he had fourteen hundred chariots and twelve thousand horses,[e] which he kept in the chariot cities and also with him in Jerusalem. 27 The king made silver as common in Jerusalem as stones, and cedar as plentiful as sycamore-fig trees in the foothills. 28 Solomon's horses were imported from Egypt[f] and from Kue[g]—the royal merchants purchased them from Kue. 29 They imported a chariot from Egypt for six hundred shekels[h] of silver, and a horse for a hundred and fifty.[c] They also exported them to all the kings of the Hittites and of the Arameans.

Solomon's Wives

11 King Solomon, however, loved many foreign women besides Pharaoh's daughter—Moabites, Ammonites, Edomites, Sidonians and Hittites. 2 They were from nations about which the LORD had told the Israelites, "You must not intermarry with them, because they will surely turn your hearts after their gods." Nevertheless, Solomon held fast to them in love. 3 He had seven hundred wives of royal birth and three hundred concubines, and his wives led him astray. 4 As Solomon grew old, his wives turned his heart after other gods, and his heart was not fully devoted to the LORD his God, as the heart of David his father had been. 5 He followed Ashtoreth the goddess of the Sidonians, and Molech[i] the detestable god of the Ammonites. 6 So Solomon did evil in the eyes of the LORD; he did not follow the LORD completely, as David his father had done.

7 On a hill east of Jerusalem, Solomon built a high place for Chemosh the detestable god of Moab, and for Molech the detestable god of the Ammonites. 8 He did the same for all his foreign wives, who burned incense and offered sacrifices to their gods.

9 The LORD became angry with Solomon because his heart had turned away from the LORD, the God of Israel, who had appeared to him twice. 10 Although he had forbidden Solomon to follow other gods, Solomon did not keep the LORD's command. 11 So the LORD said to Solomon, "Since this is your attitude and you have not kept my covenant and my decrees, which I commanded you, I will most certainly tear the kingdom away from you and give it to one of your subordinates. 12 Nevertheless, for the sake of David your father, I will not do it during your lifetime. I will tear it out of the hand of your son. 13 Yet I will not tear the whole kingdom from him, but will give him one tribe for the sake of David my servant and for the sake of Jerusalem, which I have chosen."

Solomon's Adversaries

14 Then the LORD raised up against Solomon an adversary, Hadad the Edomite, from the royal line of Edom. 15 Earlier when David was fighting with Edom, Joab the commander of the army, who had gone up to bury the dead, had struck down all the men in Edom. 16 Joab and all the Israelites stayed there for six months, until they had destroyed all the men in Edom. 17 But Hadad, still only a boy, fled to Egypt with some Edomite officials who had served his father. 18 They set out from Midian and went to Paran. Then taking men from Paran with them, they went to Egypt, to Pharaoh king of Egypt, who gave Hadad a house and land and provided him with food.

[a] *14* That is, about 25 tons (about 23 metric tons) [b] *16* That is, about 7 1/2 pounds (about 3.5 kilograms)
[c] *17,29* That is, about 3 3/4 pounds (about 1.7 kilograms) [d] *22* Hebrew *of ships of Tarshish*
[e] *26* Or *charioteers* [f] *28* Or possibly *Muzur*, a region in Cilicia; also in verse 29 [g] *28* Probably *Cilicia*
[h] *29* That is, about 15 pounds (about 7 kilograms) [i] *5* Hebrew *Milcom*; also in verse 33

19Pharaoh was so pleased with Hadad that he gave him a sister of his own wife, Queen Tahpenes, in marriage. 20The sister of Tahpenes bore him a son named Genubath, whom Tahpenes brought up in the royal palace. There Genubath lived with Pharaoh's own children.

21While he was in Egypt, Hadad heard that David rested with his fathers and that Joab the commander of the army was also dead. Then Hadad said to Pharaoh, "Let me go, that I may return to my own country."

22"What have you lacked here that you want to go back to your own country?" Pharaoh asked.

"Nothing," Hadad replied, "but do let me go!"

23And God raised up against Solomon another adversary, Rezon son of Eliada, who had fled from his master, Hadadezer king of Zobah. 24He gathered men around him and became the leader of a band of rebels when David destroyed the forces[a] ⌊of Zobah⌋; the rebels went to Damascus, where they settled and took control. 25Rezon was Israel's adversary as long as Solomon lived, adding to the trouble caused by Hadad. So Rezon ruled in Aram and was hostile toward Israel.

Jeroboam Rebels Against Solomon

26Also, Jeroboam son of Nebat rebelled against the king. He was one of Solomon's officials, an Ephraimite from Zeredah, and his mother was a widow named Zeruah.

27Here is the account of how he rebelled against the king: Solomon had built the supporting terraces[b] and had filled in the gap in the wall of the city of David his father. 28Now Jeroboam was a man of standing, and when Solomon saw how well the young man did his work, he put him in charge of the whole labor force of the house of Joseph.

29About that time Jeroboam was going out of Jerusalem, and Ahijah the prophet of Shiloh met him on the way, wearing a new cloak. The two of them were alone out in the country, 30and Ahijah took hold of the new cloak he was wearing and tore it into twelve pieces. 31Then he said to Jeroboam, "Take ten pieces for yourself, for this is what the LORD, the God of Israel, says: 'See, I am going to tear the kingdom out of Solomon's hand and give you ten tribes. 32But for the sake of my servant David and the city of Jerusalem, which I have chosen out of all the tribes of Israel, he will have one tribe. 33I will do this because they have[c] forsaken me and worshiped Ashtoreth the goddess of the Sidonians, Chemosh the god of the Moabites, and Molech the god of the Ammonites, and have not walked in my ways, nor done what is right in my eyes, nor kept my statutes and laws as David, Solomon's father, did.

34" 'But I will not take the whole kingdom out of Solomon's hand; I have made him ruler all the days of his life for the sake of David my servant, whom I chose and who observed my commands and statutes. 35I will take the kingdom from his son's hands and give you ten tribes. 36I will give one tribe to his son so that David my servant may always have a lamp before me in Jerusalem, the city where I chose to put my Name. 37However, as for you, I will take you, and you will rule over all that your heart desires; you will be king over Israel. 38If you do whatever I command you and walk in my ways and do what is right in my eyes by keeping my statutes and commands, as David my servant did, I will be with you. I will build you a dynasty as enduring as the one I built for David and will give Israel to you. 39I will humble David's descendants because of this, but not forever.' "

40Solomon tried to kill Jeroboam, but Jeroboam fled to Egypt, to Shishak the king, and stayed there until Solomon's death.

Solomon's Death

41As for the other events of Solomon's reign—all he did and the wisdom he displayed—are they not written in the book of the annals of Solomon? 42Solomon reigned in Jerusalem over all Israel forty years. 43Then he rested with his fathers and was buried in the city of David his father. And Rehoboam his son succeeded him as king.

Israel Rebels Against Rehoboam

12 Rehoboam went to Shechem, for all the Israelites had gone there to make him king. 2When Jeroboam son of Nebat heard this (he was still in Egypt, where he had fled from King Solomon), he returned from[d] Egypt. 3So they sent for Jeroboam, and he and the whole assembly of Israel went to Rehoboam and said to him: 4"Your father put a heavy yoke on us, but now lighten the harsh labor and the heavy yoke he put on us, and we will serve you."

5Rehoboam answered, "Go away for three days and then come back to me." So the people went away.

6Then King Rehoboam consulted the elders who had served his father Solomon during his lifetime. "How would you advise me to answer these people?" he asked.

7They replied, "If today you will be a servant to these people and serve them and give them a favorable answer, they will always be your servants."

8But Rehoboam rejected the advice the elders gave him and consulted the young men who had grown up with him and were serving him. 9He asked them, "What is your advice? How should we answer these people who say to me, 'Lighten the yoke your father put on us'?"

10The young men who had grown up with him replied, "Tell these people who have said to you, 'Your father put a heavy yoke on us, but make our yoke lighter'—tell them, 'My

*a*24 Hebrew *destroyed them* *b*27 Or *the Millo* *c*33 Hebrew; Septuagint, Vulgate and Syriac *because he has* *d*2 Or *he remained in*

little finger is thicker than my father's waist. 11My father laid on you a heavy yoke; I will make it even heavier. My father scourged you with whips; I will scourge you with scorpions.' "

12Three days later Jeroboam and all the people returned to Rehoboam, as the king had said, "Come back to me in three days." 13The king answered the people harshly. Rejecting the advice given him by the elders, 14he followed the advice of the young men and said, "My father made your yoke heavy; I will make it even heavier. My father scourged you with whips; I will scourge you with scorpions." 15So the king did not listen to the people, for this turn of events was from the LORD, to fulfill the word the LORD had spoken to Jeroboam son of Nebat through Ahijah the Shilonite.

16When all Israel saw that the king refused to listen to them, they answered the king:

"What share do we have in David,
 what part in Jesse's son?
To your tents, O Israel!
 Look after your own house, O David!"

So the Israelites went home. 17But as for the Israelites who were living in the towns of Judah, Rehoboam still ruled over them.

18King Rehoboam sent out Adoniram,[a] who was in charge of forced labor, but all Israel stoned him to death. King Rehoboam, however, managed to get into his chariot and escape to Jerusalem. 19So Israel has been in rebellion against the house of David to this day.

20When all the Israelites heard that Jeroboam had returned, they sent and called him to the assembly and made him king over all Israel. Only the tribe of Judah remained loyal to the house of David.

21When Rehoboam arrived in Jerusalem, he mustered the whole house of Judah and the tribe of Benjamin—a hundred and eighty thousand fighting men—to make war against the house of Israel and to regain the kingdom for Rehoboam son of Solomon.

22But this word of God came to Shemaiah the man of God: 23"Say to Rehoboam son of Solomon king of Judah, to the whole house of Judah and Benjamin, and to the rest of the people, 24'This is what the LORD says: Do not go up to fight against your brothers, the Israelites. Go home, every one of you, for this is my doing.' " So they obeyed the word of the LORD and went home again, as the LORD had ordered.

Golden Calves at Bethel and Dan

25Then Jeroboam fortified Shechem in the hill country of Ephraim and lived there. From there he went out and built up Peniel.[b]

26Jeroboam thought to himself, "The kingdom will now likely revert to the house of David. 27If these people go up to offer sacrifices at the temple of the LORD in Jerusalem, they will again give their allegiance to their lord, Rehoboam king of Judah. They will kill me and return to King Rehoboam."

28After seeking advice, the king made two golden calves. He said to the people, "It is too much for you to go up to Jerusalem. Here are your gods, O Israel, who brought you up out of Egypt." 29One he set up in Bethel, and the other in Dan. 30And this thing became a sin; the people went even as far as Dan to worship the one there.

31Jeroboam built shrines on high places and appointed priests from all sorts of people, even though they were not Levites. 32He instituted a festival on the fifteenth day of the eighth month, like the festival held in Judah, and offered sacrifices on the altar. This he did in Bethel, sacrificing to the calves he had made. And at Bethel he also installed priests at the high places he had made. 33On the fifteenth day of the eighth month, a month of his own choosing, he offered sacrifices on the altar he had built at Bethel. So he instituted the festival for the Israelites and went up to the altar to make offerings.

The Man of God From Judah

13 By the word of the LORD a man of God came from Judah to Bethel, as Jeroboam was standing by the altar to make an offering. 2He cried out against the altar by the word of the LORD: "O altar, altar! This is what the LORD says: 'A son named Josiah will be born to the house of David. On you he will sacrifice the priests of the high places who now make offerings here, and human bones will be burned on you.' " 3That same day the man of God gave a sign: "This is the sign the LORD has declared: The altar will be split apart and the ashes on it will be poured out."

4When King Jeroboam heard what the man of God cried out against the altar at Bethel, he stretched out his hand from the altar and said, "Seize him!" But the hand he stretched out toward the man shriveled up, so that he could not pull it back. 5Also, the altar was split apart and its ashes poured out according to the sign given by the man of God by the word of the LORD.

6Then the king said to the man of God, "Intercede with the LORD your God and pray for me that my hand may be restored." So the man of God interceded with the LORD, and the king's hand was restored and became as it was before.

7The king said to the man of God, "Come home with me and have something to eat, and I will give you a gift."

8But the man of God answered the king, "Even if you were to give me half your possessions, I would not go with you, nor would I eat bread or drink water here. 9For I was commanded by the word of the LORD: 'You must not eat bread or drink water or return by the

[a] *18* Some Septuagint manuscripts and Syriac (see also 1 Kings 4:6 and 5:14); Hebrew *Adoram* [b] *25* Hebrew *Penuel,* a variant of *Peniel*

way you came.' " 10So he took another road and did not return by the way he had come to Bethel.

11Now there was a certain old prophet living in Bethel, whose sons came and told him all that the man of God had done there that day. They also told their father what he had said to the king. 12Their father asked them, "Which way did he go?" And his sons showed him which road the man of God from Judah had taken. 13So he said to his sons, "Saddle the donkey for me." And when they had saddled the donkey for him, he mounted it 14and rode after the man of God. He found him sitting under an oak tree and asked, "Are you the man of God who came from Judah?"

"I am," he replied.

15So the prophet said to him, "Come home with me and eat."

16The man of God said, "I cannot turn back and go with you, nor can I eat bread or drink water with you in this place. 17I have been told by the word of the LORD: 'You must not eat bread or drink water there or return by the way you came.' "

18The old prophet answered, "I too am a prophet, as you are. And an angel said to me by the word of the LORD: 'Bring him back with you to your house so that he may eat bread and drink water.' " (But he was lying to him.) 19So the man of God returned with him and ate and drank in his house.

20While they were sitting at the table, the word of the LORD came to the old prophet who had brought him back. 21He cried out to the man of God who had come from Judah, "This is what the LORD says: 'You have defied the word of the LORD and have not kept the command the LORD your God gave you. 22You came back and ate bread and drank water in the place where he told you not to eat or drink. Therefore your body will not be buried in the tomb of your fathers.' "

23When the man of God had finished eating and drinking, the prophet who had brought him back saddled his donkey for him. 24As he went on his way, a lion met him on the road and killed him, and his body was thrown down on the road, with both the donkey and the lion standing beside it. 25Some people who passed by saw the body thrown down there, with the lion standing beside the body, and they went and reported it in the city where the old prophet lived.

26When the prophet who had brought him back from his journey heard of it, he said, "It is the man of God who defied the word of the LORD. The LORD has given him over to the lion, which has mauled him and killed him, as the word of the LORD had warned him."

27The prophet said to his sons, "Saddle the donkey for me," and they did so. 28Then he went out and found the body thrown down on the road, with the donkey and the lion standing beside it. The lion had neither eaten the body nor mauled the donkey. 29So the prophet picked up the body of the man of God, laid it on the donkey, and brought it back to his own city to mourn for him and bury him. 30Then he laid the body in his own tomb, and they mourned over him and said, "Oh, my brother!"

31After burying him, he said to his sons, "When I die, bury me in the grave where the man of God is buried; lay my bones beside his bones. 32For the message he declared by the word of the LORD against the altar in Bethel and against all the shrines on the high places in the towns of Samaria will certainly come true."

33Even after this, Jeroboam did not change his evil ways, but once more appointed priests for the high places from all sorts of people. Anyone who wanted to become a priest he consecrated for the high places. 34This was the sin of the house of Jeroboam that led to its downfall and to its destruction from the face of the earth.

Ahijah's Prophecy Against Jeroboam

14 At that time Abijah son of Jeroboam became ill, 2and Jeroboam said to his wife, "Go, disguise yourself, so you won't be recognized as the wife of Jeroboam. Then go to Shiloh. Ahijah the prophet is there—the one who told me I would be king over this people. 3Take ten loaves of bread with you, some cakes and a jar of honey, and go to him. He will tell you what will happen to the boy." 4So Jeroboam's wife did what he said and went to Ahijah's house in Shiloh.

Now Ahijah could not see; his sight was gone because of his age. 5But the LORD had told Ahijah, "Jeroboam's wife is coming to ask you about her son, for he is ill, and you are to give her such and such an answer. When she arrives, she will pretend to be someone else."

6So when Ahijah heard the sound of her footsteps at the door, he said, "Come in, wife of Jeroboam. Why this pretense? I have been sent to you with bad news. 7Go, tell Jeroboam that this is what the LORD, the God of Israel, says: 'I raised you up from among the people and made you a leader over my people Israel. 8I tore the kingdom away from the house of David and gave it to you, but you have not been like my servant David, who kept my commands and followed me with all his heart, doing only what was right in my eyes. 9You have done more evil than all who lived before you. You have made for yourself other gods, idols made of metal; you have provoked me to anger and thrust me behind your back.

10" 'Because of this, I am going to bring disaster on the house of Jeroboam. I will cut off from Jeroboam every last male in Israel—slave or free. I will burn up the house of Jeroboam as one burns dung, until it is all gone. 11Dogs will eat those belonging to Jeroboam who die in the city, and the birds of the air will feed on those who die in the country. The LORD has spoken!'

12"As for you, go back home. When you set foot in your city, the boy will die. 13All Israel will mourn for him and bury him. He is the only one belonging to Jeroboam who will be

buried, because he is the only one in the house
of Jeroboam in whom the LORD, the God of
Israel, has found anything good.
14“The LORD will raise up for himself a king
over Israel who will cut off the family of Jeroboam. This is the day! What? Yes, even now.[a]
15And the LORD will strike Israel, so that it will
be like a reed swaying in the water. He will
uproot Israel from this good land that he gave
to their forefathers and scatter them beyond the
River,[b] because they provoked the LORD to
anger by making Asherah poles.[c] 16And he
will give Israel up because of the sins Jeroboam has committed and has caused Israel to
commit.”
17Then Jeroboam’s wife got up and left and
went to Tirzah. As soon as she stepped over
the threshold of the house, the boy died.
18They buried him, and all Israel mourned for
him, as the LORD had said through his servant
the prophet Ahijah.
19The other events of Jeroboam’s reign, his
wars and how he ruled, are written in the book
of the annals of the kings of Israel. 20He
reigned for twenty-two years and then rested
with his fathers. And Nadab his son succeeded
him as king.

Rehoboam King of Judah

21Rehoboam son of Solomon was king in
Judah. He was forty-one years old when he
became king, and he reigned seventeen years
in Jerusalem, the city the LORD had chosen out
of all the tribes of Israel in which to put his
Name. His mother’s name was Naamah; she
was an Ammonite.
22Judah did evil in the eyes of the LORD. By
the sins they committed they stirred up his
jealous anger more than their fathers had done.
23They also set up for themselves high places,
sacred stones and Asherah poles on every high
hill and under every spreading tree. 24There
were even male shrine prostitutes in the land;
the people engaged in all the detestable practices of the nations the LORD had driven out
before the Israelites.
25In the fifth year of King Rehoboam, Shishak king of Egypt attacked Jerusalem. 26He
carried off the treasures of the temple of the
LORD and the treasures of the royal palace. He
took everything, including all the gold shields
Solomon had made. 27So King Rehoboam
made bronze shields to replace them and assigned these to the commanders of the guard
on duty at the entrance to the royal palace.
28Whenever the king went to the LORD’s temple, the guards bore the shields, and afterward
they returned them to the guardroom.
29As for the other events of Rehoboam’s
reign, and all he did, are they not written in the
book of the annals of the kings of Judah?
30There was continual warfare between Rehoboam and Jeroboam. 31And Rehoboam rested
with his fathers and was buried with them in
the City of David. His mother’s name was Naamah; she was an Ammonite. And Abijah[d] his
son succeeded him as king.

Abijah King of Judah

15 In the eighteenth year of the reign of
Jeroboam son of Nebat, Abijah[e] became king of Judah, 2and he reigned in Jerusalem three years. His mother’s name was Maacah daughter of Abishalom.[f]
3He committed all the sins his father had
done before him; his heart was not fully devoted to the LORD his God, as the heart of David
his forefather had been. 4Nevertheless, for David’s sake the LORD his God gave him a lamp
in Jerusalem by raising up a son to succeed
him and by making Jerusalem strong. 5For David had done what was right in the eyes of the
LORD and had not failed to keep any of the
LORD’s commands all the days of his life—except in the case of Uriah the Hittite.
6There was war between Rehoboam[g] and
Jeroboam throughout ⌞Abijah’s⌟ lifetime. 7As
for the other events of Abijah’s reign, and all
he did, are they not written in the book of the
annals of the kings of Judah? There was war
between Abijah and Jeroboam. 8And Abijah
rested with his fathers and was buried in the
City of David. And Asa his son succeeded him
as king.

Asa King of Judah

9In the twentieth year of Jeroboam king of
Israel, Asa became king of Judah, 10and he
reigned in Jerusalem forty-one years. His
grandmother’s name was Maacah daughter of
Abishalom.
11Asa did what was right in the eyes of the
LORD, as his father David had done. 12He expelled the male shrine prostitutes from the land
and got rid of all the idols his fathers had
made. 13He even deposed his grandmother
Maacah from her position as queen mother,
because she had made a repulsive Asherah
pole. Asa cut the pole down and burned it in
the Kidron Valley. 14Although he did not remove the high places, Asa’s heart was fully
committed to the LORD all his life. 15He
brought into the temple of the LORD the silver
and gold and the articles that he and his father
had dedicated.
16There was war between Asa and Baasha
king of Israel throughout their reigns. 17Baasha
king of Israel went up against Judah and fortified Ramah to prevent anyone from leaving or
entering the territory of Asa king of Judah.
18Asa then took all the silver and gold that
was left in the treasuries of the LORD’s temple

[a] *14* The meaning of the Hebrew for this sentence is uncertain. [b] *15* That is, the Euphrates [c] *15* That is, symbols of the goddess Asherah; here and elsewhere in 1 Kings [d] *31* Some Hebrew manuscripts and Septuagint (see also 2 Chron. 12:16); most Hebrew manuscripts *Abijam* [e] *1* Some Hebrew manuscripts and Septuagint (see also 2 Chron. 12:16); most Hebrew manuscripts *Abijam*; also in verses 7 and 8 [f] *2* A variant of *Absalom*; also in verse 10 [g] *6* Most Hebrew manuscripts; some Hebrew manuscripts and Syriac *Abijam* (that is, Abijah)

and of his own palace. He entrusted it to his
officials and sent them to Ben-Hadad son of
Tabrimmon, the son of Hezion, the king of
Aram, who was ruling in Damascus. 19"Let
there be a treaty between me and you," he said,
"as there was between my father and your father. See, I am sending you a gift of silver and
gold. Now break your treaty with Baasha king
of Israel so he will withdraw from me."

20Ben-Hadad agreed with King Asa and
sent the commanders of his forces against the
towns of Israel. He conquered Ijon, Dan, Abel
Beth Maacah and all Kinnereth in addition
to Naphtali. 21When Baasha heard this, he
stopped building Ramah and withdrew to Tirzah. 22Then King Asa issued an order to all
Judah—no one was exempt—and they carried
away from Ramah the stones and timber Baasha had been using there. With them King Asa
built up Geba in Benjamin, and also Mizpah.

23As for all the other events of Asa's reign,
all his achievements, all he did and the cities
he built, are they not written in the book of the
annals of the kings of Judah? In his old age,
however, his feet became diseased. 24Then Asa
rested with his fathers and was buried with
them in the city of his father David. And Jehoshaphat his son succeeded him as king.

Nadab King of Israel

25Nadab son of Jeroboam became king of
Israel in the second year of Asa king of Judah,
and he reigned over Israel two years. 26He did
evil in the eyes of the LORD, walking in the
ways of his father and in his sin, which he had
caused Israel to commit.

27Baasha son of Ahijah of the house of Issachar plotted against him, and he struck him
down at Gibbethon, a Philistine town, while
Nadab and all Israel were besieging it. 28Baa-
sha killed Nadab in the third year of Asa king
of Judah and succeeded him as king.

29As soon as he began to reign, he killed
Jeroboam's whole family. He did not leave
Jeroboam anyone that breathed, but destroyed
them all, according to the word of the LORD
given through his servant Ahijah the Shilonite— 30because of the sins Jeroboam had
committed and had caused Israel to commit,
and because he provoked the LORD, the God of
Israel, to anger.

31As for the other events of Nadab's reign,
and all he did, are they not written in the book
of the annals of the kings of Israel? 32There
was war between Asa and Baasha king of Israel throughout their reigns.

Baasha King of Israel

33In the third year of Asa king of Judah,
Baasha son of Ahijah became king of all Israel
in Tirzah, and he reigned twenty-four years.
34He did evil in the eyes of the LORD, walking
in the ways of Jeroboam and in his sin, which
he had caused Israel to commit.

16 Then the word of the LORD came to
Jehu son of Hanani against Baasha: 2"I
lifted you up from the dust and made you leader of my people Israel, but you walked in the
ways of Jeroboam and caused my people Israel
to sin and to provoke me to anger by their sins.
3So I am about to consume Baasha and his
house, and I will make your house like that of
Jeroboam son of Nebat. 4Dogs will eat those
belonging to Baasha who die in the city, and
the birds of the air will feed on those who die
in the country."

5As for the other events of Baasha's reign,
what he did and his achievements, are they not
written in the book of the annals of the kings
of Israel? 6Baasha rested with his fathers and
was buried in Tirzah. And Elah his son succeeded him as king.

7Moreover, the word of the LORD came
through the prophet Jehu son of Hanani to Baasha and his house, because of all the evil he
had done in the eyes of the LORD, provoking
him to anger by the things he did, and becoming like the house of Jeroboam—and also because he destroyed it.

Elah King of Israel

8In the twenty-sixth year of Asa king of Judah, Elah son of Baasha became king of Israel,
and he reigned in Tirzah two years.

9Zimri, one of his officials, who had command of half his chariots, plotted against him.
Elah was in Tirzah at the time, getting drunk in
the home of Arza, the man in charge of the
palace at Tirzah. 10Zimri came in, struck him
down and killed him in the twenty-seventh
year of Asa king of Judah. Then he succeeded
him as king.

11As soon as he began to reign and was seated on the throne, he killed off Baasha's whole
family. He did not spare a single male, whether
relative or friend. 12So Zimri destroyed the
whole family of Baasha, in accordance with
the word of the LORD spoken against Baasha
through the prophet Jehu— 13because of all
the sins Baasha and his son Elah had committed and had caused Israel to commit, so that
they provoked the LORD, the God of Israel, to
anger by their worthless idols.

14As for the other events of Elah's reign,
and all he did, are they not written in the book
of the annals of the kings of Israel?

Zimri King of Israel

15In the twenty-seventh year of Asa king of
Judah, Zimri reigned in Tirzah seven days. The
army was encamped near Gibbethon, a Philistine town. 16When the Israelites in the camp
heard that Zimri had plotted against the king
and murdered him, they proclaimed Omri, the
commander of the army, king over Israel that
very day there in the camp. 17Then Omri and
all the Israelites with him withdrew from Gibbethon and laid siege to Tirzah. 18When Zimri
saw that the city was taken, he went into the
citadel of the royal palace and set the palace on
fire around him. So he died, 19because of the
sins he had committed, doing evil in the eyes
of the LORD and walking in the ways of Jero-

boam and in the sin he had committed and had caused Israel to commit.

20As for the other events of Zimri's reign, and the rebellion he carried out, are they not written in the book of the annals of the kings of Israel?

Omri King of Israel

21Then the people of Israel were split into two factions; half supported Tibni son of Ginath for king, and the other half supported Omri. 22But Omri's followers proved stronger than those of Tibni son of Ginath. So Tibni died and Omri became king.

23In the thirty-first year of Asa king of Judah, Omri became king of Israel, and he reigned twelve years, six of them in Tirzah. 24He bought the hill of Samaria from Shemer for two talents[a] of silver and built a city on the hill, calling it Samaria, after Shemer, the name of the former owner of the hill.

25But Omri did evil in the eyes of the LORD and sinned more than all those before him. 26He walked in all the ways of Jeroboam son of Nebat and in his sin, which he had caused Israel to commit, so that they provoked the LORD, the God of Israel, to anger by their worthless idols.

27As for the other events of Omri's reign, what he did and the things he achieved, are they not written in the book of the annals of the kings of Israel? 28Omri rested with his fathers and was buried in Samaria. And Ahab his son succeeded him as king.

Ahab Becomes King of Israel

29In the thirty-eighth year of Asa king of Judah, Ahab son of Omri became king of Israel, and he reigned in Samaria over Israel twenty-two years. 30Ahab son of Omri did more evil in the eyes of the LORD than any of those before him. 31He not only considered it trivial to commit the sins of Jeroboam son of Nebat, but he also married Jezebel daughter of Ethbaal king of the Sidonians, and began to serve Baal and worship him. 32He set up an altar for Baal in the temple of Baal that he built in Samaria. 33Ahab also made an Asherah pole and did more to provoke the LORD, the God of Israel, to anger than did all the kings of Israel before him.

34In Ahab's time, Hiel of Bethel rebuilt Jericho. He laid its foundations at the cost of his firstborn son Abiram, and he set up its gates at the cost of his youngest son Segub, in accordance with the word of the LORD spoken by Joshua son of Nun.

Elijah Fed by Ravens

17 Now Elijah the Tishbite, from Tishbe[b] in Gilead, said to Ahab, "As the LORD, the God of Israel, lives, whom I serve, there will be neither dew nor rain in the next few years except at my word."

2Then the word of the LORD came to Elijah: 3"Leave here, turn eastward and hide in the Kerith Ravine, east of the Jordan. 4You will drink from the brook, and I have ordered the ravens to feed you there."

5So he did what the LORD had told him. He went to the Kerith Ravine, east of the Jordan, and stayed there. 6The ravens brought him bread and meat in the morning and bread and meat in the evening, and he drank from the brook.

The Widow at Zarephath

7Some time later the brook dried up because there had been no rain in the land. 8Then the word of the LORD came to him: 9"Go at once to Zarephath of Sidon and stay there. I have commanded a widow in that place to supply you with food." 10So he went to Zarephath. When he came to the town gate, a widow was there gathering sticks. He called to her and asked, "Would you bring me a little water in a jar so I may have a drink?" 11As she was going to get it, he called, "And bring me, please, a piece of bread."

12"As surely as the LORD your God lives," she replied, "I don't have any bread—only a handful of flour in a jar and a little oil in a jug. I am gathering a few sticks to take home and make a meal for myself and my son, that we may eat it—and die."

13Elijah said to her, "Don't be afraid. Go home and do as you have said. But first make a small cake of bread for me from what you have and bring it to me, and then make something for yourself and your son. 14For this is what the LORD, the God of Israel, says: 'The jar of flour will not be used up and the jug of oil will not run dry until the day the LORD gives rain on the land.' "

15She went away and did as Elijah had told her. So there was food every day for Elijah and for the woman and her family. 16For the jar of flour was not used up and the jug of oil did not run dry, in keeping with the word of the LORD spoken by Elijah.

17Some time later the son of the woman who owned the house became ill. He grew worse and worse, and finally stopped breathing. 18She said to Elijah, "What do you have against me, man of God? Did you come to remind me of my sin and kill my son?"

19"Give me your son," Elijah replied. He took him from her arms, carried him to the upper room where he was staying, and laid him on his bed. 20Then he cried out to the LORD, "O LORD my God, have you brought tragedy also upon this widow I am staying with, by causing her son to die?" 21Then he stretched himself out on the boy three times and cried to the LORD, "O LORD my God, let this boy's life return to him!"

22The LORD heard Elijah's cry, and the boy's life returned to him, and he lived. 23Elijah picked up the child and carried him down from the room into the house. He gave him to his mother and said, "Look, your son is alive!"

[a]24 That is, about 150 pounds (about 70 kilograms) [b]1 Or *Tishbite, of the settlers*

24Then the woman said to Elijah, "Now I know that you are a man of God and that the word of the LORD from your mouth is the truth."

Elijah and Obadiah

18 After a long time, in the third year, the word of the LORD came to Elijah: "Go and present yourself to Ahab, and I will send rain on the land." 2So Elijah went to present himself to Ahab.

Now the famine was severe in Samaria, 3and Ahab had summoned Obadiah, who was in charge of his palace. (Obadiah was a devout believer in the LORD. 4While Jezebel was killing off the LORD's prophets, Obadiah had taken a hundred prophets and hidden them in two caves, fifty in each, and had supplied them with food and water.) 5Ahab had said to Obadiah, "Go through the land to all the springs and valleys. Maybe we can find some grass to keep the horses and mules alive so we will not have to kill any of our animals." 6So they divided the land they were to cover, Ahab going in one direction and Obadiah in another.

7As Obadiah was walking along, Elijah met him. Obadiah recognized him, bowed down to the ground, and said, "Is it really you, my lord Elijah?"

8"Yes," he replied. "Go tell your master, 'Elijah is here.' "

9"What have I done wrong," asked Obadiah, "that you are handing your servant over to Ahab to be put to death? 10As surely as the LORD your God lives, there is not a nation or kingdom where my master has not sent someone to look for you. And whenever a nation or kingdom claimed you were not there, he made them swear they could not find you. 11But now you tell me to go to my master and say, 'Elijah is here.' 12I don't know where the Spirit of the LORD may carry you when I leave you. If I go and tell Ahab and he doesn't find you, he will kill me. Yet I your servant have worshiped the LORD since my youth. 13Haven't you heard, my lord, what I did while Jezebel was killing the prophets of the LORD? I hid a hundred of the LORD's prophets in two caves, fifty in each, and supplied them with food and water. 14And now you tell me to go to my master and say, 'Elijah is here.' He will kill me!"

15Elijah said, "As the LORD Almighty lives, whom I serve, I will surely present myself to Ahab today."

Elijah on Mount Carmel

16So Obadiah went to meet Ahab and told him, and Ahab went to meet Elijah. 17When he saw Elijah, he said to him, "Is that you, you troubler of Israel?"

18"I have not made trouble for Israel," Elijah replied. "But you and your father's family have. You have abandoned the LORD's commands and have followed the Baals. 19Now summon the people from all over Israel to meet me on Mount Carmel. And bring the four hundred and fifty prophets of Baal and the four hundred prophets of Asherah, who eat at Jezebel's table."

20So Ahab sent word throughout all Israel and assembled the prophets on Mount Carmel. 21Elijah went before the people and said, "How long will you waver between two opinions? If the LORD is God, follow him; but if Baal is God, follow him."

But the people said nothing.

22Then Elijah said to them, "I am the only one of the LORD's prophets left, but Baal has four hundred and fifty prophets. 23Get two bulls for us. Let them choose one for themselves, and let them cut it into pieces and put it on the wood but not set fire to it. I will prepare the other bull and put it on the wood but not set fire to it. 24Then you call on the name of your god, and I will call on the name of the LORD. The god who answers by fire—he is God."

Then all the people said, "What you say is good."

25Elijah said to the prophets of Baal, "Choose one of the bulls and prepare it first, since there are so many of you. Call on the name of your god, but do not light the fire." 26So they took the bull given them and prepared it.

Then they called on the name of Baal from morning till noon. "O Baal, answer us!" they shouted. But there was no response; no one answered. And they danced around the altar they had made.

27At noon Elijah began to taunt them. "Shout louder!" he said. "Surely he is a god! Perhaps he is deep in thought, or busy, or traveling. Maybe he is sleeping and must be awakened." 28So they shouted louder and slashed themselves with swords and spears, as was their custom, until their blood flowed. 29Midday passed, and they continued their frantic prophesying until the time for the evening sacrifice. But there was no response, no one answered, no one paid attention.

30Then Elijah said to all the people, "Come here to me." They came to him, and he repaired the altar of the LORD, which was in ruins. 31Elijah took twelve stones, one for each of the tribes descended from Jacob, to whom the word of the LORD had come, saying, "Your name shall be Israel." 32With the stones he built an altar in the name of the LORD, and he dug a trench around it large enough to hold two seahs[a] of seed. 33He arranged the wood, cut the bull into pieces and laid it on the wood. Then he said to them, "Fill four large jars with water and pour it on the offering and on the wood."

34"Do it again," he said, and they did it again.

"Do it a third time," he ordered, and they did it the third time. 35The water ran down around the altar and even filled the trench.

[a]*32* That is, probably about 13 quarts (about 15 liters)

36 At the time of sacrifice, the prophet Elijah stepped forward and prayed: "O LORD, God of Abraham, Isaac and Israel, let it be known today that you are God in Israel and that I am your servant and have done all these things at your command. 37 Answer me, O LORD, answer me, so these people will know that you, O LORD, are God, and that you are turning their hearts back again."

38 Then the fire of the LORD fell and burned up the sacrifice, the wood, the stones and the soil, and also licked up the water in the trench.

39 When all the people saw this, they fell prostrate and cried, "The LORD—he is God! The LORD—he is God!"

40 Then Elijah commanded them, "Seize the prophets of Baal. Don't let anyone get away!" They seized them, and Elijah had them brought down to the Kishon Valley and slaughtered there.

41 And Elijah said to Ahab, "Go, eat and drink, for there is the sound of a heavy rain." 42 So Ahab went off to eat and drink, but Elijah climbed to the top of Carmel, bent down to the ground and put his face between his knees.

43 "Go and look toward the sea," he told his servant. And he went up and looked.

"There is nothing there," he said.

Seven times Elijah said, "Go back."

44 The seventh time the servant reported, "A cloud as small as a man's hand is rising from the sea."

So Elijah said, "Go and tell Ahab, 'Hitch up your chariot and go down before the rain stops you.' "

45 Meanwhile, the sky grew black with clouds, the wind rose, a heavy rain came on and Ahab rode off to Jezreel. 46 The power of the LORD came upon Elijah and, tucking his cloak into his belt, he ran ahead of Ahab all the way to Jezreel.

Elijah Flees to Horeb

19 Now Ahab told Jezebel everything Elijah had done and how he had killed all the prophets with the sword. 2 So Jezebel sent a messenger to Elijah to say, "May the gods deal with me, be it ever so severely, if by this time tomorrow I do not make your life like that of one of them."

3 Elijah was afraid[a] and ran for his life. When he came to Beersheba in Judah, he left his servant there, 4 while he himself went a day's journey into the desert. He came to a broom tree, sat down under it and prayed that he might die. "I have had enough, LORD," he said. "Take my life; I am no better than my ancestors." 5 Then he lay down under the tree and fell asleep.

All at once an angel touched him and said, "Get up and eat." 6 He looked around, and there by his head was a cake of bread baked over hot coals, and a jar of water. He ate and drank and then lay down again.

7 The angel of the LORD came back a second time and touched him and said, "Get up and eat, for the journey is too much for you." 8 So he got up and ate and drank. Strengthened by that food, he traveled forty days and forty nights until he reached Horeb, the mountain of God. 9 There he went into a cave and spent the night.

The LORD Appears to Elijah

And the word of the LORD came to him: "What are you doing here, Elijah?"

10 He replied, "I have been very zealous for the LORD God Almighty. The Israelites have rejected your covenant, broken down your altars, and put your prophets to death with the sword. I am the only one left, and now they are trying to kill me too."

11 The LORD said, "Go out and stand on the mountain in the presence of the LORD, for the LORD is about to pass by."

Then a great and powerful wind tore the mountains apart and shattered the rocks before the LORD, but the LORD was not in the wind. After the wind there was an earthquake, but the LORD was not in the earthquake. 12 After the earthquake came a fire, but the LORD was not in the fire. And after the fire came a gentle whisper. 13 When Elijah heard it, he pulled his cloak over his face and went out and stood at the mouth of the cave.

Then a voice said to him, "What are you doing here, Elijah?"

14 He replied, "I have been very zealous for the LORD God Almighty. The Israelites have rejected your covenant, broken down your altars, and put your prophets to death with the sword. I am the only one left, and now they are trying to kill me too."

15 The LORD said to him, "Go back the way you came, and go to the Desert of Damascus. When you get there, anoint Hazael king over Aram. 16 Also, anoint Jehu son of Nimshi king over Israel, and anoint Elisha son of Shaphat from Abel Meholah to succeed you as prophet. 17 Jehu will put to death any who escape the sword of Hazael, and Elisha will put to death any who escape the sword of Jehu. 18 Yet I reserve seven thousand in Israel—all whose knees have not bowed down to Baal and all whose mouths have not kissed him."

The Call of Elisha

19 So Elijah went from there and found Elisha son of Shaphat. He was plowing with twelve yoke of oxen, and he himself was driving the twelfth pair. Elijah went up to him and threw his cloak around him. 20 Elisha then left his oxen and ran after Elijah. "Let me kiss my father and mother good-by," he said, "and then I will come with you."

"Go back," Elijah replied. "What have I done to you?"

21 So Elisha left him and went back. He took his yoke of oxen and slaughtered them. He burned the plowing equipment to cook the

[a] 3 Or *Elijah saw*

meat and gave it to the people, and they ate.
Then he set out to follow Elijah and became
his attendant.

Ben-Hadad Attacks Samaria

20 Now Ben-Hadad king of Aram mustered his entire army. Accompanied by
thirty-two kings with their horses and chariots,
he went up and besieged Samaria and attacked
it. 2He sent messengers into the city to Ahab
king of Israel, saying, "This is what Ben-
Hadad says: 3'Your silver and gold are mine,
and the best of your wives and children are
mine.' "

4The king of Israel answered, "Just as you
say, my lord the king. I and all I have are
yours."

5The messengers came again and said, "This
is what Ben-Hadad says: 'I sent to demand
your silver and gold, your wives and your children. 6But about this time tomorrow I am going to send my officials to search your palace
and the houses of your officials. They will
seize everything you value and carry it
away.' "

7The king of Israel summoned all the elders
of the land and said to them, "See how this
man is looking for trouble! When he sent for
my wives and my children, my silver and my
gold, I did not refuse him."

8The elders and the people all answered,
"Don't listen to him or agree to his demands."

9So he replied to Ben-Hadad's messengers,
"Tell my lord the king, 'Your servant will do
all you demanded the first time, but this demand I cannot meet.' " They left and took the
answer back to Ben-Hadad.

10Then Ben-Hadad sent another message to
Ahab: "May the gods deal with me, be it ever
so severely, if enough dust remains in Samaria
to give each of my men a handful."

11The king of Israel answered, "Tell him:
'One who puts on his armor should not boast
like one who takes it off.' "

12Ben-Hadad heard this message while he
and the kings were drinking in their tents,[a] and
he ordered his men: "Prepare to attack." So
they prepared to attack the city.

Ahab Defeats Ben-Hadad

13Meanwhile a prophet came to Ahab king
of Israel and announced, "This is what the
LORD says: 'Do you see this vast army? I will
give it into your hand today, and then you will
know that I am the LORD.' "

14"But who will do this?" asked Ahab.

The prophet replied, "This is what the LORD
says: 'The young officers of the provincial
commanders will do it.' "

"And who will start the battle?" he asked.

The prophet answered, "You will."

15So Ahab summoned the young officers of
the provincial commanders, 232 men. Then he
assembled the rest of the Israelites, 7,000 in
all. 16They set out at noon while Ben-Hadad
and the 32 kings allied with him were in their
tents getting drunk. 17The young officers of the
provincial commanders went out first.

Now Ben-Hadad had dispatched scouts,
who reported, "Men are advancing from Samaria."

18He said, "If they have come out for peace,
take them alive; if they have come out for war,
take them alive."

19The young officers of the provincial commanders marched out of the city with the army
behind them 20and each one struck down his
opponent. At that, the Arameans fled, with the
Israelites in pursuit. But Ben-Hadad king of
Aram escaped on horseback with some of his
horsemen. 21The king of Israel advanced and
overpowered the horses and chariots and inflicted heavy losses on the Arameans.

22Afterward, the prophet came to the king of
Israel and said, "Strengthen your position and
see what must be done, because next spring the
king of Aram will attack you again."

23Meanwhile, the officials of the king of
Aram advised him, "Their gods are gods of the
hills. That is why they were too strong for us.
But if we fight them on the plains, surely we
will be stronger than they. 24Do this: Remove
all the kings from their commands and replace
them with other officers. 25You must also raise
an army like the one you lost—horse for horse
and chariot for chariot—so we can fight Israel
on the plains. Then surely we will be stronger
than they." He agreed with them and acted
accordingly.

26The next spring Ben-Hadad mustered the
Arameans and went up to Aphek to fight
against Israel. 27When the Israelites were also
mustered and given provisions, they marched
out to meet them. The Israelites camped opposite them like two small flocks of goats, while
the Arameans covered the countryside.

28The man of God came up and told the king
of Israel, "This is what the LORD says: 'Because the Arameans think the LORD is a god of
the hills and not a god of the valleys, I will
deliver this vast army into your hands, and you
will know that I am the LORD.' "

29For seven days they camped opposite each
other, and on the seventh day the battle was
joined. The Israelites inflicted a hundred thousand casualties on the Aramean foot soldiers in
one day. 30The rest of them escaped to the city
of Aphek, where the wall collapsed on twenty-
seven thousand of them. And Ben-Hadad fled
to the city and hid in an inner room.

31His officials said to him, "Look, we have
heard that the kings of the house of Israel are
merciful. Let us go to the king of Israel with
sackcloth around our waists and ropes around
our heads. Perhaps he will spare your life."

32Wearing sackcloth around their waists and
ropes around their heads, they went to the king
of Israel and said, "Your servant Ben-Hadad
says: 'Please let me live.' "

[a]12 Or *in Succoth*; also in verse 16

The king answered, "Is he still alive? He is my brother."

33The men took this as a good sign and were quick to pick up his word. "Yes, your brother Ben-Hadad!" they said.

"Go and get him," the king said. When Ben-Hadad came out, Ahab had him come up into his chariot.

34"I will return the cities my father took from your father," Ben-Hadad offered. "You may set up your own market areas in Damascus, as my father did in Samaria."

⌊Ahab said,⌋ "On the basis of a treaty I will set you free." So he made a treaty with him, and let him go.

A Prophet Condemns Ahab

35By the word of the LORD one of the sons of the prophets said to his companion, "Strike me with your weapon," but the man refused.

36So the prophet said, "Because you have not obeyed the LORD, as soon as you leave me a lion will kill you." And after the man went away, a lion found him and killed him.

37The prophet found another man and said, "Strike me, please." So the man struck him and wounded him. 38Then the prophet went and stood by the road waiting for the king. He disguised himself with his headband down over his eyes. 39As the king passed by, the prophet called out to him, "Your servant went into the thick of the battle, and someone came to me with a captive and said, 'Guard this man. If he is missing, it will be your life for his life, or you must pay a talent[a] of silver.' 40While your servant was busy here and there, the man disappeared."

"That is your sentence," the king of Israel said. "You have pronounced it yourself."

41Then the prophet quickly removed the headband from his eyes, and the king of Israel recognized him as one of the prophets. 42He said to the king, "This is what the LORD says: 'You have set free a man I had determined should die.[b] Therefore it is your life for his life, your people for his people.' " 43Sullen and angry, the king of Israel went to his palace in Samaria.

Naboth's Vineyard

21 Some time later there was an incident involving a vineyard belonging to Naboth the Jezreelite. The vineyard was in Jezreel, close to the palace of Ahab king of Samaria. 2Ahab said to Naboth, "Let me have your vineyard to use for a vegetable garden, since it is close to my palace. In exchange I will give you a better vineyard or, if you prefer, I will pay you whatever it is worth."

3But Naboth replied, "The LORD forbid that I should give you the inheritance of my fathers."

4So Ahab went home, sullen and angry because Naboth the Jezreelite had said, "I will not give you the inheritance of my fathers." He lay on his bed sulking and refused to eat.

5His wife Jezebel came in and asked him, "Why are you so sullen? Why won't you eat?"

6He answered her, "Because I said to Naboth the Jezreelite, 'Sell me your vineyard; or if you prefer, I will give you another vineyard in its place.' But he said, 'I will not give you my vineyard.' "

7Jezebel his wife said, "Is this how you act as king over Israel? Get up and eat! Cheer up. I'll get you the vineyard of Naboth the Jezreelite."

8So she wrote letters in Ahab's name, placed his seal on them, and sent them to the elders and nobles who lived in Naboth's city with him. 9In those letters she wrote:

> "Proclaim a day of fasting and seat Naboth in a prominent place among the people. 10But seat two scoundrels opposite him and have them testify that he has cursed both God and the king. Then take him out and stone him to death."

11So the elders and nobles who lived in Naboth's city did as Jezebel directed in the letters she had written to them. 12They proclaimed a fast and seated Naboth in a prominent place among the people. 13Then two scoundrels came and sat opposite him and brought charges against Naboth before the people, saying, "Naboth has cursed both God and the king." So they took him outside the city and stoned him to death. 14Then they sent word to Jezebel: "Naboth has been stoned and is dead."

15As soon as Jezebel heard that Naboth had been stoned to death, she said to Ahab, "Get up and take possession of the vineyard of Naboth the Jezreelite that he refused to sell you. He is no longer alive, but dead." 16When Ahab heard that Naboth was dead, he got up and went down to take possession of Naboth's vineyard.

17Then the word of the LORD came to Elijah the Tishbite: 18"Go down to meet Ahab king of Israel, who rules in Samaria. He is now in Naboth's vineyard, where he has gone to take possession of it. 19Say to him, 'This is what the LORD says: Have you not murdered a man and seized his property?' Then say to him, 'This is what the LORD says: In the place where dogs licked up Naboth's blood, dogs will lick up your blood—yes, yours!' "

20Ahab said to Elijah, "So you have found me, my enemy!"

"I have found you," he answered, "because you have sold yourself to do evil in the eyes of the LORD. 21'I am going to bring disaster on you. I will consume your descendants and cut off from Ahab every last male in Israel—slave or free. 22I will make your house like that of Jeroboam son of Nebat and that of Baasha son of Ahijah, because you have provoked me to anger and have caused Israel to sin.'

23"And also concerning Jezebel the LORD

[a]*39* That is, about 75 pounds (about 34 kilograms) [b]*42* The Hebrew term refers to the irrevocable giving over of things or persons to the LORD, often by totally destroying them.

says: ‘Dogs will devour Jezebel by the wall
of[a] Jezreel.’
24 “Dogs will eat those belonging to Ahab
who die in the city, and the birds of the air will
feed on those who die in the country.”
25 (There was never a man like Ahab, who
sold himself to do evil in the eyes of the LORD,
urged on by Jezebel his wife. 26 He behaved in
the vilest manner by going after idols, like the
Amorites the LORD drove out before Israel.)
27 When Ahab heard these words, he tore his
clothes, put on sackcloth and fasted. He lay in
sackcloth and went around meekly.
28 Then the word of the LORD came to Elijah
the Tishbite: 29 “Have you noticed how Ahab
has humbled himself before me? Because he
has humbled himself, I will not bring this disaster in his day, but I will bring it on his house
in the days of his son.”

Micaiah Prophesies Against Ahab

22 For three years there was no war between Aram and Israel. 2 But in the third
year Jehoshaphat king of Judah went down to
see the king of Israel. 3 The king of Israel had
said to his officials, “Don’t you know that Ramoth Gilead belongs to us and yet we are
doing nothing to retake it from the king of
Aram?”
4 So he asked Jehoshaphat, “Will you go
with me to fight against Ramoth Gilead?”
Jehoshaphat replied to the king of Israel, “I
am as you are, my people as your people, my
horses as your horses.” 5 But Jehoshaphat also
said to the king of Israel, “First seek the counsel of the LORD.”
6 So the king of Israel brought together the
prophets—about four hundred men—and
asked them, “Shall I go to war against Ramoth
Gilead, or shall I refrain?”
“Go,” they answered, “for the Lord will give
it into the king’s hand.”
7 But Jehoshaphat asked, “Is there not a
prophet of the LORD here whom we can inquire of?”
8 The king of Israel answered Jehoshaphat,
“There is still one man through whom we can
inquire of the LORD, but I hate him because he
never prophesies anything good about me, but
always bad. He is Micaiah son of Imlah.”
“The king should not say that,” Jehoshaphat
replied.
9 So the king of Israel called one of his officials and said, “Bring Micaiah son of Imlah at
once.”
10 Dressed in their royal robes, the king of
Israel and Jehoshaphat king of Judah were sitting on their thrones at the threshing floor by
the entrance of the gate of Samaria, with all the
prophets prophesying before them. 11 Now
Zedekiah son of Kenaanah had made iron
horns and he declared, “This is what the LORD
says: ‘With these you will gore the Arameans
until they are destroyed.’ ”
12 All the other prophets were prophesying
the same thing. “Attack Ramoth Gilead and be
victorious,” they said, “for the LORD will give
it into the king’s hand.”
13 The messenger who had gone to summon
Micaiah said to him, “Look, as one man the
other prophets are predicting success for the
king. Let your word agree with theirs, and
speak favorably.”
14 But Micaiah said, “As surely as the LORD
lives, I can tell him only what the LORD
tells me.”
15 When he arrived, the king asked him, “Micaiah, shall we go to war against Ramoth Gilead, or shall I refrain?”
“Attack and be victorious,” he answered,
“for the LORD will give it into the king’s
hand.”
16 The king said to him, “How many times
must I make you swear to tell me nothing but
the truth in the name of the LORD?”
17 Then Micaiah answered, “I saw all Israel
scattered on the hills like sheep without a shepherd, and the LORD said, ‘These people have
no master. Let each one go home in peace.’ ”
18 The king of Israel said to Jehoshaphat,
“Didn’t I tell you that he never prophesies anything good about me, but only bad?”
19 Micaiah continued, “Therefore hear the
word of the LORD: I saw the LORD sitting on
his throne with all the host of heaven standing
around him on his right and on his left. 20 And
the LORD said, ‘Who will entice Ahab into
attacking Ramoth Gilead and going to his
death there?’
“One suggested this, and another that. 21 Finally, a spirit came forward, stood before the
LORD and said, ‘I will entice him.’
22 “ ‘By what means?’ the LORD asked.
“ ‘I will go out and be a lying spirit in the
mouths of all his prophets,’ he said.
“ ‘You will succeed in enticing him,’ said
the LORD. ‘Go and do it.’
23 “So now the LORD has put a lying spirit in
the mouths of all these prophets of yours. The
LORD has decreed disaster for you.”
24 Then Zedekiah son of Kenaanah went up
and slapped Micaiah in the face. “Which way
did the spirit from[b] the LORD go when he went
from me to speak to you?” he asked.
25 Micaiah replied, “You will find out on the
day you go to hide in an inner room.”
26 The king of Israel then ordered, “Take Micaiah and send him back to Amon the ruler of
the city and to Joash the king’s son 27 and say,
‘This is what the king says: Put this fellow in
prison and give him nothing but bread and water until I return safely.’ ”
28 Micaiah declared, “If you ever return safely, the LORD has not spoken through me.”
Then he added, “Mark my words, all you people!”

[a] *23* Most Hebrew manuscripts; a few Hebrew manuscripts, Vulgate and Syriac (see also 2 Kings 9:26) *the plot of ground at* [b] *24* Or *Spirit of*

Ahab Killed at Ramoth Gilead

29So the king of Israel and Jehoshaphat king of Judah went up to Ramoth Gilead. 30The king of Israel said to Jehoshaphat, "I will enter the battle in disguise, but you wear your royal robes." So the king of Israel disguised himself and went into battle.

31Now the king of Aram had ordered his thirty-two chariot commanders, "Do not fight with anyone, small or great, except the king of Israel." 32When the chariot commanders saw Jehoshaphat, they thought, "Surely this is the king of Israel." So they turned to attack him, but when Jehoshaphat cried out, 33the chariot commanders saw that he was not the king of Israel and stopped pursuing him.

34But someone drew his bow at random and hit the king of Israel between the sections of his armor. The king told his chariot driver, "Wheel around and get me out of the fighting. I've been wounded." 35All day long the battle raged, and the king was propped up in his chariot facing the Arameans. The blood from his wound ran onto the floor of the chariot, and that evening he died. 36As the sun was setting, a cry spread through the army: "Every man to his town; everyone to his land!"

37So the king died and was brought to Samaria, and they buried him there. 38They washed the chariot at a pool in Samaria (where the prostitutes bathed),[a] and the dogs licked up his blood, as the word of the LORD had declared.

39As for the other events of Ahab's reign, including all he did, the palace he built and inlaid with ivory, and the cities he fortified, are they not written in the book of the annals of the kings of Israel? 40Ahab rested with his fathers. And Ahaziah his son succeeded him as king.

Jehoshaphat King of Judah

41Jehoshaphat son of Asa became king of Judah in the fourth year of Ahab king of Israel. 42Jehoshaphat was thirty-five years old when he became king, and he reigned in Jerusalem twenty-five years. His mother's name was Azubah daughter of Shilhi. 43In everything he walked in the ways of his father Asa and did not stray from them; he did what was right in the eyes of the LORD. The high places, however, were not removed, and the people continued to offer sacrifices and burn incense there. 44Jehoshaphat was also at peace with the king of Israel.

45As for the other events of Jehoshaphat's reign, the things he achieved and his military exploits, are they not written in the book of the annals of the kings of Judah? 46He rid the land of the rest of the male shrine prostitutes who remained there even after the reign of his father Asa. 47There was then no king in Edom; a deputy ruled.

48Now Jehoshaphat built a fleet of trading ships[b] to go to Ophir for gold, but they never set sail—they were wrecked at Ezion Geber. 49At that time Ahaziah son of Ahab said to Jehoshaphat, "Let my men sail with your men," but Jehoshaphat refused.

50Then Jehoshaphat rested with his fathers and was buried with them in the city of David his father. And Jehoram his son succeeded him.

Ahaziah King of Israel

51Ahaziah son of Ahab became king of Israel in Samaria in the seventeenth year of Jehoshaphat king of Judah, and he reigned over Israel two years. 52He did evil in the eyes of the LORD, because he walked in the ways of his father and mother and in the ways of Jeroboam son of Nebat, who caused Israel to sin. 53He served and worshiped Baal and provoked the LORD, the God of Israel, to anger, just as his father had done.

2 Kings

The LORD's Judgment on Ahaziah

1 After Ahab's death, Moab rebelled against Israel. 2Now Ahaziah had fallen through the lattice of his upper room in Samaria and injured himself. So he sent messengers, saying to them, "Go and consult Baal-Zebub, the god of Ekron, to see if I will recover from this injury."

3But the angel of the LORD said to Elijah the Tishbite, "Go up and meet the messengers of the king of Samaria and ask them, 'Is it because there is no God in Israel that you are going off to consult Baal-Zebub, the god of Ekron?' 4Therefore this is what the LORD says: 'You will not leave the bed you are lying on. You will certainly die!' " So Elijah went.

5When the messengers returned to the king, he asked them, "Why have you come back?"

6"A man came to meet us," they replied. "And he said to us, 'Go back to the king who sent you and tell him, "This is what the LORD says: Is it because there is no God in Israel that you are sending men to consult Baal-Zebub, the god of Ekron? Therefore you will not leave the bed you are lying on. You will certainly die!" ' "

7The king asked them, "What kind of man was it who came to meet you and told you this?"

[a]38 Or *Samaria and cleaned the weapons* [b]48 Hebrew *of ships of Tarshish*

8They replied, "He was a man with a garment of hair and with a leather belt around his
waist."
The king said, "That was Elijah the Tishbite."
9Then he sent to Elijah a captain with his
company of fifty men. The captain went up to
Elijah, who was sitting on the top of a hill, and
said to him, "Man of God, the king says,
'Come down!' "
10Elijah answered the captain, "If I am a
man of God, may fire come down from heaven
and consume you and your fifty men!" Then
fire fell from heaven and consumed the captain
and his men.
11At this the king sent to Elijah another captain with his fifty men. The captain said to
him, "Man of God, this is what the king says,
'Come down at once!' "
12"If I am a man of God," Elijah replied,
"may fire come down from heaven and consume you and your fifty men!" Then the fire of
God fell from heaven and consumed him and
his fifty men.
13So the king sent a third captain with his
fifty men. This third captain went up and fell
on his knees before Elijah. "Man of God," he
begged, "please have respect for my life and
the lives of these fifty men, your servants!
14See, fire has fallen from heaven and consumed the first two captains and all their men.
But now have respect for my life!"
15The angel of the LORD said to Elijah, "Go
down with him; do not be afraid of him." So
Elijah got up and went down with him to the
king.
16He told the king, "This is what the LORD
says: Is it because there is no God in Israel for
you to consult that you have sent messengers
to consult Baal-Zebub, the god of Ekron? Because you have done this, you will never leave
the bed you are lying on. You will certainly
die!" 17So he died, according to the word of
the LORD that Elijah had spoken.
Because Ahaziah had no son, Joram[a] succeeded him as king in the second year of Jehoram son of Jehoshaphat king of Judah. 18As for
all the other events of Ahaziah's reign, and
what he did, are they not written in the book of
the annals of the kings of Israel?

Elijah Taken Up to Heaven

2 When the LORD was about to take Elijah
up to heaven in a whirlwind, Elijah and
Elisha were on their way from Gilgal. 2Elijah
said to Elisha, "Stay here; the LORD has sent
me to Bethel."
But Elisha said, "As surely as the LORD
lives and as you live, I will not leave you." So
they went down to Bethel.
3The company of the prophets at Bethel
came out to Elisha and asked, "Do you know
that the LORD is going to take your master
from you today?"
"Yes, I know," Elisha replied, "but do not
speak of it."
4Then Elijah said to him, "Stay here, Elisha;
the LORD has sent me to Jericho."
And he replied, "As surely as the LORD lives
and as you live, I will not leave you." So they
went to Jericho.
5The company of the prophets at Jericho
went up to Elisha and asked him, "Do you
know that the LORD is going to take your master from you today?"
"Yes, I know," he replied, "but do not speak
of it."
6Then Elijah said to him, "Stay here; the
LORD has sent me to the Jordan."
And he replied, "As surely as the LORD lives
and as you live, I will not leave you." So the
two of them walked on.
7Fifty men of the company of the prophets
went and stood at a distance, facing the place
where Elijah and Elisha had stopped at the
Jordan. 8Elijah took his cloak, rolled it up and
struck the water with it. The water divided to
the right and to the left, and the two of them
crossed over on dry ground.
9When they had crossed, Elijah said to Elisha, "Tell me, what can I do for you before I
am taken from you?"
"Let me inherit a double portion of your
spirit," Elisha replied.
10"You have asked a difficult thing," Elijah
said, "yet if you see me when I am taken from
you, it will be yours—otherwise not."
11As they were walking along and talking
together, suddenly a chariot of fire and horses
of fire appeared and separated the two of them,
and Elijah went up to heaven in a whirlwind.
12Elisha saw this and cried out, "My father!
My father! The chariots and horsemen of Israel!" And Elisha saw him no more. Then he
took hold of his own clothes and tore them
apart.
13He picked up the cloak that had fallen
from Elijah and went back and stood on the
bank of the Jordan. 14Then he took the cloak
that had fallen from him and struck the water
with it. "Where now is the LORD, the God of
Elijah?" he asked. When he struck the water, it
divided to the right and to the left, and he
crossed over.
15The company of the prophets from Jericho, who were watching, said, "The spirit of
Elijah is resting on Elisha." And they went to
meet him and bowed to the ground before him.
16"Look," they said, "we your servants have
fifty able men. Let them go and look for your
master. Perhaps the Spirit of the LORD has
picked him up and set him down on some
mountain or in some valley."
"No," Elisha replied, "do not send them."
17But they persisted until he was too
ashamed to refuse. So he said, "Send them."
And they sent fifty men, who searched for
three days but did not find him. 18When they

[a] 17 Hebrew *Jehoram,* a variant of *Joram*

returned to Elisha, who was staying in Jericho, he said to them, "Didn't I tell you not to go?"

Healing of the Water

19The men of the city said to Elisha, "Look, our lord, this town is well situated, as you can see, but the water is bad and the land is unproductive."

20"Bring me a new bowl," he said, "and put salt in it." So they brought it to him.

21Then he went out to the spring and threw the salt into it, saying, "This is what the LORD says: 'I have healed this water. Never again will it cause death or make the land unproductive.' " 22And the water has remained wholesome to this day, according to the word Elisha had spoken.

Elisha Is Jeered

23From there Elisha went up to Bethel. As he was walking along the road, some youths came out of the town and jeered at him. "Go on up, you baldhead!" they said. "Go on up, you baldhead!" 24He turned around, looked at them and called down a curse on them in the name of the LORD. Then two bears came out of the woods and mauled forty-two of the youths. 25And he went on to Mount Carmel and from there returned to Samaria.

Moab Revolts

3 Joram[a] son of Ahab became king of Israel in Samaria in the eighteenth year of Jehoshaphat king of Judah, and he reigned twelve years. 2He did evil in the eyes of the LORD, but not as his father and mother had done. He got rid of the sacred stone of Baal that his father had made. 3Nevertheless he clung to the sins of Jeroboam son of Nebat, which he had caused Israel to commit; he did not turn away from them.

4Now Mesha king of Moab raised sheep, and he had to supply the king of Israel with a hundred thousand lambs and with the wool of a hundred thousand rams. 5But after Ahab died, the king of Moab rebelled against the king of Israel. 6So at that time King Joram set out from Samaria and mobilized all Israel. 7He also sent this message to Jehoshaphat king of Judah: "The king of Moab has rebelled against me. Will you go with me to fight against Moab?"

"I will go with you," he replied. "I am as you are, my people as your people, my horses as your horses."

8"By what route shall we attack?" he asked.

"Through the Desert of Edom," he answered.

9So the king of Israel set out with the king of Judah and the king of Edom. After a roundabout march of seven days, the army had no more water for themselves or for the animals with them.

10"What!" exclaimed the king of Israel. "Has the LORD called us three kings together only to hand us over to Moab?"

11But Jehoshaphat asked, "Is there no prophet of the LORD here, that we may inquire of the LORD through him?"

An officer of the king of Israel answered, "Elisha son of Shaphat is here. He used to pour water on the hands of Elijah.[b]"

12Jehoshaphat said, "The word of the LORD is with him." So the king of Israel and Jehoshaphat and the king of Edom went down to him.

13Elisha said to the king of Israel, "What do we have to do with each other? Go to the prophets of your father and the prophets of your mother."

"No," the king of Israel answered, "because it was the LORD who called us three kings together to hand us over to Moab."

14Elisha said, "As surely as the LORD Almighty lives, whom I serve, if I did not have respect for the presence of Jehoshaphat king of Judah, I would not look at you or even notice you. 15But now bring me a harpist."

While the harpist was playing, the hand of the LORD came upon Elisha 16and he said, "This is what the LORD says: Make this valley full of ditches. 17For this is what the LORD says: You will see neither wind nor rain, yet this valley will be filled with water, and you, your cattle and your other animals will drink. 18This is an easy thing in the eyes of the LORD; he will also hand Moab over to you. 19You will overthrow every fortified city and every major town. You will cut down every good tree, stop up all the springs, and ruin every good field with stones."

20The next morning, about the time for offering the sacrifice, there it was—water flowing from the direction of Edom! And the land was filled with water.

21Now all the Moabites had heard that the kings had come to fight against them; so every man, young and old, who could bear arms was called up and stationed on the border. 22When they got up early in the morning, the sun was shining on the water. To the Moabites across the way, the water looked red—like blood. 23"That's blood!" they said. "Those kings must have fought and slaughtered each other. Now to the plunder, Moab!"

24But when the Moabites came to the camp of Israel, the Israelites rose up and fought them until they fled. And the Israelites invaded the land and slaughtered the Moabites. 25They destroyed the towns, and each man threw a stone on every good field until it was covered. They stopped up all the springs and cut down every good tree. Only Kir Hareseth was left with its stones in place, but men armed with slings surrounded it and attacked it as well.

26When the king of Moab saw that the battle had gone against him, he took with him seven hundred swordsmen to break through to the king of Edom, but they failed. 27Then he took his firstborn son, who was to succeed him as king, and offered him as a sacrifice on the city

a1 Hebrew *Jehoram,* a variant of *Joram*; also in verse 6

b11 That is, he was Elijah's personal servant.

wall. The fury against Israel was great; they withdrew and returned to their own land.

The Widow's Oil

4 The wife of a man from the company of the prophets cried out to Elisha, "Your servant my husband is dead, and you know that he revered the LORD. But now his creditor is coming to take my two boys as his slaves."

2Elisha replied to her, "How can I help you? Tell me, what do you have in your house?"

"Your servant has nothing there at all," she said, "except a little oil."

3Elisha said, "Go around and ask all your neighbors for empty jars. Don't ask for just a few. 4Then go inside and shut the door behind you and your sons. Pour oil into all the jars, and as each is filled, put it to one side."

5She left him and afterward shut the door behind her and her sons. They brought the jars to her and she kept pouring. 6When all the jars were full, she said to her son, "Bring me another one."

But he replied, "There is not a jar left." Then the oil stopped flowing.

7She went and told the man of God, and he said, "Go, sell the oil and pay your debts. You and your sons can live on what is left."

The Shunammite's Son Restored to Life

8One day Elisha went to Shunem. And a well-to-do woman was there, who urged him to stay for a meal. So whenever he came by, he stopped there to eat. 9She said to her husband, "I know that this man who often comes our way is a holy man of God. 10Let's make a small room on the roof and put in it a bed and a table, a chair and a lamp for him. Then he can stay there whenever he comes to us."

11One day when Elisha came, he went up to his room and lay down there. 12He said to his servant Gehazi, "Call the Shunammite." So he called her, and she stood before him. 13Elisha said to him, "Tell her, 'You have gone to all this trouble for us. Now what can be done for you? Can we speak on your behalf to the king or the commander of the army?' "

She replied, "I have a home among my own people."

14"What can be done for her?" Elisha asked.

Gehazi said, "Well, she has no son and her husband is old."

15Then Elisha said, "Call her." So he called her, and she stood in the doorway. 16"About this time next year," Elisha said, "you will hold a son in your arms."

"No, my lord," she objected. "Don't mislead your servant, O man of God!"

17But the woman became pregnant, and the next year about that same time she gave birth to a son, just as Elisha had told her.

18The child grew, and one day he went out to his father, who was with the reapers. 19"My head! My head!" he said to his father.

His father told a servant, "Carry him to his mother." 20After the servant had lifted him up and carried him to his mother, the boy sat on her lap until noon, and then he died. 21She went up and laid him on the bed of the man of God, then shut the door and went out.

22She called her husband and said, "Please send me one of the servants and a donkey so I can go to the man of God quickly and return."

23"Why go to him today?" he asked. "It's not the New Moon or the Sabbath."

"It's all right," she said.

24She saddled the donkey and said to her servant, "Lead on; don't slow down for me unless I tell you." 25So she set out and came to the man of God at Mount Carmel.

When he saw her in the distance, the man of God said to his servant Gehazi, "Look! There's the Shunammite! 26Run to meet her and ask her, 'Are you all right? Is your husband all right? Is your child all right?' "

"Everything is all right," she said.

27When she reached the man of God at the mountain, she took hold of his feet. Gehazi came over to push her away, but the man of God said, "Leave her alone! She is in bitter distress, but the LORD has hidden it from me and has not told me why."

28"Did I ask you for a son, my lord?" she said. "Didn't I tell you, 'Don't raise my hopes'?"

29Elisha said to Gehazi, "Tuck your cloak into your belt, take my staff in your hand and run. If you meet anyone, do not greet him, and if anyone greets you, do not answer. Lay my staff on the boy's face."

30But the child's mother said, "As surely as the LORD lives and as you live, I will not leave you." So he got up and followed her.

31Gehazi went on ahead and laid the staff on the boy's face, but there was no sound or response. So Gehazi went back to meet Elisha and told him, "The boy has not awakened."

32When Elisha reached the house, there was the boy lying dead on his couch. 33He went in, shut the door on the two of them and prayed to the LORD. 34Then he got on the bed and lay upon the boy, mouth to mouth, eyes to eyes, hands to hands. As he stretched himself out upon him, the boy's body grew warm. 35Elisha turned away and walked back and forth in the room and then got on the bed and stretched out upon him once more. The boy sneezed seven times and opened his eyes.

36Elisha summoned Gehazi and said, "Call the Shunammite." And he did. When she came, he said, "Take your son." 37She came in, fell at his feet and bowed to the ground. Then she took her son and went out.

Death in the Pot

38Elisha returned to Gilgal and there was a famine in that region. While the company of the prophets was meeting with him, he said to his servant, "Put on the large pot and cook some stew for these men."

39One of them went out into the fields to gather herbs and found a wild vine. He gathered some of its gourds and filled the fold of his cloak. When he returned, he cut them up into the pot of stew, though no one knew what they were. 40The stew was poured out for the men, but as they began to eat it, they cried out, "O man of God, there is death in the pot!" And they could not eat it.

41Elisha said, "Get some flour." He put it into the pot and said, "Serve it to the people to eat." And there was nothing harmful in the pot.

Feeding of a Hundred

42A man came from Baal Shalishah, bringing the man of God twenty loaves of barley bread baked from the first ripe grain, along with some heads of new grain. "Give it to the people to eat," Elisha said.

43"How can I set this before a hundred men?" his servant asked.

But Elisha answered, "Give it to the people to eat. For this is what the LORD says: 'They will eat and have some left over.' " 44Then he set it before them, and they ate and had some left over, according to the word of the LORD.

Naaman Healed of Leprosy

5 Now Naaman was commander of the army of the king of Aram. He was a great man in the sight of his master and highly regarded, because through him the LORD had given victory to Aram. He was a valiant soldier, but he had leprosy.[a]

2Now bands from Aram had gone out and had taken captive a young girl from Israel, and she served Naaman's wife. 3She said to her mistress, "If only my master would see the prophet who is in Samaria! He would cure him of his leprosy."

4Naaman went to his master and told him what the girl from Israel had said. 5"By all means, go," the king of Aram replied. "I will send a letter to the king of Israel." So Naaman left, taking with him ten talents[b] of silver, six thousand shekels[c] of gold and ten sets of clothing. 6The letter that he took to the king of Israel read: "With this letter I am sending my servant Naaman to you so that you may cure him of his leprosy."

7As soon as the king of Israel read the letter, he tore his robes and said, "Am I God? Can I kill and bring back to life? Why does this fellow send someone to me to be cured of his leprosy? See how he is trying to pick a quarrel with me!"

8When Elisha the man of God heard that the king of Israel had torn his robes, he sent him this message: "Why have you torn your robes? Have the man come to me and he will know that there is a prophet in Israel." 9So Naaman went with his horses and chariots and stopped at the door of Elisha's house. 10Elisha sent a messenger to say to him, "Go, wash yourself seven times in the Jordan, and your flesh will be restored and you will be cleansed."

11But Naaman went away angry and said, "I thought that he would surely come out to me and stand and call on the name of the LORD his God, wave his hand over the spot and cure me of my leprosy. 12Are not Abana and Pharpar, the rivers of Damascus, better than any of the waters of Israel? Couldn't I wash in them and be cleansed?" So he turned and went off in a rage.

13Naaman's servants went to him and said, "My father, if the prophet had told you to do some great thing, would you not have done it? How much more, then, when he tells you, 'Wash and be cleansed'!" 14So he went down and dipped himself in the Jordan seven times, as the man of God had told him, and his flesh was restored and became clean like that of a young boy.

15Then Naaman and all his attendants went back to the man of God. He stood before him and said, "Now I know that there is no God in all the world except in Israel. Please accept now a gift from your servant."

16The prophet answered, "As surely as the LORD lives, whom I serve, I will not accept a thing." And even though Naaman urged him, he refused.

17"If you will not," said Naaman, "please let me, your servant, be given as much earth as a pair of mules can carry, for your servant will never again make burnt offerings and sacrifices to any other god but the LORD. 18But may the LORD forgive your servant for this one thing: When my master enters the temple of Rimmon to bow down and he is leaning on my arm and I bow there also—when I bow down in the temple of Rimmon, may the LORD forgive your servant for this."

19"Go in peace," Elisha said.

After Naaman had traveled some distance, 20Gehazi, the servant of Elisha the man of God, said to himself, "My master was too easy on Naaman, this Aramean, by not accepting from him what he brought. As surely as the LORD lives, I will run after him and get something from him."

21So Gehazi hurried after Naaman. When Naaman saw him running toward him, he got down from the chariot to meet him. "Is everything all right?" he asked.

22"Everything is all right," Gehazi answered. "My master sent me to say, 'Two young men from the company of the prophets have just come to me from the hill country of Ephraim. Please give them a talent[d] of silver and two sets of clothing.' "

23"By all means, take two talents," said Naaman. He urged Gehazi to accept them, and then tied up the two talents of silver in two bags, with two sets of clothing. He gave them to two of his servants, and they carried them ahead of Gehazi. 24When Gehazi came to the hill, he took the things from the servants and put them away in the house. He sent the men

[a] *1* The Hebrew word was used for various diseases affecting the skin—not necessarily leprosy; also in verses 3, 6, 7, 11 and 27. [b] *5* That is, about 750 pounds (about 340 kilograms) [c] *5* That is, about 150 pounds (about 70 kilograms) [d] *22* That is, about 75 pounds (about 34 kilograms)

away and they left. 25Then he went in and stood before his master Elisha.

"Where have you been, Gehazi?" Elisha asked.

"Your servant didn't go anywhere," Gehazi answered.

26But Elisha said to him, "Was not my spirit with you when the man got down from his chariot to meet you? Is this the time to take money, or to accept clothes, olive groves, vineyards, flocks, herds, or menservants and maidservants? 27Naaman's leprosy will cling to you and to your descendants forever." Then Gehazi went from Elisha's presence and he was leprous, as white as snow.

An Axhead Floats

6 The company of the prophets said to Elisha, "Look, the place where we meet with you is too small for us. 2Let us go to the Jordan, where each of us can get a pole; and let us build a place there for us to live."

And he said, "Go."

3Then one of them said, "Won't you please come with your servants?"

"I will," Elisha replied. 4And he went with them.

They went to the Jordan and began to cut down trees. 5As one of them was cutting down a tree, the iron axhead fell into the water. "Oh, my lord," he cried out, "it was borrowed!"

6The man of God asked, "Where did it fall?" When he showed him the place, Elisha cut a stick and threw it there, and made the iron float. 7"Lift it out," he said. Then the man reached out his hand and took it.

Elisha Traps Blinded Arameans

8Now the king of Aram was at war with Israel. After conferring with his officers, he said, "I will set up my camp in such and such a place."

9The man of God sent word to the king of Israel: "Beware of passing that place, because the Arameans are going down there." 10So the king of Israel checked on the place indicated by the man of God. Time and again Elisha warned the king, so that he was on his guard in such places.

11This enraged the king of Aram. He summoned his officers and demanded of them, "Will you not tell me which of us is on the side of the king of Israel?"

12"None of us, my lord the king," said one of his officers, "but Elisha, the prophet who is in Israel, tells the king of Israel the very words you speak in your bedroom."

13"Go, find out where he is," the king ordered, "so I can send men and capture him." The report came back: "He is in Dothan." 14Then he sent horses and chariots and a strong force there. They went by night and surrounded the city.

15When the servant of the man of God got up and went out early the next morning, an army with horses and chariots had surrounded the city. "Oh, my lord, what shall we do?" the servant asked.

16"Don't be afraid," the prophet answered. "Those who are with us are more than those who are with them."

17And Elisha prayed, "O LORD, open his eyes so he may see." Then the LORD opened the servant's eyes, and he looked and saw the hills full of horses and chariots of fire all around Elisha.

18As the enemy came down toward him, Elisha prayed to the LORD, "Strike these people with blindness." So he struck them with blindness, as Elisha had asked.

19Elisha told them, "This is not the road and this is not the city. Follow me, and I will lead you to the man you are looking for." And he led them to Samaria.

20After they entered the city, Elisha said, "LORD, open the eyes of these men so they can see." Then the LORD opened their eyes and they looked, and there they were, inside Samaria.

21When the king of Israel saw them, he asked Elisha, "Shall I kill them, my father? Shall I kill them?"

22"Do not kill them," he answered. "Would you kill men you have captured with your own sword or bow? Set food and water before them so that they may eat and drink and then go back to their master." 23So he prepared a great feast for them, and after they had finished eating and drinking, he sent them away, and they returned to their master. So the bands from Aram stopped raiding Israel's territory.

Famine in Besieged Samaria

24Some time later, Ben-Hadad king of Aram mobilized his entire army and marched up and laid siege to Samaria. 25There was a great famine in the city; the siege lasted so long that a donkey's head sold for eighty shekels[a] of silver, and a quarter of a cab[b] of seed pods[c] for five shekels.[d]

26As the king of Israel was passing by on the wall, a woman cried to him, "Help me, my lord the king!"

27The king replied, "If the LORD does not help you, where can I get help for you? From the threshing floor? From the winepress?" 28Then he asked her, "What's the matter?"

She answered, "This woman said to me, 'Give up your son so we may eat him today, and tomorrow we'll eat my son.' 29So we cooked my son and ate him. The next day I said to her, 'Give up your son so we may eat him,' but she had hidden him."

30When the king heard the woman's words, he tore his robes. As he went along the wall, the people looked, and there, underneath, he had sackcloth on his body. 31He said, "May God deal with me, be it ever so severely, if the

[a] 25 That is, about 2 pounds (about 1 kilogram) [b] 25 That is, probably about 1/2 pint (about 0.3 liter)
[c] 25 Or *of dove's dung* [d] 25 That is, about 2 ounces (about 55 grams)

head of Elisha son of Shaphat remains on his
shoulders today!"
32 Now Elisha was sitting in his house, and
the elders were sitting with him. The king sent
a messenger ahead, but before he arrived, Elisha said to the elders, "Don't you see how this
murderer is sending someone to cut off my
head? Look, when the messenger comes, shut
the door and hold it shut against him. Is not the
sound of his master's footsteps behind him?"
33 While he was still talking to them, the
messenger came down to him. And ⌞the king⌟
said, "This disaster is from the LORD. Why
should I wait for the LORD any longer?"
7 Elisha said, "Hear the word of the LORD.
This is what the LORD says: About this
time tomorrow, a seah[a] of flour will sell for a
shekel[b] and two seahs[c] of barley for a shekel
at the gate of Samaria."
2 The officer on whose arm the king was
leaning said to the man of God, "Look, even if
the LORD should open the floodgates of the
heavens, could this happen?"
"You will see it with your own eyes," answered Elisha, "but you will not eat any of it!"

The Siege Lifted

3 Now there were four men with leprosy[d] at
the entrance of the city gate. They said to each
other, "Why stay here until we die? 4 If we say,
'We'll go into the city'—the famine is there,
and we will die. And if we stay here, we will
die. So let's go over to the camp of the Arameans and surrender. If they spare us, we live; if
they kill us, then we die."
5 At dusk they got up and went to the camp
of the Arameans. When they reached the edge
of the camp, not a man was there, 6 for the Lord
had caused the Arameans to hear the sound of
chariots and horses and a great army, so that
they said to one another, "Look, the king of
Israel has hired the Hittite and Egyptian kings
to attack us!" 7 So they got up and fled in
the dusk and abandoned their tents and their
horses and donkeys. They left the camp as it
was and ran for their lives.
8 The men who had leprosy reached the edge
of the camp and entered one of the tents. They
ate and drank, and carried away silver, gold
and clothes, and went off and hid them. They
returned and entered another tent and took
some things from it and hid them also.
9 Then they said to each other, "We're not
doing right. This is a day of good news and we
are keeping it to ourselves. If we wait until
daylight, punishment will overtake us. Let's go
at once and report this to the royal palace."
10 So they went and called out to the city
gatekeepers and told them, "We went into the
Aramean camp and not a man was there—not
a sound of anyone—only tethered horses and
donkeys, and the tents left just as they were."
11 The gatekeepers shouted the news, and it
was reported within the palace.
12 The king got up in the night and said to his
officers, "I will tell you what the Arameans
have done to us. They know we are starving;
so they have left the camp to hide in the countryside, thinking, 'They will surely come out,
and then we will take them alive and get into
the city.' "
13 One of his officers answered, "Have some
men take five of the horses that are left in the
city. Their plight will be like that of all the
Israelites left here—yes, they will only be like
all these Israelites who are doomed. So let us
send them to find out what happened."
14 So they selected two chariots with their
horses, and the king sent them after the Aramean army. He commanded the drivers, "Go and
find out what has happened." 15 They followed
them as far as the Jordan, and they found the
whole road strewn with the clothing and equipment the Arameans had thrown away in their
headlong flight. So the messengers returned
and reported to the king. 16 Then the people
went out and plundered the camp of the Arameans. So a seah of flour sold for a shekel, and
two seahs of barley sold for a shekel, as the
LORD had said.
17 Now the king had put the officer on whose
arm he leaned in charge of the gate, and the
people trampled him in the gateway, and he
died, just as the man of God had foretold when
the king came down to his house. 18 It happened as the man of God had said to the king:
"About this time tomorrow, a seah of flour will
sell for a shekel and two seahs of barley for a
shekel at the gate of Samaria."
19 The officer had said to the man of God,
"Look, even if the LORD should open the
floodgates of the heavens, could this happen?"
The man of God had replied, "You will see it
with your own eyes, but you will not eat any of
it!" 20 And that is exactly what happened to
him, for the people trampled him in the gateway, and he died.

The Shunammite's Land Restored

8 Now Elisha had said to the woman whose
son he had restored to life, "Go away with
your family and stay for a while wherever you
can, because the LORD has decreed a famine in
the land that will last seven years." 2 The woman proceeded to do as the man of God said. She
and her family went away and stayed in the
land of the Philistines seven years.
3 At the end of the seven years she came
back from the land of the Philistines and went
to the king to beg for her house and land. 4 The
king was talking to Gehazi, the servant of the
man of God, and had said, "Tell me about all
the great things Elisha has done." 5 Just as Gehazi was telling the king how Elisha had restored the dead to life, the woman whose son

[a] *1* That is, probably about 7 quarts (about 7.3 liters); also in verses 16 and 18 [b] *1* That is, about 2/5 ounce (about 11 grams); also in verses 16 and 18 [c] *1* That is, probably about 13 quarts (about 15 liters); also in verses 16 and 18 [d] *3* The Hebrew word is used for various diseases affecting the skin—not necessarily leprosy; also in verse 8.

Elisha had brought back to life came to beg the
king for her house and land.

Gehazi said, "This is the woman, my lord
the king, and this is her son whom Elisha restored to life." 6The king asked the woman
about it, and she told him.

Then he assigned an official to her case and
said to him, "Give back everything that belonged to her, including all the income from
her land from the day she left the country until
now."

Hazael Murders Ben-Hadad

7Elisha went to Damascus, and Ben-Hadad
king of Aram was ill. When the king was told,
"The man of God has come all the way up
here," 8he said to Hazael, "Take a gift with you
and go to meet the man of God. Consult the
LORD through him; ask him, 'Will I recover
from this illness?' "

9Hazael went to meet Elisha, taking with
him as a gift forty camel-loads of all the finest
wares of Damascus. He went in and stood before him, and said, "Your son Ben-Hadad king
of Aram has sent me to ask, 'Will I recover
from this illness?' "

10Elisha answered, "Go and say to him,
'You will certainly recover'; but[a] the LORD
has revealed to me that he will in fact die."
11He stared at him with a fixed gaze until Hazael felt ashamed. Then the man of God began
to weep.

12"Why is my lord weeping?" asked Hazael.

"Because I know the harm you will do to the
Israelites," he answered. "You will set fire to
their fortified places, kill their young men with
the sword, dash their little children to the
ground, and rip open their pregnant women."

13Hazael said, "How could your servant, a
mere dog, accomplish such a feat?"

"The LORD has shown me that you will become king of Aram," answered Elisha.

14Then Hazael left Elisha and returned to his
master. When Ben-Hadad asked, "What did
Elisha say to you?" Hazael replied, "He told
me that you would certainly recover." 15But
the next day he took a thick cloth, soaked it in
water and spread it over the king's face, so that
he died. Then Hazael succeeded him as king.

Jehoram King of Judah

16In the fifth year of Joram son of Ahab king
of Israel, when Jehoshaphat was king of Judah,
Jehoram son of Jehoshaphat began his reign as
king of Judah. 17He was thirty-two years old
when he became king, and he reigned in Jerusalem eight years. 18He walked in the ways of
the kings of Israel, as the house of Ahab had
done, for he married a daughter of Ahab. He
did evil in the eyes of the LORD. 19Neverthe-
less, for the sake of his servant David, the
LORD was not willing to destroy Judah. He had
promised to maintain a lamp for David and his
descendants forever.

20In the time of Jehoram, Edom rebelled
against Judah and set up its own king. 21So
Jehoram[b] went to Zair with all his chariots.
The Edomites surrounded him and his chariot
commanders, but he rose up and broke through
by night; his army, however, fled back home.
22To this day Edom has been in rebellion
against Judah. Libnah revolted at the same
time.

23As for the other events of Jehoram's reign,
and all he did, are they not written in the book
of the annals of the kings of Judah? 24Jehoram
rested with his fathers and was buried with
them in the City of David. And Ahaziah his
son succeeded him as king.

Ahaziah King of Judah

25In the twelfth year of Joram son of Ahab
king of Israel, Ahaziah son of Jehoram king of
Judah began to reign. 26Ahaziah was twenty-
two years old when he became king, and he
reigned in Jerusalem one year. His mother's
name was Athaliah, a granddaughter of Omri
king of Israel. 27He walked in the ways of the
house of Ahab and did evil in the eyes of the
LORD, as the house of Ahab had done, for he
was related by marriage to Ahab's family.

28Ahaziah went with Joram son of Ahab to
war against Hazael king of Aram at Ramoth
Gilead. The Arameans wounded Joram; 29so
King Joram returned to Jezreel to recover from
the wounds the Arameans had inflicted on him
at Ramoth[c] in his battle with Hazael king of
Aram.

Then Ahaziah son of Jehoram king of Judah
went down to Jezreel to see Joram son of
Ahab, because he had been wounded.

Jehu Anointed King of Israel

9 The prophet Elisha summoned a man from
the company of the prophets and said to
him, "Tuck your cloak into your belt, take this
flask of oil with you and go to Ramoth Gilead.
2When you get there, look for Jehu son of Jehoshaphat, the son of Nimshi. Go to him, get
him away from his companions and take him
into an inner room. 3Then take the flask and
pour the oil on his head and declare, 'This is
what the LORD says: I anoint you king over
Israel.' Then open the door and run; don't delay!"

4So the young man, the prophet, went to
Ramoth Gilead. 5When he arrived, he found
the army officers sitting together. "I have a
message for you, commander," he said.

"For which of us?" asked Jehu.

"For you, commander," he replied.

6Jehu got up and went into the house. Then
the prophet poured the oil on Jehu's head and
declared, "This is what the LORD, the God of
Israel, says: 'I anoint you king over the LORD's
people Israel. 7You are to destroy the house of
Ahab your master, and I will avenge the blood
of my servants the prophets and the blood of
all the LORD's servants shed by Jezebel. 8The
whole house of Ahab will perish. I will cut off

[a]10 The Hebrew may also be read *Go and say, 'You will certainly not recover,' for.* [b]21 Hebrew *Joram,* a variant of *Jehoram*; also in verses 23 and 24 [c]29 Hebrew *Ramah,* a variant of *Ramoth*

from Ahab every last male in Israel—slave or free. **9**I will make the house of Ahab like the house of Jeroboam son of Nebat and like the house of Baasha son of Ahijah. **10**As for Jezebel, dogs will devour her on the plot of ground at Jezreel, and no one will bury her.' " Then he opened the door and ran.

11When Jehu went out to his fellow officers, one of them asked him, "Is everything all right? Why did this madman come to you?"

"You know the man and the sort of things he says," Jehu replied.

12"That's not true!" they said. "Tell us."

Jehu said, "Here is what he told me: 'This is what the LORD says: I anoint you king over Israel.' "

13They hurried and took their cloaks and spread them under him on the bare steps. Then they blew the trumpet and shouted, "Jehu is king!"

Jehu Kills Joram and Ahaziah

14So Jehu son of Jehoshaphat, the son of Nimshi, conspired against Joram. (Now Joram and all Israel had been defending Ramoth Gilead against Hazael king of Aram, **15**but King Joram[a] had returned to Jezreel to recover from the wounds the Arameans had inflicted on him in the battle with Hazael king of Aram.) Jehu said, "If this is the way you feel, don't let anyone slip out of the city to go and tell the news in Jezreel." **16**Then he got into his chariot and rode to Jezreel, because Joram was resting there and Ahaziah king of Judah had gone down to see him.

17When the lookout standing on the tower in Jezreel saw Jehu's troops approaching, he called out, "I see some troops coming."

"Get a horseman," Joram ordered. "Send him to meet them and ask, 'Do you come in peace?' "

18The horseman rode off to meet Jehu and said, "This is what the king says: 'Do you come in peace?' "

"What do you have to do with peace?" Jehu replied. "Fall in behind me."

The lookout reported, "The messenger has reached them, but he isn't coming back."

19So the king sent out a second horseman. When he came to them he said, "This is what the king says: 'Do you come in peace?' "

Jehu replied, "What do you have to do with peace? Fall in behind me."

20The lookout reported, "He has reached them, but he isn't coming back either. The driving is like that of Jehu son of Nimshi—he drives like a madman."

21"Hitch up my chariot," Joram ordered. And when it was hitched up, Joram king of Israel and Ahaziah king of Judah rode out, each in his own chariot, to meet Jehu. They met him at the plot of ground that had belonged to Naboth the Jezreelite. **22**When Joram saw Jehu he asked, "Have you come in peace, Jehu?"

"How can there be peace," Jehu replied, "as long as all the idolatry and witchcraft of your mother Jezebel abound?"

23Joram turned about and fled, calling out to Ahaziah, "Treachery, Ahaziah!"

24Then Jehu drew his bow and shot Joram between the shoulders. The arrow pierced his heart and he slumped down in his chariot. **25**Jehu said to Bidkar, his chariot officer, "Pick him up and throw him on the field that belonged to Naboth the Jezreelite. Remember how you and I were riding together in chariots behind Ahab his father when the LORD made this prophecy about him: **26**'Yesterday I saw the blood of Naboth and the blood of his sons, declares the LORD, and I will surely make you pay for it on this plot of ground, declares the LORD.'[b] Now then, pick him up and throw him on that plot, in accordance with the word of the LORD."

27When Ahaziah king of Judah saw what had happened, he fled up the road to Beth Haggan.[c] Jehu chased him, shouting, "Kill him too!" They wounded him in his chariot on the way up to Gur near Ibleam, but he escaped to Megiddo and died there. **28**His servants took him by chariot to Jerusalem and buried him with his fathers in his tomb in the City of David. **29**(In the eleventh year of Joram son of Ahab, Ahaziah had become king of Judah.)

Jezebel Killed

30Then Jehu went to Jezreel. When Jezebel heard about it, she painted her eyes, arranged her hair and looked out of a window. **31**As Jehu entered the gate, she asked, "Have you come in peace, Zimri, you murderer of your master?"[d]

32He looked up at the window and called out, "Who is on my side? Who?" Two or three eunuchs looked down at him. **33**"Throw her down!" Jehu said. So they threw her down, and some of her blood spattered the wall and the horses as they trampled her underfoot.

34Jehu went in and ate and drank. "Take care of that cursed woman," he said, "and bury her, for she was a king's daughter." **35**But when they went out to bury her, they found nothing except her skull, her feet and her hands. **36**They went back and told Jehu, who said, "This is the word of the LORD that he spoke through his servant Elijah the Tishbite: On the plot of ground at Jezreel dogs will devour Jezebel's flesh.[e] **37**Jezebel's body will be like refuse on the ground in the plot at Jezreel, so that no one will be able to say, 'This is Jezebel.' "

Ahab's Family Killed

10 Now there were in Samaria seventy sons of the house of Ahab. So Jehu wrote letters and sent them to Samaria: to the officials of Jezreel,[f] to the elders and to the

[a] *15* Hebrew *Jehoram,* a variant of *Joram*; also in verses 17 and 21-24 [b] *26* See 1 Kings 21:19.
[c] *27* Or *fled by way of the garden house* [d] *31* Or *"Did Zimri have peace, who murdered his master?"*
[e] *36* See 1 Kings 21:23. [f] *1* Hebrew; some Septuagint manuscripts and Vulgate *of the city*

guardians of Ahab's children. He said, 2"As
soon as this letter reaches you, since your master's sons are with you and you have chariots
and horses, a fortified city and weapons,
3choose the best and most worthy of your master's sons and set him on his father's throne.
Then fight for your master's house."

4But they were terrified and said, "If two
kings could not resist him, how can we?"

5So the palace administrator, the city governor, the elders and the guardians sent this message to Jehu: "We are your servants and we
will do anything you say. We will not appoint
anyone as king; you do whatever you think
best."

6Then Jehu wrote them a second letter, saying, "If you are on my side and will obey me,
take the heads of your master's sons and come
to me in Jezreel by this time tomorrow."

Now the royal princes, seventy of them,
were with the leading men of the city, who
were rearing them. 7When the letter arrived,
these men took the princes and slaughtered all
seventy of them. They put their heads in baskets and sent them to Jehu in Jezreel. 8When
the messenger arrived, he told Jehu, "They
have brought the heads of the princes."

Then Jehu ordered, "Put them in two piles at
the entrance of the city gate until morning."

9The next morning Jehu went out. He stood
before all the people and said, "You are innocent. It was I who conspired against my master
and killed him, but who killed all these?
10Know then, that not a word the LORD has
spoken against the house of Ahab will fail. The
LORD has done what he promised through his
servant Elijah." 11So Jehu killed everyone in
Jezreel who remained of the house of Ahab, as
well as all his chief men, his close friends and
his priests, leaving him no survivor.

12Jehu then set out and went toward Samaria. At Beth Eked of the Shepherds, 13he met
some relatives of Ahaziah king of Judah and
asked, "Who are you?"

They said, "We are relatives of Ahaziah, and
we have come down to greet the families of the
king and of the queen mother."

14"Take them alive!" he ordered. So they
took them alive and slaughtered them by the
well of Beth Eked—forty-two men. He left no
survivor.

15After he left there, he came upon Jehonadab son of Recab, who was on his way to meet
him. Jehu greeted him and said, "Are you in
accord with me, as I am with you?"

"I am," Jehonadab answered.

"If so," said Jehu, "give me your hand." So
he did, and Jehu helped him up into the chariot. 16Jehu said, "Come with me and see my
zeal for the LORD." Then he had him ride along
in his chariot.

17When Jehu came to Samaria, he killed all
who were left there of Ahab's family; he destroyed them, according to the word of the
LORD spoken to Elijah.

Ministers of Baal Killed

18Then Jehu brought all the people together
and said to them, "Ahab served Baal a little;
Jehu will serve him much. 19Now summon all
the prophets of Baal, all his ministers and all
his priests. See that no one is missing, because
I am going to hold a great sacrifice for Baal.
Anyone who fails to come will no longer live."
But Jehu was acting deceptively in order to
destroy the ministers of Baal.

20Jehu said, "Call an assembly in honor of
Baal." So they proclaimed it. 21Then he sent
word throughout Israel, and all the ministers of
Baal came; not one stayed away. They crowded into the temple of Baal until it was full from
one end to the other. 22And Jehu said to the
keeper of the wardrobe, "Bring robes for all
the ministers of Baal." So he brought out robes
for them.

23Then Jehu and Jehonadab son of Recab
went into the temple of Baal. Jehu said to the
ministers of Baal, "Look around and see that
no servants of the LORD are here with you—
only ministers of Baal." 24So they went in to
make sacrifices and burnt offerings. Now Jehu
had posted eighty men outside with this warning: "If one of you lets any of the men I am
placing in your hands escape, it will be your
life for his life."

25As soon as Jehu had finished making the
burnt offering, he ordered the guards and officers: "Go in and kill them; let no one escape."
So they cut them down with the sword. The
guards and officers threw the bodies out and
then entered the inner shrine of the temple of
Baal. 26They brought the sacred stone out of
the temple of Baal and burned it. 27They demolished the sacred stone of Baal and tore
down the temple of Baal, and people have used
it for a latrine to this day.

28So Jehu destroyed Baal worship in Israel.
29However, he did not turn away from the sins
of Jeroboam son of Nebat, which he had
caused Israel to commit—the worship of the
golden calves at Bethel and Dan.

30The LORD said to Jehu, "Because you
have done well in accomplishing what is right
in my eyes and have done to the house of Ahab
all I had in mind to do, your descendants will
sit on the throne of Israel to the fourth generation." 31Yet Jehu was not careful to keep the
law of the LORD, the God of Israel, with all his
heart. He did not turn away from the sins of
Jeroboam, which he had caused Israel to commit.

32In those days the LORD began to reduce
the size of Israel. Hazael overpowered the Israelites throughout their territory 33east of the
Jordan in all the land of Gilead (the region of
Gad, Reuben and Manasseh), from Aroer by
the Arnon Gorge through Gilead to Bashan.

34As for the other events of Jehu's reign, all
he did, and all his achievements, are they not
written in the book of the annals of the kings
of Israel?

35Jehu rested with his fathers and was buried

in Samaria. And Jehoahaz his son succeeded him as king. 36The time that Jehu reigned over Israel in Samaria was twenty-eight years.

Athaliah and Joash

11 When Athaliah the mother of Ahaziah saw that her son was dead, she proceeded to destroy the whole royal family. 2But Jehosheba, the daughter of King Jehoram[a] and sister of Ahaziah, took Joash son of Ahaziah and stole him away from among the royal princes, who were about to be murdered. She put him and his nurse in a bedroom to hide him from Athaliah; so he was not killed. 3He remained hidden with his nurse at the temple of the LORD for six years while Athaliah ruled the land.

4In the seventh year Jehoiada sent for the commanders of units of a hundred, the Carites and the guards and had them brought to him at the temple of the LORD. He made a covenant with them and put them under oath at the temple of the LORD. Then he showed them the king's son. 5He commanded them, saying, "This is what you are to do: You who are in the three companies that are going on duty on the Sabbath—a third of you guarding the royal palace, 6a third at the Sur Gate, and a third at the gate behind the guard, who take turns guarding the temple— 7and you who are in the other two companies that normally go off Sabbath duty are all to guard the temple for the king. 8Station yourselves around the king, each man with his weapon in his hand. Anyone who approaches your ranks[b] must be put to death. Stay close to the king wherever he goes."

9The commanders of units of a hundred did just as Jehoiada the priest ordered. Each one took his men—those who were going on duty on the Sabbath and those who were going off duty—and came to Jehoiada the priest. 10Then he gave the commanders the spears and shields that had belonged to King David and that were in the temple of the LORD. 11The guards, each with his weapon in his hand, stationed themselves around the king—near the altar and the temple, from the south side to the north side of the temple.

12Jehoiada brought out the king's son and put the crown on him; he presented him with a copy of the covenant and proclaimed him king. They anointed him, and the people clapped their hands and shouted, "Long live the king!"

13When Athaliah heard the noise made by the guards and the people, she went to the people at the temple of the LORD. 14She looked and there was the king, standing by the pillar, as the custom was. The officers and the trumpeters were beside the king, and all the people of the land were rejoicing and blowing trumpets. Then Athaliah tore her robes and called out, "Treason! Treason!"

15Jehoiada the priest ordered the commanders of units of a hundred, who were in charge of the troops: "Bring her out between the ranks[c] and put to the sword anyone who follows her." For the priest had said, "She must not be put to death in the temple of the LORD." 16So they seized her as she reached the place where the horses enter the palace grounds, and there she was put to death.

17Jehoiada then made a covenant between the LORD and the king and people that they would be the LORD's people. He also made a covenant between the king and the people. 18All the people of the land went to the temple of Baal and tore it down. They smashed the altars and idols to pieces and killed Mattan the priest of Baal in front of the altars.

Then Jehoiada the priest posted guards at the temple of the LORD. 19He took with him the commanders of hundreds, the Carites, the guards and all the people of the land, and together they brought the king down from the temple of the LORD and went into the palace, entering by way of the gate of the guards. The king then took his place on the royal throne, 20and all the people of the land rejoiced. And the city was quiet, because Athaliah had been slain with the sword at the palace.

21Joash[d] was seven years old when he began to reign.

Joash Repairs the Temple

12 In the seventh year of Jehu, Joash[e] became king, and he reigned in Jerusalem forty years. His mother's name was Zibiah; she was from Beersheba. 2Joash did what was right in the eyes of the LORD all the years Jehoiada the priest instructed him. 3The high places, however, were not removed; the people continued to offer sacrifices and burn incense there.

4Joash said to the priests, "Collect all the money that is brought as sacred offerings to the temple of the LORD—the money collected in the census, the money received from personal vows and the money brought voluntarily to the temple. 5Let every priest receive the money from one of the treasurers, and let it be used to repair whatever damage is found in the temple."

6But by the twenty-third year of King Joash the priests still had not repaired the temple. 7Therefore King Joash summoned Jehoiada the priest and the other priests and asked them, "Why aren't you repairing the damage done to the temple? Take no more money from your treasurers, but hand it over for repairing the temple." 8The priests agreed that they would not collect any more money from the people and that they would not repair the temple themselves.

9Jehoiada the priest took a chest and bored a hole in its lid. He placed it beside the altar, on the right side as one enters the temple of the LORD. The priests who guarded the entrance

[a]2 Hebrew *Joram,* a variant of *Jehoram* [b]8 Or *approaches the precincts* [c]15 Or *out from the precincts*
[d]21 Hebrew *Jehoash,* a variant of *Joash* [e]1 Hebrew *Jehoash,* a variant of *Joash*; also in verses 2, 4, 6, 7 and 18

put into the chest all the money that was
brought to the temple of the LORD. 10When-
ever they saw that there was a large amount of
money in the chest, the royal secretary and the
high priest came, counted the money that had
been brought into the temple of the LORD and
put it into bags. 11When the amount had been
determined, they gave the money to the men
appointed to supervise the work on the temple.
With it they paid those who worked on the
temple of the LORD—the carpenters and builders, 12the masons and stonecutters. They purchased timber and dressed stone for the repair
of the temple of the LORD, and met all the
other expenses of restoring the temple.

13The money brought into the temple was
not spent for making silver basins, wick trimmers, sprinkling bowls, trumpets or any other
articles of gold or silver for the temple of the
LORD; 14it was paid to the workmen, who used
it to repair the temple. 15They did not require
an accounting from those to whom they gave
the money to pay the workers, because they
acted with complete honesty. 16The money
from the guilt offerings and sin offerings was
not brought into the temple of the LORD; it
belonged to the priests.

17About this time Hazael king of Aram went
up and attacked Gath and captured it. Then he
turned to attack Jerusalem. 18But Joash king of
Judah took all the sacred objects dedicated by
his fathers—Jehoshaphat, Jehoram and Ahaziah, the kings of Judah—and the gifts he himself had dedicated and all the gold found in the
treasuries of the temple of the LORD and of the
royal palace, and he sent them to Hazael king
of Aram, who then withdrew from Jerusalem.

19As for the other events of the reign of
Joash, and all he did, are they not written in the
book of the annals of the kings of Judah? 20His
officials conspired against him and assassinated him at Beth Millo, on the road down to
Silla. 21The officials who murdered him were
Jozabad son of Shimeath and Jehozabad son of
Shomer. He died and was buried with his fathers in the City of David. And Amaziah his
son succeeded him as king.

Jehoahaz King of Israel

13 In the twenty-third year of Joash son of
Ahaziah king of Judah, Jehoahaz son of
Jehu became king of Israel in Samaria, and he
reigned seventeen years. 2He did evil in the
eyes of the LORD by following the sins of Jeroboam son of Nebat, which he had caused Israel
to commit, and he did not turn away from
them. 3So the LORD's anger burned against Israel, and for a long time he kept them under the
power of Hazael king of Aram and Ben-Hadad
his son.

4Then Jehoahaz sought the LORD's favor,
and the LORD listened to him, for he saw how
severely the king of Aram was oppressing Israel. 5The LORD provided a deliverer for Israel,
and they escaped from the power of Aram. So
the Israelites lived in their own homes as they
had before. 6But they did not turn away from
the sins of the house of Jeroboam, which he
had caused Israel to commit; they continued in
them. Also, the Asherah pole[a] remained standing in Samaria.

7Nothing had been left of the army of Jehoahaz except fifty horsemen, ten chariots and ten
thousand foot soldiers, for the king of Aram
had destroyed the rest and made them like the
dust at threshing time.

8As for the other events of the reign of Jehoahaz, all he did and his achievements, are they
not written in the book of the annals of the
kings of Israel? 9Jehoahaz rested with his fathers and was buried in Samaria. And Jehoash[b] his son succeeded him as king.

Jehoash King of Israel

10In the thirty-seventh year of Joash king of
Judah, Jehoash son of Jehoahaz became king
of Israel in Samaria, and he reigned sixteen
years. 11He did evil in the eyes of the LORD
and did not turn away from any of the sins of
Jeroboam son of Nebat, which he had caused
Israel to commit; he continued in them.

12As for the other events of the reign of
Jehoash, all he did and his achievements, including his war against Amaziah king of Judah, are they not written in the book of the
annals of the kings of Israel? 13Jehoash rested
with his fathers, and Jeroboam succeeded him
on the throne. Jehoash was buried in Samaria
with the kings of Israel.

14Now Elisha was suffering from the illness
from which he died. Jehoash king of Israel
went down to see him and wept over him. "My
father! My father!" he cried. "The chariots and
horsemen of Israel!"

15Elisha said, "Get a bow and some arrows,"
and he did so. 16"Take the bow in your hands,"
he said to the king of Israel. When he had
taken it, Elisha put his hands on the king's
hands.

17"Open the east window," he said, and he
opened it. "Shoot!" Elisha said, and he shot.
"The LORD's arrow of victory, the arrow of
victory over Aram!" Elisha declared. "You
will completely destroy the Arameans at
Aphek."

18Then he said, "Take the arrows," and the
king took them. Elisha told him, "Strike the
ground." He struck it three times and stopped.
19The man of God was angry with him and
said, "You should have struck the ground five
or six times; then you would have defeated
Aram and completely destroyed it. But now
you will defeat it only three times."

20Elisha died and was buried.

Now Moabite raiders used to enter the country every spring. 21Once while some Israelites
were burying a man, suddenly they saw a band
of raiders; so they threw the man's body into

[a]6 That is, a symbol of the goddess Asherah; here and elsewhere in 2 Kings [b]9 Hebrew *Joash,* a variant of *Jehoash*; also in verses 12-14 and 25

Elisha's tomb. When the body touched Elisha's bones, the man came to life and stood up on his feet.

22Hazael king of Aram oppressed Israel throughout the reign of Jehoahaz. 23But the LORD was gracious to them and had compassion and showed concern for them because of his covenant with Abraham, Isaac and Jacob. To this day he has been unwilling to destroy them or banish them from his presence.

24Hazael king of Aram died, and Ben-Hadad his son succeeded him as king. 25Then Jehoash son of Jehoahaz recaptured from Ben-Hadad son of Hazael the towns he had taken in battle from his father Jehoahaz. Three times Jehoash defeated him, and so he recovered the Israelite towns.

Amaziah King of Judah

14 In the second year of Jehoash[a] son of Jehoahaz king of Israel, Amaziah son of Joash king of Judah began to reign. 2He was twenty-five years old when he became king, and he reigned in Jerusalem twenty-nine years. His mother's name was Jehoaddin; she was from Jerusalem. 3He did what was right in the eyes of the LORD, but not as his father David had done. In everything he followed the example of his father Joash. 4The high places, however, were not removed; the people continued to offer sacrifices and burn incense there.

5After the kingdom was firmly in his grasp, he executed the officials who had murdered his father the king. 6Yet he did not put the sons of the assassins to death, in accordance with what is written in the Book of the Law of Moses where the LORD commanded: "Fathers shall not be put to death for their children, nor children put to death for their fathers; each is to die for his own sins."[b]

7He was the one who defeated ten thousand Edomites in the Valley of Salt and captured Sela in battle, calling it Joktheel, the name it has to this day.

8Then Amaziah sent messengers to Jehoash son of Jehoahaz, the son of Jehu, king of Israel, with the challenge: "Come, meet me face to face."

9But Jehoash king of Israel replied to Amaziah king of Judah: "A thistle in Lebanon sent a message to a cedar in Lebanon, 'Give your daughter to my son in marriage.' Then a wild beast in Lebanon came along and trampled the thistle underfoot. 10You have indeed defeated Edom and now you are arrogant. Glory in your victory, but stay at home! Why ask for trouble and cause your own downfall and that of Judah also?"

11Amaziah, however, would not listen, so Jehoash king of Israel attacked. He and Amaziah king of Judah faced each other at Beth Shemesh in Judah. 12Judah was routed by Israel, and every man fled to his home. 13Jehoash king of Israel captured Amaziah king of Judah, the son of Joash, the son of Ahaziah, at Beth Shemesh. Then Jehoash went to Jerusalem and broke down the wall of Jerusalem from the Ephraim Gate to the Corner Gate—a section about six hundred feet long.[c] 14He took all the gold and silver and all the articles found in the temple of the LORD and in the treasuries of the royal palace. He also took hostages and returned to Samaria.

15As for the other events of the reign of Jehoash, what he did and his achievements, including his war against Amaziah king of Judah, are they not written in the book of the annals of the kings of Israel? 16Jehoash rested with his fathers and was buried in Samaria with the kings of Israel. And Jeroboam his son succeeded him as king.

17Amaziah son of Joash king of Judah lived for fifteen years after the death of Jehoash son of Jehoahaz king of Israel. 18As for the other events of Amaziah's reign, are they not written in the book of the annals of the kings of Judah?

19They conspired against him in Jerusalem, and he fled to Lachish, but they sent men after him to Lachish and killed him there. 20He was brought back by horse and was buried in Jerusalem with his fathers, in the City of David.

21Then all the people of Judah took Azariah,[d] who was sixteen years old, and made him king in place of his father Amaziah. 22He was the one who rebuilt Elath and restored it to Judah after Amaziah rested with his fathers.

Jeroboam II King of Israel

23In the fifteenth year of Amaziah son of Joash king of Judah, Jeroboam son of Jehoash king of Israel became king in Samaria, and he reigned forty-one years. 24He did evil in the eyes of the LORD and did not turn away from any of the sins of Jeroboam son of Nebat, which he had caused Israel to commit. 25He was the one who restored the boundaries of Israel from Lebo[e] Hamath to the Sea of the Arabah,[f] in accordance with the word of the LORD, the God of Israel, spoken through his servant Jonah son of Amittai, the prophet from Gath Hepher.

26The LORD had seen how bitterly everyone in Israel, whether slave or free, was suffering; there was no one to help them. 27And since the LORD had not said he would blot out the name of Israel from under heaven, he saved them by the hand of Jeroboam son of Jehoash.

28As for the other events of Jeroboam's reign, all he did, and his military achievements, including how he recovered for Israel both Damascus and Hamath, which had belonged to Yaudi,[g] are they not written in the book of the annals of the kings of Israel? 29Jeroboam rested with his fathers, the kings of Israel. And Zechariah his son succeeded him as king.

[a] *1* Hebrew *Joash*, a variant of *Jehoash*; also in verses 13, 23 and 27 [b] *6* Deut. 24:16 [c] *13* Hebrew *four hundred cubits* (about 180 meters) [d] *21* Also called *Uzziah* [e] *25* Or *from the entrance to* [f] *25* That is, the Dead Sea [g] *28* Or *Judah*

Azariah King of Judah

15 In the twenty-seventh year of Jeroboam
king of Israel, Azariah son of Amaziah
king of Judah began to reign. 2He was sixteen
years old when he became king, and he reigned
in Jerusalem fifty-two years. His mother's
name was Jecoliah; she was from Jerusalem.
3He did what was right in the eyes of the
LORD, just as his father Amaziah had done.
4The high places, however, were not removed;
the people continued to offer sacrifices and
burn incense there.

5The LORD afflicted the king with leprosy[a]
until the day he died, and he lived in a separate
house.[b] Jotham the king's son had charge of
the palace and governed the people of the land.

6As for the other events of Azariah's reign,
and all he did, are they not written in the book
of the annals of the kings of Judah? 7Azariah
rested with his fathers and was buried near
them in the City of David. And Jotham his son
succeeded him as king.

Zechariah King of Israel

8In the thirty-eighth year of Azariah king
of Judah, Zechariah son of Jeroboam became
king of Israel in Samaria, and he reigned six
months. 9He did evil in the eyes of the LORD,
as his fathers had done. He did not turn away
from the sins of Jeroboam son of Nebat, which
he had caused Israel to commit.

10Shallum son of Jabesh conspired against
Zechariah. He attacked him in front of the people,[c] assassinated him and succeeded him as
king. 11The other events of Zechariah's reign
are written in the book of the annals of the
kings of Israel. 12So the word of the LORD
spoken to Jehu was fulfilled: "Your descendants will sit on the throne of Israel to the
fourth generation."[d]

Shallum King of Israel

13Shallum son of Jabesh became king in the
thirty-ninth year of Uzziah king of Judah, and
he reigned in Samaria one month. 14Then
Menahem son of Gadi went from Tirzah up to
Samaria. He attacked Shallum son of Jabesh in
Samaria, assassinated him and succeeded him
as king.

15The other events of Shallum's reign, and
the conspiracy he led, are written in the book
of the annals of the kings of Israel.

16At that time Menahem, starting out from
Tirzah, attacked Tiphsah and everyone in the
city and its vicinity, because they refused to
open their gates. He sacked Tiphsah and ripped
open all the pregnant women.

Menahem King of Israel

17In the thirty-ninth year of Azariah king of
Judah, Menahem son of Gadi became king of
Israel, and he reigned in Samaria ten years.
18He did evil in the eyes of the LORD. During
his entire reign he did not turn away from the
sins of Jeroboam son of Nebat, which he had
caused Israel to commit.

19Then Pul[e] king of Assyria invaded the
land, and Menahem gave him a thousand talents[f] of silver to gain his support and strength-
en his own hold on the kingdom. 20Menahem
exacted this money from Israel. Every wealthy
man had to contribute fifty shekels[g] of silver
to be given to the king of Assyria. So the king
of Assyria withdrew and stayed in the land no
longer.

21As for the other events of Menahem's
reign, and all he did, are they not written in the
book of the annals of the kings of Israel?
22Menahem rested with his fathers. And Pekahiah his son succeeded him as king.

Pekahiah King of Israel

23In the fiftieth year of Azariah king of Judah, Pekahiah son of Menahem became king
of Israel in Samaria, and he reigned two years.
24Pekahiah did evil in the eyes of the LORD. He
did not turn away from the sins of Jeroboam
son of Nebat, which he had caused Israel to
commit. 25One of his chief officers, Pekah son
of Remaliah, conspired against him. Taking
fifty men of Gilead with him, he assassinated
Pekahiah, along with Argob and Arieh, in the
citadel of the royal palace at Samaria. So Pekah killed Pekahiah and succeeded him as
king.

26The other events of Pekahiah's reign, and
all he did, are written in the book of the annals
of the kings of Israel.

Pekah King of Israel

27In the fifty-second year of Azariah king of
Judah, Pekah son of Remaliah became king of
Israel in Samaria, and he reigned twenty years.
28He did evil in the eyes of the LORD. He did
not turn away from the sins of Jeroboam son of
Nebat, which he had caused Israel to commit.

29In the time of Pekah king of Israel,
Tiglath-Pileser king of Assyria came and took
Ijon, Abel Beth Maacah, Janoah, Kedesh and
Hazor. He took Gilead and Galilee, including
all the land of Naphtali, and deported the people to Assyria. 30Then Hoshea son of Elah conspired against Pekah son of Remaliah. He attacked and assassinated him, and then
succeeded him as king in the twentieth year of
Jotham son of Uzziah.

31As for the other events of Pekah's reign,
and all he did, are they not written in the book
of the annals of the kings of Israel?

Jotham King of Judah

32In the second year of Pekah son of Remaliah king of Israel, Jotham son of Uzziah king
of Judah began to reign. 33He was twenty-five
years old when he became king, and he reigned
in Jerusalem sixteen years. His mother's name

[a] *5* The Hebrew word was used for various diseases affecting the skin—not necessarily leprosy. [b] *5* Or *in a house where he was relieved of responsibility* [c] *10* Hebrew; some Septuagint manuscripts *in Ibleam* [d] *12* 2 Kings 10:30 [e] *19* Also called *Tiglath-Pileser* [f] *19* That is, about 37 tons (about 34 metric tons) [g] *20* That is, about 1 1/4 pounds (about 0.6 kilogram)

was Jerusha daughter of Zadok. 34He did what was right in the eyes of the LORD, just as his father Uzziah had done. 35The high places, however, were not removed; the people continued to offer sacrifices and burn incense there. Jotham rebuilt the Upper Gate of the temple of the LORD.

36As for the other events of Jotham's reign, and what he did, are they not written in the book of the annals of the kings of Judah? 37(In those days the LORD began to send Rezin king of Aram and Pekah son of Remaliah against Judah.) 38Jotham rested with his fathers and was buried with them in the City of David, the city of his father. And Ahaz his son succeeded him as king.

Ahaz King of Judah

16 In the seventeenth year of Pekah son of Remaliah, Ahaz son of Jotham king of Judah began to reign. 2Ahaz was twenty years old when he became king, and he reigned in Jerusalem sixteen years. Unlike David his father, he did not do what was right in the eyes of the LORD his God. 3He walked in the ways of the kings of Israel and even sacrificed his son in[a] the fire, following the detestable ways of the nations the LORD had driven out before the Israelites. 4He offered sacrifices and burned incense at the high places, on the hilltops and under every spreading tree.

5Then Rezin king of Aram and Pekah son of Remaliah king of Israel marched up to fight against Jerusalem and besieged Ahaz, but they could not overpower him. 6At that time, Rezin king of Aram recovered Elath for Aram by driving out the men of Judah. Edomites then moved into Elath and have lived there to this day.

7Ahaz sent messengers to say to Tiglath-Pileser king of Assyria, "I am your servant and vassal. Come up and save me out of the hand of the king of Aram and of the king of Israel, who are attacking me." 8And Ahaz took the silver and gold found in the temple of the LORD and in the treasuries of the royal palace and sent it as a gift to the king of Assyria. 9The king of Assyria complied by attacking Damascus and capturing it. He deported its inhabitants to Kir and put Rezin to death.

10Then King Ahaz went to Damascus to meet Tiglath-Pileser king of Assyria. He saw an altar in Damascus and sent to Uriah the priest a sketch of the altar, with detailed plans for its construction. 11So Uriah the priest built an altar in accordance with all the plans that King Ahaz had sent from Damascus and finished it before King Ahaz returned. 12When the king came back from Damascus and saw the altar, he approached it and presented offerings[b] on it. 13He offered up his burnt offering and grain offering, poured out his drink offering, and sprinkled the blood of his fellowship offerings[c] on the altar. 14The bronze altar that stood before the LORD he brought from the front of the temple—from between the new altar and the temple of the LORD—and put it on the north side of the new altar.

15King Ahaz then gave these orders to Uriah the priest: "On the large new altar, offer the morning burnt offering and the evening grain offering, the king's burnt offering and his grain offering, and the burnt offering of all the people of the land, and their grain offering and their drink offering. Sprinkle on the altar all the blood of the burnt offerings and sacrifices. But I will use the bronze altar for seeking guidance." 16And Uriah the priest did just as King Ahaz had ordered.

17King Ahaz took away the side panels and removed the basins from the movable stands. He removed the Sea from the bronze bulls that supported it and set it on a stone base. 18He took away the Sabbath canopy[d] that had been built at the temple and removed the royal entryway outside the temple of the LORD, in deference to the king of Assyria.

19As for the other events of the reign of Ahaz, and what he did, are they not written in the book of the annals of the kings of Judah? 20Ahaz rested with his fathers and was buried with them in the City of David. And Hezekiah his son succeeded him as king.

Hoshea Last King of Israel

17 In the twelfth year of Ahaz king of Judah, Hoshea son of Elah became king of Israel in Samaria, and he reigned nine years. 2He did evil in the eyes of the LORD, but not like the kings of Israel who preceded him.

3Shalmaneser king of Assyria came up to attack Hoshea, who had been Shalmaneser's vassal and had paid him tribute. 4But the king of Assyria discovered that Hoshea was a traitor, for he had sent envoys to So[e] king of Egypt, and he no longer paid tribute to the king of Assyria, as he had done year by year. Therefore Shalmaneser seized him and put him in prison. 5The king of Assyria invaded the entire land, marched against Samaria and laid siege to it for three years. 6In the ninth year of Hoshea, the king of Assyria captured Samaria and deported the Israelites to Assyria. He settled them in Halah, in Gozan on the Habor River and in the towns of the Medes.

Israel Exiled Because of Sin

7All this took place because the Israelites had sinned against the LORD their God, who had brought them up out of Egypt from under the power of Pharaoh king of Egypt. They worshiped other gods 8and followed the practices of the nations the LORD had driven out before them, as well as the practices that the kings of Israel had introduced. 9The Israelites secretly did things against the LORD their God that were not right. From watchtower to forti-

[a] 3 Or *even made his son pass through* [b] 12 Or *and went up* [c] 13 Traditionally *peace offerings*
[d] 18 Or *the dais of his throne* (see Septuagint) [e] 4 Or *to Sais, to the*; *So* is possibly an abbreviation for *Osorkon.*

fied city they built themselves high places in all their towns. 10They set up sacred stones and Asherah poles on every high hill and under every spreading tree. 11At every high place they burned incense, as the nations whom the LORD had driven out before them had done. They did wicked things that provoked the LORD to anger. 12They worshiped idols, though the LORD had said, "You shall not do this."[a] 13The LORD warned Israel and Judah through all his prophets and seers: "Turn from your evil ways. Observe my commands and decrees, in accordance with the entire Law that I commanded your fathers to obey and that I delivered to you through my servants the prophets."

14But they would not listen and were as stiff-necked as their fathers, who did not trust in the LORD their God. 15They rejected his decrees and the covenant he had made with their fathers and the warnings he had given them. They followed worthless idols and themselves became worthless. They imitated the nations around them although the LORD had ordered them, "Do not do as they do," and they did the things the LORD had forbidden them to do.

16They forsook all the commands of the LORD their God and made for themselves two idols cast in the shape of calves, and an Asherah pole. They bowed down to all the starry hosts, and they worshiped Baal. 17They sacrificed their sons and daughters in[b] the fire. They practiced divination and sorcery and sold themselves to do evil in the eyes of the LORD, provoking him to anger.

18So the LORD was very angry with Israel and removed them from his presence. Only the tribe of Judah was left, 19and even Judah did not keep the commands of the LORD their God. They followed the practices Israel had introduced. 20Therefore the LORD rejected all the people of Israel; he afflicted them and gave them into the hands of plunderers, until he thrust them from his presence.

21When he tore Israel away from the house of David, they made Jeroboam son of Nebat their king. Jeroboam enticed Israel away from following the LORD and caused them to commit a great sin. 22The Israelites persisted in all the sins of Jeroboam and did not turn away from them 23until the LORD removed them from his presence, as he had warned through all his servants the prophets. So the people of Israel were taken from their homeland into exile in Assyria, and they are still there.

Samaria Resettled

24The king of Assyria brought people from Babylon, Cuthah, Avva, Hamath and Sepharvaim and settled them in the towns of Samaria to replace the Israelites. They took over Samaria and lived in its towns. 25When they first lived there, they did not worship the LORD; so he sent lions among them and they killed some of the people. 26It was reported to the king of Assyria: "The people you deported and resettled in the towns of Samaria do not know what the god of that country requires. He has sent lions among them, which are killing them off, because the people do not know what he requires."

27Then the king of Assyria gave this order: "Have one of the priests you took captive from Samaria go back to live there and teach the people what the god of the land requires." 28So one of the priests who had been exiled from Samaria came to live in Bethel and taught them how to worship the LORD.

29Nevertheless, each national group made its own gods in the several towns where they settled, and set them up in the shrines the people of Samaria had made at the high places. 30The men from Babylon made Succoth Benoth, the men from Cuthah made Nergal, and the men from Hamath made Ashima; 31the Avvites made Nibhaz and Tartak, and the Sepharvites burned their children in the fire as sacrifices to Adrammelech and Anammelech, the gods of Sepharvaim. 32They worshiped the LORD, but they also appointed all sorts of their own people to officiate for them as priests in the shrines at the high places. 33They worshiped the LORD, but they also served their own gods in accordance with the customs of the nations from which they had been brought.

34To this day they persist in their former practices. They neither worship the LORD nor adhere to the decrees and ordinances, the laws and commands that the LORD gave the descendants of Jacob, whom he named Israel. 35When the LORD made a covenant with the Israelites, he commanded them: "Do not worship any other gods or bow down to them, serve them or sacrifice to them. 36But the LORD, who brought you up out of Egypt with mighty power and outstretched arm, is the one you must worship. To him you shall bow down and to him offer sacrifices. 37You must always be careful to keep the decrees and ordinances, the laws and commands he wrote for you. Do not worship other gods. 38Do not forget the covenant I have made with you, and do not worship other gods. 39Rather, worship the LORD your God; it is he who will deliver you from the hand of all your enemies."

40They would not listen, however, but persisted in their former practices. 41Even while these people were worshiping the LORD, they were serving their idols. To this day their children and grandchildren continue to do as their fathers did.

Hezekiah King of Judah

18 In the third year of Hoshea son of Elah king of Israel, Hezekiah son of Ahaz king of Judah began to reign. 2He was twenty-five years old when he became king, and he reigned in Jerusalem twenty-nine years. His

[a] *12* Exodus 20:4, 5 [b] *17* Or *They made their sons and daughters pass through*

mother's name was Abijah[a] daughter of Zechariah. 3He did what was right in the eyes of the LORD, just as his father David had done. 4He removed the high places, smashed the sacred stones and cut down the Asherah poles. He broke into pieces the bronze snake Moses had made, for up to that time the Israelites had been burning incense to it. (It was called[b] Nehushtan.[c])

5Hezekiah trusted in the LORD, the God of Israel. There was no one like him among all the kings of Judah, either before him or after him. 6He held fast to the LORD and did not cease to follow him; he kept the commands the LORD had given Moses. 7And the LORD was with him; he was successful in whatever he undertook. He rebelled against the king of Assyria and did not serve him. 8From watchtower to fortified city, he defeated the Philistines, as far as Gaza and its territory.

9In King Hezekiah's fourth year, which was the seventh year of Hoshea son of Elah king of Israel, Shalmaneser king of Assyria marched against Samaria and laid siege to it. 10At the end of three years the Assyrians took it. So Samaria was captured in Hezekiah's sixth year, which was the ninth year of Hoshea king of Israel. 11The king of Assyria deported Israel to Assyria and settled them in Halah, in Gozan on the Habor River and in towns of the Medes. 12This happened because they had not obeyed the LORD their God, but had violated his covenant—all that Moses the servant of the LORD commanded. They neither listened to the commands nor carried them out.

13In the fourteenth year of King Hezekiah's reign, Sennacherib king of Assyria attacked all the fortified cities of Judah and captured them. 14So Hezekiah king of Judah sent this message to the king of Assyria at Lachish: "I have done wrong. Withdraw from me, and I will pay whatever you demand of me." The king of Assyria exacted from Hezekiah king of Judah three hundred talents[d] of silver and thirty talents[e] of gold. 15So Hezekiah gave him all the silver that was found in the temple of the LORD and in the treasuries of the royal palace.

16At this time Hezekiah king of Judah stripped off the gold with which he had covered the doors and doorposts of the temple of the LORD, and gave it to the king of Assyria.

Sennacherib Threatens Jerusalem

17The king of Assyria sent his supreme commander, his chief officer and his field commander with a large army, from Lachish to King Hezekiah at Jerusalem. They came up to Jerusalem and stopped at the aqueduct of the Upper Pool, on the road to the Washerman's Field. 18They called for the king; and Eliakim son of Hilkiah the palace administrator, Shebna the secretary, and Joah son of Asaph the recorder went out to them.

19The field commander said to them, "Tell Hezekiah:

> " 'This is what the great king, the king of Assyria, says: On what are you basing this confidence of yours? 20You say you have strategy and military strength—but you speak only empty words. On whom are you depending, that you rebel against me? 21Look now, you are depending on Egypt, that splintered reed of a staff, which pierces a man's hand and wounds him if he leans on it! Such is Pharaoh king of Egypt to all who depend on him. 22And if you say to me, "We are depending on the LORD our God"—isn't he the one whose high places and altars Hezekiah removed, saying to Judah and Jerusalem, "You must worship before this altar in Jerusalem"?
>
> 23" 'Come now, make a bargain with my master, the king of Assyria: I will give you two thousand horses—if you can put riders on them! 24How can you repulse one officer of the least of my master's officials, even though you are depending on Egypt for chariots and horsemen[f]? 25Furthermore, have I come to attack and destroy this place without word from the LORD? The LORD himself told me to march against this country and destroy it.' "

26Then Eliakim son of Hilkiah, and Shebna and Joah said to the field commander, "Please speak to your servants in Aramaic, since we understand it. Don't speak to us in Hebrew in the hearing of the people on the wall."

27But the commander replied, "Was it only to your master and you that my master sent me to say these things, and not to the men sitting on the wall—who, like you, will have to eat their own filth and drink their own urine?"

28Then the commander stood and called out in Hebrew: "Hear the word of the great king, the king of Assyria! 29This is what the king says: Do not let Hezekiah deceive you. He cannot deliver you from my hand. 30Do not let Hezekiah persuade you to trust in the LORD when he says, 'The LORD will surely deliver us; this city will not be given into the hand of the king of Assyria.'

31"Do not listen to Hezekiah. This is what the king of Assyria says: Make peace with me and come out to me. Then every one of you will eat from his own vine and fig tree and drink water from his own cistern, 32until I come and take you to a land like your own, a land of grain and new wine, a land of bread and vineyards, a land of olive trees and honey. Choose life and not death!

"Do not listen to Hezekiah, for he is misleading you when he says, 'The LORD will deliver us.' 33Has the god of any nation ever

[a]2 Hebrew *Abi*, a variant of *Abijah* [b]4 Or *He called it* [c]4 *Nehushtan* sounds like the Hebrew for *bronze* and *snake* and *unclean thing*. [d]14 That is, about 11 tons (about 10 metric tons) [e]14 That is, about 1 ton (about 1 metric ton) [f]24 Or *charioteers*

delivered his land from the hand of the king of
Assyria? 34Where are the gods of Hamath and
Arpad? Where are the gods of Sepharvaim,
Hena and Ivvah? Have they rescued Samaria
from my hand? 35Who of all the gods of these
countries has been able to save his land from
me? How then can the LORD deliver Jerusalem
from my hand?"
36But the people remained silent and said
nothing in reply, because the king had commanded, "Do not answer him."
37Then Eliakim son of Hilkiah the palace
administrator, Shebna the secretary and Joah
son of Asaph the recorder went to Hezekiah,
with their clothes torn, and told him what the
field commander had said.

Jerusalem's Deliverance Foretold

19 When King Hezekiah heard this, he tore
his clothes and put on sackcloth and
went into the temple of the LORD. 2He sent
Eliakim the palace administrator, Shebna the
secretary and the leading priests, all wearing
sackcloth, to the prophet Isaiah son of Amoz.
3They told him, "This is what Hezekiah says:
This day is a day of distress and rebuke and
disgrace, as when children come to the point of
birth and there is no strength to deliver them.
4It may be that the LORD your God will hear all
the words of the field commander, whom his
master, the king of Assyria, has sent to ridicule
the living God, and that he will rebuke him
for the words the LORD your God has heard.
Therefore pray for the remnant that still survives."
5When King Hezekiah's officials came to
Isaiah, 6Isaiah said to them, "Tell your master,
'This is what the LORD says: Do not be afraid
of what you have heard—those words with
which the underlings of the king of Assyria
have blasphemed me. 7Listen! I am going to
put such a spirit in him that when he hears a
certain report, he will return to his own country, and there I will have him cut down with
the sword.' "
8When the field commander heard that the
king of Assyria had left Lachish, he withdrew
and found the king fighting against Libnah.
9Now Sennacherib received a report that
Tirhakah, the Cushite[a] king ⌞of Egypt⌟, was
marching out to fight against him. So he again
sent messengers to Hezekiah with this word:
10"Say to Hezekiah king of Judah: Do not let
the god you depend on deceive you when he
says, 'Jerusalem will not be handed over to the
king of Assyria.' 11Surely you have heard what
the kings of Assyria have done to all the countries, destroying them completely. And will
you be delivered? 12Did the gods of the nations
that were destroyed by my forefathers deliver
them: the gods of Gozan, Haran, Rezeph and
the people of Eden who were in Tel Assar?
13Where is the king of Hamath, the king of
Arpad, the king of the city of Sepharvaim, or
of Hena or Ivvah?"

Hezekiah's Prayer

14Hezekiah received the letter from the messengers and read it. Then he went up to the
temple of the LORD and spread it out before the
LORD. 15And Hezekiah prayed to the LORD:
"O LORD, God of Israel, enthroned between
the cherubim, you alone are God over all the
kingdoms of the earth. You have made heaven
and earth. 16Give ear, O LORD, and hear; open
your eyes, O LORD, and see; listen to the
words Sennacherib has sent to insult the living
God.
17"It is true, O LORD, that the Assyrian
kings have laid waste these nations and their
lands. 18They have thrown their gods into the
fire and destroyed them, for they were not gods
but only wood and stone, fashioned by men's
hands. 19Now, O LORD our God, deliver us
from his hand, so that all kingdoms on earth
may know that you alone, O LORD, are God."

Isaiah Prophesies Sennacherib's Fall

20Then Isaiah son of Amoz sent a message
to Hezekiah: "This is what the LORD, the God
of Israel, says: I have heard your prayer concerning Sennacherib king of Assyria. 21This is
the word that the LORD has spoken against
him:

" 'The Virgin Daughter of Zion
despises you and mocks you.
The Daughter of Jerusalem
tosses her head as you flee.
22Who is it you have insulted and
blasphemed?
Against whom have you raised your
voice
and lifted your eyes in pride?
Against the Holy One of Israel!
23By your messengers
you have heaped insults on the Lord.
And you have said,
"With my many chariots
I have ascended the heights of the
mountains,
the utmost heights of Lebanon.
I have cut down its tallest cedars,
the choicest of its pines.
I have reached its remotest parts,
the finest of its forests.
24I have dug wells in foreign lands
and drunk the water there.
With the soles of my feet
I have dried up all the streams of
Egypt."

25" 'Have you not heard?
Long ago I ordained it.
In days of old I planned it;
now I have brought it to pass,
that you have turned fortified cities
into piles of stone.
26Their people, drained of power,
are dismayed and put to shame.
They are like plants in the field,
like tender green shoots,

[a]9 That is, from the upper Nile region

like grass sprouting on the roof,
scorched before it grows up.

27“ ‘But I know where you stay
and when you come and go
and how you rage against me.
28Because you rage against me
and your insolence has reached my ears,
I will put my hook in your nose
and my bit in your mouth,
and I will make you return
by the way you came.’

29“This will be the sign for you,
O Hezekiah:

“This year you will eat what grows by
itself,
and the second year what springs from
that.
But in the third year sow and reap,
plant vineyards and eat their fruit.
30Once more a remnant of the house of
Judah
will take root below and bear fruit
above.
31For out of Jerusalem will come a remnant,
and out of Mount Zion a band of
survivors.

The zeal of the LORD Almighty will accomplish this.

32“Therefore this is what the LORD says concerning the king of Assyria:

“He will not enter this city
or shoot an arrow here.
He will not come before it with shield
or build a siege ramp against it.
33By the way that he came he will return;
he will not enter this city,
declares the LORD.
34I will defend this city and save it,
for my sake and for the sake of David
my servant.”

35That night the angel of the LORD went out
and put to death a hundred and eighty-five
thousand men in the Assyrian camp. When the
people got up the next morning—there were
all the dead bodies! 36So Sennacherib king
of Assyria broke camp and withdrew. He returned to Nineveh and stayed there.
37One day, while he was worshiping in the
temple of his god Nisroch, his sons Adrammelech and Sharezer cut him down with the
sword, and they escaped to the land of Ararat.
And Esarhaddon his son succeeded him as
king.

Hezekiah's Illness

20 In those days Hezekiah became ill and
was at the point of death. The prophet
Isaiah son of Amoz went to him and said,
“This is what the LORD says: Put your house in
order, because you are going to die; you will
not recover.”
2Hezekiah turned his face to the wall and
prayed to the LORD, 3“Remember, O LORD,
how I have walked before you faithfully and
with wholehearted devotion and have done
what is good in your eyes.” And Hezekiah
wept bitterly.
4Before Isaiah had left the middle court, the
word of the LORD came to him: 5“Go back and
tell Hezekiah, the leader of my people, ‘This is
what the LORD, the God of your father David,
says: I have heard your prayer and seen your
tears; I will heal you. On the third day from
now you will go up to the temple of the LORD.
6I will add fifteen years to your life. And I will
deliver you and this city from the hand of the
king of Assyria. I will defend this city for my
sake and for the sake of my servant David.’ ”
7Then Isaiah said, “Prepare a poultice of
figs.” They did so and applied it to the boil,
and he recovered.
8Hezekiah had asked Isaiah, “What will be
the sign that the LORD will heal me and that I
will go up to the temple of the LORD on the
third day from now?”
9Isaiah answered, “This is the LORD's sign
to you that the LORD will do what he has promised: Shall the shadow go forward ten steps, or
shall it go back ten steps?”
10“It is a simple matter for the shadow to go
forward ten steps,” said Hezekiah. “Rather,
have it go back ten steps.”
11Then the prophet Isaiah called upon the
LORD, and the LORD made the shadow go back
the ten steps it had gone down on the stairway
of Ahaz.

Envoys From Babylon

12At that time Merodach-Baladan son of
Baladan king of Babylon sent Hezekiah letters
and a gift, because he had heard of Hezekiah's
illness. 13Hezekiah received the messengers
and showed them all that was in his storehouses—the silver, the gold, the spices and the
fine oil—his armory and everything found
among his treasures. There was nothing in his
palace or in all his kingdom that Hezekiah did
not show them.
14Then Isaiah the prophet went to King Hezekiah and asked, “What did those men say, and
where did they come from?”
“From a distant land,” Hezekiah replied.
“They came from Babylon.”
15The prophet asked, “What did they see in
your palace?”
“They saw everything in my palace,” Hezekiah said. “There is nothing among my treasures that I did not show them.”
16Then Isaiah said to Hezekiah, “Hear the
word of the LORD: 17The time will surely come
when everything in your palace, and all that
your fathers have stored up until this day, will
be carried off to Babylon. Nothing will be left,
says the LORD. 18And some of your descendants, your own flesh and blood, that will be
born to you, will be taken away, and they will
become eunuchs in the palace of the king of
Babylon.”
19“The word of the LORD you have spoken
is good,” Hezekiah replied. For he thought,

"Will there not be peace and security in my lifetime?"

20As for the other events of Hezekiah's reign, all his achievements and how he made the pool and the tunnel by which he brought water into the city, are they not written in the book of the annals of the kings of Judah? 21Hezekiah rested with his fathers. And Manasseh his son succeeded him as king.

Manasseh King of Judah

21 Manasseh was twelve years old when he became king, and he reigned in Jerusalem fifty-five years. His mother's name was Hephzibah. 2He did evil in the eyes of the LORD, following the detestable practices of the nations the LORD had driven out before the Israelites. 3He rebuilt the high places his father Hezekiah had destroyed; he also erected altars to Baal and made an Asherah pole, as Ahab king of Israel had done. He bowed down to all the starry hosts and worshiped them. 4He built altars in the temple of the LORD, of which the LORD had said, "In Jerusalem I will put my Name." 5In both courts of the temple of the LORD, he built altars to all the starry hosts. 6He sacrificed his own son in[a] the fire, practiced sorcery and divination, and consulted mediums and spiritists. He did much evil in the eyes of the LORD, provoking him to anger.

7He took the carved Asherah pole he had made and put it in the temple, of which the LORD had said to David and to his son Solomon, "In this temple and in Jerusalem, which I have chosen out of all the tribes of Israel, I will put my Name forever. 8I will not again make the feet of the Israelites wander from the land I gave their forefathers, if only they will be careful to do everything I commanded them and will keep the whole Law that my servant Moses gave them." 9But the people did not listen. Manasseh led them astray, so that they did more evil than the nations the LORD had destroyed before the Israelites.

10The LORD said through his servants the prophets: 11"Manasseh king of Judah has committed these detestable sins. He has done more evil than the Amorites who preceded him and has led Judah into sin with his idols. 12Therefore this is what the LORD, the God of Israel, says: I am going to bring such disaster on Jerusalem and Judah that the ears of everyone who hears of it will tingle. 13I will stretch out over Jerusalem the measuring line used against Samaria and the plumb line used against the house of Ahab. I will wipe out Jerusalem as one wipes a dish, wiping it and turning it upside down. 14I will forsake the remnant of my inheritance and hand them over to their enemies. They will be looted and plundered by all their foes, 15because they have done evil in my eyes and have provoked me to anger from the day their forefathers came out of Egypt until this day."

16Moreover, Manasseh also shed so much innocent blood that he filled Jerusalem from end to end—besides the sin that he had caused Judah to commit, so that they did evil in the eyes of the LORD.

17As for the other events of Manasseh's reign, and all he did, including the sin he committed, are they not written in the book of the annals of the kings of Judah? 18Manasseh rested with his fathers and was buried in his palace garden, the garden of Uzza. And Amon his son succeeded him as king.

Amon King of Judah

19Amon was twenty-two years old when he became king, and he reigned in Jerusalem two years. His mother's name was Meshullemeth daughter of Haruz; she was from Jotbah. 20He did evil in the eyes of the LORD, as his father Manasseh had done. 21He walked in all the ways of his father; he worshiped the idols his father had worshiped, and bowed down to them. 22He forsook the LORD, the God of his fathers, and did not walk in the way of the LORD.

23Amon's officials conspired against him and assassinated the king in his palace. 24Then the people of the land killed all who had plotted against King Amon, and they made Josiah his son king in his place.

25As for the other events of Amon's reign, and what he did, are they not written in the book of the annals of the kings of Judah? 26He was buried in his grave in the garden of Uzza. And Josiah his son succeeded him as king.

The Book of the Law Found

22 Josiah was eight years old when he became king, and he reigned in Jerusalem thirty-one years. His mother's name was Jedidah daughter of Adaiah; she was from Bozkath. 2He did what was right in the eyes of the LORD and walked in all the ways of his father David, not turning aside to the right or to the left.

3In the eighteenth year of his reign, King Josiah sent the secretary, Shaphan son of Azaliah, the son of Meshullam, to the temple of the LORD. He said: 4"Go up to Hilkiah the high priest and have him get ready the money that has been brought into the temple of the LORD, which the doorkeepers have collected from the people. 5Have them entrust it to the men appointed to supervise the work on the temple. And have these men pay the workers who repair the temple of the LORD— 6the carpenters, the builders and the masons. Also have them purchase timber and dressed stone to repair the temple. 7But they need not account for the money entrusted to them, because they are acting faithfully."

8Hilkiah the high priest said to Shaphan the secretary, "I have found the Book of the Law in the temple of the LORD." He gave it to Shaphan, who read it. 9Then Shaphan the secretary went to the king and reported to him: "Your

[a]6 Or *He made his own son pass through*

officials have paid out the money that was in the temple of the LORD and have entrusted it to the workers and supervisors at the temple." 10Then Shaphan the secretary informed the king, "Hilkiah the priest has given me a book." And Shaphan read from it in the presence of the king.

11When the king heard the words of the Book of the Law, he tore his robes. 12He gave these orders to Hilkiah the priest, Ahikam son of Shaphan, Acbor son of Micaiah, Shaphan the secretary and Asaiah the king's attendant: 13"Go and inquire of the LORD for me and for the people and for all Judah about what is written in this book that has been found. Great is the LORD's anger that burns against us because our fathers have not obeyed the words of this book; they have not acted in accordance with all that is written there concerning us."

14Hilkiah the priest, Ahikam, Acbor, Shaphan and Asaiah went to speak to the prophetess Huldah, who was the wife of Shallum son of Tikvah, the son of Harhas, keeper of the wardrobe. She lived in Jerusalem, in the Second District.

15She said to them, "This is what the LORD, the God of Israel, says: Tell the man who sent you to me, 16'This is what the LORD says: I am going to bring disaster on this place and its people, according to everything written in the book the king of Judah has read. 17Because they have forsaken me and burned incense to other gods and provoked me to anger by all the idols their hands have made,[a] my anger will burn against this place and will not be quenched.' 18Tell the king of Judah, who sent you to inquire of the LORD, 'This is what the LORD, the God of Israel, says concerning the words you heard: 19Because your heart was responsive and you humbled yourself before the LORD when you heard what I have spoken against this place and its people, that they would become accursed and laid waste, and because you tore your robes and wept in my presence, I have heard you, declares the LORD. 20Therefore I will gather you to your fathers, and you will be buried in peace. Your eyes will not see all the disaster I am going to bring on this place.' "

So they took her answer back to the king.

Josiah Renews the Covenant

23 Then the king called together all the elders of Judah and Jerusalem. 2He went up to the temple of the LORD with the men of Judah, the people of Jerusalem, the priests and the prophets—all the people from the least to the greatest. He read in their hearing all the words of the Book of the Covenant, which had been found in the temple of the LORD. 3The king stood by the pillar and renewed the covenant in the presence of the LORD—to follow the LORD and keep his commands, regulations and decrees with all his heart and all his soul, thus confirming the words of the covenant written in this book. Then all the people pledged themselves to the covenant.

4The king ordered Hilkiah the high priest, the priests next in rank and the doorkeepers to remove from the temple of the LORD all the articles made for Baal and Asherah and all the starry hosts. He burned them outside Jerusalem in the fields of the Kidron Valley and took the ashes to Bethel. 5He did away with the pagan priests appointed by the kings of Judah to burn incense on the high places of the towns of Judah and on those around Jerusalem—those who burned incense to Baal, to the sun and moon, to the constellations and to all the starry hosts. 6He took the Asherah pole from the temple of the LORD to the Kidron Valley outside Jerusalem and burned it there. He ground it to powder and scattered the dust over the graves of the common people. 7He also tore down the quarters of the male shrine prostitutes, which were in the temple of the LORD and where women did weaving for Asherah.

8Josiah brought all the priests from the towns of Judah and desecrated the high places, from Geba to Beersheba, where the priests had burned incense. He broke down the shrines[b] at the gates—at the entrance to the Gate of Joshua, the city governor, which is on the left of the city gate. 9Although the priests of the high places did not serve at the altar of the LORD in Jerusalem, they ate unleavened bread with their fellow priests.

10He desecrated Topheth, which was in the Valley of Ben Hinnom, so no one could use it to sacrifice his son or daughter in[c] the fire to Molech. 11He removed from the entrance to the temple of the LORD the horses that the kings of Judah had dedicated to the sun. They were in the court near the room of an official named Nathan-Melech. Josiah then burned the chariots dedicated to the sun.

12He pulled down the altars the kings of Judah had erected on the roof near the upper room of Ahaz, and the altars Manasseh had built in the two courts of the temple of the LORD. He removed them from there, smashed them to pieces and threw the rubble into the Kidron Valley. 13The king also desecrated the high places that were east of Jerusalem on the south of the Hill of Corruption—the ones Solomon king of Israel had built for Ashtoreth the vile goddess of the Sidonians, for Chemosh the vile god of Moab, and for Molech[d] the detestable god of the people of Ammon. 14Josiah smashed the sacred stones and cut down the Asherah poles and covered the sites with human bones.

15Even the altar at Bethel, the high place made by Jeroboam son of Nebat, who had caused Israel to sin—even that altar and high place he demolished. He burned the high place and ground it to powder, and burned the Asherah pole also. 16Then Josiah looked around,

[a] *17* Or *by everything they have done* [b] *8* Or *high places* [c] *10* Or *to make his son or daughter pass through* [d] *13* Hebrew *Milcom*

and when he saw the tombs that were there on
the hillside, he had the bones removed from
them and burned on the altar to defile it, in
accordance with the word of the LORD proclaimed by the man of God who foretold these
things.
17 The king asked, "What is that tombstone I
see?"
The men of the city said, "It marks the tomb
of the man of God who came from Judah and
pronounced against the altar of Bethel the very
things you have done to it."
18 "Leave it alone," he said. "Don't let anyone disturb his bones." So they spared his
bones and those of the prophet who had come
from Samaria.
19 Just as he had done at Bethel, Josiah removed and defiled all the shrines at the high
places that the kings of Israel had built in the
towns of Samaria that had provoked the LORD
to anger. 20 Josiah slaughtered all the priests of
those high places on the altars and burned human bones on them. Then he went back to
Jerusalem.
21 The king gave this order to all the people:
"Celebrate the Passover to the LORD your God,
as it is written in this Book of the Covenant."
22 Not since the days of the judges who led
Israel, nor throughout the days of the kings of
Israel and the kings of Judah, had any such
Passover been observed. 23 But in the eighteenth year of King Josiah, this Passover was
celebrated to the LORD in Jerusalem.
24 Furthermore, Josiah got rid of the mediums and spiritists, the household gods, the
idols and all the other detestable things seen in
Judah and Jerusalem. This he did to fulfill the
requirements of the law written in the book
that Hilkiah the priest had discovered in the
temple of the LORD. 25 Neither before nor after
Josiah was there a king like him who turned to
the LORD as he did—with all his heart and
with all his soul and with all his strength, in
accordance with all the Law of Moses.
26 Nevertheless, the LORD did not turn away
from the heat of his fierce anger, which burned
against Judah because of all that Manasseh had
done to provoke him to anger. 27 So the LORD
said, "I will remove Judah also from my presence as I removed Israel, and I will reject Jerusalem, the city I chose, and this temple, about
which I said, 'There shall my Name be.'[a]"
28 As for the other events of Josiah's reign,
and all he did, are they not written in the book
of the annals of the kings of Judah?
29 While Josiah was king, Pharaoh Neco
king of Egypt went up to the Euphrates River
to help the king of Assyria. King Josiah
marched out to meet him in battle, but Neco
faced him and killed him at Megiddo. 30 Josiah's servants brought his body in a chariot
from Megiddo to Jerusalem and buried him in
his own tomb. And the people of the land took
Jehoahaz son of Josiah and anointed him and
made him king in place of his father.

Jehoahaz King of Judah

31 Jehoahaz was twenty-three years old
when he became king, and he reigned in Jerusalem three months. His mother's name was
Hamutal daughter of Jeremiah; she was from
Libnah. 32 He did evil in the eyes of the LORD,
just as his fathers had done. 33 Pharaoh Neco
put him in chains at Riblah in the land of Hamath[b] so that he might not reign in Jerusalem,
and he imposed on Judah a levy of a hundred
talents[c] of silver and a talent[d] of gold. 34 Pharaoh Neco made Eliakim son of Josiah king in
place of his father Josiah and changed Eliakim's name to Jehoiakim. But he took Jehoahaz and carried him off to Egypt, and there he
died. 35 Jehoiakim paid Pharaoh Neco the silver
and gold he demanded. In order to do so, he
taxed the land and exacted the silver and gold
from the people of the land according to their
assessments.

Jehoiakim King of Judah

36 Jehoiakim was twenty-five years old
when he became king, and he reigned in Jerusalem eleven years. His mother's name was
Zebidah daughter of Pedaiah; she was from
Rumah. 37 And he did evil in the eyes of the
LORD, just as his fathers had done.
24 During Jehoiakim's reign, Nebuchadnezzar king of Babylon invaded the
land, and Jehoiakim became his vassal for
three years. But then he changed his mind and
rebelled against Nebuchadnezzar. 2 The LORD
sent Babylonian,[e] Aramean, Moabite and Ammonite raiders against him. He sent them to
destroy Judah, in accordance with the word
of the LORD proclaimed by his servants the
prophets. 3 Surely these things happened to Judah according to the LORD's command, in order to remove them from his presence because
of the sins of Manasseh and all he had done,
4 including the shedding of innocent blood. For
he had filled Jerusalem with innocent blood,
and the LORD was not willing to forgive.
5 As for the other events of Jehoiakim's
reign, and all he did, are they not written in the
book of the annals of the kings of Judah? 6 Jehoiakim rested with his fathers. And Jehoiachin his son succeeded him as king.
7 The king of Egypt did not march out from
his own country again, because the king of
Babylon had taken all his territory, from the
Wadi of Egypt to the Euphrates River.

Jehoiachin King of Judah

8 Jehoiachin was eighteen years old when
he became king, and he reigned in Jerusalem
three months. His mother's name was Nehush-
ta daughter of Elnathan; she was from Jerusalem. 9 He did evil in the eyes of the LORD, just
as his father had done.

[a] 27 1 Kings 8:29 [b] 33 Hebrew; Septuagint (see also 2 Chron. 36:3) *Neco at Riblah in Hamath removed him*
[c] 33 That is, about 3 3/4 tons (about 3.4 metric tons) [d] 33 That is, about 75 pounds (about 34 kilograms)
[e] 2 Or *Chaldean*

10At that time the officers of Nebuchadnezzar king of Babylon advanced on Jerusalem
and laid siege to it, 11and Nebuchadnezzar
himself came up to the city while his officers
were besieging it. 12Jehoiachin king of Judah,
his mother, his attendants, his nobles and his
officials all surrendered to him.

In the eighth year of the reign of the king of
Babylon, he took Jehoiachin prisoner. 13As the
LORD had declared, Nebuchadnezzar removed
all the treasures from the temple of the LORD
and from the royal palace, and took away all
the gold articles that Solomon king of Israel
had made for the temple of the LORD. 14He
carried into exile all Jerusalem: all the officers
and fighting men, and all the craftsmen and
artisans—a total of ten thousand. Only the
poorest people of the land were left.

15Nebuchadnezzar took Jehoiachin captive
to Babylon. He also took from Jerusalem to
Babylon the king's mother, his wives, his officials and the leading men of the land. 16The
king of Babylon also deported to Babylon the
entire force of seven thousand fighting men,
strong and fit for war, and a thousand craftsmen and artisans. 17He made Mattaniah, Jehoiachin's uncle, king in his place and changed
his name to Zedekiah.

Zedekiah King of Judah

18Zedekiah was twenty-one years old when
he became king, and he reigned in Jerusalem
eleven years. His mother's name was Hamutal
daughter of Jeremiah; she was from Libnah.
19He did evil in the eyes of the LORD, just as
Jehoiakim had done. 20It was because of the
LORD's anger that all this happened to Jerusalem and Judah, and in the end he thrust them
from his presence.

The Fall of Jerusalem

Now Zedekiah rebelled against the king of
Babylon.

25 So in the ninth year of Zedekiah's reign,
on the tenth day of the tenth month,
Nebuchadnezzar king of Babylon marched
against Jerusalem with his whole army. He encamped outside the city and built siege works
all around it. 2The city was kept under siege
until the eleventh year of King Zedekiah. 3By
the ninth day of the ⌞fourth⌟[a] month the famine
in the city had become so severe that there was
no food for the people to eat. 4Then the city
wall was broken through, and the whole army
fled at night through the gate between the two
walls near the king's garden, though the Babylonians[b] were surrounding the city. They fled
toward the Arabah,[c] 5but the Babylonian[d]
army pursued the king and overtook him in the
plains of Jericho. All his soldiers were separated from him and scattered, 6and he was captured. He was taken to the king of Babylon at
Riblah, where sentence was pronounced on
him. 7They killed the sons of Zedekiah before
his eyes. Then they put out his eyes, bound
him with bronze shackles and took him to Babylon.

8On the seventh day of the fifth month, in
the nineteenth year of Nebuchadnezzar king of
Babylon, Nebuzaradan commander of the imperial guard, an official of the king of Babylon,
came to Jerusalem. 9He set fire to the temple of
the LORD, the royal palace and all the houses
of Jerusalem. Every important building he
burned down. 10The whole Babylonian army,
under the commander of the imperial guard,
broke down the walls around Jerusalem.
11Nebuzaradan the commander of the guard
carried into exile the people who remained in
the city, along with the rest of the populace and
those who had gone over to the king of Babylon. 12But the commander left behind some of
the poorest people of the land to work the vineyards and fields.

13The Babylonians broke up the bronze pillars, the movable stands and the bronze Sea
that were at the temple of the LORD and they
carried the bronze to Babylon. 14They also
took away the pots, shovels, wick trimmers,
dishes and all the bronze articles used in the
temple service. 15The commander of the imperial guard took away the censers and sprinkling
bowls—all that were made of pure gold or
silver.

16The bronze from the two pillars, the Sea
and the movable stands, which Solomon had
made for the temple of the LORD, was more
than could be weighed. 17Each pillar was
twenty-seven feet[e] high. The bronze capital
on top of one pillar was four and a half feet[f]
high and was decorated with a network and
pomegranates of bronze all around. The other
pillar, with its network, was similar.

18The commander of the guard took as prisoners Seraiah the chief priest, Zephaniah the
priest next in rank and the three doorkeepers.
19Of those still in the city, he took the officer
in charge of the fighting men and five royal
advisers. He also took the secretary who was
chief officer in charge of conscripting the people of the land and sixty of his men who were
found in the city. 20Nebuzaradan the commander took them all and brought them to the
king of Babylon at Riblah. 21There at Riblah,
in the land of Hamath, the king had them executed.

So Judah went into captivity, away from her
land.

22Nebuchadnezzar king of Babylon appointed Gedaliah son of Ahikam, the son of Shaphan, to be over the people he had left behind
in Judah. 23When all the army officers and
their men heard that the king of Babylon had
appointed Gedaliah as governor, they came to
Gedaliah at Mizpah—Ishmael son of Nethaniah, Johanan son of Kareah, Seraiah son of Tanhumeth the Netophathite, Jaazaniah the son of

a3 See Jer. 52:6. b4 Or *Chaldeans*; also in verses 13, 25 and 26 c4 Or *the Jordan Valley*
d5 Or *Chaldean*; also in verses 10 and 24 e17 Hebrew *eighteen cubits* (about 8.1 meters) f17 Hebrew
three cubits (about 1.3 meters)

the Maacathite, and their men. 24Gedaliah took
an oath to reassure them and their men. "Do
not be afraid of the Babylonian officials," he
said. "Settle down in the land and serve the
king of Babylon, and it will go well with you."
25In the seventh month, however, Ishmael
son of Nethaniah, the son of Elishama, who
was of royal blood, came with ten men and
assassinated Gedaliah and also the men of Judah and the Babylonians who were with him at
Mizpah. 26At this, all the people from the least
to the greatest, together with the army officers,
fled to Egypt for fear of the Babylonians.

Jehoiachin Released

27In the thirty-seventh year of the exile of
Jehoiachin king of Judah, in the year Evil-
Merodach[a] became king of Babylon, he released Jehoiachin from prison on the twenty-
seventh day of the twelfth month. 28He spoke
kindly to him and gave him a seat of honor
higher than those of the other kings who were
with him in Babylon. 29So Jehoiachin put aside
his prison clothes and for the rest of his life ate
regularly at the king's table. 30Day by day the
king gave Jehoiachin a regular allowance as
long as he lived.

1 Chronicles

Historical Records From Adam to Abraham

To Noah's Sons

1 Adam, Seth, Enosh, 2Kenan, Mahalalel,
Jared, 3Enoch, Methuselah, Lamech,
Noah.

4The sons of Noah:[b]
Shem, Ham and Japheth.

The Japhethites

5The sons[c] of Japheth:
Gomer, Magog, Madai, Javan, Tubal,
Meshech and Tiras.
6The sons of Gomer:
Ashkenaz, Riphath[d] and Togarmah.
7The sons of Javan:
Elishah, Tarshish, the Kittim and the
Rodanim.

The Hamites

8The sons of Ham:
Cush, Mizraim,[e] Put and Canaan.
9The sons of Cush:
Seba, Havilah, Sabta, Raamah and
Sabteca.
The sons of Raamah:
Sheba and Dedan.
10Cush was the father[f] of
Nimrod, who grew to be a mighty
warrior on earth.
11Mizraim was the father of
the Ludites, Anamites, Lehabites,
Naphtuhites, 12Pathrusites, Casluhites
(from whom the Philistines came) and
Caphtorites.
13Canaan was the father of
Sidon his firstborn,[g] and of the Hittites, 14Jebusites, Amorites, Girgashites, 15Hivites, Arkites, Sinites,
16Arvadites, Zemarites and Hamathites.

The Semites

17The sons of Shem:
Elam, Asshur, Arphaxad, Lud and
Aram.
The sons of Aram[h]:
Uz, Hul, Gether and Meshech.
18Arphaxad was the father of Shelah,
and Shelah the father of Eber.
19Two sons were born to Eber:
One was named Peleg,[i] because in
his time the earth was divided; his
brother was named Joktan.
20Joktan was the father of
Almodad, Sheleph, Hazarmaveth, Jerah, 21Hadoram, Uzal, Diklah,
22Obal,[j] Abimael, Sheba, 23Ophir,
Havilah and Jobab. All these were
sons of Joktan.

24Shem, Arphaxad,[k] Shelah,
25Eber, Peleg, Reu,
26Serug, Nahor, Terah
27and Abram (that is, Abraham).

The Family of Abraham

28The sons of Abraham:
Isaac and Ishmael.

Descendants of Hagar

29These were their descendants:
Nebaioth the firstborn of Ishmael, Kedar, Adbeel, Mibsam, 30Mishma, Dumah, Massa, Hadad, Tema, 31Jetur,

[a]27 Also called *Amel-Marduk* [b]4 Septuagint; Hebrew does not have *The sons of Noah:* [c]5 *Sons* may mean *descendants* or *successors* or *nations*; also in verses 6-10, 17 and 20. [d]6 Many Hebrew manuscripts and Vulgate (see also Septuagint and Gen. 10:3); most Hebrew manuscripts *Diphath* [e]8 That is, Egypt; also in verse 11 [f]10 *Father* may mean *ancestor* or *predecessor* or *founder*; also in verses 11, 13, 18 and 20. [g]13 Or *of the Sidonians, the foremost* [h]17 One Hebrew manuscript and some Septuagint manuscripts (see also Gen. 10:23); most Hebrew manuscripts do not have this line. [i]19 *Peleg* means *division.* [j]22 Some Hebrew manuscripts and Syriac (see also Gen. 10:28); most Hebrew manuscripts *Ebal* [k]24 Hebrew; some Septuagint manuscripts *Arphaxad, Cainan* (see also note at Gen. 11:10)

Naphish and Kedemah. These were the sons of Ishmael.

Descendants of Keturah

32The sons born to Keturah, Abraham's concubine:
Zimran, Jokshan, Medan, Midian, Ishbak and Shuah.
The sons of Jokshan:
Sheba and Dedan.
33The sons of Midian:
Ephah, Epher, Hanoch, Abida and Eldaah.
All these were descendants of Keturah.

Descendants of Sarah

34Abraham was the father of Isaac.
The sons of Isaac:
Esau and Israel.

Esau's Sons

35The sons of Esau:
Eliphaz, Reuel, Jeush, Jalam and Korah.
36The sons of Eliphaz:
Teman, Omar, Zepho,[a] Gatam and Kenaz;
by Timna: Amalek.[b]
37The sons of Reuel:
Nahath, Zerah, Shammah and Mizzah.

The People of Seir in Edom

38The sons of Seir:
Lotan, Shobal, Zibeon, Anah, Dishon, Ezer and Dishan.
39The sons of Lotan:
Hori and Homam. Timna was Lotan's sister.
40The sons of Shobal:
Alvan,[c] Manahath, Ebal, Shepho and Onam.
The sons of Zibeon:
Aiah and Anah.
41The son of Anah:
Dishon.
The sons of Dishon:
Hemdan,[d] Eshban, Ithran and Keran.
42The sons of Ezer:
Bilhan, Zaavan and Akan.[e]
The sons of Dishan[f]:
Uz and Aran.

The Rulers of Edom

43These were the kings who reigned in Edom before any Israelite king reigned[g]:
Bela son of Beor, whose city was named Dinhabah.
44When Bela died, Jobab son of Zerah from Bozrah succeeded him as king.
45When Jobab died, Husham from the land of the Temanites succeeded him as king.
46When Husham died, Hadad son of Bedad, who defeated Midian in the country of Moab, succeeded him as king. His city was named Avith.
47When Hadad died, Samlah from Masrekah succeeded him as king.
48When Samlah died, Shaul from Rehoboth on the river[h] succeeded him as king.
49When Shaul died, Baal-Hanan son of Acbor succeeded him as king.
50When Baal-Hanan died, Hadad succeeded him as king. His city was named Pau,[i] and his wife's name was Mehetabel daughter of Matred, the daughter of Me-Zahab. 51Hadad also died.

The chiefs of Edom were:
Timna, Alvah, Jetheth, 52Oholibamah, Elah, Pinon, 53Kenaz, Teman, Mibzar, 54Magdiel and Iram. These were the chiefs of Edom.

Israel's Sons

2 These were the sons of Israel:
Reuben, Simeon, Levi, Judah, Issachar, Zebulun, 2Dan, Joseph, Benjamin, Naphtali, Gad and Asher.

Judah

To Hezron's Sons

3The sons of Judah:
Er, Onan and Shelah. These three were born to him by a Canaanite woman, the daughter of Shua. Er, Judah's firstborn, was wicked in the LORD's sight; so the LORD put him to death. 4Tamar, Judah's daughter-in-law, bore him Perez and Zerah. Judah had five sons in all.

5The sons of Perez:
Hezron and Hamul.
6The sons of Zerah:
Zimri, Ethan, Heman, Calcol and Darda[j]—five in all.
7The son of Carmi:
Achar,[k] who brought trouble on Israel

[a] *36* Many Hebrew manuscripts, some Septuagint manuscripts and Syriac (see also Gen. 36:11); most Hebrew manuscripts *Zephi* [b] *36* Some Septuagint manuscripts (see also Gen. 36:12); Hebrew *Gatam, Kenaz, Timna and Amalek* [c] *40* Many Hebrew manuscripts and some Septuagint manuscripts (see also Gen. 36:23); most Hebrew manuscripts *Alian* [d] *41* Many Hebrew manuscripts and some Septuagint manuscripts (see also Gen. 36:26); most Hebrew manuscripts *Hamran* [e] *42* Many Hebrew and Septuagint manuscripts (see also Gen. 36:27); most Hebrew manuscripts *Zaavan, Jaakan* [f] *42* Hebrew *Dishon,* a variant of *Dishan* [g] *43* Or *before an Israelite king reigned over them* [h] *48* Possibly the Euphrates [i] *50* Many Hebrew manuscripts, some Septuagint manuscripts, Vulgate and Syriac (see also Gen. 36:39); most Hebrew manuscripts *Pai* [j] *6* Many Hebrew manuscripts, some Septuagint manuscripts and Syriac (see also 1 Kings 4:31); most Hebrew manuscripts *Dara* [k] *7* *Achar* means *trouble*; *Achar* is called *Achan* in Joshua.

by violating the ban on taking devoted things.[a]

8The son of Ethan:
Azariah.

9The sons born to Hezron were:
Jerahmeel, Ram and Caleb.[b]

From Ram Son of Hezron

10Ram was the father of
Amminadab, and Amminadab the father of Nahshon, the leader of the people of Judah. 11Nahshon was the father of Salmon,[c] Salmon the father of Boaz, 12Boaz the father of Obed and Obed the father of Jesse.

13Jesse was the father of
Eliab his firstborn; the second son was
Abinadab, the third Shimea, 14the
fourth Nethanel, the fifth Raddai,
15the sixth Ozem and the seventh David.
16Their sisters were Zeruiah and
Abigail. Zeruiah's three sons were
Abishai, Joab and Asahel. 17Abigail
was the mother of Amasa, whose father was Jether the Ishmaelite.

Caleb Son of Hezron

18Caleb son of Hezron had children by his
wife Azubah (and by Jerioth). These
were her sons: Jesher, Shobab and Ardon.
19When Azubah died, Caleb
married Ephrath, who bore him Hur.
20Hur was the father of Uri, and Uri
the father of Bezalel.

21Later, Hezron lay with the daughter of
Makir the father of Gilead (he had
married her when he was sixty years
old), and she bore him Segub. 22Segub
was the father of Jair, who controlled twenty-three towns in Gilead.
23(But Geshur and Aram captured
Havvoth Jair,[d] as well as Kenath with its surrounding settlements—sixty towns.) All these were descendants of Makir the father of Gilead.

24After Hezron died in Caleb Ephrathah, Abijah the wife of Hezron bore him Ashhur the father[e] of Tekoa.

Jerahmeel Son of Hezron

25The sons of Jerahmeel the firstborn of Hezron:
Ram his firstborn, Bunah, Oren,
Ozem and[f] Ahijah. 26Jerahmeel had
another wife, whose name was Atarah; she was the mother of Onam.

27The sons of Ram the firstborn of Jerahmeel:
Maaz, Jamin and Eker.

28The sons of Onam:
Shammai and Jada.
The sons of Shammai:
Nadab and Abishur.

29Abishur's wife was named Abihail, who bore him Ahban and Molid.

30The sons of Nadab:
Seled and Appaim. Seled died without children.

31The son of Appaim:
Ishi, who was the father of Sheshan.
Sheshan was the father of Ahlai.

32The sons of Jada, Shammai's brother:
Jether and Jonathan. Jether died without children.

33The sons of Jonathan:
Peleth and Zaza.
These were the descendants of Jerahmeel.

34Sheshan had no sons—only daughters.
He had an Egyptian servant named
Jarha. 35Sheshan gave his daughter in
marriage to his servant Jarha, and she bore him Attai.

36Attai was the father of Nathan,
Nathan the father of Zabad,
37Zabad the father of Ephlal,
Ephlal the father of Obed,
38Obed the father of Jehu,
Jehu the father of Azariah,
39Azariah the father of Helez,
Helez the father of Eleasah,
40Eleasah the father of Sismai,
Sismai the father of Shallum,
41Shallum the father of Jekamiah,
and Jekamiah the father of Elishama.

The Clans of Caleb

42The sons of Caleb the brother of Jerahmeel:
Mesha his firstborn, who was the father of Ziph, and his son Mareshah,[g] who was the father of Hebron.

43The sons of Hebron:
Korah, Tappuah, Rekem and Shema.
44Shema was the father of Raham,
and Raham the father of Jorkeam. Rekem was the father of Shammai.
45The son of Shammai was Maon, and
Maon was the father of Beth Zur.

46Caleb's concubine Ephah was the mother of Haran, Moza and Gazez. Haran was the father of Gazez.

47The sons of Jahdai:
Regem, Jotham, Geshan, Pelet, Ephah and Shaaph.

48Caleb's concubine Maacah was the
mother of Sheber and Tirhanah. 49She
also gave birth to Shaaph the father of
Madmannah and to Sheva the father
of Macbenah and Gibea. Caleb's
daughter was Acsah. 50These were the
descendants of Caleb.

[a]7 The Hebrew term refers to the irrevocable giving over of things or persons to the LORD, often by totally destroying them. [b]9 Hebrew *Kelubai*, a variant of *Caleb* [c]11 Septuagint (see also Ruth 4:21); Hebrew *Salma* [d]23 Or *captured the settlements of Jair* [e]24 *Father* may mean *civic leader* or *military leader*; also in verses 42, 45, 49-52 and possibly elsewhere. [f]25 Or *Oren and Ozem, by* [g]42 The meaning of the Hebrew for this phrase is uncertain.

The sons of Hur the firstborn of Ephrathah:
Shobal the father of Kiriath Jearim,
51 Salma the father of Bethlehem, and
Hareph the father of Beth Gader.
52 The descendants of Shobal the father of
Kiriath Jearim were:
Haroeh, half the Manahathites, 53 and
the clans of Kiriath Jearim: the Ithrites, Puthites, Shumathites and Mishraites. From these descended the Zorathites and Eshtaolites.
54 The descendants of Salma:
Bethlehem, the Netophathites, Atroth Beth Joab, half the Manahathites, the
Zorites, 55 and the clans of scribes[a]
who lived at Jabez: the Tirathites, Shimeathites and Sucathites. These are the Kenites who came from Hammath, the father of the house of Recab.[b]

The Sons of David

3 These were the sons of David born to him in Hebron:
The firstborn was Amnon the son of Ahinoam of Jezreel;
the second, Daniel the son of Abigail of Carmel;
2 the third, Absalom the son of Maacah daughter of Talmai king of Geshur;
the fourth, Adonijah the son of Haggith;
3 the fifth, Shephatiah the son of Abital;
and the sixth, Ithream, by his wife Eglah.
4 These six were born to David in Hebron, where he reigned seven years and six months.
David reigned in Jerusalem thirty-three years,
5 and these were the children born to him there:
Shammua,[c] Shobab, Nathan and Solomon. These four were by Bathsheba[d] daughter of Ammiel.
6 There were
also Ibhar, Elishua,[e] Eliphelet, 7 Nogah, Nepheg, Japhia,
8 Elishama, Eliada and Eliphelet—nine in all.
9 All
these were the sons of David, besides his sons by his concubines. And Tamar was their sister.

The Kings of Judah

10 Solomon's son was Rehoboam,
Abijah his son,
Asa his son,
Jehoshaphat his son,
11 Jehoram[f] his son,
Ahaziah his son,
Joash his son,
12 Amaziah his son,
Azariah his son,
Jotham his son,
13 Ahaz his son,
Hezekiah his son,
Manasseh his son,
14 Amon his son,
Josiah his son.
15 The sons of Josiah:
Johanan the firstborn,
Jehoiakim the second son,
Zedekiah the third,
Shallum the fourth.
16 The successors of Jehoiakim:
Jehoiachin[g] his son,
and Zedekiah.

The Royal Line After the Exile

17 The descendants of Jehoiachin the captive:
Shealtiel his son, 18 Malkiram, Pedaiah, Shenazzar, Jekamiah, Hoshama and Nedabiah.
19 The sons of Pedaiah:
Zerubbabel and Shimei.
The sons of Zerubbabel:
Meshullam and Hananiah.
Shelomith was their sister.
20 There were also five others:
Hashubah, Ohel, Berekiah, Hasadiah and Jushab-Hesed.
21 The descendants of Hananiah:
Pelatiah and Jeshaiah, and the sons of Rephaiah, of Arnan, of Obadiah and of Shecaniah.
22 The descendants of Shecaniah:
Shemaiah and his sons:
Hattush, Igal, Bariah, Neariah and Shaphat—six in all.
23 The sons of Neariah:
Elioenai, Hizkiah and Azrikam—three in all.
24 The sons of Elioenai:
Hodaviah, Eliashib, Pelaiah, Akkub, Johanan, Delaiah and Anani—seven in all.

Other Clans of Judah

4 The descendants of Judah:
Perez, Hezron, Carmi, Hur and Shobal.
2 Reaiah son of Shobal was the father of Jahath, and Jahath the father of Ahumai and Lahad. These were the clans of the Zorathites.
3 These were the sons[h] of Etam:
Jezreel, Ishma and Idbash. Their sister was named Hazzelelponi.
4 Penuel
was the father of Gedor, and Ezer the father of Hushah.
These were the descendants of Hur, the firstborn of Ephrathah and father[i] of Bethlehem.

[a] 55 Or *of the Sopherites* [b] 55 Or *father of Beth Recab* [c] 5 Hebrew *Shimea,* a variant of *Shammua*
[d] 5 One Hebrew manuscript and Vulgate (see also Septuagint and 2 Samuel 11:3); most Hebrew manuscripts *Bathshua* [e] 6 Two Hebrew manuscripts (see also 2 Samuel 5:15 and 1 Chron. 14:5); most Hebrew manuscripts *Elishama* [f] 11 Hebrew *Joram,* a variant of *Jehoram* [g] 16 Hebrew *Jeconiah,* a variant of *Jehoiachin*; also in verse 17 [h] 3 Some Septuagint manuscripts (see also Vulgate); Hebrew *father*
[i] 4 *Father* may mean *civic leader* or *military leader*; also in verses 12, 14, 17, 18 and possibly elsewhere.

[5]Ashhur the father of Tekoa had two wives, Helah and Naarah.
[6]Naarah bore him Ahuzzam, Hepher, Temeni and Haahashtari. These were the descendants of Naarah.
[7]The sons of Helah:
Zereth, Zohar, Ethnan, [8]and Koz, who was the father of Anub and Hazzobebah and of the clans of Aharhel son of Harum.

[9]Jabez was more honorable than his brothers. His mother had named him Jabez,[a] saying, "I gave birth to him in pain." [10]Jabez cried out to the God of Israel, "Oh, that you would bless me and enlarge my territory! Let your hand be with me, and keep me from harm so that I will be free from pain." And God granted his request.

[11]Kelub, Shuhah's brother, was the father of Mehir, who was the father of Eshton. [12]Eshton was the father of Beth Rapha, Paseah and Tehinnah the father of Ir Nahash.[b] These were the men of Recah.

[13]The sons of Kenaz:
Othniel and Seraiah.
The sons of Othniel:
Hathath and Meonothai.[c] [14]Meonothai was the father of Ophrah.
Seraiah was the father of Joab,
the father of Ge Harashim.[d] It was called this because its people were craftsmen.
[15]The sons of Caleb son of Jephunneh:
Iru, Elah and Naam.
The son of Elah:
Kenaz.
[16]The sons of Jehallelel:
Ziph, Ziphah, Tiria and Asarel.
[17]The sons of Ezrah:
Jether, Mered, Epher and Jalon. One of Mered's wives gave birth to Miriam, Shammai and Ishbah the father of Eshtemoa. [18](His Judean wife gave birth to Jered the father of Gedor, Heber the father of Soco, and Jekuthiel the father of Zanoah.) These were the children of Pharaoh's daughter Bithiah, whom Mered had married.
[19]The sons of Hodiah's wife, the sister of Naham:
the father of Keilah the Garmite, and Eshtemoa the Maacathite.
[20]The sons of Shimon:
Amnon, Rinnah, Ben-Hanan and Tilon.
The descendants of Ishi:
Zoheth and Ben-Zoheth.
[21]The sons of Shelah son of Judah:
Er the father of Lecah, Laadah the father of Mareshah and the clans of the linen workers at Beth Ashbea, [22]Jokim, the men of Cozeba, and Joash and Saraph, who ruled in Moab and Jashubi Lehem. (These records are from ancient times.) [23]They were the potters who lived at Netaim and Gederah; they stayed there and worked for the king.

Simeon

[24]The descendants of Simeon:
Nemuel, Jamin, Jarib, Zerah and Shaul;
[25]Shallum was Shaul's son, Mibsam his son and Mishma his son.
[26]The descendants of Mishma:
Hammuel his son, Zaccur his son and Shimei his son.

[27]Shimei had sixteen sons and six daughters, but his brothers did not have many children; so their entire clan did not become as numerous as the people of Judah. [28]They lived in Beersheba, Moladah, Hazar Shual, [29]Bilhah, Ezem, Tolad, [30]Bethuel, Hormah, Ziklag, [31]Beth Marcaboth, Hazar Susim, Beth Biri and Shaaraim. These were their towns until the reign of David. [32]Their surrounding villages were Etam, Ain, Rimmon, Token and Ashan—five towns— [33]and all the villages around these towns as far as Baalath.[e] These were their settlements. And they kept a genealogical record.

[34]Meshobab, Jamlech, Joshah son of Amaziah, [35]Joel, Jehu son of Joshibiah, the son of Seraiah, the son of Asiel, [36]also Elioenai, Jaakobah, Jeshohaiah, Asaiah, Adiel, Jesimiel, Benaiah, [37]and Ziza son of Shiphi, the son of Allon, the son of Jedaiah, the son of Shimri, the son of Shemaiah.

[38]The men listed above by name were leaders of their clans. Their families increased greatly, [39]and they went to the outskirts of Gedor to the east of the valley in search of pasture for their flocks. [40]They found rich, good pasture, and the land was spacious, peaceful and quiet. Some Hamites had lived there formerly.

[41]The men whose names were listed came in the days of Hezekiah king of Judah. They attacked the Hamites in their dwellings and also the Meunites who were there and completely destroyed[f] them, as is evident to this day. Then they settled in their place, because there was pasture for their flocks. [42]And five hundred of these Simeonites, led by Pelatiah, Neariah, Rephaiah and Uzziel, the sons of Ishi, invaded the hill country of Seir. [43]They killed the remaining Amalekites who had escaped, and they have lived there to this day.

Reuben

5 The sons of Reuben the firstborn of Israel (he was the firstborn, but when he defiled

[a]9 *Jabez* sounds like the Hebrew for *pain.* [b]12 Or *of the city of Nahash* [c]13 Some Septuagint manuscripts and Vulgate; Hebrew does not have *and Meonothai.* [d]14 *Ge Harashim* means *valley of craftsmen.* [e]33 Some Septuagint manuscripts (see also Joshua 19:8); Hebrew *Baal* [f]41 The Hebrew term refers to the irrevocable giving over of things or persons to the LORD, often by totally destroying them.

his father's marriage bed, his rights as firstborn
were given to the sons of Joseph son of Israel;
so he could not be listed in the genealogical
record in accordance with his birthright, 2and
though Judah was the strongest of his brothers
and a ruler came from him, the rights of the
firstborn belonged to Joseph)— 3the sons of
Reuben the firstborn of Israel:

Hanoch, Pallu, Hezron and Carmi.

4The descendants of Joel:

Shemaiah his son, Gog his son,
Shimei his son, 5Micah his son,
Reaiah his son, Baal his son,
6and Beerah his son, whom Tiglath-
Pileser[a] king of Assyria took into exile. Beerah was a leader of the Reubenites.

7Their relatives by clans, listed according
to their genealogical records:

Jeiel the chief, Zechariah, 8and Bela
son of Azaz, the son of Shema, the
son of Joel. They settled in the area
from Aroer to Nebo and Baal Meon.
9To the east they occupied the land up
to the edge of the desert that extends
to the Euphrates River, because their
livestock had increased in Gilead.

10During Saul's reign they waged war
against the Hagrites, who were defeated
at their hands; they occupied the dwellings of the Hagrites throughout the entire region east of Gilead.

Gad

11The Gadites lived next to them in Bashan, as far as Salecah:

12Joel was the chief, Shapham the second, then Janai and Shaphat, in Bashan.

13Their relatives, by families, were:

Michael, Meshullam, Sheba, Jorai, Ja-
can, Zia and Eber—seven in all.

14These were the sons of Abihail son of
Huri, the son of Jaroah, the son of
Gilead, the son of Michael, the son of
Jeshishai, the son of Jahdo, the son of
Buz.

15Ahi son of Abdiel, the son of Guni,
was head of their family.

16The Gadites lived in Gilead, in Bashan
and its outlying villages, and on all
the pasturelands of Sharon as far as
they extended.

17All these were entered in the genealogical
records during the reigns of Jotham king of
Judah and Jeroboam king of Israel.

18The Reubenites, the Gadites and the half-
tribe of Manasseh had 44,760 men ready for
military service—able-bodied men who could
handle shield and sword, who could use a bow,
and who were trained for battle. 19They waged
war against the Hagrites, Jetur, Naphish and
Nodab. 20They were helped in fighting them,
and God handed the Hagrites and all their allies over to them, because they cried out to him
during the battle. He answered their prayers,
because they trusted in him. 21They seized the
livestock of the Hagrites—fifty thousand camels, two hundred fifty thousand sheep and two
thousand donkeys. They also took one hundred
thousand people captive, 22and many others
fell slain, because the battle was God's. And
they occupied the land until the exile.

The Half-Tribe of Manasseh

23The people of the half-tribe of Manasseh
were numerous; they settled in the land from
Bashan to Baal Hermon, that is, to Senir
(Mount Hermon).

24These were the heads of their families:
Epher, Ishi, Eliel, Azriel, Jeremiah, Hodaviah
and Jahdiel. They were brave warriors, famous
men, and heads of their families. 25But they
were unfaithful to the God of their fathers and
prostituted themselves to the gods of the peoples of the land, whom God had destroyed before them. 26So the God of Israel stirred up the
spirit of Pul king of Assyria (that is, Tiglath-
Pileser king of Assyria), who took the Reubenites, the Gadites and the half-tribe of Manasseh into exile. He took them to Halah, Habor,
Hara and the river of Gozan, where they are to
this day.

Levi

6 The sons of Levi:

Gershon, Kohath and Merari.

2The sons of Kohath:

Amram, Izhar, Hebron and Uzziel.

3The children of Amram:

Aaron, Moses and Miriam.

The sons of Aaron:

Nadab, Abihu, Eleazar and Ithamar.
4Eleazar was the father of Phinehas,
Phinehas the father of Abishua,
5Abishua the father of Bukki,
Bukki the father of Uzzi,
6Uzzi the father of Zerahiah,
Zerahiah the father of Meraioth,
7Meraioth the father of Amariah,
Amariah the father of Ahitub,
8Ahitub the father of Zadok,
Zadok the father of Ahimaaz,
9Ahimaaz the father of Azariah,
Azariah the father of Johanan,
10Johanan the father of Azariah (it was
he who served as priest in the temple
Solomon built in Jerusalem),
11Azariah the father of Amariah,
Amariah the father of Ahitub,
12Ahitub the father of Zadok,
Zadok the father of Shallum,
13Shallum the father of Hilkiah,
Hilkiah the father of Azariah,
14Azariah the father of Seraiah,
and Seraiah the father of Jehozadak.

15Jehozadak was deported when the LORD
sent Judah and Jerusalem into exile by
the hand of Nebuchadnezzar.

16The sons of Levi:

[a]6 Hebrew *Tilgath-Pilneser,* a variant of *Tiglath-Pileser*; also in verse 26

Gershon,[a] Kohath and Merari.
17These are the names of the sons of Gershon:
Libni and Shimei.
18The sons of Kohath:
Amram, Izhar, Hebron and Uzziel.
19The sons of Merari:
Mahli and Mushi.
These are the clans of the Levites listed according to their fathers:
20Of Gershon:
Libni his son, Jehath his son,
Zimmah his son, 21Joah his son,
Iddo his son, Zerah his son
and Jeatherai his son.
22The descendants of Kohath:
Amminadab his son, Korah his son,
Assir his son, 23Elkanah his son,
Ebiasaph his son, Assir his son,
24Tahath his son, Uriel his son,
Uzziah his son and Shaul his son.
25The descendants of Elkanah:
Amasai, Ahimoth,
26Elkanah his son,[b] Zophai his son,
Nahath his son, 27Eliab his son,
Jeroham his son, Elkanah his son
and Samuel his son.[c]
28The sons of Samuel:
Joel[d] the firstborn
and Abijah the second son.
29The descendants of Merari:
Mahli, Libni his son,
Shimei his son, Uzzah his son,
30Shimea his son, Haggiah his son
and Asaiah his son.

The Temple Musicians

31These are the men David put in charge of
the music in the house of the LORD after the
ark came to rest there. 32They ministered with
music before the tabernacle, the Tent of Meeting, until Solomon built the temple of the LORD in Jerusalem. They performed their duties according to the regulations laid down for them.
33Here are the men who served, together with their sons:
From the Kohathites:
Heman, the musician,
the son of Joel, the son of Samuel,
34the son of Elkanah, the son of Jeroham,
the son of Eliel, the son of Toah,
35the son of Zuph, the son of Elkanah,
the son of Mahath, the son of Amasai,
36the son of Elkanah, the son of Joel,
the son of Azariah, the son of Zephaniah,
37the son of Tahath, the son of Assir,
the son of Ebiasaph, the son of Korah,
38the son of Izhar, the son of Kohath,
the son of Levi, the son of Israel;
39and Heman's associate Asaph, who served at his right hand:
Asaph son of Berekiah, the son of Shimea,
40the son of Michael, the son of Baaseiah,[e]
the son of Malkijah, 41the son of Ethni,
the son of Zerah, the son of Adaiah,
42the son of Ethan, the son of Zimmah,
the son of Shimei, 43the son of Jahath,
the son of Gershon, the son of Levi;
44and from their associates, the Merarites, at his left hand:
Ethan son of Kishi, the son of Abdi,
the son of Malluch, 45the son of Hashabiah,
the son of Amaziah, the son of Hilkiah,
46the son of Amzi, the son of Bani,
the son of Shemer, 47the son of Mahli,
the son of Mushi, the son of Merari,
the son of Levi.

48Their fellow Levites were assigned to all
the other duties of the tabernacle, the house of
God. 49But Aaron and his descendants were
the ones who presented offerings on the altar of burnt offering and on the altar of incense in connection with all that was done in the Most Holy Place, making atonement for Israel, in accordance with all that Moses the servant of God had commanded.

50These were the descendants of Aaron:
Eleazar his son, Phinehas his son,
Abishua his son, 51Bukki his son,
Uzzi his son, Zerahiah his son,
52Meraioth his son, Amariah his son,
Ahitub his son, 53Zadok his son
and Ahimaaz his son.

54These were the locations of their settlements allotted as their territory (they were assigned to the descendants of Aaron who were from the Kohathite clan, because the first lot was for them):

55They were given Hebron in Judah
with its surrounding pasturelands. 56But
the fields and villages around the city were given to Caleb son of Jephunneh.

57So the descendants of Aaron were
given Hebron (a city of refuge), and Libnah,[f] Jattir, Eshtemoa, 58Hilen, Debir,
59Ashan, Juttah[g] and Beth Shemesh, together with their pasturelands. 60And
from the tribe of Benjamin they were giv-

[a] *16* Hebrew *Gershom,* a variant of *Gershon*; also in verses 17, 20, 43, 62 and 71 [b] *26* Some Hebrew manuscripts, Septuagint and Syriac; most Hebrew manuscripts *Ahimoth* [26] *and Elkanah. The sons of Elkanah:* [c] *27* Some Septuagint manuscripts (see also 1 Samuel 1:19,20 and 1 Chron. 6:33,34); Hebrew does not have *and Samuel his son.* [d] *28* Some Septuagint manuscripts and Syriac (see also 1 Samuel 8:2 and 1 Chron. 6:33); Hebrew does not have *Joel.* [e] *40* Most Hebrew manuscripts; some Hebrew manuscripts, one Septuagint manuscript and Syriac *Maaseiah* [f] *57* See Joshua 21:13; Hebrew *given the cities of refuge: Hebron, Libnah.* [g] *59* Syriac (see also Septuagint and Joshua 21:16); Hebrew does not have *Juttah.*

en Gibeon,[a] Geba, Alemeth and Anathoth, together with their pasturelands.
These towns, which were distributed
among the Kohathite clans, were thirteen
in all.
61The rest of Kohath's descendants were allotted ten towns from the clans of half the tribe
of Manasseh.
62The descendants of Gershon, clan by clan,
were allotted thirteen towns from the tribes of
Issachar, Asher and Naphtali, and from the
part of the tribe of Manasseh that is in Bashan.
63The descendants of Merari, clan by clan,
were allotted twelve towns from the tribes of
Reuben, Gad and Zebulun.
64So the Israelites gave the Levites these
towns and their pasturelands. 65From the tribes
of Judah, Simeon and Benjamin they allotted
the previously named towns.
66Some of the Kohathite clans were given as
their territory towns from the tribe of Ephraim.
67In the hill country of Ephraim they
were given Shechem (a city of refuge),
and Gezer,[b] 68Jokmeam, Beth Horon,
69Aijalon and Gath Rimmon, together
with their pasturelands.
70And from half the tribe of Manasseh
the Israelites gave Aner and Bileam, together with their pasturelands, to the rest
of the Kohathite clans.

71The Gershonites received the following:
From the clan of the half-tribe of Manasseh
they received Golan in Bashan and
also Ashtaroth, together with their
pasturelands;
72from the tribe of Issachar
they received Kedesh, Daberath,
73Ramoth and Anem, together with
their pasturelands;
74from the tribe of Asher
they received Mashal, Abdon, 75Hu-
kok and Rehob, together with their
pasturelands;
76and from the tribe of Naphtali
they received Kedesh in Galilee,
Hammon and Kiriathaim, together
with their pasturelands.

77The Merarites (the rest of the Levites)
received the following:
From the tribe of Zebulun
they received Jokneam, Kartah,[c]
Rimmono and Tabor, together with
their pasturelands;
78from the tribe of Reuben across the Jordan east of Jericho
they received Bezer in the desert, Jahzah, 79Kedemoth and Mephaath, together with their pasturelands;
80and from the tribe of Gad
they received Ramoth in Gilead, Mahanaim, 81Heshbon and Jazer, together with their pasturelands.

Issachar

7 The sons of Issachar:
Tola, Puah, Jashub and Shimron—
four in all.
2The sons of Tola:
Uzzi, Rephaiah, Jeriel, Jahmai, Ibsam
and Samuel—heads of their families.
During the reign of David, the descendants of Tola listed as fighting men in
their genealogy numbered 22,600.
3The son of Uzzi:
Izrahiah.
The sons of Izrahiah:
Michael, Obadiah, Joel and Isshiah.
All five of them were chiefs. 4Accord-
ing to their family genealogy, they
had 36,000 men ready for battle, for
they had many wives and children.
5The relatives who were fighting men belonging to all the clans of Issachar, as
listed in their genealogy, were 87,000
in all.

Benjamin

6Three sons of Benjamin:
Bela, Beker and Jediael.
7The sons of Bela:
Ezbon, Uzzi, Uzziel, Jerimoth and Iri,
heads of families—five in all. Their
genealogical record listed 22,034
fighting men.
8The sons of Beker:
Zemirah, Joash, Eliezer, Elioenai,
Omri, Jeremoth, Abijah, Anathoth
and Alemeth. All these were the sons
of Beker. 9Their genealogical record
listed the heads of families and 20,200
fighting men.
10The son of Jediael:
Bilhan.
The sons of Bilhan:
Jeush, Benjamin, Ehud, Kenaanah,
Zethan, Tarshish and Ahishahar. 11All
these sons of Jediael were heads of
families. There were 17,200 fighting
men ready to go out to war.
12The Shuppites and Huppites were the
descendants of Ir, and the Hushites
the descendants of Aher.

Naphtali

13The sons of Naphtali:
Jahziel, Guni, Jezer and Shillem[d]—
the descendants of Bilhah.

Manasseh

14The descendants of Manasseh:
Asriel was his descendant through his
Aramean concubine. She gave birth to
Makir the father of Gilead. 15Makir took

[a]60 See Joshua 21:17; Hebrew does not have *Gibeon.* [b]67 See Joshua 21:21; Hebrew *given the cities of refuge: Shechem, Gezer.* [c]77 See Septuagint and Joshua 21:34; Hebrew does not have *Jokneam, Kartah.* [d]13 Some Hebrew and Septuagint manuscripts (see also Gen. 46:24 and Num. 26:49); most Hebrew manuscripts *Shallum*

a wife from among the Huppites and Shuppites. His sister's name was Maacah.

Another descendant was named Zelophehad, who had only daughters.

16Makir's wife Maacah gave birth to a son and named him Peresh. His brother was named Sheresh, and his sons were Ulam and Rakem.

17The son of Ulam:
Bedan.

These were the sons of Gilead son of Makir, the son of Manasseh. 18His sister Hammoleketh gave birth to Ishhod, Abiezer and Mahlah.

19The sons of Shemida were:
Ahian, Shechem, Likhi and Aniam.

Ephraim

20The descendants of Ephraim:
Shuthelah, Bered his son,
Tahath his son, Eleadah his son,
Tahath his son, 21Zabad his son
and Shuthelah his son.

Ezer and Elead were killed by the native-born men of Gath, when they went down to seize their livestock. 22Their father Ephraim mourned for them many days, and his relatives came to comfort him. 23Then he lay with his wife again, and she became pregnant and gave birth to a son. He named him Beriah,[a] because there had been misfortune in his family. 24His daughter was Sheerah, who built Lower and Upper Beth Horon as well as Uzzen Sheerah.

25Rephah was his son, Resheph his son,[b]
Telah his son, Tahan his son,
26Ladan his son, Ammihud his son,
Elishama his son, 27Nun his son
and Joshua his son.

28Their lands and settlements included Bethel and its surrounding villages, Naaran to the east, Gezer and its villages to the west, and Shechem and its villages all the way to Ayyah and its villages. 29Along the borders of Manasseh were Beth Shan, Taanach, Megiddo and Dor, together with their villages. The descendants of Joseph son of Israel lived in these towns.

Asher

30The sons of Asher:
Imnah, Ishvah, Ishvi and Beriah.
Their sister was Serah.

31The sons of Beriah:
Heber and Malkiel, who was the father of Birzaith.

32Heber was the father of Japhlet, Shomer and Hotham and of their sister Shua.

33The sons of Japhlet:
Pasach, Bimhal and Ashvath.
These were Japhlet's sons.

34The sons of Shomer:
Ahi, Rohgah,[c] Hubbah and Aram.

35The sons of his brother Helem:
Zophah, Imna, Shelesh and Amal.

36The sons of Zophah:
Suah, Harnepher, Shual, Beri, Imrah,
37Bezer, Hod, Shamma, Shilshah, Ithran[d] and Beera.

38The sons of Jether:
Jephunneh, Pispah and Ara.

39The sons of Ulla:
Arah, Hanniel and Rizia.

40All these were descendants of Asher—heads of families, choice men, brave warriors and outstanding leaders. The number of men ready for battle, as listed in their genealogy, was 26,000.

The Genealogy of Saul the Benjamite

8 Benjamin was the father of Bela his firstborn,
Ashbel the second son, Aharah the third,
2Nohah the fourth and Rapha the fifth.

3The sons of Bela were:
Addar, Gera, Abihud,[e] 4Abishua, Naaman, Ahoah, 5Gera, Shephuphan and Huram.

6These were the descendants of Ehud, who were heads of families of those living in Geba and were deported to Manahath:

7Naaman, Ahijah, and Gera, who deported them and who was the father of Uzza and Ahihud.

8Sons were born to Shaharaim in Moab after he had divorced his wives Hushim and Baara. 9By his wife Hodesh he had Jobab, Zibia, Mesha, Malcam, 10Jeuz, Sakia and Mirmah. These were his sons, heads of families. 11By Hushim he had Abitub and Elpaal.

12The sons of Elpaal:
Eber, Misham, Shemed (who built Ono and Lod with its surrounding villages), 13and Beriah and Shema, who were heads of families of those living in Aijalon and who drove out the inhabitants of Gath.

14Ahio, Shashak, Jeremoth, 15Zebadiah, Arad, Eder, 16Michael, Ishpah and Joha were the sons of Beriah.

17Zebadiah, Meshullam, Hizki, Heber, 18Ishmerai, Izliah and Jobab were the sons of Elpaal.

19Jakim, Zicri, Zabdi, 20Elienai, Zillethai, Eliel, 21Adaiah, Beraiah and Shimrath were the sons of Shimei.

22Ishpan, Eber, Eliel, 23Abdon, Zicri, Hanan, 24Hananiah, Elam, Anthothijah, 25Iphdeiah and Penuel were the sons of Shashak.

26Shamsherai, Shehariah, Athaliah, 27Jaa-

[a]*23 Beriah* sounds like the Hebrew for *misfortune.* [b]*25* Some Septuagint manuscripts; Hebrew does not have *his son.* [c]*34* Or *of his brother Shomer: Rohgah* [d]*37* Possibly a variant of *Jether* [e]*3* Or *Gera the father of Ehud*

reshiah, Elijah and Zicri were the sons of Jeroham.

[28]All these were heads of families, chiefs as listed in their genealogy, and they lived in Jerusalem.

[29]Jeiel[a] the father[b] of Gibeon lived in Gibeon.
His wife's name was Maacah, [30]and
his firstborn son was Abdon, followed
by Zur, Kish, Baal, Ner,[c] Nadab,
[31]Gedor, Ahio, Zeker [32]and Mikloth,
who was the father of Shimeah. They
too lived near their relatives in Jerusalem.

[33]Ner was the father of Kish, Kish the father of Saul, and Saul the father of Jonathan, Malki-Shua, Abinadab and Esh-Baal.[d]

[34]The son of Jonathan:
Merib-Baal,[e] who was the father of Micah.

[35]The sons of Micah:
Pithon, Melech, Tarea and Ahaz.

[36]Ahaz was the father of Jehoaddah, Jehoaddah was the father of Alemeth,
Azmaveth and Zimri, and Zimri was
the father of Moza. [37]Moza was the
father of Binea; Raphah was his son,
Eleasah his son and Azel his son.

[38]Azel had six sons, and these were their names:
Azrikam, Bokeru, Ishmael, Sheariah, Obadiah and Hanan. All these were the sons of Azel.

[39]The sons of his brother Eshek:
Ulam his firstborn, Jeush the second
son and Eliphelet the third. [40]The sons
of Ulam were brave warriors who
could handle the bow. They had many sons and grandsons—150 in all.

All these were the descendants of Benjamin.

9 All Israel was listed in the genealogies recorded in the book of the kings of Israel.

The People in Jerusalem

The people of Judah were taken captive to Babylon because of their unfaithfulness. [2]Now
the first to resettle on their own property in their own towns were some Israelites, priests, Levites and temple servants.

[3]Those from Judah, from Benjamin, and from Ephraim and Manasseh who lived in Jerusalem were:

[4]Uthai son of Ammihud, the son of Omri, the son of Imri, the son of Bani, a descendant of Perez son of Judah.

[5]Of the Shilonites:
Asaiah the firstborn and his sons.

[6]Of the Zerahites:
Jeuel.
The people from Judah numbered 690.

[7]Of the Benjamites:
Sallu son of Meshullam, the son of Hodaviah, the son of Hassenuah;

[8]Ibneiah son of Jeroham; Elah son of Uzzi, the son of Micri; and Meshullam son of Shephatiah, the son of Reuel, the son of Ibnijah.

[9]The people from Benjamin, as listed in their genealogy, numbered 956. All these men were heads of their families.

[10]Of the priests:
Jedaiah; Jehoiarib; Jakin;

[11]Azariah son of Hilkiah, the son of Meshullam, the son of Zadok, the son of Meraioth, the son of Ahitub, the official in charge of the house of God;

[12]Adaiah son of Jeroham, the son of Pashhur, the son of Malkijah; and Maasai son of Adiel, the son of Jahzerah, the son of Meshullam, the son of Meshillemith, the son of Immer.

[13]The priests, who were heads of families, numbered 1,760. They were able men, responsible for ministering in the house of God.

[14]Of the Levites:
Shemaiah son of Hasshub, the son of
Azrikam, the son of Hashabiah, a Merarite; [15]Bakbakkar, Heresh, Galal
and Mattaniah son of Mica, the son of
Zicri, the son of Asaph; [16]Obadiah
son of Shemaiah, the son of Galal, the son of Jeduthun; and Berekiah son of Asa, the son of Elkanah, who lived in the villages of the Netophathites.

[17]The gatekeepers:
Shallum, Akkub, Talmon, Ahiman
and their brothers, Shallum their chief
[18]being stationed at the King's Gate
on the east, up to the present time.
These were the gatekeepers belonging
to the camp of the Levites. [19]Shallum
son of Kore, the son of Ebiasaph, the son of Korah, and his fellow gatekeepers from his family (the Korahites) were responsible for guarding the thresholds of the Tent[f] just as their fathers had been responsible for guarding the entrance to the dwelling
of the LORD. [20]In earlier times Phine-
has son of Eleazar was in charge of the gatekeepers, and the LORD was
with him. [21]Zechariah son of Meshelemiah was the gatekeeper at the entrance to the Tent of Meeting.

[22]Altogether, those chosen to be gatekeepers at the thresholds numbered 212. They were registered by genealogy in their villages. The gatekeepers had been assigned to their posi-

[a]*29* Some Septuagint manuscripts (see also 1 Chron. 9:35); Hebrew does not have *Jeiel.* [b]*29* *Father* may mean *civic leader* or *military leader.* [c]*30* Some Septuagint manuscripts (see also 1 Chron. 9:36); Hebrew does not have *Ner.* [d]*33* Also known as *Ish-Bosheth* [e]*34* Also known as *Mephibosheth* [f]*19* That is, the temple; also in verses 21 and 23

tions of trust by David and Samuel the seer. 23They and their descendants were in charge of guarding the gates of the house of the LORD—the house called the Tent. 24The gatekeepers were on the four sides: east, west, north and south. 25Their brothers in their villages had to come from time to time and share their duties for seven-day periods. 26But the four principal gatekeepers, who were Levites, were entrusted with the responsibility for the rooms and treasuries in the house of God. 27They would spend the night stationed around the house of God, because they had to guard it; and they had charge of the key for opening it each morning.

28Some of them were in charge of the articles used in the temple service; they counted them when they were brought in and when they were taken out. 29Others were assigned to take care of the furnishings and all the other articles of the sanctuary, as well as the flour and wine, and the oil, incense and spices. 30But some of the priests took care of mixing the spices. 31A Levite named Mattithiah, the firstborn son of Shallum the Korahite, was entrusted with the responsibility for baking the offering bread. 32Some of their Kohathite brothers were in charge of preparing for every Sabbath the bread set out on the table.

33Those who were musicians, heads of Levite families, stayed in the rooms of the temple and were exempt from other duties because they were responsible for the work day and night.

34All these were heads of Levite families, chiefs as listed in their genealogy, and they lived in Jerusalem.

The Genealogy of Saul

35Jeiel the father[a] of Gibeon lived in Gibeon.
His wife's name was Maacah, 36and his firstborn son was Abdon, followed by Zur, Kish, Baal, Ner, Nadab, 37Gedor, Ahio, Zechariah and Mikloth. 38Mikloth was the father of Shimeam. They too lived near their relatives in Jerusalem.

39Ner was the father of Kish, Kish the father of Saul, and Saul the father of Jonathan, Malki-Shua, Abinadab and Esh-Baal.[b]

40The son of Jonathan:
Merib-Baal,[c] who was the father of Micah.

41The sons of Micah:
Pithon, Melech, Tahrea and Ahaz.[d]
42Ahaz was the father of Jadah, Jadah[e] was the father of Alemeth, Azmaveth and Zimri, and Zimri was the father of Moza. 43Moza was the father of Binea; Rephaiah was his son, Eleasah his son and Azel his son.

44Azel had six sons, and these were their names:
Azrikam, Bokeru, Ishmael, Sheariah, Obadiah and Hanan. These were the sons of Azel.

Saul Takes His Life

10 Now the Philistines fought against Israel; the Israelites fled before them, and many fell slain on Mount Gilboa. 2The Philistines pressed hard after Saul and his sons, and they killed his sons Jonathan, Abinadab and Malki-Shua. 3The fighting grew fierce around Saul, and when the archers overtook him, they wounded him.

4Saul said to his armor-bearer, "Draw your sword and run me through, or these uncircumcised fellows will come and abuse me."

But his armor-bearer was terrified and would not do it; so Saul took his own sword and fell on it. 5When the armor-bearer saw that Saul was dead, he too fell on his sword and died. 6So Saul and his three sons died, and all his house died together.

7When all the Israelites in the valley saw that the army had fled and that Saul and his sons had died, they abandoned their towns and fled. And the Philistines came and occupied them.

8The next day, when the Philistines came to strip the dead, they found Saul and his sons fallen on Mount Gilboa. 9They stripped him and took his head and his armor, and sent messengers throughout the land of the Philistines to proclaim the news among their idols and their people. 10They put his armor in the temple of their gods and hung up his head in the temple of Dagon.

11When all the inhabitants of Jabesh Gilead heard of everything the Philistines had done to Saul, 12all their valiant men went and took the bodies of Saul and his sons and brought them to Jabesh. Then they buried their bones under the great tree in Jabesh, and they fasted seven days.

13Saul died because he was unfaithful to the LORD; he did not keep the word of the LORD and even consulted a medium for guidance, 14and did not inquire of the LORD. So the LORD put him to death and turned the kingdom over to David son of Jesse.

David Becomes King Over Israel

11 All Israel came together to David at Hebron and said, "We are your own flesh and blood. 2In the past, even while Saul was king, you were the one who led Israel on their military campaigns. And the LORD your God said to you, 'You will shepherd my people Israel, and you will become their ruler.' "

3When all the elders of Israel had come to King David at Hebron, he made a compact with them at Hebron before the LORD, and they

[a]35 *Father* may mean *civic leader* or *military leader.* [b]39 Also known as *Ish-Bosheth* [c]40 Also known as *Mephibosheth* [d]41 Vulgate and Syriac (see also Septuagint and 1 Chron. 8:35); Hebrew does not have *and Ahaz.* [e]42 Some Hebrew manuscripts and Septuagint (see also 1 Chron. 8:36); most Hebrew manuscripts *Jarah, Jarah*

anointed David king over Israel, as the LORD
had promised through Samuel.

David Conquers Jerusalem

4David and all the Israelites marched to Jerusalem (that is, Jebus). The Jebusites who
lived there 5said to David, "You will not get in
here." Nevertheless, David captured the fortress of Zion, the City of David.
6David had said, "Whoever leads the attack
on the Jebusites will become commander-in-
chief." Joab son of Zeruiah went up first, and
so he received the command.
7David then took up residence in the fortress, and so it was called the City of David.
8He built up the city around it, from the supporting terraces[a] to the surrounding wall,
while Joab restored the rest of the city. 9And
David became more and more powerful, because the LORD Almighty was with him.

David's Mighty Men

10These were the chiefs of David's mighty
men—they, together with all Israel, gave his
kingship strong support to extend it over the
whole land, as the LORD had promised—
11this is the list of David's mighty men:
Jashobeam,[b] a Hacmonite, was chief of the
officers[c]; he raised his spear against three hundred men, whom he killed in one encounter.
12Next to him was Eleazar son of Dodai the
Ahohite, one of the three mighty men. 13He
was with David at Pas Dammim when the Philistines gathered there for battle. At a place
where there was a field full of barley, the
troops fled from the Philistines. 14But they
took their stand in the middle of the field. They
defended it and struck the Philistines down,
and the LORD brought about a great victory.
15Three of the thirty chiefs came down to
David to the rock at the cave of Adullam,
while a band of Philistines was encamped in
the Valley of Rephaim. 16At that time David
was in the stronghold, and the Philistine garrison was at Bethlehem. 17David longed for water and said, "Oh, that someone would get me
a drink of water from the well near the gate of
Bethlehem!" 18So the Three broke through the
Philistine lines, drew water from the well near
the gate of Bethlehem and carried it back to
David. But he refused to drink it; instead, he
poured it out before the LORD. 19"God forbid
that I should do this!" he said. "Should I drink
the blood of these men who went at the risk of
their lives?" Because they risked their lives to
bring it back, David would not drink it.
Such were the exploits of the three mighty
men.
20Abishai the brother of Joab was chief of
the Three. He raised his spear against three
hundred men, whom he killed, and so he became as famous as the Three. 21He was doubly
honored above the Three and became their
commander, even though he was not included
among them.
22Benaiah son of Jehoiada was a valiant
fighter from Kabzeel, who performed great exploits. He struck down two of Moab's best
men. He also went down into a pit on a snowy
day and killed a lion. 23And he struck down an
Egyptian who was seven and a half feet[d] tall.
Although the Egyptian had a spear like a
weaver's rod in his hand, Benaiah went against
him with a club. He snatched the spear from
the Egyptian's hand and killed him with his
own spear. 24Such were the exploits of Benaiah son of Jehoiada; he too was as famous as
the three mighty men. 25He was held in greater
honor than any of the Thirty, but he was not
included among the Three. And David put him
in charge of his bodyguard.

26The mighty men were:
Asahel the brother of Joab,
Elhanan son of Dodo from Bethlehem,
27Shammoth the Harorite,
Helez the Pelonite,
28Ira son of Ikkesh from Tekoa,
Abiezer from Anathoth,
29Sibbecai the Hushathite,
Ilai the Ahohite,
30Maharai the Netophathite,
Heled son of Baanah the Netopha-
thite,
31Ithai son of Ribai from Gibeah in
Benjamin,
Benaiah the Pirathonite,
32Hurai from the ravines of Gaash,
Abiel the Arbathite,
33Azmaveth the Baharumite,
Eliahba the Shaalbonite,
34the sons of Hashem the Gizonite,
Jonathan son of Shagee the Hararite,
35Ahiam son of Sacar the Hararite,
Eliphal son of Ur,
36Hepher the Mekerathite,
Ahijah the Pelonite,
37Hezro the Carmelite,
Naarai son of Ezbai,
38Joel the brother of Nathan,
Mibhar son of Hagri,
39Zelek the Ammonite,
Naharai the Berothite, the armor-
bearer of Joab son of Zeruiah,
40Ira the Ithrite,
Gareb the Ithrite,
41Uriah the Hittite,
Zabad son of Ahlai,
42Adina son of Shiza the Reubenite,
who was chief of the Reubenites, and
the thirty with him,
43Hanan son of Maacah,
Joshaphat the Mithnite,
44Uzzia the Ashterathite,
Shama and Jeiel the sons of Hotham
the Aroerite,
45Jediael son of Shimri,
his brother Joha the Tizite,
46Eliel the Mahavite,

[a]*8* Or *the Millo* [b]*11* Possibly a variant of *Jashob-Baal* [c]*11* Or *Thirty*; some Septuagint manuscripts *Three* (see also 2 Samuel 23:8) [d]*23* Hebrew *five cubits* (about 2.3 meters)

Jeribai and Joshaviah the sons of Elnaam,
Ithmah the Moabite,
47Eliel, Obed and Jaasiel the Mezobaite.

Warriors Join David

12 These were the men who came to David at Ziklag, while he was banished from the presence of Saul son of Kish (they were among the warriors who helped him in battle; 2they were armed with bows and were able to shoot arrows or to sling stones right-handed or left-handed; they were kinsmen of Saul from the tribe of Benjamin):

3Ahiezer their chief and Joash the sons of Shemaah the Gibeathite; Jeziel and Pelet the sons of Azmaveth; Beracah, Jehu the Anathothite, 4and Ishmaiah the Gibeonite, a mighty man among the Thirty, who was a leader of the Thirty; Jeremiah, Jahaziel, Johanan, Jozabad the Gederathite, 5Eluzai, Jerimoth, Bealiah, Shemariah and Shephatiah the Haruphite; 6Elkanah, Isshiah, Azarel, Joezer and Jashobeam the Korahites; 7and Joelah and Zebadiah the sons of Jeroham from Gedor.

8Some Gadites defected to David at his stronghold in the desert. They were brave warriors, ready for battle and able to handle the shield and spear. Their faces were the faces of lions, and they were as swift as gazelles in the mountains.

9Ezer was the chief,
Obadiah the second in command, Eliab the third,
10Mishmannah the fourth, Jeremiah the fifth,
11Attai the sixth, Eliel the seventh,
12Johanan the eighth, Elzabad the ninth,
13Jeremiah the tenth and Macbannai the eleventh.

14These Gadites were army commanders; the least was a match for a hundred, and the greatest for a thousand. 15It was they who crossed the Jordan in the first month when it was overflowing all its banks, and they put to flight everyone living in the valleys, to the east and to the west.

16Other Benjamites and some men from Judah also came to David in his stronghold. 17David went out to meet them and said to them, "If you have come to me in peace, to help me, I am ready to have you unite with me. But if you have come to betray me to my enemies when my hands are free from violence, may the God of our fathers see it and judge you."

18Then the Spirit came upon Amasai, chief of the Thirty, and he said:

"We are yours, O David!
We are with you, O son of Jesse!
Success, success to you,
and success to those who help you,
for your God will help you."

So David received them and made them leaders of his raiding bands.

19Some of the men of Manasseh defected to David when he went with the Philistines to fight against Saul. (He and his men did not help the Philistines because, after consultation, their rulers sent him away. They said, "It will cost us our heads if he deserts to his master Saul.") 20When David went to Ziklag, these were the men of Manasseh who defected to him: Adnah, Jozabad, Jediael, Michael, Jozabad, Elihu and Zillethai, leaders of units of a thousand in Manasseh. 21They helped David against raiding bands, for all of them were brave warriors, and they were commanders in his army. 22Day after day men came to help David, until he had a great army, like the army of God.[a]

Others Join David at Hebron

23These are the numbers of the men armed for battle who came to David at Hebron to turn Saul's kingdom over to him, as the LORD had said:

24men of Judah, carrying shield and spear—6,800 armed for battle;
25men of Simeon, warriors ready for battle—7,100;
26men of Levi—4,600, 27including Jehoiada, leader of the family of Aaron, with 3,700 men, 28and Zadok, a brave young warrior, with 22 officers from his family;
29men of Benjamin, Saul's kinsmen—3,000, most of whom had remained loyal to Saul's house until then;
30men of Ephraim, brave warriors, famous in their own clans—20,800;
31men of half the tribe of Manasseh, designated by name to come and make David king—18,000;
32men of Issachar, who understood the times and knew what Israel should do—200 chiefs, with all their relatives under their command;
33men of Zebulun, experienced soldiers prepared for battle with every type of weapon, to help David with undivided loyalty—50,000;
34men of Naphtali—1,000 officers, together with 37,000 men carrying shields and spears;
35men of Dan, ready for battle—28,600;
36men of Asher, experienced soldiers prepared for battle—40,000;
37and from east of the Jordan, men of Reuben, Gad and the half-tribe of Manasseh, armed with every type of weapon—120,000.

38All these were fighting men who volunteered to serve in the ranks. They came to Hebron fully determined to make David king over all Israel. All the rest of the Israelites were also of one mind to make David king. 39The men spent three days there with David, eating and

[a]22 Or *a great and mighty army*

drinking, for their families had supplied provisions for them. 40Also, their neighbors from as far away as Issachar, Zebulun and Naphtali came bringing food on donkeys, camels, mules and oxen. There were plentiful supplies of flour, fig cakes, raisin cakes, wine, oil, cattle and sheep, for there was joy in Israel.

Bringing Back the Ark

13 David conferred with each of his officers, the commanders of thousands and commanders of hundreds. 2He then said to the whole assembly of Israel, "If it seems good to you and if it is the will of the LORD our God, let us send word far and wide to the rest of our brothers throughout the territories of Israel, and also to the priests and Levites who are with them in their towns and pasturelands, to come and join us. 3Let us bring the ark of our God back to us, for we did not inquire of[a] it[b] during the reign of Saul." 4The whole assembly agreed to do this, because it seemed right to all the people.

5So David assembled all the Israelites, from the Shihor River in Egypt to Lebo[c] Hamath, to bring the ark of God from Kiriath Jearim. 6David and all the Israelites with him went to Baalah of Judah (Kiriath Jearim) to bring up from there the ark of God the LORD, who is enthroned between the cherubim—the ark that is called by the Name.

7They moved the ark of God from Abinadab's house on a new cart, with Uzzah and Ahio guiding it. 8David and all the Israelites were celebrating with all their might before God, with songs and with harps, lyres, tambourines, cymbals and trumpets.

9When they came to the threshing floor of Kidon, Uzzah reached out his hand to steady the ark, because the oxen stumbled. 10The LORD's anger burned against Uzzah, and he struck him down because he had put his hand on the ark. So he died there before God.

11Then David was angry because the LORD's wrath had broken out against Uzzah, and to this day that place is called Perez Uzzah.[d]

12David was afraid of God that day and asked, "How can I ever bring the ark of God to me?" 13He did not take the ark to be with him in the City of David. Instead, he took it aside to the house of Obed-Edom the Gittite. 14The ark of God remained with the family of Obed-Edom in his house for three months, and the LORD blessed his household and everything he had.

David's House and Family

14 Now Hiram king of Tyre sent messengers to David, along with cedar logs, stonemasons and carpenters to build a palace for him. 2And David knew that the LORD had established him as king over Israel and that his kingdom had been highly exalted for the sake of his people Israel.

3In Jerusalem David took more wives and became the father of more sons and daughters. 4These are the names of the children born to him there: Shammua, Shobab, Nathan, Solomon, 5Ibhar, Elishua, Elpelet, 6Nogah, Nepheg, Japhia, 7Elishama, Beeliada[e] and Eliphelet.

David Defeats the Philistines

8When the Philistines heard that David had been anointed king over all Israel, they went up in full force to search for him, but David heard about it and went out to meet them. 9Now the Philistines had come and raided the Valley of Rephaim; 10so David inquired of God: "Shall I go and attack the Philistines? Will you hand them over to me?"

The LORD answered him, "Go, I will hand them over to you."

11So David and his men went up to Baal Perazim, and there he defeated them. He said, "As waters break out, God has broken out against my enemies by my hand." So that place was called Baal Perazim.[f] 12The Philistines had abandoned their gods there, and David gave orders to burn them in the fire.

13Once more the Philistines raided the valley; 14so David inquired of God again, and God answered him, "Do not go straight up, but circle around them and attack them in front of the balsam trees. 15As soon as you hear the sound of marching in the tops of the balsam trees, move out to battle, because that will mean God has gone out in front of you to strike the Philistine army." 16So David did as God commanded him, and they struck down the Philistine army, all the way from Gibeon to Gezer.

17So David's fame spread throughout every land, and the LORD made all the nations fear him.

The Ark Brought to Jerusalem

15 After David had constructed buildings for himself in the City of David, he prepared a place for the ark of God and pitched a tent for it. 2Then David said, "No one but the Levites may carry the ark of God, because the LORD chose them to carry the ark of the LORD and to minister before him forever."

3David assembled all Israel in Jerusalem to bring up the ark of the LORD to the place he had prepared for it. 4He called together the descendants of Aaron and the Levites:

5From the descendants of Kohath,
  Uriel the leader and 120 relatives;
6from the descendants of Merari,
  Asaiah the leader and 220 relatives;
7from the descendants of Gershon,[g]
  Joel the leader and 130 relatives;
8from the descendants of Elizaphan,

[a]3 Or *we neglected* [b]3 Or *him* [c]5 Or *to the entrance to* [d]11 *Perez Uzzah* means *outbreak against Uzzah.* [e]7 A variant of *Eliada* [f]11 *Baal Perazim* means *the lord who breaks out.* [g]7 Hebrew *Gershom,* a variant of *Gershon*

Shemaiah the leader and 200 relatives;
9from the descendants of Hebron,
Eliel the leader and 80 relatives;
10from the descendants of Uzziel,
Amminadab the leader and 112 relatives.

11Then David summoned Zadok and Abiathar the priests, and Uriel, Asaiah, Joel, Shemaiah, Eliel and Amminadab the Levites. 12He
said to them, "You are the heads of the Levitical families; you and your fellow Levites are to
consecrate yourselves and bring up the ark of
the LORD, the God of Israel, to the place I have
prepared for it. 13It was because you, the Levites, did not bring it up the first time that the
LORD our God broke out in anger against us.
We did not inquire of him about how to do it
in the prescribed way." 14So the priests and
Levites consecrated themselves in order to
bring up the ark of the LORD, the God of Israel.
15And the Levites carried the ark of God with
the poles on their shoulders, as Moses had
commanded in accordance with the word of
the LORD.

16David told the leaders of the Levites to
appoint their brothers as singers to sing joyful
songs, accompanied by musical instruments:
lyres, harps and cymbals.

17So the Levites appointed Heman son of
Joel; from his brothers, Asaph son of Berekiah;
and from their brothers the Merarites, Ethan
son of Kushaiah; 18and with them their brothers next in rank: Zechariah,[a] Jaaziel, Shemiramoth, Jehiel, Unni, Eliab, Benaiah, Maaseiah,
Mattithiah, Eliphelehu, Mikneiah, Obed-Edom
and Jeiel,[b] the gatekeepers.

19The musicians Heman, Asaph and Ethan
were to sound the bronze cymbals; 20Zechari-
ah, Aziel, Shemiramoth, Jehiel, Unni, Eliab,
Maaseiah and Benaiah were to play the lyres
according to *alamoth*,[c] 21and Mattithiah,
Eliphelehu, Mikneiah, Obed-Edom, Jeiel and
Azaziah were to play the harps, directing according to *sheminith*.[c] 22Kenaniah the head
Levite was in charge of the singing; that was
his responsibility because he was skillful at it.
23Berekiah and Elkanah were to be doorkeepers for the ark. 24Shebaniah, Joshaphat,
Nethanel, Amasai, Zechariah, Benaiah and Eliezer the priests were to blow trumpets before
the ark of God. Obed-Edom and Jehiah were
also to be doorkeepers for the ark.

25So David and the elders of Israel and the
commanders of units of a thousand went to
bring up the ark of the covenant of the LORD
from the house of Obed-Edom, with rejoicing.
26Because God had helped the Levites who
were carrying the ark of the covenant of the
LORD, seven bulls and seven rams were sacrificed. 27Now David was clothed in a robe of
fine linen, as were all the Levites who were
carrying the ark, and as were the singers, and
Kenaniah, who was in charge of the singing of
the choirs. David also wore a linen ephod. 28So
all Israel brought up the ark of the covenant of
the LORD with shouts, with the sounding of
rams' horns and trumpets, and of cymbals, and
the playing of lyres and harps.

29As the ark of the covenant of the LORD
was entering the City of David, Michal daughter of Saul watched from a window. And when
she saw King David dancing and celebrating,
she despised him in her heart.

16 They brought the ark of God and set it
inside the tent that David had pitched
for it, and they presented burnt offerings and
fellowship offerings[d] before God. 2After David had finished sacrificing the burnt offerings
and fellowship offerings, he blessed the people
in the name of the LORD. 3Then he gave a loaf
of bread, a cake of dates and a cake of raisins
to each Israelite man and woman.

4He appointed some of the Levites to minister before the ark of the LORD, to make petition, to give thanks, and to praise the LORD, the
God of Israel: 5Asaph was the chief, Zechariah
second, then Jeiel, Shemiramoth, Jehiel, Mattithiah, Eliab, Benaiah, Obed-Edom and Jeiel.
They were to play the lyres and harps, Asaph
was to sound the cymbals, 6and Benaiah and
Jahaziel the priests were to blow the trumpets
regularly before the ark of the covenant of
God.

David's Psalm of Thanks

7That day David first committed to Asaph
and his associates this psalm of thanks to the
LORD:

8Give thanks to the LORD, call on his name;
make known among the nations what he has done.
9Sing to him, sing praise to him;
tell of all his wonderful acts.
10Glory in his holy name;
let the hearts of those who seek the LORD rejoice.
11Look to the LORD and his strength;
seek his face always.
12Remember the wonders he has done,
his miracles, and the judgments he pronounced,
13O descendants of Israel his servant,
O sons of Jacob, his chosen ones.

14He is the LORD our God;
his judgments are in all the earth.
15He remembers[e] his covenant forever,
the word he commanded, for a thousand generations,
16the covenant he made with Abraham,
the oath he swore to Isaac.
17He confirmed it to Jacob as a decree,
to Israel as an everlasting covenant:

[a] *18* Three Hebrew manuscripts and most Septuagint manuscripts (see also verse 20 and 1 Chron. 16:5); most Hebrew manuscripts *Zechariah son and* or *Zechariah, Ben and* [b] *18* Hebrew; Septuagint (see also verse 21) *Jeiel and Azaziah* [c] *20,21* Probably a musical term [d] *1* Traditionally *peace offerings*; also in verse 2
[e] *15* Some Septuagint manuscripts (see also Psalm 105:8); Hebrew *Remember*

18 "To you I will give the land of Canaan
as the portion you will inherit."

19 When they were but few in number,
few indeed, and strangers in it,
20 they[a] wandered from nation to nation,
from one kingdom to another.
21 He allowed no man to oppress them;
for their sake he rebuked kings:
22 "Do not touch my anointed ones;
do my prophets no harm."

23 Sing to the LORD, all the earth;
proclaim his salvation day after day.
24 Declare his glory among the nations,
his marvelous deeds among all peoples.
25 For great is the LORD and most worthy of
praise;
he is to be feared above all gods.
26 For all the gods of the nations are idols,
but the LORD made the heavens.
27 Splendor and majesty are before him;
strength and joy in his dwelling place.
28 Ascribe to the LORD, O families of
nations,
ascribe to the LORD glory and strength,
29 ascribe to the LORD the glory due his
name.
Bring an offering and come before him;
worship the LORD in the splendor of
his[b] holiness.
30 Tremble before him, all the earth!
The world is firmly established; it
cannot be moved.
31 Let the heavens rejoice, let the earth be
glad;
let them say among the nations, "The
LORD reigns!"
32 Let the sea resound, and all that is in it;
let the fields be jubilant, and everything
in them!
33 Then the trees of the forest will sing,
they will sing for joy before the LORD,
for he comes to judge the earth.

34 Give thanks to the LORD, for he is good;
his love endures forever.
35 Cry out, "Save us, O God our Savior;
gather us and deliver us from the
nations,
that we may give thanks to your holy
name,
that we may glory in your praise."
36 Praise be to the LORD, the God of Israel,
from everlasting to everlasting.

Then all the people said "Amen" and "Praise
the LORD."

37 David left Asaph and his associates before
the ark of the covenant of the LORD to minister
there regularly, according to each day's requirements. 38 He also left Obed-Edom and his
sixty-eight associates to minister with them.
Obed-Edom son of Jeduthun, and also Hosah,
were gatekeepers.

39 David left Zadok the priest and his fellow
priests before the tabernacle of the LORD at the
high place in Gibeon 40 to present burnt offerings to the LORD on the altar of burnt offering
regularly, morning and evening, in accordance
with everything written in the Law of the
LORD, which he had given Israel. 41 With them
were Heman and Jeduthun and the rest of those
chosen and designated by name to give thanks
to the LORD, "for his love endures forever."
42 Heman and Jeduthun were responsible for
the sounding of the trumpets and cymbals and
for the playing of the other instruments for
sacred song. The sons of Jeduthun were stationed at the gate.

43 Then all the people left, each for his own
home, and David returned home to bless his
family.

God's Promise to David

17 After David was settled in his palace, he
said to Nathan the prophet, "Here I am,
living in a palace of cedar, while the ark of the
covenant of the LORD is under a tent."

2 Nathan replied to David, "Whatever you
have in mind, do it, for God is with you."

3 That night the word of God came to Nathan, saying:

4 "Go and tell my servant David, 'This
is what the LORD says: You are not the
one to build me a house to dwell in. 5 I
have not dwelt in a house from the day I
brought Israel up out of Egypt to this day.
I have moved from one tent site to another, from one dwelling place to another.
6 Wherever I have moved with all the Israelites, did I ever say to any of their leaders[c] whom I commanded to shepherd my
people, "Why have you not built me a
house of cedar?" '

7 "Now then, tell my servant David,
'This is what the LORD Almighty says: I
took you from the pasture and from following the flock, to be ruler over my people Israel. 8 I have been with you wherever
you have gone, and I have cut off all your
enemies from before you. Now I will
make your name like the names of the
greatest men of the earth. 9 And I will provide a place for my people Israel and will
plant them so that they can have a home
of their own and no longer be disturbed.
Wicked people will not oppress them anymore, as they did at the beginning 10 and
have done ever since the time I appointed
leaders over my people Israel. I will also
subdue all your enemies.

" 'I declare to you that the LORD will
build a house for you: 11 When your days
are over and you go to be with your fathers, I will raise up your offspring to succeed you, one of your own sons, and I will
establish his kingdom. 12 He is the one

[a] *18-20* One Hebrew manuscript, Septuagint and Vulgate (see also Psalm 105:12); most Hebrew manuscripts *inherit, / 19 though you are but few in number, / few indeed, and strangers in it." / 20 They* [b] *29* Or *LORD with the splendor of* [c] *6* Traditionally *judges*; also in verse 10

who will build a house for me, and I will establish his throne forever. **13**I will be his father, and he will be my son. I will never take my love away from him, as I took it away from your predecessor. **14**I will set him over my house and my kingdom forever; his throne will be established forever.' "

15Nathan reported to David all the words of this entire revelation.

David's Prayer

16Then King David went in and sat before the LORD, and he said:

"Who am I, O LORD God, and what is my family, that you have brought me this far? **17**And as if this were not enough in your sight, O God, you have spoken about the future of the house of your servant. You have looked on me as though I were the most exalted of men, O LORD God.

18"What more can David say to you for honoring your servant? For you know your servant, **19**O LORD. For the sake of your servant and according to your will, you have done this great thing and made known all these great promises.

20"There is no one like you, O LORD, and there is no God but you, as we have heard with our own ears. **21**And who is like your people Israel—the one nation on earth whose God went out to redeem a people for himself, and to make a name for yourself, and to perform great and awesome wonders by driving out nations from before your people, whom you redeemed from Egypt? **22**You made your people Israel your very own forever, and you, O LORD, have become their God.

23"And now, LORD, let the promise you have made concerning your servant and his house be established forever. Do as you promised, **24**so that it will be established and that your name will be great forever. Then men will say, 'The LORD Almighty, the God over Israel, is Israel's God!' And the house of your servant David will be established before you.

25"You, my God, have revealed to your servant that you will build a house for him. So your servant has found courage to pray to you. **26**O LORD, you are God! You have promised these good things to your servant. **27**Now you have been pleased to bless the house of your servant, that it may continue forever in your sight; for you, O LORD, have blessed it, and it will be blessed forever."

David's Victories

18 In the course of time, David defeated the Philistines and subdued them, and he took Gath and its surrounding villages from the control of the Philistines.

2David also defeated the Moabites, and they became subject to him and brought tribute.

3Moreover, David fought Hadadezer king of Zobah, as far as Hamath, when he went to establish his control along the Euphrates River. **4**David captured a thousand of his chariots, seven thousand charioteers and twenty thousand foot soldiers. He hamstrung all but a hundred of the chariot horses.

5When the Arameans of Damascus came to help Hadadezer king of Zobah, David struck down twenty-two thousand of them. **6**He put garrisons in the Aramean kingdom of Damascus, and the Arameans became subject to him and brought tribute. The LORD gave David victory everywhere he went.

7David took the gold shields carried by the officers of Hadadezer and brought them to Jerusalem. **8**From Tebah[a] and Cun, towns that belonged to Hadadezer, David took a great quantity of bronze, which Solomon used to make the bronze Sea, the pillars and various bronze articles.

9When Tou king of Hamath heard that David had defeated the entire army of Hadadezer king of Zobah, **10**he sent his son Hadoram to King David to greet him and congratulate him on his victory in battle over Hadadezer, who had been at war with Tou. Hadoram brought all kinds of articles of gold and silver and bronze.

11King David dedicated these articles to the LORD, as he had done with the silver and gold he had taken from all these nations: Edom and Moab, the Ammonites and the Philistines, and Amalek.

12Abishai son of Zeruiah struck down eighteen thousand Edomites in the Valley of Salt. **13**He put garrisons in Edom, and all the Edomites became subject to David. The LORD gave David victory everywhere he went.

David's Officials

14David reigned over all Israel, doing what was just and right for all his people. **15**Joab son of Zeruiah was over the army; Jehoshaphat son of Ahilud was recorder; **16**Zadok son of Ahitub and Ahimelech[b] son of Abiathar were priests; Shavsha was secretary; **17**Benaiah son of Jehoiada was over the Kerethites and Pelethites; and David's sons were chief officials at the king's side.

The Battle Against the Ammonites

19 In the course of time, Nahash king of the Ammonites died, and his son succeeded him as king. **2**David thought, "I will show kindness to Hanun son of Nahash, because his father showed kindness to me." So David sent a delegation to express his sympathy to Hanun concerning his father.

When David's men came to Hanun in the land of the Ammonites to express sympathy to

[a] *8* Hebrew *Tibhath,* a variant of *Tebah* [b] *16* Some Hebrew manuscripts, Vulgate and Syriac (see also 2 Samuel 8:17); most Hebrew manuscripts *Abimelech*

him, 3the Ammonite nobles said to Hanun, "Do you think David is honoring your father by sending men to you to express sympathy? Haven't his men come to you to explore and spy out the country and overthrow it?" 4So Hanun seized David's men, shaved them, cut off their garments in the middle at the buttocks, and sent them away.

5When someone came and told David about the men, he sent messengers to meet them, for they were greatly humiliated. The king said, "Stay at Jericho till your beards have grown, and then come back."

6When the Ammonites realized that they had become a stench in David's nostrils, Hanun and the Ammonites sent a thousand talents[a] of silver to hire chariots and charioteers from Aram Naharaim,[b] Aram Maacah and Zobah. 7They hired thirty-two thousand chariots and charioteers, as well as the king of Maacah with his troops, who came and camped near Medeba, while the Ammonites were mustered from their towns and moved out for battle.

8On hearing this, David sent Joab out with the entire army of fighting men. 9The Ammonites came out and drew up in battle formation at the entrance to their city, while the kings who had come were by themselves in the open country.

10Joab saw that there were battle lines in front of him and behind him; so he selected some of the best troops in Israel and deployed them against the Arameans. 11He put the rest of the men under the command of Abishai his brother, and they were deployed against the Ammonites. 12Joab said, "If the Arameans are too strong for me, then you are to rescue me; but if the Ammonites are too strong for you, then I will rescue you. 13Be strong and let us fight bravely for our people and the cities of our God. The LORD will do what is good in his sight."

14Then Joab and the troops with him advanced to fight the Arameans, and they fled before him. 15When the Ammonites saw that the Arameans were fleeing, they too fled before his brother Abishai and went inside the city. So Joab went back to Jerusalem.

16After the Arameans saw that they had been routed by Israel, they sent messengers and had Arameans brought from beyond the River,[c] with Shophach the commander of Hadadezer's army leading them.

17When David was told of this, he gathered all Israel and crossed the Jordan; he advanced against them and formed his battle lines opposite them. David formed his lines to meet the Arameans in battle, and they fought against him. 18But they fled before Israel, and David killed seven thousand of their charioteers and forty thousand of their foot soldiers. He also killed Shophach the commander of their army.

19When the vassals of Hadadezer saw that they had been defeated by Israel, they made peace with David and became subject to him.

So the Arameans were not willing to help the Ammonites anymore.

The Capture of Rabbah

20 In the spring, at the time when kings go off to war, Joab led out the armed forces. He laid waste the land of the Ammonites and went to Rabbah and besieged it, but David remained in Jerusalem. Joab attacked Rabbah and left it in ruins. 2David took the crown from the head of their king[d]—its weight was found to be a talent[e] of gold, and it was set with precious stones—and it was placed on David's head. He took a great quantity of plunder from the city 3and brought out the people who were there, consigning them to labor with saws and with iron picks and axes. David did this to all the Ammonite towns. Then David and his entire army returned to Jerusalem.

War With the Philistines

4In the course of time, war broke out with the Philistines, at Gezer. At that time Sibbecai the Hushathite killed Sippai, one of the descendants of the Rephaites, and the Philistines were subjugated.

5In another battle with the Philistines, Elhanan son of Jair killed Lahmi the brother of Goliath the Gittite, who had a spear with a shaft like a weaver's rod.

6In still another battle, which took place at Gath, there was a huge man with six fingers on each hand and six toes on each foot—twenty-four in all. He also was descended from Rapha. 7When he taunted Israel, Jonathan son of Shimea, David's brother, killed him.

8These were descendants of Rapha in Gath, and they fell at the hands of David and his men.

David Numbers the Fighting Men

21 Satan rose up against Israel and incited David to take a census of Israel. 2So David said to Joab and the commanders of the troops, "Go and count the Israelites from Beersheba to Dan. Then report back to me so that I may know how many there are."

3But Joab replied, "May the LORD multiply his troops a hundred times over. My lord the king, are they not all my lord's subjects? Why does my lord want to do this? Why should he bring guilt on Israel?"

4The king's word, however, overruled Joab; so Joab left and went throughout Israel and then came back to Jerusalem. 5Joab reported the number of the fighting men to David: In all Israel there were one million one hundred thousand men who could handle a sword, including four hundred and seventy thousand in Judah.

6But Joab did not include Levi and Benjamin in the numbering, because the king's command was repulsive to him. 7This command

[a]6 That is, about 37 tons (about 34 metric tons) [b]6 That is, Northwest Mesopotamia [c]16 That is, the Euphrates [d]2 Or *of Milcom,* that is, Molech [e]2 That is, about 75 pounds (about 34 kilograms)

was also evil in the sight of God; so he punished Israel.

8Then David said to God, "I have sinned greatly by doing this. Now, I beg you, take away the guilt of your servant. I have done a very foolish thing."

9The LORD said to Gad, David's seer, 10"Go and tell David, 'This is what the LORD says: I am giving you three options. Choose one of them for me to carry out against you.' "

11So Gad went to David and said to him, "This is what the LORD says: 'Take your choice: 12three years of famine, three months of being swept away[a] before your enemies, with their swords overtaking you, or three days of the sword of the LORD—days of plague in the land, with the angel of the LORD ravaging every part of Israel.' Now then, decide how I should answer the one who sent me."

13David said to Gad, "I am in deep distress. Let me fall into the hands of the LORD, for his mercy is very great; but do not let me fall into the hands of men."

14So the LORD sent a plague on Israel, and seventy thousand men of Israel fell dead. 15And God sent an angel to destroy Jerusalem. But as the angel was doing so, the LORD saw it and was grieved because of the calamity and said to the angel who was destroying the people, "Enough! Withdraw your hand." The angel of the LORD was then standing at the threshing floor of Araunah[b] the Jebusite.

16David looked up and saw the angel of the LORD standing between heaven and earth, with a drawn sword in his hand extended over Jerusalem. Then David and the elders, clothed in sackcloth, fell facedown.

17David said to God, "Was it not I who ordered the fighting men to be counted? I am the one who has sinned and done wrong. These are but sheep. What have they done? O LORD my God, let your hand fall upon me and my family, but do not let this plague remain on your people."

18Then the angel of the LORD ordered Gad to tell David to go up and build an altar to the LORD on the threshing floor of Araunah the Jebusite. 19So David went up in obedience to the word that Gad had spoken in the name of the LORD.

20While Araunah was threshing wheat, he turned and saw the angel; his four sons who were with him hid themselves. 21Then David approached, and when Araunah looked and saw him, he left the threshing floor and bowed down before David with his face to the ground.

22David said to him, "Let me have the site of your threshing floor so I can build an altar to the LORD, that the plague on the people may be stopped. Sell it to me at the full price."

23Araunah said to David, "Take it! Let my lord the king do whatever pleases him. Look, I will give the oxen for the burnt offerings, the threshing sledges for the wood, and the wheat for the grain offering. I will give all this."

24But King David replied to Araunah, "No, I insist on paying the full price. I will not take for the LORD what is yours, or sacrifice a burnt offering that costs me nothing."

25So David paid Araunah six hundred shekels[c] of gold for the site. 26David built an altar to the LORD there and sacrificed burnt offerings and fellowship offerings.[d] He called on the LORD, and the LORD answered him with fire from heaven on the altar of burnt offering.

27Then the LORD spoke to the angel, and he put his sword back into its sheath. 28At that time, when David saw that the LORD had answered him on the threshing floor of Araunah the Jebusite, he offered sacrifices there. 29The tabernacle of the LORD, which Moses had made in the desert, and the altar of burnt offering were at that time on the high place at Gibeon. 30But David could not go before it to inquire of God, because he was afraid of the sword of the angel of the LORD.

22 Then David said, "The house of the LORD God is to be here, and also the altar of burnt offering for Israel."

Preparations for the Temple

2So David gave orders to assemble the aliens living in Israel, and from among them he appointed stonecutters to prepare dressed stone for building the house of God. 3He provided a large amount of iron to make nails for the doors of the gateways and for the fittings, and more bronze than could be weighed. 4He also provided more cedar logs than could be counted, for the Sidonians and Tyrians had brought large numbers of them to David.

5David said, "My son Solomon is young and inexperienced, and the house to be built for the LORD should be of great magnificence and fame and splendor in the sight of all the nations. Therefore I will make preparations for it." So David made extensive preparations before his death.

6Then he called for his son Solomon and charged him to build a house for the LORD, the God of Israel. 7David said to Solomon: "My son, I had it in my heart to build a house for the Name of the LORD my God. 8But this word of the LORD came to me: 'You have shed much blood and have fought many wars. You are not to build a house for my Name, because you have shed much blood on the earth in my sight. 9But you will have a son who will be a man of peace and rest, and I will give him rest from all his enemies on every side. His name will be Solomon,[e] and I will grant Israel peace and quiet during his reign. 10He is the one who will build a house for my Name. He will be my son, and I will be his father. And I will establish the throne of his kingdom over Israel forever.'

11"Now, my son, the LORD be with you, and

[a] *12* Hebrew; Septuagint and Vulgate (see also 2 Samuel 24:13) *of fleeing* [b] *15* Hebrew *Ornan,* a variant of *Araunah*; also in verses 18-28 [c] *25* That is, about 15 pounds (about 7 kilograms) [d] *26* Traditionally *peace offerings* [e] *9* *Solomon* sounds like and may be derived from the Hebrew for *peace.*

may you have success and build the house of
the LORD your God, as he said you would.
12May the LORD give you discretion and understanding when he puts you in command
over Israel, so that you may keep the law of the
LORD your God. 13Then you will have success
if you are careful to observe the decrees and
laws that the LORD gave Moses for Israel. Be
strong and courageous. Do not be afraid or
discouraged.

14"I have taken great pains to provide for the
temple of the LORD a hundred thousand talents[a] of gold, a million talents[b] of silver,
quantities of bronze and iron too great to be
weighed, and wood and stone. And you may
add to them. 15You have many workmen:
stonecutters, masons and carpenters, as well as
men skilled in every kind of work 16in gold
and silver, bronze and iron—craftsmen beyond number. Now begin the work, and the
LORD be with you."

17Then David ordered all the leaders of Israel to help his son Solomon. 18He said to them,
"Is not the LORD your God with you? And has
he not granted you rest on every side? For he
has handed the inhabitants of the land over to
me, and the land is subject to the LORD and to
his people. 19Now devote your heart and soul
to seeking the LORD your God. Begin to build
the sanctuary of the LORD God, so that you
may bring the ark of the covenant of the LORD
and the sacred articles belonging to God into
the temple that will be built for the Name of
the LORD."

The Levites

23 When David was old and full of years,
he made his son Solomon king over Israel.

2He also gathered together all the leaders of
Israel, as well as the priests and Levites. 3The
Levites thirty years old or more were counted,
and the total number of men was thirty-eight
thousand. 4David said, "Of these, twenty-four
thousand are to supervise the work of the temple of the LORD and six thousand are to be
officials and judges. 5Four thousand are to be
gatekeepers and four thousand are to praise the
LORD with the musical instruments I have provided for that purpose."

6David divided the Levites into groups corresponding to the sons of Levi: Gershon, Kohath and Merari.

Gershonites

7Belonging to the Gershonites:
Ladan and Shimei.
8The sons of Ladan:
Jehiel the first, Zetham and Joel—
three in all.
9The sons of Shimei:
Shelomoth, Haziel and Haran—three
in all.
These were the heads of the families
of Ladan.
10And the sons of Shimei:
Jahath, Ziza,[c] Jeush and Beriah.
These were the sons of Shimei—four
in all.
11Jahath was the first and Ziza the second, but Jeush and Beriah did not
have many sons; so they were counted
as one family with one assignment.

Kohathites

12The sons of Kohath:
Amram, Izhar, Hebron and Uzziel—
four in all.
13The sons of Amram:
Aaron and Moses.
Aaron was set apart, he and his
descendants forever, to consecrate the
most holy things, to offer sacrifices
before the LORD, to minister before
him and to pronounce blessings in his
name forever. 14The sons of Moses
the man of God were counted as part
of the tribe of Levi.
15The sons of Moses:
Gershom and Eliezer.
16The descendants of Gershom:
Shubael was the first.
17The descendants of Eliezer:
Rehabiah was the first.
Eliezer had no other sons, but the sons
of Rehabiah were very numerous.
18The sons of Izhar:
Shelomith was the first.
19The sons of Hebron:
Jeriah the first, Amariah the second,
Jahaziel the third and Jekameam the
fourth.
20The sons of Uzziel:
Micah the first and Isshiah the second.

Merarites

21The sons of Merari:
Mahli and Mushi.
The sons of Mahli:
Eleazar and Kish.
22Eleazar died without having sons: he
had only daughters. Their cousins, the
sons of Kish, married them.
23The sons of Mushi:
Mahli, Eder and Jerimoth—three in
all.

24These were the descendants of Levi by
their families—the heads of families as they
were registered under their names and counted
individually, that is, the workers twenty years
old or more who served in the temple of the
LORD. 25For David had said, "Since the LORD,
the God of Israel, has granted rest to his people
and has come to dwell in Jerusalem forever,
26the Levites no longer need to carry the tabernacle or any of the articles used in its service."

[a] *14* That is, about 3,750 tons (about 3,450 metric tons) [b] *14* That is, about 37,500 tons (about 34,500 metric tons) [c] *10* One Hebrew manuscript, Septuagint and Vulgate (see also verse 11); most Hebrew manuscripts *Zina*

27According to the last instructions of David,
the Levites were counted from those twenty
years old or more.

28The duty of the Levites was to help Aaron's descendants in the service of the temple
of the LORD: to be in charge of the courtyards,
the side rooms, the purification of all sacred
things and the performance of other duties at
the house of God. 29They were in charge of the
bread set out on the table, the flour for the
grain offerings, the unleavened wafers,
the baking and the mixing, and all measurements of quantity and size. 30They were also to
stand every morning to thank and praise the
LORD. They were to do the same in the evening
31and whenever burnt offerings were presented
to the LORD on Sabbaths and at New Moon
festivals and at appointed feasts. They were to
serve before the LORD regularly in the proper
number and in the way prescribed for them.

32And so the Levites carried out their responsibilities for the Tent of Meeting, for the
Holy Place and, under their brothers the
descendants of Aaron, for the service of
the temple of the LORD.

The Divisions of Priests

24 These were the divisions of the sons of Aaron:
The sons of Aaron were Nadab, Abihu, Eleazar and Ithamar. 2But Nadab and Abihu died
before their father did, and they had no sons;
so Eleazar and Ithamar served as the priests.
3With the help of Zadok a descendant of Eleazar and Ahimelech a descendant of Ithamar,
David separated them into divisions for their
appointed order of ministering. 4A larger number of leaders were found among Eleazar's
descendants than among Ithamar's, and they
were divided accordingly: sixteen heads of
families from Eleazar's descendants and eight
heads of families from Ithamar's descendants.
5They divided them impartially by drawing
lots, for there were officials of the sanctuary
and officials of God among the descendants of
both Eleazar and Ithamar.

6The scribe Shemaiah son of Nethanel, a
Levite, recorded their names in the presence of
the king and of the officials: Zadok the priest,
Ahimelech son of Abiathar and the heads of
families of the priests and of the Levites—one
family being taken from Eleazar and then one
from Ithamar.

7The first lot fell to Jehoiarib,
the second to Jedaiah,
8the third to Harim,
the fourth to Seorim,
9the fifth to Malkijah,
the sixth to Mijamin,
10the seventh to Hakkoz,
the eighth to Abijah,
11the ninth to Jeshua,
the tenth to Shecaniah,
12the eleventh to Eliashib,
the twelfth to Jakim,
13the thirteenth to Huppah,
the fourteenth to Jeshebeab,
14the fifteenth to Bilgah,
the sixteenth to Immer,
15the seventeenth to Hezir,
the eighteenth to Happizzez,
16the nineteenth to Pethahiah,
the twentieth to Jehezkel,
17the twenty-first to Jakin,
the twenty-second to Gamul,
18the twenty-third to Delaiah
and the twenty-fourth to Maaziah.

19This was their appointed order of ministering when they entered the temple of the LORD,
according to the regulations prescribed for
them by their forefather Aaron, as the LORD,
the God of Israel, had commanded him.

The Rest of the Levites

20As for the rest of the descendants of Levi:
from the sons of Amram: Shubael;
from the sons of Shubael: Jehdeiah.
21As for Rehabiah, from his sons:
Isshiah was the first.
22From the Izharites: Shelomoth;
from the sons of Shelomoth: Jahath.
23The sons of Hebron: Jeriah the first,[a]
Amariah the second, Jahaziel the third
and Jekameam the fourth.
24The son of Uzziel: Micah;
from the sons of Micah: Shamir.
25The brother of Micah: Isshiah;
from the sons of Isshiah: Zechariah.
26The sons of Merari: Mahli and Mushi.
The son of Jaaziah: Beno.
27The sons of Merari:
from Jaaziah: Beno, Shoham, Zaccur
and Ibri.
28From Mahli: Eleazar, who had no sons.
29From Kish: the son of Kish:
Jerahmeel.
30And the sons of Mushi: Mahli, Eder and
Jerimoth.

These were the Levites, according to their
families. 31They also cast lots, just as their
brothers the descendants of Aaron did, in the
presence of King David and of Zadok, Ahimelech, and the heads of families of the priests
and of the Levites. The families of the oldest
brother were treated the same as those of the
youngest.

The Singers

25 David, together with the commanders of the army, set apart some of the sons of
Asaph, Heman and Jeduthun for the ministry
of prophesying, accompanied by harps, lyres
and cymbals. Here is the list of the men who
performed this service:

2From the sons of Asaph:
Zaccur, Joseph, Nethaniah and Asarelah.
The sons of Asaph were under the super-

[a]23 Two Hebrew manuscripts and some Septuagint manuscripts (see also 1 Chron. 23:19); most Hebrew manuscripts *The sons of Jeriah:*

vision of Asaph, who prophesied under
the king's supervision.
3 As for Jeduthun, from his sons:
Gedaliah, Zeri, Jeshaiah, Shimei,[a] Hashabiah and Mattithiah, six in all, under the supervision of their father Jeduthun, who prophesied, using the harp in thanking and praising the LORD.
4 As for Heman, from his sons:
Bukkiah, Mattaniah, Uzziel, Shubael and Jerimoth; Hananiah, Hanani, Eliathah, Giddalti and Romamti-Ezer; Joshbekashah, Mallothi, Hothir and Mahazioth.
5 All these were sons of Heman the king's seer. They were given him through the promises of God to exalt him.[b] God gave Heman fourteen sons and three daughters.

6 All these men were under the supervision of their fathers for the music of the temple of the LORD, with cymbals, lyres and harps, for the ministry at the house of God. Asaph, Jeduthun and Heman were under the supervision of
the king. 7 Along with their relatives—all of them trained and skilled in music for the
LORD—they numbered 288. 8 Young and old alike, teacher as well as student, cast lots for their duties.

9 The first lot, which was for Asaph,
fell to Joseph,
his sons and relatives,[c] 12[d]
the second to Gedaliah,
he and his relatives and sons, 12
10 the third to Zaccur,
his sons and relatives, 12
11 the fourth to Izri,[e]
his sons and relatives, 12
12 the fifth to Nethaniah,
his sons and relatives, 12
13 the sixth to Bukkiah,
his sons and relatives, 12
14 the seventh to Jesarelah,[f]
his sons and relatives, 12
15 the eighth to Jeshaiah,
his sons and relatives, 12
16 the ninth to Mattaniah,
his sons and relatives, 12
17 the tenth to Shimei,
his sons and relatives, 12
18 the eleventh to Azarel,[g]
his sons and relatives, 12
19 the twelfth to Hashabiah,
his sons and relatives, 12
20 the thirteenth to Shubael,
his sons and relatives, 12
21 the fourteenth to Mattithiah,
his sons and relatives, 12
22 the fifteenth to Jerimoth,
his sons and relatives, 12
23 the sixteenth to Hananiah,
his sons and relatives, 12
24 the seventeenth to
Joshbekashah,
his sons and relatives, 12
25 the eighteenth to Hanani,
his sons and relatives, 12
26 the nineteenth to Mallothi,
his sons and relatives, 12
27 the twentieth to Eliathah,
his sons and relatives, 12
28 the twenty-first to Hothir,
his sons and relatives, 12
29 the twenty-second to Giddalti,
his sons and relatives, 12
30 the twenty-third to Mahazioth,
his sons and relatives, 12
31 the twenty-fourth to Romamti-Ezer,
his sons and relatives, 12

The Gatekeepers

26 The divisions of the gatekeepers:

From the Korahites: Meshelemiah son of Kore, one of the sons of Asaph.
2 Meshelemiah had sons:
Zechariah the firstborn,
Jediael the second,
Zebadiah the third,
Jathniel the fourth,
3 Elam the fifth,
Jehohanan the sixth
and Eliehoenai the seventh.
4 Obed-Edom also had sons:
Shemaiah the firstborn,
Jehozabad the second,
Joah the third,
Sacar the fourth,
Nethanel the fifth,
5 Ammiel the sixth,
Issachar the seventh
and Peullethai the eighth.
(For God had blessed Obed-Edom.)

6 His son Shemaiah also had sons, who were leaders in their father's family because they were very capable men.
7 The sons of Shemaiah: Othni, Rephael, Obed and Elzabad; his relatives Elihu and Semakiah were also able
men. 8 All these were descendants of Obed-Edom; they and their sons and their relatives were capable men with the strength to do the work—descendants of Obed-Edom, 62 in all.
9 Meshelemiah had sons and relatives, who were able men—18 in all.

10 Hosah the Merarite had sons: Shimri the first (although he was not the firstborn, his father had appointed him the
first), 11 Hilkiah the second, Tabaliah the third and Zechariah the fourth. The sons and relatives of Hosah were 13 in all.
12 These divisions of the gatekeepers,

[a] 3 One Hebrew manuscript and some Septuagint manuscripts (see also verse 17); most Hebrew manuscripts do not have *Shimei.* [b] 5 Hebrew *exalt the horn* [c] 9 See Septuagint; Hebrew does not have *his sons and relatives.* [d] 9 See the total in verse 7; Hebrew does not have *twelve.* [e] 11 A variant of *Zeri*
[f] 14 A variant of *Asarelah* [g] 18 A variant of *Uzziel*

through their chief men, had duties for ministering in the temple of the LORD, just as their relatives had. 13Lots were cast for each gate, according to their families, young and old alike.

14The lot for the East Gate fell to Shelemiah.[a] Then lots were cast for his son Zechariah, a wise counselor, and the lot for the North Gate fell to him. 15The lot for the South Gate fell to Obed-Edom, and the lot for the storehouse fell to his sons. 16The lots for the West Gate and the Shalleketh Gate on the upper road fell to Shuppim and Hosah.

Guard was alongside of guard: 17There were six Levites a day on the east, four a day on the north, four a day on the south and two at a time at the storehouse. 18As for the court to the west, there were four at the road and two at the court itself.

19These were the divisions of the gatekeepers who were descendants of Korah and Merari.

The Treasurers and Other Officials

20Their fellow Levites were[b] in charge of the treasuries of the house of God and the treasuries for the dedicated things.

21The descendants of Ladan, who were Gershonites through Ladan and who were heads of families belonging to Ladan the Gershonite, were Jehieli, 22the sons of Jehieli, Zetham and his brother Joel. They were in charge of the treasuries of the temple of the LORD.

23From the Amramites, the Izharites, the Hebronites and the Uzzielites:

24Shubael, a descendant of Gershom son of Moses, was the officer in charge of the treasuries. 25His relatives through Eliezer: Rehabiah his son, Jeshaiah his son, Joram his son, Zicri his son and Shelomith his son. 26Shelomith and his relatives were in charge of all the treasuries for the things dedicated by King David, by the heads of families who were the commanders of thousands and commanders of hundreds, and by the other army commanders. 27Some of the plunder taken in battle they dedicated for the repair of the temple of the LORD. 28And everything dedicated by Samuel the seer and by Saul son of Kish, Abner son of Ner and Joab son of Zeruiah, and all the other dedicated things were in the care of Shelomith and his relatives.

29From the Izharites: Kenaniah and his sons were assigned duties away from the temple, as officials and judges over Israel.

30From the Hebronites: Hashabiah and his relatives—seventeen hundred able men—were responsible in Israel west of the Jordan for all the work of the LORD and for the king's service. 31As for the Hebronites, Jeriah was their chief according to the genealogical records of their families. In the fortieth year of David's reign a search was made in the records, and capable men among the Hebronites were found at Jazer in Gilead. 32Jeriah had twenty-seven hundred relatives, who were able men and heads of families, and King David put them in charge of the Reubenites, the Gadites and the half-tribe of Manasseh for every matter pertaining to God and for the affairs of the king.

Army Divisions

27 This is the list of the Israelites—heads of families, commanders of thousands and commanders of hundreds, and their officers, who served the king in all that concerned the army divisions that were on duty month by month throughout the year. Each division consisted of 24,000 men.

2In charge of the first division, for the first month, was Jashobeam son of Zabdiel. There were 24,000 men in his division. 3He was a descendant of Perez and chief of all the army officers for the first month.

4In charge of the division for the second month was Dodai the Ahohite; Mikloth was the leader of his division. There were 24,000 men in his division.

5The third army commander, for the third month, was Benaiah son of Jehoiada the priest. He was chief and there were 24,000 men in his division. 6This was the Benaiah who was a mighty man among the Thirty and was over the Thirty. His son Ammizabad was in charge of his division.

7The fourth, for the fourth month, was Asahel the brother of Joab; his son Zebadiah was his successor. There were 24,000 men in his division.

8The fifth, for the fifth month, was the commander Shamhuth the Izrahite. There were 24,000 men in his division.

9The sixth, for the sixth month, was Ira the son of Ikkesh the Tekoite. There were 24,000 men in his division.

10The seventh, for the seventh month, was Helez the Pelonite, an Ephraimite. There were 24,000 men in his division.

11The eighth, for the eighth month, was Sibbecai the Hushathite, a Zerahite. There were 24,000 men in his division.

12The ninth, for the ninth month, was Abiezer the Anathothite, a Benjamite. There were 24,000 men in his division.

13The tenth, for the tenth month, was Maharai the Netophathite, a Zerahite. There were 24,000 men in his division.

14The eleventh, for the eleventh month, was Benaiah the Pirathonite, an Ephraimite. There were 24,000 men in his division.

15The twelfth, for the twelfth month, was Hel-

[a] *14* A variant of *Meshelemiah* [b] *20* Septuagint; Hebrew *As for the Levites, Ahijah was*

dai the Netophathite, from the family of
Othniel. There were 24,000 men in his division.

Officers of the Tribes

16 The officers over the tribes of Israel:

over the Reubenites: Eliezer son of
Zicri;
over the Simeonites: Shephatiah son of
Maacah;
17 over Levi: Hashabiah son of Kemuel;
over Aaron: Zadok;
18 over Judah: Elihu, a brother of David;
over Issachar: Omri son of Michael;
19 over Zebulun: Ishmaiah son of Obadiah;
over Naphtali: Jerimoth son of Azriel;
20 over the Ephraimites: Hoshea son of Azaziah;
over half the tribe of Manasseh: Joel son
of Pedaiah;
21 over the half-tribe of Manasseh in Gilead: Iddo son of Zechariah;
over Benjamin: Jaasiel son of Abner;
22 over Dan: Azarel son of Jeroham.

These were the officers over the tribes of
Israel.

23 David did not take the number of the men
twenty years old or less, because the LORD had
promised to make Israel as numerous as the
stars in the sky. 24 Joab son of Zeruiah began to
count the men but did not finish. Wrath came
on Israel on account of this numbering, and the
number was not entered in the book[a] of the
annals of King David.

The King's Overseers

25 Azmaveth son of Adiel was in charge of
the royal storehouses.

Jonathan son of Uzziah was in charge of the
storehouses in the outlying districts, in the
towns, the villages and the watchtowers.

26 Ezri son of Kelub was in charge of the
field workers who farmed the land.

27 Shimei the Ramathite was in charge of the
vineyards.

Zabdi the Shiphmite was in charge of the
produce of the vineyards for the wine vats.

28 Baal-Hanan the Gederite was in charge of
the olive and sycamore-fig trees in the western
foothills.

Joash was in charge of the supplies of olive
oil.

29 Shitrai the Sharonite was in charge of the
herds grazing in Sharon.

Shaphat son of Adlai was in charge of the
herds in the valleys.

30 Obil the Ishmaelite was in charge of the
camels.

Jehdeiah the Meronothite was in charge of
the donkeys.

31 Jaziz the Hagrite was in charge of the
flocks.

All these were the officials in charge of
King David's property.

32 Jonathan, David's uncle, was a counselor,
a man of insight and a scribe. Jehiel son of
Hacmoni took care of the king's sons.

33 Ahithophel was the king's counselor.

Hushai the Arkite was the king's friend.
34 Ahithophel was succeeded by Jehoiada son
of Benaiah and by Abiathar.

Joab was the commander of the royal army.

David's Plans for the Temple

28 David summoned all the officials of Israel to assemble at Jerusalem: the officers over the tribes, the commanders of the
divisions in the service of the king, the commanders of thousands and commanders of
hundreds, and the officials in charge of all the
property and livestock belonging to the king
and his sons, together with the palace officials,
the mighty men and all the brave warriors.

2 King David rose to his feet and said: "Listen to me, my brothers and my people. I had it
in my heart to build a house as a place of rest
for the ark of the covenant of the LORD, for the
footstool of our God, and I made plans to build
it. 3 But God said to me, 'You are not to build
a house for my Name, because you are a warrior and have shed blood.'

4 "Yet the LORD, the God of Israel, chose me
from my whole family to be king over Israel
forever. He chose Judah as leader, and from
the house of Judah he chose my family, and
from my father's sons he was pleased to make
me king over all Israel. 5 Of all my sons—and
the LORD has given me many—he has chosen
my son Solomon to sit on the throne of the
kingdom of the LORD over Israel. 6 He said to
me: 'Solomon your son is the one who will
build my house and my courts, for I have chosen him to be my son, and I will be his father.
7 I will establish his kingdom forever if he is
unswerving in carrying out my commands and
laws, as is being done at this time.'

8 "So now I charge you in the sight of all
Israel and of the assembly of the LORD, and in
the hearing of our God: Be careful to follow all
the commands of the LORD your God, that you
may possess this good land and pass it on as an
inheritance to your descendants forever.

9 "And you, my son Solomon, acknowledge
the God of your father, and serve him with
wholehearted devotion and with a willing
mind, for the LORD searches every heart and
understands every motive behind the thoughts.
If you seek him, he will be found by you; but
if you forsake him, he will reject you forever.
10 Consider now, for the LORD has chosen you
to build a temple as a sanctuary. Be strong and
do the work."

11 Then David gave his son Solomon the
plans for the portico of the temple, its buildings, its storerooms, its upper parts, its inner
rooms and the place of atonement. 12 He gave
him the plans of all that the Spirit had put in
his mind for the courts of the temple of the
LORD and all the surrounding rooms, for the

[a] 24 Septuagint; Hebrew *number*

treasuries of the temple of God and for
the treasuries for the dedicated things. 13He
gave him instructions for the divisions of the
priests and Levites, and for all the work of
serving in the temple of the LORD, as well as
for all the articles to be used in its service.
14He designated the weight of gold for all the
gold articles to be used in various kinds of
service, and the weight of silver for all the
silver articles to be used in various kinds of
service: 15the weight of gold for the gold lampstands and their lamps, with the weight for
each lampstand and its lamps; and the weight
of silver for each silver lampstand and its
lamps, according to the use of each lampstand;
16the weight of gold for each table for consecrated bread; the weight of silver for the silver
tables; 17the weight of pure gold for the forks,
sprinkling bowls and pitchers; the weight of
gold for each gold dish; the weight of silver for
each silver dish; 18and the weight of the refined gold for the altar of incense. He also gave
him the plan for the chariot, that is, the cherubim of gold that spread their wings and shelter
the ark of the covenant of the LORD.

19"All this," David said, "I have in writing
from the hand of the LORD upon me, and he
gave me understanding in all the details of the
plan."

20David also said to Solomon his son, "Be
strong and courageous, and do the work. Do
not be afraid or discouraged, for the LORD
God, my God, is with you. He will not fail you
or forsake you until all the work for the service
of the temple of the LORD is finished. 21The
divisions of the priests and Levites are ready
for all the work on the temple of God, and
every willing man skilled in any craft will help
you in all the work. The officials and all the
people will obey your every command."

Gifts for Building the Temple

29 Then King David said to the whole assembly: "My son Solomon, the one
whom God has chosen, is young and inexperienced. The task is great, because this palatial
structure is not for man but for the LORD God.
2With all my resources I have provided for the
temple of my God—gold for the gold work,
silver for the silver, bronze for the bronze, iron
for the iron and wood for the wood, as well as
onyx for the settings, turquoise,[a] stones of various colors, and all kinds of fine stone and
marble—all of these in large quantities. 3Be-
sides, in my devotion to the temple of my God
I now give my personal treasures of gold and
silver for the temple of my God, over and
above everything I have provided for this holy
temple: 4three thousand talents[b] of gold (gold
of Ophir) and seven thousand talents[c] of refined silver, for the overlaying of the walls of
the buildings, 5for the gold work and the silver
work, and for all the work to be done by the
craftsmen. Now, who is willing to consecrate
himself today to the LORD?"

6Then the leaders of families, the officers of
the tribes of Israel, the commanders of thousands and commanders of hundreds, and the
officials in charge of the king's work gave
willingly. 7They gave toward the work on the
temple of God five thousand talents[d] and ten
thousand darics[e] of gold, ten thousand talents[f]
of silver, eighteen thousand talents[g] of bronze
and a hundred thousand talents[h] of iron. 8Any
who had precious stones gave them to the treasury of the temple of the LORD in the custody
of Jehiel the Gershonite. 9The people rejoiced
at the willing response of their leaders, for they
had given freely and wholeheartedly to the
LORD. David the king also rejoiced greatly.

David's Prayer

10David praised the LORD in the presence of
the whole assembly, saying,

"Praise be to you, O LORD,
God of our father Israel,
from everlasting to everlasting.
11Yours, O LORD, is the greatness and the
power
and the glory and the majesty and the
splendor,
for everything in heaven and earth is
yours.
Yours, O LORD, is the kingdom;
you are exalted as head over all.
12Wealth and honor come from you;
you are the ruler of all things.
In your hands are strength and power
to exalt and give strength to all.
13Now, our God, we give you thanks,
and praise your glorious name.

14"But who am I, and who are my people,
that we should be able to give as generously as
this? Everything comes from you, and we have
given you only what comes from your hand.
15We are aliens and strangers in your sight, as
were all our forefathers. Our days on earth are
like a shadow, without hope. 16O LORD our
God, as for all this abundance that we have
provided for building you a temple for your
Holy Name, it comes from your hand, and all
of it belongs to you. 17I know, my God, that
you test the heart and are pleased with integrity. All these things have I given willingly and
with honest intent. And now I have seen with
joy how willingly your people who are here
have given to you. 18O LORD, God of our fathers Abraham, Isaac and Israel, keep this desire in the hearts of your people forever, and
keep their hearts loyal to you. 19And give my
son Solomon the wholehearted devotion to
keep your commands, requirements and de-

[a]2 The meaning of the Hebrew for this word is uncertain. [b]4 That is, about 110 tons (about 100 metric tons) [c]4 That is, about 260 tons (about 240 metric tons) [d]7 That is, about 190 tons (about 170 metric tons) [e]7 That is, about 185 pounds (about 84 kilograms) [f]7 That is, about 375 tons (about 345 metric tons) [g]7 That is, about 675 tons (about 610 metric tons) [h]7 That is, about 3,750 tons (about 3,450 metric tons)

crees and to do everything to build the palatial structure for which I have provided."

20Then David said to the whole assembly, "Praise the LORD your God." So they all praised the LORD, the God of their fathers; they bowed low and fell prostrate before the LORD and the king.

Solomon Acknowledged as King

21The next day they made sacrifices to the LORD and presented burnt offerings to him: a thousand bulls, a thousand rams and a thousand male lambs, together with their drink offerings, and other sacrifices in abundance for all Israel. 22They ate and drank with great joy in the presence of the LORD that day.

Then they acknowledged Solomon son of David as king a second time, anointing him before the LORD to be ruler and Zadok to be priest. 23So Solomon sat on the throne of the LORD as king in place of his father David. He prospered and all Israel obeyed him. 24All the officers and mighty men, as well as all of King David's sons, pledged their submission to King Solomon.

25The LORD highly exalted Solomon in the sight of all Israel and bestowed on him royal splendor such as no king over Israel ever had before.

The Death of David

26David son of Jesse was king over all Israel. 27He ruled over Israel forty years—seven in Hebron and thirty-three in Jerusalem. 28He died at a good old age, having enjoyed long life, wealth and honor. His son Solomon succeeded him as king.

29As for the events of King David's reign, from beginning to end, they are written in the records of Samuel the seer, the records of Nathan the prophet and the records of Gad the seer, 30together with the details of his reign and power, and the circumstances that surrounded him and Israel and the kingdoms of all the other lands.

2 Chronicles

Solomon Asks for Wisdom

1 Solomon son of David established himself firmly over his kingdom, for the LORD his God was with him and made him exceedingly great.

2Then Solomon spoke to all Israel—to the commanders of thousands and commanders of hundreds, to the judges and to all the leaders in Israel, the heads of families— 3and Solomon and the whole assembly went to the high place at Gibeon, for God's Tent of Meeting was there, which Moses the LORD's servant had made in the desert. 4Now David had brought up the ark of God from Kiriath Jearim to the place he had prepared for it, because he had pitched a tent for it in Jerusalem. 5But the bronze altar that Bezalel son of Uri, the son of Hur, had made was in Gibeon in front of the tabernacle of the LORD; so Solomon and the assembly inquired of him there. 6Solomon went up to the bronze altar before the LORD in the Tent of Meeting and offered a thousand burnt offerings on it.

7That night God appeared to Solomon and said to him, "Ask for whatever you want me to give you."

8Solomon answered God, "You have shown great kindness to David my father and have made me king in his place. 9Now, LORD God, let your promise to my father David be confirmed, for you have made me king over a people who are as numerous as the dust of the earth. 10Give me wisdom and knowledge, that I may lead this people, for who is able to govern this great people of yours?"

11God said to Solomon, "Since this is your heart's desire and you have not asked for wealth, riches or honor, nor for the death of your enemies, and since you have not asked for a long life but for wisdom and knowledge to govern my people over whom I have made you king, 12therefore wisdom and knowledge will be given you. And I will also give you wealth, riches and honor, such as no king who was before you ever had and none after you will have."

13Then Solomon went to Jerusalem from the high place at Gibeon, from before the Tent of Meeting. And he reigned over Israel.

14Solomon accumulated chariots and horses; he had fourteen hundred chariots and twelve thousand horses,[a] which he kept in the chariot cities and also with him in Jerusalem. 15The king made silver and gold as common in Jerusalem as stones, and cedar as plentiful as sycamore-fig trees in the foothills. 16Solomon's horses were imported from Egypt[b] and from Kue[c]—the royal merchants purchased them from Kue. 17They imported a chariot from Egypt for six hundred shekels[d] of silver, and a horse for a hundred and fifty.[e] They also exported them to all the kings of the Hittites and of the Arameans.

Preparations for Building the Temple

2 Solomon gave orders to build a temple for the Name of the LORD and a royal palace

[a]14 Or *charioteers* [b]16 Or possibly *Muzur,* a region in Cilicia; also in verse 17 [c]16 Probably Cilicia
[d]17 That is, about 15 pounds (about 7 kilograms) [e]17 That is, about 3 3/4 pounds (about 1.7 kilograms)

for himself. 2He conscripted seventy thousand men as carriers and eighty thousand as stonecutters in the hills and thirty-six hundred as foremen over them.

3Solomon sent this message to Hiram[a] king of Tyre:

"Send me cedar logs as you did for my father David when you sent him cedar to build a palace to live in. 4Now I am about to build a temple for the Name of the LORD my God and to dedicate it to him for burning fragrant incense before him, for setting out the consecrated bread regularly, and for making burnt offerings every morning and evening and on Sabbaths and New Moons and at the appointed feasts of the LORD our God. This is a lasting ordinance for Israel.

5"The temple I am going to build will be great, because our God is greater than all other gods. 6But who is able to build a temple for him, since the heavens, even the highest heavens, cannot contain him? Who then am I to build a temple for him, except as a place to burn sacrifices before him?

7"Send me, therefore, a man skilled to work in gold and silver, bronze and iron, and in purple, crimson and blue yarn, and experienced in the art of engraving, to work in Judah and Jerusalem with my skilled craftsmen, whom my father David provided.

8"Send me also cedar, pine and algum[b] logs from Lebanon, for I know that your men are skilled in cutting timber there. My men will work with yours 9to provide me with plenty of lumber, because the temple I build must be large and magnificent. 10I will give your servants, the woodsmen who cut the timber, twenty thousand cors[c] of ground wheat, twenty thousand cors of barley, twenty thousand baths[d] of wine and twenty thousand baths of olive oil."

11Hiram king of Tyre replied by letter to Solomon:

"Because the LORD loves his people, he has made you their king."

12And Hiram added:

"Praise be to the LORD, the God of Israel, who made heaven and earth! He has given King David a wise son, endowed with intelligence and discernment, who will build a temple for the LORD and a palace for himself.

13"I am sending you Huram-Abi, a man of great skill, 14whose mother was from Dan and whose father was from Tyre. He is trained to work in gold and silver, bronze and iron, stone and wood, and with purple and blue and crimson yarn and fine linen. He is experienced in all kinds of engraving and can execute any design given to him. He will work with your craftsmen and with those of my lord, David your father.

15"Now let my lord send his servants the wheat and barley and the olive oil and wine he promised, 16and we will cut all the logs from Lebanon that you need and will float them in rafts by sea down to Joppa. You can then take them up to Jerusalem."

17Solomon took a census of all the aliens who were in Israel, after the census his father David had taken; and they were found to be 153,600. 18He assigned 70,000 of them to be carriers and 80,000 to be stonecutters in the hills, with 3,600 foremen over them to keep the people working.

Solomon Builds the Temple

3 Then Solomon began to build the temple of the LORD in Jerusalem on Mount Moriah, where the LORD had appeared to his father David. It was on the threshing floor of Araunah[e] the Jebusite, the place provided by David. 2He began building on the second day of the second month in the fourth year of his reign.

3The foundation Solomon laid for building the temple of God was sixty cubits long and twenty cubits wide[f] (using the cubit of the old standard). 4The portico at the front of the temple was twenty cubits[g] long across the width of the building and twenty cubits[h] high.

He overlaid the inside with pure gold. 5He paneled the main hall with pine and covered it with fine gold and decorated it with palm tree and chain designs. 6He adorned the temple with precious stones. And the gold he used was gold of Parvaim. 7He overlaid the ceiling beams, doorframes, walls and doors of the temple with gold, and he carved cherubim on the walls.

8He built the Most Holy Place, its length corresponding to the width of the temple—twenty cubits long and twenty cubits wide. He overlaid the inside with six hundred talents[i] of fine gold. 9The gold nails weighed fifty shekels.[j] He also overlaid the upper parts with gold.

10In the Most Holy Place he made a pair of sculptured cherubim and overlaid them with gold. 11The total wingspan of the cherubim was twenty cubits. One wing of the first cherub

[a] *3* Hebrew *Huram,* a variant of *Hiram;* also in verses 11 and 12 [b] *8* Probably a variant of *almug;* possibly juniper [c] *10* That is, probably about 125,000 bushels (about 4,400 kiloliters) [d] *10* That is, probably about 115,000 gallons (about 440 kiloliters) [e] *1* Hebrew *Ornan,* a variant of *Araunah* [f] *3* That is, about 90 feet (about 27 meters) long and 30 feet (about 9 meters) wide [g] *4* That is, about 30 feet (about 9 meters); also in verses 8, 11 and 13 [h] *4* Some Septuagint and Syriac manuscripts; Hebrew *and a hundred and twenty* [i] *8* That is, about 23 tons (about 21 metric tons) [j] *9* That is, about 1 1/4 pounds (about 0.6 kilogram)

was five cubits[a] long and touched the temple
wall, while its other wing, also five cubits
long, touched the wing of the other cherub.
12Similarly one wing of the second cherub was
five cubits long and touched the other temple
wall, and its other wing, also five cubits long,
touched the wing of the first cherub. 13The
wings of these cherubim extended twenty cubits. They stood on their feet, facing the main
hall.[b]

14He made the curtain of blue, purple and
crimson yarn and fine linen, with cherubim
worked into it.

15In the front of the temple he made two
pillars, which ⌞together⌟ were thirty-five cubits[c] long, each with a capital on top measuring five cubits. 16He made interwoven chains[d]
and put them on top of the pillars. He also
made a hundred pomegranates and attached
them to the chains. 17He erected the pillars in
the front of the temple, one to the south and
one to the north. The one to the south he
named Jakin[e] and the one to the north Boaz.[f]

The Temple's Furnishings

4 He made a bronze altar twenty cubits long,
twenty cubits wide and ten cubits high.[g]
2He made the Sea of cast metal, circular in
shape, measuring ten cubits from rim to rim
and five cubits[h] high. It took a line of thirty
cubits[i] to measure around it. 3Below the rim,
figures of bulls encircled it—ten to a cubit.[j]
The bulls were cast in two rows in one piece
with the Sea.

4The Sea stood on twelve bulls, three facing
north, three facing west, three facing south and
three facing east. The Sea rested on top of
them, and their hindquarters were toward the
center. 5It was a handbreadth[k] in thickness,
and its rim was like the rim of a cup, like a lily
blossom. It held three thousand baths.[l]

6He then made ten basins for washing and
placed five on the south side and five on the
north. In them the things to be used for the
burnt offerings were rinsed, but the Sea was to
be used by the priests for washing.

7He made ten gold lampstands according to
the specifications for them and placed them in
the temple, five on the south side and five on
the north.

8He made ten tables and placed them in the
temple, five on the south side and five on the
north. He also made a hundred gold sprinkling
bowls.

9He made the courtyard of the priests, and
the large court and the doors for the court, and
overlaid the doors with bronze. 10He placed
the Sea on the south side, at the southeast corner.

11He also made the pots and shovels and
sprinkling bowls.

So Huram finished the work he had undertaken for King Solomon in the temple of God:

12the two pillars;
the two bowl-shaped capitals on top of the pillars;
the two sets of network decorating the two bowl-shaped capitals on top of the pillars;
13the four hundred pomegranates for the two sets of network (two rows of pomegranates for each network, decorating the bowl-shaped capitals on top of the pillars);
14the stands with their basins;
15the Sea and the twelve bulls under it;
16the pots, shovels, meat forks and all related articles.

All the objects that Huram-Abi made for
King Solomon for the temple of the LORD
were of polished bronze. 17The king had them
cast in clay molds in the plain of the Jordan
between Succoth and Zarethan.[m] 18All these
things that Solomon made amounted to so
much that the weight of the bronze was not
determined.

19Solomon also made all the furnishings that
were in God's temple:

the golden altar;
the tables on which was the bread of the Presence;
20the lampstands of pure gold with their lamps, to burn in front of the inner sanctuary as prescribed;
21the gold floral work and lamps and tongs (they were solid gold);
22the pure gold wick trimmers, sprinkling bowls, dishes and censers; and the gold doors of the temple: the inner doors to the Most Holy Place and the doors of the main hall.

5 When all the work Solomon had done for
the temple of the LORD was finished, he
brought in the things his father David had dedicated—the silver and gold and all the furnishings—and he placed them in the treasuries of
God's temple.

The Ark Brought to the Temple

2Then Solomon summoned to Jerusalem the
elders of Israel, all the heads of the tribes and
the chiefs of the Israelite families, to bring up
the ark of the LORD's covenant from Zion, the
City of David. 3And all the men of Israel came
together to the king at the time of the festival
in the seventh month.

4When all the elders of Israel had arrived,

[a] *11* That is, about 7 1/2 feet (about 2.3 meters); also in verse 15 [b] *13* Or *facing inward* [c] *15* That is, about 52 feet (about 16 meters) [d] *16* Or possibly *made chains in the inner sanctuary*; the meaning of the Hebrew for this phrase is uncertain. [e] *17* *Jakin* probably means *he establishes.* [f] *17* *Boaz* probably means *in him is strength.* [g] *1* That is, about 30 feet (about 9 meters) long and wide, and about 15 feet (about 4.5 meters) high [h] *2* That is, about 7 1/2 feet (about 2.3 meters) [i] *2* That is, about 45 feet (about 13.5 meters) [j] *3* That is, about 1 1/2 feet (about 0.5 meter) [k] *5* That is, about 3 inches (about 8 centimeters) [l] *5* That is, about 17,500 gallons (about 66 kiloliters) [m] *17* Hebrew *Zeredatha,* a variant of *Zarethan*

the Levites took up the ark, 5and they brought up the ark and the Tent of Meeting and all the sacred furnishings in it. The priests, who were Levites, carried them up; 6and King Solomon and the entire assembly of Israel that had gathered about him were before the ark, sacrificing so many sheep and cattle that they could not be recorded or counted.

7The priests then brought the ark of the LORD's covenant to its place in the inner sanctuary of the temple, the Most Holy Place, and put it beneath the wings of the cherubim. 8The cherubim spread their wings over the place of the ark and covered the ark and its carrying poles. 9These poles were so long that their ends, extending from the ark, could be seen from in front of the inner sanctuary, but not from outside the Holy Place; and they are still there today. 10There was nothing in the ark except the two tablets that Moses had placed in it at Horeb, where the LORD made a covenant with the Israelites after they came out of Egypt.

11The priests then withdrew from the Holy Place. All the priests who were there had consecrated themselves, regardless of their divisions. 12All the Levites who were musicians—Asaph, Heman, Jeduthun and their sons and relatives—stood on the east side of the altar, dressed in fine linen and playing cymbals, harps and lyres. They were accompanied by 120 priests sounding trumpets. 13The trumpeters and singers joined in unison, as with one voice, to give praise and thanks to the LORD. Accompanied by trumpets, cymbals and other instruments, they raised their voices in praise to the LORD and sang:

"He is good;
his love endures forever."

Then the temple of the LORD was filled with a cloud, 14and the priests could not perform their service because of the cloud, for the glory of the LORD filled the temple of God.

6 Then Solomon said, "The LORD has said that he would dwell in a dark cloud; 2I have built a magnificent temple for you, a place for you to dwell forever."

3While the whole assembly of Israel was standing there, the king turned around and blessed them. 4Then he said:

"Praise be to the LORD, the God of Israel, who with his hands has fulfilled what he promised with his mouth to my father David. For he said, 5'Since the day I brought my people out of Egypt, I have not chosen a city in any tribe of Israel to have a temple built for my Name to be there, nor have I chosen anyone to be the leader over my people Israel. 6But now I have chosen Jerusalem for my Name to be there, and I have chosen David to rule my people Israel.'

7"My father David had it in his heart to build a temple for the Name of the LORD, the God of Israel. 8But the LORD said to my father David, 'Because it was in your heart to build a temple for my Name, you did well to have this in your heart. 9Nevertheless, you are not the one to build the temple, but your son, who is your own flesh and blood—he is the one who will build the temple for my Name.'

10"The LORD has kept the promise he made. I have succeeded David my father and now I sit on the throne of Israel, just as the LORD promised, and I have built the temple for the Name of the LORD, the God of Israel. 11There I have placed the ark, in which is the covenant of the LORD that he made with the people of Israel."

Solomon's Prayer of Dedication

12Then Solomon stood before the altar of the LORD in front of the whole assembly of Israel and spread out his hands. 13Now he had made a bronze platform, five cubits[a] long, five cubits wide and three cubits[b] high, and had placed it in the center of the outer court. He stood on the platform and then knelt down before the whole assembly of Israel and spread out his hands toward heaven. 14He said:

"O LORD, God of Israel, there is no God like you in heaven or on earth—you who keep your covenant of love with your servants who continue wholeheartedly in your way. 15You have kept your promise to your servant David my father; with your mouth you have promised and with your hand you have fulfilled it—as it is today.

16"Now LORD, God of Israel, keep for your servant David my father the promises you made to him when you said, 'You shall never fail to have a man to sit before me on the throne of Israel, if only your sons are careful in all they do to walk before me according to my law, as you have done.' 17And now, O LORD, God of Israel, let your word that you promised your servant David come true.

18"But will God really dwell on earth with men? The heavens, even the highest heavens, cannot contain you. How much less this temple I have built! 19Yet give attention to your servant's prayer and his plea for mercy, O LORD my God. Hear the cry and the prayer that your servant is praying in your presence. 20May your eyes be open toward this temple day and night, this place of which you said you would put your Name there. May you hear the prayer your servant prays toward this place. 21Hear the supplications of your servant and of your people Israel when they pray toward this place. Hear from heaven, your dwelling place; and when you hear, forgive.

22"When a man wrongs his neighbor

[a] *13* That is, about 7 1/2 feet (about 2.3 meters) [b] *13* That is, about 4 1/2 feet (about 1.3 meters)

and is required to take an oath and he
comes and swears the oath before your
altar in this temple, 23then hear from
heaven and act. Judge between your servants, repaying the guilty by bringing
down on his own head what he has done.
Declare the innocent not guilty and so establish his innocence.

24"When your people Israel have been
defeated by an enemy because they have
sinned against you and when they turn
back and confess your name, praying and
making supplication before you in this
temple, 25then hear from heaven and forgive the sin of your people Israel and
bring them back to the land you gave to
them and their fathers.

26"When the heavens are shut up and
there is no rain because your people have
sinned against you, and when they pray
toward this place and confess your name
and turn from their sin because you have
afflicted them, 27then hear from heaven
and forgive the sin of your servants, your
people Israel. Teach them the right way to
live, and send rain on the land you gave
your people for an inheritance.

28"When famine or plague comes to the
land, or blight or mildew, locusts or grasshoppers, or when enemies besiege them
in any of their cities, whatever disaster or
disease may come, 29and when a prayer or
plea is made by any of your people Israel—each one aware of his afflictions and
pains, and spreading out his hands toward
this temple— 30then hear from heaven,
your dwelling place. Forgive, and deal
with each man according to all he does,
since you know his heart (for you alone
know the hearts of men), 31so that they
will fear you and walk in your ways all
the time they live in the land you gave our
fathers.

32"As for the foreigner who does not
belong to your people Israel but has come
from a distant land because of your great
name and your mighty hand and your outstretched arm—when he comes and prays
toward this temple, 33then hear from
heaven, your dwelling place, and do
whatever the foreigner asks of you, so
that all the peoples of the earth may know
your name and fear you, as do your own
people Israel, and may know that this
house I have built bears your Name.

34"When your people go to war against
their enemies, wherever you send them,
and when they pray to you toward this
city you have chosen and the temple I
have built for your Name, 35then hear
from heaven their prayer and their plea,
and uphold their cause.

36"When they sin against you—for
there is no one who does not sin—and
you become angry with them and give
them over to the enemy, who takes them
captive to a land far away or near; 37and
if they have a change of heart in the land
where they are held captive, and repent
and plead with you in the land of their
captivity and say, 'We have sinned, we
have done wrong and acted wickedly';
38and if they turn back to you with all
their heart and soul in the land of their
captivity where they were taken, and pray
toward the land you gave their fathers,
toward the city you have chosen and toward the temple I have built for your
Name; 39then from heaven, your dwelling
place, hear their prayer and their pleas,
and uphold their cause. And forgive your
people, who have sinned against you.

40"Now, my God, may your eyes be
open and your ears attentive to the prayers
offered in this place.

41"Now arise, O LORD God, and come
to your resting place,
you and the ark of your might.
May your priests, O LORD God, be
clothed with salvation,
may your saints rejoice in your
goodness.
42O LORD God, do not reject your
anointed one.
Remember the great love promised
to David your servant."

The Dedication of the Temple

7 When Solomon finished praying, fire came
down from heaven and consumed the burnt
offering and the sacrifices, and the glory of the
LORD filled the temple. 2The priests could not
enter the temple of the LORD because the glory
of the LORD filled it. 3When all the Israelites
saw the fire coming down and the glory of the
LORD above the temple, they knelt on the
pavement with their faces to the ground, and
they worshiped and gave thanks to the LORD,
saying,

"He is good;
his love endures forever."

4Then the king and all the people offered sacrifices before the LORD. 5And King Solomon
offered a sacrifice of twenty-two thousand
head of cattle and a hundred and twenty thousand sheep and goats. So the king and all the
people dedicated the temple of God. 6The
priests took their positions, as did the Levites
with the LORD's musical instruments, which
King David had made for praising the LORD
and which were used when he gave thanks,
saying, "His love endures forever." Opposite
the Levites, the priests blew their trumpets,
and all the Israelites were standing.

7Solomon consecrated the middle part of the
courtyard in front of the temple of the LORD,
and there he offered burnt offerings and the
fat of the fellowship offerings,[a] because the
bronze altar he had made could not hold the

[a]7 Traditionally *peace offerings*

burnt offerings, the grain offerings and the fat portions.

8So Solomon observed the festival at that time for seven days, and all Israel with him—a vast assembly, people from Lebo[a] Hamath to the Wadi of Egypt. 9On the eighth day they held an assembly, for they had celebrated the dedication of the altar for seven days and the festival for seven days more. 10On the twenty-third day of the seventh month he sent the people to their homes, joyful and glad in heart for the good things the LORD had done for David and Solomon and for his people Israel.

The LORD Appears to Solomon

11When Solomon had finished the temple of the LORD and the royal palace, and had succeeded in carrying out all he had in mind to do in the temple of the LORD and in his own palace, 12the LORD appeared to him at night and said:

> "I have heard your prayer and have chosen this place for myself as a temple for sacrifices.
>
> 13"When I shut up the heavens so that there is no rain, or command locusts to devour the land or send a plague among my people, 14if my people, who are called by my name, will humble themselves and pray and seek my face and turn from their wicked ways, then will I hear from heaven and will forgive their sin and will heal their land. 15Now my eyes will be open and my ears attentive to the prayers offered in this place. 16I have chosen and consecrated this temple so that my Name may be there forever. My eyes and my heart will always be there.
>
> 17"As for you, if you walk before me as David your father did, and do all I command, and observe my decrees and laws, 18I will establish your royal throne, as I covenanted with David your father when I said, 'You shall never fail to have a man to rule over Israel.'
>
> 19"But if you[b] turn away and forsake the decrees and commands I have given you[b] and go off to serve other gods and worship them, 20then I will uproot Israel from my land, which I have given them, and will reject this temple I have consecrated for my Name. I will make it a byword and an object of ridicule among all peoples. 21And though this temple is now so imposing, all who pass by will be appalled and say, 'Why has the LORD done such a thing to this land and to this temple?' 22People will answer, 'Because they have forsaken the LORD, the God of their fathers, who brought them out of Egypt, and have embraced other gods, worshiping and serving them—that is why he brought all this disaster on them.' "

Solomon's Other Activities

8 At the end of twenty years, during which Solomon built the temple of the LORD and his own palace, 2Solomon rebuilt the villages that Hiram[c] had given him, and settled Israelites in them. 3Solomon then went to Hamath Zobah and captured it. 4He also built up Tadmor in the desert and all the store cities he had built in Hamath. 5He rebuilt Upper Beth Horon and Lower Beth Horon as fortified cities, with walls and with gates and bars, 6as well as Baalath and all his store cities, and all the cities for his chariots and for his horses[d]—whatever he desired to build in Jerusalem, in Lebanon and throughout all the territory he ruled.

7All the people left from the Hittites, Amorites, Perizzites, Hivites and Jebusites (these peoples were not Israelites), 8that is, their descendants remaining in the land, whom the Israelites had not destroyed—these Solomon conscripted for his slave labor force, as it is to this day. 9But Solomon did not make slaves of the Israelites for his work; they were his fighting men, commanders of his captains, and commanders of his chariots and charioteers. 10They were also King Solomon's chief officials—two hundred and fifty officials supervising the men.

11Solomon brought Pharaoh's daughter up from the City of David to the palace he had built for her, for he said, "My wife must not live in the palace of David king of Israel, because the places the ark of the LORD has entered are holy."

12On the altar of the LORD that he had built in front of the portico, Solomon sacrificed burnt offerings to the LORD, 13according to the daily requirement for offerings commanded by Moses for Sabbaths, New Moons and the three annual feasts—the Feast of Unleavened Bread, the Feast of Weeks and the Feast of Tabernacles. 14In keeping with the ordinance of his father David, he appointed the divisions of the priests for their duties, and the Levites to lead the praise and to assist the priests according to each day's requirement. He also appointed the gatekeepers by divisions for the various gates, because this was what David the man of God had ordered. 15They did not deviate from the king's commands to the priests or to the Levites in any matter, including that of the treasuries.

16All Solomon's work was carried out, from the day the foundation of the temple of the LORD was laid until its completion. So the temple of the LORD was finished.

17Then Solomon went to Ezion Geber and Elath on the coast of Edom. 18And Hiram sent him ships commanded by his own officers, men who knew the sea. These, with Solomon's men, sailed to Ophir and brought back four hundred and fifty talents[e] of gold, which they delivered to King Solomon.

[a] *8* Or *from the entrance to* [b] *19* The Hebrew is plural. [c] *2* Hebrew *Huram,* a variant of *Hiram;* also in verse 18 [d] *6* Or *charioteers* [e] *18* That is, about 17 tons (about 16 metric tons)

The Queen of Sheba Visits Solomon

9 When the queen of Sheba heard of Solomon's fame, she came to Jerusalem to test him with hard questions. Arriving with a very great caravan—with camels carrying spices, large quantities of gold, and precious stones—she came to Solomon and talked with him about all she had on her mind. 2Solomon answered all her questions; nothing was too hard for him to explain to her. 3When the queen of Sheba saw the wisdom of Solomon, as well as the palace he had built, 4the food on his table, the seating of his officials, the attending servants in their robes, the cupbearers in their robes and the burnt offerings he made at[a] the temple of the LORD, she was overwhelmed.

5She said to the king, "The report I heard in my own country about your achievements and your wisdom is true. 6But I did not believe what they said until I came and saw with my own eyes. Indeed, not even half the greatness of your wisdom was told me; you have far exceeded the report I heard. 7How happy your men must be! How happy your officials, who continually stand before you and hear your wisdom! 8Praise be to the LORD your God, who has delighted in you and placed you on his throne as king to rule for the LORD your God. Because of the love of your God for Israel and his desire to uphold them forever, he has made you king over them, to maintain justice and righteousness."

9Then she gave the king 120 talents[b] of gold, large quantities of spices, and precious stones. There had never been such spices as those the queen of Sheba gave to King Solomon.

10(The men of Hiram and the men of Solomon brought gold from Ophir; they also brought algumwood[c] and precious stones. 11The king used the algumwood to make steps for the temple of the LORD and for the royal palace, and to make harps and lyres for the musicians. Nothing like them had ever been seen in Judah.)

12King Solomon gave the queen of Sheba all she desired and asked for; he gave her more than she had brought to him. Then she left and returned with her retinue to her own country.

Solomon's Splendor

13The weight of the gold that Solomon received yearly was 666 talents,[d] 14not including the revenues brought in by merchants and traders. Also all the kings of Arabia and the governors of the land brought gold and silver to Solomon.

15King Solomon made two hundred large shields of hammered gold; six hundred bekas[e] of hammered gold went into each shield. 16He also made three hundred small shields of hammered gold, with three hundred bekas[f] of gold in each shield. The king put them in the Palace of the Forest of Lebanon.

17Then the king made a great throne inlaid with ivory and overlaid with pure gold. 18The throne had six steps, and a footstool of gold was attached to it. On both sides of the seat were armrests, with a lion standing beside each of them. 19Twelve lions stood on the six steps, one at either end of each step. Nothing like it had ever been made for any other kingdom. 20All King Solomon's goblets were gold, and all the household articles in the Palace of the Forest of Lebanon were pure gold. Nothing was made of silver, because silver was considered of little value in Solomon's day. 21The king had a fleet of trading ships[g] manned by Hiram's[h] men. Once every three years it returned, carrying gold, silver and ivory, and apes and baboons.

22King Solomon was greater in riches and wisdom than all the other kings of the earth. 23All the kings of the earth sought audience with Solomon to hear the wisdom God had put in his heart. 24Year after year, everyone who came brought a gift—articles of silver and gold, and robes, weapons and spices, and horses and mules.

25Solomon had four thousand stalls for horses and chariots, and twelve thousand horses,[i] which he kept in the chariot cities and also with him in Jerusalem. 26He ruled over all the kings from the River[j] to the land of the Philistines, as far as the border of Egypt. 27The king made silver as common in Jerusalem as stones, and cedar as plentiful as sycamore-fig trees in the foothills. 28Solomon's horses were imported from Egypt[k] and from all other countries.

Solomon's Death

29As for the other events of Solomon's reign, from beginning to end, are they not written in the records of Nathan the prophet, in the prophecy of Ahijah the Shilonite and in the visions of Iddo the seer concerning Jeroboam son of Nebat? 30Solomon reigned in Jerusalem over all Israel forty years. 31Then he rested with his fathers and was buried in the city of David his father. And Rehoboam his son succeeded him as king.

Israel Rebels Against Rehoboam

10 Rehoboam went to Shechem, for all the Israelites had gone there to make him king. 2When Jeroboam son of Nebat heard this (he was in Egypt, where he had fled from King Solomon), he returned from Egypt. 3So they sent for Jeroboam, and he and all Israel went to Rehoboam and said to him: 4"Your father put a heavy yoke on us, but now lighten the harsh

[a]4 Or *the ascent by which he went up to* [b]9 That is, about 4 1/2 tons (about 4 metric tons) [c]10 Probably a variant of *almugwood* [d]13 That is, about 25 tons (about 23 metric tons) [e]15 That is, about 7 1/2 pounds (about 3.5 kilograms) [f]16 That is, about 3 3/4 pounds (about 1.7 kilograms) [g]21 Hebrew *of ships that could go to Tarshish* [h]21 Hebrew *Huram,* a variant of *Hiram* [i]25 Or *charioteers* [j]26 That is, the Euphrates [k]28 Or possibly *Muzur,* a region in Cilicia

labor and the heavy yoke he put on us, and we will serve you."

5 Rehoboam answered, "Come back to me in three days." So the people went away.

6 Then King Rehoboam consulted the elders who had served his father Solomon during his lifetime. "How would you advise me to answer these people?" he asked.

7 They replied, "If you will be kind to these people and please them and give them a favorable answer, they will always be your servants."

8 But Rehoboam rejected the advice the elders gave him and consulted the young men who had grown up with him and were serving him. 9 He asked them, "What is your advice? How should we answer these people who say to me, 'Lighten the yoke your father put on us'?"

10 The young men who had grown up with him replied, "Tell the people who have said to you, 'Your father put a heavy yoke on us, but make our yoke lighter'—tell them, 'My little finger is thicker than my father's waist. 11 My father laid on you a heavy yoke; I will make it even heavier. My father scourged you with whips; I will scourge you with scorpions.' "

12 Three days later Jeroboam and all the people returned to Rehoboam, as the king had said, "Come back to me in three days." 13 The king answered them harshly. Rejecting the advice of the elders, 14 he followed the advice of the young men and said, "My father made your yoke heavy; I will make it even heavier. My father scourged you with whips; I will scourge you with scorpions." 15 So the king did not listen to the people, for this turn of events was from God, to fulfill the word the LORD had spoken to Jeroboam son of Nebat through Ahijah the Shilonite.

16 When all Israel saw that the king refused to listen to them, they answered the king:

"What share do we have in David,
  what part in Jesse's son?
To your tents, O Israel!
  Look after your own house, O David!"

So all the Israelites went home. 17 But as for the Israelites who were living in the towns of Judah, Rehoboam still ruled over them.

18 King Rehoboam sent out Adoniram,[a] who was in charge of forced labor, but the Israelites stoned him to death. King Rehoboam, however, managed to get into his chariot and escape to Jerusalem. 19 So Israel has been in rebellion against the house of David to this day.

11 When Rehoboam arrived in Jerusalem, he mustered the house of Judah and Benjamin—a hundred and eighty thousand fighting men—to make war against Israel and to regain the kingdom for Rehoboam.

2 But this word of the LORD came to Shemaiah the man of God: 3 "Say to Rehoboam son of Solomon king of Judah and to all the Israelites in Judah and Benjamin, 4 'This is what the LORD says: Do not go up to fight against your brothers. Go home, every one of you, for this is my doing.' " So they obeyed the words of the LORD and turned back from marching against Jeroboam.

Rehoboam Fortifies Judah

5 Rehoboam lived in Jerusalem and built up towns for defense in Judah: 6 Bethlehem, Etam, Tekoa, 7 Beth Zur, Soco, Adullam, 8 Gath, Mareshah, Ziph, 9 Adoraim, Lachish, Azekah, 10 Zorah, Aijalon and Hebron. These were fortified cities in Judah and Benjamin. 11 He strengthened their defenses and put commanders in them, with supplies of food, olive oil and wine. 12 He put shields and spears in all the cities, and made them very strong. So Judah and Benjamin were his.

13 The priests and Levites from all their districts throughout Israel sided with him. 14 The Levites even abandoned their pasturelands and property, and came to Judah and Jerusalem because Jeroboam and his sons had rejected them as priests of the LORD. 15 And he appointed his own priests for the high places and for the goat and calf idols he had made. 16 Those from every tribe of Israel who set their hearts on seeking the LORD, the God of Israel, followed the Levites to Jerusalem to offer sacrifices to the LORD, the God of their fathers. 17 They strengthened the kingdom of Judah and supported Rehoboam son of Solomon three years, walking in the ways of David and Solomon during this time.

Rehoboam's Family

18 Rehoboam married Mahalath, who was the daughter of David's son Jerimoth and of Abihail, the daughter of Jesse's son Eliab. 19 She bore him sons: Jeush, Shemariah and Zaham. 20 Then he married Maacah daughter of Absalom, who bore him Abijah, Attai, Ziza and Shelomith. 21 Rehoboam loved Maacah daughter of Absalom more than any of his other wives and concubines. In all, he had eighteen wives and sixty concubines, twenty-eight sons and sixty daughters.

22 Rehoboam appointed Abijah son of Maacah to be the chief prince among his brothers, in order to make him king. 23 He acted wisely, dispersing some of his sons throughout the districts of Judah and Benjamin, and to all the fortified cities. He gave them abundant provisions and took many wives for them.

Shishak Attacks Jerusalem

12 After Rehoboam's position as king was established and he had become strong, he and all Israel[b] with him abandoned the law of the LORD. 2 Because they had been unfaithful to the LORD, Shishak king of Egypt attacked Jerusalem in the fifth year of King Rehoboam. 3 With twelve hundred chariots and sixty thousand horsemen and the innumerable

[a] *18* Hebrew *Hadoram*, a variant of *Adoniram* [b] *1* That is, Judah, as frequently in 2 Chronicles

troops of Libyans, Sukkites and Cushites[a] that came with him from Egypt, 4he captured the fortified cities of Judah and came as far as Jerusalem.

5Then the prophet Shemaiah came to Rehoboam and to the leaders of Judah who had assembled in Jerusalem for fear of Shishak, and he said to them, "This is what the LORD says, 'You have abandoned me; therefore, I now abandon you to Shishak.' "

6The leaders of Israel and the king humbled themselves and said, "The LORD is just."

7When the LORD saw that they humbled themselves, this word of the LORD came to Shemaiah: "Since they have humbled themselves, I will not destroy them but will soon give them deliverance. My wrath will not be poured out on Jerusalem through Shishak. 8They will, however, become subject to him, so that they may learn the difference between serving me and serving the kings of other lands."

9When Shishak king of Egypt attacked Jerusalem, he carried off the treasures of the temple of the LORD and the treasures of the royal palace. He took everything, including the gold shields Solomon had made. 10So King Rehoboam made bronze shields to replace them and assigned these to the commanders of the guard on duty at the entrance to the royal palace. 11Whenever the king went to the LORD's temple, the guards went with him, bearing the shields, and afterward they returned them to the guardroom.

12Because Rehoboam humbled himself, the LORD's anger turned from him, and he was not totally destroyed. Indeed, there was some good in Judah.

13King Rehoboam established himself firmly in Jerusalem and continued as king. He was forty-one years old when he became king, and he reigned seventeen years in Jerusalem, the city the LORD had chosen out of all the tribes of Israel in which to put his Name. His mother's name was Naamah; she was an Ammonite. 14He did evil because he had not set his heart on seeking the LORD.

15As for the events of Rehoboam's reign, from beginning to end, are they not written in the records of Shemaiah the prophet and of Iddo the seer that deal with genealogies? There was continual warfare between Rehoboam and Jeroboam. 16Rehoboam rested with his fathers and was buried in the City of David. And Abijah his son succeeded him as king.

Abijah King of Judah

13 In the eighteenth year of the reign of Jeroboam, Abijah became king of Judah, 2and he reigned in Jerusalem three years. His mother's name was Maacah,[b] a daughter[c] of Uriel of Gibeah.

There was war between Abijah and Jeroboam. 3Abijah went into battle with a force of four hundred thousand able fighting men, and Jeroboam drew up a battle line against him with eight hundred thousand able troops.

4Abijah stood on Mount Zemaraim, in the hill country of Ephraim, and said, "Jeroboam and all Israel, listen to me! 5Don't you know that the LORD, the God of Israel, has given the kingship of Israel to David and his descendants forever by a covenant of salt? 6Yet Jeroboam son of Nebat, an official of Solomon son of David, rebelled against his master. 7Some worthless scoundrels gathered around him and opposed Rehoboam son of Solomon when he was young and indecisive and not strong enough to resist them.

8"And now you plan to resist the kingdom of the LORD, which is in the hands of David's descendants. You are indeed a vast army and have with you the golden calves that Jeroboam made to be your gods. 9But didn't you drive out the priests of the LORD, the sons of Aaron, and the Levites, and make priests of your own as the peoples of other lands do? Whoever comes to consecrate himself with a young bull and seven rams may become a priest of what are not gods.

10"As for us, the LORD is our God, and we have not forsaken him. The priests who serve the LORD are sons of Aaron, and the Levites assist them. 11Every morning and evening they present burnt offerings and fragrant incense to the LORD. They set out the bread on the ceremonially clean table and light the lamps on the gold lampstand every evening. We are observing the requirements of the LORD our God. But you have forsaken him. 12God is with us; he is our leader. His priests with their trumpets will sound the battle cry against you. Men of Israel, do not fight against the LORD, the God of your fathers, for you will not succeed."

13Now Jeroboam had sent troops around to the rear, so that while he was in front of Judah the ambush was behind them. 14Judah turned and saw that they were being attacked at both front and rear. Then they cried out to the LORD. The priests blew their trumpets 15and the men of Judah raised the battle cry. At the sound of their battle cry, God routed Jeroboam and all Israel before Abijah and Judah. 16The Israelites fled before Judah, and God delivered them into their hands. 17Abijah and his men inflicted heavy losses on them, so that there were five hundred thousand casualties among Israel's able men. 18The men of Israel were subdued on that occasion, and the men of Judah were victorious because they relied on the LORD, the God of their fathers.

19Abijah pursued Jeroboam and took from him the towns of Bethel, Jeshanah and Ephron, with their surrounding villages. 20Jeroboam did not regain power during the time of Abijah. And the LORD struck him down and he died.

21But Abijah grew in strength. He married

[a]3 That is, people from the upper Nile region [b]2 Most Septuagint manuscripts and Syriac (see also 2 Chron. 11:20 and 1 Kings 15:2); Hebrew *Micaiah* [c]2 Or *granddaughter*

fourteen wives and had twenty-two sons and
sixteen daughters.
22The other events of Abijah's reign, what
he did and what he said, are written in the
annotations of the prophet Iddo.

14 And Abijah rested with his fathers and
was buried in the City of David. Asa his
son succeeded him as king, and in his days the
country was at peace for ten years.

Asa King of Judah

2Asa did what was good and right in the
eyes of the LORD his God. 3He removed the
foreign altars and the high places, smashed
the sacred stones and cut down the Asherah
poles.[a] 4He commanded Judah to seek the
LORD, the God of their fathers, and to obey his
laws and commands. 5He removed the high
places and incense altars in every town in Judah, and the kingdom was at peace under him.
6He built up the fortified cities of Judah, since
the land was at peace. No one was at war with
him during those years, for the LORD gave him
rest.
7"Let us build up these towns," he said to
Judah, "and put walls around them, with towers, gates and bars. The land is still ours, because we have sought the LORD our God; we
sought him and he has given us rest on every
side." So they built and prospered.
8Asa had an army of three hundred thousand
men from Judah, equipped with large shields
and with spears, and two hundred and eighty
thousand from Benjamin, armed with small
shields and with bows. All these were brave
fighting men.
9Zerah the Cushite marched out against
them with a vast army[b] and three hundred
chariots, and came as far as Mareshah. 10Asa
went out to meet him, and they took up battle
positions in the Valley of Zephathah near Mareshah.
11Then Asa called to the LORD his God and
said, "LORD, there is no one like you to help
the powerless against the mighty. Help us,
O LORD our God, for we rely on you, and in
your name we have come against this vast
army. O LORD, you are our God; do not let
man prevail against you."
12The LORD struck down the Cushites before Asa and Judah. The Cushites fled, 13and
Asa and his army pursued them as far as Gerar.
Such a great number of Cushites fell that they
could not recover; they were crushed before
the LORD and his forces. The men of Judah
carried off a large amount of plunder. 14They
destroyed all the villages around Gerar, for the
terror of the LORD had fallen upon them. They
plundered all these villages, since there was
much booty there. 15They also attacked the
camps of the herdsmen and carried off droves
of sheep and goats and camels. Then they returned to Jerusalem.

Asa's Reform

15 The Spirit of God came upon Azariah
son of Oded. 2He went out to meet Asa
and said to him, "Listen to me, Asa and all
Judah and Benjamin. The LORD is with you
when you are with him. If you seek him, he
will be found by you, but if you forsake him,
he will forsake you. 3For a long time Israel was
without the true God, without a priest to teach
and without the law. 4But in their distress they
turned to the LORD, the God of Israel, and
sought him, and he was found by them. 5In
those days it was not safe to travel about, for
all the inhabitants of the lands were in great
turmoil. 6One nation was being crushed by another and one city by another, because God
was troubling them with every kind of distress.
7But as for you, be strong and do not give up,
for your work will be rewarded."
8When Asa heard these words and the
prophecy of Azariah son of[c] Oded the prophet,
he took courage. He removed the detestable
idols from the whole land of Judah and Benjamin and from the towns he had captured in the
hills of Ephraim. He repaired the altar of the
LORD that was in front of the portico of
the LORD's temple.
9Then he assembled all Judah and Benjamin
and the people from Ephraim, Manasseh and
Simeon who had settled among them, for large
numbers had come over to him from Israel
when they saw that the LORD his God was with
him.
10They assembled at Jerusalem in the third
month of the fifteenth year of Asa's reign. 11At
that time they sacrificed to the LORD seven
hundred head of cattle and seven thousand
sheep and goats from the plunder they had
brought back. 12They entered into a covenant
to seek the LORD, the God of their fathers, with
all their heart and soul. 13All who would not
seek the LORD, the God of Israel, were to be
put to death, whether small or great, man or
woman. 14They took an oath to the LORD with
loud acclamation, with shouting and with
trumpets and horns. 15All Judah rejoiced about
the oath because they had sworn it wholeheartedly. They sought God eagerly, and he was
found by them. So the LORD gave them rest on
every side.
16King Asa also deposed his grandmother
Maacah from her position as queen mother,
because she had made a repulsive Asherah
pole. Asa cut the pole down, broke it up and
burned it in the Kidron Valley. 17Although he
did not remove the high places from Israel,
Asa's heart was fully committed ⌊to the LORD⌋
all his life. 18He brought into the temple of
God the silver and gold and the articles that he
and his father had dedicated.
19There was no more war until the thirty-
fifth year of Asa's reign.

[a] *3* That is, symbols of the goddess Asherah; here and elsewhere in 2 Chronicles [b] *9* Hebrew *with an army of a thousand thousands* or *with an army of thousands upon thousands* [c] *8* Vulgate and Syriac (see also Septuagint and verse 1); Hebrew does not have *Azariah son of.*

Asa's Last Years

16 In the thirty-sixth year of Asa's reign Baasha king of Israel went up against Judah and fortified Ramah to prevent anyone from leaving or entering the territory of Asa king of Judah.

2Asa then took the silver and gold out of the treasuries of the LORD's temple and of his own palace and sent it to Ben-Hadad king of Aram, who was ruling in Damascus. 3"Let there be a treaty between me and you," he said, "as there was between my father and your father. See, I am sending you silver and gold. Now break your treaty with Baasha king of Israel so he will withdraw from me."

4Ben-Hadad agreed with King Asa and sent the commanders of his forces against the towns of Israel. They conquered Ijon, Dan, Abel Maim[a] and all the store cities of Naphtali. 5When Baasha heard this, he stopped building Ramah and abandoned his work. 6Then King Asa brought all the men of Judah, and they carried away from Ramah the stones and timber Baasha had been using. With them he built up Geba and Mizpah.

7At that time Hanani the seer came to Asa king of Judah and said to him: "Because you relied on the king of Aram and not on the LORD your God, the army of the king of Aram has escaped from your hand. 8Were not the Cushites[b] and Libyans a mighty army with great numbers of chariots and horsemen[c]? Yet when you relied on the LORD, he delivered them into your hand. 9For the eyes of the LORD range throughout the earth to strengthen those whose hearts are fully committed to him. You have done a foolish thing, and from now on you will be at war."

10Asa was angry with the seer because of this; he was so enraged that he put him in prison. At the same time Asa brutally oppressed some of the people.

11The events of Asa's reign, from beginning to end, are written in the book of the kings of Judah and Israel. 12In the thirty-ninth year of his reign Asa was afflicted with a disease in his feet. Though his disease was severe, even in his illness he did not seek help from the LORD, but only from the physicians. 13Then in the forty-first year of his reign Asa died and rested with his fathers. 14They buried him in the tomb that he had cut out for himself in the City of David. They laid him on a bier covered with spices and various blended perfumes, and they made a huge fire in his honor.

Jehoshaphat King of Judah

17 Jehoshaphat his son succeeded him as king and strengthened himself against Israel. 2He stationed troops in all the fortified cities of Judah and put garrisons in Judah and in the towns of Ephraim that his father Asa had captured.

3The LORD was with Jehoshaphat because in his early years he walked in the ways his father David had followed. He did not consult the Baals 4but sought the God of his father and followed his commands rather than the practices of Israel. 5The LORD established the kingdom under his control; and all Judah brought gifts to Jehoshaphat, so that he had great wealth and honor. 6His heart was devoted to the ways of the LORD; furthermore, he removed the high places and the Asherah poles from Judah.

7In the third year of his reign he sent his officials Ben-Hail, Obadiah, Zechariah, Nethanel and Micaiah to teach in the towns of Judah. 8With them were certain Levites—Shemaiah, Nethaniah, Zebadiah, Asahel, Shemiramoth, Jehonathan, Adonijah, Tobijah and Tob-Adonijah—and the priests Elishama and Jehoram. 9They taught throughout Judah, taking with them the Book of the Law of the LORD; they went around to all the towns of Judah and taught the people.

10The fear of the LORD fell on all the kingdoms of the lands surrounding Judah, so that they did not make war with Jehoshaphat. 11Some Philistines brought Jehoshaphat gifts and silver as tribute, and the Arabs brought him flocks: seven thousand seven hundred rams and seven thousand seven hundred goats.

12Jehoshaphat became more and more powerful; he built forts and store cities in Judah 13and had large supplies in the towns of Judah. He also kept experienced fighting men in Jerusalem. 14Their enrollment by families was as follows:

From Judah, commanders of units of 1,000:
Adnah the commander, with 300,000 fighting men;
15next, Jehohanan the commander, with 280,000;
16next, Amasiah son of Zicri, who volunteered himself for the service of the LORD, with 200,000.
17From Benjamin:
Eliada, a valiant soldier, with 200,000 men armed with bows and shields;
18next, Jehozabad, with 180,000 men armed for battle.

19These were the men who served the king, besides those he stationed in the fortified cities throughout Judah.

Micaiah Prophesies Against Ahab

18 Now Jehoshaphat had great wealth and honor, and he allied himself with Ahab by marriage. 2Some years later he went down to visit Ahab in Samaria. Ahab slaughtered many sheep and cattle for him and the people with him and urged him to attack Ramoth Gilead. 3Ahab king of Israel asked Jehoshaphat king of Judah, "Will you go with me against Ramoth Gilead?"

Jehoshaphat replied, "I am as you are, and my people as your people; we will join you in

[a] 4 Also known as *Abel Beth Maacah* [b] 8 That is, people from the upper Nile region [c] 8 Or *charioteers*

the war." 4But Jehoshaphat also said to the
king of Israel, "First seek the counsel of the
LORD."
5So the king of Israel brought together the
prophets—four hundred men—and asked
them, "Shall we go to war against Ramoth Gilead, or shall I refrain?"
"Go," they answered, "for God will give it
into the king's hand."
6But Jehoshaphat asked, "Is there not a
prophet of the LORD here whom we can inquire of?"
7The king of Israel answered Jehoshaphat,
"There is still one man through whom we can
inquire of the LORD, but I hate him because he
never prophesies anything good about me, but
always bad. He is Micaiah son of Imlah."
"The king should not say that," Jehoshaphat
replied.
8So the king of Israel called one of his officials and said, "Bring Micaiah son of Imlah at
once."
9Dressed in their royal robes, the king of
Israel and Jehoshaphat king of Judah were sitting on their thrones at the threshing floor by
the entrance to the gate of Samaria, with all the
prophets prophesying before them. 10Now
Zedekiah son of Kenaanah had made iron
horns, and he declared, "This is what the LORD
says: 'With these you will gore the Arameans
until they are destroyed.' "
11All the other prophets were prophesying
the same thing. "Attack Ramoth Gilead and be
victorious," they said, "for the LORD will give
it into the king's hand."
12The messenger who had gone to summon
Micaiah said to him, "Look, as one man the
other prophets are predicting success for the
king. Let your word agree with theirs, and
speak favorably."
13But Micaiah said, "As surely as the LORD
lives, I can tell him only what my God says."
14When he arrived, the king asked him, "Micaiah, shall we go to war against Ramoth Gilead, or shall I refrain?"
"Attack and be victorious," he answered,
"for they will be given into your hand."
15The king said to him, "How many times
must I make you swear to tell me nothing but
the truth in the name of the LORD?"
16Then Micaiah answered, "I saw all Israel
scattered on the hills like sheep without a shepherd, and the LORD said, 'These people have
no master. Let each one go home in peace.' "
17The king of Israel said to Jehoshaphat,
"Didn't I tell you that he never prophesies anything good about me, but only bad?"
18Micaiah continued, "Therefore hear the
word of the LORD: I saw the LORD sitting on
his throne with all the host of heaven standing
on his right and on his left. 19And the LORD
said, 'Who will entice Ahab king of Israel into
attacking Ramoth Gilead and going to his
death there?'
"One suggested this, and another that. 20Fi-
nally, a spirit came forward, stood before the
LORD and said, 'I will entice him.'
" 'By what means?' the LORD asked.
21" 'I will go and be a lying spirit in the
mouths of all his prophets,' he said.
" 'You will succeed in enticing him,' said
the LORD. 'Go and do it.'
22"So now the LORD has put a lying spirit in
the mouths of these prophets of yours. The
LORD has decreed disaster for you."
23Then Zedekiah son of Kenaanah went up
and slapped Micaiah in the face. "Which way
did the spirit from[a] the LORD go when he went
from me to speak to you?" he asked.
24Micaiah replied, "You will find out on the
day you go to hide in an inner room."
25The king of Israel then ordered, "Take Micaiah and send him back to Amon the ruler of
the city and to Joash the king's son, 26and say,
'This is what the king says: Put this fellow in
prison and give him nothing but bread and water until I return safely.' "
27Micaiah declared, "If you ever return safely, the LORD has not spoken through me."
Then he added, "Mark my words, all you people!"

Ahab Killed at Ramoth Gilead

28So the king of Israel and Jehoshaphat king
of Judah went up to Ramoth Gilead. 29The
king of Israel said to Jehoshaphat, "I will enter
the battle in disguise, but you wear your royal
robes." So the king of Israel disguised himself
and went into battle.
30Now the king of Aram had ordered his
chariot commanders, "Do not fight with anyone, small or great, except the king of Israel."
31When the chariot commanders saw Jehoshaphat, they thought, "This is the king of Israel."
So they turned to attack him, but Jehoshaphat
cried out, and the LORD helped him. God drew
them away from him, 32for when the chariot
commanders saw that he was not the king of
Israel, they stopped pursuing him.
33But someone drew his bow at random and
hit the king of Israel between the sections of
his armor. The king told the chariot driver,
"Wheel around and get me out of the fighting.
I've been wounded." 34All day long the battle
raged, and the king of Israel propped himself
up in his chariot facing the Arameans until
evening. Then at sunset he died.

19 When Jehoshaphat king of Judah returned safely to his palace in Jerusalem,
2Jehu the seer, the son of Hanani, went out to
meet him and said to the king, "Should you
help the wicked and love[b] those who hate the
LORD? Because of this, the wrath of the LORD
is upon you. 3There is, however, some good in
you, for you have rid the land of the Asherah
poles and have set your heart on seeking God."

Jehoshaphat Appoints Judges

4Jehoshaphat lived in Jerusalem, and he
went out again among the people from Beer-

[a]23 Or *Spirit of* [b]2 Or *and make alliances with*

sheba to the hill country of Ephraim and turned
them back to the LORD, the God of their fathers. 5He appointed judges in the land, in each
of the fortified cities of Judah. 6He told them,
"Consider carefully what you do, because you
are not judging for man but for the LORD, who
is with you whenever you give a verdict. 7Now
let the fear of the LORD be upon you. Judge
carefully, for with the LORD our God there is
no injustice or partiality or bribery."
8In Jerusalem also, Jehoshaphat appointed
some of the Levites, priests and heads of Israelite families to administer the law of the LORD
and to settle disputes. And they lived in Jerusalem. 9He gave them these orders: "You must
serve faithfully and wholeheartedly in the fear
of the LORD. 10In every case that comes before
you from your fellow countrymen who live in
the cities—whether bloodshed or other concerns of the law, commands, decrees or ordinances—you are to warn them not to sin
against the LORD; otherwise his wrath will
come on you and your brothers. Do this, and
you will not sin.
11"Amariah the chief priest will be over you
in any matter concerning the LORD, and Zebadiah son of Ishmael, the leader of the tribe of
Judah, will be over you in any matter concerning the king, and the Levites will serve as officials before you. Act with courage, and may
the LORD be with those who do well."

Jehoshaphat Defeats Moab and Ammon

20 After this, the Moabites and Ammonites
with some of the Meunites[a] came to
make war on Jehoshaphat.
2Some men came and told Jehoshaphat, "A
vast army is coming against you from Edom,[b]
from the other side of the Sea.[c] It is already in
Hazazon Tamar" (that is, En Gedi). 3Alarmed,
Jehoshaphat resolved to inquire of the LORD,
and he proclaimed a fast for all Judah. 4The
people of Judah came together to seek help
from the LORD; indeed, they came from every
town in Judah to seek him.
5Then Jehoshaphat stood up in the assembly
of Judah and Jerusalem at the temple of the
LORD in the front of the new courtyard 6and
said:

"O LORD, God of our fathers, are you
not the God who is in heaven? You rule
over all the kingdoms of the nations.
Power and might are in your hand, and no
one can withstand you. 7O our God, did
you not drive out the inhabitants of this
land before your people Israel and give it
forever to the descendants of Abraham
your friend? 8They have lived in it and
have built in it a sanctuary for your Name,
saying, 9'If calamity comes upon us,
whether the sword of judgment, or plague
or famine, we will stand in your presence
before this temple that bears your Name
and will cry out to you in our distress, and
you will hear us and save us.'
10"But now here are men from Ammon, Moab and Mount Seir, whose territory you would not allow Israel to invade
when they came from Egypt; so they
turned away from them and did not destroy them. 11See how they are repaying
us by coming to drive us out of the possession you gave us as an inheritance.
12O our God, will you not judge them?
For we have no power to face this vast
army that is attacking us. We do not know
what to do, but our eyes are upon you."

13All the men of Judah, with their wives and
children and little ones, stood there before the
LORD.
14Then the Spirit of the LORD came upon
Jahaziel son of Zechariah, the son of Benaiah,
the son of Jeiel, the son of Mattaniah, a Levite
and descendant of Asaph, as he stood in the
assembly.
15He said: "Listen, King Jehoshaphat and all
who live in Judah and Jerusalem! This is what
the LORD says to you: 'Do not be afraid or
discouraged because of this vast army. For the
battle is not yours, but God's. 16Tomorrow
march down against them. They will be climb-
ing up by the Pass of Ziz, and you will find
them at the end of the gorge in the Desert of
Jeruel. 17You will not have to fight this battle.
Take up your positions; stand firm and see the
deliverance the LORD will give you, O Judah
and Jerusalem. Do not be afraid; do not be
discouraged. Go out to face them tomorrow,
and the LORD will be with you.' "
18Jehoshaphat bowed with his face to the
ground, and all the people of Judah and Jerusalem fell down in worship before the LORD.
19Then some Levites from the Kohathites and
Korahites stood up and praised the LORD, the
God of Israel, with very loud voice.
20Early in the morning they left for the
Desert of Tekoa. As they set out, Jehoshaphat
stood and said, "Listen to me, Judah and people of Jerusalem! Have faith in the LORD your
God and you will be upheld; have faith in his
prophets and you will be successful." 21After
consulting the people, Jehoshaphat appointed
men to sing to the LORD and to praise him for
the splendor of his[d] holiness as they went out
at the head of the army, saying:

"Give thanks to the LORD,
for his love endures forever."

22As they began to sing and praise, the
LORD set ambushes against the men of Ammon and Moab and Mount Seir who were invading Judah, and they were defeated. 23The
men of Ammon and Moab rose up against the
men from Mount Seir to destroy and annihilate
them. After they finished slaughtering the men
from Seir, they helped to destroy one another.
24When the men of Judah came to the place

[a]*1* Some Septuagint manuscripts; Hebrew *Ammonites* [b]*2* One Hebrew manuscript; most Hebrew manuscripts, Septuagint and Vulgate *Aram* [c]*2* That is, the Dead Sea [d]*21* Or *him with the splendor of*

that overlooks the desert and looked toward
the vast army, they saw only dead bodies lying
on the ground; no one had escaped. 25So Jehoshaphat and his men went to carry off their
plunder, and they found among them a great
amount of equipment and clothing[a] and also
articles of value—more than they could take
away. There was so much plunder that it took
three days to collect it. 26On the fourth day
they assembled in the Valley of Beracah,
where they praised the LORD. This is why it is
called the Valley of Beracah[b] to this day.

27Then, led by Jehoshaphat, all the men of
Judah and Jerusalem returned joyfully to Jerusalem, for the LORD had given them cause to
rejoice over their enemies. 28They entered Jerusalem and went to the temple of the LORD
with harps and lutes and trumpets.

29The fear of God came upon all the kingdoms of the countries when they heard how the
LORD had fought against the enemies of Israel.
30And the kingdom of Jehoshaphat was at
peace, for his God had given him rest on every
side.

The End of Jehoshaphat's Reign

31So Jehoshaphat reigned over Judah. He
was thirty-five years old when he became king
of Judah, and he reigned in Jerusalem twenty-
five years. His mother's name was Azubah
daughter of Shilhi. 32He walked in the ways of
his father Asa and did not stray from them; he
did what was right in the eyes of the LORD.
33The high places, however, were not removed, and the people still had not set their
hearts on the God of their fathers.

34The other events of Jehoshaphat's reign,
from beginning to end, are written in the annals of Jehu son of Hanani, which are recorded
in the book of the kings of Israel.

35Later, Jehoshaphat king of Judah made an
alliance with Ahaziah king of Israel, who was
guilty of wickedness. 36He agreed with him to
construct a fleet of trading ships.[c] After these
were built at Ezion Geber, 37Eliezer son of
Dodavahu of Mareshah prophesied against Jehoshaphat, saying, "Because you have made
an alliance with Ahaziah, the LORD will destroy what you have made." The ships were
wrecked and were not able to set sail to trade.[d]

21 Then Jehoshaphat rested with his fathers and was buried with them in the
City of David. And Jehoram his son succeeded
him as king. 2Jehoram's brothers, the sons of
Jehoshaphat, were Azariah, Jehiel, Zechariah,
Azariahu, Michael and Shephatiah. All these
were sons of Jehoshaphat king of Israel.[e]
3Their father had given them many gifts of
silver and gold and articles of value, as well as
fortified cities in Judah, but he had given the
kingdom to Jehoram because he was his firstborn son.

Jehoram King of Judah

4When Jehoram established himself firmly
over his father's kingdom, he put all his brothers to the sword along with some of the princes
of Israel. 5Jehoram was thirty-two years old
when he became king, and he reigned in Jerusalem eight years. 6He walked in the ways of
the kings of Israel, as the house of Ahab had
done, for he married a daughter of Ahab. He
did evil in the eyes of the LORD. 7Nevertheless,
because of the covenant the LORD had made
with David, the LORD was not willing to destroy the house of David. He had promised to
maintain a lamp for him and his descendants
forever.

8In the time of Jehoram, Edom rebelled
against Judah and set up its own king. 9So
Jehoram went there with his officers and all his
chariots. The Edomites surrounded him and his
chariot commanders, but he rose up and broke
through by night. 10To this day Edom has been
in rebellion against Judah.

Libnah revolted at the same time, because
Jehoram had forsaken the LORD, the God of his
fathers. 11He had also built high places on the
hills of Judah and had caused the people of
Jerusalem to prostitute themselves and had led
Judah astray.

12Jehoram received a letter from Elijah the
prophet, which said:

> "This is what the LORD, the God of your
> father David, says: 'You have not walked
> in the ways of your father Jehoshaphat or
> of Asa king of Judah. 13But you have
> walked in the ways of the kings of Israel,
> and you have led Judah and the people of
> Jerusalem to prostitute themselves, just as
> the house of Ahab did. You have also
> murdered your own brothers, members of
> your father's house, men who were better
> than you. 14So now the LORD is about to
> strike your people, your sons, your wives
> and everything that is yours, with a heavy
> blow. 15You yourself will be very ill with
> a lingering disease of the bowels, until
> the disease causes your bowels to come
> out.' "

16The LORD aroused against Jehoram the
hostility of the Philistines and of the Arabs
who lived near the Cushites. 17They attacked
Judah, invaded it and carried off all the goods
found in the king's palace, together with his
sons and wives. Not a son was left to him
except Ahaziah,[f] the youngest.

18After all this, the LORD afflicted Jehoram
with an incurable disease of the bowels. 19In
the course of time, at the end of the second
year, his bowels came out because of the disease, and he died in great pain. His people
made no fire in his honor, as they had for his
fathers.

20Jehoram was thirty-two years old when

[a] *25* Some Hebrew manuscripts and Vulgate; most Hebrew manuscripts *corpses* [b] *26* *Beracah* means *praise.* [c] *36* Hebrew *of ships that could go to Tarshish* [d] *37* Hebrew *sail for Tarshish* [e] *2* That is, Judah, as frequently in 2 Chronicles [f] *17* Hebrew *Jehoahaz,* a variant of *Ahaziah*

he became king, and he reigned in Jerusalem eight years. He passed away, to no one's regret, and was buried in the City of David, but not in the tombs of the kings.

Ahaziah King of Judah

22 The people of Jerusalem made Ahaziah, Jehoram's youngest son, king in his place, since the raiders, who came with the Arabs into the camp, had killed all the older sons. So Ahaziah son of Jehoram king of Judah began to reign.

2 Ahaziah was twenty-two[a] years old when he became king, and he reigned in Jerusalem one year. His mother's name was Athaliah, a granddaughter of Omri.

3 He too walked in the ways of the house of Ahab, for his mother encouraged him in doing wrong. 4 He did evil in the eyes of the LORD, as the house of Ahab had done, for after his father's death they became his advisers, to his undoing. 5 He also followed their counsel when he went with Joram[b] son of Ahab king of Israel to war against Hazael king of Aram at Ramoth Gilead. The Arameans wounded Joram; 6 so he returned to Jezreel to recover from the wounds they had inflicted on him at Ramoth[c] in his battle with Hazael king of Aram.

Then Ahaziah[d] son of Jehoram king of Judah went down to Jezreel to see Joram son of Ahab because he had been wounded.

7 Through Ahaziah's visit to Joram, God brought about Ahaziah's downfall. When Ahaziah arrived, he went out with Joram to meet Jehu son of Nimshi, whom the LORD had anointed to destroy the house of Ahab. 8 While Jehu was executing judgment on the house of Ahab, he found the princes of Judah and the sons of Ahaziah's relatives, who had been attending Ahaziah, and he killed them. 9 He then went in search of Ahaziah, and his men captured him while he was hiding in Samaria. He was brought to Jehu and put to death. They buried him, for they said, "He was a son of Jehoshaphat, who sought the LORD with all his heart." So there was no one in the house of Ahaziah powerful enough to retain the kingdom.

Athaliah and Joash

10 When Athaliah the mother of Ahaziah saw that her son was dead, she proceeded to destroy the whole royal family of the house of Judah. 11 But Jehosheba,[e] the daughter of King Jehoram, took Joash son of Ahaziah and stole him away from among the royal princes who were about to be murdered and put him and his nurse in a bedroom. Because Jehosheba,[e] the daughter of King Jehoram and wife of the priest Jehoiada, was Ahaziah's sister, she hid the child from Athaliah so she could not kill him. 12 He remained hidden with them at the temple of God for six years while Athaliah ruled the land.

23 In the seventh year Jehoiada showed his strength. He made a covenant with the commanders of units of a hundred: Azariah son of Jeroham, Ishmael son of Jehohanan, Azariah son of Obed, Maaseiah son of Adaiah, and Elishaphat son of Zicri. 2 They went throughout Judah and gathered the Levites and the heads of Israelite families from all the towns. When they came to Jerusalem, 3 the whole assembly made a covenant with the king at the temple of God.

Jehoiada said to them, "The king's son shall reign, as the LORD promised concerning the descendants of David. 4 Now this is what you are to do: A third of you priests and Levites who are going on duty on the Sabbath are to keep watch at the doors, 5 a third of you at the royal palace and a third at the Foundation Gate, and all the other men are to be in the courtyards of the temple of the LORD. 6 No one is to enter the temple of the LORD except the priests and Levites on duty; they may enter because they are consecrated, but all the other men are to guard what the LORD has assigned to them.[f] 7 The Levites are to station themselves around the king, each man with his weapons in his hand. Anyone who enters the temple must be put to death. Stay close to the king wherever he goes."

8 The Levites and all the men of Judah did just as Jehoiada the priest ordered. Each one took his men—those who were going on duty on the Sabbath and those who were going off duty—for Jehoiada the priest had not released any of the divisions. 9 Then he gave the commanders of units of a hundred the spears and the large and small shields that had belonged to King David and that were in the temple of God. 10 He stationed all the men, each with his weapon in his hand, around the king—near the altar and the temple, from the south side to the north side of the temple.

11 Jehoiada and his sons brought out the king's son and put the crown on him; they presented him with a copy of the covenant and proclaimed him king. They anointed him and shouted, "Long live the king!"

12 When Athaliah heard the noise of the people running and cheering the king, she went to them at the temple of the LORD. 13 She looked, and there was the king, standing by his pillar at the entrance. The officers and the trumpeters were beside the king, and all the people of the land were rejoicing and blowing trumpets, and singers with musical instruments were leading the praises. Then Athaliah tore her robes and shouted, "Treason! Treason!"

14 Jehoiada the priest sent out the commanders of units of a hundred, who were in charge of the troops, and said to them: "Bring her out

[a]2 Some Septuagint manuscripts and Syriac (see also 2 Kings 8:26); Hebrew *forty-two* [b]5 Hebrew *Jehoram,* a variant of *Joram*; also in verses 6 and 7 [c]6 Hebrew *Ramah,* a variant of *Ramoth* [d]6 Some Hebrew manuscripts, Septuagint, Vulgate and Syriac (see also 2 Kings 8:29); most Hebrew manuscripts *Azariah* [e]11 Hebrew *Jehoshabeath,* a variant of *Jehosheba* [f]6 Or *to observe the LORD's command ⌊not to enter⌋*

between the ranks[a] and put to the sword anyone who follows her." For the priest had said, "Do not put her to death at the temple of the LORD." **15**So they seized her as she reached the entrance of the Horse Gate on the palace grounds, and there they put her to death.

16Jehoiada then made a covenant that he and the people and the king[b] would be the LORD's people. **17**All the people went to the temple of Baal and tore it down. They smashed the altars and idols and killed Mattan the priest of Baal in front of the altars.

18Then Jehoiada placed the oversight of the temple of the LORD in the hands of the priests, who were Levites, to whom David had made assignments in the temple, to present the burnt offerings of the LORD as written in the Law of Moses, with rejoicing and singing, as David had ordered. **19**He also stationed doorkeepers at the gates of the LORD's temple so that no one who was in any way unclean might enter.

20He took with him the commanders of hundreds, the nobles, the rulers of the people and all the people of the land and brought the king down from the temple of the LORD. They went into the palace through the Upper Gate and seated the king on the royal throne, **21**and all the people of the land rejoiced. And the city was quiet, because Athaliah had been slain with the sword.

Joash Repairs the Temple

24 Joash was seven years old when he became king, and he reigned in Jerusalem forty years. His mother's name was Zibiah; she was from Beersheba. **2**Joash did what was right in the eyes of the LORD all the years of Jehoiada the priest. **3**Jehoiada chose two wives for him, and he had sons and daughters.

4Some time later Joash decided to restore the temple of the LORD. **5**He called together the priests and Levites and said to them, "Go to the towns of Judah and collect the money due annually from all Israel, to repair the temple of your God. Do it now." But the Levites did not act at once.

6Therefore the king summoned Jehoiada the chief priest and said to him, "Why haven't you required the Levites to bring in from Judah and Jerusalem the tax imposed by Moses the servant of the LORD and by the assembly of Israel for the Tent of the Testimony?"

7Now the sons of that wicked woman Athaliah had broken into the temple of God and had used even its sacred objects for the Baals.

8At the king's command, a chest was made and placed outside, at the gate of the temple of the LORD. **9**A proclamation was then issued in Judah and Jerusalem that they should bring to the LORD the tax that Moses the servant of God had required of Israel in the desert. **10**All the officials and all the people brought their contributions gladly, dropping them into the chest until it was full. **11**Whenever the chest was brought in by the Levites to the king's officials and they saw that there was a large amount of money, the royal secretary and the officer of the chief priest would come and empty the chest and carry it back to its place. They did this regularly and collected a great amount of money. **12**The king and Jehoiada gave it to the men who carried out the work required for the temple of the LORD. They hired masons and carpenters to restore the LORD's temple, and also workers in iron and bronze to repair the temple.

13The men in charge of the work were diligent, and the repairs progressed under them. They rebuilt the temple of God according to its original design and reinforced it. **14**When they had finished, they brought the rest of the money to the king and Jehoiada, and with it were made articles for the LORD's temple: articles for the service and for the burnt offerings, and also dishes and other objects of gold and silver. As long as Jehoiada lived, burnt offerings were presented continually in the temple of the LORD.

15Now Jehoiada was old and full of years, and he died at the age of a hundred and thirty. **16**He was buried with the kings in the City of David, because of the good he had done in Israel for God and his temple.

The Wickedness of Joash

17After the death of Jehoiada, the officials of Judah came and paid homage to the king, and he listened to them. **18**They abandoned the temple of the LORD, the God of their fathers, and worshiped Asherah poles and idols. Because of their guilt, God's anger came upon Judah and Jerusalem. **19**Although the LORD sent prophets to the people to bring them back to him, and though they testified against them, they would not listen.

20Then the Spirit of God came upon Zechariah son of Jehoiada the priest. He stood before the people and said, "This is what God says: 'Why do you disobey the LORD's commands? You will not prosper. Because you have forsaken the LORD, he has forsaken you.' "

21But they plotted against him, and by order of the king they stoned him to death in the courtyard of the LORD's temple. **22**King Joash did not remember the kindness Zechariah's father Jehoiada had shown him but killed his son, who said as he lay dying, "May the LORD see this and call you to account."

23At the turn of the year,[c] the army of Aram marched against Joash; it invaded Judah and Jerusalem and killed all the leaders of the people. They sent all the plunder to their king in Damascus. **24**Although the Aramean army had come with only a few men, the LORD delivered into their hands a much larger army. Because Judah had forsaken the LORD, the God of their fathers, judgment was executed on Joash. **25**When the Arameans withdrew, they left Jo-

[a]14 Or *out from the precincts* [b]16 Or *covenant between* ⌊*the LORD*⌋ *and the people and the king that they* (see 2 Kings 11:17) [c]23 Probably in the spring

ash severely wounded. His officials conspired against him for murdering the son of Jehoiada the priest, and they killed him in his bed. So he died and was buried in the City of David, but not in the tombs of the kings.

26Those who conspired against him were Zabad,[a] son of Shimeath an Ammonite woman, and Jehozabad, son of Shimrith[b] a Moabite woman. 27The account of his sons, the many prophecies about him, and the record of the restoration of the temple of God are written in the annotations on the book of the kings. And Amaziah his son succeeded him as king.

Amaziah King of Judah

25 Amaziah was twenty-five years old when he became king, and he reigned in Jerusalem twenty-nine years. His mother's name was Jehoaddin[c]; she was from Jerusalem. 2He did what was right in the eyes of the LORD, but not wholeheartedly. 3After the kingdom was firmly in his control, he executed the officials who had murdered his father the king. 4Yet he did not put their sons to death, but acted in accordance with what is written in the Law, in the Book of Moses, where the LORD commanded: "Fathers shall not be put to death for their children, nor children put to death for their fathers; each is to die for his own sins."[d]

5Amaziah called the people of Judah together and assigned them according to their families to commanders of thousands and commanders of hundreds for all Judah and Benjamin. He then mustered those twenty years old or more and found that there were three hundred thousand men ready for military service, able to handle the spear and shield. 6He also hired a hundred thousand fighting men from Israel for a hundred talents[e] of silver.

7But a man of God came to him and said, "O king, these troops from Israel must not march with you, for the LORD is not with Israel—not with any of the people of Ephraim. 8Even if you go and fight courageously in battle, God will overthrow you before the enemy, for God has the power to help or to overthrow."

9Amaziah asked the man of God, "But what about the hundred talents I paid for these Israelite troops?"

The man of God replied, "The LORD can give you much more than that."

10So Amaziah dismissed the troops who had come to him from Ephraim and sent them home. They were furious with Judah and left for home in a great rage.

11Amaziah then marshaled his strength and led his army to the Valley of Salt, where he killed ten thousand men of Seir. 12The army of Judah also captured ten thousand men alive, took them to the top of a cliff and threw them down so that all were dashed to pieces.

13Meanwhile the troops that Amaziah had sent back and had not allowed to take part in the war raided Judean towns from Samaria to Beth Horon. They killed three thousand people and carried off great quantities of plunder.

14When Amaziah returned from slaughtering the Edomites, he brought back the gods of the people of Seir. He set them up as his own gods, bowed down to them and burned sacrifices to them. 15The anger of the LORD burned against Amaziah, and he sent a prophet to him, who said, "Why do you consult this people's gods, which could not save their own people from your hand?"

16While he was still speaking, the king said to him, "Have we appointed you an adviser to the king? Stop! Why be struck down?"

So the prophet stopped but said, "I know that God has determined to destroy you, because you have done this and have not listened to my counsel."

17After Amaziah king of Judah consulted his advisers, he sent this challenge to Jehoash[f] son of Jehoahaz, the son of Jehu, king of Israel: "Come, meet me face to face."

18But Jehoash king of Israel replied to Amaziah king of Judah: "A thistle in Lebanon sent a message to a cedar in Lebanon, 'Give your daughter to my son in marriage.' Then a wild beast in Lebanon came along and trampled the thistle underfoot. 19You say to yourself that you have defeated Edom, and now you are arrogant and proud. But stay at home! Why ask for trouble and cause your own downfall and that of Judah also?"

20Amaziah, however, would not listen, for God so worked that he might hand them over to ⌊Jehoash⌋, because they sought the gods of Edom. 21So Jehoash king of Israel attacked. He and Amaziah king of Judah faced each other at Beth Shemesh in Judah. 22Judah was routed by Israel, and every man fled to his home. 23Jehoash king of Israel captured Amaziah king of Judah, the son of Joash, the son of Ahaziah,[g] at Beth Shemesh. Then Jehoash brought him to Jerusalem and broke down the wall of Jerusalem from the Ephraim Gate to the Corner Gate—a section about six hundred feet[h] long. 24He took all the gold and silver and all the articles found in the temple of God that had been in the care of Obed-Edom, together with the palace treasures and the hostages, and returned to Samaria.

25Amaziah son of Joash king of Judah lived for fifteen years after the death of Jehoash son of Jehoahaz king of Israel. 26As for the other events of Amaziah's reign, from beginning to end, are they not written in the book of the kings of Judah and Israel? 27From the time that Amaziah turned away from following the LORD, they conspired against him in Jerusalem and he fled to Lachish, but they sent men after him to Lachish and killed him there. 28He was

[a] *26* A variant of *Jozabad* [b] *26* A variant of *Shomer* [c] *1* Hebrew *Jehoaddan,* a variant of *Jehoaddin* [d] *4* Deut. 24:16 [e] *6* That is, about 3 3/4 tons (about 3.4 metric tons); also in verse 9 [f] *17* Hebrew *Joash,* a variant of *Jehoash*; also in verses 18, 21, 23 and 25 [g] *23* Hebrew *Jehoahaz,* a variant of *Ahaziah* [h] *23* Hebrew *four hundred cubits* (about 180 meters)

brought back by horse and was buried with his fathers in the City of Judah.

Uzziah King of Judah

26 Then all the people of Judah took Uzziah,[a] who was sixteen years old, and made him king in place of his father Amaziah. 2He was the one who rebuilt Elath and restored it to Judah after Amaziah rested with his fathers.

3Uzziah was sixteen years old when he became king, and he reigned in Jerusalem fifty-two years. His mother's name was Jecoliah; she was from Jerusalem. 4He did what was right in the eyes of the LORD, just as his father Amaziah had done. 5He sought God during the days of Zechariah, who instructed him in the fear[b] of God. As long as he sought the LORD, God gave him success.

6He went to war against the Philistines and broke down the walls of Gath, Jabneh and Ashdod. He then rebuilt towns near Ashdod and elsewhere among the Philistines. 7God helped him against the Philistines and against the Arabs who lived in Gur Baal and against the Meunites. 8The Ammonites brought tribute to Uzziah, and his fame spread as far as the border of Egypt, because he had become very powerful.

9Uzziah built towers in Jerusalem at the Corner Gate, at the Valley Gate and at the angle of the wall, and he fortified them. 10He also built towers in the desert and dug many cisterns, because he had much livestock in the foothills and in the plain. He had people working his fields and vineyards in the hills and in the fertile lands, for he loved the soil.

11Uzziah had a well-trained army, ready to go out by divisions according to their numbers as mustered by Jeiel the secretary and Maaseiah the officer under the direction of Hananiah, one of the royal officials. 12The total number of family leaders over the fighting men was 2,600. 13Under their command was an army of 307,500 men trained for war, a powerful force to support the king against his enemies. 14Uzziah provided shields, spears, helmets, coats of armor, bows and slingstones for the entire army. 15In Jerusalem he made machines designed by skillful men for use on the towers and on the corner defenses to shoot arrows and hurl large stones. His fame spread far and wide, for he was greatly helped until he became powerful.

16But after Uzziah became powerful, his pride led to his downfall. He was unfaithful to the LORD his God, and entered the temple of the LORD to burn incense on the altar of incense. 17Azariah the priest with eighty other courageous priests of the LORD followed him in. 18They confronted him and said, "It is not right for you, Uzziah, to burn incense to the LORD. That is for the priests, the descendants of Aaron, who have been consecrated to burn incense. Leave the sanctuary, for you have been unfaithful; and you will not be honored by the LORD God."

19Uzziah, who had a censer in his hand ready to burn incense, became angry. While he was raging at the priests in their presence before the incense altar in the LORD's temple, leprosy[c] broke out on his forehead. 20When Azariah the chief priest and all the other priests looked at him, they saw that he had leprosy on his forehead, so they hurried him out. Indeed, he himself was eager to leave, because the LORD had afflicted him.

21King Uzziah had leprosy until the day he died. He lived in a separate house[d]—leprous, and excluded from the temple of the LORD. Jotham his son had charge of the palace and governed the people of the land.

22The other events of Uzziah's reign, from beginning to end, are recorded by the prophet Isaiah son of Amoz. 23Uzziah rested with his fathers and was buried near them in a field for burial that belonged to the kings, for people said, "He had leprosy." And Jotham his son succeeded him as king.

Jotham King of Judah

27 Jotham was twenty-five years old when he became king, and he reigned in Jerusalem sixteen years. His mother's name was Jerusha daughter of Zadok. 2He did what was right in the eyes of the LORD, just as his father Uzziah had done, but unlike him he did not enter the temple of the LORD. The people, however, continued their corrupt practices. 3Jotham rebuilt the Upper Gate of the temple of the LORD and did extensive work on the wall at the hill of Ophel. 4He built towns in the Judean hills and forts and towers in the wooded areas.

5Jotham made war on the king of the Ammonites and conquered them. That year the Ammonites paid him a hundred talents[e] of silver, ten thousand cors[f] of wheat and ten thousand cors of barley. The Ammonites brought him the same amount also in the second and third years.

6Jotham grew powerful because he walked steadfastly before the LORD his God.

7The other events in Jotham's reign, including all his wars and the other things he did, are written in the book of the kings of Israel and Judah. 8He was twenty-five years old when he became king, and he reigned in Jerusalem sixteen years. 9Jotham rested with his fathers and was buried in the City of David. And Ahaz his son succeeded him as king.

Ahaz King of Judah

28 Ahaz was twenty years old when he became king, and he reigned in Jerusalem sixteen years. Unlike David his father, he did

[a] *1* Also called *Azariah* [b] *5* Many Hebrew manuscripts, Septuagint and Syriac; other Hebrew manuscripts *vision* [c] *19* The Hebrew word was used for various diseases affecting the skin—not necessarily leprosy; also in verses 20, 21 and 23. [d] *21* Or *in a house where he was relieved of responsibilities* [e] *5* That is, about 3 3/4 tons (about 3.4 metric tons) [f] *5* That is, probably about 62,000 bushels (about 2,200 kiloliters)

not do what was right in the eyes of the LORD. 2He walked in the ways of the kings of Israel and also made cast idols for worshiping the Baals. 3He burned sacrifices in the Valley of Ben Hinnom and sacrificed his sons in the fire, following the detestable ways of the nations the LORD had driven out before the Israelites. 4He offered sacrifices and burned incense at the high places, on the hilltops and under every spreading tree.

5Therefore the LORD his God handed him over to the king of Aram. The Arameans defeated him and took many of his people as prisoners and brought them to Damascus.

He was also given into the hands of the king of Israel, who inflicted heavy casualties on him. 6In one day Pekah son of Remaliah killed a hundred and twenty thousand soldiers in Judah—because Judah had forsaken the LORD, the God of their fathers. 7Zicri, an Ephraimite warrior, killed Maaseiah the king's son, Azrikam the officer in charge of the palace, and Elkanah, second to the king. 8The Israelites took captive from their kinsmen two hundred thousand wives, sons and daughters. They also took a great deal of plunder, which they carried back to Samaria.

9But a prophet of the LORD named Oded was there, and he went out to meet the army when it returned to Samaria. He said to them, "Because the LORD, the God of your fathers, was angry with Judah, he gave them into your hand. But you have slaughtered them in a rage that reaches to heaven. 10And now you intend to make the men and women of Judah and Jerusalem your slaves. But aren't you also guilty of sins against the LORD your God? 11Now listen to me! Send back your fellow countrymen you have taken as prisoners, for the LORD's fierce anger rests on you."

12Then some of the leaders in Ephraim—Azariah son of Jehohanan, Berekiah son of Meshillemoth, Jehizkiah son of Shallum, and Amasa son of Hadlai—confronted those who were arriving from the war. 13"You must not bring those prisoners here," they said, "or we will be guilty before the LORD. Do you intend to add to our sin and guilt? For our guilt is already great, and his fierce anger rests on Israel."

14So the soldiers gave up the prisoners and plunder in the presence of the officials and all the assembly. 15The men designated by name took the prisoners, and from the plunder they clothed all who were naked. They provided them with clothes and sandals, food and drink, and healing balm. All those who were weak they put on donkeys. So they took them back to their fellow countrymen at Jericho, the City of Palms, and returned to Samaria.

16At that time King Ahaz sent to the king[a] of Assyria for help. 17The Edomites had again come and attacked Judah and carried away prisoners, 18while the Philistines had raided towns in the foothills and in the Negev of Judah. They captured and occupied Beth Shemesh, Aijalon and Gederoth, as well as Soco, Timnah and Gimzo, with their surrounding villages. 19The LORD had humbled Judah because of Ahaz king of Israel,[b] for he had promoted wickedness in Judah and had been most unfaithful to the LORD. 20Tiglath-Pileser[c] king of Assyria came to him, but he gave him trouble instead of help. 21Ahaz took some of the things from the temple of the LORD and from the royal palace and from the princes and presented them to the king of Assyria, but that did not help him.

22In his time of trouble King Ahaz became even more unfaithful to the LORD. 23He offered sacrifices to the gods of Damascus, who had defeated him; for he thought, "Since the gods of the kings of Aram have helped them, I will sacrifice to them so they will help me." But they were his downfall and the downfall of all Israel.

24Ahaz gathered together the furnishings from the temple of God and took them away.[d] He shut the doors of the LORD's temple and set up altars at every street corner in Jerusalem. 25In every town in Judah he built high places to burn sacrifices to other gods and provoked the LORD, the God of his fathers, to anger.

26The other events of his reign and all his ways, from beginning to end, are written in the book of the kings of Judah and Israel. 27Ahaz rested with his fathers and was buried in the city of Jerusalem, but he was not placed in the tombs of the kings of Israel. And Hezekiah his son succeeded him as king.

Hezekiah Purifies the Temple

29 Hezekiah was twenty-five years old when he became king, and he reigned in Jerusalem twenty-nine years. His mother's name was Abijah daughter of Zechariah. 2He did what was right in the eyes of the LORD, just as his father David had done.

3In the first month of the first year of his reign, he opened the doors of the temple of the LORD and repaired them. 4He brought in the priests and the Levites, assembled them in the square on the east side 5and said: "Listen to me, Levites! Consecrate yourselves now and consecrate the temple of the LORD, the God of your fathers. Remove all defilement from the sanctuary. 6Our fathers were unfaithful; they did evil in the eyes of the LORD our God and forsook him. They turned their faces away from the LORD's dwelling place and turned their backs on him. 7They also shut the doors of the portico and put out the lamps. They did not burn incense or present any burnt offerings at the sanctuary to the God of Israel. 8Therefore, the anger of the LORD has fallen on Judah and Jerusalem; he has made them an object of

[a]*16* One Hebrew manuscript, Septuagint and Vulgate (see also 2 Kings 16:7); most Hebrew manuscripts *kings*
[b]*19* That is, Judah, as frequently in 2 Chronicles [c]*20* Hebrew *Tilgath-Pilneser,* a variant of *Tiglath-Pileser*
[d]*24* Or *and cut them up*

dread and horror and scorn, as you can see with your own eyes. 9This is why our fathers have fallen by the sword and why our sons and daughters and our wives are in captivity. 10Now I intend to make a covenant with the LORD, the God of Israel, so that his fierce anger will turn away from us. 11My sons, do not be negligent now, for the LORD has chosen you to stand before him and serve him, to minister before him and to burn incense."

12Then these Levites set to work:
from the Kohathites,
Mahath son of Amasai and Joel son of Azariah;
from the Merarites,
Kish son of Abdi and Azariah son of Jehallelel;
from the Gershonites,
Joah son of Zimmah and Eden son of Joah;
13from the descendants of Elizaphan,
Shimri and Jeiel;
from the descendants of Asaph,
Zechariah and Mattaniah;
14from the descendants of Heman,
Jehiel and Shimei;
from the descendants of Jeduthun,
Shemaiah and Uzziel.

15When they had assembled their brothers and consecrated themselves, they went in to purify the temple of the LORD, as the king had ordered, following the word of the LORD. 16The priests went into the sanctuary of the LORD to purify it. They brought out to the courtyard of the LORD's temple everything unclean that they found in the temple of the LORD. The Levites took it and carried it out to the Kidron Valley. 17They began the consecration on the first day of the first month, and by the eighth day of the month they reached the portico of the LORD. For eight more days they consecrated the temple of the LORD itself, finishing on the sixteenth day of the first month.

18Then they went in to King Hezekiah and reported: "We have purified the entire temple of the LORD, the altar of burnt offering with all its utensils, and the table for setting out the consecrated bread, with all its articles. 19We have prepared and consecrated all the articles that King Ahaz removed in his unfaithfulness while he was king. They are now in front of the LORD's altar."

20Early the next morning King Hezekiah gathered the city officials together and went up to the temple of the LORD. 21They brought seven bulls, seven rams, seven male lambs and seven male goats as a sin offering for the kingdom, for the sanctuary and for Judah. The king commanded the priests, the descendants of Aaron, to offer these on the altar of the LORD. 22So they slaughtered the bulls, and the priests took the blood and sprinkled it on the altar; next they slaughtered the rams and sprinkled their blood on the altar; then they slaughtered the lambs and sprinkled their blood on the altar. 23The goats for the sin offering were brought before the king and the assembly, and they laid their hands on them. 24The priests then slaughtered the goats and presented their blood on the altar for a sin offering to atone for all Israel, because the king had ordered the burnt offering and the sin offering for all Israel.

25He stationed the Levites in the temple of the LORD with cymbals, harps and lyres in the way prescribed by David and Gad the king's seer and Nathan the prophet; this was commanded by the LORD through his prophets. 26So the Levites stood ready with David's instruments, and the priests with their trumpets.

27Hezekiah gave the order to sacrifice the burnt offering on the altar. As the offering began, singing to the LORD began also, accompanied by trumpets and the instruments of David king of Israel. 28The whole assembly bowed in worship, while the singers sang and the trumpeters played. All this continued until the sacrifice of the burnt offering was completed.

29When the offerings were finished, the king and everyone present with him knelt down and worshiped. 30King Hezekiah and his officials ordered the Levites to praise the LORD with the words of David and of Asaph the seer. So they sang praises with gladness and bowed their heads and worshiped.

31Then Hezekiah said, "You have now dedicated yourselves to the LORD. Come and bring sacrifices and thank offerings to the temple of the LORD." So the assembly brought sacrifices and thank offerings, and all whose hearts were willing brought burnt offerings.

32The number of burnt offerings the assembly brought was seventy bulls, a hundred rams and two hundred male lambs—all of them for burnt offerings to the LORD. 33The animals consecrated as sacrifices amounted to six hundred bulls and three thousand sheep and goats. 34The priests, however, were too few to skin all the burnt offerings; so their kinsmen the Levites helped them until the task was finished and until other priests had been consecrated, for the Levites had been more conscientious in consecrating themselves than the priests had been. 35There were burnt offerings in abundance, together with the fat of the fellowship offerings[a] and the drink offerings that accompanied the burnt offerings.

So the service of the temple of the LORD was reestablished. 36Hezekiah and all the people rejoiced at what God had brought about for his people, because it was done so quickly.

Hezekiah Celebrates the Passover

30 Hezekiah sent word to all Israel and Judah and also wrote letters to Ephraim and Manasseh, inviting them to come to the temple of the LORD in Jerusalem and celebrate the Passover to the LORD, the God of Israel. 2The king and his officials and the whole assembly in Jerusalem decided to celebrate the

[a]35 Traditionally *peace offerings*

Passover in the second month. 3They had not
been able to celebrate it at the regular time
because not enough priests had consecrated
themselves and the people had not assembled
in Jerusalem. 4The plan seemed right both to
the king and to the whole assembly. 5They
decided to send a proclamation throughout Israel, from Beersheba to Dan, calling the people
to come to Jerusalem and celebrate the Passover to the LORD, the God of Israel. It had not
been celebrated in large numbers according to
what was written.

6At the king's command, couriers went
throughout Israel and Judah with letters from
the king and from his officials, which read:

> "People of Israel, return to the LORD,
> the God of Abraham, Isaac and Israel, that
> he may return to you who are left, who
> have escaped from the hand of the kings
> of Assyria. 7Do not be like your fathers
> and brothers, who were unfaithful to the
> LORD, the God of their fathers, so that he
> made them an object of horror, as you see.
> 8Do not be stiff-necked, as your fathers
> were; submit to the LORD. Come to the
> sanctuary, which he has consecrated for-
> ever. Serve the LORD your God, so that
> his fierce anger will turn away from you.
> 9If you return to the LORD, then your
> brothers and your children will be shown
> compassion by their captors and will
> come back to this land, for the LORD your
> God is gracious and compassionate. He
> will not turn his face from you if you
> return to him."

10The couriers went from town to town in
Ephraim and Manasseh, as far as Zebulun, but
the people scorned and ridiculed them. 11Nev-
ertheless, some men of Asher, Manasseh and
Zebulun humbled themselves and went to Jerusalem. 12Also in Judah the hand of God was
on the people to give them unity of mind to
carry out what the king and his officials had
ordered, following the word of the LORD.

13A very large crowd of people assembled in
Jerusalem to celebrate the Feast of Unleavened
Bread in the second month. 14They removed
the altars in Jerusalem and cleared away the
incense altars and threw them into the Kidron
Valley.

15They slaughtered the Passover lamb on
the fourteenth day of the second month. The
priests and the Levites were ashamed and consecrated themselves and brought burnt offerings to the temple of the LORD. 16Then they
took up their regular positions as prescribed in
the Law of Moses the man of God. The priests
sprinkled the blood handed to them by the Levites. 17Since many in the crowd had not consecrated themselves, the Levites had to kill the
Passover lambs for all those who were not ceremonially clean and could not consecrate ⌞their
lambs⌟ to the LORD. 18Although most of the
many people who came from Ephraim, Manasseh, Issachar and Zebulun had not purified
themselves, yet they ate the Passover, contrary
to what was written. But Hezekiah prayed for
them, saying, "May the LORD, who is good,
pardon everyone 19who sets his heart on seeking God—the LORD, the God of his fathers—
even if he is not clean according to the rules of
the sanctuary." 20And the LORD heard Hezekiah and healed the people.

21The Israelites who were present in Jerusalem celebrated the Feast of Unleavened Bread
for seven days with great rejoicing, while the
Levites and priests sang to the LORD every
day, accompanied by the LORD's instruments
of praise.[a]

22Hezekiah spoke encouragingly to all the
Levites, who showed good understanding of
the service of the LORD. For the seven days
they ate their assigned portion and offered fellowship offerings[b] and praised the LORD, the
God of their fathers.

23The whole assembly then agreed to celebrate the festival seven more days; so for another seven days they celebrated joyfully.
24Hezekiah king of Judah provided a thousand
bulls and seven thousand sheep and goats for
the assembly, and the officials provided them
with a thousand bulls and ten thousand sheep
and goats. A great number of priests consecrated themselves. 25The entire assembly of Judah
rejoiced, along with the priests and Levites and
all who had assembled from Israel, including
the aliens who had come from Israel and those
who lived in Judah. 26There was great joy in
Jerusalem, for since the days of Solomon son
of David king of Israel there had been nothing
like this in Jerusalem. 27The priests and the
Levites stood to bless the people, and God
heard them, for their prayer reached heaven,
his holy dwelling place.

31 When all this had ended, the Israelites
who were there went out to the towns of
Judah, smashed the sacred stones and cut down
the Asherah poles. They destroyed the high
places and the altars throughout Judah and
Benjamin and in Ephraim and Manasseh. After
they had destroyed all of them, the Israelites
returned to their own towns and to their own
property.

Contributions for Worship

2Hezekiah assigned the priests and Levites
to divisions—each of them according to their
duties as priests or Levites—to offer burnt offerings and fellowship offerings,[b] to minister,
to give thanks and to sing praises at the gates
of the LORD's dwelling. 3The king contributed
from his own possessions for the morning and
evening burnt offerings and for the burnt offerings on the Sabbaths, New Moons and appointed feasts as written in the Law of the LORD.
4He ordered the people living in Jerusalem to
give the portion due the priests and Levites so

[a] *21* Or *priests praised the LORD every day with resounding instruments belonging to the LORD*
[b] *22,2* Traditionally *peace offerings*

they could devote themselves to the Law of the
LORD. 5As soon as the order went out, the
Israelites generously gave the firstfruits of
their grain, new wine, oil and honey and all
that the fields produced. They brought a great
amount, a tithe of everything. 6The men of
Israel and Judah who lived in the towns of
Judah also brought a tithe of their herds and
flocks and a tithe of the holy things dedicated
to the LORD their God, and they piled them in
heaps. 7They began doing this in the third
month and finished in the seventh month.
8When Hezekiah and his officials came and
saw the heaps, they praised the LORD and
blessed his people Israel.

9Hezekiah asked the priests and Levites
about the heaps; 10and Azariah the chief priest,
from the family of Zadok, answered, "Since
the people began to bring their contributions to
the temple of the LORD, we have had enough
to eat and plenty to spare, because the LORD
has blessed his people, and this great amount is
left over."

11Hezekiah gave orders to prepare storerooms in the temple of the LORD, and this was
done. 12Then they faithfully brought in the
contributions, tithes and dedicated gifts. Conaniah, a Levite, was in charge of these things,
and his brother Shimei was next in rank. 13Je-
hiel, Azaziah, Nahath, Asahel, Jerimoth, Jozabad, Eliel, Ismakiah, Mahath and Benaiah
were supervisors under Conaniah and Shimei
his brother, by appointment of King Hezekiah
and Azariah the official in charge of the temple
of God.

14Kore son of Imnah the Levite, keeper of
the East Gate, was in charge of the freewill
offerings given to God, distributing the contributions made to the LORD and also the consecrated gifts. 15Eden, Miniamin, Jeshua, Shemaiah, Amariah and Shecaniah assisted him
faithfully in the towns of the priests, distributing to their fellow priests according to their
divisions, old and young alike.

16In addition, they distributed to the males
three years old or more whose names were in
the genealogical records—all who would enter
the temple of the LORD to perform the daily
duties of their various tasks, according to their
responsibilities and their divisions. 17And they
distributed to the priests enrolled by their families in the genealogical records and likewise to
the Levites twenty years old or more, according to their responsibilities and their divisions.
18They included all the little ones, the wives,
and the sons and daughters of the whole community listed in these genealogical records.
For they were faithful in consecrating themselves.

19As for the priests, the descendants of Aaron, who lived on the farm lands around their
towns or in any other towns, men were designated by name to distribute portions to every
male among them and to all who were recorded in the genealogies of the Levites.

20This is what Hezekiah did throughout Judah, doing what was good and right and faithful before the LORD his God. 21In everything
that he undertook in the service of God's temple and in obedience to the law and the commands, he sought his God and worked wholeheartedly. And so he prospered.

Sennacherib Threatens Jerusalem

32 After all that Hezekiah had so faithfully
done, Sennacherib king of Assyria came
and invaded Judah. He laid siege to the fortified cities, thinking to conquer them for himself. 2When Hezekiah saw that Sennacherib
had come and that he intended to make war on
Jerusalem, 3he consulted with his officials and
military staff about blocking off the water
from the springs outside the city, and they
helped him. 4A large force of men assembled,
and they blocked all the springs and the stream
that flowed through the land. "Why should the
kings[a] of Assyria come and find plenty of water?" they said. 5Then he worked hard repairing all the broken sections of the wall and
building towers on it. He built another wall
outside that one and reinforced the supporting
terraces[b] of the City of David. He also made
large numbers of weapons and shields.

6He appointed military officers over the
people and assembled them before him in the
square at the city gate and encouraged them
with these words: 7"Be strong and courageous.
Do not be afraid or discouraged because of the
king of Assyria and the vast army with him, for
there is a greater power with us than with him.
8With him is only the arm of flesh, but with us
is the LORD our God to help us and to fight our
battles." And the people gained confidence
from what Hezekiah the king of Judah said.

9Later, when Sennacherib king of Assyria
and all his forces were laying siege to Lachish,
he sent his officers to Jerusalem with this message for Hezekiah king of Judah and for all the
people of Judah who were there:

10"This is what Sennacherib king of
Assyria says: On what are you basing
your confidence, that you remain in Jerusalem under siege? 11When Hezekiah
says, 'The LORD our God will save us
from the hand of the king of Assyria,' he
is misleading you, to let you die of hunger
and thirst. 12Did not Hezekiah himself remove this god's high places and altars,
saying to Judah and Jerusalem, 'You must
worship before one altar and burn sacrifices on it'?

13"Do you not know what I and my
fathers have done to all the peoples of the
other lands? Were the gods of those nations ever able to deliver their land from
my hand? 14Who of all the gods of these
nations that my fathers destroyed has
been able to save his people from me?
How then can your god deliver you from
my hand? 15Now do not let Hezekiah de-

a4 Hebrew; Septuagint and Syriac *king*   b5 Or *the Millo* ceive you and mislead you like this. Do not believe him, for no god of any nation or kingdom has been able to deliver his people from my hand or the hand of my fathers. How much less will your god deliver you from my hand!"

16Sennacherib's officers spoke further against the LORD God and against his servant Hezekiah. 17The king also wrote letters insulting the LORD, the God of Israel, and saying this against him: "Just as the gods of the peoples of the other lands did not rescue their people from my hand, so the god of Hezekiah will not rescue his people from my hand." 18Then they called out in Hebrew to the people of Jerusalem who were on the wall, to terrify them and make them afraid in order to capture the city. 19They spoke about the God of Jerusalem as they did about the gods of the other peoples of the world—the work of men's hands.

20King Hezekiah and the prophet Isaiah son of Amoz cried out in prayer to heaven about this. 21And the LORD sent an angel, who annihilated all the fighting men and the leaders and officers in the camp of the Assyrian king. So he withdrew to his own land in disgrace. And when he went into the temple of his god, some of his sons cut him down with the sword.

22So the LORD saved Hezekiah and the people of Jerusalem from the hand of Sennacherib king of Assyria and from the hand of all others. He took care of them[a] on every side. 23Many brought offerings to Jerusalem for the LORD and valuable gifts for Hezekiah king of Judah. From then on he was highly regarded by all the nations.

Hezekiah's Pride, Success and Death

24In those days Hezekiah became ill and was at the point of death. He prayed to the LORD, who answered him and gave him a miraculous sign. 25But Hezekiah's heart was proud and he did not respond to the kindness shown him; therefore the LORD's wrath was on him and on Judah and Jerusalem. 26Then Hezekiah repented of the pride of his heart, as did the people of Jerusalem; therefore the LORD's wrath did not come upon them during the days of Hezekiah.

27Hezekiah had very great riches and honor, and he made treasuries for his silver and gold and for his precious stones, spices, shields and all kinds of valuables. 28He also made buildings to store the harvest of grain, new wine and oil; and he made stalls for various kinds of cattle, and pens for the flocks. 29He built villages and acquired great numbers of flocks and herds, for God had given him very great riches.

30It was Hezekiah who blocked the upper outlet of the Gihon spring and channeled the water down to the west side of the City of David. He succeeded in everything he undertook. 31But when envoys were sent by the rulers of Babylon to ask him about the miraculous sign that had occurred in the land, God left him to test him and to know everything that was in his heart.

32The other events of Hezekiah's reign and his acts of devotion are written in the vision of the prophet Isaiah son of Amoz in the book of the kings of Judah and Israel. 33Hezekiah rested with his fathers and was buried on the hill where the tombs of David's descendants are. All Judah and the people of Jerusalem honored him when he died. And Manasseh his son succeeded him as king.

Manasseh King of Judah

33 Manasseh was twelve years old when he became king, and he reigned in Jerusalem fifty-five years. 2He did evil in the eyes of the LORD, following the detestable practices of the nations the LORD had driven out before the Israelites. 3He rebuilt the high places his father Hezekiah had demolished; he also erected altars to the Baals and made Asherah poles. He bowed down to all the starry hosts and worshiped them. 4He built altars in the temple of the LORD, of which the LORD had said, "My Name will remain in Jerusalem forever." 5In both courts of the temple of the LORD, he built altars to all the starry hosts. 6He sacrificed his sons in[b] the fire in the Valley of Ben Hinnom, practiced sorcery, divination and witchcraft, and consulted mediums and spiritists. He did much evil in the eyes of the LORD, provoking him to anger.

7He took the carved image he had made and put it in God's temple, of which God had said to David and to his son Solomon, "In this temple and in Jerusalem, which I have chosen out of all the tribes of Israel, I will put my Name forever. 8I will not again make the feet of the Israelites leave the land I assigned to your forefathers, if only they will be careful to do everything I commanded them concerning all the laws, decrees and ordinances given through Moses." 9But Manasseh led Judah and the people of Jerusalem astray, so that they did more evil than the nations the LORD had destroyed before the Israelites.

10The LORD spoke to Manasseh and his people, but they paid no attention. 11So the LORD brought against them the army commanders of the king of Assyria, who took Manasseh prisoner, put a hook in his nose, bound him with bronze shackles and took him to Babylon. 12In his distress he sought the favor of the LORD his God and humbled himself greatly before the God of his fathers. 13And when he prayed to him, the LORD was moved by his entreaty and listened to his plea; so he brought him back to Jerusalem and to his kingdom. Then Manasseh knew that the LORD is God.

14Afterward he rebuilt the outer wall of the City of David, west of the Gihon spring in the valley, as far as the entrance of the Fish Gate and encircling the hill of Ophel; he also made

[a]22 Hebrew; Septuagint and Vulgate *He gave them rest*

[b]6 Or *He made his sons pass through*

it much higher. He stationed military commanders in all the fortified cities in Judah.
15He got rid of the foreign gods and removed the image from the temple of the LORD,
as well as all the altars he had built on the
temple hill and in Jerusalem; and he threw
them out of the city. 16Then he restored the
altar of the LORD and sacrificed fellowship offerings[a] and thank offerings on it, and told
Judah to serve the LORD, the God of Israel.
17The people, however, continued to sacrifice
at the high places, but only to the LORD their
God.
18The other events of Manasseh's reign, including his prayer to his God and the words the
seers spoke to him in the name of the LORD,
the God of Israel, are written in the annals of
the kings of Israel.[b] 19His prayer and how God
was moved by his entreaty, as well as all his
sins and unfaithfulness, and the sites where he
built high places and set up Asherah poles and
idols before he humbled himself—all are written in the records of the seers.[c] 20Manasseh
rested with his fathers and was buried in his
palace. And Amon his son succeeded him as
king.

Amon King of Judah

21Amon was twenty-two years old when he
became king, and he reigned in Jerusalem two
years. 22He did evil in the eyes of the LORD, as
his father Manasseh had done. Amon worshiped and offered sacrifices to all the idols
Manasseh had made. 23But unlike his father
Manasseh, he did not humble himself before
the LORD; Amon increased his guilt.
24Amon's officials conspired against him
and assassinated him in his palace. 25Then the
people of the land killed all who had plotted
against King Amon, and they made Josiah his
son king in his place.

Josiah's Reforms

34 Josiah was eight years old when he became king, and he reigned in Jerusalem
thirty-one years. 2He did what was right in the
eyes of the LORD and walked in the ways of his
father David, not turning aside to the right or
to the left.
3In the eighth year of his reign, while he was
still young, he began to seek the God of his
father David. In his twelfth year he began to
purge Judah and Jerusalem of high places,
Asherah poles, carved idols and cast images.
4Under his direction the altars of the Baals
were torn down; he cut to pieces the incense
altars that were above them, and smashed the
Asherah poles, the idols and the images. These
he broke to pieces and scattered over the
graves of those who had sacrificed to them.
5He burned the bones of the priests on their
altars, and so he purged Judah and Jerusalem.
6In the towns of Manasseh, Ephraim and Simeon, as far as Naphtali, and in the ruins around
them, 7he tore down the altars and the Asherah
poles and crushed the idols to powder and cut
to pieces all the incense altars throughout Israel. Then he went back to Jerusalem.
8In the eighteenth year of Josiah's reign, to
purify the land and the temple, he sent Shaphan son of Azaliah and Maaseiah the ruler of
the city, with Joah son of Joahaz, the recorder,
to repair the temple of the LORD his God.
9They went to Hilkiah the high priest and
gave him the money that had been brought into
the temple of God, which the Levites who
were the doorkeepers had collected from the
people of Manasseh, Ephraim and the entire
remnant of Israel and from all the people of
Judah and Benjamin and the inhabitants of Jerusalem. 10Then they entrusted it to the men
appointed to supervise the work on the LORD's
temple. These men paid the workers who repaired and restored the temple. 11They also
gave money to the carpenters and builders to
purchase dressed stone, and timber for joists
and beams for the buildings that the kings of
Judah had allowed to fall into ruin.
12The men did the work faithfully. Over
them to direct them were Jahath and Obadiah,
Levites descended from Merari, and Zechariah
and Meshullam, descended from Kohath. The
Levites—all who were skilled in playing musical instruments— 13had charge of the laborers
and supervised all the workers from job to job.
Some of the Levites were secretaries, scribes
and doorkeepers.

The Book of the Law Found

14While they were bringing out the money
that had been taken into the temple of the
LORD, Hilkiah the priest found the Book of the
Law of the LORD that had been given through
Moses. 15Hilkiah said to Shaphan the secretary, "I have found the Book of the Law in the
temple of the LORD." He gave it to Shaphan.
16Then Shaphan took the book to the king
and reported to him: "Your officials are doing
everything that has been committed to them.
17They have paid out the money that was in the
temple of the LORD and have entrusted it to the
supervisors and workers." 18Then Shaphan
the secretary informed the king, "Hilkiah the
priest has given me a book." And Shaphan
read from it in the presence of the king.
19When the king heard the words of the
Law, he tore his robes. 20He gave these orders
to Hilkiah, Ahikam son of Shaphan, Abdon
son of Micah,[d] Shaphan the secretary and Asaiah the king's attendant: 21"Go and inquire of
the LORD for me and for the remnant in Israel
and Judah about what is written in this book
that has been found. Great is the LORD's anger
that is poured out on us because our fathers
have not kept the word of the LORD; they have
not acted in accordance with all that is written
in this book."
22Hilkiah and those the king had sent with

[a] *16* Traditionally *peace offerings* [b] *18* That is, Judah, as frequently in 2 Chronicles [c] *19* One Hebrew manuscript and Septuagint; most Hebrew manuscripts *of Hozai* [d] *20* Also called *Acbor son of Micaiah*

him[a] went to speak to the prophetess Huldah, who was the wife of Shallum son of Tokhath,[b] the son of Hasrah,[c] keeper of the wardrobe. She lived in Jerusalem, in the Second District.

23She said to them, "This is what the LORD, the God of Israel, says: Tell the man who sent you to me, 24'This is what the LORD says: I am going to bring disaster on this place and its people—all the curses written in the book that has been read in the presence of the king of Judah. 25Because they have forsaken me and burned incense to other gods and provoked me to anger by all that their hands have made,[d] my anger will be poured out on this place and will not be quenched.' 26Tell the king of Judah, who sent you to inquire of the LORD, 'This is what the LORD, the God of Israel, says concerning the words you heard: 27Because your heart was responsive and you humbled yourself before God when you heard what he spoke against this place and its people, and because you humbled yourself before me and tore your robes and wept in my presence, I have heard you, declares the LORD. 28Now I will gather you to your fathers, and you will be buried in peace. Your eyes will not see all the disaster I am going to bring on this place and on those who live here.' "

So they took her answer back to the king.

29Then the king called together all the elders of Judah and Jerusalem. 30He went up to the temple of the LORD with the men of Judah, the people of Jerusalem, the priests and the Levites—all the people from the least to the greatest. He read in their hearing all the words of the Book of the Covenant, which had been found in the temple of the LORD. 31The king stood by his pillar and renewed the covenant in the presence of the LORD—to follow the LORD and keep his commands, regulations and decrees with all his heart and all his soul, and to obey the words of the covenant written in this book.

32Then he had everyone in Jerusalem and Benjamin pledge themselves to it; the people of Jerusalem did this in accordance with the covenant of God, the God of their fathers.

33Josiah removed all the detestable idols from all the territory belonging to the Israelites, and he had all who were present in Israel serve the LORD their God. As long as he lived, they did not fail to follow the LORD, the God of their fathers.

Josiah Celebrates the Passover

35 Josiah celebrated the Passover to the LORD in Jerusalem, and the Passover lamb was slaughtered on the fourteenth day of the first month. 2He appointed the priests to their duties and encouraged them in the service of the LORD's temple. 3He said to the Levites, who instructed all Israel and who had been consecrated to the LORD: "Put the sacred ark in the temple that Solomon son of David king of Israel built. It is not to be carried about on your shoulders. Now serve the LORD your God and his people Israel. 4Prepare yourselves by families in your divisions, according to the directions written by David king of Israel and by his son Solomon.

5"Stand in the holy place with a group of Levites for each subdivision of the families of your fellow countrymen, the lay people. 6Slaughter the Passover lambs, consecrate yourselves and prepare ⌞the lambs⌟ for your fellow countrymen, doing what the LORD commanded through Moses."

7Josiah provided for all the lay people who were there a total of thirty thousand sheep and goats for the Passover offerings, and also three thousand cattle—all from the king's own possessions.

8His officials also contributed voluntarily to the people and the priests and Levites. Hilkiah, Zechariah and Jehiel, the administrators of God's temple, gave the priests twenty-six hundred Passover offerings and three hundred cattle. 9Also Conaniah along with Shemaiah and Nethanel, his brothers, and Hashabiah, Jeiel and Jozabad, the leaders of the Levites, provided five thousand Passover offerings and five hundred head of cattle for the Levites.

10The service was arranged and the priests stood in their places with the Levites in their divisions as the king had ordered. 11The Passover lambs were slaughtered, and the priests sprinkled the blood handed to them, while the Levites skinned the animals. 12They set aside the burnt offerings to give them to the subdivisions of the families of the people to offer to the LORD, as is written in the Book of Moses. They did the same with the cattle. 13They roasted the Passover animals over the fire as prescribed, and boiled the holy offerings in pots, caldrons and pans and served them quickly to all the people. 14After this, they made preparations for themselves and for the priests, because the priests, the descendants of Aaron, were sacrificing the burnt offerings and the fat portions until nightfall. So the Levites made preparations for themselves and for the Aaronic priests.

15The musicians, the descendants of Asaph, were in the places prescribed by David, Asaph, Heman and Jeduthun the king's seer. The gatekeepers at each gate did not need to leave their posts, because their fellow Levites made the preparations for them.

16So at that time the entire service of the LORD was carried out for the celebration of the Passover and the offering of burnt offerings on the altar of the LORD, as King Josiah had ordered. 17The Israelites who were present celebrated the Passover at that time and observed the Feast of Unleavened Bread for seven days. 18The Passover had not been observed like this in Israel since the days of the prophet Samuel; and none of the kings of Israel had ever cele-

[a]22 One Hebrew manuscript, Vulgate and Syriac; most Hebrew manuscripts do not have *had sent with him.*
[b]22 Also called *Tikvah* [c]22 Also called *Harhas* [d]25 Or *by everything they have done*

brated such a Passover as did Josiah, with the priests, the Levites and all Judah and Israel who were there with the people of Jerusalem. [19]This Passover was celebrated in the eighteenth year of Josiah's reign.

The Death of Josiah

[20]After all this, when Josiah had set the temple in order, Neco king of Egypt went up to fight at Carchemish on the Euphrates, and Josiah marched out to meet him in battle. [21]But Neco sent messengers to him, saying, "What quarrel is there between you and me, O king of Judah? It is not you I am attacking at this time, but the house with which I am at war. God has told me to hurry; so stop opposing God, who is with me, or he will destroy you."

[22]Josiah, however, would not turn away from him, but disguised himself to engage him in battle. He would not listen to what Neco had said at God's command but went to fight him on the plain of Megiddo.

[23]Archers shot King Josiah, and he told his officers, "Take me away; I am badly wounded." [24]So they took him out of his chariot, put him in the other chariot he had and brought him to Jerusalem, where he died. He was buried in the tombs of his fathers, and all Judah and Jerusalem mourned for him.

[25]Jeremiah composed laments for Josiah, and to this day all the men and women singers commemorate Josiah in the laments. These became a tradition in Israel and are written in the Laments.

[26]The other events of Josiah's reign and his acts of devotion, according to what is written in the Law of the LORD— [27]all the events, from beginning to end, are written in the book of the kings of Israel and Judah.

36 [1]And the people of the land took Jehoahaz son of Josiah and made him king in Jerusalem in place of his father.

Jehoahaz King of Judah

[2]Jehoahaz[a] was twenty-three years old when he became king, and he reigned in Jerusalem three months. [3]The king of Egypt dethroned him in Jerusalem and imposed on Judah a levy of a hundred talents[b] of silver and a talent[c] of gold. [4]The king of Egypt made Eliakim, a brother of Jehoahaz, king over Judah and Jerusalem and changed Eliakim's name to Jehoiakim. But Neco took Eliakim's brother Jehoahaz and carried him off to Egypt.

Jehoiakim King of Judah

[5]Jehoiakim was twenty-five years old when he became king, and he reigned in Jerusalem eleven years. He did evil in the eyes of the LORD his God. [6]Nebuchadnezzar king of Babylon attacked him and bound him with bronze shackles to take him to Babylon. [7]Nebuchadnezzar also took to Babylon articles from the temple of the LORD and put them in his temple[d] there.

[8]The other events of Jehoiakim's reign, the detestable things he did and all that was found against him, are written in the book of the kings of Israel and Judah. And Jehoiachin his son succeeded him as king.

Jehoiachin King of Judah

[9]Jehoiachin was eighteen[e] years old when he became king, and he reigned in Jerusalem three months and ten days. He did evil in the eyes of the LORD. [10]In the spring, King Nebuchadnezzar sent for him and brought him to Babylon, together with articles of value from the temple of the LORD, and he made Jehoiachin's uncle,[f] Zedekiah, king over Judah and Jerusalem.

Zedekiah King of Judah

[11]Zedekiah was twenty-one years old when he became king, and he reigned in Jerusalem eleven years. [12]He did evil in the eyes of the LORD his God and did not humble himself before Jeremiah the prophet, who spoke the word of the LORD. [13]He also rebelled against King Nebuchadnezzar, who had made him take an oath in God's name. He became stiff-necked and hardened his heart and would not turn to the LORD, the God of Israel. [14]Furthermore, all the leaders of the priests and the people became more and more unfaithful, following all the detestable practices of the nations and defiling the temple of the LORD, which he had consecrated in Jerusalem.

The Fall of Jerusalem

[15]The LORD, the God of their fathers, sent word to them through his messengers again and again, because he had pity on his people and on his dwelling place. [16]But they mocked God's messengers, despised his words and scoffed at his prophets until the wrath of the LORD was aroused against his people and there was no remedy. [17]He brought up against them the king of the Babylonians,[g] who killed their young men with the sword in the sanctuary, and spared neither young man nor young woman, old man or aged. God handed all of them over to Nebuchadnezzar. [18]He carried to Babylon all the articles from the temple of God, both large and small, and the treasures of the LORD's temple and the treasures of the king and his officials. [19]They set fire to God's temple and broke down the wall of Jerusalem; they burned all the palaces and destroyed everything of value there.

[20]He carried into exile to Babylon the remnant, who escaped from the sword, and they became servants to him and his sons until the kingdom of Persia came to power. [21]The land enjoyed its sabbath rests; all the time of its

[a]2 Hebrew *Joahaz,* a variant of *Jehoahaz*; also in verse 4 [b]3 That is, about 3 3/4 tons (about 3.4 metric tons) [c]3 That is, about 75 pounds (about 34 kilograms) [d]7 Or *palace* [e]9 One Hebrew manuscript, some Septuagint manuscripts and Syriac (see also 2 Kings 24:8); most Hebrew manuscripts *eight* [f]10 Hebrew *brother,* that is, relative (see 2 Kings 24:17) [g]17 Or *Chaldeans*

desolation it rested, until the seventy years
were completed in fulfillment of the word of
the LORD spoken by Jeremiah.
22 In the first year of Cyrus king of Persia, in
order to fulfill the word of the LORD spoken by
Jeremiah, the LORD moved the heart of Cyrus
king of Persia to make a proclamation throughout his realm and to put it in writing:

23 "This is what Cyrus king of Persia says:
" 'The LORD, the God of heaven, has
given me all the kingdoms of the earth
and he has appointed me to build a temple
for him at Jerusalem in Judah. Anyone of
his people among you—may the LORD
his God be with him, and let him
go up.' "

Ezra

Cyrus Helps the Exiles to Return

1 In the first year of Cyrus king of Persia, in
order to fulfill the word of the LORD spoken by Jeremiah, the LORD moved the heart of
Cyrus king of Persia to make a proclamation
throughout his realm and to put it in writing:

2 "This is what Cyrus king of Persia says:
" 'The LORD, the God of heaven, has
given me all the kingdoms of the earth
and he has appointed me to build a temple
for him at Jerusalem in Judah. 3 Anyone of
his people among you—may his God be
with him, and let him go up to Jerusalem
in Judah and build the temple of the
LORD, the God of Israel, the God who
is in Jerusalem. 4 And the people of any
place where survivors may now be living
are to provide him with silver and gold,
with goods and livestock, and with freewill offerings for the temple of God in
Jerusalem.' "

5 Then the family heads of Judah and Benjamin, and the priests and Levites—everyone
whose heart God had moved—prepared to go
up and build the house of the LORD in Jerusalem. 6 All their neighbors assisted them with
articles of silver and gold, with goods and livestock, and with valuable gifts, in addition to all
the freewill offerings. 7 Moreover, King Cyrus
brought out the articles belonging to the temple of the LORD, which Nebuchadnezzar had
carried away from Jerusalem and had placed in
the temple of his god.[a] 8 Cyrus king of Persia
had them brought by Mithredath the treasurer,
who counted them out to Sheshbazzar the
prince of Judah.
9 This was the inventory:

gold dishes	30
silver dishes	1,000
silver pans[b]	29
10 gold bowls	30
matching silver bowls	410
other articles	1,000

11 In all, there were 5,400 articles of gold and
of silver. Sheshbazzar brought all these along
when the exiles came up from Babylon to Jerusalem.

The List of the Exiles Who Returned

2 Now these are the people of the province
who came up from the captivity of the exiles, whom Nebuchadnezzar king of Babylon
had taken captive to Babylon (they returned to
Jerusalem and Judah, each to his own town, 2 in
company with Zerubbabel, Jeshua, Nehemiah,
Seraiah, Reelaiah, Mordecai, Bilshan, Mispar,
Bigvai, Rehum and Baanah):

The list of the men of the people of Israel:

3 the descendants of Parosh	2,172
4 of Shephatiah	372
5 of Arah	775
6 of Pahath-Moab (through the line of Jeshua and Joab)	2,812
7 of Elam	1,254
8 of Zattu	945
9 of Zaccai	760
10 of Bani	642
11 of Bebai	623
12 of Azgad	1,222
13 of Adonikam	666
14 of Bigvai	2,056
15 of Adin	454
16 of Ater (through Hezekiah)	98
17 of Bezai	323
18 of Jorah	112
19 of Hashum	223
20 of Gibbar	95
21 the men of Bethlehem	123
22 of Netophah	56
23 of Anathoth	128
24 of Azmaveth	42
25 of Kiriath Jearim,[c] Kephirah and Beeroth	743
26 of Ramah and Geba	621
27 of Micmash	122
28 of Bethel and Ai	223
29 of Nebo	52
30 of Magbish	156
31 of the other Elam	1,254
32 of Harim	320
33 of Lod, Hadid and Ono	725

[a] *7* Or *gods* [b] *9* The meaning of the Hebrew for this word is uncertain. [c] *25* See Septuagint (see also Neh. 7:29); Hebrew *Kiriath Arim*.

34of Jericho 345
35of Senaah 3,630

36The priests:

the descendants of Jedaiah
(through the family of Jeshua) 973
37of Immer 1,052
38of Pashhur 1,247
39of Harim 1,017

40The Levites:

the descendants of Jeshua and
Kadmiel (through the line of
Hodaviah) 74

41The singers:

the descendants of Asaph 128

42The gatekeepers of the temple:

the descendants of
Shallum, Ater, Talmon,
Akkub, Hatita and Shobai 139

43The temple servants:

the descendants of
Ziha, Hasupha, Tabbaoth,
44Keros, Siaha, Padon,
45Lebanah, Hagabah, Akkub,
46Hagab, Shalmai, Hanan,
47Giddel, Gahar, Reaiah,
48Rezin, Nekoda, Gazzam,
49Uzza, Paseah, Besai,
50Asnah, Meunim, Nephussim,
51Bakbuk, Hakupha, Harhur,
52Bazluth, Mehida, Harsha,
53Barkos, Sisera, Temah,
54Neziah and Hatipha

55The descendants of the servants of Solomon:

the descendants of
Sotai, Hassophereth, Peruda,
56Jaala, Darkon, Giddel,
57Shephatiah, Hattil,
Pokereth-Hazzebaim and Ami

58The temple servants and the
descendants of the servants of
Solomon 392

59The following came up from the
towns of Tel Melah, Tel Harsha, Kerub,
Addon and Immer, but they could not
show that their families were descended
from Israel:

60The descendants of
Delaiah, Tobiah and Nekoda 652

61And from among the priests:

The descendants of
Hobaiah, Hakkoz and Barzillai (a
man who had married a daughter
of Barzillai the Gileadite and was
called by that name).

62These searched for their family
records, but they could not find them and
so were excluded from the priesthood as
unclean. 63The governor ordered them not
to eat any of the most sacred food until
there was a priest ministering with the
Urim and Thummim.

64The whole company numbered
42,360, 65besides their 7,337 menservants
and maidservants; and they also had 200
men and women singers. 66They had 736
horses, 245 mules, 67435 camels and
6,720 donkeys.

68When they arrived at the house of the
LORD in Jerusalem, some of the heads of the
families gave freewill offerings toward the rebuilding of the house of God on its site. 69Ac-
cording to their ability they gave to the treasury for this work 61,000 drachmas[a] of gold,
5,000 minas[b] of silver and 100 priestly garments.

70The priests, the Levites, the singers, the
gatekeepers and the temple servants settled in
their own towns, along with some of the other
people, and the rest of the Israelites settled in
their towns.

Rebuilding the Altar

3 When the seventh month came and the Israelites had settled in their towns, the people assembled as one man in Jerusalem. 2Then
Jeshua son of Jozadak and his fellow priests
and Zerubbabel son of Shealtiel and his associates began to build the altar of the God of
Israel to sacrifice burnt offerings on it, in accordance with what is written in the Law of
Moses the man of God. 3Despite their fear of
the peoples around them, they built the altar on
its foundation and sacrificed burnt offerings on
it to the LORD, both the morning and evening
sacrifices. 4Then in accordance with what is
written, they celebrated the Feast of Tabernacles with the required number of burnt offerings prescribed for each day. 5After that, they
presented the regular burnt offerings, the New
Moon sacrifices and the sacrifices for all the
appointed sacred feasts of the LORD, as well
as those brought as freewill offerings to the
LORD. 6On the first day of the seventh month
they began to offer burnt offerings to the
LORD, though the foundation of the LORD's
temple had not yet been laid.

Rebuilding the Temple

7Then they gave money to the masons and
carpenters, and gave food and drink and oil to
the people of Sidon and Tyre, so that they
would bring cedar logs by sea from Lebanon to
Joppa, as authorized by Cyrus king of Persia.
8In the second month of the second year
after their arrival at the house of God in Jerusalem, Zerubbabel son of Shealtiel, Jeshua son
of Jozadak and the rest of their brothers (the
priests and the Levites and all who had returned from the captivity to Jerusalem) began

[a] *69* That is, about 1,100 pounds (about 500 kilograms)
[b] *69* That is, about 3 tons (about 2.9 metric tons)

the work, appointing Levites twenty years of
age and older to supervise the building of the
house of the LORD. 9Jeshua and his sons and
brothers and Kadmiel and his sons (descendants of Hodaviah[a]) and the sons of Henadad
and their sons and brothers—all Levites—
joined together in supervising those working
on the house of God.
10When the builders laid the foundation of
the temple of the LORD, the priests in their
vestments and with trumpets, and the Levites
(the sons of Asaph) with cymbals, took their
places to praise the LORD, as prescribed by
David king of Israel. 11With praise and thanksgiving they sang to the LORD:

"He is good;
his love to Israel endures forever."

And all the people gave a great shout of praise
to the LORD, because the foundation of the
house of the LORD was laid. 12But many of the
older priests and Levites and family heads,
who had seen the former temple, wept aloud
when they saw the foundation of this temple
being laid, while many others shouted for joy.
13No one could distinguish the sound of the
shouts of joy from the sound of weeping, because the people made so much noise. And the
sound was heard far away.

Opposition to the Rebuilding

4 When the enemies of Judah and Benjamin
heard that the exiles were building a temple for the LORD, the God of Israel, 2they came
to Zerubbabel and to the heads of the families
and said, "Let us help you build because, like
you, we seek your God and have been sacrificing to him since the time of Esarhaddon king
of Assyria, who brought us here."
3But Zerubbabel, Jeshua and the rest of the
heads of the families of Israel answered, "You
have no part with us in building a temple to our
God. We alone will build it for the LORD, the
God of Israel, as King Cyrus, the king of Persia, commanded us."
4Then the peoples around them set out to
discourage the people of Judah and make them
afraid to go on building.[b] 5They hired counselors to work against them and frustrate their
plans during the entire reign of Cyrus king of
Persia and down to the reign of Darius king of
Persia.

Later Opposition Under Xerxes and Artaxerxes

6At the beginning of the reign of Xerxes,[c]
they lodged an accusation against the people of
Judah and Jerusalem.
7And in the days of Artaxerxes king of Persia, Bishlam, Mithredath, Tabeel and the rest
of his associates wrote a letter to Artaxerxes.
The letter was written in Aramaic script and in
the Aramaic language.[d, e]

8Rehum the commanding officer and Shimshai the secretary wrote a letter against Jerusalem to Artaxerxes the king as follows:

9Rehum the commanding officer and
Shimshai the secretary, together with the
rest of their associates—the judges and
officials over the men from Tripolis, Persia,[f] Erech and Babylon, the Elamites of
Susa, 10and the other people whom the
great and honorable Ashurbanipal[g] deported and settled in the city of Samaria
and elsewhere in Trans-Euphrates.

11(This is a copy of the letter they sent him.)

To King Artaxerxes,

From your servants, the men of Trans-
Euphrates:

12The king should know that the Jews
who came up to us from you have gone to
Jerusalem and are rebuilding that rebellious and wicked city. They are restoring
the walls and repairing the foundations.
13Furthermore, the king should know
that if this city is built and its walls are
restored, no more taxes, tribute or duty
will be paid, and the royal revenues will
suffer. 14Now since we are under obligation to the palace and it is not proper for
us to see the king dishonored, we are
sending this message to inform the king,
15so that a search may be made in the
archives of your predecessors. In these
records you will find that this city is a
rebellious city, troublesome to kings and
provinces, a place of rebellion from ancient times. That is why this city was destroyed. 16We inform the king that if this
city is built and its walls are restored,
you will be left with nothing in Trans-
Euphrates.

17The king sent this reply:

To Rehum the commanding officer,
Shimshai the secretary and the rest of
their associates living in Samaria and
elsewhere in Trans-Euphrates:

Greetings.

18The letter you sent us has been read
and translated in my presence. 19I issued
an order and a search was made, and it
was found that this city has a long history
of revolt against kings and has been a
place of rebellion and sedition. 20Jerusa-
lem has had powerful kings ruling over
the whole of Trans-Euphrates, and taxes,
tribute and duty were paid to them. 21Now
issue an order to these men to stop work,
so that this city will not be rebuilt until I
so order. 22Be careful not to neglect this

[a]*9* Hebrew *Yehudah,* probably a variant of *Hodaviah* [b]*4* Or *and troubled them as they built* [c]*6* Hebrew *Ahasuerus,* a variant of Xerxes' Persian name [d]*7* Or *written in Aramaic and translated* [e]*7* The text of Ezra 4:8—6:18 is in Aramaic. [f]*9* Or *officials, magistrates and governors over the men from* [g]*10* Aramaic *Osnappar,* a variant of *Ashurbanipal*

matter. Why let this threat grow, to the
detriment of the royal interests?

23As soon as the copy of the letter of King
Artaxerxes was read to Rehum and Shimshai
the secretary and their associates, they went
immediately to the Jews in Jerusalem and
compelled them by force to stop.

24Thus the work on the house of God in
Jerusalem came to a standstill until the second
year of the reign of Darius king of Persia.

Tattenai's Letter to Darius

5 Now Haggai the prophet and Zechariah the
prophet, a descendant of Iddo, prophesied
to the Jews in Judah and Jerusalem in the name
of the God of Israel, who was over them.
2Then Zerubbabel son of Shealtiel and Jeshua
son of Jozadak set to work to rebuild the house
of God in Jerusalem. And the prophets of God
were with them, helping them.
3At that time Tattenai, governor of Trans-
Euphrates, and Shethar-Bozenai and their associates went to them and asked, "Who authorized you to rebuild this temple and restore this
structure?" 4They also asked, "What are the
names of the men constructing this building?"[a] 5But the eye of their God was watching
over the elders of the Jews, and they were not
stopped until a report could go to Darius and
his written reply be received.
6This is a copy of the letter that Tattenai,
governor of Trans-Euphrates, and Shethar-
Bozenai and their associates, the officials of
Trans-Euphrates, sent to King Darius. 7The report they sent him read as follows:

To King Darius:

Cordial greetings.

8The king should know that we went to
the district of Judah, to the temple of the
great God. The people are building it with
large stones and placing the timbers in the
walls. The work is being carried on with
diligence and is making rapid progress
under their direction.
9We questioned the elders and asked
them, "Who authorized you to rebuild this
temple and restore this structure?" 10We
also asked them their names, so that we
could write down the names of their leaders for your information.
11This is the answer they gave us:

"We are the servants of the God of
heaven and earth, and we are rebuilding
the temple that was built many years ago,
one that a great king of Israel built and
finished. 12But because our fathers angered the God of heaven, he handed them
over to Nebuchadnezzar the Chaldean,
king of Babylon, who destroyed this temple and deported the people to Babylon.
13"However, in the first year of Cyrus
king of Babylon, King Cyrus issued a decree to rebuild this house of God. 14He
even removed from the temple[b] of Babylon the gold and silver articles of the
house of God, which Nebuchadnezzar
had taken from the temple in Jerusalem
and brought to the temple[b] in Babylon.
"Then King Cyrus gave them to a man
named Sheshbazzar, whom he had appointed governor, 15and he told him,
'Take these articles and go and deposit
them in the temple in Jerusalem. And rebuild the house of God on its site.' 16So
this Sheshbazzar came and laid the foundations of the house of God in Jerusalem.
From that day to the present it has been
under construction but is not yet finished."

17Now if it pleases the king, let a search
be made in the royal archives of Babylon
to see if King Cyrus did in fact issue a
decree to rebuild this house of God in
Jerusalem. Then let the king send us his
decision in this matter.

The Decree of Darius

6 King Darius then issued an order, and they
searched in the archives stored in the treasury at Babylon. 2A scroll was found in the
citadel of Ecbatana in the province of Media,
and this was written on it:

Memorandum:

3In the first year of King Cyrus, the
king issued a decree concerning the temple of God in Jerusalem:

Let the temple be rebuilt as a place to
present sacrifices, and let its foundations
be laid. It is to be ninety feet[c] high and
ninety feet wide, 4with three courses of
large stones and one of timbers. The costs
are to be paid by the royal treasury. 5Also,
the gold and silver articles of the house of
God, which Nebuchadnezzar took from
the temple in Jerusalem and brought to
Babylon, are to be returned to their places
in the temple in Jerusalem; they are to be
deposited in the house of God.

6Now then, Tattenai, governor of
Trans-Euphrates, and Shethar-Bozenai
and you, their fellow officials of that
province, stay away from there. 7Do not
interfere with the work on this temple of
God. Let the governor of the Jews and the
Jewish elders rebuild this house of God
on its site.
8Moreover, I hereby decree what you
are to do for these elders of the Jews in
the construction of this house of God:
The expenses of these men are to be
fully paid out of the royal treasury, from
the revenues of Trans-Euphrates, so that

[a] *4* See Septuagint; Aramaic *4We told them the names of the men constructing this building.* [b] *14* Or *palace*
[c] *3* Aramaic *sixty cubits* (about 27 meters)

the work will not stop. 9Whatever is needed—young bulls, rams, male lambs for
burnt offerings to the God of heaven, and
wheat, salt, wine and oil, as requested by
the priests in Jerusalem—must be given
them daily without fail, 10so that they
may offer sacrifices pleasing to the God
of heaven and pray for the well-being of
the king and his sons.

11Furthermore, I decree that if anyone
changes this edict, a beam is to be pulled
from his house and he is to be lifted up
and impaled on it. And for this crime his
house is to be made a pile of rubble.
12May God, who has caused his Name to
dwell there, overthrow any king or people
who lifts a hand to change this decree or
to destroy this temple in Jerusalem.

I Darius have decreed it. Let it be carried out with diligence.

Completion and Dedication of the Temple

13Then, because of the decree King Darius
had sent, Tattenai, governor of Trans-
Euphrates, and Shethar-Bozenai and their associates carried it out with diligence. 14So the
elders of the Jews continued to build and prosper under the preaching of Haggai the prophet
and Zechariah, a descendant of Iddo. They
finished building the temple according to the
command of the God of Israel and the decrees
of Cyrus, Darius and Artaxerxes, kings of Persia. 15The temple was completed on the third
day of the month Adar, in the sixth year of the
reign of King Darius.

16Then the people of Israel—the priests, the
Levites and the rest of the exiles—celebrated
the dedication of the house of God with joy.
17For the dedication of this house of God they
offered a hundred bulls, two hundred rams,
four hundred male lambs and, as a sin offering
for all Israel, twelve male goats, one for each
of the tribes of Israel. 18And they installed the
priests in their divisions and the Levites in
their groups for the service of God at Jerusalem, according to what is written in the Book
of Moses.

The Passover

19On the fourteenth day of the first month,
the exiles celebrated the Passover. 20The
priests and Levites had purified themselves
and were all ceremonially clean. The Levites
slaughtered the Passover lamb for all the exiles, for their brothers the priests and for themselves. 21So the Israelites who had returned
from the exile ate it, together with all who had
separated themselves from the unclean practices of their Gentile neighbors in order to seek
the LORD, the God of Israel. 22For seven days
they celebrated with joy the Feast of Unleavened Bread, because the LORD had filled them
with joy by changing the attitude of the king of
Assyria, so that he assisted them in the work
on the house of God, the God of Israel.

Ezra Comes to Jerusalem

7 After these things, during the reign of Artaxerxes king of Persia, Ezra son of Seraiah, the son of Azariah, the son of Hilkiah, 2the
son of Shallum, the son of Zadok, the son of
Ahitub, 3the son of Amariah, the son of Azariah, the son of Meraioth, 4the son of Zerahiah,
the son of Uzzi, the son of Bukki, 5the son of
Abishua, the son of Phinehas, the son of Eleazar, the son of Aaron the chief priest— 6this
Ezra came up from Babylon. He was a teacher
well versed in the Law of Moses, which the
LORD, the God of Israel, had given. The king
had granted him everything he asked, for the
hand of the LORD his God was on him. 7Some
of the Israelites, including priests, Levites,
singers, gatekeepers and temple servants, also
came up to Jerusalem in the seventh year of
King Artaxerxes.

8Ezra arrived in Jerusalem in the fifth month
of the seventh year of the king. 9He had begun
his journey from Babylon on the first day of
the first month, and he arrived in Jerusalem on
the first day of the fifth month, for the gracious
hand of his God was on him. 10For Ezra had
devoted himself to the study and observance of
the Law of the LORD, and to teaching its decrees and laws in Israel.

King Artaxerxes' Letter to Ezra

11This is a copy of the letter King Artaxerxes had given to Ezra the priest and teacher, a
man learned in matters concerning the commands and decrees of the LORD for Israel:

12[a]Artaxerxes, king of kings,

To Ezra the priest, a teacher of the Law of the God of heaven:

Greetings.

13Now I decree that any of the Israelites in my kingdom, including priests and
Levites, who wish to go to Jerusalem with
you, may go. 14You are sent by the king
and his seven advisers to inquire about
Judah and Jerusalem with regard to the
Law of your God, which is in your hand.
15Moreover, you are to take with you the
silver and gold that the king and his advisers have freely given to the God of Israel,
whose dwelling is in Jerusalem, 16togeth-
er with all the silver and gold you may
obtain from the province of Babylon, as
well as the freewill offerings of the people
and priests for the temple of their God in
Jerusalem. 17With this money be sure to
buy bulls, rams and male lambs, together
with their grain offerings and drink offerings, and sacrifice them on the altar of the
temple of your God in Jerusalem.

18You and your brother Jews may then
do whatever seems best with the rest of

[a] 12 The text of Ezra 7:12-26 is in Aramaic.

the silver and gold, in accordance with the
will of your God. 19Deliver to the God of
Jerusalem all the articles entrusted to you
for worship in the temple of your God.
20And anything else needed for the temple of your God that you may have occasion to supply, you may provide from the
royal treasury.

21Now I, King Artaxerxes, order all the
treasurers of Trans-Euphrates to provide
with diligence whatever Ezra the priest, a
teacher of the Law of the God of heaven,
may ask of you— 22up to a hundred talents[a] of silver, a hundred cors[b] of wheat,
a hundred baths[c] of wine, a hundred
baths[c] of olive oil, and salt without limit.
23Whatever the God of heaven has prescribed, let it be done with diligence for
the temple of the God of heaven. Why
should there be wrath against the realm of
the king and of his sons? 24You are also
to know that you have no authority to impose taxes, tribute or duty on any of the
priests, Levites, singers, gatekeepers,
temple servants or other workers at this
house of God.

25And you, Ezra, in accordance with
the wisdom of your God, which you possess, appoint magistrates and judges to
administer justice to all the people of
Trans-Euphrates—all who know the laws
of your God. And you are to teach any
who do not know them. 26Whoever does
not obey the law of your God and the law
of the king must surely be punished by
death, banishment, confiscation of property, or imprisonment.

27Praise be to the LORD, the God of our
fathers, who has put it into the king's heart to
bring honor to the house of the LORD in Jerusalem in this way 28and who has extended his
good favor to me before the king and his advisers and all the king's powerful officials. Because the hand of the LORD my God was on
me, I took courage and gathered leading men
from Israel to go up with me.

List of the Family Heads Returning With Ezra

8 These are the family heads and those registered with them who came up with me
from Babylon during the reign of King Artaxerxes:

2of the descendants of Phinehas, Gershom;
of the descendants of Ithamar, Daniel;
of the descendants of David, Hattush 3of
the descendants of Shecaniah;

of the descendants of Parosh, Zechariah,
and with him were registered 150
men;
4of the descendants of Pahath-Moab, Eliehoenai son of Zerahiah, and with him
200 men;
5of the descendants of Zattu,[d] Shecaniah
son of Jahaziel, and with him 300
men;
6of the descendants of Adin, Ebed son of
Jonathan, and with him 50 men;
7of the descendants of Elam, Jeshaiah son
of Athaliah, and with him 70 men;
8of the descendants of Shephatiah, Zebadiah son of Michael, and with him 80
men;
9of the descendants of Joab, Obadiah son
of Jehiel, and with him 218 men;
10of the descendants of Bani,[e] Shelomith
son of Josiphiah, and with him 160
men;
11of the descendants of Bebai, Zechariah
son of Bebai, and with him 28 men;
12of the descendants of Azgad, Johanan
son of Hakkatan, and with him 110
men;
13of the descendants of Adonikam, the last
ones, whose names were Eliphelet, Jeuel and Shemaiah, and with them 60
men;
14of the descendants of Bigvai, Uthai and
Zaccur, and with them 70 men.

The Return to Jerusalem

15I assembled them at the canal that flows
toward Ahava, and we camped there three
days. When I checked among the people and
the priests, I found no Levites there. 16So I
summoned Eliezer, Ariel, Shemaiah, Elnathan,
Jarib, Elnathan, Nathan, Zechariah and Meshullam, who were leaders, and Joiarib and
Elnathan, who were men of learning, 17and I
sent them to Iddo, the leader in Casiphia. I told
them what to say to Iddo and his kinsmen, the
temple servants in Casiphia, so that they might
bring attendants to us for the house of our God.
18Because the gracious hand of our God was
on us, they brought us Sherebiah, a capable
man, from the descendants of Mahli son of
Levi, the son of Israel, and Sherebiah's sons
and brothers, 18 men; 19and Hashabiah, together with Jeshaiah from the descendants of
Merari, and his brothers and nephews, 20 men.
20They also brought 220 of the temple servants—a body that David and the officials had
established to assist the Levites. All were registered by name.

21There, by the Ahava Canal, I proclaimed a
fast, so that we might humble ourselves before
our God and ask him for a safe journey for us
and our children, with all our possessions. 22I
was ashamed to ask the king for soldiers and
horsemen to protect us from enemies on the
road, because we had told the king, "The gracious hand of our God is on everyone who
looks to him, but his great anger is against all

[a]22 That is, about 3 3/4 tons (about 3.4 metric tons) [b]22 That is, probably about 600 bushels (about 22 kiloliters) [c]22 That is, probably about 600 gallons (about 2.2 kiloliters) [d]5 Some Septuagint manuscripts (also 1 Esdras 8:32); Hebrew does not have *Zattu.* [e]10 Some Septuagint manuscripts (also 1 Esdras 8:36); Hebrew does not have *Bani.*

who forsake him." 23So we fasted and petitioned our God about this, and he answered our prayer.

24Then I set apart twelve of the leading priests, together with Sherebiah, Hashabiah and ten of their brothers, 25and I weighed out to them the offering of silver and gold and the articles that the king, his advisers, his officials and all Israel present there had donated for the house of our God. 26I weighed out to them 650 talents[a] of silver, silver articles weighing 100 talents,[b] 100 talents[b] of gold, 2720 bowls of gold valued at 1,000 darics,[c] and two fine articles of polished bronze, as precious as gold.

28I said to them, "You as well as these articles are consecrated to the LORD. The silver and gold are a freewill offering to the LORD, the God of your fathers. 29Guard them carefully until you weigh them out in the chambers of the house of the LORD in Jerusalem before the leading priests and the Levites and the family heads of Israel." 30Then the priests and Levites received the silver and gold and sacred articles that had been weighed out to be taken to the house of our God in Jerusalem.

31On the twelfth day of the first month we set out from the Ahava Canal to go to Jerusalem. The hand of our God was on us, and he protected us from enemies and bandits along the way. 32So we arrived in Jerusalem, where we rested three days.

33On the fourth day, in the house of our God, we weighed out the silver and gold and the sacred articles into the hands of Meremoth son of Uriah, the priest. Eleazar son of Phinehas was with him, and so were the Levites Jozabad son of Jeshua and Noadiah son of Binnui. 34Everything was accounted for by number and weight, and the entire weight was recorded at that time.

35Then the exiles who had returned from captivity sacrificed burnt offerings to the God of Israel: twelve bulls for all Israel, ninety-six rams, seventy-seven male lambs and, as a sin offering, twelve male goats. All this was a burnt offering to the LORD. 36They also delivered the king's orders to the royal satraps and to the governors of Trans-Euphrates, who then gave assistance to the people and to the house of God.

Ezra's Prayer About Intermarriage

9 After these things had been done, the leaders came to me and said, "The people of Israel, including the priests and the Levites, have not kept themselves separate from the neighboring peoples with their detestable practices, like those of the Canaanites, Hittites, Perizzites, Jebusites, Ammonites, Moabites, Egyptians and Amorites. 2They have taken some of their daughters as wives for themselves and their sons, and have mingled the holy race with the peoples around them. And the leaders and officials have led the way in this unfaithfulness."

3When I heard this, I tore my tunic and cloak, pulled hair from my head and beard and sat down appalled. 4Then everyone who trembled at the words of the God of Israel gathered around me because of this unfaithfulness of the exiles. And I sat there appalled until the evening sacrifice.

5Then, at the evening sacrifice, I rose from my self-abasement, with my tunic and cloak torn, and fell on my knees with my hands spread out to the LORD my God 6and prayed:

> "O my God, I am too ashamed and disgraced to lift up my face to you, my God, because our sins are higher than our heads and our guilt has reached to the heavens. 7From the days of our forefathers until now, our guilt has been great. Because of our sins, we and our kings and our priests have been subjected to the sword and captivity, to pillage and humiliation at the hand of foreign kings, as it is today.
>
> 8"But now, for a brief moment, the LORD our God has been gracious in leaving us a remnant and giving us a firm place in his sanctuary, and so our God gives light to our eyes and a little relief in our bondage. 9Though we are slaves, our God has not deserted us in our bondage. He has shown us kindness in the sight of the kings of Persia: He has granted us new life to rebuild the house of our God and repair its ruins, and he has given us a wall of protection in Judah and Jerusalem.
>
> 10"But now, O our God, what can we say after this? For we have disregarded the commands 11you gave through your servants the prophets when you said: 'The land you are entering to possess is a land polluted by the corruption of its peoples. By their detestable practices they have filled it with their impurity from one end to the other. 12Therefore, do not give your daughters in marriage to their sons or take their daughters for your sons. Do not seek a treaty of friendship with them at any time, that you may be strong and eat the good things of the land and leave it to your children as an everlasting inheritance.'
>
> 13"What has happened to us is a result of our evil deeds and our great guilt, and yet, our God, you have punished us less than our sins have deserved and have given us a remnant like this. 14Shall we again break your commands and intermarry with the peoples who commit such detestable practices? Would you not be angry enough with us to destroy us, leaving us no remnant or survivor? 15O LORD, God of Israel, you are righteous! We are left this day as a remnant. Here we are before

[a]26 That is, about 25 tons (about 22 metric tons) [b]26 That is, about 3 3/4 tons (about 3.4 metric tons)
[c]27 That is, about 19 pounds (about 8.5 kilograms)

you in our guilt, though because of it not one of us can stand in your presence."

The People's Confession of Sin

10 While Ezra was praying and confessing, weeping and throwing himself down before the house of God, a large crowd of Israelites—men, women and children—gathered around him. They too wept bitterly. 2Then Shecaniah son of Jehiel, one of the descendants of Elam, said to Ezra, "We have been unfaithful to our God by marrying foreign women from the peoples around us. But in spite of this, there is still hope for Israel. 3Now let us make a covenant before our God to send away all these women and their children, in accordance with the counsel of my lord and of those who fear the commands of our God. Let it be done according to the Law. 4Rise up; this matter is in your hands. We will support you, so take courage and do it."

5So Ezra rose up and put the leading priests and Levites and all Israel under oath to do what had been suggested. And they took the oath. 6Then Ezra withdrew from before the house of God and went to the room of Jehohanan son of Eliashib. While he was there, he ate no food and drank no water, because he continued to mourn over the unfaithfulness of the exiles.

7A proclamation was then issued throughout Judah and Jerusalem for all the exiles to assemble in Jerusalem. 8Anyone who failed to appear within three days would forfeit all his property, in accordance with the decision of the officials and elders, and would himself be expelled from the assembly of the exiles.

9Within the three days, all the men of Judah and Benjamin had gathered in Jerusalem. And on the twentieth day of the ninth month, all the people were sitting in the square before the house of God, greatly distressed by the occasion and because of the rain. 10Then Ezra the priest stood up and said to them, "You have been unfaithful; you have married foreign women, adding to Israel's guilt. 11Now make confession to the LORD, the God of your fathers, and do his will. Separate yourselves from the peoples around you and from your foreign wives."

12The whole assembly responded with a loud voice: "You are right! We must do as you say. 13But there are many people here and it is the rainy season; so we cannot stand outside. Besides, this matter cannot be taken care of in a day or two, because we have sinned greatly in this thing. 14Let our officials act for the whole assembly. Then let everyone in our towns who has married a foreign woman come at a set time, along with the elders and judges of each town, until the fierce anger of our God in this matter is turned away from us." 15Only Jonathan son of Asahel and Jahzeiah son of Tikvah, supported by Meshullam and Shabbethai the Levite, opposed this.

16So the exiles did as was proposed. Ezra the priest selected men who were family heads, one from each family division, and all of them designated by name. On the first day of the tenth month they sat down to investigate the cases, 17and by the first day of the first month they finished dealing with all the men who had married foreign women.

Those Guilty of Intermarriage

18Among the descendants of the priests, the following had married foreign women:

From the descendants of Jeshua son of Jozadak, and his brothers: Maaseiah, Eliezer, Jarib and Gedaliah. 19(They all gave their hands in pledge to put away their wives, and for their guilt they each presented a ram from the flock as a guilt offering.)

20From the descendants of Immer:
Hanani and Zebadiah.

21From the descendants of Harim:
Maaseiah, Elijah, Shemaiah, Jehiel and Uzziah.

22From the descendants of Pashhur:
Elioenai, Maaseiah, Ishmael, Nethanel, Jozabad and Elasah.

23Among the Levites:

Jozabad, Shimei, Kelaiah (that is, Kelita), Pethahiah, Judah and Eliezer.

24From the singers:
Eliashib.

From the gatekeepers:
Shallum, Telem and Uri.

25And among the other Israelites:

From the descendants of Parosh:
Ramiah, Izziah, Malkijah, Mijamin, Eleazar, Malkijah and Benaiah.

26From the descendants of Elam:
Mattaniah, Zechariah, Jehiel, Abdi, Jeremoth and Elijah.

27From the descendants of Zattu:
Elioenai, Eliashib, Mattaniah, Jeremoth, Zabad and Aziza.

28From the descendants of Bebai:
Jehohanan, Hananiah, Zabbai and Athlai.

29From the descendants of Bani:
Meshullam, Malluch, Adaiah, Jashub, Sheal and Jeremoth.

30From the descendants of Pahath-Moab:
Adna, Kelal, Benaiah, Maaseiah, Mattaniah, Bezalel, Binnui and Manasseh.

31From the descendants of Harim:
Eliezer, Ishijah, Malkijah, Shemaiah, Shimeon, 32Benjamin, Malluch and Shemariah.

33From the descendants of Hashum:
Mattenai, Mattattah, Zabad, Eliphelet, Jeremai, Manasseh and Shimei.

34From the descendants of Bani:
Maadai, Amram, Uel, 35Benaiah, Be-
deiah, Keluhi, 36Vaniah, Meremoth,
Eliashib, 37Mattaniah, Mattenai and
Jaasu.
38From the descendants of Binnui:[a]
Shimei, 39Shelemiah, Nathan, Adaiah,
40Macnadebai, Shashai, Sharai, 41Az-
arel, Shelemiah, Shemariah, 42Shal-
lum, Amariah and Joseph.
43From the descendants of Nebo:
Jeiel, Mattithiah, Zabad, Zebina, Jad-
dai, Joel and Benaiah.

44All these had married foreign women, and
some of them had children by these wives.[b]

Nehemiah

Nehemiah's Prayer

1 The words of Nehemiah son of Hacaliah:

In the month of Kislev in the twentieth year,
while I was in the citadel of Susa, 2Hanani, one
of my brothers, came from Judah with some
other men, and I questioned them about the
Jewish remnant that survived the exile, and
also about Jerusalem.

3They said to me, "Those who survived the
exile and are back in the province are in great
trouble and disgrace. The wall of Jerusalem is
broken down, and its gates have been burned
with fire."

4When I heard these things, I sat down and
wept. For some days I mourned and fasted and
prayed before the God of heaven. 5Then I
said:

> "O LORD, God of heaven, the great and
> awesome God, who keeps his covenant of
> love with those who love him and obey
> his commands, 6let your ear be attentive
> and your eyes open to hear the prayer
> your servant is praying before you day
> and night for your servants, the people of
> Israel. I confess the sins we Israelites, in-
> cluding myself and my father's house,
> have committed against you. 7We have
> acted very wickedly toward you. We have
> not obeyed the commands, decrees and
> laws you gave your servant Moses.
>
> 8"Remember the instruction you gave
> your servant Moses, saying, 'If you are
> unfaithful, I will scatter you among the
> nations, 9but if you return to me and obey
> my commands, then even if your exiled
> people are at the farthest horizon, I will
> gather them from there and bring them to
> the place I have chosen as a dwelling for
> my Name.'
>
> 10"They are your servants and your
> people, whom you redeemed by your
> great strength and your mighty hand.
> 11O Lord, let your ear be attentive to the
> prayer of this your servant and to the
> prayer of your servants who delight in re-
> vering your name. Give your servant suc-
> cess today by granting him favor in the
> presence of this man."

I was cupbearer to the king.

Artaxerxes Sends Nehemiah to Jerusalem

2 In the month of Nisan in the twentieth
year of King Artaxerxes, when wine was
brought for him, I took the wine and gave it to
the king. I had not been sad in his presence
before; 2so the king asked me, "Why does your
face look so sad when you are not ill? This can
be nothing but sadness of heart."

I was very much afraid, 3but I said to the
king, "May the king live forever! Why should
my face not look sad when the city where my
fathers are buried lies in ruins, and its gates
have been destroyed by fire?"

4The king said to me, "What is it you want?"

Then I prayed to the God of heaven, 5and I
answered the king, "If it pleases the king and
if your servant has found favor in his sight, let
him send me to the city in Judah where my
fathers are buried so that I can rebuild it."

6Then the king, with the queen sitting beside
him, asked me, "How long will your journey
take, and when will you get back?" It pleased
the king to send me; so I set a time.

7I also said to him, "If it pleases the king,
may I have letters to the governors of Trans-
Euphrates, so that they will provide me safe-
conduct until I arrive in Judah? 8And may I
have a letter to Asaph, keeper of the king's
forest, so he will give me timber to make
beams for the gates of the citadel by the temple
and for the city wall and for the residence I
will occupy?" And because the gracious hand
of my God was upon me, the king granted my
requests. 9So I went to the governors of Trans-
Euphrates and gave them the king's letters.
The king had also sent army officers and cavalry with me.

10When Sanballat the Horonite and Tobiah
the Ammonite official heard about this, they
were very much disturbed that someone had
come to promote the welfare of the Israelites.

Nehemiah Inspects Jerusalem's Walls

11I went to Jerusalem, and after staying

[a] *37,38* See Septuagint (also 1 Esdras 9:34); Hebrew *Jaasu 38and Bani and Binnui,* [b] *44* Or *and they sent them away with their children*

there three days 12I set out during the night with a few men. I had not told anyone what my God had put in my heart to do for Jerusalem. There were no mounts with me except the one I was riding on.

13By night I went out through the Valley Gate toward the Jackal[a] Well and the Dung Gate, examining the walls of Jerusalem, which had been broken down, and its gates, which had been destroyed by fire. 14Then I moved on toward the Fountain Gate and the King's Pool, but there was not enough room for my mount to get through; 15so I went up the valley by night, examining the wall. Finally, I turned back and reentered through the Valley Gate. 16The officials did not know where I had gone or what I was doing, because as yet I had said nothing to the Jews or the priests or nobles or officials or any others who would be doing the work.

17Then I said to them, "You see the trouble we are in: Jerusalem lies in ruins, and its gates have been burned with fire. Come, let us rebuild the wall of Jerusalem, and we will no longer be in disgrace." 18I also told them about the gracious hand of my God upon me and what the king had said to me.

They replied, "Let us start rebuilding." So they began this good work.

19But when Sanballat the Horonite, Tobiah the Ammonite official and Geshem the Arab heard about it, they mocked and ridiculed us. "What is this you are doing?" they asked. "Are you rebelling against the king?"

20I answered them by saying, "The God of heaven will give us success. We his servants will start rebuilding, but as for you, you have no share in Jerusalem or any claim or historic right to it."

Builders of the Wall

3 Eliashib the high priest and his fellow priests went to work and rebuilt the Sheep Gate. They dedicated it and set its doors in place, building as far as the Tower of the Hundred, which they dedicated, and as far as the Tower of Hananel. 2The men of Jericho built the adjoining section, and Zaccur son of Imri built next to them.

3The Fish Gate was rebuilt by the sons of Hassenaah. They laid its beams and put its doors and bolts and bars in place. 4Meremoth son of Uriah, the son of Hakkoz, repaired the next section. Next to him Meshullam son of Berekiah, the son of Meshezabel, made repairs, and next to him Zadok son of Baana also made repairs. 5The next section was repaired by the men of Tekoa, but their nobles would not put their shoulders to the work under their supervisors.[b]

6The Jeshanah[c] Gate was repaired by Joiada son of Paseah and Meshullam son of Besodeiah. They laid its beams and put its doors and bolts and bars in place. 7Next to them, repairs were made by men from Gibeon and Mizpah—Melatiah of Gibeon and Jadon of Meronoth—places under the authority of the governor of Trans-Euphrates. 8Uzziel son of Harhaiah, one of the goldsmiths, repaired the next section; and Hananiah, one of the perfume-makers, made repairs next to that. They restored[d] Jerusalem as far as the Broad Wall. 9Rephaiah son of Hur, ruler of a half-district of Jerusalem, repaired the next section. 10Adjoining this, Jedaiah son of Harumaph made repairs opposite his house, and Hattush son of Hashabneiah made repairs next to him. 11Malkijah son of Harim and Hasshub son of Pahath-Moab repaired another section and the Tower of the Ovens. 12Shallum son of Hallohesh, ruler of a half-district of Jerusalem, repaired the next section with the help of his daughters.

13The Valley Gate was repaired by Hanun and the residents of Zanoah. They rebuilt it and put its doors and bolts and bars in place. They also repaired five hundred yards[e] of the wall as far as the Dung Gate.

14The Dung Gate was repaired by Malkijah son of Recab, ruler of the district of Beth Hakkerem. He rebuilt it and put its doors and bolts and bars in place.

15The Fountain Gate was repaired by Shallun son of Col-Hozeh, ruler of the district of Mizpah. He rebuilt it, roofing it over and putting its doors and bolts and bars in place. He also repaired the wall of the Pool of Siloam,[f] by the King's Garden, as far as the steps going down from the City of David. 16Beyond him, Nehemiah son of Azbuk, ruler of a half-district of Beth Zur, made repairs up to a point opposite the tombs[g] of David, as far as the artificial pool and the House of the Heroes.

17Next to him, the repairs were made by the Levites under Rehum son of Bani. Beside him, Hashabiah, ruler of half the district of Keilah, carried out repairs for his district. 18Next to him, the repairs were made by their countrymen under Binnui[h] son of Henadad, ruler of the other half-district of Keilah. 19Next to him, Ezer son of Jeshua, ruler of Mizpah, repaired another section, from a point facing the ascent to the armory as far as the angle. 20Next to him, Baruch son of Zabbai zealously repaired another section, from the angle to the entrance of the house of Eliashib the high priest. 21Next to him, Meremoth son of Uriah, the son of Hakkoz, repaired another section, from the entrance of Eliashib's house to the end of it.

22The repairs next to him were made by the priests from the surrounding region. 23Beyond them, Benjamin and Hasshub made repairs in front of their house; and next to them, Azariah

[a] *13* Or *Serpent* or *Fig* [b] *5* Or *their Lord* or *the governor* [c] *6* Or *Old* [d] *8* Or *They left out part of*
[e] *13* Hebrew *a thousand cubits* (about 450 meters) [f] *15* Hebrew *Shelah,* a variant of *Shiloah,* that is, Siloam
[g] *16* Hebrew; Septuagint, some Vulgate manuscripts and Syriac *tomb* [h] *18* Two Hebrew manuscripts and Syriac (see also Septuagint and verse 24); most Hebrew manuscripts *Bavvai*

son of Maaseiah, the son of Ananiah, made
repairs beside his house. 24Next to him, Binnui
son of Henadad repaired another section, from
Azariah's house to the angle and the corner,
25and Palal son of Uzai worked opposite the
angle and the tower projecting from the upper
palace near the court of the guard. Next to him,
Pedaiah son of Parosh 26and the temple servants living on the hill of Ophel made repairs
up to a point opposite the Water Gate toward
the east and the projecting tower. 27Next to
them, the men of Tekoa repaired another section, from the great projecting tower to the
wall of Ophel.

28Above the Horse Gate, the priests made
repairs, each in front of his own house. 29Next
to them, Zadok son of Immer made repairs
opposite his house. Next to him, Shemaiah son
of Shecaniah, the guard at the East Gate, made
repairs. 30Next to him, Hananiah son of Shelemiah, and Hanun, the sixth son of Zalaph, repaired another section. Next to them, Meshullam son of Berekiah made repairs opposite his
living quarters. 31Next to him, Malkijah, one
of the goldsmiths, made repairs as far as the
house of the temple servants and the merchants, opposite the Inspection Gate, and as far
as the room above the corner; 32and between
the room above the corner and the Sheep Gate
the goldsmiths and merchants made repairs.

Opposition to the Rebuilding

4 When Sanballat heard that we were rebuilding the wall, he became angry and
was greatly incensed. He ridiculed the Jews,
2and in the presence of his associates and the
army of Samaria, he said, "What are those feeble Jews doing? Will they restore their wall?
Will they offer sacrifices? Will they finish in a
day? Can they bring the stones back to life
from those heaps of rubble—burned as they
are?"

3Tobiah the Ammonite, who was at his side,
said, "What they are building—if even a fox
climbed up on it, he would break down their
wall of stones!"

4Hear us, O our God, for we are despised.
Turn their insults back on their own heads.
Give them over as plunder in a land of captivity. 5Do not cover up their guilt or blot out their
sins from your sight, for they have thrown insults in the face of[a] the builders.

6So we rebuilt the wall till all of it reached
half its height, for the people worked with all
their heart.

7But when Sanballat, Tobiah, the Arabs, the
Ammonites and the men of Ashdod heard that
the repairs to Jerusalem's walls had gone
ahead and that the gaps were being closed,
they were very angry. 8They all plotted together to come and fight against Jerusalem and stir
up trouble against it. 9But we prayed to our
God and posted a guard day and night to meet
this threat.

10Meanwhile, the people in Judah said, "The
strength of the laborers is giving out, and there
is so much rubble that we cannot rebuild the
wall."

11Also our enemies said, "Before they know
it or see us, we will be right there among them
and will kill them and put an end to the work."

12Then the Jews who lived near them came
and told us ten times over, "Wherever you
turn, they will attack us."

13Therefore I stationed some of the people
behind the lowest points of the wall at the exposed places, posting them by families, with
their swords, spears and bows. 14After I looked
things over, I stood up and said to the nobles,
the officials and the rest of the people, "Don't
be afraid of them. Remember the Lord, who is
great and awesome, and fight for your brothers, your sons and your daughters, your wives
and your homes."

15When our enemies heard that we were
aware of their plot and that God had frustrated
it, we all returned to the wall, each to his own
work.

16From that day on, half of my men did the
work, while the other half were equipped with
spears, shields, bows and armor. The officers
posted themselves behind all the people of Judah 17who were building the wall. Those who
carried materials did their work with one hand
and held a weapon in the other, 18and each of
the builders wore his sword at his side as he
worked. But the man who sounded the trumpet
stayed with me.

19Then I said to the nobles, the officials and
the rest of the people, "The work is extensive
and spread out, and we are widely separated
from each other along the wall. 20Wherever
you hear the sound of the trumpet, join us
there. Our God will fight for us!"

21So we continued the work with half the
men holding spears, from the first light of
dawn till the stars came out. 22At that time I
also said to the people, "Have every man and
his helper stay inside Jerusalem at night, so
they can serve us as guards by night and workmen by day." 23Neither I nor my brothers nor
my men nor the guards with me took off our
clothes; each had his weapon, even when he
went for water.[b]

Nehemiah Helps the Poor

5 Now the men and their wives raised a great
outcry against their Jewish brothers.
2Some were saying, "We and our sons and
daughters are numerous; in order for us to eat
and stay alive, we must get grain."

3Others were saying, "We are mortgaging
our fields, our vineyards and our homes to get
grain during the famine."

4Still others were saying, "We have had to
borrow money to pay the king's tax on our
fields and vineyards. 5Although we are of the
same flesh and blood as our countrymen and
though our sons are as good as theirs, yet we

[a]5 Or *have provoked you to anger before* [b]23 The meaning of the Hebrew for this clause is uncertain.

have to subject our sons and daughters to slavery. Some of our daughters have already been enslaved, but we are powerless, because our fields and our vineyards belong to others."

6When I heard their outcry and these charges, I was very angry. 7I pondered them in my mind and then accused the nobles and officials. I told them, "You are exacting usury from your own countrymen!" So I called together a large meeting to deal with them 8and said: "As far as possible, we have bought back our Jewish brothers who were sold to the Gentiles. Now you are selling your brothers, only for them to be sold back to us!" They kept quiet, because they could find nothing to say.

9So I continued, "What you are doing is not right. Shouldn't you walk in the fear of our God to avoid the reproach of our Gentile enemies? 10I and my brothers and my men are also lending the people money and grain. But let the exacting of usury stop! 11Give back to them immediately their fields, vineyards, olive groves and houses, and also the usury you are charging them—the hundredth part of the money, grain, new wine and oil."

12"We will give it back," they said. "And we will not demand anything more from them. We will do as you say."

Then I summoned the priests and made the nobles and officials take an oath to do what they had promised. 13I also shook out the folds of my robe and said, "In this way may God shake out of his house and possessions every man who does not keep this promise. So may such a man be shaken out and emptied!"

At this the whole assembly said, "Amen," and praised the LORD. And the people did as they had promised.

14Moreover, from the twentieth year of King Artaxerxes, when I was appointed to be their governor in the land of Judah, until his thirty-second year—twelve years—neither I nor my brothers ate the food allotted to the governor. 15But the earlier governors—those preceding me—placed a heavy burden on the people and took forty shekels[a] of silver from them in addition to food and wine. Their assistants also lorded it over the people. But out of reverence for God I did not act like that. 16Instead, I devoted myself to the work on this wall. All my men were assembled there for the work; we[b] did not acquire any land.

17Furthermore, a hundred and fifty Jews and officials ate at my table, as well as those who came to us from the surrounding nations. 18Each day one ox, six choice sheep and some poultry were prepared for me, and every ten days an abundant supply of wine of all kinds. In spite of all this, I never demanded the food allotted to the governor, because the demands were heavy on these people.

19Remember me with favor, O my God, for all I have done for these people.

Further Opposition to the Rebuilding

6 When word came to Sanballat, Tobiah, Geshem the Arab and the rest of our enemies that I had rebuilt the wall and not a gap was left in it—though up to that time I had not set the doors in the gates— 2Sanballat and Geshem sent me this message: "Come, let us meet together in one of the villages[c] on the plain of Ono."

But they were scheming to harm me; 3so I sent messengers to them with this reply: "I am carrying on a great project and cannot go down. Why should the work stop while I leave it and go down to you?" 4Four times they sent me the same message, and each time I gave them the same answer.

5Then, the fifth time, Sanballat sent his aide to me with the same message, and in his hand was an unsealed letter 6in which was written:

> "It is reported among the nations—and Geshem[d] says it is true—that you and the Jews are plotting to revolt, and therefore you are building the wall. Moreover, according to these reports you are about to become their king 7and have even appointed prophets to make this proclamation about you in Jerusalem: 'There is a king in Judah!' Now this report will get back to the king; so come, let us confer together."

8I sent him this reply: "Nothing like what you are saying is happening; you are just making it up out of your head."

9They were all trying to frighten us, thinking, "Their hands will get too weak for the work, and it will not be completed."

⌞But I prayed,⌟ "Now strengthen my hands."

10One day I went to the house of Shemaiah son of Delaiah, the son of Mehetabel, who was shut in at his home. He said, "Let us meet in the house of God, inside the temple, and let us close the temple doors, because men are coming to kill you—by night they are coming to kill you."

11But I said, "Should a man like me run away? Or should one like me go into the temple to save his life? I will not go!" 12I realized that God had not sent him, but that he had prophesied against me because Tobiah and Sanballat had hired him. 13He had been hired to intimidate me so that I would commit a sin by doing this, and then they would give me a bad name to discredit me.

14Remember Tobiah and Sanballat, O my God, because of what they have done; remember also the prophetess Noadiah and the rest of the prophets who have been trying to intimidate me.

The Completion of the Wall

15So the wall was completed on the twenty-fifth of Elul, in fifty-two days. 16When all our enemies heard about this, all the surrounding

[a] *15* That is, about 1 pound (about 0.5 kilogram) [b] *16* Most Hebrew manuscripts; some Hebrew manuscripts, Septuagint, Vulgate and Syriac *I* [c] *2* Or *in Kephirim* [d] *6* Hebrew *Gashmu,* a variant of *Geshem*

nations were afraid and lost their self-
confidence, because they realized that this
work had been done with the help of our God.
[17]Also, in those days the nobles of Judah
were sending many letters to Tobiah, and replies from Tobiah kept coming to them. [18]For
many in Judah were under oath to him, since
he was son-in-law to Shecaniah son of Arah,
and his son Jehohanan had married the daughter of Meshullam son of Berekiah. [19]Moreover,
they kept reporting to me his good deeds and
then telling him what I said. And Tobiah sent
letters to intimidate me.

7 After the wall had been rebuilt and I had
set the doors in place, the gatekeepers and
the singers and the Levites were appointed. [2]I
put in charge of Jerusalem my brother Hanani,
along with[a] Hananiah the commander of the
citadel, because he was a man of integrity and
feared God more than most men do. [3]I said to
them, "The gates of Jerusalem are not to be
opened until the sun is hot. While the gatekeepers are still on duty, have them shut the
doors and bar them. Also appoint residents of
Jerusalem as guards, some at their posts and
some near their own houses."

The List of the Exiles Who Returned

[4]Now the city was large and spacious, but
there were few people in it, and the houses had
not yet been rebuilt. [5]So my God put it into my
heart to assemble the nobles, the officials and
the common people for registration by families. I found the genealogical record of those
who had been the first to return. This is what
I found written there:

[6]These are the people of the province
who came up from the captivity of the
exiles whom Nebuchadnezzar king of
Babylon had taken captive (they returned
to Jerusalem and Judah, each to his own
town, [7]in company with Zerubbabel,
Jeshua, Nehemiah, Azariah, Raamiah,
Nahamani, Mordecai, Bilshan, Mispereth,
Bigvai, Nehum and Baanah):

The list of the men of Israel:

[8]the descendants of Parosh 2,172
[9]of Shephatiah 372
[10]of Arah 652
[11]of Pahath-Moab (through the
line of Jeshua and Joab) 2,818
[12]of Elam 1,254
[13]of Zattu 845
[14]of Zaccai 760
[15]of Binnui 648
[16]of Bebai 628
[17]of Azgad 2,322
[18]of Adonikam 667
[19]of Bigvai 2,067
[20]of Adin 655
[21]of Ater (through Hezekiah) 98
[22]of Hashum 328
[23]of Bezai 324
[24]of Hariph 112
[25]of Gibeon 95

[26]the men of Bethlehem and
Netophah 188
[27]of Anathoth 128
[28]of Beth Azmaveth 42
[29]of Kiriath Jearim, Kephirah and
Beeroth 743
[30]of Ramah and Geba 621
[31]of Micmash 122
[32]of Bethel and Ai 123
[33]of the other Nebo 52
[34]of the other Elam 1,254
[35]of Harim 320
[36]of Jericho 345
[37]of Lod, Hadid and Ono 721
[38]of Senaah 3,930

[39]The priests:

the descendants of Jedaiah
(through the family of Jeshua) 973
[40]of Immer 1,052
[41]of Pashhur 1,247
[42]of Harim 1,017

[43]The Levites:

the descendants of Jeshua (through
Kadmiel through the line of
Hodaviah) 74

[44]The singers:

the descendants of Asaph 148

[45]The gatekeepers:

the descendants of
Shallum, Ater, Talmon, Akkub,
Hatita and Shobai 138

[46]The temple servants:

the descendants of
Ziha, Hasupha, Tabbaoth,
[47]Keros, Sia, Padon,
[48]Lebana, Hagaba, Shalmai,
[49]Hanan, Giddel, Gahar,
[50]Reaiah, Rezin, Nekoda,
[51]Gazzam, Uzza, Paseah,
[52]Besai, Meunim, Nephussim,
[53]Bakbuk, Hakupha, Harhur,
[54]Bazluth, Mehida, Harsha,
[55]Barkos, Sisera, Temah,
[56]Neziah and Hatipha

[57]The descendants of the servants of Solomon:

the descendants of
Sotai, Sophereth, Perida,
[58]Jaala, Darkon, Giddel,
[59]Shephatiah, Hattil,
Pokereth-Hazzebaim and Amon

[60]The temple servants and the
descendants of the servants of
Solomon 392

[61]The following came up from the
towns of Tel Melah, Tel Harsha, Kerub,

[a]2 Or *Hanani, that is,*

Addon and Immer, but they could not
show that their families were descended
from Israel:

62the descendants of
Delaiah, Tobiah and Nekoda 642

63And from among the priests:

the descendants of
Hobaiah, Hakkoz and Barzillai (a
man who had married a daughter
of Barzillai the Gileadite and was
called by that name).

64These searched for their family
records, but they could not find them and
so were excluded from the priesthood as
unclean. 65The governor, therefore, ordered them not to eat any of the most
sacred food until there should be a priest
ministering with the Urim and Thummim.

66The whole company numbered
42,360, 67besides their 7,337 menservants
and maidservants; and they also had 245
men and women singers. 68There were
736 horses, 245 mules,[a] 69435 camels
and 6,720 donkeys.

70Some of the heads of the families
contributed to the work. The governor
gave to the treasury 1,000 drachmas[b] of
gold, 50 bowls and 530 garments for
priests. 71Some of the heads of the families gave to the treasury for the work
20,000 drachmas[c] of gold and 2,200 minas[d] of silver. 72The total given by the
rest of the people was 20,000 drachmas of
gold, 2,000 minas[e] of silver and 67 garments for priests.

73The priests, the Levites, the gatekeepers, the singers and the temple servants, along with certain of the people
and the rest of the Israelites, settled in
their own towns.

Ezra Reads the Law

When the seventh month came and the Isra-
8 elites had settled in their towns, 1all the
people assembled as one man in the square
before the Water Gate. They told Ezra the
scribe to bring out the Book of the Law of
Moses, which the LORD had commanded for
Israel.

2So on the first day of the seventh month
Ezra the priest brought the Law before the assembly, which was made up of men and wom-
en and all who were able to understand. 3He
read it aloud from daybreak till noon as he
faced the square before the Water Gate in the
presence of the men, women and others who
could understand. And all the people listened
attentively to the Book of the Law.

4Ezra the scribe stood on a high wooden
platform built for the occasion. Beside him on
his right stood Mattithiah, Shema, Anaiah, Uriah, Hilkiah and Maaseiah; and on his left were
Pedaiah, Mishael, Malkijah, Hashum, Hash-
baddanah, Zechariah and Meshullam.

5Ezra opened the book. All the people could
see him because he was standing above them;
and as he opened it, the people all stood up.
6Ezra praised the LORD, the great God; and all
the people lifted their hands and responded,
"Amen! Amen!" Then they bowed down and
worshiped the LORD with their faces to the
ground.

7The Levites—Jeshua, Bani, Sherebiah, Jamin, Akkub, Shabbethai, Hodiah, Maaseiah,
Kelita, Azariah, Jozabad, Hanan and Pelaiah—
instructed the people in the Law while the people were standing there. 8They read from the
Book of the Law of God, making it clear[f] and
giving the meaning so that the people could
understand what was being read.

9Then Nehemiah the governor, Ezra the
priest and scribe, and the Levites who were
instructing the people said to them all, "This
day is sacred to the LORD your God. Do not
mourn or weep." For all the people had been
weeping as they listened to the words of the
Law.

10Nehemiah said, "Go and enjoy choice
food and sweet drinks, and send some to those
who have nothing prepared. This day is sacred
to our Lord. Do not grieve, for the joy of the
LORD is your strength."

11The Levites calmed all the people, saying,
"Be still, for this is a sacred day. Do not
grieve."

12Then all the people went away to eat and
drink, to send portions of food and to celebrate
with great joy, because they now understood
the words that had been made known to them.

13On the second day of the month, the heads
of all the families, along with the priests and
the Levites, gathered around Ezra the scribe to
give attention to the words of the Law. 14They
found written in the Law, which the LORD had
commanded through Moses, that the Israelites
were to live in booths during the feast of the
seventh month 15and that they should proclaim
this word and spread it throughout their towns
and in Jerusalem: "Go out into the hill country
and bring back branches from olive and wild
olive trees, and from myrtles, palms and shade
trees, to make booths"—as it is written.[g]

16So the people went out and brought back
branches and built themselves booths on their
own roofs, in their courtyards, in the courts of
the house of God and in the square by the
Water Gate and the one by the Gate of Ephraim. 17The whole company that had returned
from exile built booths and lived in them.
From the days of Joshua son of Nun until that
day, the Israelites had not celebrated it like
this. And their joy was very great.

[a] *68* Some Hebrew manuscripts (see also Ezra 2:66); most Hebrew manuscripts do not have this verse.
[b] *70* That is, about 19 pounds (about 8.5 kilograms) [c] *71* That is, about 375 pounds (about 170 kilograms);
also in verse 72 [d] *71* That is, about 1 1/3 tons (about 1.2 metric tons) [e] *72* That is, about 1 1/4 tons (about
1.1 metric tons) [f] *8* Or *God, translating it* [g] *15* See Lev. 23:37-40.

18 Day after day, from the first day to the
last, Ezra read from the Book of the Law of
God. They celebrated the feast for seven days,
and on the eighth day, in accordance with the
regulation, there was an assembly.

The Israelites Confess Their Sins

9 On the twenty-fourth day of the same
month, the Israelites gathered together,
fasting and wearing sackcloth and having dust
on their heads. 2 Those of Israelite descent had
separated themselves from all foreigners. They
stood in their places and confessed their sins
and the wickedness of their fathers. 3 They
stood where they were and read from the Book
of the Law of the LORD their God for a quarter
of the day, and spent another quarter in confession and in worshiping the LORD their God.
4 Standing on the stairs were the Levites—
Jeshua, Bani, Kadmiel, Shebaniah, Bunni,
Sherebiah, Bani and Kenani—who called with
loud voices to the LORD their God. 5 And the
Levites—Jeshua, Kadmiel, Bani, Hashabneiah, Sherebiah, Hodiah, Shebaniah and Pethahiah—said: "Stand up and praise the LORD your
God, who is from everlasting to everlasting.[a]"

"Blessed be your glorious name, and
may it be exalted above all blessing and
praise. 6 You alone are the LORD. You
made the heavens, even the highest heavens, and all their starry host, the earth and
all that is on it, the seas and all that is in
them. You give life to everything, and the
multitudes of heaven worship you.

7 "You are the LORD God, who chose
Abram and brought him out of Ur of the
Chaldeans and named him Abraham.
8 You found his heart faithful to you, and
you made a covenant with him to give to
his descendants the land of the Canaanites, Hittites, Amorites, Perizzites, Jebusites and Girgashites. You have kept your
promise because you are righteous.

9 "You saw the suffering of our forefathers in Egypt; you heard their cry at the
Red Sea.[b] 10 You sent miraculous signs
and wonders against Pharaoh, against all
his officials and all the people of his land,
for you knew how arrogantly the Egyptians treated them. You made a name for
yourself, which remains to this day.
11 You divided the sea before them, so that
they passed through it on dry ground, but
you hurled their pursuers into the depths,
like a stone into mighty waters. 12 By day
you led them with a pillar of cloud, and
by night with a pillar of fire to give them
light on the way they were to take.

13 "You came down on Mount Sinai;
you spoke to them from heaven. You
gave them regulations and laws that are
just and right, and decrees and commands
that are good. 14 You made known to them
your holy Sabbath and gave them commands, decrees and laws through your
servant Moses. 15 In their hunger you gave
them bread from heaven and in their thirst
you brought them water from the rock;
you told them to go in and take possession
of the land you had sworn with uplifted
hand to give them.

16 "But they, our forefathers, became
arrogant and stiff-necked, and did not
obey your commands. 17 They refused to
listen and failed to remember the miracles
you performed among them. They became stiff-necked and in their rebellion
appointed a leader in order to return to
their slavery. But you are a forgiving
God, gracious and compassionate, slow to
anger and abounding in love. Therefore
you did not desert them, 18 even when they
cast for themselves an image of a calf and
said, 'This is your god, who brought you
up out of Egypt,' or when they committed
awful blasphemies.

19 "Because of your great compassion
you did not abandon them in the desert.
By day the pillar of cloud did not cease to
guide them on their path, nor the pillar of
fire by night to shine on the way they
were to take. 20 You gave your good Spirit
to instruct them. You did not withhold
your manna from their mouths, and you
gave them water for their thirst. 21 For forty years you sustained them in the desert;
they lacked nothing, their clothes did not
wear out nor did their feet become swollen.

22 "You gave them kingdoms and nations, allotting to them even the remotest
frontiers. They took over the country of
Sihon[c] king of Heshbon and the country
of Og king of Bashan. 23 You made their
sons as numerous as the stars in the sky,
and you brought them into the land that
you told their fathers to enter and possess.
24 Their sons went in and took possession
of the land. You subdued before them the
Canaanites, who lived in the land; you
handed the Canaanites over to them,
along with their kings and the peoples
of the land, to deal with them as they
pleased. 25 They captured fortified cities
and fertile land; they took possession of
houses filled with all kinds of good
things, wells already dug, vineyards, olive
groves and fruit trees in abundance. They
ate to the full and were well-nourished;
they reveled in your great goodness.

26 "But they were disobedient and rebelled against you; they put your law behind their backs. They killed your prophets, who had admonished them in order to
turn them back to you; they committed
awful blasphemies. 27 So you handed

[a] *5* Or *God for ever and ever* [b] *9* Hebrew *Yam Suph*; that is, Sea of Reeds [c] *22* One Hebrew manuscript and Septuagint; most Hebrew manuscripts *Sihon, that is, the country of the*

them over to their enemies, who oppressed them. But when they were oppressed they cried out to you. From heav-
en you heard them, and in your great
compassion you gave them deliverers,
who rescued them from the hand of their
enemies.
28“But as soon as they were at rest, they
again did what was evil in your sight.
Then you abandoned them to the hand
of their enemies so that they ruled over
them. And when they cried out to you
again, you heard from heaven, and in your
compassion you delivered them time after
time.
29“You warned them to return to your
law, but they became arrogant and disobeyed your commands. They sinned
against your ordinances, by which a man
will live if he obeys them. Stubbornly
they turned their backs on you, became
stiff-necked and refused to listen. 30For
many years you were patient with them.
By your Spirit you admonished them
through your prophets. Yet they paid no
attention, so you handed them over to the
neighboring peoples. 31But in your great
mercy you did not put an end to them or
abandon them, for you are a gracious and
merciful God.
32“Now therefore, O our God, the
great, mighty and awesome God, who
keeps his covenant of love, do not let all
this hardship seem trifling in your eyes—
the hardship that has come upon us, upon
our kings and leaders, upon our priests
and prophets, upon our fathers and all
your people, from the days of the kings of
Assyria until today. 33In all that has happened to us, you have been just; you have
acted faithfully, while we did wrong.
34Our kings, our leaders, our priests and
our fathers did not follow your law; they
did not pay attention to your commands
or the warnings you gave them. 35Even
while they were in their kingdom, enjoying your great goodness to them in the
spacious and fertile land you gave them,
they did not serve you or turn from their
evil ways.
36“But see, we are slaves today, slaves
in the land you gave our forefathers so
they could eat its fruit and the other good
things it produces. 37Because of our sins,
its abundant harvest goes to the kings you
have placed over us. They rule over our
bodies and our cattle as they please. We
are in great distress.

The Agreement of the People

38“In view of all this, we are making a binding agreement, putting it in writing, and our
leaders, our Levites and our priests are affixing
their seals to it.”

10 Those who sealed it were:

Nehemiah the governor, the son of Hacaliah.

Zedekiah, 2Seraiah, Azariah, Jeremiah,
3Pashhur, Amariah, Malkijah,
4Hattush, Shebaniah, Malluch,
5Harim, Meremoth, Obadiah,
6Daniel, Ginnethon, Baruch,
7Meshullam, Abijah, Mijamin,
8Maaziah, Bilgai and Shemaiah.
These were the priests.

9The Levites:

Jeshua son of Azaniah, Binnui of the sons of Henadad, Kadmiel,
10and their associates: Shebaniah,
Hodiah, Kelita, Pelaiah, Hanan,
11Mica, Rehob, Hashabiah,
12Zaccur, Sherebiah, Shebaniah,
13Hodiah, Bani and Beninu.

14The leaders of the people:

Parosh, Pahath-Moab, Elam, Zattu, Bani,
15Bunni, Azgad, Bebai,
16Adonijah, Bigvai, Adin,
17Ater, Hezekiah, Azzur,
18Hodiah, Hashum, Bezai,
19Hariph, Anathoth, Nebai,
20Magpiash, Meshullam, Hezir,
21Meshezabel, Zadok, Jaddua,
22Pelatiah, Hanan, Anaiah,
23Hoshea, Hananiah, Hasshub,
24Hallohesh, Pilha, Shobek,
25Rehum, Hashabnah, Maaseiah,
26Ahiah, Hanan, Anan,
27Malluch, Harim and Baanah.

28“The rest of the people—priests, Levites, gatekeepers, singers, temple servants and all who separated themselves
from the neighboring peoples for the sake
of the Law of God, together with their
wives and all their sons and daughters
who are able to understand— 29all these
now join their brothers the nobles, and
bind themselves with a curse and an oath
to follow the Law of God given through
Moses the servant of God and to obey
carefully all the commands, regulations
and decrees of the LORD our Lord.
30“We promise not to give our daughters in marriage to the peoples around us
or take their daughters for our sons.
31“When the neighboring peoples bring
merchandise or grain to sell on the Sabbath, we will not buy from them on the
Sabbath or on any holy day. Every seventh year we will forgo working the land
and will cancel all debts.
32“We assume the responsibility for
carrying out the commands to give a third
of a shekel[a] each year for the service of

[a]32 That is, about 1/8 ounce (about 4 grams)

the house of our God: 33for the bread set out on the table; for the regular grain offerings and burnt offerings; for the offerings on the Sabbaths, New Moon festivals and appointed feasts; for the holy offerings; for sin offerings to make atonement for Israel; and for all the duties of the house of our God.

34"We—the priests, the Levites and the people—have cast lots to determine when each of our families is to bring to the house of our God at set times each year a contribution of wood to burn on the altar of the LORD our God, as it is written in the Law.

35"We also assume responsibility for bringing to the house of the LORD each year the firstfruits of our crops and of every fruit tree.

36"As it is also written in the Law, we will bring the firstborn of our sons and of our cattle, of our herds and of our flocks to the house of our God, to the priests ministering there.

37"Moreover, we will bring to the storerooms of the house of our God, to the priests, the first of our ground meal, of our ⌊grain⌋ offerings, of the fruit of all our trees and of our new wine and oil. And we will bring a tithe of our crops to the Levites, for it is the Levites who collect the tithes in all the towns where we work. 38A priest descended from Aaron is to accompany the Levites when they receive the tithes, and the Levites are to bring a tenth of the tithes up to the house of our God, to the storerooms of the treasury. 39The people of Israel, including the Levites, are to bring their contributions of grain, new wine and oil to the storerooms where the articles for the sanctuary are kept and where the ministering priests, the gatekeepers and the singers stay.

"We will not neglect the house of our God."

The New Residents of Jerusalem

11 Now the leaders of the people settled in Jerusalem, and the rest of the people cast lots to bring one out of every ten to live in Jerusalem, the holy city, while the remaining nine were to stay in their own towns. 2The people commended all the men who volunteered to live in Jerusalem.

3These are the provincial leaders who settled in Jerusalem (now some Israelites, priests, Levites, temple servants and descendants of Solomon's servants lived in the towns of Judah, each on his own property in the various towns, 4while other people from both Judah and Benjamin lived in Jerusalem):

From the descendants of Judah:

Athaiah son of Uzziah, the son of Zechariah, the son of Amariah, the son of Shephatiah, the son of Mahalalel, a descendant of Perez; 5and Maaseiah son of Baruch, the son of Col-Hozeh, the son of Hazaiah, the son of Adaiah, the son of Joiarib, the son of Zechariah, a descendant of Shelah. 6The descendants of Perez who lived in Jerusalem totaled 468 able men.

7From the descendants of Benjamin:

Sallu son of Meshullam, the son of Joed, the son of Pedaiah, the son of Kolaiah, the son of Maaseiah, the son of Ithiel, the son of Jeshaiah, 8and his followers, Gabbai and Sallai—928 men. 9Joel son of Zicri was their chief officer, and Judah son of Hassenuah was over the Second District of the city.

10From the priests:

Jedaiah; the son of Joiarib; Jakin; 11Seraiah son of Hilkiah, the son of Meshullam, the son of Zadok, the son of Meraioth, the son of Ahitub, supervisor in the house of God, 12and their associates, who carried on work for the temple—822 men; Adaiah son of Jeroham, the son of Pelaliah, the son of Amzi, the son of Zechariah, the son of Pashhur, the son of Malkijah, 13and his associates, who were heads of families—242 men; Amashsai son of Azarel, the son of Ahzai, the son of Meshillemoth, the son of Immer, 14and his[a] associates, who were able men—128. Their chief officer was Zabdiel son of Haggedolim.

15From the Levites:

Shemaiah son of Hasshub, the son of Azrikam, the son of Hashabiah, the son of Bunni; 16Shabbethai and Jozabad, two of the heads of the Levites, who had charge of the outside work of the house of God; 17Mattaniah son of Mica, the son of Zabdi, the son of Asaph, the director who led in thanksgiving and prayer; Bakbukiah, second among his associates; and Abda son of Shammua, the son of Galal, the son of Jeduthun. 18The Levites in the holy city totaled 284.

19The gatekeepers:

Akkub, Talmon and their associates, who kept watch at the gates—172 men.

20The rest of the Israelites, with the priests and Levites, were in all the towns of Judah, each on his ancestral property.

21The temple servants lived on the hill of Ophel, and Ziha and Gishpa were in charge of them.

22The chief officer of the Levites in Jerusalem was Uzzi son of Bani, the son of Hashabiah, the son of Mattaniah, the son of Mica. Uzzi was one of Asaph's descendants, who were the

[a] 14 Most Septuagint manuscripts; Hebrew *their*

singers responsible for the service of the house
of God. 23The singers were under the king's
orders, which regulated their daily activity.
24Pethahiah son of Meshezabel, one of the
descendants of Zerah son of Judah, was the
king's agent in all affairs relating to the people.
25As for the villages with their fields, some
of the people of Judah lived in Kiriath Arba
and its surrounding settlements, in Dibon and
its settlements, in Jekabzeel and its villages,
26in Jeshua, in Moladah, in Beth Pelet, 27in
Hazar Shual, in Beersheba and its settlements,
28in Ziklag, in Meconah and its settlements,
29in En Rimmon, in Zorah, in Jarmuth, 30Za-
noah, Adullam and their villages, in Lachish
and its fields, and in Azekah and its settlements. So they were living all the way from
Beersheba to the Valley of Hinnom.
31The descendants of the Benjamites from
Geba lived in Micmash, Aija, Bethel and its
settlements, 32in Anathoth, Nob and Ananiah,
33in Hazor, Ramah and Gittaim, 34in Hadid,
Zeboim and Neballat, 35in Lod and Ono, and in
the Valley of the Craftsmen.
36Some of the divisions of the Levites of
Judah settled in Benjamin.

Priests and Levites

12 These were the priests and Levites who
returned with Zerubbabel son of Shealtiel and with Jeshua:
Seraiah, Jeremiah, Ezra,
2Amariah, Malluch, Hattush,
3Shecaniah, Rehum, Meremoth,
4Iddo, Ginnethon,[a] Abijah,
5Mijamin,[b] Moadiah, Bilgah,
6Shemaiah, Joiarib, Jedaiah,
7Sallu, Amok, Hilkiah and Jedaiah.
These were the leaders of the priests and their
associates in the days of Jeshua.
8The Levites were Jeshua, Binnui, Kadmiel,
Sherebiah, Judah, and also Mattaniah, who, together with his associates, was in charge of the
songs of thanksgiving. 9Bakbukiah and Unni,
their associates, stood opposite them in the services.
10Jeshua was the father of Joiakim, Joiakim
the father of Eliashib, Eliashib the father of
Joiada, 11Joiada the father of Jonathan, and
Jonathan the father of Jaddua.
12In the days of Joiakim, these were the
heads of the priestly families:
of Seraiah's family, Meraiah;
of Jeremiah's, Hananiah;
13of Ezra's, Meshullam;
of Amariah's, Jehohanan;
14of Malluch's, Jonathan;
of Shecaniah's,[c] Joseph;
15of Harim's, Adna;
of Meremoth's,[d] Helkai;
16of Iddo's, Zechariah;
of Ginnethon's, Meshullam;
17of Abijah's, Zicri;
of Miniamin's and of Moadiah's, Piltai;
18of Bilgah's, Shammua;
of Shemaiah's, Jehonathan;
19of Joiarib's, Mattenai;
of Jedaiah's, Uzzi;
20of Sallu's, Kallai;
of Amok's, Eber;
21of Hilkiah's, Hashabiah;
of Jedaiah's, Nethanel.
22The family heads of the Levites in the
days of Eliashib, Joiada, Johanan and Jaddua,
as well as those of the priests, were recorded in
the reign of Darius the Persian. 23The family
heads among the descendants of Levi up to the
time of Johanan son of Eliashib were recorded
in the book of the annals. 24And the leaders of
the Levites were Hashabiah, Sherebiah, Jeshua
son of Kadmiel, and their associates, who
stood opposite them to give praise and thanksgiving, one section responding to the other, as
prescribed by David the man of God.
25Mattaniah, Bakbukiah, Obadiah, Meshullam, Talmon and Akkub were gatekeepers who
guarded the storerooms at the gates. 26They
served in the days of Joiakim son of Jeshua,
the son of Jozadak, and in the days of Nehemiah the governor and of Ezra the priest and
scribe.

Dedication of the Wall of Jerusalem

27At the dedication of the wall of Jerusalem,
the Levites were sought out from where they
lived and were brought to Jerusalem to celebrate joyfully the dedication with songs of
thanksgiving and with the music of cymbals,
harps and lyres. 28The singers also were
brought together from the region around Jerusalem—from the villages of the Netophathites,
29from Beth Gilgal, and from the area of Geba
and Azmaveth, for the singers had built villages for themselves around Jerusalem.
30When the priests and Levites had purified
themselves ceremonially, they purified the
people, the gates and the wall.
31I had the leaders of Judah go up on top[e] of
the wall. I also assigned two large choirs to
give thanks. One was to proceed on top[f] of the
wall to the right, toward the Dung Gate. 32Ho-
shaiah and half the leaders of Judah followed
them, 33along with Azariah, Ezra, Meshullam,
34Judah, Benjamin, Shemaiah, Jeremiah, 35as
well as some priests with trumpets, and also
Zechariah son of Jonathan, the son of Shemaiah, the son of Mattaniah, the son of Micaiah,
the son of Zaccur, the son of Asaph, 36and his
associates—Shemaiah, Azarel, Milalai, Gila-
lai, Maai, Nethanel, Judah and Hanani—with
musical instruments ⌞prescribed by⌟ David the
man of God. Ezra the scribe led the procession.
37At the Fountain Gate they continued directly
up the steps of the City of David on the ascent
to the wall and passed above the house of David to the Water Gate on the east.

[a]4 Many Hebrew manuscripts and Vulgate (see also Neh. 12:16); most Hebrew manuscripts *Ginnethoi*
[b]5 A variant of *Miniamin* [c]14 Very many Hebrew manuscripts, some Septuagint manuscripts and Syriac (see also Neh. 12:3); most Hebrew manuscripts *Shebaniah's* [d]15 Some Septuagint manuscripts (see also Neh. 12:3); Hebrew *Meraioth's* [e]31 Or *go alongside* [f]31 Or *proceed alongside*

38The second choir proceeded in the opposite direction. I followed them on top[a] of the
wall, together with half the people—past the
Tower of the Ovens to the Broad Wall, 39over
the Gate of Ephraim, the Jeshanah[b] Gate, the
Fish Gate, the Tower of Hananel and the Tower of the Hundred, as far as the Sheep Gate. At
the Gate of the Guard they stopped.

40The two choirs that gave thanks then took
their places in the house of God; so did I, together with half the officials, 41as well as the
priests—Eliakim, Maaseiah, Miniamin, Micaiah, Elioenai, Zechariah and Hananiah with
their trumpets— 42and also Maaseiah, Shemaiah, Eleazar, Uzzi, Jehohanan, Malkijah, Elam
and Ezer. The choirs sang under the direction
of Jezrahiah. 43And on that day they offered
great sacrifices, rejoicing because God had
given them great joy. The women and children
also rejoiced. The sound of rejoicing in Jerusalem could be heard far away.

44At that time men were appointed to be in
charge of the storerooms for the contributions,
firstfruits and tithes. From the fields around the
towns they were to bring into the storerooms
the portions required by the Law for the priests
and the Levites, for Judah was pleased with the
ministering priests and Levites. 45They performed the service of their God and the service
of purification, as did also the singers and gatekeepers, according to the commands of David
and his son Solomon. 46For long ago, in the
days of David and Asaph, there had been di-
rectors for the singers and for the songs of
praise and thanksgiving to God. 47So in the
days of Zerubbabel and of Nehemiah, all Israel
contributed the daily portions for the singers
and gatekeepers. They also set aside the portion for the other Levites, and the Levites set
aside the portion for the descendants of Aaron.

Nehemiah's Final Reforms

13 On that day the Book of Moses was
read aloud in the hearing of the people
and there it was found written that no Ammonite or Moabite should ever be admitted into the
assembly of God, 2because they had not met
the Israelites with food and water but had hired
Balaam to call a curse down on them. (Our
God, however, turned the curse into a blessing.) 3When the people heard this law, they
excluded from Israel all who were of foreign
descent.

4Before this, Eliashib the priest had been put
in charge of the storerooms of the house of our
God. He was closely associated with Tobiah,
5and he had provided him with a large room
formerly used to store the grain offerings and
incense and temple articles, and also the tithes
of grain, new wine and oil prescribed for the
Levites, singers and gatekeepers, as well as the
contributions for the priests.

6But while all this was going on, I was not
in Jerusalem, for in the thirty-second year of
Artaxerxes king of Babylon I had returned to
the king. Some time later I asked his permission 7and came back to Jerusalem. Here I
learned about the evil thing Eliashib had done
in providing Tobiah a room in the courts of the
house of God. 8I was greatly displeased and
threw all Tobiah's household goods out of the
room. 9I gave orders to purify the rooms, and
then I put back into them the equipment of the
house of God, with the grain offerings and the
incense.

10I also learned that the portions assigned to
the Levites had not been given to them, and
that all the Levites and singers responsible for
the service had gone back to their own fields.
11So I rebuked the officials and asked them,
"Why is the house of God neglected?" Then I
called them together and stationed them at
their posts.

12All Judah brought the tithes of grain, new
wine and oil into the storerooms. 13I put Shelemiah the priest, Zadok the scribe, and a Levite
named Pedaiah in charge of the storerooms
and made Hanan son of Zaccur, the son of
Mattaniah, their assistant, because these men
were considered trustworthy. They were made
responsible for distributing the supplies to
their brothers.

14Remember me for this, O my God, and do
not blot out what I have so faithfully done for
the house of my God and its services.

15In those days I saw men in Judah treading
winepresses on the Sabbath and bringing in
grain and loading it on donkeys, together with
wine, grapes, figs and all other kinds of loads.
And they were bringing all this into Jerusalem
on the Sabbath. Therefore I warned them
against selling food on that day. 16Men from
Tyre who lived in Jerusalem were bringing in
fish and all kinds of merchandise and selling
them in Jerusalem on the Sabbath to the people
of Judah. 17I rebuked the nobles of Judah and
said to them, "What is this wicked thing you
are doing—desecrating the Sabbath day?
18Didn't your forefathers do the same things,
so that our God brought all this calamity upon
us and upon this city? Now you are stirring up
more wrath against Israel by desecrating the
Sabbath."

19When evening shadows fell on the gates of
Jerusalem before the Sabbath, I ordered the
doors to be shut and not opened until the Sabbath was over. I stationed some of my own
men at the gates so that no load could be
brought in on the Sabbath day. 20Once or twice
the merchants and sellers of all kinds of goods
spent the night outside Jerusalem. 21But I
warned them and said, "Why do you spend the
night by the wall? If you do this again, I will
lay hands on you." From that time on they no
longer came on the Sabbath. 22Then I commanded the Levites to purify themselves and
go and guard the gates in order to keep the
Sabbath day holy.

[a]38 Or *them alongside* [b]39 Or *Old*

Remember me for this also, O my God, and
show mercy to me according to your great
love.

23Moreover, in those days I saw men of Judah who had married women from Ashdod,
Ammon and Moab. 24Half of their children
spoke the language of Ashdod or the language
of one of the other peoples, and did not know
how to speak the language of Judah. 25I rebuked them and called curses down on them. I
beat some of the men and pulled out their hair.
I made them take an oath in God's name and
said: "You are not to give your daughters in
marriage to their sons, nor are you to take their
daughters in marriage for your sons or for
yourselves. 26Was it not because of marriages
like these that Solomon king of Israel sinned?
Among the many nations there was no king
like him. He was loved by his God, and God
made him king over all Israel, but even he was
led into sin by foreign women. 27Must we hear
now that you too are doing all this terrible
wickedness and are being unfaithful to our
God by marrying foreign women?"
28One of the sons of Joiada son of Eliashib
the high priest was son-in-law to Sanballat the
Horonite. And I drove him away from me.

29Remember them, O my God, because they
defiled the priestly office and the covenant of
the priesthood and of the Levites.

30So I purified the priests and the Levites of
everything foreign, and assigned them duties,
each to his own task. 31I also made provision
for contributions of wood at designated times,
and for the firstfruits.

Remember me with favor, O my God.

Esther

Queen Vashti Deposed

1 This is what happened during the time of
Xerxes,[a] the Xerxes who ruled over 127
provinces stretching from India to Cush[b]: 2At
that time King Xerxes reigned from his royal
throne in the citadel of Susa, 3and in the third
year of his reign he gave a banquet for all his
nobles and officials. The military leaders of
Persia and Media, the princes, and the nobles
of the provinces were present.
4For a full 180 days he displayed the vast
wealth of his kingdom and the splendor and
glory of his majesty. 5When these days were
over, the king gave a banquet, lasting seven
days, in the enclosed garden of the king's palace, for all the people from the least to the
greatest, who were in the citadel of Susa. 6The
garden had hangings of white and blue linen,
fastened with cords of white linen and purple
material to silver rings on marble pillars. There
were couches of gold and silver on a mosaic
pavement of porphyry, marble, mother-of-
pearl and other costly stones. 7Wine was
served in goblets of gold, each one different
from the other, and the royal wine was abundant, in keeping with the king's liberality. 8By
the king's command each guest was allowed to
drink in his own way, for the king instructed
all the wine stewards to serve each man what
he wished.
9Queen Vashti also gave a banquet for the
women in the royal palace of King Xerxes.
10On the seventh day, when King Xerxes
was in high spirits from wine, he commanded
the seven eunuchs who served him—Mehu-
man, Biztha, Harbona, Bigtha, Abagtha, Ze-
thar and Carcas— 11to bring before him Queen
Vashti, wearing her royal crown, in order to
display her beauty to the people and nobles, for
she was lovely to look at. 12But when the attendants delivered the king's command, Queen
Vashti refused to come. Then the king became
furious and burned with anger.
13Since it was customary for the king to consult experts in matters of law and justice, he
spoke with the wise men who understood the
times 14and were closest to the king—Carshe-
na, Shethar, Admatha, Tarshish, Meres, Mar-
sena and Memucan, the seven nobles of Persia
and Media who had special access to the king
and were highest in the kingdom.
15"According to law, what must be done to
Queen Vashti?" he asked. "She has not obeyed
the command of King Xerxes that the eunuchs
have taken to her."
16Then Memucan replied in the presence of
the king and the nobles, "Queen Vashti has
done wrong, not only against the king but also
against all the nobles and the peoples of all the
provinces of King Xerxes. 17For the queen's
conduct will become known to all the women,
and so they will despise their husbands and
say, 'King Xerxes commanded Queen Vashti
to be brought before him, but she would not
come.' 18This very day the Persian and Median
women of the nobility who have heard about
the queen's conduct will respond to all the
king's nobles in the same way. There will be
no end of disrespect and discord.
19"Therefore, if it pleases the king, let him
issue a royal decree and let it be written in the
laws of Persia and Media, which cannot be
repealed, that Vashti is never again to enter the

[a] *1* Hebrew *Ahasuerus,* a variant of Xerxes' Persian name; here and throughout Esther [b] *1* That is, the upper Nile region

presence of King Xerxes. Also let the king give her royal position to someone else who is better than she. 20Then when the king's edict is proclaimed throughout all his vast realm, all the women will respect their husbands, from the least to the greatest."

21The king and his nobles were pleased with this advice, so the king did as Memucan proposed. 22He sent dispatches to all parts of the kingdom, to each province in its own script and to each people in its own language, proclaiming in each people's tongue that every man should be ruler over his own household.

Esther Made Queen

2 Later when the anger of King Xerxes had subsided, he remembered Vashti and what she had done and what he had decreed about her. 2Then the king's personal attendants proposed, "Let a search be made for beautiful young virgins for the king. 3Let the king appoint commissioners in every province of his realm to bring all these beautiful girls into the harem at the citadel of Susa. Let them be placed under the care of Hegai, the king's eunuch, who is in charge of the women; and let beauty treatments be given to them. 4Then let the girl who pleases the king be queen instead of Vashti." This advice appealed to the king, and he followed it.

5Now there was in the citadel of Susa a Jew of the tribe of Benjamin, named Mordecai son of Jair, the son of Shimei, the son of Kish, 6who had been carried into exile from Jerusalem by Nebuchadnezzar king of Babylon, among those taken captive with Jehoiachin[a] king of Judah. 7Mordecai had a cousin named Hadassah, whom he had brought up because she had neither father nor mother. This girl, who was also known as Esther, was lovely in form and features, and Mordecai had taken her as his own daughter when her father and mother died.

8When the king's order and edict had been proclaimed, many girls were brought to the citadel of Susa and put under the care of Hegai. Esther also was taken to the king's palace and entrusted to Hegai, who had charge of the harem. 9The girl pleased him and won his favor. Immediately he provided her with her beauty treatments and special food. He assigned to her seven maids selected from the king's palace and moved her and her maids into the best place in the harem.

10Esther had not revealed her nationality and family background, because Mordecai had forbidden her to do so. 11Every day he walked back and forth near the courtyard of the harem to find out how Esther was and what was happening to her.

12Before a girl's turn came to go in to King Xerxes, she had to complete twelve months of beauty treatments prescribed for the women, six months with oil of myrrh and six with perfumes and cosmetics. 13And this is how she would go to the king: Anything she wanted was given her to take with her from the harem to the king's palace. 14In the evening she would go there and in the morning return to another part of the harem to the care of Shaashgaz, the king's eunuch who was in charge of the concubines. She would not return to the king unless he was pleased with her and summoned her by name.

15When the turn came for Esther (the girl Mordecai had adopted, the daughter of his uncle Abihail) to go to the king, she asked for nothing other than what Hegai, the king's eunuch who was in charge of the harem, suggested. And Esther won the favor of everyone who saw her. 16She was taken to King Xerxes in the royal residence in the tenth month, the month of Tebeth, in the seventh year of his reign.

17Now the king was attracted to Esther more than to any of the other women, and she won his favor and approval more than any of the other virgins. So he set a royal crown on her head and made her queen instead of Vashti. 18And the king gave a great banquet, Esther's banquet, for all his nobles and officials. He proclaimed a holiday throughout the provinces and distributed gifts with royal liberality.

Mordecai Uncovers a Conspiracy

19When the virgins were assembled a second time, Mordecai was sitting at the king's gate. 20But Esther had kept secret her family background and nationality just as Mordecai had told her to do, for she continued to follow Mordecai's instructions as she had done when he was bringing her up.

21During the time Mordecai was sitting at the king's gate, Bigthana[b] and Teresh, two of the king's officers who guarded the doorway, became angry and conspired to assassinate King Xerxes. 22But Mordecai found out about the plot and told Queen Esther, who in turn reported it to the king, giving credit to Mordecai. 23And when the report was investigated and found to be true, the two officials were hanged on a gallows.[c] All this was recorded in the book of the annals in the presence of the king.

Haman's Plot to Destroy the Jews

3 After these events, King Xerxes honored Haman son of Hammedatha, the Agagite, elevating him and giving him a seat of honor higher than that of all the other nobles. 2All the royal officials at the king's gate knelt down and paid honor to Haman, for the king had commanded this concerning him. But Mordecai would not kneel down or pay him honor.

3Then the royal officials at the king's gate asked Mordecai, "Why do you disobey the king's command?" 4Day after day they spoke to him but he refused to comply. Therefore they told Haman about it to see whether Mor-

[a]6 Hebrew *Jeconiah,* a variant of *Jehoiachin* [b]21 Hebrew *Bigthan,* a variant of *Bigthana* [c]23 Or *were hung* (or *impaled*) *on poles*; similarly elsewhere in Esther

decai's behavior would be tolerated, for he had
told them he was a Jew.
5When Haman saw that Mordecai would not
kneel down or pay him honor, he was enraged.
6Yet having learned who Mordecai's people
were, he scorned the idea of killing only Mordecai. Instead Haman looked for a way to destroy all Mordecai's people, the Jews, throughout the whole kingdom of Xerxes.
7In the twelfth year of King Xerxes, in the
first month, the month of Nisan, they cast the
pur (that is, the lot) in the presence of Haman
to select a day and month. And the lot fell on[a]
the twelfth month, the month of Adar.
8Then Haman said to King Xerxes, "There
is a certain people dispersed and scattered
among the peoples in all the provinces of your
kingdom whose customs are different from
those of all other people and who do not obey
the king's laws; it is not in the king's best
interest to tolerate them. 9If it pleases the king,
let a decree be issued to destroy them, and I
will put ten thousand talents[b] of silver into the
royal treasury for the men who carry out this
business."
10So the king took his signet ring from his
finger and gave it to Haman son of Hammedatha, the Agagite, the enemy of the Jews.
11"Keep the money," the king said to Haman,
"and do with the people as you please."
12Then on the thirteenth day of the first
month the royal secretaries were summoned.
They wrote out in the script of each province
and in the language of each people all Haman's orders to the king's satraps, the governors of the various provinces and the nobles of
the various peoples. These were written in the
name of King Xerxes himself and sealed with
his own ring. 13Dispatches were sent by couriers to all the king's provinces with the order
to destroy, kill and annihilate all the Jews—
young and old, women and little children—on
a single day, the thirteenth day of the twelfth
month, the month of Adar, and to plunder their
goods. 14A copy of the text of the edict was to
be issued as law in every province and made
known to the people of every nationality so
they would be ready for that day.
15Spurred on by the king's command, the
couriers went out, and the edict was issued in
the citadel of Susa. The king and Haman sat
down to drink, but the city of Susa was bewildered.

Mordecai Persuades Esther to Help

4 When Mordecai learned of all that had
been done, he tore his clothes, put on sackcloth and ashes, and went out into the city,
wailing loudly and bitterly. 2But he went only
as far as the king's gate, because no one
clothed in sackcloth was allowed to enter it.
3In every province to which the edict and order
of the king came, there was great mourning
among the Jews, with fasting, weeping and
wailing. Many lay in sackcloth and ashes.
4When Esther's maids and eunuchs came
and told her about Mordecai, she was in great
distress. She sent clothes for him to put on
instead of his sackcloth, but he would not accept them. 5Then Esther summoned Hathach,
one of the king's eunuchs assigned to attend
her, and ordered him to find out what was troubling Mordecai and why.
6So Hathach went out to Mordecai in the
open square of the city in front of the king's
gate. 7Mordecai told him everything that had
happened to him, including the exact amount
of money Haman had promised to pay into the
royal treasury for the destruction of the Jews.
8He also gave him a copy of the text of the
edict for their annihilation, which had been
published in Susa, to show to Esther and explain it to her, and he told him to urge her to
go into the king's presence to beg for mercy
and plead with him for her people.
9Hathach went back and reported to Esther
what Mordecai had said. 10Then she instructed
him to say to Mordecai, 11"All the king's officials and the people of the royal provinces
know that for any man or woman who approaches the king in the inner court without
being summoned the king has but one law: that
he be put to death. The only exception to this
is for the king to extend the gold scepter to him
and spare his life. But thirty days have passed
since I was called to go to the king."
12When Esther's words were reported to
Mordecai, 13he sent back this answer: "Do not
think that because you are in the king's house
you alone of all the Jews will escape. 14For if
you remain silent at this time, relief and deliverance for the Jews will arise from another
place, but you and your father's family will
perish. And who knows but that you have
come to royal position for such a time as this?"
15Then Esther sent this reply to Mordecai:
16"Go, gather together all the Jews who are in
Susa, and fast for me. Do not eat or drink for
three days, night or day. I and my maids will
fast as you do. When this is done, I will go to
the king, even though it is against the law. And
if I perish, I perish."
17So Mordecai went away and carried out all
of Esther's instructions.

Esther's Request to the King

5 On the third day Esther put on her royal
robes and stood in the inner court of the
palace, in front of the king's hall. The king was
sitting on his royal throne in the hall, facing the
entrance. 2When he saw Queen Esther standing in the court, he was pleased with her and
held out to her the gold scepter that was in his
hand. So Esther approached and touched the
tip of the scepter.
3Then the king asked, "What is it, Queen

[a]7 Septuagint; Hebrew does not have *And the lot fell on.*
[b]9 That is, about 375 tons (about 345 metric tons)

Esther? What is your request? Even up to half the kingdom, it will be given you."

4"If it pleases the king," replied Esther, "let the king, together with Haman, come today to a banquet I have prepared for him."

5"Bring Haman at once," the king said, "so that we may do what Esther asks."

So the king and Haman went to the banquet Esther had prepared. 6As they were drinking wine, the king again asked Esther, "Now what is your petition? It will be given you. And what is your request? Even up to half the kingdom, it will be granted."

7Esther replied, "My petition and my request is this: 8If the king regards me with favor and if it pleases the king to grant my petition and fulfill my request, let the king and Haman come tomorrow to the banquet I will prepare for them. Then I will answer the king's question."

Haman's Rage Against Mordecai

9Haman went out that day happy and in high spirits. But when he saw Mordecai at the king's gate and observed that he neither rose nor showed fear in his presence, he was filled with rage against Mordecai. 10Nevertheless, Haman restrained himself and went home.

Calling together his friends and Zeresh, his wife, 11Haman boasted to them about his vast wealth, his many sons, and all the ways the king had honored him and how he had elevated him above the other nobles and officials. 12"And that's not all," Haman added. "I'm the only person Queen Esther invited to accompany the king to the banquet she gave. And she has invited me along with the king tomorrow. 13But all this gives me no satisfaction as long as I see that Jew Mordecai sitting at the king's gate."

14His wife Zeresh and all his friends said to him, "Have a gallows built, seventy-five feet[a] high, and ask the king in the morning to have Mordecai hanged on it. Then go with the king to the dinner and be happy." This suggestion delighted Haman, and he had the gallows built.

Mordecai Honored

6 That night the king could not sleep; so he ordered the book of the chronicles, the record of his reign, to be brought in and read to him. 2It was found recorded there that Mordecai had exposed Bigthana and Teresh, two of the king's officers who guarded the doorway, who had conspired to assassinate King Xerxes.

3"What honor and recognition has Mordecai received for this?" the king asked.

"Nothing has been done for him," his attendants answered.

4The king said, "Who is in the court?" Now Haman had just entered the outer court of the palace to speak to the king about hanging Mordecai on the gallows he had erected for him.

5His attendants answered, "Haman is standing in the court."

"Bring him in," the king ordered.

6When Haman entered, the king asked him, "What should be done for the man the king delights to honor?"

Now Haman thought to himself, "Who is there that the king would rather honor than me?" 7So he answered the king, "For the man the king delights to honor, 8have them bring a royal robe the king has worn and a horse the king has ridden, one with a royal crest placed on its head. 9Then let the robe and horse be entrusted to one of the king's most noble princes. Let them robe the man the king delights to honor, and lead him on the horse through the city streets, proclaiming before him, 'This is what is done for the man the king delights to honor!' "

10"Go at once," the king commanded Haman. "Get the robe and the horse and do just as you have suggested for Mordecai the Jew, who sits at the king's gate. Do not neglect anything you have recommended."

11So Haman got the robe and the horse. He robed Mordecai, and led him on horseback through the city streets, proclaiming before him, "This is what is done for the man the king delights to honor!"

12Afterward Mordecai returned to the king's gate. But Haman rushed home, with his head covered in grief, 13and told Zeresh his wife and all his friends everything that had happened to him.

His advisers and his wife Zeresh said to him, "Since Mordecai, before whom your downfall has started, is of Jewish origin, you cannot stand against him—you will surely come to ruin!" 14While they were still talking with him, the king's eunuchs arrived and hurried Haman away to the banquet Esther had prepared.

Haman Hanged

7 So the king and Haman went to dine with Queen Esther, 2and as they were drinking wine on that second day, the king again asked, "Queen Esther, what is your petition? It will be given you. What is your request? Even up to half the kingdom, it will be granted."

3Then Queen Esther answered, "If I have found favor with you, O king, and if it pleases your majesty, grant me my life—this is my petition. And spare my people—this is my request. 4For I and my people have been sold for destruction and slaughter and annihilation. If we had merely been sold as male and female slaves, I would have kept quiet, because no such distress would justify disturbing the king.[b]"

5King Xerxes asked Queen Esther, "Who is he? Where is the man who has dared to do such a thing?"

6Esther said, "The adversary and enemy is this vile Haman."

Then Haman was terrified before the king and queen. 7The king got up in a rage, left his

[a] *14* Hebrew *fifty cubits* (about 23 meters) [b] *4* Or *quiet, but the compensation our adversary offers cannot be compared with the loss the king would suffer*

wine and went out into the palace garden. But
Haman, realizing that the king had already decided his fate, stayed behind to beg Queen Esther for his life.

[8]Just as the king returned from the palace
garden to the banquet hall, Haman was falling
on the couch where Esther was reclining.

The king exclaimed, "Will he even molest
the queen while she is with me in the house?"

As soon as the word left the king's mouth,
they covered Haman's face. [9]Then Harbona,
one of the eunuchs attending the king, said, "A
gallows seventy-five feet[a] high stands by Haman's house. He had it made for Mordecai,
who spoke up to help the king."

The king said, "Hang him on it!" [10]So they
hanged Haman on the gallows he had prepared
for Mordecai. Then the king's fury subsided.

The King's Edict in Behalf of the Jews

8 That same day King Xerxes gave Queen
Esther the estate of Haman, the enemy of
the Jews. And Mordecai came into the presence of the king, for Esther had told how he
was related to her. [2]The king took off his signet ring, which he had reclaimed from Haman,
and presented it to Mordecai. And Esther appointed him over Haman's estate.

[3]Esther again pleaded with the king, falling
at his feet and weeping. She begged him to put
an end to the evil plan of Haman the Agagite,
which he had devised against the Jews. [4]Then
the king extended the gold scepter to Esther
and she arose and stood before him.

[5]"If it pleases the king," she said, "and if he
regards me with favor and thinks it the right
thing to do, and if he is pleased with me, let an
order be written overruling the dispatches that
Haman son of Hammedatha, the Agagite, devised and wrote to destroy the Jews in all the
king's provinces. [6]For how can I bear to see
disaster fall on my people? How can I bear to
see the destruction of my family?"

[7]King Xerxes replied to Queen Esther and to
Mordecai the Jew, "Because Haman attacked
the Jews, I have given his estate to Esther, and
they have hanged him on the gallows. [8]Now
write another decree in the king's name in behalf of the Jews as seems best to you, and seal
it with the king's signet ring—for no docu-
ment written in the king's name and sealed
with his ring can be revoked."

[9]At once the royal secretaries were summoned—on the twenty-third day of the third
month, the month of Sivan. They wrote out all
Mordecai's orders to the Jews, and to the satraps, governors and nobles of the 127 provinces stretching from India to Cush.[b] These
orders were written in the script of each province and the language of each people and also
to the Jews in their own script and language.
[10]Mordecai wrote in the name of King Xerxes,
sealed the dispatches with the king's signet
ring, and sent them by mounted couriers, who
rode fast horses especially bred for the king.

[11]The king's edict granted the Jews in every
city the right to assemble and protect themselves; to destroy, kill and annihilate any
armed force of any nationality or province that
might attack them and their women and children; and to plunder the property of their enemies. [12]The day appointed for the Jews to do
this in all the provinces of King Xerxes was
the thirteenth day of the twelfth month, the
month of Adar. [13]A copy of the text of the
edict was to be issued as law in every province
and made known to the people of every nationality so that the Jews would be ready on that
day to avenge themselves on their enemies.

[14]The couriers, riding the royal horses, raced
out, spurred on by the king's command. And
the edict was also issued in the citadel of Susa.

[15]Mordecai left the king's presence wearing
royal garments of blue and white, a large
crown of gold and a purple robe of fine linen.
And the city of Susa held a joyous celebration.
[16]For the Jews it was a time of happiness and
joy, gladness and honor. [17]In every province
and in every city, wherever the edict of the
king went, there was joy and gladness among
the Jews, with feasting and celebrating. And
many people of other nationalities became
Jews because fear of the Jews had seized them.

Triumph of the Jews

9 On the thirteenth day of the twelfth month,
the month of Adar, the edict commanded
by the king was to be carried out. On this day
the enemies of the Jews had hoped to overpower them, but now the tables were turned
and the Jews got the upper hand over those
who hated them. [2]The Jews assembled in their
cities in all the provinces of King Xerxes to
attack those seeking their destruction. No one
could stand against them, because the people
of all the other nationalities were afraid of
them. [3]And all the nobles of the provinces, the
satraps, the governors and the king's administrators helped the Jews, because fear of Mordecai had seized them. [4]Mordecai was prominent
in the palace; his reputation spread throughout
the provinces, and he became more and more
powerful.

[5]The Jews struck down all their enemies
with the sword, killing and destroying them,
and they did what they pleased to those who
hated them. [6]In the citadel of Susa, the Jews
killed and destroyed five hundred men. [7]They
also killed Parshandatha, Dalphon, Aspatha,
[8]Poratha, Adalia, Aridatha, [9]Parmashta, Arisai,
Aridai and Vaizatha, [10]the ten sons of Haman
son of Hammedatha, the enemy of the Jews.
But they did not lay their hands on the plunder.

[11]The number of those slain in the citadel of
Susa was reported to the king that same day.
[12]The king said to Queen Esther, "The Jews
have killed and destroyed five hundred men
and the ten sons of Haman in the citadel of
Susa. What have they done in the rest of the
king's provinces? Now what is your petition?

[a]9 Hebrew *fifty cubits* (about 23 meters)   [b]9 That is, the upper Nile region

It will be given you. What is your request? It
will also be granted."
13"If it pleases the king," Esther answered,
"give the Jews in Susa permission to carry out
this day's edict tomorrow also, and let Haman's ten sons be hanged on gallows."
14So the king commanded that this be done.
An edict was issued in Susa, and they hanged
the ten sons of Haman. 15The Jews in Susa
came together on the fourteenth day of the
month of Adar, and they put to death in Susa
three hundred men, but they did not lay their
hands on the plunder.
16Meanwhile, the remainder of the Jews
who were in the king's provinces also assembled to protect themselves and get relief from
their enemies. They killed seventy-five thousand of them but did not lay their hands on the
plunder. 17This happened on the thirteenth day
of the month of Adar, and on the fourteenth
they rested and made it a day of feasting and
joy.

Purim Celebrated

18The Jews in Susa, however, had assembled on the thirteenth and fourteenth, and then
on the fifteenth they rested and made it a day
of feasting and joy.
19That is why rural Jews—those living in
villages—observe the fourteenth of the month
of Adar as a day of joy and feasting, a day for
giving presents to each other.
20Mordecai recorded these events, and he
sent letters to all the Jews throughout the provinces of King Xerxes, near and far, 21to have
them celebrate annually the fourteenth and fifteenth days of the month of Adar 22as the time
when the Jews got relief from their enemies,
and as the month when their sorrow was turned
into joy and their mourning into a day of celebration. He wrote them to observe the days as
days of feasting and joy and giving presents of
food to one another and gifts to the poor.
23So the Jews agreed to continue the celebration they had begun, doing what Mordecai
had written to them. 24For Haman son of Hammedatha, the Agagite, the enemy of all the
Jews, had plotted against the Jews to destroy
them and had cast the *pur* (that is, the lot) for
their ruin and destruction. 25But when the plot
came to the king's attention,[a] he issued written
orders that the evil scheme Haman had devised
against the Jews should come back onto his
own head, and that he and his sons should be
hanged on the gallows. 26(Therefore these days
were called Purim, from the word *pur*.) Because of everything written in this letter and
because of what they had seen and what had
happened to them, 27the Jews took it upon
themselves to establish the custom that they
and their descendants and all who join them
should without fail observe these two days every year, in the way prescribed and at the time
appointed. 28These days should be remembered and observed in every generation by every family, and in every province and in every
city. And these days of Purim should never
cease to be celebrated by the Jews, nor should
the memory of them die out among their
descendants.
29So Queen Esther, daughter of Abihail,
along with Mordecai the Jew, wrote with full
authority to confirm this second letter concerning Purim. 30And Mordecai sent letters to all
the Jews in the 127 provinces of the kingdom
of Xerxes—words of goodwill and assurance— 31to establish these days of Purim at
their designated times, as Mordecai the Jew
and Queen Esther had decreed for them, and as
they had established for themselves and their
descendants in regard to their times of fasting
and lamentation. 32Esther's decree confirmed
these regulations about Purim, and it was written down in the records.

The Greatness of Mordecai

10 King Xerxes imposed tribute throughout the empire, to its distant shores.
2And all his acts of power and might, together
with a full account of the greatness of Mordecai to which the king had raised him, are they
not written in the book of the annals of the
kings of Media and Persia? 3Mordecai the Jew
was second in rank to King Xerxes, preemi-
nent among the Jews, and held in high esteem
by his many fellow Jews, because he worked
for the good of his people and spoke up for the
welfare of all the Jews.

Job

Prologue

1 In the land of Uz there lived a man whose
name was Job. This man was blameless
and upright; he feared God and shunned evil.
2He had seven sons and three daughters, 3and
he owned seven thousand sheep, three thousand camels, five hundred yoke of oxen and
five hundred donkeys, and had a large number
of servants. He was the greatest man among all
the people of the East.
4His sons used to take turns holding feasts in
their homes, and they would invite their three
sisters to eat and drink with them. 5When a
period of feasting had run its course, Job
would send and have them purified. Early in
the morning he would sacrifice a burnt offer-

[a]25 Or *when Esther came before the king*

ing for each of them, thinking, "Perhaps my
children have sinned and cursed God in their
hearts." This was Job's regular custom.

Job's First Test

6One day the angels[a] came to present themselves before the LORD, and Satan[b] also came
with them. 7The LORD said to Satan, "Where
have you come from?"

Satan answered the LORD, "From roaming
through the earth and going back and forth
in it."

8Then the LORD said to Satan, "Have you
considered my servant Job? There is no one on
earth like him; he is blameless and upright, a
man who fears God and shuns evil."

9"Does Job fear God for nothing?" Satan
replied. 10"Have you not put a hedge around
him and his household and everything he has?
You have blessed the work of his hands, so
that his flocks and herds are spread throughout
the land. 11But stretch out your hand and strike
everything he has, and he will surely curse you
to your face."

12The LORD said to Satan, "Very well, then,
everything he has is in your hands, but on the
man himself do not lay a finger."

Then Satan went out from the presence of
the LORD.

13One day when Job's sons and daughters
were feasting and drinking wine at the oldest
brother's house, 14a messenger came to Job
and said, "The oxen were plowing and the donkeys were grazing nearby, 15and the Sabeans
attacked and carried them off. They put the
servants to the sword, and I am the only one
who has escaped to tell you!"

16While he was still speaking, another messenger came and said, "The fire of God fell
from the sky and burned up the sheep and the
servants, and I am the only one who has escaped to tell you!"

17While he was still speaking, another messenger came and said, "The Chaldeans formed
three raiding parties and swept down on your
camels and carried them off. They put the servants to the sword, and I am the only one who
has escaped to tell you!"

18While he was still speaking, yet another
messenger came and said, "Your sons and
daughters were feasting and drinking wine at
the oldest brother's house, 19when suddenly a
mighty wind swept in from the desert and
struck the four corners of the house. It collapsed on them and they are dead, and I am the
only one who has escaped to tell you!"

20At this, Job got up and tore his robe and
shaved his head. Then he fell to the ground in
worship 21and said:

"Naked I came from my mother's womb,
and naked I will depart.[c]
The LORD gave and the LORD has taken
away;
may the name of the LORD be praised."

22In all this, Job did not sin by charging God
with wrongdoing.

Job's Second Test

2 On another day the angels[a] came to
present themselves before the LORD, and
Satan also came with them to present himself
before him. 2And the LORD said to Satan,
"Where have you come from?"

Satan answered the LORD, "From roaming
through the earth and going back and forth
in it."

3Then the LORD said to Satan, "Have you
considered my servant Job? There is no one on
earth like him; he is blameless and upright, a
man who fears God and shuns evil. And he still
maintains his integrity, though you incited me
against him to ruin him without any reason."

4"Skin for skin!" Satan replied. "A man will
give all he has for his own life. 5But stretch out
your hand and strike his flesh and bones, and
he will surely curse you to your face."

6The LORD said to Satan, "Very well, then,
he is in your hands; but you must spare his
life."

7So Satan went out from the presence of the
LORD and afflicted Job with painful sores from
the soles of his feet to the top of his head.
8Then Job took a piece of broken pottery and
scraped himself with it as he sat among the
ashes.

9His wife said to him, "Are you still holding
on to your integrity? Curse God and die!"

10He replied, "You are talking like a foolish[d] woman. Shall we accept good from God,
and not trouble?"

In all this, Job did not sin in what he said.

Job's Three Friends

11When Job's three friends, Eliphaz the Temanite, Bildad the Shuhite and Zophar the Naamathite, heard about all the troubles that had
come upon him, they set out from their homes
and met together by agreement to go and sympathize with him and comfort him. 12When
they saw him from a distance, they could hardly recognize him; they began to weep aloud,
and they tore their robes and sprinkled dust on
their heads. 13Then they sat on the ground with
him for seven days and seven nights. No one
said a word to him, because they saw how
great his suffering was.

Job Speaks

3 After this, Job opened his mouth and
cursed the day of his birth. 2He said:

3"May the day of my birth perish,
and the night it was said, 'A boy is
born!'
4That day—may it turn to darkness;
may God above not care about it;
may no light shine upon it.
5May darkness and deep shadow[e] claim it
once more;

[a]6,1 Hebrew *the sons of God* [b]6 *Satan* means *accuser.* [c]21 Or *will return there* [d]10 The Hebrew
word rendered *foolish* denotes moral deficiency. [e]5 Or *and the shadow of death*

may a cloud settle over it;
may blackness overwhelm its light.
6That night—may thick darkness seize it;
may it not be included among the days of the year
nor be entered in any of the months.
7May that night be barren;
may no shout of joy be heard in it.
8May those who curse days[a] curse that day,
those who are ready to rouse Leviathan.
9May its morning stars become dark;
may it wait for daylight in vain
and not see the first rays of dawn,
10for it did not shut the doors of the womb on me
to hide trouble from my eyes.

11"Why did I not perish at birth,
and die as I came from the womb?
12Why were there knees to receive me
and breasts that I might be nursed?
13For now I would be lying down in peace;
I would be asleep and at rest
14with kings and counselors of the earth,
who built for themselves places now lying in ruins,
15with rulers who had gold,
who filled their houses with silver.
16Or why was I not hidden in the ground like a stillborn child,
like an infant who never saw the light of day?
17There the wicked cease from turmoil,
and there the weary are at rest.
18Captives also enjoy their ease;
they no longer hear the slave driver's shout.
19The small and the great are there,
and the slave is freed from his master.

20"Why is light given to those in misery,
and life to the bitter of soul,
21to those who long for death that does not come,
who search for it more than for hidden treasure,
22who are filled with gladness
and rejoice when they reach the grave?
23Why is life given to a man
whose way is hidden,
whom God has hedged in?
24For sighing comes to me instead of food;
my groans pour out like water.
25What I feared has come upon me;
what I dreaded has happened to me.
26I have no peace, no quietness;
I have no rest, but only turmoil."

Eliphaz

4 Then Eliphaz the Temanite replied:

2"If someone ventures a word with you,
will you be impatient?
But who can keep from speaking?
3Think how you have instructed many,
how you have strengthened feeble hands.
4Your words have supported those who stumbled;
you have strengthened faltering knees.
5But now trouble comes to you, and you are discouraged;
it strikes you, and you are dismayed.
6Should not your piety be your confidence
and your blameless ways your hope?

7"Consider now: Who, being innocent, has ever perished?
Where were the upright ever destroyed?
8As I have observed, those who plow evil
and those who sow trouble reap it.
9At the breath of God they are destroyed;
at the blast of his anger they perish.
10The lions may roar and growl,
yet the teeth of the great lions are broken.
11The lion perishes for lack of prey,
and the cubs of the lioness are scattered.

12"A word was secretly brought to me,
my ears caught a whisper of it.
13Amid disquieting dreams in the night,
when deep sleep falls on men,
14fear and trembling seized me
and made all my bones shake.
15A spirit glided past my face,
and the hair on my body stood on end.
16It stopped,
but I could not tell what it was.
A form stood before my eyes,
and I heard a hushed voice:
17'Can a mortal be more righteous than God?
Can a man be more pure than his Maker?
18If God places no trust in his servants,
if he charges his angels with error,
19how much more those who live in houses of clay,
whose foundations are in the dust,
who are crushed more readily than a moth!
20Between dawn and dusk they are broken to pieces;
unnoticed, they perish forever.
21Are not the cords of their tent pulled up,
so that they die without wisdom?'[b]

5 "Call if you will, but who will answer you?
To which of the holy ones will you turn?
2Resentment kills a fool,
and envy slays the simple.
3I myself have seen a fool taking root,
but suddenly his house was cursed.
4His children are far from safety,
crushed in court without a defender.
5The hungry consume his harvest,
taking it even from among thorns,
and the thirsty pant after his wealth.

[a] *8* Or *the sea* [b] *21* Some interpreters end the quotation after verse 17.

6For hardship does not spring from the soil,
nor does trouble sprout from the ground.
7Yet man is born to trouble
as surely as sparks fly upward.

8"But if it were I, I would appeal to God;
I would lay my cause before him.
9He performs wonders that cannot be fathomed,
miracles that cannot be counted.
10He bestows rain on the earth;
he sends water upon the countryside.
11The lowly he sets on high,
and those who mourn are lifted to safety.
12He thwarts the plans of the crafty,
so that their hands achieve no success.
13He catches the wise in their craftiness,
and the schemes of the wily are swept away.
14Darkness comes upon them in the daytime;
at noon they grope as in the night.
15He saves the needy from the sword in their mouth;
he saves them from the clutches of the powerful.
16So the poor have hope,
and injustice shuts its mouth.

17"Blessed is the man whom God corrects;
so do not despise the discipline of the Almighty.[a]
18For he wounds, but he also binds up;
he injures, but his hands also heal.
19From six calamities he will rescue you;
in seven no harm will befall you.
20In famine he will ransom you from death,
and in battle from the stroke of the sword.
21You will be protected from the lash of the tongue,
and need not fear when destruction comes.
22You will laugh at destruction and famine,
and need not fear the beasts of the earth.
23For you will have a covenant with the stones of the field,
and the wild animals will be at peace with you.
24You will know that your tent is secure;
you will take stock of your property and find nothing missing.
25You will know that your children will be many,
and your descendants like the grass of the earth.
26You will come to the grave in full vigor,
like sheaves gathered in season.

27"We have examined this, and it is true.
So hear it and apply it to yourself."

Job

6 Then Job replied:

2"If only my anguish could be weighed
and all my misery be placed on the scales!
3It would surely outweigh the sand of the seas—
no wonder my words have been impetuous.
4The arrows of the Almighty are in me,
my spirit drinks in their poison;
God's terrors are marshaled against me.
5Does a wild donkey bray when it has grass,
or an ox bellow when it has fodder?
6Is tasteless food eaten without salt,
or is there flavor in the white of an egg[b]?
7I refuse to touch it;
such food makes me ill.

8"Oh, that I might have my request,
that God would grant what I hope for,
9that God would be willing to crush me,
to let loose his hand and cut me off!
10Then I would still have this consolation—
my joy in unrelenting pain—
that I had not denied the words of the Holy One.

11"What strength do I have, that I should still hope?
What prospects, that I should be patient?
12Do I have the strength of stone?
Is my flesh bronze?
13Do I have any power to help myself,
now that success has been driven from me?

14"A despairing man should have the devotion of his friends,
even though he forsakes the fear of the Almighty.
15But my brothers are as undependable as intermittent streams,
as the streams that overflow
16when darkened by thawing ice
and swollen with melting snow,
17but that cease to flow in the dry season,
and in the heat vanish from their channels.
18Caravans turn aside from their routes;
they go up into the wasteland and perish.
19The caravans of Tema look for water,
the traveling merchants of Sheba look in hope.
20They are distressed, because they had been confident;
they arrive there, only to be disappointed.
21Now you too have proved to be of no help;

[a]17 Hebrew *Shaddai*; here and throughout Job [b]6 The meaning of the Hebrew for this phrase is uncertain.

you see something dreadful and are afraid.
22Have I ever said, 'Give something on my behalf,
pay a ransom for me from your wealth,
23deliver me from the hand of the enemy,
ransom me from the clutches of the ruthless'?

24"Teach me, and I will be quiet;
show me where I have been wrong.
25How painful are honest words!
But what do your arguments prove?
26Do you mean to correct what I say,
and treat the words of a despairing man as wind?
27You would even cast lots for the fatherless
and barter away your friend.

28"But now be so kind as to look at me.
Would I lie to your face?
29Relent, do not be unjust;
reconsider, for my integrity is at stake.[a]
30Is there any wickedness on my lips?
Can my mouth not discern malice?

7 "Does not man have hard service on earth?
Are not his days like those of a hired man?
2Like a slave longing for the evening shadows,
or a hired man waiting eagerly for his wages,
3so I have been allotted months of futility,
and nights of misery have been assigned to me.
4When I lie down I think, 'How long before I get up?'
The night drags on, and I toss till dawn.
5My body is clothed with worms and scabs,
my skin is broken and festering.

6"My days are swifter than a weaver's shuttle,
and they come to an end without hope.
7Remember, O God, that my life is but a breath;
my eyes will never see happiness again.
8The eye that now sees me will see me no longer;
you will look for me, but I will be no more.
9As a cloud vanishes and is gone,
so he who goes down to the grave[b]
does not return.
10He will never come to his house again;
his place will know him no more.

11"Therefore I will not keep silent;
I will speak out in the anguish of my spirit,
I will complain in the bitterness of my soul.
12Am I the sea, or the monster of the deep,
that you put me under guard?
13When I think my bed will comfort me
and my couch will ease my complaint,
14even then you frighten me with dreams
and terrify me with visions,
15so that I prefer strangling and death,
rather than this body of mine.
16I despise my life; I would not live forever.
Let me alone; my days have no meaning.

17"What is man that you make so much of him,
that you give him so much attention,
18that you examine him every morning
and test him every moment?
19Will you never look away from me,
or let me alone even for an instant?
20If I have sinned, what have I done to you,
O watcher of men?
Why have you made me your target?
Have I become a burden to you?[c]
21Why do you not pardon my offenses
and forgive my sins?
For I will soon lie down in the dust;
you will search for me, but I will be no more."

Bildad

8 Then Bildad the Shuhite replied:

2"How long will you say such things?
Your words are a blustering wind.
3Does God pervert justice?
Does the Almighty pervert what is right?
4When your children sinned against him,
he gave them over to the penalty of their sin.
5But if you will look to God
and plead with the Almighty,
6if you are pure and upright,
even now he will rouse himself on your behalf
and restore you to your rightful place.
7Your beginnings will seem humble,
so prosperous will your future be.

8"Ask the former generations
and find out what their fathers learned,
9for we were born only yesterday and know nothing,
and our days on earth are but a shadow.
10Will they not instruct you and tell you?
Will they not bring forth words from their understanding?
11Can papyrus grow tall where there is no marsh?
Can reeds thrive without water?
12While still growing and uncut,
they wither more quickly than grass.
13Such is the destiny of all who forget God;
so perishes the hope of the godless.
14What he trusts in is fragile[d];

[a]29 Or *my righteousness still stands* [b]9 Hebrew *Sheol* [c]20 A few manuscripts of the Masoretic Text, an ancient Hebrew scribal tradition and Septuagint; most manuscripts of the Masoretic Text *I have become a burden to myself.* [d]14 The meaning of the Hebrew for this word is uncertain.

what he relies on is a spider's web.
15He leans on his web, but it gives way,
he clings to it, but it does not hold.
16He is like a well-watered plant in the sunshine,
spreading its shoots over the garden;
17it entwines its roots around a pile of rocks
and looks for a place among the stones.
18But when it is torn from its spot,
that place disowns it and says, 'I never saw you.'
19Surely its life withers away,
and[a] from the soil other plants grow.

20"Surely God does not reject a blameless man
or strengthen the hands of evildoers.
21He will yet fill your mouth with laughter
and your lips with shouts of joy.
22Your enemies will be clothed in shame,
and the tents of the wicked will be no more."

Job

9 Then Job replied:

2"Indeed, I know that this is true.
But how can a mortal be righteous before God?
3Though one wished to dispute with him,
he could not answer him one time out of a thousand.
4His wisdom is profound, his power is vast.
Who has resisted him and come out unscathed?
5He moves mountains without their knowing it
and overturns them in his anger.
6He shakes the earth from its place
and makes its pillars tremble.
7He speaks to the sun and it does not shine;
he seals off the light of the stars.
8He alone stretches out the heavens
and treads on the waves of the sea.
9He is the Maker of the Bear and Orion,
the Pleiades and the constellations of the south.
10He performs wonders that cannot be fathomed,
miracles that cannot be counted.
11When he passes me, I cannot see him;
when he goes by, I cannot perceive him.
12If he snatches away, who can stop him?
Who can say to him, 'What are you doing?'
13God does not restrain his anger;
even the cohorts of Rahab cowered at his feet.

14"How then can I dispute with him?
How can I find words to argue with him?
15Though I were innocent, I could not answer him;
I could only plead with my Judge for mercy.
16Even if I summoned him and he responded,
I do not believe he would give me a hearing.
17He would crush me with a storm
and multiply my wounds for no reason.
18He would not let me regain my breath
but would overwhelm me with misery.
19If it is a matter of strength, he is mighty!
And if it is a matter of justice, who will summon him[b]?
20Even if I were innocent, my mouth would condemn me;
if I were blameless, it would pronounce me guilty.

21"Although I am blameless,
I have no concern for myself;
I despise my own life.
22It is all the same; that is why I say,
'He destroys both the blameless and the wicked.'
23When a scourge brings sudden death,
he mocks the despair of the innocent.
24When a land falls into the hands of the wicked,
he blindfolds its judges.
If it is not he, then who is it?

25"My days are swifter than a runner;
they fly away without a glimpse of joy.
26They skim past like boats of papyrus,
like eagles swooping down on their prey.
27If I say, 'I will forget my complaint,
I will change my expression, and smile,'
28I still dread all my sufferings,
for I know you will not hold me innocent.
29Since I am already found guilty,
why should I struggle in vain?
30Even if I washed myself with soap[c]
and my hands with washing soda,
31you would plunge me into a slime pit
so that even my clothes would detest me.

32"He is not a man like me that I might answer him,
that we might confront each other in court.
33If only there were someone to arbitrate between us,
to lay his hand upon us both,
34someone to remove God's rod from me,
so that his terror would frighten me no more.
35Then I would speak up without fear of him,
but as it now stands with me, I cannot.

10 "I loathe my very life;
therefore I will give free rein to my complaint

[a] 19 Or *Surely all the joy it has / is that* [b] 19 See Septuagint; Hebrew *me.* [c] 30 Or *snow*

and speak out in the bitterness of my
soul.
2I will say to God: Do not condemn me,
but tell me what charges you have
against me.
3Does it please you to oppress me,
to spurn the work of your hands,
while you smile on the schemes of the
wicked?
4Do you have eyes of flesh?
Do you see as a mortal sees?
5Are your days like those of a mortal
or your years like those of a man,
6that you must search out my faults
and probe after my sin—
7though you know that I am not guilty
and that no one can rescue me from
your hand?

8"Your hands shaped me and made me.
Will you now turn and destroy me?
9Remember that you molded me like clay.
Will you now turn me to dust again?
10Did you not pour me out like milk
and curdle me like cheese,
11clothe me with skin and flesh
and knit me together with bones and
sinews?
12You gave me life and showed me
kindness,
and in your providence watched over
my spirit.

13"But this is what you concealed in your
heart,
and I know that this was in your mind:
14If I sinned, you would be watching me
and would not let my offense go
unpunished.
15If I am guilty—woe to me!
Even if I am innocent, I cannot lift my
head,
for I am full of shame
and drowned in[a] my affliction.
16If I hold my head high, you stalk me like
a lion
and again display your awesome power
against me.
17You bring new witnesses against me
and increase your anger toward me;
your forces come against me wave upon
wave.

18"Why then did you bring me out of the
womb?
I wish I had died before any eye saw
me.
19If only I had never come into being,
or had been carried straight from the
womb to the grave!
20Are not my few days almost over?
Turn away from me so I can have a
moment's joy
21before I go to the place of no return,
to the land of gloom and deep shadow,[b]
22to the land of deepest night,
of deep shadow and disorder,
where even the light is like darkness."

Zophar

11 Then Zophar the Naamathite replied:

2"Are all these words to go unanswered?
Is this talker to be vindicated?
3Will your idle talk reduce men to silence?
Will no one rebuke you when you
mock?
4You say to God, 'My beliefs are flawless
and I am pure in your sight.'
5Oh, how I wish that God would speak,
that he would open his lips against you
6and disclose to you the secrets of wisdom,
for true wisdom has two sides.
Know this: God has even forgotten
some of your sin.

7"Can you fathom the mysteries of God?
Can you probe the limits of the
Almighty?
8They are higher than the heavens—what
can you do?
They are deeper than the depths of the
grave[c]—what can you know?
9Their measure is longer than the earth
and wider than the sea.

10"If he comes along and confines you in
prison
and convenes a court, who can oppose
him?
11Surely he recognizes deceitful men;
and when he sees evil, does he not take
note?
12But a witless man can no more become
wise
than a wild donkey's colt can be born a
man.[d]

13"Yet if you devote your heart to him
and stretch out your hands to him,
14if you put away the sin that is in your
hand
and allow no evil to dwell in your tent,
15then you will lift up your face without
shame;
you will stand firm and without fear.
16You will surely forget your trouble,
recalling it only as waters gone by.
17Life will be brighter than noonday,
and darkness will become like morning.
18You will be secure, because there is hope;
you will look about you and take your
rest in safety.
19You will lie down, with no one to make
you afraid,
and many will court your favor.
20But the eyes of the wicked will fail,
and escape will elude them;
their hope will become a dying gasp."

[a] *15* Or *and aware of* [b] *21* Or *and the shadow of death*; also in verse 22 [c] *8* Hebrew *than Sheol*
[d] *12* Or *wild donkey can be born tame*

Job

12 Then Job replied:

2"Doubtless you are the people,
and wisdom will die with you!
3But I have a mind as well as you;
I am not inferior to you.
Who does not know all these things?

4"I have become a laughingstock to my friends,
though I called upon God and he answered—
a mere laughingstock, though righteous and blameless!
5Men at ease have contempt for misfortune
as the fate of those whose feet are slipping.
6The tents of marauders are undisturbed,
and those who provoke God are secure—
those who carry their god in their hands.[a]

7"But ask the animals, and they will teach you,
or the birds of the air, and they will tell you;
8or speak to the earth, and it will teach you,
or let the fish of the sea inform you.
9Which of all these does not know
that the hand of the LORD has done this?
10In his hand is the life of every creature
and the breath of all mankind.
11Does not the ear test words
as the tongue tastes food?
12Is not wisdom found among the aged?
Does not long life bring understanding?

13"To God belong wisdom and power;
counsel and understanding are his.
14What he tears down cannot be rebuilt;
the man he imprisons cannot be released.
15If he holds back the waters, there is drought;
if he lets them loose, they devastate the land.
16To him belong strength and victory;
both deceived and deceiver are his.
17He leads counselors away stripped
and makes fools of judges.
18He takes off the shackles put on by kings
and ties a loincloth[b] around their waist.
19He leads priests away stripped
and overthrows men long established.
20He silences the lips of trusted advisers
and takes away the discernment of elders.
21He pours contempt on nobles
and disarms the mighty.
22He reveals the deep things of darkness
and brings deep shadows into the light.
23He makes nations great, and destroys them;
he enlarges nations, and disperses them.
24He deprives the leaders of the earth of their reason;
he sends them wandering through a trackless waste.
25They grope in darkness with no light;
he makes them stagger like drunkards.

13 "My eyes have seen all this,
my ears have heard and understood it.
2What you know, I also know;
I am not inferior to you.
3But I desire to speak to the Almighty
and to argue my case with God.
4You, however, smear me with lies;
you are worthless physicians, all of you!
5If only you would be altogether silent!
For you, that would be wisdom.
6Hear now my argument;
listen to the plea of my lips.
7Will you speak wickedly on God's behalf?
Will you speak deceitfully for him?
8Will you show him partiality?
Will you argue the case for God?
9Would it turn out well if he examined you?
Could you deceive him as you might deceive men?
10He would surely rebuke you
if you secretly showed partiality.
11Would not his splendor terrify you?
Would not the dread of him fall on you?
12Your maxims are proverbs of ashes;
your defenses are defenses of clay.

13"Keep silent and let me speak;
then let come to me what may.
14Why do I put myself in jeopardy
and take my life in my hands?
15Though he slay me, yet will I hope in him;
I will surely[c] defend my ways to his face.
16Indeed, this will turn out for my deliverance,
for no godless man would dare come before him!
17Listen carefully to my words;
let your ears take in what I say.
18Now that I have prepared my case,
I know I will be vindicated.
19Can anyone bring charges against me?
If so, I will be silent and die.

20"Only grant me these two things, O God,
and then I will not hide from you:
21Withdraw your hand far from me,
and stop frightening me with your terrors.
22Then summon me and I will answer,
or let me speak, and you reply.

[a]6 Or *secure / in what God's hand brings them* [b]18 Or *shackles of kings / and ties a belt* [c]15 Or *He will surely slay me; I have no hope — / yet I will*

23How many wrongs and sins have I
committed?
Show me my offense and my sin.
24Why do you hide your face
and consider me your enemy?
25Will you torment a windblown leaf?
Will you chase after dry chaff?
26For you write down bitter things against
me
and make me inherit the sins of my
youth.
27You fasten my feet in shackles;
you keep close watch on all my paths
by putting marks on the soles of my
feet.

28"So man wastes away like something
rotten,
like a garment eaten by moths.

14 "Man born of woman
is of few days and full of trouble.
2He springs up like a flower and withers
away;
like a fleeting shadow, he does not
endure.
3Do you fix your eye on such a one?
Will you bring him[a] before you for
judgment?
4Who can bring what is pure from the
impure?
No one!
5Man's days are determined;
you have decreed the number of his
months
and have set limits he cannot exceed.
6So look away from him and let him alone,
till he has put in his time like a hired
man.

7"At least there is hope for a tree:
If it is cut down, it will sprout again,
and its new shoots will not fail.
8Its roots may grow old in the ground
and its stump die in the soil,
9yet at the scent of water it will bud
and put forth shoots like a plant.
10But man dies and is laid low;
he breathes his last and is no more.
11As water disappears from the sea
or a riverbed becomes parched and dry,
12so man lies down and does not rise;
till the heavens are no more, men will
not awake
or be roused from their sleep.

13"If only you would hide me in the grave[b]
and conceal me till your anger has
passed!
If only you would set me a time
and then remember me!
14If a man dies, will he live again?
All the days of my hard service
I will wait for my renewal[c] to come.
15You will call and I will answer you;
you will long for the creature your
hands have made.
16Surely then you will count my steps
but not keep track of my sin.
17My offenses will be sealed up in a bag;
you will cover over my sin.

18"But as a mountain erodes and crumbles
and as a rock is moved from its place,
19as water wears away stones
and torrents wash away the soil,
so you destroy man's hope.
20You overpower him once for all, and he is
gone;
you change his countenance and send
him away.
21If his sons are honored, he does not know
it;
if they are brought low, he does not see
it.
22He feels but the pain of his own body
and mourns only for himself."

Eliphaz

15 Then Eliphaz the Temanite replied:

2"Would a wise man answer with empty
notions
or fill his belly with the hot east wind?
3Would he argue with useless words,
with speeches that have no value?
4But you even undermine piety
and hinder devotion to God.
5Your sin prompts your mouth;
you adopt the tongue of the crafty.
6Your own mouth condemns you, not mine;
your own lips testify against you.

7"Are you the first man ever born?
Were you brought forth before the hills?
8Do you listen in on God's council?
Do you limit wisdom to yourself?
9What do you know that we do not know?
What insights do you have that we do
not have?
10The gray-haired and the aged are on our
side,
men even older than your father.
11Are God's consolations not enough for
you,
words spoken gently to you?
12Why has your heart carried you away,
and why do your eyes flash,
13so that you vent your rage against God
and pour out such words from your
mouth?

14"What is man, that he could be pure,
or one born of woman, that he could be
righteous?
15If God places no trust in his holy ones,
if even the heavens are not pure in his
eyes,
16how much less man, who is vile and
corrupt,
who drinks up evil like water!

17"Listen to me and I will explain to you;
let me tell you what I have seen,

[a] 3 Septuagint, Vulgate and Syriac; Hebrew *me* [b] 13 Hebrew *Sheol* [c] 14 Or *release*

18what wise men have declared,
hiding nothing received from their fathers
19(to whom alone the land was given
when no alien passed among them):
20All his days the wicked man suffers torment,
the ruthless through all the years stored up for him.
21Terrifying sounds fill his ears;
when all seems well, marauders attack him.
22He despairs of escaping the darkness;
he is marked for the sword.
23He wanders about—food for vultures[a];
he knows the day of darkness is at hand.
24Distress and anguish fill him with terror;
they overwhelm him, like a king poised to attack,
25because he shakes his fist at God
and vaunts himself against the Almighty,
26defiantly charging against him
with a thick, strong shield.

27"Though his face is covered with fat
and his waist bulges with flesh,
28he will inhabit ruined towns
and houses where no one lives,
houses crumbling to rubble.
29He will no longer be rich and his wealth will not endure,
nor will his possessions spread over the land.
30He will not escape the darkness;
a flame will wither his shoots,
and the breath of God's mouth will carry him away.
31Let him not deceive himself by trusting what is worthless,
for he will get nothing in return.
32Before his time he will be paid in full,
and his branches will not flourish.
33He will be like a vine stripped of its unripe grapes,
like an olive tree shedding its blossoms.
34For the company of the godless will be barren,
and fire will consume the tents of those who love bribes.
35They conceive trouble and give birth to evil;
their womb fashions deceit."

Job

16 Then Job replied:

2"I have heard many things like these;
miserable comforters are you all!
3Will your long-winded speeches never end?
What ails you that you keep on arguing?
4I also could speak like you,
if you were in my place;
I could make fine speeches against you
and shake my head at you.
5But my mouth would encourage you;
comfort from my lips would bring you relief.

6"Yet if I speak, my pain is not relieved;
and if I refrain, it does not go away.
7Surely, O God, you have worn me out;
you have devastated my entire household.
8You have bound me—and it has become a witness;
my gauntness rises up and testifies against me.
9God assails me and tears me in his anger
and gnashes his teeth at me;
my opponent fastens on me his piercing eyes.
10Men open their mouths to jeer at me;
they strike my cheek in scorn
and unite together against me.
11God has turned me over to evil men
and thrown me into the clutches of the wicked.
12All was well with me, but he shattered me;
he seized me by the neck and crushed me.
He has made me his target;
13 his archers surround me.
Without pity, he pierces my kidneys
and spills my gall on the ground.
14Again and again he bursts upon me;
he rushes at me like a warrior.

15"I have sewed sackcloth over my skin
and buried my brow in the dust.
16My face is red with weeping,
deep shadows ring my eyes;
17yet my hands have been free of violence
and my prayer is pure.

18"O earth, do not cover my blood;
may my cry never be laid to rest!
19Even now my witness is in heaven;
my advocate is on high.
20My intercessor is my friend[b]
as my eyes pour out tears to God;
21on behalf of a man he pleads with God
as a man pleads for his friend.

22"Only a few years will pass
before I go on the journey of no return.

17 1My spirit is broken,
my days are cut short,
the grave awaits me.
2Surely mockers surround me;
my eyes must dwell on their hostility.

3"Give me, O God, the pledge you demand.
Who else will put up security for me?
4You have closed their minds to understanding;
therefore you will not let them triumph.

[a]23 Or *about, looking for food* [b]20 Or *My friends treat me with scorn*

5If a man denounces his friends for reward,
the eyes of his children will fail.

6"God has made me a byword to everyone,
a man in whose face people spit.
7My eyes have grown dim with grief;
my whole frame is but a shadow.
8Upright men are appalled at this;
the innocent are aroused against the ungodly.
9Nevertheless, the righteous will hold to their ways,
and those with clean hands will grow stronger.

10"But come on, all of you, try again!
I will not find a wise man among you.
11My days have passed, my plans are shattered,
and so are the desires of my heart.
12These men turn night into day;
in the face of darkness they say, 'Light is near.'
13If the only home I hope for is the grave,[a]
if I spread out my bed in darkness,
14if I say to corruption, 'You are my father,'
and to the worm, 'My mother' or 'My sister,'
15where then is my hope?
Who can see any hope for me?
16Will it go down to the gates of death[a]?
Will we descend together into the dust?"

Bildad

18 Then Bildad the Shuhite replied:

2"When will you end these speeches?
Be sensible, and then we can talk.
3Why are we regarded as cattle
and considered stupid in your sight?
4You who tear yourself to pieces in your anger,
is the earth to be abandoned for your sake?
Or must the rocks be moved from their place?

5"The lamp of the wicked is snuffed out;
the flame of his fire stops burning.
6The light in his tent becomes dark;
the lamp beside him goes out.
7The vigor of his step is weakened;
his own schemes throw him down.
8His feet thrust him into a net
and he wanders into its mesh.
9A trap seizes him by the heel;
a snare holds him fast.
10A noose is hidden for him on the ground;
a trap lies in his path.
11Terrors startle him on every side
and dog his every step.
12Calamity is hungry for him;
disaster is ready for him when he falls.
13It eats away parts of his skin;
death's firstborn devours his limbs.
14He is torn from the security of his tent
and marched off to the king of terrors.
15Fire resides[b] in his tent;
burning sulfur is scattered over his dwelling.
16His roots dry up below
and his branches wither above.
17The memory of him perishes from the earth;
he has no name in the land.
18He is driven from light into darkness
and is banished from the world.
19He has no offspring or descendants among his people,
no survivor where once he lived.
20Men of the west are appalled at his fate;
men of the east are seized with horror.
21Surely such is the dwelling of an evil man;
such is the place of one who knows not God."

Job

19 Then Job replied:

2"How long will you torment me
and crush me with words?
3Ten times now you have reproached me;
shamelessly you attack me.
4If it is true that I have gone astray,
my error remains my concern alone.
5If indeed you would exalt yourselves above me
and use my humiliation against me,
6then know that God has wronged me
and drawn his net around me.

7"Though I cry, 'I've been wronged!' I get no response;
though I call for help, there is no justice.
8He has blocked my way so I cannot pass;
he has shrouded my paths in darkness.
9He has stripped me of my honor
and removed the crown from my head.
10He tears me down on every side till I am gone;
he uproots my hope like a tree.
11His anger burns against me;
he counts me among his enemies.
12His troops advance in force;
they build a siege ramp against me
and encamp around my tent.

13"He has alienated my brothers from me;
my acquaintances are completely estranged from me.
14My kinsmen have gone away;
my friends have forgotten me.
15My guests and my maidservants count me a stranger;
they look upon me as an alien.
16I summon my servant, but he does not answer,
though I beg him with my own mouth.
17My breath is offensive to my wife;
I am loathsome to my own brothers.

[a] *13,16* Hebrew *Sheol* [b] *15* Or *Nothing he had remains*

18Even the little boys scorn me;
when I appear, they ridicule me.
19All my intimate friends detest me;
those I love have turned against me.
20I am nothing but skin and bones;
I have escaped with only the skin of my teeth.[a]

21"Have pity on me, my friends, have pity,
for the hand of God has struck me.
22Why do you pursue me as God does?
Will you never get enough of my flesh?

23"Oh, that my words were recorded,
that they were written on a scroll,
24that they were inscribed with an iron tool on[b] lead,
or engraved in rock forever!
25I know that my Redeemer[c] lives,
and that in the end he will stand upon the earth.[d]
26And after my skin has been destroyed,
yet[e] in[f] my flesh I will see God;
27I myself will see him
with my own eyes—I, and not another.
How my heart yearns within me!

28"If you say, 'How we will hound him,
since the root of the trouble lies in him,[g]'
29you should fear the sword yourselves;
for wrath will bring punishment by the sword,
and then you will know that there is judgment.[h]"

Zophar

20 Then Zophar the Naamathite replied:

2"My troubled thoughts prompt me to answer
because I am greatly disturbed.
3I hear a rebuke that dishonors me,
and my understanding inspires me to reply.

4"Surely you know how it has been from of old,
ever since man[i] was placed on the earth,
5that the mirth of the wicked is brief,
the joy of the godless lasts but a moment.
6Though his pride reaches to the heavens
and his head touches the clouds,
7he will perish forever, like his own dung;
those who have seen him will say,
'Where is he?'
8Like a dream he flies away, no more to be found,
banished like a vision of the night.
9The eye that saw him will not see him again;
his place will look on him no more.
10His children must make amends to the poor;
his own hands must give back his wealth.
11The youthful vigor that fills his bones
will lie with him in the dust.

12"Though evil is sweet in his mouth
and he hides it under his tongue,
13though he cannot bear to let it go
and keeps it in his mouth,
14yet his food will turn sour in his stomach;
it will become the venom of serpents within him.
15He will spit out the riches he swallowed;
God will make his stomach vomit them up.
16He will suck the poison of serpents;
the fangs of an adder will kill him.
17He will not enjoy the streams,
the rivers flowing with honey and cream.
18What he toiled for he must give back uneaten;
he will not enjoy the profit from his trading.
19For he has oppressed the poor and left them destitute;
he has seized houses he did not build.

20"Surely he will have no respite from his craving;
he cannot save himself by his treasure.
21Nothing is left for him to devour;
his prosperity will not endure.
22In the midst of his plenty, distress will overtake him;
the full force of misery will come upon him.
23When he has filled his belly,
God will vent his burning anger against him
and rain down his blows upon him.
24Though he flees from an iron weapon,
a bronze-tipped arrow pierces him.
25He pulls it out of his back,
the gleaming point out of his liver.
Terrors will come over him;
26 total darkness lies in wait for his treasures.
A fire unfanned will consume him
and devour what is left in his tent.
27The heavens will expose his guilt;
the earth will rise up against him.
28A flood will carry off his house,
rushing waters[j] on the day of God's wrath.
29Such is the fate God allots the wicked,
the heritage appointed for them by God."

[a]20 Or *only my gums* [b]24 Or *and* [c]25 Or *defender* [d]25 Or *upon my grave* [e]26 Or *And after I awake, / though this ⌊body⌋ has been destroyed, / then* [f]26 Or */ apart from* [g]28 Many Hebrew manuscripts, Septuagint and Vulgate; most Hebrew manuscripts *me* [h]29 Or */ that you may come to know the Almighty* [i]4 Or *Adam* [j]28 Or *The possessions in his house will be carried off, / washed away*

Job

21 Then Job replied:

2"Listen carefully to my words;
let this be the consolation you give me.
3Bear with me while I speak,
and after I have spoken, mock on.

4"Is my complaint directed to man?
Why should I not be impatient?
5Look at me and be astonished;
clap your hand over your mouth.
6When I think about this, I am terrified;
trembling seizes my body.
7Why do the wicked live on,
growing old and increasing in power?
8They see their children established around them,
their offspring before their eyes.
9Their homes are safe and free from fear;
the rod of God is not upon them.
10Their bulls never fail to breed;
their cows calve and do not miscarry.
11They send forth their children as a flock;
their little ones dance about.
12They sing to the music of tambourine and harp;
they make merry to the sound of the flute.
13They spend their years in prosperity
and go down to the grave[a] in peace.[b]
14Yet they say to God, 'Leave us alone!
We have no desire to know your ways.
15Who is the Almighty, that we should serve him?
What would we gain by praying to him?'
16But their prosperity is not in their own hands,
so I stand aloof from the counsel of the wicked.

17"Yet how often is the lamp of the wicked snuffed out?
How often does calamity come upon them,
the fate God allots in his anger?
18How often are they like straw before the wind,
like chaff swept away by a gale?
19⌊It is said,⌋ 'God stores up a man's punishment for his sons.'
Let him repay the man himself, so that he will know it!
20Let his own eyes see his destruction;
let him drink of the wrath of the Almighty.[c]
21For what does he care about the family he leaves behind
when his allotted months come to an end?

22"Can anyone teach knowledge to God,
since he judges even the highest?
23One man dies in full vigor,
completely secure and at ease,
24his body[d] well nourished,
his bones rich with marrow.
25Another man dies in bitterness of soul,
never having enjoyed anything good.
26Side by side they lie in the dust,
and worms cover them both.

27"I know full well what you are thinking,
the schemes by which you would wrong me.
28You say, 'Where now is the great man's house,
the tents where wicked men lived?'
29Have you never questioned those who travel?
Have you paid no regard to their accounts—
30that the evil man is spared from the day of calamity,
that he is delivered from[e] the day of wrath?
31Who denounces his conduct to his face?
Who repays him for what he has done?
32He is carried to the grave,
and watch is kept over his tomb.
33The soil in the valley is sweet to him;
all men follow after him,
and a countless throng goes[f] before him.

34"So how can you console me with your nonsense?
Nothing is left of your answers but falsehood!"

Eliphaz

22 Then Eliphaz the Temanite replied:

2"Can a man be of benefit to God?
Can even a wise man benefit him?
3What pleasure would it give the Almighty if you were righteous?
What would he gain if your ways were blameless?

4"Is it for your piety that he rebukes you
and brings charges against you?
5Is not your wickedness great?
Are not your sins endless?
6You demanded security from your brothers for no reason;
you stripped men of their clothing, leaving them naked.
7You gave no water to the weary
and you withheld food from the hungry,
8though you were a powerful man, owning land—
an honored man, living on it.
9And you sent widows away empty-handed
and broke the strength of the fatherless.
10That is why snares are all around you,
why sudden peril terrifies you,

[a] *13* Hebrew *Sheol* [b] *13* Or *in an instant* [c] *17-20* Verses 17 and 18 may be taken as exclamations and 19 and 20 as declarations. [d] *24* The meaning of the Hebrew for this word is uncertain. [e] *30* Or *man is reserved for the day of calamity, / that he is brought forth to* [f] *33* Or */ as a countless throng went*

11why it is so dark you cannot see,
and why a flood of water covers you.

12"Is not God in the heights of heaven?
And see how lofty are the highest stars!
13Yet you say, 'What does God know?
Does he judge through such darkness?
14Thick clouds veil him, so he does not see
us
as he goes about in the vaulted
heavens.'
15Will you keep to the old path
that evil men have trod?
16They were carried off before their time,
their foundations washed away by a
flood.
17They said to God, 'Leave us alone!
What can the Almighty do to us?'
18Yet it was he who filled their houses with
good things,
so I stand aloof from the counsel of the
wicked.

19"The righteous see their ruin and rejoice;
the innocent mock them, saying,
20'Surely our foes are destroyed,
and fire devours their wealth.'

21"Submit to God and be at peace with him;
in this way prosperity will come to you.
22Accept instruction from his mouth
and lay up his words in your heart.
23If you return to the Almighty, you will be
restored:
If you remove wickedness far from your
tent
24and assign your nuggets to the dust,
your gold of Ophir to the rocks in the
ravines,
25then the Almighty will be your gold,
the choicest silver for you.
26Surely then you will find delight in the
Almighty
and will lift up your face to God.
27You will pray to him, and he will hear
you,
and you will fulfill your vows.
28What you decide on will be done,
and light will shine on your ways.
29When men are brought low and you say,
'Lift them up!'
then he will save the downcast.
30He will deliver even one who is not
innocent,
who will be delivered through the
cleanness of your hands."

Job

23 Then Job replied:

2"Even today my complaint is bitter;
his hand[a] is heavy in spite of[b] my
groaning.
3If only I knew where to find him;
if only I could go to his dwelling!
4I would state my case before him
and fill my mouth with arguments.
5I would find out what he would answer
me,
and consider what he would say.
6Would he oppose me with great power?
No, he would not press charges against
me.
7There an upright man could present his
case before him,
and I would be delivered forever from
my judge.

8"But if I go to the east, he is not there;
if I go to the west, I do not find him.
9When he is at work in the north, I do not
see him;
when he turns to the south, I catch no
glimpse of him.
10But he knows the way that I take;
when he has tested me, I will come
forth as gold.
11My feet have closely followed his steps;
I have kept to his way without turning
aside.
12I have not departed from the commands of
his lips;
I have treasured the words of his mouth
more than my daily bread.

13"But he stands alone, and who can oppose
him?
He does whatever he pleases.
14He carries out his decree against me,
and many such plans he still has in
store.
15That is why I am terrified before him;
when I think of all this, I fear him.
16God has made my heart faint;
the Almighty has terrified me.
17Yet I am not silenced by the darkness,
by the thick darkness that covers my
face.

24 "Why does the Almighty not set times
for judgment?
Why must those who know him look in
vain for such days?
2Men move boundary stones;
they pasture flocks they have stolen.
3They drive away the orphan's donkey
and take the widow's ox in pledge.
4They thrust the needy from the path
and force all the poor of the land into
hiding.
5Like wild donkeys in the desert,
the poor go about their labor of
foraging food;
the wasteland provides food for their
children.
6They gather fodder in the fields
and glean in the vineyards of the
wicked.
7Lacking clothes, they spend the night
naked;
they have nothing to cover themselves
in the cold.
8They are drenched by mountain rains

[a]2 Septuagint and Syriac; Hebrew / *the hand on me* [b]2 Or *heavy on me in*

and hug the rocks for lack of shelter.
9The fatherless child is snatched from the breast;
the infant of the poor is seized for a debt.
10Lacking clothes, they go about naked;
they carry the sheaves, but still go hungry.
11They crush olives among the terraces[a];
they tread the winepresses, yet suffer thirst.
12The groans of the dying rise from the city,
and the souls of the wounded cry out for help.
But God charges no one with wrongdoing.

13"There are those who rebel against the light,
who do not know its ways
or stay in its paths.
14When daylight is gone, the murderer rises up
and kills the poor and needy;
in the night he steals forth like a thief.
15The eye of the adulterer watches for dusk;
he thinks, 'No eye will see me,'
and he keeps his face concealed.
16In the dark, men break into houses,
but by day they shut themselves in;
they want nothing to do with the light.
17For all of them, deep darkness is their morning[b];
they make friends with the terrors of darkness.[c]

18"Yet they are foam on the surface of the water;
their portion of the land is cursed,
so that no one goes to the vineyards.
19As heat and drought snatch away the melted snow,
so the grave[d] snatches away those who have sinned.
20The womb forgets them,
the worm feasts on them;
evil men are no longer remembered
but are broken like a tree.
21They prey on the barren and childless woman,
and to the widow show no kindness.
22But God drags away the mighty by his power;
though they become established, they have no assurance of life.
23He may let them rest in a feeling of security,
but his eyes are on their ways.
24For a little while they are exalted, and then they are gone;
they are brought low and gathered up like all others;
they are cut off like heads of grain.
25"If this is not so, who can prove me false
and reduce my words to nothing?"

Bildad

25 Then Bildad the Shuhite replied:

2"Dominion and awe belong to God;
he establishes order in the heights of heaven.
3Can his forces be numbered?
Upon whom does his light not rise?
4How then can a man be righteous before God?
How can one born of woman be pure?
5If even the moon is not bright
and the stars are not pure in his eyes,
6how much less man, who is but a maggot—
a son of man, who is only a worm!"

Job

26 Then Job replied:

2"How you have helped the powerless!
How you have saved the arm that is feeble!
3What advice you have offered to one without wisdom!
And what great insight you have displayed!
4Who has helped you utter these words?
And whose spirit spoke from your mouth?

5"The dead are in deep anguish,
those beneath the waters and all that live in them.
6Death[d] is naked before God;
Destruction[e] lies uncovered.
7He spreads out the northern ⌊skies⌋ over empty space;
he suspends the earth over nothing.
8He wraps up the waters in his clouds,
yet the clouds do not burst under their weight.
9He covers the face of the full moon,
spreading his clouds over it.
10He marks out the horizon on the face of the waters
for a boundary between light and darkness.
11The pillars of the heavens quake,
aghast at his rebuke.
12By his power he churned up the sea;
by his wisdom he cut Rahab to pieces.
13By his breath the skies became fair;
his hand pierced the gliding serpent.
14And these are but the outer fringe of his works;
how faint the whisper we hear of him!
Who then can understand the thunder of his power?"

[a] *11* Or *olives between the millstones*; the meaning of the Hebrew for this word is uncertain. [b] *17* Or *them, their morning is like the shadow of death* [c] *17* Or *of the shadow of death* [d] *19,6* Hebrew *Sheol*
[e] *6* Hebrew *Abaddon*

27 And Job continued his discourse:
2"As surely as God lives, who has denied me justice,
the Almighty, who has made me taste bitterness of soul,
3as long as I have life within me,
the breath of God in my nostrils,
4my lips will not speak wickedness,
and my tongue will utter no deceit.
5I will never admit you are in the right;
till I die, I will not deny my integrity.
6I will maintain my righteousness and never let go of it;
my conscience will not reproach me as long as I live.

7"May my enemies be like the wicked,
my adversaries like the unjust!
8For what hope has the godless when he is cut off,
when God takes away his life?
9Does God listen to his cry
when distress comes upon him?
10Will he find delight in the Almighty?
Will he call upon God at all times?

11"I will teach you about the power of God;
the ways of the Almighty I will not conceal.
12You have all seen this yourselves.
Why then this meaningless talk?

13"Here is the fate God allots to the wicked,
the heritage a ruthless man receives from the Almighty:
14However many his children, their fate is the sword;
his offspring will never have enough to eat.
15The plague will bury those who survive him,
and their widows will not weep for them.
16Though he heaps up silver like dust
and clothes like piles of clay,
17what he lays up the righteous will wear,
and the innocent will divide his silver.
18The house he builds is like a moth's cocoon,
like a hut made by a watchman.
19He lies down wealthy, but will do so no more;
when he opens his eyes, all is gone.
20Terrors overtake him like a flood;
a tempest snatches him away in the night.
21The east wind carries him off, and he is gone;
it sweeps him out of his place.
22It hurls itself against him without mercy
as he flees headlong from its power.
23It claps its hands in derision
and hisses him out of his place.

28 "There is a mine for silver
and a place where gold is refined.
2Iron is taken from the earth,
and copper is smelted from ore.
3Man puts an end to the darkness;
he searches the farthest recesses
for ore in the blackest darkness.
4Far from where people dwell he cuts a shaft,
in places forgotten by the foot of man;
far from men he dangles and sways.
5The earth, from which food comes,
is transformed below as by fire;
6sapphires[a] come from its rocks,
and its dust contains nuggets of gold.
7No bird of prey knows that hidden path,
no falcon's eye has seen it.
8Proud beasts do not set foot on it,
and no lion prowls there.
9Man's hand assaults the flinty rock
and lays bare the roots of the mountains.
10He tunnels through the rock;
his eyes see all its treasures.
11He searches[b] the sources of the rivers
and brings hidden things to light.

12"But where can wisdom be found?
Where does understanding dwell?
13Man does not comprehend its worth;
it cannot be found in the land of the living.
14The deep says, 'It is not in me';
the sea says, 'It is not with me.'
15It cannot be bought with the finest gold,
nor can its price be weighed in silver.
16It cannot be bought with the gold of Ophir,
with precious onyx or sapphires.
17Neither gold nor crystal can compare with it,
nor can it be had for jewels of gold.
18Coral and jasper are not worthy of mention;
the price of wisdom is beyond rubies.
19The topaz of Cush cannot compare with it;
it cannot be bought with pure gold.

20"Where then does wisdom come from?
Where does understanding dwell?
21It is hidden from the eyes of every living thing,
concealed even from the birds of the air.
22Destruction[c] and Death say,
'Only a rumor of it has reached our ears.'
23God understands the way to it
and he alone knows where it dwells,
24for he views the ends of the earth
and sees everything under the heavens.
25When he established the force of the wind
and measured out the waters,
26when he made a decree for the rain
and a path for the thunderstorm,

[a]6 Or *lapis lazuli*; also in verse 16 [b]11 Septuagint, Aquila and Vulgate; Hebrew *He dams up*
[c]22 Hebrew *Abaddon*

27then he looked at wisdom and appraised
it;
he confirmed it and tested it.
28And he said to man,
'The fear of the Lord—that is wisdom,
and to shun evil is understanding.' "

29 Job continued his discourse:

2"How I long for the months gone by,
for the days when God watched over
me,
3when his lamp shone upon my head
and by his light I walked through
darkness!
4Oh, for the days when I was in my prime,
when God's intimate friendship blessed
my house,
5when the Almighty was still with me
and my children were around me,
6when my path was drenched with cream
and the rock poured out for me streams
of olive oil.

7"When I went to the gate of the city
and took my seat in the public square,
8the young men saw me and stepped aside
and the old men rose to their feet;
9the chief men refrained from speaking
and covered their mouths with their
hands;
10the voices of the nobles were hushed,
and their tongues stuck to the roof of
their mouths.
11Whoever heard me spoke well of me,
and those who saw me commended me,
12because I rescued the poor who cried for
help,
and the fatherless who had none to
assist him.
13The man who was dying blessed me;
I made the widow's heart sing.
14I put on righteousness as my clothing;
justice was my robe and my turban.
15I was eyes to the blind
and feet to the lame.
16I was a father to the needy;
I took up the case of the stranger.
17I broke the fangs of the wicked
and snatched the victims from their
teeth.

18"I thought, 'I will die in my own house,
my days as numerous as the grains of
sand.
19My roots will reach to the water,
and the dew will lie all night on my
branches.
20My glory will remain fresh in me,
the bow ever new in my hand.'

21"Men listened to me expectantly,
waiting in silence for my counsel.
22After I had spoken, they spoke no more;
my words fell gently on their ears.
23They waited for me as for showers
and drank in my words as the spring
rain.
24When I smiled at them, they scarcely
believed it;
the light of my face was precious to
them.[a]
25I chose the way for them and sat as their
chief;
I dwelt as a king among his troops;
I was like one who comforts mourners.

30 "But now they mock me,
men younger than I,
whose fathers I would have disdained
to put with my sheep dogs.
2Of what use was the strength of their
hands to me,
since their vigor had gone from them?
3Haggard from want and hunger,
they roamed[b] the parched land
in desolate wastelands at night.
4In the brush they gathered salt herbs,
and their food[c] was the root of the
broom tree.
5They were banished from their fellow
men,
shouted at as if they were thieves.
6They were forced to live in the dry stream
beds,
among the rocks and in holes in the
ground.
7They brayed among the bushes
and huddled in the undergrowth.
8A base and nameless brood,
they were driven out of the land.

9"And now their sons mock me in song;
I have become a byword among them.
10They detest me and keep their distance;
they do not hesitate to spit in my face.
11Now that God has unstrung my bow and
afflicted me,
they throw off restraint in my presence.
12On my right the tribe[d] attacks;
they lay snares for my feet,
they build their siege ramps against me
13They break up my road;
they succeed in destroying me—
without anyone's helping them.[e]
14They advance as through a gaping breach
amid the ruins they come rolling in.
15Terrors overwhelm me;
my dignity is driven away as by the
wind,
my safety vanishes like a cloud.

16"And now my life ebbs away;
days of suffering grip me.
17Night pierces my bones;
my gnawing pains never rest.
18In his great power ⌞God⌟ becomes like
clothing to me[f];
he binds me like the neck of my
garment.

[a]24 The meaning of the Hebrew for this clause is uncertain. [b]3 Or *gnawed* [c]4 Or *fuel*
[d]12 The meaning of the Hebrew for this word is uncertain. [e]13 Or *me. / 'No one can help him,' ⌞they say⌟.*
[f]18 Hebrew; Septuagint *⌞God⌟ grasps my clothing*

19He throws me into the mud,
and I am reduced to dust and ashes.

20"I cry out to you, O God, but you do not answer;
I stand up, but you merely look at me.
21You turn on me ruthlessly;
with the might of your hand you attack me.
22You snatch me up and drive me before the wind;
you toss me about in the storm.
23I know you will bring me down to death,
to the place appointed for all the living.

24"Surely no one lays a hand on a broken man
when he cries for help in his distress.
25Have I not wept for those in trouble?
Has not my soul grieved for the poor?
26Yet when I hoped for good, evil came;
when I looked for light, then came darkness.
27The churning inside me never stops;
days of suffering confront me.
28I go about blackened, but not by the sun;
I stand up in the assembly and cry for help.
29I have become a brother of jackals,
a companion of owls.
30My skin grows black and peels;
my body burns with fever.
31My harp is tuned to mourning,
and my flute to the sound of wailing.

31 "I made a covenant with my eyes
not to look lustfully at a girl.
2For what is man's lot from God above,
his heritage from the Almighty on high?
3Is it not ruin for the wicked,
disaster for those who do wrong?
4Does he not see my ways
and count my every step?

5"If I have walked in falsehood
or my foot has hurried after deceit—
6let God weigh me in honest scales
and he will know that I am blameless—
7if my steps have turned from the path,
if my heart has been led by my eyes,
or if my hands have been defiled,
8then may others eat what I have sown,
and may my crops be uprooted.

9"If my heart has been enticed by a woman,
or if I have lurked at my neighbor's door,
10then may my wife grind another man's grain,
and may other men sleep with her.
11For that would have been shameful,
a sin to be judged.
12It is a fire that burns to Destruction[a];
it would have uprooted my harvest.

13"If I have denied justice to my menservants and maidservants
when they had a grievance against me,
14what will I do when God confronts me?
What will I answer when called to account?
15Did not he who made me in the womb make them?
Did not the same one form us both within our mothers?

16"If I have denied the desires of the poor
or let the eyes of the widow grow weary,
17if I have kept my bread to myself,
not sharing it with the fatherless—
18but from my youth I reared him as would a father,
and from my birth I guided the widow—
19if I have seen anyone perishing for lack of clothing,
or a needy man without a garment,
20and his heart did not bless me
for warming him with the fleece from my sheep,
21if I have raised my hand against the fatherless,
knowing that I had influence in court,
22then let my arm fall from the shoulder,
let it be broken off at the joint.
23For I dreaded destruction from God,
and for fear of his splendor I could not do such things.

24"If I have put my trust in gold
or said to pure gold, 'You are my security,'
25if I have rejoiced over my great wealth,
the fortune my hands had gained,
26if I have regarded the sun in its radiance
or the moon moving in splendor,
27so that my heart was secretly enticed
and my hand offered them a kiss of homage,
28then these also would be sins to be judged,
for I would have been unfaithful to God on high.

29"If I have rejoiced at my enemy's misfortune
or gloated over the trouble that came to him—
30I have not allowed my mouth to sin
by invoking a curse against his life—
31if the men of my household have never said,
'Who has not had his fill of Job's meat?'—
32but no stranger had to spend the night in the street,
for my door was always open to the traveler—
33if I have concealed my sin as men do,[b]
by hiding my guilt in my heart
34because I so feared the crowd

[a] 12 Hebrew *Abaddon* [b] 33 Or *as Adam did*

and so dreaded the contempt of the
clans
that I kept silent and would not go
outside

35("Oh, that I had someone to hear me!
I sign now my defense—let the
Almighty answer me;
let my accuser put his indictment in
writing.
36Surely I would wear it on my shoulder,
I would put it on like a crown.
37I would give him an account of my every
step;
like a prince I would approach him.)—

38"if my land cries out against me
and all its furrows are wet with tears,
39if I have devoured its yield without
payment
or broken the spirit of its tenants,
40then let briers come up instead of wheat
and weeds instead of barley."

The words of Job are ended.

Elihu

32 So these three men stopped answering
Job, because he was righteous in his
own eyes. 2But Elihu son of Barakel the Buzite, of the family of Ram, became very angry
with Job for justifying himself rather than
God. 3He was also angry with the three
friends, because they had found no way to refute Job, and yet had condemned him.[a] 4Now
Elihu had waited before speaking to Job because they were older than he. 5But when he
saw that the three men had nothing more to
say, his anger was aroused.

6So Elihu son of Barakel the Buzite said:

"I am young in years,
and you are old;
that is why I was fearful,
not daring to tell you what I know.
7I thought, 'Age should speak;
advanced years should teach wisdom.'
8But it is the spirit[b] in a man,
the breath of the Almighty, that gives
him understanding.
9It is not only the old[c] who are wise,
not only the aged who understand what
is right.

10"Therefore I say: Listen to me;
I too will tell you what I know.
11I waited while you spoke,
I listened to your reasoning;
while you were searching for words,
12 I gave you my full attention.
But not one of you has proved Job wrong;
none of you has answered his
arguments.
13Do not say, 'We have found wisdom;
let God refute him, not man.'
14But Job has not marshaled his words
against me,
and I will not answer him with your
arguments.

15"They are dismayed and have no more to
say;
words have failed them.
16Must I wait, now that they are silent,
now that they stand there with no reply?
17I too will have my say;
I too will tell what I know.
18For I am full of words,
and the spirit within me compels me;
19inside I am like bottled-up wine,
like new wineskins ready to burst.
20I must speak and find relief;
I must open my lips and reply.
21I will show partiality to no one,
nor will I flatter any man;
22for if I were skilled in flattery,
my Maker would soon take me away.

33 "But now, Job, listen to my words;
pay attention to everything I say.
2I am about to open my mouth;
my words are on the tip of my tongue.
3My words come from an upright heart;
my lips sincerely speak what I know.
4The Spirit of God has made me;
the breath of the Almighty gives me
life.
5Answer me then, if you can;
prepare yourself and confront me.
6I am just like you before God;
I too have been taken from clay.
7No fear of me should alarm you,
nor should my hand be heavy upon you.

8"But you have said in my hearing—
I heard the very words—
9'I am pure and without sin;
I am clean and free from guilt.
10Yet God has found fault with me;
he considers me his enemy.
11He fastens my feet in shackles;
he keeps close watch on all my paths.'

12"But I tell you, in this you are not right,
for God is greater than man.
13Why do you complain to him
that he answers none of man's words[d]?
14For God does speak—now one way, now
another—
though man may not perceive it.
15In a dream, in a vision of the night,
when deep sleep falls on men
as they slumber in their beds,
16he may speak in their ears
and terrify them with warnings,
17to turn man from wrongdoing
and keep him from pride,
18to preserve his soul from the pit,[e]
his life from perishing by the sword.[f]

[a]3 Masoretic Text; an ancient Hebrew scribal tradition *Job, and so had condemned God* [b]8 Or *Spirit*; also in verse 18 [c]9 Or *many*; or *great* [d]13 Or *that he does not answer for any of his actions* [e]18 Or *preserve him from the grave* [f]18 Or *from crossing the River*

19Or a man may be chastened on a bed of
pain
with constant distress in his bones,
20so that his very being finds food repulsive
and his soul loathes the choicest meal.
21His flesh wastes away to nothing,
and his bones, once hidden, now stick
out.
22His soul draws near to the pit,[a]
and his life to the messengers of death.[b]

23"Yet if there is an angel on his side
as a mediator, one out of a thousand,
to tell a man what is right for him,
24to be gracious to him and say,
'Spare him from going down to the
pit[c];
I have found a ransom for him'—
25then his flesh is renewed like a child's;
it is restored as in the days of his youth.
26He prays to God and finds favor with him,
he sees God's face and shouts for joy;
he is restored by God to his righteous
state.
27Then he comes to men and says,
'I sinned, and perverted what was right,
but I did not get what I deserved.
28He redeemed my soul from going down to
the pit,[d]
and I will live to enjoy the light.'

29"God does all these things to a man—
twice, even three times—
30to turn back his soul from the pit,[e]
that the light of life may shine on him.

31"Pay attention, Job, and listen to me;
be silent, and I will speak.
32If you have anything to say, answer me;
speak up, for I want you to be cleared.
33But if not, then listen to me;
be silent, and I will teach you wisdom."

34 Then Elihu said:

2"Hear my words, you wise men;
listen to me, you men of learning.
3For the ear tests words
as the tongue tastes food.
4Let us discern for ourselves what is right;
let us learn together what is good.

5"Job says, 'I am innocent,
but God denies me justice.
6Although I am right,
I am considered a liar;
although I am guiltless,
his arrow inflicts an incurable wound.'
7What man is like Job,
who drinks scorn like water?
8He keeps company with evildoers;
he associates with wicked men.
9For he says, 'It profits a man nothing
when he tries to please God.'

10"So listen to me, you men of
understanding.
Far be it from God to do evil,
from the Almighty to do wrong.
11He repays a man for what he has done;
he brings upon him what his conduct
deserves.
12It is unthinkable that God would do
wrong,
that the Almighty would pervert justice.
13Who appointed him over the earth?
Who put him in charge of the whole
world?
14If it were his intention
and he withdrew his spirit[f] and breath,
15all mankind would perish together
and man would return to the dust.

16"If you have understanding, hear this;
listen to what I say.
17Can he who hates justice govern?
Will you condemn the just and mighty
One?
18Is he not the One who says to kings, 'You
are worthless,'
and to nobles, 'You are wicked,'
19who shows no partiality to princes
and does not favor the rich over the
poor,
for they are all the work of his hands?
20They die in an instant, in the middle of
the night;
the people are shaken and they pass
away;
the mighty are removed without human
hand.

21"His eyes are on the ways of men;
he sees their every step.
22There is no dark place, no deep shadow,
where evildoers can hide.
23God has no need to examine men further,
that they should come before him for
judgment.
24Without inquiry he shatters the mighty
and sets up others in their place.
25Because he takes note of their deeds,
he overthrows them in the night and
they are crushed.
26He punishes them for their wickedness
where everyone can see them,
27because they turned from following him
and had no regard for any of his ways.
28They caused the cry of the poor to come
before him,
so that he heard the cry of the needy.
29But if he remains silent, who can
condemn him?
If he hides his face, who can see him?
Yet he is over man and nation alike,
30 to keep a godless man from ruling,
from laying snares for the people.

31"Suppose a man says to God,
'I am guilty but will offend no more.
32Teach me what I cannot see;
if I have done wrong, I will not do so
again.'

[a]22 Or *He draws near to the grave* [b]22 Or *to the dead down to the grave* [e]30 Or *turn him back from the grave* [c]24 Or *grave* [d]28 Or *redeemed me from going* [f]14 Or *Spirit*

33Should God then reward you on your terms,
when you refuse to repent?
You must decide, not I;
so tell me what you know.

34"Men of understanding declare,
wise men who hear me say to me,
35'Job speaks without knowledge;
his words lack insight.'
36Oh, that Job might be tested to the utmost
for answering like a wicked man!
37To his sin he adds rebellion;
scornfully he claps his hands among us
and multiplies his words against God."

35 Then Elihu said:

2"Do you think this is just?
You say, 'I will be cleared by God.[a]'
3Yet you ask him, 'What profit is it to me,[b]
and what do I gain by not sinning?'

4"I would like to reply to you
and to your friends with you.
5Look up at the heavens and see;
gaze at the clouds so high above you.
6If you sin, how does that affect him?
If your sins are many, what does that do to him?
7If you are righteous, what do you give to him,
or what does he receive from your hand?
8Your wickedness affects only a man like yourself,
and your righteousness only the sons of men.

9"Men cry out under a load of oppression;
they plead for relief from the arm of the powerful.
10But no one says, 'Where is God my Maker,
who gives songs in the night,
11who teaches more to us than to[c] the beasts of the earth
and makes us wiser than[d] the birds of the air?'
12He does not answer when men cry out
because of the arrogance of the wicked.
13Indeed, God does not listen to their empty plea;
the Almighty pays no attention to it.
14How much less, then, will he listen
when you say that you do not see him,
that your case is before him
and you must wait for him,
15and further, that his anger never punishes
and he does not take the least notice of wickedness.[e]
16So Job opens his mouth with empty talk;
without knowledge he multiplies words."

36 Elihu continued:

2"Bear with me a little longer and I will show you
that there is more to be said in God's behalf.
3I get my knowledge from afar;
I will ascribe justice to my Maker.
4Be assured that my words are not false;
one perfect in knowledge is with you.

5"God is mighty, but does not despise men;
he is mighty, and firm in his purpose.
6He does not keep the wicked alive
but gives the afflicted their rights.
7He does not take his eyes off the righteous;
he enthrones them with kings
and exalts them forever.
8But if men are bound in chains,
held fast by cords of affliction,
9he tells them what they have done—
that they have sinned arrogantly.
10He makes them listen to correction
and commands them to repent of their evil.
11If they obey and serve him,
they will spend the rest of their days in prosperity
and their years in contentment.
12But if they do not listen,
they will perish by the sword[f]
and die without knowledge.

13"The godless in heart harbor resentment;
even when he fetters them, they do not cry for help.
14They die in their youth,
among male prostitutes of the shrines.
15But those who suffer he delivers in their suffering;
he speaks to them in their affliction.

16"He is wooing you from the jaws of distress
to a spacious place free from restriction,
to the comfort of your table laden with choice food.
17But now you are laden with the judgment due the wicked;
judgment and justice have taken hold of you.
18Be careful that no one entices you by riches;
do not let a large bribe turn you aside.
19Would your wealth
or even all your mighty efforts
sustain you so you would not be in distress?
20Do not long for the night,
to drag people away from their homes.[g]
21Beware of turning to evil,
which you seem to prefer to affliction.

22"God is exalted in his power.

[a]2 Or *My righteousness is more than God's* [b]3 Or *you* [c]11 Or *teaches us by* [d]11 Or *us wise by*
[e]15 Symmachus, Theodotion and Vulgate; the meaning of the Hebrew for this word is uncertain.
[f]12 Or *will cross the River* [g]20 The meaning of the Hebrew for verses 18-20 is uncertain.

Who is a teacher like him?
23Who has prescribed his ways for him,
or said to him, 'You have done wrong'?
24Remember to extol his work,
which men have praised in song.
25All mankind has seen it;
men gaze on it from afar.
26How great is God—beyond our understanding!
The number of his years is past finding out.

27"He draws up the drops of water,
which distill as rain to the streams[a];
28the clouds pour down their moisture
and abundant showers fall on mankind.
29Who can understand how he spreads out the clouds,
how he thunders from his pavilion?
30See how he scatters his lightning about him,
bathing the depths of the sea.
31This is the way he governs[b] the nations
and provides food in abundance.
32He fills his hands with lightning
and commands it to strike its mark.
33His thunder announces the coming storm;
even the cattle make known its approach.[c]

37 "At this my heart pounds
and leaps from its place.
2Listen! Listen to the roar of his voice,
to the rumbling that comes from his mouth.
3He unleashes his lightning beneath the whole heaven
and sends it to the ends of the earth.
4After that comes the sound of his roar;
he thunders with his majestic voice.
When his voice resounds,
he holds nothing back.
5God's voice thunders in marvelous ways;
he does great things beyond our understanding.
6He says to the snow, 'Fall on the earth,'
and to the rain shower, 'Be a mighty downpour.'
7So that all men he has made may know his work,
he stops every man from his labor.[d]
8The animals take cover;
they remain in their dens.
9The tempest comes out from its chamber,
the cold from the driving winds.
10The breath of God produces ice,
and the broad waters become frozen.
11He loads the clouds with moisture;
he scatters his lightning through them.
12At his direction they swirl around
over the face of the whole earth
to do whatever he commands them.
13He brings the clouds to punish men,
or to water his earth[e] and show his love.

14"Listen to this, Job;
stop and consider God's wonders.
15Do you know how God controls the clouds
and makes his lightning flash?
16Do you know how the clouds hang poised,
those wonders of him who is perfect in knowledge?
17You who swelter in your clothes
when the land lies hushed under the south wind,
18can you join him in spreading out the skies,
hard as a mirror of cast bronze?

19"Tell us what we should say to him;
we cannot draw up our case because of our darkness.
20Should he be told that I want to speak?
Would any man ask to be swallowed up?
21Now no one can look at the sun,
bright as it is in the skies
after the wind has swept them clean.
22Out of the north he comes in golden splendor;
God comes in awesome majesty.
23The Almighty is beyond our reach and exalted in power;
in his justice and great righteousness, he does not oppress.
24Therefore, men revere him,
for does he not have regard for all the wise in heart?[f]"

The LORD Speaks

38 Then the LORD answered Job out of the storm. He said:

2"Who is this that darkens my counsel
with words without knowledge?
3Brace yourself like a man;
I will question you,
and you shall answer me.

4"Where were you when I laid the earth's foundation?
Tell me, if you understand.
5Who marked off its dimensions? Surely you know!
Who stretched a measuring line across it?
6On what were its footings set,
or who laid its cornerstone—
7while the morning stars sang together
and all the angels[g] shouted for joy?

8"Who shut up the sea behind doors
when it burst forth from the womb,
9when I made the clouds its garment
and wrapped it in thick darkness,
10when I fixed limits for it
and set its doors and bars in place,

[a]27 Or *distill from the mist as rain* [b]31 Or *nourishes* [c]33 Or *announces his coming—/ the One zealous against evil* [d]7 Or */ he fills all men with fear by his power* [e]13 Or *to favor them* [f]24 Or *for he does not have regard for any who think they are wise.* [g]7 Hebrew *the sons of God*

11when I said, 'This far you may come and
no farther;
here is where your proud waves halt'?

12"Have you ever given orders to the
morning,
or shown the dawn its place,
13that it might take the earth by the edges
and shake the wicked out of it?
14The earth takes shape like clay under a
seal;
its features stand out like those of a
garment.
15The wicked are denied their light,
and their upraised arm is broken.

16"Have you journeyed to the springs of the
sea
or walked in the recesses of the deep?
17Have the gates of death been shown to
you?
Have you seen the gates of the shadow
of death[a]?
18Have you comprehended the vast expanses
of the earth?
Tell me, if you know all this.

19"What is the way to the abode of light?
And where does darkness reside?
20Can you take them to their places?
Do you know the paths to their
dwellings?
21Surely you know, for you were already
born!
You have lived so many years!

22"Have you entered the storehouses of the
snow
or seen the storehouses of the hail,
23which I reserve for times of trouble,
for days of war and battle?
24What is the way to the place where the
lightning is dispersed,
or the place where the east winds are
scattered over the earth?
25Who cuts a channel for the torrents of
rain,
and a path for the thunderstorm,
26to water a land where no man lives,
a desert with no one in it,
27to satisfy a desolate wasteland
and make it sprout with grass?
28Does the rain have a father?
Who fathers the drops of dew?
29From whose womb comes the ice?
Who gives birth to the frost from the
heavens
30when the waters become hard as stone,
when the surface of the deep is frozen?

31"Can you bind the beautiful[b] Pleiades?
Can you loose the cords of Orion?
32Can you bring forth the constellations in
their seasons[c]
or lead out the Bear[d] with its cubs?
33Do you know the laws of the heavens?
Can you set up ⌊God's[e]⌋ dominion over
the earth?

34"Can you raise your voice to the clouds
and cover yourself with a flood of
water?
35Do you send the lightning bolts on their
way?
Do they report to you, 'Here we are'?
36Who endowed the heart[f] with wisdom
or gave understanding to the mind[f]?
37Who has the wisdom to count the clouds?
Who can tip over the water jars of the
heavens
38when the dust becomes hard
and the clods of earth stick together?

39"Do you hunt the prey for the lioness
and satisfy the hunger of the lions
40when they crouch in their dens
or lie in wait in a thicket?
41Who provides food for the raven
when its young cry out to God
and wander about for lack of food?

39 "Do you know when the mountain
goats give birth?
Do you watch when the doe bears her
fawn?
2Do you count the months till they bear?
Do you know the time they give birth?
3They crouch down and bring forth their
young;
their labor pains are ended.
4Their young thrive and grow strong in the
wilds;
they leave and do not return.

5"Who let the wild donkey go free?
Who untied his ropes?
6I gave him the wasteland as his home,
the salt flats as his habitat.
7He laughs at the commotion in the town;
he does not hear a driver's shout.
8He ranges the hills for his pasture
and searches for any green thing.

9"Will the wild ox consent to serve you?
Will he stay by your manger at night?
10Can you hold him to the furrow with a
harness?
Will he till the valleys behind you?
11Will you rely on him for his great
strength?
Will you leave your heavy work to
him?
12Can you trust him to bring in your grain
and gather it to your threshing floor?

13"The wings of the ostrich flap joyfully,
but they cannot compare with the
pinions and feathers of the stork.
14She lays her eggs on the ground
and lets them warm in the sand,
15unmindful that a foot may crush them,
that some wild animal may trample
them.

[a] 17 Or *gates of deep shadows* [b] 31 Or *the twinkling*; or *the chains of the* [c] 32 Or *the morning star in its season* [d] 32 Or *out Leo* [e] 33 Or *his*; or *their* [f] 36 The meaning of the Hebrew for this word is uncertain.

[16]She treats her young harshly, as if they
were not hers;
she cares not that her labor was in vain,
[17]for God did not endow her with wisdom
or give her a share of good sense.
[18]Yet when she spreads her feathers to run,
she laughs at horse and rider.

[19]"Do you give the horse his strength
or clothe his neck with a flowing mane?
[20]Do you make him leap like a locust,
striking terror with his proud snorting?
[21]He paws fiercely, rejoicing in his strength,
and charges into the fray.
[22]He laughs at fear, afraid of nothing;
he does not shy away from the sword.
[23]The quiver rattles against his side,
along with the flashing spear and lance.
[24]In frenzied excitement he eats up the
ground;
he cannot stand still when the trumpet
sounds.
[25]At the blast of the trumpet he snorts,
'Aha!'
He catches the scent of battle from afar,
the shout of commanders and the battle
cry.

[26]"Does the hawk take flight by your
wisdom
and spread his wings toward the south?
[27]Does the eagle soar at your command
and build his nest on high?
[28]He dwells on a cliff and stays there at
night;
a rocky crag is his stronghold.
[29]From there he seeks out his food;
his eyes detect it from afar.
[30]His young ones feast on blood,
and where the slain are, there is he."

40

The LORD said to Job:

[2]"Will the one who contends with the
Almighty correct him?
Let him who accuses God answer him!"

[3]Then Job answered the LORD:

[4]"I am unworthy—how can I reply to you?
I put my hand over my mouth.
[5]I spoke once, but I have no answer—
twice, but I will say no more."

[6]Then the LORD spoke to Job out of the
storm:

[7]"Brace yourself like a man;
I will question you,
and you shall answer me.

[8]"Would you discredit my justice?
Would you condemn me to justify
yourself?
[9]Do you have an arm like God's,
and can your voice thunder like his?
[10]Then adorn yourself with glory and
splendor,
and clothe yourself in honor and
majesty.
[11]Unleash the fury of your wrath,
look at every proud man and bring him
low,
[12]look at every proud man and humble him,
crush the wicked where they stand.
[13]Bury them all in the dust together;
shroud their faces in the grave.
[14]Then I myself will admit to you
that your own right hand can save you.

[15]"Look at the behemoth,[a]
which I made along with you
and which feeds on grass like an ox.
[16]What strength he has in his loins,
what power in the muscles of his belly!
[17]His tail[b] sways like a cedar;
the sinews of his thighs are close-knit.
[18]His bones are tubes of bronze,
his limbs like rods of iron.
[19]He ranks first among the works of God,
yet his Maker can approach him with
his sword.
[20]The hills bring him their produce,
and all the wild animals play nearby.
[21]Under the lotus plants he lies,
hidden among the reeds in the marsh.
[22]The lotuses conceal him in their shadow;
the poplars by the stream surround him.
[23]When the river rages, he is not alarmed;
he is secure, though the Jordan should
surge against his mouth.
[24]Can anyone capture him by the eyes,[c]
or trap him and pierce his nose?

41

"Can you pull in the leviathan[d] with a
fishhook
or tie down his tongue with a rope?
[2]Can you put a cord through his nose
or pierce his jaw with a hook?
[3]Will he keep begging you for mercy?
Will he speak to you with gentle
words?
[4]Will he make an agreement with you
for you to take him as your slave for
life?
[5]Can you make a pet of him like a bird
or put him on a leash for your girls?
[6]Will traders barter for him?
Will they divide him up among the
merchants?
[7]Can you fill his hide with harpoons
or his head with fishing spears?
[8]If you lay a hand on him,
you will remember the struggle and
never do it again!
[9]Any hope of subduing him is false;
the mere sight of him is overpowering.
[10]No one is fierce enough to rouse him.
Who then is able to stand against me?
[11]Who has a claim against me that I must
pay?
Everything under heaven belongs to me.

[12]"I will not fail to speak of his limbs,

[a] *15* Possibly the hippopotamus or the elephant [b] *17* Possibly trunk [c] *24* Or *by a water hole*
[d] *1* Possibly the crocodile

his strength and his graceful form.
13 Who can strip off his outer coat?
Who would approach him with a bridle?
14 Who dares open the doors of his mouth,
ringed about with his fearsome teeth?
15 His back has[a] rows of shields
tightly sealed together;
16 each is so close to the next
that no air can pass between.
17 They are joined fast to one another;
they cling together and cannot be
parted.
18 His snorting throws out flashes of light;
his eyes are like the rays of dawn.
19 Firebrands stream from his mouth;
sparks of fire shoot out.
20 Smoke pours from his nostrils
as from a boiling pot over a fire of
reeds.
21 His breath sets coals ablaze,
and flames dart from his mouth.
22 Strength resides in his neck;
dismay goes before him.
23 The folds of his flesh are tightly joined;
they are firm and immovable.
24 His chest is hard as rock,
hard as a lower millstone.
25 When he rises up, the mighty are terrified;
they retreat before his thrashing.
26 The sword that reaches him has no effect,
nor does the spear or the dart or the
javelin.
27 Iron he treats like straw
and bronze like rotten wood.
28 Arrows do not make him flee;
slingstones are like chaff to him.
29 A club seems to him but a piece of straw;
he laughs at the rattling of the lance.
30 His undersides are jagged potsherds,
leaving a trail in the mud like a
threshing sledge.
31 He makes the depths churn like a boiling
caldron
and stirs up the sea like a pot of
ointment.
32 Behind him he leaves a glistening wake;
one would think the deep had white
hair.
33 Nothing on earth is his equal—
a creature without fear.
34 He looks down on all that are haughty;
he is king over all that are proud."

Job

42 Then Job replied to the LORD:

2 "I know that you can do all things;
no plan of yours can be thwarted.
3 ⌞You asked,⌟ 'Who is this that obscures my
counsel without knowledge?'
Surely I spoke of things I did not
understand,
things too wonderful for me to know.

4 ⌞"You said,⌟ 'Listen now, and I will
speak;
I will question you,
and you shall answer me.'
5 My ears had heard of you
but now my eyes have seen you.
6 Therefore I despise myself
and repent in dust and ashes."

Epilogue

7 After the LORD had said these things to Job,
he said to Eliphaz the Temanite, "I am angry
with you and your two friends, because you
have not spoken of me what is right, as my
servant Job has. 8 So now take seven bulls and
seven rams and go to my servant Job and sacrifice a burnt offering for yourselves. My servant Job will pray for you, and I will accept his
prayer and not deal with you according to your
folly. You have not spoken of me what is right,
as my servant Job has." 9 So Eliphaz the Temanite, Bildad the Shuhite and Zophar the Naamathite did what the LORD told them; and the
LORD accepted Job's prayer.

10 After Job had prayed for his friends, the
LORD made him prosperous again and gave
him twice as much as he had before. 11 All his
brothers and sisters and everyone who had
known him before came and ate with him in
his house. They comforted and consoled him
over all the trouble the LORD had brought upon
him, and each one gave him a piece of silver[b]
and a gold ring.

12 The LORD blessed the latter part of Job's
life more than the first. He had fourteen thousand sheep, six thousand camels, a thousand
yoke of oxen and a thousand donkeys. 13 And
he also had seven sons and three daughters.
14 The first daughter he named Jemimah, the
second Keziah and the third Keren-Happuch.
15 Nowhere in all the land were there found
women as beautiful as Job's daughters, and
their father granted them an inheritance along
with their brothers.

16 After this, Job lived a hundred and forty
years; he saw his children and their children to
the fourth generation. 17 And so he died, old
and full of years.

[a] *15* Or *His pride is his* [b] *11* Hebrew *him a kesitah*; a kesitah was a unit of money of unknown weight and value.

Psalms

BOOK I

Psalms 1–41

Psalm 1

1Blessed is the man
who does not walk in the counsel of the wicked
or stand in the way of sinners
or sit in the seat of mockers.
2But his delight is in the law of the LORD,
and on his law he meditates day and night.
3He is like a tree planted by streams of water,
which yields its fruit in season
and whose leaf does not wither.
Whatever he does prospers.

4Not so the wicked!
They are like chaff
that the wind blows away.
5Therefore the wicked will not stand in the judgment,
nor sinners in the assembly of the righteous.

6For the LORD watches over the way of the righteous,
but the way of the wicked will perish.

Psalm 2

1Why do the nations conspire[a]
and the peoples plot in vain?
2The kings of the earth take their stand
and the rulers gather together
against the LORD
and against his Anointed One.[b]
3"Let us break their chains," they say,
"and throw off their fetters."

4The One enthroned in heaven laughs;
the Lord scoffs at them.
5Then he rebukes them in his anger
and terrifies them in his wrath, saying,
6"I have installed my King[c]
on Zion, my holy hill."

7I will proclaim the decree of the LORD:

He said to me, "You are my Son[d];
today I have become your Father.[e]
8Ask of me,
and I will make the nations your inheritance,
the ends of the earth your possession.
9You will rule them with an iron scepter[f];
you will dash them to pieces like pottery."

10Therefore, you kings, be wise;
be warned, you rulers of the earth.
11Serve the LORD with fear
and rejoice with trembling.
12Kiss the Son, lest he be angry
and you be destroyed in your way,
for his wrath can flare up in a moment.
Blessed are all who take refuge in him.

Psalm 3

A psalm of David. When he fled from his son Absalom.

1O LORD, how many are my foes!
How many rise up against me!
2Many are saying of me,
"God will not deliver him." *Selah*[g]

3But you are a shield around me, O LORD;
you bestow glory on me and lift[h] up my head.
4To the LORD I cry aloud,
and he answers me from his holy hill. *Selah*

5I lie down and sleep;
I wake again, because the LORD sustains me.
6I will not fear the tens of thousands
drawn up against me on every side.

7Arise, O LORD!
Deliver me, O my God!
Strike all my enemies on the jaw;
break the teeth of the wicked.

8From the LORD comes deliverance.
May your blessing be on your people. *Selah*

Psalm 4

For the director of music. With stringed instruments. A psalm of David.

1Answer me when I call to you,
O my righteous God.
Give me relief from my distress;
be merciful to me and hear my prayer.

2How long, O men, will you turn my glory into shame[i]?
How long will you love delusions and seek false gods[j]? *Selah*
3Know that the LORD has set apart the godly for himself;
the LORD will hear when I call to him.

4In your anger do not sin;
when you are on your beds,
search your hearts and be silent. *Selah*

[a] 1 Hebrew; Septuagint *rage* [b] 2 Or *anointed one* [c] 6 Or *king* [d] 7 Or *son*; also in verse 12 [e] 7 Or *have begotten you* [f] 9 Or *will break them with a rod of iron* [g] 2 A word of uncertain meaning, occurring frequently in the Psalms; possibly a musical term [h] 3 Or *LORD, / my Glorious One, who lifts* [i] 2 Or *you dishonor my Glorious One* [j] 2 Or *seek lies*

5Offer right sacrifices
and trust in the LORD.

6Many are asking, "Who can show us any good?"
Let the light of your face shine upon us, O LORD.
7You have filled my heart with greater joy
than when their grain and new wine abound.
8I will lie down and sleep in peace,
for you alone, O LORD,
make me dwell in safety.

Psalm 5

For the director of music. For flutes. A psalm of David.

1Give ear to my words, O LORD,
consider my sighing.
2Listen to my cry for help,
my King and my God,
for to you I pray.
3In the morning, O LORD, you hear my voice;
in the morning I lay my requests before you
and wait in expectation.

4You are not a God who takes pleasure in evil;
with you the wicked cannot dwell.
5The arrogant cannot stand in your presence;
you hate all who do wrong.
6You destroy those who tell lies;
bloodthirsty and deceitful men
the LORD abhors.

7But I, by your great mercy,
will come into your house;
in reverence will I bow down
toward your holy temple.
8Lead me, O LORD, in your righteousness
because of my enemies—
make straight your way before me.

9Not a word from their mouth can be trusted;
their heart is filled with destruction.
Their throat is an open grave;
with their tongue they speak deceit.
10Declare them guilty, O God!
Let their intrigues be their downfall.
Banish them for their many sins,
for they have rebelled against you.

11But let all who take refuge in you be glad;
let them ever sing for joy.
Spread your protection over them,
that those who love your name may rejoice in you.
12For surely, O LORD, you bless the righteous;
you surround them with your favor as with a shield.

Psalm 6

For the director of music. With stringed instruments. According to *sheminith.*[a] A psalm of David.

1O LORD, do not rebuke me in your anger
or discipline me in your wrath.
2Be merciful to me, LORD, for I am faint;
O LORD, heal me, for my bones are in agony.
3My soul is in anguish.
How long, O LORD, how long?

4Turn, O LORD, and deliver me;
save me because of your unfailing love.
5No one remembers you when he is dead.
Who praises you from the grave[b]?

6I am worn out from groaning;
all night long I flood my bed with weeping
and drench my couch with tears.
7My eyes grow weak with sorrow;
they fail because of all my foes.

8Away from me, all you who do evil,
for the LORD has heard my weeping.
9The LORD has heard my cry for mercy;
the LORD accepts my prayer.
10All my enemies will be ashamed and dismayed;
they will turn back in sudden disgrace.

Psalm 7

A *shiggaion*[c] of David, which he sang to the LORD concerning Cush, a Benjamite.

1O LORD my God, I take refuge in you;
save and deliver me from all who pursue me,
2or they will tear me like a lion
and rip me to pieces with no one to rescue me.

3O LORD my God, if I have done this
and there is guilt on my hands—
4if I have done evil to him who is at peace with me
or without cause have robbed my foe—
5then let my enemy pursue and overtake me;
let him trample my life to the ground
and make me sleep in the dust. *Selah*

6Arise, O LORD, in your anger;
rise up against the rage of my enemies.
Awake, my God; decree justice.
7Let the assembled peoples gather around you.
Rule over them from on high;
8 let the LORD judge the peoples.
Judge me, O LORD, according to my righteousness,
according to my integrity, O Most High.
9O righteous God,
who searches minds and hearts,

[a]Title: Probably a musical term [b]5 Hebrew *Sheol* [c]Title: Probably a literary or musical term

bring to an end the violence of the wicked
and make the righteous secure.
10My shield[a] is God Most High,
who saves the upright in heart.
11God is a righteous judge,
a God who expresses his wrath every day.
12If he does not relent,
he[b] will sharpen his sword;
he will bend and string his bow.
13He has prepared his deadly weapons;
he makes ready his flaming arrows.

14He who is pregnant with evil
and conceives trouble gives birth to disillusionment.
15He who digs a hole and scoops it out
falls into the pit he has made.
16The trouble he causes recoils on himself;
his violence comes down on his own head.

17I will give thanks to the LORD because of his righteousness
and will sing praise to the name of the LORD Most High.

Psalm 8

For the director of music. According to *gittith*.[c] A psalm of David.

1O LORD, our Lord,
how majestic is your name in all the earth!

You have set your glory
above the heavens.
2From the lips of children and infants
you have ordained praise[d]
because of your enemies,
to silence the foe and the avenger.

3When I consider your heavens,
the work of your fingers,
the moon and the stars,
which you have set in place,
4what is man that you are mindful of him,
the son of man that you care for him?
5You made him a little lower than the heavenly beings[e]
and crowned him with glory and honor.

6You made him ruler over the works of your hands;
you put everything under his feet:
7all flocks and herds,
and the beasts of the field,
8the birds of the air,
and the fish of the sea,
all that swim the paths of the seas.

9O LORD, our Lord,
how majestic is your name in all the earth!

Psalm 9[f]

For the director of music. To ⌊the tune of⌋ "The Death of the Son." A psalm of David.

1I will praise you, O LORD, with all my heart;
I will tell of all your wonders.
2I will be glad and rejoice in you;
I will sing praise to your name, O Most High.

3My enemies turn back;
they stumble and perish before you.
4For you have upheld my right and my cause;
you have sat on your throne, judging righteously.
5You have rebuked the nations and destroyed the wicked;
you have blotted out their name for ever and ever.
6Endless ruin has overtaken the enemy,
you have uprooted their cities;
even the memory of them has perished.

7The LORD reigns forever;
he has established his throne for judgment.
8He will judge the world in righteousness;
he will govern the peoples with justice.
9The LORD is a refuge for the oppressed,
a stronghold in times of trouble.
10Those who know your name will trust in you,
for you, LORD, have never forsaken those who seek you.

11Sing praises to the LORD, enthroned in Zion;
proclaim among the nations what he has done.
12For he who avenges blood remembers;
he does not ignore the cry of the afflicted.

13O LORD, see how my enemies persecute me!
Have mercy and lift me up from the gates of death,
14that I may declare your praises
in the gates of the Daughter of Zion
and there rejoice in your salvation.
15The nations have fallen into the pit they have dug;
their feet are caught in the net they have hidden.
16The LORD is known by his justice;
the wicked are ensnared by the work of their hands. *Higgaion.*[g] *Selah*
17The wicked return to the grave,[h]
all the nations that forget God.
18But the needy will not always be forgotten,
nor the hope of the afflicted ever perish.

[a] *10* Or *sovereign* [b] *12* Or *If a man does not repent, / God* [c] Title: Probably a musical term
[d] *2* Or *strength* [e] *5* Or *than God* [f] Psalms 9 and 10 may have been originally a single acrostic poem, the stanzas of which begin with the successive letters of the Hebrew alphabet. In the Septuagint they constitute one psalm. [g] *16* Or *Meditation*; possibly a musical notation [h] *17* Hebrew *Sheol*

19Arise, O LORD, let not man triumph;
let the nations be judged in your presence.
20Strike them with terror, O LORD;
let the nations know they are but men. *Selah*

Psalm 10[a]

1Why, O LORD, do you stand far off?
Why do you hide yourself in times of trouble?

2In his arrogance the wicked man hunts down the weak,
who are caught in the schemes he devises.
3He boasts of the cravings of his heart;
he blesses the greedy and reviles the LORD.
4In his pride the wicked does not seek him;
in all his thoughts there is no room for God.
5His ways are always prosperous;
he is haughty and your laws are far from him;
he sneers at all his enemies.
6He says to himself, "Nothing will shake me;
I'll always be happy and never have trouble."
7His mouth is full of curses and lies and threats;
trouble and evil are under his tongue.
8He lies in wait near the villages;
from ambush he murders the innocent,
watching in secret for his victims.
9He lies in wait like a lion in cover;
he lies in wait to catch the helpless;
he catches the helpless and drags them off in his net.
10His victims are crushed, they collapse;
they fall under his strength.
11He says to himself, "God has forgotten;
he covers his face and never sees."

12Arise, LORD! Lift up your hand, O God.
Do not forget the helpless.
13Why does the wicked man revile God?
Why does he say to himself,
"He won't call me to account"?
14But you, O God, do see trouble and grief;
you consider it to take it in hand.
The victim commits himself to you;
you are the helper of the fatherless.
15Break the arm of the wicked and evil man;
call him to account for his wickedness
that would not be found out.

16The LORD is King for ever and ever;
the nations will perish from his land.
17You hear, O LORD, the desire of the afflicted;
you encourage them, and you listen to their cry,
18defending the fatherless and the oppressed,
in order that man, who is of the earth,
may terrify no more.

Psalm 11

For the director of music. Of David.

1In the LORD I take refuge.
How then can you say to me:
"Flee like a bird to your mountain.
2For look, the wicked bend their bows;
they set their arrows against the strings
to shoot from the shadows
at the upright in heart.
3When the foundations are being destroyed,
what can the righteous do[b]?"

4The LORD is in his holy temple;
the LORD is on his heavenly throne.
He observes the sons of men;
his eyes examine them.
5The LORD examines the righteous,
but the wicked[c] and those who love violence
his soul hates.
6On the wicked he will rain
fiery coals and burning sulfur;
a scorching wind will be their lot.

7For the LORD is righteous,
he loves justice;
upright men will see his face.

Psalm 12

For the director of music. According to *sheminith*.[d] A psalm of David.

1Help, LORD, for the godly are no more;
the faithful have vanished from among men.
2Everyone lies to his neighbor;
their flattering lips speak with deception.

3May the LORD cut off all flattering lips
and every boastful tongue
4that says, "We will triumph with our tongues;
we own our lips[e]—who is our master?"

5"Because of the oppression of the weak
and the groaning of the needy,
I will now arise," says the LORD.
"I will protect them from those who malign them."
6And the words of the LORD are flawless,
like silver refined in a furnace of clay,
purified seven times.

7O LORD, you will keep us safe
and protect us from such people forever.

[a]Psalms 9 and 10 may have been originally a single acrostic poem, the stanzas of which begin with the successive letters of the Hebrew alphabet. In the Septuagint they constitute one psalm. [b]3 Or *what is the Righteous One doing* [c]5 Or *The LORD, the Righteous One, examines the wicked, /* [d]Title: Probably a musical term [e]4 Or */ our lips are our plowshares*

8The wicked freely strut about
when what is vile is honored among men.

Psalm 13

For the director of music. A psalm of David.

1How long, O LORD? Will you forget me forever?
How long will you hide your face from me?
2How long must I wrestle with my thoughts
and every day have sorrow in my heart?
How long will my enemy triumph over me?
3Look on me and answer, O LORD my God.
Give light to my eyes, or I will sleep in death;
4my enemy will say, "I have overcome him,"
and my foes will rejoice when I fall.

5But I trust in your unfailing love;
my heart rejoices in your salvation.
6I will sing to the LORD,
for he has been good to me.

Psalm 14

For the director of music. Of David.

1The fool[a] says in his heart,
"There is no God."
They are corrupt, their deeds are vile;
there is no one who does good.

2The LORD looks down from heaven
on the sons of men
to see if there are any who understand,
any who seek God.
3All have turned aside,
they have together become corrupt;
there is no one who does good,
not even one.

4Will evildoers never learn—
those who devour my people as men eat bread
and who do not call on the LORD?
5There they are, overwhelmed with dread,
for God is present in the company of the righteous.
6You evildoers frustrate the plans of the poor,
but the LORD is their refuge.

7Oh, that salvation for Israel would come out of Zion!
When the LORD restores the fortunes of his people,
let Jacob rejoice and Israel be glad!

Psalm 15

A psalm of David.

1LORD, who may dwell in your sanctuary?
Who may live on your holy hill?

2He whose walk is blameless
and who does what is righteous,
who speaks the truth from his heart
3 and has no slander on his tongue,
who does his neighbor no wrong
and casts no slur on his fellowman,
4who despises a vile man
but honors those who fear the LORD,
who keeps his oath
even when it hurts,
5who lends his money without usury
and does not accept a bribe against the innocent.

He who does these things
will never be shaken.

Psalm 16

A *miktam*[b] of David.

1Keep me safe, O God,
for in you I take refuge.

2I said to the LORD, "You are my Lord;
apart from you I have no good thing."
3As for the saints who are in the land,
they are the glorious ones in whom is all my delight.[c]
4The sorrows of those will increase
who run after other gods.
I will not pour out their libations of blood
or take up their names on my lips.

5LORD, you have assigned me my portion and my cup;
you have made my lot secure.
6The boundary lines have fallen for me in pleasant places;
surely I have a delightful inheritance.

7I will praise the LORD, who counsels me;
even at night my heart instructs me.
8I have set the LORD always before me.
Because he is at my right hand,
I will not be shaken.

9Therefore my heart is glad and my tongue rejoices;
my body also will rest secure,
10because you will not abandon me to the grave,[d]
nor will you let your Holy One[e] see decay.
11You have made[f] known to me the path of life;

[a] *1* The Hebrew words rendered *fool* in Psalms denote one who is morally deficient. [b] Title: Probably a literary or musical term [c] *3* Or *As for the pagan priests who are in the land / and the nobles in whom all delight, I said:* [d] *10* Hebrew *Sheol* [e] *10* Or *your faithful one* [f] *11* Or *You will make*

you will fill me with joy in your
presence,
with eternal pleasures at your right
hand.

Psalm 17

A prayer of David.

1Hear, O LORD, my righteous plea;
listen to my cry.
Give ear to my prayer—
it does not rise from deceitful lips.
2May my vindication come from you;
may your eyes see what is right.

3Though you probe my heart and examine
me at night,
though you test me, you will find
nothing;
I have resolved that my mouth will not
sin.
4As for the deeds of men—
by the word of your lips
I have kept myself
from the ways of the violent.
5My steps have held to your paths;
my feet have not slipped.

6I call on you, O God, for you will answer
me;
give ear to me and hear my prayer.
7Show the wonder of your great love,
you who save by your right hand
those who take refuge in you from their
foes.
8Keep me as the apple of your eye;
hide me in the shadow of your wings
9from the wicked who assail me,
from my mortal enemies who surround
me.

10They close up their callous hearts,
and their mouths speak with arrogance.
11They have tracked me down, they now
surround me,
with eyes alert, to throw me to the
ground.
12They are like a lion hungry for prey,
like a great lion crouching in cover.

13Rise up, O LORD, confront them, bring
them down;
rescue me from the wicked by your
sword.
14O LORD, by your hand save me from such
men,
from men of this world whose reward is
in this life.

You still the hunger of those you cherish;
their sons have plenty,
and they store up wealth for their
children.
15And I—in righteousness I will see your
face;
when I awake, I will be satisfied with
seeing your likeness.

Psalm 18

For the director of music. Of David the
servant of the LORD. He sang to the LORD
the words of this song when the LORD
delivered him from the hand of all his
enemies and from the hand of Saul.
He said:

1I love you, O LORD, my strength.

2The LORD is my rock, my fortress and my
deliverer;
my God is my rock, in whom I take
refuge.
He is my shield and the horn[a] of my
salvation, my stronghold.
3I call to the LORD, who is worthy of
praise,
and I am saved from my enemies.

4The cords of death entangled me;
the torrents of destruction overwhelmed
me.
5The cords of the grave[b] coiled around me;
the snares of death confronted me.
6In my distress I called to the LORD;
I cried to my God for help.
From his temple he heard my voice;
my cry came before him, into his ears.

7The earth trembled and quaked,
and the foundations of the mountains
shook;
they trembled because he was angry.
8Smoke rose from his nostrils;
consuming fire came from his mouth,
burning coals blazed out of it.
9He parted the heavens and came down;
dark clouds were under his feet.
10He mounted the cherubim and flew;
he soared on the wings of the wind.
11He made darkness his covering, his
canopy around him—
the dark rain clouds of the sky.
12Out of the brightness of his presence
clouds advanced,
with hailstones and bolts of lightning.
13The LORD thundered from heaven;
the voice of the Most High resounded.[c]
14He shot his arrows and scattered ⌊the
enemies⌋,
great bolts of lightning and routed them.
15The valleys of the sea were exposed
and the foundations of the earth laid
bare
at your rebuke, O LORD,
at the blast of breath from your nostrils.

16He reached down from on high and took
hold of me;
he drew me out of deep waters.
17He rescued me from my powerful enemy,
from my foes, who were too strong for
me.
18They confronted me in the day of my
disaster,
but the LORD was my support.

[a]2 *Horn* here symbolizes strength. [b]5 Hebrew *Sheol* [c]13 Some Hebrew manuscripts and Septuagint (see also 2 Samuel 22:14); most Hebrew manuscripts *resounded, / amid hailstones and bolts of lightning*

19He brought me out into a spacious place;
he rescued me because he delighted in me.

20The LORD has dealt with me according to my righteousness;
according to the cleanness of my hands he has rewarded me.
21For I have kept the ways of the LORD;
I have not done evil by turning from my God.
22All his laws are before me;
I have not turned away from his decrees.
23I have been blameless before him
and have kept myself from sin.
24The LORD has rewarded me according to my righteousness,
according to the cleanness of my hands in his sight.

25To the faithful you show yourself faithful,
to the blameless you show yourself blameless,
26to the pure you show yourself pure,
but to the crooked you show yourself shrewd.
27You save the humble
but bring low those whose eyes are haughty.
28You, O LORD, keep my lamp burning;
my God turns my darkness into light.
29With your help I can advance against a troop[a];
with my God I can scale a wall.

30As for God, his way is perfect;
the word of the LORD is flawless.
He is a shield
for all who take refuge in him.
31For who is God besides the LORD?
And who is the Rock except our God?
32It is God who arms me with strength
and makes my way perfect.
33He makes my feet like the feet of a deer;
he enables me to stand on the heights.
34He trains my hands for battle;
my arms can bend a bow of bronze.
35You give me your shield of victory,
and your right hand sustains me;
you stoop down to make me great.
36You broaden the path beneath me,
so that my ankles do not turn.

37I pursued my enemies and overtook them;
I did not turn back till they were destroyed.
38I crushed them so that they could not rise;
they fell beneath my feet.
39You armed me with strength for battle;
you made my adversaries bow at my feet.
40You made my enemies turn their backs in flight,
and I destroyed my foes.
41They cried for help, but there was no one to save them—
to the LORD, but he did not answer.
42I beat them as fine as dust borne on the wind;
I poured them out like mud in the streets.

43You have delivered me from the attacks of the people;
you have made me the head of nations;
people I did not know are subject to me.
44As soon as they hear me, they obey me;
foreigners cringe before me.
45They all lose heart;
they come trembling from their strongholds.

46The LORD lives! Praise be to my Rock!
Exalted be God my Savior!
47He is the God who avenges me,
who subdues nations under me,
48 who saves me from my enemies.
You exalted me above my foes;
from violent men you rescued me.
49Therefore I will praise you among the nations, O LORD;
I will sing praises to your name.
50He gives his king great victories;
he shows unfailing kindness to his anointed,
to David and his descendants forever.

Psalm 19

For the director of music. A psalm of David.

1The heavens declare the glory of God;
the skies proclaim the work of his hands.
2Day after day they pour forth speech;
night after night they display knowledge.
3There is no speech or language
where their voice is not heard.[b]
4Their voice[c] goes out into all the earth,
their words to the ends of the world.

In the heavens he has pitched a tent for the sun,
5 which is like a bridegroom coming forth from his pavilion,
like a champion rejoicing to run his course.
6It rises at one end of the heavens
and makes its circuit to the other;
nothing is hidden from its heat.

7The law of the LORD is perfect,
reviving the soul.
The statutes of the LORD are trustworthy,
making wise the simple.
8The precepts of the LORD are right,
giving joy to the heart.
The commands of the LORD are radiant,

[a]29 Or *can run through a barricade* [b]3 Or *They have no speech, there are no words; / no sound is heard from them* [c]4 Septuagint, Jerome and Syriac; Hebrew *line*

giving light to the eyes.
9The fear of the LORD is pure,
enduring forever.
The ordinances of the LORD are sure
and altogether righteous.
10They are more precious than gold,
than much pure gold;
they are sweeter than honey,
than honey from the comb.
11By them is your servant warned;
in keeping them there is great reward.

12Who can discern his errors?
Forgive my hidden faults.
13Keep your servant also from willful sins;
may they not rule over me.
Then will I be blameless,
innocent of great transgression.

14May the words of my mouth and the meditation of my heart
be pleasing in your sight,
O LORD, my Rock and my Redeemer.

Psalm 20

For the director of music. A psalm of David.

1May the LORD answer you when you are in distress;
may the name of the God of Jacob protect you.
2May he send you help from the sanctuary
and grant you support from Zion.
3May he remember all your sacrifices
and accept your burnt offerings. *Selah*
4May he give you the desire of your heart
and make all your plans succeed.
5We will shout for joy when you are victorious
and will lift up our banners in the name of our God.
May the LORD grant all your requests.

6Now I know that the LORD saves his anointed;
he answers him from his holy heaven
with the saving power of his right hand.
7Some trust in chariots and some in horses,
but we trust in the name of the LORD our God.
8They are brought to their knees and fall,
but we rise up and stand firm.

9O LORD, save the king!
Answer[a] us when we call!

Psalm 21

For the director of music. A psalm of David.

1O LORD, the king rejoices in your strength.
How great is his joy in the victories you give!
2You have granted him the desire of his heart
and have not withheld the request of his lips. *Selah*
3You welcomed him with rich blessings
and placed a crown of pure gold on his head.
4He asked you for life, and you gave it to him—
length of days, for ever and ever.
5Through the victories you gave, his glory is great;
you have bestowed on him splendor and majesty.
6Surely you have granted him eternal blessings
and made him glad with the joy of your presence.
7For the king trusts in the LORD;
through the unfailing love of the Most High
he will not be shaken.

8Your hand will lay hold on all your enemies;
your right hand will seize your foes.
9At the time of your appearing
you will make them like a fiery furnace.
In his wrath the LORD will swallow them up,
and his fire will consume them.
10You will destroy their descendants from the earth,
their posterity from mankind.
11Though they plot evil against you
and devise wicked schemes, they cannot succeed;
12for you will make them turn their backs
when you aim at them with drawn bow.

13Be exalted, O LORD, in your strength;
we will sing and praise your might.

Psalm 22

For the director of music. To ⌊the tune of⌋ "The Doe of the Morning." A psalm of David.

1My God, my God, why have you forsaken me?
Why are you so far from saving me,
so far from the words of my groaning?
2O my God, I cry out by day, but you do not answer,
by night, and am not silent.

3Yet you are enthroned as the Holy One;
you are the praise of Israel.[b]
4In you our fathers put their trust;
they trusted and you delivered them.
5They cried to you and were saved;
in you they trusted and were not disappointed.

6But I am a worm and not a man,
scorned by men and despised by the people.
7All who see me mock me;
they hurl insults, shaking their heads:

[a]9 Or *save! / O King, answer* [b]3 Or *Yet you are holy, / enthroned on the praises of Israel*

8"He trusts in the LORD;
let the LORD rescue him.
Let him deliver him,
since he delights in him."

9Yet you brought me out of the womb;
you made me trust in you
even at my mother's breast.
10From birth I was cast upon you;
from my mother's womb you have been my God.
11Do not be far from me,
for trouble is near
and there is no one to help.

12Many bulls surround me;
strong bulls of Bashan encircle me.
13Roaring lions tearing their prey
open their mouths wide against me.
14I am poured out like water,
and all my bones are out of joint.
My heart has turned to wax;
it has melted away within me.
15My strength is dried up like a potsherd,
and my tongue sticks to the roof of my mouth;
you lay me[a] in the dust of death.
16Dogs have surrounded me;
a band of evil men has encircled me,
they have pierced[b] my hands and my feet.
17I can count all my bones;
people stare and gloat over me.
18They divide my garments among them
and cast lots for my clothing.

19But you, O LORD, be not far off;
O my Strength, come quickly to help me.
20Deliver my life from the sword,
my precious life from the power of the dogs.
21Rescue me from the mouth of the lions;
save[c] me from the horns of the wild oxen.

22I will declare your name to my brothers;
in the congregation I will praise you.
23You who fear the LORD, praise him!
All you descendants of Jacob, honor him!
Revere him, all you descendants of Israel!
24For he has not despised or disdained
the suffering of the afflicted one;
he has not hidden his face from him
but has listened to his cry for help.

25From you comes the theme of my praise
in the great assembly;
before those who fear you[d] will I fulfill my vows.
26The poor will eat and be satisfied;
they who seek the LORD will praise him—
may your hearts live forever!
27All the ends of the earth
will remember and turn to the LORD,
and all the families of the nations
will bow down before him,
28for dominion belongs to the LORD
and he rules over the nations.

29All the rich of the earth will feast and worship;
all who go down to the dust will kneel before him—
those who cannot keep themselves alive.
30Posterity will serve him;
future generations will be told about the Lord.
31They will proclaim his righteousness
to a people yet unborn—
for he has done it.

Psalm 23

A psalm of David.

1The LORD is my shepherd, I shall not be in want.
2 He makes me lie down in green pastures,
he leads me beside quiet waters,
3 he restores my soul.
He guides me in paths of righteousness
for his name's sake.
4Even though I walk
through the valley of the shadow of death,[e]
I will fear no evil,
for you are with me;
your rod and your staff,
they comfort me.

5You prepare a table before me
in the presence of my enemies.
You anoint my head with oil;
my cup overflows.
6Surely goodness and love will follow me
all the days of my life,
and I will dwell in the house of the LORD
forever.

Psalm 24

Of David. A psalm.

1The earth is the LORD's, and everything in it,
the world, and all who live in it;
2for he founded it upon the seas
and established it upon the waters.

3Who may ascend the hill of the LORD?
Who may stand in his holy place?
4He who has clean hands and a pure heart,
who does not lift up his soul to an idol
or swear by what is false.[f]
5He will receive blessing from the LORD
and vindication from God his Savior.
6Such is the generation of those who seek him,

[a] 15 Or */I am laid* [b] 16 Some Hebrew manuscripts, Septuagint and Syriac; most Hebrew manuscripts */like the lion,* [c] 21 Or */ you have heard* [d] 25 Hebrew *him* [e] 4 Or *through the darkest valley* [f] 4 Or *swear falsely*

who seek your face, O God of Jacob.[a] *Selah*

7Lift up your heads, O you gates;
be lifted up, you ancient doors,
that the King of glory may come in.
8Who is this King of glory?
The LORD strong and mighty,
the LORD mighty in battle.
9Lift up your heads, O you gates;
lift them up, you ancient doors,
that the King of glory may come in.
10Who is he, this King of glory?
The LORD Almighty—
he is the King of glory. *Selah*

Psalm 25[b]

Of David.

1To you, O LORD, I lift up my soul;
2 in you I trust, O my God.
Do not let me be put to shame,
nor let my enemies triumph over me.
3No one whose hope is in you
will ever be put to shame,
but they will be put to shame
who are treacherous without excuse.

4Show me your ways, O LORD,
teach me your paths;
5guide me in your truth and teach me,
for you are God my Savior,
and my hope is in you all day long.
6Remember, O LORD, your great mercy and love,
for they are from of old.
7Remember not the sins of my youth
and my rebellious ways;
according to your love remember me,
for you are good, O LORD.

8Good and upright is the LORD;
therefore he instructs sinners in his ways.
9He guides the humble in what is right
and teaches them his way.
10All the ways of the LORD are loving and faithful
for those who keep the demands of his covenant.
11For the sake of your name, O LORD,
forgive my iniquity, though it is great.
12Who, then, is the man that fears the LORD?
He will instruct him in the way chosen for him.
13He will spend his days in prosperity,
and his descendants will inherit the land.
14The LORD confides in those who fear him;
he makes his covenant known to them.
15My eyes are ever on the LORD,
for only he will release my feet from the snare.
16Turn to me and be gracious to me,
for I am lonely and afflicted.
17The troubles of my heart have multiplied;
free me from my anguish.
18Look upon my affliction and my distress
and take away all my sins.
19See how my enemies have increased
and how fiercely they hate me!
20Guard my life and rescue me;
let me not be put to shame,
for I take refuge in you.
21May integrity and uprightness protect me,
because my hope is in you.

22Redeem Israel, O God,
from all their troubles!

Psalm 26

Of David.

1Vindicate me, O LORD,
for I have led a blameless life;
I have trusted in the LORD
without wavering.
2Test me, O LORD, and try me,
examine my heart and my mind;
3for your love is ever before me,
and I walk continually in your truth.
4I do not sit with deceitful men,
nor do I consort with hypocrites;
5I abhor the assembly of evildoers
and refuse to sit with the wicked.
6I wash my hands in innocence,
and go about your altar, O LORD,
7proclaiming aloud your praise
and telling of all your wonderful deeds.
8I love the house where you live, O LORD,
the place where your glory dwells.

9Do not take away my soul along with sinners,
my life with bloodthirsty men,
10in whose hands are wicked schemes,
whose right hands are full of bribes.
11But I lead a blameless life;
redeem me and be merciful to me.

12My feet stand on level ground;
in the great assembly I will praise the LORD.

Psalm 27

Of David.

1The LORD is my light and my salvation—
whom shall I fear?
The LORD is the stronghold of my life—
of whom shall I be afraid?
2When evil men advance against me
to devour my flesh,[c]
when my enemies and my foes attack me,
they will stumble and fall.
3Though an army besiege me,
my heart will not fear;

[a]6 Two Hebrew manuscripts and Syriac (see also Septuagint); most Hebrew manuscripts *face, Jacob* [b]This psalm is an acrostic poem, the verses of which begin with the successive letters of the Hebrew alphabet.
[c]2 Or *to slander me*

though war break out against me,
even then will I be confident.

4One thing I ask of the LORD,
this is what I seek:
that I may dwell in the house of the LORD
all the days of my life,
to gaze upon the beauty of the LORD
and to seek him in his temple.
5For in the day of trouble
he will keep me safe in his dwelling;
he will hide me in the shelter of his tabernacle
and set me high upon a rock.
6Then my head will be exalted
above the enemies who surround me;
at his tabernacle will I sacrifice with shouts of joy;
I will sing and make music to the LORD.

7Hear my voice when I call, O LORD;
be merciful to me and answer me.
8My heart says of you, "Seek his[a] face!"
Your face, LORD, I will seek.
9Do not hide your face from me,
do not turn your servant away in anger;
you have been my helper.
Do not reject me or forsake me,
O God my Savior.
10Though my father and mother forsake me,
the LORD will receive me.
11Teach me your way, O LORD;
lead me in a straight path
because of my oppressors.
12Do not turn me over to the desire of my foes,
for false witnesses rise up against me,
breathing out violence.

13I am still confident of this:
I will see the goodness of the LORD
in the land of the living.
14Wait for the LORD;
be strong and take heart
and wait for the LORD.

Psalm 28

Of David.

1To you I call, O LORD my Rock;
do not turn a deaf ear to me.
For if you remain silent,
I will be like those who have gone down to the pit.
2Hear my cry for mercy
as I call to you for help,
as I lift up my hands
toward your Most Holy Place.

3Do not drag me away with the wicked,
with those who do evil,
who speak cordially with their neighbors
but harbor malice in their hearts.
4Repay them for their deeds
and for their evil work;
repay them for what their hands have done
and bring back upon them what they deserve.
5Since they show no regard for the works of the LORD
and what his hands have done,
he will tear them down
and never build them up again.

6Praise be to the LORD,
for he has heard my cry for mercy.
7The LORD is my strength and my shield;
my heart trusts in him, and I am helped.
My heart leaps for joy
and I will give thanks to him in song.

8The LORD is the strength of his people,
a fortress of salvation for his anointed one.
9Save your people and bless your inheritance;
be their shepherd and carry them forever.

Psalm 29

A psalm of David.

1Ascribe to the LORD, O mighty ones,
ascribe to the LORD glory and strength.
2Ascribe to the LORD the glory due his name;
worship the LORD in the splendor of his[b] holiness.

3The voice of the LORD is over the waters;
the God of glory thunders,
the LORD thunders over the mighty waters.
4The voice of the LORD is powerful;
the voice of the LORD is majestic.
5The voice of the LORD breaks the cedars;
the LORD breaks in pieces the cedars of Lebanon.
6He makes Lebanon skip like a calf,
Sirion[c] like a young wild ox.
7The voice of the LORD strikes
with flashes of lightning.
8The voice of the LORD shakes the desert;
the LORD shakes the Desert of Kadesh.
9The voice of the LORD twists the oaks[d]
and strips the forests bare.
And in his temple all cry, "Glory!"

10The LORD sits[e] enthroned over the flood;
the LORD is enthroned as King forever.
11The LORD gives strength to his people;
the LORD blesses his people with peace.

Psalm 30

A psalm. A song. For the dedication of the temple.[f] Of David.

1I will exalt you, O LORD,
for you lifted me out of the depths
and did not let my enemies gloat over me.

[a] 8 Or *To you, O my heart, he has said, "Seek my* [b] 2 Or *LORD with the splendor of* [c] 6 That is, Mount Hermon [d] 9 Or *LORD makes the deer give birth* [e] 10 Or *sat* [f] Title: Or *palace*

2O LORD my God, I called to you for help
and you healed me.
3O LORD, you brought me up from the grave[a];
you spared me from going down into the pit.

4Sing to the LORD, you saints of his;
praise his holy name.
5For his anger lasts only a moment,
but his favor lasts a lifetime;
weeping may remain for a night,
but rejoicing comes in the morning.

6When I felt secure, I said,
"I will never be shaken."
7O LORD, when you favored me,
you made my mountain[b] stand firm;
but when you hid your face,
I was dismayed.

8To you, O LORD, I called;
to the Lord I cried for mercy:
9"What gain is there in my destruction,[c]
in my going down into the pit?
Will the dust praise you?
Will it proclaim your faithfulness?
10Hear, O LORD, and be merciful to me;
O LORD, be my help."

11You turned my wailing into dancing;
you removed my sackcloth and clothed me with joy,
12that my heart may sing to you and not be silent.
O LORD my God, I will give you thanks forever.

Psalm 31

For the director of music. A psalm of David.

1In you, O LORD, I have taken refuge;
let me never be put to shame;
deliver me in your righteousness.
2Turn your ear to me,
come quickly to my rescue;
be my rock of refuge,
a strong fortress to save me.
3Since you are my rock and my fortress,
for the sake of your name lead and guide me.
4Free me from the trap that is set for me,
for you are my refuge.
5Into your hands I commit my spirit;
redeem me, O LORD, the God of truth.

6I hate those who cling to worthless idols;
I trust in the LORD.
7I will be glad and rejoice in your love,
for you saw my affliction
and knew the anguish of my soul.
8You have not handed me over to the enemy
but have set my feet in a spacious place.

9Be merciful to me, O LORD, for I am in distress;
my eyes grow weak with sorrow,
my soul and my body with grief.
10My life is consumed by anguish
and my years by groaning;
my strength fails because of my affliction,[d]
and my bones grow weak.
11Because of all my enemies,
I am the utter contempt of my neighbors;
I am a dread to my friends—
those who see me on the street flee from me.
12I am forgotten by them as though I were dead;
I have become like broken pottery.
13For I hear the slander of many;
there is terror on every side;
they conspire against me
and plot to take my life.

14But I trust in you, O LORD;
I say, "You are my God."
15My times are in your hands;
deliver me from my enemies
and from those who pursue me.
16Let your face shine on your servant;
save me in your unfailing love.
17Let me not be put to shame, O LORD,
for I have cried out to you;
but let the wicked be put to shame
and lie silent in the grave.[a]
18Let their lying lips be silenced,
for with pride and contempt
they speak arrogantly against the righteous.

19How great is your goodness,
which you have stored up for those who fear you,
which you bestow in the sight of men
on those who take refuge in you.
20In the shelter of your presence you hide them
from the intrigues of men;
in your dwelling you keep them safe
from accusing tongues.

21Praise be to the LORD,
for he showed his wonderful love to me
when I was in a besieged city.
22In my alarm I said,
"I am cut off from your sight!"
Yet you heard my cry for mercy
when I called to you for help.

23Love the LORD, all his saints!
The LORD preserves the faithful,
but the proud he pays back in full.
24Be strong and take heart,
all you who hope in the LORD.

[a]*3,17* Hebrew *Sheol* [b]*7* Or *hill country* [c]*9* Or *there if I am silenced* [d]*10* Or *guilt*

Psalm 32

Of David. A *maskil.*[a]

1Blessed is he
whose transgressions are forgiven,
whose sins are covered.
2Blessed is the man
whose sin the LORD does not count
against him
and in whose spirit is no deceit.

3When I kept silent,
my bones wasted away
through my groaning all day long.
4For day and night
your hand was heavy upon me;
my strength was sapped
as in the heat of summer. *Selah*
5Then I acknowledged my sin to you
and did not cover up my iniquity.
I said, "I will confess
my transgressions to the LORD"—
and you forgave
the guilt of my sin. *Selah*

6Therefore let everyone who is godly pray
to you
while you may be found;
surely when the mighty waters rise,
they will not reach him.
7You are my hiding place;
you will protect me from trouble
and surround me with songs of
deliverance. *Selah*

8I will instruct you and teach you in the
way you should go;
I will counsel you and watch over you.
9Do not be like the horse or the mule,
which have no understanding
but must be controlled by bit and bridle
or they will not come to you.
10Many are the woes of the wicked,
but the LORD's unfailing love
surrounds the man who trusts in him.

11Rejoice in the LORD and be glad, you
righteous;
sing, all you who are upright in heart!

Psalm 33

1Sing joyfully to the LORD, you righteous;
it is fitting for the upright to praise him.
2Praise the LORD with the harp;
make music to him on the ten-stringed
lyre.
3Sing to him a new song;
play skillfully, and shout for joy.

4For the word of the LORD is right and
true;
he is faithful in all he does.
5The LORD loves righteousness and justice;
the earth is full of his unfailing love.

6By the word of the LORD were the
heavens made,
their starry host by the breath of his
mouth.
7He gathers the waters of the sea into
jars[b];
he puts the deep into storehouses.
8Let all the earth fear the LORD;
let all the people of the world revere
him.
9For he spoke, and it came to be;
he commanded, and it stood firm.
10The LORD foils the plans of the nations;
he thwarts the purposes of the peoples.
11But the plans of the LORD stand firm
forever,
the purposes of his heart through all
generations.

12Blessed is the nation whose God is the
LORD,
the people he chose for his inheritance.
13From heaven the LORD looks down
and sees all mankind;
14from his dwelling place he watches
all who live on earth—
15he who forms the hearts of all,
who considers everything they do.
16No king is saved by the size of his army;
no warrior escapes by his great strength.
17A horse is a vain hope for deliverance;
despite all its great strength it cannot
save.
18But the eyes of the LORD are on those
who fear him,
on those whose hope is in his unfailing
love,
19to deliver them from death
and keep them alive in famine.

20We wait in hope for the LORD;
he is our help and our shield.
21In him our hearts rejoice,
for we trust in his holy name.
22May your unfailing love rest upon us,
O LORD,
even as we put our hope in you.

Psalm 34[c]

Of David. When he pretended to be insane
before Abimelech, who drove him away,
and he left.

1I will extol the LORD at all times;
his praise will always be on my lips.
2My soul will boast in the LORD;
let the afflicted hear and rejoice.
3Glorify the LORD with me;
let us exalt his name together.

4I sought the LORD, and he answered me;
he delivered me from all my fears.
5Those who look to him are radiant;
their faces are never covered with
shame.
6This poor man called, and the LORD heard
him;
he saved him out of all his troubles.

[a]Title: Probably a literary or musical term [b]7 Or *sea as into a heap* [c]This psalm is an acrostic poem, the verses of which begin with the successive letters of the Hebrew alphabet.

7The angel of the LORD encamps around
those who fear him,
and he delivers them.

8Taste and see that the LORD is good;
blessed is the man who takes refuge in
him.
9Fear the LORD, you his saints,
for those who fear him lack nothing.
10The lions may grow weak and hungry,
but those who seek the LORD lack no
good thing.

11Come, my children, listen to me;
I will teach you the fear of the LORD.
12Whoever of you loves life
and desires to see many good days,
13keep your tongue from evil
and your lips from speaking lies.
14Turn from evil and do good;
seek peace and pursue it.

15The eyes of the LORD are on the righteous
and his ears are attentive to their cry;
16the face of the LORD is against those who
do evil,
to cut off the memory of them from the
earth.

17The righteous cry out, and the LORD hears
them;
he delivers them from all their troubles.
18The LORD is close to the brokenhearted
and saves those who are crushed in
spirit.

19A righteous man may have many troubles,
but the LORD delivers him from them
all;
20he protects all his bones,
not one of them will be broken.

21Evil will slay the wicked;
the foes of the righteous will be
condemned.
22The LORD redeems his servants;
no one will be condemned who takes
refuge in him.

Psalm 35

Of David.

1Contend, O LORD, with those who contend
with me;
fight against those who fight against
me.
2Take up shield and buckler;
arise and come to my aid.
3Brandish spear and javelin[a]
against those who pursue me.
Say to my soul,
"I am your salvation."

4May those who seek my life
be disgraced and put to shame;
may those who plot my ruin
be turned back in dismay.
5May they be like chaff before the wind,
with the angel of the LORD driving
them away;
6may their path be dark and slippery,
with the angel of the LORD pursuing
them.
7Since they hid their net for me without
cause
and without cause dug a pit for me,
8may ruin overtake them by surprise—
may the net they hid entangle them,
may they fall into the pit, to their ruin.
9Then my soul will rejoice in the LORD
and delight in his salvation.
10My whole being will exclaim,
"Who is like you, O LORD?
You rescue the poor from those too strong
for them,
the poor and needy from those who rob
them."

11Ruthless witnesses come forward;
they question me on things I know
nothing about.
12They repay me evil for good
and leave my soul forlorn.
13Yet when they were ill, I put on sackcloth
and humbled myself with fasting.
When my prayers returned to me
unanswered,
14 I went about mourning
as though for my friend or brother.
I bowed my head in grief
as though weeping for my mother.
15But when I stumbled, they gathered in
glee;
attackers gathered against me when I
was unaware.
They slandered me without ceasing.
16Like the ungodly they maliciously
mocked[b];
they gnashed their teeth at me.
17O Lord, how long will you look on?
Rescue my life from their ravages,
my precious life from these lions.
18I will give you thanks in the great
assembly;
among throngs of people I will praise
you.

19Let not those gloat over me
who are my enemies without cause;
let not those who hate me without reason
maliciously wink the eye.
20They do not speak peaceably,
but devise false accusations
against those who live quietly in the
land.
21They gape at me and say, "Aha! Aha!
With our own eyes we have seen it."

22O LORD, you have seen this; be not silent.
Do not be far from me, O Lord.
23Awake, and rise to my defense!
Contend for me, my God and Lord.
24Vindicate me in your righteousness,
O LORD my God;

[a] 3 Or *and block the way* [b] 16 Septuagint; Hebrew may mean *ungodly circle of mockers.*

do not let them gloat over me.
25Do not let them think, "Aha, just what we wanted!"
or say, "We have swallowed him up."

26May all who gloat over my distress
be put to shame and confusion;
may all who exalt themselves over me
be clothed with shame and disgrace.
27May those who delight in my vindication
shout for joy and gladness;
may they always say, "The LORD be exalted,
who delights in the well-being of his servant."
28My tongue will speak of your righteousness
and of your praises all day long.

Psalm 36

For the director of music. Of David the servant of the LORD.

1An oracle is within my heart
concerning the sinfulness of the wicked:[a]
There is no fear of God
before his eyes.
2For in his own eyes he flatters himself
too much to detect or hate his sin.
3The words of his mouth are wicked and deceitful;
he has ceased to be wise and to do good.
4Even on his bed he plots evil;
he commits himself to a sinful course
and does not reject what is wrong.

5Your love, O LORD, reaches to the heavens,
your faithfulness to the skies.
6Your righteousness is like the mighty mountains,
your justice like the great deep.
O LORD, you preserve both man and beast.
7 How priceless is your unfailing love!
Both high and low among men
find[b] refuge in the shadow of your wings.
8They feast on the abundance of your house;
you give them drink from your river of delights.
9For with you is the fountain of life;
in your light we see light.

10Continue your love to those who know you,
your righteousness to the upright in heart.
11May the foot of the proud not come against me,
nor the hand of the wicked drive me away.
12See how the evildoers lie fallen—
thrown down, not able to rise!

Psalm 37[c]

Of David.

1Do not fret because of evil men
or be envious of those who do wrong;
2for like the grass they will soon wither,
like green plants they will soon die away.

3Trust in the LORD and do good;
dwell in the land and enjoy safe pasture.
4Delight yourself in the LORD
and he will give you the desires of your heart.

5Commit your way to the LORD;
trust in him and he will do this:
6He will make your righteousness shine like the dawn,
the justice of your cause like the noonday sun.

7Be still before the LORD and wait patiently for him;
do not fret when men succeed in their ways,
when they carry out their wicked schemes.

8Refrain from anger and turn from wrath;
do not fret—it leads only to evil.
9For evil men will be cut off,
but those who hope in the LORD will inherit the land.

10A little while, and the wicked will be no more;
though you look for them, they will not be found.
11But the meek will inherit the land
and enjoy great peace.

12The wicked plot against the righteous
and gnash their teeth at them;
13but the Lord laughs at the wicked,
for he knows their day is coming.

14The wicked draw the sword
and bend the bow
to bring down the poor and needy,
to slay those whose ways are upright.
15But their swords will pierce their own hearts,
and their bows will be broken.

16Better the little that the righteous have
than the wealth of many wicked;
17for the power of the wicked will be broken,
but the LORD upholds the righteous.

18The days of the blameless are known to the LORD,
and their inheritance will endure forever.

[a] 1 Or *heart: / Sin proceeds from the wicked.* [b] 7 Or *love, O God! / Men find*; or *love! / Both heavenly beings and men / find* [c] This psalm is an acrostic poem, the stanzas of which begin with the successive letters of the Hebrew alphabet.

19In times of disaster they will not wither;
in days of famine they will enjoy plenty.

20But the wicked will perish:
The LORD's enemies will be like the beauty of the fields,
they will vanish—vanish like smoke.

21The wicked borrow and do not repay,
but the righteous give generously;
22those the LORD blesses will inherit the land,
but those he curses will be cut off.

23If the LORD delights in a man's way,
he makes his steps firm;
24though he stumble, he will not fall,
for the LORD upholds him with his hand.

25I was young and now I am old,
yet I have never seen the righteous forsaken
or their children begging bread.
26They are always generous and lend freely;
their children will be blessed.

27Turn from evil and do good;
then you will dwell in the land forever.
28For the LORD loves the just
and will not forsake his faithful ones.

They will be protected forever,
but the offspring of the wicked will be cut off;
29the righteous will inherit the land
and dwell in it forever.

30The mouth of the righteous man utters wisdom,
and his tongue speaks what is just.
31The law of his God is in his heart;
his feet do not slip.

32The wicked lie in wait for the righteous,
seeking their very lives;
33but the LORD will not leave them in their power
or let them be condemned when brought to trial.

34Wait for the LORD
and keep his way.
He will exalt you to inherit the land;
when the wicked are cut off, you will see it.

35I have seen a wicked and ruthless man
flourishing like a green tree in its native soil,
36but he soon passed away and was no more;
though I looked for him, he could not be found.

37Consider the blameless, observe the upright;
there is a future[a] for the man of peace.
38But all sinners will be destroyed;
the future[b] of the wicked will be cut off.

39The salvation of the righteous comes from the LORD;
he is their stronghold in time of trouble.
40The LORD helps them and delivers them;
he delivers them from the wicked and saves them,
because they take refuge in him.

Psalm 38

A psalm of David. A petition.

1O LORD, do not rebuke me in your anger
or discipline me in your wrath.
2For your arrows have pierced me,
and your hand has come down upon me.
3Because of your wrath there is no health in my body;
my bones have no soundness because of my sin.
4My guilt has overwhelmed me
like a burden too heavy to bear.

5My wounds fester and are loathsome
because of my sinful folly.
6I am bowed down and brought very low;
all day long I go about mourning.
7My back is filled with searing pain;
there is no health in my body.
8I am feeble and utterly crushed;
I groan in anguish of heart.

9All my longings lie open before you, O Lord;
my sighing is not hidden from you.
10My heart pounds, my strength fails me;
even the light has gone from my eyes.
11My friends and companions avoid me
because of my wounds;
my neighbors stay far away.
12Those who seek my life set their traps,
those who would harm me talk of my ruin;
all day long they plot deception.

13I am like a deaf man, who cannot hear,
like a mute, who cannot open his mouth;
14I have become like a man who does not hear,
whose mouth can offer no reply.
15I wait for you, O LORD;
you will answer, O Lord my God.
16For I said, "Do not let them gloat
or exalt themselves over me when my foot slips."

17For I am about to fall,
and my pain is ever with me.
18I confess my iniquity;
I am troubled by my sin.
19Many are those who are my vigorous enemies;
those who hate me without reason are numerous.

[a]37 Or *there will be posterity* [b]38 Or *posterity*

20Those who repay my good with evil
slander me when I pursue what is good.

21O LORD, do not forsake me;
be not far from me, O my God.
22Come quickly to help me,
O Lord my Savior.

Psalm 39

For the director of music. For Jeduthun.
A psalm of David.

1I said, "I will watch my ways
and keep my tongue from sin;
I will put a muzzle on my mouth
as long as the wicked are in my
presence."
2But when I was silent and still,
not even saying anything good,
my anguish increased.
3My heart grew hot within me,
and as I meditated, the fire burned;
then I spoke with my tongue:

4"Show me, O LORD, my life's end
and the number of my days;
let me know how fleeting is my life.
5You have made my days a mere
handbreadth;
the span of my years is as nothing
before you.
Each man's life is but a breath. *Selah*
6Man is a mere phantom as he goes to and
fro:
He bustles about, but only in vain;
he heaps up wealth, not knowing who
will get it.

7"But now, Lord, what do I look for?
My hope is in you.
8Save me from all my transgressions;
do not make me the scorn of fools.
9I was silent; I would not open my mouth,
for you are the one who has done this.
10Remove your scourge from me;
I am overcome by the blow of your
hand.
11You rebuke and discipline men for their
sin;
you consume their wealth like a moth—
each man is but a breath. *Selah*

12"Hear my prayer, O LORD,
listen to my cry for help;
be not deaf to my weeping.
For I dwell with you as an alien,
a stranger, as all my fathers were.
13Look away from me, that I may rejoice
again
before I depart and am no more."

Psalm 40

For the director of music. Of David.
A psalm.

1I waited patiently for the LORD;
he turned to me and heard my cry.
2He lifted me out of the slimy pit,
out of the mud and mire;
he set my feet on a rock
and gave me a firm place to stand.
3He put a new song in my mouth,
a hymn of praise to our God.
Many will see and fear
and put their trust in the LORD.

4Blessed is the man
who makes the LORD his trust,
who does not look to the proud,
to those who turn aside to false gods.[a]
5Many, O LORD my God,
are the wonders you have done.
The things you planned for us
no one can recount to you;
were I to speak and tell of them,
they would be too many to declare.

6Sacrifice and offering you did not desire,
but my ears you have pierced[b, c];
burnt offerings and sin offerings
you did not require.
7Then I said, "Here I am, I have come—
it is written about me in the scroll.[d]
8I desire to do your will, O my God;
your law is within my heart."

9I proclaim righteousness in the great
assembly;
I do not seal my lips,
as you know, O LORD.
10I do not hide your righteousness in my
heart;
I speak of your faithfulness and
salvation.
I do not conceal your love and your truth
from the great assembly.

11Do not withhold your mercy from me,
O LORD;
may your love and your truth always
protect me.
12For troubles without number surround me;
my sins have overtaken me, and I
cannot see.
They are more than the hairs of my head,
and my heart fails within me.

13Be pleased, O LORD, to save me;
O LORD, come quickly to help me.
14May all who seek to take my life
be put to shame and confusion;
may all who desire my ruin
be turned back in disgrace.
15May those who say to me, "Aha! Aha!"
be appalled at their own shame.
16But may all who seek you
rejoice and be glad in you;
may those who love your salvation always
say,
"The LORD be exalted!"

17Yet I am poor and needy;
may the Lord think of me.

[a]4 Or *to falsehood* [b]6 Hebrew; Septuagint *but a body you have prepared for me* (see also Symmachus and Theodotion) [c]6 Or *opened* [d]7 Or *come / with the scroll written for me*

You are my help and my deliverer;
O my God, do not delay.

Psalm 41

For the director of music. A psalm of David.

1Blessed is he who has regard for the weak;
the LORD delivers him in times of trouble.
2The LORD will protect him and preserve his life;
he will bless him in the land
and not surrender him to the desire of his foes.
3The LORD will sustain him on his sickbed
and restore him from his bed of illness.

4I said, "O LORD, have mercy on me;
heal me, for I have sinned against you."
5My enemies say of me in malice,
"When will he die and his name perish?"
6Whenever one comes to see me,
he speaks falsely, while his heart gathers slander;
then he goes out and spreads it abroad.

7All my enemies whisper together against me;
they imagine the worst for me, saying,
8"A vile disease has beset him;
he will never get up from the place where he lies."
9Even my close friend, whom I trusted,
he who shared my bread,
has lifted up his heel against me.

10But you, O LORD, have mercy on me;
raise me up, that I may repay them.
11I know that you are pleased with me,
for my enemy does not triumph over me.
12In my integrity you uphold me
and set me in your presence forever.

13Praise be to the LORD, the God of Israel,
from everlasting to everlasting.
Amen and Amen.

BOOK II

Psalms 42–72

Psalm 42[a]

For the director of music. A *maskil*[b] of the Sons of Korah.

1As the deer pants for streams of water,
so my soul pants for you, O God.
2My soul thirsts for God, for the living God.
When can I go and meet with God?
3My tears have been my food
day and night,
while men say to me all day long,
"Where is your God?"
4These things I remember
as I pour out my soul:
how I used to go with the multitude,
leading the procession to the house of God,
with shouts of joy and thanksgiving
among the festive throng.

5Why are you downcast, O my soul?
Why so disturbed within me?
Put your hope in God,
for I will yet praise him,
my Savior and 6my God.

My[c] soul is downcast within me;
therefore I will remember you
from the land of the Jordan,
the heights of Hermon—from Mount Mizar.
7Deep calls to deep
in the roar of your waterfalls;
all your waves and breakers
have swept over me.

8By day the LORD directs his love,
at night his song is with me—
a prayer to the God of my life.

9I say to God my Rock,
"Why have you forgotten me?
Why must I go about mourning,
oppressed by the enemy?"
10My bones suffer mortal agony
as my foes taunt me,
saying to me all day long,
"Where is your God?"

11Why are you downcast, O my soul?
Why so disturbed within me?
Put your hope in God,
for I will yet praise him,
my Savior and my God.

Psalm 43[a]

1Vindicate me, O God,
and plead my cause against an ungodly nation;
rescue me from deceitful and wicked men.
2You are God my stronghold.
Why have you rejected me?
Why must I go about mourning,
oppressed by the enemy?
3Send forth your light and your truth,
let them guide me;
let them bring me to your holy mountain,
to the place where you dwell.
4Then will I go to the altar of God,
to God, my joy and my delight.
I will praise you with the harp,
O God, my God.

5Why are you downcast, O my soul?
Why so disturbed within me?

[a]In many Hebrew manuscripts Psalms 42 and 43 constitute one psalm. [b]Title: Probably a literary or musical term [c]*5,6* A few Hebrew manuscripts, Septuagint and Syriac; most Hebrew manuscripts *praise him for his saving help. / [6]O my God, my*

Put your hope in God,
for I will yet praise him,
my Savior and my God.

Psalm 44

For the director of music. Of the Sons of Korah. A *maskil.* [a]

1We have heard with our ears, O God;
our fathers have told us
what you did in their days,
in days long ago.
2With your hand you drove out the nations
and planted our fathers;
you crushed the peoples
and made our fathers flourish.
3It was not by their sword that they won
the land,
nor did their arm bring them victory;
it was your right hand, your arm,
and the light of your face, for you loved
them.

4You are my King and my God,
who decrees[b] victories for Jacob.
5Through you we push back our enemies;
through your name we trample our foes.
6I do not trust in my bow,
my sword does not bring me victory;
7but you give us victory over our enemies,
you put our adversaries to shame.
8In God we make our boast all day long,
and we will praise your name forever.
Selah

9But now you have rejected and humbled
us;
you no longer go out with our armies.
10You made us retreat before the enemy,
and our adversaries have plundered us.
11You gave us up to be devoured like sheep
and have scattered us among the
nations.
12You sold your people for a pittance,
gaining nothing from their sale.

13You have made us a reproach to our
neighbors,
the scorn and derision of those around
us.
14You have made us a byword among the
nations;
the peoples shake their heads at us.
15My disgrace is before me all day long,
and my face is covered with shame
16at the taunts of those who reproach and
revile me,
because of the enemy, who is bent on
revenge.

17All this happened to us,
though we had not forgotten you
or been false to your covenant.
18Our hearts had not turned back;
our feet had not strayed from your path.
19But you crushed us and made us a haunt
for jackals
and covered us over with deep darkness.

20If we had forgotten the name of our God
or spread out our hands to a foreign
god,
21would not God have discovered it,
since he knows the secrets of the heart?
22Yet for your sake we face death all day
long;
we are considered as sheep to be
slaughtered.

23Awake, O Lord! Why do you sleep?
Rouse yourself! Do not reject us
forever.
24Why do you hide your face
and forget our misery and oppression?

25We are brought down to the dust;
our bodies cling to the ground.
26Rise up and help us;
redeem us because of your unfailing
love.

Psalm 45

For the director of music. To ⌊the tune of⌋ "Lilies." Of the Sons of Korah. A *maskil.* [a] A wedding song.

1My heart is stirred by a noble theme
as I recite my verses for the king;
my tongue is the pen of a skillful
writer.

2You are the most excellent of men
and your lips have been anointed with
grace,
since God has blessed you forever.
3Gird your sword upon your side,
O mighty one;
clothe yourself with splendor and
majesty.
4In your majesty ride forth victoriously
in behalf of truth, humility and
righteousness;
let your right hand display awesome
deeds.
5Let your sharp arrows pierce the hearts of
the king's enemies;
let the nations fall beneath your feet.
6Your throne, O God, will last for ever and
ever;
a scepter of justice will be the scepter
of your kingdom.
7You love righteousness and hate
wickedness;
therefore God, your God, has set you
above your companions
by anointing you with the oil of joy.
8All your robes are fragrant with myrrh and
aloes and cassia;
from palaces adorned with ivory
the music of the strings makes you glad.
9Daughters of kings are among your
honored women;

[a]Title: Probably a literary or musical term [b]4 Septuagint, Aquila and Syriac; Hebrew *King, O God; / command*

at your right hand is the royal bride in
gold of Ophir.

10 Listen, O daughter, consider and give ear:
Forget your people and your father's
house.
11 The king is enthralled by your beauty;
honor him, for he is your lord.
12 The Daughter of Tyre will come with a
gift,[a]
men of wealth will seek your favor.

13 All glorious is the princess within ⌊her
chamber⌋;
her gown is interwoven with gold.
14 In embroidered garments she is led to the
king;
her virgin companions follow her
and are brought to you.
15 They are led in with joy and gladness;
they enter the palace of the king.

16 Your sons will take the place of your
fathers;
you will make them princes throughout
the land.
17 I will perpetuate your memory through all
generations;
therefore the nations will praise you for
ever and ever.

Psalm 46

For the director of music. Of the Sons of Korah. According to *alamoth*.[b] A song.

1 God is our refuge and strength,
an ever-present help in trouble.
2 Therefore we will not fear, though the
earth give way
and the mountains fall into the heart of
the sea,
3 though its waters roar and foam
and the mountains quake with their
surging. *Selah*

4 There is a river whose streams make glad
the city of God,
the holy place where the Most High
dwells.
5 God is within her, she will not fall;
God will help her at break of day.
6 Nations are in uproar, kingdoms fall;
he lifts his voice, the earth melts.

7 The LORD Almighty is with us;
the God of Jacob is our fortress. *Selah*

8 Come and see the works of the LORD,
the desolations he has brought on the
earth.
9 He makes wars cease to the ends of the
earth;
he breaks the bow and shatters the
spear,
he burns the shields[c] with fire.
10 "Be still, and know that I am God;
I will be exalted among the nations,
I will be exalted in the earth."
11 The LORD Almighty is with us;
the God of Jacob is our fortress. *Selah*

Psalm 47

For the director of music. Of the Sons of Korah. A psalm.

1 Clap your hands, all you nations;
shout to God with cries of joy.
2 How awesome is the LORD Most High,
the great King over all the earth!
3 He subdued nations under us,
peoples under our feet.
4 He chose our inheritance for us,
the pride of Jacob, whom he loved.
Selah

5 God has ascended amid shouts of joy,
the LORD amid the sounding of
trumpets.
6 Sing praises to God, sing praises;
sing praises to our King, sing praises.

7 For God is the King of all the earth;
sing to him a psalm[d] of praise.
8 God reigns over the nations;
God is seated on his holy throne.
9 The nobles of the nations assemble
as the people of the God of Abraham,
for the kings[e] of the earth belong to God;
he is greatly exalted.

Psalm 48

A song. A psalm of the Sons of Korah.

1 Great is the LORD, and most worthy of
praise,
in the city of our God, his holy
mountain.
2 It is beautiful in its loftiness,
the joy of the whole earth.
Like the utmost heights of Zaphon[f] is
Mount Zion,
the[g] city of the Great King.
3 God is in her citadels;
he has shown himself to be her fortress.

4 When the kings joined forces,
when they advanced together,
5 they saw ⌊her⌋ and were astounded;
they fled in terror.
6 Trembling seized them there,
pain like that of a woman in labor.
7 You destroyed them like ships of Tarshish
shattered by an east wind.

8 As we have heard,
so have we seen
in the city of the LORD Almighty,
in the city of our God:
God makes her secure forever. *Selah*

9 Within your temple, O God,
we meditate on your unfailing love.

[a] 12 Or *A Tyrian robe is among the gifts* [b] Title: Probably a musical term [c] 9 Or *chariots* [d] 7 Or *a maskil* (probably a literary or musical term) [e] 9 Or *shields* [f] 2 *Zaphon* can refer to a sacred mountain or the direction north. [g] 2 Or *earth, / Mount Zion, on the northern side / of the*

10Like your name, O God,
your praise reaches to the ends of the earth;
your right hand is filled with righteousness.
11Mount Zion rejoices,
the villages of Judah are glad
because of your judgments.

12Walk about Zion, go around her,
count her towers,
13consider well her ramparts,
view her citadels,
that you may tell of them to the next generation.
14For this God is our God for ever and ever;
he will be our guide even to the end.

Psalm 49

For the director of music. Of the Sons of Korah. A psalm.

1Hear this, all you peoples;
listen, all who live in this world,
2both low and high,
rich and poor alike:
3My mouth will speak words of wisdom;
the utterance from my heart will give understanding.
4I will turn my ear to a proverb;
with the harp I will expound my riddle:

5Why should I fear when evil days come,
when wicked deceivers surround me—
6those who trust in their wealth
and boast of their great riches?
7No man can redeem the life of another
or give to God a ransom for him—
8the ransom for a life is costly,
no payment is ever enough—
9that he should live on forever
and not see decay.

10For all can see that wise men die;
the foolish and the senseless alike perish
and leave their wealth to others.
11Their tombs will remain their houses[a] forever,
their dwellings for endless generations,
though they had[b] named lands after themselves.

12But man, despite his riches, does not endure;
he is[c] like the beasts that perish.

13This is the fate of those who trust in themselves,
and of their followers, who approve their sayings. *Selah*
14Like sheep they are destined for the grave,[d]
and death will feed on them.
The upright will rule over them in the morning;
their forms will decay in the grave,[d]
far from their princely mansions.
15But God will redeem my life[e] from the grave;
he will surely take me to himself. *Selah*

16Do not be overawed when a man grows rich,
when the splendor of his house increases;
17for he will take nothing with him when he dies,
his splendor will not descend with him.
18Though while he lived he counted himself blessed—
and men praise you when you prosper—
19he will join the generation of his fathers,
who will never see the light ⌊of life⌋.

20A man who has riches without understanding
is like the beasts that perish.

Psalm 50

A psalm of Asaph.

1The Mighty One, God, the LORD,
speaks and summons the earth
from the rising of the sun to the place where it sets.
2From Zion, perfect in beauty,
God shines forth.
3Our God comes and will not be silent;
a fire devours before him,
and around him a tempest rages.
4He summons the heavens above,
and the earth, that he may judge his people:
5"Gather to me my consecrated ones,
who made a covenant with me by sacrifice."
6And the heavens proclaim his righteousness,
for God himself is judge. *Selah*

7"Hear, O my people, and I will speak,
O Israel, and I will testify against you:
I am God, your God.
8I do not rebuke you for your sacrifices
or your burnt offerings, which are ever before me.
9I have no need of a bull from your stall
or of goats from your pens,
10for every animal of the forest is mine,
and the cattle on a thousand hills.
11I know every bird in the mountains,
and the creatures of the field are mine.
12If I were hungry I would not tell you,
for the world is mine, and all that is in it.
13Do I eat the flesh of bulls
or drink the blood of goats?
14Sacrifice thank offerings to God,
fulfill your vows to the Most High,
15and call upon me in the day of trouble;

[a] *11* Septuagint and Syriac; Hebrew *In their thoughts their houses will remain* [b] *11* Or */for they have*
[c] *12* Hebrew; Septuagint and Syriac read verse 12 the same as verse 20. [d] *14* Hebrew *Sheol*; also in verse 15
[e] *15* Or *soul*

I will deliver you, and you will honor
me."

16But to the wicked, God says:

"What right have you to recite my laws
or take my covenant on your lips?
17You hate my instruction
and cast my words behind you.
18When you see a thief, you join with him;
you throw in your lot with adulterers.
19You use your mouth for evil
and harness your tongue to deceit.
20You speak continually against your brother
and slander your own mother's son.
21These things you have done and I kept
silent;
you thought I was altogether[a] like you.
But I will rebuke you
and accuse you to your face.

22"Consider this, you who forget God,
or I will tear you to pieces, with none
to rescue:
23He who sacrifices thank offerings honors
me,
and he prepares the way
so that I may show him[b] the salvation
of God."

Psalm 51

For the director of music. A psalm of David. When the prophet Nathan came to him after David had committed adultery with Bathsheba.

1Have mercy on me, O God,
according to your unfailing love;
according to your great compassion
blot out my transgressions.
2Wash away all my iniquity
and cleanse me from my sin.

3For I know my transgressions,
and my sin is always before me.
4Against you, you only, have I sinned
and done what is evil in your sight,
so that you are proved right when you
speak
and justified when you judge.
5Surely I was sinful at birth,
sinful from the time my mother
conceived me.
6Surely you desire truth in the inner parts[c];
you teach[d] me wisdom in the inmost
place.

7Cleanse me with hyssop, and I will be
clean;
wash me, and I will be whiter than
snow.
8Let me hear joy and gladness;
let the bones you have crushed rejoice.
9Hide your face from my sins
and blot out all my iniquity.

10Create in me a pure heart, O God,
and renew a steadfast spirit within me.
11Do not cast me from your presence
or take your Holy Spirit from me.
12Restore to me the joy of your salvation
and grant me a willing spirit, to sustain
me.

13Then I will teach transgressors your ways,
and sinners will turn back to you.
14Save me from bloodguilt, O God,
the God who saves me,
and my tongue will sing of your
righteousness.
15O Lord, open my lips,
and my mouth will declare your praise.
16You do not delight in sacrifice, or I would
bring it;
you do not take pleasure in burnt
offerings.
17The sacrifices of God are[e] a broken spirit;
a broken and contrite heart,
O God, you will not despise.

18In your good pleasure make Zion prosper;
build up the walls of Jerusalem.
19Then there will be righteous sacrifices,
whole burnt offerings to delight you;
then bulls will be offered on your altar.

Psalm 52

For the director of music. A *maskil*[f] of David. When Doeg the Edomite had gone to Saul and told him: "David has gone to the house of Ahimelech."

1Why do you boast of evil, you mighty
man?
Why do you boast all day long,
you who are a disgrace in the eyes of
God?
2Your tongue plots destruction;
it is like a sharpened razor,
you who practice deceit.
3You love evil rather than good,
falsehood rather than speaking the truth.
Selah
4You love every harmful word,
O you deceitful tongue!

5Surely God will bring you down to
everlasting ruin:
He will snatch you up and tear you
from your tent;
he will uproot you from the land of the
living. *Selah*
6The righteous will see and fear;
they will laugh at him, saying,
7"Here now is the man
who did not make God his stronghold
but trusted in his great wealth
and grew strong by destroying others!"

8But I am like an olive tree
flourishing in the house of God;
I trust in God's unfailing love
for ever and ever.

[a]21 Or *thought the 'I AM' was* [b]23 Or *and to him who considers his way / I will show* [c]6 The meaning of the Hebrew for this phrase is uncertain. [d]6 Or *you desired . . . ; / you taught* [e]17 Or *My sacrifice, O God, is* [f]Title: Probably a literary or musical term

9I will praise you forever for what you
have done;
in your name I will hope, for your
name is good.
I will praise you in the presence of your
saints.

Psalm 53

For the director of music. According to *mahalath.*[a] A *maskil*[b] of David.

1The fool says in his heart,
"There is no God."
They are corrupt, and their ways are vile;
there is no one who does good.

2God looks down from heaven
on the sons of men
to see if there are any who understand,
any who seek God.
3Everyone has turned away,
they have together become corrupt;
there is no one who does good,
not even one.

4Will the evildoers never learn—
those who devour my people as men eat
bread
and who do not call on God?
5There they were, overwhelmed with dread,
where there was nothing to dread.
God scattered the bones of those who
attacked you;
you put them to shame, for God
despised them.

6Oh, that salvation for Israel would come
out of Zion!
When God restores the fortunes of his
people,
let Jacob rejoice and Israel be glad!

Psalm 54

For the director of music. With stringed instruments. A *maskil*[b] of David. When the Ziphites had gone to Saul and said, "Is not David hiding among us?"

1Save me, O God, by your name;
vindicate me by your might.
2Hear my prayer, O God;
listen to the words of my mouth.

3Strangers are attacking me;
ruthless men seek my life—
men without regard for God. *Selah*

4Surely God is my help;
the Lord is the one who sustains me.

5Let evil recoil on those who slander me;
in your faithfulness destroy them.

6I will sacrifice a freewill offering to you;
I will praise your name, O LORD,
for it is good.

7For he has delivered me from all my
troubles,
and my eyes have looked in triumph on
my foes.

Psalm 55

For the director of music. With stringed instruments. A *maskil*[b] of David.

1Listen to my prayer, O God,
do not ignore my plea;
2 hear me and answer me.
My thoughts trouble me and I am
distraught
3 at the voice of the enemy,
at the stares of the wicked;
for they bring down suffering upon me
and revile me in their anger.

4My heart is in anguish within me;
the terrors of death assail me.
5Fear and trembling have beset me;
horror has overwhelmed me.
6I said, "Oh, that I had the wings of a
dove!
I would fly away and be at rest—
7I would flee far away
and stay in the desert; *Selah*
8I would hurry to my place of shelter,
far from the tempest and storm."

9Confuse the wicked, O Lord, confound
their speech,
for I see violence and strife in the city.
10Day and night they prowl about on its
walls;
malice and abuse are within it.
11Destructive forces are at work in the city;
threats and lies never leave its streets.

12If an enemy were insulting me,
I could endure it;
if a foe were raising himself against me,
I could hide from him.
13But it is you, a man like myself,
my companion, my close friend,
14with whom I once enjoyed sweet
fellowship
as we walked with the throng at the
house of God.

15Let death take my enemies by surprise;
let them go down alive to the grave,[c]
for evil finds lodging among them.

16But I call to God,
and the LORD saves me.
17Evening, morning and noon
I cry out in distress,
and he hears my voice.
18He ransoms me unharmed
from the battle waged against me,
even though many oppose me.
19God, who is enthroned forever,
will hear them and afflict them— *Selah*

[a]Title: Probably a musical term [b]Title: Probably a literary or musical term [c]*15* Hebrew *Sheol*

men who never change their ways
and have no fear of God.

20My companion attacks his friends;
he violates his covenant.
21His speech is smooth as butter,
yet war is in his heart;
his words are more soothing than oil,
yet they are drawn swords.

22Cast your cares on the LORD
and he will sustain you;
he will never let the righteous fall.
23But you, O God, will bring down the wicked
into the pit of corruption;
bloodthirsty and deceitful men
will not live out half their days.

But as for me, I trust in you.

Psalm 56

For the director of music. To ⌊the tune of⌋ "A Dove on Distant Oaks." Of David. A *miktam.*[a] When the Philistines had seized him in Gath.

1Be merciful to me, O God, for men hotly pursue me;
all day long they press their attack.
2My slanderers pursue me all day long;
many are attacking me in their pride.

3When I am afraid,
I will trust in you.
4In God, whose word I praise,
in God I trust; I will not be afraid.
What can mortal man do to me?

5All day long they twist my words;
they are always plotting to harm me.
6They conspire, they lurk,
they watch my steps,
eager to take my life.

7On no account let them escape;
in your anger, O God, bring down the nations.
8Record my lament;
list my tears on your scroll[b]—
are they not in your record?

9Then my enemies will turn back
when I call for help.
By this I will know that God is for me.
10In God, whose word I praise,
in the LORD, whose word I praise—
11in God I trust; I will not be afraid.
What can man do to me?

12I am under vows to you, O God;
I will present my thank offerings to you.
13For you have delivered me[c] from death
and my feet from stumbling,
that I may walk before God
in the light of life.[d]

Psalm 57

For the director of music. ⌊To the tune of⌋ "Do Not Destroy." Of David. A *miktam.*[a] When he had fled from Saul into the cave.

1Have mercy on me, O God, have mercy on me,
for in you my soul takes refuge.
I will take refuge in the shadow of your wings
until the disaster has passed.

2I cry out to God Most High,
to God, who fulfills ⌊his purpose⌋ for me.
3He sends from heaven and saves me,
rebuking those who hotly pursue me; *Selah*
God sends his love and his faithfulness.

4I am in the midst of lions;
I lie among ravenous beasts—
men whose teeth are spears and arrows,
whose tongues are sharp swords.

5Be exalted, O God, above the heavens;
let your glory be over all the earth.

6They spread a net for my feet—
I was bowed down in distress.
They dug a pit in my path—
but they have fallen into it themselves. *Selah*

7My heart is steadfast, O God,
my heart is steadfast;
I will sing and make music.
8Awake, my soul!
Awake, harp and lyre!
I will awaken the dawn.

9I will praise you, O Lord, among the nations;
I will sing of you among the peoples.
10For great is your love, reaching to the heavens;
your faithfulness reaches to the skies.

11Be exalted, O God, above the heavens;
let your glory be over all the earth.

Psalm 58

For the director of music. ⌊To the tune of⌋ "Do Not Destroy." Of David. A *miktam.*[a]

1Do you rulers indeed speak justly?
Do you judge uprightly among men?
2No, in your heart you devise injustice,
and your hands mete out violence on the earth.
3Even from birth the wicked go astray;
from the womb they are wayward and speak lies.
4Their venom is like the venom of a snake,
like that of a cobra that has stopped its ears,
5that will not heed the tune of the charmer,
however skillful the enchanter may be.

[a]Title: Probably a literary or musical term [b]8 Or *I put my tears in your wineskin* [c]13 Or *my soul*
[d]13 Or *the land of the living*

6Break the teeth in their mouths, O God;
tear out, O LORD, the fangs of the lions!
7Let them vanish like water that flows away;
when they draw the bow, let their arrows be blunted.
8Like a slug melting away as it moves along,
like a stillborn child, may they not see the sun.

9Before your pots can feel ⌞the heat of⌟ the thorns—
whether they be green or dry—the wicked will be swept away.[a]
10The righteous will be glad when they are avenged,
when they bathe their feet in the blood of the wicked.
11Then men will say,
"Surely the righteous still are rewarded;
surely there is a God who judges the earth."

12For the sins of their mouths,
for the words of their lips,
let them be caught in their pride.
For the curses and lies they utter,
13 consume them in wrath,
consume them till they are no more.
Then it will be known to the ends of the earth
that God rules over Jacob. *Selah*

14They return at evening,
snarling like dogs,
and prowl about the city.
15They wander about for food
and howl if not satisfied.
16But I will sing of your strength,
in the morning I will sing of your love;
for you are my fortress,
my refuge in times of trouble.

17O my Strength, I sing praise to you;
you, O God, are my fortress, my loving God.

Psalm 59

For the director of music. ⌞To the tune of⌟ "Do Not Destroy." Of David. A *miktam.*[b] When Saul had sent men to watch David's house in order to kill him.

1Deliver me from my enemies, O God;
protect me from those who rise up against me.
2Deliver me from evildoers
and save me from bloodthirsty men.

3See how they lie in wait for me!
Fierce men conspire against me
for no offense or sin of mine, O LORD.
4I have done no wrong, yet they are ready to attack me.
Arise to help me; look on my plight!
5O LORD God Almighty, the God of Israel,
rouse yourself to punish all the nations;
show no mercy to wicked traitors. *Selah*

6They return at evening,
snarling like dogs,
and prowl about the city.
7See what they spew from their mouths—
they spew out swords from their lips,
and they say, "Who can hear us?"
8But you, O LORD, laugh at them;
you scoff at all those nations.

9O my Strength, I watch for you;
you, O God, are my fortress, 10my loving God.

God will go before me
and will let me gloat over those who slander me.
11But do not kill them, O Lord our shield,[c]
or my people will forget.
In your might make them wander about,
and bring them down.

Psalm 60

For the director of music. To ⌞the tune of⌟ "The Lily of the Covenant." A *miktam*[b] of David. For teaching. When he fought Aram Naharaim[d] and Aram Zobah,[e] and when Joab returned and struck down twelve thousand Edomites in the Valley of Salt.

1You have rejected us, O God, and burst forth upon us;
you have been angry—now restore us!
2You have shaken the land and torn it open;
mend its fractures, for it is quaking.
3You have shown your people desperate times;
you have given us wine that makes us stagger.

4But for those who fear you, you have raised a banner
to be unfurled against the bow. *Selah*

5Save us and help us with your right hand,
that those you love may be delivered.
6God has spoken from his sanctuary:
"In triumph I will parcel out Shechem
and measure off the Valley of Succoth.
7Gilead is mine, and Manasseh is mine;
Ephraim is my helmet,
Judah my scepter.
8Moab is my washbasin,
upon Edom I toss my sandal;
over Philistia I shout in triumph."

9Who will bring me to the fortified city?
Who will lead me to Edom?
10Is it not you, O God, you who have rejected us
and no longer go out with our armies?
11Give us aid against the enemy,
for the help of man is worthless.

[a]9 The meaning of the Hebrew for this verse is uncertain. [b]Title: Probably a literary or musical term
[c]11 Or *sovereign* [d]Title: That is, Arameans of Northwest Mesopotamia [e]Title: That is, Arameans of central Syria

12With God we will gain the victory,
and he will trample down our enemies.

Psalm 61

For the director of music. With stringed instruments. Of David.

1Hear my cry, O God;
listen to my prayer.

2From the ends of the earth I call to you,
I call as my heart grows faint;
lead me to the rock that is higher than I.
3For you have been my refuge,
a strong tower against the foe.

4I long to dwell in your tent forever
and take refuge in the shelter of your wings. *Selah*
5For you have heard my vows, O God;
you have given me the heritage of those who fear your name.

6Increase the days of the king's life,
his years for many generations.
7May he be enthroned in God's presence forever;
appoint your love and faithfulness to protect him.

8Then will I ever sing praise to your name
and fulfill my vows day after day.

Psalm 62

For the director of music. For Jeduthun. A psalm of David.

1My soul finds rest in God alone;
my salvation comes from him.
2He alone is my rock and my salvation;
he is my fortress, I will never be shaken.

3How long will you assault a man?
Would all of you throw him down—
this leaning wall, this tottering fence?
4They fully intend to topple him
from his lofty place;
they take delight in lies.
With their mouths they bless,
but in their hearts they curse. *Selah*

5Find rest, O my soul, in God alone;
my hope comes from him.
6He alone is my rock and my salvation;
he is my fortress, I will not be shaken.
7My salvation and my honor depend on God[a];
he is my mighty rock, my refuge.
8Trust in him at all times, O people;
pour out your hearts to him,
for God is our refuge. *Selah*

9Lowborn men are but a breath,
the highborn are but a lie;
if weighed on a balance, they are nothing;
together they are only a breath.
10Do not trust in extortion
or take pride in stolen goods;
though your riches increase,
do not set your heart on them.

11One thing God has spoken,
two things have I heard:
that you, O God, are strong,
12 and that you, O Lord, are loving.
Surely you will reward each person
according to what he has done.

Psalm 63

A psalm of David. When he was in the Desert of Judah.

1O God, you are my God,
earnestly I seek you;
my soul thirsts for you,
my body longs for you,
in a dry and weary land
where there is no water.

2I have seen you in the sanctuary
and beheld your power and your glory.
3Because your love is better than life,
my lips will glorify you.
4I will praise you as long as I live,
and in your name I will lift up my hands.
5My soul will be satisfied as with the richest of foods;
with singing lips my mouth will praise you.

6On my bed I remember you;
I think of you through the watches of the night.
7Because you are my help,
I sing in the shadow of your wings.
8My soul clings to you;
your right hand upholds me.

9They who seek my life will be destroyed;
they will go down to the depths of the earth.
10They will be given over to the sword
and become food for jackals.

11But the king will rejoice in God;
all who swear by God's name will praise him,
while the mouths of liars will be silenced.

Psalm 64

For the director of music. A psalm of David.

1Hear me, O God, as I voice my complaint;
protect my life from the threat of the enemy.
2Hide me from the conspiracy of the wicked,
from that noisy crowd of evildoers.

3They sharpen their tongues like swords
and aim their words like deadly arrows.
4They shoot from ambush at the innocent man;

[a] 7 Or *I God Most High is my salvation and my honor*

they shoot at him suddenly, without
fear.

5They encourage each other in evil plans,
they talk about hiding their snares;
they say, "Who will see them[a]?"
6They plot injustice and say,
"We have devised a perfect plan!"
Surely the mind and heart of man are
cunning.

7But God will shoot them with arrows;
suddenly they will be struck down.
8He will turn their own tongues against
them
and bring them to ruin;
all who see them will shake their heads
in scorn.

9All mankind will fear;
they will proclaim the works of God
and ponder what he has done.
10Let the righteous rejoice in the LORD
and take refuge in him;
let all the upright in heart praise him!

Psalm 65

For the director of music. A psalm of David. A song.

1Praise awaits[b] you, O God, in Zion;
to you our vows will be fulfilled.
2O you who hear prayer,
to you all men will come.
3When we were overwhelmed by sins,
you forgave[c] our transgressions.
4Blessed are those you choose
and bring near to live in your courts!
We are filled with the good things of your
house,
of your holy temple.

5You answer us with awesome deeds of
righteousness,
O God our Savior,
the hope of all the ends of the earth
and of the farthest seas,
6who formed the mountains by your power,
having armed yourself with strength,
7who stilled the roaring of the seas,
the roaring of their waves,
and the turmoil of the nations.
8Those living far away fear your wonders;
where morning dawns and evening
fades
you call forth songs of joy.

9You care for the land and water it;
you enrich it abundantly.
The streams of God are filled with water
to provide the people with grain,
for so you have ordained it.[d]
10You drench its furrows
and level its ridges;
you soften it with showers
and bless its crops.
11You crown the year with your bounty,
and your carts overflow with
abundance.
12The grasslands of the desert overflow;
the hills are clothed with gladness.
13The meadows are covered with flocks
and the valleys are mantled with grain;
they shout for joy and sing.

Psalm 66

For the director of music. A song. A psalm.

1Shout with joy to God, all the earth!
2 Sing the glory of his name;
make his praise glorious!
3Say to God, "How awesome are your
deeds!
So great is your power
that your enemies cringe before you.
4All the earth bows down to you;
they sing praise to you,
they sing praise to your name." *Selah*

5Come and see what God has done,
how awesome his works in man's
behalf!
6He turned the sea into dry land,
they passed through the waters on
foot—
come, let us rejoice in him.
7He rules forever by his power,
his eyes watch the nations—
let not the rebellious rise up against
him. *Selah*

8Praise our God, O peoples,
let the sound of his praise be heard;
9he has preserved our lives
and kept our feet from slipping.
10For you, O God, tested us;
you refined us like silver.
11You brought us into prison
and laid burdens on our backs.
12You let men ride over our heads;
we went through fire and water,
but you brought us to a place of
abundance.

13I will come to your temple with burnt
offerings
and fulfill my vows to you—
14vows my lips promised and my mouth
spoke
when I was in trouble.
15I will sacrifice fat animals to you
and an offering of rams;
I will offer bulls and goats. *Selah*

16Come and listen, all you who fear God;
let me tell you what he has done for
me.
17I cried out to him with my mouth;
his praise was on my tongue.
18If I had cherished sin in my heart,
the Lord would not have listened;
19but God has surely listened

[a] *5* Or *us* [b] *1* Or *befits*; the meaning of the Hebrew for this word is uncertain. [c] *3* Or *made atonement for*
[d] *9* Or *for that is how you prepare the land*

and heard my voice in prayer.
20Praise be to God,
who has not rejected my prayer
or withheld his love from me!

Psalm 67

For the director of music. With stringed instruments. A psalm. A song.

1May God be gracious to us and bless us
and make his face shine upon us, *Selah*
2that your ways may be known on earth,
your salvation among all nations.

3May the peoples praise you, O God;
may all the peoples praise you.
4May the nations be glad and sing for joy,
for you rule the peoples justly
and guide the nations of the earth. *Selah*
5May the peoples praise you, O God;
may all the peoples praise you.

6Then the land will yield its harvest,
and God, our God, will bless us.
7God will bless us,
and all the ends of the earth will fear him.

Psalm 68

For the director of music. Of David. A psalm. A song.

1May God arise, may his enemies be scattered;
may his foes flee before him.
2As smoke is blown away by the wind,
may you blow them away;
as wax melts before the fire,
may the wicked perish before God.
3But may the righteous be glad
and rejoice before God;
may they be happy and joyful.

4Sing to God, sing praise to his name,
extol him who rides on the clouds[a]—
his name is the LORD—
and rejoice before him.
5A father to the fatherless, a defender of widows,
is God in his holy dwelling.
6God sets the lonely in families,[b]
he leads forth the prisoners with singing;
but the rebellious live in a sun-scorched land.

7When you went out before your people, O God,
when you marched through the wasteland, *Selah*
8the earth shook,
the heavens poured down rain,
before God, the One of Sinai,
before God, the God of Israel.
9You gave abundant showers, O God;
you refreshed your weary inheritance.
10Your people settled in it,
and from your bounty, O God, you provided for the poor.

11The Lord announced the word,
and great was the company of those who proclaimed it:
12"Kings and armies flee in haste;
in the camps men divide the plunder.
13Even while you sleep among the campfires,[c]
the wings of ⌊my⌋ dove are sheathed with silver,
its feathers with shining gold."
14When the Almighty[d] scattered the kings in the land,
it was like snow fallen on Zalmon.

15The mountains of Bashan are majestic mountains;
rugged are the mountains of Bashan.
16Why gaze in envy, O rugged mountains,
at the mountain where God chooses to reign,
where the LORD himself will dwell forever?
17The chariots of God are tens of thousands
and thousands of thousands;
the Lord ⌊has come⌋ from Sinai into his sanctuary.
18When you ascended on high,
you led captives in your train;
you received gifts from men,
even from[e] the rebellious—
that you,[f] O LORD God, might dwell there.

19Praise be to the Lord, to God our Savior,
who daily bears our burdens. *Selah*
20Our God is a God who saves;
from the Sovereign LORD comes escape from death.

21Surely God will crush the heads of his enemies,
the hairy crowns of those who go on in their sins.
22The Lord says, "I will bring them from Bashan;
I will bring them from the depths of the sea,
23that you may plunge your feet in the blood of your foes,
while the tongues of your dogs have their share."

24Your procession has come into view, O God,
the procession of my God and King into the sanctuary.
25In front are the singers, after them the musicians;
with them are the maidens playing tambourines.
26Praise God in the great congregation;
praise the LORD in the assembly of Israel.

a4 Or / *prepare the way for him who rides through the deserts* b6 Or *the desolate in a homeland*
c13 Or *saddlebags* d14 Hebrew *Shaddai* e18 Or *gifts for men, / even* f18 Or *they*

27There is the little tribe of Benjamin,
leading them,
there the great throng of Judah's
princes,
and there the princes of Zebulun and of
Naphtali.

28Summon your power, O God[a];
show us your strength, O God, as you
have done before.
29Because of your temple at Jerusalem
kings will bring you gifts.
30Rebuke the beast among the reeds,
the herd of bulls among the calves of
the nations.
Humbled, may it bring bars of silver.
Scatter the nations who delight in war.
31Envoys will come from Egypt;
Cush[b] will submit herself to God.

32Sing to God, O kingdoms of the earth,
sing praise to the Lord, *Selah*
33to him who rides the ancient skies above,
who thunders with mighty voice.
34Proclaim the power of God,
whose majesty is over Israel,
whose power is in the skies.
35You are awesome, O God, in your
sanctuary;
the God of Israel gives power and
strength to his people.

Praise be to God!

Psalm 69

For the director of music. To ⌊the tune of⌋ "Lilies." Of David.

1Save me, O God,
for the waters have come up to my
neck.
2I sink in the miry depths,
where there is no foothold.
I have come into the deep waters;
the floods engulf me.
3I am worn out calling for help;
my throat is parched.
My eyes fail,
looking for my God.
4Those who hate me without reason
outnumber the hairs of my head;
many are my enemies without cause,
those who seek to destroy me.
I am forced to restore
what I did not steal.

5You know my folly, O God;
my guilt is not hidden from you.

6May those who hope in you
not be disgraced because of me,
O Lord, the LORD Almighty;
may those who seek you
not be put to shame because of me,
O God of Israel.
7For I endure scorn for your sake,
and shame covers my face.
8I am a stranger to my brothers,
an alien to my own mother's sons;
9for zeal for your house consumes me,
and the insults of those who insult you
fall on me.
10When I weep and fast,
I must endure scorn;
11when I put on sackcloth,
people make sport of me.
12Those who sit at the gate mock me,
and I am the song of the drunkards.

13But I pray to you, O LORD,
in the time of your favor;
in your great love, O God,
answer me with your sure salvation.
14Rescue me from the mire,
do not let me sink;
deliver me from those who hate me,
from the deep waters.
15Do not let the floodwaters engulf me
or the depths swallow me up
or the pit close its mouth over me.
16Answer me, O LORD, out of the goodness
of your love;
in your great mercy turn to me.
17Do not hide your face from your servant;
answer me quickly, for I am in trouble.
18Come near and rescue me;
redeem me because of my foes.

19You know how I am scorned, disgraced
and shamed;
all my enemies are before you.
20Scorn has broken my heart
and has left me helpless;
I looked for sympathy, but there was
none,
for comforters, but I found none.
21They put gall in my food
and gave me vinegar for my thirst.

22May the table set before them become a
snare;
may it become retribution and[c] a trap.
23May their eyes be darkened so they cannot
see,
and their backs be bent forever.
24Pour out your wrath on them;
let your fierce anger overtake them.
25May their place be deserted;
let there be no one to dwell in their
tents.
26For they persecute those you wound
and talk about the pain of those you
hurt.
27Charge them with crime upon crime;
do not let them share in your salvation.
28May they be blotted out of the book of
life
and not be listed with the righteous.

29I am in pain and distress;
may your salvation, O God, protect me.

30I will praise God's name in song
and glorify him with thanksgiving.

[a]28 Many Hebrew manuscripts, Septuagint and Syriac; most Hebrew manuscripts *Your God has summoned power for you* [b]31 That is, the upper Nile region [c]22 Or *snare / and their fellowship become*

31This will please the LORD more than an ox,
more than a bull with its horns and hoofs.
32The poor will see and be glad—
you who seek God, may your hearts live!
33The LORD hears the needy
and does not despise his captive people.

34Let heaven and earth praise him,
the seas and all that move in them,
35for God will save Zion
and rebuild the cities of Judah.
Then people will settle there and possess it;
36 the children of his servants will inherit it,
and those who love his name will dwell there.

Psalm 70

For the director of music. Of David.
A petition.

1Hasten, O God, to save me;
O LORD, come quickly to help me.
2May those who seek my life
be put to shame and confusion;
may all who desire my ruin
be turned back in disgrace.
3May those who say to me, "Aha! Aha!"
turn back because of their shame.
4But may all who seek you
rejoice and be glad in you;
may those who love your salvation always say,
"Let God be exalted!"

5Yet I am poor and needy;
come quickly to me, O God.
You are my help and my deliverer;
O LORD, do not delay.

Psalm 71

1In you, O LORD, I have taken refuge;
let me never be put to shame.
2Rescue me and deliver me in your righteousness;
turn your ear to me and save me.
3Be my rock of refuge,
to which I can always go;
give the command to save me,
for you are my rock and my fortress.
4Deliver me, O my God, from the hand of the wicked,
from the grasp of evil and cruel men.

5For you have been my hope, O Sovereign LORD,
my confidence since my youth.
6From birth I have relied on you;
you brought me forth from my mother's womb.
I will ever praise you.
7I have become like a portent to many,
but you are my strong refuge.
8My mouth is filled with your praise,
declaring your splendor all day long.

9Do not cast me away when I am old;
do not forsake me when my strength is gone.
10For my enemies speak against me;
those who wait to kill me conspire together.
11They say, "God has forsaken him;
pursue him and seize him,
for no one will rescue him."
12Be not far from me, O God;
come quickly, O my God, to help me.
13May my accusers perish in shame;
may those who want to harm me
be covered with scorn and disgrace.

14But as for me, I will always have hope;
I will praise you more and more.
15My mouth will tell of your righteousness,
of your salvation all day long,
though I know not its measure.
16I will come and proclaim your mighty acts, O Sovereign LORD;
I will proclaim your righteousness, yours alone.
17Since my youth, O God, you have taught me,
and to this day I declare your marvelous deeds.
18Even when I am old and gray,
do not forsake me, O God,
till I declare your power to the next generation,
your might to all who are to come.

19Your righteousness reaches to the skies, O God,
you who have done great things.
Who, O God, is like you?
20Though you have made me see troubles, many and bitter,
you will restore my life again;
from the depths of the earth
you will again bring me up.
21You will increase my honor
and comfort me once again.

22I will praise you with the harp
for your faithfulness, O my God;
I will sing praise to you with the lyre,
O Holy One of Israel.
23My lips will shout for joy
when I sing praise to you—
I, whom you have redeemed.
24My tongue will tell of your righteous acts all day long,
for those who wanted to harm me
have been put to shame and confusion.

Psalm 72

Of Solomon.

1Endow the king with your justice, O God,
the royal son with your righteousness.

2He will[a] judge your people in
righteousness,
your afflicted ones with justice.
3The mountains will bring prosperity to the
people,
the hills the fruit of righteousness.
4He will defend the afflicted among the
people
and save the children of the needy;
he will crush the oppressor.

5He will endure[b] as long as the sun,
as long as the moon, through all
generations.
6He will be like rain falling on a mown
field,
like showers watering the earth.
7In his days the righteous will flourish;
prosperity will abound till the moon is
no more.

8He will rule from sea to sea
and from the River[c] to the ends of the
earth.[d]
9The desert tribes will bow before him
and his enemies will lick the dust.
10The kings of Tarshish and of distant
shores
will bring tribute to him;
the kings of Sheba and Seba
will present him gifts.
11All kings will bow down to him
and all nations will serve him.

12For he will deliver the needy who cry out,
the afflicted who have no one to help.
13He will take pity on the weak and the
needy
and save the needy from death.
14He will rescue them from oppression and
violence,
for precious is their blood in his sight.

15Long may he live!
May gold from Sheba be given him.
May people ever pray for him
and bless him all day long.
16Let grain abound throughout the land;
on the tops of the hills may it sway.
Let its fruit flourish like Lebanon;
let it thrive like the grass of the field.
17May his name endure forever;
may it continue as long as the sun.

All nations will be blessed through him,
and they will call him blessed.

18Praise be to the LORD God, the God of
Israel,
who alone does marvelous deeds.
19Praise be to his glorious name forever;
may the whole earth be filled with his
glory.
Amen and Amen.

20This concludes the prayers of David son
of Jesse.

BOOK III

Psalms 73–89

Psalm 73

A psalm of Asaph.

1Surely God is good to Israel,
to those who are pure in heart.

2But as for me, my feet had almost slipped;
I had nearly lost my foothold.
3For I envied the arrogant
when I saw the prosperity of the
wicked.

4They have no struggles;
their bodies are healthy and strong.[e]
5They are free from the burdens common
to man;
they are not plagued by human ills.
6Therefore pride is their necklace;
they clothe themselves with violence.
7From their callous hearts comes iniquity[f];
the evil conceits of their minds know no
limits.
8They scoff, and speak with malice;
in their arrogance they threaten
oppression.
9Their mouths lay claim to heaven,
and their tongues take possession of the
earth.
10Therefore their people turn to them
and drink up waters in abundance.[g]
11They say, "How can God know?
Does the Most High have knowledge?"

12This is what the wicked are like—
always carefree, they increase in wealth.

13Surely in vain have I kept my heart pure;
in vain have I washed my hands in
innocence.
14All day long I have been plagued;
I have been punished every morning.

15If I had said, "I will speak thus,"
I would have betrayed your children.
16When I tried to understand all this,
it was oppressive to me
17till I entered the sanctuary of God;
then I understood their final destiny.

18Surely you place them on slippery ground;
you cast them down to ruin.
19How suddenly are they destroyed,
completely swept away by terrors!
20As a dream when one awakes,
so when you arise, O Lord,
you will despise them as fantasies.

21When my heart was grieved
and my spirit embittered,

[a]2 Or *May he*; similarly in verses 3-11 and 17 [b]5 Septuagint; Hebrew *You will be feared* [c]8 That is, the Euphrates [d]8 Or *the end of the land* [e]4 With a different word division of the Hebrew; Masoretic Text *struggles at their death; / their bodies are healthy* [f]7 Syriac (see also Septuagint); Hebrew *Their eyes bulge with fat* [g]10 The meaning of the Hebrew for this verse is uncertain.

22I was senseless and ignorant;
I was a brute beast before you.

23Yet I am always with you;
you hold me by my right hand.
24You guide me with your counsel,
and afterward you will take me into glory.
25Whom have I in heaven but you?
And earth has nothing I desire besides you.
26My flesh and my heart may fail,
but God is the strength of my heart
and my portion forever.

27Those who are far from you will perish;
you destroy all who are unfaithful to you.
28But as for me, it is good to be near God.
I have made the Sovereign LORD my refuge;
I will tell of all your deeds.

Psalm 74

A *maskil*[a] of Asaph.

1Why have you rejected us forever, O God?
Why does your anger smolder against the sheep of your pasture?
2Remember the people you purchased of old,
the tribe of your inheritance, whom you redeemed—
Mount Zion, where you dwelt.
3Turn your steps toward these everlasting ruins,
all this destruction the enemy has brought on the sanctuary.

4Your foes roared in the place where you met with us;
they set up their standards as signs.
5They behaved like men wielding axes
to cut through a thicket of trees.
6They smashed all the carved paneling
with their axes and hatchets.
7They burned your sanctuary to the ground;
they defiled the dwelling place of your Name.
8They said in their hearts, "We will crush them completely!"
They burned every place where God was worshiped in the land.
9We are given no miraculous signs;
no prophets are left,
and none of us knows how long this will be.

10How long will the enemy mock you, O God?
Will the foe revile your name forever?
11Why do you hold back your hand, your right hand?
Take it from the folds of your garment and destroy them!

12But you, O God, are my king from of old;
you bring salvation upon the earth.
13It was you who split open the sea by your power;
you broke the heads of the monster in the waters.
14It was you who crushed the heads of Leviathan
and gave him as food to the creatures of the desert.
15It was you who opened up springs and streams;
you dried up the ever flowing rivers.
16The day is yours, and yours also the night;
you established the sun and moon.
17It was you who set all the boundaries of the earth;
you made both summer and winter.

18Remember how the enemy has mocked you, O LORD,
how foolish people have reviled your name.
19Do not hand over the life of your dove to wild beasts;
do not forget the lives of your afflicted people forever.
20Have regard for your covenant,
because haunts of violence fill the dark places of the land.
21Do not let the oppressed retreat in disgrace;
may the poor and needy praise your name.

22Rise up, O God, and defend your cause;
remember how fools mock you all day long.
23Do not ignore the clamor of your adversaries,
the uproar of your enemies, which rises continually.

Psalm 75

For the director of music. ⌞To the tune of⌟ "Do Not Destroy." A psalm of Asaph. A song.

1We give thanks to you, O God,
we give thanks, for your Name is near;
men tell of your wonderful deeds.

2You say, "I choose the appointed time;
it is I who judge uprightly.
3When the earth and all its people quake,
it is I who hold its pillars firm. *Selah*
4To the arrogant I say, 'Boast no more,'
and to the wicked, 'Do not lift up your horns.
5Do not lift your horns against heaven;
do not speak with outstretched neck.' "

6No one from the east or the west
or from the desert can exalt a man.
7But it is God who judges:
He brings one down, he exalts another.
8In the hand of the LORD is a cup
full of foaming wine mixed with spices;

[a]Title: Probably a literary or musical term

he pours it out, and all the wicked of the
earth
drink it down to its very dregs.

9As for me, I will declare this forever;
I will sing praise to the God of Jacob.
10I will cut off the horns of all the wicked,
but the horns of the righteous will be
lifted up.

Psalm 76

For the director of music. With stringed instruments. A psalm of Asaph. A song.

1In Judah God is known;
his name is great in Israel.
2His tent is in Salem,
his dwelling place in Zion.
3There he broke the flashing arrows,
the shields and the swords, the weapons
of war. *Selah*

4You are resplendent with light,
more majestic than mountains rich with
game.
5Valiant men lie plundered,
they sleep their last sleep;
not one of the warriors
can lift his hands.
6At your rebuke, O God of Jacob,
both horse and chariot lie still.
7You alone are to be feared.
Who can stand before you when you
are angry?
8From heaven you pronounced judgment,
and the land feared and was quiet—
9when you, O God, rose up to judge,
to save all the afflicted of the land.
Selah
10Surely your wrath against men brings you
praise,
and the survivors of your wrath are
restrained.[a]

11Make vows to the LORD your God and
fulfill them;
let all the neighboring lands
bring gifts to the One to be feared.
12He breaks the spirit of rulers;
he is feared by the kings of the earth.

Psalm 77

For the director of music. For Jeduthun. Of Asaph. A psalm.

1I cried out to God for help;
I cried out to God to hear me.
2When I was in distress, I sought the Lord;
at night I stretched out untiring hands
and my soul refused to be comforted.

3I remembered you, O God, and I groaned;
I mused, and my spirit grew faint. *Selah*
4You kept my eyes from closing;
I was too troubled to speak.
5I thought about the former days,
the years of long ago;
6I remembered my songs in the night.
My heart mused and my spirit inquired:

7"Will the Lord reject forever?
Will he never show his favor again?
8Has his unfailing love vanished forever?
Has his promise failed for all time?
9Has God forgotten to be merciful?
Has he in anger withheld his
compassion?" *Selah*

10Then I thought, "To this I will appeal:
the years of the right hand of the Most
High."
11I will remember the deeds of the LORD;
yes, I will remember your miracles of
long ago.
12I will meditate on all your works
and consider all your mighty deeds.

13Your ways, O God, are holy.
What god is so great as our God?
14You are the God who performs miracles;
you display your power among the
peoples.
15With your mighty arm you redeemed your
people,
the descendants of Jacob and Joseph.
Selah

16The waters saw you, O God,
the waters saw you and writhed;
the very depths were convulsed.
17The clouds poured down water,
the skies resounded with thunder;
your arrows flashed back and forth.
18Your thunder was heard in the whirlwind,
your lightning lit up the world;
the earth trembled and quaked.
19Your path led through the sea,
your way through the mighty waters,
though your footprints were not seen.

20You led your people like a flock
by the hand of Moses and Aaron.

Psalm 78

A *maskil*[b] of Asaph.

1O my people, hear my teaching;
listen to the words of my mouth.
2I will open my mouth in parables,
I will utter hidden things, things from of
old—
3what we have heard and known,
what our fathers have told us.
4We will not hide them from their children;
we will tell the next generation
the praiseworthy deeds of the LORD,
his power, and the wonders he has
done.
5He decreed statutes for Jacob
and established the law in Israel,
which he commanded our forefathers
to teach their children,
6so the next generation would know them,
even the children yet to be born,

[a]10 Or *Surely the wrath of men brings you praise, / and with the remainder of wrath you arm yourself*
[b]Title: Probably a literary or musical term

and they in turn would tell their
children.
7Then they would put their trust in God
and would not forget his deeds
but would keep his commands.
8They would not be like their forefathers—
a stubborn and rebellious generation,
whose hearts were not loyal to God,
whose spirits were not faithful to him.

9The men of Ephraim, though armed with
bows,
turned back on the day of battle;
10they did not keep God's covenant
and refused to live by his law.
11They forgot what he had done,
the wonders he had shown them.
12He did miracles in the sight of their
fathers
in the land of Egypt, in the region of
Zoan.
13He divided the sea and led them through;
he made the water stand firm like a
wall.
14He guided them with the cloud by day
and with light from the fire all night.
15He split the rocks in the desert
and gave them water as abundant as the
seas;
16he brought streams out of a rocky crag
and made water flow down like rivers.

17But they continued to sin against him,
rebelling in the desert against the Most
High.
18They willfully put God to the test
by demanding the food they craved.
19They spoke against God, saying,
"Can God spread a table in the desert?
20When he struck the rock, water gushed
out,
and streams flowed abundantly.
But can he also give us food?
Can he supply meat for his people?"
21When the LORD heard them, he was very
angry;
his fire broke out against Jacob,
and his wrath rose against Israel,
22for they did not believe in God
or trust in his deliverance.
23Yet he gave a command to the skies
above
and opened the doors of the heavens;
24he rained down manna for the people to
eat,
he gave them the grain of heaven.
25Men ate the bread of angels;
he sent them all the food they could eat.
26He let loose the east wind from the
heavens
and led forth the south wind by his
power.
27He rained meat down on them like dust,
flying birds like sand on the seashore.
28He made them come down inside their
camp,
all around their tents.
29They ate till they had more than enough,
for he had given them what they craved.
30But before they turned from the food they
craved,
even while it was still in their mouths,
31God's anger rose against them;
he put to death the sturdiest among
them,
cutting down the young men of Israel.

32In spite of all this, they kept on sinning;
in spite of his wonders, they did not
believe.
33So he ended their days in futility
and their years in terror.
34Whenever God slew them, they would
seek him;
they eagerly turned to him again.
35They remembered that God was their
Rock,
that God Most High was their
Redeemer.
36But then they would flatter him with their
mouths,
lying to him with their tongues;
37their hearts were not loyal to him,
they were not faithful to his covenant.
38Yet he was merciful;
he forgave their iniquities
and did not destroy them.
Time after time he restrained his anger
and did not stir up his full wrath.
39He remembered that they were but flesh,
a passing breeze that does not return.

40How often they rebelled against him in the
desert
and grieved him in the wasteland!
41Again and again they put God to the test;
they vexed the Holy One of Israel.
42They did not remember his power—
the day he redeemed them from the
oppressor,
43the day he displayed his miraculous signs
in Egypt,
his wonders in the region of Zoan.
44He turned their rivers to blood;
they could not drink from their streams.
45He sent swarms of flies that devoured
them,
and frogs that devastated them.
46He gave their crops to the grasshopper,
their produce to the locust.
47He destroyed their vines with hail
and their sycamore-figs with sleet.
48He gave over their cattle to the hail,
their livestock to bolts of lightning.
49He unleashed against them his hot anger,
his wrath, indignation and hostility—
a band of destroying angels.
50He prepared a path for his anger;
he did not spare them from death
but gave them over to the plague.
51He struck down all the firstborn of Egypt,
the firstfruits of manhood in the tents of
Ham.
52But he brought his people out like a flock;
he led them like sheep through the
desert.

53He guided them safely, so they were
unafraid;
but the sea engulfed their enemies.
54Thus he brought them to the border of his
holy land,
to the hill country his right hand had
taken.
55He drove out nations before them
and allotted their lands to them as an
inheritance;
he settled the tribes of Israel in their
homes.

56But they put God to the test
and rebelled against the Most High;
they did not keep his statutes.
57Like their fathers they were disloyal and
faithless,
as unreliable as a faulty bow.
58They angered him with their high places;
they aroused his jealousy with their
idols.
59When God heard them, he was very
angry;
he rejected Israel completely.
60He abandoned the tabernacle of Shiloh,
the tent he had set up among men.
61He sent ⌊the ark of⌋ his might into
captivity,
his splendor into the hands of the
enemy.
62He gave his people over to the sword;
he was very angry with his inheritance.
63Fire consumed their young men,
and their maidens had no wedding
songs;
64their priests were put to the sword,
and their widows could not weep.

65Then the Lord awoke as from sleep,
as a man wakes from the stupor of
wine.
66He beat back his enemies;
he put them to everlasting shame.
67Then he rejected the tents of Joseph,
he did not choose the tribe of Ephraim;
68but he chose the tribe of Judah,
Mount Zion, which he loved.
69He built his sanctuary like the heights,
like the earth that he established
forever.
70He chose David his servant
and took him from the sheep pens;
71from tending the sheep he brought him
to be the shepherd of his people Jacob,
of Israel his inheritance.
72And David shepherded them with integrity
of heart;
with skillful hands he led them.

Psalm 79

A psalm of Asaph.

1O God, the nations have invaded your
inheritance;
they have defiled your holy temple,
they have reduced Jerusalem to rubble.
2They have given the dead bodies of your
servants
as food to the birds of the air,
the flesh of your saints to the beasts of
the earth.
3They have poured out blood like water
all around Jerusalem,
and there is no one to bury the dead.
4We are objects of reproach to our
neighbors,
of scorn and derision to those around
us.

5How long, O LORD? Will you be angry
forever?
How long will your jealousy burn like
fire?
6Pour out your wrath on the nations
that do not acknowledge you,
on the kingdoms
that do not call on your name;
7for they have devoured Jacob
and destroyed his homeland.
8Do not hold against us the sins of the
fathers;
may your mercy come quickly to meet
us,
for we are in desperate need.

9Help us, O God our Savior,
for the glory of your name;
deliver us and forgive our sins
for your name's sake.
10Why should the nations say,
"Where is their God?"
Before our eyes, make known among the
nations
that you avenge the outpoured blood of
your servants.
11May the groans of the prisoners come
before you;
by the strength of your arm
preserve those condemned to die.

12Pay back into the laps of our neighbors
seven times
the reproach they have hurled at you,
O Lord.
13Then we your people, the sheep of your
pasture,
will praise you forever;
from generation to generation
we will recount your praise.

Psalm 80

For the director of music. To ⌊the tune of⌋
"The Lilies of the Covenant." Of Asaph.
A psalm.

1Hear us, O Shepherd of Israel,
you who lead Joseph like a flock;
you who sit enthroned between the
cherubim, shine forth
2 before Ephraim, Benjamin and
Manasseh.
Awaken your might;
come and save us.

3Restore us, O God;

make your face shine upon us,
that we may be saved.

4O LORD God Almighty,
how long will your anger smolder
against the prayers of your people?
5You have fed them with the bread of
tears;
you have made them drink tears by the
bowlful.
6You have made us a source of contention
to our neighbors,
and our enemies mock us.

7Restore us, O God Almighty;
make your face shine upon us,
that we may be saved.

8You brought a vine out of Egypt;
you drove out the nations and planted it.
9You cleared the ground for it,
and it took root and filled the land.
10The mountains were covered with its
shade,
the mighty cedars with its branches.
11It sent out its boughs to the Sea,[a]
its shoots as far as the River.[b]

12Why have you broken down its walls
so that all who pass by pick its grapes?
13Boars from the forest ravage it
and the creatures of the field feed on it.
14Return to us, O God Almighty!
Look down from heaven and see!
Watch over this vine,
15 the root your right hand has planted,
the son[c] you have raised up for
yourself.

16Your vine is cut down, it is burned with
fire;
at your rebuke your people perish.
17Let your hand rest on the man at your
right hand,
the son of man you have raised up for
yourself.
18Then we will not turn away from you;
revive us, and we will call on your
name.

19Restore us, O LORD God Almighty;
make your face shine upon us,
that we may be saved.

Psalm 81

For the director of music. According to *gittith*.[d] Of Asaph.

1Sing for joy to God our strength;
shout aloud to the God of Jacob!
2Begin the music, strike the tambourine,
play the melodious harp and lyre.

3Sound the ram's horn at the New Moon,
and when the moon is full, on the day
of our Feast;
4this is a decree for Israel,
an ordinance of the God of Jacob.
5He established it as a statute for Joseph
when he went out against Egypt,
where we heard a language we did not
understand.[e]

6He says, "I removed the burden from their
shoulders;
their hands were set free from the
basket.
7In your distress you called and I rescued
you,
I answered you out of a thundercloud;
I tested you at the waters of Meribah.
Selah

8"Hear, O my people, and I will warn
you—
if you would but listen to me, O Israel!
9You shall have no foreign god among
you;
you shall not bow down to an alien
god.
10I am the LORD your God,
who brought you up out of Egypt.
Open wide your mouth and I will fill it.

11"But my people would not listen to me;
Israel would not submit to me.
12So I gave them over to their stubborn
hearts
to follow their own devices.

13"If my people would but listen to me,
if Israel would follow my ways,
14how quickly would I subdue their enemies
and turn my hand against their foes!
15Those who hate the LORD would cringe
before him,
and their punishment would last forever.
16But you would be fed with the finest of
wheat;
with honey from the rock I would
satisfy you."

Psalm 82

A psalm of Asaph.

1God presides in the great assembly;
he gives judgment among the "gods":

2"How long will you[f] defend the unjust
and show partiality to the wicked? *Selah*
3Defend the cause of the weak and
fatherless;
maintain the rights of the poor and
oppressed.
4Rescue the weak and needy;
deliver them from the hand of the
wicked.

5"They know nothing, they understand
nothing.
They walk about in darkness;
all the foundations of the earth are
shaken.

6"I said, 'You are "gods";
you are all sons of the Most High.'

[a] *11* Probably the Mediterranean [b] *11* That is, the Euphrates [c] *15* Or *branch* [d] Title: Probably a musical term [e] *5* Or / *and we heard a voice we had not known* [f] *2* The Hebrew is plural.

7But you will die like mere men;
you will fall like every other ruler."

8Rise up, O God, judge the earth,
for all the nations are your inheritance.

Psalm 83

A song. A psalm of Asaph.

1O God, do not keep silent;
be not quiet, O God, be not still.
2See how your enemies are astir,
how your foes rear their heads.
3With cunning they conspire against your people;
they plot against those you cherish.
4"Come," they say, "let us destroy them as a nation,
that the name of Israel be remembered no more."

5With one mind they plot together;
they form an alliance against you—
6the tents of Edom and the Ishmaelites,
of Moab and the Hagrites,
7Gebal,[a] Ammon and Amalek,
Philistia, with the people of Tyre.
8Even Assyria has joined them
to lend strength to the descendants of Lot. *Selah*

9Do to them as you did to Midian,
as you did to Sisera and Jabin at the river Kishon,
10who perished at Endor
and became like refuse on the ground.
11Make their nobles like Oreb and Zeeb,
all their princes like Zebah and Zalmunna,
12who said, "Let us take possession
of the pasturelands of God."

13Make them like tumbleweed, O my God,
like chaff before the wind.
14As fire consumes the forest
or a flame sets the mountains ablaze,
15so pursue them with your tempest
and terrify them with your storm.
16Cover their faces with shame
so that men will seek your name, O LORD.

17May they ever be ashamed and dismayed;
may they perish in disgrace.
18Let them know that you, whose name is the LORD—
that you alone are the Most High over all the earth.

Psalm 84

For the director of music. According to *gittith.*[b] Of the Sons of Korah. A psalm.

1How lovely is your dwelling place,
O LORD Almighty!
2My soul yearns, even faints,
for the courts of the LORD;
my heart and my flesh cry out
for the living God.

3Even the sparrow has found a home,
and the swallow a nest for herself,
where she may have her young—
a place near your altar,
O LORD Almighty, my King and my God.
4Blessed are those who dwell in your house;
they are ever praising you. *Selah*

5Blessed are those whose strength is in you,
who have set their hearts on pilgrimage.
6As they pass through the Valley of Baca,
they make it a place of springs;
the autumn rains also cover it with pools.[c]
7They go from strength to strength,
till each appears before God in Zion.

8Hear my prayer, O LORD God Almighty;
listen to me, O God of Jacob. *Selah*
9Look upon our shield,[d] O God;
look with favor on your anointed one.

10Better is one day in your courts
than a thousand elsewhere;
I would rather be a doorkeeper in the house of my God
than dwell in the tents of the wicked.
11For the LORD God is a sun and shield;
the LORD bestows favor and honor;
no good thing does he withhold
from those whose walk is blameless.

12O LORD Almighty,
blessed is the man who trusts in you.

Psalm 85

For the director of music. Of the Sons of Korah. A psalm.

1You showed favor to your land, O LORD;
you restored the fortunes of Jacob.
2You forgave the iniquity of your people
and covered all their sins. *Selah*
3You set aside all your wrath
and turned from your fierce anger.

4Restore us again, O God our Savior,
and put away your displeasure toward us.
5Will you be angry with us forever?
Will you prolong your anger through all generations?
6Will you not revive us again,
that your people may rejoice in you?
7Show us your unfailing love, O LORD,
and grant us your salvation.

8I will listen to what God the LORD will say;
he promises peace to his people, his saints—
but let them not return to folly.

[a]7 That is, Byblos [b]Title: Probably a musical term [c]6 Or *blessings* [d]9 Or *sovereign*

9Surely his salvation is near those who fear
him,
that his glory may dwell in our land.

10Love and faithfulness meet together;
righteousness and peace kiss each other.
11Faithfulness springs forth from the earth,
and righteousness looks down from
heaven.
12The LORD will indeed give what is good,
and our land will yield its harvest.
13Righteousness goes before him
and prepares the way for his steps.

Psalm 86

A prayer of David.

1Hear, O LORD, and answer me,
for I am poor and needy.
2Guard my life, for I am devoted to you.
You are my God; save your servant
who trusts in you.
3Have mercy on me, O Lord,
for I call to you all day long.
4Bring joy to your servant,
for to you, O Lord,
I lift up my soul.

5You are forgiving and good, O Lord,
abounding in love to all who call to
you.
6Hear my prayer, O LORD;
listen to my cry for mercy.
7In the day of my trouble I will call to you,
for you will answer me.

8Among the gods there is none like you,
O Lord;
no deeds can compare with yours.
9All the nations you have made
will come and worship before you,
O Lord;
they will bring glory to your name.
10For you are great and do marvelous deeds;
you alone are God.

11Teach me your way, O LORD,
and I will walk in your truth;
give me an undivided heart,
that I may fear your name.
12I will praise you, O Lord my God, with
all my heart;
I will glorify your name forever.
13For great is your love toward me;
you have delivered me from the depths
of the grave.[a]

14The arrogant are attacking me, O God;
a band of ruthless men seeks my life—
men without regard for you.
15But you, O Lord, are a compassionate and
gracious God,
slow to anger, abounding in love and
faithfulness.
16Turn to me and have mercy on me;
grant your strength to your servant
and save the son of your maidservant.[b]
17Give me a sign of your goodness,
that my enemies may see it and be put
to shame,
for you, O LORD, have helped me and
comforted me.

Psalm 87

Of the Sons of Korah. A psalm. A song.

1He has set his foundation on the holy
mountain;
2 the LORD loves the gates of Zion
more than all the dwellings of Jacob.
3Glorious things are said of you,
O city of God: *Selah*
4"I will record Rahab[c] and Babylon
among those who acknowledge me—
Philistia too, and Tyre, along with
Cush[d]—
and will say, 'This[e] one was born in
Zion.' "

5Indeed, of Zion it will be said,
"This one and that one were born in
her,
and the Most High himself will
establish her."
6The LORD will write in the register of the
peoples:
"This one was born in Zion." *Selah*
7As they make music they will sing,
"All my fountains are in you."

Psalm 88

A song. A psalm of the Sons of Korah.
For the director of music. According to
mahalath leannoth.[f] A *maskil*[g] of
Heman the Ezrahite.

1O LORD, the God who saves me,
day and night I cry out before you.
2May my prayer come before you;
turn your ear to my cry.

3For my soul is full of trouble
and my life draws near the grave.[a]
4I am counted among those who go down
to the pit;
I am like a man without strength.
5I am set apart with the dead,
like the slain who lie in the grave,
whom you remember no more,
who are cut off from your care.

6You have put me in the lowest pit,
in the darkest depths.
7Your wrath lies heavily upon me;
you have overwhelmed me with all your
waves. *Selah*
8You have taken from me my closest
friends
and have made me repulsive to them.

[a] *13,3* Hebrew *Sheol* [b] *16* Or *save your faithful son* [c] *4* A poetic name for Egypt [d] *4* That is, the upper Nile region [e] *4* Or *"O Rahab and Babylon, / Philistia, Tyre and Cush, / I will record concerning those who acknowledge me: / 'This* [f] Title: Possibly a tune, "The Suffering of Affliction" [g] Title: Probably a literary or musical term

I am confined and cannot escape;
9 my eyes are dim with grief.

I call to you, O LORD, every day;
I spread out my hands to you.
10 Do you show your wonders to the dead?
Do those who are dead rise up and
praise you? *Selah*
11 Is your love declared in the grave,
your faithfulness in Destruction[a]?
12 Are your wonders known in the place of
darkness,
or your righteous deeds in the land of
oblivion?

13 But I cry to you for help, O LORD;
in the morning my prayer comes before
you.
14 Why, O LORD, do you reject me
and hide your face from me?

15 From my youth I have been afflicted and
close to death;
I have suffered your terrors and am in
despair.
16 Your wrath has swept over me;
your terrors have destroyed me.
17 All day long they surround me like a
flood;
they have completely engulfed me.
18 You have taken my companions and loved
ones from me;
the darkness is my closest friend.

Psalm 89

A *maskil*[b] of Ethan the Ezrahite.

1 I will sing of the LORD's great love
forever;
with my mouth I will make your
faithfulness known through all
generations.
2 I will declare that your love stands firm
forever,
that you established your faithfulness in
heaven itself.

3 You said, "I have made a covenant with
my chosen one,
I have sworn to David my servant,
4 'I will establish your line forever
and make your throne firm through all
generations.' " *Selah*

5 The heavens praise your wonders,
O LORD,
your faithfulness too, in the assembly of
the holy ones.
6 For who in the skies above can compare
with the LORD?
Who is like the LORD among the
heavenly beings?
7 In the council of the holy ones God is
greatly feared;
he is more awesome than all who
surround him.
8 O LORD God Almighty, who is like you?
You are mighty, O LORD, and your
faithfulness surrounds you.

9 You rule over the surging sea;
when its waves mount up, you still
them.
10 You crushed Rahab like one of the slain;
with your strong arm you scattered your
enemies.
11 The heavens are yours, and yours also the
earth;
you founded the world and all that is in
it.
12 You created the north and the south;
Tabor and Hermon sing for joy at your
name.
13 Your arm is endued with power;
your hand is strong, your right hand
exalted.

14 Righteousness and justice are the
foundation of your throne;
love and faithfulness go before you.
15 Blessed are those who have learned to
acclaim you,
who walk in the light of your presence,
O LORD.
16 They rejoice in your name all day long;
they exult in your righteousness.
17 For you are their glory and strength,
and by your favor you exalt our horn.[c]
18 Indeed, our shield[d] belongs to the LORD,
our king to the Holy One of Israel.

19 Once you spoke in a vision,
to your faithful people you said:
"I have bestowed strength on a warrior;
I have exalted a young man from
among the people.
20 I have found David my servant;
with my sacred oil I have anointed him.
21 My hand will sustain him;
surely my arm will strengthen him.
22 No enemy will subject him to tribute;
no wicked man will oppress him.
23 I will crush his foes before him
and strike down his adversaries.
24 My faithful love will be with him,
and through my name his horn[e] will be
exalted.
25 I will set his hand over the sea,
his right hand over the rivers.
26 He will call out to me, 'You are my
Father,
my God, the Rock my Savior.'
27 I will also appoint him my firstborn,
the most exalted of the kings of the
earth.
28 I will maintain my love to him forever,
and my covenant with him will never
fail.
29 I will establish his line forever,
his throne as long as the heavens
endure.

30 "If his sons forsake my law

[a] *11* Hebrew *Abaddon* [b] Title: Probably a literary or musical term [c] *17* *Horn* here symbolizes strong one.
[d] *18* Or *sovereign* [e] *24* *Horn* here symbolizes strength.

and do not follow my statutes,
31 if they violate my decrees
and fail to keep my commands,
32 I will punish their sin with the rod,
their iniquity with flogging;
33 but I will not take my love from him,
nor will I ever betray my faithfulness.
34 I will not violate my covenant
or alter what my lips have uttered.
35 Once for all, I have sworn by my holiness—
and I will not lie to David—
36 that his line will continue forever
and his throne endure before me like the sun;
37 it will be established forever like the moon,
the faithful witness in the sky." *Selah*

38 But you have rejected, you have spurned,
you have been very angry with your anointed one.
39 You have renounced the covenant with your servant
and have defiled his crown in the dust.
40 You have broken through all his walls
and reduced his strongholds to ruins.
41 All who pass by have plundered him;
he has become the scorn of his neighbors.
42 You have exalted the right hand of his foes;
you have made all his enemies rejoice.
43 You have turned back the edge of his sword
and have not supported him in battle.
44 You have put an end to his splendor
and cast his throne to the ground.
45 You have cut short the days of his youth;
you have covered him with a mantle of shame. *Selah*

46 How long, O LORD? Will you hide yourself forever?
How long will your wrath burn like fire?
47 Remember how fleeting is my life.
For what futility you have created all men!
48 What man can live and not see death,
or save himself from the power of the grave[a]? *Selah*
49 O Lord, where is your former great love,
which in your faithfulness you swore to David?
50 Remember, Lord, how your servant has[b] been mocked,
how I bear in my heart the taunts of all the nations,
51 the taunts with which your enemies have mocked, O LORD,
with which they have mocked every step of your anointed one.

52 Praise be to the LORD forever!
Amen and Amen.

BOOK IV

Psalms 90–106

Psalm 90

A prayer of Moses the man of God.

1 Lord, you have been our dwelling place
throughout all generations.
2 Before the mountains were born
or you brought forth the earth and the world,
from everlasting to everlasting you are God.

3 You turn men back to dust,
saying, "Return to dust, O sons of men."
4 For a thousand years in your sight
are like a day that has just gone by,
or like a watch in the night.
5 You sweep men away in the sleep of death;
they are like the new grass of the morning—
6 though in the morning it springs up new,
by evening it is dry and withered.

7 We are consumed by your anger
and terrified by your indignation.
8 You have set our iniquities before you,
our secret sins in the light of your presence.
9 All our days pass away under your wrath;
we finish our years with a moan.
10 The length of our days is seventy years—
or eighty, if we have the strength;
yet their span[c] is but trouble and sorrow,
for they quickly pass, and we fly away.

11 Who knows the power of your anger?
For your wrath is as great as the fear that is due you.
12 Teach us to number our days aright,
that we may gain a heart of wisdom.

13 Relent, O LORD! How long will it be?
Have compassion on your servants.
14 Satisfy us in the morning with your unfailing love,
that we may sing for joy and be glad all our days.
15 Make us glad for as many days as you have afflicted us,
for as many years as we have seen trouble.
16 May your deeds be shown to your servants,
your splendor to their children.

17 May the favor[d] of the Lord our God rest upon us;
establish the work of our hands for us—
yes, establish the work of our hands.

[a] *48* Hebrew *Sheol* [b] *50* Or *your servants have* [c] *10* Or *yet the best of them* [d] *17* Or *beauty*

Psalm 91

1He who dwells in the shelter of the Most High
will rest in the shadow of the Almighty.[a]
2I will say[b] of the LORD, "He is my refuge and my fortress,
my God, in whom I trust."

3Surely he will save you from the fowler's snare
and from the deadly pestilence.
4He will cover you with his feathers,
and under his wings you will find refuge;
his faithfulness will be your shield and rampart.
5You will not fear the terror of night,
nor the arrow that flies by day,
6nor the pestilence that stalks in the darkness,
nor the plague that destroys at midday.
7A thousand may fall at your side,
ten thousand at your right hand,
but it will not come near you.
8You will only observe with your eyes
and see the punishment of the wicked.

9If you make the Most High your dwelling—
even the LORD, who is my refuge—
10then no harm will befall you,
no disaster will come near your tent.
11For he will command his angels concerning you
to guard you in all your ways;
12they will lift you up in their hands,
so that you will not strike your foot against a stone.
13You will tread upon the lion and the cobra;
you will trample the great lion and the serpent.

14"Because he loves me," says the LORD, "I will rescue him;
I will protect him, for he acknowledges my name.
15He will call upon me, and I will answer him;
I will be with him in trouble,
I will deliver him and honor him.
16With long life will I satisfy him
and show him my salvation."

Psalm 92

A psalm. A song. For the Sabbath day.

1It is good to praise the LORD
and make music to your name, O Most High,
2to proclaim your love in the morning
and your faithfulness at night,
3to the music of the ten-stringed lyre
and the melody of the harp.
4For you make me glad by your deeds, O LORD;
I sing for joy at the works of your hands.
5How great are your works, O LORD,
how profound your thoughts!
6The senseless man does not know,
fools do not understand,
7that though the wicked spring up like grass
and all evildoers flourish,
they will be forever destroyed.

8But you, O LORD, are exalted forever.

9For surely your enemies, O LORD,
surely your enemies will perish;
all evildoers will be scattered.
10You have exalted my horn[c] like that of a wild ox;
fine oils have been poured upon me.
11My eyes have seen the defeat of my adversaries;
my ears have heard the rout of my wicked foes.

12The righteous will flourish like a palm tree,
they will grow like a cedar of Lebanon;
13planted in the house of the LORD,
they will flourish in the courts of our God.
14They will still bear fruit in old age,
they will stay fresh and green,
15proclaiming, "The LORD is upright;
he is my Rock, and there is no wickedness in him."

Psalm 93

1The LORD reigns, he is robed in majesty;
the LORD is robed in majesty
and is armed with strength.
The world is firmly established;
it cannot be moved.
2Your throne was established long ago;
you are from all eternity.

3The seas have lifted up, O LORD,
the seas have lifted up their voice;
the seas have lifted up their pounding waves.
4Mightier than the thunder of the great waters,
mightier than the breakers of the sea—
the LORD on high is mighty.

5Your statutes stand firm;
holiness adorns your house
for endless days, O LORD.

Psalm 94

1O LORD, the God who avenges,
O God who avenges, shine forth.
2Rise up, O Judge of the earth;
pay back to the proud what they deserve.

[a] *1* Hebrew *Shaddai* [b] *2* Or *He says* [c] *10* *Horn* here symbolizes strength.

3How long will the wicked, O LORD,
how long will the wicked be jubilant?

4They pour out arrogant words;
all the evildoers are full of boasting.
5They crush your people, O LORD;
they oppress your inheritance.
6They slay the widow and the alien;
they murder the fatherless.
7They say, "The LORD does not see;
the God of Jacob pays no heed."

8Take heed, you senseless ones among the people;
you fools, when will you become wise?
9Does he who implanted the ear not hear?
Does he who formed the eye not see?
10Does he who disciplines nations not punish?
Does he who teaches man lack knowledge?
11The LORD knows the thoughts of man;
he knows that they are futile.

12Blessed is the man you discipline, O LORD,
the man you teach from your law;
13you grant him relief from days of trouble,
till a pit is dug for the wicked.
14For the LORD will not reject his people;
he will never forsake his inheritance.
15Judgment will again be founded on righteousness,
and all the upright in heart will follow it.

16Who will rise up for me against the wicked?
Who will take a stand for me against evildoers?
17Unless the LORD had given me help,
I would soon have dwelt in the silence of death.
18When I said, "My foot is slipping,"
your love, O LORD, supported me.
19When anxiety was great within me,
your consolation brought joy to my soul.

20Can a corrupt throne be allied with you—
one that brings on misery by its decrees?
21They band together against the righteous
and condemn the innocent to death.
22But the LORD has become my fortress,
and my God the rock in whom I take refuge.
23He will repay them for their sins
and destroy them for their wickedness;
the LORD our God will destroy them.

Psalm 95

1Come, let us sing for joy to the LORD;
let us shout aloud to the Rock of our salvation.
2Let us come before him with thanksgiving
and extol him with music and song.
3For the LORD is the great God,
the great King above all gods.
4In his hand are the depths of the earth,
and the mountain peaks belong to him.
5The sea is his, for he made it,
and his hands formed the dry land.

6Come, let us bow down in worship,
let us kneel before the LORD our Maker;
7for he is our God
and we are the people of his pasture,
the flock under his care.

Today, if you hear his voice,
8 do not harden your hearts as you did at Meribah,[a]
as you did that day at Massah[b] in the desert,
9where your fathers tested and tried me,
though they had seen what I did.
10For forty years I was angry with that generation;
I said, "They are a people whose hearts go astray,
and they have not known my ways."
11So I declared on oath in my anger,
"They shall never enter my rest."

Psalm 96

1Sing to the LORD a new song;
sing to the LORD, all the earth.
2Sing to the LORD, praise his name;
proclaim his salvation day after day.
3Declare his glory among the nations,
his marvelous deeds among all peoples.

4For great is the LORD and most worthy of praise;
he is to be feared above all gods.
5For all the gods of the nations are idols,
but the LORD made the heavens.
6Splendor and majesty are before him;
strength and glory are in his sanctuary.

7Ascribe to the LORD, O families of nations,
ascribe to the LORD glory and strength.
8Ascribe to the LORD the glory due his name;
bring an offering and come into his courts.
9Worship the LORD in the splendor of his[c] holiness;
tremble before him, all the earth.

10Say among the nations, "The LORD reigns."
The world is firmly established, it cannot be moved;
he will judge the peoples with equity.
11Let the heavens rejoice, let the earth be glad;
let the sea resound, and all that is in it;
12 let the fields be jubilant, and everything in them.
Then all the trees of the forest will sing for joy;

[a]8 *Meribah* means *quarreling.* [b]8 *Massah* means *testing.* [c]9 Or *LORD with the splendor of*

13 they will sing before the LORD, for he comes,
he comes to judge the earth.
He will judge the world in righteousness
and the peoples in his truth.

Psalm 97

1 The LORD reigns, let the earth be glad;
let the distant shores rejoice.

2 Clouds and thick darkness surround him;
righteousness and justice are the foundation of his throne.
3 Fire goes before him
and consumes his foes on every side.
4 His lightning lights up the world;
the earth sees and trembles.
5 The mountains melt like wax before the LORD,
before the Lord of all the earth.
6 The heavens proclaim his righteousness,
and all the peoples see his glory.

7 All who worship images are put to shame,
those who boast in idols—
worship him, all you gods!

8 Zion hears and rejoices
and the villages of Judah are glad
because of your judgments, O LORD.
9 For you, O LORD, are the Most High over all the earth;
you are exalted far above all gods.

10 Let those who love the LORD hate evil,
for he guards the lives of his faithful ones
and delivers them from the hand of the wicked.
11 Light is shed upon the righteous
and joy on the upright in heart.
12 Rejoice in the LORD, you who are righteous,
and praise his holy name.

Psalm 98

A psalm.

1 Sing to the LORD a new song,
for he has done marvelous things;
his right hand and his holy arm
have worked salvation for him.
2 The LORD has made his salvation known
and revealed his righteousness to the nations.
3 He has remembered his love
and his faithfulness to the house of Israel;
all the ends of the earth have seen
the salvation of our God.

4 Shout for joy to the LORD, all the earth,
burst into jubilant song with music;
5 make music to the LORD with the harp,
with the harp and the sound of singing,
6 with trumpets and the blast of the ram's horn—
shout for joy before the LORD, the King.

7 Let the sea resound, and everything in it,
the world, and all who live in it.
8 Let the rivers clap their hands,
let the mountains sing together for joy;
9 let them sing before the LORD,
for he comes to judge the earth.
He will judge the world in righteousness
and the peoples with equity.

Psalm 99

1 The LORD reigns,
let the nations tremble;
he sits enthroned between the cherubim,
let the earth shake.
2 Great is the LORD in Zion;
he is exalted over all the nations.
3 Let them praise your great and awesome name—
he is holy.

4 The King is mighty, he loves justice—
you have established equity;
in Jacob you have done
what is just and right.
5 Exalt the LORD our God
and worship at his footstool;
he is holy.

6 Moses and Aaron were among his priests,
Samuel was among those who called on his name;
they called on the LORD
and he answered them.
7 He spoke to them from the pillar of cloud;
they kept his statutes and the decrees he gave them.

8 O LORD our God,
you answered them;
you were to Israel[a] a forgiving God,
though you punished their misdeeds.[b]
9 Exalt the LORD our God
and worship at his holy mountain,
for the LORD our God is holy.

Psalm 100

A psalm. For giving thanks.

1 Shout for joy to the LORD, all the earth.
2 Worship the LORD with gladness;
come before him with joyful songs.
3 Know that the LORD is God.
It is he who made us, and we are his[c];
we are his people, the sheep of his pasture.

4 Enter his gates with thanksgiving
and his courts with praise;
give thanks to him and praise his name.

[a] 8 Hebrew *them* [b] 8 Or / *an avenger of the wrongs done to them* [c] 3 Or *and not we ourselves*

5For the LORD is good and his love endures
forever;
his faithfulness continues through all
generations.

Psalm 101

Of David. A psalm.

1I will sing of your love and justice;
to you, O LORD, I will sing praise.
2I will be careful to lead a blameless life—
when will you come to me?

I will walk in my house
with blameless heart.
3I will set before my eyes
no vile thing.

The deeds of faithless men I hate;
they will not cling to me.
4Men of perverse heart shall be far from
me;
I will have nothing to do with evil.

5Whoever slanders his neighbor in secret,
him will I put to silence;
whoever has haughty eyes and a proud
heart,
him will I not endure.

6My eyes will be on the faithful in the
land,
that they may dwell with me;
he whose walk is blameless
will minister to me.

7No one who practices deceit
will dwell in my house;
no one who speaks falsely
will stand in my presence.

8Every morning I will put to silence
all the wicked in the land;
I will cut off every evildoer
from the city of the LORD.

Psalm 102

A prayer of an afflicted man. When he is
faint and pours out his lament
before the LORD.

1Hear my prayer, O LORD;
let my cry for help come to you.
2Do not hide your face from me
when I am in distress.
Turn your ear to me;
when I call, answer me quickly.

3For my days vanish like smoke;
my bones burn like glowing embers.
4My heart is blighted and withered like
grass;
I forget to eat my food.
5Because of my loud groaning
I am reduced to skin and bones.
6I am like a desert owl,
like an owl among the ruins.
7I lie awake; I have become
like a bird alone on a roof.
8All day long my enemies taunt me;
those who rail against me use my name
as a curse.
9For I eat ashes as my food
and mingle my drink with tears
10because of your great wrath,
for you have taken me up and thrown
me aside.
11My days are like the evening shadow;
I wither away like grass.

12But you, O LORD, sit enthroned forever;
your renown endures through all
generations.
13You will arise and have compassion on
Zion,
for it is time to show favor to her;
the appointed time has come.
14For her stones are dear to your servants;
her very dust moves them to pity.
15The nations will fear the name of the
LORD,
all the kings of the earth will revere
your glory.
16For the LORD will rebuild Zion
and appear in his glory.
17He will respond to the prayer of the
destitute;
he will not despise their plea.

18Let this be written for a future generation,
that a people not yet created may praise
the LORD:
19"The LORD looked down from his
sanctuary on high,
from heaven he viewed the earth,
20to hear the groans of the prisoners
and release those condemned to death."
21So the name of the LORD will be declared
in Zion
and his praise in Jerusalem
22when the peoples and the kingdoms
assemble to worship the LORD.

23In the course of my life[a] he broke my
strength;
he cut short my days.
24So I said:
"Do not take me away, O my God, in
the midst of my days;
your years go on through all
generations.
25In the beginning you laid the foundations
of the earth,
and the heavens are the work of your
hands.
26They will perish, but you remain;
they will all wear out like a garment.
Like clothing you will change them
and they will be discarded.
27But you remain the same,
and your years will never end.
28The children of your servants will live in
your presence;
their descendants will be established
before you."

[a]23 Or *By his power*

Psalm 103

Of David.

[1]Praise the LORD, O my soul;
all my inmost being, praise his holy name.
[2]Praise the LORD, O my soul,
and forget not all his benefits—
[3]who forgives all your sins
and heals all your diseases,
[4]who redeems your life from the pit
and crowns you with love and compassion,
[5]who satisfies your desires with good things
so that your youth is renewed like the eagle's.

[6]The LORD works righteousness
and justice for all the oppressed.

[7]He made known his ways to Moses,
his deeds to the people of Israel:
[8]The LORD is compassionate and gracious,
slow to anger, abounding in love.
[9]He will not always accuse,
nor will he harbor his anger forever;
[10]he does not treat us as our sins deserve
or repay us according to our iniquities.
[11]For as high as the heavens are above the earth,
so great is his love for those who fear him;
[12]as far as the east is from the west,
so far has he removed our transgressions from us.
[13]As a father has compassion on his children,
so the LORD has compassion on those who fear him;
[14]for he knows how we are formed,
he remembers that we are dust.
[15]As for man, his days are like grass,
he flourishes like a flower of the field;
[16]the wind blows over it and it is gone,
and its place remembers it no more.
[17]But from everlasting to everlasting
the LORD's love is with those who fear him,
and his righteousness with their children's children—
[18]with those who keep his covenant
and remember to obey his precepts.

[19]The LORD has established his throne in heaven,
and his kingdom rules over all.

[20]Praise the LORD, you his angels,
you mighty ones who do his bidding,
who obey his word.
[21]Praise the LORD, all his heavenly hosts,
you his servants who do his will.
[22]Praise the LORD, all his works
everywhere in his dominion.

Praise the LORD, O my soul.

Psalm 104

[1]Praise the LORD, O my soul.

O LORD my God, you are very great;
you are clothed with splendor and majesty.
[2]He wraps himself in light as with a garment;
he stretches out the heavens like a tent
[3] and lays the beams of his upper chambers on their waters.
He makes the clouds his chariot
and rides on the wings of the wind.
[4]He makes winds his messengers,[a]
flames of fire his servants.

[5]He set the earth on its foundations;
it can never be moved.
[6]You covered it with the deep as with a garment;
the waters stood above the mountains.
[7]But at your rebuke the waters fled,
at the sound of your thunder they took to flight;
[8]they flowed over the mountains,
they went down into the valleys,
to the place you assigned for them.
[9]You set a boundary they cannot cross;
never again will they cover the earth.

[10]He makes springs pour water into the ravines;
it flows between the mountains.
[11]They give water to all the beasts of the field;
the wild donkeys quench their thirst.
[12]The birds of the air nest by the waters;
they sing among the branches.
[13]He waters the mountains from his upper chambers;
the earth is satisfied by the fruit of his work.
[14]He makes grass grow for the cattle,
and plants for man to cultivate—
bringing forth food from the earth:
[15]wine that gladdens the heart of man,
oil to make his face shine,
and bread that sustains his heart.
[16]The trees of the LORD are well watered,
the cedars of Lebanon that he planted.
[17]There the birds make their nests;
the stork has its home in the pine trees.
[18]The high mountains belong to the wild goats;
the crags are a refuge for the coneys.[b]

[19]The moon marks off the seasons,
and the sun knows when to go down.
[20]You bring darkness, it becomes night,
and all the beasts of the forest prowl.
[21]The lions roar for their prey
and seek their food from God.
[22]The sun rises, and they steal away;
they return and lie down in their dens.
[23]Then man goes out to his work,
to his labor until evening.

[a]4 Or *angels* [b]18 That is, the hyrax or rock badger

24How many are your works, O LORD!
In wisdom you made them all;
the earth is full of your creatures.
25There is the sea, vast and spacious,
teeming with creatures beyond number—
living things both large and small.
26There the ships go to and fro,
and the leviathan, which you formed to frolic there.

27These all look to you
to give them their food at the proper time.
28When you give it to them,
they gather it up;
when you open your hand,
they are satisfied with good things.
29When you hide your face,
they are terrified;
when you take away their breath,
they die and return to the dust.
30When you send your Spirit,
they are created,
and you renew the face of the earth.

31May the glory of the LORD endure forever;
may the LORD rejoice in his works—
32he who looks at the earth, and it trembles,
who touches the mountains, and they smoke.

33I will sing to the LORD all my life;
I will sing praise to my God as long as I live.
34May my meditation be pleasing to him,
as I rejoice in the LORD.
35But may sinners vanish from the earth
and the wicked be no more.

Praise the LORD, O my soul.

Praise the LORD.[a]

Psalm 105

1Give thanks to the LORD, call on his name;
make known among the nations what he has done.
2Sing to him, sing praise to him;
tell of all his wonderful acts.
3Glory in his holy name;
let the hearts of those who seek the LORD rejoice.
4Look to the LORD and his strength;
seek his face always.

5Remember the wonders he has done,
his miracles, and the judgments he pronounced,
6O descendants of Abraham his servant,
O sons of Jacob, his chosen ones.
7He is the LORD our God;
his judgments are in all the earth.

8He remembers his covenant forever,
the word he commanded, for a thousand generations,
9the covenant he made with Abraham,
the oath he swore to Isaac.
10He confirmed it to Jacob as a decree,
to Israel as an everlasting covenant:
11"To you I will give the land of Canaan
as the portion you will inherit."

12When they were but few in number,
few indeed, and strangers in it,
13they wandered from nation to nation,
from one kingdom to another.
14He allowed no one to oppress them;
for their sake he rebuked kings:
15"Do not touch my anointed ones;
do my prophets no harm."

16He called down famine on the land
and destroyed all their supplies of food;
17and he sent a man before them—
Joseph, sold as a slave.
18They bruised his feet with shackles,
his neck was put in irons,
19till what he foretold came to pass,
till the word of the LORD proved him true.
20The king sent and released him,
the ruler of peoples set him free.
21He made him master of his household,
ruler over all he possessed,
22to instruct his princes as he pleased
and teach his elders wisdom.

23Then Israel entered Egypt;
Jacob lived as an alien in the land of Ham.
24The LORD made his people very fruitful;
he made them too numerous for their foes,
25whose hearts he turned to hate his people,
to conspire against his servants.
26He sent Moses his servant,
and Aaron, whom he had chosen.
27They performed his miraculous signs among them,
his wonders in the land of Ham.
28He sent darkness and made the land dark—
for had they not rebelled against his words?
29He turned their waters into blood,
causing their fish to die.
30Their land teemed with frogs,
which went up into the bedrooms of their rulers.
31He spoke, and there came swarms of flies,
and gnats throughout their country.
32He turned their rain into hail,
with lightning throughout their land;
33he struck down their vines and fig trees
and shattered the trees of their country.
34He spoke, and the locusts came,
grasshoppers without number;
35they ate up every green thing in their land,
ate up the produce of their soil.

[a]35 Hebrew *Hallelu Yah*; in the Septuagint this line stands at the beginning of Psalm 105.

36Then he struck down all the firstborn in
their land,
the firstfruits of all their manhood.

37He brought out Israel, laden with silver
and gold,
and from among their tribes no one
faltered.
38Egypt was glad when they left,
because dread of Israel had fallen on
them.
39He spread out a cloud as a covering,
and a fire to give light at night.
40They asked, and he brought them quail
and satisfied them with the bread of
heaven.
41He opened the rock, and water gushed out;
like a river it flowed in the desert.

42For he remembered his holy promise
given to his servant Abraham.
43He brought out his people with rejoicing,
his chosen ones with shouts of joy;
44he gave them the lands of the nations,
and they fell heir to what others had
toiled for—
45that they might keep his precepts
and observe his laws.

Praise the LORD.[a]

Psalm 106

1Praise the LORD.[b]

Give thanks to the LORD, for he is good;
his love endures forever.
2Who can proclaim the mighty acts of the
LORD
or fully declare his praise?
3Blessed are they who maintain justice,
who constantly do what is right.
4Remember me, O LORD, when you show
favor to your people,
come to my aid when you save them,
5that I may enjoy the prosperity of your
chosen ones,
that I may share in the joy of your
nation
and join your inheritance in giving
praise.

6We have sinned, even as our fathers did;
we have done wrong and acted
wickedly.
7When our fathers were in Egypt,
they gave no thought to your miracles;
they did not remember your many
kindnesses,
and they rebelled by the sea, the Red
Sea.[c]
8Yet he saved them for his name's sake,
to make his mighty power known.
9He rebuked the Red Sea, and it dried up;
he led them through the depths as
through a desert.
10He saved them from the hand of the foe;
from the hand of the enemy he
redeemed them.
11The waters covered their adversaries;
not one of them survived.
12Then they believed his promises
and sang his praise.

13But they soon forgot what he had done
and did not wait for his counsel.
14In the desert they gave in to their craving;
in the wasteland they put God to the
test.
15So he gave them what they asked for,
but sent a wasting disease upon them.

16In the camp they grew envious of Moses
and of Aaron, who was consecrated to
the LORD.
17The earth opened up and swallowed
Dathan;
it buried the company of Abiram.
18Fire blazed among their followers;
a flame consumed the wicked.

19At Horeb they made a calf
and worshiped an idol cast from metal.
20They exchanged their Glory
for an image of a bull, which eats grass.
21They forgot the God who saved them,
who had done great things in Egypt,
22miracles in the land of Ham
and awesome deeds by the Red Sea.
23So he said he would destroy them—
had not Moses, his chosen one,
stood in the breach before him
to keep his wrath from destroying them.

24Then they despised the pleasant land;
they did not believe his promise.
25They grumbled in their tents
and did not obey the LORD.
26So he swore to them with uplifted hand
that he would make them fall in the
desert,
27make their descendants fall among the
nations
and scatter them throughout the lands.

28They yoked themselves to the Baal of
Peor
and ate sacrifices offered to lifeless
gods;
29they provoked the LORD to anger by their
wicked deeds,
and a plague broke out among them.
30But Phinehas stood up and intervened,
and the plague was checked.
31This was credited to him as righteousness
for endless generations to come.

32By the waters of Meribah they angered the
LORD,
and trouble came to Moses because of
them;
33for they rebelled against the Spirit of God,
and rash words came from Moses'
lips.[d]

[a]45 Hebrew *Hallelu Yah* [b]1 Hebrew *Hallelu Yah*; also in verse 48 [c]7 Hebrew *Yam Suph*; that is, Sea of Reeds; also in verses 9 and 22 [d]33 Or *against his spirit, / and rash words came from his lips*

34They did not destroy the peoples
as the LORD had commanded them,
35but they mingled with the nations
and adopted their customs.
36They worshiped their idols,
which became a snare to them.
37They sacrificed their sons
and their daughters to demons.
38They shed innocent blood,
the blood of their sons and daughters,
whom they sacrificed to the idols of Canaan,
and the land was desecrated by their blood.
39They defiled themselves by what they did;
by their deeds they prostituted themselves.

40Therefore the LORD was angry with his people
and abhorred his inheritance.
41He handed them over to the nations,
and their foes ruled over them.
42Their enemies oppressed them
and subjected them to their power.
43Many times he delivered them,
but they were bent on rebellion
and they wasted away in their sin.

44But he took note of their distress
when he heard their cry;
45for their sake he remembered his covenant
and out of his great love he relented.
46He caused them to be pitied
by all who held them captive.

47Save us, O LORD our God,
and gather us from the nations,
that we may give thanks to your holy name
and glory in your praise.

48Praise be to the LORD, the God of Israel,
from everlasting to everlasting.
Let all the people say, "Amen!"

Praise the LORD.

BOOK V

Psalms 107–150

Psalm 107

1Give thanks to the LORD, for he is good;
his love endures forever.
2Let the redeemed of the LORD say this—
those he redeemed from the hand of the foe,
3those he gathered from the lands,
from east and west, from north and south.[a]

4Some wandered in desert wastelands,
finding no way to a city where they could settle.
5They were hungry and thirsty,
and their lives ebbed away.
6Then they cried out to the LORD in their trouble,
and he delivered them from their distress.
7He led them by a straight way
to a city where they could settle.
8Let them give thanks to the LORD for his unfailing love
and his wonderful deeds for men,
9for he satisfies the thirsty
and fills the hungry with good things.

10Some sat in darkness and the deepest gloom,
prisoners suffering in iron chains,
11for they had rebelled against the words of God
and despised the counsel of the Most High.
12So he subjected them to bitter labor;
they stumbled, and there was no one to help.
13Then they cried to the LORD in their trouble,
and he saved them from their distress.
14He brought them out of darkness and the deepest gloom
and broke away their chains.
15Let them give thanks to the LORD for his unfailing love
and his wonderful deeds for men,
16for he breaks down gates of bronze
and cuts through bars of iron.

17Some became fools through their rebellious ways
and suffered affliction because of their iniquities.
18They loathed all food
and drew near the gates of death.
19Then they cried to the LORD in their trouble,
and he saved them from their distress.
20He sent forth his word and healed them;
he rescued them from the grave.
21Let them give thanks to the LORD for his unfailing love
and his wonderful deeds for men.
22Let them sacrifice thank offerings
and tell of his works with songs of joy.

23Others went out on the sea in ships;
they were merchants on the mighty waters.
24They saw the works of the LORD,
his wonderful deeds in the deep.
25For he spoke and stirred up a tempest
that lifted high the waves.
26They mounted up to the heavens and went down to the depths;
in their peril their courage melted away.
27They reeled and staggered like drunken men;
they were at their wits' end.
28Then they cried out to the LORD in their trouble,

[a] 3 Hebrew *north and the sea*

and he brought them out of their
distress.
29He stilled the storm to a whisper;
the waves of the sea were hushed.
30They were glad when it grew calm,
and he guided them to their desired
haven.
31Let them give thanks to the LORD for his
unfailing love
and his wonderful deeds for men.
32Let them exalt him in the assembly of the
people
and praise him in the council of the
elders.

33He turned rivers into a desert,
flowing springs into thirsty ground,
34and fruitful land into a salt waste,
because of the wickedness of those who
lived there.
35He turned the desert into pools of water
and the parched ground into flowing
springs;
36there he brought the hungry to live,
and they founded a city where they
could settle.
37They sowed fields and planted vineyards
that yielded a fruitful harvest;
38he blessed them, and their numbers greatly
increased,
and he did not let their herds diminish.

39Then their numbers decreased, and they
were humbled
by oppression, calamity and sorrow;
40he who pours contempt on nobles
made them wander in a trackless waste.
41But he lifted the needy out of their
affliction
and increased their families like flocks.
42The upright see and rejoice,
but all the wicked shut their mouths.

43Whoever is wise, let him heed these
things
and consider the great love of the LORD.

Psalm 108

A song. A psalm of David.

1My heart is steadfast, O God;
I will sing and make music with all my
soul.
2Awake, harp and lyre!
I will awaken the dawn.
3I will praise you, O LORD, among the
nations;
I will sing of you among the peoples.
4For great is your love, higher than the
heavens;
your faithfulness reaches to the skies.
5Be exalted, O God, above the heavens,
and let your glory be over all the earth.

6Save us and help us with your right hand,
that those you love may be delivered.
7God has spoken from his sanctuary:
"In triumph I will parcel out Shechem
and measure off the Valley of Succoth.
8Gilead is mine, Manasseh is mine;
Ephraim is my helmet,
Judah my scepter.
9Moab is my washbasin,
upon Edom I toss my sandal;
over Philistia I shout in triumph."

10Who will bring me to the fortified city?
Who will lead me to Edom?
11Is it not you, O God, you who have
rejected us
and no longer go out with our armies?
12Give us aid against the enemy,
for the help of man is worthless.
13With God we will gain the victory,
and he will trample down our enemies.

Psalm 109

For the director of music. Of David.
A psalm.

1O God, whom I praise,
do not remain silent,
2for wicked and deceitful men
have opened their mouths against me;
they have spoken against me with lying
tongues.
3With words of hatred they surround me;
they attack me without cause.
4In return for my friendship they accuse
me,
but I am a man of prayer.
5They repay me evil for good,
and hatred for my friendship.

6Appoint[a] an evil man[b] to oppose him;
let an accuser[c] stand at his right hand.
7When he is tried, let him be found guilty,
and may his prayers condemn him.
8May his days be few;
may another take his place of
leadership.
9May his children be fatherless
and his wife a widow.
10May his children be wandering beggars;
may they be driven[d] from their ruined
homes.
11May a creditor seize all he has;
may strangers plunder the fruits of his
labor.
12May no one extend kindness to him
or take pity on his fatherless children.
13May his descendants be cut off,
their names blotted out from the next
generation.
14May the iniquity of his fathers be
remembered before the LORD;
may the sin of his mother never be
blotted out.
15May their sins always remain before the
LORD,

[a]6 Or ⌊*They say:*⌋ *"Appoint* (with quotation marks at the end of verse 19) [b]6 Or *the Evil One* [c]6 Or *let Satan* [d]10 Septuagint; Hebrew *sought*

that he may cut off the memory of them
from the earth.

16For he never thought of doing a kindness,
but hounded to death the poor
and the needy and the brokenhearted.
17He loved to pronounce a curse—
may it[a] come on him;
he found no pleasure in blessing—
may it be[b] far from him.
18He wore cursing as his garment;
it entered into his body like water,
into his bones like oil.
19May it be like a cloak wrapped about him,
like a belt tied forever around him.
20May this be the LORD's payment to my accusers,
to those who speak evil of me.

21But you, O Sovereign LORD,
deal well with me for your name's sake;
out of the goodness of your love,
deliver me.
22For I am poor and needy,
and my heart is wounded within me.
23I fade away like an evening shadow;
I am shaken off like a locust.
24My knees give way from fasting;
my body is thin and gaunt.
25I am an object of scorn to my accusers;
when they see me, they shake their heads.

26Help me, O LORD my God;
save me in accordance with your love.
27Let them know that it is your hand,
that you, O LORD, have done it.
28They may curse, but you will bless;
when they attack they will be put to shame,
but your servant will rejoice.
29My accusers will be clothed with disgrace
and wrapped in shame as in a cloak.

30With my mouth I will greatly extol the LORD;
in the great throng I will praise him.
31For he stands at the right hand of the needy one,
to save his life from those who
condemn him.

Psalm 110

Of David. A psalm.

1The LORD says to my Lord:
"Sit at my right hand
until I make your enemies
a footstool for your feet."

2The LORD will extend your mighty scepter
from Zion;
you will rule in the midst of your
enemies.
3Your troops will be willing
on your day of battle.
Arrayed in holy majesty,
from the womb of the dawn
you will receive the dew of your
youth.[c]

4The LORD has sworn
and will not change his mind:
"You are a priest forever,
in the order of Melchizedek."

5The Lord is at your right hand;
he will crush kings on the day of his
wrath.
6He will judge the nations, heaping up the dead
and crushing the rulers of the whole
earth.
7He will drink from a brook beside the way[d];
therefore he will lift up his head.

Psalm 111[e]

1Praise the LORD.[f]

I will extol the LORD with all my heart
in the council of the upright and in the
assembly.

2Great are the works of the LORD;
they are pondered by all who delight in
them.
3Glorious and majestic are his deeds,
and his righteousness endures forever.
4He has caused his wonders to be
remembered;
the LORD is gracious and
compassionate.
5He provides food for those who fear him;
he remembers his covenant forever.
6He has shown his people the power of his works,
giving them the lands of other nations.
7The works of his hands are faithful and just;
all his precepts are trustworthy.
8They are steadfast for ever and ever,
done in faithfulness and uprightness.
9He provided redemption for his people;
he ordained his covenant forever—
holy and awesome is his name.

10The fear of the LORD is the beginning of
wisdom;
all who follow his precepts have good
understanding.
To him belongs eternal praise.

Psalm 112[e]

1Praise the LORD.[f]

Blessed is the man who fears the LORD,
who finds great delight in his
commands.

2His children will be mighty in the land;

[a]17 Or *curse, / and it has* [b]17 Or *blessing, / and it is* [c]3 Or / *your young men will come to you like the dew* [d]7 Or / *The One who grants succession will set him in authority* [e]This psalm is an acrostic poem, the lines of which begin with the successive letters of the Hebrew alphabet. [f]1 Hebrew *Hallelu Yah*

the generation of the upright will be
blessed.
3Wealth and riches are in his house,
and his righteousness endures forever.
4Even in darkness light dawns for the
upright,
for the gracious and compassionate and
righteous man.[a]
5Good will come to him who is generous
and lends freely,
who conducts his affairs with justice.
6Surely he will never be shaken;
a righteous man will be remembered
forever.
7He will have no fear of bad news;
his heart is steadfast, trusting in the
LORD.
8His heart is secure, he will have no fear;
in the end he will look in triumph on
his foes.
9He has scattered abroad his gifts to the
poor,
his righteousness endures forever;
his horn[b] will be lifted high in honor.

10The wicked man will see and be vexed,
he will gnash his teeth and waste away;
the longings of the wicked will come to
nothing.

Psalm 113

1Praise the LORD.[c]

Praise, O servants of the LORD,
praise the name of the LORD.
2Let the name of the LORD be praised,
both now and forevermore.
3From the rising of the sun to the place
where it sets,
the name of the LORD is to be praised.

4The LORD is exalted over all the nations,
his glory above the heavens.
5Who is like the LORD our God,
the One who sits enthroned on high,
6who stoops down to look
on the heavens and the earth?

7He raises the poor from the dust
and lifts the needy from the ash heap;
8he seats them with princes,
with the princes of their people.
9He settles the barren woman in her home
as a happy mother of children.

Praise the LORD.

Psalm 114

1When Israel came out of Egypt,
the house of Jacob from a people of
foreign tongue,
2Judah became God's sanctuary,
Israel his dominion.

3The sea looked and fled,
the Jordan turned back;
4the mountains skipped like rams,
the hills like lambs.

5Why was it, O sea, that you fled,
O Jordan, that you turned back,
6you mountains, that you skipped like
rams,
you hills, like lambs?

7Tremble, O earth, at the presence of the
Lord,
at the presence of the God of Jacob,
8who turned the rock into a pool,
the hard rock into springs of water.

Psalm 115

1Not to us, O LORD, not to us
but to your name be the glory,
because of your love and faithfulness.

2Why do the nations say,
"Where is their God?"
3Our God is in heaven;
he does whatever pleases him.
4But their idols are silver and gold,
made by the hands of men.
5They have mouths, but cannot speak,
eyes, but they cannot see;
6they have ears, but cannot hear,
noses, but they cannot smell;
7they have hands, but cannot feel,
feet, but they cannot walk;
nor can they utter a sound with their
throats.
8Those who make them will be like them,
and so will all who trust in them.

9O house of Israel, trust in the LORD—
he is their help and shield.
10O house of Aaron, trust in the LORD—
he is their help and shield.
11You who fear him, trust in the LORD—
he is their help and shield.

12The LORD remembers us and will bless us:
He will bless the house of Israel,
he will bless the house of Aaron,
13he will bless those who fear the LORD—
small and great alike.

14May the LORD make you increase,
both you and your children.
15May you be blessed by the LORD,
the Maker of heaven and earth.

16The highest heavens belong to the LORD,
but the earth he has given to man.
17It is not the dead who praise the LORD,
those who go down to silence;
18it is we who extol the LORD,
both now and forevermore.

Praise the LORD.[d]

Psalm 116

1I love the LORD, for he heard my voice;
he heard my cry for mercy.

[a]4 Or */ for ⌞the LORD⌟ is gracious and compassionate and righteous* [b]9 *Horn* here symbolizes dignity.
[c]1 Hebrew *Hallelu Yah*; also in verse 9 [d]18 Hebrew *Hallelu Yah*

2Because he turned his ear to me,
I will call on him as long as I live.

3The cords of death entangled me,
the anguish of the grave[a] came upon me;
I was overcome by trouble and sorrow.
4Then I called on the name of the LORD:
"O LORD, save me!"

5The LORD is gracious and righteous;
our God is full of compassion.
6The LORD protects the simplehearted;
when I was in great need, he saved me.

7Be at rest once more, O my soul,
for the LORD has been good to you.

8For you, O LORD, have delivered my soul from death,
my eyes from tears,
my feet from stumbling,
9that I may walk before the LORD
in the land of the living.
10I believed; therefore[b] I said,
"I am greatly afflicted."
11And in my dismay I said,
"All men are liars."

12How can I repay the LORD
for all his goodness to me?
13I will lift up the cup of salvation
and call on the name of the LORD.
14I will fulfill my vows to the LORD
in the presence of all his people.

15Precious in the sight of the LORD
is the death of his saints.
16O LORD, truly I am your servant;
I am your servant, the son of your maidservant[c];
you have freed me from my chains.

17I will sacrifice a thank offering to you
and call on the name of the LORD.
18I will fulfill my vows to the LORD
in the presence of all his people,
19in the courts of the house of the LORD—
in your midst, O Jerusalem.

Praise the LORD.[d]

Psalm 117

1Praise the LORD, all you nations;
extol him, all you peoples.
2For great is his love toward us,
and the faithfulness of the LORD endures forever.

Praise the LORD.[d]

Psalm 118

1Give thanks to the LORD, for he is good;
his love endures forever.

2Let Israel say:
"His love endures forever."
3Let the house of Aaron say:
"His love endures forever."
4Let those who fear the LORD say:
"His love endures forever."

5In my anguish I cried to the LORD,
and he answered by setting me free.
6The LORD is with me; I will not be afraid.
What can man do to me?
7The LORD is with me; he is my helper.
I will look in triumph on my enemies.

8It is better to take refuge in the LORD
than to trust in man.
9It is better to take refuge in the LORD
than to trust in princes.

10All the nations surrounded me,
but in the name of the LORD I cut them off.
11They surrounded me on every side,
but in the name of the LORD I cut them off.
12They swarmed around me like bees,
but they died out as quickly as burning thorns;
in the name of the LORD I cut them off.

13I was pushed back and about to fall,
but the LORD helped me.
14The LORD is my strength and my song;
he has become my salvation.

15Shouts of joy and victory
resound in the tents of the righteous:
"The LORD's right hand has done mighty things!
16 The LORD's right hand is lifted high;
the LORD's right hand has done mighty things!"

17I will not die but live,
and will proclaim what the LORD has done.
18The LORD has chastened me severely,
but he has not given me over to death.

19Open for me the gates of righteousness;
I will enter and give thanks to the LORD.
20This is the gate of the LORD
through which the righteous may enter.
21I will give you thanks, for you answered me;
you have become my salvation.

22The stone the builders rejected
has become the capstone;
23the LORD has done this,
and it is marvelous in our eyes.
24This is the day the LORD has made;
let us rejoice and be glad in it.

25O LORD, save us;
O LORD, grant us success.
26Blessed is he who comes in the name of the LORD.
From the house of the LORD we bless you.[e]
27The LORD is God,

[a]3 Hebrew *Sheol* [b]10 Or *believed even when* [c]16 Or *servant, your faithful son* [d]19,2 Hebrew *Hallelu Yah* [e]26 The Hebrew is plural.

and he has made his light shine upon us.
With boughs in hand, join in the festal procession
up[a] to the horns of the altar.

28You are my God, and I will give you thanks;
you are my God, and I will exalt you.

29Give thanks to the LORD, for he is good;
his love endures forever.

Psalm 119[b]

א Aleph

1Blessed are they whose ways are blameless,
who walk according to the law of the LORD.
2Blessed are they who keep his statutes
and seek him with all their heart.
3They do nothing wrong;
they walk in his ways.
4You have laid down precepts
that are to be fully obeyed.
5Oh, that my ways were steadfast
in obeying your decrees!
6Then I would not be put to shame
when I consider all your commands.
7I will praise you with an upright heart
as I learn your righteous laws.
8I will obey your decrees;
do not utterly forsake me.

ב Beth

9How can a young man keep his way pure?
By living according to your word.
10I seek you with all my heart;
do not let me stray from your commands.
11I have hidden your word in my heart
that I might not sin against you.
12Praise be to you, O LORD;
teach me your decrees.
13With my lips I recount
all the laws that come from your mouth.
14I rejoice in following your statutes
as one rejoices in great riches.
15I meditate on your precepts
and consider your ways.
16I delight in your decrees;
I will not neglect your word.

ג Gimel

17Do good to your servant, and I will live;
I will obey your word.
18Open my eyes that I may see
wonderful things in your law.
19I am a stranger on earth;
do not hide your commands from me.
20My soul is consumed with longing
for your laws at all times.
21You rebuke the arrogant, who are cursed
and who stray from your commands.
22Remove from me scorn and contempt,
for I keep your statutes.
23Though rulers sit together and slander me,
your servant will meditate on your decrees.
24Your statutes are my delight;
they are my counselors.

ד Daleth

25I am laid low in the dust;
preserve my life according to your word.
26I recounted my ways and you answered me;
teach me your decrees.
27Let me understand the teaching of your precepts;
then I will meditate on your wonders.
28My soul is weary with sorrow;
strengthen me according to your word.
29Keep me from deceitful ways;
be gracious to me through your law.
30I have chosen the way of truth;
I have set my heart on your laws.
31I hold fast to your statutes, O LORD;
do not let me be put to shame.
32I run in the path of your commands,
for you have set my heart free.

ה He

33Teach me, O LORD, to follow your decrees;
then I will keep them to the end.
34Give me understanding, and I will keep your law
and obey it with all my heart.
35Direct me in the path of your commands,
for there I find delight.
36Turn my heart toward your statutes
and not toward selfish gain.
37Turn my eyes away from worthless things;
preserve my life according to your word.[c]
38Fulfill your promise to your servant,
so that you may be feared.
39Take away the disgrace I dread,
for your laws are good.
40How I long for your precepts!
Preserve my life in your righteousness.

ו Waw

41May your unfailing love come to me, O LORD,
your salvation according to your promise;
42then I will answer the one who taunts me,
for I trust in your word.
43Do not snatch the word of truth from my mouth,
for I have put my hope in your laws.
44I will always obey your law,
for ever and ever.

[a]27 Or *Bind the festal sacrifice with ropes / and take it* [b]This psalm is an acrostic poem; the verses of each stanza begin with the same letter of the Hebrew alphabet. [c]37 Two manuscripts of the Masoretic Text and Dead Sea Scrolls; most manuscripts of the Masoretic Text *life in your way*

45I will walk about in freedom,
for I have sought out your precepts.
46I will speak of your statutes before kings
and will not be put to shame,
47for I delight in your commands
because I love them.
48I lift up my hands to[a] your commands,
which I love,
and I meditate on your decrees.

ז Zayin

49Remember your word to your servant,
for you have given me hope.
50My comfort in my suffering is this:
Your promise preserves my life.
51The arrogant mock me without restraint,
but I do not turn from your law.
52I remember your ancient laws, O LORD,
and I find comfort in them.
53Indignation grips me because of the wicked,
who have forsaken your law.
54Your decrees are the theme of my song
wherever I lodge.
55In the night I remember your name, O LORD,
and I will keep your law.
56This has been my practice:
I obey your precepts.

ח Heth

57You are my portion, O LORD;
I have promised to obey your words.
58I have sought your face with all my heart;
be gracious to me according to your promise.
59I have considered my ways
and have turned my steps to your statutes.
60I will hasten and not delay
to obey your commands.
61Though the wicked bind me with ropes,
I will not forget your law.
62At midnight I rise to give you thanks
for your righteous laws.
63I am a friend to all who fear you,
to all who follow your precepts.
64The earth is filled with your love, O LORD;
teach me your decrees.

ט Teth

65Do good to your servant
according to your word, O LORD.
66Teach me knowledge and good judgment,
for I believe in your commands.
67Before I was afflicted I went astray,
but now I obey your word.
68You are good, and what you do is good;
teach me your decrees.
69Though the arrogant have smeared me with lies,
I keep your precepts with all my heart.
70Their hearts are callous and unfeeling,
but I delight in your law.
71It was good for me to be afflicted
so that I might learn your decrees.
72The law from your mouth is more precious to me
than thousands of pieces of silver and gold.

י Yodh

73Your hands made me and formed me;
give me understanding to learn your commands.
74May those who fear you rejoice when they see me,
for I have put my hope in your word.
75I know, O LORD, that your laws are righteous,
and in faithfulness you have afflicted me.
76May your unfailing love be my comfort,
according to your promise to your servant.
77Let your compassion come to me that I may live,
for your law is my delight.
78May the arrogant be put to shame for wronging me without cause;
but I will meditate on your precepts.
79May those who fear you turn to me,
those who understand your statutes.
80May my heart be blameless toward your decrees,
that I may not be put to shame.

כ Kaph

81My soul faints with longing for your salvation,
but I have put my hope in your word.
82My eyes fail, looking for your promise;
I say, "When will you comfort me?"
83Though I am like a wineskin in the smoke,
I do not forget your decrees.
84How long must your servant wait?
When will you punish my persecutors?
85The arrogant dig pitfalls for me,
contrary to your law.
86All your commands are trustworthy;
help me, for men persecute me without cause.
87They almost wiped me from the earth,
but I have not forsaken your precepts.
88Preserve my life according to your love,
and I will obey the statutes of your mouth.

ל Lamedh

89Your word, O LORD, is eternal;
it stands firm in the heavens.
90Your faithfulness continues through all generations;
you established the earth, and it endures.
91Your laws endure to this day,
for all things serve you.
92If your law had not been my delight,

[a]48 Or *for*

I would have perished in my affliction.
93I will never forget your precepts,
for by them you have preserved my life.
94Save me, for I am yours;
I have sought out your precepts.
95The wicked are waiting to destroy me,
but I will ponder your statutes.
96To all perfection I see a limit;
but your commands are boundless.

מ Mem

97Oh, how I love your law!
I meditate on it all day long.
98Your commands make me wiser than my enemies,
for they are ever with me.
99I have more insight than all my teachers,
for I meditate on your statutes.
100I have more understanding than the elders,
for I obey your precepts.
101I have kept my feet from every evil path
so that I might obey your word.
102I have not departed from your laws,
for you yourself have taught me.
103How sweet are your words to my taste,
sweeter than honey to my mouth!
104I gain understanding from your precepts;
therefore I hate every wrong path.

נ Nun

105Your word is a lamp to my feet
and a light for my path.
106I have taken an oath and confirmed it,
that I will follow your righteous laws.
107I have suffered much;
preserve my life, O LORD, according to your word.
108Accept, O LORD, the willing praise of my mouth,
and teach me your laws.
109Though I constantly take my life in my hands,
I will not forget your law.
110The wicked have set a snare for me,
but I have not strayed from your precepts.
111Your statutes are my heritage forever;
they are the joy of my heart.
112My heart is set on keeping your decrees
to the very end.

ס Samekh

113I hate double-minded men,
but I love your law.
114You are my refuge and my shield;
I have put my hope in your word.
115Away from me, you evildoers,
that I may keep the commands of my God!
116Sustain me according to your promise,
and I will live;
do not let my hopes be dashed.
117Uphold me, and I will be delivered;
I will always have regard for your decrees.
118You reject all who stray from your decrees,
for their deceitfulness is in vain.
119All the wicked of the earth you discard like dross;
therefore I love your statutes.
120My flesh trembles in fear of you;
I stand in awe of your laws.

ע Ayin

121I have done what is righteous and just;
do not leave me to my oppressors.
122Ensure your servant's well-being;
let not the arrogant oppress me.
123My eyes fail, looking for your salvation,
looking for your righteous promise.
124Deal with your servant according to your love
and teach me your decrees.
125I am your servant; give me discernment
that I may understand your statutes.
126It is time for you to act, O LORD;
your law is being broken.
127Because I love your commands
more than gold, more than pure gold,
128and because I consider all your precepts right,
I hate every wrong path.

פ Pe

129Your statutes are wonderful;
therefore I obey them.
130The unfolding of your words gives light;
it gives understanding to the simple.
131I open my mouth and pant,
longing for your commands.
132Turn to me and have mercy on me,
as you always do to those who love your name.
133Direct my footsteps according to your word;
let no sin rule over me.
134Redeem me from the oppression of men,
that I may obey your precepts.
135Make your face shine upon your servant
and teach me your decrees.
136Streams of tears flow from my eyes,
for your law is not obeyed.

צ Tsadhe

137Righteous are you, O LORD,
and your laws are right.
138The statutes you have laid down are righteous;
they are fully trustworthy.
139My zeal wears me out,
for my enemies ignore your words.
140Your promises have been thoroughly tested,
and your servant loves them.
141Though I am lowly and despised,
I do not forget your precepts.
142Your righteousness is everlasting
and your law is true.
143Trouble and distress have come upon me,
but your commands are my delight.

144Your statutes are forever right;
give me understanding that I may live.

ק Qoph

145I call with all my heart; answer me, O LORD,
and I will obey your decrees.
146I call out to you; save me
and I will keep your statutes.
147I rise before dawn and cry for help;
I have put my hope in your word.
148My eyes stay open through the watches of the night,
that I may meditate on your promises.
149Hear my voice in accordance with your love;
preserve my life, O LORD, according to your laws.
150Those who devise wicked schemes are near,
but they are far from your law.
151Yet you are near, O LORD,
and all your commands are true.
152Long ago I learned from your statutes
that you established them to last forever.

ר Resh

153Look upon my suffering and deliver me,
for I have not forgotten your law.
154Defend my cause and redeem me;
preserve my life according to your promise.
155Salvation is far from the wicked,
for they do not seek out your decrees.
156Your compassion is great, O LORD;
preserve my life according to your laws.
157Many are the foes who persecute me,
but I have not turned from your statutes.
158I look on the faithless with loathing,
for they do not obey your word.
159See how I love your precepts;
preserve my life, O LORD, according to your love.
160All your words are true;
all your righteous laws are eternal.

ש Sin and Shin

161Rulers persecute me without cause,
but my heart trembles at your word.
162I rejoice in your promise
like one who finds great spoil.
163I hate and abhor falsehood
but I love your law.
164Seven times a day I praise you
for your righteous laws.
165Great peace have they who love your law,
and nothing can make them stumble.
166I wait for your salvation, O LORD,
and I follow your commands.
167I obey your statutes,
for I love them greatly.
168I obey your precepts and your statutes,
for all my ways are known to you.

ת Taw

169May my cry come before you, O LORD;
give me understanding according to your word.
170May my supplication come before you;
deliver me according to your promise.
171May my lips overflow with praise,
for you teach me your decrees.
172May my tongue sing of your word,
for all your commands are righteous.
173May your hand be ready to help me,
for I have chosen your precepts.
174I long for your salvation, O LORD,
and your law is my delight.
175Let me live that I may praise you,
and may your laws sustain me.
176I have strayed like a lost sheep.
Seek your servant,
for I have not forgotten your commands.

Psalm 120

A song of ascents.

1I call on the LORD in my distress,
and he answers me.
2Save me, O LORD, from lying lips
and from deceitful tongues.

3What will he do to you,
and what more besides, O deceitful tongue?
4He will punish you with a warrior's sharp arrows,
with burning coals of the broom tree.

5Woe to me that I dwell in Meshech,
that I live among the tents of Kedar!
6Too long have I lived
among those who hate peace.
7I am a man of peace;
but when I speak, they are for war.

Psalm 121

A song of ascents.

1I lift up my eyes to the hills—
where does my help come from?
2My help comes from the LORD,
the Maker of heaven and earth.

3He will not let your foot slip—
he who watches over you will not slumber;
4indeed, he who watches over Israel
will neither slumber nor sleep.

5The LORD watches over you—
the LORD is your shade at your right hand;
6the sun will not harm you by day,
nor the moon by night.

7The LORD will keep you from all harm—
he will watch over your life;
8the LORD will watch over your coming and going
both now and forevermore.

Psalm 122

A song of ascents. Of David.

1I rejoiced with those who said to me,
"Let us go to the house of the LORD."
2Our feet are standing
in your gates, O Jerusalem.

3Jerusalem is built like a city
that is closely compacted together.
4That is where the tribes go up,
the tribes of the LORD,
to praise the name of the LORD
according to the statute given to Israel.
5There the thrones for judgment stand,
the thrones of the house of David.

6Pray for the peace of Jerusalem:
"May those who love you be secure.
7May there be peace within your walls
and security within your citadels."
8For the sake of my brothers and friends,
I will say, "Peace be within you."
9For the sake of the house of the LORD our God,
I will seek your prosperity.

Psalm 123

A song of ascents.

1I lift up my eyes to you,
to you whose throne is in heaven.
2As the eyes of slaves look to the hand of their master,
as the eyes of a maid look to the hand of her mistress,
so our eyes look to the LORD our God,
till he shows us his mercy.

3Have mercy on us, O LORD, have mercy on us,
for we have endured much contempt.
4We have endured much ridicule from the proud,
much contempt from the arrogant.

Psalm 124

A song of ascents. Of David.

1If the LORD had not been on our side—
let Israel say—
2if the LORD had not been on our side
when men attacked us,
3when their anger flared against us,
they would have swallowed us alive;
4the flood would have engulfed us,
the torrent would have swept over us,
5the raging waters
would have swept us away.

6Praise be to the LORD,
who has not let us be torn by their teeth.
7We have escaped like a bird
out of the fowler's snare;
the snare has been broken,
and we have escaped.
8Our help is in the name of the LORD,
the Maker of heaven and earth.

Psalm 125

A song of ascents.

1Those who trust in the LORD are like Mount Zion,
which cannot be shaken but endures forever.
2As the mountains surround Jerusalem,
so the LORD surrounds his people
both now and forevermore.

3The scepter of the wicked will not remain
over the land allotted to the righteous,
for then the righteous might use
their hands to do evil.

4Do good, O LORD, to those who are good,
to those who are upright in heart.
5But those who turn to crooked ways
the LORD will banish with the evildoers.

Peace be upon Israel.

Psalm 126

A song of ascents.

1When the LORD brought back the captives to[a] Zion,
we were like men who dreamed.[b]
2Our mouths were filled with laughter,
our tongues with songs of joy.
Then it was said among the nations,
"The LORD has done great things for them."
3The LORD has done great things for us,
and we are filled with joy.

4Restore our fortunes,[c] O LORD,
like streams in the Negev.
5Those who sow in tears
will reap with songs of joy.
6He who goes out weeping,
carrying seed to sow,
will return with songs of joy,
carrying sheaves with him.

Psalm 127

A song of ascents. Of Solomon.

1Unless the LORD builds the house,
its builders labor in vain.
Unless the LORD watches over the city,
the watchmen stand guard in vain.
2In vain you rise early
and stay up late,
toiling for food to eat—
for he grants sleep to[d] those he loves.

3Sons are a heritage from the LORD,
children a reward from him.
4Like arrows in the hands of a warrior
are sons born in one's youth.
5Blessed is the man
whose quiver is full of them.

[a] *1* Or *LORD restored the fortunes of* [b] *1* Or *men restored to health* [c] *4* Or *Bring back our captives*
[d] *2* Or *eat—/for while they sleep he provides for*

They will not be put to shame
when they contend with their enemies in the gate.

Psalm 128

A song of ascents.

1Blessed are all who fear the LORD,
who walk in his ways.
2You will eat the fruit of your labor;
blessings and prosperity will be yours.
3Your wife will be like a fruitful vine
within your house;
your sons will be like olive shoots
around your table.
4Thus is the man blessed
who fears the LORD.

5May the LORD bless you from Zion
all the days of your life;
may you see the prosperity of Jerusalem,
6 and may you live to see your children's children.

Peace be upon Israel.

Psalm 129

A song of ascents.

1They have greatly oppressed me from my youth—
let Israel say—
2they have greatly oppressed me from my youth,
but they have not gained the victory over me.
3Plowmen have plowed my back
and made their furrows long.
4But the LORD is righteous;
he has cut me free from the cords of the wicked.

5May all who hate Zion
be turned back in shame.
6May they be like grass on the roof,
which withers before it can grow;
7with it the reaper cannot fill his hands,
nor the one who gathers fill his arms.
8May those who pass by not say,
"The blessing of the LORD be upon you;
we bless you in the name of the LORD."

Psalm 130

A song of ascents.

1Out of the depths I cry to you, O LORD;
2 O Lord, hear my voice.
Let your ears be attentive
to my cry for mercy.

3If you, O LORD, kept a record of sins,
O Lord, who could stand?
4But with you there is forgiveness;
therefore you are feared.

5I wait for the LORD, my soul waits,
and in his word I put my hope.
6My soul waits for the Lord
more than watchmen wait for the morning,
more than watchmen wait for the morning.

7O Israel, put your hope in the LORD,
for with the LORD is unfailing love
and with him is full redemption.
8He himself will redeem Israel
from all their sins.

Psalm 131

A song of ascents. Of David.

1My heart is not proud, O LORD,
my eyes are not haughty;
I do not concern myself with great matters
or things too wonderful for me.
2But I have stilled and quieted my soul;
like a weaned child with its mother,
like a weaned child is my soul within me.

3O Israel, put your hope in the LORD
both now and forevermore.

Psalm 132

A song of ascents.

1O LORD, remember David
and all the hardships he endured.

2He swore an oath to the LORD
and made a vow to the Mighty One of Jacob:
3"I will not enter my house
or go to my bed—
4I will allow no sleep to my eyes,
no slumber to my eyelids,
5till I find a place for the LORD,
a dwelling for the Mighty One of Jacob."

6We heard it in Ephrathah,
we came upon it in the fields of Jaar[a]:[b]
7"Let us go to his dwelling place;
let us worship at his footstool—
8arise, O LORD, and come to your resting place,
you and the ark of your might.
9May your priests be clothed with righteousness;
may your saints sing for joy."

10For the sake of David your servant,
do not reject your anointed one.

11The LORD swore an oath to David,
a sure oath that he will not revoke:
"One of your own descendants
I will place on your throne—
12if your sons keep my covenant
and the statutes I teach them,
then their sons will sit
on your throne for ever and ever."

13For the LORD has chosen Zion,

[a]*6* That is, Kiriath Jearim [b]*6* Or *heard of it in Ephrathah, / we found it in the fields of Jaar.* (And no quotes around verses 7-9)

he has desired it for his dwelling:
14"This is my resting place for ever and ever;
here I will sit enthroned, for I have desired it—
15I will bless her with abundant provisions;
her poor will I satisfy with food.
16I will clothe her priests with salvation,
and her saints will ever sing for joy.

17"Here I will make a horn[a] grow for David
and set up a lamp for my anointed one.
18I will clothe his enemies with shame,
but the crown on his head will be resplendent."

Psalm 133

A song of ascents. Of David.

1How good and pleasant it is
when brothers live together in unity!
2It is like precious oil poured on the head,
running down on the beard,
running down on Aaron's beard,
down upon the collar of his robes.
3It is as if the dew of Hermon
were falling on Mount Zion.
For there the LORD bestows his blessing,
even life forevermore.

Psalm 134

A song of ascents.

1Praise the LORD, all you servants of the LORD
who minister by night in the house of the LORD.
2Lift up your hands in the sanctuary
and praise the LORD.

3May the LORD, the Maker of heaven and earth,
bless you from Zion.

Psalm 135

1Praise the LORD.[b]

Praise the name of the LORD;
praise him, you servants of the LORD,
2you who minister in the house of the LORD,
in the courts of the house of our God.

3Praise the LORD, for the LORD is good;
sing praise to his name, for that is pleasant.
4For the LORD has chosen Jacob to be his own,
Israel to be his treasured possession.

5I know that the LORD is great,
that our Lord is greater than all gods.
6The LORD does whatever pleases him,
in the heavens and on the earth,
in the seas and all their depths.
7He makes clouds rise from the ends of the earth;
he sends lightning with the rain
and brings out the wind from his storehouses.

8He struck down the firstborn of Egypt,
the firstborn of men and animals.
9He sent his signs and wonders into your midst, O Egypt,
against Pharaoh and all his servants.
10He struck down many nations
and killed mighty kings—
11Sihon king of the Amorites,
Og king of Bashan
and all the kings of Canaan—
12and he gave their land as an inheritance,
an inheritance to his people Israel.

13Your name, O LORD, endures forever,
your renown, O LORD, through all generations.
14For the LORD will vindicate his people
and have compassion on his servants.

15The idols of the nations are silver and gold,
made by the hands of men.
16They have mouths, but cannot speak,
eyes, but they cannot see;
17they have ears, but cannot hear,
nor is there breath in their mouths.
18Those who make them will be like them,
and so will all who trust in them.

19O house of Israel, praise the LORD;
O house of Aaron, praise the LORD;
20O house of Levi, praise the LORD;
you who fear him, praise the LORD.
21Praise be to the LORD from Zion,
to him who dwells in Jerusalem.

Praise the LORD.

Psalm 136

1Give thanks to the LORD, for he is good.
His love endures forever.
2Give thanks to the God of gods.
His love endures forever.
3Give thanks to the Lord of lords:
His love endures forever.

4to him who alone does great wonders,
His love endures forever.
5who by his understanding made the heavens,
His love endures forever.
6who spread out the earth upon the waters,
His love endures forever.
7who made the great lights—
His love endures forever.
8the sun to govern the day,
His love endures forever.
9the moon and stars to govern the night;
His love endures forever.

10to him who struck down the firstborn of Egypt
His love endures forever.

[a] *17* *Horn* here symbolizes strong one, that is, king.
[b] *1* Hebrew *Hallelu Yah*; also in verses 3 and 21

11and brought Israel out from among them
His love endures forever.
12with a mighty hand and outstretched arm;
His love endures forever.

13to him who divided the Red Sea[a] asunder
His love endures forever.
14and brought Israel through the midst of it,
His love endures forever.
15but swept Pharaoh and his army into the
Red Sea;
His love endures forever.

16to him who led his people through the
desert,
His love endures forever.
17who struck down great kings,
His love endures forever.
18and killed mighty kings—
His love endures forever.
19Sihon king of the Amorites
His love endures forever.
20and Og king of Bashan—
His love endures forever.
21and gave their land as an inheritance,
His love endures forever.
22an inheritance to his servant Israel;
His love endures forever.

23to the One who remembered us in our low
estate
His love endures forever.
24and freed us from our enemies,
His love endures forever.
25and who gives food to every creature.
His love endures forever.

26Give thanks to the God of heaven.
His love endures forever.

Psalm 137

1By the rivers of Babylon we sat and wept
when we remembered Zion.
2There on the poplars
we hung our harps,
3for there our captors asked us for songs,
our tormentors demanded songs of joy;
they said, "Sing us one of the songs of
Zion!"

4How can we sing the songs of the LORD
while in a foreign land?
5If I forget you, O Jerusalem,
may my right hand forget ⌊its skill⌋.
6May my tongue cling to the roof of my
mouth
if I do not remember you,
if I do not consider Jerusalem
my highest joy.

7Remember, O LORD, what the Edomites
did
on the day Jerusalem fell.
"Tear it down," they cried,
"tear it down to its foundations!"

8O Daughter of Babylon, doomed to
destruction,
happy is he who repays you
for what you have done to us—
9he who seizes your infants
and dashes them against the rocks.

Psalm 138

Of David.

1I will praise you, O LORD, with all my
heart;
before the "gods" I will sing your
praise.
2I will bow down toward your holy temple
and will praise your name
for your love and your faithfulness,
for you have exalted above all things
your name and your word.
3When I called, you answered me;
you made me bold and stouthearted.

4May all the kings of the earth praise you,
O LORD,
when they hear the words of your
mouth.
5May they sing of the ways of the LORD,
for the glory of the LORD is great.

6Though the LORD is on high, he looks
upon the lowly,
but the proud he knows from afar.
7Though I walk in the midst of trouble,
you preserve my life;
you stretch out your hand against the
anger of my foes,
with your right hand you save me.
8The LORD will fulfill ⌊his purpose⌋ for me;
your love, O LORD, endures forever—
do not abandon the works of your
hands.

Psalm 139

For the director of music. Of David.
A psalm.

1O LORD, you have searched me
and you know me.
2You know when I sit and when I rise;
you perceive my thoughts from afar.
3You discern my going out and my lying
down;
you are familiar with all my ways.
4Before a word is on my tongue
you know it completely, O LORD.

5You hem me in—behind and before;
you have laid your hand upon me.
6Such knowledge is too wonderful for me,
too lofty for me to attain.

7Where can I go from your Spirit?
Where can I flee from your presence?
8If I go up to the heavens, you are there;
if I make my bed in the depths,[b] you
are there.
9If I rise on the wings of the dawn,
if I settle on the far side of the sea,

[a]*13* Hebrew *Yam Suph*; that is, Sea of Reeds; also in verse 15 [b]*8* Hebrew *Sheol*

10even there your hand will guide me,
your right hand will hold me fast.

11If I say, "Surely the darkness will hide me
and the light become night around me,"
12even the darkness will not be dark to you;
the night will shine like the day,
for darkness is as light to you.

13For you created my inmost being;
you knit me together in my mother's
womb.
14I praise you because I am fearfully and
wonderfully made;
your works are wonderful,
I know that full well.
15My frame was not hidden from you
when I was made in the secret place.
When I was woven together in the depths
of the earth,
16 your eyes saw my unformed body.
All the days ordained for me
were written in your book
before one of them came to be.

17How precious to[a] me are your thoughts,
O God!
How vast is the sum of them!
18Were I to count them,
they would outnumber the grains of
sand.
When I awake,
I am still with you.

19If only you would slay the wicked,
O God!
Away from me, you bloodthirsty men!
20They speak of you with evil intent;
your adversaries misuse your name.
21Do I not hate those who hate you,
O LORD,
and abhor those who rise up against
you?
22I have nothing but hatred for them;
I count them my enemies.

23Search me, O God, and know my heart;
test me and know my anxious thoughts.
24See if there is any offensive way in me,
and lead me in the way everlasting.

Psalm 140

For the director of music. A psalm of David.

1Rescue me, O LORD, from evil men;
protect me from men of violence,
2who devise evil plans in their hearts
and stir up war every day.
3They make their tongues as sharp as a
serpent's;
the poison of vipers is on their lips.
Selah

4Keep me, O LORD, from the hands of the
wicked;
protect me from men of violence
who plan to trip my feet.
5Proud men have hidden a snare for me;
they have spread out the cords of their
net
and have set traps for me along my
path. *Selah*

6O LORD, I say to you, "You are my God."
Hear, O LORD, my cry for mercy.
7O Sovereign LORD, my strong deliverer,
who shields my head in the day of
battle—
8do not grant the wicked their desires,
O LORD;
do not let their plans succeed,
or they will become proud. *Selah*

9Let the heads of those who surround me
be covered with the trouble their lips
have caused.
10Let burning coals fall upon them;
may they be thrown into the fire,
into miry pits, never to rise.
11Let slanderers not be established in the
land;
may disaster hunt down men of
violence.

12I know that the LORD secures justice for
the poor
and upholds the cause of the needy.
13Surely the righteous will praise your name
and the upright will live before you.

Psalm 141

A psalm of David.

1O LORD, I call to you; come quickly to
me.
Hear my voice when I call to you.
2May my prayer be set before you like
incense;
may the lifting up of my hands be like
the evening sacrifice.

3Set a guard over my mouth, O LORD;
keep watch over the door of my lips.
4Let not my heart be drawn to what is evil,
to take part in wicked deeds
with men who are evildoers;
let me not eat of their delicacies.

5Let a righteous man[b] strike me—it is a
kindness;
let him rebuke me—it is oil on my
head.
My head will not refuse it.

Yet my prayer is ever against the deeds of
evildoers;
6 their rulers will be thrown down from
the cliffs,
and the wicked will learn that my words
were well spoken.
7⌊They will say,⌋ "As one plows and breaks
up the earth,
so our bones have been scattered at the
mouth of the grave.[c]"

[a]17 Or *concerning* [b]5 Or *Let the Righteous One* [c]7 Hebrew *Sheol*

8But my eyes are fixed on you,
O Sovereign LORD;
in you I take refuge—do not give me
over to death.
9Keep me from the snares they have laid
for me,
from the traps set by evildoers.
10Let the wicked fall into their own nets,
while I pass by in safety.

Psalm 142

A *maskil*[a] of David. When he was in the cave. A prayer.

1I cry aloud to the LORD;
I lift up my voice to the LORD for
mercy.
2I pour out my complaint before him;
before him I tell my trouble.

3When my spirit grows faint within me,
it is you who know my way.
In the path where I walk
men have hidden a snare for me.
4Look to my right and see;
no one is concerned for me.
I have no refuge;
no one cares for my life.

5I cry to you, O LORD;
I say, "You are my refuge,
my portion in the land of the living."
6Listen to my cry,
for I am in desperate need;
rescue me from those who pursue me,
for they are too strong for me.
7Set me free from my prison,
that I may praise your name.

Then the righteous will gather about me
because of your goodness to me.

Psalm 143

A psalm of David.

1O LORD, hear my prayer,
listen to my cry for mercy;
in your faithfulness and righteousness
come to my relief.
2Do not bring your servant into judgment,
for no one living is righteous before
you.

3The enemy pursues me,
he crushes me to the ground;
he makes me dwell in darkness
like those long dead.
4So my spirit grows faint within me;
my heart within me is dismayed.

5I remember the days of long ago;
I meditate on all your works
and consider what your hands have
done.
6I spread out my hands to you;
my soul thirsts for you like a parched
land. *Selah*

7Answer me quickly, O LORD;
my spirit fails.
Do not hide your face from me
or I will be like those who go down to
the pit.
8Let the morning bring me word of your
unfailing love,
for I have put my trust in you.
Show me the way I should go,
for to you I lift up my soul.
9Rescue me from my enemies, O LORD,
for I hide myself in you.
10Teach me to do your will,
for you are my God;
may your good Spirit
lead me on level ground.

11For your name's sake, O LORD, preserve
my life;
in your righteousness, bring me out of
trouble.
12In your unfailing love, silence my
enemies;
destroy all my foes,
for I am your servant.

Psalm 144

Of David.

1Praise be to the LORD my Rock,
who trains my hands for war,
my fingers for battle.
2He is my loving God and my fortress,
my stronghold and my deliverer,
my shield, in whom I take refuge,
who subdues peoples[b] under me.

3O LORD, what is man that you care for
him,
the son of man that you think of him?
4Man is like a breath;
his days are like a fleeting shadow.

5Part your heavens, O LORD, and come
down;
touch the mountains, so that they
smoke.
6Send forth lightning and scatter ⌞the
enemies⌟;
shoot your arrows and rout them.
7Reach down your hand from on high;
deliver me and rescue me
from the mighty waters,
from the hands of foreigners
8whose mouths are full of lies,
whose right hands are deceitful.

9I will sing a new song to you, O God;
on the ten-stringed lyre I will make
music to you,
10to the One who gives victory to kings,
who delivers his servant David from the
deadly sword.

11Deliver me and rescue me
from the hands of foreigners

[a]Title: Probably a literary or musical term [b]2 Many manuscripts of the Masoretic Text, Dead Sea Scrolls, Aquila, Jerome and Syriac; most manuscripts of the Masoretic Text *subdues my people*

whose mouths are full of lies,
whose right hands are deceitful.

12Then our sons in their youth
will be like well-nurtured plants,
and our daughters will be like pillars
carved to adorn a palace.
13Our barns will be filled
with every kind of provision.
Our sheep will increase by thousands,
by tens of thousands in our fields;
14 our oxen will draw heavy loads.[a]
There will be no breaching of walls,
no going into captivity,
no cry of distress in our streets.

15Blessed are the people of whom this is true;
blessed are the people whose God is the LORD.

Psalm 145[b]

A psalm of praise. Of David.

1I will exalt you, my God the King;
I will praise your name for ever and ever.
2Every day I will praise you
and extol your name for ever and ever.

3Great is the LORD and most worthy of praise;
his greatness no one can fathom.
4One generation will commend your works to another;
they will tell of your mighty acts.
5They will speak of the glorious splendor of your majesty,
and I will meditate on your wonderful works.[c]
6They will tell of the power of your awesome works,
and I will proclaim your great deeds.
7They will celebrate your abundant goodness
and joyfully sing of your righteousness.

8The LORD is gracious and compassionate,
slow to anger and rich in love.
9The LORD is good to all;
he has compassion on all he has made.
10All you have made will praise you, O LORD;
your saints will extol you.
11They will tell of the glory of your kingdom
and speak of your might,
12so that all men may know of your mighty acts
and the glorious splendor of your kingdom.
13Your kingdom is an everlasting kingdom,
and your dominion endures through all generations.

The LORD is faithful to all his promises
and loving toward all he has made.[d]
14The LORD upholds all those who fall
and lifts up all who are bowed down.
15The eyes of all look to you,
and you give them their food at the proper time.
16You open your hand
and satisfy the desires of every living thing.

17The LORD is righteous in all his ways
and loving toward all he has made.
18The LORD is near to all who call on him,
to all who call on him in truth.
19He fulfills the desires of those who fear him;
he hears their cry and saves them.
20The LORD watches over all who love him,
but all the wicked he will destroy.

21My mouth will speak in praise of the LORD.
Let every creature praise his holy name
for ever and ever.

Psalm 146

1Praise the LORD.[e]

Praise the LORD, O my soul.
2 I will praise the LORD all my life;
I will sing praise to my God as long as I live.

3Do not put your trust in princes,
in mortal men, who cannot save.
4When their spirit departs, they return to the ground;
on that very day their plans come to nothing.

5Blessed is he whose help is the God of Jacob,
whose hope is in the LORD his God,
6the Maker of heaven and earth,
the sea, and everything in them—
the LORD, who remains faithful forever.
7He upholds the cause of the oppressed
and gives food to the hungry.
The LORD sets prisoners free,
8 the LORD gives sight to the blind,
the LORD lifts up those who are bowed down,
the LORD loves the righteous.
9The LORD watches over the alien
and sustains the fatherless and the widow,
but he frustrates the ways of the wicked.

[a]*14* Or *our chieftains will be firmly established* [b]This psalm is an acrostic poem, the verses of which (including verse 13b) begin with the successive letters of the Hebrew alphabet. [c]*5* Dead Sea Scrolls and Syriac (see also Septuagint); Masoretic Text *On the glorious splendor of your majesty / and on your wonderful works I will meditate* [d]*13* One manuscript of the Masoretic Text, Dead Sea Scrolls and Syriac (see also Septuagint); most manuscripts of the Masoretic Text do not have the last two lines of verse 13. [e]*1* Hebrew *Hallelu Yah*; also in verse 10

10The LORD reigns forever,
your God, O Zion, for all generations.

Praise the LORD.

Psalm 147

1Praise the LORD.[a]

How good it is to sing praises to our God,
how pleasant and fitting to praise him!

2The LORD builds up Jerusalem;
he gathers the exiles of Israel.
3He heals the brokenhearted
and binds up their wounds.

4He determines the number of the stars
and calls them each by name.
5Great is our Lord and mighty in power;
his understanding has no limit.
6The LORD sustains the humble
but casts the wicked to the ground.

7Sing to the LORD with thanksgiving;
make music to our God on the harp.
8He covers the sky with clouds;
he supplies the earth with rain
and makes grass grow on the hills.
9He provides food for the cattle
and for the young ravens when they call.

10His pleasure is not in the strength of the horse,
nor his delight in the legs of a man;
11the LORD delights in those who fear him,
who put their hope in his unfailing love.

12Extol the LORD, O Jerusalem;
praise your God, O Zion,
13for he strengthens the bars of your gates
and blesses your people within you.
14He grants peace to your borders
and satisfies you with the finest of wheat.

15He sends his command to the earth;
his word runs swiftly.
16He spreads the snow like wool
and scatters the frost like ashes.
17He hurls down his hail like pebbles.
Who can withstand his icy blast?
18He sends his word and melts them;
he stirs up his breezes, and the waters flow.

19He has revealed his word to Jacob,
his laws and decrees to Israel.
20He has done this for no other nation;
they do not know his laws.

Praise the LORD.

Psalm 148

1Praise the LORD.[b]

Praise the LORD from the heavens,
praise him in the heights above.
2Praise him, all his angels,
praise him, all his heavenly hosts.
3Praise him, sun and moon,
praise him, all you shining stars.
4Praise him, you highest heavens
and you waters above the skies.
5Let them praise the name of the LORD,
for he commanded and they were created.
6He set them in place for ever and ever;
he gave a decree that will never pass away.

7Praise the LORD from the earth,
you great sea creatures and all ocean depths,
8lightning and hail, snow and clouds,
stormy winds that do his bidding,
9you mountains and all hills,
fruit trees and all cedars,
10wild animals and all cattle,
small creatures and flying birds,
11kings of the earth and all nations,
you princes and all rulers on earth,
12young men and maidens,
old men and children.

13Let them praise the name of the LORD,
for his name alone is exalted;
his splendor is above the earth and the heavens.
14He has raised up for his people a horn,[c]
the praise of all his saints,
of Israel, the people close to his heart.

Praise the LORD.

Psalm 149

1Praise the LORD.[d]

Sing to the LORD a new song,
his praise in the assembly of the saints.

2Let Israel rejoice in their Maker;
let the people of Zion be glad in their King.
3Let them praise his name with dancing
and make music to him with tambourine and harp.
4For the LORD takes delight in his people;
he crowns the humble with salvation.
5Let the saints rejoice in this honor
and sing for joy on their beds.

6May the praise of God be in their mouths
and a double-edged sword in their hands,
7to inflict vengeance on the nations
and punishment on the peoples,
8to bind their kings with fetters,
their nobles with shackles of iron,
9to carry out the sentence written against them.
This is the glory of all his saints.

Praise the LORD.

a1 Hebrew *Hallelu Yah*; also in verse 20   b1 Hebrew *Hallelu Yah*; also in verse 14   c14 *Horn* here symbolizes strong one, that is, king.   d1 Hebrew *Hallelu Yah*; also in verse 9

Psalm 150

1Praise the LORD.[a]

Praise God in his sanctuary;
praise him in his mighty heavens.
2Praise him for his acts of power;
praise him for his surpassing greatness.
3Praise him with the sounding of the trumpet,
praise him with the harp and lyre,
4praise him with tambourine and dancing,
praise him with the strings and flute,
5praise him with the clash of cymbals,
praise him with resounding cymbals.

6Let everything that has breath praise the LORD.

Praise the LORD.

Proverbs

Prologue: Purpose and Theme

1 The proverbs of Solomon son of David, king of Israel:

2for attaining wisdom and discipline;
for understanding words of insight;
3for acquiring a disciplined and prudent life,
doing what is right and just and fair;
4for giving prudence to the simple,
knowledge and discretion to the young—
5let the wise listen and add to their learning,
and let the discerning get guidance—
6for understanding proverbs and parables,
the sayings and riddles of the wise.

7The fear of the LORD is the beginning of knowledge,
but fools[b] despise wisdom and discipline.

Exhortations to Embrace Wisdom

Warning Against Enticement

8Listen, my son, to your father's instruction
and do not forsake your mother's teaching.
9They will be a garland to grace your head
and a chain to adorn your neck.

10My son, if sinners entice you,
do not give in to them.
11If they say, "Come along with us;
let's lie in wait for someone's blood,
let's waylay some harmless soul;
12let's swallow them alive, like the grave,[c]
and whole, like those who go down to the pit;
13we will get all sorts of valuable things
and fill our houses with plunder;
14throw in your lot with us,
and we will share a common purse"—
15my son, do not go along with them,
do not set foot on their paths;
16for their feet rush into sin,
they are swift to shed blood.
17How useless to spread a net
in full view of all the birds!
18These men lie in wait for their own blood;
they waylay only themselves!
19Such is the end of all who go after ill-gotten gain;
it takes away the lives of those who get it.

Warning Against Rejecting Wisdom

20Wisdom calls aloud in the street,
she raises her voice in the public squares;
21at the head of the noisy streets[d] she cries out,
in the gateways of the city she makes her speech:

22"How long will you simple ones[e] love your simple ways?
How long will mockers delight in mockery
and fools hate knowledge?
23If you had responded to my rebuke,
I would have poured out my heart to you
and made my thoughts known to you.
24But since you rejected me when I called
and no one gave heed when I stretched out my hand,
25since you ignored all my advice
and would not accept my rebuke,
26I in turn will laugh at your disaster;
I will mock when calamity overtakes you—
27when calamity overtakes you like a storm,
when disaster sweeps over you like a whirlwind,
when distress and trouble overwhelm you.

28"Then they will call to me but I will not answer;
they will look for me but will not find me.

[a] *1* Hebrew *Hallelu Yah*; also in verse 6 [b] *7* The Hebrew words rendered *fool* in Proverbs, and often elsewhere in the Old Testament, denote one who is morally deficient. [c] *12* Hebrew *Sheol* [d] *21* Hebrew; Septuagint / *on the tops of the walls* [e] *22* The Hebrew word rendered *simple* in Proverbs generally denotes one without moral direction and inclined to evil.

29Since they hated knowledge
and did not choose to fear the LORD,
30since they would not accept my advice
and spurned my rebuke,
31they will eat the fruit of their ways
and be filled with the fruit of their schemes.
32For the waywardness of the simple will kill them,
and the complacency of fools will destroy them;
33but whoever listens to me will live in safety
and be at ease, without fear of harm."

Moral Benefits of Wisdom

2 My son, if you accept my words
and store up my commands within you,
2turning your ear to wisdom
and applying your heart to understanding,
3and if you call out for insight
and cry aloud for understanding,
4and if you look for it as for silver
and search for it as for hidden treasure,
5then you will understand the fear of the LORD
and find the knowledge of God.
6For the LORD gives wisdom,
and from his mouth come knowledge and understanding.
7He holds victory in store for the upright,
he is a shield to those whose walk is blameless,
8for he guards the course of the just
and protects the way of his faithful ones.

9Then you will understand what is right and just
and fair—every good path.
10For wisdom will enter your heart,
and knowledge will be pleasant to your soul.
11Discretion will protect you,
and understanding will guard you.

12Wisdom will save you from the ways of wicked men,
from men whose words are perverse,
13who leave the straight paths
to walk in dark ways,
14who delight in doing wrong
and rejoice in the perverseness of evil,
15whose paths are crooked
and who are devious in their ways.

16It will save you also from the adulteress,
from the wayward wife with her seductive words,
17who has left the partner of her youth
and ignored the covenant she made before God.[a]
18For her house leads down to death
and her paths to the spirits of the dead.
19None who go to her return
or attain the paths of life.

20Thus you will walk in the ways of good men
and keep to the paths of the righteous.
21For the upright will live in the land,
and the blameless will remain in it;
22but the wicked will be cut off from the land,
and the unfaithful will be torn from it.

Further Benefits of Wisdom

3 My son, do not forget my teaching,
but keep my commands in your heart,
2for they will prolong your life many years
and bring you prosperity.

3Let love and faithfulness never leave you;
bind them around your neck,
write them on the tablet of your heart.
4Then you will win favor and a good name
in the sight of God and man.

5Trust in the LORD with all your heart
and lean not on your own understanding;
6in all your ways acknowledge him,
and he will make your paths straight.[b]

7Do not be wise in your own eyes;
fear the LORD and shun evil.
8This will bring health to your body
and nourishment to your bones.

9Honor the LORD with your wealth,
with the firstfruits of all your crops;
10then your barns will be filled to overflowing,
and your vats will brim over with new wine.

11My son, do not despise the LORD's discipline
and do not resent his rebuke,
12because the LORD disciplines those he loves,
as a father[c] the son he delights in.

13Blessed is the man who finds wisdom,
the man who gains understanding,
14for she is more profitable than silver
and yields better returns than gold.
15She is more precious than rubies;
nothing you desire can compare with her.
16Long life is in her right hand;
in her left hand are riches and honor.
17Her ways are pleasant ways,
and all her paths are peace.
18She is a tree of life to those who embrace her;
those who lay hold of her will be blessed.

19By wisdom the LORD laid the earth's foundations,
by understanding he set the heavens in place;
20by his knowledge the deeps were divided,
and the clouds let drop the dew.

a17 Or *covenant of her God* b6 Or *will direct your paths* c12 Hebrew; Septuagint / *and he punishes*

[21]My son, preserve sound judgment and discernment,
do not let them out of your sight;
[22]they will be life for you,
an ornament to grace your neck.
[23]Then you will go on your way in safety,
and your foot will not stumble;
[24]when you lie down, you will not be afraid;
when you lie down, your sleep will be sweet.
[25]Have no fear of sudden disaster
or of the ruin that overtakes the wicked,
[26]for the LORD will be your confidence
and will keep your foot from being snared.

[27]Do not withhold good from those who deserve it,
when it is in your power to act.
[28]Do not say to your neighbor,
"Come back later; I'll give it tomorrow"—
when you now have it with you.

[29]Do not plot harm against your neighbor,
who lives trustfully near you.
[30]Do not accuse a man for no reason—
when he has done you no harm.

[31]Do not envy a violent man
or choose any of his ways,
[32]for the LORD detests a perverse man
but takes the upright into his confidence.

[33]The LORD's curse is on the house of the wicked,
but he blesses the home of the righteous.
[34]He mocks proud mockers
but gives grace to the humble.
[35]The wise inherit honor,
but fools he holds up to shame.

Wisdom Is Supreme

4 Listen, my sons, to a father's instruction;
pay attention and gain understanding.
[2]I give you sound learning,
so do not forsake my teaching.
[3]When I was a boy in my father's house,
still tender, and an only child of my mother,
[4]he taught me and said,
"Lay hold of my words with all your heart;
keep my commands and you will live.
[5]Get wisdom, get understanding;
do not forget my words or swerve from them.
[6]Do not forsake wisdom, and she will protect you;
love her, and she will watch over you.
[7]Wisdom is supreme; therefore get wisdom.
Though it cost all you have,[a] get understanding.
[8]Esteem her, and she will exalt you;
embrace her, and she will honor you.
[9]She will set a garland of grace on your head
and present you with a crown of splendor."

[10]Listen, my son, accept what I say,
and the years of your life will be many.
[11]I guide you in the way of wisdom
and lead you along straight paths.
[12]When you walk, your steps will not be hampered;
when you run, you will not stumble.
[13]Hold on to instruction, do not let it go;
guard it well, for it is your life.
[14]Do not set foot on the path of the wicked
or walk in the way of evil men.
[15]Avoid it, do not travel on it;
turn from it and go on your way.
[16]For they cannot sleep till they do evil;
they are robbed of slumber till they make someone fall.
[17]They eat the bread of wickedness
and drink the wine of violence.

[18]The path of the righteous is like the first gleam of dawn,
shining ever brighter till the full light of day.
[19]But the way of the wicked is like deep darkness;
they do not know what makes them stumble.

[20]My son, pay attention to what I say;
listen closely to my words.
[21]Do not let them out of your sight,
keep them within your heart;
[22]for they are life to those who find them
and health to a man's whole body.
[23]Above all else, guard your heart,
for it is the wellspring of life.
[24]Put away perversity from your mouth;
keep corrupt talk far from your lips.
[25]Let your eyes look straight ahead,
fix your gaze directly before you.
[26]Make level[b] paths for your feet
and take only ways that are firm.
[27]Do not swerve to the right or the left;
keep your foot from evil.

Warning Against Adultery

5 My son, pay attention to my wisdom,
listen well to my words of insight,
[2]that you may maintain discretion
and your lips may preserve knowledge.
[3]For the lips of an adulteress drip honey,
and her speech is smoother than oil;
[4]but in the end she is bitter as gall,
sharp as a double-edged sword.
[5]Her feet go down to death;
her steps lead straight to the grave.[c]
[6]She gives no thought to the way of life;
her paths are crooked, but she knows it not.

[7]Now then, my sons, listen to me;

[a]7 Or *Whatever else you get* [b]26 Or *Consider the* [c]5 Hebrew *Sheol*

do not turn aside from what I say.
8Keep to a path far from her,
do not go near the door of her house,
9lest you give your best strength to others
and your years to one who is cruel,
10lest strangers feast on your wealth
and your toil enrich another man's house.
11At the end of your life you will groan,
when your flesh and body are spent.
12You will say, "How I hated discipline!
How my heart spurned correction!
13I would not obey my teachers
or listen to my instructors.
14I have come to the brink of utter ruin
in the midst of the whole assembly."

15Drink water from your own cistern,
running water from your own well.
16Should your springs overflow in the streets,
your streams of water in the public squares?
17Let them be yours alone,
never to be shared with strangers.
18May your fountain be blessed,
and may you rejoice in the wife of your youth.
19A loving doe, a graceful deer—
may her breasts satisfy you always,
may you ever be captivated by her love.
20Why be captivated, my son, by an adulteress?
Why embrace the bosom of another man's wife?

21For a man's ways are in full view of the LORD,
and he examines all his paths.
22The evil deeds of a wicked man ensnare him;
the cords of his sin hold him fast.
23He will die for lack of discipline,
led astray by his own great folly.

Warnings Against Folly

6 My son, if you have put up security for your neighbor,
if you have struck hands in pledge for another,
2if you have been trapped by what you said,
ensnared by the words of your mouth,
3then do this, my son, to free yourself,
since you have fallen into your neighbor's hands:
Go and humble yourself;
press your plea with your neighbor!
4Allow no sleep to your eyes,
no slumber to your eyelids.
5Free yourself, like a gazelle from the hand of the hunter,
like a bird from the snare of the fowler.

6Go to the ant, you sluggard;
consider its ways and be wise!
7It has no commander,
no overseer or ruler,
8yet it stores its provisions in summer
and gathers its food at harvest.

9How long will you lie there, you sluggard?
When will you get up from your sleep?
10A little sleep, a little slumber,
a little folding of the hands to rest—
11and poverty will come on you like a bandit
and scarcity like an armed man.[a]

12A scoundrel and villain,
who goes about with a corrupt mouth,
13 who winks with his eye,
signals with his feet
and motions with his fingers,
14 who plots evil with deceit in his heart—
he always stirs up dissension.
15Therefore disaster will overtake him in an instant;
he will suddenly be destroyed—without remedy.

16There are six things the LORD hates,
seven that are detestable to him:
17 haughty eyes,
a lying tongue,
hands that shed innocent blood,
18 a heart that devises wicked schemes,
feet that are quick to rush into evil,
19 a false witness who pours out lies
and a man who stirs up dissension among brothers.

Warning Against Adultery

20My son, keep your father's commands
and do not forsake your mother's teaching.
21Bind them upon your heart forever;
fasten them around your neck.
22When you walk, they will guide you;
when you sleep, they will watch over you;
when you awake, they will speak to you.
23For these commands are a lamp,
this teaching is a light,
and the corrections of discipline
are the way to life,
24keeping you from the immoral woman,
from the smooth tongue of the wayward wife.
25Do not lust in your heart after her beauty
or let her captivate you with her eyes,
26for the prostitute reduces you to a loaf of bread,
and the adulteress preys upon your very life.
27Can a man scoop fire into his lap
without his clothes being burned?
28Can a man walk on hot coals
without his feet being scorched?
29So is he who sleeps with another man's wife;

a 11 Or *like a vagrant / and scarcity like a beggar*

no one who touches her will go
unpunished.

30Men do not despise a thief if he steals
to satisfy his hunger when he is
starving.
31Yet if he is caught, he must pay
sevenfold,
though it costs him all the wealth of his
house.
32But a man who commits adultery lacks
judgment;
whoever does so destroys himself.
33Blows and disgrace are his lot,
and his shame will never be wiped
away;
34for jealousy arouses a husband's fury,
and he will show no mercy when he
takes revenge.
35He will not accept any compensation;
he will refuse the bribe, however great
it is.

Warning Against the Adulteress

7 My son, keep my words
and store up my commands within you.
2Keep my commands and you will live;
guard my teachings as the apple of your
eye.
3Bind them on your fingers;
write them on the tablet of your heart.
4Say to wisdom, "You are my sister,"
and call understanding your kinsman;
5they will keep you from the adulteress,
from the wayward wife with her
seductive words.

6At the window of my house
I looked out through the lattice.
7I saw among the simple,
I noticed among the young men,
a youth who lacked judgment.
8He was going down the street near her
corner,
walking along in the direction of her
house
9at twilight, as the day was fading,
as the dark of night set in.

10Then out came a woman to meet him,
dressed like a prostitute and with crafty
intent.
11(She is loud and defiant,
her feet never stay at home;
12now in the street, now in the squares,
at every corner she lurks.)
13She took hold of him and kissed him
and with a brazen face she said:

14"I have fellowship offerings[a] at home;
today I fulfilled my vows.
15So I came out to meet you;
I looked for you and have found you!
16I have covered my bed
with colored linens from Egypt.
17I have perfumed my bed
with myrrh, aloes and cinnamon.
18Come, let's drink deep of love till
morning;
let's enjoy ourselves with love!
19My husband is not at home;
he has gone on a long journey.
20He took his purse filled with money
and will not be home till full moon."

21With persuasive words she led him astray;
she seduced him with her smooth talk.
22All at once he followed her
like an ox going to the slaughter,
like a deer[b] stepping into a noose[c]
23 till an arrow pierces his liver,
like a bird darting into a snare,
little knowing it will cost him his life.

24Now then, my sons, listen to me;
pay attention to what I say.
25Do not let your heart turn to her ways
or stray into her paths.
26Many are the victims she has brought
down;
her slain are a mighty throng.
27Her house is a highway to the grave,[d]
leading down to the chambers of death.

Wisdom's Call

8 Does not wisdom call out?
Does not understanding raise her voice?
2On the heights along the way,
where the paths meet, she takes her
stand;
3beside the gates leading into the city,
at the entrances, she cries aloud:
4"To you, O men, I call out;
I raise my voice to all mankind.
5You who are simple, gain prudence;
you who are foolish, gain
understanding.
6Listen, for I have worthy things to say;
I open my lips to speak what is right.
7My mouth speaks what is true,
for my lips detest wickedness.
8All the words of my mouth are just;
none of them is crooked or perverse.
9To the discerning all of them are right;
they are faultless to those who have
knowledge.
10Choose my instruction instead of silver,
knowledge rather than choice gold,
11for wisdom is more precious than rubies,
and nothing you desire can compare
with her.

12"I, wisdom, dwell together with prudence;
I possess knowledge and discretion.
13To fear the LORD is to hate evil;
I hate pride and arrogance,
evil behavior and perverse speech.
14Counsel and sound judgment are mine;
I have understanding and power.
15By me kings reign
and rulers make laws that are just;
16by me princes govern,

[a]*14* Traditionally *peace offerings* [b]*22* Syriac (see also Septuagint); Hebrew *fool* [c]*22* The meaning of the Hebrew for this line is uncertain. [d]*27* Hebrew *Sheol*

and all nobles who rule on earth.[a]
17 I love those who love me,
and those who seek me find me.
18 With me are riches and honor,
enduring wealth and prosperity.
19 My fruit is better than fine gold;
what I yield surpasses choice silver.
20 I walk in the way of righteousness,
along the paths of justice,
21 bestowing wealth on those who love me
and making their treasures full.

22 "The LORD brought me forth as the first
of his works,[b,c]
before his deeds of old;
23 I was appointed[d] from eternity,
from the beginning, before the world
began.
24 When there were no oceans, I was given
birth,
when there were no springs abounding
with water;
25 before the mountains were settled in place,
before the hills, I was given birth,
26 before he made the earth or its fields
or any of the dust of the world.
27 I was there when he set the heavens in
place,
when he marked out the horizon on the
face of the deep,
28 when he established the clouds above
and fixed securely the fountains of the
deep,
29 when he gave the sea its boundary
so the waters would not overstep his
command,
and when he marked out the foundations
of the earth.
30 Then I was the craftsman at his side.
I was filled with delight day after day,
rejoicing always in his presence,
31 rejoicing in his whole world
and delighting in mankind.

32 "Now then, my sons, listen to me;
blessed are those who keep my ways.
33 Listen to my instruction and be wise;
do not ignore it.
34 Blessed is the man who listens to me,
watching daily at my doors,
waiting at my doorway.
35 For whoever finds me finds life
and receives favor from the LORD.
36 But whoever fails to find me harms
himself;
all who hate me love death."

Invitations of Wisdom and of Folly

9 Wisdom has built her house;
she has hewn out its seven pillars.
2 She has prepared her meat and mixed her
wine;
she has also set her table.
3 She has sent out her maids, and she calls
from the highest point of the city.
4 "Let all who are simple come in here!"
she says to those who lack judgment.
5 "Come, eat my food
and drink the wine I have mixed.
6 Leave your simple ways and you will live;
walk in the way of understanding.

7 "Whoever corrects a mocker invites insult;
whoever rebukes a wicked man incurs
abuse.
8 Do not rebuke a mocker or he will hate
you;
rebuke a wise man and he will love
you.
9 Instruct a wise man and he will be wiser
still;
teach a righteous man and he will add
to his learning.

10 "The fear of the LORD is the beginning of
wisdom,
and knowledge of the Holy One is
understanding.
11 For through me your days will be many,
and years will be added to your life.
12 If you are wise, your wisdom will reward
you;
if you are a mocker, you alone will
suffer."

13 The woman Folly is loud;
she is undisciplined and without
knowledge.
14 She sits at the door of her house,
on a seat at the highest point of the
city,
15 calling out to those who pass by,
who go straight on their way.
16 "Let all who are simple come in here!"
she says to those who lack judgment.
17 "Stolen water is sweet;
food eaten in secret is delicious!"
18 But little do they know that the dead are
there,
that her guests are in the depths of the
grave.[e]

Proverbs of Solomon

10 The proverbs of Solomon:

A wise son brings joy to his father,
but a foolish son grief to his mother.

2 Ill-gotten treasures are of no value,
but righteousness delivers from death.

3 The LORD does not let the righteous go
hungry
but he thwarts the craving of the
wicked.

4 Lazy hands make a man poor,
but diligent hands bring wealth.

[a] *16* Many Hebrew manuscripts and Septuagint; most Hebrew manuscripts *and nobles—all righteous rulers*
[b] *22* Or *way*; or *dominion* [c] *22* Or *The LORD possessed me at the beginning of his work*; or *The LORD brought forth at the beginning of his work* [d] *23* Or *fashioned* [e] *18* Hebrew *Sheol*

5He who gathers crops in summer is a wise son,
but he who sleeps during harvest is a disgraceful son.

6Blessings crown the head of the righteous,
but violence overwhelms the mouth of the wicked.[a]

7The memory of the righteous will be a blessing,
but the name of the wicked will rot.

8The wise in heart accept commands,
but a chattering fool comes to ruin.

9The man of integrity walks securely,
but he who takes crooked paths will be found out.

10He who winks maliciously causes grief,
and a chattering fool comes to ruin.

11The mouth of the righteous is a fountain of life,
but violence overwhelms the mouth of the wicked.

12Hatred stirs up dissension,
but love covers over all wrongs.

13Wisdom is found on the lips of the discerning,
but a rod is for the back of him who lacks judgment.

14Wise men store up knowledge,
but the mouth of a fool invites ruin.

15The wealth of the rich is their fortified city,
but poverty is the ruin of the poor.

16The wages of the righteous bring them life,
but the income of the wicked brings them punishment.

17He who heeds discipline shows the way to life,
but whoever ignores correction leads others astray.

18He who conceals his hatred has lying lips,
and whoever spreads slander is a fool.

19When words are many, sin is not absent,
but he who holds his tongue is wise.

20The tongue of the righteous is choice silver,
but the heart of the wicked is of little value.

21The lips of the righteous nourish many,
but fools die for lack of judgment.

22The blessing of the LORD brings wealth,
and he adds no trouble to it.

23A fool finds pleasure in evil conduct,
but a man of understanding delights in wisdom.

24What the wicked dreads will overtake him;
what the righteous desire will be granted.

25When the storm has swept by, the wicked are gone,
but the righteous stand firm forever.

26As vinegar to the teeth and smoke to the eyes,
so is a sluggard to those who send him.

27The fear of the LORD adds length to life,
but the years of the wicked are cut short.

28The prospect of the righteous is joy,
but the hopes of the wicked come to nothing.

29The way of the LORD is a refuge for the righteous,
but it is the ruin of those who do evil.

30The righteous will never be uprooted,
but the wicked will not remain in the land.

31The mouth of the righteous brings forth wisdom,
but a perverse tongue will be cut out.

32The lips of the righteous know what is fitting,
but the mouth of the wicked only what is perverse.

11 The LORD abhors dishonest scales,
but accurate weights are his delight.

2When pride comes, then comes disgrace,
but with humility comes wisdom.

3The integrity of the upright guides them,
but the unfaithful are destroyed by their duplicity.

4Wealth is worthless in the day of wrath,
but righteousness delivers from death.

5The righteousness of the blameless makes a straight way for them,
but the wicked are brought down by their own wickedness.

6The righteousness of the upright delivers them,
but the unfaithful are trapped by evil desires.

7When a wicked man dies, his hope perishes;
all he expected from his power comes to nothing.

8The righteous man is rescued from trouble,
and it comes on the wicked instead.

9With his mouth the godless destroys his neighbor,

[a]6 Or *but the mouth of the wicked conceals violence*; also in verse 11

but through knowledge the righteous
escape.

10When the righteous prosper, the city
rejoices;
when the wicked perish, there are
shouts of joy.

11Through the blessing of the upright a city
is exalted,
but by the mouth of the wicked it is
destroyed.

12A man who lacks judgment derides his
neighbor,
but a man of understanding holds his
tongue.

13A gossip betrays a confidence,
but a trustworthy man keeps a secret.

14For lack of guidance a nation falls,
but many advisers make victory sure.

15He who puts up security for another will
surely suffer,
but whoever refuses to strike hands in
pledge is safe.

16A kindhearted woman gains respect,
but ruthless men gain only wealth.

17A kind man benefits himself,
but a cruel man brings trouble on
himself.

18The wicked man earns deceptive wages,
but he who sows righteousness reaps a
sure reward.

19The truly righteous man attains life,
but he who pursues evil goes to his
death.

20The LORD detests men of perverse heart
but he delights in those whose ways are
blameless.

21Be sure of this: The wicked will not go
unpunished,
but those who are righteous will go
free.

22Like a gold ring in a pig's snout
is a beautiful woman who shows no
discretion.

23The desire of the righteous ends only in
good,
but the hope of the wicked only in
wrath.

24One man gives freely, yet gains even
more;
another withholds unduly, but comes to
poverty.

25A generous man will prosper;
he who refreshes others will himself be
refreshed.

26People curse the man who hoards grain,
but blessing crowns him who is willing
to sell.

[illegible]e who seeks good finds goodwill,
but evil comes to him who searches for
it.

28Whoever trusts in his riches will fall,
but the righteous will thrive like a green
leaf.

29He who brings trouble on his family will
inherit only wind,
and the fool will be servant to the wise.

30The fruit of the righteous is a tree of life,
and he who wins souls is wise.

31If the righteous receive their due on earth,
how much more the ungodly and the
sinner!

12 Whoever loves discipline loves
knowledge,
but he who hates correction is stupid.

2A good man obtains favor from the LORD,
but the LORD condemns a crafty man.

3A man cannot be established through
wickedness,
but the righteous cannot be uprooted.

4A wife of noble character is her husband's
crown,
but a disgraceful wife is like decay in
his bones.

5The plans of the righteous are just,
but the advice of the wicked is
deceitful.

6The words of the wicked lie in wait for
blood,
but the speech of the upright rescues
them.

7Wicked men are overthrown and are no
more,
but the house of the righteous stands
firm.

8A man is praised according to his wisdom,
but men with warped minds are
despised.

9Better to be a nobody and yet have a
servant
than pretend to be somebody and have
no food.

10A righteous man cares for the needs of his
animal,
but the kindest acts of the wicked are
cruel.

11He who works his land will have abundant
food,
but he who chases fantasies lacks
judgment.

12The wicked desire the plunder of evil
men,
but the root of the righteous flourishes.

13An evil man is trapped by his sinful talk,
but a righteous man escapes trouble.

14From the fruit of his lips a man is filled
with good things

as surely as the work of his hands
rewards him.

15The way of a fool seems right to him,
but a wise man listens to advice.

16A fool shows his annoyance at once,
but a prudent man overlooks an insult.

17A truthful witness gives honest testimony,
but a false witness tells lies.

18Reckless words pierce like a sword,
but the tongue of the wise brings
healing.

19Truthful lips endure forever,
but a lying tongue lasts only a moment.

20There is deceit in the hearts of those who
plot evil,
but joy for those who promote peace.

21No harm befalls the righteous,
but the wicked have their fill of trouble.

22The LORD detests lying lips,
but he delights in men who are truthful.

23A prudent man keeps his knowledge to
himself,
but the heart of fools blurts out folly.

24Diligent hands will rule,
but laziness ends in slave labor.

25An anxious heart weighs a man down,
but a kind word cheers him up.

26A righteous man is cautious in
friendship,[a]
but the way of the wicked leads them
astray.

27The lazy man does not roast[b] his game,
but the diligent man prizes his
possessions.

28In the way of righteousness there is life;
along that path is immortality.

13 A wise son heeds his father's
instruction,
but a mocker does not listen to rebuke.

2From the fruit of his lips a man enjoys
good things,
but the unfaithful have a craving for
violence.

3He who guards his lips guards his life,
but he who speaks rashly will come to
ruin.

4The sluggard craves and gets nothing,
but the desires of the diligent are fully
satisfied.

5The righteous hate what is false,
but the wicked bring shame and
disgrace.

6Righteousness guards the man of integrity,
but wickedness overthrows the sinner.

7One man pretends to be rich, yet has
nothing;
another pretends to be poor, yet has
great wealth.

8A man's riches may ransom his life,
but a poor man hears no threat.

9The light of the righteous shines brightly,
but the lamp of the wicked is snuffed
out.

10Pride only breeds quarrels,
but wisdom is found in those who take
advice.

11Dishonest money dwindles away,
but he who gathers money little by little
makes it grow.

12Hope deferred makes the heart sick,
but a longing fulfilled is a tree of life.

13He who scorns instruction will pay
for it,
but he who respects a command is
rewarded.

14The teaching of the wise is a fountain of
life,
turning a man from the snares of death.

15Good understanding wins favor,
but the way of the unfaithful is hard.[c]

16Every prudent man acts out of knowledge,
but a fool exposes his folly.

17A wicked messenger falls into trouble,
but a trustworthy envoy brings healing.

18He who ignores discipline comes to
poverty and shame,
but whoever heeds correction is
honored.

19A longing fulfilled is sweet to the soul,
but fools detest turning from evil.

20He who walks with the wise grows wise,
but a companion of fools suffers harm.

21Misfortune pursues the sinner,
but prosperity is the reward of the
righteous.

22A good man leaves an inheritance for his
children's children,
but a sinner's wealth is stored up for
the righteous.

23A poor man's field may produce abundant
food,
but injustice sweeps it away.

24He who spares the rod hates his son,
but he who loves him is careful to
discipline him.

25The righteous eat to their hearts' content,
but the stomach of the wicked goes
hungry.

[a]26 Or *man is a guide to his neighbor* [b]27 The meaning of the Hebrew for this word is uncertain.
[c]15 Or *unfaithful does not endure*

14 The wise woman builds her house,
but with her own hands the foolish one tears hers down.

2 He whose walk is upright fears the LORD,
but he whose ways are devious despises him.

3 A fool's talk brings a rod to his back,
but the lips of the wise protect them.

4 Where there are no oxen, the manger is empty,
but from the strength of an ox comes an abundant harvest.

5 A truthful witness does not deceive,
but a false witness pours out lies.

6 The mocker seeks wisdom and finds none,
but knowledge comes easily to the discerning.

7 Stay away from a foolish man,
for you will not find knowledge on his lips.

8 The wisdom of the prudent is to give thought to their ways,
but the folly of fools is deception.

9 Fools mock at making amends for sin,
but goodwill is found among the upright.

10 Each heart knows its own bitterness,
and no one else can share its joy.

11 The house of the wicked will be destroyed,
but the tent of the upright will flourish.

12 There is a way that seems right to a man,
but in the end it leads to death.

13 Even in laughter the heart may ache,
and joy may end in grief.

14 The faithless will be fully repaid for their ways,
and the good man rewarded for his.

15 A simple man believes anything,
but a prudent man gives thought to his steps.

16 A wise man fears the LORD and shuns evil,
but a fool is hotheaded and reckless.

17 A quick-tempered man does foolish things,
and a crafty man is hated.

18 The simple inherit folly,
but the prudent are crowned with knowledge.

19 Evil men will bow down in the presence of the good,
and the wicked at the gates of the righteous.

20 The poor are shunned even by their neighbors,
but the rich have many friends.

21 He who despises his neighbor sins,
but blessed is he who is kind to the needy.

22 Do not those who plot evil go astray?
But those who plan what is good find[a] love and faithfulness.

23 All hard work brings a profit,
but mere talk leads only to poverty.

24 The wealth of the wise is their crown,
but the folly of fools yields folly.

25 A truthful witness saves lives,
but a false witness is deceitful.

26 He who fears the LORD has a secure fortress,
and for his children it will be a refuge.

27 The fear of the LORD is a fountain of life,
turning a man from the snares of death.

28 A large population is a king's glory,
but without subjects a prince is ruined.

29 A patient man has great understanding,
but a quick-tempered man displays folly.

30 A heart at peace gives life to the body,
but envy rots the bones.

31 He who oppresses the poor shows contempt for their Maker,
but whoever is kind to the needy honors God.

32 When calamity comes, the wicked are brought down,
but even in death the righteous have a refuge.

33 Wisdom reposes in the heart of the discerning
and even among fools she lets herself be known.[b]

34 Righteousness exalts a nation,
but sin is a disgrace to any people.

35 A king delights in a wise servant,
but a shameful servant incurs his wrath.

15 A gentle answer turns away wrath,
but a harsh word stirs up anger.

2 The tongue of the wise commends knowledge,
but the mouth of the fool gushes folly.

3 The eyes of the LORD are everywhere,
keeping watch on the wicked and the good.

4 The tongue that brings healing is a tree of life,
but a deceitful tongue crushes the spirit.

5 A fool spurns his father's discipline,

[a] Or *show* [b] 33 Hebrew; Septuagint and Syriac / *but in the heart of fools she is not known*

but whoever heeds correction shows
prudence.

6The house of the righteous contains great
treasure,
but the income of the wicked brings
them trouble.

7The lips of the wise spread knowledge;
not so the hearts of fools.

8The LORD detests the sacrifice of the
wicked,
but the prayer of the upright pleases
him.

9The LORD detests the way of the wicked
but he loves those who pursue
righteousness.

10Stern discipline awaits him who leaves the
path;
he who hates correction will die.

11Death and Destruction[a] lie open before
the LORD—
how much more the hearts of men!

12A mocker resents correction;
he will not consult the wise.

13A happy heart makes the face cheerful,
but heartache crushes the spirit.

14The discerning heart seeks knowledge,
but the mouth of a fool feeds on folly.

15All the days of the oppressed are
wretched,
but the cheerful heart has a continual
feast.

16Better a little with the fear of the LORD
than great wealth with turmoil.

17Better a meal of vegetables where there is
love
than a fattened calf with hatred.

18A hot-tempered man stirs up dissension,
but a patient man calms a quarrel.

19The way of the sluggard is blocked with
thorns,
but the path of the upright is a highway.

20A wise son brings joy to his father,
but a foolish man despises his mother.

21Folly delights a man who lacks judgment,
but a man of understanding keeps a
straight course.

22Plans fail for lack of counsel,
but with many advisers they succeed.

23A man finds joy in giving an apt reply—
and how good is a timely word!

24The path of life leads upward for the wise
to keep him from going down to the
grave.[b]

25The LORD tears down the proud man's
house
but he keeps the widow's boundaries
intact.

26The LORD detests the thoughts of the
wicked,
but those of the pure are pleasing to
him.

27A greedy man brings trouble to his family,
but he who hates bribes will live.

28The heart of the righteous weighs its
answers,
but the mouth of the wicked gushes
evil.

29The LORD is far from the wicked
but he hears the prayer of the righteous.

30A cheerful look brings joy to the heart,
and good news gives health to the
bones.

31He who listens to a life-giving rebuke
will be at home among the wise.

32He who ignores discipline despises
himself,
but whoever heeds correction gains
understanding.

33The fear of the LORD teaches a man
wisdom,[c]
and humility comes before honor.

16 To man belong the plans of the heart,
but from the LORD comes the reply of
the tongue.

2All a man's ways seem innocent to him,
but motives are weighed by the LORD.

3Commit to the LORD whatever you do,
and your plans will succeed.

4The LORD works out everything for his
own ends—
even the wicked for a day of disaster.

5The LORD detests all the proud of heart.
Be sure of this: They will not go
unpunished.

6Through love and faithfulness sin is
atoned for;
through the fear of the LORD a man
avoids evil.

7When a man's ways are pleasing to the
LORD,
he makes even his enemies live at peace
with him.

8Better a little with righteousness
than much gain with injustice.

9In his heart a man plans his course,
but the LORD determines his steps.

10The lips of a king speak as an oracle,
and his mouth should not betray justice.

11Honest scales and balances are from the
LORD;

[a] *11* Hebrew *Sheol and Abaddon* [b] *24* Hebrew *Sheol* [c] *33* Or *Wisdom teaches the fear of the LORD*

all the weights in the bag are of his
making.

12 Kings detest wrongdoing,
for a throne is established through
righteousness.

13 Kings take pleasure in honest lips;
they value a man who speaks the truth.

14 A king's wrath is a messenger of death,
but a wise man will appease it.

15 When a king's face brightens, it means
life;
his favor is like a rain cloud in spring.

16 How much better to get wisdom than
gold,
to choose understanding rather than
silver!

17 The highway of the upright avoids evil;
he who guards his way guards his life.

18 Pride goes before destruction,
a haughty spirit before a fall.

19 Better to be lowly in spirit and among the
oppressed
than to share plunder with the proud.

20 Whoever gives heed to instruction
prospers,
and blessed is he who trusts in the
LORD.

21 The wise in heart are called discerning,
and pleasant words promote
instruction.[a]

22 Understanding is a fountain of life to
those who have it,
but folly brings punishment to fools.

23 A wise man's heart guides his mouth,
and his lips promote instruction.[b]

24 Pleasant words are a honeycomb,
sweet to the soul and healing to the
bones.

25 There is a way that seems right to a man,
but in the end it leads to death.

26 The laborer's appetite works for him;
his hunger drives him on.

27 A scoundrel plots evil,
and his speech is like a scorching fire.

28 A perverse man stirs up dissension,
and a gossip separates close friends.

29 A violent man entices his neighbor
and leads him down a path that is not
good.

30 He who winks with his eye is plotting
perversity;
he who purses his lips is bent on evil.

31 Gray hair is a crown of splendor;
it is attained by a righteous life.

32 Better a patient man than a warrior,
a man who controls his temper than one
who takes a city.

33 The lot is cast into the lap,
but its every decision is from the LORD.

17 Better a dry crust with peace and
quiet
than a house full of feasting,[c] with
strife.

2 A wise servant will rule over a disgraceful
son,
and will share the inheritance as one of
the brothers.

3 The crucible for silver and the furnace for
gold,
but the LORD tests the heart.

4 A wicked man listens to evil lips;
a liar pays attention to a malicious
tongue.

5 He who mocks the poor shows contempt
for their Maker;
whoever gloats over disaster will not go
unpunished.

6 Children's children are a crown to the
aged,
and parents are the pride of their
children.

7 Arrogant[d] lips are unsuited to a fool—
how much worse lying lips to a ruler!

8 A bribe is a charm to the one who gives
it;
wherever he turns, he succeeds.

9 He who covers over an offense promotes
love,
but whoever repeats the matter separates
close friends.

10 A rebuke impresses a man of discernment
more than a hundred lashes a fool.

11 An evil man is bent only on rebellion;
a merciless official will be sent against
him.

12 Better to meet a bear robbed of her cubs
than a fool in his folly.

13 If a man pays back evil for good,
evil will never leave his house.

14 Starting a quarrel is like breaching a
dam;
so drop the matter before a dispute
breaks out.

15 Acquitting the guilty and condemning the
innocent—
the LORD detests them both.

16 Of what use is money in the hand of a
fool,
since he has no desire to get wisdom?

[a]21 Or *words make a man persuasive* [b]23 Or *mouth / and makes his lips persuasive* [c]1 Hebrew *sacrifices* [d]7 Or *Eloquent*

17 A friend loves at all times,
and a brother is born for adversity.

18 A man lacking in judgment strikes hands
in pledge
and puts up security for his neighbor.

19 He who loves a quarrel loves sin;
he who builds a high gate invites
destruction.

20 A man of perverse heart does not prosper;
he whose tongue is deceitful falls into
trouble.

21 To have a fool for a son brings grief;
there is no joy for the father of a fool.

22 A cheerful heart is good medicine,
but a crushed spirit dries up the bones.

23 A wicked man accepts a bribe in secret
to pervert the course of justice.

24 A discerning man keeps wisdom in view,
but a fool's eyes wander to the ends of
the earth.

25 A foolish son brings grief to his father
and bitterness to the one who bore him.

26 It is not good to punish an innocent man,
or to flog officials for their integrity.

27 A man of knowledge uses words with
restraint,
and a man of understanding is
even-tempered.

28 Even a fool is thought wise if he keeps
silent,
and discerning if he holds his tongue.

18 An unfriendly man pursues selfish
ends;
he defies all sound judgment.

2 A fool finds no pleasure in understanding
but delights in airing his own opinions.

3 When wickedness comes, so does
contempt,
and with shame comes disgrace.

4 The words of a man's mouth are deep
waters,
but the fountain of wisdom is a
bubbling brook.

5 It is not good to be partial to the wicked
or to deprive the innocent of justice.

6 A fool's lips bring him strife,
and his mouth invites a beating.

7 A fool's mouth is his undoing,
and his lips are a snare to his soul.

8 The words of a gossip are like choice
morsels;
they go down to a man's inmost parts.

9 One who is slack in his work
is brother to one who destroys.

10 The name of the LORD is a strong tower;
the righteous run to it and are safe.

11 The wealth of the rich is their fortified
city;
they imagine it an unscalable wall.

12 Before his downfall a man's heart is
proud,
but humility comes before honor.

13 He who answers before listening—
that is his folly and his shame.

14 A man's spirit sustains him in sickness,
but a crushed spirit who can bear?

15 The heart of the discerning acquires
knowledge;
the ears of the wise seek it out.

16 A gift opens the way for the giver
and ushers him into the presence of the
great.

17 The first to present his case seems right,
till another comes forward and questions
him.

18 Casting the lot settles disputes
and keeps strong opponents apart.

19 An offended brother is more unyielding
than a fortified city,
and disputes are like the barred gates of
a citadel.

20 From the fruit of his mouth a man's
stomach is filled;
with the harvest from his lips he is
satisfied.

21 The tongue has the power of life and
death,
and those who love it will eat its fruit.

22 He who finds a wife finds what is good
and receives favor from the LORD.

23 A poor man pleads for mercy,
but a rich man answers harshly.

24 A man of many companions may come to
ruin,
but there is a friend who sticks closer
than a brother.

19 Better a poor man whose walk is
blameless
than a fool whose lips are perverse.

2 It is not good to have zeal without
knowledge,
nor to be hasty and miss the way.

3 A man's own folly ruins his life,
yet his heart rages against the LORD.

4 Wealth brings many friends,
but a poor man's friend deserts him.

5 A false witness will not go unpunished,
and he who pours out lies will not go
free.

6 Many curry favor with a ruler,
and everyone is the friend of a man
who gives gifts.

7 A poor man is shunned by all his relatives—
how much more do his friends avoid him!
Though he pursues them with pleading,
they are nowhere to be found.[a]

8 He who gets wisdom loves his own soul;
he who cherishes understanding prospers.

9 A false witness will not go unpunished,
and he who pours out lies will perish.

10 It is not fitting for a fool to live in luxury—
how much worse for a slave to rule over princes!

11 A man's wisdom gives him patience;
it is to his glory to overlook an offense.

12 A king's rage is like the roar of a lion,
but his favor is like dew on the grass.

13 A foolish son is his father's ruin,
and a quarrelsome wife is like a constant dripping.

14 Houses and wealth are inherited from parents,
but a prudent wife is from the LORD.

15 Laziness brings on deep sleep,
and the shiftless man goes hungry.

16 He who obeys instructions guards his life,
but he who is contemptuous of his ways will die.

17 He who is kind to the poor lends to the LORD,
and he will reward him for what he has done.

18 Discipline your son, for in that there is hope;
do not be a willing party to his death.

19 A hot-tempered man must pay the penalty;
if you rescue him, you will have to do it again.

20 Listen to advice and accept instruction,
and in the end you will be wise.

21 Many are the plans in a man's heart,
but it is the LORD's purpose that prevails.

22 What a man desires is unfailing love[b];
better to be poor than a liar.

23 The fear of the LORD leads to life:
Then one rests content, untouched by trouble.

24 The sluggard buries his hand in the dish;
he will not even bring it back to his mouth!

Flog a mocker, and the simple will learn prudence;
rebuke a discerning man, and he will gain knowledge.

26 He who robs his father and drives out his mother
is a son who brings shame and disgrace.

27 Stop listening to instruction, my son,
and you will stray from the words of knowledge.

28 A corrupt witness mocks at justice,
and the mouth of the wicked gulps down evil.

29 Penalties are prepared for mockers,
and beatings for the backs of fools.

20 Wine is a mocker and beer a brawler;
whoever is led astray by them is not wise.

2 A king's wrath is like the roar of a lion;
he who angers him forfeits his life.

3 It is to a man's honor to avoid strife,
but every fool is quick to quarrel.

4 A sluggard does not plow in season;
so at harvest time he looks but finds nothing.

5 The purposes of a man's heart are deep waters,
but a man of understanding draws them out.

6 Many a man claims to have unfailing love,
but a faithful man who can find?

7 The righteous man leads a blameless life;
blessed are his children after him.

8 When a king sits on his throne to judge,
he winnows out all evil with his eyes.

9 Who can say, "I have kept my heart pure;
I am clean and without sin"?

10 Differing weights and differing measures—
the LORD detests them both.

11 Even a child is known by his actions,
by whether his conduct is pure and right.

12 Ears that hear and eyes that see—
the LORD has made them both.

13 Do not love sleep or you will grow poor;
stay awake and you will have food to spare.

14 "It's no good, it's no good!" says the buyer;
then off he goes and boasts about his purchase.

15 Gold there is, and rubies in abundance,
but lips that speak knowledge are a rare jewel.

meaning of the Hebrew for this sentence is uncertain. [b]22 Or *A man's greed is his shame*

[16]Take the garment of one who puts up
security for a stranger;
hold it in pledge if he does it for a
wayward woman.

[17]Food gained by fraud tastes sweet to a
man,
but he ends up with a mouth full of
gravel.

[18]Make plans by seeking advice;
if you wage war, obtain guidance.

[19]A gossip betrays a confidence;
so avoid a man who talks too much.

[20]If a man curses his father or mother,
his lamp will be snuffed out in pitch
darkness.

[21]An inheritance quickly gained at the
beginning
will not be blessed at the end.

[22]Do not say, "I'll pay you back for this
wrong!"
Wait for the LORD, and he will deliver
you.

[23]The LORD detests differing weights,
and dishonest scales do not please him.

[24]A man's steps are directed by the LORD.
How then can anyone understand his
own way?

[25]It is a trap for a man to dedicate
something rashly
and only later to consider his vows.

[26]A wise king winnows out the wicked;
he drives the threshing wheel over
them.

[27]The lamp of the LORD searches the spirit
of a man[a];
it searches out his inmost being.

[28]Love and faithfulness keep a king safe;
through love his throne is made secure.

[29]The glory of young men is their strength,
gray hair the splendor of the old.

[30]Blows and wounds cleanse away evil,
and beatings purge the inmost being.

21 The king's heart is in the hand of the
LORD;
he directs it like a watercourse wherever
he pleases.

[2]All a man's ways seem right to him,
but the LORD weighs the heart.

[3]To do what is right and just
is more acceptable to the LORD than
sacrifice.

[4]Haughty eyes and a proud heart,
the lamp of the wicked, are sin!

[5]The plans of the diligent lead to profit
as surely as haste leads to poverty.

[6]A fortune made by a lying tongue
is a fleeting vapor and a deadly snare.[b]

[7]The violence of the wicked will drag them
away,
for they refuse to do what is right.

[8]The way of the guilty is devious,
but the conduct of the innocent is
upright.

[9]Better to live on a corner of the roof
than share a house with a quarrelsome
wife.

[10]The wicked man craves evil;
his neighbor gets no mercy from him.

[11]When a mocker is punished, the simple
gain wisdom;
when a wise man is instructed, he gets
knowledge.

[12]The Righteous One[c] takes note of the
house of the wicked
and brings the wicked to ruin.

[13]If a man shuts his ears to the cry of the
poor,
he too will cry out and not be
answered.

[14]A gift given in secret soothes anger,
and a bribe concealed in the cloak
pacifies great wrath.

[15]When justice is done, it brings joy to the
righteous
but terror to evildoers.

[16]A man who strays from the path of
understanding
comes to rest in the company of the
dead.

[17]He who loves pleasure will become
poor;
whoever loves wine and oil will never
be rich.

[18]The wicked become a ransom for the
righteous,
and the unfaithful for the upright.

[19]Better to live in a desert
than with a quarrelsome and
ill-tempered wife.

[20]In the house of the wise are stores of
choice food and oil,
but a foolish man devours all he has.

[21]He who pursues righteousness and love
finds life, prosperity[d] and honor.

[22]A wise man attacks the city of the mighty
and pulls down the stronghold in which
they trust.

[23]He who guards his mouth and his tongu
keeps himself from calamity.

[a]27 Or *The spirit of man is the LORD's lamp* [b]6 Some Hebrew manuscripts, Septuagint and Vulgate; m
Hebrew manuscripts *vapor for those who seek death* [c]12 Or *The righteous man* [d]21 Or *righteousn*

24 The proud and arrogant man—"Mocker" is his name;
he behaves with overweening pride.

25 The sluggard's craving will be the death of him,
because his hands refuse to work.
26 All day long he craves for more,
but the righteous give without sparing.

27 The sacrifice of the wicked is detestable—
how much more so when brought with evil intent!

28 A false witness will perish,
and whoever listens to him will be destroyed forever.[a]

29 A wicked man puts up a bold front,
but an upright man gives thought to his ways.

30 There is no wisdom, no insight, no plan
that can succeed against the LORD.

31 The horse is made ready for the day of battle,
but victory rests with the LORD.

22 A good name is more desirable than great riches;
to be esteemed is better than silver or gold.

2 Rich and poor have this in common:
The LORD is the Maker of them all.

3 A prudent man sees danger and takes refuge,
but the simple keep going and suffer for it.

4 Humility and the fear of the LORD
bring wealth and honor and life.

5 In the paths of the wicked lie thorns and snares,
but he who guards his soul stays far from them.

6 Train[b] a child in the way he should go,
and when he is old he will not turn from it.

7 The rich rule over the poor,
and the borrower is servant to the lender.

8 He who sows wickedness reaps trouble,
and the rod of his fury will be destroyed.

9 A generous man will himself be blessed,
for he shares his food with the poor.

10 Drive out the mocker, and out goes strife;
quarrels and insults are ended.

11 He who loves a pure heart and whose speech is gracious
will have the king for his friend.

12 The eyes of the LORD keep watch over knowledge,
but he frustrates the words of the unfaithful.

13 The sluggard says, "There is a lion outside!"
or, "I will be murdered in the streets!"

14 The mouth of an adulteress is a deep pit;
he who is under the LORD's wrath will fall into it.

15 Folly is bound up in the heart of a child,
but the rod of discipline will drive it far from him.

16 He who oppresses the poor to increase his wealth
and he who gives gifts to the rich—
both come to poverty.

Sayings of the Wise

17 Pay attention and listen to the sayings of the wise;
apply your heart to what I teach,
18 for it is pleasing when you keep them in your heart
and have all of them ready on your lips.
19 So that your trust may be in the LORD,
I teach you today, even you.
20 Have I not written thirty[c] sayings for you,
sayings of counsel and knowledge,
21 teaching you true and reliable words,
so that you can give sound answers
to him who sent you?

22 Do not exploit the poor because they are poor
and do not crush the needy in court,
23 for the LORD will take up their case
and will plunder those who plunder them.

24 Do not make friends with a hot-tempered man,
do not associate with one easily angered,
25 or you may learn his ways
and get yourself ensnared.

26 Do not be a man who strikes hands in pledge
or puts up security for debts;
27 if you lack the means to pay,
your very bed will be snatched from under you.

28 Do not move an ancient boundary stone
set up by your forefathers.

29 Do you see a man skilled in his work?
He will serve before kings;
he will not serve before obscure men.

23 When you sit to dine with a ruler,
note well what[d] is before you,
2 and put a knife to your throat

[a] 28 Or *but the words of an obedient man will live on*
[b] 6 Or *Start*
[c] 20 Or *not formerly written*; or *not written excellent*
[d] 1 Or *who*

if you are given to gluttony.
3Do not crave his delicacies,
for that food is deceptive.

4Do not wear yourself out to get rich;
have the wisdom to show restraint.
5Cast but a glance at riches, and they are gone,
for they will surely sprout wings
and fly off to the sky like an eagle.

6Do not eat the food of a stingy man,
do not crave his delicacies;
7for he is the kind of man
who is always thinking about the cost.[a]
"Eat and drink," he says to you,
but his heart is not with you.
8You will vomit up the little you have eaten
and will have wasted your compliments.

9Do not speak to a fool,
for he will scorn the wisdom of your words.

10Do not move an ancient boundary stone
or encroach on the fields of the fatherless,
11for their Defender is strong;
he will take up their case against you.

12Apply your heart to instruction
and your ears to words of knowledge.

13Do not withhold discipline from a child;
if you punish him with the rod, he will not die.
14Punish him with the rod
and save his soul from death.[b]

15My son, if your heart is wise,
then my heart will be glad;
16my inmost being will rejoice
when your lips speak what is right.

17Do not let your heart envy sinners,
but always be zealous for the fear of the LORD.
18There is surely a future hope for you,
and your hope will not be cut off.

19Listen, my son, and be wise,
and keep your heart on the right path.
20Do not join those who drink too much wine
or gorge themselves on meat,
21for drunkards and gluttons become poor,
and drowsiness clothes them in rags.

22Listen to your father, who gave you life,
and do not despise your mother when she is old.
23Buy the truth and do not sell it;
get wisdom, discipline and understanding.
24The father of a righteous man has great joy;
he who has a wise son delights in him.
25May your father and mother be glad;
may she who gave you birth rejoice!

26My son, give me your heart
and let your eyes keep to my ways,
27for a prostitute is a deep pit
and a wayward wife is a narrow well.
28Like a bandit she lies in wait,
and multiplies the unfaithful among men.

29Who has woe? Who has sorrow?
Who has strife? Who has complaints?
Who has needless bruises? Who has bloodshot eyes?
30Those who linger over wine,
who go to sample bowls of mixed wine.
31Do not gaze at wine when it is red,
when it sparkles in the cup,
when it goes down smoothly!
32In the end it bites like a snake
and poisons like a viper.
33Your eyes will see strange sights
and your mind imagine confusing things.
34You will be like one sleeping on the high seas,
lying on top of the rigging.
35"They hit me," you will say, "but I'm not hurt!
They beat me, but I don't feel it!
When will I wake up
so I can find another drink?"

24 Do not envy wicked men,
do not desire their company;
2for their hearts plot violence,
and their lips talk about making trouble.

3By wisdom a house is built,
and through understanding it is established;
4through knowledge its rooms are filled
with rare and beautiful treasures.

5A wise man has great power,
and a man of knowledge increases strength;
6for waging war you need guidance,
and for victory many advisers.

7Wisdom is too high for a fool;
in the assembly at the gate he has nothing to say.

8He who plots evil
will be known as a schemer.
9The schemes of folly are sin,
and men detest a mocker.

10If you falter in times of trouble,
how small is your strength!

11Rescue those being led away to death;
hold back those staggering toward slaughter.
12If you say, "But we knew nothing about this,"
does not he who weighs the heart perceive it?
Does not he who guards your life know it?

[a]7 Or *for as he thinks within himself, / so he is*; or *for as he puts on a feast, / so he is* [b]14 Hebrew *Sheol*

Will he not repay each person according
to what he has done?

13Eat honey, my son, for it is good;
honey from the comb is sweet to your
taste.
14Know also that wisdom is sweet to your
soul;
if you find it, there is a future hope for
you,
and your hope will not be cut off.

15Do not lie in wait like an outlaw against a
righteous man's house,
do not raid his dwelling place;
16for though a righteous man falls seven
times, he rises again,
but the wicked are brought down by
calamity.

17Do not gloat when your enemy falls;
when he stumbles, do not let your heart
rejoice,
18or the LORD will see and disapprove
and turn his wrath away from him.

19Do not fret because of evil men
or be envious of the wicked,
20for the evil man has no future hope,
and the lamp of the wicked will be
snuffed out.

21Fear the LORD and the king, my son,
and do not join with the rebellious,
22for those two will send sudden destruction
upon them,
and who knows what calamities they
can bring?

Further Sayings of the Wise

23These also are sayings of the wise:

To show partiality in judging is not good:
24Whoever says to the guilty, "You are
innocent"—
peoples will curse him and nations
denounce him.
25But it will go well with those who convict
the guilty,
and rich blessing will come upon them.

26An honest answer
is like a kiss on the lips.

27Finish your outdoor work
and get your fields ready;
after that, build your house.

28Do not testify against your neighbor
without cause,
or use your lips to deceive.
29Do not say, "I'll do to him as he has done
to me;
I'll pay that man back for what he did."

30I went past the field of the sluggard,
past the vineyard of the man who lacks
judgment;
31thorns had come up everywhere,
the ground was covered with weeds,
and the stone wall was in ruins.
32I applied my heart to what I observed
and learned a lesson from what I saw:
33A little sleep, a little slumber,
a little folding of the hands to rest—
34and poverty will come on you like a
bandit
and scarcity like an armed man.[a]

More Proverbs of Solomon

25 These are more proverbs of Solomon,
copied by the men of Hezekiah king of
Judah:

2It is the glory of God to conceal a matter;
to search out a matter is the glory of
kings.

3As the heavens are high and the earth is
deep,
so the hearts of kings are unsearchable.

4Remove the dross from the silver,
and out comes material for[b] the
silversmith;
5remove the wicked from the king's
presence,
and his throne will be established
through righteousness.

6Do not exalt yourself in the king's
presence,
and do not claim a place among great
men;
7it is better for him to say to you, "Come
up here,"
than for him to humiliate you before a
nobleman.

What you have seen with your eyes
8 do not bring[c] hastily to court,
for what will you do in the end
if your neighbor puts you to shame?

9If you argue your case with a neighbor,
do not betray another man's confidence,
10or he who hears it may shame you
and you will never lose your bad
reputation.

11A word aptly spoken
is like apples of gold in settings of
silver.

12Like an earring of gold or an ornament of
fine gold
is a wise man's rebuke to a listening
ear.

13Like the coolness of snow at harvest time
is a trustworthy messenger to those who
send him;
he refreshes the spirit of his masters.

14Like clouds and wind without rain
is a man who boasts of gifts he does
not give.

[a]34 Or *like a vagrant / and scarcity like a beggar* [b]4 Or *comes a vessel from* [c]7,8 Or *nobleman / on you had set your eyes. / [8]Do not go*

15Through patience a ruler can be
persuaded,
and a gentle tongue can break a bone.

16If you find honey, eat just enough—
too much of it, and you will vomit.
17Seldom set foot in your neighbor's
house—
too much of you, and he will hate
you.

18Like a club or a sword or a sharp arrow
is the man who gives false testimony
against his neighbor.

19Like a bad tooth or a lame foot
is reliance on the unfaithful in times of
trouble.

20Like one who takes away a garment on a
cold day,
or like vinegar poured on soda,
is one who sings songs to a heavy
heart.

21If your enemy is hungry, give him food to
eat;
if he is thirsty, give him water to drink.
22In doing this, you will heap burning coals
on his head,
and the LORD will reward you.

23As a north wind brings rain,
so a sly tongue brings angry looks.

24Better to live on a corner of the roof
than share a house with a quarrelsome
wife.

25Like cold water to a weary soul
is good news from a distant land.

26Like a muddied spring or a polluted well
is a righteous man who gives way to
the wicked.

27It is not good to eat too much honey,
nor is it honorable to seek one's own
honor.

28Like a city whose walls are broken down
is a man who lacks self-control.

26 Like snow in summer or rain in
harvest,
honor is not fitting for a fool.

2Like a fluttering sparrow or a darting
swallow,
an undeserved curse does not come to
rest.

3A whip for the horse, a halter for the
donkey,
and a rod for the backs of fools!

4Do not answer a fool according to his
folly,
or you will be like him yourself.

5Answer a fool according to his folly,
or he will be wise in his own eyes.

6Like cutting off one's feet or drinking
violence
is the sending of a message by the hand
of a fool.

7Like a lame man's legs that hang limp
is a proverb in the mouth of a fool.

8Like tying a stone in a sling
is the giving of honor to a fool.

9Like a thornbush in a drunkard's hand
is a proverb in the mouth of a fool.

10Like an archer who wounds at random
is he who hires a fool or any passer-by.

11As a dog returns to its vomit,
so a fool repeats his folly.

12Do you see a man wise in his own eyes?
There is more hope for a fool than for
him.

13The sluggard says, "There is a lion in the
road,
a fierce lion roaming the streets!"

14As a door turns on its hinges,
so a sluggard turns on his bed.

15The sluggard buries his hand in the dish;
he is too lazy to bring it back to his
mouth.

16The sluggard is wiser in his own eyes
than seven men who answer discreetly.

17Like one who seizes a dog by the ears
is a passer-by who meddles in a quarrel
not his own.

18Like a madman shooting
firebrands or deadly arrows
19is a man who deceives his neighbor
and says, "I was only joking!"

20Without wood a fire goes out;
without gossip a quarrel dies down.

21As charcoal to embers and as wood to
fire,
so is a quarrelsome man for kindling
strife.

22The words of a gossip are like choice
morsels;
they go down to a man's inmost parts.

23Like a coating of glaze[a] over earthenware
are fervent lips with an evil heart.

24A malicious man disguises himself with
his lips,
but in his heart he harbors deceit.
25Though his speech is charming, do not
believe him,
for seven abominations fill his heart.
26His malice may be concealed by
deception,
but his wickedness will be exposed in
the assembly.

27If a man digs a pit, he will fall into it;

[a]23 With a different word division of the Hebrew; Masoretic Text *of silver dross*

if a man rolls a stone, it will roll back
on him.

28A lying tongue hates those it hurts,
and a flattering mouth works ruin.

27 Do not boast about tomorrow,
for you do not know what a day may
bring forth.

2Let another praise you, and not your own
mouth;
someone else, and not your own lips.

3Stone is heavy and sand a burden,
but provocation by a fool is heavier
than both.

4Anger is cruel and fury overwhelming,
but who can stand before jealousy?

5Better is open rebuke
than hidden love.

6Wounds from a friend can be trusted,
but an enemy multiplies kisses.

7He who is full loathes honey,
but to the hungry even what is bitter
tastes sweet.

8Like a bird that strays from its nest
is a man who strays from his home.

9Perfume and incense bring joy to the
heart,
and the pleasantness of one's friend
springs from his earnest counsel.

10Do not forsake your friend and the friend
of your father,
and do not go to your brother's house
when disaster strikes you—
better a neighbor nearby than a brother
far away.

11Be wise, my son, and bring joy to my
heart;
then I can answer anyone who treats me
with contempt.

12The prudent see danger and take refuge,
but the simple keep going and suffer for
it.

13Take the garment of one who puts up
security for a stranger;
hold it in pledge if he does it for a
wayward woman.

14If a man loudly blesses his neighbor early
in the morning,
it will be taken as a curse.

15A quarrelsome wife is like
a constant dripping on a rainy day;
16restraining her is like restraining the wind
or grasping oil with the hand.

17As iron sharpens iron,
so one man sharpens another.

18He who tends a fig tree will eat its fruit,
and he who looks after his master will
be honored.

19As water reflects a face,
so a man's heart reflects the man.

20Death and Destruction[a] are never
satisfied,
and neither are the eyes of man.

21The crucible for silver and the furnace for
gold,
but man is tested by the praise he
receives.

22Though you grind a fool in a mortar,
grinding him like grain with a pestle,
you will not remove his folly from him.

23Be sure you know the condition of your
flocks,
give careful attention to your herds;
24for riches do not endure forever,
and a crown is not secure for all
generations.
25When the hay is removed and new growth
appears
and the grass from the hills is gathered
in,
26the lambs will provide you with clothing,
and the goats with the price of a field.
27You will have plenty of goats' milk
to feed you and your family
and to nourish your servant girls.

28 The wicked man flees though no one
pursues,
but the righteous are as bold as a lion.

2When a country is rebellious, it has many
rulers,
but a man of understanding and
knowledge maintains order.

3A ruler[b] who oppresses the poor
is like a driving rain that leaves no
crops.

4Those who forsake the law praise the
wicked,
but those who keep the law resist them.

5Evil men do not understand justice,
but those who seek the LORD
understand it fully.

6Better a poor man whose walk is
blameless
than a rich man whose ways are
perverse.

7He who keeps the law is a discerning son,
but a companion of gluttons disgraces
his father.

8He who increases his wealth by exorbitant
interest
amasses it for another, who will be kind
to the poor.

9If anyone turns a deaf ear to the law,
even his prayers are detestable.

[a]20 Hebrew *Sheol and Abaddon* [b]3 Or *A poor man*

10He who leads the upright along an evil path
will fall into his own trap,
but the blameless will receive a good inheritance.

11A rich man may be wise in his own eyes,
but a poor man who has discernment sees through him.

12When the righteous triumph, there is great elation;
but when the wicked rise to power, men go into hiding.

13He who conceals his sins does not prosper,
but whoever confesses and renounces them finds mercy.

14Blessed is the man who always fears the LORD,
but he who hardens his heart falls into trouble.

15Like a roaring lion or a charging bear
is a wicked man ruling over a helpless people.

16A tyrannical ruler lacks judgment,
but he who hates ill-gotten gain will enjoy a long life.

17A man tormented by the guilt of murder
will be a fugitive till death;
let no one support him.

18He whose walk is blameless is kept safe,
but he whose ways are perverse will suddenly fall.

19He who works his land will have abundant food,
but the one who chases fantasies will have his fill of poverty.

20A faithful man will be richly blessed,
but one eager to get rich will not go unpunished.

21To show partiality is not good—
yet a man will do wrong for a piece of bread.

22A stingy man is eager to get rich
and is unaware that poverty awaits him.

23He who rebukes a man will in the end gain more favor
than he who has a flattering tongue.

24He who robs his father or mother
and says, "It's not wrong"—
he is partner to him who destroys.

25A greedy man stirs up dissension,
but he who trusts in the LORD will prosper.

26He who trusts in himself is a fool,
but he who walks in wisdom is kept safe.

27He who gives to the poor will lack nothing,
but he who closes his eyes to them receives many curses.

28When the wicked rise to power, people go into hiding;
but when the wicked perish, the righteous thrive.

29 A man who remains stiff-necked after many rebukes
will suddenly be destroyed—without remedy.

2When the righteous thrive, the people rejoice;
when the wicked rule, the people groan.

3A man who loves wisdom brings joy to his father,
but a companion of prostitutes squanders his wealth.

4By justice a king gives a country stability,
but one who is greedy for bribes tears it down.

5Whoever flatters his neighbor
is spreading a net for his feet.

6An evil man is snared by his own sin,
but a righteous one can sing and be glad.

7The righteous care about justice for the poor,
but the wicked have no such concern.

8Mockers stir up a city,
but wise men turn away anger.

9If a wise man goes to court with a fool,
the fool rages and scoffs, and there is no peace.

10Bloodthirsty men hate a man of integrity
and seek to kill the upright.

11A fool gives full vent to his anger,
but a wise man keeps himself under control.

12If a ruler listens to lies,
all his officials become wicked.

13The poor man and the oppressor have this in common:
The LORD gives sight to the eyes of both.

14If a king judges the poor with fairness,
his throne will always be secure.

15The rod of correction imparts wisdom,
but a child left to himself disgraces his mother.

16When the wicked thrive, so does sin,
but the righteous will see their downfall.

17Discipline your son, and he will give you peace;
he will bring delight to your soul.

18Where there is no revelation, the people cast off restraint;
but blessed is he who keeps the law.

19 A servant cannot be corrected by mere words;
though he understands, he will not respond.

20 Do you see a man who speaks in haste?
There is more hope for a fool than for him.

21 If a man pampers his servant from youth,
he will bring grief[a] in the end.

22 An angry man stirs up dissension,
and a hot-tempered one commits many sins.

23 A man's pride brings him low,
but a man of lowly spirit gains honor.

24 The accomplice of a thief is his own enemy;
he is put under oath and dare not testify.

25 Fear of man will prove to be a snare,
but whoever trusts in the LORD is kept safe.

26 Many seek an audience with a ruler,
but it is from the LORD that man gets justice.

27 The righteous detest the dishonest;
the wicked detest the upright.

Sayings of Agur

30 The sayings of Agur son of Jakeh—an oracle[b]:

This man declared to Ithiel,
to Ithiel and to Ucal:[c]

2 "I am the most ignorant of men;
I do not have a man's understanding.
3 I have not learned wisdom,
nor have I knowledge of the Holy One.
4 Who has gone up to heaven and come down?
Who has gathered up the wind in the hollow of his hands?
Who has wrapped up the waters in his cloak?
Who has established all the ends of the earth?
What is his name, and the name of his son?
Tell me if you know!

5 "Every word of God is flawless;
he is a shield to those who take refuge in him.
6 Do not add to his words,
or he will rebuke you and prove you a liar.

7 "Two things I ask of you, O LORD;
do not refuse me before I die:
8 Keep falsehood and lies far from me;
give me neither poverty nor riches,
but give me only my daily bread.
9 Otherwise, I may have too much and disown you
and say, 'Who is the LORD?'
Or I may become poor and steal,
and so dishonor the name of my God.

10 "Do not slander a servant to his master,
or he will curse you, and you will pay for it.

11 "There are those who curse their fathers
and do not bless their mothers;
12 those who are pure in their own eyes
and yet are not cleansed of their filth;
13 those whose eyes are ever so haughty,
whose glances are so disdainful;
14 those whose teeth are swords
and whose jaws are set with knives
to devour the poor from the earth,
the needy from among mankind.

15 "The leech has two daughters.
'Give! Give!' they cry.

"There are three things that are never satisfied,
four that never say, 'Enough!':
16 the grave,[d] the barren womb,
land, which is never satisfied with water,
and fire, which never says, 'Enough!'

17 "The eye that mocks a father,
that scorns obedience to a mother,
will be pecked out by the ravens of the valley,
will be eaten by the vultures.

18 "There are three things that are too amazing for me,
four that I do not understand:
19 the way of an eagle in the sky,
the way of a snake on a rock,
the way of a ship on the high seas,
and the way of a man with a maiden.

20 "This is the way of an adulteress:
She eats and wipes her mouth
and says, 'I've done nothing wrong.'

21 "Under three things the earth trembles,
under four it cannot bear up:
22 a servant who becomes king,
a fool who is full of food,
23 an unloved woman who is married,
and a maidservant who displaces her mistress.

24 "Four things on earth are small,
yet they are extremely wise:
25 Ants are creatures of little strength,
yet they store up their food in the summer;
26 coneys[e] are creatures of little power,
yet they make their home in the crags;
27 locusts have no king,

[a] *21* The meaning of the Hebrew for this word is uncertain. [b] *1* Or *Jakeh of Massa* [c] *1* Masoretic Text; with a different word division of the Hebrew *declared, "I am weary, O God; / I am weary, O God, and faint.*
[d] *16* Hebrew *Sheol* [e] *26* That is, the hyrax or rock badger

yet they advance together in ranks;
28 a lizard can be caught with the hand,
yet it is found in kings' palaces.

29 "There are three things that are stately in their stride,
four that move with stately bearing:
30 a lion, mighty among beasts,
who retreats before nothing;
31 a strutting rooster, a he-goat,
and a king with his army around him.[a]

32 "If you have played the fool and exalted yourself,
or if you have planned evil,
clap your hand over your mouth!
33 For as churning the milk produces butter,
and as twisting the nose produces blood,
so stirring up anger produces strife."

Sayings of King Lemuel

31 The sayings of King Lemuel—an oracle[b] his mother taught him:

2 "O my son, O son of my womb,
O son of my vows,[c]
3 do not spend your strength on women,
your vigor on those who ruin kings.

4 "It is not for kings, O Lemuel—
not for kings to drink wine,
not for rulers to crave beer,
5 lest they drink and forget what the law decrees,
and deprive all the oppressed of their rights.
6 Give beer to those who are perishing,
wine to those who are in anguish;
7 let them drink and forget their poverty
and remember their misery no more.

8 "Speak up for those who cannot speak for themselves,
for the rights of all who are destitute.
9 Speak up and judge fairly;
defend the rights of the poor and needy."

Epilogue: The Wife of Noble Character

10 [d]A wife of noble character who can find?
She is worth far more than rubies.
11 Her husband has full confidence in her
and lacks nothing of value.
12 She brings him good, not harm,
all the days of her life.
13 She selects wool and flax
and works with eager hands.
14 She is like the merchant ships,
bringing her food from afar.
15 She gets up while it is still dark;
she provides food for her family
and portions for her servant girls.
16 She considers a field and buys it;
out of her earnings she plants a vineyard.
17 She sets about her work vigorously;
her arms are strong for her tasks.
18 She sees that her trading is profitable,
and her lamp does not go out at night.
19 In her hand she holds the distaff
and grasps the spindle with her fingers.
20 She opens her arms to the poor
and extends her hands to the needy.
21 When it snows, she has no fear for her household;
for all of them are clothed in scarlet.
22 She makes coverings for her bed;
she is clothed in fine linen and purple.
23 Her husband is respected at the city gate,
where he takes his seat among the elders of the land.
24 She makes linen garments and sells them,
and supplies the merchants with sashes.
25 She is clothed with strength and dignity;
she can laugh at the days to come.
26 She speaks with wisdom,
and faithful instruction is on her tongue.
27 She watches over the affairs of her household
and does not eat the bread of idleness.
28 Her children arise and call her blessed;
her husband also, and he praises her:
29 "Many women do noble things,
but you surpass them all."
30 Charm is deceptive, and beauty is fleeting;
but a woman who fears the LORD is to be praised.
31 Give her the reward she has earned,
and let her works bring her praise at the city gate.

[a] *31* Or *king secure against revolt* [b] *1* Or *of Lemuel king of Massa, which* [c] *2* Or */ the answer to my prayers* [d] *10* Verses 10-31 are an acrostic, each verse beginning with a successive letter of the Hebrew alphabet.

Ecclesiastes

Everything Is Meaningless

1 The words of the Teacher,[a] son of David,
king in Jerusalem:

2"Meaningless! Meaningless!"
says the Teacher.
"Utterly meaningless!
Everything is meaningless."

3What does man gain from all his labor
at which he toils under the sun?
4Generations come and generations go,
but the earth remains forever.
5The sun rises and the sun sets,
and hurries back to where it rises.
6The wind blows to the south
and turns to the north;
round and round it goes,
ever returning on its course.
7All streams flow into the sea,
yet the sea is never full.
To the place the streams come from,
there they return again.
8All things are wearisome,
more than one can say.
The eye never has enough of seeing,
nor the ear its fill of hearing.
9What has been will be again,
what has been done will be done again;
there is nothing new under the sun.
10Is there anything of which one can say,
"Look! This is something new"?
It was here already, long ago;
it was here before our time.
11There is no remembrance of men of old,
and even those who are yet to come
will not be remembered
by those who follow.

Wisdom Is Meaningless

12I, the Teacher, was king over Israel in Jerusalem. 13I devoted myself to study and to
explore by wisdom all that is done under heav-
en. What a heavy burden God has laid on men!
14I have seen all the things that are done under
the sun; all of them are meaningless, a chasing
after the wind.

15What is twisted cannot be straightened;
what is lacking cannot be counted.

16I thought to myself, "Look, I have grown
and increased in wisdom more than anyone
who has ruled over Jerusalem before me; I
have experienced much of wisdom and knowledge." 17Then I applied myself to the understanding of wisdom, and also of madness and
folly, but I learned that this, too, is a chasing
after the wind.

18For with much wisdom comes much
sorrow;
the more knowledge, the more grief.

Pleasures Are Meaningless

2 I thought in my heart, "Come now, I will
test you with pleasure to find out what is
good." But that also proved to be meaningless.
2"Laughter," I said, "is foolish. And what does
pleasure accomplish?" 3I tried cheering myself
with wine, and embracing folly—my mind
still guiding me with wisdom. I wanted to see
what was worthwhile for men to do under
heaven during the few days of their lives.
4I undertook great projects: I built houses
for myself and planted vineyards. 5I made gardens and parks and planted all kinds of fruit
trees in them. 6I made reservoirs to water
groves of flourishing trees. 7I bought male and
female slaves and had other slaves who were
born in my house. I also owned more herds and
flocks than anyone in Jerusalem before me. 8I
amassed silver and gold for myself, and the
treasure of kings and provinces. I acquired
men and women singers, and a harem[b] as
well—the delights of the heart of man. 9I became greater by far than anyone in Jerusalem
before me. In all this my wisdom stayed
with me.

10I denied myself nothing my eyes desired;
I refused my heart no pleasure.
My heart took delight in all my work,
and this was the reward for all my
labor.
11Yet when I surveyed all that my hands
had done
and what I had toiled to achieve,
everything was meaningless, a chasing
after the wind;
nothing was gained under the sun.

Wisdom and Folly Are Meaningless

12Then I turned my thoughts to consider
wisdom,
and also madness and folly.
What more can the king's successor do
than what has already been done?
13I saw that wisdom is better than folly,
just as light is better than darkness.
14The wise man has eyes in his head,
while the fool walks in the darkness;
but I came to realize
that the same fate overtakes them both.

15Then I thought in my heart,

"The fate of the fool will overtake me
also.
What then do I gain by being wise?"
I said in my heart,

[a] *1* Or *leader of the assembly*; also in verses 2 and 12 uncertain.
[b] *8* The meaning of the Hebrew for this phrase is

"This too is meaningless."
16For the wise man, like the fool, will not
be long remembered;
in days to come both will be forgotten.
Like the fool, the wise man too must die!

Toil Is Meaningless

17So I hated life, because the work that is
done under the sun was grievous to me. All of
it is meaningless, a chasing after the wind. 18I
hated all the things I had toiled for under the
sun, because I must leave them to the one who
comes after me. 19And who knows whether he
will be a wise man or a fool? Yet he will have
control over all the work into which I have
poured my effort and skill under the sun. This
too is meaningless. 20So my heart began to
despair over all my toilsome labor under the
sun. 21For a man may do his work with wisdom, knowledge and skill, and then he must
leave all he owns to someone who has not
worked for it. This too is meaningless and a
great misfortune. 22What does a man get for all
the toil and anxious striving with which he
labors under the sun? 23All his days his work
is pain and grief; even at night his mind does
not rest. This too is meaningless.
24A man can do nothing better than to eat
and drink and find satisfaction in his work.
This too, I see, is from the hand of God, 25for
without him, who can eat or find enjoyment?
26To the man who pleases him, God gives wisdom, knowledge and happiness, but to the sinner he gives the task of gathering and storing
up wealth to hand it over to the one who
pleases God. This too is meaningless, a chasing after the wind.

A Time for Everything

3 There is a time for everything,
and a season for every activity under
heaven:

2 a time to be born and a time to die,
a time to plant and a time to uproot,
3 a time to kill and a time to heal,
a time to tear down and a time to build,
4 a time to weep and a time to laugh,
a time to mourn and a time to dance,
5 a time to scatter stones and a time to
gather them,
a time to embrace and a time to refrain,
6 a time to search and a time to give up,
a time to keep and a time to throw
away,
7 a time to tear and a time to mend,
a time to be silent and a time to speak,
8 a time to love and a time to hate,
a time for war and a time for peace.

9What does the worker gain from his toil?
10I have seen the burden God has laid on men.
11He has made everything beautiful in its time.
He has also set eternity in the hearts of men;
yet they cannot fathom what God has done
from beginning to end. 12I know that there is
nothing better for men than to be happy and do
good while they live. 13That everyone may eat
and drink, and find satisfaction in all his toil—
this is the gift of God. 14I know that everything
God does will endure forever; nothing can be
added to it and nothing taken from it. God does
it so that men will revere him.

15Whatever is has already been,
and what will be has been before;
and God will call the past to account.[a]

16And I saw something else under the sun:

In the place of judgment—wickedness was
there,
in the place of justice—wickedness was
there.

17I thought in my heart,

"God will bring to judgment
both the righteous and the wicked,
for there will be a time for every activity,
a time for every deed."

18I also thought, "As for men, God tests
them so that they may see that they are like the
animals. 19Man's fate is like that of the animals; the same fate awaits them both: As one
dies, so dies the other. All have the same
breath[b]; man has no advantage over the animal. Everything is meaningless. 20All go to the
same place; all come from dust, and to dust all
return. 21Who knows if the spirit of man rises
upward and if the spirit of the animal[c] goes
down into the earth?"
22So I saw that there is nothing better for a
man than to enjoy his work, because that is his
lot. For who can bring him to see what will
happen after him?

Oppression, Toil, Friendlessness

4 Again I looked and saw all the oppression
that was taking place under the sun:

I saw the tears of the oppressed—
and they have no comforter;
power was on the side of their
oppressors—
and they have no comforter.
2And I declared that the dead,
who had already died,
are happier than the living,
who are still alive.
3But better than both
is he who has not yet been,
who has not seen the evil
that is done under the sun.

4And I saw that all labor and all achieve-
ment spring from man's envy of his neighbor.
This too is meaningless, a chasing after the
wind.

5The fool folds his hands
and ruins himself.
6Better one handful with tranquillity

[a]*15* Or *God calls back the past* [b]*19* Or *spirit* [c]*21* Or *Who knows the spirit of man, which rises upward, or the spirit of the animal, which*

than two handfuls with toil
and chasing after the wind.

7Again I saw something meaningless under
the sun:

8There was a man all alone;
he had neither son nor brother.
There was no end to his toil,
yet his eyes were not content with his wealth.
"For whom am I toiling," he asked,
"and why am I depriving myself of enjoyment?"
This too is meaningless—
a miserable business!

9Two are better than one,
because they have a good return for their work:
10If one falls down,
his friend can help him up.
But pity the man who falls
and has no one to help him up!
11Also, if two lie down together, they will keep warm.
But how can one keep warm alone?
12Though one may be overpowered,
two can defend themselves.
A cord of three strands is not quickly broken.

Advancement Is Meaningless

13Better a poor but wise youth than an old
but foolish king who no longer knows how to
take warning. 14The youth may have come
from prison to the kingship, or he may have
been born in poverty within his kingdom. 15I
saw that all who lived and walked under the
sun followed the youth, the king's successor.
16There was no end to all the people who were
before them. But those who came later were
not pleased with the successor. This too is
meaningless, a chasing after the wind.

Stand in Awe of God

5 Guard your steps when you go to the house
of God. Go near to listen rather than to
offer the sacrifice of fools, who do not know
that they do wrong.

2Do not be quick with your mouth,
do not be hasty in your heart
to utter anything before God.
God is in heaven
and you are on earth,
so let your words be few.
3As a dream comes when there are many cares,
so the speech of a fool when there are many words.

4When you make a vow to God, do not delay in fulfilling it. He has no pleasure in fools;
fulfill your vow. 5It is better not to vow than to
make a vow and not fulfill it. 6Do not let your
mouth lead you into sin. And do not protest to
the ⌊temple⌋ messenger, "My vow was a mistake." Why should God be angry at what you
say and destroy the work of your hands?
7Much dreaming and many words are meaningless. Therefore stand in awe of God.

Riches Are Meaningless

8If you see the poor oppressed in a district,
and justice and rights denied, do not be surprised at such things; for one official is eyed
by a higher one, and over them both are others
higher still. 9The increase from the land is tak-
en by all; the king himself profits from the
fields.

10Whoever loves money never has money enough;
whoever loves wealth is never satisfied with his income.
This too is meaningless.

11As goods increase,
so do those who consume them.
And what benefit are they to the owner
except to feast his eyes on them?

12The sleep of a laborer is sweet,
whether he eats little or much,
but the abundance of a rich man
permits him no sleep.

13I have seen a grievous evil under the sun:

wealth hoarded to the harm of its owner,
14 or wealth lost through some misfortune,
so that when he has a son
there is nothing left for him.
15Naked a man comes from his mother's womb,
and as he comes, so he departs.
He takes nothing from his labor
that he can carry in his hand.

16This too is a grievous evil:

As a man comes, so he departs,
and what does he gain,
since he toils for the wind?
17All his days he eats in darkness,
with great frustration, affliction and anger.

18Then I realized that it is good and proper
for a man to eat and drink, and to find satisfaction in his toilsome labor under the sun during
the few days of life God has given him—for
this is his lot. 19Moreover, when God gives any
man wealth and possessions, and enables him
to enjoy them, to accept his lot and be happy
in his work—this is a gift of God. 20He seldom
reflects on the days of his life, because God
keeps him occupied with gladness of heart.

6 I have seen another evil under the sun, and
it weighs heavily on men: 2God gives a
man wealth, possessions and honor, so that he
lacks nothing his heart desires, but God does
not enable him to enjoy them, and a stranger
enjoys them instead. This is meaningless, a
grievous evil.

3A man may have a hundred children and
live many years; yet no matter how long he
lives, if he cannot enjoy his prosperity and
does not receive proper burial, I say that a

stillborn child is better off than he. [4]It comes
without meaning, it departs in darkness, and in
darkness its name is shrouded. [5]Though it never saw the sun or knew anything, it has more
rest than does that man— [6]even if he lives a
thousand years twice over but fails to enjoy his
prosperity. Do not all go to the same place?

[7]All man's efforts are for his mouth,
yet his appetite is never satisfied.
[8]What advantage has a wise man
over a fool?
What does a poor man gain
by knowing how to conduct himself
before others?
[9]Better what the eye sees
than the roving of the appetite.
This too is meaningless,
a chasing after the wind.

[10]Whatever exists has already been named,
and what man is has been known;
no man can contend
with one who is stronger than he.
[11]The more the words,
the less the meaning,
and how does that profit anyone?

[12]For who knows what is good for a man in
life, during the few and meaningless days he
passes through like a shadow? Who can tell
him what will happen under the sun after he is
gone?

Wisdom

7 A good name is better than fine perfume,
and the day of death better than the day
of birth.
[2]It is better to go to a house of mourning
than to go to a house of feasting,
for death is the destiny of every man;
the living should take this to heart.
[3]Sorrow is better than laughter,
because a sad face is good for the heart.
[4]The heart of the wise is in the house of
mourning,
but the heart of fools is in the house of
pleasure.
[5]It is better to heed a wise man's rebuke
than to listen to the song of fools.
[6]Like the crackling of thorns under the pot,
so is the laughter of fools.
This too is meaningless.

[7]Extortion turns a wise man into a fool,
and a bribe corrupts the heart.

[8]The end of a matter is better than its
beginning,
and patience is better than pride.
[9]Do not be quickly provoked in your spirit,
for anger resides in the lap of fools.

[10]Do not say, "Why were the old days
better than these?"
For it is not wise to ask such questions.

[11]Wisdom, like an inheritance, is a good
thing
and benefits those who see the sun.
[12]Wisdom is a shelter
as money is a shelter,
but the advantage of knowledge is this:
that wisdom preserves the life of its
possessor.

[13]Consider what God has done:

Who can straighten
what he has made crooked?
[14]When times are good, be happy;
but when times are bad, consider:
God has made the one
as well as the other.
Therefore, a man cannot discover
anything about his future.

[15]In this meaningless life of mine I have
seen both of these:

a righteous man perishing in his
righteousness,
and a wicked man living long in his
wickedness.
[16]Do not be overrighteous,
neither be overwise—
why destroy yourself?
[17]Do not be overwicked,
and do not be a fool—
why die before your time?
[18]It is good to grasp the one
and not let go of the other.
The man who fears God will avoid all
⌊extremes⌋.[a]

[19]Wisdom makes one wise man more
powerful
than ten rulers in a city.

[20]There is not a righteous man on earth
who does what is right and never sins.

[21]Do not pay attention to every word people
say,
or you may hear your servant cursing
you—
[22]for you know in your heart
that many times you yourself have
cursed others.

[23]All this I tested by wisdom and I said,

"I am determined to be wise"—
but this was beyond me.
[24]Whatever wisdom may be,
it is far off and most profound—
who can discover it?
[25]So I turned my mind to understand,
to investigate and to search out wisdom
and the scheme of things
and to understand the stupidity of
wickedness
and the madness of folly.

[26]I find more bitter than death
the woman who is a snare,
whose heart is a trap
and whose hands are chains.
The man who pleases God will escape her,

[a] *18* Or *will follow them both*

but the sinner she will ensnare.

27“Look,” says the Teacher,[a] “this is what I
have discovered:

“Adding one thing to another to discover
the scheme of things—
28 while I was still searching
but not finding—
I found one ⌊upright⌋ man among a
thousand,
but not one ⌊upright⌋ woman among
them all.
29This only have I found:
God made mankind upright,
but men have gone in search of many
schemes.”

8 Who is like the wise man?
Who knows the explanation of things?
Wisdom brightens a man’s face
and changes its hard appearance.

Obey the King

2Obey the king’s command, I say, because
you took an oath before God. 3Do not be in a
hurry to leave the king’s presence. Do not
stand up for a bad cause, for he will do whatever he pleases. 4Since a king’s word is supreme, who can say to him, “What are you
doing?”

5Whoever obeys his command will come to
no harm,
and the wise heart will know the proper
time and procedure.
6For there is a proper time and procedure
for every matter,
though a man’s misery weighs heavily
upon him.

7Since no man knows the future,
who can tell him what is to come?
8No man has power over the wind to
contain it[b];
so no one has power over the day of his
death.
As no one is discharged in time of war,
so wickedness will not release those
who practice it.

9All this I saw, as I applied my mind to
everything done under the sun. There is a time
when a man lords it over others to his own[c]
hurt. 10Then too, I saw the wicked buried—
those who used to come and go from the holy
place and receive praise[d] in the city where
they did this. This too is meaningless.
11When the sentence for a crime is not
quickly carried out, the hearts of the people are
filled with schemes to do wrong. 12Although a
wicked man commits a hundred crimes and
still lives a long time, I know that it will go
better with God-fearing men, who are reverent
before God. 13Yet because the wicked do not
fear God, it will not go well with them, and
their days will not lengthen like a shadow.
14There is something else meaningless that
occurs on earth: righteous men who get what
the wicked deserve, and wicked men who get
what the righteous deserve. This too, I say, is
meaningless. 15So I commend the enjoyment
of life, because nothing is better for a man
under the sun than to eat and drink and be glad.
Then joy will accompany him in his work all
the days of the life God has given him under
the sun.
16When I applied my mind to know wisdom
and to observe man’s labor on earth—his eyes
not seeing sleep day or night— 17then I saw all
that God has done. No one can comprehend
what goes on under the sun. Despite all his
efforts to search it out, man cannot discover its
meaning. Even if a wise man claims he knows,
he cannot really comprehend it.

A Common Destiny for All

9 So I reflected on all this and concluded that
the righteous and the wise and what they
do are in God’s hands, but no man knows
whether love or hate awaits him. 2All share a
common destiny—the righteous and the wicked, the good and the bad,[e] the clean and the
unclean, those who offer sacrifices and those
who do not.

As it is with the good man,
so with the sinner;
as it is with those who take oaths,
so with those who are afraid to take
them.

3This is the evil in everything that happens
under the sun: The same destiny overtakes all.
The hearts of men, moreover, are full of evil
and there is madness in their hearts while they
live, and afterward they join the dead. 4Any-
one who is among the living has hope[f]—even
a live dog is better off than a dead lion!

5For the living know that they will die,
but the dead know nothing;
they have no further reward,
and even the memory of them is
forgotten.
6Their love, their hate
and their jealousy have long since
vanished;
never again will they have a part
in anything that happens under the sun.

7Go, eat your food with gladness, and drink
your wine with a joyful heart, for it is now that
God favors what you do. 8Always be clothed
in white, and always anoint your head with oil.
9Enjoy life with your wife, whom you love, all
the days of this meaningless life that God has
given you under the sun—all your meaningless days. For this is your lot in life and in your
toilsome labor under the sun. 10Whatever your

[a]27 Or *leader of the assembly* [b]8 Or *over his spirit to retain it* [c]9 Or *to their* [d]10 Some Hebrew manuscripts and Septuagint (Aquila); most Hebrew manuscripts *and are forgotten* [e]2 Septuagint (Aquila), Vulgate and Syriac; Hebrew does not have *and the bad.* [f]4 Or *What then is to be chosen? With all who live, there is hope*

hand finds to do, do it with all your might, for in the grave,[a] where you are going, there is neither working nor planning nor knowledge nor wisdom.

11I have seen something else under the sun:

The race is not to the swift
or the battle to the strong,
nor does food come to the wise
or wealth to the brilliant
or favor to the learned;
but time and chance happen to them all.

12Moreover, no man knows when his hour will come:

As fish are caught in a cruel net,
or birds are taken in a snare,
so men are trapped by evil times
that fall unexpectedly upon them.

Wisdom Better Than Folly

13I also saw under the sun this example of
wisdom that greatly impressed me: 14There
was once a small city with only a few people
in it. And a powerful king came against it,
surrounded it and built huge siegeworks
against it. 15Now there lived in that city a man
poor but wise, and he saved the city by his
wisdom. But nobody remembered that poor
man. 16So I said, "Wisdom is better than
strength." But the poor man's wisdom is despised, and his words are no longer heeded.

17The quiet words of the wise are more to be heeded
than the shouts of a ruler of fools.
18Wisdom is better than weapons of war,
but one sinner destroys much good.

10 As dead flies give perfume a bad smell,
so a little folly outweighs wisdom and honor.
2The heart of the wise inclines to the right,
but the heart of the fool to the left.
3Even as he walks along the road,
the fool lacks sense
and shows everyone how stupid he is.
4If a ruler's anger rises against you,
do not leave your post;
calmness can lay great errors to rest.

5There is an evil I have seen under the sun,
the sort of error that arises from a ruler:
6Fools are put in many high positions,
while the rich occupy the low ones.
7I have seen slaves on horseback,
while princes go on foot like slaves.

8Whoever digs a pit may fall into it;
whoever breaks through a wall may be bitten by a snake.
9Whoever quarries stones may be injured by them;
whoever splits logs may be endangered by them.

10If the ax is dull
and its edge unsharpened,
more strength is needed
but skill will bring success.

11If a snake bites before it is charmed,
there is no profit for the charmer.

12Words from a wise man's mouth are gracious,
but a fool is consumed by his own lips.
13At the beginning his words are folly;
at the end they are wicked madness—
14 and the fool multiplies words.

No one knows what is coming—
who can tell him what will happen after him?

15A fool's work wearies him;
he does not know the way to town.

16Woe to you, O land whose king was a servant[b]
and whose princes feast in the morning.
17Blessed are you, O land whose king is of noble birth
and whose princes eat at a proper time—
for strength and not for drunkenness.

18If a man is lazy, the rafters sag;
if his hands are idle, the house leaks.

19A feast is made for laughter,
and wine makes life merry,
but money is the answer for everything.

20Do not revile the king even in your thoughts,
or curse the rich in your bedroom,
because a bird of the air may carry your words,
and a bird on the wing may report what you say.

Bread Upon the Waters

11 Cast your bread upon the waters,
for after many days you will find it again.
2Give portions to seven, yes to eight,
for you do not know what disaster may come upon the land.

3If clouds are full of water,
they pour rain upon the earth.
Whether a tree falls to the south or to the north,
in the place where it falls, there will it lie.
4Whoever watches the wind will not plant;
whoever looks at the clouds will not reap.

5As you do not know the path of the wind,
or how the body is formed[c] in a mother's womb,

[a] *10* Hebrew *Sheol* [b] *16* Or *king is a child* [c] *5* Or *know how life* (or *the spirit*) / *enters the body being formed*

so you cannot understand the work of
God,
the Maker of all things.

6Sow your seed in the morning,
and at evening let not your hands be
idle,
for you do not know which will succeed,
whether this or that,
or whether both will do equally well.

Remember Your Creator While Young

7Light is sweet,
and it pleases the eyes to see the sun.
8However many years a man may live,
let him enjoy them all.
But let him remember the days of
darkness,
for they will be many.
Everything to come is meaningless.

9Be happy, young man, while you are
young,
and let your heart give you joy in the
days of your youth.
Follow the ways of your heart
and whatever your eyes see,
but know that for all these things
God will bring you to judgment.
10So then, banish anxiety from your heart
and cast off the troubles of your body,
for youth and vigor are meaningless.

12 Remember your Creator
in the days of your youth,
before the days of trouble come
and the years approach when you will
say,
"I find no pleasure in them"—
2before the sun and the light
and the moon and the stars grow dark,
and the clouds return after the rain;
3when the keepers of the house tremble,
and the strong men stoop,
when the grinders cease because they are
few,
and those looking through the windows
grow dim;
4when the doors to the street are closed
and the sound of grinding fades;
when men rise up at the sound of birds,
but all their songs grow faint;
5when men are afraid of heights
and of dangers in the streets;
when the almond tree blossoms
and the grasshopper drags himself along
and desire no longer is stirred.
Then man goes to his eternal home
and mourners go about the streets.

6Remember him—before the silver cord is
severed,
or the golden bowl is broken;
before the pitcher is shattered at the
spring,
or the wheel broken at the well,
7and the dust returns to the ground it came
from,
and the spirit returns to God who gave
it.

8"Meaningless! Meaningless!" says the
Teacher.[a]
"Everything is meaningless!"

The Conclusion of the Matter

9Not only was the Teacher wise, but also he
imparted knowledge to the people. He pondered and searched out and set in order many
proverbs. 10The Teacher searched to find just
the right words, and what he wrote was upright
and true.

11The words of the wise are like goads,
their collected sayings like firmly embedded
nails—given by one Shepherd. 12Be warned,
my son, of anything in addition to them.

Of making many books there is no end, and much study wearies the body.

13Now all has been heard;
here is the conclusion of the matter:
Fear God and keep his commandments,
for this is the whole ⌊duty⌋ of man.
14For God will bring every deed into
judgment,
including every hidden thing,
whether it is good or evil.

Song of Songs

1 Solomon's Song of Songs.

Beloved[b]

2Let him kiss me with the kisses of his
mouth—
for your love is more delightful than
wine.
3Pleasing is the fragrance of your
perfumes;
your name is like perfume poured out.
No wonder the maidens love you!
4Take me away with you—let us hurry!
Let the king bring me into his
chambers.

[a]8 Or *the leader of the assembly*; also in verses 9 and 10 [b]Primarily on the basis of the gender of the Hebrew pronouns used, male and female speakers are indicated in the margins by the captions *Lover* and *Beloved* respectively. The words of others are marked *Friends*. In some instances the divisions and their captions are debatable.

Friends

We rejoice and delight in you[a];
we will praise your love more than
wine.

Beloved

How right they are to adore you!

5Dark am I, yet lovely,
O daughters of Jerusalem,
dark like the tents of Kedar,
like the tent curtains of Solomon.[b]
6Do not stare at me because I am dark,
because I am darkened by the sun.
My mother's sons were angry with me
and made me take care of the
vineyards;
my own vineyard I have neglected.
7Tell me, you whom I love, where you
graze your flock
and where you rest your sheep at
midday.
Why should I be like a veiled woman
beside the flocks of your friends?

Friends

8If you do not know, most beautiful of
women,
follow the tracks of the sheep
and graze your young goats
by the tents of the shepherds.

Lover

9I liken you, my darling, to a mare
harnessed to one of the chariots of
Pharaoh.
10Your cheeks are beautiful with earrings,
your neck with strings of jewels.
11We will make you earrings of gold,
studded with silver.

Beloved

12While the king was at his table,
my perfume spread its fragrance.
13My lover is to me a sachet of myrrh
resting between my breasts.
14My lover is to me a cluster of henna
blossoms
from the vineyards of En Gedi.

Lover

15How beautiful you are, my darling!
Oh, how beautiful!
Your eyes are doves.

Beloved

16How handsome you are, my lover!
Oh, how charming!
And our bed is verdant.

Lover

17The beams of our house are cedars;
our rafters are firs.

Beloved[c]

2 I am a rose[d] of Sharon,
a lily of the valleys.

Lover

2Like a lily among thorns
is my darling among the maidens.

Beloved

3Like an apple tree among the trees of the
forest
is my lover among the young men.
I delight to sit in his shade,
and his fruit is sweet to my taste.
4He has taken me to the banquet hall,
and his banner over me is love.
5Strengthen me with raisins,
refresh me with apples,
for I am faint with love.
6His left arm is under my head,
and his right arm embraces me.
7Daughters of Jerusalem, I charge you
by the gazelles and by the does of the
field:
Do not arouse or awaken love
until it so desires.

8Listen! My lover!
Look! Here he comes,
leaping across the mountains,
bounding over the hills.
9My lover is like a gazelle or a young stag.
Look! There he stands behind our wall,
gazing through the windows,
peering through the lattice.
10My lover spoke and said to me,
"Arise, my darling,
my beautiful one, and come with me.
11See! The winter is past;
the rains are over and gone.
12Flowers appear on the earth;
the season of singing has come,
the cooing of doves
is heard in our land.
13The fig tree forms its early fruit;
the blossoming vines spread their
fragrance.
Arise, come, my darling;
my beautiful one, come with me."

Lover

14My dove in the clefts of the rock,
in the hiding places on the
mountainside,
show me your face,
let me hear your voice;
for your voice is sweet,
and your face is lovely.
15Catch for us the foxes,
the little foxes
that ruin the vineyards,
our vineyards that are in bloom.

Beloved

16My lover is mine and I am his;

[a] *4* The Hebrew is masculine singular. [b] *5* Or *Salma* [c] *1* Or *Lover* [d] *1* Possibly a member of the crocus family

he browses among the lilies.
17Until the day breaks
and the shadows flee,
turn, my lover,
and be like a gazelle
or like a young stag
on the rugged hills.[a]

3 All night long on my bed
I looked for the one my heart loves;
I looked for him but did not find him.
2I will get up now and go about the city,
through its streets and squares;
I will search for the one my heart loves.
So I looked for him but did not find him.
3The watchmen found me
as they made their rounds in the city.
"Have you seen the one my heart loves?"
4Scarcely had I passed them
when I found the one my heart loves.
I held him and would not let him go
till I had brought him to my mother's house,
to the room of the one who conceived me.
5Daughters of Jerusalem, I charge you
by the gazelles and by the does of the field:
Do not arouse or awaken love
until it so desires.

6Who is this coming up from the desert
like a column of smoke,
perfumed with myrrh and incense
made from all the spices of the merchant?
7Look! It is Solomon's carriage,
escorted by sixty warriors,
the noblest of Israel,
8all of them wearing the sword,
all experienced in battle,
each with his sword at his side,
prepared for the terrors of the night.
9King Solomon made for himself the carriage;
he made it of wood from Lebanon.
10Its posts he made of silver,
its base of gold.
Its seat was upholstered with purple,
its interior lovingly inlaid
by[b] the daughters of Jerusalem.
11Come out, you daughters of Zion,
and look at King Solomon wearing the crown,
the crown with which his mother crowned him
on the day of his wedding,
the day his heart rejoiced.

Lover

4 How beautiful you are, my darling!
Oh, how beautiful!
Your eyes behind your veil are doves.
Your hair is like a flock of goats
descending from Mount Gilead.
2Your teeth are like a flock of sheep just shorn,
coming up from the washing.
Each has its twin;
not one of them is alone.
3Your lips are like a scarlet ribbon;
your mouth is lovely.
Your temples behind your veil
are like the halves of a pomegranate.
4Your neck is like the tower of David,
built with elegance[c];
on it hang a thousand shields,
all of them shields of warriors.
5Your two breasts are like two fawns,
like twin fawns of a gazelle
that browse among the lilies.
6Until the day breaks
and the shadows flee,
I will go to the mountain of myrrh
and to the hill of incense.
7All beautiful you are, my darling;
there is no flaw in you.

8Come with me from Lebanon, my bride,
come with me from Lebanon.
Descend from the crest of Amana,
from the top of Senir, the summit of Hermon,
from the lions' dens
and the mountain haunts of the leopards.
9You have stolen my heart, my sister, my bride;
you have stolen my heart
with one glance of your eyes,
with one jewel of your necklace.
10How delightful is your love, my sister, my bride!
How much more pleasing is your love than wine,
and the fragrance of your perfume than any spice!
11Your lips drop sweetness as the honeycomb, my bride;
milk and honey are under your tongue.
The fragrance of your garments is like that of Lebanon.
12You are a garden locked up, my sister, my bride;
you are a spring enclosed, a sealed fountain.
13Your plants are an orchard of pomegranates
with choice fruits,
with henna and nard,
14 nard and saffron,
calamus and cinnamon,
with every kind of incense tree,
with myrrh and aloes
and all the finest spices.
15You are[d] a garden fountain,
a well of flowing water
streaming down from Lebanon.

[a]17 Or *the hills of Bether* [b]10 Or *its inlaid interior a gift of love / from* [c]4 The meaning of the Hebrew for this word is uncertain. [d]15 Or *I am* (spoken by the *Beloved*)

Beloved

16Awake, north wind,
and come, south wind!
Blow on my garden,
that its fragrance may spread abroad.
Let my lover come into his garden
and taste its choice fruits.

Lover

5 I have come into my garden, my sister,
my bride;
I have gathered my myrrh with my
spice.
I have eaten my honeycomb and my
honey;
I have drunk my wine and my milk.

Friends

Eat, O friends, and drink;
drink your fill, O lovers.

Beloved

2I slept but my heart was awake.
Listen! My lover is knocking:
"Open to me, my sister, my darling,
my dove, my flawless one.
My head is drenched with dew,
my hair with the dampness of the
night."
3I have taken off my robe—
must I put it on again?
I have washed my feet—
must I soil them again?
4My lover thrust his hand through the
latch-opening;
my heart began to pound for him.
5I arose to open for my lover,
and my hands dripped with myrrh,
my fingers with flowing myrrh,
on the handles of the lock.
6I opened for my lover,
but my lover had left; he was gone.
My heart sank at his departure.[a]
I looked for him but did not find him.
I called him but he did not answer.
7The watchmen found me
as they made their rounds in the city.
They beat me, they bruised me;
they took away my cloak,
those watchmen of the walls!
8O daughters of Jerusalem, I charge you—
if you find my lover,
what will you tell him?
Tell him I am faint with love.

Friends

9How is your beloved better than others,
most beautiful of women?
How is your beloved better than others,
that you charge us so?

Beloved

10My lover is radiant and ruddy,
outstanding among ten thousand.
11His head is purest gold;
his hair is wavy
and black as a raven.
12His eyes are like doves
by the water streams,
washed in milk,
mounted like jewels.
13His cheeks are like beds of spice
yielding perfume.
His lips are like lilies
dripping with myrrh.
14His arms are rods of gold
set with chrysolite.
His body is like polished ivory
decorated with sapphires.[b]
15His legs are pillars of marble
set on bases of pure gold.
His appearance is like Lebanon,
choice as its cedars.
16His mouth is sweetness itself;
he is altogether lovely.
This is my lover, this my friend,
O daughters of Jerusalem.

Friends

6 Where has your lover gone,
most beautiful of women?
Which way did your lover turn,
that we may look for him with you?

Beloved

2My lover has gone down to his garden,
to the beds of spices,
to browse in the gardens
and to gather lilies.
3I am my lover's and my lover is mine;
he browses among the lilies.

Lover

4You are beautiful, my darling, as Tirzah,
lovely as Jerusalem,
majestic as troops with banners.
5Turn your eyes from me;
they overwhelm me.
Your hair is like a flock of goats
descending from Gilead.
6Your teeth are like a flock of sheep
coming up from the washing.
Each has its twin,
not one of them is alone.
7Your temples behind your veil
are like the halves of a pomegranate.
8Sixty queens there may be,
and eighty concubines,
and virgins beyond number;
9but my dove, my perfect one, is unique,
the only daughter of her mother,
the favorite of the one who bore her.
The maidens saw her and called her
blessed;
the queens and concubines praised her.

Friends

10Who is this that appears like the dawn,
fair as the moon, bright as the sun,
majestic as the stars in procession?

[a]6 Or *heart had gone out to him when he spoke* [b]14 Or *lapis lazuli*

Lover

11I went down to the grove of nut trees
to look at the new growth in the valley,
to see if the vines had budded
or the pomegranates were in bloom.
12Before I realized it,
my desire set me among the royal
chariots of my people.[a]

Friends

13Come back, come back, O Shulammite;
come back, come back, that we may
gaze on you!

Lover

Why would you gaze on the Shulammite
as on the dance of Mahanaim?

7 How beautiful your sandaled feet,
O prince's daughter!
Your graceful legs are like jewels,
the work of a craftsman's hands.
2Your navel is a rounded goblet
that never lacks blended wine.
Your waist is a mound of wheat
encircled by lilies.
3Your breasts are like two fawns,
twins of a gazelle.
4Your neck is like an ivory tower.
Your eyes are the pools of Heshbon
by the gate of Bath Rabbim.
Your nose is like the tower of Lebanon
looking toward Damascus.
5Your head crowns you like Mount Carmel.
Your hair is like royal tapestry;
the king is held captive by its tresses.
6How beautiful you are and how pleasing,
O love, with your delights!
7Your stature is like that of the palm,
and your breasts like clusters of fruit.
8I said, "I will climb the palm tree;
I will take hold of its fruit."
May your breasts be like the clusters of
the vine,
the fragrance of your breath like apples,
9 and your mouth like the best wine.

Beloved

May the wine go straight to my lover,
flowing gently over lips and teeth.[b]
10I belong to my lover,
and his desire is for me.
11Come, my lover, let us go to the
countryside,
let us spend the night in the villages.[c]
12Let us go early to the vineyards
to see if the vines have budded,
if their blossoms have opened,
and if the pomegranates are in bloom—
there I will give you my love.
13The mandrakes send out their fragrance,
and at our door is every delicacy,
both new and old,
that I have stored up for you, my lover.

8 If only you were to me like a brother,
who was nursed at my mother's breasts!
Then, if I found you outside,
I would kiss you,
and no one would despise me.
2I would lead you
and bring you to my mother's house—
she who has taught me.
I would give you spiced wine to drink,
the nectar of my pomegranates.
3His left arm is under my head
and his right arm embraces me.
4Daughters of Jerusalem, I charge you:
Do not arouse or awaken love
until it so desires.

Friends

5Who is this coming up from the desert
leaning on her lover?

Beloved

Under the apple tree I roused you;
there your mother conceived you,
there she who was in labor gave you
birth.
6Place me like a seal over your heart,
like a seal on your arm;
for love is as strong as death,
its jealousy[d] unyielding as the grave.[e]
It burns like blazing fire,
like a mighty flame.[f]
7Many waters cannot quench love;
rivers cannot wash it away.
If one were to give
all the wealth of his house for love,
it[g] would be utterly scorned.

Friends

8We have a young sister,
and her breasts are not yet grown.
What shall we do for our sister
for the day she is spoken for?
9If she is a wall,
we will build towers of silver on her.
If she is a door,
we will enclose her with panels of
cedar.

Beloved

10I am a wall,
and my breasts are like towers.
Thus I have become in his eyes
like one bringing contentment.
11Solomon had a vineyard in Baal Hamon;
he let out his vineyard to tenants.
Each was to bring for its fruit
a thousand shekels[h] of silver.

[a] *12* Or *among the chariots of Amminadab*; or *among the chariots of the people of the prince* [b] *9* Septuagint, Aquila, Vulgate and Syriac; Hebrew *lips of sleepers* [c] *11* Or *henna bushes* [d] *6* Or *ardor* [e] *6* Hebrew *Sheol* [f] *6* Or */ like the very flame of the LORD* [g] *7* Or *he* [h] *11* That is, about 25 pounds (about 11.5 kilograms); also in verse 12

12But my own vineyard is mine to give;
the thousand shekels are for you,
O Solomon,
and two hundred[a] are for those who
tend its fruit.

Lover

13You who dwell in the gardens
with friends in attendance,
let me hear your voice!

Beloved

14Come away, my lover,
and be like a gazelle
or like a young stag
on the spice-laden mountains.

Isaiah

1 The vision concerning Judah and Jerusalem that Isaiah son of Amoz saw during the
reigns of Uzziah, Jotham, Ahaz and Hezekiah,
kings of Judah.

A Rebellious Nation

2Hear, O heavens! Listen, O earth!
For the LORD has spoken:
"I reared children and brought them up,
but they have rebelled against me.
3The ox knows his master,
the donkey his owner's manger,
but Israel does not know,
my people do not understand."

4Ah, sinful nation,
a people loaded with guilt,
a brood of evildoers,
children given to corruption!
They have forsaken the LORD;
they have spurned the Holy One of
Israel
and turned their backs on him.

5Why should you be beaten anymore?
Why do you persist in rebellion?
Your whole head is injured,
your whole heart afflicted.
6From the sole of your foot to the top of
your head
there is no soundness—
only wounds and welts
and open sores,
not cleansed or bandaged
or soothed with oil.

7Your country is desolate,
your cities burned with fire;
your fields are being stripped by
foreigners
right before you,
laid waste as when overthrown by
strangers.
8The Daughter of Zion is left
like a shelter in a vineyard,
like a hut in a field of melons,
like a city under siege.
9Unless the LORD Almighty
had left us some survivors,
we would have become like Sodom,
we would have been like Gomorrah.

10Hear the word of the LORD,
you rulers of Sodom;
listen to the law of our God,
you people of Gomorrah!
11"The multitude of your sacrifices—
what are they to me?" says the LORD.
"I have more than enough of burnt
offerings,
of rams and the fat of fattened animals;
I have no pleasure
in the blood of bulls and lambs and
goats.
12When you come to appear before me,
who has asked this of you,
this trampling of my courts?
13Stop bringing meaningless offerings!
Your incense is detestable to me.
New Moons, Sabbaths and convocations—
I cannot bear your evil assemblies.
14Your New Moon festivals and your
appointed feasts
my soul hates.
They have become a burden to me;
I am weary of bearing them.
15When you spread out your hands in
prayer,
I will hide my eyes from you;
even if you offer many prayers,
I will not listen.
Your hands are full of blood;
16 wash and make yourselves clean.
Take your evil deeds
out of my sight!
Stop doing wrong,
17 learn to do right!
Seek justice,
encourage the oppressed.[b]
Defend the cause of the fatherless,
plead the case of the widow.

18"Come now, let us reason together,"
says the LORD.
"Though your sins are like scarlet,
they shall be as white as snow;
though they are red as crimson,
they shall be like wool.
19If you are willing and obedient,
you will eat the best from the land;
20but if you resist and rebel,
you will be devoured by the sword."
For the mouth of the LORD
has spoken.

21See how the faithful city
has become a harlot!

[a]12 That is, about 5 pounds (about 2.3 kilograms)
[b]17 Or / *rebuke the oppressor*

She once was full of justice;
righteousness used to dwell in her—
but now murderers!
22Your silver has become dross,
your choice wine is diluted with water.
23Your rulers are rebels,
companions of thieves;
they all love bribes
and chase after gifts.
They do not defend the cause of the fatherless;
the widow's case does not come before them.
24Therefore the Lord, the LORD Almighty,
the Mighty One of Israel, declares:
"Ah, I will get relief from my foes
and avenge myself on my enemies.
25I will turn my hand against you;
I will thoroughly purge away your dross
and remove all your impurities.
26I will restore your judges as in days of old,
your counselors as at the beginning.
Afterward you will be called
the City of Righteousness,
the Faithful City."

27Zion will be redeemed with justice,
her penitent ones with righteousness.
28But rebels and sinners will both be broken,
and those who forsake the LORD will perish.

29"You will be ashamed because of the sacred oaks
in which you have delighted;
you will be disgraced because of the gardens
that you have chosen.
30You will be like an oak with fading leaves,
like a garden without water.
31The mighty man will become tinder
and his work a spark;
both will burn together,
with no one to quench the fire."

The Mountain of the LORD

2 This is what Isaiah son of Amoz saw concerning Judah and Jerusalem:

2In the last days

the mountain of the LORD's temple will be established
as chief among the mountains;
it will be raised above the hills,
and all nations will stream to it.

3Many peoples will come and say,

"Come, let us go up to the mountain of the LORD,
to the house of the God of Jacob.
He will teach us his ways,
so that we may walk in his paths."
The law will go out from Zion,
the word of the LORD from Jerusalem.
4He will judge between the nations
and will settle disputes for many peoples.
They will beat their swords into plowshares
and their spears into pruning hooks.
Nation will not take up sword against nation,
nor will they train for war anymore.

5Come, O house of Jacob,
let us walk in the light of the LORD.

The Day of the LORD

6You have abandoned your people,
the house of Jacob.
They are full of superstitions from the East;
they practice divination like the Philistines
and clasp hands with pagans.
7Their land is full of silver and gold;
there is no end to their treasures.
Their land is full of horses;
there is no end to their chariots.
8Their land is full of idols;
they bow down to the work of their hands,
to what their fingers have made.
9So man will be brought low
and mankind humbled—
do not forgive them.[a]

10Go into the rocks,
hide in the ground
from dread of the LORD
and the splendor of his majesty!
11The eyes of the arrogant man will be humbled
and the pride of men brought low;
the LORD alone will be exalted in that day.

12The LORD Almighty has a day in store
for all the proud and lofty,
for all that is exalted
(and they will be humbled),
13for all the cedars of Lebanon, tall and lofty,
and all the oaks of Bashan,
14for all the towering mountains
and all the high hills,
15for every lofty tower
and every fortified wall,
16for every trading ship[b]
and every stately vessel.
17The arrogance of man will be brought low
and the pride of men humbled;
the LORD alone will be exalted in that day,
18 and the idols will totally disappear.

19Men will flee to caves in the rocks
and to holes in the ground
from dread of the LORD
and the splendor of his majesty,

[a]9 Or *not raise them up* [b]16 Hebrew *every ship of Tarshish*

when he rises to shake the earth.
20In that day men will throw away
to the rodents and bats
their idols of silver and idols of gold,
which they made to worship.
21They will flee to caverns in the rocks
and to the overhanging crags
from dread of the LORD
and the splendor of his majesty,
when he rises to shake the earth.

22Stop trusting in man,
who has but a breath in his nostrils.
Of what account is he?

Judgment on Jerusalem and Judah

3 See now, the Lord,
the LORD Almighty,
is about to take from Jerusalem and Judah
both supply and support:
all supplies of food and all supplies of water,
2 the hero and warrior,
the judge and prophet,
the soothsayer and elder,
3the captain of fifty and man of rank,
the counselor, skilled craftsman and clever enchanter.

4I will make boys their officials;
mere children will govern them.
5People will oppress each other—
man against man, neighbor against neighbor.
The young will rise up against the old,
the base against the honorable.

6A man will seize one of his brothers
at his father's home, and say,
"You have a cloak, you be our leader;
take charge of this heap of ruins!"
7But in that day he will cry out,
"I have no remedy.
I have no food or clothing in my house;
do not make me the leader of the people."

8Jerusalem staggers,
Judah is falling;
their words and deeds are against the LORD,
defying his glorious presence.
9The look on their faces testifies against them;
they parade their sin like Sodom;
they do not hide it.
Woe to them!
They have brought disaster upon themselves.

10Tell the righteous it will be well with them,
for they will enjoy the fruit of their deeds.
11Woe to the wicked! Disaster is upon them!
They will be paid back for what their hands have done.

12Youths oppress my people,
women rule over them.
O my people, your guides lead you astray;
they turn you from the path.

13The LORD takes his place in court;
he rises to judge the people.
14The LORD enters into judgment
against the elders and leaders of his people:
"It is you who have ruined my vineyard;
the plunder from the poor is in your houses.
15What do you mean by crushing my people
and grinding the faces of the poor?"
declares the Lord,
the LORD Almighty.

16The LORD says,
"The women of Zion are haughty,
walking along with outstretched necks,
flirting with their eyes,
tripping along with mincing steps,
with ornaments jingling on their ankles.
17Therefore the Lord will bring sores on the heads of the women of Zion;
the LORD will make their scalps bald."

18In that day the Lord will snatch away their
finery: the bangles and headbands and crescent
necklaces, 19the earrings and bracelets and
veils, 20the headdresses and ankle chains and
sashes, the perfume bottles and charms, 21the
signet rings and nose rings, 22the fine robes
and the capes and cloaks, the purses 23and mirrors, and the linen garments and tiaras and
shawls.

24Instead of fragrance there will be a stench;
instead of a sash, a rope;
instead of well-dressed hair, baldness;
instead of fine clothing, sackcloth;
instead of beauty, branding.
25Your men will fall by the sword,
your warriors in battle.
26The gates of Zion will lament and mourn;
destitute, she will sit on the ground.

4 In that day seven women
will take hold of one man
and say, "We will eat our own food
and provide our own clothes;
only let us be called by your name.
Take away our disgrace!"

The Branch of the LORD

2In that day the Branch of the LORD will be
beautiful and glorious, and the fruit of the land
will be the pride and glory of the survivors in
Israel. 3Those who are left in Zion, who remain in Jerusalem, will be called holy, all who
are recorded among the living in Jerusalem.
4The Lord will wash away the filth of the
women of Zion; he will cleanse the bloodstains
from Jerusalem by a spirit[a] of judgment and a
spirit[a] of fire. 5Then the LORD will create over
all of Mount Zion and over those who assemble there a cloud of smoke by day and a glow

[a]4 Or *the Spirit*

of flaming fire by night; over all the glory will
be a canopy. 6It will be a shelter and shade
from the heat of the day, and a refuge and
hiding place from the storm and rain.

The Song of the Vineyard

5 I will sing for the one I love
a song about his vineyard:
My loved one had a vineyard
on a fertile hillside.
2He dug it up and cleared it of stones
and planted it with the choicest vines.
He built a watchtower in it
and cut out a winepress as well.
Then he looked for a crop of good grapes,
but it yielded only bad fruit.

3"Now you dwellers in Jerusalem and men
of Judah,
judge between me and my vineyard.
4What more could have been done for my
vineyard
than I have done for it?
When I looked for good grapes,
why did it yield only bad?
5Now I will tell you
what I am going to do to my vineyard:
I will take away its hedge,
and it will be destroyed;
I will break down its wall,
and it will be trampled.
6I will make it a wasteland,
neither pruned nor cultivated,
and briers and thorns will grow there.
I will command the clouds
not to rain on it."

7The vineyard of the LORD Almighty
is the house of Israel,
and the men of Judah
are the garden of his delight.
And he looked for justice, but saw
bloodshed;
for righteousness, but heard cries of
distress.

Woes and Judgments

8Woe to you who add house to house
and join field to field
till no space is left
and you live alone in the land.

9The LORD Almighty has declared in my
hearing:

"Surely the great houses will become
desolate,
the fine mansions left without
occupants.
10A ten-acre[a] vineyard will produce only a
bath[b] of wine,
a homer[c] of seed only an ephah[d] of
grain."

11Woe to those who rise early in the
morning
to run after their drinks,
who stay up late at night
till they are inflamed with wine.
12They have harps and lyres at their
banquets,
tambourines and flutes and wine,
but they have no regard for the deeds of
the LORD,
no respect for the work of his hands.
13Therefore my people will go into exile
for lack of understanding;
their men of rank will die of hunger
and their masses will be parched with
thirst.
14Therefore the grave[e] enlarges its appetite
and opens its mouth without limit;
into it will descend their nobles and
masses
with all their brawlers and revelers.
15So man will be brought low
and mankind humbled,
the eyes of the arrogant humbled.
16But the LORD Almighty will be exalted by
his justice,
and the holy God will show himself
holy by his righteousness.
17Then sheep will graze as in their own
pasture;
lambs will feed[f] among the ruins of the
rich.

18Woe to those who draw sin along with
cords of deceit,
and wickedness as with cart ropes,
19to those who say, "Let God hurry,
let him hasten his work
so we may see it.
Let it approach,
let the plan of the Holy One of Israel
come,
so we may know it."

20Woe to those who call evil good
and good evil,
who put darkness for light
and light for darkness,
who put bitter for sweet
and sweet for bitter.

21Woe to those who are wise in their own
eyes
and clever in their own sight.

22Woe to those who are heroes at drinking
wine
and champions at mixing drinks,
23who acquit the guilty for a bribe,
but deny justice to the innocent.
24Therefore, as tongues of fire lick up straw
and as dry grass sinks down in the
flames,
so their roots will decay
and their flowers blow away like dust;
for they have rejected the law of the LORD
Almighty

[a]10 Hebrew *ten-yoke,* that is, the land plowed by 10 yoke of oxen in one day [b]10 That is, probably about 6 gallons (about 22 liters) [c]10 That is, probably about 6 bushels (about 220 liters) [d]10 That is, probably about 3/5 bushel (about 22 liters) [e]14 Hebrew *Sheol* [f]17 Septuagint; Hebrew / *strangers will eat*

and spurned the word of the Holy One of Israel.
25 Therefore the LORD's anger burns against his people;
his hand is raised and he strikes them down.
The mountains shake,
and the dead bodies are like refuse in the streets.

Yet for all this, his anger is not turned away,
his hand is still upraised.

26 He lifts up a banner for the distant nations,
he whistles for those at the ends of the earth.
Here they come,
swiftly and speedily!
27 Not one of them grows tired or stumbles,
not one slumbers or sleeps;
not a belt is loosened at the waist,
not a sandal thong is broken.
28 Their arrows are sharp,
all their bows are strung;
their horses' hoofs seem like flint,
their chariot wheels like a whirlwind.
29 Their roar is like that of the lion,
they roar like young lions;
they growl as they seize their prey
and carry it off with no one to rescue.
30 In that day they will roar over it
like the roaring of the sea.
And if one looks at the land,
he will see darkness and distress;
even the light will be darkened by the clouds.

Isaiah's Commission

6 In the year that King Uzziah died, I saw the
Lord seated on a throne, high and exalted,
and the train of his robe filled the temple.
2 Above him were seraphs, each with six
wings: With two wings they covered their
faces, with two they covered their feet, and
with two they were flying. 3 And they were
calling to one another:

"Holy, holy, holy is the LORD Almighty;
the whole earth is full of his glory."

4 At the sound of their voices the doorposts and
thresholds shook and the temple was filled
with smoke.
5 "Woe to me!" I cried. "I am ruined! For I
am a man of unclean lips, and I live among a
people of unclean lips, and my eyes have seen
the King, the LORD Almighty."
6 Then one of the seraphs flew to me with a
live coal in his hand, which he had taken with
tongs from the altar. 7 With it he touched my
mouth and said, "See, this has touched your
lips; your guilt is taken away and your sin
atoned for."
8 Then I heard the voice of the Lord saying,
"Whom shall I send? And who will go for us?"
And I said, "Here am I. Send me!"
9 He said, "Go and tell this people:

" 'Be ever hearing, but never understanding;
be ever seeing, but never perceiving.'
10 Make the heart of this people calloused;
make their ears dull
and close their eyes.[a]
Otherwise they might see with their eyes,
hear with their ears,
understand with their hearts,
and turn and be healed."

11 Then I said, "For how long, O Lord?"
And he answered:

"Until the cities lie ruined
and without inhabitant,
until the houses are left deserted
and the fields ruined and ravaged,
12 until the LORD has sent everyone far away
and the land is utterly forsaken.
13 And though a tenth remains in the land,
it will again be laid waste.
But as the terebinth and oak
leave stumps when they are cut down,
so the holy seed will be the stump in the land."

The Sign of Immanuel

7 When Ahaz son of Jotham, the son of Uzziah, was king of Judah, King Rezin of
Aram and Pekah son of Remaliah king of Israel marched up to fight against Jerusalem, but
they could not overpower it.
2 Now the house of David was told, "Aram
has allied itself with[b] Ephraim"; so the hearts
of Ahaz and his people were shaken, as the
trees of the forest are shaken by the wind.
3 Then the LORD said to Isaiah, "Go out, you
and your son Shear-Jashub,[c] to meet Ahaz at
the end of the aqueduct of the Upper Pool, on
the road to the Washerman's Field. 4 Say to
him, 'Be careful, keep calm and don't be
afraid. Do not lose heart because of these two
smoldering stubs of firewood—because of the
fierce anger of Rezin and Aram and of the son
of Remaliah. 5 Aram, Ephraim and Remaliah's
son have plotted your ruin, saying, 6 "Let us
invade Judah; let us tear it apart and divide it
among ourselves, and make the son of Tabeel
king over it." 7 Yet this is what the Sovereign
LORD says:

" 'It will not take place,
it will not happen,
8 for the head of Aram is Damascus,
and the head of Damascus is only Rezin.
Within sixty-five years
Ephraim will be too shattered to be a people.

[a] 9,10 Hebrew; Septuagint *'You will be ever hearing, but never understanding; / you will be ever seeing, but never perceiving.' / 10This people's heart has become calloused; / they hardly hear with their ears, / and they have closed their eyes* [b] 2 Or *has set up camp in* [c] 3 *Shear-Jashub* means *a remnant will return.*

9The head of Ephraim is Samaria,
and the head of Samaria is only
Remaliah's son.
If you do not stand firm in your faith,
you will not stand at all.' "

10Again the LORD spoke to Ahaz, 11"Ask
the LORD your God for a sign, whether in the
deepest depths or in the highest heights."
12But Ahaz said, "I will not ask; I will not
put the LORD to the test."
13Then Isaiah said, "Hear now, you house of
David! Is it not enough to try the patience of
men? Will you try the patience of my God
also? 14Therefore the Lord himself will give
you[a] a sign: The virgin will be with child and
will give birth to a son, and[b] will call him
Immanuel.[c] 15He will eat curds and honey
when he knows enough to reject the wrong and
choose the right. 16But before the boy knows
enough to reject the wrong and choose the
right, the land of the two kings you dread will
be laid waste. 17The LORD will bring on you
and on your people and on the house of your
father a time unlike any since Ephraim broke
away from Judah—he will bring the king of
Assyria."
18In that day the LORD will whistle for flies
from the distant streams of Egypt and for bees
from the land of Assyria. 19They will all come
and settle in the steep ravines and in the crevices in the rocks, on all the thornbushes and at
all the water holes. 20In that day the Lord will
use a razor hired from beyond the River[d]—the
king of Assyria—to shave your head and the
hair of your legs, and to take off your beards
also. 21In that day, a man will keep alive a
young cow and two goats. 22And because of
the abundance of the milk they give, he will
have curds to eat. All who remain in the land
will eat curds and honey. 23In that day, in every place where there were a thousand vines
worth a thousand silver shekels,[e] there will be
only briers and thorns. 24Men will go there
with bow and arrow, for the land will be covered with briers and thorns. 25As for all the
hills once cultivated by the hoe, you will no
longer go there for fear of the briers and
thorns; they will become places where cattle
are turned loose and where sheep run.

Assyria, the LORD's Instrument

8 The LORD said to me, "Take a large scroll
and write on it with an ordinary pen:
Maher-Shalal-Hash-Baz.[f] 2And I will call in
Uriah the priest and Zechariah son of Jebereki-
ah as reliable witnesses for me."
3Then I went to the prophetess, and she conceived and gave birth to a son. And the LORD
said to me, "Name him Maher-Shalal-Hash-
Baz. 4Before the boy knows how to say 'My
father' or 'My mother,' the wealth of Damascus and the plunder of Samaria will be carried
off by the king of Assyria."
5The LORD spoke to me again:

6"Because this people has rejected
the gently flowing waters of Shiloah
and rejoices over Rezin
and the son of Remaliah,
7therefore the Lord is about to bring
against them
the mighty floodwaters of the River[d]—
the king of Assyria with all his pomp.
It will overflow all its channels,
run over all its banks
8and sweep on into Judah, swirling over it,
passing through it and reaching up to
the neck.
Its outspread wings will cover the breadth
of your land,
O Immanuel[c]!"

9Raise the war cry,[g] you nations, and be
shattered!
Listen, all you distant lands.
Prepare for battle, and be shattered!
Prepare for battle, and be shattered!
10Devise your strategy, but it will be
thwarted;
propose your plan, but it will not stand,
for God is with us.[h]

Fear God

11The LORD spoke to me with his strong
hand upon me, warning me not to follow the
way of this people. He said:

12"Do not call conspiracy
everything that these people call
conspiracy[i];
do not fear what they fear,
and do not dread it.
13The LORD Almighty is the one you are to
regard as holy,
he is the one you are to fear,
he is the one you are to dread,
14and he will be a sanctuary;
but for both houses of Israel he will be
a stone that causes men to stumble
and a rock that makes them fall.
And for the people of Jerusalem he will
be
a trap and a snare.
15Many of them will stumble;
they will fall and be broken,
they will be snared and captured."

16Bind up the testimony
and seal up the law among my
disciples.
17I will wait for the LORD,
who is hiding his face from the house
of Jacob.
I will put my trust in him.

18Here am I, and the children the LORD has

[a] *14* The Hebrew is plural. [b] *14* Masoretic Text; Dead Sea Scrolls *and he* or *and they* [c] *14,8 Immanuel* means *God with us.* [d] *20,7* That is, the Euphrates [e] *23* That is, about 25 pounds (about 11.5 kilograms) [f] *1 Maher-Shalal-Hash-Baz* means *quick to the plunder, swift to the spoil*; also in verse 3. [g] *9* Or *Do your worst* [h] *10* Hebrew *Immanuel* [i] *12* Or *Do not call for a treaty / every time these people call for a treaty*

given me. We are signs and symbols in Israel
from the LORD Almighty, who dwells on
Mount Zion.
19When men tell you to consult mediums
and spiritists, who whisper and mutter, should
not a people inquire of their God? Why consult
the dead on behalf of the living? 20To the law
and to the testimony! If they do not speak according to this word, they have no light of
dawn. 21Distressed and hungry, they will roam
through the land; when they are famished, they
will become enraged and, looking upward, will
curse their king and their God. 22Then they
will look toward the earth and see only distress
and darkness and fearful gloom, and they will
be thrust into utter darkness.

To Us a Child Is Born

9 Nevertheless, there will be no more gloom for those who were in distress. In the past he humbled the land of Zebulun and the land of Naphtali, but in the future he will honor Galilee of the Gentiles, by the way of the sea, along the Jordan—

2The people walking in darkness
have seen a great light;
on those living in the land of the shadow of death[a]
a light has dawned.
3You have enlarged the nation
and increased their joy;
they rejoice before you
as people rejoice at the harvest,
as men rejoice
when dividing the plunder.
4For as in the day of Midian's defeat,
you have shattered
the yoke that burdens them,
the bar across their shoulders,
the rod of their oppressor.
5Every warrior's boot used in battle
and every garment rolled in blood
will be destined for burning,
will be fuel for the fire.
6For to us a child is born,
to us a son is given,
and the government will be on his shoulders.
And he will be called
Wonderful Counselor,[b] Mighty God,
Everlasting Father, Prince of Peace.
7Of the increase of his government and peace
there will be no end.
He will reign on David's throne
and over his kingdom,
establishing and upholding it
with justice and righteousness
from that time on and forever.
The zeal of the LORD Almighty
will accomplish this.

The LORD's Anger Against Israel

8The Lord has sent a message against Jacob;
it will fall on Israel.
9All the people will know it—
Ephraim and the inhabitants of Samaria—
who say with pride
and arrogance of heart,
10"The bricks have fallen down,
but we will rebuild with dressed stone;
the fig trees have been felled,
but we will replace them with cedars."
11But the LORD has strengthened Rezin's foes against them
and has spurred their enemies on.
12Arameans from the east and Philistines from the west
have devoured Israel with open mouth.

Yet for all this, his anger is not turned away,
his hand is still upraised.

13But the people have not returned to him who struck them,
nor have they sought the LORD Almighty.
14So the LORD will cut off from Israel both head and tail,
both palm branch and reed in a single day;
15the elders and prominent men are the head,
the prophets who teach lies are the tail.
16Those who guide this people mislead them,
and those who are guided are led astray.
17Therefore the Lord will take no pleasure in the young men,
nor will he pity the fatherless and widows,
for everyone is ungodly and wicked,
every mouth speaks vileness.

Yet for all this, his anger is not turned away,
his hand is still upraised.

18Surely wickedness burns like a fire;
it consumes briers and thorns,
it sets the forest thickets ablaze,
so that it rolls upward in a column of smoke.
19By the wrath of the LORD Almighty
the land will be scorched
and the people will be fuel for the fire;
no one will spare his brother.
20On the right they will devour,
but still be hungry;
on the left they will eat,
but not be satisfied.
Each will feed on the flesh of his own offspring[c]:
21 Manasseh will feed on Ephraim, and Ephraim on Manasseh;
together they will turn against Judah.

Yet for all this, his anger is not turned away,

[a]2 Or *land of darkness* [b]6 Or *Wonderful, Counselor* [c]20 Or *arm*

his hand is still upraised.

10 Woe to those who make unjust laws,
to those who issue oppressive decrees,
2to deprive the poor of their rights
and withhold justice from the oppressed
of my people,
making widows their prey
and robbing the fatherless.
3What will you do on the day of reckoning,
when disaster comes from afar?
To whom will you run for help?
Where will you leave your riches?
4Nothing will remain but to cringe among
the captives
or fall among the slain.

Yet for all this, his anger is not turned
away,
his hand is still upraised.

God's Judgment on Assyria

5"Woe to the Assyrian, the rod of my
anger,
in whose hand is the club of my wrath!
6I send him against a godless nation,
I dispatch him against a people who
anger me,
to seize loot and snatch plunder,
and to trample them down like mud in
the streets.
7But this is not what he intends,
this is not what he has in mind;
his purpose is to destroy,
to put an end to many nations.
8'Are not my commanders all kings?' he
says.
9 'Has not Calno fared like Carchemish?
Is not Hamath like Arpad,
and Samaria like Damascus?
10As my hand seized the kingdoms of the
idols,
kingdoms whose images excelled those
of Jerusalem and Samaria—
11shall I not deal with Jerusalem and her
images
as I dealt with Samaria and her idols?' "

12When the Lord has finished all his work
against Mount Zion and Jerusalem, he will say,
"I will punish the king of Assyria for the willful pride of his heart and the haughty look in
his eyes. 13For he says:

" 'By the strength of my hand I have done
this,
and by my wisdom, because I have
understanding.
I removed the boundaries of nations,
I plundered their treasures;
like a mighty one I subdued[a] their
kings.
14As one reaches into a nest,
so my hand reached for the wealth of
the nations;
as men gather abandoned eggs,
so I gathered all the countries;
not one flapped a wing,
or opened its mouth to chirp.' "

15Does the ax raise itself above him who
swings it,
or the saw boast against him who uses
it?
As if a rod were to wield him who lifts it
up,
or a club brandish him who is not
wood!
16Therefore, the Lord, the LORD Almighty,
will send a wasting disease upon his
sturdy warriors;
under his pomp a fire will be kindled
like a blazing flame.
17The Light of Israel will become a fire,
their Holy One a flame;
in a single day it will burn and consume
his thorns and his briers.
18The splendor of his forests and fertile
fields
it will completely destroy,
as when a sick man wastes away.
19And the remaining trees of his forests will
be so few
that a child could write them down.

The Remnant of Israel

20In that day the remnant of Israel,
the survivors of the house of Jacob,
will no longer rely on him
who struck them down
but will truly rely on the LORD,
the Holy One of Israel.
21A remnant will return,[b] a remnant of
Jacob
will return to the Mighty God.
22Though your people, O Israel, be like the
sand by the sea,
only a remnant will return.
Destruction has been decreed,
overwhelming and righteous.
23The Lord, the LORD Almighty, will carry
out
the destruction decreed upon the whole
land.

24Therefore, this is what the Lord, the LORD
Almighty, says:

"O my people who live in Zion,
do not be afraid of the Assyrians,
who beat you with a rod
and lift up a club against you, as Egypt
did.
25Very soon my anger against you will end
and my wrath will be directed to their
destruction."
26The LORD Almighty will lash them with a
whip,
as when he struck down Midian at the
rock of Oreb;
and he will raise his staff over the waters,
as he did in Egypt.

[a]13 Or / I subdued the mighty, [b]21 Hebrew *shear-jashub*; also in verse 22

27In that day their burden will be lifted from
your shoulders,
their yoke from your neck;
the yoke will be broken
because you have grown so fat.[a]

28They enter Aiath;
they pass through Migron;
they store supplies at Micmash.
29They go over the pass, and say,
"We will camp overnight at Geba."
Ramah trembles;
Gibeah of Saul flees.
30Cry out, O Daughter of Gallim!
Listen, O Laishah!
Poor Anathoth!
31Madmenah is in flight;
the people of Gebim take cover.
32This day they will halt at Nob;
they will shake their fist
at the mount of the Daughter of Zion,
at the hill of Jerusalem.

33See, the Lord, the LORD Almighty,
will lop off the boughs with great
power.
The lofty trees will be felled,
the tall ones will be brought low.
34He will cut down the forest thickets with
an ax;
Lebanon will fall before the Mighty
One.

The Branch From Jesse

11 A shoot will come up from the stump
of Jesse;
from his roots a Branch will bear fruit.
2The Spirit of the LORD will rest on him—
the Spirit of wisdom and of
understanding,
the Spirit of counsel and of power,
the Spirit of knowledge and of the fear
of the LORD—
3and he will delight in the fear of the
LORD.

He will not judge by what he sees with
his eyes,
or decide by what he hears with his
ears;
4but with righteousness he will judge the
needy,
with justice he will give decisions for
the poor of the earth.
He will strike the earth with the rod of his
mouth;
with the breath of his lips he will slay
the wicked.
5Righteousness will be his belt
and faithfulness the sash around his
waist.

6The wolf will live with the lamb,
the leopard will lie down with the goat,
the calf and the lion and the yearling[b]
together;
and a little child will lead them.
7The cow will feed with the bear,
their young will lie down together,
and the lion will eat straw like the ox.
8The infant will play near the hole of the
cobra,
and the young child put his hand into
the viper's nest.
9They will neither harm nor destroy
on all my holy mountain,
for the earth will be full of the knowledge
of the LORD
as the waters cover the sea.

10In that day the Root of Jesse will stand as
a banner for the peoples; the nations will rally
to him, and his place of rest will be glorious.
11In that day the Lord will reach out his hand
a second time to reclaim the remnant that is
left of his people from Assyria, from Lower
Egypt, from Upper Egypt,[c] from Cush,[d] from
Elam, from Babylonia,[e] from Hamath and
from the islands of the sea.

12He will raise a banner for the nations
and gather the exiles of Israel;
he will assemble the scattered people of
Judah
from the four quarters of the earth.
13Ephraim's jealousy will vanish,
and Judah's enemies[f] will be cut off;
Ephraim will not be jealous of Judah,
nor Judah hostile toward Ephraim.
14They will swoop down on the slopes of
Philistia to the west;
together they will plunder the people to
the east.
They will lay hands on Edom and Moab,
and the Ammonites will be subject to
them.
15The LORD will dry up
the gulf of the Egyptian sea;
with a scorching wind he will sweep his
hand
over the Euphrates River.[g]
He will break it up into seven streams
so that men can cross over in sandals.
16There will be a highway for the remnant
of his people
that is left from Assyria,
as there was for Israel
when they came up from Egypt.

Songs of Praise

12 In that day you will say:

"I will praise you, O LORD.
Although you were angry with me,
your anger has turned away
and you have comforted me.
2Surely God is my salvation;
I will trust and not be afraid.

[a]27 Hebrew; Septuagint *broken / from your shoulders* [b]6 Hebrew; Septuagint *lion will feed* [c]11 Hebrew *from Pathros* [d]11 That is, the upper Nile region [e]11 Hebrew *Shinar* [f]13 Or *hostility* [g]15 Hebrew *the River*

The LORD, the LORD, is my strength and
my song;
he has become my salvation."
3With joy you will draw water
from the wells of salvation.

4In that day you will say:

"Give thanks to the LORD, call on his
name;
make known among the nations what he
has done,
and proclaim that his name is exalted.
5Sing to the LORD, for he has done
glorious things;
let this be known to all the world.
6Shout aloud and sing for joy, people of
Zion,
for great is the Holy One of Israel
among you."

A Prophecy Against Babylon

13 An oracle concerning Babylon that Isaiah son of Amoz saw:

2Raise a banner on a bare hilltop,
shout to them;
beckon to them
to enter the gates of the nobles.
3I have commanded my holy ones;
I have summoned my warriors to carry
out my wrath—
those who rejoice in my triumph.

4Listen, a noise on the mountains,
like that of a great multitude!
Listen, an uproar among the kingdoms,
like nations massing together!
The LORD Almighty is mustering
an army for war.
5They come from faraway lands,
from the ends of the heavens—
the LORD and the weapons of his wrath—
to destroy the whole country.

6Wail, for the day of the LORD is near;
it will come like destruction from the
Almighty.[a]
7Because of this, all hands will go limp,
every man's heart will melt.
8Terror will seize them,
pain and anguish will grip them;
they will writhe like a woman in labor.
They will look aghast at each other,
their faces aflame.

9See, the day of the LORD is coming
—a cruel day, with wrath and fierce
anger—
to make the land desolate
and destroy the sinners within it.
10The stars of heaven and their
constellations
will not show their light.
The rising sun will be darkened
and the moon will not give its light.
11I will punish the world for its evil,
the wicked for their sins.
I will put an end to the arrogance of the
haughty
and will humble the pride of the
ruthless.
12I will make man scarcer than pure gold,
more rare than the gold of Ophir.
13Therefore I will make the heavens
tremble;
and the earth will shake from its place
at the wrath of the LORD Almighty,
in the day of his burning anger.

14Like a hunted gazelle,
like sheep without a shepherd,
each will return to his own people,
each will flee to his native land.
15Whoever is captured will be thrust
through;
all who are caught will fall by the
sword.
16Their infants will be dashed to pieces
before their eyes;
their houses will be looted and their
wives ravished.

17See, I will stir up against them the Medes,
who do not care for silver
and have no delight in gold.
18Their bows will strike down the young
men;
they will have no mercy on infants
nor will they look with compassion on
children.
19Babylon, the jewel of kingdoms,
the glory of the Babylonians'[b] pride,
will be overthrown by God
like Sodom and Gomorrah.
20She will never be inhabited
or lived in through all generations;
no Arab will pitch his tent there,
no shepherd will rest his flocks there.
21But desert creatures will lie there,
jackals will fill her houses;
there the owls will dwell,
and there the wild goats will leap about.
22Hyenas will howl in her strongholds,
jackals in her luxurious palaces.
Her time is at hand,
and her days will not be prolonged.

14 The LORD will have compassion on
Jacob;
once again he will choose Israel
and will settle them in their own land.
Aliens will join them
and unite with the house of Jacob.
2Nations will take them
and bring them to their own place.
And the house of Israel will possess the
nations
as menservants and maidservants in the
LORD's land.
They will make captives of their captors
and rule over their oppressors.

3On the day the LORD gives you relief from

[a]6 Hebrew *Shaddai* [b]19 Or *Chaldeans'*

suffering and turmoil and cruel bondage, 4you
will take up this taunt against the king of Babylon:

How the oppressor has come to an end!
How his fury[a] has ended!
5The LORD has broken the rod of the wicked,
the scepter of the rulers,
6which in anger struck down peoples
with unceasing blows,
and in fury subdued nations
with relentless aggression.
7All the lands are at rest and at peace;
they break into singing.
8Even the pine trees and the cedars of Lebanon
exult over you and say,
"Now that you have been laid low,
no woodsman comes to cut us down."

9The grave[b] below is all astir
to meet you at your coming;
it rouses the spirits of the departed to greet you—
all those who were leaders in the world;
it makes them rise from their thrones—
all those who were kings over the nations.
10They will all respond,
they will say to you,
"You also have become weak, as we are;
you have become like us."
11All your pomp has been brought down to the grave,
along with the noise of your harps;
maggots are spread out beneath you
and worms cover you.

12How you have fallen from heaven,
O morning star, son of the dawn!
You have been cast down to the earth,
you who once laid low the nations!
13You said in your heart,
"I will ascend to heaven;
I will raise my throne
above the stars of God;
I will sit enthroned on the mount of assembly,
on the utmost heights of the sacred mountain.[c]
14I will ascend above the tops of the clouds;
I will make myself like the Most High."
15But you are brought down to the grave,
to the depths of the pit.

16Those who see you stare at you,
they ponder your fate:
"Is this the man who shook the earth
and made kingdoms tremble,
17the man who made the world a desert,
who overthrew its cities
and would not let his captives go home?"

18All the kings of the nations lie in state,
each in his own tomb.
19But you are cast out of your tomb
like a rejected branch;
you are covered with the slain,
with those pierced by the sword,
those who descend to the stones of the pit.
Like a corpse trampled underfoot,
20 you will not join them in burial,
for you have destroyed your land
and killed your people.

The offspring of the wicked
will never be mentioned again.
21Prepare a place to slaughter his sons
for the sins of their forefathers;
they are not to rise to inherit the land
and cover the earth with their cities.

22"I will rise up against them,"
declares the LORD Almighty.
"I will cut off from Babylon her name and survivors,
her offspring and descendants,"
declares the LORD.
23"I will turn her into a place for owls
and into swampland;
I will sweep her with the broom of destruction,"
declares the LORD Almighty.

A Prophecy Against Assyria

24The LORD Almighty has sworn,

"Surely, as I have planned, so it will be,
and as I have purposed, so it will stand.
25I will crush the Assyrian in my land;
on my mountains I will trample him down.
His yoke will be taken from my people,
and his burden removed from their shoulders."

26This is the plan determined for the whole world;
this is the hand stretched out over all nations.
27For the LORD Almighty has purposed, and who can thwart him?
His hand is stretched out, and who can turn it back?

A Prophecy Against the Philistines

28This oracle came in the year King Ahaz
died:

29Do not rejoice, all you Philistines,
that the rod that struck you is broken;
from the root of that snake will spring up a viper,
its fruit will be a darting, venomous serpent.
30The poorest of the poor will find pasture,
and the needy will lie down in safety.
But your root I will destroy by famine;
it will slay your survivors.

31Wail, O gate! Howl, O city!

[a]4 Dead Sea Scrolls, Septuagint and Syriac; the meaning of the word in the Masoretic Text is uncertain.
[b]9 Hebrew *Sheol*; also in verses 11 and 15 [c]13 Or *the north*; Hebrew *Zaphon*

Melt away, all you Philistines!
A cloud of smoke comes from the north,
and there is not a straggler in its ranks.
32 What answer shall be given
to the envoys of that nation?
"The LORD has established Zion,
and in her his afflicted people will find refuge."

A Prophecy Against Moab

15 An oracle concerning Moab:

Ar in Moab is ruined,
destroyed in a night!
Kir in Moab is ruined,
destroyed in a night!
2 Dibon goes up to its temple,
to its high places to weep;
Moab wails over Nebo and Medeba.
Every head is shaved
and every beard cut off.
3 In the streets they wear sackcloth;
on the roofs and in the public squares
they all wail,
prostrate with weeping.
4 Heshbon and Elealeh cry out,
their voices are heard all the way to Jahaz.
Therefore the armed men of Moab cry out,
and their hearts are faint.

5 My heart cries out over Moab;
her fugitives flee as far as Zoar,
as far as Eglath Shelishiyah.
They go up the way to Luhith,
weeping as they go;
on the road to Horonaim
they lament their destruction.
6 The waters of Nimrim are dried up
and the grass is withered;
the vegetation is gone
and nothing green is left.
7 So the wealth they have acquired and stored up
they carry away over the Ravine of the Poplars.
8 Their outcry echoes along the border of Moab;
their wailing reaches as far as Eglaim,
their lamentation as far as Beer Elim.
9 Dimon's[a] waters are full of blood,
but I will bring still more upon Dimon[a]—
a lion upon the fugitives of Moab
and upon those who remain in the land.

16 Send lambs as tribute
to the ruler of the land,
from Sela, across the desert,
to the mount of the Daughter of Zion.
2 Like fluttering birds
pushed from the nest,
so are the women of Moab
at the fords of the Arnon.

3 "Give us counsel,
render a decision.
Make your shadow like night—
at high noon.
Hide the fugitives,
do not betray the refugees.
4 Let the Moabite fugitives stay with you;
be their shelter from the destroyer."

The oppressor will come to an end,
and destruction will cease;
the aggressor will vanish from the land.
5 In love a throne will be established;
in faithfulness a man will sit on it—
one from the house[b] of David—
one who in judging seeks justice
and speeds the cause of righteousness.

6 We have heard of Moab's pride—
her overweening pride and conceit,
her pride and her insolence—
but her boasts are empty.
7 Therefore the Moabites wail,
they wail together for Moab.
Lament and grieve
for the men[c] of Kir Hareseth.
8 The fields of Heshbon wither,
the vines of Sibmah also.
The rulers of the nations
have trampled down the choicest vines,
which once reached Jazer
and spread toward the desert.
Their shoots spread out
and went as far as the sea.
9 So I weep, as Jazer weeps,
for the vines of Sibmah.
O Heshbon, O Elealeh,
I drench you with tears!
The shouts of joy over your ripened fruit
and over your harvests have been stilled.
10 Joy and gladness are taken away from the orchards;
no one sings or shouts in the vineyards;
no one treads out wine at the presses,
for I have put an end to the shouting.
11 My heart laments for Moab like a harp,
my inmost being for Kir Hareseth.
12 When Moab appears at her high place,
she only wears herself out;
when she goes to her shrine to pray,
it is to no avail.

13 This is the word the LORD has already spoken concerning Moab. 14 But now the LORD
says: "Within three years, as a servant bound
by contract would count them, Moab's splendor and all her many people will be despised,
and her survivors will be very few and feeble."

An Oracle Against Damascus

17 An oracle concerning Damascus:

"See, Damascus will no longer be a city
but will become a heap of ruins.
2 The cities of Aroer will be deserted

[a] 9 Masoretic Text; Dead Sea Scrolls, some Septuagint manuscripts and Vulgate *Dibon* [b] 5 Hebrew *tent*
[c] 7 Or "*raisin cakes*," a wordplay

and left to flocks, which will lie down,
with no one to make them afraid.
3The fortified city will disappear from
Ephraim,
and royal power from Damascus;
the remnant of Aram will be
like the glory of the Israelites,"
declares the LORD Almighty.

4"In that day the glory of Jacob will fade;
the fat of his body will waste away.
5It will be as when a reaper gathers the
standing grain
and harvests the grain with his arm—
as when a man gleans heads of grain
in the Valley of Rephaim.
6Yet some gleanings will remain,
as when an olive tree is beaten,
leaving two or three olives on the topmost
branches,
four or five on the fruitful boughs,"
declares the LORD, the God
of Israel.

7In that day men will look to their Maker
and turn their eyes to the Holy One of
Israel.
8They will not look to the altars,
the work of their hands,
and they will have no regard for the
Asherah poles[a]
and the incense altars their fingers have
made.

9In that day their strong cities, which they
left because of the Israelites, will be like places
abandoned to thickets and undergrowth. And
all will be desolation.

10You have forgotten God your Savior;
you have not remembered the Rock,
your fortress.
Therefore, though you set out the finest
plants
and plant imported vines,
11though on the day you set them out, you
make them grow,
and on the morning when you plant
them, you bring them to bud,
yet the harvest will be as nothing
in the day of disease and incurable pain.

12Oh, the raging of many nations—
they rage like the raging sea!
Oh, the uproar of the peoples—
they roar like the roaring of great
waters!
13Although the peoples roar like the roar of
surging waters,
when he rebukes them they flee far
away,
driven before the wind like chaff on the
hills,
like tumbleweed before a gale.
14In the evening, sudden terror!
Before the morning, they are gone!
This is the portion of those who loot us,
the lot of those who plunder us.

A Prophecy Against Cush

18 Woe to the land of whirring wings[b]
along the rivers of Cush,[c]
2which sends envoys by sea
in papyrus boats over the water.

Go, swift messengers,
to a people tall and smooth-skinned,
to a people feared far and wide,
an aggressive nation of strange speech,
whose land is divided by rivers.

3All you people of the world,
you who live on the earth,
when a banner is raised on the mountains,
you will see it,
and when a trumpet sounds,
you will hear it.
4This is what the LORD says to me:
"I will remain quiet and will look on
from my dwelling place,
like shimmering heat in the sunshine,
like a cloud of dew in the heat of
harvest."
5For, before the harvest, when the blossom
is gone
and the flower becomes a ripening
grape,
he will cut off the shoots with pruning
knives,
and cut down and take away the
spreading branches.
6They will all be left to the mountain birds
of prey
and to the wild animals;
the birds will feed on them all summer,
the wild animals all winter.

7At that time gifts will be brought to the
LORD Almighty

from a people tall and smooth-skinned,
from a people feared far and wide,
an aggressive nation of strange speech,
whose land is divided by rivers—

the gifts will be brought to Mount Zion, the
place of the Name of the LORD Almighty.

A Prophecy About Egypt

19 An oracle concerning Egypt:

See, the LORD rides on a swift cloud
and is coming to Egypt.
The idols of Egypt tremble before him,
and the hearts of the Egyptians melt
within them.

2"I will stir up Egyptian against
Egyptian—
brother will fight against brother,
neighbor against neighbor,
city against city,
kingdom against kingdom.
3The Egyptians will lose heart,

[a] 8 That is, symbols of the goddess Asherah [b] 1 Or *of locusts* [c] 1 That is, the upper Nile region

and I will bring their plans to nothing;
they will consult the idols and the spirits
of the dead,
the mediums and the spiritists.
4 I will hand the Egyptians over
to the power of a cruel master,
and a fierce king will rule over them,"
declares the Lord, the LORD Almighty.

5 The waters of the river will dry up,
and the riverbed will be parched and
dry.
6 The canals will stink;
the streams of Egypt will dwindle and
dry up.
The reeds and rushes will wither,
7 also the plants along the Nile,
at the mouth of the river.
Every sown field along the Nile
will become parched, will blow away
and be no more.
8 The fishermen will groan and lament,
all who cast hooks into the Nile;
those who throw nets on the water
will pine away.
9 Those who work with combed flax will
despair,
the weavers of fine linen will lose hope.
10 The workers in cloth will be dejected,
and all the wage earners will be sick at
heart.

11 The officials of Zoan are nothing but
fools;
the wise counselors of Pharaoh give
senseless advice.
How can you say to Pharaoh,
"I am one of the wise men,
a disciple of the ancient kings"?

12 Where are your wise men now?
Let them show you and make known
what the LORD Almighty
has planned against Egypt.
13 The officials of Zoan have become fools,
the leaders of Memphis[a] are deceived;
the cornerstones of her peoples
have led Egypt astray.
14 The LORD has poured into them
a spirit of dizziness;
they make Egypt stagger in all that she
does,
as a drunkard staggers around in his
vomit.
15 There is nothing Egypt can do—
head or tail, palm branch or reed.

16 In that day the Egyptians will be like
women. They will shudder with fear at the
uplifted hand that the LORD Almighty raises
against them. 17 And the land of Judah will
bring terror to the Egyptians; everyone to
whom Judah is mentioned will be terrified, because of what the LORD Almighty is planning
against them.

18 In that day five cities in Egypt will speak
the language of Canaan and swear allegiance
to the LORD Almighty. One of them will be
called the City of Destruction.[b]

19 In that day there will be an altar to the
LORD in the heart of Egypt, and a monument to
the LORD at its border. 20 It will be a sign and
witness to the LORD Almighty in the land of
Egypt. When they cry out to the LORD because
of their oppressors, he will send them a savior
and defender, and he will rescue them. 21 So the
LORD will make himself known to the Egyptians, and in that day they will acknowledge
the LORD. They will worship with sacrifices
and grain offerings; they will make vows to the
LORD and keep them. 22 The LORD will strike
Egypt with a plague; he will strike them and
heal them. They will turn to the LORD, and he
will respond to their pleas and heal them.

23 In that day there will be a highway from
Egypt to Assyria. The Assyrians will go to
Egypt and the Egyptians to Assyria. The Egyptians and Assyrians will worship together. 24 In
that day Israel will be the third, along with
Egypt and Assyria, a blessing on the earth.
25 The LORD Almighty will bless them, saying,
"Blessed be Egypt my people, Assyria my
handiwork, and Israel my inheritance."

A Prophecy Against Egypt and Cush

20 In the year that the supreme commander, sent by Sargon king of Assyria,
came to Ashdod and attacked and captured
it— 2 at that time the LORD spoke through Isaiah son of Amoz. He said to him, "Take off
the sackcloth from your body and the sandals
from your feet." And he did so, going around
stripped and barefoot.

3 Then the LORD said, "Just as my servant
Isaiah has gone stripped and barefoot for three
years, as a sign and portent against Egypt and
Cush,[c] 4 so the king of Assyria will lead away
stripped and barefoot the Egyptian captives
and Cushite exiles, young and old, with buttocks bared—to Egypt's shame. 5 Those who
trusted in Cush and boasted in Egypt will be
afraid and put to shame. 6 In that day the people
who live on this coast will say, 'See what has
happened to those we relied on, those we fled
to for help and deliverance from the king of
Assyria! How then can we escape?' "

A Prophecy Against Babylon

21 An oracle concerning the Desert by the
Sea:

Like whirlwinds sweeping through the
southland,
an invader comes from the desert,
from a land of terror.

2 A dire vision has been shown to me:
The traitor betrays, the looter takes loot.
Elam, attack! Media, lay siege!

[a] *13* Hebrew *Noph* [b] *18* Most manuscripts of the Masoretic Text; some manuscripts of the Masoretic Text, Dead Sea Scrolls and Vulgate *City of the Sun* (that is, Heliopolis) [c] *3* That is, the upper Nile region; also in verse 5

I will bring to an end all the groaning
she caused.

3At this my body is racked with pain,
pangs seize me, like those of a woman
in labor;
I am staggered by what I hear,
I am bewildered by what I see.
4My heart falters,
fear makes me tremble;
the twilight I longed for
has become a horror to me.

5They set the tables,
they spread the rugs,
they eat, they drink!
Get up, you officers,
oil the shields!

6This is what the Lord says to me:

"Go, post a lookout
and have him report what he sees.
7When he sees chariots
with teams of horses,
riders on donkeys
or riders on camels,
let him be alert,
fully alert."

8And the lookout[a] shouted,

"Day after day, my lord, I stand on the
watchtower;
every night I stay at my post.
9Look, here comes a man in a chariot
with a team of horses.
And he gives back the answer:
'Babylon has fallen, has fallen!
All the images of its gods
lie shattered on the ground!' "

10O my people, crushed on the threshing
floor,
I tell you what I have heard
from the LORD Almighty,
from the God of Israel.

A Prophecy Against Edom

11An oracle concerning Dumah[b]:

Someone calls to me from Seir,
"Watchman, what is left of the night?
Watchman, what is left of the night?"
12The watchman replies,
"Morning is coming, but also the night.
If you would ask, then ask;
and come back yet again."

A Prophecy Against Arabia

13An oracle concerning Arabia:

You caravans of Dedanites,
who camp in the thickets of Arabia,
14 bring water for the thirsty;
you who live in Tema,
bring food for the fugitives.
15They flee from the sword,
from the drawn sword,
from the bent bow
and from the heat of battle.

16This is what the Lord says to me: "Within
one year, as a servant bound by contract would
count it, all the pomp of Kedar will come to an
end. 17The survivors of the bowmen, the warriors of Kedar, will be few." The LORD, the
God of Israel, has spoken.

A Prophecy About Jerusalem

22 An oracle concerning the Valley of Vision:

What troubles you now,
that you have all gone up on the roofs,
2O town full of commotion,
O city of tumult and revelry?
Your slain were not killed by the sword,
nor did they die in battle.
3All your leaders have fled together;
they have been captured without using
the bow.
All you who were caught were taken
prisoner together,
having fled while the enemy was still
far away.
4Therefore I said, "Turn away from me;
let me weep bitterly.
Do not try to console me
over the destruction of my people."

5The Lord, the LORD Almighty, has a day
of tumult and trampling and terror
in the Valley of Vision,
a day of battering down walls
and of crying out to the mountains.
6Elam takes up the quiver,
with her charioteers and horses;
Kir uncovers the shield.
7Your choicest valleys are full of chariots,
and horsemen are posted at the city
gates;
8 the defenses of Judah are stripped
away.

And you looked in that day
to the weapons in the Palace of the
Forest;
9you saw that the City of David
had many breaches in its defenses;
you stored up water
in the Lower Pool.
10You counted the buildings in Jerusalem
and tore down houses to strengthen the
wall.
11You built a reservoir between the two
walls
for the water of the Old Pool,
but you did not look to the One who
made it,
or have regard for the One who planned
it long ago.

12The Lord, the LORD Almighty,
called you on that day
to weep and to wail,

[a]*8* Dead Sea Scrolls and Syriac; Masoretic Text *A lion*
[b]*11* *Dumah* means *silence* or *stillness,* a wordplay on *Edom.*

to tear out your hair and put on
sackcloth.
13 But see, there is joy and revelry,
slaughtering of cattle and killing of
sheep,
eating of meat and drinking of wine!
"Let us eat and drink," you say,
"for tomorrow we die!"

14 The LORD Almighty has revealed this in
my hearing: "Till your dying day this sin will
not be atoned for," says the Lord, the LORD
Almighty.

15 This is what the Lord, the LORD Almighty,
says:

"Go, say to this steward,
to Shebna, who is in charge of the
palace:
16 What are you doing here and who gave
you permission
to cut out a grave for yourself here,
hewing your grave on the height
and chiseling your resting place in the
rock?

17 "Beware, the LORD is about to take firm
hold of you
and hurl you away, O you mighty man.
18 He will roll you up tightly like a ball
and throw you into a large country.
There you will die
and there your splendid chariots will
remain—
you disgrace to your master's house!
19 I will depose you from your office,
and you will be ousted from your
position.

20 "In that day I will summon my servant,
Eliakim son of Hilkiah. 21 I will clothe him
with your robe and fasten your sash around
him and hand your authority over to him. He
will be a father to those who live in Jerusalem
and to the house of Judah. 22 I will place on his
shoulder the key to the house of David; what
he opens no one can shut, and what he shuts no
one can open. 23 I will drive him like a peg into
a firm place; he will be a seat[a] of honor for the
house of his father. 24 All the glory of his family will hang on him: its offspring and off-
shoots—all its lesser vessels, from the bowls
to all the jars.

25 "In that day," declares the LORD Almighty, "the peg driven into the firm place will
give way; it will be sheared off and will fall,
and the load hanging on it will be cut down."
The LORD has spoken.

A Prophecy About Tyre

23 An oracle concerning Tyre:

Wail, O ships of Tarshish!
For Tyre is destroyed
and left without house or harbor.
From the land of Cyprus[b]
word has come to them.

2 Be silent, you people of the island
and you merchants of Sidon,
whom the seafarers have enriched.
3 On the great waters
came the grain of the Shihor;
the harvest of the Nile[c] was the revenue
of Tyre,
and she became the marketplace of the
nations.

4 Be ashamed, O Sidon, and you, O fortress
of the sea,
for the sea has spoken:
"I have neither been in labor nor given
birth;
I have neither reared sons nor brought
up daughters."
5 When word comes to Egypt,
they will be in anguish at the report
from Tyre.

6 Cross over to Tarshish;
wail, you people of the island.
7 Is this your city of revelry,
the old, old city,
whose feet have taken her
to settle in far-off lands?
8 Who planned this against Tyre,
the bestower of crowns,
whose merchants are princes,
whose traders are renowned in the
earth?
9 The LORD Almighty planned it,
to bring low the pride of all glory
and to humble all who are renowned on
the earth.

10 Till[d] your land as along the Nile,
O Daughter of Tarshish,
for you no longer have a harbor.
11 The LORD has stretched out his hand over
the sea
and made its kingdoms tremble.
He has given an order concerning
Phoenicia[e]
that her fortresses be destroyed.
12 He said, "No more of your reveling,
O Virgin Daughter of Sidon, now
crushed!

"Up, cross over to Cyprus[b];
even there you will find no rest."
13 Look at the land of the Babylonians,[f]
this people that is now of no account!
The Assyrians have made it
a place for desert creatures;
they raised up their siege towers,
they stripped its fortresses bare
and turned it into a ruin.

[a] *23* Or *throne* [b] *1,12* Hebrew *Kittim* [c] *2,3* Masoretic Text; one Dead Sea Scroll *Sidon, / who cross over the sea; / your envoys* [3] *are on the great waters. / The grain of the Shihor, / the harvest of the Nile,*
[d] *10* Dead Sea Scrolls and some Septuagint manuscripts; Masoretic Text *Go through* [e] *11* Hebrew *Canaan*
[f] *13* Or *Chaldeans*

14Wail, you ships of Tarshish;
your fortress is destroyed!

15At that time Tyre will be forgotten for seventy years, the span of a king's life. But at the
end of these seventy years, it will happen to
Tyre as in the song of the prostitute:

16"Take up a harp, walk through the city,
O prostitute forgotten;
play the harp well, sing many a song,
so that you will be remembered."

17At the end of seventy years, the LORD will
deal with Tyre. She will return to her hire as a
prostitute and will ply her trade with all the
kingdoms on the face of the earth. 18Yet her
profit and her earnings will be set apart for the
LORD; they will not be stored up or hoarded.
Her profits will go to those who live before the
LORD, for abundant food and fine clothes.

The LORD's Devastation of the Earth

24 See, the LORD is going to lay waste
the earth
and devastate it;
he will ruin its face
and scatter its inhabitants—
2it will be the same
for priest as for people,
for master as for servant,
for mistress as for maid,
for seller as for buyer,
for borrower as for lender,
for debtor as for creditor.
3The earth will be completely laid waste
and totally plundered.
The LORD has spoken this word.

4The earth dries up and withers,
the world languishes and withers,
the exalted of the earth languish.
5The earth is defiled by its people;
they have disobeyed the laws,
violated the statutes
and broken the everlasting covenant.
6Therefore a curse consumes the earth;
its people must bear their guilt.
Therefore earth's inhabitants are burned
up,
and very few are left.
7The new wine dries up and the vine
withers;
all the merrymakers groan.
8The gaiety of the tambourines is stilled,
the noise of the revelers has stopped,
the joyful harp is silent.
9No longer do they drink wine with a song;
the beer is bitter to its drinkers.
10The ruined city lies desolate;
the entrance to every house is barred.
11In the streets they cry out for wine;
all joy turns to gloom,
all gaiety is banished from the earth.
12The city is left in ruins,
its gate is battered to pieces.
13So will it be on the earth
and among the nations,
as when an olive tree is beaten,
or as when gleanings are left after the
grape harvest.

14They raise their voices, they shout for joy;
from the west they acclaim the LORD's
majesty.
15Therefore in the east give glory to the
LORD;
exalt the name of the LORD, the God of
Israel,
in the islands of the sea.
16From the ends of the earth we hear
singing:
"Glory to the Righteous One."

But I said, "I waste away, I waste away!
Woe to me!
The treacherous betray!
With treachery the treacherous betray!"
17Terror and pit and snare await you,
O people of the earth.
18Whoever flees at the sound of terror
will fall into a pit;
whoever climbs out of the pit
will be caught in a snare.

The floodgates of the heavens are opened,
the foundations of the earth shake.
19The earth is broken up,
the earth is split asunder,
the earth is thoroughly shaken.
20The earth reels like a drunkard,
it sways like a hut in the wind;
so heavy upon it is the guilt of its
rebellion
that it falls—never to rise again.

21In that day the LORD will punish
the powers in the heavens above
and the kings on the earth below.
22They will be herded together
like prisoners bound in a dungeon;
they will be shut up in prison
and be punished[a] after many days.
23The moon will be abashed, the sun
ashamed;
for the LORD Almighty will reign
on Mount Zion and in Jerusalem,
and before its elders, gloriously.

Praise to the LORD

25 O LORD, you are my God;
I will exalt you and praise your name,
for in perfect faithfulness
you have done marvelous things,
things planned long ago.
2You have made the city a heap of rubble,
the fortified town a ruin,
the foreigners' stronghold a city no more;
it will never be rebuilt.
3Therefore strong peoples will honor you;
cities of ruthless nations will revere
you.
4You have been a refuge for the poor,
a refuge for the needy in his distress,

[a]22 Or *released*

a shelter from the storm
and a shade from the heat.
For the breath of the ruthless
is like a storm driving against a wall
5 and like the heat of the desert.
You silence the uproar of foreigners;
as heat is reduced by the shadow of a cloud,
so the song of the ruthless is stilled.

6On this mountain the LORD Almighty will prepare
a feast of rich food for all peoples,
a banquet of aged wine—
the best of meats and the finest of wines.
7On this mountain he will destroy
the shroud that enfolds all peoples,
the sheet that covers all nations;
8 he will swallow up death forever.
The Sovereign LORD will wipe away the tears
from all faces;
he will remove the disgrace of his people
from all the earth.
The LORD has spoken.

9In that day they will say,

"Surely this is our God;
we trusted in him, and he saved us.
This is the LORD, we trusted in him;
let us rejoice and be glad in his salvation."

10The hand of the LORD will rest on this mountain;
but Moab will be trampled under him
as straw is trampled down in the manure.
11They will spread out their hands in it,
as a swimmer spreads out his hands to swim.
God will bring down their pride
despite the cleverness[a] of their hands.
12He will bring down your high fortified walls
and lay them low;
he will bring them down to the ground,
to the very dust.

A Song of Praise

26 In that day this song will be sung in the land of Judah:

We have a strong city;
God makes salvation
its walls and ramparts.
2Open the gates
that the righteous nation may enter,
the nation that keeps faith.
3You will keep in perfect peace
him whose mind is steadfast,
because he trusts in you.
4Trust in the LORD forever,
for the LORD, the LORD, is the Rock eternal.
5He humbles those who dwell on high,
he lays the lofty city low;
he levels it to the ground
and casts it down to the dust.
6Feet trample it down—
the feet of the oppressed,
the footsteps of the poor.

7The path of the righteous is level;
O upright One, you make the way of the righteous smooth.
8Yes, LORD, walking in the way of your laws,[b]
we wait for you;
your name and renown
are the desire of our hearts.
9My soul yearns for you in the night;
in the morning my spirit longs for you.
When your judgments come upon the earth,
the people of the world learn righteousness.
10Though grace is shown to the wicked,
they do not learn righteousness;
even in a land of uprightness they go on doing evil
and regard not the majesty of the LORD.
11O LORD, your hand is lifted high,
but they do not see it.
Let them see your zeal for your people
and be put to shame;
let the fire reserved for your enemies
consume them.

12LORD, you establish peace for us;
all that we have accomplished you have done for us.
13O LORD, our God, other lords besides you
have ruled over us,
but your name alone do we honor.
14They are now dead, they live no more;
those departed spirits do not rise.
You punished them and brought them to ruin;
you wiped out all memory of them.
15You have enlarged the nation, O LORD;
you have enlarged the nation.
You have gained glory for yourself;
you have extended all the borders of the land.

16LORD, they came to you in their distress;
when you disciplined them,
they could barely whisper a prayer.[c]
17As a woman with child and about to give birth
writhes and cries out in her pain,
so were we in your presence, O LORD.
18We were with child, we writhed in pain,
but we gave birth to wind.
We have not brought salvation to the earth;
we have not given birth to people of the world.

19But your dead will live;

[a] *11* The meaning of the Hebrew for this word is uncertain. [b] *8* Or *judgments* [c] *16* The meaning of the Hebrew for this clause is uncertain.

their bodies will rise.
You who dwell in the dust,
wake up and shout for joy.
Your dew is like the dew of the morning;
the earth will give birth to her dead.

20 Go, my people, enter your rooms
and shut the doors behind you;
hide yourselves for a little while
until his wrath has passed by.
21 See, the LORD is coming out of his dwelling
to punish the people of the earth for their sins.
The earth will disclose the blood shed upon her;
she will conceal her slain no longer.

Deliverance of Israel

27 In that day,

the LORD will punish with his sword,
his fierce, great and powerful sword,
Leviathan the gliding serpent,
Leviathan the coiling serpent;
he will slay the monster of the sea.

2 In that day—

"Sing about a fruitful vineyard:
3 I, the LORD, watch over it;
I water it continually.
I guard it day and night
so that no one may harm it.
4 I am not angry.
If only there were briers and thorns confronting me!
I would march against them in battle;
I would set them all on fire.
5 Or else let them come to me for refuge;
let them make peace with me,
yes, let them make peace with me."

6 In days to come Jacob will take root,
Israel will bud and blossom
and fill all the world with fruit.

7 Has ⌊the LORD⌋ struck her
as he struck down those who struck her?
Has she been killed
as those were killed who killed her?
8 By warfare[a] and exile you contend with her—
with his fierce blast he drives her out,
as on a day the east wind blows.
9 By this, then, will Jacob's guilt be atoned for,
and this will be the full fruitage of the removal of his sin:
When he makes all the altar stones
to be like chalk stones crushed to pieces,
no Asherah poles[b] or incense altars
will be left standing.
10 The fortified city stands desolate,
an abandoned settlement, forsaken like the desert;
there the calves graze,
there they lie down;
they strip its branches bare.
11 When its twigs are dry, they are broken off
and women come and make fires with them.
For this is a people without understanding;
so their Maker has no compassion on them,
and their Creator shows them no favor.

12 In that day the LORD will thresh from the
flowing Euphrates[c] to the Wadi of Egypt, and
you, O Israelites, will be gathered up one by
one. 13 And in that day a great trumpet will
sound. Those who were perishing in Assyria
and those who were exiled in Egypt will come
and worship the LORD on the holy mountain in
Jerusalem.

Woe to Ephraim

28 Woe to that wreath, the pride of Ephraim's drunkards,
to the fading flower, his glorious beauty,
set on the head of a fertile valley—
to that city, the pride of those laid low by wine!
2 See, the Lord has one who is powerful and strong.
Like a hailstorm and a destructive wind,
like a driving rain and a flooding downpour,
he will throw it forcefully to the ground.
3 That wreath, the pride of Ephraim's drunkards,
will be trampled underfoot.
4 That fading flower, his glorious beauty,
set on the head of a fertile valley,
will be like a fig ripe before harvest—
as soon as someone sees it and takes it in his hand,
he swallows it.

5 In that day the LORD Almighty
will be a glorious crown,
a beautiful wreath
for the remnant of his people.
6 He will be a spirit of justice
to him who sits in judgment,
a source of strength
to those who turn back the battle at the gate.

7 And these also stagger from wine
and reel from beer:
Priests and prophets stagger from beer
and are befuddled with wine;
they reel from beer,
they stagger when seeing visions,
they stumble when rendering decisions.

[a] 8 See Septuagint; the meaning of the Hebrew for this word is uncertain. [b] 9 That is, symbols of the goddess Asherah [c] 12 Hebrew *River*

8All the tables are covered with vomit
and there is not a spot without filth.

9"Who is it he is trying to teach?
To whom is he explaining his message?
To children weaned from their milk,
to those just taken from the breast?
10For it is:
Do and do, do and do,
rule on rule, rule on rule[a];
a little here, a little there."

11Very well then, with foreign lips and strange tongues
God will speak to this people,
12to whom he said,
"This is the resting place, let the weary rest";
and, "This is the place of repose"—
but they would not listen.
13So then, the word of the LORD to them will become:
Do and do, do and do,
rule on rule, rule on rule;
a little here, a little there—
so that they will go and fall backward,
be injured and snared and captured.

14Therefore hear the word of the LORD, you scoffers
who rule this people in Jerusalem.
15You boast, "We have entered into a covenant with death,
with the grave[b] we have made an agreement.
When an overwhelming scourge sweeps by,
it cannot touch us,
for we have made a lie our refuge
and falsehood[c] our hiding place."

16So this is what the Sovereign LORD says:

"See, I lay a stone in Zion,
a tested stone,
a precious cornerstone for a sure foundation;
the one who trusts will never be dismayed.
17I will make justice the measuring line
and righteousness the plumb line;
hail will sweep away your refuge, the lie,
and water will overflow your hiding place.
18Your covenant with death will be annulled;
your agreement with the grave will not stand.
When the overwhelming scourge sweeps by,
you will be beaten down by it.
19As often as it comes it will carry you away;
morning after morning, by day and by night,
it will sweep through."

The understanding of this message
will bring sheer terror.
20The bed is too short to stretch out on,
the blanket too narrow to wrap around you.
21The LORD will rise up as he did at Mount Perazim,
he will rouse himself as in the Valley of Gibeon—
to do his work, his strange work,
and perform his task, his alien task.
22Now stop your mocking,
or your chains will become heavier;
the Lord, the LORD Almighty, has told me
of the destruction decreed against the whole land.

23Listen and hear my voice;
pay attention and hear what I say.
24When a farmer plows for planting, does he plow continually?
Does he keep on breaking up and harrowing the soil?
25When he has leveled the surface,
does he not sow caraway and scatter cummin?
Does he not plant wheat in its place,[d]
barley in its plot,[d]
and spelt in its field?
26His God instructs him
and teaches him the right way.

27Caraway is not threshed with a sledge,
nor is a cartwheel rolled over cummin;
caraway is beaten out with a rod,
and cummin with a stick.
28Grain must be ground to make bread;
so one does not go on threshing it forever.
Though he drives the wheels of his threshing cart over it,
his horses do not grind it.
29All this also comes from the LORD Almighty,
wonderful in counsel and magnificent in wisdom.

Woe to David's City

29 Woe to you, Ariel, Ariel,
the city where David settled!
Add year to year
and let your cycle of festivals go on.
2Yet I will besiege Ariel;
she will mourn and lament,
she will be to me like an altar hearth.[e]
3I will encamp against you all around;
I will encircle you with towers
and set up my siege works against you.
4Brought low, you will speak from the ground;

[a] *10* Hebrew / *sav lasav sav lasav / kav lakav kav lakav* (possibly meaningless sounds; perhaps a mimicking of the prophet's words); also in verse 13 [b] *15* Hebrew *Sheol*; also in verse 18 [c] *15* Or *false gods*
[d] *25* The meaning of the Hebrew for this word is uncertain. [e] *2* The Hebrew for *altar hearth* sounds like the Hebrew for *Ariel*.

your speech will mumble out of the dust.
Your voice will come ghostlike from the earth;
out of the dust your speech will whisper.

5 But your many enemies will become like fine dust,
the ruthless hordes like blown chaff.
Suddenly, in an instant,
6 the LORD Almighty will come
with thunder and earthquake and great noise,
with windstorm and tempest and flames of a devouring fire.
7 Then the hordes of all the nations that fight against Ariel,
that attack her and her fortress and besiege her,
will be as it is with a dream,
with a vision in the night—
8 as when a hungry man dreams that he is eating,
but he awakens, and his hunger remains;
as when a thirsty man dreams that he is drinking,
but he awakens faint, with his thirst unquenched.
So will it be with the hordes of all the nations
that fight against Mount Zion.

9 Be stunned and amazed,
blind yourselves and be sightless;
be drunk, but not from wine,
stagger, but not from beer.
10 The LORD has brought over you a deep sleep:
He has sealed your eyes (the prophets);
he has covered your heads (the seers).

11 For you this whole vision is nothing but
words sealed in a scroll. And if you give the
scroll to someone who can read, and say to
him, "Read this, please," he will answer, "I
can't; it is sealed." 12 Or if you give the scroll
to someone who cannot read, and say, "Read
this, please," he will answer, "I don't know
how to read."

13 The Lord says:

"These people come near to me with their mouth
and honor me with their lips,
but their hearts are far from me.
Their worship of me
is made up only of rules taught by men.[a]
14 Therefore once more I will astound these people
with wonder upon wonder;
the wisdom of the wise will perish,
the intelligence of the intelligent will vanish."
15 Woe to those who go to great depths
to hide their plans from the LORD,
who do their work in darkness and think,
"Who sees us? Who will know?"
16 You turn things upside down,
as if the potter were thought to be like the clay!
Shall what is formed say to him who formed it,
"He did not make me"?
Can the pot say of the potter,
"He knows nothing"?

17 In a very short time, will not Lebanon be turned into a fertile field
and the fertile field seem like a forest?
18 In that day the deaf will hear the words of the scroll,
and out of gloom and darkness
the eyes of the blind will see.
19 Once more the humble will rejoice in the LORD;
the needy will rejoice in the Holy One of Israel.
20 The ruthless will vanish,
the mockers will disappear,
and all who have an eye for evil will be cut down—
21 those who with a word make a man out to be guilty,
who ensnare the defender in court
and with false testimony deprive the innocent of justice.

22 Therefore this is what the LORD, who redeemed Abraham, says to the house of Jacob:

"No longer will Jacob be ashamed;
no longer will their faces grow pale.
23 When they see among them their children,
the work of my hands,
they will keep my name holy;
they will acknowledge the holiness of the Holy One of Jacob,
and will stand in awe of the God of Israel.
24 Those who are wayward in spirit will gain understanding;
those who complain will accept instruction."

Woe to the Obstinate Nation

30 "Woe to the obstinate children,"
declares the LORD,
"to those who carry out plans that are not mine,
forming an alliance, but not by my Spirit,
heaping sin upon sin;
2 who go down to Egypt
without consulting me;
who look for help to Pharaoh's protection,
to Egypt's shade for refuge.
3 But Pharaoh's protection will be to your shame,
Egypt's shade will bring you disgrace.
4 Though they have officials in Zoan

[a] 13 Hebrew; Septuagint *They worship me in vain; / their teachings are but rules taught by men*

and their envoys have arrived in Hanes,
5 everyone will be put to shame
because of a people useless to them,
who bring neither help nor advantage,
but only shame and disgrace."

6 An oracle concerning the animals of the Negev:

Through a land of hardship and distress,
of lions and lionesses,
of adders and darting snakes,
the envoys carry their riches on donkeys' backs,
their treasures on the humps of camels,
to that unprofitable nation,
7 to Egypt, whose help is utterly useless.
Therefore I call her
Rahab the Do-Nothing.

8 Go now, write it on a tablet for them,
inscribe it on a scroll,
that for the days to come
it may be an everlasting witness.
9 These are rebellious people, deceitful children,
children unwilling to listen to the LORD's instruction.
10 They say to the seers,
"See no more visions!"
and to the prophets,
"Give us no more visions of what is right!
Tell us pleasant things,
prophesy illusions.
11 Leave this way,
get off this path,
and stop confronting us
with the Holy One of Israel!"

12 Therefore, this is what the Holy One of Israel says:

"Because you have rejected this message,
relied on oppression
and depended on deceit,
13 this sin will become for you
like a high wall, cracked and bulging,
that collapses suddenly, in an instant.
14 It will break in pieces like pottery,
shattered so mercilessly
that among its pieces not a fragment will be found
for taking coals from a hearth
or scooping water out of a cistern."

15 This is what the Sovereign LORD, the Holy One of Israel, says:

"In repentance and rest is your salvation,
in quietness and trust is your strength,
but you would have none of it.
16 You said, 'No, we will flee on horses.'
Therefore you will flee!
You said, 'We will ride off on swift horses.'
Therefore your pursuers will be swift!
17 A thousand will flee
at the threat of one;
at the threat of five
you will all flee away,
till you are left
like a flagstaff on a mountaintop,
like a banner on a hill."

18 Yet the LORD longs to be gracious to you;
he rises to show you compassion.
For the LORD is a God of justice.
Blessed are all who wait for him!

19 O people of Zion, who live in Jerusalem,
you will weep no more. How gracious he will
be when you cry for help! As soon as he hears,
he will answer you. 20 Although the Lord gives
you the bread of adversity and the water of
affliction, your teachers will be hidden no
more; with your own eyes you will see them.
21 Whether you turn to the right or to the left,
your ears will hear a voice behind you, saying,
"This is the way; walk in it." 22 Then you will
defile your idols overlaid with silver and your
images covered with gold; you will throw
them away like a menstrual cloth and say to
them, "Away with you!"

23 He will also send you rain for the seed you
sow in the ground, and the food that comes
from the land will be rich and plentiful. In that
day your cattle will graze in broad meadows.
24 The oxen and donkeys that work the soil will
eat fodder and mash, spread out with fork and
shovel. 25 In the day of great slaughter, when
the towers fall, streams of water will flow
on every high mountain and every lofty hill.
26 The moon will shine like the sun, and the
sunlight will be seven times brighter, like the
light of seven full days, when the LORD binds
up the bruises of his people and heals the
wounds he inflicted.

27 See, the Name of the LORD comes from afar,
with burning anger and dense clouds of smoke;
his lips are full of wrath,
and his tongue is a consuming fire.
28 His breath is like a rushing torrent,
rising up to the neck.
He shakes the nations in the sieve of destruction;
he places in the jaws of the peoples
a bit that leads them astray.
29 And you will sing
as on the night you celebrate a holy festival;
your hearts will rejoice
as when people go up with flutes
to the mountain of the LORD,
to the Rock of Israel.
30 The LORD will cause men to hear his majestic voice
and will make them see his arm coming down
with raging anger and consuming fire,
with cloudburst, thunderstorm and hail.
31 The voice of the LORD will shatter Assyria;
with his scepter he will strike them down.

32Every stroke the LORD lays on them
with his punishing rod
will be to the music of tambourines and
harps,
as he fights them in battle with the
blows of his arm.
33Topheth has long been prepared;
it has been made ready for the king.
Its fire pit has been made deep and wide,
with an abundance of fire and wood;
the breath of the LORD,
like a stream of burning sulfur,
sets it ablaze.

Woe to Those Who Rely on Egypt

31 Woe to those who go down to Egypt
for help,
who rely on horses,
who trust in the multitude of their chariots
and in the great strength of their
horsemen,
but do not look to the Holy One of Israel,
or seek help from the LORD.
2Yet he too is wise and can bring disaster;
he does not take back his words.
He will rise up against the house of the
wicked,
against those who help evildoers.
3But the Egyptians are men and not God;
their horses are flesh and not spirit.
When the LORD stretches out his hand,
he who helps will stumble,
he who is helped will fall;
both will perish together.

4This is what the LORD says to me:

"As a lion growls,
a great lion over his prey—
and though a whole band of shepherds
is called together against him,
he is not frightened by their shouts
or disturbed by their clamor—
so the LORD Almighty will come down
to do battle on Mount Zion and on its
heights.
5Like birds hovering overhead,
the LORD Almighty will shield
Jerusalem;
he will shield it and deliver it,
he will 'pass over' it and will rescue
it."

6Return to him you have so greatly revolted
against, O Israelites. 7For in that day every one
of you will reject the idols of silver and gold
your sinful hands have made.

8"Assyria will fall by a sword that is not of
man;
a sword, not of mortals, will devour
them.
They will flee before the sword
and their young men will be put to
forced labor.
9Their stronghold will fall because of
terror;
at sight of the battle standard their
commanders will panic,"
declares the LORD,
whose fire is in Zion,
whose furnace is in Jerusalem.

The Kingdom of Righteousness

32 See, a king will reign in righteousness
and rulers will rule with justice.
2Each man will be like a shelter from the
wind
and a refuge from the storm,
like streams of water in the desert
and the shadow of a great rock in a
thirsty land.

3Then the eyes of those who see will no
longer be closed,
and the ears of those who hear will
listen.
4The mind of the rash will know and
understand,
and the stammering tongue will be
fluent and clear.
5No longer will the fool be called noble
nor the scoundrel be highly respected.
6For the fool speaks folly,
his mind is busy with evil:
He practices ungodliness
and spreads error concerning the LORD;
the hungry he leaves empty
and from the thirsty he withholds water.
7The scoundrel's methods are wicked,
he makes up evil schemes
to destroy the poor with lies,
even when the plea of the needy is just.
8But the noble man makes noble plans,
and by noble deeds he stands.

The Women of Jerusalem

9You women who are so complacent,
rise up and listen to me;
you daughters who feel secure,
hear what I have to say!
10In little more than a year
you who feel secure will tremble;
the grape harvest will fail,
and the harvest of fruit will not come.
11Tremble, you complacent women;
shudder, you daughters who feel secure!
Strip off your clothes,
put sackcloth around your waists.
12Beat your breasts for the pleasant fields,
for the fruitful vines
13and for the land of my people,
a land overgrown with thorns and
briers—
yes, mourn for all houses of merriment
and for this city of revelry.
14The fortress will be abandoned,
the noisy city deserted;
citadel and watchtower will become a
wasteland forever,
the delight of donkeys, a pasture for
flocks,
15till the Spirit is poured upon us from on
high,
and the desert becomes a fertile field,
and the fertile field seems like a forest.

[16]Justice will dwell in the desert
and righteousness live in the fertile field.
[17]The fruit of righteousness will be peace;
the effect of righteousness will be quietness and confidence forever.
[18]My people will live in peaceful dwelling places,
in secure homes,
in undisturbed places of rest.
[19]Though hail flattens the forest
and the city is leveled completely,
[20]how blessed you will be,
sowing your seed by every stream,
and letting your cattle and donkeys range free.

Distress and Help

33 Woe to you, O destroyer,
you who have not been destroyed!
Woe to you, O traitor,
you who have not been betrayed!
When you stop destroying,
you will be destroyed;
when you stop betraying,
you will be betrayed.

[2]O LORD, be gracious to us;
we long for you.
Be our strength every morning,
our salvation in time of distress.
[3]At the thunder of your voice, the peoples flee;
when you rise up, the nations scatter.
[4]Your plunder, O nations, is harvested as by young locusts;
like a swarm of locusts men pounce on it.

[5]The LORD is exalted, for he dwells on high;
he will fill Zion with justice and righteousness.
[6]He will be the sure foundation for your times,
a rich store of salvation and wisdom and knowledge;
the fear of the LORD is the key to this treasure.[a]

[7]Look, their brave men cry aloud in the streets;
the envoys of peace weep bitterly.
[8]The highways are deserted,
no travelers are on the roads.
The treaty is broken,
its witnesses[b] are despised,
no one is respected.
[9]The land mourns[c] and wastes away,
Lebanon is ashamed and withers;
Sharon is like the Arabah,
and Bashan and Carmel drop their leaves.

[10]"Now will I arise," says the LORD.
"Now will I be exalted;
now will I be lifted up.
[11]You conceive chaff,
you give birth to straw;
your breath is a fire that consumes you.
[12]The peoples will be burned as if to lime;
like cut thornbushes they will be set ablaze."

[13]You who are far away, hear what I have done;
you who are near, acknowledge my power!
[14]The sinners in Zion are terrified;
trembling grips the godless:
"Who of us can dwell with the consuming fire?
Who of us can dwell with everlasting burning?"
[15]He who walks righteously
and speaks what is right,
who rejects gain from extortion
and keeps his hand from accepting bribes,
who stops his ears against plots of murder
and shuts his eyes against contemplating evil—
[16]this is the man who will dwell on the heights,
whose refuge will be the mountain fortress.
His bread will be supplied,
and water will not fail him.

[17]Your eyes will see the king in his beauty
and view a land that stretches afar.
[18]In your thoughts you will ponder the former terror:
"Where is that chief officer?
Where is the one who took the revenue?
Where is the officer in charge of the towers?"
[19]You will see those arrogant people no more,
those people of an obscure speech,
with their strange, incomprehensible tongue.

[20]Look upon Zion, the city of our festivals;
your eyes will see Jerusalem,
a peaceful abode, a tent that will not be moved;
its stakes will never be pulled up,
nor any of its ropes broken.
[21]There the LORD will be our Mighty One.
It will be like a place of broad rivers and streams.
No galley with oars will ride them,
no mighty ship will sail them.
[22]For the LORD is our judge,
the LORD is our lawgiver,
the LORD is our king;
it is he who will save us.

[23]Your rigging hangs loose:
The mast is not held secure,
the sail is not spread.
Then an abundance of spoils will be divided

[a]6 Or *is a treasure from him* [b]8 Dead Sea Scrolls; Masoretic Text / *the cities* [c]9 Or *dries up*

and even the lame will carry off
plunder.
24No one living in Zion will say, "I am ill";
and the sins of those who dwell there
will be forgiven.

Judgment Against the Nations

34 Come near, you nations, and listen;
pay attention, you peoples!
Let the earth hear, and all that is in it,
the world, and all that comes out of it!
2The LORD is angry with all nations;
his wrath is upon all their armies.
He will totally destroy[a] them,
he will give them over to slaughter.
3Their slain will be thrown out,
their dead bodies will send up a stench;
the mountains will be soaked with their
blood.
4All the stars of the heavens will be
dissolved
and the sky rolled up like a scroll;
all the starry host will fall
like withered leaves from the vine,
like shriveled figs from the fig tree.

5My sword has drunk its fill in the
heavens;
see, it descends in judgment on Edom,
the people I have totally destroyed.
6The sword of the LORD is bathed in blood,
it is covered with fat—
the blood of lambs and goats,
fat from the kidneys of rams.
For the LORD has a sacrifice in Bozrah
and a great slaughter in Edom.
7And the wild oxen will fall with them,
the bull calves and the great bulls.
Their land will be drenched with blood,
and the dust will be soaked with fat.

8For the LORD has a day of vengeance,
a year of retribution, to uphold Zion's
cause.
9Edom's streams will be turned into pitch,
her dust into burning sulfur;
her land will become blazing pitch!
10It will not be quenched night and day;
its smoke will rise forever.
From generation to generation it will lie
desolate;
no one will ever pass through it again.
11The desert owl[b] and screech owl[b] will
possess it;
the great owl[b] and the raven will nest
there.
God will stretch out over Edom
the measuring line of chaos
and the plumb line of desolation.
12Her nobles will have nothing there to be
called a kingdom,
all her princes will vanish away.
13Thorns will overrun her citadels,
nettles and brambles her strongholds.
She will become a haunt for jackals,
a home for owls.
14Desert creatures will meet with hyenas,
and wild goats will bleat to each other;
there the night creatures will also repose
and find for themselves places of rest.
15The owl will nest there and lay eggs,
she will hatch them, and care for her
young under the shadow of her
wings;
there also the falcons will gather,
each with its mate.

16Look in the scroll of the LORD and read:

None of these will be missing,
not one will lack her mate.
For it is his mouth that has given the
order,
and his Spirit will gather them together.
17He allots their portions;
his hand distributes them by measure.
They will possess it forever
and dwell there from generation to
generation.

Joy of the Redeemed

35 The desert and the parched land will
be glad;
the wilderness will rejoice and blossom.
Like the crocus, 2it will burst into bloom;
it will rejoice greatly and shout for joy.
The glory of Lebanon will be given to it,
the splendor of Carmel and Sharon;
they will see the glory of the LORD,
the splendor of our God.

3Strengthen the feeble hands,
steady the knees that give way;
4say to those with fearful hearts,
"Be strong, do not fear;
your God will come,
he will come with vengeance;
with divine retribution
he will come to save you."

5Then will the eyes of the blind be opened
and the ears of the deaf unstopped.
6Then will the lame leap like a deer,
and the mute tongue shout for joy.
Water will gush forth in the wilderness
and streams in the desert.
7The burning sand will become a pool,
the thirsty ground bubbling springs.
In the haunts where jackals once lay,
grass and reeds and papyrus will grow.

8And a highway will be there;
it will be called the Way of Holiness.
The unclean will not journey on it;
it will be for those who walk in that
Way;
wicked fools will not go about on it.[c]
9No lion will be there,
nor will any ferocious beast get up on
it;

[a]2 The Hebrew term refers to the irrevocable giving over of things or persons to the LORD, often by totally destroying them; also in verse 5. [b]11 The precise identification of these birds is uncertain. [c]8 Or / *the simple will not stray from it*

they will not be found there.
But only the redeemed will walk there,
10 and the ransomed of the LORD will return.
They will enter Zion with singing;
everlasting joy will crown their heads.
Gladness and joy will overtake them,
and sorrow and sighing will flee away.

Sennacherib Threatens Jerusalem

36 In the fourteenth year of King Hezekiah's reign, Sennacherib king of Assyria attacked all the fortified cities of Judah and captured them. 2Then the king of Assyria sent his field commander with a large army from Lachish to King Hezekiah at Jerusalem. When the commander stopped at the aqueduct of the Upper Pool, on the road to the Washerman's Field, 3Eliakim son of Hilkiah the palace administrator, Shebna the secretary, and Joah son of Asaph the recorder went out to him.

4The field commander said to them, "Tell Hezekiah,

" 'This is what the great king, the king of Assyria, says: On what are you basing this confidence of yours? 5You say you have strategy and military strength—but you speak only empty words. On whom are you depending, that you rebel against me? 6Look now, you are depending on Egypt, that splintered reed of a staff, which pierces a man's hand and wounds him if he leans on it! Such is Pharaoh king of Egypt to all who depend on him. 7And if you say to me, "We are depending on the LORD our God"—isn't he the one whose high places and altars Hezekiah removed, saying to Judah and Jerusalem, "You must worship before this altar"?

8" 'Come now, make a bargain with my master, the king of Assyria: I will give you two thousand horses—if you can put riders on them! 9How then can you repulse one officer of the least of my master's officials, even though you are depending on Egypt for chariots and horsemen? 10Furthermore, have I come to attack and destroy this land without the LORD? The LORD himself told me to march against this country and destroy it.' "

11Then Eliakim, Shebna and Joah said to the field commander, "Please speak to your servants in Aramaic, since we understand it. Don't speak to us in Hebrew in the hearing of the people on the wall."

12But the commander replied, "Was it only to your master and you that my master sent me to say these things, and not to the men sitting on the wall—who, like you, will have to eat their own filth and drink their own urine?"

13Then the commander stood and called out in Hebrew, "Hear the words of the great king, the king of Assyria! 14This is what the king says: Do not let Hezekiah deceive you. He cannot deliver you! 15Do not let Hezekiah persuade you to trust in the LORD when he says, 'The LORD will surely deliver us; this city will not be given into the hand of the king of Assyria.'

16"Do not listen to Hezekiah. This is what the king of Assyria says: Make peace with me and come out to me. Then every one of you will eat from his own vine and fig tree and drink water from his own cistern, 17until I come and take you to a land like your own—a land of grain and new wine, a land of bread and vineyards.

18"Do not let Hezekiah mislead you when he says, 'The LORD will deliver us.' Has the god of any nation ever delivered his land from the hand of the king of Assyria? 19Where are the gods of Hamath and Arpad? Where are the gods of Sepharvaim? Have they rescued Samaria from my hand? 20Who of all the gods of these countries has been able to save his land from me? How then can the LORD deliver Jerusalem from my hand?"

21But the people remained silent and said nothing in reply, because the king had commanded, "Do not answer him."

22Then Eliakim son of Hilkiah the palace administrator, Shebna the secretary, and Joah son of Asaph the recorder went to Hezekiah, with their clothes torn, and told him what the field commander had said.

Jerusalem's Deliverance Foretold

37 When King Hezekiah heard this, he tore his clothes and put on sackcloth and went into the temple of the LORD. 2He sent Eliakim the palace administrator, Shebna the secretary, and the leading priests, all wearing sackcloth, to the prophet Isaiah son of Amoz. 3They told him, "This is what Hezekiah says: This day is a day of distress and rebuke and disgrace, as when children come to the point of birth and there is no strength to deliver them. 4It may be that the LORD your God will hear the words of the field commander, whom his master, the king of Assyria, has sent to ridicule the living God, and that he will rebuke him for the words the LORD your God has heard. Therefore pray for the remnant that still survives."

5When King Hezekiah's officials came to Isaiah, 6Isaiah said to them, "Tell your master, 'This is what the LORD says: Do not be afraid of what you have heard—those words with which the underlings of the king of Assyria have blasphemed me. 7Listen! I am going to put a spirit in him so that when he hears a certain report, he will return to his own country, and there I will have him cut down with the sword.' "

8When the field commander heard that the king of Assyria had left Lachish, he withdrew and found the king fighting against Libnah.

9Now Sennacherib received a report that

Tirhakah, the Cushite[a] king ⌞of Egypt⌟, was
marching out to fight against him. When he
heard it, he sent messengers to Hezekiah with
this word: 10"Say to Hezekiah king of Judah:
Do not let the god you depend on deceive you
when he says, 'Jerusalem will not be handed
over to the king of Assyria.' 11Surely you have
heard what the kings of Assyria have done to
all the countries, destroying them completely.
And will you be delivered? 12Did the gods of
the nations that were destroyed by my forefathers deliver them—the gods of Gozan, Haran,
Rezeph and the people of Eden who were in
Tel Assar? 13Where is the king of Hamath, the
king of Arpad, the king of the city of Sepharvaim, or of Hena or Ivvah?"

Hezekiah's Prayer

14Hezekiah received the letter from the messengers and read it. Then he went up to the
temple of the LORD and spread it out before the
LORD. 15And Hezekiah prayed to the LORD:
16"O LORD Almighty, God of Israel, enthroned between the cherubim, you alone are
God over all the kingdoms of the earth. You
have made heaven and earth. 17Give ear,
O LORD, and hear; open your eyes, O LORD,
and see; listen to all the words Sennacherib has
sent to insult the living God.

18"It is true, O LORD, that the Assyrian
kings have laid waste all these peoples and
their lands. 19They have thrown their gods into
the fire and destroyed them, for they were not
gods but only wood and stone, fashioned by
human hands. 20Now, O LORD our God, deliver us from his hand, so that all kingdoms on
earth may know that you alone, O LORD, are
God.[b]"

Sennacherib's Fall

21Then Isaiah son of Amoz sent a message
to Hezekiah: "This is what the LORD, the God
of Israel, says: Because you have prayed to me
concerning Sennacherib king of Assyria, 22this
is the word the LORD has spoken against him:

"The Virgin Daughter of Zion
despises and mocks you.
The Daughter of Jerusalem
tosses her head as you flee.
23Who is it you have insulted and
blasphemed?
Against whom have you raised your
voice
and lifted your eyes in pride?
Against the Holy One of Israel!
24By your messengers
you have heaped insults on the Lord.
And you have said,
'With my many chariots
I have ascended the heights of the
mountains,
the utmost heights of Lebanon.
I have cut down its tallest cedars,
the choicest of its pines.
I have reached its remotest heights,
the finest of its forests.
25I have dug wells in foreign lands[c]
and drunk the water there.
With the soles of my feet
I have dried up all the streams of
Egypt.'

26"Have you not heard?
Long ago I ordained it.
In days of old I planned it;
now I have brought it to pass,
that you have turned fortified cities
into piles of stone.
27Their people, drained of power,
are dismayed and put to shame.
They are like plants in the field,
like tender green shoots,
like grass sprouting on the roof,
scorched[d] before it grows up.

28"But I know where you stay
and when you come and go
and how you rage against me.
29Because you rage against me
and because your insolence has reached
my ears,
I will put my hook in your nose
and my bit in your mouth,
and I will make you return
by the way you came.

30"This will be the sign for you,
O Hezekiah:

"This year you will eat what grows by
itself,
and the second year what springs from
that.
But in the third year sow and reap,
plant vineyards and eat their fruit.
31Once more a remnant of the house of
Judah
will take root below and bear fruit
above.
32For out of Jerusalem will come a remnant,
and out of Mount Zion a band of
survivors.
The zeal of the LORD Almighty
will accomplish this.

33"Therefore this is what the LORD says concerning the king of Assyria:

"He will not enter this city
or shoot an arrow here.
He will not come before it with shield
or build a siege ramp against it.
34By the way that he came he will return;
he will not enter this city,"
declares the LORD.
35"I will defend this city and save it,

[a]9 That is, from the upper Nile region [b]*20* Dead Sea Scrolls (see also 2 Kings 19:19); Masoretic Text *alone are the LORD* [c]*25* Dead Sea Scrolls (see also 2 Kings 19:24); Masoretic Text does not have *in foreign lands.* [d]*27* Some manuscripts of the Masoretic Text, Dead Sea Scrolls and some Septuagint manuscripts (see also 2 Kings 19:26); most manuscripts of the Masoretic Text *roof / and terraced fields*

for my sake and for the sake of David
my servant!"

36Then the angel of the LORD went out and
put to death a hundred and eighty-five thousand men in the Assyrian camp. When the people got up the next morning—there were all
the dead bodies! 37So Sennacherib king of Assyria broke camp and withdrew. He returned to
Nineveh and stayed there.

38One day, while he was worshiping in the
temple of his god Nisroch, his sons Adrammelech and Sharezer cut him down with the
sword, and they escaped to the land of Ararat.
And Esarhaddon his son succeeded him as
king.

Hezekiah's Illness

38 In those days Hezekiah became ill and
was at the point of death. The prophet
Isaiah son of Amoz went to him and said,
"This is what the LORD says: Put your house in
order, because you are going to die; you will
not recover."

2Hezekiah turned his face to the wall and
prayed to the LORD, 3"Remember, O LORD,
how I have walked before you faithfully and
with wholehearted devotion and have done
what is good in your eyes." And Hezekiah
wept bitterly.

4Then the word of the LORD came to Isaiah:
5"Go and tell Hezekiah, 'This is what the
LORD, the God of your father David, says: I
have heard your prayer and seen your tears; I
will add fifteen years to your life. 6And I will
deliver you and this city from the hand of the
king of Assyria. I will defend this city.

7" 'This is the LORD's sign to you that the
LORD will do what he has promised: 8I will
make the shadow cast by the sun go back the
ten steps it has gone down on the stairway of
Ahaz.' " So the sunlight went back the ten
steps it had gone down.

9A writing of Hezekiah king of Judah after
his illness and recovery:

10I said, "In the prime of my life
must I go through the gates of death[a]
and be robbed of the rest of my years?"
11I said, "I will not again see the LORD,
the LORD, in the land of the living;
no longer will I look on mankind,
or be with those who now dwell in this
world.[b]
12Like a shepherd's tent my house
has been pulled down and taken from
me.
Like a weaver I have rolled up my life,
and he has cut me off from the loom;
day and night you made an end of me.
13I waited patiently till dawn,
but like a lion he broke all my bones;
day and night you made an end of me.
14I cried like a swift or thrush,
I moaned like a mourning dove.
My eyes grew weak as I looked to the
heavens.
I am troubled; O Lord, come to my
aid!"
15But what can I say?
He has spoken to me, and he himself
has done this.
I will walk humbly all my years
because of this anguish of my soul.
16Lord, by such things men live;
and my spirit finds life in them too.
You restored me to health
and let me live.
17Surely it was for my benefit
that I suffered such anguish.
In your love you kept me
from the pit of destruction;
you have put all my sins
behind your back.
18For the grave[a] cannot praise you,
death cannot sing your praise;
those who go down to the pit
cannot hope for your faithfulness.
19The living, the living—they praise you,
as I am doing today;
fathers tell their children
about your faithfulness.

20The LORD will save me,
and we will sing with stringed
instruments
all the days of our lives
in the temple of the LORD.

21Isaiah had said, "Prepare a poultice of figs
and apply it to the boil, and he will recover."
22Hezekiah had asked, "What will be the
sign that I will go up to the temple of the
LORD?"

Envoys From Babylon

39 At that time Merodach-Baladan son of
Baladan king of Babylon sent Hezekiah
letters and a gift, because he had heard of his
illness and recovery. 2Hezekiah received the
envoys gladly and showed them what was in
his storehouses—the silver, the gold, the
spices, the fine oil, his entire armory and everything found among his treasures. There was
nothing in his palace or in all his kingdom that
Hezekiah did not show them.

3Then Isaiah the prophet went to King Hezekiah and asked, "What did those men say, and
where did they come from?"

"From a distant land," Hezekiah replied.
"They came to me from Babylon."

4The prophet asked, "What did they see in
your palace?"

"They saw everything in my palace," Hezekiah said. "There is nothing among my treasures that I did not show them."

5Then Isaiah said to Hezekiah, "Hear the
word of the LORD Almighty: 6The time will
surely come when everything in your palace,
and all that your fathers have stored up until
this day, will be carried off to Babylon. Noth-

[a] *10,18* Hebrew *Sheol* [b] *11* A few Hebrew manuscripts; most Hebrew manuscripts *in the place of cessation*

ing will be left, says the LORD. 7And some of
your descendants, your own flesh and blood
who will be born to you, will be taken away,
and they will become eunuchs in the palace of
the king of Babylon."
8"The word of the LORD you have spoken
is good," Hezekiah replied. For he thought,
"There will be peace and security in my lifetime."

Comfort for God's People

40 Comfort, comfort my people,
says your God.
2Speak tenderly to Jerusalem,
and proclaim to her
that her hard service has been completed,
that her sin has been paid for,
that she has received from the LORD's
hand
double for all her sins.

3A voice of one calling:
"In the desert prepare
the way for the LORD[a];
make straight in the wilderness
a highway for our God.[b]
4Every valley shall be raised up,
every mountain and hill made low;
the rough ground shall become level,
the rugged places a plain.
5And the glory of the LORD will be
revealed,
and all mankind together will see it.
For the mouth of the LORD
has spoken."

6A voice says, "Cry out."
And I said, "What shall I cry?"

"All men are like grass,
and all their glory is like the flowers of
the field.
7The grass withers and the flowers fall,
because the breath of the LORD blows
on them.
Surely the people are grass.
8The grass withers and the flowers fall,
but the word of our God stands
forever."

9You who bring good tidings to Zion,
go up on a high mountain.
You who bring good tidings to
Jerusalem,[c]
lift up your voice with a shout,
lift it up, do not be afraid;
say to the towns of Judah,
"Here is your God!"
10See, the Sovereign LORD comes with
power,
and his arm rules for him.
See, his reward is with him,
and his recompense accompanies him.
11He tends his flock like a shepherd:
He gathers the lambs in his arms
and carries them close to his heart;
he gently leads those that have young.

12Who has measured the waters in the
hollow of his hand,
or with the breadth of his hand marked
off the heavens?
Who has held the dust of the earth in a
basket,
or weighed the mountains on the scales
and the hills in a balance?
13Who has understood the mind[d] of the
LORD,
or instructed him as his counselor?
14Whom did the LORD consult to enlighten
him,
and who taught him the right way?
Who was it that taught him knowledge
or showed him the path of
understanding?

15Surely the nations are like a drop in a
bucket;
they are regarded as dust on the scales;
he weighs the islands as though they
were fine dust.
16Lebanon is not sufficient for altar fires,
nor its animals enough for burnt
offerings.
17Before him all the nations are as nothing;
they are regarded by him as worthless
and less than nothing.

18To whom, then, will you compare God?
What image will you compare him to?
19As for an idol, a craftsman casts it,
and a goldsmith overlays it with gold
and fashions silver chains for it.
20A man too poor to present such an
offering
selects wood that will not rot.
He looks for a skilled craftsman
to set up an idol that will not topple.

21Do you not know?
Have you not heard?
Has it not been told you from the
beginning?
Have you not understood since the earth
was founded?
22He sits enthroned above the circle of the
earth,
and its people are like grasshoppers.
He stretches out the heavens like a
canopy,
and spreads them out like a tent to live
in.
23He brings princes to naught
and reduces the rulers of this world to
nothing.
24No sooner are they planted,
no sooner are they sown,
no sooner do they take root in the
ground,
than he blows on them and they wither,

[a] 3 Or *A voice of one calling in the desert: / "Prepare the way for the LORD* [b] 3 Hebrew; Septuagint *make straight the paths of our God* [c] 9 Or *O Zion, bringer of good tidings, / go up on a high mountain. / O Jerusalem, bringer of good tidings* [d] 13 Or *Spirit*; or *spirit*

and a whirlwind sweeps them away like
chaff.

25"To whom will you compare me?
Or who is my equal?" says the Holy
One.
26Lift your eyes and look to the heavens:
Who created all these?
He who brings out the starry host one by
one,
and calls them each by name.
Because of his great power and mighty
strength,
not one of them is missing.

27Why do you say, O Jacob,
and complain, O Israel,
"My way is hidden from the LORD;
my cause is disregarded by my God"?
28Do you not know?
Have you not heard?
The LORD is the everlasting God,
the Creator of the ends of the earth.
He will not grow tired or weary,
and his understanding no one can
fathom.
29He gives strength to the weary
and increases the power of the weak.
30Even youths grow tired and weary,
and young men stumble and fall;
31but those who hope in the LORD
will renew their strength.
They will soar on wings like eagles;
they will run and not grow weary,
they will walk and not be faint.

The Helper of Israel

41 "Be silent before me, you islands!
Let the nations renew their strength!
Let them come forward and speak;
let us meet together at the place of
judgment.

2"Who has stirred up one from the east,
calling him in righteousness to his
service[a]?
He hands nations over to him
and subdues kings before him.
He turns them to dust with his sword,
to windblown chaff with his bow.
3He pursues them and moves on unscathed,
by a path his feet have not traveled
before.
4Who has done this and carried it through,
calling forth the generations from the
beginning?
I, the LORD—with the first of them
and with the last—I am he."

5The islands have seen it and fear;
the ends of the earth tremble.
They approach and come forward;
6 each helps the other
and says to his brother, "Be strong!"
7The craftsman encourages the goldsmith,
and he who smooths with the hammer
spurs on him who strikes the anvil.
He says of the welding, "It is good."
He nails down the idol so it will not
topple.

8"But you, O Israel, my servant,
Jacob, whom I have chosen,
you descendants of Abraham my friend,
9I took you from the ends of the earth,
from its farthest corners I called you.
I said, 'You are my servant';
I have chosen you and have not rejected
you.
10So do not fear, for I am with you;
do not be dismayed, for I am your God.
I will strengthen you and help you;
I will uphold you with my righteous
right hand.

11"All who rage against you
will surely be ashamed and disgraced;
those who oppose you
will be as nothing and perish.
12Though you search for your enemies,
you will not find them.
Those who wage war against you
will be as nothing at all.
13For I am the LORD, your God,
who takes hold of your right hand
and says to you, Do not fear;
I will help you.
14Do not be afraid, O worm Jacob,
O little Israel,
for I myself will help you," declares the
LORD,
your Redeemer, the Holy One of Israel.
15"See, I will make you into a threshing
sledge,
new and sharp, with many teeth.
You will thresh the mountains and crush
them,
and reduce the hills to chaff.
16You will winnow them, the wind will pick
them up,
and a gale will blow them away.
But you will rejoice in the LORD
and glory in the Holy One of Israel.

17"The poor and needy search for water,
but there is none;
their tongues are parched with thirst.
But I the LORD will answer them;
I, the God of Israel, will not forsake
them.
18I will make rivers flow on barren heights,
and springs within the valleys.
I will turn the desert into pools of water,
and the parched ground into springs.
19I will put in the desert
the cedar and the acacia, the myrtle and
the olive.
I will set pines in the wasteland,
the fir and the cypress together,
20so that people may see and know,
may consider and understand,
that the hand of the LORD has done this,

[a]2 Or / *whom victory meets at every step*

that the Holy One of Israel has created
it.

21"Present your case," says the LORD.
"Set forth your arguments," says
Jacob's King.
22"Bring in ⌊your idols⌋ to tell us
what is going to happen.
Tell us what the former things were,
so that we may consider them
and know their final outcome.
Or declare to us the things to come,
23 tell us what the future holds,
so we may know that you are gods.
Do something, whether good or bad,
so that we will be dismayed and filled
with fear.
24But you are less than nothing
and your works are utterly worthless;
he who chooses you is detestable.

25"I have stirred up one from the north, and
he comes—
one from the rising sun who calls on
my name.
He treads on rulers as if they were mortar,
as if he were a potter treading the clay.
26Who told of this from the beginning, so
we could know,
or beforehand, so we could say, 'He
was right'?
No one told of this,
no one foretold it,
no one heard any words from you.
27I was the first to tell Zion, 'Look, here
they are!'
I gave to Jerusalem a messenger of
good tidings.
28I look but there is no one—
no one among them to give counsel,
no one to give answer when I ask them.
29See, they are all false!
Their deeds amount to nothing;
their images are but wind and
confusion.

The Servant of the LORD

42 "Here is my servant, whom I uphold,
my chosen one in whom I delight;
I will put my Spirit on him
and he will bring justice to the nations.
2He will not shout or cry out,
or raise his voice in the streets.
3A bruised reed he will not break,
and a smoldering wick he will not snuff
out.
In faithfulness he will bring forth justice;
4 he will not falter or be discouraged
till he establishes justice on earth.
In his law the islands will put their
hope."

5This is what God the LORD says—
he who created the heavens and stretched
them out,
who spread out the earth and all that
comes out of it,
who gives breath to its people,
and life to those who walk on it:
6"I, the LORD, have called you in
righteousness;
I will take hold of your hand.
I will keep you and will make you
to be a covenant for the people
and a light for the Gentiles,
7to open eyes that are blind,
to free captives from prison
and to release from the dungeon those
who sit in darkness.

8"I am the LORD; that is my name!
I will not give my glory to another
or my praise to idols.
9See, the former things have taken place,
and new things I declare;
before they spring into being
I announce them to you."

Song of Praise to the LORD

10Sing to the LORD a new song,
his praise from the ends of the earth,
you who go down to the sea, and all that
is in it,
you islands, and all who live in them.
11Let the desert and its towns raise their
voices;
let the settlements where Kedar lives
rejoice.
Let the people of Sela sing for joy;
let them shout from the mountaintops.
12Let them give glory to the LORD
and proclaim his praise in the islands.
13The LORD will march out like a mighty
man,
like a warrior he will stir up his zeal;
with a shout he will raise the battle cry
and will triumph over his enemies.

14"For a long time I have kept silent,
I have been quiet and held myself back.
But now, like a woman in childbirth,
I cry out, I gasp and pant.
15I will lay waste the mountains and hills
and dry up all their vegetation;
I will turn rivers into islands
and dry up the pools.
16I will lead the blind by ways they have
not known,
along unfamiliar paths I will guide
them;
I will turn the darkness into light before
them
and make the rough places smooth.
These are the things I will do;
I will not forsake them.
17But those who trust in idols,
who say to images, 'You are our gods,'
will be turned back in utter shame.

Israel Blind and Deaf

18"Hear, you deaf;
look, you blind, and see!
19Who is blind but my servant,
and deaf like the messenger I send?
Who is blind like the one committed to
me,

blind like the servant of the LORD?
20You have seen many things, but have paid no attention;
your ears are open, but you hear nothing."
21It pleased the LORD
for the sake of his righteousness
to make his law great and glorious.
22But this is a people plundered and looted,
all of them trapped in pits
or hidden away in prisons.
They have become plunder,
with no one to rescue them;
they have been made loot,
with no one to say, "Send them back."

23Which of you will listen to this
or pay close attention in time to come?
24Who handed Jacob over to become loot,
and Israel to the plunderers?
Was it not the LORD,
against whom we have sinned?
For they would not follow his ways;
they did not obey his law.
25So he poured out on them his burning anger,
the violence of war.
It enveloped them in flames, yet they did not understand;
it consumed them, but they did not take it to heart.

Israel's Only Savior

43 But now, this is what the LORD says—
he who created you, O Jacob,
he who formed you, O Israel:
"Fear not, for I have redeemed you;
I have summoned you by name; you are mine.
2When you pass through the waters,
I will be with you;
and when you pass through the rivers,
they will not sweep over you.
When you walk through the fire,
you will not be burned;
the flames will not set you ablaze.
3For I am the LORD, your God,
the Holy One of Israel, your Savior;
I give Egypt for your ransom,
Cush[a] and Seba in your stead.
4Since you are precious and honored in my sight,
and because I love you,
I will give men in exchange for you,
and people in exchange for your life.
5Do not be afraid, for I am with you;
I will bring your children from the east
and gather you from the west.
6I will say to the north, 'Give them up!'
and to the south, 'Do not hold them back.'
Bring my sons from afar
and my daughters from the ends of the earth—
7everyone who is called by my name,
whom I created for my glory,
whom I formed and made."

8Lead out those who have eyes but are blind,
who have ears but are deaf.
9All the nations gather together
and the peoples assemble.
Which of them foretold this
and proclaimed to us the former things?
Let them bring in their witnesses to prove they were right,
so that others may hear and say, "It is true."
10"You are my witnesses," declares the LORD,
"and my servant whom I have chosen,
so that you may know and believe me
and understand that I am he.
Before me no god was formed,
nor will there be one after me.
11I, even I, am the LORD,
and apart from me there is no savior.
12I have revealed and saved and proclaimed—
I, and not some foreign god among you.
You are my witnesses," declares the LORD, "that I am God.
13 Yes, and from ancient days I am he.
No one can deliver out of my hand.
When I act, who can reverse it?"

God's Mercy and Israel's Unfaithfulness

14This is what the LORD says—
your Redeemer, the Holy One of Israel:
"For your sake I will send to Babylon
and bring down as fugitives all the Babylonians,[b]
in the ships in which they took pride.
15I am the LORD, your Holy One,
Israel's Creator, your King."

16This is what the LORD says—
he who made a way through the sea,
a path through the mighty waters,
17who drew out the chariots and horses,
the army and reinforcements together,
and they lay there, never to rise again,
extinguished, snuffed out like a wick:
18"Forget the former things;
do not dwell on the past.
19See, I am doing a new thing!
Now it springs up; do you not perceive it?
I am making a way in the desert
and streams in the wasteland.
20The wild animals honor me,
the jackals and the owls,
because I provide water in the desert
and streams in the wasteland,
to give drink to my people, my chosen,
21 the people I formed for myself
that they may proclaim my praise.

[a]3 That is, the upper Nile region [b]14 Or *Chaldeans*

22"Yet you have not called upon me,
O Jacob,
you have not wearied yourselves for
me, O Israel.
23You have not brought me sheep for burnt
offerings,
nor honored me with your sacrifices.
I have not burdened you with grain
offerings
nor wearied you with demands for
incense.
24You have not bought any fragrant calamus
for me,
or lavished on me the fat of your
sacrifices.
But you have burdened me with your sins
and wearied me with your offenses.

25"I, even I, am he who blots out
your transgressions, for my own sake,
and remembers your sins no more.
26Review the past for me,
let us argue the matter together;
state the case for your innocence.
27Your first father sinned;
your spokesmen rebelled against me.
28So I will disgrace the dignitaries of your
temple,
and I will consign Jacob to destruction[a]
and Israel to scorn.

Israel the Chosen

44 "But now listen, O Jacob, my servant,
Israel, whom I have chosen.
2This is what the LORD says—
he who made you, who formed you in
the womb,
and who will help you:
Do not be afraid, O Jacob, my servant,
Jeshurun, whom I have chosen.
3For I will pour water on the thirsty land,
and streams on the dry ground;
I will pour out my Spirit on your
offspring,
and my blessing on your descendants.
4They will spring up like grass in a
meadow,
like poplar trees by flowing streams.
5One will say, 'I belong to the LORD';
another will call himself by the name of
Jacob;
still another will write on his hand, 'The
LORD's,'
and will take the name Israel.

The LORD, Not Idols

6"This is what the LORD says—
Israel's King and Redeemer, the LORD
Almighty:
I am the first and I am the last;
apart from me there is no God.
7Who then is like me? Let him proclaim it.
Let him declare and lay out before me
what has happened since I established my
ancient people,
and what is yet to come—
yes, let him foretell what will come.
8Do not tremble, do not be afraid.
Did I not proclaim this and foretell it
long ago?
You are my witnesses. Is there any God
besides me?
No, there is no other Rock; I know not
one."

9All who make idols are nothing,
and the things they treasure are
worthless.
Those who would speak up for them are
blind;
they are ignorant, to their own shame.
10Who shapes a god and casts an idol,
which can profit him nothing?
11He and his kind will be put to shame;
craftsmen are nothing but men.
Let them all come together and take their
stand;
they will be brought down to terror and
infamy.

12The blacksmith takes a tool
and works with it in the coals;
he shapes an idol with hammers,
he forges it with the might of his arm.
He gets hungry and loses his strength;
he drinks no water and grows faint.
13The carpenter measures with a line
and makes an outline with a marker;
he roughs it out with chisels
and marks it with compasses.
He shapes it in the form of man,
of man in all his glory,
that it may dwell in a shrine.
14He cut down cedars,
or perhaps took a cypress or oak.
He let it grow among the trees of the
forest,
or planted a pine, and the rain made it
grow.
15It is man's fuel for burning;
some of it he takes and warms himself,
he kindles a fire and bakes bread.
But he also fashions a god and worships
it;
he makes an idol and bows down to it.
16Half of the wood he burns in the fire;
over it he prepares his meal,
he roasts his meat and eats his fill.
He also warms himself and says,
"Ah! I am warm; I see the fire."
17From the rest he makes a god, his idol;
he bows down to it and worships.
He prays to it and says,
"Save me; you are my god."
18They know nothing, they understand
nothing;
their eyes are plastered over so they
cannot see,
and their minds closed so they cannot
understand.

[a]28 The Hebrew term refers to the irrevocable giving over of things or persons to the LORD, often by totally destroying them.

19No one stops to think,
no one has the knowledge or understanding to say,
"Half of it I used for fuel;
I even baked bread over its coals,
I roasted meat and I ate.
Shall I make a detestable thing from what is left?
Shall I bow down to a block of wood?"
20He feeds on ashes, a deluded heart misleads him;
he cannot save himself, or say,
"Is not this thing in my right hand a lie?"

21"Remember these things, O Jacob,
for you are my servant, O Israel.
I have made you, you are my servant;
O Israel, I will not forget you.
22I have swept away your offenses like a cloud,
your sins like the morning mist.
Return to me,
for I have redeemed you."

23Sing for joy, O heavens, for the LORD has done this;
shout aloud, O earth beneath.
Burst into song, you mountains,
you forests and all your trees,
for the LORD has redeemed Jacob,
he displays his glory in Israel.

Jerusalem to Be Inhabited

24"This is what the LORD says—
your Redeemer, who formed you in the womb:

I am the LORD,
who has made all things,
who alone stretched out the heavens,
who spread out the earth by myself,

25who foils the signs of false prophets
and makes fools of diviners,
who overthrows the learning of the wise
and turns it into nonsense,
26who carries out the words of his servants
and fulfills the predictions of his messengers,

who says of Jerusalem, 'It shall be inhabited,'
of the towns of Judah, 'They shall be built,'
and of their ruins, 'I will restore them,'
27who says to the watery deep, 'Be dry,
and I will dry up your streams,'
28who says of Cyrus, 'He is my shepherd
and will accomplish all that I please;
he will say of Jerusalem, "Let it be rebuilt,"
and of the temple, "Let its foundations be laid." '

45 "This is what the LORD says to his anointed,
to Cyrus, whose right hand I take hold of
to subdue nations before him
and to strip kings of their armor,
to open doors before him
so that gates will not be shut:
2I will go before you
and will level the mountains[a];
I will break down gates of bronze
and cut through bars of iron.
3I will give you the treasures of darkness,
riches stored in secret places,
so that you may know that I am the LORD,
the God of Israel, who summons you by name.
4For the sake of Jacob my servant,
of Israel my chosen,
I summon you by name
and bestow on you a title of honor,
though you do not acknowledge me.
5I am the LORD, and there is no other;
apart from me there is no God.
I will strengthen you,
though you have not acknowledged me,
6so that from the rising of the sun
to the place of its setting
men may know there is none besides me.
I am the LORD, and there is no other.
7I form the light and create darkness,
I bring prosperity and create disaster;
I, the LORD, do all these things.

8"You heavens above, rain down righteousness;
let the clouds shower it down.
Let the earth open wide,
let salvation spring up,
let righteousness grow with it;
I, the LORD, have created it.

9"Woe to him who quarrels with his Maker,
to him who is but a potsherd among the potsherds on the ground.
Does the clay say to the potter,
'What are you making?'
Does your work say,
'He has no hands'?
10Woe to him who says to his father,
'What have you begotten?'
or to his mother,
'What have you brought to birth?'

11"This is what the LORD says—
the Holy One of Israel, and its Maker:
Concerning things to come,
do you question me about my children,
or give me orders about the work of my hands?
12It is I who made the earth
and created mankind upon it.
My own hands stretched out the heavens;
I marshaled their starry hosts.
13I will raise up Cyrus[b] in my righteousness:
I will make all his ways straight.

[a]2 Dead Sea Scrolls and Septuagint; the meaning of the word in the Masoretic Text is uncertain.
[b]13 Hebrew *him*

He will rebuild my city
and set my exiles free,
but not for a price or reward,
says the LORD Almighty."

14This is what the LORD says:

"The products of Egypt and the merchandise of Cush,[a]
and those tall Sabeans—
they will come over to you
and will be yours;
they will trudge behind you,
coming over to you in chains.
They will bow down before you
and plead with you, saying,
'Surely God is with you, and there is no other;
there is no other god.' "

15Truly you are a God who hides himself,
O God and Savior of Israel.
16All the makers of idols will be put to shame and disgraced;
they will go off into disgrace together.
17But Israel will be saved by the LORD
with an everlasting salvation;
you will never be put to shame or disgraced,
to ages everlasting.

18For this is what the LORD says—
he who created the heavens,
he is God;
he who fashioned and made the earth,
he founded it;
he did not create it to be empty,
but formed it to be inhabited—
he says:
"I am the LORD,
and there is no other.
19I have not spoken in secret,
from somewhere in a land of darkness;
I have not said to Jacob's descendants,
'Seek me in vain.'
I, the LORD, speak the truth;
I declare what is right.

20"Gather together and come;
assemble, you fugitives from the nations.
Ignorant are those who carry about idols of wood,
who pray to gods that cannot save.
21Declare what is to be, present it—
let them take counsel together.
Who foretold this long ago,
who declared it from the distant past?
Was it not I, the LORD?
And there is no God apart from me,
a righteous God and a Savior;
there is none but me.

22"Turn to me and be saved,
all you ends of the earth;
for I am God, and there is no other.
23By myself I have sworn,
my mouth has uttered in all integrity
a word that will not be revoked:
Before me every knee will bow;
by me every tongue will swear.
24They will say of me, 'In the LORD alone
are righteousness and strength.' "
All who have raged against him
will come to him and be put to shame.
25But in the LORD all the descendants of Israel
will be found righteous and will exult.

Gods of Babylon

46 Bel bows down, Nebo stoops low;
their idols are borne by beasts of burden.[b]
The images that are carried about are burdensome,
a burden for the weary.
2They stoop and bow down together;
unable to rescue the burden,
they themselves go off into captivity.

3"Listen to me, O house of Jacob,
all you who remain of the house of Israel,
you whom I have upheld since you were conceived,
and have carried since your birth.
4Even to your old age and gray hairs
I am he, I am he who will sustain you.
I have made you and I will carry you;
I will sustain you and I will rescue you.

5"To whom will you compare me or count me equal?
To whom will you liken me that we may be compared?
6Some pour out gold from their bags
and weigh out silver on the scales;
they hire a goldsmith to make it into a god,
and they bow down and worship it.
7They lift it to their shoulders and carry it;
they set it up in its place, and there it stands.
From that spot it cannot move.
Though one cries out to it, it does not answer;
it cannot save him from his troubles.

8"Remember this, fix it in mind,
take it to heart, you rebels.
9Remember the former things, those of long ago;
I am God, and there is no other;
I am God, and there is none like me.
10I make known the end from the beginning,
from ancient times, what is still to come.
I say: My purpose will stand,
and I will do all that I please.
11From the east I summon a bird of prey;
from a far-off land, a man to fulfill my purpose.
What I have said, that will I bring about;
what I have planned, that will I do.
12Listen to me, you stubborn-hearted,

[a] *14* That is, the upper Nile region [b] *1* Or *are but beasts and cattle*

you who are far from righteousness.
13I am bringing my righteousness near,
it is not far away;
and my salvation will not be delayed.
I will grant salvation to Zion,
my splendor to Israel.

The Fall of Babylon

47 "Go down, sit in the dust,
Virgin Daughter of Babylon;
sit on the ground without a throne,
Daughter of the Babylonians.[a]
No more will you be called
tender or delicate.
2Take millstones and grind flour;
take off your veil.
Lift up your skirts, bare your legs,
and wade through the streams.
3Your nakedness will be exposed
and your shame uncovered.
I will take vengeance;
I will spare no one."

4Our Redeemer—the LORD Almighty is his
name—
is the Holy One of Israel.

5"Sit in silence, go into darkness,
Daughter of the Babylonians;
no more will you be called
queen of kingdoms.
6I was angry with my people
and desecrated my inheritance;
I gave them into your hand,
and you showed them no mercy.
Even on the aged
you laid a very heavy yoke.
7You said, 'I will continue forever—
the eternal queen!'
But you did not consider these things
or reflect on what might happen.

8"Now then, listen, you wanton creature,
lounging in your security
and saying to yourself,
'I am, and there is none besides me.
I will never be a widow
or suffer the loss of children.'
9Both of these will overtake you
in a moment, on a single day:
loss of children and widowhood.
They will come upon you in full measure,
in spite of your many sorceries
and all your potent spells.
10You have trusted in your wickedness
and have said, 'No one sees me.'
Your wisdom and knowledge mislead you
when you say to yourself,
'I am, and there is none besides me.'
11Disaster will come upon you,
and you will not know how to conjure
it away.
A calamity will fall upon you
that you cannot ward off with a ransom;
a catastrophe you cannot foresee
will suddenly come upon you.

12"Keep on, then, with your magic spells
and with your many sorceries,
which you have labored at since
childhood.
Perhaps you will succeed,
perhaps you will cause terror.
13All the counsel you have received has
only worn you out!
Let your astrologers come forward,
those stargazers who make predictions
month by month,
let them save you from what is coming
upon you.
14Surely they are like stubble;
the fire will burn them up.
They cannot even save themselves
from the power of the flame.
Here are no coals to warm anyone;
here is no fire to sit by.
15That is all they can do for you—
these you have labored with
and trafficked with since childhood.
Each of them goes on in his error;
there is not one that can save you.

Stubborn Israel

48 "Listen to this, O house of Jacob,
you who are called by the name of
Israel
and come from the line of Judah,
you who take oaths in the name of the
LORD
and invoke the God of Israel—
but not in truth or righteousness—
2you who call yourselves citizens of the
holy city
and rely on the God of Israel—
the LORD Almighty is his name:
3I foretold the former things long ago,
my mouth announced them and I made
them known;
then suddenly I acted, and they came to
pass.
4For I knew how stubborn you were;
the sinews of your neck were iron,
your forehead was bronze.
5Therefore I told you these things long ago;
before they happened I announced them
to you
so that you could not say,
'My idols did them;
my wooden image and metal god
ordained them.'
6You have heard these things; look at them
all.
Will you not admit them?

"From now on I will tell you of new
things,
of hidden things unknown to you.
7They are created now, and not long ago;
you have not heard of them before
today.
So you cannot say,
'Yes, I knew of them.'
8You have neither heard nor understood;

[a] *1* Or *Chaldeans*: also in verse 5

from of old your ear has not been open.
Well do I know how treacherous you are;
you were called a rebel from birth.
9For my own name's sake I delay my wrath;
for the sake of my praise I hold it back from you,
so as not to cut you off.
10See, I have refined you, though not as silver;
I have tested you in the furnace of affliction.
11For my own sake, for my own sake, I do this.
How can I let myself be defamed?
I will not yield my glory to another.

Israel Freed

12"Listen to me, O Jacob,
Israel, whom I have called:
I am he;
I am the first and I am the last.
13My own hand laid the foundations of the earth,
and my right hand spread out the heavens;
when I summon them,
they all stand up together.

14"Come together, all of you, and listen:
Which of ⌞the idols⌟ has foretold these things?
The LORD's chosen ally
will carry out his purpose against Babylon;
his arm will be against the Babylonians.[a]
15I, even I, have spoken;
yes, I have called him.
I will bring him,
and he will succeed in his mission.

16"Come near me and listen to this:

"From the first announcement I have not spoken in secret;
at the time it happens, I am there."

And now the Sovereign LORD has sent me,
with his Spirit.

17This is what the LORD says—
your Redeemer, the Holy One of Israel:
"I am the LORD your God,
who teaches you what is best for you,
who directs you in the way you should go.
18If only you had paid attention to my commands,
your peace would have been like a river,
your righteousness like the waves of the sea.
19Your descendants would have been like the sand,
your children like its numberless grains;
their name would never be cut off
nor destroyed from before me."

20Leave Babylon,
flee from the Babylonians!
Announce this with shouts of joy
and proclaim it.
Send it out to the ends of the earth;
say, "The LORD has redeemed his servant Jacob."
21They did not thirst when he led them through the deserts;
he made water flow for them from the rock;
he split the rock
and water gushed out.

22"There is no peace," says the LORD, "for the wicked."

The Servant of the LORD

49 Listen to me, you islands;
hear this, you distant nations:
Before I was born the LORD called me;
from my birth he has made mention of my name.
2He made my mouth like a sharpened sword,
in the shadow of his hand he hid me;
he made me into a polished arrow
and concealed me in his quiver.
3He said to me, "You are my servant,
Israel, in whom I will display my splendor."
4But I said, "I have labored to no purpose;
I have spent my strength in vain and for nothing.
Yet what is due me is in the LORD's hand,
and my reward is with my God."

5And now the LORD says—
he who formed me in the womb to be his servant
to bring Jacob back to him
and gather Israel to himself,
for I am honored in the eyes of the LORD
and my God has been my strength—
6he says:
"It is too small a thing for you to be my servant
to restore the tribes of Jacob
and bring back those of Israel I have kept.
I will also make you a light for the Gentiles,
that you may bring my salvation to the ends of the earth."

7This is what the LORD says—
the Redeemer and Holy One of Israel—
to him who was despised and abhorred by the nation,
to the servant of rulers:
"Kings will see you and rise up,
princes will see and bow down,
because of the LORD, who is faithful,

[a] 14 Or *Chaldeans*; also in verse 20

the Holy One of Israel, who has chosen
you."

Restoration of Israel

8This is what the LORD says:

"In the time of my favor I will answer
you,
and in the day of salvation I will help
you;
I will keep you and will make you
to be a covenant for the people,
to restore the land
and to reassign its desolate inheritances,
9to say to the captives, 'Come out,'
and to those in darkness, 'Be free!'

"They will feed beside the roads
and find pasture on every barren hill.
10They will neither hunger nor thirst,
nor will the desert heat or the sun beat
upon them.
He who has compassion on them will
guide them
and lead them beside springs of water.
11I will turn all my mountains into roads,
and my highways will be raised up.
12See, they will come from afar—
some from the north, some from the
west,
some from the region of Aswan.[a]"

13Shout for joy, O heavens;
rejoice, O earth;
burst into song, O mountains!
For the LORD comforts his people
and will have compassion on his
afflicted ones.

14But Zion said, "The LORD has forsaken
me,
the Lord has forgotten me."

15"Can a mother forget the baby at her
breast
and have no compassion on the child
she has borne?
Though she may forget,
I will not forget you!
16See, I have engraved you on the palms of
my hands;
your walls are ever before me.
17Your sons hasten back,
and those who laid you waste depart
from you.
18Lift up your eyes and look around;
all your sons gather and come to you.
As surely as I live," declares the LORD,
"you will wear them all as ornaments;
you will put them on, like a bride.

19"Though you were ruined and made
desolate
and your land laid waste,
now you will be too small for your
people,
and those who devoured you will be far
away.
20The children born during your
bereavement
will yet say in your hearing,
'This place is too small for us;
give us more space to live in.'
21Then you will say in your heart,
'Who bore me these?
I was bereaved and barren;
I was exiled and rejected.
Who brought these up?
I was left all alone,
but these—where have they come
from?' "

22This is what the Sovereign LORD says:

"See, I will beckon to the Gentiles,
I will lift up my banner to the peoples;
they will bring your sons in their arms
and carry your daughters on their
shoulders.
23Kings will be your foster fathers,
and their queens your nursing mothers.
They will bow down before you with their
faces to the ground;
they will lick the dust at your feet.
Then you will know that I am the LORD;
those who hope in me will not be
disappointed."

24Can plunder be taken from warriors,
or captives rescued from the fierce[b]?

25But this is what the LORD says:

"Yes, captives will be taken from
warriors,
and plunder retrieved from the fierce;
I will contend with those who contend
with you,
and your children I will save.
26I will make your oppressors eat their own
flesh;
they will be drunk on their own blood,
as with wine.
Then all mankind will know
that I, the LORD, am your Savior,
your Redeemer, the Mighty One of
Jacob."

Israel's Sin and the Servant's Obedience

50 This is what the LORD says:

"Where is your mother's certificate of
divorce
with which I sent her away?
Or to which of my creditors
did I sell you?
Because of your sins you were sold;
because of your transgressions your
mother was sent away.
2When I came, why was there no one?
When I called, why was there no one to
answer?

[a]12 Dead Sea Scrolls; Masoretic Text *Sinim* [b]24 Dead Sea Scrolls, Vulgate and Syriac (see also Septuagint and verse 25); Masoretic Text *righteous*

Was my arm too short to ransom you?
Do I lack the strength to rescue you?
By a mere rebuke I dry up the sea,
I turn rivers into a desert;
their fish rot for lack of water
and die of thirst.
3I clothe the sky with darkness
and make sackcloth its covering."

4The Sovereign LORD has given me an
instructed tongue,
to know the word that sustains the
weary.
He wakens me morning by morning,
wakens my ear to listen like one being
taught.
5The Sovereign LORD has opened my ears,
and I have not been rebellious;
I have not drawn back.
6I offered my back to those who beat me,
my cheeks to those who pulled out my
beard;
I did not hide my face
from mocking and spitting.
7Because the Sovereign LORD helps me,
I will not be disgraced.
Therefore have I set my face like flint,
and I know I will not be put to shame.
8He who vindicates me is near.
Who then will bring charges against
me?
Let us face each other!
Who is my accuser?
Let him confront me!
9It is the Sovereign LORD who helps me.
Who is he that will condemn me?
They will all wear out like a garment;
the moths will eat them up.

10Who among you fears the LORD
and obeys the word of his servant?
Let him who walks in the dark,
who has no light,
trust in the name of the LORD
and rely on his God.
11But now, all you who light fires
and provide yourselves with flaming
torches,
go, walk in the light of your fires
and of the torches you have set ablaze.
This is what you shall receive from my
hand:
You will lie down in torment.

Everlasting Salvation for Zion

51 "Listen to me, you who pursue
righteousness
and who seek the LORD:
Look to the rock from which you were cut
and to the quarry from which you were
hewn;
2look to Abraham, your father,
and to Sarah, who gave you birth.
When I called him he was but one,
and I blessed him and made him many.
3The LORD will surely comfort Zion
and will look with compassion on all
her ruins;
he will make her deserts like Eden,
her wastelands like the garden of the
LORD.
Joy and gladness will be found in her,
thanksgiving and the sound of singing.

4"Listen to me, my people;
hear me, my nation:
The law will go out from me;
my justice will become a light to the
nations.
5My righteousness draws near speedily,
my salvation is on the way,
and my arm will bring justice to the
nations.
The islands will look to me
and wait in hope for my arm.
6Lift up your eyes to the heavens,
look at the earth beneath;
the heavens will vanish like smoke,
the earth will wear out like a garment
and its inhabitants die like flies.
But my salvation will last forever,
my righteousness will never fail.

7"Hear me, you who know what is right,
you people who have my law in your
hearts:
Do not fear the reproach of men
or be terrified by their insults.
8For the moth will eat them up like a
garment;
the worm will devour them like wool.
But my righteousness will last forever,
my salvation through all generations."

9Awake, awake! Clothe yourself with
strength,
O arm of the LORD;
awake, as in days gone by,
as in generations of old.
Was it not you who cut Rahab to pieces,
who pierced that monster through?
10Was it not you who dried up the sea,
the waters of the great deep,
who made a road in the depths of the sea
so that the redeemed might cross over?
11The ransomed of the LORD will return.
They will enter Zion with singing;
everlasting joy will crown their heads.
Gladness and joy will overtake them,
and sorrow and sighing will flee away.

12"I, even I, am he who comforts you.
Who are you that you fear mortal men,
the sons of men, who are but grass,
13that you forget the LORD your Maker,
who stretched out the heavens
and laid the foundations of the earth,
that you live in constant terror every day
because of the wrath of the oppressor,
who is bent on destruction?
For where is the wrath of the oppressor?
14 The cowering prisoners will soon be
set free;
they will not die in their dungeon,
nor will they lack bread.
15For I am the LORD your God,

who churns up the sea so that its waves
roar—
the LORD Almighty is his name.
16I have put my words in your mouth
and covered you with the shadow of my
hand—
I who set the heavens in place,
who laid the foundations of the earth,
and who say to Zion, 'You are my
people.' "

The Cup of the LORD's Wrath

17Awake, awake!
Rise up, O Jerusalem,
you who have drunk from the hand of the
LORD
the cup of his wrath,
you who have drained to its dregs
the goblet that makes men stagger.
18Of all the sons she bore
there was none to guide her;
of all the sons she reared
there was none to take her by the hand.
19These double calamities have come upon
you—
who can comfort you?—
ruin and destruction, famine and sword—
who can[a] console you?
20Your sons have fainted;
they lie at the head of every street,
like antelope caught in a net.
They are filled with the wrath of the LORD
and the rebuke of your God.

21Therefore hear this, you afflicted one,
made drunk, but not with wine.
22This is what your Sovereign LORD says,
your God, who defends his people:
"See, I have taken out of your hand
the cup that made you stagger;
from that cup, the goblet of my wrath,
you will never drink again.
23I will put it into the hands of your
tormentors,
who said to you,
'Fall prostrate that we may walk over
you.'
And you made your back like the ground,
like a street to be walked over."

52 Awake, awake, O Zion,
clothe yourself with strength.
Put on your garments of splendor,
O Jerusalem, the holy city.
The uncircumcised and defiled
will not enter you again.
2Shake off your dust;
rise up, sit enthroned, O Jerusalem.
Free yourself from the chains on your
neck,
O captive Daughter of Zion.

3For this is what the LORD says:

"You were sold for nothing,
and without money you will be
redeemed."

4For this is what the Sovereign LORD says:

"At first my people went down to Egypt
to live;
lately, Assyria has oppressed them.

5"And now what do I have here?" declares
the LORD.

"For my people have been taken away for
nothing,
and those who rule them mock,[b]"
declares the LORD.
"And all day long
my name is constantly blasphemed.
6Therefore my people will know my name;
therefore in that day they will know
that it is I who foretold it.
Yes, it is I."

7How beautiful on the mountains
are the feet of those who bring good
news,
who proclaim peace,
who bring good tidings,
who proclaim salvation,
who say to Zion,
"Your God reigns!"
8Listen! Your watchmen lift up their
voices;
together they shout for joy.
When the LORD returns to Zion,
they will see it with their own eyes.
9Burst into songs of joy together,
you ruins of Jerusalem,
for the LORD has comforted his people,
he has redeemed Jerusalem.
10The LORD will lay bare his holy arm
in the sight of all the nations,
and all the ends of the earth will see
the salvation of our God.

11Depart, depart, go out from there!
Touch no unclean thing!
Come out from it and be pure,
you who carry the vessels of the LORD.
12But you will not leave in haste
or go in flight;
for the LORD will go before you,
the God of Israel will be your rear
guard.

The Suffering and Glory of the Servant

13See, my servant will act wisely[c];
he will be raised and lifted up and
highly exalted.
14Just as there were many who were
appalled at him[d]—
his appearance was so disfigured
beyond that of any man
and his form marred beyond human
likeness—
15so will he sprinkle many nations,[e]

[a] *19* Dead Sea Scrolls, Septuagint, Vulgate and Syriac; Masoretic Text / *how can I* [b] *5* Dead Sea Scrolls and Vulgate; Masoretic Text *wail* [c] *13* Or *will prosper* [d] *14* Hebrew *you* [e] *15* Hebrew; Septuagint *so will many nations marvel at him*

and kings will shut their mouths
because of him.
For what they were not told, they will see,
and what they have not heard, they will
understand.

53 Who has believed our message
and to whom has the arm of the LORD
been revealed?
2He grew up before him like a tender
shoot,
and like a root out of dry ground.
He had no beauty or majesty to attract us
to him,
nothing in his appearance that we
should desire him.
3He was despised and rejected by men,
a man of sorrows, and familiar with
suffering.
Like one from whom men hide their faces
he was despised, and we esteemed him
not.

4Surely he took up our infirmities
and carried our sorrows,
yet we considered him stricken by God,
smitten by him, and afflicted.
5But he was pierced for our transgressions,
he was crushed for our iniquities;
the punishment that brought us peace was
upon him,
and by his wounds we are healed.
6We all, like sheep, have gone astray,
each of us has turned to his own way;
and the LORD has laid on him
the iniquity of us all.

7He was oppressed and afflicted,
yet he did not open his mouth;
he was led like a lamb to the slaughter,
and as a sheep before her shearers is
silent,
so he did not open his mouth.
8By oppression[a] and judgment he was
taken away.
And who can speak of his descendants?
For he was cut off from the land of the
living;
for the transgression of my people he
was stricken.[b]
9He was assigned a grave with the wicked,
and with the rich in his death,
though he had done no violence,
nor was any deceit in his mouth.

10Yet it was the LORD's will to crush him
and cause him to suffer,
and though the LORD makes[c] his life a
guilt offering,
he will see his offspring and prolong his
days,
and the will of the LORD will prosper in
his hand.
11After the suffering of his soul,
he will see the light ⌞of life⌟[d] and be
satisfied[e];
by his knowledge[f] my righteous servant
will justify many,
and he will bear their iniquities.
12Therefore I will give him a portion among
the great,[g]
and he will divide the spoils with the
strong,[h]
because he poured out his life unto death,
and was numbered with the
transgressors.
For he bore the sin of many,
and made intercession for the
transgressors.

The Future Glory of Zion

54 "Sing, O barren woman,
you who never bore a child;
burst into song, shout for joy,
you who were never in labor;
because more are the children of the
desolate woman
than of her who has a husband,"
says the LORD.
2"Enlarge the place of your tent,
stretch your tent curtains wide,
do not hold back;
lengthen your cords,
strengthen your stakes.
3For you will spread out to the right and to
the left;
your descendants will dispossess nations
and settle in their desolate cities.

4"Do not be afraid; you will not suffer
shame.
Do not fear disgrace; you will not be
humiliated.
You will forget the shame of your youth
and remember no more the reproach of
your widowhood.
5For your Maker is your husband—
the LORD Almighty is his name—
the Holy One of Israel is your Redeemer;
he is called the God of all the earth.
6The LORD will call you back
as if you were a wife deserted and
distressed in spirit—
a wife who married young,
only to be rejected," says your God.
7"For a brief moment I abandoned you,
but with deep compassion I will bring
you back.
8In a surge of anger
I hid my face from you for a moment,
but with everlasting kindness
I will have compassion on you,"
says the LORD your Redeemer.

9"To me this is like the days of Noah,
when I swore that the waters of Noah
would never again cover the earth.

[a]8 Or *From arrest* [b]8 Or *away. / Yet who of his generation considered / that he was cut off from the land of the living / for the transgression of my people, / to whom the blow was due?* [c]10 Hebrew *though you make* [d]11 Dead Sea Scrolls (see also Septuagint); Masoretic Text does not have *the light ⌞of life⌟*
[e]11 Or (with Masoretic Text) *11He will see the result of the suffering of his soul / and be satisfied*
[f]11 Or *by knowledge of him* [g]12 Or *many* [h]12 Or *numerous*

So now I have sworn not to be angry with you,
never to rebuke you again.
10Though the mountains be shaken
and the hills be removed,
yet my unfailing love for you will not be shaken
nor my covenant of peace be removed,"
says the LORD, who has compassion on you.

11"O afflicted city, lashed by storms and not comforted,
I will build you with stones of turquoise,[a]
your foundations with sapphires.[b]
12I will make your battlements of rubies,
your gates of sparkling jewels,
and all your walls of precious stones.
13All your sons will be taught by the LORD,
and great will be your children's peace.
14In righteousness you will be established:
Tyranny will be far from you;
you will have nothing to fear.
Terror will be far removed;
it will not come near you.
15If anyone does attack you, it will not be my doing;
whoever attacks you will surrender to you.

16"See, it is I who created the blacksmith
who fans the coals into flame
and forges a weapon fit for its work.
And it is I who have created the destroyer to work havoc;
17 no weapon forged against you will prevail,
and you will refute every tongue that accuses you.
This is the heritage of the servants of the LORD,
and this is their vindication from me,"
declares the LORD.

Invitation to the Thirsty

55 "Come, all you who are thirsty,
come to the waters;
and you who have no money,
come, buy and eat!
Come, buy wine and milk
without money and without cost.
2Why spend money on what is not bread,
and your labor on what does not satisfy?
Listen, listen to me, and eat what is good,
and your soul will delight in the richest of fare.
3Give ear and come to me;
hear me, that your soul may live.
I will make an everlasting covenant with you,
my faithful love promised to David.
4See, I have made him a witness to the peoples,
a leader and commander of the peoples.
5Surely you will summon nations you know not,
and nations that do not know you will hasten to you,
because of the LORD your God,
the Holy One of Israel,
for he has endowed you with splendor."

6Seek the LORD while he may be found;
call on him while he is near.
7Let the wicked forsake his way
and the evil man his thoughts.
Let him turn to the LORD, and he will have mercy on him,
and to our God, for he will freely pardon.

8"For my thoughts are not your thoughts,
neither are your ways my ways,"
declares the LORD.
9"As the heavens are higher than the earth,
so are my ways higher than your ways
and my thoughts than your thoughts.
10As the rain and the snow
come down from heaven,
and do not return to it
without watering the earth
and making it bud and flourish,
so that it yields seed for the sower and bread for the eater,
11so is my word that goes out from my mouth:
It will not return to me empty,
but will accomplish what I desire
and achieve the purpose for which I sent it.
12You will go out in joy
and be led forth in peace;
the mountains and hills
will burst into song before you,
and all the trees of the field
will clap their hands.
13Instead of the thornbush will grow the pine tree,
and instead of briers the myrtle will grow.
This will be for the LORD's renown,
for an everlasting sign,
which will not be destroyed."

Salvation for Others

56 This is what the LORD says:

"Maintain justice
and do what is right,
for my salvation is close at hand
and my righteousness will soon be revealed.
2Blessed is the man who does this,
the man who holds it fast,
who keeps the Sabbath without desecrating it,
and keeps his hand from doing any evil."

3Let no foreigner who has bound himself to the LORD say,

[a] *11* The meaning of the Hebrew for this word is uncertain. [b] *11* Or *lapis lazuli*

"The LORD will surely exclude me from
his people."
And let not any eunuch complain,
"I am only a dry tree."

4For this is what the LORD says:

"To the eunuchs who keep my Sabbaths,
who choose what pleases me
and hold fast to my covenant—
5to them I will give within my temple and
its walls
a memorial and a name
better than sons and daughters;
I will give them an everlasting name
that will not be cut off.
6And foreigners who bind themselves to
the LORD
to serve him,
to love the name of the LORD,
and to worship him,
all who keep the Sabbath without
desecrating it
and who hold fast to my covenant—
7these I will bring to my holy mountain
and give them joy in my house of
prayer.
Their burnt offerings and sacrifices
will be accepted on my altar;
for my house will be called
a house of prayer for all nations."
8The Sovereign LORD declares—
he who gathers the exiles of Israel:
"I will gather still others to them
besides those already gathered."

God's Accusation Against the Wicked

9Come, all you beasts of the field,
come and devour, all you beasts of the
forest!
10Israel's watchmen are blind,
they all lack knowledge;
they are all mute dogs,
they cannot bark;
they lie around and dream,
they love to sleep.
11They are dogs with mighty appetites;
they never have enough.
They are shepherds who lack
understanding;
they all turn to their own way,
each seeks his own gain.
12"Come," each one cries, "let me get wine!
Let us drink our fill of beer!
And tomorrow will be like today,
or even far better."

57 The righteous perish,
and no one ponders it in his heart;
devout men are taken away,
and no one understands
that the righteous are taken away
to be spared from evil.
2Those who walk uprightly
enter into peace;
they find rest as they lie in death.

3"But you—come here, you sons of a
sorceress,
you offspring of adulterers and
prostitutes!
4Whom are you mocking?
At whom do you sneer
and stick out your tongue?
Are you not a brood of rebels,
the offspring of liars?
5You burn with lust among the oaks
and under every spreading tree;
you sacrifice your children in the ravines
and under the overhanging crags.
6⌊The idols⌋ among the smooth stones of the
ravines are your portion;
they, they are your lot.
Yes, to them you have poured out drink
offerings
and offered grain offerings.
In the light of these things, should I
relent?
7You have made your bed on a high and
lofty hill;
there you went up to offer your
sacrifices.
8Behind your doors and your doorposts
you have put your pagan symbols.
Forsaking me, you uncovered your bed,
you climbed into it and opened it wide;
you made a pact with those whose beds
you love,
and you looked on their nakedness.
9You went to Molech[a] with olive oil
and increased your perfumes.
You sent your ambassadors[b] far away;
you descended to the grave[c] itself!
10You were wearied by all your ways,
but you would not say, 'It is hopeless.'
You found renewal of your strength,
and so you did not faint.

11"Whom have you so dreaded and feared
that you have been false to me,
and have neither remembered me
nor pondered this in your hearts?
Is it not because I have long been silent
that you do not fear me?
12I will expose your righteousness and your
works,
and they will not benefit you.
13When you cry out for help,
let your collection ⌊of idols⌋ save you!
The wind will carry all of them off,
a mere breath will blow them away.
But the man who makes me his refuge
will inherit the land
and possess my holy mountain."

Comfort for the Contrite

14And it will be said:

"Build up, build up, prepare the road!
Remove the obstacles out of the way of
my people."
15For this is what the high and lofty One
says—

[a]9 Or *to the king* [b]9 Or *idols* [c]9 Hebrew *Sheol*

he who lives forever, whose name is holy:
"I live in a high and holy place,
but also with him who is contrite and lowly in spirit,
to revive the spirit of the lowly
and to revive the heart of the contrite.
16I will not accuse forever,
nor will I always be angry,
for then the spirit of man would grow faint before me—
the breath of man that I have created.
17I was enraged by his sinful greed;
I punished him, and hid my face in anger,
yet he kept on in his willful ways.
18I have seen his ways, but I will heal him;
I will guide him and restore comfort to him,
19 creating praise on the lips of the mourners in Israel.
Peace, peace, to those far and near,"
says the LORD. "And I will heal them."
20But the wicked are like the tossing sea,
which cannot rest,
whose waves cast up mire and mud.
21"There is no peace," says my God, "for the wicked."

True Fasting

58 "Shout it aloud, do not hold back.
Raise your voice like a trumpet.
Declare to my people their rebellion
and to the house of Jacob their sins.
2For day after day they seek me out;
they seem eager to know my ways,
as if they were a nation that does what is right
and has not forsaken the commands of its God.
They ask me for just decisions
and seem eager for God to come near them.
3'Why have we fasted,' they say,
'and you have not seen it?
Why have we humbled ourselves,
and you have not noticed?'

"Yet on the day of your fasting, you do as you please
and exploit all your workers.
4Your fasting ends in quarreling and strife,
and in striking each other with wicked fists.
You cannot fast as you do today
and expect your voice to be heard on high.
5Is this the kind of fast I have chosen,
only a day for a man to humble himself?
Is it only for bowing one's head like a reed
and for lying on sackcloth and ashes?
Is that what you call a fast,
a day acceptable to the LORD?

6"Is not this the kind of fasting I have chosen:
to loose the chains of injustice
and untie the cords of the yoke,
to set the oppressed free
and break every yoke?
7Is it not to share your food with the hungry
and to provide the poor wanderer with shelter—
when you see the naked, to clothe him,
and not to turn away from your own flesh and blood?
8Then your light will break forth like the dawn,
and your healing will quickly appear;
then your righteousness[a] will go before you,
and the glory of the LORD will be your rear guard.
9Then you will call, and the LORD will answer;
you will cry for help, and he will say: Here am I.

"If you do away with the yoke of oppression,
with the pointing finger and malicious talk,
10and if you spend yourselves in behalf of the hungry
and satisfy the needs of the oppressed,
then your light will rise in the darkness,
and your night will become like the noonday.
11The LORD will guide you always;
he will satisfy your needs in a sun-scorched land
and will strengthen your frame.
You will be like a well-watered garden,
like a spring whose waters never fail.
12Your people will rebuild the ancient ruins
and will raise up the age-old foundations;
you will be called Repairer of Broken Walls,
Restorer of Streets with Dwellings.

13"If you keep your feet from breaking the Sabbath
and from doing as you please on my holy day,
if you call the Sabbath a delight
and the LORD's holy day honorable,
and if you honor it by not going your own way
and not doing as you please or speaking idle words,
14then you will find your joy in the LORD,
and I will cause you to ride on the heights of the land
and to feast on the inheritance of your father Jacob."
The mouth of the LORD has spoken.

[a]8 Or *your righteous One*

Sin, Confession and Redemption

59 Surely the arm of the LORD is not too short to save,
nor his ear too dull to hear.
2But your iniquities have separated you from your God;
your sins have hidden his face from you,
so that he will not hear.
3For your hands are stained with blood,
your fingers with guilt.
Your lips have spoken lies,
and your tongue mutters wicked things.
4No one calls for justice;
no one pleads his case with integrity.
They rely on empty arguments and speak lies;
they conceive trouble and give birth to evil.
5They hatch the eggs of vipers
and spin a spider's web.
Whoever eats their eggs will die,
and when one is broken, an adder is hatched.
6Their cobwebs are useless for clothing;
they cannot cover themselves with what they make.
Their deeds are evil deeds,
and acts of violence are in their hands.
7Their feet rush into sin;
they are swift to shed innocent blood.
Their thoughts are evil thoughts;
ruin and destruction mark their ways.
8The way of peace they do not know;
there is no justice in their paths.
They have turned them into crooked roads;
no one who walks in them will know peace.

9So justice is far from us,
and righteousness does not reach us.
We look for light, but all is darkness;
for brightness, but we walk in deep shadows.
10Like the blind we grope along the wall,
feeling our way like men without eyes.
At midday we stumble as if it were twilight;
among the strong, we are like the dead.
11We all growl like bears;
we moan mournfully like doves.
We look for justice, but find none;
for deliverance, but it is far away.

12For our offenses are many in your sight,
and our sins testify against us.
Our offenses are ever with us,
and we acknowledge our iniquities:
13rebellion and treachery against the LORD,
turning our backs on our God,
fomenting oppression and revolt,
uttering lies our hearts have conceived.
14So justice is driven back,
and righteousness stands at a distance;
truth has stumbled in the streets,
honesty cannot enter.
15Truth is nowhere to be found,
and whoever shuns evil becomes a prey.

The LORD looked and was displeased
that there was no justice.
16He saw that there was no one,
he was appalled that there was no one to intervene;
so his own arm worked salvation for him,
and his own righteousness sustained him.
17He put on righteousness as his breastplate,
and the helmet of salvation on his head;
he put on the garments of vengeance
and wrapped himself in zeal as in a cloak.
18According to what they have done,
so will he repay
wrath to his enemies
and retribution to his foes;
he will repay the islands their due.
19From the west, men will fear the name of the LORD,
and from the rising of the sun, they will revere his glory.
For he will come like a pent-up flood
that the breath of the LORD drives along.[a]

20"The Redeemer will come to Zion,
to those in Jacob who repent of their sins,"
declares the LORD.

21"As for me, this is my covenant with
them," says the LORD. "My Spirit, who is on
you, and my words that I have put in your
mouth will not depart from your mouth, or
from the mouths of your children, or from the
mouths of their descendants from this time on
and forever," says the LORD.

The Glory of Zion

60 "Arise, shine, for your light has come,
and the glory of the LORD rises upon you.
2See, darkness covers the earth
and thick darkness is over the peoples,
but the LORD rises upon you
and his glory appears over you.
3Nations will come to your light,
and kings to the brightness of your dawn.

4"Lift up your eyes and look about you:
All assemble and come to you;
your sons come from afar,
and your daughters are carried on the arm.
5Then you will look and be radiant,
your heart will throb and swell with joy;
the wealth on the seas will be brought to you,
to you the riches of the nations will come.
6Herds of camels will cover your land,

[a] 19 Or *When the enemy comes in like a flood, / the Spirit of the LORD will put him to flight*

young camels of Midian and Ephah.
And all from Sheba will come,
bearing gold and incense
and proclaiming the praise of the LORD.
7All Kedar's flocks will be gathered to you,
the rams of Nebaioth will serve you;
they will be accepted as offerings on my altar,
and I will adorn my glorious temple.

8"Who are these that fly along like clouds,
like doves to their nests?
9Surely the islands look to me;
in the lead are the ships of Tarshish,[a]
bringing your sons from afar,
with their silver and gold,
to the honor of the LORD your God,
the Holy One of Israel,
for he has endowed you with splendor.

10"Foreigners will rebuild your walls,
and their kings will serve you.
Though in anger I struck you,
in favor I will show you compassion.
11Your gates will always stand open,
they will never be shut, day or night,
so that men may bring you the wealth of the nations—
their kings led in triumphal procession.
12For the nation or kingdom that will not serve you will perish;
it will be utterly ruined.

13"The glory of Lebanon will come to you,
the pine, the fir and the cypress together,
to adorn the place of my sanctuary;
and I will glorify the place of my feet.
14The sons of your oppressors will come bowing before you;
all who despise you will bow down at your feet
and will call you the City of the LORD,
Zion of the Holy One of Israel.

15"Although you have been forsaken and hated,
with no one traveling through,
I will make you the everlasting pride
and the joy of all generations.
16You will drink the milk of nations
and be nursed at royal breasts.
Then you will know that I, the LORD, am your Savior,
your Redeemer, the Mighty One of Jacob.
17Instead of bronze I will bring you gold,
and silver in place of iron.
Instead of wood I will bring you bronze,
and iron in place of stones.
I will make peace your governor
and righteousness your ruler.
18No longer will violence be heard in your land,
nor ruin or destruction within your borders,
but you will call your walls Salvation
and your gates Praise.
19The sun will no more be your light by day,
nor will the brightness of the moon shine on you,
for the LORD will be your everlasting light,
and your God will be your glory.
20Your sun will never set again,
and your moon will wane no more;
the LORD will be your everlasting light,
and your days of sorrow will end.
21Then will all your people be righteous
and they will possess the land forever.
They are the shoot I have planted,
the work of my hands,
for the display of my splendor.
22The least of you will become a thousand,
the smallest a mighty nation.
I am the LORD;
in its time I will do this swiftly."

The Year of the LORD's Favor

61 The Spirit of the Sovereign LORD is on me,
because the LORD has anointed me
to preach good news to the poor.
He has sent me to bind up the brokenhearted,
to proclaim freedom for the captives
and release from darkness for the prisoners,[b]
2to proclaim the year of the LORD's favor
and the day of vengeance of our God,
to comfort all who mourn,
3 and provide for those who grieve in Zion—
to bestow on them a crown of beauty
instead of ashes,
the oil of gladness
instead of mourning,
and a garment of praise
instead of a spirit of despair.
They will be called oaks of righteousness,
a planting of the LORD
for the display of his splendor.

4They will rebuild the ancient ruins
and restore the places long devastated;
they will renew the ruined cities
that have been devastated for generations.
5Aliens will shepherd your flocks;
foreigners will work your fields and vineyards.
6And you will be called priests of the LORD,
you will be named ministers of our God.
You will feed on the wealth of nations,
and in their riches you will boast.

7Instead of their shame

[a] 9 Or *the trading ships* [b] 1 Hebrew; Septuagint *the blind*

my people will receive a double portion,
and instead of disgrace
they will rejoice in their inheritance;
and so they will inherit a double portion
in their land,
and everlasting joy will be theirs.

8 "For I, the LORD, love justice;
I hate robbery and iniquity.
In my faithfulness I will reward them
and make an everlasting covenant with
them.
9 Their descendants will be known among
the nations
and their offspring among the peoples.
All who see them will acknowledge
that they are a people the LORD has
blessed."

10 I delight greatly in the LORD;
my soul rejoices in my God.
For he has clothed me with garments of
salvation
and arrayed me in a robe of
righteousness,
as a bridegroom adorns his head like a
priest,
and as a bride adorns herself with her
jewels.
11 For as the soil makes the sprout come up
and a garden causes seeds to grow,
so the Sovereign LORD will make
righteousness and praise
spring up before all nations.

Zion's New Name

62 For Zion's sake I will not keep silent,
for Jerusalem's sake I will not remain
quiet,
till her righteousness shines out like the
dawn,
her salvation like a blazing torch.
2 The nations will see your righteousness,
and all kings your glory;
you will be called by a new name
that the mouth of the LORD will bestow.
3 You will be a crown of splendor in the
LORD's hand,
a royal diadem in the hand of your
God.
4 No longer will they call you Deserted,
or name your land Desolate.
But you will be called Hephzibah,[a]
and your land Beulah[b];
for the LORD will take delight in you,
and your land will be married.
5 As a young man marries a maiden,
so will your sons[c] marry you;
as a bridegroom rejoices over his bride,
so will your God rejoice over you.

6 I have posted watchmen on your walls,
O Jerusalem;
they will never be silent day or night.
You who call on the LORD,
give yourselves no rest,
7 and give him no rest till he establishes
Jerusalem
and makes her the praise of the earth.

8 The LORD has sworn by his right hand
and by his mighty arm:
"Never again will I give your grain
as food for your enemies,
and never again will foreigners drink the
new wine
for which you have toiled;
9 but those who harvest it will eat it
and praise the LORD,
and those who gather the grapes will drink
it
in the courts of my sanctuary."

10 Pass through, pass through the gates!
Prepare the way for the people.
Build up, build up the highway!
Remove the stones.
Raise a banner for the nations.

11 The LORD has made proclamation
to the ends of the earth:
"Say to the Daughter of Zion,
'See, your Savior comes!
See, his reward is with him,
and his recompense accompanies him.' "
12 They will be called the Holy People,
the Redeemed of the LORD;
and you will be called Sought After,
the City No Longer Deserted.

God's Day of Vengeance and Redemption

63 Who is this coming from Edom,
from Bozrah, with his garments
stained crimson?
Who is this, robed in splendor,
striding forward in the greatness of his
strength?

"It is I, speaking in righteousness,
mighty to save."

2 Why are your garments red,
like those of one treading the
winepress?

3 "I have trodden the winepress alone;
from the nations no one was with me.
I trampled them in my anger
and trod them down in my wrath;
their blood spattered my garments,
and I stained all my clothing.
4 For the day of vengeance was in my heart,
and the year of my redemption has
come.
5 I looked, but there was no one to help,
I was appalled that no one gave
support;
so my own arm worked salvation for me,
and my own wrath sustained me.
6 I trampled the nations in my anger;
in my wrath I made them drunk
and poured their blood on the ground."

[a]4 *Hephzibah* means *my delight is in her.* [b]4 *Beulah* means *married.* [c]5 Or *Builder*

Praise and Prayer

[7]I will tell of the kindnesses of the LORD,
the deeds for which he is to be praised,
according to all the LORD has done for us—
yes, the many good things he has done
for the house of Israel,
according to his compassion and many kindnesses.
[8]He said, "Surely they are my people,
sons who will not be false to me";
and so he became their Savior.
[9]In all their distress he too was distressed,
and the angel of his presence saved them.
In his love and mercy he redeemed them;
he lifted them up and carried them
all the days of old.
[10]Yet they rebelled
and grieved his Holy Spirit.
So he turned and became their enemy
and he himself fought against them.

[11]Then his people recalled[a] the days of old,
the days of Moses and his people—
where is he who brought them through the sea,
with the shepherd of his flock?
Where is he who set
his Holy Spirit among them,
[12]who sent his glorious arm of power
to be at Moses' right hand,
who divided the waters before them,
to gain for himself everlasting renown,
[13]who led them through the depths?
Like a horse in open country,
they did not stumble;
[14]like cattle that go down to the plain,
they were given rest by the Spirit of the LORD.
This is how you guided your people
to make for yourself a glorious name.

[15]Look down from heaven and see
from your lofty throne, holy and glorious.
Where are your zeal and your might?
Your tenderness and compassion are withheld from us.
[16]But you are our Father,
though Abraham does not know us
or Israel acknowledge us;
you, O LORD, are our Father,
our Redeemer from of old is your name.
[17]Why, O LORD, do you make us wander
from your ways
and harden our hearts so we do not revere you?
Return for the sake of your servants,
the tribes that are your inheritance.
[18]For a little while your people possessed
your holy place,
but now our enemies have trampled
down your sanctuary.
[19]We are yours from of old;
but you have not ruled over them,
they have not been called by your name.[b]

64 Oh, that you would rend the heavens
and come down,
that the mountains would tremble before you!
[2]As when fire sets twigs ablaze
and causes water to boil,
come down to make your name known to
your enemies
and cause the nations to quake before you!
[3]For when you did awesome things that we
did not expect,
you came down, and the mountains
trembled before you.
[4]Since ancient times no one has heard,
no ear has perceived,
no eye has seen any God besides you,
who acts on behalf of those who wait
for him.
[5]You come to the help of those who gladly
do right,
who remember your ways.
But when we continued to sin against them,
you were angry.
How then can we be saved?
[6]All of us have become like one who is
unclean,
and all our righteous acts are like filthy rags;
we all shrivel up like a leaf,
and like the wind our sins sweep us away.
[7]No one calls on your name
or strives to lay hold of you;
for you have hidden your face from us
and made us waste away because of our sins.

[8]Yet, O LORD, you are our Father.
We are the clay, you are the potter;
we are all the work of your hand.
[9]Do not be angry beyond measure,
O LORD;
do not remember our sins forever.
Oh, look upon us, we pray,
for we are all your people.
[10]Your sacred cities have become a desert;
even Zion is a desert, Jerusalem a
desolation.
[11]Our holy and glorious temple, where our
fathers praised you,
has been burned with fire,
and all that we treasured lies in ruins.
[12]After all this, O LORD, will you hold
yourself back?
Will you keep silent and punish us
beyond measure?

[a] *11* Or *But may he recall* [b] *19* Or *We are like those you have never ruled, / like those never called by your name*

Judgment and Salvation

65 "I revealed myself to those who did not ask for me;
I was found by those who did not seek me.
To a nation that did not call on my name,
I said, 'Here am I, here am I.'
2All day long I have held out my hands
to an obstinate people,
who walk in ways not good,
pursuing their own imaginations—
3a people who continually provoke me
to my very face,
offering sacrifices in gardens
and burning incense on altars of brick;
4who sit among the graves
and spend their nights keeping secret vigil;
who eat the flesh of pigs,
and whose pots hold broth of unclean meat;
5who say, 'Keep away; don't come near me,
for I am too sacred for you!'
Such people are smoke in my nostrils,
a fire that keeps burning all day.

6"See, it stands written before me:
I will not keep silent but will pay back in full;
I will pay it back into their laps—
7both your sins and the sins of your fathers,"
says the LORD.
"Because they burned sacrifices on the mountains
and defied me on the hills,
I will measure into their laps
the full payment for their former deeds."

8This is what the LORD says:

"As when juice is still found in a cluster of grapes
and men say, 'Don't destroy it,
there is yet some good in it,'
so will I do in behalf of my servants;
I will not destroy them all.
9I will bring forth descendants from Jacob,
and from Judah those who will possess my mountains;
my chosen people will inherit them,
and there will my servants live.
10Sharon will become a pasture for flocks,
and the Valley of Achor a resting place for herds,
for my people who seek me.

11"But as for you who forsake the LORD
and forget my holy mountain,
who spread a table for Fortune
and fill bowls of mixed wine for Destiny,
12I will destine you for the sword,
and you will all bend down for the slaughter;
for I called but you did not answer,
I spoke but you did not listen.
You did evil in my sight
and chose what displeases me."

13Therefore this is what the Sovereign LORD says:

"My servants will eat,
but you will go hungry;
my servants will drink,
but you will go thirsty;
my servants will rejoice,
but you will be put to shame.
14My servants will sing
out of the joy of their hearts,
but you will cry out
from anguish of heart
and wail in brokenness of spirit.
15You will leave your name
to my chosen ones as a curse;
the Sovereign LORD will put you to death,
but to his servants he will give another name.
16Whoever invokes a blessing in the land
will do so by the God of truth;
he who takes an oath in the land
will swear by the God of truth.
For the past troubles will be forgotten
and hidden from my eyes.

New Heavens and a New Earth

17"Behold, I will create
new heavens and a new earth.
The former things will not be remembered,
nor will they come to mind.
18But be glad and rejoice forever
in what I will create,
for I will create Jerusalem to be a delight
and its people a joy.
19I will rejoice over Jerusalem
and take delight in my people;
the sound of weeping and of crying
will be heard in it no more.

20"Never again will there be in it
an infant who lives but a few days,
or an old man who does not live out his years;
he who dies at a hundred
will be thought a mere youth;
he who fails to reach[a] a hundred
will be considered accursed.
21They will build houses and dwell in them;
they will plant vineyards and eat their fruit.
22No longer will they build houses and others live in them,
or plant and others eat
For as the days of a tree,
so will be the days of my people;
my chosen ones will long enjoy
the works of their hands.
23They will not toil in vain
or bear children doomed to misfortune;

[a]20 Or / *the sinner who reaches*

for they will be a people blessed by the
LORD,
they and their descendants with them.
24Before they call I will answer;
while they are still speaking I will hear.
25The wolf and the lamb will feed together,
and the lion will eat straw like the ox,
but dust will be the serpent's food.
They will neither harm nor destroy
on all my holy mountain,"
says the LORD.

Judgment and Hope

66 This is what the LORD says:

"Heaven is my throne,
and the earth is my footstool.
Where is the house you will build for me?
Where will my resting place be?
2Has not my hand made all these things,
and so they came into being?"
declares the LORD.

"This is the one I esteem:
he who is humble and contrite in spirit,
and trembles at my word.
3But whoever sacrifices a bull
is like one who kills a man,
and whoever offers a lamb,
like one who breaks a dog's neck;
whoever makes a grain offering
is like one who presents pig's blood,
and whoever burns memorial incense,
like one who worships an idol.
They have chosen their own ways,
and their souls delight in their
abominations;
4so I also will choose harsh treatment for
them
and will bring upon them what they
dread.
For when I called, no one answered,
when I spoke, no one listened.
They did evil in my sight
and chose what displeases me."

5Hear the word of the LORD,
you who tremble at his word:
"Your brothers who hate you,
and exclude you because of my name,
have said,
'Let the LORD be glorified,
that we may see your joy!'
Yet they will be put to shame.
6Hear that uproar from the city,
hear that noise from the temple!
It is the sound of the LORD
repaying his enemies all they deserve.

7"Before she goes into labor,
she gives birth;
before the pains come upon her,
she delivers a son.
8Who has ever heard of such a thing?
Who has ever seen such things?
Can a country be born in a day
or a nation be brought forth in a
moment?
Yet no sooner is Zion in labor
than she gives birth to her children.
9Do I bring to the moment of birth
and not give delivery?" says the LORD.
"Do I close up the womb
when I bring to delivery?" says your
God.
10"Rejoice with Jerusalem and be glad for
her,
all you who love her;
rejoice greatly with her,
all you who mourn over her.
11For you will nurse and be satisfied
at her comforting breasts;
you will drink deeply
and delight in her overflowing
abundance."

12For this is what the LORD says:

"I will extend peace to her like a river,
and the wealth of nations like a
flooding stream;
you will nurse and be carried on her arm
and dandled on her knees.
13As a mother comforts her child,
so will I comfort you;
and you will be comforted over
Jerusalem."

14When you see this, your heart will rejoice
and you will flourish like grass;
the hand of the LORD will be made known
to his servants,
but his fury will be shown to his foes.
15See, the LORD is coming with fire,
and his chariots are like a whirlwind;
he will bring down his anger with fury,
and his rebuke with flames of fire.
16For with fire and with his sword
the LORD will execute judgment upon
all men,
and many will be those slain by the
LORD.

17"Those who consecrate and purify themselves to go into the gardens, following the one
in the midst of[a] those who eat the flesh of pigs
and rats and other abominable things—they
will meet their end together," declares the
LORD.
18"And I, because of their actions and their
imaginations, am about to come[b] and gather
all nations and tongues, and they will come
and see my glory.
19"I will set a sign among them, and I will
send some of those who survive to the nations—to Tarshish, to the Libyans[c] and Lydi-
ans (famous as archers), to Tubal and Greece,
and to the distant islands that have not heard of
my fame or seen my glory. They will proclaim
my glory among the nations. 20And they will
bring all your brothers, from all the nations, to
my holy mountain in Jerusalem as an offering

[a] *17* Or *gardens behind one of your temples, and* [b] *18* The meaning of the Hebrew for this clause is uncertain. [c] *19* Some Septuagint manuscripts *Put* (Libyans); Hebrew *Pul*

to the LORD—on horses, in chariots and wagons, and on mules and camels," says the LORD.
"They will bring them, as the Israelites bring
their grain offerings, to the temple of the LORD
in ceremonially clean vessels. 21And I will select some of them also to be priests and Levites," says the LORD.

22"As the new heavens and the new earth
that I make will endure before me," declares
the LORD, "so will your name and descendants
endure. 23From one New Moon to another and
from one Sabbath to another, all mankind will
come and bow down before me," says the
LORD. 24"And they will go out and look upon
the dead bodies of those who rebelled against
me; their worm will not die, nor will their fire
be quenched, and they will be loathsome to all
mankind."

Jeremiah

1 The words of Jeremiah son of Hilkiah, one
of the priests at Anathoth in the territory of
Benjamin. 2The word of the LORD came to him
in the thirteenth year of the reign of Josiah son
of Amon king of Judah, 3and through the reign
of Jehoiakim son of Josiah king of Judah,
down to the fifth month of the eleventh year of
Zedekiah son of Josiah king of Judah, when
the people of Jerusalem went into exile.

The Call of Jeremiah

4The word of the LORD came to me, saying,

5"Before I formed you in the womb I
knew[a] you,
before you were born I set you apart;
I appointed you as a prophet to the
nations."

6"Ah, Sovereign LORD," I said, "I do not
know how to speak; I am only a child."
7But the LORD said to me, "Do not say, 'I
am only a child.' You must go to everyone I
send you to and say whatever I command you.
8Do not be afraid of them, for I am with you
and will rescue you," declares the LORD.
9Then the LORD reached out his hand and
touched my mouth and said to me, "Now, I
have put my words in your mouth. 10See, today
I appoint you over nations and kingdoms to
uproot and tear down, to destroy and overthrow, to build and to plant."
11The word of the LORD came to me: "What
do you see, Jeremiah?"
"I see the branch of an almond tree," I replied.
12The LORD said to me, "You have seen
correctly, for I am watching[b] to see that my
word is fulfilled."
13The word of the LORD came to me again:
"What do you see?"
"I see a boiling pot, tilting away from the
north," I answered.
14The LORD said to me, "From the north
disaster will be poured out on all who live in
the land. 15I am about to summon all the peoples of the northern kingdoms," declares the
LORD.

"Their kings will come and set up their
thrones
in the entrance of the gates of
Jerusalem;
they will come against all her surrounding
walls
and against all the towns of Judah.
16I will pronounce my judgments on my
people
because of their wickedness in forsaking
me,
in burning incense to other gods
and in worshiping what their hands have
made.

17"Get yourself ready! Stand up and say to
them whatever I command you. Do not be terrified by them, or I will terrify you before
them. 18Today I have made you a fortified city,
an iron pillar and a bronze wall to stand against
the whole land—against the kings of Judah, its
officials, its priests and the people of the land.
19They will fight against you but will not overcome you, for I am with you and will rescue
you," declares the LORD.

Israel Forsakes God

2 The word of the LORD came to me: 2"Go
and proclaim in the hearing of Jerusalem:

" 'I remember the devotion of your youth,
how as a bride you loved me
and followed me through the desert,
through a land not sown.
3Israel was holy to the LORD,
the firstfruits of his harvest;
all who devoured her were held guilty,
and disaster overtook them,' "
declares the LORD.

4Hear the word of the LORD, O house of
Jacob,
all you clans of the house of Israel.

5This is what the LORD says:

"What fault did your fathers find in me,
that they strayed so far from me?
They followed worthless idols
and became worthless themselves.

[a]5 Or *chose* [b]12 The Hebrew for *watching* sounds like the Hebrew for *almond tree.*

6They did not ask, 'Where is the LORD,
who brought us up out of Egypt
and led us through the barren wilderness,
through a land of deserts and rifts,
a land of drought and darkness,[a]
a land where no one travels and no one lives?'
7I brought you into a fertile land
to eat its fruit and rich produce.
But you came and defiled my land
and made my inheritance detestable.
8The priests did not ask,
'Where is the LORD?'
Those who deal with the law did not know me;
the leaders rebelled against me.
The prophets prophesied by Baal,
following worthless idols.

9"Therefore I bring charges against you again,"
declares the LORD.
"And I will bring charges against your children's children.
10Cross over to the coasts of Kittim[b] and look,
send to Kedar[c] and observe closely;
see if there has ever been anything like this:
11Has a nation ever changed its gods?
(Yet they are not gods at all.)
But my people have exchanged their[d] Glory
for worthless idols.
12Be appalled at this, O heavens,
and shudder with great horror,"
declares the LORD.
13"My people have committed two sins:
They have forsaken me,
the spring of living water,
and have dug their own cisterns,
broken cisterns that cannot hold water.
14Is Israel a servant, a slave by birth?
Why then has he become plunder?
15Lions have roared;
they have growled at him.
They have laid waste his land;
his towns are burned and deserted.
16Also, the men of Memphis[e] and Tahpanhes
have shaved the crown of your head.[f]
17Have you not brought this on yourselves
by forsaking the LORD your God
when he led you in the way?
18Now why go to Egypt
to drink water from the Shihor[g]?
And why go to Assyria
to drink water from the River[h]?
19Your wickedness will punish you;
your backsliding will rebuke you.
Consider then and realize
how evil and bitter it is for you
when you forsake the LORD your God
and have no awe of me,"
declares the Lord,
the LORD Almighty.

20"Long ago you broke off your yoke
and tore off your bonds;
you said, 'I will not serve you!'
Indeed, on every high hill
and under every spreading tree
you lay down as a prostitute.
21I had planted you like a choice vine
of sound and reliable stock.
How then did you turn against me
into a corrupt, wild vine?
22Although you wash yourself with soda
and use an abundance of soap,
the stain of your guilt is still before me,"
declares the Sovereign LORD.
23"How can you say, 'I am not defiled;
I have not run after the Baals'?
See how you behaved in the valley;
consider what you have done.
You are a swift she-camel
running here and there,
24a wild donkey accustomed to the desert,
sniffing the wind in her craving—
in her heat who can restrain her?
Any males that pursue her need not tire themselves;
at mating time they will find her.
25Do not run until your feet are bare
and your throat is dry.
But you said, 'It's no use!
I love foreign gods,
and I must go after them.'

26"As a thief is disgraced when he is caught,
so the house of Israel is disgraced—
they, their kings and their officials,
their priests and their prophets.
27They say to wood, 'You are my father,'
and to stone, 'You gave me birth.'
They have turned their backs to me
and not their faces;
yet when they are in trouble, they say,
'Come and save us!'
28Where then are the gods you made for yourselves?
Let them come if they can save you
when you are in trouble!
For you have as many gods
as you have towns, O Judah.

29"Why do you bring charges against me?
You have all rebelled against me,"
declares the LORD.
30"In vain I punished your people;
they did not respond to correction.
Your sword has devoured your prophets
like a ravening lion.

[a]6 Or *and the shadow of death* [b]10 That is, Cyprus and western coastlands [c]10 The home of Bedouin tribes in the Syro-Arabian desert [d]11 Masoretic Text; an ancient Hebrew scribal tradition *my* [e]16 Hebrew *Noph* [f]16 Or *have cracked your skull* [g]18 That is, a branch of the Nile [h]18 That is, the Euphrates

31“You of this generation, consider the word
of the LORD:

“Have I been a desert to Israel
or a land of great darkness?
Why do my people say, ‘We are free to
roam;
we will come to you no more’?
32Does a maiden forget her jewelry,
a bride her wedding ornaments?
Yet my people have forgotten me,
days without number.
33How skilled you are at pursuing love!
Even the worst of women can learn
from your ways.
34On your clothes men find
the lifeblood of the innocent poor,
though you did not catch them breaking
in.
Yet in spite of all this
35 you say, ‘I am innocent;
he is not angry with me.’
But I will pass judgment on you
because you say, ‘I have not sinned.’
36Why do you go about so much,
changing your ways?
You will be disappointed by Egypt
as you were by Assyria.
37You will also leave that place
with your hands on your head,
for the LORD has rejected those you trust;
you will not be helped by them.

3 “If a man divorces his wife
and she leaves him and marries another
man,
should he return to her again?
Would not the land be completely
defiled?
But you have lived as a prostitute with
many lovers—
would you now return to me?”
declares the LORD.
2“Look up to the barren heights and see.
Is there any place where you have not
been ravished?
By the roadside you sat waiting for lovers,
sat like a nomad[a] in the desert.
You have defiled the land
with your prostitution and wickedness.
3Therefore the showers have been withheld,
and no spring rains have fallen.
Yet you have the brazen look of a
prostitute;
you refuse to blush with shame.
4Have you not just called to me:
‘My Father, my friend from my youth,
5will you always be angry?
Will your wrath continue forever?’
This is how you talk,
but you do all the evil you can.”

Unfaithful Israel

6During the reign of King Josiah, the LORD
said to me, “Have you seen what faithless Israel has done? She has gone up on every high
hill and under every spreading tree and has
committed adultery there. 7I thought that after
she had done all this she would return to me
but she did not, and her unfaithful sister Judah
saw it. 8I gave faithless Israel her certificate of
divorce and sent her away because of all her
adulteries. Yet I saw that her unfaithful sister
Judah had no fear; she also went out and committed adultery. 9Because Israel's immorality
mattered so little to her, she defiled the land
and committed adultery with stone and wood.
10In spite of all this, her unfaithful sister Judah
did not return to me with all her heart, but only
in pretense,” declares the LORD.
11The LORD said to me, “Faithless Israel is
more righteous than unfaithful Judah. 12Go,
proclaim this message toward the north:

“ ‘Return, faithless Israel,’ declares the
LORD,
‘I will frown on you no longer,
for I am merciful,’ declares the LORD,
‘I will not be angry forever.
13Only acknowledge your guilt—
you have rebelled against the LORD
your God,
you have scattered your favors to foreign
gods
under every spreading tree,
and have not obeyed me,’ ”
declares the LORD.

14“Return, faithless people,” declares the
LORD, “for I am your husband. I will choose
you—one from a town and two from a clan—
and bring you to Zion. 15Then I will give you
shepherds after my own heart, who will lead
you with knowledge and understanding. 16In
those days, when your numbers have increased
greatly in the land,” declares the LORD, “men
will no longer say, ‘The ark of the covenant of
the LORD.’ It will never enter their minds or be
remembered; it will not be missed, nor will
another one be made. 17At that time they will
call Jerusalem The Throne of the LORD, and all
nations will gather in Jerusalem to honor the
name of the LORD. No longer will they follow
the stubbornness of their evil hearts. 18In those
days the house of Judah will join the house of
Israel, and together they will come from a
northern land to the land I gave your forefathers as an inheritance.
19“I myself said,

“ ‘How gladly would I treat you like sons
and give you a desirable land,
the most beautiful inheritance of any
nation.’
I thought you would call me ‘Father’
and not turn away from following me.
20But like a woman unfaithful to her
husband,
so you have been unfaithful to me,
O house of Israel,”
declares the LORD.

21A cry is heard on the barren heights,

[a]2 Or *an Arab*

the weeping and pleading of the people
of Israel,
because they have perverted their ways
and have forgotten the LORD their God.

22"Return, faithless people;
I will cure you of backsliding."

"Yes, we will come to you,
for you are the LORD our God.
23Surely the ⌊idolatrous⌋ commotion on the
hills
and mountains is a deception;
surely in the LORD our God
is the salvation of Israel.
24From our youth shameful gods have
consumed
the fruits of our fathers' labor—
their flocks and herds,
their sons and daughters.
25Let us lie down in our shame,
and let our disgrace cover us.
We have sinned against the LORD our
God,
both we and our fathers;
from our youth till this day
we have not obeyed the LORD our
God."

4 "If you will return, O Israel,
return to me,"
declares the LORD.
"If you put your detestable idols out of
my sight
and no longer go astray,
2and if in a truthful, just and righteous way
you swear, 'As surely as the LORD
lives,'
then the nations will be blessed by him
and in him they will glory."

3This is what the LORD says to the men of
Judah and to Jerusalem:

"Break up your unplowed ground
and do not sow among thorns.
4Circumcise yourselves to the LORD,
circumcise your hearts,
you men of Judah and people of
Jerusalem,
or my wrath will break out and burn like
fire
because of the evil you have done—
burn with no one to quench it.

Disaster From the North

5"Announce in Judah and proclaim in
Jerusalem and say:
'Sound the trumpet throughout the
land!'
Cry aloud and say:
'Gather together!
Let us flee to the fortified cities!'
6Raise the signal to go to Zion!
Flee for safety without delay!
For I am bringing disaster from the north,
even terrible destruction."

7A lion has come out of his lair;
a destroyer of nations has set out.
He has left his place
to lay waste your land.
Your towns will lie in ruins
without inhabitant.
8So put on sackcloth,
lament and wail,
for the fierce anger of the LORD
has not turned away from us.

9"In that day," declares the LORD,
"the king and the officials will lose
heart,
the priests will be horrified,
and the prophets will be appalled."

10Then I said, "Ah, Sovereign LORD, how
completely you have deceived this people and
Jerusalem by saying, 'You will have peace,'
when the sword is at our throats."
11At that time this people and Jerusalem will
be told, "A scorching wind from the barren
heights in the desert blows toward my people,
but not to winnow or cleanse; 12a wind too
strong for that comes from me.[a] Now I pronounce my judgments against them."

13Look! He advances like the clouds,
his chariots come like a whirlwind,
his horses are swifter than eagles.
Woe to us! We are ruined!
14O Jerusalem, wash the evil from your
heart and be saved.
How long will you harbor wicked
thoughts?
15A voice is announcing from Dan,
proclaiming disaster from the hills of
Ephraim.
16"Tell this to the nations,
proclaim it to Jerusalem:
'A besieging army is coming from a
distant land,
raising a war cry against the cities of
Judah.
17They surround her like men guarding a
field,
because she has rebelled against me,' "
declares the LORD.
18"Your own conduct and actions
have brought this upon you.
This is your punishment.
How bitter it is!
How it pierces to the heart!"

19Oh, my anguish, my anguish!
I writhe in pain.
Oh, the agony of my heart!
My heart pounds within me,
I cannot keep silent.
For I have heard the sound of the trumpet;
I have heard the battle cry.
20Disaster follows disaster;
the whole land lies in ruins.
In an instant my tents are destroyed,
my shelter in a moment.

[a]12 Or *comes at my command*

21How long must I see the battle standard
and hear the sound of the trumpet?

22"My people are fools;
they do not know me.
They are senseless children;
they have no understanding.
They are skilled in doing evil;
they know not how to do good."

23I looked at the earth,
and it was formless and empty;
and at the heavens,
and their light was gone.
24I looked at the mountains,
and they were quaking;
all the hills were swaying.
25I looked, and there were no people;
every bird in the sky had flown away.
26I looked, and the fruitful land was a desert;
all its towns lay in ruins
before the LORD, before his fierce anger.

27This is what the LORD says:

"The whole land will be ruined,
though I will not destroy it completely.
28Therefore the earth will mourn
and the heavens above grow dark,
because I have spoken and will not relent,
I have decided and will not turn back."

29At the sound of horsemen and archers
every town takes to flight.
Some go into the thickets;
some climb up among the rocks.
All the towns are deserted;
no one lives in them.

30What are you doing, O devastated one?
Why dress yourself in scarlet
and put on jewels of gold?
Why shade your eyes with paint?
You adorn yourself in vain.
Your lovers despise you;
they seek your life.

31I hear a cry as of a woman in labor,
a groan as of one bearing her first child—
the cry of the Daughter of Zion gasping for breath,
stretching out her hands and saying,
"Alas! I am fainting;
my life is given over to murderers."

Not One Is Upright

5 "Go up and down the streets of Jerusalem,
look around and consider,
search through her squares.
If you can find but one person
who deals honestly and seeks the truth,
I will forgive this city.
2Although they say, 'As surely as the LORD lives,'
still they are swearing falsely."

3O LORD, do not your eyes look for truth?
You struck them, but they felt no pain;
you crushed them, but they refused correction.
They made their faces harder than stone
and refused to repent.
4I thought, "These are only the poor;
they are foolish,
for they do not know the way of the LORD,
the requirements of their God.
5So I will go to the leaders
and speak to them;
surely they know the way of the LORD,
the requirements of their God."
But with one accord they too had broken off the yoke
and torn off the bonds.
6Therefore a lion from the forest will attack them,
a wolf from the desert will ravage them,
a leopard will lie in wait near their towns
to tear to pieces any who venture out,
for their rebellion is great
and their backslidings many.

7"Why should I forgive you?
Your children have forsaken me
and sworn by gods that are not gods.
I supplied all their needs,
yet they committed adultery
and thronged to the houses of prostitutes.
8They are well-fed, lusty stallions,
each neighing for another man's wife.
9Should I not punish them for this?"
declares the LORD.
"Should I not avenge myself
on such a nation as this?

10"Go through her vineyards and ravage them,
but do not destroy them completely.
Strip off her branches,
for these people do not belong to the LORD.
11The house of Israel and the house of Judah
have been utterly unfaithful to me,"
declares the LORD.

12They have lied about the LORD;
they said, "He will do nothing!
No harm will come to us;
we will never see sword or famine.
13The prophets are but wind
and the word is not in them;
so let what they say be done to them."

14Therefore this is what the LORD God Almighty says:

"Because the people have spoken these words,
I will make my words in your mouth a fire
and these people the wood it consumes.
15O house of Israel," declares the LORD,
"I am bringing a distant nation against you—

an ancient and enduring nation,
a people whose language you do not know,
whose speech you do not understand.
16Their quivers are like an open grave;
all of them are mighty warriors.
17They will devour your harvests and food,
devour your sons and daughters;
they will devour your flocks and herds,
devour your vines and fig trees.
With the sword they will destroy
the fortified cities in which you trust.

18"Yet even in those days," declares the
LORD, "I will not destroy you completely.
19And when the people ask, 'Why has the
LORD our God done all this to us?' you will tell
them, 'As you have forsaken me and served
foreign gods in your own land, so now you will
serve foreigners in a land not your own.'

20"Announce this to the house of Jacob
and proclaim it in Judah:
21Hear this, you foolish and senseless people,
who have eyes but do not see,
who have ears but do not hear:
22Should you not fear me?" declares the LORD.
"Should you not tremble in my presence?
I made the sand a boundary for the sea,
an everlasting barrier it cannot cross.
The waves may roll, but they cannot prevail;
they may roar, but they cannot cross it.
23But these people have stubborn and rebellious hearts;
they have turned aside and gone away.
24They do not say to themselves,
'Let us fear the LORD our God,
who gives autumn and spring rains in season,
who assures us of the regular weeks of harvest.'
25Your wrongdoings have kept these away;
your sins have deprived you of good.

26"Among my people are wicked men
who lie in wait like men who snare birds
and like those who set traps to catch men.
27Like cages full of birds,
their houses are full of deceit;
they have become rich and powerful
28 and have grown fat and sleek.
Their evil deeds have no limit;
they do not plead the case of the fatherless to win it,
they do not defend the rights of the poor.
29Should I not punish them for this?"
declares the LORD.
"Should I not avenge myself
on such a nation as this?

30"A horrible and shocking thing
has happened in the land:
31The prophets prophesy lies,
the priests rule by their own authority,
and my people love it this way.
But what will you do in the end?

Jerusalem Under Siege

6 "Flee for safety, people of Benjamin!
Flee from Jerusalem!
Sound the trumpet in Tekoa!
Raise the signal over Beth Hakkerem!
For disaster looms out of the north,
even terrible destruction.
2I will destroy the Daughter of Zion,
so beautiful and delicate.
3Shepherds with their flocks will come against her;
they will pitch their tents around her,
each tending his own portion."

4"Prepare for battle against her!
Arise, let us attack at noon!
But, alas, the daylight is fading,
and the shadows of evening grow long.
5So arise, let us attack at night
and destroy her fortresses!"

6This is what the LORD Almighty says:

"Cut down the trees
and build siege ramps against Jerusalem.
This city must be punished;
it is filled with oppression.
7As a well pours out its water,
so she pours out her wickedness.
Violence and destruction resound in her;
her sickness and wounds are ever before me.
8Take warning, O Jerusalem,
or I will turn away from you
and make your land desolate
so no one can live in it."

9This is what the LORD Almighty says:

"Let them glean the remnant of Israel
as thoroughly as a vine;
pass your hand over the branches again,
like one gathering grapes."

10To whom can I speak and give warning?
Who will listen to me?
Their ears are closed[a]
so they cannot hear.
The word of the LORD is offensive to them;
they find no pleasure in it.
11But I am full of the wrath of the LORD,
and I cannot hold it in.

"Pour it out on the children in the street
and on the young men gathered together;
both husband and wife will be caught in it,
and the old, those weighed down with years.

[a]10 Hebrew *uncircumcised*

[12]Their houses will be turned over to others,
together with their fields and their wives,
when I stretch out my hand
against those who live in the land,"
declares the LORD.
[13]"From the least to the greatest,
all are greedy for gain;
prophets and priests alike,
all practice deceit.
[14]They dress the wound of my people
as though it were not serious.
'Peace, peace,' they say,
when there is no peace.
[15]Are they ashamed of their loathsome conduct?
No, they have no shame at all;
they do not even know how to blush.
So they will fall among the fallen;
they will be brought down when I punish them,"
says the LORD.

[16]This is what the LORD says:

"Stand at the crossroads and look;
ask for the ancient paths,
ask where the good way is, and walk in it,
and you will find rest for your souls.
But you said, 'We will not walk in it.'
[17]I appointed watchmen over you and said,
'Listen to the sound of the trumpet!'
But you said, 'We will not listen.'
[18]Therefore hear, O nations;
observe, O witnesses,
what will happen to them.
[19]Hear, O earth:
I am bringing disaster on this people,
the fruit of their schemes,
because they have not listened to my words
and have rejected my law.
[20]What do I care about incense from Sheba
or sweet calamus from a distant land?
Your burnt offerings are not acceptable;
your sacrifices do not please me."

[21]Therefore this is what the LORD says:

"I will put obstacles before this people.
Fathers and sons alike will stumble over them;
neighbors and friends will perish."

[22]This is what the LORD says:

"Look, an army is coming
from the land of the north;
a great nation is being stirred up
from the ends of the earth.
[23]They are armed with bow and spear;
they are cruel and show no mercy.
They sound like the roaring sea
as they ride on their horses;
they come like men in battle formation
to attack you, O Daughter of Zion."

[24]We have heard reports about them,
and our hands hang limp.
Anguish has gripped us,
pain like that of a woman in labor.
[25]Do not go out to the fields
or walk on the roads,
for the enemy has a sword,
and there is terror on every side.
[26]O my people, put on sackcloth
and roll in ashes;
mourn with bitter wailing
as for an only son,
for suddenly the destroyer
will come upon us.

[27]"I have made you a tester of metals
and my people the ore,
that you may observe
and test their ways.
[28]They are all hardened rebels,
going about to slander.
They are bronze and iron;
they all act corruptly.
[29]The bellows blow fiercely
to burn away the lead with fire,
but the refining goes on in vain;
the wicked are not purged out.
[30]They are called rejected silver,
because the LORD has rejected them."

False Religion Worthless

7 This is the word that came to Jeremiah
from the LORD: [2]"Stand at the gate of the
LORD's house and there proclaim this message:

" 'Hear the word of the LORD, all you people
of Judah who come through these gates to worship the LORD. [3]This is what the LORD Almighty, the God of Israel, says: Reform your
ways and your actions, and I will let you live
in this place. [4]Do not trust in deceptive words
and say, "This is the temple of the LORD, the
temple of the LORD, the temple of the LORD!"
[5]If you really change your ways and your actions and deal with each other justly, [6]if you do
not oppress the alien, the fatherless or the widow and do not shed innocent blood in this
place, and if you do not follow other gods to
your own harm, [7]then I will let you live in this
place, in the land I gave your forefathers for
ever and ever. [8]But look, you are trusting in
deceptive words that are worthless.

[9]" 'Will you steal and murder, commit adultery and perjury,[a] burn incense to Baal and
follow other gods you have not known, [10]and
then come and stand before me in this house,
which bears my Name, and say, "We are
safe"—safe to do all these detestable things?
[11]Has this house, which bears my Name, become a den of robbers to you? But I have been
watching! declares the LORD.

[12]" 'Go now to the place in Shiloh where I
first made a dwelling for my Name, and see
what I did to it because of the wickedness of
my people Israel. [13]While you were doing all
these things, declares the LORD, I spoke to you
again and again, but you did not listen; I called

[a]9 Or *and swear by false gods*

you, but you did not answer. 14Therefore, what
I did to Shiloh I will now do to the house that
bears my Name, the temple you trust in, the
place I gave to you and your fathers. 15I will
thrust you from my presence, just as I did all
your brothers, the people of Ephraim.'

16"So do not pray for this people nor offer
any plea or petition for them; do not plead with
me, for I will not listen to you. 17Do you not
see what they are doing in the towns of Judah
and in the streets of Jerusalem? 18The children
gather wood, the fathers light the fire, and the
women knead the dough and make cakes of
bread for the Queen of Heaven. They pour out
drink offerings to other gods to provoke me to
anger. 19But am I the one they are provoking?
declares the LORD. Are they not rather harming
themselves, to their own shame?

20" 'Therefore this is what the Sovereign
LORD says: My anger and my wrath will be
poured out on this place, on man and beast, on
the trees of the field and on the fruit of the
ground, and it will burn and not be quenched.

21" 'This is what the LORD Almighty, the
God of Israel, says: Go ahead, add your burnt
offerings to your other sacrifices and eat the
meat yourselves! 22For when I brought your
forefathers out of Egypt and spoke to them, I
did not just give them commands about burnt
offerings and sacrifices, 23but I gave them this
command: Obey me, and I will be your God
and you will be my people. Walk in all the
ways I command you, that it may go well with
you. 24But they did not listen or pay attention;
instead, they followed the stubborn inclina-
tions of their evil hearts. They went backward
and not forward. 25From the time your forefathers left Egypt until now, day after day, again
and again I sent you my servants the prophets.
26But they did not listen to me or pay attention.
They were stiff-necked and did more evil than
their forefathers.'

27"When you tell them all this, they will not
listen to you; when you call to them, they will
not answer. 28Therefore say to them, 'This is
the nation that has not obeyed the LORD its
God or responded to correction. Truth has perished; it has vanished from their lips. 29Cut off
your hair and throw it away; take up a lament
on the barren heights, for the LORD has rejected and abandoned this generation that is under
his wrath.

The Valley of Slaughter

30" 'The people of Judah have done evil in
my eyes, declares the LORD. They have set up
their detestable idols in the house that bears
my Name and have defiled it. 31They have
built the high places of Topheth in the Valley
of Ben Hinnom to burn their sons and daughters in the fire—something I did not command,
nor did it enter my mind. 32So beware, the days
are coming, declares the LORD, when people
will no longer call it Topheth or the Valley of
Ben Hinnom, but the Valley of Slaughter, for
they will bury the dead in Topheth until there
is no more room. 33Then the carcasses of this
people will become food for the birds of the air
and the beasts of the earth, and there will be no
one to frighten them away. 34I will bring an
end to the sounds of joy and gladness and to
the voices of bride and bridegroom in the
towns of Judah and the streets of Jerusalem,
for the land will become desolate.

8 " 'At that time, declares the LORD, the
bones of the kings and officials of Judah,
the bones of the priests and prophets, and the
bones of the people of Jerusalem will be removed from their graves. 2They will be exposed to the sun and the moon and all the stars
of the heavens, which they have loved and
served and which they have followed and consulted and worshiped. They will not be gathered up or buried, but will be like refuse lying
on the ground. 3Wherever I banish them, all
the survivors of this evil nation will prefer
death to life, declares the LORD Almighty.'

Sin and Punishment

4"Say to them, 'This is what the LORD says:

" 'When men fall down, do they not get
up?
When a man turns away, does he not
return?
5Why then have these people turned away?
Why does Jerusalem always turn away?
They cling to deceit;
they refuse to return.
6I have listened attentively,
but they do not say what is right.
No one repents of his wickedness,
saying, "What have I done?"
Each pursues his own course
like a horse charging into battle.
7Even the stork in the sky
knows her appointed seasons,
and the dove, the swift and the thrush
observe the time of their migration.
But my people do not know
the requirements of the LORD.

8" 'How can you say, "We are wise,
for we have the law of the LORD,"
when actually the lying pen of the scribes
has handled it falsely?
9The wise will be put to shame;
they will be dismayed and trapped.
Since they have rejected the word of the
LORD,
what kind of wisdom do they have?
10Therefore I will give their wives to other
men
and their fields to new owners.
From the least to the greatest,
all are greedy for gain;
prophets and priests alike,
all practice deceit.
11They dress the wound of my people
as though it were not serious.
"Peace, peace," they say,
when there is no peace.
12Are they ashamed of their loathsome
conduct?
No, they have no shame at all;

they do not even know how to blush.
So they will fall among the fallen;
they will be brought down when they are punished,
says the LORD.

13" 'I will take away their harvest,
declares the LORD.
There will be no grapes on the vine.
There will be no figs on the tree,
and their leaves will wither.
What I have given them
will be taken from them.[a]' "

14"Why are we sitting here?
Gather together!
Let us flee to the fortified cities
and perish there!
For the LORD our God has doomed us to perish
and given us poisoned water to drink,
because we have sinned against him.
15We hoped for peace
but no good has come,
for a time of healing
but there was only terror.
16The snorting of the enemy's horses
is heard from Dan;
at the neighing of their stallions
the whole land trembles.
They have come to devour
the land and everything in it,
the city and all who live there."

17"See, I will send venomous snakes among you,
vipers that cannot be charmed,
and they will bite you,"
declares the LORD.

18O my Comforter[b] in sorrow,
my heart is faint within me.
19Listen to the cry of my people
from a land far away:
"Is the LORD not in Zion?
Is her King no longer there?"

"Why have they provoked me to anger
with their images,
with their worthless foreign idols?"

20"The harvest is past,
the summer has ended,
and we are not saved."

21Since my people are crushed, I am crushed;
I mourn, and horror grips me.
22Is there no balm in Gilead?
Is there no physician there?
Why then is there no healing
for the wound of my people?

9 1Oh, that my head were a spring of water
and my eyes a fountain of tears!
I would weep day and night
for the slain of my people.
2Oh, that I had in the desert
a lodging place for travelers,
so that I might leave my people
and go away from them;
for they are all adulterers,
a crowd of unfaithful people.

3"They make ready their tongue
like a bow, to shoot lies;
it is not by truth
that they triumph[c] in the land.
They go from one sin to another;
they do not acknowledge me,"
declares the LORD.
4"Beware of your friends;
do not trust your brothers.
For every brother is a deceiver,[d]
and every friend a slanderer.
5Friend deceives friend,
and no one speaks the truth.
They have taught their tongues to lie;
they weary themselves with sinning.
6You[e] live in the midst of deception;
in their deceit they refuse to acknowledge me,"
declares the LORD.

7Therefore this is what the LORD Almighty says:

"See, I will refine and test them,
for what else can I do
because of the sin of my people?
8Their tongue is a deadly arrow;
it speaks with deceit.
With his mouth each speaks cordially to his neighbor,
but in his heart he sets a trap for him.
9Should I not punish them for this?"
declares the LORD.
"Should I not avenge myself
on such a nation as this?"

10I will weep and wail for the mountains
and take up a lament concerning the desert pastures.
They are desolate and untraveled,
and the lowing of cattle is not heard.
The birds of the air have fled
and the animals are gone.

11"I will make Jerusalem a heap of ruins,
a haunt of jackals;
and I will lay waste the towns of Judah
so no one can live there."

12What man is wise enough to understand
this? Who has been instructed by the LORD and
can explain it? Why has the land been ruined
and laid waste like a desert that no one can
cross?
13The LORD said, "It is because they have
forsaken my law, which I set before them; they
have not obeyed me or followed my law. 14In-
stead, they have followed the stubbornness of
their hearts; they have followed the Baals, as

[a]13 The meaning of the Hebrew for this sentence is uncertain. [b]18 The meaning of the Hebrew for this word is uncertain. [c]3 Or *lies; / they are not valiant for truth* [d]4 Or *a deceiving Jacob* [e]6 That is, Jeremiah (the Hebrew is singular)

their fathers taught them." 15Therefore, this is
what the LORD Almighty, the God of Israel,
says: "See, I will make this people eat bitter
food and drink poisoned water. 16I will scatter
them among nations that neither they nor their
fathers have known, and I will pursue them
with the sword until I have destroyed them."

17This is what the LORD Almighty says:

"Consider now! Call for the wailing
women to come;
send for the most skillful of them.
18Let them come quickly
and wail over us
till our eyes overflow with tears
and water streams from our eyelids.
19The sound of wailing is heard from Zion:
'How ruined we are!
How great is our shame!
We must leave our land
because our houses are in ruins.' "

20Now, O women, hear the word of the
LORD;
open your ears to the words of his
mouth.
Teach your daughters how to wail;
teach one another a lament.
21Death has climbed in through our
windows
and has entered our fortresses;
it has cut off the children from the streets
and the young men from the public
squares.

22Say, "This is what the LORD declares:

" 'The dead bodies of men will lie
like refuse on the open field,
like cut grain behind the reaper,
with no one to gather them.' "

23This is what the LORD says:

"Let not the wise man boast of his
wisdom
or the strong man boast of his strength
or the rich man boast of his riches,
24but let him who boasts boast about this:
that he understands and knows me,
that I am the LORD, who exercises
kindness,
justice and righteousness on earth,
for in these I delight,"
declares the LORD.

25"The days are coming," declares the
LORD, "when I will punish all who are circumcised only in the flesh— 26Egypt, Judah,
Edom, Ammon, Moab and all who live in the
desert in distant places.[a] For all these nations
are really uncircumcised, and even the whole
house of Israel is uncircumcised in heart."

God and Idols

10 Hear what the LORD says to you,
O house of Israel. 2This is what the
LORD says:

"Do not learn the ways of the nations
or be terrified by signs in the sky,
though the nations are terrified by them.
3For the customs of the peoples are
worthless;
they cut a tree out of the forest,
and a craftsman shapes it with his
chisel.
4They adorn it with silver and gold;
they fasten it with hammer and nails
so it will not totter.
5Like a scarecrow in a melon patch,
their idols cannot speak;
they must be carried
because they cannot walk.
Do not fear them;
they can do no harm
nor can they do any good."

6No one is like you, O LORD;
you are great,
and your name is mighty in power.
7Who should not revere you,
O King of the nations?
This is your due.
Among all the wise men of the nations
and in all their kingdoms,
there is no one like you.
8They are all senseless and foolish;
they are taught by worthless wooden
idols.
9Hammered silver is brought from Tarshish
and gold from Uphaz.
What the craftsman and goldsmith have
made
is then dressed in blue and purple—
all made by skilled workers.
10But the LORD is the true God;
he is the living God, the eternal King.
When he is angry, the earth trembles;
the nations cannot endure his wrath.

11"Tell them this: 'These gods, who did not
make the heavens and the earth, will perish
from the earth and from under the heavens.' "[b]

12But God made the earth by his power;
he founded the world by his wisdom
and stretched out the heavens by his
understanding.
13When he thunders, the waters in the
heavens roar;
he makes clouds rise from the ends of
the earth.
He sends lightning with the rain
and brings out the wind from his
storehouses.

14Everyone is senseless and without
knowledge;
every goldsmith is shamed by his idols.
His images are a fraud;
they have no breath in them.
15They are worthless, the objects of
mockery;
when their judgment comes, they will
perish.

[a]26 Or *desert and who clip the hair by their foreheads*
[b]11 The text of this verse is in Aramaic.

16He who is the Portion of Jacob is not like
these,
for he is the Maker of all things,
including Israel, the tribe of his
inheritance—
the LORD Almighty is his name.

Coming Destruction

17Gather up your belongings to leave the
land,
you who live under siege.
18For this is what the LORD says:
"At this time I will hurl out
those who live in this land;
I will bring distress on them
so that they may be captured."

19Woe to me because of my injury!
My wound is incurable!
Yet I said to myself,
"This is my sickness, and I must endure
it."
20My tent is destroyed;
all its ropes are snapped.
My sons are gone from me and are no
more;
no one is left now to pitch my tent
or to set up my shelter.
21The shepherds are senseless
and do not inquire of the LORD;
so they do not prosper
and all their flock is scattered.
22Listen! The report is coming—
a great commotion from the land of the
north!
It will make the towns of Judah desolate,
a haunt of jackals.

Jeremiah's Prayer

23I know, O LORD, that a man's life is not
his own;
it is not for man to direct his steps.
24Correct me, LORD, but only with justice—
not in your anger,
lest you reduce me to nothing.
25Pour out your wrath on the nations
that do not acknowledge you,
on the peoples who do not call on your
name.
For they have devoured Jacob;
they have devoured him completely
and destroyed his homeland.

The Covenant Is Broken

11 This is the word that came to Jeremiah
from the LORD: 2"Listen to the terms of
this covenant and tell them to the people of
Judah and to those who live in Jerusalem. 3Tell
them that this is what the LORD, the God of
Israel, says: 'Cursed is the man who does not
obey the terms of this covenant— 4the terms I
commanded your forefathers when I brought
them out of Egypt, out of the iron-smelting
furnace.' I said, 'Obey me and do everything I
command you, and you will be my people, and
I will be your God. 5Then I will fulfill the oath
I swore to your forefathers, to give them a land
flowing with milk and honey'—the land you
possess today."

I answered, "Amen, LORD."

6The LORD said to me, "Proclaim all these
words in the towns of Judah and in the streets
of Jerusalem: 'Listen to the terms of this covenant and follow them. 7From the time I
brought your forefathers up from Egypt until
today, I warned them again and again, saying,
"Obey me." 8But they did not listen or pay
attention; instead, they followed the stubbornness of their evil hearts. So I brought on them
all the curses of the covenant I had commanded them to follow but that they did not keep.' "

9Then the LORD said to me, "There is a conspiracy among the people of Judah and those
who live in Jerusalem. 10They have returned to
the sins of their forefathers, who refused to
listen to my words. They have followed other
gods to serve them. Both the house of Israel
and the house of Judah have broken the covenant I made with their forefathers. 11There-
fore this is what the LORD says: 'I will bring on
them a disaster they cannot escape. Although
they cry out to me, I will not listen to them.
12The towns of Judah and the people of Jerusalem will go and cry out to the gods to whom
they burn incense, but they will not help them
at all when disaster strikes. 13You have as
many gods as you have towns, O Judah; and
the altars you have set up to burn incense to
that shameful god Baal are as many as the
streets of Jerusalem.'

14"Do not pray for this people nor offer any
plea or petition for them, because I will not
listen when they call to me in the time of their
distress.

15"What is my beloved doing in my temple
as she works out her evil schemes with
many?
Can consecrated meat avert ⌊your
punishment⌋?
When you engage in your wickedness,
then you rejoice.[a]"

16The LORD called you a thriving olive tree
with fruit beautiful in form.
But with the roar of a mighty storm
he will set it on fire,
and its branches will be broken.

17The LORD Almighty, who planted you, has
decreed disaster for you, because the house of
Israel and the house of Judah have done evil
and provoked me to anger by burning incense
to Baal.

Plot Against Jeremiah

18Because the LORD revealed their plot to
me, I knew it, for at that time he showed me
what they were doing. 19I had been like a gentle lamb led to the slaughter; I did not realize
that they had plotted against me, saying,

"Let us destroy the tree and its fruit;

[a]*15* Or *Could consecrated meat avert your punishment? / Then you would rejoice*

let us cut him off from the land of the living,
that his name be remembered no more."
20But, O LORD Almighty, you who judge righteously
and test the heart and mind,
let me see your vengeance upon them,
for to you I have committed my cause.

21"Therefore this is what the LORD says
about the men of Anathoth who are seeking
your life and saying, 'Do not prophesy in the
name of the LORD or you will die by our
hands'— 22therefore this is what the LORD Almighty says: 'I will punish them. Their young
men will die by the sword, their sons and
daughters by famine. 23Not even a remnant
will be left to them, because I will bring disaster on the men of Anathoth in the year of their
punishment.' "

Jeremiah's Complaint

12 You are always righteous, O LORD,
when I bring a case before you.
Yet I would speak with you about your justice:
Why does the way of the wicked prosper?
Why do all the faithless live at ease?
2You have planted them, and they have taken root;
they grow and bear fruit.
You are always on their lips
but far from their hearts.
3Yet you know me, O LORD;
you see me and test my thoughts about you.
Drag them off like sheep to be butchered!
Set them apart for the day of slaughter!
4How long will the land lie parched[a]
and the grass in every field be withered?
Because those who live in it are wicked,
the animals and birds have perished.
Moreover, the people are saying,
"He will not see what happens to us."

God's Answer

5"If you have raced with men on foot
and they have worn you out,
how can you compete with horses?
If you stumble in safe country,[b]
how will you manage in the thickets by[c] the Jordan?
6Your brothers, your own family—
even they have betrayed you;
they have raised a loud cry against you.
Do not trust them,
though they speak well of you.

7"I will forsake my house,
abandon my inheritance;
I will give the one I love
into the hands of her enemies.
8My inheritance has become to me
like a lion in the forest.
She roars at me;
therefore I hate her.
9Has not my inheritance become to me
like a speckled bird of prey
that other birds of prey surround and attack?
Go and gather all the wild beasts;
bring them to devour.
10Many shepherds will ruin my vineyard
and trample down my field;
they will turn my pleasant field
into a desolate wasteland.
11It will be made a wasteland,
parched and desolate before me;
the whole land will be laid waste
because there is no one who cares.
12Over all the barren heights in the desert
destroyers will swarm,
for the sword of the LORD will devour
from one end of the land to the other;
no one will be safe.
13They will sow wheat but reap thorns;
they will wear themselves out but gain nothing.
So bear the shame of your harvest
because of the LORD's fierce anger."

14This is what the LORD says: "As for all my
wicked neighbors who seize the inheritance I
gave my people Israel, I will uproot them from
their lands and I will uproot the house of Judah
from among them. 15But after I uproot them, I
will again have compassion and will bring
each of them back to his own inheritance and
his own country. 16And if they learn well the
ways of my people and swear by my name,
saying, 'As surely as the LORD lives'—even
as they once taught my people to swear by
Baal—then they will be established among my
people. 17But if any nation does not listen, I
will completely uproot and destroy it," declares the LORD.

A Linen Belt

13 This is what the LORD said to me: "Go
and buy a linen belt and put it around
your waist, but do not let it touch water." 2So
I bought a belt, as the LORD directed, and put
it around my waist.

3Then the word of the LORD came to me a
second time: 4"Take the belt you bought and
are wearing around your waist, and go now to
Perath[d] and hide it there in a crevice in the
rocks." 5So I went and hid it at Perath, as the
LORD told me.

6Many days later the LORD said to me, "Go
now to Perath and get the belt I told you to
hide there." 7So I went to Perath and dug up
the belt and took it from the place where I had
hidden it, but now it was ruined and completely useless.

8Then the word of the LORD came to me:
9"This is what the LORD says: 'In the same
way I will ruin the pride of Judah and the great
pride of Jerusalem. 10These wicked people,

[a]4 Or *land mourn* [b]5 Or *If you put your trust in a land of safety* [c]5 Or *the flooding of* [d]4 Or possibly *the Euphrates*; also in verses 5-7

who refuse to listen to my words, who follow
the stubbornness of their hearts and go after
other gods to serve and worship them, will be
like this belt—completely useless! 11For as a
belt is bound around a man's waist, so I bound
the whole house of Israel and the whole house
of Judah to me,' declares the LORD, 'to be my
people for my renown and praise and honor.
But they have not listened.'

Wineskins

12"Say to them: 'This is what the LORD, the
God of Israel, says: Every wineskin should be
filled with wine.' And if they say to you,
'Don't we know that every wineskin should be
filled with wine?' 13then tell them, 'This is
what the LORD says: I am going to fill with
drunkenness all who live in this land, including
the kings who sit on David's throne, the
priests, the prophets and all those living in Jerusalem. 14I will smash them one against the
other, fathers and sons alike, declares the
LORD. I will allow no pity or mercy or compassion to keep me from destroying them.' "

Threat of Captivity

15Hear and pay attention,
do not be arrogant,
for the LORD has spoken.
16Give glory to the LORD your God
before he brings the darkness,
before your feet stumble
on the darkening hills.
You hope for light,
but he will turn it to thick darkness
and change it to deep gloom.
17But if you do not listen,
I will weep in secret
because of your pride;
my eyes will weep bitterly,
overflowing with tears,
because the LORD's flock will be taken
captive.

18Say to the king and to the queen mother,
"Come down from your thrones,
for your glorious crowns
will fall from your heads."
19The cities in the Negev will be shut up,
and there will be no one to open them.
All Judah will be carried into exile,
carried completely away.

20Lift up your eyes and see
those who are coming from the north.
Where is the flock that was entrusted to
you,
the sheep of which you boasted?
21What will you say when ⌊the LORD⌋ sets
over you
those you cultivated as your special
allies?
Will not pain grip you
like that of a woman in labor?
22And if you ask yourself,
"Why has this happened to me?"—
it is because of your many sins
that your skirts have been torn off
and your body mistreated.
23Can the Ethiopian[a] change his skin
or the leopard its spots?
Neither can you do good
who are accustomed to doing evil.

24"I will scatter you like chaff
driven by the desert wind.
25This is your lot,
the portion I have decreed for you,"
declares the LORD,
"because you have forgotten me
and trusted in false gods.
26I will pull up your skirts over your face
that your shame may be seen—
27your adulteries and lustful neighings,
your shameless prostitution!
I have seen your detestable acts
on the hills and in the fields.
Woe to you, O Jerusalem!
How long will you be unclean?"

Drought, Famine, Sword

14 This is the word of the LORD to Jeremiah concerning the drought:

2"Judah mourns,
her cities languish;
they wail for the land,
and a cry goes up from Jerusalem.
3The nobles send their servants for water;
they go to the cisterns
but find no water.
They return with their jars unfilled;
dismayed and despairing,
they cover their heads.
4The ground is cracked
because there is no rain in the land;
the farmers are dismayed
and cover their heads.
5Even the doe in the field
deserts her newborn fawn
because there is no grass.
6Wild donkeys stand on the barren heights
and pant like jackals;
their eyesight fails
for lack of pasture."

7Although our sins testify against us,
O LORD, do something for the sake of
your name.
For our backsliding is great;
we have sinned against you.
8O Hope of Israel,
its Savior in times of distress,
why are you like a stranger in the land,
like a traveler who stays only a night?
9Why are you like a man taken by surprise,
like a warrior powerless to save?
You are among us, O LORD,
and we bear your name;
do not forsake us!

10This is what the LORD says about this people:

[a]23 Hebrew *Cushite* (probably a person from the upper Nile region)

"They greatly love to wander;
they do not restrain their feet.
So the LORD does not accept them;
he will now remember their wickedness
and punish them for their sins."

11 Then the LORD said to me, "Do not pray
for the well-being of this people. 12 Although
they fast, I will not listen to their cry; though
they offer burnt offerings and grain offerings,
I will not accept them. Instead, I will destroy
them with the sword, famine and plague."

13 But I said, "Ah, Sovereign LORD, the
prophets keep telling them, 'You will not see
the sword or suffer famine. Indeed, I will give
you lasting peace in this place.' "

14 Then the LORD said to me, "The prophets
are prophesying lies in my name. I have not
sent them or appointed them or spoken to
them. They are prophesying to you false visions, divinations, idolatries[a] and the delusions of their own minds. 15 Therefore, this is
what the LORD says about the prophets who
are prophesying in my name: I did not send
them, yet they are saying, 'No sword or famine
will touch this land.' Those same prophets will
perish by sword and famine. 16 And the people
they are prophesying to will be thrown out into
the streets of Jerusalem because of the famine
and sword. There will be no one to bury them
or their wives, their sons or their daughters. I
will pour out on them the calamity they deserve.

17 "Speak this word to them:

" 'Let my eyes overflow with tears
night and day without ceasing;
for my virgin daughter—my people—
has suffered a grievous wound,
a crushing blow.
18 If I go into the country,
I see those slain by the sword;
if I go into the city,
I see the ravages of famine.
Both prophet and priest
have gone to a land they know not.' "

19 Have you rejected Judah completely?
Do you despise Zion?
Why have you afflicted us
so that we cannot be healed?
We hoped for peace
but no good has come,
for a time of healing
but there is only terror.
20 O LORD, we acknowledge our wickedness
and the guilt of our fathers;
we have indeed sinned against you.
21 For the sake of your name do not despise
us;
do not dishonor your glorious throne.
Remember your covenant with us
and do not break it.
22 Do any of the worthless idols of the
nations bring rain?
Do the skies themselves send down
showers?
No, it is you, O LORD our God.
Therefore our hope is in you,
for you are the one who does all this.

15 Then the LORD said to me: "Even if
Moses and Samuel were to stand before
me, my heart would not go out to this people.
Send them away from my presence! Let them
go! 2 And if they ask you, 'Where shall we go?'
tell them, 'This is what the LORD says:

" 'Those destined for death, to death;
those for the sword, to the sword;
those for starvation, to starvation;
those for captivity, to captivity.'

3 "I will send four kinds of destroyers against
them," declares the LORD, "the sword to kill
and the dogs to drag away and the birds of the
air and the beasts of the earth to devour and
destroy. 4 I will make them abhorrent to all the
kingdoms of the earth because of what Manasseh son of Hezekiah king of Judah did in Jerusalem.

5 "Who will have pity on you, O Jerusalem?
Who will mourn for you?
Who will stop to ask how you are?
6 You have rejected me," declares the
LORD.
"You keep on backsliding.
So I will lay hands on you and destroy
you;
I can no longer show compassion.
7 I will winnow them with a winnowing
fork
at the city gates of the land.
I will bring bereavement and destruction
on my people,
for they have not changed their ways.
8 I will make their widows more numerous
than the sand of the sea.
At midday I will bring a destroyer
against the mothers of their young men;
suddenly I will bring down on them
anguish and terror.
9 The mother of seven will grow faint
and breathe her last.
Her sun will set while it is still day;
she will be disgraced and humiliated.
I will put the survivors to the sword
before their enemies,"
declares the LORD.

10 Alas, my mother, that you gave me birth,
a man with whom the whole land
strives and contends!
I have neither lent nor borrowed,
yet everyone curses me.

11 The LORD said,

"Surely I will deliver you for a good
purpose;
surely I will make your enemies plead
with you

[a] 14 Or *visions, worthless divinations*

in times of disaster and times of
distress.

12"Can a man break iron—
iron from the north—or bronze?
13Your wealth and your treasures
I will give as plunder, without charge,
because of all your sins
throughout your country.
14I will enslave you to your enemies
in[a] a land you do not know,
for my anger will kindle a fire
that will burn against you."

15You understand, O LORD;
remember me and care for me.
Avenge me on my persecutors.
You are long-suffering—do not take me
away;
think of how I suffer reproach for your
sake.
16When your words came, I ate them;
they were my joy and my heart's
delight,
for I bear your name,
O LORD God Almighty.
17I never sat in the company of revelers,
never made merry with them;
I sat alone because your hand was on me
and you had filled me with indignation.
18Why is my pain unending
and my wound grievous and incurable?
Will you be to me like a deceptive brook,
like a spring that fails?

19Therefore this is what the LORD says:

"If you repent, I will restore you
that you may serve me;
if you utter worthy, not worthless, words,
you will be my spokesman.
Let this people turn to you,
but you must not turn to them.
20I will make you a wall to this people,
a fortified wall of bronze;
they will fight against you
but will not overcome you,
for I am with you
to rescue and save you,"
declares the LORD.
21"I will save you from the hands of the
wicked
and redeem you from the grasp of the
cruel."

Day of Disaster

16 Then the word of the LORD came to me:
2"You must not marry and have sons or
daughters in this place." 3For this is what the
LORD says about the sons and daughters born
in this land and about the women who are their
mothers and the men who are their fathers:
4"They will die of deadly diseases. They will
not be mourned or buried but will be like refuse lying on the ground. They will perish by
sword and famine, and their dead bodies will
become food for the birds of the air and the
beasts of the earth."
5For this is what the LORD says: "Do not
enter a house where there is a funeral meal; do
not go to mourn or show sympathy, because I
have withdrawn my blessing, my love and my
pity from this people," declares the LORD.
6"Both high and low will die in this land. They
will not be buried or mourned, and no one will
cut himself or shave his head for them. 7No
one will offer food to comfort those who
mourn for the dead—not even for a father or a
mother—nor will anyone give them a drink to
console them.
8"And do not enter a house where there is
feasting and sit down to eat and drink. 9For this
is what the LORD Almighty, the God of Israel,
says: Before your eyes and in your days I will
bring an end to the sounds of joy and gladness
and to the voices of bride and bridegroom in
this place.
10"When you tell these people all this and
they ask you, 'Why has the LORD decreed such
a great disaster against us? What wrong have
we done? What sin have we committed against
the LORD our God?' 11then say to them, 'It is
because your fathers forsook me,' declares the
LORD, 'and followed other gods and served
and worshiped them. They forsook me and did
not keep my law. 12But you have behaved
more wickedly than your fathers. See how
each of you is following the stubbornness of
his evil heart instead of obeying me. 13So I will
throw you out of this land into a land neither
you nor your fathers have known, and there
you will serve other gods day and night, for I
will show you no favor.'
14"However, the days are coming," declares
the LORD, "when men will no longer say, 'As
surely as the LORD lives, who brought the Israelites up out of Egypt,' 15but they will say, 'As
surely as the LORD lives, who brought the Israelites up out of the land of the north and out of
all the countries where he had banished them.'
For I will restore them to the land I gave their
forefathers.
16"But now I will send for many fishermen,"
declares the LORD, "and they will catch them.
After that I will send for many hunters, and
they will hunt them down on every mountain
and hill and from the crevices of the rocks.
17My eyes are on all their ways; they are not
hidden from me, nor is their sin concealed
from my eyes. 18I will repay them double for
their wickedness and their sin, because they
have defiled my land with the lifeless forms of
their vile images and have filled my inheritance with their detestable idols."

19O LORD, my strength and my fortress,
my refuge in time of distress,
to you the nations will come
from the ends of the earth and say,
"Our fathers possessed nothing but false
gods,

[a]14 Some Hebrew manuscripts, Septuagint and Syriac (see also Jer. 17:4); most Hebrew manuscripts *I will cause your enemies to bring you / into*

worthless idols that did them no good.
20 Do men make their own gods?
Yes, but they are not gods!"

21 "Therefore I will teach them—
this time I will teach them
my power and might.
Then they will know
that my name is the LORD.

17 "Judah's sin is engraved with an iron tool,
inscribed with a flint point,
on the tablets of their hearts
and on the horns of their altars.
2 Even their children remember
their altars and Asherah poles[a]
beside the spreading trees
and on the high hills.
3 My mountain in the land
and your[b] wealth and all your treasures
I will give away as plunder,
together with your high places,
because of sin throughout your country.
4 Through your own fault you will lose
the inheritance I gave you.
I will enslave you to your enemies
in a land you do not know,
for you have kindled my anger,
and it will burn forever."

5 This is what the LORD says:

"Cursed is the one who trusts in man,
who depends on flesh for his strength
and whose heart turns away from the LORD.
6 He will be like a bush in the wastelands;
he will not see prosperity when it comes.
He will dwell in the parched places of the desert,
in a salt land where no one lives.

7 "But blessed is the man who trusts in the LORD,
whose confidence is in him.
8 He will be like a tree planted by the water
that sends out its roots by the stream.
It does not fear when heat comes;
its leaves are always green.
It has no worries in a year of drought
and never fails to bear fruit."

9 The heart is deceitful above all things
and beyond cure.
Who can understand it?

10 "I the LORD search the heart
and examine the mind,
to reward a man according to his conduct,
according to what his deeds deserve."

11 Like a partridge that hatches eggs it did not lay
is the man who gains riches by unjust means.
When his life is half gone, they will desert him,
and in the end he will prove to be a fool.

12 A glorious throne, exalted from the beginning,
is the place of our sanctuary.
13 O LORD, the hope of Israel,
all who forsake you will be put to shame.
Those who turn away from you will be written in the dust
because they have forsaken the LORD,
the spring of living water.

14 Heal me, O LORD, and I will be healed;
save me and I will be saved,
for you are the one I praise.
15 They keep saying to me,
"Where is the word of the LORD?
Let it now be fulfilled!"
16 I have not run away from being your shepherd;
you know I have not desired the day of despair.
What passes my lips is open before you.
17 Do not be a terror to me;
you are my refuge in the day of disaster.
18 Let my persecutors be put to shame,
but keep me from shame;
let them be terrified,
but keep me from terror.
Bring on them the day of disaster;
destroy them with double destruction.

Keeping the Sabbath Holy

19 This is what the LORD said to me: "Go and
stand at the gate of the people, through which
the kings of Judah go in and out; stand also at
all the other gates of Jerusalem. 20 Say to them,
'Hear the word of the LORD, O kings of Judah
and all people of Judah and everyone living
in Jerusalem who come through these gates.
21 This is what the LORD says: Be careful not to
carry a load on the Sabbath day or bring it
through the gates of Jerusalem. 22 Do not bring
a load out of your houses or do any work on
the Sabbath, but keep the Sabbath day holy, as
I commanded your forefathers. 23 Yet they did
not listen or pay attention; they were stiff-
necked and would not listen or respond to discipline. 24 But if you are careful to obey me,
declares the LORD, and bring no load through
the gates of this city on the Sabbath, but keep
the Sabbath day holy by not doing any work on
it, 25 then kings who sit on David's throne will
come through the gates of this city with their
officials. They and their officials will come
riding in chariots and on horses, accompanied
by the men of Judah and those living in Jerusalem, and this city will be inhabited forever.
26 People will come from the towns of Judah
and the villages around Jerusalem, from the
territory of Benjamin and the western foothills,
from the hill country and the Negev, bringing
burnt offerings and sacrifices, grain offerings,

[a] 2 That is, symbols of the goddess Asherah [b] *2,3* Or *hills / 3 and the mountains of the land. / Your*

incense and thank offerings to the house of the
LORD. 27But if you do not obey me to keep the
Sabbath day holy by not carrying any load as
you come through the gates of Jerusalem on
the Sabbath day, then I will kindle an unquenchable fire in the gates of Jerusalem that
will consume her fortresses.' "

At the Potter's House

18 This is the word that came to Jeremiah
from the LORD: 2"Go down to the potter's house, and there I will give you my message." 3So I went down to the potter's house,
and I saw him working at the wheel. 4But the
pot he was shaping from the clay was marred
in his hands; so the potter formed it into another pot, shaping it as seemed best to him.
5Then the word of the LORD came to me:
6"O house of Israel, can I not do with you as
this potter does?" declares the LORD. "Like
clay in the hand of the potter, so are you in my
hand, O house of Israel. 7If at any time I announce that a nation or kingdom is to be uprooted, torn down and destroyed, 8and if that
nation I warned repents of its evil, then I will
relent and not inflict on it the disaster I had
planned. 9And if at another time I announce
that a nation or kingdom is to be built up and
planted, 10and if it does evil in my sight and
does not obey me, then I will reconsider the
good I had intended to do for it.
11"Now therefore say to the people of Judah
and those living in Jerusalem, 'This is what the
LORD says: Look! I am preparing a disaster for
you and devising a plan against you. So turn
from your evil ways, each one of you, and
reform your ways and your actions.' 12But
they will reply, 'It's no use. We will continue
with our own plans; each of us will follow the
stubbornness of his evil heart.' "

13Therefore this is what the LORD says:

"Inquire among the nations:
  Who has ever heard anything like this?
A most horrible thing has been done
  by Virgin Israel.
14Does the snow of Lebanon
  ever vanish from its rocky slopes?
Do its cool waters from distant sources
  ever cease to flow?[a]
15Yet my people have forgotten me;
  they burn incense to worthless idols,
which made them stumble in their ways
  and in the ancient paths.
They made them walk in bypaths
  and on roads not built up.
16Their land will be laid waste,
  an object of lasting scorn;
all who pass by will be appalled
  and will shake their heads.
17Like a wind from the east,
  I will scatter them before their enemies;
I will show them my back and not my
    face
  in the day of their disaster."

18They said, "Come, let's make plans
against Jeremiah; for the teaching of the law
by the priest will not be lost, nor will counsel
from the wise, nor the word from the prophets.
So come, let's attack him with our tongues and
pay no attention to anything he says."

19Listen to me, O LORD;
  hear what my accusers are saying!
20Should good be repaid with evil?
  Yet they have dug a pit for me.
Remember that I stood before you
  and spoke in their behalf
  to turn your wrath away from them.
21So give their children over to famine;
  hand them over to the power of the
    sword.
Let their wives be made childless and
    widows;
  let their men be put to death,
  their young men slain by the sword in
    battle.
22Let a cry be heard from their houses
  when you suddenly bring invaders
    against them,
for they have dug a pit to capture me
  and have hidden snares for my feet.
23But you know, O LORD,
  all their plots to kill me.
Do not forgive their crimes
  or blot out their sins from your sight.
Let them be overthrown before you;
  deal with them in the time of your
    anger.

19 This is what the LORD says: "Go and
buy a clay jar from a potter. Take along
some of the elders of the people and of the
priests 2and go out to the Valley of Ben Hinnom, near the entrance of the Potsherd Gate.
There proclaim the words I tell you, 3and say,
'Hear the word of the LORD, O kings of Judah
and people of Jerusalem. This is what the
LORD Almighty, the God of Israel, says: Listen! I am going to bring a disaster on this place
that will make the ears of everyone who hears
of it tingle. 4For they have forsaken me and
made this a place of foreign gods; they have
burned sacrifices in it to gods that neither they
nor their fathers nor the kings of Judah ever
knew, and they have filled this place with the
blood of the innocent. 5They have built the
high places of Baal to burn their sons in
the fire as offerings to Baal—something I did
not command or mention, nor did it enter my
mind. 6So beware, the days are coming, declares the LORD, when people will no longer
call this place Topheth or the Valley of Ben
Hinnom, but the Valley of Slaughter.
7" 'In this place I will ruin[b] the plans of
Judah and Jerusalem. I will make them fall by

[a] *14* The meaning of the Hebrew for this sentence is uncertain. [b] *7* The Hebrew for *ruin* sounds like the Hebrew for *jar* (see verses 1 and 10).

the sword before their enemies, at the hands of
those who seek their lives, and I will give their
carcasses as food to the birds of the air and the
beasts of the earth. 8I will devastate this city
and make it an object of scorn; all who pass by
will be appalled and will scoff because of all
its wounds. 9I will make them eat the flesh of
their sons and daughters, and they will eat one
another's flesh during the stress of the siege
imposed on them by the enemies who seek
their lives.'

10"Then break the jar while those who go
with you are watching, 11and say to them,
'This is what the LORD Almighty says: I will
smash this nation and this city just as this potter's jar is smashed and cannot be repaired.
They will bury the dead in Topheth until there
is no more room. 12This is what I will do to
this place and to those who live here, declares
the LORD. I will make this city like Topheth.
13The houses in Jerusalem and those of the
kings of Judah will be defiled like this place,
Topheth—all the houses where they burned
incense on the roofs to all the starry hosts and
poured out drink offerings to other gods.' "

14Jeremiah then returned from Topheth,
where the LORD had sent him to prophesy, and
stood in the court of the LORD's temple and
said to all the people, 15"This is what the LORD
Almighty, the God of Israel, says: 'Listen! I
am going to bring on this city and the villages
around it every disaster I pronounced against
them, because they were stiff-necked and
would not listen to my words.' "

Jeremiah and Pashhur

20 When the priest Pashhur son of Immer,
the chief officer in the temple of the
LORD, heard Jeremiah prophesying these
things, 2he had Jeremiah the prophet beaten
and put in the stocks at the Upper Gate of
Benjamin at the LORD's temple. 3The next day,
when Pashhur released him from the stocks,
Jeremiah said to him, "The LORD's name for
you is not Pashhur, but Magor-Missabib.[a]
4For this is what the LORD says: 'I will make
you a terror to yourself and to all your friends;
with your own eyes you will see them fall by
the sword of their enemies. I will hand all Judah over to the king of Babylon, who will carry them away to Babylon or put them to the
sword. 5I will hand over to their enemies all
the wealth of this city—all its products, all its
valuables and all the treasures of the kings of
Judah. They will take it away as plunder and
carry it off to Babylon. 6And you, Pashhur, and
all who live in your house will go into exile to
Babylon. There you will die and be buried, you
and all your friends to whom you have prophesied lies.' "

Jeremiah's Complaint

7O LORD, you deceived[b] me, and I was
deceived[b];
you overpowered me and prevailed.
I am ridiculed all day long;
everyone mocks me.
8Whenever I speak, I cry out
proclaiming violence and destruction.
So the word of the LORD has brought me
insult and reproach all day long.
9But if I say, "I will not mention him
or speak any more in his name,"
his word is in my heart like a fire,
a fire shut up in my bones.
I am weary of holding it in;
indeed, I cannot.
10I hear many whispering,
"Terror on every side!
Report him! Let's report him!"
All my friends
are waiting for me to slip, saying,
"Perhaps he will be deceived;
then we will prevail over him
and take our revenge on him."

11But the LORD is with me like a mighty
warrior;
so my persecutors will stumble and not
prevail.
They will fail and be thoroughly
disgraced;
their dishonor will never be forgotten.
12O LORD Almighty, you who examine the
righteous
and probe the heart and mind,
let me see your vengeance upon them,
for to you I have committed my cause.

13Sing to the LORD!
Give praise to the LORD!
He rescues the life of the needy
from the hands of the wicked.

14Cursed be the day I was born!
May the day my mother bore me not be
blessed!
15Cursed be the man who brought my father
the news,
who made him very glad, saying,
"A child is born to you—a son!"
16May that man be like the towns
the LORD overthrew without pity.
May he hear wailing in the morning,
a battle cry at noon.
17For he did not kill me in the womb,
with my mother as my grave,
her womb enlarged forever.
18Why did I ever come out of the womb
to see trouble and sorrow
and to end my days in shame?

God Rejects Zedekiah's Request

21 The word came to Jeremiah from the
LORD when King Zedekiah sent to him
Pashhur son of Malkijah and the priest Zephaniah son of Maaseiah. They said: 2"Inquire
now of the LORD for us because Nebuchadnezzar[c] king of Babylon is attacking us. Perhaps
the LORD will perform wonders for us as in
times past so that he will withdraw from us."

[a]3 *Magor-Missabib* means *terror on every side.* [b]7 Or *persuaded* [c]2 Hebrew *Nebuchadrezzar,* of which *Nebuchadnezzar* is a variant; here and often in Jeremiah and Ezekiel

3But Jeremiah answered them, "Tell Zedekiah, 4'This is what the LORD, the God of Israel,
says: I am about to turn against you the weapons of war that are in your hands, which you
are using to fight the king of Babylon and the
Babylonians[a] who are outside the wall besieging you. And I will gather them inside this city.
5I myself will fight against you with an outstretched hand and a mighty arm in anger and
fury and great wrath. 6I will strike down those
who live in this city—both men and animals—
and they will die of a terrible plague. 7After
that, declares the LORD, I will hand over Zedekiah king of Judah, his officials and the people
in this city who survive the plague, sword and
famine, to Nebuchadnezzar king of Babylon
and to their enemies who seek their lives. He
will put them to the sword; he will show them
no mercy or pity or compassion.'

8"Furthermore, tell the people, 'This is what
the LORD says: See, I am setting before you the
way of life and the way of death. 9Whoever
stays in this city will die by the sword, famine
or plague. But whoever goes out and surrenders to the Babylonians who are besieging you
will live; he will escape with his life. 10I have
determined to do this city harm and not good,
declares the LORD. It will be given into the
hands of the king of Babylon, and he will destroy it with fire.'

11"Moreover, say to the royal house of Judah, 'Hear the word of the LORD; 12O house of
David, this is what the LORD says:

" 'Administer justice every morning;
rescue from the hand of his oppressor
the one who has been robbed,
or my wrath will break out and burn like
fire
because of the evil you have done—
burn with no one to quench it.
13I am against you, ⌊Jerusalem,⌋
you who live above this valley
on the rocky plateau,
declares the LORD—
you who say, "Who can come against us?
Who can enter our refuge?"
14I will punish you as your deeds deserve,
declares the LORD.
I will kindle a fire in your forests
that will consume everything around
you.' "

Judgment Against Evil Kings

22 This is what the LORD says: "Go down
to the palace of the king of Judah and
proclaim this message there: 2'Hear the word
of the LORD, O king of Judah, you who sit on
David's throne—you, your officials and your
people who come through these gates. 3This is
what the LORD says: Do what is just and right.
Rescue from the hand of his oppressor the one
who has been robbed. Do no wrong or violence
to the alien, the fatherless or the widow, and do
not shed innocent blood in this place. 4For if
you are careful to carry out these commands,
then kings who sit on David's throne will
come through the gates of this palace, riding in
chariots and on horses, accompanied by their
officials and their people. 5But if you do not
obey these commands, declares the LORD, I
swear by myself that this palace will become a
ruin.' "

6For this is what the LORD says about the
palace of the king of Judah:

"Though you are like Gilead to me,
like the summit of Lebanon,
I will surely make you like a desert,
like towns not inhabited.
7I will send destroyers against you,
each man with his weapons,
and they will cut up your fine cedar
beams
and throw them into the fire.

8"People from many nations will pass by
this city and will ask one another, 'Why has
the LORD done such a thing to this great city?'
9And the answer will be: 'Because they have
forsaken the covenant of the LORD their God
and have worshiped and served other gods.' "

10Do not weep for the dead ⌊king⌋ or mourn
his loss;
rather, weep bitterly for him who is
exiled,
because he will never return
nor see his native land again.

11For this is what the LORD says about Shallum[b] son of Josiah, who succeeded his father
as king of Judah but has gone from this place:
"He will never return. 12He will die in the
place where they have led him captive; he will
not see this land again."

13"Woe to him who builds his palace by
unrighteousness,
his upper rooms by injustice,
making his countrymen work for nothing,
not paying them for their labor.
14He says, 'I will build myself a great
palace
with spacious upper rooms.'
So he makes large windows in it,
panels it with cedar
and decorates it in red.

15"Does it make you a king
to have more and more cedar?
Did not your father have food and drink?
He did what was right and just,
so all went well with him.
16He defended the cause of the poor and
needy,
and so all went well.
Is that not what it means to know me?"
declares the LORD.
17"But your eyes and your heart
are set only on dishonest gain,
on shedding innocent blood
and on oppression and extortion."

[a]4 Or *Chaldeans*; also in verse 9 [b]11 Also called *Jehoahaz*

18 Therefore this is what the LORD says about
Jehoiakim son of Josiah king of Judah:

“They will not mourn for him:
‘Alas, my brother! Alas, my sister!’
They will not mourn for him:
‘Alas, my master! Alas, his splendor!’
19 He will have the burial of a donkey—
dragged away and thrown
outside the gates of Jerusalem.”

20 “Go up to Lebanon and cry out,
let your voice be heard in Bashan,
cry out from Abarim,
for all your allies are crushed.
21 I warned you when you felt secure,
but you said, ‘I will not listen!’
This has been your way from your youth;
you have not obeyed me.
22 The wind will drive all your shepherds
away,
and your allies will go into exile.
Then you will be ashamed and disgraced
because of all your wickedness.
23 You who live in ‘Lebanon,[a]’
who are nestled in cedar buildings,
how you will groan when pangs come
upon you,
pain like that of a woman in labor!

24 “As surely as I live,” declares the LORD,
“even if you, Jehoiachin[b] son of Jehoiakim
king of Judah, were a signet ring on my right
hand, I would still pull you off. 25 I will hand
you over to those who seek your life, those you
fear—to Nebuchadnezzar king of Babylon and
to the Babylonians.[c] 26 I will hurl you and the
mother who gave you birth into another country, where neither of you was born, and there
you both will die. 27 You will never come back
to the land you long to return to.”

28 Is this man Jehoiachin a despised, broken
pot,
an object no one wants?
Why will he and his children be hurled
out,
cast into a land they do not know?
29 O land, land, land,
hear the word of the LORD!
30 This is what the LORD says:
“Record this man as if childless,
a man who will not prosper in his
lifetime,
for none of his offspring will prosper,
none will sit on the throne of David
or rule anymore in Judah.”

The Righteous Branch

23 “Woe to the shepherds who are destroying and scattering the sheep of my pasture!” declares the LORD. 2 Therefore this is
what the LORD, the God of Israel, says to the
shepherds who tend my people: “Because you
have scattered my flock and driven them away
and have not bestowed care on them, I will
bestow punishment on you for the evil you
have done,” declares the LORD. 3 “I myself will
gather the remnant of my flock out of all the
countries where I have driven them and will
bring them back to their pasture, where they
will be fruitful and increase in number. 4 I will
place shepherds over them who will tend them,
and they will no longer be afraid or terrified,
nor will any be missing,” declares the LORD.

5 “The days are coming,” declares the
LORD,
“when I will raise up to David[d] a
righteous Branch,
a King who will reign wisely
and do what is just and right in the
land.
6 In his days Judah will be saved
and Israel will live in safety.
This is the name by which he will be
called:
The LORD Our Righteousness.

7 “So then, the days are coming,” declares the
LORD, “when people will no longer say, ‘As
surely as the LORD lives, who brought the Israelites up out of Egypt,’ 8 but they will say, ‘As
surely as the LORD lives, who brought the
descendants of Israel up out of the land of the
north and out of all the countries where he had
banished them.’ Then they will live in their
own land.”

Lying Prophets

9 Concerning the prophets:

My heart is broken within me;
all my bones tremble.
I am like a drunken man,
like a man overcome by wine,
because of the LORD
and his holy words.
10 The land is full of adulterers;
because of the curse[e] the land lies
parched[f]
and the pastures in the desert are
withered.
The ⌞prophets⌟ follow an evil course
and use their power unjustly.

11 “Both prophet and priest are godless;
even in my temple I find their
wickedness,”
declares the LORD.
12 “Therefore their path will become
slippery;
they will be banished to darkness
and there they will fall.
I will bring disaster on them
in the year they are punished,”
declares the LORD.

13 “Among the prophets of Samaria
I saw this repulsive thing:
They prophesied by Baal

[a] *23* That is, the palace in Jerusalem (see 1 Kings 7:2) [b] *24* Hebrew *Coniah,* a variant of *Jehoiachin*; also in verse 28 [c] *25* Or *Chaldeans* [d] *5* Or *up from David's line* [e] *10* Or *because of these things* [f] *10* Or *land mourns*

and led my people Israel astray.
14And among the prophets of Jerusalem
I have seen something horrible:
They commit adultery and live a lie.
They strengthen the hands of evildoers,
so that no one turns from his
wickedness.
They are all like Sodom to me;
the people of Jerusalem are like
Gomorrah."

15Therefore, this is what the LORD Almighty says concerning the prophets:

"I will make them eat bitter food
and drink poisoned water,
because from the prophets of Jerusalem
ungodliness has spread throughout the
land."

16This is what the LORD Almighty says:

"Do not listen to what the prophets are
prophesying to you;
they fill you with false hopes.
They speak visions from their own minds,
not from the mouth of the LORD.
17They keep saying to those who despise
me,
'The LORD says: You will have peace.'
And to all who follow the stubbornness of
their hearts
they say, 'No harm will come to you.'
18But which of them has stood in the
council of the LORD
to see or to hear his word?
Who has listened and heard his word?
19See, the storm of the LORD
will burst out in wrath,
a whirlwind swirling down
on the heads of the wicked.
20The anger of the LORD will not turn back
until he fully accomplishes
the purposes of his heart.
In days to come
you will understand it clearly.
21I did not send these prophets,
yet they have run with their message;
I did not speak to them,
yet they have prophesied.
22But if they had stood in my council,
they would have proclaimed my words
to my people
and would have turned them from their
evil ways
and from their evil deeds.

23"Am I only a God nearby,"
declares the LORD,
"and not a God far away?
24Can anyone hide in secret places
so that I cannot see him?"
declares the LORD.
"Do not I fill heaven and earth?"
declares the LORD.

25"I have heard what the prophets say who
prophesy lies in my name. They say, 'I had a
dream! I had a dream!' 26How long will this
continue in the hearts of these lying prophets,
who prophesy the delusions of their own
minds? 27They think the dreams they tell one
another will make my people forget my name,
just as their fathers forgot my name through
Baal worship. 28Let the prophet who has a
dream tell his dream, but let the one who has
my word speak it faithfully. For what has straw
to do with grain?" declares the LORD. 29"Is not
my word like fire," declares the LORD, "and
like a hammer that breaks a rock in pieces?

30"Therefore," declares the LORD, "I am
against the prophets who steal from one another words supposedly from me. 31Yes," declares
the LORD, "I am against the prophets who wag
their own tongues and yet declare, 'The LORD
declares.' 32Indeed, I am against those who
prophesy false dreams," declares the LORD.
"They tell them and lead my people astray
with their reckless lies, yet I did not send or
appoint them. They do not benefit these people
in the least," declares the LORD.

False Oracles and False Prophets

33"When these people, or a prophet or a
priest, ask you, 'What is the oracle[a] of the
LORD?' say to them, 'What oracle?[b] I will forsake you, declares the LORD.' 34If a prophet or
a priest or anyone else claims, 'This is the
oracle of the LORD,' I will punish that man and
his household. 35This is what each of you
keeps on saying to his friend or relative: 'What
is the LORD's answer?' or 'What has the LORD
spoken?' 36But you must not mention 'the oracle of the LORD' again, because every man's
own word becomes his oracle and so you distort the words of the living God, the LORD
Almighty, our God. 37This is what you keep
saying to a prophet: 'What is the LORD's answer to you?' or 'What has the LORD spoken?'
38Although you claim, 'This is the oracle of
the LORD,' this is what the LORD says: You
used the words, 'This is the oracle of the
LORD,' even though I told you that you must
not claim, 'This is the oracle of the LORD.'
39Therefore, I will surely forget you and cast
you out of my presence along with the city I
gave to you and your fathers. 40I will bring
upon you everlasting disgrace—everlasting
shame that will not be forgotten."

Two Baskets of Figs

24 After Jehoiachin[c] son of Jehoiakim
king of Judah and the officials, the
craftsmen and the artisans of Judah were carried into exile from Jerusalem to Babylon by
Nebuchadnezzar king of Babylon, the LORD
showed me two baskets of figs placed in front
of the temple of the LORD. 2One basket had
very good figs, like those that ripen early; the
other basket had very poor figs, so bad they
could not be eaten.

[a]*33* Or *burden* (see Septuagint and Vulgate) [b]*33* Hebrew; Septuagint and Vulgate *'You are the burden.* (The Hebrew for *oracle* and *burden* is the same.) [c]*1* Hebrew *Jeconiah,* a variant of *Jehoiachin*

3Then the LORD asked me, "What do you see, Jeremiah?"

"Figs," I answered. "The good ones are very good, but the poor ones are so bad they cannot be eaten."

4Then the word of the LORD came to me: 5"This is what the LORD, the God of Israel, says: 'Like these good figs, I regard as good the exiles from Judah, whom I sent away from this place to the land of the Babylonians.[a] 6My eyes will watch over them for their good, and I will bring them back to this land. I will build them up and not tear them down; I will plant them and not uproot them. 7I will give them a heart to know me, that I am the LORD. They will be my people, and I will be their God, for they will return to me with all their heart.

8" 'But like the poor figs, which are so bad they cannot be eaten,' says the LORD, 'so will I deal with Zedekiah king of Judah, his officials and the survivors from Jerusalem, whether they remain in this land or live in Egypt. 9I will make them abhorrent and an offense to all the kingdoms of the earth, a reproach and a byword, an object of ridicule and cursing, wherever I banish them. 10I will send the sword, famine and plague against them until they are destroyed from the land I gave to them and their fathers.' "

Seventy Years of Captivity

25 The word came to Jeremiah concerning all the people of Judah in the fourth year of Jehoiakim son of Josiah king of Judah, which was the first year of Nebuchadnezzar king of Babylon. 2So Jeremiah the prophet said to all the people of Judah and to all those living in Jerusalem: 3For twenty-three years—from the thirteenth year of Josiah son of Amon king of Judah until this very day—the word of the LORD has come to me and I have spoken to you again and again, but you have not listened.

4And though the LORD has sent all his servants the prophets to you again and again, you have not listened or paid any attention. 5They said, "Turn now, each of you, from your evil ways and your evil practices, and you can stay in the land the LORD gave to you and your fathers for ever and ever. 6Do not follow other gods to serve and worship them; do not provoke me to anger with what your hands have made. Then I will not harm you."

7"But you did not listen to me," declares the LORD, "and you have provoked me with what your hands have made, and you have brought harm to yourselves."

8Therefore the LORD Almighty says this: "Because you have not listened to my words, 9I will summon all the peoples of the north and my servant Nebuchadnezzar king of Babylon," declares the LORD, "and I will bring them against this land and its inhabitants and against all the surrounding nations. I will completely destroy[b] them and make them an object of horror and scorn, and an everlasting ruin. 10I will banish from them the sounds of joy and gladness, the voices of bride and bridegroom, the sound of millstones and the light of the lamp. 11This whole country will become a desolate wasteland, and these nations will serve the king of Babylon seventy years.

12"But when the seventy years are fulfilled, I will punish the king of Babylon and his nation, the land of the Babylonians,[a] for their guilt," declares the LORD, "and will make it desolate forever. 13I will bring upon that land all the things I have spoken against it, all that are written in this book and prophesied by Jeremiah against all the nations. 14They themselves will be enslaved by many nations and great kings; I will repay them according to their deeds and the work of their hands."

The Cup of God's Wrath

15This is what the LORD, the God of Israel, said to me: "Take from my hand this cup filled with the wine of my wrath and make all the nations to whom I send you drink it. 16When they drink it, they will stagger and go mad because of the sword I will send among them."

17So I took the cup from the LORD's hand and made all the nations to whom he sent me drink it: 18Jerusalem and the towns of Judah, its kings and officials, to make them a ruin and an object of horror and scorn and cursing, as they are today; 19Pharaoh king of Egypt, his attendants, his officials and all his people, 20and all the foreign people there; all the kings of Uz; all the kings of the Philistines (those of Ashkelon, Gaza, Ekron, and the people left at Ashdod); 21Edom, Moab and Ammon; 22all the kings of Tyre and Sidon; the kings of the coastlands across the sea; 23Dedan, Tema, Buz and all who are in distant places[c]; 24all the kings of Arabia and all the kings of the foreign people who live in the desert; 25all the kings of Zimri, Elam and Media; 26and all the kings of the north, near and far, one after the other—all the kingdoms on the face of the earth. And after all of them, the king of Sheshach[d] will drink it too.

27"Then tell them, 'This is what the LORD Almighty, the God of Israel, says: Drink, get drunk and vomit, and fall to rise no more because of the sword I will send among you.' 28But if they refuse to take the cup from your hand and drink, tell them, 'This is what the LORD Almighty says: You must drink it! 29See, I am beginning to bring disaster on the city that bears my Name, and will you indeed go unpunished? You will not go unpunished, for I am calling down a sword upon all who live on the earth, declares the LORD Almighty.'

30"Now prophesy all these words against them and say to them:

" 'The LORD will roar from on high;

[a]5,12 Or *Chaldeans* [b]9 The Hebrew term refers to the irrevocable giving over of things or persons to the LORD, often by totally destroying them. [c]23 Or *who clip the hair by their foreheads* [d]26 *Sheshach* is a cryptogram for Babylon.

he will thunder from his holy dwelling
and roar mightily against his land.
He will shout like those who tread the grapes,
shout against all who live on the earth.
31The tumult will resound to the ends of the earth,
for the LORD will bring charges against the nations;
he will bring judgment on all mankind
and put the wicked to the sword,' "
declares the LORD.

32This is what the LORD Almighty says:

"Look! Disaster is spreading
from nation to nation;
a mighty storm is rising
from the ends of the earth."

33At that time those slain by the LORD will be
everywhere—from one end of the earth to the
other. They will not be mourned or gathered up
or buried, but will be like refuse lying on the
ground.

34Weep and wail, you shepherds;
roll in the dust, you leaders of the flock.
For your time to be slaughtered has come;
you will fall and be shattered like fine pottery.
35The shepherds will have nowhere to flee,
the leaders of the flock no place to escape.
36Hear the cry of the shepherds,
the wailing of the leaders of the flock,
for the LORD is destroying their pasture.
37The peaceful meadows will be laid waste
because of the fierce anger of the LORD.
38Like a lion he will leave his lair,
and their land will become desolate
because of the sword[a] of the oppressor
and because of the LORD's fierce anger.

Jeremiah Threatened With Death

26 Early in the reign of Jehoiakim son of
Josiah king of Judah, this word came
from the LORD: 2"This is what the LORD says:
Stand in the courtyard of the LORD's house and
speak to all the people of the towns of Judah
who come to worship in the house of the
LORD. Tell them everything I command you;
do not omit a word. 3Perhaps they will listen
and each will turn from his evil way. Then I
will relent and not bring on them the disaster I
was planning because of the evil they have
done. 4Say to them, 'This is what the LORD
says: If you do not listen to me and follow my
law, which I have set before you, 5and if you
do not listen to the words of my servants the
prophets, whom I have sent to you again and
again (though you have not listened), 6then I
will make this house like Shiloh and this city
an object of cursing among all the nations of
the earth.' "

7The priests, the prophets and all the people
heard Jeremiah speak these words in the house
of the LORD. 8But as soon as Jeremiah finished
telling all the people everything the LORD had
commanded him to say, the priests, the prophets and all the people seized him and said,
"You must die! 9Why do you prophesy in the
LORD's name that this house will be like Shiloh and this city will be desolate and deserted?" And all the people crowded around Jeremiah in the house of the LORD.

10When the officials of Judah heard about
these things, they went up from the royal palace to the house of the LORD and took their
places at the entrance of the New Gate of
the LORD's house. 11Then the priests and the
prophets said to the officials and all the people,
"This man should be sentenced to death because he has prophesied against this city. You
have heard it with your own ears!"

12Then Jeremiah said to all the officials and
all the people: "The LORD sent me to prophesy
against this house and this city all the things
you have heard. 13Now reform your ways and
your actions and obey the LORD your God.
Then the LORD will relent and not bring the
disaster he has pronounced against you. 14As
for me, I am in your hands; do with me whatever you think is good and right. 15Be assured,
however, that if you put me to death, you will
bring the guilt of innocent blood on yourselves
and on this city and on those who live in it, for
in truth the LORD has sent me to you to speak
all these words in your hearing."

16Then the officials and all the people said
to the priests and the prophets, "This man
should not be sentenced to death! He has spoken to us in the name of the LORD our God."

17Some of the elders of the land stepped
forward and said to the entire assembly of people, 18"Micah of Moresheth prophesied in the
days of Hezekiah king of Judah. He told all the
people of Judah, 'This is what the LORD Almighty says:

" 'Zion will be plowed like a field,
Jerusalem will become a heap of rubble,
the temple hill a mound overgrown with thickets.'[b]

19"Did Hezekiah king of Judah or anyone else
in Judah put him to death? Did not Hezekiah
fear the LORD and seek his favor? And did not
the LORD relent, so that he did not bring the
disaster he pronounced against them? We are
about to bring a terrible disaster on ourselves!"

20(Now Uriah son of Shemaiah from Kiriath
Jearim was another man who prophesied in the
name of the LORD; he prophesied the same
things against this city and this land as Jeremiah did. 21When King Jehoiakim and all his
officers and officials heard his words, the king
sought to put him to death. But Uriah heard of
it and fled in fear to Egypt. 22King Jehoiakim,
however, sent Elnathan son of Acbor to Egypt,
along with some other men. 23They brought

[a] *38* Some Hebrew manuscripts and Septuagint (see also Jer. 46:16 and 50:16); most Hebrew manuscripts *anger* [b] *18* Micah 3:12

Uriah out of Egypt and took him to King Jehoiakim, who had him struck down with a sword and his body thrown into the burial place of the common people.)

24Furthermore, Ahikam son of Shaphan supported Jeremiah, and so he was not handed over to the people to be put to death.

Judah to Serve Nebuchadnezzar

27 Early in the reign of Zedekiah[a] son of Josiah king of Judah, this word came to Jeremiah from the LORD: 2This is what the LORD said to me: "Make a yoke out of straps and crossbars and put it on your neck. 3Then send word to the kings of Edom, Moab, Ammon, Tyre and Sidon through the envoys who have come to Jerusalem to Zedekiah king of Judah. 4Give them a message for their masters and say, 'This is what the LORD Almighty, the God of Israel, says: "Tell this to your masters: 5With my great power and outstretched arm I made the earth and its people and the animals that are on it, and I give it to anyone I please. 6Now I will hand all your countries over to my servant Nebuchadnezzar king of Babylon; I will make even the wild animals subject to him. 7All nations will serve him and his son and his grandson until the time for his land comes; then many nations and great kings will subjugate him.

8" ' "If, however, any nation or kingdom will not serve Nebuchadnezzar king of Babylon or bow its neck under his yoke, I will punish that nation with the sword, famine and plague, declares the LORD, until I destroy it by his hand. 9So do not listen to your prophets, your diviners, your interpreters of dreams, your mediums or your sorcerers who tell you, 'You will not serve the king of Babylon.' 10They prophesy lies to you that will only serve to remove you far from your lands; I will banish you and you will perish. 11But if any nation will bow its neck under the yoke of the king of Babylon and serve him, I will let that nation remain in its own land to till it and to live there, declares the LORD." ' "

12I gave the same message to Zedekiah king of Judah. I said, "Bow your neck under the yoke of the king of Babylon; serve him and his people, and you will live. 13Why will you and your people die by the sword, famine and plague with which the LORD has threatened any nation that will not serve the king of Babylon? 14Do not listen to the words of the prophets who say to you, 'You will not serve the king of Babylon,' for they are prophesying lies to you. 15'I have not sent them,' declares the LORD. 'They are prophesying lies in my name. Therefore, I will banish you and you will perish, both you and the prophets who prophesy to you.' "

16Then I said to the priests and all these people, "This is what the LORD says: Do not listen to the prophets who say, 'Very soon now the articles from the LORD's house will be brought back from Babylon.' They are prophesying lies to you. 17Do not listen to them. Serve the king of Babylon, and you will live. Why should this city become a ruin? 18If they are prophets and have the word of the LORD, let them plead with the LORD Almighty that the furnishings remaining in the house of the LORD and in the palace of the king of Judah and in Jerusalem not be taken to Babylon. 19For this is what the LORD Almighty says about the pillars, the Sea, the movable stands and the other furnishings that are left in this city, 20which Nebuchadnezzar king of Babylon did not take away when he carried Jehoiachin[b] son of Jehoiakim king of Judah into exile from Jerusalem to Babylon, along with all the nobles of Judah and Jerusalem— 21yes, this is what the LORD Almighty, the God of Israel, says about the things that are left in the house of the LORD and in the palace of the king of Judah and in Jerusalem: 22'They will be taken to Babylon and there they will remain until the day I come for them,' declares the LORD. 'Then I will bring them back and restore them to this place.' "

The False Prophet Hananiah

28 In the fifth month of that same year, the fourth year, early in the reign of Zedekiah king of Judah, the prophet Hananiah son of Azzur, who was from Gibeon, said to me in the house of the LORD in the presence of the priests and all the people: 2"This is what the LORD Almighty, the God of Israel, says: 'I will break the yoke of the king of Babylon. 3Within two years I will bring back to this place all the articles of the LORD's house that Nebuchadnezzar king of Babylon removed from here and took to Babylon. 4I will also bring back to this place Jehoiachin[b] son of Jehoiakim king of Judah and all the other exiles from Judah who went to Babylon,' declares the LORD, 'for I will break the yoke of the king of Babylon.' "

5Then the prophet Jeremiah replied to the prophet Hananiah before the priests and all the people who were standing in the house of the LORD. 6He said, "Amen! May the LORD do so! May the LORD fulfill the words you have prophesied by bringing the articles of the LORD's house and all the exiles back to this place from Babylon. 7Nevertheless, listen to what I have to say in your hearing and in the hearing of all the people: 8From early times the prophets who preceded you and me have prophesied war, disaster and plague against many countries and great kingdoms. 9But the prophet who prophesies peace will be recognized as one truly sent by the LORD only if his prediction comes true."

10Then the prophet Hananiah took the yoke

a1 A few Hebrew manuscripts and Syriac (see also Jer. 27:3, 12 and 28:1); most Hebrew manuscripts *Jehoiakim* (Most Septuagint manuscripts do not have this verse.) *b20,4* Hebrew *Jeconiah,* a variant of *Jehoiachin*

off the neck of the prophet Jeremiah and broke
it, 11and he said before all the people, "This is
what the LORD says: 'In the same way will I
break the yoke of Nebuchadnezzar king of
Babylon off the neck of all the nations within
two years.' " At this, the prophet Jeremiah
went on his way.
12Shortly after the prophet Hananiah had
broken the yoke off the neck of the prophet
Jeremiah, the word of the LORD came to Jeremiah: 13"Go and tell Hananiah, 'This is what
the LORD says: You have broken a wooden
yoke, but in its place you will get a yoke of
iron. 14This is what the LORD Almighty, the
God of Israel, says: I will put an iron yoke on
the necks of all these nations to make them
serve Nebuchadnezzar king of Babylon, and
they will serve him. I will even give him control over the wild animals.' "
15Then the prophet Jeremiah said to Hananiah the prophet, "Listen, Hananiah! The LORD
has not sent you, yet you have persuaded this
nation to trust in lies. 16Therefore, this is what
the LORD says: 'I am about to remove you
from the face of the earth. This very year you
are going to die, because you have preached
rebellion against the LORD.' "
17In the seventh month of that same year,
Hananiah the prophet died.

A Letter to the Exiles

29 This is the text of the letter that the
prophet Jeremiah sent from Jerusalem
to the surviving elders among the exiles and to
the priests, the prophets and all the other people Nebuchadnezzar had carried into exile
from Jerusalem to Babylon. 2(This was after
King Jehoiachin[a] and the queen mother, the
court officials and the leaders of Judah and
Jerusalem, the craftsmen and the artisans had
gone into exile from Jerusalem.) 3He entrusted
the letter to Elasah son of Shaphan and to
Gemariah son of Hilkiah, whom Zedekiah king
of Judah sent to King Nebuchadnezzar in Babylon. It said:

4This is what the LORD Almighty, the
God of Israel, says to all those I carried
into exile from Jerusalem to Babylon:
5"Build houses and settle down; plant gardens and eat what they produce. 6Marry
and have sons and daughters; find wives
for your sons and give your daughters in
marriage, so that they too may have sons
and daughters. Increase in number there;
do not decrease. 7Also, seek the peace and
prosperity of the city to which I have carried you into exile. Pray to the LORD for
it, because if it prospers, you too will
prosper." 8Yes, this is what the LORD Almighty, the God of Israel, says: "Do not
let the prophets and diviners among you
deceive you. Do not listen to the dreams
you encourage them to have. 9They are
prophesying lies to you in my name. I
have not sent them," declares the LORD.
10This is what the LORD says: "When
seventy years are completed for Babylon,
I will come to you and fulfill my gracious
promise to bring you back to this place.
11For I know the plans I have for you,"
declares the LORD, "plans to prosper you
and not to harm you, plans to give
you hope and a future. 12Then you will
call upon me and come and pray to me,
and I will listen to you. 13You will seek
me and find me when you seek me with
all your heart. 14I will be found by you,"
declares the LORD, "and will bring you
back from captivity.[b] I will gather
you from all the nations and places where
I have banished you," declares the LORD,
"and will bring you back to the place from
which I carried you into exile."
15You may say, "The LORD has raised
up prophets for us in Babylon," 16but this
is what the LORD says about the king who
sits on David's throne and all the people
who remain in this city, your countrymen
who did not go with you into exile—
17yes, this is what the LORD Almighty
says: "I will send the sword, famine and
plague against them and I will make them
like poor figs that are so bad they cannot
be eaten. 18I will pursue them with the
sword, famine and plague and will make
them abhorrent to all the kingdoms of the
earth and an object of cursing and horror,
of scorn and reproach, among all the nations where I drive them. 19For they have
not listened to my words," declares the
LORD, "words that I sent to them again
and again by my servants the prophets.
And you exiles have not listened either,"
declares the LORD.
20Therefore, hear the word of the
LORD, all you exiles whom I have sent
away from Jerusalem to Babylon. 21This
is what the LORD Almighty, the God of
Israel, says about Ahab son of Kolaiah
and Zedekiah son of Maaseiah, who are
prophesying lies to you in my name: "I
will hand them over to Nebuchadnezzar
king of Babylon, and he will put them to
death before your very eyes. 22Because of
them, all the exiles from Judah who are in
Babylon will use this curse: 'The LORD
treat you like Zedekiah and Ahab, whom
the king of Babylon burned in the fire.'
23For they have done outrageous things in
Israel; they have committed adultery with
their neighbors' wives and in my name
have spoken lies, which I did not tell them
to do. I know it and am a witness to it,"
declares the LORD.

Message to Shemaiah

24Tell Shemaiah the Nehelamite, 25"This is
what the LORD Almighty, the God of Israel,
says: You sent letters in your own name to all
the people in Jerusalem, to Zephaniah son of

[a]2 Hebrew *Jeconiah,* a variant of *Jehoiachin* [b]14 Or *will restore your fortunes*

Maaseiah the priest, and to all the other priests.
You said to Zephaniah, 26'The LORD has appointed you priest in place of Jehoiada to be in
charge of the house of the LORD; you should
put any madman who acts like a prophet into
the stocks and neck-irons. 27So why have you
not reprimanded Jeremiah from Anathoth, who
poses as a prophet among you? 28He has sent
this message to us in Babylon: It will be a long
time. Therefore build houses and settle down;
plant gardens and eat what they produce.' "

29Zephaniah the priest, however, read the
letter to Jeremiah the prophet. 30Then the word
of the LORD came to Jeremiah: 31"Send this
message to all the exiles: 'This is what the
LORD says about Shemaiah the Nehelamite:
Because Shemaiah has prophesied to you, even
though I did not send him, and has led you to
believe a lie, 32this is what the LORD says: I
will surely punish Shemaiah the Nehelamite
and his descendants. He will have no one left
among this people, nor will he see the good
things I will do for my people, declares the
LORD, because he has preached rebellion
against me.' "

Restoration of Israel

30 This is the word that came to Jeremiah
from the LORD: 2"This is what the
LORD, the God of Israel, says: 'Write in a book
all the words I have spoken to you. 3The days
are coming,' declares the LORD, 'when I will
bring my people Israel and Judah back from
captivity[a] and restore them to the land I gave
their forefathers to possess,' says the LORD."

4These are the words the LORD spoke concerning Israel and Judah: 5"This is what the
LORD says:

" 'Cries of fear are heard—
terror, not peace.
6Ask and see:
Can a man bear children?
Then why do I see every strong man
with his hands on his stomach like a
woman in labor,
every face turned deathly pale?
7How awful that day will be!
None will be like it.
It will be a time of trouble for Jacob,
but he will be saved out of it.

8" 'In that day,' declares the LORD
Almighty,
'I will break the yoke off their necks
and will tear off their bonds;
no longer will foreigners enslave them.
9Instead, they will serve the LORD their
God
and David their king,
whom I will raise up for them.

10" 'So do not fear, O Jacob my servant;
do not be dismayed, O Israel,'
declares the LORD.
'I will surely save you out of a distant
place,
your descendants from the land of their
exile.
Jacob will again have peace and security,
and no one will make him afraid.
11I am with you and will save you,'
declares the LORD.
'Though I completely destroy all the
nations
among which I scatter you,
I will not completely destroy you.
I will discipline you but only with justice;
I will not let you go entirely
unpunished.'

12"This is what the LORD says:

" 'Your wound is incurable,
your injury beyond healing.
13There is no one to plead your cause,
no remedy for your sore,
no healing for you.
14All your allies have forgotten you;
they care nothing for you.
I have struck you as an enemy would
and punished you as would the cruel,
because your guilt is so great
and your sins so many.
15Why do you cry out over your wound,
your pain that has no cure?
Because of your great guilt and many sins
I have done these things to you.

16" 'But all who devour you will be
devoured;
all your enemies will go into exile.
Those who plunder you will be plundered;
all who make spoil of you I will
despoil.
17But I will restore you to health
and heal your wounds,'
declares the LORD,
'because you are called an outcast,
Zion for whom no one cares.'

18"This is what the LORD says:

" 'I will restore the fortunes of Jacob's
tents
and have compassion on his dwellings;
the city will be rebuilt on her ruins,
and the palace will stand in its proper
place.
19From them will come songs of
thanksgiving
and the sound of rejoicing.
I will add to their numbers,
and they will not be decreased;
I will bring them honor,
and they will not be disdained.
20Their children will be as in days of old,
and their community will be established
before me;
I will punish all who oppress them.
21Their leader will be one of their own;
their ruler will arise from among them.
I will bring him near and he will come
close to me,

[a]3 Or *will restore the fortunes of my people Israel and Judah*

for who is he who will devote himself
to be close to me?'
declares the LORD.
22" 'So you will be my people,
and I will be your God.' "

23See, the storm of the LORD
will burst out in wrath,
a driving wind swirling down
on the heads of the wicked.
24The fierce anger of the LORD will not turn back
until he fully accomplishes
the purposes of his heart.
In days to come
you will understand this.

31 "At that time," declares the LORD, "I
will be the God of all the clans of Israel,
and they will be my people."
2This is what the LORD says:

"The people who survive the sword
will find favor in the desert;
I will come to give rest to Israel."

3The LORD appeared to us in the past,[a] saying:

"I have loved you with an everlasting love;
I have drawn you with loving-kindness.
4I will build you up again
and you will be rebuilt, O Virgin Israel.
Again you will take up your tambourines
and go out to dance with the joyful.
5Again you will plant vineyards
on the hills of Samaria;
the farmers will plant them
and enjoy their fruit.
6There will be a day when watchmen cry out
on the hills of Ephraim,
'Come, let us go up to Zion,
to the LORD our God.' "

7This is what the LORD says:

"Sing with joy for Jacob;
shout for the foremost of the nations.
Make your praises heard, and say,
'O LORD, save your people,
the remnant of Israel.'
8See, I will bring them from the land of the north
and gather them from the ends of the earth.
Among them will be the blind and the lame,
expectant mothers and women in labor;
a great throng will return.
9They will come with weeping;
they will pray as I bring them back.
I will lead them beside streams of water
on a level path where they will not stumble,
because I am Israel's father,
and Ephraim is my firstborn son.

10"Hear the word of the LORD, O nations;
proclaim it in distant coastlands:
'He who scattered Israel will gather them
and will watch over his flock like a shepherd.'
11For the LORD will ransom Jacob
and redeem them from the hand of those stronger than they.
12They will come and shout for joy on the heights of Zion;
they will rejoice in the bounty of the LORD—
the grain, the new wine and the oil,
the young of the flocks and herds.
They will be like a well-watered garden,
and they will sorrow no more.
13Then maidens will dance and be glad,
young men and old as well.
I will turn their mourning into gladness;
I will give them comfort and joy instead of sorrow.
14I will satisfy the priests with abundance,
and my people will be filled with my bounty,"
declares the LORD.

15This is what the LORD says:

"A voice is heard in Ramah,
mourning and great weeping,
Rachel weeping for her children
and refusing to be comforted,
because her children are no more."

16This is what the LORD says:

"Restrain your voice from weeping
and your eyes from tears,
for your work will be rewarded,"
declares the LORD.
"They will return from the land of the enemy.
17So there is hope for your future,"
declares the LORD.
"Your children will return to their own land.

18"I have surely heard Ephraim's moaning:
'You disciplined me like an unruly calf,
and I have been disciplined.
Restore me, and I will return,
because you are the LORD my God.
19After I strayed,
I repented;
after I came to understand,
I beat my breast.
I was ashamed and humiliated
because I bore the disgrace of my youth.'
20Is not Ephraim my dear son,
the child in whom I delight?
Though I often speak against him,
I still remember him.
Therefore my heart yearns for him;
I have great compassion for him,"
declares the LORD.

21"Set up road signs;

[a]3 Or *LORD has appeared to us from afar*

put up guideposts.
Take note of the highway,
the road that you take.
Return, O Virgin Israel,
return to your towns.
22How long will you wander,
O unfaithful daughter?
The LORD will create a new thing on earth—
a woman will surround[a] a man."

23This is what the LORD Almighty, the God
of Israel, says: "When I bring them back from
captivity,[b] the people in the land of Judah and
in its towns will once again use these words:
'The LORD bless you, O righteous dwelling,
O sacred mountain.' 24People will live together in Judah and all its towns—farmers and
those who move about with their flocks. 25I
will refresh the weary and satisfy the faint."
26At this I awoke and looked around. My
sleep had been pleasant to me.
27"The days are coming," declares the
LORD, "when I will plant the house of Israel
and the house of Judah with the offspring of
men and of animals. 28Just as I watched over
them to uproot and tear down, and to overthrow, destroy and bring disaster, so I will
watch over them to build and to plant," declares the LORD. 29"In those days people will
no longer say,

'The fathers have eaten sour grapes,
and the children's teeth are set on edge.'

30Instead, everyone will die for his own sin;
whoever eats sour grapes—his own teeth will
be set on edge.

31"The time is coming," declares the LORD,
"when I will make a new covenant
with the house of Israel
and with the house of Judah.
32It will not be like the covenant
I made with their forefathers
when I took them by the hand
to lead them out of Egypt,
because they broke my covenant,
though I was a husband to[c] them,[d]"
declares the LORD.
33"This is the covenant I will make with the house of Israel
after that time," declares the LORD.
"I will put my law in their minds
and write it on their hearts.
I will be their God,
and they will be my people.
34No longer will a man teach his neighbor,
or a man his brother, saying, 'Know the LORD,'
because they will all know me,
from the least of them to the greatest,"
declares the LORD.
"For I will forgive their wickedness
and will remember their sins no more."

35This is what the LORD says,

he who appoints the sun
to shine by day,
who decrees the moon and stars
to shine by night,
who stirs up the sea
so that its waves roar—
the LORD Almighty is his name:
36"Only if these decrees vanish from my sight,"
declares the LORD,
"will the descendants of Israel ever cease
to be a nation before me."

37This is what the LORD says:

"Only if the heavens above can be measured
and the foundations of the earth below
be searched out
will I reject all the descendants of Israel
because of all they have done,"
declares the LORD.

38"The days are coming," declares the
LORD, "when this city will be rebuilt for me
from the Tower of Hananel to the Corner Gate.
39The measuring line will stretch from there
straight to the hill of Gareb and then turn to
Goah. 40The whole valley where dead bodies
and ashes are thrown, and all the terraces out
to the Kidron Valley on the east as far as the
corner of the Horse Gate, will be holy to the
LORD. The city will never again be uprooted or
demolished."

Jeremiah Buys a Field

32 This is the word that came to Jeremiah
from the LORD in the tenth year of Zedekiah king of Judah, which was the eighteenth
year of Nebuchadnezzar. 2The army of the
king of Babylon was then besieging Jerusalem,
and Jeremiah the prophet was confined in the
courtyard of the guard in the royal palace of
Judah.
3Now Zedekiah king of Judah had imprisoned him there, saying, "Why do you prophesy
as you do? You say, 'This is what the LORD
says: I am about to hand this city over to the
king of Babylon, and he will capture it. 4Zede-
kiah king of Judah will not escape out of the
hands of the Babylonians[e] but will certainly
be handed over to the king of Babylon, and
will speak with him face to face and see him
with his own eyes. 5He will take Zedekiah to
Babylon, where he will remain until I deal with
him, declares the LORD. If you fight against the
Babylonians, you will not succeed.' "
6Jeremiah said, "The word of the LORD
came to me: 7Hanamel son of Shallum your
uncle is going to come to you and say, 'Buy

[a]22 Or *will go about* ⌊*seeking*⌋; or *will protect* [b]23 Or *I restore their fortunes* [c]32 Hebrew; Septuagint and Syriac */ and I turned away from* [d]32 Or *was their master* [e]4 Or *Chaldeans*; also in verses 5, 24, 25, 28, 29 and 43

my field at Anathoth, because as nearest relative it is your right and duty to buy it.’
8“Then, just as the LORD had said, my cousin Hanamel came to me in the courtyard of the
guard and said, ‘Buy my field at Anathoth in
the territory of Benjamin. Since it is your right
to redeem it and possess it, buy it for yourself.’
“I knew that this was the word of the LORD;
9so I bought the field at Anathoth from my
cousin Hanamel and weighed out for him seventeen shekels[a] of silver. 10I signed and sealed
the deed, had it witnessed, and weighed out the
silver on the scales. 11I took the deed of purchase—the sealed copy containing the terms
and conditions, as well as the unsealed copy—
12and I gave this deed to Baruch son of Neriah,
the son of Mahseiah, in the presence of my
cousin Hanamel and of the witnesses who had
signed the deed and of all the Jews sitting in
the courtyard of the guard.
13“In their presence I gave Baruch these instructions: 14‘This is what the LORD Almighty,
the God of Israel, says: Take these documents,
both the sealed and unsealed copies of the deed
of purchase, and put them in a clay jar so they
will last a long time. 15For this is what the
LORD Almighty, the God of Israel, says:
Houses, fields and vineyards will again be
bought in this land.’
16“After I had given the deed of purchase to
Baruch son of Neriah, I prayed to the LORD:

17“Ah, Sovereign LORD, you have made
the heavens and the earth by your great
power and outstretched arm. Nothing is
too hard for you. 18You show love to
thousands but bring the punishment for
the fathers’ sins into the laps of their children after them. O great and powerful
God, whose name is the LORD Almighty,
19great are your purposes and mighty are
your deeds. Your eyes are open to all the
ways of men; you reward everyone according to his conduct and as his deeds
deserve. 20You performed miraculous
signs and wonders in Egypt and have continued them to this day, both in Israel and
among all mankind, and have gained the
renown that is still yours. 21You brought
your people Israel out of Egypt with signs
and wonders, by a mighty hand and an
outstretched arm and with great terror.
22You gave them this land you had sworn
to give their forefathers, a land flowing
with milk and honey. 23They came in and
took possession of it, but they did not
obey you or follow your law; they did not
do what you commanded them to do. So
you brought all this disaster upon them.
24“See how the siege ramps are built up
to take the city. Because of the sword,
famine and plague, the city will be handed over to the Babylonians who are attacking it. What you said has happened,
as you now see. 25And though the city
will be handed over to the Babylonians,
you, O Sovereign LORD, say to me, ‘Buy
the field with silver and have the transac-
tion witnessed.’ ”

26Then the word of the LORD came to Jeremiah: 27“I am the LORD, the God of all mankind. Is anything too hard for me? 28Therefore,
this is what the LORD says: I am about to hand
this city over to the Babylonians and to Nebuchadnezzar king of Babylon, who will capture
it. 29The Babylonians who are attacking this
city will come in and set it on fire; they will
burn it down, along with the houses where the
people provoked me to anger by burning incense on the roofs to Baal and by pouring out
drink offerings to other gods.
30“The people of Israel and Judah have done
nothing but evil in my sight from their youth;
indeed, the people of Israel have done nothing
but provoke me with what their hands have
made, declares the LORD. 31From the day it
was built until now, this city has so aroused my
anger and wrath that I must remove it from my
sight. 32The people of Israel and Judah have
provoked me by all the evil they have done—
they, their kings and officials, their priests and
prophets, the men of Judah and the people of
Jerusalem. 33They turned their backs to me and
not their faces; though I taught them again and
again, they would not listen or respond to discipline. 34They set up their abominable idols in
the house that bears my Name and defiled it.
35They built high places for Baal in the Valley
of Ben Hinnom to sacrifice their sons and
daughters[b] to Molech, though I never commanded, nor did it enter my mind, that they
should do such a detestable thing and so make
Judah sin.
36“You are saying about this city, ‘By the
sword, famine and plague it will be handed
over to the king of Babylon’; but this is what
the LORD, the God of Israel, says: 37I will surely gather them from all the lands where I banish them in my furious anger and great wrath;
I will bring them back to this place and let
them live in safety. 38They will be my people,
and I will be their God. 39I will give them
singleness of heart and action, so that they will
always fear me for their own good and the
good of their children after them. 40I will make
an everlasting covenant with them: I will never
stop doing good to them, and I will inspire
them to fear me, so that they will never turn
away from me. 41I will rejoice in doing them
good and will assuredly plant them in this land
with all my heart and soul.
42“This is what the LORD says: As I have
brought all this great calamity on this people,
so I will give them all the prosperity I have
promised them. 43Once more fields will be
bought in this land of which you say, ‘It is a
desolate waste, without men or animals, for it
has been handed over to the Babylonians.’
44Fields will be bought for silver, and deeds

[a]9 That is, about 7 ounces (about 200 grams)   [b]35 Or *to make their sons and daughters pass through ⌊the fire⌋*

will be signed, sealed and witnessed in the territory of Benjamin, in the villages around Jerusalem, in the towns of Judah and in the towns
of the hill country, of the western foothills and
of the Negev, because I will restore their fortunes,[a] declares the LORD."

Promise of Restoration

33 While Jeremiah was still confined in the
courtyard of the guard, the word of the
LORD came to him a second time: **2**"This is
what the LORD says, he who made the earth,
the LORD who formed it and established it—
the LORD is his name: **3**'Call to me and I will
answer you and tell you great and unsearchable things you do not know.' **4**For this is what
the LORD, the God of Israel, says about the
houses in this city and the royal palaces of
Judah that have been torn down to be used
against the siege ramps and the sword **5**in the
fight with the Babylonians[b]: 'They will be
filled with the dead bodies of the men I will
slay in my anger and wrath. I will hide my face
from this city because of all its wickedness.

6" 'Nevertheless, I will bring health and
healing to it; I will heal my people and will let
them enjoy abundant peace and security. **7**I
will bring Judah and Israel back from captivity[c] and will rebuild them as they were before.
8I will cleanse them from all the sin they have
committed against me and will forgive all their
sins of rebellion against me. **9**Then this city
will bring me renown, joy, praise and honor
before all nations on earth that hear of all the
good things I do for it; and they will be in awe
and will tremble at the abundant prosperity and
peace I provide for it.'

10"This is what the LORD says: 'You say
about this place, "It is a desolate waste, without men or animals." Yet in the towns of Judah
and the streets of Jerusalem that are deserted,
inhabited by neither men nor animals, there
will be heard once more **11**the sounds of joy
and gladness, the voices of bride and bridegroom, and the voices of those who bring
thank offerings to the house of the LORD, saying,

"Give thanks to the LORD Almighty,
for the LORD is good;
his love endures forever."

For I will restore the fortunes of the land as
they were before,' says the LORD.

12"This is what the LORD Almighty says: 'In
this place, desolate and without men or animals—in all its towns there will again be pastures for shepherds to rest their flocks. **13**In the
towns of the hill country, of the western foothills and of the Negev, in the territory of Benjamin, in the villages around Jerusalem and in
the towns of Judah, flocks will again pass under the hand of the one who counts them,' says
the LORD.

14" 'The days are coming,' declares the
LORD, 'when I will fulfill the gracious promise
I made to the house of Israel and to the house
of Judah.

15" 'In those days and at that time
I will make a righteous Branch sprout
from David's line;
he will do what is just and right in the
land.
16In those days Judah will be saved
and Jerusalem will live in safety.
This is the name by which it[d] will be
called:
The LORD Our Righteousness.'

17For this is what the LORD says: 'David will
never fail to have a man to sit on the throne of
the house of Israel, **18**nor will the priests, who
are Levites, ever fail to have a man to stand
before me continually to offer burnt offerings,
to burn grain offerings and to present sacrifices.' "

19The word of the LORD came to Jeremiah:
20"This is what the LORD says: 'If you can
break my covenant with the day and my covenant with the night, so that day and night no
longer come at their appointed time, **21**then my
covenant with David my servant—and my
covenant with the Levites who are priests ministering before me—can be broken and David
will no longer have a descendant to reign on
his throne. **22**I will make the descendants of
David my servant and the Levites who minister before me as countless as the stars of the
sky and as measureless as the sand on the seashore.' "

23The word of the LORD came to Jeremiah:
24"Have you not noticed that these people are
saying, 'The LORD has rejected the two kingdoms[e] he chose'? So they despise my people
and no longer regard them as a nation. **25**This
is what the LORD says: 'If I have not established my covenant with day and night and the
fixed laws of heaven and earth, **26**then I will
reject the descendants of Jacob and David my
servant and will not choose one of his sons to
rule over the descendants of Abraham, Isaac
and Jacob. For I will restore their fortunes[a]
and have compassion on them.' "

Warning to Zedekiah

34 While Nebuchadnezzar king of Babylon
and all his army and all the kingdoms
and peoples in the empire he ruled were fighting against Jerusalem and all its surrounding
towns, this word came to Jeremiah from the
LORD: **2**"This is what the LORD, the God of
Israel, says: Go to Zedekiah king of Judah and
tell him, 'This is what the LORD says: I am
about to hand this city over to the king of
Babylon, and he will burn it down. **3**You will
not escape from his grasp but will surely be
captured and handed over to him. You will see
the king of Babylon with your own eyes, and

[a]44,26 Or *will bring them back from captivity* [b]5 Or *Chaldeans* [c]7 Or *will restore the fortunes of Judah and Israel* [d]16 Or *he* [e]24 Or *families*

he will speak with you face to face. And you will go to Babylon.

4" 'Yet hear the promise of the LORD, O Zedekiah king of Judah. This is what the LORD says concerning you: You will not die by the sword; 5you will die peacefully. As people made a funeral fire in honor of your fathers, the former kings who preceded you, so they will make a fire in your honor and lament, "Alas, O master!" I myself make this promise, declares the LORD.' "

6Then Jeremiah the prophet told all this to Zedekiah king of Judah, in Jerusalem, 7while the army of the king of Babylon was fighting against Jerusalem and the other cities of Judah that were still holding out—Lachish and Azekah. These were the only fortified cities left in Judah.

Freedom for Slaves

8The word came to Jeremiah from the LORD after King Zedekiah had made a covenant with all the people in Jerusalem to proclaim freedom for the slaves. 9Everyone was to free his Hebrew slaves, both male and female; no one was to hold a fellow Jew in bondage. 10So all the officials and people who entered into this covenant agreed that they would free their male and female slaves and no longer hold them in bondage. They agreed, and set them free. 11But afterward they changed their minds and took back the slaves they had freed and enslaved them again.

12Then the word of the LORD came to Jeremiah: 13"This is what the LORD, the God of Israel, says: I made a covenant with your forefathers when I brought them out of Egypt, out of the land of slavery. I said, 14'Every seventh year each of you must free any fellow Hebrew who has sold himself to you. After he has served you six years, you must let him go free.'[a] Your fathers, however, did not listen to me or pay attention to me. 15Recently you repented and did what is right in my sight: Each of you proclaimed freedom to his countrymen. You even made a covenant before me in the house that bears my Name. 16But now you have turned around and profaned my name; each of you has taken back the male and female slaves you had set free to go where they wished. You have forced them to become your slaves again.

17"Therefore, this is what the LORD says: You have not obeyed me; you have not proclaimed freedom for your fellow countrymen. So I now proclaim 'freedom' for you, declares the LORD—'freedom' to fall by the sword, plague and famine. I will make you abhorrent to all the kingdoms of the earth. 18The men who have violated my covenant and have not fulfilled the terms of the covenant they made before me, I will treat like the calf they cut in two and then walked between its pieces. 19The leaders of Judah and Jerusalem, the court officials, the priests and all the people of the land who walked between the pieces of the calf, 20I will hand over to their enemies who seek their lives. Their dead bodies will become food for the birds of the air and the beasts of the earth.

21"I will hand Zedekiah king of Judah and his officials over to their enemies who seek their lives, to the army of the king of Babylon, which has withdrawn from you. 22I am going to give the order, declares the LORD, and I will bring them back to this city. They will fight against it, take it and burn it down. And I will lay waste the towns of Judah so no one can live there."

The Recabites

35 This is the word that came to Jeremiah from the LORD during the reign of Jehoiakim son of Josiah king of Judah: 2"Go to the Recabite family and invite them to come to one of the side rooms of the house of the LORD and give them wine to drink."

3So I went to get Jaazaniah son of Jeremiah, the son of Habazziniah, and his brothers and all his sons—the whole family of the Recabites. 4I brought them into the house of the LORD, into the room of the sons of Hanan son of Igdaliah the man of God. It was next to the room of the officials, which was over that of Maaseiah son of Shallum the doorkeeper. 5Then I set bowls full of wine and some cups before the men of the Recabite family and said to them, "Drink some wine."

6But they replied, "We do not drink wine, because our forefather Jonadab son of Recab gave us this command: 'Neither you nor your descendants must ever drink wine. 7Also you must never build houses, sow seed or plant vineyards; you must never have any of these things, but must always live in tents. Then you will live a long time in the land where you are nomads.' 8We have obeyed everything our forefather Jonadab son of Recab commanded us. Neither we nor our wives nor our sons and daughters have ever drunk wine 9or built houses to live in or had vineyards, fields or crops. 10We have lived in tents and have fully obeyed everything our forefather Jonadab commanded us. 11But when Nebuchadnezzar king of Babylon invaded this land, we said, 'Come, we must go to Jerusalem to escape the Babylonian[b] and Aramean armies.' So we have remained in Jerusalem."

12Then the word of the LORD came to Jeremiah, saying: 13"This is what the LORD Almighty, the God of Israel, says: Go and tell the men of Judah and the people of Jerusalem, 'Will you not learn a lesson and obey my words?' declares the LORD. 14'Jonadab son of Recab ordered his sons not to drink wine and this command has been kept. To this day they do not drink wine, because they obey their forefather's command. But I have spoken to you again and again, yet you have not obeyed me. 15Again and again I sent all my servants the prophets to you. They said, "Each of you

[a] 14 Deut. 15:12 [b] 11 Or *Chaldean*

must turn from your wicked ways and reform your actions; do not follow other gods to serve them. Then you will live in the land I have given to you and your fathers." But you have not paid attention or listened to me. 16The descendants of Jonadab son of Recab have carried out the command their forefather gave them, but these people have not obeyed me.'

17"Therefore, this is what the LORD God Almighty, the God of Israel, says: 'Listen! I am going to bring on Judah and on everyone living in Jerusalem every disaster I pronounced against them. I spoke to them, but they did not listen; I called to them, but they did not answer.' "

18Then Jeremiah said to the family of the Recabites, "This is what the LORD Almighty, the God of Israel, says: 'You have obeyed the command of your forefather Jonadab and have followed all his instructions and have done everything he ordered.' 19Therefore, this is what the LORD Almighty, the God of Israel, says: 'Jonadab son of Recab will never fail to have a man to serve me.' "

Jehoiakim Burns Jeremiah's Scroll

36 In the fourth year of Jehoiakim son of Josiah king of Judah, this word came to Jeremiah from the LORD: 2"Take a scroll and write on it all the words I have spoken to you concerning Israel, Judah and all the other nations from the time I began speaking to you in the reign of Josiah till now. 3Perhaps when the people of Judah hear about every disaster I plan to inflict on them, each of them will turn from his wicked way; then I will forgive their wickedness and their sin."

4So Jeremiah called Baruch son of Neriah, and while Jeremiah dictated all the words the LORD had spoken to him, Baruch wrote them on the scroll. 5Then Jeremiah told Baruch, "I am restricted; I cannot go to the LORD's temple. 6So you go to the house of the LORD on a day of fasting and read to the people from the scroll the words of the LORD that you wrote as I dictated. Read them to all the people of Judah who come in from their towns. 7Perhaps they will bring their petition before the LORD, and each will turn from his wicked ways, for the anger and wrath pronounced against this people by the LORD are great."

8Baruch son of Neriah did everything Jeremiah the prophet told him to do; at the LORD's temple he read the words of the LORD from the scroll. 9In the ninth month of the fifth year of Jehoiakim son of Josiah king of Judah, a time of fasting before the LORD was proclaimed for all the people in Jerusalem and those who had come from the towns of Judah. 10From the room of Gemariah son of Shaphan the secretary, which was in the upper courtyard at the entrance of the New Gate of the temple, Baruch read to all the people at the LORD's temple the words of Jeremiah from the scroll.

11When Micaiah son of Gemariah, the son of Shaphan, heard all the words of the LORD from the scroll, 12he went down to the secretary's room in the royal palace, where all the officials were sitting: Elishama the secretary, Delaiah son of Shemaiah, Elnathan son of Acbor, Gemariah son of Shaphan, Zedekiah son of Hananiah, and all the other officials. 13After Micaiah told them everything he had heard Baruch read to the people from the scroll, 14all the officials sent Jehudi son of Nethaniah, the son of Shelemiah, the son of Cushi, to say to Baruch, "Bring the scroll from which you have read to the people and come." So Baruch son of Neriah went to them with the scroll in his hand. 15They said to him, "Sit down, please, and read it to us."

So Baruch read it to them. 16When they heard all these words, they looked at each other in fear and said to Baruch, "We must report all these words to the king." 17Then they asked Baruch, "Tell us, how did you come to write all this? Did Jeremiah dictate it?"

18"Yes," Baruch replied, "he dictated all these words to me, and I wrote them in ink on the scroll."

19Then the officials said to Baruch, "You and Jeremiah, go and hide. Don't let anyone know where you are."

20After they put the scroll in the room of Elishama the secretary, they went to the king in the courtyard and reported everything to him. 21The king sent Jehudi to get the scroll, and Jehudi brought it from the room of Elishama the secretary and read it to the king and all the officials standing beside him. 22It was the ninth month and the king was sitting in the winter apartment, with a fire burning in the firepot in front of him. 23Whenever Jehudi had read three or four columns of the scroll, the king cut them off with a scribe's knife and threw them into the firepot, until the entire scroll was burned in the fire. 24The king and all his attendants who heard all these words showed no fear, nor did they tear their clothes. 25Even though Elnathan, Delaiah and Gemariah urged the king not to burn the scroll, he would not listen to them. 26Instead, the king commanded Jerahmeel, a son of the king, Seraiah son of Azriel and Shelemiah son of Abdeel to arrest Baruch the scribe and Jeremiah the prophet. But the LORD had hidden them.

27After the king burned the scroll containing the words that Baruch had written at Jeremiah's dictation, the word of the LORD came to Jeremiah: 28"Take another scroll and write on it all the words that were on the first scroll, which Jehoiakim king of Judah burned up. 29Also tell Jehoiakim king of Judah, 'This is what the LORD says: You burned that scroll and said, "Why did you write on it that the king of Babylon would certainly come and destroy this land and cut off both men and animals from it?" 30Therefore, this is what the LORD says about Jehoiakim king of Judah: He will have no one to sit on the throne of David; his body will be thrown out and exposed to the heat by day and the frost by night. 31I will punish him and his children and his attendants for their wickedness; I will bring on them and those living in Jerusalem and the people of Judah every disaster I pronounced against them, because they have not listened.' "

32 So Jeremiah took another scroll and gave it to the scribe Baruch son of Neriah, and as Jeremiah dictated, Baruch wrote on it all the words of the scroll that Jehoiakim king of Judah had burned in the fire. And many similar words were added to them.

Jeremiah in Prison

37 Zedekiah son of Josiah was made king of Judah by Nebuchadnezzar king of Babylon; he reigned in place of Jehoiachin[a] son of Jehoiakim. 2 Neither he nor his attendants nor the people of the land paid any attention to the words the LORD had spoken through Jeremiah the prophet.

3 King Zedekiah, however, sent Jehucal son of Shelemiah with the priest Zephaniah son of Maaseiah to Jeremiah the prophet with this message: "Please pray to the LORD our God for us."

4 Now Jeremiah was free to come and go among the people, for he had not yet been put in prison. 5 Pharaoh's army had marched out of Egypt, and when the Babylonians[b] who were besieging Jerusalem heard the report about them, they withdrew from Jerusalem.

6 Then the word of the LORD came to Jeremiah the prophet: 7 "This is what the LORD, the God of Israel, says: Tell the king of Judah, who sent you to inquire of me, 'Pharaoh's army, which has marched out to support you, will go back to its own land, to Egypt. 8 Then the Babylonians will return and attack this city; they will capture it and burn it down.'

9 "This is what the LORD says: Do not deceive yourselves, thinking, 'The Babylonians will surely leave us.' They will not! 10 Even if you were to defeat the entire Babylonian[c] army that is attacking you and only wounded men were left in their tents, they would come out and burn this city down."

11 After the Babylonian army had withdrawn from Jerusalem because of Pharaoh's army, 12 Jeremiah started to leave the city to go to the territory of Benjamin to get his share of the property among the people there. 13 But when he reached the Benjamin Gate, the captain of the guard, whose name was Irijah son of Shelemiah, the son of Hananiah, arrested him and said, "You are deserting to the Babylonians!"

14 "That's not true!" Jeremiah said. "I am not deserting to the Babylonians." But Irijah would not listen to him; instead, he arrested Jeremiah and brought him to the officials. 15 They were angry with Jeremiah and had him beaten and imprisoned in the house of Jonathan the secretary, which they had made into a prison.

16 Jeremiah was put into a vaulted cell in a dungeon, where he remained a long time. 17 Then King Zedekiah sent for him and had him brought to the palace, where he asked him privately, "Is there any word from the LORD?"

"Yes," Jeremiah replied, "you will be handed over to the king of Babylon."

18 Then Jeremiah said to King Zedekiah, "What crime have I committed against you or your officials or this people, that you have put me in prison? 19 Where are your prophets who prophesied to you, 'The king of Babylon will not attack you or this land'? 20 But now, my lord the king, please listen. Let me bring my petition before you: Do not send me back to the house of Jonathan the secretary, or I will die there."

21 King Zedekiah then gave orders for Jeremiah to be placed in the courtyard of the guard and given bread from the street of the bakers each day until all the bread in the city was gone. So Jeremiah remained in the courtyard of the guard.

Jeremiah Thrown Into a Cistern

38 Shephatiah son of Mattan, Gedaliah son of Pashhur, Jehucal[d] son of Shelemiah, and Pashhur son of Malkijah heard what Jeremiah was telling all the people when he said, 2 "This is what the LORD says: 'Whoever stays in this city will die by the sword, famine or plague, but whoever goes over to the Babylonians[e] will live. He will escape with his life; he will live.' 3 And this is what the LORD says: 'This city will certainly be handed over to the army of the king of Babylon, who will capture it.' "

4 Then the officials said to the king, "This man should be put to death. He is discouraging the soldiers who are left in this city, as well as all the people, by the things he is saying to them. This man is not seeking the good of these people but their ruin."

5 "He is in your hands," King Zedekiah answered. "The king can do nothing to oppose you."

6 So they took Jeremiah and put him into the cistern of Malkijah, the king's son, which was in the courtyard of the guard. They lowered Jeremiah by ropes into the cistern; it had no water in it, only mud, and Jeremiah sank down into the mud.

7 But Ebed-Melech, a Cushite,[f] an official[g] in the royal palace, heard that they had put Jeremiah into the cistern. While the king was sitting in the Benjamin Gate, 8 Ebed-Melech went out of the palace and said to him, 9 "My lord the king, these men have acted wickedly in all they have done to Jeremiah the prophet. They have thrown him into a cistern, where he will starve to death when there is no longer any bread in the city."

10 Then the king commanded Ebed-Melech the Cushite, "Take thirty men from here with

[a] *1* Hebrew *Coniah,* a variant of *Jehoiachin* [b] *5* Or *Chaldeans*; also in verses 8, 9, 13 and 14 [c] *10* Or *Chaldean*; also in verse 11 [d] *1* Hebrew *Jucal,* a variant of *Jehucal* [e] *2* Or *Chaldeans*; also in verses 18, 19 and 23 [f] *7* Probably from the upper Nile region [g] *7* Or *a eunuch*

you and lift Jeremiah the prophet out of the cistern before he dies."

11So Ebed-Melech took the men with him and went to a room under the treasury in the palace. He took some old rags and worn-out clothes from there and let them down with ropes to Jeremiah in the cistern. 12Ebed-Melech the Cushite said to Jeremiah, "Put these old rags and worn-out clothes under your arms to pad the ropes." Jeremiah did so, 13and they pulled him up with the ropes and lifted him out of the cistern. And Jeremiah remained in the courtyard of the guard.

Zedekiah Questions Jeremiah Again

14Then King Zedekiah sent for Jeremiah the prophet and had him brought to the third entrance to the temple of the LORD. "I am going to ask you something," the king said to Jeremiah. "Do not hide anything from me."

15Jeremiah said to Zedekiah, "If I give you an answer, will you not kill me? Even if I did give you counsel, you would not listen to me."

16But King Zedekiah swore this oath secretly to Jeremiah: "As surely as the LORD lives, who has given us breath, I will neither kill you nor hand you over to those who are seeking your life."

17Then Jeremiah said to Zedekiah, "This is what the LORD God Almighty, the God of Israel, says: 'If you surrender to the officers of the king of Babylon, your life will be spared and this city will not be burned down; you and your family will live. 18But if you will not surrender to the officers of the king of Babylon, this city will be handed over to the Babylonians and they will burn it down; you yourself will not escape from their hands.' "

19King Zedekiah said to Jeremiah, "I am afraid of the Jews who have gone over to the Babylonians, for the Babylonians may hand me over to them and they will mistreat me."

20"They will not hand you over," Jeremiah replied. "Obey the LORD by doing what I tell you. Then it will go well with you, and your life will be spared. 21But if you refuse to surrender, this is what the LORD has revealed to me: 22All the women left in the palace of the king of Judah will be brought out to the officials of the king of Babylon. Those women will say to you:

" 'They misled you and overcame you—
    those trusted friends of yours.
Your feet are sunk in the mud;
    your friends have deserted you.'

23"All your wives and children will be brought out to the Babylonians. You yourself will not escape from their hands but will be captured by the king of Babylon; and this city will[a] be burned down."

24Then Zedekiah said to Jeremiah, "Do not let anyone know about this conversation, or you may die. 25If the officials hear that I talked with you, and they come to you and say, 'Tell us what you said to the king and what the king said to you; do not hide it from us or we will kill you,' 26then tell them, 'I was pleading with the king not to send me back to Jonathan's house to die there.' "

27All the officials did come to Jeremiah and question him, and he told them everything the king had ordered him to say. So they said no more to him, for no one had heard his conversation with the king.

28And Jeremiah remained in the courtyard of the guard until the day Jerusalem was captured.

The Fall of Jerusalem

39 This is how Jerusalem was taken: 1In the ninth year of Zedekiah king of Judah, in the tenth month, Nebuchadnezzar king of Babylon marched against Jerusalem with his whole army and laid siege to it. 2And on the ninth day of the fourth month of Zedekiah's eleventh year, the city wall was broken through. 3Then all the officials of the king of Babylon came and took seats in the Middle Gate: Nergal-Sharezer of Samgar, Nebo-Sarsekim[b] a chief officer, Nergal-Sharezer a high official and all the other officials of the king of Babylon. 4When Zedekiah king of Judah and all the soldiers saw them, they fled; they left the city at night by way of the king's garden, through the gate between the two walls, and headed toward the Arabah.[c]

5But the Babylonian[d] army pursued them and overtook Zedekiah in the plains of Jericho. They captured him and took him to Nebuchadnezzar king of Babylon at Riblah in the land of Hamath, where he pronounced sentence on him. 6There at Riblah the king of Babylon slaughtered the sons of Zedekiah before his eyes and also killed all the nobles of Judah. 7Then he put out Zedekiah's eyes and bound him with bronze shackles to take him to Babylon.

8The Babylonians[e] set fire to the royal palace and the houses of the people and broke down the walls of Jerusalem. 9Nebuzaradan commander of the imperial guard carried into exile to Babylon the people who remained in the city, along with those who had gone over to him, and the rest of the people. 10But Nebuzaradan the commander of the guard left behind in the land of Judah some of the poor people, who owned nothing; and at that time he gave them vineyards and fields.

11Now Nebuchadnezzar king of Babylon had given these orders about Jeremiah through Nebuzaradan commander of the imperial guard: 12"Take him and look after him; don't harm him but do for him whatever he asks." 13So Nebuzaradan the commander of the guard, Nebushazban a chief officer, Nergal-Sharezer a high official and all the other officers of the king of Babylon 14sent and had

[a]23 Or *and you will cause this city to* [b]3 Or *Nergal-Sharezer, Samgar-Nebo, Sarsekim* [c]4 Or *the Jordan Valley* [d]5 Or *Chaldean* [e]8 Or *Chaldeans*

Jeremiah taken out of the courtyard of the guard. They turned him over to Gedaliah son of Ahikam, the son of Shaphan, to take him back to his home. So he remained among his own people.

15While Jeremiah had been confined in the courtyard of the guard, the word of the LORD came to him: 16"Go and tell Ebed-Melech the Cushite, 'This is what the LORD Almighty, the God of Israel, says: I am about to fulfill my words against this city through disaster, not prosperity. At that time they will be fulfilled before your eyes. 17But I will rescue you on that day, declares the LORD; you will not be handed over to those you fear. 18I will save you; you will not fall by the sword but will escape with your life, because you trust in me, declares the LORD.' "

Jeremiah Freed

40 The word came to Jeremiah from the LORD after Nebuzaradan commander of the imperial guard had released him at Ramah. He had found Jeremiah bound in chains among all the captives from Jerusalem and Judah who were being carried into exile to Babylon. 2When the commander of the guard found Jeremiah, he said to him, "The LORD your God decreed this disaster for this place. 3And now the LORD has brought it about; he has done just as he said he would. All this happened because you people sinned against the LORD and did not obey him. 4But today I am freeing you from the chains on your wrists. Come with me to Babylon, if you like, and I will look after you; but if you do not want to, then don't come. Look, the whole country lies before you; go wherever you please." 5However, before Jeremiah turned to go,[a] Nebuzaradan added, "Go back to Gedaliah son of Ahikam, the son of Shaphan, whom the king of Babylon has appointed over the towns of Judah, and live with him among the people, or go anywhere else you please."

Then the commander gave him provisions and a present and let him go. 6So Jeremiah went to Gedaliah son of Ahikam at Mizpah and stayed with him among the people who were left behind in the land.

Gedaliah Assassinated

7When all the army officers and their men who were still in the open country heard that the king of Babylon had appointed Gedaliah son of Ahikam as governor over the land and had put him in charge of the men, women and children who were the poorest in the land and who had not been carried into exile to Babylon, 8they came to Gedaliah at Mizpah—Ishmael son of Nethaniah, Johanan and Jonathan the sons of Kareah, Seraiah son of Tanhumeth, the sons of Ephai the Netophathite, and Jaazaniah[b] the son of the Maacathite, and their men. 9Gedaliah son of Ahikam, the son of Shaphan, took an oath to reassure them and their men. "Do not be afraid to serve the Babylonians,[c]" he said. "Settle down in the land and serve the king of Babylon, and it will go well with you. 10I myself will stay at Mizpah to represent you before the Babylonians who come to us, but you are to harvest the wine, summer fruit and oil, and put them in your storage jars, and live in the towns you have taken over."

11When all the Jews in Moab, Ammon, Edom and all the other countries heard that the king of Babylon had left a remnant in Judah and had appointed Gedaliah son of Ahikam, the son of Shaphan, as governor over them, 12they all came back to the land of Judah, to Gedaliah at Mizpah, from all the countries where they had been scattered. And they harvested an abundance of wine and summer fruit.

13Johanan son of Kareah and all the army officers still in the open country came to Gedaliah at Mizpah 14and said to him, "Don't you know that Baalis king of the Ammonites has sent Ishmael son of Nethaniah to take your life?" But Gedaliah son of Ahikam did not believe them.

15Then Johanan son of Kareah said privately to Gedaliah in Mizpah, "Let me go and kill Ishmael son of Nethaniah, and no one will know it. Why should he take your life and cause all the Jews who are gathered around you to be scattered and the remnant of Judah to perish?"

16But Gedaliah son of Ahikam said to Johanan son of Kareah, "Don't do such a thing! What you are saying about Ishmael is not true."

41 In the seventh month Ishmael son of Nethaniah, the son of Elishama, who was of royal blood and had been one of the king's officers, came with ten men to Gedaliah son of Ahikam at Mizpah. While they were eating together there, 2Ishmael son of Nethaniah and the ten men who were with him got up and struck down Gedaliah son of Ahikam, the son of Shaphan, with the sword, killing the one whom the king of Babylon had appointed as governor over the land. 3Ishmael also killed all the Jews who were with Gedaliah at Mizpah, as well as the Babylonian[d] soldiers who were there.

4The day after Gedaliah's assassination, before anyone knew about it, 5eighty men who had shaved off their beards, torn their clothes and cut themselves came from Shechem, Shiloh and Samaria, bringing grain offerings and incense with them to the house of the LORD. 6Ishmael son of Nethaniah went out from Mizpah to meet them, weeping as he went. When he met them, he said, "Come to Gedaliah son of Ahikam." 7When they went into the city, Ishmael son of Nethaniah and the men who were with him slaughtered them and threw them into a cistern. 8But ten of them said to Ishmael, "Don't kill us! We have wheat and

[a]5 Or *Jeremiah answered* [b]8 Hebrew *Jezaniah*, a variant of *Jaazaniah* [c]9 Or *Chaldeans*; also in verse 10
[d]3 Or *Chaldean*

barley, oil and honey, hidden in a field." So he
let them alone and did not kill them with the
others. 9Now the cistern where he threw all the
bodies of the men he had killed along with
Gedaliah was the one King Asa had made as
part of his defense against Baasha king of Israel. Ishmael son of Nethaniah filled it with the
dead.
10Ishmael made captives of all the rest of
the people who were in Mizpah—the king's
daughters along with all the others who were
left there, over whom Nebuzaradan commander of the imperial guard had appointed Gedaliah son of Ahikam. Ishmael son of Nethaniah
took them captive and set out to cross over to
the Ammonites.
11When Johanan son of Kareah and all the
army officers who were with him heard about
all the crimes Ishmael son of Nethaniah had
committed, 12they took all their men and went
to fight Ishmael son of Nethaniah. They caught
up with him near the great pool in Gibeon.
13When all the people Ishmael had with him
saw Johanan son of Kareah and the army officers who were with him, they were glad. 14All
the people Ishmael had taken captive at Mizpah turned and went over to Johanan son of
Kareah. 15But Ishmael son of Nethaniah and
eight of his men escaped from Johanan and
fled to the Ammonites.

Flight to Egypt

16Then Johanan son of Kareah and all the
army officers who were with him led away all
the survivors from Mizpah whom he had recovered from Ishmael son of Nethaniah after
he had assassinated Gedaliah son of Ahikam:
the soldiers, women, children and court officials he had brought from Gibeon. 17And they
went on, stopping at Geruth Kimham near
Bethlehem on their way to Egypt 18to escape
the Babylonians.[a] They were afraid of them
because Ishmael son of Nethaniah had killed
Gedaliah son of Ahikam, whom the king of
Babylon had appointed as governor over the
land.

42 Then all the army officers, including Johanan son of Kareah and Jezaniah[b] son
of Hoshaiah, and all the people from the least
to the greatest approached 2Jeremiah the
prophet and said to him, "Please hear our petition and pray to the LORD your God for this
entire remnant. For as you now see, though we
were once many, now only a few are left.
3Pray that the LORD your God will tell us
where we should go and what we should do."
4"I have heard you," replied Jeremiah the
prophet. "I will certainly pray to the LORD
your God as you have requested; I will tell you
everything the LORD says and will keep nothing back from you."
5Then they said to Jeremiah, "May the LORD
be a true and faithful witness against us if we
do not act in accordance with everything the
LORD your God sends you to tell us. 6Whether
it is favorable or unfavorable, we will obey the
LORD our God, to whom we are sending you,
so that it will go well with us, for we will obey
the LORD our God."
7Ten days later the word of the LORD came
to Jeremiah. 8So he called together Johanan
son of Kareah and all the army officers who
were with him and all the people from the least
to the greatest. 9He said to them, "This is what
the LORD, the God of Israel, to whom you sent
me to present your petition, says: 10'If you stay
in this land, I will build you up and not tear
you down; I will plant you and not uproot you,
for I am grieved over the disaster I have inflicted on you. 11Do not be afraid of the king of
Babylon, whom you now fear. Do not be afraid
of him, declares the LORD, for I am with you
and will save you and deliver you from his
hands. 12I will show you compassion so that he
will have compassion on you and restore you
to your land.'
13"However, if you say, 'We will not stay in
this land,' and so disobey the LORD your God,
14and if you say, 'No, we will go and live in
Egypt, where we will not see war or hear the
trumpet or be hungry for bread,' 15then hear
the word of the LORD, O remnant of Judah.
This is what the LORD Almighty, the God of
Israel, says: 'If you are determined to go to
Egypt and you do go to settle there, 16then the
sword you fear will overtake you there, and the
famine you dread will follow you into Egypt,
and there you will die. 17Indeed, all who are
determined to go to Egypt to settle there will
die by the sword, famine and plague; not one
of them will survive or escape the disaster I
will bring on them.' 18This is what the LORD
Almighty, the God of Israel, says: 'As my anger and wrath have been poured out on those
who lived in Jerusalem, so will my wrath be
poured out on you when you go to Egypt. You
will be an object of cursing and horror, of condemnation and reproach; you will never see
this place again.'
19"O remnant of Judah, the LORD has told
you, 'Do not go to Egypt.' Be sure of this: I
warn you today 20that you made a fatal mistake[c] when you sent me to the LORD your God
and said, 'Pray to the LORD our God for us; tell
us everything he says and we will do it.' 21I
have told you today, but you still have not
obeyed the LORD your God in all he sent me to
tell you. 22So now, be sure of this: You will die
by the sword, famine and plague in the place
where you want to go to settle."

43 When Jeremiah finished telling the people all the words of the LORD their
God—everything the LORD had sent him to
tell them— 2Azariah son of Hoshaiah and Johanan son of Kareah and all the arrogant men
said to Jeremiah, "You are lying! The LORD
our God has not sent you to say, 'You must not
go to Egypt to settle there.' 3But Baruch son of
Neriah is inciting you against us to hand us

[a] *18* Or *Chaldeans* [b] *1* Hebrew; Septuagint (see also 43:2) *Azariah* [c] *20* Or *you erred in your hearts*

over to the Babylonians,[a] so they may kill us or carry us into exile to Babylon."

4So Johanan son of Kareah and all the army officers and all the people disobeyed the LORD's command to stay in the land of Judah. 5Instead, Johanan son of Kareah and all the army officers led away all the remnant of Judah who had come back to live in the land of Judah from all the nations where they had been scattered. 6They also led away all the men, women and children and the king's daughters whom Nebuzaradan commander of the imperial guard had left with Gedaliah son of Ahikam, the son of Shaphan, and Jeremiah the prophet and Baruch son of Neriah. 7So they entered Egypt in disobedience to the LORD and went as far as Tahpanhes.

8In Tahpanhes the word of the LORD came to Jeremiah: 9"While the Jews are watching, take some large stones with you and bury them in clay in the brick pavement at the entrance to Pharaoh's palace in Tahpanhes. 10Then say to them, 'This is what the LORD Almighty, the God of Israel, says: I will send for my servant Nebuchadnezzar king of Babylon, and I will set his throne over these stones I have buried here; he will spread his royal canopy above them. 11He will come and attack Egypt, bringing death to those destined for death, captivity to those destined for captivity, and the sword to those destined for the sword. 12He[b] will set fire to the temples of the gods of Egypt; he will burn their temples and take their gods captive. As a shepherd wraps his garment around him, so will he wrap Egypt around himself and depart from there unscathed. 13There in the temple of the sun[c] in Egypt he will demolish the sacred pillars and will burn down the temples of the gods of Egypt.' "

Disaster Because of Idolatry

44 This word came to Jeremiah concerning all the Jews living in Lower Egypt—in Migdol, Tahpanhes and Memphis[d]—and in Upper Egypt[e]: 2"This is what the LORD Almighty, the God of Israel, says: You saw the great disaster I brought on Jerusalem and on all the towns of Judah. Today they lie deserted and in ruins 3because of the evil they have done. They provoked me to anger by burning incense and by worshiping other gods that neither they nor you nor your fathers ever knew. 4Again and again I sent my servants the prophets, who said, 'Do not do this detestable thing that I hate!' 5But they did not listen or pay attention; they did not turn from their wickedness or stop burning incense to other gods. 6Therefore, my fierce anger was poured out; it raged against the towns of Judah and the streets of Jerusalem and made them the desolate ruins they are today.

7"Now this is what the LORD God Almighty, the God of Israel, says: Why bring such great disaster on yourselves by cutting off from Judah the men and women, the children and infants, and so leave yourselves without a remnant? 8Why provoke me to anger with what your hands have made, burning incense to other gods in Egypt, where you have come to live? You will destroy yourselves and make yourselves an object of cursing and reproach among all the nations on earth. 9Have you forgotten the wickedness committed by your fathers and by the kings and queens of Judah and the wickedness committed by you and your wives in the land of Judah and the streets of Jerusalem? 10To this day they have not humbled themselves or shown reverence, nor have they followed my law and the decrees I set before you and your fathers.

11"Therefore, this is what the LORD Almighty, the God of Israel, says: I am determined to bring disaster on you and to destroy all Judah. 12I will take away the remnant of Judah who were determined to go to Egypt to settle there. They will all perish in Egypt; they will fall by the sword or die from famine. From the least to the greatest, they will die by sword or famine. They will become an object of cursing and horror, of condemnation and reproach. 13I will punish those who live in Egypt with the sword, famine and plague, as I punished Jerusalem. 14None of the remnant of Judah who have gone to live in Egypt will escape or survive to return to the land of Judah, to which they long to return and live; none will return except a few fugitives."

15Then all the men who knew that their wives were burning incense to other gods, along with all the women who were present—a large assembly—and all the people living in Lower and Upper Egypt,[f] said to Jeremiah, 16"We will not listen to the message you have spoken to us in the name of the LORD! 17We will certainly do everything we said we would: We will burn incense to the Queen of Heaven and will pour out drink offerings to her just as we and our fathers, our kings and our officials did in the towns of Judah and in the streets of Jerusalem. At that time we had plenty of food and were well off and suffered no harm. 18But ever since we stopped burning incense to the Queen of Heaven and pouring out drink offerings to her, we have had nothing and have been perishing by sword and famine."

19The women added, "When we burned incense to the Queen of Heaven and poured out drink offerings to her, did not our husbands know that we were making cakes like her image and pouring out drink offerings to her?"

20Then Jeremiah said to all the people, both men and women, who were answering him, 21"Did not the LORD remember and think about the incense burned in the towns of Judah and the streets of Jerusalem by you and your fathers, your kings and your officials and the people of the land? 22When the LORD could no longer endure your wicked actions and the de-

[a] 3 Or *Chaldeans* [b] 12 Or *I* [c] 13 Or *in Heliopolis* [d] 1 Hebrew *Noph* [e] 1 Hebrew *in Pathros*
[f] 15 Hebrew *in Egypt and Pathros*

testable things you did, your land became an
object of cursing and a desolate waste without
inhabitants, as it is today. 23Because you have
burned incense and have sinned against the
LORD and have not obeyed him or followed his
law or his decrees or his stipulations, this disaster has come upon you, as you now see."

24Then Jeremiah said to all the people, including the women, "Hear the word of the
LORD, all you people of Judah in Egypt. 25This
is what the LORD Almighty, the God of Israel,
says: You and your wives have shown by your
actions what you promised when you said,
'We will certainly carry out the vows we made
to burn incense and pour out drink offerings to
the Queen of Heaven.'

"Go ahead then, do what you promised!
Keep your vows! 26But hear the word of the
LORD, all Jews living in Egypt: 'I swear by my
great name,' says the LORD, 'that no one from
Judah living anywhere in Egypt will ever again
invoke my name or swear, "As surely as the
Sovereign LORD lives." 27For I am watching
over them for harm, not for good; the Jews in
Egypt will perish by sword and famine until
they are all destroyed. 28Those who escape the
sword and return to the land of Judah from
Egypt will be very few. Then the whole remnant of Judah who came to live in Egypt will
know whose word will stand—mine or theirs.

29" 'This will be the sign to you that I will
punish you in this place,' declares the LORD,
'so that you will know that my threats of harm
against you will surely stand.' 30This is what
the LORD says: 'I am going to hand Pharaoh
Hophra king of Egypt over to his enemies who
seek his life, just as I handed Zedekiah king of
Judah over to Nebuchadnezzar king of Babylon, the enemy who was seeking his life.' "

A Message to Baruch

45 This is what Jeremiah the prophet told
Baruch son of Neriah in the fourth year
of Jehoiakim son of Josiah king of Judah, after
Baruch had written on a scroll the words Jeremiah was then dictating: 2"This is what the
LORD, the God of Israel, says to you, Baruch:
3You said, 'Woe to me! The LORD has added
sorrow to my pain; I am worn out with groaning and find no rest.' "

4⌊The LORD said,⌋ "Say this to him: 'This is
what the LORD says: I will overthrow what I
have built and uproot what I have planted,
throughout the land. 5Should you then seek
great things for yourself? Seek them not. For
I will bring disaster on all people, declares the
LORD, but wherever you go I will let you escape with your life.' "

A Message About Egypt

46 This is the word of the LORD that came
to Jeremiah the prophet concerning the
nations:

2Concerning Egypt:

This is the message against the army of
Pharaoh Neco king of Egypt, which was defeated at Carchemish on the Euphrates River
by Nebuchadnezzar king of Babylon in the
fourth year of Jehoiakim son of Josiah king of
Judah:

3"Prepare your shields, both large and
small,
and march out for battle!
4Harness the horses,
mount the steeds!
Take your positions
with helmets on!
Polish your spears,
put on your armor!
5What do I see?
They are terrified,
they are retreating,
their warriors are defeated.
They flee in haste
without looking back,
and there is terror on every side,"
declares the LORD.

6"The swift cannot flee
nor the strong escape.
In the north by the River Euphrates
they stumble and fall.

7"Who is this that rises like the Nile,
like rivers of surging waters?
8Egypt rises like the Nile,
like rivers of surging waters.
She says, 'I will rise and cover the earth;
I will destroy cities and their people.'
9Charge, O horses!
Drive furiously, O charioteers!
March on, O warriors—
men of Cush[a] and Put who carry
shields,
men of Lydia who draw the bow.
10But that day belongs to the Lord, the
LORD Almighty—
a day of vengeance, for vengeance on
his foes.
The sword will devour till it is satisfied,
till it has quenched its thirst with blood.
For the Lord, the LORD Almighty, will
offer sacrifice
in the land of the north by the River
Euphrates.

11"Go up to Gilead and get balm,
O Virgin Daughter of Egypt.
But you multiply remedies in vain;
there is no healing for you.
12The nations will hear of your shame;
your cries will fill the earth.
One warrior will stumble over another;
both will fall down together."

13This is the message the LORD spoke to
Jeremiah the prophet about the coming of Nebuchadnezzar king of Babylon to attack Egypt:

14"Announce this in Egypt, and proclaim it
in Migdol;

a9 That is, the upper Nile region

proclaim it also in Memphis[a] and
Tahpanhes:
'Take your positions and get ready,
for the sword devours those around
you.'
15Why will your warriors be laid low?
They cannot stand, for the LORD will
push them down.
16They will stumble repeatedly;
they will fall over each other.
They will say, 'Get up, let us go back
to our own people and our native lands,
away from the sword of the oppressor.'
17There they will exclaim,
'Pharaoh king of Egypt is only a loud
noise;
he has missed his opportunity.'

18"As surely as I live," declares the King,
whose name is the LORD Almighty,
"one will come who is like Tabor among
the mountains,
like Carmel by the sea.
19Pack your belongings for exile,
you who live in Egypt,
for Memphis will be laid waste
and lie in ruins without inhabitant.

20"Egypt is a beautiful heifer,
but a gadfly is coming
against her from the north.
21The mercenaries in her ranks
are like fattened calves.
They too will turn and flee together,
they will not stand their ground,
for the day of disaster is coming upon
them,
the time for them to be punished.
22Egypt will hiss like a fleeing serpent
as the enemy advances in force;
they will come against her with axes,
like men who cut down trees.
23They will chop down her forest,"
declares the LORD,
"dense though it be.
They are more numerous than locusts,
they cannot be counted.
24The Daughter of Egypt will be put to
shame,
handed over to the people of the north."

25The LORD Almighty, the God of Israel,
says: "I am about to bring punishment on
Amon god of Thebes,[b] on Pharaoh, on Egypt
and her gods and her kings, and on those who
rely on Pharaoh. 26I will hand them over to
those who seek their lives, to Nebuchadnezzar
king of Babylon and his officers. Later, however, Egypt will be inhabited as in times past,"
declares the LORD.

27"Do not fear, O Jacob my servant;
do not be dismayed, O Israel.
I will surely save you out of a distant
place,
your descendants from the land of their
exile.
Jacob will again have peace and security,
and no one will make him afraid.
28Do not fear, O Jacob my servant,
for I am with you," declares the LORD.
"Though I completely destroy all the
nations
among which I scatter you,
I will not completely destroy you.
I will discipline you but only with justice;
I will not let you go entirely
unpunished."

A Message About the Philistines

47 This is the word of the LORD that came
to Jeremiah the prophet concerning the
Philistines before Pharaoh attacked Gaza:

2This is what the LORD says:

"See how the waters are rising in the
north;
they will become an overflowing
torrent.
They will overflow the land and
everything in it,
the towns and those who live in them.
The people will cry out;
all who dwell in the land will wail
3at the sound of the hoofs of galloping
steeds,
at the noise of enemy chariots
and the rumble of their wheels.
Fathers will not turn to help their children;
their hands will hang limp.
4For the day has come
to destroy all the Philistines
and to cut off all survivors
who could help Tyre and Sidon.
The LORD is about to destroy the
Philistines,
the remnant from the coasts of
Caphtor.[c]
5Gaza will shave her head in mourning;
Ashkelon will be silenced.
O remnant on the plain,
how long will you cut yourselves?

6" 'Ah, sword of the LORD,' ⌞you cry,⌟
'how long till you rest?
Return to your scabbard;
cease and be still.'
7But how can it rest
when the LORD has commanded it,
when he has ordered it
to attack Ashkelon and the coast?"

A Message About Moab

48 Concerning Moab:

This is what the LORD Almighty, the God of
Israel, says:

"Woe to Nebo, for it will be ruined.
Kiriathaim will be disgraced and
captured;
the stronghold[d] will be disgraced and
shattered.

[a] 14 Hebrew *Noph*; also in verse 19 [b] 25 Hebrew *No* [c] 4 That is, Crete [d] 1 Or */Misgab*

2 Moab will be praised no more;
in Heshbon[a] men will plot her downfall:
'Come, let us put an end to that nation.'
You too, O Madmen,[b] will be silenced;
the sword will pursue you.
3 Listen to the cries from Horonaim,
cries of great havoc and destruction.
4 Moab will be broken;
her little ones will cry out.[c]
5 They go up the way to Luhith,
weeping bitterly as they go;
on the road down to Horonaim
anguished cries over the destruction are heard.
6 Flee! Run for your lives;
become like a bush[d] in the desert.
7 Since you trust in your deeds and riches,
you too will be taken captive,
and Chemosh will go into exile,
together with his priests and officials.
8 The destroyer will come against every town,
and not a town will escape.
The valley will be ruined
and the plateau destroyed,
because the LORD has spoken.
9 Put salt on Moab,
for she will be laid waste[e];
her towns will become desolate,
with no one to live in them.

10 "A curse on him who is lax in doing the LORD's work!
A curse on him who keeps his sword from bloodshed!

11 "Moab has been at rest from youth,
like wine left on its dregs,
not poured from one jar to another—
she has not gone into exile.
So she tastes as she did,
and her aroma is unchanged.
12 But days are coming,"
declares the LORD,
"when I will send men who pour from jars,
and they will pour her out;
they will empty her jars
and smash her jugs.
13 Then Moab will be ashamed of Chemosh,
as the house of Israel was ashamed
when they trusted in Bethel.

14 "How can you say, 'We are warriors,
men valiant in battle'?
15 Moab will be destroyed and her towns invaded;
her finest young men will go down in the slaughter,"
declares the King, whose name is the LORD Almighty.
16 "The fall of Moab is at hand;
her calamity will come quickly.
17 Mourn for her, all who live around her,
all who know her fame;
say, 'How broken is the mighty scepter,
how broken the glorious staff!'

18 "Come down from your glory
and sit on the parched ground,
O inhabitants of the Daughter of Dibon,
for he who destroys Moab
will come up against you
and ruin your fortified cities.
19 Stand by the road and watch,
you who live in Aroer.
Ask the man fleeing and the woman escaping,
ask them, 'What has happened?'
20 Moab is disgraced, for she is shattered.
Wail and cry out!
Announce by the Arnon
that Moab is destroyed.
21 Judgment has come to the plateau—
to Holon, Jahzah and Mephaath,
22 to Dibon, Nebo and Beth Diblathaim,
23 to Kiriathaim, Beth Gamul and Beth Meon,
24 to Kerioth and Bozrah—
to all the towns of Moab, far and near.
25 Moab's horn[f] is cut off;
her arm is broken,"
declares the LORD.

26 "Make her drunk,
for she has defied the LORD.
Let Moab wallow in her vomit;
let her be an object of ridicule.
27 Was not Israel the object of your ridicule?
Was she caught among thieves,
that you shake your head in scorn
whenever you speak of her?
28 Abandon your towns and dwell among the rocks,
you who live in Moab.
Be like a dove that makes its nest
at the mouth of a cave.

29 "We have heard of Moab's pride—
her overweening pride and conceit,
her pride and arrogance
and the haughtiness of her heart.
30 I know her insolence but it is futile,"
declares the LORD,
"and her boasts accomplish nothing.
31 Therefore I wail over Moab,
for all Moab I cry out,
I moan for the men of Kir Hareseth.
32 I weep for you, as Jazer weeps,
O vines of Sibmah.
Your branches spread as far as the sea;
they reached as far as the sea of Jazer.
The destroyer has fallen
on your ripened fruit and grapes.
33 Joy and gladness are gone
from the orchards and fields of Moab.
I have stopped the flow of wine from the presses;
no one treads them with shouts of joy.

[a]2 The Hebrew for *Heshbon* sounds like the Hebrew for *plot.* [b]2 The name of the Moabite town Madmen sounds like the Hebrew for *be silenced.* [c]4 Hebrew; Septuagint */ proclaim it to Zoar* [d]6 Or *like Aroer* [e]9 Or *Give wings to Moab, / for she will fly away* [f]25 *Horn* here symbolizes strength.

Although there are shouts,
they are not shouts of joy.

34"The sound of their cry rises
from Heshbon to Elealeh and Jahaz,
from Zoar as far as Horonaim and Eglath Shelishiyah,
for even the waters of Nimrim are dried up.
35In Moab I will put an end
to those who make offerings on the high places
and burn incense to their gods,"
declares the LORD.
36"So my heart laments for Moab like a flute;
it laments like a flute for the men of Kir Hareseth.
The wealth they acquired is gone.
37Every head is shaved
and every beard cut off;
every hand is slashed
and every waist is covered with sackcloth.
38On all the roofs in Moab
and in the public squares
there is nothing but mourning,
for I have broken Moab
like a jar that no one wants,"
declares the LORD.
39"How shattered she is! How they wail!
How Moab turns her back in shame!
Moab has become an object of ridicule,
an object of horror to all those around her."

40This is what the LORD says:

"Look! An eagle is swooping down,
spreading its wings over Moab.
41Kerioth[a] will be captured
and the strongholds taken.
In that day the hearts of Moab's warriors
will be like the heart of a woman in labor.
42Moab will be destroyed as a nation
because she defied the LORD.
43Terror and pit and snare await you,
O people of Moab,"
declares the LORD.
44"Whoever flees from the terror
will fall into a pit,
whoever climbs out of the pit
will be caught in a snare;
for I will bring upon Moab
the year of her punishment,"
declares the LORD.

45"In the shadow of Heshbon
the fugitives stand helpless,
for a fire has gone out from Heshbon,
a blaze from the midst of Sihon;
it burns the foreheads of Moab,
the skulls of the noisy boasters.
46Woe to you, O Moab!
The people of Chemosh are destroyed;
your sons are taken into exile
and your daughters into captivity.

47"Yet I will restore the fortunes of Moab
in days to come,"
declares the LORD.

Here ends the judgment on Moab.

A Message About Ammon

49 Concerning the Ammonites:

This is what the LORD says:

"Has Israel no sons?
Has she no heirs?
Why then has Molech[b] taken possession of Gad?
Why do his people live in its towns?
2But the days are coming,"
declares the LORD,
"when I will sound the battle cry
against Rabbah of the Ammonites;
it will become a mound of ruins,
and its surrounding villages will be set on fire.
Then Israel will drive out
those who drove her out,"
says the LORD.
3"Wail, O Heshbon, for Ai is destroyed!
Cry out, O inhabitants of Rabbah!
Put on sackcloth and mourn;
rush here and there inside the walls,
for Molech will go into exile,
together with his priests and officials.
4Why do you boast of your valleys,
boast of your valleys so fruitful?
O unfaithful daughter,
you trust in your riches and say,
'Who will attack me?'
5I will bring terror on you
from all those around you,"
declares the Lord,
the LORD Almighty.
"Every one of you will be driven away,
and no one will gather the fugitives.

6"Yet afterward, I will restore the fortunes of the Ammonites,"
declares the LORD.

A Message About Edom

7Concerning Edom:

This is what the LORD Almighty says:

"Is there no longer wisdom in Teman?
Has counsel perished from the prudent?
Has their wisdom decayed?
8Turn and flee, hide in deep caves,
you who live in Dedan,
for I will bring disaster on Esau
at the time I punish him.
9If grape pickers came to you,
would they not leave a few grapes?
If thieves came during the night,
would they not steal only as much as they wanted?

[a] 41 Or *The cities* [b] 1 Or *their king*; Hebrew *malcam*; also in verse 3

10But I will strip Esau bare;
I will uncover his hiding places,
so that he cannot conceal himself.
His children, relatives and neighbors will perish,
and he will be no more.
11Leave your orphans; I will protect their lives.
Your widows too can trust in me."

12This is what the LORD says: "If those who
do not deserve to drink the cup must drink it,
why should you go unpunished? You will not
go unpunished, but must drink it. 13I swear by
myself," declares the LORD, "that Bozrah will
become a ruin and an object of horror, of reproach and of cursing; and all its towns will be
in ruins forever."

14I have heard a message from the LORD:
An envoy was sent to the nations to say,
"Assemble yourselves to attack it!
Rise up for battle!"

15"Now I will make you small among the nations,
despised among men.
16The terror you inspire
and the pride of your heart have deceived you,
you who live in the clefts of the rocks,
who occupy the heights of the hill.
Though you build your nest as high as the eagle's,
from there I will bring you down,"
declares the LORD.
17"Edom will become an object of horror;
all who pass by will be appalled and will scoff
because of all its wounds.
18As Sodom and Gomorrah were overthrown,
along with their neighboring towns,"
says the LORD,
"so no one will live there;
no man will dwell in it.

19"Like a lion coming up from Jordan's thickets
to a rich pastureland,
I will chase Edom from its land in an instant.
Who is the chosen one I will appoint for this?
Who is like me and who can challenge me?
And what shepherd can stand against me?"
20Therefore, hear what the LORD has planned against Edom,
what he has purposed against those who live in Teman:
The young of the flock will be dragged away;
he will completely destroy their pasture because of them.
21At the sound of their fall the earth will tremble;
their cry will resound to the Red Sea.[a]
22Look! An eagle will soar and swoop down,
spreading its wings over Bozrah.
In that day the hearts of Edom's warriors
will be like the heart of a woman in labor.

A Message About Damascus

23Concerning Damascus:

"Hamath and Arpad are dismayed,
for they have heard bad news.
They are disheartened,
troubled like[b] the restless sea.
24Damascus has become feeble,
she has turned to flee
and panic has gripped her;
anguish and pain have seized her,
pain like that of a woman in labor.
25Why has the city of renown not been abandoned,
the town in which I delight?
26Surely, her young men will fall in the streets;
all her soldiers will be silenced in that day,"
declares the LORD Almighty.
27"I will set fire to the walls of Damascus;
it will consume the fortresses of Ben-Hadad."

A Message About Kedar and Hazor

28Concerning Kedar and the kingdoms of
Hazor, which Nebuchadnezzar king of Babylon attacked:

This is what the LORD says:

"Arise, and attack Kedar
and destroy the people of the East.
29Their tents and their flocks will be taken;
their shelters will be carried off
with all their goods and camels.
Men will shout to them,
'Terror on every side!'

30"Flee quickly away!
Stay in deep caves, you who live in Hazor,"
declares the LORD.
"Nebuchadnezzar king of Babylon has plotted against you;
he has devised a plan against you.

31"Arise and attack a nation at ease,
which lives in confidence,"
declares the LORD,
"a nation that has neither gates nor bars;
its people live alone.
32Their camels will become plunder,
and their large herds will be booty.

[a]21 Hebrew *Yam Suph*; that is, Sea of Reeds [b]23 Hebrew *on* or *by*

I will scatter to the winds those who are
in distant places[a]
and will bring disaster on them from
every side,"
declares the LORD.
33"Hazor will become a haunt of jackals,
a desolate place forever.
No one will live there;
no man will dwell in it."

A Message About Elam

34This is the word of the LORD that came to
Jeremiah the prophet concerning Elam, early
in the reign of Zedekiah king of Judah:

35This is what the LORD Almighty says:

"See, I will break the bow of Elam,
the mainstay of their might.
36I will bring against Elam the four winds
from the four quarters of the heavens;
I will scatter them to the four winds,
and there will not be a nation
where Elam's exiles do not go.
37I will shatter Elam before their foes,
before those who seek their lives;
I will bring disaster upon them,
even my fierce anger,"
declares the LORD.
"I will pursue them with the sword
until I have made an end of them.
38I will set my throne in Elam
and destroy her king and officials,"
declares the LORD.

39"Yet I will restore the fortunes of Elam
in days to come,"
declares the LORD.

A Message About Babylon

50 This is the word the LORD spoke
through Jeremiah the prophet concerning Babylon and the land of the Babylonians[b]:

2"Announce and proclaim among the
nations,
lift up a banner and proclaim it;
keep nothing back, but say,
'Babylon will be captured;
Bel will be put to shame,
Marduk filled with terror.
Her images will be put to shame
and her idols filled with terror.'
3A nation from the north will attack her
and lay waste her land.
No one will live in it;
both men and animals will flee away.

4"In those days, at that time,"
declares the LORD,
"the people of Israel and the people of
Judah together
will go in tears to seek the LORD their
God.
5They will ask the way to Zion
and turn their faces toward it.
They will come and bind themselves to
the LORD
in an everlasting covenant
that will not be forgotten.

6"My people have been lost sheep;
their shepherds have led them astray
and caused them to roam on the
mountains.
They wandered over mountain and hill
and forgot their own resting place.
7Whoever found them devoured them;
their enemies said, 'We are not guilty,
for they sinned against the LORD, their
true pasture,
the LORD, the hope of their fathers.'

8"Flee out of Babylon;
leave the land of the Babylonians,
and be like the goats that lead the flock.
9For I will stir up and bring against
Babylon
an alliance of great nations from the
land of the north.
They will take up their positions against
her,
and from the north she will be captured.
Their arrows will be like skilled warriors
who do not return empty-handed.
10So Babylonia[c] will be plundered;
all who plunder her will have their fill,"
declares the LORD.

11"Because you rejoice and are glad,
you who pillage my inheritance,
because you frolic like a heifer threshing
grain
and neigh like stallions,
12your mother will be greatly ashamed;
she who gave you birth will be
disgraced.
She will be the least of the nations—
a wilderness, a dry land, a desert.
13Because of the LORD's anger she will not
be inhabited
but will be completely desolate.
All who pass Babylon will be horrified
and scoff
because of all her wounds.

14"Take up your positions around Babylon,
all you who draw the bow.
Shoot at her! Spare no arrows,
for she has sinned against the LORD.
15Shout against her on every side!
She surrenders, her towers fall,
her walls are torn down.
Since this is the vengeance of the LORD,
take vengeance on her;
do to her as she has done to others.
16Cut off from Babylon the sower,
and the reaper with his sickle at harvest.
Because of the sword of the oppressor
let everyone return to his own people,
let everyone flee to his own land.

17"Israel is a scattered flock

[a]32 Or *who clip the hair by their foreheads* [b]1 Or *Chaldeans*; also in verses 8, 25, 35 and 45
[c]10 Or *Chaldea*

that lions have chased away.
The first to devour him
was the king of Assyria;
the last to crush his bones
was Nebuchadnezzar king of Babylon."

18Therefore this is what the LORD Almighty, the God of Israel, says:

"I will punish the king of Babylon and his land
as I punished the king of Assyria.
19But I will bring Israel back to his own pasture
and he will graze on Carmel and Bashan;
his appetite will be satisfied
on the hills of Ephraim and Gilead.
20In those days, at that time,"
declares the LORD,
"search will be made for Israel's guilt,
but there will be none,
and for the sins of Judah,
but none will be found,
for I will forgive the remnant I spare.

21"Attack the land of Merathaim
and those who live in Pekod.
Pursue, kill and completely destroy[a] them,"
declares the LORD.
"Do everything I have commanded you.
22The noise of battle is in the land,
the noise of great destruction!
23How broken and shattered
is the hammer of the whole earth!
How desolate is Babylon
among the nations!
24I set a trap for you, O Babylon,
and you were caught before you knew it;
you were found and captured
because you opposed the LORD.
25The LORD has opened his arsenal
and brought out the weapons of his wrath,
for the Sovereign LORD Almighty has work to do
in the land of the Babylonians.
26Come against her from afar.
Break open her granaries;
pile her up like heaps of grain.
Completely destroy her
and leave her no remnant.
27Kill all her young bulls;
let them go down to the slaughter!
Woe to them! For their day has come,
the time for them to be punished.
28Listen to the fugitives and refugees from Babylon
declaring in Zion
how the LORD our God has taken vengeance,
vengeance for his temple.

29"Summon archers against Babylon,
all those who draw the bow.
Encamp all around her;
let no one escape.
Repay her for her deeds;
do to her as she has done.
For she has defied the LORD,
the Holy One of Israel.
30Therefore, her young men will fall in the streets;
all her soldiers will be silenced in that day,"
declares the LORD.
31"See, I am against you, O arrogant one,"
declares the Lord, the LORD Almighty,
"for your day has come,
the time for you to be punished.
32The arrogant one will stumble and fall
and no one will help her up;
I will kindle a fire in her towns
that will consume all who are around her."

33This is what the LORD Almighty says:

"The people of Israel are oppressed,
and the people of Judah as well.
All their captors hold them fast,
refusing to let them go.
34Yet their Redeemer is strong;
the LORD Almighty is his name.
He will vigorously defend their cause
so that he may bring rest to their land,
but unrest to those who live in Babylon.

35"A sword against the Babylonians!"
declares the LORD—
"against those who live in Babylon
and against her officials and wise men!
36A sword against her false prophets!
They will become fools.
A sword against her warriors!
They will be filled with terror.
37A sword against her horses and chariots
and all the foreigners in her ranks!
They will become women.
A sword against her treasures!
They will be plundered.
38A drought on[b] her waters!
They will dry up.
For it is a land of idols,
idols that will go mad with terror.

39"So desert creatures and hyenas will live there,
and there the owl will dwell.
It will never again be inhabited
or lived in from generation to generation.
40As God overthrew Sodom and Gomorrah
along with their neighboring towns,"
declares the LORD,
"so no one will live there;
no man will dwell in it.

41"Look! An army is coming from the north;
a great nation and many kings

[a]21 The Hebrew term refers to the irrevocable giving over of things or persons to the LORD, often by totally destroying them; also in verse 26. [b]38 Or *A sword against*

are being stirred up from the ends of
the earth.
42They are armed with bows and spears;
they are cruel and without mercy.
They sound like the roaring sea
as they ride on their horses;
they come like men in battle formation
to attack you, O Daughter of Babylon.
43The king of Babylon has heard reports
about them,
and his hands hang limp.
Anguish has gripped him,
pain like that of a woman in labor.
44Like a lion coming up from Jordan's
thickets
to a rich pastureland,
I will chase Babylon from its land in an
instant.
Who is the chosen one I will appoint
for this?
Who is like me and who can challenge
me?
And what shepherd can stand against
me?"
45Therefore, hear what the LORD has
planned against Babylon,
what he has purposed against the land
of the Babylonians:
The young of the flock will be dragged
away;
he will completely destroy their pasture
because of them.
46At the sound of Babylon's capture the
earth will tremble;
its cry will resound among the nations.

51 This is what the LORD says:

"See, I will stir up the spirit of a destroyer
against Babylon and the people of Leb
Kamai.[a]
2I will send foreigners to Babylon
to winnow her and to devastate her
land;
they will oppose her on every side
in the day of her disaster.
3Let not the archer string his bow,
nor let him put on his armor.
Do not spare her young men;
completely destroy[b] her army.
4They will fall down slain in Babylon,[c]
fatally wounded in her streets.
5For Israel and Judah have not been
forsaken
by their God, the LORD Almighty,
though their land[d] is full of guilt
before the Holy One of Israel.

6"Flee from Babylon!
Run for your lives!
Do not be destroyed because of her
sins.
It is time for the LORD's vengeance;
he will pay her what she deserves.
7Babylon was a gold cup in the LORD's
hand;
she made the whole earth drunk.
The nations drank her wine;
therefore they have now gone mad.
8Babylon will suddenly fall and be broken.
Wail over her!
Get balm for her pain;
perhaps she can be healed.

9" 'We would have healed Babylon,
but she cannot be healed;
let us leave her and each go to his own
land,
for her judgment reaches to the skies,
it rises as high as the clouds.'

10" 'The LORD has vindicated us;
come, let us tell in Zion
what the LORD our God has done.'

11"Sharpen the arrows,
take up the shields!
The LORD has stirred up the kings of the
Medes,
because his purpose is to destroy
Babylon.
The LORD will take vengeance,
vengeance for his temple.
12Lift up a banner against the walls of
Babylon!
Reinforce the guard,
station the watchmen,
prepare an ambush!
The LORD will carry out his purpose,
his decree against the people of
Babylon.
13You who live by many waters
and are rich in treasures,
your end has come,
the time for you to be cut off.
14The LORD Almighty has sworn by
himself:
I will surely fill you with men, as with
a swarm of locusts,
and they will shout in triumph over you.

15"He made the earth by his power;
he founded the world by his wisdom
and stretched out the heavens by his
understanding.
16When he thunders, the waters in the
heavens roar;
he makes clouds rise from the ends of
the earth.
He sends lightning with the rain
and brings out the wind from his
storehouses.

17"Every man is senseless and without
knowledge;
every goldsmith is shamed by his idols.
His images are a fraud;
they have no breath in them.
18They are worthless, the objects of
mockery;

[a] *1 Leb Kamai* is a cryptogram for Chaldea, that is, Babylonia. [b] *3* The Hebrew term refers to the irrevocable giving over of things or persons to the LORD, often by totally destroying them. [c] *4* Or *Chaldea*
[d] *5* Or / *and the land ⌞of the Babylonians⌟*

when their judgment comes, they will
perish.
19He who is the Portion of Jacob is not like
these,
for he is the Maker of all things,
including the tribe of his inheritance—
the LORD Almighty is his name.

20"You are my war club,
my weapon for battle—
with you I shatter nations,
with you I destroy kingdoms,
21with you I shatter horse and rider,
with you I shatter chariot and driver,
22with you I shatter man and woman,
with you I shatter old man and youth,
with you I shatter young man and
maiden,
23with you I shatter shepherd and flock,
with you I shatter farmer and oxen,
with you I shatter governors and
officials.

24"Before your eyes I will repay Babylon
and all who live in Babylonia[a] for all the
wrong they have done in Zion," declares the
LORD.

25"I am against you, O destroying mountain,
you who destroy the whole earth,"
declares the LORD.
"I will stretch out my hand against you,
roll you off the cliffs,
and make you a burned-out mountain.
26No rock will be taken from you for a
cornerstone,
nor any stone for a foundation,
for you will be desolate forever,"
declares the LORD.

27"Lift up a banner in the land!
Blow the trumpet among the nations!
Prepare the nations for battle against her;
summon against her these kingdoms:
Ararat, Minni and Ashkenaz.
Appoint a commander against her;
send up horses like a swarm of locusts.
28Prepare the nations for battle against
her—
the kings of the Medes,
their governors and all their officials,
and all the countries they rule.
29The land trembles and writhes,
for the LORD's purposes against
Babylon stand—
to lay waste the land of Babylon
so that no one will live there.
30Babylon's warriors have stopped fighting;
they remain in their strongholds.
Their strength is exhausted;
they have become like women.
Her dwellings are set on fire;
the bars of her gates are broken.
31One courier follows another
and messenger follows messenger
to announce to the king of Babylon
that his entire city is captured,
32the river crossings seized,
the marshes set on fire,
and the soldiers terrified."

33This is what the LORD Almighty, the God
of Israel, says:

"The Daughter of Babylon is like a
threshing floor
at the time it is trampled;
the time to harvest her will soon come."

34"Nebuchadnezzar king of Babylon has
devoured us,
he has thrown us into confusion,
he has made us an empty jar.
Like a serpent he has swallowed us
and filled his stomach with our
delicacies,
and then has spewed us out.
35May the violence done to our flesh[b] be
upon Babylon,"
say the inhabitants of Zion.
"May our blood be on those who live in
Babylonia,"
says Jerusalem.

36Therefore, this is what the LORD says:

"See, I will defend your cause
and avenge you;
I will dry up her sea
and make her springs dry.
37Babylon will be a heap of ruins,
a haunt of jackals,
an object of horror and scorn,
a place where no one lives.
38Her people all roar like young lions,
they growl like lion cubs.
39But while they are aroused,
I will set out a feast for them
and make them drunk,
so that they shout with laughter—
then sleep forever and not awake,"
declares the LORD.
40"I will bring them down
like lambs to the slaughter,
like rams and goats.

41"How Sheshach[c] will be captured,
the boast of the whole earth seized!
What a horror Babylon will be
among the nations!
42The sea will rise over Babylon;
its roaring waves will cover her.
43Her towns will be desolate,
a dry and desert land,
a land where no one lives,
through which no man travels.
44I will punish Bel in Babylon
and make him spew out what he has
swallowed.
The nations will no longer stream to him.
And the wall of Babylon will fall.

45"Come out of her, my people!
Run for your lives!

[a]24 Or *Chaldea*; also in verse 35 [b]35 Or *done to us and to our children* [c]41 *Sheshach* is a cryptogram for Babylon.

Run from the fierce anger of the LORD.
46Do not lose heart or be afraid
when rumors are heard in the land;
one rumor comes this year, another the
next,
rumors of violence in the land
and of ruler against ruler.
47For the time will surely come
when I will punish the idols of
Babylon;
her whole land will be disgraced
and her slain will all lie fallen within
her.
48Then heaven and earth and all that is in
them
will shout for joy over Babylon,
for out of the north
destroyers will attack her,"
declares the LORD.

49"Babylon must fall because of Israel's
slain,
just as the slain in all the earth
have fallen because of Babylon.
50You who have escaped the sword,
leave and do not linger!
Remember the LORD in a distant land,
and think on Jerusalem."

51"We are disgraced,
for we have been insulted
and shame covers our faces,
because foreigners have entered
the holy places of the LORD's house."

52"But days are coming," declares the LORD,
"when I will punish her idols,
and throughout her land
the wounded will groan.
53Even if Babylon reaches the sky
and fortifies her lofty stronghold,
I will send destroyers against her,"
declares the LORD.

54"The sound of a cry comes from Babylon,
the sound of great destruction
from the land of the Babylonians.[a]
55The LORD will destroy Babylon;
he will silence her noisy din.
Waves ⌊of enemies⌋ will rage like great
waters;
the roar of their voices will resound.
56A destroyer will come against Babylon;
her warriors will be captured,
and their bows will be broken.
For the LORD is a God of retribution;
he will repay in full.
57I will make her officials and wise men
drunk,
her governors, officers and warriors as
well;
they will sleep forever and not awake,"
declares the King, whose name is the
LORD Almighty.

58This is what the LORD Almighty says:

"Babylon's thick wall will be leveled
and her high gates set on fire;
the peoples exhaust themselves for
nothing,
the nations' labor is only fuel for the
flames."

59This is the message Jeremiah gave to the
staff officer Seraiah son of Neriah, the son of
Mahseiah, when he went to Babylon with Zedekiah king of Judah in the fourth year of his
reign. 60Jeremiah had written on a scroll about
all the disasters that would come upon Babylon—all that had been recorded concerning
Babylon. 61He said to Seraiah, "When you get
to Babylon, see that you read all these words
aloud. 62Then say, 'O LORD, you have said
you will destroy this place, so that neither man
nor animal will live in it; it will be desolate
forever.' 63When you finish reading this scroll,
tie a stone to it and throw it into the Euphrates.
64Then say, 'So will Babylon sink to rise no
more because of the disaster I will bring upon
her. And her people will fall.' "

The words of Jeremiah end here.

The Fall of Jerusalem

52 Zedekiah was twenty-one years old
when he became king, and he reigned in
Jerusalem eleven years. His mother's name
was Hamutal daughter of Jeremiah; she was
from Libnah. 2He did evil in the eyes of the
LORD, just as Jehoiakim had done. 3It was because of the LORD's anger that all this happened to Jerusalem and Judah, and in the end
he thrust them from his presence.

Now Zedekiah rebelled against the king of
Babylon.

4So in the ninth year of Zedekiah's reign, on
the tenth day of the tenth month, Nebuchadnezzar king of Babylon marched against Jerusalem with his whole army. They camped outside the city and built siege works all around it.
5The city was kept under siege until the eleventh year of King Zedekiah.

6By the ninth day of the fourth month the
famine in the city had become so severe that
there was no food for the people to eat. 7Then
the city wall was broken through, and the
whole army fled. They left the city at night
through the gate between the two walls near
the king's garden, though the Babylonians[b]
were surrounding the city. They fled toward
the Arabah,[c] 8but the Babylonian[d] army pursued King Zedekiah and overtook him in the
plains of Jericho. All his soldiers were separated from him and scattered, 9and he was captured.

He was taken to the king of Babylon at
Riblah in the land of Hamath, where he pronounced sentence on him. 10There at Riblah
the king of Babylon slaughtered the sons of
Zedekiah before his eyes; he also killed all the
officials of Judah. 11Then he put out Zedeki-

[a]54 Or *Chaldeans* [b]7 Or *Chaldeans*; also in verse 17 [c]7 Or *the Jordan Valley* [d]8 Or *Chaldean*; also in verse 14

ah's eyes, bound him with bronze shackles and
took him to Babylon, where he put him in prison till the day of his death.
12On the tenth day of the fifth month, in the
nineteenth year of Nebuchadnezzar king of
Babylon, Nebuzaradan commander of the imperial guard, who served the king of Babylon,
came to Jerusalem. 13He set fire to the temple
of the LORD, the royal palace and all the
houses of Jerusalem. Every important building
he burned down. 14The whole Babylonian
army under the commander of the imperial
guard broke down all the walls around Jerusalem. 15Nebuzaradan the commander of the
guard carried into exile some of the poorest
people and those who remained in the city,
along with the rest of the craftsmen[a] and those
who had gone over to the king of Babylon.
16But Nebuzaradan left behind the rest of the
poorest people of the land to work the vineyards and fields.
17The Babylonians broke up the bronze pillars, the movable stands and the bronze Sea
that were at the temple of the LORD and they
carried all the bronze to Babylon. 18They also
took away the pots, shovels, wick trimmers,
sprinkling bowls, dishes and all the bronze articles used in the temple service. 19The commander of the imperial guard took away the
basins, censers, sprinkling bowls, pots, lampstands, dishes and bowls used for drink offerings—all that were made of pure gold or silver.
20The bronze from the two pillars, the Sea
and the twelve bronze bulls under it, and the
movable stands, which King Solomon had
made for the temple of the LORD, was more
than could be weighed. 21Each of the pillars
was eighteen cubits high and twelve cubits in
circumference[b]; each was four fingers thick,
and hollow. 22The bronze capital on top of the
one pillar was five cubits[c] high and was decorated with a network and pomegranates of
bronze all around. The other pillar, with its
pomegranates, was similar. 23There were
ninety-six pomegranates on the sides; the total
number of pomegranates above the surrounding network was a hundred.
24The commander of the guard took as prisoners Seraiah the chief priest, Zephaniah the
priest next in rank and the three doorkeepers.
25Of those still in the city, he took the officer
in charge of the fighting men, and seven royal
advisers. He also took the secretary who was
chief officer in charge of conscripting the people of the land and sixty of his men who were
found in the city. 26Nebuzaradan the commander took them all and brought them to the
king of Babylon at Riblah. 27There at Riblah,
in the land of Hamath, the king had them executed.
So Judah went into captivity, away from her
land. 28This is the number of the people Nebuchadnezzar carried into exile:

in the seventh year, 3,023 Jews;
29in Nebuchadnezzar's eighteenth year,
832 people from Jerusalem;
30in his twenty-third year,
745 Jews taken into exile by Nebuzaradan the commander of the imperial guard.
There were 4,600 people in all.

Jehoiachin Released

31In the thirty-seventh year of the exile of
Jehoiachin king of Judah, in the year Evil-
Merodach[d] became king of Babylon, he released Jehoiachin king of Judah and freed him
from prison on the twenty-fifth day of the
twelfth month. 32He spoke kindly to him and
gave him a seat of honor higher than those of
the other kings who were with him in Babylon.
33So Jehoiachin put aside his prison clothes
and for the rest of his life ate regularly at the
king's table. 34Day by day the king of Babylon
gave Jehoiachin a regular allowance as long as
he lived, till the day of his death.

Lamentations

1 [e]How deserted lies the city,
once so full of people!
How like a widow is she,
who once was great among the nations!
She who was queen among the provinces
has now become a slave.

2Bitterly she weeps at night,
tears are upon her cheeks.
Among all her lovers
there is none to comfort her.
All her friends have betrayed her;
they have become her enemies.

3After affliction and harsh labor,
Judah has gone into exile.
She dwells among the nations;
she finds no resting place.
All who pursue her have overtaken her
in the midst of her distress.

4The roads to Zion mourn,

[a]15 Or *populace* [b]21 That is, about 27 feet (about 8.1 meters) high and 18 feet (about 5.4 meters) in circumference [c]22 That is, about 7 1/2 feet (about 2.3 meters) [d]31 Also called *Amel-Marduk* [e]This chapter is an acrostic poem, the verses of which begin with the successive letters of the Hebrew alphabet.

for no one comes to her appointed
feasts.
All her gateways are desolate,
her priests groan,
her maidens grieve,
and she is in bitter anguish.

5Her foes have become her masters;
her enemies are at ease.
The LORD has brought her grief
because of her many sins.
Her children have gone into exile,
captive before the foe.

6All the splendor has departed
from the Daughter of Zion.
Her princes are like deer
that find no pasture;
in weakness they have fled
before the pursuer.

7In the days of her affliction and wandering
Jerusalem remembers all the treasures
that were hers in days of old.
When her people fell into enemy hands,
there was no one to help her.
Her enemies looked at her
and laughed at her destruction.

8Jerusalem has sinned greatly
and so has become unclean.
All who honored her despise her,
for they have seen her nakedness;
she herself groans
and turns away.

9Her filthiness clung to her skirts;
she did not consider her future.
Her fall was astounding;
there was none to comfort her.
"Look, O LORD, on my affliction,
for the enemy has triumphed."

10The enemy laid hands
on all her treasures;
she saw pagan nations
enter her sanctuary—
those you had forbidden
to enter your assembly.

11All her people groan
as they search for bread;
they barter their treasures for food
to keep themselves alive.
"Look, O LORD, and consider,
for I am despised."

12"Is it nothing to you, all you who pass
by?
Look around and see.
Is any suffering like my suffering
that was inflicted on me,
that the LORD brought on me
in the day of his fierce anger?

13"From on high he sent fire,
sent it down into my bones.
He spread a net for my feet
and turned me back.
He made me desolate,
faint all the day long.

14"My sins have been bound into a yoke[a];
by his hands they were woven together.
They have come upon my neck
and the Lord has sapped my strength.
He has handed me over
to those I cannot withstand.

15"The Lord has rejected
all the warriors in my midst;
he has summoned an army against me
to[b] crush my young men.
In his winepress the Lord has trampled
the Virgin Daughter of Judah.

16"This is why I weep
and my eyes overflow with tears.
No one is near to comfort me,
no one to restore my spirit.
My children are destitute
because the enemy has prevailed."

17Zion stretches out her hands,
but there is no one to comfort her.
The LORD has decreed for Jacob
that his neighbors become his foes;
Jerusalem has become
an unclean thing among them.

18"The LORD is righteous,
yet I rebelled against his command.
Listen, all you peoples;
look upon my suffering.
My young men and maidens
have gone into exile.

19"I called to my allies
but they betrayed me.
My priests and my elders
perished in the city
while they searched for food
to keep themselves alive.

20"See, O LORD, how distressed I am!
I am in torment within,
and in my heart I am disturbed,
for I have been most rebellious.
Outside, the sword bereaves;
inside, there is only death.

21"People have heard my groaning,
but there is no one to comfort me.
All my enemies have heard of my distress;
they rejoice at what you have done.
May you bring the day you have
announced
so they may become like me.

22"Let all their wickedness come before
you;
deal with them
as you have dealt with me
because of all my sins.
My groans are many
and my heart is faint."

[a]14 Most Hebrew manuscripts; Septuagint *He kept watch over my sins* [b]15 Or *has set a time for me / when he will*

2[a] How the Lord has covered the Daughter of Zion
with the cloud of his anger[b]!
He has hurled down the splendor of Israel
from heaven to earth;
he has not remembered his footstool
in the day of his anger.

2Without pity the Lord has swallowed up
all the dwellings of Jacob;
in his wrath he has torn down
the strongholds of the Daughter of Judah.
He has brought her kingdom and its princes
down to the ground in dishonor.

3In fierce anger he has cut off
every horn[c] of Israel.
He has withdrawn his right hand
at the approach of the enemy.
He has burned in Jacob like a flaming fire
that consumes everything around it.

4Like an enemy he has strung his bow;
his right hand is ready.
Like a foe he has slain
all who were pleasing to the eye;
he has poured out his wrath like fire
on the tent of the Daughter of Zion.

5The Lord is like an enemy;
he has swallowed up Israel.
He has swallowed up all her palaces
and destroyed her strongholds.
He has multiplied mourning and lamentation
for the Daughter of Judah.

6He has laid waste his dwelling like a garden;
he has destroyed his place of meeting.
The LORD has made Zion forget
her appointed feasts and her Sabbaths;
in his fierce anger he has spurned
both king and priest.

7The Lord has rejected his altar
and abandoned his sanctuary.
He has handed over to the enemy
the walls of her palaces;
they have raised a shout in the house of the LORD
as on the day of an appointed feast.

8The LORD determined to tear down
the wall around the Daughter of Zion.
He stretched out a measuring line
and did not withhold his hand from destroying.
He made ramparts and walls lament;
together they wasted away.

9Her gates have sunk into the ground;
their bars he has broken and destroyed.
Her king and her princes are exiled among the nations,
the law is no more,
and her prophets no longer find
visions from the LORD.

10The elders of the Daughter of Zion
sit on the ground in silence;
they have sprinkled dust on their heads
and put on sackcloth.
The young women of Jerusalem
have bowed their heads to the ground.

11My eyes fail from weeping,
I am in torment within,
my heart is poured out on the ground
because my people are destroyed,
because children and infants faint
in the streets of the city.

12They say to their mothers,
"Where is bread and wine?"
as they faint like wounded men
in the streets of the city,
as their lives ebb away
in their mothers' arms.

13What can I say for you?
With what can I compare you,
O Daughter of Jerusalem?
To what can I liken you,
that I may comfort you,
O Virgin Daughter of Zion?
Your wound is as deep as the sea.
Who can heal you?

14The visions of your prophets
were false and worthless;
they did not expose your sin
to ward off your captivity.
The oracles they gave you
were false and misleading.

15All who pass your way
clap their hands at you;
they scoff and shake their heads
at the Daughter of Jerusalem:
"Is this the city that was called
the perfection of beauty,
the joy of the whole earth?"

16All your enemies open their mouths
wide against you;
they scoff and gnash their teeth
and say, "We have swallowed her up.
This is the day we have waited for;
we have lived to see it."

17The LORD has done what he planned;
he has fulfilled his word,
which he decreed long ago.
He has overthrown you without pity,
he has let the enemy gloat over you,
he has exalted the horn[d] of your foes.

18The hearts of the people
cry out to the Lord.
O wall of the Daughter of Zion,
let your tears flow like a river
day and night;

[a]This chapter is an acrostic poem, the verses of which begin with the successive letters of the Hebrew alphabet. [b]*1* Or *How the Lord in his anger / has treated the Daughter of Zion with contempt* [c]*3* Or */ all the strength*; or *every king*; *horn* here symbolizes strength. [d]*17* *Horn* here symbolizes strength.

give yourself no relief,
your eyes no rest.

19 Arise, cry out in the night,
as the watches of the night begin;
pour out your heart like water
in the presence of the Lord.
Lift up your hands to him
for the lives of your children,
who faint from hunger
at the head of every street.

20 "Look, O LORD, and consider:
Whom have you ever treated like this?
Should women eat their offspring,
the children they have cared for?
Should priest and prophet be killed
in the sanctuary of the Lord?

21 "Young and old lie together
in the dust of the streets;
my young men and maidens
have fallen by the sword.
You have slain them in the day of your
anger;
you have slaughtered them without pity.

22 "As you summon to a feast day,
so you summoned against me terrors on
every side.
In the day of the LORD's anger
no one escaped or survived;
those I cared for and reared,
my enemy has destroyed."

3 [a] I am the man who has seen affliction
by the rod of his wrath.
2 He has driven me away and made me
walk
in darkness rather than light;
3 indeed, he has turned his hand against me
again and again, all day long.

4 He has made my skin and my flesh grow
old
and has broken my bones.
5 He has besieged me and surrounded me
with bitterness and hardship.
6 He has made me dwell in darkness
like those long dead.

7 He has walled me in so I cannot escape;
he has weighed me down with chains.
8 Even when I call out or cry for help,
he shuts out my prayer.
9 He has barred my way with blocks of
stone;
he has made my paths crooked.

10 Like a bear lying in wait,
like a lion in hiding,
11 he dragged me from the path and mangled
me
and left me without help.
12 He drew his bow
and made me the target for his arrows.

13 He pierced my heart
with arrows from his quiver.
14 I became the laughingstock of all my
people;
they mock me in song all day long.
15 He has filled me with bitter herbs
and sated me with gall.

16 He has broken my teeth with gravel;
he has trampled me in the dust.
17 I have been deprived of peace;
I have forgotten what prosperity is.
18 So I say, "My splendor is gone
and all that I had hoped from the
LORD."

19 I remember my affliction and my
wandering,
the bitterness and the gall.
20 I well remember them,
and my soul is downcast within me.
21 Yet this I call to mind
and therefore I have hope:

22 Because of the LORD's great love we are
not consumed,
for his compassions never fail.
23 They are new every morning;
great is your faithfulness.
24 I say to myself, "The LORD is my portion;
therefore I will wait for him."

25 The LORD is good to those whose hope is
in him,
to the one who seeks him;
26 it is good to wait quietly
for the salvation of the LORD.
27 It is good for a man to bear the yoke
while he is young.

28 Let him sit alone in silence,
for the LORD has laid it on him.
29 Let him bury his face in the dust—
there may yet be hope.
30 Let him offer his cheek to one who would
strike him,
and let him be filled with disgrace.

31 For men are not cast off
by the Lord forever.
32 Though he brings grief, he will show
compassion,
so great is his unfailing love.
33 For he does not willingly bring affliction
or grief to the children of men.

34 To crush underfoot
all prisoners in the land,
35 to deny a man his rights
before the Most High,
36 to deprive a man of justice—
would not the Lord see such things?

37 Who can speak and have it happen
if the Lord has not decreed it?
38 Is it not from the mouth of the Most High
that both calamities and good things
come?

[a] This chapter is an acrostic poem; the verses of each stanza begin with the successive letters of the Hebrew alphabet, and the verses within each stanza begin with the same letter.

39Why should any living man complain
when punished for his sins?

40Let us examine our ways and test them,
and let us return to the LORD.
41Let us lift up our hearts and our hands
to God in heaven, and say:
42"We have sinned and rebelled
and you have not forgiven.

43"You have covered yourself with anger
and pursued us;
you have slain without pity.
44You have covered yourself with a cloud
so that no prayer can get through.
45You have made us scum and refuse
among the nations.

46"All our enemies have opened their
mouths
wide against us.
47We have suffered terror and pitfalls,
ruin and destruction."
48Streams of tears flow from my eyes
because my people are destroyed.

49My eyes will flow unceasingly,
without relief,
50until the LORD looks down
from heaven and sees.
51What I see brings grief to my soul
because of all the women of my city.

52Those who were my enemies without
cause
hunted me like a bird.
53They tried to end my life in a pit
and threw stones at me;
54the waters closed over my head,
and I thought I was about to be cut off.

55I called on your name, O LORD,
from the depths of the pit.
56You heard my plea: "Do not close your
ears
to my cry for relief."
57You came near when I called you,
and you said, "Do not fear."

58O Lord, you took up my case;
you redeemed my life.
59You have seen, O LORD, the wrong done
to me.
Uphold my cause!
60You have seen the depth of their
vengeance,
all their plots against me.

61O LORD, you have heard their insults,
all their plots against me—
62what my enemies whisper and mutter
against me all day long.
63Look at them! Sitting or standing,
they mock me in their songs.

64Pay them back what they deserve,
O LORD,
for what their hands have done.
65Put a veil over their hearts,
and may your curse be on them!
66Pursue them in anger and destroy them
from under the heavens of the LORD.

4 [a] How the gold has lost its luster,
the fine gold become dull!
The sacred gems are scattered
at the head of every street.

2How the precious sons of Zion,
once worth their weight in gold,
are now considered as pots of clay,
the work of a potter's hands!

3Even jackals offer their breasts
to nurse their young,
but my people have become heartless
like ostriches in the desert.

4Because of thirst the infant's tongue
sticks to the roof of its mouth;
the children beg for bread,
but no one gives it to them.

5Those who once ate delicacies
are destitute in the streets.
Those nurtured in purple
now lie on ash heaps.

6The punishment of my people
is greater than that of Sodom,
which was overthrown in a moment
without a hand turned to help her.

7Their princes were brighter than snow
and whiter than milk,
their bodies more ruddy than rubies,
their appearance like sapphires.[b]

8But now they are blacker than soot;
they are not recognized in the streets.
Their skin has shriveled on their bones;
it has become as dry as a stick.

9Those killed by the sword are better off
than those who die of famine;
racked with hunger, they waste away
for lack of food from the field.

10With their own hands compassionate
women
have cooked their own children,
who became their food
when my people were destroyed.

11The LORD has given full vent to his wrath;
he has poured out his fierce anger.
He kindled a fire in Zion
that consumed her foundations.

12The kings of the earth did not believe,
nor did any of the world's people,
that enemies and foes could enter
the gates of Jerusalem.

13But it happened because of the sins of her
prophets
and the iniquities of her priests,
who shed within her
the blood of the righteous.

[a]This chapter is an acrostic poem, the verses of which begin with the successive letters of the Hebrew alphabet. [b]7 Or *lapis lazuli*

14Now they grope through the streets
like men who are blind.
They are so defiled with blood
that no one dares to touch their
garments.

15"Go away! You are unclean!" men cry to
them.
"Away! Away! Don't touch us!"
When they flee and wander about,
people among the nations say,
"They can stay here no longer."

16The LORD himself has scattered them;
he no longer watches over them.
The priests are shown no honor,
the elders no favor.

17Moreover, our eyes failed,
looking in vain for help;
from our towers we watched
for a nation that could not save us.

18Men stalked us at every step,
so we could not walk in our streets.
Our end was near, our days were
numbered,
for our end had come.

19Our pursuers were swifter
than eagles in the sky;
they chased us over the mountains
and lay in wait for us in the desert.

20The LORD's anointed, our very life breath,
was caught in their traps.
We thought that under his shadow
we would live among the nations.

21Rejoice and be glad, O Daughter of Edom,
you who live in the land of Uz.
But to you also the cup will be passed;
you will be drunk and stripped naked.

22O Daughter of Zion, your punishment will
end;
he will not prolong your exile.
But, O Daughter of Edom, he will punish
your sin
and expose your wickedness.

5 Remember, O LORD, what has happened
to us;
look, and see our disgrace.
2Our inheritance has been turned over to
aliens,
our homes to foreigners.
3We have become orphans and fatherless,
our mothers like widows.
4We must buy the water we drink;
our wood can be had only at a price.
5Those who pursue us are at our heels;
we are weary and find no rest.
6We submitted to Egypt and Assyria
to get enough bread.
7Our fathers sinned and are no more,
and we bear their punishment.
8Slaves rule over us,
and there is none to free us from their
hands.
9We get our bread at the risk of our lives
because of the sword in the desert.
10Our skin is hot as an oven,
feverish from hunger.
11Women have been ravished in Zion,
and virgins in the towns of Judah.
12Princes have been hung up by their hands;
elders are shown no respect.
13Young men toil at the millstones;
boys stagger under loads of wood.
14The elders are gone from the city gate;
the young men have stopped their
music.
15Joy is gone from our hearts;
our dancing has turned to mourning.
16The crown has fallen from our head.
Woe to us, for we have sinned!
17Because of this our hearts are faint,
because of these things our eyes grow
dim
18for Mount Zion, which lies desolate,
with jackals prowling over it.

19You, O LORD, reign forever;
your throne endures from generation to
generation.
20Why do you always forget us?
Why do you forsake us so long?
21Restore us to yourself, O LORD, that we
may return;
renew our days as of old
22unless you have utterly rejected us
and are angry with us beyond measure.

Ezekiel

The Living Creatures and the Glory of the LORD

1 In the[a] thirtieth year, in the fourth month
on the fifth day, while I was among the
exiles by the Kebar River, the heavens were
opened and I saw visions of God.
2On the fifth of the month—it was the fifth
year of the exile of King Jehoiachin— 3the
word of the LORD came to Ezekiel the priest,
the son of Buzi,[b] by the Kebar River in the
land of the Babylonians.[c] There the hand of
the LORD was upon him.
4I looked, and I saw a windstorm coming
out of the north—an immense cloud with
flashing lightning and surrounded by brilliant

[a]1 Or ⌊my⌋ [b]3 Or *Ezekiel son of Buzi the priest* [c]3 Or *Chaldeans*

light. The center of the fire looked like glowing metal, 5and in the fire was what looked like four living creatures. In appearance their form was that of a man, 6but each of them had four faces and four wings. 7Their legs were straight; their feet were like those of a calf and gleamed like burnished bronze. 8Under their wings on their four sides they had the hands of a man. All four of them had faces and wings, 9and their wings touched one another. Each one went straight ahead; they did not turn as they moved.

10Their faces looked like this: Each of the four had the face of a man, and on the right side each had the face of a lion, and on the left the face of an ox; each also had the face of an eagle. 11Such were their faces. Their wings were spread out upward; each had two wings, one touching the wing of another creature on either side, and two wings covering its body. 12Each one went straight ahead. Wherever the spirit would go, they would go, without turning as they went. 13The appearance of the living creatures was like burning coals of fire or like torches. Fire moved back and forth among the creatures; it was bright, and lightning flashed out of it. 14The creatures sped back and forth like flashes of lightning.

15As I looked at the living creatures, I saw a wheel on the ground beside each creature with its four faces. 16This was the appearance and structure of the wheels: They sparkled like chrysolite, and all four looked alike. Each appeared to be made like a wheel intersecting a wheel. 17As they moved, they would go in any one of the four directions the creatures faced; the wheels did not turn about[a] as the creatures went. 18Their rims were high and awesome, and all four rims were full of eyes all around.

19When the living creatures moved, the wheels beside them moved; and when the living creatures rose from the ground, the wheels also rose. 20Wherever the spirit would go, they would go, and the wheels would rise along with them, because the spirit of the living creatures was in the wheels. 21When the creatures moved, they also moved; when the creatures stood still, they also stood still; and when the creatures rose from the ground, the wheels rose along with them, because the spirit of the living creatures was in the wheels.

22Spread out above the heads of the living creatures was what looked like an expanse, sparkling like ice, and awesome. 23Under the expanse their wings were stretched out one toward the other, and each had two wings covering its body. 24When the creatures moved, I heard the sound of their wings, like the roar of rushing waters, like the voice of the Almighty,[b] like the tumult of an army. When they stood still, they lowered their wings.

25Then there came a voice from above the expanse over their heads as they stood with lowered wings. 26Above the expanse over their heads was what looked like a throne of sapphire,[c] and high above on the throne was a figure like that of a man. 27I saw that from what appeared to be his waist up he looked like glowing metal, as if full of fire, and that from there down he looked like fire; and brilliant light surrounded him. 28Like the appearance of a rainbow in the clouds on a rainy day, so was the radiance around him.

This was the appearance of the likeness of the glory of the LORD. When I saw it, I fell facedown, and I heard the voice of one speaking.

Ezekiel's Call

2 He said to me, "Son of man, stand up on your feet and I will speak to you." 2As he spoke, the Spirit came into me and raised me to my feet, and I heard him speaking to me.

3He said: "Son of man, I am sending you to the Israelites, to a rebellious nation that has rebelled against me; they and their fathers have been in revolt against me to this very day. 4The people to whom I am sending you are obstinate and stubborn. Say to them, 'This is what the Sovereign LORD says.' 5And whether they listen or fail to listen—for they are a rebellious house—they will know that a prophet has been among them. 6And you, son of man, do not be afraid of them or their words. Do not be afraid, though briers and thorns are all around you and you live among scorpions. Do not be afraid of what they say or terrified by them, though they are a rebellious house. 7You must speak my words to them, whether they listen or fail to listen, for they are rebellious. 8But you, son of man, listen to what I say to you. Do not rebel like that rebellious house; open your mouth and eat what I give you."

9Then I looked, and I saw a hand stretched out to me. In it was a scroll, 10which he unrolled before me. On both sides of it were written words of lament and mourning and woe.

3 And he said to me, "Son of man, eat what is before you, eat this scroll; then go and speak to the house of Israel." 2So I opened my mouth, and he gave me the scroll to eat.

3Then he said to me, "Son of man, eat this scroll I am giving you and fill your stomach with it." So I ate it, and it tasted as sweet as honey in my mouth.

4He then said to me: "Son of man, go now to the house of Israel and speak my words to them. 5You are not being sent to a people of obscure speech and difficult language, but to the house of Israel— 6not to many peoples of obscure speech and difficult language, whose words you cannot understand. Surely if I had sent you to them, they would have listened to you. 7But the house of Israel is not willing to listen to you because they are not willing to listen to me, for the whole house of Israel is hardened and obstinate. 8But I will make you as unyielding and hardened as they are. 9I will make your forehead like the hardest stone,

[a] *17* Or *aside* [b] *24* Hebrew *Shaddai* [c] *26* Or *lapis lazuli*

harder than flint. Do not be afraid of them or
terrified by them, though they are a rebellious
house."
10And he said to me, "Son of man, listen
carefully and take to heart all the words I speak
to you. 11Go now to your countrymen in exile
and speak to them. Say to them, 'This is what
the Sovereign LORD says,' whether they listen
or fail to listen."
12Then the Spirit lifted me up, and I heard
behind me a loud rumbling sound—May the
glory of the LORD be praised in his dwelling
place!— 13the sound of the wings of the living
creatures brushing against each other and the
sound of the wheels beside them, a loud rumbling sound. 14The Spirit then lifted me up and
took me away, and I went in bitterness and in
the anger of my spirit, with the strong hand of
the LORD upon me. 15I came to the exiles who
lived at Tel Abib near the Kebar River. And
there, where they were living, I sat among
them for seven days—overwhelmed.

Warning to Israel

16At the end of seven days the word of the
LORD came to me: 17"Son of man, I have made
you a watchman for the house of Israel; so hear
the word I speak and give them warning from
me. 18When I say to a wicked man, 'You will
surely die,' and you do not warn him or speak
out to dissuade him from his evil ways in order
to save his life, that wicked man will die for[a]
his sin, and I will hold you accountable for his
blood. 19But if you do warn the wicked man
and he does not turn from his wickedness or
from his evil ways, he will die for his sin; but
you will have saved yourself.
20"Again, when a righteous man turns from
his righteousness and does evil, and I put a
stumbling block before him, he will die. Since
you did not warn him, he will die for his sin.
The righteous things he did will not be remembered, and I will hold you accountable for his
blood. 21But if you do warn the righteous man
not to sin and he does not sin, he will surely
live because he took warning, and you will
have saved yourself."
22The hand of the LORD was upon me there,
and he said to me, "Get up and go out to the
plain, and there I will speak to you." 23So I got
up and went out to the plain. And the glory of
the LORD was standing there, like the glory I
had seen by the Kebar River, and I fell facedown.
24Then the Spirit came into me and raised
me to my feet. He spoke to me and said: "Go,
shut yourself inside your house. 25And you,
son of man, they will tie with ropes; you will
be bound so that you cannot go out among the
people. 26I will make your tongue stick to the
roof of your mouth so that you will be silent
and unable to rebuke them, though they are a
rebellious house. 27But when I speak to you, I
will open your mouth and you shall say to
them, 'This is what the Sovereign LORD says.'
Whoever will listen let him listen, and whoever will refuse let him refuse; for they are a
rebellious house.

Siege of Jerusalem Symbolized

4 "Now, son of man, take a clay tablet, put it
in front of you and draw the city of Jerusalem on it. 2Then lay siege to it: Erect siege
works against it, build a ramp up to it, set up
camps against it and put battering rams around
it. 3Then take an iron pan, place it as an iron
wall between you and the city and turn your
face toward it. It will be under siege, and you
shall besiege it. This will be a sign to the house
of Israel.
4"Then lie on your left side and put the sin
of the house of Israel upon yourself.[b] You are
to bear their sin for the number of days you lie
on your side. 5I have assigned you the same
number of days as the years of their sin. So for
390 days you will bear the sin of the house of
Israel.
6"After you have finished this, lie down
again, this time on your right side, and bear the
sin of the house of Judah. I have assigned you
40 days, a day for each year. 7Turn your face
toward the siege of Jerusalem and with bared
arm prophesy against her. 8I will tie you up
with ropes so that you cannot turn from one
side to the other until you have finished the
days of your siege.
9"Take wheat and barley, beans and lentils,
millet and spelt; put them in a storage jar and
use them to make bread for yourself. You are
to eat it during the 390 days you lie on your
side. 10Weigh out twenty shekels[c] of food to
eat each day and eat it at set times. 11Also
measure out a sixth of a hin[d] of water and
drink it at set times. 12Eat the food as you
would a barley cake; bake it in the sight of
the people, using human excrement for fuel."
13The LORD said, "In this way the people of
Israel will eat defiled food among the nations
where I will drive them."
14Then I said, "Not so, Sovereign LORD! I
have never defiled myself. From my youth until now I have never eaten anything found dead
or torn by wild animals. No unclean meat has
ever entered my mouth."
15"Very well," he said, "I will let you bake
your bread over cow manure instead of human
excrement."
16He then said to me: "Son of man, I will cut
off the supply of food in Jerusalem. The people
will eat rationed food in anxiety and drink rationed water in despair, 17for food and water
will be scarce. They will be appalled at the
sight of each other and will waste away because of[e] their sin.

5 "Now, son of man, take a sharp sword and
use it as a barber's razor to shave your
head and your beard. Then take a set of scales
and divide up the hair. 2When the days of your

[a] *18* Or *in*; also in verses 19 and 20 [b] *4* Or *your side* [c] *10* That is, about 8 ounces (about 0.2 kilogram)
[d] *11* That is, about 2/3 quart (about 0.6 liter) [e] *17* Or *away in*

siege come to an end, burn a third of the hair with fire inside the city. Take a third and strike it with the sword all around the city. And scatter a third to the wind. For I will pursue them with drawn sword. 3 But take a few strands of hair and tuck them away in the folds of your garment. 4 Again, take a few of these and throw them into the fire and burn them up. A fire will spread from there to the whole house of Israel.

5 "This is what the Sovereign LORD says: This is Jerusalem, which I have set in the center of the nations, with countries all around her. 6 Yet in her wickedness she has rebelled against my laws and decrees more than the nations and countries around her. She has rejected my laws and has not followed my decrees.

7 "Therefore this is what the Sovereign LORD says: You have been more unruly than the nations around you and have not followed my decrees or kept my laws. You have not even[a] conformed to the standards of the nations around you.

8 "Therefore this is what the Sovereign LORD says: I myself am against you, Jerusalem, and I will inflict punishment on you in the sight of the nations. 9 Because of all your detestable idols, I will do to you what I have never done before and will never do again. 10 Therefore in your midst fathers will eat their children, and children will eat their fathers. I will inflict punishment on you and will scatter all your survivors to the winds. 11 Therefore as surely as I live, declares the Sovereign LORD, because you have defiled my sanctuary with all your vile images and detestable practices, I myself will withdraw my favor; I will not look on you with pity or spare you. 12 A third of your people will die of the plague or perish by famine inside you; a third will fall by the sword outside your walls; and a third I will scatter to the winds and pursue with drawn sword.

13 "Then my anger will cease and my wrath against them will subside, and I will be avenged. And when I have spent my wrath upon them, they will know that I the LORD have spoken in my zeal.

14 "I will make you a ruin and a reproach among the nations around you, in the sight of all who pass by. 15 You will be a reproach and a taunt, a warning and an object of horror to the nations around you when I inflict punishment on you in anger and in wrath and with stinging rebuke. I the LORD have spoken. 16 When I shoot at you with my deadly and destructive arrows of famine, I will shoot to destroy you. I will bring more and more famine upon you and cut off your supply of food. 17 I will send famine and wild beasts against you, and they will leave you childless. Plague and bloodshed will sweep through you, and I will bring the sword against you. I the LORD have spoken."

A Prophecy Against the Mountains of Israel

6 The word of the LORD came to me: 2 "Son of man, set your face against the mountains of Israel; prophesy against them 3 and say: 'O mountains of Israel, hear the word of the Sovereign LORD. This is what the Sovereign LORD says to the mountains and hills, to the ravines and valleys: I am about to bring a sword against you, and I will destroy your high places. 4 Your altars will be demolished and your incense altars will be smashed; and I will slay your people in front of your idols. 5 I will lay the dead bodies of the Israelites in front of their idols, and I will scatter your bones around your altars. 6 Wherever you live, the towns will be laid waste and the high places demolished, so that your altars will be laid waste and devastated, your idols smashed and ruined, your incense altars broken down, and what you have made wiped out. 7 Your people will fall slain among you, and you will know that I am the LORD.

8 " 'But I will spare some, for some of you will escape the sword when you are scattered among the lands and nations. 9 Then in the nations where they have been carried captive, those who escape will remember me—how I have been grieved by their adulterous hearts, which have turned away from me, and by their eyes, which have lusted after their idols. They will loathe themselves for the evil they have done and for all their detestable practices. 10 And they will know that I am the LORD; I did not threaten in vain to bring this calamity on them.

11 " 'This is what the Sovereign LORD says: Strike your hands together and stamp your feet and cry out "Alas!" because of all the wicked and detestable practices of the house of Israel, for they will fall by the sword, famine and plague. 12 He that is far away will die of the plague, and he that is near will fall by the sword, and he that survives and is spared will die of famine. So will I spend my wrath upon them. 13 And they will know that I am the LORD, when their people lie slain among their idols around their altars, on every high hill and on all the mountaintops, under every spreading tree and every leafy oak—places where they offered fragrant incense to all their idols. 14 And I will stretch out my hand against them and make the land a desolate waste from the desert to Diblah[b]—wherever they live. Then they will know that I am the LORD.' "

The End Has Come

7 The word of the LORD came to me: 2 "Son of man, this is what the Sovereign LORD says to the land of Israel: The end! The end has come upon the four corners of the land. 3 The end is now upon you and I will unleash my anger against you. I will judge you according to your conduct and repay you for all your

[a] 7 Most Hebrew manuscripts; some Hebrew manuscripts and Syriac *You have* [b] 14 Most Hebrew manuscripts; a few Hebrew manuscripts *Riblah*

detestable practices. 4I will not look on you
with pity or spare you; I will surely repay you
for your conduct and the detestable practices
among you. Then you will know that I am the
LORD.

5"This is what the Sovereign LORD says:
Disaster! An unheard-of[a] disaster is coming.
6The end has come! The end has come! It has
roused itself against you. It has come! 7Doom
has come upon you—you who dwell in the
land. The time has come, the day is near; there
is panic, not joy, upon the mountains. 8I am
about to pour out my wrath on you and spend
my anger against you; I will judge you according to your conduct and repay you for all your
detestable practices. 9I will not look on you
with pity or spare you; I will repay you in
accordance with your conduct and the detestable practices among you. Then you will know
that it is I the LORD who strikes the blow.

10"The day is here! It has come! Doom has
burst forth, the rod has budded, arrogance has
blossomed! 11Violence has grown into[b] a rod
to punish wickedness; none of the people will
be left, none of that crowd—no wealth, nothing of value. 12The time has come, the day has
arrived. Let not the buyer rejoice nor the seller
grieve, for wrath is upon the whole crowd.
13The seller will not recover the land he has
sold as long as both of them live, for the vision
concerning the whole crowd will not be re-
versed. Because of their sins, not one of them
will preserve his life. 14Though they blow the
trumpet and get everything ready, no one will
go into battle, for my wrath is upon the whole
crowd.

15"Outside is the sword, inside are plague
and famine; those in the country will die by the
sword, and those in the city will be devoured
by famine and plague. 16All who survive and
escape will be in the mountains, moaning like
doves of the valleys, each because of his sins.
17Every hand will go limp, and every knee will
become as weak as water. 18They will put on
sackcloth and be clothed with terror. Their
faces will be covered with shame and their
heads will be shaved. 19They will throw their
silver into the streets, and their gold will be an
unclean thing. Their silver and gold will not be
able to save them in the day of the LORD's
wrath. They will not satisfy their hunger or fill
their stomachs with it, for it has made them
stumble into sin. 20They were proud of their
beautiful jewelry and used it to make their detestable idols and vile images. Therefore I will
turn these into an unclean thing for them. 21I
will hand it all over as plunder to foreigners
and as loot to the wicked of the earth, and they
will defile it. 22I will turn my face away from
them, and they will desecrate my treasured
place; robbers will enter it and desecrate it.

23"Prepare chains, because the land is full of
bloodshed and the city is full of violence. 24I
will bring the most wicked of the nations to
take possession of their houses; I will put an
end to the pride of the mighty, and their sanctuaries will be desecrated. 25When terror
comes, they will seek peace, but there will be
none. 26Calamity upon calamity will come,
and rumor upon rumor. They will try to get a
vision from the prophet; the teaching of the
law by the priest will be lost, as will the counsel of the elders. 27The king will mourn, the
prince will be clothed with despair, and the
hands of the people of the land will tremble. I
will deal with them according to their conduct,
and by their own standards I will judge them.
Then they will know that I am the LORD."

Idolatry in the Temple

8 In the sixth year, in the sixth month on the
fifth day, while I was sitting in my house
and the elders of Judah were sitting before me,
the hand of the Sovereign LORD came upon me
there. 2I looked, and I saw a figure like that of
a man.[c] From what appeared to be his waist
down he was like fire, and from there up his
appearance was as bright as glowing metal.
3He stretched out what looked like a hand and
took me by the hair of my head. The Spirit
lifted me up between earth and heaven and in
visions of God he took me to Jerusalem, to the
entrance to the north gate of the inner court,
where the idol that provokes to jealousy stood.
4And there before me was the glory of the God
of Israel, as in the vision I had seen in the
plain.

5Then he said to me, "Son of man, look
toward the north." So I looked, and in the entrance north of the gate of the altar I saw this
idol of jealousy.

6And he said to me, "Son of man, do you see
what they are doing—the utterly detestable
things the house of Israel is doing here, things
that will drive me far from my sanctuary? But
you will see things that are even more detestable."

7Then he brought me to the entrance to the
court. I looked, and I saw a hole in the wall.
8He said to me, "Son of man, now dig into the
wall." So I dug into the wall and saw a doorway there.

9And he said to me, "Go in and see the
wicked and detestable things they are doing
here." 10So I went in and looked, and I saw
portrayed all over the walls all kinds of crawling things and detestable animals and all the
idols of the house of Israel. 11In front of them
stood seventy elders of the house of Israel, and
Jaazaniah son of Shaphan was standing among
them. Each had a censer in his hand, and a
fragrant cloud of incense was rising.

12He said to me, "Son of man, have you seen
what the elders of the house of Israel are doing
in the darkness, each at the shrine of his own
idol? They say, 'The LORD does not see us; the
LORD has forsaken the land.' " 13Again, he

[a]5 Most Hebrew manuscripts; some Hebrew manuscripts and Syriac *Disaster after* [b]11 Or *The violent one has become* [c]2 Or *saw a fiery figure*

said, "You will see them doing things that are even more detestable."

14Then he brought me to the entrance to the north gate of the house of the LORD, and I saw women sitting there, mourning for Tammuz. 15He said to me, "Do you see this, son of man? You will see things that are even more detestable than this."

16He then brought me into the inner court of the house of the LORD, and there at the entrance to the temple, between the portico and the altar, were about twenty-five men. With their backs toward the temple of the LORD and their faces toward the east, they were bowing down to the sun in the east.

17He said to me, "Have you seen this, son of man? Is it a trivial matter for the house of Judah to do the detestable things they are doing here? Must they also fill the land with violence and continually provoke me to anger? Look at them putting the branch to their nose! 18Therefore I will deal with them in anger; I will not look on them with pity or spare them. Although they shout in my ears, I will not listen to them."

Idolaters Killed

9 Then I heard him call out in a loud voice, "Bring the guards of the city here, each with a weapon in his hand." 2And I saw six men coming from the direction of the upper gate, which faces north, each with a deadly weapon in his hand. With them was a man clothed in linen who had a writing kit at his side. They came in and stood beside the bronze altar.

3Now the glory of the God of Israel went up from above the cherubim, where it had been, and moved to the threshold of the temple. Then the LORD called to the man clothed in linen who had the writing kit at his side 4and said to him, "Go throughout the city of Jerusalem and put a mark on the foreheads of those who grieve and lament over all the detestable things that are done in it."

5As I listened, he said to the others, "Follow him through the city and kill, without showing pity or compassion. 6Slaughter old men, young men and maidens, women and children, but do not touch anyone who has the mark. Begin at my sanctuary." So they began with the elders who were in front of the temple.

7Then he said to them, "Defile the temple and fill the courts with the slain. Go!" So they went out and began killing throughout the city. 8While they were killing and I was left alone, I fell facedown, crying out, "Ah, Sovereign LORD! Are you going to destroy the entire remnant of Israel in this outpouring of your wrath on Jerusalem?"

9He answered me, "The sin of the house of Israel and Judah is exceedingly great; the land is full of bloodshed and the city is full of injustice. They say, 'The LORD has forsaken the land; the LORD does not see.' 10So I will not look on them with pity or spare them, but I will bring down on their own heads what they have done."

11Then the man in linen with the writing kit at his side brought back word, saying, "I have done as you commanded."

The Glory Departs From the Temple

10 I looked, and I saw the likeness of a throne of sapphire[a] above the expanse that was over the heads of the cherubim. 2The LORD said to the man clothed in linen, "Go in among the wheels beneath the cherubim. Fill your hands with burning coals from among the cherubim and scatter them over the city." And as I watched, he went in.

3Now the cherubim were standing on the south side of the temple when the man went in, and a cloud filled the inner court. 4Then the glory of the LORD rose from above the cherubim and moved to the threshold of the temple. The cloud filled the temple, and the court was full of the radiance of the glory of the LORD. 5The sound of the wings of the cherubim could be heard as far away as the outer court, like the voice of God Almighty[b] when he speaks.

6When the LORD commanded the man in linen, "Take fire from among the wheels, from among the cherubim," the man went in and stood beside a wheel. 7Then one of the cherubim reached out his hand to the fire that was among them. He took up some of it and put it into the hands of the man in linen, who took it and went out. 8(Under the wings of the cherubim could be seen what looked like the hands of a man.)

9I looked, and I saw beside the cherubim four wheels, one beside each of the cherubim; the wheels sparkled like chrysolite. 10As for their appearance, the four of them looked alike; each was like a wheel intersecting a wheel. 11As they moved, they would go in any one of the four directions the cherubim faced; the wheels did not turn about[c] as the cherubim went. The cherubim went in whatever direction the head faced, without turning as they went. 12Their entire bodies, including their backs, their hands and their wings, were completely full of eyes, as were their four wheels. 13I heard the wheels being called "the whirling wheels." 14Each of the cherubim had four faces: One face was that of a cherub, the second the face of a man, the third the face of a lion, and the fourth the face of an eagle.

15Then the cherubim rose upward. These were the living creatures I had seen by the Kebar River. 16When the cherubim moved, the wheels beside them moved; and when the cherubim spread their wings to rise from the ground, the wheels did not leave their side. 17When the cherubim stood still, they also stood still; and when the cherubim rose, they rose with them, because the spirit of the living creatures was in them.

18Then the glory of the LORD departed from

a *1* Or *lapis lazuli* b *5* Hebrew *El-Shaddai* c *11* Or *aside* over the threshold of the temple and stopped above the cherubim. 19While I watched, the cherubim spread their wings and rose from the ground, and as they went, the wheels went with them. They stopped at the entrance to the east gate of the LORD's house, and the glory of the God of Israel was above them.

20These were the living creatures I had seen beneath the God of Israel by the Kebar River, and I realized that they were cherubim. 21Each had four faces and four wings, and under their wings was what looked like the hands of a man. 22Their faces had the same appearance as those I had seen by the Kebar River. Each one went straight ahead.

Judgment on Israel's Leaders

11 Then the Spirit lifted me up and brought me to the gate of the house of the LORD that faces east. There at the entrance to the gate were twenty-five men, and I saw among them Jaazaniah son of Azzur and Pelatiah son of Benaiah, leaders of the people. 2The LORD said to me, "Son of man, these are the men who are plotting evil and giving wicked advice in this city. 3They say, 'Will it not soon be time to build houses?[a] This city is a cooking pot, and we are the meat.' 4Therefore prophesy against them; prophesy, son of man."

5Then the Spirit of the LORD came upon me, and he told me to say: "This is what the LORD says: That is what you are saying, O house of Israel, but I know what is going through your mind. 6You have killed many people in this city and filled its streets with the dead.

7"Therefore this is what the Sovereign LORD says: The bodies you have thrown there are the meat and this city is the pot, but I will drive you out of it. 8You fear the sword, and the sword is what I will bring against you, declares the Sovereign LORD. 9I will drive you out of the city and hand you over to foreigners and inflict punishment on you. 10You will fall by the sword, and I will execute judgment on you at the borders of Israel. Then you will know that I am the LORD. 11This city will not be a pot for you, nor will you be the meat in it; I will execute judgment on you at the borders of Israel. 12And you will know that I am the LORD, for you have not followed my decrees or kept my laws but have conformed to the standards of the nations around you."

13Now as I was prophesying, Pelatiah son of Benaiah died. Then I fell facedown and cried out in a loud voice, "Ah, Sovereign LORD! Will you completely destroy the remnant of Israel?"

14The word of the LORD came to me: 15"Son of man, your brothers—your brothers who are your blood relatives[b] and the whole house of Israel—are those of whom the people of Jerusalem have said, 'They are[c] far away from the LORD; this land was given to us as our possession.'

Promised Return of Israel

16"Therefore say: 'This is what the Sovereign LORD says: Although I sent them far away among the nations and scattered them among the countries, yet for a little while I have been a sanctuary for them in the countries where they have gone.'

17"Therefore say: 'This is what the Sovereign LORD says: I will gather you from the nations and bring you back from the countries where you have been scattered, and I will give you back the land of Israel again.'

18"They will return to it and remove all its vile images and detestable idols. 19I will give them an undivided heart and put a new spirit in them; I will remove from them their heart of stone and give them a heart of flesh. 20Then they will follow my decrees and be careful to keep my laws. They will be my people, and I will be their God. 21But as for those whose hearts are devoted to their vile images and detestable idols, I will bring down on their own heads what they have done, declares the Sovereign LORD."

22Then the cherubim, with the wheels beside them, spread their wings, and the glory of the God of Israel was above them. 23The glory of the LORD went up from within the city and stopped above the mountain east of it. 24The Spirit lifted me up and brought me to the exiles in Babylonia[d] in the vision given by the Spirit of God.

Then the vision I had seen went up from me, 25and I told the exiles everything the LORD had shown me.

The Exile Symbolized

12 The word of the LORD came to me: 2"Son of man, you are living among a rebellious people. They have eyes to see but do not see and ears to hear but do not hear, for they are a rebellious people.

3"Therefore, son of man, pack your belongings for exile and in the daytime, as they watch, set out and go from where you are to another place. Perhaps they will understand, though they are a rebellious house. 4During the daytime, while they watch, bring out your belongings packed for exile. Then in the evening, while they are watching, go out like those who go into exile. 5While they watch, dig through the wall and take your belongings out through it. 6Put them on your shoulder as they are watching and carry them out at dusk. Cover your face so that you cannot see the land, for I have made you a sign to the house of Israel."

7So I did as I was commanded. During the day I brought out my things packed for exile. Then in the evening I dug through the wall with my hands. I took my belongings out at dusk, carrying them on my shoulders while they watched.

8In the morning the word of the LORD came to me: 9"Son of man, did not that rebellious

[a] *3* Or *This is not the time to build houses.* [b] *15* Or *are in exile with you* (see Septuagint and Syriac)
[c] *15* Or *those to whom the people of Jerusalem have said, 'Stay* [d] *24* Or *Chaldea*

house of Israel ask you, ‘What are you doing?’
10“Say to them, ‘This is what the Sovereign
LORD says: This oracle concerns the prince in
Jerusalem and the whole house of Israel who
are there.’ 11Say to them, ‘I am a sign to you.’
“As I have done, so it will be done to them.
They will go into exile as captives.
12“The prince among them will put his
things on his shoulder at dusk and leave, and a
hole will be dug in the wall for him to go
through. He will cover his face so that he cannot see the land. 13I will spread my net for him,
and he will be caught in my snare; I will bring
him to Babylonia, the land of the Chaldeans,
but he will not see it, and there he will die. 14I
will scatter to the winds all those around
him—his staff and all his troops—and I will
pursue them with drawn sword.
15“They will know that I am the LORD,
when I disperse them among the nations and
scatter them through the countries. 16But I will
spare a few of them from the sword, famine
and plague, so that in the nations where they
go they may acknowledge all their detestable
practices. Then they will know that I am the
LORD.”
17The word of the LORD came to me: 18“Son
of man, tremble as you eat your food, and
shudder in fear as you drink your water. 19Say
to the people of the land: ‘This is what the
Sovereign LORD says about those living in Jerusalem and in the land of Israel: They will eat
their food in anxiety and drink their water in
despair, for their land will be stripped of everything in it because of the violence of all who
live there. 20The inhabited towns will be laid
waste and the land will be desolate. Then you
will know that I am the LORD.’ ”
21The word of the LORD came to me: 22“Son
of man, what is this proverb you have in the
land of Israel: ‘The days go by and every vision comes to nothing’? 23Say to them, ‘This is
what the Sovereign LORD says: I am going to
put an end to this proverb, and they will no
longer quote it in Israel.’ Say to them, ‘The
days are near when every vision will be fulfilled. 24For there will be no more false visions
or flattering divinations among the people of
Israel. 25But I the LORD will speak what I will,
and it shall be fulfilled without delay. For
in your days, you rebellious house, I will fulfill whatever I say, declares the Sovereign
LORD.’ ”
26The word of the LORD came to me: 27“Son
of man, the house of Israel is saying, ‘The
vision he sees is for many years from now, and
he prophesies about the distant future.’
28“Therefore say to them, ‘This is what the
Sovereign LORD says: None of my words will
be delayed any longer; whatever I say will be
fulfilled, declares the Sovereign LORD.’ ”

False Prophets Condemned

13 The word of the LORD came to me:
2“Son of man, prophesy against the
prophets of Israel who are now prophesying.
Say to those who prophesy out of their own
imagination: ‘Hear the word of the LORD!
3This is what the Sovereign LORD says: Woe
to the foolish[a] prophets who follow their own
spirit and have seen nothing! 4Your prophets,
O Israel, are like jackals among ruins. 5You
have not gone up to the breaks in the wall to
repair it for the house of Israel so that it will
stand firm in the battle on the day of the LORD.
6Their visions are false and their divinations a
lie. They say, “The LORD declares,” when the
LORD has not sent them; yet they expect their
words to be fulfilled. 7Have you not seen false
visions and uttered lying divinations when you
say, “The LORD declares,” though I have not
spoken?
8“ ‘Therefore this is what the Sovereign
LORD says: Because of your false words and
lying visions, I am against you, declares the
Sovereign LORD. 9My hand will be against the
prophets who see false visions and utter lying
divinations. They will not belong to the council of my people or be listed in the records of
the house of Israel, nor will they enter the land
of Israel. Then you will know that I am the
Sovereign LORD.
10“ ‘Because they lead my people astray,
saying, “Peace,” when there is no peace, and
because, when a flimsy wall is built, they cover it with whitewash, 11therefore tell those who
cover it with whitewash that it is going to fall.
Rain will come in torrents, and I will send
hailstones hurtling down, and violent winds
will burst forth. 12When the wall collapses,
will people not ask you, “Where is the whitewash you covered it with?”
13“ ‘Therefore this is what the Sovereign
LORD says: In my wrath I will unleash a violent wind, and in my anger hailstones and torrents of rain will fall with destructive fury. 14I
will tear down the wall you have covered with
whitewash and will level it to the ground so
that its foundation will be laid bare. When it[b]
falls, you will be destroyed in it; and you will
know that I am the LORD. 15So I will spend my
wrath against the wall and against those who
covered it with whitewash. I will say to you,
“The wall is gone and so are those who whitewashed it, 16those prophets of Israel who
prophesied to Jerusalem and saw visions of
peace for her when there was no peace, declares the Sovereign LORD.” ’
17“Now, son of man, set your face against
the daughters of your people who prophesy out
of their own imagination. Prophesy against
them 18and say, ‘This is what the Sovereign
LORD says: Woe to the women who sew magic
charms on all their wrists and make veils of
various lengths for their heads in order to ensnare people. Will you ensnare the lives of my
people but preserve your own? 19You have
profaned me among my people for a few handfuls of barley and scraps of bread. By lying to
my people, who listen to lies, you have killed

[a]3 Or *wicked* [b]14 Or *the city*

those who should not have died and have spared those who should not live.

20“ ‘Therefore this is what the Sovereign LORD says: I am against your magic charms with which you ensnare people like birds and I will tear them from your arms; I will set free the people that you ensnare like birds. 21I will tear off your veils and save my people from your hands, and they will no longer fall prey to your power. Then you will know that I am the LORD. 22Because you disheartened the righteous with your lies, when I had brought them no grief, and because you encouraged the wicked not to turn from their evil ways and so save their lives, 23therefore you will no longer see false visions or practice divination. I will save my people from your hands. And then you will know that I am the LORD.’ ”

Idolaters Condemned

14 Some of the elders of Israel came to me and sat down in front of me. 2Then the word of the LORD came to me: 3“Son of man, these men have set up idols in their hearts and put wicked stumbling blocks before their faces. Should I let them inquire of me at all? 4Therefore speak to them and tell them, ‘This is what the Sovereign LORD says: When any Israelite sets up idols in his heart and puts a wicked stumbling block before his face and then goes to a prophet, I the LORD will answer him myself in keeping with his great idolatry. 5I will do this to recapture the hearts of the people of Israel, who have all deserted me for their idols.’

6“Therefore say to the house of Israel, ‘This is what the Sovereign LORD says: Repent! Turn from your idols and renounce all your detestable practices!

7“ ‘When any Israelite or any alien living in Israel separates himself from me and sets up idols in his heart and puts a wicked stumbling block before his face and then goes to a prophet to inquire of me, I the LORD will answer him myself. 8I will set my face against that man and make him an example and a byword. I will cut him off from my people. Then you will know that I am the LORD.

9“ ‘And if the prophet is enticed to utter a prophecy, I the LORD have enticed that prophet, and I will stretch out my hand against him and destroy him from among my people Israel. 10They will bear their guilt—the prophet will be as guilty as the one who consults him. 11Then the people of Israel will no longer stray from me, nor will they defile themselves anymore with all their sins. They will be my people, and I will be their God, declares the Sovereign LORD.’ ”

Judgment Inescapable

12The word of the LORD came to me: 13“Son of man, if a country sins against me by being unfaithful and I stretch out my hand against it to cut off its food supply and send famine upon it and kill its men and their animals, 14even if these three men—Noah, Daniel[a] and Job—were in it, they could save only themselves by their righteousness, declares the Sovereign LORD.

15“Or if I send wild beasts through that country and they leave it childless and it becomes desolate so that no one can pass through it because of the beasts, 16as surely as I live, declares the Sovereign LORD, even if these three men were in it, they could not save their own sons or daughters. They alone would be saved, but the land would be desolate.

17“Or if I bring a sword against that country and say, ‘Let the sword pass throughout the land,’ and I kill its men and their animals, 18as surely as I live, declares the Sovereign LORD, even if these three men were in it, they could not save their own sons or daughters. They alone would be saved.

19“Or if I send a plague into that land and pour out my wrath upon it through bloodshed, killing its men and their animals, 20as surely as I live, declares the Sovereign LORD, even if Noah, Daniel and Job were in it, they could save neither son nor daughter. They would save only themselves by their righteousness.

21“For this is what the Sovereign LORD says: How much worse will it be when I send against Jerusalem my four dreadful judgments—sword and famine and wild beasts and plague—to kill its men and their animals! 22Yet there will be some survivors—sons and daughters who will be brought out of it. They will come to you, and when you see their conduct and their actions, you will be consoled regarding the disaster I have brought upon Jerusalem—every disaster I have brought upon it. 23You will be consoled when you see their conduct and their actions, for you will know that I have done nothing in it without cause, declares the Sovereign LORD.”

Jerusalem, A Useless Vine

15 The word of the LORD came to me: 2“Son of man, how is the wood of a vine better than that of a branch on any of the trees in the forest? 3Is wood ever taken from it to make anything useful? Do they make pegs from it to hang things on? 4And after it is thrown on the fire as fuel and the fire burns both ends and chars the middle, is it then useful for anything? 5If it was not useful for anything when it was whole, how much less can it be made into something useful when the fire has burned it and it is charred?

6“Therefore this is what the Sovereign LORD says: As I have given the wood of the vine among the trees of the forest as fuel for the fire, so will I treat the people living in Jerusalem. 7I will set my face against them. Although they have come out of the fire, the fire will yet consume them. And when I set my face against them, you will know that I am the LORD. 8I

[a] *14* Or *Danel*; the Hebrew spelling may suggest a person other than the prophet Daniel; also in verse 20.

will make the land desolate because they have been unfaithful, declares the Sovereign LORD."

An Allegory of Unfaithful Jerusalem

16 The word of the LORD came to me: 2"Son of man, confront Jerusalem with her detestable practices 3and say, 'This is what the Sovereign LORD says to Jerusalem: Your ancestry and birth were in the land of the Canaanites; your father was an Amorite and your mother a Hittite. 4On the day you were born your cord was not cut, nor were you washed with water to make you clean, nor were you rubbed with salt or wrapped in cloths. 5No one looked on you with pity or had compassion enough to do any of these things for you. Rather, you were thrown out into the open field, for on the day you were born you were despised.

6" 'Then I passed by and saw you kicking about in your blood, and as you lay there in your blood I said to you, "Live!"[a] 7I made you grow like a plant of the field. You grew up and developed and became the most beautiful of jewels.[b] Your breasts were formed and your hair grew, you who were naked and bare.

8" 'Later I passed by, and when I looked at you and saw that you were old enough for love, I spread the corner of my garment over you and covered your nakedness. I gave you my solemn oath and entered into a covenant with you, declares the Sovereign LORD, and you became mine.

9" 'I bathed[c] you with water and washed the blood from you and put ointments on you. 10I clothed you with an embroidered dress and put leather sandals on you. I dressed you in fine linen and covered you with costly garments. 11I adorned you with jewelry: I put bracelets on your arms and a necklace around your neck, 12and I put a ring on your nose, earrings on your ears and a beautiful crown on your head. 13So you were adorned with gold and silver; your clothes were of fine linen and costly fabric and embroidered cloth. Your food was fine flour, honey and olive oil. You became very beautiful and rose to be a queen. 14And your fame spread among the nations on account of your beauty, because the splendor I had given you made your beauty perfect, declares the Sovereign LORD.

15" 'But you trusted in your beauty and used your fame to become a prostitute. You lavished your favors on anyone who passed by and your beauty became his.[d] 16You took some of your garments to make gaudy high places, where you carried on your prostitution. Such things should not happen, nor should they ever occur. 17You also took the fine jewelry I gave you, the jewelry made of my gold and silver, and you made for yourself male idols and engaged in prostitution with them. 18And you took your embroidered clothes to put on them, and you offered my oil and incense before them. 19Also the food I provided for you—the fine flour, olive oil and honey I gave you to eat—you offered as fragrant incense before them. That is what happened, declares the Sovereign LORD.

20" 'And you took your sons and daughters whom you bore to me and sacrificed them as food to the idols. Was your prostitution not enough? 21You slaughtered my children and sacrificed them[e] to the idols. 22In all your detestable practices and your prostitution you did not remember the days of your youth, when you were naked and bare, kicking about in your blood.

23" 'Woe! Woe to you, declares the Sovereign LORD. In addition to all your other wickedness, 24you built a mound for yourself and made a lofty shrine in every public square. 25At the head of every street you built your lofty shrines and degraded your beauty, offering your body with increasing promiscuity to anyone who passed by. 26You engaged in prostitution with the Egyptians, your lustful neighbors, and provoked me to anger with your increasing promiscuity. 27So I stretched out my hand against you and reduced your territory; I gave you over to the greed of your enemies, the daughters of the Philistines, who were shocked by your lewd conduct. 28You engaged in prostitution with the Assyrians too, because you were insatiable; and even after that, you still were not satisfied. 29Then you increased your promiscuity to include Babylonia,[f] a land of merchants, but even with this you were not satisfied.

30" 'How weak-willed you are, declares the Sovereign LORD, when you do all these things, acting like a brazen prostitute! 31When you built your mounds at the head of every street and made your lofty shrines in every public square, you were unlike a prostitute, because you scorned payment.

32" 'You adulterous wife! You prefer strangers to your own husband! 33Every prostitute receives a fee, but you give gifts to all your lovers, bribing them to come to you from everywhere for your illicit favors. 34So in your prostitution you are the opposite of others; no one runs after you for your favors. You are the very opposite, for you give payment and none is given to you.

35" 'Therefore, you prostitute, hear the word of the LORD! 36This is what the Sovereign LORD says: Because you poured out your wealth[g] and exposed your nakedness in your promiscuity with your lovers, and because of all your detestable idols, and because you gave them your children's blood, 37therefore I am going to gather all your lovers, with whom you found pleasure, those you loved as well as those you hated. I will gather them against you from all around and will strip you in front of

[a] 6 A few Hebrew manuscripts, Septuagint and Syriac; most Hebrew manuscripts *"Live!" And as you lay there in your blood I said to you, "Live!"* [b] 7 Or *became mature* [c] 9 Or *I had bathed* [d] 15 Most Hebrew manuscripts; one Hebrew manuscript (see some Septuagint manuscripts) *by. Such a thing should not happen* [e] 21 Or *and made them pass through ⌞the fire⌟* [f] 29 Or *Chaldea* [g] 36 Or *lust*

them, and they will see all your nakedness. 38I will sentence you to the punishment of women who commit adultery and who shed blood; I will bring upon you the blood vengeance of my wrath and jealous anger. 39Then I will hand you over to your lovers, and they will tear down your mounds and destroy your lofty shrines. They will strip you of your clothes and take your fine jewelry and leave you naked and bare. 40They will bring a mob against you, who will stone you and hack you to pieces with their swords. 41They will burn down your houses and inflict punishment on you in the sight of many women. I will put a stop to your prostitution, and you will no longer pay your lovers. 42Then my wrath against you will subside and my jealous anger will turn away from you; I will be calm and no longer angry.

43" 'Because you did not remember the days of your youth but enraged me with all these things, I will surely bring down on your head what you have done, declares the Sovereign LORD. Did you not add lewdness to all your other detestable practices?

44" 'Everyone who quotes proverbs will quote this proverb about you: "Like mother, like daughter." 45You are a true daughter of your mother, who despised her husband and her children; and you are a true sister of your sisters, who despised their husbands and their children. Your mother was a Hittite and your father an Amorite. 46Your older sister was Samaria, who lived to the north of you with her daughters; and your younger sister, who lived to the south of you with her daughters, was Sodom. 47You not only walked in their ways and copied their detestable practices, but in all your ways you soon became more depraved than they. 48As surely as I live, declares the Sovereign LORD, your sister Sodom and her daughters never did what you and your daughters have done.

49" 'Now this was the sin of your sister Sodom: She and her daughters were arrogant, overfed and unconcerned; they did not help the poor and needy. 50They were haughty and did detestable things before me. Therefore I did away with them as you have seen. 51Samaria did not commit half the sins you did. You have done more detestable things than they, and have made your sisters seem righteous by all these things you have done. 52Bear your disgrace, for you have furnished some justification for your sisters. Because your sins were more vile than theirs, they appear more righteous than you. So then, be ashamed and bear your disgrace, for you have made your sisters appear righteous.

53" 'However, I will restore the fortunes of Sodom and her daughters and of Samaria and her daughters, and your fortunes along with them, 54so that you may bear your disgrace and be ashamed of all you have done in giving them comfort. 55And your sisters, Sodom with her daughters and Samaria with her daughters, will return to what they were before; and you and your daughters will return to what you were before. 56You would not even mention your sister Sodom in the day of your pride, 57before your wickedness was uncovered. Even so, you are now scorned by the daughters of Edom[a] and all her neighbors and the daughters of the Philistines—all those around you who despise you. 58You will bear the consequences of your lewdness and your detestable practices, declares the LORD.

59" 'This is what the Sovereign LORD says: I will deal with you as you deserve, because you have despised my oath by breaking the covenant. 60Yet I will remember the covenant I made with you in the days of your youth, and I will establish an everlasting covenant with you. 61Then you will remember your ways and be ashamed when you receive your sisters, both those who are older than you and those who are younger. I will give them to you as daughters, but not on the basis of my covenant with you. 62So I will establish my covenant with you, and you will know that I am the LORD. 63Then, when I make atonement for you for all you have done, you will remember and be ashamed and never again open your mouth because of your humiliation, declares the Sovereign LORD.' "

Two Eagles and a Vine

17 The word of the LORD came to me: 2"Son of man, set forth an allegory and tell the house of Israel a parable. 3Say to them, 'This is what the Sovereign LORD says: A great eagle with powerful wings, long feathers and full plumage of varied colors came to Lebanon. Taking hold of the top of a cedar, 4he broke off its topmost shoot and carried it away to a land of merchants, where he planted it in a city of traders.

5" 'He took some of the seed of your land and put it in fertile soil. He planted it like a willow by abundant water, 6and it sprouted and became a low, spreading vine. Its branches turned toward him, but its roots remained under it. So it became a vine and produced branches and put out leafy boughs.

7" 'But there was another great eagle with powerful wings and full plumage. The vine now sent out its roots toward him from the plot where it was planted and stretched out its branches to him for water. 8It had been planted in good soil by abundant water so that it would produce branches, bear fruit and become a splendid vine.'

9"Say to them, 'This is what the Sovereign LORD says: Will it thrive? Will it not be uprooted and stripped of its fruit so that it withers? All its new growth will wither. It will not take a strong arm or many people to pull it up by the roots. 10Even if it is transplanted, will it thrive? Will it not wither completely when the east wind strikes it—wither away in the plot where it grew?' "

[a]57 Many Hebrew manuscripts and Syriac; most Hebrew manuscripts, Septuagint and Vulgate *Aram*

11Then the word of the LORD came to me:
12"Say to this rebellious house, 'Do you not
know what these things mean?' Say to them:
'The king of Babylon went to Jerusalem and
carried off her king and her nobles, bringing
them back with him to Babylon. 13Then he
took a member of the royal family and made a
treaty with him, putting him under oath. He
also carried away the leading men of the land,
14so that the kingdom would be brought low,
unable to rise again, surviving only by keeping
his treaty. 15But the king rebelled against him
by sending his envoys to Egypt to get horses
and a large army. Will he succeed? Will he
who does such things escape? Will he break
the treaty and yet escape?

16" 'As surely as I live, declares the Sovereign LORD, he shall die in Babylon, in the land
of the king who put him on the throne, whose
oath he despised and whose treaty he broke.
17Pharaoh with his mighty army and great
horde will be of no help to him in war, when
ramps are built and siege works erected to destroy many lives. 18He despised the oath by
breaking the covenant. Because he had given
his hand in pledge and yet did all these things,
he shall not escape.

19" 'Therefore this is what the Sovereign
LORD says: As surely as I live, I will bring
down on his head my oath that he despised and
my covenant that he broke. 20I will spread my
net for him, and he will be caught in my snare.
I will bring him to Babylon and execute judgment upon him there because he was unfaithful
to me. 21All his fleeing troops will fall by the
sword, and the survivors will be scattered to
the winds. Then you will know that I the LORD
have spoken.

22" 'This is what the Sovereign LORD says:
I myself will take a shoot from the very top of
a cedar and plant it; I will break off a tender
sprig from its topmost shoots and plant it on a
high and lofty mountain. 23On the mountain
heights of Israel I will plant it; it will produce
branches and bear fruit and become a splendid
cedar. Birds of every kind will nest in it; they
will find shelter in the shade of its branches.
24All the trees of the field will know that I the
LORD bring down the tall tree and make the
low tree grow tall. I dry up the green tree and
make the dry tree flourish.

" 'I the LORD have spoken, and I will
do it.' "

The Soul Who Sins Will Die

18 The word of the LORD came to me:
2"What do you people mean by quoting
this proverb about the land of Israel:

" 'The fathers eat sour grapes,
and the children's teeth are set on
edge'?

3"As surely as I live, declares the Sovereign
LORD, you will no longer quote this proverb in
Israel. 4For every living soul belongs to me,
the father as well as the son—both alike belong to me. The soul who sins is the one who
will die.

5"Suppose there is a righteous man
who does what is just and right.
6He does not eat at the mountain shrines
or look to the idols of the house of
Israel.
He does not defile his neighbor's wife
or lie with a woman during her period.
7He does not oppress anyone,
but returns what he took in pledge for a
loan.
He does not commit robbery
but gives his food to the hungry
and provides clothing for the naked.
8He does not lend at usury
or take excessive interest.[a]
He withholds his hand from doing wrong
and judges fairly between man and man.
9He follows my decrees
and faithfully keeps my laws.
That man is righteous;
he will surely live,
declares the Sovereign LORD.

10"Suppose he has a violent son, who sheds
blood or does any of these other things[b]
11(though the father has done none of them):

"He eats at the mountain shrines.
He defiles his neighbor's wife.
12He oppresses the poor and needy.
He commits robbery.
He does not return what he took in
pledge.
He looks to the idols.
He does detestable things.
13He lends at usury and takes excessive
interest.

Will such a man live? He will not! Because he
has done all these detestable things, he will
surely be put to death and his blood will be on
his own head.

14"But suppose this son has a son who sees
all the sins his father commits, and though he
sees them, he does not do such things:

15"He does not eat at the mountain shrines
or look to the idols of the house of
Israel.
He does not defile his neighbor's wife.
16He does not oppress anyone
or require a pledge for a loan.
He does not commit robbery
but gives his food to the hungry
and provides clothing for the naked.
17He withholds his hand from sin[c]
and takes no usury or excessive interest.
He keeps my laws and follows my
decrees.

He will not die for his father's sin; he will
surely live. 18But his father will die for his own

[a]8 Or *take interest*; similarly in verses 13 and 17 [b]10 Or *things to a brother* [c]17 Septuagint (see also verse 8); Hebrew *from the poor*

sin, because he practiced extortion, robbed his
brother and did what was wrong among his
people.
19“Yet you ask, ‘Why does the son not share
the guilt of his father?’ Since the son has done
what is just and right and has been careful to
keep all my decrees, he will surely live. 20The
soul who sins is the one who will die. The son
will not share the guilt of the father, nor will
the father share the guilt of the son. The righteousness of the righteous man will be credited
to him, and the wickedness of the wicked will
be charged against him.
21“But if a wicked man turns away from all
the sins he has committed and keeps all my
decrees and does what is just and right, he will
surely live; he will not die. 22None of the offenses he has committed will be remembered
against him. Because of the righteous things he
has done, he will live. 23Do I take any pleasure
in the death of the wicked? declares the Sovereign LORD. Rather, am I not pleased when they
turn from their ways and live?
24“But if a righteous man turns from his
righteousness and commits sin and does the
same detestable things the wicked man does,
will he live? None of the righteous things he
has done will be remembered. Because of the
unfaithfulness he is guilty of and because of
the sins he has committed, he will die.
25“Yet you say, ‘The way of the Lord is not
just.’ Hear, O house of Israel: Is my way unjust? Is it not your ways that are unjust? 26If a
righteous man turns from his righteousness
and commits sin, he will die for it; because of
the sin he has committed he will die. 27But if
a wicked man turns away from the wickedness
he has committed and does what is just and
right, he will save his life. 28Because he considers all the offenses he has committed and
turns away from them, he will surely live; he
will not die. 29Yet the house of Israel says,
‘The way of the Lord is not just.’ Are my ways
unjust, O house of Israel? Is it not your ways
that are unjust?
30“Therefore, O house of Israel, I will judge
you, each one according to his ways, declares
the Sovereign LORD. Repent! Turn away from
all your offenses; then sin will not be your
downfall. 31Rid yourselves of all the offenses
you have committed, and get a new heart and
a new spirit. Why will you die, O house of
Israel? 32For I take no pleasure in the death of
anyone, declares the Sovereign LORD. Repent
and live!

A Lament for Israel’s Princes

19 “Take up a lament concerning the
princes of Israel 2and say:

“ ‘What a lioness was your mother
among the lions!
She lay down among the young lions
and reared her cubs.
3She brought up one of her cubs,
and he became a strong lion.
He learned to tear the prey
and he devoured men.
4The nations heard about him,
and he was trapped in their pit.
They led him with hooks
to the land of Egypt.

5“ ‘When she saw her hope unfulfilled,
her expectation gone,
she took another of her cubs
and made him a strong lion.
6He prowled among the lions,
for he was now a strong lion.
He learned to tear the prey
and he devoured men.
7He broke down[a] their strongholds
and devastated their towns.
The land and all who were in it
were terrified by his roaring.
8Then the nations came against him,
those from regions round about.
They spread their net for him,
and he was trapped in their pit.
9With hooks they pulled him into a cage
and brought him to the king of Babylon.
They put him in prison,
so his roar was heard no longer
on the mountains of Israel.

10“ ‘Your mother was like a vine in your
vineyard[b]
planted by the water;
it was fruitful and full of branches
because of abundant water.
11Its branches were strong,
fit for a ruler’s scepter.
It towered high
above the thick foliage,
conspicuous for its height
and for its many branches.
12But it was uprooted in fury
and thrown to the ground.
The east wind made it shrivel,
it was stripped of its fruit;
its strong branches withered
and fire consumed them.
13Now it is planted in the desert,
in a dry and thirsty land.
14Fire spread from one of its main[c]
branches
and consumed its fruit.
No strong branch is left on it
fit for a ruler’s scepter.’

This is a lament and is to be used as a lament.”

Rebellious Israel

20 In the seventh year, in the fifth month
on the tenth day, some of the elders of
Israel came to inquire of the LORD, and they
sat down in front of me.
2Then the word of the LORD came to me:
3“Son of man, speak to the elders of Israel and
say to them, ‘This is what the Sovereign LORD
says: Have you come to inquire of me? As

[a]7 Targum (see Septuagint); Hebrew *He knew your blood* [b]10 Two Hebrew manuscripts; most Hebrew manuscripts *your blood* [c]14 Or *from under its*

surely as I live, I will not let you inquire of me, declares the Sovereign LORD.’

4“Will you judge them? Will you judge them, son of man? Then confront them with the detestable practices of their fathers 5and say to them: ‘This is what the Sovereign LORD says: On the day I chose Israel, I swore with uplifted hand to the descendants of the house of Jacob and revealed myself to them in Egypt. With uplifted hand I said to them, “I am the LORD your God.” 6On that day I swore to them that I would bring them out of Egypt into a land I had searched out for them, a land flowing with milk and honey, the most beautiful of all lands. 7And I said to them, “Each of you, get rid of the vile images you have set your eyes on, and do not defile yourselves with the idols of Egypt. I am the LORD your God.”

8“ ‘But they rebelled against me and would not listen to me; they did not get rid of the vile images they had set their eyes on, nor did they forsake the idols of Egypt. So I said I would pour out my wrath on them and spend my anger against them in Egypt. 9But for the sake of my name I did what would keep it from being profaned in the eyes of the nations they lived among and in whose sight I had revealed myself to the Israelites by bringing them out of Egypt. 10Therefore I led them out of Egypt and brought them into the desert. 11I gave them my decrees and made known to them my laws, for the man who obeys them will live by them. 12Also I gave them my Sabbaths as a sign between us, so they would know that I the LORD made them holy.

13“ ‘Yet the people of Israel rebelled against me in the desert. They did not follow my decrees but rejected my laws—although the man who obeys them will live by them—and they utterly desecrated my Sabbaths. So I said I would pour out my wrath on them and destroy them in the desert. 14But for the sake of my name I did what would keep it from being profaned in the eyes of the nations in whose sight I had brought them out. 15Also with uplifted hand I swore to them in the desert that I would not bring them into the land I had given them—a land flowing with milk and honey, most beautiful of all lands— 16because they rejected my laws and did not follow my decrees and desecrated my Sabbaths. For their hearts were devoted to their idols. 17Yet I looked on them with pity and did not destroy them or put an end to them in the desert. 18I said to their children in the desert, “Do not follow the statutes of your fathers or keep their laws or defile yourselves with their idols. 19I am the LORD your God; follow my decrees and be careful to keep my laws. 20Keep my Sabbaths holy, that they may be a sign between us. Then you will know that I am the LORD your God.”

21“ ‘But the children rebelled against me: They did not follow my decrees, they were not careful to keep my laws—although the man who obeys them will live by them—and they desecrated my Sabbaths. So I said I would pour out my wrath on them and spend my anger against them in the desert. 22But I withheld my hand, and for the sake of my name I did what would keep it from being profaned in the eyes of the nations in whose sight I had brought them out. 23Also with uplifted hand I swore to them in the desert that I would disperse them among the nations and scatter them through the countries, 24because they had not obeyed my laws but had rejected my decrees and desecrated my Sabbaths, and their eyes ⌊lusted⌋ after their fathers’ idols. 25I also gave them over to statutes that were not good and laws they could not live by; 26I let them become defiled through their gifts—the sacrifice of every firstborn[a]—that I might fill them with horror so they would know that I am the LORD.’

27“Therefore, son of man, speak to the people of Israel and say to them, ‘This is what the Sovereign LORD says: In this also your fathers blasphemed me by forsaking me: 28When I brought them into the land I had sworn to give them and they saw any high hill or any leafy tree, there they offered their sacrifices, made offerings that provoked me to anger, presented their fragrant incense and poured out their drink offerings. 29Then I said to them: What is this high place you go to?’ ” (It is called Bamah[b] to this day.)

Judgment and Restoration

30“Therefore say to the house of Israel: ‘This is what the Sovereign LORD says: Will you defile yourselves the way your fathers did and lust after their vile images? 31When you offer your gifts—the sacrifice of your sons in[c] the fire—you continue to defile yourselves with all your idols to this day. Am I to let you inquire of me, O house of Israel? As surely as I live, declares the Sovereign LORD, I will not let you inquire of me.

32“ ‘You say, “We want to be like the nations, like the peoples of the world, who serve wood and stone.” But what you have in mind will never happen. 33As surely as I live, declares the Sovereign LORD, I will rule over you with a mighty hand and an outstretched arm and with outpoured wrath. 34I will bring you from the nations and gather you from the countries where you have been scattered—with a mighty hand and an outstretched arm and with outpoured wrath. 35I will bring you into the desert of the nations and there, face to face, I will execute judgment upon you. 36As I judged your fathers in the desert of the land of Egypt, so I will judge you, declares the Sovereign LORD. 37I will take note of you as you pass under my rod, and I will bring you into the bond of the covenant. 38I will purge you of those who revolt and rebel against me. Al-

[a]26 Or *—making every firstborn pass through ⌊the fire⌋*
[b]29 *Bamah* means *high place.*
[c]31 Or *—making your sons pass through*

though I will bring them out of the land where
they are living, yet they will not enter the land
of Israel. Then you will know that I am the
LORD.
39“ ‘As for you, O house of Israel, this is
what the Sovereign LORD says: Go and serve
your idols, every one of you! But afterward
you will surely listen to me and no longer profane my holy name with your gifts and idols.
40For on my holy mountain, the high mountain
of Israel, declares the Sovereign LORD, there in
the land the entire house of Israel will serve
me, and there I will accept them. There I will
require your offerings and your choice gifts,[a]
along with all your holy sacrifices. 41I will
accept you as fragrant incense when I bring
you out from the nations and gather you from
the countries where you have been scattered,
and I will show myself holy among you in the
sight of the nations. 42Then you will know that
I am the LORD, when I bring you into the land
of Israel, the land I had sworn with uplifted
hand to give to your fathers. 43There you will
remember your conduct and all the actions by
which you have defiled yourselves, and you
will loathe yourselves for all the evil you have
done. 44You will know that I am the LORD,
when I deal with you for my name's sake and
not according to your evil ways and your corrupt practices, O house of Israel, declares the
Sovereign LORD.' ”

Prophecy Against the South

45The word of the LORD came to me: 46“Son
of man, set your face toward the south; preach
against the south and prophesy against the forest of the southland. 47Say to the southern forest: 'Hear the word of the LORD. This is what
the Sovereign LORD says: I am about to set fire
to you, and it will consume all your trees, both
green and dry. The blazing flame will not be
quenched, and every face from south to north
will be scorched by it. 48Everyone will see that
I the LORD have kindled it; it will not be
quenched.' ”
49Then I said, “Ah, Sovereign LORD! They
are saying of me, 'Isn't he just telling parables?' ”

Babylon, God's Sword of Judgment

21 The word of the LORD came to me:
2“Son of man, set your face against Jerusalem and preach against the sanctuary.
Prophesy against the land of Israel 3and say to
her: 'This is what the LORD says: I am against
you. I will draw my sword from its scabbard
and cut off from you both the righteous and the
wicked. 4Because I am going to cut off the
righteous and the wicked, my sword will be
unsheathed against everyone from south to
north. 5Then all people will know that I the
LORD have drawn my sword from its scabbard;
it will not return again.'
6“Therefore groan, son of man! Groan before them with broken heart and bitter grief.
7And when they ask you, 'Why are you groaning?' you shall say, 'Because of the news that
is coming. Every heart will melt and every
hand go limp; every spirit will become faint
and every knee become as weak as water.' It is
coming! It will surely take place, declares the
Sovereign LORD.”
8The word of the LORD came to me: 9“Son
of man, prophesy and say, 'This is what the
Lord says:

“ 'A sword, a sword,
sharpened and polished—
10sharpened for the slaughter,
polished to flash like lightning!

“ 'Shall we rejoice in the scepter of my son
⌊Judah⌋? The sword despises every such stick.

11“ 'The sword is appointed to be polished,
to be grasped with the hand;
it is sharpened and polished,
made ready for the hand of the slayer.
12Cry out and wail, son of man,
for it is against my people;
it is against all the princes of Israel.
They are thrown to the sword
along with my people.
Therefore beat your breast.

13“ 'Testing will surely come. And what if
the scepter ⌊of Judah⌋, which the sword despises, does not continue? declares the Sovereign LORD.'

14“So then, son of man, prophesy
and strike your hands together.
Let the sword strike twice,
even three times.
It is a sword for slaughter—
a sword for great slaughter,
closing in on them from every side.
15So that hearts may melt
and the fallen be many,
I have stationed the sword for slaughter[b]
at all their gates.
Oh! It is made to flash like lightning,
it is grasped for slaughter.
16O sword, slash to the right,
then to the left,
wherever your blade is turned.
17I too will strike my hands together,
and my wrath will subside.
I the LORD have spoken.”

18The word of the LORD came to me: 19“Son
of man, mark out two roads for the sword of
the king of Babylon to take, both starting from
the same country. Make a signpost where the
road branches off to the city. 20Mark out one
road for the sword to come against Rabbah of
the Ammonites and another against Judah and
fortified Jerusalem. 21For the king of Babylon
will stop at the fork in the road, at the junction
of the two roads, to seek an omen: He will cast
lots with arrows, he will consult his idols, he
will examine the liver. 22Into his right hand

[a]40 Or *and the gifts of your firstfruits* [b]15 Septuagint; the meaning of the Hebrew for this word is uncertain.

will come the lot for Jerusalem, where he is to
set up battering rams, to give the command to
slaughter, to sound the battle cry, to set battering rams against the gates, to build a ramp and
to erect siege works. 23It will seem like a false
omen to those who have sworn allegiance to
him, but he will remind them of their guilt and
take them captive.
24"Therefore this is what the Sovereign
LORD says: 'Because you people have brought
to mind your guilt by your open rebellion, revealing your sins in all that you do—because
you have done this, you will be taken captive.
25" 'O profane and wicked prince of Israel,
whose day has come, whose time of punishment has reached its climax, 26this is what the
Sovereign LORD says: Take off the turban, remove the crown. It will not be as it was: The
lowly will be exalted and the exalted will be
brought low. 27A ruin! A ruin! I will make it a
ruin! It will not be restored until he comes
to whom it rightfully belongs; to him I will
give it.'
28"And you, son of man, prophesy and say,
'This is what the Sovereign LORD says about
the Ammonites and their insults:

" 'A sword, a sword,
drawn for the slaughter,
polished to consume
and to flash like lightning!
29Despite false visions concerning you
and lying divinations about you,
it will be laid on the necks
of the wicked who are to be slain,
whose day has come,
whose time of punishment has reached
its climax.
30Return the sword to its scabbard.
In the place where you were created,
in the land of your ancestry,
I will judge you.
31I will pour out my wrath upon you
and breathe out my fiery anger against
you;
I will hand you over to brutal men,
men skilled in destruction.
32You will be fuel for the fire,
your blood will be shed in your land,
you will be remembered no more;
for I the LORD have spoken.' "

Jerusalem's Sins

22 The word of the LORD came to me:
2"Son of man, will you judge her? Will
you judge this city of bloodshed? Then confront her with all her detestable practices 3and
say: 'This is what the Sovereign LORD says:
O city that brings on herself doom by shedding
blood in her midst and defiles herself by making idols, 4you have become guilty because of
the blood you have shed and have become defiled by the idols you have made. You have
brought your days to a close, and the end of
your years has come. Therefore I will make
you an object of scorn to the nations and a
laughingstock to all the countries. 5Those who
are near and those who are far away will mock
you, O infamous city, full of turmoil.
6" 'See how each of the princes of Israel
who are in you uses his power to shed blood.
7In you they have treated father and mother
with contempt; in you they have oppressed the
alien and mistreated the fatherless and the widow. 8You have despised my holy things and
desecrated my Sabbaths. 9In you are slanderous men bent on shedding blood; in you are
those who eat at the mountain shrines and
commit lewd acts. 10In you are those who dishonor their fathers' bed; in you are those who
violate women during their period, when they
are ceremonially unclean. 11In you one man
commits a detestable offense with his neighbor's wife, another shamefully defiles his
daughter-in-law, and another violates his sister, his own father's daughter. 12In you men
accept bribes to shed blood; you take usury
and excessive interest[a] and make unjust gain
from your neighbors by extortion. And you
have forgotten me, declares the Sovereign
LORD.
13" 'I will surely strike my hands together at
the unjust gain you have made and at the blood
you have shed in your midst. 14Will your courage endure or your hands be strong in the day
I deal with you? I the LORD have spoken, and
I will do it. 15I will disperse you among the
nations and scatter you through the countries;
and I will put an end to your uncleanness.
16When you have been defiled[b] in the eyes
of the nations, you will know that I am the
LORD.' "
17Then the word of the LORD came to me:
18"Son of man, the house of Israel has become
dross to me; all of them are the copper, tin,
iron and lead left inside a furnace. They are but
the dross of silver. 19Therefore this is what the
Sovereign LORD says: 'Because you have all
become dross, I will gather you into Jerusalem.
20As men gather silver, copper, iron, lead and
tin into a furnace to melt it with a fiery blast,
so will I gather you in my anger and my wrath
and put you inside the city and melt you. 21I
will gather you and I will blow on you with my
fiery wrath, and you will be melted inside her.
22As silver is melted in a furnace, so you will
be melted inside her, and you will know that I
the LORD have poured out my wrath upon
you.' "
23Again the word of the LORD came to me:
24"Son of man, say to the land, 'You are a land
that has had no rain or showers[c] in the day of
wrath.' 25There is a conspiracy of her princes[d]
within her like a roaring lion tearing its prey;
they devour people, take treasures and precious things and make many widows within
her. 26Her priests do violence to my law and
profane my holy things; they do not distinguish between the holy and the common; they

[a] *12* Or *usury and interest* [b] *16* Or *When I have allotted you your inheritance* [c] *24* Septuagint; Hebrew *has not been cleansed or rained on* [d] *25* Septuagint; Hebrew *prophets*

teach that there is no difference between the
unclean and the clean; and they shut their eyes
to the keeping of my Sabbaths, so that I am
profaned among them. 27Her officials within
her are like wolves tearing their prey; they
shed blood and kill people to make unjust gain.
28Her prophets whitewash these deeds for
them by false visions and lying divinations.
They say, 'This is what the Sovereign LORD
says'—when the LORD has not spoken. 29The
people of the land practice extortion and commit robbery; they oppress the poor and needy
and mistreat the alien, denying them justice.

30"I looked for a man among them who
would build up the wall and stand before me in
the gap on behalf of the land so I would not
have to destroy it, but I found none. 31So I will
pour out my wrath on them and consume them
with my fiery anger, bringing down on their
own heads all they have done, declares the
Sovereign LORD."

Two Adulterous Sisters

23 The word of the LORD came to me:
2"Son of man, there were two women,
daughters of the same mother. 3They became
prostitutes in Egypt, engaging in prostitution
from their youth. In that land their breasts were
fondled and their virgin bosoms caressed. 4The
older was named Oholah, and her sister was
Oholibah. They were mine and gave birth to
sons and daughters. Oholah is Samaria, and
Oholibah is Jerusalem.

5"Oholah engaged in prostitution while she
was still mine; and she lusted after her lovers,
the Assyrians—warriors 6clothed in blue, governors and commanders, all of them handsome
young men, and mounted horsemen. 7She gave
herself as a prostitute to all the elite of the
Assyrians and defiled herself with all the idols
of everyone she lusted after. 8She did not give
up the prostitution she began in Egypt, when
during her youth men slept with her, caressed
her virgin bosom and poured out their lust
upon her.

9"Therefore I handed her over to her lovers,
the Assyrians, for whom she lusted. 10They
stripped her naked, took away her sons and
daughters and killed her with the sword. She
became a byword among women, and punishment was inflicted on her.

11"Her sister Oholibah saw this, yet in her
lust and prostitution she was more depraved
than her sister. 12She too lusted after the Assyrians—governors and commanders, warriors
in full dress, mounted horsemen, all handsome
young men. 13I saw that she too defiled herself; both of them went the same way.

14"But she carried her prostitution still further. She saw men portrayed on a wall, figures
of Chaldeans[a] portrayed in red, 15with belts
around their waists and flowing turbans on
their heads; all of them looked like Babylonian
chariot officers, natives of Chaldea.[b] 16As
soon as she saw them, she lusted after them
and sent messengers to them in Chaldea.
17Then the Babylonians came to her, to the bed
of love, and in their lust they defiled her. After
she had been defiled by them, she turned away
from them in disgust. 18When she carried on
her prostitution openly and exposed her nakedness, I turned away from her in disgust, just as
I had turned away from her sister. 19Yet she
became more and more promiscuous as she
recalled the days of her youth, when she was a
prostitute in Egypt. 20There she lusted after her
lovers, whose genitals were like those of donkeys and whose emission was like that of
horses. 21So you longed for the lewdness of
your youth, when in Egypt your bosom was
caressed and your young breasts fondled.[c]

22"Therefore, Oholibah, this is what the
Sovereign LORD says: I will stir up your lovers
against you, those you turned away from in
disgust, and I will bring them against you from
every side— 23the Babylonians and all the
Chaldeans, the men of Pekod and Shoa and
Koa, and all the Assyrians with them, handsome young men, all of them governors and
commanders, chariot officers and men of high
rank, all mounted on horses. 24They will come
against you with weapons,[d] chariots and wagons and with a throng of people; they will take
up positions against you on every side with
large and small shields and with helmets. I will
turn you over to them for punishment, and they
will punish you according to their standards.
25I will direct my jealous anger against you,
and they will deal with you in fury. They will
cut off your noses and your ears, and those of
you who are left will fall by the sword. They
will take away your sons and daughters, and
those of you who are left will be consumed by
fire. 26They will also strip you of your clothes
and take your fine jewelry. 27So I will put a
stop to the lewdness and prostitution you began in Egypt. You will not look on these things
with longing or remember Egypt anymore.

28"For this is what the Sovereign LORD says:
I am about to hand you over to those you hate,
to those you turned away from in disgust.
29They will deal with you in hatred and take
away everything you have worked for. They
will leave you naked and bare, and the shame
of your prostitution will be exposed. Your
lewdness and promiscuity 30have brought this
upon you, because you lusted after the nations
and defiled yourself with their idols. 31You
have gone the way of your sister; so I will put
her cup into your hand.

32"This is what the Sovereign LORD says:

"You will drink your sister's cup,
a cup large and deep;
it will bring scorn and derision,
for it holds so much.
33You will be filled with drunkenness and
sorrow,
the cup of ruin and desolation,

[a]14 Or *Babylonians* [b]15 Or *Babylonia*; also in verse 16 [c]21 Syriac (see also verse 3); Hebrew *caressed because of your young breasts* [d]24 The meaning of the Hebrew for this word is uncertain.

the cup of your sister Samaria.
34 You will drink it and drain it dry;
you will dash it to pieces
and tear your breasts.

I have spoken, declares the Sovereign LORD.

35 "Therefore this is what the Sovereign
LORD says: Since you have forgotten me and
thrust me behind your back, you must bear the
consequences of your lewdness and prostitution."
36 The LORD said to me: "Son of man, will
you judge Oholah and Oholibah? Then confront them with their detestable practices, 37 for
they have committed adultery and blood is on
their hands. They committed adultery with
their idols; they even sacrificed their children,
whom they bore to me,[a] as food for them.
38 They have also done this to me: At that same
time they defiled my sanctuary and desecrated
my Sabbaths. 39 On the very day they sacrificed
their children to their idols, they entered my
sanctuary and desecrated it. That is what they
did in my house.
40 "They even sent messengers for men who
came from far away, and when they arrived
you bathed yourself for them, painted your
eyes and put on your jewelry. 41 You sat on an
elegant couch, with a table spread before it on
which you had placed the incense and oil that
belonged to me.
42 "The noise of a carefree crowd was around
her; Sabeans[b] were brought from the desert
along with men from the rabble, and they put
bracelets on the arms of the woman and her
sister and beautiful crowns on their heads.
43 Then I said about the one worn out by adultery, 'Now let them use her as a prostitute, for
that is all she is.' 44 And they slept with her. As
men sleep with a prostitute, so they slept with
those lewd women, Oholah and Oholibah.
45 But righteous men will sentence them to the
punishment of women who commit adultery
and shed blood, because they are adulterous
and blood is on their hands.
46 "This is what the Sovereign LORD says:
Bring a mob against them and give them over
to terror and plunder. 47 The mob will stone
them and cut them down with their swords;
they will kill their sons and daughters and burn
down their houses.
48 "So I will put an end to lewdness in the
land, that all women may take warning and not
imitate you. 49 You will suffer the penalty for
your lewdness and bear the consequences of
your sins of idolatry. Then you will know that
I am the Sovereign LORD."

The Cooking Pot

24 In the ninth year, in the tenth month on
the tenth day, the word of the LORD
came to me: 2 "Son of man, record this date,
this very date, because the king of Babylon has
laid siege to Jerusalem this very day. 3 Tell this
rebellious house a parable and say to them:
'This is what the Sovereign LORD says:

" 'Put on the cooking pot; put it on
and pour water into it.
4 Put into it the pieces of meat,
all the choice pieces—the leg and the shoulder.
Fill it with the best of these bones;
5 take the pick of the flock.
Pile wood beneath it for the bones;
bring it to a boil
and cook the bones in it.

6 " 'For this is what the Sovereign LORD says:

" 'Woe to the city of bloodshed,
to the pot now encrusted,
whose deposit will not go away!
Empty it piece by piece
without casting lots for them.

7 " 'For the blood she shed is in her midst:
She poured it on the bare rock;
she did not pour it on the ground,
where the dust would cover it.
8 To stir up wrath and take revenge
I put her blood on the bare rock,
so that it would not be covered.

9 " 'Therefore this is what the Sovereign LORD
says:

" 'Woe to the city of bloodshed!
I, too, will pile the wood high.
10 So heap on the wood
and kindle the fire.
Cook the meat well,
mixing in the spices;
and let the bones be charred.
11 Then set the empty pot on the coals
till it becomes hot and its copper glows
so its impurities may be melted
and its deposit burned away.
12 It has frustrated all efforts;
its heavy deposit has not been removed,
not even by fire.

13 " 'Now your impurity is lewdness. Because I tried to cleanse you but you would not
be cleansed from your impurity, you will not
be clean again until my wrath against you has
subsided.

14 " 'I the LORD have spoken. The time has
come for me to act. I will not hold back; I will
not have pity, nor will I relent. You will be
judged according to your conduct and your actions, declares the Sovereign LORD.' "

Ezekiel's Wife Dies

15 The word of the LORD came to me: 16 "Son
of man, with one blow I am about to take away
from you the delight of your eyes. Yet do not
lament or weep or shed any tears. 17 Groan quietly; do not mourn for the dead. Keep your
turban fastened and your sandals on your feet;
do not cover the lower part of your face or eat
the customary food ⌊of mourners⌋."

[a] 37 Or *even made the children they bore to me pass through ⌊the fire⌋* [b] 42 Or *drunkards*

18So I spoke to the people in the morning, and in the evening my wife died. The next morning I did as I had been commanded.

19Then the people asked me, "Won't you tell us what these things have to do with us?"

20So I said to them, "The word of the LORD came to me: 21Say to the house of Israel, 'This is what the Sovereign LORD says: I am about to desecrate my sanctuary—the stronghold in which you take pride, the delight of your eyes, the object of your affection. The sons and daughters you left behind will fall by the sword. 22And you will do as I have done. You will not cover the lower part of your face or eat the customary food ⌊of mourners⌋. 23You will keep your turbans on your heads and your sandals on your feet. You will not mourn or weep but will waste away because of[a] your sins and groan among yourselves. 24Ezekiel will be a sign to you; you will do just as he has done. When this happens, you will know that I am the Sovereign LORD.'

25"And you, son of man, on the day I take away their stronghold, their joy and glory, the delight of their eyes, their heart's desire, and their sons and daughters as well— 26on that day a fugitive will come to tell you the news. 27At that time your mouth will be opened; you will speak with him and will no longer be silent. So you will be a sign to them, and they will know that I am the LORD."

A Prophecy Against Ammon

25 The word of the LORD came to me: 2"Son of man, set your face against the Ammonites and prophesy against them. 3Say to them, 'Hear the word of the Sovereign LORD. This is what the Sovereign LORD says: Because you said "Aha!" over my sanctuary when it was desecrated and over the land of Israel when it was laid waste and over the people of Judah when they went into exile, 4therefore I am going to give you to the people of the East as a possession. They will set up their camps and pitch their tents among you; they will eat your fruit and drink your milk. 5I will turn Rabbah into a pasture for camels and Ammon into a resting place for sheep. Then you will know that I am the LORD. 6For this is what the Sovereign LORD says: Because you have clapped your hands and stamped your feet, rejoicing with all the malice of your heart against the land of Israel, 7therefore I will stretch out my hand against you and give you as plunder to the nations. I will cut you off from the nations and exterminate you from the countries. I will destroy you, and you will know that I am the LORD.' "

A Prophecy Against Moab

8"This is what the Sovereign LORD says: 'Because Moab and Seir said, "Look, the house of Judah has become like all the other nations," 9therefore I will expose the flank of Moab, beginning at its frontier towns—Beth Jeshimoth, Baal Meon and Kiriathaim—the glory of that land. 10I will give Moab along with the Ammonites to the people of the East as a possession, so that the Ammonites will not be remembered among the nations; 11and I will inflict punishment on Moab. Then they will know that I am the LORD.' "

A Prophecy Against Edom

12"This is what the Sovereign LORD says: 'Because Edom took revenge on the house of Judah and became very guilty by doing so, 13therefore this is what the Sovereign LORD says: I will stretch out my hand against Edom and kill its men and their animals. I will lay it waste, and from Teman to Dedan they will fall by the sword. 14I will take vengeance on Edom by the hand of my people Israel, and they will deal with Edom in accordance with my anger and my wrath; they will know my vengeance, declares the Sovereign LORD.' "

A Prophecy Against Philistia

15"This is what the Sovereign LORD says: 'Because the Philistines acted in vengeance and took revenge with malice in their hearts, and with ancient hostility sought to destroy Judah, 16therefore this is what the Sovereign LORD says: I am about to stretch out my hand against the Philistines, and I will cut off the Kerethites and destroy those remaining along the coast. 17I will carry out great vengeance on them and punish them in my wrath. Then they will know that I am the LORD, when I take vengeance on them.' "

A Prophecy Against Tyre

26 In the eleventh year, on the first day of the month, the word of the LORD came to me: 2"Son of man, because Tyre has said of Jerusalem, 'Aha! The gate to the nations is broken, and its doors have swung open to me; now that she lies in ruins I will prosper,' 3therefore this is what the Sovereign LORD says: I am against you, O Tyre, and I will bring many nations against you, like the sea casting up its waves. 4They will destroy the walls of Tyre and pull down her towers; I will scrape away her rubble and make her a bare rock. 5Out in the sea she will become a place to spread fishnets, for I have spoken, declares the Sovereign LORD. She will become plunder for the nations, 6and her settlements on the mainland will be ravaged by the sword. Then they will know that I am the LORD.

7"For this is what the Sovereign LORD says: From the north I am going to bring against Tyre Nebuchadnezzar[b] king of Babylon, king of kings, with horses and chariots, with horsemen and a great army. 8He will ravage your settlements on the mainland with the sword; he will set up siege works against you, build a ramp up to your walls and raise his shields against you. 9He will direct the blows of his battering rams against your walls and demolish

[a]23 Or *away in* [b]7 Hebrew *Nebuchadrezzar,* of which *Nebuchadnezzar* is a variant; here and often in Ezekiel and Jeremiah

your towers with his weapons. 10His horses
will be so many that they will cover you with
dust. Your walls will tremble at the noise of
the war horses, wagons and chariots when he
enters your gates as men enter a city whose
walls have been broken through. 11The hoofs
of his horses will trample all your streets; he
will kill your people with the sword, and your
strong pillars will fall to the ground. 12They
will plunder your wealth and loot your merchandise; they will break down your walls and
demolish your fine houses and throw your
stones, timber and rubble into the sea. 13I will
put an end to your noisy songs, and the music
of your harps will be heard no more. 14I will
make you a bare rock, and you will become a
place to spread fishnets. You will never be
rebuilt, for I the LORD have spoken, declares
the Sovereign LORD.

15"This is what the Sovereign LORD says to
Tyre: Will not the coastlands tremble at the
sound of your fall, when the wounded groan
and the slaughter takes place in you? 16Then
all the princes of the coast will step down from
their thrones and lay aside their robes and take
off their embroidered garments. Clothed with
terror, they will sit on the ground, trembling
every moment, appalled at you. 17Then they
will take up a lament concerning you and say
to you:

" 'How you are destroyed, O city of
renown,
peopled by men of the sea!
You were a power on the seas,
you and your citizens;
you put your terror
on all who lived there.
18Now the coastlands tremble
on the day of your fall;
the islands in the sea
are terrified at your collapse.'

19"This is what the Sovereign LORD says:
When I make you a desolate city, like cities no
longer inhabited, and when I bring the ocean
depths over you and its vast waters cover you,
20then I will bring you down with those who
go down to the pit, to the people of long ago.
I will make you dwell in the earth below, as in
ancient ruins, with those who go down to the
pit, and you will not return or take your place[a]
in the land of the living. 21I will bring you to
a horrible end and you will be no more. You
will be sought, but you will never again be
found, declares the Sovereign LORD."

A Lament for Tyre

27 The word of the LORD came to me:
2"Son of man, take up a lament concerning Tyre. 3Say to Tyre, situated at the
gateway to the sea, merchant of peoples on
many coasts, 'This is what the Sovereign LORD
says:

" 'You say, O Tyre,
"I am perfect in beauty."
4Your domain was on the high seas;
your builders brought your beauty to
perfection.
5They made all your timbers
of pine trees from Senir[b];
they took a cedar from Lebanon
to make a mast for you.
6Of oaks from Bashan
they made your oars;
of cypress wood[c] from the coasts of
Cyprus[d]
they made your deck, inlaid with ivory.
7Fine embroidered linen from Egypt was
your sail
and served as your banner;
your awnings were of blue and purple
from the coasts of Elishah.
8Men of Sidon and Arvad were your
oarsmen;
your skilled men, O Tyre, were aboard
as your seamen.
9Veteran craftsmen of Gebal[e] were on
board
as shipwrights to caulk your seams.
All the ships of the sea and their sailors
came alongside to trade for your wares.

10" 'Men of Persia, Lydia and Put
served as soldiers in your army.
They hung their shields and helmets on
your walls,
bringing you splendor.
11Men of Arvad and Helech
manned your walls on every side;
men of Gammad
were in your towers.
They hung their shields around your walls;
they brought your beauty to perfection.

12" 'Tarshish did business with you because
of your great wealth of goods; they exchanged
silver, iron, tin and lead for your merchandise.

13" 'Greece, Tubal and Meshech traded with
you; they exchanged slaves and articles of
bronze for your wares.

14" 'Men of Beth Togarmah exchanged
work horses, war horses and mules for your
merchandise.

15" 'The men of Rhodes[f] traded with you,
and many coastlands were your customers;
they paid you with ivory tusks and ebony.

16" 'Aram[g] did business with you because
of your many products; they exchanged turquoise, purple fabric, embroidered work, fine
linen, coral and rubies for your merchandise.

17" 'Judah and Israel traded with you; they
exchanged wheat from Minnith and confec-
tions,[h] honey, oil and balm for your wares.

18" 'Damascus, because of your many products and great wealth of goods, did business

[a]20 Septuagint; Hebrew *return, and I will give glory* [b]5 That is, Hermon [c]6 Targum; the Masoretic Text has a different division of the consonants. [d]6 Hebrew *Kittim* [e]9 That is, Byblos [f]15 Septuagint; Hebrew *Dedan* [g]16 Most Hebrew manuscripts; some Hebrew manuscripts and Syriac *Edom*
[h]17 The meaning of the Hebrew for this word is uncertain.

with you in wine from Helbon and wool from
Zahar.
19" 'Danites and Greeks from Uzal bought
your merchandise; they exchanged wrought
iron, cassia and calamus for your wares.
20" 'Dedan traded in saddle blankets with
you.
21" 'Arabia and all the princes of Kedar
were your customers; they did business with
you in lambs, rams and goats.
22" 'The merchants of Sheba and Raamah
traded with you; for your merchandise they
exchanged the finest of all kinds of spices and
precious stones, and gold.
23" 'Haran, Canneh and Eden and merchants
of Sheba, Asshur and Kilmad traded with you.
24In your marketplace they traded with you
beautiful garments, blue fabric, embroidered
work and multicolored rugs with cords twisted
and tightly knotted.

25" 'The ships of Tarshish serve
as carriers for your wares.
You are filled with heavy cargo
in the heart of the sea.
26Your oarsmen take you
out to the high seas.
But the east wind will break you to pieces
in the heart of the sea.
27Your wealth, merchandise and wares,
your mariners, seamen and shipwrights,
your merchants and all your soldiers,
and everyone else on board
will sink into the heart of the sea
on the day of your shipwreck.
28The shorelands will quake
when your seamen cry out.
29All who handle the oars
will abandon their ships;
the mariners and all the seamen
will stand on the shore.
30They will raise their voice
and cry bitterly over you;
they will sprinkle dust on their heads
and roll in ashes.
31They will shave their heads because of
you
and will put on sackcloth.
They will weep over you with anguish of
soul
and with bitter mourning.
32As they wail and mourn over you,
they will take up a lament concerning
you:
"Who was ever silenced like Tyre,
surrounded by the sea?"
33When your merchandise went out on the
seas,
you satisfied many nations;
with your great wealth and your wares
you enriched the kings of the earth.
34Now you are shattered by the sea
in the depths of the waters;
your wares and all your company
have gone down with you.
35All who live in the coastlands
are appalled at you;
their kings shudder with horror
and their faces are distorted with fear.
36The merchants among the nations hiss at
you;
you have come to a horrible end
and will be no more.' "

A Prophecy Against the King of Tyre

28 The word of the LORD came to me:
2"Son of man, say to the ruler of Tyre,
'This is what the Sovereign LORD says:

" 'In the pride of your heart
you say, "I am a god;
I sit on the throne of a god
in the heart of the seas."
But you are a man and not a god,
though you think you are as wise as a
god.
3Are you wiser than Daniel[a]?
Is no secret hidden from you?
4By your wisdom and understanding
you have gained wealth for yourself
and amassed gold and silver
in your treasuries.
5By your great skill in trading
you have increased your wealth,
and because of your wealth
your heart has grown proud.

6" 'Therefore this is what the Sovereign
LORD says:

" 'Because you think you are wise,
as wise as a god,
7I am going to bring foreigners against
you,
the most ruthless of nations;
they will draw their swords against your
beauty and wisdom
and pierce your shining splendor.
8They will bring you down to the pit,
and you will die a violent death
in the heart of the seas.
9Will you then say, "I am a god,"
in the presence of those who kill you?
You will be but a man, not a god,
in the hands of those who slay you.
10You will die the death of the
uncircumcised
at the hands of foreigners.

I have spoken, declares the Sovereign LORD.' "

11The word of the LORD came to me: 12"Son
of man, take up a lament concerning the king
of Tyre and say to him: 'This is what the Sovereign LORD says:

" 'You were the model of perfection,
full of wisdom and perfect in beauty.
13You were in Eden,
the garden of God;
every precious stone adorned you:
ruby, topaz and emerald,
chrysolite, onyx and jasper,

a3 Or *Danel*; the Hebrew spelling may suggest a person other than the prophet Daniel.

sapphire,[a] turquoise and beryl.[b]
Your settings and mountings[c] were made
of gold;
on the day you were created they were
prepared.
14You were anointed as a guardian cherub,
for so I ordained you.
You were on the holy mount of God;
you walked among the fiery stones.
15You were blameless in your ways
from the day you were created
till wickedness was found in you.
16Through your widespread trade
you were filled with violence,
and you sinned.
So I drove you in disgrace from the mount
of God,
and I expelled you, O guardian cherub,
from among the fiery stones.
17Your heart became proud
on account of your beauty,
and you corrupted your wisdom
because of your splendor.
So I threw you to the earth;
I made a spectacle of you before kings.
18By your many sins and dishonest trade
you have desecrated your sanctuaries.
So I made a fire come out from you,
and it consumed you,
and I reduced you to ashes on the ground
in the sight of all who were watching.
19All the nations who knew you
are appalled at you;
you have come to a horrible end
and will be no more.' "

A Prophecy Against Sidon

20The word of the LORD came to me: 21"Son
of man, set your face against Sidon; prophesy
against her 22and say: 'This is what the Sovereign LORD says:

" 'I am against you, O Sidon,
and I will gain glory within you.
They will know that I am the LORD,
when I inflict punishment on her
and show myself holy within her.
23I will send a plague upon her
and make blood flow in her streets.
The slain will fall within her,
with the sword against her on every
side.
Then they will know that I am the LORD.

24" 'No longer will the people of Israel have
malicious neighbors who are painful briers and
sharp thorns. Then they will know that I am the
Sovereign LORD.

25" 'This is what the Sovereign LORD says:
When I gather the people of Israel from the
nations where they have been scattered, I will
show myself holy among them in the sight of
the nations. Then they will live in their own
land, which I gave to my servant Jacob. 26They
will live there in safety and will build houses
and plant vineyards; they will live in safety
when I inflict punishment on all their neighbors who maligned them. Then they will know
that I am the LORD their God.' "

A Prophecy Against Egypt

29 In the tenth year, in the tenth month on
the twelfth day, the word of the LORD
came to me: 2"Son of man, set your face
against Pharaoh king of Egypt and prophesy
against him and against all Egypt. 3Speak to
him and say: 'This is what the Sovereign LORD
says:

" 'I am against you, Pharaoh king of
Egypt,
you great monster lying among your
streams.
You say, "The Nile is mine;
I made it for myself."
4But I will put hooks in your jaws
and make the fish of your streams stick
to your scales.
I will pull you out from among your
streams,
with all the fish sticking to your scales.
5I will leave you in the desert,
you and all the fish of your streams.
You will fall on the open field
and not be gathered or picked up.
I will give you as food
to the beasts of the earth and the birds
of the air.

6Then all who live in Egypt will know that I
am the LORD.

" 'You have been a staff of reed for the
house of Israel. 7When they grasped you with
their hands, you splintered and you tore open
their shoulders; when they leaned on you, you
broke and their backs were wrenched.[d]

8" 'Therefore this is what the Sovereign
LORD says: I will bring a sword against you
and kill your men and their animals. 9Egypt
will become a desolate wasteland. Then they
will know that I am the LORD.

" 'Because you said, "The Nile is mine; I
made it," 10therefore I am against you and
against your streams, and I will make the land
of Egypt a ruin and a desolate waste from Migdol to Aswan, as far as the border of Cush.[e]
11No foot of man or animal will pass through
it; no one will live there for forty years. 12I will
make the land of Egypt desolate among devastated lands, and her cities will lie desolate forty
years among ruined cities. And I will disperse
the Egyptians among the nations and scatter
them through the countries.

13" 'Yet this is what the Sovereign LORD
says: At the end of forty years I will gather the
Egyptians from the nations where they were
scattered. 14I will bring them back from captivity and return them to Upper Egypt,[f] the land

[a] *13* Or *lapis lazuli* [b] *13* The precise identification of some of these precious stones is uncertain.
[c] *13* The meaning of the Hebrew for this phrase is uncertain. [d] *7* Syriac (see also Septuagint and Vulgate); Hebrew *and you caused their backs to stand* [e] *10* That is, the upper Nile region [f] *14* Hebrew *to Pathros*

of their ancestry. There they will be a lowly
kingdom. 15It will be the lowliest of kingdoms
and will never again exalt itself above the other nations. I will make it so weak that it will
never again rule over the nations. 16Egypt will
no longer be a source of confidence for the
people of Israel but will be a reminder of their
sin in turning to her for help. Then they will
know that I am the Sovereign LORD.' "

17In the twenty-seventh year, in the first
month on the first day, the word of the LORD
came to me: 18"Son of man, Nebuchadnezzar
king of Babylon drove his army in a hard campaign against Tyre; every head was rubbed
bare and every shoulder made raw. Yet he and
his army got no reward from the campaign he
led against Tyre. 19Therefore this is what the
Sovereign LORD says: I am going to give
Egypt to Nebuchadnezzar king of Babylon,
and he will carry off its wealth. He will loot
and plunder the land as pay for his army. 20I
have given him Egypt as a reward for his efforts because he and his army did it for me,
declares the Sovereign LORD.

21"On that day I will make a horn[a] grow for
the house of Israel, and I will open your mouth
among them. Then they will know that I am
the LORD."

A Lament for Egypt

30 The word of the LORD came to me:
2"Son of man, prophesy and say: 'This
is what the Sovereign LORD says:

" 'Wail and say,
"Alas for that day!"
3For the day is near,
the day of the LORD is near—
a day of clouds,
a time of doom for the nations.
4A sword will come against Egypt,
and anguish will come upon Cush.[b]
When the slain fall in Egypt,
her wealth will be carried away
and her foundations torn down.

5Cush and Put, Lydia and all Arabia, Libya[c]
and the people of the covenant land will fall by
the sword along with Egypt.

6" 'This is what the LORD says:

" 'The allies of Egypt will fall
and her proud strength will fail.
From Migdol to Aswan
they will fall by the sword within her,
declares the Sovereign LORD.
7" 'They will be desolate
among desolate lands,
and their cities will lie
among ruined cities.
8Then they will know that I am the LORD,
when I set fire to Egypt
and all her helpers are crushed.

9" 'On that day messengers will go out from
me in ships to frighten Cush out of her complacency. Anguish will take hold of them on the
day of Egypt's doom, for it is sure to come.

10" 'This is what the Sovereign LORD says:

" 'I will put an end to the hordes of Egypt
by the hand of Nebuchadnezzar king of
Babylon.
11He and his army—the most ruthless of
nations—
will be brought in to destroy the land.
They will draw their swords against Egypt
and fill the land with the slain.
12I will dry up the streams of the Nile
and sell the land to evil men;
by the hand of foreigners
I will lay waste the land and everything
in it.

I the LORD have spoken.

13" 'This is what the Sovereign LORD says:

" 'I will destroy the idols
and put an end to the images in
Memphis.[d]
No longer will there be a prince in Egypt,
and I will spread fear throughout the
land.
14I will lay waste Upper Egypt,[e]
set fire to Zoan
and inflict punishment on Thebes.[f]
15I will pour out my wrath on Pelusium,[g]
the stronghold of Egypt,
and cut off the hordes of Thebes.
16I will set fire to Egypt;
Pelusium will writhe in agony.
Thebes will be taken by storm;
Memphis will be in constant distress.
17The young men of Heliopolis[h] and
Bubastis[i]
will fall by the sword,
and the cities themselves will go into
captivity.
18Dark will be the day at Tahpanhes
when I break the yoke of Egypt;
there her proud strength will come to an
end.
She will be covered with clouds,
and her villages will go into captivity.
19So I will inflict punishment on Egypt,
and they will know that I am the
LORD.' "

20In the eleventh year, in the first month on
the seventh day, the word of the LORD came to
me: 21"Son of man, I have broken the arm of
Pharaoh king of Egypt. It has not been bound
up for healing or put in a splint so as to become
strong enough to hold a sword. 22Therefore
this is what the Sovereign LORD says: I am
against Pharaoh king of Egypt. I will break
both his arms, the good arm as well as the
broken one, and make the sword fall from his
hand. 23I will disperse the Egyptians among

[a]21 *Horn* here symbolizes strength. [b]4 That is, the upper Nile region; also in verses 5 and 9 [c]5 Hebrew *Cub* [d]13 Hebrew *Noph*; also in verse 16 [e]14 Hebrew *waste Pathros* [f]14 Hebrew *No*; also in verses 15 and 16 [g]15 Hebrew *Sin*; also in verse 16 [h]17 Hebrew *Awen* (or *On*) [i]17 Hebrew *Pi Beseth*

the nations and scatter them through the countries. [24]I will strengthen the arms of the king of
Babylon and put my sword in his hand, but I
will break the arms of Pharaoh, and he will
groan before him like a mortally wounded
man. [25]I will strengthen the arms of the king of
Babylon, but the arms of Pharaoh will fall
limp. Then they will know that I am the LORD,
when I put my sword into the hand of the king
of Babylon and he brandishes it against Egypt.
[26]I will disperse the Egyptians among the nations and scatter them through the countries.
Then they will know that I am the LORD."

A Cedar in Lebanon

31 In the eleventh year, in the third month
on the first day, the word of the LORD
came to me: [2]"Son of man, say to Pharaoh king
of Egypt and to his hordes:

" 'Who can be compared with you in
majesty?
[3]Consider Assyria, once a cedar in
Lebanon,
with beautiful branches overshadowing
the forest;
it towered on high,
its top above the thick foliage.
[4]The waters nourished it,
deep springs made it grow tall;
their streams flowed
all around its base
and sent their channels
to all the trees of the field.
[5]So it towered higher
than all the trees of the field;
its boughs increased
and its branches grew long,
spreading because of abundant waters.
[6]All the birds of the air
nested in its boughs,
all the beasts of the field
gave birth under its branches;
all the great nations
lived in its shade.
[7]It was majestic in beauty,
with its spreading boughs,
for its roots went down
to abundant waters.
[8]The cedars in the garden of God
could not rival it,
nor could the pine trees
equal its boughs,
nor could the plane trees
compare with its branches—
no tree in the garden of God
could match its beauty.
[9]I made it beautiful
with abundant branches,
the envy of all the trees of Eden
in the garden of God.

[10]" 'Therefore this is what the Sovereign
LORD says: Because it towered on high, lifting
its top above the thick foliage, and because it
was proud of its height, [11]I handed it over to
the ruler of the nations, for him to deal with
according to its wickedness. I cast it aside,
[12]and the most ruthless of foreign nations cut
it down and left it. Its boughs fell on the mountains and in all the valleys; its branches lay
broken in all the ravines of the land. All the
nations of the earth came out from under its
shade and left it. [13]All the birds of the air settled on the fallen tree, and all the beasts of the
field were among its branches. [14]Therefore no
other trees by the waters are ever to tower
proudly on high, lifting their tops above the
thick foliage. No other trees so well-watered
are ever to reach such a height; they are all
destined for death, for the earth below, among
mortal men, with those who go down to the pit.
[15]" 'This is what the Sovereign LORD says:
On the day it was brought down to the grave[a]
I covered the deep springs with mourning for
it; I held back its streams, and its abundant
waters were restrained. Because of it I clothed
Lebanon with gloom, and all the trees of the
field withered away. [16]I made the nations
tremble at the sound of its fall when I brought
it down to the grave with those who go down
to the pit. Then all the trees of Eden, the choicest and best of Lebanon, all the trees that were
well-watered, were consoled in the earth below. [17]Those who lived in its shade, its allies
among the nations, had also gone down to the
grave with it, joining those killed by the sword.
[18]" 'Which of the trees of Eden can be compared with you in splendor and majesty? Yet
you, too, will be brought down with the trees
of Eden to the earth below; you will lie among
the uncircumcised, with those killed by the
sword.

" 'This is Pharaoh and all his hordes, declares the Sovereign LORD.' "

A Lament for Pharaoh

32 In the twelfth year, in the twelfth month
on the first day, the word of the LORD
came to me: [2]"Son of man, take up a lament
concerning Pharaoh king of Egypt and say to
him:

" 'You are like a lion among the nations;
you are like a monster in the seas
thrashing about in your streams,
churning the water with your feet
and muddying the streams.

[3]" 'This is what the Sovereign LORD says:

" 'With a great throng of people
I will cast my net over you,
and they will haul you up in my net.
[4]I will throw you on the land
and hurl you on the open field.
I will let all the birds of the air settle on
you
and all the beasts of the earth gorge
themselves on you.
[5]I will spread your flesh on the mountains
and fill the valleys with your remains.

[a]15 Hebrew *Sheol*; also in verses 16 and 17

6I will drench the land with your flowing
blood
all the way to the mountains,
and the ravines will be filled with your
flesh.
7When I snuff you out, I will cover the
heavens
and darken their stars;
I will cover the sun with a cloud,
and the moon will not give its light.
8All the shining lights in the heavens
I will darken over you;
I will bring darkness over your land,
declares the Sovereign LORD.
9I will trouble the hearts of many peoples
when I bring about your destruction
among the nations,
among[a] lands you have not known.
10I will cause many peoples to be appalled
at you,
and their kings will shudder with horror
because of you
when I brandish my sword before them.
On the day of your downfall
each of them will tremble
every moment for his life.

11" 'For this is what the Sovereign LORD
says:

" 'The sword of the king of Babylon
will come against you.
12I will cause your hordes to fall
by the swords of mighty men—
the most ruthless of all nations.
They will shatter the pride of Egypt,
and all her hordes will be overthrown.
13I will destroy all her cattle
from beside abundant waters
no longer to be stirred by the foot of man
or muddied by the hoofs of cattle.
14Then I will let her waters settle
and make her streams flow like oil,
declares the Sovereign LORD.
15When I make Egypt desolate
and strip the land of everything in it,
when I strike down all who live there,
then they will know that I am the
LORD.'

16"This is the lament they will chant for her.
The daughters of the nations will chant it; for
Egypt and all her hordes they will chant it,
declares the Sovereign LORD."

17In the twelfth year, on the fifteenth day of
the month, the word of the LORD came to me:
18"Son of man, wail for the hordes of Egypt
and consign to the earth below both her and the
daughters of mighty nations, with those who
go down to the pit. **19**Say to them, 'Are you
more favored than others? Go down and be
laid among the uncircumcised.' **20**They will
fall among those killed by the sword. The
sword is drawn; let her be dragged off with
all her hordes. **21**From within the grave[b] the
mighty leaders will say of Egypt and her allies,
'They have come down and they lie with the
uncircumcised, with those killed by the
sword.'

22"Assyria is there with her whole army; she
is surrounded by the graves of all her slain, all
who have fallen by the sword. **23**Their graves
are in the depths of the pit and her army lies
around her grave. All who had spread terror in
the land of the living are slain, fallen by the
sword.

24"Elam is there, with all her hordes around
her grave. All of them are slain, fallen by the
sword. All who had spread terror in the land of
the living went down uncircumcised to the
earth below. They bear their shame with those
who go down to the pit. **25**A bed is made for
her among the slain, with all her hordes around
her grave. All of them are uncircumcised,
killed by the sword. Because their terror had
spread in the land of the living, they bear their
shame with those who go down to the pit; they
are laid among the slain.

26"Meshech and Tubal are there, with all
their hordes around their graves. All of them
are uncircumcised, killed by the sword because
they spread their terror in the land of the living.
27Do they not lie with the other uncircumcised
warriors who have fallen, who went down to
the grave with their weapons of war, whose
swords were placed under their heads? The
punishment for their sins rested on their bones,
though the terror of these warriors had stalked
through the land of the living.

28"You too, O Pharaoh, will be broken and
will lie among the uncircumcised, with those
killed by the sword.

29"Edom is there, her kings and all her
princes; despite their power, they are laid with
those killed by the sword. They lie with the
uncircumcised, with those who go down to the
pit.

30"All the princes of the north and all the
Sidonians are there; they went down with the
slain in disgrace despite the terror caused by
their power. They lie uncircumcised with those
killed by the sword and bear their shame with
those who go down to the pit.

31"Pharaoh—he and all his army—will see
them and he will be consoled for all his hordes
that were killed by the sword, declares the
Sovereign LORD. **32**Although I had him spread
terror in the land of the living, Pharaoh and all
his hordes will be laid among the uncircumcised, with those killed by the sword, declares
the Sovereign LORD."

Ezekiel a Watchman

33 The word of the LORD came to me:
2"Son of man, speak to your countrymen and say to them: 'When I bring the sword
against a land, and the people of the land
choose one of their men and make him their
watchman, **3**and he sees the sword coming
against the land and blows the trumpet to warn
the people, **4**then if anyone hears the trumpet

[a]9 Hebrew; Septuagint *bring you into captivity among the nations, / to* [b]21 Hebrew *Sheol*; also in verse 27

but does not take warning and the sword
comes and takes his life, his blood will be on
his own head. 5Since he heard the sound of the
trumpet but did not take warning, his blood
will be on his own head. If he had taken warning, he would have saved himself. 6But if the
watchman sees the sword coming and does not
blow the trumpet to warn the people and the
sword comes and takes the life of one of them,
that man will be taken away because of his sin,
but I will hold the watchman accountable for
his blood.'

7"Son of man, I have made you a watchman
for the house of Israel; so hear the word I
speak and give them warning from me. 8When
I say to the wicked, 'O wicked man, you will
surely die,' and you do not speak out to dissuade him from his ways, that wicked man will
die for[a] his sin, and I will hold you accountable for his blood. 9But if you do warn the
wicked man to turn from his ways and he does
not do so, he will die for his sin, but you will
have saved yourself.

10"Son of man, say to the house of Israel,
'This is what you are saying: "Our offenses
and sins weigh us down, and we are wasting
away because of[b] them. How then can we
live?" ' 11Say to them, 'As surely as I live,
declares the Sovereign LORD, I take no pleasure in the death of the wicked, but rather that
they turn from their ways and live. Turn! Turn
from your evil ways! Why will you die,
O house of Israel?'

12"Therefore, son of man, say to your countrymen, 'The righteousness of the righteous
man will not save him when he disobeys, and
the wickedness of the wicked man will not
cause him to fall when he turns from it. The
righteous man, if he sins, will not be allowed
to live because of his former righteousness.'
13If I tell the righteous man that he will surely
live, but then he trusts in his righteousness and
does evil, none of the righteous things he has
done will be remembered; he will die for the
evil he has done. 14And if I say to the wicked
man, 'You will surely die,' but he then turns
away from his sin and does what is just and
right— 15if he gives back what he took in
pledge for a loan, returns what he has stolen,
follows the decrees that give life, and does no
evil, he will surely live; he will not die. 16None
of the sins he has committed will be remembered against him. He has done what is just
and right; he will surely live.

17"Yet your countrymen say, 'The way of
the Lord is not just.' But it is their way that is
not just. 18If a righteous man turns from his
righteousness and does evil, he will die for it.
19And if a wicked man turns away from his
wickedness and does what is just and right, he
will live by doing so. 20Yet, O house of Israel,
you say, 'The way of the Lord is not just.' But
I will judge each of you according to his own
ways."

Jerusalem's Fall Explained

21In the twelfth year of our exile, in the tenth
month on the fifth day, a man who had escaped
from Jerusalem came to me and said, "The city
has fallen!" 22Now the evening before the man
arrived, the hand of the LORD was upon me,
and he opened my mouth before the man came
to me in the morning. So my mouth was
opened and I was no longer silent.

23Then the word of the LORD came to me:
24"Son of man, the people living in those ruins
in the land of Israel are saying, 'Abraham was
only one man, yet he possessed the land. But
we are many; surely the land has been given to
us as our possession.' 25Therefore say to them,
'This is what the Sovereign LORD says: Since
you eat meat with the blood still in it and look
to your idols and shed blood, should you then
possess the land? 26You rely on your sword,
you do detestable things, and each of you defiles his neighbor's wife. Should you then possess the land?'

27"Say this to them: 'This is what the Sovereign LORD says: As surely as I live, those who
are left in the ruins will fall by the sword, those
out in the country I will give to the wild animals to be devoured, and those in strongholds
and caves will die of a plague. 28I will make
the land a desolate waste, and her proud
strength will come to an end, and the mountains of Israel will become desolate so that no
one will cross them. 29Then they will know
that I am the LORD, when I have made the land
a desolate waste because of all the detestable
things they have done.'

30"As for you, son of man, your countrymen
are talking together about you by the walls and
at the doors of the houses, saying to each other,
'Come and hear the message that has come
from the LORD.' 31My people come to you, as
they usually do, and sit before you to listen to
your words, but they do not put them into practice. With their mouths they express devotion,
but their hearts are greedy for unjust gain. 32In-
deed, to them you are nothing more than one
who sings love songs with a beautiful voice
and plays an instrument well, for they hear
your words but do not put them into practice.

33"When all this comes true—and it surely
will—then they will know that a prophet has
been among them."

Shepherds and Sheep

34 The word of the LORD came to me:
2"Son of man, prophesy against the
shepherds of Israel; prophesy and say to them:
'This is what the Sovereign LORD says: Woe to
the shepherds of Israel who only take care of
themselves! Should not shepherds take care of
the flock? 3You eat the curds, clothe yourselves with the wool and slaughter the choice
animals, but you do not take care of the flock.
4You have not strengthened the weak or healed
the sick or bound up the injured. You have not
brought back the strays or searched for the lost.

[a]8 Or *in*; also in verse 9 [b]10 Or *away in*

You have ruled them harshly and brutally. 5So they were scattered because there was no shepherd, and when they were scattered they became food for all the wild animals. 6My sheep wandered over all the mountains and on every high hill. They were scattered over the whole earth, and no one searched or looked for them.

7" 'Therefore, you shepherds, hear the word of the LORD: 8As surely as I live, declares the Sovereign LORD, because my flock lacks a shepherd and so has been plundered and has become food for all the wild animals, and because my shepherds did not search for my flock but cared for themselves rather than for my flock, 9therefore, O shepherds, hear the word of the LORD: 10This is what the Sovereign LORD says: I am against the shepherds and will hold them accountable for my flock. I will remove them from tending the flock so that the shepherds can no longer feed themselves. I will rescue my flock from their mouths, and it will no longer be food for them.

11" 'For this is what the Sovereign LORD says: I myself will search for my sheep and look after them. 12As a shepherd looks after his scattered flock when he is with them, so will I look after my sheep. I will rescue them from all the places where they were scattered on a day of clouds and darkness. 13I will bring them out from the nations and gather them from the countries, and I will bring them into their own land. I will pasture them on the mountains of Israel, in the ravines and in all the settlements in the land. 14I will tend them in a good pasture, and the mountain heights of Israel will be their grazing land. There they will lie down in good grazing land, and there they will feed in a rich pasture on the mountains of Israel. 15I myself will tend my sheep and have them lie down, declares the Sovereign LORD. 16I will search for the lost and bring back the strays. I will bind up the injured and strengthen the weak, but the sleek and the strong I will destroy. I will shepherd the flock with justice.

17" 'As for you, my flock, this is what the Sovereign LORD says: I will judge between one sheep and another, and between rams and goats. 18Is it not enough for you to feed on the good pasture? Must you also trample the rest of your pasture with your feet? Is it not enough for you to drink clear water? Must you also muddy the rest with your feet? 19Must my flock feed on what you have trampled and drink what you have muddied with your feet?

20" 'Therefore this is what the Sovereign LORD says to them: See, I myself will judge between the fat sheep and the lean sheep. 21Because you shove with flank and shoulder, butting all the weak sheep with your horns until you have driven them away, 22I will save my flock, and they will no longer be plundered. I will judge between one sheep and another. 23I will place over them one shepherd, my servant David, and he will tend them; he will tend them and be their shepherd. 24I the LORD will be their God, and my servant David will be prince among them. I the LORD have spoken.

25" 'I will make a covenant of peace with them and rid the land of wild beasts so that they may live in the desert and sleep in the forests in safety. 26I will bless them and the places surrounding my hill.[a] I will send down showers in season; there will be showers of blessing. 27The trees of the field will yield their fruit and the ground will yield its crops; the people will be secure in their land. They will know that I am the LORD, when I break the bars of their yoke and rescue them from the hands of those who enslaved them. 28They will no longer be plundered by the nations, nor will wild animals devour them. They will live in safety, and no one will make them afraid. 29I will provide for them a land renowned for its crops, and they will no longer be victims of famine in the land or bear the scorn of the nations. 30Then they will know that I, the LORD their God, am with them and that they, the house of Israel, are my people, declares the Sovereign LORD. 31You my sheep, the sheep of my pasture, are people, and I am your God, declares the Sovereign LORD.' "

A Prophecy Against Edom

35 The word of the LORD came to me: 2"Son of man, set your face against Mount Seir; prophesy against it 3and say: 'This is what the Sovereign LORD says: I am against you, Mount Seir, and I will stretch out my hand against you and make you a desolate waste. 4I will turn your towns into ruins and you will be desolate. Then you will know that I am the LORD.

5" 'Because you harbored an ancient hostility and delivered the Israelites over to the sword at the time of their calamity, the time their punishment reached its climax, 6therefore as surely as I live, declares the Sovereign LORD, I will give you over to bloodshed and it will pursue you. Since you did not hate bloodshed, bloodshed will pursue you. 7I will make Mount Seir a desolate waste and cut off from it all who come and go. 8I will fill your mountains with the slain; those killed by the sword will fall on your hills and in your valleys and in all your ravines. 9I will make you desolate forever; your towns will not be inhabited. Then you will know that I am the LORD.

10" 'Because you have said, "These two nations and countries will be ours and we will take possession of them," even though I the LORD was there, 11therefore as surely as I live, declares the Sovereign LORD, I will treat you in accordance with the anger and jealousy you showed in your hatred of them and I will make myself known among them when I judge you. 12Then you will know that I the LORD have heard all the contemptible things you have said against the mountains of Israel. You said, "They have been laid waste and have been given over to us to devour." 13You boasted

[a]26 Or *I will make them and the places surrounding my hill a blessing*

against me and spoke against me without restraint, and I heard it. 14This is what the Sovereign LORD says: While the whole earth rejoices, I will make you desolate. 15Because
you rejoiced when the inheritance of the house
of Israel became desolate, that is how I will
treat you. You will be desolate, O Mount Seir,
you and all of Edom. Then they will know that
I am the LORD.' "

A Prophecy to the Mountains of Israel

36 "Son of man, prophesy to the mountains
of Israel and say, 'O mountains of Israel, hear the word of the LORD. 2This is what
the Sovereign LORD says: The enemy said of
you, "Aha! The ancient heights have become
our possession." ' 3Therefore prophesy and
say, 'This is what the Sovereign LORD says:
Because they ravaged and hounded you from
every side so that you became the possession
of the rest of the nations and the object of
people's malicious talk and slander, 4therefore,
O mountains of Israel, hear the word of the
Sovereign LORD: This is what the Sovereign
LORD says to the mountains and hills, to the
ravines and valleys, to the desolate ruins and
the deserted towns that have been plundered
and ridiculed by the rest of the nations around
you— 5this is what the Sovereign LORD says:
In my burning zeal I have spoken against the
rest of the nations, and against all Edom, for
with glee and with malice in their hearts they
made my land their own possession so that
they might plunder its pastureland.' 6Therefore
prophesy concerning the land of Israel and say
to the mountains and hills, to the ravines and
valleys: 'This is what the Sovereign LORD
says: I speak in my jealous wrath because you
have suffered the scorn of the nations. 7There-
fore this is what the Sovereign LORD says: I
swear with uplifted hand that the nations
around you will also suffer scorn.

8" 'But you, O mountains of Israel, will produce branches and fruit for my people Israel,
for they will soon come home. 9I am concerned for you and will look on you with favor; you will be plowed and sown, 10and I will
multiply the number of people upon you, even
the whole house of Israel. The towns will be
inhabited and the ruins rebuilt. 11I will increase
the number of men and animals upon you, and
they will be fruitful and become numerous. I
will settle people on you as in the past and will
make you prosper more than before. Then you
will know that I am the LORD. 12I will cause
people, my people Israel, to walk upon you.
They will possess you, and you will be their
inheritance; you will never again deprive them
of their children.

13" 'This is what the Sovereign LORD says:
Because people say to you, "You devour men
and deprive your nation of its children,"
14therefore you will no longer devour men or
make your nation childless, declares the Sovereign LORD. 15No longer will I make you hear
the taunts of the nations, and no longer will
you suffer the scorn of the peoples or cause
your nation to fall, declares the Sovereign
LORD.' "

16Again the word of the LORD came to me:
17"Son of man, when the people of Israel were
living in their own land, they defiled it by their
conduct and their actions. Their conduct was
like a woman's monthly uncleanness in my
sight. 18So I poured out my wrath on them
because they had shed blood in the land and
because they had defiled it with their idols. 19I
dispersed them among the nations, and they
were scattered through the countries; I judged
them according to their conduct and their actions. 20And wherever they went among the
nations they profaned my holy name, for it was
said of them, 'These are the LORD's people,
and yet they had to leave his land.' 21I had
concern for my holy name, which the house of
Israel profaned among the nations where they
had gone.

22"Therefore say to the house of Israel,
'This is what the Sovereign LORD says: It is
not for your sake, O house of Israel, that I am
going to do these things, but for the sake of my
holy name, which you have profaned among
the nations where you have gone. 23I will show
the holiness of my great name, which has been
profaned among the nations, the name you
have profaned among them. Then the nations
will know that I am the LORD, declares the
Sovereign LORD, when I show myself holy
through you before their eyes.

24" 'For I will take you out of the nations; I
will gather you from all the countries and bring
you back into your own land. 25I will sprinkle
clean water on you, and you will be clean; I
will cleanse you from all your impurities and
from all your idols. 26I will give you a new
heart and put a new spirit in you; I will remove
from you your heart of stone and give you a
heart of flesh. 27And I will put my Spirit in you
and move you to follow my decrees and be
careful to keep my laws. 28You will live in the
land I gave your forefathers; you will be my
people, and I will be your God. 29I will save
you from all your uncleanness. I will call for
the grain and make it plentiful and will not
bring famine upon you. 30I will increase the
fruit of the trees and the crops of the field, so
that you will no longer suffer disgrace among
the nations because of famine. 31Then you will
remember your evil ways and wicked deeds,
and you will loathe yourselves for your sins
and detestable practices. 32I want you to know
that I am not doing this for your sake, declares
the Sovereign LORD. Be ashamed and disgraced for your conduct, O house of Israel!

33" 'This is what the Sovereign LORD says:
On the day I cleanse you from all your sins, I
will resettle your towns, and the ruins will be
rebuilt. 34The desolate land will be cultivated
instead of lying desolate in the sight of all who
pass through it. 35They will say, "This land
that was laid waste has become like the garden
of Eden; the cities that were lying in ruins,
desolate and destroyed, are now fortified and
inhabited." 36Then the nations around you that

remain will know that I the LORD have rebuilt what was destroyed and have replanted what was desolate. I the LORD have spoken, and I will do it.'

37"This is what the Sovereign LORD says: Once again I will yield to the plea of the house of Israel and do this for them: I will make their people as numerous as sheep, 38as numerous as the flocks for offerings at Jerusalem during her appointed feasts. So will the ruined cities be filled with flocks of people. Then they will know that I am the LORD."

The Valley of Dry Bones

37 The hand of the LORD was upon me, and he brought me out by the Spirit of the LORD and set me in the middle of a valley; it was full of bones. 2He led me back and forth among them, and I saw a great many bones on the floor of the valley, bones that were very dry. 3He asked me, "Son of man, can these bones live?"

I said, "O Sovereign LORD, you alone know."

4Then he said to me, "Prophesy to these bones and say to them, 'Dry bones, hear the word of the LORD! 5This is what the Sovereign LORD says to these bones: I will make breath[a] enter you, and you will come to life. 6I will attach tendons to you and make flesh come upon you and cover you with skin; I will put breath in you, and you will come to life. Then you will know that I am the LORD.' "

7So I prophesied as I was commanded. And as I was prophesying, there was a noise, a rattling sound, and the bones came together, bone to bone. 8I looked, and tendons and flesh appeared on them and skin covered them, but there was no breath in them.

9Then he said to me, "Prophesy to the breath; prophesy, son of man, and say to it, 'This is what the Sovereign LORD says: Come from the four winds, O breath, and breathe into these slain, that they may live.' " 10So I prophesied as he commanded me, and breath entered them; they came to life and stood up on their feet—a vast army.

11Then he said to me: "Son of man, these bones are the whole house of Israel. They say, 'Our bones are dried up and our hope is gone; we are cut off.' 12Therefore prophesy and say to them: 'This is what the Sovereign LORD says: O my people, I am going to open your graves and bring you up from them; I will bring you back to the land of Israel. 13Then you, my people, will know that I am the LORD, when I open your graves and bring you up from them. 14I will put my Spirit in you and you will live, and I will settle you in your own land. Then you will know that I the LORD have spoken, and I have done it, declares the LORD.' "

One Nation Under One King

15The word of the LORD came to me: 16"Son of man, take a stick of wood and write on it, 'Belonging to Judah and the Israelites associated with him.' Then take another stick of wood, and write on it, 'Ephraim's stick, belonging to Joseph and all the house of Israel associated with him.' 17Join them together into one stick so that they will become one in your hand.

18"When your countrymen ask you, 'Won't you tell us what you mean by this?' 19say to them, 'This is what the Sovereign LORD says: I am going to take the stick of Joseph—which is in Ephraim's hand—and of the Israelite tribes associated with him, and join it to Judah's stick, making them a single stick of wood, and they will become one in my hand.' 20Hold before their eyes the sticks you have written on 21and say to them, 'This is what the Sovereign LORD says: I will take the Israelites out of the nations where they have gone. I will gather them from all around and bring them back into their own land. 22I will make them one nation in the land, on the mountains of Israel. There will be one king over all of them and they will never again be two nations or be divided into two kingdoms. 23They will no longer defile themselves with their idols and vile images or with any of their offenses, for I will save them from all their sinful backsliding,[b] and I will cleanse them. They will be my people, and I will be their God.

24" 'My servant David will be king over them, and they will all have one shepherd. They will follow my laws and be careful to keep my decrees. 25They will live in the land I gave to my servant Jacob, the land where your fathers lived. They and their children and their children's children will live there forever, and David my servant will be their prince forever. 26I will make a covenant of peace with them; it will be an everlasting covenant. I will establish them and increase their numbers, and I will put my sanctuary among them forever. 27My dwelling place will be with them; I will be their God, and they will be my people. 28Then the nations will know that I the LORD make Israel holy, when my sanctuary is among them forever.' "

A Prophecy Against Gog

38 The word of the LORD came to me: 2"Son of man, set your face against Gog, of the land of Magog, the chief prince of[c] Meshech and Tubal; prophesy against him 3and say: 'This is what the Sovereign LORD says: I am against you, O Gog, chief prince of[d] Meshech and Tubal. 4I will turn you around, put hooks in your jaws and bring you out with your whole army—your horses, your horsemen fully armed, and a great horde with large and small shields, all of them brandishing their swords. 5Persia, Cush[e] and Put will be

[a]5 The Hebrew for this word can also mean *wind* or *spirit* (see verses 6-14). [b]23 Many Hebrew manuscripts (see also Septuagint); most Hebrew manuscripts *all their dwelling places where they sinned*
[c]2 Or *the prince of Rosh,* [d]3 Or *Gog, prince of Rosh,* [e]5 That is, the upper Nile region

with them, all with shields and helmets, 6also
Gomer with all its troops, and Beth Togarmah
from the far north with all its troops—the
many nations with you.
7“ ‘Get ready; be prepared, you and all the
hordes gathered about you, and take command
of them. 8After many days you will be called
to arms. In future years you will invade a land
that has recovered from war, whose people
were gathered from many nations to the mountains of Israel, which had long been desolate.
They had been brought out from the nations,
and now all of them live in safety. 9You and all
your troops and the many nations with you will
go up, advancing like a storm; you will be like
a cloud covering the land.
10“ ‘This is what the Sovereign LORD says:
On that day thoughts will come into your mind
and you will devise an evil scheme. 11You will
say, “I will invade a land of unwalled villages;
I will attack a peaceful and unsuspecting people—all of them living without walls and without gates and bars. 12I will plunder and loot
and turn my hand against the resettled ruins
and the people gathered from the nations, rich
in livestock and goods, living at the center of
the land.” 13Sheba and Dedan and the merchants of Tarshish and all her villages[a] will
say to you, “Have you come to plunder? Have
you gathered your hordes to loot, to carry off
silver and gold, to take away livestock and
goods and to seize much plunder?” ’
14“Therefore, son of man, prophesy and say
to Gog: ‘This is what the Sovereign LORD
says: In that day, when my people Israel are
living in safety, will you not take notice of it?
15You will come from your place in the far
north, you and many nations with you, all of
them riding on horses, a great horde, a mighty
army. 16You will advance against my people
Israel like a cloud that covers the land. In days
to come, O Gog, I will bring you against my
land, so that the nations may know me when I
show myself holy through you before their
eyes.
17“ ‘This is what the Sovereign LORD says:
Are you not the one I spoke of in former days
by my servants the prophets of Israel? At that
time they prophesied for years that I would
bring you against them. 18This is what will
happen in that day: When Gog attacks the land
of Israel, my hot anger will be aroused, declares the Sovereign LORD. 19In my zeal and
fiery wrath I declare that at that time there
shall be a great earthquake in the land of Israel.
20The fish of the sea, the birds of the air, the
beasts of the field, every creature that moves
along the ground, and all the people on the face
of the earth will tremble at my presence. The
mountains will be overturned, the cliffs will
crumble and every wall will fall to the ground.
21I will summon a sword against Gog on all
my mountains, declares the Sovereign LORD.
Every man’s sword will be against his brother.
22I will execute judgment upon him with
plague and bloodshed; I will pour down torrents of rain, hailstones and burning sulfur on
him and on his troops and on the many nations
with him. 23And so I will show my greatness
and my holiness, and I will make myself
known in the sight of many nations. Then they
will know that I am the LORD.’

39 “Son of man, prophesy against Gog and
say: ‘This is what the Sovereign LORD
says: I am against you, O Gog, chief prince
of[b] Meshech and Tubal. 2I will turn you
around and drag you along. I will bring you
from the far north and send you against the
mountains of Israel. 3Then I will strike your
bow from your left hand and make your arrows
drop from your right hand. 4On the mountains
of Israel you will fall, you and all your troops
and the nations with you. I will give you as
food to all kinds of carrion birds and to the
wild animals. 5You will fall in the open field,
for I have spoken, declares the Sovereign
LORD. 6I will send fire on Magog and on those
who live in safety in the coastlands, and they
will know that I am the LORD.
7“ ‘I will make known my holy name among
my people Israel. I will no longer let my holy
name be profaned, and the nations will know
that I the LORD am the Holy One in Israel. 8It
is coming! It will surely take place, declares
the Sovereign LORD. This is the day I have
spoken of.
9“ ‘Then those who live in the towns of Israel will go out and use the weapons for fuel and
burn them up—the small and large shields, the
bows and arrows, the war clubs and spears. For
seven years they will use them for fuel. 10They
will not need to gather wood from the fields or
cut it from the forests, because they will use
the weapons for fuel. And they will plunder
those who plundered them and loot those who
looted them, declares the Sovereign LORD.
11“ ‘On that day I will give Gog a burial
place in Israel, in the valley of those who travel
east toward[c] the Sea.[d] It will block the way of
travelers, because Gog and all his hordes will
be buried there. So it will be called the Valley
of Hamon Gog.[e]
12“ ‘For seven months the house of Israel
will be burying them in order to cleanse the
land. 13All the people of the land will bury
them, and the day I am glorified will be a
memorable day for them, declares the Sovereign LORD.
14“ ‘Men will be regularly employed to
cleanse the land. Some will go throughout the
land and, in addition to them, others will bury
those that remain on the ground. At the end of
the seven months they will begin their search.
15As they go through the land and one of them
sees a human bone, he will set up a marker
beside it until the gravediggers have buried it
in the Valley of Hamon Gog. 16(Also a town

[a]13 Or *her strong lions* [b]1 Or *Gog, prince of Rosh,* [c]11 Or *of* [d]11 That is, the Dead Sea
[e]11 *Hamon Gog* means *hordes of Gog.*

called Hamonah[a] will be there.) And so they will cleanse the land.'

17"Son of man, this is what the Sovereign LORD says: Call out to every kind of bird and all the wild animals: 'Assemble and come together from all around to the sacrifice I am preparing for you, the great sacrifice on the mountains of Israel. There you will eat flesh and drink blood. 18You will eat the flesh of mighty men and drink the blood of the princes of the earth as if they were rams and lambs, goats and bulls—all of them fattened animals from Bashan. 19At the sacrifice I am preparing for you, you will eat fat till you are glutted and drink blood till you are drunk. 20At my table you will eat your fill of horses and riders, mighty men and soldiers of every kind,' declares the Sovereign LORD.

21"I will display my glory among the nations, and all the nations will see the punishment I inflict and the hand I lay upon them. 22From that day forward the house of Israel will know that I am the LORD their God. 23And the nations will know that the people of Israel went into exile for their sin, because they were unfaithful to me. So I hid my face from them and handed them over to their enemies, and they all fell by the sword. 24I dealt with them according to their uncleanness and their offenses, and I hid my face from them.

25"Therefore this is what the Sovereign LORD says: I will now bring Jacob back from captivity[b] and will have compassion on all the people of Israel, and I will be zealous for my holy name. 26They will forget their shame and all the unfaithfulness they showed toward me when they lived in safety in their land with no one to make them afraid. 27When I have brought them back from the nations and have gathered them from the countries of their enemies, I will show myself holy through them in the sight of many nations. 28Then they will know that I am the LORD their God, for though I sent them into exile among the nations, I will gather them to their own land, not leaving any behind. 29I will no longer hide my face from them, for I will pour out my Spirit on the house of Israel, declares the Sovereign LORD."

The New Temple Area

40 In the twenty-fifth year of our exile, at the beginning of the year, on the tenth of the month, in the fourteenth year after the fall of the city—on that very day the hand of the LORD was upon me and he took me there. 2In visions of God he took me to the land of Israel and set me on a very high mountain, on whose south side were some buildings that looked like a city. 3He took me there, and I saw a man whose appearance was like bronze; he was standing in the gateway with a linen cord and a measuring rod in his hand. 4The man said to me, "Son of man, look with your eyes and hear with your ears and pay attention to everything I am going to show you, for that is why you have been brought here. Tell the house of Israel everything you see."

The East Gate to the Outer Court

5I saw a wall completely surrounding the temple area. The length of the measuring rod in the man's hand was six long cubits, each of which was a cubit[c] and a handbreadth.[d] He measured the wall; it was one measuring rod thick and one rod high.

6Then he went to the gate facing east. He climbed its steps and measured the threshold of the gate; it was one rod deep.[e] 7The alcoves for the guards were one rod long and one rod wide, and the projecting walls between the alcoves were five cubits thick. And the threshold of the gate next to the portico facing the temple was one rod deep.

8Then he measured the portico of the gateway; 9it[f] was eight cubits deep and its jambs were two cubits thick. The portico of the gateway faced the temple.

10Inside the east gate were three alcoves on each side; the three had the same measurements, and the faces of the projecting walls on each side had the same measurements. 11Then he measured the width of the entrance to the gateway; it was ten cubits and its length was thirteen cubits. 12In front of each alcove was a wall one cubit high, and the alcoves were six cubits square. 13Then he measured the gateway from the top of the rear wall of one alcove to the top of the opposite one; the distance was twenty-five cubits from one parapet opening to the opposite one. 14He measured along the faces of the projecting walls all around the inside of the gateway—sixty cubits. The measurement was up to the portico[g] facing the courtyard.[h] 15The distance from the entrance of the gateway to the far end of its portico was fifty cubits. 16The alcoves and the projecting walls inside the gateway were surmounted by narrow parapet openings all around, as was the portico; the openings all around faced inward. The faces of the projecting walls were decorated with palm trees.

The Outer Court

17Then he brought me into the outer court. There I saw some rooms and a pavement that had been constructed all around the court; there were thirty rooms along the pavement. 18It abutted the sides of the gateways and was as wide as they were long; this was the lower pavement. 19Then he measured the distance from the inside of the lower gateway to the

[a]16 *Hamonah* means *horde.* [b]25 Or *now restore the fortunes of Jacob* [c]5 The common cubit was about 1 1/2 feet (about 0.5 meter). [d]5 That is, about 3 inches (about 8 centimeters) [e]6 Septuagint; Hebrew *deep, the first threshold, one rod deep* [f]8,9 Many Hebrew manuscripts, Septuagint, Vulgate and Syriac; most Hebrew manuscripts *gateway facing the temple; it was one rod deep. 9Then he measured the portico of the gateway; it* [g]14 Septuagint; Hebrew *projecting wall* [h]14 The meaning of the Hebrew for this verse is uncertain.

outside of the inner court; it was a hundred cubits on the east side as well as on the north.

The North Gate

20Then he measured the length and width of the gate facing north, leading into the outer court. 21Its alcoves—three on each side—its projecting walls and its portico had the same measurements as those of the first gateway. It was fifty cubits long and twenty-five cubits wide. 22Its openings, its portico and its palm tree decorations had the same measurements as those of the gate facing east. Seven steps led up to it, with its portico opposite them. 23There was a gate to the inner court facing the north gate, just as there was on the east. He measured from one gate to the opposite one; it was a hundred cubits.

The South Gate

24Then he led me to the south side and I saw a gate facing south. He measured its jambs and its portico, and they had the same measurements as the others. 25The gateway and its portico had narrow openings all around, like the openings of the others. It was fifty cubits long and twenty-five cubits wide. 26Seven steps led up to it, with its portico opposite them; it had palm tree decorations on the faces of the projecting walls on each side. 27The inner court also had a gate facing south, and he measured from this gate to the outer gate on the south side; it was a hundred cubits.

Gates to the Inner Court

28Then he brought me into the inner court through the south gate, and he measured the south gate; it had the same measurements as the others. 29Its alcoves, its projecting walls and its portico had the same measurements as the others. The gateway and its portico had openings all around. It was fifty cubits long and twenty-five cubits wide. 30(The porticoes of the gateways around the inner court were twenty-five cubits wide and five cubits deep.) 31Its portico faced the outer court; palm trees decorated its jambs, and eight steps led up to it.

32Then he brought me to the inner court on the east side, and he measured the gateway; it had the same measurements as the others. 33Its alcoves, its projecting walls and its portico had the same measurements as the others. The gateway and its portico had openings all around. It was fifty cubits long and twenty-five cubits wide. 34Its portico faced the outer court; palm trees decorated the jambs on either side, and eight steps led up to it.

35Then he brought me to the north gate and measured it. It had the same measurements as the others, 36as did its alcoves, its projecting walls and its portico, and it had openings all around. It was fifty cubits long and twenty-five cubits wide. 37Its portico[a] faced the outer court; palm trees decorated the jambs on either side, and eight steps led up to it.

The Rooms for Preparing Sacrifices

38A room with a doorway was by the portico in each of the inner gateways, where the burnt offerings were washed. 39In the portico of the gateway were two tables on each side, on which the burnt offerings, sin offerings and guilt offerings were slaughtered. 40By the outside wall of the portico of the gateway, near the steps at the entrance to the north gateway were two tables, and on the other side of the steps were two tables. 41So there were four tables on one side of the gateway and four on the other—eight tables in all—on which the sacrifices were slaughtered. 42There were also four tables of dressed stone for the burnt offerings, each a cubit and a half long, a cubit and a half wide and a cubit high. On them were placed the utensils for slaughtering the burnt offerings and the other sacrifices. 43And double-pronged hooks, each a handbreadth long, were attached to the wall all around. The tables were for the flesh of the offerings.

Rooms for the Priests

44Outside the inner gate, within the inner court, were two rooms, one[b] at the side of the north gate and facing south, and another at the side of the south[c] gate and facing north. 45He said to me, "The room facing south is for the priests who have charge of the temple, 46and the room facing north is for the priests who have charge of the altar. These are the sons of Zadok, who are the only Levites who may draw near to the LORD to minister before him."

47Then he measured the court: It was square—a hundred cubits long and a hundred cubits wide. And the altar was in front of the temple.

The Temple

48He brought me to the portico of the temple and measured the jambs of the portico; they were five cubits wide on either side. The width of the entrance was fourteen cubits and its projecting walls were[d] three cubits wide on either side. 49The portico was twenty cubits wide, and twelve[e] cubits from front to back. It was reached by a flight of stairs,[f] and there were pillars on each side of the jambs.

41 Then the man brought me to the outer sanctuary and measured the jambs; the width of the jambs was six cubits[g] on each side.[h] 2The entrance was ten cubits wide, and the projecting walls on each side of it were five cubits wide. He also measured the outer sanctuary; it was forty cubits long and twenty cubits wide.

[a]*37* Septuagint (see also verses 31 and 34); Hebrew *jambs* [b]*44* Septuagint; Hebrew *were rooms for singers, which were* [c]*44* Septuagint; Hebrew *east* [d]*48* Septuagint; Hebrew *entrance was* [e]*49* Septuagint; Hebrew *eleven* [f]*49* Hebrew; Septuagint *Ten steps led up to it* [g]*1* The common cubit was about 1 1/2 feet (about 0.5 meter). [h]*1* One Hebrew manuscript and Septuagint; most Hebrew manuscripts *side, the width of the tent*

3 Then he went into the inner sanctuary and measured the jambs of the entrance; each was two cubits wide. The entrance was six cubits wide, and the projecting walls on each side of it were seven cubits wide. 4 And he measured the length of the inner sanctuary; it was twenty cubits, and its width was twenty cubits across the end of the outer sanctuary. He said to me, "This is the Most Holy Place."

5 Then he measured the wall of the temple; it was six cubits thick, and each side room around the temple was four cubits wide. 6 The side rooms were on three levels, one above another, thirty on each level. There were ledges all around the wall of the temple to serve as supports for the side rooms, so that the supports were not inserted into the wall of the temple. 7 The side rooms all around the temple were wider at each successive level. The structure surrounding the temple was built in ascending stages, so that the rooms widened as one went upward. A stairway went up from the lowest floor to the top floor through the middle floor.

8 I saw that the temple had a raised base all around it, forming the foundation of the side rooms. It was the length of the rod, six long cubits. 9 The outer wall of the side rooms was five cubits thick. The open area between the side rooms of the temple 10 and the ⌊priests'⌋ rooms was twenty cubits wide all around the temple. 11 There were entrances to the side rooms from the open area, one on the north and another on the south; and the base adjoining the open area was five cubits wide all around.

12 The building facing the temple courtyard on the west side was seventy cubits wide. The wall of the building was five cubits thick all around, and its length was ninety cubits.

13 Then he measured the temple; it was a hundred cubits long, and the temple courtyard and the building with its walls were also a hundred cubits long. 14 The width of the temple courtyard on the east, including the front of the temple, was a hundred cubits.

15 Then he measured the length of the building facing the courtyard at the rear of the temple, including its galleries on each side; it was a hundred cubits.

The outer sanctuary, the inner sanctuary and the portico facing the court, 16 as well as the thresholds and the narrow windows and galleries around the three of them—everything beyond and including the threshold was covered with wood. The floor, the wall up to the windows, and the windows were covered. 17 In the space above the outside of the entrance to the inner sanctuary and on the walls at regular intervals all around the inner and outer sanctuary 18 were carved cherubim and palm trees. Palm trees alternated with cherubim. Each cherub had two faces: 19 the face of a man toward the palm tree on one side and the face of a lion toward the palm tree on the other. They were carved all around the whole temple. 20 From the floor to the area above the entrance, cherubim and palm trees were carved on the wall of the outer sanctuary.

21 The outer sanctuary had a rectangular doorframe, and the one at the front of the Most Holy Place was similar. 22 There was a wooden altar three cubits high and two cubits square[a]; its corners, its base[b] and its sides were of wood. The man said to me, "This is the table that is before the LORD." 23 Both the outer sanctuary and the Most Holy Place had double doors. 24 Each door had two leaves—two hinged leaves for each door. 25 And on the doors of the outer sanctuary were carved cherubim and palm trees like those carved on the walls, and there was a wooden overhang on the front of the portico. 26 On the sidewalls of the portico were narrow windows with palm trees carved on each side. The side rooms of the temple also had overhangs.

Rooms for the Priests

42 Then the man led me northward into the outer court and brought me to the rooms opposite the temple courtyard and opposite the outer wall on the north side. 2 The building whose door faced north was a hundred cubits[c] long and fifty cubits wide. 3 Both in the section twenty cubits from the inner court and in the section opposite the pavement of the outer court, gallery faced gallery at the three levels. 4 In front of the rooms was an inner passageway ten cubits wide and a hundred cubits[d] long. Their doors were on the north. 5 Now the upper rooms were narrower, for the galleries took more space from them than from the rooms on the lower and middle floors of the building. 6 The rooms on the third floor had no pillars, as the courts had; so they were smaller in floor space than those on the lower and middle floors. 7 There was an outer wall parallel to the rooms and the outer court; it extended in front of the rooms for fifty cubits. 8 While the row of rooms on the side next to the outer court was fifty cubits long, the row on the side nearest the sanctuary was a hundred cubits long. 9 The lower rooms had an entrance on the east side as one enters them from the outer court.

10 On the south side[e] along the length of the wall of the outer court, adjoining the temple courtyard and opposite the outer wall, were rooms 11 with a passageway in front of them. These were like the rooms on the north; they had the same length and width, with similar exits and dimensions. Similar to the doorways on the north 12 were the doorways of the rooms on the south. There was a doorway at the beginning of the passageway that was parallel to the corresponding wall extending eastward, by which one enters the rooms.

13 Then he said to me, "The north and south rooms facing the temple courtyard are the

[a] *22* Septuagint; Hebrew *long* [b] *22* Septuagint; Hebrew *length* [c] *2* The common cubit was about 1 1/2 feet (about 0.5 meter). [d] *4* Septuagint and Syriac; Hebrew *and one cubit* [e] *10* Septuagint; Hebrew *Eastward*

priests' rooms, where the priests who approach
the LORD will eat the most holy offerings.
There they will put the most holy offerings—
the grain offerings, the sin offerings and the
guilt offerings—for the place is holy. 14Once
the priests enter the holy precincts, they are not
to go into the outer court until they leave behind the garments in which they minister, for
these are holy. They are to put on other clothes
before they go near the places that are for the
people."

15When he had finished measuring what was
inside the temple area, he led me out by the
east gate and measured the area all around:
16He measured the east side with the measuring rod; it was five hundred cubits.[a] 17He measured the north side; it was five hundred cubits[b] by the measuring rod. 18He measured the
south side; it was five hundred cubits by the
measuring rod. 19Then he turned to the west
side and measured; it was five hundred cubits
by the measuring rod. 20So he measured the
area on all four sides. It had a wall around it,
five hundred cubits long and five hundred cubits wide, to separate the holy from the common.

The Glory Returns to the Temple

43 Then the man brought me to the gate
facing east, 2and I saw the glory of the
God of Israel coming from the east. His voice
was like the roar of rushing waters, and the
land was radiant with his glory. 3The vision I
saw was like the vision I had seen when he[c]
came to destroy the city and like the visions I
had seen by the Kebar River, and I fell facedown. 4The glory of the LORD entered the temple through the gate facing east. 5Then the
Spirit lifted me up and brought me into the
inner court, and the glory of the LORD filled
the temple.

6While the man was standing beside me, I
heard someone speaking to me from inside the
temple. 7He said: "Son of man, this is the place
of my throne and the place for the soles of my
feet. This is where I will live among the Israelites forever. The house of Israel will never
again defile my holy name—neither they nor
their kings—by their prostitution[d] and the lifeless idols[e] of their kings at their high places.
8When they placed their threshold next to my
threshold and their doorposts beside my doorposts, with only a wall between me and them,
they defiled my holy name by their detestable
practices. So I destroyed them in my anger.
9Now let them put away from me their prostitution and the lifeless idols of their kings, and
I will live among them forever.

10"Son of man, describe the temple to the
people of Israel, that they may be ashamed of
their sins. Let them consider the plan, 11and if
they are ashamed of all they have done, make
known to them the design of the temple—its
arrangement, its exits and entrances—its
whole design and all its regulations[f] and laws.
Write these down before them so that they may
be faithful to its design and follow all its regulations.

12"This is the law of the temple: All the
surrounding area on top of the mountain will
be most holy. Such is the law of the temple.

The Altar

13"These are the measurements of the altar
in long cubits, that cubit being a cubit[g] and a
handbreadth[h]: Its gutter is a cubit deep and a
cubit wide, with a rim of one span[i] around the
edge. And this is the height of the altar: 14From
the gutter on the ground up to the lower ledge
it is two cubits high and a cubit wide, and from
the smaller ledge up to the larger ledge it is
four cubits high and a cubit wide. 15The altar
hearth is four cubits high, and four horns
project upward from the hearth. 16The altar
hearth is square, twelve cubits long and twelve
cubits wide. 17The upper ledge also is square,
fourteen cubits long and fourteen cubits wide,
with a rim of half a cubit and a gutter of a cubit
all around. The steps of the altar face east."

18Then he said to me, "Son of man, this is
what the Sovereign LORD says: These will be
the regulations for sacrificing burnt offerings
and sprinkling blood upon the altar when it is
built: 19You are to give a young bull as a sin
offering to the priests, who are Levites, of the
family of Zadok, who come near to minister
before me, declares the Sovereign LORD.
20You are to take some of its blood and put it
on the four horns of the altar and on the four
corners of the upper ledge and all around the
rim, and so purify the altar and make atonement for it. 21You are to take the bull for the
sin offering and burn it in the designated part
of the temple area outside the sanctuary.

22"On the second day you are to offer a male
goat without defect for a sin offering, and the
altar is to be purified as it was purified with the
bull. 23When you have finished purifying it,
you are to offer a young bull and a ram from
the flock, both without defect. 24You are to
offer them before the LORD, and the priests are
to sprinkle salt on them and sacrifice them as
a burnt offering to the LORD.

25"For seven days you are to provide a male
goat daily for a sin offering; you are also to
provide a young bull and a ram from the flock,
both without defect. 26For seven days they are
to make atonement for the altar and cleanse it;
thus they will dedicate it. 27At the end of these
days, from the eighth day on, the priests are to
present your burnt offerings and fellowship of-

[a] *16* See Septuagint of verse 17; Hebrew *rods*; also in verses 18 and 19. [b] *17* Septuagint; Hebrew *rods*
[c] *3* Some Hebrew manuscripts and Vulgate; most Hebrew manuscripts *I* [d] *7* Or *their spiritual adultery*; also in verse 9 [e] *7* Or *the corpses*; also in verse 9 [f] *11* Some Hebrew manuscripts and Septuagint; most Hebrew manuscripts *regulations and its whole design* [g] *13* The common cubit was about 1 1/2 feet (about 0.5 meter).
[h] *13* That is, about 3 inches (about 8 centimeters) [i] *13* That is, about 9 inches (about 22 centimeters)

ferings[a] on the altar. Then I will accept you, declares the Sovereign LORD."

The Prince, the Levites, the Priests

44 Then the man brought me back to the outer gate of the sanctuary, the one facing east, and it was shut. 2The LORD said to me, "This gate is to remain shut. It must not be opened; no one may enter through it. It is to remain shut because the LORD, the God of Israel, has entered through it. 3The prince himself is the only one who may sit inside the gateway to eat in the presence of the LORD. He is to enter by way of the portico of the gateway and go out the same way."

4Then the man brought me by way of the north gate to the front of the temple. I looked and saw the glory of the LORD filling the temple of the LORD, and I fell facedown.

5The LORD said to me, "Son of man, look carefully, listen closely and give attention to everything I tell you concerning all the regulations regarding the temple of the LORD. Give attention to the entrance of the temple and all the exits of the sanctuary. 6Say to the rebellious house of Israel, 'This is what the Sovereign LORD says: Enough of your detestable practices, O house of Israel! 7In addition to all your other detestable practices, you brought foreigners uncircumcised in heart and flesh into my sanctuary, desecrating my temple while you offered me food, fat and blood, and you broke my covenant. 8Instead of carrying out your duty in regard to my holy things, you put others in charge of my sanctuary. 9This is what the Sovereign LORD says: No foreigner uncircumcised in heart and flesh is to enter my sanctuary, not even the foreigners who live among the Israelites.

10" 'The Levites who went far from me when Israel went astray and who wandered from me after their idols must bear the consequences of their sin. 11They may serve in my sanctuary, having charge of the gates of the temple and serving in it; they may slaughter the burnt offerings and sacrifices for the people and stand before the people and serve them. 12But because they served them in the presence of their idols and made the house of Israel fall into sin, therefore I have sworn with uplifted hand that they must bear the consequences of their sin, declares the Sovereign LORD. 13They are not to come near to serve me as priests or come near any of my holy things or my most holy offerings; they must bear the shame of their detestable practices. 14Yet I will put them in charge of the duties of the temple and all the work that is to be done in it.

15" 'But the priests, who are Levites and descendants of Zadok and who faithfully carried out the duties of my sanctuary when the Israelites went astray from me, are to come near to minister before me; they are to stand before me to offer sacrifices of fat and blood, declares the Sovereign LORD. 16They alone are to enter my sanctuary; they alone are to come near my table to minister before me and perform my service.

17" 'When they enter the gates of the inner court, they are to wear linen clothes; they must not wear any woolen garment while ministering at the gates of the inner court or inside the temple. 18They are to wear linen turbans on their heads and linen undergarments around their waists. They must not wear anything that makes them perspire. 19When they go out into the outer court where the people are, they are to take off the clothes they have been ministering in and are to leave them in the sacred rooms, and put on other clothes, so that they do not consecrate the people by means of their garments.

20" 'They must not shave their heads or let their hair grow long, but they are to keep the hair of their heads trimmed. 21No priest is to drink wine when he enters the inner court. 22They must not marry widows or divorced women; they may marry only virgins of Israelite descent or widows of priests. 23They are to teach my people the difference between the holy and the common and show them how to distinguish between the unclean and the clean.

24" 'In any dispute, the priests are to serve as judges and decide it according to my ordinances. They are to keep my laws and my decrees for all my appointed feasts, and they are to keep my Sabbaths holy.

25" 'A priest must not defile himself by going near a dead person; however, if the dead person was his father or mother, son or daughter, brother or unmarried sister, then he may defile himself. 26After he is cleansed, he must wait seven days. 27On the day he goes into the inner court of the sanctuary to minister in the sanctuary, he is to offer a sin offering for himself, declares the Sovereign LORD.

28" 'I am to be the only inheritance the priests have. You are to give them no possession in Israel; I will be their possession. 29They will eat the grain offerings, the sin offerings and the guilt offerings; and everything in Israel devoted[b] to the LORD will belong to them. 30The best of all the firstfruits and of all your special gifts will belong to the priests. You are to give them the first portion of your ground meal so that a blessing may rest on your household. 31The priests must not eat anything, bird or animal, found dead or torn by wild animals.

Division of the Land

45 " 'When you allot the land as an inheritance, you are to present to the LORD a portion of the land as a sacred district, 25,000 cubits long and 20,000[c] cubits wide; the entire area will be holy. 2Of this, a section 500 cubits square is to be for the sanctuary, with 50 cubits around it for open land. 3In the sacred district,

[a]27 Traditionally *peace offerings* [b]29 The Hebrew term refers to the irrevocable giving over of things or persons to the LORD. [c]1 Septuagint (see also verses 3 and 5 and 48:9); Hebrew *10,000*

measure off a section 25,000 cubits[a] long and
10,000 cubits[b] wide. In it will be the sanctuary, the Most Holy Place. 4It will be the sacred
portion of the land for the priests, who minister
in the sanctuary and who draw near to minister
before the LORD. It will be a place for their
houses as well as a holy place for the sanctuary. 5An area 25,000 cubits long and 10,000
cubits wide will belong to the Levites, who
serve in the temple, as their possession for
towns to live in.[c]

6" 'You are to give the city as its property an
area 5,000 cubits wide and 25,000 cubits long,
adjoining the sacred portion; it will belong to
the whole house of Israel.

7" 'The prince will have the land bordering
each side of the area formed by the sacred
district and the property of the city. It will
extend westward from the west side and eastward from the east side, running lengthwise
from the western to the eastern border parallel
to one of the tribal portions. 8This land will be
his possession in Israel. And my princes will
no longer oppress my people but will allow the
house of Israel to possess the land according to
their tribes.

9" 'This is what the Sovereign LORD says:
You have gone far enough, O princes of Israel!
Give up your violence and oppression and do
what is just and right. Stop dispossessing my
people, declares the Sovereign LORD. 10You
are to use accurate scales, an accurate ephah[d]
and an accurate bath.[e] 11The ephah and the
bath are to be the same size, the bath containing a tenth of a homer[f] and the ephah a tenth
of a homer; the homer is to be the standard
measure for both. 12The shekel[g] is to consist
of twenty gerahs. Twenty shekels plus twenty-
five shekels plus fifteen shekels equal one
mina.[h]

Offerings and Holy Days

13" 'This is the special gift you are to offer:
a sixth of an ephah from each homer of wheat
and a sixth of an ephah from each homer of
barley. 14The prescribed portion of oil, measured by the bath, is a tenth of a bath from each
cor (which consists of ten baths or one homer,
for ten baths are equivalent to a homer). 15Also
one sheep is to be taken from every flock of
two hundred from the well-watered pastures of
Israel. These will be used for the grain offerings, burnt offerings and fellowship offerings[i]
to make atonement for the people, declares the
Sovereign LORD. 16All the people of the land
will participate in this special gift for the use of
the prince in Israel. 17It will be the duty of the
prince to provide the burnt offerings, grain offerings and drink offerings at the festivals, the
New Moons and the Sabbaths—at all the appointed feasts of the house of Israel. He will
provide the sin offerings, grain offerings, burnt
offerings and fellowship offerings to make
atonement for the house of Israel.

18" 'This is what the Sovereign LORD says:
In the first month on the first day you are to
take a young bull without defect and purify the
sanctuary. 19The priest is to take some of the
blood of the sin offering and put it on the doorposts of the temple, on the four corners of the
upper ledge of the altar and on the gateposts of
the inner court. 20You are to do the same on
the seventh day of the month for anyone who
sins unintentionally or through ignorance; so
you are to make atonement for the temple.

21" 'In the first month on the fourteenth day
you are to observe the Passover, a feast lasting
seven days, during which you shall eat bread
made without yeast. 22On that day the prince is
to provide a bull as a sin offering for himself
and for all the people of the land. 23Every day
during the seven days of the Feast he is to
provide seven bulls and seven rams without
defect as a burnt offering to the LORD, and a
male goat for a sin offering. 24He is to provide
as a grain offering an ephah for each bull and
an ephah for each ram, along with a hin[j] of oil
for each ephah.

25" 'During the seven days of the Feast,
which begins in the seventh month on the fifteenth day, he is to make the same provision
for sin offerings, burnt offerings, grain offerings and oil.

46 " 'This is what the Sovereign LORD
says: The gate of the inner court facing
east is to be shut on the six working days, but
on the Sabbath day and on the day of the New
Moon it is to be opened. 2The prince is to enter
from the outside through the portico of the
gateway and stand by the gatepost. The priests
are to sacrifice his burnt offering and his fellowship offerings.[k] He is to worship at the
threshold of the gateway and then go out, but
the gate will not be shut until evening. 3On the
Sabbaths and New Moons the people of the
land are to worship in the presence of
the LORD at the entrance to that gateway. 4The
burnt offering the prince brings to the LORD on
the Sabbath day is to be six male lambs and a
ram, all without defect. 5The grain offering
given with the ram is to be an ephah,[l] and the
grain offering with the lambs is to be as much
as he pleases, along with a hin[j] of oil for each
ephah. 6On the day of the New Moon he is to
offer a young bull, six lambs and a ram, all
without defect. 7He is to provide as a grain
offering one ephah with the bull, one ephah
with the ram, and with the lambs as much as he
wants to give, along with a hin of oil with each
ephah. 8When the prince enters, he is to go in
through the portico of the gateway, and he is to
come out the same way.

[a] *3* That is, about 7 miles (about 12 kilometers) [b] *3* That is, about 3 miles (about 5 kilometers)
[c] *5* Septuagint; Hebrew *temple; they will have as their possession 20 rooms* [d] *10* An ephah was a dry
measure. [e] *10* A bath was a liquid measure. [f] *11* A homer was a dry measure. [g] *12* A shekel weighed
about 2/5 ounce (about 11.5 grams). [h] *12* That is, 60 shekels; the common mina was 50 shekels.
[i] *15* Traditionally *peace offerings*; also in verse 17 [j] *24,5* That is, probably about 4 quarts (about 4 liters)
[k] *2* Traditionally *peace offerings*; also in verse 12 [l] *5* That is, probably about 3/5 bushel (about 22 liters)

9“ ‘When the people of the land come before the LORD at the appointed feasts, whoever enters by the north gate to worship is to go out the south gate; and whoever enters by the south gate is to go out the north gate. No one is to return through the gate by which he entered, but each is to go out the opposite gate. 10The prince is to be among them, going in when they go in and going out when they go out.

11“ ‘At the festivals and the appointed feasts, the grain offering is to be an ephah with a bull, an ephah with a ram, and with the lambs as much as one pleases, along with a hin of oil for each ephah. 12When the prince provides a freewill offering to the LORD—whether a burnt offering or fellowship offerings—the gate facing east is to be opened for him. He shall offer his burnt offering or his fellowship offerings as he does on the Sabbath day. Then he shall go out, and after he has gone out, the gate will be shut.

13“ ‘Every day you are to provide a year-old lamb without defect for a burnt offering to the LORD; morning by morning you shall provide it. 14You are also to provide with it morning by morning a grain offering, consisting of a sixth of an ephah with a third of a hin of oil to moisten the flour. The presenting of this grain offering to the LORD is a lasting ordinance. 15So the lamb and the grain offering and the oil shall be provided morning by morning for a regular burnt offering.

16“ ‘This is what the Sovereign LORD says: If the prince makes a gift from his inheritance to one of his sons, it will also belong to his descendants; it is to be their property by inheritance. 17If, however, he makes a gift from his inheritance to one of his servants, the servant may keep it until the year of freedom; then it will revert to the prince. His inheritance belongs to his sons only; it is theirs. 18The prince must not take any of the inheritance of the people, driving them off their property. He is to give his sons their inheritance out of his own property, so that none of my people will be separated from his property.’ ”

19Then the man brought me through the entrance at the side of the gate to the sacred rooms facing north, which belonged to the priests, and showed me a place at the western end. 20He said to me, “This is the place where the priests will cook the guilt offering and the sin offering and bake the grain offering, to avoid bringing them into the outer court and consecrating the people.”

21He then brought me to the outer court and led me around to its four corners, and I saw in each corner another court. 22In the four corners of the outer court were enclosed[a] courts, forty cubits long and thirty cubits wide; each of the courts in the four corners was the same size. 23Around the inside of each of the four courts was a ledge of stone, with places for fire built all around under the ledge. 24He said to me, “These are the kitchens where those who minister at the temple will cook the sacrifices of the people.”

The River From the Temple

47 The man brought me back to the entrance of the temple, and I saw water coming out from under the threshold of the temple toward the east (for the temple faced east). The water was coming down from under the south side of the temple, south of the altar. 2He then brought me out through the north gate and led me around the outside to the outer gate facing east, and the water was flowing from the south side.

3As the man went eastward with a measuring line in his hand, he measured off a thousand cubits[b] and then led me through water that was ankle-deep. 4He measured off another thousand cubits and led me through water that was knee-deep. He measured off another thousand and led me through water that was up to the waist. 5He measured off another thousand, but now it was a river that I could not cross, because the water had risen and was deep enough to swim in—a river that no one could cross. 6He asked me, “Son of man, do you see this?”

Then he led me back to the bank of the river. 7When I arrived there, I saw a great number of trees on each side of the river. 8He said to me, “This water flows toward the eastern region and goes down into the Arabah,[c] where it enters the Sea.[d] When it empties into the Sea,[d] the water there becomes fresh. 9Swarms of living creatures will live wherever the river flows. There will be large numbers of fish, because this water flows there and makes the salt water fresh; so where the river flows everything will live. 10Fishermen will stand along the shore; from En Gedi to En Eglaim there will be places for spreading nets. The fish will be of many kinds—like the fish of the Great Sea.[e] 11But the swamps and marshes will not become fresh; they will be left for salt. 12Fruit trees of all kinds will grow on both banks of the river. Their leaves will not wither, nor will their fruit fail. Every month they will bear, because the water from the sanctuary flows to them. Their fruit will serve for food and their leaves for healing.”

The Boundaries of the Land

13This is what the Sovereign LORD says: “These are the boundaries by which you are to divide the land for an inheritance among the twelve tribes of Israel, with two portions for Joseph. 14You are to divide it equally among them. Because I swore with uplifted hand to give it to your forefathers, this land will become your inheritance.

[a] *22* The meaning of the Hebrew for this word is uncertain. [b] *3* That is, about 1,500 feet (about 450 meters)
[c] *8* Or *the Jordan Valley* [d] *8* That is, the Dead Sea [e] *10* That is, the Mediterranean; also in verses 15, 19 and 20

15 “This is to be the boundary of the land:

“On the north side it will run from the Great
Sea by the Hethlon road past Lebo[a] Hamath to Zedad, 16 Berothah[b] and Sibraim
(which lies on the border between Damascus and Hamath), as far as Hazer Hatticon,
which is on the border of Hauran. 17 The
boundary will extend from the sea to Hazar
Enan,[c] along the northern border of Damascus, with the border of Hamath to the
north. This will be the north boundary.

18 “On the east side the boundary will run between Hauran and Damascus, along the
Jordan between Gilead and the land of Israel, to the eastern sea and as far as Tamar.[d]
This will be the east boundary.

19 “On the south side it will run from Tamar as
far as the waters of Meribah Kadesh, then
along the Wadi ⌊of Egypt⌋ to the Great Sea.
This will be the south boundary.

20 “On the west side, the Great Sea will be the
boundary to a point opposite Lebo[e] Hamath. This will be the west boundary.

21 “You are to distribute this land among
yourselves according to the tribes of Israel.
22 You are to allot it as an inheritance for yourselves and for the aliens who have settled
among you and who have children. You are to
consider them as native-born Israelites; along
with you they are to be allotted an inheritance
among the tribes of Israel. 23 In whatever tribe
the alien settles, there you are to give him his
inheritance,” declares the Sovereign LORD.

The Division of the Land

48 “These are the tribes, listed by name: At
the northern frontier, Dan will have one
portion; it will follow the Hethlon road to
Lebo[f] Hamath; Hazar Enan and the northern
border of Damascus next to Hamath will be
part of its border from the east side to the west
side.

2 “Asher will have one portion; it will border
the territory of Dan from east to west.

3 “Naphtali will have one portion; it will border the territory of Asher from east to west.

4 “Manasseh will have one portion; it will
border the territory of Naphtali from east to
west.

5 “Ephraim will have one portion; it will border the territory of Manasseh from east to west.

6 “Reuben will have one portion; it will border the territory of Ephraim from east to west.

7 “Judah will have one portion; it will border
the territory of Reuben from east to west.

8 “Bordering the territory of Judah from east
to west will be the portion you are to present
as a special gift. It will be 25,000 cubits[g] wide,
and its length from east to west will equal one
of the tribal portions; the sanctuary will be in
the center of it.

9 “The special portion you are to offer to the
LORD will be 25,000 cubits long and 10,000
cubits[h] wide. 10 This will be the sacred portion
for the priests. It will be 25,000 cubits long on
the north side, 10,000 cubits wide on the west
side, 10,000 cubits wide on the east side and
25,000 cubits long on the south side. In the
center of it will be the sanctuary of the LORD.
11 This will be for the consecrated priests, the
Zadokites, who were faithful in serving me and
did not go astray as the Levites did when the
Israelites went astray. 12 It will be a special gift
to them from the sacred portion of the land, a
most holy portion, bordering the territory of
the Levites.

13 “Alongside the territory of the priests, the
Levites will have an allotment 25,000 cubits
long and 10,000 cubits wide. Its total length
will be 25,000 cubits and its width 10,000 cubits. 14 They must not sell or exchange any of
it. This is the best of the land and must not pass
into other hands, because it is holy to the
LORD.

15 “The remaining area, 5,000 cubits wide
and 25,000 cubits long, will be for the common use of the city, for houses and for pastureland. The city will be in the center of it 16 and
will have these measurements: the north side
4,500 cubits, the south side 4,500 cubits, the
east side 4,500 cubits, and the west side 4,500
cubits. 17 The pastureland for the city will be
250 cubits on the north, 250 cubits on the
south, 250 cubits on the east, and 250 cubits on
the west. 18 What remains of the area, bordering on the sacred portion and running the
length of it, will be 10,000 cubits on the east
side and 10,000 cubits on the west side. Its
produce will supply food for the workers of the
city. 19 The workers from the city who farm it
will come from all the tribes of Israel. 20 The
entire portion will be a square, 25,000 cubits
on each side. As a special gift you will set
aside the sacred portion, along with the property of the city.

21 “What remains on both sides of the area
formed by the sacred portion and the city property will belong to the prince. It will extend
eastward from the 25,000 cubits of the sacred
portion to the eastern border, and westward
from the 25,000 cubits to the western border.
Both these areas running the length of the tribal portions will belong to the prince, and the
sacred portion with the temple sanctuary will
be in the center of them. 22 So the property of
the Levites and the property of the city will lie
in the center of the area that belongs to the
prince. The area belonging to the prince will
lie between the border of Judah and the border
of Benjamin.

23 “As for the rest of the tribes: Benjamin
will have one portion; it will extend from the
east side to the west side.

24 “Simeon will have one portion; it will bor-

[a]15 Or *past the entrance to* [b]15,16 See Septuagint and Ezekiel 48:1; Hebrew *road to go into Zedad, 16Hamath, Berothah* [c]17 Hebrew *Enon,* a variant of *Enan* [d]18 Septuagint and Syriac; Hebrew *Israel. You will measure to the eastern sea* [e]20 Or *opposite the entrance to* [f]1 Or *to the entrance to* [g]8 That is, about 7 miles (about 12 kilometers) [h]9 That is, about 3 miles (about 5 kilometers)

der the territory of Benjamin from east to west.
25"Issachar will have one portion; it will
border the territory of Simeon from east to
west.
26"Zebulun will have one portion; it will
border the territory of Issachar from east to
west.
27"Gad will have one portion; it will border
the territory of Zebulun from east to west.
28"The southern boundary of Gad will run
south from Tamar to the waters of Meribah
Kadesh, then along the Wadi ⌞of Egypt⌟ to the
Great Sea.[a]
29"This is the land you are to allot as an
inheritance to the tribes of Israel, and these
will be their portions," declares the Sovereign
LORD.

The Gates of the City

30"These will be the exits of the city: Beginning on the north side, which is 4,500 cubits
long, 31the gates of the city will be named after
the tribes of Israel. The three gates on the north
side will be the gate of Reuben, the gate of
Judah and the gate of Levi.
32"On the east side, which is 4,500 cubits
long, will be three gates: the gate of Joseph,
the gate of Benjamin and the gate of Dan.
33"On the south side, which measures 4,500
cubits, will be three gates: the gate of Simeon,
the gate of Issachar and the gate of Zebulun.
34"On the west side, which is 4,500 cubits
long, will be three gates: the gate of Gad, the
gate of Asher and the gate of Naphtali.
35"The distance all around will be 18,000
cubits.

"And the name of the city from that time on
will be:

THE LORD IS THERE."

Daniel

Daniel's Training in Babylon

1 In the third year of the reign of Jehoiakim
king of Judah, Nebuchadnezzar king of
Babylon came to Jerusalem and besieged it.
2And the Lord delivered Jehoiakim king of Judah into his hand, along with some of the articles from the temple of God. These he carried
off to the temple of his god in Babylonia[b] and
put in the treasure house of his god.
3Then the king ordered Ashpenaz, chief of
his court officials, to bring in some of the Israelites from the royal family and the nobility—
4young men without any physical defect, handsome, showing aptitude for every kind of
learning, well informed, quick to understand,
and qualified to serve in the king's palace. He
was to teach them the language and literature
of the Babylonians.[c] 5The king assigned them
a daily amount of food and wine from the
king's table. They were to be trained for three
years, and after that they were to enter the
king's service.
6Among these were some from Judah: Daniel, Hananiah, Mishael and Azariah. 7The chief
official gave them new names: to Daniel, the
name Belteshazzar; to Hananiah, Shadrach; to
Mishael, Meshach; and to Azariah, Abednego.
8But Daniel resolved not to defile himself
with the royal food and wine, and he asked the
chief official for permission not to defile himself this way. 9Now God had caused the official to show favor and sympathy to Daniel,
10but the official told Daniel, "I am afraid of
my lord the king, who has assigned your[d] food
and drink. Why should he see you looking
worse than the other young men your age? The
king would then have my head because of
you."
11Daniel then said to the guard whom the
chief official had appointed over Daniel, Hananiah, Mishael and Azariah, 12"Please test your
servants for ten days: Give us nothing but vegetables to eat and water to drink. 13Then compare our appearance with that of the young
men who eat the royal food, and treat your
servants in accordance with what you see."
14So he agreed to this and tested them for ten
days.
15At the end of the ten days they looked
healthier and better nourished than any of the
young men who ate the royal food. 16So the
guard took away their choice food and
the wine they were to drink and gave them
vegetables instead.
17To these four young men God gave
knowledge and understanding of all kinds of
literature and learning. And Daniel could understand visions and dreams of all kinds.
18At the end of the time set by the king to
bring them in, the chief official presented them
to Nebuchadnezzar. 19The king talked with
them, and he found none equal to Daniel, Hananiah, Mishael and Azariah; so they entered
the king's service. 20In every matter of wisdom
and understanding about which the king questioned them, he found them ten times better
than all the magicians and enchanters in his
whole kingdom.
21And Daniel remained there until the first
year of King Cyrus.

[a] *28* That is, the Mediterranean [b] *2* Hebrew *Shinar* [c] *4* Or *Chaldeans* [d] *10* The Hebrew for *your* and *you* in this verse is plural.

Nebuchadnezzar's Dream

2 In the second year of his reign, Nebuchadnezzar had dreams; his mind was troubled
and he could not sleep. 2So the king summoned the magicians, enchanters, sorcerers
and astrologers[a] to tell him what he had
dreamed. When they came in and stood before
the king, 3he said to them, "I have had a dream
that troubles me and I want to know what it
means.[b]"

4Then the astrologers answered the king in
Aramaic,[c] "O king, live forever! Tell your
servants the dream, and we will interpret it."

5The king replied to the astrologers, "This is
what I have firmly decided: If you do not tell
me what my dream was and interpret it, I will
have you cut into pieces and your houses
turned into piles of rubble. 6But if you tell me
the dream and explain it, you will receive from
me gifts and rewards and great honor. So tell
me the dream and interpret it for me."

7Once more they replied, "Let the king tell
his servants the dream, and we will interpret it."

8Then the king answered, "I am certain that
you are trying to gain time, because you realize
that this is what I have firmly decided: 9If you
do not tell me the dream, there is just one
penalty for you. You have conspired to tell me
misleading and wicked things, hoping the situation will change. So then, tell me the dream,
and I will know that you can interpret it
for me."

10The astrologers answered the king, "There
is not a man on earth who can do what the king
asks! No king, however great and mighty, has
ever asked such a thing of any magician or
enchanter or astrologer. 11What the king asks
is too difficult. No one can reveal it to the king
except the gods, and they do not live among
men."

12This made the king so angry and furious
that he ordered the execution of all the wise
men of Babylon. 13So the decree was issued to
put the wise men to death, and men were sent
to look for Daniel and his friends to put them
to death.

14When Arioch, the commander of the
king's guard, had gone out to put to death the
wise men of Babylon, Daniel spoke to him
with wisdom and tact. 15He asked the king's
officer, "Why did the king issue such a harsh
decree?" Arioch then explained the matter to
Daniel. 16At this, Daniel went in to the king
and asked for time, so that he might interpret
the dream for him.

17Then Daniel returned to his house and explained the matter to his friends Hananiah,
Mishael and Azariah. 18He urged them to
plead for mercy from the God of heaven concerning this mystery, so that he and his friends
might not be executed with the rest of the wise
men of Babylon. 19During the night the mystery was revealed to Daniel in a vision. Then
Daniel praised the God of heaven 20and said:

"Praise be to the name of God for ever
and ever;
wisdom and power are his.
21He changes times and seasons;
he sets up kings and deposes them.
He gives wisdom to the wise
and knowledge to the discerning.
22He reveals deep and hidden things;
he knows what lies in darkness,
and light dwells with him.
23I thank and praise you, O God of my
fathers:
You have given me wisdom and power,
you have made known to me what we
asked of you,
you have made known to us the dream
of the king."

Daniel Interprets the Dream

24Then Daniel went to Arioch, whom the
king had appointed to execute the wise men of
Babylon, and said to him, "Do not execute the
wise men of Babylon. Take me to the king, and
I will interpret his dream for him."

25Arioch took Daniel to the king at once and
said, "I have found a man among the exiles
from Judah who can tell the king what his
dream means."

26The king asked Daniel (also called Belteshazzar), "Are you able to tell me what I saw
in my dream and interpret it?"

27Daniel replied, "No wise man, enchanter,
magician or diviner can explain to the king the
mystery he has asked about, 28but there is a
God in heaven who reveals mysteries. He has
shown King Nebuchadnezzar what will happen in days to come. Your dream and the visions that passed through your mind as you lay
on your bed are these:

29"As you were lying there, O king, your
mind turned to things to come, and the revealer
of mysteries showed you what is going to happen. 30As for me, this mystery has been revealed to me, not because I have greater wisdom than other living men, but so that you,
O king, may know the interpretation and that
you may understand what went through your
mind.

31"You looked, O king, and there before
you stood a large statue—an enormous, dazzling statue, awesome in appearance. 32The
head of the statue was made of pure gold, its
chest and arms of silver, its belly and thighs of
bronze, 33its legs of iron, its feet partly of iron
and partly of baked clay. 34While you were
watching, a rock was cut out, but not by human
hands. It struck the statue on its feet of iron and
clay and smashed them. 35Then the iron, the
clay, the bronze, the silver and the gold were
broken to pieces at the same time and became
like chaff on a threshing floor in the summer.
The wind swept them away without leaving a
trace. But the rock that struck the statue be-

[a]2 Or *Chaldeans*; also in verses 4, 5 and 10 [b]3 Or *was* [c]4 The text from here through chapter 7 is in Aramaic.

came a huge mountain and filled the whole earth.

36“This was the dream, and now we will interpret it to the king. 37You, O king, are the king of kings. The God of heaven has given you dominion and power and might and glory; 38in your hands he has placed mankind and the beasts of the field and the birds of the air. Wherever they live, he has made you ruler over them all. You are that head of gold.

39“After you, another kingdom will rise, inferior to yours. Next, a third kingdom, one of bronze, will rule over the whole earth. 40Finally, there will be a fourth kingdom, strong as iron—for iron breaks and smashes everything—and as iron breaks things to pieces, so it will crush and break all the others. 41Just as you saw that the feet and toes were partly of baked clay and partly of iron, so this will be a divided kingdom; yet it will have some of the strength of iron in it, even as you saw iron mixed with clay. 42As the toes were partly iron and partly clay, so this kingdom will be partly strong and partly brittle. 43And just as you saw the iron mixed with baked clay, so the people will be a mixture and will not remain united, any more than iron mixes with clay.

44“In the time of those kings, the God of heaven will set up a kingdom that will never be destroyed, nor will it be left to another people. It will crush all those kingdoms and bring them to an end, but it will itself endure forever. 45This is the meaning of the vision of the rock cut out of a mountain, but not by human hands—a rock that broke the iron, the bronze, the clay, the silver and the gold to pieces.

“The great God has shown the king what will take place in the future. The dream is true and the interpretation is trustworthy.”

46Then King Nebuchadnezzar fell prostrate before Daniel and paid him honor and ordered that an offering and incense be presented to him. 47The king said to Daniel, “Surely your God is the God of gods and the Lord of kings and a revealer of mysteries, for you were able to reveal this mystery.”

48Then the king placed Daniel in a high position and lavished many gifts on him. He made him ruler over the entire province of Babylon and placed him in charge of all its wise men. 49Moreover, at Daniel’s request the king appointed Shadrach, Meshach and Abednego administrators over the province of Babylon, while Daniel himself remained at the royal court.

The Image of Gold and the Fiery Furnace

3 King Nebuchadnezzar made an image of gold, ninety feet high and nine feet[a] wide, and set it up on the plain of Dura in the province of Babylon. 2He then summoned the satraps, prefects, governors, advisers, treasurers, judges, magistrates and all the other provincial officials to come to the dedication of the image he had set up. 3So the satraps, prefects, governors, advisers, treasurers, judges, magistrates and all the other provincial officials assembled for the dedication of the image that King Nebuchadnezzar had set up, and they stood before it.

4Then the herald loudly proclaimed, “This is what you are commanded to do, O peoples, nations and men of every language: 5As soon as you hear the sound of the horn, flute, zither, lyre, harp, pipes and all kinds of music, you must fall down and worship the image of gold that King Nebuchadnezzar has set up. 6Whoever does not fall down and worship will immediately be thrown into a blazing furnace.”

7Therefore, as soon as they heard the sound of the horn, flute, zither, lyre, harp and all kinds of music, all the peoples, nations and men of every language fell down and worshiped the image of gold that King Nebuchadnezzar had set up.

8At this time some astrologers[b] came forward and denounced the Jews. 9They said to King Nebuchadnezzar, “O king, live forever! 10You have issued a decree, O king, that everyone who hears the sound of the horn, flute, zither, lyre, harp, pipes and all kinds of music must fall down and worship the image of gold, 11and that whoever does not fall down and worship will be thrown into a blazing furnace. 12But there are some Jews whom you have set over the affairs of the province of Babylon—Shadrach, Meshach and Abednego—who pay no attention to you, O king. They neither serve your gods nor worship the image of gold you have set up.”

13Furious with rage, Nebuchadnezzar summoned Shadrach, Meshach and Abednego. So these men were brought before the king, 14and Nebuchadnezzar said to them, “Is it true, Shadrach, Meshach and Abednego, that you do not serve my gods or worship the image of gold I have set up? 15Now when you hear the sound of the horn, flute, zither, lyre, harp, pipes and all kinds of music, if you are ready to fall down and worship the image I made, very good. But if you do not worship it, you will be thrown immediately into a blazing furnace. Then what god will be able to rescue you from my hand?”

16Shadrach, Meshach and Abednego replied to the king, “O Nebuchadnezzar, we do not need to defend ourselves before you in this matter. 17If we are thrown into the blazing furnace, the God we serve is able to save us from it, and he will rescue us from your hand, O king. 18But even if he does not, we want you to know, O king, that we will not serve your gods or worship the image of gold you have set up.”

19Then Nebuchadnezzar was furious with Shadrach, Meshach and Abednego, and his attitude toward them changed. He ordered the furnace heated seven times hotter than usual

[a]*1* Aramaic *sixty cubits high and six cubits wide* (about 27 meters high and 2.7 meters wide)
[b]*8* Or *Chaldeans*

20and commanded some of the strongest soldiers in his army to tie up Shadrach, Meshach
and Abednego and throw them into the blazing
furnace. 21So these men, wearing their robes,
trousers, turbans and other clothes, were bound
and thrown into the blazing furnace. 22The
king's command was so urgent and the furnace
so hot that the flames of the fire killed the
soldiers who took up Shadrach, Meshach and
Abednego, 23and these three men, firmly tied,
fell into the blazing furnace.

24Then King Nebuchadnezzar leaped to his
feet in amazement and asked his advisers,
"Weren't there three men that we tied up and
threw into the fire?"

They replied, "Certainly, O king."

25He said, "Look! I see four men walking
around in the fire, unbound and unharmed, and
the fourth looks like a son of the gods."

26Nebuchadnezzar then approached the
opening of the blazing furnace and shouted,
"Shadrach, Meshach and Abednego, servants
of the Most High God, come out! Come here!"

So Shadrach, Meshach and Abednego came
out of the fire, 27and the satraps, prefects, governors and royal advisers crowded around
them. They saw that the fire had not harmed
their bodies, nor was a hair of their heads
singed; their robes were not scorched, and
there was no smell of fire on them.

28Then Nebuchadnezzar said, "Praise be to
the God of Shadrach, Meshach and Abednego,
who has sent his angel and rescued his servants! They trusted in him and defied the
king's command and were willing to give up
their lives rather than serve or worship any god
except their own God. 29Therefore I decree
that the people of any nation or language who
say anything against the God of Shadrach, Meshach and Abednego be cut into pieces and
their houses be turned into piles of rubble, for
no other god can save in this way."

30Then the king promoted Shadrach, Meshach and Abednego in the province of Babylon.

Nebuchadnezzar's Dream of a Tree

4 King Nebuchadnezzar,

To the peoples, nations and men of every language, who live in all the world:

May you prosper greatly!

2It is my pleasure to tell you about the
miraculous signs and wonders that the
Most High God has performed for me.

3How great are his signs,
how mighty his wonders!
His kingdom is an eternal kingdom;
his dominion endures from
generation to generation.

4I, Nebuchadnezzar, was at home in my
palace, contented and prosperous. 5I had a
dream that made me afraid. As I was lying in my bed, the images and visions that
passed through my mind terrified me. 6So
I commanded that all the wise men of
Babylon be brought before me to interpret
the dream for me. 7When the magicians,
enchanters, astrologers[a] and diviners
came, I told them the dream, but they
could not interpret it for me. 8Finally,
Daniel came into my presence and I told
him the dream. (He is called Belteshazzar,
after the name of my god, and the spirit of
the holy gods is in him.)

9I said, "Belteshazzar, chief of the magicians, I know that the spirit of the holy
gods is in you, and no mystery is too difficult for you. Here is my dream; interpret
it for me. 10These are the visions I saw
while lying in my bed: I looked, and there
before me stood a tree in the middle of the
land. Its height was enormous. 11The tree
grew large and strong and its top touched
the sky; it was visible to the ends of the
earth. 12Its leaves were beautiful, its fruit
abundant, and on it was food for all. Under it the beasts of the field found shelter,
and the birds of the air lived in its
branches; from it every creature was fed.

13"In the visions I saw while lying in
my bed, I looked, and there before me
was a messenger,[b] a holy one, coming
down from heaven. 14He called in a loud
voice: 'Cut down the tree and trim off its
branches; strip off its leaves and scatter its
fruit. Let the animals flee from under it
and the birds from its branches. 15But let
the stump and its roots, bound with iron
and bronze, remain in the ground, in the
grass of the field.

" 'Let him be drenched with the dew of
heaven, and let him live with the animals
among the plants of the earth. 16Let his
mind be changed from that of a man and
let him be given the mind of an animal,
till seven times[c] pass by for him.

17" 'The decision is announced by messengers, the holy ones declare the verdict,
so that the living may know that the Most
High is sovereign over the kingdoms of
men and gives them to anyone he wishes
and sets over them the lowliest of men.'

18"This is the dream that I, King Nebuchadnezzar, had. Now, Belteshazzar, tell
me what it means, for none of the wise
men in my kingdom can interpret it for
me. But you can, because the spirit of the
holy gods is in you."

Daniel Interprets the Dream

19Then Daniel (also called Belteshazzar) was greatly perplexed for a time, and
his thoughts terrified him. So the king
said, "Belteshazzar, do not let the dream
or its meaning alarm you."

Belteshazzar answered, "My lord, if
only the dream applied to your enemies

[a]7 Or *Chaldeans* [b]13 Or *watchman*; also in verses 17 and 23 [c]16 Or *years*; also in verses 23, 25 and 32

and its meaning to your adversaries! 20The tree you saw, which grew large and strong, with its top touching the sky, visible to the whole earth, 21with beautiful leaves and abundant fruit, providing food for all, giving shelter to the beasts of the field, and having nesting places in its branches for the birds of the air— 22you, O king, are that tree! You have become great and strong; your greatness has grown until it reaches the sky, and your dominion extends to distant parts of the earth.

23"You, O king, saw a messenger, a holy one, coming down from heaven and saying, 'Cut down the tree and destroy it, but leave the stump, bound with iron and bronze, in the grass of the field, while its roots remain in the ground. Let him be drenched with the dew of heaven; let him live like the wild animals, until seven times pass by for him.'

24"This is the interpretation, O king, and this is the decree the Most High has issued against my lord the king: 25You will be driven away from people and will live with the wild animals; you will eat grass like cattle and be drenched with the dew of heaven. Seven times will pass by for you until you acknowledge that the Most High is sovereign over the kingdoms of men and gives them to anyone he wishes. 26The command to leave the stump of the tree with its roots means that your kingdom will be restored to you when you acknowledge that Heaven rules. 27Therefore, O king, be pleased to accept my advice: Renounce your sins by doing what is right, and your wickedness by being kind to the oppressed. It may be that then your prosperity will continue."

The Dream Is Fulfilled

28All this happened to King Nebuchadnezzar. 29Twelve months later, as the king was walking on the roof of the royal palace of Babylon, 30he said, "Is not this the great Babylon I have built as the royal residence, by my mighty power and for the glory of my majesty?"

31The words were still on his lips when a voice came from heaven, "This is what is decreed for you, King Nebuchadnezzar: Your royal authority has been taken from you. 32You will be driven away from people and will live with the wild animals; you will eat grass like cattle. Seven times will pass by for you until you acknowledge that the Most High is sovereign over the kingdoms of men and gives them to anyone he wishes."

33Immediately what had been said about Nebuchadnezzar was fulfilled. He was driven away from people and ate grass like cattle. His body was drenched with the dew of heaven until his hair grew like the feathers of an eagle and his nails like the claws of a bird.

34At the end of that time, I, Nebuchadnezzar, raised my eyes toward heaven, and my sanity was restored. Then I praised the Most High; I honored and glorified him who lives forever.

His dominion is an eternal dominion;
  his kingdom endures from generation to generation.
35All the peoples of the earth
  are regarded as nothing.
He does as he pleases
  with the powers of heaven
  and the peoples of the earth.
No one can hold back his hand
  or say to him: "What have you done?"

36At the same time that my sanity was restored, my honor and splendor were returned to me for the glory of my kingdom. My advisers and nobles sought me out, and I was restored to my throne and became even greater than before. 37Now I, Nebuchadnezzar, praise and exalt and glorify the King of heaven, because everything he does is right and all his ways are just. And those who walk in pride he is able to humble.

The Writing on the Wall

5 King Belshazzar gave a great banquet for a thousand of his nobles and drank wine with them. 2While Belshazzar was drinking his wine, he gave orders to bring in the gold and silver goblets that Nebuchadnezzar his father[a] had taken from the temple in Jerusalem, so that the king and his nobles, his wives and his concubines might drink from them. 3So they brought in the gold goblets that had been taken from the temple of God in Jerusalem, and the king and his nobles, his wives and his concubines drank from them. 4As they drank the wine, they praised the gods of gold and silver, of bronze, iron, wood and stone.

5Suddenly the fingers of a human hand appeared and wrote on the plaster of the wall, near the lampstand in the royal palace. The king watched the hand as it wrote. 6His face turned pale and he was so frightened that his knees knocked together and his legs gave way.

7The king called out for the enchanters, astrologers[b] and diviners to be brought and said to these wise men of Babylon, "Whoever reads this writing and tells me what it means will be clothed in purple and have a gold chain placed around his neck, and he will be made the third highest ruler in the kingdom."

8Then all the king's wise men came in, but they could not read the writing or tell the king what it meant. 9So King Belshazzar became even more terrified and his face grew more pale. His nobles were baffled.

[a]2 Or *ancestor*; or *predecessor*; also in verses 11, 13 and 18 [b]7 Or *Chaldeans*; also in verse 11

10The queen,[a] hearing the voices of the king
and his nobles, came into the banquet hall.
"O king, live forever!" she said. "Don't be
alarmed! Don't look so pale! 11There is a man
in your kingdom who has the spirit of the holy
gods in him. In the time of your father he was
found to have insight and intelligence and wisdom like that of the gods. King Nebuchadnezzar your father—your father the king, I say—
appointed him chief of the magicians,
enchanters, astrologers and diviners. 12This
man Daniel, whom the king called Belteshazzar, was found to have a keen mind and knowledge and understanding, and also the ability to
interpret dreams, explain riddles and solve difficult problems. Call for Daniel, and he will
tell you what the writing means."

13So Daniel was brought before the king,
and the king said to him, "Are you Daniel, one
of the exiles my father the king brought from
Judah? 14I have heard that the spirit of the gods
is in you and that you have insight, intelligence
and outstanding wisdom. 15The wise men and
enchanters were brought before me to read this
writing and tell me what it means, but they
could not explain it. 16Now I have heard that
you are able to give interpretations and to
solve difficult problems. If you can read this
writing and tell me what it means, you will be
clothed in purple and have a gold chain placed
around your neck, and you will be made the
third highest ruler in the kingdom."

17Then Daniel answered the king, "You may
keep your gifts for yourself and give your rewards to someone else. Nevertheless, I will
read the writing for the king and tell him what
it means.

18"O king, the Most High God gave your
father Nebuchadnezzar sovereignty and greatness and glory and splendor. 19Because of the
high position he gave him, all the peoples and
nations and men of every language dreaded
and feared him. Those the king wanted to put
to death, he put to death; those he wanted to
spare, he spared; those he wanted to promote,
he promoted; and those he wanted to humble,
he humbled. 20But when his heart became arrogant and hardened with pride, he was deposed from his royal throne and stripped of his
glory. 21He was driven away from people and
given the mind of an animal; he lived with the
wild donkeys and ate grass like cattle; and his
body was drenched with the dew of heaven,
until he acknowledged that the Most High God
is sovereign over the kingdoms of men and
sets over them anyone he wishes.

22"But you his son,[b] O Belshazzar, have not
humbled yourself, though you knew all this.
23Instead, you have set yourself up against the
Lord of heaven. You had the goblets from his
temple brought to you, and you and your nobles, your wives and your concubines drank
wine from them. You praised the gods of silver
and gold, of bronze, iron, wood and stone,
which cannot see or hear or understand. But
you did not honor the God who holds in his
hand your life and all your ways. 24Therefore
he sent the hand that wrote the inscription.

25"This is the inscription that was written:

MENE, MENE, TEKEL, PARSIN[c]

26"This is what these words mean:

Mene[d]: God has numbered the days
of your reign and brought it to
an end.
27*Tekel*[e]: You have been weighed on
the scales and found wanting.
28*Peres*[f]: Your kingdom is divided
and given to the Medes and
Persians."

29Then at Belshazzar's command, Daniel
was clothed in purple, a gold chain was placed
around his neck, and he was proclaimed the
third highest ruler in the kingdom.

30That very night Belshazzar, king of the
Babylonians,[g] was slain, 31and Darius the
Mede took over the kingdom, at the age of
sixty-two.

Daniel in the Den of Lions

6 It pleased Darius to appoint 120 satraps to
rule throughout the kingdom, 2with three
administrators over them, one of whom was
Daniel. The satraps were made accountable to
them so that the king might not suffer loss.
3Now Daniel so distinguished himself among
the administrators and the satraps by his ex-
ceptional qualities that the king planned to set
him over the whole kingdom. 4At this, the
administrators and the satraps tried to find
grounds for charges against Daniel in his conduct of government affairs, but they were unable to do so. They could find no corruption in
him, because he was trustworthy and neither
corrupt nor negligent. 5Finally these men said,
"We will never find any basis for charges
against this man Daniel unless it has something to do with the law of his God."

6So the administrators and the satraps went
as a group to the king and said: "O King Darius, live forever! 7The royal administrators,
prefects, satraps, advisers and governors have
all agreed that the king should issue an edict
and enforce the decree that anyone who prays
to any god or man during the next thirty days,
except to you, O king, shall be thrown into the
lions' den. 8Now, O king, issue the decree and
put it in writing so that it cannot be altered—in
accordance with the laws of the Medes and
Persians, which cannot be repealed." 9So King
Darius put the decree in writing.

10Now when Daniel learned that the decree
had been published, he went home to his upstairs room where the windows opened toward

[a]10 Or *queen mother* [b]22 Or *descendant*; or *successor* [c]25 Aramaic *UPARSIN* (that is, *AND PARSIN*)
[d]26 *Mene* can mean *numbered* or *mina* (a unit of money). [e]27 *Tekel* can mean *weighed* or *shekel*.
[f]28 *Peres* (the singular of *Parsin*) can mean *divided* or *Persia* or *a half mina* or *a half shekel*.
[g]30 Or *Chaldeans*

Jerusalem. Three times a day he got down on
his knees and prayed, giving thanks to his God,
just as he had done before. 11Then these men
went as a group and found Daniel praying and
asking God for help. 12So they went to the king
and spoke to him about his royal decree: "Did
you not publish a decree that during the next
thirty days anyone who prays to any god or
man except to you, O king, would be thrown
into the lions' den?"

The king answered, "The decree stands—in
accordance with the laws of the Medes and
Persians, which cannot be repealed."

13Then they said to the king, "Daniel, who is
one of the exiles from Judah, pays no attention
to you, O king, or to the decree you put in
writing. He still prays three times a day."
14When the king heard this, he was greatly
distressed; he was determined to rescue Daniel
and made every effort until sundown to save
him.

15Then the men went as a group to the king
and said to him, "Remember, O king, that according to the law of the Medes and Persians
no decree or edict that the king issues can be
changed."

16So the king gave the order, and they
brought Daniel and threw him into the lions'
den. The king said to Daniel, "May your God,
whom you serve continually, rescue you!"

17A stone was brought and placed over the
mouth of the den, and the king sealed it with
his own signet ring and with the rings of his
nobles, so that Daniel's situation might not be
changed. 18Then the king returned to his palace and spent the night without eating and
without any entertainment being brought to
him. And he could not sleep.

19At the first light of dawn, the king got up
and hurried to the lions' den. 20When he came
near the den, he called to Daniel in an anguished voice, "Daniel, servant of the living
God, has your God, whom you serve continually, been able to rescue you from the lions?"

21Daniel answered, "O king, live forever!
22My God sent his angel, and he shut the
mouths of the lions. They have not hurt me,
because I was found innocent in his sight.
Nor have I ever done any wrong before you,
O king."

23The king was overjoyed and gave orders
to lift Daniel out of the den. And when Daniel
was lifted from the den, no wound was found
on him, because he had trusted in his God.

24At the king's command, the men who had
falsely accused Daniel were brought in and
thrown into the lions' den, along with their
wives and children. And before they reached
the floor of the den, the lions overpowered
them and crushed all their bones.

25Then King Darius wrote to all the peoples,
nations and men of every language throughout
the land:

"May you prosper greatly!

26"I issue a decree that in every part of
my kingdom people must fear and reverence the God of Daniel.

"For he is the living God
and he endures forever;
his kingdom will not be destroyed,
his dominion will never end.
27He rescues and he saves;
he performs signs and wonders
in the heavens and on the earth.
He has rescued Daniel
from the power of the lions."

28So Daniel prospered during the reign of
Darius and the reign of Cyrus[a] the Persian.

Daniel's Dream of Four Beasts

7 In the first year of Belshazzar king of Babylon, Daniel had a dream, and visions
passed through his mind as he was lying on
his bed. He wrote down the substance of his
dream.

2Daniel said: "In my vision at night I
looked, and there before me were the four
winds of heaven churning up the great sea.
3Four great beasts, each different from the others, came up out of the sea.

4"The first was like a lion, and it had the
wings of an eagle. I watched until its wings
were torn off and it was lifted from the ground
so that it stood on two feet like a man, and the
heart of a man was given to it.

5"And there before me was a second beast,
which looked like a bear. It was raised up on
one of its sides, and it had three ribs in its
mouth between its teeth. It was told, 'Get up
and eat your fill of flesh!'

6"After that, I looked, and there before me
was another beast, one that looked like a leopard. And on its back it had four wings like
those of a bird. This beast had four heads, and
it was given authority to rule.

7"After that, in my vision at night I looked,
and there before me was a fourth beast—terrifying and frightening and very powerful. It had
large iron teeth; it crushed and devoured its
victims and trampled underfoot whatever was
left. It was different from all the former beasts,
and it had ten horns.

8"While I was thinking about the horns,
there before me was another horn, a little one,
which came up among them; and three of the
first horns were uprooted before it. This horn
had eyes like the eyes of a man and a mouth
that spoke boastfully.

9"As I looked,

"thrones were set in place,
and the Ancient of Days took his seat.
His clothing was as white as snow;
the hair of his head was white like
wool.
His throne was flaming with fire,
and its wheels were all ablaze.
10A river of fire was flowing,
coming out from before him.

[a]28 Or *Darius, that is, the reign of Cyrus*

Thousands upon thousands attended him;
 ten thousand times ten thousand stood
  before him.
The court was seated,
 and the books were opened.

11“Then I continued to watch because of the boastful words the horn was speaking. I kept looking until the beast was slain and its body destroyed and thrown into the blazing fire. 12(The other beasts had been stripped of their authority, but were allowed to live for a period of time.)

13“In my vision at night I looked, and there before me was one like a son of man, coming with the clouds of heaven. He approached the Ancient of Days and was led into his presence. 14He was given authority, glory and sovereign power; all peoples, nations and men of every language worshiped him. His dominion is an everlasting dominion that will not pass away, and his kingdom is one that will never be destroyed.

The Interpretation of the Dream

15“I, Daniel, was troubled in spirit, and the visions that passed through my mind disturbed me. 16I approached one of those standing there and asked him the true meaning of all this.

“So he told me and gave me the interpretation of these things: 17‘The four great beasts are four kingdoms that will rise from the earth. 18But the saints of the Most High will receive the kingdom and will possess it forever—yes, for ever and ever.’

19“Then I wanted to know the true meaning of the fourth beast, which was different from all the others and most terrifying, with its iron teeth and bronze claws—the beast that crushed and devoured its victims and trampled underfoot whatever was left. 20I also wanted to know about the ten horns on its head and about the other horn that came up, before which three of them fell—the horn that looked more imposing than the others and that had eyes and a mouth that spoke boastfully. 21As I watched, this horn was waging war against the saints and defeating them, 22until the Ancient of Days came and pronounced judgment in favor of the saints of the Most High, and the time came when they possessed the kingdom.

23“He gave me this explanation: ‘The fourth beast is a fourth kingdom that will appear on earth. It will be different from all the other kingdoms and will devour the whole earth, trampling it down and crushing it. 24The ten horns are ten kings who will come from this kingdom. After them another king will arise, different from the earlier ones; he will subdue three kings. 25He will speak against the Most High and oppress his saints and try to change the set times and the laws. The saints will be handed over to him for a time, times and half a time.[a]

26“ ‘But the court will sit, and his power will be taken away and completely destroyed forever. 27Then the sovereignty, power and greatness of the kingdoms under the whole heaven will be handed over to the saints, the people of the Most High. His kingdom will be an everlasting kingdom, and all rulers will worship and obey him.’

28“This is the end of the matter. I, Daniel, was deeply troubled by my thoughts, and my face turned pale, but I kept the matter to myself.”

Daniel’s Vision of a Ram and a Goat

8 In the third year of King Belshazzar’s reign, I, Daniel, had a vision, after the one that had already appeared to me. 2In my vision I saw myself in the citadel of Susa in the province of Elam; in the vision I was beside the Ulai Canal. 3I looked up, and there before me was a ram with two horns, standing beside the canal, and the horns were long. One of the horns was longer than the other but grew up later. 4I watched the ram as he charged toward the west and the north and the south. No animal could stand against him, and none could rescue from his power. He did as he pleased and became great.

5As I was thinking about this, suddenly a goat with a prominent horn between his eyes came from the west, crossing the whole earth without touching the ground. 6He came toward the two-horned ram I had seen standing beside the canal and charged at him in great rage. 7I saw him attack the ram furiously, striking the ram and shattering his two horns. The ram was powerless to stand against him; the goat knocked him to the ground and trampled on him, and none could rescue the ram from his power. 8The goat became very great, but at the height of his power his large horn was broken off, and in its place four prominent horns grew up toward the four winds of heaven.

9Out of one of them came another horn, which started small but grew in power to the south and to the east and toward the Beautiful Land. 10It grew until it reached the host of the heavens, and it threw some of the starry host down to the earth and trampled on them. 11It set itself up to be as great as the Prince of the host; it took away the daily sacrifice from him, and the place of his sanctuary was brought low. 12Because of rebellion, the host ⌞of the saints⌟[b] and the daily sacrifice were given over to it. It prospered in everything it did, and truth was thrown to the ground.

13Then I heard a holy one speaking, and another holy one said to him, “How long will it take for the vision to be fulfilled—the vision concerning the daily sacrifice, the rebellion that causes desolation, and the surrender of the sanctuary and of the host that will be trampled underfoot?”

14He said to me, “It will take 2,300 evenings and mornings; then the sanctuary will be reconsecrated.”

[a]25 Or *for a year, two years and half a year* [b]12 Or *rebellion, the armies*

The Interpretation of the Vision

15While I, Daniel, was watching the vision and trying to understand it, there before me stood one who looked like a man. 16And I heard a man's voice from the Ulai calling, "Gabriel, tell this man the meaning of the vision."

17As he came near the place where I was standing, I was terrified and fell prostrate. "Son of man," he said to me, "understand that the vision concerns the time of the end."

18While he was speaking to me, I was in a deep sleep, with my face to the ground. Then he touched me and raised me to my feet.

19He said: "I am going to tell you what will happen later in the time of wrath, because the vision concerns the appointed time of the end.[a] 20The two-horned ram that you saw represents the kings of Media and Persia. 21The shaggy goat is the king of Greece, and the large horn between his eyes is the first king. 22The four horns that replaced the one that was broken off represent four kingdoms that will emerge from his nation but will not have the same power.

23"In the latter part of their reign, when rebels have become completely wicked, a stern-faced king, a master of intrigue, will arise. 24He will become very strong, but not by his own power. He will cause astounding devastation and will succeed in whatever he does. He will destroy the mighty men and the holy people. 25He will cause deceit to prosper, and he will consider himself superior. When they feel secure, he will destroy many and take his stand against the Prince of princes. Yet he will be destroyed, but not by human power.

26"The vision of the evenings and mornings that has been given you is true, but seal up the vision, for it concerns the distant future."

27I, Daniel, was exhausted and lay ill for several days. Then I got up and went about the king's business. I was appalled by the vision; it was beyond understanding.

Daniel's Prayer

9 In the first year of Darius son of Xerxes[b] (a Mede by descent), who was made ruler over the Babylonian[c] kingdom— 2in the first year of his reign, I, Daniel, understood from the Scriptures, according to the word of the LORD given to Jeremiah the prophet, that the desolation of Jerusalem would last seventy years. 3So I turned to the Lord God and pleaded with him in prayer and petition, in fasting, and in sackcloth and ashes.

4I prayed to the LORD my God and confessed:

> "O Lord, the great and awesome God, who keeps his covenant of love with all who love him and obey his commands, 5we have sinned and done wrong. We have been wicked and have rebelled; we have turned away from your commands and laws. 6We have not listened to your servants the prophets, who spoke in your name to our kings, our princes and our fathers, and to all the people of the land.
>
> 7"Lord, you are righteous, but this day we are covered with shame—the men of Judah and people of Jerusalem and all Israel, both near and far, in all the countries where you have scattered us because of our unfaithfulness to you. 8O LORD, we and our kings, our princes and our fathers are covered with shame because we have sinned against you. 9The Lord our God is merciful and forgiving, even though we have rebelled against him; 10we have not obeyed the LORD our God or kept the laws he gave us through his servants the prophets. 11All Israel has transgressed your law and turned away, refusing to obey you.
>
> "Therefore the curses and sworn judgments written in the Law of Moses, the servant of God, have been poured out on us, because we have sinned against you. 12You have fulfilled the words spoken against us and against our rulers by bringing upon us great disaster. Under the whole heaven nothing has ever been done like what has been done to Jerusalem. 13Just as it is written in the Law of Moses, all this disaster has come upon us, yet we have not sought the favor of the LORD our God by turning from our sins and giving attention to your truth. 14The LORD did not hesitate to bring the disaster upon us, for the LORD our God is righteous in everything he does; yet we have not obeyed him.
>
> 15"Now, O Lord our God, who brought your people out of Egypt with a mighty hand and who made for yourself a name that endures to this day, we have sinned, we have done wrong. 16O Lord, in keeping with all your righteous acts, turn away your anger and your wrath from Jerusalem, your city, your holy hill. Our sins and the iniquities of our fathers have made Jerusalem and your people an object of scorn to all those around us.
>
> 17"Now, our God, hear the prayers and petitions of your servant. For your sake, O Lord, look with favor on your desolate sanctuary. 18Give ear, O God, and hear; open your eyes and see the desolation of the city that bears your Name. We do not make requests of you because we are righteous, but because of your great mercy. 19O Lord, listen! O Lord, forgive! O Lord, hear and act! For your sake, O my God, do not delay, because your city and your people bear your Name."

The Seventy "Sevens"

20While I was speaking and praying, confessing my sin and the sin of my people Israel

[a] 19 Or *because the end will be at the appointed time* [b] 1 Hebrew *Ahasuerus* [c] 1 Or *Chaldean*

and making my request to the LORD my God
for his holy hill— 21while I was still in prayer,
Gabriel, the man I had seen in the earlier vision, came to me in swift flight about the time
of the evening sacrifice. 22He instructed me
and said to me, "Daniel, I have now come to
give you insight and understanding. 23As soon
as you began to pray, an answer was given,
which I have come to tell you, for you are
highly esteemed. Therefore, consider the message and understand the vision:

24"Seventy 'sevens'[a] are decreed for your
people and your holy city to finish[b] transgression, to put an end to sin, to atone for wickedness, to bring in everlasting righteousness, to
seal up vision and prophecy and to anoint the
most holy.[c]

25"Know and understand this: From the is-
suing of the decree[d] to restore and rebuild Jerusalem until the Anointed One,[e] the ruler,
comes, there will be seven 'sevens,' and sixty-
two 'sevens.' It will be rebuilt with streets and
a trench, but in times of trouble. 26After the
sixty-two 'sevens,' the Anointed One will be
cut off and will have nothing.[f] The people of
the ruler who will come will destroy the city
and the sanctuary. The end will come like a
flood: War will continue until the end, and
desolations have been decreed. 27He will confirm a covenant with many for one 'seven.'[g] In
the middle of the 'seven'[g] he will put an end
to sacrifice and offering. And on a wing ⌊of the
temple⌋ he will set up an abomination that
causes desolation, until the end that is decreed
is poured out on him.[h]"[i]

Daniel's Vision of a Man

10 In the third year of Cyrus king of Persia,
a revelation was given to Daniel (who
was called Belteshazzar). Its message was true
and it concerned a great war.[j] The understanding of the message came to him in a vision.

2At that time I, Daniel, mourned for three
weeks. 3I ate no choice food; no meat or wine
touched my lips; and I used no lotions at all
until the three weeks were over.

4On the twenty-fourth day of the first
month, as I was standing on the bank of the
great river, the Tigris, 5I looked up and there
before me was a man dressed in linen, with a
belt of the finest gold around his waist. 6His
body was like chrysolite, his face like lightning, his eyes like flaming torches, his arms
and legs like the gleam of burnished bronze,
and his voice like the sound of a multitude.

7I, Daniel, was the only one who saw the
vision; the men with me did not see it, but such
terror overwhelmed them that they fled and hid
themselves. 8So I was left alone, gazing at this
great vision; I had no strength left, my face
turned deathly pale and I was helpless. 9Then
I heard him speaking, and as I listened to him,
I fell into a deep sleep, my face to the ground.

10A hand touched me and set me trembling
on my hands and knees. 11He said, "Daniel,
you who are highly esteemed, consider carefully the words I am about to speak to you, and
stand up, for I have now been sent to you."
And when he said this to me, I stood up trembling.

12Then he continued, "Do not be afraid,
Daniel. Since the first day that you set your
mind to gain understanding and to humble
yourself before your God, your words were
heard, and I have come in response to them.
13But the prince of the Persian kingdom resisted me twenty-one days. Then Michael, one of
the chief princes, came to help me, because I
was detained there with the king of Persia.
14Now I have come to explain to you what will
happen to your people in the future, for the
vision concerns a time yet to come."

15While he was saying this to me, I bowed
with my face toward the ground and was
speechless. 16Then one who looked like a
man[k] touched my lips, and I opened my mouth
and began to speak. I said to the one standing
before me, "I am overcome with anguish because of the vision, my lord, and I am helpless.
17How can I, your servant, talk with you, my
lord? My strength is gone and I can hardly
breathe."

18Again the one who looked like a man
touched me and gave me strength. 19"Do not
be afraid, O man highly esteemed," he said.
"Peace! Be strong now; be strong."

When he spoke to me, I was strengthened
and said, "Speak, my lord, since you have giv-
en me strength."

20So he said, "Do you know why I have
come to you? Soon I will return to fight against
the prince of Persia, and when I go, the prince
of Greece will come; 21but first I will tell you
what is written in the Book of Truth. (No one
supports me against them except Michael, your
11 prince. 1And in the first year of Darius
the Mede, I took my stand to support
and protect him.)

The Kings of the South and the North

2"Now then, I tell you the truth: Three more
kings will appear in Persia, and then a fourth,
who will be far richer than all the others. When
he has gained power by his wealth, he will stir
up everyone against the kingdom of Greece.
3Then a mighty king will appear, who will rule
with great power and do as he pleases. 4After
he has appeared, his empire will be broken up
and parceled out toward the four winds of
heaven. It will not go to his descendants, nor
will it have the power he exercised, because

[a]24 Or *'weeks'*; also in verses 25 and 26 [b]24 Or *restrain* [c]24 Or *Most Holy Place*; or *most holy One*
[d]25 Or *word* [e]25 Or *an anointed one*; also in verse 26 [f]26 Or *off and will have no one*; or *off, but not for himself* [g]27 Or *'week'* [h]27 Or *it* [i]27 Or *And one who causes desolation will come upon the pinnacle of the abominable ⌊temple⌋, until the end that is decreed is poured out on the desolated ⌊city⌋*
[j]1 Or *true and burdensome* [k]16 Most manuscripts of the Masoretic Text; one manuscript of the Masoretic Text, Dead Sea Scrolls and Septuagint *Then something that looked like a man's hand*

his empire will be uprooted and given to others.

5"The king of the South will become strong, but one of his commanders will become even stronger than he and will rule his own kingdom with great power. 6After some years, they will become allies. The daughter of the king of the South will go to the king of the North to make an alliance, but she will not retain her power, and he and his power[a] will not last. In those days she will be handed over, together with her royal escort and her father[b] and the one who supported her.

7"One from her family line will arise to take her place. He will attack the forces of the king of the North and enter his fortress; he will fight against them and be victorious. 8He will also seize their gods, their metal images and their valuable articles of silver and gold and carry them off to Egypt. For some years he will leave the king of the North alone. 9Then the king of the North will invade the realm of the king of the South but will retreat to his own country. 10His sons will prepare for war and assemble a great army, which will sweep on like an irresistible flood and carry the battle as far as his fortress.

11"Then the king of the South will march out in a rage and fight against the king of the North, who will raise a large army, but it will be defeated. 12When the army is carried off, the king of the South will be filled with pride and will slaughter many thousands, yet he will not remain triumphant. 13For the king of the North will muster another army, larger than the first; and after several years, he will advance with a huge army fully equipped.

14"In those times many will rise against the king of the South. The violent men among your own people will rebel in fulfillment of the vision, but without success. 15Then the king of the North will come and build up siege ramps and will capture a fortified city. The forces of the South will be powerless to resist; even their best troops will not have the strength to stand. 16The invader will do as he pleases; no one will be able to stand against him. He will establish himself in the Beautiful Land and will have the power to destroy it. 17He will determine to come with the might of his entire kingdom and will make an alliance with the king of the South. And he will give him a daughter in marriage in order to overthrow the kingdom, but his plans[c] will not succeed or help him. 18Then he will turn his attention to the coastlands and will take many of them, but a commander will put an end to his insolence and will turn his insolence back upon him. 19After this, he will turn back toward the fortresses of his own country but will stumble and fall, to be seen no more.

20"His successor will send out a tax collector to maintain the royal splendor. In a few years, however, he will be destroyed, yet not in anger or in battle.

21"He will be succeeded by a contemptible person who has not been given the honor of royalty. He will invade the kingdom when its people feel secure, and he will seize it through intrigue. 22Then an overwhelming army will be swept away before him; both it and a prince of the covenant will be destroyed. 23After coming to an agreement with him, he will act deceitfully, and with only a few people he will rise to power. 24When the richest provinces feel secure, he will invade them and will achieve what neither his fathers nor his forefathers did. He will distribute plunder, loot and wealth among his followers. He will plot the overthrow of fortresses—but only for a time.

25"With a large army he will stir up his strength and courage against the king of the South. The king of the South will wage war with a large and very powerful army, but he will not be able to stand because of the plots devised against him. 26Those who eat from the king's provisions will try to destroy him; his army will be swept away, and many will fall in battle. 27The two kings, with their hearts bent on evil, will sit at the same table and lie to each other, but to no avail, because an end will still come at the appointed time. 28The king of the North will return to his own country with great wealth, but his heart will be set against the holy covenant. He will take action against it and then return to his own country.

29"At the appointed time he will invade the South again, but this time the outcome will be different from what it was before. 30Ships of the western coastlands[d] will oppose him, and he will lose heart. Then he will turn back and vent his fury against the holy covenant. He will return and show favor to those who forsake the holy covenant.

31"His armed forces will rise up to desecrate the temple fortress and will abolish the daily sacrifice. Then they will set up the abomination that causes desolation. 32With flattery he will corrupt those who have violated the covenant, but the people who know their God will firmly resist him.

33"Those who are wise will instruct many, though for a time they will fall by the sword or be burned or captured or plundered. 34When they fall, they will receive a little help, and many who are not sincere will join them. 35Some of the wise will stumble, so that they may be refined, purified and made spotless until the time of the end, for it will still come at the appointed time.

The King Who Exalts Himself

36"The king will do as he pleases. He will exalt and magnify himself above every god and will say unheard-of things against the God of gods. He will be successful until the time of wrath is completed, for what has been determined must take place. 37He will show no regard for the gods of his fathers or for the one desired by women, nor will he regard any god,

[a]6 Or *offspring* [b]6 Or *child* (see Vulgate and Syriac) [c]17 Or *but she* [d]30 Hebrew *of Kittim*

but will exalt himself above them all. 38Instead
of them, he will honor a god of fortresses; a
god unknown to his fathers he will honor with
gold and silver, with precious stones and costly
gifts. 39He will attack the mightiest fortresses
with the help of a foreign god and will greatly
honor those who acknowledge him. He will
make them rulers over many people and will
distribute the land at a price.[a]

40"At the time of the end the king of the
South will engage him in battle, and the king
of the North will storm out against him with
chariots and cavalry and a great fleet of ships.
He will invade many countries and sweep
through them like a flood. 41He will also invade the Beautiful Land. Many countries will
fall, but Edom, Moab and the leaders of Ammon will be delivered from his hand. 42He will
extend his power over many countries; Egypt
will not escape. 43He will gain control of the
treasures of gold and silver and all the riches of
Egypt, with the Libyans and Nubians in submission. 44But reports from the east and the
north will alarm him, and he will set out in
a great rage to destroy and annihilate many.
45He will pitch his royal tents between the seas
at[b] the beautiful holy mountain. Yet he will
come to his end, and no one will help him.

The End Times

12 "At that time Michael, the great prince
who protects your people, will arise.
There will be a time of distress such as has not
happened from the beginning of nations until
then. But at that time your people—everyone
whose name is found written in the book—will
be delivered. 2Multitudes who sleep in the dust
of the earth will awake: some to everlasting
life, others to shame and everlasting contempt.
3Those who are wise[c] will shine like the
brightness of the heavens, and those who lead
many to righteousness, like the stars for ever
and ever. 4But you, Daniel, close up and seal
the words of the scroll until the time of the end.
Many will go here and there to increase knowledge."

5Then I, Daniel, looked, and there before me
stood two others, one on this bank of the river
and one on the opposite bank. 6One of them
said to the man clothed in linen, who was
above the waters of the river, "How long will
it be before these astonishing things are fulfilled?"

7The man clothed in linen, who was above
the waters of the river, lifted his right hand and
his left hand toward heaven, and I heard him
swear by him who lives forever, saying, "It
will be for a time, times and half a time.[d]
When the power of the holy people has been
finally broken, all these things will be completed."

8I heard, but I did not understand. So I
asked, "My lord, what will the outcome of all
this be?"

9He replied, "Go your way, Daniel, because
the words are closed up and sealed until the
time of the end. 10Many will be purified, made
spotless and refined, but the wicked will continue to be wicked. None of the wicked will
understand, but those who are wise will understand.

11"From the time that the daily sacrifice is
abolished and the abomination that causes desolation is set up, there will be 1,290 days.
12Blessed is the one who waits for and reaches
the end of the 1,335 days.

13"As for you, go your way till the end. You
will rest, and then at the end of the days you
will rise to receive your allotted inheritance."

Hosea

1 The word of the LORD that came to Hosea
son of Beeri during the reigns of Uzziah,
Jotham, Ahaz and Hezekiah, kings of Judah,
and during the reign of Jeroboam son of Jehoash[e] king of Israel:

Hosea's Wife and Children

2When the LORD began to speak through
Hosea, the LORD said to him, "Go, take to
yourself an adulterous wife and children of unfaithfulness, because the land is guilty of the
vilest adultery in departing from the LORD."
3So he married Gomer daughter of Diblaim,
and she conceived and bore him a son.

4Then the LORD said to Hosea, "Call him
Jezreel, because I will soon punish the house of
Jehu for the massacre at Jezreel, and I will
put an end to the kingdom of Israel. 5In that
day I will break Israel's bow in the Valley of
Jezreel."

6Gomer conceived again and gave birth to a
daughter. Then the LORD said to Hosea, "Call
her Lo-Ruhamah,[f] for I will no longer show
love to the house of Israel, that I should at all
forgive them. 7Yet I will show love to the
house of Judah; and I will save them—not by
bow, sword or battle, or by horses and horsemen, but by the LORD their God."

8After she had weaned Lo-Ruhamah, Gomer had another son. 9Then the LORD said,

[a]*39* Or *land for a reward* [b]*45* Or *the sea and* [c]*3* Or *who impart wisdom* [d]*7* Or *a year, two years and half a year* [e]*1* Hebrew *Joash,* a variant of *Jehoash* [f]*6* *Lo-Ruhamah* means *not loved.*

"Call him Lo-Ammi,[a] for you are not my people, and I am not your God.
10"Yet the Israelites will be like the sand on
the seashore, which cannot be measured or
counted. In the place where it was said to
them, 'You are not my people,' they will be
called 'sons of the living God.' 11The people
of Judah and the people of Israel will be reunit-
ed, and they will appoint one leader and will
come up out of the land, for great will be the
day of Jezreel.
2 "Say of your brothers, 'My people,' and of
your sisters, 'My loved one.'

Israel Punished and Restored

2"Rebuke your mother, rebuke her,
for she is not my wife,
and I am not her husband.
Let her remove the adulterous look from her face
and the unfaithfulness from between her breasts.
3Otherwise I will strip her naked
and make her as bare as on the day she was born;
I will make her like a desert,
turn her into a parched land,
and slay her with thirst.
4I will not show my love to her children,
because they are the children of adultery.
5Their mother has been unfaithful
and has conceived them in disgrace.
She said, 'I will go after my lovers,
who give me my food and my water,
my wool and my linen, my oil and my drink.'
6Therefore I will block her path with thornbushes;
I will wall her in so that she cannot find her way.
7She will chase after her lovers but not catch them;
she will look for them but not find them.
Then she will say,
'I will go back to my husband as at first,
for then I was better off than now.'
8She has not acknowledged that I was the one
who gave her the grain, the new wine and oil,
who lavished on her the silver and gold—
which they used for Baal.

9"Therefore I will take away my grain when it ripens,
and my new wine when it is ready.
I will take back my wool and my linen,
intended to cover her nakedness.
10So now I will expose her lewdness
before the eyes of her lovers;
no one will take her out of my hands.
11I will stop all her celebrations:
her yearly festivals, her New Moons,
her Sabbath days—all her appointed feasts.
12I will ruin her vines and her fig trees,
which she said were her pay from her lovers;
I will make them a thicket,
and wild animals will devour them.
13I will punish her for the days
she burned incense to the Baals;
she decked herself with rings and jewelry,
and went after her lovers,
but me she forgot,"
declares the LORD.

14"Therefore I am now going to allure her;
I will lead her into the desert
and speak tenderly to her.
15There I will give her back her vineyards,
and will make the Valley of Achor[b] a door of hope.
There she will sing[c] as in the days of her youth,
as in the day she came up out of Egypt.

16"In that day," declares the LORD,
"you will call me 'my husband';
you will no longer call me 'my master.[d]'
17I will remove the names of the Baals from her lips;
no longer will their names be invoked.
18In that day I will make a covenant for them
with the beasts of the field and the birds of the air
and the creatures that move along the ground.
Bow and sword and battle
I will abolish from the land,
so that all may lie down in safety.
19I will betroth you to me forever;
I will betroth you in[e] righteousness and justice,
in[f] love and compassion.
20I will betroth you in faithfulness,
and you will acknowledge the LORD.

21"In that day I will respond,"
declares the LORD—
"I will respond to the skies,
and they will respond to the earth;
22and the earth will respond to the grain,
the new wine and oil,
and they will respond to Jezreel.[g]
23I will plant her for myself in the land;
I will show my love to the one I called 'Not my loved one.[h]'
I will say to those called 'Not my people,[i]' 'You are my people';
and they will say, 'You are my God.' "

[a]9 *Lo-Ammi* means *not my people.* [b]15 *Achor* means *trouble.* [c]15 Or *respond* [d]16 Hebrew *baal* [e]19 Or *with*; also in verse 20 [f]19 Or *with* [g]22 *Jezreel* means *God plants.* [h]23 Hebrew *Lo-Ruhamah* [i]23 Hebrew *Lo-Ammi*

Hosea's Reconciliation With His Wife

3 The LORD said to me, "Go, show your love
to your wife again, though she is loved by
another and is an adulteress. Love her as the
LORD loves the Israelites, though they turn to
other gods and love the sacred raisin cakes."
2So I bought her for fifteen shekels[a] of silver and about a homer and a lethek[b] of barley.
3Then I told her, "You are to live with[c] me
many days; you must not be a prostitute or be
intimate with any man, and I will live with[c]
you."
4For the Israelites will live many days without king or prince, without sacrifice or sacred
stones, without ephod or idol. 5Afterward the
Israelites will return and seek the LORD their
God and David their king. They will come
trembling to the LORD and to his blessings in
the last days.

The Charge Against Israel

4 Hear the word of the LORD, you
Israelites,
because the LORD has a charge to bring
against you who live in the land:
"There is no faithfulness, no love,
no acknowledgment of God in the land.
2There is only cursing,[d] lying and murder,
stealing and adultery;
they break all bounds,
and bloodshed follows bloodshed.
3Because of this the land mourns,[e]
and all who live in it waste away;
the beasts of the field and the birds of the
air
and the fish of the sea are dying.

4"But let no man bring a charge,
let no man accuse another,
for your people are like those
who bring charges against a priest.
5You stumble day and night,
and the prophets stumble with you.
So I will destroy your mother—
6 my people are destroyed from lack of
knowledge.

"Because you have rejected knowledge,
I also reject you as my priests;
because you have ignored the law of your
God,
I also will ignore your children.
7The more the priests increased,
the more they sinned against me;
they exchanged[f] their[g] Glory for
something disgraceful.
8They feed on the sins of my people
and relish their wickedness.
9And it will be: Like people, like priests.
I will punish both of them for their
ways
and repay them for their deeds.

10"They will eat but not have enough;
they will engage in prostitution but not
increase,
because they have deserted the LORD
to give themselves 11to prostitution,
to old wine and new,
which take away the understanding 12of
my people.
They consult a wooden idol
and are answered by a stick of wood.
A spirit of prostitution leads them astray;
they are unfaithful to their God.
13They sacrifice on the mountaintops
and burn offerings on the hills,
under oak, poplar and terebinth,
where the shade is pleasant.
Therefore your daughters turn to
prostitution
and your daughters-in-law to adultery.

14"I will not punish your daughters
when they turn to prostitution,
nor your daughters-in-law
when they commit adultery,
because the men themselves consort with
harlots
and sacrifice with shrine prostitutes—
a people without understanding will
come to ruin!

15"Though you commit adultery, O Israel,
let not Judah become guilty.

"Do not go to Gilgal;
do not go up to Beth Aven.[h]
And do not swear, 'As surely as the
LORD lives!'
16The Israelites are stubborn,
like a stubborn heifer.
How then can the LORD pasture them
like lambs in a meadow?
17Ephraim is joined to idols;
leave him alone!
18Even when their drinks are gone,
they continue their prostitution;
their rulers dearly love shameful ways.
19A whirlwind will sweep them away,
and their sacrifices will bring them
shame.

Judgment Against Israel

5 "Hear this, you priests!
Pay attention, you Israelites!
Listen, O royal house!
This judgment is against you:
You have been a snare at Mizpah,
a net spread out on Tabor.
2The rebels are deep in slaughter.
I will discipline all of them.
3I know all about Ephraim;
Israel is not hidden from me.
Ephraim, you have now turned to
prostitution;
Israel is corrupt.

4"Their deeds do not permit them

[a]2 That is, about 6 ounces (about 170 grams) [b]2 That is, probably about 10 bushels (about 330 liters)
[c]3 Or *wait for* [d]2 That is, to pronounce a curse upon [e]3 Or *dries up* [f]7 Syriac and an ancient Hebrew scribal tradition; Masoretic Text *I will exchange* [g]7 Masoretic Text; an ancient Hebrew scribal tradition *my*
[h]15 *Beth Aven* means *house of wickedness* (a name for Bethel, which means *house of God*).

to return to their God.
A spirit of prostitution is in their heart;
they do not acknowledge the LORD.
5Israel's arrogance testifies against them;
the Israelites, even Ephraim, stumble in their sin;
Judah also stumbles with them.
6When they go with their flocks and herds
to seek the LORD,
they will not find him;
he has withdrawn himself from them.
7They are unfaithful to the LORD;
they give birth to illegitimate children.
Now their New Moon festivals
will devour them and their fields.

8"Sound the trumpet in Gibeah,
the horn in Ramah.
Raise the battle cry in Beth Aven[a];
lead on, O Benjamin.
9Ephraim will be laid waste
on the day of reckoning.
Among the tribes of Israel
I proclaim what is certain.
10Judah's leaders are like those
who move boundary stones.
I will pour out my wrath on them
like a flood of water.
11Ephraim is oppressed,
trampled in judgment,
intent on pursuing idols.[b]
12I am like a moth to Ephraim,
like rot to the people of Judah.

13"When Ephraim saw his sickness,
and Judah his sores,
then Ephraim turned to Assyria,
and sent to the great king for help.
But he is not able to cure you,
not able to heal your sores.
14For I will be like a lion to Ephraim,
like a great lion to Judah.
I will tear them to pieces and go away;
I will carry them off, with no one to rescue them.
15Then I will go back to my place
until they admit their guilt.
And they will seek my face;
in their misery they will earnestly seek me."

Israel Unrepentant

6 "Come, let us return to the LORD.
He has torn us to pieces
but he will heal us;
he has injured us
but he will bind up our wounds.
2After two days he will revive us;
on the third day he will restore us,
that we may live in his presence.
3Let us acknowledge the LORD;
let us press on to acknowledge him.
As surely as the sun rises,
he will appear;
he will come to us like the winter rains,
like the spring rains that water the earth."

4"What can I do with you, Ephraim?
What can I do with you, Judah?
Your love is like the morning mist,
like the early dew that disappears.
5Therefore I cut you in pieces with my prophets,
I killed you with the words of my mouth;
my judgments flashed like lightning upon you.
6For I desire mercy, not sacrifice,
and acknowledgment of God rather than burnt offerings.
7Like Adam,[c] they have broken the covenant—
they were unfaithful to me there.
8Gilead is a city of wicked men,
stained with footprints of blood.
9As marauders lie in ambush for a man,
so do bands of priests;
they murder on the road to Shechem,
committing shameful crimes.
10I have seen a horrible thing
in the house of Israel.
There Ephraim is given to prostitution
and Israel is defiled.

11"Also for you, Judah,
a harvest is appointed.

"Whenever I would restore the fortunes of my people,
7 1whenever I would heal Israel,
the sins of Ephraim are exposed
and the crimes of Samaria revealed.
They practice deceit,
thieves break into houses,
bandits rob in the streets;
2but they do not realize
that I remember all their evil deeds.
Their sins engulf them;
they are always before me.

3"They delight the king with their wickedness,
the princes with their lies.
4They are all adulterers,
burning like an oven
whose fire the baker need not stir
from the kneading of the dough till it rises.
5On the day of the festival of our king
the princes become inflamed with wine,
and he joins hands with the mockers.
6Their hearts are like an oven;
they approach him with intrigue.
Their passion smolders all night;
in the morning it blazes like a flaming fire.
7All of them are hot as an oven;
they devour their rulers.
All their kings fall,
and none of them calls on me.

[a]8 *Beth Aven* means *house of wickedness* (a name for Bethel, which means *house of God*).
[b]11 The meaning of the Hebrew for this word is uncertain.
[c]7 Or *As at Adam*; or *Like men*

8"Ephraim mixes with the nations;
Ephraim is a flat cake not turned over.
9Foreigners sap his strength,
but he does not realize it.
His hair is sprinkled with gray,
but he does not notice.
10Israel's arrogance testifies against him,
but despite all this
he does not return to the LORD his God
or search for him.

11"Ephraim is like a dove,
easily deceived and senseless—
now calling to Egypt,
now turning to Assyria.
12When they go, I will throw my net over them;
I will pull them down like birds of the air.
When I hear them flocking together,
I will catch them.
13Woe to them,
because they have strayed from me!
Destruction to them,
because they have rebelled against me!
I long to redeem them
but they speak lies against me.
14They do not cry out to me from their hearts
but wail upon their beds.
They gather together[a] for grain and new wine
but turn away from me.
15I trained them and strengthened them,
but they plot evil against me.
16They do not turn to the Most High;
they are like a faulty bow.
Their leaders will fall by the sword
because of their insolent words.
For this they will be ridiculed
in the land of Egypt.

Israel to Reap the Whirlwind

8 "Put the trumpet to your lips!
An eagle is over the house of the LORD
because the people have broken my covenant
and rebelled against my law.
2Israel cries out to me,
'O our God, we acknowledge you!'
3But Israel has rejected what is good;
an enemy will pursue him.
4They set up kings without my consent;
they choose princes without my approval.
With their silver and gold
they make idols for themselves
to their own destruction.
5Throw out your calf-idol, O Samaria!
My anger burns against them.
How long will they be incapable of purity?
6 They are from Israel!
This calf—a craftsman has made it;
it is not God.
It will be broken in pieces,
that calf of Samaria.

7"They sow the wind
and reap the whirlwind.
The stalk has no head;
it will produce no flour.
Were it to yield grain,
foreigners would swallow it up.
8Israel is swallowed up;
now she is among the nations
like a worthless thing.
9For they have gone up to Assyria
like a wild donkey wandering alone.
Ephraim has sold herself to lovers.
10Although they have sold themselves among the nations,
I will now gather them together.
They will begin to waste away
under the oppression of the mighty king.

11"Though Ephraim built many altars for sin offerings,
these have become altars for sinning.
12I wrote for them the many things of my law,
but they regarded them as something alien.
13They offer sacrifices given to me
and they eat the meat,
but the LORD is not pleased with them.
Now he will remember their wickedness
and punish their sins:
They will return to Egypt.
14Israel has forgotten his Maker
and built palaces;
Judah has fortified many towns.
But I will send fire upon their cities
that will consume their fortresses."

Punishment for Israel

9 Do not rejoice, O Israel;
do not be jubilant like the other nations.
For you have been unfaithful to your God;
you love the wages of a prostitute
at every threshing floor.
2Threshing floors and winepresses will not feed the people;
the new wine will fail them.
3They will not remain in the LORD's land;
Ephraim will return to Egypt
and eat unclean[b] food in Assyria.
4They will not pour out wine offerings to the LORD,
nor will their sacrifices please him.
Such sacrifices will be to them like the bread of mourners;
all who eat them will be unclean.
This food will be for themselves;
it will not come into the temple of the LORD.

5What will you do on the day of your appointed feasts,
on the festival days of the LORD?

[a] 14 Most Hebrew manuscripts; some Hebrew manuscripts and Septuagint *They slash themselves* [b] 3 That is, ceremonially unclean

6Even if they escape from destruction,
Egypt will gather them,
and Memphis will bury them.
Their treasures of silver will be taken over by briers,
and thorns will overrun their tents.
7The days of punishment are coming,
the days of reckoning are at hand.
Let Israel know this.
Because your sins are so many
and your hostility so great,
the prophet is considered a fool,
the inspired man a maniac.
8The prophet, along with my God,
is the watchman over Ephraim,[a]
yet snares await him on all his paths,
and hostility in the house of his God.
9They have sunk deep into corruption,
as in the days of Gibeah.
God will remember their wickedness
and punish them for their sins.

10"When I found Israel,
it was like finding grapes in the desert;
when I saw your fathers,
it was like seeing the early fruit on the fig tree.
But when they came to Baal Peor,
they consecrated themselves to that shameful idol
and became as vile as the thing they loved.
11Ephraim's glory will fly away like a bird—
no birth, no pregnancy, no conception.
12Even if they rear children,
I will bereave them of every one.
Woe to them
when I turn away from them!
13I have seen Ephraim, like Tyre,
planted in a pleasant place.
But Ephraim will bring out
their children to the slayer."

14Give them, O LORD—
what will you give them?
Give them wombs that miscarry
and breasts that are dry.

15"Because of all their wickedness in Gilgal,
I hated them there.
Because of their sinful deeds,
I will drive them out of my house.
I will no longer love them;
all their leaders are rebellious.
16Ephraim is blighted,
their root is withered,
they yield no fruit.
Even if they bear children,
I will slay their cherished offspring."

17My God will reject them
because they have not obeyed him;
they will be wanderers among the nations.

10 Israel was a spreading vine;
he brought forth fruit for himself.
As his fruit increased,
he built more altars;
as his land prospered,
he adorned his sacred stones.
2Their heart is deceitful,
and now they must bear their guilt.
The LORD will demolish their altars
and destroy their sacred stones.

3Then they will say, "We have no king
because we did not revere the LORD.
But even if we had a king,
what could he do for us?"
4They make many promises,
take false oaths
and make agreements;
therefore lawsuits spring up
like poisonous weeds in a plowed field.
5The people who live in Samaria fear
for the calf-idol of Beth Aven.[b]
Its people will mourn over it,
and so will its idolatrous priests,
those who had rejoiced over its splendor,
because it is taken from them into exile.
6It will be carried to Assyria
as tribute for the great king.
Ephraim will be disgraced;
Israel will be ashamed of its wooden idols.[c]
7Samaria and its king will float away
like a twig on the surface of the waters.
8The high places of wickedness[d] will be destroyed—
it is the sin of Israel.
Thorns and thistles will grow up
and cover their altars.
Then they will say to the mountains,
"Cover us!"
and to the hills, "Fall on us!"

9"Since the days of Gibeah, you have sinned, O Israel,
and there you have remained.[e]
Did not war overtake
the evildoers in Gibeah?
10When I please, I will punish them;
nations will be gathered against them
to put them in bonds for their double sin.
11Ephraim is a trained heifer
that loves to thresh;
so I will put a yoke
on her fair neck.
I will drive Ephraim,
Judah must plow,
and Jacob must break up the ground.
12Sow for yourselves righteousness,
reap the fruit of unfailing love,
and break up your unplowed ground;
for it is time to seek the LORD,
until he comes
and showers righteousness on you.

[a]8 Or *The prophet is the watchman over Ephraim, / the people of my God* [b]5 *Beth Aven* means *house of wickedness* (a name for Bethel, which means *house of God*). [c]6 Or *its counsel* [d]8 Hebrew *aven*, a reference to Beth Aven (a derogatory name for Bethel) [e]9 Or *there a stand was taken*

13But you have planted wickedness,
you have reaped evil,
you have eaten the fruit of deception.
Because you have depended on your own strength
and on your many warriors,
14the roar of battle will rise against your people,
so that all your fortresses will be devastated—
as Shalman devastated Beth Arbel on the day of battle,
when mothers were dashed to the ground with their children.
15Thus will it happen to you, O Bethel,
because your wickedness is great.
When that day dawns,
the king of Israel will be completely destroyed.

God's Love for Israel

11 "When Israel was a child, I loved him,
and out of Egypt I called my son.
2But the more I[a] called Israel,
the further they went from me.[b]
They sacrificed to the Baals
and they burned incense to images.
3It was I who taught Ephraim to walk,
taking them by the arms;
but they did not realize
it was I who healed them.
4I led them with cords of human kindness,
with ties of love;
I lifted the yoke from their neck
and bent down to feed them.

5"Will they not return to Egypt
and will not Assyria rule over them
because they refuse to repent?
6Swords will flash in their cities,
will destroy the bars of their gates
and put an end to their plans.
7My people are determined to turn from me.
Even if they call to the Most High,
he will by no means exalt them.

8"How can I give you up, Ephraim?
How can I hand you over, Israel?
How can I treat you like Admah?
How can I make you like Zeboiim?
My heart is changed within me;
all my compassion is aroused.
9I will not carry out my fierce anger,
nor will I turn and devastate Ephraim.
For I am God, and not man—
the Holy One among you.
I will not come in wrath.[c]
10They will follow the LORD;
he will roar like a lion.
When he roars,
his children will come trembling from the west.
11They will come trembling
like birds from Egypt,
like doves from Assyria.
I will settle them in their homes,"
declares the LORD.

Israel's Sin

12Ephraim has surrounded me with lies,
the house of Israel with deceit.
And Judah is unruly against God,
even against the faithful Holy One.

12 1Ephraim feeds on the wind;
he pursues the east wind all day
and multiplies lies and violence.
He makes a treaty with Assyria
and sends olive oil to Egypt.
2The LORD has a charge to bring against Judah;
he will punish Jacob[d] according to his ways
and repay him according to his deeds.
3In the womb he grasped his brother's heel;
as a man he struggled with God.
4He struggled with the angel and overcame him;
he wept and begged for his favor.
He found him at Bethel
and talked with him there—
5the LORD God Almighty,
the LORD is his name of renown!
6But you must return to your God;
maintain love and justice,
and wait for your God always.

7The merchant uses dishonest scales;
he loves to defraud.
8Ephraim boasts,
"I am very rich; I have become wealthy.
With all my wealth they will not find in me
any iniquity or sin."

9"I am the LORD your God,
⌊who brought you⌋ out of[e] Egypt;
I will make you live in tents again,
as in the days of your appointed feasts.
10I spoke to the prophets,
gave them many visions
and told parables through them."

11Is Gilead wicked?
Its people are worthless!
Do they sacrifice bulls in Gilgal?
Their altars will be like piles of stones
on a plowed field.
12Jacob fled to the country of Aram[f];
Israel served to get a wife,
and to pay for her he tended sheep.
13The LORD used a prophet to bring Israel up from Egypt,
by a prophet he cared for him.
14But Ephraim has bitterly provoked him to anger;

[a]2 Some Septuagint manuscripts; Hebrew *they* [b]2 Septuagint; Hebrew *them* [c]9 Or *come against any city*
[d]2 *Jacob* means *he grasps the heel* (figuratively, *he deceives*). [e]9 Or *God / ever since you were in*
[f]12 That is, Northwest Mesopotamia

his Lord will leave upon him the guilt
of his bloodshed
and will repay him for his contempt.

The LORD's Anger Against Israel

13 When Ephraim spoke, men trembled;
he was exalted in Israel.
But he became guilty of Baal worship
and died.
2Now they sin more and more;
they make idols for themselves from
their silver,
cleverly fashioned images,
all of them the work of craftsmen.
It is said of these people,
"They offer human sacrifice
and kiss[a] the calf-idols."
3Therefore they will be like the morning
mist,
like the early dew that disappears,
like chaff swirling from a threshing
floor,
like smoke escaping through a window.

4"But I am the LORD your God,
⌊who brought you⌋ out of[b] Egypt.
You shall acknowledge no God but me,
no Savior except me.
5I cared for you in the desert,
in the land of burning heat.
6When I fed them, they were satisfied;
when they were satisfied, they became
proud;
then they forgot me.
7So I will come upon them like a lion,
like a leopard I will lurk by the path.
8Like a bear robbed of her cubs,
I will attack them and rip them open.
Like a lion I will devour them;
a wild animal will tear them apart.

9"You are destroyed, O Israel,
because you are against me, against
your helper.
10Where is your king, that he may save
you?
Where are your rulers in all your towns,
of whom you said,
'Give me a king and princes'?
11So in my anger I gave you a king,
and in my wrath I took him away.
12The guilt of Ephraim is stored up,
his sins are kept on record.
13Pains as of a woman in childbirth come to
him,
but he is a child without wisdom;
when the time arrives,
he does not come to the opening of the
womb.

14"I will ransom them from the power of the
grave[c];
I will redeem them from death.
Where, O death, are your plagues?
Where, O grave,[c] is your destruction?

"I will have no compassion,
15 even though he thrives among his
brothers.
An east wind from the LORD will come,
blowing in from the desert;
his spring will fail
and his well dry up.
His storehouse will be plundered
of all its treasures.
16The people of Samaria must bear their
guilt,
because they have rebelled against their
God.
They will fall by the sword;
their little ones will be dashed to the
ground,
their pregnant women ripped open."

Repentance to Bring Blessing

14 Return, O Israel, to the LORD your
God.
Your sins have been your downfall!
2Take words with you
and return to the LORD.
Say to him:
"Forgive all our sins
and receive us graciously,
that we may offer the fruit of our lips.[d]
3Assyria cannot save us;
we will not mount war-horses.
We will never again say 'Our gods'
to what our own hands have made,
for in you the fatherless find
compassion."

4"I will heal their waywardness
and love them freely,
for my anger has turned away from
them.
5I will be like the dew to Israel;
he will blossom like a lily.
Like a cedar of Lebanon
he will send down his roots;
6 his young shoots will grow.
His splendor will be like an olive tree,
his fragrance like a cedar of Lebanon.
7Men will dwell again in his shade.
He will flourish like the grain.
He will blossom like a vine,
and his fame will be like the wine from
Lebanon.
8O Ephraim, what more have I[e] to do with
idols?
I will answer him and care for him.
I am like a green pine tree;
your fruitfulness comes from me."

9Who is wise? He will realize these things.
Who is discerning? He will understand
them.
The ways of the LORD are right;
the righteous walk in them,
but the rebellious stumble in them.

[a]2 Or *"Men who sacrifice / kiss* [b]4 Or *God / ever since you were in* [c]14 Hebrew *Sheol* [d]2 Or *offer our lips as sacrifices of bulls* [e]8 Or *What more has Ephraim*

Joel

1 The word of the LORD that came to Joel son of Pethuel.

An Invasion of Locusts

2Hear this, you elders;
listen, all who live in the land.
Has anything like this ever happened in your days
or in the days of your forefathers?
3Tell it to your children,
and let your children tell it to their children,
and their children to the next generation.
4What the locust swarm has left
the great locusts have eaten;
what the great locusts have left
the young locusts have eaten;
what the young locusts have left
other locusts[a] have eaten.

5Wake up, you drunkards, and weep!
Wail, all you drinkers of wine;
wail because of the new wine,
for it has been snatched from your lips.
6A nation has invaded my land,
powerful and without number;
it has the teeth of a lion,
the fangs of a lioness.
7It has laid waste my vines
and ruined my fig trees.
It has stripped off their bark
and thrown it away,
leaving their branches white.

8Mourn like a virgin[b] in sackcloth
grieving for the husband[c] of her youth.
9Grain offerings and drink offerings
are cut off from the house of the LORD.
The priests are in mourning,
those who minister before the LORD.
10The fields are ruined,
the ground is dried up[d];
the grain is destroyed,
the new wine is dried up,
the oil fails.
11Despair, you farmers,
wail, you vine growers;
grieve for the wheat and the barley,
because the harvest of the field is destroyed.
12The vine is dried up
and the fig tree is withered;
the pomegranate, the palm and the apple tree—
all the trees of the field—are dried up.
Surely the joy of mankind
is withered away.

A Call to Repentance

13Put on sackcloth, O priests, and mourn;
wail, you who minister before the altar.
Come, spend the night in sackcloth,
you who minister before my God;
for the grain offerings and drink offerings
are withheld from the house of your God.
14Declare a holy fast;
call a sacred assembly.
Summon the elders
and all who live in the land
to the house of the LORD your God,
and cry out to the LORD.

15Alas for that day!
For the day of the LORD is near;
it will come like destruction from the Almighty.[e]

16Has not the food been cut off
before our very eyes—
joy and gladness
from the house of our God?
17The seeds are shriveled
beneath the clods.[f]
The storehouses are in ruins,
the granaries have been broken down,
for the grain has dried up.
18How the cattle moan!
The herds mill about
because they have no pasture;
even the flocks of sheep are suffering.

19To you, O LORD, I call,
for fire has devoured the open pastures
and flames have burned up all the trees of the field.
20Even the wild animals pant for you;
the streams of water have dried up
and fire has devoured the open pastures.

An Army of Locusts

2 Blow the trumpet in Zion;
sound the alarm on my holy hill.
Let all who live in the land tremble,
for the day of the LORD is coming.
It is close at hand—
2 a day of darkness and gloom,
a day of clouds and blackness.
Like dawn spreading across the mountains
a large and mighty army comes,
such as never was of old
nor ever will be in ages to come.

3Before them fire devours,
behind them a flame blazes.
Before them the land is like the garden of Eden,
behind them, a desert waste—

[a]4 The precise meaning of the four Hebrew words used here for locusts is uncertain. [b]8 Or *young woman* [c]8 Or *betrothed* [d]10 Or *ground mourns* [e]15 Hebrew *Shaddai* [f]17 The meaning of the Hebrew for this word is uncertain.

nothing escapes them.
4They have the appearance of horses;
they gallop along like cavalry.
5With a noise like that of chariots
they leap over the mountaintops,
like a crackling fire consuming stubble,
like a mighty army drawn up for battle.

6At the sight of them, nations are in anguish;
every face turns pale.
7They charge like warriors;
they scale walls like soldiers.
They all march in line,
not swerving from their course.
8They do not jostle each other;
each marches straight ahead.
They plunge through defenses
without breaking ranks.
9They rush upon the city;
they run along the wall.
They climb into the houses;
like thieves they enter through the windows.

10Before them the earth shakes,
the sky trembles,
the sun and moon are darkened,
and the stars no longer shine.
11The LORD thunders
at the head of his army;
his forces are beyond number,
and mighty are those who obey his command.
The day of the LORD is great;
it is dreadful.
Who can endure it?

Rend Your Heart

12"Even now," declares the LORD,
"return to me with all your heart,
with fasting and weeping and mourning."

13Rend your heart
and not your garments.
Return to the LORD your God,
for he is gracious and compassionate,
slow to anger and abounding in love,
and he relents from sending calamity.
14Who knows? He may turn and have pity
and leave behind a blessing—
grain offerings and drink offerings
for the LORD your God.

15Blow the trumpet in Zion,
declare a holy fast,
call a sacred assembly.
16Gather the people,
consecrate the assembly;
bring together the elders,
gather the children,
those nursing at the breast.
Let the bridegroom leave his room
and the bride her chamber.
17Let the priests, who minister before the LORD,
weep between the temple porch and the altar.
Let them say, "Spare your people, O LORD.
Do not make your inheritance an object of scorn,
a byword among the nations.
Why should they say among the peoples,
'Where is their God?' "

The LORD's Answer

18Then the LORD will be jealous for his land
and take pity on his people.

19The LORD will reply[a] to them:

"I am sending you grain, new wine and oil,
enough to satisfy you fully;
never again will I make you
an object of scorn to the nations.

20"I will drive the northern army far from you,
pushing it into a parched and barren land,
with its front columns going into the eastern sea[b]
and those in the rear into the western sea.[c]
And its stench will go up;
its smell will rise."

Surely he has done great things.[d]
21 Be not afraid, O land;
be glad and rejoice.
Surely the LORD has done great things.
22 Be not afraid, O wild animals,
for the open pastures are becoming green.
The trees are bearing their fruit;
the fig tree and the vine yield their riches.
23Be glad, O people of Zion,
rejoice in the LORD your God,
for he has given you
the autumn rains in righteousness.[e]
He sends you abundant showers,
both autumn and spring rains, as before.
24The threshing floors will be filled with grain;
the vats will overflow with new wine and oil.

25"I will repay you for the years the locusts have eaten—
the great locust and the young locust,
the other locusts and the locust swarm[f]—
my great army that I sent among you.
26You will have plenty to eat, until you are full,
and you will praise the name of the LORD your God,

[a] 18,19 Or *LORD was jealous . . . / and took pity . . . / 19The LORD replied* [b] 20 That is, the Dead Sea [c] 20 That is, the Mediterranean [d] 20 Or *rise. / Surely it has done great things."* [e] 23 Or / *the teacher for righteousness:* [f] 25 The precise meaning of the four Hebrew words used here for locusts is uncertain.

who has worked wonders for you;
never again will my people be shamed.
27Then you will know that I am in Israel,
that I am the LORD your God,
and that there is no other;
never again will my people be shamed.

The Day of the LORD

28"And afterward,
I will pour out my Spirit on all people.
Your sons and daughters will prophesy,
your old men will dream dreams,
your young men will see visions.
29Even on my servants, both men and women,
I will pour out my Spirit in those days.
30I will show wonders in the heavens
and on the earth,
blood and fire and billows of smoke.
31The sun will be turned to darkness
and the moon to blood
before the coming of the great and dreadful day of the LORD.
32And everyone who calls
on the name of the LORD will be saved;
for on Mount Zion and in Jerusalem
there will be deliverance,
as the LORD has said,
among the survivors
whom the LORD calls.

The Nations Judged

3 "In those days and at that time,
when I restore the fortunes of Judah and Jerusalem,
2I will gather all nations
and bring them down to the Valley of Jehoshaphat.[a]
There I will enter into judgment against them
concerning my inheritance, my people Israel,
for they scattered my people among the nations
and divided up my land.
3They cast lots for my people
and traded boys for prostitutes;
they sold girls for wine
that they might drink.

4"Now what have you against me, O Tyre
and Sidon and all you regions of Philistia? Are
you repaying me for something I have done? If
you are paying me back, I will swiftly and
speedily return on your own heads what you
have done. 5For you took my silver and my
gold and carried off my finest treasures to your
temples. 6You sold the people of Judah and
Jerusalem to the Greeks, that you might send
them far from their homeland.

7"See, I am going to rouse them out of the
places to which you sold them, and I will return on your own heads what you have done.
8I will sell your sons and daughters to the people of Judah, and they will sell them to the
Sabeans, a nation far away." The LORD has
spoken.

9Proclaim this among the nations:
Prepare for war!
Rouse the warriors!
Let all the fighting men draw near and attack.
10Beat your plowshares into swords
and your pruning hooks into spears.
Let the weakling say,
"I am strong!"
11Come quickly, all you nations from every side,
and assemble there.

Bring down your warriors, O LORD!

12"Let the nations be roused;
let them advance into the Valley of Jehoshaphat,
for there I will sit
to judge all the nations on every side.
13Swing the sickle,
for the harvest is ripe.
Come, trample the grapes,
for the winepress is full
and the vats overflow—
so great is their wickedness!"

14Multitudes, multitudes
in the valley of decision!
For the day of the LORD is near
in the valley of decision.
15The sun and moon will be darkened,
and the stars no longer shine.
16The LORD will roar from Zion
and thunder from Jerusalem;
the earth and the sky will tremble.
But the LORD will be a refuge for his people,
a stronghold for the people of Israel.

Blessings for God's People

17"Then you will know that I, the LORD your God,
dwell in Zion, my holy hill.
Jerusalem will be holy;
never again will foreigners invade her.

18"In that day the mountains will drip new wine,
and the hills will flow with milk;
all the ravines of Judah will run with water.
A fountain will flow out of the LORD's house
and will water the valley of acacias.[b]
19But Egypt will be desolate,
Edom a desert waste,
because of violence done to the people of Judah,
in whose land they shed innocent blood.
20Judah will be inhabited forever
and Jerusalem through all generations.
21Their bloodguilt, which I have not pardoned,
I will pardon."

The LORD dwells in Zion!

[a] 2 *Jehoshaphat* means *the LORD judges*; also in verse 12.
[b] 18 Or *Valley of Shittim*

Amos

1 The words of Amos, one of the shepherds of Tekoa—what he saw concerning Israel two years before the earthquake, when Uzziah was king of Judah and Jeroboam son of Jehoash[a] was king of Israel.
2He said:

"The LORD roars from Zion
and thunders from Jerusalem;
the pastures of the shepherds dry up,[b]
and the top of Carmel withers."

Judgment on Israel's Neighbors

3This is what the LORD says:

"For three sins of Damascus,
even for four, I will not turn back ⌊my wrath⌋.
Because she threshed Gilead
with sledges having iron teeth,
4I will send fire upon the house of Hazael
that will consume the fortresses of Ben-Hadad.
5I will break down the gate of Damascus;
I will destroy the king who is in[c] the Valley of Aven[d]
and the one who holds the scepter in Beth Eden.
The people of Aram will go into exile to Kir,"
says the LORD.

6This is what the LORD says:

"For three sins of Gaza,
even for four, I will not turn back ⌊my wrath⌋.
Because she took captive whole communities
and sold them to Edom,
7I will send fire upon the walls of Gaza
that will consume her fortresses.
8I will destroy the king[e] of Ashdod
and the one who holds the scepter in Ashkelon.
I will turn my hand against Ekron,
till the last of the Philistines is dead,"
says the Sovereign LORD.

9This is what the LORD says:

"For three sins of Tyre,
even for four, I will not turn back ⌊my wrath⌋.
Because she sold whole communities of captives to Edom,
disregarding a treaty of brotherhood,
10I will send fire upon the walls of Tyre
that will consume her fortresses."

11This is what the LORD says:

"For three sins of Edom,
even for four, I will not turn back ⌊my wrath⌋.
Because he pursued his brother with a sword,
stifling all compassion,[f]
because his anger raged continually
and his fury flamed unchecked,
12I will send fire upon Teman
that will consume the fortresses of Bozrah."

13This is what the LORD says:

"For three sins of Ammon,
even for four, I will not turn back ⌊my wrath⌋.
Because he ripped open the pregnant women of Gilead
in order to extend his borders,
14I will set fire to the walls of Rabbah
that will consume her fortresses
amid war cries on the day of battle,
amid violent winds on a stormy day.
15Her king[g] will go into exile,
he and his officials together,"
says the LORD.

2 This is what the LORD says:

"For three sins of Moab,
even for four, I will not turn back ⌊my wrath⌋.
Because he burned, as if to lime,
the bones of Edom's king,
2I will send fire upon Moab
that will consume the fortresses of Kerioth.[h]
Moab will go down in great tumult
amid war cries and the blast of the trumpet.
3I will destroy her ruler
and kill all her officials with him,"
says the LORD.

4This is what the LORD says:

"For three sins of Judah,
even for four, I will not turn back ⌊my wrath⌋.
Because they have rejected the law of the LORD

[a] 1 Hebrew *Joash,* a variant of *Jehoash* [b] 2 Or *shepherds mourn* [c] 5 Or *the inhabitants of* [d] 5 *Aven* means *wickedness.* [e] 8 Or *inhabitants* [f] 11 Or *sword / and destroyed his allies* [g] 15 Or / *Molech*; Hebrew *malcam* [h] 2 Or *of her cities*

and have not kept his decrees,
because they have been led astray by false gods,[a]
the gods[b] their ancestors followed,
5I will send fire upon Judah
that will consume the fortresses of Jerusalem."

Judgment on Israel

6This is what the LORD says:

"For three sins of Israel,
even for four, I will not turn back ⌊my wrath⌋.
They sell the righteous for silver,
and the needy for a pair of sandals.
7They trample on the heads of the poor
as upon the dust of the ground
and deny justice to the oppressed.
Father and son use the same girl
and so profane my holy name.
8They lie down beside every altar
on garments taken in pledge.
In the house of their god
they drink wine taken as fines.

9"I destroyed the Amorite before them,
though he was tall as the cedars
and strong as the oaks.
I destroyed his fruit above
and his roots below.

10"I brought you up out of Egypt,
and I led you forty years in the desert
to give you the land of the Amorites.
11I also raised up prophets from among your sons
and Nazirites from among your young men.
Is this not true, people of Israel?"
declares the LORD.
12"But you made the Nazirites drink wine
and commanded the prophets not to prophesy.

13"Now then, I will crush you
as a cart crushes when loaded with grain.
14The swift will not escape,
the strong will not muster their strength,
and the warrior will not save his life.
15The archer will not stand his ground,
the fleet-footed soldier will not get away,
and the horseman will not save his life.
16Even the bravest warriors
will flee naked on that day,"
declares the LORD.

Witnesses Summoned Against Israel

3 Hear this word the LORD has spoken
against you, O people of Israel—against
the whole family I brought up out of Egypt:

2"You only have I chosen
of all the families of the earth;
therefore I will punish you
for all your sins."

3Do two walk together
unless they have agreed to do so?
4Does a lion roar in the thicket
when he has no prey?
Does he growl in his den
when he has caught nothing?
5Does a bird fall into a trap on the ground
where no snare has been set?
Does a trap spring up from the earth
when there is nothing to catch?
6When a trumpet sounds in a city,
do not the people tremble?
When disaster comes to a city,
has not the LORD caused it?

7Surely the Sovereign LORD does nothing
without revealing his plan
to his servants the prophets.

8The lion has roared—
who will not fear?
The Sovereign LORD has spoken—
who can but prophesy?

9Proclaim to the fortresses of Ashdod
and to the fortresses of Egypt:
"Assemble yourselves on the mountains of Samaria;
see the great unrest within her
and the oppression among her people."

10"They do not know how to do right,"
declares the LORD,
"who hoard plunder and loot in their fortresses."

11Therefore this is what the Sovereign LORD
says:

"An enemy will overrun the land;
he will pull down your strongholds
and plunder your fortresses."

12This is what the LORD says:

"As a shepherd saves from the lion's mouth
only two leg bones or a piece of an ear,
so will the Israelites be saved,
those who sit in Samaria
on the edge of their beds
and in Damascus on their couches.[c]"

13"Hear this and testify against the house of
Jacob," declares the Lord, the LORD God Almighty.

14"On the day I punish Israel for her sins,
I will destroy the altars of Bethel;
the horns of the altar will be cut off
and fall to the ground.
15I will tear down the winter house
along with the summer house;
the houses adorned with ivory will be destroyed

[a]4 Or *by lies* [b]4 Or *lies* [c]12 The meaning of the Hebrew for this line is uncertain.

and the mansions will be demolished,"
declares the LORD.

Israel Has Not Returned to God

4 Hear this word, you cows of Bashan on
Mount Samaria,
you women who oppress the poor and
crush the needy
and say to your husbands, "Bring us
some drinks!"
2The Sovereign LORD has sworn by his
holiness:
"The time will surely come
when you will be taken away with hooks,
the last of you with fishhooks.
3You will each go straight out
through breaks in the wall,
and you will be cast out toward
Harmon,[a]"
declares the LORD.
4"Go to Bethel and sin;
go to Gilgal and sin yet more.
Bring your sacrifices every morning,
your tithes every three years.[b]
5Burn leavened bread as a thank offering
and brag about your freewill
offerings—
boast about them, you Israelites,
for this is what you love to do,"
declares the Sovereign LORD.

6"I gave you empty stomachs[c] in every
city
and lack of bread in every town,
yet you have not returned to me,"
declares the LORD.

7"I also withheld rain from you
when the harvest was still three months
away.
I sent rain on one town,
but withheld it from another.
One field had rain;
another had none and dried up.
8People staggered from town to town for
water
but did not get enough to drink,
yet you have not returned to me,"
declares the LORD.

9"Many times I struck your gardens and
vineyards,
I struck them with blight and mildew.
Locusts devoured your fig and olive trees,
yet you have not returned to me,"
declares the LORD.

10"I sent plagues among you
as I did to Egypt.
I killed your young men with the sword,
along with your captured horses.
I filled your nostrils with the stench of
your camps,
yet you have not returned to me,"
declares the LORD.

11"I overthrew some of you
as I[d] overthrew Sodom and Gomorrah.
You were like a burning stick snatched
from the fire,
yet you have not returned to me,"
declares the LORD.

12"Therefore this is what I will do to you,
Israel,
and because I will do this to you,
prepare to meet your God, O Israel."

13He who forms the mountains,
creates the wind,
and reveals his thoughts to man,
he who turns dawn to darkness,
and treads the high places of the
earth—
the LORD God Almighty is his name.

A Lament and Call to Repentance

5 Hear this word, O house of Israel, this lament I take up concerning you:

2"Fallen is Virgin Israel,
never to rise again,
deserted in her own land,
with no one to lift her up."

3This is what the Sovereign LORD says:

"The city that marches out a thousand
strong for Israel
will have only a hundred left;
the town that marches out a hundred
strong
will have only ten left."

4This is what the LORD says to the house of
Israel:

"Seek me and live;
5 do not seek Bethel,
do not go to Gilgal,
do not journey to Beersheba.
For Gilgal will surely go into exile,
and Bethel will be reduced to
nothing.[e]"
6Seek the LORD and live,
or he will sweep through the house of
Joseph like a fire;
it will devour,
and Bethel will have no one to quench
it.

7You who turn justice into bitterness
and cast righteousness to the ground
8(he who made the Pleiades and Orion,
who turns blackness into dawn
and darkens day into night,
who calls for the waters of the sea
and pours them out over the face of the
land—
the LORD is his name—
9he flashes destruction on the stronghold
and brings the fortified city to ruin),

[a]3 Masoretic Text; with a different word division of the Hebrew (see Septuagint) *out, O mountain of oppression* [b]4 Or *tithes on the third day* [c]6 Hebrew *you cleanness of teeth* [d]11 Hebrew *God*
[e]5 Or *grief*; or *wickedness*; Hebrew *aven*, a reference to Beth Aven (a derogatory name for Bethel)

10you hate the one who reproves in court
and despise him who tells the truth.

11You trample on the poor
and force him to give you grain.
Therefore, though you have built stone mansions,
you will not live in them;
though you have planted lush vineyards,
you will not drink their wine.
12For I know how many are your offenses
and how great your sins.

You oppress the righteous and take bribes
and you deprive the poor of justice in the courts.
13Therefore the prudent man keeps quiet in such times,
for the times are evil.

14Seek good, not evil,
that you may live.
Then the LORD God Almighty will be with you,
just as you say he is.
15Hate evil, love good;
maintain justice in the courts.
Perhaps the LORD God Almighty will have mercy
on the remnant of Joseph.

16Therefore this is what the Lord, the LORD
God Almighty, says:

"There will be wailing in all the streets
and cries of anguish in every public square.
The farmers will be summoned to weep
and the mourners to wail.
17There will be wailing in all the vineyards,
for I will pass through your midst,"
says the LORD.

The Day of the LORD

18Woe to you who long
for the day of the LORD!
Why do you long for the day of the LORD?
That day will be darkness, not light.
19It will be as though a man fled from a lion
only to meet a bear,
as though he entered his house
and rested his hand on the wall
only to have a snake bite him.
20Will not the day of the LORD be darkness, not light—
pitch-dark, without a ray of brightness?

21"I hate, I despise your religious feasts;
I cannot stand your assemblies.
22Even though you bring me burnt offerings
and grain offerings,
I will not accept them.
Though you bring choice fellowship offerings,[a]
I will have no regard for them.
23Away with the noise of your songs!
I will not listen to the music of your harps.
24But let justice roll on like a river,
righteousness like a never-failing stream!

25"Did you bring me sacrifices and offerings
forty years in the desert, O house of Israel?
26You have lifted up the shrine of your king,
the pedestal of your idols,
the star of your god[b]—
which you made for yourselves.
27Therefore I will send you into exile
beyond Damascus,"
says the LORD, whose name is God Almighty.

Woe to the Complacent

6 Woe to you who are complacent in Zion,
and to you who feel secure on Mount Samaria,
you notable men of the foremost nation,
to whom the people of Israel come!
2Go to Calneh and look at it;
go from there to great Hamath,
and then go down to Gath in Philistia.
Are they better off than your two kingdoms?
Is their land larger than yours?
3You put off the evil day
and bring near a reign of terror.
4You lie on beds inlaid with ivory
and lounge on your couches.
You dine on choice lambs
and fattened calves.
5You strum away on your harps like David
and improvise on musical instruments.
6You drink wine by the bowlful
and use the finest lotions,
but you do not grieve over the ruin of Joseph.
7Therefore you will be among the first to go into exile;
your feasting and lounging will end.

The LORD Abhors the Pride of Israel

8The Sovereign LORD has sworn by himself—the LORD God Almighty declares:

"I abhor the pride of Jacob
and detest his fortresses;
I will deliver up the city
and everything in it."

9If ten men are left in one house, they too
will die. 10And if a relative who is to burn the
bodies comes to carry them out of the house
and asks anyone still hiding there, "Is anyone
with you?" and he says, "No," then he will say,
"Hush! We must not mention the name of the
LORD."

11For the LORD has given the command,

[a]22 Traditionally *peace offerings* [b]26 Or *lifted up Sakkuth your king / and Kaiwan your idols, / your star-gods*; Septuagint *lifted up the shrine of Molech / and the star of your god Rephan, / their idols*

and he will smash the great house into pieces
and the small house into bits.

12Do horses run on the rocky crags?
Does one plow there with oxen?
But you have turned justice into poison
and the fruit of righteousness into bitterness—
13you who rejoice in the conquest of Lo Debar[a]
and say, "Did we not take Karnaim[b] by our own strength?"

14For the LORD God Almighty declares,
"I will stir up a nation against you,
O house of Israel,
that will oppress you all the way
from Lebo[c] Hamath to the valley of the Arabah."

Locusts, Fire and a Plumb Line

7 This is what the Sovereign LORD showed
me: He was preparing swarms of locusts
after the king's share had been harvested and
just as the second crop was coming up. 2When
they had stripped the land clean, I cried out,
"Sovereign LORD, forgive! How can Jacob survive? He is so small!"
3So the LORD relented.
"This will not happen," the LORD said.
4This is what the Sovereign LORD showed
me: The Sovereign LORD was calling for judgment by fire; it dried up the great deep and
devoured the land. 5Then I cried out, "Sovereign LORD, I beg you, stop! How can Jacob
survive? He is so small!"
6So the LORD relented.
"This will not happen either," the Sovereign
LORD said.

7This is what he showed me: The Lord was
standing by a wall that had been built true to
plumb, with a plumb line in his hand. 8And the
LORD asked me, "What do you see, Amos?"
"A plumb line," I replied.
Then the Lord said, "Look, I am setting a
plumb line among my people Israel; I will
spare them no longer.

9"The high places of Isaac will be destroyed
and the sanctuaries of Israel will be ruined;
with my sword I will rise against the house of Jeroboam."

Amos and Amaziah

10Then Amaziah the priest of Bethel sent a
message to Jeroboam king of Israel: "Amos is
raising a conspiracy against you in the very
heart of Israel. The land cannot bear all his
words. 11For this is what Amos is saying:

" 'Jeroboam will die by the sword,
and Israel will surely go into exile,
away from their native land.' "

12Then Amaziah said to Amos, "Get out,
you seer! Go back to the land of Judah. Earn
your bread there and do your prophesying
there. 13Don't prophesy anymore at Bethel, because this is the king's sanctuary and the temple of the kingdom."
14Amos answered Amaziah, "I was neither a
prophet nor a prophet's son, but I was a shepherd, and I also took care of sycamore-fig
trees. 15But the LORD took me from tending
the flock and said to me, 'Go, prophesy to my
people Israel.' 16Now then, hear the word of
the LORD. You say,

" 'Do not prophesy against Israel,
and stop preaching against the house of Isaac.'

17"Therefore this is what the LORD says:

" 'Your wife will become a prostitute in the city,
and your sons and daughters will fall by the sword.
Your land will be measured and divided up,
and you yourself will die in a pagan[d] country.
And Israel will certainly go into exile,
away from their native land.' "

A Basket of Ripe Fruit

8 This is what the Sovereign LORD showed
me: a basket of ripe fruit. 2"What do you
see, Amos?" he asked.
"A basket of ripe fruit," I answered.
Then the LORD said to me, "The time is ripe
for my people Israel; I will spare them no
longer.
3"In that day," declares the Sovereign LORD,
"the songs in the temple will turn to wailing.[e]
Many, many bodies—flung everywhere! Silence!"

4Hear this, you who trample the needy
and do away with the poor of the land,

5saying,

"When will the New Moon be over
that we may sell grain,
and the Sabbath be ended
that we may market wheat?"—
skimping the measure,
boosting the price
and cheating with dishonest scales,
6buying the poor with silver
and the needy for a pair of sandals,
selling even the sweepings with the wheat.

7The LORD has sworn by the Pride of Jacob:
"I will never forget anything they have done.

8"Will not the land tremble for this,
and all who live in it mourn?
The whole land will rise like the Nile;

[a] *13 Lo Debar* means *nothing.* [b] *13 Karnaim* means *horns*; *horn* here symbolizes strength. [c] *14* Or *from the entrance to* [d] *17* Hebrew *an unclean* [e] *3* Or *"the temple singers will wail*

it will be stirred up and then sink
like the river of Egypt.

9"In that day," declares the Sovereign LORD,

"I will make the sun go down at noon
and darken the earth in broad daylight.
10I will turn your religious feasts into mourning
and all your singing into weeping.
I will make all of you wear sackcloth
and shave your heads.
I will make that time like mourning for an only son
and the end of it like a bitter day.

11"The days are coming," declares the Sovereign LORD,
"when I will send a famine through the land—
not a famine of food or a thirst for water,
but a famine of hearing the words of the LORD.
12Men will stagger from sea to sea
and wander from north to east,
searching for the word of the LORD,
but they will not find it.

13"In that day

"the lovely young women and strong young men
will faint because of thirst.
14They who swear by the shame[a] of Samaria,
or say, 'As surely as your god lives, O Dan,'
or, 'As surely as the god[b] of Beersheba lives'—
they will fall,
never to rise again."

Israel to Be Destroyed

9 I saw the Lord standing by the altar, and he said:

"Strike the tops of the pillars
so that the thresholds shake.
Bring them down on the heads of all the people;
those who are left I will kill with the sword.
Not one will get away,
none will escape.
2Though they dig down to the depths of the grave,[c]
from there my hand will take them.
Though they climb up to the heavens,
from there I will bring them down.
3Though they hide themselves on the top of Carmel,
there I will hunt them down and seize them.
Though they hide from me at the bottom of the sea,
there I will command the serpent to bite them.
4Though they are driven into exile by their enemies,
there I will command the sword to slay them.
I will fix my eyes upon them
for evil and not for good."

5The Lord, the LORD Almighty,
he who touches the earth and it melts,
and all who live in it mourn—
the whole land rises like the Nile,
then sinks like the river of Egypt—
6he who builds his lofty palace[d] in the heavens
and sets its foundation[e] on the earth,
who calls for the waters of the sea
and pours them out over the face of the land—
the LORD is his name.

7"Are not you Israelites
the same to me as the Cushites[f]?"
declares the LORD.
"Did I not bring Israel up from Egypt,
the Philistines from Caphtor[g]
and the Arameans from Kir?

8"Surely the eyes of the Sovereign LORD
are on the sinful kingdom.
I will destroy it
from the face of the earth—
yet I will not totally destroy
the house of Jacob,"
declares the LORD.
9"For I will give the command,
and I will shake the house of Israel
among all the nations
as grain is shaken in a sieve,
and not a pebble will reach the ground.
10All the sinners among my people
will die by the sword,
all those who say,
'Disaster will not overtake or meet us.'

Israel's Restoration

11"In that day I will restore
David's fallen tent.
I will repair its broken places,
restore its ruins,
and build it as it used to be,
12so that they may possess the remnant of Edom
and all the nations that bear my name,[h]"
declares the LORD,
who will do these things.

13"The days are coming," declares the LORD,

[a] 14 Or *by Ashima*; or *by the idol* [b] 14 Or *power* [c] 2 Hebrew *to Sheol* [d] 6 The meaning of the Hebrew for this phrase is uncertain. [e] 6 The meaning of the Hebrew for this word is uncertain. [f] 7 That is, people from the upper Nile region [g] 7 That is, Crete [h] 12 Hebrew; Septuagint *so that the remnant of men / and all the nations that bear my name may seek ⌊the Lord⌋*

"when the reaper will be overtaken by the
plowman
and the planter by the one treading
grapes.
New wine will drip from the mountains
and flow from all the hills.
14I will bring back my exiled[a] people Israel;
they will rebuild the ruined cities and
live in them.
They will plant vineyards and drink their
wine;
they will make gardens and eat their
fruit.
15I will plant Israel in their own land,
never again to be uprooted
from the land I have given them,"

says the LORD your God.

Obadiah

1The vision of Obadiah.

This is what the Sovereign LORD says about Edom—

We have heard a message from the LORD:
An envoy was sent to the nations to
say,
"Rise, and let us go against her for
battle"—

2"See, I will make you small among the
nations;
you will be utterly despised.
3The pride of your heart has deceived you,
you who live in the clefts of the rocks[b]
and make your home on the heights,
you who say to yourself,
'Who can bring me down to the
ground?'
4Though you soar like the eagle
and make your nest among the stars,
from there I will bring you down,"
declares the LORD.
5"If thieves came to you,
if robbers in the night—
Oh, what a disaster awaits you—
would they not steal only as much as
they wanted?
If grape pickers came to you,
would they not leave a few grapes?
6But how Esau will be ransacked,
his hidden treasures pillaged!
7All your allies will force you to the
border;
your friends will deceive and overpower
you;
those who eat your bread will set a trap
for you,[c]
but you will not detect it.

8"In that day," declares the LORD,
"will I not destroy the wise men of
Edom,
men of understanding in the mountains
of Esau?
9Your warriors, O Teman, will be terrified,
and everyone in Esau's mountains
will be cut down in the slaughter.
10Because of the violence against your
brother Jacob,
you will be covered with shame;
you will be destroyed forever.
11On the day you stood aloof
while strangers carried off his wealth
and foreigners entered his gates
and cast lots for Jerusalem,
you were like one of them.
12You should not look down on your
brother
in the day of his misfortune,
nor rejoice over the people of Judah
in the day of their destruction,
nor boast so much
in the day of their trouble.
13You should not march through the gates
of my people
in the day of their disaster,
nor look down on them in their calamity
in the day of their disaster,
nor seize their wealth
in the day of their disaster.
14You should not wait at the crossroads
to cut down their fugitives,
nor hand over their survivors
in the day of their trouble.

15"The day of the LORD is near
for all nations.
As you have done, it will be done to you;
your deeds will return upon your own
head.
16Just as you drank on my holy hill,
so all the nations will drink continually;
they will drink and drink
and be as if they had never been.
17But on Mount Zion will be deliverance;
it will be holy,
and the house of Jacob
will possess its inheritance.
18The house of Jacob will be a fire
and the house of Joseph a flame;
the house of Esau will be stubble,
and they will set it on fire and consume
it.

[a]14 Or *will restore the fortunes of my* [b]3 Or *of Sela* [c]7 The meaning of the Hebrew for this clause is uncertain.

There will be no survivors
from the house of Esau."
The LORD has spoken.

19People from the Negev will occupy
the mountains of Esau,
and people from the foothills will possess
the land of the Philistines.
They will occupy the fields of Ephraim
and Samaria,
and Benjamin will possess Gilead.

20This company of Israelite exiles who are
in Canaan
will possess ⌊the land⌋ as far as
Zarephath;
the exiles from Jerusalem who are in
Sepharad
will possess the towns of the Negev.
21Deliverers will go up on[a] Mount Zion
to govern the mountains of Esau.
And the kingdom will be the LORD's.

Jonah

Jonah Flees From the LORD

1 The word of the LORD came to Jonah son
of Amittai: 2"Go to the great city of Nineveh and preach against it, because its wickedness has come up before me."
3But Jonah ran away from the LORD and
headed for Tarshish. He went down to Joppa,
where he found a ship bound for that port.
After paying the fare, he went aboard and
sailed for Tarshish to flee from the LORD.
4Then the LORD sent a great wind on the sea,
and such a violent storm arose that the ship
threatened to break up. 5All the sailors were
afraid and each cried out to his own god. And
they threw the cargo into the sea to lighten the
ship.
But Jonah had gone below deck, where he
lay down and fell into a deep sleep. 6The captain went to him and said, "How can you
sleep? Get up and call on your god! Maybe he
will take notice of us, and we will not perish."
7Then the sailors said to each other, "Come,
let us cast lots to find out who is responsible
for this calamity." They cast lots and the lot
fell on Jonah.
8So they asked him, "Tell us, who is responsible for making all this trouble for us? What
do you do? Where do you come from? What is
your country? From what people are you?"
9He answered, "I am a Hebrew and I worship the LORD, the God of heaven, who made
the sea and the land."
10This terrified them and they asked, "What
have you done?" (They knew he was running
away from the LORD, because he had already
told them so.)
11The sea was getting rougher and rougher.
So they asked him, "What should we do to you
to make the sea calm down for us?"
12"Pick me up and throw me into the sea,"
he replied, "and it will become calm. I know
that it is my fault that this great storm has
come upon you."
13Instead, the men did their best to row back
to land. But they could not, for the sea grew
even wilder than before. 14Then they cried to
the LORD, "O LORD, please do not let us die
for taking this man's life. Do not hold us accountable for killing an innocent man, for you,
O LORD, have done as you pleased." 15Then
they took Jonah and threw him overboard, and
the raging sea grew calm. 16At this the men
greatly feared the LORD, and they offered a
sacrifice to the LORD and made vows to him.
17But the LORD provided a great fish to
swallow Jonah, and Jonah was inside the fish
three days and three nights.

Jonah's Prayer

2 From inside the fish Jonah prayed to the
LORD his God. 2He said:

"In my distress I called to the LORD,
and he answered me.
From the depths of the grave[b] I called for
help,
and you listened to my cry.
3You hurled me into the deep,
into the very heart of the seas,
and the currents swirled about me;
all your waves and breakers
swept over me.
4I said, 'I have been banished
from your sight;
yet I will look again
toward your holy temple.'
5The engulfing waters threatened me,[c]
the deep surrounded me;
seaweed was wrapped around my head.
6To the roots of the mountains I sank
down;
the earth beneath barred me in forever.
But you brought my life up from the pit,
O LORD my God.

7"When my life was ebbing away,
I remembered you, LORD,
and my prayer rose to you,
to your holy temple.

8"Those who cling to worthless idols
forfeit the grace that could be theirs.
9But I, with a song of thanksgiving,

[a]21 Or *from* [b]2 Hebrew *Sheol* [c]5 Or *waters were at my throat*

will sacrifice to you.
What I have vowed I will make good.
Salvation comes from the LORD."

10And the LORD commanded the fish, and it vomited Jonah onto dry land.

Jonah Goes to Nineveh

3 Then the word of the LORD came to Jonah a second time: 2"Go to the great city of Nineveh and proclaim to it the message I give you."

3Jonah obeyed the word of the LORD and went to Nineveh. Now Nineveh was a very important city—a visit required three days. 4On the first day, Jonah started into the city. He proclaimed: "Forty more days and Nineveh will be overturned." 5The Ninevites believed God. They declared a fast, and all of them, from the greatest to the least, put on sackcloth.

6When the news reached the king of Nineveh, he rose from his throne, took off his royal robes, covered himself with sackcloth and sat down in the dust. 7Then he issued a proclamation in Nineveh:

"By the decree of the king and his nobles:

Do not let any man or beast, herd or flock, taste anything; do not let them eat or drink. 8But let man and beast be covered with sackcloth. Let everyone call urgently on God. Let them give up their evil ways and their violence. 9Who knows? God may yet relent and with compassion turn from his fierce anger so that we will not perish."

10When God saw what they did and how they turned from their evil ways, he had compassion and did not bring upon them the destruction he had threatened.

Jonah's Anger at the LORD's Compassion

4 But Jonah was greatly displeased and became angry. 2He prayed to the LORD, "O LORD, is this not what I said when I was still at home? That is why I was so quick to flee to Tarshish. I knew that you are a gracious and compassionate God, slow to anger and abounding in love, a God who relents from sending calamity. 3Now, O LORD, take away my life, for it is better for me to die than to live."

4But the LORD replied, "Have you any right to be angry?"

5Jonah went out and sat down at a place east of the city. There he made himself a shelter, sat in its shade and waited to see what would happen to the city. 6Then the LORD God provided a vine and made it grow up over Jonah to give shade for his head to ease his discomfort, and Jonah was very happy about the vine. 7But at dawn the next day God provided a worm, which chewed the vine so that it withered. 8When the sun rose, God provided a scorching east wind, and the sun blazed on Jonah's head so that he grew faint. He wanted to die, and said, "It would be better for me to die than to live."

9But God said to Jonah, "Do you have a right to be angry about the vine?"

"I do," he said. "I am angry enough to die."

10But the LORD said, "You have been concerned about this vine, though you did not tend it or make it grow. It sprang up overnight and died overnight. 11But Nineveh has more than a hundred and twenty thousand people who cannot tell their right hand from their left, and many cattle as well. Should I not be concerned about that great city?"

Micah

1 The word of the LORD that came to Micah of Moresheth during the reigns of Jotham, Ahaz and Hezekiah, kings of Judah—the vision he saw concerning Samaria and Jerusalem.

2Hear, O peoples, all of you,
listen, O earth and all who are in it,
that the Sovereign LORD may witness against you,
the Lord from his holy temple.

Judgment Against Samaria and Jerusalem

3Look! The LORD is coming from his dwelling place;
he comes down and treads the high places of the earth.
4The mountains melt beneath him
and the valleys split apart,
like wax before the fire,
like water rushing down a slope.
5All this is because of Jacob's transgression,
because of the sins of the house of Israel.
What is Jacob's transgression?
Is it not Samaria?
What is Judah's high place?
Is it not Jerusalem?

6"Therefore I will make Samaria a heap of rubble,
a place for planting vineyards.
I will pour her stones into the valley
and lay bare her foundations.
7All her idols will be broken to pieces;
all her temple gifts will be burned with fire;

I will destroy all her images.
Since she gathered her gifts from the wages of prostitutes,
as the wages of prostitutes they will again be used."

Weeping and Mourning

8Because of this I will weep and wail;
I will go about barefoot and naked.
I will howl like a jackal
and moan like an owl.
9For her wound is incurable;
it has come to Judah.
It[a] has reached the very gate of my people,
even to Jerusalem itself.
10Tell it not in Gath[b];
weep not at all.[c]
In Beth Ophrah[d]
roll in the dust.
11Pass on in nakedness and shame,
you who live in Shaphir.[e]
Those who live in Zaanan[f]
will not come out.
Beth Ezel is in mourning;
its protection is taken from you.
12Those who live in Maroth[g] writhe in pain,
waiting for relief,
because disaster has come from the LORD,
even to the gate of Jerusalem.
13You who live in Lachish,[h]
harness the team to the chariot.
You were the beginning of sin
to the Daughter of Zion,
for the transgressions of Israel
were found in you.
14Therefore you will give parting gifts
to Moresheth Gath.
The town of Aczib[i] will prove deceptive
to the kings of Israel.
15I will bring a conqueror against you
who live in Mareshah.[j]
He who is the glory of Israel
will come to Adullam.
16Shave your heads in mourning
for the children in whom you delight;
make yourselves as bald as the vulture,
for they will go from you into exile.

Man's Plans and God's

2 Woe to those who plan iniquity,
to those who plot evil on their beds!
At morning's light they carry it out
because it is in their power to do it.
2They covet fields and seize them,
and houses, and take them.
They defraud a man of his home,
a fellowman of his inheritance.

3Therefore, the LORD says:

"I am planning disaster against this people,
from which you cannot save yourselves.
You will no longer walk proudly,
for it will be a time of calamity.
4In that day men will ridicule you;
they will taunt you with this mournful song:
'We are utterly ruined;
my people's possession is divided up.
He takes it from me!
He assigns our fields to traitors.' "

5Therefore you will have no one in the assembly of the LORD
to divide the land by lot.

False Prophets

6"Do not prophesy," their prophets say.
"Do not prophesy about these things;
disgrace will not overtake us."
7Should it be said, O house of Jacob:
"Is the Spirit of the LORD angry?
Does he do such things?"

"Do not my words do good
to him whose ways are upright?
8Lately my people have risen up
like an enemy.
You strip off the rich robe
from those who pass by without a care,
like men returning from battle.
9You drive the women of my people
from their pleasant homes.
You take away my blessing
from their children forever.
10Get up, go away!
For this is not your resting place,
because it is defiled,
it is ruined, beyond all remedy.
11If a liar and deceiver comes and says,
'I will prophesy for you plenty of wine and beer,'
he would be just the prophet for this people!

Deliverance Promised

12"I will surely gather all of you, O Jacob;
I will surely bring together the remnant of Israel.
I will bring them together like sheep in a pen,
like a flock in its pasture;
the place will throng with people.
13One who breaks open the way will go up before them;
they will break through the gate and go out.
Their king will pass through before them,
the LORD at their head."

Leaders and Prophets Rebuked

3 Then I said,

"Listen, you leaders of Jacob,

[a] 9 Or *He* [b] 10 *Gath* sounds like the Hebrew for *tell.* [c] 10 Hebrew; Septuagint may suggest *not in Acco.* The Hebrew for *in Acco* sounds like the Hebrew for *weep.* [d] 10 *Beth Ophrah* means *house of dust.* [e] 11 *Shaphir* means *pleasant.* [f] 11 *Zaanan* sounds like the Hebrew for *come out.* [g] 12 *Maroth* sounds like the Hebrew for *bitter.* [h] 13 *Lachish* sounds like the Hebrew for *team.* [i] 14 *Aczib* means *deception.* [j] 15 *Mareshah* sounds like the Hebrew for *conqueror.*

you rulers of the house of Israel.
Should you not know justice,
2 you who hate good and love evil;
who tear the skin from my people
and the flesh from their bones;
3who eat my people's flesh,
strip off their skin
and break their bones in pieces;
who chop them up like meat for the pan,
like flesh for the pot?"

4Then they will cry out to the LORD,
but he will not answer them.
At that time he will hide his face from them
because of the evil they have done.

5This is what the LORD says:

"As for the prophets
who lead my people astray,
if one feeds them,
they proclaim 'peace';
if he does not,
they prepare to wage war against him.
6Therefore night will come over you,
without visions,
and darkness, without divination.
The sun will set for the prophets,
and the day will go dark for them.
7The seers will be ashamed
and the diviners disgraced.
They will all cover their faces
because there is no answer from God."

8But as for me, I am filled with power,
with the Spirit of the LORD,
and with justice and might,
to declare to Jacob his transgression,
to Israel his sin.
9Hear this, you leaders of the house of Jacob,
you rulers of the house of Israel,
who despise justice
and distort all that is right;
10who build Zion with bloodshed,
and Jerusalem with wickedness.
11Her leaders judge for a bribe,
her priests teach for a price,
and her prophets tell fortunes for money.
Yet they lean upon the LORD and say,
"Is not the LORD among us?
No disaster will come upon us."
12Therefore because of you,
Zion will be plowed like a field,
Jerusalem will become a heap of rubble,
the temple hill a mound overgrown with thickets.

The Mountain of the LORD

4 In the last days

the mountain of the LORD's temple will be established
as chief among the mountains;
it will be raised above the hills,
and peoples will stream to it.

2Many nations will come and say,

"Come, let us go up to the mountain of the LORD,
to the house of the God of Jacob.
He will teach us his ways,
so that we may walk in his paths."
The law will go out from Zion,
the word of the LORD from Jerusalem.
3He will judge between many peoples
and will settle disputes for strong nations far and wide.
They will beat their swords into plowshares
and their spears into pruning hooks.
Nation will not take up sword against nation,
nor will they train for war anymore.
4Every man will sit under his own vine
and under his own fig tree,
and no one will make them afraid,
for the LORD Almighty has spoken.
5All the nations may walk
in the name of their gods;
we will walk in the name of the LORD
our God for ever and ever.

The LORD's Plan

6"In that day," declares the LORD,

"I will gather the lame;
I will assemble the exiles
and those I have brought to grief.
7I will make the lame a remnant,
those driven away a strong nation.
The LORD will rule over them in Mount Zion
from that day and forever.
8As for you, O watchtower of the flock,
O stronghold[a] of the Daughter of Zion,
the former dominion will be restored to you;
kingship will come to the Daughter of Jerusalem."

9Why do you now cry aloud—
have you no king?
Has your counselor perished,
that pain seizes you like that of a woman in labor?
10Writhe in agony, O Daughter of Zion,
like a woman in labor,
for now you must leave the city
to camp in the open field.
You will go to Babylon;
there you will be rescued.
There the LORD will redeem you
out of the hand of your enemies.

11But now many nations
are gathered against you.
They say, "Let her be defiled,
let our eyes gloat over Zion!"
12But they do not know
the thoughts of the LORD;

[a]8 Or *hill*

they do not understand his plan,
he who gathers them like sheaves to the threshing floor.

13"Rise and thresh, O Daughter of Zion,
for I will give you horns of iron;
I will give you hoofs of bronze
and you will break to pieces many nations."

You will devote their ill-gotten gains to the LORD,
their wealth to the Lord of all the earth.

A Promised Ruler From Bethlehem

5 Marshal your troops, O city of troops,[a]
for a siege is laid against us.
They will strike Israel's ruler
on the cheek with a rod.

2"But you, Bethlehem Ephrathah,
though you are small among the clans[b] of Judah,
out of you will come for me
one who will be ruler over Israel,
whose origins[c] are from of old,
from ancient times.[d]"

3Therefore Israel will be abandoned
until the time when she who is in labor gives birth
and the rest of his brothers return
to join the Israelites.

4He will stand and shepherd his flock
in the strength of the LORD,
in the majesty of the name of the LORD his God.
And they will live securely, for then his greatness
will reach to the ends of the earth.
5 And he will be their peace.

Deliverance and Destruction

When the Assyrian invades our land
and marches through our fortresses,
we will raise against him seven shepherds,
even eight leaders of men.
6They will rule[e] the land of Assyria with the sword,
the land of Nimrod with drawn sword.[f]
He will deliver us from the Assyrian
when he invades our land
and marches into our borders.

7The remnant of Jacob will be
in the midst of many peoples
like dew from the LORD,
like showers on the grass,
which do not wait for man
or linger for mankind.
8The remnant of Jacob will be among the nations,
in the midst of many peoples,
like a lion among the beasts of the forest,
like a young lion among flocks of sheep,
which mauls and mangles as it goes,
and no one can rescue.
9Your hand will be lifted up in triumph over your enemies,
and all your foes will be destroyed.

10"In that day," declares the LORD,

"I will destroy your horses from among you
and demolish your chariots.
11I will destroy the cities of your land
and tear down all your strongholds.
12I will destroy your witchcraft
and you will no longer cast spells.
13I will destroy your carved images
and your sacred stones from among you;
you will no longer bow down
to the work of your hands.
14I will uproot from among you your Asherah poles[g]
and demolish your cities.
15I will take vengeance in anger and wrath
upon the nations that have not obeyed me."

The LORD's Case Against Israel

6 Listen to what the LORD says:

"Stand up, plead your case before the mountains;
let the hills hear what you have to say.
2Hear, O mountains, the LORD's accusation;
listen, you everlasting foundations of the earth.
For the LORD has a case against his people;
he is lodging a charge against Israel.

3"My people, what have I done to you?
How have I burdened you? Answer me.
4I brought you up out of Egypt
and redeemed you from the land of slavery.
I sent Moses to lead you,
also Aaron and Miriam.
5My people, remember
what Balak king of Moab counseled
and what Balaam son of Beor answered.
Remember ⌊your journey⌋ from Shittim to Gilgal,
that you may know the righteous acts of the LORD."

6With what shall I come before the LORD
and bow down before the exalted God?
Shall I come before him with burnt offerings,
with calves a year old?
7Will the LORD be pleased with thousands of rams,
with ten thousand rivers of oil?
Shall I offer my firstborn for my transgression,
the fruit of my body for the sin of my soul?

[a]1 Or *Strengthen your walls, O walled city* [b]2 Or *rulers* [c]2 Hebrew *goings out* [d]2 Or *from days of eternity* [e]6 Or *crush* [f]6 Or *Nimrod in its gates* [g]14 That is, symbols of the goddess Asherah

8He has showed you, O man, what is good.
And what does the LORD require of you?
To act justly and to love mercy
and to walk humbly with your God.

Israel's Guilt and Punishment

9Listen! The LORD is calling to the city—
and to fear your name is wisdom—
"Heed the rod and the One who appointed it.[a]
10Am I still to forget, O wicked house,
your ill-gotten treasures
and the short ephah,[b] which is accursed?
11Shall I acquit a man with dishonest scales,
with a bag of false weights?
12Her rich men are violent;
her people are liars
and their tongues speak deceitfully.
13Therefore, I have begun to destroy you,
to ruin you because of your sins.
14You will eat but not be satisfied;
your stomach will still be empty.[c]
You will store up but save nothing,
because what you save I will give to the sword.
15You will plant but not harvest;
you will press olives but not use the oil on yourselves,
you will crush grapes but not drink the wine.
16You have observed the statutes of Omri
and all the practices of Ahab's house,
and you have followed their traditions.
Therefore I will give you over to ruin
and your people to derision;
you will bear the scorn of the nations.[d]"

Israel's Misery

7 What misery is mine!
I am like one who gathers summer fruit
at the gleaning of the vineyard;
there is no cluster of grapes to eat,
none of the early figs that I crave.
2The godly have been swept from the land;
not one upright man remains.
All men lie in wait to shed blood;
each hunts his brother with a net.
3Both hands are skilled in doing evil;
the ruler demands gifts,
the judge accepts bribes,
the powerful dictate what they desire—
they all conspire together.
4The best of them is like a brier,
the most upright worse than a thorn hedge.
The day of your watchmen has come,
the day God visits you.
Now is the time of their confusion.
5Do not trust a neighbor;
put no confidence in a friend.
Even with her who lies in your embrace
be careful of your words.
6For a son dishonors his father,
a daughter rises up against her mother,
a daughter-in-law against her mother-in-law—
a man's enemies are the members of his own household.

7But as for me, I watch in hope for the LORD,
I wait for God my Savior;
my God will hear me.

Israel Will Rise

8Do not gloat over me, my enemy!
Though I have fallen, I will rise.
Though I sit in darkness,
the LORD will be my light.
9Because I have sinned against him,
I will bear the LORD's wrath,
until he pleads my case
and establishes my right.
He will bring me out into the light;
I will see his righteousness.
10Then my enemy will see it
and will be covered with shame,
she who said to me,
"Where is the LORD your God?"
My eyes will see her downfall;
even now she will be trampled underfoot
like mire in the streets.

11The day for building your walls will come,
the day for extending your boundaries.
12In that day people will come to you
from Assyria and the cities of Egypt,
even from Egypt to the Euphrates
and from sea to sea
and from mountain to mountain.
13The earth will become desolate because of its inhabitants,
as the result of their deeds.

Prayer and Praise

14Shepherd your people with your staff,
the flock of your inheritance,
which lives by itself in a forest,
in fertile pasturelands.[e]
Let them feed in Bashan and Gilead
as in days long ago.

15"As in the days when you came out of Egypt,
I will show them my wonders."

16Nations will see and be ashamed,
deprived of all their power.
They will lay their hands on their mouths
and their ears will become deaf.
17They will lick dust like a snake,
like creatures that crawl on the ground.
They will come trembling out of their dens;

[a] *9* The meaning of the Hebrew for this line is uncertain.
[b] *10* An ephah was a dry measure.
[c] *14* The meaning of the Hebrew for this word is uncertain.
[d] *16* Septuagint; Hebrew *scorn due my people*
[e] *14* Or *in the middle of Carmel*

they will turn in fear to the LORD our God
and will be afraid of you.
18Who is a God like you,
who pardons sin and forgives the transgression
of the remnant of his inheritance?
You do not stay angry forever
but delight to show mercy.
19You will again have compassion on us;
you will tread our sins underfoot
and hurl all our iniquities into the depths of the sea.
20You will be true to Jacob,
and show mercy to Abraham,
as you pledged on oath to our fathers
in days long ago.

Nahum

1 An oracle concerning Nineveh. The book
of the vision of Nahum the Elkoshite.

The LORD's Anger Against Nineveh

2The LORD is a jealous and avenging God;
the LORD takes vengeance and is filled with wrath.
The LORD takes vengeance on his foes
and maintains his wrath against his enemies.
3The LORD is slow to anger and great in power;
the LORD will not leave the guilty unpunished.
His way is in the whirlwind and the storm,
and clouds are the dust of his feet.
4He rebukes the sea and dries it up;
he makes all the rivers run dry.
Bashan and Carmel wither
and the blossoms of Lebanon fade.
5The mountains quake before him
and the hills melt away.
The earth trembles at his presence,
the world and all who live in it.
6Who can withstand his indignation?
Who can endure his fierce anger?
His wrath is poured out like fire;
the rocks are shattered before him.

7The LORD is good,
a refuge in times of trouble.
He cares for those who trust in him,
8 but with an overwhelming flood
he will make an end of ⌊Nineveh⌋;
he will pursue his foes into darkness.

9Whatever they plot against the LORD
he[a] will bring to an end;
trouble will not come a second time.
10They will be entangled among thorns
and drunk from their wine;
they will be consumed like dry stubble.[b]
11From you, ⌊O Nineveh,⌋ has one come forth
who plots evil against the LORD
and counsels wickedness.

12This is what the LORD says:

"Although they have allies and are numerous,
they will be cut off and pass away.
Although I have afflicted you, ⌊O Judah,⌋
I will afflict you no more.
13Now I will break their yoke from your neck
and tear your shackles away."

14The LORD has given a command concerning you, ⌊Nineveh⌋:
"You will have no descendants to bear your name.
I will destroy the carved images and cast idols
that are in the temple of your gods.
I will prepare your grave,
for you are vile."

15Look, there on the mountains,
the feet of one who brings good news,
who proclaims peace!
Celebrate your festivals, O Judah,
and fulfill your vows.
No more will the wicked invade you;
they will be completely destroyed.

Nineveh to Fall

2 An attacker advances against you, ⌊Nineveh⌋.
Guard the fortress,
watch the road,
brace yourselves,
marshal all your strength!

2The LORD will restore the splendor of Jacob
like the splendor of Israel,
though destroyers have laid them waste
and have ruined their vines.

3The shields of his soldiers are red;
the warriors are clad in scarlet.
The metal on the chariots flashes
on the day they are made ready;
the spears of pine are brandished.[c]
4The chariots storm through the streets,

[a] 9 Or *What do you foes plot against the LORD? / He* [b] 10 The meaning of the Hebrew for this verse is uncertain. [c] 3 Hebrew; Septuagint and Syriac / *the horsemen rush to and fro*

rushing back and forth through the
squares.
They look like flaming torches;
they dart about like lightning.

5He summons his picked troops,
yet they stumble on their way.
They dash to the city wall;
the protective shield is put in place.
6The river gates are thrown open
and the palace collapses.
7It is decreed[a] that ⌞the city⌟
be exiled and carried away.
Its slave girls moan like doves
and beat upon their breasts.
8Nineveh is like a pool,
and its water is draining away.
"Stop! Stop!" they cry,
but no one turns back.
9Plunder the silver!
Plunder the gold!
The supply is endless,
the wealth from all its treasures!
10She is pillaged, plundered, stripped!
Hearts melt, knees give way,
bodies tremble, every face grows pale.

11Where now is the lions' den,
the place where they fed their young,
where the lion and lioness went,
and the cubs, with nothing to fear?
12The lion killed enough for his cubs
and strangled the prey for his mate,
filling his lairs with the kill
and his dens with the prey.

13"I am against you,"
declares the LORD Almighty.
"I will burn up your chariots in smoke,
and the sword will devour your young
lions.
I will leave you no prey on the earth.
The voices of your messengers
will no longer be heard."

Woe to Nineveh

3 Woe to the city of blood,
full of lies,
full of plunder,
never without victims!
2The crack of whips,
the clatter of wheels,
galloping horses
and jolting chariots!
3Charging cavalry,
flashing swords
and glittering spears!
Many casualties,
piles of dead,
bodies without number,
people stumbling over the corpses—
4all because of the wanton lust of a harlot,
alluring, the mistress of sorceries,
who enslaved nations by her prostitution
and peoples by her witchcraft.

5"I am against you," declares the LORD
Almighty.
"I will lift your skirts over your face.
I will show the nations your nakedness
and the kingdoms your shame.
6I will pelt you with filth,
I will treat you with contempt
and make you a spectacle.
7All who see you will flee from you and
say,
'Nineveh is in ruins—who will mourn
for her?'
Where can I find anyone to comfort
you?"

8Are you better than Thebes,[b]
situated on the Nile,
with water around her?
The river was her defense,
the waters her wall.
9Cush[c] and Egypt were her boundless
strength;
Put and Libya were among her allies.
10Yet she was taken captive
and went into exile.
Her infants were dashed to pieces
at the head of every street.
Lots were cast for her nobles,
and all her great men were put in
chains.
11You too will become drunk;
you will go into hiding
and seek refuge from the enemy.

12All your fortresses are like fig trees
with their first ripe fruit;
when they are shaken,
the figs fall into the mouth of the eater.
13Look at your troops—
they are all women!
The gates of your land
are wide open to your enemies;
fire has consumed their bars.

14Draw water for the siege,
strengthen your defenses!
Work the clay,
tread the mortar,
repair the brickwork!
15There the fire will devour you;
the sword will cut you down
and, like grasshoppers, consume you.
Multiply like grasshoppers,
multiply like locusts!
16You have increased the number of your
merchants
till they are more than the stars of the
sky,
but like locusts they strip the land
and then fly away.
17Your guards are like locusts,
your officials like swarms of locusts
that settle in the walls on a cold day—
but when the sun appears they fly away,
and no one knows where.

[a]7 The meaning of the Hebrew for this word is uncertain. [b]8 Hebrew *No Amon* [c]9 That is, the upper Nile region

18O king of Assyria, your shepherds[a]
slumber;
your nobles lie down to rest.
Your people are scattered on the
mountains
with no one to gather them.
19Nothing can heal your wound;
your injury is fatal.
Everyone who hears the news about you
claps his hands at your fall,
for who has not felt
your endless cruelty?

Habakkuk

1 The oracle that Habakkuk the prophet received.

Habakkuk's Complaint

2How long, O LORD, must I call for help,
but you do not listen?
Or cry out to you, "Violence!"
but you do not save?
3Why do you make me look at injustice?
Why do you tolerate wrong?
Destruction and violence are before me;
there is strife, and conflict abounds.
4Therefore the law is paralyzed,
and justice never prevails.
The wicked hem in the righteous,
so that justice is perverted.

The LORD's Answer

5"Look at the nations and watch—
and be utterly amazed.
For I am going to do something in your
days
that you would not believe,
even if you were told.
6I am raising up the Babylonians,[b]
that ruthless and impetuous people,
who sweep across the whole earth
to seize dwelling places not their own.
7They are a feared and dreaded people;
they are a law to themselves
and promote their own honor.
8Their horses are swifter than leopards,
fiercer than wolves at dusk.
Their cavalry gallops headlong;
their horsemen come from afar.
They fly like a vulture swooping to
devour;
9 they all come bent on violence.
Their hordes[c] advance like a desert wind
and gather prisoners like sand.
10They deride kings
and scoff at rulers.
They laugh at all fortified cities;
they build earthen ramps and capture
them.
11Then they sweep past like the wind and
go on—
guilty men, whose own strength is their
god."

Habakkuk's Second Complaint

12O LORD, are you not from everlasting?
My God, my Holy One, we will not
die.
O LORD, you have appointed them to
execute judgment;
O Rock, you have ordained them to
punish.
13Your eyes are too pure to look on evil;
you cannot tolerate wrong.
Why then do you tolerate the treacherous?
Why are you silent while the wicked
swallow up those more righteous than
themselves?
14You have made men like fish in the sea,
like sea creatures that have no ruler.
15The wicked foe pulls all of them up with
hooks,
he catches them in his net,
he gathers them up in his dragnet;
and so he rejoices and is glad.
16Therefore he sacrifices to his net
and burns incense to his dragnet,
for by his net he lives in luxury
and enjoys the choicest food.
17Is he to keep on emptying his net,
destroying nations without mercy?

2 I will stand at my watch
and station myself on the ramparts;
I will look to see what he will say to me,
and what answer I am to give to this
complaint.[d]

The LORD's Answer

2Then the LORD replied:

"Write down the revelation
and make it plain on tablets
so that a herald[e] may run with it.
3For the revelation awaits an appointed
time;
it speaks of the end
and will not prove false.
Though it linger, wait for it;
it[f] will certainly come and will not
delay.

4"See, he is puffed up;
his desires are not upright—

[a]18 Or *rulers* [b]6 Or *Chaldeans* [c]9 The meaning of the Hebrew for this word is uncertain. [d]1 Or *and what to answer when I am rebuked* [e]2 Or *so that whoever reads it* [f]3 Or *Though he linger, wait for him; / he*

but the righteous will live by his
faith[a]—
5indeed, wine betrays him;
he is arrogant and never at rest.
Because he is as greedy as the grave[b]
and like death is never satisfied,
he gathers to himself all the nations
and takes captive all the peoples.

6"Will not all of them taunt him with ridicule and scorn, saying,

" 'Woe to him who piles up stolen goods
and makes himself wealthy by
extortion!
How long must this go on?'
7Will not your debtors[c] suddenly arise?
Will they not wake up and make you
tremble?
Then you will become their victim.
8Because you have plundered many
nations,
the peoples who are left will plunder
you.
For you have shed man's blood;
you have destroyed lands and cities and
everyone in them.

9"Woe to him who builds his realm by
unjust gain
to set his nest on high,
to escape the clutches of ruin!
10You have plotted the ruin of many
peoples,
shaming your own house and forfeiting
your life.
11The stones of the wall will cry out,
and the beams of the woodwork will
echo it.

12"Woe to him who builds a city with
bloodshed
and establishes a town by crime!
13Has not the LORD Almighty determined
that the people's labor is only fuel for
the fire,
that the nations exhaust themselves for
nothing?
14For the earth will be filled with the
knowledge of the glory of the
LORD,
as the waters cover the sea.

15"Woe to him who gives drink to his
neighbors,
pouring it from the wineskin till they
are drunk,
so that he can gaze on their naked
bodies.
16You will be filled with shame instead of
glory.
Now it is your turn! Drink and be
exposed[d]!
The cup from the LORD's right hand is
coming around to you,
and disgrace will cover your glory.
17The violence you have done to Lebanon
will overwhelm you,
and your destruction of animals will
terrify you.
For you have shed man's blood;
you have destroyed lands and cities and
everyone in them.

18"Of what value is an idol, since a man has
carved it?
Or an image that teaches lies?
For he who makes it trusts in his own
creation;
he makes idols that cannot speak.
19Woe to him who says to wood, 'Come to
life!'
Or to lifeless stone, 'Wake up!'
Can it give guidance?
It is covered with gold and silver;
there is no breath in it.
20But the LORD is in his holy temple;
let all the earth be silent before him."

Habakkuk's Prayer

3 A prayer of Habakkuk the prophet. On
shigionoth.[e]

2LORD, I have heard of your fame;
I stand in awe of your deeds, O LORD.
Renew them in our day,
in our time make them known;
in wrath remember mercy.

3God came from Teman,
the Holy One from Mount Paran.
Selah[f]
His glory covered the heavens
and his praise filled the earth.
4His splendor was like the sunrise;
rays flashed from his hand,
where his power was hidden.
5Plague went before him;
pestilence followed his steps.
6He stood, and shook the earth;
he looked, and made the nations
tremble.
The ancient mountains crumbled
and the age-old hills collapsed.
His ways are eternal.
7I saw the tents of Cushan in distress,
the dwellings of Midian in anguish.

8Were you angry with the rivers, O LORD?
Was your wrath against the streams?
Did you rage against the sea
when you rode with your horses
and your victorious chariots?
9You uncovered your bow,
you called for many arrows. *Selah*
You split the earth with rivers;
10 the mountains saw you and writhed.
Torrents of water swept by;
the deep roared
and lifted its waves on high.

11Sun and moon stood still in the heavens

[a]4 Or *faithfulness* [b]5 Hebrew *Sheol* [c]7 Or *creditors* [d]16 Masoretic Text; Dead Sea Scrolls, Aquila, Vulgate and Syriac (see also Septuagint) *and stagger* [e]1 Probably a literary or musical term [f]3 A word of uncertain meaning; possibly a musical term; also in verses 9 and 13

at the glint of your flying arrows,
at the lightning of your flashing spear.
12 In wrath you strode through the earth
and in anger you threshed the nations.
13 You came out to deliver your people,
to save your anointed one.
You crushed the leader of the land of wickedness,
you stripped him from head to foot.
Selah
14 With his own spear you pierced his head
when his warriors stormed out to scatter us,
gloating as though about to devour
the wretched who were in hiding.
15 You trampled the sea with your horses,
churning the great waters.

16 I heard and my heart pounded,
my lips quivered at the sound;
decay crept into my bones,
and my legs trembled.
Yet I will wait patiently for the day of calamity
to come on the nation invading us.
17 Though the fig tree does not bud
and there are no grapes on the vines,
though the olive crop fails
and the fields produce no food,
though there are no sheep in the pen
and no cattle in the stalls,
18 yet I will rejoice in the LORD,
I will be joyful in God my Savior.

19 The Sovereign LORD is my strength;
he makes my feet like the feet of a deer,
he enables me to go on the heights.

For the director of music. On my stringed instruments.

Zephaniah

1 The word of the LORD that came to Zephaniah son of Cushi, the son of Gedaliah, the
son of Amariah, the son of Hezekiah, during
the reign of Josiah son of Amon king of Judah:

Warning of Coming Destruction

2 "I will sweep away everything
from the face of the earth,"
declares the LORD.
3 "I will sweep away both men and animals;
I will sweep away the birds of the air
and the fish of the sea.
The wicked will have only heaps of rubble[a]
when I cut off man from the face of the earth,"
declares the LORD.

Against Judah

4 "I will stretch out my hand against Judah
and against all who live in Jerusalem.
I will cut off from this place every remnant of Baal,
the names of the pagan and the idolatrous priests—
5 those who bow down on the roofs
to worship the starry host,
those who bow down and swear by the LORD
and who also swear by Molech,[b]
6 those who turn back from following the LORD
and neither seek the LORD nor inquire of him.
7 Be silent before the Sovereign LORD,
for the day of the LORD is near.
The LORD has prepared a sacrifice;
he has consecrated those he has invited.
8 On the day of the LORD's sacrifice
I will punish the princes
and the king's sons
and all those clad
in foreign clothes.
9 On that day I will punish
all who avoid stepping on the threshold,[c]
who fill the temple of their gods
with violence and deceit.

10 "On that day," declares the LORD,
"a cry will go up from the Fish Gate,
wailing from the New Quarter,
and a loud crash from the hills.
11 Wail, you who live in the market district[d];
all your merchants will be wiped out,
all who trade with[e] silver will be ruined.
12 At that time I will search Jerusalem with lamps
and punish those who are complacent,
who are like wine left on its dregs,
who think, 'The LORD will do nothing,
either good or bad.'
13 Their wealth will be plundered,
their houses demolished.
They will build houses
but not live in them;
they will plant vineyards
but not drink the wine.

The Great Day of the LORD

14 "The great day of the LORD is near—

[a] 3 The meaning of the Hebrew for this line is uncertain. [b] 5 Hebrew *Malcam,* that is, Milcom
[c] 9 See 1 Samuel 5:5. [d] 11 Or *the Mortar* [e] 11 Or *in*

near and coming quickly.
Listen! The cry on the day of the LORD
will be bitter,
the shouting of the warrior there.
15That day will be a day of wrath,
a day of distress and anguish,
a day of trouble and ruin,
a day of darkness and gloom,
a day of clouds and blackness,
16a day of trumpet and battle cry
against the fortified cities
and against the corner towers.
17I will bring distress on the people
and they will walk like blind men,
because they have sinned against the
LORD.
Their blood will be poured out like dust
and their entrails like filth.
18Neither their silver nor their gold
will be able to save them
on the day of the LORD's wrath.
In the fire of his jealousy
the whole world will be consumed,
for he will make a sudden end
of all who live in the earth."

2 Gather together, gather together,
O shameful nation,
2before the appointed time arrives
and that day sweeps on like chaff,
before the fierce anger of the LORD comes
upon you,
before the day of the LORD's wrath
comes upon you.
3Seek the LORD, all you humble of the
land,
you who do what he commands.
Seek righteousness, seek humility;
perhaps you will be sheltered
on the day of the LORD's anger.

Against Philistia

4Gaza will be abandoned
and Ashkelon left in ruins.
At midday Ashdod will be emptied
and Ekron uprooted.
5Woe to you who live by the sea,
O Kerethite people;
the word of the LORD is against you,
O Canaan, land of the Philistines.

"I will destroy you,
and none will be left."

6The land by the sea, where the Kerethites[a]
dwell,
will be a place for shepherds and sheep
pens.
7It will belong to the remnant of the house
of Judah;
there they will find pasture.
In the evening they will lie down
in the houses of Ashkelon.
The LORD their God will care for them;
he will restore their fortunes.[b]

Against Moab and Ammon

8"I have heard the insults of Moab
and the taunts of the Ammonites,
who insulted my people
and made threats against their land.
9Therefore, as surely as I live,"
declares the LORD Almighty, the God of
Israel,
"surely Moab will become like Sodom,
the Ammonites like Gomorrah—
a place of weeds and salt pits,
a wasteland forever.
The remnant of my people will plunder
them;
the survivors of my nation will inherit
their land."

10This is what they will get in return for
their pride,
for insulting and mocking the people of
the LORD Almighty.
11The LORD will be awesome to them
when he destroys all the gods of the
land.
The nations on every shore will worship
him,
every one in its own land.

Against Cush

12"You too, O Cushites,[c]
will be slain by my sword."

Against Assyria

13He will stretch out his hand against the
north
and destroy Assyria,
leaving Nineveh utterly desolate
and dry as the desert.
14Flocks and herds will lie down there,
creatures of every kind.
The desert owl and the screech owl
will roost on her columns.
Their calls will echo through the windows,
rubble will be in the doorways,
the beams of cedar will be exposed.
15This is the carefree city
that lived in safety.
She said to herself,
"I am, and there is none besides me."
What a ruin she has become,
a lair for wild beasts!
All who pass by her scoff
and shake their fists.

The Future of Jerusalem

3 Woe to the city of oppressors,
rebellious and defiled!
2She obeys no one,
she accepts no correction.
She does not trust in the LORD,
she does not draw near to her God.
3Her officials are roaring lions,
her rulers are evening wolves,
who leave nothing for the morning.
4Her prophets are arrogant;

[a]*6* The meaning of the Hebrew for this word is uncertain. [b]*7* Or *will bring back their captives* [c]*12* That is, people from the upper Nile region

they are treacherous men.
Her priests profane the sanctuary
and do violence to the law.
5The LORD within her is righteous;
he does no wrong.
Morning by morning he dispenses his justice,
and every new day he does not fail,
yet the unrighteous know no shame.

6"I have cut off nations;
their strongholds are demolished.
I have left their streets deserted,
with no one passing through.
Their cities are destroyed;
no one will be left—no one at all.
7I said to the city,
'Surely you will fear me
and accept correction!'
Then her dwelling would not be cut off,
nor all my punishments come upon her.
But they were still eager
to act corruptly in all they did.
8Therefore wait for me," declares the LORD,
"for the day I will stand up to testify.[a]
I have decided to assemble the nations,
to gather the kingdoms
and to pour out my wrath on them—
all my fierce anger.
The whole world will be consumed
by the fire of my jealous anger.

9"Then will I purify the lips of the peoples,
that all of them may call on the name of the LORD
and serve him shoulder to shoulder.
10From beyond the rivers of Cush[b]
my worshipers, my scattered people,
will bring me offerings.
11On that day you will not be put to shame
for all the wrongs you have done to me,
because I will remove from this city
those who rejoice in their pride.
Never again will you be haughty
on my holy hill.
12But I will leave within you
the meek and humble,
who trust in the name of the LORD.
13The remnant of Israel will do no wrong;
they will speak no lies,
nor will deceit be found in their mouths.
They will eat and lie down
and no one will make them afraid."

14Sing, O Daughter of Zion;
shout aloud, O Israel!
Be glad and rejoice with all your heart,
O Daughter of Jerusalem!
15The LORD has taken away your punishment,
he has turned back your enemy.
The LORD, the King of Israel, is with you;
never again will you fear any harm.
16On that day they will say to Jerusalem,
"Do not fear, O Zion;
do not let your hands hang limp.
17The LORD your God is with you,
he is mighty to save.
He will take great delight in you,
he will quiet you with his love,
he will rejoice over you with singing."

18"The sorrows for the appointed feasts
I will remove from you;
they are a burden and a reproach to you.[c]
19At that time I will deal
with all who oppressed you;
I will rescue the lame
and gather those who have been scattered.
I will give them praise and honor
in every land where they were put to shame.
20At that time I will gather you;
at that time I will bring you home.
I will give you honor and praise
among all the peoples of the earth
when I restore your fortunes[d]
before your very eyes,"
says the LORD.

Haggai

A Call to Build the House of the LORD

1 In the second year of King Darius, on the
first day of the sixth month, the word of the
LORD came through the prophet Haggai to Zerubbabel son of Shealtiel, governor of Judah,
and to Joshua[e] son of Jehozadak, the high
priest:
2This is what the LORD Almighty says:
"These people say, 'The time has not yet come
for the LORD's house to be built.' "
3Then the word of the LORD came through
the prophet Haggai: 4"Is it a time for you yourselves to be living in your paneled houses,
while this house remains a ruin?"
5Now this is what the LORD Almighty says:
"Give careful thought to your ways. 6You have
planted much, but have harvested little. You

[a]8 Septuagint and Syriac; Hebrew *will rise up to plunder* [b]10 That is, the upper Nile region [c]18 Or *"I will gather you who mourn for the appointed feasts; / your reproach is a burden to you* [d]20 Or *I bring back your captives* [e]1 A variant of *Jeshua*; here and elsewhere in Haggai

eat, but never have enough. You drink, but
never have your fill. You put on clothes, but
are not warm. You earn wages, only to put
them in a purse with holes in it."
7This is what the LORD Almighty says:
"Give careful thought to your ways. 8Go up
into the mountains and bring down timber and
build the house, so that I may take pleasure in
it and be honored," says the LORD. 9"You expected much, but see, it turned out to be little.
What you brought home, I blew away. Why?"
declares the LORD Almighty. "Because of my
house, which remains a ruin, while each of you
is busy with his own house. 10Therefore, because of you the heavens have withheld their
dew and the earth its crops. 11I called for a
drought on the fields and the mountains, on the
grain, the new wine, the oil and whatever the
ground produces, on men and cattle, and on
the labor of your hands."

12Then Zerubbabel son of Shealtiel, Joshua
son of Jehozadak, the high priest, and the
whole remnant of the people obeyed the voice
of the LORD their God and the message of the
prophet Haggai, because the LORD their God
had sent him. And the people feared the LORD.
13Then Haggai, the LORD's messenger, gave
this message of the LORD to the people: "I am
with you," declares the LORD. 14So the LORD
stirred up the spirit of Zerubbabel son of Shealtiel, governor of Judah, and the spirit of Joshua son of Jehozadak, the high priest, and the
spirit of the whole remnant of the people. They
came and began to work on the house of the
LORD Almighty, their God, 15on the twenty-
fourth day of the sixth month in the second
year of King Darius.

The Promised Glory of the New House

2 On the twenty-first day of the seventh
month, the word of the LORD came through
the prophet Haggai: 2"Speak to Zerubbabel
son of Shealtiel, governor of Judah, to Joshua
son of Jehozadak, the high priest, and to the
remnant of the people. Ask them, 3'Who of
you is left who saw this house in its former
glory? How does it look to you now? Does it
not seem to you like nothing? 4But now be
strong, O Zerubbabel,' declares the LORD. 'Be
strong, O Joshua son of Jehozadak, the high
priest. Be strong, all you people of the land,'
declares the LORD, 'and work. For I am with
you,' declares the LORD Almighty. 5'This is
what I covenanted with you when you came
out of Egypt. And my Spirit remains among
you. Do not fear.'
6"This is what the LORD Almighty says: 'In
a little while I will once more shake the heavens and the earth, the sea and the dry land. 7I
will shake all nations, and the desired of all
nations will come, and I will fill this house
with glory,' says the LORD Almighty. 8'The
silver is mine and the gold is mine,' declares
the LORD Almighty. 9'The glory of this present
house will be greater than the glory of the former house,' says the LORD Almighty. 'And
in this place I will grant peace,' declares the
LORD Almighty."

Blessings for a Defiled People

10On the twenty-fourth day of the ninth
month, in the second year of Darius, the word
of the LORD came to the prophet Haggai:
11"This is what the LORD Almighty says: 'Ask
the priests what the law says: 12If a person
carries consecrated meat in the fold of his garment, and that fold touches some bread or
stew, some wine, oil or other food, does it
become consecrated?' "
The priests answered, "No."
13Then Haggai said, "If a person defiled by
contact with a dead body touches one of these
things, does it become defiled?"
"Yes," the priests replied, "it becomes defiled."
14Then Haggai said, " 'So it is with this people and this nation in my sight,' declares the
LORD. 'Whatever they do and whatever they
offer there is defiled.
15" 'Now give careful thought to this from
this day on[a]—consider how things were before one stone was laid on another in the
LORD's temple. 16When anyone came to a
heap of twenty measures, there were only ten.
When anyone went to a wine vat to draw fifty
measures, there were only twenty. 17I struck all
the work of your hands with blight, mildew
and hail, yet you did not turn to me,' declares
the LORD. 18'From this day on, from this
twenty-fourth day of the ninth month, give
careful thought to the day when the foundation
of the LORD's temple was laid. Give careful
thought: 19Is there yet any seed left in the
barn? Until now, the vine and the fig tree, the
pomegranate and the olive tree have not borne
fruit.
" 'From this day on I will bless you.' "

Zerubbabel the LORD's Signet Ring

20The word of the LORD came to Haggai a
second time on the twenty-fourth day of the
month: 21"Tell Zerubbabel governor of Judah
that I will shake the heavens and the earth. 22I
will overturn royal thrones and shatter the
power of the foreign kingdoms. I will overthrow chariots and their drivers; horses and
their riders will fall, each by the sword of his
brother.
23" 'On that day,' declares the LORD Almighty, 'I will take you, my servant Zerubbabel son of Shealtiel,' declares the LORD, 'and
I will make you like my signet ring, for I have
chosen you,' declares the LORD Almighty."

[a] 15 Or *to the days past*

Zechariah

A Call to Return to the LORD

1 In the eighth month of the second year of Darius, the word of the LORD came to the prophet Zechariah son of Berekiah, the son of Iddo:

2“The LORD was very angry with your forefathers. 3Therefore tell the people: This is what the LORD Almighty says: ‘Return to me,’ declares the LORD Almighty, ‘and I will return to you,’ says the LORD Almighty. 4Do not be like your forefathers, to whom the earlier prophets proclaimed: This is what the LORD Almighty says: ‘Turn from your evil ways and your evil practices.’ But they would not listen or pay attention to me, declares the LORD. 5Where are your forefathers now? And the prophets, do they live forever? 6But did not my words and my decrees, which I commanded my servants the prophets, overtake your forefathers?

“Then they repented and said, ‘The LORD Almighty has done to us what our ways and practices deserve, just as he determined to do.’ ”

The Man Among the Myrtle Trees

7On the twenty-fourth day of the eleventh month, the month of Shebat, in the second year of Darius, the word of the LORD came to the prophet Zechariah son of Berekiah, the son of Iddo.

8During the night I had a vision—and there before me was a man riding a red horse! He was standing among the myrtle trees in a ravine. Behind him were red, brown and white horses.

9I asked, “What are these, my lord?”

The angel who was talking with me answered, “I will show you what they are.”

10Then the man standing among the myrtle trees explained, “They are the ones the LORD has sent to go throughout the earth.”

11And they reported to the angel of the LORD, who was standing among the myrtle trees, “We have gone throughout the earth and found the whole world at rest and in peace.”

12Then the angel of the LORD said, “LORD Almighty, how long will you withhold mercy from Jerusalem and from the towns of Judah, which you have been angry with these seventy years?” 13So the LORD spoke kind and comforting words to the angel who talked with me.

14Then the angel who was speaking to me said, “Proclaim this word: This is what the LORD Almighty says: ‘I am very jealous for Jerusalem and Zion, 15but I am very angry with the nations that feel secure. I was only a little angry, but they added to the calamity.’

16“Therefore, this is what the LORD says: ‘I will return to Jerusalem with mercy, and there my house will be rebuilt. And the measuring line will be stretched out over Jerusalem,’ declares the LORD Almighty.

17“Proclaim further: This is what the LORD Almighty says: ‘My towns will again overflow with prosperity, and the LORD will again comfort Zion and choose Jerusalem.’ ”

Four Horns and Four Craftsmen

18Then I looked up—and there before me were four horns! 19I asked the angel who was speaking to me, “What are these?”

He answered me, “These are the horns that scattered Judah, Israel and Jerusalem.”

20Then the LORD showed me four craftsmen. 21I asked, “What are these coming to do?”

He answered, “These are the horns that scattered Judah so that no one could raise his head, but the craftsmen have come to terrify them and throw down these horns of the nations who lifted up their horns against the land of Judah to scatter its people.”

A Man With a Measuring Line

2 Then I looked up—and there before me was a man with a measuring line in his hand! 2I asked, “Where are you going?”

He answered me, “To measure Jerusalem, to find out how wide and how long it is.”

3Then the angel who was speaking to me left, and another angel came to meet him 4and said to him: “Run, tell that young man, ‘Jerusalem will be a city without walls because of the great number of men and livestock in it. 5And I myself will be a wall of fire around it,’ declares the LORD, ‘and I will be its glory within.’

6“Come! Come! Flee from the land of the north,” declares the LORD, “for I have scattered you to the four winds of heaven,” declares the LORD.

7“Come, O Zion! Escape, you who live in the Daughter of Babylon!” 8For this is what the LORD Almighty says: “After he has honored me and has sent me against the nations that have plundered you—for whoever touches you touches the apple of his eye— 9I will surely raise my hand against them so that their slaves will plunder them.[a] Then you will know that the LORD Almighty has sent me.

10“Shout and be glad, O Daughter of Zion. For I am coming, and I will live among you,” declares the LORD. 11“Many nations will be joined with the LORD in that day and will become my people. I will live among you and you will know that the LORD Almighty has sent me to you. 12The LORD will inherit Judah as his portion in the holy land and will again choose Jerusalem. 13Be still before the LORD,

[a]8,9 Or *says after . . . eye: 9“I . . . plunder them.”*

all mankind, because he has roused himself from his holy dwelling."

Clean Garments for the High Priest

3 Then he showed me Joshua[a] the high priest standing before the angel of the LORD, and Satan[b] standing at his right side to accuse him. 2The LORD said to Satan, "The LORD rebuke you, Satan! The LORD, who has chosen Jerusalem, rebuke you! Is not this man a burning stick snatched from the fire?"

3Now Joshua was dressed in filthy clothes as he stood before the angel. 4The angel said to those who were standing before him, "Take off his filthy clothes."

Then he said to Joshua, "See, I have taken away your sin, and I will put rich garments on you."

5Then I said, "Put a clean turban on his head." So they put a clean turban on his head and clothed him, while the angel of the LORD stood by.

6The angel of the LORD gave this charge to Joshua: 7"This is what the LORD Almighty says: 'If you will walk in my ways and keep my requirements, then you will govern my house and have charge of my courts, and I will give you a place among these standing here.

8" 'Listen, O high priest Joshua and your associates seated before you, who are men symbolic of things to come: I am going to bring my servant, the Branch. 9See, the stone I have set in front of Joshua! There are seven eyes[c] on that one stone, and I will engrave an inscription on it,' says the LORD Almighty, 'and I will remove the sin of this land in a single day.

10" 'In that day each of you will invite his neighbor to sit under his vine and fig tree,' declares the LORD Almighty."

The Gold Lampstand and the Two Olive Trees

4 Then the angel who talked with me returned and wakened me, as a man is wakened from his sleep. 2He asked me, "What do you see?"

I answered, "I see a solid gold lampstand with a bowl at the top and seven lights on it, with seven channels to the lights. 3Also there are two olive trees by it, one on the right of the bowl and the other on its left."

4I asked the angel who talked with me, "What are these, my lord?"

5He answered, "Do you not know what these are?"

"No, my lord," I replied.

6So he said to me, "This is the word of the LORD to Zerubbabel: 'Not by might nor by power, but by my Spirit,' says the LORD Almighty.

7"What[d] are you, O mighty mountain? Before Zerubbabel you will become level ground. Then he will bring out the capstone to shouts of 'God bless it! God bless it!' "

8Then the word of the LORD came to me: 9"The hands of Zerubbabel have laid the foundation of this temple; his hands will also complete it. Then you will know that the LORD Almighty has sent me to you.

10"Who despises the day of small things? Men will rejoice when they see the plumb line in the hand of Zerubbabel.

"(These seven are the eyes of the LORD, which range throughout the earth.)"

11Then I asked the angel, "What are these two olive trees on the right and the left of the lampstand?"

12Again I asked him, "What are these two olive branches beside the two gold pipes that pour out golden oil?"

13He replied, "Do you not know what these are?"

"No, my lord," I said.

14So he said, "These are the two who are anointed to[e] serve the Lord of all the earth."

The Flying Scroll

5 I looked again—and there before me was a flying scroll!

2He asked me, "What do you see?"

I answered, "I see a flying scroll, thirty feet long and fifteen feet wide.[f]"

3And he said to me, "This is the curse that is going out over the whole land; for according to what it says on one side, every thief will be banished, and according to what it says on the other, everyone who swears falsely will be banished. 4The LORD Almighty declares, 'I will send it out, and it will enter the house of the thief and the house of him who swears falsely by my name. It will remain in his house and destroy it, both its timbers and its stones.' "

The Woman in a Basket

5Then the angel who was speaking to me came forward and said to me, "Look up and see what this is that is appearing."

6I asked, "What is it?"

He replied, "It is a measuring basket.[g]" And he added, "This is the iniquity[h] of the people throughout the land."

7Then the cover of lead was raised, and there in the basket sat a woman! 8He said, "This is wickedness," and he pushed her back into the basket and pushed the lead cover down over its mouth.

9Then I looked up—and there before me were two women, with the wind in their wings! They had wings like those of a stork, and they lifted up the basket between heaven and earth.

10"Where are they taking the basket?" I asked the angel who was speaking to me.

11He replied, "To the country of Babylonia[i]

[a] *1* A variant of *Jeshua*; here and elsewhere in Zechariah [b] *1* *Satan* means *accuser.* [c] *9* Or *facets*
[d] *7* Or *Who* [e] *14* Or *two who bring oil and* [f] *2* Hebrew *twenty cubits long and ten cubits wide* (about 9 meters long and 4.5 meters wide) [g] *6* Hebrew *an ephah*; also in verses 7-11 [h] *6* Or *appearance*
[i] *11* Hebrew *Shinar*

to build a house for it. When it is ready, the
basket will be set there in its place."

Four Chariots

6 I looked up again—and there before me
were four chariots coming out from between two mountains—mountains of bronze!
2The first chariot had red horses, the second
black, 3the third white, and the fourth dappled—all of them powerful. 4I asked the angel
who was speaking to me, "What are these, my
lord?"
5The angel answered me, "These are the
four spirits[a] of heaven, going out from standing in the presence of the Lord of the whole
world. 6The one with the black horses is going
toward the north country, the one with the
white horses toward the west,[b] and the one
with the dappled horses toward the south."
7When the powerful horses went out, they
were straining to go throughout the earth. And
he said, "Go throughout the earth!" So they
went throughout the earth.
8Then he called to me, "Look, those going
toward the north country have given my Spirit[c] rest in the land of the north."

A Crown for Joshua

9The word of the LORD came to me: 10"Take
⌞silver and gold⌟ from the exiles Heldai, Tobijah and Jedaiah, who have arrived from Babylon. Go the same day to the house of Josiah
son of Zephaniah. 11Take the silver and gold
and make a crown, and set it on the head of the
high priest, Joshua son of Jehozadak. 12Tell
him this is what the LORD Almighty says:
'Here is the man whose name is the Branch,
and he will branch out from his place and build
the temple of the LORD. 13It is he who will
build the temple of the LORD, and he will be
clothed with majesty and will sit and rule on
his throne. And he will be a priest on his
throne. And there will be harmony between the
two.' 14The crown will be given to Heldai,[d]
Tobijah, Jedaiah and Hen[e] son of Zephaniah
as a memorial in the temple of the LORD.
15Those who are far away will come and help
to build the temple of the LORD, and you will
know that the LORD Almighty has sent me to
you. This will happen if you diligently obey
the LORD your God."

Justice and Mercy, Not Fasting

7 In the fourth year of King Darius, the word
of the LORD came to Zechariah on the
fourth day of the ninth month, the month of
Kislev. 2The people of Bethel had sent Sharezer and Regem-Melech, together with their
men, to entreat the LORD 3by asking the priests
of the house of the LORD Almighty and the
prophets, "Should I mourn and fast in the fifth
month, as I have done for so many years?"
4Then the word of the LORD Almighty came
to me: 5"Ask all the people of the land and the
priests, 'When you fasted and mourned in the
fifth and seventh months for the past seventy
years, was it really for me that you fasted?
6And when you were eating and drinking, were
you not just feasting for yourselves? 7Are
these not the words the LORD proclaimed
through the earlier prophets when Jerusalem
and its surrounding towns were at rest and
prosperous, and the Negev and the western
foothills were settled?' "
8And the word of the LORD came again to
Zechariah: 9"This is what the LORD Almighty
says: 'Administer true justice; show mercy and
compassion to one another. 10Do not oppress
the widow or the fatherless, the alien or the
poor. In your hearts do not think evil of each
other.'
11"But they refused to pay attention; stubbornly they turned their backs and stopped up
their ears. 12They made their hearts as hard as
flint and would not listen to the law or to the
words that the LORD Almighty had sent by
his Spirit through the earlier prophets. So the
LORD Almighty was very angry.
13" 'When I called, they did not listen; so
when they called, I would not listen,' says the
LORD Almighty. 14'I scattered them with a
whirlwind among all the nations, where they
were strangers. The land was left so desolate
behind them that no one could come or go.
This is how they made the pleasant land desolate.' "

The LORD Promises to Bless Jerusalem

8 Again the word of the LORD Almighty
came to me. 2This is what the LORD Almighty says: "I am very jealous for Zion; I am
burning with jealousy for her."
3This is what the LORD says: "I will return
to Zion and dwell in Jerusalem. Then Jerusalem will be called the City of Truth, and the
mountain of the LORD Almighty will be called
the Holy Mountain."
4This is what the LORD Almighty says:
"Once again men and women of ripe old age
will sit in the streets of Jerusalem, each with
cane in hand because of his age. 5The city
streets will be filled with boys and girls playing there."
6This is what the LORD Almighty says: "It
may seem marvelous to the remnant of this
people at that time, but will it seem marvelous
to me?" declares the LORD Almighty.
7This is what the LORD Almighty says: "I
will save my people from the countries of the
east and the west. 8I will bring them back to
live in Jerusalem; they will be my people, and
I will be faithful and righteous to them as their
God."
9This is what the LORD Almighty says:
"You who now hear these words spoken by the
prophets who were there when the foundation
was laid for the house of the LORD Almighty,
let your hands be strong so that the temple may
be built. 10Before that time there were no

[a]5 Or *winds* [b]6 Or *horses after them* [c]8 Or *spirit* [d]14 Syriac; Hebrew *Helem* [e]14 Or *and the gracious one, the*

wages for man or beast. No one could go about
his business safely because of his enemy, for I
had turned every man against his neighbor.
11But now I will not deal with the remnant of
this people as I did in the past," declares the
LORD Almighty.

12"The seed will grow well, the vine will
yield its fruit, the ground will produce its
crops, and the heavens will drop their dew. I
will give all these things as an inheritance to
the remnant of this people. 13As you have
been an object of cursing among the nations,
O Judah and Israel, so will I save you, and you
will be a blessing. Do not be afraid, but let
your hands be strong."

14This is what the LORD Almighty says:
"Just as I had determined to bring disaster
upon you and showed no pity when your fathers angered me," says the LORD Almighty,
15"so now I have determined to do good again
to Jerusalem and Judah. Do not be afraid.
16These are the things you are to do: Speak the
truth to each other, and render true and sound
judgment in your courts; 17do not plot evil
against your neighbor, and do not love to
swear falsely. I hate all this," declares the
LORD.

18Again the word of the LORD Almighty
came to me. 19This is what the LORD Almighty
says: "The fasts of the fourth, fifth, seventh
and tenth months will become joyful and glad
occasions and happy festivals for Judah.
Therefore love truth and peace."

20This is what the LORD Almighty says:
"Many peoples and the inhabitants of many
cities will yet come, 21and the inhabitants of
one city will go to another and say, 'Let us go
at once to entreat the LORD and seek the LORD
Almighty. I myself am going.' 22And many
peoples and powerful nations will come to Jerusalem to seek the LORD Almighty and to
entreat him."

23This is what the LORD Almighty says: "In
those days ten men from all languages and
nations will take firm hold of one Jew by the
hem of his robe and say, 'Let us go with you,
because we have heard that God is with you.' "

Judgment on Israel's Enemies

An Oracle

9 The word of the LORD is against the land
of Hadrach
and will rest upon Damascus—
for the eyes of men and all the tribes of
Israel
are on the LORD—[a]
2and upon Hamath too, which borders on
it,
and upon Tyre and Sidon, though they
are very skillful.
3Tyre has built herself a stronghold;
she has heaped up silver like dust,
and gold like the dirt of the streets.
4But the Lord will take away her
possessions
and destroy her power on the sea,
and she will be consumed by fire.
5Ashkelon will see it and fear;
Gaza will writhe in agony,
and Ekron too, for her hope will wither.
Gaza will lose her king
and Ashkelon will be deserted.
6Foreigners will occupy Ashdod,
and I will cut off the pride of the
Philistines.
7I will take the blood from their mouths,
the forbidden food from between their
teeth.
Those who are left will belong to our God
and become leaders in Judah,
and Ekron will be like the Jebusites.
8But I will defend my house
against marauding forces.
Never again will an oppressor overrun my
people,
for now I am keeping watch.

The Coming of Zion's King

9Rejoice greatly, O Daughter of Zion!
Shout, Daughter of Jerusalem!
See, your king[b] comes to you,
righteous and having salvation,
gentle and riding on a donkey,
on a colt, the foal of a donkey.
10I will take away the chariots from
Ephraim
and the war-horses from Jerusalem,
and the battle bow will be broken.
He will proclaim peace to the nations.
His rule will extend from sea to sea
and from the River[c] to the ends of the
earth.[d]
11As for you, because of the blood of my
covenant with you,
I will free your prisoners from the
waterless pit.
12Return to your fortress, O prisoners of
hope;
even now I announce that I will restore
twice as much to you.
13I will bend Judah as I bend my bow
and fill it with Ephraim.
I will rouse your sons, O Zion,
against your sons, O Greece,
and make you like a warrior's sword.

The LORD Will Appear

14Then the LORD will appear over them;
his arrow will flash like lightning.
The Sovereign LORD will sound the
trumpet;
he will march in the storms of the
south,
15 and the LORD Almighty will shield
them.
They will destroy
and overcome with slingstones.
They will drink and roar as with wine;

[a] *1* Or *Damascus. / For the eye of the LORD is on all mankind, / as well as on the tribes of Israel,*
[b] *9* Or *King* [c] *10* That is, the Euphrates [d] *10* Or *the end of the land*

they will be full like a bowl
used for sprinkling[a] the corners of the altar.
16The LORD their God will save them on that day
as the flock of his people.
They will sparkle in his land
like jewels in a crown.
17How attractive and beautiful they will be!
Grain will make the young men thrive,
and new wine the young women.

The LORD Will Care for Judah

10 Ask the LORD for rain in the springtime;
it is the LORD who makes the storm clouds.
He gives showers of rain to men,
and plants of the field to everyone.
2The idols speak deceit,
diviners see visions that lie;
they tell dreams that are false,
they give comfort in vain.
Therefore the people wander like sheep
oppressed for lack of a shepherd.

3"My anger burns against the shepherds,
and I will punish the leaders;
for the LORD Almighty will care
for his flock, the house of Judah,
and make them like a proud horse in battle.
4From Judah will come the cornerstone,
from him the tent peg,
from him the battle bow,
from him every ruler.
5Together they[b] will be like mighty men
trampling the muddy streets in battle.
Because the LORD is with them,
they will fight and overthrow the horsemen.

6"I will strengthen the house of Judah
and save the house of Joseph.
I will restore them
because I have compassion on them.
They will be as though
I had not rejected them,
for I am the LORD their God
and I will answer them.
7The Ephraimites will become like mighty men,
and their hearts will be glad as with wine.
Their children will see it and be joyful;
their hearts will rejoice in the LORD.
8I will signal for them
and gather them in.
Surely I will redeem them;
they will be as numerous as before.
9Though I scatter them among the peoples,
yet in distant lands they will remember me.
They and their children will survive,
and they will return.
10I will bring them back from Egypt
and gather them from Assyria.
I will bring them to Gilead and Lebanon,
and there will not be room enough for them.
11They will pass through the sea of trouble;
the surging sea will be subdued
and all the depths of the Nile will dry up.
Assyria's pride will be brought down
and Egypt's scepter will pass away.
12I will strengthen them in the LORD
and in his name they will walk,"
declares the LORD.

11 Open your doors, O Lebanon,
so that fire may devour your cedars!
2Wail, O pine tree, for the cedar has fallen;
the stately trees are ruined!
Wail, oaks of Bashan;
the dense forest has been cut down!
3Listen to the wail of the shepherds;
their rich pastures are destroyed!
Listen to the roar of the lions;
the lush thicket of the Jordan is ruined!

Two Shepherds

4This is what the LORD my God says: "Pasture the flock marked for slaughter. 5Their
buyers slaughter them and go unpunished.
Those who sell them say, 'Praise the LORD, I
am rich!' Their own shepherds do not spare
them. 6For I will no longer have pity on the
people of the land," declares the LORD. "I will
hand everyone over to his neighbor and his
king. They will oppress the land, and I will not
rescue them from their hands."

7So I pastured the flock marked for slaughter, particularly the oppressed of the flock.
Then I took two staffs and called one Favor
and the other Union, and I pastured the flock.
8In one month I got rid of the three shepherds.

The flock detested me, and I grew weary of
them 9and said, "I will not be your shepherd.
Let the dying die, and the perishing perish. Let
those who are left eat one another's flesh."

10Then I took my staff called Favor and
broke it, revoking the covenant I had made
with all the nations. 11It was revoked on that
day, and so the afflicted of the flock who were
watching me knew it was the word of the
LORD.

12I told them, "If you think it best, give me
my pay; but if not, keep it." So they paid me
thirty pieces of silver.

13And the LORD said to me, "Throw it to the
potter"—the handsome price at which they
priced me! So I took the thirty pieces of silver
and threw them into the house of the LORD to
the potter.

14Then I broke my second staff called
Union, breaking the brotherhood between Judah and Israel.

15Then the LORD said to me, "Take again
the equipment of a foolish shepherd. 16For I
am going to raise up a shepherd over the land
who will not care for the lost, or seek the

[a] 15 Or *bowl, / like* [b] 4,5 Or *ruler, all of them together. / 5They*

young, or heal the injured, or feed the healthy,
but will eat the meat of the choice sheep, tearing off their hoofs.

17 "Woe to the worthless shepherd,
  who deserts the flock!
 May the sword strike his arm and his right
   eye!
  May his arm be completely withered,
  his right eye totally blinded!"

Jerusalem's Enemies to Be Destroyed

An Oracle

12 This is the word of the LORD concerning Israel. The LORD, who stretches out
the heavens, who lays the foundation of the
earth, and who forms the spirit of man within
him, declares: 2 "I am going to make Jerusalem
a cup that sends all the surrounding peoples
reeling. Judah will be besieged as well as Jerusalem. 3 On that day, when all the nations of the
earth are gathered against her, I will make Jerusalem an immovable rock for all the nations.
All who try to move it will injure themselves.
4 On that day I will strike every horse with
panic and its rider with madness," declares the
LORD. "I will keep a watchful eye over the
house of Judah, but I will blind all the horses
of the nations. 5 Then the leaders of Judah will
say in their hearts, 'The people of Jerusalem
are strong, because the LORD Almighty is their
God.'

6 "On that day I will make the leaders of
Judah like a firepot in a woodpile, like a flaming torch among sheaves. They will consume
right and left all the surrounding peoples, but
Jerusalem will remain intact in her place.

7 "The LORD will save the dwellings of Judah first, so that the honor of the house of
David and of Jerusalem's inhabitants may not
be greater than that of Judah. 8 On that day the
LORD will shield those who live in Jerusalem,
so that the feeblest among them will be like
David, and the house of David will be like
God, like the Angel of the LORD going before
them. 9 On that day I will set out to destroy all
the nations that attack Jerusalem.

Mourning for the One They Pierced

10 "And I will pour out on the house of David
and the inhabitants of Jerusalem a spirit[a] of
grace and supplication. They will look on[b] me,
the one they have pierced, and they will mourn
for him as one mourns for an only child, and
grieve bitterly for him as one grieves for a
firstborn son. 11 On that day the weeping in
Jerusalem will be great, like the weeping of
Hadad Rimmon in the plain of Megiddo. 12 The
land will mourn, each clan by itself, with their
wives by themselves: the clan of the house of
David and their wives, the clan of the house of
Nathan and their wives, 13 the clan of the house
of Levi and their wives, the clan of Shimei and
their wives, 14 and all the rest of the clans and
their wives.

Cleansing From Sin

13 "On that day a fountain will be opened
to the house of David and the inhabitants of Jerusalem, to cleanse them from sin
and impurity.

2 "On that day, I will banish the names of the
idols from the land, and they will be remembered no more," declares the LORD Almighty.
"I will remove both the prophets and the spirit
of impurity from the land. 3 And if anyone still
prophesies, his father and mother, to whom he
was born, will say to him, 'You must die, because you have told lies in the LORD's name.'
When he prophesies, his own parents will stab
him.

4 "On that day every prophet will be
ashamed of his prophetic vision. He will not
put on a prophet's garment of hair in order to
deceive. 5 He will say, 'I am not a prophet. I am
a farmer; the land has been my livelihood since
my youth.[c]' 6 If someone asks him, 'What are
these wounds on your body[d]?' he will answer,
'The wounds I was given at the house of my
friends.'

The Shepherd Struck, the Sheep Scattered

7 "Awake, O sword, against my shepherd,
  against the man who is close to me!"
  declares the LORD Almighty.
 "Strike the shepherd,
  and the sheep will be scattered,
  and I will turn my hand against the
   little ones.
8 In the whole land," declares the LORD,
  "two-thirds will be struck down and
   perish;
  yet one-third will be left in it.
9 This third I will bring into the fire;
  I will refine them like silver
  and test them like gold.
 They will call on my name
  and I will answer them;
 I will say, 'They are my people,'
  and they will say, 'The LORD is our
   God.' "

The LORD Comes and Reigns

14 A day of the LORD is coming when your
plunder will be divided among you.

2 I will gather all the nations to Jerusalem to
fight against it; the city will be captured, the
houses ransacked, and the women raped. Half
of the city will go into exile, but the rest of the
people will not be taken from the city.

3 Then the LORD will go out and fight against
those nations, as he fights in the day of battle.
4 On that day his feet will stand on the Mount
of Olives, east of Jerusalem, and the Mount of
Olives will be split in two from east to west,
forming a great valley, with half of the mountain moving north and half moving south.
5 You will flee by my mountain valley, for it
will extend to Azel. You will flee as you fled

[a] 10 Or *the Spirit* [b] 10 Or *to* [c] 5 Or *farmer; a man sold me in my youth* [d] 6 Or *wounds between your hands*

from the earthquake[a] in the days of Uzziah king of Judah. Then the LORD my God will come, and all the holy ones with him.

6On that day there will be no light, no cold or frost. 7It will be a unique day, without daytime or nighttime—a day known to the LORD. When evening comes, there will be light.

8On that day living water will flow out from Jerusalem, half to the eastern sea[b] and half to the western sea,[c] in summer and in winter.

9The LORD will be king over the whole earth. On that day there will be one LORD, and his name the only name.

10The whole land, from Geba to Rimmon, south of Jerusalem, will become like the Arabah. But Jerusalem will be raised up and remain in its place, from the Benjamin Gate to the site of the First Gate, to the Corner Gate, and from the Tower of Hananel to the royal winepresses. 11It will be inhabited; never again will it be destroyed. Jerusalem will be secure.

12This is the plague with which the LORD will strike all the nations that fought against Jerusalem: Their flesh will rot while they are still standing on their feet, their eyes will rot in their sockets, and their tongues will rot in their mouths. 13On that day men will be stricken by the LORD with great panic. Each man will seize the hand of another, and they will attack each other. 14Judah too will fight at Jerusalem. The wealth of all the surrounding nations will be collected—great quantities of gold and silver and clothing. 15A similar plague will strike the horses and mules, the camels and donkeys, and all the animals in those camps.

16Then the survivors from all the nations that have attacked Jerusalem will go up year after year to worship the King, the LORD Almighty, and to celebrate the Feast of Tabernacles. 17If any of the peoples of the earth do not go up to Jerusalem to worship the King, the LORD Almighty, they will have no rain. 18If the Egyptian people do not go up and take part, they will have no rain. The LORD[d] will bring on them the plague he inflicts on the nations that do not go up to celebrate the Feast of Tabernacles. 19This will be the punishment of Egypt and the punishment of all the nations that do not go up to celebrate the Feast of Tabernacles.

20On that day HOLY TO THE LORD will be inscribed on the bells of the horses, and the cooking pots in the LORD's house will be like the sacred bowls in front of the altar. 21Every pot in Jerusalem and Judah will be holy to the LORD Almighty, and all who come to sacrifice will take some of the pots and cook in them. And on that day there will no longer be a Canaanite[e] in the house of the LORD Almighty.

Malachi

1 An oracle: The word of the LORD to Israel through Malachi.[f]

Jacob Loved, Esau Hated

2"I have loved you," says the LORD.

"But you ask, 'How have you loved us?'

"Was not Esau Jacob's brother?" the LORD says. "Yet I have loved Jacob, 3but Esau I have hated, and I have turned his mountains into a wasteland and left his inheritance to the desert jackals."

4Edom may say, "Though we have been crushed, we will rebuild the ruins."

But this is what the LORD Almighty says: "They may build, but I will demolish. They will be called the Wicked Land, a people always under the wrath of the LORD. 5You will see it with your own eyes and say, 'Great is the LORD—even beyond the borders of Israel!'

Blemished Sacrifices

6"A son honors his father, and a servant his master. If I am a father, where is the honor due me? If I am a master, where is the respect due me?" says the LORD Almighty. "It is you, O priests, who show contempt for my name.

"But you ask, 'How have we shown contempt for your name?'

7"You place defiled food on my altar.

"But you ask, 'How have we defiled you?'

"By saying that the LORD's table is contemptible. 8When you bring blind animals for sacrifice, is that not wrong? When you sacrifice crippled or diseased animals, is that not wrong? Try offering them to your governor! Would he be pleased with you? Would he accept you?" says the LORD Almighty.

9"Now implore God to be gracious to us. With such offerings from your hands, will he accept you?"—says the LORD Almighty.

10"Oh, that one of you would shut the temple doors, so that you would not light useless fires on my altar! I am not pleased with you," says the LORD Almighty, "and I will accept no offering from your hands. 11My name will be great among the nations, from the rising to the setting of the sun. In every place incense and pure offerings will be brought to my name, because my name will be great among the nations," says the LORD Almighty.

[a]*5* Or *5My mountain valley will be blocked and will extend to Azel. It will be blocked as it was blocked because of the earthquake* [b]*8* That is, the Dead Sea [c]*8* That is, the Mediterranean [d]*18* Or *part, then the LORD* [e]*21* Or *merchant* [f]*1* *Malachi* means *my messenger.*

12“But you profane it by saying of the
Lord’s table, ‘It is defiled,’ and of its food, ‘It
is contemptible.’ 13And you say, ‘What a burden!’ and you sniff at it contemptuously,” says
the LORD Almighty.

“When you bring injured, crippled or diseased animals and offer them as sacrifices,
should I accept them from your hands?” says
the LORD. 14“Cursed is the cheat who has an
acceptable male in his flock and vows to give
it, but then sacrifices a blemished animal to the
Lord. For I am a great king,” says the LORD
Almighty, “and my name is to be feared
among the nations.

Admonition for the Priests

2 “And now this admonition is for you,
O priests. 2If you do not listen, and if you
do not set your heart to honor my name,” says
the LORD Almighty, “I will send a curse upon
you, and I will curse your blessings. Yes, I
have already cursed them, because you have
not set your heart to honor me.

3“Because of you I will rebuke[a] your
descendants[b]; I will spread on your faces the
offal from your festival sacrifices, and you will
be carried off with it. 4And you will know that
I have sent you this admonition so that my
covenant with Levi may continue,” says the
LORD Almighty. 5“My covenant was with him,
a covenant of life and peace, and I gave them
to him; this called for reverence and he revered
me and stood in awe of my name. 6True instruction was in his mouth and nothing false
was found on his lips. He walked with me in
peace and uprightness, and turned many from
sin.

7“For the lips of a priest ought to preserve
knowledge, and from his mouth men should
seek instruction—because he is the messenger
of the LORD Almighty. 8But you have turned
from the way and by your teaching have
caused many to stumble; you have violated the
covenant with Levi,” says the LORD Almighty.
9“So I have caused you to be despised and
humiliated before all the people, because you
have not followed my ways but have shown
partiality in matters of the law.”

Judah Unfaithful

10Have we not all one Father[c]? Did not one
God create us? Why do we profane the covenant of our fathers by breaking faith with one
another?

11Judah has broken faith. A detestable thing
has been committed in Israel and in Jerusalem:
Judah has desecrated the sanctuary the LORD
loves, by marrying the daughter of a foreign
god. 12As for the man who does this, whoever
he may be, may the LORD cut him off from the
tents of Jacob[d]—even though he brings offerings to the LORD Almighty.

13Another thing you do: You flood the
LORD’s altar with tears. You weep and wail
because he no longer pays attention to your
offerings or accepts them with pleasure from
your hands. 14You ask, “Why?” It is because
the LORD is acting as the witness between you
and the wife of your youth, because you have
broken faith with her, though she is your partner, the wife of your marriage covenant.

15Has not ⌞the LORD⌟ made them one? In
flesh and spirit they are his. And why one?
Because he was seeking godly offspring.[e] So
guard yourself in your spirit, and do not break
faith with the wife of your youth.

16“I hate divorce,” says the LORD God of
Israel, “and I hate a man’s covering himself[f]
with violence as well as with his garment,”
says the LORD Almighty.

So guard yourself in your spirit, and do not
break faith.

The Day of Judgment

17You have wearied the LORD with your
words.

“How have we wearied him?” you ask.

By saying, “All who do evil are good in the
eyes of the LORD, and he is pleased with them”
or “Where is the God of justice?”

3 “See, I will send my messenger, who will
prepare the way before me. Then suddenly
the Lord you are seeking will come to his temple; the messenger of the covenant, whom you
desire, will come,” says the LORD Almighty.

2But who can endure the day of his coming?
Who can stand when he appears? For he will
be like a refiner’s fire or a launderer’s soap.
3He will sit as a refiner and purifier of silver;
he will purify the Levites and refine them like
gold and silver. Then the LORD will have men
who will bring offerings in righteousness, 4and
the offerings of Judah and Jerusalem will be
acceptable to the LORD, as in days gone by, as
in former years.

5“So I will come near to you for judgment.
I will be quick to testify against sorcerers,
adulterers and perjurers, against those who defraud laborers of their wages, who oppress the
widows and the fatherless, and deprive aliens
of justice, but do not fear me,” says the LORD
Almighty.

Robbing God

6“I the LORD do not change. So you,
O descendants of Jacob, are not destroyed.
7Ever since the time of your forefathers you
have turned away from my decrees and have
not kept them. Return to me, and I will return
to you,” says the LORD Almighty.

“But you ask, ‘How are we to return?’

8“Will a man rob God? Yet you rob me.

“But you ask, ‘How do we rob you?’

“In tithes and offerings. 9You are under a
curse—the whole nation of you—because you
are robbing me. 10Bring the whole tithe into

[a]3 Or *cut off* (see Septuagint) [b]3 Or *will blight your grain* [c]10 Or *father* [d]12 Or *12May the LORD cut off from the tents of Jacob anyone who gives testimony in behalf of the man who does this* [e]15 Or *15But the one ⌞who is our father⌟ did not do this, not as long as life remained in him. And what was he seeking? An offspring from God* [f]16 Or *his wife*

the storehouse, that there may be food in my
house. Test me in this," says the LORD Almighty, "and see if I will not throw open the
floodgates of heaven and pour out so much
blessing that you will not have room enough
for it. 11I will prevent pests from devouring
your crops, and the vines in your fields will not
cast their fruit," says the LORD Almighty.
12"Then all the nations will call you blessed,
for yours will be a delightful land," says the
LORD Almighty.

13"You have said harsh things against me,"
says the LORD.

"Yet you ask, 'What have we said against
you?'

14"You have said, 'It is futile to serve God.
What did we gain by carrying out his requirements and going about like mourners before
the LORD Almighty? 15But now we call the
arrogant blessed. Certainly the evildoers prosper, and even those who challenge God escape.' "

16Then those who feared the LORD talked
with each other, and the LORD listened and
heard. A scroll of remembrance was written in
his presence concerning those who feared the
LORD and honored his name.

17"They will be mine," says the LORD Almighty, "in the day when I make up my treasured possession.[a] I will spare them, just as in
compassion a man spares his son who serves
him. 18And you will again see the distinction
between the righteous and the wicked, between
those who serve God and those who do not.

The Day of the LORD

4 "Surely the day is coming; it will burn like
a furnace. All the arrogant and every evildoer will be stubble, and that day that is coming will set them on fire," says the LORD Almighty. "Not a root or a branch will be left to
them. 2But for you who revere my name, the
sun of righteousness will rise with healing in
its wings. And you will go out and leap like
calves released from the stall. 3Then you will
trample down the wicked; they will be ashes
under the soles of your feet on the day when I
do these things," says the LORD Almighty.

4"Remember the law of my servant Moses,
the decrees and laws I gave him at Horeb for
all Israel.

5"See, I will send you the prophet Elijah
before that great and dreadful day of the LORD
comes. 6He will turn the hearts of the fathers to
their children, and the hearts of the children to
their fathers; or else I will come and strike the
land with a curse."

[a]17 Or *Almighty, "my treasured possession, in the day when I act*

The New Testament

Matthew

The Genealogy of Jesus

1 A record of the genealogy of Jesus Christ the son of David, the son of Abraham:

2Abraham was the father of Isaac,
Isaac the father of Jacob,
Jacob the father of Judah and his brothers,
3Judah the father of Perez and Zerah, whose mother was Tamar,
Perez the father of Hezron,
Hezron the father of Ram,
4Ram the father of Amminadab,
Amminadab the father of Nahshon,
Nahshon the father of Salmon,
5Salmon the father of Boaz, whose mother was Rahab,
Boaz the father of Obed, whose mother was Ruth,
Obed the father of Jesse,
6and Jesse the father of King David.

David was the father of Solomon, whose mother had been Uriah's wife,
7Solomon the father of Rehoboam,
Rehoboam the father of Abijah,
Abijah the father of Asa,
8Asa the father of Jehoshaphat,
Jehoshaphat the father of Jehoram,
Jehoram the father of Uzziah,
9Uzziah the father of Jotham,
Jotham the father of Ahaz,
Ahaz the father of Hezekiah,
10Hezekiah the father of Manasseh,
Manasseh the father of Amon,
Amon the father of Josiah,
11and Josiah the father of Jeconiah[a] and his brothers at the time of the exile to Babylon.

12After the exile to Babylon:
Jeconiah was the father of Shealtiel,
Shealtiel the father of Zerubbabel,
13Zerubbabel the father of Abiud,
Abiud the father of Eliakim,
Eliakim the father of Azor,
14Azor the father of Zadok,
Zadok the father of Akim,
Akim the father of Eliud,
15Eliud the father of Eleazar,
Eleazar the father of Matthan,
Matthan the father of Jacob,
16and Jacob the father of Joseph, the husband of Mary, of whom was born Jesus, who is called Christ.

17Thus there were fourteen generations in all from Abraham to David, fourteen from David to the exile to Babylon, and fourteen from the exile to the Christ.[b]

The Birth of Jesus Christ

18This is how the birth of Jesus Christ came about: His mother Mary was pledged to be married to Joseph, but before they came together, she was found to be with child through the Holy Spirit. 19Because Joseph her husband was a righteous man and did not want to expose her to public disgrace, he had in mind to divorce her quietly.

20But after he had considered this, an angel of the Lord appeared to him in a dream and said, "Joseph son of David, do not be afraid to take Mary home as your wife, because what is conceived in her is from the Holy Spirit. 21She will give birth to a son, and you are to give him the name Jesus,[c] because he will save his people from their sins."

22All this took place to fulfill what the Lord had said through the prophet: 23"The virgin will be with child and will give birth to a son, and they will call him Immanuel"[d]—which means, "God with us."

24When Joseph woke up, he did what the angel of the Lord had commanded him and took Mary home as his wife. 25But he had no union with her until she gave birth to a son. And he gave him the name Jesus.

The Visit of the Magi

2 After Jesus was born in Bethlehem in Judea, during the time of King Herod, Magi[e] from the east came to Jerusalem 2and asked, "Where is the one who has been born king of the Jews? We saw his star in the east[f] and have come to worship him."

3When King Herod heard this he was disturbed, and all Jerusalem with him. 4When he had called together all the people's chief priests and teachers of the law, he asked them where the Christ[g] was to be born. 5"In Bethlehem in Judea," they replied, "for this is what the prophet has written:

6" 'But you, Bethlehem, in the land of Judah,
are by no means least among the rulers of Judah;
for out of you will come a ruler
who will be the shepherd of my people Israel.'[h]"

7Then Herod called the Magi secretly and found out from them the exact time the star had appeared. 8He sent them to Bethlehem and said, "Go and make a careful search for the

[a] *11* That is, Jehoiachin; also in verse 12 [b] *17* Or *Messiah.* "The Christ" (Greek) and "the Messiah" (Hebrew) both mean "the Anointed One." [c] *21* *Jesus* is the Greek form of *Joshua,* which means *the LORD saves.* [d] *23* Isaiah 7:14 [e] *1* Traditionally *Wise Men* [f] *2* Or *star when it rose* [g] *4* Or *Messiah* [h] *6* Micah 5:2

child. As soon as you find him, report to me,
so that I too may go and worship him."
9After they had heard the king, they went on
their way, and the star they had seen in the
east[a] went ahead of them until it stopped over
the place where the child was. 10When they
saw the star, they were overjoyed. 11On coming to the house, they saw the child with his
mother Mary, and they bowed down and worshiped him. Then they opened their treasures
and presented him with gifts of gold and of
incense and of myrrh. 12And having been
warned in a dream not to go back to Herod,
they returned to their country by another route.

The Escape to Egypt

13When they had gone, an angel of the Lord
appeared to Joseph in a dream. "Get up," he
said, "take the child and his mother and escape
to Egypt. Stay there until I tell you, for Herod
is going to search for the child to kill him."
14So he got up, took the child and his mother
during the night and left for Egypt, 15where he
stayed until the death of Herod. And so was
fulfilled what the Lord had said through the
prophet: "Out of Egypt I called my son."[b]
16When Herod realized that he had been out-
witted by the Magi, he was furious, and he
gave orders to kill all the boys in Bethlehem
and its vicinity who were two years old and
under, in accordance with the time he had
learned from the Magi. 17Then what was said
through the prophet Jeremiah was fulfilled:

18"A voice is heard in Ramah,
weeping and great mourning,
Rachel weeping for her children
and refusing to be comforted,
because they are no more."[c]

The Return to Nazareth

19After Herod died, an angel of the Lord
appeared in a dream to Joseph in Egypt 20and
said, "Get up, take the child and his mother
and go to the land of Israel, for those who were
trying to take the child's life are dead."
21So he got up, took the child and his mother
and went to the land of Israel. 22But when he
heard that Archelaus was reigning in Judea in
place of his father Herod, he was afraid to go
there. Having been warned in a dream, he
withdrew to the district of Galilee, 23and he
went and lived in a town called Nazareth. So
was fulfilled what was said through the prophets: "He will be called a Nazarene."

John the Baptist Prepares the Way

3 In those days John the Baptist came,
preaching in the Desert of Judea 2and saying, "Repent, for the kingdom of heaven is
near." 3This is he who was spoken of through
the prophet Isaiah:

"A voice of one calling in the desert,
'Prepare the way for the Lord,
make straight paths for him.' "[d]

4John's clothes were made of camel's hair,
and he had a leather belt around his waist. His
food was locusts and wild honey. 5People went
out to him from Jerusalem and all Judea and
the whole region of the Jordan. 6Confessing
their sins, they were baptized by him in the
Jordan River.
7But when he saw many of the Pharisees
and Sadducees coming to where he was baptizing, he said to them: "You brood of vipers!
Who warned you to flee from the coming
wrath? 8Produce fruit in keeping with repentance. 9And do not think you can say to yourselves, 'We have Abraham as our father.' I tell
you that out of these stones God can raise up
children for Abraham. 10The ax is already at
the root of the trees, and every tree that does
not produce good fruit will be cut down and
thrown into the fire.
11"I baptize you with[e] water for repentance.
But after me will come one who is more powerful than I, whose sandals I am not fit to carry.
He will baptize you with the Holy Spirit and
with fire. 12His winnowing fork is in his hand,
and he will clear his threshing floor, gathering
his wheat into the barn and burning up the
chaff with unquenchable fire."

The Baptism of Jesus

13Then Jesus came from Galilee to the Jordan to be baptized by John. 14But John tried to
deter him, saying, "I need to be baptized by
you, and do you come to me?"
15Jesus replied, "Let it be so now; it is proper for us to do this to fulfill all righteousness."
Then John consented.
16As soon as Jesus was baptized, he went up
out of the water. At that moment heaven was
opened, and he saw the Spirit of God descending like a dove and lighting on him. 17And a
voice from heaven said, "This is my Son,
whom I love; with him I am well pleased."

The Temptation of Jesus

4 Then Jesus was led by the Spirit into the
desert to be tempted by the devil. 2After
fasting forty days and forty nights, he was hungry. 3The tempter came to him and said, "If
you are the Son of God, tell these stones to
become bread."
4Jesus answered, "It is written: 'Man does
not live on bread alone, but on every word that
comes from the mouth of God.'[f]"
5Then the devil took him to the holy city and
had him stand on the highest point of the temple. 6"If you are the Son of God," he said,
"throw yourself down. For it is written:

" 'He will command his angels concerning
you,
and they will lift you up in their hands,
so that you will not strike your foot
against a stone.'[g]"

7Jesus answered him, "It is also written: 'Do
not put the Lord your God to the test.'[h]"

[a] 9 Or *seen when it rose* [b] 15 Hosea 11:1 [c] 18 Jer. 31:15 [d] 3 Isaiah 40:3 [e] 11 Or *in* [f] 4 Deut. 8:3
[g] 6 Psalm 91:11,12 [h] 7 Deut. 6:16

8 Again, the devil took him to a very high
mountain and showed him all the kingdoms of
the world and their splendor. 9 "All this I will
give you," he said, "if you will bow down and
worship me."

10 Jesus said to him, "Away from me, Satan!
For it is written: 'Worship the Lord your God,
and serve him only.'[a]"

11 Then the devil left him, and angels came
and attended him.

Jesus Begins to Preach

12 When Jesus heard that John had been put
in prison, he returned to Galilee. 13 Leaving
Nazareth, he went and lived in Capernaum,
which was by the lake in the area of Zebulun
and Naphtali— 14 to fulfill what was said
through the prophet Isaiah:

15 "Land of Zebulun and land of Naphtali,
the way to the sea, along the Jordan,
Galilee of the Gentiles—
16 the people living in darkness
have seen a great light;
on those living in the land of the shadow
of death
a light has dawned."[b]

17 From that time on Jesus began to preach,
"Repent, for the kingdom of heaven is near."

The Calling of the First Disciples

18 As Jesus was walking beside the Sea of
Galilee, he saw two brothers, Simon called Peter and his brother Andrew. They were casting
a net into the lake, for they were fishermen.
19 "Come, follow me," Jesus said, "and I will
make you fishers of men." 20 At once they left
their nets and followed him.

21 Going on from there, he saw two other
brothers, James son of Zebedee and his brother
John. They were in a boat with their father
Zebedee, preparing their nets. Jesus called
them, 22 and immediately they left the boat and
their father and followed him.

Jesus Heals the Sick

23 Jesus went throughout Galilee, teaching in
their synagogues, preaching the good news of
the kingdom, and healing every disease and
sickness among the people. 24 News about him
spread all over Syria, and people brought to
him all who were ill with various diseases,
those suffering severe pain, the demon-
possessed, those having seizures, and the paralyzed, and he healed them. 25 Large crowds
from Galilee, the Decapolis,[c] Jerusalem, Judea
and the region across the Jordan followed him.

The Beatitudes

5 Now when he saw the crowds, he went up
on a mountainside and sat down. His disciples came to him, 2 and he began to teach them,
saying:

3 "Blessed are the poor in spirit,
for theirs is the kingdom of heaven.
4 Blessed are those who mourn,
for they will be comforted.
5 Blessed are the meek,
for they will inherit the earth.
6 Blessed are those who hunger and thirst
for righteousness,
for they will be filled.
7 Blessed are the merciful,
for they will be shown mercy.
8 Blessed are the pure in heart,
for they will see God.
9 Blessed are the peacemakers,
for they will be called sons of God.
10 Blessed are those who are persecuted
because of righteousness,
for theirs is the kingdom of heaven.

11 "Blessed are you when people insult you,
persecute you and falsely say all kinds of evil
against you because of me. 12 Rejoice and be
glad, because great is your reward in heaven,
for in the same way they persecuted the prophets who were before you.

Salt and Light

13 "You are the salt of the earth. But if the
salt loses its saltiness, how can it be made salty
again? It is no longer good for anything, except
to be thrown out and trampled by men.

14 "You are the light of the world. A city on
a hill cannot be hidden. 15 Neither do people
light a lamp and put it under a bowl. Instead
they put it on its stand, and it gives light to
everyone in the house. 16 In the same way, let
your light shine before men, that they may see
your good deeds and praise your Father in
heaven.

The Fulfillment of the Law

17 "Do not think that I have come to abolish
the Law or the Prophets; I have not come to
abolish them but to fulfill them. 18 I tell you the
truth, until heaven and earth disappear, not the
smallest letter, not the least stroke of a pen,
will by any means disappear from the Law
until everything is accomplished. 19 Anyone
who breaks one of the least of these commandments and teaches others to do the same will
be called least in the kingdom of heaven, but
whoever practices and teaches these commands will be called great in the kingdom of
heaven. 20 For I tell you that unless your righteousness surpasses that of the Pharisees and
the teachers of the law, you will certainly not
enter the kingdom of heaven.

Murder

21 "You have heard that it was said to the
people long ago, 'Do not murder,[d] and anyone
who murders will be subject to judgment.'
22 But I tell you that anyone who is angry with
his brother[e] will be subject to judgment.
Again, anyone who says to his brother,
'Raca,[f]' is answerable to the Sanhedrin. But

a10 Deut. 6:13 *b16* Isaiah 9:1,2 *c25* That is, the Ten Cities *d21* Exodus 20:13 *e22* Some manuscripts *brother without cause* *f22* An Aramaic term of contempt

anyone who says, 'You fool!' will be in danger of the fire of hell.

23"Therefore, if you are offering your gift at the altar and there remember that your brother has something against you, 24leave your gift there in front of the altar. First go and be reconciled to your brother; then come and offer your gift.

25"Settle matters quickly with your adversary who is taking you to court. Do it while you are still with him on the way, or he may hand you over to the judge, and the judge may hand you over to the officer, and you may be thrown into prison. 26I tell you the truth, you will not get out until you have paid the last penny.[a]

Adultery

27"You have heard that it was said, 'Do not commit adultery.'[b] 28But I tell you that anyone who looks at a woman lustfully has already committed adultery with her in his heart. 29If your right eye causes you to sin, gouge it out and throw it away. It is better for you to lose one part of your body than for your whole body to be thrown into hell. 30And if your right hand causes you to sin, cut it off and throw it away. It is better for you to lose one part of your body than for your whole body to go into hell.

Divorce

31"It has been said, 'Anyone who divorces his wife must give her a certificate of divorce.'[c] 32But I tell you that anyone who divorces his wife, except for marital unfaithfulness, causes her to become an adulteress, and anyone who marries the divorced woman commits adultery.

Oaths

33"Again, you have heard that it was said to the people long ago, 'Do not break your oath, but keep the oaths you have made to the Lord.' 34But I tell you, Do not swear at all: either by heaven, for it is God's throne; 35or by the earth, for it is his footstool; or by Jerusalem, for it is the city of the Great King. 36And do not swear by your head, for you cannot make even one hair white or black. 37Simply let your 'Yes' be 'Yes,' and your 'No,' 'No'; anything beyond this comes from the evil one.

An Eye for an Eye

38"You have heard that it was said, 'Eye for eye, and tooth for tooth.'[d] 39But I tell you, Do not resist an evil person. If someone strikes you on the right cheek, turn to him the other also. 40And if someone wants to sue you and take your tunic, let him have your cloak as well. 41If someone forces you to go one mile, go with him two miles. 42Give to the one who asks you, and do not turn away from the one who wants to borrow from you.

Love for Enemies

43"You have heard that it was said, 'Love your neighbor[e] and hate your enemy.' 44But I tell you: Love your enemies[f] and pray for those who persecute you, 45that you may be sons of your Father in heaven. He causes his sun to rise on the evil and the good, and sends rain on the righteous and the unrighteous. 46If you love those who love you, what reward will you get? Are not even the tax collectors doing that? 47And if you greet only your brothers, what are you doing more than others? Do not even pagans do that? 48Be perfect, therefore, as your heavenly Father is perfect.

Giving to the Needy

6 "Be careful not to do your 'acts of righteousness' before men, to be seen by them. If you do, you will have no reward from your Father in heaven.

2"So when you give to the needy, do not announce it with trumpets, as the hypocrites do in the synagogues and on the streets, to be honored by men. I tell you the truth, they have received their reward in full. 3But when you give to the needy, do not let your left hand know what your right hand is doing, 4so that your giving may be in secret. Then your Father, who sees what is done in secret, will reward you.

Prayer

5"And when you pray, do not be like the hypocrites, for they love to pray standing in the synagogues and on the street corners to be seen by men. I tell you the truth, they have received their reward in full. 6But when you pray, go into your room, close the door and pray to your Father, who is unseen. Then your Father, who sees what is done in secret, will reward you. 7And when you pray, do not keep on babbling like pagans, for they think they will be heard because of their many words. 8Do not be like them, for your Father knows what you need before you ask him.

9"This, then, is how you should pray:

" 'Our Father in heaven,
hallowed be your name,
10your kingdom come,
your will be done
on earth as it is in heaven.
11Give us today our daily bread.
12Forgive us our debts,
as we also have forgiven our debtors.
13And lead us not into temptation,
but deliver us from the evil one.[g] '

14For if you forgive men when they sin against you, your heavenly Father will also forgive

[a] *26* Greek *kodrantes* [b] *27* Exodus 20:14 [c] *31* Deut. 24:1 [d] *38* Exodus 21:24; Lev. 24:20; Deut. 19:21
[e] *43* Lev. 19:18 [f] *44* Some late manuscripts *enemies, bless those who curse you, do good to those who hate you* [g] *13* Or *from evil*; some late manuscripts *one, / for yours is the kingdom and the power and the glory forever. Amen.*

you. 15But if you do not forgive men their sins,
your Father will not forgive your sins.

Fasting

16“When you fast, do not look somber as the
hypocrites do, for they disfigure their faces to
show men they are fasting. I tell you the truth,
they have received their reward in full. 17But
when you fast, put oil on your head and wash
your face, 18so that it will not be obvious to
men that you are fasting, but only to your Father, who is unseen; and your Father, who sees
what is done in secret, will reward you.

Treasures in Heaven

19“Do not store up for yourselves treasures
on earth, where moth and rust destroy, and
where thieves break in and steal. 20But store up
for yourselves treasures in heaven, where moth
and rust do not destroy, and where thieves do
not break in and steal. 21For where your treasure is, there your heart will be also.

22“The eye is the lamp of the body. If your
eyes are good, your whole body will be full of
light. 23But if your eyes are bad, your whole
body will be full of darkness. If then the light
within you is darkness, how great is that darkness!

24“No one can serve two masters. Either he
will hate the one and love the other, or he will
be devoted to the one and despise the other.
You cannot serve both God and Money.

Do Not Worry

25“Therefore I tell you, do not worry about
your life, what you will eat or drink; or about
your body, what you will wear. Is not life more
important than food, and the body more important than clothes? 26Look at the birds of the air;
they do not sow or reap or store away in barns,
and yet your heavenly Father feeds them. Are
you not much more valuable than they? 27Who
of you by worrying can add a single hour to his
life[a]?

28“And why do you worry about clothes?
See how the lilies of the field grow. They do
not labor or spin. 29Yet I tell you that not even
Solomon in all his splendor was dressed like
one of these. 30If that is how God clothes the
grass of the field, which is here today and tomorrow is thrown into the fire, will he not
much more clothe you, O you of little faith?
31So do not worry, saying, ‘What shall we
eat?’ or ‘What shall we drink?’ or ‘What shall
we wear?’ 32For the pagans run after all these
things, and your heavenly Father knows that
you need them. 33But seek first his kingdom
and his righteousness, and all these things will
be given to you as well. 34Therefore do not
worry about tomorrow, for tomorrow will worry about itself. Each day has enough trouble of
its own.

Judging Others

7 “Do not judge, or you too will be judged.
2For in the same way you judge others, you
will be judged, and with the measure you use,
it will be measured to you.

3“Why do you look at the speck of sawdust
in your brother’s eye and pay no attention to
the plank in your own eye? 4How can you say
to your brother, ‘Let me take the speck out of
your eye,’ when all the time there is a plank in
your own eye? 5You hypocrite, first take the
plank out of your own eye, and then you will
see clearly to remove the speck from your
brother’s eye.

6“Do not give dogs what is sacred; do not
throw your pearls to pigs. If you do, they may
trample them under their feet, and then turn
and tear you to pieces.

Ask, Seek, Knock

7“Ask and it will be given to you; seek and
you will find; knock and the door will be
opened to you. 8For everyone who asks receives; he who seeks finds; and to him who
knocks, the door will be opened.

9“Which of you, if his son asks for bread,
will give him a stone? 10Or if he asks for a fish,
will give him a snake? 11If you, then, though
you are evil, know how to give good gifts to
your children, how much more will your Father in heaven give good gifts to those who ask
him! 12So in everything, do to others what you
would have them do to you, for this sums up
the Law and the Prophets.

The Narrow and Wide Gates

13“Enter through the narrow gate. For wide
is the gate and broad is the road that leads to
destruction, and many enter through it. 14But
small is the gate and narrow the road that leads
to life, and only a few find it.

A Tree and Its Fruit

15“Watch out for false prophets. They come
to you in sheep’s clothing, but inwardly they
are ferocious wolves. 16By their fruit you will
recognize them. Do people pick grapes from
thornbushes, or figs from thistles? 17Likewise
every good tree bears good fruit, but a bad tree
bears bad fruit. 18A good tree cannot bear bad
fruit, and a bad tree cannot bear good fruit.
19Every tree that does not bear good fruit is cut
down and thrown into the fire. 20Thus, by their
fruit you will recognize them.

21“Not everyone who says to me, ‘Lord,
Lord,’ will enter the kingdom of heaven, but
only he who does the will of my Father who is
in heaven. 22Many will say to me on that day,
‘Lord, Lord, did we not prophesy in your
name, and in your name drive out demons and
perform many miracles?’ 23Then I will tell
them plainly, ‘I never knew you. Away from
me, you evildoers!’

The Wise and Foolish Builders

24“Therefore everyone who hears these
words of mine and puts them into practice is
like a wise man who built his house on the
rock. 25The rain came down, the streams rose,

[a]27 Or *single cubit to his height*

and the winds blew and beat against that house; yet it did not fall, because it had its foundation on the rock. 26But everyone who hears these words of mine and does not put them into practice is like a foolish man who built his house on sand. 27The rain came down, the streams rose, and the winds blew and beat against that house, and it fell with a great crash."

28When Jesus had finished saying these things, the crowds were amazed at his teaching, 29because he taught as one who had authority, and not as their teachers of the law.

The Man With Leprosy

8 When he came down from the mountainside, large crowds followed him. 2A man with leprosy[a] came and knelt before him and said, "Lord, if you are willing, you can make me clean."

3Jesus reached out his hand and touched the man. "I am willing," he said. "Be clean!" Immediately he was cured[b] of his leprosy. 4Then Jesus said to him, "See that you don't tell anyone. But go, show yourself to the priest and offer the gift Moses commanded, as a testimony to them."

The Faith of the Centurion

5When Jesus had entered Capernaum, a centurion came to him, asking for help. 6"Lord," he said, "my servant lies at home paralyzed and in terrible suffering."

7Jesus said to him, "I will go and heal him."

8The centurion replied, "Lord, I do not deserve to have you come under my roof. But just say the word, and my servant will be healed. 9For I myself am a man under authority, with soldiers under me. I tell this one, 'Go,' and he goes; and that one, 'Come,' and he comes. I say to my servant, 'Do this,' and he does it."

10When Jesus heard this, he was astonished and said to those following him, "I tell you the truth, I have not found anyone in Israel with such great faith. 11I say to you that many will come from the east and the west, and will take their places at the feast with Abraham, Isaac and Jacob in the kingdom of heaven. 12But the subjects of the kingdom will be thrown outside, into the darkness, where there will be weeping and gnashing of teeth."

13Then Jesus said to the centurion, "Go! It will be done just as you believed it would." And his servant was healed at that very hour.

Jesus Heals Many

14When Jesus came into Peter's house, he saw Peter's mother-in-law lying in bed with a fever. 15He touched her hand and the fever left her, and she got up and began to wait on him.

16When evening came, many who were demon-possessed were brought to him, and he drove out the spirits with a word and healed all the sick. 17This was to fulfill what was spoken through the prophet Isaiah:

"He took up our infirmities
and carried our diseases."[c]

The Cost of Following Jesus

18When Jesus saw the crowd around him, he gave orders to cross to the other side of the lake. 19Then a teacher of the law came to him and said, "Teacher, I will follow you wherever you go."

20Jesus replied, "Foxes have holes and birds of the air have nests, but the Son of Man has no place to lay his head."

21Another disciple said to him, "Lord, first let me go and bury my father."

22But Jesus told him, "Follow me, and let the dead bury their own dead."

Jesus Calms the Storm

23Then he got into the boat and his disciples followed him. 24Without warning, a furious storm came up on the lake, so that the waves swept over the boat. But Jesus was sleeping. 25The disciples went and woke him, saying, "Lord, save us! We're going to drown!"

26He replied, "You of little faith, why are you so afraid?" Then he got up and rebuked the winds and the waves, and it was completely calm.

27The men were amazed and asked, "What kind of man is this? Even the winds and the waves obey him!"

The Healing of Two Demon-possessed Men

28When he arrived at the other side in the region of the Gadarenes,[d] two demon-possessed men coming from the tombs met him. They were so violent that no one could pass that way. 29"What do you want with us, Son of God?" they shouted. "Have you come here to torture us before the appointed time?"

30Some distance from them a large herd of pigs was feeding. 31The demons begged Jesus, "If you drive us out, send us into the herd of pigs."

32He said to them, "Go!" So they came out and went into the pigs, and the whole herd rushed down the steep bank into the lake and died in the water. 33Those tending the pigs ran off, went into the town and reported all this, including what had happened to the demon-possessed men. 34Then the whole town went out to meet Jesus. And when they saw him, they pleaded with him to leave their region.

Jesus Heals a Paralytic

9 Jesus stepped into a boat, crossed over and came to his own town. 2Some men brought to him a paralytic, lying on a mat. When Jesus saw their faith, he said to the paralytic, "Take heart, son; your sins are forgiven."

3At this, some of the teachers of the law said

[a]2 The Greek word was used for various diseases affecting the skin—not necessarily leprosy. [b]3 Greek *made clean* [c]17 Isaiah 53:4 [d]28 Some manuscripts *Gergesenes*; others *Gerasenes*

to themselves, "This fellow is blaspheming!"

4Knowing their thoughts, Jesus said, "Why do you entertain evil thoughts in your hearts? 5Which is easier: to say, 'Your sins are forgiven,' or to say, 'Get up and walk'? 6But so that you may know that the Son of Man has authority on earth to forgive sins . . ." Then he said to the paralytic, "Get up, take your mat and go home." 7And the man got up and went home. 8When the crowd saw this, they were filled with awe; and they praised God, who had given such authority to men.

The Calling of Matthew

9As Jesus went on from there, he saw a man named Matthew sitting at the tax collector's booth. "Follow me," he told him, and Matthew got up and followed him.

10While Jesus was having dinner at Matthew's house, many tax collectors and "sinners" came and ate with him and his disciples. 11When the Pharisees saw this, they asked his disciples, "Why does your teacher eat with tax collectors and 'sinners'?"

12On hearing this, Jesus said, "It is not the healthy who need a doctor, but the sick. 13But go and learn what this means: 'I desire mercy, not sacrifice.'[a] For I have not come to call the righteous, but sinners."

Jesus Questioned About Fasting

14Then John's disciples came and asked him, "How is it that we and the Pharisees fast, but your disciples do not fast?"

15Jesus answered, "How can the guests of the bridegroom mourn while he is with them? The time will come when the bridegroom will be taken from them; then they will fast.

16"No one sews a patch of unshrunk cloth on an old garment, for the patch will pull away from the garment, making the tear worse. 17Neither do men pour new wine into old wineskins. If they do, the skins will burst, the wine will run out and the wineskins will be ruined. No, they pour new wine into new wineskins, and both are preserved."

A Dead Girl and a Sick Woman

18While he was saying this, a ruler came and knelt before him and said, "My daughter has just died. But come and put your hand on her, and she will live." 19Jesus got up and went with him, and so did his disciples.

20Just then a woman who had been subject to bleeding for twelve years came up behind him and touched the edge of his cloak. 21She said to herself, "If I only touch his cloak, I will be healed."

22Jesus turned and saw her. "Take heart, daughter," he said, "your faith has healed you." And the woman was healed from that moment.

23When Jesus entered the ruler's house and saw the flute players and the noisy crowd, 24he said, "Go away. The girl is not dead but asleep." But they laughed at him. 25After the crowd had been put outside, he went in and took the girl by the hand, and she got up. 26News of this spread through all that region.

Jesus Heals the Blind and Mute

27As Jesus went on from there, two blind men followed him, calling out, "Have mercy on us, Son of David!"

28When he had gone indoors, the blind men came to him, and he asked them, "Do you believe that I am able to do this?"

"Yes, Lord," they replied.

29Then he touched their eyes and said, "According to your faith will it be done to you"; 30and their sight was restored. Jesus warned them sternly, "See that no one knows about this." 31But they went out and spread the news about him all over that region.

32While they were going out, a man who was demon-possessed and could not talk was brought to Jesus. 33And when the demon was driven out, the man who had been mute spoke. The crowd was amazed and said, "Nothing like this has ever been seen in Israel."

34But the Pharisees said, "It is by the prince of demons that he drives out demons."

The Workers Are Few

35Jesus went through all the towns and villages, teaching in their synagogues, preaching the good news of the kingdom and healing every disease and sickness. 36When he saw the crowds, he had compassion on them, because they were harassed and helpless, like sheep without a shepherd. 37Then he said to his disciples, "The harvest is plentiful but the workers are few. 38Ask the Lord of the harvest, therefore, to send out workers into his harvest field."

Jesus Sends Out the Twelve

10 He called his twelve disciples to him and gave them authority to drive out evil[b] spirits and to heal every disease and sickness.

2These are the names of the twelve apostles: first, Simon (who is called Peter) and his brother Andrew; James son of Zebedee, and his brother John; 3Philip and Bartholomew; Thomas and Matthew the tax collector; James son of Alphaeus, and Thaddaeus; 4Simon the Zealot and Judas Iscariot, who betrayed him.

5These twelve Jesus sent out with the following instructions: "Do not go among the Gentiles or enter any town of the Samaritans. 6Go rather to the lost sheep of Israel. 7As you go, preach this message: 'The kingdom of heaven is near.' 8Heal the sick, raise the dead, cleanse those who have leprosy,[c] drive out demons. Freely you have received, freely give. 9Do not take along any gold or silver or copper in your belts; 10take no bag for the journey, or extra tunic, or sandals or a staff; for the worker is worth his keep.

[a] *13* Hosea 6:6 [b] *1* Greek *unclean* [c] *8* The Greek word was used for various diseases affecting the skin—not necessarily leprosy.

11 “Whatever town or village you enter, search for some worthy person there and stay at his house until you leave. 12 As you enter the home, give it your greeting. 13 If the home is deserving, let your peace rest on it; if it is not, let your peace return to you. 14 If anyone will not welcome you or listen to your words, shake the dust off your feet when you leave that home or town. 15 I tell you the truth, it will be more bearable for Sodom and Gomorrah on the day of judgment than for that town. 16 I am sending you out like sheep among wolves. Therefore be as shrewd as snakes and as innocent as doves.

17 “Be on your guard against men; they will hand you over to the local councils and flog you in their synagogues. 18 On my account you will be brought before governors and kings as witnesses to them and to the Gentiles. 19 But when they arrest you, do not worry about what to say or how to say it. At that time you will be given what to say, 20 for it will not be you speaking, but the Spirit of your Father speaking through you.

21 “Brother will betray brother to death, and a father his child; children will rebel against their parents and have them put to death. 22 All men will hate you because of me, but he who stands firm to the end will be saved. 23 When you are persecuted in one place, flee to another. I tell you the truth, you will not finish going through the cities of Israel before the Son of Man comes.

24 “A student is not above his teacher, nor a servant above his master. 25 It is enough for the student to be like his teacher, and the servant like his master. If the head of the house has been called Beelzebub,[a] how much more the members of his household!

26 “So do not be afraid of them. There is nothing concealed that will not be disclosed, or hidden that will not be made known. 27 What I tell you in the dark, speak in the daylight; what is whispered in your ear, proclaim from the roofs. 28 Do not be afraid of those who kill the body but cannot kill the soul. Rather, be afraid of the One who can destroy both soul and body in hell. 29 Are not two sparrows sold for a penny[b]? Yet not one of them will fall to the ground apart from the will of your Father. 30 And even the very hairs of your head are all numbered. 31 So don’t be afraid; you are worth more than many sparrows.

32 “Whoever acknowledges me before men, I will also acknowledge him before my Father in heaven. 33 But whoever disowns me before men, I will disown him before my Father in heaven.

34 “Do not suppose that I have come to bring peace to the earth. I did not come to bring peace, but a sword. 35 For I have come to turn

“ ‘a man against his father,
a daughter against her mother,
a daughter-in-law against her
mother-in-law—
36 a man’s enemies will be the members
of his own household.’[c]

37 “Anyone who loves his father or mother more than me is not worthy of me; anyone who loves his son or daughter more than me is not worthy of me; 38 and anyone who does not take his cross and follow me is not worthy of me. 39 Whoever finds his life will lose it, and whoever loses his life for my sake will find it.

40 “He who receives you receives me, and he who receives me receives the one who sent me. 41 Anyone who receives a prophet because he is a prophet will receive a prophet’s reward, and anyone who receives a righteous man because he is a righteous man will receive a righteous man’s reward. 42 And if anyone gives even a cup of cold water to one of these little ones because he is my disciple, I tell you the truth, he will certainly not lose his reward.”

Jesus and John the Baptist

11 After Jesus had finished instructing his twelve disciples, he went on from there to teach and preach in the towns of Galilee.[d]

2 When John heard in prison what Christ was doing, he sent his disciples 3 to ask him, “Are you the one who was to come, or should we expect someone else?”

4 Jesus replied, “Go back and report to John what you hear and see: 5 The blind receive sight, the lame walk, those who have leprosy[e] are cured, the deaf hear, the dead are raised, and the good news is preached to the poor. 6 Blessed is the man who does not fall away on account of me.”

7 As John’s disciples were leaving, Jesus began to speak to the crowd about John: “What did you go out into the desert to see? A reed swayed by the wind? 8 If not, what did you go out to see? A man dressed in fine clothes? No, those who wear fine clothes are in kings’ palaces. 9 Then what did you go out to see? A prophet? Yes, I tell you, and more than a prophet. 10 This is the one about whom it is written:

“ ‘I will send my messenger ahead of you,
who will prepare your way before
you.’[f]

11 I tell you the truth: Among those born of women there has not risen anyone greater than John the Baptist; yet he who is least in the kingdom of heaven is greater than he. 12 From the days of John the Baptist until now, the kingdom of heaven has been forcefully advancing, and forceful men lay hold of it. 13 For all the Prophets and the Law prophesied until John. 14 And if you are willing to accept it, he is the Elijah who was to come. 15 He who has ears, let him hear.

16 “To what can I compare this generation?

[a] *25* Greek *Beezeboul* or *Beelzeboul* [b] *29* Greek *an assarion* [c] *36* Micah 7:6 [d] *1* Greek *in their towns*
[e] *5* The Greek word was used for various diseases affecting the skin—not necessarily leprosy. [f] *10* Mal. 3:1

They are like children sitting in the marketplaces and calling out to others:

17" 'We played the flute for you,
and you did not dance;
we sang a dirge,
and you did not mourn.'

18For John came neither eating nor drinking,
and they say, 'He has a demon.' 19The Son of
Man came eating and drinking, and they say,
'Here is a glutton and a drunkard, a friend of
tax collectors and "sinners." ' But wisdom is
proved right by her actions."

Woe on Unrepentant Cities

20Then Jesus began to denounce the cities
in which most of his miracles had been performed, because they did not repent. 21"Woe to
you, Korazin! Woe to you, Bethsaida! If the
miracles that were performed in you had been
performed in Tyre and Sidon, they would have
repented long ago in sackcloth and ashes.
22But I tell you, it will be more bearable for
Tyre and Sidon on the day of judgment than
for you. 23And you, Capernaum, will you be
lifted up to the skies? No, you will go down to
the depths.[a] If the miracles that were performed in you had been performed in Sodom,
it would have remained to this day. 24But I tell
you that it will be more bearable for Sodom on
the day of judgment than for you."

Rest for the Weary

25At that time Jesus said, "I praise you, Father, Lord of heaven and earth, because you
have hidden these things from the wise and
learned, and revealed them to little children.
26Yes, Father, for this was your good pleasure.
27"All things have been committed to me by
my Father. No one knows the Son except the
Father, and no one knows the Father except the
Son and those to whom the Son chooses to
reveal him.
28"Come to me, all you who are weary and
burdened, and I will give you rest. 29Take my
yoke upon you and learn from me, for I am
gentle and humble in heart, and you will find
rest for your souls. 30For my yoke is easy and
my burden is light."

Lord of the Sabbath

12 At that time Jesus went through the
grainfields on the Sabbath. His disciples
were hungry and began to pick some heads of
grain and eat them. 2When the Pharisees saw
this, they said to him, "Look! Your disciples
are doing what is unlawful on the Sabbath."
3He answered, "Haven't you read what David did when he and his companions were hungry? 4He entered the house of God, and he and
his companions ate the consecrated bread—
which was not lawful for them to do, but only
for the priests. 5Or haven't you read in the Law
that on the Sabbath the priests in the temple
desecrate the day and yet are innocent? 6I tell
you that one[b] greater than the temple is here.
7If you had known what these words mean, 'I
desire mercy, not sacrifice,'[c] you would not
have condemned the innocent. 8For the Son of
Man is Lord of the Sabbath."
9Going on from that place, he went into their
synagogue, 10and a man with a shriveled hand
was there. Looking for a reason to accuse
Jesus, they asked him, "Is it lawful to heal on
the Sabbath?"
11He said to them, "If any of you has a sheep
and it falls into a pit on the Sabbath, will you
not take hold of it and lift it out? 12How much
more valuable is a man than a sheep! Therefore it is lawful to do good on the Sabbath."
13Then he said to the man, "Stretch out your
hand." So he stretched it out and it was completely restored, just as sound as the other.
14But the Pharisees went out and plotted how
they might kill Jesus.

God's Chosen Servant

15Aware of this, Jesus withdrew from that
place. Many followed him, and he healed all
their sick, 16warning them not to tell who he
was. 17This was to fulfill what was spoken
through the prophet Isaiah:

18"Here is my servant whom I have chosen,
the one I love, in whom I delight;
I will put my Spirit on him,
and he will proclaim justice to the
nations.
19He will not quarrel or cry out;
no one will hear his voice in the streets.
20A bruised reed he will not break,
and a smoldering wick he will not snuff
out,
till he leads justice to victory.
21 In his name the nations will put their
hope."[d]

Jesus and Beelzebub

22Then they brought him a demon-
possessed man who was blind and mute, and
Jesus healed him, so that he could both talk
and see. 23All the people were astonished and
said, "Could this be the Son of David?"
24But when the Pharisees heard this, they
said, "It is only by Beelzebub,[e] the prince of
demons, that this fellow drives out demons."
25Jesus knew their thoughts and said to
them, "Every kingdom divided against itself
will be ruined, and every city or household
divided against itself will not stand. 26If Satan
drives out Satan, he is divided against himself.
How then can his kingdom stand? 27And if I
drive out demons by Beelzebub, by whom do
your people drive them out? So then, they will
be your judges. 28But if I drive out demons by
the Spirit of God, then the kingdom of God has
come upon you.
29"Or again, how can anyone enter a strong
man's house and carry off his possessions un-

[a] *23* Greek *Hades* [b] *6* Or *something*; also in verses 41 and 42 [c] *7* Hosea 6:6 [d] *21* Isaiah 42:1-4
[e] *24* Greek *Beezeboul* or *Beelzeboul*; also in verse 27

less he first ties up the strong man? Then he
can rob his house.
30“He who is not with me is against me, and
he who does not gather with me scatters.
31And so I tell you, every sin and blasphemy
will be forgiven men, but the blasphemy
against the Spirit will not be forgiven. 32Any-
one who speaks a word against the Son of Man
will be forgiven, but anyone who speaks
against the Holy Spirit will not be forgiven,
either in this age or in the age to come.
33“Make a tree good and its fruit will be
good, or make a tree bad and its fruit will be
bad, for a tree is recognized by its fruit. 34You
brood of vipers, how can you who are evil say
anything good? For out of the overflow of
the heart the mouth speaks. 35The good man
brings good things out of the good stored up in
him, and the evil man brings evil things out of
the evil stored up in him. 36But I tell you that
men will have to give account on the day of
judgment for every careless word they have
spoken. 37For by your words you will be ac-
quitted, and by your words you will be condemned.”

The Sign of Jonah

38Then some of the Pharisees and teachers
of the law said to him, “Teacher, we want to
see a miraculous sign from you.”
39He answered, “A wicked and adulterous
generation asks for a miraculous sign! But
none will be given it except the sign of the
prophet Jonah. 40For as Jonah was three days
and three nights in the belly of a huge fish, so
the Son of Man will be three days and three
nights in the heart of the earth. 41The men of
Nineveh will stand up at the judgment with
this generation and condemn it; for they repented at the preaching of Jonah, and now
one[a] greater than Jonah is here. 42The Queen
of the South will rise at the judgment with this
generation and condemn it; for she came from
the ends of the earth to listen to Solomon’s
wisdom, and now one greater than Solomon is
here.
43“When an evil[b] spirit comes out of a man,
it goes through arid places seeking rest and
does not find it. 44Then it says, ‘I will return to
the house I left.’ When it arrives, it finds the
house unoccupied, swept clean and put in order. 45Then it goes and takes with it seven
other spirits more wicked than itself, and they
go in and live there. And the final condition of
that man is worse than the first. That is how it
will be with this wicked generation.”

Jesus’ Mother and Brothers

46While Jesus was still talking to the crowd,
his mother and brothers stood outside, wanting
to speak to him. 47Someone told him, “Your
mother and brothers are standing outside,
wanting to speak to you.”[c]
48He replied to him, “Who is my mother,
and who are my brothers?” 49Pointing to his
disciples, he said, “Here are my mother and
my brothers. 50For whoever does the will of
my Father in heaven is my brother and sister
and mother.”

The Parable of the Sower

13 That same day Jesus went out of the
house and sat by the lake. 2Such large
crowds gathered around him that he got into a
boat and sat in it, while all the people stood on
the shore. 3Then he told them many things in
parables, saying: “A farmer went out to sow
his seed. 4As he was scattering the seed, some
fell along the path, and the birds came and ate
it up. 5Some fell on rocky places, where it did
not have much soil. It sprang up quickly, because the soil was shallow. 6But when the sun
came up, the plants were scorched, and they
withered because they had no root. 7Other seed
fell among thorns, which grew up and choked
the plants. 8Still other seed fell on good soil,
where it produced a crop—a hundred, sixty or
thirty times what was sown. 9He who has ears,
let him hear.”
10The disciples came to him and asked,
“Why do you speak to the people in parables?”
11He replied, “The knowledge of the secrets
of the kingdom of heaven has been given to
you, but not to them. 12Whoever has will be
given more, and he will have an abundance.
Whoever does not have, even what he has will
be taken from him. 13This is why I speak to
them in parables:

“Though seeing, they do not see;
 though hearing, they do not hear or
  understand.

14In them is fulfilled the prophecy of Isaiah:

“ ‘You will be ever hearing but never
  understanding;
 you will be ever seeing but never
  perceiving.
15For this people’s heart has become
  calloused;
 they hardly hear with their ears,
 and they have closed their eyes.
Otherwise they might see with their eyes,
 hear with their ears,
 understand with their hearts
and turn, and I would heal them.’[d]

16But blessed are your eyes because they see,
and your ears because they hear. 17For I tell
you the truth, many prophets and righteous
men longed to see what you see but did not
see it, and to hear what you hear but did not
hear it.
18“Listen then to what the parable of the
sower means: 19When anyone hears the message about the kingdom and does not understand it, the evil one comes and snatches away
what was sown in his heart. This is the seed
sown along the path. 20The one who received
the seed that fell on rocky places is the man

[a] *41* Or *something*; also in verse 42 [b] *43* Greek *unclean* [c] *47* Some manuscripts do not have verse 47.
[d] *15* Isaiah 6:9,10

who hears the word and at once receives it
with joy. 21But since he has no root, he lasts
only a short time. When trouble or persecution
comes because of the word, he quickly falls
away. 22The one who received the seed that
fell among the thorns is the man who hears the
word, but the worries of this life and the deceitfulness of wealth choke it, making it unfruitful. 23But the one who received the seed
that fell on good soil is the man who hears the
word and understands it. He produces a crop,
yielding a hundred, sixty or thirty times what
was sown."

The Parable of the Weeds

24Jesus told them another parable: "The
kingdom of heaven is like a man who sowed
good seed in his field. 25But while everyone
was sleeping, his enemy came and sowed
weeds among the wheat, and went away.
26When the wheat sprouted and formed heads,
then the weeds also appeared.

27"The owner's servants came to him and
said, 'Sir, didn't you sow good seed in your
field? Where then did the weeds come from?'

28" 'An enemy did this,' he replied.

"The servants asked him, 'Do you want us
to go and pull them up?'

29" 'No,' he answered, 'because while you
are pulling the weeds, you may root up the
wheat with them. 30Let both grow together until the harvest. At that time I will tell the harvesters: First collect the weeds and tie them in
bundles to be burned; then gather the wheat
and bring it into my barn.' "

The Parables of the Mustard Seed and the Yeast

31He told them another parable: "The kingdom of heaven is like a mustard seed, which a
man took and planted in his field. 32Though it
is the smallest of all your seeds, yet when it
grows, it is the largest of garden plants and
becomes a tree, so that the birds of the air
come and perch in its branches."

33He told them still another parable: "The
kingdom of heaven is like yeast that a woman
took and mixed into a large amount[a] of flour
until it worked all through the dough."

34Jesus spoke all these things to the crowd in
parables; he did not say anything to them without using a parable. 35So was fulfilled what
was spoken through the prophet:

"I will open my mouth in parables,
I will utter things hidden since the
creation of the world."[b]

The Parable of the Weeds Explained

36Then he left the crowd and went into the
house. His disciples came to him and said,
"Explain to us the parable of the weeds in the
field."

37He answered, "The one who sowed the
good seed is the Son of Man. 38The field is the
world, and the good seed stands for the sons of
the kingdom. The weeds are the sons of the
evil one, 39and the enemy who sows them is
the devil. The harvest is the end of the age, and
the harvesters are angels.

40"As the weeds are pulled up and burned in
the fire, so it will be at the end of the age.
41The Son of Man will send out his angels, and
they will weed out of his kingdom everything
that causes sin and all who do evil. 42They will
throw them into the fiery furnace, where there
will be weeping and gnashing of teeth. 43Then
the righteous will shine like the sun in the
kingdom of their Father. He who has ears, let
him hear.

The Parables of the Hidden Treasure and the Pearl

44"The kingdom of heaven is like treasure
hidden in a field. When a man found it, he hid
it again, and then in his joy went and sold all
he had and bought that field.

45"Again, the kingdom of heaven is like a
merchant looking for fine pearls. 46When he
found one of great value, he went away and
sold everything he had and bought it.

The Parable of the Net

47"Once again, the kingdom of heaven is
like a net that was let down into the lake and
caught all kinds of fish. 48When it was full, the
fishermen pulled it up on the shore. Then they
sat down and collected the good fish in baskets, but threw the bad away. 49This is how it
will be at the end of the age. The angels will
come and separate the wicked from the righteous 50and throw them into the fiery furnace,
where there will be weeping and gnashing of
teeth.

51"Have you understood all these things?"
Jesus asked.

"Yes," they replied.

52He said to them, "Therefore every teacher
of the law who has been instructed about the
kingdom of heaven is like the owner of a house
who brings out of his storeroom new treasures
as well as old."

A Prophet Without Honor

53When Jesus had finished these parables,
he moved on from there. 54Coming to his
hometown, he began teaching the people in
their synagogue, and they were amazed.
"Where did this man get this wisdom and these
miraculous powers?" they asked. 55"Isn't this
the carpenter's son? Isn't his mother's name
Mary, and aren't his brothers James, Joseph,
Simon and Judas? 56Aren't all his sisters with
us? Where then did this man get all these
things?" 57And they took offense at him.

But Jesus said to them, "Only in his hometown and in his own house is a prophet without
honor."

58And he did not do many miracles there
because of their lack of faith.

[a]33 Greek *three satas* (probably about 1/2 bushel or 22 liters) [b]35 Psalm 78:2

John the Baptist Beheaded

14 At that time Herod the tetrarch heard the reports about Jesus, 2and he said to his attendants, "This is John the Baptist; he has risen from the dead! That is why miraculous powers are at work in him."

3Now Herod had arrested John and bound him and put him in prison because of Herodias, his brother Philip's wife, 4for John had been saying to him: "It is not lawful for you to have her." 5Herod wanted to kill John, but he was afraid of the people, because they considered him a prophet.

6On Herod's birthday the daughter of Herodias danced for them and pleased Herod so much 7that he promised with an oath to give her whatever she asked. 8Prompted by her mother, she said, "Give me here on a platter the head of John the Baptist." 9The king was distressed, but because of his oaths and his dinner guests, he ordered that her request be granted 10and had John beheaded in the prison. 11His head was brought in on a platter and given to the girl, who carried it to her mother. 12John's disciples came and took his body and buried it. Then they went and told Jesus.

Jesus Feeds the Five Thousand

13When Jesus heard what had happened, he withdrew by boat privately to a solitary place. Hearing of this, the crowds followed him on foot from the towns. 14When Jesus landed and saw a large crowd, he had compassion on them and healed their sick.

15As evening approached, the disciples came to him and said, "This is a remote place, and it's already getting late. Send the crowds away, so they can go to the villages and buy themselves some food."

16Jesus replied, "They do not need to go away. You give them something to eat."

17"We have here only five loaves of bread and two fish," they answered.

18"Bring them here to me," he said. 19And he directed the people to sit down on the grass. Taking the five loaves and the two fish and looking up to heaven, he gave thanks and broke the loaves. Then he gave them to the disciples, and the disciples gave them to the people. 20They all ate and were satisfied, and the disciples picked up twelve basketfuls of broken pieces that were left over. 21The number of those who ate was about five thousand men, besides women and children.

Jesus Walks on the Water

22Immediately Jesus made the disciples get into the boat and go on ahead of him to the other side, while he dismissed the crowd. 23After he had dismissed them, he went up on a mountainside by himself to pray. When evening came, he was there alone, 24but the boat was already a considerable distance[a] from land, buffeted by the waves because the wind was against it.

25During the fourth watch of the night Jesus went out to them, walking on the lake. 26When the disciples saw him walking on the lake, they were terrified. "It's a ghost," they said, and cried out in fear.

27But Jesus immediately said to them: "Take courage! It is I. Don't be afraid."

28"Lord, if it's you," Peter replied, "tell me to come to you on the water."

29"Come," he said.

Then Peter got down out of the boat, walked on the water and came toward Jesus. 30But when he saw the wind, he was afraid and, beginning to sink, cried out, "Lord, save me!"

31Immediately Jesus reached out his hand and caught him. "You of little faith," he said, "why did you doubt?"

32And when they climbed into the boat, the wind died down. 33Then those who were in the boat worshiped him, saying, "Truly you are the Son of God."

34When they had crossed over, they landed at Gennesaret. 35And when the men of that place recognized Jesus, they sent word to all the surrounding country. People brought all their sick to him 36and begged him to let the sick just touch the edge of his cloak, and all who touched him were healed.

Clean and Unclean

15 Then some Pharisees and teachers of the law came to Jesus from Jerusalem and asked, 2"Why do your disciples break the tradition of the elders? They don't wash their hands before they eat!"

3Jesus replied, "And why do you break the command of God for the sake of your tradition? 4For God said, 'Honor your father and mother'[b] and 'Anyone who curses his father or mother must be put to death.'[c] 5But you say that if a man says to his father or mother, 'Whatever help you might otherwise have received from me is a gift devoted to God,' 6he is not to 'honor his father[d]' with it. Thus you nullify the word of God for the sake of your tradition. 7You hypocrites! Isaiah was right when he prophesied about you:

8" 'These people honor me with their lips,
  but their hearts are far from me.
9They worship me in vain;
  their teachings are but rules taught by
    men.'[e]"

10Jesus called the crowd to him and said, "Listen and understand. 11What goes into a man's mouth does not make him 'unclean,' but what comes out of his mouth, that is what makes him 'unclean.' "

12Then the disciples came to him and asked, "Do you know that the Pharisees were offended when they heard this?"

13He replied, "Every plant that my heavenly

[a]24 Greek *many stadia* [b]4 Exodus 20:12; Deut. 5:16 [c]4 Exodus 21:17; Lev. 20:9 [d]6 Some manuscripts *father or his mother* [e]9 Isaiah 29:13

Father has not planted will be pulled up by the roots. 14Leave them; they are blind guides.[a] If a blind man leads a blind man, both will fall into a pit."

15Peter said, "Explain the parable to us."

16"Are you still so dull?" Jesus asked them. 17"Don't you see that whatever enters the mouth goes into the stomach and then out of the body? 18But the things that come out of the mouth come from the heart, and these make a man 'unclean.' 19For out of the heart come evil thoughts, murder, adultery, sexual immorality, theft, false testimony, slander. 20These are what make a man 'unclean'; but eating with unwashed hands does not make him 'unclean.' "

The Faith of the Canaanite Woman

21Leaving that place, Jesus withdrew to the region of Tyre and Sidon. 22A Canaanite woman from that vicinity came to him, crying out, "Lord, Son of David, have mercy on me! My daughter is suffering terribly from demon-possession."

23Jesus did not answer a word. So his disciples came to him and urged him, "Send her away, for she keeps crying out after us."

24He answered, "I was sent only to the lost sheep of Israel."

25The woman came and knelt before him. "Lord, help me!" she said.

26He replied, "It is not right to take the children's bread and toss it to their dogs."

27"Yes, Lord," she said, "but even the dogs eat the crumbs that fall from their masters' table."

28Then Jesus answered, "Woman, you have great faith! Your request is granted." And her daughter was healed from that very hour.

Jesus Feeds the Four Thousand

29Jesus left there and went along the Sea of Galilee. Then he went up on a mountainside and sat down. 30Great crowds came to him, bringing the lame, the blind, the crippled, the mute and many others, and laid them at his feet; and he healed them. 31The people were amazed when they saw the mute speaking, the crippled made well, the lame walking and the blind seeing. And they praised the God of Israel.

32Jesus called his disciples to him and said, "I have compassion for these people; they have already been with me three days and have nothing to eat. I do not want to send them away hungry, or they may collapse on the way."

33His disciples answered, "Where could we get enough bread in this remote place to feed such a crowd?"

34"How many loaves do you have?" Jesus asked.

"Seven," they replied, "and a few small fish."

35He told the crowd to sit down on the ground. 36Then he took the seven loaves and the fish, and when he had given thanks, he broke them and gave them to the disciples, and they in turn to the people. 37They all ate and were satisfied. Afterward the disciples picked up seven basketfuls of broken pieces that were left over. 38The number of those who ate was four thousand, besides women and children. 39After Jesus had sent the crowd away, he got into the boat and went to the vicinity of Magadan.

The Demand for a Sign

16 The Pharisees and Sadducees came to Jesus and tested him by asking him to show them a sign from heaven.

2He replied,[b] "When evening comes, you say, 'It will be fair weather, for the sky is red,' 3and in the morning, 'Today it will be stormy, for the sky is red and overcast.' You know how to interpret the appearance of the sky, but you cannot interpret the signs of the times. 4A wicked and adulterous generation looks for a miraculous sign, but none will be given it except the sign of Jonah." Jesus then left them and went away.

The Yeast of the Pharisees and Sadducees

5When they went across the lake, the disciples forgot to take bread. 6"Be careful," Jesus said to them. "Be on your guard against the yeast of the Pharisees and Sadducees."

7They discussed this among themselves and said, "It is because we didn't bring any bread."

8Aware of their discussion, Jesus asked, "You of little faith, why are you talking among yourselves about having no bread? 9Do you still not understand? Don't you remember the five loaves for the five thousand, and how many basketfuls you gathered? 10Or the seven loaves for the four thousand, and how many basketfuls you gathered? 11How is it you don't understand that I was not talking to you about bread? But be on your guard against the yeast of the Pharisees and Sadducees." 12Then they understood that he was not telling them to guard against the yeast used in bread, but against the teaching of the Pharisees and Sadducees.

Peter's Confession of Christ

13When Jesus came to the region of Caesarea Philippi, he asked his disciples, "Who do people say the Son of Man is?"

14They replied, "Some say John the Baptist; others say Elijah; and still others, Jeremiah or one of the prophets."

15"But what about you?" he asked. "Who do you say I am?"

16Simon Peter answered, "You are the Christ,[c] the Son of the living God."

17Jesus replied, "Blessed are you, Simon son of Jonah, for this was not revealed to you by man, but by my Father in heaven. 18And I tell you that you are Peter,[d] and on this rock I will

[a]14 Some manuscripts *guides of the blind* [b]2 Some early manuscripts do not have the rest of verse 2 and all of verse 3. [c]16 Or *Messiah*; also in verse 20 [d]18 *Peter* means *rock*.

build my church, and the gates of Hades[a] will not overcome it.[b] 19I will give you the keys of the kingdom of heaven; whatever you bind on earth will be[c] bound in heaven, and whatever you loose on earth will be[c] loosed in heaven." 20Then he warned his disciples not to tell anyone that he was the Christ.

Jesus Predicts His Death

21From that time on Jesus began to explain to his disciples that he must go to Jerusalem and suffer many things at the hands of the elders, chief priests and teachers of the law, and that he must be killed and on the third day be raised to life.

22Peter took him aside and began to rebuke him. "Never, Lord!" he said. "This shall never happen to you!"

23Jesus turned and said to Peter, "Get behind me, Satan! You are a stumbling block to me; you do not have in mind the things of God, but the things of men."

24Then Jesus said to his disciples, "If anyone would come after me, he must deny himself and take up his cross and follow me. 25For whoever wants to save his life[d] will lose it, but whoever loses his life for me will find it. 26What good will it be for a man if he gains the whole world, yet forfeits his soul? Or what can a man give in exchange for his soul? 27For the Son of Man is going to come in his Father's glory with his angels, and then he will reward each person according to what he has done. 28I tell you the truth, some who are standing here will not taste death before they see the Son of Man coming in his kingdom."

The Transfiguration

17 After six days Jesus took with him Peter, James and John the brother of James, and led them up a high mountain by themselves. 2There he was transfigured before them. His face shone like the sun, and his clothes became as white as the light. 3Just then there appeared before them Moses and Elijah, talking with Jesus.

4Peter said to Jesus, "Lord, it is good for us to be here. If you wish, I will put up three shelters—one for you, one for Moses and one for Elijah."

5While he was still speaking, a bright cloud enveloped them, and a voice from the cloud said, "This is my Son, whom I love; with him I am well pleased. Listen to him!"

6When the disciples heard this, they fell facedown to the ground, terrified. 7But Jesus came and touched them. "Get up," he said. "Don't be afraid." 8When they looked up, they saw no one except Jesus.

9As they were coming down the mountain, Jesus instructed them, "Don't tell anyone what you have seen, until the Son of Man has been raised from the dead."

10The disciples asked him, "Why then do the teachers of the law say that Elijah must come first?"

11Jesus replied, "To be sure, Elijah comes and will restore all things. 12But I tell you, Elijah has already come, and they did not recognize him, but have done to him everything they wished. In the same way the Son of Man is going to suffer at their hands." 13Then the disciples understood that he was talking to them about John the Baptist.

The Healing of a Boy With a Demon

14When they came to the crowd, a man approached Jesus and knelt before him. 15"Lord, have mercy on my son," he said. "He has seizures and is suffering greatly. He often falls into the fire or into the water. 16I brought him to your disciples, but they could not heal him."

17"O unbelieving and perverse generation," Jesus replied, "how long shall I stay with you? How long shall I put up with you? Bring the boy here to me." 18Jesus rebuked the demon, and it came out of the boy, and he was healed from that moment.

19Then the disciples came to Jesus in private and asked, "Why couldn't we drive it out?"

20He replied, "Because you have so little faith. I tell you the truth, if you have faith as small as a mustard seed, you can say to this mountain, 'Move from here to there' and it will move. Nothing will be impossible for you.[e]"

22When they came together in Galilee, he said to them, "The Son of Man is going to be betrayed into the hands of men. 23They will kill him, and on the third day he will be raised to life." And the disciples were filled with grief.

The Temple Tax

24After Jesus and his disciples arrived in Capernaum, the collectors of the two-drachma tax came to Peter and asked, "Doesn't your teacher pay the temple tax[f]?"

25"Yes, he does," he replied.

When Peter came into the house, Jesus was the first to speak. "What do you think, Simon?" he asked. "From whom do the kings of the earth collect duty and taxes—from their own sons or from others?"

26"From others," Peter answered.

"Then the sons are exempt," Jesus said to him. 27"But so that we may not offend them, go to the lake and throw out your line. Take the first fish you catch; open its mouth and you will find a four-drachma coin. Take it and give it to them for my tax and yours."

The Greatest in the Kingdom of Heaven

18 At that time the disciples came to Jesus and asked, "Who is the greatest in the kingdom of heaven?"

2He called a little child and had him stand

[a] *18* Or *hell* [b] *18* Or *not prove stronger than it* [c] *19* Or *have been* [d] *25* The Greek word means either *life* or *soul*; also in verse 26. [e] *20* Some manuscripts *you.* [21] *But this kind does not go out except by prayer and fasting.* [f] *24* Greek *the two drachmas*

among them. 3And he said: "I tell you the
truth, unless you change and become like little
children, you will never enter the kingdom of
heaven. 4Therefore, whoever humbles himself
like this child is the greatest in the kingdom of
heaven.

5"And whoever welcomes a little child like
this in my name welcomes me. 6But if anyone
causes one of these little ones who believe in
me to sin, it would be better for him to have a
large millstone hung around his neck and to be
drowned in the depths of the sea.

7"Woe to the world because of the things
that cause people to sin! Such things must
come, but woe to the man through whom they
come! 8If your hand or your foot causes you to
sin, cut it off and throw it away. It is better for
you to enter life maimed or crippled than to
have two hands or two feet and be thrown into
eternal fire. 9And if your eye causes you to sin,
gouge it out and throw it away. It is better for
you to enter life with one eye than to have two
eyes and be thrown into the fire of hell.

The Parable of the Lost Sheep

10"See that you do not look down on one of
these little ones. For I tell you that their angels
in heaven always see the face of my Father in
heaven.[a]

12"What do you think? If a man owns a hundred sheep, and one of them wanders away,
will he not leave the ninety-nine on the hills
and go to look for the one that wandered off?
13And if he finds it, I tell you the truth, he is
happier about that one sheep than about the
ninety-nine that did not wander off. 14In the
same way your Father in heaven is not willing
that any of these little ones should be lost.

A Brother Who Sins Against You

15"If your brother sins against you,[b] go and
show him his fault, just between the two of
you. If he listens to you, you have won your
brother over. 16But if he will not listen, take
one or two others along, so that 'every matter
may be established by the testimony of two or
three witnesses.'[c] 17If he refuses to listen to
them, tell it to the church; and if he refuses to
listen even to the church, treat him as you
would a pagan or a tax collector.

18"I tell you the truth, whatever you bind on
earth will be[d] bound in heaven, and whatever
you loose on earth will be[d] loosed in heaven.

19"Again, I tell you that if two of you on
earth agree about anything you ask for, it will
be done for you by my Father in heaven. 20For
where two or three come together in my name,
there am I with them."

The Parable of the Unmerciful Servant

21Then Peter came to Jesus and asked,
"Lord, how many times shall I forgive my
brother when he sins against me? Up to seven
times?"

22Jesus answered, "I tell you, not seven
times, but seventy-seven times.[e]

23"Therefore, the kingdom of heaven is like
a king who wanted to settle accounts with his
servants. 24As he began the settlement, a man
who owed him ten thousand talents[f] was
brought to him. 25Since he was not able to pay,
the master ordered that he and his wife and his
children and all that he had be sold to repay the
debt.

26"The servant fell on his knees before him.
'Be patient with me,' he begged, 'and I will
pay back everything.' 27The servant's master
took pity on him, canceled the debt and let
him go.

28"But when that servant went out, he found
one of his fellow servants who owed him a
hundred denarii.[g] He grabbed him and began
to choke him. 'Pay back what you owe me!' he
demanded.

29"His fellow servant fell to his knees and
begged him, 'Be patient with me, and I will
pay you back.'

30"But he refused. Instead, he went off and
had the man thrown into prison until he could
pay the debt. 31When the other servants saw
what had happened, they were greatly distressed and went and told their master everything that had happened.

32"Then the master called the servant in.
'You wicked servant,' he said, 'I canceled all
that debt of yours because you begged me to.
33Shouldn't you have had mercy on your fellow servant just as I had on you?' 34In anger
his master turned him over to the jailers to be
tortured, until he should pay back all he owed.

35"This is how my heavenly Father will treat
each of you unless you forgive your brother
from your heart."

Divorce

19 When Jesus had finished saying these
things, he left Galilee and went into the
region of Judea to the other side of the Jordan.
2Large crowds followed him, and he healed
them there.

3Some Pharisees came to him to test him.
They asked, "Is it lawful for a man to divorce
his wife for any and every reason?"

4"Haven't you read," he replied, "that at the
beginning the Creator 'made them male and
female,'[h] 5and said, 'For this reason a man
will leave his father and mother and be united
to his wife, and the two will become one
flesh'[i]? 6So they are no longer two, but one.
Therefore what God has joined together, let
man not separate."

7"Why then," they asked, "did Moses command that a man give his wife a certificate of
divorce and send her away?"

8Jesus replied, "Moses permitted you to divorce your wives because your hearts were
hard. But it was not this way from the begin-

[a] *10* Some manuscripts *heaven. 11The Son of Man came to save what was lost.* [b] *15* Some manuscripts do not have *against you.* [c] *16* Deut. 19:15 [d] *18* Or *have been* [e] *22* Or *seventy times seven* [f] *24* That is, millions of dollars [g] *28* That is, a few dollars [h] *4* Gen. 1:27 [i] *5* Gen. 2:24

ning. 9I tell you that anyone who divorces his wife, except for marital unfaithfulness, and marries another woman commits adultery."

10The disciples said to him, "If this is the situation between a husband and wife, it is better not to marry."

11Jesus replied, "Not everyone can accept this word, but only those to whom it has been given. 12For some are eunuchs because they were born that way; others were made that way by men; and others have renounced marriage[a] because of the kingdom of heaven. The one who can accept this should accept it."

The Little Children and Jesus

13Then little children were brought to Jesus for him to place his hands on them and pray for them. But the disciples rebuked those who brought them.

14Jesus said, "Let the little children come to me, and do not hinder them, for the kingdom of heaven belongs to such as these." 15When he had placed his hands on them, he went on from there.

The Rich Young Man

16Now a man came up to Jesus and asked, "Teacher, what good thing must I do to get eternal life?"

17"Why do you ask me about what is good?" Jesus replied. "There is only One who is good. If you want to enter life, obey the commandments."

18"Which ones?" the man inquired.

Jesus replied, " 'Do not murder, do not commit adultery, do not steal, do not give false testimony, 19honor your father and mother,'[b] and 'love your neighbor as yourself.'[c]"

20"All these I have kept," the young man said. "What do I still lack?"

21Jesus answered, "If you want to be perfect, go, sell your possessions and give to the poor, and you will have treasure in heaven. Then come, follow me."

22When the young man heard this, he went away sad, because he had great wealth.

23Then Jesus said to his disciples, "I tell you the truth, it is hard for a rich man to enter the kingdom of heaven. 24Again I tell you, it is easier for a camel to go through the eye of a needle than for a rich man to enter the kingdom of God."

25When the disciples heard this, they were greatly astonished and asked, "Who then can be saved?"

26Jesus looked at them and said, "With man this is impossible, but with God all things are possible."

27Peter answered him, "We have left everything to follow you! What then will there be for us?"

28Jesus said to them, "I tell you the truth, at the renewal of all things, when the Son of Man sits on his glorious throne, you who have followed me will also sit on twelve thrones, judging the twelve tribes of Israel. 29And everyone who has left houses or brothers or sisters or father or mother[d] or children or fields for my sake will receive a hundred times as much and will inherit eternal life. 30But many who are first will be last, and many who are last will be first.

The Parable of the Workers in the Vineyard

20 "For the kingdom of heaven is like a landowner who went out early in the morning to hire men to work in his vineyard. 2He agreed to pay them a denarius for the day and sent them into his vineyard.

3"About the third hour he went out and saw others standing in the marketplace doing nothing. 4He told them, 'You also go and work in my vineyard, and I will pay you whatever is right.' 5So they went.

"He went out again about the sixth hour and the ninth hour and did the same thing. 6About the eleventh hour he went out and found still others standing around. He asked them, 'Why have you been standing here all day long doing nothing?'

7" 'Because no one has hired us,' they answered.

"He said to them, 'You also go and work in my vineyard.'

8"When evening came, the owner of the vineyard said to his foreman, 'Call the workers and pay them their wages, beginning with the last ones hired and going on to the first.'

9"The workers who were hired about the eleventh hour came and each received a denarius. 10So when those came who were hired first, they expected to receive more. But each one of them also received a denarius. 11When they received it, they began to grumble against the landowner. 12'These men who were hired last worked only one hour,' they said, 'and you have made them equal to us who have borne the burden of the work and the heat of the day.'

13"But he answered one of them, 'Friend, I am not being unfair to you. Didn't you agree to work for a denarius? 14Take your pay and go. I want to give the man who was hired last the same as I gave you. 15Don't I have the right to do what I want with my own money? Or are you envious because I am generous?'

16"So the last will be first, and the first will be last."

Jesus Again Predicts His Death

17Now as Jesus was going up to Jerusalem, he took the twelve disciples aside and said to them, 18"We are going up to Jerusalem, and the Son of Man will be betrayed to the chief priests and the teachers of the law. They will condemn him to death 19and will turn him over to the Gentiles to be mocked and flogged and crucified. On the third day he will be raised to life!"

[a]12 Or *have made themselves eunuchs* [b]19 Exodus 20:12-16; Deut. 5:16-20 [c]19 Lev. 19:18 [d]29 Some manuscripts *mother or wife*

A Mother's Request

20Then the mother of Zebedee's sons came
to Jesus with her sons and, kneeling down,
asked a favor of him.

21"What is it you want?" he asked.

She said, "Grant that one of these two sons
of mine may sit at your right and the other at
your left in your kingdom."

22"You don't know what you are asking,"
Jesus said to them. "Can you drink the cup I
am going to drink?"

"We can," they answered.

23Jesus said to them, "You will indeed drink
from my cup, but to sit at my right or left is not
for me to grant. These places belong to those
for whom they have been prepared by my Father."

24When the ten heard about this, they were
indignant with the two brothers. 25Jesus called
them together and said, "You know that the
rulers of the Gentiles lord it over them, and
their high officials exercise authority over
them. 26Not so with you. Instead, whoever
wants to become great among you must be
your servant, 27and whoever wants to be first
must be your slave— 28just as the Son of Man
did not come to be served, but to serve, and to
give his life as a ransom for many."

Two Blind Men Receive Sight

29As Jesus and his disciples were leaving
Jericho, a large crowd followed him. 30Two
blind men were sitting by the roadside, and
when they heard that Jesus was going by, they
shouted, "Lord, Son of David, have mercy
on us!"

31The crowd rebuked them and told them to
be quiet, but they shouted all the louder, "Lord,
Son of David, have mercy on us!"

32Jesus stopped and called them. "What do
you want me to do for you?" he asked.

33"Lord," they answered, "we want our
sight."

34Jesus had compassion on them and
touched their eyes. Immediately they received
their sight and followed him.

The Triumphal Entry

21 As they approached Jerusalem and
came to Bethphage on the Mount of Olives, Jesus sent two disciples, 2saying to them,
"Go to the village ahead of you, and at once
you will find a donkey tied there, with her colt
by her. Untie them and bring them to me. 3If
anyone says anything to you, tell him that the
Lord needs them, and he will send them right
away."

4This took place to fulfill what was spoken
through the prophet:

5"Say to the Daughter of Zion,
'See, your king comes to you,
gentle and riding on a donkey,
on a colt, the foal of a donkey.' "[a]

6The disciples went and did as Jesus had
instructed them. 7They brought the donkey and
the colt, placed their cloaks on them, and Jesus
sat on them. 8A very large crowd spread their
cloaks on the road, while others cut branches
from the trees and spread them on the road.
9The crowds that went ahead of him and those
that followed shouted,

"Hosanna[b] to the Son of David!"

"Blessed is he who comes in the name of
the Lord!"[c]

"Hosanna[b] in the highest!"

10When Jesus entered Jerusalem, the whole
city was stirred and asked, "Who is this?"

11The crowds answered, "This is Jesus, the
prophet from Nazareth in Galilee."

Jesus at the Temple

12Jesus entered the temple area and drove
out all who were buying and selling there. He
overturned the tables of the money changers
and the benches of those selling doves. 13"It is
written," he said to them, " 'My house will be
called a house of prayer,'[d] but you are making
it a 'den of robbers.'[e]"

14The blind and the lame came to him at the
temple, and he healed them. 15But when the
chief priests and the teachers of the law saw
the wonderful things he did and the children
shouting in the temple area, "Hosanna to the
Son of David," they were indignant.

16"Do you hear what these children are saying?" they asked him.

"Yes," replied Jesus, "have you never read,

" 'From the lips of children and infants
you have ordained praise'[f]?"

17And he left them and went out of the city
to Bethany, where he spent the night.

The Fig Tree Withers

18Early in the morning, as he was on his way
back to the city, he was hungry. 19Seeing a fig
tree by the road, he went up to it but found
nothing on it except leaves. Then he said to it,
"May you never bear fruit again!" Immediately the tree withered.

20When the disciples saw this, they were
amazed. "How did the fig tree wither so quickly?" they asked.

21Jesus replied, "I tell you the truth, if you
have faith and do not doubt, not only can you
do what was done to the fig tree, but also you
can say to this mountain, 'Go, throw yourself
into the sea,' and it will be done. 22If you believe, you will receive whatever you ask for in
prayer."

The Authority of Jesus Questioned

23Jesus entered the temple courts, and, while
he was teaching, the chief priests and the elders of the people came to him. "By what

[a]*5* Zech. 9:9 [b]*9* A Hebrew expression meaning "Save!" which became an exclamation of praise; also in verse 15 [c]*9* Psalm 118:26 [d]*13* Isaiah 56:7 [e]*13* Jer. 7:11 [f]*16* Psalm 8:2

authority are you doing these things?" they asked. "And who gave you this authority?"

24Jesus replied, "I will also ask you one question. If you answer me, I will tell you by what authority I am doing these things. 25John's baptism—where did it come from? Was it from heaven, or from men?"

They discussed it among themselves and said, "If we say, 'From heaven,' he will ask, 'Then why didn't you believe him?' 26But if we say, 'From men'—we are afraid of the people, for they all hold that John was a prophet."

27So they answered Jesus, "We don't know."

Then he said, "Neither will I tell you by what authority I am doing these things.

The Parable of the Two Sons

28"What do you think? There was a man who had two sons. He went to the first and said, 'Son, go and work today in the vineyard.'

29" 'I will not,' he answered, but later he changed his mind and went.

30"Then the father went to the other son and said the same thing. He answered, 'I will, sir,' but he did not go.

31"Which of the two did what his father wanted?"

"The first," they answered.

Jesus said to them, "I tell you the truth, the tax collectors and the prostitutes are entering the kingdom of God ahead of you. 32For John came to you to show you the way of righteousness, and you did not believe him, but the tax collectors and the prostitutes did. And even after you saw this, you did not repent and believe him.

The Parable of the Tenants

33"Listen to another parable: There was a landowner who planted a vineyard. He put a wall around it, dug a winepress in it and built a watchtower. Then he rented the vineyard to some farmers and went away on a journey. 34When the harvest time approached, he sent his servants to the tenants to collect his fruit.

35"The tenants seized his servants; they beat one, killed another, and stoned a third. 36Then he sent other servants to them, more than the first time, and the tenants treated them the same way. 37Last of all, he sent his son to them. 'They will respect my son,' he said.

38"But when the tenants saw the son, they said to each other, 'This is the heir. Come, let's kill him and take his inheritance.' 39So they took him and threw him out of the vineyard and killed him.

40"Therefore, when the owner of the vineyard comes, what will he do to those tenants?"

41"He will bring those wretches to a wretched end," they replied, "and he will rent the vineyard to other tenants, who will give him his share of the crop at harvest time."

42Jesus said to them, "Have you never read in the Scriptures:

" 'The stone the builders rejected
has become the capstone[a];
the Lord has done this,
and it is marvelous in our eyes'[b]?

43"Therefore I tell you that the kingdom of God will be taken away from you and given to a people who will produce its fruit. 44He who falls on this stone will be broken to pieces, but he on whom it falls will be crushed."[c]

45When the chief priests and the Pharisees heard Jesus' parables, they knew he was talking about them. 46They looked for a way to arrest him, but they were afraid of the crowd because the people held that he was a prophet.

The Parable of the Wedding Banquet

22 Jesus spoke to them again in parables, saying: 2"The kingdom of heaven is like a king who prepared a wedding banquet for his son. 3He sent his servants to those who had been invited to the banquet to tell them to come, but they refused to come.

4"Then he sent some more servants and said, 'Tell those who have been invited that I have prepared my dinner: My oxen and fattened cattle have been butchered, and everything is ready. Come to the wedding banquet.'

5"But they paid no attention and went off—one to his field, another to his business. 6The rest seized his servants, mistreated them and killed them. 7The king was enraged. He sent his army and destroyed those murderers and burned their city.

8"Then he said to his servants, 'The wedding banquet is ready, but those I invited did not deserve to come. 9Go to the street corners and invite to the banquet anyone you find.' 10So the servants went out into the streets and gathered all the people they could find, both good and bad, and the wedding hall was filled with guests.

11"But when the king came in to see the guests, he noticed a man there who was not wearing wedding clothes. 12'Friend,' he asked, 'how did you get in here without wedding clothes?' The man was speechless.

13"Then the king told the attendants, 'Tie him hand and foot, and throw him outside, into the darkness, where there will be weeping and gnashing of teeth.'

14"For many are invited, but few are chosen."

Paying Taxes to Caesar

15Then the Pharisees went out and laid plans to trap him in his words. 16They sent their disciples to him along with the Herodians. "Teacher," they said, "we know you are a man of integrity and that you teach the way of God in accordance with the truth. You aren't swayed by men, because you pay no attention to who they are. 17Tell us then, what is your opinion? Is it right to pay taxes to Caesar or not?"

18But Jesus, knowing their evil intent, said,

[a]42 Or *cornerstone* [b]42 Psalm 118:22,23 [c]44 Some manuscripts do not have verse 44.

"You hypocrites, why are you trying to trap me? 19Show me the coin used for paying the tax." They brought him a denarius, 20and he asked them, "Whose portrait is this? And whose inscription?"

21"Caesar's," they replied.

Then he said to them, "Give to Caesar what is Caesar's, and to God what is God's."

22When they heard this, they were amazed. So they left him and went away.

Marriage at the Resurrection

23That same day the Sadducees, who say there is no resurrection, came to him with a question. 24"Teacher," they said, "Moses told us that if a man dies without having children, his brother must marry the widow and have children for him. 25Now there were seven brothers among us. The first one married and died, and since he had no children, he left his wife to his brother. 26The same thing happened to the second and third brother, right on down to the seventh. 27Finally, the woman died. 28Now then, at the resurrection, whose wife will she be of the seven, since all of them were married to her?"

29Jesus replied, "You are in error because you do not know the Scriptures or the power of God. 30At the resurrection people will neither marry nor be given in marriage; they will be like the angels in heaven. 31But about the resurrection of the dead—have you not read what God said to you, 32'I am the God of Abraham, the God of Isaac, and the God of Jacob'[a]? He is not the God of the dead but of the living."

33When the crowds heard this, they were astonished at his teaching.

The Greatest Commandment

34Hearing that Jesus had silenced the Sadducees, the Pharisees got together. 35One of them, an expert in the law, tested him with this question: 36"Teacher, which is the greatest commandment in the Law?"

37Jesus replied: " 'Love the Lord your God with all your heart and with all your soul and with all your mind.'[b] 38This is the first and greatest commandment. 39And the second is like it: 'Love your neighbor as yourself.'[c] 40All the Law and the Prophets hang on these two commandments."

Whose Son Is the Christ?

41While the Pharisees were gathered together, Jesus asked them, 42"What do you think about the Christ[d]? Whose son is he?"

"The son of David," they replied.

43He said to them, "How is it then that David, speaking by the Spirit, calls him 'Lord'? For he says,

44" 'The Lord said to my Lord:
"Sit at my right hand
until I put your enemies
under your feet." '[e]

45If then David calls him 'Lord,' how can he be his son?" 46No one could say a word in reply, and from that day on no one dared to ask him any more questions.

Seven Woes

23 Then Jesus said to the crowds and to his disciples: 2"The teachers of the law and the Pharisees sit in Moses' seat. 3So you must obey them and do everything they tell you. But do not do what they do, for they do not practice what they preach. 4They tie up heavy loads and put them on men's shoulders, but they themselves are not willing to lift a finger to move them.

5"Everything they do is done for men to see: They make their phylacteries[f] wide and the tassels on their garments long; 6they love the place of honor at banquets and the most important seats in the synagogues; 7they love to be greeted in the marketplaces and to have men call them 'Rabbi.'

8"But you are not to be called 'Rabbi,' for you have only one Master and you are all brothers. 9And do not call anyone on earth 'father,' for you have one Father, and he is in heaven. 10Nor are you to be called 'teacher,' for you have one Teacher, the Christ.[d] 11The greatest among you will be your servant. 12For whoever exalts himself will be humbled, and whoever humbles himself will be exalted.

13"Woe to you, teachers of the law and Pharisees, you hypocrites! You shut the kingdom of heaven in men's faces. You yourselves do not enter, nor will you let those enter who are trying to.[g]

15"Woe to you, teachers of the law and Pharisees, you hypocrites! You travel over land and sea to win a single convert, and when he becomes one, you make him twice as much a son of hell as you are.

16"Woe to you, blind guides! You say, 'If anyone swears by the temple, it means nothing; but if anyone swears by the gold of the temple, he is bound by his oath.' 17You blind fools! Which is greater: the gold, or the temple that makes the gold sacred? 18You also say, 'If anyone swears by the altar, it means nothing; but if anyone swears by the gift on it, he is bound by his oath.' 19You blind men! Which is greater: the gift, or the altar that makes the gift sacred? 20Therefore, he who swears by the altar swears by it and by everything on it. 21And he who swears by the temple swears by it and by the one who dwells in it. 22And he who swears by heaven swears by God's throne and by the one who sits on it.

23"Woe to you, teachers of the law and Pharisees, you hypocrites! You give a tenth of your spices—mint, dill and cummin. But you

[a] *32* Exodus 3:6 [b] *37* Deut. 6:5 [c] *39* Lev. 19:18 [d] *42,10* Or *Messiah* [e] *44* Psalm 110:1 [f] *5* That is, boxes containing Scripture verses, worn on forehead and arm [g] *13* Some manuscripts *to. 14Woe to you, teachers of the law and Pharisees, you hypocrites! You devour widows' houses and for a show make lengthy prayers. Therefore you will be punished more severely.*

have neglected the more important matters of
the law—justice, mercy and faithfulness. You
should have practiced the latter, without ne-
glecting the former. 24You blind guides! You
strain out a gnat but swallow a camel.

25"Woe to you, teachers of the law and
Pharisees, you hypocrites! You clean the outside of the cup and dish, but inside they are full
of greed and self-indulgence. 26Blind Pharisee! First clean the inside of the cup and dish,
and then the outside also will be clean.

27"Woe to you, teachers of the law and
Pharisees, you hypocrites! You are like whitewashed tombs, which look beautiful on the
outside but on the inside are full of dead men's
bones and everything unclean. 28In the same
way, on the outside you appear to people as
righteous but on the inside you are full of hypocrisy and wickedness.

29"Woe to you, teachers of the law and
Pharisees, you hypocrites! You build tombs for
the prophets and decorate the graves of the
righteous. 30And you say, 'If we had lived in
the days of our forefathers, we would not have
taken part with them in shedding the blood of
the prophets.' 31So you testify against yourselves that you are the descendants of those
who murdered the prophets. 32Fill up, then, the
measure of the sin of your forefathers!

33"You snakes! You brood of vipers! How
will you escape being condemned to hell?
34Therefore I am sending you prophets and
wise men and teachers. Some of them you will
kill and crucify; others you will flog in your
synagogues and pursue from town to town.
35And so upon you will come all the righteous
blood that has been shed on earth, from the
blood of righteous Abel to the blood of Zechariah son of Berekiah, whom you murdered between the temple and the altar. 36I tell you the
truth, all this will come upon this generation.

37"O Jerusalem, Jerusalem, you who kill the
prophets and stone those sent to you, how often I have longed to gather your children together, as a hen gathers her chicks under her
wings, but you were not willing. 38Look, your
house is left to you desolate. 39For I tell you,
you will not see me again until you say,
'Blessed is he who comes in the name of the
Lord.'[a]"

Signs of the End of the Age

24 Jesus left the temple and was walking
away when his disciples came up to him
to call his attention to its buildings. 2"Do you
see all these things?" he asked. "I tell you the
truth, not one stone here will be left on another; every one will be thrown down."

3As Jesus was sitting on the Mount of Olives, the disciples came to him privately. "Tell
us," they said, "when will this happen, and
what will be the sign of your coming and of the
end of the age?"

4Jesus answered: "Watch out that no one
deceives you. 5For many will come in my
name, claiming, 'I am the Christ,[b]' and will
deceive many. 6You will hear of wars and rumors of wars, but see to it that you are not
alarmed. Such things must happen, but the end
is still to come. 7Nation will rise against nation, and kingdom against kingdom. There will
be famines and earthquakes in various places.
8All these are the beginning of birth pains.

9"Then you will be handed over to be persecuted and put to death, and you will be hated
by all nations because of me. 10At that time
many will turn away from the faith and will
betray and hate each other, 11and many false
prophets will appear and deceive many people.
12Because of the increase of wickedness, the
love of most will grow cold, 13but he who
stands firm to the end will be saved. 14And this
gospel of the kingdom will be preached in the
whole world as a testimony to all nations, and
then the end will come.

15"So when you see standing in the holy
place 'the abomination that causes desolation,'[c] spoken of through the prophet Daniel—let the reader understand— 16then let
those who are in Judea flee to the mountains.
17Let no one on the roof of his house go down
to take anything out of the house. 18Let no one
in the field go back to get his cloak. 19How
dreadful it will be in those days for pregnant
women and nursing mothers! 20Pray that your
flight will not take place in winter or on the
Sabbath. 21For then there will be great distress,
unequaled from the beginning of the world until now—and never to be equaled again. 22If
those days had not been cut short, no one
would survive, but for the sake of the elect
those days will be shortened. 23At that time if
anyone says to you, 'Look, here is the Christ!'
or, 'There he is!' do not believe it. 24For false
Christs and false prophets will appear and perform great signs and miracles to deceive even
the elect—if that were possible. 25See, I have
told you ahead of time.

26"So if anyone tells you, 'There he is, out
in the desert,' do not go out; or, 'Here he is, in
the inner rooms,' do not believe it. 27For as
lightning that comes from the east is visible
even in the west, so will be the coming of the
Son of Man. 28Wherever there is a carcass,
there the vultures will gather.

29"Immediately after the distress of those
days

" 'the sun will be darkened,
  and the moon will not give its light;
the stars will fall from the sky,
  and the heavenly bodies will be
    shaken.'[d]

30"At that time the sign of the Son of Man
will appear in the sky, and all the nations of the
earth will mourn. They will see the Son of Man
coming on the clouds of the sky, with power
and great glory. 31And he will send his angels

[a]39 Psalm 118:26 [b]5 Or *Messiah*; also in verse 23 [c]15 Daniel 9:27; 11:31; 12:11 [d]29 Isaiah 13:10; 34:4

with a loud trumpet call, and they will gather his elect from the four winds, from one end of the heavens to the other.

32“Now learn this lesson from the fig tree: As soon as its twigs get tender and its leaves come out, you know that summer is near. 33Even so, when you see all these things, you know that it[a] is near, right at the door. 34I tell you the truth, this generation[b] will certainly not pass away until all these things have happened. 35Heaven and earth will pass away, but my words will never pass away.

The Day and Hour Unknown

36“No one knows about that day or hour, not even the angels in heaven, nor the Son,[c] but only the Father. 37As it was in the days of Noah, so it will be at the coming of the Son of Man. 38For in the days before the flood, people were eating and drinking, marrying and giving in marriage, up to the day Noah entered the ark; 39and they knew nothing about what would happen until the flood came and took them all away. That is how it will be at the coming of the Son of Man. 40Two men will be in the field; one will be taken and the other left. 41Two women will be grinding with a hand mill; one will be taken and the other left.

42“Therefore keep watch, because you do not know on what day your Lord will come. 43But understand this: If the owner of the house had known at what time of night the thief was coming, he would have kept watch and would not have let his house be broken into. 44So you also must be ready, because the Son of Man will come at an hour when you do not expect him.

45“Who then is the faithful and wise servant, whom the master has put in charge of the servants in his household to give them their food at the proper time? 46It will be good for that servant whose master finds him doing so when he returns. 47I tell you the truth, he will put him in charge of all his possessions. 48But suppose that servant is wicked and says to himself, ‘My master is staying away a long time,’ 49and he then begins to beat his fellow servants and to eat and drink with drunkards. 50The master of that servant will come on a day when he does not expect him and at an hour he is not aware of. 51He will cut him to pieces and assign him a place with the hypocrites, where there will be weeping and gnashing of teeth.

The Parable of the Ten Virgins

25 “At that time the kingdom of heaven will be like ten virgins who took their lamps and went out to meet the bridegroom. 2Five of them were foolish and five were wise. 3The foolish ones took their lamps but did not take any oil with them. 4The wise, however, took oil in jars along with their lamps. 5The bridegroom was a long time in coming, and they all became drowsy and fell asleep.

6“At midnight the cry rang out: ‘Here’s the bridegroom! Come out to meet him!’

7“Then all the virgins woke up and trimmed their lamps. 8The foolish ones said to the wise, ‘Give us some of your oil; our lamps are going out.’

9“ ‘No,’ they replied, ‘there may not be enough for both us and you. Instead, go to those who sell oil and buy some for yourselves.’

10“But while they were on their way to buy the oil, the bridegroom arrived. The virgins who were ready went in with him to the wedding banquet. And the door was shut.

11“Later the others also came. ‘Sir! Sir!’ they said. ‘Open the door for us!’

12“But he replied, ‘I tell you the truth, I don’t know you.’

13“Therefore keep watch, because you do not know the day or the hour.

The Parable of the Talents

14“Again, it will be like a man going on a journey, who called his servants and entrusted his property to them. 15To one he gave five talents[d] of money, to another two talents, and to another one talent, each according to his ability. Then he went on his journey. 16The man who had received the five talents went at once and put his money to work and gained five more. 17So also, the one with the two talents gained two more. 18But the man who had received the one talent went off, dug a hole in the ground and hid his master’s money.

19“After a long time the master of those servants returned and settled accounts with them. 20The man who had received the five talents brought the other five. ‘Master,’ he said, ‘you entrusted me with five talents. See, I have gained five more.’

21“His master replied, ‘Well done, good and faithful servant! You have been faithful with a few things; I will put you in charge of many things. Come and share your master’s happiness!’

22“The man with the two talents also came. ‘Master,’ he said, ‘you entrusted me with two talents; see, I have gained two more.’

23“His master replied, ‘Well done, good and faithful servant! You have been faithful with a few things; I will put you in charge of many things. Come and share your master’s happiness!’

24“Then the man who had received the one talent came. ‘Master,’ he said, ‘I knew that you are a hard man, harvesting where you have not sown and gathering where you have not scattered seed. 25So I was afraid and went out and hid your talent in the ground. See, here is what belongs to you.’

26“His master replied, ‘You wicked, lazy servant! So you knew that I harvest where I have not sown and gather where I have not scattered seed? 27Well then, you should have

[a] *33* Or *he* [b] *34* Or *race* [c] *36* Some manuscripts do not have *nor the Son.* [d] *15* A talent was worth more than a thousand dollars.

put my money on deposit with the bankers, so
that when I returned I would have received it
back with interest.
28" 'Take the talent from him and give it to
the one who has the ten talents. 29For everyone
who has will be given more, and he will have
an abundance. Whoever does not have, even
what he has will be taken from him. 30And
throw that worthless servant outside, into the
darkness, where there will be weeping and
gnashing of teeth.'

The Sheep and the Goats

31"When the Son of Man comes in his glory,
and all the angels with him, he will sit on his
throne in heavenly glory. 32All the nations will
be gathered before him, and he will separate
the people one from another as a shepherd separates the sheep from the goats. 33He will put
the sheep on his right and the goats on his left.
34"Then the King will say to those on his
right, 'Come, you who are blessed by my Father; take your inheritance, the kingdom prepared for you since the creation of the world.
35For I was hungry and you gave me something to eat, I was thirsty and you gave me
something to drink, I was a stranger and you
invited me in, 36I needed clothes and you
clothed me, I was sick and you looked after
me, I was in prison and you came to visit me.'
37"Then the righteous will answer him,
'Lord, when did we see you hungry and feed
you, or thirsty and give you something to
drink? 38When did we see you a stranger and
invite you in, or needing clothes and clothe
you? 39When did we see you sick or in prison
and go to visit you?'
40"The King will reply, 'I tell you the truth,
whatever you did for one of the least of these
brothers of mine, you did for me.'
41"Then he will say to those on his left, 'Depart from me, you who are cursed, into the
eternal fire prepared for the devil and his angels. 42For I was hungry and you gave me
nothing to eat, I was thirsty and you gave me
nothing to drink, 43I was a stranger and you did
not invite me in, I needed clothes and you did
not clothe me, I was sick and in prison and you
did not look after me.'
44"They also will answer, 'Lord, when did
we see you hungry or thirsty or a stranger or
needing clothes or sick or in prison, and did
not help you?'
45"He will reply, 'I tell you the truth, whatever you did not do for one of the least of
these, you did not do for me.'
46"Then they will go away to eternal punishment, but the righteous to eternal life."

The Plot Against Jesus

26 When Jesus had finished saying all
these things, he said to his disciples,
2"As you know, the Passover is two days
away—and the Son of Man will be handed
over to be crucified."
3Then the chief priests and the elders of the
people assembled in the palace of the high
priest, whose name was Caiaphas, 4and they
plotted to arrest Jesus in some sly way and kill
him. 5"But not during the Feast," they said, "or
there may be a riot among the people."

Jesus Anointed at Bethany

6While Jesus was in Bethany in the home of
a man known as Simon the Leper, 7a woman
came to him with an alabaster jar of very
expensive perfume, which she poured on his
head as he was reclining at the table.
8When the disciples saw this, they were indignant. "Why this waste?" they asked. 9"This
perfume could have been sold at a high price
and the money given to the poor."
10Aware of this, Jesus said to them, "Why
are you bothering this woman? She has done a
beautiful thing to me. 11The poor you will always have with you, but you will not always
have me. 12When she poured this perfume on
my body, she did it to prepare me for burial. 13I
tell you the truth, wherever this gospel is
preached throughout the world, what she has
done will also be told, in memory of her."

Judas Agrees to Betray Jesus

14Then one of the Twelve—the one called
Judas Iscariot—went to the chief priests 15and
asked, "What are you willing to give me if I
hand him over to you?" So they counted out
for him thirty silver coins. 16From then on Judas watched for an opportunity to hand him
over.

The Lord's Supper

17On the first day of the Feast of Unleavened Bread, the disciples came to Jesus and
asked, "Where do you want us to make preparations for you to eat the Passover?"
18He replied, "Go into the city to a certain
man and tell him, 'The Teacher says: My appointed time is near. I am going to celebrate
the Passover with my disciples at your
house.' " 19So the disciples did as Jesus had
directed them and prepared the Passover.
20When evening came, Jesus was reclining
at the table with the Twelve. 21And while they
were eating, he said, "I tell you the truth, one
of you will betray me."
22They were very sad and began to say to
him one after the other, "Surely not I, Lord?"
23Jesus replied, "The one who has dipped
his hand into the bowl with me will betray me.
24The Son of Man will go just as it is written
about him. But woe to that man who betrays
the Son of Man! It would be better for him if
he had not been born."
25Then Judas, the one who would betray
him, said, "Surely not I, Rabbi?"
Jesus answered, "Yes, it is you."[a]
26While they were eating, Jesus took bread,
gave thanks and broke it, and gave it to his
disciples, saying, "Take and eat; this is my
body."

[a]25 Or *"You yourself have said it"*

27Then he took the cup, gave thanks and
offered it to them, saying, "Drink from it, all of
you. 28This is my blood of the[a] covenant,
which is poured out for many for the forgiveness of sins. 29I tell you, I will not drink of this
fruit of the vine from now on until that day
when I drink it anew with you in my Father's
kingdom."

30When they had sung a hymn, they went
out to the Mount of Olives.

Jesus Predicts Peter's Denial

31Then Jesus told them, "This very night
you will all fall away on account of me, for it
is written:

" 'I will strike the shepherd,
and the sheep of the flock will be
scattered.'[b]

32But after I have risen, I will go ahead of you
into Galilee."

33Peter replied, "Even if all fall away on
account of you, I never will."

34"I tell you the truth," Jesus answered, "this
very night, before the rooster crows, you will
disown me three times."

35But Peter declared, "Even if I have to die
with you, I will never disown you." And all the
other disciples said the same.

Gethsemane

36Then Jesus went with his disciples to a
place called Gethsemane, and he said to them,
"Sit here while I go over there and pray." 37He
took Peter and the two sons of Zebedee along
with him, and he began to be sorrowful and
troubled. 38Then he said to them, "My soul
is overwhelmed with sorrow to the point of
death. Stay here and keep watch with me."

39Going a little farther, he fell with his face
to the ground and prayed, "My Father, if it is
possible, may this cup be taken from me. Yet
not as I will, but as you will."

40Then he returned to his disciples and
found them sleeping. "Could you men not keep
watch with me for one hour?" he asked Peter.
41"Watch and pray so that you will not fall into
temptation. The spirit is willing, but the body
is weak."

42He went away a second time and prayed,
"My Father, if it is not possible for this cup to
be taken away unless I drink it, may your will
be done."

43When he came back, he again found them
sleeping, because their eyes were heavy. 44So
he left them and went away once more and
prayed the third time, saying the same thing.

45Then he returned to the disciples and said
to them, "Are you still sleeping and resting?
Look, the hour is near, and the Son of Man is
betrayed into the hands of sinners. 46Rise, let
us go! Here comes my betrayer!"

Jesus Arrested

47While he was still speaking, Judas, one of
the Twelve, arrived. With him was a large
crowd armed with swords and clubs, sent from
the chief priests and the elders of the people.
48Now the betrayer had arranged a signal with
them: "The one I kiss is the man; arrest him."
49Going at once to Jesus, Judas said, "Greetings, Rabbi!" and kissed him.

50Jesus replied, "Friend, do what you came
for."[c]

Then the men stepped forward, seized Jesus
and arrested him. 51With that, one of Jesus'
companions reached for his sword, drew it out
and struck the servant of the high priest, cutting off his ear.

52"Put your sword back in its place," Jesus
said to him, "for all who draw the sword will
die by the sword. 53Do you think I cannot call
on my Father, and he will at once put at my
disposal more than twelve legions of angels?
54But how then would the Scriptures be fulfilled that say it must happen in this way?"

55At that time Jesus said to the crowd,
"Am I leading a rebellion, that you have come
out with swords and clubs to capture me? Every day I sat in the temple courts teaching, and
you did not arrest me. 56But this has all taken
place that the writings of the prophets might be
fulfilled." Then all the disciples deserted him
and fled.

Before the Sanhedrin

57Those who had arrested Jesus took him to
Caiaphas, the high priest, where the teachers of
the law and the elders had assembled. 58But
Peter followed him at a distance, right up to the
courtyard of the high priest. He entered and sat
down with the guards to see the outcome.

59The chief priests and the whole Sanhedrin
were looking for false evidence against Jesus
so that they could put him to death. 60But they
did not find any, though many false witnesses
came forward.

Finally two came forward 61and declared,
"This fellow said, 'I am able to destroy the
temple of God and rebuild it in three days.' "

62Then the high priest stood up and said to
Jesus, "Are you not going to answer? What
is this testimony that these men are bringing
against you?" 63But Jesus remained silent.

The high priest said to him, "I charge you
under oath by the living God: Tell us if you are
the Christ,[d] the Son of God."

64"Yes, it is as you say," Jesus replied. "But
I say to all of you: In the future you will see the
Son of Man sitting at the right hand of the
Mighty One and coming on the clouds of
heaven."

65Then the high priest tore his clothes and
said, "He has spoken blasphemy! Why do we
need any more witnesses? Look, now you have
heard the blasphemy. 66What do you think?"

"He is worthy of death," they answered.

67Then they spit in his face and struck him

[a] *28* Some manuscripts *the new* [b] *31* Zech. 13:7 [c] *50* Or *"Friend, why have you come?"*
[d] *63* Or *Messiah*; also in verse 68

with their fists. Others slapped him 68and said,
"Prophesy to us, Christ. Who hit you?"

Peter Disowns Jesus

69Now Peter was sitting out in the courtyard,
and a servant girl came to him. "You also were
with Jesus of Galilee," she said.
70But he denied it before them all. "I don't
know what you're talking about," he said.
71Then he went out to the gateway, where
another girl saw him and said to the people
there, "This fellow was with Jesus of Nazareth."
72He denied it again, with an oath: "I don't
know the man!"
73After a little while, those standing there
went up to Peter and said, "Surely you are one
of them, for your accent gives you away."
74Then he began to call down curses on himself and he swore to them, "I don't know the
man!"
Immediately a rooster crowed. 75Then Peter
remembered the word Jesus had spoken: "Before the rooster crows, you will disown me
three times." And he went outside and wept
bitterly.

Judas Hangs Himself

27 Early in the morning, all the chief
priests and the elders of the people
came to the decision to put Jesus to death.
2They bound him, led him away and handed
him over to Pilate, the governor.
3When Judas, who had betrayed him, saw
that Jesus was condemned, he was seized with
remorse and returned the thirty silver coins
to the chief priests and the elders. 4"I have
sinned," he said, "for I have betrayed innocent
blood."
"What is that to us?" they replied. "That's
your responsibility."
5So Judas threw the money into the temple
and left. Then he went away and hanged himself.
6The chief priests picked up the coins and
said, "It is against the law to put this into the
treasury, since it is blood money." 7So they
decided to use the money to buy the potter's
field as a burial place for foreigners. 8That is
why it has been called the Field of Blood to
this day. 9Then what was spoken by Jeremiah
the prophet was fulfilled: "They took the thirty
silver coins, the price set on him by the people
of Israel, 10and they used them to buy the potter's field, as the Lord commanded me."[a]

Jesus Before Pilate

11Meanwhile Jesus stood before the governor, and the governor asked him, "Are you the
king of the Jews?"
"Yes, it is as you say," Jesus replied.
12When he was accused by the chief priests
and the elders, he gave no answer. 13Then Pilate asked him, "Don't you hear the testimony
they are bringing against you?" 14But Jesus
made no reply, not even to a single charge—to
the great amazement of the governor.
15Now it was the governor's custom at the
Feast to release a prisoner chosen by the
crowd. 16At that time they had a notorious
prisoner, called Barabbas. 17So when the
crowd had gathered, Pilate asked them,
"Which one do you want me to release to you:
Barabbas, or Jesus who is called Christ?" 18For
he knew it was out of envy that they had handed Jesus over to him.
19While Pilate was sitting on the judge's
seat, his wife sent him this message: "Don't
have anything to do with that innocent man,
for I have suffered a great deal today in a
dream because of him."
20But the chief priests and the elders persuaded the crowd to ask for Barabbas and to
have Jesus executed.
21"Which of the two do you want me to
release to you?" asked the governor.
"Barabbas," they answered.
22"What shall I do, then, with Jesus who is
called Christ?" Pilate asked.
They all answered, "Crucify him!"
23"Why? What crime has he committed?"
asked Pilate.
But they shouted all the louder, "Crucify
him!"
24When Pilate saw that he was getting nowhere, but that instead an uproar was starting,
he took water and washed his hands in front
of the crowd. "I am innocent of this man's
blood," he said. "It is your responsibility!"
25All the people answered, "Let his blood be
on us and on our children!"
26Then he released Barabbas to them. But he
had Jesus flogged, and handed him over to be
crucified.

The Soldiers Mock Jesus

27Then the governor's soldiers took Jesus
into the Praetorium and gathered the whole
company of soldiers around him. 28They
stripped him and put a scarlet robe on him,
29and then twisted together a crown of thorns
and set it on his head. They put a staff in
his right hand and knelt in front of him and
mocked him. "Hail, king of the Jews!" they
said. 30They spit on him, and took the staff and
struck him on the head again and again. 31Af-
ter they had mocked him, they took off the
robe and put his own clothes on him. Then
they led him away to crucify him.

The Crucifixion

32As they were going out, they met a man
from Cyrene, named Simon, and they forced
him to carry the cross. 33They came to a place
called Golgotha (which means The Place of
the Skull). 34There they offered Jesus wine to
drink, mixed with gall; but after tasting it, he
refused to drink it. 35When they had crucified
him, they divided up his clothes by casting

[a] *10* See Zech. 11:12,13; Jer. 19:1-13; 32:6-9.

lots.[a] 36And sitting down, they kept watch
over him there. 37Above his head they placed
the written charge against him: THIS IS JESUS,
THE KING OF THE JEWS. 38Two robbers were
crucified with him, one on his right and one on
his left. 39Those who passed by hurled insults
at him, shaking their heads 40and saying, "You
who are going to destroy the temple and build
it in three days, save yourself! Come down
from the cross, if you are the Son of God!"

41In the same way the chief priests, the
teachers of the law and the elders mocked him.
42"He saved others," they said, "but he can't
save himself! He's the King of Israel! Let him
come down now from the cross, and we will
believe in him. 43He trusts in God. Let God
rescue him now if he wants him, for he said, 'I
am the Son of God.' " 44In the same way the
robbers who were crucified with him also
heaped insults on him.

The Death of Jesus

45From the sixth hour until the ninth hour
darkness came over all the land. 46About the
ninth hour Jesus cried out in a loud voice,
"Eloi, Eloi,[b] *lama sabachthani?"*—which
means, "My God, my God, why have you forsaken me?"[c]

47When some of those standing there heard
this, they said, "He's calling Elijah."

48Immediately one of them ran and got a
sponge. He filled it with wine vinegar, put it on
a stick, and offered it to Jesus to drink. 49The
rest said, "Now leave him alone. Let's see if
Elijah comes to save him."

50And when Jesus had cried out again in a
loud voice, he gave up his spirit.

51At that moment the curtain of the temple
was torn in two from top to bottom. The earth
shook and the rocks split. 52The tombs broke
open and the bodies of many holy people who
had died were raised to life. 53They came out
of the tombs, and after Jesus' resurrection they
went into the holy city and appeared to many
people.

54When the centurion and those with him
who were guarding Jesus saw the earthquake
and all that had happened, they were terrified,
and exclaimed, "Surely he was the Son[d] of
God!"

55Many women were there, watching from a
distance. They had followed Jesus from Galilee to care for his needs. 56Among them were
Mary Magdalene, Mary the mother of James
and Joses, and the mother of Zebedee's sons.

The Burial of Jesus

57As evening approached, there came a rich
man from Arimathea, named Joseph, who had
himself become a disciple of Jesus. 58Going to
Pilate, he asked for Jesus' body, and Pilate
ordered that it be given to him. 59Joseph took
the body, wrapped it in a clean linen cloth,
60and placed it in his own new tomb that he
had cut out of the rock. He rolled a big stone
in front of the entrance to the tomb and went
away. 61Mary Magdalene and the other Mary
were sitting there opposite the tomb.

The Guard at the Tomb

62The next day, the one after Preparation
Day, the chief priests and the Pharisees went to
Pilate. 63"Sir," they said, "we remember that
while he was still alive that deceiver said, 'After three days I will rise again.' 64So give the
order for the tomb to be made secure until the
third day. Otherwise, his disciples may come
and steal the body and tell the people that he
has been raised from the dead. This last deception will be worse than the first."

65"Take a guard," Pilate answered. "Go,
make the tomb as secure as you know how."
66So they went and made the tomb secure by
putting a seal on the stone and posting the
guard.

The Resurrection

28 After the Sabbath, at dawn on the first
day of the week, Mary Magdalene and
the other Mary went to look at the tomb.

2There was a violent earthquake, for an angel of the Lord came down from heaven and,
going to the tomb, rolled back the stone and sat
on it. 3His appearance was like lightning, and
his clothes were white as snow. 4The guards
were so afraid of him that they shook and became like dead men.

5The angel said to the women, "Do not be
afraid, for I know that you are looking for
Jesus, who was crucified. 6He is not here; he
has risen, just as he said. Come and see the
place where he lay. 7Then go quickly and tell
his disciples: 'He has risen from the dead and
is going ahead of you into Galilee. There you
will see him.' Now I have told you."

8So the women hurried away from the tomb,
afraid yet filled with joy, and ran to tell his
disciples. 9Suddenly Jesus met them. "Greetings," he said. They came to him, clasped his
feet and worshiped him. 10Then Jesus said to
them, "Do not be afraid. Go and tell my brothers to go to Galilee; there they will see me."

The Guards' Report

11While the women were on their way, some
of the guards went into the city and reported to
the chief priests everything that had happened.
12When the chief priests had met with the elders and devised a plan, they gave the soldiers
a large sum of money, 13telling them, "You are
to say, 'His disciples came during the night
and stole him away while we were asleep.' 14If
this report gets to the governor, we will satisfy
him and keep you out of trouble." 15So the
soldiers took the money and did as they were
instructed. And this story has been widely cir-
culated among the Jews to this very day.

[a] *35* A few late manuscripts *lots that the word spoken by the prophet might be fulfilled: "They divided my garments among themselves and cast lots for my clothing"* (Psalm 22:18) [b] *46* Some manuscripts *Eli, Eli*
[c] *46* Psalm 22:1 [d] *54* Or *a son*

The Great Commission

16Then the eleven disciples went to Galilee,
to the mountain where Jesus had told them to
go. 17When they saw him, they worshiped him;
but some doubted. 18Then Jesus came to them
and said, "All authority in heaven and on earth
has been given to me. 19Therefore go and
make disciples of all nations, baptizing them
in[a] the name of the Father and of the Son and
of the Holy Spirit, 20and teaching them to obey
everything I have commanded you. And surely
I am with you always, to the very end of the
age."

Mark

John the Baptist Prepares the Way

1 The beginning of the gospel about Jesus
Christ, the Son of God.[b]

2It is written in Isaiah the prophet:

"I will send my messenger ahead of you,
who will prepare your way"[c]—
3"a voice of one calling in the desert,
'Prepare the way for the Lord,
make straight paths for him.' "[d]

4And so John came, baptizing in the desert
region and preaching a baptism of repentance
for the forgiveness of sins. 5The whole Judean
countryside and all the people of Jerusalem
went out to him. Confessing their sins, they
were baptized by him in the Jordan River.
6John wore clothing made of camel's hair,
with a leather belt around his waist, and he ate
locusts and wild honey. 7And this was his message: "After me will come one more powerful
than I, the thongs of whose sandals I am not
worthy to stoop down and untie. 8I baptize you
with[e] water, but he will baptize you with the
Holy Spirit."

The Baptism and Temptation of Jesus

9At that time Jesus came from Nazareth in
Galilee and was baptized by John in the Jordan. 10As Jesus was coming up out of the water, he saw heaven being torn open and the
Spirit descending on him like a dove. 11And a
voice came from heaven: "You are my Son,
whom I love; with you I am well pleased."

12At once the Spirit sent him out into the
desert, 13and he was in the desert forty days,
being tempted by Satan. He was with the wild
animals, and angels attended him.

The Calling of the First Disciples

14After John was put in prison, Jesus went
into Galilee, proclaiming the good news of
God. 15"The time has come," he said. "The
kingdom of God is near. Repent and believe
the good news!"

16As Jesus walked beside the Sea of Galilee,
he saw Simon and his brother Andrew casting
a net into the lake, for they were fishermen.
17"Come, follow me," Jesus said, "and I will
make you fishers of men." 18At once they left
their nets and followed him.

19When he had gone a little farther, he saw
James son of Zebedee and his brother John in
a boat, preparing their nets. 20Without delay he
called them, and they left their father Zebedee
in the boat with the hired men and followed
him.

Jesus Drives Out an Evil Spirit

21They went to Capernaum, and when the
Sabbath came, Jesus went into the synagogue
and began to teach. 22The people were amazed
at his teaching, because he taught them as one
who had authority, not as the teachers of the
law. 23Just then a man in their synagogue who
was possessed by an evil[f] spirit cried out,
24"What do you want with us, Jesus of Nazareth? Have you come to destroy us? I know
who you are—the Holy One of God!"

25"Be quiet!" said Jesus sternly. "Come out
of him!" 26The evil spirit shook the man violently and came out of him with a shriek.

27The people were all so amazed that they
asked each other, "What is this? A new teaching—and with authority! He even gives orders
to evil spirits and they obey him." 28News
about him spread quickly over the whole region of Galilee.

Jesus Heals Many

29As soon as they left the synagogue, they
went with James and John to the home of Simon and Andrew. 30Simon's mother-in-law
was in bed with a fever, and they told Jesus
about her. 31So he went to her, took her hand
and helped her up. The fever left her and she
began to wait on them.

32That evening after sunset the people
brought to Jesus all the sick and demon-
possessed. 33The whole town gathered at the
door, 34and Jesus healed many who had various diseases. He also drove out many demons,
but he would not let the demons speak because
they knew who he was.

Jesus Prays in a Solitary Place

35Very early in the morning, while it was

[a] *19* Or *into*; see Acts 8:16; 19:5; Romans 6:3; 1 Cor. 1:13; 10:2 and Gal. 3:27. [b] *1* Some manuscripts do not have *the Son of God.* [c] *2* Mal. 3:1 [d] *3* Isaiah 40:3 [e] *8* Or *in* [f] *23* Greek *unclean*; also in verses 26 and 27

still dark, Jesus got up, left the house and went
off to a solitary place, where he prayed. 36Si-
mon and his companions went to look for him,
37and when they found him, they exclaimed:
"Everyone is looking for you!"
38Jesus replied, "Let us go somewhere
else—to the nearby villages—so I can preach
there also. That is why I have come." 39So he
traveled throughout Galilee, preaching in their
synagogues and driving out demons.

A Man With Leprosy

40A man with leprosy[a] came to him and
begged him on his knees, "If you are willing,
you can make me clean."
41Filled with compassion, Jesus reached out
his hand and touched the man. "I am willing,"
he said. "Be clean!" 42Immediately the leprosy
left him and he was cured.
43Jesus sent him away at once with a strong
warning: 44"See that you don't tell this to anyone. But go, show yourself to the priest and
offer the sacrifices that Moses commanded for
your cleansing, as a testimony to them." 45In-
stead he went out and began to talk freely,
spreading the news. As a result, Jesus could no
longer enter a town openly but stayed outside
in lonely places. Yet the people still came to
him from everywhere.

Jesus Heals a Paralytic

2 A few days later, when Jesus again entered
Capernaum, the people heard that he had
come home. 2So many gathered that there was
no room left, not even outside the door, and he
preached the word to them. 3Some men came,
bringing to him a paralytic, carried by four of
them. 4Since they could not get him to Jesus
because of the crowd, they made an opening in
the roof above Jesus and, after digging through
it, lowered the mat the paralyzed man was lying on. 5When Jesus saw their faith, he said to
the paralytic, "Son, your sins are forgiven."
6Now some teachers of the law were sitting
there, thinking to themselves, 7"Why does this
fellow talk like that? He's blaspheming! Who
can forgive sins but God alone?"
8Immediately Jesus knew in his spirit that
this was what they were thinking in their
hearts, and he said to them, "Why are you
thinking these things? 9Which is easier: to say
to the paralytic, 'Your sins are forgiven,' or to
say, 'Get up, take your mat and walk'? 10But
that you may know that the Son of Man has
authority on earth to forgive sins . . ." He said
to the paralytic, 11"I tell you, get up, take your
mat and go home." 12He got up, took his mat
and walked out in full view of them all. This
amazed everyone and they praised God, saying, "We have never seen anything like this!"

The Calling of Levi

13Once again Jesus went out beside the lake.
A large crowd came to him, and he began to
teach them. 14As he walked along, he saw Levi
son of Alphaeus sitting at the tax collector's
booth. "Follow me," Jesus told him, and Levi
got up and followed him.
15While Jesus was having dinner at Levi's
house, many tax collectors and "sinners" were
eating with him and his disciples, for there
were many who followed him. 16When the
teachers of the law who were Pharisees saw
him eating with the "sinners" and tax collectors, they asked his disciples: "Why does he
eat with tax collectors and 'sinners'?"
17On hearing this, Jesus said to them, "It is
not the healthy who need a doctor, but the sick.
I have not come to call the righteous, but sinners."

Jesus Questioned About Fasting

18Now John's disciples and the Pharisees
were fasting. Some people came and asked
Jesus, "How is it that John's disciples and the
disciples of the Pharisees are fasting, but yours
are not?"
19Jesus answered, "How can the guests of
the bridegroom fast while he is with them?
They cannot, so long as they have him with
them. 20But the time will come when the bridegroom will be taken from them, and on that
day they will fast.
21"No one sews a patch of unshrunk cloth on
an old garment. If he does, the new piece will
pull away from the old, making the tear worse.
22And no one pours new wine into old wineskins. If he does, the wine will burst the skins,
and both the wine and the wineskins will be
ruined. No, he pours new wine into new wineskins."

Lord of the Sabbath

23One Sabbath Jesus was going through the
grainfields, and as his disciples walked along,
they began to pick some heads of grain. 24The
Pharisees said to him, "Look, why are they
doing what is unlawful on the Sabbath?"
25He answered, "Have you never read what
David did when he and his companions were
hungry and in need? 26In the days of Abiathar
the high priest, he entered the house of God
and ate the consecrated bread, which is lawful
only for priests to eat. And he also gave some
to his companions."
27Then he said to them, "The Sabbath was
made for man, not man for the Sabbath. 28So
the Son of Man is Lord even of the Sabbath."
3 Another time he went into the synagogue,
and a man with a shriveled hand was there.
2Some of them were looking for a reason to
accuse Jesus, so they watched him closely to
see if he would heal him on the Sabbath. 3Jesus
said to the man with the shriveled hand, "Stand
up in front of everyone."
4Then Jesus asked them, "Which is lawful
on the Sabbath: to do good or to do evil, to
save life or to kill?" But they remained silent.
5He looked around at them in anger and,
deeply distressed at their stubborn hearts, said
to the man, "Stretch out your hand." He

[a]40 The Greek word was used for various diseases affecting the skin—not necessarily leprosy.

stretched it out, and his hand was completely restored. 6Then the Pharisees went out and began to plot with the Herodians how they might kill Jesus.

Crowds Follow Jesus

7Jesus withdrew with his disciples to the lake, and a large crowd from Galilee followed. 8When they heard all he was doing, many people came to him from Judea, Jerusalem, Idumea, and the regions across the Jordan and around Tyre and Sidon. 9Because of the crowd he told his disciples to have a small boat ready for him, to keep the people from crowding him. 10For he had healed many, so that those with diseases were pushing forward to touch him. 11Whenever the evil[a] spirits saw him, they fell down before him and cried out, "You are the Son of God." 12But he gave them strict orders not to tell who he was.

The Appointing of the Twelve Apostles

13Jesus went up on a mountainside and called to him those he wanted, and they came to him. 14He appointed twelve—designating them apostles[b]—that they might be with him and that he might send them out to preach 15and to have authority to drive out demons. 16These are the twelve he appointed: Simon (to whom he gave the name Peter); 17James son of Zebedee and his brother John (to them he gave the name Boanerges, which means Sons of Thunder); 18Andrew, Philip, Bartholomew, Matthew, Thomas, James son of Alphaeus, Thaddaeus, Simon the Zealot 19and Judas Iscariot, who betrayed him.

Jesus and Beelzebub

20Then Jesus entered a house, and again a crowd gathered, so that he and his disciples were not even able to eat. 21When his family heard about this, they went to take charge of him, for they said, "He is out of his mind."

22And the teachers of the law who came down from Jerusalem said, "He is possessed by Beelzebub[c]! By the prince of demons he is driving out demons."

23So Jesus called them and spoke to them in parables: "How can Satan drive out Satan? 24If a kingdom is divided against itself, that kingdom cannot stand. 25If a house is divided against itself, that house cannot stand. 26And if Satan opposes himself and is divided, he cannot stand; his end has come. 27In fact, no one can enter a strong man's house and carry off his possessions unless he first ties up the strong man. Then he can rob his house. 28I tell you the truth, all the sins and blasphemies of men will be forgiven them. 29But whoever blasphemes against the Holy Spirit will never be forgiven; he is guilty of an eternal sin."

30He said this because they were saying, "He has an evil spirit."

Jesus' Mother and Brothers

31Then Jesus' mother and brothers arrived. Standing outside, they sent someone in to call him. 32A crowd was sitting around him, and they told him, "Your mother and brothers are outside looking for you."

33"Who are my mother and my brothers?" he asked.

34Then he looked at those seated in a circle around him and said, "Here are my mother and my brothers! 35Whoever does God's will is my brother and sister and mother."

The Parable of the Sower

4 Again Jesus began to teach by the lake. The crowd that gathered around him was so large that he got into a boat and sat in it out on the lake, while all the people were along the shore at the water's edge. 2He taught them many things by parables, and in his teaching said: 3"Listen! A farmer went out to sow his seed. 4As he was scattering the seed, some fell along the path, and the birds came and ate it up. 5Some fell on rocky places, where it did not have much soil. It sprang up quickly, because the soil was shallow. 6But when the sun came up, the plants were scorched, and they withered because they had no root. 7Other seed fell among thorns, which grew up and choked the plants, so that they did not bear grain. 8Still other seed fell on good soil. It came up, grew and produced a crop, multiplying thirty, sixty, or even a hundred times."

9Then Jesus said, "He who has ears to hear, let him hear."

10When he was alone, the Twelve and the others around him asked him about the parables. 11He told them, "The secret of the kingdom of God has been given to you. But to those on the outside everything is said in parables 12so that,

" 'they may be ever seeing but never
 perceiving,
and ever hearing but never
 understanding;
otherwise they might turn and be
 forgiven!'[d]"

13Then Jesus said to them, "Don't you understand this parable? How then will you understand any parable? 14The farmer sows the word. 15Some people are like seed along the path, where the word is sown. As soon as they hear it, Satan comes and takes away the word that was sown in them. 16Others, like seed sown on rocky places, hear the word and at once receive it with joy. 17But since they have no root, they last only a short time. When trouble or persecution comes because of the word, they quickly fall away. 18Still others, like seed sown among thorns, hear the word; 19but the worries of this life, the deceitfulness of wealth and the desires for other things come in and choke the word, making it unfruitful. 20Others,

[a]11 Greek *unclean*; also in verse 30 [b]14 Some manuscripts do not have *designating them apostles.*
[c]22 Greek *Beezeboul* or *Beelzeboul* [d]12 Isaiah 6:9,10

like seed sown on good soil, hear the word,
accept it, and produce a crop—thirty, sixty or
even a hundred times what was sown."

A Lamp on a Stand

21He said to them, "Do you bring in a lamp
to put it under a bowl or a bed? Instead, don't
you put it on its stand? 22For whatever is hidden is meant to be disclosed, and whatever is
concealed is meant to be brought out into the
open. 23If anyone has ears to hear, let him
hear."

24"Consider carefully what you hear," he
continued. "With the measure you use, it will
be measured to you—and even more. 25Who-
ever has will be given more; whoever does not
have, even what he has will be taken from
him."

The Parable of the Growing Seed

26He also said, "This is what the kingdom of
God is like. A man scatters seed on the ground.
27Night and day, whether he sleeps or gets up,
the seed sprouts and grows, though he does not
know how. 28All by itself the soil produces
grain—first the stalk, then the head, then the
full kernel in the head. 29As soon as the grain
is ripe, he puts the sickle to it, because the
harvest has come."

The Parable of the Mustard Seed

30Again he said, "What shall we say the
kingdom of God is like, or what parable shall
we use to describe it? 31It is like a mustard
seed, which is the smallest seed you plant in
the ground. 32Yet when planted, it grows and
becomes the largest of all garden plants, with
such big branches that the birds of the air can
perch in its shade."

33With many similar parables Jesus spoke
the word to them, as much as they could understand. 34He did not say anything to them without using a parable. But when he was alone
with his own disciples, he explained everything.

Jesus Calms the Storm

35That day when evening came, he said to
his disciples, "Let us go over to the other side."
36Leaving the crowd behind, they took him
along, just as he was, in the boat. There were
also other boats with him. 37A furious squall
came up, and the waves broke over the boat, so
that it was nearly swamped. 38Jesus was in the
stern, sleeping on a cushion. The disciples
woke him and said to him, "Teacher, don't you
care if we drown?"

39He got up, rebuked the wind and said to
the waves, "Quiet! Be still!" Then the wind
died down and it was completely calm.

40He said to his disciples, "Why are you so
afraid? Do you still have no faith?"

41They were terrified and asked each other,
"Who is this? Even the wind and the waves
obey him!"

The Healing of a Demon-possessed Man

5 They went across the lake to the region of
the Gerasenes.[a] 2When Jesus got out of the
boat, a man with an evil[b] spirit came from the
tombs to meet him. 3This man lived in
the tombs, and no one could bind him any
more, not even with a chain. 4For he had often
been chained hand and foot, but he tore the
chains apart and broke the irons on his feet. No
one was strong enough to subdue him. 5Night
and day among the tombs and in the hills he
would cry out and cut himself with stones.

6When he saw Jesus from a distance, he ran
and fell on his knees in front of him. 7He
shouted at the top of his voice, "What do you
want with me, Jesus, Son of the Most High
God? Swear to God that you won't torture
me!" 8For Jesus had said to him, "Come out of
this man, you evil spirit!"

9Then Jesus asked him, "What is your
name?"

"My name is Legion," he replied, "for we
are many." 10And he begged Jesus again and
again not to send them out of the area.

11A large herd of pigs was feeding on the
nearby hillside. 12The demons begged Jesus,
"Send us among the pigs; allow us to go into
them." 13He gave them permission, and the
evil spirits came out and went into the pigs.
The herd, about two thousand in number,
rushed down the steep bank into the lake and
were drowned.

14Those tending the pigs ran off and reported this in the town and countryside, and the
people went out to see what had happened.
15When they came to Jesus, they saw the man
who had been possessed by the legion of demons, sitting there, dressed and in his right
mind; and they were afraid. 16Those who had
seen it told the people what had happened to
the demon-possessed man—and told about the
pigs as well. 17Then the people began to plead
with Jesus to leave their region.

18As Jesus was getting into the boat, the
man who had been demon-possessed begged
to go with him. 19Jesus did not let him, but
said, "Go home to your family and tell them
how much the Lord has done for you, and how
he has had mercy on you." 20So the man went
away and began to tell in the Decapolis[c] how
much Jesus had done for him. And all the people were amazed.

A Dead Girl and a Sick Woman

21When Jesus had again crossed over by
boat to the other side of the lake, a large crowd
gathered around him while he was by the lake.
22Then one of the synagogue rulers, named
Jairus, came there. Seeing Jesus, he fell at his
feet 23and pleaded earnestly with him, "My
little daughter is dying. Please come and put
your hands on her so that she will be healed
and live." 24So Jesus went with him.

[a] *1* Some manuscripts *Gadarenes*; other manuscripts *Gergesenes* [b] *2* Greek *unclean*; also in verses 8 and 13
[c] *20* That is, the Ten Cities

A large crowd followed and pressed around
him. 25And a woman was there who had been
subject to bleeding for twelve years. 26She had
suffered a great deal under the care of many
doctors and had spent all she had, yet instead
of getting better she grew worse. 27When she
heard about Jesus, she came up behind him in
the crowd and touched his cloak, 28because she
thought, "If I just touch his clothes, I will be
healed." 29Immediately her bleeding stopped
and she felt in her body that she was freed
from her suffering.

30At once Jesus realized that power had
gone out from him. He turned around in the
crowd and asked, "Who touched my clothes?"

31"You see the people crowding against
you," his disciples answered, "and yet you can
ask, 'Who touched me?' "

32But Jesus kept looking around to see who
had done it. 33Then the woman, knowing what
had happened to her, came and fell at his feet
and, trembling with fear, told him the whole
truth. 34He said to her, "Daughter, your faith
has healed you. Go in peace and be freed from
your suffering."

35While Jesus was still speaking, some men
came from the house of Jairus, the synagogue
ruler. "Your daughter is dead," they said.
"Why bother the teacher any more?"

36Ignoring what they said, Jesus told the
synagogue ruler, "Don't be afraid; just believe."

37He did not let anyone follow him except
Peter, James and John the brother of James.
38When they came to the home of the synagogue ruler, Jesus saw a commotion, with people crying and wailing loudly. 39He went in
and said to them, "Why all this commotion and
wailing? The child is not dead but asleep."
40But they laughed at him.

After he put them all out, he took the child's
father and mother and the disciples who were
with him, and went in where the child was.
41He took her by the hand and said to her,
"Talitha koum!" (which means, "Little girl, I
say to you, get up!"). 42Immediately the girl
stood up and walked around (she was twelve
years old). At this they were completely astonished. 43He gave strict orders not to let anyone
know about this, and told them to give her
something to eat.

A Prophet Without Honor

6 Jesus left there and went to his hometown,
accompanied by his disciples. 2When the
Sabbath came, he began to teach in the synagogue, and many who heard him were amazed.

"Where did this man get these things?" they
asked. "What's this wisdom that has been giv-
en him, that he even does miracles! 3Isn't this
the carpenter? Isn't this Mary's son and the
brother of James, Joseph,[a] Judas and Simon?
Aren't his sisters here with us?" And they took
offense at him.

4Jesus said to them, "Only in his hometown,
among his relatives and in his own house is a
prophet without honor." 5He could not do any
miracles there, except lay his hands on a few
sick people and heal them. 6And he was
amazed at their lack of faith.

Jesus Sends Out the Twelve

Then Jesus went around teaching from village to village. 7Calling the Twelve to him, he
sent them out two by two and gave them authority over evil[b] spirits.

8These were his instructions: "Take nothing
for the journey except a staff—no bread, no
bag, no money in your belts. 9Wear sandals but
not an extra tunic. 10Whenever you enter a
house, stay there until you leave that town.
11And if any place will not welcome you or
listen to you, shake the dust off your feet when
you leave, as a testimony against them."

12They went out and preached that people
should repent. 13They drove out many demons
and anointed many sick people with oil and
healed them.

John the Baptist Beheaded

14King Herod heard about this, for Jesus'
name had become well known. Some were
saying,[c] "John the Baptist has been raised
from the dead, and that is why miraculous
powers are at work in him."

15Others said, "He is Elijah."

And still others claimed, "He is a prophet,
like one of the prophets of long ago."

16But when Herod heard this, he said, "John,
the man I beheaded, has been raised from the
dead!"

17For Herod himself had given orders to
have John arrested, and he had him bound and
put in prison. He did this because of Herodias,
his brother Philip's wife, whom he had married. 18For John had been saying to Herod, "It
is not lawful for you to have your brother's
wife." 19So Herodias nursed a grudge against
John and wanted to kill him. But she was not
able to, 20because Herod feared John and protected him, knowing him to be a righteous and
holy man. When Herod heard John, he was
greatly puzzled[d]; yet he liked to listen to him.

21Finally the opportune time came. On his
birthday Herod gave a banquet for his high
officials and military commanders and the
leading men of Galilee. 22When the daughter
of Herodias came in and danced, she pleased
Herod and his dinner guests.

The king said to the girl, "Ask me for anything you want, and I'll give it to you." 23And
he promised her with an oath, "Whatever you
ask I will give you, up to half my kingdom."

24She went out and said to her mother,
"What shall I ask for?"

"The head of John the Baptist," she answered.

25At once the girl hurried in to the king with

[a]*3* Greek *Joses,* a variant of *Joseph* [b]*7* Greek *unclean* [c]*14* Some early manuscripts *He was saying*
[d]*20* Some early manuscripts *he did many things*

the request: "I want you to give me right now the head of John the Baptist on a platter."

26The king was greatly distressed, but because of his oaths and his dinner guests, he did not want to refuse her. 27So he immediately sent an executioner with orders to bring John's head. The man went, beheaded John in the prison, 28and brought back his head on a platter. He presented it to the girl, and she gave it to her mother. 29On hearing of this, John's disciples came and took his body and laid it in a tomb.

Jesus Feeds the Five Thousand

30The apostles gathered around Jesus and reported to him all they had done and taught. 31Then, because so many people were coming and going that they did not even have a chance to eat, he said to them, "Come with me by yourselves to a quiet place and get some rest."

32So they went away by themselves in a boat to a solitary place. 33But many who saw them leaving recognized them and ran on foot from all the towns and got there ahead of them. 34When Jesus landed and saw a large crowd, he had compassion on them, because they were like sheep without a shepherd. So he began teaching them many things.

35By this time it was late in the day, so his disciples came to him. "This is a remote place," they said, "and it's already very late. 36Send the people away so they can go to the surrounding countryside and villages and buy themselves something to eat."

37But he answered, "You give them something to eat."

They said to him, "That would take eight months of a man's wages[a]! Are we to go and spend that much on bread and give it to them to eat?"

38"How many loaves do you have?" he asked. "Go and see."

When they found out, they said, "Five—and two fish."

39Then Jesus directed them to have all the people sit down in groups on the green grass. 40So they sat down in groups of hundreds and fifties. 41Taking the five loaves and the two fish and looking up to heaven, he gave thanks and broke the loaves. Then he gave them to his disciples to set before the people. He also divided the two fish among them all. 42They all ate and were satisfied, 43and the disciples picked up twelve basketfuls of broken pieces of bread and fish. 44The number of the men who had eaten was five thousand.

Jesus Walks on the Water

45Immediately Jesus made his disciples get into the boat and go on ahead of him to Bethsaida, while he dismissed the crowd. 46After leaving them, he went up on a mountainside to pray.

47When evening came, the boat was in the middle of the lake, and he was alone on land. 48He saw the disciples straining at the oars, because the wind was against them. About the fourth watch of the night he went out to them, walking on the lake. He was about to pass by them, 49but when they saw him walking on the lake, they thought he was a ghost. They cried out, 50because they all saw him and were terrified.

Immediately he spoke to them and said, "Take courage! It is I. Don't be afraid." 51Then he climbed into the boat with them, and the wind died down. They were completely amazed, 52for they had not understood about the loaves; their hearts were hardened.

53When they had crossed over, they landed at Gennesaret and anchored there. 54As soon as they got out of the boat, people recognized Jesus. 55They ran throughout that whole region and carried the sick on mats to wherever they heard he was. 56And wherever he went—into villages, towns or countryside—they placed the sick in the marketplaces. They begged him to let them touch even the edge of his cloak, and all who touched him were healed.

Clean and Unclean

7 The Pharisees and some of the teachers of the law who had come from Jerusalem gathered around Jesus and 2saw some of his disciples eating food with hands that were "unclean," that is, unwashed. 3(The Pharisees and all the Jews do not eat unless they give their hands a ceremonial washing, holding to the tradition of the elders. 4When they come from the marketplace they do not eat unless they wash. And they observe many other traditions, such as the washing of cups, pitchers and kettles.[b])

5So the Pharisees and teachers of the law asked Jesus, "Why don't your disciples live according to the tradition of the elders instead of eating their food with 'unclean' hands?"

6He replied, "Isaiah was right when he prophesied about you hypocrites; as it is written:

" 'These people honor me with their lips,
but their hearts are far from me.
7They worship me in vain;
their teachings are but rules taught by men.'[c]

8You have let go of the commands of God and are holding on to the traditions of men."

9And he said to them: "You have a fine way of setting aside the commands of God in order to observe[d] your own traditions! 10For Moses said, 'Honor your father and your mother,'[e] and, 'Anyone who curses his father or mother must be put to death.'[f] 11But you say that if a man says to his father or mother: 'Whatever help you might otherwise have received from me is Corban' (that is, a gift devoted to God),

[a]37 Greek *take two hundred denarii* [b]4 Some early manuscripts *pitchers, kettles and dining couches* [c]6,7 Isaiah 29:13 [d]9 Some manuscripts *set up* [e]10 Exodus 20:12; Deut. 5:16 [f]10 Exodus 21:17; Lev. 20:9

12then you no longer let him do anything for his father or mother. 13Thus you nullify the word of God by your tradition that you have handed down. And you do many things like that."

14Again Jesus called the crowd to him and said, "Listen to me, everyone, and understand this. 15Nothing outside a man can make him 'unclean' by going into him. Rather, it is what comes out of a man that makes him 'unclean.'[a]"

17After he had left the crowd and entered the house, his disciples asked him about this parable. 18"Are you so dull?" he asked. "Don't you see that nothing that enters a man from the outside can make him 'unclean'? 19For it doesn't go into his heart but into his stomach, and then out of his body." (In saying this, Jesus declared all foods "clean.")

20He went on: "What comes out of a man is what makes him 'unclean.' 21For from within, out of men's hearts, come evil thoughts, sexual immorality, theft, murder, adultery, 22greed, malice, deceit, lewdness, envy, slander, arrogance and folly. 23All these evils come from inside and make a man 'unclean.' "

The Faith of a Syrophoenician Woman

24Jesus left that place and went to the vicinity of Tyre.[b] He entered a house and did not want anyone to know it; yet he could not keep his presence secret. 25In fact, as soon as she heard about him, a woman whose little daughter was possessed by an evil[c] spirit came and fell at his feet. 26The woman was a Greek, born in Syrian Phoenicia. She begged Jesus to drive the demon out of her daughter.

27"First let the children eat all they want," he told her, "for it is not right to take the children's bread and toss it to their dogs."

28"Yes, Lord," she replied, "but even the dogs under the table eat the children's crumbs."

29Then he told her, "For such a reply, you may go; the demon has left your daughter."

30She went home and found her child lying on the bed, and the demon gone.

The Healing of a Deaf and Mute Man

31Then Jesus left the vicinity of Tyre and went through Sidon, down to the Sea of Galilee and into the region of the Decapolis.[d] 32There some people brought to him a man who was deaf and could hardly talk, and they begged him to place his hand on the man.

33After he took him aside, away from the crowd, Jesus put his fingers into the man's ears. Then he spit and touched the man's tongue. 34He looked up to heaven and with a deep sigh said to him, *"Ephphatha!"* (which means, "Be opened!"). 35At this, the man's ears were opened, his tongue was loosened and he began to speak plainly.

36Jesus commanded them not to tell anyone. But the more he did so, the more they kept talking about it. 37People were overwhelmed with amazement. "He has done everything well," they said. "He even makes the deaf hear and the mute speak."

Jesus Feeds the Four Thousand

8 During those days another large crowd gathered. Since they had nothing to eat, Jesus called his disciples to him and said, 2"I have compassion for these people; they have already been with me three days and have nothing to eat. 3If I send them home hungry, they will collapse on the way, because some of them have come a long distance."

4His disciples answered, "But where in this remote place can anyone get enough bread to feed them?"

5"How many loaves do you have?" Jesus asked.

"Seven," they replied.

6He told the crowd to sit down on the ground. When he had taken the seven loaves and given thanks, he broke them and gave them to his disciples to set before the people, and they did so. 7They had a few small fish as well; he gave thanks for them also and told the disciples to distribute them. 8The people ate and were satisfied. Afterward the disciples picked up seven basketfuls of broken pieces that were left over. 9About four thousand men were present. And having sent them away, 10he got into the boat with his disciples and went to the region of Dalmanutha.

11The Pharisees came and began to question Jesus. To test him, they asked him for a sign from heaven. 12He sighed deeply and said, "Why does this generation ask for a miraculous sign? I tell you the truth, no sign will be given to it." 13Then he left them, got back into the boat and crossed to the other side.

The Yeast of the Pharisees and Herod

14The disciples had forgotten to bring bread, except for one loaf they had with them in the boat. 15"Be careful," Jesus warned them. "Watch out for the yeast of the Pharisees and that of Herod."

16They discussed this with one another and said, "It is because we have no bread."

17Aware of their discussion, Jesus asked them: "Why are you talking about having no bread? Do you still not see or understand? Are your hearts hardened? 18Do you have eyes but fail to see, and ears but fail to hear? And don't you remember? 19When I broke the five loaves for the five thousand, how many basketfuls of pieces did you pick up?"

"Twelve," they replied.

20"And when I broke the seven loaves for the four thousand, how many basketfuls of pieces did you pick up?"

They answered, "Seven."

21He said to them, "Do you still not understand?"

[a] *15* Some early manuscripts *'unclean.' 16If anyone has ears to hear, let him hear.* [b] *24* Many early manuscripts *Tyre and Sidon* [c] *25* Greek *unclean* [d] *31* That is, the Ten Cities

The Healing of a Blind Man at Bethsaida

22They came to Bethsaida, and some people brought a blind man and begged Jesus to touch him. 23He took the blind man by the hand and led him outside the village. When he had spit on the man's eyes and put his hands on him, Jesus asked, "Do you see anything?"

24He looked up and said, "I see people; they look like trees walking around."

25Once more Jesus put his hands on the man's eyes. Then his eyes were opened, his sight was restored, and he saw everything clearly. 26Jesus sent him home, saying, "Don't go into the village.[a]"

Peter's Confession of Christ

27Jesus and his disciples went on to the villages around Caesarea Philippi. On the way he asked them, "Who do people say I am?"

28They replied, "Some say John the Baptist; others say Elijah; and still others, one of the prophets."

29"But what about you?" he asked. "Who do you say I am?"

Peter answered, "You are the Christ.[b]"

30Jesus warned them not to tell anyone about him.

Jesus Predicts His Death

31He then began to teach them that the Son of Man must suffer many things and be rejected by the elders, chief priests and teachers of the law, and that he must be killed and after three days rise again. 32He spoke plainly about this, and Peter took him aside and began to rebuke him.

33But when Jesus turned and looked at his disciples, he rebuked Peter. "Get behind me, Satan!" he said. "You do not have in mind the things of God, but the things of men."

34Then he called the crowd to him along with his disciples and said: "If anyone would come after me, he must deny himself and take up his cross and follow me. 35For whoever wants to save his life[c] will lose it, but whoever loses his life for me and for the gospel will save it. 36What good is it for a man to gain the whole world, yet forfeit his soul? 37Or what can a man give in exchange for his soul? 38If anyone is ashamed of me and my words in this adulterous and sinful generation, the Son of Man will be ashamed of him when he comes in his Father's glory with the holy angels."

9 And he said to them, "I tell you the truth, some who are standing here will not taste death before they see the kingdom of God come with power."

The Transfiguration

2After six days Jesus took Peter, James and John with him and led them up a high mountain, where they were all alone. There he was transfigured before them. 3His clothes became dazzling white, whiter than anyone in the world could bleach them. 4And there appeared before them Elijah and Moses, who were talking with Jesus.

5Peter said to Jesus, "Rabbi, it is good for us to be here. Let us put up three shelters—one for you, one for Moses and one for Elijah." 6(He did not know what to say, they were so frightened.)

7Then a cloud appeared and enveloped them, and a voice came from the cloud: "This is my Son, whom I love. Listen to him!"

8Suddenly, when they looked around, they no longer saw anyone with them except Jesus.

9As they were coming down the mountain, Jesus gave them orders not to tell anyone what they had seen until the Son of Man had risen from the dead. 10They kept the matter to themselves, discussing what "rising from the dead" meant.

11And they asked him, "Why do the teachers of the law say that Elijah must come first?"

12Jesus replied, "To be sure, Elijah does come first, and restores all things. Why then is it written that the Son of Man must suffer much and be rejected? 13But I tell you, Elijah has come, and they have done to him everything they wished, just as it is written about him."

The Healing of a Boy With an Evil Spirit

14When they came to the other disciples, they saw a large crowd around them and the teachers of the law arguing with them. 15As soon as all the people saw Jesus, they were overwhelmed with wonder and ran to greet him.

16"What are you arguing with them about?" he asked.

17A man in the crowd answered, "Teacher, I brought you my son, who is possessed by a spirit that has robbed him of speech. 18Whenever it seizes him, it throws him to the ground. He foams at the mouth, gnashes his teeth and becomes rigid. I asked your disciples to drive out the spirit, but they could not."

19"O unbelieving generation," Jesus replied, "how long shall I stay with you? How long shall I put up with you? Bring the boy to me."

20So they brought him. When the spirit saw Jesus, it immediately threw the boy into a convulsion. He fell to the ground and rolled around, foaming at the mouth.

21Jesus asked the boy's father, "How long has he been like this?"

"From childhood," he answered. 22"It has often thrown him into fire or water to kill him. But if you can do anything, take pity on us and help us."

23" 'If you can'?" said Jesus. "Everything is possible for him who believes."

24Immediately the boy's father exclaimed,

[a]26 Some manuscripts *Don't go and tell anyone in the village* [b]29 Or *Messiah.* "The Christ" (Greek) and "the Messiah" (Hebrew) both mean "the Anointed One." [c]35 The Greek word means either *life* or *soul*; also in verse 36.

"I do believe; help me overcome my unbelief!"
25When Jesus saw that a crowd was running
to the scene, he rebuked the evil[a] spirit. "You
deaf and mute spirit," he said, "I command
you, come out of him and never enter him
again."
26The spirit shrieked, convulsed him violently and came out. The boy looked so much
like a corpse that many said, "He's dead."
27But Jesus took him by the hand and lifted
him to his feet, and he stood up.
28After Jesus had gone indoors, his disciples
asked him privately, "Why couldn't we drive it
out?"
29He replied, "This kind can come out only
by prayer.[b]"
30They left that place and passed through
Galilee. Jesus did not want anyone to know
where they were, 31because he was teaching
his disciples. He said to them, "The Son of
Man is going to be betrayed into the hands of
men. They will kill him, and after three days
he will rise." 32But they did not understand
what he meant and were afraid to ask him
about it.

Who Is the Greatest?

33They came to Capernaum. When he was
in the house, he asked them, "What were you
arguing about on the road?" 34But they kept
quiet because on the way they had argued
about who was the greatest.
35Sitting down, Jesus called the Twelve and
said, "If anyone wants to be first, he must be
the very last, and the servant of all."
36He took a little child and had him stand
among them. Taking him in his arms, he said
to them, 37"Whoever welcomes one of these
little children in my name welcomes me; and
whoever welcomes me does not welcome me
but the one who sent me."

Whoever Is Not Against Us Is for Us

38"Teacher," said John, "we saw a man driving out demons in your name and we told him
to stop, because he was not one of us."
39"Do not stop him," Jesus said. "No one
who does a miracle in my name can in the next
moment say anything bad about me, 40for
whoever is not against us is for us. 41I tell you
the truth, anyone who gives you a cup of water
in my name because you belong to Christ will
certainly not lose his reward.

Causing to Sin

42"And if anyone causes one of these little
ones who believe in me to sin, it would be
better for him to be thrown into the sea with a
large millstone tied around his neck. 43If your
hand causes you to sin, cut it off. It is better for
you to enter life maimed than with two hands
to go into hell, where the fire never goes out.[c]
45And if your foot causes you to sin, cut it off.
It is better for you to enter life crippled than to
have two feet and be thrown into hell.[d] 47And
if your eye causes you to sin, pluck it out. It is
better for you to enter the kingdom of God
with one eye than to have two eyes and be
thrown into hell, 48where

" 'their worm does not die,
and the fire is not quenched.'[e]

49Everyone will be salted with fire.
50"Salt is good, but if it loses its saltiness,
how can you make it salty again? Have salt in
yourselves, and be at peace with each other."

Divorce

10 Jesus then left that place and went into
the region of Judea and across the Jordan. Again crowds of people came to him, and
as was his custom, he taught them.
2Some Pharisees came and tested him by
asking, "Is it lawful for a man to divorce his
wife?"
3"What did Moses command you?" he replied.
4They said, "Moses permitted a man to write
a certificate of divorce and send her away."
5"It was because your hearts were hard that
Moses wrote you this law," Jesus replied.
6"But at the beginning of creation God 'made
them male and female.'[f] 7'For this reason a
man will leave his father and mother and be
united to his wife,[g] 8and the two will become
one flesh.'[h] So they are no longer two, but
one. 9Therefore what God has joined together,
let man not separate."
10When they were in the house again, the
disciples asked Jesus about this. 11He answered, "Anyone who divorces his wife and
marries another woman commits adultery
against her. 12And if she divorces her husband
and marries another man, she commits adultery."

The Little Children and Jesus

13People were bringing little children to
Jesus to have him touch them, but the disciples
rebuked them. 14When Jesus saw this, he was
indignant. He said to them, "Let the little children come to me, and do not hinder them, for
the kingdom of God belongs to such as these.
15I tell you the truth, anyone who will not receive the kingdom of God like a little child
will never enter it." 16And he took the children
in his arms, put his hands on them and blessed
them.

The Rich Young Man

17As Jesus started on his way, a man ran up
to him and fell on his knees before him. "Good
teacher," he asked, "what must I do to inherit
eternal life?"
18"Why do you call me good?" Jesus an-

[a] *25* Greek *unclean* [b] *29* Some manuscripts *prayer and fasting* [c] *43* Some manuscripts *out, 44where / " 'their worm does not die, / and the fire is not quenched.'* [d] *45* Some manuscripts *hell, 46where / " 'their worm does not die, / and the fire is not quenched.'* [e] *48* Isaiah 66:24 [f] *6* Gen. 1:27 [g] *7* Some early manuscripts do not have *and be united to his wife.* [h] *8* Gen. 2:24

swered. "No one is good—except God alone.
19You know the commandments: 'Do not murder, do not commit adultery, do not steal, do
not give false testimony, do not defraud, honor
your father and mother.'[a]"
20"Teacher," he declared, "all these I have
kept since I was a boy."
21Jesus looked at him and loved him. "One
thing you lack," he said. "Go, sell everything
you have and give to the poor, and you will
have treasure in heaven. Then come, follow me."
22At this the man's face fell. He went away
sad, because he had great wealth.
23Jesus looked around and said to his disciples, "How hard it is for the rich to enter the
kingdom of God!"
24The disciples were amazed at his words.
But Jesus said again, "Children, how hard it
is[b] to enter the kingdom of God! 25It is easier
for a camel to go through the eye of a needle
than for a rich man to enter the kingdom of
God."
26The disciples were even more amazed,
and said to each other, "Who then can be
saved?"
27Jesus looked at them and said, "With man
this is impossible, but not with God; all things
are possible with God."
28Peter said to him, "We have left everything to follow you!"
29"I tell you the truth," Jesus replied, "no
one who has left home or brothers or sisters or
mother or father or children or fields for me
and the gospel 30will fail to receive a hundred
times as much in this present age (homes,
brothers, sisters, mothers, children and
fields—and with them, persecutions) and in
the age to come, eternal life. 31But many who
are first will be last, and the last first."

Jesus Again Predicts His Death

32They were on their way up to Jerusalem,
with Jesus leading the way, and the disciples
were astonished, while those who followed
were afraid. Again he took the Twelve aside
and told them what was going to happen to
him. 33"We are going up to Jerusalem," he
said, "and the Son of Man will be betrayed to
the chief priests and teachers of the law. They
will condemn him to death and will hand him
over to the Gentiles, 34who will mock him and
spit on him, flog him and kill him. Three days
later he will rise."

The Request of James and John

35Then James and John, the sons of Zebedee, came to him. "Teacher," they said, "we
want you to do for us whatever we ask."
36"What do you want me to do for you?" he
asked.
37They replied, "Let one of us sit at your
right and the other at your left in your glory."
38"You don't know what you are asking,"
Jesus said. "Can you drink the cup I drink or be
baptized with the baptism I am baptized with?"
39"We can," they answered.
Jesus said to them, "You will drink the cup
I drink and be baptized with the baptism I am
baptized with, 40but to sit at my right or left is
not for me to grant. These places belong to
those for whom they have been prepared."
41When the ten heard about this, they became indignant with James and John. 42Jesus
called them together and said, "You know that
those who are regarded as rulers of the Gentiles lord it over them, and their high officials
exercise authority over them. 43Not so with
you. Instead, whoever wants to become great
among you must be your servant, 44and whoever wants to be first must be slave of all.
45For even the Son of Man did not come to be
served, but to serve, and to give his life as a
ransom for many."

Blind Bartimaeus Receives His Sight

46Then they came to Jericho. As Jesus and
his disciples, together with a large crowd, were
leaving the city, a blind man, Bartimaeus (that
is, the Son of Timaeus), was sitting by the
roadside begging. 47When he heard that it was
Jesus of Nazareth, he began to shout, "Jesus,
Son of David, have mercy on me!"
48Many rebuked him and told him to be quiet, but he shouted all the more, "Son of David,
have mercy on me!"
49Jesus stopped and said, "Call him."
So they called to the blind man, "Cheer up!
On your feet! He's calling you." 50Throwing
his cloak aside, he jumped to his feet and came
to Jesus.
51"What do you want me to do for you?"
Jesus asked him.
The blind man said, "Rabbi, I want to see."
52"Go," said Jesus, "your faith has healed
you." Immediately he received his sight and
followed Jesus along the road.

The Triumphal Entry

11 As they approached Jerusalem and
came to Bethphage and Bethany at the
Mount of Olives, Jesus sent two of his disciples, 2saying to them, "Go to the village ahead
of you, and just as you enter it, you will find
a colt tied there, which no one has ever ridden.
Untie it and bring it here. 3If anyone asks you,
'Why are you doing this?' tell him, 'The Lord
needs it and will send it back here shortly.' "
4They went and found a colt outside in the
street, tied at a doorway. As they untied it,
5some people standing there asked, "What are
you doing, untying that colt?" 6They answered
as Jesus had told them to, and the people let
them go. 7When they brought the colt to Jesus
and threw their cloaks over it, he sat on it.
8Many people spread their cloaks on the road,
while others spread branches they had cut in

[a] 19 Exodus 20:12-16; Deut. 5:16-20 [b] 24 Some manuscripts *is for those who trust in riches*

the fields. 9Those who went ahead and those
who followed shouted,

"Hosanna![a]"

"Blessed is he who comes in the name of
the Lord!"[b]

10"Blessed is the coming kingdom of our
father David!"

"Hosanna in the highest!"

11Jesus entered Jerusalem and went to the
temple. He looked around at everything, but
since it was already late, he went out to Bethany with the Twelve.

Jesus Clears the Temple

12The next day as they were leaving Bethany, Jesus was hungry. 13Seeing in the distance
a fig tree in leaf, he went to find out if it had
any fruit. When he reached it, he found nothing but leaves, because it was not the season
for figs. 14Then he said to the tree, "May no
one ever eat fruit from you again." And his
disciples heard him say it.
15On reaching Jerusalem, Jesus entered the
temple area and began driving out those who
were buying and selling there. He overturned
the tables of the money changers and the
benches of those selling doves, 16and would
not allow anyone to carry merchandise through
the temple courts. 17And as he taught them, he
said, "Is it not written:

" 'My house will be called
a house of prayer for all nations'[c]?

But you have made it 'a den of robbers.'[d]"
18The chief priests and the teachers of the
law heard this and began looking for a way
to kill him, for they feared him, because the
whole crowd was amazed at his teaching.
19When evening came, they[e] went out of
the city.

The Withered Fig Tree

20In the morning, as they went along, they
saw the fig tree withered from the roots. 21Pe-
ter remembered and said to Jesus, "Rabbi,
look! The fig tree you cursed has withered!"
22"Have[f] faith in God," Jesus answered.
23"I tell you the truth, if anyone says to this
mountain, 'Go, throw yourself into the sea,'
and does not doubt in his heart but believes
that what he says will happen, it will be done
for him. 24Therefore I tell you, whatever you
ask for in prayer, believe that you have received it, and it will be yours. 25And when you
stand praying, if you hold anything against
anyone, forgive him, so that your Father in
heaven may forgive you your sins.[g]"

The Authority of Jesus Questioned

27They arrived again in Jerusalem, and
while Jesus was walking in the temple courts,
the chief priests, the teachers of the law and the
elders came to him. 28"By what authority are
you doing these things?" they asked. "And
who gave you authority to do this?"
29Jesus replied, "I will ask you one question.
Answer me, and I will tell you by what authority I am doing these things. 30John's baptism—was it from heaven, or from men?
Tell me!"
31They discussed it among themselves and
said, "If we say, 'From heaven,' he will ask,
'Then why didn't you believe him?' 32But if
we say, 'From men' . . ." (They feared the people, for everyone held that John really was a
prophet.)
33So they answered Jesus, "We don't
know."
Jesus said, "Neither will I tell you by what
authority I am doing these things."

The Parable of the Tenants

12 He then began to speak to them in parables: "A man planted a vineyard. He put
a wall around it, dug a pit for the winepress
and built a watchtower. Then he rented the
vineyard to some farmers and went away on a
journey. 2At harvest time he sent a servant to
the tenants to collect from them some of the
fruit of the vineyard. 3But they seized him,
beat him and sent him away empty-handed.
4Then he sent another servant to them; they
struck this man on the head and treated him
shamefully. 5He sent still another, and that one
they killed. He sent many others; some of them
they beat, others they killed.
6"He had one left to send, a son, whom he
loved. He sent him last of all, saying, 'They
will respect my son.'
7"But the tenants said to one another, 'This
is the heir. Come, let's kill him, and the inheritance will be ours.' 8So they took him and
killed him, and threw him out of the vineyard.
9"What then will the owner of the vineyard
do? He will come and kill those tenants and
give the vineyard to others. 10Haven't you read
this scripture:

" 'The stone the builders rejected
has become the capstone[h];
11the Lord has done this,
and it is marvelous in our eyes'[i]?"

12Then they looked for a way to arrest him
because they knew he had spoken the parable
against them. But they were afraid of the
crowd; so they left him and went away.

Paying Taxes to Caesar

13Later they sent some of the Pharisees and
Herodians to Jesus to catch him in his words.
14They came to him and said, "Teacher, we
know you are a man of integrity. You aren't
swayed by men, because you pay no attention
to who they are; but you teach the way of God

[a]*9* A Hebrew expression meaning "Save!" which became an exclamation of praise; also in verse 10
[b]*9* Psalm 118:25,26 [c]*17* Isaiah 56:7 [d]*17* Jer. 7:11 [e]*19* Some early manuscripts *he* [f]*22* Some early manuscripts *If you have* [g]*25* Some manuscripts *sins. 26But if you do not forgive, neither will your Father who is in heaven forgive your sins.* [h]*10* Or *cornerstone* [i]*11* Psalm 118:22,23

in accordance with the truth. Is it right to pay
taxes to Caesar or not? 15Should we pay or
shouldn't we?"

But Jesus knew their hypocrisy. "Why are
you trying to trap me?" he asked. "Bring me a
denarius and let me look at it." 16They brought
the coin, and he asked them, "Whose portrait is
this? And whose inscription?"

"Caesar's," they replied.

17Then Jesus said to them, "Give to Caesar
what is Caesar's and to God what is God's."

And they were amazed at him.

Marriage at the Resurrection

18Then the Sadducees, who say there is no
resurrection, came to him with a question.
19"Teacher," they said, "Moses wrote for us
that if a man's brother dies and leaves a wife
but no children, the man must marry the widow and have children for his brother. 20Now
there were seven brothers. The first one married and died without leaving any children.
21The second one married the widow, but he
also died, leaving no child. It was the same
with the third. 22In fact, none of the seven left
any children. Last of all, the woman died too.
23At the resurrection[a] whose wife will she be,
since the seven were married to her?"

24Jesus replied, "Are you not in error because you do not know the Scriptures or the
power of God? 25When the dead rise, they will
neither marry nor be given in marriage; they
will be like the angels in heaven. 26Now about
the dead rising—have you not read in the book
of Moses, in the account of the bush, how God
said to him, 'I am the God of Abraham, the
God of Isaac, and the God of Jacob'[b]? 27He is
not the God of the dead, but of the living. You
are badly mistaken!"

The Greatest Commandment

28One of the teachers of the law came and
heard them debating. Noticing that Jesus had
given them a good answer, he asked him, "Of
all the commandments, which is the most important?"

29"The most important one," answered
Jesus, "is this: 'Hear, O Israel, the Lord our
God, the Lord is one.[c] 30Love the Lord your
God with all your heart and with all your soul
and with all your mind and with all your
strength.'[d] 31The second is this: 'Love your
neighbor as yourself.'[e] There is no commandment greater than these."

32"Well said, teacher," the man replied.
"You are right in saying that God is one and
there is no other but him. 33To love him with
all your heart, with all your understanding and
with all your strength, and to love your neighbor as yourself is more important than all burnt
offerings and sacrifices."

34When Jesus saw that he had answered
wisely, he said to him, "You are not far from
the kingdom of God." And from then on no
one dared ask him any more questions.

Whose Son Is the Christ?

35While Jesus was teaching in the temple
courts, he asked, "How is it that the teachers of
the law say that the Christ[f] is the son of David? 36David himself, speaking by the Holy
Spirit, declared:

" 'The Lord said to my Lord:
"Sit at my right hand
until I put your enemies
under your feet." '[g]

37David himself calls him 'Lord.' How then
can he be his son?"

The large crowd listened to him with delight.

38As he taught, Jesus said, "Watch out for
the teachers of the law. They like to walk
around in flowing robes and be greeted in the
marketplaces, 39and have the most important
seats in the synagogues and the places of honor
at banquets. 40They devour widows' houses
and for a show make lengthy prayers. Such
men will be punished most severely."

The Widow's Offering

41Jesus sat down opposite the place where
the offerings were put and watched the crowd
putting their money into the temple treasury.
Many rich people threw in large amounts.
42But a poor widow came and put in two very
small copper coins,[h] worth only a fraction of a
penny.[i]

43Calling his disciples to him, Jesus said, "I
tell you the truth, this poor widow has put
more into the treasury than all the others.
44They all gave out of their wealth; but she, out
of her poverty, put in everything—all she had
to live on."

Signs of the End of the Age

13 As he was leaving the temple, one of his
disciples said to him, "Look, Teacher!
What massive stones! What magnificent buildings!"

2"Do you see all these great buildings?" replied Jesus. "Not one stone here will be left on
another; every one will be thrown down."

3As Jesus was sitting on the Mount of Olives opposite the temple, Peter, James, John
and Andrew asked him privately, 4"Tell us,
when will these things happen? And what will
be the sign that they are all about to be fulfilled?"

5Jesus said to them: "Watch out that no one
deceives you. 6Many will come in my name,
claiming, 'I am he,' and will deceive many.
7When you hear of wars and rumors of wars,
do not be alarmed. Such things must happen,
but the end is still to come. 8Nation will rise
against nation, and kingdom against kingdom.
There will be earthquakes in various places,

[a]23 Some manuscripts *resurrection, when men rise from the dead,* [b]26 Exodus 3:6 [c]29 Or *the Lord our God is one Lord* [d]30 Deut. 6:4,5 [e]31 Lev. 19:18 [f]35 Or *Messiah* [g]36 Psalm 110:1 [h]42 Greek *two lepta* [i]42 Greek *kodrantes*

and famines. These are the beginning of birth pains.

9“You must be on your guard. You will be handed over to the local councils and flogged in the synagogues. On account of me you will stand before governors and kings as witnesses to them. 10And the gospel must first be preached to all nations. 11Whenever you are arrested and brought to trial, do not worry beforehand about what to say. Just say whatever is given you at the time, for it is not you speaking, but the Holy Spirit.

12“Brother will betray brother to death, and a father his child. Children will rebel against their parents and have them put to death. 13All men will hate you because of me, but he who stands firm to the end will be saved.

14“When you see ‘the abomination that causes desolation’[a] standing where it[b] does not belong—let the reader understand—then let those who are in Judea flee to the mountains. 15Let no one on the roof of his house go down or enter the house to take anything out. 16Let no one in the field go back to get his cloak. 17How dreadful it will be in those days for pregnant women and nursing mothers! 18Pray that this will not take place in winter, 19because those will be days of distress unequaled from the beginning, when God created the world, until now—and never to be equaled again. 20If the Lord had not cut short those days, no one would survive. But for the sake of the elect, whom he has chosen, he has shortened them. 21At that time if anyone says to you, ‘Look, here is the Christ[c]!’ or, ‘Look, there he is!’ do not believe it. 22For false Christs and false prophets will appear and perform signs and miracles to deceive the elect—if that were possible. 23So be on your guard; I have told you everything ahead of time.

24“But in those days, following that distress,

“ ‘the sun will be darkened,
and the moon will not give its light;
25the stars will fall from the sky,
and the heavenly bodies will be
shaken.’[d]

26“At that time men will see the Son of Man coming in clouds with great power and glory. 27And he will send his angels and gather his elect from the four winds, from the ends of the earth to the ends of the heavens.

28“Now learn this lesson from the fig tree: As soon as its twigs get tender and its leaves come out, you know that summer is near. 29Even so, when you see these things happening, you know that it is near, right at the door. 30I tell you the truth, this generation[e] will certainly not pass away until all these things have happened. 31Heaven and earth will pass away, but my words will never pass away.

The Day and Hour Unknown

32“No one knows about that day or hour, not even the angels in heaven, nor the Son, but only the Father. 33Be on guard! Be alert[f]! You do not know when that time will come. 34It’s like a man going away: He leaves his house and puts his servants in charge, each with his assigned task, and tells the one at the door to keep watch.

35“Therefore keep watch because you do not know when the owner of the house will come back—whether in the evening, or at midnight, or when the rooster crows, or at dawn. 36If he comes suddenly, do not let him find you sleeping. 37What I say to you, I say to everyone: ‘Watch!’ ”

Jesus Anointed at Bethany

14 Now the Passover and the Feast of Unleavened Bread were only two days away, and the chief priests and the teachers of the law were looking for some sly way to arrest Jesus and kill him. 2“But not during the Feast,” they said, “or the people may riot.”

3While he was in Bethany, reclining at the table in the home of a man known as Simon the Leper, a woman came with an alabaster jar of very expensive perfume, made of pure nard. She broke the jar and poured the perfume on his head.

4Some of those present were saying indignantly to one another, “Why this waste of perfume? 5It could have been sold for more than a year’s wages[g] and the money given to the poor.” And they rebuked her harshly.

6“Leave her alone,” said Jesus. “Why are you bothering her? She has done a beautiful thing to me. 7The poor you will always have with you, and you can help them any time you want. But you will not always have me. 8She did what she could. She poured perfume on my body beforehand to prepare for my burial. 9I tell you the truth, wherever the gospel is preached throughout the world, what she has done will also be told, in memory of her.”

10Then Judas Iscariot, one of the Twelve, went to the chief priests to betray Jesus to them. 11They were delighted to hear this and promised to give him money. So he watched for an opportunity to hand him over.

The Lord’s Supper

12On the first day of the Feast of Unleavened Bread, when it was customary to sacrifice the Passover lamb, Jesus’ disciples asked him, “Where do you want us to go and make preparations for you to eat the Passover?”

13So he sent two of his disciples, telling them, “Go into the city, and a man carrying a jar of water will meet you. Follow him. 14Say to the owner of the house he enters, ‘The Teacher asks: Where is my guest room, where I may eat the Passover with my disciples?’ 15He will show you a large upper room, furnished and ready. Make preparations for us there.”

16The disciples left, went into the city and

[a] *14* Daniel 9:27; 11:31; 12:11 [b] *14* Or *he*; also in verse 29 [c] *21* Or *Messiah* [d] *25* Isaiah 13:10; 34:4
[e] *30* Or *race* [f] *33* Some manuscripts *alert and pray* [g] *5* Greek *than three hundred denarii*

found things just as Jesus had told them. So
they prepared the Passover.
17When evening came, Jesus arrived with
the Twelve. 18While they were reclining at the
table eating, he said, "I tell you the truth, one
of you will betray me—one who is eating
with me."
19They were saddened, and one by one they
said to him, "Surely not I?"
20"It is one of the Twelve," he replied, "one
who dips bread into the bowl with me. 21The
Son of Man will go just as it is written about
him. But woe to that man who betrays the Son
of Man! It would be better for him if he had
not been born."
22While they were eating, Jesus took bread,
gave thanks and broke it, and gave it to his
disciples, saying, "Take it; this is my body."
23Then he took the cup, gave thanks and
offered it to them, and they all drank from it.
24"This is my blood of the[a] covenant, which
is poured out for many," he said to them. 25"I
tell you the truth, I will not drink again of the
fruit of the vine until that day when I drink it
anew in the kingdom of God."
26When they had sung a hymn, they went
out to the Mount of Olives.

Jesus Predicts Peter's Denial

27"You will all fall away," Jesus told them,
"for it is written:

" 'I will strike the shepherd,
and the sheep will be scattered.'[b]

28But after I have risen, I will go ahead of you
into Galilee."
29Peter declared, "Even if all fall away, I
will not."
30"I tell you the truth," Jesus answered, "today—yes, tonight—before the rooster crows
twice[c] you yourself will disown me three
times."
31But Peter insisted emphatically, "Even if I
have to die with you, I will never disown you."
And all the others said the same.

Gethsemane

32They went to a place called Gethsemane,
and Jesus said to his disciples, "Sit here while
I pray." 33He took Peter, James and John along
with him, and he began to be deeply distressed
and troubled. 34"My soul is overwhelmed with
sorrow to the point of death," he said to them.
"Stay here and keep watch."
35Going a little farther, he fell to the ground
and prayed that if possible the hour might pass
from him. 36"*Abba*,[d] Father," he said, "everything is possible for you. Take this cup from
me. Yet not what I will, but what you will."
37Then he returned to his disciples and
found them sleeping. "Simon," he said to Peter, "are you asleep? Could you not keep watch
for one hour? 38Watch and pray so that you
will not fall into temptation. The spirit is willing, but the body is weak."
39Once more he went away and prayed the
same thing. 40When he came back, he again
found them sleeping, because their eyes were
heavy. They did not know what to say to him.
41Returning the third time, he said to them,
"Are you still sleeping and resting? Enough!
The hour has come. Look, the Son of Man is
betrayed into the hands of sinners. 42Rise! Let
us go! Here comes my betrayer!"

Jesus Arrested

43Just as he was speaking, Judas, one of the
Twelve, appeared. With him was a crowd
armed with swords and clubs, sent from the
chief priests, the teachers of the law, and the
elders.
44Now the betrayer had arranged a signal
with them: "The one I kiss is the man; arrest
him and lead him away under guard." 45Going
at once to Jesus, Judas said, "Rabbi!" and
kissed him. 46The men seized Jesus and arrested him. 47Then one of those standing near
drew his sword and struck the servant of the
high priest, cutting off his ear.
48"Am I leading a rebellion," said Jesus,
"that you have come out with swords and clubs
to capture me? 49Every day I was with you,
teaching in the temple courts, and you did not
arrest me. But the Scriptures must be fulfilled." 50Then everyone deserted him and fled.
51A young man, wearing nothing but a linen
garment, was following Jesus. When they
seized him, 52he fled naked, leaving his garment behind.

Before the Sanhedrin

53They took Jesus to the high priest, and all
the chief priests, elders and teachers of the law
came together. 54Peter followed him at a distance, right into the courtyard of the high
priest. There he sat with the guards and
warmed himself at the fire.
55The chief priests and the whole Sanhedrin
were looking for evidence against Jesus so that
they could put him to death, but they did not
find any. 56Many testified falsely against him,
but their statements did not agree.
57Then some stood up and gave this false
testimony against him: 58"We heard him say,
'I will destroy this man-made temple and in
three days will build another, not made by
man.' " 59Yet even then their testimony did not
agree.
60Then the high priest stood up before them
and asked Jesus, "Are you not going to answer? What is this testimony that these men
are bringing against you?" 61But Jesus remained silent and gave no answer.
Again the high priest asked him, "Are you
the Christ,[e] the Son of the Blessed One?"
62"I am," said Jesus. "And you will see the
Son of Man sitting at the right hand of the
Mighty One and coming on the clouds of
heaven."
63The high priest tore his clothes. "Why

[a]24 Some manuscripts *the new* [b]27 Zech. 13:7 [c]30 Some early manuscripts do not have *twice.*
[d]36 Aramaic for *Father* [e]61 Or *Messiah*

do we need any more witnesses?" he asked. 64"You have heard the blasphemy. What do you think?"

They all condemned him as worthy of death. 65Then some began to spit at him; they blindfolded him, struck him with their fists, and said, "Prophesy!" And the guards took him and beat him.

Peter Disowns Jesus

66While Peter was below in the courtyard, one of the servant girls of the high priest came by. 67When she saw Peter warming himself, she looked closely at him.

"You also were with that Nazarene, Jesus," she said.

68But he denied it. "I don't know or understand what you're talking about," he said, and went out into the entryway.[a]

69When the servant girl saw him there, she said again to those standing around, "This fellow is one of them." 70Again he denied it.

After a little while, those standing near said to Peter, "Surely you are one of them, for you are a Galilean."

71He began to call down curses on himself, and he swore to them, "I don't know this man you're talking about."

72Immediately the rooster crowed the second time.[b] Then Peter remembered the word Jesus had spoken to him: "Before the rooster crows twice[c] you will disown me three times." And he broke down and wept.

Jesus Before Pilate

15 Very early in the morning, the chief priests, with the elders, the teachers of the law and the whole Sanhedrin, reached a decision. They bound Jesus, led him away and handed him over to Pilate.

2"Are you the king of the Jews?" asked Pilate.

"Yes, it is as you say," Jesus replied.

3The chief priests accused him of many things. 4So again Pilate asked him, "Aren't you going to answer? See how many things they are accusing you of."

5But Jesus still made no reply, and Pilate was amazed.

6Now it was the custom at the Feast to release a prisoner whom the people requested. 7A man called Barabbas was in prison with the insurrectionists who had committed murder in the uprising. 8The crowd came up and asked Pilate to do for them what he usually did.

9"Do you want me to release to you the king of the Jews?" asked Pilate, 10knowing it was out of envy that the chief priests had handed Jesus over to him. 11But the chief priests stirred up the crowd to have Pilate release Barabbas instead.

12"What shall I do, then, with the one you call the king of the Jews?" Pilate asked them.

13"Crucify him!" they shouted.

14"Why? What crime has he committed?" asked Pilate.

But they shouted all the louder, "Crucify him!"

15Wanting to satisfy the crowd, Pilate released Barabbas to them. He had Jesus flogged, and handed him over to be crucified.

The Soldiers Mock Jesus

16The soldiers led Jesus away into the palace (that is, the Praetorium) and called together the whole company of soldiers. 17They put a purple robe on him, then twisted together a crown of thorns and set it on him. 18And they began to call out to him, "Hail, king of the Jews!" 19Again and again they struck him on the head with a staff and spit on him. Falling on their knees, they paid homage to him. 20And when they had mocked him, they took off the purple robe and put his own clothes on him. Then they led him out to crucify him.

The Crucifixion

21A certain man from Cyrene, Simon, the father of Alexander and Rufus, was passing by on his way in from the country, and they forced him to carry the cross. 22They brought Jesus to the place called Golgotha (which means The Place of the Skull). 23Then they offered him wine mixed with myrrh, but he did not take it. 24And they crucified him. Dividing up his clothes, they cast lots to see what each would get.

25It was the third hour when they crucified him. 26The written notice of the charge against him read: THE KING OF THE JEWS. 27They crucified two robbers with him, one on his right and one on his left.[d] 29Those who passed by hurled insults at him, shaking their heads and saying, "So! You who are going to destroy the temple and build it in three days, 30come down from the cross and save yourself!"

31In the same way the chief priests and the teachers of the law mocked him among themselves. "He saved others," they said, "but he can't save himself! 32Let this Christ,[e] this King of Israel, come down now from the cross, that we may see and believe." Those crucified with him also heaped insults on him.

The Death of Jesus

33At the sixth hour darkness came over the whole land until the ninth hour. 34And at the ninth hour Jesus cried out in a loud voice, *"Eloi, Eloi, lama sabachthani?"*—which means, "My God, my God, why have you forsaken me?"[f]

35When some of those standing near heard this, they said, "Listen, he's calling Elijah."

36One man ran, filled a sponge with wine vinegar, put it on a stick, and offered it to Jesus

[a] *68* Some early manuscripts *entryway and the rooster crowed* [b] *72* Some early manuscripts do not have *the second time.* [c] *72* Some early manuscripts do not have *twice.* [d] *27* Some manuscripts *left, [28]and the scripture was fulfilled which says, "He was counted with the lawless ones"* (Isaiah 53:12) [e] *32* Or *Messiah* [f] *34* Psalm 22:1

to drink. "Now leave him alone. Let's see if Elijah comes to take him down," he said.

37With a loud cry, Jesus breathed his last.

38The curtain of the temple was torn in two from top to bottom. 39And when the centurion, who stood there in front of Jesus, heard his cry and[a] saw how he died, he said, "Surely this man was the Son[b] of God!"

40Some women were watching from a distance. Among them were Mary Magdalene, Mary the mother of James the younger and of Joses, and Salome. 41In Galilee these women had followed him and cared for his needs. Many other women who had come up with him to Jerusalem were also there.

The Burial of Jesus

42It was Preparation Day (that is, the day before the Sabbath). So as evening approached, 43Joseph of Arimathea, a prominent member of the Council, who was himself waiting for the kingdom of God, went boldly to Pilate and asked for Jesus' body. 44Pilate was surprised to hear that he was already dead. Summoning the centurion, he asked him if Jesus had already died. 45When he learned from the centurion that it was so, he gave the body to Joseph. 46So Joseph bought some linen cloth, took down the body, wrapped it in the linen, and placed it in a tomb cut out of rock. Then he rolled a stone against the entrance of the tomb. 47Mary Magdalene and Mary the mother of Joses saw where he was laid.

The Resurrection

16 When the Sabbath was over, Mary Magdalene, Mary the mother of James, and Salome bought spices so that they might go to anoint Jesus' body. 2Very early on the first day of the week, just after sunrise, they were on their way to the tomb 3and they asked each other, "Who will roll the stone away from the entrance of the tomb?"

4But when they looked up, they saw that the stone, which was very large, had been rolled away. 5As they entered the tomb, they saw a young man dressed in a white robe sitting on the right side, and they were alarmed.

6"Don't be alarmed," he said. "You are looking for Jesus the Nazarene, who was crucified. He has risen! He is not here. See the place where they laid him. 7But go, tell his disciples and Peter, 'He is going ahead of you into Galilee. There you will see him, just as he told you.' "

8Trembling and bewildered, the women went out and fled from the tomb. They said nothing to anyone, because they were afraid.

[The earliest manuscripts and some other ancient witnesses do not have Mark 16:9–20.]

9When Jesus rose early on the first day of the week, he appeared first to Mary Magdalene, out of whom he had driven seven demons. 10She went and told those who had been with him and who were mourning and weeping. 11When they heard that Jesus was alive and that she had seen him, they did not believe it.

12Afterward Jesus appeared in a different form to two of them while they were walking in the country. 13These returned and reported it to the rest; but they did not believe them either.

14Later Jesus appeared to the Eleven as they were eating; he rebuked them for their lack of faith and their stubborn refusal to believe those who had seen him after he had risen.

15He said to them, "Go into all the world and preach the good news to all creation. 16Whoever believes and is baptized will be saved, but whoever does not believe will be condemned. 17And these signs will accompany those who believe: In my name they will drive out demons; they will speak in new tongues; 18they will pick up snakes with their hands; and when they drink deadly poison, it will not hurt them at all; they will place their hands on sick people, and they will get well."

19After the Lord Jesus had spoken to them, he was taken up into heaven and he sat at the right hand of God. 20Then the disciples went out and preached everywhere, and the Lord worked with them and confirmed his word by the signs that accompanied it.

Luke

Introduction

1 Many have undertaken to draw up an account of the things that have been fulfilled[c] among us, 2just as they were handed down to us by those who from the first were eyewitnesses and servants of the word. 3Therefore, since I myself have carefully investigated everything from the beginning, it seemed good also to me to write an orderly account for you, most excellent Theophilus, 4so that you may know the certainty of the things you have been taught.

The Birth of John the Baptist Foretold

5In the time of Herod king of Judea there was a priest named Zechariah, who belonged to the priestly division of Abijah; his wife Eliz-

[a]39 Some manuscripts do not have *heard his cry and*   [b]39 Or *a son*   [c]1 Or *been surely believed*

abeth was also a descendant of Aaron. 6Both of
them were upright in the sight of God, observing all the Lord's commandments and regulations blamelessly. 7But they had no children,
because Elizabeth was barren; and they were
both well along in years.

8Once when Zechariah's division was on
duty and he was serving as priest before God,
9he was chosen by lot, according to the custom
of the priesthood, to go into the temple of the
Lord and burn incense. 10And when the time
for the burning of incense came, all the assembled worshipers were praying outside.

11Then an angel of the Lord appeared to
him, standing at the right side of the altar of
incense. 12When Zechariah saw him, he was
startled and was gripped with fear. 13But the
angel said to him: "Do not be afraid, Zechariah; your prayer has been heard. Your wife
Elizabeth will bear you a son, and you are to
give him the name John. 14He will be a joy and
delight to you, and many will rejoice because
of his birth, 15for he will be great in the sight
of the Lord. He is never to take wine or other
fermented drink, and he will be filled with the
Holy Spirit even from birth.[a] 16Many of the
people of Israel will he bring back to the Lord
their God. 17And he will go on before the Lord,
in the spirit and power of Elijah, to turn the
hearts of the fathers to their children and the
disobedient to the wisdom of the righteous—to
make ready a people prepared for the Lord."

18Zechariah asked the angel, "How can I be
sure of this? I am an old man and my wife is
well along in years."

19The angel answered, "I am Gabriel. I stand
in the presence of God, and I have been sent to
speak to you and to tell you this good news.
20And now you will be silent and not able to
speak until the day this happens, because you
did not believe my words, which will come
true at their proper time."

21Meanwhile, the people were waiting for
Zechariah and wondering why he stayed so
long in the temple. 22When he came out, he
could not speak to them. They realized he had
seen a vision in the temple, for he kept making
signs to them but remained unable to speak.

23When his time of service was completed,
he returned home. 24After this his wife Elizabeth became pregnant and for five months remained in seclusion. 25"The Lord has done this
for me," she said. "In these days he has shown
his favor and taken away my disgrace among
the people."

The Birth of Jesus Foretold

26In the sixth month, God sent the angel
Gabriel to Nazareth, a town in Galilee, 27to a
virgin pledged to be married to a man named
Joseph, a descendant of David. The virgin's
name was Mary. 28The angel went to her and
said, "Greetings, you who are highly favored!
The Lord is with you."

29Mary was greatly troubled at his words
and wondered what kind of greeting this might
be. 30But the angel said to her, "Do not be
afraid, Mary, you have found favor with God.
31You will be with child and give birth to a
son, and you are to give him the name Jesus.
32He will be great and will be called the Son of
the Most High. The Lord God will give him
the throne of his father David, 33and he will
reign over the house of Jacob forever; his kingdom will never end."

34"How will this be," Mary asked the angel,
"since I am a virgin?"

35The angel answered, "The Holy Spirit will
come upon you, and the power of the Most
High will overshadow you. So the holy one to
be born will be called[b] the Son of God. 36Even
Elizabeth your relative is going to have a child
in her old age, and she who was said to be
barren is in her sixth month. 37For nothing is
impossible with God."

38"I am the Lord's servant," Mary answered.
"May it be to me as you have said." Then the
angel left her.

Mary Visits Elizabeth

39At that time Mary got ready and hurried to
a town in the hill country of Judea, 40where she
entered Zechariah's home and greeted Elizabeth. 41When Elizabeth heard Mary's greeting,
the baby leaped in her womb, and Elizabeth
was filled with the Holy Spirit. 42In a loud
voice she exclaimed: "Blessed are you among
women, and blessed is the child you will bear!
43But why am I so favored, that the mother of
my Lord should come to me? 44As soon as the
sound of your greeting reached my ears, the
baby in my womb leaped for joy. 45Blessed is
she who has believed that what the Lord has
said to her will be accomplished!"

Mary's Song

46And Mary said:

"My soul glorifies the Lord
47 and my spirit rejoices in God my
Savior,
48for he has been mindful
of the humble state of his servant.
From now on all generations will call me
blessed,
49 for the Mighty One has done great
things for me—
holy is his name.
50His mercy extends to those who fear him,
from generation to generation.
51He has performed mighty deeds with his
arm;
he has scattered those who are proud in
their inmost thoughts.
52He has brought down rulers from their
thrones
but has lifted up the humble.
53He has filled the hungry with good things
but has sent the rich away empty.
54He has helped his servant Israel,
remembering to be merciful

[a]15 Or *from his mother's womb* [b]35 Or *So the child to be born will be called holy,*

55to Abraham and his descendants forever,
even as he said to our fathers."

56Mary stayed with Elizabeth for about three
months and then returned home.

The Birth of John the Baptist

57When it was time for Elizabeth to have her
baby, she gave birth to a son. 58Her neighbors
and relatives heard that the Lord had shown
her great mercy, and they shared her joy.
59On the eighth day they came to circumcise
the child, and they were going to name him
after his father Zechariah, 60but his mother
spoke up and said, "No! He is to be called
John."
61They said to her, "There is no one among
your relatives who has that name."
62Then they made signs to his father, to find
out what he would like to name the child. 63He
asked for a writing tablet, and to everyone's
astonishment he wrote, "His name is John."
64Immediately his mouth was opened and his
tongue was loosed, and he began to speak,
praising God. 65The neighbors were all filled
with awe, and throughout the hill country of
Judea people were talking about all these
things. 66Everyone who heard this wondered
about it, asking, "What then is this child going
to be?" For the Lord's hand was with him.

Zechariah's Song

67His father Zechariah was filled with the
Holy Spirit and prophesied:

68"Praise be to the Lord, the God of Israel,
because he has come and has redeemed
his people.
69He has raised up a horn[a] of salvation for
us
in the house of his servant David
70(as he said through his holy prophets of
long ago),
71salvation from our enemies
and from the hand of all who hate us—
72to show mercy to our fathers
and to remember his holy covenant,
73 the oath he swore to our father
Abraham:
74to rescue us from the hand of our
enemies,
and to enable us to serve him without
fear
75 in holiness and righteousness before
him all our days.

76And you, my child, will be called a
prophet of the Most High;
for you will go on before the Lord to
prepare the way for him,
77to give his people the knowledge of
salvation
through the forgiveness of their sins,
78because of the tender mercy of our God,
by which the rising sun will come to us
from heaven
79to shine on those living in darkness
and in the shadow of death,
to guide our feet into the path of peace."

80And the child grew and became strong in
spirit; and he lived in the desert until he appeared publicly to Israel.

The Birth of Jesus

2 In those days Caesar Augustus issued a decree that a census should be taken of the
entire Roman world. 2(This was the first census that took place while Quirinius was governor of Syria.) 3And everyone went to his own
town to register.
4So Joseph also went up from the town of
Nazareth in Galilee to Judea, to Bethlehem the
town of David, because he belonged to the
house and line of David. 5He went there to
register with Mary, who was pledged to be
married to him and was expecting a child.
6While they were there, the time came for the
baby to be born, 7and she gave birth to her
firstborn, a son. She wrapped him in cloths and
placed him in a manger, because there was no
room for them in the inn.

The Shepherds and the Angels

8And there were shepherds living out in the
fields nearby, keeping watch over their flocks
at night. 9An angel of the Lord appeared to
them, and the glory of the Lord shone around
them, and they were terrified. 10But the angel
said to them, "Do not be afraid. I bring you
good news of great joy that will be for all the
people. 11Today in the town of David a Savior
has been born to you; he is Christ[b] the Lord.
12This will be a sign to you: You will find a
baby wrapped in cloths and lying in a manger."
13Suddenly a great company of the heavenly
host appeared with the angel, praising God and
saying,

14"Glory to God in the highest,
and on earth peace to men on whom his
favor rests."

15When the angels had left them and gone
into heaven, the shepherds said to one another,
"Let's go to Bethlehem and see this thing that
has happened, which the Lord has told us
about."
16So they hurried off and found Mary and
Joseph, and the baby, who was lying in the
manger. 17When they had seen him, they
spread the word concerning what had been told
them about this child, 18and all who heard it
were amazed at what the shepherds said to
them. 19But Mary treasured up all these things
and pondered them in her heart. 20The shepherds returned, glorifying and praising God for
all the things they had heard and seen, which
were just as they had been told.

Jesus Presented in the Temple

21On the eighth day, when it was time to

[a]69 *Horn* here symbolizes strength. [b]11 Or *Messiah.* "The Christ" (Greek) and "the Messiah" (Hebrew) both mean "the Anointed One"; also in verse 26.

circumcise him, he was named Jesus, the name
the angel had given him before he had been
conceived.
22When the time of their purification according to the Law of Moses had been completed, Joseph and Mary took him to Jerusalem
to present him to the Lord 23(as it is written in
the Law of the Lord, "Every firstborn male is
to be consecrated to the Lord"[a]), 24and to offer a sacrifice in keeping with what is said in
the Law of the Lord: "a pair of doves or two
young pigeons."[b]
25Now there was a man in Jerusalem called
Simeon, who was righteous and devout. He
was waiting for the consolation of Israel, and
the Holy Spirit was upon him. 26It had been
revealed to him by the Holy Spirit that he
would not die before he had seen the Lord's
Christ. 27Moved by the Spirit, he went into the
temple courts. When the parents brought in the
child Jesus to do for him what the custom of
the Law required, 28Simeon took him in his
arms and praised God, saying:

29"Sovereign Lord, as you have promised,
you now dismiss[c] your servant in
peace.
30For my eyes have seen your salvation,
31 which you have prepared in the sight
of all people,
32a light for revelation to the Gentiles
and for glory to your people Israel."

33The child's father and mother marveled
at what was said about him. 34Then Simeon
blessed them and said to Mary, his mother:
"This child is destined to cause the falling and
rising of many in Israel, and to be a sign that
will be spoken against, 35so that the thoughts
of many hearts will be revealed. And a sword
will pierce your own soul too."
36There was also a prophetess, Anna, the
daughter of Phanuel, of the tribe of Asher. She
was very old; she had lived with her husband
seven years after her marriage, 37and then was
a widow until she was eighty-four.[d] She never
left the temple but worshiped night and day,
fasting and praying. 38Coming up to them at
that very moment, she gave thanks to God and
spoke about the child to all who were looking
forward to the redemption of Jerusalem.
39When Joseph and Mary had done everything required by the Law of the Lord, they
returned to Galilee to their own town of Nazareth. 40And the child grew and became strong;
he was filled with wisdom, and the grace of
God was upon him.

The Boy Jesus at the Temple

41Every year his parents went to Jerusalem
for the Feast of the Passover. 42When he was
twelve years old, they went up to the Feast,
according to the custom. 43After the Feast was
over, while his parents were returning home,
the boy Jesus stayed behind in Jerusalem, but
they were unaware of it. 44Thinking he was in
their company, they traveled on for a day.
Then they began looking for him among their
relatives and friends. 45When they did not find
him, they went back to Jerusalem to look for
him. 46After three days they found him in the
temple courts, sitting among the teachers, listening to them and asking them questions.
47Everyone who heard him was amazed at his
understanding and his answers. 48When his
parents saw him, they were astonished. His
mother said to him, "Son, why have you treated us like this? Your father and I have been
anxiously searching for you."
49"Why were you searching for me?" he
asked. "Didn't you know I had to be in my
Father's house?" 50But they did not understand
what he was saying to them.
51Then he went down to Nazareth with them
and was obedient to them. But his mother treasured all these things in her heart. 52And Jesus
grew in wisdom and stature, and in favor with
God and men.

John the Baptist Prepares the Way

3 In the fifteenth year of the reign of Tiberius
Caesar—when Pontius Pilate was governor of Judea, Herod tetrarch of Galilee, his
brother Philip tetrarch of Iturea and Traconitis,
and Lysanias tetrarch of Abilene— 2during the
high priesthood of Annas and Caiaphas, the
word of God came to John son of Zechariah in
the desert. 3He went into all the country around
the Jordan, preaching a baptism of repentance
for the forgiveness of sins. 4As is written in the
book of the words of Isaiah the prophet:

"A voice of one calling in the desert,
'Prepare the way for the Lord,
make straight paths for him.
5Every valley shall be filled in,
every mountain and hill made low.
The crooked roads shall become straight,
the rough ways smooth.
6And all mankind will see God's
salvation.' "[e]

7John said to the crowds coming out to be
baptized by him, "You brood of vipers! Who
warned you to flee from the coming wrath?
8Produce fruit in keeping with repentance. And
do not begin to say to yourselves, 'We have
Abraham as our father.' For I tell you that out
of these stones God can raise up children for
Abraham. 9The ax is already at the root of the
trees, and every tree that does not produce
good fruit will be cut down and thrown into the
fire."
10"What should we do then?" the crowd
asked.
11John answered, "The man with two tunics
should share with him who has none, and the
one who has food should do the same."
12Tax collectors also came to be baptized.
"Teacher," they asked, "what should we do?"

[a]*23* Exodus 13:2,12 [b]*24* Lev. 12:8 [c]*29* Or *promised, / now dismiss* [d]*37* Or *widow for eighty-four years* [e]*6* Isaiah 40:3-5

13“Don't collect any more than you are required to,” he told them.

14Then some soldiers asked him, “And what should we do?”

He replied, “Don't extort money and don't accuse people falsely—be content with your pay.”

15The people were waiting expectantly and were all wondering in their hearts if John might possibly be the Christ.[a] 16John answered them all, “I baptize you with[b] water. But one more powerful than I will come, the thongs of whose sandals I am not worthy to untie. He will baptize you with the Holy Spirit and with fire. 17His winnowing fork is in his hand to clear his threshing floor and to gather the wheat into his barn, but he will burn up the chaff with unquenchable fire.” 18And with many other words John exhorted the people and preached the good news to them.

19But when John rebuked Herod the tetrarch because of Herodias, his brother's wife, and all the other evil things he had done, 20Herod added this to them all: He locked John up in prison.

The Baptism and Genealogy of Jesus

21When all the people were being baptized, Jesus was baptized too. And as he was praying, heaven was opened 22and the Holy Spirit descended on him in bodily form like a dove. And a voice came from heaven: “You are my Son, whom I love; with you I am well pleased.”

23Now Jesus himself was about thirty years old when he began his ministry. He was the son, so it was thought, of Joseph,

the son of Heli, 24the son of Matthat,
the son of Levi, the son of Melki,
the son of Jannai, the son of Joseph,
25the son of Mattathias, the son of Amos,
the son of Nahum, the son of Esli,
the son of Naggai, 26the son of Maath,
the son of Mattathias, the son of Semein,
the son of Josech, the son of Joda,
27the son of Joanan, the son of Rhesa,
the son of Zerubbabel, the son of Shealtiel,
the son of Neri, 28the son of Melki,
the son of Addi, the son of Cosam,
the son of Elmadam, the son of Er,
29the son of Joshua, the son of Eliezer,
the son of Jorim, the son of Matthat,
the son of Levi, 30the son of Simeon,
the son of Judah, the son of Joseph,
the son of Jonam, the son of Eliakim,
31the son of Melea, the son of Menna,
the son of Mattatha, the son of Nathan,
the son of David, 32the son of Jesse,
the son of Obed, the son of Boaz,
the son of Salmon,[c] the son of Nahshon,
33the son of Amminadab, the son of Ram,[d]
the son of Hezron, the son of Perez,
the son of Judah, 34the son of Jacob,
the son of Isaac, the son of Abraham,
the son of Terah, the son of Nahor,
35the son of Serug, the son of Reu,
the son of Peleg, the son of Eber,
the son of Shelah, 36the son of Cainan,
the son of Arphaxad, the son of Shem,
the son of Noah, the son of Lamech,
37the son of Methuselah, the son of Enoch,
the son of Jared, the son of Mahalalel,
the son of Kenan, 38the son of Enosh,
the son of Seth, the son of Adam,
the son of God.

The Temptation of Jesus

4 Jesus, full of the Holy Spirit, returned from the Jordan and was led by the Spirit in the desert, 2where for forty days he was tempted by the devil. He ate nothing during those days, and at the end of them he was hungry.

3The devil said to him, “If you are the Son of God, tell this stone to become bread.”

4Jesus answered, “It is written: ‘Man does not live on bread alone.’[e]”

5The devil led him up to a high place and showed him in an instant all the kingdoms of the world. 6And he said to him, “I will give you all their authority and splendor, for it has been given to me, and I can give it to anyone I want to. 7So if you worship me, it will all be yours.”

8Jesus answered, “It is written: ‘Worship the Lord your God and serve him only.’[f]”

9The devil led him to Jerusalem and had him stand on the highest point of the temple. “If you are the Son of God,” he said, “throw yourself down from here. 10For it is written:

“ ‘He will command his angels concerning you
to guard you carefully;
11they will lift you up in their hands,
so that you will not strike your foot
against a stone.’[g]”

12Jesus answered, “It says: ‘Do not put the Lord your God to the test.’[h]”

13When the devil had finished all this tempting, he left him until an opportune time.

Jesus Rejected at Nazareth

14Jesus returned to Galilee in the power of the Spirit, and news about him spread through the whole countryside. 15He taught in their synagogues, and everyone praised him.

16He went to Nazareth, where he had been brought up, and on the Sabbath day he went into the synagogue, as was his custom. And he stood up to read. 17The scroll of the prophet Isaiah was handed to him. Unrolling it, he found the place where it is written:

18“The Spirit of the Lord is on me,
because he has anointed me

[a]15 Or *Messiah* [b]16 Or *in* [c]32 Some early manuscripts *Sala* [d]33 Some manuscripts *Amminadab, the son of Admin, the son of Arni*; other manuscripts vary widely. [e]4 Deut. 8:3 [f]8 Deut. 6:13 [g]11 Psalm 91:11,12 [h]12 Deut. 6:16

to preach good news to the poor.
He has sent me to proclaim freedom for
the prisoners
and recovery of sight for the blind,
to release the oppressed,
19 to proclaim the year of the Lord's
favor."[a]

20 Then he rolled up the scroll, gave it back
to the attendant and sat down. The eyes of
everyone in the synagogue were fastened on
him, 21 and he began by saying to them, "Today
this scripture is fulfilled in your hearing."
22 All spoke well of him and were amazed at
the gracious words that came from his lips.
"Isn't this Joseph's son?" they asked.
23 Jesus said to them, "Surely you will quote
this proverb to me: 'Physician, heal yourself!
Do here in your hometown what we have
heard that you did in Capernaum.' "
24 "I tell you the truth," he continued, "no
prophet is accepted in his hometown. 25 I assure you that there were many widows in Israel
in Elijah's time, when the sky was shut for
three and a half years and there was a severe
famine throughout the land. 26 Yet Elijah was
not sent to any of them, but to a widow in
Zarephath in the region of Sidon. 27 And there
were many in Israel with leprosy[b] in the time
of Elisha the prophet, yet not one of them was
cleansed—only Naaman the Syrian."
28 All the people in the synagogue were furious when they heard this. 29 They got up, drove
him out of the town, and took him to the brow
of the hill on which the town was built, in
order to throw him down the cliff. 30 But he
walked right through the crowd and went on
his way.

Jesus Drives Out an Evil Spirit

31 Then he went down to Capernaum, a town
in Galilee, and on the Sabbath began to teach
the people. 32 They were amazed at his teaching, because his message had authority.
33 In the synagogue there was a man possessed by a demon, an evil[c] spirit. He cried out
at the top of his voice, 34 "Ha! What do you
want with us, Jesus of Nazareth? Have you
come to destroy us? I know who you are—the
Holy One of God!"
35 "Be quiet!" Jesus said sternly. "Come out
of him!" Then the demon threw the man down
before them all and came out without injuring
him.
36 All the people were amazed and said to
each other, "What is this teaching? With authority and power he gives orders to evil spirits
and they come out!" 37 And the news about him
spread throughout the surrounding area.

Jesus Heals Many

38 Jesus left the synagogue and went to the
home of Simon. Now Simon's mother-in-law
was suffering from a high fever, and they
asked Jesus to help her. 39 So he bent over her
and rebuked the fever, and it left her. She got
up at once and began to wait on them.
40 When the sun was setting, the people
brought to Jesus all who had various kinds of
sickness, and laying his hands on each one, he
healed them. 41 Moreover, demons came out of
many people, shouting, "You are the Son of
God!" But he rebuked them and would not
allow them to speak, because they knew he
was the Christ.[d]
42 At daybreak Jesus went out to a solitary
place. The people were looking for him and
when they came to where he was, they tried to
keep him from leaving them. 43 But he said, "I
must preach the good news of the kingdom of
God to the other towns also, because that is
why I was sent." 44 And he kept on preaching
in the synagogues of Judea.[e]

The Calling of the First Disciples

5 One day as Jesus was standing by the Lake
of Gennesaret,[f] with the people crowding
around him and listening to the word of God,
2 he saw at the water's edge two boats, left
there by the fishermen, who were washing
their nets. 3 He got into one of the boats, the
one belonging to Simon, and asked him to put
out a little from shore. Then he sat down and
taught the people from the boat.
4 When he had finished speaking, he said
to Simon, "Put out into deep water, and let
down[g] the nets for a catch."
5 Simon answered, "Master, we've worked
hard all night and haven't caught anything. But
because you say so, I will let down the nets."
6 When they had done so, they caught such a
large number of fish that their nets began to
break. 7 So they signaled their partners in the
other boat to come and help them, and they
came and filled both boats so full that they
began to sink.
8 When Simon Peter saw this, he fell at
Jesus' knees and said, "Go away from me,
Lord; I am a sinful man!" 9 For he and all his
companions were astonished at the catch of
fish they had taken, 10 and so were James and
John, the sons of Zebedee, Simon's partners.
Then Jesus said to Simon, "Don't be afraid;
from now on you will catch men." 11 So they
pulled their boats up on shore, left everything
and followed him.

The Man With Leprosy

12 While Jesus was in one of the towns, a
man came along who was covered with leprosy.[b] When he saw Jesus, he fell with his face
to the ground and begged him, "Lord, if you
are willing, you can make me clean."
13 Jesus reached out his hand and touched the
man. "I am willing," he said. "Be clean!" And
immediately the leprosy left him.
14 Then Jesus ordered him, "Don't tell anyone, but go, show yourself to the priest and

[a] *19* Isaiah 61:1,2 [b] *27,12* The Greek word was used for various diseases affecting the skin—not necessarily leprosy. [c] *33* Greek *unclean*; also in verse 36 [d] *41* Or *Messiah* [e] *44* Or *the land of the Jews*; some manuscripts *Galilee* [f] *1* That is, Sea of Galilee [g] *4* The Greek verb is plural.

offer the sacrifices that Moses commanded for
your cleansing, as a testimony to them."
15Yet the news about him spread all the
more, so that crowds of people came to hear
him and to be healed of their sicknesses. 16But
Jesus often withdrew to lonely places and
prayed.

Jesus Heals a Paralytic

17One day as he was teaching, Pharisees and
teachers of the law, who had come from every
village of Galilee and from Judea and Jerusalem, were sitting there. And the power of the
Lord was present for him to heal the sick.
18Some men came carrying a paralytic on a
mat and tried to take him into the house to lay
him before Jesus. 19When they could not find
a way to do this because of the crowd, they
went up on the roof and lowered him on his
mat through the tiles into the middle of the
crowd, right in front of Jesus.
20When Jesus saw their faith, he said,
"Friend, your sins are forgiven."
21The Pharisees and the teachers of the law
began thinking to themselves, "Who is this fellow who speaks blasphemy? Who can forgive
sins but God alone?"
22Jesus knew what they were thinking and
asked, "Why are you thinking these things in
your hearts? 23Which is easier: to say, 'Your
sins are forgiven,' or to say, 'Get up and
walk'? 24But that you may know that the Son
of Man has authority on earth to forgive
sins . . ." He said to the paralyzed man, "I tell
you, get up, take your mat and go home."
25Immediately he stood up in front of them,
took what he had been lying on and went home
praising God. 26Everyone was amazed and
gave praise to God. They were filled with awe
and said, "We have seen remarkable things today."

The Calling of Levi

27After this, Jesus went out and saw a tax
collector by the name of Levi sitting at his tax
booth. "Follow me," Jesus said to him, 28and
Levi got up, left everything and followed him.
29Then Levi held a great banquet for Jesus at
his house, and a large crowd of tax collectors
and others were eating with them. 30But the
Pharisees and the teachers of the law who belonged to their sect complained to his disciples, "Why do you eat and drink with tax collectors and 'sinners'?"
31Jesus answered them, "It is not the healthy
who need a doctor, but the sick. 32I have not
come to call the righteous, but sinners to repentance."

Jesus Questioned About Fasting

33They said to him, "John's disciples often
fast and pray, and so do the disciples of the
Pharisees, but yours go on eating and drinking."
34Jesus answered, "Can you make the guests
of the bridegroom fast while he is with them?
35But the time will come when the bridegroom
will be taken from them; in those days they
will fast."
36He told them this parable: "No one tears a
patch from a new garment and sews it on an
old one. If he does, he will have torn the new
garment, and the patch from the new will not
match the old. 37And no one pours new wine
into old wineskins. If he does, the new wine
will burst the skins, the wine will run out and
the wineskins will be ruined. 38No, new wine
must be poured into new wineskins. 39And no
one after drinking old wine wants the new, for
he says, 'The old is better.' "

Lord of the Sabbath

6 One Sabbath Jesus was going through the
grainfields, and his disciples began to pick
some heads of grain, rub them in their hands
and eat the kernels. 2Some of the Pharisees
asked, "Why are you doing what is unlawful
on the Sabbath?"
3Jesus answered them, "Have you never
read what David did when he and his companions were hungry? 4He entered the house of
God, and taking the consecrated bread, he ate
what is lawful only for priests to eat. And he
also gave some to his companions." 5Then
Jesus said to them, "The Son of Man is Lord of
the Sabbath."
6On another Sabbath he went into the synagogue and was teaching, and a man was there
whose right hand was shriveled. 7The Pharisees and the teachers of the law were looking
for a reason to accuse Jesus, so they watched
him closely to see if he would heal on the
Sabbath. 8But Jesus knew what they were
thinking and said to the man with the shriveled
hand, "Get up and stand in front of everyone."
So he got up and stood there.
9Then Jesus said to them, "I ask you, which
is lawful on the Sabbath: to do good or to do
evil, to save life or to destroy it?"
10He looked around at them all, and then
said to the man, "Stretch out your hand." He
did so, and his hand was completely restored.
11But they were furious and began to discuss
with one another what they might do to Jesus.

The Twelve Apostles

12One of those days Jesus went out to a
mountainside to pray, and spent the night praying to God. 13When morning came, he called
his disciples to him and chose twelve of them,
whom he also designated apostles: 14Simon
(whom he named Peter), his brother Andrew,
James, John, Philip, Bartholomew, 15Matthew,
Thomas, James son of Alphaeus, Simon who
was called the Zealot, 16Judas son of James,
and Judas Iscariot, who became a traitor.

Blessings and Woes

17He went down with them and stood on a
level place. A large crowd of his disciples was
there and a great number of people from all
over Judea, from Jerusalem, and from the coast
of Tyre and Sidon, 18who had come to hear
him and to be healed of their diseases. Those

troubled by evil[a] spirits were cured, 19and the people all tried to touch him, because power was coming from him and healing them all.

20Looking at his disciples, he said:

"Blessed are you who are poor,
for yours is the kingdom of God.
21Blessed are you who hunger now,
for you will be satisfied.
Blessed are you who weep now,
for you will laugh.
22Blessed are you when men hate you,
when they exclude you and insult you
and reject your name as evil,
because of the Son of Man.

23"Rejoice in that day and leap for joy, because great is your reward in heaven. For that is how their fathers treated the prophets.

24"But woe to you who are rich,
for you have already received your comfort.
25Woe to you who are well fed now,
for you will go hungry.
Woe to you who laugh now,
for you will mourn and weep.
26Woe to you when all men speak well of you,
for that is how their fathers treated the false prophets.

Love for Enemies

27"But I tell you who hear me: Love your enemies, do good to those who hate you, 28bless those who curse you, pray for those who mistreat you. 29If someone strikes you on one cheek, turn to him the other also. If someone takes your cloak, do not stop him from taking your tunic. 30Give to everyone who asks you, and if anyone takes what belongs to you, do not demand it back. 31Do to others as you would have them do to you.

32"If you love those who love you, what credit is that to you? Even 'sinners' love those who love them. 33And if you do good to those who are good to you, what credit is that to you? Even 'sinners' do that. 34And if you lend to those from whom you expect repayment, what credit is that to you? Even 'sinners' lend to 'sinners,' expecting to be repaid in full. 35But love your enemies, do good to them, and lend to them without expecting to get anything back. Then your reward will be great, and you will be sons of the Most High, because he is kind to the ungrateful and wicked. 36Be merciful, just as your Father is merciful.

Judging Others

37"Do not judge, and you will not be judged. Do not condemn, and you will not be condemned. Forgive, and you will be forgiven. 38Give, and it will be given to you. A good measure, pressed down, shaken together and running over, will be poured into your lap. For with the measure you use, it will be measured to you."

39He also told them this parable: "Can a blind man lead a blind man? Will they not both fall into a pit? 40A student is not above his teacher, but everyone who is fully trained will be like his teacher.

41"Why do you look at the speck of sawdust in your brother's eye and pay no attention to the plank in your own eye? 42How can you say to your brother, 'Brother, let me take the speck out of your eye,' when you yourself fail to see the plank in your own eye? You hypocrite, first take the plank out of your eye, and then you will see clearly to remove the speck from your brother's eye.

A Tree and Its Fruit

43"No good tree bears bad fruit, nor does a bad tree bear good fruit. 44Each tree is recognized by its own fruit. People do not pick figs from thornbushes, or grapes from briers. 45The good man brings good things out of the good stored up in his heart, and the evil man brings evil things out of the evil stored up in his heart. For out of the overflow of his heart his mouth speaks.

The Wise and Foolish Builders

46"Why do you call me, 'Lord, Lord,' and do not do what I say? 47I will show you what he is like who comes to me and hears my words and puts them into practice. 48He is like a man building a house, who dug down deep and laid the foundation on rock. When a flood came, the torrent struck that house but could not shake it, because it was well built. 49But the one who hears my words and does not put them into practice is like a man who built a house on the ground without a foundation. The moment the torrent struck that house, it collapsed and its destruction was complete."

The Faith of the Centurion

7 When Jesus had finished saying all this in the hearing of the people, he entered Capernaum. 2There a centurion's servant, whom his master valued highly, was sick and about to die. 3The centurion heard of Jesus and sent some elders of the Jews to him, asking him to come and heal his servant. 4When they came to Jesus, they pleaded earnestly with him, "This man deserves to have you do this, 5because he loves our nation and has built our synagogue." 6So Jesus went with them.

He was not far from the house when the centurion sent friends to say to him: "Lord, don't trouble yourself, for I do not deserve to have you come under my roof. 7That is why I did not even consider myself worthy to come to you. But say the word, and my servant will be healed. 8For I myself am a man under authority, with soldiers under me. I tell this one, 'Go,' and he goes; and that one, 'Come,' and he comes. I say to my servant, 'Do this,' and he does it."

9When Jesus heard this, he was amazed at him, and turning to the crowd following him,

[a]18 Greek *unclean*

he said, "I tell you, I have not found such great
faith even in Israel." 10Then the men who had
been sent returned to the house and found the
servant well.

Jesus Raises a Widow's Son

11Soon afterward, Jesus went to a town
called Nain, and his disciples and a large
crowd went along with him. 12As he approached the town gate, a dead person was
being carried out—the only son of his mother,
and she was a widow. And a large crowd from
the town was with her. 13When the Lord saw
her, his heart went out to her and he said,
"Don't cry."

14Then he went up and touched the coffin,
and those carrying it stood still. He said,
"Young man, I say to you, get up!" 15The dead
man sat up and began to talk, and Jesus gave
him back to his mother.

16They were all filled with awe and praised
God. "A great prophet has appeared among
us," they said. "God has come to help his people." 17This news about Jesus spread throughout Judea[a] and the surrounding country.

Jesus and John the Baptist

18John's disciples told him about all these
things. Calling two of them, 19he sent them to
the Lord to ask, "Are you the one who was to
come, or should we expect someone else?"

20When the men came to Jesus, they said,
"John the Baptist sent us to you to ask, 'Are
you the one who was to come, or should we
expect someone else?' "

21At that very time Jesus cured many who
had diseases, sicknesses and evil spirits, and
gave sight to many who were blind. 22So he
replied to the messengers, "Go back and report
to John what you have seen and heard: The
blind receive sight, the lame walk, those who
have leprosy[b] are cured, the deaf hear, the
dead are raised, and the good news is preached
to the poor. 23Blessed is the man who does not
fall away on account of me."

24After John's messengers left, Jesus began
to speak to the crowd about John: "What did
you go out into the desert to see? A reed
swayed by the wind? 25If not, what did you go
out to see? A man dressed in fine clothes? No,
those who wear expensive clothes and indulge
in luxury are in palaces. 26But what did you go
out to see? A prophet? Yes, I tell you, and
more than a prophet. 27This is the one about
whom it is written:

" 'I will send my messenger ahead of you,
who will prepare your way before
you.'[c]

28I tell you, among those born of women there
is no one greater than John; yet the one who
is least in the kingdom of God is greater
than he."

29(All the people, even the tax collectors,
when they heard Jesus' words, acknowledged
that God's way was right, because they had
been baptized by John. 30But the Pharisees and
experts in the law rejected God's purpose for
themselves, because they had not been baptized by John.)

31"To what, then, can I compare the people
of this generation? What are they like? 32They
are like children sitting in the marketplace and
calling out to each other:

" 'We played the flute for you,
and you did not dance;
we sang a dirge,
and you did not cry.'

33For John the Baptist came neither eating
bread nor drinking wine, and you say, 'He has
a demon.' 34The Son of Man came eating and
drinking, and you say, 'Here is a glutton and a
drunkard, a friend of tax collectors and "sinners." ' 35But wisdom is proved right by all her
children."

Jesus Anointed by a Sinful Woman

36Now one of the Pharisees invited Jesus to
have dinner with him, so he went to the Pharisee's house and reclined at the table. 37When a
woman who had lived a sinful life in that town
learned that Jesus was eating at the Pharisee's
house, she brought an alabaster jar of perfume,
38and as she stood behind him at his feet weeping, she began to wet his feet with her tears.
Then she wiped them with her hair, kissed
them and poured perfume on them.

39When the Pharisee who had invited him
saw this, he said to himself, "If this man were
a prophet, he would know who is touching him
and what kind of woman she is—that she is a
sinner."

40Jesus answered him, "Simon, I have something to tell you."

"Tell me, teacher," he said.

41"Two men owed money to a certain moneylender. One owed him five hundred denarii,[d] and the other fifty. 42Neither of them had
the money to pay him back, so he canceled the
debts of both. Now which of them will love
him more?"

43Simon replied, "I suppose the one who
had the bigger debt canceled."

"You have judged correctly," Jesus said.

44Then he turned toward the woman and
said to Simon, "Do you see this woman? I
came into your house. You did not give me any
water for my feet, but she wet my feet with her
tears and wiped them with her hair. 45You did
not give me a kiss, but this woman, from the
time I entered, has not stopped kissing my feet.
46You did not put oil on my head, but she has
poured perfume on my feet. 47Therefore, I tell
you, her many sins have been forgiven—for
she loved much. But he who has been forgiven
little loves little."

48Then Jesus said to her, "Your sins are forgiven."

[a]*17* Or *the land of the Jews* [b]*22* The Greek word was used for various diseases affecting the skin—not necessarily leprosy. [c]*27* Mal. 3:1 [d]*41* A denarius was a coin worth about a day's wages.

49The other guests began to say among
themselves, "Who is this who even forgives
sins?"
50Jesus said to the woman, "Your faith has
saved you; go in peace."

The Parable of the Sower

8 After this, Jesus traveled about from one
town and village to another, proclaiming
the good news of the kingdom of God. The
Twelve were with him, 2and also some women
who had been cured of evil spirits and diseases: Mary (called Magdalene) from whom
seven demons had come out; 3Joanna the wife
of Cuza, the manager of Herod's household;
Susanna; and many others. These women were
helping to support them out of their own
means.
4While a large crowd was gathering and
people were coming to Jesus from town after
town, he told this parable: 5"A farmer went out
to sow his seed. As he was scattering the seed,
some fell along the path; it was trampled on,
and the birds of the air ate it up. 6Some fell on
rock, and when it came up, the plants withered
because they had no moisture. 7Other seed fell
among thorns, which grew up with it and
choked the plants. 8Still other seed fell on good
soil. It came up and yielded a crop, a hundred
times more than was sown."
When he said this, he called out, "He who
has ears to hear, let him hear."
9His disciples asked him what this parable
meant. 10He said, "The knowledge of the secrets of the kingdom of God has been given to
you, but to others I speak in parables, so that,

" 'though seeing, they may not see;
though hearing, they may not
understand.'[a]

11"This is the meaning of the parable: The
seed is the word of God. 12Those along the
path are the ones who hear, and then the devil
comes and takes away the word from their
hearts, so that they may not believe and be
saved. 13Those on the rock are the ones who
receive the word with joy when they hear it,
but they have no root. They believe for a
while, but in the time of testing they fall away.
14The seed that fell among thorns stands for
those who hear, but as they go on their way
they are choked by life's worries, riches and
pleasures, and they do not mature. 15But the
seed on good soil stands for those with a noble
and good heart, who hear the word, retain it,
and by persevering produce a crop.

A Lamp on a Stand

16"No one lights a lamp and hides it in a jar
or puts it under a bed. Instead, he puts it on a
stand, so that those who come in can see the
light. 17For there is nothing hidden that will
not be disclosed, and nothing concealed that
will not be known or brought out into the open.
18Therefore consider carefully how you listen.
Whoever has will be given more; whoever
does not have, even what he thinks he has will
be taken from him."

Jesus' Mother and Brothers

19Now Jesus' mother and brothers came to
see him, but they were not able to get near him
because of the crowd. 20Someone told him,
"Your mother and brothers are standing outside, wanting to see you."
21He replied, "My mother and brothers are
those who hear God's word and put it into
practice."

Jesus Calms the Storm

22One day Jesus said to his disciples, "Let's
go over to the other side of the lake." So they
got into a boat and set out. 23As they sailed, he
fell asleep. A squall came down on the lake, so
that the boat was being swamped, and they
were in great danger.
24The disciples went and woke him, saying,
"Master, Master, we're going to drown!"
He got up and rebuked the wind and the
raging waters; the storm subsided, and all was
calm. 25"Where is your faith?" he asked his
disciples.
In fear and amazement they asked one another, "Who is this? He commands even the
winds and the water, and they obey him."

The Healing of a Demon-possessed Man

26They sailed to the region of the Gerasenes,[b] which is across the lake from Galilee.
27When Jesus stepped ashore, he was met by a
demon-possessed man from the town. For a
long time this man had not worn clothes or
lived in a house, but had lived in the tombs.
28When he saw Jesus, he cried out and fell at
his feet, shouting at the top of his voice, "What
do you want with me, Jesus, Son of the Most
High God? I beg you, don't torture me!" 29For
Jesus had commanded the evil[c] spirit to come
out of the man. Many times it had seized him,
and though he was chained hand and foot and
kept under guard, he had broken his chains and
had been driven by the demon into solitary
places.
30Jesus asked him, "What is your name?"
"Legion," he replied, because many demons
had gone into him. 31And they begged him
repeatedly not to order them to go into the
Abyss.
32A large herd of pigs was feeding there on
the hillside. The demons begged Jesus to let
them go into them, and he gave them permission. 33When the demons came out of the man,
they went into the pigs, and the herd rushed
down the steep bank into the lake and was
drowned.
34When those tending the pigs saw what had

[a] *10* Isaiah 6:9 [b] *26* Some manuscripts *Gadarenes*; other manuscripts *Gergesenes*; also in verse 37
[c] *29* Greek *unclean*

happened, they ran off and reported this in the
town and countryside, 35and the people went
out to see what had happened. When they
came to Jesus, they found the man from whom
the demons had gone out, sitting at Jesus' feet,
dressed and in his right mind; and they were
afraid. 36Those who had seen it told the people
how the demon-possessed man had been
cured. 37Then all the people of the region of
the Gerasenes asked Jesus to leave them, because they were overcome with fear. So he got
into the boat and left.

38The man from whom the demons had gone
out begged to go with him, but Jesus sent him
away, saying, 39"Return home and tell how
much God has done for you." So the man went
away and told all over town how much Jesus
had done for him.

A Dead Girl and a Sick Woman

40Now when Jesus returned, a crowd welcomed him, for they were all expecting him.
41Then a man named Jairus, a ruler of the synagogue, came and fell at Jesus' feet, pleading
with him to come to his house 42because his
only daughter, a girl of about twelve, was dying.

As Jesus was on his way, the crowds almost
crushed him. 43And a woman was there who
had been subject to bleeding for twelve years,[a]
but no one could heal her. 44She came up behind him and touched the edge of his cloak,
and immediately her bleeding stopped.

45"Who touched me?" Jesus asked.

When they all denied it, Peter said, "Master,
the people are crowding and pressing against
you."

46But Jesus said, "Someone touched me; I
know that power has gone out from me."

47Then the woman, seeing that she could not
go unnoticed, came trembling and fell at his
feet. In the presence of all the people, she told
why she had touched him and how she had
been instantly healed. 48Then he said to her,
"Daughter, your faith has healed you. Go in
peace."

49While Jesus was still speaking, someone
came from the house of Jairus, the synagogue
ruler. "Your daughter is dead," he said. "Don't
bother the teacher any more."

50Hearing this, Jesus said to Jairus, "Don't
be afraid; just believe, and she will be healed."

51When he arrived at the house of Jairus, he
did not let anyone go in with him except Peter,
John and James, and the child's father and
mother. 52Meanwhile, all the people were
wailing and mourning for her. "Stop wailing,"
Jesus said. "She is not dead but asleep."

53They laughed at him, knowing that she
was dead. 54But he took her by the hand and
said, "My child, get up!" 55Her spirit returned,
and at once she stood up. Then Jesus told them
to give her something to eat. 56Her parents
were astonished, but he ordered them not to
tell anyone what had happened.

Jesus Sends Out the Twelve

9 When Jesus had called the Twelve together, he gave them power and authority to
drive out all demons and to cure diseases, 2and
he sent them out to preach the kingdom of God
and to heal the sick. 3He told them: "Take
nothing for the journey—no staff, no bag, no
bread, no money, no extra tunic. 4Whatever
house you enter, stay there until you leave that
town. 5If people do not welcome you, shake
the dust off your feet when you leave their
town, as a testimony against them." 6So they
set out and went from village to village,
preaching the gospel and healing people everywhere.

7Now Herod the tetrarch heard about all that
was going on. And he was perplexed, because
some were saying that John had been raised
from the dead, 8others that Elijah had appeared, and still others that one of the prophets
of long ago had come back to life. 9But Herod
said, "I beheaded John. Who, then, is this I
hear such things about?" And he tried to see
him.

Jesus Feeds the Five Thousand

10When the apostles returned, they reported
to Jesus what they had done. Then he took
them with him and they withdrew by themselves to a town called Bethsaida, 11but the
crowds learned about it and followed him. He
welcomed them and spoke to them about the
kingdom of God, and healed those who needed
healing.

12Late in the afternoon the Twelve came to
him and said, "Send the crowd away so they
can go to the surrounding villages and countryside and find food and lodging, because we are
in a remote place here."

13He replied, "You give them something to
eat."

They answered, "We have only five loaves
of bread and two fish—unless we go and buy
food for all this crowd." 14(About five thousand men were there.)

But he said to his disciples, "Have them sit
down in groups of about fifty each." 15The
disciples did so, and everybody sat down.
16Taking the five loaves and the two fish and
looking up to heaven, he gave thanks and
broke them. Then he gave them to the disciples
to set before the people. 17They all ate and
were satisfied, and the disciples picked up
twelve basketfuls of broken pieces that were
left over.

Peter's Confession of Christ

18Once when Jesus was praying in private
and his disciples were with him, he asked
them, "Who do the crowds say I am?"

19They replied, "Some say John the Baptist;
others say Elijah; and still others, that one of
the prophets of long ago has come back to
life."

a43 Many manuscripts *years, and she had spent all she had on doctors*

20"But what about you?" he asked. "Who do
you say I am?"
Peter answered, "The Christ[a] of God."
21Jesus strictly warned them not to tell this
to anyone. 22And he said, "The Son of Man
must suffer many things and be rejected by the
elders, chief priests and teachers of the law,
and he must be killed and on the third day be
raised to life."
23Then he said to them all: "If anyone would
come after me, he must deny himself and take
up his cross daily and follow me. 24For whoever wants to save his life will lose it, but
whoever loses his life for me will save it.
25What good is it for a man to gain the whole
world, and yet lose or forfeit his very self? 26If
anyone is ashamed of me and my words, the
Son of Man will be ashamed of him when he
comes in his glory and in the glory of the Father and of the holy angels. 27I tell you the
truth, some who are standing here will not taste
death before they see the kingdom of God."

The Transfiguration

28About eight days after Jesus said this, he
took Peter, John and James with him and went
up onto a mountain to pray. 29As he was praying, the appearance of his face changed, and
his clothes became as bright as a flash of lightning. 30Two men, Moses and Elijah, 31ap-
peared in glorious splendor, talking with Jesus.
They spoke about his departure, which he was
about to bring to fulfillment at Jerusalem.
32Peter and his companions were very sleepy,
but when they became fully awake, they saw
his glory and the two men standing with him.
33As the men were leaving Jesus, Peter said to
him, "Master, it is good for us to be here. Let
us put up three shelters—one for you, one for
Moses and one for Elijah." (He did not know
what he was saying.)
34While he was speaking, a cloud appeared
and enveloped them, and they were afraid as
they entered the cloud. 35A voice came from
the cloud, saying, "This is my Son, whom I
have chosen; listen to him." 36When the voice
had spoken, they found that Jesus was alone.
The disciples kept this to themselves, and told
no one at that time what they had seen.

The Healing of a Boy With an Evil Spirit

37The next day, when they came down from
the mountain, a large crowd met him. 38A man
in the crowd called out, "Teacher, I beg you to
look at my son, for he is my only child. 39A
spirit seizes him and he suddenly screams; it
throws him into convulsions so that he foams
at the mouth. It scarcely ever leaves him and is
destroying him. 40I begged your disciples to
drive it out, but they could not."
41"O unbelieving and perverse generation,"
Jesus replied, "how long shall I stay with you
and put up with you? Bring your son here."
42Even while the boy was coming, the demon threw him to the ground in a convulsion.
But Jesus rebuked the evil[b] spirit, healed the
boy and gave him back to his father. 43And
they were all amazed at the greatness of God.
While everyone was marveling at all that
Jesus did, he said to his disciples, 44"Listen
carefully to what I am about to tell you: The
Son of Man is going to be betrayed into the
hands of men." 45But they did not understand
what this meant. It was hidden from them, so
that they did not grasp it, and they were afraid
to ask him about it.

Who Will Be the Greatest?

46An argument started among the disciples
as to which of them would be the greatest.
47Jesus, knowing their thoughts, took a little
child and had him stand beside him. 48Then he
said to them, "Whoever welcomes this little
child in my name welcomes me; and whoever
welcomes me welcomes the one who sent me.
For he who is least among you all—he is the
greatest."
49"Master," said John, "we saw a man driving out demons in your name and we tried to
stop him, because he is not one of us."
50"Do not stop him," Jesus said, "for whoever is not against you is for you."

Samaritan Opposition

51As the time approached for him to be tak-
en up to heaven, Jesus resolutely set out for
Jerusalem. 52And he sent messengers on
ahead, who went into a Samaritan village to
get things ready for him; 53but the people there
did not welcome him, because he was heading
for Jerusalem. 54When the disciples James and
John saw this, they asked, "Lord, do you want
us to call fire down from heaven to destroy
them[c]?" 55But Jesus turned and rebuked them,
56and[d] they went to another village.

The Cost of Following Jesus

57As they were walking along the road, a
man said to him, "I will follow you wherever
you go."
58Jesus replied, "Foxes have holes and birds
of the air have nests, but the Son of Man has
no place to lay his head."
59He said to another man, "Follow me."
But the man replied, "Lord, first let me go
and bury my father."
60Jesus said to him, "Let the dead bury their
own dead, but you go and proclaim the kingdom of God."
61Still another said, "I will follow you, Lord;
but first let me go back and say good-by to my
family."
62Jesus replied, "No one who puts his hand
to the plow and looks back is fit for service in
the kingdom of God."

[a] *20* Or *Messiah* [b] *42* Greek *unclean* [c] *54* Some manuscripts *them, even as Elijah did* [d] *55,56* Some manuscripts *them. And he said, "You do not know what kind of spirit you are of, for the Son of Man did not come to destroy men's lives, but to save them." 56And*

Jesus Sends Out the Seventy-two

10 After this the Lord appointed seventy-two[a] others and sent them two by two ahead of him to every town and place where he was about to go. 2He told them, "The harvest is plentiful, but the workers are few. Ask the Lord of the harvest, therefore, to send out workers into his harvest field. 3Go! I am sending you out like lambs among wolves. 4Do not take a purse or bag or sandals; and do not greet anyone on the road.

5"When you enter a house, first say, 'Peace to this house.' 6If a man of peace is there, your peace will rest on him; if not, it will return to you. 7Stay in that house, eating and drinking whatever they give you, for the worker deserves his wages. Do not move around from house to house.

8"When you enter a town and are welcomed, eat what is set before you. 9Heal the sick who are there and tell them, 'The kingdom of God is near you.' 10But when you enter a town and are not welcomed, go into its streets and say, 11'Even the dust of your town that sticks to our feet we wipe off against you. Yet be sure of this: The kingdom of God is near.' 12I tell you, it will be more bearable on that day for Sodom than for that town.

13"Woe to you, Korazin! Woe to you, Bethsaida! For if the miracles that were performed in you had been performed in Tyre and Sidon, they would have repented long ago, sitting in sackcloth and ashes. 14But it will be more bearable for Tyre and Sidon at the judgment than for you. 15And you, Capernaum, will you be lifted up to the skies? No, you will go down to the depths.[b]

16"He who listens to you listens to me; he who rejects you rejects me; but he who rejects me rejects him who sent me."

17The seventy-two returned with joy and said, "Lord, even the demons submit to us in your name."

18He replied, "I saw Satan fall like lightning from heaven. 19I have given you authority to trample on snakes and scorpions and to overcome all the power of the enemy; nothing will harm you. 20However, do not rejoice that the spirits submit to you, but rejoice that your names are written in heaven."

21At that time Jesus, full of joy through the Holy Spirit, said, "I praise you, Father, Lord of heaven and earth, because you have hidden these things from the wise and learned, and revealed them to little children. Yes, Father, for this was your good pleasure.

22"All things have been committed to me by my Father. No one knows who the Son is except the Father, and no one knows who the Father is except the Son and those to whom the Son chooses to reveal him."

23Then he turned to his disciples and said privately, "Blessed are the eyes that see what you see. 24For I tell you that many prophets and kings wanted to see what you see but did not see it, and to hear what you hear but did not hear it."

The Parable of the Good Samaritan

25On one occasion an expert in the law stood up to test Jesus. "Teacher," he asked, "what must I do to inherit eternal life?"

26"What is written in the Law?" he replied. "How do you read it?"

27He answered: " 'Love the Lord your God with all your heart and with all your soul and with all your strength and with all your mind'[c]; and, 'Love your neighbor as yourself.'[d]"

28"You have answered correctly," Jesus replied. "Do this and you will live."

29But he wanted to justify himself, so he asked Jesus, "And who is my neighbor?"

30In reply Jesus said: "A man was going down from Jerusalem to Jericho, when he fell into the hands of robbers. They stripped him of his clothes, beat him and went away, leaving him half dead. 31A priest happened to be going down the same road, and when he saw the man, he passed by on the other side. 32So too, a Levite, when he came to the place and saw him, passed by on the other side. 33But a Samaritan, as he traveled, came where the man was; and when he saw him, he took pity on him. 34He went to him and bandaged his wounds, pouring on oil and wine. Then he put the man on his own donkey, took him to an inn and took care of him. 35The next day he took out two silver coins[e] and gave them to the innkeeper. 'Look after him,' he said, 'and when I return, I will reimburse you for any extra expense you may have.'

36"Which of these three do you think was a neighbor to the man who fell into the hands of robbers?"

37The expert in the law replied, "The one who had mercy on him."

Jesus told him, "Go and do likewise."

At the Home of Martha and Mary

38As Jesus and his disciples were on their way, he came to a village where a woman named Martha opened her home to him. 39She had a sister called Mary, who sat at the Lord's feet listening to what he said. 40But Martha was distracted by all the preparations that had to be made. She came to him and asked, "Lord, don't you care that my sister has left me to do the work by myself? Tell her to help me!"

41"Martha, Martha," the Lord answered, "you are worried and upset about many things, 42but only one thing is needed.[f] Mary has chosen what is better, and it will not be taken away from her."

Jesus' Teaching on Prayer

11 One day Jesus was praying in a certain place. When he finished, one of his dis-

[a] *1* Some manuscripts *seventy*; also in verse 17 [b] *15* Greek *Hades* [c] *27* Deut. 6:5 [d] *27* Lev. 19:18
[e] *35* Greek *two denarii* [f] *42* Some manuscripts *but few things are needed—or only one*

ciples said to him, "Lord, teach us to pray, just as John taught his disciples."

2He said to them, "When you pray, say:

" 'Father,[a]
hallowed be your name,
your kingdom come.[b]
3Give us each day our daily bread.
4Forgive us our sins,
for we also forgive everyone who sins
against us.[c]
And lead us not into temptation.[d]' "

5Then he said to them, "Suppose one of you has a friend, and he goes to him at midnight and says, 'Friend, lend me three loaves of bread, 6because a friend of mine on a journey has come to me, and I have nothing to set before him.'

7"Then the one inside answers, 'Don't bother me. The door is already locked, and my children are with me in bed. I can't get up and give you anything.' 8I tell you, though he will not get up and give him the bread because he is his friend, yet because of the man's boldness[e] he will get up and give him as much as he needs.

9"So I say to you: Ask and it will be given to you; seek and you will find; knock and the door will be opened to you. 10For everyone who asks receives; he who seeks finds; and to him who knocks, the door will be opened.

11"Which of you fathers, if your son asks for[f] a fish, will give him a snake instead? 12Or if he asks for an egg, will give him a scorpion? 13If you then, though you are evil, know how to give good gifts to your children, how much more will your Father in heaven give the Holy Spirit to those who ask him!"

Jesus and Beelzebub

14Jesus was driving out a demon that was mute. When the demon left, the man who had been mute spoke, and the crowd was amazed. 15But some of them said, "By Beelzebub,[g] the prince of demons, he is driving out demons." 16Others tested him by asking for a sign from heaven.

17Jesus knew their thoughts and said to them: "Any kingdom divided against itself will be ruined, and a house divided against itself will fall. 18If Satan is divided against himself, how can his kingdom stand? I say this because you claim that I drive out demons by Beelzebub. 19Now if I drive out demons by Beelzebub, by whom do your followers drive them out? So then, they will be your judges. 20But if I drive out demons by the finger of God, then the kingdom of God has come to you.

21"When a strong man, fully armed, guards his own house, his possessions are safe. 22But when someone stronger attacks and overpowers him, he takes away the armor in which the man trusted and divides up the spoils.

23"He who is not with me is against me, and he who does not gather with me, scatters.

24"When an evil[h] spirit comes out of a man, it goes through arid places seeking rest and does not find it. Then it says, 'I will return to the house I left.' 25When it arrives, it finds the house swept clean and put in order. 26Then it goes and takes seven other spirits more wicked than itself, and they go in and live there. And the final condition of that man is worse than the first."

27As Jesus was saying these things, a woman in the crowd called out, "Blessed is the mother who gave you birth and nursed you."

28He replied, "Blessed rather are those who hear the word of God and obey it."

The Sign of Jonah

29As the crowds increased, Jesus said, "This is a wicked generation. It asks for a miraculous sign, but none will be given it except the sign of Jonah. 30For as Jonah was a sign to the Ninevites, so also will the Son of Man be to this generation. 31The Queen of the South will rise at the judgment with the men of this generation and condemn them; for she came from the ends of the earth to listen to Solomon's wisdom, and now one[i] greater than Solomon is here. 32The men of Nineveh will stand up at the judgment with this generation and condemn it; for they repented at the preaching of Jonah, and now one greater than Jonah is here.

The Lamp of the Body

33"No one lights a lamp and puts it in a place where it will be hidden, or under a bowl. Instead he puts it on its stand, so that those who come in may see the light. 34Your eye is the lamp of your body. When your eyes are good, your whole body also is full of light. But when they are bad, your body also is full of darkness. 35See to it, then, that the light within you is not darkness. 36Therefore, if your whole body is full of light, and no part of it dark, it will be completely lighted, as when the light of a lamp shines on you."

Six Woes

37When Jesus had finished speaking, a Pharisee invited him to eat with him; so he went in and reclined at the table. 38But the Pharisee, noticing that Jesus did not first wash before the meal, was surprised.

39Then the Lord said to him, "Now then, you Pharisees clean the outside of the cup and dish, but inside you are full of greed and wickedness. 40You foolish people! Did not the one who made the outside make the inside also? 41But give what is inside ⌞the dish⌟[j] to the poor, and everything will be clean for you.

[a]2 Some manuscripts *Our Father in heaven* [b]2 Some manuscripts *come. May your will be done on earth as it is in heaven.* [c]4 Greek *everyone who is indebted to us* [d]4 Some manuscripts *temptation but deliver us from the evil one* [e]8 Or *persistence* [f]11 Some manuscripts *for bread, will give him a stone; or if he asks for* [g]15 Greek *Beezeboul* or *Beelzeboul*; also in verses 18 and 19 [h]24 Greek *unclean* [i]31 Or *something*; also in verse 32 [j]41 Or *what you have*

42“Woe to you Pharisees, because you give
God a tenth of your mint, rue and all other
kinds of garden herbs, but you neglect justice
and the love of God. You should have practiced the latter without leaving the former undone.

43“Woe to you Pharisees, because you love
the most important seats in the synagogues and
greetings in the marketplaces.

44“Woe to you, because you are like un-
marked graves, which men walk over without
knowing it.”

45One of the experts in the law answered
him, “Teacher, when you say these things, you
insult us also.”

46Jesus replied, “And you experts in the law,
woe to you, because you load people down
with burdens they can hardly carry, and you
yourselves will not lift one finger to help them.

47“Woe to you, because you build tombs for
the prophets, and it was your forefathers who
killed them. 48So you testify that you approve
of what your forefathers did; they killed the
prophets, and you build their tombs. 49Because
of this, God in his wisdom said, ‘I will send
them prophets and apostles, some of whom
they will kill and others they will persecute.’
50Therefore this generation will be held responsible for the blood of all the prophets that
has been shed since the beginning of the world,
51from the blood of Abel to the blood of Zechariah, who was killed between the altar and the
sanctuary. Yes, I tell you, this generation will
be held responsible for it all.

52“Woe to you experts in the law, because
you have taken away the key to knowledge.
You yourselves have not entered, and you have
hindered those who were entering.”

53When Jesus left there, the Pharisees and
the teachers of the law began to oppose him
fiercely and to besiege him with questions,
54waiting to catch him in something he might
say.

Warnings and Encouragements

12 Meanwhile, when a crowd of many
thousands had gathered, so that they
were trampling on one another, Jesus began to
speak first to his disciples, saying: “Be on your
guard against the yeast of the Pharisees, which
is hypocrisy. 2There is nothing concealed that
will not be disclosed, or hidden that will not be
made known. 3What you have said in the dark
will be heard in the daylight, and what you
have whispered in the ear in the inner rooms
will be proclaimed from the roofs.

4“I tell you, my friends, do not be afraid of
those who kill the body and after that can do
no more. 5But I will show you whom you
should fear: Fear him who, after the killing of
the body, has power to throw you into hell.
Yes, I tell you, fear him. 6Are not five sparrows sold for two pennies[a]? Yet not one of
them is forgotten by God. 7Indeed, the very
hairs of your head are all numbered. Don’t be
afraid; you are worth more than many sparrows.

8“I tell you, whoever acknowledges me before men, the Son of Man will also acknowledge him before the angels of God. 9But he
who disowns me before men will be disowned
before the angels of God. 10And everyone who
speaks a word against the Son of Man will be
forgiven, but anyone who blasphemes against
the Holy Spirit will not be forgiven.

11“When you are brought before synagogues, rulers and authorities, do not worry
about how you will defend yourselves or what
you will say, 12for the Holy Spirit will teach
you at that time what you should say.”

The Parable of the Rich Fool

13Someone in the crowd said to him,
“Teacher, tell my brother to divide the inheritance with me.”

14Jesus replied, “Man, who appointed me a
judge or an arbiter between you?” 15Then he
said to them, “Watch out! Be on your guard
against all kinds of greed; a man’s life does not
consist in the abundance of his possessions.”

16And he told them this parable: “The
ground of a certain rich man produced a good
crop. 17He thought to himself, ‘What shall I
do? I have no place to store my crops.’

18“Then he said, ‘This is what I’ll do. I will
tear down my barns and build bigger ones, and
there I will store all my grain and my goods.
19And I’ll say to myself, “You have plenty of
good things laid up for many years. Take life
easy; eat, drink and be merry.” ’

20“But God said to him, ‘You fool! This
very night your life will be demanded from
you. Then who will get what you have prepared for yourself?’

21“This is how it will be with anyone who
stores up things for himself but is not rich toward God.”

Do Not Worry

22Then Jesus said to his disciples: “Therefore I tell you, do not worry about your life,
what you will eat; or about your body, what
you will wear. 23Life is more than food, and
the body more than clothes. 24Consider the ravens: They do not sow or reap, they have no
storeroom or barn; yet God feeds them. And
how much more valuable you are than birds!
25Who of you by worrying can add a single
hour to his life[b]? 26Since you cannot do this
very little thing, why do you worry about the
rest?

27“Consider how the lilies grow. They do
not labor or spin. Yet I tell you, not even Solomon in all his splendor was dressed like one of
these. 28If that is how God clothes the grass of
the field, which is here today, and tomorrow is
thrown into the fire, how much more will he
clothe you, O you of little faith! 29And do not
set your heart on what you will eat or drink; do
not worry about it. 30For the pagan world runs

[a]6 Greek *two assaria* [b]25 Or *single cubit to his height*

after all such things, and your Father knows that you need them. 31But seek his kingdom, and these things will be given to you as well.

32"Do not be afraid, little flock, for your Father has been pleased to give you the kingdom. 33Sell your possessions and give to the poor. Provide purses for yourselves that will not wear out, a treasure in heaven that will not be exhausted, where no thief comes near and no moth destroys. 34For where your treasure is, there your heart will be also.

Watchfulness

35"Be dressed ready for service and keep your lamps burning, 36like men waiting for their master to return from a wedding banquet, so that when he comes and knocks they can immediately open the door for him. 37It will be good for those servants whose master finds them watching when he comes. I tell you the truth, he will dress himself to serve, will have them recline at the table and will come and wait on them. 38It will be good for those servants whose master finds them ready, even if he comes in the second or third watch of the night. 39But understand this: If the owner of the house had known at what hour the thief was coming, he would not have let his house be broken into. 40You also must be ready, because the Son of Man will come at an hour when you do not expect him."

41Peter asked, "Lord, are you telling this parable to us, or to everyone?"

42The Lord answered, "Who then is the faithful and wise manager, whom the master puts in charge of his servants to give them their food allowance at the proper time? 43It will be good for that servant whom the master finds doing so when he returns. 44I tell you the truth, he will put him in charge of all his possessions. 45But suppose the servant says to himself, 'My master is taking a long time in coming,' and he then begins to beat the menservants and maidservants and to eat and drink and get drunk. 46The master of that servant will come on a day when he does not expect him and at an hour he is not aware of. He will cut him to pieces and assign him a place with the unbelievers.

47"That servant who knows his master's will and does not get ready or does not do what his master wants will be beaten with many blows. 48But the one who does not know and does things deserving punishment will be beaten with few blows. From everyone who has been given much, much will be demanded; and from the one who has been entrusted with much, much more will be asked.

Not Peace but Division

49"I have come to bring fire on the earth, and how I wish it were already kindled! 50But I have a baptism to undergo, and how distressed I am until it is completed! 51Do you think I came to bring peace on earth? No, I tell you, but division. 52From now on there will be five in one family divided against each other, three against two and two against three. 53They will be divided, father against son and son against father, mother against daughter and daughter against mother, mother-in-law against daughter-in-law and daughter-in-law against mother-in-law."

Interpreting the Times

54He said to the crowd: "When you see a cloud rising in the west, immediately you say, 'It's going to rain,' and it does. 55And when the south wind blows, you say, 'It's going to be hot,' and it is. 56Hypocrites! You know how to interpret the appearance of the earth and the sky. How is it that you don't know how to interpret this present time?

57"Why don't you judge for yourselves what is right? 58As you are going with your adversary to the magistrate, try hard to be reconciled to him on the way, or he may drag you off to the judge, and the judge turn you over to the officer, and the officer throw you into prison. 59I tell you, you will not get out until you have paid the last penny.[a]"

Repent or Perish

13 Now there were some present at that time who told Jesus about the Galileans whose blood Pilate had mixed with their sacrifices. 2Jesus answered, "Do you think that these Galileans were worse sinners than all the other Galileans because they suffered this way? 3I tell you, no! But unless you repent, you too will all perish. 4Or those eighteen who died when the tower in Siloam fell on them—do you think they were more guilty than all the others living in Jerusalem? 5I tell you, no! But unless you repent, you too will all perish."

6Then he told this parable: "A man had a fig tree, planted in his vineyard, and he went to look for fruit on it, but did not find any. 7So he said to the man who took care of the vineyard, 'For three years now I've been coming to look for fruit on this fig tree and haven't found any. Cut it down! Why should it use up the soil?'

8" 'Sir,' the man replied, 'leave it alone for one more year, and I'll dig around it and fertilize it. 9If it bears fruit next year, fine! If not, then cut it down.' "

A Crippled Woman Healed on the Sabbath

10On a Sabbath Jesus was teaching in one of the synagogues, 11and a woman was there who had been crippled by a spirit for eighteen years. She was bent over and could not straighten up at all. 12When Jesus saw her, he called her forward and said to her, "Woman, you are set free from your infirmity." 13Then he put his hands on her, and immediately she straightened up and praised God.

14Indignant because Jesus had healed on the Sabbath, the synagogue ruler said to the people, "There are six days for work. So come and

[a]59 Greek *lepton*

be healed on those days, not on the Sabbath."
15The Lord answered him, "You hypocrites!
Doesn't each of you on the Sabbath untie his
ox or donkey from the stall and lead it out to
give it water? 16Then should not this woman,
a daughter of Abraham, whom Satan has kept
bound for eighteen long years, be set free on
the Sabbath day from what bound her?"
17When he said this, all his opponents were
humiliated, but the people were delighted with
all the wonderful things he was doing.

The Parables of the Mustard Seed and the Yeast

18Then Jesus asked, "What is the kingdom
of God like? What shall I compare it to? 19It is
like a mustard seed, which a man took and
planted in his garden. It grew and became a
tree, and the birds of the air perched in its
branches."
20Again he asked, "What shall I compare the
kingdom of God to? 21It is like yeast that a
woman took and mixed into a large amount[a]
of flour until it worked all through the dough."

The Narrow Door

22Then Jesus went through the towns and
villages, teaching as he made his way to Jerusalem. 23Someone asked him, "Lord, are only
a few people going to be saved?"
He said to them, 24"Make every effort to
enter through the narrow door, because many,
I tell you, will try to enter and will not be able
to. 25Once the owner of the house gets up and
closes the door, you will stand outside knocking and pleading, 'Sir, open the door for us.'
"But he will answer, 'I don't know you or
where you come from.'
26"Then you will say, 'We ate and drank
with you, and you taught in our streets.'
27"But he will reply, 'I don't know you or
where you come from. Away from me, all you
evildoers!'
28"There will be weeping there, and gnashing of teeth, when you see Abraham, Isaac and
Jacob and all the prophets in the kingdom of
God, but you yourselves thrown out. 29People
will come from east and west and north and
south, and will take their places at the feast in
the kingdom of God. 30Indeed there are those
who are last who will be first, and first who
will be last."

Jesus' Sorrow for Jerusalem

31At that time some Pharisees came to Jesus
and said to him, "Leave this place and go
somewhere else. Herod wants to kill you."
32He replied, "Go tell that fox, 'I will drive
out demons and heal people today and tomorrow, and on the third day I will reach my goal.'
33In any case, I must keep going today and
tomorrow and the next day—for surely no
prophet can die outside Jerusalem!
34"O Jerusalem, Jerusalem, you who kill the
prophets and stone those sent to you, how often I have longed to gather your children together, as a hen gathers her chicks under her
wings, but you were not willing! 35Look, your
house is left to you desolate. I tell you, you
will not see me again until you say, 'Blessed is
he who comes in the name of the Lord.'[b]"

Jesus at a Pharisee's House

14 One Sabbath, when Jesus went to eat in
the house of a prominent Pharisee, he
was being carefully watched. 2There in front of
him was a man suffering from dropsy. 3Jesus
asked the Pharisees and experts in the law, "Is
it lawful to heal on the Sabbath or not?" 4But
they remained silent. So taking hold of the
man, he healed him and sent him away.
5Then he asked them, "If one of you has a
son[c] or an ox that falls into a well on the
Sabbath day, will you not immediately pull
him out?" 6And they had nothing to say.
7When he noticed how the guests picked the
places of honor at the table, he told them this
parable: 8"When someone invites you to a
wedding feast, do not take the place of honor,
for a person more distinguished than you may
have been invited. 9If so, the host who invited
both of you will come and say to you, 'Give
this man your seat.' Then, humiliated, you will
have to take the least important place. 10But
when you are invited, take the lowest place, so
that when your host comes, he will say to you,
'Friend, move up to a better place.' Then you
will be honored in the presence of all your
fellow guests. 11For everyone who exalts himself will be humbled, and he who humbles
himself will be exalted."
12Then Jesus said to his host, "When you
give a luncheon or dinner, do not invite your
friends, your brothers or relatives, or your rich
neighbors; if you do, they may invite you back
and so you will be repaid. 13But when you give
a banquet, invite the poor, the crippled, the
lame, the blind, 14and you will be blessed. Although they cannot repay you, you will be repaid at the resurrection of the righteous."

The Parable of the Great Banquet

15When one of those at the table with him
heard this, he said to Jesus, "Blessed is the
man who will eat at the feast in the kingdom of
God."
16Jesus replied: "A certain man was preparing a great banquet and invited many guests.
17At the time of the banquet he sent his servant
to tell those who had been invited, 'Come, for
everything is now ready.'
18"But they all alike began to make excuses.
The first said, 'I have just bought a field, and
I must go and see it. Please excuse me.'
19"Another said, 'I have just bought five
yoke of oxen, and I'm on my way to try them
out. Please excuse me.'
20"Still another said, 'I just got married, so
I can't come.'
21"The servant came back and reported this

[a]*21* Greek *three satas* (probably about 1/2 bushel or 22 liters) [b]*35* Psalm 118:26 [c]*5* Some manuscripts *donkey*

to his master. Then the owner of the house
became angry and ordered his servant, ‘Go out
quickly into the streets and alleys of the town
and bring in the poor, the crippled, the blind
and the lame.’
22“ ‘Sir,’ the servant said, ‘what you ordered
has been done, but there is still room.’
23“Then the master told his servant, ‘Go out
to the roads and country lanes and make them
come in, so that my house will be full. 24I tell
you, not one of those men who were invited
will get a taste of my banquet.’ ”

The Cost of Being a Disciple

25Large crowds were traveling with Jesus,
and turning to them he said: 26“If anyone
comes to me and does not hate his father and
mother, his wife and children, his brothers and
sisters—yes, even his own life—he cannot be
my disciple. 27And anyone who does not carry
his cross and follow me cannot be my disciple.
28“Suppose one of you wants to build a tower. Will he not first sit down and estimate the
cost to see if he has enough money to complete
it? 29For if he lays the foundation and is not
able to finish it, everyone who sees it will ridicule him, 30saying, ‘This fellow began to build
and was not able to finish.’
31“Or suppose a king is about to go to war
against another king. Will he not first sit down
and consider whether he is able with ten thousand men to oppose the one coming against
him with twenty thousand? 32If he is not able,
he will send a delegation while the other is still
a long way off and will ask for terms of peace.
33In the same way, any of you who does not
give up everything he has cannot be my disciple.
34“Salt is good, but if it loses its saltiness,
how can it be made salty again? 35It is fit neither for the soil nor for the manure pile; it is
thrown out.
“He who has ears to hear, let him hear.”

The Parable of the Lost Sheep

15 Now the tax collectors and “sinners”
were all gathering around to hear him.
2But the Pharisees and the teachers of the law
muttered, “This man welcomes sinners and
eats with them.”
3Then Jesus told them this parable: 4“Suppose one of you has a hundred sheep and loses
one of them. Does he not leave the ninety-nine
in the open country and go after the lost sheep
until he finds it? 5And when he finds it, he
joyfully puts it on his shoulders 6and goes
home. Then he calls his friends and neighbors
together and says, ‘Rejoice with me; I have
found my lost sheep.’ 7I tell you that in the
same way there will be more rejoicing in heav-
en over one sinner who repents than over
ninety-nine righteous persons who do not need
to repent.

The Parable of the Lost Coin

8“Or suppose a woman has ten silver coins[a]
and loses one. Does she not light a lamp,
sweep the house and search carefully until she
finds it? 9And when she finds it, she calls her
friends and neighbors together and says, ‘Rejoice with me; I have found my lost coin.’ 10In
the same way, I tell you, there is rejoicing in
the presence of the angels of God over one
sinner who repents.”

The Parable of the Lost Son

11Jesus continued: “There was a man who
had two sons. 12The younger one said to his
father, ‘Father, give me my share of the estate.’
So he divided his property between them.
13“Not long after that, the younger son got
together all he had, set off for a distant country
and there squandered his wealth in wild living.
14After he had spent everything, there was a
severe famine in that whole country, and he
began to be in need. 15So he went and hired
himself out to a citizen of that country, who
sent him to his fields to feed pigs. 16He longed
to fill his stomach with the pods that the pigs
were eating, but no one gave him anything.
17“When he came to his senses, he said,
‘How many of my father’s hired men have
food to spare, and here I am starving to death!
18I will set out and go back to my father and
say to him: Father, I have sinned against heav-
en and against you. 19I am no longer worthy to
be called your son; make me like one of your
hired men.’ 20So he got up and went to his
father.
“But while he was still a long way off, his
father saw him and was filled with compassion
for him; he ran to his son, threw his arms
around him and kissed him.
21“The son said to him, ‘Father, I have
sinned against heaven and against you. I am no
longer worthy to be called your son.[b]’
22“But the father said to his servants,
‘Quick! Bring the best robe and put it on him.
Put a ring on his finger and sandals on his feet.
23Bring the fattened calf and kill it. Let’s have
a feast and celebrate. 24For this son of mine
was dead and is alive again; he was lost and is
found.’ So they began to celebrate.
25“Meanwhile, the older son was in the
field. When he came near the house, he heard
music and dancing. 26So he called one of the
servants and asked him what was going on.
27‘Your brother has come,’ he replied, ‘and
your father has killed the fattened calf because
he has him back safe and sound.’
28“The older brother became angry and refused to go in. So his father went out and
pleaded with him. 29But he answered his father, ‘Look! All these years I’ve been slaving
for you and never disobeyed your orders. Yet
you never gave me even a young goat so I
could celebrate with my friends. 30But when
this son of yours who has squandered your

[a]8 Greek *ten drachmas,* each worth about a day’s wages
[b]21 Some early manuscripts *son. Make me like one of your hired men.*

property with prostitutes comes home, you kill the fattened calf for him!’

31“ ‘My son,’ the father said, ‘you are always with me, and everything I have is yours. 32But we had to celebrate and be glad, because this brother of yours was dead and is alive again; he was lost and is found.’ ”

The Parable of the Shrewd Manager

16 Jesus told his disciples: “There was a rich man whose manager was accused of wasting his possessions. 2So he called him in and asked him, ‘What is this I hear about you? Give an account of your management, because you cannot be manager any longer.’

3“The manager said to himself, ‘What shall I do now? My master is taking away my job. I’m not strong enough to dig, and I’m ashamed to beg— 4I know what I’ll do so that, when I lose my job here, people will welcome me into their houses.’

5“So he called in each one of his master’s debtors. He asked the first, ‘How much do you owe my master?’

6“ ‘Eight hundred gallons[a] of olive oil,’ he replied.

“The manager told him, ‘Take your bill, sit down quickly, and make it four hundred.’

7“Then he asked the second, ‘And how much do you owe?’

“ ‘A thousand bushels[b] of wheat,’ he replied.

“He told him, ‘Take your bill and make it eight hundred.’

8“The master commended the dishonest manager because he had acted shrewdly. For the people of this world are more shrewd in dealing with their own kind than are the people of the light. 9I tell you, use worldly wealth to gain friends for yourselves, so that when it is gone, you will be welcomed into eternal dwellings.

10“Whoever can be trusted with very little can also be trusted with much, and whoever is dishonest with very little will also be dishonest with much. 11So if you have not been trustworthy in handling worldly wealth, who will trust you with true riches? 12And if you have not been trustworthy with someone else’s property, who will give you property of your own?

13“No servant can serve two masters. Either he will hate the one and love the other, or he will be devoted to the one and despise the other. You cannot serve both God and Money.”

14The Pharisees, who loved money, heard all this and were sneering at Jesus. 15He said to them, “You are the ones who justify yourselves in the eyes of men, but God knows your hearts. What is highly valued among men is detestable in God’s sight.

Additional Teachings

16“The Law and the Prophets were proclaimed until John. Since that time, the good news of the kingdom of God is being preached, and everyone is forcing his way into it. 17It is easier for heaven and earth to disappear than for the least stroke of a pen to drop out of the Law.

18“Anyone who divorces his wife and marries another woman commits adultery, and the man who marries a divorced woman commits adultery.

The Rich Man and Lazarus

19“There was a rich man who was dressed in purple and fine linen and lived in luxury every day. 20At his gate was laid a beggar named Lazarus, covered with sores 21and longing to eat what fell from the rich man’s table. Even the dogs came and licked his sores.

22“The time came when the beggar died and the angels carried him to Abraham’s side. The rich man also died and was buried. 23In hell,[c] where he was in torment, he looked up and saw Abraham far away, with Lazarus by his side. 24So he called to him, ‘Father Abraham, have pity on me and send Lazarus to dip the tip of his finger in water and cool my tongue, because I am in agony in this fire.’

25“But Abraham replied, ‘Son, remember that in your lifetime you received your good things, while Lazarus received bad things, but now he is comforted here and you are in agony. 26And besides all this, between us and you a great chasm has been fixed, so that those who want to go from here to you cannot, nor can anyone cross over from there to us.’

27“He answered, ‘Then I beg you, father, send Lazarus to my father’s house, 28for I have five brothers. Let him warn them, so that they will not also come to this place of torment.’

29“Abraham replied, ‘They have Moses and the Prophets; let them listen to them.’

30“ ‘No, father Abraham,’ he said, ‘but if someone from the dead goes to them, they will repent.’

31“He said to him, ‘If they do not listen to Moses and the Prophets, they will not be convinced even if someone rises from the dead.’ ”

Sin, Faith, Duty

17 Jesus said to his disciples: “Things that cause people to sin are bound to come, but woe to that person through whom they come. 2It would be better for him to be thrown into the sea with a millstone tied around his neck than for him to cause one of these little ones to sin. 3So watch yourselves.

“If your brother sins, rebuke him, and if he repents, forgive him. 4If he sins against you seven times in a day, and seven times comes back to you and says, ‘I repent,’ forgive him.”

5The apostles said to the Lord, “Increase our faith!”

6He replied, “If you have faith as small as a mustard seed, you can say to this mulberry tree, ‘Be uprooted and planted in the sea,’ and it will obey you.

7“Suppose one of you had a servant plowing

[a]6 Greek *one hundred batous* (probably about 3 kiloliters)
[b]7 Greek *one hundred korous* (probably about 35 kiloliters)
[c]23 Greek *Hades*

or looking after the sheep. Would he say to the servant when he comes in from the field, 'Come along now and sit down to eat'? 8Would he not rather say, 'Prepare my supper, get yourself ready and wait on me while I eat and drink; after that you may eat and drink'? 9Would he thank the servant because he did what he was told to do? 10So you also, when you have done everything you were told to do, should say, 'We are unworthy servants; we have only done our duty.' "

Ten Healed of Leprosy

11Now on his way to Jerusalem, Jesus traveled along the border between Samaria and Galilee. 12As he was going into a village, ten men who had leprosy[a] met him. They stood at a distance 13and called out in a loud voice, "Jesus, Master, have pity on us!"

14When he saw them, he said, "Go, show yourselves to the priests." And as they went, they were cleansed.

15One of them, when he saw he was healed, came back, praising God in a loud voice. 16He threw himself at Jesus' feet and thanked him—and he was a Samaritan.

17Jesus asked, "Were not all ten cleansed? Where are the other nine? 18Was no one found to return and give praise to God except this foreigner?" 19Then he said to him, "Rise and go; your faith has made you well."

The Coming of the Kingdom of God

20Once, having been asked by the Pharisees when the kingdom of God would come, Jesus replied, "The kingdom of God does not come with your careful observation, 21nor will people say, 'Here it is,' or 'There it is,' because the kingdom of God is within[b] you."

22Then he said to his disciples, "The time is coming when you will long to see one of the days of the Son of Man, but you will not see it. 23Men will tell you, 'There he is!' or 'Here he is!' Do not go running off after them. 24For the Son of Man in his day[c] will be like the lightning, which flashes and lights up the sky from one end to the other. 25But first he must suffer many things and be rejected by this generation.

26"Just as it was in the days of Noah, so also will it be in the days of the Son of Man. 27People were eating, drinking, marrying and being given in marriage up to the day Noah entered the ark. Then the flood came and destroyed them all.

28"It was the same in the days of Lot. People were eating and drinking, buying and selling, planting and building. 29But the day Lot left Sodom, fire and sulfur rained down from heaven and destroyed them all.

30"It will be just like this on the day the Son of Man is revealed. 31On that day no one who is on the roof of his house, with his goods inside, should go down to get them. Likewise, no one in the field should go back for anything. 32Remember Lot's wife! 33Whoever tries to keep his life will lose it, and whoever loses his life will preserve it. 34I tell you, on that night two people will be in one bed; one will be taken and the other left. 35Two women will be grinding grain together; one will be taken and the other left.[d]"

37"Where, Lord?" they asked.

He replied, "Where there is a dead body, there the vultures will gather."

The Parable of the Persistent Widow

18 Then Jesus told his disciples a parable to show them that they should always pray and not give up. 2He said: "In a certain town there was a judge who neither feared God nor cared about men. 3And there was a widow in that town who kept coming to him with the plea, 'Grant me justice against my adversary.'

4"For some time he refused. But finally he said to himself, 'Even though I don't fear God or care about men, 5yet because this widow keeps bothering me, I will see that she gets justice, so that she won't eventually wear me out with her coming!' "

6And the Lord said, "Listen to what the unjust judge says. 7And will not God bring about justice for his chosen ones, who cry out to him day and night? Will he keep putting them off? 8I tell you, he will see that they get justice, and quickly. However, when the Son of Man comes, will he find faith on the earth?"

The Parable of the Pharisee and the Tax Collector

9To some who were confident of their own righteousness and looked down on everybody else, Jesus told this parable: 10"Two men went up to the temple to pray, one a Pharisee and the other a tax collector. 11The Pharisee stood up and prayed about[e] himself: 'God, I thank you that I am not like other men—robbers, evildoers, adulterers—or even like this tax collector. 12I fast twice a week and give a tenth of all I get.'

13"But the tax collector stood at a distance. He would not even look up to heaven, but beat his breast and said, 'God, have mercy on me, a sinner.'

14"I tell you that this man, rather than the other, went home justified before God. For everyone who exalts himself will be humbled, and he who humbles himself will be exalted."

The Little Children and Jesus

15People were also bringing babies to Jesus to have him touch them. When the disciples saw this, they rebuked them. 16But Jesus called the children to him and said, "Let the little children come to me, and do not hinder them, for the kingdom of God belongs to such as these. 17I tell you the truth, anyone who will not receive the kingdom of God like a little child will never enter it."

[a] *12* The Greek word was used for various diseases affecting the skin—not necessarily leprosy.
[b] *21* Or *among* [c] *24* Some manuscripts do not have *in his day.* [d] *35* Some manuscripts *left.* *36Two men will be in the field; one will be taken and the other left.* [e] *11* Or *to*

The Rich Ruler

18A certain ruler asked him, "Good teacher,
what must I do to inherit eternal life?"
19"Why do you call me good?" Jesus answered. "No one is good—except God alone.
20You know the commandments: 'Do not commit adultery, do not murder, do not steal, do
not give false testimony, honor your father and
mother.'[a]"
21"All these I have kept since I was a boy,"
he said.
22When Jesus heard this, he said to him,
"You still lack one thing. Sell everything you
have and give to the poor, and you will have
treasure in heaven. Then come, follow me."
23When he heard this, he became very sad,
because he was a man of great wealth. 24Jesus
looked at him and said, "How hard it is for the
rich to enter the kingdom of God! 25Indeed, it
is easier for a camel to go through the eye of
a needle than for a rich man to enter the kingdom of God."
26Those who heard this asked, "Who then
can be saved?"
27Jesus replied, "What is impossible with
men is possible with God."
28Peter said to him, "We have left all we had
to follow you!"
29"I tell you the truth," Jesus said to them,
"no one who has left home or wife or brothers
or parents or children for the sake of the kingdom of God 30will fail to receive many times
as much in this age and, in the age to come,
eternal life."

Jesus Again Predicts His Death

31Jesus took the Twelve aside and told them,
"We are going up to Jerusalem, and everything
that is written by the prophets about the Son of
Man will be fulfilled. 32He will be handed over
to the Gentiles. They will mock him, insult
him, spit on him, flog him and kill him. 33On
the third day he will rise again."
34The disciples did not understand any of
this. Its meaning was hidden from them, and
they did not know what he was talking about.

A Blind Beggar Receives His Sight

35As Jesus approached Jericho, a blind man
was sitting by the roadside begging. 36When
he heard the crowd going by, he asked what
was happening. 37They told him, "Jesus of
Nazareth is passing by."
38He called out, "Jesus, Son of David, have
mercy on me!"
39Those who led the way rebuked him and
told him to be quiet, but he shouted all the
more, "Son of David, have mercy on me!"
40Jesus stopped and ordered the man to be
brought to him. When he came near, Jesus
asked him, 41"What do you want me to do for
you?"
"Lord, I want to see," he replied.
42Jesus said to him, "Receive your sight;
your faith has healed you." 43Immediately he
received his sight and followed Jesus, praising
God. When all the people saw it, they also
praised God.

Zacchaeus the Tax Collector

19 Jesus entered Jericho and was passing
through. 2A man was there by the name
of Zacchaeus; he was a chief tax collector and
was wealthy. 3He wanted to see who Jesus
was, but being a short man he could not, because of the crowd. 4So he ran ahead and
climbed a sycamore-fig tree to see him, since
Jesus was coming that way.
5When Jesus reached the spot, he looked up
and said to him, "Zacchaeus, come down immediately. I must stay at your house today."
6So he came down at once and welcomed him
gladly.
7All the people saw this and began to mutter, "He has gone to be the guest of a 'sinner.' "
8But Zacchaeus stood up and said to the
Lord, "Look, Lord! Here and now I give half
of my possessions to the poor, and if I have
cheated anybody out of anything, I will pay
back four times the amount."
9Jesus said to him, "Today salvation has
come to this house, because this man, too, is a
son of Abraham. 10For the Son of Man came to
seek and to save what was lost."

The Parable of the Ten Minas

11While they were listening to this, he went
on to tell them a parable, because he was near
Jerusalem and the people thought that the
kingdom of God was going to appear at once.
12He said: "A man of noble birth went to a
distant country to have himself appointed king
and then to return. 13So he called ten of his
servants and gave them ten minas.[b] 'Put this
money to work,' he said, 'until I come back.'
14"But his subjects hated him and sent a delegation after him to say, 'We don't want this
man to be our king.'
15"He was made king, however, and returned home. Then he sent for the servants to
whom he had given the money, in order to find
out what they had gained with it.
16"The first one came and said, 'Sir, your
mina has earned ten more.'
17" 'Well done, my good servant!' his master replied. 'Because you have been trustworthy in a very small matter, take charge of ten
cities.'
18"The second came and said, 'Sir, your
mina has earned five more.'
19"His master answered, 'You take charge
of five cities.'
20"Then another servant came and said, 'Sir,
here is your mina; I have kept it laid away in
a piece of cloth. 21I was afraid of you, because
you are a hard man. You take out what you did
not put in and reap what you did not sow.'
22"His master replied, 'I will judge you by
your own words, you wicked servant! You

[a] *20* Exodus 20:12-16; Deut. 5:16-20 [b] *13* A mina was about three months' wages.

knew, did you, that I am a hard man, taking out what I did not put in, and reaping what I did not sow? 23Why then didn't you put my money on deposit, so that when I came back, I could have collected it with interest?'

24"Then he said to those standing by, 'Take his mina away from him and give it to the one who has ten minas.'

25" 'Sir,' they said, 'he already has ten!'

26"He replied, 'I tell you that to everyone who has, more will be given, but as for the one who has nothing, even what he has will be taken away. 27But those enemies of mine who did not want me to be king over them—bring them here and kill them in front of me.' "

The Triumphal Entry

28After Jesus had said this, he went on ahead, going up to Jerusalem. 29As he approached Bethphage and Bethany at the hill called the Mount of Olives, he sent two of his disciples, saying to them, 30"Go to the village ahead of you, and as you enter it, you will find a colt tied there, which no one has ever ridden. Untie it and bring it here. 31If anyone asks you, 'Why are you untying it?' tell him, 'The Lord needs it.' "

32Those who were sent ahead went and found it just as he had told them. 33As they were untying the colt, its owners asked them, "Why are you untying the colt?"

34They replied, "The Lord needs it."

35They brought it to Jesus, threw their cloaks on the colt and put Jesus on it. 36As he went along, people spread their cloaks on the road.

37When he came near the place where the road goes down the Mount of Olives, the whole crowd of disciples began joyfully to praise God in loud voices for all the miracles they had seen:

38"Blessed is the king who comes in the
name of the Lord!"[a]

"Peace in heaven and glory in the
highest!"

39Some of the Pharisees in the crowd said to Jesus, "Teacher, rebuke your disciples!"

40"I tell you," he replied, "if they keep quiet, the stones will cry out."

41As he approached Jerusalem and saw the city, he wept over it 42and said, "If you, even you, had only known on this day what would bring you peace—but now it is hidden from your eyes. 43The days will come upon you when your enemies will build an embankment against you and encircle you and hem you in on every side. 44They will dash you to the ground, you and the children within your walls. They will not leave one stone on another, because you did not recognize the time of God's coming to you."

Jesus at the Temple

45Then he entered the temple area and began driving out those who were selling. 46"It is written," he said to them, " 'My house will be a house of prayer'[b]; but you have made it 'a den of robbers.'[c]"

47Every day he was teaching at the temple. But the chief priests, the teachers of the law and the leaders among the people were trying to kill him. 48Yet they could not find any way to do it, because all the people hung on his words.

The Authority of Jesus Questioned

20 One day as he was teaching the people in the temple courts and preaching the gospel, the chief priests and the teachers of the law, together with the elders, came up to him. 2"Tell us by what authority you are doing these things," they said. "Who gave you this authority?"

3He replied, "I will also ask you a question. Tell me, 4John's baptism—was it from heaven, or from men?"

5They discussed it among themselves and said, "If we say, 'From heaven,' he will ask, 'Why didn't you believe him?' 6But if we say, 'From men,' all the people will stone us, because they are persuaded that John was a prophet."

7So they answered, "We don't know where it was from."

8Jesus said, "Neither will I tell you by what authority I am doing these things."

The Parable of the Tenants

9He went on to tell the people this parable: "A man planted a vineyard, rented it to some farmers and went away for a long time. 10At harvest time he sent a servant to the tenants so they would give him some of the fruit of the vineyard. But the tenants beat him and sent him away empty-handed. 11He sent another servant, but that one also they beat and treated shamefully and sent away empty-handed. 12He sent still a third, and they wounded him and threw him out.

13"Then the owner of the vineyard said, 'What shall I do? I will send my son, whom I love; perhaps they will respect him.'

14"But when the tenants saw him, they talked the matter over. 'This is the heir,' they said. 'Let's kill him, and the inheritance will be ours.' 15So they threw him out of the vineyard and killed him.

"What then will the owner of the vineyard do to them? 16He will come and kill those tenants and give the vineyard to others."

When the people heard this, they said, "May this never be!"

17Jesus looked directly at them and asked, "Then what is the meaning of that which is written:

" 'The stone the builders rejected
has become the capstone[d]'[e]?

18Everyone who falls on that stone will be bro-

a38 Psalm 118:26 *b46* Isaiah 56:7 *c46* Jer. 7:11 *d17* Or *cornerstone* *e17* Psalm 118:22

ken to pieces, but he on whom it falls will be crushed."

19The teachers of the law and the chief priests looked for a way to arrest him immediately, because they knew he had spoken this parable against them. But they were afraid of the people.

Paying Taxes to Caesar

20Keeping a close watch on him, they sent spies, who pretended to be honest. They hoped to catch Jesus in something he said so that they might hand him over to the power and authority of the governor. 21So the spies questioned him: "Teacher, we know that you speak and teach what is right, and that you do not show partiality but teach the way of God in accordance with the truth. 22Is it right for us to pay taxes to Caesar or not?"

23He saw through their duplicity and said to them, 24"Show me a denarius. Whose portrait and inscription are on it?"

25"Caesar's," they replied.

He said to them, "Then give to Caesar what is Caesar's, and to God what is God's."

26They were unable to trap him in what he had said there in public. And astonished by his answer, they became silent.

The Resurrection and Marriage

27Some of the Sadducees, who say there is no resurrection, came to Jesus with a question. 28"Teacher," they said, "Moses wrote for us that if a man's brother dies and leaves a wife but no children, the man must marry the widow and have children for his brother. 29Now there were seven brothers. The first one married a woman and died childless. 30The second 31and then the third married her, and in the same way the seven died, leaving no children. 32Finally, the woman died too. 33Now then, at the resurrection whose wife will she be, since the seven were married to her?"

34Jesus replied, "The people of this age marry and are given in marriage. 35But those who are considered worthy of taking part in that age and in the resurrection from the dead will neither marry nor be given in marriage, 36and they can no longer die; for they are like the angels. They are God's children, since they are children of the resurrection. 37But in the account of the bush, even Moses showed that the dead rise, for he calls the Lord 'the God of Abraham, and the God of Isaac, and the God of Jacob.'[a] 38He is not the God of the dead, but of the living, for to him all are alive."

39Some of the teachers of the law responded, "Well said, teacher!" 40And no one dared to ask him any more questions.

Whose Son Is the Christ?

41Then Jesus said to them, "How is it that they say the Christ[b] is the Son of David? 42David himself declares in the Book of Psalms:

" 'The Lord said to my Lord:
"Sit at my right hand
43until I make your enemies
a footstool for your feet." '[c]

44David calls him 'Lord.' How then can he be his son?"

45While all the people were listening, Jesus said to his disciples, 46"Beware of the teachers of the law. They like to walk around in flowing robes and love to be greeted in the marketplaces and have the most important seats in the synagogues and the places of honor at banquets. 47They devour widows' houses and for a show make lengthy prayers. Such men will be punished most severely."

The Widow's Offering

21 As he looked up, Jesus saw the rich putting their gifts into the temple treasury. 2He also saw a poor widow put in two very small copper coins.[d] 3"I tell you the truth," he said, "this poor widow has put in more than all the others. 4All these people gave their gifts out of their wealth; but she out of her poverty put in all she had to live on."

Signs of the End of the Age

5Some of his disciples were remarking about how the temple was adorned with beautiful stones and with gifts dedicated to God. But Jesus said, 6"As for what you see here, the time will come when not one stone will be left on another; every one of them will be thrown down."

7"Teacher," they asked, "when will these things happen? And what will be the sign that they are about to take place?"

8He replied: "Watch out that you are not deceived. For many will come in my name, claiming, 'I am he,' and, 'The time is near.' Do not follow them. 9When you hear of wars and revolutions, do not be frightened. These things must happen first, but the end will not come right away."

10Then he said to them: "Nation will rise against nation, and kingdom against kingdom. 11There will be great earthquakes, famines and pestilences in various places, and fearful events and great signs from heaven.

12"But before all this, they will lay hands on you and persecute you. They will deliver you to synagogues and prisons, and you will be brought before kings and governors, and all on account of my name. 13This will result in your being witnesses to them. 14But make up your mind not to worry beforehand how you will defend yourselves. 15For I will give you words and wisdom that none of your adversaries will be able to resist or contradict. 16You will be betrayed even by parents, brothers, relatives and friends, and they will put some of you to death. 17All men will hate you because of me. 18But not a hair of your head will perish. 19By standing firm you will gain life.

20"When you see Jerusalem being surrounded by armies, you will know that its desolation

[a]37 Exodus 3:6 [b]41 Or *Messiah* [c]43 Psalm 110:1 [d]2 Greek *two lepta*

is near. **21**Then let those who are in Judea flee to the mountains, let those in the city get out, and let those in the country not enter the city. **22**For this is the time of punishment in fulfillment of all that has been written. **23**How dreadful it will be in those days for pregnant women and nursing mothers! There will be great distress in the land and wrath against this people. **24**They will fall by the sword and will be taken as prisoners to all the nations. Jerusalem will be trampled on by the Gentiles until the times of the Gentiles are fulfilled.

25"There will be signs in the sun, moon and stars. On the earth, nations will be in anguish and perplexity at the roaring and tossing of the sea. **26**Men will faint from terror, apprehensive of what is coming on the world, for the heavenly bodies will be shaken. **27**At that time they will see the Son of Man coming in a cloud with power and great glory. **28**When these things begin to take place, stand up and lift up your heads, because your redemption is drawing near."

29He told them this parable: "Look at the fig tree and all the trees. **30**When they sprout leaves, you can see for yourselves and know that summer is near. **31**Even so, when you see these things happening, you know that the kingdom of God is near.

32"I tell you the truth, this generation[a] will certainly not pass away until all these things have happened. **33**Heaven and earth will pass away, but my words will never pass away.

34"Be careful, or your hearts will be weighed down with dissipation, drunkenness and the anxieties of life, and that day will close on you unexpectedly like a trap. **35**For it will come upon all those who live on the face of the whole earth. **36**Be always on the watch, and pray that you may be able to escape all that is about to happen, and that you may be able to stand before the Son of Man."

37Each day Jesus was teaching at the temple, and each evening he went out to spend the night on the hill called the Mount of Olives, **38**and all the people came early in the morning to hear him at the temple.

Judas Agrees to Betray Jesus

22 Now the Feast of Unleavened Bread, called the Passover, was approaching, **2**and the chief priests and the teachers of the law were looking for some way to get rid of Jesus, for they were afraid of the people. **3**Then Satan entered Judas, called Iscariot, one of the Twelve. **4**And Judas went to the chief priests and the officers of the temple guard and discussed with them how he might betray Jesus. **5**They were delighted and agreed to give him money. **6**He consented, and watched for an opportunity to hand Jesus over to them when no crowd was present.

The Last Supper

7Then came the day of Unleavened Bread on which the Passover lamb had to be sacrificed. **8**Jesus sent Peter and John, saying, "Go and make preparations for us to eat the Passover."

9"Where do you want us to prepare for it?" they asked.

10He replied, "As you enter the city, a man carrying a jar of water will meet you. Follow him to the house that he enters, **11**and say to the owner of the house, 'The Teacher asks: Where is the guest room, where I may eat the Passover with my disciples?' **12**He will show you a large upper room, all furnished. Make preparations there."

13They left and found things just as Jesus had told them. So they prepared the Passover.

14When the hour came, Jesus and his apostles reclined at the table. **15**And he said to them, "I have eagerly desired to eat this Passover with you before I suffer. **16**For I tell you, I will not eat it again until it finds fulfillment in the kingdom of God."

17After taking the cup, he gave thanks and said, "Take this and divide it among you. **18**For I tell you I will not drink again of the fruit of the vine until the kingdom of God comes."

19And he took bread, gave thanks and broke it, and gave it to them, saying, "This is my body given for you; do this in remembrance of me."

20In the same way, after the supper he took the cup, saying, "This cup is the new covenant in my blood, which is poured out for you. **21**But the hand of him who is going to betray me is with mine on the table. **22**The Son of Man will go as it has been decreed, but woe to that man who betrays him." **23**They began to question among themselves which of them it might be who would do this.

24Also a dispute arose among them as to which of them was considered to be greatest. **25**Jesus said to them, "The kings of the Gentiles lord it over them; and those who exercise authority over them call themselves Benefactors. **26**But you are not to be like that. Instead, the greatest among you should be like the youngest, and the one who rules like the one who serves. **27**For who is greater, the one who is at the table or the one who serves? Is it not the one who is at the table? But I am among you as one who serves. **28**You are those who have stood by me in my trials. **29**And I confer on you a kingdom, just as my Father conferred one on me, **30**so that you may eat and drink at my table in my kingdom and sit on thrones, judging the twelve tribes of Israel.

31"Simon, Simon, Satan has asked to sift you[b] as wheat. **32**But I have prayed for you, Simon, that your faith may not fail. And when you have turned back, strengthen your brothers."

33But he replied, "Lord, I am ready to go with you to prison and to death."

34Jesus answered, "I tell you, Peter, before the rooster crows today, you will deny three times that you know me."

[a] *32* Or *race* [b] *31* The Greek is plural.

35Then Jesus asked them, "When I sent you without purse, bag or sandals, did you lack anything?"

"Nothing," they answered.

36He said to them, "But now if you have a purse, take it, and also a bag; and if you don't have a sword, sell your cloak and buy one. 37It is written: 'And he was numbered with the transgressors'[a]; and I tell you that this must be fulfilled in me. Yes, what is written about me is reaching its fulfillment."

38The disciples said, "See, Lord, here are two swords."

"That is enough," he replied.

Jesus Prays on the Mount of Olives

39Jesus went out as usual to the Mount of Olives, and his disciples followed him. 40On reaching the place, he said to them, "Pray that you will not fall into temptation." 41He withdrew about a stone's throw beyond them, knelt down and prayed, 42"Father, if you are willing, take this cup from me; yet not my will, but yours be done." 43An angel from heaven appeared to him and strengthened him. 44And being in anguish, he prayed more earnestly, and his sweat was like drops of blood falling to the ground.[b]

45When he rose from prayer and went back to the disciples, he found them asleep, exhausted from sorrow. 46"Why are you sleeping?" he asked them. "Get up and pray so that you will not fall into temptation."

Jesus Arrested

47While he was still speaking a crowd came up, and the man who was called Judas, one of the Twelve, was leading them. He approached Jesus to kiss him, 48but Jesus asked him, "Judas, are you betraying the Son of Man with a kiss?"

49When Jesus' followers saw what was going to happen, they said, "Lord, should we strike with our swords?" 50And one of them struck the servant of the high priest, cutting off his right ear.

51But Jesus answered, "No more of this!" And he touched the man's ear and healed him.

52Then Jesus said to the chief priests, the officers of the temple guard, and the elders, who had come for him, "Am I leading a rebellion, that you have come with swords and clubs? 53Every day I was with you in the temple courts, and you did not lay a hand on me. But this is your hour—when darkness reigns."

Peter Disowns Jesus

54Then seizing him, they led him away and took him into the house of the high priest. Peter followed at a distance. 55But when they had kindled a fire in the middle of the courtyard and had sat down together, Peter sat down with them. 56A servant girl saw him seated there in the firelight. She looked closely at him and said, "This man was with him."

57But he denied it. "Woman, I don't know him," he said.

58A little later someone else saw him and said, "You also are one of them."

"Man, I am not!" Peter replied.

59About an hour later another asserted, "Certainly this fellow was with him, for he is a Galilean."

60Peter replied, "Man, I don't know what you're talking about!" Just as he was speaking, the rooster crowed. 61The Lord turned and looked straight at Peter. Then Peter remembered the word the Lord had spoken to him: "Before the rooster crows today, you will disown me three times." 62And he went outside and wept bitterly.

The Guards Mock Jesus

63The men who were guarding Jesus began mocking and beating him. 64They blindfolded him and demanded, "Prophesy! Who hit you?" 65And they said many other insulting things to him.

Jesus Before Pilate and Herod

66At daybreak the council of the elders of the people, both the chief priests and teachers of the law, met together, and Jesus was led before them. 67"If you are the Christ,[c]" they said, "tell us."

Jesus answered, "If I tell you, you will not believe me, 68and if I asked you, you would not answer. 69But from now on, the Son of Man will be seated at the right hand of the mighty God."

70They all asked, "Are you then the Son of God?"

He replied, "You are right in saying I am."

71Then they said, "Why do we need any more testimony? We have heard it from his own lips."

23 Then the whole assembly rose and led him off to Pilate. 2And they began to accuse him, saying, "We have found this man subverting our nation. He opposes payment of taxes to Caesar and claims to be Christ,[d] a king."

3So Pilate asked Jesus, "Are you the king of the Jews?"

"Yes, it is as you say," Jesus replied.

4Then Pilate announced to the chief priests and the crowd, "I find no basis for a charge against this man."

5But they insisted, "He stirs up the people all over Judea[e] by his teaching. He started in Galilee and has come all the way here."

6On hearing this, Pilate asked if the man was a Galilean. 7When he learned that Jesus was under Herod's jurisdiction, he sent him to Herod, who was also in Jerusalem at that time.

8When Herod saw Jesus, he was greatly pleased, because for a long time he had been wanting to see him. From what he had heard about him, he hoped to see him perform some miracle. 9He plied him with many questions,

[a]37 Isaiah 53:12 [b]44 Some early manuscripts do not have verses 43 and 44. [c]67 Or *Messiah*
[d]2 Or *Messiah*; also in verses 35 and 39 [e]5 Or *over the land of the Jews*

but Jesus gave him no answer. 10The chief
priests and the teachers of the law were standing there, vehemently accusing him. 11Then
Herod and his soldiers ridiculed and mocked
him. Dressing him in an elegant robe, they sent
him back to Pilate. 12That day Herod and Pilate became friends—before this they had been
enemies.

13Pilate called together the chief priests, the
rulers and the people, 14and said to them, "You
brought me this man as one who was inciting
the people to rebellion. I have examined him in
your presence and have found no basis for
your charges against him. 15Neither has Herod,
for he sent him back to us; as you can see, he
has done nothing to deserve death. 16There-
fore, I will punish him and then release him.[a]"

18With one voice they cried out, "Away
with this man! Release Barabbas to us!"
19(Barabbas had been thrown into prison for an
insurrection in the city, and for murder.)

20Wanting to release Jesus, Pilate appealed
to them again. 21But they kept shouting, "Crucify him! Crucify him!"

22For the third time he spoke to them:
"Why? What crime has this man committed? I
have found in him no grounds for the death
penalty. Therefore I will have him punished
and then release him."

23But with loud shouts they insistently demanded that he be crucified, and their shouts
prevailed. 24So Pilate decided to grant their
demand. 25He released the man who had been
thrown into prison for insurrection and murder,
the one they asked for, and surrendered Jesus
to their will.

The Crucifixion

26As they led him away, they seized Simon
from Cyrene, who was on his way in from the
country, and put the cross on him and made
him carry it behind Jesus. 27A large number of
people followed him, including women who
mourned and wailed for him. 28Jesus turned
and said to them, "Daughters of Jerusalem, do
not weep for me; weep for yourselves and for
your children. 29For the time will come when
you will say, 'Blessed are the barren women,
the wombs that never bore and the breasts that
never nursed!' 30Then

" 'they will say to the mountains, "Fall on
us!"
and to the hills, "Cover us!" '[b]

31For if men do these things when the tree is
green, what will happen when it is dry?"

32Two other men, both criminals, were also
led out with him to be executed. 33When they
came to the place called the Skull, there they
crucified him, along with the criminals—one
on his right, the other on his left. 34Jesus said,
"Father, forgive them, for they do not know
what they are doing."[c] And they divided up
his clothes by casting lots.

35The people stood watching, and the rulers
even sneered at him. They said, "He saved
others; let him save himself if he is the Christ
of God, the Chosen One."

36The soldiers also came up and mocked
him. They offered him wine vinegar 37and
said, "If you are the king of the Jews, save
yourself."

38There was a written notice above him,
which read: THIS IS THE KING OF THE JEWS.

39One of the criminals who hung there
hurled insults at him: "Aren't you the Christ?
Save yourself and us!"

40But the other criminal rebuked him.
"Don't you fear God," he said, "since you are
under the same sentence? 41We are punished
justly, for we are getting what our deeds deserve. But this man has done nothing wrong."

42Then he said, "Jesus, remember me when
you come into your kingdom.[d]"

43Jesus answered him, "I tell you the truth,
today you will be with me in paradise."

Jesus' Death

44It was now about the sixth hour, and darkness came over the whole land until the ninth
hour, 45for the sun stopped shining. And the
curtain of the temple was torn in two. 46Jesus
called out with a loud voice, "Father, into your
hands I commit my spirit." When he had said
this, he breathed his last.

47The centurion, seeing what had happened,
praised God and said, "Surely this was a righteous man." 48When all the people who had
gathered to witness this sight saw what took
place, they beat their breasts and went away.
49But all those who knew him, including the
women who had followed him from Galilee,
stood at a distance, watching these things.

Jesus' Burial

50Now there was a man named Joseph, a
member of the Council, a good and upright
man, 51who had not consented to their decision
and action. He came from the Judean town of
Arimathea and he was waiting for the kingdom
of God. 52Going to Pilate, he asked for Jesus'
body. 53Then he took it down, wrapped it in
linen cloth and placed it in a tomb cut in the
rock, one in which no one had yet been laid.
54It was Preparation Day, and the Sabbath was
about to begin.

55The women who had come with Jesus
from Galilee followed Joseph and saw the
tomb and how his body was laid in it. 56Then
they went home and prepared spices and perfumes. But they rested on the Sabbath in obedience to the commandment.

The Resurrection

24 On the first day of the week, very early
in the morning, the women took the

[a]16 Some manuscripts *him." 17Now he was obliged to release one man to them at the Feast.*
[b]30 Hosea 10:8 [c]34 Some early manuscripts do not have this sentence. [d]42 Some manuscripts *come with your kingly power*

spices they had prepared and went to the tomb.
2They found the stone rolled away from the
tomb, 3but when they entered, they did not find
the body of the Lord Jesus. 4While they were
wondering about this, suddenly two men in
clothes that gleamed like lightning stood beside them. 5In their fright the women bowed
down with their faces to the ground, but the
men said to them, "Why do you look for the
living among the dead? 6He is not here; he has
risen! Remember how he told you, while he
was still with you in Galilee: 7'The Son of
Man must be delivered into the hands of sinful
men, be crucified and on the third day be
raised again.' " 8Then they remembered his
words.

9When they came back from the tomb, they
told all these things to the Eleven and to all the
others. 10It was Mary Magdalene, Joanna,
Mary the mother of James, and the others with
them who told this to the apostles. 11But they
did not believe the women, because their
words seemed to them like nonsense. 12Peter,
however, got up and ran to the tomb. Bending
over, he saw the strips of linen lying by themselves, and he went away, wondering to himself what had happened.

On the Road to Emmaus

13Now that same day two of them were going to a village called Emmaus, about seven
miles[a] from Jerusalem. 14They were talking
with each other about everything that had happened. 15As they talked and discussed these
things with each other, Jesus himself came up
and walked along with them; 16but they were
kept from recognizing him.

17He asked them, "What are you discussing
together as you walk along?"

They stood still, their faces downcast. 18One
of them, named Cleopas, asked him, "Are you
only a visitor to Jerusalem and do not know
the things that have happened there in these
days?"

19"What things?" he asked.

"About Jesus of Nazareth," they replied.
"He was a prophet, powerful in word and deed
before God and all the people. 20The chief
priests and our rulers handed him over to be
sentenced to death, and they crucified him;
21but we had hoped that he was the one who
was going to redeem Israel. And what is more,
it is the third day since all this took place. 22In
addition, some of our women amazed us. They
went to the tomb early this morning 23but
didn't find his body. They came and told us
that they had seen a vision of angels, who said
he was alive. 24Then some of our companions
went to the tomb and found it just as the wom-
en had said, but him they did not see."

25He said to them, "How foolish you are,
and how slow of heart to believe all that the
prophets have spoken! 26Did not the Christ[b]
have to suffer these things and then enter his
glory?" 27And beginning with Moses and all
the Prophets, he explained to them what was
said in all the Scriptures concerning himself.

28As they approached the village to which
they were going, Jesus acted as if he were going farther. 29But they urged him strongly,
"Stay with us, for it is nearly evening; the day
is almost over." So he went in to stay with
them.

30When he was at the table with them, he
took bread, gave thanks, broke it and began to
give it to them. 31Then their eyes were opened
and they recognized him, and he disappeared
from their sight. 32They asked each other,
"Were not our hearts burning within us while
he talked with us on the road and opened the
Scriptures to us?"

33They got up and returned at once to Jerusalem. There they found the Eleven and those
with them, assembled together 34and saying,
"It is true! The Lord has risen and has appeared to Simon." 35Then the two told what
had happened on the way, and how Jesus was
recognized by them when he broke the bread.

Jesus Appears to the Disciples

36While they were still talking about this,
Jesus himself stood among them and said to
them, "Peace be with you."

37They were startled and frightened, thinking they saw a ghost. 38He said to them, "Why
are you troubled, and why do doubts rise in
your minds? 39Look at my hands and my feet.
It is I myself! Touch me and see; a ghost does
not have flesh and bones, as you see I have."

40When he had said this, he showed them
his hands and feet. 41And while they still did
not believe it because of joy and amazement,
he asked them, "Do you have anything here to
eat?" 42They gave him a piece of broiled fish,
43and he took it and ate it in their presence.

44He said to them, "This is what I told you
while I was still with you: Everything must be
fulfilled that is written about me in the Law of
Moses, the Prophets and the Psalms."

45Then he opened their minds so they could
understand the Scriptures. 46He told them,
"This is what is written: The Christ will suffer
and rise from the dead on the third day, 47and
repentance and forgiveness of sins will be
preached in his name to all nations, beginning
at Jerusalem. 48You are witnesses of these
things. 49I am going to send you what my Father has promised; but stay in the city until you
have been clothed with power from on high."

The Ascension

50When he had led them out to the vicinity
of Bethany, he lifted up his hands and blessed
them. 51While he was blessing them, he left
them and was taken up into heaven. 52Then
they worshiped him and returned to Jerusalem
with great joy. 53And they stayed continually
at the temple, praising God.

[a] *13* Greek *sixty stadia* (about 11 kilometers) [b] *26* Or *Messiah*; also in verse 46

John

The Word Became Flesh

1 In the beginning was the Word, and the
Word was with God, and the Word was
God. 2He was with God in the beginning.
3Through him all things were made; without
him nothing was made that has been made. 4In
him was life, and that life was the light of men.
5The light shines in the darkness, but the darkness has not understood[a] it.
6There came a man who was sent from God;
his name was John. 7He came as a witness to
testify concerning that light, so that through
him all men might believe. 8He himself was
not the light; he came only as a witness to the
light. 9The true light that gives light to every
man was coming into the world.[b]
10He was in the world, and though the world
was made through him, the world did not recognize him. 11He came to that which was his
own, but his own did not receive him. 12Yet to
all who received him, to those who believed in
his name, he gave the right to become children
of God— 13children born not of natural descent,[c] nor of human decision or a husband's
will, but born of God.
14The Word became flesh and made his
dwelling among us. We have seen his glory,
the glory of the One and Only,[d] who came
from the Father, full of grace and truth.
15John testifies concerning him. He cries
out, saying, "This was he of whom I said, 'He
who comes after me has surpassed me because
he was before me.' " 16From the fullness of his
grace we have all received one blessing after
another. 17For the law was given through Moses; grace and truth came through Jesus Christ.
18No one has ever seen God, but God the One
and Only,[d,e] who is at the Father's side, has
made him known.

John the Baptist Denies Being the Christ

19Now this was John's testimony when the
Jews of Jerusalem sent priests and Levites to
ask him who he was. 20He did not fail to
confess, but confessed freely, "I am not the
Christ.[f]"
21They asked him, "Then who are you? Are
you Elijah?"
He said, "I am not."
"Are you the Prophet?"
He answered, "No."
22Finally they said, "Who are you? Give us
an answer to take back to those who sent us.
What do you say about yourself?"
23John replied in the words of Isaiah the
prophet, "I am the voice of one calling in
the desert, 'Make straight the way for the
Lord.' "[g]
24Now some Pharisees who had been sent
25questioned him, "Why then do you baptize if
you are not the Christ, nor Elijah, nor the
Prophet?"
26"I baptize with[h] water," John replied, "but
among you stands one you do not know. 27He
is the one who comes after me, the thongs of
whose sandals I am not worthy to untie."
28This all happened at Bethany on the other
side of the Jordan, where John was baptizing.

Jesus the Lamb of God

29The next day John saw Jesus coming toward him and said, "Look, the Lamb of God,
who takes away the sin of the world! 30This is
the one I meant when I said, 'A man who
comes after me has surpassed me because he
was before me.' 31I myself did not know him,
but the reason I came baptizing with water was
that he might be revealed to Israel."
32Then John gave this testimony: "I saw the
Spirit come down from heaven as a dove and
remain on him. 33I would not have known him,
except that the one who sent me to baptize
with water told me, 'The man on whom you
see the Spirit come down and remain is he who
will baptize with the Holy Spirit.' 34I have
seen and I testify that this is the Son of God."

Jesus' First Disciples

35The next day John was there again with
two of his disciples. 36When he saw Jesus
passing by, he said, "Look, the Lamb of God!"
37When the two disciples heard him say this,
they followed Jesus. 38Turning around, Jesus
saw them following and asked, "What do you
want?"
They said, "Rabbi" (which means Teacher),
"where are you staying?"
39"Come," he replied, "and you will see."
So they went and saw where he was staying,
and spent that day with him. It was about the
tenth hour.
40Andrew, Simon Peter's brother, was one
of the two who heard what John had said and
who had followed Jesus. 41The first thing Andrew did was to find his brother Simon and tell
him, "We have found the Messiah" (that is, the
Christ). 42And he brought him to Jesus.
Jesus looked at him and said, "You are Simon son of John. You will be called Cephas"
(which, when translated, is Peter[i]).

[a]*5* Or *darkness, and the darkness has not overcome* [b]*9* Or *This was the true light that gives light to every man who comes into the world* [c]*13* Greek *of bloods* [d]*14,18* Or *the Only Begotten* [e]*18* Some manuscripts *but the only* (or *only begotten*) *Son* [f]*20* Or *Messiah.* "The Christ" (Greek) and "the Messiah" (Hebrew) both mean "the Anointed One"; also in verse 25. [g]*23* Isaiah 40:3 [h]*26* Or *in*; also in verses 31 and 33 [i]*42* Both *Cephas* (Aramaic) and *Peter* (Greek) mean *rock.*

Jesus Calls Philip and Nathanael

43 The next day Jesus decided to leave for Galilee. Finding Philip, he said to him, "Follow me."

44 Philip, like Andrew and Peter, was from the town of Bethsaida. 45 Philip found Nathanael and told him, "We have found the one Moses wrote about in the Law, and about whom the prophets also wrote—Jesus of Nazareth, the son of Joseph."

46 "Nazareth! Can anything good come from there?" Nathanael asked.

"Come and see," said Philip.

47 When Jesus saw Nathanael approaching, he said of him, "Here is a true Israelite, in whom there is nothing false."

48 "How do you know me?" Nathanael asked.

Jesus answered, "I saw you while you were still under the fig tree before Philip called you."

49 Then Nathanael declared, "Rabbi, you are the Son of God; you are the King of Israel."

50 Jesus said, "You believe[a] because I told you I saw you under the fig tree. You shall see greater things than that." 51 He then added, "I tell you[b] the truth, you[b] shall see heaven open, and the angels of God ascending and descending on the Son of Man."

Jesus Changes Water to Wine

2 On the third day a wedding took place at Cana in Galilee. Jesus' mother was there, 2 and Jesus and his disciples had also been invited to the wedding. 3 When the wine was gone, Jesus' mother said to him, "They have no more wine."

4 "Dear woman, why do you involve me?" Jesus replied. "My time has not yet come."

5 His mother said to the servants, "Do whatever he tells you."

6 Nearby stood six stone water jars, the kind used by the Jews for ceremonial washing, each holding from twenty to thirty gallons.[c]

7 Jesus said to the servants, "Fill the jars with water"; so they filled them to the brim.

8 Then he told them, "Now draw some out and take it to the master of the banquet."

They did so, 9 and the master of the banquet tasted the water that had been turned into wine. He did not realize where it had come from, though the servants who had drawn the water knew. Then he called the bridegroom aside 10 and said, "Everyone brings out the choice wine first and then the cheaper wine after the guests have had too much to drink; but you have saved the best till now."

11 This, the first of his miraculous signs, Jesus performed at Cana in Galilee. He thus revealed his glory, and his disciples put their faith in him.

Jesus Clears the Temple

12 After this he went down to Capernaum with his mother and brothers and his disciples. There they stayed for a few days.

13 When it was almost time for the Jewish Passover, Jesus went up to Jerusalem. 14 In the temple courts he found men selling cattle, sheep and doves, and others sitting at tables exchanging money. 15 So he made a whip out of cords, and drove all from the temple area, both sheep and cattle; he scattered the coins of the money changers and overturned their tables. 16 To those who sold doves he said, "Get these out of here! How dare you turn my Father's house into a market!"

17 His disciples remembered that it is written: "Zeal for your house will consume me."[d]

18 Then the Jews demanded of him, "What miraculous sign can you show us to prove your authority to do all this?"

19 Jesus answered them, "Destroy this temple, and I will raise it again in three days."

20 The Jews replied, "It has taken forty-six years to build this temple, and you are going to raise it in three days?" 21 But the temple he had spoken of was his body. 22 After he was raised from the dead, his disciples recalled what he had said. Then they believed the Scripture and the words that Jesus had spoken.

23 Now while he was in Jerusalem at the Passover Feast, many people saw the miraculous signs he was doing and believed in his name.[e] 24 But Jesus would not entrust himself to them, for he knew all men. 25 He did not need man's testimony about man, for he knew what was in a man.

Jesus Teaches Nicodemus

3 Now there was a man of the Pharisees named Nicodemus, a member of the Jewish ruling council. 2 He came to Jesus at night and said, "Rabbi, we know you are a teacher who has come from God. For no one could perform the miraculous signs you are doing if God were not with him."

3 In reply Jesus declared, "I tell you the truth, no one can see the kingdom of God unless he is born again.[f]"

4 "How can a man be born when he is old?" Nicodemus asked. "Surely he cannot enter a second time into his mother's womb to be born!"

5 Jesus answered, "I tell you the truth, no one can enter the kingdom of God unless he is born of water and the Spirit. 6 Flesh gives birth to flesh, but the Spirit[g] gives birth to spirit. 7 You should not be surprised at my saying, 'You[b] must be born again.' 8 The wind blows wherever it pleases. You hear its sound, but you cannot tell where it comes from or where it is going. So it is with everyone born of the Spirit."

9 "How can this be?" Nicodemus asked.

[a] 50 Or *Do you believe . . . ?* [b] 51,7 The Greek is plural. [c] 6 Greek *two to three metretes* (probably about 75 to 115 liters) [d] 17 Psalm 69:9 [e] 23 Or *and believed in him* [f] 3 Or *born from above*; also in verse 7 [g] 6 Or *but spirit*

10“You are Israel’s teacher,” said Jesus, “and do you not understand these things? 11I tell you the truth, we speak of what we know, and we testify to what we have seen, but still you people do not accept our testimony. 12I have spoken to you of earthly things and you do not believe; how then will you believe if I speak of heavenly things? 13No one has ever gone into heaven except the one who came from heaven—the Son of Man.[a] 14Just as Moses lifted up the snake in the desert, so the Son of Man must be lifted up, 15that everyone who believes in him may have eternal life.[b]

16“For God so loved the world that he gave his one and only Son,[c] that whoever believes in him shall not perish but have eternal life. 17For God did not send his Son into the world to condemn the world, but to save the world through him. 18Whoever believes in him is not condemned, but whoever does not believe stands condemned already because he has not believed in the name of God’s one and only Son.[d] 19This is the verdict: Light has come into the world, but men loved darkness instead of light because their deeds were evil. 20Everyone who does evil hates the light, and will not come into the light for fear that his deeds will be exposed. 21But whoever lives by the truth comes into the light, so that it may be seen plainly that what he has done has been done through God.”[e]

John the Baptist’s Testimony About Jesus

22After this, Jesus and his disciples went out into the Judean countryside, where he spent some time with them, and baptized. 23Now John also was baptizing at Aenon near Salim, because there was plenty of water, and people were constantly coming to be baptized. 24(This was before John was put in prison.) 25An argument developed between some of John’s disciples and a certain Jew[f] over the matter of ceremonial washing. 26They came to John and said to him, “Rabbi, that man who was with you on the other side of the Jordan—the one you testified about—well, he is baptizing, and everyone is going to him.”

27To this John replied, “A man can receive only what is given him from heaven. 28You yourselves can testify that I said, ‘I am not the Christ[g] but am sent ahead of him.’ 29The bride belongs to the bridegroom. The friend who attends the bridegroom waits and listens for him, and is full of joy when he hears the bridegroom’s voice. That joy is mine, and it is now complete. 30He must become greater; I must become less.

31“The one who comes from above is above all; the one who is from the earth belongs to the earth, and speaks as one from the earth. The one who comes from heaven is above all. 32He testifies to what he has seen and heard, but no one accepts his testimony. 33The man who has accepted it has certified that God is truthful. 34For the one whom God has sent speaks the words of God, for God[h] gives the Spirit without limit. 35The Father loves the Son and has placed everything in his hands. 36Whoever believes in the Son has eternal life, but whoever rejects the Son will not see life, for God’s wrath remains on him.”[i]

Jesus Talks With a Samaritan Woman

4 The Pharisees heard that Jesus was gaining and baptizing more disciples than John, 2although in fact it was not Jesus who baptized, but his disciples. 3When the Lord learned of this, he left Judea and went back once more to Galilee.

4Now he had to go through Samaria. 5So he came to a town in Samaria called Sychar, near the plot of ground Jacob had given to his son Joseph. 6Jacob’s well was there, and Jesus, tired as he was from the journey, sat down by the well. It was about the sixth hour.

7When a Samaritan woman came to draw water, Jesus said to her, “Will you give me a drink?” 8(His disciples had gone into the town to buy food.)

9The Samaritan woman said to him, “You are a Jew and I am a Samaritan woman. How can you ask me for a drink?” (For Jews do not associate with Samaritans.[j])

10Jesus answered her, “If you knew the gift of God and who it is that asks you for a drink, you would have asked him and he would have given you living water.”

11“Sir,” the woman said, “you have nothing to draw with and the well is deep. Where can you get this living water? 12Are you greater than our father Jacob, who gave us the well and drank from it himself, as did also his sons and his flocks and herds?”

13Jesus answered, “Everyone who drinks this water will be thirsty again, 14but whoever drinks the water I give him will never thirst. Indeed, the water I give him will become in him a spring of water welling up to eternal life.”

15The woman said to him, “Sir, give me this water so that I won’t get thirsty and have to keep coming here to draw water.”

16He told her, “Go, call your husband and come back.”

17“I have no husband,” she replied.

Jesus said to her, “You are right when you say you have no husband. 18The fact is, you have had five husbands, and the man you now have is not your husband. What you have just said is quite true.”

19“Sir,” the woman said, “I can see that you are a prophet. 20Our fathers worshiped on this mountain, but you Jews claim that the place where we must worship is in Jerusalem.”

[a]*13* Some manuscripts *Man, who is in heaven* [b]*15* Or *believes may have eternal life in him* [c]*16* Or *his only begotten Son* [d]*18* Or *God’s only begotten Son* [e]*21* Some interpreters end the quotation after verse 15. [f]*25* Some manuscripts *and certain Jews* [g]*28* Or *Messiah* [h]*34* Greek *he* [i]*36* Some interpreters end the quotation after verse 30. [j]*9* Or *do not use dishes Samaritans have used*

21Jesus declared, "Believe me, woman, a time is coming when you will worship the Father neither on this mountain nor in Jerusalem. 22You Samaritans worship what you do not know; we worship what we do know, for salvation is from the Jews. 23Yet a time is coming and has now come when the true worshipers will worship the Father in spirit and truth, for they are the kind of worshipers the Father seeks. 24God is spirit, and his worshipers must worship in spirit and in truth."

25The woman said, "I know that Messiah" (called Christ) "is coming. When he comes, he will explain everything to us."

26Then Jesus declared, "I who speak to you am he."

The Disciples Rejoin Jesus

27Just then his disciples returned and were surprised to find him talking with a woman. But no one asked, "What do you want?" or "Why are you talking with her?"

28Then, leaving her water jar, the woman went back to the town and said to the people, 29"Come, see a man who told me everything I ever did. Could this be the Christ[a]?" 30They came out of the town and made their way toward him.

31Meanwhile his disciples urged him, "Rabbi, eat something."

32But he said to them, "I have food to eat that you know nothing about."

33Then his disciples said to each other, "Could someone have brought him food?"

34"My food," said Jesus, "is to do the will of him who sent me and to finish his work. 35Do you not say, 'Four months more and then the harvest'? I tell you, open your eyes and look at the fields! They are ripe for harvest. 36Even now the reaper draws his wages, even now he harvests the crop for eternal life, so that the sower and the reaper may be glad together. 37Thus the saying 'One sows and another reaps' is true. 38I sent you to reap what you have not worked for. Others have done the hard work, and you have reaped the benefits of their labor."

Many Samaritans Believe

39Many of the Samaritans from that town believed in him because of the woman's testimony, "He told me everything I ever did." 40So when the Samaritans came to him, they urged him to stay with them, and he stayed two days. 41And because of his words many more became believers.

42They said to the woman, "We no longer believe just because of what you said; now we have heard for ourselves, and we know that this man really is the Savior of the world."

Jesus Heals the Official's Son

43After the two days he left for Galilee. 44(Now Jesus himself had pointed out that a prophet has no honor in his own country.) 45When he arrived in Galilee, the Galileans welcomed him. They had seen all that he had done in Jerusalem at the Passover Feast, for they also had been there.

46Once more he visited Cana in Galilee, where he had turned the water into wine. And there was a certain royal official whose son lay sick at Capernaum. 47When this man heard that Jesus had arrived in Galilee from Judea, he went to him and begged him to come and heal his son, who was close to death.

48"Unless you people see miraculous signs and wonders," Jesus told him, "you will never believe."

49The royal official said, "Sir, come down before my child dies."

50Jesus replied, "You may go. Your son will live."

The man took Jesus at his word and departed. 51While he was still on the way, his servants met him with the news that his boy was living. 52When he inquired as to the time when his son got better, they said to him, "The fever left him yesterday at the seventh hour."

53Then the father realized that this was the exact time at which Jesus had said to him, "Your son will live." So he and all his household believed.

54This was the second miraculous sign that Jesus performed, having come from Judea to Galilee.

The Healing at the Pool

5 Some time later, Jesus went up to Jerusalem for a feast of the Jews. 2Now there is in Jerusalem near the Sheep Gate a pool, which in Aramaic is called Bethesda[b] and which is surrounded by five covered colonnades. 3Here a great number of disabled people used to lie—the blind, the lame, the paralyzed.[c] 5One who was there had been an invalid for thirty-eight years. 6When Jesus saw him lying there and learned that he had been in this condition for a long time, he asked him, "Do you want to get well?"

7"Sir," the invalid replied, "I have no one to help me into the pool when the water is stirred. While I am trying to get in, someone else goes down ahead of me."

8Then Jesus said to him, "Get up! Pick up your mat and walk." 9At once the man was cured; he picked up his mat and walked.

The day on which this took place was a Sabbath, 10and so the Jews said to the man who had been healed, "It is the Sabbath; the law forbids you to carry your mat."

11But he replied, "The man who made me well said to me, 'Pick up your mat and walk.' "

12So they asked him, "Who is this fellow who told you to pick it up and walk?"

13The man who was healed had no idea who

[a]29 Or *Messiah* [b]2 Some manuscripts *Bethzatha*; other manuscripts *Bethsaida* [c]3 Some less important manuscripts *paralyzed—and they waited for the moving of the waters.* [4]*From time to time an angel of the Lord would come down and stir up the waters. The first one into the pool after each such disturbance would be cured of whatever disease he had.*

it was, for Jesus had slipped away into the
crowd that was there.
14Later Jesus found him at the temple and
said to him, "See, you are well again. Stop
sinning or something worse may happen to
you." 15The man went away and told the Jews
that it was Jesus who had made him well.

Life Through the Son

16So, because Jesus was doing these things
on the Sabbath, the Jews persecuted him.
17Jesus said to them, "My Father is always at
his work to this very day, and I, too, am working." 18For this reason the Jews tried all the
harder to kill him; not only was he breaking
the Sabbath, but he was even calling God his
own Father, making himself equal with God.
19Jesus gave them this answer: "I tell you
the truth, the Son can do nothing by himself;
he can do only what he sees his Father doing,
because whatever the Father does the Son also
does. 20For the Father loves the Son and shows
him all he does. Yes, to your amazement he
will show him even greater things than these.
21For just as the Father raises the dead and
gives them life, even so the Son gives life to
whom he is pleased to give it. 22Moreover, the
Father judges no one, but has entrusted all
judgment to the Son, 23that all may honor the
Son just as they honor the Father. He who does
not honor the Son does not honor the Father,
who sent him.
24"I tell you the truth, whoever hears my
word and believes him who sent me has eternal
life and will not be condemned; he has crossed
over from death to life. 25I tell you the truth, a
time is coming and has now come when the
dead will hear the voice of the Son of God and
those who hear will live. 26For as the Father
has life in himself, so he has granted the Son
to have life in himself. 27And he has given him
authority to judge because he is the Son of
Man.
28"Do not be amazed at this, for a time is
coming when all who are in their graves will
hear his voice 29and come out—those who
have done good will rise to live, and those who
have done evil will rise to be condemned. 30By
myself I can do nothing; I judge only as I hear,
and my judgment is just, for I seek not to
please myself but him who sent me.

Testimonies About Jesus

31"If I testify about myself, my testimony is
not valid. 32There is another who testifies in
my favor, and I know that his testimony about
me is valid.
33"You have sent to John and he has testified to the truth. 34Not that I accept human
testimony; but I mention it that you may be
saved. 35John was a lamp that burned and gave
light, and you chose for a time to enjoy his
light.
36"I have testimony weightier than that of
John. For the very work that the Father has
given me to finish, and which I am doing, testifies that the Father has sent me. 37And the
Father who sent me has himself testified concerning me. You have never heard his voice
nor seen his form, 38nor does his word dwell in
you, for you do not believe the one he sent.
39You diligently study[a] the Scriptures because
you think that by them you possess eternal life.
These are the Scriptures that testify about me,
40yet you refuse to come to me to have life.
41"I do not accept praise from men, 42but I
know you. I know that you do not have the
love of God in your hearts. 43I have come in
my Father's name, and you do not accept me;
but if someone else comes in his own name,
you will accept him. 44How can you believe if
you accept praise from one another, yet make
no effort to obtain the praise that comes from
the only God[b]?
45"But do not think I will accuse you before
the Father. Your accuser is Moses, on whom
your hopes are set. 46If you believed Moses,
you would believe me, for he wrote about me.
47But since you do not believe what he wrote,
how are you going to believe what I say?"

Jesus Feeds the Five Thousand

6 Some time after this, Jesus crossed to the
far shore of the Sea of Galilee (that is, the
Sea of Tiberias), 2and a great crowd of people
followed him because they saw the miraculous
signs he had performed on the sick. 3Then
Jesus went up on a mountainside and sat down
with his disciples. 4The Jewish Passover Feast
was near.
5When Jesus looked up and saw a great
crowd coming toward him, he said to Philip,
"Where shall we buy bread for these people to
eat?" 6He asked this only to test him, for he
already had in mind what he was going to do.
7Philip answered him, "Eight months'
wages[c] would not buy enough bread for each
one to have a bite!"
8Another of his disciples, Andrew, Simon
Peter's brother, spoke up, 9"Here is a boy with
five small barley loaves and two small fish, but
how far will they go among so many?"
10Jesus said, "Have the people sit down."
There was plenty of grass in that place, and the
men sat down, about five thousand of them.
11Jesus then took the loaves, gave thanks, and
distributed to those who were seated as much
as they wanted. He did the same with the fish.
12When they had all had enough to eat, he
said to his disciples, "Gather the pieces that are
left over. Let nothing be wasted." 13So they
gathered them and filled twelve baskets with
the pieces of the five barley loaves left over by
those who had eaten.
14After the people saw the miraculous sign
that Jesus did, they began to say, "Surely this
is the Prophet who is to come into the world."
15Jesus, knowing that they intended to come

[a] *39* Or *Study diligently* (the imperative) [b] *44* Some early manuscripts *the Only One* [c] *7* Greek *two hundred denarii*

and make him king by force, withdrew again to
a mountain by himself.

Jesus Walks on the Water

16When evening came, his disciples went
down to the lake, 17where they got into a boat
and set off across the lake for Capernaum. By
now it was dark, and Jesus had not yet joined
them. 18A strong wind was blowing and the
waters grew rough. 19When they had rowed
three or three and a half miles,[a] they saw Jesus
approaching the boat, walking on the water;
and they were terrified. 20But he said to them,
"It is I; don't be afraid." 21Then they were
willing to take him into the boat, and immediately the boat reached the shore where they
were heading.

22The next day the crowd that had stayed on
the opposite shore of the lake realized that only
one boat had been there, and that Jesus had not
entered it with his disciples, but that they had
gone away alone. 23Then some boats from Tiberias landed near the place where the people
had eaten the bread after the Lord had given
thanks. 24Once the crowd realized that neither
Jesus nor his disciples were there, they got into
the boats and went to Capernaum in search of
Jesus.

Jesus the Bread of Life

25When they found him on the other side of
the lake, they asked him, "Rabbi, when did you
get here?"

26Jesus answered, "I tell you the truth, you
are looking for me, not because you saw miraculous signs but because you ate the loaves
and had your fill. 27Do not work for food that
spoils, but for food that endures to eternal life,
which the Son of Man will give you. On him
God the Father has placed his seal of approval."

28Then they asked him, "What must we do
to do the works God requires?"

29Jesus answered, "The work of God is this:
to believe in the one he has sent."

30So they asked him, "What miraculous sign
then will you give that we may see it and believe you? What will you do? 31Our forefathers
ate the manna in the desert; as it is written: 'He
gave them bread from heaven to eat.'[b]"

32Jesus said to them, "I tell you the truth, it
is not Moses who has given you the bread from
heaven, but it is my Father who gives you the
true bread from heaven. 33For the bread of God
is he who comes down from heaven and gives
life to the world."

34"Sir," they said, "from now on give us this
bread."

35Then Jesus declared, "I am the bread of
life. He who comes to me will never go hungry, and he who believes in me will never be
thirsty. 36But as I told you, you have seen me
and still you do not believe. 37All that the Father gives me will come to me, and whoever
comes to me I will never drive away. 38For I
have come down from heaven not to do my
will but to do the will of him who sent me.
39And this is the will of him who sent me, that
I shall lose none of all that he has given me,
but raise them up at the last day. 40For my
Father's will is that everyone who looks to the
Son and believes in him shall have eternal life,
and I will raise him up at the last day."

41At this the Jews began to grumble about
him because he said, "I am the bread that came
down from heaven." 42They said, "Is this not
Jesus, the son of Joseph, whose father and
mother we know? How can he now say, 'I
came down from heaven'?"

43"Stop grumbling among yourselves,"
Jesus answered. 44"No one can come to me
unless the Father who sent me draws him, and
I will raise him up at the last day. 45It is written
in the Prophets: 'They will all be taught by
God.'[c] Everyone who listens to the Father and
learns from him comes to me. 46No one has
seen the Father except the one who is from
God; only he has seen the Father. 47I tell you
the truth, he who believes has everlasting life.
48I am the bread of life. 49Your forefathers ate
the manna in the desert, yet they died. 50But
here is the bread that comes down from heav-
en, which a man may eat and not die. 51I am
the living bread that came down from heaven.
If anyone eats of this bread, he will live forever. This bread is my flesh, which I will give for
the life of the world."

52Then the Jews began to argue sharply
among themselves, "How can this man give us
his flesh to eat?"

53Jesus said to them, "I tell you the truth,
unless you eat the flesh of the Son of Man
and drink his blood, you have no life in you.
54Whoever eats my flesh and drinks my blood
has eternal life, and I will raise him up at the
last day. 55For my flesh is real food and my
blood is real drink. 56Whoever eats my flesh
and drinks my blood remains in me, and I in
him. 57Just as the living Father sent me and I
live because of the Father, so the one who
feeds on me will live because of me. 58This is
the bread that came down from heaven. Your
forefathers ate manna and died, but he who
feeds on this bread will live forever." 59He said
this while teaching in the synagogue in Capernaum.

Many Disciples Desert Jesus

60On hearing it, many of his disciples said,
"This is a hard teaching. Who can accept it?"

61Aware that his disciples were grumbling
about this, Jesus said to them, "Does this offend you? 62What if you see the Son of Man
ascend to where he was before! 63The Spirit
gives life; the flesh counts for nothing. The
words I have spoken to you are spirit[d] and
they are life. 64Yet there are some of you who
do not believe." For Jesus had known from the
beginning which of them did not believe and

[a] *19* Greek *rowed twenty-five or thirty stadia* (about 5 or 6 kilometers) [b] *31* Exodus 16:4; Neh. 9:15; Psalm 78:24,25 [c] *45* Isaiah 54:13 [d] *63* Or *Spirit*

who would betray him. 65He went on to say,
"This is why I told you that no one can come
to me unless the Father has enabled him."
66From this time many of his disciples
turned back and no longer followed him.
67"You do not want to leave too, do you?"
Jesus asked the Twelve.
68Simon Peter answered him, "Lord, to
whom shall we go? You have the words of
eternal life. 69We believe and know that you
are the Holy One of God."
70Then Jesus replied, "Have I not chosen
you, the Twelve? Yet one of you is a devil!"
71(He meant Judas, the son of Simon Iscariot,
who, though one of the Twelve, was later to
betray him.)

Jesus Goes to the Feast of Tabernacles

7 After this, Jesus went around in Galilee,
purposely staying away from Judea because the Jews there were waiting to take his
life. 2But when the Jewish Feast of Tabernacles was near, 3Jesus' brothers said to him,
"You ought to leave here and go to Judea, so
that your disciples may see the miracles you
do. 4No one who wants to become a public
figure acts in secret. Since you are doing these
things, show yourself to the world." 5For even
his own brothers did not believe in him.
6Therefore Jesus told them, "The right time
for me has not yet come; for you any time is
right. 7The world cannot hate you, but it hates
me because I testify that what it does is evil.
8You go to the Feast. I am not yet[a] going up
to this Feast, because for me the right time has
not yet come." 9Having said this, he stayed in
Galilee.
10However, after his brothers had left for the
Feast, he went also, not publicly, but in secret.
11Now at the Feast the Jews were watching for
him and asking, "Where is that man?"
12Among the crowds there was widespread
whispering about him. Some said, "He is a
good man."

Others replied, "No, he deceives the people." 13But no one would say anything publicly
about him for fear of the Jews.

Jesus Teaches at the Feast

14Not until halfway through the Feast did
Jesus go up to the temple courts and begin to
teach. 15The Jews were amazed and asked,
"How did this man get such learning without
having studied?"
16Jesus answered, "My teaching is not my
own. It comes from him who sent me. 17If
anyone chooses to do God's will, he will find
out whether my teaching comes from God or
whether I speak on my own. 18He who speaks
on his own does so to gain honor for himself,
but he who works for the honor of the one who
sent him is a man of truth; there is nothing
false about him. 19Has not Moses given you
the law? Yet not one of you keeps the law.
Why are you trying to kill me?"
20"You are demon-possessed," the crowd
answered. "Who is trying to kill you?"
21Jesus said to them, "I did one miracle, and
you are all astonished. 22Yet, because Moses
gave you circumcision (though actually it did
not come from Moses, but from the patriarchs), you circumcise a child on the Sabbath.
23Now if a child can be circumcised on the
Sabbath so that the law of Moses may not be
broken, why are you angry with me for healing
the whole man on the Sabbath? 24Stop judging
by mere appearances, and make a right judgment."

Is Jesus the Christ?

25At that point some of the people of Jerusalem began to ask, "Isn't this the man they are
trying to kill? 26Here he is, speaking publicly,
and they are not saying a word to him. Have
the authorities really concluded that he is the
Christ[b]? 27But we know where this man is
from; when the Christ comes, no one will
know where he is from."
28Then Jesus, still teaching in the temple
courts, cried out, "Yes, you know me, and you
know where I am from. I am not here on my
own, but he who sent me is true. You do not
know him, 29but I know him because I am
from him and he sent me."
30At this they tried to seize him, but no one
laid a hand on him, because his time had not
yet come. 31Still, many in the crowd put their
faith in him. They said, "When the Christ
comes, will he do more miraculous signs than
this man?"
32The Pharisees heard the crowd whispering
such things about him. Then the chief priests
and the Pharisees sent temple guards to arrest
him.
33Jesus said, "I am with you for only a short
time, and then I go to the one who sent me.
34You will look for me, but you will not find
me; and where I am, you cannot come."
35The Jews said to one another, "Where
does this man intend to go that we cannot find
him? Will he go where our people live scattered among the Greeks, and teach the Greeks?
36What did he mean when he said, 'You will
look for me, but you will not find me,' and
'Where I am, you cannot come'?"
37On the last and greatest day of the Feast,
Jesus stood and said in a loud voice, "If anyone
is thirsty, let him come to me and drink.
38Whoever believes in me, as[c] the Scripture
has said, streams of living water will flow from
within him." 39By this he meant the Spirit,
whom those who believed in him were later to
receive. Up to that time the Spirit had not been
given, since Jesus had not yet been glorified.
40On hearing his words, some of the people
said, "Surely this man is the Prophet."
41Others said, "He is the Christ."

[a]8 Some early manuscripts do not have *yet.* [b]26 Or *Messiah*; also in verses 27, 31, 41 and 42
[c]37,38 Or / *If anyone is thirsty, let him come to me. / And let him drink,* 38*who believes in me. / As*

Still others asked, "How can the Christ come from Galilee? 42Does not the Scripture say that the Christ will come from David's family[a] and from Bethlehem, the town where David lived?" 43Thus the people were divided because of Jesus. 44Some wanted to seize him, but no one laid a hand on him.

Unbelief of the Jewish Leaders

45Finally the temple guards went back to the chief priests and Pharisees, who asked them, "Why didn't you bring him in?"

46"No one ever spoke the way this man does," the guards declared.

47"You mean he has deceived you also?" the Pharisees retorted. 48"Has any of the rulers or of the Pharisees believed in him? 49No! But this mob that knows nothing of the law—there is a curse on them."

50Nicodemus, who had gone to Jesus earlier and who was one of their own number, asked, 51"Does our law condemn anyone without first hearing him to find out what he is doing?"

52They replied, "Are you from Galilee, too? Look into it, and you will find that a prophet[b] does not come out of Galilee."

[The earliest manuscripts and many other ancient witnesses do not have John 7:53–8:11.]

53Then each went to his own home.

8 But Jesus went to the Mount of Olives. 2At dawn he appeared again in the temple courts, where all the people gathered around him, and he sat down to teach them. 3The teachers of the law and the Pharisees brought in a woman caught in adultery. They made her stand before the group 4and said to Jesus, "Teacher, this woman was caught in the act of adultery. 5In the Law Moses commanded us to stone such women. Now what do you say?" 6They were using this question as a trap, in order to have a basis for accusing him.

But Jesus bent down and started to write on the ground with his finger. 7When they kept on questioning him, he straightened up and said to them, "If any one of you is without sin, let him be the first to throw a stone at her." 8Again he stooped down and wrote on the ground.

9At this, those who heard began to go away one at a time, the older ones first, until only Jesus was left, with the woman still standing there. 10Jesus straightened up and asked her, "Woman, where are they? Has no one condemned you?"

11"No one, sir," she said.

"Then neither do I condemn you," Jesus declared. "Go now and leave your life of sin."

The Validity of Jesus' Testimony

12When Jesus spoke again to the people, he said, "I am the light of the world. Whoever follows me will never walk in darkness, but will have the light of life."

13The Pharisees challenged him, "Here you are, appearing as your own witness; your testimony is not valid."

14Jesus answered, "Even if I testify on my own behalf, my testimony is valid, for I know where I came from and where I am going. But you have no idea where I come from or where I am going. 15You judge by human standards; I pass judgment on no one. 16But if I do judge, my decisions are right, because I am not alone. I stand with the Father, who sent me. 17In your own Law it is written that the testimony of two men is valid. 18I am one who testifies for myself; my other witness is the Father, who sent me."

19Then they asked him, "Where is your father?"

"You do not know me or my Father," Jesus replied. "If you knew me, you would know my Father also." 20He spoke these words while teaching in the temple area near the place where the offerings were put. Yet no one seized him, because his time had not yet come.

21Once more Jesus said to them, "I am going away, and you will look for me, and you will die in your sin. Where I go, you cannot come."

22This made the Jews ask, "Will he kill himself? Is that why he says, 'Where I go, you cannot come'?"

23But he continued, "You are from below; I am from above. You are of this world; I am not of this world. 24I told you that you would die in your sins; if you do not believe that I am ⌊the one I claim to be⌋,[c] you will indeed die in your sins."

25"Who are you?" they asked.

"Just what I have been claiming all along," Jesus replied. 26"I have much to say in judgment of you. But he who sent me is reliable, and what I have heard from him I tell the world."

27They did not understand that he was telling them about his Father. 28So Jesus said, "When you have lifted up the Son of Man, then you will know that I am ⌊the one I claim to be⌋ and that I do nothing on my own but speak just what the Father has taught me. 29The one who sent me is with me; he has not left me alone, for I always do what pleases him." 30Even as he spoke, many put their faith in him.

The Children of Abraham

31To the Jews who had believed him, Jesus said, "If you hold to my teaching, you are really my disciples. 32Then you will know the truth, and the truth will set you free."

33They answered him, "We are Abraham's descendants[d] and have never been slaves of

---

[a]42 Greek *seed* [b]52 Two early manuscripts *the Prophet* [c]24 Or *I am he*; also in verse 28 [d]33 Greek *seed*; also in verse 37

anyone. How can you say that we shall be set
free?"
34Jesus replied, "I tell you the truth, everyone who sins is a slave to sin. 35Now a slave
has no permanent place in the family, but a son
belongs to it forever. 36So if the Son sets you
free, you will be free indeed. 37I know you are
Abraham's descendants. Yet you are ready to
kill me, because you have no room for my
word. 38I am telling you what I have seen in
the Father's presence, and you do what you
have heard from your father.[a]"
39"Abraham is our father," they answered.
"If you were Abraham's children," said
Jesus, "then you would[b] do the things Abraham did. 40As it is, you are determined to kill
me, a man who has told you the truth that I
heard from God. Abraham did not do such
things. 41You are doing the things your own
father does."
"We are not illegitimate children," they protested. "The only Father we have is God himself."

The Children of the Devil

42Jesus said to them, "If God were your Father, you would love me, for I came from God
and now am here. I have not come on my own;
but he sent me. 43Why is my language not
clear to you? Because you are unable to hear
what I say. 44You belong to your father, the
devil, and you want to carry out your father's
desire. He was a murderer from the beginning,
not holding to the truth, for there is no truth in
him. When he lies, he speaks his native language, for he is a liar and the father of lies.
45Yet because I tell the truth, you do not believe me! 46Can any of you prove me guilty of
sin? If I am telling the truth, why don't you
believe me? 47He who belongs to God hears
what God says. The reason you do not hear is
that you do not belong to God."

The Claims of Jesus About Himself

48The Jews answered him, "Aren't we right
in saying that you are a Samaritan and demon-
possessed?"
49"I am not possessed by a demon," said
Jesus, "but I honor my Father and you dishon-
or me. 50I am not seeking glory for myself; but
there is one who seeks it, and he is the judge.
51I tell you the truth, if anyone keeps my word,
he will never see death."
52At this the Jews exclaimed, "Now we
know that you are demon-possessed! Abraham
died and so did the prophets, yet you say that
if anyone keeps your word, he will never taste
death. 53Are you greater than our father Abraham? He died, and so did the prophets. Who
do you think you are?"
54Jesus replied, "If I glorify myself, my glory means nothing. My Father, whom you claim
as your God, is the one who glorifies me.
55Though you do not know him, I know him.
If I said I did not, I would be a liar like you, but
I do know him and keep his word. 56Your father Abraham rejoiced at the thought of seeing
my day; he saw it and was glad."
57"You are not yet fifty years old," the Jews
said to him, "and you have seen Abraham!"
58"I tell you the truth," Jesus answered, "before Abraham was born, I am!" 59At this, they
picked up stones to stone him, but Jesus hid
himself, slipping away from the temple
grounds.

Jesus Heals a Man Born Blind

9 As he went along, he saw a man blind from
birth. 2His disciples asked him, "Rabbi,
who sinned, this man or his parents, that he
was born blind?"
3"Neither this man nor his parents sinned,"
said Jesus, "but this happened so that the work
of God might be displayed in his life. 4As long
as it is day, we must do the work of him who
sent me. Night is coming, when no one can
work. 5While I am in the world, I am the light
of the world."
6Having said this, he spit on the ground,
made some mud with the saliva, and put it on
the man's eyes. 7"Go," he told him, "wash in
the Pool of Siloam" (this word means Sent). So
the man went and washed, and came home
seeing.
8His neighbors and those who had formerly
seen him begging asked, "Isn't this the same
man who used to sit and beg?" 9Some claimed
that he was.
Others said, "No, he only looks like him."
But he himself insisted, "I am the man."
10"How then were your eyes opened?" they
demanded.
11He replied, "The man they call Jesus made
some mud and put it on my eyes. He told me
to go to Siloam and wash. So I went and
washed, and then I could see."
12"Where is this man?" they asked him.
"I don't know," he said.

The Pharisees Investigate the Healing

13They brought to the Pharisees the man
who had been blind. 14Now the day on which
Jesus had made the mud and opened the man's
eyes was a Sabbath. 15Therefore the Pharisees
also asked him how he had received his sight.
"He put mud on my eyes," the man replied,
"and I washed, and now I see."
16Some of the Pharisees said, "This man is
not from God, for he does not keep the Sabbath."
But others asked, "How can a sinner do such
miraculous signs?" So they were divided.
17Finally they turned again to the blind man,
"What have you to say about him? It was your
eyes he opened."
The man replied, "He is a prophet."
18The Jews still did not believe that he had
been blind and had received his sight until they
sent for the man's parents. 19"Is this your
son?" they asked. "Is this the one you say was

[a]38 Or *presence. Therefore do what you have heard from the Father.* [b]39 Some early manuscripts *"If you are Abraham's children," said Jesus, "then*

born blind? How is it that now he can see?”

20“We know he is our son,” the parents answered, “and we know he was born blind. 21But how he can see now, or who opened his eyes, we don’t know. Ask him. He is of age; he will speak for himself.” 22His parents said this because they were afraid of the Jews, for already the Jews had decided that anyone who acknowledged that Jesus was the Christ[a] would be put out of the synagogue. 23That was why his parents said, “He is of age; ask him.”

24A second time they summoned the man who had been blind. “Give glory to God,[b]” they said. “We know this man is a sinner.”

25He replied, “Whether he is a sinner or not, I don’t know. One thing I do know. I was blind but now I see!”

26Then they asked him, “What did he do to you? How did he open your eyes?”

27He answered, “I have told you already and you did not listen. Why do you want to hear it again? Do you want to become his disciples, too?”

28Then they hurled insults at him and said, “You are this fellow’s disciple! We are disciples of Moses! 29We know that God spoke to Moses, but as for this fellow, we don’t even know where he comes from.”

30The man answered, “Now that is remarkable! You don’t know where he comes from, yet he opened my eyes. 31We know that God does not listen to sinners. He listens to the godly man who does his will. 32Nobody has ever heard of opening the eyes of a man born blind. 33If this man were not from God, he could do nothing.”

34To this they replied, “You were steeped in sin at birth; how dare you lecture us!” And they threw him out.

Spiritual Blindness

35Jesus heard that they had thrown him out, and when he found him, he said, “Do you believe in the Son of Man?”

36“Who is he, sir?” the man asked. “Tell me so that I may believe in him.”

37Jesus said, “You have now seen him; in fact, he is the one speaking with you.”

38Then the man said, “Lord, I believe,” and he worshiped him.

39Jesus said, “For judgment I have come into this world, so that the blind will see and those who see will become blind.”

40Some Pharisees who were with him heard him say this and asked, “What? Are we blind too?”

41Jesus said, “If you were blind, you would not be guilty of sin; but now that you claim you can see, your guilt remains.

The Shepherd and His Flock

10 “I tell you the truth, the man who does not enter the sheep pen by the gate, but climbs in by some other way, is a thief and a robber. 2The man who enters by the gate is the shepherd of his sheep. 3The watchman opens the gate for him, and the sheep listen to his voice. He calls his own sheep by name and leads them out. 4When he has brought out all his own, he goes on ahead of them, and his sheep follow him because they know his voice. 5But they will never follow a stranger; in fact, they will run away from him because they do not recognize a stranger’s voice.” 6Jesus used this figure of speech, but they did not understand what he was telling them.

7Therefore Jesus said again, “I tell you the truth, I am the gate for the sheep. 8All who ever came before me were thieves and robbers, but the sheep did not listen to them. 9I am the gate; whoever enters through me will be saved.[c] He will come in and go out, and find pasture. 10The thief comes only to steal and kill and destroy; I have come that they may have life, and have it to the full.

11“I am the good shepherd. The good shepherd lays down his life for the sheep. 12The hired hand is not the shepherd who owns the sheep. So when he sees the wolf coming, he abandons the sheep and runs away. Then the wolf attacks the flock and scatters it. 13The man runs away because he is a hired hand and cares nothing for the sheep.

14“I am the good shepherd; I know my sheep and my sheep know me— 15just as the Father knows me and I know the Father—and I lay down my life for the sheep. 16I have other sheep that are not of this sheep pen. I must bring them also. They too will listen to my voice, and there shall be one flock and one shepherd. 17The reason my Father loves me is that I lay down my life—only to take it up again. 18No one takes it from me, but I lay it down of my own accord. I have authority to lay it down and authority to take it up again. This command I received from my Father.”

19At these words the Jews were again divided. 20Many of them said, “He is demon-possessed and raving mad. Why listen to him?”

21But others said, “These are not the sayings of a man possessed by a demon. Can a demon open the eyes of the blind?”

The Unbelief of the Jews

22Then came the Feast of Dedication[d] at Jerusalem. It was winter, 23and Jesus was in the temple area walking in Solomon’s Colonnade. 24The Jews gathered around him, saying, “How long will you keep us in suspense? If you are the Christ,[a] tell us plainly.”

25Jesus answered, “I did tell you, but you do not believe. The miracles I do in my Father’s name speak for me, 26but you do not believe because you are not my sheep. 27My sheep listen to my voice; I know them, and they follow me. 28I give them eternal life, and they shall never perish; no one can snatch them out of my hand. 29My Father, who has given them

[a]22,24 Or *Messiah* [b]24 A solemn charge to tell the truth (see Joshua 7:19) [c]9 Or *kept safe* [d]22 That is, Hanukkah

to me, is greater than all[a]; no one can snatch
them out of my Father's hand. 30I and the Father are one."
31Again the Jews picked up stones to stone
him, 32but Jesus said to them, "I have shown
you many great miracles from the Father. For
which of these do you stone me?"
33"We are not stoning you for any of these,"
replied the Jews, "but for blasphemy, because
you, a mere man, claim to be God."
34Jesus answered them, "Is it not written in
your Law, 'I have said you are gods'[b]? 35If he
called them 'gods,' to whom the word of God
came—and the Scripture cannot be broken—
36what about the one whom the Father set apart
as his very own and sent into the world? Why
then do you accuse me of blasphemy because
I said, 'I am God's Son'? 37Do not believe me
unless I do what my Father does. 38But if I do
it, even though you do not believe me, believe
the miracles, that you may know and understand that the Father is in me, and I in the
Father." 39Again they tried to seize him, but he
escaped their grasp.
40Then Jesus went back across the Jordan to
the place where John had been baptizing in the
early days. Here he stayed 41and many people
came to him. They said, "Though John never
performed a miraculous sign, all that John said
about this man was true." 42And in that place
many believed in Jesus.

The Death of Lazarus

11 Now a man named Lazarus was sick.
He was from Bethany, the village of
Mary and her sister Martha. 2This Mary,
whose brother Lazarus now lay sick, was the
same one who poured perfume on the Lord and
wiped his feet with her hair. 3So the sisters sent
word to Jesus, "Lord, the one you love is sick."
4When he heard this, Jesus said, "This sickness will not end in death. No, it is for God's
glory so that God's Son may be glorified
through it." 5Jesus loved Martha and her sister
and Lazarus. 6Yet when he heard that Lazarus
was sick, he stayed where he was two more
days.
7Then he said to his disciples, "Let us go
back to Judea."
8"But Rabbi," they said, "a short while ago
the Jews tried to stone you, and yet you are
going back there?"
9Jesus answered, "Are there not twelve
hours of daylight? A man who walks by day
will not stumble, for he sees by this world's
light. 10It is when he walks by night that he
stumbles, for he has no light."
11After he had said this, he went on to tell
them, "Our friend Lazarus has fallen asleep;
but I am going there to wake him up."
12His disciples replied, "Lord, if he sleeps,
he will get better." 13Jesus had been speaking
of his death, but his disciples thought he meant
natural sleep.
14So then he told them plainly, "Lazarus is
dead, 15and for your sake I am glad I was not
there, so that you may believe. But let us go to
him."
16Then Thomas (called Didymus) said to the
rest of the disciples, "Let us also go, that we
may die with him."

Jesus Comforts the Sisters

17On his arrival, Jesus found that Lazarus
had already been in the tomb for four days.
18Bethany was less than two miles[c] from Jerusalem, 19and many Jews had come to Martha
and Mary to comfort them in the loss of their
brother. 20When Martha heard that Jesus was
coming, she went out to meet him, but Mary
stayed at home.
21"Lord," Martha said to Jesus, "if you had
been here, my brother would not have died.
22But I know that even now God will give you
whatever you ask."
23Jesus said to her, "Your brother will rise
again."
24Martha answered, "I know he will rise
again in the resurrection at the last day."
25Jesus said to her, "I am the resurrection
and the life. He who believes in me will live,
even though he dies; 26and whoever lives and
believes in me will never die. Do you believe
this?"
27"Yes, Lord," she told him, "I believe that
you are the Christ,[d] the Son of God, who was
to come into the world."
28And after she had said this, she went back
and called her sister Mary aside. "The Teacher
is here," she said, "and is asking for you."
29When Mary heard this, she got up quickly
and went to him. 30Now Jesus had not yet entered the village, but was still at the place
where Martha had met him. 31When the Jews
who had been with Mary in the house, comforting her, noticed how quickly she got up and
went out, they followed her, supposing she
was going to the tomb to mourn there.
32When Mary reached the place where Jesus
was and saw him, she fell at his feet and said,
"Lord, if you had been here, my brother would
not have died."
33When Jesus saw her weeping, and the
Jews who had come along with her also weeping, he was deeply moved in spirit and troubled. 34"Where have you laid him?" he asked.
"Come and see, Lord," they replied.
35Jesus wept.
36Then the Jews said, "See how he loved
him!"
37But some of them said, "Could not he who
opened the eyes of the blind man have kept
this man from dying?"

Jesus Raises Lazarus From the Dead

38Jesus, once more deeply moved, came to
the tomb. It was a cave with a stone laid across
the entrance. 39"Take away the stone," he said.
"But, Lord," said Martha, the sister of the

[a] *29* Many early manuscripts *What my Father has given me is greater than all* [b] *34* Psalm 82:6
[c] *18* Greek *fifteen stadia* (about 3 kilometers) [d] *27* Or *Messiah*

dead man, "by this time there is a bad odor, for he has been there four days."

40Then Jesus said, "Did I not tell you that if you believed, you would see the glory of God?"

41So they took away the stone. Then Jesus looked up and said, "Father, I thank you that you have heard me. 42I knew that you always hear me, but I said this for the benefit of the people standing here, that they may believe that you sent me."

43When he had said this, Jesus called in a loud voice, "Lazarus, come out!" 44The dead man came out, his hands and feet wrapped with strips of linen, and a cloth around his face.

Jesus said to them, "Take off the grave clothes and let him go."

The Plot to Kill Jesus

45Therefore many of the Jews who had come to visit Mary, and had seen what Jesus did, put their faith in him. 46But some of them went to the Pharisees and told them what Jesus had done. 47Then the chief priests and the Pharisees called a meeting of the Sanhedrin.

"What are we accomplishing?" they asked. "Here is this man performing many miraculous signs. 48If we let him go on like this, everyone will believe in him, and then the Romans will come and take away both our place[a] and our nation."

49Then one of them, named Caiaphas, who was high priest that year, spoke up, "You know nothing at all! 50You do not realize that it is better for you that one man die for the people than that the whole nation perish."

51He did not say this on his own, but as high priest that year he prophesied that Jesus would die for the Jewish nation, 52and not only for that nation but also for the scattered children of God, to bring them together and make them one. 53So from that day on they plotted to take his life.

54Therefore Jesus no longer moved about publicly among the Jews. Instead he withdrew to a region near the desert, to a village called Ephraim, where he stayed with his disciples.

55When it was almost time for the Jewish Passover, many went up from the country to Jerusalem for their ceremonial cleansing before the Passover. 56They kept looking for Jesus, and as they stood in the temple area they asked one another, "What do you think? Isn't he coming to the Feast at all?" 57But the chief priests and Pharisees had given orders that if anyone found out where Jesus was, he should report it so that they might arrest him.

Jesus Anointed at Bethany

12 Six days before the Passover, Jesus arrived at Bethany, where Lazarus lived, whom Jesus had raised from the dead. 2Here a dinner was given in Jesus' honor. Martha served, while Lazarus was among those reclining at the table with him. 3Then Mary took about a pint[b] of pure nard, an expensive perfume; she poured it on Jesus' feet and wiped his feet with her hair. And the house was filled with the fragrance of the perfume.

4But one of his disciples, Judas Iscariot, who was later to betray him, objected, 5"Why wasn't this perfume sold and the money given to the poor? It was worth a year's wages.[c]" 6He did not say this because he cared about the poor but because he was a thief; as keeper of the money bag, he used to help himself to what was put into it.

7"Leave her alone," Jesus replied. "⌊It was intended⌋ that she should save this perfume for the day of my burial. 8You will always have the poor among you, but you will not always have me."

9Meanwhile a large crowd of Jews found out that Jesus was there and came, not only because of him but also to see Lazarus, whom he had raised from the dead. 10So the chief priests made plans to kill Lazarus as well, 11for on account of him many of the Jews were going over to Jesus and putting their faith in him.

The Triumphal Entry

12The next day the great crowd that had come for the Feast heard that Jesus was on his way to Jerusalem. 13They took palm branches and went out to meet him, shouting,

"Hosanna![d]"

"Blessed is he who comes in the name of
the Lord!"[e]

"Blessed is the King of Israel!"

14Jesus found a young donkey and sat upon it, as it is written,

15"Do not be afraid, O Daughter of Zion;
see, your king is coming,
seated on a donkey's colt."[f]

16At first his disciples did not understand all this. Only after Jesus was glorified did they realize that these things had been written about him and that they had done these things to him.

17Now the crowd that was with him when he called Lazarus from the tomb and raised him from the dead continued to spread the word. 18Many people, because they had heard that he had given this miraculous sign, went out to meet him. 19So the Pharisees said to one another, "See, this is getting us nowhere. Look how the whole world has gone after him!"

Jesus Predicts His Death

20Now there were some Greeks among those who went up to worship at the Feast. 21They came to Philip, who was from Bethsaida in Galilee, with a request. "Sir," they said, "we would like to see Jesus." 22Philip went to tell Andrew; Andrew and Philip in turn told Jesus.

[a]48 Or *temple* [b]3 Greek *a litra* (probably about 0.5 liter) [c]5 Greek *three hundred denarii*
[d]13 A Hebrew expression meaning "Save!" which became an exclamation of praise [e]13 Psalm 118:25, 26
[f]15 Zech. 9:9

23Jesus replied, "The hour has come for the
Son of Man to be glorified. 24I tell you the
truth, unless a kernel of wheat falls to the
ground and dies, it remains only a single seed.
But if it dies, it produces many seeds. 25The
man who loves his life will lose it, while the
man who hates his life in this world will keep
it for eternal life. 26Whoever serves me must
follow me; and where I am, my servant also
will be. My Father will honor the one who
serves me.

27"Now my heart is troubled, and what shall
I say? 'Father, save me from this hour'? No, it
was for this very reason I came to this hour.
28Father, glorify your name!"

Then a voice came from heaven, "I have
glorified it, and will glorify it again." 29The
crowd that was there and heard it said it had
thundered; others said an angel had spoken to
him.

30Jesus said, "This voice was for your benefit, not mine. 31Now is the time for judgment
on this world; now the prince of this world will
be driven out. 32But I, when I am lifted up
from the earth, will draw all men to myself."
33He said this to show the kind of death he was
going to die.

34The crowd spoke up, "We have heard
from the Law that the Christ[a] will remain forever, so how can you say, 'The Son of Man
must be lifted up'? Who is this 'Son of Man'?"

35Then Jesus told them, "You are going to
have the light just a little while longer. Walk
while you have the light, before darkness overtakes you. The man who walks in the dark does
not know where he is going. 36Put your trust in
the light while you have it, so that you may
become sons of light." When he had finished
speaking, Jesus left and hid himself from them.

The Jews Continue in Their Unbelief

37Even after Jesus had done all these miraculous signs in their presence, they still would
not believe in him. 38This was to fulfill the
word of Isaiah the prophet:

"Lord, who has believed our message
  and to whom has the arm of the Lord
    been revealed?"[b]

39For this reason they could not believe, because, as Isaiah says elsewhere:

40"He has blinded their eyes
  and deadened their hearts,
so they can neither see with their eyes,
  nor understand with their hearts,
  nor turn—and I would heal them."[c]

41Isaiah said this because he saw Jesus' glory
and spoke about him.

42Yet at the same time many even among
the leaders believed in him. But because of the
Pharisees they would not confess their faith for
fear they would be put out of the synagogue;
43for they loved praise from men more than
praise from God.

44Then Jesus cried out, "When a man believes in me, he does not believe in me only,
but in the one who sent me. 45When he looks
at me, he sees the one who sent me. 46I have
come into the world as a light, so that no one
who believes in me should stay in darkness.

47"As for the person who hears my words
but does not keep them, I do not judge him.
For I did not come to judge the world, but to
save it. 48There is a judge for the one who
rejects me and does not accept my words; that
very word which I spoke will condemn him at
the last day. 49For I did not speak of my own
accord, but the Father who sent me commanded me what to say and how to say it. 50I know
that his command leads to eternal life. So
whatever I say is just what the Father has told
me to say."

Jesus Washes His Disciples' Feet

13 It was just before the Passover Feast.
Jesus knew that the time had come for
him to leave this world and go to the Father.
Having loved his own who were in the world,
he now showed them the full extent of his
love.[d]

2The evening meal was being served, and
the devil had already prompted Judas Iscariot,
son of Simon, to betray Jesus. 3Jesus knew that
the Father had put all things under his power,
and that he had come from God and was returning to God; 4so he got up from the meal,
took off his outer clothing, and wrapped a towel around his waist. 5After that, he poured water into a basin and began to wash his disciples' feet, drying them with the towel that was
wrapped around him.

6He came to Simon Peter, who said to him,
"Lord, are you going to wash my feet?"

7Jesus replied, "You do not realize now
what I am doing, but later you will understand."

8"No," said Peter, "you shall never wash my
feet."

Jesus answered, "Unless I wash you, you
have no part with me."

9"Then, Lord," Simon Peter replied, "not
just my feet but my hands and my head as
well!"

10Jesus answered, "A person who has had a
bath needs only to wash his feet; his whole
body is clean. And you are clean, though not
every one of you." 11For he knew who was
going to betray him, and that was why he said
not every one was clean.

12When he had finished washing their feet,
he put on his clothes and returned to his place.
"Do you understand what I have done for
you?" he asked them. 13"You call me 'Teacher' and 'Lord,' and rightly so, for that is what
I am. 14Now that I, your Lord and Teacher,
have washed your feet, you also should wash
one another's feet. 15I have set you an example
that you should do as I have done for you. 16I
tell you the truth, no servant is greater than his

[a]34 Or *Messiah* [b]38 Isaiah 53:1 [c]40 Isaiah 6:10 [d]1 Or *he loved them to the last*

master, nor is a messenger greater than the one who sent him. 17Now that you know these things, you will be blessed if you do them.

Jesus Predicts His Betrayal

18"I am not referring to all of you; I know those I have chosen. But this is to fulfill the scripture: 'He who shares my bread has lifted up his heel against me.'[a]

19"I am telling you now before it happens, so that when it does happen you will believe that I am He. 20I tell you the truth, whoever accepts anyone I send accepts me; and whoever accepts me accepts the one who sent me."

21After he had said this, Jesus was troubled in spirit and testified, "I tell you the truth, one of you is going to betray me."

22His disciples stared at one another, at a loss to know which of them he meant. 23One of them, the disciple whom Jesus loved, was reclining next to him. 24Simon Peter motioned to this disciple and said, "Ask him which one he means."

25Leaning back against Jesus, he asked him, "Lord, who is it?"

26Jesus answered, "It is the one to whom I will give this piece of bread when I have dipped it in the dish." Then, dipping the piece of bread, he gave it to Judas Iscariot, son of Simon. 27As soon as Judas took the bread, Satan entered into him.

"What you are about to do, do quickly," Jesus told him, 28but no one at the meal understood why Jesus said this to him. 29Since Judas had charge of the money, some thought Jesus was telling him to buy what was needed for the Feast, or to give something to the poor. 30As soon as Judas had taken the bread, he went out. And it was night.

Jesus Predicts Peter's Denial

31When he was gone, Jesus said, "Now is the Son of Man glorified and God is glorified in him. 32If God is glorified in him,[b] God will glorify the Son in himself, and will glorify him at once.

33"My children, I will be with you only a little longer. You will look for me, and just as I told the Jews, so I tell you now: Where I am going, you cannot come.

34"A new command I give you: Love one another. As I have loved you, so you must love one another. 35By this all men will know that you are my disciples, if you love one another."

36Simon Peter asked him, "Lord, where are you going?"

Jesus replied, "Where I am going, you cannot follow now, but you will follow later."

37Peter asked, "Lord, why can't I follow you now? I will lay down my life for you."

38Then Jesus answered, "Will you really lay down your life for me? I tell you the truth, before the rooster crows, you will disown me three times!

Jesus Comforts His Disciples

14 "Do not let your hearts be troubled. Trust in God[c]; trust also in me. 2In my Father's house are many rooms; if it were not so, I would have told you. I am going there to prepare a place for you. 3And if I go and prepare a place for you, I will come back and take you to be with me that you also may be where I am. 4You know the way to the place where I am going."

Jesus the Way to the Father

5Thomas said to him, "Lord, we don't know where you are going, so how can we know the way?"

6Jesus answered, "I am the way and the truth and the life. No one comes to the Father except through me. 7If you really knew me, you would know[d] my Father as well. From now on, you do know him and have seen him."

8Philip said, "Lord, show us the Father and that will be enough for us."

9Jesus answered: "Don't you know me, Philip, even after I have been among you such a long time? Anyone who has seen me has seen the Father. How can you say, 'Show us the Father'? 10Don't you believe that I am in the Father, and that the Father is in me? The words I say to you are not just my own. Rather, it is the Father, living in me, who is doing his work. 11Believe me when I say that I am in the Father and the Father is in me; or at least believe on the evidence of the miracles themselves. 12I tell you the truth, anyone who has faith in me will do what I have been doing. He will do even greater things than these, because I am going to the Father. 13And I will do whatever you ask in my name, so that the Son may bring glory to the Father. 14You may ask me for anything in my name, and I will do it.

Jesus Promises the Holy Spirit

15"If you love me, you will obey what I command. 16And I will ask the Father, and he will give you another Counselor to be with you forever— 17the Spirit of truth. The world cannot accept him, because it neither sees him nor knows him. But you know him, for he lives with you and will be[e] in you. 18I will not leave you as orphans; I will come to you. 19Before long, the world will not see me anymore, but you will see me. Because I live, you also will live. 20On that day you will realize that I am in my Father, and you are in me, and I am in you. 21Whoever has my commands and obeys them, he is the one who loves me. He who loves me will be loved by my Father, and I too will love him and show myself to him."

22Then Judas (not Judas Iscariot) said, "But, Lord, why do you intend to show yourself to us and not to the world?"

23Jesus replied, "If anyone loves me, he will obey my teaching. My Father will love him,

[a] *18* Psalm 41:9 [b] *32* Many early manuscripts do not have *If God is glorified in him.* [c] *1* Or *You trust in God* [d] *7* Some early manuscripts *If you really have known me, you will know* [e] *17* Some early manuscripts *and is*

and we will come to him and make our home with him. [24]He who does not love me will not obey my teaching. These words you hear are not my own; they belong to the Father who sent me.

[25]"All this I have spoken while still with you. [26]But the Counselor, the Holy Spirit, whom the Father will send in my name, will teach you all things and will remind you of everything I have said to you. [27]Peace I leave with you; my peace I give you. I do not give to you as the world gives. Do not let your hearts be troubled and do not be afraid.

[28]"You heard me say, 'I am going away and I am coming back to you.' If you loved me, you would be glad that I am going to the Father, for the Father is greater than I. [29]I have told you now before it happens, so that when it does happen you will believe. [30]I will not speak with you much longer, for the prince of this world is coming. He has no hold on me, [31]but the world must learn that I love the Father and that I do exactly what my Father has commanded me.

"Come now; let us leave.

The Vine and the Branches

15 "I am the true vine, and my Father is the gardener. [2]He cuts off every branch in me that bears no fruit, while every branch that does bear fruit he prunes[a] so that it will be even more fruitful. [3]You are already clean because of the word I have spoken to you. [4]Remain in me, and I will remain in you. No branch can bear fruit by itself; it must remain in the vine. Neither can you bear fruit unless you remain in me.

[5]"I am the vine; you are the branches. If a man remains in me and I in him, he will bear much fruit; apart from me you can do nothing. [6]If anyone does not remain in me, he is like a branch that is thrown away and withers; such branches are picked up, thrown into the fire and burned. [7]If you remain in me and my words remain in you, ask whatever you wish, and it will be given you. [8]This is to my Father's glory, that you bear much fruit, showing yourselves to be my disciples.

[9]"As the Father has loved me, so have I loved you. Now remain in my love. [10]If you obey my commands, you will remain in my love, just as I have obeyed my Father's commands and remain in his love. [11]I have told you this so that my joy may be in you and that your joy may be complete. [12]My command is this: Love each other as I have loved you. [13]Greater love has no one than this, that he lay down his life for his friends. [14]You are my friends if you do what I command. [15]I no longer call you servants, because a servant does not know his master's business. Instead, I have called you friends, for everything that I learned from my Father I have made known to you. [16]You did not choose me, but I chose you and appointed you to go and bear fruit—fruit that will last. Then the Father will give you whatever you ask in my name. [17]This is my command: Love each other.

The World Hates the Disciples

[18]"If the world hates you, keep in mind that it hated me first. [19]If you belonged to the world, it would love you as its own. As it is, you do not belong to the world, but I have chosen you out of the world. That is why the world hates you. [20]Remember the words I spoke to you: 'No servant is greater than his master.'[b] If they persecuted me, they will persecute you also. If they obeyed my teaching, they will obey yours also. [21]They will treat you this way because of my name, for they do not know the One who sent me. [22]If I had not come and spoken to them, they would not be guilty of sin. Now, however, they have no excuse for their sin. [23]He who hates me hates my Father as well. [24]If I had not done among them what no one else did, they would not be guilty of sin. But now they have seen these miracles, and yet they have hated both me and my Father. [25]But this is to fulfill what is written in their Law: 'They hated me without reason.'[c]

[26]"When the Counselor comes, whom I will send to you from the Father, the Spirit of truth who goes out from the Father, he will testify about me. [27]And you also must testify, for you have been with me from the beginning.

16 "All this I have told you so that you will not go astray. [2]They will put you out of the synagogue; in fact, a time is coming when anyone who kills you will think he is offering a service to God. [3]They will do such things because they have not known the Father or me. [4]I have told you this, so that when the time comes you will remember that I warned you. I did not tell you this at first because I was with you.

The Work of the Holy Spirit

[5]"Now I am going to him who sent me, yet none of you asks me, 'Where are you going?' [6]Because I have said these things, you are filled with grief. [7]But I tell you the truth: It is for your good that I am going away. Unless I go away, the Counselor will not come to you; but if I go, I will send him to you. [8]When he comes, he will convict the world of guilt[d] in regard to sin and righteousness and judgment: [9]in regard to sin, because men do not believe in me; [10]in regard to righteousness, because I am going to the Father, where you can see me no longer; [11]and in regard to judgment, because the prince of this world now stands condemned.

[12]"I have much more to say to you, more than you can now bear. [13]But when he, the Spirit of truth, comes, he will guide you into all truth. He will not speak on his own; he will speak only what he hears, and he will tell you what is yet to come. [14]He will bring glory to

[a]*2* The Greek for *prunes* also means *cleans.* [b]*20* John 13:16 [c]*25* Psalms 35:19; 69:4 [d]*8* Or *will expose the guilt of the world*

me by taking from what is mine and making it known to you. 15All that belongs to the Father is mine. That is why I said the Spirit will take from what is mine and make it known to you.

16"In a little while you will see me no more, and then after a little while you will see me."

The Disciples' Grief Will Turn to Joy

17Some of his disciples said to one another, "What does he mean by saying, 'In a little while you will see me no more, and then after a little while you will see me,' and 'Because I am going to the Father'?" 18They kept asking, "What does he mean by 'a little while'? We don't understand what he is saying."

19Jesus saw that they wanted to ask him about this, so he said to them, "Are you asking one another what I meant when I said, 'In a little while you will see me no more, and then after a little while you will see me'? 20I tell you the truth, you will weep and mourn while the world rejoices. You will grieve, but your grief will turn to joy. 21A woman giving birth to a child has pain because her time has come; but when her baby is born she forgets the anguish because of her joy that a child is born into the world. 22So with you: Now is your time of grief, but I will see you again and you will rejoice, and no one will take away your joy. 23In that day you will no longer ask me anything. I tell you the truth, my Father will give you whatever you ask in my name. 24Until now you have not asked for anything in my name. Ask and you will receive, and your joy will be complete.

25"Though I have been speaking figuratively, a time is coming when I will no longer use this kind of language but will tell you plainly about my Father. 26In that day you will ask in my name. I am not saying that I will ask the Father on your behalf. 27No, the Father himself loves you because you have loved me and have believed that I came from God. 28I came from the Father and entered the world; now I am leaving the world and going back to the Father."

29Then Jesus' disciples said, "Now you are speaking clearly and without figures of speech. 30Now we can see that you know all things and that you do not even need to have anyone ask you questions. This makes us believe that you came from God."

31"You believe at last!"[a] Jesus answered. 32"But a time is coming, and has come, when you will be scattered, each to his own home. You will leave me all alone. Yet I am not alone, for my Father is with me.

33"I have told you these things, so that in me you may have peace. In this world you will have trouble. But take heart! I have overcome the world."

Jesus Prays for Himself

17 After Jesus said this, he looked toward heaven and prayed:

"Father, the time has come. Glorify your Son, that your Son may glorify you. 2For you granted him authority over all people that he might give eternal life to all those you have given him. 3Now this is eternal life: that they may know you, the only true God, and Jesus Christ, whom you have sent. 4I have brought you glory on earth by completing the work you gave me to do. 5And now, Father, glorify me in your presence with the glory I had with you before the world began.

Jesus Prays for His Disciples

6"I have revealed you[b] to those whom you gave me out of the world. They were yours; you gave them to me and they have obeyed your word. 7Now they know that everything you have given me comes from you. 8For I gave them the words you gave me and they accepted them. They knew with certainty that I came from you, and they believed that you sent me. 9I pray for them. I am not praying for the world, but for those you have given me, for they are yours. 10All I have is yours, and all you have is mine. And glory has come to me through them. 11I will remain in the world no longer, but they are still in the world, and I am coming to you. Holy Father, protect them by the power of your name—the name you gave me—so that they may be one as we are one. 12While I was with them, I protected them and kept them safe by that name you gave me. None has been lost except the one doomed to destruction so that Scripture would be fulfilled.

13"I am coming to you now, but I say these things while I am still in the world, so that they may have the full measure of my joy within them. 14I have given them your word and the world has hated them, for they are not of the world any more than I am of the world. 15My prayer is not that you take them out of the world but that you protect them from the evil one. 16They are not of the world, even as I am not of it. 17Sanctify[c] them by the truth; your word is truth. 18As you sent me into the world, I have sent them into the world. 19For them I sanctify myself, that they too may be truly sanctified.

Jesus Prays for All Believers

20"My prayer is not for them alone. I pray also for those who will believe in me through their message, 21that all of them may be one, Father, just as you are in me and I am in you. May they also be in us so that the world may believe that you have sent me. 22I have given them the glory that you gave me, that they may be one as we are one: 23I in them and you in me. May they be brought to complete uni-

[a]*31* Or *"Do you now believe?"* [b]*6* Greek *your name*; also in verse 26 [c]*17* Greek *hagiazo (set apart for sacred use* or *make holy)*; also in verse 19

ty to let the world know that you sent me
and have loved them even as you have
loved me.
24“Father, I want those you have given
me to be with me where I am, and to see
my glory, the glory you have given me
because you loved me before the creation
of the world.
25“Righteous Father, though the world
does not know you, I know you, and they
know that you have sent me. 26I have
made you known to them, and will continue to make you known in order that the
love you have for me may be in them and
that I myself may be in them.”

Jesus Arrested

18 When he had finished praying, Jesus
left with his disciples and crossed the
Kidron Valley. On the other side there was an
olive grove, and he and his disciples went
into it.
2Now Judas, who betrayed him, knew the
place, because Jesus had often met there with
his disciples. 3So Judas came to the grove,
guiding a detachment of soldiers and some officials from the chief priests and Pharisees.
They were carrying torches, lanterns and
weapons.
4Jesus, knowing all that was going to happen to him, went out and asked them, “Who is
it you want?”
5“Jesus of Nazareth,” they replied.
“I am he,” Jesus said. (And Judas the traitor
was standing there with them.) 6When Jesus
said, “I am he,” they drew back and fell to the
ground.
7Again he asked them, “Who is it you
want?”
And they said, “Jesus of Nazareth.”
8“I told you that I am he,” Jesus answered.
“If you are looking for me, then let these men
go.” 9This happened so that the words he had
spoken would be fulfilled: “I have not lost one
of those you gave me.”[a]
10Then Simon Peter, who had a sword, drew
it and struck the high priest’s servant, cutting
off his right ear. (The servant’s name was Mal-
chus.)
11Jesus commanded Peter, “Put your sword
away! Shall I not drink the cup the Father has
given me?”

Jesus Taken to Annas

12Then the detachment of soldiers with its
commander and the Jewish officials arrested
Jesus. They bound him 13and brought him first
to Annas, who was the father-in-law of Caiaphas, the high priest that year. 14Caiaphas was
the one who had advised the Jews that it would
be good if one man died for the people.

Peter’s First Denial

15Simon Peter and another disciple were following Jesus. Because this disciple was known
to the high priest, he went with Jesus into the
high priest’s courtyard, 16but Peter had to wait
outside at the door. The other disciple, who
was known to the high priest, came back,
spoke to the girl on duty there and brought
Peter in.
17“You are not one of his disciples, are
you?” the girl at the door asked Peter.
He replied, “I am not.”
18It was cold, and the servants and officials
stood around a fire they had made to keep
warm. Peter also was standing with them,
warming himself.

The High Priest Questions Jesus

19Meanwhile, the high priest questioned
Jesus about his disciples and his teaching.
20“I have spoken openly to the world,” Jesus
replied. “I always taught in synagogues or at
the temple, where all the Jews come together.
I said nothing in secret. 21Why question me?
Ask those who heard me. Surely they know
what I said.”
22When Jesus said this, one of the officials
nearby struck him in the face. “Is this the way
you answer the high priest?” he demanded.
23“If I said something wrong,” Jesus replied,
“testify as to what is wrong. But if I spoke the
truth, why did you strike me?” 24Then Annas
sent him, still bound, to Caiaphas the high
priest.[b]

Peter’s Second and Third Denials

25As Simon Peter stood warming himself,
he was asked, “You are not one of his disciples, are you?”
He denied it, saying, “I am not.”
26One of the high priest’s servants, a relative
of the man whose ear Peter had cut off, challenged him, “Didn’t I see you with him in the
olive grove?” 27Again Peter denied it, and at
that moment a rooster began to crow.

Jesus Before Pilate

28Then the Jews led Jesus from Caiaphas to
the palace of the Roman governor. By now it
was early morning, and to avoid ceremonial
uncleanness the Jews did not enter the palace;
they wanted to be able to eat the Passover.
29So Pilate came out to them and asked, “What
charges are you bringing against this man?”
30“If he were not a criminal,” they replied,
“we would not have handed him over to you.”
31Pilate said, “Take him yourselves and
judge him by your own law.”
“But we have no right to execute anyone,”
the Jews objected. 32This happened so that the
words Jesus had spoken indicating the kind of
death he was going to die would be fulfilled.
33Pilate then went back inside the palace,
summoned Jesus and asked him, “Are you the
king of the Jews?”
34“Is that your own idea,” Jesus asked, “or
did others talk to you about me?”
35“Am I a Jew?” Pilate replied. “It was your
people and your chief priests who handed you
over to me. What is it you have done?”

[a]9 John 6:39 [b]24 Or *(Now Annas had sent him, still bound, to Caiaphas the high priest.)*

36Jesus said, "My kingdom is not of this
world. If it were, my servants would fight to
prevent my arrest by the Jews. But now my
kingdom is from another place."
37"You are a king, then!" said Pilate.
Jesus answered, "You are right in saying I
am a king. In fact, for this reason I was born,
and for this I came into the world, to testify to
the truth. Everyone on the side of truth listens
to me."
38"What is truth?" Pilate asked. With this he
went out again to the Jews and said, "I find no
basis for a charge against him. 39But it is your
custom for me to release to you one prisoner at
the time of the Passover. Do you want me to
release 'the king of the Jews'?"
40They shouted back, "No, not him! Give us
Barabbas!" Now Barabbas had taken part in a
rebellion.

Jesus Sentenced to Be Crucified

19 Then Pilate took Jesus and had him
flogged. 2The soldiers twisted together
a crown of thorns and put it on his head. They
clothed him in a purple robe 3and went up to
him again and again, saying, "Hail, king of the
Jews!" And they struck him in the face.
4Once more Pilate came out and said to the
Jews, "Look, I am bringing him out to you to
let you know that I find no basis for a charge
against him." 5When Jesus came out wearing
the crown of thorns and the purple robe, Pilate
said to them, "Here is the man!"
6As soon as the chief priests and their officials saw him, they shouted, "Crucify! Crucify!"
But Pilate answered, "You take him and crucify him. As for me, I find no basis for a
charge against him."
7The Jews insisted, "We have a law, and
according to that law he must die, because he
claimed to be the Son of God."
8When Pilate heard this, he was even more
afraid, 9and he went back inside the palace.
"Where do you come from?" he asked Jesus,
but Jesus gave him no answer. 10"Do you refuse to speak to me?" Pilate said. "Don't you
realize I have power either to free you or to
crucify you?"
11Jesus answered, "You would have no
power over me if it were not given to you from
above. Therefore the one who handed me over
to you is guilty of a greater sin."
12From then on, Pilate tried to set Jesus free,
but the Jews kept shouting, "If you let this man
go, you are no friend of Caesar. Anyone who
claims to be a king opposes Caesar."
13When Pilate heard this, he brought Jesus
out and sat down on the judge's seat at a place
known as the Stone Pavement (which in Aramaic is Gabbatha). 14It was the day of Preparation of Passover Week, about the sixth hour.
"Here is your king," Pilate said to the Jews.
15But they shouted, "Take him away! Take
him away! Crucify him!"
"Shall I crucify your king?" Pilate asked.
"We have no king but Caesar," the chief
priests answered.
16Finally Pilate handed him over to them to
be crucified.

The Crucifixion

So the soldiers took charge of Jesus. 17Car-
rying his own cross, he went out to the place of
the Skull (which in Aramaic is called Golgotha). 18Here they crucified him, and with him
two others—one on each side and Jesus in the
middle.
19Pilate had a notice prepared and fastened
to the cross. It read: JESUS OF NAZARETH, THE
KING OF THE JEWS. 20Many of the Jews read
this sign, for the place where Jesus was crucified was near the city, and the sign was written
in Aramaic, Latin and Greek. 21The chief
priests of the Jews protested to Pilate, "Do not
write 'The King of the Jews,' but that this man
claimed to be king of the Jews."
22Pilate answered, "What I have written, I
have written."
23When the soldiers crucified Jesus, they
took his clothes, dividing them into four
shares, one for each of them, with the under-
garment remaining. This garment was seam-
less, woven in one piece from top to bottom.
24"Let's not tear it," they said to one another. "Let's decide by lot who will get it."
This happened that the scripture might be
fulfilled which said,

> "They divided my garments among them
> and cast lots for my clothing."[a]

So this is what the soldiers did.
25Near the cross of Jesus stood his mother,
his mother's sister, Mary the wife of Clopas,
and Mary Magdalene. 26When Jesus saw his
mother there, and the disciple whom he loved
standing nearby, he said to his mother, "Dear
woman, here is your son," 27and to the disciple, "Here is your mother." From that time on,
this disciple took her into his home.

The Death of Jesus

28Later, knowing that all was now completed, and so that the Scripture would be fulfilled,
Jesus said, "I am thirsty." 29A jar of wine vinegar was there, so they soaked a sponge in it,
put the sponge on a stalk of the hyssop plant,
and lifted it to Jesus' lips. 30When he had received the drink, Jesus said, "It is finished."
With that, he bowed his head and gave up his
spirit.
31Now it was the day of Preparation, and the
next day was to be a special Sabbath. Because
the Jews did not want the bodies left on the
crosses during the Sabbath, they asked Pilate
to have the legs broken and the bodies taken
down. 32The soldiers therefore came and broke
the legs of the first man who had been crucified with Jesus, and then those of the other.
33But when they came to Jesus and found that

[a] *24* Psalm 22:18

he was already dead, they did not break his legs. 34Instead, one of the soldiers pierced Jesus' side with a spear, bringing a sudden flow of blood and water. 35The man who saw it has given testimony, and his testimony is true. He knows that he tells the truth, and he testifies so that you also may believe. 36These things happened so that the scripture would be fulfilled: "Not one of his bones will be broken,"[a] 37and, as another scripture says, "They will look on the one they have pierced."[b]

The Burial of Jesus

38Later, Joseph of Arimathea asked Pilate for the body of Jesus. Now Joseph was a disciple of Jesus, but secretly because he feared the Jews. With Pilate's permission, he came and took the body away. 39He was accompanied by Nicodemus, the man who earlier had visited Jesus at night. Nicodemus brought a mixture of myrrh and aloes, about seventy-five pounds.[c] 40Taking Jesus' body, the two of them wrapped it, with the spices, in strips of linen. This was in accordance with Jewish burial customs. 41At the place where Jesus was crucified, there was a garden, and in the garden a new tomb, in which no one had ever been laid. 42Because it was the Jewish day of Preparation and since the tomb was nearby, they laid Jesus there.

The Empty Tomb

20 Early on the first day of the week, while it was still dark, Mary Magdalene went to the tomb and saw that the stone had been removed from the entrance. 2So she came running to Simon Peter and the other disciple, the one Jesus loved, and said, "They have taken the Lord out of the tomb, and we don't know where they have put him!"

3So Peter and the other disciple started for the tomb. 4Both were running, but the other disciple outran Peter and reached the tomb first. 5He bent over and looked in at the strips of linen lying there but did not go in. 6Then Simon Peter, who was behind him, arrived and went into the tomb. He saw the strips of linen lying there, 7as well as the burial cloth that had been around Jesus' head. The cloth was folded up by itself, separate from the linen. 8Finally the other disciple, who had reached the tomb first, also went inside. He saw and believed. 9(They still did not understand from Scripture that Jesus had to rise from the dead.)

Jesus Appears to Mary Magdalene

10Then the disciples went back to their homes, 11but Mary stood outside the tomb crying. As she wept, she bent over to look into the tomb 12and saw two angels in white, seated where Jesus' body had been, one at the head and the other at the foot.

13They asked her, "Woman, why are you crying?"

"They have taken my Lord away," she said, "and I don't know where they have put him." 14At this, she turned around and saw Jesus standing there, but she did not realize that it was Jesus.

15"Woman," he said, "why are you crying? Who is it you are looking for?"

Thinking he was the gardener, she said, "Sir, if you have carried him away, tell me where you have put him, and I will get him."

16Jesus said to her, "Mary."

She turned toward him and cried out in Aramaic, "Rabboni!" (which means Teacher).

17Jesus said, "Do not hold on to me, for I have not yet returned to the Father. Go instead to my brothers and tell them, 'I am returning to my Father and your Father, to my God and your God.' "

18Mary Magdalene went to the disciples with the news: "I have seen the Lord!" And she told them that he had said these things to her.

Jesus Appears to His Disciples

19On the evening of that first day of the week, when the disciples were together, with the doors locked for fear of the Jews, Jesus came and stood among them and said, "Peace be with you!" 20After he said this, he showed them his hands and side. The disciples were overjoyed when they saw the Lord.

21Again Jesus said, "Peace be with you! As the Father has sent me, I am sending you." 22And with that he breathed on them and said, "Receive the Holy Spirit. 23If you forgive anyone his sins, they are forgiven; if you do not forgive them, they are not forgiven."

Jesus Appears to Thomas

24Now Thomas (called Didymus), one of the Twelve, was not with the disciples when Jesus came. 25So the other disciples told him, "We have seen the Lord!"

But he said to them, "Unless I see the nail marks in his hands and put my finger where the nails were, and put my hand into his side, I will not believe it."

26A week later his disciples were in the house again, and Thomas was with them. Though the doors were locked, Jesus came and stood among them and said, "Peace be with you!" 27Then he said to Thomas, "Put your finger here; see my hands. Reach out your hand and put it into my side. Stop doubting and believe."

28Thomas said to him, "My Lord and my God!"

29Then Jesus told him, "Because you have seen me, you have believed; blessed are those who have not seen and yet have believed."

30Jesus did many other miraculous signs in the presence of his disciples, which are not recorded in this book. 31But these are written that you may[d] believe that Jesus is the Christ, the Son of God, and that by believing you may have life in his name.

[a] *36* Exodus 12:46; Num. 9:12; Psalm 34:20 [b] *37* Zech. 12:10 [c] *39* Greek *a hundred litrai* (about 34 kilograms) [d] *31* Some manuscripts *may continue to*

Jesus and the Miraculous Catch of Fish

21 Afterward Jesus appeared again to his disciples, by the Sea of Tiberias.[a] It happened this way: 2Simon Peter, Thomas (called Didymus), Nathanael from Cana in Galilee, the sons of Zebedee, and two other disciples were together. 3"I'm going out to fish," Simon Peter told them, and they said, "We'll go with you." So they went out and got into the boat, but that night they caught nothing.

4Early in the morning, Jesus stood on the shore, but the disciples did not realize that it was Jesus.

5He called out to them, "Friends, haven't you any fish?"

"No," they answered.

6He said, "Throw your net on the right side of the boat and you will find some." When they did, they were unable to haul the net in because of the large number of fish.

7Then the disciple whom Jesus loved said to Peter, "It is the Lord!" As soon as Simon Peter heard him say, "It is the Lord," he wrapped his outer garment around him (for he had taken it off) and jumped into the water. 8The other disciples followed in the boat, towing the net full of fish, for they were not far from shore, about a hundred yards.[b] 9When they landed, they saw a fire of burning coals there with fish on it, and some bread.

10Jesus said to them, "Bring some of the fish you have just caught."

11Simon Peter climbed aboard and dragged the net ashore. It was full of large fish, 153, but even with so many the net was not torn. 12Jesus said to them, "Come and have breakfast." None of the disciples dared ask him, "Who are you?" They knew it was the Lord. 13Jesus came, took the bread and gave it to them, and did the same with the fish. 14This was now the third time Jesus appeared to his disciples after he was raised from the dead.

Jesus Reinstates Peter

15When they had finished eating, Jesus said to Simon Peter, "Simon son of John, do you truly love me more than these?"

"Yes, Lord," he said, "you know that I love you."

Jesus said, "Feed my lambs."

16Again Jesus said, "Simon son of John, do you truly love me?"

He answered, "Yes, Lord, you know that I love you."

Jesus said, "Take care of my sheep."

17The third time he said to him, "Simon son of John, do you love me?"

Peter was hurt because Jesus asked him the third time, "Do you love me?" He said, "Lord, you know all things; you know that I love you."

Jesus said, "Feed my sheep. 18I tell you the truth, when you were younger you dressed yourself and went where you wanted; but when you are old you will stretch out your hands, and someone else will dress you and lead you where you do not want to go." 19Jesus said this to indicate the kind of death by which Peter would glorify God. Then he said to him, "Follow me!"

20Peter turned and saw that the disciple whom Jesus loved was following them. (This was the one who had leaned back against Jesus at the supper and had said, "Lord, who is going to betray you?") 21When Peter saw him, he asked, "Lord, what about him?"

22Jesus answered, "If I want him to remain alive until I return, what is that to you? You must follow me." 23Because of this, the rumor spread among the brothers that this disciple would not die. But Jesus did not say that he would not die; he only said, "If I want him to remain alive until I return, what is that to you?"

24This is the disciple who testifies to these things and who wrote them down. We know that his testimony is true.

25Jesus did many other things as well. If every one of them were written down, I suppose that even the whole world would not have room for the books that would be written.

Acts

Jesus Taken Up Into Heaven

1 In my former book, Theophilus, I wrote about all that Jesus began to do and to teach 2until the day he was taken up to heaven, after giving instructions through the Holy Spirit to the apostles he had chosen. 3After his suffering, he showed himself to these men and gave many convincing proofs that he was alive. He appeared to them over a period of forty days and spoke about the kingdom of God. 4On one occasion, while he was eating with them, he gave them this command: "Do not leave Jerusalem, but wait for the gift my Father promised, which you have heard me speak about. 5For John baptized with[c] water, but in a few days you will be baptized with the Holy Spirit."

6So when they met together, they asked him,

[a] *1* That is, Sea of Galilee [b] *8* Greek *about two hundred cubits* (about 90 meters) [c] *5* Or *in*

"Lord, are you at this time going to restore the
kingdom to Israel?"
7He said to them: "It is not for you to know
the times or dates the Father has set by his own
authority. 8But you will receive power when
the Holy Spirit comes on you; and you will be
my witnesses in Jerusalem, and in all Judea
and Samaria, and to the ends of the earth."
9After he said this, he was taken up before
their very eyes, and a cloud hid him from their
sight.
10They were looking intently up into the sky
as he was going, when suddenly two men
dressed in white stood beside them. 11"Men of
Galilee," they said, "why do you stand here
looking into the sky? This same Jesus, who has
been taken from you into heaven, will come
back in the same way you have seen him go
into heaven."

Matthias Chosen to Replace Judas

12Then they returned to Jerusalem from the
hill called the Mount of Olives, a Sabbath
day's walk[a] from the city. 13When they arrived, they went upstairs to the room where
they were staying. Those present were Peter,
John, James and Andrew; Philip and Thomas,
Bartholomew and Matthew; James son of Alphaeus and Simon the Zealot, and Judas son of
James. 14They all joined together constantly in
prayer, along with the women and Mary the
mother of Jesus, and with his brothers.
15In those days Peter stood up among the
believers[b] (a group numbering about a hundred and twenty) 16and said, "Brothers, the
Scripture had to be fulfilled which the Holy
Spirit spoke long ago through the mouth of
David concerning Judas, who served as guide
for those who arrested Jesus— 17he was one of
our number and shared in this ministry."
18(With the reward he got for his wickedness, Judas bought a field; there he fell headlong, his body burst open and all his intestines
spilled out. 19Everyone in Jerusalem heard
about this, so they called that field in their
language Akeldama, that is, Field of Blood.)
20"For," said Peter, "it is written in the book
of Psalms,

" 'May his place be deserted;
let there be no one to dwell in it,'[c]

and,

" 'May another take his place of
leadership.'[d]

21Therefore it is necessary to choose one of the
men who have been with us the whole time the
Lord Jesus went in and out among us, 22begin-
ning from John's baptism to the time when
Jesus was taken up from us. For one of these
must become a witness with us of his resurrection."
23So they proposed two men: Joseph called
Barsabbas (also known as Justus) and Matthias. 24Then they prayed, "Lord, you know everyone's heart. Show us which of these two
you have chosen 25to take over this apostolic
ministry, which Judas left to go where he belongs." 26Then they cast lots, and the lot fell to
Matthias; so he was added to the eleven apostles.

The Holy Spirit Comes at Pentecost

2 When the day of Pentecost came, they
were all together in one place. 2Suddenly a
sound like the blowing of a violent wind came
from heaven and filled the whole house where
they were sitting. 3They saw what seemed to
be tongues of fire that separated and came to
rest on each of them. 4All of them were filled
with the Holy Spirit and began to speak in
other tongues[e] as the Spirit enabled them.
5Now there were staying in Jerusalem God-
fearing Jews from every nation under heaven.
6When they heard this sound, a crowd came
together in bewilderment, because each one
heard them speaking in his own language. 7Ut-
terly amazed, they asked: "Are not all these
men who are speaking Galileans? 8Then how
is it that each of us hears them in his own
native language? 9Parthians, Medes and Elamites; residents of Mesopotamia, Judea and Cappadocia, Pontus and Asia, 10Phrygia and Pamphylia, Egypt and the parts of Libya near
Cyrene; visitors from Rome 11(both Jews and
converts to Judaism); Cretans and Arabs—we
hear them declaring the wonders of God in our
own tongues!" 12Amazed and perplexed, they
asked one another, "What does this mean?"
13Some, however, made fun of them and
said, "They have had too much wine.[f]"

Peter Addresses the Crowd

14Then Peter stood up with the Eleven,
raised his voice and addressed the crowd: "Fellow Jews and all of you who live in Jerusalem,
let me explain this to you; listen carefully to
what I say. 15These men are not drunk, as you
suppose. It's only nine in the morning! 16No,
this is what was spoken by the prophet Joel:

17" 'In the last days, God says,
I will pour out my Spirit on all people.
Your sons and daughters will prophesy,
your young men will see visions,
your old men will dream dreams.
18Even on my servants, both men and
women,
I will pour out my Spirit in those days,
and they will prophesy.
19I will show wonders in the heaven above
and signs on the earth below,
blood and fire and billows of smoke.
20The sun will be turned to darkness
and the moon to blood
before the coming of the great and
glorious day of the Lord.
21And everyone who calls

[a] *12* That is, about 3/4 mile (about 1,100 meters) [b] *15* Greek *brothers* [c] *20* Psalm 69:25
[d] *20* Psalm 109:8 [e] *4* Or *languages*; also in verse 11 [f] *13* Or *sweet wine*

on the name of the Lord will be
saved.'[a]

22"Men of Israel, listen to this: Jesus of Nazareth was a man accredited by God to you by
miracles, wonders and signs, which God did
among you through him, as you yourselves
know. 23This man was handed over to you by
God's set purpose and foreknowledge; and
you, with the help of wicked men,[b] put him to
death by nailing him to the cross. 24But God
raised him from the dead, freeing him from the
agony of death, because it was impossible for
death to keep its hold on him. 25David said
about him:

" 'I saw the Lord always before me.
Because he is at my right hand,
I will not be shaken.
26Therefore my heart is glad and my tongue
rejoices;
my body also will live in hope,
27because you will not abandon me to the
grave,
nor will you let your Holy One see
decay.
28You have made known to me the paths of
life;
you will fill me with joy in your
presence.'[c]

29"Brothers, I can tell you confidently that
the patriarch David died and was buried, and
his tomb is here to this day. 30But he was a
prophet and knew that God had promised him
on oath that he would place one of his descendants on his throne. 31Seeing what was ahead,
he spoke of the resurrection of the Christ,[d] that
he was not abandoned to the grave, nor did his
body see decay. 32God has raised this Jesus to
life, and we are all witnesses of the fact. 33Ex-
alted to the right hand of God, he has received
from the Father the promised Holy Spirit and
has poured out what you now see and hear.
34For David did not ascend to heaven, and yet
he said,

" 'The Lord said to my Lord:
"Sit at my right hand
35until I make your enemies
a footstool for your feet." '[e]

36"Therefore let all Israel be assured of this:
God has made this Jesus, whom you crucified,
both Lord and Christ."

37When the people heard this, they were cut
to the heart and said to Peter and the other
apostles, "Brothers, what shall we do?"

38Peter replied, "Repent and be baptized, every one of you, in the name of Jesus Christ for
the forgiveness of your sins. And you will receive the gift of the Holy Spirit. 39The promise
is for you and your children and for all who are
far off—for all whom the Lord our God will
call."

40With many other words he warned them;
and he pleaded with them, "Save yourselves
from this corrupt generation." 41Those who accepted his message were baptized, and about
three thousand were added to their number that
day.

The Fellowship of the Believers

42They devoted themselves to the apostles'
teaching and to the fellowship, to the breaking
of bread and to prayer. 43Everyone was filled
with awe, and many wonders and miraculous
signs were done by the apostles. 44All the believers were together and had everything in
common. 45Selling their possessions and
goods, they gave to anyone as he had need.
46Every day they continued to meet together in
the temple courts. They broke bread in their
homes and ate together with glad and sincere
hearts, 47praising God and enjoying the favor
of all the people. And the Lord added to their
number daily those who were being saved.

Peter Heals the Crippled Beggar

3 One day Peter and John were going up to
the temple at the time of prayer—at three
in the afternoon. 2Now a man crippled from
birth was being carried to the temple gate
called Beautiful, where he was put every day
to beg from those going into the temple courts.
3When he saw Peter and John about to enter,
he asked them for money. 4Peter looked
straight at him, as did John. Then Peter said,
"Look at us!" 5So the man gave them his attention, expecting to get something from them.

6Then Peter said, "Silver or gold I do not
have, but what I have I give you. In the name
of Jesus Christ of Nazareth, walk." 7Taking
him by the right hand, he helped him up, and
instantly the man's feet and ankles became
strong. 8He jumped to his feet and began to
walk. Then he went with them into the temple
courts, walking and jumping, and praising
God. 9When all the people saw him walking
and praising God, 10they recognized him as the
same man who used to sit begging at the temple gate called Beautiful, and they were filled
with wonder and amazement at what had happened to him.

Peter Speaks to the Onlookers

11While the beggar held on to Peter and
John, all the people were astonished and came
running to them in the place called Solomon's
Colonnade. 12When Peter saw this, he said to
them: "Men of Israel, why does this surprise
you? Why do you stare at us as if by our own
power or godliness we had made this man
walk? 13The God of Abraham, Isaac and Jacob, the God of our fathers, has glorified his
servant Jesus. You handed him over to be
killed, and you disowned him before Pilate,
though he had decided to let him go. 14You
disowned the Holy and Righteous One and
asked that a murderer be released to you.

[a]*21* Joel 2:28-32 [b]*23* Or *of those not having the law* (that is, Gentiles) [c]*28* Psalm 16:8-11
[d]*31* Or *Messiah.* "The Christ" (Greek) and "the Messiah" (Hebrew) both mean "the Anointed One"; also in verse 36. [e]*35* Psalm 110:1

15You killed the author of life, but God raised
him from the dead. We are witnesses of this.
16By faith in the name of Jesus, this man
whom you see and know was made strong. It
is Jesus' name and the faith that comes through
him that has given this complete healing to
him, as you can all see.
17"Now, brothers, I know that you acted in
ignorance, as did your leaders. 18But this is
how God fulfilled what he had foretold
through all the prophets, saying that his
Christ[a] would suffer. 19Repent, then, and turn
to God, so that your sins may be wiped out,
that times of refreshing may come from the
Lord, 20and that he may send the Christ, who
has been appointed for you—even Jesus. 21He
must remain in heaven until the time comes for
God to restore everything, as he promised long
ago through his holy prophets. 22For Moses
said, 'The Lord your God will raise up for you
a prophet like me from among your own people; you must listen to everything he tells you.
23Anyone who does not listen to him will be
completely cut off from among his people.'[b]
24"Indeed, all the prophets from Samuel on,
as many as have spoken, have foretold these
days. 25And you are heirs of the prophets and
of the covenant God made with your fathers.
He said to Abraham, 'Through your offspring
all peoples on earth will be blessed.'[c] 26When
God raised up his servant, he sent him first to
you to bless you by turning each of you from
your wicked ways."

Peter and John Before the Sanhedrin

4 The priests and the captain of the temple
guard and the Sadducees came up to Peter
and John while they were speaking to the people. 2They were greatly disturbed because the
apostles were teaching the people and proclaiming in Jesus the resurrection of the dead.
3They seized Peter and John, and because it
was evening, they put them in jail until the
next day. 4But many who heard the message
believed, and the number of men grew to about
five thousand.
5The next day the rulers, elders and teachers
of the law met in Jerusalem. 6Annas the high
priest was there, and so were Caiaphas, John,
Alexander and the other men of the high
priest's family. 7They had Peter and John
brought before them and began to question
them: "By what power or what name did you
do this?"
8Then Peter, filled with the Holy Spirit, said
to them: "Rulers and elders of the people! 9If
we are being called to account today for an act
of kindness shown to a cripple and are asked
how he was healed, 10then know this, you and
all the people of Israel: It is by the name of
Jesus Christ of Nazareth, whom you crucified
but whom God raised from the dead, that this
man stands before you healed. 11He is

" 'the stone you builders rejected,
which has become the capstone.[d]'[e]

12Salvation is found in no one else, for there is
no other name under heaven given to men by
which we must be saved."
13When they saw the courage of Peter and
John and realized that they were unschooled,
ordinary men, they were astonished and they
took note that these men had been with Jesus.
14But since they could see the man who had
been healed standing there with them, there
was nothing they could say. 15So they ordered
them to withdraw from the Sanhedrin and then
conferred together. 16"What are we going to do
with these men?" they asked. "Everybody living in Jerusalem knows they have done an outstanding miracle, and we cannot deny it. 17But
to stop this thing from spreading any further
among the people, we must warn these men to
speak no longer to anyone in this name."
18Then they called them in again and commanded them not to speak or teach at all in the
name of Jesus. 19But Peter and John replied,
"Judge for yourselves whether it is right in
God's sight to obey you rather than God. 20For
we cannot help speaking about what we have
seen and heard."
21After further threats they let them go.
They could not decide how to punish them,
because all the people were praising God for
what had happened. 22For the man who was
miraculously healed was over forty years old.

The Believers' Prayer

23On their release, Peter and John went back
to their own people and reported all that the
chief priests and elders had said to them.
24When they heard this, they raised their
voices together in prayer to God. "Sovereign
Lord," they said, "you made the heaven and
the earth and the sea, and everything in them.
25You spoke by the Holy Spirit through the
mouth of your servant, our father David:

" 'Why do the nations rage
and the peoples plot in vain?
26The kings of the earth take their stand
and the rulers gather together
against the Lord
and against his Anointed One.[f]'[g]

27Indeed Herod and Pontius Pilate met together with the Gentiles and the people[h] of Israel
in this city to conspire against your holy servant Jesus, whom you anointed. 28They did
what your power and will had decided beforehand should happen. 29Now, Lord, consider
their threats and enable your servants to speak
your word with great boldness. 30Stretch out
your hand to heal and perform miraculous
signs and wonders through the name of your
holy servant Jesus."
31After they prayed, the place where they
were meeting was shaken. And they were all

[a] *18* Or *Messiah*; also in verse 20 [b] *23* Deut. 18:15,18,19 [c] *25* Gen. 22:18; 26:4 [d] *11* Or *cornerstone*
[e] *11* Psalm 118:22 [f] *26* That is, Christ or Messiah [g] *26* Psalm 2:1,2 [h] *27* The Greek is plural.

filled with the Holy Spirit and spoke the word
of God boldly.

The Believers Share Their Possessions

32All the believers were one in heart and
mind. No one claimed that any of his possessions was his own, but they shared everything
they had. 33With great power the apostles continued to testify to the resurrection of the Lord
Jesus, and much grace was upon them all.
34There were no needy persons among them.
For from time to time those who owned lands
or houses sold them, brought the money from
the sales 35and put it at the apostles' feet, and
it was distributed to anyone as he had need.

36Joseph, a Levite from Cyprus, whom the
apostles called Barnabas (which means Son of
Encouragement), 37sold a field he owned and
brought the money and put it at the apostles'
feet.

Ananias and Sapphira

5 Now a man named Ananias, together with
his wife Sapphira, also sold a piece of
property. 2With his wife's full knowledge he
kept back part of the money for himself, but
brought the rest and put it at the apostles' feet.

3Then Peter said, "Ananias, how is it that
Satan has so filled your heart that you have
lied to the Holy Spirit and have kept for yourself some of the money you received for the
land? 4Didn't it belong to you before it was
sold? And after it was sold, wasn't the money
at your disposal? What made you think of doing such a thing? You have not lied to men but
to God."

5When Ananias heard this, he fell down and
died. And great fear seized all who heard what
had happened. 6Then the young men came forward, wrapped up his body, and carried him
out and buried him.

7About three hours later his wife came in,
not knowing what had happened. 8Peter asked
her, "Tell me, is this the price you and Ananias
got for the land?"

"Yes," she said, "that is the price."

9Peter said to her, "How could you agree to
test the Spirit of the Lord? Look! The feet of
the men who buried your husband are at the
door, and they will carry you out also."

10At that moment she fell down at his feet
and died. Then the young men came in and,
finding her dead, carried her out and buried her
beside her husband. 11Great fear seized the
whole church and all who heard about these
events.

The Apostles Heal Many

12The apostles performed many miraculous
signs and wonders among the people. And all
the believers used to meet together in Solomon's Colonnade. 13No one else dared join
them, even though they were highly regarded
by the people. 14Nevertheless, more and more
men and women believed in the Lord and were
added to their number. 15As a result, people
brought the sick into the streets and laid them
on beds and mats so that at least Peter's shadow might fall on some of them as he passed by.
16Crowds gathered also from the towns around
Jerusalem, bringing their sick and those tormented by evil[a] spirits, and all of them were
healed.

The Apostles Persecuted

17Then the high priest and all his associates,
who were members of the party of the Sadducees, were filled with jealousy. 18They arrested
the apostles and put them in the public jail.
19But during the night an angel of the Lord
opened the doors of the jail and brought them
out. 20"Go, stand in the temple courts," he said,
"and tell the people the full message of this
new life."

21At daybreak they entered the temple
courts, as they had been told, and began to
teach the people.

When the high priest and his associates arrived, they called together the Sanhedrin—the
full assembly of the elders of Israel—and sent
to the jail for the apostles. 22But on arriving at
the jail, the officers did not find them there. So
they went back and reported, 23"We found the
jail securely locked, with the guards standing
at the doors; but when we opened them, we
found no one inside." 24On hearing this report,
the captain of the temple guard and the chief
priests were puzzled, wondering what would
come of this.

25Then someone came and said, "Look! The
men you put in jail are standing in the temple
courts teaching the people." 26At that, the captain went with his officers and brought the
apostles. They did not use force, because they
feared that the people would stone them.

27Having brought the apostles, they made
them appear before the Sanhedrin to be questioned by the high priest. 28"We gave you strict
orders not to teach in this name," he said. "Yet
you have filled Jerusalem with your teaching
and are determined to make us guilty of this
man's blood."

29Peter and the other apostles replied: "We
must obey God rather than men! 30The God of
our fathers raised Jesus from the dead—whom
you had killed by hanging him on a tree. 31God
exalted him to his own right hand as Prince
and Savior that he might give repentance and
forgiveness of sins to Israel. 32We are witnesses of these things, and so is the Holy Spirit, whom God has given to those who obey
him."

33When they heard this, they were furious
and wanted to put them to death. 34But a Pharisee named Gamaliel, a teacher of the law, who
was honored by all the people, stood up in the
Sanhedrin and ordered that the men be put outside for a little while. 35Then he addressed
them: "Men of Israel, consider carefully what
you intend to do to these men. 36Some time
ago Theudas appeared, claiming to be some-

[a]16 Greek *unclean*

body, and about four hundred men rallied to
him. He was killed, all his followers were dispersed, and it all came to nothing. 37After him,
Judas the Galilean appeared in the days of the
census and led a band of people in revolt. He
too was killed, and all his followers were scattered. 38Therefore, in the present case I advise
you: Leave these men alone! Let them go! For
if their purpose or activity is of human origin,
it will fail. 39But if it is from God, you will not
be able to stop these men; you will only find
yourselves fighting against God."

40His speech persuaded them. They called
the apostles in and had them flogged. Then
they ordered them not to speak in the name of
Jesus, and let them go.

41The apostles left the Sanhedrin, rejoicing
because they had been counted worthy of suffering disgrace for the Name. 42Day after day,
in the temple courts and from house to house,
they never stopped teaching and proclaiming
the good news that Jesus is the Christ.[a]

The Choosing of the Seven

6 In those days when the number of disciples
was increasing, the Grecian Jews among
them complained against the Hebraic Jews because their widows were being overlooked in
the daily distribution of food. 2So the Twelve
gathered all the disciples together and said, "It
would not be right for us to neglect the ministry of the word of God in order to wait on
tables. 3Brothers, choose seven men from
among you who are known to be full of the
Spirit and wisdom. We will turn this responsibility over to them 4and will give our attention to prayer and the ministry of the word."

5This proposal pleased the whole group.
They chose Stephen, a man full of faith and of
the Holy Spirit; also Philip, Procorus, Nicanor,
Timon, Parmenas, and Nicolas from Antioch, a
convert to Judaism. 6They presented these men
to the apostles, who prayed and laid their
hands on them.

7So the word of God spread. The number of
disciples in Jerusalem increased rapidly, and a
large number of priests became obedient to the
faith.

Stephen Seized

8Now Stephen, a man full of God's grace
and power, did great wonders and miraculous
signs among the people. 9Opposition arose,
however, from members of the Synagogue of
the Freedmen (as it was called)—Jews of Cyrene and Alexandria as well as the provinces of
Cilicia and Asia. These men began to argue
with Stephen, 10but they could not stand up
against his wisdom or the Spirit by whom he
spoke.

11Then they secretly persuaded some men to
say, "We have heard Stephen speak words of
blasphemy against Moses and against God."

12So they stirred up the people and the elders and the teachers of the law. They seized
Stephen and brought him before the Sanhedrin.
13They produced false witnesses, who testified, "This fellow never stops speaking against
this holy place and against the law. 14For we
have heard him say that this Jesus of Nazareth
will destroy this place and change the customs
Moses handed down to us."

15All who were sitting in the Sanhedrin
looked intently at Stephen, and they saw that
his face was like the face of an angel.

Stephen's Speech to the Sanhedrin

7 Then the high priest asked him, "Are these
charges true?"

2To this he replied: "Brothers and fathers,
listen to me! The God of glory appeared to our
father Abraham while he was still in Mesopotamia, before he lived in Haran. 3'Leave your
country and your people,' God said, 'and go to
the land I will show you.'[b]

4"So he left the land of the Chaldeans and
settled in Haran. After the death of his father,
God sent him to this land where you are now
living. 5He gave him no inheritance here, not
even a foot of ground. But God promised him
that he and his descendants after him would
possess the land, even though at that time
Abraham had no child. 6God spoke to him in
this way: 'Your descendants will be strangers
in a country not their own, and they will be
enslaved and mistreated four hundred years.
7But I will punish the nation they serve as
slaves,' God said, 'and afterward they will
come out of that country and worship me in
this place.'[c] 8Then he gave Abraham the covenant of circumcision. And Abraham became
the father of Isaac and circumcised him eight
days after his birth. Later Isaac became the
father of Jacob, and Jacob became the father of
the twelve patriarchs.

9"Because the patriarchs were jealous of Joseph, they sold him as a slave into Egypt. But
God was with him 10and rescued him from all
his troubles. He gave Joseph wisdom and enabled him to gain the goodwill of Pharaoh king
of Egypt; so he made him ruler over Egypt and
all his palace.

11"Then a famine struck all Egypt and Canaan, bringing great suffering, and our fathers
could not find food. 12When Jacob heard that
there was grain in Egypt, he sent our fathers on
their first visit. 13On their second visit, Joseph
told his brothers who he was, and Pharaoh
learned about Joseph's family. 14After this, Joseph sent for his father Jacob and his whole
family, seventy-five in all. 15Then Jacob went
down to Egypt, where he and our fathers died.
16Their bodies were brought back to Shechem
and placed in the tomb that Abraham had
bought from the sons of Hamor at Shechem for
a certain sum of money.

17"As the time drew near for God to fulfill
his promise to Abraham, the number of our
people in Egypt greatly increased. 18Then another king, who knew nothing about Joseph,

[a]42 Or *Messiah* [b]3 Gen. 12:1 [c]7 Gen. 15:13,14

became ruler of Egypt. 19He dealt treacherously with our people and oppressed our forefathers by forcing them to throw out their newborn babies so that they would die.

20"At that time Moses was born, and he was
no ordinary child.[a] For three months he was
cared for in his father's house. 21When he was
placed outside, Pharaoh's daughter took him
and brought him up as her own son. 22Moses
was educated in all the wisdom of the Egyptians and was powerful in speech and action.

23"When Moses was forty years old, he decided to visit his fellow Israelites. 24He saw
one of them being mistreated by an Egyptian,
so he went to his defense and avenged him by
killing the Egyptian. 25Moses thought that his
own people would realize that God was using
him to rescue them, but they did not. 26The
next day Moses came upon two Israelites who
were fighting. He tried to reconcile them by
saying, 'Men, you are brothers; why do you
want to hurt each other?'

27"But the man who was mistreating the other pushed Moses aside and said, 'Who made
you ruler and judge over us? 28Do you want to
kill me as you killed the Egyptian yesterday?'[b]
29When Moses heard this, he fled to Midian,
where he settled as a foreigner and had two
sons.

30"After forty years had passed, an angel
appeared to Moses in the flames of a burning
bush in the desert near Mount Sinai. 31When
he saw this, he was amazed at the sight. As he
went over to look more closely, he heard the
Lord's voice: 32'I am the God of your fathers,
the God of Abraham, Isaac and Jacob.'[c] Moses trembled with fear and did not dare to look.

33"Then the Lord said to him, 'Take off your
sandals; the place where you are standing is
holy ground. 34I have indeed seen the oppression of my people in Egypt. I have heard their
groaning and have come down to set them free.
Now come, I will send you back to Egypt.'[d]

35"This is the same Moses whom they had
rejected with the words, 'Who made you ruler
and judge?' He was sent to be their ruler and
deliverer by God himself, through the angel
who appeared to him in the bush. 36He led
them out of Egypt and did wonders and miraculous signs in Egypt, at the Red Sea[e] and for
forty years in the desert.

37"This is that Moses who told the Israelites,
'God will send you a prophet like me from
your own people.'[f] 38He was in the assembly
in the desert, with the angel who spoke to him
on Mount Sinai, and with our fathers; and he
received living words to pass on to us.

39"But our fathers refused to obey him. Instead, they rejected him and in their hearts
turned back to Egypt. 40They told Aaron,
'Make us gods who will go before us. As for
this fellow Moses who led us out of Egypt—
we don't know what has happened to him!'[g]
41That was the time they made an idol in the
form of a calf. They brought sacrifices to it and
held a celebration in honor of what their hands
had made. 42But God turned away and gave
them over to the worship of the heavenly bodies. This agrees with what is written in the
book of the prophets:

" 'Did you bring me sacrifices and
offerings
forty years in the desert, O house of
Israel?
43You have lifted up the shrine of Molech
and the star of your god Rephan,
the idols you made to worship.
Therefore I will send you into exile'[h]
beyond Babylon.

44"Our forefathers had the tabernacle of the
Testimony with them in the desert. It had been
made as God directed Moses, according to the
pattern he had seen. 45Having received the tabernacle, our fathers under Joshua brought it
with them when they took the land from the
nations God drove out before them. It remained in the land until the time of David,
46who enjoyed God's favor and asked that he
might provide a dwelling place for the God of
Jacob.[i] 47But it was Solomon who built the
house for him.

48"However, the Most High does not live in
houses made by men. As the prophet says:

49" 'Heaven is my throne,
and the earth is my footstool.
What kind of house will you build for
me?
says the Lord.
Or where will my resting place be?
50Has not my hand made all these things?'[j]

51"You stiff-necked people, with uncircumcised hearts and ears! You are just like your
fathers: You always resist the Holy Spirit!
52Was there ever a prophet your fathers did not
persecute? They even killed those who predicted the coming of the Righteous One. And now
you have betrayed and murdered him— 53you
who have received the law that was put into
effect through angels but have not obeyed it."

The Stoning of Stephen

54When they heard this, they were furious
and gnashed their teeth at him. 55But Stephen,
full of the Holy Spirit, looked up to heaven and
saw the glory of God, and Jesus standing at the
right hand of God. 56"Look," he said, "I see
heaven open and the Son of Man standing at
the right hand of God."

57At this they covered their ears and, yelling
at the top of their voices, they all rushed at
him, 58dragged him out of the city and began
to stone him. Meanwhile, the witnesses laid
their clothes at the feet of a young man named
Saul.

[a]20 Or *was fair in the sight of God* [b]28 Exodus 2:14 [c]32 Exodus 3:6 [d]34 Exodus 3:5,7,8,10
[e]36 That is, Sea of Reeds [f]37 Deut. 18:15 [g]40 Exodus 32:1 [h]43 Amos 5:25-27 [i]46 Some early
manuscripts *the house of Jacob* [j]50 Isaiah 66:1,2

59While they were stoning him, Stephen
prayed, "Lord Jesus, receive my spirit."
60Then he fell on his knees and cried out,
"Lord, do not hold this sin against them."
When he had said this, he fell asleep.

8 And Saul was there, giving approval to his
death.

The Church Persecuted and Scattered

On that day a great persecution broke out
against the church at Jerusalem, and all except
the apostles were scattered throughout Judea
and Samaria. 2Godly men buried Stephen and
mourned deeply for him. 3But Saul began to
destroy the church. Going from house to
house, he dragged off men and women and put
them in prison.

Philip in Samaria

4Those who had been scattered preached the
word wherever they went. 5Philip went down
to a city in Samaria and proclaimed the Christ[a]
there. 6When the crowds heard Philip and saw
the miraculous signs he did, they all paid close
attention to what he said. 7With shrieks, evil[b]
spirits came out of many, and many paralytics
and cripples were healed. 8So there was great
joy in that city.

Simon the Sorcerer

9Now for some time a man named Simon
had practiced sorcery in the city and amazed
all the people of Samaria. He boasted that he
was someone great, 10and all the people, both
high and low, gave him their attention and exclaimed, "This man is the divine power known
as the Great Power." 11They followed him because he had amazed them for a long time with
his magic. 12But when they believed Philip as
he preached the good news of the kingdom of
God and the name of Jesus Christ, they were
baptized, both men and women. 13Simon himself believed and was baptized. And he followed Philip everywhere, astonished by the
great signs and miracles he saw.

14When the apostles in Jerusalem heard that
Samaria had accepted the word of God, they
sent Peter and John to them. 15When they arrived, they prayed for them that they might
receive the Holy Spirit, 16because the Holy
Spirit had not yet come upon any of them; they
had simply been baptized into[c] the name of
the Lord Jesus. 17Then Peter and John placed
their hands on them, and they received the
Holy Spirit.

18When Simon saw that the Spirit was given
at the laying on of the apostles' hands, he offered them money 19and said, "Give me also
this ability so that everyone on whom I lay my
hands may receive the Holy Spirit."

20Peter answered: "May your money perish
with you, because you thought you could buy
the gift of God with money! 21You have no
part or share in this ministry, because your
heart is not right before God. 22Repent of this
wickedness and pray to the Lord. Perhaps he
will forgive you for having such a thought in
your heart. 23For I see that you are full of
bitterness and captive to sin."

24Then Simon answered, "Pray to the Lord
for me so that nothing you have said may happen to me."

25When they had testified and proclaimed
the word of the Lord, Peter and John returned
to Jerusalem, preaching the gospel in many
Samaritan villages.

Philip and the Ethiopian

26Now an angel of the Lord said to Philip,
"Go south to the road—the desert road—that
goes down from Jerusalem to Gaza." 27So he
started out, and on his way he met an Ethiopian[d] eunuch, an important official in charge of
all the treasury of Candace, queen of the Ethio-
pians. This man had gone to Jerusalem to worship, 28and on his way home was sitting in his
chariot reading the book of Isaiah the prophet.
29The Spirit told Philip, "Go to that chariot and
stay near it."

30Then Philip ran up to the chariot and heard
the man reading Isaiah the prophet. "Do you
understand what you are reading?" Philip
asked.

31"How can I," he said, "unless someone
explains it to me?" So he invited Philip to
come up and sit with him.

32The eunuch was reading this passage of
Scripture:

"He was led like a sheep to the slaughter,
and as a lamb before the shearer is
silent,
so he did not open his mouth.
33In his humiliation he was deprived of
justice.
Who can speak of his descendants?
For his life was taken from the earth."[e]

34The eunuch asked Philip, "Tell me, please,
who is the prophet talking about, himself or
someone else?" 35Then Philip began with that
very passage of Scripture and told him the
good news about Jesus.

36As they traveled along the road, they came
to some water and the eunuch said, "Look,
here is water. Why shouldn't I be baptized?"[f]
38And he gave orders to stop the chariot. Then
both Philip and the eunuch went down into the
water and Philip baptized him. 39When they
came up out of the water, the Spirit of the Lord
suddenly took Philip away, and the eunuch did
not see him again, but went on his way rejoicing. 40Philip, however, appeared at Azotus and
traveled about, preaching the gospel in all the
towns until he reached Caesarea.

[a] *5* Or *Messiah* [b] *7* Greek *unclean* [c] *16* Or *in* [d] *27* That is, from the upper Nile region
[e] *33* Isaiah 53:7,8 [f] *36* Some late manuscripts *baptized?" 37Philip said, "If you believe with all your heart, you may." The eunuch answered, "I believe that Jesus Christ is the Son of God."*

Saul's Conversion

9 Meanwhile, Saul was still breathing out
murderous threats against the Lord's disciples. He went to the high priest 2and asked him
for letters to the synagogues in Damascus, so
that if he found any there who belonged to the
Way, whether men or women, he might take
them as prisoners to Jerusalem. 3As he neared
Damascus on his journey, suddenly a light
from heaven flashed around him. 4He fell to
the ground and heard a voice say to him, "Saul,
Saul, why do you persecute me?"

5"Who are you, Lord?" Saul asked.

"I am Jesus, whom you are persecuting," he
replied. 6"Now get up and go into the city, and
you will be told what you must do."

7The men traveling with Saul stood there
speechless; they heard the sound but did not
see anyone. 8Saul got up from the ground, but
when he opened his eyes he could see nothing.
So they led him by the hand into Damascus.
9For three days he was blind, and did not eat or
drink anything.

10In Damascus there was a disciple named
Ananias. The Lord called to him in a vision,
"Ananias!"

"Yes, Lord," he answered.

11The Lord told him, "Go to the house of
Judas on Straight Street and ask for a man
from Tarsus named Saul, for he is praying. 12In
a vision he has seen a man named Ananias
come and place his hands on him to restore his
sight."

13"Lord," Ananias answered, "I have heard
many reports about this man and all the harm
he has done to your saints in Jerusalem. 14And
he has come here with authority from the chief
priests to arrest all who call on your name."

15But the Lord said to Ananias, "Go! This
man is my chosen instrument to carry my
name before the Gentiles and their kings and
before the people of Israel. 16I will show him
how much he must suffer for my name."

17Then Ananias went to the house and entered it. Placing his hands on Saul, he said,
"Brother Saul, the Lord—Jesus, who appeared
to you on the road as you were coming here—
has sent me so that you may see again and be
filled with the Holy Spirit." 18Immediately,
something like scales fell from Saul's eyes,
and he could see again. He got up and was
baptized, 19and after taking some food, he re-
gained his strength.

Saul in Damascus and Jerusalem

Saul spent several days with the disciples in
Damascus. 20At once he began to preach in the
synagogues that Jesus is the Son of God. 21All
those who heard him were astonished and
asked, "Isn't he the man who raised havoc in
Jerusalem among those who call on this name?
And hasn't he come here to take them as prisoners to the chief priests?" 22Yet Saul grew
more and more powerful and baffled the Jews
living in Damascus by proving that Jesus is the
Christ.[a]

23After many days had gone by, the Jews
conspired to kill him, 24but Saul learned of
their plan. Day and night they kept close watch
on the city gates in order to kill him. 25But his
followers took him by night and lowered him
in a basket through an opening in the wall.

26When he came to Jerusalem, he tried to
join the disciples, but they were all afraid of
him, not believing that he really was a disciple.
27But Barnabas took him and brought him to
the apostles. He told them how Saul on his
journey had seen the Lord and that the Lord
had spoken to him, and how in Damascus he
had preached fearlessly in the name of Jesus.
28So Saul stayed with them and moved about
freely in Jerusalem, speaking boldly in the
name of the Lord. 29He talked and debated
with the Grecian Jews, but they tried to kill
him. 30When the brothers learned of this, they
took him down to Caesarea and sent him off to
Tarsus.

31Then the church throughout Judea, Galilee
and Samaria enjoyed a time of peace. It was
strengthened; and encouraged by the Holy
Spirit, it grew in numbers, living in the fear of
the Lord.

Aeneas and Dorcas

32As Peter traveled about the country, he
went to visit the saints in Lydda. 33There he
found a man named Aeneas, a paralytic who
had been bedridden for eight years. 34"Aeneas," Peter said to him, "Jesus Christ heals you.
Get up and take care of your mat." Immediately Aeneas got up. 35All those who lived in
Lydda and Sharon saw him and turned to the
Lord.

36In Joppa there was a disciple named Tabitha (which, when translated, is Dorcas[b]), who
was always doing good and helping the poor.
37About that time she became sick and died,
and her body was washed and placed in an
upstairs room. 38Lydda was near Joppa; so
when the disciples heard that Peter was in Lydda, they sent two men to him and urged him,
"Please come at once!"

39Peter went with them, and when he arrived
he was taken upstairs to the room. All the widows stood around him, crying and showing
him the robes and other clothing that Dorcas
had made while she was still with them.

40Peter sent them all out of the room; then
he got down on his knees and prayed. Turning
toward the dead woman, he said, "Tabitha, get
up." She opened her eyes, and seeing Peter she
sat up. 41He took her by the hand and helped
her to her feet. Then he called the believers and
the widows and presented her to them alive.
42This became known all over Joppa, and
many people believed in the Lord. 43Peter
stayed in Joppa for some time with a tanner
named Simon.

[a]22 Or *Messiah* [b]36 Both *Tabitha* (Aramaic) and *Dorcas* (Greek) mean *gazelle.*

Cornelius Calls for Peter

10 At Caesarea there was a man named
Cornelius, a centurion in what was
known as the Italian Regiment. 2He and all his
family were devout and God-fearing; he gave
generously to those in need and prayed to God
regularly. 3One day at about three in the afternoon he had a vision. He distinctly saw an
angel of God, who came to him and said, "Cornelius!"

4Cornelius stared at him in fear. "What is it,
Lord?" he asked.

The angel answered, "Your prayers and gifts
to the poor have come up as a memorial offering before God. 5Now send men to Joppa to
bring back a man named Simon who is called
Peter. 6He is staying with Simon the tanner,
whose house is by the sea."

7When the angel who spoke to him had
gone, Cornelius called two of his servants and
a devout soldier who was one of his attendants.
8He told them everything that had happened
and sent them to Joppa.

Peter's Vision

9About noon the following day as they were
on their journey and approaching the city, Peter went up on the roof to pray. 10He became
hungry and wanted something to eat, and while
the meal was being prepared, he fell into a
trance. 11He saw heaven opened and something like a large sheet being let down to earth
by its four corners. 12It contained all kinds of
four-footed animals, as well as reptiles of the
earth and birds of the air. 13Then a voice told
him, "Get up, Peter. Kill and eat."

14"Surely not, Lord!" Peter replied. "I have
never eaten anything impure or unclean."

15The voice spoke to him a second time,
"Do not call anything impure that God has
made clean."

16This happened three times, and immediately the sheet was taken back to heaven.

17While Peter was wondering about the
meaning of the vision, the men sent by Cornelius found out where Simon's house was and
stopped at the gate. 18They called out, asking
if Simon who was known as Peter was staying
there.

19While Peter was still thinking about the
vision, the Spirit said to him, "Simon, three[a]
men are looking for you. 20So get up and go
downstairs. Do not hesitate to go with them,
for I have sent them."

21Peter went down and said to the men, "I'm
the one you're looking for. Why have you
come?"

22The men replied, "We have come from
Cornelius the centurion. He is a righteous and
God-fearing man, who is respected by all the
Jewish people. A holy angel told him to have
you come to his house so that he could hear
what you have to say." 23Then Peter invited
the men into the house to be his guests.

Peter at Cornelius's House

The next day Peter started out with them,
and some of the brothers from Joppa went
along. 24The following day he arrived in Caesarea. Cornelius was expecting them and had
called together his relatives and close friends.
25As Peter entered the house, Cornelius met
him and fell at his feet in reverence. 26But
Peter made him get up. "Stand up," he said, "I
am only a man myself."

27Talking with him, Peter went inside and
found a large gathering of people. 28He said to
them: "You are well aware that it is against our
law for a Jew to associate with a Gentile or
visit him. But God has shown me that I should
not call any man impure or unclean. 29So when
I was sent for, I came without raising any ob-
jection. May I ask why you sent for me?"

30Cornelius answered: "Four days ago I was
in my house praying at this hour, at three in the
afternoon. Suddenly a man in shining clothes
stood before me 31and said, 'Cornelius, God
has heard your prayer and remembered your
gifts to the poor. 32Send to Joppa for Simon
who is called Peter. He is a guest in the home
of Simon the tanner, who lives by the sea.'
33So I sent for you immediately, and it was
good of you to come. Now we are all here in
the presence of God to listen to everything the
Lord has commanded you to tell us."

34Then Peter began to speak: "I now realize
how true it is that God does not show favoritism 35but accepts men from every nation who
fear him and do what is right. 36You know the
message God sent to the people of Israel, telling the good news of peace through Jesus
Christ, who is Lord of all. 37You know what
has happened throughout Judea, beginning in
Galilee after the baptism that John preached—
38how God anointed Jesus of Nazareth with
the Holy Spirit and power, and how he went
around doing good and healing all who were
under the power of the devil, because God was
with him.

39"We are witnesses of everything he did in
the country of the Jews and in Jerusalem. They
killed him by hanging him on a tree, 40but God
raised him from the dead on the third day and
caused him to be seen. 41He was not seen by
all the people, but by witnesses whom God had
already chosen—by us who ate and drank with
him after he rose from the dead. 42He commanded us to preach to the people and to testify that he is the one whom God appointed as
judge of the living and the dead. 43All the
prophets testify about him that everyone who
believes in him receives forgiveness of sins
through his name."

44While Peter was still speaking these
words, the Holy Spirit came on all who heard
the message. 45The circumcised believers who
had come with Peter were astonished that the
gift of the Holy Spirit had been poured out
even on the Gentiles. 46For they heard them
speaking in tongues[b] and praising God.

[a] *19* One early manuscript *two*; other manuscripts do not have the number. [b] *46* Or *other languages*

Then Peter said, 47"Can anyone keep these
people from being baptized with water? They
have received the Holy Spirit just as we have."
48So he ordered that they be baptized in the
name of Jesus Christ. Then they asked Peter to
stay with them for a few days.

Peter Explains His Actions

11 The apostles and the brothers throughout Judea heard that the Gentiles also
had received the word of God. 2So when Peter
went up to Jerusalem, the circumcised believers criticized him 3and said, "You went into
the house of uncircumcised men and ate with
them."

4Peter began and explained everything to
them precisely as it had happened: 5"I was in
the city of Joppa praying, and in a trance I saw
a vision. I saw something like a large sheet
being let down from heaven by its four corners, and it came down to where I was. 6I
looked into it and saw four-footed animals of
the earth, wild beasts, reptiles, and birds of the
air. 7Then I heard a voice telling me, 'Get up,
Peter. Kill and eat.'

8"I replied, 'Surely not, Lord! Nothing impure or unclean has ever entered my mouth.'

9"The voice spoke from heaven a second
time, 'Do not call anything impure that God
has made clean.' 10This happened three times,
and then it was all pulled up to heaven again.

11"Right then three men who had been sent
to me from Caesarea stopped at the house
where I was staying. 12The Spirit told me to
have no hesitation about going with them.
These six brothers also went with me, and we
entered the man's house. 13He told us how he
had seen an angel appear in his house and say,
'Send to Joppa for Simon who is called Peter.
14He will bring you a message through which
you and all your household will be saved.'

15"As I began to speak, the Holy Spirit came
on them as he had come on us at the beginning.
16Then I remembered what the Lord had said:
'John baptized with[a] water, but you will be
baptized with the Holy Spirit.' 17So if God
gave them the same gift as he gave us, who
believed in the Lord Jesus Christ, who was I to
think that I could oppose God?"

18When they heard this, they had no further
objections and praised God, saying, "So then,
God has granted even the Gentiles repentance
unto life."

The Church in Antioch

19Now those who had been scattered by the
persecution in connection with Stephen traveled as far as Phoenicia, Cyprus and Antioch,
telling the message only to Jews. 20Some of
them, however, men from Cyprus and Cyrene,
went to Antioch and began to speak to Greeks
also, telling them the good news about the
Lord Jesus. 21The Lord's hand was with them,
and a great number of people believed and
turned to the Lord.

22News of this reached the ears of the
church at Jerusalem, and they sent Barnabas to
Antioch. 23When he arrived and saw the evidence of the grace of God, he was glad and
encouraged them all to remain true to the Lord
with all their hearts. 24He was a good man, full
of the Holy Spirit and faith, and a great number
of people were brought to the Lord.

25Then Barnabas went to Tarsus to look for
Saul, 26and when he found him, he brought
him to Antioch. So for a whole year Barnabas
and Saul met with the church and taught great
numbers of people. The disciples were called
Christians first at Antioch.

27During this time some prophets came
down from Jerusalem to Antioch. 28One of
them, named Agabus, stood up and through the
Spirit predicted that a severe famine would
spread over the entire Roman world. (This
happened during the reign of Claudius.) 29The
disciples, each according to his ability, decided
to provide help for the brothers living in Judea.
30This they did, sending their gift to the elders
by Barnabas and Saul.

Peter's Miraculous Escape From Prison

12 It was about this time that King Herod
arrested some who belonged to the
church, intending to persecute them. 2He had
James, the brother of John, put to death with
the sword. 3When he saw that this pleased the
Jews, he proceeded to seize Peter also. This
happened during the Feast of Unleavened
Bread. 4After arresting him, he put him in prison, handing him over to be guarded by four
squads of four soldiers each. Herod intended to
bring him out for public trial after the Passover.

5So Peter was kept in prison, but the church
was earnestly praying to God for him.

6The night before Herod was to bring him to
trial, Peter was sleeping between two soldiers,
bound with two chains, and sentries stood
guard at the entrance. 7Suddenly an angel of
the Lord appeared and a light shone in the cell.
He struck Peter on the side and woke him up.
"Quick, get up!" he said, and the chains fell off
Peter's wrists.

8Then the angel said to him, "Put on your
clothes and sandals." And Peter did so. "Wrap
your cloak around you and follow me," the
angel told him. 9Peter followed him out of the
prison, but he had no idea that what the angel
was doing was really happening; he thought he
was seeing a vision. 10They passed the first
and second guards and came to the iron gate
leading to the city. It opened for them by itself,
and they went through it. When they had
walked the length of one street, suddenly the
angel left him.

11Then Peter came to himself and said,
"Now I know without a doubt that the Lord
sent his angel and rescued me from Herod's

[a] *16* Or *in*

clutches and from everything the Jewish people were anticipating."

12When this had dawned on him, he went to the house of Mary the mother of John, also called Mark, where many people had gathered and were praying. 13Peter knocked at the outer entrance, and a servant girl named Rhoda came to answer the door. 14When she recognized Peter's voice, she was so overjoyed she ran back without opening it and exclaimed, "Peter is at the door!"

15"You're out of your mind," they told her. When she kept insisting that it was so, they said, "It must be his angel."

16But Peter kept on knocking, and when they opened the door and saw him, they were astonished. 17Peter motioned with his hand for them to be quiet and described how the Lord had brought him out of prison. "Tell James and the brothers about this," he said, and then he left for another place.

18In the morning, there was no small commotion among the soldiers as to what had become of Peter. 19After Herod had a thorough search made for him and did not find him, he cross-examined the guards and ordered that they be executed.

Herod's Death

Then Herod went from Judea to Caesarea and stayed there a while. 20He had been quarreling with the people of Tyre and Sidon; they now joined together and sought an audience with him. Having secured the support of Blastus, a trusted personal servant of the king, they asked for peace, because they depended on the king's country for their food supply.

21On the appointed day Herod, wearing his royal robes, sat on his throne and delivered a public address to the people. 22They shouted, "This is the voice of a god, not of a man." 23Immediately, because Herod did not give praise to God, an angel of the Lord struck him down, and he was eaten by worms and died.

24But the word of God continued to increase and spread.

25When Barnabas and Saul had finished their mission, they returned from[a] Jerusalem, taking with them John, also called Mark.

Barnabas and Saul Sent Off

13 In the church at Antioch there were prophets and teachers: Barnabas, Simeon called Niger, Lucius of Cyrene, Manaen (who had been brought up with Herod the tetrarch) and Saul. 2While they were worshiping the Lord and fasting, the Holy Spirit said, "Set apart for me Barnabas and Saul for the work to which I have called them." 3So after they had fasted and prayed, they placed their hands on them and sent them off.

On Cyprus

4The two of them, sent on their way by the Holy Spirit, went down to Seleucia and sailed from there to Cyprus. 5When they arrived at Salamis, they proclaimed the word of God in the Jewish synagogues. John was with them as their helper.

6They traveled through the whole island until they came to Paphos. There they met a Jewish sorcerer and false prophet named Bar-Jesus, 7who was an attendant of the proconsul, Sergius Paulus. The proconsul, an intelligent man, sent for Barnabas and Saul because he wanted to hear the word of God. 8But Elymas the sorcerer (for that is what his name means) opposed them and tried to turn the proconsul from the faith. 9Then Saul, who was also called Paul, filled with the Holy Spirit, looked straight at Elymas and said, 10"You are a child of the devil and an enemy of everything that is right! You are full of all kinds of deceit and trickery. Will you never stop perverting the right ways of the Lord? 11Now the hand of the Lord is against you. You are going to be blind, and for a time you will be unable to see the light of the sun."

Immediately mist and darkness came over him, and he groped about, seeking someone to lead him by the hand. 12When the proconsul saw what had happened, he believed, for he was amazed at the teaching about the Lord.

In Pisidian Antioch

13From Paphos, Paul and his companions sailed to Perga in Pamphylia, where John left them to return to Jerusalem. 14From Perga they went on to Pisidian Antioch. On the Sabbath they entered the synagogue and sat down. 15After the reading from the Law and the Prophets, the synagogue rulers sent word to them, saying, "Brothers, if you have a message of encouragement for the people, please speak."

16Standing up, Paul motioned with his hand and said: "Men of Israel and you Gentiles who worship God, listen to me! 17The God of the people of Israel chose our fathers; he made the people prosper during their stay in Egypt, with mighty power he led them out of that country, 18he endured their conduct[b] for about forty years in the desert, 19he overthrew seven nations in Canaan and gave their land to his people as their inheritance. 20All this took about 450 years.

"After this, God gave them judges until the time of Samuel the prophet. 21Then the people asked for a king, and he gave them Saul son of Kish, of the tribe of Benjamin, who ruled forty years. 22After removing Saul, he made David their king. He testified concerning him: 'I have found David son of Jesse a man after my own heart; he will do everything I want him to do.'

23"From this man's descendants God has brought to Israel the Savior Jesus, as he promised. 24Before the coming of Jesus, John preached repentance and baptism to all the people of Israel. 25As John was completing his work, he said: 'Who do you think I am? I am

[a]25 Some manuscripts *to* [b]18 Some manuscripts *and cared for them*

not that one. No, but he is coming after me,
whose sandals I am not worthy to untie.’
26 “Brothers, children of Abraham, and you
God-fearing Gentiles, it is to us that this message of salvation has been sent. 27 The people
of Jerusalem and their rulers did not recognize
Jesus, yet in condemning him they fulfilled the
words of the prophets that are read every Sabbath. 28 Though they found no proper ground
for a death sentence, they asked Pilate to have
him executed. 29 When they had carried out all
that was written about him, they took him
down from the tree and laid him in a tomb.
30 But God raised him from the dead, 31 and for
many days he was seen by those who had traveled with him from Galilee to Jerusalem. They
are now his witnesses to our people.
32 “We tell you the good news: What God
promised our fathers 33 he has fulfilled for us,
their children, by raising up Jesus. As it is
written in the second Psalm:

> “ ‘You are my Son;
> today I have become your Father.[a]’[b]

34 The fact that God raised him from the dead,
never to decay, is stated in these words:

> “ ‘I will give you the holy and sure
> blessings promised to David.’[c]

35 So it is stated elsewhere:

> “ ‘You will not let your Holy One see
> decay.’[d]

36 “For when David had served God’s purpose in his own generation, he fell asleep; he
was buried with his fathers and his body decayed. 37 But the one whom God raised from
the dead did not see decay.
38 “Therefore, my brothers, I want you to
know that through Jesus the forgiveness of sins
is proclaimed to you. 39 Through him everyone
who believes is justified from everything you
could not be justified from by the law of Moses. 40 Take care that what the prophets have
said does not happen to you:

> 41 “ ‘Look, you scoffers,
> wonder and perish,
> for I am going to do something in your
> days
> that you would never believe,
> even if someone told you.’[e]”

42 As Paul and Barnabas were leaving the
synagogue, the people invited them to speak
further about these things on the next Sabbath.
43 When the congregation was dismissed, many
of the Jews and devout converts to Judaism
followed Paul and Barnabas, who talked with
them and urged them to continue in the grace
of God.
44 On the next Sabbath almost the whole city
gathered to hear the word of the Lord. 45 When
the Jews saw the crowds, they were filled with
jealousy and talked abusively against what
Paul was saying.
46 Then Paul and Barnabas answered them
boldly: “We had to speak the word of God to
you first. Since you reject it and do not consider yourselves worthy of eternal life, we now
turn to the Gentiles. 47 For this is what the Lord
has commanded us:

> “ ‘I have made you[f] a light for the
> Gentiles,
> that you[f] may bring salvation to the
> ends of the earth.’[g]”

48 When the Gentiles heard this, they were
glad and honored the word of the Lord; and all
who were appointed for eternal life believed.
49 The word of the Lord spread through the
whole region. 50 But the Jews incited the God-
fearing women of high standing and the leading men of the city. They stirred up persecution against Paul and Barnabas, and expelled
them from their region. 51 So they shook the
dust from their feet in protest against them and
went to Iconium. 52 And the disciples were
filled with joy and with the Holy Spirit.

In Iconium

14 At Iconium Paul and Barnabas went as
usual into the Jewish synagogue. There
they spoke so effectively that a great number
of Jews and Gentiles believed. 2 But the Jews
who refused to believe stirred up the Gentiles
and poisoned their minds against the brothers.
3 So Paul and Barnabas spent considerable time
there, speaking boldly for the Lord, who confirmed the message of his grace by enabling
them to do miraculous signs and wonders.
4 The people of the city were divided; some
sided with the Jews, others with the apostles.
5 There was a plot afoot among the Gentiles
and Jews, together with their leaders, to mistreat them and stone them. 6 But they found out
about it and fled to the Lycaonian cities of
Lystra and Derbe and to the surrounding country, 7 where they continued to preach the good
news.

In Lystra and Derbe

8 In Lystra there sat a man crippled in his
feet, who was lame from birth and had never
walked. 9 He listened to Paul as he was speaking. Paul looked directly at him, saw that he
had faith to be healed 10 and called out, “Stand
up on your feet!” At that, the man jumped up
and began to walk.
11 When the crowd saw what Paul had done,
they shouted in the Lycaonian language, “The
gods have come down to us in human form!”
12 Barnabas they called Zeus, and Paul they
called Hermes because he was the chief speaker. 13 The priest of Zeus, whose temple was just
outside the city, brought bulls and wreaths to
the city gates because he and the crowd wanted
to offer sacrifices to them.
14 But when the apostles Barnabas and Paul

[a] *33* Or *have begotten you* [b] *33* Psalm 2:7 [c] *34* Isaiah 55:3 [d] *35* Psalm 16:10 [e] *41* Hab. 1:5
[f] *47* The Greek is singular. [g] *47* Isaiah 49:6

heard of this, they tore their clothes and rushed out into the crowd, shouting: 15"Men, why are you doing this? We too are only men, human like you. We are bringing you good news, telling you to turn from these worthless things to the living God, who made heaven and earth and sea and everything in them. 16In the past, he let all nations go their own way. 17Yet he has not left himself without testimony: He has shown kindness by giving you rain from heaven and crops in their seasons; he provides you with plenty of food and fills your hearts with joy." 18Even with these words, they had difficulty keeping the crowd from sacrificing to them.

19Then some Jews came from Antioch and Iconium and won the crowd over. They stoned Paul and dragged him outside the city, thinking he was dead. 20But after the disciples had gathered around him, he got up and went back into the city. The next day he and Barnabas left for Derbe.

The Return to Antioch in Syria

21They preached the good news in that city and won a large number of disciples. Then they returned to Lystra, Iconium and Antioch, 22strengthening the disciples and encouraging them to remain true to the faith. "We must go through many hardships to enter the kingdom of God," they said. 23Paul and Barnabas appointed elders[a] for them in each church and, with prayer and fasting, committed them to the Lord, in whom they had put their trust. 24After going through Pisidia, they came into Pamphylia, 25and when they had preached the word in Perga, they went down to Attalia.

26From Attalia they sailed back to Antioch, where they had been committed to the grace of God for the work they had now completed. 27On arriving there, they gathered the church together and reported all that God had done through them and how he had opened the door of faith to the Gentiles. 28And they stayed there a long time with the disciples.

The Council at Jerusalem

15 Some men came down from Judea to Antioch and were teaching the brothers: "Unless you are circumcised, according to the custom taught by Moses, you cannot be saved." 2This brought Paul and Barnabas into sharp dispute and debate with them. So Paul and Barnabas were appointed, along with some other believers, to go up to Jerusalem to see the apostles and elders about this question. 3The church sent them on their way, and as they traveled through Phoenicia and Samaria, they told how the Gentiles had been converted. This news made all the brothers very glad. 4When they came to Jerusalem, they were welcomed by the church and the apostles and elders, to whom they reported everything God had done through them.

5Then some of the believers who belonged to the party of the Pharisees stood up and said, "The Gentiles must be circumcised and required to obey the law of Moses."

6The apostles and elders met to consider this question. 7After much discussion, Peter got up and addressed them: "Brothers, you know that some time ago God made a choice among you that the Gentiles might hear from my lips the message of the gospel and believe. 8God, who knows the heart, showed that he accepted them by giving the Holy Spirit to them, just as he did to us. 9He made no distinction between us and them, for he purified their hearts by faith. 10Now then, why do you try to test God by putting on the necks of the disciples a yoke that neither we nor our fathers have been able to bear? 11No! We believe it is through the grace of our Lord Jesus that we are saved, just as they are."

12The whole assembly became silent as they listened to Barnabas and Paul telling about the miraculous signs and wonders God had done among the Gentiles through them. 13When they finished, James spoke up: "Brothers, listen to me. 14Simon[b] has described to us how God at first showed his concern by taking from the Gentiles a people for himself. 15The words of the prophets are in agreement with this, as it is written:

16" 'After this I will return
  and rebuild David's fallen tent.
Its ruins I will rebuild,
  and I will restore it,
17that the remnant of men may seek the
    Lord,
  and all the Gentiles who bear my name,
says the Lord, who does these things'[c]
18 that have been known for ages.[d]

19"It is my judgment, therefore, that we should not make it difficult for the Gentiles who are turning to God. 20Instead we should write to them, telling them to abstain from food polluted by idols, from sexual immorality, from the meat of strangled animals and from blood. 21For Moses has been preached in every city from the earliest times and is read in the synagogues on every Sabbath."

The Council's Letter to Gentile Believers

22Then the apostles and elders, with the whole church, decided to choose some of their own men and send them to Antioch with Paul and Barnabas. They chose Judas (called Barsabbas) and Silas, two men who were leaders among the brothers. 23With them they sent the following letter:

The apostles and elders, your brothers,

To the Gentile believers in Antioch, Syria and Cilicia:

[a]*23* Or *Barnabas ordained elders*; or *Barnabas had elders elected* [b]*14* Greek *Simeon*, a variant of *Simon*; that is, Peter [c]*17* Amos 9:11,12 [d]*17,18* Some manuscripts *things'—/ 18known to the Lord for ages is his work*

Greetings.

24We have heard that some went out from us without our authorization and disturbed you, troubling your minds by what they said. 25So we all agreed to choose some men and send them to you with our dear friends Barnabas and Paul— 26men who have risked their lives for the name of our Lord Jesus Christ. 27Therefore we are sending Judas and Silas to confirm by word of mouth what we are writing. 28It seemed good to the Holy Spirit and to us not to burden you with anything beyond the following requirements: 29You are to abstain from food sacrificed to idols, from blood, from the meat of strangled animals and from sexual immorality. You will do well to avoid these things.

Farewell.

30The men were sent off and went down to Antioch, where they gathered the church together and delivered the letter. 31The people read it and were glad for its encouraging message. 32Judas and Silas, who themselves were prophets, said much to encourage and strengthen the brothers. 33After spending some time there, they were sent off by the brothers with the blessing of peace to return to those who had sent them.[a] 35But Paul and Barnabas remained in Antioch, where they and many others taught and preached the word of the Lord.

Disagreement Between Paul and Barnabas

36Some time later Paul said to Barnabas, "Let us go back and visit the brothers in all the towns where we preached the word of the Lord and see how they are doing." 37Barnabas wanted to take John, also called Mark, with them, 38but Paul did not think it wise to take him, because he had deserted them in Pamphylia and had not continued with them in the work. 39They had such a sharp disagreement that they parted company. Barnabas took Mark and sailed for Cyprus, 40but Paul chose Silas and left, commended by the brothers to the grace of the Lord. 41He went through Syria and Cilicia, strengthening the churches.

Timothy Joins Paul and Silas

16 He came to Derbe and then to Lystra, where a disciple named Timothy lived, whose mother was a Jewess and a believer, but whose father was a Greek. 2The brothers at Lystra and Iconium spoke well of him. 3Paul wanted to take him along on the journey, so he circumcised him because of the Jews who lived in that area, for they all knew that his father was a Greek. 4As they traveled from town to town, they delivered the decisions reached by the apostles and elders in Jerusalem for the people to obey. 5So the churches were strengthened in the faith and grew daily in numbers.

Paul's Vision of the Man of Macedonia

6Paul and his companions traveled throughout the region of Phrygia and Galatia, having been kept by the Holy Spirit from preaching the word in the province of Asia. 7When they came to the border of Mysia, they tried to enter Bithynia, but the Spirit of Jesus would not allow them to. 8So they passed by Mysia and went down to Troas. 9During the night Paul had a vision of a man of Macedonia standing and begging him, "Come over to Macedonia and help us." 10After Paul had seen the vision, we got ready at once to leave for Macedonia, concluding that God had called us to preach the gospel to them.

Lydia's Conversion in Philippi

11From Troas we put out to sea and sailed straight for Samothrace, and the next day on to Neapolis. 12From there we traveled to Philippi, a Roman colony and the leading city of that district of Macedonia. And we stayed there several days.

13On the Sabbath we went outside the city gate to the river, where we expected to find a place of prayer. We sat down and began to speak to the women who had gathered there. 14One of those listening was a woman named Lydia, a dealer in purple cloth from the city of Thyatira, who was a worshiper of God. The Lord opened her heart to respond to Paul's message. 15When she and the members of her household were baptized, she invited us to her home. "If you consider me a believer in the Lord," she said, "come and stay at my house." And she persuaded us.

Paul and Silas in Prison

16Once when we were going to the place of prayer, we were met by a slave girl who had a spirit by which she predicted the future. She earned a great deal of money for her owners by fortune-telling. 17This girl followed Paul and the rest of us, shouting, "These men are servants of the Most High God, who are telling you the way to be saved." 18She kept this up for many days. Finally Paul became so troubled that he turned around and said to the spirit, "In the name of Jesus Christ I command you to come out of her!" At that moment the spirit left her.

19When the owners of the slave girl realized that their hope of making money was gone, they seized Paul and Silas and dragged them into the marketplace to face the authorities. 20They brought them before the magistrates and said, "These men are Jews, and are throwing our city into an uproar 21by advocating customs unlawful for us Romans to accept or practice."

22The crowd joined in the attack against Paul and Silas, and the magistrates ordered

[a]33 Some manuscripts *them, 34but Silas decided to remain there*

them to be stripped and beaten. 23After they
had been severely flogged, they were thrown
into prison, and the jailer was commanded to
guard them carefully. 24Upon receiving such
orders, he put them in the inner cell and fastened their feet in the stocks.

25About midnight Paul and Silas were praying and singing hymns to God, and the other
prisoners were listening to them. 26Suddenly
there was such a violent earthquake that the
foundations of the prison were shaken. At once
all the prison doors flew open, and everybody's chains came loose. 27The jailer woke
up, and when he saw the prison doors open, he
drew his sword and was about to kill himself
because he thought the prisoners had escaped.
28But Paul shouted, "Don't harm yourself! We
are all here!"

29The jailer called for lights, rushed in and
fell trembling before Paul and Silas. 30He then
brought them out and asked, "Sirs, what must
I do to be saved?"

31They replied, "Believe in the Lord Jesus,
and you will be saved—you and your household." 32Then they spoke the word of the Lord
to him and to all the others in his house. 33At
that hour of the night the jailer took them and
washed their wounds; then immediately he and
all his family were baptized. 34The jailer
brought them into his house and set a meal
before them; he was filled with joy because he
had come to believe in God—he and his whole
family.

35When it was daylight, the magistrates sent
their officers to the jailer with the order: "Release those men." 36The jailer told Paul, "The
magistrates have ordered that you and Silas be
released. Now you can leave. Go in peace."

37But Paul said to the officers: "They beat us
publicly without a trial, even though we are
Roman citizens, and threw us into prison. And
now do they want to get rid of us quietly? No!
Let them come themselves and escort us out."

38The officers reported this to the magistrates, and when they heard that Paul and Silas
were Roman citizens, they were alarmed.
39They came to appease them and escorted
them from the prison, requesting them to leave
the city. 40After Paul and Silas came out of the
prison, they went to Lydia's house, where they
met with the brothers and encouraged them.
Then they left.

In Thessalonica

17 When they had passed through Am-
phipolis and Apollonia, they came to
Thessalonica, where there was a Jewish synagogue. 2As his custom was, Paul went into the
synagogue, and on three Sabbath days he reasoned with them from the Scriptures, 3explain-
ing and proving that the Christ[a] had to suffer
and rise from the dead. "This Jesus I am proclaiming to you is the Christ,[a]" he said. 4Some
of the Jews were persuaded and joined Paul
and Silas, as did a large number of God-
fearing Greeks and not a few prominent
women.

5But the Jews were jealous; so they rounded
up some bad characters from the marketplace,
formed a mob and started a riot in the city.
They rushed to Jason's house in search of Paul
and Silas in order to bring them out to the
crowd.[b] 6But when they did not find them,
they dragged Jason and some other brothers
before the city officials, shouting: "These men
who have caused trouble all over the world
have now come here, 7and Jason has welcomed them into his house. They are all defying Caesar's decrees, saying that there is another king, one called Jesus." 8When they
heard this, the crowd and the city officials
were thrown into turmoil. 9Then they made
Jason and the others post bond and let
them go.

In Berea

10As soon as it was night, the brothers sent
Paul and Silas away to Berea. On arriving
there, they went to the Jewish synagogue.
11Now the Bereans were of more noble character than the Thessalonians, for they received
the message with great eagerness and examined the Scriptures every day to see if what
Paul said was true. 12Many of the Jews believed, as did also a number of prominent
Greek women and many Greek men.

13When the Jews in Thessalonica learned
that Paul was preaching the word of God at
Berea, they went there too, agitating the
crowds and stirring them up. 14The brothers
immediately sent Paul to the coast, but Silas
and Timothy stayed at Berea. 15The men who
escorted Paul brought him to Athens and then
left with instructions for Silas and Timothy to
join him as soon as possible.

In Athens

16While Paul was waiting for them in Athens, he was greatly distressed to see that the
city was full of idols. 17So he reasoned in the
synagogue with the Jews and the God-fearing
Greeks, as well as in the marketplace day by
day with those who happened to be there. 18A
group of Epicurean and Stoic philosophers began to dispute with him. Some of them asked,
"What is this babbler trying to say?" Others
remarked, "He seems to be advocating foreign
gods." They said this because Paul was preaching the good news about Jesus and the resurrection. 19Then they took him and brought him
to a meeting of the Areopagus, where they said
to him, "May we know what this new teaching
is that you are presenting? 20You are bringing
some strange ideas to our ears, and we want to
know what they mean." 21(All the Athenians
and the foreigners who lived there spent their
time doing nothing but talking about and listening to the latest ideas.)

22Paul then stood up in the meeting of the
Areopagus and said: "Men of Athens! I see

[a]3 Or *Messiah* [b]5 Or *the assembly of the people*

that in every way you are very religious. 23For
as I walked around and looked carefully at
your objects of worship, I even found an altar
with this inscription: TO AN UNKNOWN GOD.
Now what you worship as something unknown
I am going to proclaim to you.
24"The God who made the world and everything in it is the Lord of heaven and earth and
does not live in temples built by hands. 25And
he is not served by human hands, as if he needed anything, because he himself gives all men
life and breath and everything else. 26From one
man he made every nation of men, that they
should inhabit the whole earth; and he determined the times set for them and the exact
places where they should live. 27God did this
so that men would seek him and perhaps reach
out for him and find him, though he is not far
from each one of us. 28'For in him we live and
move and have our being.' As some of your
own poets have said, 'We are his offspring.'
29"Therefore since we are God's offspring,
we should not think that the divine being is
like gold or silver or stone—an image made by
man's design and skill. 30In the past God overlooked such ignorance, but now he commands
all people everywhere to repent. 31For he has
set a day when he will judge the world with
justice by the man he has appointed. He has
given proof of this to all men by raising him
from the dead."
32When they heard about the resurrection of
the dead, some of them sneered, but others
said, "We want to hear you again on this subject." 33At that, Paul left the Council. 34A few
men became followers of Paul and believed.
Among them was Dionysius, a member of the
Areopagus, also a woman named Damaris, and
a number of others.

In Corinth

18 After this, Paul left Athens and went to
Corinth. 2There he met a Jew named
Aquila, a native of Pontus, who had recently
come from Italy with his wife Priscilla, because Claudius had ordered all the Jews to
leave Rome. Paul went to see them, 3and because he was a tentmaker as they were, he
stayed and worked with them. 4Every Sabbath
he reasoned in the synagogue, trying to persuade Jews and Greeks.
5When Silas and Timothy came from Macedonia, Paul devoted himself exclusively to
preaching, testifying to the Jews that Jesus was
the Christ.[a] 6But when the Jews opposed Paul
and became abusive, he shook out his clothes
in protest and said to them, "Your blood be on
your own heads! I am clear of my responsibility. From now on I will go to the Gentiles."
7Then Paul left the synagogue and went next
door to the house of Titius Justus, a worshiper
of God. 8Crispus, the synagogue ruler, and his
entire household believed in the Lord; and
many of the Corinthians who heard him believed and were baptized.
9One night the Lord spoke to Paul in a vision: "Do not be afraid; keep on speaking, do
not be silent. 10For I am with you, and no one
is going to attack and harm you, because I have
many people in this city." 11So Paul stayed for
a year and a half, teaching them the word of
God.
12While Gallio was proconsul of Achaia, the
Jews made a united attack on Paul and brought
him into court. 13"This man," they charged, "is
persuading the people to worship God in ways
contrary to the law."
14Just as Paul was about to speak, Gallio
said to the Jews, "If you Jews were making a
complaint about some misdemeanor or serious
crime, it would be reasonable for me to listen
to you. 15But since it involves questions about
words and names and your own law—settle
the matter yourselves. I will not be a judge of
such things." 16So he had them ejected from
the court. 17Then they all turned on Sosthenes
the synagogue ruler and beat him in front of
the court. But Gallio showed no concern whatever.

Priscilla, Aquila and Apollos

18Paul stayed on in Corinth for some time.
Then he left the brothers and sailed for Syria,
accompanied by Priscilla and Aquila. Before
he sailed, he had his hair cut off at Cenchrea
because of a vow he had taken. 19They arrived
at Ephesus, where Paul left Priscilla and Aquila. He himself went into the synagogue and
reasoned with the Jews. 20When they asked
him to spend more time with them, he de-
clined. 21But as he left, he promised, "I will
come back if it is God's will." Then he set sail
from Ephesus. 22When he landed at Caesarea,
he went up and greeted the church and then
went down to Antioch.
23After spending some time in Antioch, Paul
set out from there and traveled from place to
place throughout the region of Galatia and
Phrygia, strengthening all the disciples.
24Meanwhile a Jew named Apollos, a native
of Alexandria, came to Ephesus. He was a
learned man, with a thorough knowledge of the
Scriptures. 25He had been instructed in the way
of the Lord, and he spoke with great fervor[b]
and taught about Jesus accurately, though he
knew only the baptism of John. 26He began to
speak boldly in the synagogue. When Priscilla
and Aquila heard him, they invited him to their
home and explained to him the way of God
more adequately.
27When Apollos wanted to go to Achaia, the
brothers encouraged him and wrote to the disciples there to welcome him. On arriving, he
was a great help to those who by grace had
believed. 28For he vigorously refuted the Jews
in public debate, proving from the Scriptures
that Jesus was the Christ.

[a]5 Or *Messiah;* also in verse 28 [b]25 Or *with fervor in the Spirit*

Paul in Ephesus

19 While Apollos was at Corinth, Paul took the road through the interior and arrived at Ephesus. There he found some disciples 2and asked them, "Did you receive the Holy Spirit when[a] you believed?"

They answered, "No, we have not even heard that there is a Holy Spirit."

3So Paul asked, "Then what baptism did you receive?"

"John's baptism," they replied.

4Paul said, "John's baptism was a baptism of repentance. He told the people to believe in the one coming after him, that is, in Jesus." 5On hearing this, they were baptized into[b] the name of the Lord Jesus. 6When Paul placed his hands on them, the Holy Spirit came on them, and they spoke in tongues[c] and prophesied. 7There were about twelve men in all.

8Paul entered the synagogue and spoke boldly there for three months, arguing persuasively about the kingdom of God. 9But some of them became obstinate; they refused to believe and publicly maligned the Way. So Paul left them. He took the disciples with him and had discussions daily in the lecture hall of Tyrannus. 10This went on for two years, so that all the Jews and Greeks who lived in the province of Asia heard the word of the Lord.

11God did extraordinary miracles through Paul, 12so that even handkerchiefs and aprons that had touched him were taken to the sick, and their illnesses were cured and the evil spirits left them.

13Some Jews who went around driving out evil spirits tried to invoke the name of the Lord Jesus over those who were demon-possessed. They would say, "In the name of Jesus, whom Paul preaches, I command you to come out." 14Seven sons of Sceva, a Jewish chief priest, were doing this. 15⌊One day⌋ the evil spirit answered them, "Jesus I know, and I know about Paul, but who are you?" 16Then the man who had the evil spirit jumped on them and overpowered them all. He gave them such a beating that they ran out of the house naked and bleeding.

17When this became known to the Jews and Greeks living in Ephesus, they were all seized with fear, and the name of the Lord Jesus was held in high honor. 18Many of those who believed now came and openly confessed their evil deeds. 19A number who had practiced sorcery brought their scrolls together and burned them publicly. When they calculated the value of the scrolls, the total came to fifty thousand drachmas.[d] 20In this way the word of the Lord spread widely and grew in power.

21After all this had happened, Paul decided to go to Jerusalem, passing through Macedonia and Achaia. "After I have been there," he said, "I must visit Rome also." 22He sent two of his helpers, Timothy and Erastus, to Macedonia, while he stayed in the province of Asia a little longer.

The Riot in Ephesus

23About that time there arose a great disturbance about the Way. 24A silversmith named Demetrius, who made silver shrines of Artemis, brought in no little business for the craftsmen. 25He called them together, along with the workmen in related trades, and said: "Men, you know we receive a good income from this business. 26And you see and hear how this fellow Paul has convinced and led astray large numbers of people here in Ephesus and in practically the whole province of Asia. He says that man-made gods are no gods at all. 27There is danger not only that our trade will lose its good name, but also that the temple of the great goddess Artemis will be discredited, and the goddess herself, who is worshiped throughout the province of Asia and the world, will be robbed of her divine majesty."

28When they heard this, they were furious and began shouting: "Great is Artemis of the Ephesians!" 29Soon the whole city was in an uproar. The people seized Gaius and Aristarchus, Paul's traveling companions from Macedonia, and rushed as one man into the theater. 30Paul wanted to appear before the crowd, but the disciples would not let him. 31Even some of the officials of the province, friends of Paul, sent him a message begging him not to venture into the theater.

32The assembly was in confusion: Some were shouting one thing, some another. Most of the people did not even know why they were there. 33The Jews pushed Alexander to the front, and some of the crowd shouted instructions to him. He motioned for silence in order to make a defense before the people. 34But when they realized he was a Jew, they all shouted in unison for about two hours: "Great is Artemis of the Ephesians!"

35The city clerk quieted the crowd and said: "Men of Ephesus, doesn't all the world know that the city of Ephesus is the guardian of the temple of the great Artemis and of her image, which fell from heaven? 36Therefore, since these facts are undeniable, you ought to be quiet and not do anything rash. 37You have brought these men here, though they have neither robbed temples nor blasphemed our goddess. 38If, then, Demetrius and his fellow craftsmen have a grievance against anybody, the courts are open and there are proconsuls. They can press charges. 39If there is anything further you want to bring up, it must be settled in a legal assembly. 40As it is, we are in danger of being charged with rioting because of today's events. In that case we would not be able to account for this commotion, since there is no reason for it." 41After he had said this, he dismissed the assembly.

[a]2 Or *after* [b]5 Or *in* [c]6 Or *other languages* [d]19 A drachma was a silver coin worth about a day's wages.

Through Macedonia and Greece

20 When the uproar had ended, Paul sent
for the disciples and, after encouraging
them, said good-by and set out for Macedonia.
2He traveled through that area, speaking many
words of encouragement to the people, and finally arrived in Greece, 3where he stayed three
months. Because the Jews made a plot against
him just as he was about to sail for Syria, he
decided to go back through Macedonia. 4He
was accompanied by Sopater son of Pyrrhus
from Berea, Aristarchus and Secundus from
Thessalonica, Gaius from Derbe, Timothy
also, and Tychicus and Trophimus from the
province of Asia. 5These men went on ahead
and waited for us at Troas. 6But we sailed from
Philippi after the Feast of Unleavened Bread,
and five days later joined the others at Troas,
where we stayed seven days.

Eutychus Raised From the Dead at Troas

7On the first day of the week we came together to break bread. Paul spoke to the people
and, because he intended to leave the next day,
kept on talking until midnight. 8There were
many lamps in the upstairs room where we
were meeting. 9Seated in a window was a
young man named Eutychus, who was sinking
into a deep sleep as Paul talked on and on.
When he was sound asleep, he fell to the
ground from the third story and was picked up
dead. 10Paul went down, threw himself on the
young man and put his arms around him.
"Don't be alarmed," he said. "He's alive!"
11Then he went upstairs again and broke bread
and ate. After talking until daylight, he left.
12The people took the young man home alive
and were greatly comforted.

Paul's Farewell to the Ephesian Elders

13We went on ahead to the ship and sailed
for Assos, where we were going to take Paul
aboard. He had made this arrangement because
he was going there on foot. 14When he met us
at Assos, we took him aboard and went on to
Mitylene. 15The next day we set sail from there
and arrived off Kios. The day after that we
crossed over to Samos, and on the following
day arrived at Miletus. 16Paul had decided to
sail past Ephesus to avoid spending time in the
province of Asia, for he was in a hurry to reach
Jerusalem, if possible, by the day of Pentecost.

17From Miletus, Paul sent to Ephesus for the
elders of the church. 18When they arrived, he
said to them: "You know how I lived the
whole time I was with you, from the first day
I came into the province of Asia. 19I served the
Lord with great humility and with tears, although I was severely tested by the plots of the
Jews. 20You know that I have not hesitated to
preach anything that would be helpful to you
but have taught you publicly and from house to
house. 21I have declared to both Jews and
Greeks that they must turn to God in repentance and have faith in our Lord Jesus.

22"And now, compelled by the Spirit, I am
going to Jerusalem, not knowing what will
happen to me there. 23I only know that in every
city the Holy Spirit warns me that prison and
hardships are facing me. 24However, I consider
my life worth nothing to me, if only I may
finish the race and complete the task the Lord
Jesus has given me—the task of testifying to
the gospel of God's grace.

25"Now I know that none of you among
whom I have gone about preaching the kingdom will ever see me again. 26Therefore, I declare to you today that I am innocent of the
blood of all men. 27For I have not hesitated to
proclaim to you the whole will of God. 28Keep
watch over yourselves and all the flock of
which the Holy Spirit has made you overseers.[a] Be shepherds of the church of God,[b]
which he bought with his own blood. 29I know
that after I leave, savage wolves will come in
among you and will not spare the flock. 30Even
from your own number men will arise and distort the truth in order to draw away disciples
after them. 31So be on your guard! Remember
that for three years I never stopped warning
each of you night and day with tears.

32"Now I commit you to God and to the
word of his grace, which can build you up and
give you an inheritance among all those who
are sanctified. 33I have not coveted anyone's
silver or gold or clothing. 34You yourselves
know that these hands of mine have supplied
my own needs and the needs of my companions. 35In everything I did, I showed you that
by this kind of hard work we must help the
weak, remembering the words the Lord Jesus
himself said: 'It is more blessed to give than to
receive.' "

36When he had said this, he knelt down with
all of them and prayed. 37They all wept as they
embraced him and kissed him. 38What grieved
them most was his statement that they would
never see his face again. Then they accompanied him to the ship.

On to Jerusalem

21 After we had torn ourselves away from
them, we put out to sea and sailed
straight to Cos. The next day we went to
Rhodes and from there to Patara. 2We found a
ship crossing over to Phoenicia, went on board
and set sail. 3After sighting Cyprus and passing to the south of it, we sailed on to Syria. We
landed at Tyre, where our ship was to unload
its cargo. 4Finding the disciples there, we
stayed with them seven days. Through the
Spirit they urged Paul not to go on to Jerusalem. 5But when our time was up, we left and
continued on our way. All the disciples and
their wives and children accompanied us out of
the city, and there on the beach we knelt to
pray. 6After saying good-by to each other, we
went aboard the ship, and they returned home.

[a]28 Traditionally *bishops* [b]28 Many manuscripts *of the Lord*

7We continued our voyage from Tyre and
landed at Ptolemais, where we greeted the
brothers and stayed with them for a day.
8Leaving the next day, we reached Caesarea
and stayed at the house of Philip the evangelist, one of the Seven. 9He had four unmarried
daughters who prophesied.
10After we had been there a number of days,
a prophet named Agabus came down from Judea. 11Coming over to us, he took Paul's belt,
tied his own hands and feet with it and said,
"The Holy Spirit says, 'In this way the Jews of
Jerusalem will bind the owner of this belt and
will hand him over to the Gentiles.' "
12When we heard this, we and the people
there pleaded with Paul not to go up to Jerusalem. 13Then Paul answered, "Why are you
weeping and breaking my heart? I am ready
not only to be bound, but also to die in Jerusalem for the name of the Lord Jesus." 14When
he would not be dissuaded, we gave up and
said, "The Lord's will be done."
15After this, we got ready and went up to
Jerusalem. 16Some of the disciples from Caesarea accompanied us and brought us to the
home of Mnason, where we were to stay. He
was a man from Cyprus and one of the early
disciples.

Paul's Arrival at Jerusalem

17When we arrived at Jerusalem, the brothers received us warmly. 18The next day Paul
and the rest of us went to see James, and all the
elders were present. 19Paul greeted them and
reported in detail what God had done among
the Gentiles through his ministry.
20When they heard this, they praised God.
Then they said to Paul: "You see, brother, how
many thousands of Jews have believed, and all
of them are zealous for the law. 21They have
been informed that you teach all the Jews who
live among the Gentiles to turn away from Moses, telling them not to circumcise their children or live according to our customs. 22What
shall we do? They will certainly hear that you
have come, 23so do what we tell you. There
are four men with us who have made a vow.
24Take these men, join in their purification
rites and pay their expenses, so that they can
have their heads shaved. Then everybody will
know there is no truth in these reports about
you, but that you yourself are living in obedience to the law. 25As for the Gentile believers,
we have written to them our decision that they
should abstain from food sacrificed to idols,
from blood, from the meat of strangled animals
and from sexual immorality."
26The next day Paul took the men and purified himself along with them. Then he went to
the temple to give notice of the date when the
days of purification would end and the offering
would be made for each of them.

Paul Arrested

27When the seven days were nearly over,
some Jews from the province of Asia saw Paul
at the temple. They stirred up the whole crowd
and seized him, 28shouting, "Men of Israel,
help us! This is the man who teaches all men
everywhere against our people and our law and
this place. And besides, he has brought Greeks
into the temple area and defiled this holy
place." 29(They had previously seen Trophimus the Ephesian in the city with Paul and
assumed that Paul had brought him into the
temple area.)
30The whole city was aroused, and the people came running from all directions. Seizing
Paul, they dragged him from the temple, and
immediately the gates were shut. 31While they
were trying to kill him, news reached the commander of the Roman troops that the whole
city of Jerusalem was in an uproar. 32He at
once took some officers and soldiers and ran
down to the crowd. When the rioters saw the
commander and his soldiers, they stopped
beating Paul.
33The commander came up and arrested him
and ordered him to be bound with two chains.
Then he asked who he was and what he had
done. 34Some in the crowd shouted one thing
and some another, and since the commander
could not get at the truth because of the uproar,
he ordered that Paul be taken into the barracks.
35When Paul reached the steps, the violence of
the mob was so great he had to be carried by
the soldiers. 36The crowd that followed kept
shouting, "Away with him!"

Paul Speaks to the Crowd

37As the soldiers were about to take Paul
into the barracks, he asked the commander,
"May I say something to you?"
"Do you speak Greek?" he replied.
38"Aren't you the Egyptian who started a revolt and led four thousand terrorists out into
the desert some time ago?"
39Paul answered, "I am a Jew, from Tarsus
in Cilicia, a citizen of no ordinary city. Please
let me speak to the people."
40Having received the commander's permission, Paul stood on the steps and motioned to
the crowd. When they were all silent, he said
22 to them in Aramaic[a]: 1"Brothers and
fathers, listen now to my defense."
2When they heard him speak to them in Aramaic, they became very quiet.
Then Paul said: 3"I am a Jew, born in Tarsus
of Cilicia, but brought up in this city. Under
Gamaliel I was thoroughly trained in the law
of our fathers and was just as zealous for God
as any of you are today. 4I persecuted the followers of this Way to their death, arresting
both men and women and throwing them into
prison, 5as also the high priest and all the
Council can testify. I even obtained letters
from them to their brothers in Damascus, and
went there to bring these people as prisoners to
Jerusalem to be punished.
6"About noon as I came near Damascus,

[a]40 Or possibly *Hebrew*; also in 22:2

suddenly a bright light from heaven flashed around me. 7I fell to the ground and heard a voice say to me, 'Saul! Saul! Why do you persecute me?'

8" 'Who are you, Lord?' I asked.

" 'I am Jesus of Nazareth, whom you are persecuting,' he replied. 9My companions saw the light, but they did not understand the voice of him who was speaking to me.

10" 'What shall I do, Lord?' I asked.

" 'Get up,' the Lord said, 'and go into Damascus. There you will be told all that you have been assigned to do.' 11My companions led me by the hand into Damascus, because the brilliance of the light had blinded me.

12"A man named Ananias came to see me. He was a devout observer of the law and highly respected by all the Jews living there. 13He stood beside me and said, 'Brother Saul, receive your sight!' And at that very moment I was able to see him.

14"Then he said: 'The God of our fathers has chosen you to know his will and to see the Righteous One and to hear words from his mouth. 15You will be his witness to all men of what you have seen and heard. 16And now what are you waiting for? Get up, be baptized and wash your sins away, calling on his name.'

17"When I returned to Jerusalem and was praying at the temple, I fell into a trance 18and saw the Lord speaking. 'Quick!' he said to me. 'Leave Jerusalem immediately, because they will not accept your testimony about me.'

19" 'Lord,' I replied, 'these men know that I went from one synagogue to another to imprison and beat those who believe in you. 20And when the blood of your martyr[a] Stephen was shed, I stood there giving my approval and guarding the clothes of those who were killing him.'

21"Then the Lord said to me, 'Go; I will send you far away to the Gentiles.' "

Paul the Roman Citizen

22The crowd listened to Paul until he said this. Then they raised their voices and shouted, "Rid the earth of him! He's not fit to live!"

23As they were shouting and throwing off their cloaks and flinging dust into the air, 24the commander ordered Paul to be taken into the barracks. He directed that he be flogged and questioned in order to find out why the people were shouting at him like this. 25As they stretched him out to flog him, Paul said to the centurion standing there, "Is it legal for you to flog a Roman citizen who hasn't even been found guilty?"

26When the centurion heard this, he went to the commander and reported it. "What are you going to do?" he asked. "This man is a Roman citizen."

27The commander went to Paul and asked, "Tell me, are you a Roman citizen?"

"Yes, I am," he answered.

28Then the commander said, "I had to pay a big price for my citizenship."

"But I was born a citizen," Paul replied.

29Those who were about to question him withdrew immediately. The commander himself was alarmed when he realized that he had put Paul, a Roman citizen, in chains.

Before the Sanhedrin

30The next day, since the commander wanted to find out exactly why Paul was being accused by the Jews, he released him and ordered the chief priests and all the Sanhedrin to assemble. Then he brought Paul and had him stand before them.

23 Paul looked straight at the Sanhedrin and said, "My brothers, I have fulfilled my duty to God in all good conscience to this day." 2At this the high priest Ananias ordered those standing near Paul to strike him on the mouth. 3Then Paul said to him, "God will strike you, you whitewashed wall! You sit there to judge me according to the law, yet you yourself violate the law by commanding that I be struck!"

4Those who were standing near Paul said, "You dare to insult God's high priest?"

5Paul replied, "Brothers, I did not realize that he was the high priest; for it is written: 'Do not speak evil about the ruler of your people.'[b]"

6Then Paul, knowing that some of them were Sadducees and the others Pharisees, called out in the Sanhedrin, "My brothers, I am a Pharisee, the son of a Pharisee. I stand on trial because of my hope in the resurrection of the dead." 7When he said this, a dispute broke out between the Pharisees and the Sadducees, and the assembly was divided. 8(The Sadducees say that there is no resurrection, and that there are neither angels nor spirits, but the Pharisees acknowledge them all.)

9There was a great uproar, and some of the teachers of the law who were Pharisees stood up and argued vigorously. "We find nothing wrong with this man," they said. "What if a spirit or an angel has spoken to him?" 10The dispute became so violent that the commander was afraid Paul would be torn to pieces by them. He ordered the troops to go down and take him away from them by force and bring him into the barracks.

11The following night the Lord stood near Paul and said, "Take courage! As you have testified about me in Jerusalem, so you must also testify in Rome."

The Plot to Kill Paul

12The next morning the Jews formed a conspiracy and bound themselves with an oath not to eat or drink until they had killed Paul. 13More than forty men were involved in this plot. 14They went to the chief priests and elders and said, "We have taken a solemn oath not to eat anything until we have killed Paul.

[a]20 Or *witness* [b]5 Exodus 22:28

15 Now then, you and the Sanhedrin petition the
commander to bring him before you on the
pretext of wanting more accurate information
about his case. We are ready to kill him before
he gets here."
16 But when the son of Paul's sister heard of
this plot, he went into the barracks and told
Paul.
17 Then Paul called one of the centurions and
said, "Take this young man to the commander;
he has something to tell him." 18 So he took
him to the commander.
The centurion said, "Paul, the prisoner, sent
for me and asked me to bring this young man
to you because he has something to tell you."
19 The commander took the young man by
the hand, drew him aside and asked, "What is
it you want to tell me?"
20 He said: "The Jews have agreed to ask you
to bring Paul before the Sanhedrin tomorrow
on the pretext of wanting more accurate information about him. 21 Don't give in to them,
because more than forty of them are waiting in
ambush for him. They have taken an oath not
to eat or drink until they have killed him. They
are ready now, waiting for your consent to
their request."
22 The commander dismissed the young man
and cautioned him, "Don't tell anyone that you
have reported this to me."

Paul Transferred to Caesarea

23 Then he called two of his centurions and
ordered them, "Get ready a detachment of two
hundred soldiers, seventy horsemen and two
hundred spearmen[a] to go to Caesarea at nine
tonight. 24 Provide mounts for Paul so that he
may be taken safely to Governor Felix."
25 He wrote a letter as follows:

26 Claudius Lysias,

To His Excellency, Governor Felix:

Greetings.

> 27 This man was seized by the Jews and
> they were about to kill him, but I came
> with my troops and rescued him, for I had
> learned that he is a Roman citizen. 28 I
> wanted to know why they were accusing
> him, so I brought him to their Sanhedrin.
> 29 I found that the accusation had to do
> with questions about their law, but there
> was no charge against him that deserved
> death or imprisonment. 30 When I was in-
> formed of a plot to be carried out against
> the man, I sent him to you at once. I also
> ordered his accusers to present to you
> their case against him.

31 So the soldiers, carrying out their orders,
took Paul with them during the night and
brought him as far as Antipatris. 32 The next
day they let the cavalry go on with him, while
they returned to the barracks. 33 When the cavalry arrived in Caesarea, they delivered the letter to the governor and handed Paul over to
him. 34 The governor read the letter and asked
what province he was from. Learning that he
was from Cilicia, 35 he said, "I will hear your
case when your accusers get here." Then he
ordered that Paul be kept under guard in Herod's palace.

The Trial Before Felix

24 Five days later the high priest Ananias
went down to Caesarea with some of
the elders and a lawyer named Tertullus, and
they brought their charges against Paul before
the governor. 2 When Paul was called in, Tertullus presented his case before Felix: "We
have enjoyed a long period of peace under you,
and your foresight has brought about reforms
in this nation. 3 Everywhere and in every way,
most excellent Felix, we acknowledge this
with profound gratitude. 4 But in order not to
weary you further, I would request that you be
kind enough to hear us briefly.
5 "We have found this man to be a troublemaker, stirring up riots among the Jews all
over the world. He is a ringleader of the Nazarene sect 6 and even tried to desecrate the temple; so we seized him. 8 By[b] examining him
yourself you will be able to learn the truth
about all these charges we are bringing against
him."
9 The Jews joined in the accusation, asserting
that these things were true.
10 When the governor motioned for him to
speak, Paul replied: "I know that for a number
of years you have been a judge over this nation; so I gladly make my defense. 11 You can
easily verify that no more than twelve days ago
I went up to Jerusalem to worship. 12 My accusers did not find me arguing with anyone at
the temple, or stirring up a crowd in the synagogues or anywhere else in the city. 13 And
they cannot prove to you the charges they are
now making against me. 14 However, I admit
that I worship the God of our fathers as a follower of the Way, which they call a sect. I
believe everything that agrees with the Law
and that is written in the Prophets, 15 and I have
the same hope in God as these men, that there
will be a resurrection of both the righteous and
the wicked. 16 So I strive always to keep my
conscience clear before God and man.
17 "After an absence of several years, I came
to Jerusalem to bring my people gifts for the
poor and to present offerings. 18 I was ceremonially clean when they found me in the temple courts doing this. There was no crowd with
me, nor was I involved in any disturbance.
19 But there are some Jews from the province of
Asia, who ought to be here before you and
bring charges if they have anything against me.

[a] *23* The meaning of the Greek for this word is uncertain. [b] *6-8* Some manuscripts *him and wanted to judge him according to our law. 7 But the commander, Lysias, came and with the use of much force snatched him from our hands 8 and ordered his accusers to come before you. By*

20Or these who are here should state what
crime they found in me when I stood before
the Sanhedrin— 21unless it was this one thing
I shouted as I stood in their presence: 'It is
concerning the resurrection of the dead that I
am on trial before you today.' "
22Then Felix, who was well acquainted with
the Way, adjourned the proceedings. "When
Lysias the commander comes," he said, "I will
decide your case." 23He ordered the centurion
to keep Paul under guard but to give him some
freedom and permit his friends to take care of
his needs.
24Several days later Felix came with his
wife Drusilla, who was a Jewess. He sent for
Paul and listened to him as he spoke about
faith in Christ Jesus. 25As Paul discoursed on
righteousness, self-control and the judgment
to come, Felix was afraid and said, "That's
enough for now! You may leave. When I find
it convenient, I will send for you." 26At the
same time he was hoping that Paul would offer
him a bribe, so he sent for him frequently and
talked with him.
27When two years had passed, Felix was
succeeded by Porcius Festus, but because Felix
wanted to grant a favor to the Jews, he left Paul
in prison.

The Trial Before Festus

25 Three days after arriving in the province, Festus went up from Caesarea to
Jerusalem, 2where the chief priests and Jewish
leaders appeared before him and presented the
charges against Paul. 3They urgently requested
Festus, as a favor to them, to have Paul trans-
ferred to Jerusalem, for they were preparing an
ambush to kill him along the way. 4Festus answered, "Paul is being held at Caesarea, and I
myself am going there soon. 5Let some of your
leaders come with me and press charges
against the man there, if he has done anything
wrong."
6After spending eight or ten days with them,
he went down to Caesarea, and the next day he
convened the court and ordered that Paul be
brought before him. 7When Paul appeared, the
Jews who had come down from Jerusalem
stood around him, bringing many serious
charges against him, which they could not
prove.
8Then Paul made his defense: "I have done
nothing wrong against the law of the Jews or
against the temple or against Caesar."
9Festus, wishing to do the Jews a favor, said
to Paul, "Are you willing to go up to Jerusalem
and stand trial before me there on these
charges?"
10Paul answered: "I am now standing before
Caesar's court, where I ought to be tried. I
have not done any wrong to the Jews, as you
yourself know very well. 11If, however, I am
guilty of doing anything deserving death, I do
not refuse to die. But if the charges brought
against me by these Jews are not true, no one
has the right to hand me over to them. I appeal
to Caesar!"
12After Festus had conferred with his council, he declared: "You have appealed to Caesar. To Caesar you will go!"

Festus Consults King Agrippa

13A few days later King Agrippa and Bernice arrived at Caesarea to pay their respects to
Festus. 14Since they were spending many days
there, Festus discussed Paul's case with the
king. He said: "There is a man here whom
Felix left as a prisoner. 15When I went to Jerusalem, the chief priests and elders of the Jews
brought charges against him and asked that he
be condemned.
16"I told them that it is not the Roman custom to hand over any man before he has faced
his accusers and has had an opportunity to
defend himself against their charges. 17When
they came here with me, I did not delay the
case, but convened the court the next day and
ordered the man to be brought in. 18When his
accusers got up to speak, they did not charge
him with any of the crimes I had expected.
19Instead, they had some points of dispute with
him about their own religion and about a dead
man named Jesus who Paul claimed was alive.
20I was at a loss how to investigate such matters; so I asked if he would be willing to go
to Jerusalem and stand trial there on these
charges. 21When Paul made his appeal to be
held over for the Emperor's decision, I ordered
him held until I could send him to Caesar."
22Then Agrippa said to Festus, "I would like
to hear this man myself."
He replied, "Tomorrow you will hear him."

Paul Before Agrippa

23The next day Agrippa and Bernice came
with great pomp and entered the audience
room with the high ranking officers and the
leading men of the city. At the command of
Festus, Paul was brought in. 24Festus said:
"King Agrippa, and all who are present with
us, you see this man! The whole Jewish community has petitioned me about him in Jerusalem and here in Caesarea, shouting that he
ought not to live any longer. 25I found he had
done nothing deserving of death, but because
he made his appeal to the Emperor I decided to
send him to Rome. 26But I have nothing definite to write to His Majesty about him. Therefore I have brought him before all of you, and
especially before you, King Agrippa, so that as
a result of this investigation I may have something to write. 27For I think it is unreasonable
to send on a prisoner without specifying the
charges against him."

26 Then Agrippa said to Paul, "You have
permission to speak for yourself."
So Paul motioned with his hand and began
his defense: 2"King Agrippa, I consider myself
fortunate to stand before you today as I make
my defense against all the accusations of the
Jews, 3and especially so because you are well
acquainted with all the Jewish customs and
controversies. Therefore, I beg you to listen to
me patiently.

4“The Jews all know the way I have lived
ever since I was a child, from the beginning of
my life in my own country, and also in Jerusalem. 5They have known me for a long time and
can testify, if they are willing, that according
to the strictest sect of our religion, I lived as a
Pharisee. 6And now it is because of my hope in
what God has promised our fathers that I am
on trial today. 7This is the promise our twelve
tribes are hoping to see fulfilled as they earnestly serve God day and night. O king, it is
because of this hope that the Jews are accusing
me. 8Why should any of you consider it in-
credible that God raises the dead?

9“I too was convinced that I ought to do all
that was possible to oppose the name of Jesus
of Nazareth. 10And that is just what I did in
Jerusalem. On the authority of the chief priests
I put many of the saints in prison, and when
they were put to death, I cast my vote against
them. 11Many a time I went from one synagogue to another to have them punished, and I
tried to force them to blaspheme. In my obses-
sion against them, I even went to foreign cities
to persecute them.

12“On one of these journeys I was going to
Damascus with the authority and commission
of the chief priests. 13About noon, O king, as
I was on the road, I saw a light from heaven,
brighter than the sun, blazing around me and
my companions. 14We all fell to the ground,
and I heard a voice saying to me in Aramaic,[a]
‘Saul, Saul, why do you persecute me? It is
hard for you to kick against the goads.’

15“Then I asked, ‘Who are you, Lord?’

“ ‘I am Jesus, whom you are persecuting,’
the Lord replied. 16‘Now get up and stand on
your feet. I have appeared to you to appoint
you as a servant and as a witness of what you
have seen of me and what I will show you. 17I
will rescue you from your own people and
from the Gentiles. I am sending you to them
18to open their eyes and turn them from darkness to light, and from the power of Satan to
God, so that they may receive forgiveness of
sins and a place among those who are sanctified by faith in me.’

19“So then, King Agrippa, I was not disobedient to the vision from heaven. 20First to those
in Damascus, then to those in Jerusalem and in
all Judea, and to the Gentiles also, I preached
that they should repent and turn to God and
prove their repentance by their deeds. 21That is
why the Jews seized me in the temple courts
and tried to kill me. 22But I have had God’s
help to this very day, and so I stand here and
testify to small and great alike. I am saying
nothing beyond what the prophets and Moses
said would happen— 23that the Christ[b] would
suffer and, as the first to rise from the dead,
would proclaim light to his own people and to
the Gentiles.”

24At this point Festus interrupted Paul’s defense. “You are out of your mind, Paul!” he
shouted. “Your great learning is driving you
insane.”

25“I am not insane, most excellent Festus,”
Paul replied. “What I am saying is true and
reasonable. 26The king is familiar with these
things, and I can speak freely to him. I am
convinced that none of this has escaped his
notice, because it was not done in a corner.
27King Agrippa, do you believe the prophets?
I know you do.”

28Then Agrippa said to Paul, “Do you think
that in such a short time you can persuade me
to be a Christian?”

29Paul replied, “Short time or long—I pray
God that not only you but all who are listening
to me today may become what I am, except for
these chains.”

30The king rose, and with him the governor
and Bernice and those sitting with them.
31They left the room, and while talking with
one another, they said, “This man is not doing
anything that deserves death or imprisonment.”

32Agrippa said to Festus, “This man could
have been set free if he had not appealed to
Caesar.”

Paul Sails for Rome

27 When it was decided that we would sail
for Italy, Paul and some other prisoners
were handed over to a centurion named Julius,
who belonged to the Imperial Regiment. 2We
boarded a ship from Adramyttium about to sail
for ports along the coast of the province of
Asia, and we put out to sea. Aristarchus, a
Macedonian from Thessalonica, was with us.

3The next day we landed at Sidon; and Julius, in kindness to Paul, allowed him to go to
his friends so they might provide for his needs.
4From there we put out to sea again and passed
to the lee of Cyprus because the winds were
against us. 5When we had sailed across the
open sea off the coast of Cilicia and Pamphylia, we landed at Myra in Lycia. 6There the
centurion found an Alexandrian ship sailing
for Italy and put us on board. 7We made slow
headway for many days and had difficulty arriving off Cnidus. When the wind did not allow us to hold our course, we sailed to the lee
of Crete, opposite Salmone. 8We moved along
the coast with difficulty and came to a place
called Fair Havens, near the town of Lasea.

9Much time had been lost, and sailing had
already become dangerous because by now it
was after the Fast.[c] So Paul warned them,
10“Men, I can see that our voyage is going to
be disastrous and bring great loss to ship and
cargo, and to our own lives also.” 11But the
centurion, instead of listening to what Paul
said, followed the advice of the pilot and of the
owner of the ship. 12Since the harbor was un-
suitable to winter in, the majority decided that
we should sail on, hoping to reach Phoenix and
winter there. This was a harbor in Crete, facing
both southwest and northwest.

[a]14 Or *Hebrew* [b]23 Or *Messiah* [c]9 That is, the Day of Atonement (Yom Kippur)

The Storm

13When a gentle south wind began to blow,
they thought they had obtained what they
wanted; so they weighed anchor and sailed
along the shore of Crete. 14Before very long, a
wind of hurricane force, called the "northeast-
er," swept down from the island. 15The ship
was caught by the storm and could not head
into the wind; so we gave way to it and were
driven along. 16As we passed to the lee of a
small island called Cauda, we were hardly able
to make the lifeboat secure. 17When the men
had hoisted it aboard, they passed ropes under
the ship itself to hold it together. Fearing that
they would run aground on the sandbars of
Syrtis, they lowered the sea anchor and let the
ship be driven along. 18We took such a violent
battering from the storm that the next day they
began to throw the cargo overboard. 19On the
third day, they threw the ship's tackle overboard with their own hands. 20When neither
sun nor stars appeared for many days and the
storm continued raging, we finally gave up all
hope of being saved.

21After the men had gone a long time without food, Paul stood up before them and said:
"Men, you should have taken my advice not to
sail from Crete; then you would have spared
yourselves this damage and loss. 22But now I
urge you to keep up your courage, because not
one of you will be lost; only the ship will be
destroyed. 23Last night an angel of the God
whose I am and whom I serve stood beside me
24and said, 'Do not be afraid, Paul. You must
stand trial before Caesar; and God has graciously given you the lives of all who sail with
you.' 25So keep up your courage, men, for I
have faith in God that it will happen just as he
told me. 26Nevertheless, we must run aground
on some island."

The Shipwreck

27On the fourteenth night we were still being
driven across the Adriatic[a] Sea, when about
midnight the sailors sensed they were approaching land. 28They took soundings and
found that the water was a hundred and twenty
feet[b] deep. A short time later they took soundings again and found it was ninety feet[c] deep.
29Fearing that we would be dashed against the
rocks, they dropped four anchors from the
stern and prayed for daylight. 30In an attempt
to escape from the ship, the sailors let the lifeboat down into the sea, pretending they were
going to lower some anchors from the bow.
31Then Paul said to the centurion and the soldiers, "Unless these men stay with the ship,
you cannot be saved." 32So the soldiers cut the
ropes that held the lifeboat and let it fall away.

33Just before dawn Paul urged them all to
eat. "For the last fourteen days," he said, "you
have been in constant suspense and have gone
without food—you haven't eaten anything.
34Now I urge you to take some food. You need
it to survive. Not one of you will lose a single
hair from his head." 35After he said this, he
took some bread and gave thanks to God in
front of them all. Then he broke it and began
to eat. 36They were all encouraged and ate
some food themselves. 37Altogether there were
276 of us on board. 38When they had eaten as
much as they wanted, they lightened the ship
by throwing the grain into the sea.

39When daylight came, they did not recognize the land, but they saw a bay with a sandy
beach, where they decided to run the ship
aground if they could. 40Cutting loose the anchors, they left them in the sea and at the same
time untied the ropes that held the rudders.
Then they hoisted the foresail to the wind and
made for the beach. 41But the ship struck a
sandbar and ran aground. The bow stuck fast
and would not move, and the stern was broken
to pieces by the pounding of the surf.

42The soldiers planned to kill the prisoners
to prevent any of them from swimming away
and escaping. 43But the centurion wanted to
spare Paul's life and kept them from carrying
out their plan. He ordered those who could
swim to jump overboard first and get to land.
44The rest were to get there on planks or on
pieces of the ship. In this way everyone
reached land in safety.

Ashore on Malta

28 Once safely on shore, we found out that
the island was called Malta. 2The islanders showed us unusual kindness. They
built a fire and welcomed us all because it was
raining and cold. 3Paul gathered a pile of
brushwood and, as he put it on the fire, a viper,
driven out by the heat, fastened itself on his
hand. 4When the islanders saw the snake hanging from his hand, they said to each other,
"This man must be a murderer; for though he
escaped from the sea, Justice has not allowed
him to live." 5But Paul shook the snake off into
the fire and suffered no ill effects. 6The people
expected him to swell up or suddenly fall dead,
but after waiting a long time and seeing nothing unusual happen to him, they changed their
minds and said he was a god.

7There was an estate nearby that belonged to
Publius, the chief official of the island. He
welcomed us to his home and for three days
entertained us hospitably. 8His father was sick
in bed, suffering from fever and dysentery.
Paul went in to see him and, after prayer,
placed his hands on him and healed him.
9When this had happened, the rest of the sick
on the island came and were cured. 10They
honored us in many ways and when we were
ready to sail, they furnished us with the supplies we needed.

Arrival at Rome

11After three months we put out to sea in a
ship that had wintered in the island. It was an
Alexandrian ship with the figurehead of the

[a]27 In ancient times the name referred to an area extending well south of Italy. [b]28 Greek *twenty orguias* (about 37 meters) [c]28 Greek *fifteen orguias* (about 27 meters)

twin gods Castor and Pollux. 12We put in at Syracuse and stayed there three days. 13From there we set sail and arrived at Rhegium. The next day the south wind came up, and on the following day we reached Puteoli. 14There we found some brothers who invited us to spend a week with them. And so we came to Rome. 15The brothers there had heard that we were coming, and they traveled as far as the Forum of Appius and the Three Taverns to meet us. At the sight of these men Paul thanked God and was encouraged. 16When we got to Rome, Paul was allowed to live by himself, with a soldier to guard him.

Paul Preaches at Rome Under Guard

17Three days later he called together the leaders of the Jews. When they had assembled, Paul said to them: "My brothers, although I have done nothing against our people or against the customs of our ancestors, I was arrested in Jerusalem and handed over to the Romans. 18They examined me and wanted to release me, because I was not guilty of any crime deserving death. 19But when the Jews objected, I was compelled to appeal to Caesar—not that I had any charge to bring against my own people. 20For this reason I have asked to see you and talk with you. It is because of the hope of Israel that I am bound with this chain."

21They replied, "We have not received any letters from Judea concerning you, and none of the brothers who have come from there has reported or said anything bad about you. 22But we want to hear what your views are, for we know that people everywhere are talking against this sect."

23They arranged to meet Paul on a certain day, and came in even larger numbers to the place where he was staying. From morning till evening he explained and declared to them the kingdom of God and tried to convince them about Jesus from the Law of Moses and from the Prophets. 24Some were convinced by what he said, but others would not believe. 25They disagreed among themselves and began to leave after Paul had made this final statement: "The Holy Spirit spoke the truth to your forefathers when he said through Isaiah the prophet:

26" 'Go to this people and say,
"You will be ever hearing but never understanding;
you will be ever seeing but never perceiving."
27For this people's heart has become calloused;
they hardly hear with their ears,
and they have closed their eyes.
Otherwise they might see with their eyes,
hear with their ears,
understand with their hearts
and turn, and I would heal them.'[a]

28"Therefore I want you to know that God's salvation has been sent to the Gentiles, and they will listen!"[b]

30For two whole years Paul stayed there in his own rented house and welcomed all who came to see him. 31Boldly and without hindrance he preached the kingdom of God and taught about the Lord Jesus Christ.

Romans

1 Paul, a servant of Christ Jesus, called to be an apostle and set apart for the gospel of God— 2the gospel he promised beforehand through his prophets in the Holy Scriptures 3regarding his Son, who as to his human nature was a descendant of David, 4and who through the Spirit[c] of holiness was declared with power to be the Son of God[d] by his resurrection from the dead: Jesus Christ our Lord. 5Through him and for his name's sake, we received grace and apostleship to call people from among all the Gentiles to the obedience that comes from faith. 6And you also are among those who are called to belong to Jesus Christ.

7To all in Rome who are loved by God and called to be saints:

Grace and peace to you from God our Father and from the Lord Jesus Christ.

Paul's Longing to Visit Rome

8First, I thank my God through Jesus Christ for all of you, because your faith is being reported all over the world. 9God, whom I serve with my whole heart in preaching the gospel of his Son, is my witness how constantly I remember you 10in my prayers at all times; and I pray that now at last by God's will the way may be opened for me to come to you.

11I long to see you so that I may impart to you some spiritual gift to make you strong— 12that is, that you and I may be mutually encouraged by each other's faith. 13I do not want you to be unaware, brothers, that I planned

[a]27 Isaiah 6:9,10 [b]28 Some manuscripts *listen!" 29After he said this, the Jews left, arguing vigorously among themselves.* [c]4 Or *who as to his spirit* [d]4 Or *was appointed to be the Son of God with power*

many times to come to you (but have been
prevented from doing so until now) in order
that I might have a harvest among you, just as
I have had among the other Gentiles.
14I am obligated both to Greeks and non-
Greeks, both to the wise and the foolish. 15That
is why I am so eager to preach the gospel also
to you who are at Rome.
16I am not ashamed of the gospel, because it
is the power of God for the salvation of everyone who believes: first for the Jew, then for the
Gentile. 17For in the gospel a righteousness
from God is revealed, a righteousness that is
by faith from first to last,[a] just as it is written:
"The righteous will live by faith."[b]

God's Wrath Against Mankind

18The wrath of God is being revealed from
heaven against all the godlessness and wickedness of men who suppress the truth by their
wickedness, 19since what may be known about
God is plain to them, because God has made it
plain to them. 20For since the creation of the
world God's invisible qualities—his eternal
power and divine nature—have been clearly
seen, being understood from what has been
made, so that men are without excuse.
21For although they knew God, they neither
glorified him as God nor gave thanks to him,
but their thinking became futile and their foolish hearts were darkened. 22Although they
claimed to be wise, they became fools 23and
exchanged the glory of the immortal God for
images made to look like mortal man and birds
and animals and reptiles.
24Therefore God gave them over in the sinful desires of their hearts to sexual impurity for
the degrading of their bodies with one another.
25They exchanged the truth of God for a lie,
and worshiped and served created things rather
than the Creator—who is forever praised. Amen.
26Because of this, God gave them over to
shameful lusts. Even their women exchanged
natural relations for unnatural ones. 27In the
same way the men also abandoned natural relations with women and were inflamed with
lust for one another. Men committed indecent
acts with other men, and received in themselves the due penalty for their perversion.
28Furthermore, since they did not think it
worthwhile to retain the knowledge of God, he
gave them over to a depraved mind, to do what
ought not to be done. 29They have become
filled with every kind of wickedness, evil,
greed and depravity. They are full of envy,
murder, strife, deceit and malice. They are gossips, 30slanderers, God-haters, insolent, arrogant and boastful; they invent ways of doing
evil; they disobey their parents; 31they are
senseless, faithless, heartless, ruthless. 32Al-
though they know God's righteous decree that
those who do such things deserve death, they
not only continue to do these very things but
also approve of those who practice them.

God's Righteous Judgment

2 You, therefore, have no excuse, you who
pass judgment on someone else, for at
whatever point you judge the other, you are
condemning yourself, because you who pass
judgment do the same things. 2Now we know
that God's judgment against those who do
such things is based on truth. 3So when you, a
mere man, pass judgment on them and yet do
the same things, do you think you will escape
God's judgment? 4Or do you show contempt
for the riches of his kindness, tolerance and
patience, not realizing that God's kindness
leads you toward repentance?
5But because of your stubbornness and your
unrepentant heart, you are storing up wrath
against yourself for the day of God's wrath,
when his righteous judgment will be revealed.
6God "will give to each person according to
what he has done."[c] 7To those who by persistence in doing good seek glory, honor and immortality, he will give eternal life. 8But for
those who are self-seeking and who reject the
truth and follow evil, there will be wrath and
anger. 9There will be trouble and distress for
every human being who does evil: first for the
Jew, then for the Gentile; 10but glory, honor
and peace for everyone who does good: first
for the Jew, then for the Gentile. 11For God
does not show favoritism.
12All who sin apart from the law will also
perish apart from the law, and all who sin under the law will be judged by the law. 13For it
is not those who hear the law who are righteous in God's sight, but it is those who obey
the law who will be declared righteous. 14(Indeed, when Gentiles, who do not have the law,
do by nature things required by the law, they
are a law for themselves, even though they do
not have the law, 15since they show that the
requirements of the law are written on their
hearts, their consciences also bearing witness,
and their thoughts now accusing, now even
defending them.) 16This will take place on
the day when God will judge men's secrets
through Jesus Christ, as my gospel declares.

The Jews and the Law

17Now you, if you call yourself a Jew; if you
rely on the law and brag about your relationship to God; 18if you know his will and approve of what is superior because you are instructed by the law; 19if you are convinced that
you are a guide for the blind, a light for those
who are in the dark, 20an instructor of the foolish, a teacher of infants, because you have in
the law the embodiment of knowledge and
truth— 21you, then, who teach others, do you
not teach yourself? You who preach against
stealing, do you steal? 22You who say that people should not commit adultery, do you commit adultery? You who abhor idols, do you rob
temples? 23You who brag about the law, do
you dishonor God by breaking the law? 24As it

[a] *17* Or *is from faith to faith* [b] *17* Hab. 2:4 [c] *6* Psalm 62:12; Prov. 24:12

is written: “God’s name is blasphemed among
the Gentiles because of you.”[a]
25 Circumcision has value if you observe the
law, but if you break the law, you have become
as though you had not been circumcised. 26 If
those who are not circumcised keep the law’s
requirements, will they not be regarded as
though they were circumcised? 27 The one who
is not circumcised physically and yet obeys the
law will condemn you who, even though you
have the[b] written code and circumcision, are a
lawbreaker.

28 A man is not a Jew if he is only one outwardly, nor is circumcision merely outward
and physical. 29 No, a man is a Jew if he is one
inwardly; and circumcision is circumcision of
the heart, by the Spirit, not by the written code.
Such a man’s praise is not from men, but from
God.

God’s Faithfulness

3 What advantage, then, is there in being a
Jew, or what value is there in circumcision? 2 Much in every way! First of all, they
have been entrusted with the very words of
God.

3 What if some did not have faith? Will their
lack of faith nullify God’s faithfulness? 4 Not at
all! Let God be true, and every man a liar. As
it is written:

“So that you may be proved right when
you speak
and prevail when you judge.”[c]

5 But if our unrighteousness brings out
God’s righteousness more clearly, what shall
we say? That God is unjust in bringing his
wrath on us? (I am using a human argument.)
6 Certainly not! If that were so, how could God
judge the world? 7 Someone might argue, “If
my falsehood enhances God’s truthfulness and
so increases his glory, why am I still condemned as a sinner?” 8 Why not say—as we
are being slanderously reported as saying and
as some claim that we say—“Let us do evil
that good may result”? Their condemnation is
deserved.

No One Is Righteous

9 What shall we conclude then? Are we any
better[d]? Not at all! We have already made the
charge that Jews and Gentiles alike are all under sin. 10 As it is written:

“There is no one righteous, not even one;
11 there is no one who understands,
no one who seeks God.
12 All have turned away,
they have together become worthless;
there is no one who does good,
not even one.”[e]
13 “Their throats are open graves;
their tongues practice deceit.”[f]
“The poison of vipers is on their lips.”[g]
14 “Their mouths are full of cursing and
bitterness.”[h]
15 “Their feet are swift to shed blood;
16 ruin and misery mark their ways,
17 and the way of peace they do not know.”[i]
18 “There is no fear of God before their
eyes.”[j]

19 Now we know that whatever the law says,
it says to those who are under the law, so that
every mouth may be silenced and the whole
world held accountable to God. 20 Therefore no
one will be declared righteous in his sight by
observing the law; rather, through the law we
become conscious of sin.

Righteousness Through Faith

21 But now a righteousness from God, apart
from law, has been made known, to which the
Law and the Prophets testify. 22 This righteousness from God comes through faith in Jesus
Christ to all who believe. There is no difference, 23 for all have sinned and fall short of the
glory of God, 24 and are justified freely by his
grace through the redemption that came by
Christ Jesus. 25 God presented him as a sacrifice of atonement,[k] through faith in his blood.
He did this to demonstrate his justice, because
in his forbearance he had left the sins committed beforehand unpunished— 26 he did it to
demonstrate his justice at the present time, so
as to be just and the one who justifies those
who have faith in Jesus.

27 Where, then, is boasting? It is excluded.
On what principle? On that of observing the
law? No, but on that of faith. 28 For we maintain that a man is justified by faith apart from
observing the law. 29 Is God the God of Jews
only? Is he not the God of Gentiles too? Yes,
of Gentiles too, 30 since there is only one God,
who will justify the circumcised by faith and
the uncircumcised through that same faith.
31 Do we, then, nullify the law by this faith?
Not at all! Rather, we uphold the law.

Abraham Justified by Faith

4 What then shall we say that Abraham, our
forefather, discovered in this matter? 2 If, in
fact, Abraham was justified by works, he had
something to boast about—but not before
God. 3 What does the Scripture say? “Abraham
believed God, and it was credited to him as
righteousness.”[l]

4 Now when a man works, his wages are not
credited to him as a gift, but as an obligation.
5 However, to the man who does not work but
trusts God who justifies the wicked, his faith
is credited as righteousness. 6 David says the
same thing when he speaks of the blessedness
of the man to whom God credits righteousness
apart from works:

7 “Blessed are they

[a] *24* Isaiah 52:5; Ezek. 36:22 [b] *27* Or *who, by means of a* [c] *4* Psalm 51:4 [d] *9* Or *worse* [e] *12* Psalms 14:1-3; 53:1-3; Eccles. 7:20 [f] *13* Psalm 5:9 [g] *13* Psalm 140:3 [h] *14* Psalm 10:7 [i] *17* Isaiah 59:7,8 [j] *18* Psalm 36:1 [k] *25* Or *as the one who would turn aside his wrath, taking away sin* [l] *3* Gen. 15:6; also in verse 22

whose transgressions are forgiven,
whose sins are covered.
8Blessed is the man
whose sin the Lord will never count
against him."[a]

9Is this blessedness only for the circumcised, or also for the uncircumcised? We have
been saying that Abraham's faith was credited
to him as righteousness. 10Under what circumstances was it credited? Was it after he was
circumcised, or before? It was not after, but
before! 11And he received the sign of circumcision, a seal of the righteousness that he had
by faith while he was still uncircumcised. So
then, he is the father of all who believe but
have not been circumcised, in order that righteousness might be credited to them. 12And he
is also the father of the circumcised who not
only are circumcised but who also walk in the
footsteps of the faith that our father Abraham
had before he was circumcised.

13It was not through law that Abraham and
his offspring received the promise that he
would be heir of the world, but through the
righteousness that comes by faith. 14For if
those who live by law are heirs, faith has no
value and the promise is worthless, 15because
law brings wrath. And where there is no law
there is no transgression.

16Therefore, the promise comes by faith, so
that it may be by grace and may be guaranteed
to all Abraham's offspring—not only to those
who are of the law but also to those who are of
the faith of Abraham. He is the father of us all.
17As it is written: "I have made you a father of
many nations."[b] He is our father in the sight
of God, in whom he believed—the God who
gives life to the dead and calls things that are
not as though they were.

18Against all hope, Abraham in hope believed and so became the father of many nations, just as it had been said to him, "So shall
your offspring be."[c] 19Without weakening in
his faith, he faced the fact that his body was as
good as dead—since he was about a hundred
years old—and that Sarah's womb was also
dead. 20Yet he did not waver through unbelief
regarding the promise of God, but was
strengthened in his faith and gave glory to
God, 21being fully persuaded that God had
power to do what he had promised. 22This is
why "it was credited to him as righteousness."
23The words "it was credited to him" were
written not for him alone, 24but also for us, to
whom God will credit righteousness—for us
who believe in him who raised Jesus our Lord
from the dead. 25He was delivered over to
death for our sins and was raised to life for our
justification.

Peace and Joy

5 Therefore, since we have been justified
through faith, we[d] have peace with God
through our Lord Jesus Christ, 2through whom
we have gained access by faith into this grace
in which we now stand. And we[d] rejoice in the
hope of the glory of God. 3Not only so, but
we[d] also rejoice in our sufferings, because we
know that suffering produces perseverance;
4perseverance, character; and character, hope.
5And hope does not disappoint us, because
God has poured out his love into our hearts by
the Holy Spirit, whom he has given us.

6You see, at just the right time, when we
were still powerless, Christ died for the ungodly. 7Very rarely will anyone die for a righteous
man, though for a good man someone might
possibly dare to die. 8But God demonstrates
his own love for us in this: While we were still
sinners, Christ died for us.

9Since we have now been justified by his
blood, how much more shall we be saved from
God's wrath through him! 10For if, when we
were God's enemies, we were reconciled to
him through the death of his Son, how much
more, having been reconciled, shall we be
saved through his life! 11Not only is this so,
but we also rejoice in God through our Lord
Jesus Christ, through whom we have now received reconciliation.

Death Through Adam, Life Through Christ

12Therefore, just as sin entered the world
through one man, and death through sin, and in
this way death came to all men, because all
sinned— 13for before the law was given, sin
was in the world. But sin is not taken into
account when there is no law. 14Nevertheless,
death reigned from the time of Adam to the
time of Moses, even over those who did not sin
by breaking a command, as did Adam, who
was a pattern of the one to come.

15But the gift is not like the trespass. For if
the many died by the trespass of the one man,
how much more did God's grace and the gift
that came by the grace of the one man, Jesus
Christ, overflow to the many! 16Again, the gift
of God is not like the result of the one man's
sin: The judgment followed one sin and
brought condemnation, but the gift followed
many trespasses and brought justification.
17For if, by the trespass of the one man, death
reigned through that one man, how much more
will those who receive God's abundant provision of grace and of the gift of righteousness
reign in life through the one man, Jesus Christ.

18Consequently, just as the result of one
trespass was condemnation for all men, so also
the result of one act of righteousness was justification that brings life for all men. 19For just
as through the disobedience of the one man the
many were made sinners, so also through the
obedience of the one man the many will be
made righteous.

20The law was added so that the trespass
might increase. But where sin increased, grace
increased all the more, 21so that, just as sin
reigned in death, so also grace might reign

[a]8 Psalm 32:1,2 [b]17 Gen. 17:5 [c]18 Gen. 15:5 [d]1,2,3 Or *let us*

through righteousness to bring eternal life through Jesus Christ our Lord.

Dead to Sin, Alive in Christ

6 What shall we say, then? Shall we go on sinning so that grace may increase? 2By no means! We died to sin; how can we live in it any longer? 3Or don't you know that all of us who were baptized into Christ Jesus were baptized into his death? 4We were therefore buried with him through baptism into death in order that, just as Christ was raised from the dead through the glory of the Father, we too may live a new life.

5If we have been united with him like this in his death, we will certainly also be united with him in his resurrection. 6For we know that our old self was crucified with him so that the body of sin might be done away with,[a] that we should no longer be slaves to sin— 7because anyone who has died has been freed from sin.

8Now if we died with Christ, we believe that we will also live with him. 9For we know that since Christ was raised from the dead, he cannot die again; death no longer has mastery over him. 10The death he died, he died to sin once for all; but the life he lives, he lives to God.

11In the same way, count yourselves dead to sin but alive to God in Christ Jesus. 12Therefore do not let sin reign in your mortal body so that you obey its evil desires. 13Do not offer the parts of your body to sin, as instruments of wickedness, but rather offer yourselves to God, as those who have been brought from death to life; and offer the parts of your body to him as instruments of righteousness. 14For sin shall not be your master, because you are not under law, but under grace.

Slaves to Righteousness

15What then? Shall we sin because we are not under law but under grace? By no means! 16Don't you know that when you offer yourselves to someone to obey him as slaves, you are slaves to the one whom you obey—whether you are slaves to sin, which leads to death, or to obedience, which leads to righteousness? 17But thanks be to God that, though you used to be slaves to sin, you wholeheartedly obeyed the form of teaching to which you were entrusted. 18You have been set free from sin and have become slaves to righteousness.

19I put this in human terms because you are weak in your natural selves. Just as you used to offer the parts of your body in slavery to impurity and to ever-increasing wickedness, so now offer them in slavery to righteousness leading to holiness. 20When you were slaves to sin, you were free from the control of righteousness. 21What benefit did you reap at that time from the things you are now ashamed of? Those things result in death! 22But now that you have been set free from sin and have become slaves to God, the benefit you reap leads to holiness, and the result is eternal life. 23For the wages of sin is death, but the gift of God is eternal life in[b] Christ Jesus our Lord.

An Illustration From Marriage

7 Do you not know, brothers—for I am speaking to men who know the law—that the law has authority over a man only as long as he lives? 2For example, by law a married woman is bound to her husband as long as he is alive, but if her husband dies, she is released from the law of marriage. 3So then, if she marries another man while her husband is still alive, she is called an adulteress. But if her husband dies, she is released from that law and is not an adulteress, even though she marries another man.

4So, my brothers, you also died to the law through the body of Christ, that you might belong to another, to him who was raised from the dead, in order that we might bear fruit to God. 5For when we were controlled by the sinful nature,[c] the sinful passions aroused by the law were at work in our bodies, so that we bore fruit for death. 6But now, by dying to what once bound us, we have been released from the law so that we serve in the new way of the Spirit, and not in the old way of the written code.

Struggling With Sin

7What shall we say, then? Is the law sin? Certainly not! Indeed I would not have known what sin was except through the law. For I would not have known what coveting really was if the law had not said, "Do not covet."[d] 8But sin, seizing the opportunity afforded by the commandment, produced in me every kind of covetous desire. For apart from law, sin is dead. 9Once I was alive apart from law; but when the commandment came, sin sprang to life and I died. 10I found that the very commandment that was intended to bring life actually brought death. 11For sin, seizing the opportunity afforded by the commandment, deceived me, and through the commandment put me to death. 12So then, the law is holy, and the commandment is holy, righteous and good.

13Did that which is good, then, become death to me? By no means! But in order that sin might be recognized as sin, it produced death in me through what was good, so that through the commandment sin might become utterly sinful.

14We know that the law is spiritual; but I am unspiritual, sold as a slave to sin. 15I do not understand what I do. For what I want to do I do not do, but what I hate I do. 16And if I do what I do not want to do, I agree that the law is good. 17As it is, it is no longer I myself who do it, but it is sin living in me. 18I know that nothing good lives in me, that is, in my sinful nature.[e] For I have the desire to do what is good, but I cannot carry it out. 19For what I do is not the good I want to do; no, the evil I do not want to do—this I keep on doing. 20Now

[a]6 Or *be rendered powerless* [b]23 Or *through* [c]5 Or *the flesh*; also in verse 25 [d]7 Exodus 20:17; Deut. 5:21 [e]18 Or *my flesh*

if I do what I do not want to do, it is no longer I who do it, but it is sin living in me that does it.

21So I find this law at work: When I want to do good, evil is right there with me. 22For in my inner being I delight in God's law; 23but I see another law at work in the members of my body, waging war against the law of my mind and making me a prisoner of the law of sin at work within my members. 24What a wretched man I am! Who will rescue me from this body of death? 25Thanks be to God—through Jesus Christ our Lord!

So then, I myself in my mind am a slave to God's law, but in the sinful nature a slave to the law of sin.

Life Through the Spirit

8 Therefore, there is now no condemnation for those who are in Christ Jesus,[a] 2because through Christ Jesus the law of the Spirit of life set me free from the law of sin and death. 3For what the law was powerless to do in that it was weakened by the sinful nature,[b] God did by sending his own Son in the likeness of sinful man to be a sin offering.[c] And so he condemned sin in sinful man,[d] 4in order that the righteous requirements of the law might be fully met in us, who do not live according to the sinful nature but according to the Spirit.

5Those who live according to the sinful nature have their minds set on what that nature desires; but those who live in accordance with the Spirit have their minds set on what the Spirit desires. 6The mind of sinful man[e] is death, but the mind controlled by the Spirit is life and peace; 7the sinful mind[f] is hostile to God. It does not submit to God's law, nor can it do so. 8Those controlled by the sinful nature cannot please God.

9You, however, are controlled not by the sinful nature but by the Spirit, if the Spirit of God lives in you. And if anyone does not have the Spirit of Christ, he does not belong to Christ. 10But if Christ is in you, your body is dead because of sin, yet your spirit is alive because of righteousness. 11And if the Spirit of him who raised Jesus from the dead is living in you, he who raised Christ from the dead will also give life to your mortal bodies through his Spirit, who lives in you.

12Therefore, brothers, we have an obligation—but it is not to the sinful nature, to live according to it. 13For if you live according to the sinful nature, you will die; but if by the Spirit you put to death the misdeeds of the body, you will live, 14because those who are led by the Spirit of God are sons of God. 15For you did not receive a spirit that makes you a slave again to fear, but you received the Spirit of sonship.[g] And by him we cry, "*Abba*,[h] Father." 16The Spirit himself testifies with our spirit that we are God's children. 17Now if we are children, then we are heirs—heirs of God and co-heirs with Christ, if indeed we share in his sufferings in order that we may also share in his glory.

Future Glory

18I consider that our present sufferings are not worth comparing with the glory that will be revealed in us. 19The creation waits in eager expectation for the sons of God to be revealed. 20For the creation was subjected to frustration, not by its own choice, but by the will of the one who subjected it, in hope 21that[i] the creation itself will be liberated from its bondage to decay and brought into the glorious freedom of the children of God.

22We know that the whole creation has been groaning as in the pains of childbirth right up to the present time. 23Not only so, but we ourselves, who have the firstfruits of the Spirit, groan inwardly as we wait eagerly for our adoption as sons, the redemption of our bodies. 24For in this hope we were saved. But hope that is seen is no hope at all. Who hopes for what he already has? 25But if we hope for what we do not yet have, we wait for it patiently.

26In the same way, the Spirit helps us in our weakness. We do not know what we ought to pray for, but the Spirit himself intercedes for us with groans that words cannot express. 27And he who searches our hearts knows the mind of the Spirit, because the Spirit intercedes for the saints in accordance with God's will.

More Than Conquerors

28And we know that in all things God works for the good of those who love him,[j] who[k] have been called according to his purpose. 29For those God foreknew he also predestined to be conformed to the likeness of his Son, that he might be the firstborn among many brothers. 30And those he predestined, he also called; those he called, he also justified; those he justified, he also glorified.

31What, then, shall we say in response to this? If God is for us, who can be against us? 32He who did not spare his own Son, but gave him up for us all—how will he not also, along with him, graciously give us all things? 33Who will bring any charge against those whom God has chosen? It is God who justifies. 34Who is he that condemns? Christ Jesus, who died—more than that, who was raised to life—is at the right hand of God and is also interceding for us. 35Who shall separate us from the love of Christ? Shall trouble or hardship or persecu-

[a] *1* Some later manuscripts *Jesus, who do not live according to the sinful nature but according to the Spirit,*
[b] *3* Or *the flesh*; also in verses 4, 5, 8, 9, 12 and 13 [c] *3* Or *man, for sin* [d] *3* Or *in the flesh* [e] *6* Or *mind set on the flesh* [f] *7* Or *the mind set on the flesh* [g] *15* Or *adoption* [h] *15* Aramaic for *Father*
[i] *20,21* Or *subjected it in hope. 21For* [j] *28* Some manuscripts *And we know that all things work together for good to those who love God* [k] *28* Or *works together with those who love him to bring about what is good—with those who*

tion or famine or nakedness or danger or
sword? 36As it is written:

"For your sake we face death all day long;
we are considered as sheep to be
slaughtered."[a]

37No, in all these things we are more than conquerors through him who loved us. 38For I am
convinced that neither death nor life, neither
angels nor demons,[b] neither the present nor
the future, nor any powers, 39neither height nor
depth, nor anything else in all creation, will be
able to separate us from the love of God that is
in Christ Jesus our Lord.

God's Sovereign Choice

9 I speak the truth in Christ—I am not lying,
my conscience confirms it in the Holy
Spirit— 2I have great sorrow and unceasing
anguish in my heart. 3For I could wish that I
myself were cursed and cut off from Christ for
the sake of my brothers, those of my own race,
4the people of Israel. Theirs is the adoption as
sons; theirs the divine glory, the covenants, the
receiving of the law, the temple worship and
the promises. 5Theirs are the patriarchs, and
from them is traced the human ancestry of
Christ, who is God over all, forever praised![c]
Amen.

6It is not as though God's word had failed.
For not all who are descended from Israel are
Israel. 7Nor because they are his descendants
are they all Abraham's children. On the contrary, "It is through Isaac that your offspring
will be reckoned."[d] 8In other words, it is not
the natural children who are God's children,
but it is the children of the promise who are
regarded as Abraham's offspring. 9For this
was how the promise was stated: "At the appointed time I will return, and Sarah will have
a son."[e]

10Not only that, but Rebekah's children had
one and the same father, our father Isaac.
11Yet, before the twins were born or had done
anything good or bad—in order that God's
purpose in election might stand: 12not by
works but by him who calls—she was told,
"The older will serve the younger."[f] 13Just
as it is written: "Jacob I loved, but Esau I
hated."[g]

14What then shall we say? Is God unjust?
Not at all! 15For he says to Moses,

"I will have mercy on whom I have
mercy,
and I will have compassion on whom I
have compassion."[h]

16It does not, therefore, depend on man's desire or effort, but on God's mercy. 17For the
Scripture says to Pharaoh: "I raised you up for
this very purpose, that I might display my
power in you and that my name might be proclaimed in all the earth."[i] 18Therefore God has
mercy on whom he wants to have mercy, and
he hardens whom he wants to harden.

19One of you will say to me: "Then why
does God still blame us? For who resists his
will?" 20But who are you, O man, to talk back
to God? "Shall what is formed say to him
who formed it, 'Why did you make me like
this?' "[j] 21Does not the potter have the right to
make out of the same lump of clay some pottery for noble purposes and some for common
use?

22What if God, choosing to show his wrath
and make his power known, bore with great
patience the objects of his wrath—prepared for
destruction? 23What if he did this to make the
riches of his glory known to the objects of his
mercy, whom he prepared in advance for glory— 24even us, whom he also called, not only
from the Jews but also from the Gentiles? 25As
he says in Hosea:

"I will call them 'my people' who are not
my people;
and I will call her 'my loved one' who
is not my loved one,"[k]

26and,

"It will happen that in the very place
where it was said to them,
'You are not my people,'
they will be called 'sons of the living
God.' "[l]

27Isaiah cries out concerning Israel:

"Though the number of the Israelites be
like the sand by the sea,
only the remnant will be saved.
28For the Lord will carry out
his sentence on earth with speed and
finality."[m]

29It is just as Isaiah said previously:

"Unless the Lord Almighty
had left us descendants,
we would have become like Sodom,
we would have been like Gomorrah."[n]

Israel's Unbelief

30What then shall we say? That the Gentiles,
who did not pursue righteousness, have obtained it, a righteousness that is by faith; 31but
Israel, who pursued a law of righteousness, has
not attained it. 32Why not? Because they pursued it not by faith but as if it were by works.
They stumbled over the "stumbling stone."
33As it is written:

"See, I lay in Zion a stone that causes
men to stumble
and a rock that makes them fall,
and the one who trusts in him will never
be put to shame."[o]

[a] *36* Psalm 44:22 [b] *38* Or *nor heavenly rulers* [c] *5* Or *Christ, who is over all. God be forever praised!* Or *Christ. God who is over all be forever praised!* [d] *7* Gen. 21:12 [e] *9* Gen. 18:10,14 [f] *12* Gen. 25:23 [g] *13* Mal. 1:2,3 [h] *15* Exodus 33:19 [i] *17* Exodus 9:16 [j] *20* Isaiah 29:16; 45:9 [k] *25* Hosea 2:23 [l] *26* Hosea 1:10 [m] *28* Isaiah 10:22,23 [n] *29* Isaiah 1:9 [o] *33* Isaiah 8:14; 28:16

10 Brothers, my heart's desire and prayer to God for the Israelites is that they may be saved. **2**For I can testify about them that they are zealous for God, but their zeal is not based on knowledge. **3**Since they did not know the righteousness that comes from God and sought to establish their own, they did not submit to God's righteousness. **4**Christ is the end of the law so that there may be righteousness for everyone who believes.

5Moses describes in this way the righteousness that is by the law: "The man who does these things will live by them."[a] **6**But the righteousness that is by faith says: "Do not say in your heart, 'Who will ascend into heaven?'[b]" (that is, to bring Christ down) **7**"or 'Who will descend into the deep?'[c]" (that is, to bring Christ up from the dead). **8**But what does it say? "The word is near you; it is in your mouth and in your heart,"[d] that is, the word of faith we are proclaiming: **9**That if you confess with your mouth, "Jesus is Lord," and believe in your heart that God raised him from the dead, you will be saved. **10**For it is with your heart that you believe and are justified, and it is with your mouth that you confess and are saved. **11**As the Scripture says, "Anyone who trusts in him will never be put to shame."[e] **12**For there is no difference between Jew and Gentile—the same Lord is Lord of all and richly blesses all who call on him, **13**for, "Everyone who calls on the name of the Lord will be saved."[f]

14How, then, can they call on the one they have not believed in? And how can they believe in the one of whom they have not heard? And how can they hear without someone preaching to them? **15**And how can they preach unless they are sent? As it is written, "How beautiful are the feet of those who bring good news!"[g]

16But not all the Israelites accepted the good news. For Isaiah says, "Lord, who has believed our message?"[h] **17**Consequently, faith comes from hearing the message, and the message is heard through the word of Christ. **18**But I ask: Did they not hear? Of course they did:

"Their voice has gone out into all the
earth,
their words to the ends of the world."[i]

19Again I ask: Did Israel not understand? First, Moses says,

"I will make you envious by those who
are not a nation;
I will make you angry by a nation that
has no understanding."[j]

20And Isaiah boldly says,

"I was found by those who did not seek
me;
I revealed myself to those who did not
ask for me."[k]

21But concerning Israel he says,

"All day long I have held out my hands
to a disobedient and obstinate people."[l]

The Remnant of Israel

11 I ask then: Did God reject his people? By no means! I am an Israelite myself, a descendant of Abraham, from the tribe of Benjamin. **2**God did not reject his people, whom he foreknew. Don't you know what the Scripture says in the passage about Elijah—how he appealed to God against Israel: **3**"Lord, they have killed your prophets and torn down your altars; I am the only one left, and they are trying to kill me"[m]? **4**And what was God's answer to him? "I have reserved for myself seven thousand who have not bowed the knee to Baal."[n] **5**So too, at the present time there is a remnant chosen by grace. **6**And if by grace, then it is no longer by works; if it were, grace would no longer be grace.[o]

7What then? What Israel sought so earnestly it did not obtain, but the elect did. The others were hardened, **8**as it is written:

"God gave them a spirit of stupor,
eyes so that they could not see
and ears so that they could not hear,
to this very day."[p]

9And David says:

"May their table become a snare and a
trap,
a stumbling block and a retribution for
them.
10May their eyes be darkened so they cannot
see,
and their backs be bent forever."[q]

Ingrafted Branches

11Again I ask: Did they stumble so as to fall beyond recovery? Not at all! Rather, because of their transgression, salvation has come to the Gentiles to make Israel envious. **12**But if their transgression means riches for the world, and their loss means riches for the Gentiles, how much greater riches will their fullness bring!

13I am talking to you Gentiles. Inasmuch as I am the apostle to the Gentiles, I make much of my ministry **14**in the hope that I may somehow arouse my own people to envy and save some of them. **15**For if their rejection is the reconciliation of the world, what will their acceptance be but life from the dead? **16**If the part of the dough offered as firstfruits is holy, then the whole batch is holy; if the root is holy, so are the branches.

17If some of the branches have been broken off, and you, though a wild olive shoot, have been grafted in among the others and now share in the nourishing sap from the olive root, **18**do not boast over those branches. If you do,

[a] *5* Lev. 18:5 [b] *6* Deut. 30:12 [c] *7* Deut. 30:13 [d] *8* Deut. 30:14 [e] *11* Isaiah 28:16 [f] *13* Joel 2:32
[g] *15* Isaiah 52:7 [h] *16* Isaiah 53:1 [i] *18* Psalm 19:4 [j] *19* Deut. 32:21 [k] *20* Isaiah 65:1 [l] *21* Isaiah 65:2
[m] *3* 1 Kings 19:10,14 [n] *4* 1 Kings 19:18 [o] *6* Some manuscripts *by grace. But if by works, then it is no longer grace; if it were, work would no longer be work.* [p] *8* Deut. 29:4; Isaiah 29:10 [q] *10* Psalm 69:22,23

consider this: You do not support the root, but the root supports you. 19You will say then, "Branches were broken off so that I could be grafted in." 20Granted. But they were broken off because of unbelief, and you stand by faith. Do not be arrogant, but be afraid. 21For if God did not spare the natural branches, he will not spare you either.

22Consider therefore the kindness and sternness of God: sternness to those who fell, but kindness to you, provided that you continue in his kindness. Otherwise, you also will be cut off. 23And if they do not persist in unbelief, they will be grafted in, for God is able to graft them in again. 24After all, if you were cut out of an olive tree that is wild by nature, and contrary to nature were grafted into a cultivated olive tree, how much more readily will these, the natural branches, be grafted into their own olive tree!

All Israel Will Be Saved

25I do not want you to be ignorant of this mystery, brothers, so that you may not be conceited: Israel has experienced a hardening in part until the full number of the Gentiles has come in. 26And so all Israel will be saved, as it is written:

"The deliverer will come from Zion;
he will turn godlessness away from Jacob.
27And this is[a] my covenant with them
when I take away their sins."[b]

28As far as the gospel is concerned, they are enemies on your account; but as far as election is concerned, they are loved on account of the patriarchs, 29for God's gifts and his call are irrevocable. 30Just as you who were at one time disobedient to God have now received mercy as a result of their disobedience, 31so they too have now become disobedient in order that they too may now[c] receive mercy as a result of God's mercy to you. 32For God has bound all men over to disobedience so that he may have mercy on them all.

Doxology

33Oh, the depth of the riches of the wisdom
and[d] knowledge of God!
How unsearchable his judgments,
and his paths beyond tracing out!
34"Who has known the mind of the Lord?
Or who has been his counselor?"[e]
35"Who has ever given to God,
that God should repay him?"[f]
36For from him and through him and to him
are all things.
To him be the glory forever! Amen.

Living Sacrifices

12 Therefore, I urge you, brothers, in view of God's mercy, to offer your bodies as living sacrifices, holy and pleasing to God—this is your spiritual[g] act of worship. 2Do not conform any longer to the pattern of this world, but be transformed by the renewing of your mind. Then you will be able to test and approve what God's will is—his good, pleasing and perfect will.

3For by the grace given me I say to every one of you: Do not think of yourself more highly than you ought, but rather think of yourself with sober judgment, in accordance with the measure of faith God has given you. 4Just as each of us has one body with many members, and these members do not all have the same function, 5so in Christ we who are many form one body, and each member belongs to all the others. 6We have different gifts, according to the grace given us. If a man's gift is prophesying, let him use it in proportion to his[h] faith. 7If it is serving, let him serve; if it is teaching, let him teach; 8if it is encouraging, let him encourage; if it is contributing to the needs of others, let him give generously; if it is leadership, let him govern diligently; if it is showing mercy, let him do it cheerfully.

Love

9Love must be sincere. Hate what is evil; cling to what is good. 10Be devoted to one another in brotherly love. Honor one another above yourselves. 11Never be lacking in zeal, but keep your spiritual fervor, serving the Lord. 12Be joyful in hope, patient in affliction, faithful in prayer. 13Share with God's people who are in need. Practice hospitality.

14Bless those who persecute you; bless and do not curse. 15Rejoice with those who rejoice; mourn with those who mourn. 16Live in harmony with one another. Do not be proud, but be willing to associate with people of low position.[i] Do not be conceited.

17Do not repay anyone evil for evil. Be careful to do what is right in the eyes of everybody. 18If it is possible, as far as it depends on you, live at peace with everyone. 19Do not take revenge, my friends, but leave room for God's wrath, for it is written: "It is mine to avenge; I will repay,"[j] says the Lord. 20On the contrary:

"If your enemy is hungry, feed him;
if he is thirsty, give him something to drink.
In doing this, you will heap burning coals
on his head."[k]

21Do not be overcome by evil, but overcome evil with good.

Submission to the Authorities

13 Everyone must submit himself to the governing authorities, for there is no authority except that which God has established. The authorities that exist have been established by God. 2Consequently, he who rebels against the authority is rebelling against what God has

[a]27 Or *will be* [b]27 Isaiah 59:20,21; 27:9; Jer. 31:33,34 [c]31 Some manuscripts do not have *now.* [d]33 Or *riches and the wisdom and the* [e]34 Isaiah 40:13 [f]35 Job 41:11 [g]1 Or *reasonable* [h]6 Or *in agreement with the* [i]16 Or *willing to do menial work* [j]19 Deut. 32:35 [k]20 Prov. 25:21,22

instituted, and those who do so will bring judgment on themselves. 3For rulers hold no terror for those who do right, but for those who do wrong. Do you want to be free from fear of the one in authority? Then do what is right and he will commend you. 4For he is God's servant to do you good. But if you do wrong, be afraid, for he does not bear the sword for nothing. He is God's servant, an agent of wrath to bring punishment on the wrongdoer. 5Therefore, it is necessary to submit to the authorities, not only because of possible punishment but also because of conscience.

6This is also why you pay taxes, for the authorities are God's servants, who give their full time to governing. 7Give everyone what you owe him: If you owe taxes, pay taxes; if revenue, then revenue; if respect, then respect; if honor, then honor.

Love, for the Day Is Near

8Let no debt remain outstanding, except the continuing debt to love one another, for he who loves his fellowman has fulfilled the law. 9The commandments, "Do not commit adultery," "Do not murder," "Do not steal," "Do not covet,"[a] and whatever other commandment there may be, are summed up in this one rule: "Love your neighbor as yourself."[b] 10Love does no harm to its neighbor. Therefore love is the fulfillment of the law.

11And do this, understanding the present time. The hour has come for you to wake up from your slumber, because our salvation is nearer now than when we first believed. 12The night is nearly over; the day is almost here. So let us put aside the deeds of darkness and put on the armor of light. 13Let us behave decently, as in the daytime, not in orgies and drunkenness, not in sexual immorality and debauchery, not in dissension and jealousy. 14Rather, clothe yourselves with the Lord Jesus Christ, and do not think about how to gratify the desires of the sinful nature.[c]

The Weak and the Strong

14 Accept him whose faith is weak, without passing judgment on disputable matters. 2One man's faith allows him to eat everything, but another man, whose faith is weak, eats only vegetables. 3The man who eats everything must not look down on him who does not, and the man who does not eat everything must not condemn the man who does, for God has accepted him. 4Who are you to judge someone else's servant? To his own master he stands or falls. And he will stand, for the Lord is able to make him stand.

5One man considers one day more sacred than another; another man considers every day alike. Each one should be fully convinced in his own mind. 6He who regards one day as special, does so to the Lord. He who eats meat, eats to the Lord, for he gives thanks to God; and he who abstains, does so to the Lord and gives thanks to God. 7For none of us lives to himself alone and none of us dies to himself alone. 8If we live, we live to the Lord; and if we die, we die to the Lord. So, whether we live or die, we belong to the Lord.

9For this very reason, Christ died and returned to life so that he might be the Lord of both the dead and the living. 10You, then, why do you judge your brother? Or why do you look down on your brother? For we will all stand before God's judgment seat. 11It is written:

" 'As surely as I live,' says the Lord,
'every knee will bow before me;
every tongue will confess to God.' "[d]

12So then, each of us will give an account of himself to God.

13Therefore let us stop passing judgment on one another. Instead, make up your mind not to put any stumbling block or obstacle in your brother's way. 14As one who is in the Lord Jesus, I am fully convinced that no food[e] is unclean in itself. But if anyone regards something as unclean, then for him it is unclean. 15If your brother is distressed because of what you eat, you are no longer acting in love. Do not by your eating destroy your brother for whom Christ died. 16Do not allow what you consider good to be spoken of as evil. 17For the kingdom of God is not a matter of eating and drinking, but of righteousness, peace and joy in the Holy Spirit, 18because anyone who serves Christ in this way is pleasing to God and approved by men.

19Let us therefore make every effort to do what leads to peace and to mutual edification. 20Do not destroy the work of God for the sake of food. All food is clean, but it is wrong for a man to eat anything that causes someone else to stumble. 21It is better not to eat meat or drink wine or to do anything else that will cause your brother to fall.

22So whatever you believe about these things keep between yourself and God. Blessed is the man who does not condemn himself by what he approves. 23But the man who has doubts is condemned if he eats, because his eating is not from faith; and everything that does not come from faith is sin.

15 We who are strong ought to bear with the failings of the weak and not to please ourselves. 2Each of us should please his neighbor for his good, to build him up. 3For even Christ did not please himself but, as it is written: "The insults of those who insult you have fallen on me."[f] 4For everything that was written in the past was written to teach us, so that through endurance and the encouragement of the Scriptures we might have hope.

5May the God who gives endurance and encouragement give you a spirit of unity among yourselves as you follow Christ Jesus, 6so that

[a] *9* Exodus 20:13-15,17; Deut. 5:17-19,21 [b] *9* Lev. 19:18 [c] *14* Or *the flesh* [d] *11* Isaiah 45:23
[e] *14* Or *that nothing* [f] *3* Psalm 69:9

with one heart and mouth you may glorify the
God and Father of our Lord Jesus Christ.
7Accept one another, then, just as Christ accepted you, in order to bring praise to God.
8For I tell you that Christ has become a servant
of the Jews[a] on behalf of God's truth, to confirm the promises made to the patriarchs 9so
that the Gentiles may glorify God for his mercy, as it is written:

"Therefore I will praise you among the
Gentiles;
I will sing hymns to your name."[b]

10Again, it says,

"Rejoice, O Gentiles, with his people."[c]

11And again,

"Praise the Lord, all you Gentiles,
and sing praises to him, all you
peoples."[d]

12And again, Isaiah says,

"The Root of Jesse will spring up,
one who will arise to rule over the
nations;
the Gentiles will hope in him."[e]

13May the God of hope fill you with all joy
and peace as you trust in him, so that you may
overflow with hope by the power of the Holy
Spirit.

Paul the Minister to the Gentiles

14I myself am convinced, my brothers, that
you yourselves are full of goodness, complete
in knowledge and competent to instruct one
another. 15I have written you quite boldly on
some points, as if to remind you of them again,
because of the grace God gave me 16to be a
minister of Christ Jesus to the Gentiles with
the priestly duty of proclaiming the gospel of
God, so that the Gentiles might become an
offering acceptable to God, sanctified by the
Holy Spirit.
17Therefore I glory in Christ Jesus in my
service to God. 18I will not venture to speak of
anything except what Christ has accomplished
through me in leading the Gentiles to obey
God by what I have said and done— 19by the
power of signs and miracles, through the power of the Spirit. So from Jerusalem all the way
around to Illyricum, I have fully proclaimed
the gospel of Christ. 20It has always been my
ambition to preach the gospel where Christ
was not known, so that I would not be building
on someone else's foundation. 21Rather, as it is
written:

"Those who were not told about him will
see,
and those who have not heard will
understand."[f]

22This is why I have often been hindered from
coming to you.

Paul's Plan to Visit Rome

23But now that there is no more place for me
to work in these regions, and since I have been
longing for many years to see you, 24I plan to
do so when I go to Spain. I hope to visit you
while passing through and to have you assist
me on my journey there, after I have enjoyed
your company for a while. 25Now, however, I
am on my way to Jerusalem in the service of
the saints there. 26For Macedonia and Achaia
were pleased to make a contribution for the
poor among the saints in Jerusalem. 27They
were pleased to do it, and indeed they owe it to
them. For if the Gentiles have shared in the
Jews' spiritual blessings, they owe it to the
Jews to share with them their material blessings. 28So after I have completed this task and
have made sure that they have received this
fruit, I will go to Spain and visit you on the
way. 29I know that when I come to you, I will
come in the full measure of the blessing of
Christ.
30I urge you, brothers, by our Lord Jesus
Christ and by the love of the Spirit, to join me
in my struggle by praying to God for me.
31Pray that I may be rescued from the unbelievers in Judea and that my service in Jerusalem may be acceptable to the saints there, 32so
that by God's will I may come to you with joy
and together with you be refreshed. 33The God
of peace be with you all. Amen.

Personal Greetings

16 I commend to you our sister Phoebe, a
servant[g] of the church in Cenchrea. 2I
ask you to receive her in the Lord in a way
worthy of the saints and to give her any help
she may need from you, for she has been a
great help to many people, including me.

3Greet Priscilla[h] and Aquila, my fellow
workers in Christ Jesus. 4They risked their
lives for me. Not only I but all the churches
of the Gentiles are grateful to them.
5Greet also the church that meets at their
house.
Greet my dear friend Epenetus, who was the
first convert to Christ in the province of
Asia.
6Greet Mary, who worked very hard for you.
7Greet Andronicus and Junias, my relatives
who have been in prison with me. They are
outstanding among the apostles, and they
were in Christ before I was.
8Greet Ampliatus, whom I love in the Lord.
9Greet Urbanus, our fellow worker in Christ,
and my dear friend Stachys.
10Greet Apelles, tested and approved in
Christ.
Greet those who belong to the household of
Aristobulus.
11Greet Herodion, my relative.

[a]*8* Greek *circumcision* [b]*9* 2 Samuel 22:50; Psalm 18:49 [c]*10* Deut. 32:43 [d]*11* Psalm 117:1
[e]*12* Isaiah 11:10 [f]*21* Isaiah 52:15 [g]*1* Or *deaconess* [h]*3* Greek *Prisca*, a variant of *Priscilla*

Greet those in the household of Narcissus
who are in the Lord.
12Greet Tryphena and Tryphosa, those women
who work hard in the Lord.
Greet my dear friend Persis, another woman
who has worked very hard in the Lord.
13Greet Rufus, chosen in the Lord, and his
mother, who has been a mother to me, too.
14Greet Asyncritus, Phlegon, Hermes, Patro-
bas, Hermas and the brothers with them.
15Greet Philologus, Julia, Nereus and his sister, and Olympas and all the saints with
them.
16Greet one another with a holy kiss.
All the churches of Christ send greetings.

17I urge you, brothers, to watch out for those
who cause divisions and put obstacles in your
way that are contrary to the teaching you have
learned. Keep away from them. 18For such
people are not serving our Lord Christ, but
their own appetites. By smooth talk and flattery they deceive the minds of naive people.
19Everyone has heard about your obedience, so
I am full of joy over you; but I want you to be
wise about what is good, and innocent about
what is evil.
20The God of peace will soon crush Satan
under your feet.
The grace of our Lord Jesus be with you.
21Timothy, my fellow worker, sends his
greetings to you, as do Lucius, Jason and So-
sipater, my relatives.
22I, Tertius, who wrote down this letter,
greet you in the Lord.
23Gaius, whose hospitality I and the whole
church here enjoy, sends you his greetings.
Erastus, who is the city's director of public
works, and our brother Quartus send you their
greetings.[a]
25Now to him who is able to establish you
by my gospel and the proclamation of Jesus
Christ, according to the revelation of the mystery hidden for long ages past, 26but now revealed and made known through the prophetic
writings by the command of the eternal God,
so that all nations might believe and obey
him— 27to the only wise God be glory forever
through Jesus Christ! Amen.

1 Corinthians

1 Paul, called to be an apostle of Christ Jesus
by the will of God, and our brother Sosthenes,

2To the church of God in Corinth, to those
sanctified in Christ Jesus and called to be holy,
together with all those everywhere who call on
the name of our Lord Jesus Christ—their Lord
and ours:

3Grace and peace to you from God our Father and the Lord Jesus Christ.

Thanksgiving

4I always thank God for you because of his
grace given you in Christ Jesus. 5For in him
you have been enriched in every way—in all
your speaking and in all your knowledge—
6because our testimony about Christ was confirmed in you. 7Therefore you do not lack any
spiritual gift as you eagerly wait for our Lord
Jesus Christ to be revealed. 8He will keep you
strong to the end, so that you will be blameless
on the day of our Lord Jesus Christ. 9God, who
has called you into fellowship with his Son
Jesus Christ our Lord, is faithful.

Divisions in the Church

10I appeal to you, brothers, in the name of
our Lord Jesus Christ, that all of you agree
with one another so that there may be no divisions among you and that you may be perfectly
united in mind and thought. 11My brothers,
some from Chloe's household have informed
me that there are quarrels among you. 12What
I mean is this: One of you says, "I follow
Paul"; another, "I follow Apollos"; another, "I
follow Cephas[b]"; still another, "I follow
Christ."
13Is Christ divided? Was Paul crucified for
you? Were you baptized into[c] the name of
Paul? 14I am thankful that I did not baptize any
of you except Crispus and Gaius, 15so no one
can say that you were baptized into my name.
16(Yes, I also baptized the household of Stephanas; beyond that, I don't remember if I baptized anyone else.) 17For Christ did not send
me to baptize, but to preach the gospel—not
with words of human wisdom, lest the cross of
Christ be emptied of its power.

Christ the Wisdom and Power of God

18For the message of the cross is foolishness
to those who are perishing, but to us who are
being saved it is the power of God. 19For it is
written:

"I will destroy the wisdom of the wise;
the intelligence of the intelligent I will
frustrate."[d]

20Where is the wise man? Where is the
scholar? Where is the philosopher of this age?
Has not God made foolish the wisdom of the
world? 21For since in the wisdom of God the
world through its wisdom did not know him,
God was pleased through the foolishness of

[a] 23 Some manuscripts *their greetings.* 24*May the grace of our Lord Jesus Christ be with all of you. Amen.*
[b] 12 That is, Peter [c] 13 Or *in*; also in verse 15 [d] 19 Isaiah 29:14

what was preached to save those who believe.
22Jews demand miraculous signs and Greeks
look for wisdom, 23but we preach Christ crucified: a stumbling block to Jews and foolishness
to Gentiles, 24but to those whom God has
called, both Jews and Greeks, Christ the power
of God and the wisdom of God. 25For the foolishness of God is wiser than man's wisdom,
and the weakness of God is stronger than
man's strength.
26Brothers, think of what you were when
you were called. Not many of you were wise
by human standards; not many were influen-
tial; not many were of noble birth. 27But God
chose the foolish things of the world to shame
the wise; God chose the weak things of the
world to shame the strong. 28He chose the
lowly things of this world and the despised
things—and the things that are not—to nullify
the things that are, 29so that no one may boast
before him. 30It is because of him that you are
in Christ Jesus, who has become for us wisdom
from God—that is, our righteousness, holiness
and redemption. 31Therefore, as it is written:
"Let him who boasts boast in the Lord."[a]
2 When I came to you, brothers, I did not
come with eloquence or superior wisdom
as I proclaimed to you the testimony about
God.[b] 2For I resolved to know nothing while
I was with you except Jesus Christ and him
crucified. 3I came to you in weakness and fear,
and with much trembling. 4My message and
my preaching were not with wise and persuasive words, but with a demonstration of the
Spirit's power, 5so that your faith might not
rest on men's wisdom, but on God's power.

Wisdom From the Spirit

6We do, however, speak a message of wisdom among the mature, but not the wisdom of
this age or of the rulers of this age, who are
coming to nothing. 7No, we speak of God's
secret wisdom, a wisdom that has been hidden
and that God destined for our glory before time
began. 8None of the rulers of this age understood it, for if they had, they would not have
crucified the Lord of glory. 9However, as it is
written:

"No eye has seen,
no ear has heard,
no mind has conceived
what God has prepared for those who
love him"[c]—

10but God has revealed it to us by his Spirit.
The Spirit searches all things, even the deep
things of God. 11For who among men knows
the thoughts of a man except the man's spirit
within him? In the same way no one knows the
thoughts of God except the Spirit of God.
12We have not received the spirit of the world
but the Spirit who is from God, that we may
understand what God has freely given us.
13This is what we speak, not in words taught us
by human wisdom but in words taught by the
Spirit, expressing spiritual truths in spiritual
words.[d] 14The man without the Spirit does not
accept the things that come from the Spirit of
God, for they are foolishness to him, and he
cannot understand them, because they are spiritually discerned. 15The spiritual man makes
judgments about all things, but he himself is
not subject to any man's judgment:

16"For who has known the mind of the Lord
that he may instruct him?"[e]

But we have the mind of Christ.

On Divisions in the Church

3 Brothers, I could not address you as spiritual but as worldly—mere infants in
Christ. 2I gave you milk, not solid food, for
you were not yet ready for it. Indeed, you are
still not ready. 3You are still worldly. For since
there is jealousy and quarreling among you,
are you not worldly? Are you not acting like
mere men? 4For when one says, "I follow
Paul," and another, "I follow Apollos," are you
not mere men?
5What, after all, is Apollos? And what is
Paul? Only servants, through whom you came
to believe—as the Lord has assigned to each
his task. 6I planted the seed, Apollos watered
it, but God made it grow. 7So neither he who
plants nor he who waters is anything, but only
God, who makes things grow. 8The man who
plants and the man who waters have one purpose, and each will be rewarded according to
his own labor. 9For we are God's fellow workers; you are God's field, God's building.
10By the grace God has given me, I laid a
foundation as an expert builder, and someone
else is building on it. But each one should be
careful how he builds. 11For no one can lay
any foundation other than the one already laid,
which is Jesus Christ. 12If any man builds
on this foundation using gold, silver, costly
stones, wood, hay or straw, 13his work will be
shown for what it is, because the Day will
bring it to light. It will be revealed with fire,
and the fire will test the quality of each man's
work. 14If what he has built survives, he will
receive his reward. 15If it is burned up, he will
suffer loss; he himself will be saved, but only
as one escaping through the flames.
16Don't you know that you yourselves are
God's temple and that God's Spirit lives in
you? 17If anyone destroys God's temple, God
will destroy him; for God's temple is sacred,
and you are that temple.
18Do not deceive yourselves. If any one of
you thinks he is wise by the standards of this
age, he should become a "fool" so that he may
become wise. 19For the wisdom of this world
is foolishness in God's sight. As it is written:
"He catches the wise in their craftiness"[f];
20and again, "The Lord knows that the

[a] *31* Jer. 9:24 [b] *1* Some manuscripts *as I proclaimed to you God's mystery* [c] *9* Isaiah 64:4
[d] *13* Or *Spirit, interpreting spiritual truths to spiritual men* [e] *16* Isaiah 40:13 [f] *19* Job 5:13

thoughts of the wise are futile."[a] 21So then, no
more boasting about men! All things are yours,
22whether Paul or Apollos or Cephas[b] or the
world or life or death or the present or the
future—all are yours, 23and you are of Christ,
and Christ is of God.

Apostles of Christ

4 So then, men ought to regard us as servants
of Christ and as those entrusted with the
secret things of God. 2Now it is required that
those who have been given a trust must prove
faithful. 3I care very little if I am judged by
you or by any human court; indeed, I do not
even judge myself. 4My conscience is clear,
but that does not make me innocent. It is the
Lord who judges me. 5Therefore judge nothing
before the appointed time; wait till the Lord
comes. He will bring to light what is hidden in
darkness and will expose the motives of men's
hearts. At that time each will receive his praise
from God.

6Now, brothers, I have applied these things
to myself and Apollos for your benefit, so that
you may learn from us the meaning of the
saying, "Do not go beyond what is written."
Then you will not take pride in one man over
against another. 7For who makes you different
from anyone else? What do you have that you
did not receive? And if you did receive it, why
do you boast as though you did not?

8Already you have all you want! Already
you have become rich! You have become
kings—and that without us! How I wish that
you really had become kings so that we might
be kings with you! 9For it seems to me that
God has put us apostles on display at the end
of the procession, like men condemned to die
in the arena. We have been made a spectacle to
the whole universe, to angels as well as to
men. 10We are fools for Christ, but you are so
wise in Christ! We are weak, but you are
strong! You are honored, we are dishonored!
11To this very hour we go hungry and thirsty,
we are in rags, we are brutally treated, we
are homeless. 12We work hard with our own
hands. When we are cursed, we bless; when
we are persecuted, we endure it; 13when we are
slandered, we answer kindly. Up to this moment we have become the scum of the earth,
the refuse of the world.

14I am not writing this to shame you, but to
warn you, as my dear children. 15Even though
you have ten thousand guardians in Christ, you
do not have many fathers, for in Christ Jesus
I became your father through the gospel.
16Therefore I urge you to imitate me. 17For this
reason I am sending to you Timothy, my son
whom I love, who is faithful in the Lord. He
will remind you of my way of life in Christ
Jesus, which agrees with what I teach everywhere in every church.

18Some of you have become arrogant, as if
I were not coming to you. 19But I will come to
you very soon, if the Lord is willing, and then
I will find out not only how these arrogant
people are talking, but what power they have.
20For the kingdom of God is not a matter of
talk but of power. 21What do you prefer? Shall
I come to you with a whip, or in love and with
a gentle spirit?

Expel the Immoral Brother!

5 It is actually reported that there is sexual
immorality among you, and of a kind that
does not occur even among pagans: A man
has his father's wife. 2And you are proud!
Shouldn't you rather have been filled with
grief and have put out of your fellowship the
man who did this? 3Even though I am not
physically present, I am with you in spirit. And
I have already passed judgment on the one
who did this, just as if I were present. 4When
you are assembled in the name of our Lord
Jesus and I am with you in spirit, and the power of our Lord Jesus is present, 5hand this man
over to Satan, so that the sinful nature[c] may be
destroyed and his spirit saved on the day of the
Lord.

6Your boasting is not good. Don't you know
that a little yeast works through the whole
batch of dough? 7Get rid of the old yeast that
you may be a new batch without yeast—as you
really are. For Christ, our Passover lamb, has
been sacrificed. 8Therefore let us keep the Festival, not with the old yeast, the yeast of malice
and wickedness, but with bread without yeast,
the bread of sincerity and truth.

9I have written you in my letter not to associate with sexually immoral people— 10not at
all meaning the people of this world who are
immoral, or the greedy and swindlers, or idolaters. In that case you would have to leave this
world. 11But now I am writing you that you
must not associate with anyone who calls himself a brother but is sexually immoral or
greedy, an idolater or a slanderer, a drunkard
or a swindler. With such a man do not even
eat.

12What business is it of mine to judge those
outside the church? Are you not to judge those
inside? 13God will judge those outside. "Expel
the wicked man from among you."[d]

Lawsuits Among Believers

6 If any of you has a dispute with another,
dare he take it before the ungodly for judgment instead of before the saints? 2Do you not
know that the saints will judge the world? And
if you are to judge the world, are you not competent to judge trivial cases? 3Do you not
know that we will judge angels? How much
more the things of this life! 4Therefore, if you
have disputes about such matters, appoint as
judges even men of little account in the
church![e] 5I say this to shame you. Is it possible
that there is nobody among you wise enough to
judge a dispute between believers? 6But in-

[a] *20* Psalm 94:11 [b] *22* That is, Peter [c] *5* Or *that his body*; or *that the flesh* [d] *13* Deut. 17:7; 19:19; 21:21; 22:21,24; 24:7 [e] *4* Or *matters, do you appoint as judges men of little account in the church?*

stead, one brother goes to law against another—and this in front of unbelievers!
7The very fact that you have lawsuits among
you means you have been completely defeated
already. Why not rather be wronged? Why not
rather be cheated? 8Instead, you yourselves
cheat and do wrong, and you do this to your
brothers.
9Do you not know that the wicked will not
inherit the kingdom of God? Do not be deceived: Neither the sexually immoral nor idolaters nor adulterers nor male prostitutes nor
homosexual offenders 10nor thieves nor the
greedy nor drunkards nor slanderers nor swindlers will inherit the kingdom of God. 11And
that is what some of you were. But you were
washed, you were sanctified, you were justified in the name of the Lord Jesus Christ and
by the Spirit of our God.

Sexual Immorality

12"Everything is permissible for me"—but
not everything is beneficial. "Everything is
permissible for me"—but I will not be mas-
tered by anything. 13"Food for the stomach and
the stomach for food"—but God will destroy
them both. The body is not meant for sexual
immorality, but for the Lord, and the Lord for
the body. 14By his power God raised the Lord
from the dead, and he will raise us also. 15Do
you not know that your bodies are members of
Christ himself? Shall I then take the members
of Christ and unite them with a prostitute?
Never! 16Do you not know that he who unites
himself with a prostitute is one with her in
body? For it is said, "The two will become one
flesh."[a] 17But he who unites himself with the
Lord is one with him in spirit.
18Flee from sexual immorality. All other
sins a man commits are outside his body, but
he who sins sexually sins against his own
body. 19Do you not know that your body is a
temple of the Holy Spirit, who is in you, whom
you have received from God? You are not your
own; 20you were bought at a price. Therefore
honor God with your body.

Marriage

7 Now for the matters you wrote about: It is
good for a man not to marry.[b] 2But since
there is so much immorality, each man should
have his own wife, and each woman her own
husband. 3The husband should fulfill his marital duty to his wife, and likewise the wife to
her husband. 4The wife's body does not belong
to her alone but also to her husband. In the
same way, the husband's body does not belong
to him alone but also to his wife. 5Do not deprive each other except by mutual consent and
for a time, so that you may devote yourselves
to prayer. Then come together again so that
Satan will not tempt you because of your lack
of self-control. 6I say this as a concession, not
as a command. 7I wish that all men were as I
am. But each man has his own gift from God;
one has this gift, another has that.
8Now to the unmarried and the widows I
say: It is good for them to stay unmarried, as
I am. 9But if they cannot control themselves,
they should marry, for it is better to marry than
to burn with passion.
10To the married I give this command (not I,
but the Lord): A wife must not separate from
her husband. 11But if she does, she must remain unmarried or else be reconciled to her
husband. And a husband must not divorce his
wife.
12To the rest I say this (I, not the Lord): If
any brother has a wife who is not a believer
and she is willing to live with him, he must not
divorce her. 13And if a woman has a husband
who is not a believer and he is willing to live
with her, she must not divorce him. 14For the
unbelieving husband has been sanctified
through his wife, and the unbelieving wife has
been sanctified through her believing husband.
Otherwise your children would be unclean, but
as it is, they are holy.
15But if the unbeliever leaves, let him do so.
A believing man or woman is not bound in
such circumstances; God has called us to live
in peace. 16How do you know, wife, whether
you will save your husband? Or, how do you
know, husband, whether you will save your
wife?
17Nevertheless, each one should retain the
place in life that the Lord assigned to him and
to which God has called him. This is the rule
I lay down in all the churches. 18Was a man
already circumcised when he was called? He
should not become uncircumcised. Was a man
uncircumcised when he was called? He should
not be circumcised. 19Circumcision is nothing
and uncircumcision is nothing. Keeping God's
commands is what counts. 20Each one should
remain in the situation which he was in when
God called him. 21Were you a slave when you
were called? Don't let it trouble you—although if you can gain your freedom, do so.
22For he who was a slave when he was called
by the Lord is the Lord's freedman; similarly,
he who was a free man when he was called is
Christ's slave. 23You were bought at a price;
do not become slaves of men. 24Brothers, each
man, as responsible to God, should remain in
the situation God called him to.
25Now about virgins: I have no command
from the Lord, but I give a judgment as one
who by the Lord's mercy is trustworthy. 26Be-
cause of the present crisis, I think that it is
good for you to remain as you are. 27Are you
married? Do not seek a divorce. Are you unmarried? Do not look for a wife. 28But if you
do marry, you have not sinned; and if a virgin
marries, she has not sinned. But those who
marry will face many troubles in this life, and
I want to spare you this.
29What I mean, brothers, is that the time is
short. From now on those who have wives

[a]*16* Gen. 2:24 [b]*1* Or "*It is good for a man not to have sexual relations with a woman.*"

should live as if they had none; 30those who mourn, as if they did not; those who are happy, as if they were not; those who buy something, as if it were not theirs to keep; 31those who use the things of the world, as if not engrossed in them. For this world in its present form is passing away.

32I would like you to be free from concern. An unmarried man is concerned about the Lord's affairs—how he can please the Lord. 33But a married man is concerned about the affairs of this world—how he can please his wife— 34and his interests are divided. An unmarried woman or virgin is concerned about the Lord's affairs: Her aim is to be devoted to the Lord in both body and spirit. But a married woman is concerned about the affairs of this world—how she can please her husband. 35I am saying this for your own good, not to restrict you, but that you may live in a right way in undivided devotion to the Lord.

36If anyone thinks he is acting improperly toward the virgin he is engaged to, and if she is getting along in years and he feels he ought to marry, he should do as he wants. He is not sinning. They should get married. 37But the man who has settled the matter in his own mind, who is under no compulsion but has control over his own will, and who has made up his mind not to marry the virgin—this man also does the right thing. 38So then, he who marries the virgin does right, but he who does not marry her does even better.[a]

39A woman is bound to her husband as long as he lives. But if her husband dies, she is free to marry anyone she wishes, but he must belong to the Lord. 40In my judgment, she is happier if she stays as she is—and I think that I too have the Spirit of God.

Food Sacrificed to Idols

8 Now about food sacrificed to idols: We know that we all possess knowledge.[b] Knowledge puffs up, but love builds up. 2The man who thinks he knows something does not yet know as he ought to know. 3But the man who loves God is known by God.

4So then, about eating food sacrificed to idols: We know that an idol is nothing at all in the world and that there is no God but one. 5For even if there are so-called gods, whether in heaven or on earth (as indeed there are many "gods" and many "lords"), 6yet for us there is but one God, the Father, from whom all things came and for whom we live; and there is but one Lord, Jesus Christ, through whom all things came and through whom we live.

7But not everyone knows this. Some people are still so accustomed to idols that when they eat such food they think of it as having been sacrificed to an idol, and since their conscience is weak, it is defiled. 8But food does not bring us near to God; we are no worse if we do not eat, and no better if we do.

9Be careful, however, that the exercise of your freedom does not become a stumbling block to the weak. 10For if anyone with a weak conscience sees you who have this knowledge eating in an idol's temple, won't he be emboldened to eat what has been sacrificed to idols? 11So this weak brother, for whom Christ died, is destroyed by your knowledge. 12When you sin against your brothers in this way and wound their weak conscience, you sin against Christ. 13Therefore, if what I eat causes my brother to fall into sin, I will never eat meat again, so that I will not cause him to fall.

The Rights of an Apostle

9 Am I not free? Am I not an apostle? Have I not seen Jesus our Lord? Are you not the result of my work in the Lord? 2Even though I may not be an apostle to others, surely I am to you! For you are the seal of my apostleship in the Lord.

3This is my defense to those who sit in judgment on me. 4Don't we have the right to food and drink? 5Don't we have the right to take a believing wife along with us, as do the other apostles and the Lord's brothers and Cephas[c]? 6Or is it only I and Barnabas who must work for a living?

7Who serves as a soldier at his own expense? Who plants a vineyard and does not eat of its grapes? Who tends a flock and does not drink of the milk? 8Do I say this merely from a human point of view? Doesn't the Law say the same thing? 9For it is written in the Law of Moses: "Do not muzzle an ox while it is treading out the grain."[d] Is it about oxen that God is concerned? 10Surely he says this for us, doesn't he? Yes, this was written for us, because when the plowman plows and the thresher threshes, they ought to do so in the hope of sharing in the harvest. 11If we have sown spiritual seed among you, is it too much if we reap a material harvest from you? 12If others have this right of support from you, shouldn't we have it all the more?

But we did not use this right. On the contrary, we put up with anything rather than hinder the gospel of Christ. 13Don't you know that those who work in the temple get their food from the temple, and those who serve at the altar share in what is offered on the altar? 14In the same way, the Lord has commanded that those who preach the gospel should receive their living from the gospel.

15But I have not used any of these rights. And I am not writing this in the hope that you will do such things for me. I would rather die than have anyone deprive me of this boast.

[a] *36-38* Or *36If anyone thinks he is not treating his daughter properly, and if she is getting along in years, and he feels she ought to marry, he should do as he wants. He is not sinning. He should let her get married. 37But the man who has settled the matter in his own mind, who is under no compulsion but has control over his own will, and who has made up his mind to keep the virgin unmarried—this man also does the right thing. 38So then, he who gives his virgin in marriage does right, but he who does not give her in marriage does even better.*
[b] *1* Or *"We all possess knowledge," as you say*
[c] *5* That is, Peter
[d] *9* Deut. 25:4

16Yet when I preach the gospel, I cannot boast, for I am compelled to preach. Woe to me if I do not preach the gospel! 17If I preach voluntarily, I have a reward; if not voluntarily, I am simply discharging the trust committed to me. 18What then is my reward? Just this: that in preaching the gospel I may offer it free of charge, and so not make use of my rights in preaching it.

19Though I am free and belong to no man, I make myself a slave to everyone, to win as many as possible. 20To the Jews I became like a Jew, to win the Jews. To those under the law I became like one under the law (though I myself am not under the law), so as to win those under the law. 21To those not having the law I became like one not having the law (though I am not free from God's law but am under Christ's law), so as to win those not having the law. 22To the weak I became weak, to win the weak. I have become all things to all men so that by all possible means I might save some. 23I do all this for the sake of the gospel, that I may share in its blessings.

24Do you not know that in a race all the runners run, but only one gets the prize? Run in such a way as to get the prize. 25Everyone who competes in the games goes into strict training. They do it to get a crown that will not last; but we do it to get a crown that will last forever. 26Therefore I do not run like a man running aimlessly; I do not fight like a man beating the air. 27No, I beat my body and make it my slave so that after I have preached to others, I myself will not be disqualified for the prize.

Warnings From Israel's History

10 For I do not want you to be ignorant of the fact, brothers, that our forefathers were all under the cloud and that they all passed through the sea. 2They were all baptized into Moses in the cloud and in the sea. 3They all ate the same spiritual food 4and drank the same spiritual drink; for they drank from the spiritual rock that accompanied them, and that rock was Christ. 5Nevertheless, God was not pleased with most of them; their bodies were scattered over the desert.

6Now these things occurred as examples[a] to keep us from setting our hearts on evil things as they did. 7Do not be idolaters, as some of them were; as it is written: "The people sat down to eat and drink and got up to indulge in pagan revelry."[b] 8We should not commit sexual immorality, as some of them did—and in one day twenty-three thousand of them died. 9We should not test the Lord, as some of them did—and were killed by snakes. 10And do not grumble, as some of them did—and were killed by the destroying angel.

11These things happened to them as examples and were written down as warnings for us, on whom the fulfillment of the ages has come. 12So, if you think you are standing firm, be careful that you don't fall! 13No temptation has seized you except what is common to man. And God is faithful; he will not let you be tempted beyond what you can bear. But when you are tempted, he will also provide a way out so that you can stand up under it.

Idol Feasts and the Lord's Supper

14Therefore, my dear friends, flee from idolatry. 15I speak to sensible people; judge for yourselves what I say. 16Is not the cup of thanksgiving for which we give thanks a participation in the blood of Christ? And is not the bread that we break a participation in the body of Christ? 17Because there is one loaf, we, who are many, are one body, for we all partake of the one loaf.

18Consider the people of Israel: Do not those who eat the sacrifices participate in the altar? 19Do I mean then that a sacrifice offered to an idol is anything, or that an idol is anything? 20No, but the sacrifices of pagans are offered to demons, not to God, and I do not want you to be participants with demons. 21You cannot drink the cup of the Lord and the cup of demons too; you cannot have a part in both the Lord's table and the table of demons. 22Are we trying to arouse the Lord's jealousy? Are we stronger than he?

The Believer's Freedom

23"Everything is permissible"—but not everything is beneficial. "Everything is permissible"—but not everything is constructive. 24Nobody should seek his own good, but the good of others.

25Eat anything sold in the meat market without raising questions of conscience, 26for, "The earth is the Lord's, and everything in it."[c]

27If some unbeliever invites you to a meal and you want to go, eat whatever is put before you without raising questions of conscience. 28But if anyone says to you, "This has been offered in sacrifice," then do not eat it, both for the sake of the man who told you and for conscience' sake[d]— 29the other man's conscience, I mean, not yours. For why should my freedom be judged by another's conscience? 30If I take part in the meal with thankfulness, why am I denounced because of something I thank God for?

31So whether you eat or drink or whatever you do, do it all for the glory of God. 32Do not cause anyone to stumble, whether Jews, Greeks or the church of God— 33even as I try to please everybody in every way. For I am not seeking my own good but the good of many, so that they may be saved.

11 1Follow my example, as I follow the example of Christ.

Propriety in Worship

2I praise you for remembering me in every-

[a]6 Or *types*; also in verse 11 [b]7 Exodus 32:6 [c]26 Psalm 24:1 [d]28 Some manuscripts *conscience' sake, for "the earth is the Lord's and everything in it"*

thing and for holding to the teachings,[a] just as I passed them on to you.

3Now I want you to realize that the head of every man is Christ, and the head of the woman is man, and the head of Christ is God. 4Every man who prays or prophesies with his head covered dishonors his head. 5And every woman who prays or prophesies with her head uncovered dishonors her head—it is just as though her head were shaved. 6If a woman does not cover her head, she should have her hair cut off; and if it is a disgrace for a woman to have her hair cut or shaved off, she should cover her head. 7A man ought not to cover his head,[b] since he is the image and glory of God; but the woman is the glory of man. 8For man did not come from woman, but woman from man; 9neither was man created for woman, but woman for man. 10For this reason, and because of the angels, the woman ought to have a sign of authority on her head.

11In the Lord, however, woman is not independent of man, nor is man independent of woman. 12For as woman came from man, so also man is born of woman. But everything comes from God. 13Judge for yourselves: Is it proper for a woman to pray to God with her head uncovered? 14Does not the very nature of things teach you that if a man has long hair, it is a disgrace to him, 15but that if a woman has long hair, it is her glory? For long hair is given to her as a covering. 16If anyone wants to be contentious about this, we have no other practice—nor do the churches of God.

The Lord's Supper

17In the following directives I have no praise for you, for your meetings do more harm than good. 18In the first place, I hear that when you come together as a church, there are divisions among you, and to some extent I believe it. 19No doubt there have to be differences among you to show which of you have God's approval. 20When you come together, it is not the Lord's Supper you eat, 21for as you eat, each of you goes ahead without waiting for anybody else. One remains hungry, another gets drunk. 22Don't you have homes to eat and drink in? Or do you despise the church of God and humiliate those who have nothing? What shall I say to you? Shall I praise you for this? Certainly not!

23For I received from the Lord what I also passed on to you: The Lord Jesus, on the night he was betrayed, took bread, 24and when he had given thanks, he broke it and said, "This is my body, which is for you; do this in remembrance of me." 25In the same way, after supper he took the cup, saying, "This cup is the new covenant in my blood; do this, whenever you drink it, in remembrance of me." 26For whenever you eat this bread and drink this cup, you proclaim the Lord's death until he comes.

27Therefore, whoever eats the bread or drinks the cup of the Lord in an unworthy manner will be guilty of sinning against the body and blood of the Lord. 28A man ought to examine himself before he eats of the bread and drinks of the cup. 29For anyone who eats and drinks without recognizing the body of the Lord eats and drinks judgment on himself. 30That is why many among you are weak and sick, and a number of you have fallen asleep. 31But if we judged ourselves, we would not come under judgment. 32When we are judged by the Lord, we are being disciplined so that we will not be condemned with the world.

33So then, my brothers, when you come together to eat, wait for each other. 34If anyone is hungry, he should eat at home, so that when you meet together it may not result in judgment.

And when I come I will give further directions.

Spiritual Gifts

12 Now about spiritual gifts, brothers, I do not want you to be ignorant. 2You know that when you were pagans, somehow or other you were influenced and led astray to mute idols. 3Therefore I tell you that no one who is speaking by the Spirit of God says, "Jesus be cursed," and no one can say, "Jesus is Lord," except by the Holy Spirit.

4There are different kinds of gifts, but the same Spirit. 5There are different kinds of service, but the same Lord. 6There are different kinds of working, but the same God works all of them in all men.

7Now to each one the manifestation of the Spirit is given for the common good. 8To one there is given through the Spirit the message of wisdom, to another the message of knowledge by means of the same Spirit, 9to another faith by the same Spirit, to another gifts of healing by that one Spirit, 10to another miraculous powers, to another prophecy, to another distinguishing between spirits, to another speaking in different kinds of tongues,[c] and to still another the interpretation of tongues.[c] 11All these are the work of one and the same Spirit, and he gives them to each one, just as he determines.

One Body, Many Parts

12The body is a unit, though it is made up of many parts; and though all its parts are many, they form one body. So it is with Christ. 13For we were all baptized by[d] one Spirit into one body—whether Jews or Greeks, slave or free—and we were all given the one Spirit to drink.

14Now the body is not made up of one part

[a]2 Or *traditions* [b]4-7 Or *4Every man who prays or prophesies with long hair dishonors his head. 5And every woman who prays or prophesies with no covering ⌞of hair⌟ on her head dishonors her head—she is just like one of the "shorn women." 6If a woman has no covering, let her be for now with short hair, but since it is a disgrace for a woman to have her hair shorn or shaved, she should grow it again. 7A man ought not to have long hair* [c]10 Or *languages*; also in verse 28 [d]13 Or *with*; or *in*

but of many. 15If the foot should say, "Because I am not a hand, I do not belong to the body," it would not for that reason cease to be part of the body. 16And if the ear should say, "Because I am not an eye, I do not belong to the body," it would not for that reason cease to be part of the body. 17If the whole body were an eye, where would the sense of hearing be? If the whole body were an ear, where would the sense of smell be? 18But in fact God has arranged the parts in the body, every one of them, just as he wanted them to be. 19If they were all one part, where would the body be? 20As it is, there are many parts, but one body.

21The eye cannot say to the hand, "I don't need you!" And the head cannot say to the feet, "I don't need you!" 22On the contrary, those parts of the body that seem to be weaker are indispensable, 23and the parts that we think are less honorable we treat with special honor. And the parts that are unpresentable are treated with special modesty, 24while our presentable parts need no special treatment. But God has combined the members of the body and has given greater honor to the parts that lacked it, 25so that there should be no division in the body, but that its parts should have equal concern for each other. 26If one part suffers, every part suffers with it; if one part is honored, every part rejoices with it.

27Now you are the body of Christ, and each one of you is a part of it. 28And in the church God has appointed first of all apostles, second prophets, third teachers, then workers of miracles, also those having gifts of healing, those able to help others, those with gifts of administration, and those speaking in different kinds of tongues. 29Are all apostles? Are all prophets? Are all teachers? Do all work miracles? 30Do all have gifts of healing? Do all speak in tongues[a]? Do all interpret? 31But eagerly desire[b] the greater gifts.

Love

And now I will show you the most excellent way.

13 If I speak in the tongues[c] of men and of angels, but have not love, I am only a resounding gong or a clanging cymbal. 2If I have the gift of prophecy and can fathom all mysteries and all knowledge, and if I have a faith that can move mountains, but have not love, I am nothing. 3If I give all I possess to the poor and surrender my body to the flames,[d] but have not love, I gain nothing.

4Love is patient, love is kind. It does not envy, it does not boast, it is not proud. 5It is not rude, it is not self-seeking, it is not easily angered, it keeps no record of wrongs. 6Love does not delight in evil but rejoices with the truth. 7It always protects, always trusts, always hopes, always perseveres.

8Love never fails. But where there are prophecies, they will cease; where there are tongues, they will be stilled; where there is knowledge, it will pass away. 9For we know in part and we prophesy in part, 10but when perfection comes, the imperfect disappears. 11When I was a child, I talked like a child, I thought like a child, I reasoned like a child. When I became a man, I put childish ways behind me. 12Now we see but a poor reflection as in a mirror; then we shall see face to face. Now I know in part; then I shall know fully, even as I am fully known.

13And now these three remain: faith, hope and love. But the greatest of these is love.

Gifts of Prophecy and Tongues

14 Follow the way of love and eagerly desire spiritual gifts, especially the gift of prophecy. 2For anyone who speaks in a tongue[e] does not speak to men but to God. Indeed, no one understands him; he utters mysteries with his spirit.[f] 3But everyone who prophesies speaks to men for their strengthening, encouragement and comfort. 4He who speaks in a tongue edifies himself, but he who prophesies edifies the church. 5I would like every one of you to speak in tongues,[g] but I would rather have you prophesy. He who prophesies is greater than one who speaks in tongues,[g] unless he interprets, so that the church may be edified.

6Now, brothers, if I come to you and speak in tongues, what good will I be to you, unless I bring you some revelation or knowledge or prophecy or word of instruction? 7Even in the case of lifeless things that make sounds, such as the flute or harp, how will anyone know what tune is being played unless there is a distinction in the notes? 8Again, if the trumpet does not sound a clear call, who will get ready for battle? 9So it is with you. Unless you speak intelligible words with your tongue, how will anyone know what you are saying? You will just be speaking into the air. 10Undoubtedly there are all sorts of languages in the world, yet none of them is without meaning. 11If then I do not grasp the meaning of what someone is saying, I am a foreigner to the speaker, and he is a foreigner to me. 12So it is with you. Since you are eager to have spiritual gifts, try to excel in gifts that build up the church.

13For this reason anyone who speaks in a tongue should pray that he may interpret what he says. 14For if I pray in a tongue, my spirit prays, but my mind is unfruitful. 15So what shall I do? I will pray with my spirit, but I will also pray with my mind; I will sing with my spirit, but I will also sing with my mind. 16If you are praising God with your spirit, how can one who finds himself among those who do not understand[h] say "Amen" to your thanksgiving, since he does not know what you are

[a]30 Or *other languages* [b]31 Or *But you are eagerly desiring* [c]1 Or *languages* [d]3 Some early manuscripts *body that I may boast* [e]2 Or *another language*; also in verses 4, 13, 14, 19, 26 and 27 [f]2 Or *by the Spirit* [g]5 Or *other languages*; also in verses 6, 18, 22, 23 and 39 [h]16 Or *among the inquirers*

saying? 17You may be giving thanks well enough, but the other man is not edified.

18I thank God that I speak in tongues more than all of you. 19But in the church I would rather speak five intelligible words to instruct others than ten thousand words in a tongue.

20Brothers, stop thinking like children. In regard to evil be infants, but in your thinking be adults. 21In the Law it is written:

"Through men of strange tongues
 and through the lips of foreigners
I will speak to this people,
 but even then they will not listen to
  me,"[a]
says the Lord.

22Tongues, then, are a sign, not for believers but for unbelievers; prophecy, however, is for believers, not for unbelievers. 23So if the whole church comes together and everyone speaks in tongues, and some who do not understand[b] or some unbelievers come in, will they not say that you are out of your mind? 24But if an unbeliever or someone who does not understand[c] comes in while everybody is prophesying, he will be convinced by all that he is a sinner and will be judged by all, 25and the secrets of his heart will be laid bare. So he will fall down and worship God, exclaiming, "God is really among you!"

Orderly Worship

26What then shall we say, brothers? When you come together, everyone has a hymn, or a word of instruction, a revelation, a tongue or an interpretation. All of these must be done for the strengthening of the church. 27If anyone speaks in a tongue, two—or at the most three—should speak, one at a time, and someone must interpret. 28If there is no interpreter, the speaker should keep quiet in the church and speak to himself and God.

29Two or three prophets should speak, and the others should weigh carefully what is said. 30And if a revelation comes to someone who is sitting down, the first speaker should stop. 31For you can all prophesy in turn so that everyone may be instructed and encouraged. 32The spirits of prophets are subject to the control of prophets. 33For God is not a God of disorder but of peace.

As in all the congregations of the saints, 34women should remain silent in the churches. They are not allowed to speak, but must be in submission, as the Law says. 35If they want to inquire about something, they should ask their own husbands at home; for it is disgraceful for a woman to speak in the church.

36Did the word of God originate with you? Or are you the only people it has reached? 37If anybody thinks he is a prophet or spiritually gifted, let him acknowledge that what I am writing to you is the Lord's command. 38If he ignores this, he himself will be ignored.[d]

39Therefore, my brothers, be eager to prophesy, and do not forbid speaking in tongues. 40But everything should be done in a fitting and orderly way.

The Resurrection of Christ

15 Now, brothers, I want to remind you of the gospel I preached to you, which you received and on which you have taken your stand. 2By this gospel you are saved, if you hold firmly to the word I preached to you. Otherwise, you have believed in vain.

3For what I received I passed on to you as of first importance[e]: that Christ died for our sins according to the Scriptures, 4that he was buried, that he was raised on the third day according to the Scriptures, 5and that he appeared to Peter,[f] and then to the Twelve. 6After that, he appeared to more than five hundred of the brothers at the same time, most of whom are still living, though some have fallen asleep. 7Then he appeared to James, then to all the apostles, 8and last of all he appeared to me also, as to one abnormally born.

9For I am the least of the apostles and do not even deserve to be called an apostle, because I persecuted the church of God. 10But by the grace of God I am what I am, and his grace to me was not without effect. No, I worked harder than all of them—yet not I, but the grace of God that was with me. 11Whether, then, it was I or they, this is what we preach, and this is what you believed.

The Resurrection of the Dead

12But if it is preached that Christ has been raised from the dead, how can some of you say that there is no resurrection of the dead? 13If there is no resurrection of the dead, then not even Christ has been raised. 14And if Christ has not been raised, our preaching is useless and so is your faith. 15More than that, we are then found to be false witnesses about God, for we have testified about God that he raised Christ from the dead. But he did not raise him if in fact the dead are not raised. 16For if the dead are not raised, then Christ has not been raised either. 17And if Christ has not been raised, your faith is futile; you are still in your sins. 18Then those also who have fallen asleep in Christ are lost. 19If only for this life we have hope in Christ, we are to be pitied more than all men.

20But Christ has indeed been raised from the dead, the firstfruits of those who have fallen asleep. 21For since death came through a man, the resurrection of the dead comes also through a man. 22For as in Adam all die, so in Christ all will be made alive. 23But each in his own turn: Christ, the firstfruits; then, when he comes, those who belong to him. 24Then the end will come, when he hands over the kingdom to God the Father after he has destroyed all dominion, authority and power. 25For he must reign until he has put all his enemies

[a]*21* Isaiah 28:11,12 [b]*23* Or *some inquirers* [c]*24* Or *or some inquirer* [d]*38* Some manuscripts *If he is ignorant of this, let him be ignorant* [e]*3* Or *you at the first* [f]*5* Greek *Cephas*

under his feet. 26The last enemy to be destroyed is death. 27For he "has put everything
under his feet."[a] Now when it says that "everything" has been put under him, it is clear
that this does not include God himself, who put
everything under Christ. 28When he has done
this, then the Son himself will be made subject
to him who put everything under him, so that
God may be all in all.
29Now if there is no resurrection, what will
those do who are baptized for the dead? If the
dead are not raised at all, why are people baptized for them? 30And as for us, why do we
endanger ourselves every hour? 31I die every
day—I mean that, brothers—just as surely as
I glory over you in Christ Jesus our Lord. 32If
I fought wild beasts in Ephesus for merely human reasons, what have I gained? If the dead
are not raised,

"Let us eat and drink,
for tomorrow we die."[b]

33Do not be misled: "Bad company corrupts
good character." 34Come back to your senses
as you ought, and stop sinning; for there are
some who are ignorant of God—I say this to
your shame.

The Resurrection Body

35But someone may ask, "How are the dead
raised? With what kind of body will they
come?" 36How foolish! What you sow does
not come to life unless it dies. 37When you
sow, you do not plant the body that will be, but
just a seed, perhaps of wheat or of something
else. 38But God gives it a body as he has determined, and to each kind of seed he gives its
own body. 39All flesh is not the same: Men
have one kind of flesh, animals have another,
birds another and fish another. 40There are also
heavenly bodies and there are earthly bodies;
but the splendor of the heavenly bodies is one
kind, and the splendor of the earthly bodies is
another. 41The sun has one kind of splendor,
the moon another and the stars another; and
star differs from star in splendor.
42So will it be with the resurrection of the
dead. The body that is sown is perishable, it is
raised imperishable; 43it is sown in dishonor, it
is raised in glory; it is sown in weakness, it is
raised in power; 44it is sown a natural body, it
is raised a spiritual body.
If there is a natural body, there is also a
spiritual body. 45So it is written: "The first
man Adam became a living being"[c]; the last
Adam, a life-giving spirit. 46The spiritual did
not come first, but the natural, and after that
the spiritual. 47The first man was of the dust of
the earth, the second man from heaven. 48As
was the earthly man, so are those who are of
the earth; and as is the man from heaven, so
also are those who are of heaven. 49And just as
we have borne the likeness of the earthly man,
so shall we[d] bear the likeness of the man from
heaven.
50I declare to you, brothers, that flesh and
blood cannot inherit the kingdom of God, nor
does the perishable inherit the imperishable.
51Listen, I tell you a mystery: We will not all
sleep, but we will all be changed— 52in a
flash, in the twinkling of an eye, at the last
trumpet. For the trumpet will sound, the dead
will be raised imperishable, and we will be
changed. 53For the perishable must clothe itself with the imperishable, and the mortal with
immortality. 54When the perishable has been
clothed with the imperishable, and the mortal
with immortality, then the saying that is written will come true: "Death has been swallowed
up in victory."[e]

55"Where, O death, is your victory?
Where, O death, is your sting?"[f]

56The sting of death is sin, and the power of sin
is the law. 57But thanks be to God! He gives us
the victory through our Lord Jesus Christ.
58Therefore, my dear brothers, stand firm.
Let nothing move you. Always give yourselves
fully to the work of the Lord, because you
know that your labor in the Lord is not in
vain.

The Collection for God's People

16 Now about the collection for God's
people: Do what I told the Galatian
churches to do. 2On the first day of every
week, each one of you should set aside a sum
of money in keeping with his income, saving it
up, so that when I come no collections will
have to be made. 3Then, when I arrive, I will
give letters of introduction to the men you approve and send them with your gift to Jerusalem. 4If it seems advisable for me to go also,
they will accompany me.

Personal Requests

5After I go through Macedonia, I will come
to you—for I will be going through Macedonia. 6Perhaps I will stay with you awhile, or
even spend the winter, so that you can help me
on my journey, wherever I go. 7I do not want
to see you now and make only a passing visit;
I hope to spend some time with you, if the
Lord permits. 8But I will stay on at Ephesus
until Pentecost, 9because a great door for effective work has opened to me, and there are
many who oppose me.
10If Timothy comes, see to it that he has
nothing to fear while he is with you, for he is
carrying on the work of the Lord, just as I am.
11No one, then, should refuse to accept him.
Send him on his way in peace so that he may
return to me. I am expecting him along with
the brothers.
12Now about our brother Apollos: I strongly
urged him to go to you with the brothers. He

[a] *27* Psalm 8:6 [b] *32* Isaiah 22:13 [c] *45* Gen. 2:7 [d] *49* Some early manuscripts *so let us* [e] *54* Isaiah 25:8
[f] *55* Hosea 13:14

was quite unwilling to go now, but he will go
when he has the opportunity.
13Be on your guard; stand firm in the faith;
be men of courage; be strong. 14Do everything
in love.
15You know that the household of Stephanas
were the first converts in Achaia, and they
have devoted themselves to the service of the
saints. I urge you, brothers, 16to submit to such
as these and to everyone who joins in the work,
and labors at it. 17I was glad when Stephanas,
Fortunatus and Achaicus arrived, because they
have supplied what was lacking from you.
18For they refreshed my spirit and yours also.
Such men deserve recognition.

Final Greetings

19The churches in the province of Asia send
you greetings. Aquila and Priscilla[a] greet you
warmly in the Lord, and so does the church
that meets at their house. 20All the brothers
here send you greetings. Greet one another
with a holy kiss.
21I, Paul, write this greeting in my own
hand.
22If anyone does not love the Lord—a curse
be on him. Come, O Lord[b]!
23The grace of the Lord Jesus be with you.
24My love to all of you in Christ Jesus.
Amen.[c]

2 Corinthians

1 Paul, an apostle of Christ Jesus by the will
of God, and Timothy our brother,

To the church of God in Corinth, together
with all the saints throughout Achaia:

2Grace and peace to you from God our Father and the Lord Jesus Christ.

The God of All Comfort

3Praise be to the God and Father of our Lord
Jesus Christ, the Father of compassion and the
God of all comfort, 4who comforts us in all our
troubles, so that we can comfort those in any
trouble with the comfort we ourselves have
received from God. 5For just as the sufferings
of Christ flow over into our lives, so also
through Christ our comfort overflows. 6If we
are distressed, it is for your comfort and salvation; if we are comforted, it is for your comfort, which produces in you patient endurance
of the same sufferings we suffer. 7And our
hope for you is firm, because we know that just
as you share in our sufferings, so also you
share in our comfort.
8We do not want you to be uninformed,
brothers, about the hardships we suffered in
the province of Asia. We were under great
pressure, far beyond our ability to endure, so
that we despaired even of life. 9Indeed, in our
hearts we felt the sentence of death. But this
happened that we might not rely on ourselves
but on God, who raises the dead. 10He has
delivered us from such a deadly peril, and he
will deliver us. On him we have set our hope
that he will continue to deliver us, 11as you
help us by your prayers. Then many will give
thanks on our[d] behalf for the gracious favor
granted us in answer to the prayers of many.

Paul's Change of Plans

12Now this is our boast: Our conscience testifies that we have conducted ourselves in the
world, and especially in our relations with you,
in the holiness and sincerity that are from God.
We have done so not according to worldly wisdom but according to God's grace. 13For we do
not write you anything you cannot read or understand. And I hope that, 14as you have understood us in part, you will come to understand
fully that you can boast of us just as we will
boast of you in the day of the Lord Jesus.
15Because I was confident of this, I planned
to visit you first so that you might benefit
twice. 16I planned to visit you on my way to
Macedonia and to come back to you from
Macedonia, and then to have you send me on
my way to Judea. 17When I planned this, did I
do it lightly? Or do I make my plans in a
worldly manner so that in the same breath I
say, "Yes, yes" and "No, no"?
18But as surely as God is faithful, our message to you is not "Yes" and "No." 19For the
Son of God, Jesus Christ, who was preached
among you by me and Silas[e] and Timothy,
was not "Yes" and "No," but in him it has
always been "Yes." 20For no matter how many
promises God has made, they are "Yes" in
Christ. And so through him the "Amen" is spoken by us to the glory of God. 21Now it is God
who makes both us and you stand firm in
Christ. He anointed us, 22set his seal of ownership on us, and put his Spirit in our hearts as a
deposit, guaranteeing what is to come.
23I call God as my witness that it was in
order to spare you that I did not return to Corinth. 24Not that we lord it over your faith, but
we work with you for your joy, because it is by
faith you stand firm.
2 1So I made up my
mind that I would not make another painful
visit to you. 2For if I grieve you, who is left to
make me glad but you whom I have grieved?
3I wrote as I did so that when I came I should

[a] 19 Greek *Prisca*, a variant of *Priscilla* [b] 22 In Aramaic the expression *Come, O Lord* is *Marana tha*.
[c] 24 Some manuscripts do not have *Amen*. [d] 11 Many manuscripts *your* [e] 19 Greek *Silvanus*, a variant of *Silas*

not be distressed by those who ought to make me rejoice. I had confidence in all of you, that you would all share my joy. 4For I wrote you out of great distress and anguish of heart and with many tears, not to grieve you but to let you know the depth of my love for you.

Forgiveness for the Sinner

5If anyone has caused grief, he has not so much grieved me as he has grieved all of you, to some extent—not to put it too severely. 6The punishment inflicted on him by the majority is sufficient for him. 7Now instead, you ought to forgive and comfort him, so that he will not be overwhelmed by excessive sorrow. 8I urge you, therefore, to reaffirm your love for him. 9The reason I wrote you was to see if you would stand the test and be obedient in everything. 10If you forgive anyone, I also forgive him. And what I have forgiven—if there was anything to forgive—I have forgiven in the sight of Christ for your sake, 11in order that Satan might not outwit us. For we are not unaware of his schemes.

Ministers of the New Covenant

12Now when I went to Troas to preach the gospel of Christ and found that the Lord had opened a door for me, 13I still had no peace of mind, because I did not find my brother Titus there. So I said good-by to them and went on to Macedonia.

14But thanks be to God, who always leads us in triumphal procession in Christ and through us spreads everywhere the fragrance of the knowledge of him. 15For we are to God the aroma of Christ among those who are being saved and those who are perishing. 16To the one we are the smell of death; to the other, the fragrance of life. And who is equal to such a task? 17Unlike so many, we do not peddle the word of God for profit. On the contrary, in Christ we speak before God with sincerity, like men sent from God.

3 Are we beginning to commend ourselves again? Or do we need, like some people, letters of recommendation to you or from you? 2You yourselves are our letter, written on our hearts, known and read by everybody. 3You show that you are a letter from Christ, the result of our ministry, written not with ink but with the Spirit of the living God, not on tablets of stone but on tablets of human hearts.

4Such confidence as this is ours through Christ before God. 5Not that we are competent in ourselves to claim anything for ourselves, but our competence comes from God. 6He has made us competent as ministers of a new covenant—not of the letter but of the Spirit; for the letter kills, but the Spirit gives life.

The Glory of the New Covenant

7Now if the ministry that brought death, which was engraved in letters on stone, came with glory, so that the Israelites could not look steadily at the face of Moses because of its glory, fading though it was, 8will not the ministry of the Spirit be even more glorious? 9If the ministry that condemns men is glorious, how much more glorious is the ministry that brings righteousness! 10For what was glorious has no glory now in comparison with the surpassing glory. 11And if what was fading away came with glory, how much greater is the glory of that which lasts!

12Therefore, since we have such a hope, we are very bold. 13We are not like Moses, who would put a veil over his face to keep the Israelites from gazing at it while the radiance was fading away. 14But their minds were made dull, for to this day the same veil remains when the old covenant is read. It has not been removed, because only in Christ is it taken away. 15Even to this day when Moses is read, a veil covers their hearts. 16But whenever anyone turns to the Lord, the veil is taken away. 17Now the Lord is the Spirit, and where the Spirit of the Lord is, there is freedom. 18And we, who with unveiled faces all reflect[a] the Lord's glory, are being transformed into his likeness with ever-increasing glory, which comes from the Lord, who is the Spirit.

Treasures in Jars of Clay

4 Therefore, since through God's mercy we have this ministry, we do not lose heart. 2Rather, we have renounced secret and shameful ways; we do not use deception, nor do we distort the word of God. On the contrary, by setting forth the truth plainly we commend ourselves to every man's conscience in the sight of God. 3And even if our gospel is veiled, it is veiled to those who are perishing. 4The god of this age has blinded the minds of unbelievers, so that they cannot see the light of the gospel of the glory of Christ, who is the image of God. 5For we do not preach ourselves, but Jesus Christ as Lord, and ourselves as your servants for Jesus' sake. 6For God, who said, "Let light shine out of darkness,"[b] made his light shine in our hearts to give us the light of the knowledge of the glory of God in the face of Christ.

7But we have this treasure in jars of clay to show that this all-surpassing power is from God and not from us. 8We are hard pressed on every side, but not crushed; perplexed, but not in despair; 9persecuted, but not abandoned; struck down, but not destroyed. 10We always carry around in our body the death of Jesus, so that the life of Jesus may also be revealed in our body. 11For we who are alive are always being given over to death for Jesus' sake, so that his life may be revealed in our mortal body. 12So then, death is at work in us, but life is at work in you.

13It is written: "I believed; therefore I have spoken."[c] With that same spirit of faith we also believe and therefore speak, 14because we know that the one who raised the Lord Jesus from the dead will also raise us with Jesus and

[a] *18* Or *contemplate* [b] *6* Gen. 1:3 [c] *13* Psalm 116:10

present us with you in his presence. 15All this
is for your benefit, so that the grace that is
reaching more and more people may cause
thanksgiving to overflow to the glory of God.
16Therefore we do not lose heart. Though
outwardly we are wasting away, yet inwardly
we are being renewed day by day. 17For our
light and momentary troubles are achieving for
us an eternal glory that far outweighs them all.
18So we fix our eyes not on what is seen, but
on what is unseen. For what is seen is temporary, but what is unseen is eternal.

Our Heavenly Dwelling

5 Now we know that if the earthly tent we
live in is destroyed, we have a building
from God, an eternal house in heaven, not built
by human hands. 2Meanwhile we groan, longing to be clothed with our heavenly dwelling,
3because when we are clothed, we will not be
found naked. 4For while we are in this tent, we
groan and are burdened, because we do not
wish to be unclothed but to be clothed with our
heavenly dwelling, so that what is mortal may
be swallowed up by life. 5Now it is God who
has made us for this very purpose and has giv-
en us the Spirit as a deposit, guaranteeing what
is to come.
6Therefore we are always confident and
know that as long as we are at home in the
body we are away from the Lord. 7We live by
faith, not by sight. 8We are confident, I say,
and would prefer to be away from the body
and at home with the Lord. 9So we make it our
goal to please him, whether we are at home in
the body or away from it. 10For we must all
appear before the judgment seat of Christ, that
each one may receive what is due him for the
things done while in the body, whether good or
bad.

The Ministry of Reconciliation

11Since, then, we know what it is to fear the
Lord, we try to persuade men. What we are is
plain to God, and I hope it is also plain to your
conscience. 12We are not trying to commend
ourselves to you again, but are giving you an
opportunity to take pride in us, so that you can
answer those who take pride in what is seen
rather than in what is in the heart. 13If we are
out of our mind, it is for the sake of God; if we
are in our right mind, it is for you. 14For
Christ's love compels us, because we are convinced that one died for all, and therefore all
died. 15And he died for all, that those who live
should no longer live for themselves but for
him who died for them and was raised again.
16So from now on we regard no one from a
worldly point of view. Though we once regarded Christ in this way, we do so no longer.
17Therefore, if anyone is in Christ, he is a new
creation; the old has gone, the new has come!
18All this is from God, who reconciled us to
himself through Christ and gave us the ministry of reconciliation: 19that God was reconcil-
ing the world to himself in Christ, not counting
men's sins against them. And he has committed to us the message of reconciliation. 20We
are therefore Christ's ambassadors, as though
God were making his appeal through us. We
implore you on Christ's behalf: Be reconciled
to God. 21God made him who had no sin to be
sin[a] for us, so that in him we might become
the righteousness of God.

6 As God's fellow workers we urge you not
to receive God's grace in vain. 2For he
says,

"In the time of my favor I heard you,
and in the day of salvation I helped
you."[b]

I tell you, now is the time of God's favor, now
is the day of salvation.

Paul's Hardships

3We put no stumbling block in anyone's
path, so that our ministry will not be discredited. 4Rather, as servants of God we commend
ourselves in every way: in great endurance; in
troubles, hardships and distresses; 5in beatings,
imprisonments and riots; in hard work, sleep-
less nights and hunger; 6in purity, understanding, patience and kindness; in the Holy Spirit
and in sincere love; 7in truthful speech and in
the power of God; with weapons of righteousness in the right hand and in the left; 8through
glory and dishonor, bad report and good report; genuine, yet regarded as impostors;
9known, yet regarded as unknown; dying, and
yet we live on; beaten, and yet not killed;
10sorrowful, yet always rejoicing; poor, yet
making many rich; having nothing, and yet
possessing everything.
11We have spoken freely to you, Corinthians, and opened wide our hearts to you. 12We
are not withholding our affection from you, but
you are withholding yours from us. 13As a fair
exchange—I speak as to my children—open
wide your hearts also.

Do Not Be Yoked With Unbelievers

14Do not be yoked together with unbelievers. For what do righteousness and wickedness
have in common? Or what fellowship can light
have with darkness? 15What harmony is there
between Christ and Belial[c]? What does a believer have in common with an unbeliever?
16What agreement is there between the temple
of God and idols? For we are the temple of the
living God. As God has said: "I will live with
them and walk among them, and I will be their
God, and they will be my people."[d]

17"Therefore come out from them
and be separate,
says the Lord.
Touch no unclean thing,
and I will receive you."[e]
18"I will be a Father to you,

[a]21 Or *be a sin offering* [b]2 Isaiah 49:8 [c]15 Greek *Beliar*, a variant of *Belial* [d]16 Lev. 26:12; Jer. 32:38; Ezek. 37:27 [e]17 Isaiah 52:11; Ezek. 20:34,41

and you will be my sons and daughters,
says the Lord Almighty."[a]

7 Since we have these promises, dear friends, let us purify ourselves from everything that contaminates body and spirit, perfecting holiness out of reverence for God.

Paul's Joy

2Make room for us in your hearts. We have wronged no one, we have corrupted no one, we have exploited no one. 3I do not say this to condemn you; I have said before that you have such a place in our hearts that we would live or die with you. 4I have great confidence in you; I take great pride in you. I am greatly encouraged; in all our troubles my joy knows no bounds.

5For when we came into Macedonia, this body of ours had no rest, but we were harassed at every turn—conflicts on the outside, fears within. 6But God, who comforts the downcast, comforted us by the coming of Titus, 7and not only by his coming but also by the comfort you had given him. He told us about your longing for me, your deep sorrow, your ardent concern for me, so that my joy was greater than ever.

8Even if I caused you sorrow by my letter, I do not regret it. Though I did regret it—I see that my letter hurt you, but only for a little while— 9yet now I am happy, not because you were made sorry, but because your sorrow led you to repentance. For you became sorrowful as God intended and so were not harmed in any way by us. 10Godly sorrow brings repentance that leads to salvation and leaves no regret, but worldly sorrow brings death. 11See what this godly sorrow has produced in you: what earnestness, what eagerness to clear yourselves, what indignation, what alarm, what longing, what concern, what readiness to see justice done. At every point you have proved yourselves to be innocent in this matter. 12So even though I wrote to you, it was not on account of the one who did the wrong or of the injured party, but rather that before God you could see for yourselves how devoted to us you are. 13By all this we are encouraged.

In addition to our own encouragement, we were especially delighted to see how happy Titus was, because his spirit has been refreshed by all of you. 14I had boasted to him about you, and you have not embarrassed me. But just as everything we said to you was true, so our boasting about you to Titus has proved to be true as well. 15And his affection for you is all the greater when he remembers that you were all obedient, receiving him with fear and trembling. 16I am glad I can have complete confidence in you.

Generosity Encouraged

8 And now, brothers, we want you to know about the grace that God has given the Macedonian churches. 2Out of the most severe trial, their overflowing joy and their extreme poverty welled up in rich generosity. 3For I testify that they gave as much as they were able, and even beyond their ability. Entirely on their own, 4they urgently pleaded with us for the privilege of sharing in this service to the saints. 5And they did not do as we expected, but they gave themselves first to the Lord and then to us in keeping with God's will. 6So we urged Titus, since he had earlier made a beginning, to bring also to completion this act of grace on your part. 7But just as you excel in everything—in faith, in speech, in knowledge, in complete earnestness and in your love for us[b]—see that you also excel in this grace of giving.

8I am not commanding you, but I want to test the sincerity of your love by comparing it with the earnestness of others. 9For you know the grace of our Lord Jesus Christ, that though he was rich, yet for your sakes he became poor, so that you through his poverty might become rich.

10And here is my advice about what is best for you in this matter: Last year you were the first not only to give but also to have the desire to do so. 11Now finish the work, so that your eager willingness to do it may be matched by your completion of it, according to your means. 12For if the willingness is there, the gift is acceptable according to what one has, not according to what he does not have.

13Our desire is not that others might be relieved while you are hard pressed, but that there might be equality. 14At the present time your plenty will supply what they need, so that in turn their plenty will supply what you need. Then there will be equality, 15as it is written: "He who gathered much did not have too much, and he who gathered little did not have too little."[c]

Titus Sent to Corinth

16I thank God, who put into the heart of Titus the same concern I have for you. 17For Titus not only welcomed our appeal, but he is coming to you with much enthusiasm and on his own initiative. 18And we are sending along with him the brother who is praised by all the churches for his service to the gospel. 19What is more, he was chosen by the churches to accompany us as we carry the offering, which we administer in order to honor the Lord himself and to show our eagerness to help. 20We want to avoid any criticism of the way we administer this liberal gift. 21For we are taking pains to do what is right, not only in the eyes of the Lord but also in the eyes of men.

22In addition, we are sending with them our brother who has often proved to us in many ways that he is zealous, and now even more so because of his great confidence in you. 23As for Titus, he is my partner and fellow worker among you; as for our brothers, they are representatives of the churches and an honor to Christ. 24Therefore show these men the proof

[a] *18* 2 Samuel 7:14; 7:8 [b] *7* Some manuscripts *in our love for you* [c] *15* Exodus 16:18

of your love and the reason for our pride in you, so that the churches can see it.

9 There is no need for me to write to you about this service to the saints. 2For I know your eagerness to help, and I have been boasting about it to the Macedonians, telling them that since last year you in Achaia were ready to give; and your enthusiasm has stirred most of them to action. 3But I am sending the brothers in order that our boasting about you in this matter should not prove hollow, but that you may be ready, as I said you would be. 4For if any Macedonians come with me and find you unprepared, we—not to say anything about you—would be ashamed of having been so confident. 5So I thought it necessary to urge the brothers to visit you in advance and finish the arrangements for the generous gift you had promised. Then it will be ready as a generous gift, not as one grudgingly given.

Sowing Generously

6Remember this: Whoever sows sparingly will also reap sparingly, and whoever sows generously will also reap generously. 7Each man should give what he has decided in his heart to give, not reluctantly or under compulsion, for God loves a cheerful giver. 8And God is able to make all grace abound to you, so that in all things at all times, having all that you need, you will abound in every good work. 9As it is written:

"He has scattered abroad his gifts to the
 poor;
 his righteousness endures forever."[a]

10Now he who supplies seed to the sower and bread for food will also supply and increase your store of seed and will enlarge the harvest of your righteousness. 11You will be made rich in every way so that you can be generous on every occasion, and through us your generosity will result in thanksgiving to God.

12This service that you perform is not only supplying the needs of God's people but is also overflowing in many expressions of thanks to God. 13Because of the service by which you have proved yourselves, men will praise God for the obedience that accompanies your confession of the gospel of Christ, and for your generosity in sharing with them and with everyone else. 14And in their prayers for you their hearts will go out to you, because of the surpassing grace God has given you. 15Thanks be to God for his indescribable gift!

Paul's Defense of His Ministry

10 By the meekness and gentleness of Christ, I appeal to you—I, Paul, who am "timid" when face to face with you, but "bold" when away! 2I beg you that when I come I may not have to be as bold as I expect to be toward some people who think that we live by the standards of this world. 3For though we live in the world, we do not wage war as the world does. 4The weapons we fight with are not the weapons of the world. On the contrary, they have divine power to demolish strongholds. 5We demolish arguments and every pretension that sets itself up against the knowledge of God, and we take captive every thought to make it obedient to Christ. 6And we will be ready to punish every act of disobedience, once your obedience is complete.

7You are looking only on the surface of things.[b] If anyone is confident that he belongs to Christ, he should consider again that we belong to Christ just as much as he. 8For even if I boast somewhat freely about the authority the Lord gave us for building you up rather than pulling you down, I will not be ashamed of it. 9I do not want to seem to be trying to frighten you with my letters. 10For some say, "His letters are weighty and forceful, but in person he is unimpressive and his speaking amounts to nothing." 11Such people should realize that what we are in our letters when we are absent, we will be in our actions when we are present.

12We do not dare to classify or compare ourselves with some who commend themselves. When they measure themselves by themselves and compare themselves with themselves, they are not wise. 13We, however, will not boast beyond proper limits, but will confine our boasting to the field God has assigned to us, a field that reaches even to you. 14We are not going too far in our boasting, as would be the case if we had not come to you, for we did get as far as you with the gospel of Christ. 15Neither do we go beyond our limits by boasting of work done by others.[c] Our hope is that, as your faith continues to grow, our area of activity among you will greatly expand, 16so that we can preach the gospel in the regions beyond you. For we do not want to boast about work already done in another man's territory. 17But, "Let him who boasts boast in the Lord."[d] 18For it is not the one who commends himself who is approved, but the one whom the Lord commends.

Paul and the False Apostles

11 I hope you will put up with a little of my foolishness; but you are already doing that. 2I am jealous for you with a godly jealousy. I promised you to one husband, to Christ, so that I might present you as a pure virgin to him. 3But I am afraid that just as Eve was deceived by the serpent's cunning, your minds may somehow be led astray from your sincere and pure devotion to Christ. 4For if someone comes to you and preaches a Jesus other than the Jesus we preached, or if you receive a different spirit from the one you received, or a different gospel from the one you accepted,

[a]9 Psalm 112:9 [b]7 Or *Look at the obvious facts* [c]13-15 Or *13We, however, will not boast about things that cannot be measured, but we will boast according to the standard of measurement that the God of measure has assigned us—a measurement that relates even to you. 14 . . . 15Neither do we boast about things that cannot be measured in regard to the work done by others.* [d]17 Jer. 9:24

you put up with it easily enough. 5But I do not think I am in the least inferior to those "super-apostles." 6I may not be a trained speaker, but I do have knowledge. We have made this perfectly clear to you in every way.

7Was it a sin for me to lower myself in order to elevate you by preaching the gospel of God to you free of charge? 8I robbed other churches by receiving support from them so as to serve you. 9And when I was with you and needed something, I was not a burden to anyone, for the brothers who came from Macedonia supplied what I needed. I have kept myself from being a burden to you in any way, and will continue to do so. 10As surely as the truth of Christ is in me, nobody in the regions of Achaia will stop this boasting of mine. 11Why? Because I do not love you? God knows I do! 12And I will keep on doing what I am doing in order to cut the ground from under those who want an opportunity to be considered equal with us in the things they boast about.

13For such men are false apostles, deceitful workmen, masquerading as apostles of Christ. 14And no wonder, for Satan himself masquerades as an angel of light. 15It is not surprising, then, if his servants masquerade as servants of righteousness. Their end will be what their actions deserve.

Paul Boasts About His Sufferings

16I repeat: Let no one take me for a fool. But if you do, then receive me just as you would a fool, so that I may do a little boasting. 17In this self-confident boasting I am not talking as the Lord would, but as a fool. 18Since many are boasting in the way the world does, I too will boast. 19You gladly put up with fools since you are so wise! 20In fact, you even put up with anyone who enslaves you or exploits you or takes advantage of you or pushes himself forward or slaps you in the face. 21To my shame I admit that we were too weak for that!

What anyone else dares to boast about—I am speaking as a fool—I also dare to boast about. 22Are they Hebrews? So am I. Are they Israelites? So am I. Are they Abraham's descendants? So am I. 23Are they servants of Christ? (I am out of my mind to talk like this.) I am more. I have worked much harder, been in prison more frequently, been flogged more severely, and been exposed to death again and again. 24Five times I received from the Jews the forty lashes minus one. 25Three times I was beaten with rods, once I was stoned, three times I was shipwrecked, I spent a night and a day in the open sea, 26I have been constantly on the move. I have been in danger from rivers, in danger from bandits, in danger from my own countrymen, in danger from Gentiles; in danger in the city, in danger in the country, in danger at sea; and in danger from false brothers. 27I have labored and toiled and have often gone without sleep; I have known hunger and thirst and have often gone without food; I have been cold and naked. 28Besides everything else, I face daily the pressure of my concern for all the churches. 29Who is weak, and I do not feel weak? Who is led into sin, and I do not inwardly burn?

30If I must boast, I will boast of the things that show my weakness. 31The God and Father of the Lord Jesus, who is to be praised forever, knows that I am not lying. 32In Damascus the governor under King Aretas had the city of the Damascenes guarded in order to arrest me. 33But I was lowered in a basket from a window in the wall and slipped through his hands.

Paul's Vision and His Thorn

12 I must go on boasting. Although there is nothing to be gained, I will go on to visions and revelations from the Lord. 2I know a man in Christ who fourteen years ago was caught up to the third heaven. Whether it was in the body or out of the body I do not know—God knows. 3And I know that this man—whether in the body or apart from the body I do not know, but God knows— 4was caught up to paradise. He heard inexpressible things, things that man is not permitted to tell. 5I will boast about a man like that, but I will not boast about myself, except about my weaknesses. 6Even if I should choose to boast, I would not be a fool, because I would be speaking the truth. But I refrain, so no one will think more of me than is warranted by what I do or say.

7To keep me from becoming conceited because of these surpassingly great revelations, there was given me a thorn in my flesh, a messenger of Satan, to torment me. 8Three times I pleaded with the Lord to take it away from me. 9But he said to me, "My grace is sufficient for you, for my power is made perfect in weakness." Therefore I will boast all the more gladly about my weaknesses, so that Christ's power may rest on me. 10That is why, for Christ's sake, I delight in weaknesses, in insults, in hardships, in persecutions, in difficulties. For when I am weak, then I am strong.

Paul's Concern for the Corinthians

11I have made a fool of myself, but you drove me to it. I ought to have been commended by you, for I am not in the least inferior to the "super-apostles," even though I am nothing. 12The things that mark an apostle—signs, wonders and miracles—were done among you with great perseverance. 13How were you inferior to the other churches, except that I was never a burden to you? Forgive me this wrong!

14Now I am ready to visit you for the third time, and I will not be a burden to you, because what I want is not your possessions but you. After all, children should not have to save up for their parents, but parents for their children. 15So I will very gladly spend for you everything I have and expend myself as well. If I love you more, will you love me less? 16Be that as it may, I have not been a burden to you. Yet, crafty fellow that I am, I caught you by trickery! 17Did I exploit you through any of the men I sent you? 18I urged Titus to go to you and I sent our brother with him. Titus did not exploit you, did he? Did we not act in the same spirit and follow the same course?

19Have you been thinking all along that we have been defending ourselves to you? We have been speaking in the sight of God as those in Christ; and everything we do, dear friends, is for your strengthening. 20For I am afraid that when I come I may not find you as I want you to be, and you may not find me as you want me to be. I fear that there may be quarreling, jealousy, outbursts of anger, factions, slander, gossip, arrogance and disorder. 21I am afraid that when I come again my God will humble me before you, and I will be grieved over many who have sinned earlier and have not repented of the impurity, sexual sin and debauchery in which they have indulged.

Final Warnings

13 This will be my third visit to you. "Every matter must be established by the testimony of two or three witnesses."[a] 2I already gave you a warning when I was with you the second time. I now repeat it while absent: On my return I will not spare those who sinned earlier or any of the others, 3since you are demanding proof that Christ is speaking through me. He is not weak in dealing with you, but is powerful among you. 4For to be sure, he was crucified in weakness, yet he lives by God's power. Likewise, we are weak in him, yet by God's power we will live with him to serve you.

5Examine yourselves to see whether you are in the faith; test yourselves. Do you not realize that Christ Jesus is in you—unless, of course, you fail the test? 6And I trust that you will discover that we have not failed the test. 7Now we pray to God that you will not do anything wrong. Not that people will see that we have stood the test but that you will do what is right even though we may seem to have failed. 8For we cannot do anything against the truth, but only for the truth. 9We are glad whenever we are weak but you are strong; and our prayer is for your perfection. 10This is why I write these things when I am absent, that when I come I may not have to be harsh in my use of authority—the authority the Lord gave me for building you up, not for tearing you down.

Final Greetings

11Finally, brothers, good-by. Aim for perfection, listen to my appeal, be of one mind, live in peace. And the God of love and peace will be with you.

12Greet one another with a holy kiss. 13All the saints send their greetings.

14May the grace of the Lord Jesus Christ, and the love of God, and the fellowship of the Holy Spirit be with you all.

Galatians

1 Paul, an apostle—sent not from men nor by man, but by Jesus Christ and God the Father, who raised him from the dead— 2and all the brothers with me,

To the churches in Galatia:

3Grace and peace to you from God our Father and the Lord Jesus Christ, 4who gave himself for our sins to rescue us from the present evil age, according to the will of our God and Father, 5to whom be glory for ever and ever. Amen.

No Other Gospel

6I am astonished that you are so quickly deserting the one who called you by the grace of Christ and are turning to a different gospel— 7which is really no gospel at all. Evidently some people are throwing you into confusion and are trying to pervert the gospel of Christ. 8But even if we or an angel from heaven should preach a gospel other than the one we preached to you, let him be eternally condemned! 9As we have already said, so now I say again: If anybody is preaching to you a gospel other than what you accepted, let him be eternally condemned!

10Am I now trying to win the approval of men, or of God? Or am I trying to please men? If I were still trying to please men, I would not be a servant of Christ.

Paul Called by God

11I want you to know, brothers, that the gospel I preached is not something that man made up. 12I did not receive it from any man, nor was I taught it; rather, I received it by revelation from Jesus Christ.

13For you have heard of my previous way of life in Judaism, how intensely I persecuted the church of God and tried to destroy it. 14I was advancing in Judaism beyond many Jews of my own age and was extremely zealous for the traditions of my fathers. 15But when God, who set me apart from birth[b] and called me by his grace, was pleased 16to reveal his Son in me so that I might preach him among the Gentiles, I did not consult any man, 17nor did I go up to Jerusalem to see those who were apostles before I was, but I went immediately into Arabia and later returned to Damascus.

18Then after three years, I went up to Jerusalem to get acquainted with Peter[a] and stayed

[a] *1* Deut. 19:15 [b] *15* Or *from my mother's womb*

with him fifteen days. 19I saw none of the other apostles—only James, the Lord's brother. 20I assure you before God that what I am writing you is no lie. 21Later I went to Syria and Cilicia. 22I was personally unknown to the churches of Judea that are in Christ. 23They only heard the report: "The man who formerly persecuted us is now preaching the faith he once tried to destroy." 24And they praised God because of me.

Paul Accepted by the Apostles

2 Fourteen years later I went up again to Jerusalem, this time with Barnabas. I took Titus along also. 2I went in response to a revelation and set before them the gospel that I preach among the Gentiles. But I did this privately to those who seemed to be leaders, for fear that I was running or had run my race in vain. 3Yet not even Titus, who was with me, was compelled to be circumcised, even though he was a Greek. 4⌊This matter arose⌋ because some false brothers had infiltrated our ranks to spy on the freedom we have in Christ Jesus and to make us slaves. 5We did not give in to them for a moment, so that the truth of the gospel might remain with you.

6As for those who seemed to be important—whatever they were makes no difference to me; God does not judge by external appearance—those men added nothing to my message. 7On the contrary, they saw that I had been entrusted with the task of preaching the gospel to the Gentiles,[b] just as Peter had been to the Jews.[c] 8For God, who was at work in the ministry of Peter as an apostle to the Jews, was also at work in my ministry as an apostle to the Gentiles. 9James, Peter[d] and John, those reputed to be pillars, gave me and Barnabas the right hand of fellowship when they recognized the grace given to me. They agreed that we should go to the Gentiles, and they to the Jews. 10All they asked was that we should continue to remember the poor, the very thing I was eager to do.

Paul Opposes Peter

11When Peter came to Antioch, I opposed him to his face, because he was clearly in the wrong. 12Before certain men came from James, he used to eat with the Gentiles. But when they arrived, he began to draw back and separate himself from the Gentiles because he was afraid of those who belonged to the circumcision group. 13The other Jews joined him in his hypocrisy, so that by their hypocrisy even Barnabas was led astray.

14When I saw that they were not acting in line with the truth of the gospel, I said to Peter in front of them all, "You are a Jew, yet you live like a Gentile and not like a Jew. How is it, then, that you force Gentiles to follow Jewish customs?

15"We who are Jews by birth and not 'Gentile sinners' 16know that a man is not justified by observing the law, but by faith in Jesus Christ. So we, too, have put our faith in Christ Jesus that we may be justified by faith in Christ and not by observing the law, because by observing the law no one will be justified.

17"If, while we seek to be justified in Christ, it becomes evident that we ourselves are sinners, does that mean that Christ promotes sin? Absolutely not! 18If I rebuild what I destroyed, I prove that I am a lawbreaker. 19For through the law I died to the law so that I might live for God. 20I have been crucified with Christ and I no longer live, but Christ lives in me. The life I live in the body, I live by faith in the Son of God, who loved me and gave himself for me. 21I do not set aside the grace of God, for if righteousness could be gained through the law, Christ died for nothing!"[e]

Faith or Observance of the Law

3 You foolish Galatians! Who has bewitched you? Before your very eyes Jesus Christ was clearly portrayed as crucified. 2I would like to learn just one thing from you: Did you receive the Spirit by observing the law, or by believing what you heard? 3Are you so foolish? After beginning with the Spirit, are you now trying to attain your goal by human effort? 4Have you suffered so much for nothing—if it really was for nothing? 5Does God give you his Spirit and work miracles among you because you observe the law, or because you believe what you heard?

6Consider Abraham: "He believed God, and it was credited to him as righteousness."[f] 7Understand, then, that those who believe are children of Abraham. 8The Scripture foresaw that God would justify the Gentiles by faith, and announced the gospel in advance to Abraham: "All nations will be blessed through you."[g] 9So those who have faith are blessed along with Abraham, the man of faith.

10All who rely on observing the law are under a curse, for it is written: "Cursed is everyone who does not continue to do everything written in the Book of the Law."[h] 11Clearly no one is justified before God by the law, because, "The righteous will live by faith."[i] 12The law is not based on faith; on the contrary, "The man who does these things will live by them."[j] 13Christ redeemed us from the curse of the law by becoming a curse for us, for it is written: "Cursed is everyone who is hung on a tree."[k] 14He redeemed us in order that the blessing given to Abraham might come to the Gentiles through Christ Jesus, so that by faith we might receive the promise of the Spirit.

[a] *18* Greek *Cephas* [b] *7* Greek *uncircumcised* [c] *7* Greek *circumcised*; also in verses 8 and 9 [d] *9* Greek *Cephas*; also in verses 11 and 14 [e] *21* Some interpreters end the quotation after verse 14. [f] *6* Gen. 15:6 [g] *8* Gen. 12:3; 18:18; 22:18 [h] *10* Deut. 27:26 [i] *11* Hab. 2:4 [j] *12* Lev. 18:5 [k] *13* Deut. 21:23

The Law and the Promise

15Brothers, let me take an example from everyday life. Just as no one can set aside or add
to a human covenant that has been duly established, so it is in this case. 16The promises
were spoken to Abraham and to his seed. The
Scripture does not say "and to seeds," meaning
many people, but "and to your seed,"[a] meaning one person, who is Christ. 17What I mean
is this: The law, introduced 430 years later,
does not set aside the covenant previously established by God and thus do away with the
promise. 18For if the inheritance depends on
the law, then it no longer depends on a promise; but God in his grace gave it to Abraham
through a promise.

19What, then, was the purpose of the law? It
was added because of transgressions until the
Seed to whom the promise referred had come.
The law was put into effect through angels by
a mediator. 20A mediator, however, does not
represent just one party; but God is one.

21Is the law, therefore, opposed to the promises of God? Absolutely not! For if a law had
been given that could impart life, then righteousness would certainly have come by the
law. 22But the Scripture declares that the
whole world is a prisoner of sin, so that what
was promised, being given through faith in
Jesus Christ, might be given to those who believe.

23Before this faith came, we were held prisoners by the law, locked up until faith should
be revealed. 24So the law was put in charge to
lead us to Christ[b] that we might be justified by
faith. 25Now that faith has come, we are no
longer under the supervision of the law.

Sons of God

26You are all sons of God through faith in
Christ Jesus, 27for all of you who were baptized into Christ have clothed yourselves with
Christ. 28There is neither Jew nor Greek, slave
nor free, male nor female, for you are all one
in Christ Jesus. 29If you belong to Christ, then
you are Abraham's seed, and heirs according
to the promise.

4 What I am saying is that as long as the heir
is a child, he is no different from a slave,
although he owns the whole estate. 2He is subject to guardians and trustees until the time set
by his father. 3So also, when we were children,
we were in slavery under the basic principles
of the world. 4But when the time had fully
come, God sent his Son, born of a woman,
born under law, 5to redeem those under law,
that we might receive the full rights of sons.
6Because you are sons, God sent the Spirit of
his Son into our hearts, the Spirit who calls
out, "*Abba*,[c] Father." 7So you are no longer a
slave, but a son; and since you are a son, God
has made you also an heir.

Paul's Concern for the Galatians

8Formerly, when you did not know God,
you were slaves to those who by nature are not
gods. 9But now that you know God—or rather
are known by God—how is it that you are
turning back to those weak and miserable principles? Do you wish to be enslaved by them all
over again? 10You are observing special days
and months and seasons and years! 11I fear for
you, that somehow I have wasted my efforts on
you.

12I plead with you, brothers, become like
me, for I became like you. You have done me
no wrong. 13As you know, it was because of an
illness that I first preached the gospel to you.
14Even though my illness was a trial to you,
you did not treat me with contempt or scorn.
Instead, you welcomed me as if I were an angel of God, as if I were Christ Jesus himself.
15What has happened to all your joy? I can
testify that, if you could have done so, you
would have torn out your eyes and given them
to me. 16Have I now become your enemy by
telling you the truth?

17Those people are zealous to win you over,
but for no good. What they want is to alienate
you ⌊from us⌋, so that you may be zealous for
them. 18It is fine to be zealous, provided the
purpose is good, and to be so always and not
just when I am with you. 19My dear children,
for whom I am again in the pains of childbirth
until Christ is formed in you, 20how I wish I
could be with you now and change my tone,
because I am perplexed about you!

Hagar and Sarah

21Tell me, you who want to be under the
law, are you not aware of what the law says?
22For it is written that Abraham had two sons,
one by the slave woman and the other by the
free woman. 23His son by the slave woman
was born in the ordinary way; but his son by
the free woman was born as the result of a
promise.

24These things may be taken figuratively,
for the women represent two covenants. One
covenant is from Mount Sinai and bears children who are to be slaves: This is Hagar.
25Now Hagar stands for Mount Sinai in Arabia
and corresponds to the present city of Jerusalem, because she is in slavery with her children. 26But the Jerusalem that is above is free,
and she is our mother. 27For it is written:

"Be glad, O barren woman,
who bears no children;
break forth and cry aloud,
you who have no labor pains;
because more are the children of the
desolate woman
than of her who has a husband."[d]

28Now you, brothers, like Isaac, are children
of promise. 29At that time the son born in the
ordinary way persecuted the son born by the
power of the Spirit. It is the same now. 30But
what does the Scripture say? "Get rid of the
slave woman and her son, for the slave wom-

[a] *16* Gen. 12:7; 13:15; 24:7 [b] *24* Or *charge until Christ came* [c] *6* Aramaic for *Father* [d] *27* Isaiah 54:1

an's son will never share in the inheritance
with the free woman's son."[a] 31Therefore,
brothers, we are not children of the slave woman, but of the free woman.

Freedom in Christ

5 It is for freedom that Christ has set us free.
Stand firm, then, and do not let yourselves
be burdened again by a yoke of slavery.
2Mark my words! I, Paul, tell you that if you
let yourselves be circumcised, Christ will be of
no value to you at all. 3Again I declare to every
man who lets himself be circumcised that he is
obligated to obey the whole law. 4You who are
trying to be justified by law have been alienated from Christ; you have fallen away from
grace. 5But by faith we eagerly await through
the Spirit the righteousness for which we hope.
6For in Christ Jesus neither circumcision nor
uncircumcision has any value. The only thing
that counts is faith expressing itself through
love.
7You were running a good race. Who cut in
on you and kept you from obeying the truth?
8That kind of persuasion does not come from
the one who calls you. 9"A little yeast works
through the whole batch of dough." 10I am
confident in the Lord that you will take no
other view. The one who is throwing you into
confusion will pay the penalty, whoever he
may be. 11Brothers, if I am still preaching circumcision, why am I still being persecuted? In
that case the offense of the cross has been
abolished. 12As for those agitators, I wish they
would go the whole way and emasculate themselves!
13You, my brothers, were called to be free.
But do not use your freedom to indulge the
sinful nature[b]; rather, serve one another in
love. 14The entire law is summed up in a single
command: "Love your neighbor as yourself."[c]
15If you keep on biting and devouring each
other, watch out or you will be destroyed by
each other.

Life by the Spirit

16So I say, live by the Spirit, and you will
not gratify the desires of the sinful nature.
17For the sinful nature desires what is contrary
to the Spirit, and the Spirit what is contrary to
the sinful nature. They are in conflict with each
other, so that you do not do what you want.
18But if you are led by the Spirit, you are not
under law.
19The acts of the sinful nature are obvious:
sexual immorality, impurity and debauchery;
20idolatry and witchcraft; hatred, discord, jealousy, fits of rage, selfish ambition, dissen-
sions, factions 21and envy; drunkenness, orgies, and the like. I warn you, as I did before,
that those who live like this will not inherit the
kingdom of God.
22But the fruit of the Spirit is love, joy,
peace, patience, kindness, goodness, faithfulness, 23gentleness and self-control. Against
such things there is no law. 24Those who belong to Christ Jesus have crucified the sinful
nature with its passions and desires. 25Since
we live by the Spirit, let us keep in step with
the Spirit. 26Let us not become conceited, provoking and envying each other.

Doing Good to All

6 Brothers, if someone is caught in a sin, you
who are spiritual should restore him gently. But watch yourself, or you also may be
tempted. 2Carry each other's burdens, and in
this way you will fulfill the law of Christ. 3If
anyone thinks he is something when he is
nothing, he deceives himself. 4Each one
should test his own actions. Then he can take
pride in himself, without comparing himself to
somebody else, 5for each one should carry his
own load.
6Anyone who receives instruction in the
word must share all good things with his instructor.
7Do not be deceived: God cannot be
mocked. A man reaps what he sows. 8The one
who sows to please his sinful nature, from that
nature[d] will reap destruction; the one who
sows to please the Spirit, from the Spirit will
reap eternal life. 9Let us not become weary in
doing good, for at the proper time we will reap
a harvest if we do not give up. 10Therefore, as
we have opportunity, let us do good to all people, especially to those who belong to the family of believers.

Not Circumcision but a New Creation

11See what large letters I use as I write to
you with my own hand!
12Those who want to make a good impres-
sion outwardly are trying to compel you to be
circumcised. The only reason they do this is to
avoid being persecuted for the cross of Christ.
13Not even those who are circumcised obey the
law, yet they want you to be circumcised that
they may boast about your flesh. 14May I never
boast except in the cross of our Lord Jesus
Christ, through which[e] the world has been crucified to me, and I to the world. 15Neither
circumcision nor uncircumcision means anything; what counts is a new creation. 16Peace
and mercy to all who follow this rule, even to
the Israel of God.
17Finally, let no one cause me trouble, for I
bear on my body the marks of Jesus.
18The grace of our Lord Jesus Christ be with
your spirit, brothers. Amen.

[a] *30* Gen. 21:10 [b] *13* Or *the flesh*; also in verses 16, 17, 19 and 24 [c] *14* Lev. 19:18 [d] *8* Or *his flesh, from the flesh* [e] *14* Or *whom*

Ephesians

1 Paul, an apostle of Christ Jesus by the will of God,

To the saints in Ephesus,[a] the faithful[b] in Christ Jesus:

2Grace and peace to you from God our Father and the Lord Jesus Christ.

Spiritual Blessings in Christ

3Praise be to the God and Father of our Lord Jesus Christ, who has blessed us in the heavenly realms with every spiritual blessing in Christ. 4For he chose us in him before the creation of the world to be holy and blameless in his sight. In love 5he[c] predestined us to be adopted as his sons through Jesus Christ, in accordance with his pleasure and will— 6to the praise of his glorious grace, which he has freely given us in the One he loves. 7In him we have redemption through his blood, the forgiveness of sins, in accordance with the riches of God's grace 8that he lavished on us with all wisdom and understanding. 9And he[d] made known to us the mystery of his will according to his good pleasure, which he purposed in Christ, 10to be put into effect when the times will have reached their fulfillment—to bring all things in heaven and on earth together under one head, even Christ.

11In him we were also chosen,[e] having been predestined according to the plan of him who works out everything in conformity with the purpose of his will, 12in order that we, who were the first to hope in Christ, might be for the praise of his glory. 13And you also were included in Christ when you heard the word of truth, the gospel of your salvation. Having believed, you were marked in him with a seal, the promised Holy Spirit, 14who is a deposit guaranteeing our inheritance until the redemption of those who are God's possession—to the praise of his glory.

Thanksgiving and Prayer

15For this reason, ever since I heard about your faith in the Lord Jesus and your love for all the saints, 16I have not stopped giving thanks for you, remembering you in my prayers. 17I keep asking that the God of our Lord Jesus Christ, the glorious Father, may give you the Spirit[f] of wisdom and revelation, so that you may know him better. 18I pray also that the eyes of your heart may be enlightened in order that you may know the hope to which he has called you, the riches of his glorious inheritance in the saints, 19and his incomparably great power for us who believe. That power is like the working of his mighty strength, 20which he exerted in Christ when he raised him from the dead and seated him at his right hand in the heavenly realms, 21far above all rule and authority, power and dominion, and every title that can be given, not only in the present age but also in the one to come. 22And God placed all things under his feet and appointed him to be head over everything for the church, 23which is his body, the fullness of him who fills everything in every way.

Made Alive in Christ

2 As for you, you were dead in your transgressions and sins, 2in which you used to live when you followed the ways of this world and of the ruler of the kingdom of the air, the spirit who is now at work in those who are disobedient. 3All of us also lived among them at one time, gratifying the cravings of our sinful nature[g] and following its desires and thoughts. Like the rest, we were by nature objects of wrath. 4But because of his great love for us, God, who is rich in mercy, 5made us alive with Christ even when we were dead in transgressions—it is by grace you have been saved. 6And God raised us up with Christ and seated us with him in the heavenly realms in Christ Jesus, 7in order that in the coming ages he might show the incomparable riches of his grace, expressed in his kindness to us in Christ Jesus. 8For it is by grace you have been saved, through faith—and this not from yourselves, it is the gift of God— 9not by works, so that no one can boast. 10For we are God's workmanship, created in Christ Jesus to do good works, which God prepared in advance for us to do.

One in Christ

11Therefore, remember that formerly you who are Gentiles by birth and called "uncircumcised" by those who call themselves "the circumcision" (that done in the body by the hands of men)— 12remember that at that time you were separate from Christ, excluded from citizenship in Israel and foreigners to the covenants of the promise, without hope and without God in the world. 13But now in Christ Jesus you who once were far away have been brought near through the blood of Christ.

14For he himself is our peace, who has made the two one and has destroyed the barrier, the dividing wall of hostility, 15by abolishing in his flesh the law with its commandments and regulations. His purpose was to create in himself one new man out of the two, thus making peace, 16and in this one body to reconcile both of them to God through the cross, by which he put to death their hostility. 17He came and preached peace to you who were far away and peace to those who were near. 18For through

[a] *1* Some early manuscripts do not have *in Ephesus.* [b] *1* Or *believers who are* [c] *4,5* Or *sight in love. 5He*
[d] *8,9* Or *us. With all wisdom and understanding, 9he* [e] *11* Or *were made heirs* [f] *17* Or *a spirit*
[g] *3* Or *our flesh*

him we both have access to the Father by one Spirit.

19Consequently, you are no longer foreigners and aliens, but fellow citizens with God's people and members of God's household, 20built on the foundation of the apostles and prophets, with Christ Jesus himself as the chief cornerstone. 21In him the whole building is joined together and rises to become a holy temple in the Lord. 22And in him you too are being built together to become a dwelling in which God lives by his Spirit.

Paul the Preacher to the Gentiles

3 For this reason I, Paul, the prisoner of Christ Jesus for the sake of you Gentiles—

2Surely you have heard about the administration of God's grace that was given to me for you, 3that is, the mystery made known to me by revelation, as I have already written briefly. 4In reading this, then, you will be able to understand my insight into the mystery of Christ, 5which was not made known to men in other generations as it has now been revealed by the Spirit to God's holy apostles and prophets. 6This mystery is that through the gospel the Gentiles are heirs together with Israel, members together of one body, and sharers together in the promise in Christ Jesus.

7I became a servant of this gospel by the gift of God's grace given me through the working of his power. 8Although I am less than the least of all God's people, this grace was given me: to preach to the Gentiles the unsearchable riches of Christ, 9and to make plain to everyone the administration of this mystery, which for ages past was kept hidden in God, who created all things. 10His intent was that now, through the church, the manifold wisdom of God should be made known to the rulers and authorities in the heavenly realms, 11according to his eternal purpose which he accomplished in Christ Jesus our Lord. 12In him and through faith in him we may approach God with freedom and confidence. 13I ask you, therefore, not to be discouraged because of my sufferings for you, which are your glory.

A Prayer for the Ephesians

14For this reason I kneel before the Father, 15from whom his whole family[a] in heaven and on earth derives its name. 16I pray that out of his glorious riches he may strengthen you with power through his Spirit in your inner being, 17so that Christ may dwell in your hearts through faith. And I pray that you, being rooted and established in love, 18may have power, together with all the saints, to grasp how wide and long and high and deep is the love of Christ, 19and to know this love that surpasses knowledge—that you may be filled to the measure of all the fullness of God.

20Now to him who is able to do immeasurably more than all we ask or imagine, according to his power that is at work within us, 21to him be glory in the church and in Christ Jesus throughout all generations, for ever and ever! Amen.

Unity in the Body of Christ

4 As a prisoner for the Lord, then, I urge you to live a life worthy of the calling you have received. 2Be completely humble and gentle; be patient, bearing with one another in love. 3Make every effort to keep the unity of the Spirit through the bond of peace. 4There is one body and one Spirit—just as you were called to one hope when you were called— 5one Lord, one faith, one baptism; 6one God and Father of all, who is over all and through all and in all.

7But to each one of us grace has been given as Christ apportioned it. 8This is why it[b] says:

"When he ascended on high,
he led captives in his train
and gave gifts to men."[c]

9(What does "he ascended" mean except that he also descended to the lower, earthly regions[d]? 10He who descended is the very one who ascended higher than all the heavens, in order to fill the whole universe.) 11It was he who gave some to be apostles, some to be prophets, some to be evangelists, and some to be pastors and teachers, 12to prepare God's people for works of service, so that the body of Christ may be built up 13until we all reach unity in the faith and in the knowledge of the Son of God and become mature, attaining to the whole measure of the fullness of Christ.

14Then we will no longer be infants, tossed back and forth by the waves, and blown here and there by every wind of teaching and by the cunning and craftiness of men in their deceitful scheming. 15Instead, speaking the truth in love, we will in all things grow up into him who is the Head, that is, Christ. 16From him the whole body, joined and held together by every supporting ligament, grows and builds itself up in love, as each part does its work.

Living as Children of Light

17So I tell you this, and insist on it in the Lord, that you must no longer live as the Gentiles do, in the futility of their thinking. 18They are darkened in their understanding and separated from the life of God because of the ignorance that is in them due to the hardening of their hearts. 19Having lost all sensitivity, they have given themselves over to sensuality so as to indulge in every kind of impurity, with a continual lust for more.

20You, however, did not come to know Christ that way. 21Surely you heard of him and were taught in him in accordance with the truth that is in Jesus. 22You were taught, with regard to your former way of life, to put off your old self, which is being corrupted by its deceitful desires; 23to be made new in the attitude of your minds; 24and to put on the new self, creat-

[a]15 Or *whom all fatherhood* [b]8 Or *God* [c]8 Psalm 68:18 [d]9 Or *the depths of the earth*

ed to be like God in true righteousness and
holiness.

25Therefore each of you must put off falsehood and speak truthfully to his neighbor, for
we are all members of one body. 26"In your
anger do not sin"[a]: Do not let the sun go down
while you are still angry, 27and do not give the
devil a foothold. 28He who has been stealing
must steal no longer, but must work, doing
something useful with his own hands, that he
may have something to share with those in
need.

29Do not let any unwholesome talk come out
of your mouths, but only what is helpful for
building others up according to their needs,
that it may benefit those who listen. 30And do
not grieve the Holy Spirit of God, with whom
you were sealed for the day of redemption.
31Get rid of all bitterness, rage and anger,
brawling and slander, along with every form of
malice. 32Be kind and compassionate to one
another, forgiving each other, just as in Christ
God forgave you.

5 Be imitators of God, therefore, as dearly
loved children 2and live a life of love, just
as Christ loved us and gave himself up for us
as a fragrant offering and sacrifice to God.

3But among you there must not be even a
hint of sexual immorality, or of any kind of
impurity, or of greed, because these are im-
proper for God's holy people. 4Nor should
there be obscenity, foolish talk or coarse joking, which are out of place, but rather thanksgiving. 5For of this you can be sure: No immoral, impure or greedy person—such a man
is an idolater—has any inheritance in the kingdom of Christ and of God.[b] 6Let no one deceive you with empty words, for because of
such things God's wrath comes on those who
are disobedient. 7Therefore do not be partners
with them.

8For you were once darkness, but now you
are light in the Lord. Live as children of light
9(for the fruit of the light consists in all goodness, righteousness and truth) 10and find out
what pleases the Lord. 11Have nothing to do
with the fruitless deeds of darkness, but rather
expose them. 12For it is shameful even to mention what the disobedient do in secret. 13But
everything exposed by the light becomes visible, 14for it is light that makes everything visible. This is why it is said:

"Wake up, O sleeper,
rise from the dead,
and Christ will shine on you."

15Be very careful, then, how you live—not
as unwise but as wise, 16making the most of
every opportunity, because the days are evil.
17Therefore do not be foolish, but understand
what the Lord's will is. 18Do not get drunk on
wine, which leads to debauchery. Instead, be
filled with the Spirit. 19Speak to one another
with psalms, hymns and spiritual songs. Sing
and make music in your heart to the Lord,
20always giving thanks to God the Father for
everything, in the name of our Lord Jesus
Christ.

21Submit to one another out of reverence for
Christ.

Wives and Husbands

22Wives, submit to your husbands as to the
Lord. 23For the husband is the head of the wife
as Christ is the head of the church, his body, of
which he is the Savior. 24Now as the church
submits to Christ, so also wives should submit
to their husbands in everything.

25Husbands, love your wives, just as Christ
loved the church and gave himself up for her
26to make her holy, cleansing[c] her by the
washing with water through the word, 27and to
present her to himself as a radiant church,
without stain or wrinkle or any other blemish,
but holy and blameless. 28In this same way,
husbands ought to love their wives as their
own bodies. He who loves his wife loves himself. 29After all, no one ever hated his own
body, but he feeds and cares for it, just as
Christ does the church— 30for we are members of his body. 31"For this reason a man will
leave his father and mother and be united to his
wife, and the two will become one flesh."[d]
32This is a profound mystery—but I am talking about Christ and the church. 33However,
each one of you also must love his wife as he
loves himself, and the wife must respect her
husband.

Children and Parents

6 Children, obey your parents in the Lord,
for this is right. 2"Honor your father and
mother"—which is the first commandment
with a promise— 3"that it may go well with
you and that you may enjoy long life on the
earth."[e]

4Fathers, do not exasperate your children;
instead, bring them up in the training and instruction of the Lord.

Slaves and Masters

5Slaves, obey your earthly masters with respect and fear, and with sincerity of heart, just
as you would obey Christ. 6Obey them not
only to win their favor when their eye is on
you, but like slaves of Christ, doing the will of
God from your heart. 7Serve wholeheartedly,
as if you were serving the Lord, not men, 8be-
cause you know that the Lord will reward everyone for whatever good he does, whether he
is slave or free.

9And masters, treat your slaves in the same
way. Do not threaten them, since you know
that he who is both their Master and yours is in
heaven, and there is no favoritism with him.

The Armor of God

10Finally, be strong in the Lord and in his
mighty power. 11Put on the full armor of God

[a] *26* Psalm 4:4 [b] *5* Or *kingdom of the Christ and God* [c] *26* Or *having cleansed* [d] *31* Gen. 2:24
[e] *3* Deut. 5:16

so that you can take your stand against the devil's schemes. 12For our struggle is not against flesh and blood, but against the rulers, against the authorities, against the powers of this dark world and against the spiritual forces of evil in the heavenly realms. 13Therefore put on the full armor of God, so that when the day of evil comes, you may be able to stand your ground, and after you have done everything, to stand. 14Stand firm then, with the belt of truth buckled around your waist, with the breastplate of righteousness in place, 15and with your feet fitted with the readiness that comes from the gospel of peace. 16In addition to all this, take up the shield of faith, with which you can extinguish all the flaming arrows of the evil one. 17Take the helmet of salvation and the sword of the Spirit, which is the word of God. 18And pray in the Spirit on all occasions with all kinds of prayers and requests. With this in mind, be alert and always keep on praying for all the saints.

19Pray also for me, that whenever I open my mouth, words may be given me so that I will fearlessly make known the mystery of the gospel, 20for which I am an ambassador in chains. Pray that I may declare it fearlessly, as I should.

Final Greetings

21Tychicus, the dear brother and faithful servant in the Lord, will tell you everything, so that you also may know how I am and what I am doing. 22I am sending him to you for this very purpose, that you may know how we are, and that he may encourage you.

23Peace to the brothers, and love with faith from God the Father and the Lord Jesus Christ. 24Grace to all who love our Lord Jesus Christ with an undying love.

Philippians

1 Paul and Timothy, servants of Christ Jesus,

To all the saints in Christ Jesus at Philippi, together with the overseers[a] and deacons:

2Grace and peace to you from God our Father and the Lord Jesus Christ.

Thanksgiving and Prayer

3I thank my God every time I remember you. 4In all my prayers for all of you, I always pray with joy 5because of your partnership in the gospel from the first day until now, 6being confident of this, that he who began a good work in you will carry it on to completion until the day of Christ Jesus.

7It is right for me to feel this way about all of you, since I have you in my heart; for whether I am in chains or defending and confirming the gospel, all of you share in God's grace with me. 8God can testify how I long for all of you with the affection of Christ Jesus.

9And this is my prayer: that your love may abound more and more in knowledge and depth of insight, 10so that you may be able to discern what is best and may be pure and blameless until the day of Christ, 11filled with the fruit of righteousness that comes through Jesus Christ—to the glory and praise of God.

Paul's Chains Advance the Gospel

12Now I want you to know, brothers, that what has happened to me has really served to advance the gospel. 13As a result, it has become clear throughout the whole palace guard[b] and to everyone else that I am in chains for Christ. 14Because of my chains, most of the brothers in the Lord have been encouraged to speak the word of God more courageously and fearlessly.

15It is true that some preach Christ out of envy and rivalry, but others out of goodwill. 16The latter do so in love, knowing that I am put here for the defense of the gospel. 17The former preach Christ out of selfish ambition, not sincerely, supposing that they can stir up trouble for me while I am in chains.[c] 18But what does it matter? The important thing is that in every way, whether from false motives or true, Christ is preached. And because of this I rejoice.

Yes, and I will continue to rejoice, 19for I know that through your prayers and the help given by the Spirit of Jesus Christ, what has happened to me will turn out for my deliverance.[d] 20I eagerly expect and hope that I will in no way be ashamed, but will have sufficient courage so that now as always Christ will be exalted in my body, whether by life or by death. 21For to me, to live is Christ and to die is gain. 22If I am to go on living in the body, this will mean fruitful labor for me. Yet what shall I choose? I do not know! 23I am torn between the two: I desire to depart and be with Christ, which is better by far; 24but it is more necessary for you that I remain in the body. 25Convinced of this, I know that I will remain, and I will continue with all of you for your progress and joy in the faith, 26so that through my being with you again your joy in Christ Jesus will overflow on account of me.

27Whatever happens, conduct yourselves in a manner worthy of the gospel of Christ. Then,

[a] *1* Traditionally *bishops* [b] *13* Or *whole palace* [c] *16,17* Some late manuscripts have verses 16 and 17 in reverse order. [d] *19* Or *salvation*

whether I come and see you or only hear about you in my absence, I will know that you stand firm in one spirit, contending as one man for the faith of the gospel 28without being frightened in any way by those who oppose you. This is a sign to them that they will be destroyed, but that you will be saved—and that by God. 29For it has been granted to you on behalf of Christ not only to believe on him, but also to suffer for him, 30since you are going through the same struggle you saw I had, and now hear that I still have.

Imitating Christ's Humility

2 If you have any encouragement from being united with Christ, if any comfort from his love, if any fellowship with the Spirit, if any tenderness and compassion, 2then make my joy complete by being like-minded, having the same love, being one in spirit and purpose. 3Do nothing out of selfish ambition or vain conceit, but in humility consider others better than yourselves. 4Each of you should look not only to your own interests, but also to the interests of others.

5Your attitude should be the same as that of Christ Jesus:

6Who, being in very nature[a] God,
did not consider equality with God
something to be grasped,
7but made himself nothing,
taking the very nature[b] of a servant,
being made in human likeness.
8And being found in appearance as a man,
he humbled himself
and became obedient to death—
even death on a cross!
9Therefore God exalted him to the highest
place
and gave him the name that is above
every name,
10that at the name of Jesus every knee
should bow,
in heaven and on earth and under the
earth,
11and every tongue confess that Jesus Christ
is Lord,
to the glory of God the Father.

Shining as Stars

12Therefore, my dear friends, as you have always obeyed—not only in my presence, but now much more in my absence—continue to work out your salvation with fear and trembling, 13for it is God who works in you to will and to act according to his good purpose.

14Do everything without complaining or arguing, 15so that you may become blameless and pure, children of God without fault in a crooked and depraved generation, in which you shine like stars in the universe 16as you hold out[c] the word of life—in order that I may boast on the day of Christ that I did not run or labor for nothing. 17But even if I am being poured out like a drink offering on the sacrifice and service coming from your faith, I am glad and rejoice with all of you. 18So you too should be glad and rejoice with me.

Timothy and Epaphroditus

19I hope in the Lord Jesus to send Timothy to you soon, that I also may be cheered when I receive news about you. 20I have no one else like him, who takes a genuine interest in your welfare. 21For everyone looks out for his own interests, not those of Jesus Christ. 22But you know that Timothy has proved himself, because as a son with his father he has served with me in the work of the gospel. 23I hope, therefore, to send him as soon as I see how things go with me. 24And I am confident in the Lord that I myself will come soon.

25But I think it is necessary to send back to you Epaphroditus, my brother, fellow worker and fellow soldier, who is also your messenger, whom you sent to take care of my needs. 26For he longs for all of you and is distressed because you heard he was ill. 27Indeed he was ill, and almost died. But God had mercy on him, and not on him only but also on me, to spare me sorrow upon sorrow. 28Therefore I am all the more eager to send him, so that when you see him again you may be glad and I may have less anxiety. 29Welcome him in the Lord with great joy, and honor men like him, 30because he almost died for the work of Christ, risking his life to make up for the help you could not give me.

No Confidence in the Flesh

3 Finally, my brothers, rejoice in the Lord! It is no trouble for me to write the same things to you again, and it is a safeguard for you.

2Watch out for those dogs, those men who do evil, those mutilators of the flesh. 3For it is we who are the circumcision, we who worship by the Spirit of God, who glory in Christ Jesus, and who put no confidence in the flesh—4though I myself have reasons for such confidence.

If anyone else thinks he has reasons to put confidence in the flesh, I have more: 5circumcised on the eighth day, of the people of Israel, of the tribe of Benjamin, a Hebrew of Hebrews; in regard to the law, a Pharisee; 6as for zeal, persecuting the church; as for legalistic righteousness, faultless.

7But whatever was to my profit I now consider loss for the sake of Christ. 8What is more, I consider everything a loss compared to the surpassing greatness of knowing Christ Jesus my Lord, for whose sake I have lost all things. I consider them rubbish, that I may gain Christ 9and be found in him, not having a righteousness of my own that comes from the law, but that which is through faith in Christ—the righteousness that comes from God and is by faith. 10I want to know Christ and the power of his resurrection and the fellowship of sharing in

[a]6 Or *in the form of* [b]7 Or *the form* [c]16 Or *hold on to*

his sufferings, becoming like him in his death, 11and so, somehow, to attain to the resurrection from the dead.

Pressing on Toward the Goal

12Not that I have already obtained all this, or have already been made perfect, but I press on to take hold of that for which Christ Jesus took hold of me. 13Brothers, I do not consider myself yet to have taken hold of it. But one thing I do: Forgetting what is behind and straining toward what is ahead, 14I press on toward the goal to win the prize for which God has called me heavenward in Christ Jesus.

15All of us who are mature should take such a view of things. And if on some point you think differently, that too God will make clear to you. 16Only let us live up to what we have already attained.

17Join with others in following my example, brothers, and take note of those who live according to the pattern we gave you. 18For, as I have often told you before and now say again even with tears, many live as enemies of the cross of Christ. 19Their destiny is destruction, their god is their stomach, and their glory is in their shame. Their mind is on earthly things. 20But our citizenship is in heaven. And we eagerly await a Savior from there, the Lord Jesus Christ, 21who, by the power that enables him to bring everything under his control, will transform our lowly bodies so that they will be like his glorious body.

4 Therefore, my brothers, you whom I love and long for, my joy and crown, that is how you should stand firm in the Lord, dear friends!

Exhortations

2I plead with Euodia and I plead with Syntyche to agree with each other in the Lord. 3Yes, and I ask you, loyal yokefellow,[a] help these women who have contended at my side in the cause of the gospel, along with Clement and the rest of my fellow workers, whose names are in the book of life.

4Rejoice in the Lord always. I will say it again: Rejoice! 5Let your gentleness be evident to all. The Lord is near. 6Do not be anxious about anything, but in everything, by prayer and petition, with thanksgiving, present your requests to God. 7And the peace of God, which transcends all understanding, will guard your hearts and your minds in Christ Jesus.

8Finally, brothers, whatever is true, whatever is noble, whatever is right, whatever is pure, whatever is lovely, whatever is admirable—if anything is excellent or praiseworthy—think about such things. 9Whatever you have learned or received or heard from me, or seen in me—put it into practice. And the God of peace will be with you.

Thanks for Their Gifts

10I rejoice greatly in the Lord that at last you have renewed your concern for me. Indeed, you have been concerned, but you had no opportunity to show it. 11I am not saying this because I am in need, for I have learned to be content whatever the circumstances. 12I know what it is to be in need, and I know what it is to have plenty. I have learned the secret of being content in any and every situation, whether well fed or hungry, whether living in plenty or in want. 13I can do everything through him who gives me strength.

14Yet it was good of you to share in my troubles. 15Moreover, as you Philippians know, in the early days of your acquaintance with the gospel, when I set out from Macedonia, not one church shared with me in the matter of giving and receiving, except you only; 16for even when I was in Thessalonica, you sent me aid again and again when I was in need. 17Not that I am looking for a gift, but I am looking for what may be credited to your account. 18I have received full payment and even more; I am amply supplied, now that I have received from Epaphroditus the gifts you sent. They are a fragrant offering, an acceptable sacrifice, pleasing to God. 19And my God will meet all your needs according to his glorious riches in Christ Jesus.

20To our God and Father be glory for ever and ever. Amen.

Final Greetings

21Greet all the saints in Christ Jesus. The brothers who are with me send greetings. 22All the saints send you greetings, especially those who belong to Caesar's household.

23The grace of the Lord Jesus Christ be with your spirit. Amen.[b]

Colossians

1 Paul, an apostle of Christ Jesus by the will of God, and Timothy our brother,

2To the holy and faithful[c] brothers in Christ at Colosse:

Grace and peace to you from God our Father.[d]

Thanksgiving and Prayer

3We always thank God, the Father of our

[a]3 Or *loyal Syzygus* [b]23 Some manuscripts do not have *Amen.* [c]2 Or *believing* [d]2 Some manuscripts *Father and the Lord Jesus Christ*

Lord Jesus Christ, when we pray for you, **4**because we have heard of your faith in Christ Jesus and of the love you have for all the saints— **5**the faith and love that spring from the hope that is stored up for you in heaven and that you have already heard about in the word of truth, the gospel **6**that has come to you. All over the world this gospel is bearing fruit and growing, just as it has been doing among you since the day you heard it and understood God's grace in all its truth. **7**You learned it from Epaphras, our dear fellow servant, who is a faithful minister of Christ on our[a] behalf, **8**and who also told us of your love in the Spirit.

9For this reason, since the day we heard about you, we have not stopped praying for you and asking God to fill you with the knowledge of his will through all spiritual wisdom and understanding. **10**And we pray this in order that you may live a life worthy of the Lord and may please him in every way: bearing fruit in every good work, growing in the knowledge of God, **11**being strengthened with all power according to his glorious might so that you may have great endurance and patience, and joyfully **12**giving thanks to the Father, who has qualified you[b] to share in the inheritance of the saints in the kingdom of light. **13**For he has rescued us from the dominion of darkness and brought us into the kingdom of the Son he loves, **14**in whom we have redemption,[c] the forgiveness of sins.

The Supremacy of Christ

15He is the image of the invisible God, the firstborn over all creation. **16**For by him all things were created: things in heaven and on earth, visible and invisible, whether thrones or powers or rulers or authorities; all things were created by him and for him. **17**He is before all things, and in him all things hold together. **18**And he is the head of the body, the church; he is the beginning and the firstborn from among the dead, so that in everything he might have the supremacy. **19**For God was pleased to have all his fullness dwell in him, **20**and through him to reconcile to himself all things, whether things on earth or things in heaven, by making peace through his blood, shed on the cross.

21Once you were alienated from God and were enemies in your minds because of[d] your evil behavior. **22**But now he has reconciled you by Christ's physical body through death to present you holy in his sight, without blemish and free from accusation— **23**if you continue in your faith, established and firm, not moved from the hope held out in the gospel. This is the gospel that you heard and that has been proclaimed to every creature under heaven, and of which I, Paul, have become a servant.

Paul's Labor for the Church

24Now I rejoice in what was suffered for you, and I fill up in my flesh what is still lacking in regard to Christ's afflictions, for the sake of his body, which is the church. **25**I have become its servant by the commission God gave me to present to you the word of God in its fullness— **26**the mystery that has been kept hidden for ages and generations, but is now disclosed to the saints. **27**To them God has chosen to make known among the Gentiles the glorious riches of this mystery, which is Christ in you, the hope of glory.

28We proclaim him, admonishing and teaching everyone with all wisdom, so that we may present everyone perfect in Christ. **29**To this end I labor, struggling with all his energy, which so powerfully works in me.

2 I want you to know how much I am struggling for you and for those at Laodicea, and for all who have not met me personally. **2**My purpose is that they may be encouraged in heart and united in love, so that they may have the full riches of complete understanding, in order that they may know the mystery of God, namely, Christ, **3**in whom are hidden all the treasures of wisdom and knowledge. **4**I tell you this so that no one may deceive you by fine-sounding arguments. **5**For though I am absent from you in body, I am present with you in spirit and delight to see how orderly you are and how firm your faith in Christ is.

Freedom From Human Regulations Through Life With Christ

6So then, just as you received Christ Jesus as Lord, continue to live in him, **7**rooted and built up in him, strengthened in the faith as you were taught, and overflowing with thankfulness.

8See to it that no one takes you captive through hollow and deceptive philosophy, which depends on human tradition and the basic principles of this world rather than on Christ.

9For in Christ all the fullness of the Deity lives in bodily form, **10**and you have been given fullness in Christ, who is the head over every power and authority. **11**In him you were also circumcised, in the putting off of the sinful nature,[e] not with a circumcision done by the hands of men but with the circumcision done by Christ, **12**having been buried with him in baptism and raised with him through your faith in the power of God, who raised him from the dead.

13When you were dead in your sins and in the uncircumcision of your sinful nature,[f] God made you[b] alive with Christ. He forgave us all our sins, **14**having canceled the written code, with its regulations, that was against us and that stood opposed to us; he took it away, nailing it to the cross. **15**And having disarmed the powers and authorities, he made a public spectacle of them, triumphing over them by the cross.[g]

16Therefore do not let anyone judge you by

[a] *7* Some manuscripts *your* [b] *12,13* Some manuscripts *us* [c] *14* A few late manuscripts *redemption through his blood* [d] *21* Or *minds, as shown by* [e] *11* Or *the flesh* [f] *13* Or *your flesh* [g] *15* Or *them in him*

what you eat or drink, or with regard to a religious festival, a New Moon celebration or a Sabbath day. 17These are a shadow of the things that were to come; the reality, however, is found in Christ. 18Do not let anyone who delights in false humility and the worship of angels disqualify you for the prize. Such a person goes into great detail about what he has seen, and his unspiritual mind puffs him up with idle notions. 19He has lost connection with the Head, from whom the whole body, supported and held together by its ligaments and sinews, grows as God causes it to grow.

20Since you died with Christ to the basic principles of this world, why, as though you still belonged to it, do you submit to its rules: 21"Do not handle! Do not taste! Do not touch!"? 22These are all destined to perish with use, because they are based on human commands and teachings. 23Such regulations indeed have an appearance of wisdom, with their self-imposed worship, their false humility and their harsh treatment of the body, but they lack any value in restraining sensual indulgence.

Rules for Holy Living

3 Since, then, you have been raised with Christ, set your hearts on things above, where Christ is seated at the right hand of God. 2Set your minds on things above, not on earthly things. 3For you died, and your life is now hidden with Christ in God. 4When Christ, who is your[a] life, appears, then you also will appear with him in glory.

5Put to death, therefore, whatever belongs to your earthly nature: sexual immorality, impurity, lust, evil desires and greed, which is idolatry. 6Because of these, the wrath of God is coming.[b] 7You used to walk in these ways, in the life you once lived. 8But now you must rid yourselves of all such things as these: anger, rage, malice, slander, and filthy language from your lips. 9Do not lie to each other, since you have taken off your old self with its practices 10and have put on the new self, which is being renewed in knowledge in the image of its Creator. 11Here there is no Greek or Jew, circumcised or uncircumcised, barbarian, Scythian, slave or free, but Christ is all, and is in all.

12Therefore, as God's chosen people, holy and dearly loved, clothe yourselves with compassion, kindness, humility, gentleness and patience. 13Bear with each other and forgive whatever grievances you may have against one another. Forgive as the Lord forgave you. 14And over all these virtues put on love, which binds them all together in perfect unity.

15Let the peace of Christ rule in your hearts, since as members of one body you were called to peace. And be thankful. 16Let the word of Christ dwell in you richly as you teach and admonish one another with all wisdom, and as you sing psalms, hymns and spiritual songs with gratitude in your hearts to God. 17And whatever you do, whether in word or deed, do it all in the name of the Lord Jesus, giving thanks to God the Father through him.

Rules for Christian Households

18Wives, submit to your husbands, as is fitting in the Lord.

19Husbands, love your wives and do not be harsh with them.

20Children, obey your parents in everything, for this pleases the Lord.

21Fathers, do not embitter your children, or they will become discouraged.

22Slaves, obey your earthly masters in everything; and do it, not only when their eye is on you and to win their favor, but with sincerity of heart and reverence for the Lord. 23Whatever you do, work at it with all your heart, as working for the Lord, not for men, 24since you know that you will receive an inheritance from the Lord as a reward. It is the Lord Christ you are serving. 25Anyone who does wrong will be repaid for his wrong, and there is no favoritism.

4 Masters, provide your slaves with what is right and fair, because you know that you also have a Master in heaven.

Further Instructions

2Devote yourselves to prayer, being watchful and thankful. 3And pray for us, too, that God may open a door for our message, so that we may proclaim the mystery of Christ, for which I am in chains. 4Pray that I may proclaim it clearly, as I should. 5Be wise in the way you act toward outsiders; make the most of every opportunity. 6Let your conversation be always full of grace, seasoned with salt, so that you may know how to answer everyone.

Final Greetings

7Tychicus will tell you all the news about me. He is a dear brother, a faithful minister and fellow servant in the Lord. 8I am sending him to you for the express purpose that you may know about our[c] circumstances and that he may encourage your hearts. 9He is coming with Onesimus, our faithful and dear brother, who is one of you. They will tell you everything that is happening here.

10My fellow prisoner Aristarchus sends you his greetings, as does Mark, the cousin of Barnabas. (You have received instructions about him; if he comes to you, welcome him.) 11Jesus, who is called Justus, also sends greetings. These are the only Jews among my fellow workers for the kingdom of God, and they have proved a comfort to me. 12Epaphras, who is one of you and a servant of Christ Jesus, sends greetings. He is always wrestling in prayer for you, that you may stand firm in all the will of God, mature and fully assured. 13I vouch for him that he is working hard for you

[a]4 Some manuscripts *our* [b]6 Some early manuscripts *coming on those who are disobedient* [c]8 Some manuscripts *that he may know about your*

and for those at Laodicea and Hierapolis. 14Our dear friend Luke, the doctor, and Demas send greetings. 15Give my greetings to the brothers at Laodicea, and to Nympha and the church in her house.

16After this letter has been read to you, see that it is also read in the church of the Laodiceans and that you in turn read the letter from Laodicea.

17Tell Archippus: "See to it that you complete the work you have received in the Lord."

18I, Paul, write this greeting in my own hand. Remember my chains. Grace be with you.

1 Thessalonians

1 Paul, Silas[a] and Timothy,

To the church of the Thessalonians in God the Father and the Lord Jesus Christ:

Grace and peace to you.[b]

Thanksgiving for the Thessalonians' Faith

2We always thank God for all of you, mentioning you in our prayers. 3We continually remember before our God and Father your work produced by faith, your labor prompted by love, and your endurance inspired by hope in our Lord Jesus Christ.

4For we know, brothers loved by God, that he has chosen you, 5because our gospel came to you not simply with words, but also with power, with the Holy Spirit and with deep conviction. You know how we lived among you for your sake. 6You became imitators of us and of the Lord; in spite of severe suffering, you welcomed the message with the joy given by the Holy Spirit. 7And so you became a model to all the believers in Macedonia and Achaia. 8The Lord's message rang out from you not only in Macedonia and Achaia—your faith in God has become known everywhere. Therefore we do not need to say anything about it, 9for they themselves report what kind of reception you gave us. They tell how you turned to God from idols to serve the living and true God, 10and to wait for his Son from heaven, whom he raised from the dead—Jesus, who rescues us from the coming wrath.

Paul's Ministry in Thessalonica

2 You know, brothers, that our visit to you was not a failure. 2We had previously suffered and been insulted in Philippi, as you know, but with the help of our God we dared to tell you his gospel in spite of strong opposition. 3For the appeal we make does not spring from error or impure motives, nor are we trying to trick you. 4On the contrary, we speak as men approved by God to be entrusted with the gospel. We are not trying to please men but God, who tests our hearts. 5You know we never used flattery, nor did we put on a mask to cover up greed—God is our witness. 6We were not looking for praise from men, not from you or anyone else.

As apostles of Christ we could have been a burden to you, 7but we were gentle among you, like a mother caring for her little children. 8We loved you so much that we were delighted to share with you not only the gospel of God but our lives as well, because you had become so dear to us. 9Surely you remember, brothers, our toil and hardship; we worked night and day in order not to be a burden to anyone while we preached the gospel of God to you.

10You are witnesses, and so is God, of how holy, righteous and blameless we were among you who believed. 11For you know that we dealt with each of you as a father deals with his own children, 12encouraging, comforting and urging you to live lives worthy of God, who calls you into his kingdom and glory.

13And we also thank God continually because, when you received the word of God, which you heard from us, you accepted it not as the word of men, but as it actually is, the word of God, which is at work in you who believe. 14For you, brothers, became imitators of God's churches in Judea, which are in Christ Jesus: You suffered from your own countrymen the same things those churches suffered from the Jews, 15who killed the Lord Jesus and the prophets and also drove us out. They displease God and are hostile to all men 16in their effort to keep us from speaking to the Gentiles so that they may be saved. In this way they always heap up their sins to the limit. The wrath of God has come upon them at last.[c]

Paul's Longing to See the Thessalonians

17But, brothers, when we were torn away from you for a short time (in person, not in thought), out of our intense longing we made every effort to see you. 18For we wanted to come to you—certainly I, Paul, did, again and again—but Satan stopped us. 19For what is our hope, our joy, or the crown in which we will glory in the presence of our Lord Jesus when he comes? Is it not you? 20Indeed, you are our glory and joy.

[a] *1* Greek *Silvanus*, a variant of *Silas* [b] *1* Some early manuscripts *you from God our Father and the Lord Jesus Christ* [c] *16* Or *them fully*

3 So when we could stand it no longer, we thought it best to be left by ourselves in Athens. 2We sent Timothy, who is our brother and God's fellow worker[a] in spreading the gospel of Christ, to strengthen and encourage you in your faith, 3so that no one would be unsettled by these trials. You know quite well that we were destined for them. 4In fact, when we were with you, we kept telling you that we would be persecuted. And it turned out that way, as you well know. 5For this reason, when I could stand it no longer, I sent to find out about your faith. I was afraid that in some way the tempter might have tempted you and our efforts might have been useless.

Timothy's Encouraging Report

6But Timothy has just now come to us from you and has brought good news about your faith and love. He has told us that you always have pleasant memories of us and that you long to see us, just as we also long to see you. 7Therefore, brothers, in all our distress and persecution we were encouraged about you because of your faith. 8For now we really live, since you are standing firm in the Lord. 9How can we thank God enough for you in return for all the joy we have in the presence of our God because of you? 10Night and day we pray most earnestly that we may see you again and supply what is lacking in your faith.

11Now may our God and Father himself and our Lord Jesus clear the way for us to come to you. 12May the Lord make your love increase and overflow for each other and for everyone else, just as ours does for you. 13May he strengthen your hearts so that you will be blameless and holy in the presence of our God and Father when our Lord Jesus comes with all his holy ones.

Living to Please God

4 Finally, brothers, we instructed you how to live in order to please God, as in fact you are living. Now we ask you and urge you in the Lord Jesus to do this more and more. 2For you know what instructions we gave you by the authority of the Lord Jesus.

3It is God's will that you should be sanctified: that you should avoid sexual immorality; 4that each of you should learn to control his own body[b] in a way that is holy and honorable, 5not in passionate lust like the heathen, who do not know God; 6and that in this matter no one should wrong his brother or take advantage of him. The Lord will punish men for all such sins, as we have already told you and warned you. 7For God did not call us to be impure, but to live a holy life. 8Therefore, he who rejects this instruction does not reject man but God, who gives you his Holy Spirit.

9Now about brotherly love we do not need to write to you, for you yourselves have been taught by God to love each other. 10And in fact, you do love all the brothers throughout Macedonia. Yet we urge you, brothers, to do so more and more.

11Make it your ambition to lead a quiet life, to mind your own business and to work with your hands, just as we told you, 12so that your daily life may win the respect of outsiders and so that you will not be dependent on anybody.

The Coming of the Lord

13Brothers, we do not want you to be ignorant about those who fall asleep, or to grieve like the rest of men, who have no hope. 14We believe that Jesus died and rose again and so we believe that God will bring with Jesus those who have fallen asleep in him. 15According to the Lord's own word, we tell you that we who are still alive, who are left till the coming of the Lord, will certainly not precede those who have fallen asleep. 16For the Lord himself will come down from heaven, with a loud command, with the voice of the archangel and with the trumpet call of God, and the dead in Christ will rise first. 17After that, we who are still alive and are left will be caught up together with them in the clouds to meet the Lord in the air. And so we will be with the Lord forever. 18Therefore encourage each other with these words.

5 Now, brothers, about times and dates we do not need to write to you, 2for you know very well that the day of the Lord will come like a thief in the night. 3While people are saying, "Peace and safety," destruction will come on them suddenly, as labor pains on a pregnant woman, and they will not escape.

4But you, brothers, are not in darkness so that this day should surprise you like a thief. 5You are all sons of the light and sons of the day. We do not belong to the night or to the darkness. 6So then, let us not be like others, who are asleep, but let us be alert and self-controlled. 7For those who sleep, sleep at night, and those who get drunk, get drunk at night. 8But since we belong to the day, let us be self-controlled, putting on faith and love as a breastplate, and the hope of salvation as a helmet. 9For God did not appoint us to suffer wrath but to receive salvation through our Lord Jesus Christ. 10He died for us so that, whether we are awake or asleep, we may live together with him. 11Therefore encourage one another and build each other up, just as in fact you are doing.

Final Instructions

12Now we ask you, brothers, to respect those who work hard among you, who are over you in the Lord and who admonish you. 13Hold them in the highest regard in love because of their work. Live in peace with each other. 14And we urge you, brothers, warn those who are idle, encourage the timid, help the weak, be patient with everyone. 15Make sure that nobody pays back wrong for wrong, but always

[a]2 Some manuscripts *brother and fellow worker*; other manuscripts *brother and God's servant* [b]4 Or *learn to live with his own wife*; or *learn to acquire a wife*

try to be kind to each other and to everyone else.

16 Be joyful always; 17 pray continually; 18 give thanks in all circumstances, for this is God's will for you in Christ Jesus.

19 Do not put out the Spirit's fire; 20 do not treat prophecies with contempt. 21 Test everything. Hold on to the good. 22 Avoid every kind of evil.

23 May God himself, the God of peace, sanctify you through and through. May your whole spirit, soul and body be kept blameless at the coming of our Lord Jesus Christ. 24 The one who calls you is faithful and he will do it.

25 Brothers, pray for us. 26 Greet all the brothers with a holy kiss. 27 I charge you before the Lord to have this letter read to all the brothers.

28 The grace of our Lord Jesus Christ be with you.

2 Thessalonians

1 Paul, Silas[a] and Timothy,

To the church of the Thessalonians in God our Father and the Lord Jesus Christ:

2 Grace and peace to you from God the Father and the Lord Jesus Christ.

Thanksgiving and Prayer

3 We ought always to thank God for you, brothers, and rightly so, because your faith is growing more and more, and the love every one of you has for each other is increasing. 4 Therefore, among God's churches we boast about your perseverance and faith in all the persecutions and trials you are enduring.

5 All this is evidence that God's judgment is right, and as a result you will be counted worthy of the kingdom of God, for which you are suffering. 6 God is just: He will pay back trouble to those who trouble you 7 and give relief to you who are troubled, and to us as well. This will happen when the Lord Jesus is revealed from heaven in blazing fire with his powerful angels. 8 He will punish those who do not know God and do not obey the gospel of our Lord Jesus. 9 They will be punished with everlasting destruction and shut out from the presence of the Lord and from the majesty of his power 10 on the day he comes to be glorified in his holy people and to be marveled at among all those who have believed. This includes you, because you believed our testimony to you.

11 With this in mind, we constantly pray for you, that our God may count you worthy of his calling, and that by his power he may fulfill every good purpose of yours and every act prompted by your faith. 12 We pray this so that the name of our Lord Jesus may be glorified in you, and you in him, according to the grace of our God and the Lord Jesus Christ.[b]

The Man of Lawlessness

2 Concerning the coming of our Lord Jesus Christ and our being gathered to him, we ask you, brothers, 2 not to become easily unsettled or alarmed by some prophecy, report or letter supposed to have come from us, saying that the day of the Lord has already come. 3 Don't let anyone deceive you in any way, for ⌊that day will not come⌋ until the rebellion occurs and the man of lawlessness[c] is revealed, the man doomed to destruction. 4 He will oppose and will exalt himself over everything that is called God or is worshiped, so that he sets himself up in God's temple, proclaiming himself to be God.

5 Don't you remember that when I was with you I used to tell you these things? 6 And now you know what is holding him back, so that he may be revealed at the proper time. 7 For the secret power of lawlessness is already at work; but the one who now holds it back will continue to do so till he is taken out of the way. 8 And then the lawless one will be revealed, whom the Lord Jesus will overthrow with the breath of his mouth and destroy by the splendor of his coming. 9 The coming of the lawless one will be in accordance with the work of Satan displayed in all kinds of counterfeit miracles, signs and wonders, 10 and in every sort of evil that deceives those who are perishing. They perish because they refused to love the truth and so be saved. 11 For this reason God sends them a powerful delusion so that they will believe the lie 12 and so that all will be condemned who have not believed the truth but have delighted in wickedness.

Stand Firm

13 But we ought always to thank God for you, brothers loved by the Lord, because from the beginning God chose you[d] to be saved through the sanctifying work of the Spirit and through belief in the truth. 14 He called you to this through our gospel, that you might share in the glory of our Lord Jesus Christ. 15 So then, brothers, stand firm and hold to the teachings[e] we passed on to you, whether by word of mouth or by letter.

16 May our Lord Jesus Christ himself and God our Father, who loved us and by his grace gave us eternal encouragement and good hope,

[a] *1* Greek *Silvanus,* a variant of *Silas* [b] *12* Or *God and Lord, Jesus Christ* [c] *3* Some manuscripts *sin*
[d] *13* Some manuscripts *because God chose you as his firstfruits* [e] *15* Or *traditions*

17encourage your hearts and strengthen you in
every good deed and word.

Request for Prayer

3 Finally, brothers, pray for us that the message of the Lord may spread rapidly and be
honored, just as it was with you. 2And pray
that we may be delivered from wicked and evil
men, for not everyone has faith. 3But the Lord
is faithful, and he will strengthen and protect
you from the evil one. 4We have confidence in
the Lord that you are doing and will continue
to do the things we command. 5May the Lord
direct your hearts into God's love and Christ's
perseverance.

Warning Against Idleness

6In the name of the Lord Jesus Christ, we
command you, brothers, to keep away from
every brother who is idle and does not live
according to the teaching[a] you received from
us. 7For you yourselves know how you ought
to follow our example. We were not idle when
we were with you, 8nor did we eat anyone's
food without paying for it. On the contrary, we
worked night and day, laboring and toiling so
that we would not be a burden to any of you.
9We did this, not because we do not have the
right to such help, but in order to make ourselves a model for you to follow. 10For even
when we were with you, we gave you this rule:
"If a man will not work, he shall not eat."

11We hear that some among you are idle.
They are not busy; they are busybodies. 12Such
people we command and urge in the Lord
Jesus Christ to settle down and earn the bread
they eat. 13And as for you, brothers, never tire
of doing what is right.

14If anyone does not obey our instruction in
this letter, take special note of him. Do not
associate with him, in order that he may feel
ashamed. 15Yet do not regard him as an enemy, but warn him as a brother.

Final Greetings

16Now may the Lord of peace himself give
you peace at all times and in every way. The
Lord be with all of you.

17I, Paul, write this greeting in my own
hand, which is the distinguishing mark in all
my letters. This is how I write.

18The grace of our Lord Jesus Christ be with
you all.

1 Timothy

1 Paul, an apostle of Christ Jesus by the
command of God our Savior and of Christ
Jesus our hope,

2To Timothy my true son in the faith:

Grace, mercy and peace from God the Father and Christ Jesus our Lord.

Warning Against False Teachers of the Law

3As I urged you when I went into Macedonia, stay there in Ephesus so that you may
command certain men not to teach false doctrines any longer 4nor to devote themselves to
myths and endless genealogies. These promote
controversies rather than God's work—which
is by faith. 5The goal of this command is love,
which comes from a pure heart and a good
conscience and a sincere faith. 6Some have
wandered away from these and turned to
meaningless talk. 7They want to be teachers of
the law, but they do not know what they are
talking about or what they so confidently af-
firm.

8We know that the law is good if one uses it
properly. 9We also know that law[b] is made
not for the righteous but for lawbreakers and
rebels, the ungodly and sinful, the unholy and
irreligious; for those who kill their fathers or
mothers, for murderers, 10for adulterers and
perverts, for slave traders and liars and perjurers—and for whatever else is contrary to the
sound doctrine 11that conforms to the glorious
gospel of the blessed God, which he entrusted
to me.

The Lord's Grace to Paul

12I thank Christ Jesus our Lord, who has
given me strength, that he considered me faithful, appointing me to his service. 13Even
though I was once a blasphemer and a persecu-
tor and a violent man, I was shown mercy because I acted in ignorance and unbelief. 14The
grace of our Lord was poured out on me abundantly, along with the faith and love that are in
Christ Jesus.

15Here is a trustworthy saying that deserves
full acceptance: Christ Jesus came into the
world to save sinners—of whom I am the
worst. 16But for that very reason I was shown
mercy so that in me, the worst of sinners,
Christ Jesus might display his unlimited patience as an example for those who would believe on him and receive eternal life. 17Now to
the King eternal, immortal, invisible, the only
God, be honor and glory for ever and ever.
Amen.

18Timothy, my son, I give you this instruction in keeping with the prophecies once made
about you, so that by following them you may
fight the good fight, 19holding on to faith and
a good conscience. Some have rejected these

[a]6 Or *tradition* [b]9 Or *that the law*

and so have shipwrecked their faith. 20Among them are Hymenaeus and Alexander, whom I have handed over to Satan to be taught not to blaspheme.

Instructions on Worship

2 I urge, then, first of all, that requests, prayers, intercession and thanksgiving be made for everyone— 2for kings and all those in authority, that we may live peaceful and quiet lives in all godliness and holiness. 3This is good, and pleases God our Savior, 4who wants all men to be saved and to come to a knowledge of the truth. 5For there is one God and one mediator between God and men, the man Christ Jesus, 6who gave himself as a ransom for all men—the testimony given in its proper time. 7And for this purpose I was appointed a herald and an apostle—I am telling the truth, I am not lying—and a teacher of the true faith to the Gentiles.

8I want men everywhere to lift up holy hands in prayer, without anger or disputing.

9I also want women to dress modestly, with decency and propriety, not with braided hair or gold or pearls or expensive clothes, 10but with good deeds, appropriate for women who profess to worship God.

11A woman should learn in quietness and full submission. 12I do not permit a woman to teach or to have authority over a man; she must be silent. 13For Adam was formed first, then Eve. 14And Adam was not the one deceived; it was the woman who was deceived and became a sinner. 15But women[a] will be saved[b] through childbearing—if they continue in faith, love and holiness with propriety.

Overseers and Deacons

3 Here is a trustworthy saying: If anyone sets his heart on being an overseer,[c] he desires a noble task. 2Now the overseer must be above reproach, the husband of but one wife, temperate, self-controlled, respectable, hospitable, able to teach, 3not given to drunkenness, not violent but gentle, not quarrelsome, not a lover of money. 4He must manage his own family well and see that his children obey him with proper respect. 5(If anyone does not know how to manage his own family, how can he take care of God's church?) 6He must not be a recent convert, or he may become conceited and fall under the same judgment as the devil. 7He must also have a good reputation with outsiders, so that he will not fall into disgrace and into the devil's trap.

8Deacons, likewise, are to be men worthy of respect, sincere, not indulging in much wine, and not pursuing dishonest gain. 9They must keep hold of the deep truths of the faith with a clear conscience. 10They must first be tested; and then if there is nothing against them, let them serve as deacons.

11In the same way, their wives[d] are to be women worthy of respect, not malicious talkers but temperate and trustworthy in everything.

12A deacon must be the husband of but one wife and must manage his children and his household well. 13Those who have served well gain an excellent standing and great assurance in their faith in Christ Jesus.

14Although I hope to come to you soon, I am writing you these instructions so that, 15if I am delayed, you will know how people ought to conduct themselves in God's household, which is the church of the living God, the pillar and foundation of the truth. 16Beyond all question, the mystery of godliness is great:

He[e] appeared in a body,[f]
  was vindicated by the Spirit,
was seen by angels,
  was preached among the nations,
was believed on in the world,
  was taken up in glory.

Instructions to Timothy

4 The Spirit clearly says that in later times some will abandon the faith and follow deceiving spirits and things taught by demons. 2Such teachings come through hypocritical liars, whose consciences have been seared as with a hot iron. 3They forbid people to marry and order them to abstain from certain foods, which God created to be received with thanksgiving by those who believe and who know the truth. 4For everything God created is good, and nothing is to be rejected if it is received with thanksgiving, 5because it is consecrated by the word of God and prayer.

6If you point these things out to the brothers, you will be a good minister of Christ Jesus, brought up in the truths of the faith and of the good teaching that you have followed. 7Have nothing to do with godless myths and old wives' tales; rather, train yourself to be godly. 8For physical training is of some value, but godliness has value for all things, holding promise for both the present life and the life to come.

9This is a trustworthy saying that deserves full acceptance 10(and for this we labor and strive), that we have put our hope in the living God, who is the Savior of all men, and especially of those who believe.

11Command and teach these things. 12Don't let anyone look down on you because you are young, but set an example for the believers in speech, in life, in love, in faith and in purity. 13Until I come, devote yourself to the public reading of Scripture, to preaching and to teaching. 14Do not neglect your gift, which was given you through a prophetic message when the body of elders laid their hands on you.

15Be diligent in these matters; give yourself wholly to them, so that everyone may see your progress. 16Watch your life and doctrine closely. Persevere in them, because if you do, you will save both yourself and your hearers.

[a] *15* Greek *she* [b] *15* Or *restored* [c] *1* Traditionally *bishop*; also in verse 2 [d] *11* Or *way, deaconesses*
[e] *16* Some manuscripts *God* [f] *16* Or *in the flesh*

Advice About Widows, Elders and Slaves

5 Do not rebuke an older man harshly, but exhort him as if he were your father. Treat younger men as brothers, 2older women as mothers, and younger women as sisters, with absolute purity.

3Give proper recognition to those widows who are really in need. 4But if a widow has children or grandchildren, these should learn first of all to put their religion into practice by caring for their own family and so repaying their parents and grandparents, for this is pleasing to God. 5The widow who is really in need and left all alone puts her hope in God and continues night and day to pray and to ask God for help. 6But the widow who lives for pleasure is dead even while she lives. 7Give the people these instructions, too, so that no one may be open to blame. 8If anyone does not provide for his relatives, and especially for his immediate family, he has denied the faith and is worse than an unbeliever.

9No widow may be put on the list of widows unless she is over sixty, has been faithful to her husband,[a] 10and is well known for her good deeds, such as bringing up children, showing hospitality, washing the feet of the saints, helping those in trouble and devoting herself to all kinds of good deeds.

11As for younger widows, do not put them on such a list. For when their sensual desires overcome their dedication to Christ, they want to marry. 12Thus they bring judgment on themselves, because they have broken their first pledge. 13Besides, they get into the habit of being idle and going about from house to house. And not only do they become idlers, but also gossips and busybodies, saying things they ought not to. 14So I counsel younger widows to marry, to have children, to manage their homes and to give the enemy no opportunity for slander. 15Some have in fact already turned away to follow Satan.

16If any woman who is a believer has widows in her family, she should help them and not let the church be burdened with them, so that the church can help those widows who are really in need.

17The elders who direct the affairs of the church well are worthy of double honor, especially those whose work is preaching and teaching. 18For the Scripture says, "Do not muzzle the ox while it is treading out the grain,"[b] and "The worker deserves his wages."[c] 19Do not entertain an accusation against an elder unless it is brought by two or three witnesses. 20Those who sin are to be rebuked publicly, so that the others may take warning.

21I charge you, in the sight of God and Christ Jesus and the elect angels, to keep these instructions without partiality, and to do nothing out of favoritism.

22Do not be hasty in the laying on of hands, and do not share in the sins of others. Keep yourself pure.

23Stop drinking only water, and use a little wine because of your stomach and your frequent illnesses.

24The sins of some men are obvious, reaching the place of judgment ahead of them; the sins of others trail behind them. 25In the same way, good deeds are obvious, and even those that are not cannot be hidden.

6 All who are under the yoke of slavery should consider their masters worthy of full respect, so that God's name and our teaching may not be slandered. 2Those who have believing masters are not to show less respect for them because they are brothers. Instead, they are to serve them even better, because those who benefit from their service are believers, and dear to them. These are the things you are to teach and urge on them.

Love of Money

3If anyone teaches false doctrines and does not agree to the sound instruction of our Lord Jesus Christ and to godly teaching, 4he is conceited and understands nothing. He has an unhealthy interest in controversies and quarrels about words that result in envy, strife, malicious talk, evil suspicions 5and constant friction between men of corrupt mind, who have been robbed of the truth and who think that godliness is a means to financial gain.

6But godliness with contentment is great gain. 7For we brought nothing into the world, and we can take nothing out of it. 8But if we have food and clothing, we will be content with that. 9People who want to get rich fall into temptation and a trap and into many foolish and harmful desires that plunge men into ruin and destruction. 10For the love of money is a root of all kinds of evil. Some people, eager for money, have wandered from the faith and pierced themselves with many griefs.

Paul's Charge to Timothy

11But you, man of God, flee from all this, and pursue righteousness, godliness, faith, love, endurance and gentleness. 12Fight the good fight of the faith. Take hold of the eternal life to which you were called when you made your good confession in the presence of many witnesses. 13In the sight of God, who gives life to everything, and of Christ Jesus, who while testifying before Pontius Pilate made the good confession, I charge you 14to keep this command without spot or blame until the appearing of our Lord Jesus Christ, 15which God will bring about in his own time—God, the blessed and only Ruler, the King of kings and Lord of lords, 16who alone is immortal and who lives in unapproachable light, whom no one has seen or can see. To him be honor and might forever. Amen.

17Command those who are rich in this

[a] *9* Or *has had but one husband* [b] *18* Deut. 25:4 [c] *18* Luke 10:7

present world not to be arrogant nor to put
their hope in wealth, which is so uncertain, but
to put their hope in God, who richly provides
us with everything for our enjoyment. 18Com-
mand them to do good, to be rich in good
deeds, and to be generous and willing to share.
19In this way they will lay up treasure for
themselves as a firm foundation for the coming
age, so that they may take hold of the life that
is truly life.

20Timothy, guard what has been entrusted to
your care. Turn away from godless chatter and
the opposing ideas of what is falsely called
knowledge, 21which some have professed and
in so doing have wandered from the faith.

Grace be with you.

2 Timothy

1 Paul, an apostle of Christ Jesus by the will
of God, according to the promise of life
that is in Christ Jesus,

2To Timothy, my dear son:

Grace, mercy and peace from God the Father and Christ Jesus our Lord.

Encouragement to Be Faithful

3I thank God, whom I serve, as my forefathers did, with a clear conscience, as night and
day I constantly remember you in my prayers.
4Recalling your tears, I long to see you, so that
I may be filled with joy. 5I have been reminded
of your sincere faith, which first lived in your
grandmother Lois and in your mother Eunice
and, I am persuaded, now lives in you also.
6For this reason I remind you to fan into flame
the gift of God, which is in you through the
laying on of my hands. 7For God did not give
us a spirit of timidity, but a spirit of power, of
love and of self-discipline.

8So do not be ashamed to testify about our
Lord, or ashamed of me his prisoner. But join
with me in suffering for the gospel, by the
power of God, 9who has saved us and called us
to a holy life—not because of anything we
have done but because of his own purpose and
grace. This grace was given us in Christ Jesus
before the beginning of time, 10but it has now
been revealed through the appearing of our
Savior, Christ Jesus, who has destroyed death
and has brought life and immortality to light
through the gospel. 11And of this gospel I was
appointed a herald and an apostle and a teacher. 12That is why I am suffering as I am. Yet
I am not ashamed, because I know whom I
have believed, and am convinced that he is
able to guard what I have entrusted to him for
that day.

13What you heard from me, keep as the pattern of sound teaching, with faith and love in
Christ Jesus. 14Guard the good deposit that
was entrusted to you—guard it with the help of
the Holy Spirit who lives in us.

15You know that everyone in the province of
Asia has deserted me, including Phygelus and
Hermogenes.

16May the Lord show mercy to the household of Onesiphorus, because he often refreshed me and was not ashamed of my chains.
17On the contrary, when he was in Rome, he
searched hard for me until he found me. 18May
the Lord grant that he will find mercy from the
Lord on that day! You know very well in how
many ways he helped me in Ephesus.

2 You then, my son, be strong in the grace
that is in Christ Jesus. 2And the things you
have heard me say in the presence of many
witnesses entrust to reliable men who will also
be qualified to teach others. 3Endure hardship
with us like a good soldier of Christ Jesus. 4No
one serving as a soldier gets involved in civil-
ian affairs—he wants to please his commanding officer. 5Similarly, if anyone competes as
an athlete, he does not receive the victor's
crown unless he competes according to the
rules. 6The hardworking farmer should be the
first to receive a share of the crops. 7Reflect on
what I am saying, for the Lord will give you
insight into all this.

8Remember Jesus Christ, raised from the
dead, descended from David. This is my gospel, 9for which I am suffering even to the point
of being chained like a criminal. But God's
word is not chained. 10Therefore I endure everything for the sake of the elect, that they too
may obtain the salvation that is in Christ Jesus,
with eternal glory.

11Here is a trustworthy saying:

If we died with him,
 we will also live with him;
12if we endure,
 we will also reign with him.
If we disown him,
 he will also disown us;
13if we are faithless,
 he will remain faithful,
 for he cannot disown himself.

A Workman Approved by God

14Keep reminding them of these things.
Warn them before God against quarreling
about words; it is of no value, and only ruins
those who listen. 15Do your best to present
yourself to God as one approved, a workman
who does not need to be ashamed and who
correctly handles the word of truth. 16Avoid
godless chatter, because those who indulge in
it will become more and more ungodly.
17Their teaching will spread like gangrene.

Among them are Hymenaeus and Philetus,
18who have wandered away from the truth.
They say that the resurrection has already tak-
en place, and they destroy the faith of some.
19Nevertheless, God's solid foundation stands
firm, sealed with this inscription: "The Lord
knows those who are his,"[a] and, "Everyone
who confesses the name of the Lord must turn
away from wickedness."

20In a large house there are articles not only
of gold and silver, but also of wood and clay;
some are for noble purposes and some for ig-
noble. 21If a man cleanses himself from the
latter, he will be an instrument for noble purposes, made holy, useful to the Master and
prepared to do any good work.

22Flee the evil desires of youth, and pursue
righteousness, faith, love and peace, along
with those who call on the Lord out of a pure
heart. 23Don't have anything to do with foolish
and stupid arguments, because you know they
produce quarrels. 24And the Lord's servant
must not quarrel; instead, he must be kind to
everyone, able to teach, not resentful. 25Those
who oppose him he must gently instruct, in the
hope that God will grant them repentance leading them to a knowledge of the truth, 26and
that they will come to their senses and escape
from the trap of the devil, who has taken them
captive to do his will.

Godlessness in the Last Days

3 But mark this: There will be terrible times
in the last days. 2People will be lovers of
themselves, lovers of money, boastful, proud,
abusive, disobedient to their parents, ungrateful, unholy, 3without love, unforgiving, slanderous, without self-control, brutal, not lovers
of the good, 4treacherous, rash, conceited, lovers of pleasure rather than lovers of God—
5having a form of godliness but denying its
power. Have nothing to do with them.

6They are the kind who worm their way into
homes and gain control over weak-willed
women, who are loaded down with sins and
are swayed by all kinds of evil desires, 7always
learning but never able to acknowledge the
truth. 8Just as Jannes and Jambres opposed
Moses, so also these men oppose the truth—
men of depraved minds, who, as far as the faith
is concerned, are rejected. 9But they will not
get very far because, as in the case of those
men, their folly will be clear to everyone.

Paul's Charge to Timothy

10You, however, know all about my teaching, my way of life, my purpose, faith, patience, love, endurance, 11persecutions, sufferings—what kinds of things happened to me in
Antioch, Iconium and Lystra, the persecutions
I endured. Yet the Lord rescued me from all of
them. 12In fact, everyone who wants to live a
godly life in Christ Jesus will be persecuted,
13while evil men and impostors will go from
bad to worse, deceiving and being deceived.
14But as for you, continue in what you have
learned and have become convinced of, because you know those from whom you learned
it, 15and how from infancy you have known
the holy Scriptures, which are able to make
you wise for salvation through faith in Christ
Jesus. 16All Scripture is God-breathed and is
useful for teaching, rebuking, correcting and
training in righteousness, 17so that the man of
God may be thoroughly equipped for every
good work.

4 In the presence of God and of Christ Jesus,
who will judge the living and the dead, and
in view of his appearing and his kingdom, I
give you this charge: 2Preach the Word; be
prepared in season and out of season; correct,
rebuke and encourage—with great patience
and careful instruction. 3For the time will
come when men will not put up with sound
doctrine. Instead, to suit their own desires, they
will gather around them a great number of
teachers to say what their itching ears want to
hear. 4They will turn their ears away from the
truth and turn aside to myths. 5But you, keep
your head in all situations, endure hardship, do
the work of an evangelist, discharge all the
duties of your ministry.

6For I am already being poured out like a
drink offering, and the time has come for my
departure. 7I have fought the good fight, I have
finished the race, I have kept the faith. 8Now
there is in store for me the crown of righteousness, which the Lord, the righteous Judge, will
award to me on that day—and not only to me,
but also to all who have longed for his appearing.

Personal Remarks

9Do your best to come to me quickly, 10for
Demas, because he loved this world, has deserted me and has gone to Thessalonica. Cres-
cens has gone to Galatia, and Titus to Dalma-
tia. 11Only Luke is with me. Get Mark and
bring him with you, because he is helpful to
me in my ministry. 12I sent Tychicus to Ephesus. 13When you come, bring the cloak that I
left with Carpus at Troas, and my scrolls, especially the parchments.

14Alexander the metalworker did me a great
deal of harm. The Lord will repay him for what
he has done. 15You too should be on your
guard against him, because he strongly opposed our message.

16At my first defense, no one came to my
support, but everyone deserted me. May it not
be held against them. 17But the Lord stood at
my side and gave me strength, so that through
me the message might be fully proclaimed and
all the Gentiles might hear it. And I was delivered from the lion's mouth. 18The Lord will
rescue me from every evil attack and will bring

[a] *19* Num. 16:5 (see Septuagint)

me safely to his heavenly kingdom. To him be glory for ever and ever. Amen.

Final Greetings

19Greet Priscilla[a] and Aquila and the household of Onesiphorus. 20Erastus stayed in Corinth, and I left Trophimus sick in Miletus. 21Do your best to get here before winter. Eubulus greets you, and so do Pudens, Linus, Claudia and all the brothers.

22The Lord be with your spirit. Grace be with you.

Titus

1 Paul, a servant of God and an apostle of Jesus Christ for the faith of God's elect and the knowledge of the truth that leads to godliness— 2a faith and knowledge resting on the hope of eternal life, which God, who does not lie, promised before the beginning of time, 3and at his appointed season he brought his word to light through the preaching entrusted to me by the command of God our Savior,

4To Titus, my true son in our common faith:

Grace and peace from God the Father and Christ Jesus our Savior.

Titus's Task on Crete

5The reason I left you in Crete was that you might straighten out what was left unfinished and appoint[b] elders in every town, as I directed you. 6An elder must be blameless, the husband of but one wife, a man whose children believe and are not open to the charge of being wild and disobedient. 7Since an overseer[c] is entrusted with God's work, he must be blameless—not overbearing, not quick-tempered, not given to drunkenness, not violent, not pursuing dishonest gain. 8Rather he must be hospitable, one who loves what is good, who is self-controlled, upright, holy and disciplined. 9He must hold firmly to the trustworthy message as it has been taught, so that he can encourage others by sound doctrine and refute those who oppose it.

10For there are many rebellious people, mere talkers and deceivers, especially those of the circumcision group. 11They must be silenced, because they are ruining whole households by teaching things they ought not to teach—and that for the sake of dishonest gain. 12Even one of their own prophets has said, "Cretans are always liars, evil brutes, lazy gluttons." 13This testimony is true. Therefore, rebuke them sharply, so that they will be sound in the faith 14and will pay no attention to Jewish myths or to the commands of those who reject the truth. 15To the pure, all things are pure, but to those who are corrupted and do not believe, nothing is pure. In fact, both their minds and consciences are corrupted. 16They claim to know God, but by their actions they deny him. They are detestable, disobedient and unfit for doing anything good.

What Must Be Taught to Various Groups

2 You must teach what is in accord with sound doctrine. 2Teach the older men to be temperate, worthy of respect, self-controlled, and sound in faith, in love and in endurance.

3Likewise, teach the older women to be reverent in the way they live, not to be slanderers or addicted to much wine, but to teach what is good. 4Then they can train the younger women to love their husbands and children, 5to be self-controlled and pure, to be busy at home, to be kind, and to be subject to their husbands, so that no one will malign the word of God.

6Similarly, encourage the young men to be self-controlled. 7In everything set them an example by doing what is good. In your teaching show integrity, seriousness 8and soundness of speech that cannot be condemned, so that those who oppose you may be ashamed because they have nothing bad to say about us.

9Teach slaves to be subject to their masters in everything, to try to please them, not to talk back to them, 10and not to steal from them, but to show that they can be fully trusted, so that in every way they will make the teaching about God our Savior attractive.

11For the grace of God that brings salvation has appeared to all men. 12It teaches us to say "No" to ungodliness and worldly passions, and to live self-controlled, upright and godly lives in this present age, 13while we wait for the blessed hope—the glorious appearing of our great God and Savior, Jesus Christ, 14who gave himself for us to redeem us from all wickedness and to purify for himself a people that are his very own, eager to do what is good.

15These, then, are the things you should teach. Encourage and rebuke with all authority. Do not let anyone despise you.

Doing What Is Good

3 Remind the people to be subject to rulers and authorities, to be obedient, to be ready to do whatever is good, 2to slander no one, to be peaceable and considerate, and to show true humility toward all men.

3At one time we too were foolish, disobedient, deceived and enslaved by all kinds of passions and pleasures. We lived in malice and envy, being hated and hating one another. 4But

[a] *19* Greek *Prisca,* a variant of *Priscilla* [b] *5* Or *ordain* [c] *7* Traditionally *bishop*

when the kindness and love of God our Savior
appeared, 5he saved us, not because of righteous things we had done, but because of his
mercy. He saved us through the washing of
rebirth and renewal by the Holy Spirit, 6whom
he poured out on us generously through Jesus
Christ our Savior, 7so that, having been justified by his grace, we might become heirs having the hope of eternal life. 8This is a trustworthy saying. And I want you to stress these
things, so that those who have trusted in God
may be careful to devote themselves to doing
what is good. These things are excellent and
profitable for everyone.

9But avoid foolish controversies and genealogies and arguments and quarrels about the
law, because these are unprofitable and useless. 10Warn a divisive person once, and then
warn him a second time. After that, have nothing to do with him. 11You may be sure that
such a man is warped and sinful; he is self-
condemned.

Final Remarks

12As soon as I send Artemas or Tychicus to
you, do your best to come to me at Nicopolis,
because I have decided to winter there. 13Do
everything you can to help Zenas the lawyer
and Apollos on their way and see that they
have everything they need. 14Our people must
learn to devote themselves to doing what is
good, in order that they may provide for daily
necessities and not live unproductive lives.

15Everyone with me sends you greetings.
Greet those who love us in the faith.

Grace be with you all.

Philemon

1Paul, a prisoner of Christ Jesus, and Timothy our brother,

To Philemon our dear friend and fellow
worker, 2to Apphia our sister, to Archippus our
fellow soldier and to the church that meets in
your home:

3Grace to you and peace from God our Father and the Lord Jesus Christ.

Thanksgiving and Prayer

4I always thank my God as I remember you
in my prayers, 5because I hear about your faith
in the Lord Jesus and your love for all the
saints. 6I pray that you may be active in sharing your faith, so that you will have a full
understanding of every good thing we have in
Christ. 7Your love has given me great joy and
encouragement, because you, brother, have refreshed the hearts of the saints.

Paul's Plea for Onesimus

8Therefore, although in Christ I could be
bold and order you to do what you ought to do,
9yet I appeal to you on the basis of love. I then,
as Paul—an old man and now also a prisoner
of Christ Jesus— 10I appeal to you for my son
Onesimus,[a] who became my son while I was
in chains. 11Formerly he was useless to you,
but now he has become useful both to you and
to me.

12I am sending him—who is my very
heart—back to you. 13I would have liked to
keep him with me so that he could take your
place in helping me while I am in chains for
the gospel. 14But I did not want to do anything
without your consent, so that any favor you do
will be spontaneous and not forced. 15Perhaps
the reason he was separated from you for a
little while was that you might have him back
for good— 16no longer as a slave, but better
than a slave, as a dear brother. He is very dear
to me but even dearer to you, both as a man
and as a brother in the Lord.

17So if you consider me a partner, welcome
him as you would welcome me. 18If he has
done you any wrong or owes you anything,
charge it to me. 19I, Paul, am writing this with
my own hand. I will pay it back—not to mention that you owe me your very self. 20I do
wish, brother, that I may have some benefit
from you in the Lord; refresh my heart in
Christ. 21Confident of your obedience, I write
to you, knowing that you will do even more
than I ask.

22And one thing more: Prepare a guest room
for me, because I hope to be restored to you in
answer to your prayers.

23Epaphras, my fellow prisoner in Christ
Jesus, sends you greetings. 24And so do Mark,
Aristarchus, Demas and Luke, my fellow
workers.

25The grace of the Lord Jesus Christ be with
your spirit.

[a]*10 Onesimus* means *useful.*

Hebrews

The Son Superior to Angels

1 In the past God spoke to our forefathers
through the prophets at many times and in
various ways, 2but in these last days he has
spoken to us by his Son, whom he appointed
heir of all things, and through whom he made
the universe. 3The Son is the radiance of God's
glory and the exact representation of his being,
sustaining all things by his powerful word. After he had provided purification for sins, he sat
down at the right hand of the Majesty in heav-
en. 4So he became as much superior to the
angels as the name he has inherited is superior
to theirs.
5For to which of the angels did God ever
say,

"You are my Son;
today I have become your Father[a]"[b]?

Or again,

"I will be his Father,
and he will be my Son"[c]?

6And again, when God brings his firstborn into
the world, he says,

"Let all God's angels worship him."[d]

7In speaking of the angels he says,

"He makes his angels winds,
his servants flames of fire."[e]

8But about the Son he says,

"Your throne, O God, will last for ever
and ever,
and righteousness will be the scepter of
your kingdom.
9You have loved righteousness and hated
wickedness;
therefore God, your God, has set you
above your companions
by anointing you with the oil of joy."[f]

10He also says,

"In the beginning, O Lord, you laid the
foundations of the earth,
and the heavens are the work of your
hands.
11They will perish, but you remain;
they will all wear out like a garment.
12You will roll them up like a robe;
like a garment they will be changed.
But you remain the same,
and your years will never end."[g]

13To which of the angels did God ever say,

"Sit at my right hand
until I make your enemies
a footstool for your feet"[h]?

14Are not all angels ministering spirits sent to
serve those who will inherit salvation?

Warning to Pay Attention

2 We must pay more careful attention, therefore, to what we have heard, so that we do
not drift away. 2For if the message spoken by
angels was binding, and every violation and
disobedience received its just punishment,
3how shall we escape if we ignore such a great
salvation? This salvation, which was first announced by the Lord, was confirmed to us by
those who heard him. 4God also testified to it
by signs, wonders and various miracles, and
gifts of the Holy Spirit distributed according to
his will.

Jesus Made Like His Brothers

5It is not to angels that he has subjected the
world to come, about which we are speaking.
6But there is a place where someone has testified:

"What is man that you are mindful of
him,
the son of man that you care for him?
7You made him a little[i] lower than the
angels;
you crowned him with glory and honor
8 and put everything under his feet."[j]

In putting everything under him, God left nothing that is not subject to him. Yet at present we
do not see everything subject to him. 9But we
see Jesus, who was made a little lower than the
angels, now crowned with glory and honor because he suffered death, so that by the grace of
God he might taste death for everyone.
10In bringing many sons to glory, it was fitting that God, for whom and through whom
everything exists, should make the author of
their salvation perfect through suffering.
11Both the one who makes men holy and those
who are made holy are of the same family. So
Jesus is not ashamed to call them brothers.
12He says,

"I will declare your name to my brothers;
in the presence of the congregation I
will sing your praises."[k]

13And again,

"I will put my trust in him."[l]

And again he says,

"Here am I, and the children God has
given me."[m]

[a]5 Or *have begotten you* [b]5 Psalm 2:7 [c]5 2 Samuel 7:14; 1 Chron. 17:13 [d]6 Deut. 32:43 (see Dead Sea Scrolls and Septuagint) [e]7 Psalm 104:4 [f]9 Psalm 45:6,7 [g]12 Psalm 102:25-27 [h]13 Psalm 110:1 [i]7 Or *him for a little while*; also in verse 9 [j]8 Psalm 8:4-6 [k]12 Psalm 22:22 [l]13 Isaiah 8:17 [m]13 Isaiah 8:18

14Since the children have flesh and blood, he too shared in their humanity so that by his death he might destroy him who holds the power of death—that is, the devil— 15and free those who all their lives were held in slavery by their fear of death. 16For surely it is not angels he helps, but Abraham's descendants. 17For this reason he had to be made like his brothers in every way, in order that he might become a merciful and faithful high priest in service to God, and that he might make atonement for[a] the sins of the people. 18Because he himself suffered when he was tempted, he is able to help those who are being tempted.

Jesus Greater Than Moses

3 Therefore, holy brothers, who share in the heavenly calling, fix your thoughts on Jesus, the apostle and high priest whom we confess. 2He was faithful to the one who appointed him, just as Moses was faithful in all God's house. 3Jesus has been found worthy of greater honor than Moses, just as the builder of a house has greater honor than the house itself. 4For every house is built by someone, but God is the builder of everything. 5Moses was faithful as a servant in all God's house, testifying to what would be said in the future. 6But Christ is faithful as a son over God's house. And we are his house, if we hold on to our courage and the hope of which we boast.

Warning Against Unbelief

7So, as the Holy Spirit says:

"Today, if you hear his voice,
8 do not harden your hearts
as you did in the rebellion,
during the time of testing in the desert,
9where your fathers tested and tried me
and for forty years saw what I did.
10That is why I was angry with that
generation,
and I said, 'Their hearts are always
going astray,
and they have not known my ways.'
11So I declared on oath in my anger,
'They shall never enter my rest.' "[b]

12See to it, brothers, that none of you has a sinful, unbelieving heart that turns away from the living God. 13But encourage one another daily, as long as it is called Today, so that none of you may be hardened by sin's deceitfulness. 14We have come to share in Christ if we hold firmly till the end the confidence we had at first. 15As has just been said:

"Today, if you hear his voice,
do not harden your hearts
as you did in the rebellion."[c]

16Who were they who heard and rebelled? Were they not all those Moses led out of Egypt? 17And with whom was he angry for forty years? Was it not with those who sinned, whose bodies fell in the desert? 18And to whom did God swear that they would never enter his rest if not to those who disobeyed[d]? 19So we see that they were not able to enter, because of their unbelief.

A Sabbath-Rest for the People of God

4 Therefore, since the promise of entering his rest still stands, let us be careful that none of you be found to have fallen short of it. 2For we also have had the gospel preached to us, just as they did; but the message they heard was of no value to them, because those who heard did not combine it with faith.[e] 3Now we who have believed enter that rest, just as God has said,

"So I declared on oath in my anger,
'They shall never enter my rest.' "[f]

And yet his work has been finished since the creation of the world. 4For somewhere he has spoken about the seventh day in these words: "And on the seventh day God rested from all his work."[g] 5And again in the passage above he says, "They shall never enter my rest."

6It still remains that some will enter that rest, and those who formerly had the gospel preached to them did not go in, because of their disobedience. 7Therefore God again set a certain day, calling it Today, when a long time later he spoke through David, as was said before:

"Today, if you hear his voice,
do not harden your hearts."[c]

8For if Joshua had given them rest, God would not have spoken later about another day. 9There remains, then, a Sabbath-rest for the people of God; 10for anyone who enters God's rest also rests from his own work, just as God did from his. 11Let us, therefore, make every effort to enter that rest, so that no one will fall by following their example of disobedience.

12For the word of God is living and active. Sharper than any double-edged sword, it penetrates even to dividing soul and spirit, joints and marrow; it judges the thoughts and attitudes of the heart. 13Nothing in all creation is hidden from God's sight. Everything is uncovered and laid bare before the eyes of him to whom we must give account.

Jesus the Great High Priest

14Therefore, since we have a great high priest who has gone through the heavens,[h] Jesus the Son of God, let us hold firmly to the faith we profess. 15For we do not have a high priest who is unable to sympathize with our weaknesses, but we have one who has been tempted in every way, just as we are—yet was without sin. 16Let us then approach the throne of grace with confidence, so that we may receive mercy and find grace to help us in our time of need.

[a] *17* Or *and that he might turn aside God's wrath, taking away* [b] *11* Psalm 95:7-11 [c] *15,7* Psalm 95:7,8
[d] *18* Or *disbelieved* [e] *2* Many manuscripts *because they did not share in the faith of those who obeyed*
[f] *3* Psalm 95:11; also in verse 5 [g] *4* Gen. 2:2 [h] *14* Or *gone into heaven*

5 Every high priest is selected from among men and is appointed to represent them in matters related to God, to offer gifts and sacrifices for sins. 2He is able to deal gently with those who are ignorant and are going astray, since he himself is subject to weakness. 3This is why he has to offer sacrifices for his own sins, as well as for the sins of the people.

4No one takes this honor upon himself; he must be called by God, just as Aaron was. 5So Christ also did not take upon himself the glory of becoming a high priest. But God said to him,

> "You are my Son;
> today I have become your Father.[a]"[b]

6And he says in another place,

> "You are a priest forever,
> in the order of Melchizedek."[c]

7During the days of Jesus' life on earth, he offered up prayers and petitions with loud cries and tears to the one who could save him from death, and he was heard because of his reverent submission. 8Although he was a son, he learned obedience from what he suffered 9and, once made perfect, he became the source of eternal salvation for all who obey him 10and was designated by God to be high priest in the order of Melchizedek.

Warning Against Falling Away

11We have much to say about this, but it is hard to explain because you are slow to learn. 12In fact, though by this time you ought to be teachers, you need someone to teach you the elementary truths of God's word all over again. You need milk, not solid food! 13Anyone who lives on milk, being still an infant, is not acquainted with the teaching about righteousness. 14But solid food is for the mature, who by constant use have trained themselves to distinguish good from evil.

6 Therefore let us leave the elementary teachings about Christ and go on to maturity, not laying again the foundation of repentance from acts that lead to death,[d] and of faith in God, 2instruction about baptisms, the laying on of hands, the resurrection of the dead, and eternal judgment. 3And God permitting, we will do so.

4It is impossible for those who have once been enlightened, who have tasted the heavenly gift, who have shared in the Holy Spirit, 5who have tasted the goodness of the word of God and the powers of the coming age, 6if they fall away, to be brought back to repentance, because[e] to their loss they are crucifying the Son of God all over again and subjecting him to public disgrace.

7Land that drinks in the rain often falling on it and that produces a crop useful to those for whom it is farmed receives the blessing of God. 8But land that produces thorns and thistles is worthless and is in danger of being cursed. In the end it will be burned.

9Even though we speak like this, dear friends, we are confident of better things in your case—things that accompany salvation. 10God is not unjust; he will not forget your work and the love you have shown him as you have helped his people and continue to help them. 11We want each of you to show this same diligence to the very end, in order to make your hope sure. 12We do not want you to become lazy, but to imitate those who through faith and patience inherit what has been promised.

The Certainty of God's Promise

13When God made his promise to Abraham, since there was no one greater for him to swear by, he swore by himself, 14saying, "I will surely bless you and give you many descendants."[f] 15And so after waiting patiently, Abraham received what was promised.

16Men swear by someone greater than themselves, and the oath confirms what is said and puts an end to all argument. 17Because God wanted to make the unchanging nature of his purpose very clear to the heirs of what was promised, he confirmed it with an oath. 18God did this so that, by two unchangeable things in which it is impossible for God to lie, we who have fled to take hold of the hope offered to us may be greatly encouraged. 19We have this hope as an anchor for the soul, firm and secure. It enters the inner sanctuary behind the curtain, 20where Jesus, who went before us, has entered on our behalf. He has become a high priest forever, in the order of Melchizedek.

Melchizedek the Priest

7 This Melchizedek was king of Salem and priest of God Most High. He met Abraham returning from the defeat of the kings and blessed him, 2and Abraham gave him a tenth of everything. First, his name means "king of righteousness"; then also, "king of Salem" means "king of peace." 3Without father or mother, without genealogy, without beginning of days or end of life, like the Son of God he remains a priest forever.

4Just think how great he was: Even the patriarch Abraham gave him a tenth of the plunder! 5Now the law requires the descendants of Levi who become priests to collect a tenth from the people—that is, their brothers—even though their brothers are descended from Abraham. 6This man, however, did not trace his descent from Levi, yet he collected a tenth from Abraham and blessed him who had the promises. 7And without doubt the lesser person is blessed by the greater. 8In the one case, the tenth is collected by men who die; but in the other case, by him who is declared to be living. 9One might even say that Levi, who collects the tenth, paid the tenth through Abraham,

[a] *5* Or *have begotten you* [b] *5* Psalm 2:7 [c] *6* Psalm 110:4 [d] *1* Or *from useless rituals* [e] *6* Or *repentance while* [f] *14* Gen. 22:17

10because when Melchizedek met Abraham,
Levi was still in the body of his ancestor.

Jesus Like Melchizedek

11If perfection could have been attained
through the Levitical priesthood (for on the
basis of it the law was given to the people),
why was there still need for another priest to
come—one in the order of Melchizedek, not in
the order of Aaron? 12For when there is a
change of the priesthood, there must also be a
change of the law. 13He of whom these things
are said belonged to a different tribe, and no
one from that tribe has ever served at the altar.
14For it is clear that our Lord descended from
Judah, and in regard to that tribe Moses said
nothing about priests. 15And what we have
said is even more clear if another priest like
Melchizedek appears, 16one who has become a
priest not on the basis of a regulation as to his
ancestry but on the basis of the power of an
indestructible life. 17For it is declared:

"You are a priest forever,
in the order of Melchizedek."[a]

18The former regulation is set aside because
it was weak and useless 19(for the law made
nothing perfect), and a better hope is introduced, by which we draw near to God.

20And it was not without an oath! Others
became priests without any oath, 21but he became a priest with an oath when God said to
him:

"The Lord has sworn
and will not change his mind:
'You are a priest forever.' "[a]

22Because of this oath, Jesus has become the
guarantee of a better covenant.

23Now there have been many of those
priests, since death prevented them from continuing in office; 24but because Jesus lives forever, he has a permanent priesthood. 25There-
fore he is able to save completely[b] those who
come to God through him, because he always
lives to intercede for them.

26Such a high priest meets our need—one
who is holy, blameless, pure, set apart from
sinners, exalted above the heavens. 27Unlike
the other high priests, he does not need to offer
sacrifices day after day, first for his own sins,
and then for the sins of the people. He sacrificed for their sins once for all when he offered
himself. 28For the law appoints as high priests
men who are weak; but the oath, which came
after the law, appointed the Son, who has been
made perfect forever.

The High Priest of a New Covenant

8 The point of what we are saying is this: We
do have such a high priest, who sat down
at the right hand of the throne of the Majesty
in heaven, 2and who serves in the sanctuary,
the true tabernacle set up by the Lord, not by
man.

3Every high priest is appointed to offer both
gifts and sacrifices, and so it was necessary for
this one also to have something to offer. 4If he
were on earth, he would not be a priest, for
there are already men who offer the gifts prescribed by the law. 5They serve at a sanctuary
that is a copy and shadow of what is in heaven.
This is why Moses was warned when he was
about to build the tabernacle: "See to it that
you make everything according to the pattern
shown you on the mountain."[c] 6But the ministry Jesus has received is as superior to theirs as
the covenant of which he is mediator is superi-
or to the old one, and it is founded on better
promises.

7For if there had been nothing wrong with
that first covenant, no place would have been
sought for another. 8But God found fault with
the people and said[d]:

"The time is coming, declares the Lord,
when I will make a new covenant
with the house of Israel
and with the house of Judah.
9It will not be like the covenant
I made with their forefathers
when I took them by the hand
to lead them out of Egypt,
because they did not remain faithful to my
covenant,
and I turned away from them,
declares the Lord.
10This is the covenant I will make with the
house of Israel
after that time, declares the Lord.
I will put my laws in their minds
and write them on their hearts.
I will be their God,
and they will be my people.
11No longer will a man teach his neighbor,
or a man his brother, saying, 'Know the
Lord,'
because they will all know me,
from the least of them to the greatest.
12For I will forgive their wickedness
and will remember their sins no
more."[e]

13By calling this covenant "new," he has
made the first one obsolete; and what is obsolete and aging will soon disappear.

Worship in the Earthly Tabernacle

9 Now the first covenant had regulations for
worship and also an earthly sanctuary. 2A
tabernacle was set up. In its first room were the
lampstand, the table and the consecrated bread;
this was called the Holy Place. 3Behind the
second curtain was a room called the Most
Holy Place, 4which had the golden altar of incense and the gold-covered ark of the covenant. This ark contained the gold jar of manna, Aaron's staff that had budded, and the
stone tablets of the covenant. 5Above the ark
were the cherubim of the Glory, overshadow-

[a] *17,21* Psalm 110:4 [b] *25* Or *forever* [c] *5* Exodus 25:40 [d] *8* Some manuscripts may be translated *fault and said to the people.* [e] *12* Jer. 31:31-34

ing the atonement cover.[a] But we cannot discuss these things in detail now.
6When everything had been arranged like
this, the priests entered regularly into the outer
room to carry on their ministry. 7But only the
high priest entered the inner room, and that
only once a year, and never without blood,
which he offered for himself and for the sins
the people had committed in ignorance. 8The
Holy Spirit was showing by this that the way
into the Most Holy Place had not yet been
disclosed as long as the first tabernacle was
still standing. 9This is an illustration for the
present time, indicating that the gifts and sacrifices being offered were not able to clear the
conscience of the worshiper. 10They are only a
matter of food and drink and various ceremonial washings—external regulations applying
until the time of the new order.

The Blood of Christ

11When Christ came as high priest of the
good things that are already here,[b] he went
through the greater and more perfect tabernacle that is not man-made, that is to say, not a
part of this creation. 12He did not enter by
means of the blood of goats and calves; but he
entered the Most Holy Place once for all by his
own blood, having obtained eternal redemption. 13The blood of goats and bulls and the
ashes of a heifer sprinkled on those who are
ceremonially unclean sanctify them so that
they are outwardly clean. 14How much more,
then, will the blood of Christ, who through the
eternal Spirit offered himself unblemished to
God, cleanse our consciences from acts that
lead to death,[c] so that we may serve the living
God!
15For this reason Christ is the mediator of a
new covenant, that those who are called may
receive the promised eternal inheritance—now
that he has died as a ransom to set them free
from the sins committed under the first covenant.
16In the case of a will,[d] it is necessary to
prove the death of the one who made it, 17be-
cause a will is in force only when somebody
has died; it never takes effect while the one
who made it is living. 18This is why even the
first covenant was not put into effect without
blood. 19When Moses had proclaimed every
commandment of the law to all the people, he
took the blood of calves, together with water,
scarlet wool and branches of hyssop, and
sprinkled the scroll and all the people. 20He
said, "This is the blood of the covenant, which
God has commanded you to keep."[e] 21In the
same way, he sprinkled with the blood both the
tabernacle and everything used in its ceremo-
nies. 22In fact, the law requires that nearly everything be cleansed with blood, and without
the shedding of blood there is no forgiveness.
23It was necessary, then, for the copies of
the heavenly things to be purified with these
sacrifices, but the heavenly things themselves
with better sacrifices than these. 24For Christ
did not enter a man-made sanctuary that was
only a copy of the true one; he entered heaven
itself, now to appear for us in God's presence.
25Nor did he enter heaven to offer himself
again and again, the way the high priest enters
the Most Holy Place every year with blood that
is not his own. 26Then Christ would have had
to suffer many times since the creation of the
world. But now he has appeared once for all at
the end of the ages to do away with sin by the
sacrifice of himself. 27Just as man is destined
to die once, and after that to face judgment,
28so Christ was sacrificed once to take away
the sins of many people; and he will appear a
second time, not to bear sin, but to bring salvation to those who are waiting for him.

Christ's Sacrifice Once for All

10 The law is only a shadow of the good
things that are coming—not the realities
themselves. For this reason it can never, by the
same sacrifices repeated endlessly year after
year, make perfect those who draw near to
worship. 2If it could, would they not have
stopped being offered? For the worshipers
would have been cleansed once for all, and
would no longer have felt guilty for their sins.
3But those sacrifices are an annual reminder of
sins, 4because it is impossible for the blood of
bulls and goats to take away sins.
5Therefore, when Christ came into the
world, he said:

"Sacrifice and offering you did not desire,
 but a body you prepared for me;
6with burnt offerings and sin offerings
 you were not pleased.
7Then I said, 'Here I am—it is written
 about me in the scroll—
I have come to do your will,
 O God.' "[f]

8First he said, "Sacrifices and offerings, burnt
offerings and sin offerings you did not desire,
nor were you pleased with them" (although the
law required them to be made). 9Then he said,
"Here I am, I have come to do your will." He
sets aside the first to establish the second.
10And by that will, we have been made holy
through the sacrifice of the body of Jesus
Christ once for all.
11Day after day every priest stands and performs his religious duties; again and again he
offers the same sacrifices, which can never
take away sins. 12But when this priest had offered for all time one sacrifice for sins, he sat
down at the right hand of God. 13Since that
time he waits for his enemies to be made his
footstool, 14because by one sacrifice he has
made perfect forever those who are being
made holy.
15The Holy Spirit also testifies to us about
this. First he says:

[a]5 Traditionally *the mercy seat* [b]11 Some early manuscripts *are to come* [c]14 Or *from useless rituals*
[d]16 Same Greek word as *covenant*; also in verse 17 [e]20 Exodus 24:8 [f]7 Psalm 40:6-8 (see Septuagint)

16"This is the covenant I will make with
them
after that time, says the Lord.
I will put my laws in their hearts,
and I will write them on their minds."[a]

17Then he adds:

"Their sins and lawless acts
I will remember no more."[b]

18And where these have been forgiven, there is
no longer any sacrifice for sin.

A Call to Persevere

19Therefore, brothers, since we have confidence to enter the Most Holy Place by the
blood of Jesus, 20by a new and living way
opened for us through the curtain, that is, his
body, 21and since we have a great priest over
the house of God, 22let us draw near to God
with a sincere heart in full assurance of faith,
having our hearts sprinkled to cleanse us from
a guilty conscience and having our bodies
washed with pure water. 23Let us hold un-
swervingly to the hope we profess, for he who
promised is faithful. 24And let us consider how
we may spur one another on toward love and
good deeds. 25Let us not give up meeting together, as some are in the habit of doing, but
let us encourage one another—and all the
more as you see the Day approaching.

26If we deliberately keep on sinning after we
have received the knowledge of the truth, no
sacrifice for sins is left, 27but only a fearful
expectation of judgment and of raging fire that
will consume the enemies of God. 28Anyone
who rejected the law of Moses died without
mercy on the testimony of two or three witnesses. 29How much more severely do you
think a man deserves to be punished who has
trampled the Son of God under foot, who has
treated as an unholy thing the blood of the
covenant that sanctified him, and who has insulted the Spirit of grace? 30For we know him
who said, "It is mine to avenge; I will repay,"[c]
and again, "The Lord will judge his people."[d]
31It is a dreadful thing to fall into the hands of
the living God.

32Remember those earlier days after you had
received the light, when you stood your ground
in a great contest in the face of suffering.
33Sometimes you were publicly exposed to insult and persecution; at other times you stood
side by side with those who were so treated.
34You sympathized with those in prison and
joyfully accepted the confiscation of your
property, because you knew that you yourselves had better and lasting possessions.

35So do not throw away your confidence; it
will be richly rewarded. 36You need to persevere so that when you have done the will of
God, you will receive what he has promised.
37For in just a very little while,

"He who is coming will come and will not
delay.
38 But my righteous one[e] will live by
faith.
And if he shrinks back,
I will not be pleased with him."[f]

39But we are not of those who shrink back and
are destroyed, but of those who believe and are
saved.

By Faith

11 Now faith is being sure of what we hope
for and certain of what we do not see.
2This is what the ancients were commended
for.

3By faith we understand that the universe
was formed at God's command, so that what is
seen was not made out of what was visible.

4By faith Abel offered God a better sacrifice
than Cain did. By faith he was commended as
a righteous man, when God spoke well of his
offerings. And by faith he still speaks, even
though he is dead.

5By faith Enoch was taken from this life, so
that he did not experience death; he could not
be found, because God had taken him away.
For before he was taken, he was commended
as one who pleased God. 6And without faith it
is impossible to please God, because anyone
who comes to him must believe that he exists
and that he rewards those who earnestly seek
him.

7By faith Noah, when warned about things
not yet seen, in holy fear built an ark to save
his family. By his faith he condemned the
world and became heir of the righteousness
that comes by faith.

8By faith Abraham, when called to go to a
place he would later receive as his inheritance,
obeyed and went, even though he did not know
where he was going. 9By faith he made his
home in the promised land like a stranger in a
foreign country; he lived in tents, as did Isaac
and Jacob, who were heirs with him of the
same promise. 10For he was looking forward to
the city with foundations, whose architect and
builder is God.

11By faith Abraham, even though he was
past age—and Sarah herself was barren—was
enabled to become a father because he[g] considered him faithful who had made the promise. 12And so from this one man, and he as
good as dead, came descendants as numerous
as the stars in the sky and as countless as the
sand on the seashore.

13All these people were still living by faith
when they died. They did not receive the
things promised; they only saw them and welcomed them from a distance. And they admitted that they were aliens and strangers on
earth. 14People who say such things show that
they are looking for a country of their own. 15If
they had been thinking of the country they had

[a]*16* Jer. 31:33 [b]*17* Jer. 31:34 [c]*30* Deut. 32:35 [d]*30* Deut. 32:36; Psalm 135:14 [e]*38* One early manuscript *But the righteous* [f]*38* Hab. 2:3,4 [g]*11* Or *By faith even Sarah, who was past age, was enabled to bear children because she*

left, they would have had opportunity to return. 16Instead, they were longing for a better
country—a heavenly one. Therefore God is
not ashamed to be called their God, for he has
prepared a city for them.
17By faith Abraham, when God tested him,
offered Isaac as a sacrifice. He who had received the promises was about to sacrifice his
one and only son, 18even though God had said
to him, "It is through Isaac that your offspring[a] will be reckoned."[b] 19Abraham reasoned that God could raise the dead, and figuratively speaking, he did receive Isaac back
from death.
20By faith Isaac blessed Jacob and Esau in
regard to their future.
21By faith Jacob, when he was dying,
blessed each of Joseph's sons, and worshiped
as he leaned on the top of his staff.
22By faith Joseph, when his end was near,
spoke about the exodus of the Israelites from
Egypt and gave instructions about his bones.
23By faith Moses' parents hid him for three
months after he was born, because they saw he
was no ordinary child, and they were not afraid
of the king's edict.
24By faith Moses, when he had grown up,
refused to be known as the son of Pharaoh's
daughter. 25He chose to be mistreated along
with the people of God rather than to enjoy the
pleasures of sin for a short time. 26He regarded
disgrace for the sake of Christ as of greater
value than the treasures of Egypt, because he
was looking ahead to his reward. 27By faith he
left Egypt, not fearing the king's anger; he persevered because he saw him who is invisible.
28By faith he kept the Passover and the sprinkling of blood, so that the destroyer of the
firstborn would not touch the firstborn of Israel.
29By faith the people passed through the
Red Sea[c] as on dry land; but when the Egyptians tried to do so, they were drowned.
30By faith the walls of Jericho fell, after the
people had marched around them for seven
days.
31By faith the prostitute Rahab, because she
welcomed the spies, was not killed with those
who were disobedient.[d]
32And what more shall I say? I do not have
time to tell about Gideon, Barak, Samson,
Jephthah, David, Samuel and the prophets,
33who through faith conquered kingdoms, ad-
ministered justice, and gained what was promised; who shut the mouths of lions, 34quenched
the fury of the flames, and escaped the edge
of the sword; whose weakness was turned to
strength; and who became powerful in battle
and routed foreign armies. 35Women received
back their dead, raised to life again. Others
were tortured and refused to be released, so
that they might gain a better resurrection.
36Some faced jeers and flogging, while still
others were chained and put in prison. 37They
were stoned[e]; they were sawed in two; they
were put to death by the sword. They went
about in sheepskins and goatskins, destitute,
persecuted and mistreated— 38the world was
not worthy of them. They wandered in deserts
and mountains, and in caves and holes in the
ground.
39These were all commended for their faith,
yet none of them received what had been
promised. 40God had planned something better
for us so that only together with us would they
be made perfect.

God Disciplines His Sons

12 Therefore, since we are surrounded by
such a great cloud of witnesses, let us
throw off everything that hinders and the sin
that so easily entangles, and let us run with
perseverance the race marked out for us. 2Let
us fix our eyes on Jesus, the author and per-
fecter of our faith, who for the joy set before
him endured the cross, scorning its shame, and
sat down at the right hand of the throne of God.
3Consider him who endured such opposition
from sinful men, so that you will not grow
weary and lose heart.
4In your struggle against sin, you have not
yet resisted to the point of shedding your
blood. 5And you have forgotten that word of
encouragement that addresses you as sons:

"My son, do not make light of the Lord's
discipline,
and do not lose heart when he rebukes
you,
6because the Lord disciplines those he
loves,
and he punishes everyone he accepts as
a son."[f]

7Endure hardship as discipline; God is treating you as sons. For what son is not disciplined
by his father? 8If you are not disciplined (and
everyone undergoes discipline), then you are
illegitimate children and not true sons. 9More-
over, we have all had human fathers who disciplined us and we respected them for it. How
much more should we submit to the Father of
our spirits and live! 10Our fathers disciplined
us for a little while as they thought best; but
God disciplines us for our good, that we may
share in his holiness. 11No discipline seems
pleasant at the time, but painful. Later on,
however, it produces a harvest of righteousness and peace for those who have been
trained by it.
12Therefore, strengthen your feeble arms
and weak knees. 13"Make level paths for your
feet,"[g] so that the lame may not be disabled,
but rather healed.

Warning Against Refusing God

14Make every effort to live in peace with all
men and to be holy; without holiness no one
will see the Lord. 15See to it that no one misses
the grace of God and that no bitter root grows

[a]*18* Greek *seed* [b]*18* Gen. 21:12 [c]*29* That is, Sea of Reeds [d]*31* Or *unbelieving* [e]*37* Some early manuscripts *stoned; they were put to the test;* [f]*6* Prov. 3:11,12 [g]*13* Prov. 4:26

up to cause trouble and defile many. 16See that
no one is sexually immoral, or is godless like
Esau, who for a single meal sold his inheritance rights as the oldest son. 17Afterward,
as you know, when he wanted to inherit this
blessing, he was rejected. He could bring about
no change of mind, though he sought the blessing with tears.

18You have not come to a mountain that can
be touched and that is burning with fire; to
darkness, gloom and storm; 19to a trumpet
blast or to such a voice speaking words that
those who heard it begged that no further word
be spoken to them, 20because they could not
bear what was commanded: "If even an animal
touches the mountain, it must be stoned."[a]
21The sight was so terrifying that Moses said,
"I am trembling with fear."[b]

22But you have come to Mount Zion, to the
heavenly Jerusalem, the city of the living God.
You have come to thousands upon thousands
of angels in joyful assembly, 23to the church of
the firstborn, whose names are written in heav-
en. You have come to God, the judge of all
men, to the spirits of righteous men made perfect, 24to Jesus the mediator of a new covenant,
and to the sprinkled blood that speaks a better
word than the blood of Abel.

25See to it that you do not refuse him who
speaks. If they did not escape when they refused him who warned them on earth, how
much less will we, if we turn away from him
who warns us from heaven? 26At that time his
voice shook the earth, but now he has promised, "Once more I will shake not only the
earth but also the heavens."[c] 27The words
"once more" indicate the removing of what
can be shaken—that is, created things—so
that what cannot be shaken may remain.

28Therefore, since we are receiving a kingdom that cannot be shaken, let us be thankful,
and so worship God acceptably with reverence
and awe, 29for our "God is a consuming fire."[d]

Concluding Exhortations

13 Keep on loving each other as brothers.
2Do not forget to entertain strangers, for
by so doing some people have entertained angels without knowing it. 3Remember those in
prison as if you were their fellow prisoners,
and those who are mistreated as if you yourselves were suffering.

4Marriage should be honored by all, and the
marriage bed kept pure, for God will judge the
adulterer and all the sexually immoral. 5Keep
your lives free from the love of money and be
content with what you have, because God has
said,

"Never will I leave you;
never will I forsake you."[e]

6So we say with confidence,

"The Lord is my helper; I will not be
afraid.
What can man do to me?"[f]

7Remember your leaders, who spoke the
word of God to you. Consider the outcome of
their way of life and imitate their faith. 8Jesus
Christ is the same yesterday and today and
forever.

9Do not be carried away by all kinds of
strange teachings. It is good for our hearts to
be strengthened by grace, not by ceremonial
foods, which are of no value to those who eat
them. 10We have an altar from which those
who minister at the tabernacle have no right to
eat.

11The high priest carries the blood of animals into the Most Holy Place as a sin offering, but the bodies are burned outside the
camp. 12And so Jesus also suffered outside the
city gate to make the people holy through his
own blood. 13Let us, then, go to him outside
the camp, bearing the disgrace he bore. 14For
here we do not have an enduring city, but we
are looking for the city that is to come.

15Through Jesus, therefore, let us continually offer to God a sacrifice of praise—the fruit
of lips that confess his name. 16And do not
forget to do good and to share with others, for
with such sacrifices God is pleased.

17Obey your leaders and submit to their authority. They keep watch over you as men who
must give an account. Obey them so that their
work will be a joy, not a burden, for that would
be of no advantage to you.

18Pray for us. We are sure that we have a
clear conscience and desire to live honorably
in every way. 19I particularly urge you to pray
so that I may be restored to you soon.

20May the God of peace, who through the
blood of the eternal covenant brought back
from the dead our Lord Jesus, that great Shepherd of the sheep, 21equip you with everything
good for doing his will, and may he work in us
what is pleasing to him, through Jesus Christ,
to whom be glory for ever and ever. Amen.

22Brothers, I urge you to bear with my word
of exhortation, for I have written you only a
short letter.

23I want you to know that our brother Timothy has been released. If he arrives soon, I will
come with him to see you.

24Greet all your leaders and all God's people. Those from Italy send you their greetings.

25Grace be with you all.

[a] *20* Exodus 19:12,13 [b] *21* Deut. 9:19 [c] *26* Haggai 2:6 [d] *29* Deut. 4:24 [e] *5* Deut. 31:6
[f] *6* Psalm 118:6,7

James

1 James, a servant of God and of the Lord Jesus Christ,

To the twelve tribes scattered among the nations:

Greetings.

Trials and Temptations

2Consider it pure joy, my brothers, whenever you face trials of many kinds, 3because you know that the testing of your faith develops perseverance. 4Perseverance must finish its work so that you may be mature and complete, not lacking anything. 5If any of you lacks wisdom, he should ask God, who gives generously to all without finding fault, and it will be given to him. 6But when he asks, he must believe and not doubt, because he who doubts is like a wave of the sea, blown and tossed by the wind. 7That man should not think he will receive anything from the Lord; 8he is a double-minded man, unstable in all he does.

9The brother in humble circumstances ought to take pride in his high position. 10But the one who is rich should take pride in his low position, because he will pass away like a wild flower. 11For the sun rises with scorching heat and withers the plant; its blossom falls and its beauty is destroyed. In the same way, the rich man will fade away even while he goes about his business.

12Blessed is the man who perseveres under trial, because when he has stood the test, he will receive the crown of life that God has promised to those who love him.

13When tempted, no one should say, "God is tempting me." For God cannot be tempted by evil, nor does he tempt anyone; 14but each one is tempted when, by his own evil desire, he is dragged away and enticed. 15Then, after desire has conceived, it gives birth to sin; and sin, when it is full-grown, gives birth to death.

16Don't be deceived, my dear brothers. 17Every good and perfect gift is from above, coming down from the Father of the heavenly lights, who does not change like shifting shadows. 18He chose to give us birth through the word of truth, that we might be a kind of firstfruits of all he created.

Listening and Doing

19My dear brothers, take note of this: Everyone should be quick to listen, slow to speak and slow to become angry, 20for man's anger does not bring about the righteous life that God desires. 21Therefore, get rid of all moral filth and the evil that is so prevalent and humbly accept the word planted in you, which can save you.

22Do not merely listen to the word, and so deceive yourselves. Do what it says. 23Anyone who listens to the word but does not do what it says is like a man who looks at his face in a mirror 24and, after looking at himself, goes away and immediately forgets what he looks like. 25But the man who looks intently into the perfect law that gives freedom, and continues to do this, not forgetting what he has heard, but doing it—he will be blessed in what he does.

26If anyone considers himself religious and yet does not keep a tight rein on his tongue, he deceives himself and his religion is worthless. 27Religion that God our Father accepts as pure and faultless is this: to look after orphans and widows in their distress and to keep oneself from being polluted by the world.

Favoritism Forbidden

2 My brothers, as believers in our glorious Lord Jesus Christ, don't show favoritism. 2Suppose a man comes into your meeting wearing a gold ring and fine clothes, and a poor man in shabby clothes also comes in. 3If you show special attention to the man wearing fine clothes and say, "Here's a good seat for you," but say to the poor man, "You stand there" or "Sit on the floor by my feet," 4have you not discriminated among yourselves and become judges with evil thoughts?

5Listen, my dear brothers: Has not God chosen those who are poor in the eyes of the world to be rich in faith and to inherit the kingdom he promised those who love him? 6But you have insulted the poor. Is it not the rich who are exploiting you? Are they not the ones who are dragging you into court? 7Are they not the ones who are slandering the noble name of him to whom you belong?

8If you really keep the royal law found in Scripture, "Love your neighbor as yourself,"[a] you are doing right. 9But if you show favoritism, you sin and are convicted by the law as lawbreakers. 10For whoever keeps the whole law and yet stumbles at just one point is guilty of breaking all of it. 11For he who said, "Do not commit adultery,"[b] also said, "Do not murder."[c] If you do not commit adultery but do commit murder, you have become a lawbreaker.

12Speak and act as those who are going to be judged by the law that gives freedom, 13because judgment without mercy will be shown to anyone who has not been merciful. Mercy triumphs over judgment!

Faith and Deeds

14What good is it, my brothers, if a man claims to have faith but has no deeds? Can such faith save him? 15Suppose a brother or sister is without clothes and daily food. 16If

[a]8 Lev. 19:18 [b]11 Exodus 20:14; Deut. 5:18 [c]11 Exodus 20:13; Deut. 5:17

one of you says to him, "Go, I wish you well;
keep warm and well fed," but does nothing
about his physical needs, what good is it? 17In
the same way, faith by itself, if it is not accompanied by action, is dead.

18But someone will say, "You have faith; I
have deeds."

Show me your faith without deeds, and I
will show you my faith by what I do. 19You
believe that there is one God. Good! Even the
demons believe that—and shudder.

20You foolish man, do you want evidence
that faith without deeds is useless[a]? 21Was not
our ancestor Abraham considered righteous for
what he did when he offered his son Isaac on
the altar? 22You see that his faith and his actions were working together, and his faith was
made complete by what he did. 23And the
scripture was fulfilled that says, "Abraham believed God, and it was credited to him as righteousness,"[b] and he was called God's friend.
24You see that a person is justified by what he
does and not by faith alone.

25In the same way, was not even Rahab the
prostitute considered righteous for what she
did when she gave lodging to the spies and
sent them off in a different direction? 26As the
body without the spirit is dead, so faith without
deeds is dead.

Taming the Tongue

3 Not many of you should presume to be
teachers, my brothers, because you know
that we who teach will be judged more strictly.
2We all stumble in many ways. If anyone is
never at fault in what he says, he is a perfect
man, able to keep his whole body in check.

3When we put bits into the mouths of horses
to make them obey us, we can turn the whole
animal. 4Or take ships as an example. Although they are so large and are driven by
strong winds, they are steered by a very small
rudder wherever the pilot wants to go. 5Like-
wise the tongue is a small part of the body, but
it makes great boasts. Consider what a great
forest is set on fire by a small spark. 6The
tongue also is a fire, a world of evil among the
parts of the body. It corrupts the whole person,
sets the whole course of his life on fire, and is
itself set on fire by hell.

7All kinds of animals, birds, reptiles and
creatures of the sea are being tamed and have
been tamed by man, 8but no man can tame the
tongue. It is a restless evil, full of deadly poison.

9With the tongue we praise our Lord and
Father, and with it we curse men, who have
been made in God's likeness. 10Out of the
same mouth come praise and cursing. My
brothers, this should not be. 11Can both fresh
water and salt[c] water flow from the same
spring? 12My brothers, can a fig tree bear olives, or a grapevine bear figs? Neither can a
salt spring produce fresh water.

Two Kinds of Wisdom

13Who is wise and understanding among
you? Let him show it by his good life, by deeds
done in the humility that comes from wisdom.
14But if you harbor bitter envy and selfish ambition in your hearts, do not boast about it or
deny the truth. 15Such "wisdom" does not
come down from heaven but is earthly, unspiritual, of the devil. 16For where you have envy
and selfish ambition, there you find disorder
and every evil practice.

17But the wisdom that comes from heaven is
first of all pure; then peace-loving, considerate, submissive, full of mercy and good fruit,
impartial and sincere. 18Peacemakers who sow
in peace raise a harvest of righteousness.

Submit Yourselves to God

4 What causes fights and quarrels among
you? Don't they come from your desires
that battle within you? 2You want something
but don't get it. You kill and covet, but you
cannot have what you want. You quarrel and
fight. You do not have, because you do not ask
God. 3When you ask, you do not receive, because you ask with wrong motives, that you
may spend what you get on your pleasures.

4You adulterous people, don't you know
that friendship with the world is hatred toward
God? Anyone who chooses to be a friend of
the world becomes an enemy of God. 5Or do
you think Scripture says without reason that
the spirit he caused to live in us envies intensely?[d] 6But he gives us more grace. That is why
Scripture says:

"God opposes the proud
but gives grace to the humble."[e]

7Submit yourselves, then, to God. Resist the
devil, and he will flee from you. 8Come near to
God and he will come near to you. Wash your
hands, you sinners, and purify your hearts, you
double-minded. 9Grieve, mourn and wail.
Change your laughter to mourning and your
joy to gloom. 10Humble yourselves before the
Lord, and he will lift you up.

11Brothers, do not slander one another. Anyone who speaks against his brother or judges
him speaks against the law and judges it. When
you judge the law, you are not keeping it, but
sitting in judgment on it. 12There is only one
Lawgiver and Judge, the one who is able to
save and destroy. But you—who are you to
judge your neighbor?

Boasting About Tomorrow

13Now listen, you who say, "Today or tomorrow we will go to this or that city, spend a
year there, carry on business and make money." 14Why, you do not even know what will
happen tomorrow. What is your life? You are

[a]*20* Some early manuscripts *dead* [b]*23* Gen. 15:6 [c]*11* Greek *bitter* (see also verse 14) [d]*5* Or *that God jealously longs for the spirit that he made to live in us*; or *that the Spirit he caused to live in us longs jealously* [e]*6* Prov. 3:34

a mist that appears for a little while and then
vanishes. **15**Instead, you ought to say, "If it is
the Lord's will, we will live and do this or
that." **16**As it is, you boast and brag. All such
boasting is evil. **17**Anyone, then, who knows
the good he ought to do and doesn't do it, sins.

Warning to Rich Oppressors

5 Now listen, you rich people, weep and wail
because of the misery that is coming upon
you. **2**Your wealth has rotted, and moths have
eaten your clothes. **3**Your gold and silver are
corroded. Their corrosion will testify against
you and eat your flesh like fire. You have
hoarded wealth in the last days. **4**Look! The
wages you failed to pay the workmen who
mowed your fields are crying out against you.
The cries of the harvesters have reached the
ears of the Lord Almighty. **5**You have lived on
earth in luxury and self-indulgence. You have
fattened yourselves in the day of slaughter.[a]
6You have condemned and murdered innocent
men, who were not opposing you.

Patience in Suffering

7Be patient, then, brothers, until the Lord's
coming. See how the farmer waits for the land
to yield its valuable crop and how patient he is
for the autumn and spring rains. **8**You too,
be patient and stand firm, because the Lord's
coming is near. **9**Don't grumble against each
other, brothers, or you will be judged. The
Judge is standing at the door!

10Brothers, as an example of patience in the
face of suffering, take the prophets who spoke
in the name of the Lord. **11**As you know, we
consider blessed those who have persevered.
You have heard of Job's perseverance and
have seen what the Lord finally brought about.
The Lord is full of compassion and mercy.

12Above all, my brothers, do not swear—
not by heaven or by earth or by anything else.
Let your "Yes" be yes, and your "No," no, or
you will be condemned.

The Prayer of Faith

13Is any one of you in trouble? He should
pray. Is anyone happy? Let him sing songs of
praise. **14**Is any one of you sick? He should call
the elders of the church to pray over him and
anoint him with oil in the name of the Lord.
15And the prayer offered in faith will make the
sick person well; the Lord will raise him up. If
he has sinned, he will be forgiven. **16**Therefore
confess your sins to each other and pray for
each other so that you may be healed. The
prayer of a righteous man is powerful and effective.

17Elijah was a man just like us. He prayed
earnestly that it would not rain, and it did not
rain on the land for three and a half years.
18Again he prayed, and the heavens gave rain,
and the earth produced its crops.

19My brothers, if one of you should wander
from the truth and someone should bring him
back, **20**remember this: Whoever turns a sinner
from the error of his way will save him from
death and cover over a multitude of sins.

1 Peter

1 Peter, an apostle of Jesus Christ,

To God's elect, strangers in the world, scattered throughout Pontus, Galatia, Cappadocia,
Asia and Bithynia, **2**who have been chosen according to the foreknowledge of God the Father, through the sanctifying work of the Spirit,
for obedience to Jesus Christ and sprinkling by
his blood:

Grace and peace be yours in abundance.

Praise to God for a Living Hope

3Praise be to the God and Father of our Lord
Jesus Christ! In his great mercy he has given
us new birth into a living hope through the
resurrection of Jesus Christ from the dead,
4and into an inheritance that can never perish,
spoil or fade—kept in heaven for you, **5**who
through faith are shielded by God's power until the coming of the salvation that is ready to
be revealed in the last time. **6**In this you greatly
rejoice, though now for a little while you may
have had to suffer grief in all kinds of trials.
7These have come so that your faith—of greater worth than gold, which perishes even
though refined by fire—may be proved genuine and may result in praise, glory and honor
when Jesus Christ is revealed. **8**Though you
have not seen him, you love him; and even
though you do not see him now, you believe in
him and are filled with an inexpressible and
glorious joy, **9**for you are receiving the goal of
your faith, the salvation of your souls.

10Concerning this salvation, the prophets,
who spoke of the grace that was to come to
you, searched intently and with the greatest
care, **11**trying to find out the time and circumstances to which the Spirit of Christ in them
was pointing when he predicted the sufferings
of Christ and the glories that would follow. **12**It
was revealed to them that they were not serving themselves but you, when they spoke of
the things that have now been told you by
those who have preached the gospel to you by

[a]5 Or *yourselves as in a day of feasting*

the Holy Spirit sent from heaven. Even angels
long to look into these things.

Be Holy

13Therefore, prepare your minds for action;
be self-controlled; set your hope fully on the
grace to be given you when Jesus Christ is
revealed. 14As obedient children, do not conform to the evil desires you had when you
lived in ignorance. 15But just as he who called
you is holy, so be holy in all you do; 16for it is
written: "Be holy, because I am holy."[a]
17Since you call on a Father who judges
each man's work impartially, live your lives as
strangers here in reverent fear. 18For you know
that it was not with perishable things such as
silver or gold that you were redeemed from the
empty way of life handed down to you from
your forefathers, 19but with the precious blood
of Christ, a lamb without blemish or defect.
20He was chosen before the creation of the
world, but was revealed in these last times for
your sake. 21Through him you believe in God,
who raised him from the dead and glorified
him, and so your faith and hope are in God.
22Now that you have purified yourselves by
obeying the truth so that you have sincere love
for your brothers, love one another deeply,
from the heart.[b] 23For you have been born
again, not of perishable seed, but of imperishable, through the living and enduring word of
God. 24For,

"All men are like grass,
and all their glory is like the flowers of
the field;
the grass withers and the flowers fall,
25 but the word of the Lord stands
forever."[c]

And this is the word that was preached to you.

2 Therefore, rid yourselves of all malice and
all deceit, hypocrisy, envy, and slander of
every kind. 2Like newborn babies, crave pure
spiritual milk, so that by it you may grow up in
your salvation, 3now that you have tasted that
the Lord is good.

The Living Stone and a Chosen People

4As you come to him, the living Stone—rejected by men but chosen by God and precious
to him— 5you also, like living stones, are being built into a spiritual house to be a holy
priesthood, offering spiritual sacrifices acceptable to God through Jesus Christ. 6For in
Scripture it says:

"See, I lay a stone in Zion,
a chosen and precious cornerstone,
and the one who trusts in him
will never be put to shame."[d]

7Now to you who believe, this stone is precious. But to those who do not believe,

"The stone the builders rejected
has become the capstone,[e]"[f]

8and,

"A stone that causes men to stumble
and a rock that makes them fall."[g]

They stumble because they disobey the message—which is also what they were destined
for.

9But you are a chosen people, a royal priesthood, a holy nation, a people belonging to
God, that you may declare the praises of him
who called you out of darkness into his wonderful light. 10Once you were not a people, but
now you are the people of God; once you had
not received mercy, but now you have received
mercy.

11Dear friends, I urge you, as aliens and
strangers in the world, to abstain from sinful
desires, which war against your soul. 12Live
such good lives among the pagans that, though
they accuse you of doing wrong, they may see
your good deeds and glorify God on the day he
visits us.

Submission to Rulers and Masters

13Submit yourselves for the Lord's sake to
every authority instituted among men: whether
to the king, as the supreme authority, 14or to
governors, who are sent by him to punish those
who do wrong and to commend those who do
right. 15For it is God's will that by doing good
you should silence the ignorant talk of foolish
men. 16Live as free men, but do not use your
freedom as a cover-up for evil; live as servants
of God. 17Show proper respect to everyone:
Love the brotherhood of believers, fear God,
honor the king.
18Slaves, submit yourselves to your masters
with all respect, not only to those who are good
and considerate, but also to those who are
harsh. 19For it is commendable if a man bears
up under the pain of unjust suffering because
he is conscious of God. 20But how is it to your
credit if you receive a beating for doing wrong
and endure it? But if you suffer for doing good
and you endure it, this is commendable before
God. 21To this you were called, because Christ
suffered for you, leaving you an example, that
you should follow in his steps.

22"He committed no sin,
and no deceit was found in his
mouth."[h]

23When they hurled their insults at him, he did
not retaliate; when he suffered, he made no
threats. Instead, he entrusted himself to him
who judges justly. 24He himself bore our sins
in his body on the tree, so that we might die to
sins and live for righteousness; by his wounds
you have been healed. 25For you were like
sheep going astray, but now you have returned
to the Shepherd and Overseer of your souls.

Wives and Husbands

3 Wives, in the same way be submissive to
your husbands so that, if any of them do

[a]16 Lev. 11:44,45; 19:2; 20:7 [b]22 Some early manuscripts *from a pure heart* [c]25 Isaiah 40:6-8
[d]6 Isaiah 28:16 [e]7 Or *cornerstone* [f]7 Psalm 118:22 [g]8 Isaiah 8:14 [h]22 Isaiah 53:9

not believe the word, they may be won over without words by the behavior of their wives, 2when they see the purity and reverence of your lives. 3Your beauty should not come from outward adornment, such as braided hair and the wearing of gold jewelry and fine clothes. 4Instead, it should be that of your inner self, the unfading beauty of a gentle and quiet spirit, which is of great worth in God's sight. 5For this is the way the holy women of the past who put their hope in God used to make themselves beautiful. They were submissive to their own husbands, 6like Sarah, who obeyed Abraham and called him her master. You are her daughters if you do what is right and do not give way to fear.

7Husbands, in the same way be considerate as you live with your wives, and treat them with respect as the weaker partner and as heirs with you of the gracious gift of life, so that nothing will hinder your prayers.

Suffering for Doing Good

8Finally, all of you, live in harmony with one another; be sympathetic, love as brothers, be compassionate and humble. 9Do not repay evil with evil or insult with insult, but with blessing, because to this you were called so that you may inherit a blessing. 10For,

"Whoever would love life
and see good days
must keep his tongue from evil
and his lips from deceitful speech.
11He must turn from evil and do good;
he must seek peace and pursue it.
12For the eyes of the Lord are on the righteous
and his ears are attentive to their prayer,
but the face of the Lord is against those who do evil."[a]

13Who is going to harm you if you are eager to do good? 14But even if you should suffer for what is right, you are blessed. "Do not fear what they fear[b]; do not be frightened."[c] 15But in your hearts set apart Christ as Lord. Always be prepared to give an answer to everyone who asks you to give the reason for the hope that you have. But do this with gentleness and respect, 16keeping a clear conscience, so that those who speak maliciously against your good behavior in Christ may be ashamed of their slander. 17It is better, if it is God's will, to suffer for doing good than for doing evil. 18For Christ died for sins once for all, the righteous for the unrighteous, to bring you to God. He was put to death in the body but made alive by the Spirit, 19through whom[d] also he went and preached to the spirits in prison 20who disobeyed long ago when God waited patiently in the days of Noah while the ark was being built. In it only a few people, eight in all, were saved through water, 21and this water symbolizes baptism that now saves you also—not the removal of dirt from the body but the pledge[e] of a good conscience toward God. It saves you by the resurrection of Jesus Christ, 22who has gone into heaven and is at God's right hand—with angels, authorities and powers in submission to him.

Living for God

4 Therefore, since Christ suffered in his body, arm yourselves also with the same attitude, because he who has suffered in his body is done with sin. 2As a result, he does not live the rest of his earthly life for evil human desires, but rather for the will of God. 3For you have spent enough time in the past doing what pagans choose to do—living in debauchery, lust, drunkenness, orgies, carousing and detestable idolatry. 4They think it strange that you do not plunge with them into the same flood of dissipation, and they heap abuse on you. 5But they will have to give account to him who is ready to judge the living and the dead. 6For this is the reason the gospel was preached even to those who are now dead, so that they might be judged according to men in regard to the body, but live according to God in regard to the spirit.

7The end of all things is near. Therefore be clear minded and self-controlled so that you can pray. 8Above all, love each other deeply, because love covers over a multitude of sins. 9Offer hospitality to one another without grumbling. 10Each one should use whatever gift he has received to serve others, faithfully administering God's grace in its various forms. 11If anyone speaks, he should do it as one speaking the very words of God. If anyone serves, he should do it with the strength God provides, so that in all things God may be praised through Jesus Christ. To him be the glory and the power for ever and ever. Amen.

Suffering for Being a Christian

12Dear friends, do not be surprised at the painful trial you are suffering, as though something strange were happening to you. 13But rejoice that you participate in the sufferings of Christ, so that you may be overjoyed when his glory is revealed. 14If you are insulted because of the name of Christ, you are blessed, for the Spirit of glory and of God rests on you. 15If you suffer, it should not be as a murderer or thief or any other kind of criminal, or even as a meddler. 16However, if you suffer as a Christian, do not be ashamed, but praise God that you bear that name. 17For it is time for judgment to begin with the family of God; and if it begins with us, what will the outcome be for those who do not obey the gospel of God? 18And,

"If it is hard for the righteous to be saved,
what will become of the ungodly and the sinner?"[f]

19So then, those who suffer according to

[a] *12* Psalm 34:12-16 [b] *14* Or *not fear their threats* [c] *14* Isaiah 8:12 [d] *18,19* Or *alive in the spirit, 19through which* [e] *21* Or *response* [f] *18* Prov. 11:31

God's will should commit themselves to their faithful Creator and continue to do good.

To Elders and Young Men

5 To the elders among you, I appeal as a fellow elder, a witness of Christ's sufferings and one who also will share in the glory to be revealed: [2]Be shepherds of God's flock that is under your care, serving as overseers—not because you must, but because you are willing, as God wants you to be; not greedy for money, but eager to serve; [3]not lording it over those entrusted to you, but being examples to the flock. [4]And when the Chief Shepherd appears, you will receive the crown of glory that will never fade away.

[5]Young men, in the same way be submissive to those who are older. All of you, clothe yourselves with humility toward one another, because,

> "God opposes the proud
> but gives grace to the humble."[a]

[6]Humble yourselves, therefore, under God's mighty hand, that he may lift you up in due time. [7]Cast all your anxiety on him because he cares for you.

[8]Be self-controlled and alert. Your enemy the devil prowls around like a roaring lion looking for someone to devour. [9]Resist him, standing firm in the faith, because you know that your brothers throughout the world are undergoing the same kind of sufferings.

[10]And the God of all grace, who called you to his eternal glory in Christ, after you have suffered a little while, will himself restore you and make you strong, firm and steadfast. [11]To him be the power for ever and ever. Amen.

Final Greetings

[12]With the help of Silas,[b] whom I regard as a faithful brother, I have written to you briefly, encouraging you and testifying that this is the true grace of God. Stand fast in it.

[13]She who is in Babylon, chosen together with you, sends you her greetings, and so does my son Mark. [14]Greet one another with a kiss of love.

Peace to all of you who are in Christ.

2 Peter

1 Simon Peter, a servant and apostle of Jesus Christ,

To those who through the righteousness of our God and Savior Jesus Christ have received a faith as precious as ours:

[2]Grace and peace be yours in abundance through the knowledge of God and of Jesus our Lord.

Making One's Calling and Election Sure

[3]His divine power has given us everything we need for life and godliness through our knowledge of him who called us by his own glory and goodness. [4]Through these he has given us his very great and precious promises, so that through them you may participate in the divine nature and escape the corruption in the world caused by evil desires.

[5]For this very reason, make every effort to add to your faith goodness; and to goodness, knowledge; [6]and to knowledge, self-control; and to self-control, perseverance; and to perseverance, godliness; [7]and to godliness, brotherly kindness; and to brotherly kindness, love. [8]For if you possess these qualities in increasing measure, they will keep you from being ineffective and unproductive in your knowledge of our Lord Jesus Christ. [9]But if anyone does not have them, he is nearsighted and blind, and has forgotten that he has been cleansed from his past sins.

[10]Therefore, my brothers, be all the more eager to make your calling and election sure. For if you do these things, you will never fall, [11]and you will receive a rich welcome into the eternal kingdom of our Lord and Savior Jesus Christ.

Prophecy of Scripture

[12]So I will always remind you of these things, even though you know them and are firmly established in the truth you now have. [13]I think it is right to refresh your memory as long as I live in the tent of this body, [14]because I know that I will soon put it aside, as our Lord Jesus Christ has made clear to me. [15]And I will make every effort to see that after my departure you will always be able to remember these things.

[16]We did not follow cleverly invented stories when we told you about the power and coming of our Lord Jesus Christ, but we were eyewitnesses of his majesty. [17]For he received honor and glory from God the Father when the voice came to him from the Majestic Glory, saying, "This is my Son, whom I love; with him I am well pleased."[c] [18]We ourselves heard this voice that came from heaven when we were with him on the sacred mountain.

[19]And we have the word of the prophets made more certain, and you will do well to pay

[a]5 Prov. 3:34 [b]12 Greek *Silvanus*, a variant of *Silas* [c]17 Matt. 17:5; Mark 9:7; Luke 9:35

attention to it, as to a light shining in a dark
place, until the day dawns and the morning star
rises in your hearts. 20 Above all, you must understand that no prophecy of Scripture came
about by the prophet's own interpretation.
21 For prophecy never had its origin in the will
of man, but men spoke from God as they were
carried along by the Holy Spirit.

False Teachers and Their Destruction

2 But there were also false prophets among
the people, just as there will be false teachers among you. They will secretly introduce
destructive heresies, even denying the sovereign Lord who bought them—bringing swift
destruction on themselves. 2 Many will follow
their shameful ways and will bring the way of
truth into disrepute. 3 In their greed these teachers will exploit you with stories they have
made up. Their condemnation has long been
hanging over them, and their destruction has
not been sleeping.
4 For if God did not spare angels when they
sinned, but sent them to hell,[a] putting them
into gloomy dungeons[b] to be held for judgment; 5 if he did not spare the ancient world
when he brought the flood on its ungodly people, but protected Noah, a preacher of righteousness, and seven others; 6 if he condemned
the cities of Sodom and Gomorrah by burning
them to ashes, and made them an example of
what is going to happen to the ungodly; 7 and if
he rescued Lot, a righteous man, who was distressed by the filthy lives of lawless men 8 (for
that righteous man, living among them day after day, was tormented in his righteous soul by
the lawless deeds he saw and heard)— 9 if this
is so, then the Lord knows how to rescue godly
men from trials and to hold the unrighteous for
the day of judgment, while continuing their
punishment.[c] 10 This is especially true of those
who follow the corrupt desire of the sinful nature[d] and despise authority.
Bold and arrogant, these men are not afraid
to slander celestial beings; 11 yet even angels,
although they are stronger and more powerful,
do not bring slanderous accusations against
such beings in the presence of the Lord. 12 But
these men blaspheme in matters they do not
understand. They are like brute beasts, creatures of instinct, born only to be caught and
destroyed, and like beasts they too will perish.
13 They will be paid back with harm for the
harm they have done. Their idea of pleasure is
to carouse in broad daylight. They are blots
and blemishes, reveling in their pleasures
while they feast with you.[e] 14 With eyes full of
adultery, they never stop sinning; they seduce
the unstable; they are experts in greed—an accursed brood! 15 They have left the straight way
and wandered off to follow the way of Balaam
son of Beor, who loved the wages of wickedness. 16 But he was rebuked for his wrongdoing
by a donkey—a beast without speech—who
spoke with a man's voice and restrained the
prophet's madness.
17 These men are springs without water and
mists driven by a storm. Blackest darkness is
reserved for them. 18 For they mouth empty,
boastful words and, by appealing to the lustful
desires of sinful human nature, they entice
people who are just escaping from those who
live in error. 19 They promise them freedom,
while they themselves are slaves of depravity—for a man is a slave to whatever has mas-
tered him. 20 If they have escaped the corruption of the world by knowing our Lord and
Savior Jesus Christ and are again entangled in
it and overcome, they are worse off at the end
than they were at the beginning. 21 It would
have been better for them not to have known
the way of righteousness, than to have known
it and then to turn their backs on the sacred
command that was passed on to them. 22 Of
them the proverbs are true: "A dog returns to
its vomit,"[f] and, "A sow that is washed goes
back to her wallowing in the mud."

The Day of the Lord

3 Dear friends, this is now my second letter
to you. I have written both of them as re-
minders to stimulate you to wholesome thinking. 2 I want you to recall the words spoken in
the past by the holy prophets and the command
given by our Lord and Savior through your
apostles.
3 First of all, you must understand that in the
last days scoffers will come, scoffing and following their own evil desires. 4 They will say,
"Where is this 'coming' he promised? Ever
since our fathers died, everything goes on as it
has since the beginning of creation." 5 But they
deliberately forget that long ago by God's
word the heavens existed and the earth was
formed out of water and by water. 6 By these
waters also the world of that time was deluged
and destroyed. 7 By the same word the present
heavens and earth are reserved for fire, being
kept for the day of judgment and destruction of
ungodly men.
8 But do not forget this one thing, dear
friends: With the Lord a day is like a thousand
years, and a thousand years are like a day.
9 The Lord is not slow in keeping his promise,
as some understand slowness. He is patient
with you, not wanting anyone to perish, but
everyone to come to repentance.
10 But the day of the Lord will come like a
thief. The heavens will disappear with a roar;
the elements will be destroyed by fire, and the
earth and everything in it will be laid bare.[g]
11 Since everything will be destroyed in this
way, what kind of people ought you to be?
You ought to live holy and godly lives 12 as you
look forward to the day of God and speed its
coming.[h] That day will bring about the de-

[a] 4 Greek *Tartarus* [b] 4 Some manuscripts *into chains of darkness* [c] 9 Or *unrighteous for punishment until the day of judgment* [d] 10 Or *the flesh* [e] 13 Some manuscripts *in their love feasts* [f] 22 Prov. 26:11 [g] 10 Some manuscripts *be burned up* [h] 12 Or *as you wait eagerly for the day of God to come*

struction of the heavens by fire, and the elements will melt in the heat. 13But in keeping with his promise we are looking forward to a new heaven and a new earth, the home of righteousness.

14So then, dear friends, since you are looking forward to this, make every effort to be found spotless, blameless and at peace with him. 15Bear in mind that our Lord's patience means salvation, just as our dear brother Paul also wrote you with the wisdom that God gave him. 16He writes the same way in all his letters, speaking in them of these matters. His letters contain some things that are hard to understand, which ignorant and unstable people distort, as they do the other Scriptures, to their own destruction.

17Therefore, dear friends, since you already know this, be on your guard so that you may not be carried away by the error of lawless men and fall from your secure position. 18But grow in the grace and knowledge of our Lord and Savior Jesus Christ. To him be glory both now and forever! Amen.

1 John

The Word of Life

1 That which was from the beginning, which we have heard, which we have seen with our eyes, which we have looked at and our hands have touched—this we proclaim concerning the Word of life. 2The life appeared; we have seen it and testify to it, and we proclaim to you the eternal life, which was with the Father and has appeared to us. 3We proclaim to you what we have seen and heard, so that you also may have fellowship with us. And our fellowship is with the Father and with his Son, Jesus Christ. 4We write this to make our[a] joy complete.

Walking in the Light

5This is the message we have heard from him and declare to you: God is light; in him there is no darkness at all. 6If we claim to have fellowship with him yet walk in the darkness, we lie and do not live by the truth. 7But if we walk in the light, as he is in the light, we have fellowship with one another, and the blood of Jesus, his Son, purifies us from all[b] sin.

8If we claim to be without sin, we deceive ourselves and the truth is not in us. 9If we confess our sins, he is faithful and just and will forgive us our sins and purify us from all unrighteousness. 10If we claim we have not sinned, we make him out to be a liar and his word has no place in our lives.

2 My dear children, I write this to you so that you will not sin. But if anybody does sin, we have one who speaks to the Father in our defense—Jesus Christ, the Righteous One. 2He is the atoning sacrifice for our sins, and not only for ours but also for[c] the sins of the whole world.

3We know that we have come to know him if we obey his commands. 4The man who says, "I know him," but does not do what he commands is a liar, and the truth is not in him. 5But if anyone obeys his word, God's love[d] is truly made complete in him. This is how we know we are in him: 6Whoever claims to live in him must walk as Jesus did.

7Dear friends, I am not writing you a new command but an old one, which you have had since the beginning. This old command is the message you have heard. 8Yet I am writing you a new command; its truth is seen in him and you, because the darkness is passing and the true light is already shining.

9Anyone who claims to be in the light but hates his brother is still in the darkness. 10Whoever loves his brother lives in the light, and there is nothing in him[e] to make him stumble. 11But whoever hates his brother is in the darkness and walks around in the darkness; he does not know where he is going, because the darkness has blinded him.

12I write to you, dear children,
because your sins have been forgiven on account of his name.
13I write to you, fathers,
because you have known him who is from the beginning.
I write to you, young men,
because you have overcome the evil one.
I write to you, dear children,
because you have known the Father.
14I write to you, fathers,
because you have known him who is from the beginning.
I write to you, young men,
because you are strong,
and the word of God lives in you,
and you have overcome the evil one.

Do Not Love the World

15Do not love the world or anything in the world. If anyone loves the world, the love of the Father is not in him. 16For everything in the world—the cravings of sinful man, the lust of his eyes and the boasting of what he has and does—comes not from the Father but from the world. 17The world and its desires pass away,

[a]4 Some manuscripts *your* [b]7 Or *every* [c]2 Or *He is the one who turns aside God's wrath, taking away our sins, and not only ours but also* [d]5 Or *word, love for God* [e]10 Or *it*

but the man who does the will of God lives forever.

Warning Against Antichrists

18Dear children, this is the last hour; and as you have heard that the antichrist is coming, even now many antichrists have come. This is how we know it is the last hour. 19They went out from us, but they did not really belong to us. For if they had belonged to us, they would have remained with us; but their going showed that none of them belonged to us.

20But you have an anointing from the Holy One, and all of you know the truth.[a] 21I do not write to you because you do not know the truth, but because you do know it and because no lie comes from the truth. 22Who is the liar? It is the man who denies that Jesus is the Christ. Such a man is the antichrist—he denies the Father and the Son. 23No one who denies the Son has the Father; whoever acknowledges the Son has the Father also.

24See that what you have heard from the beginning remains in you. If it does, you also will remain in the Son and in the Father. 25And this is what he promised us—even eternal life.

26I am writing these things to you about those who are trying to lead you astray. 27As for you, the anointing you received from him remains in you, and you do not need anyone to teach you. But as his anointing teaches you about all things and as that anointing is real, not counterfeit—just as it has taught you, remain in him.

Children of God

28And now, dear children, continue in him, so that when he appears we may be confident and unashamed before him at his coming.

29If you know that he is righteous, you know that everyone who does what is right has been born of him.

3 How great is the love the Father has lavished on us, that we should be called children of God! And that is what we are! The reason the world does not know us is that it did not know him. 2Dear friends, now we are children of God, and what we will be has not yet been made known. But we know that when he appears,[b] we shall be like him, for we shall see him as he is. 3Everyone who has this hope in him purifies himself, just as he is pure.

4Everyone who sins breaks the law; in fact, sin is lawlessness. 5But you know that he appeared so that he might take away our sins. And in him is no sin. 6No one who lives in him keeps on sinning. No one who continues to sin has either seen him or known him.

7Dear children, do not let anyone lead you astray. He who does what is right is righteous, just as he is righteous. 8He who does what is sinful is of the devil, because the devil has been sinning from the beginning. The reason the Son of God appeared was to destroy the devil's work. 9No one who is born of God will continue to sin, because God's seed remains in him; he cannot go on sinning, because he has been born of God. 10This is how we know who the children of God are and who the children of the devil are: Anyone who does not do what is right is not a child of God; nor is anyone who does not love his brother.

Love One Another

11This is the message you heard from the beginning: We should love one another. 12Do not be like Cain, who belonged to the evil one and murdered his brother. And why did he murder him? Because his own actions were evil and his brother's were righteous. 13Do not be surprised, my brothers, if the world hates you. 14We know that we have passed from death to life, because we love our brothers. Anyone who does not love remains in death. 15Anyone who hates his brother is a murderer, and you know that no murderer has eternal life in him.

16This is how we know what love is: Jesus Christ laid down his life for us. And we ought to lay down our lives for our brothers. 17If anyone has material possessions and sees his brother in need but has no pity on him, how can the love of God be in him? 18Dear children, let us not love with words or tongue but with actions and in truth. 19This then is how we know that we belong to the truth, and how we set our hearts at rest in his presence 20whenever our hearts condemn us. For God is greater than our hearts, and he knows everything.

21Dear friends, if our hearts do not condemn us, we have confidence before God 22and receive from him anything we ask, because we obey his commands and do what pleases him. 23And this is his command: to believe in the name of his Son, Jesus Christ, and to love one another as he commanded us. 24Those who obey his commands live in him, and he in them. And this is how we know that he lives in us: We know it by the Spirit he gave us.

Test the Spirits

4 Dear friends, do not believe every spirit, but test the spirits to see whether they are from God, because many false prophets have gone out into the world. 2This is how you can recognize the Spirit of God: Every spirit that acknowledges that Jesus Christ has come in the flesh is from God, 3but every spirit that does not acknowledge Jesus is not from God. This is the spirit of the antichrist, which you have heard is coming and even now is already in the world.

4You, dear children, are from God and have overcome them, because the one who is in you is greater than the one who is in the world. 5They are from the world and therefore speak from the viewpoint of the world, and the world listens to them. 6We are from God, and whoever knows God listens to us; but whoever is

[a] 20 Some manuscripts *and you know all things*   [b] 2 Or *when it is made known*

not from God does not listen to us. This is how we recognize the Spirit[a] of truth and the spirit of falsehood.

God's Love and Ours

7Dear friends, let us love one another, for love comes from God. Everyone who loves has been born of God and knows God. 8Whoever does not love does not know God, because God is love. 9This is how God showed his love among us: He sent his one and only Son[b] into the world that we might live through him. 10This is love: not that we loved God, but that he loved us and sent his Son as an atoning sacrifice for[c] our sins. 11Dear friends, since God so loved us, we also ought to love one another. 12No one has ever seen God; but if we love one another, God lives in us and his love is made complete in us.

13We know that we live in him and he in us, because he has given us of his Spirit. 14And we have seen and testify that the Father has sent his Son to be the Savior of the world. 15If anyone acknowledges that Jesus is the Son of God, God lives in him and he in God. 16And so we know and rely on the love God has for us.

God is love. Whoever lives in love lives in God, and God in him. 17In this way, love is made complete among us so that we will have confidence on the day of judgment, because in this world we are like him. 18There is no fear in love. But perfect love drives out fear, because fear has to do with punishment. The one who fears is not made perfect in love.

19We love because he first loved us. 20If anyone says, "I love God," yet hates his brother, he is a liar. For anyone who does not love his brother, whom he has seen, cannot love God, whom he has not seen. 21And he has given us this command: Whoever loves God must also love his brother.

Faith in the Son of God

5 Everyone who believes that Jesus is the Christ is born of God, and everyone who loves the father loves his child as well. 2This is how we know that we love the children of God: by loving God and carrying out his commands. 3This is love for God: to obey his commands. And his commands are not burdensome, 4for everyone born of God overcomes the world. This is the victory that has overcome the world, even our faith. 5Who is it that overcomes the world? Only he who believes that Jesus is the Son of God.

6This is the one who came by water and blood—Jesus Christ. He did not come by water only, but by water and blood. And it is the Spirit who testifies, because the Spirit is the truth. 7For there are three that testify: 8the[d] Spirit, the water and the blood; and the three are in agreement. 9We accept man's testimony, but God's testimony is greater because it is the testimony of God, which he has given about his Son. 10Anyone who believes in the Son of God has this testimony in his heart. Anyone who does not believe God has made him out to be a liar, because he has not believed the testimony God has given about his Son. 11And this is the testimony: God has given us eternal life, and this life is in his Son. 12He who has the Son has life; he who does not have the Son of God does not have life.

Concluding Remarks

13I write these things to you who believe in the name of the Son of God so that you may know that you have eternal life. 14This is the confidence we have in approaching God: that if we ask anything according to his will, he hears us. 15And if we know that he hears us—whatever we ask—we know that we have what we asked of him.

16If anyone sees his brother commit a sin that does not lead to death, he should pray and God will give him life. I refer to those whose sin does not lead to death. There is a sin that leads to death. I am not saying that he should pray about that. 17All wrongdoing is sin, and there is sin that does not lead to death.

18We know that anyone born of God does not continue to sin; the one who was born of God keeps him safe, and the evil one cannot harm him. 19We know that we are children of God, and that the whole world is under the control of the evil one. 20We know also that the Son of God has come and has given us understanding, so that we may know him who is true. And we are in him who is true—even in his Son Jesus Christ. He is the true God and eternal life.

21Dear children, keep yourselves from idols.

[a]*6* Or *spirit* [b]*9* Or *his only begotten Son* [c]*10* Or *as the one who would turn aside his wrath, taking away*
[d]*7,8* Late manuscripts of the Vulgate *testify in heaven: the Father, the Word and the Holy Spirit, and these three are one. 8And there are three that testify on earth: the* (not found in any Greek manuscript before the sixteenth century)

2 John

1The elder,

To the chosen lady and her children, whom
I love in the truth—and not I only, but also all
who know the truth— 2because of the truth,
which lives in us and will be with us forever:

3Grace, mercy and peace from God the Father and from Jesus Christ, the Father's Son,
will be with us in truth and love.

4It has given me great joy to find some of
your children walking in the truth, just as the
Father commanded us. 5And now, dear lady, I
am not writing you a new command but one
we have had from the beginning. I ask that we
love one another. 6And this is love: that we
walk in obedience to his commands. As you
have heard from the beginning, his command
is that you walk in love.

7Many deceivers, who do not acknowledge
Jesus Christ as coming in the flesh, have gone
out into the world. Any such person is the deceiver and the antichrist. 8Watch out that you
do not lose what you have worked for, but that
you may be rewarded fully. 9Anyone who runs
ahead and does not continue in the teaching of
Christ does not have God; whoever continues
in the teaching has both the Father and the Son.
10If anyone comes to you and does not bring
this teaching, do not take him into your house
or welcome him. 11Anyone who welcomes
him shares in his wicked work.

12I have much to write to you, but I do not
want to use paper and ink. Instead, I hope to
visit you and talk with you face to face, so that
our joy may be complete.

13The children of your chosen sister send
their greetings.

3 John

1The elder,

To my dear friend Gaius, whom I love in the
truth.

2Dear friend, I pray that you may enjoy
good health and that all may go well with you,
even as your soul is getting along well. 3It gave
me great joy to have some brothers come and
tell about your faithfulness to the truth and
how you continue to walk in the truth. 4I have
no greater joy than to hear that my children are
walking in the truth.

5Dear friend, you are faithful in what you
are doing for the brothers, even though they
are strangers to you. 6They have told the
church about your love. You will do well to
send them on their way in a manner worthy of
God. 7It was for the sake of the Name that they
went out, receiving no help from the pagans.
8We ought therefore to show hospitality to
such men so that we may work together for the
truth.

9I wrote to the church, but Diotrephes, who
loves to be first, will have nothing to do with
us. 10So if I come, I will call attention to what
he is doing, gossiping maliciously about us.
Not satisfied with that, he refuses to welcome
the brothers. He also stops those who want to
do so and puts them out of the church.

11Dear friend, do not imitate what is evil but
what is good. Anyone who does what is good
is from God. Anyone who does what is evil has
not seen God. 12Demetrius is well spoken of
by everyone—and even by the truth itself. We
also speak well of him, and you know that our
testimony is true.

13I have much to write you, but I do not
want to do so with pen and ink. 14I hope to see
you soon, and we will talk face to face.

Peace to you. The friends here send their
greetings. Greet the friends there by name.

Jude

1Jude, a servant of Jesus Christ and a brother of James,

To those who have been called, who are loved by God the Father and kept by[a] Jesus Christ:

2Mercy, peace and love be yours in abundance.

The Sin and Doom of Godless Men

3Dear friends, although I was very eager to write to you about the salvation we share, I felt I had to write and urge you to contend for the faith that was once for all entrusted to the saints. 4For certain men whose condemnation was written about[b] long ago have secretly slipped in among you. They are godless men, who change the grace of our God into a license for immorality and deny Jesus Christ our only Sovereign and Lord.

5Though you already know all this, I want to remind you that the Lord[c] delivered his people out of Egypt, but later destroyed those who did not believe. 6And the angels who did not keep their positions of authority but abandoned their own home—these he has kept in darkness, bound with everlasting chains for judgment on the great Day. 7In a similar way, Sodom and Gomorrah and the surrounding towns gave themselves up to sexual immorality and perversion. They serve as an example of those who suffer the punishment of eternal fire.

8In the very same way, these dreamers pollute their own bodies, reject authority and slander celestial beings. 9But even the archangel Michael, when he was disputing with the devil about the body of Moses, did not dare to bring a slanderous accusation against him, but said, "The Lord rebuke you!" 10Yet these men speak abusively against whatever they do not understand; and what things they do understand by instinct, like unreasoning animals—these are the very things that destroy them.

11Woe to them! They have taken the way of Cain; they have rushed for profit into Balaam's error; they have been destroyed in Korah's rebellion.

12These men are blemishes at your love feasts, eating with you without the slightest qualm—shepherds who feed only themselves. They are clouds without rain, blown along by the wind; autumn trees, without fruit and uprooted—twice dead. 13They are wild waves of the sea, foaming up their shame; wandering stars, for whom blackest darkness has been reserved forever.

14Enoch, the seventh from Adam, prophesied about these men: "See, the Lord is coming with thousands upon thousands of his holy ones 15to judge everyone, and to convict all the ungodly of all the ungodly acts they have done in the ungodly way, and of all the harsh words ungodly sinners have spoken against him." 16These men are grumblers and faultfinders; they follow their own evil desires; they boast about themselves and flatter others for their own advantage.

A Call to Persevere

17But, dear friends, remember what the apostles of our Lord Jesus Christ foretold. 18They said to you, "In the last times there will be scoffers who will follow their own ungodly desires." 19These are the men who divide you, who follow mere natural instincts and do not have the Spirit.

20But you, dear friends, build yourselves up in your most holy faith and pray in the Holy Spirit. 21Keep yourselves in God's love as you wait for the mercy of our Lord Jesus Christ to bring you to eternal life.

22Be merciful to those who doubt; 23snatch others from the fire and save them; to others show mercy, mixed with fear—hating even the clothing stained by corrupted flesh.

Doxology

24To him who is able to keep you from falling and to present you before his glorious presence without fault and with great joy— 25to the only God our Savior be glory, majesty, power and authority, through Jesus Christ our Lord, before all ages, now and forevermore! Amen.

Revelation

Prologue

1 The revelation of Jesus Christ, which God gave him to show his servants what must soon take place. He made it known by sending his angel to his servant John, 2who testifies to everything he saw—that is, the word of God and the testimony of Jesus Christ. 3Blessed is the one who reads the words of this prophecy,

[a] *1* Or *for*; or *in* [b] *4* Or *men who were marked out for condemnation* [c] *5* Some early manuscripts *Jesus*

and blessed are those who hear it and take to
heart what is written in it, because the time is
near.

Greetings and Doxology

4John,

To the seven churches in the province of
Asia:

Grace and peace to you from him who is,
and who was, and who is to come, and from
the seven spirits[a] before his throne, 5and from
Jesus Christ, who is the faithful witness, the
firstborn from the dead, and the ruler of the
kings of the earth.

To him who loves us and has freed us from
our sins by his blood, 6and has made us to be
a kingdom and priests to serve his God and
Father—to him be glory and power for ever
and ever! Amen.

7Look, he is coming with the clouds,
and every eye will see him,
even those who pierced him;
and all the peoples of the earth will
mourn because of him.
So shall it be! Amen.

8"I am the Alpha and the Omega," says the
Lord God, "who is, and who was, and who is
to come, the Almighty."

One Like a Son of Man

9I, John, your brother and companion in the
suffering and kingdom and patient endurance
that are ours in Jesus, was on the island of
Patmos because of the word of God and the
testimony of Jesus. 10On the Lord's Day I was
in the Spirit, and I heard behind me a loud
voice like a trumpet, 11which said: "Write on a
scroll what you see and send it to the seven
churches: to Ephesus, Smyrna, Pergamum,
Thyatira, Sardis, Philadelphia and Laodicea."
12I turned around to see the voice that was
speaking to me. And when I turned I saw seven
golden lampstands, 13and among the lampstands was someone "like a son of man,"[b]
dressed in a robe reaching down to his feet and
with a golden sash around his chest. 14His head
and hair were white like wool, as white as
snow, and his eyes were like blazing fire. 15His
feet were like bronze glowing in a furnace, and
his voice was like the sound of rushing waters.
16In his right hand he held seven stars, and
out of his mouth came a sharp double-edged
sword. His face was like the sun shining in all
its brilliance.
17When I saw him, I fell at his feet as though
dead. Then he placed his right hand on me and
said: "Do not be afraid. I am the First and the
Last. 18I am the Living One; I was dead, and
behold I am alive for ever and ever! And I hold
the keys of death and Hades.
19"Write, therefore, what you have seen,
what is now and what will take place later.
20The mystery of the seven stars that you saw
in my right hand and of the seven golden lampstands is this: The seven stars are the angels[c]
of the seven churches, and the seven lampstands are the seven churches.

To the Church in Ephesus

2 "To the angel[d] of the church in Ephesus
write:

These are the words of him who holds
the seven stars in his right hand and walks
among the seven golden lampstands: 2I
know your deeds, your hard work and
your perseverance. I know that you cannot tolerate wicked men, that you have
tested those who claim to be apostles but
are not, and have found them false. 3You
have persevered and have endured hardships for my name, and have not grown
weary.
4Yet I hold this against you: You have
forsaken your first love. 5Remember the
height from which you have fallen! Repent and do the things you did at first. If
you do not repent, I will come to you and
remove your lampstand from its place.
6But you have this in your favor: You
hate the practices of the Nicolaitans,
which I also hate.
7He who has an ear, let him hear what
the Spirit says to the churches. To him
who overcomes, I will give the right to eat
from the tree of life, which is in the paradise of God.

To the Church in Smyrna

8"To the angel of the church in Smyrna write:

These are the words of him who is the
First and the Last, who died and came to
life again. 9I know your afflictions and
your poverty—yet you are rich! I know
the slander of those who say they are Jews
and are not, but are a synagogue of Satan.
10Do not be afraid of what you are about
to suffer. I tell you, the devil will put
some of you in prison to test you, and you
will suffer persecution for ten days. Be
faithful, even to the point of death, and I
will give you the crown of life.
11He who has an ear, let him hear what
the Spirit says to the churches. He who
overcomes will not be hurt at all by the
second death.

To the Church in Pergamum

12"To the angel of the church in Pergamum
write:

These are the words of him who has the
sharp, double-edged sword. 13I know
where you live—where Satan has his
throne. Yet you remain true to my name.
You did not renounce your faith in me,

[a]4 Or *the sevenfold Spirit* [b]13 Daniel 7:13 [c]20 Or *messengers* [d]1 Or *messenger*; also in verses 8, 12 and 18

even in the days of Antipas, my faithful
witness, who was put to death in your
city—where Satan lives.
14 Nevertheless, I have a few things
against you: You have people there who
hold to the teaching of Balaam, who
taught Balak to entice the Israelites to sin
by eating food sacrificed to idols and by
committing sexual immorality. 15 Likewise you also have those who hold to the
teaching of the Nicolaitans. 16 Repent
therefore! Otherwise, I will soon come to
you and will fight against them with the
sword of my mouth.
17 He who has an ear, let him hear what
the Spirit says to the churches. To him
who overcomes, I will give some of the
hidden manna. I will also give him a
white stone with a new name written on
it, known only to him who receives it.

To the Church in Thyatira

18 "To the angel of the church in Thyatira write:

These are the words of the Son of God,
whose eyes are like blazing fire and
whose feet are like burnished bronze. 19 I
know your deeds, your love and faith,
your service and perseverance, and that
you are now doing more than you did at
first.
20 Nevertheless, I have this against you:
You tolerate that woman Jezebel, who
calls herself a prophetess. By her teaching
she misleads my servants into sexual immorality and the eating of food sacrificed
to idols. 21 I have given her time to repent
of her immorality, but she is unwilling.
22 So I will cast her on a bed of suffering,
and I will make those who commit adultery with her suffer intensely, unless they
repent of her ways. 23 I will strike her children dead. Then all the churches will
know that I am he who searches hearts
and minds, and I will repay each of you
according to your deeds. 24 Now I say to
the rest of you in Thyatira, to you who do
not hold to her teaching and have not
learned Satan's so-called deep secrets (I
will not impose any other burden on you):
25 Only hold on to what you have until I
come.
26 To him who overcomes and does my
will to the end, I will give authority over
the nations—

27 'He will rule them with an iron
scepter;
he will dash them to pieces like
pottery'[a]—

just as I have received authority from my
Father. 28 I will also give him the morning
star. 29 He who has an ear, let him hear
what the Spirit says to the churches.

To the Church in Sardis

3 "To the angel[b] of the church in Sardis
write:

These are the words of him who holds
the seven spirits[c] of God and the seven
stars. I know your deeds; you have a reputation of being alive, but you are dead.
2 Wake up! Strengthen what remains and
is about to die, for I have not found your
deeds complete in the sight of my God.
3 Remember, therefore, what you have received and heard; obey it, and repent. But
if you do not wake up, I will come like a
thief, and you will not know at what time
I will come to you.
4 Yet you have a few people in Sardis
who have not soiled their clothes. They
will walk with me, dressed in white, for
they are worthy. 5 He who overcomes will,
like them, be dressed in white. I will never blot out his name from the book of life,
but will acknowledge his name before my
Father and his angels. 6 He who has an ear,
let him hear what the Spirit says to the
churches.

To the Church in Philadelphia

7 "To the angel of the church in Philadelphia
write:

These are the words of him who is holy
and true, who holds the key of David.
What he opens no one can shut, and what
he shuts no one can open. 8 I know your
deeds. See, I have placed before you an
open door that no one can shut. I know
that you have little strength, yet you have
kept my word and have not denied my
name. 9 I will make those who are of the
synagogue of Satan, who claim to be Jews
though they are not, but are liars—I will
make them come and fall down at your
feet and acknowledge that I have loved
you. 10 Since you have kept my command
to endure patiently, I will also keep you
from the hour of trial that is going to
come upon the whole world to test those
who live on the earth.
11 I am coming soon. Hold on to what
you have, so that no one will take your
crown. 12 Him who overcomes I will make
a pillar in the temple of my God. Never
again will he leave it. I will write on him
the name of my God and the name of the
city of my God, the new Jerusalem, which
is coming down out of heaven from my
God; and I will also write on him my new
name. 13 He who has an ear, let him hear
what the Spirit says to the churches.

To the Church in Laodicea

14 "To the angel of the church in Laodicea
write:

These are the words of the Amen, the
faithful and true witness, the ruler of

[a] *27* Psalm 2:9 [b] *1* Or *messenger*; also in verses 7 and 14 [c] *1* Or *the sevenfold Spirit*

God's creation. 15I know your deeds, that
you are neither cold nor hot. I wish you
were either one or the other! 16So, because you are lukewarm—neither hot nor
cold—I am about to spit you out of my
mouth. 17You say, 'I am rich; I have acquired wealth and do not need a thing.'
But you do not realize that you are
wretched, pitiful, poor, blind and naked.
18I counsel you to buy from me gold refined in the fire, so you can become rich;
and white clothes to wear, so you can
cover your shameful nakedness; and salve
to put on your eyes, so you can see.

19Those whom I love I rebuke and discipline. So be earnest, and repent. 20Here
I am! I stand at the door and knock. If
anyone hears my voice and opens the
door, I will come in and eat with him, and
he with me.

21To him who overcomes, I will give
the right to sit with me on my throne, just
as I overcame and sat down with my Father on his throne. 22He who has an ear,
let him hear what the Spirit says to the
churches."

The Throne in Heaven

4 After this I looked, and there before me
was a door standing open in heaven. And
the voice I had first heard speaking to me like
a trumpet said, "Come up here, and I will show
you what must take place after this." 2At once
I was in the Spirit, and there before me was a
throne in heaven with someone sitting on it.
3And the one who sat there had the appearance
of jasper and carnelian. A rainbow, resembling
an emerald, encircled the throne. 4Surrounding
the throne were twenty-four other thrones, and
seated on them were twenty-four elders. They
were dressed in white and had crowns of gold
on their heads. 5From the throne came flashes
of lightning, rumblings and peals of thunder.
Before the throne, seven lamps were blazing.
These are the seven spirits[a] of God. 6Also before the throne there was what looked like a
sea of glass, clear as crystal.

In the center, around the throne, were four
living creatures, and they were covered with
eyes, in front and in back. 7The first living
creature was like a lion, the second was like an
ox, the third had a face like a man, the fourth
was like a flying eagle. 8Each of the four living
creatures had six wings and was covered with
eyes all around, even under his wings. Day and
night they never stop saying:

"Holy, holy, holy
is the Lord God Almighty,
who was, and is, and is to come."

9Whenever the living creatures give glory,
honor and thanks to him who sits on the throne
and who lives for ever and ever, 10the twenty-
four elders fall down before him who sits on
the throne, and worship him who lives for ever
and ever. They lay their crowns before the
throne and say:

11"You are worthy, our Lord and God,
to receive glory and honor and power,
for you created all things,
and by your will they were created
and have their being."

The Scroll and the Lamb

5 Then I saw in the right hand of him who sat
on the throne a scroll with writing on both
sides and sealed with seven seals. 2And I saw
a mighty angel proclaiming in a loud voice,
"Who is worthy to break the seals and open the
scroll?" 3But no one in heaven or on earth or
under the earth could open the scroll or even
look inside it. 4I wept and wept because no one
was found who was worthy to open the scroll
or look inside. 5Then one of the elders said to
me, "Do not weep! See, the Lion of the tribe of
Judah, the Root of David, has triumphed. He is
able to open the scroll and its seven seals."

6Then I saw a Lamb, looking as if it had
been slain, standing in the center of the throne,
encircled by the four living creatures and the
elders. He had seven horns and seven eyes,
which are the seven spirits[a] of God sent out
into all the earth. 7He came and took the scroll
from the right hand of him who sat on the
throne. 8And when he had taken it, the four
living creatures and the twenty-four elders fell
down before the Lamb. Each one had a harp
and they were holding golden bowls full of
incense, which are the prayers of the saints.
9And they sang a new song:

"You are worthy to take the scroll
and to open its seals,
because you were slain,
and with your blood you purchased men
for God
from every tribe and language and
people and nation.
10You have made them to be a kingdom and
priests to serve our God,
and they will reign on the earth."

11Then I looked and heard the voice of many
angels, numbering thousands upon thousands,
and ten thousand times ten thousand. They encircled the throne and the living creatures and
the elders. 12In a loud voice they sang:

"Worthy is the Lamb, who was slain,
to receive power and wealth and wisdom
and strength
and honor and glory and praise!"

13Then I heard every creature in heaven and
on earth and under the earth and on the sea,
and all that is in them, singing:

"To him who sits on the throne and to the
Lamb
be praise and honor and glory and power,
for ever and ever!"

[a]5,6 Or *the sevenfold Spirit*

14The four living creatures said, "Amen," and
the elders fell down and worshiped.

The Seals

6 I watched as the Lamb opened the first of
the seven seals. Then I heard one of the
four living creatures say in a voice like thunder, "Come!" 2I looked, and there before me
was a white horse! Its rider held a bow, and he
was given a crown, and he rode out as a conqueror bent on conquest.

3When the Lamb opened the second seal, I
heard the second living creature say, "Come!"
4Then another horse came out, a fiery red one.
Its rider was given power to take peace from
the earth and to make men slay each other. To
him was given a large sword.

5When the Lamb opened the third seal, I
heard the third living creature say, "Come!" I
looked, and there before me was a black horse!
Its rider was holding a pair of scales in his
hand. 6Then I heard what sounded like a voice
among the four living creatures, saying, "A
quart[a] of wheat for a day's wages,[b] and three
quarts of barley for a day's wages,[b] and do not
damage the oil and the wine!"

7When the Lamb opened the fourth seal, I
heard the voice of the fourth living creature
say, "Come!" 8I looked, and there before me
was a pale horse! Its rider was named Death,
and Hades was following close behind him.
They were given power over a fourth of the
earth to kill by sword, famine and plague, and
by the wild beasts of the earth.

9When he opened the fifth seal, I saw under
the altar the souls of those who had been slain
because of the word of God and the testimony
they had maintained. 10They called out in a
loud voice, "How long, Sovereign Lord, holy
and true, until you judge the inhabitants of the
earth and avenge our blood?" 11Then each of
them was given a white robe, and they were
told to wait a little longer, until the number of
their fellow servants and brothers who were to
be killed as they had been was completed.

12I watched as he opened the sixth seal.
There was a great earthquake. The sun turned
black like sackcloth made of goat hair, the
whole moon turned blood red, 13and the stars
in the sky fell to earth, as late figs drop from
a fig tree when shaken by a strong wind. 14The
sky receded like a scroll, rolling up, and every
mountain and island was removed from its
place.

15Then the kings of the earth, the princes,
the generals, the rich, the mighty, and every
slave and every free man hid in caves and
among the rocks of the mountains. 16They
called to the mountains and the rocks, "Fall on
us and hide us from the face of him who sits on
the throne and from the wrath of the Lamb!
17For the great day of their wrath has come,
and who can stand?"

144,000 Sealed

7 After this I saw four angels standing at the
four corners of the earth, holding back the
four winds of the earth to prevent any wind
from blowing on the land or on the sea or on
any tree. 2Then I saw another angel coming up
from the east, having the seal of the living
God. He called out in a loud voice to the four
angels who had been given power to harm the
land and the sea: 3"Do not harm the land or the
sea or the trees until we put a seal on the foreheads of the servants of our God." 4Then I
heard the number of those who were sealed:
144,000 from all the tribes of Israel.

5From the tribe of Judah 12,000 were
sealed,
from the tribe of Reuben 12,000,
from the tribe of Gad 12,000,
6from the tribe of Asher 12,000,
from the tribe of Naphtali 12,000,
from the tribe of Manasseh 12,000,
7from the tribe of Simeon 12,000,
from the tribe of Levi 12,000,
from the tribe of Issachar 12,000,
8from the tribe of Zebulun 12,000,
from the tribe of Joseph 12,000,
from the tribe of Benjamin 12,000.

The Great Multitude in White Robes

9After this I looked and there before me was
a great multitude that no one could count, from
every nation, tribe, people and language,
standing before the throne and in front of the
Lamb. They were wearing white robes and
were holding palm branches in their hands.
10And they cried out in a loud voice:

"Salvation belongs to our God,
who sits on the throne,
and to the Lamb."

11All the angels were standing around the
throne and around the elders and the four living creatures. They fell down on their faces
before the throne and worshiped God, 12say-
ing:

"Amen!
Praise and glory
and wisdom and thanks and honor
and power and strength
be to our God for ever and ever.
Amen!"

13Then one of the elders asked me, "These
in white robes—who are they, and where did
they come from?"

14I answered, "Sir, you know."

And he said, "These are they who have
come out of the great tribulation; they have
washed their robes and made them white in the
blood of the Lamb. 15Therefore,

"they are before the throne of God
and serve him day and night in his
temple;

[a]6 Greek *a choinix* (probably about a liter) [b]6 Greek *a denarius*

and he who sits on the throne will spread
his tent over them.
16Never again will they hunger;
never again will they thirst.
The sun will not beat upon them,
nor any scorching heat.
17For the Lamb at the center of the throne
will be their shepherd;
he will lead them to springs of living
water.
And God will wipe away every tear from
their eyes."

The Seventh Seal and the Golden Censer

8 When he opened the seventh seal, there was silence in heaven for about half an hour.

2And I saw the seven angels who stand before God, and to them were given seven trumpets.

3Another angel, who had a golden censer, came and stood at the altar. He was given much incense to offer, with the prayers of all the saints, on the golden altar before the throne. 4The smoke of the incense, together with the prayers of the saints, went up before God from the angel's hand. 5Then the angel took the censer, filled it with fire from the altar, and hurled it on the earth; and there came peals of thunder, rumblings, flashes of lightning and an earthquake.

The Trumpets

6Then the seven angels who had the seven trumpets prepared to sound them.

7The first angel sounded his trumpet, and there came hail and fire mixed with blood, and it was hurled down upon the earth. A third of the earth was burned up, a third of the trees were burned up, and all the green grass was burned up.

8The second angel sounded his trumpet, and something like a huge mountain, all ablaze, was thrown into the sea. A third of the sea turned into blood, 9a third of the living creatures in the sea died, and a third of the ships were destroyed.

10The third angel sounded his trumpet, and a great star, blazing like a torch, fell from the sky on a third of the rivers and on the springs of water— 11the name of the star is Wormwood.[a] A third of the waters turned bitter, and many people died from the waters that had become bitter.

12The fourth angel sounded his trumpet, and a third of the sun was struck, a third of the moon, and a third of the stars, so that a third of them turned dark. A third of the day was without light, and also a third of the night.

13As I watched, I heard an eagle that was flying in midair call out in a loud voice: "Woe! Woe! Woe to the inhabitants of the earth, because of the trumpet blasts about to be sounded by the other three angels!"

9 The fifth angel sounded his trumpet, and I saw a star that had fallen from the sky to the earth. The star was given the key to the shaft of the Abyss. 2When he opened the Abyss, smoke rose from it like the smoke from a gigantic furnace. The sun and sky were darkened by the smoke from the Abyss. 3And out of the smoke locusts came down upon the earth and were given power like that of scorpions of the earth. 4They were told not to harm the grass of the earth or any plant or tree, but only those people who did not have the seal of God on their foreheads. 5They were not given power to kill them, but only to torture them for five months. And the agony they suffered was like that of the sting of a scorpion when it strikes a man. 6During those days men will seek death, but will not find it; they will long to die, but death will elude them.

7The locusts looked like horses prepared for battle. On their heads they wore something like crowns of gold, and their faces resembled human faces. 8Their hair was like women's hair, and their teeth were like lions' teeth. 9They had breastplates like breastplates of iron, and the sound of their wings was like the thundering of many horses and chariots rushing into battle. 10They had tails and stings like scorpions, and in their tails they had power to torment people for five months. 11They had as king over them the angel of the Abyss, whose name in Hebrew is Abaddon, and in Greek, Apollyon.[b]

12The first woe is past; two other woes are yet to come.

13The sixth angel sounded his trumpet, and I heard a voice coming from the horns[c] of the golden altar that is before God. 14It said to the sixth angel who had the trumpet, "Release the four angels who are bound at the great river Euphrates." 15And the four angels who had been kept ready for this very hour and day and month and year were released to kill a third of mankind. 16The number of the mounted troops was two hundred million. I heard their number.

17The horses and riders I saw in my vision looked like this: Their breastplates were fiery red, dark blue, and yellow as sulfur. The heads of the horses resembled the heads of lions, and out of their mouths came fire, smoke and sulfur. 18A third of mankind was killed by the three plagues of fire, smoke and sulfur that came out of their mouths. 19The power of the horses was in their mouths and in their tails; for their tails were like snakes, having heads with which they inflict injury.

20The rest of mankind that were not killed by these plagues still did not repent of the work of their hands; they did not stop worshiping demons, and idols of gold, silver, bronze, stone and wood—idols that cannot see or hear or walk. 21Nor did they repent of their murders, their magic arts, their sexual immorality or their thefts.

[a] *11* That is, Bitterness [b] *11* *Abaddon* and *Apollyon* mean *Destroyer.* [c] *13* That is, projections

The Angel and the Little Scroll

10 Then I saw another mighty angel coming down from heaven. He was robed in a cloud, with a rainbow above his head; his face was like the sun, and his legs were like fiery pillars. 2He was holding a little scroll, which lay open in his hand. He planted his right foot on the sea and his left foot on the land, 3and he gave a loud shout like the roar of a lion. When he shouted, the voices of the seven thunders spoke. 4And when the seven thunders spoke, I was about to write; but I heard a voice from heaven say, "Seal up what the seven thunders have said and do not write it down."

5Then the angel I had seen standing on the sea and on the land raised his right hand to heaven. 6And he swore by him who lives for ever and ever, who created the heavens and all that is in them, the earth and all that is in it, and the sea and all that is in it, and said, "There will be no more delay! 7But in the days when the seventh angel is about to sound his trumpet, the mystery of God will be accomplished, just as he announced to his servants the prophets."

8Then the voice that I had heard from heaven spoke to me once more: "Go, take the scroll that lies open in the hand of the angel who is standing on the sea and on the land."

9So I went to the angel and asked him to give me the little scroll. He said to me, "Take it and eat it. It will turn your stomach sour, but in your mouth it will be as sweet as honey." 10I took the little scroll from the angel's hand and ate it. It tasted as sweet as honey in my mouth, but when I had eaten it, my stomach turned sour. 11Then I was told, "You must prophesy again about many peoples, nations, languages and kings."

The Two Witnesses

11 I was given a reed like a measuring rod and was told, "Go and measure the temple of God and the altar, and count the worshipers there. 2But exclude the outer court; do not measure it, because it has been given to the Gentiles. They will trample on the holy city for 42 months. 3And I will give power to my two witnesses, and they will prophesy for 1,260 days, clothed in sackcloth." 4These are the two olive trees and the two lampstands that stand before the Lord of the earth. 5If anyone tries to harm them, fire comes from their mouths and devours their enemies. This is how anyone who wants to harm them must die. 6These men have power to shut up the sky so that it will not rain during the time they are prophesying; and they have power to turn the waters into blood and to strike the earth with every kind of plague as often as they want.

7Now when they have finished their testimony, the beast that comes up from the Abyss will attack them, and overpower and kill them. 8Their bodies will lie in the street of the great city, which is figuratively called Sodom and Egypt, where also their Lord was crucified. 9For three and a half days men from every people, tribe, language and nation will gaze on their bodies and refuse them burial. 10The inhabitants of the earth will gloat over them and will celebrate by sending each other gifts, because these two prophets had tormented those who live on the earth.

11But after the three and a half days a breath of life from God entered them, and they stood on their feet, and terror struck those who saw them. 12Then they heard a loud voice from heaven saying to them, "Come up here." And they went up to heaven in a cloud, while their enemies looked on.

13At that very hour there was a severe earthquake and a tenth of the city collapsed. Seven thousand people were killed in the earthquake, and the survivors were terrified and gave glory to the God of heaven.

14The second woe has passed; the third woe is coming soon.

The Seventh Trumpet

15The seventh angel sounded his trumpet, and there were loud voices in heaven, which said:

"The kingdom of the world has become
the kingdom of our Lord and of his Christ,
and he will reign for ever and ever."

16And the twenty-four elders, who were seated on their thrones before God, fell on their faces and worshiped God, 17saying:

"We give thanks to you, Lord God Almighty,
the One who is and who was,
because you have taken your great power
and have begun to reign.
18The nations were angry;
and your wrath has come.
The time has come for judging the dead,
and for rewarding your servants the prophets
and your saints and those who reverence your name,
both small and great—
and for destroying those who destroy the earth."

19Then God's temple in heaven was opened, and within his temple was seen the ark of his covenant. And there came flashes of lightning, rumblings, peals of thunder, an earthquake and a great hailstorm.

The Woman and the Dragon

12 A great and wondrous sign appeared in heaven: a woman clothed with the sun, with the moon under her feet and a crown of twelve stars on her head. 2She was pregnant and cried out in pain as she was about to give birth. 3Then another sign appeared in heaven: an enormous red dragon with seven heads and ten horns and seven crowns on his heads. 4His tail swept a third of the stars out of the sky and

flung them to the earth. The dragon stood in front of the woman who was about to give birth, so that he might devour her child the moment it was born. 5She gave birth to a son, a male child, who will rule all the nations with an iron scepter. And her child was snatched up to God and to his throne. 6The woman fled into the desert to a place prepared for her by God, where she might be taken care of for 1,260 days.

7And there was war in heaven. Michael and his angels fought against the dragon, and the dragon and his angels fought back. 8But he was not strong enough, and they lost their place in heaven. 9The great dragon was hurled down—that ancient serpent called the devil, or Satan, who leads the whole world astray. He was hurled to the earth, and his angels with him.

10Then I heard a loud voice in heaven say:

"Now have come the salvation and the
power and the kingdom of our
God,
and the authority of his Christ.
For the accuser of our brothers,
who accuses them before our God day
and night,
has been hurled down.
11They overcame him
by the blood of the Lamb
and by the word of their testimony;
they did not love their lives so much
as to shrink from death.
12Therefore rejoice, you heavens
and you who dwell in them!
But woe to the earth and the sea,
because the devil has gone down to
you!
He is filled with fury,
because he knows that his time is
short."

13When the dragon saw that he had been hurled to the earth, he pursued the woman who had given birth to the male child. 14The woman was given the two wings of a great eagle, so that she might fly to the place prepared for her in the desert, where she would be taken care of for a time, times and half a time, out of the serpent's reach. 15Then from his mouth the serpent spewed water like a river, to overtake the woman and sweep her away with the torrent. 16But the earth helped the woman by opening its mouth and swallowing the river that the dragon had spewed out of his mouth. 17Then the dragon was enraged at the woman and went off to make war against the rest of her offspring—those who obey God's commandments and hold to the testimony of Jesus.

13 1And the dragon[a] stood on the shore of the sea.

The Beast out of the Sea

And I saw a beast coming out of the sea. He had ten horns and seven heads, with ten crowns on his horns, and on each head a blasphemous name. 2The beast I saw resembled a leopard, but had feet like those of a bear and a mouth like that of a lion. The dragon gave the beast his power and his throne and great authority. 3One of the heads of the beast seemed to have had a fatal wound, but the fatal wound had been healed. The whole world was astonished and followed the beast. 4Men worshiped the dragon because he had given authority to the beast, and they also worshiped the beast and asked, "Who is like the beast? Who can make war against him?"

5The beast was given a mouth to utter proud words and blasphemies and to exercise his authority for forty-two months. 6He opened his mouth to blaspheme God, and to slander his name and his dwelling place and those who live in heaven. 7He was given power to make war against the saints and to conquer them. And he was given authority over every tribe, people, language and nation. 8All inhabitants of the earth will worship the beast—all whose names have not been written in the book of life belonging to the Lamb that was slain from the creation of the world.[b]

9He who has an ear, let him hear.

10If anyone is to go into captivity,
into captivity he will go.
If anyone is to be killed[c] with the sword,
with the sword he will be killed.

This calls for patient endurance and faithfulness on the part of the saints.

The Beast out of the Earth

11Then I saw another beast, coming out of the earth. He had two horns like a lamb, but he spoke like a dragon. 12He exercised all the authority of the first beast on his behalf, and made the earth and its inhabitants worship the first beast, whose fatal wound had been healed. 13And he performed great and miraculous signs, even causing fire to come down from heaven to earth in full view of men. 14Because of the signs he was given power to do on behalf of the first beast, he deceived the inhabitants of the earth. He ordered them to set up an image in honor of the beast who was wounded by the sword and yet lived. 15He was given power to give breath to the image of the first beast, so that it could speak and cause all who refused to worship the image to be killed. 16He also forced everyone, small and great, rich and poor, free and slave, to receive a mark on his right hand or on his forehead, 17so that no one could buy or sell unless he had the mark, which is the name of the beast or the number of his name.

18This calls for wisdom. If anyone has insight, let him calculate the number of the beast, for it is man's number. His number is 666.

[a] *1* Some late manuscripts *And I* [b] *8* Or *written from the creation of the world in the book of life belonging to the Lamb that was slain* [c] *10* Some manuscripts *anyone kills*

The Lamb and the 144,000

14 Then I looked, and there before me was the Lamb, standing on Mount Zion, and with him 144,000 who had his name and his Father's name written on their foreheads. 2And I heard a sound from heaven like the roar of rushing waters and like a loud peal of thunder. The sound I heard was like that of harpists playing their harps. 3And they sang a new song before the throne and before the four living creatures and the elders. No one could learn the song except the 144,000 who had been redeemed from the earth. 4These are those who did not defile themselves with women, for they kept themselves pure. They follow the Lamb wherever he goes. They were purchased from among men and offered as firstfruits to God and the Lamb. 5No lie was found in their mouths; they are blameless.

The Three Angels

6Then I saw another angel flying in midair, and he had the eternal gospel to proclaim to those who live on the earth—to every nation, tribe, language and people. 7He said in a loud voice, "Fear God and give him glory, because the hour of his judgment has come. Worship him who made the heavens, the earth, the sea and the springs of water."

8A second angel followed and said, "Fallen! Fallen is Babylon the Great, which made all the nations drink the maddening wine of her adulteries."

9A third angel followed them and said in a loud voice: "If anyone worships the beast and his image and receives his mark on the forehead or on the hand, 10he, too, will drink of the wine of God's fury, which has been poured full strength into the cup of his wrath. He will be tormented with burning sulfur in the presence of the holy angels and of the Lamb. 11And the smoke of their torment rises for ever and ever. There is no rest day or night for those who worship the beast and his image, or for anyone who receives the mark of his name." 12This calls for patient endurance on the part of the saints who obey God's commandments and remain faithful to Jesus.

13Then I heard a voice from heaven say, "Write: Blessed are the dead who die in the Lord from now on."

"Yes," says the Spirit, "they will rest from their labor, for their deeds will follow them."

The Harvest of the Earth

14I looked, and there before me was a white cloud, and seated on the cloud was one "like a son of man"[a] with a crown of gold on his head and a sharp sickle in his hand. 15Then another angel came out of the temple and called in a loud voice to him who was sitting on the cloud, "Take your sickle and reap, because the time to reap has come, for the harvest of the earth is ripe." 16So he who was seated on the cloud swung his sickle over the earth, and the earth was harvested.

17Another angel came out of the temple in heaven, and he too had a sharp sickle. 18Still another angel, who had charge of the fire, came from the altar and called in a loud voice to him who had the sharp sickle, "Take your sharp sickle and gather the clusters of grapes from the earth's vine, because its grapes are ripe." 19The angel swung his sickle on the earth, gathered its grapes and threw them into the great winepress of God's wrath. 20They were trampled in the winepress outside the city, and blood flowed out of the press, rising as high as the horses' bridles for a distance of 1,600 stadia.[b]

Seven Angels With Seven Plagues

15 I saw in heaven another great and marvelous sign: seven angels with the seven last plagues—last, because with them God's wrath is completed. 2And I saw what looked like a sea of glass mixed with fire and, standing beside the sea, those who had been victorious over the beast and his image and over the number of his name. They held harps given them by God 3and sang the song of Moses the servant of God and the song of the Lamb:

"Great and marvelous are your deeds,
  Lord God Almighty.
Just and true are your ways,
  King of the ages.
4Who will not fear you, O Lord,
  and bring glory to your name?
For you alone are holy.
All nations will come
  and worship before you,
for your righteous acts have been
    revealed."

5After this I looked and in heaven the temple, that is, the tabernacle of the Testimony, was opened. 6Out of the temple came the seven angels with the seven plagues. They were dressed in clean, shining linen and wore golden sashes around their chests. 7Then one of the four living creatures gave to the seven angels seven golden bowls filled with the wrath of God, who lives for ever and ever. 8And the temple was filled with smoke from the glory of God and from his power, and no one could enter the temple until the seven plagues of the seven angels were completed.

The Seven Bowls of God's Wrath

16 Then I heard a loud voice from the temple saying to the seven angels, "Go, pour out the seven bowls of God's wrath on the earth."

2The first angel went and poured out his bowl on the land, and ugly and painful sores broke out on the people who had the mark of the beast and worshiped his image.

3The second angel poured out his bowl on the sea, and it turned into blood like that of a

[a] *14* Daniel 7:13 [b] *20* That is, about 180 miles (about 300 kilometers)

dead man, and every living thing in the sea
died.
4The third angel poured out his bowl on the
rivers and springs of water, and they became
blood. 5Then I heard the angel in charge of the
waters say:

"You are just in these judgments,
you who are and who were, the Holy
One,
because you have so judged;
6for they have shed the blood of your
saints and prophets,
and you have given them blood to drink
as they deserve."

7And I heard the altar respond:

"Yes, Lord God Almighty,
true and just are your judgments."

8The fourth angel poured out his bowl on
the sun, and the sun was given power to scorch
people with fire. 9They were seared by the intense heat and they cursed the name of God,
who had control over these plagues, but they
refused to repent and glorify him.
10The fifth angel poured out his bowl on
the throne of the beast, and his kingdom was
plunged into darkness. Men gnawed their
tongues in agony 11and cursed the God of
heaven because of their pains and their sores,
but they refused to repent of what they had
done.
12The sixth angel poured out his bowl on the
great river Euphrates, and its water was dried
up to prepare the way for the kings from the
East. 13Then I saw three evil[a] spirits that
looked like frogs; they came out of the mouth
of the dragon, out of the mouth of the beast and
out of the mouth of the false prophet. 14They
are spirits of demons performing miraculous
signs, and they go out to the kings of the whole
world, to gather them for the battle on the great
day of God Almighty.
15"Behold, I come like a thief! Blessed is he
who stays awake and keeps his clothes with
him, so that he may not go naked and be
shamefully exposed."
16Then they gathered the kings together to
the place that in Hebrew is called Armaged-
don.
17The seventh angel poured out his bowl
into the air, and out of the temple came a loud
voice from the throne, saying, "It is done!"
18Then there came flashes of lightning, rumblings, peals of thunder and a severe earthquake. No earthquake like it has ever occurred
since man has been on earth, so tremendous
was the quake. 19The great city split into three
parts, and the cities of the nations collapsed.
God remembered Babylon the Great and gave
her the cup filled with the wine of the fury of
his wrath. 20Every island fled away and the
mountains could not be found. 21From the sky
huge hailstones of about a hundred pounds
each fell upon men. And they cursed God on
account of the plague of hail, because the
plague was so terrible.

The Woman on the Beast

17 One of the seven angels who had the
seven bowls came and said to me,
"Come, I will show you the punishment of the
great prostitute, who sits on many waters.
2With her the kings of the earth committed
adultery and the inhabitants of the earth were
intoxicated with the wine of her adulteries."
3Then the angel carried me away in the Spirit into a desert. There I saw a woman sitting on
a scarlet beast that was covered with blasphemous names and had seven heads and ten
horns. 4The woman was dressed in purple and
scarlet, and was glittering with gold, precious
stones and pearls. She held a golden cup in her
hand, filled with abominable things and the
filth of her adulteries. 5This title was written
on her forehead:

MYSTERY
BABYLON THE GREAT
THE MOTHER OF PROSTITUTES
AND OF THE ABOMINATIONS OF THE EARTH.

6I saw that the woman was drunk with the
blood of the saints, the blood of those who
bore testimony to Jesus.
When I saw her, I was greatly astonished.
7Then the angel said to me: "Why are you
astonished? I will explain to you the mystery
of the woman and of the beast she rides, which
has the seven heads and ten horns. 8The beast,
which you saw, once was, now is not, and will
come up out of the Abyss and go to his destruction. The inhabitants of the earth whose
names have not been written in the book of life
from the creation of the world will be astonished when they see the beast, because he once
was, now is not, and yet will come.
9"This calls for a mind with wisdom. The
seven heads are seven hills on which the woman sits. 10They are also seven kings. Five have
fallen, one is, the other has not yet come; but
when he does come, he must remain for a little
while. 11The beast who once was, and now is
not, is an eighth king. He belongs to the seven
and is going to his destruction.
12"The ten horns you saw are ten kings who
have not yet received a kingdom, but who for
one hour will receive authority as kings along
with the beast. 13They have one purpose and
will give their power and authority to the beast.
14They will make war against the Lamb, but
the Lamb will overcome them because he is
Lord of lords and King of kings—and with
him will be his called, chosen and faithful followers."
15Then the angel said to me, "The waters
you saw, where the prostitute sits, are peoples,
multitudes, nations and languages. 16The beast
and the ten horns you saw will hate the prostitute. They will bring her to ruin and leave her

[a]13 Greek *unclean*

naked; they will eat her flesh and burn her with
fire. 17For God has put it into their hearts to
accomplish his purpose by agreeing to give the
beast their power to rule, until God's words are
fulfilled. 18The woman you saw is the great
city that rules over the kings of the earth."

The Fall of Babylon

18 After this I saw another angel coming
down from heaven. He had great authority, and the earth was illuminated by his
splendor. 2With a mighty voice he shouted:

"Fallen! Fallen is Babylon the Great!
She has become a home for demons
and a haunt for every evil[a] spirit,
a haunt for every unclean and detestable
bird.
3For all the nations have drunk
the maddening wine of her adulteries.
The kings of the earth committed adultery
with her,
and the merchants of the earth grew
rich from her excessive luxuries."

4Then I heard another voice from heaven
say:

"Come out of her, my people,
so that you will not share in her sins,
so that you will not receive any of her
plagues;
5for her sins are piled up to heaven,
and God has remembered her crimes.
6Give back to her as she has given;
pay her back double for what she has
done.
Mix her a double portion from her own
cup.
7Give her as much torture and grief
as the glory and luxury she gave
herself.
In her heart she boasts,
'I sit as queen; I am not a widow,
and I will never mourn.'
8Therefore in one day her plagues will
overtake her:
death, mourning and famine.
She will be consumed by fire,
for mighty is the Lord God who judges
her.

9"When the kings of the earth who committed adultery with her and shared her luxury see
the smoke of her burning, they will weep and
mourn over her. 10Terrified at her torment,
they will stand far off and cry:

" 'Woe! Woe, O great city,
O Babylon, city of power!
In one hour your doom has come!'

11"The merchants of the earth will weep and
mourn over her because no one buys their cargoes any more— 12cargoes of gold, silver, precious stones and pearls; fine linen, purple, silk
and scarlet cloth; every sort of citron wood,
and articles of every kind made of ivory, costly
wood, bronze, iron and marble; 13cargoes of
cinnamon and spice, of incense, myrrh and
frankincense, of wine and olive oil, of fine
flour and wheat; cattle and sheep; horses and
carriages; and bodies and souls of men.

14"They will say, 'The fruit you longed for
is gone from you. All your riches and splendor
have vanished, never to be recovered.' 15The
merchants who sold these things and gained
their wealth from her will stand far off, terrified at her torment. They will weep and mourn
16and cry out:

" 'Woe! Woe, O great city,
dressed in fine linen, purple and scarlet,
and glittering with gold, precious stones
and pearls!
17In one hour such great wealth has been
brought to ruin!'

"Every sea captain, and all who travel by
ship, the sailors, and all who earn their living
from the sea, will stand far off. 18When they
see the smoke of her burning, they will exclaim, 'Was there ever a city like this great
city?' 19They will throw dust on their heads,
and with weeping and mourning cry out:

" 'Woe! Woe, O great city,
where all who had ships on the sea
became rich through her wealth!
In one hour she has been brought to ruin!
20Rejoice over her, O heaven!
Rejoice, saints and apostles and
prophets!
God has judged her for the way she
treated you.' "

21Then a mighty angel picked up a boulder
the size of a large millstone and threw it into
the sea, and said:

"With such violence
the great city of Babylon will be thrown
down,
never to be found again.
22The music of harpists and musicians, flute
players and trumpeters,
will never be heard in you again.
No workman of any trade
will ever be found in you again.
The sound of a millstone
will never be heard in you again.
23The light of a lamp
will never shine in you again.
The voice of bridegroom and bride
will never be heard in you again.
Your merchants were the world's great
men.
By your magic spell all the nations
were led astray.
24In her was found the blood of prophets
and of the saints,
and of all who have been killed on the
earth."

[a]2 Greek *unclean*

Hallelujah!

19 After this I heard what sounded like
the roar of a great multitude in heaven
shouting:

"Hallelujah!
Salvation and glory and power belong to
our God,
2 for true and just are his judgments.
He has condemned the great prostitute
who corrupted the earth by her
adulteries.
He has avenged on her the blood of his
servants."

3And again they shouted:

"Hallelujah!
The smoke from her goes up for ever and
ever."

4The twenty-four elders and the four living
creatures fell down and worshiped God, who
was seated on the throne. And they cried:

"Amen, Hallelujah!"

5Then a voice came from the throne, saying:

"Praise our God,
all you his servants,
you who fear him,
both small and great!"

6Then I heard what sounded like a great
multitude, like the roar of rushing waters and
like loud peals of thunder, shouting:

"Hallelujah!
For our Lord God Almighty reigns.
7Let us rejoice and be glad
and give him glory!
For the wedding of the Lamb has come,
and his bride has made herself ready.
8Fine linen, bright and clean,
was given her to wear."
(Fine linen stands for the righteous acts of the
saints.)

9Then the angel said to me, "Write: 'Blessed
are those who are invited to the wedding supper of the Lamb!' " And he added, "These are
the true words of God."
10At this I fell at his feet to worship him. But
he said to me, "Do not do it! I am a fellow
servant with you and with your brothers who
hold to the testimony of Jesus. Worship God!
For the testimony of Jesus is the spirit of
prophecy."

The Rider on the White Horse

11I saw heaven standing open and there before me was a white horse, whose rider is
called Faithful and True. With justice he
judges and makes war. 12His eyes are like
blazing fire, and on his head are many crowns.
He has a name written on him that no one
knows but he himself. 13He is dressed in a robe
dipped in blood, and his name is the Word of
God. 14The armies of heaven were following
him, riding on white horses and dressed in fine
linen, white and clean. 15Out of his mouth
comes a sharp sword with which to strike
down the nations. "He will rule them with an
iron scepter."[a] He treads the winepress of the
fury of the wrath of God Almighty. 16On his
robe and on his thigh he has this name written:

KING OF KINGS AND LORD OF LORDS.

17And I saw an angel standing in the sun,
who cried in a loud voice to all the birds flying
in midair, "Come, gather together for the great
supper of God, 18so that you may eat the flesh
of kings, generals, and mighty men, of horses
and their riders, and the flesh of all people, free
and slave, small and great."
19Then I saw the beast and the kings of the
earth and their armies gathered together to
make war against the rider on the horse and his
army. 20But the beast was captured, and with
him the false prophet who had performed the
miraculous signs on his behalf. With these
signs he had deluded those who had received
the mark of the beast and worshiped his image.
The two of them were thrown alive into the
fiery lake of burning sulfur. 21The rest of them
were killed with the sword that came out of the
mouth of the rider on the horse, and all the
birds gorged themselves on their flesh.

The Thousand Years

20 And I saw an angel coming down out of
heaven, having the key to the Abyss and
holding in his hand a great chain. 2He seized
the dragon, that ancient serpent, who is the
devil, or Satan, and bound him for a thousand
years. 3He threw him into the Abyss, and
locked and sealed it over him, to keep him
from deceiving the nations anymore until the
thousand years were ended. After that, he must
be set free for a short time.
4I saw thrones on which were seated those
who had been given authority to judge. And I
saw the souls of those who had been beheaded
because of their testimony for Jesus and because of the word of God. They had not worshiped the beast or his image and had not received his mark on their foreheads or their
hands. They came to life and reigned with
Christ a thousand years. 5(The rest of the dead
did not come to life until the thousand years
were ended.) This is the first resurrection.
6Blessed and holy are those who have part in
the first resurrection. The second death has no
power over them, but they will be priests of
God and of Christ and will reign with him for
a thousand years.

Satan's Doom

7When the thousand years are over, Satan
will be released from his prison 8and will go
out to deceive the nations in the four corners of
the earth—Gog and Magog—to gather them
for battle. In number they are like the sand

[a]15 Psalm 2:9

on the seashore. 9They marched across the breadth of the earth and surrounded the camp of God's people, the city he loves. But fire came down from heaven and devoured them. 10And the devil, who deceived them, was thrown into the lake of burning sulfur, where the beast and the false prophet had been thrown. They will be tormented day and night for ever and ever.

The Dead Are Judged

11Then I saw a great white throne and him who was seated on it. Earth and sky fled from his presence, and there was no place for them. 12And I saw the dead, great and small, standing before the throne, and books were opened. Another book was opened, which is the book of life. The dead were judged according to what they had done as recorded in the books. 13The sea gave up the dead that were in it, and death and Hades gave up the dead that were in them, and each person was judged according to what he had done. 14Then death and Hades were thrown into the lake of fire. The lake of fire is the second death. 15If anyone's name was not found written in the book of life, he was thrown into the lake of fire.

The New Jerusalem

21 Then I saw a new heaven and a new earth, for the first heaven and the first earth had passed away, and there was no longer any sea. 2I saw the Holy City, the new Jerusalem, coming down out of heaven from God, prepared as a bride beautifully dressed for her husband. 3And I heard a loud voice from the throne saying, "Now the dwelling of God is with men, and he will live with them. They will be his people, and God himself will be with them and be their God. 4He will wipe every tear from their eyes. There will be no more death or mourning or crying or pain, for the old order of things has passed away."

5He who was seated on the throne said, "I am making everything new!" Then he said, "Write this down, for these words are trustworthy and true."

6He said to me: "It is done. I am the Alpha and the Omega, the Beginning and the End. To him who is thirsty I will give to drink without cost from the spring of the water of life. 7He who overcomes will inherit all this, and I will be his God and he will be my son. 8But the cowardly, the unbelieving, the vile, the murderers, the sexually immoral, those who practice magic arts, the idolaters and all liars—their place will be in the fiery lake of burning sulfur. This is the second death."

9One of the seven angels who had the seven bowls full of the seven last plagues came and said to me, "Come, I will show you the bride, the wife of the Lamb." 10And he carried me away in the Spirit to a mountain great and high, and showed me the Holy City, Jerusalem, coming down out of heaven from God. 11It shone with the glory of God, and its brilliance was like that of a very precious jewel, like a jasper, clear as crystal. 12It had a great, high wall with twelve gates, and with twelve angels at the gates. On the gates were written the names of the twelve tribes of Israel. 13There were three gates on the east, three on the north, three on the south and three on the west. 14The wall of the city had twelve foundations, and on them were the names of the twelve apostles of the Lamb.

15The angel who talked with me had a measuring rod of gold to measure the city, its gates and its walls. 16The city was laid out like a square, as long as it was wide. He measured the city with the rod and found it to be 12,000 stadia[a] in length, and as wide and high as it is long. 17He measured its wall and it was 144 cubits[b] thick,[c] by man's measurement, which the angel was using. 18The wall was made of jasper, and the city of pure gold, as pure as glass. 19The foundations of the city walls were decorated with every kind of precious stone. The first foundation was jasper, the second sapphire, the third chalcedony, the fourth emerald, 20the fifth sardonyx, the sixth carnelian, the seventh chrysolite, the eighth beryl, the ninth topaz, the tenth chrysoprase, the eleventh jacinth, and the twelfth amethyst.[d] 21The twelve gates were twelve pearls, each gate made of a single pearl. The great street of the city was of pure gold, like transparent glass.

22I did not see a temple in the city, because the Lord God Almighty and the Lamb are its temple. 23The city does not need the sun or the moon to shine on it, for the glory of God gives it light, and the Lamb is its lamp. 24The nations will walk by its light, and the kings of the earth will bring their splendor into it. 25On no day will its gates ever be shut, for there will be no night there. 26The glory and honor of the nations will be brought into it. 27Nothing impure will ever enter it, nor will anyone who does what is shameful or deceitful, but only those whose names are written in the Lamb's book of life.

The River of Life

22 Then the angel showed me the river of the water of life, as clear as crystal, flowing from the throne of God and of the Lamb 2down the middle of the great street of the city. On each side of the river stood the tree of life, bearing twelve crops of fruit, yielding its fruit every month. And the leaves of the tree are for the healing of the nations. 3No longer will there be any curse. The throne of God and of the Lamb will be in the city, and his servants will serve him. 4They will see his face, and his name will be on their foreheads. 5There will be no more night. They will not need the light of a lamp or the light of the sun, for the Lord God

[a] *16* That is, about 1,400 miles (about 2,200 kilometers) [b] *17* That is, about 200 feet (about 65 meters)
[c] *17* Or *high* [d] *20* The precise identification of some of these precious stones is uncertain.

will give them light. And they will reign for ever and ever.

6 The angel said to me, "These words are trustworthy and true. The Lord, the God of the spirits of the prophets, sent his angel to show his servants the things that must soon take place."

Jesus Is Coming

7 "Behold, I am coming soon! Blessed is he who keeps the words of the prophecy in this book."

8 I, John, am the one who heard and saw these things. And when I had heard and seen them, I fell down to worship at the feet of the angel who had been showing them to me. 9 But he said to me, "Do not do it! I am a fellow servant with you and with your brothers the prophets and of all who keep the words of this book. Worship God!"

10 Then he told me, "Do not seal up the words of the prophecy of this book, because the time is near. 11 Let him who does wrong continue to do wrong; let him who is vile continue to be vile; let him who does right continue to do right; and let him who is holy continue to be holy."

12 "Behold, I am coming soon! My reward is with me, and I will give to everyone according to what he has done. 13 I am the Alpha and the Omega, the First and the Last, the Beginning and the End.

14 "Blessed are those who wash their robes, that they may have the right to the tree of life and may go through the gates into the city. 15 Outside are the dogs, those who practice magic arts, the sexually immoral, the murderers, the idolaters and everyone who loves and practices falsehood.

16 "I, Jesus, have sent my angel to give you[a] this testimony for the churches. I am the Root and the Offspring of David, and the bright Morning Star."

17 The Spirit and the bride say, "Come!" And let him who hears say, "Come!" Whoever is thirsty, let him come; and whoever wishes, let him take the free gift of the water of life.

18 I warn everyone who hears the words of the prophecy of this book: If anyone adds anything to them, God will add to him the plagues described in this book. 19 And if anyone takes words away from this book of prophecy, God will take away from him his share in the tree of life and in the holy city, which are described in this book.

20 He who testifies to these things says, "Yes, I am coming soon."

Amen. Come, Lord Jesus.

21 The grace of the Lord Jesus be with God's people. Amen.

[a] *16* The Greek is plural.

Table of Weights and Measures

BIBLICAL UNIT		APPROXIMATE AMERICAN EQUIVALENT	APPROXIMATE METRIC EQUIVALENT
		WEIGHTS	
talent	*(60 minas)*	75 pounds	34 kilograms
mina	*(50 shekels)*	1 1/4 pounds	0.6 kilogram
shekel	*(2 bekas)*	2/5 ounce	11.5 grams
pim	*(2/3 shekel)*	1/3 ounce	7.6 grams
beka	*(10 gerahs)*	1/5 ounce	5.5 grams
gerah		1/50 ounce	0.6 gram
		LENGTH	
cubit		18 inches	0.5 meter
span		9 inches	23 centimeters
handbreadth		3 inches	8 centimeters
		CAPACITY	
		Dry Measure	
cor [homer]	*(10 ephahs)*	6 bushels	220 liters
lethek	*(5 ephahs)*	3 bushels	110 liters
ephah	*(10 omers)*	3/5 bushel	22 liters
seah	*(1/3 ephah)*	7 quarts	7.3 liters
omer	*(1/10 ephah)*	2 quarts	2 liters
cab	*(1/18 ephah)*	1 quart	1 liter
		Liquid Measure	
bath	*(1 ephah)*	6 gallons	22 liters
hin	*(1/6 bath)*	4 quarts	4 liters
log	*(1/72 bath)*	1/3 quart	0.3 liter

The figures of the table are calculated on the basis of a shekel equaling 11.5 grams, a cubit equaling 18 inches and an ephah equaling 22 liters. The quart referred to is either a dry quart (slightly larger than a liter) or a liquid quart (slightly smaller than a liter), whichever is applicable. The ton referred to in the footnotes is the American ton of 2,000 pounds.

This table is based upon the best available information, but it is not intended to be mathematically precise; like the measurement equivalents in the footnotes, it merely gives approximate amounts and distances. Weights and measures differed somewhat at various times and places in the ancient world. There is uncertainty particularly about the ephah and the bath; further discoveries may give more light on these units of capacity.

What Does It Mean and Where Do I Find It?

A Bible Dictionary and Concordance

This dictionary will help you learn the meaning of some important words in the Bible. It will also tell you where in the Bible to read about that subject or person.

A

Abraham—the father of the Jewish nation. See Genesis 12–25 (pp 8–10). God called Abraham out of his home country and promised to give him the land of Canaan.
Genesis 12:1 (p 8)
Genesis 15 (p 9)
Genesis 17:1–8 (p 10)
God also promised that all the people on earth would be blessed through Abraham.
Genesis 12:3 (p 10)
God's people today can learn from Abraham what true faith is.
Romans 4 (p 782–83)
Hebrews 11:8–19 (p 834)

Adam—the first man God created. He did not obey God and brought sin and death into the world.
Genesis 1–5 (pp 1–4)
Jesus is compared to Adam because Jesus is a new beginning for the human race. Jesus brings new life to those who believe in him.
Romans 5:12–21 (p 783)
1 Corinthians 15:20–22,42–49 (pp 799–800)

adultery—breaking the marriage promise by having sexual relations with someone other than your spouse.
Exodus 20:14 (p 53)
2 Samuel 11–12 (pp 217–19)
Matthew 5:27–30 (p 672)
John 8:1–11 (p 743)

alien—a person from another country; a stranger.
Deuteronomy 10:17–19 (p 131)
Ephesians 2:11–22 (p 811–12)

altar—a place where people would bring gifts to God. Altars were usually flat on top. They were made of dirt, rocks, wood or metal.
1 Kings 18:30–39 (p 249–50)
Revelation 8:1–5 (p 853)

amen—means "Yes, this is true!" or "Let it be so!"
Nehemiah 8:6 (p 341)
Revelation 7:11–12 (p 852)

anoint—to pour oil on a person's head. It meant that God's Spirit was helping that person do a special job.
1 Samuel 16:1–13 (p 198)
1 John 2:20–21 (p 845)

antichrist—means "against Christ." In the last days a great evil power called the antichrist will rule over the world and pretend to be like Christ. But Jesus Christ will come and destroy him.
2 Thessalonians 2:1–12 (p 821)
Revelation 11–13 (pp 854–55)

apostles—the special leaders Jesus chose to bring the message about Jesus to the world. First, Jesus chose 12 men, and then later Paul and some others became apostles.
Mark 3:13–19 (p 696)
Acts 1:12–26 (p 756)
Ephesians 2:19–22 (p 812)

Ark of the Covenant—a special box made of wood and covered with gold. It had two gold angels on top of it. The written copy of the Ten Commandments was kept inside the box.
The Ark of the Covenant was a sign to the people of Israel that God was with them.
Exodus 25:10–22 (p 57)
Joshua 3:1–17 (p 150)
2 Samuel 6 (p 214)

Asherah—the name of a fertility goddess that the people of Canaan worshiped. Often wooden poles were set up as symbols of Asherah for people to worship at.
Exodus 34:12–14 (p 64)
2 Chronicles 34:1–7 (p 325)
Micah 5:10–15 (p 648)

atonement—a payment of offering to remove or forgive sins.
In the Old Testament, the people of Israel sacrificed animals to show that atonement must be made for the sins of the people.
Leviticus 16:1–34 (p 81)
When Jesus came, he gave up his own life to make atonement for the sins of his people.
Romans 3:21–26 (p 782)
Hebrews 10:1–18 (p 833–34)

B

Baal—the name of a false god that means "master." The people of Canaan believed Baal had power over the land, crops and animals.
Judges 2:10–15 (p 167–68)
1 Kings 18:16–39 (p 249–50)
Jeremiah 11:13 (p 535)

Babylon—the capital city of Babylonia. The Babylonians captured and destroyed Jerusalem and took many people as prisoners.
2 Chronicles 36:15–21 (p 327–28)
Jeremiah 50–51 (p 567–71)
Later in the Bible, Babylon becomes a symbol for evil forces that are against God.
Revelation 17–18 (p 857–58)

baptize—to wash, dip or immerse in water. Baptism shows that a person's sins are washed away. He or she has joined the family of God and is united with Jesus in dying to sin and rising to new life.
Acts 2:36–41 (p 757)
Romans 6:1–14 (p 784)
1 Corinthians 12:13 (p 797)
Ephesians 4:4–6 (p 812)
Titus 3:5 (p 828)

bless, blessing—when God blesses someone, he makes things go well for him or her. A blessing is a good gift from God.
Genesis 12:1–3 (p 8)
Numbers 6:22–27 (p 97)
Deuteronomy 28:1–14 (p 141–42)
When people bless, they ask God to bring good to someone.
Ruth 2:4 (p 185)
Romans 12:14–21 (p 788)
1 Corinthians 4:12 (p 793)

blood—in the Bible, represents the life of something. It was the blood of a sacrifice that made it effective.
Leviticus 17:11 (p 82)
Romans 5:9–11 (p 783)
Hebrews 9:11–28 (p 833)
Revelation 5:9–10 (p 851)

C

Canaan—the land God promised to give to Israel. Canaan is at the eastern end of the Mediterranean Sea where Asia, Europe and Africa come together.
Genesis 17:1–8 (p 10)
Joshua 21:43–45 (p 164)
Psalm 105:8–11 (p 422)

centurion—an officer in the Roman army in charge of 100 soldiers.
Mark 15:39 (p 709)
Luke 7:1–10 (p 716–17)

Christ—the title of Jesus which means "anointed" or "chosen one" in Greek. The Hebrew word for Christ is "Messiah." Jesus Christ is God's chosen one to bring salvation to his people.
Matthew 16:13–20 (p 681–82)
John 1:40–42 (p 736)
Acts 3:17–26 (p 758)
1 John 5:1 (p 846)

church—a group of the followers of Jesus that meets in a certain place. Jesus calls the church his body. Most of the books of the New Testament are letters to churches.
Matthew 18:15–20 (p 683)
Acts 11:19–26 (p 765)
Romans 12:3–8 (p 788)
1 Corinthians 12:12–31 (p 797–98)
Colossians 1:15–20 (p 817)

circumcise—to remove the foreskin of the male sex organ. This was done to symbolize the removal of evil. It was also a sign of the covenant or agreement between God and the people of Israel.
Genesis 17:9–14 (p 10–11)
Romans 2:25–29 (p 782)
Colossians 2:9–13 (p 817)

city of refuge—a place of safety for someone who had accidentally killed someone.
Deuteronomy 19:1–21 (p 136)

commandment—a rule or teaching that people should obey. God gives his people commandments to help them live a good life.
Proverbs 2:1–15 (p 442)
Matthew 22:34–40 (p 687)
See also the word law in this dictionary.

covenant—an agreement or set of promises, usually between God and his people.
Genesis 9:8–17 (p 6)
Deuteronomy 29:1–29 (p 143–44)
Galatians 3:15–29 (p 809)
Hebrews 8:1–13 (p 832)
One of the most important covenant promises in the Bible is when God says, "I will be your God, and you will be my people."
Exodus 6:6–8 (p 43)
Jeremiah 11:1–5 (p 535)
2 Corinthians 6:16 (p 803)
Revelation 21:3 (p 860)
There is trouble if either side breaks the covenant promises that bind them together.
Jeremiah 34:8–20 (p 555)
Genesis 15 (p 9–10)

creation—God created, or made, the world and the entire universe. It is all his creation. The Bible says everything God made was very good.
Genesis 1–2 (p 1–2)
Psalm 65 (p 403)
Psalm 104 (p 421–22)
Revelation 4:9–11 (p 851)
All creation is now hurt by the sin in the world. But one day God will make creation perfect again.
Romans 8:18–25 (p 785)

crucify—to nail or tie a person to a cross until that person died. A cross was made of rough beams of wood nailed together in a ✝ shape. Jesus died by this method, which was usually used for criminals.
Luke 22:66–23:56 (p 733–34)
1 Corinthians 1:18–25 (p 791–92)
Galatians 2:20 (p 808)

curse—to wish that bad things happen to someone or something. God curses, or makes bad things happen, only as a punishment for not obeying him.
Genesis 3:8–19 (p 2–3)
Deuteronomy 27–30 (p 141–44)
1 Corinthians 4:12 (p 793)

D

David—a great king of Israel.
1 Samuel 16–31 (p 198–210)
2 Samuel 1–24 (p 210–31)
God promised that members of David's family would rule a kingdom that lasts forever.
2 Samuel 7:1–16 (p 215)
Psalm 132:11–12 (p 434)
Jesus was born from the family of David. He is the "Son of David" who will rule God's kingdom forever.
Luke 1:31–33 (p 710)
Acts 2:22–36 (p 757)
Romans 1:1–4 (p 780)

Day of the Lord—a phrase used in the Bible for the time in the future when God will destroy evil.
Isaiah 24:1–23 (p 491)
Zephaniah 1:14–2:3 (p 654–55)
2 Peter 3:1–13 (p 843–44)

demon—a powerful evil spirit that works for Satan. Demons can sometimes control people. But Jesus has power over demons. He can make them come out of people.
Mark 1:21–28 (p 694)
Mark 9:14–32 (p 701–02)
Acts 16:16–18 (p 769)
Ephesians 6:10–18 (p 813–14)

disciple—a follower; someone who believes and does what his or her leader teaches.
Jesus had 12 disciples to be his special helpers. Today, anyone who follows Jesus is his disciple.
Matthew 28:16–20 (p 694)
Luke 6:12–16 (p 715)
Luke 14:25–35 (p 726)
John 15:1–17 (p 750)

E

elders—older men who were leaders of God's people.
Ruth 4:1–12 (p 186)
Acts 20:13–38 (p 773)
Titus 1:5–9 (p 827)

eternal—forever; with no end. God is eternal.
Deuteronomy 33:27 (p 148)
Isaiah 26:4 (p 492)
Followers of Jesus are given the gift of eternal life.
John 6:66–69 (p 742)
John 10:10,27–28 (p 745)
2 Corinthians 4:16–18 (p 803)

F

faith—sure belief and trust. Faith is being sure of what you hope for and certain of things even if you cannot see them. To have faith in Jesus means to trust him and believe what the Bible says about him.
Romans 3:21–26 (p 782)
Ephesians 2:8–9 (p 811)
Philippians 3:7–11 (p 815–16)
Hebrews 11:1–12:3 (p 834–35)
1 John 5:1–5 (p 846)

famine—a time when there is not enough food for people. A famine can happen for many reasons. Maybe not enough rain falls, or insects destroy the crops. Sometimes people are fighting a war instead of growing things to eat.
Genesis 41:46–57 (p 31–32)
Psalm 33:18–22 (p 389)
Amos 8:11–12 (p 642)
Mark 13:8 (p 705–06)

fasting—going without food for a period of time. In the Bible, fasting was usually done by people during a special time of praying to God, or to show sadness.
2 Chronicles 20:1–30 (p 314–15)
Isaiah 58:1–14 (p 518)
Acts 13:1–3 (p 766)

firstfruits—the first crops that God's people would collect from their fields and give to God. This was a sign that everything the land produced belong to God.
Deuteronomy 26:1–15 (p 140)
In the New Testament, firstfruits is the first part of a blessing that is received as a promise of more to come.
Romans 8:23–25 (p 785)
1 Corinthians 15:20–23 (p 799)

feast—a special time of celebration and eating. In the Bible, feasts celebrated the ways God helped his people.
Leviticus 23:1–44 (p 86–87)
Isaiah 25:6–8 (p 492)
Luke 14:15–24 (p 725–26)
Luke 22:14–19 (p 732)

forgive—to not punish a person for something wrong he or she has done; to pardon someone.
The great message of the Bible is that God forgives us. Jesus took the punishment for the things we have done wrong.
Psalm 32:1–5 (p 389)
Psalm 130 (p 434)
Matthew 18:15–35 (p 683)
Colossians 3:12–14 (p 818)
1 John 1:9 (p 844)

G

Galilee—the northern part of the land of Palestine. Jesus grew up in the town of Nazareth, in Galilee. He did a lot of his ministry in Galilee.
Matthew 4:12–25 (p 671)
Mark 1:9–28 (p 694)
Luke 4:14–19 (p 713–14)

Gentiles—means "nations." A Gentile is anyone who is not a Jew. God's plan of salvation begins with the chosen nation of Israel, and then moves to include all the nations of the earth.
Isaiah 49:5–6 (p 511)
Acts 10:1–48 (p 764–65)
Romans 15:7–13 (p 790)
Ephesians 2:11–3:6 (p 811–12)
Revelation 5:9–10 (p 860)

glory—greatness and majesty that people can see or sense; usually of God.
Exodus 24:1–18 (p 56–57)
2 Chronicles 7:1–3 (p 306)
Luke 2:8–14 (p 711)
John 1:14 (p 736)
2 Corinthians 3:7–18 (p 802)
Revelation 21:22–27 (p 860)

gospel—means "good news." The gospel is the message about how Jesus defeated evil. He died and then became alive again to make us new and give us hope for the future.
The job of Jesus' followers is to share the gospel with people all over the world.
Matthew 24:14 (p 688)
Romans 1:16–17 (p 781)
2 Corinthians 4:1–6 (p 802)
Galatians 3:6–9 (p 808)
Colossians 1:3–8 (p 816–17)
1 Thessalonians 1:4–5 (p 819)

grace—showing love and kindness to someone who does not deserve it.
The heart of the Bible's message is God's grace. He loves people and saves them even while they are still fighting against him.
Numbers 6:24–26 (p 97)
2 Corinthians 12:7–10 (p 806)
Ephesians 1:1–10 (p 811)
1 Timothy 1:12–17 (p 822)
Hebrews 4:14–16 (p 830)

H

Hades—the place of the dead.
Matthew 16:13–20 (p 681–82)
Revelation 1:12–18 (p 849)
Revelation 20:11–15 (p 860)

Hallelujah—means "Praise the LORD!" This word is made by putting together two Hebrew words: Hallelu (meaning "praise") and Yah (for the name of God, "Yahweh," or "the LORD").
Psalm 146:1 (p 439)
Revelation 19:1–8 (p 859)

heaven—the place where God is, and where other spiritual beings live.
The followers of Jesus have their loyalty, or citizenship, in heaven because Jesus is there.
Philippians 3:12–21 (p 816)
But this does not mean that God has given up on the earth. According to the Bible, the struggle against evil is now taking place in both heaven and earth.
Ephesians 6:12 (p 814)
Revelation 12:1–12 (p 860–61)
One day God will destroy this heaven and earth.
Isaiah 51:4–6 (p 513)
Hebrews 12:25–29 (p 836)
He will "shake" out all evil. Then he will make a wonderful place where everyone does what is right—a new heaven and new earth.
2 Peter 3:3–13 (p 843–44)
Revelation 21:1–22:5 (p 860–61)

heir—the person who receives or inherits what belongs to a relative. The heir usually inherited these things when the relative died. In the Old Testament, Israel was the heir of God. Israel received the Promised Land as an inheritance from God.
Genesis 15:1–21 (p 1–14)
In the New Testament, God's people are also called heirs of God. They receive the gifts of righteousness, eternal life and the kingdom of God.
Romans 8:15–17 (p 785)
Galatians 3:26–4:7 (p 809)
Titus 3:3–7 (p 827–28)

high place—a place of worship built on top of a hill. High places were altars, stones or wood poles usually used for worshiping false gods.
1 Kings 11:1–13 (p 242)
1 Kings 14:22–24 (p 246)
Jeremiah 17:1–4 (p 540)
Jeremiah 19:1–6 (p 541)

holy—pure, set apart for God. God is holy. He is perfect. He does not do anything wrong.
Psalm 99 (p 419)
Isaiah 6:13 (p 479)
Zechariah 2:10–12 (p 658–59)
God also wants his people to be holy. One day, God will make them perfect.
Exodus 19:3–6 (p 52)
Romans 12:1–2 (p 788)
1 Peter 1:13–16 (p 840)

Holy Spirit—one of the three persons of God. In the Old Testament we see the Holy Spirit active in the creation of the world.
Genesis 1:1–2 (p 1)
Psalm 104:30 (p 422)
The Spirit also filled certain people with power at special times.
Numbers 11:16–17,24–30 (p 101–02)
Judges 14:1–6 (p 177–78)
It is the Holy Spirit that worked through men to produce the Scriptures.
2 Peter 1:19–21 (p 842–43)

Because Jesus died and rose to new life, the Holy Spirit now lives in all God's people. He is the One who makes them new, teaches them and gives them freedom for a new life.
John 14:15–31 (p 749–50)
Acts 2:1–21 (p 756)
Romans 8:1–27 (p 785)
1 Corinthians 2:6–16 (p 792)
Galatians 5:16–26 (p 810)

I

idol—anything that is worshiped instead of the true God. In Bible times, idols were often statues of false gods made of wood, stone or metal. Idolatry is the worship of idols.
Deuteronomy 4:15–31 (p 126)
2 Kings 17:7–23 (p 268–69)
Acts 17:16–34 (p 770–71)
1 Thessalonians 1:9–10 (p 891)

incense—a collection of spices that is burned to worship God. Incense produces a sweet smell.
Exodus 30:1–10 (p 61)
Matthew 2:7–12 (p 669–70)
The Bible teaches that the prayers of God's people are like incense to him.
Psalm 141:1–2 (p 437)
Revelation 8:1–5 (p 853)

Israel—a name meaning "he struggles with God." God gave this name to Jacob, after he fought with an angel of God.
Genesis 32:22–32 (p 24)
The 12 tribes of the nation of Israel are from the family of Jacob (Israel).
Genesis 49:1–28 (p 38)
Psalm 105 (p 422–23)
Romans 9–11 (p 786–88)
A member of the nation of Israel is called an Israelite. See also the word Jew in this dictionary.

J

Jacob—son of Isaac, grandson of Abraham.
Jacob was the father of the 12 tribes of Israel.
Genesis 25:19–35:29 (p 17–26)
Genesis 46:1–50:14 (p 35–39)
Hebrews 11:20–21 (p 835)

Jerusalem—the most important city in Israel. In Bible times, Jerusalem was the capital and also the place where the temple of God was built. Jerusalem is sometimes called "Zion," "City of David" or "City of God."
2 Samuel 5–6 (p 213–14)
Psalm 122 (p 433)
Jeremiah 4:5–31 (p 528–29)
Joel 3:17–21 (p 636)
Zechariah 8 (p 660–61)
Jesus cried about Jerusalem because the people did not know he was the Messiah.
Luke 13:31–35 (p 725)
Luke 19:28–44 (p 730)
In the future, God will show us a New Jerusalem.
Revelation 21:1–22:6 (p 860–61)

Jesus—a Greek name which means "savior." Jesus is a form of the Hebrew name "Joshua" which means "the LORD saves."
When the Son of God was born as a human being, he was named Jesus. This is because he came to save his people from their sins.
Isaiah 53 (p 515)
Matthew 1 (p 669)
Luke 1:26–38 (p 710)
Jesus is one of the three persons of God.
John 1:1–18 (p 736)
Philippians 2:1–11 (p 815)
Colossians 1:15–20 (p 817)
Jesus is also a real human person.
Hebrews 2:10–18 (p 829–30)
Hebrews 4:14–15 (p 830)

Jew—at first, this was a name for someone from the tribe of Judah. Later it came to be used for anyone who was from the family of Jacob (Israel).
Esther 2 (p 348)
Zechariah 8:23 (p 661)
Romans 10:11–13 (p 787)
Galatians 3:26–29 (p 809)

Joshua—a leader of the people of Israel. Joshua led the Israelites into the land God had promised them.
Numbers 27:12–23 (p 115)
Joshua 1–11 (p 149–157)
Joshua 23–24 (p 165–166)

Judah—one of the sons of Jacob, and father of one of the tribes of Israel.
Genesis 49:8–12 (p 38)
The tribe of Judah was the main one in the southern part of the nation of Israel. When the nation split into two parts, the southern part was called Judah.
1 Kings 12:1–24 (p 243–44)
2 Kings 24:18–25:21 (p 276)
Zechariah 12:1–9 (p 663)
Jesus was born from the tribe of Judah.
Revelation 5:5 (p 851)

judge—a strong leader of the people of Israel before Israel had kings. God brought judges to power to save the people from their enemies.
Judges 2:6–23 (p 167–68)
1 Samuel 8:1–9 (p 191–92)

justify—to make a person right with God. To justify is to say that someone's sins will not be held against him. The followers of Jesus are justified because Jesus died and rose again for them.
Luke 18:9–14 (p 728)
Romans 3:21–31 (p 782)
Romans 4:25 (p 783)
Galatians 2:15–16 (p 808)

K

kingdom of God, kingdom of heaven—God's rule, or reign, over everything he has made.
Psalm 145:11–13 (p 439)
The kingdom of God comes when God removes evil and brings real peace and justice. The main subject of Jesus' teaching was the kingdom of God.
Matthew 13:1–52 (p 678–79)
Mark 1:14–34 (p 694)
By becoming a follower of Jesus, a person becomes part of the kingdom of God.
Colossians 1:9–14 (p 817)
When God's rule over the world is complete, the kingdom will last forever.
Revelation 11:15–18 (p 854)

L

Lamb of God—Jesus is called the Lamb of God. He was sacrificed like a lamb to take away the sins of God's people.
Exodus 12:1–30 (p 47)
John 1:29 (p 736)
1 Corinthians 5:6–8 (p 793)
1 Peter 1:17–21 (p 840)
Revelation 7:9–17 (p 852–53)
See also the word Passover in this dictionary.

law—this word is used in different ways in the Bible:
1) The first five books of the Old Testament are called the Law. They contain all God's rules for how Israel was to worship him and live together as his people.
Nehemiah 8 (p 341–42)
Matthew 5:17–20 (p 671)
2) All the moral rules God gave his people in the Old Testament are called the law. Because of the sinful nature of all people, this holy law of God could not produce righteousness. So Jesus gives a right standing with God as a gift to his people.
Romans 7:1–8:17 (p 784–85)
Galatians 3:15–25 (p 809)
Philippians 3:7–11 (p 815–16)
3) Law can refer to all the practical instruction God still wants his people to obey. This law helps people show their love for God. It tells them how to live together peacefully.
Deuteronomy 5 (p 127–28)
Psalm 119 (p 429–32)
Romans 13:8–10 (p 789)
Galatians 5:13–15 (p 810)
Real freedom is found in keeping God's perfect law. This is the new command to love one another.
John 13:34–35 (p 749)
James 1:19–25 (p 837)

The Law and the Prophets—a name for the entire Old Testament.
Romans 3:21 (p 782)

leprosy—the word used in the Bible for different skin diseases and infections.
2 Kings 5 (p 258–59)
Luke 5:12–16 (p 714–15)

Levite—a member of the family line of Levi, one of the sons of Jacob. All priests came from the tribe of Levi. Other Levites worked in the temple and were teachers of the law.
Numbers 1:47–54 (p 92)

Numbers 8:5–26 (p 99)
Nehemiah 12:27–30 (p 345)
Jeremiah 33:17–22 (p 554)
Luke 10:25–37 (p 721)

lord, Lord—(in small letters or initial capital) is used in this Bible to mean "master" or someone who is in control. Sometimes this can be a title of respect for a human being.
Genesis 23:11 (p 15)
But usually it is used for God as a title showing his power over all things.
Psalm 136:3 (p 435)
Matthew 11:25 (p 677)
The early followers of Jesus said "Jesus is Lord" to mean that he has authority over everything.
Romans 10:9–13 (p 787)
1 Corinthians 12:3 (p 797)
Philippians 2:9–11 (p 815)

LORD—(in all capital letters) is used in this Bible to refer to the personal name of God.
The Hebrew word for this name is Yahweh, which means "I AM WHO I AM." This name tells us that God is always with his people.
Exodus 3:13–17 (p 41)
Exodus 6:1–8 (p 42–43)
Psalm 135 (p 435)
Isaiah 42:8 (p 505)
Jeremiah 10:6–10 (p 534)
Micah 4:5 (p 647)

Lord's Supper—a meal shared together by the followers of Jesus. Bread is shared to remember the body of Jesus that he gave up for them. Wine is shared to remember his blood that was poured out for the forgiveness of their sins.
Matthew 26:17–30 (p 690)
Luke 22:7–30 (p 732)
The Lord's Supper helps the followers of Jesus remember three things:
1) Jesus died for them;
2) Jesus is alive and is with them now through his Spirit; and
3) Jesus will eat and drink with them again when he returns.
John 6:25–59 (p 741)
1 Corinthians 10:14–17 (p 796)
1 Corinthians 11:17–34 (p 797)
Revelation 19:9 (p 859)
Sometimes, the New Testament uses the words "breaking bread" for the Lord's Supper.
Acts 20:7 (p 773)
The Lord's Supper is also called Communion or the Eucharist by some followers of Jesus.

M

manna—means "What is it?" Manna was the name the Israelites gave the special food God provided to them in the desert. It was a white, bread-like, sweet-tasting food that would show up on the ground in the morning.
Exodus 16 (p 50–51)
Numbers 11:4–35 (p 101–02)
Deuteronomy 8:2–3 (p 129)
Psalm 78:23–25 (p 410)
Jesus says he is like manna. He is the bread of life that can truly fulfill God's people.
John 6:30–35,57–58 (p 741)

mediator—a person who helps bring peace between two or more people who are having a conflict. Jesus is the mediator between God and people.
1 Timothy 2:5–6 (p 823)
Hebrews 9:15 (p 833)
Hebrews 12:22–24 (p 836)

Messiah—a Hebrew word meaning "anointed" or "chosen one." The Greek word used in the New Testament for "anointed" is Christ.
In the Old Testament, God promised to send a special person called the Messiah. This new king would save God's people.
Psalm 2 (p 377)
Isaiah 9:6–7 (p 481)
Isaiah 11:1–9 (p 483)
Daniel 7:13–14 (p 622)
The New Testament shows us that Jesus is the Messiah. He is God's chosen one to save his people.
Matthew 11:1–6 (p 676)
John 1:40–42 (p 736)
Acts 10:34–43 (p 764)

miracle—any great show of power that goes beyond the usual laws of nature. God's miracles are wonderful signs of his power to make things right.

Psalm 77:11–15 (p 409)
Luke 7:11–17 (p 717)
John 10:22–42 (p 745)
Acts 2:22 (p 757)
Hebrews 2:1–4 (p 829)

Satan and his helpers sometimes do miracles to fool people.

2 Thessalonians 2:9–12 (p 821)
Revelation 13:11–17 (p 855)

Moses—a great leader of the people of Israel in the Old Testament.
Moses led the people out of slavery in Egypt and brought God's law to them. See Exodus 1–20 (p 39–54). Later, he directed them through the desert. See Numbers 10–14 (p 100–04). Moses died just before the Israelites entered the Promised Land. See Deuteronomy 34 (p 148).
The New Testament writes about Moses as a faithful leader who pointed forward to the time of Christ.

Matthew 17:1–13 (p 682)
Luke 24:44–49 (p 735)
Hebrews 3 (p 830)
Hebrews 11:23–29 (p 835)

mystery—a secret, or something too difficult to understand, that is revealed or explained by God.

Daniel 2 (p 616–17)
Romans 16:25–27 (p 791)
Ephesians 3:1–13 (p 812)
Colossians 1:24–29 (p 817)

N

Noah—a righteous man who believed God. He obeyed when God told him to build a huge boat (the ark) because a flood was coming.

Genesis 6–9 (p 4–6)
Isaiah 54:9–10 (p 515–16)
Matthew 24:36–44 (p 689)
Hebrews 11:7 (p 834)

O

offering—something given to God to worship him. In the Old Testament, God's people offered food and animals to God.

Deuteronomy 12 (p 132)
Psalm 50:7–23 (p 397–98)
Amos 5:18–27 (p 640)
Micah 6:6–8 (p 648–49)
Mark 12:28–34 (p 705)

In the New Testament, Jesus offered himself as a sacrifice to God for us.

Ephesians 5:1–2 (p 813)
Hebrews 10:1–18 (p 833)

The followers of Jesus serve God with their whole lives as an offering of praise to God.

1 Peter 2:4–5 (p 840)

See also the word sacrifice in this dictionary.

P

parable—a short story that is told to show how one thing is like another.
Most of the parables in the Bible are stories used by Jesus. These parables teach us what the kingdom of God is like.

Mark 4:1–34 (p 696–97)
Luke 10:25–37 (p 721)
Luke 14:15–24 (p 725–26)
Luke 15 (p 726–27)
Luke 18:1–14 (p 728)

Passover—a Jewish celebration feast.
It reminds the people how God saved them from slavery in Egypt. Part of the meal includes the Passover lamb.
At the first Passover a lamb was killed and its blood was placed on the people's door frames. This is so God would "pass over" the homes of his people and spare the lives of their firstborn sons.

Exodus 12 (p 47–49)
2 Chronicles 35:1–19 (p 326–27)

Jesus is the Passover lamb for all of God's people. He was sacrificed so his people could be saved from sin and death.

Luke 22:7–16 (p 732)
1 Corinthians 5:6–8 (p 793)

Paul—a great apostle and leader among the first followers of Jesus.
Paul was known first as Saul. His name was changed to Paul after Jesus appeared to him and he became a follower of Jesus.

Acts 7:54–8:3 (p 761–62)
Acts 9:1–31 (p 763)

Paul had a special job of bringing the good news of Jesus to the Gentiles.

Acts 13–28 (p 766–80)

Paul wrote many of the letters that make up the New Testament.
2 Corinthians 12:1–10 (p 806)
Galatians 1–2 (p 807–08)
Philippians 1:12–30 (p 814–15)
1 Thessalonians 1:1–2:16 (p 819)
1 Timothy 1:12–17 (p 822)
2 Peter 3:15–16 (p 844)

Peter—one of Jesus' 12 disciples. He later became an apostle and leader in the church at Jerusalem.
Jesus changed Peter's name from Simon to Cephas (which in Greek is Peter).
Matthew 14:22–33 (p 680)
Matthew 16:13–20 (p 681–82)
John 1:35–42 (p 736)
Peter once denied that he knew Jesus.
Luke 22:31–62 (p 732–33)
John 21 (p 755)
He later became a bold leader and was thrown in jail for his faith.
Acts 1–4 (p 755–59)
Acts 9:32–12:19 (p 763–66)
Galatians 2:7–9 (p 808)

Pharisees—means "the separate ones." In New Testament times, the Pharisees were the main religious leaders of the Jews.
The Pharisees believed in following the Old Testament laws very carefully. They also added many of their own rules. Jesus often had trouble with the Pharisees.
Matthew 23 (p 687–88)
Mark 7:1–23 (p 699–700)
Luke 18:9–14 (p 728)
Acts 26:4–5 (p 778)

priest—a person who brought sacrifices and prayers to God for all the people. In Israel, a priest had to be from the tribe of Levi.
Exodus 28–29 (p 59–61)
Leviticus 1 (p 69–70)
2 Chronicles 29 (p 320–21)
The high priest had special jobs to do. He was the most important religious leader.
Leviticus 16:29–34 (p 82)
Leviticus 21:10–12 (p 85)
The New Testament tells us that Jesus is the high priest for his followers. He gave himself as a sacrifice.
Hebrews 4:14–5:10 (p 830–31)
Hebrews 10:19–25 (p 834)
Now, all the followers of Jesus are priests. They can freely bring their sacrifice of praise to God.
1 Peter 2:9–10 (p 840)

prophet—a person God has chosen to bring his message to the people.
Deuteronomy 18:14–22 (p 136)
2 Peter 1:19–21 (p 840)
God often called the prophets "my servants."
2 Kings 17:13 (p 269)
Sometimes God gave the prophets a message about what would happen in the future.
Isaiah 2:1–5 (p 476)
Zephaniah 1:1–3 (p 654)
Acts 11:27–28 (p 765)
1 Peter 1:10–12 (p 839)
False prophets gave the people a message that really was not from God.
Jeremiah 29:8–9 (p 549)
True prophets always said that God was faithful to his promises. They told the people to be faithful.
Jeremiah 3:11–20 (p 527)
Jesus came to earth as a great prophet.
Mark 13 (p 705–06)
John 6:14 (p 740)

Psalm—means "song." In the Bible, God's people used psalms to:
1) praise God (Psalm 47, p 396);
2) cry out to God for help during trouble (Psalm 13, p 381);
3) thank God (Psalm 118, p 428–29).
The people often sang the psalms when they were together to worship God.
Colossians 3:16 (p 818)

Q–R

ransom—the price paid to free someone who has been condemned. Jesus gave himself as a ransom. He set his people free from slavery to sin and its death penalty.
Isaiah 51:11 (p 513)
Hosea 13:14 (p 633)
Mark 10:45 (p 703)
Hebrews 9:15 (p 833)
See also the word redeem in this dictionary.

reap—to gather a crop at harvest time.
Leviticus 19:9–10 (p 83)
Revelation 14:14–20 (p 856)
Reap can also refer to what will happen to someone as a result of their own actions.
Psalm 126:5–6 (p 433)
2 Corinthians 9:6–15 (p 805)
Galatians 6:7–10 (p 810)

reconcile, reconciliation—to bring peace between two people who have been enemies.
Luke 12:57–59 (p 724)
The world sinned and was hostile toward God. Then God sent Jesus to reconcile the world to God.
Romans 5:10–11 (p 783)
2 Corinthians 5:16–21 (p 803)
Ephesians 2:11–18 (p 811)
Colossians 1:19–23 (p 817)

redeem, redemption—when a family member pays a price to buy someone or something back from slavery or ownership by someone else.
Leviticus 25:23–55 (p 88–89)
Ruth 3:1–4:12 (p 185–86)
In the New Testament, our brother Jesus redeems us from sin, or sets us free, by his death on the cross.
Galatians 3:10–14 (p 808)
Galatians 4:1–7 (p 809)
Ephesians 1:7–8 (p 811)
Colossians 1:13–14 (p 817)
Hebrews 2:11–15 (p 829–30)
See also the word ransom in this dictionary.

remnant—a few people who are left over from a bigger group.
Genesis 45:4–7 (p 34)
Ezra 9:5–15 (p 334–35)
The Bible says many people will fall away from serving God. But God promises always to keep a faithful remnant who are true to him.
Isaiah 10:20–23 (p 482–83)
Zephaniah 3:11–13 (p 656)
Romans 11:1–6 (p 787)

repent, repentance—to turn away from sin and start to follow God completely. To repent means to change the direction of one's life.
Jeremiah 5:3–4 (p 529)
Matthew 3:1–12 (p 670)
Mark 1:4–15 (p 694)
Acts 20:21 (p 733)
2 Corinthians 7:10 (p 804)

resurrection—coming back to life after being dead. Death came into the world because of sin.
Romans 5:12 (p 783)
Jesus raised people from the dead as a sign of God's power over sin.
Luke 7:11–17 (p 717)
John 11:1–44 (p 746–47)
The resurrection of Jesus is the key victory over death.
Matthew 28 (p 693–94)
Luke 24 (p 734–35)
Acts 2:22–39 (p 757)
Because Jesus rose from the dead, his followers have a new life now. They will also rise again with new bodies when Jesus comes again.
Romans 6:1–10 (p 784)
1 Corinthians 15 (p 799–800)
Philippians 3:7–21 (p 815–16)
At the final resurrection, all people will rise from the dead to be judged by God.
Daniel 12:1–2 (p 626)
Matthew 22:23–33 (p 687)
Revelation 20:11–15 (p 860)

reveal, revelation—to show someone something or teach them something they did not know.
Deuteronomy 29:29 (p 144)
1 Corinthians 2:6–16 (p 792)
In the Bible, God reveals the truth about us and our world. By his great acts of salvation, God shows his people his power and love. God sometimes revealed things to certain people (prophets or apostles).
Amos 3:7 (p 638)
Romans 16:25–27 (p 791)
Ephesians 3:2–5 (p 812)
When Jesus came he revealed who God is and how much he loved us.
John 1:1–18 (p 736)
Hebrews 1:1–2 (p 829)

righteous, righteousness—doing what is right or holy; being faithful to the promises of a covenant. God is the only purely righteous one.
Psalm 11 (p 380)
Psalm 119:137–144 (p 431–32)

Daniel 9:4–19 (p 623)
Romans 10:1–3 (p 782)
1 John 2:1 (p 844)

God expects his people also to be righteous. But they do not always live by God's law. God sent Jesus so that those who believe in Jesus will have his righteousness given to them.

Romans 3:9–24 (p 782)
Romans 4:1–8 (p 782–83)
2 Corinthians 5:21 (p 803)
Philippians 3:4–9 (p 815)

The Holy Spirit now works in the followers of Jesus so they can live righteously.

Romans 8:1–11 (p 785)
Galatians 5:16–26 (p 810)
Ephesians 4:17–24 (p 812–13)

S

Sabbath—a time of rest or ceasing to work.

In the Old Testament, God told his people to celebrate Sabbath days (the seventh day of the week and other holidays).

Exodus 20:8 (p 53)
Exodus 31:12–17 (p 62)
Deuteronomy 5:12–15 (p 127)

The land was to have a Sabbath year of rest every seventh year.

Leviticus 25:1–7 (p 87–88)

Jesus often had conflict with the religious leaders of his day about the Sabbath. They had added many rules about what people should not do on the Sabbath.

Mark 2:23–3:6 (p 695)
John 5:1–15 (p 739–40)

The Sabbath is a picture of the rest and peace Jesus' followers have because of his work for them.

John 5:16–17 (p 740)
Colossians 2:16–17 (p 817–18)
Hebrews 4:1–11 (p 830)

sacrifice—an offering or gift given to God to remove the guilt of sin.

Throughout the Old Testament, God's people brought sacrifices to God.

Genesis 46:1 (p 35)
Leviticus 9 (p 75)
Ezra 3:1–6 (p 329)

The greatest sacrifice was when Jesus gave his own life to pay for sin, once and for all.

Isaiah 53 (p 515)
Hebrews 7:23–28 (p 832)
Hebrews 9:23–28 (p 833)

God's people today give themselves as "living sacrifices" to serve and praise God.

Romans 12:1–2 (p 788)
Hebrews 13:15–16 (p 836)

See also the word offering in this dictionary.

Sadducees—a small but powerful group of religious leaders at the time of Jesus. The Sadducees were mostly priests who followed only the Old Testament law. They did not obey the rules added by the Pharisees. The Sadducees did not believe in any life after death. Like the Pharisees, they were often in conflict with Jesus.

Matthew 16:1–12 (p 681)
Mark 12:18–27 (p 705)
Acts 5:12–42 (p 759)

salvation, save—to be rescued from danger or evil. Salvation is a main idea in the Bible. God will take away all the results of sin. He will bring his creation to a peaceful and friendly relationship with him.

In the Old Testament, God saved his people from their enemies many times.

Exodus 15:1–21 (p 49–50)
Psalm 98 (p 419)
Isaiah 12:1–3 (p 438–84)
Isaiah 51:4–8 (p 513)

The New Testament shows us that Jesus is the Savior. Only he can save us and our world.

Matthew 1:18–21 (p 669)
Acts 4:8–12 (p 758)
Acts 16:16–34 (p 769–770)
Romans 1:16–17 (p 781)
Romans 10:9–13 (p 787)
Ephesians 2:1–10 (p 811)

Samaritan—a person from the country of Samaria (part of Palestine). The Samaritans were hated by the Jews because they had married non-Jews. They also worshiped God differently from the Jews. But Jesus showed his love for the Samaritans by going to them and teaching them about the kingdom of God.

Luke 10:25–37 (p 721)

Luke 17:11–19 (p 728)
John 4:1–42 (p 738–39)

sanctify—to make holy; to set apart to be used by God. The followers of Jesus are made holy by Jesus' sacrifice for them.

1 Corinthians 6:9–11 (p 794)
Hebrews 10:10 (p 833)

But they must also keep on working to be sanctified. The Holy Spirit helps God's people live holy lives.

John 17:15–19 (p 759)
1 Thessalonians 4:3–8 (p 820)
2 Thessalonians 2:13–15 (p 821)
Hebrews 12:14 (p 835)

Satan—means "enemy." Satan is the enemy of God. He wants to destroy everything God has created. He is also called the devil (James 4:7, p 838), the evil one (1 John 5:18–19, page 846), the prince of this world (John 14:30, page 750) and the god of this age (2 Corinthians 4:4, p 802).
Satan brought evil into the world. He lies, destroys and attacks the people of God.

Genesis 3:1–15 (p 2)
Job 1–2 (p 352–53)
John 8:42–47 (p 744)
2 Corinthians 11:13–15 (p 806)
Revelation 12 (p 854–55)

Jesus came into the world to renew what Satan had destroyed. Satan tried to stop Jesus. But Jesus is God's Son, and he has more power than Satan.

Matthew 4:1–11 (p 670–71)
Mark 3:20–30 (p 696)
Acts 26:15–18 (p 778)
1 John 3:7–8 (p 845)

The followers of Jesus can resist Satan by asking for the power of the Lord.

Ephesians 6:10–18 (p 813–14)
1 Peter 5:8–11 (p 842)

God will one day win a complete victory over Satan.

Revelation 20:1–10 (p 859–60)

sin—breaking God's law. Sin comes from a broken relationship with God. Sin is not a part of our original human nature. God created the first people with the ability to choose whether or not to trust and obey God.

Genesis 2–3 (p 1–3)

But now, all people are born with a sinful nature that holds them in slavery. This leads to all kinds of law-breaking.

Genesis 6:5–7 (p 4)
Psalm 58:1–5 (p 400)
Mark 7:20–23 (p 700)
Romans 1:18–32 (p 781)
Romans 3:9–20,23 (p 782)
Ephesians 2:1–3 (p 811)

God sent Jesus to defeat the power of sin and remove the punishment for sin.

Romans 5–6 (p 783–84)
2 Corinthians 5:21 (p 803)
Colossians 2:13–15 (p 817)
1 Timothy 1:15–16 (p 822)
Hebrews 9:11–10:18 (p 833)
1 John 1:5–2:2 (p 844)
1 John 3:1–10 (p 845)

When God's people confess their sins, God will forgive them.

Psalm 32 (p 389)
Psalm 51 (p 398)
Luke 18:9–14 (p 728)
1 John 1:9 (p 844)

In the future, God will take away all the results of sin from his creation.

2 Peter 3:10–13 (p 843)
Revelation 21:1–5 (p 849)

Son of Man—a title Jesus used for himself during his ministry on earth. In the Old Testament, there is a prophecy about a divine person—"one like a son of man." This person would receive an everlasting kingdom and be worshiped by all nations.

Daniel 7:13–14 (p 622)
Revelation 1:12–18 (p 849)

Jesus called himself "the Son of Man." This showed that he had the authority and power of a divine person, and yet also was a man.

Matthew 26:64 (p 691)
Mark 2:1–12 (p 695)
Luke 9:26 (p 720)
John 3:13–15 (p 738)
John 5:26–27 (p 740)
John 12:20–36 (p 747–48)

synagogue—a Greek word meaning "to gather." The Jews gathered at buildings called synagogues to worship God and to study the Scriptures. Each Jewish community also used the synagogue to teach young people.
Jesus went to the synagogue to worship. He also taught there.

Mark 1:21–28 (p 695)
Luke 4:14–30 (p 713–14)
John 12:37–43 (p 748)
John 18:19–21 (p 752)

Paul used the synagogue as a place to preach the gospel to the Jews.

Acts 17:1–4,10–12 (p 770)
Acts 18:1–11 (p 771)

T

tabernacles, Tent of Meeting—tabernacle means "dwelling place." It was a special tent where the Israelites worshiped God. It is sometimes called the Tent of Meeting. It was the place where god would meet his people. The Israelites used the tabernacle until Solomon built the temple.

Exodus 25–27 (p 57–59)
Exodus 39:32–40:38 (p 68–69)
2 Chronicles 1:1–13 (p 302)
Acts 7:44–47 (p 671)

The tabernacle built on earth was a copy of the true tabernacle in heaven. Now, because of Jesus' sacrifice, his followers can enter the heavenly tabernacle. They can truly meet God.

Hebrews 8–9 (p 832–33)

When Jesus came to earth, God was again dwelling with his people.

Matthew 1:18–23 (p 669)
John 1:14 (p 736)

Jesus brought peace between God and his people. So God will one day make his home with them again.

Revelation 21:3 (p 860)

teacher of the law (also called a scribe)—an expert in the law; a person with special training to read and write well. At first, scribes were people who wrote papers for others.

Nehemiah 8 (p 341–42)
Nehemiah 10:37–39 (p 344)
Jeremiah 36 (p 556–57)
Malachi 3:6–12 (p 665–66)

By the time of Jesus, they were like lawyers. They were experts in using and teaching the Jewish law.

Matthew 8:18–20 (p 674)
Matthew 15:1–20 (p 680–80)
Mark 1:21–22 (p 699)
Mark 12:28–40 (p 740)
Luke 5:17–32 (p 715)
Luke 19:45–48 (p 730)
Luke 23:8–11 (p 733–34)

temple—a building where people worship divine beings. God told Israel to build him a temple and worship him there. God showed his people that he was with them by having his presence in the temple.

1 Kings 5–6 (p 235–37)
1 Kings 8 (p 238–40)
1 Chronicles 28:11–19 (p 300–301)
Ezra 3:10–13 (p 330)
Ezra 6:13–18 (p 332)
Psalm 11:4 (p 380)
Mark 11:15–17 (p 704)

In the New Testament, we learn that the new temple is not a building. God's people are now the temple of God. God's Spirit lives within them.

1 Corinthians 3:16–17 (p 792)
2 Corinthians 6:16 (p 803)
Ephesians 2:19–22 (p 812)
Revelation 21:22 (p 860)

tithe—means "a tenth." In the Old Testament, God's people would give a tenth of their crops or animals to God. This was a sign that God owned the land and had blessed his people. Also, the tithe would be used to support the priests and Levites, and to help the poor.

Leviticus 27:30 (p 91)
Deuteronomy 14:22–29 (p 133–34)

U

unclean—a person or thing that did not meet certain conditions.
Something unclean could not be part of religious services. God set the conditions for people and things to be included in worshiping him. People who were unclean could be cleansed. Then they could worship again. To be unclean was a symbol for not being spiritually pure.

Leviticus 11–15 (p 76–81)
Isaiah 64:6 (p 522)
Lamentations 1:8 (p 573)

The sacrifice of Jesus makes his followers spiritually clean. So they do not follow the Old Testament laws about unclean conditions.

Mark 7:1–23 (p 699–700)
Acts 10 (p 764–65)
Romans 14:13–18 (p 789)

V

vision—a dream-like experience that God uses to bring a message to someone.

Numbers 12:1–8 (p 102)
Ezekiel 8:1–4 (p 581)
Zechariah 1:7–17 (p 658)
Acts 10:1–23 (p 764)

W

woe—great suffering, pain or sadness.

Jeremiah 4:13–14 (p 528)
Lamentations 5:15–16 (p 577)
Matthew 23 (p 687–88)
Revelation 12:12 (p 855)

worship—means "to bow down." Worship is an act of highest respect.

Psalm 95:6 (p 418)

Worship is praising and serving someone who is worthy. The Bible teaches that only God is worthy of worship. The heart of human sin is worshipping and serving something instead of the true God.

Deuteronomy 30:15–18 (p 144)
Matthew 4:8–10 (p 671)
Romans 1:25 (p 781)
Revelation 14:6–12 (p 856)

God's people joyfully praise and thank God when they are in his presence.

Psalm 96 (p 418–19)
Psalm 100 (p 419–420)
John 4:23–24 (p 739)
Revelation 7:9–17 (p 852–853)

The followers of Jesus give their whole lives as worship to God.

Romans 12:1–2 (p 788)

wrath—strong anger. God's wrath is his great anger that comes when people will not stop sinning.

This wrath leads to punishment of sin.

Deuteronomy 29:18–29 (p 143–44)
Psalm 78 (p 409–11)
Romans 1:18 (p 781)
Colossians 3:5–6 (p 818)

God's people are saved from the wrath of God. They trust in his mercy, and are faithful followers of Jesus.

Psalm 103:8–13 (p 421)
Jeremiah 32:36–41 (p 553)
Romans 5:9 (p 783)
1 Thessalonians 1:9b–10 (p 819)

For now, God is patiently holding back his wrath. This is the time for people to repent.

2 Peter 3:9 (p 843)

But one day, the great wrath of God against sin will be fully unleashed.

Romans 2:1–11 (p 781)
2 Thessalonians 1:6–10 (p 821)
Revelation 19:11–21 (p 859)

Z

Zion—a hill within the city of Jerusalem. God's temple was built on Zion.

2 Samuel 5:6–10 (p 213)
Psalm 132:13–14 (p 434–35)
Joel 2:32 (p 636)

Sometimes Zion or Daughter of Zion is used to refer to the whole city of Jerusalem, or to the people of God.

Isaiah 52:1–10 (p 514)
Micah 4 (p 647–48)

The New Testament refers to Mount Zion as the New Jerusalem. It is part of the new heaven and new earth that we will see in the future.

Hebrews 12:22–24 (p 836)
Revelation 14:1 (p 856)
Revelation 21:1–2 (p 860)